The Top 6000 Companies in Inner London

Companies with assets exceeding £100,000,000

John D Blackburn
Editor

dp

First Edition

Spring 2019

ISBN-13: 978-1-912736-24-9

ISBN-10: 1-912736-24-1

Printed in 8pt Nimbus Sans L

Designed by URW++ Design and Development GmbH

Dellam Publishing Limited

2 Heath Drive, Sutton, Surrey, SM2 5RP

Fax: 020 8770 7478 email: enquiries@dellam.com

SAN: 0177881 EAN/GLN: 5030670177882

Table of Contents

Acknowledgements

This is a long and detailed publication containing thousands of facts and figures. It is only to be expected, despite continuous and repeated editing and checking, that errors may occur. In such cases, once we are aware of any, we publish a correction on our website.

Readers are encouraged to check regularly at www.dellam.com/books for any corrections and updates.

Although we take extreme care to ensure accuracy and being up-to-date, we cannot accept responsibility for any errors or omissions.

We appreciate your interest in our publications, and your comments and suggestions are always welcome. Please contact us at enquiries@dellam.com.

Scotland
Northern Ireland
North East (England)
North West (England)
Yorkshire and The Humber
East Midlands (England)
West Midlands (England)
Wales
East of England
See London Inset
South East (England)
South West (England)
Outer London East and North East
Outer London West and North West
Inner London East
Inner London West
Inner London East
Outer London East and North East
Outer London South

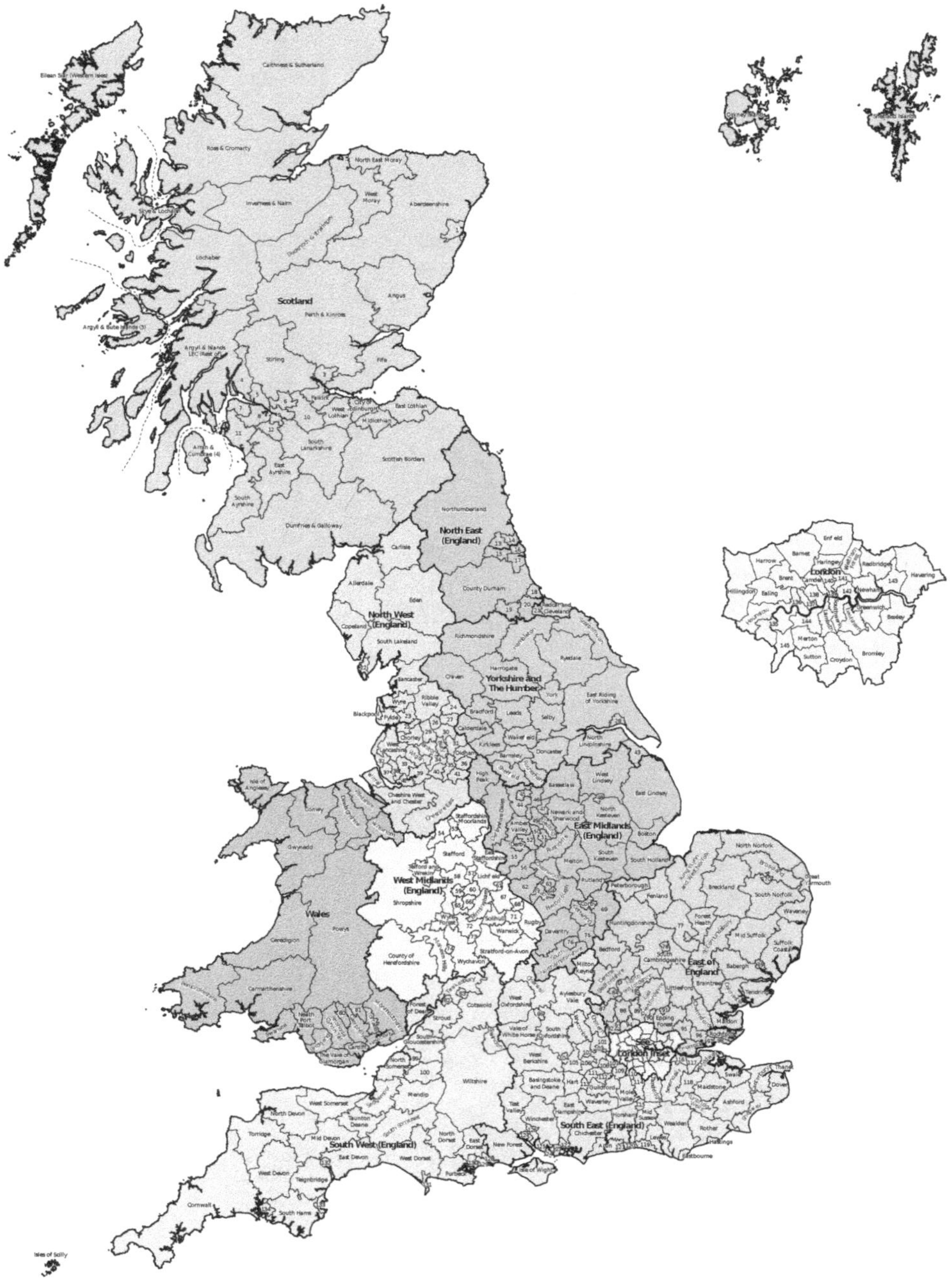
Scotland
North East (England)
North West (England)
Yorkshire and The Humber
East Midlands (England)
West Midlands (England)
Wales
East of England
London
South East (England)
South West (England)

Introduction

This study looks at all companies registered in Inner London and where their total assets are more than £100,000,000.

The statutory Inner London boroughs are: Camden, Greenwich, Hackney, Hammersmith and Fulham, Islington, Kensington and Chelsea, Lambeth, Lewisham, Southwark, Tower Hamlets, Wandsworth and Westminster. The population in 2011 was 3,232,000.

The aim of this study is to provide an overview of the key movers and shakers in the Inner London corporate sector. Only key data has been isolated, particularly the company's net worth and total assets, but also its full name, date incorporated, registered office, activities, shareholders, directors (with date of birth, occupation and nationality) and number of employees.

Two indicators of size are used: net worth and total assets. These are preferable to turnover which is influenced by profit margins and whether the companies are capital or labour intensive.

For Inner London, there are approximately 288,000 businesses with around 2 million employees. Most commercial activity is focused on Central London and Canary Wharf and 10% of public sector employment is in Westminster. Over two-thirds of all London's GVA was produced in Inner London. 39% of all jobs are in four highly specialised, high value sectors (information and communication; finance and insurance; real estate; professional, scientific and technical). In 2015, there were 55,295 new businesses and 30,785 businesses ceased trading.

Regarding both Inner and Outer London:

The population is 9 million (UK 66 million). The total output (GVA), in 2016, was £408 billion (UK £1,748 billion). The total output (GVA) per head, in 2016, was £46,482 (UK £26,621). Economic Growth (GVA), 2010-2016, was 3.2% (UK 1.9%).

Jobs in Manufacturing experienced a rapid decline from 872,000 in 1971 to 128,000 in 2015. The number employed, May-July 2018, was 4,735,000 (UK 32,397,000) with an employment rate of 74.7% (UK 75.5%). The number unemployed was 235,000 (UK 1,361,000) with an unemployment rate of 4.7% (UK 4%). In 2017, there were 140,000 jobs in manufacturing (UK 2,685,000). Manufacturing employment, January-March 2018, was 2.4% of total jobs (UK 7.7%) Public sector employment was 13.6% (UK 16.6%).

The number of VAT/PAYE businesses were in 2016: 477,000 (18.7%); in 2017: 506,000 (18.9%) and in 2018: 506,000 (19%).

London at 1.1 million and South East England at 874,000 had the most private sector businesses, accounting for 35% of the UK.

In 2017, there were 92,300 new businesses (up 15%) and 86,270 businesses ceased trading (up 14%). In 2018, there were 1,096,000 businesses (UK 5,668,000) and 239,000 employers (UK 1,360,000). In the UK, in 2018, there were 1,059 businesses per 10,000 resident adults. In London there were 1,563 businesses per 10,000 residents, the highest number of business density in the UK.

Standard cataloguing guidelines for company names in the profile section have been used, but there will be occurrences when the name may not be strictly alphabetical. A certain licence was adopted where it was felt that strictly alphabetical could lead to improper cataloguing. Some company names have been shortened in the league tables for aesthetic reasons.

John D Blackburn
Editor

This page is intentionally left blank

Total Assets League Table

Company	Value
HSBC Holdings PLC	£1,797,029,101,568
Barclays PLC	£1,133,247,987,712
Barclays Bank PLC	£1,129,342,959,616
Lloyds Bank PLC	£823,029,989,376
HSBC Bank PLC	£818,867,994,624
London Stock Exchange Group PLC	£741,979,979,776
Goldman Sachs International	£682,632,085,504
P & O Dover (Holdings) Limited	£677,548,326,912
LCH Group Holdings Limited	£612,180,426,752
Bank of England Asset Purchase Facility Fund	£605,167,026,176
Legal & General Group PLC	£505,877,004,288
Standard Chartered PLC	£499,812,433,920
Prudential Public Limited Company	£493,940,998,144
J.P. Morgan Capital Holdings Limited	£482,353,741,824
J.P. Morgan Securities PLC	£450,722,070,528
Aviva PLC	£442,684,997,632
LCH Limited	£359,171,260,416
Morgan Stanley & Co. International PLC	£347,541,995,520
National Westminster Bank PLC	£340,843,003,904
Legal & General Assurance Pensions Mngmt	£315,446,099,968
Santander UK PLC	£314,764,984,320
Santander UK Group Holdings PLC	£314,760,003,584
Citigroup Global Markets Limited	£287,517,671,424
Merrill Lynch International	£280,847,286,272
Nomura International PLC	£203,614,633,984
BP P.L.C.	£200,722,268,160
The Prudential Assurance Company Limited	£198,531,006,464
OM Residual UK Limited	£181,832,007,680
Credit Suisse International	£177,752,440,832
Scottish Widows Limited	£147,307,003,904
Legal and General Assurance Society Ltd	£141,413,007,360
British American Tobacco P.L.C.	£141,037,993,984
Blackrock Life Limited	£111,044,689,920
P & O Overseas Holdings Limited	£99,695,878,144
Royal London Mutual Insurance Society Ltd	£99,318,996,992
Credit Suisse Securities (Europe) Limited	£88,207,794,176
BHP Group PLC	£86,321,102,848
British American Tobacco (2012) Limited	£80,639,148,032
Abbey National Treasury Services PLC	£80,088,997,888
Rio Tinto PLC	£69,487,517,696
Network Rail Limited	£68,860,002,304
Network Rail Infrastructure Limited	£67,720,998,912
Shell Treasury Centre Limited	£65,824,321,536
British American Tobacco (2009) Limited	£63,439,478,784
National Grid PLC	£58,787,000,320
MUFG Securities EMEA PLC	£57,118,375,936
British Telecommunications PLC	£56,277,999,616
Aviva International Insurance Limited	£56,064,999,424
Barclays Capital Securities Limited	£55,123,898,368
HSBC Asia Holdings B.V.	£51,143,344,128
UDV (SJ) Limited	£51,027,001,344
Sumitomo Mitsui Banking Corporation Europe Ltd	£46,017,851,392
B.A.T. International Finance P.L.C.	£46,015,000,576
Goldman Sachs Group UK Limited	£44,642,377,728
Grand Metropolitan Limited	£44,032,999,424
Shell Petroleum Company Limited (The)	£43,931,176,960
BT Group PLC	£42,759,000,064
Liberty Global PLC	£41,762,631,680
Rio Tinto International Holdings Limited	£41,757,265,920
Diageo Finance PLC	£41,414,000,640
Shell Treasury Dollar Company Limited	£41,182,162,944
TSB Banking Group PLC	£41,161,601,024
WPP Jubilee Limited	£40,654,798,848
RBC Europe Limited	£40,034,942,976
Anglo American PLC	£39,605,837,824
Goldman Sachs International Bank	£39,522,959,360
John Swire & Sons Limited	£38,939,000,832
Rothesay Holdco UK Limited	£38,373,998,592
Rothesay Life PLC	£38,265,999,360
Pension Insurance Corporation Group Limited	£37,405,999,104
Pension Insurance Corporation PLC	£37,387,001,856
TP ICAP PLC	£37,373,001,728

Company	Value
Societe Generale International Limited	£37,335,166,976
Managed Pension Funds Limited	£37,302,767,616
Transport Trading Limited	£36,950,999,040
AON Global Holdings Limited	£36,046,557,184
BG Energy Holdings Limited	£35,939,594,240
Morgan Stanley Investments (UK)	£35,662,630,912
Morgan Stanley International Limited	£34,516,549,632
Louisville Securities Limited	£34,172,938,240
Aviva Group Holdings Limited	£34,008,000,512
EDF Energy Holdings Limited	£33,383,999,488
Weston (2009) Limited	£33,144,428,544
British American Tobacco (1998) Limited	£32,152,942,592
B.A.T Industries P.L.C.	£32,012,267,520
Rolls-Royce PLC	£31,794,999,296
Rio Tinto Finance PLC	£31,661,467,648
HSBC Overseas Holdings (UK) Limited	£31,377,111,040
Coutts & Company	£31,217,485,824
Rolls-Royce Holdings PLC	£30,001,999,872
Diageo PLC	£29,714,999,296
Eskom Holdings SOC Limited	£28,049,713,152
ML UK Capital Holdings Limited	£28,004,702,208
Network Rail Infrastructure Finance PLC	£27,595,999,232
Diageo Holdings Limited	£27,000,000,512
Softbank Group Capital Limited	£26,728,237,056
Bank of Ireland (UK) PLC	£26,235,000,832
British-American Tobacco (Holdings) Limited	£25,918,191,616
MCD Europe Limited	£25,501,835,264
Superior Holdings Limited	£25,416,304,640
HSBC Asia Holdings (UK) Limited	£24,768,167,936
Anglo American Capital PLC	£24,489,158,656
Anglo American Investments (UK) Limited	£24,025,305,088
Xstrata Limited	£24,004,446,208
Shell Overseas Holdings Limited	£23,419,246,592
Liberty Global Broadband I Limited	£23,129,763,840
Rio Tinto South East Asia Limited	£23,109,890,048
HSBC Finance (Netherlands)	£23,077,050,368
BAE Systems PLC	£22,453,000,192
Vedanta Resources Limited	£22,416,928,768
J Sainsbury PLC	£22,001,000,448
Standard Chartered Holdings Limited	£21,421,469,696
Investec PLC	£20,611,751,936
RSA Insurance Group PLC	£20,600,000,512
London Underground Limited	£20,205,099,008
Investec Bank PLC	£20,100,284,416
Diageo Investment Holdings Limited	£20,069,316,608
National Grid Holdings One PLC	£19,753,000,960
AON PLC	£19,713,746,944
Euroclear Limited	£19,288,576,000
Lloyds Bank Covered Bonds LLP	£18,900,615,168
Scotiabank Europe PLC	£18,754,246,656
BT Group Investments Limited	£18,603,681,792
Ice Clear Europe Limited	£18,150,565,888
Abbey Covered Bonds LLP	£18,127,405,056
Visa International Holdings Limited	£17,259,573,248
EDF Energy (UK) Limited	£17,011,545,088
ICBC Standard Bank PLC	£16,998,289,408
LME Clear Limited	£16,732,098,560
Bestway (Holdings) Limited	£16,662,303,744
Johnson & Johnson Swiss Finance Co Ltd	£16,535,329,792
Metro Bank PLC	£16,355,354,624
Low Carbon Contracts Company Ltd	£16,010,862,592
National Grid Holdings Limited	£15,676,999,680
Mizuho International PLC	£15,517,299,712
BL Intermediate Holding Company Limited	£15,475,297,280
BGEO Group Limited	£15,168,668,672
Cable & Wireless Limited	£15,156,789,248
British United Provident Association Ltd	£15,057,699,840
HSBC Securities (Japan) Limited	£14,962,477,056
Weston Investment Company Limited	£14,743,345,152
Grand Metropolitan International Holdings Ltd	£14,670,177,280
Telenor (UK) Limited	£14,483,332,096
Land Securities Group PLC	£14,469,000,192

Company	Value
Bupa Finance PLC.	£14,465,399,808
Shell QGC Holdings Limited	£14,394,172,416
Alliance Boots Holdings Limited	£14,366,999,552
Wittington Investments Limited	£14,330,000,384
National Grid Electricity Transmission PLC	£14,156,000,256
National Grid (US) Investments 4 Limited	£14,143,995,904
MCD Global Franchising Limited	£14,030,362,624
Liberty Global Europe 2 Limited	£14,027,634,688
Anglo American Services (UK) Ltd.	£14,008,655,872
Shell U.K. Limited	£13,854,000,128
BHP Billiton Group Limited	£13,768,595,456
BG Overseas Holdings Limited	£13,725,650,944
UK Power Networks Holdings Limited	£13,513,100,288
Barclays CCP Funding LLP	£13,299,495,936
WBA Acquisitions UK Holdco 7 Limited	£13,294,699,520
National Grid (US) Holdings Limited	£13,182,314,496
British Land Company PLC	£13,180,000,256
Associated British Foods PLC	£13,112,999,936
E D & F Man Holdings Limited	£13,064,151,040
ConocoPhillips Holdings Limited	£12,829,800,448
Rio Tinto Australian Holdings Limited	£12,598,478,848
E D F Trading Limited	£12,557,363,200
AON US & International Holdings Limited	£12,531,481,600
Goal Acquisitions (Holdings) Limited	£12,403,410,944
Allied Domecq (Holdings) Limited	£12,382,331,904
Prudential Pensions Limited	£12,351,028,224
RELX PLC	£12,282,999,808
RELX Group PLC	£12,282,999,808
Dentsu Aegis Network Ltd.	£12,277,799,936
Blackrock Finco UK Ltd	£12,214,462,464
Mercury UK Holdco Limited	£12,177,212,416
RELX (Holdings) Limited	£12,146,595,840
Integrafin Holdings PLC	£12,129,095,680
Trinity Acquisition PLC	£12,031,638,528
McKesson UK Finance I Limited	£11,790,977,024
ConocoPhillips (U.K.) Limited	£11,660,699,648
Mobius Life Limited	£11,614,778,368
Mobius Life Holdings Limited	£11,614,446,592
SMBC Nikko Capital Markets Limited	£11,464,048,640
Crossrail Limited	£11,418,099,712
Shell Trading International Limited	£11,342,779,392
WPP US Investments Limited	£11,302,666,240
Superior Acquisitions Limited	£11,281,999,872
Sable Holding Limited	£11,236,747,264
National Grid Gas PLC	£11,230,000,128
National Grid (US) Partner 1 Limited	£11,225,111,552
Daiwa Capital Markets Europe Limited	£11,171,809,280
Beaubien UK Finance Limited	£11,166,404,608
Shell Energy Investments Limited	£11,099,362,304
Guardian Royal Exchange PLC	£11,036,999,680
TA I Limited	£11,025,833,984
International Game Technology PLC	£11,004,070,912
UDV (SJ) Holdings Limited	£10,873,380,864
Intu Properties PLC	£10,794,500,096
Integralife UK Limited	£10,780,856,320
Antofagasta PLC	£10,704,105,472
IHS Markit Group Holdings Limited	£10,650,873,856
Schroder Pension Management Limited	£10,618,825,728
J.P. Morgan Europe Limited	£10,488,334,336
Kingfisher PLC	£10,346,999,808
Priceline. Com International Limited	£10,280,983,552
Close Brothers Group PLC	£10,251,799,552
Beaubien Finance Limited	£10,190,167,040
Bank of New York Mellon (International) Ltd	£10,117,220,352
Marks and Spencer P.L.C.	£10,109,400,064
WPP Global	£10,027,397,120
Sainsbury's Supermarkets Ltd	£10,021,999,616
GS Funding Europe III Ltd	£9,989,707,776
Smith & Nephew USD Limited	£9,945,561,088
Hammerson PLC	£9,875,699,712
Smiths Group International Holdings Limited	£9,764,216,832
Willis Investment UK Holdings Limited	£9,730,360,320
Credit Suisse Investments (UK)	£9,725,370,368
Ripon Mortgages PLC	£9,675,343,872
Unilever U.K. Central Resources Limited	£9,612,857,344
QHG Investment LLP	£9,611,516,928
TechnipFMC Holdings Limited	£9,496,069,120
Diageo US Holdings	£9,411,539,968
Close Brothers Limited	£9,396,200,448
QHG Holding LLP	£9,363,457,024
BBA Overseas Holdings Limited	£9,264,089,088
WBA Financial Services Limited	£9,258,130,432
Lombard North Central PLC	£9,217,000,448
Orange Participations UK Limited	£9,191,870,464
Ensco Universal Limited	£9,130,490,880
Rio Tinto European Holdings Limited	£9,062,165,504
BL Retail Holding Company Limited	£9,051,018,240
SVF Holdings (UK) LLP	£9,019,357,184
Mastercard/Europay U.K. Limited	£8,975,220,736
Partnership Life Assurance Company Limited	£8,944,087,040
WBA Financial Limited	£8,908,972,032
Canary Wharf Group Investment Holdings PLC	£8,883,000,320
Sheldon Holdings Limited	£8,861,050,880
BT Holdings Limited	£8,844,659,712
UBS Asset Management Life Ltd	£8,780,994,560
WPP Sphinx Limited	£8,692,347,904
Allied Domecq Spirits & Wine Holdings Limited	£8,618,527,744
Diageo US Investments	£8,586,552,832
HSBC Asset Finance (UK) Limited	£8,576,399,872
Unilever US Investments Limited	£8,564,141,056
Schroders PLC	£8,501,499,904
Glencore Energy UK Ltd.	£8,398,569,472
Land Securities (Finance) Limited	£8,340,336,128
Willis Towers Watson UK Holdings Limited	£8,311,111,168
Motability Operations Group PLC	£8,308,700,160
Lake Acquisitions Limited	£8,182,000,128
Worldpay Group Limited	£8,142,600,192
Legal & General Insurance Holdings No.2 Limited	£8,114,500,096
Barclays Covered Bonds LLP	£8,069,573,120
Catlin Syndicate Limited	£8,039,814,144
GS Funding Europe V Limited	£8,021,595,136
Babcock Holdings Limited	£8,015,947,776
Markit Group Limited	£7,994,546,176
MMC Treasury Holdings (UK) Limited	£7,964,472,320
Gracechurch Card Programme Funding PLC	£7,949,421,056
Barclaycard Funding PLC	£7,949,395,968
Segro Public Limited Company	£7,936,300,032
Axa Insurance UK PLC	£7,932,000,256
3i Group PLC	£7,898,999,808
Pearson PLC	£7,888,000,000
Tullow Oil PLC	£7,858,975,232
EVRAZ PLC	£7,819,209,216
Sainsbury's Bank PLC	£7,765,000,192
Shell QGC Upstream 1 Limited	£7,750,784,512
Land Securities P L C	£7,710,180,864
International Power (Zebra) Limited	£7,682,992,640
Ensco PLC	£7,659,516,928
Tata Steel UK Holdings Limited	£7,656,999,936
Bupa Investments Overseas Limited	£7,654,800,384
Tata Steel Europe Limited	£7,632,000,000
Delta 3 (UK) Limited	£7,626,900,992
MMC Holdings (UK) Limited	£7,612,199,936
Marks and Spencer Group P.L.C.	£7,552,699,904
Motability Operations Limited	£7,522,599,936
Jefferies International Limited	£7,499,702,784
National Grid Gas Holdings Limited	£7,464,999,936
International Power Ltd.	£7,463,030,272
NatWest Covered Bonds LLP	£7,456,384,000
BG UK Holdings Limited	£7,408,128,512
United Finance Limited	£7,359,420,928
BG Group Limited	£7,313,903,616
Dixons Carphone PLC	£7,296,000,000
Annington Limited	£7,285,855,232
Royal Mail PLC	£7,256,999,936

KAZ Minerals Investments Limited £7,212,806,144
Allied Domecq Limited £7,146,972,160
MCD Investments Limited £7,135,839,232
BG Energy Capital PLC £7,090,577,920
Anglo American International Holdings Limited £7,084,498,432
Aether IOS Limited £7,008,297,984
Credit Suisse Investment Holdings (UK) £6,927,594,496
EDF Energy Lake Limited £6,896,000,000
Annington Property Limited £6,880,119,808
Chanel Limited £6,879,171,584
Cadogan Settled Estates Limited £6,875,872,768
Kingfisher Holdings Limited £6,848,625,152
Royal Mail Group Limited £6,848,000,000
American Express Services Europe Limited £6,830,564,864
Heineken (Orange) 1 Limited £6,764,737,024
Ashtead Group Public Limited Company £6,743,000,064
Grosvenor Group Limited £6,730,200,064
Pool Reinsurance Company Limited £6,717,011,968
Beazley Group Limited £6,711,261,696
Bombardier Transportation (Global Holding) UK £6,686,582,272
ENRC Finance Limited £6,643,820,032
Anglo American Holdings Limited £6,637,677,568
Cable & Wireless Communications Limited £6,591,843,840
Nomura Europe Holdings PLC £6,571,153,920
Thomas Cook Group PLC £6,568,999,936
Blackrock UK (Alpha) Limited £6,528,287,744
National Grid Thirty Five Limited £6,412,739,072
HSBC Private Bank (UK) Limited £6,404,240,896
Ensco Holdco Limited £6,377,086,464
Ice Europe Parent Limited £6,344,938,496
Mediclinic International PLC £6,343,000,064
DS Smith PLC £6,328,999,936
Babcock International Group PLC £6,320,999,936
Intermediate Capital Group PLC £6,306,400,256
Beazley Underwriting Limited £6,304,180,736
John Lewis PLC £6,281,399,808
John Lewis Partnership PLC £6,251,200,000
Cadogan Group Limited £6,228,353,024
Hawkins Funding Limited £6,178,557,440
Barclays Services Limited £6,021,302,784
Barclays Aldersgate Investments Limited £5,976,604,160
Nomura Bank International PLC. £5,967,992,320
Balderton Aviation Holdings Limited £5,952,214,016
BHP Billiton Holdings Limited £5,941,719,552
Itau BBA International PLC £5,941,576,192
Moody's International (UK) Limited £5,928,298,496
UBMG Holdings £5,912,000,000
Rio Tinto Western Holdings Limited £5,898,169,856
Enterprise Oil Limited £5,823,799,808
Cadogan Estates Limited £5,780,406,784
RELX (UK) Limited £5,768,024,064
Willis Group Limited £5,745,924,096
QBE UK Limited £5,711,200,768
Smith & Nephew PLC £5,709,930,496
National Grid Twenty Three Limited £5,707,447,808
AD Overseas (Europe) Limited £5,703,238,144
EMI Group Finance Limited £5,670,162,944
Informa Group Holdings Limited £5,655,541,760
Cummins EMEA Holdings Limited £5,645,561,856
Tudor Minstrel £5,633,908,224
Lex Autolease Limited £5,612,012,032
WPP LN Limited £5,582,645,760
Liberty Corporate Capital Limited £5,554,416,640
Great Lakes Reinsurance (UK) SE £5,518,255,104
BG International Limited £5,517,000,192
Ladbrokes Group Finance PLC £5,485,705,216
Gulf International Bank (UK) Limited £5,470,513,664
WBAD Holdings Limited £5,464,866,304
Annington Homes Limited £5,441,652,224
MS Amlin Corporate Member Limited £5,426,899,968
National Grid Twelve Limited £5,425,227,776
G4S PLC £5,421,000,192
QBE Corporate Limited £5,393,604,096
Smith & Nephew (Overseas) Limited £5,393,190,912
AON UK Holdings Intermediaries Limited £5,389,986,816
UBMG Limited £5,385,268,224
ABPA Holdings Limited £5,373,700,096
Morgan Stanley Bank International Limited £5,321,350,144
Willis Limited £5,299,796,992
Black Horse Limited £5,286,018,048
Essar Energy Limited £5,280,370,176
AIG Holdings Europe Limited £5,273,476,096
KAZ Minerals Finance PLC £5,248,210,944
SG Leasing (March) Limited £5,237,285,376
RBS Invoice Finance Limited £5,221,587,968
Permanent Master Issuer PLC £5,215,036,928
Places for People Group Limited £5,197,100,032
AON Delta UK Limited £5,196,163,072
Bunzl Public Limited Company £5,189,600,256
Coral Group Limited £5,180,214,784
Smiths Group PLC £5,173,000,192
The Shell Transport and Trading Company Limited £5,162,565,120
Permanent Funding (No.2) Limited £5,143,396,864
Danone Holdings (UK) £5,112,710,144
Pearson Dollar Finance Two Limited £5,098,252,800
CDC Group PLC £5,084,700,160
VTB Capital PLC £5,084,092,416
Viacom Camden Lock Limited £5,074,217,984
Intercontinentalexchange Holdings £5,069,827,584
Financial Services Compensation Scheme Ltd £5,067,403,776
EDF Energy Limited £5,056,000,000
ConocoPhillips Treasury Limited £5,049,383,936
Cater Allen Limited £5,046,842,880
Inmarsat Global Limited £5,042,091,520
Derwent London PLC £5,038,099,968
WBA International Limited £5,027,800,064
NNB Generation Company (HPC) Limited £5,010,699,776
Brit Limited £5,006,056,960
Eastern Power Networks PLC £4,975,200,256
Visa Europe Limited £4,939,637,760
Informa PLC £4,892,100,096
Balfour Beatty PLC £4,877,000,192
Inchcape PLC £4,876,199,936
London & Regional Group Holdings Limited £4,872,999,936
Lloyds Bank Asset Finance Limited £4,846,000,128
LS Property Finance Company Limited £4,837,088,256
Johnson Matthey PLC £4,817,999,872
Prudential (US Holdco 1) Limited £4,807,709,184
Channel 5 Broadcasting Limited £4,793,490,944
Bombardier Transportation (Investment) UK Ltd £4,793,449,472
DNB (UK) Limited £4,793,042,944
Betjeman Holdings JVCO Limited £4,766,799,872
Betjeman Holdings Limited £4,766,799,872
Lloyds Bank Pension ABCS (No 1) LLP £4,756,259,840
HSBC Latin America Holdings (UK) Limited £4,751,256,576
Towd Point Mortgage Funding 2016-Granite1 PLC £4,730,587,136
Babcock (UK) Holdings Limited £4,726,946,816
Canary Wharf Limited £4,721,550,848
Lanark Funding Limited £4,714,863,104
Pearson Overseas Holdings Limited £4,661,514,240
Barclays Long Island Limited £4,652,858,368
Aspen Insurance UK Limited £4,643,386,368
NHS Property Services Limited £4,613,486,080
Virgin Music Group £4,610,822,144
S & N Finland Limited £4,606,000,128
Wells Fargo Securities International Limited £4,601,052,160
Lanark Master Issuer PLC £4,600,932,864
Land Securities Capital Markets PLC £4,581,364,224
C. Hoare & Co. £4,573,112,832
BG North Sea Holdings Limited £4,567,176,192
HS1 Limited £4,560,699,904
WPP Group (UK) Ltd £4,558,473,216
Howard de Walden Estates Holdings Limited £4,556,026,880
NNB Holding Company (HPC) Limited £4,542,014,976

Company	Value	Company	Value
Brit UW Limited	£4,536,346,624	Inmarsat PLC	£3,735,969,792
Shell Treasury UK Limited	£4,529,800,192	Quadgas Investments Bidco Limited	£3,735,307,008
Howard de Walden Estates Limited	£4,521,849,856	Anglo American Diamond Holdings Limited	£3,719,691,520
WPP 2005 Limited	£4,518,000,128	Heineken (Orange) 2 Limited	£3,709,016,320
Equitas Holdings Limited	£4,502,000,128	Grosvenor Limited	£3,708,600,064
Equitas Limited	£4,470,000,128	Arcadia Group Limited	£3,708,280,064
Equitas Reinsurance Limited	£4,464,999,936	Capco Group Treasury Limited	£3,707,228,928
Huawei Global Finance (UK) Limited	£4,441,466,880	London Power Networks PLC	£3,695,699,968
The Children's Investment Fund Foundation (UK)	£4,433,676,288	Shell QGC Midstream 1 Limited	£3,673,281,536
MAN Investments Finance Limited	£4,433,313,792	Total Gas & Power Limited	£3,668,352,000
BNP Paribas Commodity Futures Limited	£4,430,562,816	G4S Corporate Services Limited	£3,667,202,048
Newfound Bay Limited	£4,430,040,064	Orange Brand Services Limited	£3,663,056,128
Noble Corporation PLC	£4,427,305,984	Walt Disney Company Limited (The)	£3,651,851,008
Capita PLC	£4,421,199,872	Blackrock UK 4 LLP	£3,647,077,120
DLJ UK Holding	£4,377,460,224	NatgridTW1 Limited	£3,642,069,248
Land Securities Portfolio Management Limited	£4,374,756,864	Fiat Chrysler UK LLP	£3,637,008,640
CE Acquisition 1 Limited	£4,373,700,096	Coral Eurobet Holdings Limited	£3,634,161,920
Finco Omaha Ltd	£4,367,323,648	Liberty UK and Europe Holdings Limited	£3,627,690,496
Axa UK PLC	£4,328,999,936	Enquest Heather Limited	£3,623,812,096
Tata Steel UK Limited	£4,328,000,000	Vesuvius Holdings Limited	£3,621,038,080
Hammerson International Holdings Limited	£4,325,985,792	Commerzbank Finance Limited	£3,614,480,896
Annington Subsidiary Holdings Limited	£4,281,799,936	Thistleclub Limited	£3,614,221,056
WPP 1178	£4,266,067,712	Threadneedle Pensions Limited	£3,595,792,896
General Dynamics Global Holdings Limited	£4,261,932,800	William Hill Organization Limited	£3,592,499,968
Liberty GR Holding Company Limited	£4,260,072,960	Eurasian Natural Resources Corporation Limited	£3,585,147,136
Liberty GR Acquisition Company Limited	£4,260,072,960	Fresnillo PLC	£3,569,088,512
Morgan Stanley Langton Limited	£4,237,922,816	Shell Holdings (U.K.) Limited	£3,559,500,032
ENI Investments PLC	£4,212,641,792	Canary Wharf Group PLC	£3,555,894,016
Mixhold Investments Limited	£4,207,941,888	Inmarsat Group Limited	£3,553,908,736
INTL FCStone Ltd	£4,185,970,944	Sheldon Euro Investments 2 Limited	£3,546,684,672
Hiscox Dedicated Corporate Member Limited.	£4,182,275,072	BBA Holdings Limited	£3,541,129,984
ITV Holdings Limited	£4,177,444,096	WPP Magic Limited	£3,531,806,976
QBE European Operations PLC	£4,151,699,968	British American Tobacco Western Europe Ltd	£3,531,469,824
Prudential Capital Public Limited Company	£4,136,003,072	AD Investment Holdings Limited	£3,508,251,136
Bunzl Finance Public Limited Company	£4,129,700,096	William Hill Investments Limited	£3,502,823,936
Hellen Holdings Limited	£4,127,237,120	Valero Energy Ltd	£3,494,400,000
Weybourne Group Limited	£4,112,000,000	Ladbrokes Investments Holdings Limited	£3,490,473,984
Walgreens Boots Alliance Limited	£4,097,999,872	Nadezhda Limited	£3,487,471,104
Penarth Master Issuer PLC	£4,092,088,064	HSBC Equipment Finance (UK) Limited	£3,480,096,000
KAZ Minerals PLC	£4,081,010,432	ADSW Investment Holdings Limited	£3,476,164,352
CWG Newco Limited	£4,079,311,616	Alpha Prema UK Limited	£3,473,385,728
ABF Overseas Limited	£4,073,630,976	DLJ UK Investment Holdings Limited	£3,448,834,304
Clydesdale Financial Services Limited	£4,045,036,032	Ivy Midco Limited	£3,444,499,968
Shaftesbury PLC	£4,022,400,000	Affordable Housing Finance PLC	£3,438,377,984
International Power Consolidated Holdings Ltd	£4,005,031,168	Diageo Great Britain Limited	£3,436,999,936
GM Global Treasury Centre Limited	£4,004,572,416	Clarion Treasury Limited	£3,435,504,128
Silverstone Master Issuer PLC	£4,002,244,096	WPP North Atlantic Limited	£3,416,218,112
Hinduja Automotive Limited	£3,992,753,920	Annington Funding PLC	£3,408,953,088
Anyslam Investments	£3,986,516,736	HNVR Holdco Limited	£3,398,304,256
F & C Investment Trust PLC	£3,970,356,992	LS London Holdings One Limited	£3,392,847,104
Capital & Counties Properties PLC	£3,961,200,128	Ivy Holdco Limited	£3,392,699,904
Worldpay (UK) Limited	£3,931,000,064	Chrysaor Limited	£3,390,341,888
GS Funding Europe	£3,915,727,104	CLEF Holdings Limited	£3,385,960,192
Phillips 66 Limited	£3,900,176,384	Deva Financing PLC	£3,379,876,096
Total UK Finance Limited	£3,864,538,880	HNVR Topco Limited	£3,376,453,120
Chivas Brothers (Holdings) Limited	£3,864,496,128	HNVR Midco Limited	£3,371,208,704
Aviva Employment Services Limited	£3,860,999,936	RIT Capital Partners PLC	£3,366,299,904
ABP Bonds UK Limited	£3,857,100,032	WPP Pearls Limited	£3,361,861,888
ConocoPhillips (U.K.) Sigma Limited	£3,841,976,064	Helix Acquisition Limited	£3,352,600,064
Prudential Corporation Holdings Limited	£3,821,992,960	ITV PLC	£3,351,000,064
ABP Subholdings UK Limited	£3,813,600,000	Veolia UK Limited	£3,350,782,976
Synlab BondCo PLC	£3,797,325,056	Lloyds Bank Financial Services (Holdings) Limited	£3,344,986,112
Enquest PLC	£3,795,458,304	Credit Suisse (UK) Limited	£3,334,735,872
UBM (UK) Limited	£3,795,151,872	Blackrock Group Limited	£3,321,967,104
Coral Limited	£3,794,546,944	Chivas Atlantic Holdings Limited	£3,319,808,768
Synlab Limited	£3,792,979,968	Brooke Bond South India Estates Limited	£3,314,214,912
Rowan Companies PLC	£3,778,735,872	Total E & P North Sea UK Limited	£3,306,544,384
Inmarsat Investments Limited	£3,773,860,608	Eaton Square Limited	£3,304,667,904
WPP Beans Limited	£3,770,113,024	Bombardier UK Holding Limited	£3,299,273,472
Kingfisher International Holdings Limited	£3,768,948,992	Pearson Education Investments Limited	£3,297,648,384
Silverstone Funding (No.1) Limited	£3,761,101,056	ENI Lasmo PLC	£3,297,575,936
Long Island Assets Limited	£3,746,043,904	G4S Finance Limited	£3,293,779,968

Company	Value
Vedanta Resources Holdings Limited	£3,290,351,360
Shop Direct Holdings Limited	£3,280,199,936
ContourGlobal PLC	£3,277,815,552
Will Hill Limited	£3,276,499,968
Moody's Group (Holdings) Unlimited	£3,251,386,112
Hammerson UK Properties PLC	£3,248,049,920
ICAP Securities Limited	£3,245,105,920
Allianz Europe Limited	£3,241,573,632
Gazprom Marketing & Trading Limited	£3,240,242,944
Equinor UK Limited	£3,237,627,904
Batif Dollar Limited	£3,229,317,888
Total E & P UK Limited	£3,227,180,032
Kingfisher France Limited	£3,224,738,048
South Eastern Power Networks PLC	£3,223,699,968
Telereal Securitisation PLC	£3,218,255,104
Telereal Securitisation Holdings Limited	£3,218,255,104
Lingfield 2014 I PLC	£3,214,054,912
BMI Healthcare Limited	£3,205,789,952
WPP Dutch Holdings Limited	£3,199,870,976
McKesson Global Procurement & Sourcing Limited	£3,192,374,272
Intu (SGS) Holdco Limited	£3,188,699,904
Mitsubishi Corporation Finance PLC	£3,181,845,504
QBE Holdings (EO) Limited	£3,181,549,056
Capita Holdings Limited	£3,175,472,896
IBM North Region Holdings	£3,164,149,248
ABP Acquisitions UK Limited	£3,150,000,128
BT SLE USD Limited	£3,143,931,136
BMI Group Holdings UK Limited	£3,141,145,856
MAN Group UK Limited	£3,134,629,888
Great Portland Estates P L C	£3,120,000,000
The Medical Protection Society Limited	£3,107,610,880
Pearl Group Holdings (No. 1) Limited	£3,104,300,032
Ladbrokes Coral Group Limited	£3,096,800,000
Shell Energy Europe Limited	£3,093,540,352
Blackrock UK A LLP	£3,085,823,232
J.P. Morgan Markets Limited	£3,067,082,496
Ricoh Europe Holdings PLC	£3,065,400,064
Birchgree Limited	£3,056,826,112
LHC4 (UK) Limited	£3,056,537,344
Sinochem International Oil (London) Co., Limited	£3,056,467,712
Liberty International Group Treasury Limited	£3,034,299,904
Lazari Investments Limited	£3,032,346,112
BHP Billiton Petroleum Great Britain Limited	£3,031,198,464
AON Overseas Holdings Limited	£3,026,712,832
AON UK Limited	£3,026,394,880
ABF Investments PLC	£3,022,000,128
Grand Metropolitan Capital Company Limited	£3,007,181,056
Barclays Covered Bond Funding LLP	£3,006,658,048
Accenture (UK) Limited	£3,000,485,120
Aegis Group Holdings Limited	£2,997,874,944
Australian Gas Networks UK Limited	£2,997,041,152
WPP Finance Co. Limited	£2,985,154,048
MAN Group PLC	£2,976,999,936
Land Securities Properties Limited	£2,973,893,888
Morgan Stanley Mallard Investments Limited	£2,963,236,608
Lloyds Bank Subsidiaries Limited	£2,963,000,064
Lattice Group Limited	£2,956,000,000
ABC International Bank PLC	£2,955,578,112
Chaucer Corporate Capital (No. 3) Limited	£2,955,379,968
BBA Aviation PLC	£2,954,776,320
British Arab Commercial Bank PLC	£2,952,856,064
QHG Trading LLP	£2,946,301,952
Starbucks EMEA Holdings Ltd	£2,939,917,056
ICAP Global Broking Holdings Limited	£2,928,928,000
ICICI Bank UK PLC	£2,925,615,616
FIA UK Funding Limited	£2,917,246,464
Europe Arab Bank PLC	£2,913,797,888
Diamond Offshore Limited	£2,892,802,304
NGG Finance PLC	£2,887,589,888
Tate & Lyle Investments Limited	£2,882,418,944
Duncan Funding 2016-1 PLC	£2,878,428,928
National Grid Seventeen Limited	£2,869,391,104
Debenhams Retail PLC	£2,868,999,936
MPI (London) Limited	£2,856,695,040
WPP Compete	£2,848,218,880
Waitrose Limited	£2,839,099,904
SBWW Investments Limited	£2,836,770,560
Coach Stores Limited	£2,835,601,920
Tronox International Finance LLP	£2,828,649,472
MMC International Treasury Centre Limited	£2,824,343,808
WBA Acquisitions UK Topco Limited	£2,824,169,984
Granada Media Limited	£2,820,999,936
Waymark Asset Investments Limited	£2,818,491,904
Aegon UK PLC	£2,817,200,128
SG Kleinwort Hambros Bank Limited	£2,812,984,064
Worldpay Finance PLC	£2,807,803,904
Apache North Sea Limited	£2,804,731,648
Charter Central Finance Limited	£2,799,216,896
Tronox UK Holdings Limited	£2,799,163,904
MAN Strategic Holdings Limited	£2,796,930,048
Atlassian (UK) Limited	£2,780,529,664
Ronin Trading Europe LLP	£2,767,977,472
LCR Finance PLC	£2,763,379,968
WBA Finance 2 Limited	£2,756,532,992
KAZ Minerals Copper Finance Limited	£2,754,049,024
Daily Mail and General Holdings Limited	£2,745,842,944
The Trafford Centre Limited	£2,740,600,064
Rathbone Brothers Public Limited Company	£2,738,850,048
EFG Private Bank Limited	£2,728,581,120
Eversholt Rail Limited	£2,725,143,040
DS Smith Holdings Limited	£2,721,798,912
FBN Bank (UK) Limited	£2,717,581,056
DMGB Limited	£2,717,094,656
G4S International Holdings Limited	£2,716,150,016
Rowan No.1 Limited	£2,715,499,520
Jardine Lloyd Thompson Group PLC	£2,708,623,872
MGM Advantage Holdings Limited	£2,701,523,968
MS Amlin PLC	£2,699,699,968
Marsh Limited	£2,699,399,936
CGI Group Holdings Europe Limited	£2,697,449,984
Moody's Group UK Ltd	£2,690,549,760
Football Association Premier League Limited	£2,690,025,984
DSG Retail Limited	£2,681,499,904
EDF Energy Customers Limited	£2,673,600,000
State Grid Europe Limited	£2,667,261,952
Jane Street Europe Limited	£2,662,740,992
CKI Gas Infrastructure Limited	£2,657,058,048
EDF Energy Group Holdings Limited	£2,655,899,904
AD Westport Limited	£2,654,544,896
Brass No.6 PLC	£2,649,346,048
Babcock Investments Limited	£2,647,686,912
Phillips 66 UK Holdings Limited	£2,641,619,968
International Finance Facility for Immunisation Co	£2,637,988,608
CWCB Finance II Limited	£2,632,645,376
Harrods Limited	£2,630,700,032
CEVA Group PLC	£2,627,032,576
BG Global Energy Limited	£2,625,355,008
Cable & Wireless International HQ Limited	£2,610,723,840
HSBC Asia Pacific Holdings (UK) Limited	£2,591,429,888
Novae Corporate Underwriting Limited	£2,585,100,032
Cascade Regional Holdings Limited	£2,583,450,880
ADIUK	£2,578,682,880
William Hill Holdings Limited	£2,575,843,072
Tate & Lyle Public Limited Company	£2,571,000,064
Elite Gemstones Properties Limited	£2,570,065,920
Chevron North Sea Limited	£2,568,000,000
Covent Garden Group Holdings Limited	£2,566,700,032
Dana Petroleum Limited	£2,566,415,104
Carlton Communications Limited	£2,558,000,128
ELQ Holdings (UK) Ltd	£2,553,020,672
Babcock Overseas Investments Limited	£2,537,028,096
Daejan Holdings PLC	£2,535,004,928
Orsted Power (UK) Limited	£2,526,134,272
Beta Centauri Limited	£2,525,975,040

Company	Value
Betelgeuse Limited	£2,525,975,040
Taveta Investments (No.2) Limited	£2,525,287,936
BNY Mellon Investment Management (Europe) Ltd	£2,520,593,920
Aegon Holdings (UK) Limited	£2,519,556,096
Cigna Walnut Holdings, Ltd.	£2,519,239,168
Eversholt Rail Leasing Limited	£2,518,537,984
Repsol Sinopec Resources UK Limited	£2,514,711,808
Associated British Ports Holdings Limited	£2,513,999,872
WPP Sparky Limited	£2,497,462,016
Blackrock UK 2 LLP	£2,496,730,880
Brookfield Global Subinvestments Limited	£2,496,358,144
Aequor Investments Limited	£2,494,335,744
BL Office (Non-City) Holding Company Limited	£2,492,558,080
RTA Holdco 4 Limited	£2,488,492,032
AON Benfield Limited	£2,485,278,976
Blackrock UK 3 LLP	£2,477,234,432
WPP Headline	£2,477,144,064
Universal Music Holdings Limited	£2,462,113,024
Nakano Asset Global Ltd.	£2,459,655,424
Hikma Pharmaceuticals Public Limited Company	£2,459,349,504
Omnicom Europe Limited	£2,455,342,848
Arches Holdings Limited	£2,442,524,672
Enquest Britain Limited	£2,441,362,432
Johnson Matthey Investments Limited	£2,440,176,128
ITV Services Limited	£2,437,592,064
Quilter PLC	£2,437,400,064
Delamare Cards Funding 1 Limited	£2,437,082,112
Clearstone Holdings (International) Ltd	£2,436,870,400
Atos IT Services UK Limited	£2,435,673,088
H.J. Heinz Company Limited	£2,435,106,048
Tripadvisor UK Holdco Limited	£2,431,966,208
Pearl Income Holdings UK Limited	£2,429,190,912
Cigna Chestnut Holdings, Ltd	£2,424,423,424
Intu Shopping Centres PLC	£2,409,600,000
BIIF Holdco Limited	£2,403,419,904
National Grid (US) Investments 2 Limited	£2,397,646,080
UK Holdings CAP (Commonwealth, Asia & Pacific)	£2,387,190,784
Langton Funding (No.1) Limited	£2,385,041,920
DB Group Services (UK) Limited	£2,371,000,064
Ensco Worldwide Investments Limited	£2,370,854,912
Rowan No.2 Limited	£2,370,541,568
Starbucks International (Holdings) Ltd	£2,365,995,008
Investec 1 Limited	£2,365,828,096
Delamare Cards MTN Issuer PLC	£2,363,154,944
William Hill PLC	£2,361,999,872
Colfax UK Holdings Ltd	£2,358,837,760
Fall Ridge Partners LLP	£2,357,430,016
Axa Insurance PLC	£2,357,380,096
Bunzl American Holdings (No.1) Limited	£2,356,565,504
Schroder Financial Services Limited	£2,348,472,064
ASOS Intermediate Holdings Limited	£2,346,115,072
Workspace Group PLC	£2,339,200,000
Schroder & Co. Limited	£2,332,116,992
Alpha Partners Leasing Limited	£2,331,942,656
Proxima GR Properties Limited	£2,330,184,960
EYGS LLP	£2,327,863,808
BL Residual Holding Company Limited	£2,325,138,176
Molineux RMBS 2016-1 PLC	£2,322,417,920
Veolia Environmental Services (UK) PLC	£2,317,003,008
Fern Trading Limited	£2,303,143,936
SHEL Holdings Europe Limited	£2,301,700,096
Legal & General Pensions Limited	£2,300,456,960
Ladbroke & Co., Limited	£2,293,805,056
Rolls-Royce Group PLC	£2,285,015,040
DLJ International Group Limited	£2,283,652,608
Diageo Overseas Holdings Limited	£2,283,339,008
National Bank of Kuwait (International) PLC	£2,278,753,280
Noble Holding Land Support Limited	£2,274,169,088
Camelot UK Bidco Limited	£2,271,803,392
Markel Capital Limited	£2,269,119,744
Tulip UK Holdings (No.3) Limited	£2,267,000,064
DS Smith International Limited	£2,255,659,008
Sainsbury Propco A Limited	£2,255,000,064
The Great Rolling Stock Company Limited	£2,251,412,992
Global Prime Partners Ltd	£2,247,709,184
Witan Investment Trust PLC	£2,230,278,912
Pentland Group PLC	£2,229,199,872
Burberry Group PLC	£2,223,000,064
EVRAZ North America PLC	£2,222,204,928
Rail for London Limited	£2,221,100,032
Standard Chartered NEA Limited	£2,220,448,256
Dorchester Group Limited	£2,217,145,088
Marsh & McLennan Companies UK Limited	£2,214,318,592
The Mercantile Investment Trust PLC	£2,210,979,072
Blackrock Investment Management (UK) Limited	£2,208,962,048
AON UK Group Limited	£2,189,932,032
WPP Finance 2010	£2,185,954,816
Benton Finance Limited	£2,185,212,672
Unilever UK & CN Holdings Limited	£2,183,439,872
Heineken (Orange) 3 Limited	£2,182,822,400
Granada Group Limited	£2,180,000,000
Mercantile Leasing Company (No.132) Limited	£2,178,737,920
G4S International Finance PLC	£2,175,000,064
South32 SA Investments Limited	£2,167,046,144
Relative Value Investments UK LLLP	£2,166,709,248
JPMorgan Life Limited	£2,164,753,920
Aldermanbury Investments Limited	£2,164,326,400
Balfour Beatty Investment Holdings Limited	£2,161,743,104
Vosper Thornycroft (UK) Limited	£2,157,466,112
CLS Holdings PLC	£2,157,400,064
BG Karachaganak Limited	£2,151,838,720
Dixons Carphone Holdings Limited	£2,149,748,992
Tokio Marine Underwriting Limited	£2,147,926,016
Labcorp UK Holdings, Ltd.	£2,146,331,648
Bazalgette Tunnel Limited	£2,146,200,064
Bazalgette Equity Limited	£2,146,099,968
Bazalgette Holdings Limited	£2,146,099,968
Granada Limited	£2,142,000,000
JX Nippon Exploration and Production (U.K.) Ltd	£2,139,213,568
BCP IV UK Fuel Holdings III Limited	£2,137,484,160
BMI Healthcare Holdings Limited	£2,136,446,976
Intu (SGS) Finco Limited	£2,133,100,032
UPP Group Holdings Limited	£2,126,075,008
Hikma Acquisitions (UK) Limited	£2,125,187,968
EMI Group Worldwide	£2,121,426,944
Grosvenor Estate Holdings	£2,115,403,008
Legal & General Finance PLC	£2,106,899,968
WPP Finance 2013	£2,104,328,704
Balfour Beatty Group Limited	£2,104,000,000
NEX International Limited	£2,103,000,064
Diageo Eire Finance & Co	£2,092,270,720
Tate & Lyle International Finance PLC	£2,089,197,056
Axa Equity & Law Public Limited Company	£2,087,686,016
Bupa Insurance Limited	£2,076,237,056
Hitachi Rail Europe Limited	£2,075,116,032
Harrods Group (Holding) Limited	£2,073,299,968
Vesuvius PLC	£2,072,400,000
Inchcape International Holdings Limited	£2,070,939,008
Logica Limited	£2,069,613,056
Universal Studios Limited	£2,069,363,328
Beta Holdings Limited	£2,063,187,968
Income Contingent Student Loans 1 (2002-2006)	£2,056,414,976
NEX Group Holdings Limited	£2,054,000,000
Element Materials Technology Limited	£2,053,361,920
Element Materials Technology Group Limited	£2,053,285,248
Intertek Group PLC	£2,052,400,000
Universal Music Operations Limited	£2,048,248,064
Daily Mail and General Trust P L C	£2,048,199,936
TD Bank Europe Limited	£2,047,341,952
Atos IT Services Limited	£2,046,624,000
Cast Limited	£2,039,469,056
Union Property Holdings (London) Limited	£2,027,437,568
Bunzl Overseas Holdings (No. 2) Limited	£2,024,051,584
D B Investments (GB) Limited	£2,023,958,016

Company	Value
Ahli United Bank (UK) PLC	£2,021,229,312
Hawksmoor Mortgages 2016-1 PLC	£2,008,933,376
Starbucks EMEA Ltd	£2,004,648,576
Constantin Investment Limited	£1,999,371,264
Punch Partnerships (PTL) Limited	£1,999,080,960
Eversholt Funding PLC	£1,995,033,984
Berkshire Hathaway International Insurance Ltd	£1,995,023,744
News Corp UK & Ireland Limited	£1,985,889,024
DLJ Group	£1,985,705,216
Babcock Support Services (Investments) Limited	£1,983,122,944
Macquarie Aerospace Finance UK Limited	£1,974,771,200
Legal & General Insurance Holdings Limited	£1,973,299,968
Lloyds Development Capital (Holdings) Limited	£1,972,082,944
Priory Group UK 1 Limited	£1,970,803,968
Primark Stores Limited	£1,969,549,952
Edgbaston RMBS 2010-1 PLC	£1,968,989,056
Debenhams PLC	£1,967,900,032
Kiwara UK Limited	£1,966,322,304
London Wall Outsourcing Limited	£1,964,824,960
Pacific Life RE Holdings Limited	£1,961,270,016
ELQ Investors II Ltd	£1,957,196,160
Dana Petroleum (E & P) Limited	£1,956,797,952
MMC UK Group Limited	£1,955,831,040
Sony Interactive Entertainment Europe Limited	£1,953,571,840
SCOR Underwriting Limited	£1,947,105,024
QBE RE (Europe) Limited	£1,946,952,832
Michael Kors (UK) Intermediate Ltd.	£1,945,752,320
MSC Property Intermediate Holdings Limited	£1,941,668,096
Ashtead Financing Limited	£1,940,051,584
Regent's Place Holding Company Limited	£1,936,865,536
Amazon UK Services Ltd.	£1,930,919,040
British American Tobacco (Investments) Limited	£1,930,866,944
Babcock Management Limited	£1,926,109,952
BT Fifty-One	£1,923,838,080
Flectat Limited	£1,921,375,488
Brass No.5 PLC	£1,920,653,056
White City Acquisitions Limited	£1,915,339,008
Pacific Life RE Limited	£1,913,273,984
Cars Alliance UK 2015 Limited	£1,912,724,096
Race Bank Wind Farm Limited	£1,909,658,112
Taqa Bratani Limited	£1,909,399,680
Derwent Valley Limited	£1,906,819,328
Charter Limited	£1,905,538,944
Atlassian Corporation PLC	£1,903,520,512
Santander Asset Finance PLC	£1,895,448,960
Songbird Finance Limited	£1,895,356,800
Pontegadea UK Ltd	£1,895,106,944
Colt Technology Services Group Limited	£1,890,084,224
Ladbrokes Betting & Gaming Limited	£1,889,208,064
Harben Finance 2017-1 PLC	£1,886,124,672
HGI Group Limited	£1,884,700,032
Informa Group Limited	£1,880,099,968
Chubb Capital I Limited	£1,877,490,944
Cynergy Bank Limited	£1,877,117,952
Secure Income REIT PLC	£1,872,829,952
Caledonia Investments PLC	£1,872,099,968
Greenergy Fuels Holdings Limited	£1,870,023,040
Livanova PLC	£1,868,007,552
Centro Holdings (UK) Limited	£1,867,877,760
The Carphone Warehouse Limited	£1,865,100,032
Magical Cruise Company, Limited	£1,863,322,240
NEX Markets Limited	£1,857,302,016
E D & F Man Treasury Management PLC	£1,853,746,048
Arbuthnot Banking Group PLC	£1,853,232,000
General Healthcare Holdings (2) Limited	£1,853,044,992
Principal Financial Services I (UK) LLP	£1,841,471,744
ICBC (London) PLC	£1,831,441,792
Londonmetric Property PLC	£1,826,616,064
LMS Finance Limited	£1,825,535,744
State Street International Holdings UK Limited	£1,824,482,432
Bupa Investments Limited	£1,824,108,032
Trillium Holdings Limited	£1,823,208,960
Talbot 2002 Underwriting Capital Ltd	£1,820,064,768
ITW UK Finance Limited	£1,816,972,800
DB UK Bank Limited	£1,816,420,992
Ashtead Holdings Public Limited Company	£1,810,540,032
Mitsui Fudosan (U.K.) Ltd.	£1,809,905,280
RELX Overseas Holdings Limited	£1,806,772,992
Al Rayan Bank PLC	£1,806,307,968
DSG International Holdings Limited	£1,805,773,952
Algeco Global Finance PLC	£1,802,126,208
Endell Properties Limited	£1,801,531,776
Methane Services Limited	£1,795,226,112
Holmes Master Issuer PLC	£1,794,055,040
Broadgate Financing PLC	£1,783,904,768
Arbuthnot Latham & Co., Limited	£1,783,675,008
Agility Trains West (Holdings) Limited	£1,782,455,040
Agility Trains West Limited	£1,782,455,040
Dixons Retail Group Limited	£1,782,000,000
MMC International Limited	£1,781,133,568
American Express Payment Services Limited	£1,776,193,664
L-3 Global Holding UK Ltd	£1,772,999,296
Inchcape Finance PLC	£1,770,499,968
London Merchant Securities Limited	£1,766,908,160
HKEX Investment (UK) Limited	£1,764,817,792
EMI Group Worldwide Holdings Limited	£1,764,120,064
Monks Investment Trust PLC	£1,762,496,000
Burberry Limited	£1,761,968,000
Chiquita Holdings Limited	£1,760,657,024
El Ventures Limited	£1,760,199,936
Smith & Nephew ARTC Limited	£1,757,681,536
Bank of Montreal Capital Markets (Holdings) Ltd	£1,756,530,048
Omnicom Finance Limited	£1,754,459,008
Walney Extension Limited	£1,752,125,696
Real Estate Participation Services Limited	£1,747,502,336
Shell EP Offshore Ventures Limited	£1,743,800,064
Emerson USD Finance Company Limited	£1,740,362,240
Unilever Overseas Holdings Limited	£1,739,591,936
BL Office Holding Company Limited	£1,737,938,304
Spire Healthcare Group PLC	£1,734,099,968
AIB UK Loan Management Limited	£1,732,000,000
Spire Healthcare Holdings 3 Limited	£1,731,436,032
Tanqueray Gordon and Company Limited	£1,730,615,040
Sagittarius International Limited	£1,728,063,360
Ascential Financing Limited	£1,725,799,936
India Infrastructure Finance Company (UK) Limited	£1,724,697,088
International Nuclear Investment Limited	£1,723,886,080
S & N Angel Investments Ltd.	£1,721,977,856
Prudential Capital Holding Company Limited	£1,720,482,944
M & G Group Limited	£1,720,452,992
Land Securities Property Holdings Limited	£1,720,057,984
Ascential Group Limited	£1,717,900,032
Holmes Funding Limited	£1,711,021,952
Nostrum Oil & Gas PLC	£1,706,296,064
Leathbond Limited	£1,706,120,960
Transport for London Finance Limited	£1,702,926,976
Harrods (UK) Limited	£1,698,200,064
SSP Financing Limited	£1,697,709,056
Hikma UK Limited	£1,696,593,792
Paramount Pictures International Limited	£1,692,887,680
Diageo Finance US Limited	£1,691,309,056
London Stock Exchange Group Holdings (Italy)	£1,690,054,400
Intu Lakeside Limited	£1,685,600,000
BMO Capital Markets Limited	£1,682,835,968
Shire Global Finance	£1,682,692,608
BBP Bandenia PLC	£1,680,799,488
Allied Domecq Spirits & Wine Limited	£1,680,000,000
Duncan Funding 2015-1 PLC	£1,678,760,960
Reach Shared Services Limited	£1,677,395,968
H.J. Heinz Manufacturing UK Limited	£1,670,899,968
EMI Group (Newco) Limited	£1,670,873,984
Hikma Holdings (UK) Limited	£1,670,646,784
Perenco UK Limited	£1,670,051,968
Pips Asset Investments Limited	£1,668,941,952

Company	Value
Pricewaterhousecoopers LLP	£1,662,000,000
IP Group PLC	£1,660,499,968
Portswood Investments Limited	£1,660,224,000
OTE PLC	£1,656,523,392
The City of London Investment Trust PLC	£1,652,814,976
ERM Worldwide Group Limited	£1,651,917,440
EMI Group Limited	£1,650,844,032
Atlassian (Australia) Limited	£1,648,656,000
Greenergy Fuels Limited	£1,647,969,024
HSBC Global Services (China) Holdings Limited	£1,645,356,672
Smith & Williamson Holdings Limited	£1,645,234,048
Total Holdings UK Limited	£1,644,979,968
Ardonagh Midco 3 PLC	£1,642,659,968
Omnicom Europe Subholdings Limited	£1,640,310,656
CW Lending II Limited	£1,639,175,168
Grosvenor West End Properties	£1,635,565,952
Epihiro PLC	£1,631,506,432
Paysafe Holdings UK Limited	£1,631,395,328
Anglo American Prefco Limited	£1,630,970,240
Libra International Limited	£1,624,870,784
Canary Wharf Finance II PLC	£1,623,979,776
Brightsphere UK, Ltd.	£1,621,716,608
Mastercard Europe Services Limited	£1,621,655,424
Deutsche Holdings No.3 Limited	£1,619,823,360
Westminster Acquisition Limited	£1,618,704,000
Aberdeen Asset Management Life and Pensions	£1,617,616,000
V Acquisition Limited	£1,615,800,960
G4S Investment London Limited	£1,613,858,944
Zeus Land Investments Limited	£1,610,893,952
McDonald's Restaurants Limited	£1,605,803,008
Polar Capital Technology Trust PLC	£1,604,515,968
AIG Life Limited	£1,600,385,024
British American Tobacco International Hldgs (UK)	£1,599,456,000
Interoute Communications Limited	£1,594,560,768
Liberty Global Incorporated Limited	£1,592,778,624
Southern Pacific Mortgage Limited	£1,590,978,944
Angel Trains Limited	£1,590,300,032
Macquarie Lending & Investment Partners LLP	£1,590,259,840
Markel International Insurance Company Limited	£1,588,570,368
Broadgate (Funding) 2005 Limited	£1,583,732,480
Vertex Pharmaceuticals (Europe) Limited	£1,581,478,144
Matthey Holdings Limited	£1,580,434,048
Capita Business Services Ltd	£1,579,714,048
Citadel Securities (Europe) Limited	£1,577,947,520
Salesforce.Com EMEA Limited	£1,577,490,176
The Medical Defence Union Limited	£1,575,585,024
Infund LLP	£1,572,931,456
Polyus Finance PLC	£1,568,725,376
Southbank Media Ltd	£1,567,190,912
ABF US Holdings Limited	£1,563,617,024
Elementis Holdings Limited	£1,562,000,000
PAH Gas Infrastructure Limited	£1,558,784,000
Bank Leumi (U.K.) P.L.C.	£1,558,582,016
Pearl Income Investments UK Limited	£1,557,207,808
Ricoh Europe Finance Limited	£1,556,859,392
Atos UK IT Holdings Limited	£1,556,670,976
Gates Finance Limited	£1,553,783,680
Jane Street Financial Limited	£1,553,337,472
IBM Global Asset Management Limited	£1,550,872,192
Howden Joinery Limited	£1,548,800,000
Synlab Unsecured BondCo PLC	£1,546,060,544
Talktalk Telecom Group PLC	£1,542,000,000
KPMG LLP	£1,542,000,000
Bank of China (UK) Limited	£1,539,220,992
Shell Tunisia Upstream Limited	£1,539,091,072
CB/TCC Global Holdings Limited	£1,537,160,960
Colfax UK Finance Ltd	£1,531,834,880
Universal Music (UK) Holdings Limited	£1,529,686,016
XL Catlin Insurance Company UK Limited	£1,525,981,056
Bertelsmann UK Limited	£1,523,984,000
AB Acquisitions FX Inter Limited	£1,520,721,024
Greene King Finance Parent Limited	£1,519,115,008
Greene King Finance PLC	£1,519,115,008
Coutts Finance Co.	£1,517,250,944
Primary Health Properties PLC	£1,514,000,000
Barclays Mercantile Business Finance Limited	£1,511,600,000
Ship Midco Limited	£1,511,101,952
Discovery Communications Europe Limited	£1,510,935,040
Informa US Holdings Limited	£1,509,158,016
ELQ Investors VIII Ltd	£1,508,769,408
Hays PLC	£1,508,700,032
Renaissancere Corporate Capital (UK) Limited	£1,508,586,240
Ace European Holdings Limited	£1,501,934,976
HSBC Life (UK) Limited	£1,498,814,976
RVT CLO Investments LLP	£1,497,573,760
National Grid Twenty-Five Limited	£1,497,356,416
Newgate Funding PLC	£1,494,880,000
Sam UK Investment Holdings Limited	£1,494,655,744
Spire Healthcare Finance Limited	£1,493,936,000
Whitewell UK Investments 1 Limited	£1,492,259,968
BNY Mellon International Asset Management Group	£1,491,335,040
Sony Music Entertainment International Limited	£1,488,807,040
Balfour Beatty Overseas Investments Limited	£1,483,891,968
Post Office Limited	£1,480,999,936
CWBC Properties (BP1) Limited	£1,476,261,760
Newday Funding Transferor Ltd	£1,476,162,944
Antares Underwriting Limited	£1,472,182,016
National Bank of Egypt (UK) Limited	£1,471,021,440
Charter Consolidated Holdings Limited	£1,470,809,984
Petrochina International (London) Co., Limited	£1,470,448,128
Dudgeon Offshore Wind Limited	£1,469,698,944
Docklands Light Railway Limited	£1,465,100,032
Barclays Principal Investments Limited	£1,462,649,984
Bitstamp Limited	£1,462,374,528
National Power International Holdings	£1,461,725,568
WPP Spike Limited	£1,461,515,008
York UK Holdco International Limited	£1,457,842,560
O & H Holdings Limited	£1,454,804,992
Canary Wharf Holdings Limited	£1,453,844,992
J.P. Morgan Limited	£1,451,663,232
Ebay KTA (UK) Ltd	£1,450,932,352
BBA Aviation Finance	£1,449,742,848
Ophir Energy PLC	£1,448,106,880
Henderson Administration Limited	£1,448,064,000
MC Resource Development Ltd.	£1,447,123,456
SSP Group PLC	£1,443,800,064
Global Switch Estates 2 Limited	£1,442,770,048
Babcock Aviation Services (Holdings) Limited	£1,442,179,968
Shire Biopharmaceuticals Holdings	£1,441,087,232
Rolls-Royce & Partners Finance Limited	£1,439,967,616
Lazari Properties 1 Limited	£1,438,514,816
Axa PPP Healthcare Limited	£1,437,799,936
RRPF Engine Leasing Limited	£1,437,367,168
Time Warner London Limited	£1,437,228,032
Equity Release Holdings Limited	£1,436,112,000
ITW UK Finance Gamma Limited	£1,435,109,504
BL Leisure and Industrial Holding Co Ltd	£1,433,863,296
DNI Foreign Holdings Limited	£1,433,177,216
Justerini & Brooks,Limited	£1,432,017,024
Vue International Bidco PLC	£1,431,779,968
Itochu Treasury Centre Europe PLC	£1,431,687,936
Valero Holdco UK Ltd	£1,428,976,000
Softbank Group Capital Europe Limited	£1,428,270,976
P2P Global Investments PLC	£1,427,292,672
IPP Bond Limited	£1,424,407,808
Bestway Securities Limited	£1,424,306,048
SFP Holdings Limited	£1,423,500,032
Selfridges Properties Limited	£1,423,299,968
SCOR UK Company Limited	£1,422,754,048
Slough Trading Estate Limited	£1,421,524,992
ITW UK Finance Beta Limited	£1,419,807,232
Leggett & Platt UK Holdings LLP	£1,418,586,880
Black Horse Finance Holdings Limited	£1,418,000,000
BG Delta Limited	£1,417,797,632

Company	Value
Langton Securities (2008-1) PLC.	£1,417,760,000
Aegis Triton Limited	£1,415,796,992
Taveta Investments Limited	£1,415,104,000
Grosvenor Overseas Holdings Limited	£1,414,027,008
BG General Holdings Limited	£1,413,924,992
Greencoat UK Wind PLC	£1,413,127,936
Greencoat UK Wind Holdco Limited	£1,412,962,944
Pearson Funding Five PLC	£1,407,681,024
William Pears Group Limited	£1,404,701,056
Henderson Group Holdings Asset Management	£1,403,885,056
London and Regional Properties Limited	£1,403,138,560
Fujitsu Services Holdings PLC	£1,402,700,032
HCC International Insurance Company PLC	£1,400,646,272
Misys International Limited	£1,395,958,784
DTZ UK Guarantor Limited	£1,395,609,088
Sony Entertainment Holdings Europe Limited	£1,391,933,952
Newriver REIT PLC	£1,390,360,960
Workspace 14 Limited	£1,389,096,064
Hyperion Insurance Group Limited	£1,388,800,000
Nixes Six PLC	£1,387,321,088
Aegis International Limited	£1,385,091,968
Keller Group PLC	£1,384,999,936
SNC Securities Limited	£1,384,677,760
Eagle Financial and Leasing Services (UK) Ltd	£1,380,973,952
Vivo Energy PLC	£1,378,502,144
Argo Underwriting Agency Limited	£1,377,100,032
Nomura European Investment Limited	£1,376,929,024
Pearson Dollar Finance PLC	£1,375,620,352
L51N Limited	£1,375,600,000
Enterprise Oil Middle East Limited	£1,374,418,944
HCA International Limited	£1,373,726,976
Liberty Corporate Capital (Two) Ltd	£1,371,415,040
Pontsarn Investments Limited	£1,370,111,872
TR Property Investment Trust PLC	£1,366,977,024
Hiscox Insurance Company Limited	£1,366,727,040
Relative Value Trading Limited	£1,365,087,872
Unilever UK Group Limited	£1,364,880,000
John Laing Investments Limited	£1,363,699,968
CTRL Section 1 Finance PLC	£1,363,539,968
BT Fifty-Three Limited	£1,363,487,104
HP Foods Limited	£1,363,459,968
Goldman Sachs International Investments Limited	£1,363,080,576
BG Atlantic Finance Limited	£1,361,799,936
Merrill Lynch UK Finance	£1,358,928,000
John Laing Group PLC	£1,357,100,032
Acacia Mining PLC	£1,356,600,320
Electricinvest Acquisitions Limited	£1,351,200,000
VUR Investment (UK) Limited	£1,344,334,976
Reach PLC	£1,342,899,968
PhillipCapital UK Ltd	£1,342,800,128
Fairhold Finance Limited	£1,342,543,104
MDU Investments Limited	£1,342,523,008
BT SLE Euro Limited	£1,341,618,816
Rio Tinto Finance (USA) PLC	£1,341,607,168
King & Shaxson Limited	£1,341,111,040
BGF Group PLC	£1,339,766,016
Business Growth Fund Limited	£1,338,998,016
Australian Gas Networks UK 2 Limited	£1,337,191,936
Barfair Limited	£1,336,989,952
SIG PLC	£1,335,800,064
CGI IT UK Limited	£1,335,243,008
GBG International Holding Company Limited	£1,332,350,976
Harrods Holdings Limited	£1,330,499,968
Barbican Corporate Member Limited	£1,330,300,032
Travelex Holdings Limited	£1,329,500,032
Sheldon Sterling Investments Limited	£1,328,867,968
Virgin Management Limited	£1,328,526,976
ENI UK Holding PLC	£1,328,149,120
Multiplex Global Limited	£1,327,984,896
Warwick Finance Residential Mortgages No Two	£1,325,796,992
Assured Guaranty (Europe) PLC	£1,318,460,032
Globalgrange Limited	£1,316,551,040
Recruit Global Treasury Services Ltd	£1,313,774,464
Cummins Ltd.	£1,313,540,992
East Village London LLP	£1,312,467,968
QDD Athletes Village UK Limited	£1,312,434,944
Normanclose 2 LLP	£1,311,547,904
Worldwide Healthcare Trust PLC	£1,311,150,976
Gosforth Funding 2016-1 PLC	£1,309,976,064
JIB Group Limited	£1,309,075,968
Walney Extension Holdings Limited	£1,308,828,032
Deutsche Holdings Limited	£1,308,632,320
City Football Group Limited	£1,308,027,008
Sirius International UK Holdings Ltd	£1,306,228,608
Ark Corporate Member Limited	£1,305,682,816
LYB Treasury Services Ltd.	£1,301,045,376
Chepstow Blue PLC	£1,300,295,936
Katanalotika PLC	£1,299,683,840
Hochschild Mining Holdings Limited	£1,292,860,544
QVC UK Holdings Limited	£1,291,952,000
Natgrid One Limited	£1,286,078,976
AD Atlantic Finance Limited	£1,283,705,600
Baker Hughes Limited	£1,281,250,944
Shell Clair UK Limited	£1,279,323,008
Top Shop/Top Man Limited	£1,279,303,936
Sainsbury Propco B Limited	£1,278,000,000
Technip UK Limited	£1,277,932,032
Aviva Investors Pensions Limited	£1,276,999,936
Savills PLC	£1,270,599,936
Burbo Extension Ltd	£1,270,321,664
Mitsubishi Estate London Limited	£1,269,094,016
Transre London Limited	£1,267,958,016
A.S. Watson (Health & Beauty UK) Limited	£1,267,885,056
Precis (1814) Limited	£1,267,864,960
Fujitsu Services Limited	£1,267,299,968
Ravenseft Properties Limited	£1,267,293,952
Berrington UK	£1,264,963,968
Unilever U.K. Holdings Limited	£1,262,872,960
Camelot UK Holdco Limited	£1,261,558,656
Camelot UK Top Holdco Limited	£1,261,558,528
Newday Funding Loan Note Issuer Ltd	£1,256,936,960
Travelers Insurance Company Limited	£1,256,849,024
Ascot Underwriting Group Limited	£1,255,400,192
Faraday Capital Limited	£1,255,332,992
Columbia Pictures Corporation Limited	£1,254,567,936
CGI Corporate Holdings Limited	£1,254,360,064
Morgan Sindall Group PLC	£1,252,800,000
QH Participations Limited	£1,249,634,944
CBRE Holdings Limited	£1,247,320,320
Tesnik Holdings Limited	£1,246,130,688
Nando's Group Holdings Limited	£1,245,709,056
Coral Racing Limited	£1,241,900,032
Upfield Spreads UK Limited	£1,241,015,040
Cubico Sustainable Investments Limited	£1,240,590,464
BNP Paribas U.K. Holdings Limited	£1,239,750,016
UK Power Networks Services (South East) Ltd	£1,238,899,968
Interoute Communications Holdings Limited	£1,238,397,184
Bakkavor Finance (2) Limited	£1,233,699,968
Allianz Renewable Energy Partners IV Limited	£1,233,590,912
Sainsbury's Intermediate Holdings Limited	£1,233,517,056
Bakkavor Group PLC	£1,233,100,032
Ventient Energy Limited	£1,232,311,040
Priory Group No. 3 Limited	£1,231,181,056
Canada Square Investments Limited	£1,229,089,024
McKesson UK Finance II Limited	£1,228,445,312
R.B. Bishopsgate Investments Limited	£1,228,057,984
Bein IP Limited	£1,227,884,032
Britannia Steam Ship Insurance Association	£1,227,281,664
Bazalgette Ventures Limited	£1,224,099,968
Ladbroke US Investments Limited	£1,223,794,048
Synlab Holdco Limited	£1,222,679,936
Lloyd's Register Foundation	£1,222,445,056
Auto ABS UK Loans PLC	£1,221,537,280
China Construction Bank (London) Limited	£1,220,489,088

Company	Amount
Airbnb Payments UK Limited	£1,220,094,208
Clifford Chance LLP	£1,220,000,000
Premier Oil Holdings Limited	£1,218,181,760
BBC Commercial Holdings Limited	£1,217,600,000
Talktalk Communications Limited	£1,216,727,040
Zenith Bank (UK) Limited	£1,216,435,968
Anmercosa Finance Limited	£1,215,576,704
Bakkavor Invest Limited	£1,212,955,008
Smith & Williamson Investment Services Limited	£1,212,504,064
Nomura Capital Markets Limited	£1,212,168,192
Marubeni Finance Europe PLC	£1,211,043,328
Legal & General Resources Limited	£1,210,182,016
BL Retail Warehousing Holding Company Ltd	£1,209,484,160
ConocoPhillips Petroleum Company U.K. Ltd	£1,209,287,936
Jones Lang Lasalle Capital Investments, Limited	£1,207,898,240
BL Bluebutton 2014 Limited	£1,207,562,368
Morgan Stanley Swallow Limited	£1,207,240,960
MMS UK Holdings Limited	£1,207,149,952
Glencore Commodities Ltd	£1,204,430,976
General Dynamics Swiss Financial Management	£1,203,788,288
Centremanor Limited	£1,202,200,960
Mitie Treasury Management Limited	£1,201,356,032
Chrysaor E & P Finance Limited	£1,200,201,088
Macquarie Bank International Limited	£1,199,666,048
JPMorgan Emerging Markets Investment Trust PLC	£1,199,570,048
Bunge Corporation Limited	£1,198,570,112
Guinness Limited	£1,198,080,000
B.L.Holdings Limited	£1,192,749,824
Bakkavor (London) Limited	£1,191,655,040
World Fuel Services Europe, Ltd.	£1,190,469,888
I-Logic Technologies Bidco Limited	£1,188,963,456
I-Logic Holdings Limited	£1,188,963,456
Aviva Investors Holdings Limited	£1,188,899,968
Warwick Finance Residential Mortgages No One	£1,188,629,504
PSP Britannia Ltd	£1,186,223,744
Canary Wharf Contractors Limited	£1,185,198,848
Shell Upstream Overseas Services (I) Limited	£1,182,359,296
Michael Kors (UK) Holdings Limited	£1,180,764,672
BT Sixty-Four Limited	£1,180,393,984
Brookfield Global Corporate Investments Ltd	£1,178,971,904
Morgan Stanley UK Limited	£1,178,667,392
ELQ Investors VI Ltd	£1,176,619,904
DMG Atlantic Limited	£1,176,072,064
Catalina Holdings UK Limited	£1,175,658,752
IPGL (Holdings) Limited	£1,175,111,936
Slate No.1 PLC	£1,170,697,984
Anyslam Limited	£1,170,464,000
Trinity Square 2015-1 PLC	£1,168,448,000
Axiata Investments (UK) Limited	£1,168,223,616
Eurostar International Limited	£1,166,099,968
Mercia No.1 PLC	£1,165,888,000
Bestway UK Holdco Limited	£1,165,021,056
London Gateway Port Limited	£1,164,696,064
BTG PLC	£1,164,600,064
Evergreen Marine (UK) Limited	£1,162,165,888
Griffon Funding Limited	£1,161,046,656
Al Mistral Topco Limited	£1,158,996,864
Bakkavor Finance (3) Limited	£1,157,843,968
Bowbell No. 1 PLC	£1,157,815,040
Private Oil Holdings Oman Limited	£1,157,691,904
Intu (SGS) Finance PLC	£1,157,463,552
Vesuvius Overseas Limited	£1,155,239,040
HQCB Investments Limited	£1,153,777,024
London Wall Outsourcing Freeholds Limited	£1,152,864,000
The Bankers Investment Trust PLC	£1,151,830,016
Finastra Group Holdings Limited	£1,149,005,056
Emerald 2 Limited	£1,147,504,384
Classboss Limited	£1,146,635,008
British Land Fund Management Limited	£1,146,279,296
Tombac No.1 PLC	£1,146,140,032
Dialog Semiconductor PLC	£1,144,589,184
HQCB Properties (HQ5 (2)) Limited	£1,143,172,992
Lendlease Europe Holdings Limited	£1,142,829,952
Debenhams Group Holdings Limited	£1,141,100,032
Kufpec UK Limited	£1,140,575,104
Towd Point Mortgage Funding 2016 - Auburn 10	£1,140,260,992
Sony Corporate Services Europe Limited	£1,140,171,008
United Dominions Trust Limited	£1,140,125,056
CNA Insurance Company Limited	£1,139,515,008
Macquarie Euro Limited	£1,139,362,688
Ernst & Young LLP	£1,138,000,000
Richemont Holdings (UK) Limited	£1,137,566,976
Diageo UK Turkey Limited	£1,133,721,216
Tullett Prebon (Securities) Limited	£1,133,606,016
Hochschild Mining PLC	£1,131,694,208
L-3 Communications Limited	£1,130,516,992
ENI UK Limited	£1,128,280,960
LS Cardinal Limited	£1,128,208,000
Allen & Overy LLP	£1,127,699,968
Principal Financial Services V (UK) Ltd	£1,126,968,064
Freshfields Bruckhaus Deringer LLP	£1,125,600,000
Brightsphere Investment Group PLC	£1,124,143,104
Charles Street Conduit Asset Backed Securitisation 1	£1,123,976,704
Mavenir Private Finance Ltd	£1,123,801,472
Project Leopard Acquireco Limited	£1,122,965,120
Eagle 4 Limited	£1,120,092,288
Amtrust Corporate Member Limited	£1,119,700,992
Laird Limited	£1,119,500,032
Macquarie Commodities (UK) Limited	£1,118,053,376
Sova Capital Limited	£1,113,623,296
Talktalk Group Limited	£1,113,172,992
Ascot Corporate Name Limited	£1,112,865,024
British American Tobacco (2009 Pca) Limited	£1,112,381,952
Brooke Bond Assam Estates Limited	£1,111,694,976
Brunel Residential Mortgage Securitisation No.1	£1,111,590,016
Bluebottle UK Limited	£1,110,945,024
Cognizant Worldwide Limited	£1,109,720,064
Electrocomponents Public Limited Company	£1,107,399,936
Snap International I Limited	£1,107,347,328
Eversholt UK Rails (Holding) Limited	£1,107,275,008
Snap International II Limited	£1,107,267,840
John Laing Limited	£1,106,400,000
Sumitomo Corporation Capital Europe PLC	£1,105,428,224
Eversholt UK Rails Limited	£1,105,244,032
Total Energy (MEUK) Ltd.	£1,103,911,680
GHG Intermediate Holdings Limited	£1,103,768,064
Henderson Global Investors (Holdings) Limited	£1,103,132,032
News Corp Investments II Limited	£1,100,397,696
Deutsche Holdings No.2 Limited	£1,100,027,776
London Wall Capital Investments LLP	£1,099,951,488
Aspen Underwriting Limited	£1,099,101,056
Fleet Finco Limited	£1,099,036,032
Goldman Sachs Funding International Limited	£1,098,740,352
Semperian PPP Investment Partners Limited	£1,097,780,992
Mercer Limited	£1,096,000,000
Marubeni Oil & Gas (U.K.) Limited	£1,095,623,040
Macquarie Capital (Europe) Limited	£1,094,912,128
Betfair Group Limited	£1,094,590,976
Burbo Extension Holding Ltd	£1,092,881,664
Petropavlovsk PLC	£1,092,428,288
Allen & Ginter (UK) Limited	£1,090,668,032
City of London Real Property Company Limited	£1,090,621,952
Tesco Property Finance 3 PLC	£1,090,515,712
Passaic Issuer Holdco Limited	£1,090,515,712
Nord Anglia Education (UK) Holdings PLC	£1,089,372,288
Howden Broking Group Limited	£1,088,606,976
Ruthenium Investments Limited	£1,088,129,920
Priory Group No. 1 Limited	£1,087,517,952
Mitsui & Co. Financial Services (Europe) PLC	£1,086,739,072
JPMorgan American Investment Trust PLC	£1,086,210,048
Royal Mail Investments Limited	£1,084,999,936
Munich RE Capital Limited	£1,084,914,048
Aegis London Holdings Limited	£1,084,300,032
BMCE International (Holdings) PLC	£1,083,602,944

Company	Value
DCC Limited	£1,083,148,544
Validus Holdings (UK) Ltd	£1,082,492,288
Virgin UK Holdings Limited	£1,082,000,000
Renewables Infrastructure Group UK Investments	£1,081,892,992
IPG Holdings (UK) Limited	£1,080,169,984
Endeavour Resources Limited	£1,077,647,104
Omnicom EMEA Holdings Limited	£1,077,181,696
Odeon and UCI Cinemas Holdings Limited	£1,076,899,968
Selfridges Financing Limited	£1,076,700,032
Sony Interactive Entertainment Network Europe	£1,075,750,144
Dentsu Aegis London Limited	£1,074,704,000
Biz Finance PLC	£1,073,280,192
UK Renewable Holdco 1 Limited	£1,070,545,280
Iron Mountain Europe (Group) Limited	£1,066,531,008
Tokio Marine Kiln Group Limited	£1,066,392,000
Prutec Limited	£1,066,272,000
EMI Music Publishing Finance (UK) Limited	£1,066,124,992
Chevron Products UK Limited	£1,063,958,016
Esterline Technologies Holdings Limited	£1,063,425,216
Weldcure Limited	£1,063,419,008
Burlingtown LLP	£1,062,984,000
Inmarsat Finance PLC	£1,062,212,864
Macquarie (UK) Group Services Limited	£1,062,174,720
Aspen Managing Agency Limited	£1,061,209,984
IG Group Holdings PLC	£1,061,100,032
Docklands Aviation Group Limited	£1,060,457,984
BMO Global Asset Management (Europe) Limited	£1,060,049,024
Pic Holdings Limited	£1,059,910,016
BIIF Bidco Limited	£1,059,534,016
Marston's Issuer PLC	£1,059,299,968
CNR International (U.K.) Limited	£1,058,984,000
ELQ Investors, Ltd	£1,058,372,096
G4S US Holdings Limited	£1,056,648,000
Guardian Media Group PLC	£1,056,099,968
Bakkavor Foods Limited	£1,055,966,016
The Scott Trust Limited	£1,055,600,000
John Laing Holdco Limited	£1,053,600,000
BNY Mellon Intern'l Asset Management Hldgs No 1	£1,053,241,024
Great Hall Mortgages No.1 PLC	£1,052,625,984
DNI Europe Holdings Limited	£1,052,553,344
Temple Bar Investment Trust PLC	£1,051,443,968
Helix Midco Limited	£1,050,400,000
Helix Bufferco Limited	£1,050,400,000
Google UK Limited	£1,050,065,728
Leadenhall Securities Corporation Limited	£1,049,675,008
Hanover Acceptances Limited	£1,049,590,016
Angel Trains Group Limited	£1,049,128,000
John Lewis Properties PLC	£1,049,000,000
HSBC Investment Bank Holdings Limited	£1,048,858,816
Aegis Group Participations Limited	£1,048,617,984
ICG Global Investment UK Limited	£1,048,268,992
The Health Foundation	£1,048,235,008
PCL Asset Trustee Limited	£1,048,204,992
G4S UK Holdings Limited	£1,047,446,016
Derwent Valley Central Limited	£1,044,385,536
Gosforth Holdings 2015-1 Limited	£1,043,129,984
ITV Studios Limited	£1,042,483,008
Virgin Models Limited	£1,041,555,968
Quintain Limited	£1,040,300,032
Asos.Com Limited	£1,039,616,000
Virgin Records Limited	£1,039,337,024
Phoenix Distribution Holdings Limited	£1,039,100,032
Soho Estates Holdings Limited	£1,039,068,992
Linklaters LLP	£1,038,499,968
Aspen European Holdings Limited	£1,038,195,840
Union Property Corporation Limited	£1,037,218,496
CKI Number 3 Limited	£1,036,926,016
Phillips 66 Treasury Limited	£1,036,897,856
Babcock Defence & Security Holdings LLP	£1,036,844,992
Intu Investments Limited	£1,035,299,968
Noble Holding UK Limited	£1,034,073,792
Travelex Limited	£1,034,035,968
Barchester Healthcare Homes Limited	£1,033,468,032
Gosforth Funding 2015-1 PLC	£1,032,249,984
Sabah Shell Petroleum Company Limited	£1,031,010,176
Arsenal Holdings Limited	£1,029,056,000
Markel Capital Holdings Limited	£1,028,029,632
BLME Holdings PLC	£1,027,534,016
Meadowhall Shopping Centre Limited	£1,026,838,656
Dunwilco (1847) Limited	£1,026,764,032
Bank of London and The Middle East PLC	£1,025,888,000
Brookfield BBP UK Holdings III Limited	£1,025,368,768
GFI Holdings Limited	£1,024,769,600
Bunzl American Holdings (No.2) Limited	£1,024,547,840
BG Gas Supply (UK) Limited	£1,024,257,920
Helical PLC	£1,024,110,976
Macquarie Meters 3 (UK) Limited	£1,023,539,968
Chevron Energy Limited	£1,023,069,824
Langton Securities (2010-1) PLC	£1,022,577,984
Lloyds Bank General Insurance Limited	£1,021,953,024
The Golden Charter Trust Limited	£1,021,179,008
Naxos Investments Limited	£1,021,158,784
Premier Oil E & P UK Limited	£1,021,145,600
Macquarie Investments (UK) Limited	£1,020,599,360
BTG Management Services Limited	£1,019,619,968
MGL2 Limited	£1,018,627,968
Hawksmoor Mortgages 2016-2 PLC	£1,016,599,744
Lombard Business Leasing Limited	£1,016,168,000
Tullett Prebon Group Holdings PLC	£1,015,715,968
ENI ULX Limited	£1,015,713,728
Endurance Worldwide Insurance Limited	£1,015,262,016
EY Global Services Limited	£1,015,152,704
BG Singapore Limited	£1,014,964,992
Just Eat PLC	£1,014,700,032
United Trust Bank Limited	£1,013,899,008
UTB Partners Limited	£1,013,899,008
Goldman Sachs Group Holdings (U.K.) Limited	£1,012,618,432
Talktalk Telecom Limited	£1,012,142,976
Arsenal Football Club Public Limited Company	£1,011,310,016
Citigroup Participation Luxembourg Limited	£1,010,713,792
Pinnacle Resources Limited	£1,009,340,992
British Land Broadgate 2005 Limited	£1,008,889,664
AV Equity Trading Limited	£1,008,718,976
V2 Music Group Limited	£1,008,476,032
Capital & Regional PLC	£1,007,900,032
Veolia ES Holdings (UK) Limited	£1,007,881,984
Portman Square US Holdings Limited	£1,007,092,608
SSB No. 1 PLC	£1,007,020,224
ASOS PLC	£1,007,000,000
Legal & General Overseas Operations Ltd	£1,006,400,000
Soho Estates Limited	£1,003,897,984
Boeing European Holdings Limited	£1,001,482,688
United Kingdom Mutual Steam Ship Assurance	£1,000,043,136
Vattenfall Wind Power Ltd	£998,950,976
Liberty International Holdings Limited	£998,899,968
Noble Resources UK Holdings Limited	£997,345,600
Tullett Prebon Group Limited	£997,297,024
Lloyd's Register Group Limited	£997,294,976
Trillium (Prime) Property GP Limited	£996,601,024
JPMorgan Asset Management (UK) Limited	£995,660,032
Newday Partnership Transferor PLC	£995,265,024
Intelsat Global Sales & Marketing Ltd.	£994,452,992
Principal Financial Services IV (UK) LLP	£992,834,816
Spire Healthcare Holdings 1	£991,774,016
Anglo American Marketing Limited	£989,921,664
CGI Nordic Investments Limited	£989,649,984
Mace Finance Limited	£989,419,008
Perenco Overseas Holdings Limited	£988,140,736
Marubeni Copper Holdings Limited	£987,988,736
Ascential PLC	£987,400,000
Fitch Ratings Ltd	£986,675,008
Schroder Administration Limited	£982,630,976
LEH Global Ltd	£978,256,256
BBC Studios Distribution Limited	£977,500,032

Company	Value
Principal Financial Services III (UK) Ltd	£977,335,360
SITI 1 Limited	£975,936,000
MF Bidco Limited	£975,293,824
Empiric Student Property PLC	£972,993,984
Elementis PLC	£972,488,384
Nautical Petroleum Limited	£971,502,976
DCC Treasury 2014 Limited	£970,175,488
Herald Investment Trust PLC	£969,092,992
Bluebutton (5 Broadgate) UK Limited	£968,969,664
CFL Auto Receivables Limited	£968,964,480
Haut Investments Limited	£967,409,024
Mercury Holding Limited	£966,606,336
Statkraft UK Ltd	£966,356,992
LS Victoria Properties Limited	£963,771,008
MF Midco Limited	£963,459,008
Wellcome Trust Finance PLC	£963,444,672
Apache UK Investment Limited	£962,152,384
CGI Nordic Holdings Limited	£960,323,008
IP Fibre Devices (UK) Limited	£960,196,736
Penguin Random House Limited	£960,153,984
Towd Point Mortgage Funding 2017 - Auburn 11 PLC	£959,894,976
DTZ UK Newco Limited	£959,593,280
Aztech Advantage Ltd	£959,379,968
Ernst & Young (EMEIA) Services Limited	£958,624,448
DTEK Finance PLC	£958,607,936
Tullett Prebon Investment Holdings Limited	£958,499,968
Legal & General Investment Management Hldgs Ltd	£958,400,000
Accor Hotelinvest UK Limited	£957,522,880
Time Warner Holdings Limited	£957,379,008
Catlin (North American) Holdings Ltd	£956,544,576
BG Netherlands	£955,337,024
Total Oil GB Limited	£952,974,016
Smiths Detection Group Limited	£949,803,008
Jupiter European Opportunities Trust PLC	£948,438,976
Tilney Group Limited	£948,124,992
Wedco EMEA Ventures Limited	£947,934,016
Reach Network Media Limited	£947,798,016
TA Mfg Limited	£947,218,496
Structadene Limited	£946,374,912
MF Intermediate Limited	£946,333,376
Kypris Acquisitions Ltd	£946,319,424
WM SA Investments Limited	£945,702,336
MLEIH Funding	£944,490,496
Violin Topco Limited	£944,281,024
Mace Limited	£944,235,008
Virgin Active International Limited	£944,099,968
Sterling UK Holdco Limited	£943,811,328
Concord Resources Limited	£943,126,272
J.P. Morgan Capital Financing Limited	£942,744,768
Agility Trains East (Holdings) Limited	£941,915,008
Agility Trains East Limited	£941,915,008
Esterline Technologies Europe Limited	£941,664,512
London & Regional (Baker Street) Limited	£941,305,024
CKI Number 2 Limited	£941,014,016
Sodexo Holdings Limited	£940,289,984
Ingenious Media Holdings Limited	£939,628,032
Hess Malaysia and Thailand Limited	£939,230,272
Aegis Electric & Gas International Services Limited	£938,700,032
Marubeni North Sea Limited	£938,316,288
High Speed Rail Finance PLC	£938,000,000
Dellmes GR Limited	£937,774,336
Ramchez GR Limited	£937,773,440
Cerro Dominador UK, LLP	£937,003,072
JPMorgan Asset Management Holdings (UK) Ltd	£936,790,016
Starr Syndicate Limited	£936,635,008
De Beers UK Limited	£934,226,816
Virgin Active Health Club Holdings Limited	£934,118,016
WPG Finance Limited	£933,070,208
Intercapital Limited	£931,644,992
Mergermarket Bidco Limited	£930,537,024
Dorrington PLC	£930,150,016
ITW UK	£930,108,992
BL City Offices Holding Company Limited	£930,006,528
Informa UK Limited	£929,913,984
Stanbic Africa Holdings Limited	£929,189,568
Legal & General Capital Investments Limited	£928,761,984
AI Mistral Limited	£928,568,512
Grosvenor Properties	£927,049,024
Apple Bidco Limited	£925,400,576
Principal Financial Services II (UK) Ltd	£924,107,648
London Trocadero (2015) LLP	£923,785,408
Henderson Holdings Group Limited	£920,793,024
Ferrexpo PLC	£920,370,624
UK Power Networks Services (Development) Ltd	£920,038,016
Betjeman Holdings Midco Limited	£920,000,000
Principal International Latin America Ltd	£919,632,448
Newday UK Limited	£919,100,032
Principal Financial Services Latin America Ltd	£918,830,720
Lannraig Funding Limited	£918,337,984
SSP Group Holdings Limited	£918,065,024
Gosforth Holdings 2014-1 Limited	£917,940,992
CBRE Finance Europe LLP	£917,908,288
Sodexo Limited	£917,420,992
Arup Group Limited	£916,700,032
Royal Mail Estates Limited	£916,000,000
LR Baker St Senior Holdco Limited	£915,821,888
DVB Transport Finance Limited	£914,629,120
Brixton Limited	£914,547,008
Punjab National Bank (International) Limited	£914,431,360
Kellas Topco Limited	£913,841,024
L & Q New Homes Limited	£913,772,032
Infrastructure Investments Trafalgar Limited	£913,590,016
Ivy Bidco Limited	£913,500,032
KAZ Minerals Projects Finance Limited	£913,193,344
Lionrai Investments No.1 Limited	£912,745,984
Hunting PLC	£912,563,264
Shell Exploration and Production Tanzania Ltd	£912,468,480
Cable and Wireless (West Indies) Limited	£911,741,952
Blackrock World Mining Trust PLC	£911,721,984
High Speed Rail Finance (1) PLC	£911,600,000
Kellas Midstream Limited	£911,534,976
Hansteen Holdings PLC	£910,000,000
Debenhams Properties Limited	£909,686,016
CNH Industrial UK Limited	£908,967,360
Ashmore Group PLC	£908,000,000
Ixellion Technologies Ltd	£907,070,592
KAZ Minerals Aktogay Finance Limited	£905,461,376
Lannraig Master Issuer PLC	£904,920,000
NSC Europe Limited	£903,430,976
Artesian Finance PLC	£901,300,992
Noble Europe Limited	£899,918,720
DTEK Investments Limited	£899,817,728
Cancer Research UK	£899,100,032
Esterline Technologies Limited	£897,778,560
APR Energy Holdings Limited	£896,947,712
Jimmy Choo (Holdings) Limited	£896,396,992
Knight Dragon Investments Limited	£896,361,664
Earls Court Partnership Limited	£896,339,968
Warner Media International Limited	£893,763,968
Ashtead Plant Hire Company Limited	£893,281,024
Pam Acquisitionco Limited	£892,049,024
Virgin Holdings Limited	£892,000,000
AI Perform Holdings LLP	£891,635,968
Firmdale Holdings Limited	£891,068,992
Dunwilco (1784) Limited	£891,054,016
Dunwilco (1783) Limited	£890,947,008
CL Intermediate (UK) Limited	£890,522,560
Jupiter Fund Management PLC	£890,200,000
Rio Tinto London Limited	£888,339,008
Avation PLC	£888,087,744
Yianis Holdings Limited	£887,897,344
Shell Malaysia Limited	£887,786,304
Intu Trafford Centre Group (UK) Limited	£886,937,024
Esab Holdings Limited	£886,091,008

Brokertec Investments	£885,843,584	Castle Trust Capital PLC	£835,164,032
State Grid Europe Development (2014) PLC	£885,205,056	Cantor Fitzgerald Services LLP	£834,406,912
Time Warner International Finance Limited	£885,070,912	Topland Group PLC	£834,398,336
Clear Channel International Limited	£884,860,032	Cantor Fitzgerald Europe	£834,325,632
CKI Number 1 Limited	£884,486,016	Fortune Oil Limited	£832,443,008
Law Debenture Corporation PLC (The)	£884,427,008	Babcock Investments (Number Eight) Limited	£831,596,032
Willis Faber Limited	£884,000,000	Arthur J. Gallagher (UK) Limited	£831,446,976
Guy's and St Thomas' Charity	£883,937,024	Deutsche Morgan Grenfell Group PLC	£831,026,880
CWCB Properties (DS7) Limited	£883,276,928	South Hook Gas Company Ltd.	£830,753,024
Vivo Energy Namibia Limited	£882,790,976	Graff Diamonds International Limited	£830,131,840
Odeon Cinemas Group Limited	£880,899,968	Calypso Group UK Limited	£830,091,264
Gosforth Funding 2014-1 PLC	£880,702,016	Brit Insurance Holdings Limited	£829,856,960
BMO Global Smaller Companies PLC	£880,344,000	Mastercard Payment Gateway Services Group Ltd	£829,390,976
Match.Com Foreign Holdings Limited	£879,188,736	Westfield UK & Europe Finance PLC	£827,535,872
RBS AA Holdings (UK) Limited	£879,020,992	Babcock Southern Holdings Limited	£826,769,984
Spire Healthcare Limited	£878,553,984	Colt Telecom Finance Euro	£825,897,152
ABP Finance PLC	£878,200,000	Spirit Issuer Parent Limited	£825,761,984
Atos UK IT Limited	£877,448,000	Spirit Issuer PLC	£825,761,984
HSBC Latin America B.V.	£877,330,560	Selectuser Limited	£823,937,984
Laird Overseas Holdings Limited	£877,224,000	Pearson Education Holdings Limited	£822,945,984
KCG Europe Limited	£877,106,496	MC Ocean Holdings Limited	£822,750,784
IP Karugamo Holdings (UK) Limited	£877,011,968	Community Finance Company 1 PLC	£822,089,984
Mastercard UK Holdco Limited	£875,022,976	COFCO Holdings 1 Limited	£822,089,984
National Grid Commercial Holdings Limited	£874,000,000	Semperian PPP Investment Partners No.2 Limited	£821,650,816
Schroder AsiaPacific Fund PLC	£873,598,016	Ellerman Investments Limited	£821,326,976
Gallagher Holdings (UK) Limited	£870,972,992	Genting Worldwide Services Limited	£819,277,888
National Grid Grain LNG Limited	£870,526,016	Informa Finance USA Limited	£818,830,016
Shaftesbury Covent Garden Limited	£870,398,016	British Land Acquisitions Limited	£816,109,312
Motorola Solutions Finance EMEA Limited	£867,403,328	Lloyds UDT Limited	£815,451,008
Selene Holdings Limited	£867,201,984	Premier Lotteries Investments UK Limited	£815,200,000
TCI Fund Holdings Limited	£867,146,048	Oasis Charitable Trust	£815,022,976
Lonmin Public Limited Company	£866,473,152	Alpha Bank London Limited	£814,126,016
Beacon Rail Finance (Europe) Limited	£865,273,024	Trendcycle Limited	£811,398,976
WPP 2323 Limited	£864,050,560	WFS UK Holding Company II Limited	£811,068,544
Newline Corporate Name Limited	£863,665,024	Neptune E & P UKCS Limited	£810,516,992
MGN Limited	£862,868,992	Balfour Beatty Infrastructure Investments Limited	£809,683,968
Ceridian Global UK Holding Company Limited	£859,831,232	Ship Holdco Limited	£809,654,016
Blaxmill (Ten) Limited	£858,918,656	VAM Bidco Limited	£809,517,184
News Group Newspapers Limited	£857,824,000	U.K.& European Investments Limited	£809,400,000
Sumitomo Corporation Europe Limited	£857,546,112	Nord Anglia Education Limited	£808,990,016
N. M. Rothschild & Sons Limited	£857,472,000	Opodo Limited	£808,578,048
Henderson Smaller Co's Investment Trust PLC	£856,572,032	Howden Joinery Group PLC	£808,499,968
DLG Acquisitions Limited	£855,846,016	Belmond Finance Services Limited	£808,343,744
Power Leisure Bookmakers Limited	£855,336,512	The Wolfson Foundation	£808,065,984
Navigators Corporate Underwriters Limited	£853,934,016	William Pears Group Investments Limited	£806,517,376
Gosforth Holdings 2016-2 Limited	£853,489,024	Market Data Limited	£806,152,000
IP2IPO Limited	£853,177,024	General Healthcare Holdings (3) Limited	£804,883,008
Marsh Services Limited	£853,000,000	Omnicom Management Europe	£804,806,272
FC Skyfall Bidco Ltd	£852,417,344	Gosforth Funding 2016-2 PLC	£804,118,016
Dinosaur Merchant Bank Limited	£852,285,120	Finance for Residential Social Housing PLC	£803,032,000
Carphone Warehouse Europe Limited	£852,049,024	British Land Industrial Limited	£802,235,968
Hiscox PLC	£851,043,968	Young & Co's Brewery PLC	£800,600,000
Electricinvest Holding Company Limited	£850,800,000	DCC Holdings (UK) Limited	£799,668,608
OSW Co Holdings 2 Limited	£850,518,336	Greenham Trading Limited	£799,017,024
Elf Petroleum UK Limited	£850,377,984	FIL Holdings (UK) Limited	£798,444,992
BT Fleet Limited	£849,057,984	Keller Holdings Limited	£798,325,376
Ralph US Holdings	£848,661,376	JPMorgan European Smaller Companies Trust PLC	£798,044,992
CWIGroup Limited	£847,876,992	Sirius Minerals PLC	£796,924,992
APR Energy Limited	£847,778,752	BW Publishing Limited	£796,069,056
Meadowhall Centre (1999) Limited	£847,686,464	Oakwood Global Assets Limited	£795,537,024
HGI Asset Management Group Limited	£847,400,000	BHP Billiton (UK) Limited	£795,286,080
National Car Parks Limited	£847,369,984	Fleet Midco Limited	£795,054,016
Iron Mountain (UK) PLC	£846,876,992	Fleet Midco I Limited	£795,054,016
Endurance Corporate Capital Limited	£844,979,968	ENI ULT Limited	£794,444,416
Bruning Limited	£843,220,864	Ravenside Investments Limited	£794,372,992
Tottenham Hotspur Limited	£840,729,984	International Entertainment Holdings Limited	£794,190,016
Derwent Valley Finance Limited	£839,914,176	Reach Publishing Group Limited	£794,000,000
M & G Limited	£839,422,016	General Healthcare Holdings (4) Limited	£793,024,000
Infrastructure Investments Holdings Limited	£838,348,992	Electra Private Equity PLC	£793,000,000
ITV Broadcasting Limited	£838,264,000	Real Estate Participation Management Limited	£792,962,368
London School of Economics & Political Science	£838,145,984	Segro Overseas Holdings Limited	£791,814,016
Firstbus Investments Limited	£836,089,984	ERM Emilion Limited	£791,106,432

Company	Value	Company	Value
Orsted Race Bank (Holding) Limited	£790,390,464	Chelsea FC PLC	£755,345,984
Estee Lauder Cosmetics Limited	£789,843,008	Lloyds Bank Pension ABCS (No 2) LLP	£755,296,000
Newday Partnership Loan Note Issuer Ltd	£789,769,024	PE Pioneer Holding II Limited	£755,217,984
BGC Global Limited	£789,716,544	Westfield Stratford City Finance PLC	£753,980,544
T.H.F.C. (Funding No.3) PLC	£788,900,224	Aegis GPS Holdings Limited	£753,484,992
ERPE Topco Limited	£787,892,480	Daily Mail and General Investments Limited	£753,390,976
Praesidiad Group Limited	£787,892,480	Arthur J. Gallagher Holdings (UK) Limited	£752,902,976
Marex Spectron Group Limited	£787,351,936	TRU Taj Holdings 2 Limited	£752,862,016
Schroder Investment Management Limited	£787,299,968	Otter Ports Limited	£752,239,744
Barclays (Barley) Limited	£786,381,824	Axis Bank UK Limited	£751,414,912
Juturna (European Loan Conduit No. 16) PLC	£785,574,016	PFI Senior Funding Limited	£751,164,992
SB Energy Three Holdings Limited	£785,131,904	XL Gracechurch Limited	£750,604,096
Casper UK Bidco Limited	£785,103,552	Qatar Airways Investments (UK) Ltd	£750,490,432
Brown Shipley & Co. Limited	£784,942,976	Prometheon Enterprise Limited	£750,300,032
Intelsat UK Financial Services Ltd.	£784,788,032	Burberry Haymarket Limited	£748,966,016
Consort Healthcare (Birmingham) Limited	£782,716,032	HarperCollins (UK)	£748,902,976
Consort Healthcare (Birmingham) Holdings Ltd	£782,716,032	Fleet Bidco Limited	£748,424,000
Babcock Marine Holdings (UK) Limited	£782,388,992	Consort Healthcare (Birmingham) Funding PLC	£748,032,000
EMT 2 Holdings Limited	£782,225,472	Priory Group UK 2 Limited	£747,990,976
Ghana International Bank PLC	£781,577,984	GGR Capital Limited	£747,928,000
Euromoney Institutional Investor PLC	£781,281,984	Diageo UK Turkey Holdings Limited	£747,438,208
ADM Investor Services International Limited	£781,050,240	Morgan Stanley Employment Services UK Limited	£746,849,728
Mavenir Private Holdings II Ltd	£780,737,600	Comet Bidco Limited	£746,640,000
VTB Capital Trading Limited	£780,438,016	Comet Midco Limited	£746,640,000
Itochu Fibre Limited	£779,686,400	International Power (Fawkes)	£745,605,184
JPMorgan Japanese Investment Trust PLC	£778,545,984	Halcyon Finance Limited	£745,393,984
Paul Hamlyn Foundation	£778,419,968	Hoggant Limited	£745,190,016
XL Insurance (UK) Holdings Limited	£777,950,016	Shaftesbury AV Limited	£745,068,992
Taylor Nelson Sofres International Limited	£776,883,968	McDonald's Real Estate LLP	£743,952,000
Dornoch Limited	£776,259,008	International Power Holdings Limited	£743,276,352
Omnicom EMEA Investments Limited	£775,176,896	Faroe Petroleum PLC	£743,065,984
Shionogi Limited	£774,479,232	Hardy Underwriting Group Limited	£742,731,008
Bendler Investments II Ltd	£774,318,016	Shire Holdings UK Limited	£742,684,672
Wells Fargo Capital Finance (UK) Limited	£774,174,656	Hampshire Trust Bank PLC	£742,259,968
British American Tobacco (Brands) Limited	£773,982,016	Towd Point Mortgage Funding 2016-Vantage1 PLC	£741,123,008
CBRE Limited	£773,142,016	UPP Bond 1 Holdings Limited	£740,257,024
Intu Finance MH Limited	£772,600,000	Equinor New Energy Limited	£740,041,984
General Healthcare Mixer Partnership LLP	£772,556,032	Wilkes-Lucas Limited	£738,737,984
GLH Hotels Limited	£772,536,000	Vue International Midco Limited	£738,563,008
Artesian Finance II PLC	£771,998,016	Homebase (UK & I) Holdings Limited	£738,116,992
Fleet Midco II Limited	£771,267,008	Wittington Investments Finance Limited	£737,468,992
Shell International Petroleum Company Limited	£771,200,000	PR Goal 3 Limited	£737,426,304
Instinet Europe Limited	£771,105,024	Vue International Finco Limited	£737,393,984
Oaknorth Bank PLC	£770,944,000	Angel Leasing Company Limited	£737,321,984
Reebok International Limited	£770,678,528	Abbott Mead Vickers Group Limited	£736,813,440
JPMorgan Indian Investment Trust PLC	£770,302,976	Equity Release Funding (No.4) PLC	£736,700,992
Carestream Dental Technology Holdings 1 Limited	£770,097,920	Smithfield Limited	£736,334,592
Rothmans International Enterprises Limited	£769,108,992	BF Properties (No.5) Ltd	£735,228,352
Vue Holdings (UK) Limited	£768,684,992	River Island Clothing Co. Limited	£735,200,000
Nexteer UK Holding Ltd.	£765,838,976	Merchants Trust PLC (The)	£734,629,632
Coroin Limited	£765,742,016	Sandown 2012-2 PLC	£734,204,992
CK William Midco 2 Limited	£765,137,536	Steamship Mutual Underwriting Association Limited	£732,111,168
Sahara Hospitality Operations LLP	£764,899,008	Domestic & General Services Limited	£732,024,000
Knighton Estates Limited	£764,434,432	GroupBT Limited	£730,985,792
Coral Group Trading Limited	£764,088,000	Christie Manson & Woods Limited	£730,792,000
SIR Hospitals Propco Limited	£762,089,024	EDF Energy (Thermal Generation) Limited	£730,721,984
Atos UK Holdings Limited	£762,073,216	BNY Mellon Interna'l Asset Management (Hldgs) Ltd	£730,529,024
Shine Acquisition Co Limited	£761,961,024	Beefeater Gin Limited	£730,520,384
BG Overseas Investments Limited	£760,928,000	Danone Financing UK Limited	£730,302,784
HSBC Global Asset Management Limited	£760,737,024	Canary Wharf Retail Funding Limited	£730,293,824
CGI Eurofin UK Limited	£760,523,328	Bristol Water Group Limited	£729,400,000
Hess Finance	£760,014,336	M & G. Securities Limited	£729,380,992
Halliburton Manufacturing and Services Limited	£759,612,992	Segro Properties Limited	£729,344,000
CD & R Firefly 4 Limited	£759,217,984	Skrill Limited	£729,160,704
CD & R Firefly Holdco Limited	£759,217,984	Bupa Care Homes (CFG) PLC	£729,148,032
OMFS (GGP) Limited	£758,268,032	Equinix (UK) Limited	£729,064,000
Socar Trading (UK) Limited	£758,045,504	CMC Markets Holdings Limited	£728,499,456
Discovery Group Europe Limited	£756,391,936	Titan Financing Holdco Limited	£725,359,936
TP Holdings Limited	£756,340,992	Atrato Issuer Holdco Limited	£725,238,144
Walney (UK) Offshore Windfarms Limited	£756,060,160	Tesco Property Finance 2 PLC	£725,238,144
Inmarsat Holdings Limited	£756,007,552	Hellenic Petroleum Finance PLC	£723,469,440
WMG Acquisition (UK) Limited	£755,628,032	Longstone Finance PLC	£723,367,168

Company	Value
Castle Trust Treasury Limited	£723,344,000
Pillar Property Group Limited	£723,151,808
HgCapital Trust PLC	£722,788,992
Castle Trust Direct PLC	£722,684,032
Metropolitan Properties Company Limited	£721,740,992
Bunzl UK Limited	£721,240,000
Eddystone Finance Holdings Limited	£721,154,048
Loopsign No.2 Limited	£720,650,944
Formula One World Championship Limited	£718,209,024
Adecco UK Limited	£717,968,000
CMI Canada Financing Ltd	£717,343,872
Petrofac (Malaysia-PM 304) Limited	£717,077,376
DTZ UK Holdco Limited	£716,638,528
Grosvenor Continental Europe Holdings Limited	£715,541,120
Shaftesbury Carnaby PLC	£713,144,000
IG Markets Limited	£712,600,000
Fordstam Limited	£712,243,968
Partnership Assurance Group Limited	£711,953,984
Electrocomponents U.K. Limited	£711,860,992
MF Debtco Limited	£711,783,040
VPI Holding Limited	£710,097,024
Scania Finance Great Britain Limited	£709,678,976
Spire Healthcare Holdings 2 Limited	£709,414,976
A & N Media Finance Services Limited	£709,387,008
LR Baker St Mezz Borrower Limited	£709,154,688
Partnerships in Care Investments 1 Limited	£708,550,016
Willis Group Services Limited	£708,000,000
Willis GS UK Limited	£707,781,952
Extraclick Limited	£707,752,704
Tizir Limited	£706,950,784
Thomson Reuters (Professional) UK Limited	£706,771,968
Macquarie European Investment Holdings Ltd	£706,162,048
Howard Investments Limited	£706,067,008
UK Power Networks Services Holdings Limited	£706,000,000
Lazari Financial Holdings Limited	£705,792,512
Lazari Finance Limited	£705,782,528
London Stock Exchange PLC	£704,899,968
Engelhart CTP Holding (UK) Limited	£703,991,040
MSI Corporate Capital Limited	£703,907,968
GMS Estates Limited	£703,354,624
Pearson PRH Holdings Limited	£703,046,016
Hyperion Development UK Limited	£703,024,448
Navona Issuer Holdco Limited	£702,495,488
Tesco Property Finance 4 PLC	£702,495,488
Atos International IT Limited	£702,401,024
Jimmy Choo Group Limited	£702,265,024
ERS DGB Limited	£702,006,976
BBA Finance No.1	£701,956,992
Herbert Smith Freehills Global LLP	£700,200,000
GLA Land and Property Limited	£700,180,992
Greater London Authority Holdings Limited	£700,180,992
Intergen Holdings (UK) Limited	£699,899,584
Graff Diamonds Limited	£699,510,336
IBM Global Financing UK Company	£699,363,008
News Corp Holdings UK & Ireland	£699,219,008
JPMorgan Asset Management International Limited	£698,505,984
Akelius Residential Limited	£698,351,296
Lloyd's Register Group Services Limited	£698,243,968
Tyman PLC	£697,913,984
Unite (USAF) II PLC	£697,769,984
Pearson Loan Finance Unlimited	£697,345,984
OMV Supply & Trading Limited	£697,013,184
3i Holdings PLC	£697,000,000
Clear Channel Holdings Limited	£696,900,992
Willis GS UK Holdings Limited	£696,611,072
Viners Energy Limited	£696,017,024
Baltic Sea Offshore Holdco Limited	£695,065,792
Sandown Gold 2012-1 PLC	£694,273,024
Hardy Underwriting Limited	£692,849,984
CWBC Finance Two (BP1) Limited	£692,275,328
Charter Consolidated Limited	£692,246,016
LGH Hotels Management Limited	£691,736,000
Marks and Spencer International Holdings Limited	£691,219,008
Simec Lochaber Hydropower 2 Limited	£690,625,984
Argo (No. 604) Limited	£690,510,528
ABF Grain Products Limited	£690,345,024
DLA Piper International LLP	£690,200,000
Howden Joinery Holdings Limited	£689,209,024
Lewis Trust Group Limited	£688,754,624
Standard Chartered I H Limited	£688,096,320
Winterflood Securities Limited	£688,042,752
AON Global Operations PLC	£687,973,312
PA Consulting Group Limited	£687,870,016
Eaton Towers Limited	£686,630,400
Ribbon Holdco Limited	£685,795,008
Ribbon Midco Limited	£685,670,016
BIIF Parentco Limited	£685,653,696
GLH Hotels Holdings Limited	£685,366,976
Intergen Projects (UK) Limited	£684,550,976
ENI Oil Algeria Limited	£683,906,048
Envol Investments Limited	£682,898,688
ERS Corporate Member Limited	£682,003,008
SMBC Aviation Capital (UK) Limited	£681,355,904
Macquarie Group Investments (UK) No.2 Limited	£681,241,984
Intu Debenture PLC	£680,700,032
SCMB Overseas Limited	£680,016,128
Arch Insurance Company (Europe) Limited	£679,980,992
Cliffrange Limited	£679,932,992
London and Regional Group Finance Limited	£679,730,624
River Island Holdings Limited	£679,699,968
VPI Immingham LLP	£678,916,992
MS Amlin Corporate Services Limited	£678,390,976
Talisman Colombia Holdco Limited	£677,987,456
Saavi Energia (UK) Ltd	£677,936,000
Jupiter Asset Management Group Limited	£677,843,008
Fuller Smith & Turner PLC	£677,299,968
Victoria Investments Finco Limited	£677,012,992
Tombac No.2 PLC	£676,579,008
3i PLC	£676,505,984
EMI Music Publishing Limited	£676,472,320
Arcus Tivana Investor Vehicle 2 LLP	£675,675,712
Arcus Tivana Investor Vehicle 1 LLP	£675,673,984
Morgan Sindall Construction & Infrastructure Ltd	£675,254,016
BMG Rights Management (UK) Limited	£675,192,000
Petroineos Europe Limited	£674,768,064
Inchcape Shipping Services Holdings Limited	£674,154,688
DB UK Holdings Limited	£673,542,592
ENI Elgin/Franklin Limited	£673,075,008
Reclaim Fund Ltd	£672,713,984
HBL Bank UK Limited	£672,680,000
Habib Allied Holding Limited	£672,569,024
Atos International IT Holdings Limited	£672,391,296
Aviva Investors Global Services Limited	£672,200,000
Stena Icemax Limited	£671,847,552
WPP Fitzroy Square	£671,606,720
VUR Holdings (UK) Limited	£671,553,984
British Sugar PLC	£670,600,000
ITE Group PLC	£669,209,984
Spire UK Holdco 4 Limited	£669,118,976
Moly-Cop UK Holdings Limited	£668,905,152
Circle Anglia Social Housing PLC	£668,187,008
The Shell Company of Thailand Limited	£668,028,480
Berkley Estates London Limited	£668,023,168
Temese Funding 2 PLC	£667,886,976
LS One New Change Limited	£667,859,008
Springer Nature Limited	£667,692,992
Vitality Health Limited	£667,292,992
National Grid Interconnector Holdings Limited	£666,958,016
BL Chess Limited	£666,869,440
Discovery Holdings Europe Limited	£665,985,024
ICG Enterprise Trust PLC	£665,286,016
LTG Treasury Limited	£664,675,072
U and I Group PLC	£664,147,968
Friary Intermediate Limited	£663,510,976

Company	Value	Company	Value
Virgin Active Group Limited	£663,260,032	Just Eat Holding Limited	£629,600,000
Bal Global Finance (UK) Limited	£663,104,000	Swiss Re Specialised Investments Holdings (UK) Ltd	£628,750,016
Anglo Platinum Marketing Limited	£662,708,096	TR European Growth Trust PLC	£628,348,032
British American Tobacco Italy Limited	£661,716,992	Babcock2 Limited	£627,622,016
PA Consulting Management Services Limited	£661,130,496	Canary Wharf Developments Limited	£627,006,976
Close Brothers Finance PLC	£660,564,928	Salamander Energy PLC	£626,995,520
IPM Peacock Limited	£660,259,136	EFT Investments SE	£626,471,680
Yorse No. 3 Limited	£658,830,720	Green Park Reading No. 1 LLP	£626,145,344
Miller Insurance Services LLP	£657,651,008	Quantoil Limited	£625,209,472
Foresight Solar (UK Holdco) Limited	£657,509,248	Ribbon Acquisition Limited	£624,860,032
Hoebridge LLP	£657,385,792	The Net-a-Porter Group Limited	£624,489,024
Cathexis UK Holdings Limited	£655,900,032	Broadgate Property Holdings Limited	£623,849,984
L3 Commercial Training Solutions Limited	£655,654,016	Cheetah Holdco Limited	£623,660,992
Das Europe Limited	£655,641,984	Core Laboratories Interests One Limited	£623,090,368
Smith & Nephew Investment Holdings Limited	£655,462,016	Best Buy China UK, LLP	£623,003,008
ISG PLC	£654,600,000	Fosse Funding (No.1) Limited	£622,299,008
Bestway Wholesale Limited	£654,392,000	Colt Technology Services Europe Limited	£621,708,160
Triland Metals Limited	£653,182,592	Abengoa Concessions Investments Limited	£621,620,480
Nando's Finance Limited	£653,094,976	Kaspersky Labs Limited	£620,440,448
General Dynamics European Finance Limited	£652,667,840	Babcock Investments (Number Four) Limited	£620,320,000
E D & F Man Capital Markets Limited	£652,302,080	Canary Wharf Estate Limited	£620,297,728
Meadowhall Finance PLC	£652,292,736	Anglo American (London)	£619,418,560
Gulf Marine Services PLC	£652,228,992	RELX (Investments) PLC	£619,366,016
DMG Media Limited	£652,225,984	Reach Magazines Publishing PLC	£619,148,992
Ambac Assurance UK Limited	£652,200,000	Motor 2017-1 PLC	£619,067,840
Close Brothers Holdings Limited	£652,102,976	Thanet Offshore Wind Limited	£618,955,008
Carrington Power Limited	£650,667,008	Blueco Limited	£618,804,992
Derwent Valley London Limited	£650,484,096	Cameron Petroleum (UK) Limited	£616,990,976
Telehouse Holdings Limited	£650,107,008	ZPG Limited	£615,939,968
Associated Newspapers Limited	£649,889,024	Allianz Renewable Energy Partners V PLC	£615,602,752
T. Rowe Price International Ltd	£649,670,080	TransDigm European Holdings Limited	£615,044,288
JLT Specialty Limited	£649,588,992	European Fintyre Distribution Limited	£615,039,424
Equity Release Funding (No.3) PLC	£649,414,016	Orsted West of Duddon Sands (UK) Limited	£614,502,464
East Anglia One Limited	£649,299,968	Daejan Properties Limited	£614,441,280
Nordic Entertainment Group UK Limited	£648,895,360	National Grid Twenty Seven Limited	£614,417,984
Spire Healthcare (Holdings) Limited	£648,798,016	Chambertin (Holdings) Limited	£614,148,992
BIIF Issuerco Limited	£648,602,944	Lazari Properties 3 Limited	£613,906,816
Fosse Master Issuer PLC	£648,595,968	Choo Luxury Finance Limited	£613,603,968
EMT Holdings Limited	£647,828,736	Nando's Chickenland Limited	£613,513,984
Boreas (Investment) Limited	£647,022,016	Delamare Finance PLC	£613,328,768
Boreas Holdco Limited	£647,022,016	Delamare Group Holdings Limited	£613,328,768
LBG Capital Holdings Limited	£646,334,016	Advent Capital (No. 3) Limited	£613,207,552
Legal & General Insurance Limited	£646,302,976	DMG Charles Limited	£613,156,096
Engelhart CTP Group (UK) Limited	£646,261,760	Equitix Capital Eurobond 2 Limited	£612,945,024
London Stock Exchange (C) Limited	£645,733,184	BL Sainsbury Superstores Limited	£612,800,000
Victoria Investments Bidco Limited	£644,963,968	Neo (BC) UK Limited	£611,671,424
Pearson Education Limited	£644,780,992	ANV Corporate Name Limited	£611,125,248
Tomkins Overseas Investments Limited	£644,658,432	Ludgate Funding PLC	£611,078,016
GHG 1 (Hospital Operations) Limited	£644,283,008	Eaton Square Properties Limited	£610,966,976
Hawthorn Asset Co Limited	£644,088,000	BTG International (Holdings) Limited	£610,744,000
British American Tobacco (GLP) Limited	£643,197,120	Wyelands Holdings Limited	£610,633,024
Liberty Global Finance I (UK) Limited	£642,418,304	Petronas Energy Trading Limited	£610,454,016
Blue Finco Limited	£640,165,376	Bumper 8 (UK) Finance PLC	£610,081,792
Ferrexpo Finance PLC	£639,993,216	IPGL Limited	£609,936,000
Axis Specialty Finance PLC	£639,217,344	Silchester Capital Limited	£609,525,504
Spire Healthcare Group UK Limited	£638,585,984	Cory Riverside (Holdings) Ltd	£609,470,976
Prudential Group Holdings Limited	£637,800,000	SVF Investments (UK) Limited	£609,386,112
Ariel Corporate Member Limited	£637,393,216	Core Laboratories Interests Two Limited	£609,115,136
Greenrock Bidco Limited	£636,700,032	Meadowhall Shopping Centre Property Holdings Ltd	£609,113,216
EMI Group Global Limited	£635,157,440	G4S Regional Management (UK & I) Limited	£608,891,008
TSMUK Ltd	£635,094,080	Longman Group (Overseas Holdings) Limited	£608,614,016
Red Star Pub Company (WR III) Limited	£634,699,008	Craegmoor Limited	£608,579,968
US Real Estate Holdings No.1 Limited	£634,552,512	Viking Consortium Acquisition Limited	£608,558,976
WPP Group Holdings Limited	£634,384,000	Ensco Deepwater Drilling Limited	£608,295,616
British American Tobacco (NGP) Limited	£634,000,000	Touchstone Innovations PLC	£607,612,992
Selfridges Retail Limited	£633,400,000	L & Q PRS Co Limited	£607,241,024
Vue Entertainment Limited	£632,769,984	Ramsay Health Care (UK) Limited	£607,214,976
The Francis Crick Institute Limited	£632,203,008	Smiths Group Finance US Limited	£606,636,928
Axis Corporate Capital UK Limited	£631,026,752	Shell China Exploration and Production Co Ltd	£606,241,920
Feldspar 2016-1 PLC	£630,382,080	SIR Theme Park Subholdco Limited	£605,110,016
Equitix Capital Eurobond 3 Limited	£629,918,976	Rontec Roadside Retail Limited	£604,984,000
Inspired Education Holdings Limited	£629,913,088	Mitsubishi Corporation International (Europe) PLC	£604,982,016

Habib Bank Zurich PLC £604,948,096
Central Asia Metals PLC £604,878,016
Sanford C. Bernstein Limited £604,549,184
Telecom New Zealand (UK) Enterprises Limited £604,340,992
Horizon Bidco Limited £603,552,000
Marex Financial £603,389,888
Otis Limited £603,323,008
Match.Com Europe Limited £602,343,104
Westfield UK Finance Limited £602,275,712
Tullow Oil Finance Limited £601,784,064
Aspen (UK) Holdings Limited £601,392,832
Liquid Telecommunications Financing PLC £600,374,848
Avanti Communications Group PLC £600,222,080
Veolia ES (UK) Limited £598,864,000
DMG Investment Holdings Limited £598,732,992
Babcock Marine & Technology Holdings Limited £598,502,016
Cheniere Marketing International LLP £597,477,568
General Dynamics United Kingdom Limited £597,075,008
FS Holdco Limited £596,767,680
Petropavlovsk Mining Treasury UK Limited £596,645,632
Motorola Solutions UK Acquisition Co Ltd £595,780,992
Global Media & Entertainment Limited £594,673,984
Gresham Receivables (No.36) UK Limited £594,585,344
MAN Group Holdings Limited £594,125,504
Omnicom Media Group UK Limited £593,902,848
Concordia Investment Holdings (UK) Limited £593,745,536
Genel Energy Miran Bina Bawi Limited £593,602,496
KAZ Minerals Aktogay Project Finance Limited £593,343,872
Smart DCC Limited £593,134,016
GMR Capital Limited £592,974,016
Diamond Topco Limited £592,360,832
Advent Capital (Holdings) Ltd £592,307,712
Riverside Resource Recovery Limited £591,950,016
Alstom Transport UK (Holdings) Limited £591,600,000
ELQ Investors IX Ltd £591,273,536
Aggregator Vehicle PLC £590,856,000
LR Baker St Mezz Holdco Limited £589,860,032
Emerald 3 Limited £589,701,120
Northwharf Investments Limited £589,313,984
Principal International South America I Ltd £589,181,888
Sterling Midco Limited £588,585,024
Orsted Burbo Extension Holding Ltd £587,620,672
St Martins Healthcare Limited £587,046,016
Tokio Marine Kiln Insurance Limited £587,022,016
The Guthrie Corporation Limited £586,305,024
Hogan Lovells International LLP £585,950,976
Chime Group Holdings Limited £585,772,032
Clarkson PLC £585,299,968
Touchstone Innovations Businesses LLP £584,473,088
Chime Group Limited £583,385,984
Virgin Active Group Investments Limited £581,766,976
Colt Technology Services £581,110,976
Westfield UK Acquisitions Finance Limited £581,109,568
Pricewaterhousecoopers Services Limited £580,878,016
Entertainment One UK Holdings Limited £579,206,016
Pearson Services Limited £578,584,000
Gower Place Investments Limited £578,492,224
Land Securities Trinity Limited £577,961,984
Euromoney Canada Limited £577,207,040
Praesidiad Limited £577,007,552
Gyrus Group Limited £576,972,224
Pernod Ricard UK Limited £576,435,968
Gunwharf Quays Limited £576,248,000
Ashmore Investments (UK) Limited £575,611,008
Mergermarket Topco Limited £575,283,008
WPP UK Torre £575,240,384
NEX Optimisation Limited £574,574,016
Diamond Bidco Limited £574,081,088
Verisk UK Holdco Limited £573,934,976
Snap Group Limited £573,907,200
Shaftesbury CL Limited £573,478,016
Mavenir Private Holdings I Ltd £573,469,248
Interoute Finco Limited £573,395,392
CWBC Finance (BP1) Limited £573,174,016
Shaftesbury Chinatown PLC £572,806,976
Dollar Financial U.K. Limited £572,625,984
DSG Overseas Investments Limited £572,396,992
Omnicom DDB Holdings Limited £571,212,288
Blackrock Fund Managers Limited £571,065,024
Norlake Hospitality Limited £569,768,896
MIPL Holdings Limited £569,579,008
MIPL Group Limited £569,194,560
Lightsource BP Renewable Energy Investments £569,163,008
Cardinia Europe Limited £568,850,048
Facebook UK Ltd £568,161,024
Sulawesi LNG Development Limited £566,709,120
Equitix Offshore 5 Limited £566,507,008
Primetals Technologies, Limited £565,897,024
Mergermarket Midco 2 Limited £565,339,008
Lancashire Insurance Company (UK) Limited £565,273,088
T.H.F.C. (Capital) PLC £564,777,024
Mitsui Bussan Commodities Ltd £564,504,384
Close Invoice Finance Limited £564,080,896
Guardian Digital Communications Limited £563,625,984
Autovista Group Limited £563,246,912
Prestmade Limited £562,833,024
Sedgwick UK Holdings II Limited £562,665,344
NMC Health PLC £562,635,008
Broadgate PHC 2010 Limited £561,745,664
Morgan Stanley UK Group £561,694,144
UK Group Finance Holdco Limited £561,500,800
L'Oreal (U.K.) Limited £561,248,000
Shell Hasdrubal Limited £561,027,392
LS Mirage Limited £559,720,000
Vetco Gray Holding £559,470,912
Vetco International Holding 4 £558,971,840
Dorchester Hotel Limited £558,947,968
Schroder International Holdings Limited £558,392,000
Repsol Sinopec North Sea Limited £557,872,256
Baxalta UK Investments Ltd. £557,806,848
Virgin Records Overseas Limited £556,294,016
Trinity Financing PLC £556,001,024
CIBC World Markets PLC £555,850,944
QH Partners Limited £555,601,984
Equitix Capital Eurobond 4 Limited £555,246,016
BCS Prime Brokerage Limited £554,758,528
Blackrock Advisors (UK) Limited £554,667,008
Equity Release Funding (No.5) PLC £554,608,000
Equity Release Holdings (No. 5) Limited £554,595,008
Shell International Trading and Shipping Co Ltd £554,585,280
Jones Lang Lasalle Limited £554,233,024
Diamond Midco Limited £553,668,608
Ribbon Bidco Limited £553,521,024
Green Bidco Limited £553,352,000
Daunus Limited £551,070,976
GWI UK Acquisition Company Limited £550,174,016
A.B.F.Holdings Limited £548,924,992
Dorney Issuer Holdco Limited £548,355,264
Tesco Property Finance 6 PLC £548,355,264
Hotel (PL Property) Holding Limited £547,171,008
Babcock Mission Critical Services UK Limited £546,681,984
SHC Holdings Limited £546,337,984
SDN Limited £546,171,008
MV Werften Holdings Limited £546,103,040
Global Ports Holding PLC £545,603,968
Malmaison and Hotel du Vin Property Holdings Ltd £545,097,984
E D & F Man Sugar Limited £544,923,776
Grosvenor Americas Holdings Limited £544,366,976
MCX Dunlin (UK) Limited £544,252,032
Lakeside MWS Limited Liability Partnership £544,158,976
Pret A Manger (Europe) Limited £543,872,000
Canaccord Genuity Limited £543,500,032
Enrichment Holdings Ltd. £543,422,016
Chime Finance Limited £543,316,992

Company	Value
Stena (UK) Limited	£543,296,704
UPP Bond 1 Issuer PLC	£543,244,992
JLT Management Services Limited	£542,601,024
Heron International Holdings	£542,595,008
DTZ UK Bidco Limited	£542,468,928
Telehouse International Corporation of Europe Ltd	£542,392,000
ODH Investments Limited	£542,241,984
HSBC Global Services Limited	£541,986,048
The Girls' Day School Trust	£541,883,008
Jasper Acquisition Holdings Limited	£541,630,976
Numis Corporation PLC	£541,248,000
Select Service Partner UK Limited	£540,833,984
Mediacom UK Limited	£540,497,984
General Healthcare Holding Partnership LLP	£540,470,144
Estia Mortgage Finance II PLC	£539,654,080
Mirion Technologies (HoldingSub1), Ltd.	£538,679,296
Kellas Holdco Limited	£537,846,976
Pontoon Europe Limited	£537,817,024
Impax Environmental Markets PLC	£537,734,016
London Wall Mortgage Capital PLC	£537,627,008
Numis Securities Limited	£537,101,120
FC Skyfall Upper Midco Ltd	£536,985,984
SBWW Investments Asia Limited	£536,686,336
Olsten (U.K.) Holdings Limited	£536,075,008
Black Horse Group Limited	£535,860,992
Patina Rail LLP	£535,208,320
Bavarian Sky UK 1 PLC	£535,042,816
Soco International PLC	£534,689,280
SIR Healthcare 2 Limited	£534,009,984
Standard Bank London Holdings Limited	£533,765,920
Normanglade 4 LLP	£533,096,672
Canary Wharf Finance Leasing (BP1) Limited	£533,058,816
Allianz Renewable Energy Partners VI Limited	£532,901,472
Bana One Limited	£531,905,984
Brewin Dolphin Limited	£531,753,984
The Big Society Trust	£531,660,992
Pam Group Limited	£531,600,000
OSW Co Holdings 1 Limited	£531,573,408
Investec Investments (UK) Limited	£531,236,000
Threadneedle Asset Management Holdings Limited	£530,095,008
Herbert Smith Freehills LLP	£529,800,000
New Green Interim Holdco Limited	£529,785,312
QIB (UK) PLC	£529,767,552
Crown Financial & Merchant Bank PLC	£529,517,760
Sony Music Entertainment UK Limited	£529,380,000
Paramount British Pictures Limited	£529,103,008
Semperian PPP Investment Partners Group Ltd	£528,796,896
House of Fraser (UK & Ireland) Acquisitions Limited	£528,400,000
Arch Syndicate Investments Ltd	£528,316,000
B.A.T (U.K. and Export) Limited	£527,912,992
Universal Music Publishing International Limited	£527,726,016
Titanium UK Holdco 1 Limited	£527,658,304
Express Newspapers	£526,648,000
Residential Mortgage Securities 29 PLC	£526,536,000
Spire UK Holdco 2A Limited	£526,416,000
PSPA Topco Limited	£526,369,984
Multiplex Construction Europe Limited	£526,220,992
Priory Finance Property LLP	£526,184,000
Elementis Securities Limited	£526,135,008
Virgin Active Investment Holdings Limited	£524,923,008
Sony DADC Europe Limited	£524,750,016
Millward Brown No.2337 Limited	£524,694,016
London Bus Services Limited	£524,000,000
Broadgate (PHC 8) 2008 Limited	£523,813,408
Marks & Spencer Simply Foods Limited	£522,369,984
Holidaybreak Limited	£522,100,000
United National Bank Limited	£522,062,240
Google Payment Limited	£521,829,504
ITV Rights Limited	£521,532,992
Bank of Beirut (UK) Ltd	£520,774,112
Mirion Technologies (HoldingRep), Ltd.	£520,683,744
BF Properties (No.4) Ltd	£520,585,440
Uropa Securities PLC	£520,148,000
Uropa Holdings Limited	£520,148,000
A.T. Kearney Holdings Limited	£520,147,648
Weybourne Finance Limited	£520,072,992
Howden Joinery Corporate Services Limited	£519,907,008
Equitix Infrastructure 4 Limited	£519,571,008
WTI/EFW Holdings Ltd	£519,338,400
Threadneedle Investment Services Limited	£519,276,000
Eponymousco Limited	£519,028,768
Investec Group (UK) Limited	£518,907,008
London & Regional (Baker Street) Holdings Ltd	£518,684,992
Lewis Trust Holdings Limited	£518,577,984
Brookfield BBP UK Holdings II Limited	£518,492,128
Fred. Olsen Renewables Limited	£518,380,992
Pisti 2010-1 PLC	£517,854,656
Titan Acquisition Limited	£517,767,648
LMS Offices Limited	£516,957,312
Hess NWE Holdings	£516,650,592
Pacific Life RE Services Limited	£514,976,000
HCA UK Holdings Limited	£514,615,008
Choo Luxury Holdings Limited	£514,512,000
Heron Corporation	£514,127,008
Investec Wealth & Investment Limited	£513,784,992
Land Securities (Hotels) Limited	£513,580,000
Neon Capital Limited	£513,561,984
Westermost Rough Limited	£513,143,840
Harrods Property Limited	£512,872,000
Garden Finance Limited	£512,707,808
Garden Midco 2 Limited	£512,697,888
Universal Music Publishing Limited	£512,600,992
Pelham Capital Investments Ltd	£512,441,696
Petroineos Fuels Limited	£511,922,112
PA Group Treasury Services Limited	£510,671,392
Prometheon Holdings (UK) Limited	£510,200,000
Sunblest Bakeries Limited	£510,161,984
Guthrie Overseas Investments Limited	£509,856,000
TH Holdings Limited	£509,678,016
Friary No.4 PLC	£509,367,008
WSP UK Limited	£508,828,000
Picture Holdco Limited	£508,604,000
Diversified Agency Services Limited	£508,600,960
Bupa Care Homes (ANS) Limited	£508,508,992
Canary Wharf Properties (FC2) Limited	£506,999,264
JC Overseas Ltd	£506,699,008
Docomo Digital Limited	£506,635,616
Sumitomo Electric Finance UK Limited	£506,555,808
SG Kleinwort Hambros Limited	£506,212,960
Investors in Private Capital Limited	£504,670,016
Satellite Financing PLC	£504,411,232
Satellite Financing (Holdings) Limited	£504,411,232
North Atlantic Smaller Co's Investment Trust PLC	£503,508,000
TNS Group Holdings Limited	£503,308,000
Finantia UK Limited	£502,953,664
Pearson Management Services Limited	£502,767,008
ICAP Holdings Limited	£502,540,992
Casual Dining Group Limited	£502,500,000
Bupa Care Homes (Holdings) Limited	£501,759,008
Virgin Active Holdings Limited	£501,740,992
Macquarie International Holdings Limited	£501,500,736
Sarum Issuer Holdco Limited	£501,483,392
Tesco Property Finance 5 PLC	£501,483,392
Macquarie Commodities Finance (UK) Limited	£501,151,776
Trailfinders Group Limited	£501,131,008
The Ocean Marine Insurance Company Limited	£501,000,000
LS QAM Limited	£500,934,016
UCC Europe Limited	£500,802,848
Affinity Sutton Funding Limited	£500,611,008
Affinity Sutton Capital Markets PLC	£500,574,016
Abbey National Property Investments	£500,529,216
Phoenix Global Resources PLC	£500,506,976
Doubleplay III Limited	£500,127,008
Mitie Limited	£499,351,008

Company	Value
Westfield Europe Limited	£498,988,992
Gates Acquisitions Limited	£498,964,960
Mako Global Derivatives Partnership LLP	£498,951,168
Willis International Limited	£498,000,000
UPP Group Limited	£497,760,000
JIB UK Holdings Limited	£497,720,992
BL Superstores Holding Company Limited	£497,491,808
Otter Ports I Limited	£497,233,024
Otter Ports II Limited	£497,069,792
Lazari Properties 2 Limited	£496,940,512
BBA Finance No. 4 Limited	£496,925,056
PCL Funding I Limited	£496,924,992
Springer Nature Publishers Holdings Limited	£496,536,992
BIS (Postal Services Act 2011) CoLtd	£496,387,008
Hubbell (UK) Gulfmex Limited	£496,363,552
Alpha Shipping Finance Limited	£496,321,568
Daejan (UK) Limited	£495,504,352
Mirion Technologies (Global), Ltd.	£495,010,784
Capital & Counties Limited	£495,000,000
McKechnie Aerospace (Europe) Ltd	£494,852,640
Henry Schein Animal Health Holdings Limited	£494,477,600
Le Creuset Holding Limited	£494,433,216
JPMorgan Claverhouse Investment Trust PLC	£494,184,992
NYK Investments Limited	£494,075,616
The All England Lawn Tennis Ground PLC	£493,776,992
Spirit Aerosystems (Europe) Limited	£493,632,000
WPP Brands Development Holdings (UK) Limited	£493,630,016
CGI Finance Holdco Two Limited	£493,419,008
S & P Global Finance Europe Limited	£492,707,008
Wellington Pub Company PLC	£492,552,000
Hays International Holdings Limited	£492,432,992
Kaspersky Lab UK Limited	£492,121,664
Tandem Bank Limited	£492,037,600
ING Services Limited	£491,972,992
Harrods Corporate Management Limited	£491,600,000
First Hydro Company	£491,545,984
BMCE Bank International PLC	£490,960,000
Sumisho Osaka Gas Water UK Limited	£490,910,016
Dialog Semiconductor (UK) Limited	£490,619,808
Salic (UK) Limited	£490,574,752
London Stock Exchange Group Holdings Limited	£490,449,984
Trailfinders Limited	£490,404,992
ABP Mezzanine Holdco UK Limited	£489,700,000
Shine Holdco I Limited	£489,689,984
Shine Holdco II Limited	£489,689,984
Shine Holdco III Limited	£489,689,984
Additional Securities Limited	£488,889,984
Hess Limited	£488,840,864
International Power Luxembourg Finance Limited	£488,660,576
Aberdeen Standard Asia Focus PLC	£488,532,000
McDonald's Real Estate Company No.1 Limited	£488,444,992
Orsted London Array II Limited	£487,599,840
BT Limited	£487,292,000
Lenlyn Holdings Limited	£486,863,008
Academies Enterprise Trust	£486,832,992
Nemo Link Limited	£486,769,856
AON Hewitt Limited	£486,351,008
Rocco Forte Hotels Limited	£486,287,008
Talktalk Telecom Holdings Limited	£486,219,008
Gates Worldwide Limited	£485,624,480
Ark Schools	£485,255,008
Big Society Capital Limited	£485,216,000
British Land Department Stores Limited	£484,833,472
First Hydro Holdings Company	£484,804,000
Intu Metrocentre Finance PLC	£484,724,288
JPMorgan European Investment Trust PLC	£483,779,008
Lendlease Europe Finance PLC	£483,627,008
Maven Investment Partners Ltd	£483,179,360
Photobox Holdco Beta Limited	£482,839,008
HCA Swiss Capital 1 LLP	£482,504,000
Chrysaor North Sea Limited	£481,476,992
TES Global Holdings Direct Limited	£481,471,008
London Diocesan Fund (The)	£481,300,000
Hunting Energy Holdings Limited	£481,165,184
Guildford No.1 PLC	£480,937,984
Burlingtown UK Limited	£480,930,016
Lowland Investment Company P L C	£480,911,008
FTSE International Limited	£480,563,008
Mitie Holdings Limited	£480,476,992
Stena North Sea Limited	£480,460,448
Sheldon Poland Investments Limited	£480,404,000
Premier Oil Exploration and Production Limited	£479,706,976
Colt Telecom Holdings Limited	£479,659,552
Pepsico Holdings	£479,164,992
Jones Lang Lasalle Europe Limited	£479,134,848
J. Murphy & Sons Limited	£478,782,048
Apple Europe Limited	£478,473,984
Mitsui & Co. Europe PLC	£478,259,008
Cushman & Wakefield UK USD Holdco Limited	£478,010,080
Northern & Shell Properties Limited	£477,919,008
Frontier Agriculture Limited	£477,916,000
JLT Insurance Group Holdings Limited	£477,795,008
Corus International (Overseas Holdings) Limited	£477,591,008
Drilton Limited	£477,515,872
Morgan Stanley Montgomerie Investments Ltd	£477,116,256
Octopus Titan VCT PLC	£477,111,008
INEOS Offshore BCS Limited	£477,012,000
Cathedral Capital Holdings Limited	£476,714,880
Turner Broadcasting System Europe Limited	£476,681,056
Principal International South America II Ltd	£476,603,584
Domestic & General Insurance PLC	£476,196,992
Food Investments Limited	£475,087,008
COP Holdings Limited	£474,897,984
Savills Holding Company Limited	£474,801,984
GFI EMEA Holdings Limited	£474,752,384
Worldpay Ecommerce Limited	£474,294,016
TransDigm UK Holdings PLC	£474,105,696
Onesubsea Investments UK Limited	£474,073,376
Romulus Holdings Limited	£474,067,744
Linestair Limited	£473,866,144
Stallergenes Greer PLC	£473,830,016
Cambian Group Holdings Limited	£473,517,440
Mergermarket Midco 1 Limited	£473,171,008
Chubb Market Company Limited	£473,139,008
Conde Nast International Limited	£472,932,000
WSP Group Holdings Limited	£472,518,016
IBC Fourteen Limited	£472,457,984
Spring Technology Staffing Services Limited	£472,331,008
J. Choo Limited	£472,080,992
St. Martins Ltd.	£471,756,992
Babcock Integrated Technology Limited	£471,657,984
Luminus Group Limited	£471,321,984
News Corp Investments UK & Ireland	£470,968,992
Resloc UK 2007-1 PLC	£470,531,104
Babcock International Limited	£470,164,000
R.E.A. Holdings PLC	£469,868,608
Expedia.Com Limited	£469,166,080
International Entertainment Investments Limited	£468,416,000
Bunzl Overseas Holdings Limited	£468,146,784
Canary Wharf Investments (BP4) Limited	£468,023,040
Guaranty Trust Bank (UK) Limited	£467,793,856
10 Brock Street Limited	£466,966,272
Longmartin Properties Limited	£466,899,008
William Pears Group of Companies Limited (The)	£466,644,384
Accor Hotelservices UK Limited	£466,252,000
Global Switch Estates 1 Limited	£465,592,000
Equity Release Funding (No.2) PLC	£465,556,992
Total Oil UK Limited	£465,144,512
The Random House Group Limited	£464,781,536
Canary Finco Limited	£464,684,736
HBOS Financial Services Limited	£464,252,000
Workspace 13 Limited	£463,794,240
Blue Transmission London Array Limited	£463,172,000
Adamant Investment Corporation Limited	£463,083,424

Company	Value
Endemol Shine Group Holding UK Limited	£462,212,992
Ophir Holdings & Ventures Limited	£462,155,936
Clarion Events Limited	£462,028,992
Nesta	£461,948,000
Marfrig Beef (UK) Limited	£461,645,952
Worldpay Limited	£461,369,984
Cummins PGI Holdings Ltd	£460,811,008
Canyon UK Americas Limited	£460,016,864
Farfetch UK Limited	£459,999,008
Heron Property Corporation Limited	£459,950,016
Frasers Hospitality UK Holdings Limited	£459,904,000
Avanti Hylas 2 Limited	£459,201,184
The University of Westminster	£458,990,016
Littonace HMF Limited	£458,935,744
All England Lawn Tennis & Croquet Club Limited	£458,886,016
H.J. Heinz Foods UK Limited	£458,700,000
Sky Holdco Limited	£458,186,976
Hunting Knightsbridge Holdings Limited	£458,136,640
LS White Rose Limited	£458,056,000
Horizon Midco Limited	£457,556,992
Horizon Holdco Limited	£457,500,992
Gabriel International Holdings Limited	£456,810,144
Gabriel International Assets Limited	£456,810,016
GS Sapphire Investment Limited	£456,725,408
Exova Treasury Limited	£456,400,000
Brewin Dolphin Holdings PLC	£456,368,992
Finastra UK Limited	£456,341,312
BMO AM Group (Holdings) Limited	£455,584,992
Priory Securitisation Limited	£455,556,992
Selene Midco Limited	£455,049,984
Sach 2 Ltd	£454,923,008
TPD Investments Limited	£454,883,008
WMR JV Holdco Limited	£454,693,504
WMR JV Investco Limited	£454,693,504
Wheel Bidco Limited	£454,691,840
Schroder Investment Company Limited	£454,628,000
Silchester Partners Limited	£454,588,448
Fantfoot Limited	£454,420,832
Premier Oil Group Holdings Limited	£454,201,248
Tibra Equities Europe Limited	£453,772,128
Moody's Group Finance Limited	£453,686,560
New River Company Limited (The)	£453,612,928
Schweppes International Limited	£453,451,424
NTT Data EMEA Ltd.	£453,437,152
RI Income UK Holdings Limited	£452,668,992
Petra Diamonds US$ Treasury PLC	£452,656,192
Marfrig NBM Holdings Limited	£452,466,304
Violin Debtco Limited	£452,353,984
MHG Senior Borrower Limited	£452,097,984
Renbuff Investments Limited	£452,034,880
Hathber GR Limited	£452,034,880
Santander Lending Limited	£451,748,192
Miracle Nova (UK) Limited	£451,574,016
Barbados Enterprises PLC	£451,490,016
Clyde & Co LLP	£451,137,984
Indigo Parent Limited	£450,963,008
Oxhauth Limited	£450,840,192
Al Mistral Holdco Limited	£450,705,568
Selfridges Holdings Limited	£450,700,000
Al Mistral Parentco Limited	£450,694,688
Ogilvy & Mather Group (Holdings) Limited	£450,340,000
Addison Lee Holdings Limited	£450,331,008
Seadrill Mexico UK Ltd.	£450,155,232
Partnerships in Care Property 1 Limited	£449,929,984
Alstom Transport UK Limited	£449,700,000
Sucden Financial Limited	£449,468,544
Repsol Sinopec Oil Trading Limited	£449,388,416
Ted Baker PLC	£449,164,000
Rosequake Ltd	£449,122,432
ECOM Agrotrade Holdings Limited	£449,119,392
TTL Earls Court Properties Limited	£448,424,992
Motorola Solutions International Holding Limited	£448,356,288
Worldpay AP Ltd.	£448,169,984
Aprilgrange Limited	£447,809,088
London & Regional Group Investments Limited	£447,792,000
Allied World Capital (Europe) Limited	£447,351,840
SSP Financing UK Limited	£447,025,984
Mitsubishi Hitachi Power Systems Europe, Ltd.	£446,872,992
Shell Foundation	£446,822,048
N.B.S.A. Limited	£446,610,400
Enrichment Investments Limited	£446,264,000
Telereal Services Limited	£446,231,008
The Biotech Growth Trust PLC	£446,073,984
Cadogan Holdings Limited	£446,046,016
Britned Development Limited	£445,836,992
Violin Equityco Limited	£445,712,000
Equion Energia Limited	£445,565,440
Oat Hill No.1 PLC	£445,222,272
Mortgage Funding 2008-1 PLC	£444,988,992
IP2IPO Innovations Limited	£444,518,400
JPMorgan Global Growth & Income PLC	£444,516,992
Grand Metropolitan Estates Limited	£444,339,008
Campaign Monitor Holdings (UK) Limited	£444,028,416
Finsbury Square 2017-1 PLC	£444,004,992
Norland Holdings Ltd	£443,864,000
Onesubsea UK Limited	£443,526,816
Nicoventures Holdings Limited	£443,483,008
CWG (Wood Wharf Two) Limited	£443,313,344
Tronox UK Limited	£443,276,352
Gresham Receivables (No.40) UK Limited	£443,018,336
Tonstate Metropole Hotels Limited	£442,838,848
Westermost Rough (Holding) Limited	£442,623,872
Stobart Holdings Limited	£442,312,992
Paysafe Financial Services Limited	£442,009,120
Goldman Sachs Property Management	£441,571,008
CBRE Managed Services Limited	£441,544,000
Addison Lee Midco II Limited	£441,407,008
A-Gas Group Limited	£440,728,000
Vedanta Resources Finance Limited	£440,369,376
E. F. Oil and Gas Limited	£439,857,984
Car Giant Limited	£439,583,008
Koch Commodities Europe Limited	£439,546,880
Great Ormond Street Hospital Children's Charity	£439,535,008
Public Power Corporation Finance PLC	£439,496,064
DIVX Express Limited	£439,371,008
Oasis Community Learning	£439,065,984
Octopus Capital Limited	£438,481,984
HLG Holdings Limited	£438,038,016
Telecom Plus PLC	£437,920,000
Cabot Place Holdings Limited	£437,870,112
Menzies Distribution Limited	£437,800,000
Canary Wharf Properties (FC4) Limited	£437,415,296
John Laing Environmental Assets Group (UK) Ltd	£437,097,984
JIB Group Holdings Limited	£437,011,008
Auburn Securities 9 PLC	£436,812,000
AD INV Limited	£436,667,840
London & Birmingham Hotels Limited	£436,500,000
Broadgate (PHC 11) 2005 Limited	£436,293,856
The Financial Conduct Authority	£436,200,000
Brass No.4 PLC	£436,132,992
Kingfisher Information Technology Services (UK) Ltd	£435,916,992
Babcock Mission Critical Services Ltd	£435,751,008
The Ritz Hotel, Limited	£435,534,336
Newday BondCo PLC	£435,500,000
Infrared Infrastructure Yield Holdings Limited	£435,332,000
TTT Moneycorp Limited	£435,222,016
DS Smith Paper Limited	£434,996,000
Abbey National Treasury Services Overseas Holdings	£434,657,824
INEOS UK SNS Limited	£434,639,008
Koch Fertilizer International Limited	£434,382,752
Salamander Energy Group Limited	£434,304,288
British American Tobacco Malaysia (Investments) Ltd	£434,211,008
Corus Group Limited	£434,000,000
Retina Finance UK Limited	£433,771,008

Company	Value
James River Group Holdings UK Limited	£433,645,568
Smiths Finance Limited	£433,520,992
Mitsui E & P UK Limited	£433,462,016
Mirion Technologies (HoldingSub2), Ltd.	£432,825,920
Gam (U.K.) Limited	£432,663,008
BASF Metals Limited	£432,035,744
Cone Investments UK Limited	£431,731,264
Tokio Millennium RE (UK) Limited	£431,465,984
JPMorgan Global Emerging Markets Income Trust	£431,252,000
EMI Group International Holdings Limited	£430,889,984
British Heart Foundation	£430,300,000
Airport Group Investments Limited	£429,530,720
Burford Capital PLC	£429,369,984
BCP IV UK Fuel Holdings V Limited	£429,251,424
Primount LLP	£429,203,392
Interactive Brokers (U.K.) Limited	£428,656,000
Mobius Wind Holdings Limited	£428,632,000
Arsenal (Emirates Stadium) Limited	£428,489,984
Gresham Receivables (No.46) UK Limited	£428,380,736
Morgan Stanley Investment Management Limited	£428,167,840
Slater & Gordon (UK) 1 Limited	£427,860,992
State Street Europe Limited	£427,441,984
Northern & Shell PLC	£427,102,016
Chesterlodge Limited	£426,804,288
BT European Investments Limited	£426,212,128
Tabletop London Limited	£426,151,552
MEIF II CP SPV 2 Limited	£426,132,000
BG Netherlands Financing Unlimited	£425,758,080
Larch (Nursing Homes) Ltd	£425,367,584
Q Holdco Limited	£425,344,576
Thistle Investments (AMC) Limited	£424,992,000
OM Group (UK) Limited	£424,896,000
S & P Global Commodities UK Limited	£424,832,000
SSC Holdco (UK) Limited	£424,753,472
Tramlink Nottingham (Holdings) Limited	£424,684,992
Tramlink Nottingham Limited	£424,684,992
Grifonas Finance No.1 PLC	£424,332,320
Grifonas Holdings Limited	£424,316,000
LS 62 Buckingham Gate Limited	£424,100,000
Ipek Investment Limited	£423,582,240
Tullett Prebon (Europe) Limited	£423,468,000
Victoria Investments Midco Limited	£423,276,000
Park Tower Investments Limited	£423,218,784
Anglo-Eastern Plantations PLC	£423,065,920
Lion-Shoes Midco Limited	£422,659,136
H & M Hennes & Mauritz UK Limited	£422,466,624
Auto ABS UK Loans 2017 PLC	£422,271,840
Majority Kingdom Investment Limited	£421,737,280
Gresham Receivables (No. 26) UK Limited	£421,650,592
Residential Mortgage Securities 30 PLC	£421,236,992
HCA UK Capital Limited	£421,072,000
Commercial Acceptances Limited	£420,788,192
BG Rosetta Limited	£420,110,720
Bombardier Aerospace (Holdings) UK Limited	£419,972,000
Claridge's Hotel Holdings Limited	£419,864,000
Pharm Research Associates (UK) Limited	£419,205,120
Brunner Investment Trust PLC (The)	£419,014,432
General Healthcare Group Limited	£418,748,000
Total E & P International Ltd.	£418,298,912
Divisional Finance UK Limited	£418,187,584
Alba 2007-1 PLC	£417,871,008
Russneft (UK) Limited	£417,847,072
Newton Investment Management Limited	£417,651,008
DCC Energy Finance UK Limited	£417,610,272
Woodside Energy Holdings (Senegal) Limited	£415,598,752
Close PF Funding I Limited	£415,344,288
First Hydro Finance PLC	£415,268,000
Telesat International Limited	£415,014,688
Casual Dining Bidco Limited	£414,800,000
Tiso Blackstar Group SE	£414,774,240
London & Continental Railways Limited	£414,127,008
The Cranemere Group Limited	£414,117,184
London & Regional Trading Holdings Limited	£414,024,064
Mountview Estates PLC	£413,702,016
Irida PLC	£413,628,384
Computer Patent Annuities International Limited	£413,412,000
Redwood Partnership Ventures 2 Limited	£413,273,984
A2dominion Developments Limited	£412,836,000
Derwent Valley Property Developments Limited	£412,683,616
SK Energy Europe Limited	£412,422,336
Maritime Drilling Holdings Limited	£412,209,312
T & L Sugars Limited	£412,118,432
CWCB Properties (DS6) Limited	£412,080,288
334 Ramsbury Oxford Limited	£412,050,944
Foxland 20FS (UK) Limited	£411,830,464
Monsoon Accessorize Limited	£411,822,016
Saka Indonesia Pangkah Limited	£411,649,920
Sears Limited	£411,600,000
Macquarie Aerospace Holdings UK Limited	£411,140,000
Ashurst LLP	£411,132,992
CenturyLink Impsat Holdings II Limited	£411,103,264
The Savoy Hotel Limited	£410,927,008
OIC Run-Off Limited	£410,925,408
Ove Arup & Partners International Limited	£410,400,000
Shire Pharmaceuticals Group	£410,338,112
Tronox UK Finance Limited	£410,245,984
Lochside Asset Purchaser No.1 PLC	£409,990,016
Ernst & Young Nederland LLP	£409,903,776
KRF Holdings Limited	£409,898,176
Keele Residential Funding PLC	£409,898,176
Largenta Limited	£409,771,008
P & O Properties International Limited	£408,416,160
Unisys Limited	£408,195,008
Northern Trust Management Services Limited	£407,932,512
C.C. Licensing	£407,750,432
Global Radio Holdings Limited	£407,246,016
IAG UK Holdings Limited	£407,060,896
Tam Investment Limited	£406,943,456
VEL Holdings Limited	£406,824,000
Finastra International Limited	£406,431,008
Blackrock Throgmorton Trust PLC	£406,383,008
Addison Lee Financing Limited	£406,199,008
Gazprom Marketing & Trading Retail Limited	£405,369,984
Chilean Northern Mines Limited	£405,213,536
WBA UK Finance Limited	£405,197,440
Hammerson (Value Retail Investments) Limited	£405,153,984
Paragon Group Limited	£404,930,528
Cleveland Clinic UK Holdings Ltd	£404,692,000
Diploma PLC	£404,400,000
Reed Business Information (Holdings) Limited	£404,247,008
National Grid Interconnectors Limited	£403,448,992
RELX Finance Limited	£403,285,120
Financial Times Group Limited	£403,223,008
Equitix Infrastructure 3 Limited	£403,036,000
Fred. Olsen Wind Limited	£402,726,016
R. Raphael & Sons PLC	£402,428,992
Hutchison Whampoa Finance UK PLC	£402,392,480
SCMI Limited	£402,256,832
T.H.F.C. (Funding No.2) PLC	£402,146,176
Telereal 112 Limited	£401,929,984
Bond Mission Critical Services PLC	£401,480,992
Nobel Oil Services (UK) Limited	£401,217,728
Telereal Secured Finance Holdings Limited	£401,185,984
Telereal Secured Finance PLC	£401,183,008
Tronox Sands UK Holdings Limited	£401,132,896
Aegis Finance	£400,807,008
Bupa Care Homes (Cfhcare) Limited	£400,664,000
Barchester Healthcare Limited	£400,609,984
Drillgreat Limited	£400,352,992
RL Finance Bonds No. 2 PLC	£400,349,536
Just Eat (Acquisitions) Holding Limited	£400,210,304
P & P Spearhead UK Holdings, Ltd	£399,981,184
Knight Frank LLP	£399,896,000
Khodorkovsky Foundation	£399,837,536

Company	Value
UK Power Networks Services (Contracting) Limited	£399,351,008
Bechtel Holdings Limited	£398,604,000
CKH Gas Infrastructure Limited	£398,563,008
Axa Partners Holdings Limited	£398,516,992
EDF Development Company Limited	£398,390,016
LIH UK Topco Limited	£397,861,728
Axa Partners CLP UK Holdings Limited	£397,800,992
Rockhopper Exploration PLC	£397,789,088
Honeycomb Investment Trust PLC	£397,782,016
AMS Midco Ltd	£397,456,000
Cambian Group Limited	£397,052,992
VPC Specialty Lending Investments PLC	£397,013,376
Shell U.K. North Atlantic Limited	£396,984,992
Old Oak Holdings Limited	£396,797,184
Koch Industries International Limited	£396,620,416
London Clubs Management Limited	£396,465,984
Barclays Funds Investments Limited	£396,382,496
Institute of Cancer Research: Royal Cancer Hospital	£396,222,016
Catlin Finance (UK) Ltd.	£396,145,696
Bupa Insurance Services Limited	£396,067,008
No Ordinary Designer Label Limited	£396,052,000
Quadrant Construction Services Limited	£396,022,016
Werner European Holding Limited	£395,419,008
TI Magazines Holdings Limited	£395,024,000
The Office Group Midco Limited	£394,288,000
ICG-Longbow Senior Debt Investments No. 1 LLP	£394,285,056
Amore Group (Holdings) Limited	£394,257,984
Omega Leasing (No. 12) Limited	£394,210,336
IPM Energy Trading Limited	£393,924,000
Inmarsat Solutions Limited	£393,781,344
Tottenham Hotspur Stadium Limited	£393,239,424
Jordan International Bank PLC	£393,107,008
Tradition London Clearing Limited	£392,339,008
ADCG (UK) Limited	£392,136,000
Spring Group Limited	£391,708,000
LCI Helicopters (UK) Limited	£391,545,664
London & Regional Overseas Limited	£391,469,312
Big Bus Tours Group Holdings Limited	£391,107,872
DMGZ Limited	£390,674,464
Stanlow Receivables Funding Limited	£390,517,856
Hiscox Underwriting Group Services Limited	£390,224,992
West-Ward Holdings Limited	£390,027,360
Galaxy Group Midco Limited	£389,920,000
DS Smith Packaging Limited	£389,876,000
Guinness Overseas Limited	£389,788,000
CenturyLink Communications UK Limited	£389,547,008
Odeon Cinemas Limited	£389,348,000
E-Carat 8 PLC	£389,287,488
Nando's Group Limited	£389,044,000
News UK & Ireland Limited	£389,009,984
Shell International Limited	£388,148,992
Green Midco Limited	£387,833,984
Chelwood Trading & Investment Company Limited	£387,374,016
GCP (UK) Holdings Limited	£387,252,384
Globaldrive Auto Receivables UK 2017 -A PLC	£387,080,512
Redcastle Limited	£386,992,992
NC Shine Acquisition Ltd.	£386,897,984
Kuoni Holdings Limited	£386,754,880
Sotheby's	£386,742,016
ICE Overseas Limited	£386,730,048
Exova 2014 Limited	£386,700,000
Bouygues (U.K.) Limited	£386,499,008
Consolidated Developments Limited	£386,464,288
Goldman Sachs Group U.K. Finance Limited	£386,361,280
Gresham Receivables (No. 34) UK Limited	£386,315,296
Thomson Legal & Professional Group Limited	£386,249,568
Queensgate Bow Opco Limited	£385,856,000
Bioenergy Infrastructure Limited	£385,801,664
SSP Euro Holdings Limited	£385,417,664
Performing Right Society,Limited	£385,148,000
Fremantlemedia Limited	£385,035,008
Moorgate Funding 2014-1 PLC	£385,007,008
MAN Mash Limited	£384,989,824
Korn Ferry Global Holdings (UK) Limited	£384,886,944
Hammerson (Brent Cross) Limited	£384,833,984
LS Zig Zag Limited	£384,790,016
Cityfibre Infrastructure Holdings Limited	£384,441,984
The Thomson Organisation (No.23)	£384,252,320
Toscafund Limited	£384,173,728
Tennants Consolidated Limited	£383,999,008
Precise Mortgage Funding 2015-3R PLC	£383,940,992
London Wall Investment Warehouse 01 Limited	£383,393,984
Odeon Cinemas Holdings Limited	£382,784,992
CK William Midco 3 Limited	£382,568,768
Chelsea Football Club Limited	£382,318,016
Digital London Limited	£382,056,000
UBMG Services Limited	£381,823,008
Gates European Holdings Limited	£381,603,200
A-Gas Bidco Limited	£381,399,008
White City Property Finance PLC	£381,210,336
White City Property Holdings Limited	£381,197,856
Cathedral Capital (1998) Limited	£381,147,264
Koch Metals Trading Limited	£381,076,448
J.P. Morgan Chase International Financing Limited	£380,692,288
Island Gas Limited	£380,665,984
Photobox Holdco Alpha Limited	£380,443,008
Breezeroad Limited	£380,140,000
FirstGroup Holdings Limited	£380,044,992
Tronox Sands LLP	£379,758,784
Ansco Finance 2011 Limited	£379,688,000
Solarwinds MSP Holdings Limited	£379,050,400
United Dominions Leasing Limited	£379,001,984
Aviva International Holdings Limited	£379,000,000
SEC Lighting Services Trading Limited	£378,683,008
Endurance Worldwide Holdings Limited	£377,993,760
280 Bishopsgate Finance Limited	£377,992,000
Elbon Holdings (3) Limited	£377,729,984
Queensgate Bow UK Topco Limited	£377,627,008
Queensgate Bow UK Parent Limited	£377,615,008
UBM (GP) No1 Limited	£377,396,000
TT Club Mutual Insurance Limited	£377,373,248
Daejan Investments Limited	£376,934,688
Sir Hospital Holdings Limited	£376,676,992
St Andrew's Insurance PLC	£376,388,992
20 Triton Street Limited	£375,995,328
Rutherfurd Acquisitions Limited	£375,680,544
SG Leasing (Gems) Limited	£375,521,312
SIR Theme Parks Limited	£375,456,992
DLA Piper UK LLP	£375,000,000
The Sporting Exchange Limited	£374,878,016
Arunvill Global Equity Trading Limited	£374,113,760
Anchorage Ports LLP	£374,000,000
Lendlease Residential (CG) Limited	£373,705,984
Claranet Group Limited	£373,600,000
Marfrig Beef International Limited	£373,517,472
Laser Hotels One Limited	£373,488,992
BT (International) Holdings Limited	£373,079,008
Punch Taverns Holdings Limited	£373,036,000
University of Greenwich	£372,940,992
GNI (UK) Limited	£372,643,008
Goldman Sachs Asset Management International	£372,600,896
BTG International Limited	£372,600,000
Civica UK Limited	£372,212,000
EBS Group Limited	£372,206,016
York Potash Ltd	£372,072,992
Dukinfield PLC	£371,998,656
Collinson International Limited	£371,536,000
LR Office Developments Limited	£371,424,000
Bounty Brands Holdings Limited	£370,997,824
BOCI Global Commodities (UK) Limited	£370,902,336
Londonmetric Retail Distribution I Limited	£370,769,760
Greenergy International Limited	£370,756,992
Amco Investments Limited	£370,623,008
Amalgamated Metal Corporation PLC	£370,615,008

Company	Value
Financial Models Corporation Limited	£370,591,008
BCP IV UK Fuel Holdings IV Limited	£370,521,120
Kusuma Trust UK	£370,414,688
ICAP Global Broking Investments	£370,399,200
FIA Foundation	£370,140,768
Foseco Holding Limited	£369,887,008
Alberto-Culver Group Limited	£369,865,984
Babcock International Support Services Limited	£369,835,008
Cove Energy Limited	£369,359,040
WRBC Corporate Member Limited	£369,292,352
Puretech Health PLC	£369,228,640
London & Regional Dormant Holdings Limited	£369,081,696
Alberto-Culver UK Products Limited	£368,592,000
BCG UK1 Limited	£368,172,800
Norton Rose Fulbright LLP	£368,057,984
Shortline PLC	£367,979,008
Warner Bros. Entertainment UK Limited	£367,608,992
British Sugar (Overseas) Limited	£367,560,000
SIR Umbrella Limited	£367,551,008
Fremantlemedia Group Limited	£367,287,008
Victoria Investments Intermediate Holdco Limited	£367,176,000
NRG Victory Reinsurance Limited	£367,152,000
WIG Holdings I Limited	£366,838,016
Motorola Solutions UK Limited	£366,800,000
Wright Express International Holdings Limited	£366,444,832
WBA Latin America Limited	£365,959,936
Smiths Group Finance EU Limited	£365,820,896
Marsh & McLennan Companies Acquisition Ltd	£365,533,696
Peabody Capital No 2 PLC	£364,937,984
CIB Properties Limited	£364,287,008
Uropa Assets No. 1 Limited	£364,286,016
UBM Shared Services Limited	£364,011,008
Moussaieff Jewellers Limited	£363,709,760
Cubico Sustainable Investments Holdings Limited	£363,536,576
Creditex Holdco Limited	£363,413,312
Interservefm Ltd	£363,403,008
Finventures UK Limited	£363,097,440
SMBC Leasing (UK) Limited	£363,096,448
Towd Point Mortgage Funding 2016-Granite2 PLC	£362,950,016
Savills (UK) Limited	£362,920,000
Indigo Bidco Limited	£362,772,992
Mitsubishi Estate Europe Limited	£362,456,256
Hurricane Bidco Limited	£362,300,128
Kirkbi Burbo Extension Holding (UK) Limited	£362,230,560
BGL Receivables Financing (1) Limited	£362,109,184
Barclays Capital Asia Holdings Limited	£362,039,552
Euromoney Consortium Limited	£361,844,416
SCDM Energy Limited	£361,823,200
CDW International Holdings Limited	£361,466,592
Coral (Holdings) Limited	£361,332,000
Azzurri Group Limited	£361,200,000
Garden Midco 1 Limited	£361,164,608
Arsenal Securities PLC	£361,136,000
Babcock Land Limited	£360,987,008
The Renewables Infrastructure Group (UK) Limited	£360,944,000
Virgin Active Limited	£360,310,016
Conegate Developments Limited	£360,082,240
Project Lake Holdings Limited	£359,741,696
WPP Toronto Ltd	£359,520,000
Hanover Insurance International Holdings Limited	£359,455,456
Nextenergy Solar Holdings Limited	£359,341,024
Barclays Capital Japan Securities Holdings Limited	£359,312,064
Intu The Hayes Limited	£359,200,000
Karta II PLC	£358,730,176
Burlington Resources (Irish Sea) Limited	£358,432,000
WPP 2318 Limited	£358,289,536
Privilege Holdings Limited	£357,695,008
Flavia Holdco Limited	£357,539,904
Masdar Energy UK Limited	£357,498,400
PG (April) Limited	£357,452,000
Crosby Worldwide Limited	£357,417,760
Roder Investments No. 1 Limited	£357,398,944
Roder Investments No. 2 Limited	£357,398,944
HIG Finance Limited	£357,382,720
Gwynt y Mor OFTO PLC	£357,168,992
Gwynt y Mor OFTO Holdings Limited	£357,168,992
Omnicom Finance Brazil Limited	£357,046,112
PGIM Financial Limited	£356,924,960
Thomson Business Information Holdings Limited	£356,915,072
Sir Richard Sutton Limited	£356,275,008
Privilege Project Finance Limited	£356,260,000
Hachette UK (Holdings) Limited	£356,115,840
Queensgate Bow Propco Limited	£356,014,016
Henderson Global Investors Limited	£355,976,000
Wilphoenix (UK) Limited	£355,793,152
Sedgwick Morden Acquisitions	£355,240,480
WBA Acquisitions UK Holdco 5 Limited	£355,188,992
FIS UK Holdings Limited	£354,972,832
Rampion Investco Limited	£354,662,336
ECOM Agrotrade Limited	£354,628,992
Threadneedle Holdings Limited	£354,388,000
JPMorgan Elect PLC	£354,339,008
Reach Regionals Limited	£354,289,984
JPMorgan Asian Investment Trust PLC	£354,265,984
MSCI Limited	£354,198,240
Diamond Generating Europe Limited	£354,196,256
Finastra Holdings Limited	£353,934,336
PKA Burbo Extension Holding (UK) Limited	£353,897,568
Lanterndew Limited	£353,883,360
Wellcome Trust Investments 1 Unlimited	£353,874,720
Macquarie Factoring (UK) Limited	£353,697,632
Take-Two Interactive Software UK Limited	£353,369,696
Bunzl Overseas Holdings (No. 3) Limited	£353,134,912
Globaldrive Auto Receivables UK 2016-A PLC	£353,116,032
RL Finance Bonds No. 3 PLC	£352,890,784
Insight Investment Management (Global) Limited	£352,744,992
BHF Group UK Limited	£352,742,016
Babcock Integration LLP	£352,720,000
Biocon Biologics Limited	£352,694,368
British Land (Joint Ventures) Limited	£352,564,992
TAI Investments Limited	£352,400,000
Fidelis Underwriting Limited	£352,085,216
Versum Materials UK Limited	£351,856,992
Telereal 112 Investments Limited	£351,784,000
PG Media Services Limited	£351,304,000
Informa Finance UK Limited	£351,220,992
BTGP-BSI Limited	£351,137,152
Parkcare Homes (No.2) Limited	£350,968,000
TES Finance Limited	£350,660,000
Derwent Central Cross Limited	£350,491,808
Zayo Group International Limited	£350,401,984
Smith & Nephew UK Limited	£350,328,992
UPP (Reading I) Holdings Limited	£350,255,008
Wellcome Trust Investments 2 Unlimited	£350,151,584
Gabriel International Limited	£350,121,952
Acquisition Company Finance Limited	£349,780,704
Envol Midco Limited	£349,720,608
UK Power Networks (Operations) Limited	£349,600,000
CRF Health Group Limited	£349,517,120
Tenecom Limited	£349,472,256
Fairhold Services Limited	£349,458,400
Turbo Finance 7 PLC	£349,453,824
Howden Holdings Limited	£349,372,992
Babcock Corporate Services Limited	£349,182,016
Corus International Limited	£349,176,000
Sumitomo Corporation Global Commodities Ltd	£349,153,696
AH UK Animal Health (PVT) Ltd	£348,898,784
Brass No.3 PLC	£348,886,016
Smartestenergy Limited	£348,436,000
Friary No.3 PLC	£348,408,992
TM Media Holdings Limited	£348,332,992
Entertainment One UK Limited	£348,175,008
BMO Capital and Income Investment Trust PLC	£347,862,016
CLSA (UK)	£347,772,992

Company	Value	Company	Value
ERPE Finco Limited	£347,744,864	Addison Lee Group Limited	£337,360,000
Doughty Hanson & Co Managers Limited	£347,649,984	BBDO European Holdings Limited	£337,139,200
Offa No.1 PLC	£347,432,992	Antofagasta Railway Company PLC	£337,045,568
Kazphosphate Limited	£347,144,288	Perpetual Power (UK) Limited	£336,728,224
Energean Oil & Gas PLC	£347,033,664	ITV Enterprises Limited	£336,728,000
Airwave Solutions Limited	£346,984,000	Dunnhumby Limited	£336,665,984
Sach 1 Ltd	£346,892,992	Big Bus Tours Holdings 2 Limited	£336,289,952
Broadgate (PHC 7) Limited	£346,756,768	Drift Properties Limited	£336,155,424
Ophir Thailand (E & P) Limited	£346,719,328	The Doctors Laboratory Limited	£335,769,984
Greater Gabbard OFTO PLC	£346,494,016	R & F One (UK) Limited	£335,727,808
Greater Gabbard OFTO Holdings Limited	£346,494,016	Rome Topco Limited	£335,646,016
Aker Solutions Limited	£346,300,000	Craegmoor Group Limited	£335,324,992
Acquisition Fine Art	£346,102,208	Polar Capital Global Healthcare Trust PLC	£335,188,000
LMS (City Road) Limited	£345,816,256	Cardnet Merchant Services Limited	£335,000,000
Device Finance Collections Limited	£345,774,304	Georgia Healthcare Group PLC	£334,708,992
Uniqlo Europe Ltd	£345,626,208	Holbud Group Limited	£334,627,552
Henderson European Focus Trust PLC	£345,360,992	Schroder Japan Growth Fund PLC	£334,451,008
Truworths UK Holdco 1 Limited	£345,216,992	Gamesys Limited	£334,330,944
AMC Networks International Zone Holdings Limited	£344,959,008	Saturn UK Holdco Limited	£334,280,096
WPP Marketing Communications Spain	£344,875,680	Itochu Europe PLC	£334,200,992
Truworths UK Holdco 2 Limited	£344,678,016	State Street Global Advisors Limited	£334,152,352
Williams Lea Holdings Limited	£344,531,296	Rock Rail East Anglia PLC	£333,846,912
DSG European Investments Limited	£344,328,000	ICP Capital Limited	£333,624,992
LS 1 New Street Square Limited	£344,327,008	Rochester Financing No.2 PLC	£333,255,168
Shell Aviation Limited	£343,973,792	Urban & Civic Central Funding Limited	£333,050,432
JPMorgan Mid Cap Investment Trust PLC	£343,873,984	Pinsent Masons International LLP	£332,936,000
EFT International Investments Holdings Limited	£343,732,320	WSP Group Limited	£332,639,008
Circadian Limited	£343,647,264	Vitality Health Insurance Limited	£332,577,984
Alcentra Limited	£343,567,008	K Line Bulk Shipping (UK) Limited	£332,273,856
Kookmin Bank International Limited	£343,546,016	C. Czarnikow Limited	£332,236,864
DSG Card Handling Services Limited	£343,423,008	Czarnikow Group Limited	£332,222,624
Olympus Finance UK Limited	£343,194,016	Prepay Technologies Limited	£332,164,544
EBS Investments	£343,033,696	Martin's Family Holdings Ltd	£332,118,144
Sedgwick Overseas Limited	£342,951,296	Tam UK Holdings Limited	£332,051,008
Ramsay Health Care UK Operations Limited	£342,732,992	Lionrai Investments No.2 Limited	£332,015,008
Sedgwick UK Holdings Limited	£342,694,624	Praxis II APC Limited	£331,909,920
WMG Finance Limited	£342,334,880	Instinet Global Services Limited	£331,760,000
First Corporate Consultants Ltd	£342,036,000	First Corporate Shipping Limited	£331,729,984
Jeco 2 Ltd	£341,908,704	Shell Pension Reserve Company (UK) Limited	£331,726,592
Chambertin Finance Limited	£341,884,000	Cory Environmental Holdings Limited	£331,579,008
SREP Holdings Ltd	£341,784,992	ICAP Global Broking Finance Limited	£331,522,176
Lebara Limited	£341,635,360	Cory Riverside Energy Finance Limited	£331,468,000
E-Carat 7 PLC	£341,596,864	KAZ Minerals Sales Limited	£331,450,080
Care Homes 2 Limited	£341,372,960	Lovell Partnerships Limited	£331,323,008
Chambertin Midco Limited	£341,305,984	Colliers International EMEA Holdings Limited	£330,942,272
Garban Group Holdings Limited	£341,184,992	Ruspetro Limited	£330,735,168
CP Co Borrower Limited	£341,170,176	Martin's Properties Holdings Limited	£330,562,336
Gemfields Limited	£341,119,904	Ansco Arena Limited	£330,484,000
ICP Holdings Limited	£341,024,992	Nero Holdings Limited	£330,273,984
INEOS E & P (UK) Limited	£340,828,992	Broad Street Principal Investments UK Ltd	£330,222,464
Vesuvius Investments Limited	£340,753,984	ITW Holdings UK	£330,011,008
AECOM Limited	£340,448,992	CMC Markets PLC	£329,871,008
Halliburton Global Holdings Limited	£340,324,000	Praxis II Finance PLC	£329,855,680
Braddell Limited	£340,278,016	Macsco 22 Limited	£329,846,016
Aberdeen New Dawn Investment Trust PLC	£340,276,992	BOC Aviation (UK) Limited	£329,803,392
London & Regional (HC Properties) Limited	£340,204,832	Jupiter Asset Management Limited	£329,800,000
General Motors Europe Limited	£340,200,000	Johnson Matthey (CM) Limited	£329,774,016
UPP (Reading I) Limited	£340,072,992	Annington Rentals (Holdings) Limited	£329,748,992
Broadgate (PHC 3) Limited	£339,584,832	Rensburg Sheppards PLC	£329,575,008
The Book Service Limited	£339,552,288	CBRE UK Acquisition Company Limited	£329,545,440
Beta Central Profits Limited	£339,535,008	Peel Hunt LLP	£329,436,000
Northern Trust Holdings Limited	£339,387,392	Tomori E & P Limited	£328,864,192
Intu Watford Limited	£339,300,000	Doubleplay II Limited	£328,696,000
Marubeni Europe PLC	£339,178,240	Residential Mortgage Securities 28 PLC	£328,656,000
CMS Cameron McKenna Nabarro Olswang LLP	£339,129,984	China Navigation Company Limited (The)	£328,622,016
Cameron Mackintosh Limited	£339,015,136	Union Bank UK PLC	£328,466,304
Blackrock Greater Europe Investment Trust PLC	£338,467,008	Lloyds Bank Hill Samuel Holding Company Ltd	£328,404,992
Donvand Limited	£338,311,712	Legal & General (Unit Trust Managers) Limited	£328,400,000
Capita IT Services Holdings Limited	£337,994,208	Pillar City PLC	£328,173,952
IG Communications Limited	£337,876,992	Wates City of London Properties Limited	£328,102,112
Traveljigsaw Limited	£337,835,008	Ballymore Properties Limited	£327,999,424
Betfair Limited	£337,767,008	LXI Property Holdings 1 Limited	£327,915,328

Company	Value
Radianz Limited	£327,771,008
Retirement Bridge Investments Limited	£327,768,000
Yunnan Limited	£327,691,296
LS Cardiff Limited	£327,521,984
Daily Mail International Limited	£327,368,736
Hammerson (Bristol Investments) Limited	£327,256,992
Ofto Superholdco Limited	£326,990,016
CDW Limited	£326,784,192
Williams Lea Group Limited	£326,702,016
Link Fund Solutions Limited	£326,603,488
Rome Bidco Limited	£326,511,008
Tube Lines Limited	£326,500,000
Mercury Midco 1 Limited	£326,497,984
Hectagon Assets Limited	£326,477,504
Global World-Check	£326,098,048
Stockton Retail Park Limited	£325,927,136
IQVIA Solutions UK Limited	£325,131,008
FIL Investment Management Limited	£325,124,992
National Grid Property Holdings Limited	£325,055,008
The Berkeley Hotel Limited	£325,016,000
Star Pubs & Bars (Property) Limited	£324,868,000
Baillie Gifford UK Growth Fund PLC	£324,745,984
ESBII UK Limited	£324,580,992
Cola Holdings Limited	£324,363,008
Cushman & Wakefield Debenham Tie Leung Limited	£324,272,992
Hansa Trust PLC	£324,108,000
WPP Unicorn Limited	£323,854,016
Robert Walters PLC	£323,680,000
Doubleplay I Limited	£323,665,984
The Office Group Properties Limited	£323,596,992
Valeo Foods UK Limited	£323,568,000
Perenco CUU Long Limited	£323,560,544
Enbridge UK Holdings Ltd	£323,476,352
Trillium (Prime) Holdings Limited	£322,815,008
Rhythmone PLC	£322,566,912
Conning Holdings Limited	£322,362,560
Vanta Education Holdings Limited	£322,304,160
Melli Bank PLC	£322,174,400
London International Exhibition Centre PLC	£322,095,008
China RE UK Limited	£322,030,016
Progressive Global Energy Kurdistan Limited	£322,000,000
Shell Trinidad and Tobago Limited	£321,853,088
Hays Specialist Recruitment Limited	£321,428,992
Ascential UK Holdings Limited	£321,156,000
Equity Release Funding (No.1) PLC	£321,140,992
Chel (Shares) LLP	£321,064,000
Laudico Limited	£321,017,408
BT Global Services Limited	£320,956,992
Chelsea Harbour Estates Limited	£320,928,992
Chambertin Acquisition Limited	£320,928,000
GA HC REIT II CH U.K. Senior Housing Portfolio	£320,859,008
Trainline.Com Limited	£320,743,008
Faist Limited	£320,560,864
Precise Mortgage Funding 2017-1B PLC	£320,159,136
Caffe Nero Group Holdings Ltd	£320,116,992
GWW UK Holdings Ltd	£320,046,048
Beaufort Dedicated No 2 Limited	£320,003,968
AMG Plymouth UK Holdings (1) Limited	£319,957,088
Cheetah Bidco Limited	£319,846,016
Eurosail-UK 2007-4BL PLC	£319,808,992
BLD Property Holdings Limited	£319,718,624
ABF (No.1) Limited	£319,444,000
Sodexo Services Group Limited	£319,384,000
Bank Sepah International PLC	£319,288,064
Avara Pharma Services Ltd	£319,280,512
Cedar Project Holdco Limited	£319,058,560
Elios Energy Holdings Limited	£318,988,992
Clear Channel Overseas Limited	£318,904,992
DS Smith Sudbrook Limited	£318,823,008
Hachette UK Limited	£318,445,280
Oliver Wyman Limited	£318,327,008
Building Energy 1 Holdings PLC	£317,840,352
JIB Overseas Holdings Limited	£317,294,016
IOCL Exploration and Production Oman Limited	£317,222,272
City and Country Properties Limited	£316,945,536
Diageo Financing Turkey Limited	£316,836,992
Kexim Bank (UK) Limited	£316,801,824
Tianqi UK Limited	£316,678,528
Bakkavor Holdings Limited	£316,670,016
Enbridge Rampion UK Ltd	£316,585,952
CELF Advisors LLP	£316,320,992
Element Materials Technology Group Holdings CC2	£316,226,336
CMC Markets UK PLC	£315,727,008
BL Piccadilly Residential Limited	£315,688,608
Ipsos EMEA Holdings Ltd	£315,311,008
Bakkavor Finance (1) Limited	£315,254,016
LS Ashdown Limited	£315,142,016
Primary Health Investment Properties Limited	£315,049,824
Partnership Holdings Limited	£315,001,984
Schroder Asian Total Return Investment Co PLC	£314,976,000
IG Group Limited	£314,800,000
Pinsent Masons LLP	£314,792,000
Allianz Technology Trust PLC	£314,789,312
Winton Group Limited	£314,668,000
Sirius Minerals Holdings Limited	£314,515,008
York Potash Holdings Limited	£314,510,016
Rio 587 Limited	£314,392,992
Christie's International PLC	£314,270,016
Henderson High Income Trust PLC	£314,220,000
Liberty International Financial Services Limited	£314,200,000
Northrop Grumman Global Holdings Limited	£313,907,008
TS Property Lending Limited	£313,885,600
Bluebutton Properties UK Limited	£313,840,096
Travelex Financing PLC	£313,600,000
Fidessa Group Holdings Limited	£313,540,992
Henderson Investment Funds Limited	£313,404,992
DWS Alternatives Global Limited	£313,280,992
Bakkavor Limited	£313,177,984
LSEG (M) Financing Limited	£312,862,720
Horizon RE Limited	£312,594,336
Ernst & Young (Asia-Pacific) Services Limited	£312,475,456
F & G UK Underwriters Limited	£312,447,424
BNP Paribas UK Limited	£312,344,000
Universal Music Leisure Limited	£312,329,984
Fundsmith Emerging Equities Trust PLC	£312,295,008
International Publishing Corporation Limited	£312,148,000
TI Magazines (UK) Limited	£312,147,008
Apple Retail UK Limited	£312,116,000
Tate & Lyle Industries Limited	£312,000,000
Enquest ENS Limited	£311,715,488
S32 Leasing Company Ltd	£311,637,248
Sojitz Europe PLC	£311,593,984
Lendlease Construction (Europe) Limited	£311,507,008
Arcus A1 Investor Vehicle LLP	£311,387,360
CenturyLink EMEA Holdings Limited	£311,319,008
The Kennedy Trust for Rheumatology Research	£311,222,016
Tribeca Square LLP	£311,086,624
Dealogic (Holdings) Limited	£311,071,072
LXI REIT PLC	£310,739,008
Hiscox Holdings Limited	£310,040,992
The Economist Group (US Holdings) Limited	£309,729,376
Global Fashion Group Middle East Holdings (UK) Ltd	£309,625,440
Wind UK Invest Limited	£309,574,016
Intact Limited	£309,339,008
A2dominion Residential Limited	£309,292,000
EC Finance PLC	£309,141,056
BMO AM Group (Management) Limited	£309,137,984
Lifeways Finance Limited	£309,086,816
Newton Management Limited	£308,958,016
ELQ Investors VII Ltd	£308,706,080
Insight Investment Management Limited	£308,249,984
RBS SME Investments Limited	£307,941,952
Wework International Limited	£307,729,440
Credit Suisse Asset Management Limited	£307,521,984

Company	Value
Jones Lang Lasalle European Holdings Limited	£307,476,576
Berry Bros. & Rudd Limited	£307,287,008
Sensis Holding Limited	£307,040,544
Accord Topco Limited	£306,535,008
Priceline.Com Holdco U.K. Limited	£306,015,616
Gunfleet Sands Holding Ltd	£305,772,960
Chapelfield LP Limited	£305,652,000
Babcock Mission Critical Services Topco Ltd	£305,343,008
Deloitte MCS Limited	£305,003,008
Mercer Africa Limited	£305,000,000
BTG International Healthcare Limited	£304,991,168
Omega Leasing (No.9) Limited	£304,946,144
Care Homes 3 Limited	£304,854,976
Kensington Mortgage Securities PLC	£304,827,008
EDF Energy (Energy Branch) Limited	£304,444,992
Freepoint Commodities Holdings Ltd	£304,436,096
Liberty Commodities Limited	£304,431,328
CB-SDG Limited	£304,323,008
HSBC (BGF) Investments Limited	£304,295,328
HSB Engineering Insurance Limited	£304,249,984
Motor Oil Finance PLC	£304,020,864
Henderson International Income Trust PLC	£303,836,000
Interserve (Facilities Management) Ltd	£303,823,008
Discovery Networks International Holdings Ltd	£303,777,984
A2dominion Treasury Limited	£303,657,984
ConocoPhillips (U.K.) Theta Limited	£303,548,000
JPMorgan Russian Securities PLC	£303,319,008
Mansard Mortgages 2007-2 PLC	£303,262,912
Investec Holding Company Limited	£303,216,000
Chubb Capital Ltd	£303,180,992
AHL Partners LLP	£303,114,496
Glen Turner Company Limited	£302,870,016
Cory Riverside Energy Holdings Limited	£302,660,992
Hatton Garden Properties Limited	£302,539,488
Virtus Holdco Limited	£302,497,984
Royal Opera House Covent Garden Foundation	£302,470,016
QW Rail Leasing Limited	£302,383,008
South London Church Fund & Southwark Diocesan	£302,356,000
Chime Holdco Limited	£302,156,000
Elementis UK Limited	£302,100,000
Aberdeen Infrastructure (No.3) Limited	£301,975,008
UK Renewable Holdco 2 Limited	£301,524,128
Big Bus Tours Limited	£301,372,000
Kas No.8 Limited	£301,302,464
Lear Corporation (UK) Limited	£301,100,992
Global Switch Limited	£300,907,008
GB Social Housing PLC	£300,839,968
CWCB Investments (Rt2) Limited	£300,461,376
Trillium (Prime) Project Holdings Limited	£300,000,000
McKesson UK Finance IV Limited	£299,837,376
Ormonde Energy Limited	£299,820,000
Dukinfield II PLC	£299,349,536
Chime Midco Limited	£298,808,000
Wembley Park Limited	£298,687,008
WGC (UK) Limited	£298,472,736
Legal & General Overseas Holdings Limited	£298,400,000
Chime Communications Limited	£298,358,016
PGIM Limited	£298,342,080
Hurricane Cleanco Limited	£298,314,912
Greencoat Solar Assets I Limited	£298,301,216
Hurricane Noteco Limited	£298,236,384
Just Eat Central Holdings Limited	£297,600,000
JLT Reinsurance Brokers Limited	£297,419,008
Oceaneering International Services Limited	£297,031,008
Elios Energy Holdings 3 Limited	£297,017,984
Jupiter Fund Management Group Limited	£297,000,000
Big Bus Tours Group Limited	£296,720,064
AMS Bidco Ltd	£296,640,992
Polar Capital Global Financials Trust PLC	£296,440,000
Keller Investments LLP	£296,062,880
Virgin Active South Africa Holdings Limited	£296,040,544
UK Green Investment Lyle Limited	£295,997,216
IIR Exhibitions Limited	£295,873,984
Tiffany & Co. (UK) Holdings Limited	£295,855,232
Coralglade Limited	£295,748,736
Kirkglade Limited	£295,748,640
OHI UK Healthcare Properties Ltd	£295,727,776
Bank of Scotland Structured Asset Finance Limited	£295,648,000
Freepoint Commodities Europe LLP	£295,441,984
NM Money Holdings Limited	£295,284,992
ITV2 Limited	£295,028,000
Grant Thornton UK LLP	£295,001,984
JLIF Investments Limited	£294,927,008
MYI UK Holdings (No.1) Limited	£294,833,152
Primetals Technologies Financial Services Limited	£294,796,768
Consolidated Developments Holdings Limited	£294,449,536
Metroline Limited	£294,353,984
Forex Capital Markets Limited	£294,042,016
Citibank Investments Limited	£294,000,000
Carolia Tower Hotel Limited	£293,547,008
BL CW Holdings Limited	£293,298,624
Triplereason Limited	£293,268,352
Virgin Gyms Limited	£292,941,664
Workspace 12 Limited	£292,848,896
Taikoo Limited	£292,812,000
WB/TT Holdings Limited	£292,805,344
The Cayzer Trust Company Limited	£292,804,768
Gresham Receivables (No. 31) UK Limited	£292,653,344
Charter Mortgage Funding 2017-1 PLC	£292,532,992
ADG Market Making LLP	£292,496,480
Gresham Receivables (No.27) UK Limited	£292,197,536
Starbucks Coffee Holdings (UK) Limited	£292,150,144
GAM Systematic Holding Limited	£292,132,992
Dobbies Garden Centres Group Limited	£292,004,000
Rothmans International Limited	£291,668,992
Orsted Westermost Rough Limited	£291,576,960
Greenland (United Kingdom) Investment Limited	£291,287,040
Holbud Limited	£291,019,808
JPMorgan Japan Smaller Companies Trust PLC	£290,960,992
GTA Holdco Limited	£290,944,480
GWI UK Holding Limited	£290,752,000
UK Renewable Holdco 3 Limited	£290,605,152
Aamby Valley (UK) Limited	£290,600,480
Intu Metrocentre Limited	£290,600,000
GBT Travel Services UK Limited	£290,376,448
Aberdeen New India Investment Trust PLC	£289,847,008
Transfercom Limited	£289,822,144
Lazari Properties 7 Limited	£289,747,488
WBA Propco C LLP	£289,744,992
North Colonnade Limited	£289,416,768
21CF Shine Holdings UK Limited	£289,287,008
Chelsea Harbour Limited	£289,268,000
Trinity Mirror Media Limited	£289,183,008
HSBC Global Asset Management (UK) Limited	£289,171,008
Eagle 3 Limited	£289,106,272
Foster + Partners Group Limited	£288,990,016
Advanced Payment Solutions Limited	£288,976,928
Mitie Technical Facilities Management Limited	£288,719,008
BNP PUK Holding Limited	£288,488,992
Eurosail-UK 2007-1NC PLC	£288,403,008
WPG Treasury Limited	£288,321,600
Folio London Limited	£288,177,984
Mindshare Media UK Limited	£288,172,000
Chubb Services UK Limited	£288,137,984
PTTEP SP Limited	£288,041,408
Malmaison Hotel du Vin Holdings Limited	£288,036,000
Shaftesbury AV Investment Limited	£287,864,992
London South Bank University	£287,739,008
Harewood Holdings Limited	£287,736,992
Esterline Technologies Global Limited	£287,315,648
Jockey Club Racecourses (Holdings) Limited	£287,300,000
Jockey Club Racecourses Limited	£287,300,000
Agincourt (1) LLP	£287,267,264
Vancor Ltd	£287,055,392

Company	Value
Consolidated Insurance Group Limited	£286,825,984
HGPE FRWL Holdco Limited	£286,798,304
Intu Milton Keynes Limited	£286,700,000
PCF Group PLC	£286,470,016
CDW Finance Bidco Limited	£286,459,040
Greenland Ram (London) Limited	£286,207,872
IQVIA Solutions Finance UK V Ltd.	£286,200,960
Amdipharm Mercury UK Limited	£286,048,608
Deloitte Global Services Holdings Limited	£286,040,320
PIL Investments LLP	£285,891,136
The Stage Shoreditch LLP	£285,726,496
Eversheds Sutherland (International) LLP	£285,665,984
Batleys Properties Limited	£285,641,984
Domestic & General Acquisitions 1 Limited	£285,609,664
Argenta Holdings Limited	£285,520,000
HICP Holdings Limited	£285,406,016
PA Holdings Limited	£285,297,184
10 Trinity Square Residences Limited	£285,265,856
Euston Tower Limited	£285,184,928
Homer Newco Limited	£284,965,952
Dudgeon Holdings Ltd	£284,827,424
Tronox Sands Investment Funding Limited	£284,691,712
Shaftesbury Soho Limited	£284,689,984
GF Financial Markets (UK) Limited	£284,516,544
Pelican Point Power Limited	£284,506,816
Global Starnet Limited	£284,477,760
SHG Acquisition (UK) Limited	£284,444,000
Financial Ombudsman Service Limited	£284,353,984
WPP UK Germany Holdings	£284,348,800
Laird Asia Holdings Limited	£284,280,992
Tolmar Holding Limited	£284,213,632
Elm Trading Limited	£284,190,304
Canary Wharf Investments Limited	£284,075,776
Arca Bidco Limited	£284,056,992
DLG Financing 1 Limited	£283,967,424
OMD Group Limited	£283,872,096
Macmillan Cancer Support	£283,772,000
Korn Ferry GH1 Limited	£283,652,096
Salix Finance Ltd	£283,619,424
Ticketmaster Europe Holdco Limited	£283,597,504
The Restaurant Group (UK) Limited	£283,492,992
Renewable Energy Income Partnership Holdings	£283,285,088
Newday Funding 2015-1 PLC	£283,228,992
Johnson Matthey Precious Metals Limited	£283,208,896
Lloyds Bank Leasing Limited	£283,139,008
Eastlink Lanker PLC	£282,955,488
Phoenix Natural Gas PP Finance PLC	£282,944,992
Newday Funding 2015-2 PLC	£282,388,992
Gazeley UK Limited	£282,299,392
LS Ludgate (No.2) Limited	£281,847,008
Charles Stanley Group PLC	£281,575,008
Fair Isaac Software Holdings Limited	£281,556,352
BL Ealing Limited	£281,541,536
Braehead Glasgow Limited	£281,400,000
Cavendish Nuclear Limited	£281,270,016
Seminole Hard Rock UK Limited	£281,200,992
SPX European Holding Limited	£281,107,008
Agman Investments Limited	£280,990,560
Esporta Health & Fitness Limited	£280,932,000
Montserrat Acquisitions Ltd	£280,834,720
Mandarin Oriental Hyde Park Limited	£280,643,008
Cedar Project Bidco Limited	£280,545,824
Gatehouse Bank PLC	£280,526,240
Chaucer Holdings Limited	£280,480,992
London and City Group Holdings Limited	£280,388,736
Huntsworth PLC	£280,356,992
Mabel Topco Limited	£280,056,992
Mabel Mezzco Limited	£279,979,008
Azzurri Trading Limited	£279,788,000
London Metropolitan University	£279,728,000
Omnicom Holdings Limited	£279,608,960
Schroder Unit Trusts Limited	£279,406,016
Tintagel Castle Limited	£279,398,208
Happybadge Projects Limited	£278,820,672
Equitix Healthcare 2 Limited	£278,769,984
Unisys Europe Limited	£278,650,976
Atrium 5 Limited	£278,579,488
Renewable Energy Income Partnership Holdings 1	£278,375,488
Finlay Group Limited	£278,329,984
Save The Children International	£278,284,128
DCC Technology Limited	£278,057,056
Limited Life Assets Master Limited	£277,453,184
Braehead Park Investments Limited	£277,400,000
Melton Renewable Energy UK Limited	£277,388,000
Bridge Petroleum 3 Limited	£277,386,336
Cranefield Limited	£277,384,000
Orsted Power (Gunfleet Sands) Ltd	£277,132,864
Dorrington Investment P L C	£277,083,776
London & Regional Group Trading No.3 Limited	£277,039,296
Investec Asset Management Limited	£276,782,016
Moody's Analytics UK Limited	£276,720,000
Miller 2015 Limited	£276,464,992
Tarsus Group Limited	£276,295,744
STV News Services Limited	£276,295,008
BTC Islands Limited	£276,275,008
Edenred (UK Group) Limited	£276,148,992
IPP Gas Holdings Limited	£276,008,256
PE QIQ Holding Limited	£275,857,536
Project Quill Holding Limited	£275,825,504
Martin Pecheur Sterling Investments Limited	£275,713,984
Bakethin Finance PLC	£275,513,984
Investcorp Credit Management EU Limited	£275,499,008
Renewable Energy Income Partnership Holdings 2	£275,413,152
Bridge Petroleum 4 Limited	£275,281,760
Brixton Premier Park Limited	£275,022,016
LS Buchanan Limited	£274,824,000
RSL Finance (No. 1) PLC	£274,515,008
Monex Europe Limited	£274,497,568
Brit Group Finance Limited	£274,325,536
Gazeley Blue UK Limited	£274,312,000
CBRE Global Investors Europe Holdings Limited	£274,260,480
ConocoPhillips (U.K.) Zeta Limited	£273,900,992
Bifurcate Funding Limited	£273,885,696
International General Insurance Company (UK)	£273,796,096
SThree PLC	£273,526,016
DHE Regional Limited	£273,427,552
Charles Stanley & Co. Limited	£273,304,992
Daejan Traders Limited	£273,240,448
Communications Networking Services (UK)	£273,144,992
Sainsbury Property Investments Limited	£273,072,992
Subsea Leasing Limited	£272,916,320
Seadrill UK Ltd.	£272,841,344
Henares Limited	£272,633,312
BBA Finance	£272,423,008
AB Agri Limited	£272,384,000
Livanova IP Limited	£272,070,016
Icebox Bidco Limited	£271,952,160
Premiertel PLC	£271,939,808
Marble Arch Residential Securitisation No. 4 PLC	£271,896,992
TechnipFMC Umbilicals Ltd	£271,892,000
Macquarie UK Passenger Leasing Limited	£271,819,008
Press Acquisitions Limited	£271,500,000
Claridge's Hotel Limited	£271,292,992
AGF Insurance Limited	£270,728,992
MF White Television City Limited	£270,412,448
GS Finco Limited	£270,194,976
Tullow Oil SPE Limited	£270,039,936
Aberdeen Standard Equity Income Trust PLC	£270,012,992
Pall Mall Investments (London) Limited	£269,763,552
Legal & General International Limited	£269,700,000
Truworths UK Holdco 3 Limited	£269,256,000
Friary No.2 PLC	£268,963,008
Societe Generale Investments (U.K.) Limited	£268,892,896
GFI Securities Limited	£268,811,136

Company	Value
Gates Holdings Limited	£268,790,144
Imagination Industries Ltd	£268,537,984
Nameco (No.808) Limited	£268,418,000
Novae Group Limited	£268,199,008
Empiric Investments (Four) Limited	£268,000,608
Kajima Europe Limited	£267,948,992
Bestway Northern Limited	£267,483,008
BG Gas Marketing Ltd	£267,350,816
CFC Group Limited	£267,292,992
Corsair Mint III Limited	£267,107,008
Blackrock Frontiers Investment Trust PLC	£267,097,248
Maref Topco Ltd	£267,028,992
Grantchester Holdings Limited	£267,011,008
Osnaburgh Street Limited	£266,898,016
Vocalink Limited	£266,700,000
Cyan Auto Receivables Limited	£266,576,944
Lombard Technology Services Limited	£266,254,000
Lendlease (Elephant & Castle) Limited	£266,116,000
Lanesborough Management Limited	£266,096,480
Burberry International Holdings Limited	£265,968,000
Westpac Europe Limited	£265,950,128
Mitsui Sumitomo Insurance Co (Europe) Ltd	£265,940,000
VIL Ltd	£265,902,832
Diamond Transmission Corporation Limited	£265,720,400
Road Management Group Limited	£265,700,992
Punch Taverns (Chiltern) Limited	£265,568,000
The Tudor Trust	£265,531,008
Pyrenees Acquisitions Limited	£265,519,440
Pan African Resources PLC	£265,342,112
Reach Printing Services Limited	£265,234,000
Trinity Mirror Finance Limited	£265,186,000
Regus Group Limited	£264,931,008
Eskmuir Properties Limited	£264,882,000
Henderson Eurotrust PLC	£264,792,992
CNR International (U.K.) Developments Limited	£264,780,000
Canonical Group Limited	£264,696,960
M & C Saatchi PLC	£264,628,992
Rail Settlement Plan Limited	£264,544,000
Darrowby No. 4 PLC	£264,507,008
Chesterfield Properties Limited	£264,465,888
Debussy DTC PLC	£264,278,832
YOA Holdco Limited	£264,146,400
Interconnector (UK) Limited	£264,088,992
Revcap Finance Limited	£263,825,504
Avanti Communications Infrastructure Limited	£263,243,008
ITW CS (UK) Ltd	£263,220,992
Deloitte Global Services Limited	£263,217,952
International Biotechnology Trust PLC	£263,216,992
Osaka Gas UK, Ltd.	£263,109,536
Diageo Treasury Australia LLP	£263,008,000
The Office Group Holdings Limited	£263,000,000
Heron Quays Investments (RT3) Limited	£262,956,432
Best Buy Distributions Limited	£262,927,024
Alliance Automotive Procurement Limited	£262,744,832
Caesars Entertainment UK Limited	£262,598,000
Eurosail-UK 2007-2NP PLC	£262,463,008
Choicezone Limited	£262,394,000
Lloyds Bank Insurance Services Limited	£262,320,992
Morgan Stanley Longcross Limited	£262,255,616
American Express Holdings Limited	£262,031,008
BTG Pactual UK Holdco Limited	£262,024,000
BDO LLP	£262,000,000
Eurosail-UK 2007-5NP PLC	£261,942,000
Central Equity Limited	£261,877,744
ICF Debt Pool LLP	£261,841,776
G.H. Financials Limited	£261,379,952
BL Retail Investments Limited	£261,227,280
MEPC (1946) Limited	£261,100,000
Trustees of The London Clinic Limited	£261,098,000
BL Superstores Finance PLC	£261,046,432
BL Superstores (Funding) Ltd	£260,975,808
NBG Finance (Dollar) PLC	£260,890,496

Company	Value
TRG (Holdings) Limited	£260,793,040
Dress Holdco A Limited	£260,760,000
Young Street Holdings Limited	£260,710,928
Imperial London Hotels Group Limited	£260,678,272
Prepaid Financial Services Limited	£260,460,720
Petroceltic Holdings Limited	£260,352,672
10 Gresham Street LLP	£260,140,992
NCR Limited	£260,072,000
Balfour Beatty Group Employment Limited	£260,028,992
Macquarie Infrastructure and Real Assets Investments	£259,832,144
Sponsio Limited	£259,806,000
Stepstone UK Holding Limited	£259,645,008
National Grid International Limited	£259,355,008
Abbey Commercial Ltd	£259,263,952
BMO AM Treasury Limited	£259,263,008
Hammerson (Leeds Investments) Limited	£259,208,000
Pharmadeals Limited	£259,192,992
Norwegian Sextant Ltd	£259,151,472
Cubcall Limited	£259,131,696
Bear Stearns UK Holdings Limited	£259,109,920
CLS UK Intermediate Holdings Ltd.	£259,032,992
Bridging Trading LLP	£259,024,000
GFI Markets Limited	£258,980,288
XTX Markets Limited	£258,720,992
Haven Funding PLC	£258,643,488
Kantar UK Limited	£258,600,992
Better Properties Limited	£258,540,416
Cameron Flow Control Technology (UK) Limited	£258,540,000
Theatre (Hospitals) No.1 PLC	£258,527,664
HCA International Holdings Limited	£258,515,008
Omnicom Media Group Europe Limited	£258,506,032
Treimco Limited	£258,423,008
Ham Yard Investment Limited	£258,308,000
Santander Private Banking UK Limited	£258,157,104
Rank Foundation Limited (The)	£258,116,000
Accord Bidco Limited	£257,920,992
IIR Management Limited	£257,799,008
GenFinance II PLC	£257,730,000
Xerium Technologies Limited	£257,579,040
Connect Bidco Limited	£257,380,000
Thameswey Limited	£257,317,360
Fisher Island Limited	£257,087,008
Square Enix Limited	£256,988,000
Travelex Banknotes Limited	£256,947,008
Finastra Global Limited	£256,901,760
British Land Leisure Limited	£256,898,032
Taste Bidco Limited	£256,824,000
UPP Bond 1 Limited	£256,740,000
Telit Communications PLC	£256,675,536
Charity Projects	£256,515,008
Inchcape Corporate Services Limited	£256,512,992
The Lancaster Landmark Hotel Company Limited	£256,484,992
Global Radio Acquisitions Limited	£256,482,000
Noble Clean Fuels Limited	£256,477,360
Kellen Acquisitions Limited	£256,438,000
DLG Financing 2 Limited	£256,346,816
ITV Global Entertainment Limited	£255,998,000
Clarusone Sourcing Services LLP	£255,661,328
Schawk Wace Group	£255,654,624
Pictet Asset Management Limited	£255,614,496
UD Europe Limited	£255,606,656
Diamond Bank (UK) PLC	£255,525,328
Rockrose UKCS4 Limited	£255,492,608
Stratford City Business District Limited	£255,488,992
IGas Energy PLC	£254,926,000
BB & R Limited	£254,874,000
Lockton Companies LLP	£254,708,208
Hiscox Underwriting Ltd	£254,584,000
Endemol Shine UK Limited	£254,548,000
Canyon UK Investments Ltd.	£254,546,432
Belmond Dollar Treasury Limited	£254,479,024
Marathon Oil West of Shetlands Limited	£254,471,648

Company	Value	Company	Value
Morgan Stanley Group (Europe)	£254,409,264	Estates & Agency Holdings Limited	£247,903,008
RPOW UK Limited	£254,321,424	The Phone House Holdings (UK) Limited	£247,812,000
Shine Limited	£254,308,000	Sager House (Almeida) Limited	£247,620,912
Uropa Assets No.2 Limited	£254,236,000	ICAP Holdings (UK) Limited	£247,348,000
Rome PIK Holdco Limited	£254,214,000	Vertus NFL Limited	£247,151,248
ISS Group Holdings Limited	£253,964,576	Highdorn Co. Limited	£247,083,008
Medical Centre Holdings Limited	£253,825,792	Pitch International LLP	£247,011,232
Intu Eldon Square Limited	£253,800,000	GAP (UK Holdings) Limited	£246,929,248
European Express Enterprises Limited	£253,755,520	Pace Topco Limited	£246,798,272
JPMorgan Smaller Companies Investment Trust PLC	£253,543,008	Emerson Electric U.K. Limited	£246,712,000
LS Ludgate (No.1) Limited	£253,495,008	Eurosail-UK 2007-3BL PLC	£246,550,000
Anglo Pacific Group PLC	£253,362,000	80 Charlotte Street Limited	£246,540,480
TNS-NFO UK Limited	£253,229,776	Agman Holdings Limited	£246,521,040
Axel Springer International Limited	£253,048,400	Caledonian Rail Leasing Limited	£246,472,928
T.H.F.C. (Funding No. 1) PLC	£253,020,928	Euromoney Charles Limited	£246,377,120
Artesian Finance III PLC	£252,884,992	Lazard & Co., Holdings Limited	£246,362,000
Marsh Treasury Services Limited	£252,600,000	Shell Trinidad 5(A) Limited	£246,320,624
Rothschild & Co Continuation Limited	£252,591,008	Ansco UK Finance Co. 2 Ltd.	£246,295,008
Thrones 2015-1 PLC	£252,474,016	Vibe Corporate Member Limited	£246,222,000
Lockton International Holdings Limited	£252,444,704	B.A.T Uzbekistan (Investments) Limited	£246,196,992
East Finance PLC	£252,320,000	Surgical Specialties Corporation Limited	£246,160,832
Financial Times Limited (The)	£252,068,000	O & H Properties Limited	£246,090,224
Allianz Renewable Energy Partners II Limited	£252,027,536	Elementis US Limited	£246,078,128
Arena Racing Corporation Limited	£251,999,008	Triathlon Homes LLP	£245,935,008
IMG Media Limited	£251,994,256	Lanespace Limited	£245,840,576
APS Financial Limited	£251,991,120	Opet International Limited	£245,744,000
DMG Loanco Limited	£251,888,000	Segro Industrial Estates Limited	£245,743,008
Mabel Bidco Limited	£251,844,992	Redwood Partnership Ventures Limited	£245,708,000
Lexadon Limited	£251,702,176	Interpublic Limited	£245,632,992
Fred. Olsen Wind Holdings Limited	£251,660,992	Slater & Gordon (UK) 2 LLP	£245,571,776
Mitsui E & P Mozambique Area 1 Limited	£251,497,792	LW Theatres Group Limited	£245,442,000
Mercury Acquisitions Limited	£251,474,000	Gresham Receivables (No. 32) UK Limited	£245,321,952
WPP 2709 Limited	£251,386,000	CB-SDG Topco Limited	£245,208,992
Currencies Direct Holdings Limited	£251,304,992	CB-SDG Midco Limited	£245,136,000
Total E & P International K2 Ltd.	£251,288,736	Sirius (Korea) Limited	£245,060,000
Electrocomponents US Finance Limited	£251,275,008	XL London Market Group Limited	£244,859,008
Intermediate Capital Managers Limited	£251,123,008	Lloyds Bank Equipment Leasing (No. 1) Limited	£244,838,000
Diamond Rig Investments Limited	£251,072,608	Shell Gas Holdings (Malaysia) Limited	£244,753,920
Bedford Estates London Estates LLP	£250,849,664	Newday Funding 2017-1 PLC	£244,504,000
JPMorgan Chinese Investment Trust PLC	£250,552,000	Newday Partnership Funding 2015-1 PLC	£244,454,000
Dow Jones Business Interactive (U.K.), Limited	£250,481,280	Quilter Investors Limited	£244,436,992
Precis (1789) Limited	£250,468,992	Danataugusta Propco1 Limited	£244,316,992
Max Recovery Limited	£250,420,304	Accantia Group Holdings	£244,275,008
Metdist Limited	£250,398,688	Threadneedle Asset Management Limited	£244,072,992
Schroder Financial Holdings Limited	£250,094,000	Simmons & Simmons LLP	£244,031,008
Awilco Drilling PLC	£250,017,328	Taste Midco 2 Limited	£243,928,000
United Cinemas International (UK) Limited	£249,984,000	Urban & Civic Alconbury Limited	£243,914,512
Alixpartners Ltd	£249,976,000	Advantage Sales & Marketing Limited	£243,774,000
Chrysaor E & P Services Limited	£249,932,000	Ensco Finance Limited	£243,765,232
Canary Wharf Properties (Crossrail) Limited	£249,887,808	Danataugusta Propco3 Limited	£243,531,008
Arena Leisure Limited	£249,826,032	Arlington House Investments Limited	£243,493,280
Oranje-Nassau Energie Resources Limited	£249,782,000	Babcock Critical Assets Holdings LLP	£243,492,000
Aviva Investors Realm Infrastructure No.1 Limited	£249,686,352	Shire Holdings Europe Limited	£243,420,304
Orsted Lincs (UK) Ltd	£249,480,352	Dauphine Holdings (UK) Limited	£243,208,864
Sojitz Global Finance PLC	£249,431,344	Santander Asset Management UK Holdings Limited	£243,189,888
Cornwall Bidco Limited	£249,374,000	3i Assets LLP	£243,089,632
Ribbon Mezzco Limited	£249,370,000	Craegmoor Group (No.3) Limited	£243,035,008
Conduit Insurance Holdings Limited	£249,200,000	TES Global Limited	£242,991,008
Bedford Estates Bloomsbury Limited	£249,090,080	Almack Ltd	£242,607,008
Monsoon Holdings (No.1) Limited	£248,830,336	Pipesafe Limited	£242,335,328
Gazeley Limited	£248,722,288	United Cinemas International Acquisitions Limited	£242,300,000
Travel Document Service	£248,644,992	Punch Taverns Holdco (A) Limited	£242,174,000
Economist Newspaper Limited (The)	£248,560,992	Punch Taverns Intermediate Holdco (A) Limited	£242,174,000
Aberforth Split Level Income Trust PLC	£248,230,000	Amesbury Holdings Limited	£242,070,816
Newday Funding 2016-1 PLC	£248,188,000	Malmaison Hotel du Vin Brand Services Limited	£241,928,000
PIMCO Europe Ltd	£248,174,000	Tower Bridge Funding No.1 PLC	£241,896,928
WTI Ferrybridge Limited	£248,105,824	Antham 1 Limited	£241,783,008
Nectar Loyalty Limited	£248,076,000	Vue Entertainment Investment Limited	£241,616,000
MMC Middle East Holdings Limited	£248,050,960	Lightsource Radiate 2 Limited	£241,353,520
Shenda Investment UK Limited	£248,003,696	Falck Renewables Wind Limited	£241,327,008
Antalis Limited	£247,910,000	Slate No.2 PLC	£241,276,384
Brixton Greenford Park Limited	£247,908,992	Thistle Investments (ERM) Limited	£241,243,008

Company	Amount
Capita Life & Pensions Regulated Services Limited	£241,236,640
TIAA International Holdings 2 Limited	£241,177,152
Beazley Furlonge Holdings Limited	£240,979,280
Sampford Underwriting Limited	£240,958,000
Carestream Dental Technology Holdings 2 Limited	£240,825,504
International Power (Genco) Limited	£240,790,752
International Power Australia Holdings Limited	£240,671,856
Modernelite Limited	£240,596,832
Liberty Zeta Limited	£240,586,000
Infrastructure Investments (Affinity) Limited	£240,562,304
Broadgate (PHC 9) Limited	£240,521,392
TFS Derivatives Limited	£240,331,008
Digital River UK Holdings II Ltd	£240,324,416
GC Campden Hill LLP	£240,168,080
West London & Suburban Property Investments Ltd	£240,080,768
Sonali Bank (UK) Limited	£240,077,552
Thrones 2014-1 PLC	£239,963,856
FPI (UK) 1 Limited	£239,892,064
Prudential Services Limited	£239,867,008
Vouvray Midco Limited	£239,769,888
Aetna Insurance Company Limited	£239,318,032
Rio Tinto Diamonds Limited	£239,263,200
Howden UK Group Limited	£239,256,000
Castell 2017-1 PLC	£239,197,824
Dress Holdco 4 Limited	£239,168,000
Premier Place Finance Limited	£239,100,992
Deutsche Alternative Asset Management (UK) Ltd	£239,092,992
Warner Bros. Studios Leavesden Limited	£239,048,000
Hakkasan Limited	£239,011,792
BCI UK Holdings Limited	£239,008,048
Babcock DSG Ltd	£239,002,000
Morgan Stanley Gamma Investments	£238,896,992
Bunzl Retail & Healthcare Supplies Limited	£238,888,992
Imperial London Hotels Limited (The)	£238,855,712
FTI Consulting LLP	£238,742,000
CBRE GWS Limited	£238,648,000
Hammerson (Leicester) Limited.	£238,427,008
Esselco Group Limited	£237,924,000
Ping Petroleum UK Limited	£237,891,680
Arca Topco Limited	£237,848,000
Arca Midco Limited	£237,848,000
WFL (UK) Limited	£237,782,000
Schroder Income Growth Fund PLC	£237,619,008
Citigroup Global Markets Europe Finance Limited	£237,482,176
Phoenix Energy Holdings Limited	£237,426,000
Admiral Taverns Limited	£237,404,000
Vouvray Finance Limited	£237,180,608
Westone Hotel Acquisitions Company	£237,096,000
The Foundry Topco No.2 Limited	£236,972,000
ITV Consumer Limited	£236,518,000
International Entertainment Finance Limited	£236,472,000
The Tower Hotel (London) Limited	£236,366,000
Together Asset Backed Securitisation 1 PLC	£236,310,448
Broad Gain (UK) Limited	£236,256,000
British American Tobacco Global Travel Retail Limited	£236,178,800
International Entertainment Midco Limited	£236,128,992
Gazeley Holdings UK Limited	£236,044,848
Eurohome UK Mortgages 2007-2 PLC	£235,976,720
Otis UK Holding Limited	£235,964,992
Greif UK International Holding Ltd	£235,953,968
Hunter Up 1 Limited	£235,827,264
MEIF II CP Holdings 1 Limited	£235,586,000
Waldorf Hotel Investment Limited	£235,574,000
Weston Aerospace Limited	£235,542,000
Lakeside Asset Backed Securitisation 1 Limited	£235,501,472
Catalina Echo Limited	£235,451,536
SThree Overseas Holdings Limited	£234,876,992
UKTV Media Limited	£234,824,992
UKTV Media Holdings Limited	£234,824,992
Universal Music Publishing MGB Limited	£234,824,000
Terido LLP	£234,794,560
Liberty Living Investments II Limited	£234,742,000

Company	Amount
Ritz Hotel (London) Limited (The)	£234,716,000
Halifax Leasing (September) Limited	£234,614,000
Knightsbridge Asset Management Limited	£234,496,992
PZ Cussons Beauty LLP	£234,435,008
Exova Group Limited	£234,300,000
Sinochem Resources UK Limited	£234,224,496
Harvey Nash Group Limited	£234,156,992
Electra Investments Limited	£234,050,000
Bayeast Property Co Limited	£233,956,160
Lonrho Holdings Limited	£233,548,880
Bodiam Hill Limited	£233,356,000
Chaucer Capital Investments Limited	£233,311,008
Lavenham Underwriting Limited	£233,280,000
DHCM Holdco Limited	£233,235,008
Tomkins Engineering Limited	£233,224,000
Deco 8 - UK Conduit 2 PLC	£233,217,856
Vedanta Finance UK Limited	£232,788,144
Farmcare Trading Limited	£232,788,000
Element Materials Technology Group Holdings CC1	£232,769,120
Sumi Agro Europe Limited	£232,749,680
China Merchants Securities (UK) Limited	£232,548,272
Benesco Charity Limited	£232,532,992
Vue Entertainment Holdings (UK) Limited	£232,246,000
Consolidated Holdings Limited	£232,203,568
Savers Health and Beauty Limited	£231,971,008
Equifax EUA Limited	£231,827,008
Freightliner Limited	£231,786,000
Lendlease Construction Holdings (Europe) Limited	£231,532,000
Exane Limited	£231,505,600
Eurosail 2006-4NP PLC	£231,500,992
Marken Limited	£231,155,008
Proserv Operations Limited	£231,134,000
All3media Finance Limited	£231,122,992
Endeavour Acquisition UK Limited	£231,079,472
Centurycomm Limited	£231,010,000
Luminus Finance Limited	£230,976,000
ITWP Acquisitions Limited	£230,632,000
Tottenham Hotspur Stadium Development Limited	£230,498,896
Livn UK Holdco Limited	£230,488,480
Horizon Groupco Limited	£230,488,000
Metropolitan Properties Co. (F.G.C.) Limited	£230,389,968
NGC Europe Limited	£230,372,992
WPP Rocky Ltd	£230,320,992
EII (Ventures) Limited	£230,260,832
Horizon Debtco Limited	£230,171,008
Colgems Productions Limited	£230,024,672
Blackrock Latin American Investment Trust PLC	£229,985,680
Canada Square Operations Limited	£229,907,008
GCM Global Energy PLC	£229,834,272
DDB UK Investments Limited	£229,576,656
IQVIA Holdings (UK) Ltd.	£229,368,992
Folgate Holdings Limited	£229,219,760
Boeing Defence UK Limited	£229,212,000
Marks and Spencer Guernsey Investments LLP	£229,047,536
Vectura Group Services Limited	£229,000,000
R.Twining and Company Limited	£228,972,000
Topland Jupiter Limited	£228,901,472
UK Green Investment Sheringham Shoal Limited	£228,822,144
Stow Real Estate PLC	£228,770,512
Project Leopard Topco Limited	£228,740,992
Marlbray Limited	£228,660,992
WGC (UK) Finance Limited	£228,504,176
London & Regional (St. Georges Court) Limited	£228,207,872
Bradley Hall Holdings Limited	£228,177,776
Build King Construction Limited	£228,167,264
CB & I UK Limited	£228,016,992
Wagamama Finance PLC	£227,991,008
Triplog Holdings Limited	£227,880,032
UK Group of Hotels PLC	£227,820,992
Babcock Rail Limited	£227,783,008
Mezqual Limited	£227,753,104
Hubbell Holdings Europe Limited	£227,494,000

Company	Value
Babcock Mission Critical Services Leasing Limited	£227,423,008
Moody's Investors Service Limited	£227,268,992
RDL Realisation PLC	£227,264,160
TFG Brands (London) Limited	£227,236,992
Structadene (LBG) Properties Limited	£227,176,336
WP R Midco 1 Limited	£226,974,000
QVC UK	£226,948,000
Redrock Investment Limited	£226,744,384
Vitol Services Limited	£226,713,120
UKEI (Finance) Limited	£226,623,104
Clear Channel UK Limited	£226,330,000
Iron Mountain Europe Limited	£226,174,000
Redquince Limited	£225,825,200
Borders & Southern Petroleum PLC	£225,633,152
Pacific Horizon Investment Trust PLC	£225,630,000
The Robert Hitchins Group Limited	£225,528,000
Elios Renewable Energy Limited	£225,274,000
Arig Capital Limited	£225,170,000
A.S. Watson (P & C UK) Ltd	£225,150,528
West Quay Shopping Centre Limited	£225,128,992
Encore Oil Limited	£225,123,472
Omnicom Latam Holdings Limited	£225,021,744
Wilhunter (UK) Limited	£224,941,344
LTG International Limited	£224,694,928
J. Leon & Company Limited	£224,655,776
Accor UK Business & Leisure Hotels Limited	£224,406,000
Liberty Managing Agency Limited	£224,357,808
Endeavour Energy UK Limited	£224,295,600
Quilter Cheviot Limited	£224,292,992
Vertice Pharma UK Parent Limited	£224,279,200
Burford Capital Holdings (UK) Limited	£224,224,000
FHH No.1 Limited	£224,200,992
GFS Renewable Energy Limited	£224,136,000
DEKA Energy Associates Limited	£224,066,144
Overbury PLC	£224,016,000
Total UK Limited	£224,000,000
Legal & General RE Holdings Limited	£223,900,000
UK Green Investment Lid Limited	£223,881,440
Structadene (LBG) Holdings Limited	£223,737,488
RSM UK Holdings Limited	£223,715,008
Aggregator of Loans Backed By Assets 2015-1 PLC	£223,713,136
MC GFS Investment Company Limited	£223,534,000
Intelligent Processing Solutions Limited	£223,436,000
GAI Indemnity, Ltd.	£223,340,000
Vaultex UK Limited	£223,322,000
USAA Limited	£223,315,008
Eurosail 2006-2BL PLC	£223,304,000
Stanlington No. 1 PLC	£223,148,992
Broadgate (PHC 15A) Limited	£223,081,264
Carros Sensors Topco Limited	£223,031,504
Axia Finance PLC	£223,002,048
Muirgold Limited	£222,958,000
Symphony Bidco Limited	£222,767,776
WGSN Group Limited	£222,760,992
Just Eat.co.uk Ltd	£222,700,000
Winton Capital Management Limited	£222,671,008
Citigroup Capital UK Limited	£222,632,992
Praxis I Finance PLC	£222,494,512
JLT EB Holdings Limited	£222,424,992
Blackmead Infrastructure Limited	£222,214,144
Oncilla Mortgage Funding 2016-1 PLC	£222,107,280
Six Degrees Holdings Limited	£221,875,008
The Blackstone Group International Partners LLP	£221,812,560
Trenport Property Holdings Limited	£221,800,000
Orosi (UK) 2 Limited	£221,709,584
South Downs Waste Services Limited	£221,548,000
Linklaters Business Services	£221,436,000
Grosvenor Europe Limited	£221,304,992
PGI Acquisition Limited	£221,287,296
Macquarie Commodities Factoring Holdings UK Ltd	£221,276,720
Firoka (Kings Cross) Limited	£221,164,800
Schroder Wealth Holdings Limited	£221,148,992
ANZ Europe Limited	£221,103,808
Lotus Group Ltd	£221,102,176
Peer Group PLC	£221,015,984
ABF HK Finance Limited	£221,011,472
Revcap UK Holdings Limited	£220,593,568
Campaign Monitor (UK) Limited	£220,476,560
Road Management Services (A13) Holdings Ltd	£220,472,000
Road Management Services (A13) PLC	£220,468,992
Mitie Technical Facilities Management Holdings Ltd	£220,376,992
Fair Isaac UK Group Limited	£220,262,000
Fair Isaac UK International Holdings Ltd.	£220,240,928
The Endeavour Company Holdings Limited	£220,228,000
PIAS Holding (UK) Limited	£220,131,008
Metroline Travel Limited	£220,036,000
Shaftesbury CL Investment Limited	£220,000,096
IQVIA Solutions Finance UK I Ltd.	£219,706,352
Telegraph Media Group Limited	£219,600,000
HCUK Auto Funding 2017-1 Ltd	£219,543,664
The Tannen Group Limited	£219,398,000
MacTaggart Heritable Limited	£219,180,992
Lynwood Retail UK Limited	£219,124,992
The Motability Tenth Anniversary Trust	£219,122,000
Nuveen Real Estate Limited	£219,097,312
Borders & Southern Falkland Islands Limited	£219,044,256
BBPF LLP	£218,965,296
Eclipse Film Partners No. 26 LLP	£218,908,176
Big Bus Tours Holdings 1 Limited	£218,801,664
LSEG Business Services Limited	£218,517,408
Argo International Holdings Limited	£218,255,920
Parvus Asset Management Limited	£218,240,144
Axa Services Limited	£218,198,000
Loch Lomond Holdings 1 Limited	£217,984,992
Veolia ES Staffordshire Limited	£217,980,000
Seven Capital PLC	£217,924,528
BNY Mellon Investment Management Seed Capital	£217,843,744
Bupa Global Holdings Limited	£217,828,624
Grange (Prescot Street) Limited	£217,765,552
Babcock Education & Training Holdings LLP	£217,600,992
Boeing Commercial Aviation Services Europe Ltd	£217,568,432
6 Bevis Marks Limited	£217,454,736
McLaren Construction Group PLC	£217,452,480
FFP Investment UK Ltd	£217,436,064
Northstar Investments Limited	£217,340,992
Land Securities Management Limited	£217,275,008
Bear Stearns Holdings Limited	£217,240,768
Birch Sites Limited	£217,200,000
Loch Lomond Distillers Limited	£217,186,000
Diamond Offshore Drilling (UK) Limited.	£217,183,936
Babcock US Investments Limited	£217,003,424
Fox Healthcare Acquisitions Limited	£216,858,000
Fletcher Bay Group Limited	£216,684,992
IQVIA Solutions HQ Ltd.	£216,478,000
Catalyst Finance Limited	£216,312,000
Sunderland (SHG) Finance PLC	£216,307,760
Victoria Asset Finance Limited	£216,208,992
Acturis Group Limited	£216,196,288
Global Reach Group Ltd	£216,135,008
BLSSP Property Holdings Limited	£216,090,912
Endowment Investment Holdings Limited	£216,078,656
Baker & McKenzie LLP	£216,012,000
DWS Group Services UK Limited	£215,908,000
SVF Holdco (UK) Limited	£215,639,008
Prepaid Services Company Limited	£215,474,144
CGN Europe Energy Green Power Holding Limited	£215,406,816
Boots Propco B Limited	£215,360,992
Student Finance PLC	£215,315,040
UPP (Lancaster) Limited	£215,283,008
UPP (Lancaster) Holdings Limited	£215,271,008
Primepanel Limited	£215,256,992
Wagamama Limited	£215,190,000
Avanade Europe Services Ltd.	£215,186,000
INCJ SJ Investment Limited	£215,121,136

Company	Value
WPP Brands Holdings (UK) Limited	£214,995,008
Amazon Video Limited	£214,974,000
SSC Intermediateco Limited	£214,955,120
Livn UK 3 Co Limited	£214,929,328
Chapelcrest Investments Limited	£214,915,120
Lion/Heaven UK II Limited	£214,896,000
Sumitomo Corporation Europe Holding Limited	£214,714,704
Walworth Investment Properties Limited	£214,502,032
Globaldata PLC	£214,491,008
MEIF II CP Holdings 3 Limited	£214,474,000
LHA London Ltd	£214,467,536
Citadel Enterprise Europe Limited	£214,428,992
UBS Asset Management (UK) Ltd	£214,412,000
NYK International PLC	£214,367,872
Penguin Books Limited	£214,134,000
Equitix Offshore 3 Limited	£213,960,000
Equitix Offshore 4 Limited	£213,960,000
Corbiere Asset Investments Ltd	£213,904,000
Tripadvisor Limited	£213,870,272
ABF Funding	£213,490,672
121333 Limited	£213,436,992
CBI UK Cayman Acquisition Limited	£213,430,480
XDG Limited	£213,344,992
The Mary Street Estate Limited	£213,343,136
GFG UK 1 Limited	£213,191,680
Pangaea Funding 1 PLC	£213,079,200
Genome Research Limited	£212,844,992
Realreed Limited	£212,824,672
Cobalt Data Centres Limited	£212,815,536
London Town Group of Companies Holdings Limited	£212,605,552
London Town Group of Companies Limited	£212,601,248
Rational Foreign Exchange Limited	£212,371,088
J O Hambro Capital Management Holdings Limited	£212,330,000
Digital River UK Holdings I Ltd	£212,294,240
Rational Group Limited	£212,271,904
CenturyLink Impsat Holdings I Limited	£212,247,184
Oval (2041) Limited	£212,232,992
GIP II (Vista) Holdco 1, Limited	£212,228,240
Sableknight Limited	£212,104,368
BNY Mellon Investment Management EMEA Limited	£212,078,000
Broadgate (PHC 2) Limited	£212,060,016
Barts Square First Limited	£211,913,808
Pendal UK Limited	£211,656,992
International Schools Partnership Limited	£211,641,856
Granada Television Overseas Limited	£211,452,992
Gresham Receivables (No.11) UK Limited	£211,310,544
Ladbroke Group	£211,304,000
Metinvest Capital UK Limited	£211,210,656
Alpha Plus Holdings PLC	£211,120,992
Axia III APC Limited	£211,100,784
Accorinvest UK BCT Limited	£210,838,000
Aviva Europe SE	£210,793,312
Liberty Living Investments II Holdco 2 Limited	£210,779,008
Grosvenor UK Finance PLC	£210,688,000
Broadgate (PHC 6) 2005 Limited	£210,261,824
PACG2 Limited	£210,219,568
Chugai Pharma Europe Limited	£210,165,520
QHotels Services Limited	£210,163,008
ATK Finance Limited	£210,140,336
ED Broking Holdings (London) Limited	£210,126,000
Omnicom Network Holdings Limited	£210,119,296
Kobalt Music Group Limited	£209,967,936
GLIL Corporate Holdings Limited	£209,760,592
Bond Aviation Topco Limited	£209,743,008
Axia III Finance PLC	£209,728,976
Informa Telecoms & Media Limited	£209,708,000
Tomahawk Capital Partners I LLP	£209,683,968
Tonicstar Limited	£209,659,008
Morgan Stanley Alpha Investments LLP	£209,626,000
Semperian Senior Funding PLC	£209,622,752
Ambassador Square	£209,503,008
RMC Estates Co. LLP	£209,492,800
Independent Clinical Services Limited	£209,484,000
ENI Australia Limited	£209,467,424
TI UK Publishing Holdings Limited	£209,391,008
Axa PPP Healthcare Group Limited	£209,379,008
Coral Eurobet Limited	£209,348,000
Metinvest Investments Limited	£209,282,384
Clavis Securities PLC	£209,260,992
First State Investments (UK) Limited	£209,244,000
Reliance Bank Limited	£209,158,800
Axa Investment Managers UK Limited	£208,891,840
Harbour Funding PLC	£208,878,320
Tokai Tokyo Securities Europe Limited	£208,778,224
Charles Tyrwhitt Shirts Limited	£208,734,000
Triple Point Social Housing REIT PLC	£208,699,008
Global Radio Limited	£208,648,000
Tate & Lyle Technology Limited	£208,627,008
121222 Holdco Limited	£208,571,008
Argent Foods Limited	£208,456,992
Alexander Mann Group Limited	£208,446,000
1 & 4 & 7 Triton Limited	£208,425,360
Vesuvius Ceramics Limited	£208,358,000
Quilter Cheviot Holdings Limited	£208,314,000
Fitzroy Property Limited	£208,244,576
Matthey Finance Limited	£208,238,000
BMO Real Estate Partners LLP	£208,183,008
URS Corporation Group Limited	£207,976,000
Babcock Mission Critical Services Design	£207,899,008
Old Mutual Financial Services (UK) Limited	£207,808,992
Peabody Capital PLC	£207,799,008
Intervefm (Holdings) Ltd	£207,708,992
East Slope Residencies Student Accommodation LLP	£207,660,400
SIR ATP Limited	£207,650,000
ESB Asset Development UK Limited	£207,644,992
OMD EMEA Limited	£207,590,304
Tullow Group Services Limited	£207,573,280
Titan Financing Limited	£207,556,592
Perenco Oil and Gas Colombia Limited	£207,525,376
Amdocs (UK) Limited	£207,408,256
Titan Acquisition Holdco Limited	£207,284,576
British Alcan Aluminium Limited	£207,267,008
Capita Customer Management Limited	£207,211,248
Constellation Barclay UK Limited	£207,200,800
SG (Maritime) Leasing Limited	£207,173,008
Transkey Limited	£207,157,712
PHP Primary Properties Limited	£207,092,016
Pearson Funding Four PLC	£206,896,000
PHD Media Limited	£206,538,624
BPP Holdings Limited	£206,478,000
JLEAG Wind Holding Limited	£206,254,000
JLEAG Wind Limited	£206,254,000
Palace Holdco UK Limited	£206,224,000
Veolia ES Landfill Limited	£205,944,000
TIAA International Holdings 3 Limited	£205,911,488
Zavarco PLC	£205,853,232
Transworld Petroleum (U.K.) Limited	£205,773,136
Broadgate (PHC 5) 2005 Limited	£205,735,184
Digital Appliance Controls (UK) Limited	£205,712,000
Kurt Geiger Limited	£205,622,000
Landmark Mortgage Securities No.3 PLC	£205,514,208
Larch Funding (UK) Ltd	£205,470,720
Jupiter Unit Trust Managers Limited	£205,200,000
Vale Europe Limited	£205,186,000
Fleet Trade & Transport Limited	£205,062,480
Marken Services Limited	£204,914,848
Genting Americas Holdings Limited	£204,783,152
SPIE UK Limited	£204,720,000
Wittington Investments (Properties) Limited	£204,649,504
Equitix Capital Eurobond Limited	£204,604,992
G4S Care and Justice Services (UK) Limited	£204,506,000
Orbita Funding 2017-1 PLC	£204,474,736
Collin Estates Limited	£204,352,480
BCP IV UK Fuel Holdings II Limited	£204,174,208

Company	Value
Keybridge House LLP	£204,074,000
Crops Holdings (UK) Limited	£204,028,496
Reed Overseas Corporation Limited	£204,028,000
Daejan Investments (Grove Hall) Limited	£204,019,360
Babcock Investments (Number Three) Limited	£204,003,008
Hartree Partners Power & Gas Company (UK) Ltd	£203,917,984
Ediston Property Investment Company PLC	£203,707,008
Tilbury Green Power Limited	£203,592,352
Springer Nature Holdings Limited	£203,584,992
Dress Holdco C Limited	£203,584,992
Henderson Diversified Income Trust PLC	£203,546,000
AECOM Holdings Limited	£203,543,008
WIG Holdings II Limited	£203,500,000
Ember Overseas Holdings Limited	£203,330,000
WP R Holdco Limited	£203,222,624
Brook Funding (No.1) Limited	£203,195,456
Euromoney Trading Limited	£202,932,000
Delfont Mackintosh Theatres Limited	£202,895,536
PIP Infrastructure Investments (No 6) Limited	£202,841,984
Firmdale Hotels PLC	£202,732,992
Daytona Midco 1 Limited	£202,711,008
UK Green Investment Gwynt y Mor Limited	£202,671,216
Anasuria Hibiscus UK Limited	£202,650,496
Clothworkers' Foundation (The)	£202,635,632
Landmark Hotel London Limited	£202,462,000
Mercury Pharma Group Limited	£202,432,240
Bird & Bird LLP	£202,318,848
CNR International (U.K.) Investments Limited	£202,100,000
Roehampton University	£202,070,000
ULiving@Hertfordshire Holdco Limited	£201,738,000
ULiving@Hertfordshire PLC	£201,738,000
AMC Networks International Broadcasting Limited	£201,522,000
Real Estate Venture Capital Partners LLP	£201,511,952
Arrow Bidco Limited	£201,467,008
Jac Travel Group (Holdings) Limited	£201,336,000
Anthology Group Limited	£201,248,992
HM Treasury UK Sovereign Sukuk PLC	£200,842,000
Instant Cash Loans Limited	£200,831,008
Smith & Nephew Trading Group Limited	£200,747,008
Towd Point Mortgage Funding 2016-Granite3 PLC	£200,714,000
Knight Dragon Developments Limited	£200,678,384
The Foundry Holdco Limited	£200,596,992
First Olsen (Holdings) Limited	£200,520,000
Marble Arch Hotel (London) Limited	£200,411,008
HBOS Insurance & Investment Group Limited	£200,300,000
Majedie Investments PLC	£200,248,000
Craegmoor Group (No.6) Limited	£200,202,000
The Foundry Midco 3 Limited	£200,200,000
PA Consulting Services Limited	£200,071,008
TNS UK Holdings Limited	£200,000,000
Macquarie Holdings (UK) No.1 Limited	£200,000,000
DIF Tamblin Limited	£199,993,920
Cambian Heritage II Limited	£199,812,304
New Ventures II (UK) Limited	£199,789,264
EMP Exploration (Kangean) Limited	£199,706,896
Arena Leisure Racing Limited	£199,672,784
Blue Transmission Sheringham Shoal Limited	£199,590,000
Yianis Hotels Limited	£199,508,240
Finlay Extracts & Ingredients UK Limited	£199,493,232
Inpex Angola Block 14 Ltd.	£199,425,456
Stena Ropax Limited	£199,340,000
Bank Saderat PLC	£199,185,312
AEW UK REIT PLC	£199,076,000
Goodenough College	£199,046,000
Ascend Overseas Limited	£198,950,000
Allianz Renewable Energy Partners VIII Limited	£198,925,344
Hirecorp Limited	£198,891,008
Epic (No. 1) Limited	£198,796,000
Lloyds Bank Equipment Leasing (No. 7) Limited	£198,743,008
Petra Diamonds UK Treasury Limited	£198,697,792
Hunting Oil Holdings Limited	£198,666,864
HSBC Specialist Investments Limited	£198,632,992
Swan National Limited	£198,463,552
TES Global Holdings Limited	£198,426,000
Marie Stopes International	£198,422,000
Aviva Investors Realm Infrastructure No.5 Limited	£198,292,272
Renault Retail Group UK Limited	£198,159,008
Group Miki Holdings Limited	£198,067,696
Huntsworth Holdings Limited	£198,031,232
Elexon Limited	£197,979,008
WBA Acquisitions UK Holdco 2 Limited	£197,946,000
VUR Mezzanine I (UK) Limited	£197,886,000
NRG Victory Holdings Limited	£197,782,000
UBS Asset Management Holding Ltd	£197,776,000
Greenrock Topco Limited	£197,712,176
Ticketmaster UK Limited	£197,638,000
EP Langage Limited	£197,620,992
Forum Worldwide Holdings Limited	£197,505,168
TC Financing Limited	£197,476,000
Smyths Toys UK Limited	£197,444,992
Dorrington Properties PLC	£197,053,888
Bloomsbury Publishing PLC	£196,991,008
Macquarie Internationale Investments Limited	£196,987,936
Sensis Holding II Limited	£196,972,896
East Slope Residencies PLC	£196,904,000
VUR Mezzanine II (UK) Limited	£196,824,000
I2 Holdco Limited	£196,745,360
Macquarie Infrastructure and Real Assets Core Ltd	£196,680,848
Soho House UK Limited	£196,620,016
London Forfaiting Company Limited	£196,454,640
Impact Healthcare REIT PLC	£196,383,008
HCA UK Services Limited	£196,370,000
P & O Property Accounts Limited	£196,275,808
Azzurri Restaurants Limited	£196,214,000
Factset UK Limited	£196,191,344
Liquid Telecommunications Investments Limited	£196,159,392
Rickleford Ltd	£196,131,360
Firstclear Limited	£196,068,992
Glencore UK Ltd.	£196,032,752
Sextant Consolidated Limited	£195,960,176
Capital Hill Hotels Limited	£195,903,008
Harvey Nichols and Company Limited	£195,892,000
European Policy Exchange Limited	£195,889,216
Tiso Blackstar Holdings SE	£195,748,336
FET Global Holdings Limited	£195,666,000
Next Fifteen Communications Group PLC	£195,330,000
Office Holdings Limited	£195,231,008
FS Debtco Limited	£195,203,872
The London Metal Exchange	£195,007,264
Limited Life Assets Services Limited	£194,991,216
Brookfield Renewable UK Hydro Limited	£194,964,000
FS Senior Co Limited	£194,787,008
UK Green Investment Gym Participant Limited	£194,683,184
Standard Chartered Apr Limited	£194,617,808
4 Howley Place Limited	£194,409,472
Orchard Street UK Prime Property GP Limited	£194,395,808
CP Co 7 Limited	£194,292,048
Norsea Pipeline Limited	£194,191,008
Telereal (London Wall) Limited	£194,176,992
EFL Futures Limited	£193,832,064
Get Living London EV2 Holdco Limited	£193,824,992
I2 Bidco Limited	£193,781,888
Autovista Limited	£193,373,008
M7 Real Estate Ltd	£193,203,008
Freston Ventures Investments LLP	£193,018,112
Gunfleet Sands Limited	£192,744,208
Collinson Finance Limited	£192,612,960
Premier Oil E & P UK EU Limited	£192,364,000
Taylor Clark Limited	£192,220,992
XXIII Capital A Limited	£192,074,736
CBRE Acquisition Company 3 Limited	£191,939,696
Sanne Group (UK) Limited	£191,900,192
CBRE Acquisition Company 2 Limited	£191,792,784
ICG Carbon Funding Limited	£191,791,760

Kin and Carta PLC	£191,692,992	Capita Justice & Secure Services Holdings Limited	£186,609,360
Minmetals (U.K) Limited	£191,641,648	Multiplex Construction Europe Holding Limited	£186,554,672
Clarion Acquisition Limited	£191,635,008	Places for People Ventures Limited	£186,551,008
Broadgate (PHC 16) 2005 Limited	£191,478,800	Christie's Private Sales Limited	£186,428,992
CPA Global Management Services Ltd	£191,424,784	Maxus Communications (UK) Limited	£186,423,008
Throgmorton Assets PLC	£191,411,504	SOL Aviation Services Limited	£186,393,232
IG Index Limited	£191,400,000	Darrowby No. 3 PLC	£186,372,000
Metals Exploration PLC	£191,138,832	D-Clear Europe Limited	£186,273,856
Legal & General Investment Management Limited	£191,000,000	Retail Centres V (Sweden) Investment Limited	£186,266,512
Pearson Shared Services Limited	£190,968,000	Teesside Gas & Liquids Processing	£186,182,000
ICAP Management Services Limited	£190,948,992	Belgrave Square	£186,160,992
Electricity First Limited	£190,930,000	Principal Global Financial Services (Europe) II Ltd	£185,976,512
De Facto 1341 Limited	£190,927,008	Aberdeen Standard European Logistics Income PLC	£185,884,544
Zero Bypass Limited	£190,867,152	DTZ UK Bidco 2 Limited	£185,642,080
Zero Bypass (Holdings) Limited	£190,867,152	Stifel Nicolaus Europe Limited	£185,580,992
Babcock Services Group Limited	£190,847,008	Tarsus Holdings Limited	£185,500,352
Macquarie European Rail Limited	£190,833,952	Olekit Investments Ltd	£185,385,536
Ardmore Group Limited	£190,794,784	Shire Pharmaceutical Development Limited	£185,380,992
PFI Infrastructure Finance Limited	£190,701,936	Creation Communications Limited	£185,195,008
Thanet OFTO Holdco Limited	£190,670,000	Marsh Corporate Services Limited	£185,100,000
Thanet OFTO Limited	£190,670,000	FS JV Co Limited	£185,018,000
Westark Properties Limited	£190,420,000	British Medical Association	£184,960,000
Lendlease Europe Limited	£190,400,000	NCR UK Group Limited	£184,904,000
Tallwood Investments Ltd	£190,124,000	Business Mortgage Finance 6 PLC	£184,736,992
Alstom NL Service Provision Ltd	£190,082,000	Laura Ashley Limited	£184,608,000
York House W1 Limited	£190,038,064	Garban-Intercapital US Investments (Holdings) Ltd	£184,587,008
Gresham Receivables (No. 33) UK Limited	£189,987,152	Garban-Intercapital US Investments (No 1) Limited	£184,587,008
O & H (NBS) Limited	£189,986,464	C & C Alpha Group Limited	£184,533,264
Veolia Water UK Limited	£189,986,000	Markitserv Holdings Limited	£184,435,552
Shire Europe Limited	£189,961,200	LW Theatres Holdings Limited	£184,374,000
Midasplayer.Com Ltd.	£189,846,208	West Ham United Football Club Limited	£184,198,000
Swire Oilfield Services (Holdings) Limited	£189,808,992	WH Holding Limited	£184,198,000
CPB Residential Finance Limited	£189,780,000	First Property Group PLC	£184,080,000
Hammerson Bull Ring Limited	£189,732,992	State Street Global Markets International Limited	£184,004,000
Promontoria Gyle Holdings (2) Ltd	£189,705,072	Willis Overseas Investments Limited	£184,000,000
Promontoria Gyle Holding Ltd	£189,608,512	Admiral Taverns (Chester) Limited	£183,964,992
Promontoria Gyle Top Holding Ltd	£189,574,912	MAN Investments Limited	£183,859,888
RW Wentworth UK Limited	£189,490,000	CP Co 3 Limited	£183,760,976
MBC Europe Limited	£189,214,880	Milton Magna Limited	£183,753,344
Murderme Limited	£189,014,832	Laser Tradeco Limited	£183,639,008
Waterstones Booksellers Limited	£188,808,000	Ruffer LLP	£183,574,688
Multiplex Europe Limited	£188,801,088	Integro Insurance Brokers Holdings Limited	£183,511,008
Accor UK Economy Hotels Limited	£188,771,008	Rio Tinto Metals Limited	£183,489,488
Promontoria Gyle 2 Ltd	£188,713,904	Perenco Rang Dong Limited	£183,365,792
Octagon Assets Limited	£188,632,448	Repsol Sinopec Alpha Limited	£183,322,288
LDC (Managers) Limited	£188,614,000	Albion No.3 PLC	£183,232,000
J O Hambro Capital Management Limited	£188,600,000	Hansteen Property Investments Limited	£183,161,696
C.I. Property & Investments Limited	£188,548,000	Tokio Marine HCC Insurance Holdings (Int) Ltd	£183,125,744
London City Airport Limited	£188,496,000	ENI Pakistan Limited	£183,039,552
Citywide Trading (UK) Limited	£188,416,976	ENI JPDA 03-13 Limited	£182,843,696
LS City & West End Limited	£188,348,000	Cityfibre Limited	£182,655,008
Liberty Plaza (London) Limited	£188,347,008	Muse Developments Limited	£182,604,992
UIG Holdings (No 4) Ltd	£188,285,200	HSBC Trust Company (UK) Limited	£182,564,992
Folgate Estates Limited	£188,258,720	MAN UK Strategies Limited	£182,472,704
Baronsmead Second Venture Trust PLC	£188,139,008	Turbo Finance 6 PLC	£182,386,352
ICG FMC Limited	£188,100,000	Argo (Alpha) Limited	£182,182,592
Garban-Intercapital (2001) Limited	£188,096,992	Management Consortium Bid Limited	£182,166,000
ICAP America Investments Limited	£188,094,000	H P Bulmer Limited	£182,007,008
Unilever Australia Investments Limited	£187,936,992	IQVIA Solutions Finance UK II Ltd.	£181,862,304
Unilever Australia Partnership Limited	£187,919,008	RG Engagement Group Limited	£181,836,944
Mastercard Payment Gateway Services Limited	£187,836,000	Savills (Overseas Holdings) Limited	£181,804,992
Caparo Holdings (US) Limited	£187,760,128	Cubico Holdings (UK) 4 Limited	£181,750,000
PP Oil & Gas (Indonesia-Jabung) Limited	£187,739,824	UBS Asset Management Holding (No.2) Ltd	£181,616,992
DEKA Energy Enterprises Limited	£187,691,888	JPMorgan US Smaller Co's Investment Trust PLC	£181,596,992
Inremco 26 Limited	£187,550,368	LS (Finchley Road) Limited	£181,532,992
TBWA EMEA Limited	£187,193,536	MPG Finco Limited	£181,406,880
Hawk Newco Limited	£187,156,000	Technip-Coflexip UK Holdings Limited	£181,336,992
Foxtons Intermediate Holdings Limited	£186,956,000	DMGV Limited	£181,328,000
Mithras Leasing (No.1) Ltd	£186,901,072	Cedar Project Midco Limited	£181,277,136
Citadel Europe LLP	£186,844,000	IQVIA Solutions Global Holdings UK Ltd.	£181,260,000
Aberdeen Infrastructure (No 2) LLP	£186,786,640	Congregation of The Daughters of Cross of Liege	£181,168,000
SRE Portfolios UK Ltd	£186,668,912	BG Overseas Limited	£181,099,808

Company	Value
Q Intermediate Holdco Limited	£180,994,960
The Perfume Shop Limited	£180,992,000
Hanover House Limited	£180,947,376
Dolphin Drilling Limited	£180,943,040
Transocean UK Limited	£180,771,296
Agrichrome Limited	£180,684,000
IG Finance Three	£180,648,992
Humber Gateway OFTO Holdings Limited	£180,614,000
Humber Gateway OFTO Limited	£180,614,000
Trainline Group Investments Limited	£180,560,000
Portman Investments (Baker Street) Limited	£180,434,128
Pearl Income Investments II UK Limited	£180,432,720
Alexander Mann Solutions Limited	£180,336,992
Lion/Jenga Midco Limited	£180,247,008
Greenland Hertsmere (London) Limited	£180,215,008
Smartstream Technologies Group Limited	£180,135,008
CDCH Limited	£180,078,896
BG LNG Investments Limited	£179,831,584
Equitix Orbital Holdings Limited	£179,810,000
STA Travel International Limited	£179,776,960
Sirius GR Limited	£179,664,000
Partnership Group Holdings Limited	£179,640,992
Malt Hill No.1 PLC	£179,566,752
Centro Asset Management Limited	£179,540,464
LR (Baker St) Limited	£179,504,432
BG Trinidad LNG Limited	£179,470,160
Stradawood Limited	£179,359,520
The Stage Shoreditch Residential Limited	£179,344,176
Wallis Retail Limited	£179,298,000
PL Hotel Limited	£179,250,240
Robert Brett & Sons Limited	£179,131,008
Places for People Developments Limited	£179,003,008
Val TM Limited	£178,974,000
Priory Securitisation Holdings Limited	£178,936,000
Lockton International Limited	£178,931,104
Sunshine Purchaser Limited	£178,874,848
Arup Treasury Limited	£178,856,848
Lockfold Communications Limited	£178,831,904
Stamford Properties Three Limited	£178,750,048
Shell Chemicals U.K. Limited	£178,708,000
Cambian Properties (U.K.) Limited	£178,375,632
LS Retail Warehouses Limited	£178,248,000
Atrium 100 Properties Limited	£178,160,992
Motor 2015-1 PLC	£178,130,752
Exterion Holdings (UK) Limited	£178,120,000
Engine Partners UK LLP	£178,080,992
Alba 2006-2 PLC	£178,004,992
Rock Rail South Western PLC	£177,962,208
John Laing Investments Overseas Holdings Limited	£177,937,104
Rock Rail South Western (Holdings) 2 Limited	£177,925,328
Compart Systems Limited	£177,897,568
Farmont Baker Street Limited	£177,823,728
E-Act	£177,783,008
Castle Lane Securities Limited	£177,702,000
The Foundry Bidco No.2 Limited	£177,700,000
Bluebay Asset Management (Services) Ltd	£177,651,008
British American Tobacco Peru Holdings Limited	£177,632,000
Turkish Bank (UK) Limited	£177,603,008
I2 Holdco 2 Limited	£177,586,976
ED Broking Group Limited	£177,487,536
Newline Insurance Company Limited	£177,358,000
Civica Group Limited	£177,324,992
MPS Group International Limited	£177,271,008
IPC Information Systems UK Limited	£177,269,616
Foxtons Group PLC	£177,220,000
Guildhall Asset Purchasing Company (No.11) UK Ltd	£177,166,000
IDCO Overseas Holdings Limited	£177,159,008
Haymarket Capital Ventures LLP	£177,007,600
EP SHB Limited	£176,960,992
Cofunds Limited	£176,955,008
Ocubis Financing Limited	£176,886,752
BMO AM Holdings Limited	£176,805,888
European Investments Solar Holdings Limited	£176,799,008
The Connaught Hotel Limited	£176,734,000
Alliancebernstein Limited	£176,594,160
G. Modiano Limited	£176,384,000
British American Tobacco Italy Investments Limited	£176,382,000
Finsbury Square 2016-1 PLC	£176,378,000
ITV Digital Channels Limited	£176,362,000
EMF-UK 2008-1 PLC	£176,348,992
Colt Telecom Finance Switzerland	£176,216,768
NGC UK Holdings Company Limited	£175,928,000
L-3 Technology & Services UK Ltd	£175,921,952
Monaco Topco Limited	£175,892,992
Springer Nature Two Limited	£175,883,840
Council for World Mission (UK)	£175,721,152
Kensington & Global Limited	£175,701,584
4 Imprint USA Limited	£175,503,008
Halcrow Holdings Limited	£175,463,008
Project Leopard Intermediateco Limited	£175,374,528
Lycamobile UK Limited	£175,298,000
Strategic Equity Capital PLC	£175,224,000
LN-Gaiety Holdings Limited	£175,027,744
SB Investment Advisers (UK) Limited	£174,971,472
AMS Holdco Ltd	£174,967,008
Local Trust	£174,896,992
Chiquita Finance Company Limited	£174,886,960
MSCI UK Holdings Limited	£174,812,000
Orsted Sales (UK) Limited	£174,792,992
Admiral Taverns Bidco Limited	£174,655,008
E-Carat 6 PLC	£174,593,264
Aston Lark (Topco) Limited	£174,550,144
Semperian No.21 Limited	£174,434,896
Marston Properties Holdings Limited	£174,338,784
Artemis Alpha Trust PLC	£174,279,008
GH Holdings 1 Limited	£174,251,008
Zegona Communications PLC	£174,181,728
Clifford Chance London Limited	£174,024,992
West India Quay (Eastern) Limited	£173,968,016
Grosvenor Europe Investments Limited	£173,923,728
Burford Investments Limited	£173,872,112
NEX Services Limited	£173,660,000
Aston Lark (Bidco) Limited	£173,620,800
Thomas Pocklington Trust	£173,430,000
IPM Holdings (UK) Limited	£173,415,008
Total E & P International K3 Ltd.	£173,341,296
Diploma Holdings PLC	£173,316,992
Newport Holdings Limited	£173,277,792
Kddi Europe Limited	£173,164,992
Babcock IP Management (Number Two) Limited	£173,144,000
Val TM (Holdings) Limited	£173,100,992
Awin Ltd	£173,036,000
Listrac Midco Limited	£172,901,600
Havin Bank Ltd	£172,801,360
Masdar Offshore Wind UK Limited	£172,735,680
MP Granite Ltd	£172,681,760
Heron Treasury Services Limited	£172,657,856
Addison Lee Limited	£172,598,000
Fred Perry (Holdings) Limited	£172,592,000
Iranian Oil Company (U.K.) Limited	£172,479,008
CD & R Firefly 2 Limited	£172,466,000
Theatre (Hospitals) No.2 PLC	£172,415,632
Havana Holdings (UK) Limited	£172,412,992
J. & J. Denholm Limited	£172,316,000
SMBC Derivative Products Limited	£172,315,616
Virgin Rail Group Holdings Limited	£172,272,000
Telstra Limited	£172,111,008
Spotify Finance Limited	£172,063,216
Dynamic Estates Limited	£172,042,912
Nimbus Acquisitions Holdings Limited	£172,004,000
Nimbus Acquisitions Midco 1 Limited	£171,996,000
Lightsource Pumpkin 4 Limited	£171,909,584
Ash8 Group Holdings Limited	£171,883,008
Veladail Hotels Limited	£171,877,040

Company	Value
Indigo Intermediate Limited	£171,832,000
Indigo Cleanco Limited	£171,831,008
Fevertree Drinks PLC	£171,789,328
Pulford Trading Limited	£171,779,008
Experis Limited	£171,770,000
MC GIP-UK Ltd.	£171,764,784
PRA Corporate Capital Limited	£171,761,376
Dashwood House Limited	£171,760,992
Zealburg Holdings Limited	£171,712,000
Ansell (U.K.) Limited	£171,663,248
Beaufort Wind Limited	£171,656,000
KPMG UK Limited	£171,638,000
Tramtrack Croydon Limited	£171,624,000
Newsprinters (Broxbourne) Limited	£171,608,992
PRACCL Limited	£171,567,600
JKX Oil & Gas PLC	£171,476,480
Jupiter US Smaller Companies PLC	£171,474,000
Burford Global Investments Limited	£171,358,736
Ricoh Capital Limited	£171,324,992
West Coast Trains Limited	£171,311,008
CX Holdco Limited	£170,819,008
Pandora Jewellery UK Limited	£170,668,992
Sonic Healthcare Holding Company	£170,646,000
Race Bank Wind Farm (Holding) Limited	£170,586,480
Beverage Services Limited	£170,562,224
The Boston Consulting Group UK LLP	£170,407,232
ENI AEP Limited	£170,364,992
Hotel (PL Property) Holdco Limited	£170,295,840
Metric Property Investments Limited	£170,276,832
Eurohome UK Mortgages 2007 - 1 PLC	£170,231,984
Worldline IT Services UK Limited	£170,230,000
PLJ Chelsea Limited	£170,220,656
Fox Networks Group (UK) Limited	£170,126,816
PHP Investments No.2 Limited	£170,074,384
La Perla Global Management (UK) Limited	£170,024,048
MT Property Investments LLP	£169,778,000
Acturis International Limited	£169,753,968
Ludgate Northumberland Holdings Limited	£169,693,456
Castile Acquisitions Ltd	£169,663,904
Building Schools for The Future Investments LLP	£169,624,992
Building Energy Ltd	£169,609,104
Brixton (Metropolitan Park) 1 Limited	£169,571,008
Zeuss Childcare Limited	£169,438,880
Addleshaw Goddard LLP	£169,376,992
Fence Topco Limited	£169,283,008
Threadneedle Asset Management Finance Limited	£169,256,992
Eurosail-UK 2007-6NC PLC	£169,180,992
E & A Property Investment Company Limited	£169,096,992
Exterion Media (UK) Limited	£169,055,008
Galloper Holdco Limited	£169,036,480
Vauxhall Square (Nominee 1) Limited	£168,955,008
Marston Properties Limited	£168,913,168
Sinclair Pharma Limited	£168,876,992
Argus Media Limited	£168,795,008
Enterprise Oil U.K. Limited	£168,672,992
Royal London Asset Management Limited	£168,578,000
Onyx Germany (1) Ltd	£168,472,240
East End Homes Limited	£168,460,992
Credit Suisse Asset Management (UK) Holding Ltd	£168,392,992
Paysafe Processing Limited	£168,041,024
Funding Circle Holdings PLC	£167,900,000
PHP Glen Spean Limited	£167,723,712
Royal Brompton and Harefield Hospitals Charity	£167,691,008
Derwent Valley Property Investments Limited	£167,599,120
Bupa Care Homes (CFChomes) Limited	£167,564,992
Apollo Management International LLP	£167,545,984
Jasper Acquisition Limited	£167,443,312
10 Triton Street Limited	£167,356,464
Palace Capital PLC	£167,254,000
Royal Mencap Society	£167,220,000
KMC Stirling Square Limited	£167,152,000
Tyrion Security Bidco Limited	£167,042,000
Nintex Global Limited	£167,022,144
RQIH Limited	£167,022,000
Legal & General International (Holdings) Limited	£167,016,000
Blind Veterans UK	£167,004,000
IDCO Worldwide Holdings Limited	£166,948,000
Liberty Living Investments Limited	£166,920,992
BBC Studios Limited	£166,864,000
Alberto-Culver (Europe) Limited	£166,860,000
Jupiter Properties 2011 UK Limited	£166,739,008
Be Offices Limited	£166,703,312
Instinet International Limited	£166,624,992
Babcock UK Finance	£166,624,000
UPP (Hull) Holdings Limited	£166,520,000
UPP (Hull) Limited	£166,468,992
Jester Bidco Limited	£166,330,496
Third New Court Limited	£166,222,432
Ropemaker RB Holdings Limited	£166,148,720
British American Shared Services (GSD) Limited	£166,020,992
MAN Investments Holdings Limited	£165,920,128
DS Smith Display Holding Limited	£165,900,000
Wellington Management International Limited	£165,862,000
TBL (Milton Keynes) Limited	£165,782,672
ESB Group (UK) Limited	£165,744,000
Argo (No. 703) Limited	£165,595,296
Trainline Holdings Limited	£165,575,008
AIG Transaction Execution Limited	£165,512,000
Raphael Freshwater Memorial Association Limited	£165,399,008
Firmdale Property Investments Limited	£165,288,000
The Great Beer Company Limited	£165,237,680
Guardian News & Media Limited	£165,096,992
Brixton (Axis Park) Limited	£165,063,008
Idex UK Investment Ltd	£165,039,488
Amyn Hotels Limited	£165,033,328
CWE SPV HCO Limited	£164,957,472
Carolia Westminster Hotel Limited	£164,868,992
Warwick & Esplen Limited	£164,788,736
CMC Markets UK Holdings Limited	£164,719,088
CLS Spring Gardens Limited	£164,513,184
P2P BL-3 PLC	£164,493,504
Angus Dundee Distillers PLC	£164,446,112
Lakenorth Limited	£164,390,944
LR Skipton House Limited	£164,367,824
Capita International Limited	£164,326,544
Vocalink Holdings Limited	£164,300,000
Persia International Bank PLC	£164,217,744
Henderson Global Investors Asset Management Ltd	£164,206,000
Fairhold Homes (No.2) Limited	£164,189,712
WFS UK Holding Company III Limited	£164,162,816
UPP (Cartwright Gardens) Holdings Limited	£163,999,008
LS Victoria Circle Lp2 Limited	£163,964,992
LS Victoria Circle Lp1 Limited	£163,964,992
Neuberger Berman Europe Limited	£163,933,056
Euromoney Consortium 2 Limited	£163,837,984
Axelos Limited	£163,806,416
Interpayment Services Limited	£163,666,000
Phonographic Performance Limited	£163,624,992
URBN Holdings UK Limited	£163,606,176
Frontier Finance PLC	£163,600,000
Smartstream Technologies Limited	£163,484,992
British American Tobacco (AIT) Limited	£163,287,008
AMV BBDO Investments Limited	£163,261,952
Anzef Limited	£163,244,000
Ernst & Young Accountants LLP	£163,074,656
Antalis Group (Holdings) Limited	£162,997,136
Redcastle (214 Oxford Street) Limited	£162,828,992
Eros International Limited	£162,765,424
Hadley Shipping Group Limited	£162,737,472
Mithras Leasing (No.4) Limited	£162,723,392
Listrac Finance Limited	£162,387,424
Building & Property (Holdings) Limited	£162,330,000
Pearson International Finance Limited	£162,056,000
GH Holdings 2 Limited	£161,795,008

Company	Amount
Toyota Tsusho Metals Limited	£161,736,000
Octagon Overseas Limited	£161,707,136
Creative Education Trust	£161,703,008
Broadgate (PHC 14) Limited	£161,597,040
I-Environment Investments Limited	£161,582,352
Braemar Shipping Services PLC	£161,504,992
Dan Regents Place Finance Limited	£161,483,008
Sarti Holdings (UK) Limited	£161,327,712
Yianis Investments Limited	£161,298,496
Stratton Metal Resources Limited	£160,976,032
Midcorp Limited	£160,922,000
Arcadis LLP	£160,904,000
Sparrows Offshore Services Limited	£160,888,992
Ricoh Europe ASP Limited	£160,772,160
Barclays Investment Management Limited	£160,731,008
Baronsmead Venture Trust PLC	£160,714,000
Childcare Vouchers Limited	£160,538,000
Slater and Gordon UK Limited	£160,450,000
Pace Bidco Limited	£160,434,400
BIH Holdings Limited	£160,379,744
Lexton Investments Limited	£160,345,488
Integral UK Limited	£160,264,000
Veolia Water Enterprise Limited	£160,223,008
Fairhold Homes Investment (No.16) AL Limited	£160,106,496
Rio 588 Limited	£160,050,000
Marks and Spencer Investments	£160,011,008
Amber Infrastructure Group Holdings Limited	£159,983,008
Connect Midco Limited	£159,948,000
Sunshine Midco Limited	£159,835,936
ISG Construction Limited	£159,767,008
Due West Investments Limited	£159,738,000
Shell Company of The Philippines Limited (The)	£159,611,008
Caledonia Thames Holdings Limited	£159,567,008
Caledonia Thames Group Limited	£159,567,008
Trebuchet Investments (UK) Limited	£159,480,992
Gresham Receivables (No.16) UK Limited	£159,470,352
Vector Industries Limited	£159,312,992
Rapiscan Systems Limited	£159,289,440
Gresham Receivables (No. 19) UK Limited	£159,275,472
R & Q Capital No. 6 Limited	£159,264,992
Landmark Mortgage Securities No.2 PLC	£159,127,568
Sunshine Topco Limited	£159,102,560
Save The Children Fund	£158,814,000
Otis Investments Limited	£158,804,992
Catlin Insurance Company (UK) Holdings Ltd.	£158,785,696
Monopro Limited	£158,728,016
LMS Capital Holdings Limited	£158,597,616
Dreof II Europe Holdings Limited	£158,526,176
Permasteelisa (UK) Limited	£158,510,128
2 & 3 Triton Limited	£158,380,000
Fence Bidco Limited	£158,350,000
Thameswey Housing Limited	£158,349,888
CF Sparks Limited	£158,341,936
WGA (UK) Holdings Limited	£158,320,000
Southampton Container Terminals Limited	£158,175,008
A.G. Clothing Limited	£158,147,008
Gresham Receivables (No.37) UK Limited	£158,132,608
SYND Holdco Limited	£158,074,000
Urban Exposure PLC	£157,940,992
Aspect Capital Limited	£157,919,008
Get Living London EV N01 Limited	£157,888,000
Skyscanner Holdings Limited	£157,814,000
NTT Europe Ltd.	£157,788,992
IG Finance Two	£157,706,544
Bryan Cave Leighton Paisner LLP	£157,702,000
Howden Group Limited	£157,644,000
Derwent London Oliver's Yard Limited	£157,612,816
DIF Infra 3 UK Limited	£157,554,192
Burlington Resources (UK) Holdings Limited	£157,346,000
Frenchgate Interchange Limited	£157,288,384
BBDO EMEA Limited	£157,273,904
Lloyds Bank Corporate Asset Finance (No. 4) Limited	£157,175,008
Rockhopper Exploration (Hydrocarbons) Limited	£157,159,328
Coca-Cola Holdings (United Kingdom) Limited	£157,000,608
Luxtail Limited	£156,941,264
Babcock Training Limited	£156,920,000
London & Regional Group Securitisation No.1 Limited	£156,911,824
Newco NHL UK (17) Limited	£156,904,544
Live Nation Limited	£156,889,136
Williams Lea Limited	£156,864,000
Carnival Film & Television Limited	£156,852,000
DAC Beachcroft LLP	£156,846,000
HHT PLC	£156,792,992
Millennium Capital Management Ltd.	£156,736,000
Interoute Managed Services UK Limited	£156,608,000
Capita Property and Infrastructure Holdings Limited	£156,460,992
Lur Berri International Limited	£156,197,440
Ruffer Management Limited	£156,156,880
Max Credit Investment Limited	£156,131,056
Colas Rail Limited	£156,060,000
Grantchester Limited	£156,024,992
St. Stephens Shopping Centre Limited	£155,995,776
Cavendish Fluor Partnership Limited	£155,970,000
European Financial Services Limited	£155,894,064
Bluefin Insurance Services Limited	£155,800,000
Leonard Cheshire Disability	£155,668,000
Rothschild & Co Holdings UK Limited	£155,591,008
BPG Global Holdings UK Limited	£155,550,256
TT Games Limited	£155,408,512
Pall Mall 3 Limited	£155,333,520
QBE Management Services (UK) Limited	£155,267,008
EIS Group Public Limited Company	£155,248,000
Road Management Services (Peterborough) Limited	£155,243,008
Enquest NNS Limited	£155,212,752
H.A. Funding Limited	£155,181,392
BL Department Stores Holding Company Limited	£155,151,536
Avaya UK Holdings Limited	£155,136,800
LIH Financing Limited	£155,128,992
MATW UK Holding LLP	£154,924,304
Alpha Offshore International Leasing Limited	£154,897,680
OSW LP Holdco Limited	£154,769,680
Nexa Resources UK Limited	£154,760,176
Interserve (Defence) Ltd	£154,714,000
Gold Quay Assets Limited	£154,710,608
Touchstone Innovations Investments Limited	£154,591,216
TS Structured Finance Limited	£154,569,392
Global Radio Services Limited	£154,532,000
St. John Ambulance	£154,500,000
Romulus Securities Limited	£154,326,400
Loch Lomond Distillery Company Limited	£154,226,000
Glen Scotia Distillery Company Limited	£154,226,000
Annington Rentals (No. 6) Limited	£154,203,888
Wise Conclusion	£154,083,008
Hermes Fund Managers Limited	£154,072,000
Wavemaker Limited	£154,024,992
EMI Songs Limited	£153,923,536
Alpha Plus Group Limited	£153,844,000
PA Topco Limited	£153,832,992
Aldwych Finance Limited	£153,744,992
Yorker Holdings PKR Limited	£153,723,008
Cubico Holdings (UK) 2 Limited	£153,710,000
WBA Holdings 1 Limited	£153,700,000
TBL (Peterborough) Limited	£153,614,160
Sureserve Group PLC	£153,612,000
Lonrho Limited	£153,518,448
European Legacy Holdings Limited	£153,510,000
Semperian (Community Health) Limited	£153,490,592
SIR Rivers Limited	£153,480,000
Mergermarket Limited	£153,466,000
Sixmoor Limited	£153,397,920
UBS UK Properties Limited	£153,223,008
Badger Property Partners LLP	£153,142,800
Virtus IMH 2 Limited	£153,124,992
Jewish Care	£153,118,000

Company	Amount	Company	Amount
PRS for Music Limited	£153,044,992	A2D Funding II PLC	£149,524,992
RKH Group Limited	£153,036,992	BL HB Investments Limited	£149,483,104
John Laing Infrastructure Limited	£153,028,992	Oaktree Capital Management (UK) LLP	£149,300,000
Mesoblast UK Limited	£153,025,392	ADIB (UK) Limited	£149,294,912
Eucalyptus Energy Limited	£152,976,992	Syco Entertainment Limited	£149,280,864
The Westbury Hotel Limited	£152,935,008	Dollar Financial UK Holding Ltd	£149,279,008
CB-SDG Holdco Limited	£152,903,008	NYOP Education (Aberdeen) Limited	£149,156,384
Kingfisher UK Limited	£152,871,008	The Belvedere Realty Investments Limited	£149,146,544
A2D Funding PLC	£152,859,008	Warner Music International Services Limited	£148,956,000
Close Asset Management Holdings Limited	£152,844,000	AECOM Corporation Holdings (UK) Limited	£148,936,000
CWCB Leasing (DS6) Limited	£152,836,288	Zara U.K. Limited	£148,931,008
Control Risks Group Holdings Limited	£152,832,832	Mountain Warehouse International Limited	£148,916,000
Universal Coal PLC	£152,829,088	Reed Specialist Recruitment Limited	£148,875,008
Cboe Worldwide Holdings Limited	£152,806,800	Granada UK Rental and Retail Limited	£148,840,992
Integro Insurance Brokers Limited	£152,787,008	C J O'Shea Group Limited	£148,816,352
Sensburg Finance Ltd	£152,771,504	SCP Acquisition Topco Limited	£148,703,008
Greenway Infrastructure Capital PLC	£152,689,392	The Lankellychase Foundation	£148,635,408
The Foundation for Social Entrepreneurs	£152,688,976	Canary Wharf Properties (WF9) Limited	£148,581,264
Ardmore Construction Limited	£152,448,640	Firestone Diamonds PLC	£148,522,432
CLS UK Properties PLC	£152,427,376	JLT Benefit Solutions Limited	£148,500,000
Edgen Murray Europe Limited	£152,426,000	International Transport Intermediaries Club Ltd	£148,480,784
SIR TP Limited	£152,426,000	Precise Mortgage Funding 2015-2B PLC	£148,449,120
Phillips 66 CS Limited	£152,253,152	SK Shipping Europe PLC	£148,238,240
Cath Kidston Group Limited	£152,238,000	Vacant Property Security Limited	£148,160,000
Lime Street (Funding) Limited	£152,163,008	Doyle London Hotels Limited	£148,151,008
Circle Anglia Social Housing 2 PLC	£152,120,000	National Magazine Company Limited (The)	£148,028,000
Flint Nominees Limited	£152,085,344	Agilisys Holdings Limited	£147,944,000
T-Systems Limited	£151,955,008	AD (Europe) Finance	£147,925,488
Reed Smith LLP	£151,831,888	Warner Music UK Limited	£147,519,008
Bechtel Limited	£151,756,992	TIGI Holdings Limited	£147,452,992
Lawn Tennis Association Limited	£151,703,008	CAN Holdings Limited	£147,444,000
HPI UK Holding Ltd.	£151,700,992	Castle Trust Finance Limited	£147,420,992
Hydrasun Group Acquisitions Ltd	£151,675,008	Palmbest Limited	£147,404,000
Jurys Inns (UK) Limited	£151,672,992	4imprint UK Holdings Limited	£147,308,992
Eucalyptus Energy Holdings Limited	£151,603,008	Watch Tower Bible and Tract Society of Britain	£147,207,760
BC Capital Management Services Limited	£151,590,000	Element Materials Technology Holding UK Ltd	£147,136,368
Foseco Limited	£151,562,000	Closerstill Media Holdings Limited	£147,109,504
The Campden Charities Trustee	£151,531,120	Closerstill Acquisitions Limited	£147,109,424
AMT Mortgage Insurance Limited	£151,412,032	BDCG Holdings Limited	£147,023,008
Total Midstream Holdings UK Limited	£151,348,992	Scottish Sea Farms Limited	£147,022,000
Priority Pass Limited	£151,347,904	All3media USA Limited	£146,994,176
Trainline Investments Holdings Limited	£151,338,000	Eurosail 2006-1 PLC	£146,992,000
Aberdeen Asset Investments Limited	£151,239,008	Arndale Properties Limited	£146,936,000
IW Group Services (UK) Limited	£151,212,992	ISG Fit Out Limited	£146,807,008
The Dunhill Medical Trust	£151,119,184	Canary Wharf (North Quay) Limited	£146,509,936
Quest Diagnostics Holdings Ltd.	£151,055,216	338 Euston Road Limited	£146,504,688
Interior Services Group (UK Holdings) Limited	£150,950,000	Zoopla Limited	£146,314,000
IG Finance	£150,916,576	McGraw-Hill Education (UK) Limited	£146,300,000
Gresham Receivables (No.38) UK Limited	£150,916,368	Dana Petroleum (BvUK) Limited	£146,280,992
Aitch Group Limited	£150,867,088	Eurosail 2006-3NC PLC	£146,248,000
Aegis Media Pacific Ltd	£150,866,000	Western Union Business Solutions (UK) Limited	£146,196,992
CP Global Trading LLP	£150,842,192	Emerson Holding Company Limited	£145,986,000
Amber Bidco Limited	£150,803,008	Freightliner Heavy Haul Limited	£145,808,992
350 Euston Road Limited	£150,800,496	Casual Dining Limited	£145,763,008
Wilmington PLC	£150,780,992	Lancashire Insurance Holdings (UK) Limited	£145,699,936
New Star Asset Management Group Limited	£150,724,000	Cello Health PLC	£145,608,000
Ontic Engineering & Manufacturing UK Limited	£150,695,568	Monecor (London) Limited	£145,507,008
Origin Invest Limited	£150,511,520	Fairhold Homes (No.9) Limited	£145,416,416
PA International Consulting Group Limited	£150,501,104	Vanguard Asset Services, Ltd.	£145,336,000
Veolia ES Leeds Limited	£150,388,000	J.P. Boden & Co. Limited	£145,334,064
Harwood Capital Management Limited	£150,366,464	Larch Life No.1 (UK) Ltd	£145,305,568
Diageo DV Limited	£150,331,008	GB Railfreight Limited	£145,156,000
Rosediamond LLP	£150,262,224	Rolex Watch Company,Limited (The)	£145,143,008
Artemis Investment Management LLP	£150,216,000	Starstone Finance Limited	£145,138,672
Onefinestay (Holdings) Limited	£150,174,048	National Grid Metering Limited	£145,119,008
RG Engagement Group 5 Limited	£150,111,920	PA Overseas Holdings Limited	£145,051,168
CLS One Limited	£150,046,208	FGIC UK Limited	£145,016,000
MF Finco1 Limited	£150,000,000	Deco 11 - UK Conduit 3 P.L.C.	£144,981,360
Stephenson Harwood LLP	£150,000,000	PHP SB Limited	£144,948,960
CLH Pipeline System (CLH-PS) Ltd	£149,832,480	T Clarke Public Limited Company	£144,900,000
CLDN UK Limited	£149,799,936	London & Associated Properties PLC	£144,791,008
A V Co 1 Limited	£149,696,000	Honours (Holdings) Limited	£144,787,008

Company	Value
Dagger Holdings Limited	£144,759,008
Yougov PLC	£144,754,000
G4S US Investments Limited	£144,669,728
CenturyLink Communications Europe Limited	£144,563,152
LMS Capital PLC	£144,528,000
H.R.Owen PLC	£144,499,008
TI Media Limited	£144,431,008
Fairhold Homes Limited	£144,352,960
Launcelot Investments (UK) Limited	£144,271,248
4 Ventures Limited	£144,200,000
Residential Mortgage Securities 23 PLC	£144,196,992
Jupiter Hotels Limited	£144,003,008
Houlihan Lokey Capital (Holdings) Limited	£143,973,808
Collins Stewart Former Holdings Limited	£143,963,040
Reuters Transaction Services Limited	£143,959,552
Connect M77/GSO Holdings Limited	£143,916,992
Connect M77/GSO PLC	£143,916,992
LXI Property Holdings 2 Limited	£143,816,928
Miki Travel Limited	£143,779,952
M I Investment Holding Limited	£143,740,992
American Express Group Services Limited	£143,676,992
UPP (Exeter) Limited	£143,560,000
Derwent London Farringdon Limited	£143,530,624
Travelex Group Investments Limited	£143,500,000
Victoria Investments PIKco Limited	£143,482,000
New Printing House Square Limited	£143,443,120
B.A.T. China Limited	£143,436,992
Infrastructure Investments (Colorado) Limited	£143,421,536
WP R Midco 2 Limited	£143,381,936
Elegant Hotels Group PLC	£143,341,792
Fitch Solutions Group Limited	£143,330,720
Shanti Hospitality Group Limited	£143,324,400
Tungsten Corporation PLC	£143,247,008
Hindwain Limited	£143,228,000
PSPA Midco Limited	£143,224,992
URBN UK Limited	£143,220,672
Phillips 66 UK Funding Limited	£143,127,504
Noerr LLP	£143,096,640
Brown-Forman Beverages, Europe, Ltd	£143,020,992
Conduent Business Process Solutions Limited	£142,926,000
Heven Limited	£142,915,040
Babcock Group International Limited	£142,884,992
Flodrive Holdings Limited	£142,803,728
New Topco Limited	£142,792,000
Diamond Offshore Enterprises Limited	£142,771,600
BL HC PH LLP	£142,766,368
CGN Europe Energy UK Holding Limited	£142,559,008
Mortar No.1 Limited	£142,548,000
ITE Holdings Limited	£142,483,008
MCX Osprey (UK) Limited	£142,362,000
Schroder Private Assets Holdings Limited	£142,330,000
Morgan Stanley Corporate Trader	£142,304,688
Tullett Prebon (No. 1)	£142,296,448
Eunetworks Fiber UK Limited	£142,258,368
Rotch Property Group Limited	£142,250,432
Ecofin Global Utilities and Infrastructure Trust PLC	£142,244,992
Emperador Holdings (GB) Ltd	£142,009,056
AB Mauri (UK) Limited	£141,970,000
Raznoimport (UK) Limited	£141,846,352
Firmus Energy (Distribution) Limited	£141,770,624
Zayo Group UK Limited	£141,668,992
Valero Energy UK Ltd	£141,668,000
Shell Caribbean Investments Limited	£141,664,784
Istithmar P & O Estates (UK) Limited	£141,541,984
J. Walter Thompson Group Limited	£141,492,000
Webhelp UK Holdings Ltd	£141,452,000
Cambian Education Services Limited	£141,435,424
L.E.K. Consulting Group Limited	£141,356,288
L.E.K. International Group Limited	£141,356,288
Cath Kidston Acquisitions Limited	£141,278,000
DS Smith Corrugated Packaging Limited	£141,236,992
Gamma Communications PLC	£141,200,000

Company	Value
Hampshire Waste Services Limited	£141,144,992
PSPA Holdco Limited	£141,144,992
Soho Estates Portfolio Limited	£141,135,008
Selligent Holdings Limited	£141,117,888
Chelsea Land Limited	£140,944,992
Foresight VCT PLC	£140,848,992
Skuld I Limited	£140,800,992
Bath Road Cheltenham Limited	£140,701,168
Mizkan Euro Ltd.	£140,630,000
URBN International Operations Limited	£140,417,920
Mizkan Euro Holdings Limited	£140,286,000
Gresham Receivables (No. 15) UK Limited	£140,219,600
Aldea UK Holdco Limited	£140,161,440
LMS Capital Group Limited	£140,141,744
Mediaedge:cia (UK) Holdings Limited	£140,019,008
Allied SX Ltd	£140,000,032
Intu Properties Investments Limited	£140,000,000
Dunhill Tobacco of London Limited	£139,982,000
Firstbus (North) Limited	£139,876,992
Zetar Limited	£139,816,000
Vancouver Topco Limited	£139,754,000
Cathedral Capital Limited	£139,736,784
Hydrasun Group Holdings Ltd	£139,722,000
Gulfmark UK Ltd	£139,647,008
Beazley Management Limited	£139,600,000
Portobar Capital Limited	£139,587,040
Kenon Limited	£139,547,232
BIIF Holdco III Limited	£139,514,128
DS Smith Recycling UK Limited	£139,506,000
Giltbrook Retail Park Nottingham Limited	£139,503,408
Poplar HARCA Capital PLC	£139,500,992
JLT UK Investment Holdings Limited	£139,474,000
PA Group Holdings Limited	£139,315,008
Aberdeen Sidecar LLP	£139,247,008
M & G Investment Management Limited	£139,242,000
Fairhold Homes (No.6) Limited	£139,234,192
Mastcraft Limited	£138,994,880
Kensington Close Hotel Limited	£138,818,000
Syco Holdings Limited	£138,807,456
Capita Secure Information Solutions Limited	£138,790,800
Oath (UK) Limited	£138,679,008
Wilsonart Limited	£138,668,176
EDF Energy (Cottam Power) Limited	£138,663,008
SIR Hotels 1 Limited	£138,648,992
Talktalk Brands Limited	£138,647,008
Veolia Water Outsourcing Limited	£138,582,000
Londonmetric Saturn Limited	£138,567,088
E-Rewards Bidco Limited	£138,483,088
Business Design Centre Limited	£138,468,992
Mphasis UK Limited	£138,376,544
QHotels Holdings Limited	£138,276,000
Canary Wharf Holdings (PB) Limited	£138,263,120
Hostelworld Group PLC	£138,240,656
Blackrock UK Holdco Limited	£138,075,008
Tyrion Security Midco Limited	£138,040,992
Jump Trading International Limited	£137,980,528
HSIL Investments Limited	£137,914,000
Lapsent Limited	£137,910,000
Tyrion Security Topco Limited	£137,823,008
AHK International LLP	£137,821,104
Nobel Oil E & P (UK) Limited	£137,818,176
EDF Energy Services Limited	£137,666,000
Tullow Oil SK Limited	£137,587,008
Fred Perry Limited	£137,563,008
Aberdeen Investments Limited	£137,438,000
Mount Anvil Limited	£137,276,992
Stemcor Holdings 2 Limited	£137,268,992
Resource Solutions Limited	£137,035,008
Rooftop Funding Limited	£136,982,464
Gain Capital Holdings Ltd	£136,943,008
Glyn Hopkin Holdings Limited	£136,939,008
Clifford Chance International LLP	£136,927,872

Company	Value
The Conygar Investment Company PLC	£136,874,000
Mountsfield Park Finance Limited	£136,804,000
Henry Davies (Holborn) Limited	£136,755,296
The Wireless Infrastructure Company Limited	£136,674,320
Unifund PLC	£136,634,944
International Bible Students Association	£136,628,640
FTSE Global Debt Capital Markets Limited	£136,558,000
Clarion UK Midco Limited	£136,423,008
Minerva Corporation Limited	£136,396,592
Millennium Capital Partners LLP	£136,392,000
TS Real Estate Limited	£136,248,768
Chubb Capital V Limited	£136,230,000
Khoo Teck Puat UK Foundation	£136,156,224
Deltatre Holdings Limited	£136,043,680
Mercury Midco 2 Limited	£136,006,000
Mondrian Investment Partners Limited	£135,975,648
Openbet Technologies Limited	£135,924,000
Discovery Lightning Investments Ltd	£135,875,184
AD European Investments Limited	£135,870,432
Priory Group Limited	£135,636,992
Lion/Heaven UK Limited	£135,630,000
Starstone Corporate Capital 1 Limited	£135,595,136
Santos (UK) Limited	£135,567,616
Internetq Group Limited	£135,561,648
Royal London Management Services Limited	£135,504,992
Ascential Prefco Limited	£135,478,000
Antalis Group	£135,456,000
E D & F Man Limited	£135,442,768
Elbon Holdings (2) Limited	£135,216,176
Sapient Limited	£135,204,992
PSPA Finance Limited	£135,199,008
Lloyds Bank Corporate Asset Finance (No. 1) Ltd	£135,082,000
Old Hall Street Properties Limited	£135,034,000
Ground Rents Income Fund PLC	£134,971,632
Zenith UK (Media) Limited	£134,800,992
CGI Finance (UK) Limited	£134,748,992
Valero Logistics UK Ltd	£134,712,000
Almacantar (Centre Point) Limited	£134,637,392
BMA Investments Limited	£134,632,992
Cote Restaurants Group Holdings Limited	£134,610,000
Raymond Estates Ltd	£134,571,280
Siblu Holdings Limited	£134,535,120
Marie Curie	£134,504,000
JLL 2002	£134,414,928
Lazard & Co., Limited	£134,359,008
Equitix Offshore 2 Limited	£134,352,000
Brent Co-Efficient Limited	£134,298,000
Lok'n Store Limited	£134,286,240
Legal & General Homes Communities Limited	£134,239,456
Maestro (Holdings 1) Limited	£134,235,008
Empiric Investments (One) Limited	£134,220,960
Canary Holdco Limited	£134,190,168
Discovery Finance Company Europe Limited	£133,961,240
Red Bee Media Limited	£133,907,000
Intu Potteries Limited	£133,900,000
C & C Topco Limited	£133,836,000
Securitas Services Holding UK Limited	£133,834,496
Unisys Finance Limited	£133,671,704
EGX Credit Liquidity Ltd	£133,670,704
Patriot Topco Limited	£133,635,600
Yianis Docklands Hotels Limited	£133,626,960
Rothschild & Co Continuation Finance PLC	£133,593,280
Residential Mortgage Securities 26 PLC	£133,593,000
SEI Investments (Europe) Ltd	£133,589,000
Priory Education Services Limited	£133,549,000
HGHL Holdings Ltd	£133,546,920
Thomson Information & Publishing Holdings Limited	£133,493,960
Labuan RE Underwriting Limited	£133,380,520
Mabel Midco Limited	£133,375,000
Gresham Receivables (No.39) UK Limited	£133,372,992
St. Paul's School	£133,338,000
London & Regional (Empire) Limited	£133,285,672
Apple (UK) Limited	£133,259,000
Nomura Properties PLC	£133,219,384
The Mission Marketing Group PLC	£133,134,000
K Line LNG Shipping (UK) Limited	£133,127,656
BHP Billiton Marketing UK Limited	£133,068,704
Norwegian Compass Ltd	£133,051,584
Friary Court Investments Limited	£132,979,000
Smith & Williamson LLP	£132,956,000
H.J. Heinz Finance UK PLC	£132,950,000
Capita Resourcing Limited	£132,935,080
Salamander Energy (S.E. Asia) Limited	£132,920,504
Sunshine Finco Limited	£132,909,272
MacFarlanes LLP	£132,864,000
Aviva Investors UK Fund Services Limited	£132,788,000
Freepoint Commodities Enterprises Ltd.	£132,784,632
Office Retail Limited	£132,731,000
Omega Leasing (No.10) Limited	£132,679,752
London International Exhibition Centre Holdings PLC	£132,635,000
Mabanaft Limited	£132,602,000
O & H Q7 Limited	£132,492,352
Auria Solutions UK I Ltd.	£132,468,000
Dunbar Assets PLC	£132,355,000
Brookfield Global Property Advisor Limited	£132,324,336
Octopus Apollo VCT PLC	£132,324,000
Sunshine Holdco Limited	£132,228,800
John Laing Social Infrastructure Limited	£132,219,000
C & C Properties UK Limited	£132,105,000
Rothschild Foundation (Hanadiv) Europe	£132,054,384
Victoria's Secret UK Limited	£131,980,000
Vouvray Acquisition Limited	£131,961,384
Centro Europe Limited	£131,916,208
Oak No.1 PLC	£131,839,000
Recruit Global Treasury Services AUD Ltd	£131,713,040
Gabelli Value Plus + Trust PLC	£131,696,000
Gazprom Global LNG Limited	£131,593,192
Wireless Infrastructure Group Limited	£131,551,000
Barnsley SPV Three Limited	£131,438,000
APG (KE) Ltd.	£131,418,272
Lazard Asset Management (UK) Holdings Limited	£131,322,200
Equitix Healthcare Limited	£131,300,000
London Kensington Hotel Limited	£131,277,344
FS Holdco 2 Limited	£131,274,024
London Southend Airport Company Limited	£131,213,856
Irobot UK Ltd.	£131,196,800
European Wind Investments Group Limited	£131,152,000
Donnelley Financial Solutions Holdings UK Limited	£131,138,792
Catlin Holdings Limited	£131,135,720
3i International Holdings	£131,113,000
Springer Nature One Limited	£131,092,760
Aston Bidco Limited	£131,089,000
Tay Valley Lighting (Hampshire) Limited	£131,071,000
Time Out Group PLC	£131,047,000
Burberry Beauty Limited	£130,843,000
Chemchina UK Limited	£130,738,240
Bluecrest Capital Management (UK) LLP	£130,618,000
KG Group Holdings Limited	£130,610,000
Wellcome Trust Residential 1 Limited	£130,192,656
BIG Legolas Holdings Limited	£130,082,000
Trayport Holdings Limited	£130,080,504
Babcock Brazil Investments Limited	£130,061,000
Black Star Holdings Limited	£130,029,448
Point Dume Holdings Limited	£130,020,280
M7 Real Estate Investment Holdings Holdco Ltd	£129,836,336
EMGH Limited	£129,781,536
Technicolor Disc Services International Limited	£129,710,000
Ly Holding Limited	£129,641,072
Bracken Holdings Limited	£129,633,864
JLIF Holdings (Barcelona Metro) Limited	£129,598,000
LS Lewisham Limited	£129,509,000
Onyx Germany (2) Ltd	£129,501,704
Biomed Central Limited	£129,479,000
Alberto-Culver UK Holdings Limited	£129,455,000

Company	Value
Saatchi & Saatchi Holdings Limited	£129,396,000
FFI Holdings PLC	£129,362,168
The Royal Marsden Cancer Charity	£129,362,000
Omega Leasing (No.11) Limited	£129,311,648
Leconport Estates	£129,300,000
W. R. Berkley London Holdings, Limited	£129,274,000
Aspers Group Limited	£129,103,000
Dentons UK and Middle East LLP	£129,053,000
Ensco U.K. Limited	£129,047,224
Monaco Bidco Limited	£129,028,000
Infrastructure Investments Betjeman Limited	£128,959,440
Polar Capital Holdings PLC.	£128,914,000
Monument Containers Limited	£128,887,000
Autovista Holdco UK Limited	£128,722,992
Hammerson (Rugby) Limited	£128,691,000
LR (City Road) Ltd	£128,679,616
All3media Limited	£128,633,720
Get Living London EV N07 Limited	£128,541,000
Miller Freeman Worldwide Limited	£128,476,000
Foster + Partners Limited	£128,467,000
Ferrovial Agroman Limited	£128,450,000
Stewardship Services (UKET) Limited	£128,446,000
Lloyd's Register Inspection Limited	£128,296,000
Bampton Property Group Limited (The)	£128,270,568
Virtus IMH Limited	£128,266,000
IO Investment 2 LLP	£128,207,992
IO2 Propco LLP	£128,206,944
Claranet Limited	£128,200,000
Jones Lang Lasalle Dorchester Ltd	£128,121,680
Avanade Europe Holdings Ltd.	£128,089,000
Big Box Midco UK Limited	£128,050,040
Octopus AIM VCT PLC	£128,033,000
TKG-Storagemart Partners UK Limited	£128,012,696
Universal Publishing Production Music Limited	£127,741,000
Lightsource Simba Limited	£127,723,552
World Fuel Services European Holding Company I, Ltd.	£127,679,784
Snacks International Development UK Limited	£127,669,168
BNY Mellon Fund Managers Limited	£127,617,000
Bank and Clients PLC	£127,438,000
Hammerson (Merthyr) Limited	£127,404,000
Top Shop / Top Man Properties Limited	£127,400,000
Bluebay Asset Management LLP	£127,369,000
Deutsche Holdings No.4 Limited	£127,315,248
The Royal Masonic Benevolent Institution Care Co	£127,270,000
Harrods Commercial Property Limited	£127,200,000
EBS Dealing Resources International Limited	£127,190,000
Canary Wharf Properties (RT5) Limited	£127,083,304
Gulfmark North Sea Limited	£127,062,000
Lightsource Pumbaa Limited	£127,031,608
Lightsource Timon Limited	£127,031,288
Tangguh Hiri Finance Limited	£126,913,568
The Griffin Insurance Association Limited	£126,896,792
Henderson Asset Management Limited	£126,787,000
D & P International Holdings (UK) Limited	£126,703,000
Gorkana Group Holdings Limited	£126,666,696
C & C Bidco Limited	£126,634,000
Enquest Global Limited	£126,513,840
Belmont Green Funding 3 Limited	£126,401,728
Care Homes 1 Limited	£126,376,504
Simca LLP	£126,360,168
AD Fin Services Limited	£126,333,304
Northern & Shell Enterprises Limited	£126,314,000
Kellen Investments Limited	£126,200,000
Ensco Offshore U.K. Limited	£126,134,648
Infrastructure Investments (A63) Holdings Limited	£126,093,936
Barchester Finco 2017 UK Limited	£126,074,000
Blue Transmission Walney 2 Limited	£125,943,000
Puente Holding Limited	£125,933,896
E D & F Man Capital Markets Treasury Management	£125,916,544
Westminster Topco Limited	£125,833,000
Alba 2006-1 PLC	£125,823,000
Majedie Asset Management Limited	£125,762,688
Tangguh Sago Finance Limited	£125,751,456
Zeal Network SE	£125,722,560
International Hoteliers (UK) Limited	£125,541,000
Brooks MacDonald Group PLC	£125,531,000
Exelvia Company	£125,474,000
BTIG Limited	£125,385,592
The British Museum Trust Limited	£125,357,528
Merrill Lynch (Camberley) Limited	£125,357,000
Pall Mall and Woodcote Park Clubhouses Limited	£125,341,000
Emerald Acquisition Limited	£125,318,368
P & O Property Holdings Limited	£125,312,000
Global Fashion Group UK Finance Limited	£125,245,648
Area Estates Limited	£125,209,992
Nine United Properties UK Ltd	£125,140,520
TC Ormonde OFTO Limited	£125,122,000
Aberdeen New Thai Investment Trust PLC	£125,112,000
Dorrington London Flats Limited	£125,003,632
Star Energy Group Limited	£124,864,000
SGO Corporation Limited	£124,794,144
Veolia ES Shropshire Limited	£124,645,000
Laura Ashley Holdings PLC	£124,600,000
Fox Healthcare Holdco 2 Limited	£124,576,000
Mayfair Charities Limited	£124,514,000
Ingenious Media Limited	£124,513,000
Methodist Independent Schools Trust	£124,512,000
Antalis Holdings Limited	£124,468,000
P1 Reversions Limited	£124,364,000
Coppid Farming Enterprises LLP	£124,322,400
Pepsico International Limited	£124,306,000
Convoys Properties Limited	£124,282,808
Derwent London Page Street Limited	£124,268,920
DS Smith Perch Limited	£124,230,000
CACI Limited	£124,144,832
Securitisation of Consumer Agreements Limited	£124,123,120
Fred. Olsen Cruise Lines Limited	£124,028,000
Equitix Highways 2 Limited	£124,025,000
Pacific Quay Finance PLC	£124,023,088
KAS No.2 Limited	£124,022,112
Pacific Quay Holdings Limited	£124,010,584
Tyman Financial Services Limited	£124,001,000
Rabai Power Holdings Limited	£123,984,224
Capital & Regional Holdings Limited	£123,891,560
Firstplus Financial Group Limited	£123,882,000
Aberdeen Infrastructure Limited	£123,847,320
Searchmap Limited	£123,790,000
Hayabusa Limited	£123,756,000
IEP Infrastructure Holdco Limited	£123,751,448
Oikia (UK) Limited	£123,657,744
IBC (Ten) Limited	£123,641,000
Flemings Hotel Mayfair Ltd	£123,590,456
BM Manchester Limited	£123,481,800
Simon Group Limited	£123,476,264
Disney Magic Company Limited	£123,432,248
St Ermin's Property Co.Limited	£123,394,552
Shams Maan Solar UK Limited	£123,360,920
Queensgate Bow UK Midco Limited	£123,355,000
BPP Services Limited	£123,319,000
Canonsfield Estates Limited	£123,261,712
Publicis Media Limited	£123,208,000
International Trade and Exhibitions Overseas Ltd	£123,048,816
Civica Holdings Limited	£122,956,000
Maurice Investments Limited	£122,935,592
Fujitsu EMEA PLC	£122,880,000
Charcoal Midco 2 Limited	£122,849,000
EMR Capital RF II LLP	£122,688,216
SThree UK Holdings Limited	£122,673,000
Aberdeen Infrastructure II Limited	£122,559,000
Larch (Nursing Homes) Holdco Ltd	£122,488,504
Cummins Power Generation Limited	£122,393,000
Third Point RE (UK) Holdings Ltd	£122,350,792
Sage Publications Limited	£122,282,000
Blackrock North American Income Trust PLC	£122,209,000

Company	Value
Inn on BW (UK) Limited	£122,157,744
All Saints Retail Limited	£122,146,000
Mishcon de Reya LLP	£122,107,000
Northstar Midco Limited	£122,020,000
Brixton (Origin) Limited	£121,964,000
Insight Group Limited	£121,857,896
Limited Life Assets Issuance PLC	£121,844,256
Innocent Limited	£121,799,000
Nando's Limited	£121,780,000
New England Paint Company Limited	£121,772,000
Quest Diagnostics Subsidiary Holdings Ltd.	£121,754,760
North Row Estates Limited	£121,680,792
Capital Hill Hotels Group London Limited	£121,616,000
The Royal Automobile Club Limited	£121,616,000
Akelius UK One Limited	£121,488,040
CMS Distribution Limited	£121,463,128
Immediate Media Company Limited	£121,460,000
VM Receivables Financing PLC	£121,323,632
NH2 Limited	£121,306,992
Origin Finance Limited	£121,264,000
Glyn Hopkin Limited	£121,245,000
Kin and Carta Marketing Services Limited	£121,201,872
Nimbus Acquisitions Midco Limited	£121,169,000
Greencoat Solar Assets II Limited	£121,079,816
DMG Information Limited	£121,054,208
Elbon Holdings (1) Limited	£121,041,304
Lazari Properties 5 Limited	£121,035,280
Alopuc Limited	£120,886,496
General Alumina Holdings Limited	£120,839,944
Dayshape Limited	£120,826,464
LS Hill House Limited	£120,818,000
Hunt Amber London 2 Ltd	£120,805,328
Burren Energy PLC	£120,753,296
Grainmarket Properties Limited	£120,736,744
Hammerson Oracle Investments Limited	£120,632,000
Meurice Limited	£120,557,688
First State Investment Services (UK) Limited	£120,554,000
Jester Debtco Limited	£120,460,664
Jester Midco Limited	£120,460,664
Control Risks Capital Limited	£120,452,000
Azzurri Midco 1 Limited	£120,400,000
Glen Water (Holdings) Limited	£120,197,000
Glen Water Limited	£120,197,000
Esselco Estates Limited	£120,163,000
Harvey Nichols Group Limited	£120,159,000
Old Mutual Business Services Limited	£120,147,000
Mansard Mortgages 2006-1 PLC	£120,133,064
Total Upstream UK Limited	£120,015,000
Outsourcing UK Limited	£119,970,000
Enquest Heather Leasing Limited	£119,805,256
Leopard UK Kensington Propco Limited	£119,797,000
OM Zimbabwe Holdco Limited	£119,726,000
Gowling WLG (UK) LLP	£119,517,000
Mount Anvil New Holdings Limited	£119,508,000
Bridges Business Space LLP	£119,443,648
Gresham Receivables (No.45) UK Limited	£119,433,736
ICE Asia Holdings Limited	£119,354,816
BG Great Britain Limited	£119,328,000
Solitaire Group Limited	£119,204,560
Mount Anvil Group Limited	£119,105,000
Global Aerospace Underwriting Managers Limited	£119,051,000
Hunt Amber London 1 Ltd	£118,923,536
Liberty Theta Limited	£118,897,000
TSL Education SPV 2 Limited	£118,889,000
Prophaven Limited	£118,849,000
First Rail Holdings Limited	£118,814,000
Amarin Corporation PLC	£118,798,544
Catlin Syndicate 6112 Limited	£118,770,000
Hector Rail Holding UK Limited	£118,748,000
JS Information Systems Limited	£118,649,000
Kantar Media UK Ltd	£118,646,456
Canary Wharf Investments (Three)	£118,623,608

Company	Value
Tamoa Limited	£118,464,464
Hull Esteem Consortium PSP Limited	£118,459,232
Cornwall Midco Limited	£118,452,000
PA Netherlands Treasury Services Limited	£118,376,616
Sony Pictures Television Production UK Limited	£118,343,000
Infopro Digital Holding (UK) Limited	£118,319,840
ICAP WCLK Limited	£118,228,000
Frasers Property (UK) Limited	£118,165,000
CGIS Group (No. 3) Limited	£118,034,000
Helios Underwriting PLC	£117,920,000
Victoria Oil & Gas PLC	£117,908,848
Borealis Infrastructure Europe (UK) Limited	£117,617,152
U-Pol Holdings Limited	£117,569,000
The Economist Intelligence Unit Limited	£117,545,000
OTPPB Investments (U.K.) Limited	£117,528,312
Laird (Finance) Limited	£117,504,000
ISG Central Services Limited	£117,498,000
Finance Holdings Limited	£117,486,000
G.I. Globinvestment Limited	£117,459,888
Eurosail Prime-UK 2007-A PLC	£117,366,000
Tremco Illbruck Limited	£117,303,544
Snowdon Leasing Company Limited	£117,300,536
Concierge Holding Company Limited	£117,286,992
Gosling Foundation Limited (The)	£117,223,544
ML Invest Holdings	£117,222,000
Tullett Prebon (No. 3) Limited	£117,176,320
Constitution Bidco 2 Limited	£117,131,000
Kinapse Holdco Limited	£117,114,000
Maybourne Hotels Limited	£117,095,000
Sectormatch Limited	£117,013,464
Ensono Opco Holdings Limited	£116,985,000
Mitie Security Holdings Limited	£116,945,000
Kinapse Midco Limited	£116,916,000
Scimco Limited	£116,849,000
Instron International Limited	£116,844,000
The Bernard Sunley Charitable Foundation	£116,820,000
Euroclear UK & Ireland Limited	£116,665,424
Housing Association Funding PLC	£116,543,848
Arca Holdco Limited	£116,462,000
Arcadis UK (Holdings) Limited	£116,387,000
Eskmuir Securities Limited	£116,250,000
The Cavendish Hotel (London) Limited	£116,209,000
UK SPV Credit Finance PLC	£116,083,512
Bridgepoint Funding III A Limited	£115,978,200
Wipro Holdings (UK) Limited	£115,971,912
Closerstill Finance Limited	£115,940,112
Legal & General Homes Communities (Crowthorne)	£115,905,120
Primary Medical Property Investments Limited	£115,803,672
WMR Holdco Limited	£115,739,320
Optimum Three Limited	£115,703,760
CII Holdco Ltd	£115,541,824
DMEP Holdco Limited	£115,396,448
Nuveen Real Estate Management Limited	£115,361,584
Gartmore Investment Management Limited	£115,358,000
St Mungo Community Housing Association	£115,348,000
London & Regional Hotel Finance Limited	£115,264,000
Maestro (Holdings 2) Limited	£115,230,000
Riverland Holdings Limited	£115,220,112
Meininger Hotels Limited	£115,179,000
Bonhams 1793 Limited	£115,112,000
Summit Exploration and Production Limited	£115,015,440
GWR Group Limited	£114,711,000
Anglo Asian Mining PLC	£114,649,344
Christopher Moran Holdings Limited	£114,635,184
Santa Fe Group Limited	£114,546,736
WR Midco Limited	£114,531,816
Hard Rock International Limited	£114,406,000
Kore Potash PLC	£114,374,544
Hines Europe Limited	£114,340,144
Babcock Communications Limited	£114,298,000
Maintel Holdings PLC	£114,285,000
Global Reach Partners Limited	£114,260,000

MHDV Holdings (UK) Limited	£114,223,000
Inn on the Park (London) Limited	£114,185,000
Really Useful Theatres Entertainment Limited	£114,163,000
Factset Europe Limited	£114,113,000
One Fleet Realty Ltd	£114,065,960
Gracechurch Bellyard Limited	£114,060,368
Cote Group (Financing) Limited	£113,900,000
Nintex UK Limited	£113,899,128
Connect M1-A1 Limited	£113,886,000
Vine Acquisitions Limited	£113,883,000
Crawford & Company Risk Services Investments Ltd	£113,856,000
Eurasia Finance Management Limited	£113,828,280
WBA Finance 1 Limited	£113,748,552
Travelex Central Services Limited	£113,746,000
Centaur Media PLC	£113,700,000
O & H Capital Limited	£113,653,016
Blue Transmission Walney 1 Limited	£113,530,000
Fiberweb Limited	£113,488,000
AAA UK Acquisition Co. Limited	£113,211,576
Nuveen FCACO Limited	£113,090,352
Ebiquity PLC	£113,012,000
Selfridges & Co. Limited	£113,000,000
Qwest Communications International Ltd.	£112,951,032
Eclectic Capital Limited	£112,840,168
Connect M1-A1 Holdings Limited	£112,769,000
Assembled Productions III UK Limited	£112,739,160
Partnerships in Care Limited	£112,737,000
Lancer Square Limited	£112,717,840
UPP (Duncan House) Holdings Limited	£112,697,000
UPP (Duncan House) Limited	£112,696,000
Time Warner Entertainment Limited	£112,660,000
Land Securities Buchanan Street Developments Ltd	£112,608,000
Avenell Property PLC	£112,519,000
LS Shepherds Bush Limited	£112,435,000
St. James Court Hotel Limited	£112,399,848
Hammerson (60 Threadneedle Street) Limited	£112,342,000
Maxwell Asset Management Ltd	£112,269,376
Rogers Chapman UK Limited	£112,168,856
The Sports Council Trust Company	£112,139,000
United Bank for Africa (UK) Limited	£112,132,800
Energy Power Resources Limited	£112,098,000
Leadiant Biosciences Limited	£112,069,976
Tenneco Management (Europe) Limited	£112,064,000
Aberdeen Japan Investment Trust PLC	£112,038,000
Quarto Publishing PLC	£112,034,000
Percy Village Limited	£111,998,152
Finance for Higher Education Limited	£111,980,000
Donnelley Financial Solutions Group UK Limited	£111,754,936
Bank Mandiri (Europe) Limited	£111,691,728
Verdoso Holdings Limited	£111,656,312
Residential Mortgage Securities 25 PLC	£111,644,000
Chello Zone Holdings Limited	£111,612,000
Hanover & Oxford Property Limited	£111,581,608
Spotify Limited	£111,565,200
UPP (Nottingham) Ltd	£111,490,000
Marks and Spencer (Bradford) Limited	£111,417,000
HCA Global Capital LLP	£111,401,520
AAA UK Holding Co. Limited	£111,399,136
Calypso FX USD Limited	£111,346,320
Harding Midco Limited	£111,287,000
Idex UK Ltd.	£111,252,568
Ocubis Limited	£111,199,664
Meteogroup Limited	£111,165,504
Harewood Helena 2 Limited	£111,071,424
Kinapse Bidco Limited	£111,062,000
Merrill Lynch Europe Limited	£111,040,000
Road Management Services (Gloucester) Limited	£111,040,000
Besso Insurance Group Limited	£111,030,632
Greenwich BSF SPV Limited	£111,013,000
Blue Manchester Limited	£111,008,600
Fintry 3 Limited	£110,966,000
Nugent Shopping Park Limited	£110,924,584
McKesson Global Sourcing UK Limited	£110,886,528
Venaglass Limited	£110,882,160
Daisy 2015 Topco Limited	£110,776,936
ELQ Omega UK Ltd	£110,744,832
Kinapse Topco Limited	£110,639,000
Sojitz Energy Development Limited	£110,634,936
PA Consulting Holdings Limited	£110,613,072
British Land in Town Retail Limited	£110,586,856
London Leasehold Flats Limited	£110,577,192
Fox Investments Limited	£110,564,472
Charles Russell Speechlys LLP	£110,557,000
PA Group Limited	£110,545,000
Amcol (Holdings) Ltd.	£110,531,000
Daisy 2015 Holdco Limited	£110,507,632
Daejan (US) Limited	£110,447,024
Metallon Corporation Limited	£110,404,520
Dragonglass UK Holding Limited	£110,354,352
Mycitydeal Limited	£110,278,000
Nbcuniversal International Limited	£110,231,000
Cordiant Communications Group Limited	£110,223,000
Cambian Heritage I Limited	£110,217,280
Ferrari Group Limited	£110,162,824
Engine Acquisition Limited	£110,072,000
Element Materials Technology Group Holdings Ltd	£110,008,368
Thames Quay Properties Limited	£109,986,000
Thames Quay Properties II Limited	£109,986,000
Thames Quay Properties Holdings Limited	£109,986,000
Thames Quay Properties III Limited	£109,986,000
FirstGroup Canadian Finance Limited	£109,928,568
MS Amlin Underwriting Limited	£109,857,000
Petroceltic Resources Limited	£109,813,696
NYSE Holdings UK Limited	£109,811,720
MAP Capital Limited	£109,810,000
Livn UK 2 Co Limited	£109,799,216
LGPL Cornwall Limited	£109,756,152
Abbotstar Trading Ltd	£109,755,680
Whiteacre Resources Ltd	£109,755,680
Clearmoon Commercial Ltd	£109,754,976
Henwick Ventures Ltd	£109,753,608
FDL Holdings Limited	£109,666,792
Ashmore Investment Management Limited	£109,592,000
111 Group Holdings Limited	£109,547,000
Grey Communications Group Limited	£109,474,000
The Engine Group Limited	£109,472,000
Cortina Race LLP	£109,470,600
Lloyds Bank General Leasing (No. 3) Limited	£109,409,000
Ferrovial Agroman (UK) Limited	£109,373,000
International Power Australia Holdings (1) Limited	£109,345,056
The Economist Overseas (Holdings) Limited	£109,260,904
Craegmoor Group (No.5) Limited	£109,253,000
12 Smithfield General Partner Limited	£109,237,664
Gardaworld Consulting (UK) Limited	£109,235,168
IDR Finance UK II Limited	£109,176,384
Rocco Forte & Family (Luxury Hotels) Limited	£108,852,000
Orsted Burbo (UK) Limited	£108,847,736
Punter Southall Group Limited	£108,744,800
Cloudreach Acquisitions Limited	£108,571,000
Landesk Holdco UK Ltd	£108,552,472
Unlimited Marketing Group Ltd	£108,474,000
Upfield Foods UK Limited	£108,406,800
Fairhold Homes (No.7) Limited	£108,357,104
OCHL (Globe) Limited	£108,212,000
Ash8 Group Limited	£108,211,080
The Education Endowment Foundation	£108,149,400
Ove Arup & Partners Hong Kong Limited	£108,145,000
LS Harbour Exchange Option Limited	£108,122,000
Werner US Holding Limited	£108,119,296
Psygnosis Limited	£108,104,952
Vale Inco Europe Holdings	£108,081,000
Lloyds General Leasing Limited	£108,056,000
Faroe Petroleum (U.K.) Limited	£107,885,000
BMO Asset Management Limited	£107,828,000

Citifinancial Europe Limited	£107,788,000
Scottish & Newcastle India Limited	£107,743,000
Palace Midco UK Limited	£107,725,000
Kili Topco Limited	£107,722,920
Tritax REIT Acquisition 16 Limited	£107,710,048
London & Regional Portfolio Finance Limited	£107,706,032
G4S Facilities Management (UK) Limited	£107,704,000
G. Costa (Holdings) Limited	£107,624,904
SCP Acquisition Bidco Limited	£107,581,000
Verbena Investment Limited	£107,566,376
Swiss Re Services Limited	£107,513,000
Rocco Forte & Family (London) Limited	£107,404,000
Corob Consolidated Limited	£107,223,784
Tudehope Ltd	£107,169,504
Prudential Financial Services Limited	£107,153,000
TBWA UK Group Limited	£107,099,520
Rosleb Limited	£107,043,808
Nyraff Limited	£107,023,584
Primeairo Limited	£107,006,000
Voice Topco Limited	£106,773,224
Spitalfields Developments Limited	£106,620,000
Capita Property and Infrastructure Limited	£106,589,376
Sigma Pharmaceuticals PLC	£106,546,000
SB Energy Holdings Limited	£106,514,464
Minova Insurance Holdings Limited	£106,488,000
Admiral Taverns (780) Limited	£106,379,000
Orbital Shopping Park Swindon Limited	£106,377,408
National Australia Finance (Vessel Leasing No.5) Ltd	£106,231,072
Wisdom Profit (UK) Development Limited	£106,229,608
Cityfibre Holdings Limited	£106,221,000
Stena Spey Services Limited	£106,191,912
European Ferries Limited	£106,183,032
National Grid William Limited	£106,176,000
PKA Teesrep Holding (UK) Limited	£106,046,328
Louis Vuitton UK Limited	£106,022,000
Dialight PLC	£106,000,000
Iridium Midco Limited	£105,888,000
GESB PLC	£105,860,096
Conde Nast Publications Limited (The)	£105,794,000
Enovert Management Limited	£105,769,000
De Beers Jewellers Limited	£105,679,792
Corfe Hill Limited	£105,617,000
Clarion UK Topco Limited	£105,558,000
Bond Propco Limited	£105,550,000
Syncbeam Limited	£105,484,032
Central London Commercial Estates Limited	£105,457,264
GPS (Great Britain) Limited	£105,428,000
Suzaku Aviation One Limited	£105,291,064
Mandarin Oriental Hyde Park (Investment) Limited	£105,221,000
Rio Tinto Minerals Development Limited	£105,142,728
Clarion UK Holdco Limited	£105,135,000
TES Global Group Limited	£104,998,000
Merchant Retail Group Limited	£104,989,000
Elephant and Castle LLP	£104,916,360
Minerva Limited	£104,863,456
AWP Assistance UK Ltd	£104,735,600
Interserve FS (UK) Limited	£104,651,000
Prestbury Investment Holdings Limited	£104,603,000
UPP (Broadgate Park) Holdings Limited	£104,556,000
Hodson Holdings (Ashford) Limited	£104,535,480
Network Rail (High Speed) Limited	£104,460,000
The London and Overseas Insurance Company Ltd	£104,422,296
Hestok Limited	£104,373,024
Cote Group (Bidco) Limited	£104,286,000
LDC (Care Homes) Finco Limited	£104,226,664
Northstar Holding Limited	£104,162,000
Thinc UK Group Limited	£104,136,000
TI European Holdings Limited	£104,088,248
Union Lifestyle Holdings Limited	£103,947,872
Capita Employee Benefits Limited	£103,912,152
Tallwood Limited	£103,910,400
EDM Business Services Holdings Limited	£103,821,000
Navigator Gas Invest Limited	£103,760,824
Listrac Bidco Limited	£103,717,488
Calypso FX EUR Limited	£103,703,904
6-10 Cambridge Terrace Developments LLP	£103,701,472
Henderson Holdings Limited	£103,665,000
Nextpower Radius Limited	£103,606,280
Questor Properties Ltd	£103,543,440
Formpart (HPL) Limited	£103,435,000
Jupiter Emerging & Frontier Income Trust PLC	£103,387,000
Lions Gate International Media Limited	£103,299,856
Eastern & Oriental PLC	£103,218,912
CW Properties DS7B Limited	£103,216,496
Capital Hill Hotels Group Europe Limited	£103,211,000
Cerner Limited	£103,180,280
British American Tobacco China Holdings Limited	£102,995,000
Gresham Receivables (No. 30) UK Limited	£102,889,752
Live Nation (Music) UK Limited	£102,734,032
Lonrho Africa (Holdings) Limited	£102,728,032
FC Skyfall TA Limited	£102,684,560
WEX Europe UK Limited	£102,597,920
Kenmin (HP) Limited	£102,574,864
TI Atlantic Europe Holdings Limited	£102,559,912
Derwent London Angel Square Limited	£102,433,216
Tilfen Land Limited	£102,415,000
Fern Renewable Energy Limited	£102,386,000
Road Management Consolidated PLC	£102,270,000
Caledonia Thames Acquisitions Limited	£102,120,000
CWCB Finance Leasing (DS7B) Limited	£102,088,496
David Morris International Limited	£101,921,632
Noble Resources UK Limited	£101,881,472
WIC (UK) Ltd	£101,821,696
Orsted London Array Limited	£101,779,464
CNA Europe Holdings Limited	£101,722,000
Pearson Australia Finance Unlimited	£101,672,000
Music Sales Group Limited	£101,640,912
JC No. 3 (UK) Limited	£101,566,048
Crawford & Company EMEA/A-P Holdings Limited	£101,390,000
Shake UK Newco Limited	£101,374,040
Deltatre Group Limited	£101,373,424
Busyexport Limited	£101,354,000
Colart International Holdings Limited	£101,276,000
Cosmo Oil (U.K.) Limited	£101,203,544
Pillar Denton Limited	£101,191,728
Canary Wharf Investments (DS8) Limited	£101,142,640
A & L CF June (3) Limited	£101,126,472
Bluefin Insurance Group Limited	£100,800,000
Belmont Green Funding 1 Limited	£100,781,344
Jupiter Acquisitions (Holdings) Limited	£100,654,000
TRS Group (UK) Limited	£100,450,704
Spire Property 5 Limited	£100,384,000
Equitix MA 2 Capital Eurobond Limited	£100,230,000
Hydrasun Group Finance Ltd	£100,178,000
Anchor Carehomes Limited	£100,163,136
Nordson London Limited	£100,139,728
IFG UK Holdings Limited	£100,124,000
PTT International Trading London Ltd	£100,062,504
Margolis and Ridley Limited	£100,000,000

This page is intentionally left blank

Age of Companies

1800s [65]

Antofagasta Railway Company PLC
Aviva International Insurance Ltd
B.L.Holdings Limited
BBA Aviation PLC
BMO Global Smaller Companies PLC
Bankers Investment Trust PLC
Barclays PLC
Britannia Steam Ship Insurance Association
British Medical Association
Bunzl Retail & Healthcare Supplies
CNA Insurance Co Ltd
Cable and Wireless (West Indies) Ltd
China Navigation Co Ltd
City of London Investment Trust PLC
City of London Real Property Co Ltd
Claridge's Hotel Limited
Coutts & Company
Diageo DV Limited
Diageo PLC
EIS Group PLC
Electra Investments Limited
F & C Investment Trust PLC
Girls' Day School Trust
HSBC Bank PLC
Harrods Limited
Henderson Smaller Companies Investment Trust
Insight Group Limited
JPMorgan American Investment Trust PLC
JPMorgan Global Growth & Income PLC
Johnson Matthey PLC
LCH Limited
Ladbrokes Investments Holdings Ltd
Laird Limited
Law Debenture Corporation PLC
Lloyds Bank PLC
London Merchant Securities Ltd
London and Overseas Insurance Co Ltd
Mary Street Estate Limited
Medical Defence Union Limited
Medical Protection Society Ltd
Mercantile Investment Trust PLC
Merchants Trust PLC
Metropolitan Properties Co Ltd
NCR Limited
Ocean Marine Insurance Co Ltd
Ogilvy & Mather Group (Holdings) Ltd
PA Group Limited
Pearson PLC
Prudential Assurance Co Ltd
Reed Business Information (Holdings)
Rio Tinto Western Holdings Ltd
Ritz Hotel (London) Limited
Ritz Hotel, Limited
Shell Transport and Trading Co Ltd
Simon Group Limited
DS Smith Corrugated Packaging Ltd
DS Smith Paper Limited
Springer Nature Holdings Ltd
Charles Stanley Group PLC
TI Media Limited
Tanqueray Gordon and Co Ltd
Unilever U.K. Central Resources Ltd
Unilever U.K. Holdings Limited
United Kingdom Mutual Steam Ship Assurance Association (Europe)
Young & Co's Brewery PLC

1900-1909 [41]

ABF Grain Products Limited
Associated Newspapers Limited
Axa Insurance UK PLC
BP P.L.C.
Babcock International Limited
Babcock UK Finance
Balfour Beatty Group Limited
British American Tobacco (Investments)
British American Tobacco International Holdings (UK)
Debenhams Retail PLC
Elementis Holdings Limited
Fujitsu Services Limited
Guardian Media Group PLC
HSBC Life (UK) Limited
HSBC Trust Company (UK) Ltd
Harvey Nichols Group Limited
Hiscox Insurance Co Ltd
Justerini & Brooks,Limited
London School of Economics & Political Science
Lonmin PLC
M & G. Securities Limited
New River Co Ltd
News Corp UK & Ireland Limited
Otis Investments Limited
Pearson Management Services Ltd
RELX PLC
Reach PLC
Reliance Bank Limited
Royal London Mutual Insurance Society,Limited
Selfridges Retail Limited
Shell Petroleum Co Ltd
Steamship Mutual Underwriting Association
Stewardship Services (UKET) Ltd
TR Property Investment Trust PLC
Tate & Lyle PLC
Unilever UK & CN Holdings Ltd
Unisys Limited
Vosper Thornycroft (UK) Ltd
Waitrose Limited
West Ham United Football Club Ltd
Witan Investment Trust PLC

1910-1919 [48]

Antalis Group
Arsenal Football Club PLC
B.A.T. China Limited
Babcock Management Limited
H P Bulmer Limited
Chelwood Trading & Investment Co Ltd
Chilean Northern Mines Limited
T Clarke PLC
ENI Pakistan Limited
Eastern & Oriental PLC
Express Newspapers
Fujitsu Services Holdings PLC
Guthrie Overseas Investments Ltd
Hansa Trust PLC
H.J. Heinz Manufacturing UK Ltd
Helical PLC
Hinduja Automotive Limited
International Bible Students Association
Investec 1 Limited
JLT EB Holdings Limited
Lazard & Co., Limited
Lloyds Bank Subsidiaries Ltd
London Diocesan Fund
Majedie Investments PLC
NRG Victory Reinsurance Ltd
National Magazine Co Ltd
Otis Limited
Paramount British Pictures Ltd
Pearson Overseas Holdings Ltd
Performing Right Society,Limited
Rio Tinto Metals Limited
Rolex Watch Co Ltd
Sears Limited
Shell Company of Thailand Ltd
Shell Company of The Philippines Ltd
Shell Malaysia Limited
Shell U.K. Limited
Smiths Group PLC
John Swire & Sons Limited
Tomkins Engineering Limited
UBMG Holdings
Unilever Australia Investments Ltd
VTB Capital PLC
Vale Europe Limited
Valero Energy UK Ltd
Vectura Group Services Limited
Vesuvius Ceramics Limited
Warwick & Esplen Limited

1920-1929 [70]

AB Agri Limited
AON UK Limited
Adamant Investment Corporation Ltd
All England Lawn Tennis Ground PLC
Alpha Bank London Limited
Amalgamated Metal Corporation PLC
Arcadia Group Limited
B.A.T (U.K. and Export) Ltd
B.A.T Industries P.L.C.
Babcock Investments Limited
Batif Dollar Limited
Batleys Properties Limited
Blind Veterans UK
Robert Brett & Sons Limited
British American Tobacco Malaysia (Investments)
Brixton Limited
Brunner Investment Trust PLC
Burberry Limited
Cable & Wireless Limited
Caledonia Investments PLC
Chanel Limited
Close Brothers Limited
Columbia Pictures Corporation Ltd
Conde Nast Publications Ltd
Daily Mail and General Trust P L C
Derwent Valley Central Limited
Derwent Valley London Limited
Diageo Finance PLC
EMI Group Limited
Economist Newspaper Limited
Financial Times Limited
Fuller Smith & Turner PLC
GMS Estates Limited
Gates Worldwide Limited
HSBC Asset Finance (UK) Ltd
C. Hoare & Co.
ITV Services Limited
Investec Investments (UK) Ltd
JPMorgan European Investment Trust PLC
JPMorgan Japanese Investment Trust PLC
Ladbroke & Co., Limited
Legal and General Assurance Society
Lendlease Construction Holdings (Europe)
J. Leon & Co Ltd
John Lewis PLC
John Lewis Partnership PLC
Liberty International Financial Services
Lloyds Bank General Insurance Ltd

Lloyds Bank Hill Samuel Holding Co Ltd
Lloyds UDT Limited
Marks and Spencer P.L.C.
Merrill Lynch Europe Limited
Monks Investment Trust PLC
Pearson Education Holdings Ltd
J Sainsbury PLC
Save The Children Fund
Schweppes International Ltd
Segro PLC
DS Smith Recycling UK Limited
Societe Generale Investments (U.K.)
South London Church Fund & Southwark Diocesan Board of Finance
Star Pubs & Bars (Property) Ltd
Technip UK Limited
Temple Bar Investment Trust PLC
Unilever Overseas Holdings Ltd
United Dominions Trust Limited
Vesuvius Overseas Limited
Wembley Park Limited
Weston Investment Co Ltd
Willis Limited

1930-1939 [68]

A.B.F.Holdings Limited
ABF Investments PLC
Additional Securities Limited
Antalis Holdings Limited
Anzef Limited
Artemis Alpha Trust PLC
Associated British Foods PLC
British Sugar PLC
British-American Tobacco (Holdings)
Capital & Counties Limited
Carlton Communications Limited
Castle Lane Securities Limited
Clear Channel International Ltd
Collin Estates Limited
Cummins Power Generation Ltd
DB UK Bank Limited
DMGZ Limited
Daejan Holdings PLC
Debenhams Properties Limited
Diploma Holdings PLC
Dorrington London Flats Ltd
ENI AEP Limited
ENI ULT Limited
Electra Private Equity PLC
European Ferries Limited
Folgate Estates Limited
Fremantlemedia Group Limited
Fremantlemedia Limited
GLH Hotels Limited
Goodenough College
Granada Group Limited
Granada UK Rental and Retail Ltd
Grand Metropolitan Limited
Hammerson UK Properties PLC
Henderson Administration Ltd
William Hill Organization Ltd
Kantar Media UK Ltd
L'Oreal (U.K.) Limited
Leadenhall Securities Corporation
John Lewis Properties PLC
Lombard North Central PLC
London & Associated Properties PLC
Marston Properties Limited
Matthey Finance Limited
J.P. Morgan Limited
Mountview Estates PLC
N.B.S.A. Limited
National Car Parks Limited
OIC Run-Off Limited
P & O Property Holdings Ltd
Phonographic Performance Ltd
Private Oil Holdings Oman Ltd
Rio Tinto Minerals Development Ltd
Sabah Shell Petroleum Co Ltd
Smith & Nephew PLC
Sir Richard Sutton Limited
Tate & Lyle Investments Ltd
Taylor Clark Limited
Tennants Consolidated Limited
Tomkins Overseas Investments Ltd
Travel Document Service
Tremco Illbruck Limited
Trustees of The London Clinic Ltd
Unilever Australia Partnership Ltd
Vesuvius Holdings Limited
Virgin Records Overseas Ltd
Warner Bros. Entertainment UK Ltd
Warner Bros. Studios Leavesden Ltd

1940-1949 [57]

3i International Holdings
3i PLC
Alpha Plus Group Limited
Anglo American Marketing Ltd
Ascential Group Limited
Ashtead Plant Hire Co Ltd
Axa Services Limited
Balfour Beatty Infrastructure Investments
Balfour Beatty PLC
Book Service Limited
British Alcan Aluminium Ltd
British United Provident Association
Brown Shipley & Co. Limited
Bunzl PLC
Cater Allen Limited
Chesterfield Properties Ltd
Clarion Events Limited
Derwent Valley Limited
Eaton Square Properties Ltd
Food Investments Limited
G4S Care and Justice Services (UK)
Grand Metropolitan Estates Ltd
Hammerson PLC
Henderson European Focus Trust PLC
Howden Group Limited
ISG Construction Limited
Imperial London Hotels Limited
Knighton Estates Limited
LHA London Ltd
Legal & General Insurance Ltd
Lendlease Construction (Europe) Ltd
MEPC (1946) Limited
Marsh Corporate Services Ltd
Onesubsea UK Limited
PA Consulting Services Limited
Primark Stores Limited
Ravenseft Properties Limited
Rio Tinto Australian Holdings Ltd
Rio Tinto Finance PLC
Rio Tinto International Holdings Ltd
Rio Tinto London Limited
Rothschild & Co Continuation Ltd
Segro Industrial Estates Ltd
Segro Properties Limited
Shell Chemicals U.K. Limited
Smith & Nephew Investment Holdings
DS Smith Display Holding Ltd
Soho Estates Limited
St Martins Healthcare Limited
Sunblest Bakeries Limited
Telegraph Media Group Limited
Tower Hotel (London) Limited
UBM (UK) Limited
Union Property Holdings (London) Ltd
Vesuvius Investments Limited
Wilkes-Lucas Limited
Wittington Investments Limited

1950-1959 [93]

AD INV Limited
Adecco UK Limited
Angus Dundee Distillers PLC
Ascential UK Holdings Limited
Laura Ashley Limited
BBA Holdings Limited
BMO Asset Management Limited
Bank Leumi (U.K.) P.L.C.
Bayeast Property Co Limited
Bechtel Limited
Blackrock Throgmorton Trust PLC
British Land Company PLC
British Land Industrial Ltd
Charter Central Finance Ltd
Chelsea Harbour Limited
Leonard Cheshire Disability
City and Country Properties Ltd
Close Brothers Group PLC
Commerzbank Finance Limited
ConocoPhillips (U.K.) Limited
Coral Racing Limited
Cummins Ltd.
Marie Curie
DSG Retail Limited
Daejan Investments (Grove Hall) Ltd
Daejan Investments Limited
Daejan Properties Limited
Henry Davies (Holborn) Ltd
Diageo Great Britain Limited
Walt Disney Co Ltd
Domestic & General Insurance PLC
Dorrington Investment P L C
EMI Music Publishing Limited
Edenred (UK Group) Limited
Elementis Securities Limited
Equion Energia Limited
Estates & Agency Holdings Ltd
Formpart (HPL) Limited
Great Portland Estates P L C
Guinness Limited
HSBC Holdings PLC
HSBC Private Bank (UK) Limited
Halliburton Manufacturing and Services
Highdorn Co. Limited
Howden Joinery Limited
ICAP Securities Limited
IQVIA Solutions UK Limited
Inchcape PLC
Institute of Cancer Research: Royal Cancer Hospital
Investec Bank PLC
JPMorgan US Smaller Companies Investment Trust
Ladbroke US Investments Ltd
Ladbrokes Coral Group Limited
Land Securities P L C
Linklaters Business Services
Lloyds Bank Asset Finance Ltd
M & G Group Limited
E D & F Man Sugar Limited
Margolis and Ridley Limited
Midcorp Limited

Morgan Sindall Group PLC
J. Murphy & Sons Limited
P & O Overseas Holdings Ltd
William Pears Group of Companies
Phillips 66 Limited
Pontsarn Investments Limited
Primary Medical Property Investments
Queensgate Bow Propco Limited
Rank Foundation Limited
River Island Clothing Co. Ltd
Royal Mencap Society
Royal Opera House Covent Garden Foundation
S & N Angel Investments Ltd.
Santander Asset Management UK Holdings
Schroder International Holdings Ltd
Shell International Petroleum Co Ltd
Shell International Trading and Shipping Co
Shell Overseas Holdings Ltd
DS Smith Packaging Limited
DS Smith Sudbrook Limited
Spring Group Limited
Tannen Group Limited
Threadneedle Asset Management Ltd
Total UK Limited
R.Twining and Co Ltd
United Trust Bank Limited
WFL (UK) Limited
Waterstones Booksellers Ltd
West London & Suburban Property Investments
West Quay Shopping Centre Ltd
Willis Group Limited
XDG Limited
Zeus Land Investments Limited

1960-1969 [172]

A.G. Clothing Limited
AGF Insurance Limited
Aberdeen Asset Investments Ltd
Ahli United Bank (UK) PLC
Allied Domecq (Holdings) Ltd
Allied Domecq Spirits & Wine Ltd
Amcol (Holdings) Ltd.
Anglo Pacific Group PLC
Anmercosa Finance Limited
Arbuthnot Latham & Co., Ltd
Arena Leisure Limited
Axa Insurance PLC
BBA Overseas Holdings Limited
BG Great Britain Limited
BG International Limited
BHP Billiton Petroleum Great Britain
BLD Property Holdings Limited
Bampton Property Group Limited
Barclays Mercantile Business Finance
Black Horse Limited
Blackrock Advisors (UK) Ltd
Blackrock Group Limited
Bluefin Insurance Services Ltd
British American Tobacco (AIT) Ltd
British Heart Foundation
Bupa Investments Limited
CBRE GWS Limited
CGI IT UK Limited
CNR International (U.K.) Ltd
Cadogan Estates Limited
Cadogan Holdings Limited
Cardnet Merchant Services Ltd
Central London Commercial Estates
Charter Consolidated Limited
Chelsea Land Limited
Chrysaor North Sea Limited
Clear Channel UK Limited
Close Invoice Finance Limited
ConocoPhillips Petroleum Company U.K.
Coral (Holdings) Limited
Corus International Limited
Coutts Finance Co.
Credit Suisse Securities (Europe)
J. & J. Denholm Limited
Diamond Offshore Limited
Drift Properties Limited
Dunbar Assets PLC
EMI Group Finance Limited
EMI Songs Limited
EMP Exploration (Kangean) Ltd
ENI UK Limited
ENI ULX Limited
Electrocomponents PLC
Elementis UK Limited
Emerson Electric U.K. Limited
Euromoney Institutional Investor PLC
Financial Times Group Limited
Finastra Holdings Limited
GWR Group Limited
Gartmore Investment Management Ltd
Kurt Geiger Limited
Global Radio Limited
Graff Diamonds Limited
Granada Television Overseas Ltd
Greenham Trading Limited
Grosvenor Properties
Grosvenor West End Properties
Guardian News & Media Limited
Guinness Overseas Limited
Guthrie Corporation Limited
HCA International Holdings Ltd
Hammerson International Holdings Ltd
Henderson Global Investors Ltd
Heron Corporation
Heron International Holdings
Hess Limited
The Robert Hitchins Group Ltd
Howard de Walden Estates Ltd
Howden UK Group Limited
IOCL Exploration and Production Oman
ITV Broadcasting Limited
Insight Investment Management (Global)
Integralife UK Limited
International Publishing Corporation
Interpublic Limited
JPMorgan Claverhouse Investment Trust
Jockey Club Racecourses (Holdings)
Kennedy Trust for Rheumatology Research
King & Shaxson Limited
Ladbrokes Betting & Gaming Ltd
John Laing Investments Ltd
Land Securities (Finance) Ltd
Land Securities Properties Ltd
Estee Lauder Cosmetics Ltd
Lewis Trust Group Limited
Lloyds Bank Insurance Services Ltd
Lockfold Communications Ltd
Longman Group (Overseas Holdings)
Lowland Investment Company P L C
M & G Investment Management Ltd
Markel International Insurance Co Ltd
Marsh Treasury Services Ltd
Martin's Properties Holdings Ltd
Mayfair Charities Limited
Methane Services Limited
Metropolitan Properties Co. (F.G.C.)
Mitie Technical Facilities Management
G. Modiano Limited
Monecor (London) Limited
Monopro Limited
J.P. Morgan Europe Limited
Motorola Solutions UK Limited
Moussaieff Jewellers Limited
Music Sales Group Limited
National Westminster Bank PLC
News Group Newspapers Limited
Ove Arup & Partners International
Overbury PLC
P & O Property Accounts Ltd
PA International Consulting Group
PG Media Services Limited
Pacific Life RE Limited
Pearson Education Limited
Penguin Books Limited
Penguin Random House Limited
Pentland Group PLC
Portman Investments (Baker Street)
Pricewaterhousecoopers Services Ltd
Prudential Group Holdings Ltd
R.E.A. Holdings PLC
RBS Invoice Finance Limited
Random House Group Limited
Raphael Freshwater Memorial Association
Reed Overseas Corporation Ltd
Repsol Sinopec Resources UK Ltd
Restaurant Group (UK) Limited
Ricoh Europe Finance Limited
Rio Tinto PLC
N. M. Rothschild & Sons Ltd
SG Kleinwort Hambros Bank Ltd
SG Leasing (March) Limited
Schawk Wace Group
Schroder Investment Co Ltd
Scotiabank Europe PLC
Scottish Sea Farms Limited
Simec Lochaber Hydropower 2 Ltd
Smith & Nephew (Overseas) Ltd
Smith & Nephew Trading Group Ltd
Sodexo Limited
Sotheby's
Sparrows Offshore Services Ltd
Springer Nature Limited
St Ermin's Property Co.Limited
Stanbic Africa Holdings Ltd
Standard Chartered PLC
TNS Group Holdings Limited
TTT Moneycorp Limited
Tandem Bank Limited
Tate & Lyle Industries Limited
Total E & P UK Limited
Total Oil UK Limited
Travelex Group Investments Ltd
Tullett Prebon (Europe) Ltd
U.K.& European Investments Ltd
USAA Limited
Union Property Corporation Ltd
United Dominions Leasing Ltd
United Finance Limited
Universal Music Operations Ltd
Universal Music Publishing Ltd
Universal Music Publishing MGB Ltd
Warner Music UK Limited

1970-1979 [214]

3i Group PLC
Abbott Mead Vickers Group Ltd
Accor UK Business & Leisure Hotels
Accor UK Economy Hotels Ltd
Addison Lee Limited

Amyn Hotels Limited
Ansell (U.K.) Limited
Antalis Group (Holdings) Ltd
Antalis Limited
Ardmore Construction Limited
Arup Group Limited
Laura Ashley Holdings PLC
Aspen Insurance UK Limited
Atos IT Services Limited
Atos IT Services UK Limited
Aviva Investors Global Services Ltd
Aviva Investors Pensions Ltd
Axa Investment Managers UK Ltd
B.A.T. International Finance P.L.C.
BAE Systems PLC
BBC Studios Distribution Ltd
BG Global Energy Limited
BNY Mellon Investment Management EMEA
BPP Holdings Limited
Baker Hughes Limited
Bakkavor Foods Limited
Balfour Beatty Investment Holdings
Balfour Beatty Overseas Investments
Bank Saderat PLC
Bank and Clients PLC
Bank of Montreal Capital Markets (Holdings)
Barclays Bank PLC
Benesco Charity Limited
Bestway (Holdings) Limited
Bestway Wholesale Limited
Blackrock Fund Managers Ltd
Boeing Defence UK Limited
British Arab Commercial Bank PLC
Build King Construction Ltd
Bunzl Finance PLC
CLSA (UK)
CNR International (U.K.) Developments
CNR International (U.K.) Investments
Canonsfield Estates Limited
Capita Customer Management Ltd
Capital & Regional PLC
Car Giant Limited
Carnival Film & Television Ltd
Centremanor Limited
Christie Manson & Woods Ltd
Christie's International PLC
Citifinancial Europe Limited
Clarkson PLC
Clear Channel Overseas Limited
Clothworkers' Foundation
Cola Holdings Limited
Conegate Developments Limited
Cordiant Communications Group Ltd
Cubcall Limited
Das Europe Limited
Dentsu Aegis Network Ltd.
Deutsche Morgan Grenfell Group PLC
Dolphin Drilling Limited
Donvand Limited
Dorchester Hotel Limited
Doyle London Hotels Limited
ED Broking Holdings (London) Ltd
EMI Group International Holdings Ltd
ENI Australia Limited
ENI Lasmo PLC
Edgen Murray Europe Limited
Elf Petroleum UK Limited
Equinor UK Limited
Euroclear Limited
Evergreen Marine (UK) Limited
Finastra Group Holdings Ltd
Finastra International Limited
Fitch Ratings Ltd
GF Financial Markets (UK) Ltd
Arthur J. Gallagher (UK) Ltd
Glencore UK Ltd.
Goldman Sachs International Bank
Graff Diamonds International Ltd
Grand Metropolitan International Holdings
Grosvenor Estate Holdings
Group Miki Holdings Limited
Gulf International Bank (UK) Ltd
HSBC Asia Pacific Holdings (UK) Ltd
Hampshire Trust Bank PLC
Hanover Acceptances Limited
Hard Rock International Ltd
Havin Bank Ltd
Hays Specialist Recruitment Ltd
Henderson Holdings Limited
H & M Hennes & Mauritz UK Ltd
Hindwain Limited
Holbud Limited
Hunting Energy Holdings Ltd
Hunting Knightsbridge Holdings Ltd
Hunting Oil Holdings Limited
Hunting PLC
IG Index Limited
INEOS UK SNS Limited
ING Services Limited
Inchcape Corporate Services Ltd
Informa Telecoms & Media Ltd
Informa UK Limited
Instinet International Limited
Instron International Limited
Intercapital Limited
Iranian Oil Company (U.K.) Ltd
JPMorgan Asset Management (UK) Ltd
JPMorgan Mid Cap Investment Trust PLC
Johnson Matthey Investments Ltd
Jones Lang Lasalle European Holdings
Jones Lang Lasalle Limited
Ladbrokes Group Finance PLC
John Laing Limited
Legal & General (Unit Trust Managers)
Legal & General Group PLC
Legal & General International Ltd
Legal & General Overseas Holdings
Legal and General Assurance (Pensions Management)
Lex Autolease Limited
Link Fund Solutions Limited
Lloyd's Register Inspection Ltd
Lloyds Bank Financial Services (Holdings)
Lloyds Bank Leasing Limited
Lloyds Development Capital (Holdings)
London Metropolitan University
London South Bank University
Lonrho Africa (Holdings) Ltd
M & G Limited
E D & F Man Capital Markets Ltd
E D & F Man Limited
McDonald's Restaurants Limited
Mediacom UK Limited
Menzies Distribution Limited
Mercer Limited
Merchant Retail Group Limited
Metdist Limited
Mitsui Sumitomo Insurance Company (Europe),
Mizuho International PLC
Monsoon Accessorize Limited
Christopher Moran Holdings Ltd
Morgan Stanley UK Group
Motability Operations Limited
Muirgold Limited
News Corp Investments UK & Ireland
Newton Investment Management Ltd
Norsea Pipeline Limited
North Atlantic Smaller Companies Investment Trust
Oceaneering International Services
Omnicom Finance Limited
Ove Arup & Partners Hong Kong Ltd
P & O Properties International Ltd
PGIM Financial Limited
Pall Mall and Woodcote Park Clubhouses
Pearson Services Limited
Peer Group PLC
Prudential Corporation Holdings Ltd
Prudential Pensions Limited
Prudential PLC
Psygnosis Limited
QBE RE (Europe) Limited
Quarto Publishing PLC
RBC Europe Limited
R. Raphael & Sons PLC
Rathbone Brothers PLC
Ravenside Investments Limited
Repsol Sinopec North Sea Ltd
Rio Tinto European Holdings Ltd
Rolls-Royce PLC
Romulus Securities Limited
Royal Masonic Benevolent Institution Care Company
SCOR UK Co Ltd
SIG PLC
SNC Securities Limited
Sableknight Limited
Sage Publications Limited
Segro Overseas Holdings Ltd
Shell China Exploration and Production Co
Slough Trading Estate Limited
Smith & Nephew USD Limited
Smith & Williamson Investment Services
DS Smith PLC
Smiths Group International Holdings
Stena Ropax Limited
Marie Stopes International
Structadene Limited
Sucden Financial Limited
Tamoa Limited
Tate & Lyle International Finance PLC
Tenecom Limited
Threadneedle Pensions Limited
Tokio Marine Kiln Insurance Ltd
Trailfinders Limited
Transworld Petroleum (U.K.) Ltd
Travelers Insurance Co Ltd
Triland Metals Limited
Tullett Prebon Group Limited
UDV (SJ) Limited
University of Greenwich
University of Westminster
Veladail Hotels Limited
Venaglass Limited
Veolia ES Landfill Limited
Virgin Records Limited
Vivo Energy Namibia Limited
WPP 2005 Limited
WSP UK Limited
Willis Faber Limited
Willis Group Services Limited
Willis International Limited

1980-1989 [506]

A & L CF June (3) Limited

AB Mauri (UK) Limited
AD Overseas (Europe) Limited
AECOM Limited
AIB UK Loan Management Limited
AMV BBDO Investments Limited
ANZ Europe Limited
AON UK Group Limited
AWP Assistance UK Ltd
Abbey National Property Investments
Abbey National Treasury Services PLC
Aberdeen New Dawn Investment Trust PLC
Aberdeen New Thai Investment Trust PLC
Aegis Group Holdings Limited
Agrichrome Limited
Alberto-Culver Group Limited
Allen & Ginter (UK) Limited
Allianz Europe Limited
Amarin Corporation PLC
American Express Services Europe Ltd
Anglo American Investments (UK) Ltd
Anglo American Services (UK) Ltd.
Anglo-Eastern Plantations PLC
Antofagasta PLC
Apple (UK) Limited
Arbuthnot Banking Group PLC
Argus Media Limited
Ashtead Group PLC
Associated British Ports Holdings
Atos International IT Limited
Aviva Group Holdings Limited
Aviva International Holdings Ltd
Aviva Investors Holdings Ltd
Aviva Investors UK Fund Services Ltd
Axa Equity & Law PLC
BASF Metals Limited
BBDO EMEA Limited
BG North Sea Holdings Limited
BG Overseas Holdings Limited
BG UK Holdings Limited
BMI Healthcare Limited
BMO AM Group (Holdings) Ltd
BMO AM Group (Management) Ltd
BMO AM Holdings Limited
BNP PUK Holding Limited
BNP Paribas Commodity Futures Ltd
BNP Paribas U.K. Holdings Ltd
BNP Paribas UK Limited
BNY Mellon Fund Managers Ltd
BT (International) Holdings Ltd
BT Global Services Limited
BT Holdings Limited
BT Limited
Babcock International Group PLC
Babcock Investments (Number Eight)
Babcock Southern Holdings Ltd
Bakkavor Limited
Ballymore Properties Limited
Bank of Scotland Structured Asset Finance
Barclays Aldersgate Investments Ltd
Barclays Capital Securities Ltd
Barclays Investment Management Ltd
Barclays Services Limited
Bear Stearns Holdings Limited
Better Properties Limited
Beverage Services Limited
Birchgree Limited
Blackrock Investment Management (UK)
Blackrock Life Limited
Blackrock UK Holdco Limited
Bloomsbury Publishing PLC
Braemar Shipping Services PLC
Brewin Dolphin Limited
British Sugar (Overseas) Ltd
British Telecommunications PLC
Brooke Bond Assam Estates Ltd
Brooke Bond South India Estates Ltd
Bunzl Overseas Holdings (No. 2) Ltd
Bupa Care Homes (ANS) Limited
Bupa Care Homes (CFChomes) Ltd
Bupa Care Homes (CFG) PLC
Business Design Centre Limited
C.C. Licensing
C.I. Property & Investments Ltd
CACI Limited
CAN Holdings Limited
CBRE Managed Services Limited
CIB Properties Limited
CMC Markets UK PLC
CMS Distribution Limited
Canaccord Genuity Limited
Canary Wharf Contractors Ltd
Canary Wharf Finance Leasing (BP1)
Canary Wharf Investments (Three)
Canary Wharf Investments Ltd
Canary Wharf Limited
Caparo Holdings (US) Limited
Capita Business Services Ltd
Capita Employee Benefits Ltd
Capita Life & Pensions Regulated Services
Capita PLC
Capita Property and Infrastructure
Capita Secure Information Solutions
Carphone Warehouse Limited
Cast Limited
Catlin Holdings Limited
Centro Europe Limited
Charity Projects
Chelsea Football Club Limited
Chesterlodge Limited
Chevron North Sea Limited
Childcare Vouchers Limited
Chime Communications Limited
Chubb Services UK Limited
Citibank Investments Limited
Citigroup Global Markets Ltd
Civica Holdings Limited
Civica UK Limited
Cliffrange Limited
Coca-Cola Holdings (United Kingdom)
Colgems Productions Limited
Colt Technology Services
Commercial Acceptances Limited
Conduit Insurance Holdings Ltd
ConocoPhillips (U.K.) Theta Ltd
ConocoPhillips (U.K.) Zeta Ltd
Consolidated Insurance Group Ltd
Control Risks Group Holdings Ltd
Corob Consolidated Limited
Credit Suisse (UK) Limited
Credit Suisse Asset Management Ltd
D B Investments (GB) Limited
DCC Technology Limited
DWS Group Services UK Limited
Daily Mail International Ltd
Daily Mail and General Holdings Ltd
Daily Mail and General Investments
Daiwa Capital Markets Europe Ltd
Dana Petroleum (E & P) Limited
Danone Holdings (UK)
De Beers UK Limited
Dentsu Aegis London Limited
Derwent London PLC
Derwent Valley Property Developments
Derwent Valley Property Investments
Dialog Semiconductor (UK) Ltd
Diversified Agency Services Ltd
Docklands Light Railway Ltd
Doctors Laboratory Limited
Domestic & General Services Ltd
Dorchester Group Limited
Dorrington PLC
Dorrington Properties PLC
Dunnhumby Limited
EDF Energy (Energy Branch) Ltd
EDF Energy Customers Limited
EDF Energy Limited
EFG Private Bank Limited
EFL Futures Limited
ENI Oil Algeria Limited
Eastern Power Networks PLC
Economist Intelligence Unit Ltd
Economist Overseas (Holdings) Ltd
Electrocomponents U.K. Limited
Element Materials Technology Holding UK
Ellerman Investments Limited
Emerson Holding Co Ltd
Endemol Shine UK Limited
Enterprise Oil Limited
Enterprise Oil U.K. Limited
Eros International Limited
Esab Holdings Limited
Euromoney Canada Limited
Experis Limited
FIL Investment Management Ltd
Fair Isaac UK International Holdings Ltd.
Faist Limited
Financial Conduct Authority
Financial Models Corporation Ltd
Finastra UK Limited
Firmdale Hotels PLC
First Corporate Consultants Ltd
First Hydro Company
First State Investments (UK) Ltd
FirstGroup Holdings Limited
Firstbus Investments Limited
Fleet Trade & Transport Ltd
Fortune Oil Limited
Foster + Partners Limited
Fujitsu EMEA PLC
GPS (Great Britain) Limited
Gain Capital Holdings Ltd
Gam (U.K.) Limited
Gazeley Limited
Gazeley UK Limited
General Dynamics United Kingdom Ltd
Glencore Commodities Ltd
Globalgrange Limited
Goldman Sachs International
Goldman Sachs Property Management
Gosling Foundation Limited
Grey Communications Group Ltd
Griffin Insurance Association Ltd
Guardian Royal Exchange PLC
HBL Bank UK Limited
HCC International Insurance Company PLC
HGI Group Limited
HP Foods Limited
HSB Engineering Insurance Ltd
HSBC Equipment Finance (UK) Ltd
HSBC Global Asset Management (UK)
HSBC Global Asset Management Ltd
HSBC Latin America Holdings (UK) Ltd
HSBC Overseas Holdings (UK) Ltd
HSBC Securities (Japan) Ltd
Hachette UK Limited
Halcrow Holdings Limited

Halcyon Finance Limited
J O Hambro Capital Management Ltd
HarperCollins (UK)
Harrods (UK) Limited
Harrods Holdings Limited
Harvey Nichols and Co Ltd
Hays PLC
Health Foundation
Henderson Global Investors (Holdings)
Henderson Global Investors Asset Management
Henderson High Income Trust PLC
Hermes Fund Managers Limited
Heron Property Corporation Ltd
Heron Treasury Services Ltd
HgCapital Trust PLC
Hiscox Holdings Limited
Hiscox Underwriting Ltd
Holidaybreak Limited
Howden Joinery Corporate Services
Howden Joinery Group PLC
Huntsworth PLC
IBC (Ten) Limited
ICAP Management Services Ltd
ICAP WCLK Limited
ICBC Standard Bank PLC
ICG Enterprise Trust PLC
IG Communications Limited
IP2IPO Innovations Limited
IPG Holdings (UK) Limited
IPGL Limited
IQVIA Holdings (UK) Ltd.
ITE Group PLC
ITV Global Entertainment Ltd
ITV2 Limited
Inchcape Finance PLC
Inn on the Park (London) Ltd
Inremco 26 Limited
Insight Investment Management Ltd
Instinet Europe Limited
Intermediate Capital Group PLC
Intermediate Capital Managers Ltd
International Hoteliers (UK) Ltd
International Power Ltd.
Interpayment Services Limited
Interserve FS (UK) Limited
Investec Asset Management Ltd
Investec Group (UK) Limited
Investec Wealth & Investment Ltd
Iron Mountain (UK) PLC
Iron Mountain Europe Limited
Itochu Europe PLC
JC No. 3 (UK) Limited
JIB Group Limited
JLT Benefit Solutions Limited
JLT Management Services Ltd
JLT Specialty Limited
JPMorgan Asset Management Holdings (UK)
JPMorgan European Smaller Companies Trust
Jardine Lloyd Thompson Group PLC
Jefferies International Ltd
Jewish Care
Jordan International Bank PLC
Jupiter Asset Management Ltd
Jupiter Unit Trust Managers Ltd
Kddi Europe Limited
Keller Group PLC
Kin and Carta PLC
Kingfisher Information Technology Services (UK)
Kingfisher PLC
Koch Industries International Ltd
LS Buchanan Limited
LS Lewisham Limited
LS Shepherds Bush Limited
Lanesborough Management Ltd
Lapsent Limited
Leathbond Limited
Legal & General Finance PLC
Legal & General Investment Management
Legal & General Resources Ltd
Lendlease Residential (CG) Ltd
Lexadon Limited
Lexton Investments Limited
Liberty International Group Treasury
Liberty International Holdings Ltd
Live Nation (Music) UK Limited
Logica Limited
Lombard Technology Services Ltd
London City Airport Limited
London Forfaiting Co Ltd
London Metal Exchange
London Stock Exchange PLC
London Town Group of Companies Ltd
London Underground Limited
Lotus Group Ltd
Lovell Partnerships Limited
MAN Investments Holdings Ltd
MAN Investments Limited
MS Amlin Corporate Services Ltd
MS Amlin Underwriting Limited
MUFG Securities EMEA PLC
Mace Limited
Cameron Mackintosh Limited
Macmillan Cancer Support
Alexander Mann Solutions Ltd
Marken Limited
Marsh Limited
Marubeni Europe PLC
Mastcraft Limited
Mastercard/Europay U.K. Ltd
Meadowhall Centre (1999) Ltd
Mercury Pharma Group Limited
Merrill Lynch International
Metroline Travel Limited
Miki Travel Limited
Miller Freeman Worldwide Ltd
Minerva Corporation Limited
Minmetals (U.K) Limited
Minova Insurance Holdings Ltd
Mithras Leasing (No.4) Limited
Mitsubishi Corporation Finance PLC
Mitsubishi Corporation International (Europe)
Mitsubishi Estate London Ltd
Mitsui & Co. Europe PLC
Moody's Investors Service Ltd
J.P. Morgan Capital Financing Ltd
J.P. Morgan Markets Limited
Morgan Stanley & Co. International PLC
Morgan Stanley Group (Europe)
Morgan Stanley Investment Management
Motability Tenth Anniversary Trust
NRG Victory Holdings Limited
NTT Europe Ltd.
NYK International PLC
National Grid Electricity Transmission
National Grid Gas PLC
National Grid Holdings One PLC
News UK & Ireland Limited
Next Fifteen Communications Group PLC
Nomura Bank International PLC.
Nomura International PLC
Nomura Properties PLC
Nord Anglia Education Limited
Nordic Entertainment Group UK Ltd
Numis Corporation PLC
Numis Securities Limited
Nuveen Real Estate Management Ltd
Nyraff Limited
O & H Properties Limited
OMD Group Limited
OMFS (GGP) Limited
Odeon Cinemas Limited
Office Holdings Limited
Omnicom Media Group Europe Ltd
Orange Brand Services Limited
Orsted Sales (UK) Limited
H.R.Owen PLC
PA Group Treasury Services Ltd
PA Holdings Limited
PA Overseas Holdings Limited
PHD Media Limited
Pacific Horizon Investment Trust PLC
Pacific Life RE Services Ltd
Pall Mall Investments (London) Ltd
Pepsico Holdings
Pepsico International Limited
Perenco Oil and Gas Colombia Ltd
Permasteelisa (UK) Limited
Pernod Ricard UK Limited
Post Office Limited
Pret A Manger (Europe) Limited
Primeairo Limited
Prophaven Limited
Prudential Capital PLC
Prudential Financial Services Ltd
Prudential Services Limited
Prutec Limited
QBE UK Limited
Quilter Cheviot Limited
RIT Capital Partners PLC
RSA Insurance Group PLC
Ramsay Health Care UK Operations Ltd
Raznoimport (UK) Limited
Reach Magazines Publishing PLC
Reach Printing Services Ltd
Really Useful Theatres Entertainment
Realreed Limited
Reebok International Limited
Renault Retail Group UK Ltd
Rensburg Sheppards PLC
Repsol Sinopec Oil Trading Ltd
Resource Solutions Limited
Reuters Transaction Services Ltd
Rogers Chapman UK Limited
Rolls-Royce & Partners Finance Ltd
Rotch Property Group Limited
Royal London Asset Management Ltd
SCMB Overseas Limited
SMBC Leasing (UK) Limited
SMBC Nikko Capital Markets Ltd
Saatchi & Saatchi Holdings Ltd
Sainsbury Property Investments Ltd
Santander Asset Finance PLC
Santander UK PLC
Savers Health and Beauty Ltd
Savills (Overseas Holdings) Ltd
Savills PLC
Scania Finance Great Britain Ltd
Schroder & Co. Limited
Schroder Asian Total Return Investment Company
Schroder Financial Services Ltd
Schroder Investment Management Ltd
Sedgwick Overseas Limited

Shaftesbury Carnaby PLC
Shaftesbury Chinatown PLC
Shaftesbury PLC
Shell EP Offshore Ventures Ltd
Shell Holdings (U.K.) Limited
Shell Trinidad and Tobago Ltd
Sigma Pharmaceuticals PLC
Smartstream Technologies Ltd
Sony Corporate Services Europe Ltd
Sony Music Entertainment International
Sony Music Entertainment UK Ltd
Southampton Container Terminals Ltd
Spire Healthcare Limited
Spitalfields Developments Ltd
Spring Technology Staffing Services
Square Enix Limited
Standard Bank London Holdings Ltd
Standard Chartered Holdings Ltd
Charles Stanley & Co. Limited
Subsea Leasing Limited
Sumitomo Corporation Capital Europe PLC
Sumitomo Corporation Europe Ltd
Sumitomo Electric Finance UK Ltd
Swan National Limited
T-Systems Limited
TA Mfg Limited
TAI Investments Limited
TES Global Limited
Taikoo Limited
Tarsus Group Limited
Tata Steel UK Limited
Taylor Nelson Sofres International
Technip-Coflexip UK Holdings Ltd
TechnipFMC Umbilicals Ltd
Telehouse International Corporation of Europe
Thistleclub Limited
J. Walter Thompson Group Ltd
Thomson Legal & Professional Group
Thomson Organisation (No.23)
Thomson Reuters (Professional) UK
Tokio Marine HCC Insurance Holdings (International)
Top Shop/Top Man Limited
Total Gas & Power Limited
Total Holdings UK Limited
Total Upstream UK Limited
Tottenham Hotspur Limited
Turner Broadcasting System Europe
Glen Turner Co Ltd
U and I Group PLC
UBMG Limited
UBS Asset Management (UK) Ltd
UBS Asset Management Holding Ltd
UBS UK Properties Limited
UK Power Networks Services (Contracting)
UK Power Networks Services (South East)
United Cinemas International (UK)
Universal Music Publishing International
Universal Publishing Production Music
Veolia Environmental Services (UK) PLC
Veolia Water UK Limited
Virgin Management Limited
Virgin Models Limited
Virgin Music Group
Vitality Health Insurance Ltd
Louis Vuitton UK Limited
WPP Brands Holdings (UK) Ltd
WSP Group Limited
Warner Music International Services
Wates City of London Properties Ltd
Williams Lea Group Limited
Williams Lea Limited
Winterflood Securities Limited
Workspace Group PLC
XL London Market Group Limited
Yorse No. 3 Limited
Zara U.K. Limited
Zenith UK (Media) Limited

1990-1994 [354]

338 Euston Road Limited
350 Euston Road Limited
3i Holdings PLC
4 Imprint USA Limited
ABC International Bank PLC
AD European Investments Ltd
AD Fin Services Limited
ADM Investor Services International
AH UK Animal Health (PVT) Ltd
AMT Mortgage Insurance Limited
Abbey National Treasury Services Overseas Holdings
Aberdeen Investments Limited
Aberdeen New India Investment Trust PLC
Aberdeen Standard Equity Income Trust
Aegon Holdings (UK) Limited
Alcentra Limited
Alliancebernstein Limited
Allied Domecq Spirits & Wine Holdings
Alstom NL Service Provision Ltd
Angel Trains Limited
Arlington House Investments Ltd
Arup Treasury Limited
Assured Guaranty (Europe) PLC
Atos UK IT Limited
Atrium 5 Limited
Aviva PLC
Axa UK PLC
Azzurri Restaurants Limited
B.A.T Uzbekistan (Investments) Ltd
BG Overseas Investments Ltd
BG Trinidad LNG Limited
BHP Billiton (UK) Limited
BMA Investments Limited
BMO Capital Markets Limited
BMO Capital and Income Investment Trust
BTG International Limited
BTG Management Services Ltd
BTG PLC
Babcock Group International Ltd
Babcock Holdings Limited
Babcock Overseas Investments Ltd
Babcock Rail Limited
Babcock Training Limited
Babcock2 Limited
Baillie Gifford UK Growth Fund PLC
Bal Global Finance (UK) Ltd
Barchester Healthcare Homes Ltd
Barchester Healthcare Limited
Barclaycard Funding PLC
Beazley Furlonge Holdings Ltd
Bechtel Holdings Limited
Berkley Estates London Limited
Besso Insurance Group Limited
Bestway Northern Limited
Black Horse Group Limited
Blackrock Latin American Investment Trust
Blackrock World Mining Trust PLC
J.P. Boden & Co. Limited
Braehead Glasgow Limited
Braehead Park Investments Ltd
Brewin Dolphin Holdings PLC
Bunzl American Holdings (No.1) Ltd
Bunzl Overseas Holdings Ltd
Bunzl UK Limited
Bupa Care Homes (Cfhcare) Ltd
Bupa Finance PLC.
Bupa Investments Overseas Ltd
CDW Limited
CIBC World Markets PLC
CLS Holdings PLC
Cadogan Group Limited
Caesars Entertainment UK Ltd
Canada Square Operations Ltd
Canary Wharf Holdings Limited
Cantor Fitzgerald Europe
Capita International Limited
Catlin Syndicate Limited
CenturyLink Communications UK Ltd
Cerner Limited
Charter Limited
Chaucer Holdings Limited
Chelsea FC PLC
Chubb Capital V Limited
Clydesdale Financial Services Ltd
Colas Rail Limited
Collinson International Ltd
Communications Networking Services (UK)
Connect M1-A1 Limited
Consolidated Developments Ltd
Corus International (Overseas Holdings)
Cosmo Oil (U.K.) Limited
Craegmoor Limited
Crawford & Company Risk Services Investments
Credit Suisse International
Cushman & Wakefield Debenham Tie Leung
Czarnikow Group Limited
DCC Holdings (UK) Limited
DLJ Group
DSG Overseas Investments Ltd
Dashwood House Limited
Delfont Mackintosh Theatres Ltd
Deutsche Alternative Asset Management (UK)
Diageo Investment Holdings Ltd
Dialight PLC
Diamond Offshore Drilling (UK) Ltd
Digital Appliance Controls (UK) Ltd
Drilton Limited
Dunhill Tobacco of London Ltd
EBS Dealing Resources International
EBS Group Limited
EDF Energy (UK) Limited
ENI JPDA 03-13 Limited
EP SHB Limited
ERS Corporate Member Limited
Eagle Financial and Leasing Services (UK)
Eastlink Lanker PLC
Enquest Heather Limited
Ensco Offshore U.K. Limited
Enterprise Oil Middle East Ltd
Entertainment One UK Limited
Eponymousco Limited
Eskmuir Properties Limited
Esporta Health & Fitness Ltd
Euroclear UK & Ireland Limited
Eurostar International Limited
Eversholt Rail Leasing Limited
Exane Limited
Exterion Media (UK) Limited
Fair Isaac Software Holdings Ltd
Fairhold Homes Limited
Faraday Capital Limited
Finantia UK Limited

Firoka (Kings Cross) Limited
First Corporate Shipping Ltd
First Property Group PLC
Flint Nominees Limited
Flodrive Holdings Limited
Folgate Holdings Limited
Football Association Premier League
G.H. Financials Limited
GESB PLC
GMR Capital Limited
GNI (UK) Limited
Genome Research Limited
Global Aerospace Underwriting Managers
Goldman Sachs Asset Management International
Grantchester Limited
Greenergy International Ltd
Grosvenor Limited
Grosvenor Overseas Holdings Ltd
Gulfmark North Sea Limited
Gulfmark UK Ltd
HSBC Finance (Netherlands)
Hampshire Waste Services Ltd
Happybadge Projects Limited
Hardy Underwriting Limited
Henderson Eurotrust PLC
Henderson Investment Funds Ltd
Herald Investment Trust PLC
Hiscox Dedicated Corporate Member
Hiscox PLC
Glyn Hopkin Limited
Hyperion Insurance Group Ltd
IIR Exhibitions Limited
IIR Management Limited
IP Fibre Devices (UK) Limited
IPM Energy Trading Limited
ISG Central Services Limited
ITV Consumer Limited
IW Group Services (UK) Limited
Instant Cash Loans Limited
Instinet Global Services Ltd
Integro Insurance Brokers Ltd
Interconnector (UK) Limited
International Biotechnology Trust PLC
International Trade and Exhibitions Overseas
International Transport Intermediaries Club
Interserve (Defence) Ltd
Interservefm Ltd
Intu Investments Limited
Intu Shopping Centres PLC
JIB Group Holdings Limited
JIB Overseas Holdings Limited
JIB UK Holdings Limited
JPMorgan Chinese Investment Trust PLC
JPMorgan Emerging Markets Investment Trust
JPMorgan Indian Investment Trust PLC
JPMorgan Smaller Companies Investment Trust
Jockey Club Racecourses Ltd
Johnson Matthey (CM) Limited
Jupiter US Smaller Companies PLC
Keller Holdings Limited
Kexim Bank (UK) Limited
Kingfisher International Holdings
Kookmin Bank International Ltd
LDC (Managers) Limited
LTG International Limited
Lancaster Landmark Hotel Co Ltd
Lear Corporation (UK) Limited
Legal & General Insurance Holdings
Legal & General International (Holdings)
Lendlease Europe Holdings Ltd
Lenlyn Holdings Limited
Liberty Corporate Capital Ltd
Liberty Managing Agency Ltd
Lloyds General Leasing Limited
Lockton International Limited
Lok'n Store Limited
London & Continental Railways Ltd
London Clubs Management Ltd
London Southend Airport Co Ltd
London and Regional Properties Ltd
Lonrho Limited
MAN Group Holdings Limited
MAN Mash Limited
MAN Strategic Holdings Limited
MGN Limited
MPI (London) Limited
MS Amlin Corporate Member Ltd
MS Amlin PLC
Mabanaft Limited
Management Consortium Bid Ltd
Marks and Spencer International Holdings
Maxus Communications (UK) Ltd
Mediaedge:cia (UK) Holdings Ltd
Medical Centre Holdings Ltd
Mercantile Leasing Company (No.132)
Meteogroup Limited
Metroline Limited
Minerva Limited
Mitie Limited
Mitsui Fudosan (U.K.) Ltd.
Mondrian Investment Partners Ltd
Monsoon Holdings (No.1) Ltd
J.P. Morgan Securities PLC
David Morris International Ltd
Mount Anvil Limited
Muse Developments Limited
NYK Investments Limited
Nando's Chickenland Limited
National Bank of Egypt (UK) Ltd
National Bank of Kuwait (International)
National Grid (US) Holdings Ltd
National Grid International Ltd
National Power International Holdings
Network Rail Infrastructure Ltd
New Printing House Square Ltd
Newport Holdings Limited
Newton Management Limited
No Ordinary Designer Label Ltd
Noble Europe Limited
OMV Supply & Trading Limited
Oasis Charitable Trust
Old Hall Street Properties Ltd
Fred. Olsen Cruise Lines Ltd
Fred. Olsen Renewables Ltd
Olsten (U.K.) Holdings Limited
PCF Group PLC
PIMCO Europe Ltd
Palmbest Limited
Park Tower Investments Limited
Partnerships in Care Limited
Pearson International Finance Ltd
Pelican Point Power Limited
Perfume Shop Limited
PhillipCapital UK Ltd
Phillips 66 CS Limited
Pillar Denton Limited
Pillar Property Group Limited
Pool Reinsurance Co Ltd
Premier Oil E & P UK EU Ltd
Premier Oil E & P UK Limited
Primary Health Investment Properties
Priority Pass Limited
QBE European Operations PLC
QVC UK
Quintain Limited
R.B. Bishopsgate Investments Ltd
RBS AA Holdings (UK) Limited
RELX (UK) Limited
RELX Group PLC
RRPF Engine Leasing Limited
Rapiscan Systems Limited
Richemont Holdings (UK) Ltd
Ricoh Capital Limited
Riverland Holdings Limited
Road Management Group Limited
Road Management Services (Peterborough)
Rockrose UKCS4 Limited
Rothmans International Enterprises
Royal London Management Services Ltd
Ruffer Management Limited
SMBC Derivative Products Ltd
SVF Holdco (UK) Limited
Santander Private Banking UK Ltd
Savills (UK) Limited
Schroder Japan Growth Fund PLC
Sectormatch Limited
Sheldon Holdings Limited
Shell Tunisia Upstream Limited
Shire Pharmaceutical Development Ltd
Shire Pharmaceuticals Group
Silchester Partners Limited
Sinochem International Oil (London) Co.,
DS Smith International Ltd
Smithfield Limited
Sodexo Holdings Limited
Sodexo Services Group Limited
Soho House UK Limited
Sojitz Europe PLC
Solitaire Group Limited
Sports Council Trust Company
State Street Global Advisors Ltd
Stena (UK) Limited
TD Bank Europe Limited
TIGI Holdings Limited
TR European Growth Trust PLC
TT Club Mutual Insurance Ltd
Teesside Gas & Liquids Processing
Telecom New Zealand (UK) Enterprises
Telehouse Holdings Limited
Tenneco Management (Europe) Ltd
Thomson Business Information Holdings
Thomson Information & Publishing Holdings
Ticketmaster UK Limited
Time Warner Entertainment Ltd
Tokio Marine Kiln Group Ltd
Tokio Millennium RE (UK) Ltd
Topland Group PLC
Total Midstream Holdings UK Ltd
Triplereason Limited
Tullett Prebon (Securities) Ltd
Turkish Bank (UK) Limited
Tyman PLC
Charles Tyrwhitt Shirts Ltd
Vacant Property Security Ltd
Vector Industries Limited
Veolia ES (UK) Limited
Veolia UK Limited
Veolia Water Outsourcing Ltd
Vertex Pharmaceuticals (Europe) Ltd
Virgin Active Group Limited
WBA Holdings 1 Limited
WPP 1178
WPP Group (UK) Ltd

WPP Group Holdings Limited
WPP North Atlantic Limited
Wagamama Limited
Warner Media International Ltd
Wells Fargo Capital Finance (UK) Ltd
Western Union Business Solutions (UK)
Wise Conclusion
Oliver Wyman Limited
York House W1 Limited

1995 [85]

AECOM Corporation Holdings (UK) Ltd
Aberdeen Standard Asia Focus PLC
Advent Capital (Holdings) Ltd
Aegis International Limited
Allianz Technology Trust PLC
Amdocs (UK) Limited
Angel Leasing Co Ltd
Angel Trains Group Limited
Brit Insurance Holdings Ltd
Bunge Corporation Limited
CWCB Finance Leasing (DS7B) Ltd
CWE SPV HCO Limited
CWIGroup Limited
Cadogan Settled Estates Ltd
Canary Wharf Estate Limited
Chubb Capital I Limited
Connect M1-A1 Holdings Limited
Credit Suisse Asset Management (UK) Holding
Credit Suisse Investment Holdings (UK)
DB Group Services (UK) Limited
DMG Loanco Limited
Dornoch Limited
Doughty Hanson & Co Managers Ltd
Eaton Square Limited
Equitas Holdings Limited
Equitas Reinsurance Limited
F & G UK Underwriters Limited
FTSE International Limited
First Hydro Finance PLC
First Hydro Holdings Company
Flectat Limited
Freightliner Limited
Grainmarket Properties Limited
Granada Media Limited
Great Rolling Stock Co Ltd
HCA International Limited
HSBC Investment Bank Holdings Ltd
Haven Funding PLC
IBC Fourteen Limited
ITV Digital Channels Limited
ITV Studios Limited
Informa Group Limited
Intact Limited
JKX Oil & Gas PLC
Kantar UK Limited
Knightsbridge Asset Management Ltd
Louisville Securities Limited
Markel Capital Limited
Marsh & McLennan Companies UK Ltd
Marsh Services Limited
Matthey Holdings Limited
Mobius Life Limited
National Grid Holdings Limited
Northern & Shell Enterprises Ltd
Novae Corporate Underwriting Ltd
PTTEP SP Limited
Fred Perry (Holdings) Limited
Fred Perry Limited
Pictet Asset Management Ltd
Primary Health Properties PLC
QBE Corporate Limited
Quantoil Limited
Rail Settlement Plan Limited
Road Management Consolidated PLC
Road Management Services (Gloucester)
Rothmans International Limited
Saka Indonesia Pangkah Limited
Schroder AsiaPacific Fund PLC
Schroder Income Growth Fund PLC
Scottish & Newcastle India Ltd
Shell International Limited
Softbank Group Capital Europe Ltd
South Eastern Power Networks PLC
Springer Nature Publishers Holdings
St Andrew's Insurance PLC
Sumi Agro Europe Limited
TP Holdings Limited
Time Warner Holdings Limited
Trafford Centre Limited
Tramtrack Croydon Limited
URBN UK Limited
United Bank for Africa (UK) Ltd
West Coast Trains Limited
Wilmington PLC
Worldwide Healthcare Trust PLC

1996 [107]

Aegis Electric & Gas International Services
Amazon UK Services Ltd.
Ambac Assurance UK Limited
Ambassador Square
Annington Homes Limited
Annington Property Limited
Aviva Employment Services Ltd
Axa PPP Healthcare Group Ltd
Axa PPP Healthcare Limited
BG Delta Limited
BG Karachaganak Limited
BHP Group PLC
Babcock Communications Limited
Bank of New York Mellon (International)
Belgrave Square
Berkshire Hathaway International Insurance
Berrington UK
Bertelsmann UK Limited
Bluebay Asset Management (Services) Ltd
Blueco Limited
Bluefin Insurance Group Ltd
Brit UW Limited
Building & Property (Holdings) Ltd
CGI Group Holdings Europe Ltd
Capital Hill Hotels Group Europe Ltd
Channel 5 Broadcasting Limited
Chaucer Capital Investments Ltd
J. Choo Limited
Claranet Limited
Colt Technology Services Europe Ltd
Colt Technology Services Group Ltd
C. Czarnikow Limited
DIVX Express Limited
DMG Investment Holdings Ltd
EDF Energy Group Holdings Ltd
EMI Group Worldwide
Enovert Management Limited
Equitas Limited
Exelvia Company
Fidessa Group Holdings Limited
Firstbus (North) Limited
Rocco Forte Hotels Limited
G4S Regional Management (UK & I) Ltd
Global Radio Services Limited
Grand Metropolitan Capital Co Ltd
Grosvenor Group Limited
Gyrus Group Limited
H.A. Funding Limited
HBOS Insurance & Investment Group
HCA UK Holdings Limited
Halifax Leasing (September) Ltd
Hammerson Oracle Investments Ltd
Hardy Underwriting Group Ltd
Housing Association Funding PLC
ITW Holdings UK
Interserve (Facilities Management) Ltd
Intu Properties Investments Ltd
JLL 2002
JLT Insurance Group Holdings Ltd
JPMorgan Life Limited
JX Nippon Exploration and Production (U.K.)
Lendlease Europe Limited
MDU Investments Limited
Magical Cruise Company, Ltd
Maintel Holdings PLC
Mandarin Oriental Hyde Park (Investment)
Mastercard Payment Gateway Services Group
Munich RE Capital Limited
NCR UK Group Limited
Navigators Corporate Underwriters
Nero Holdings Limited
Newline Corporate Name Limited
Nomura European Investment Ltd
Opet International Limited
PP Oil & Gas (Indonesia-Jabung) Ltd
Paysafe Holdings UK Limited
Paysafe Processing Limited
Petroceltic Resources Limited
Pharm Research Associates (UK) Ltd
Polar Capital Technology Trust PLC
QBE Management Services (UK) Ltd
RPOW UK Limited
Redcastle Limited
Royal Mail Investments Limited
SEC Lighting Services Trading Ltd
SThree Overseas Holdings Ltd
Sainsbury's Bank PLC
Sainsbury's Supermarkets Ltd
Sapient Limited
Scimco Limited
Scottish Widows Limited
Shaftesbury Covent Garden Ltd
Shire Holdings Europe Limited
Sony Interactive Entertainment Europe
Sony Pictures Television Production UK
Southern Pacific Mortgage Ltd
Stow Real Estate PLC
Sumitomo Corporation Europe Holding
Talktalk Telecom Holdings Ltd
Telecom Plus PLC
Telenor (UK) Limited
UBM (GP) No1 Limited
UBS Asset Management Life Ltd
UK Power Networks Services (Development)
V2 Music Group Limited
Virgin UK Holdings Limited
White City Acquisitions Ltd

1997 [106]

ABF Overseas Limited
Annington Subsidiary Holdings Ltd
Anyslam Limited
Ashmore Investment Management Ltd
Ashmore Investments (UK) Ltd
BHP Billiton Group Limited
BHP Billiton Holdings Limited

Babcock International Support Services
Ted Baker PLC
Biotech Growth Trust PLC
Bouygues (U.K.) Limited
British American Tobacco (1998) Ltd
British American Tobacco P.L.C.
British Land in Town Retail Ltd
Burberry Group PLC
Burlington Resources (Irish Sea) Ltd
Burlington Resources (UK) Holdings
CLS UK Intermediate Holdings Ltd.
CW Properties DS7B Limited
CWCB Investments (Rt2) Limited
Cabot Place Holdings Limited
Capital Hill Hotels Group London Ltd
Cathedral Capital (1998) Ltd
Cathedral Capital Holdings Ltd
Centurycomm Limited
Chugai Pharma Europe Limited
Classboss Limited
Clifford Chance London Limited
DLJ International Group Ltd
DLJ UK Holding
DLJ UK Investment Holdings Ltd
DNB (UK) Limited
Dana Petroleum (BvUK) Limited
Dana Petroleum Limited
Dayshape Limited
Debenhams Group Holdings Ltd
Deloitte MCS Limited
Diageo Overseas Holdings Ltd
E. F. Oil and Gas Limited
EP Langage Limited
Elementis PLC
Encore Oil Limited
Energy Power Resources Limited
Fairhold Homes (No.2) Limited
Finance for Higher Education Ltd
Finance for Residential Social Housing
FirstGroup Canadian Finance Ltd
Firstplus Financial Group Ltd
Foresight VCT PLC
G4S Facilities Management (UK) Ltd
GFI Holdings Limited
GFI Securities Limited
Ghana International Bank PLC
Gracechurch Bellyard Limited
HBOS Financial Services Ltd
Hammerson (Brent Cross) Ltd
Will Hill Limited
Howden Joinery Holdings Ltd
JPMorgan Asian Investment Trust PLC
Koch Metals Trading Limited
Liberty Commodities Limited
London & Regional (St. Georges Court)
London International Exhibition Centre
ML Invest Holdings
MPS Group International Ltd
Mastercard Payment Gateway Services
Maurice Investments Limited
Meurice Limited
Mindshare Media UK Limited
Harvey Nash Group Limited
National Grid Interconnectors Ltd
Neptune E & P UKCS Limited
Oath (UK) Limited
Octopus AIM VCT PLC
Old Mutual Financial Services (UK)
PRS for Music Limited
Paramount Pictures International Ltd
Petrofac (Malaysia-PM 304) Ltd
Petronas Energy Trading Ltd
Pontoon Europe Limited
Qwest Communications International Ltd.
Rothschild & Co Holdings UK Ltd
SDN Limited
SG Kleinwort Hambros Limited
Shell Aviation Limited
Shell Treasury Centre Limited
Shell Treasury Dollar Co Ltd
Soco International PLC
Starbucks Coffee Holdings (UK) Ltd
State Street Europe Limited
State Street Global Markets International
TI Magazines (UK) Limited
TI Magazines Holdings Limited
Trillium (Prime) Property GP Ltd
Trillium Holdings Limited
Universal Music (UK) Holdings Ltd
Universal Music Leisure Ltd
Veolia ES Holdings (UK) Ltd
Virgin Active Limited
Wellington Pub Company PLC
Wells Fargo Securities International
West India Quay (Eastern) Ltd
Willis Overseas Investments Ltd
Winton Capital Management Ltd
Wireless Infrastructure Co Ltd
Worldpay Limited

1998 [115]

Aberdeen Asset Management Life and Pensions
Aberdeen Japan Investment Trust PLC
Aegon UK PLC
Amtrust Corporate Member Ltd
Anglo American PLC
Ashmore Group PLC
Asos.Com Limited
Aspect Capital Limited
BG Group Limited
BT Fifty-One
BT Fifty-Three Limited
Babcock Land Limited
Barfair Limited
Baronsmead Venture Trust PLC
Berkeley Hotel Limited
Biomed Central Limited
British American Tobacco (Brands)
Burren Energy PLC
CBRE Limited
CLS One Limited
CNA Europe Holdings Limited
CWCB Finance II Limited
Chevron Products UK Limited
Chubb Market Co Ltd
Citadel Enterprise Europe Ltd
Citigroup Capital UK Limited
Claridge's Hotel Holdings Ltd
Clear Channel Holdings Limited
Colart International Holdings Ltd
Congregation of The Daughters of The Cross of Liege
Connaught Hotel Limited
ConocoPhillips Holdings Ltd
ConocoPhillips Treasury Ltd
Coral Group Trading Limited
G. Costa (Holdings) Limited
Credit Suisse Investments (UK)
DB UK Holdings Limited
DVB Transport Finance Limited
Diageo Holdings Limited
Dialog Semiconductor PLC
Disney Magic Co Ltd
ECOM Agrotrade Limited
Enquest Britain Limited
Equinix (UK) Limited
Firestone Diamonds PLC
Garban Group Holdings Limited
HS1 Limited
HSBC Specialist Investments Ltd
Hakkasan Limited
Havana Holdings (UK) Limited
William Hill Holdings Limited
IQVIA Solutions HQ Ltd.
ISS Group Holdings Limited
ITW UK
Inchcape International Holdings Ltd
Ingenious Media Limited
Inmarsat Global Limited
Intu Properties PLC
Investec PLC
Johnson Matthey Precious Metals Ltd
KCG Europe Limited
KPMG UK Limited
Kaspersky Lab UK Limited
Kuoni Holdings Limited
LCR Finance PLC
John Laing Social Infrastructure
London International Exhibition Centre Holdings
Alexander Mann Group Limited
Maybourne Hotels Limited
Morgan Stanley International Ltd
NEX International Limited
National Grid Gas Holdings Ltd
Nomura Europe Holdings PLC
O & H Capital Limited
OM Group (UK) Limited
OM Residual UK Limited
Old Mutual Business Services Ltd
Orange Participations UK Ltd
Oranje-Nassau Energie Resources Ltd
P & O Dover (Holdings) Limited
PIAS Holding (UK) Limited
Pearl Group Holdings (No. 1) Ltd
Phone House Holdings (UK) Ltd
Premier Oil Holdings Limited
Prestmade Limited
Punch Partnerships (PTL) Ltd
Punch Taverns Holdings Limited
Questor Properties Ltd
RKH Group Limited
RQIH Limited
RSL Finance (No. 1) PLC
Royal Automobile Club Limited
Savoy Hotel Limited
Sedgwick Morden Acquisitions
Selfridges & Co. Limited
Shell Trading International Ltd
Sony Entertainment Holdings Europe
TA I Limited
Threadneedle Asset Management Holdings
Tilfen Land Limited
Total E & P North Sea UK Ltd
Total Oil GB Limited
Toyota Tsusho Metals Limited
Tradition London Clearing Ltd
Trillium (Prime) Project Holdings
Trinity Acquisition PLC
UBMG Services Limited
UBS Asset Management Holding (No.2) Ltd
Unisys Finance Limited
Virgin Active Holdings Limited
Virgin Holdings Limited
WPP Dutch Holdings Limited

Weldcure Limited
Westone Hotel Acquisitions Company
Yougov PLC

1999 [157]

A & N Media Finance Services Ltd
AECOM Holdings Limited
AMC Networks International Broadcasting
Agilisys Holdings Limited
Agman Holdings Limited
Allied Domecq Limited
Anglo American Holdings Ltd
Anglo American Prefco Limited
Annington Rentals (Holdings) Ltd
Argo Underwriting Agency Ltd
Avenell Property PLC
BG Energy Holdings Limited
BG Gas Supply (UK) Limited
BG General Holdings Limited
BNY Mellon International Asset Management Group
Bank Mandiri (Europe) Limited
Bath Road Cheltenham Limited
Bendler Investments II Ltd
Sanford C. Bernstein Limited
Black Horse Finance Holdings Ltd
Bluebottle UK Limited
Braddell Limited
British American Tobacco China Holdings
Broadgate (PHC 14) Limited
Broadgate (PHC 15A) Limited
Broadgate (PHC 2) Limited
Broadgate (PHC 3) Limited
Broadgate (PHC 7) Limited
Broadgate (PHC 9) Limited
Broadgate Property Holdings Ltd
Bupa Insurance Services Ltd
CDC Group PLC
Cambian Heritage II Limited
Capita Property and Infrastructure Holdings
Catalina Holdings UK Limited
Centro Asset Management Ltd
Centro Holdings (UK) Limited
CenturyLink Communications Europe
CenturyLink EMEA Holdings Ltd
Chelsea Harbour Estates Ltd
Circadian Limited
Close Asset Management Holdings Ltd
Colt Telecom Holdings Limited
Corus Group Limited
DMG Information Limited
DSG European Investments Ltd
DSG International Holdings Ltd
Diploma PLC
Dixons Retail Group Limited
Dollar Financial U.K. Limited
E D F Trading Limited
ENI Elgin/Franklin Limited
Elexon Limited
Esterline Technologies Limited
Euromoney Consortium 2 Limited
Expedia.Com Limited
Factset Europe Limited
Fairhold Homes (No.6) Limited
Fairhold Homes (No.7) Limited
Fairhold Homes (No.9) Limited
Financial Ombudsman Service Ltd
Freightliner Heavy Haul Ltd
G4S UK Holdings Limited
GAP (UK Holdings) Limited
GB Railfreight Limited
Gazprom Marketing & Trading Ltd
Goldman Sachs Group Holdings (U.K.)
Hachette UK (Holdings) Limited
H.J. Heinz Finance UK PLC
William Hill Investments Ltd
Honours (Holdings) Limited
Howard Investments Limited
JPMorgan Elect PLC
Johnson & Johnson Swiss Finance Co Ltd
Jones Lang Lasalle Europe Ltd
KRF Holdings Limited
Keele Residential Funding PLC
Ladbroke Group
Lattice Group Limited
Lazard & Co., Holdings Limited
Legal & General Overseas Operations
Live Nation Limited
London & Regional Overseas Ltd
MMC International Limited
MMC UK Group Limited
Macquarie Capital (Europe) Ltd
Mergermarket Limited
Moody's Analytics UK Limited
J.P. Morgan Capital Holdings Ltd
Morgan Stanley Bank International
Mphasis UK Limited
Multiplex Construction Europe Ltd
National Grid (US) Investments 2 Ltd
National Grid (US) Investments 4 Ltd
National Grid Metering Limited
National Grid Property Holdings Ltd
Net-a-Porter Group Limited
Northrop Grumman Global Holdings Ltd
OTE PLC
Octagon Assets Limited
Odeon Cinemas Holdings Limited
Orsted London Array Limited
PGIM Limited
Perenco Rang Dong Limited
Pipesafe Limited
Places for People Group Ltd
Power Leisure Bookmakers Ltd
Precis (1789) Limited
Precis (1814) Limited
Proxima GR Properties Limited
Reach Publishing Group Limited
Reach Regionals Limited
Reach Shared Services Limited
Redcastle (214 Oxford Street) Ltd
Rio Tinto South East Asia Ltd
Riverside Resource Recovery Ltd
Romulus Holdings Limited
SEI Investments (Europe) Ltd
SK Shipping Europe PLC
STV News Services Limited
SThree PLC
SThree UK Holdings Limited
Save The Children International
Searchmap Limited
Selectuser Limited
Sinclair Pharma Limited
Sirius (Korea) Limited
Sonali Bank (UK) Limited
Sporting Exchange Limited
St. James Court Hotel Limited
St. John Ambulance
St. Martins Ltd.
Stamford Properties Three Ltd
Starstone Corporate Capital 1 Ltd
Stifel Nicolaus Europe Limited
Swire Oilfield Services (Holdings)
Syncbeam Limited
TBL (Milton Keynes) Limited
TBL (Peterborough) Limited
Talktalk Communications Ltd
Telstra Limited
Thameswey Limited
Threadneedle Investment Services Ltd
Trainline Holdings Limited
Trainline.Com Limited
Tudor Minstrel
UK Power Networks (Operations) Ltd
Urban & Civic Central Funding Ltd
Vale Inco Europe Holdings
Vitol Services Limited
Vue Entertainment Holdings (UK) Ltd
WPP Beans Limited
WPP Brands Development Holdings (UK)
WPP Pearls Limited
Watch Tower Bible and Tract Society of Britain
Zayo Group International Ltd
Zayo Group UK Limited

2000 [172]

4 Ventures Limited
ASOS PLC
Admiral Taverns (Chester) Ltd
Agman Investments Limited
Airwave Solutions Limited
Aldermanbury Investments Ltd
All Saints Retail Limited
Alpha Partners Leasing Limited
Anyslam Investments
Arsenal (Emirates Stadium) Ltd
Avaya UK Holdings Limited
Awin Ltd
BBA Finance
BBDO European Holdings Limited
BC Capital Management Services Ltd
BG Atlantic Finance Limited
BGC Global Limited
BLSSP Property Holdings Ltd
BT Sixty-Four Limited
BTG International (Holdings) Ltd
Babcock Services Group Limited
Barclays (Barley) Limited
Barclays Funds Investments Ltd
Baronsmead Second Venture Trust PLC
Bear Stearns UK Holdings Ltd
Beazley Group Limited
Belvedere Realty Investments Ltd
Brown-Forman Beverages, Europe, Ltd
Bupa Insurance Limited
CPA Global Management Services Ltd
CW Lending II Limited
CWCB Leasing (DS6) Limited
CWCB Properties (DS6) Limited
Canary Wharf Finance II PLC
Capita Resourcing Limited
Cavendish Nuclear Limited
Chapelfield LP Limited
Claranet Group Limited
Cofunds Limited
Computer Patent Annuities International
Conduent Business Process Solutions
De Beers Jewellers Limited
Diageo Finance US Limited
EDF Energy (Cottam Power) Ltd
ENI Investments PLC
ESBII UK Limited
Ebiquity PLC
Endeavour Company Holdings Ltd
Equity Release Funding (No.1) PLC
Equity Release Holdings Ltd

Euromoney Charles Limited
Euromoney Consortium Limited
Financial Services Compensation Scheme
First State Investment Services (UK)
Firstclear Limited
Forex Capital Markets Limited
Fox Investments Limited
Gamesys Limited
Gazprom Marketing & Trading Retail
General Healthcare Group Ltd
General Healthcare Holdings (2) Ltd
General Healthcare Holdings (3) Ltd
General Healthcare Holdings (4) Ltd
Global Radio Holdings Limited
Globaldata PLC
Google UK Limited
Granada Limited
Grantchester Holdings Limited
Greenergy Fuels Limited
Grosvenor Europe Limited
Gunfleet Sands Limited
Gunwharf Quays Limited
Habib Allied Holding Limited
Henderson Asset Management Ltd
Hess Finance
Hess NWE Holdings
Holmes Funding Limited
IG Group Limited
IG Markets Limited
IP2IPO Limited
Innocent Limited
Integro Insurance Brokers Holdings
Intelligent Processing Solutions Ltd
Intelsat Global Sales & Marketing Ltd.
Interactive Brokers (U.K.) Ltd
International Power Holdings Ltd
Interservefm (Holdings) Ltd
Intu Metrocentre Limited
Investec Holding Co Ltd
JLT UK Investment Holdings Ltd
JPMorgan Japan Smaller Companies Trust
Jupiter European Opportunities Trust PLC
Kobalt Music Group Limited
LMS Capital Holdings Limited
LS QAM Limited
LW Theatres Group Limited
Land Securities Portfolio Management
Leconport Estates
Lendlease Europe Finance PLC
London Bus Services Limited
London Power Networks PLC
MAP Capital Limited
MSCI Limited
MSI Corporate Capital Limited
Macquarie International Holdings Ltd
Macquarie Investments (UK) Ltd
Malmaison Hotel du Vin Holdings Ltd
E D & F Man Holdings Limited
E D & F Man Treasury Management PLC
Marathon Oil West of Shetlands Ltd
Marston Properties Holdings Ltd
Marubeni Oil & Gas (U.K.) Ltd
J.P. Morgan Chase International Financing
Morgan Stanley Mallard Investments
Morgan Stanley Montgomerie Investments
Morgan Stanley UK Limited
Murderme Limited
National Grid Commercial Holdings
National Grid PLC
New England Paint Co Ltd
North Row Estates Limited
Northern & Shell PLC
Northern & Shell Properties Ltd
OMD EMEA Limited
Octopus Capital Limited
Ocubis Limited
Opodo Limited
Orsted Burbo (UK) Limited
Pan African Resources PLC
Parkcare Homes (No.2) Limited
Pillar City PLC
Pinnacle Resources Limited
Places for People Developments Ltd
Prepay Technologies Limited
Prestbury Investment Holdings Ltd
Priory Securitisation Limited
Punter Southall Group Limited
Radianz Limited
Reach Network Media Limited
Red Star Pub Company (WR III) Ltd
Ricoh Europe ASP Limited
Road Management Services (A13) Holdings
Road Management Services (A13) PLC
Rothschild & Co Continuation Finance PLC
Rothschild Foundation (Hanadiv) Europe
T. Rowe Price International Ltd
Schroders PLC
Shell Foundation
Shine Limited
Smartestenergy Limited
TFS Derivatives Limited
TM Media Holdings Limited
Tallwood Limited
Technicolor Disc Services International
Tonicstar Limited
Toscafund Limited
Total UK Finance Limited
Transocean UK Limited
Transport Trading Limited
Travelex Limited
Trillium (Prime) Holdings Ltd
Trinity Mirror Media Limited
Tube Lines Limited
Tullett Prebon Group Holdings PLC
Tullow Oil PLC
Verdoso Holdings Limited
WPP Finance Co. Limited
WPP LN Limited
Robert Walters PLC
A.S. Watson (Health & Beauty UK)
Wavemaker Limited
Westfield Europe Limited

2001 [167]

AON UK Holdings Intermediaries Ltd
Argo (No. 604) Limited
Arsenal Holdings Limited
Ascot Corporate Name Limited
BBA Finance No.1
BCG UK1 Limited
BG Energy Capital PLC
BG Gas Marketing Ltd
BG Singapore Limited
BT European Investments Ltd
BT Group Investments Limited
BT Group PLC
Bakkavor (London) Limited
Bank Sepah International PLC
Beaufort Dedicated No 2 Ltd
Bonhams 1793 Limited
Britned Development Limited
Burberry International Holdings Ltd
C & C Properties UK Limited
Canary Wharf Group PLC
Cancer Research UK
Catalyst Finance Limited
Central Equity Limited
Chivas Brothers (Holdings) Ltd
Citigroup Participation Luxembourg
Close Brothers Finance PLC
Coralglade Limited
Craegmoor Group (No.5) Limited
Craegmoor Group (No.6) Limited
Crossrail Limited
DMG Charles Limited
DSG Card Handling Services Ltd
Daejan (UK) Limited
Daejan (US) Limited
Daejan Traders Limited
Dealogic (Holdings) Limited
Diageo US Holdings
EDF Energy (Thermal Generation) Ltd
ESB Group (UK) Limited
EYGS LLP
Ebay KTA (UK) Ltd
Electrocomponents US Finance Ltd
Endeavour Resources Limited
Enrichment Investments Limited
Ernst & Young LLP
FIA Foundation
Finlay Group Limited
Finventures UK Limited
Formula One World Championship Ltd
Foseco Holding Limited
Foundation for Social Entrepreneurs
GA HC REIT II CH U.K. Senior Housing Portfolio
GHG Intermediate Holdings Ltd
Gabriel International Limited
Garban-Intercapital (2001) Ltd
Garban-Intercapital US Investments (Holdings)
Garban-Intercapital US Investments (No 1)
Gates Holdings Limited
Global Reach Partners Limited
Grosvenor Continental Europe Holdings
Grosvenor UK Finance PLC
GroupBT Limited
HSBC Asia Holdings (UK) Ltd
HSBC Global Services (China) Holdings
Hammerson (Leeds Investments) Ltd
Hammerson (Rugby) Limited
Hartree Partners Power & Gas Company (UK)
William Hill PLC
Hiscox Underwriting Group Services
Hotel (PL Property) Holding Ltd
IBM Global Financing UK Company
IBM North Region Holdings
IP Group PLC
ITV Holdings Limited
Intertek Group PLC
Intu Lakeside Limited
Intu The Hayes Limited
JPMorgan Asset Management International
JS Information Systems Limited
Kaspersky Labs Limited
Kingfisher France Limited
Kirkglade Limited
Knight Dragon Developments Ltd
LR Skipton House Limited
LS Ashdown Limited
LS Cardiff Limited
LS Hill House Limited
LS One New Change Limited
Lebara Limited

Legal & General Investment Management (Holdings)
Lloyds Bank Equipment Leasing (No. 1)
Lombard Business Leasing Ltd
London Gateway Port Limited
London and Regional Group Finance
MSC Property Intermediate Holdings
Marble Arch Hotel (London) Ltd
Markit Group Limited
Marks and Spencer Group P.L.C.
Meadowhall Shopping Centre Ltd
Meadowhall Shopping Centre Property Holdings
Melli Bank PLC
Modernelite Limited
Morgan Sindall Construction & Infrastructure
NGG Finance PLC
Nakano Asset Global Ltd.
National Grid (US) Partner 1 Ltd
Nectar Loyalty Limited
Oxhauth Limited
PFI Senior Funding Limited
PHP Glen Spean Limited
Persia International Bank PLC
Petropavlovsk PLC
Phoenix Energy Holdings Ltd
Polar Capital Holdings PLC.
Privilege Project Finance Ltd
Publicis Media Limited
Quilter Investors Limited
Red Bee Media Limited
Royal Mail Group Limited
Russneft (UK) Limited
S & N Finland Limited
S & P Global Commodities UK Ltd
SCOR Underwriting Limited
SG (Maritime) Leasing Limited
SHC Holdings Limited
SITI 1 Limited
SK Energy Europe Limited
Sager House (Almeida) Limited
Schroder Unit Trusts Limited
Sheldon Sterling Investments Ltd
Shell Caribbean Investments Ltd
Shell Energy Europe Limited
Skrill Limited
Sonic Healthcare Holding Company
Spire Healthcare (Holdings) Ltd
Sponsio Limited
Sunderland (SHG) Finance PLC
Swiss Re Services Limited
T.H.F.C. (Capital) PLC
TBWA UK Group Limited
TI UK Publishing Holdings Ltd
Talbot 2002 Underwriting Capital Ltd
Telereal 112 Limited
Telereal Securitisation Holdings Ltd
Telereal Securitisation PLC
Telereal Services Limited
Telesat International Limited
Trailfinders Group Limited
TransDigm European Holdings Ltd
Trinity Mirror Finance Limited
UKTV Media Limited
UPP (Nottingham) Ltd
United National Bank Limited
VPI Immingham LLP
Virgin Rail Group Holdings Ltd
WPP 2318 Limited
WPP 2323 Limited
WPP Marketing Communications Spain
WPP Sparky Limited
WPP Spike Limited
WRBC Corporate Member Limited
Waldorf Hotel Investment Ltd
Wallis Retail Limited
Wellington Management International
Westbury Hotel Limited
XL Insurance (UK) Holdings Ltd
Xstrata Limited

2002 [154]

AD (Europe) Finance
AON Hewitt Limited
Aegis Finance
Al Rayan Bank PLC
Alixpartners Ltd
Alliance Boots Holdings Ltd
Alpha Plus Holdings PLC
Anchor Carehomes Limited
Ansco Arena Limited
Apache North Sea Limited
Argo (No. 703) Limited
Artesian Finance PLC
Atos UK IT Holdings Limited
Atrium 100 Properties Limited
BBC Commercial Holdings Ltd
BBC Studios Limited
BMO AM Treasury Limited
BT Fleet Limited
Babcock Brazil Investments Ltd
Babcock Corporate Services Ltd
Babcock Marine & Technology Holdings
Babcock Support Services (Investments)
Bank of Beirut (UK) Ltd
Baxalta UK Investments Ltd.
Beazley Underwriting Limited
Beefeater Gin Limited
British Land Fund Management Ltd
Brixton (Axis Park) Limited
Broad Gain (UK) Limited
Brooks MacDonald Group PLC
Busyexport Limited
C & C Alpha Group Limited
CB & I UK Limited
CGIS Group (No. 3) Limited
COP Holdings Limited
CWBC Finance (BP1) Limited
CWBC Properties (BP1) Limited
Cameron Petroleum (UK) Limited
Canary Wharf Investments (DS8) Ltd
Casual Dining Limited
Children's Investment Fund Foundation (UK)
Christie's Private Sales Ltd
Colt Telecom Finance Euro
Colt Telecom Finance Switzerland
Coral Eurobet Holdings Limited
DMG Atlantic Limited
DMGB Limited
Dudgeon Offshore Wind Limited
East End Homes Limited
Endurance Worldwide Holdings Ltd
Endurance Worldwide Insurance Ltd
Ensco U.K. Limited
Equity Release Funding (No.2) PLC
Extraclick Limited
FBN Bank (UK) Limited
Falck Renewables Wind Limited
Faroe Petroleum PLC
Rocco Forte & Family (Luxury Hotels)
Fox Networks Group (UK) Ltd
Friary Intermediate Limited
GLH Hotels Holdings Limited
Glencore Energy UK Ltd.
HCA UK Services Limited
HQCB Investments Limited
HQCB Properties (HQ5 (2)) Ltd
HSIL Investments Limited
Hammerson (Leicester) Limited.
Hawkins Funding Limited
Howden Holdings Limited
ICBC (London) PLC
IDCO Overseas Holdings Limited
IDCO Worldwide Holdings Ltd
IMG Media Limited
INEOS E & P (UK) Limited
Impax Environmental Markets PLC
Intercontinentalexchange Holdings
Interior Services Group (UK Holdings)
Interoute Communications Ltd
Intu Potteries Limited
JPMorgan Russian Securities PLC
KPMG LLP
Kensington Close Hotel Limited
LR Office Developments Limited
John Laing Infrastructure Ltd
Land Securities Group PLC
Lanespace Limited
Lavenham Underwriting Limited
Lazard Asset Management (UK) Holdings
Lime Street (Funding) Limited
Lloyds Bank Equipment Leasing (No. 7)
London & Regional (Baker Street) Holdings
London & Regional (Empire) Ltd
London & Regional Dormant Holdings
London & Regional Group Holdings Ltd
London & Regional Hotel Finance Ltd
London & Regional Trading Holdings
Majedie Asset Management Ltd
Managed Pension Funds Limited
McDonald's Real Estate Company No.1
McDonald's Real Estate LLP
Merrill Lynch UK Finance
Midasplayer.Com Ltd.
Millennium Capital Management Ltd.
Miller Insurance Services LLP
Mitsui Bussan Commodities Ltd
Mixhold Investments Limited
Mount Anvil Group Limited
NSC Europe Limited
National Grid Grain LNG Ltd
National Grid Seventeen Ltd
National Grid Twelve Limited
Nautical Petroleum Limited
Nbcuniversal International Ltd
Neon Capital Limited
Network Rail (High Speed) Ltd
Network Rail Limited
Newline Insurance Co Ltd
Omnicom Media Group UK Limited
Paysafe Financial Services Ltd
Pearson Shared Services Ltd
Percy Village Limited
Permanent Funding (No.2) Ltd
Petrochina International (London) Co.,
Pharmadeals Limited
Pricewaterhousecoopers LLP
Primepanel Limited
Priory Group Limited
Reed Smith LLP
Rosleb Limited
Royal Marsden Cancer Charity
S & P Global Finance Europe Ltd
Shell Energy Investments Ltd
Shell Exploration and Production Tanzania
Shell Gas Holdings (Malaysia) Ltd

Smith & Nephew UK Limited
Smith & Williamson Holdings Ltd
South Downs Waste Services Ltd
South32 SA Investments Limited
Sova Capital Limited
Stena North Sea Limited
Stratton Metal Resources Ltd
Swiss Re Specialised Investments Holdings (UK)
Taveta Investments Limited
Thanet Offshore Wind Limited
Top Shop / Top Man Properties Ltd
Trendcycle Limited
Tullow Oil SPE Limited
UPP (Lancaster) Limited
Universal Coal PLC
Virgin Active Group Investments Ltd
WPP Magic Limited
WPP Unicorn Limited
Wipro Holdings (UK) Limited
Young Street Holdings Limited

2003 [176]

ABF (No.1) Limited
Abbey Commercial Ltd
Accantia Group Holdings
Accenture (UK) Limited
Advanced Payment Solutions Ltd
Aker Solutions Limited
Aldwych Finance Limited
All3media Limited
Amco Investments Limited
Anglo American Capital PLC
Apple Retail UK Limited
Aprilgrange Limited
Arch Insurance Company (Europe) Ltd
Area Estates Limited
Argenta Holdings Limited
Arndale Properties Limited
Artesian Finance II PLC
Ashtead Holdings PLC
Aspen (UK) Holdings Limited
Axa Partners CLP UK Holdings Ltd
Axa Partners Holdings Limited
BBA Finance No. 4 Limited
BBP Bandenia PLC
BDO LLP
BTC Islands Limited
Babcock Mission Critical Services Leasing
Beaufort Wind Limited
W. R. Berkley London Holdings, Ltd
Blaxmill (Ten) Limited
Borealis Infrastructure Europe (UK)
British American Tobacco Italy Investments
British American Tobacco Italy Ltd
British American Tobacco Peru Holdings
British Land (Joint Ventures) Ltd
Bruning Limited
Burberry Haymarket Limited
CBRE Finance Europe LLP
CGI Corporate Holdings Limited
CTRL Section 1 Finance PLC
Capita Justice & Secure Services Holdings
Carrington Power Limited
Cayzer Trust Co Ltd
Centaur Media PLC
Citigroup Global Markets Europe Finance
Civica Group Limited
Connect M77/GSO Holdings Ltd
Connect M77/GSO PLC
Conygar Investment Company PLC
Council for World Mission (UK)
Cove Energy Limited
Cynergy Bank Limited
DCC Limited
DLA Piper International LLP
Daunus Limited
Dinosaur Merchant Bank Limited
ELQ Investors, Ltd
Equity Release Funding (No.3) PLC
Equity Release Funding (No.4) PLC
Eunetworks Fiber UK Limited
European Policy Exchange Ltd
Eversheds Sutherland (International) LLP
FHH No.1 Limited
Faroe Petroleum (U.K.) Limited
Ferrexpo Finance PLC
Firmdale Holdings Limited
Firmdale Property Investments Ltd
Fordstam Limited
Rocco Forte & Family (London) Ltd
G4S PLC
GS Finco Limited
Gates Finance Limited
Global Switch Estates 1 Ltd
Global Switch Estates 2 Ltd
Gowling WLG (UK) LLP
HCA UK Capital Limited
Ham Yard Investment Limited
Harbour Funding PLC
Hirecorp Limited
ICAP America Investments Ltd
ICICI Bank UK PLC
IG Group Holdings PLC
IGas Energy PLC
ITV PLC
Inchcape Shipping Services Holdings
Independent Clinical Services Ltd
Infund LLP
Inmarsat Finance PLC
Inmarsat Group Limited
Inmarsat Holdings Limited
Inmarsat Investments Limited
Inmarsat PLC
International Power (Fawkes)
International Power (Genco) Ltd
International Power Australia Holdings (1)
International Power Australia Holdings
International Power Luxembourg Finance
Interoute Communications Holdings
Ipsos EMEA Holdings Ltd
Island Gas Limited
Just Eat.co.uk Ltd
Juturna (European Loan Conduit No. 16)
K Line Bulk Shipping (UK) Ltd
Khodorkovsky Foundation
Knight Frank LLP
L & Q New Homes Limited
LCH Group Holdings Limited
LS (Finchley Road) Limited
Laudico Limited
Lloyds Bank Corporate Asset Finance (No. 1)
Lloyds Bank Corporate Asset Finance (No. 4)
Luminus Group Limited
ML UK Capital Holdings Limited
MMS UK Holdings Limited
Macquarie Internationale Investments
Marks & Spencer Simply Foods Ltd
Marks and Spencer Investments
Marlbray Limited
Max Recovery Limited
Millward Brown No.2337 Limited
Morgan Stanley Alpha Investments LLP
Morgan Stanley Gamma Investments
Multiplex Construction Europe Holding
Nameco (No.808) Limited
News Corp Holdings UK & Ireland
Northern Trust Holdings Ltd
Northern Trust Management Services
Octagon Overseas Limited
Omnicom Europe Limited
Omnicom Holdings Limited
Ormonde Energy Limited
Orsted Power (UK) Limited
Perenco CUU Long Limited
Perenco UK Limited
Premiertel PLC
Priory Securitisation Holdings Ltd
QHotels Services Limited
QIB (UK) PLC
Quadrant Construction Services Ltd
Regus Group Limited
Repsol Sinopec Alpha Limited
Revcap UK Holdings Limited
Rolls-Royce Group PLC
Rooftop Funding Limited
Ruffer LLP
SIR Hospitals Propco Limited
SMBC Aviation Capital (UK) Ltd
Sable Holding Limited
Sampford Underwriting Limited
Schroder Administration Ltd
Selfridges Holdings Limited
Selfridges Properties Limited
Shell U.K. North Atlantic Ltd
Shire Holdings UK Limited
Sirius Minerals PLC
South Hook Gas Co Ltd.
St. Stephens Shopping Centre Ltd
Sumitomo Mitsui Banking Corporation Europe
Talktalk Telecom Limited
Time Warner London Limited
UBM Shared Services Limited
UPP (Broadgate Park) Holdings Ltd
UPP (Lancaster) Holdings Ltd
UTB Partners Limited
Union Bank UK PLC
Uniqlo Europe Ltd
Vedanta Resources Holdings Ltd
Vedanta Resources Limited
Vetco International Holding 4
Vue Entertainment Limited
WMG Acquisition (UK) Limited
WPP 2709 Limited
Weston Aerospace Limited
World Fuel Services Europe, Ltd.
World Fuel Services European Holding Company I, Ltd.
XL Gracechurch Limited
Yianis Holdings Limited

2004 [187]

280 Bishopsgate Finance Ltd
334 Ramsbury Oxford Limited
A2dominion Residential Limited
AD Atlantic Finance Limited
AD Investment Holdings Limited
AD Westport Limited
ADSW Investment Holdings Ltd
Ace European Holdings Limited
Allen & Overy LLP
American Express Holdings Ltd
Anglo Asian Mining PLC
Apple Europe Limited
Ark Schools

Aspers Group Limited
Avanade Europe Holdings Ltd.
Avanade Europe Services Ltd.
Avanti Communications Infrastructure
BF Properties (No.4) Ltd
BF Properties (No.5) Ltd
BG Rosetta Limited
BMCE Bank International PLC
BMCE International (Holdings) PLC
Babcock Investments (Number Four)
Babcock Investments (Number Three)
Babcock Marine Holdings (UK) Ltd
Babcock Mission Critical Services Design and Completions
Bakethin Finance PLC
Bakkavor Invest Limited
Beazley Management Limited
Betfair Limited
Blackrock Greater Europe Investment Trust
Borders & Southern Petroleum PLC
Breezeroad Limited
British American Shared Services (GSD)
British American Tobacco Western Europe Commercial Trading
British Land Broadgate 2005 Ltd
British Land Department Stores Ltd
British Land Leisure Limited
Brixton (Metropolitan Park) 1 Ltd
Brixton (Origin) Limited
Brixton Greenford Park Limited
Brixton Premier Park Limited
Broadgate (Funding) 2005 Ltd
Broadgate (PHC 11) 2005 Ltd
Broadgate (PHC 16) 2005 Ltd
Broadgate (PHC 5) 2005 Limited
Broadgate (PHC 6) 2005 Limited
Broadgate Financing PLC
Bunzl American Holdings (No.2) Ltd
CBRE Global Investors Europe Holdings
CE Acquisition 1 Limited
CMC Markets PLC
CMS Cameron McKenna Nabarro Olswang LLP
Cambian Heritage I Limited
Campden Charities Trustee
Canary Wharf Group Investment Holdings
Cello Health PLC
Chaucer Corporate Capital (No. 3)
Chello Zone Holdings Limited
Chevron Energy Limited
Coral Eurobet Limited
Coral Group Limited
Coral Limited
Coroin Limited
DLA Piper UK LLP
Delamare Finance PLC
Delamare Group Holdings Ltd
Diageo Eire Finance & Co
Discovery Communications Europe Ltd
Discovery Group Europe Limited
Endeavour Energy UK Limited
Engine Group Limited
Esterline Technologies Holdings Ltd
FGIC UK Limited
Fair Isaac UK Group Limited
Fintry 3 Limited
First Rail Holdings Limited
Frontier Agriculture Limited
GS Funding Europe
Gemfields Limited
Grant Thornton UK LLP
Greene King Finance Parent Ltd
HSBC (BGF) Investments Limited
Paul Hamlyn Foundation
IG Finance
IG Finance Three
IG Finance Two
Integral UK Limited
Intu Trafford Centre Group (UK) Ltd
Investors in Private Capital Ltd
KAS No.2 Limited
KAZ Minerals PLC
LMS Offices Limited
LN-Gaiety Holdings Limited
LS 62 Buckingham Gate Limited
LS City & West End Limited
LS Property Finance Co Ltd
LS Retail Warehouses Limited
Land Securities Capital Markets PLC
Land Securities Property Holdings
Lankellychase Foundation
Lanterndew Limited
Larch (Nursing Homes) Ltd
Larch Funding (UK) Ltd
Larch Life No.1 (UK) Ltd
Lloyds Bank General Leasing (No. 3)
London and City Group Holdings Ltd
Longmartin Properties Limited
Lur Berri International Ltd
MCD Europe Limited
Macquarie Commodities (UK) Ltd
Macquarie Commodities Finance (UK)
Mako Global Derivatives Partnership LLP
Market Data Limited
Marston's Issuer PLC
Marubeni North Sea Limited
Metals Exploration PLC
Monument Containers Limited
Morgan Stanley Corporate Trader
Morgan Stanley Employment Services UK
National Grid Thirty Five Ltd
Network Rail Infrastructure Finance PLC
Newsprinters (Broxbourne) Ltd
Nine United Properties UK Ltd
Normanclose 2 LLP
Normanglade 4 LLP
Northwharf Investments Limited
O & H Q7 Limited
OTPPB Investments (U.K.) Ltd
Old Oak Holdings Limited
Omnicom Management Europe
Ophir Energy PLC
PFI Infrastructure Finance Ltd
PL Hotel Limited
Pacific Quay Finance PLC
Pacific Quay Holdings Limited
Paragon Group Limited
Parvus Asset Management Ltd
Pearson Dollar Finance PLC
Pearson Loan Finance Unlimited
Petroineos Europe Limited
Phoenix Global Resources PLC
Pitch International LLP
Premier Place Finance Limited
Press Acquisitions Limited
Priceline.Com Holdco U.K. Ltd
Race Bank Wind Farm Limited
Real Estate Venture Capital Partners LLP
Rio Tinto Diamonds Limited
Rockhopper Exploration PLC
Roehampton University
SG Leasing (Gems) Limited
SOL Aviation Services Limited
STA Travel International Ltd
M & C Saatchi PLC
Salamander Energy Group Ltd
Salesforce.Com EMEA Limited
Salix Finance Ltd
Shaftesbury CL Limited
Shaftesbury Soho Limited
Shanti Hospitality Group Ltd
Shop Direct Holdings Limited
Smiths Detection Group Limited
Spirit Issuer PLC
Spirit Issuer Parent Limited
Standard Chartered Apr Limited
Star Energy Group Limited
T.H.F.C. (Funding No. 1) PLC
Tarsus Holdings Limited
Taveta Investments (No.2) Ltd
Telit Communications PLC
Traveljigsaw Limited
Tudor Trust
Tullow Oil SK Limited
UK Group of Hotels PLC
UPP Group Holdings Limited
Unilever US Investments Ltd
United Cinemas International Acquisitions
Vedanta Resources Finance Ltd
Victoria Oil & Gas PLC
Visa Europe Limited
Vitality Health Limited
Walney (UK) Offshore Windfarms Ltd
Westark Properties Limited
Westfield UK Acquisitions Finance
Xerium Technologies Limited
Zetar Limited

2005 [212]

A2dominion Developments Ltd
ABF Funding
ABF US Holdings Limited
ADIUK
ATK Finance Limited
Abbey Covered Bonds LLP
Admiral Taverns Limited
Advent Capital (No. 3) Limited
Affinity Sutton Funding Ltd
Almacantar (Centre Point) Ltd
Alpha Prema UK Limited
Anglo American (London)
Anglo American International Holdings
Apollo Management International LLP
Arcadis UK (Holdings) Limited
Arsenal Securities PLC
Artesian Finance III PLC
BB & R Limited
BL Superstores (Funding) Ltd
BL Superstores Finance PLC
Badger Property Partners LLP
Baker & McKenzie LLP
Balderton Aviation Holdings Ltd
Barclays Capital Asia Holdings Ltd
Barclays Capital Japan Securities Holdings
Berry Bros. & Rudd Limited
Borders & Southern Falkland Islands
British Land Acquisitions Ltd
Bryan Cave Leighton Paisner LLP
Bupa Global Holdings Limited
CGI Nordic Investments Limited
CMC Markets UK Holdings Ltd
CWCB Properties (DS7) Limited
Cambian Education Services Ltd
Cambian Properties (U.K.) Ltd
Canary Wharf Properties (FC2) Ltd
Canary Wharf Properties (FC4) Ltd

Capital & Regional Holdings Ltd
Catlin (North American) Holdings Ltd
Catlin Finance (UK) Ltd.
Catlin Insurance Company (UK) Holdings Ltd.
Central Asia Metals PLC
Citadel Securities (Europe) Ltd
Cobalt Data Centres Limited
Conde Nast International Ltd
Consort Healthcare (Birmingham) Funding
Consort Healthcare (Birmingham) Holdings
Consort Healthcare (Birmingham) Ltd
Convoys Properties Limited
Cory Environmental Holdings Ltd
Creation Communications Ltd
DWS Alternatives Global Ltd
Debenhams PLC
Derwent Valley Finance Limited
Deutsche Holdings Limited
Divisional Finance UK Limited
EY Global Services Limited
Eagle 3 Limited
Eagle 4 Limited
Eclipse Film Partners No. 26 LLP
Eddystone Finance Holdings Ltd
Elbon Holdings (1) Limited
Elbon Holdings (2) Limited
Elbon Holdings (3) Limited
Equity Release Funding (No.5) PLC
Equity Release Holdings (No. 5) Ltd
Europe Arab Bank PLC
European Express Enterprises Ltd
FIS UK Holdings Limited
Factset UK Limited
Fairhold Finance Limited
Fantfoot Limited
Farmont Baker Street Limited
Ferrexpo PLC
Finance Holdings Limited
Firmus Energy (Distribution) Ltd
Foseco Limited
Frasers Property (UK) Limited
G4S Finance Limited
G4S International Holdings Ltd
Giltbrook Retail Park Nottingham Ltd
Glen Water (Holdings) Limited
Glen Water Limited
Goal Acquisitions (Holdings) Ltd
Grange (Prescot Street) Ltd
Greene King Finance PLC
Grifonas Finance No.1 PLC
HLG Holdings Limited
HPI UK Holding Ltd.
HSBC Global Services Limited
Hammerson Bull Ring Limited
Hansteen Holdings PLC
Hansteen Property Investments Ltd
Hays International Holdings Ltd
Hellenic Petroleum Finance PLC
Herbert Smith Freehills LLP
Heron Quays Investments (RT3) Ltd
Hikma Pharmaceuticals PLC
Hikma UK Limited
Hitachi Rail Europe Limited
Horizon RE Limited
Hunter Up 1 Limited
Huntsworth Holdings Limited
ICP Capital Limited
INTL FCStone Ltd
Intelsat UK Financial Services Ltd.
Intu Eldon Square Limited
Intu Watford Limited
Investcorp Credit Management EU Ltd
JLT Reinsurance Brokers Ltd
Jones Lang Lasalle Capital Investments,
Just Eat Holding Limited
K Line LNG Shipping (UK) Ltd
A.T. Kearney Holdings Limited
Kellen Acquisitions Limited
Kellen Investments Limited
Kypris Acquisitions Ltd
LMS (City Road) Limited
LMS Capital Group Limited
LMS Finance Limited
LR (Baker St) Limited
Laird (Finance) Limited
Lakenorth Limited
Linestair Limited
Littonace HMF Limited
London Leasehold Flats Limited
London Stock Exchange Group PLC
Longstone Finance PLC
Ludgate Northumberland Holdings Ltd
M I Investment Holding Limited
Macquarie UK Passenger Leasing Ltd
Marex Financial
Marex Spectron Group Limited
McLaren Construction Group PLC
Merrill Lynch (Camberley) Ltd
Millennium Capital Partners LLP
Mithras Leasing (No.1) Ltd
Morgan Stanley Swallow Limited
Motorola Solutions Finance EMEA Ltd
Nando's Finance Limited
Natgrid One Limited
Naxos Investments Limited
Neuberger Berman Europe Ltd
Newfound Bay Limited
Norland Holdings Ltd
O & H (NBS) Limited
Oakwood Global Assets Limited
Oasis Community Learning
Onyx Germany (1) Ltd
Ophir Thailand (E & P) Limited
Orbital Shopping Park Swindon Ltd
Oval (2041) Limited
PHP Primary Properties Limited
PR Goal 3 Limited
Palace Capital PLC
Partnership Group Holdings Ltd
Partnership Life Assurance Co Ltd
Partnerships in Care Property 1 Ltd
Pearson Australia Finance Unlimited
Thomas Pocklington Trust
Priceline. Com International Ltd
Priory Finance Property LLP
Rational Foreign Exchange Ltd
Retina Finance UK Limited
Ribbon Acquisition Limited
Rockhopper Exploration (Hydrocarbons)
Charles Russell Speechlys LLP
Ruthenium Investments Limited
Sainsbury Propco A Limited
Sainsbury Propco B Limited
Salamander Energy (S.E. Asia) Ltd
Santa Fe Group Limited
Satellite Financing (Holdings) Ltd
Satellite Financing PLC
Schroder Pension Management Ltd
Sensburg Finance Ltd
Shell Trinidad 5(A) Limited
Shire Biopharmaceuticals Holdings
Shire Global Finance
Societe Generale International Ltd
Sony DADC Europe Limited
Spirit Aerosystems (Europe) Ltd
Standard Chartered NEA Limited
Stockton Retail Park Limited
Strategic Equity Capital PLC
The Bernard Sunley Charitable Foundation
TNS-NFO UK Limited
TRG (Holdings) Limited
TT Games Limited
Thameswey Housing Limited
Threadneedle Asset Management Finance
Time Warner International Finance
Total Energy (MEUK) Ltd.
Travelex Banknotes Limited
Travelex Central Services Ltd
Travelex Holdings Limited
Tripadvisor Limited
Tullow Group Services Limited
UK Holdings CAP (Commonwealth, Asia and Pacific)
URS Corporation Group Limited
Universal Music Holdings Ltd
VEL Holdings Limited
WGA (UK) Holdings Limited
WPP Compete
A.S. Watson (P & C UK) Ltd
Westpac Europe Limited
White City Property Finance PLC
White City Property Holdings Ltd
Wireless Infrastructure Group Ltd
Worldpay AP Ltd.
XL Catlin Insurance Company UK Ltd
Yianis Hotels Limited

2006 [253]

1 & 4 & 7 Triton Limited
2 & 3 Triton Limited
4imprint UK Holdings Limited
A V Co 1 Limited
ABP Acquisitions UK Limited
ABP Bonds UK Limited
ABP Mezzanine Holdco UK Ltd
ABP Subholdings UK Limited
ADG Market Making LLP
APS Financial Limited
Abbotstar Trading Ltd
Addleshaw Goddard LLP
Admiral Taverns (780) Limited
Aetna Insurance Co Ltd
Alba 2006-1 PLC
Alba 2006-2 PLC
Alba 2007-1 PLC
All3media Finance Limited
Amber Bidco Limited
Annington Rentals (No. 6) Ltd
Ansco UK Finance Co. 2 Ltd.
Arena Leisure Racing Limited
Autovista Group Limited
Autovista Holdco UK Limited
Autovista Limited
Avation PLC
BG Netherlands
BL City Offices Holding Co Ltd
BL Department Stores Holding Co Ltd
BL HC PH LLP
BL Intermediate Holding Co Ltd
BL Leisure and Industrial Holding Co Ltd
BL Office (Non-City) Holding Co Ltd
BL Office Holding Co Ltd
BL Residual Holding Co Ltd
BL Retail Holding Co Ltd
BL Retail Warehousing Holding Co Ltd

BL Superstores Holding Co Ltd
BMI Healthcare Holdings Ltd
BPP Services Limited
Bank of London and The Middle East PLC
Beta Holdings Limited
Blackrock Finco UK Ltd
Brunel Residential Mortgage Securitisation No. 1
Building Schools for The Future Investments LLP
Burlingtown LLP
CB/TCC Global Holdings Limited
CEVA Group PLC
Cable & Wireless International HQ
Caffe Nero Group Holdings Ltd
Capita Holdings Limited
Capita IT Services Holdings Ltd
Care Homes 1 Limited
Care Homes 2 Limited
Care Homes 3 Limited
Casual Dining Bidco Limited
Cathedral Capital Limited
Cavendish Hotel (London) Ltd
Charcoal Midco 2 Limited
Chivas Atlantic Holdings Ltd
Clavis Securities PLC
Clearmoon Commercial Ltd
Clifford Chance LLP
DAC Beachcroft LLP
DMG Media Limited
DMGV Limited
Dagger Holdings Limited
De Facto 1341 Limited
Deco 11 - UK Conduit 3 P.L.C.
Deco 8 - UK Conduit 2 PLC
Delta 3 (UK) Limited
Dentons UK and Middle East LLP
Deutsche Holdings No.2 Limited
Deutsche Holdings No.3 Limited
Diageo US Investments
Discovery Holdings Europe Ltd
Docklands Aviation Group Ltd
Dow Jones Business Interactive (U.K.),
EI Ventures Limited
EII (Ventures) Limited
Electricinvest Acquisitions Ltd
Electricinvest Holding Co Ltd
Eskom Holdings SOC Limited
Eurasian Natural Resources Corporation
Eurohome UK Mortgages 2007 - 1 PLC
Euromoney Trading Limited
Eurosail 2006-1 PLC
Eurosail 2006-2BL PLC
Eurosail 2006-3NC PLC
Eurosail 2006-4NP PLC
Eurosail-UK 2007-1NC PLC
Eurosail-UK 2007-2NP PLC
Euston Tower Limited
FET Global Holdings Limited
Ferrovial Agroman (UK) Limited
Fiberweb Limited
Fisher Island Limited
Fosse Funding (No.1) Limited
Fosse Master Issuer PLC
Foster + Partners Group Ltd
Frenchgate Interchange Limited
GGR Capital Limited
GHG 1 (Hospital Operations) Ltd
Gabriel International Assets Ltd
Gabriel International Holdings Ltd
Gallagher Holdings (UK) Ltd
Gates European Holdings Ltd
General Healthcare Holding Partnership LLP
General Healthcare Mixer Partnership LLP
Global Starnet Limited
Google Payment Limited
Great Hall Mortgages No.1 PLC
Greenway Infrastructure Capital PLC
Gresham Receivables (No. 15) UK Ltd
Gresham Receivables (No.11) UK Ltd
Grifonas Holdings Limited
Guaranty Trust Bank (UK) Ltd
Harewood Holdings Limited
Harrods Group (Holding) Ltd
Harrods Property Limited
Hatton Garden Properties Ltd
Hawthorn Asset Co Limited
Helios Underwriting PLC
Henwick Ventures Ltd
Hikma Acquisitions (UK) Ltd
Hikma Holdings (UK) Limited
Hochschild Mining Holdings Ltd
Hochschild Mining PLC
Hogan Lovells International LLP
Holmes Master Issuer PLC
House of Fraser (UK & Ireland) Acquisitions
Hutchison Whampoa Finance UK PLC
IAG UK Holdings Limited
ICP Holdings Limited
IFG UK Holdings Limited
International Finance Facility for Immunisation Company
International Power Consolidated Holdings
Intu Debenture PLC
Iron Mountain Europe (Group) Ltd
Jane Street Europe Limited
Jump Trading International Ltd
Kazphosphate Limited
L-3 Communications Limited
L3 Commercial Training Solutions Ltd
LIH UK Topco Limited
LMS Capital PLC
Labuan RE Underwriting Limited
John Laing Group PLC
John Laing Holdco Limited
Lancashire Insurance Company (UK)
Lancashire Insurance Holdings (UK)
Laser Hotels One Limited
Laser Tradeco Limited
Legal & General Pensions Ltd
Lockton International Holdings Ltd
London & Regional (HC Properties)
London & Regional Portfolio Finance
London Trocadero (2015) LLP
Ludgate Funding PLC
Lycamobile UK Limited
MAN Group UK Limited
MAN Investments Finance Ltd
MMC International Treasury Centre
Malmaison and Hotel du Vin Property Holdings
Mansard Mortgages 2006-1 PLC
Marble Arch Residential Securitisation No. 4
Meadowhall Finance PLC
Mission Marketing Group PLC
Mitie Holdings Limited
Mitie Security Holdings Ltd
Monex Europe Limited
Morgan Stanley Langton Limited
Morgan Stanley Longcross Ltd
Newgate Funding PLC
Novae Group Limited
O & H Holdings Limited
Octopus Apollo VCT PLC
Osnaburgh Street Limited
Otis UK Holding Limited
PA Netherlands Treasury Services Ltd
Pension Insurance Corporation PLC
Permanent Master Issuer PLC
Pic Holdings Limited
Portman Square US Holdings Ltd
Portobar Capital Limited
Prepaid Services Co Ltd
Prudential (US Holdco 1) Ltd
Prudential Capital Holding Co Ltd
Punjab National Bank (International)
QH Partners Limited
RELX (Holdings) Limited
RELX (Investments) PLC
RSM UK Holdings Limited
Rail for London Limited
Rational Group Limited
Redquince Limited
Rome Bidco Limited
Rome PIK Holdco Limited
Rome Topco Limited
Rosediamond LLP
Royal Mail Estates Limited
S32 Leasing Co Ltd
SIR Theme Park Subholdco Ltd
SSP Financing Limited
SSP Financing UK Limited
SSP Group Holdings Limited
SSP Group PLC
Salamander Energy PLC
Sanne Group (UK) Limited
Santander Lending Limited
Securitas Services Holding UK Ltd
Select Service Partner UK Ltd
Semperian (Community Health) Ltd
Shell Treasury UK Limited
Siblu Holdings Limited
Sir Hospital Holdings Limited
Smartstream Technologies Group Ltd
Sony Interactive Entertainment Network Europe
Starr Syndicate Limited
Statkraft UK Ltd
Sumitomo Corporation Global Commodities
TH Holdings Limited
TP ICAP PLC
TPD Investments Limited
Talktalk Brands Limited
Taqa Bratani Limited
Tata Steel Europe Limited
Tata Steel UK Holdings Limited
Tate & Lyle Technology Limited
Thinc UK Group Limited
Tokai Tokyo Securities Europe Ltd
Tonstate Metropole Hotels Ltd
Touchstone Innovations PLC
Trainline Group Investments Ltd
Trainline Investments Holdings Ltd
Transfercom Limited
Tulip UK Holdings (No.3) Ltd
VTB Capital Trading Limited
Vetco Gray Holding
Vibe Corporate Member Limited
Virgin Gyms Limited
Vue Entertainment Investment Ltd
WH Holding Limited
Wellcome Trust Finance PLC
Whiteacre Resources Ltd
Williams Lea Holdings Limited
Workspace 12 Limited
Workspace 13 Limited

Workspace 14 Limited
Yianis Docklands Hotels Ltd
Yorker Holdings PKR Limited
Zealburg Holdings Limited
Zenith Bank (UK) Limited

2007 [267]

12 Smithfield General Partner Ltd
4 Howley Place Limited
AB Acquisitions FX Inter Ltd
AIG Life Limited
Airport Group Investments Ltd
Allianz Renewable Energy Partners V PLC
American Express Payment Services
Antares Underwriting Limited
Antham 1 Limited
Ariel Corporate Member Limited
Ark Corporate Member Limited
Ashurst LLP
Aspen Managing Agency Limited
Aspen Underwriting Limited
Avanti Communications Group PLC
BBA Aviation Finance
BDCG Holdings Limited
BTIG Limited
Babcock (UK) Holdings Limited
Bakkavor Holdings Limited
Bank of China (UK) Limited
Barbican Corporate Member Ltd
Barclays Covered Bonds Limited Liability Partnership
Beta Central Profits Limited
Birch Sites Limited
Bodiam Hill Limited
Boots Propco B Limited
Bracken Holdings Limited
Bradley Hall Holdings Limited
Brent Co-Efficient Limited
Brit Group Finance Limited
British American Tobacco (GLP) Ltd
Burlingtown UK Limited
Business Mortgage Finance 6 PLC
CLEF Holdings Limited
Canary Wharf Developments Ltd
Capco Group Treasury Limited
CenturyLink Impsat Holdings I Ltd
CenturyLink Impsat Holdings II Ltd
Charles Street Conduit Asset Backed Securitisation 1
China Construction Bank (London) Ltd
Choicezone Limited
Chrysaor Limited
Circle Anglia Social Housing PLC
Clarion Treasury Limited
Clifford Chance International LLP
Clyde & Co LLP
Thomas Cook Group PLC
Corfe Hill Limited
Crown Financial & Merchant Bank PLC
Currencies Direct Holdings Ltd
D-Clear Europe Limited
Deutsche Holdings No.4 Limited
Diamond Bank (UK) PLC
Discovery Networks International Holdings
Domestic & General Acquisitions 1
Drillgreat Limited
EDF Development Co Ltd
ELQ Holdings (UK) Ltd
ELQ Investors II Ltd
EMI Group Worldwide Holdings Ltd
EMI Music Publishing Finance (UK)
ENI UK Holding PLC
ENRC Finance Limited
Ember Overseas Holdings Ltd
Endell Properties Limited
Endemol Shine Group Holding UK Ltd
Endurance Corporate Capital Ltd
Enquest ENS Limited
Enrichment Holdings Ltd.
Entertainment One UK Holdings Ltd
Equitix Healthcare Limited
Estia Mortgage Finance II PLC
Eurohome UK Mortgages 2007-2 PLC
Eurosail Prime-UK 2007-A PLC
Eurosail-UK 2007-3BL PLC
Eurosail-UK 2007-4BL PLC
Eurosail-UK 2007-5NP PLC
Eurosail-UK 2007-6NC PLC
Exterion Holdings (UK) Limited
Facebook UK Ltd
Fairhold Services Limited
Farfetch UK Limited
Fern Trading Limited
Finlay Extracts & Ingredients UK Ltd
First Olsen (Holdings) Limited
Folio London Limited
Foxtons Intermediate Holdings Ltd
Fresnillo PLC
G4S US Holdings Limited
GAI Indemnity, Ltd.
GCM Global Energy PLC
Gatehouse Bank PLC
Global Media & Entertainment Ltd
Global Radio Acquisitions Ltd
Global Switch Limited
Global World-Check
Gresham Receivables (No. 19) UK Ltd
Gresham Receivables (No.16) UK Ltd
Guardian Digital Communications Ltd
Heineken (Orange) 1 Limited
Heineken (Orange) 2 Limited
Henares Limited
Heven Limited
Houlihan Lokey Capital (Holdings)
Howard de Walden Estates Holdings
Howden Broking Group Limited
I2 Bidco Limited
I2 Holdco 2 Limited
I2 Holdco Limited
IHS Markit Group Holdings Ltd
IPP Bond Limited
Ice Clear Europe Limited
Inmarsat Solutions Limited
Intergen Holdings (UK) Limited
Intergen Projects (UK) Limited
Istithmar P & O Estates (UK) Ltd
Jane Street Financial Limited
Jasper Acquisition Holdings Ltd
Jasper Acquisition Limited
Jupiter Asset Management Group Ltd
Jupiter Fund Management Group Ltd
Jupiter Fund Management PLC
Jurys Inns (UK) Limited
KAZ Minerals Investments Ltd
KAZ Minerals Sales Limited
Kensington Mortgage Securities PLC
Knight Dragon Investments Ltd
LBG Capital Holdings Limited
LS Harbour Exchange Option Ltd
LS London Holdings One Limited
LS Victoria Properties Limited
LS White Rose Limited
Laird Overseas Holdings Ltd
Lanark Funding Limited
Lanark Master Issuer PLC
Land Securities (Hotels) Ltd
Land Securities Buchanan Street Developments
Land Securities Management Ltd
Land Securities Trinity Ltd
Landmark Mortgage Securities No.2 PLC
Landmark Mortgage Securities No.3 PLC
Langton Funding (No.1) Limited
Langton Securities (2008-1) PLC.
Legal & General Insurance Holdings No.2
Lifeways Finance Limited
Linklaters LLP
Lloyd's Register Group Services Ltd
Luminus Finance Limited
MCX Dunlin (UK) Limited
MCX Osprey (UK) Limited
MEIF II CP Holdings 1 Limited
MEIF II CP Holdings 3 Limited
MGL2 Limited
MLEIH Funding
Macquarie (UK) Group Services Ltd
Macquarie Bank International Ltd
Macquarie European Investment Holdings
Macquarie Holdings (UK) No.1 Ltd
Mandarin Oriental Hyde Park Ltd
Mansard Mortgages 2007-2 PLC
Maxwell Asset Management Ltd
McKechnie Aerospace (Europe) Ltd
Metallon Corporation Limited
Metro Bank PLC
Mitsui E & P Mozambique Area 1 Ltd
Moody's Group UK Ltd
NGC UK Holdings Co Ltd
NYOP Education (Aberdeen) Ltd
NYSE Holdings UK Limited
Nando's Group Holdings Limited
National Australia Finance (Vessel Leasing No.5)
New Star Asset Management Group Ltd
Nomura Capital Markets Limited
North Colonnade Limited
Norton Rose Fulbright LLP
Nugent Shopping Park Limited
Octopus Titan VCT PLC
Odeon and UCI Cinemas Holdings Ltd
Onyx Germany (2) Ltd
Origin Finance Limited
P1 Reversions Limited
PG (April) Limited
Pam Group Limited
Phoenix Distribution Holdings Ltd
Pinsent Masons LLP
Prepaid Financial Services Ltd
Priory Education Services Ltd
Proserv Operations Limited
QW Rail Leasing Limited
Quilter PLC
RTA Holdco 4 Limited
Ralph US Holdings
Ramsay Health Care (UK) Ltd
Redwood Partnership Ventures Ltd
Resloc UK 2007-1 PLC
Rhythmone PLC
Ricoh Europe Holdings PLC
Rio Tinto Finance (USA) PLC
Rothesay Life PLC
SHG Acquisition (UK) Limited
SIR ATP Limited
SIR Rivers Limited
SIR TP Limited
SIR Theme Parks Limited

Secure Income REIT PLC
Sedgwick UK Holdings II Ltd
Sedgwick UK Holdings Limited
Seminole Hard Rock UK Limited
Semperian No.21 Limited
Semperian PPP Investment Partners
Semperian PPP Investment Partners No.2
Semperian Senior Funding PLC
Shell Hasdrubal Limited
Smyths Toys UK Limited
Snowdon Leasing Co Ltd
Songbird Finance Limited
Spire Healthcare Holdings 1
Spire Healthcare Holdings 2 Ltd
Spire Healthcare Holdings 3 Ltd
Spire Property 5 Limited
Spire UK Holdco 4 Limited
Spotify Limited
St. Paul's School
Starstone Finance Limited
Superior Acquisitions Limited
TES Global Holdings Limited
TNS UK Holdings Limited
TSL Education SPV 2 Limited
Tabletop London Limited
Tangguh Hiri Finance Limited
Tangguh Sago Finance Limited
Theatre (Hospitals) No.1 PLC
Theatre (Hospitals) No.2 PLC
Tilbury Green Power Limited
Touchstone Innovations Businesses LLP
Touchstone Innovations Investments
Tullett Prebon (No. 1)
Tullett Prebon (No. 3) Limited
UK SPV Credit Finance PLC
UPP Group Limited
Unifund PLC
Uropa Assets No. 1 Limited
Uropa Holdings Limited
Uropa Securities PLC
Vattenfall Wind Power Ltd
Vaultex UK Limited
Veolia ES Shropshire Limited
Veolia Water Enterprise Ltd
Viking Consortium Acquisition Ltd
Virgin Active Investment Holdings
Vocalink Holdings Limited
Vocalink Limited
WB/TT Holdings Limited
WBA Acquisitions UK Holdco 2 Ltd
WBA Acquisitions UK Topco Ltd
WBA International Limited
WBA Propco C LLP
WPP Global
WPP Headline
WPP Rocky Ltd
WPP Toronto Ltd
Walgreens Boots Alliance Ltd
Wellcome Trust Residential 1 Ltd
Westermost Rough Limited
Yianis Investments Limited
Zoopla Limited

2008 [171]

A2dominion Treasury Limited
ADCG (UK) Limited
ANV Corporate Name Limited
AON Benfield Limited
Aberdeen Infrastructure (No 2) LLP
Aberdeen Infrastructure (No.3) Ltd
Aberdeen Infrastructure Ltd
Academies Enterprise Trust
Aegis GPS Holdings Limited
Aegis Group Participations Ltd
Affinity Sutton Capital Markets PLC
Alliance Automotive Procurement Ltd
Amazon Video Limited
American Express Group Services Ltd
Amore Group (Holdings) Limited
Anglo Platinum Marketing Ltd
Arch Syndicate Investments Ltd
Argo International Holdings Ltd
Ashtead Financing Limited
Axia Finance PLC
BIIF Bidco Limited
BIIF Holdco Limited
BIIF Issuerco Limited
BIIF Parentco Limited
BL Sainsbury Superstores Ltd
BMG Rights Management (UK) Ltd
BMO Real Estate Partners LLP
Babcock Integrated Technology Ltd
Barclays Long Island Limited
Best Buy China UK, LLP
Best Buy Distributions Limited
Betfair Group Limited
Bird & Bird LLP
Broadgate (PHC 8) 2008 Limited
Canary Wharf (North Quay) Ltd
Canary Wharf Properties (Crossrail)
Canary Wharf Properties (RT5) Ltd
Carphone Warehouse Europe Ltd
Charter Consolidated Holdings Ltd
Citadel Europe LLP
Citywide Trading (UK) Limited
Clarion Acquisition Limited
Clarion UK Holdco Limited
Clarion UK Midco Limited
Clarion UK Topco Limited
Close Brothers Holdings Ltd
Cornwall Bidco Limited
Cornwall Midco Limited
Cory Riverside (Holdings) Ltd
Craegmoor Group (No.3) Limited
Craegmoor Group Limited
Creditex Holdco Limited
DHCM Holdco Limited
Delamare Cards MTN Issuer PLC
Deva Financing PLC
Diamond Offshore Enterprises Ltd
Diamond Rig Investments Ltd
Dynamic Estates Limited
E-Act
EMF-UK 2008-1 PLC
Economist Group (US Holdings) Ltd
Equitix Capital Eurobond Ltd
Ernst & Young (EMEIA) Services Ltd
Ernst & Young Accountants LLP
Ernst & Young Nederland LLP
Exova 2014 Limited
Exova Treasury Limited
FIL Holdings (UK) Limited
Fairhold Homes Investment (No.16) AL
Fox Healthcare Acquisitions Ltd
Fox Healthcare Holdco 2 Ltd
Freshfields Bruckhaus Deringer LLP
G4S US Investments Limited
Arthur J. Gallagher Holdings (UK)
Gazeley Holdings UK Limited
Gazprom Global LNG Limited
Goldman Sachs Group U.K. Finance Ltd
Gracechurch Card Programme Funding PLC
Hammerson (60 Threadneedle Street)
Hammerson (Bristol Investments) Ltd
Hammerson (Merthyr) Limited
Hammerson (Value Retail Investments)
Harewood Helena 2 Limited
Haymarket Capital Ventures LLP
Heineken (Orange) 3 Limited
Henderson Holdings Group Ltd
Hestok Limited
Hotel (PL Property) Holdco Ltd
ICAP Holdings (UK) Limited
ICAP Holdings Limited
IQVIA Solutions Global Holdings UK Ltd.
ITV Rights Limited
Idex UK Ltd.
India Infrastructure Finance Company (UK)
Infrastructure Investments Holdings
Ingenious Media Holdings Ltd
Itochu Treasury Centre Europe PLC
KAZ Minerals Finance PLC
KG Group Holdings Limited
Kajima Europe Limited
Katanalotika PLC
Kingfisher UK Limited
Kusuma Trust UK
Lake Acquisitions Limited
Landmark Hotel London Limited
Larch (Nursing Homes) Holdco Ltd
Liberty Corporate Capital (Two) Ltd
Lloyds Bank Covered Bonds LLP
London & Regional Group Investments
London & Regional Group Securitisation No.1
London & Regional Group Trading No.3
London Wall Outsourcing Ltd
Loopsign No.2 Limited
MacFarlanes LLP
Markel Capital Holdings Ltd
Max Credit Investment Limited
Morgan Stanley Investments (UK)
Mortgage Funding 2008-1 PLC
Motability Operations Group PLC
NBG Finance (Dollar) PLC
NEX Group Holdings Limited
Nando's Group Limited
Nord Anglia Education (UK) Holdings PLC
Fred. Olsen Wind Holdings Ltd
Fred. Olsen Wind Limited
Ontic Engineering & Manufacturing UK
Openbet Technologies Limited
Orsted London Array II Limited
Orsted West of Duddon Sands (UK) Ltd
PACG2 Limited
Pacific Life RE Holdings Ltd
Pam Acquisitionco Limited
Pandora Jewellery UK Limited
Partnership Holdings Limited
Pearson Dollar Finance Two Ltd
Penarth Master Issuer PLC
QBE Holdings (EO) Limited
QH Participations Limited
QVC UK Holdings Limited
Rabai Power Holdings Limited
Residential Mortgage Securities 23 PLC
Rio 587 Limited
Rio 588 Limited
Savills Holding Co Ltd
Scott Trust Limited
Seadrill UK Ltd.
Shell QGC Holdings Limited
Shell QGC Midstream 1 Limited
Shell QGC Upstream 1 Limited
Shire Europe Limited
Silverstone Funding (No.1) Ltd

Silverstone Master Issuer PLC
DS Smith Holdings Limited
Spire Healthcare Group UK Ltd
Spire UK Holdco 2A Limited
Talktalk Group Limited
Tam UK Holdings Limited
Third New Court Limited
Ticketmaster Europe Holdco Ltd
Tiffany & Co. (UK) Holdings Ltd
Tokio Marine Underwriting Ltd
Transport for London Finance Ltd
Trayport Holdings Limited
Triathlon Homes LLP
Trinity Financing PLC
UDV (SJ) Holdings Limited
Uropa Assets No.2 Limited
Wellcome Trust Investments 1 Unlimited
Wellcome Trust Investments 2 Unlimited
Westfield UK Finance Limited
Willis Investment UK Holdings Ltd

2009 [126]

APR Energy Holdings Limited
APR Energy Limited
Admiral Taverns Bidco Limited
Aegis Media Pacific Ltd
Alberto-Culver (Europe) Ltd
Alberto-Culver UK Products Ltd
Allianz Renewable Energy Partners II
Allianz Renewable Energy Partners IV
Argent Foods Limited
Argo (Alpha) Limited
Atrato Issuer Holdco Limited
Avanti Hylas 2 Limited
Awilco Drilling PLC
Axia III APC Limited
Axia III Finance PLC
BG LNG Investments Limited
BHF Group UK Limited
Bank of England Asset Purchase Facility Fund
Bank of Ireland (UK) PLC
Barclays Covered Bond Funding LLP
Bluebutton Properties UK Ltd
Bluecrest Capital Management (UK) LLP
British American Tobacco (2009 Pca)
British American Tobacco (2009) Ltd
Canonical Group Limited
Chapelcrest Investments Ltd
Chepstow Blue PLC
Crawford & Company EMEA/A-P Holdings
The Francis Crick Institute Ltd
Dixons Carphone PLC
E-Rewards Bidco Limited
EDF Energy Holdings Limited
EMGH Limited
ESB Asset Development UK Ltd
Edgbaston RMBS 2010-1 PLC
Ensco Finance Limited
Ensco Holdco Limited
Ensco PLC
Ensco Universal Limited
Ensco Worldwide Investments Ltd
Epihiro PLC
Equinor New Energy Limited
Essar Energy Limited
Esterline Technologies Europe Ltd
Eversholt Rail Limited
Fletcher Bay Group Limited
Foxtons Group PLC
GC Campden Hill LLP
GenFinance II PLC
Global Prime Partners Ltd
Greenwich BSF SPV Limited
Hoebridge LLP
Homer Newco Limited
Hull Esteem Consortium PSP Ltd
ICF Debt Pool LLP
ISG Fit Out Limited
ITE Holdings Limited
ITW CS (UK) Ltd
Imagination Industries Ltd
Informa Group Holdings Limited
International General Insurance Company (UK)
Irida PLC
Ivy Bidco Limited
Ivy Midco Limited
Just Eat PLC
Kenmin (HP) Limited
Koch Commodities Europe Ltd
L51N Limited
LW Theatres Holdings Limited
Laird Asia Holdings Limited
Liberty UK and Europe Holdings Ltd
Lloyds Bank Pension ABCS (No 1) LLP
Lloyds Bank Pension ABCS (No 2) LLP
London Stock Exchange Group Holdings (Italy)
London Stock Exchange Group Holdings
MT Property Investments LLP
Macquarie Commodities Factoring Holdings (UK)
Macquarie Factoring (UK) Ltd
Markitserv Holdings Limited
Marks and Spencer Guernsey Investments Limited Liability Partnership
Masdar Energy UK Limited
Mitie Technical Facilities Management Holdings
Mitsubishi Estate Europe Ltd
Mobius Wind Holdings Limited
Mycitydeal Limited
NNB Generation Company (HPC) Ltd
NNB Holding Company (HPC) Ltd
NatWest Covered Bonds Limited Liability Partnership
National Grid Twenty Three Ltd
Noble Clean Fuels Limited
Noble Resources UK Limited
Noerr LLP
Origin Invest Limited
Petroineos Fuels Limited
Petropavlovsk Mining Treasury UK Ltd
Praxis I Finance PLC
Praxis II APC Limited
Praxis II Finance PLC
Public Power Corporation Finance PLC
R & Q Capital No. 6 Limited
RBS SME Investments Limited
Reed Specialist Recruitment Ltd
Relative Value Investments UK Limited Liability Partnership
Relative Value Trading Limited
Renaissancere Corporate Capital (UK)
Semperian PPP Investment Partners Group
Seven Capital PLC
Shell Clair UK Limited
Simca LLP
Sinochem Resources UK Limited
T.H.F.C. (Funding No.2) PLC
Talktalk Telecom Group PLC
Tam Investment Limited
Tay Valley Lighting (Hampshire) Ltd
Tesco Property Finance 2 PLC
Tintagel Castle Limited
Tomori E & P Limited
Treimco Limited
Tullett Prebon Investment Holdings
UD Europe Limited
UPP (Exeter) Limited
Vanta Education Holdings Ltd
Weston (2009) Limited
Wilhunter (UK) Limited
Wilphoenix (UK) Limited
Wittington Investments (Properties)

January-June 2010 [81]

AMG Plymouth UK Holdings (1) Ltd
Acacia Mining PLC
Acturis Group Limited
Acturis International Limited
Aether IOS Limited
Allied World Capital (Europe) Ltd
Alpha Offshore International Leasing
Arrow Bidco Limited
Artemis Investment Management LLP
Biz Finance PLC
Blackstone Group International Partners LLP
Bowbell No. 1 PLC
Broadgate PHC 2010 Limited
CKI Number 1 Limited
CKI Number 2 Limited
CKI Number 3 Limited
Capital & Counties Properties PLC
Chubb Capital Ltd
Close PF Funding I Limited
Coach Stores Limited
Cognizant Worldwide Limited
Deloitte Global Services Holdings
Deloitte Global Services Ltd
EC Finance PLC
ED Broking Group Limited
Electricity First Limited
Elios Renewable Energy Limited
Enquest PLC
Equifax EUA Limited
Ernst & Young (Asia-Pacific) Services
Friary Court Investments Ltd
Funding Circle Holdings PLC
G4S International Finance PLC
GB Social Housing PLC
GFI Markets Limited
Gorkana Group Holdings Limited
Gresham Receivables (No. 26) UK Ltd
ICG FMC Limited
Ice Europe Parent Limited
JPMorgan Global Emerging Markets Income Trust
Jeco 2 Ltd
Cath Kidston Acquisitions Ltd
Cath Kidston Group Limited
Kufpec UK Limited
La Perla Global Management (UK) Ltd
Lakeside MWS Limited Liability Partnership
Largenta Limited
Lendlease (Elephant & Castle) Ltd
Lockton Companies LLP
London Town Group of Companies Holdings
Londonmetric Property PLC
Macsco 22 Limited
Metric Property Investments Ltd
Mount Anvil New Holdings Ltd
NGC Europe Limited
National Grid Twenty-Five Ltd
National Grid William Limited

Navigator Gas Invest Limited
Olympus Finance UK Limited
Osaka Gas UK, Ltd.
Passaic Issuer Holdco Limited
Pisti 2010-1 PLC
Polar Capital Global Healthcare Trust
Premier Lotteries Investments UK Ltd
Raymond Estates Ltd
Rutherfurd Acquisitions Ltd
SPIE UK Limited
Simmons & Simmons LLP
Stobart Holdings Limited
Sulawesi LNG Development Ltd
Syco Entertainment Limited
TCI Fund Holdings Limited
Tesco Property Finance 3 PLC
Tibra Equities Europe Limited
UK Green Investment Gym Participant
UK Power Networks Holdings Ltd
Vanguard Asset Services, Ltd.
Veolia ES Staffordshire Ltd
Viacom Camden Lock Limited
Victoria's Secret UK Limited
York Potash Ltd

July-December 2010 [110]

10 Brock Street Limited
10 Gresham Street LLP
ADIB (UK) Limited
AIG Transaction Execution Ltd
Arig Capital Limited
BM Manchester Limited
Babcock Integration LLP
Babcock US Investments Limited
Bana One Limited
Barclays CCP Funding LLP
Barnsley SPV Three Limited
Be Offices Limited
Blackrock Frontiers Investment Trust PLC
Blue Manchester Limited
Blue Transmission Walney 1 Ltd
Bluebutton (5 Broadgate) UK Ltd
Boston Consulting Group UK LLP
Bridging Trading LLP
Burbo Extension Ltd
Burford Capital Holdings (UK) Ltd
CELF Advisors LLP
CGI Eurofin UK Limited
CWG (Wood Wharf Two) Limited
Castle Trust Capital PLC
Catalina Echo Limited
Chel (Shares) LLP
Community Finance Company 1 PLC
Derwent Central Cross Limited
Dunhill Medical Trust
EFT International Investments Holdings
East Anglia One Limited
Emerald 3 Limited
Equitix Capital Eurobond 2 Ltd
Equitix Highways 2 Limited
Eversholt Funding PLC
Freston Ventures Investments LLP
G4S Corporate Services Limited
GS Sapphire Investment Limited
Gates Acquisitions Limited
Greenergy Fuels Holdings Ltd
Gresham Receivables (No.27) UK Ltd
Guildhall Asset Purchasing Company (No.11) UK
Helix Acquisition Limited
Helix Bufferco Limited
Helix Midco Limited
Imperial London Hotels Group Ltd
International Power (Zebra) Ltd
Itau BBA International PLC
KAZ Minerals Copper Finance Ltd
KAZ Minerals Projects Finance Ltd
LS Cardinal Limited
Langton Securities (2010-1) PLC
Lannraig Master Issuer PLC
Lawn Tennis Association Ltd
Long Island Assets Limited
MPG Finco Limited
Macquarie Group Investments (UK) No.2
Macquarie Meters 3 (UK) Ltd
Maestro (Holdings 1) Limited
Maestro (Holdings 2) Limited
Mitie Treasury Management Ltd
Moly-Cop UK Holdings Limited
Multiplex Europe Limited
Nando's Limited
Navona Issuer Holdco Limited
Nordson London Limited
Office Group Midco Limited
Office Group Properties Ltd
Office Retail Limited
Peel Hunt LLP
Pelham Capital Investments Ltd
Priory Group No. 1 Limited
Priory Group No. 3 Limited
RVT CLO Investments LLP
Reclaim Fund Ltd
Residential Mortgage Securities 25 PLC
Ronin Trading Europe LLP
SGO Corporation Limited
SSB No. 1 PLC
Henry Schein Animal Health Holdings
Ship Holdco Limited
Ship Midco Limited
Six Degrees Holdings Limited
Skuld I Limited
Soho Estates Holdings Limited
Southbank Media Ltd
Stratford City Business District Ltd
T & L Sugars Limited
TC Financing Limited
TC Ormonde OFTO Limited
TSMUK Ltd
Talisman Colombia Holdco Ltd
Tesco Property Finance 4 PLC
Thanet OFTO Holdco Limited
Thanet OFTO Limited
Threadneedle Holdings Limited
Time Out Group PLC
Topland Jupiter Limited
Tudehope Ltd
U-Pol Holdings Limited
UK Power Networks Services Holdings
Vouvray Finance Limited
Vue Holdings (UK) Limited
WBA Acquisitions UK Holdco 5 Ltd
WFS UK Holding Company II Ltd
WPP Finance 2010
Walney Extension Limited
Worldpay (UK) Limited
Worldpay Ecommerce Limited
Worldpay Finance PLC

January-June 2011 [121]

Aequor Investments Limited
All England Lawn Tennis & Croquet Club
Amesbury Holdings Limited
Ansco Finance 2011 Limited
Apache UK Investment Limited
Axis Bank UK Limited
BT SLE Euro Limited
BT SLE USD Limited
Babcock Mission Critical Services UK
Bakkavor Finance (1) Limited
Bakkavor Finance (2) Limited
Bakkavor Finance (3) Limited
Bifurcate Funding Limited
Big Bus Tours Limited
Big Society Capital Limited
Big Society Trust
Bristol Water Group Limited
British Museum Trust Limited
Brook Funding (No.1) Limited
Business Growth Fund Limited
COFCO Holdings 1 Limited
Choo Luxury Finance Limited
Choo Luxury Holdings Limited
Cityfibre Holdings Limited
Clearstone Holdings (International) Ltd
Core Laboratories Interests One Ltd
Core Laboratories Interests Two Ltd
Creative Education Trust
DNI Europe Holdings Limited
Derwent London Page Street Ltd
EDM Business Services Holdings Ltd
EMI Group Global Limited
Education Endowment Foundation
Emerald 2 Limited
Emerson USD Finance Co Ltd
Engine Partners UK LLP
Equitix Healthcare 2 Limited
Eskmuir Securities Limited
GTA Holdco Limited
General Motors Europe Limited
Gresham Receivables (No. 30) UK Ltd
Gresham Receivables (No. 31) UK Ltd
Gunfleet Sands Holding Ltd
Hadley Shipping Group Limited
J O Hambro Capital Management Holdings
Hanover Insurance International Holdings
Harwood Capital Management Ltd
Henderson International Income Trust PLC
I-Environment Investments Ltd
ICG Global Investment UK Ltd
ITWP Acquisitions Limited
Idex UK Investment Ltd
Immediate Media Co Ltd
Ivy Holdco Limited
Jones Lang Lasalle Dorchester Ltd
Jupiter Acquisitions (Holdings) Ltd
Jupiter Hotels Limited
Jupiter Properties 2011 UK Ltd
KAZ Minerals Aktogay Finance Ltd
Khoo Teck Puat UK Foundation
LME Clear Limited
LS Ludgate (No.1) Limited
LS Ludgate (No.2) Limited
John Laing Investments Overseas Holdings
Lannraig Funding Limited
Limited Life Assets Issuance PLC
Limited Life Assets Master Ltd
Limited Life Assets Services Ltd
Lion/Heaven UK II Limited
Lion/Heaven UK Limited
Lynwood Retail UK Limited
MC Resource Development Ltd.
MIPL Group Limited
MIPL Holdings Limited
Mabel Bidco Limited
Mabel Mezzco Limited
Mabel Midco Limited

Mabel Topco Limited
Macquarie Lending & Investment Partners LLP
Match.Com Europe Limited
Maven Investment Partners Ltd
Mesoblast UK Limited
Methodist Independent Schools Trust
Mitsui E & P UK Limited
NC Shine Acquisition Ltd.
NatgridTW1 Limited
Noble Resources UK Holdings Ltd
Oaktree Capital Management (UK) LLP
Ofto Superholdco Limited
Orsted Lincs (UK) Ltd
Orsted Power (Gunfleet Sands) Ltd
Otter Ports I Limited
Otter Ports II Limited
Otter Ports Limited
PCL Funding I Limited
PHP Investments No.2 Limited
PZ Cussons Beauty LLP
Peabody Capital PLC
Pendal UK Limited
Perenco Overseas Holdings Ltd
Photobox Holdco Alpha Limited
Photobox Holdco Beta Limited
Prometheon Holdings (UK) Ltd
QDD Athletes Village UK Ltd
Redwood Partnership Ventures 2 Ltd
Rolls-Royce Holdings PLC
Saavi Energia (UK) Ltd
Shell Upstream Overseas Services (I)
Spotify Finance Limited
TRS Group (UK) Limited
Tramlink Nottingham (Holdings) Ltd
Tramlink Nottingham Limited
UKTV Media Holdings Limited
UPP (Reading I) Holdings Ltd
UPP (Reading I) Limited
Valero Holdco UK Ltd
Vancouver Topco Limited
Virtus Holdco Limited
WM SA Investments Limited
WTI/EFW Holdings Ltd
Zavarco PLC

July-December 2011 [89]

6 Bevis Marks Limited
ABF HK Finance Limited
ABP Finance PLC
ABPA Holdings Limited
AON PLC
Aitch Group Limited
Arcadis LLP
Aviva Europe SE
BGEO Group Limited
BOCI Global Commodities (UK) Ltd
BW Publishing Limited
Blackrock UK 2 LLP
Blackrock UK 3 LLP
Blackrock UK 4 LLP
Blue Transmission Walney 2 Ltd
Bluebay Asset Management LLP
Bridgepoint Funding III A Ltd
CGI Nordic Holdings Limited
Canary Wharf Investments (BP4) Ltd
Cantor Fitzgerald Services LLP
Capital Hill Hotels Limited
Catlin Syndicate 6112 Limited
China RE UK Limited
Colfax UK Finance Ltd
Colfax UK Holdings Ltd
ConocoPhillips (U.K.) Sigma Ltd
Coppid Farming Enterprises LLP
Cummins EMEA Holdings Limited
DMEP Holdco Limited
Dixons Carphone Holdings Ltd
EMI Group (Newco) Limited
EVRAZ PLC
Eaton Towers Limited
Enquest Heather Leasing Ltd
Finastra Global Limited
Freepoint Commodities Enterprises Ltd.
Freepoint Commodities Europe LLP
Freepoint Commodities Holdings Ltd
G4S Investment London Limited
GFS Renewable Energy Limited
Genel Energy Miran Bina Bawi Ltd
Green Park Reading No. 1 LLP
Gresham Receivables (No. 32) UK Ltd
Gresham Receivables (No. 33) UK Ltd
Gresham Receivables (No. 34) UK Ltd
Harrods Commercial Property Ltd
ICE Overseas Limited
Karta II PLC
LS Victoria Circle Lp1 Limited
LS Victoria Circle Lp2 Limited
Liberty Plaza (London) Limited
Local Trust
MC GFS Investment Co Ltd
MYI UK Holdings (No.1) Limited
Macquarie Euro Limited
Mountsfield Park Finance Ltd
NHS Property Services Limited
NMC Health PLC
Nesta
Ocubis Financing Limited
Partnerships in Care Investments 1
Phillips 66 Treasury Limited
Phillips 66 UK Funding Limited
Phillips 66 UK Holdings Ltd
Prometheon Enterprise Limited
Rowan Companies PLC
Royal Brompton and Harefield Hospitals Charity
Ruspetro Limited
SHEL Holdings Europe Limited
SRE Portfolios UK Ltd
Sarum Issuer Holdco Limited
Sheldon Euro Investments 2 Ltd
Skyscanner Holdings Limited
Smith & Williamson LLP
Smiths Finance Limited
State Grid Europe Limited
Stena Spey Services Limited
T.H.F.C. (Funding No.3) PLC
Tesco Property Finance 5 PLC
Tizir Limited
Vancor Ltd
Veolia ES Leeds Limited
Virgin Active Health Club Holdings
Virgin Active International Ltd
Virgin Active South Africa Holdings
Vouvray Acquisition Limited
Vouvray Midco Limited
WGC (UK) Limited
WSP Group Holdings Limited

January-March 2012 [55]

10 Triton Street Limited
20 Triton Street Limited
3i Assets LLP
AV Equity Trading Limited
Aegis London Holdings Limited
Agility Trains East (Holdings) Ltd
Agility Trains East Limited
Agility Trains West (Holdings) Ltd
Agility Trains West Limited
Akelius Residential Limited
Alberto-Culver UK Holdings Ltd
Anglo American Diamond Holdings Ltd
Arena Racing Corporation Ltd
Aviva Investors Realm Infrastructure No.1
BIS (Postal Services Act 2011) Co Ltd
Babcock Mission Critical Services Ltd
Collins Stewart Former Holdings Ltd
Diageo Treasury Australia LLP
East Finance PLC
Elementis US Limited
FTI Consulting LLP
GLA Land and Property Limited
Greater London Authority Holdings
Green Bidco Limited
Green Midco Limited
HCA Global Capital LLP
IDR Finance UK II Limited
INCJ SJ Investment Limited
LS Mirage Limited
Lloyd's Register Foundation
London Stock Exchange (C) Ltd
MEIF II CP SPV 2 Limited
Marubeni Finance Europe PLC
McGraw-Hill Education (UK) Ltd
Misys International Limited
Mitsui & Co. Financial Services (Europe)
Mizkan Euro Holdings Limited
Moody's Group (Holdings) Unlimited
Moody's Group Finance Limited
Moody's International (UK) Ltd
NTT Data EMEA Ltd.
National Grid Twenty Seven Ltd
New Ventures II (UK) Limited
Pearson Funding Four PLC
Sandown Gold 2012-1 PLC
Shionogi Limited
Slater & Gordon (UK) 1 Limited
Slater & Gordon (UK) 2 LLP
Slater and Gordon UK Limited
Soho Estates Portfolio Limited
Stephenson Harwood LLP
Tungsten Corporation PLC
Unilever UK Group Limited
Validus Holdings (UK) Ltd
Wright Express International Holdings

April-June 2012 [46]

10 Trinity Square Residences Ltd
AON Global Operations PLC
BCS Prime Brokerage Limited
BTG International Healthcare Ltd
Barclays Principal Investments Ltd
Blue Transmission Sheringham Shoal
CLS UK Properties PLC
Corsair Mint III Limited
DIF Infra 3 UK Limited
FIA UK Funding Limited
Ground Rents Income Fund PLC
HKEX Investment (UK) Limited
Harrods Corporate Management Ltd
Herbert Smith Freehills Global LLP
Infrared Infrastructure Yield Holdings
Inpex Angola Block 14 Ltd.
Itochu Fibre Limited
Listrac Bidco Limited
Listrac Finance Limited
Listrac Midco Limited

MF White Television City Ltd
MP Granite Ltd
Mace Finance Limited
Mizkan Euro Ltd.
NM Money Holdings Limited
Nintex UK Limited
Norlake Hospitality Limited
Omega Leasing (No.9) Limited
PIP Infrastructure Investments (No 6)
Pips Asset Investments Limited
Real Estate Participation Management
Real Estate Participation Services
Rowan No.1 Limited
Rowan No.2 Limited
Sandown 2012-2 PLC
Stena Icemax Limited
TI Atlantic Europe Holdings Ltd
Tronox International Finance LLP
Tronox Sands Investment Funding Ltd
Tronox Sands LLP
Tronox UK Finance Limited
Tullow Oil Finance Limited
UCC Europe Limited
Virtus IMH Limited
Westfield UK & Europe Finance PLC
York UK Holdco International Ltd

July-September 2012 [60]
AON Overseas Holdings Limited
Aamby Valley (UK) Limited
Algeco Global Finance PLC
Amdipharm Mercury UK Limited
BIIF Holdco III Limited
Babcock Critical Assets Holdings LLP
Babcock Defence & Security Holdings LLP
Babcock Education & Training Holdings LLP
Bitstamp Limited
Blackrock North American Income Trust
Boeing Commercial Aviation Services Europe
Bunzl Overseas Holdings (No. 3) Ltd
CGI Finance (UK) Limited
CGI Finance Holdco Two Limited
CL Intermediate (UK) Limited
CP Co 3 Limited
CP Co 7 Limited
CP Co Borrower Limited
Diageo Financing Turkey Ltd
Diamond Generating Europe Ltd
Dorney Issuer Holdco Limited
Greater Gabbard OFTO Holdings Ltd
Greater Gabbard OFTO PLC
HGI Asset Management Group Ltd
Henderson Group Holdings Asset Management
Hess Malaysia and Thailand Ltd
High Speed Rail Finance PLC
Intu Milton Keynes Limited
LS 1 New Street Square Limited
Lloyd's Register Group Limited
MAN Group PLC
MSCI UK Holdings Limited
Milton Magna Limited
Motorola Solutions International Holding
National Grid Interconnector Holdings
Nemo Link Limited
Newday Funding Transferor Ltd
OCHL (Globe) Limited
PA Group Holdings Limited
PA Topco Limited
Premier Oil Exploration and Production
Principal Financial Services I (UK) LLP
Principal Financial Services II (UK) Ltd
Principal Financial Services III (UK)
Principal Financial Services Latin America
Principal International Latin America
Principal International South America I
Principal International South America II
Residential Mortgage Securities 26 PLC
Rickleford Ltd
Rosequake Ltd
Sahara Hospitality Operations LLP
DS Smith Perch Limited
St Mungo Community Housing Association
TS Property Lending Limited
Terido LLP
Tesco Property Finance 6 PLC
Vesuvius PLC
WBA Acquisitions UK Holdco 7 Ltd
Wilsonart Limited

October-December 2012 [73]
AHL Partners LLP
Aegis Triton Limited
All3media USA Limited
Annington Limited
Arunvill Global Equity Trading Ltd
Auto ABS UK Loans PLC
BNY Mellon International Asset Management (Holdings)
BNY Mellon International Asset Management (Holdings) No. 1
BNY Mellon Investment Management (Europe)
Babcock Mission Critical Services Topco
Balfour Beatty Group Employment Ltd
Blue Transmission London Array Ltd
British American Tobacco (2012) Ltd
Burberry Beauty Limited
Canary Wharf Properties (WF9) Ltd
Canary Wharf Retail Funding Ltd
Cranemere Group Limited
Cummins PGI Holdings Ltd
Dunwilco (1783) Limited
Dunwilco (1784) Limited
ERS DGB Limited
EVRAZ North America PLC
Elm Trading Limited
Eurasia Finance Management Ltd
FTSE Global Debt Capital Markets Ltd
Fall Ridge Partners LLP
Ferrovial Agroman Limited
Flemings Hotel Mayfair Ltd
Greencoat UK Wind PLC
HGHL Holdings Ltd
H.J. Heinz Co Ltd
H.J. Heinz Foods UK Limited
KAZ Minerals Aktogay Project Finance
Kas No.8 Limited
Lewis Trust Holdings Limited
Londonmetric Saturn Limited
MHDV Holdings (UK) Limited
MHG Senior Borrower Limited
Macquarie European Rail Ltd
Macquarie Infrastructure and Real Assets Investments
Maritime Drilling Holdings Ltd
Martin Pecheur Sterling Investments
Mediclinic International PLC
Mercia No.1 PLC
Newday Partnership Transferor PLC
Nicoventures Holdings Limited
OM Zimbabwe Holdco Limited
PA Consulting Holdings Limited
Portswood Investments Limited
Principal Financial Services IV (UK) LLP
Principal Financial Services V (UK) Ltd
Progressive Global Energy Kurdistan
Quilter Cheviot Holdings Ltd
Roder Investments No. 1 Ltd
Roder Investments No. 2 Ltd
SCMI Limited
Sirius Minerals Holdings Ltd
Tripadvisor UK Holdco Limited
ULiving@Hertfordshire Holdco Ltd
ULiving@Hertfordshire PLC
UPP Bond 1 Holdings Limited
UPP Bond 1 Issuer PLC
UPP Bond 1 Limited
WBA Latin America Limited
WGC (UK) Finance Limited
WGSN Group Limited
WMG Finance Limited
WPP Jubilee Limited
WPP US Investments Limited
Waymark Asset Investments Ltd
Webhelp UK Holdings Ltd
York Potash Holdings Limited
Yunnan Limited

January-March 2013 [55]
Affordable Housing Finance PLC
Alstom Transport UK Limited
BHP Billiton Marketing UK Ltd
Bedford Estates London Estates LLP
Brookfield Global Property Advisor
CBRE Holdings Limited
Cameron Flow Control Technology (UK)
Canada Square Investments Ltd
City Football Group Limited
DTEK Finance PLC
DTEK Investments Limited
Debussy DTC PLC
Delamare Cards Funding 1 Ltd
Diageo UK Turkey Holdings Ltd
Diageo UK Turkey Limited
Equitix Capital Eurobond 3 Ltd
European Investments Solar Holdings
Fevertree Drinks PLC
GFI EMEA Holdings Limited
Greencoat UK Wind Holdco Ltd
Haut Investments Limited
High Speed Rail Finance (1) PLC
Hydrasun Group Acquisitions Ltd
Hydrasun Group Finance Ltd
Hydrasun Group Holdings Ltd
Interoute Managed Services UK Ltd
Intu (SGS) Finance PLC
Intu (SGS) Finco Limited
Intu (SGS) Holdco Limited
Intu Finance MH Limited
JLIF Investments Limited
Kenon Limited
Kin and Carta Marketing Services Ltd
LS Zig Zag Limited
Legal & General Capital Investments
Liberty Global Europe 2 Ltd
Liberty Global Incorporated Ltd
Liberty Global PLC
MGM Advantage Holdings Limited
Marken Services Limited
Noble Corporation PLC
Onesubsea Investments UK Ltd
Partnership Assurance Group Ltd
Pearson Education Investments Ltd
Pearson Funding Five PLC

Pulford Trading Limited
QHotels Holdings Limited
Sheldon Poland Investments Ltd
Shortline PLC
Standard Chartered I H Limited
Sumisho Osaka Gas Water UK Ltd
UKEI (Finance) Limited
Walworth Investment Properties Ltd
Weybourne Finance Limited
Weybourne Group Limited

April-June 2013 [67]

AON US & International Holdings Ltd
ASOS Intermediate Holdings Ltd
Addison Lee Financing Limited
Addison Lee Group Limited
Addison Lee Holdings Limited
Addison Lee Midco II Limited
Alopuc Limited
Axelos Limited
BL Chess Limited
BLME Holdings PLC
Beacon Rail Finance (Europe) Ltd
Bond Aviation Topco Limited
Bond Mission Critical Services PLC
Brass No.3 PLC
CP Global Trading LLP
CPB Residential Finance Ltd
Canary Wharf Holdings (PB) Ltd
Chambertin (Holdings) Limited
Chambertin Acquisition Limited
Chambertin Finance Limited
Chambertin Midco Limited
Diamond Transmission Corporation Ltd
ELQ Investors VI Ltd
Eclectic Capital Limited
Engelhart CTP Holding (UK) Ltd
Enquest Global Limited
Ensco Deepwater Drilling Ltd
Foresight Solar (UK Holdco) Ltd
Gazeley Blue UK Limited
Gresham Receivables (No.36) UK Ltd
HCA Swiss Capital 1 LLP
Hubbell Holdings Europe Ltd
IBM Global Asset Management Ltd
Korn Ferry GH1 Limited
Korn Ferry Global Holdings (UK) Ltd
Londonmetric Retail Distribution I
Lonrho Holdings Limited
MC GIP-UK Ltd.
Match.Com Foreign Holdings Ltd
Mobius Life Holdings Limited
Nuveen Real Estate Limited
ODH Investments Limited
William Pears Group Investments Ltd
William Pears Group Limited
Pearson PRH Holdings Limited
Polar Capital Global Financials Trust
Poplar HARCA Capital PLC
Renewables Infrastructure Group (UK)
Sam UK Investment Holdings Ltd
Santos (UK) Limited
Shake UK Newco Limited
Stepstone UK Holding Limited
Telereal Secured Finance Holdings
Telereal Secured Finance PLC
Transkey Limited
Transre London Limited
Travelex Financing PLC
Unite (USAF) II PLC
VPI Holding Limited
Valero Energy Ltd
Valero Logistics UK Ltd
Vue International Bidco PLC
Vue International Finco Ltd
Vue International Midco Ltd
WPG Finance Limited
WPG Treasury Limited
Worldline IT Services UK Ltd

July-September 2013 [53]

A2D Funding PLC
Axis Corporate Capital UK Ltd
BL Piccadilly Residential Ltd
Boreas (Investment) Limited
Boreas Holdco Limited
British American Tobacco (NGP) Ltd
CWBC Finance Two (BP1) Limited
Cote Group (Bidco) Limited
Cote Group (Financing) Limited
Cote Restaurants Group Holdings Ltd
DNI Foreign Holdings Limited
Darrowby No. 3 PLC
Device Finance Collections Ltd
Doubleplay I Limited
Doubleplay II Limited
Doubleplay III Limited
Get Living London EV N01 Ltd
Get Living London EV N07 Ltd
Get Living London EV2 Holdco Ltd
Glen Scotia Distillery Co Ltd
Goldman Sachs Group UK Limited
Gower Place Investments Ltd
Hoggant Limited
Intu Metrocentre Finance PLC
Legal & General RE Holdings Ltd
Lionrai Investments No.1 Ltd
Lionrai Investments No.2 Ltd
Loch Lomond Distillers Limited
Loch Lomond Distillery Co Ltd
Loch Lomond Holdings 1 Limited
M7 Real Estate Ltd
Nixes Six PLC
Norwegian Compass Ltd
Norwegian Sextant Ltd
Nuveen FCACO Limited
Oaknorth Bank PLC
One Fleet Realty Ltd
PGI Acquisition Limited
PRA Corporate Capital Limited
PRACCL Limited
Pontegadea UK Ltd
R & F One (UK) Limited
Rothesay Holdco UK Limited
Royal Mail PLC
SSP Euro Holdings Limited
Santander UK Group Holdings PLC
Smart DCC Limited
TES Global Group Limited
TES Global Holdings Direct Ltd
TIAA International Holdings 2 Ltd
TIAA International Holdings 3 Ltd
Telereal 112 Investments Ltd
Thames Quay Properties Limited

October-December 2013 [114]

AMC Networks International Zone Holdings
AMS Bidco Ltd
AMS Holdco Ltd
AMS Midco Ltd
AON Delta UK Limited
Abengoa Concessions Investments Ltd
Aberdeen Sidecar LLP
Alstom Transport UK (Holdings) Ltd
Ascend Overseas Limited
Atlassian (Australia) Limited
Atlassian (UK) Limited
Atlassian Corporation PLC
Auburn Securities 9 PLC
BG Overseas Limited
BNY Mellon Investment Management Seed Capital
Belmond Finance Services Ltd
Brit Limited
Brookfield Global Corporate Investments
Brookfield Global Subinvestments Ltd
C & C Bidco Limited
C & C Topco Limited
CBRE UK Acquisition Co Ltd
CII Holdco Ltd
Cheniere Marketing International LLP
China Merchants Securities (UK) Ltd
Cigna Chestnut Holdings, Ltd
Cityfibre Infrastructure Holdings
Constellation Barclay UK Ltd
Crosby Worldwide Limited
DDB UK Investments Limited
Danone Financing UK Limited
Dollar Financial UK Holding Ltd
Duncan Funding 2015-1 PLC
Elephant and Castle LLP
Elite Gemstones Properties Ltd
Equitix Infrastructure 3 Ltd
Esselco Estates Limited
Esselco Group Limited
Fitch Solutions Group Limited
Fundsmith Emerging Equities Trust PLC
GBG International Holding Co Ltd
GBT Travel Services UK Limited
General Dynamics European Finance
General Dynamics Global Holdings Ltd
Goldman Sachs International Investments
Grosvenor Americas Holdings Ltd
Gwynt y Mor OFTO Holdings Ltd
Gwynt y Mor OFTO PLC
HGPE FRWL Holdco Limited
HIG Finance Limited
HSBC Asia Holdings B.V.
HSBC Latin America B.V.
Halliburton Global Holdings Ltd
Hanover & Oxford Property Ltd
Hayabusa Limited
Holbud Group Limited
ICE Asia Holdings Limited
ICG Carbon Funding Limited
IQVIA Solutions Finance UK I Ltd.
IQVIA Solutions Finance UK II Ltd.
IQVIA Solutions Finance UK V Ltd.
Informa Finance UK Limited
International Entertainment Finance
International Entertainment Holdings
International Entertainment Investments
International Entertainment Midco
LCI Helicopters (UK) Limited
LEH Global Ltd
Liberty Theta Limited
Liberty Zeta Limited
London Wall Outsourcing Freeholds
Low Carbon Contracts Co Ltd
Majority Kingdom Investment Ltd
McKesson Global Procurement & Sourcing
McKesson UK Finance I Limited
McKesson UK Finance II Limited
Mergermarket Bidco Limited
Mergermarket Midco 1 Limited

Mergermarket Midco 2 Limited
Mergermarket Topco Limited
Metinvest Capital UK Limited
Metinvest Investments Limited
Mountain Warehouse International Ltd
Nostrum Oil & Gas PLC
Oak No.1 PLC
Orchard Street UK Prime Property GP
P2P Global Investments PLC
Peabody Capital No 2 PLC
Primount LLP
RL Finance Bonds No. 2 PLC
Revcap Finance Limited
Seadrill Mexico UK Ltd.
Shaftesbury CL Investment Ltd
Stallergenes Greer PLC
Stemcor Holdings 2 Limited
Sunshine Finco Limited
Sunshine Midco Limited
Sunshine Purchaser Limited
Sunshine Topco Limited
TS Real Estate Limited
Thames Quay Properties Holdings Ltd
Thames Quay Properties II Ltd
Thames Quay Properties III Ltd
Tilney Group Limited
Tomahawk Capital Partners I LLP
Tribeca Square LLP
Verbena Investment Limited
Violin Debtco Limited
Violin Equityco Limited
Violin Topco Limited
WPP Finance 2013
WPP Sphinx Limited
Winton Group Limited
Worldpay Group Limited

January-March 2014 [67]

21CF Shine Holdings UK Limited
Akelius UK One Limited
Axis Specialty Finance PLC
BMO Global Asset Management (Europe)
Belmond Dollar Treasury Ltd
Blackmead Infrastructure Ltd
Blue Finco Limited
Cambian Group Holdings Limited
Cambian Group Limited
Carros Sensors Topco Limited
DCC Treasury 2014 Limited
DEKA Energy Associates Limited
DEKA Energy Enterprises Ltd
Earls Court Partnership Ltd
Empiric Student Property PLC
Exova Group Limited
GIP II (Vista) Holdco 1, Ltd
Gamma Communications PLC
Gold Quay Assets Limited
Greenland (United Kingdom) Investment
Greenland Hertsmere (London) Ltd
Greenland Ram (London) Limited
Gulf Marine Services PLC
HHT PLC
Habib Bank Zurich PLC
Hectagon Assets Limited
ICG-Longbow Senior Debt Investments No. 1 LLP
Informa Finance USA Limited
Informa PLC
Integrafin Holdings PLC
LR (City Road) Ltd
John Laing Environmental Assets Group (UK)
London & Birmingham Hotels Ltd
MBC Europe Limited
Malmaison Hotel du Vin Brand Services
Meininger Hotels Limited
Mercury Holding Limited
Mezqual Limited
Moorgate Funding 2014-1 PLC
Newday Partnership Loan Note Issuer Ltd
Nextenergy Solar Holdings Ltd
Nobel Oil E & P (UK) Limited
Orsted Westermost Rough Ltd
PLJ Chelsea Limited
Sextant Consolidated Limited
Shell Pension Reserve Company (UK)
Summit Exploration and Production
Sunshine Holdco Limited
TSB Banking Group PLC
TTL Earls Court Properties Ltd
Tianqi UK Limited
Tombac No.1 PLC
Tyrion Security Topco Limited
UPP (Cartwright Gardens) Holdings
Val TM (Holdings) Limited
Val TM Limited
Valeo Foods UK Limited
Vedanta Finance UK Limited
WFS UK Holding Company III Ltd
WMR JV Holdco Limited
WMR JV Investco Limited
Westermost Rough (Holding) Ltd
Wheel Bidco Limited
Wind UK Invest Limited
Wittington Investments Finance Ltd
Wolfson Foundation
Zeal Network SE

April-June 2014 [84]

Alpha Shipping Finance Limited
Aston Bidco Limited
Australian Gas Networks UK Ltd
Axel Springer International Ltd
BL Bluebutton 2014 Limited
BOC Aviation (UK) Limited
Babcock Aviation Services (Holdings)
Barts Square First Limited
Bein IP Limited
Bestway Securities Limited
Bestway UK Holdco Limited
Brightsphere Investment Group PLC
Brightsphere UK, Ltd.
Brokertec Investments
Burford Capital PLC
CKH Gas Infrastructure Limited
CKI Gas Infrastructure Limited
CLDN UK Limited
Canyon UK Investments Ltd.
Castle Trust Direct PLC
Cavendish Fluor Partnership Ltd
Cigna Walnut Holdings, Ltd.
DLG Acquisitions Limited
EBS Investments
ECOM Agrotrade Holdings Ltd
ELQ Investors VII Ltd
Ediston Property Investment Company PLC
Emperador Holdings (GB) Ltd
Engine Acquisition Limited
Epic (No. 1) Limited
Esterline Technologies Global Ltd
FC Skyfall Bidco Ltd
FC Skyfall Upper Midco Ltd
Fern Renewable Energy Limited
Finco Omaha Ltd
Friary No.2 PLC
HM Treasury UK Sovereign Sukuk PLC
ICAP Global Broking Holdings Ltd
ICAP Global Broking Investments
IP Karugamo Holdings (UK) Ltd
IPGL (Holdings) Limited
IPM Holdings (UK) Limited
Indigo Bidco Limited
Indigo Cleanco Limited
Indigo Intermediate Limited
Indigo Parent Limited
Inn on BW (UK) Limited
Jac Travel Group (Holdings) Ltd
Kellas Holdco Limited
Kellas Midstream Limited
Kellas Topco Limited
Michael Kors (UK) Holdings Ltd
LSEG Business Services Limited
Ly Holding Limited
Masdar Offshore Wind UK Ltd
Mercer Africa Limited
Motor Oil Finance PLC
NEX Markets Limited
NEX Optimisation Limited
Nadezhda Limited
Newday Partnership Funding 2015-1 PLC
Nobel Oil Services (UK) Ltd
PAH Gas Infrastructure Limited
Pangaea Funding 1 PLC
Priory Group UK 1 Limited
Priory Group UK 2 Limited
Shams Maan Solar UK Limited
Spire Healthcare Finance Ltd
Spire Healthcare Group PLC
Starbucks EMEA Ltd
Sterling UK Holdco Limited
TES Finance Limited
TI European Holdings Limited
Throgmorton Assets PLC
Thrones 2014-1 PLC
Tyrion Security Bidco Limited
Tyrion Security Midco Limited
Universal Studios Limited
Urban & Civic Alconbury Ltd
VAM Bidco Limited
Wedco EMEA Ventures Limited
Westfield Stratford City Finance PLC
YOA Holdco Limited
ZPG Limited

July-September 2014 [71]

A2D Funding II PLC
AON Global Holdings Limited
Aberdeen Infrastructure II Ltd
Advantage Sales & Marketing Ltd
Aggregator Vehicle PLC
Aspen European Holdings Ltd
Australian Gas Networks UK 2 Ltd
Azzurri Group Limited
Azzurri Midco 1 Limited
Brass No.4 PLC
Casper UK Bidco Limited
Casual Dining Group Limited
Chiquita Holdings Limited
Jimmy Choo (Holdings) Limited
Jimmy Choo Group Limited
Collinson Finance Limited
DLG Financing 1 Limited
DLG Financing 2 Limited
DTZ UK Bidco Limited
DTZ UK Guarantor Limited
DTZ UK Holdco Limited

Dunwilco (1847) Limited
EDF Energy Lake Limited
ELQ Investors VIII Ltd
Element Materials Technology Group Holdings CC1
Element Materials Technology Group Holdings CC2
Element Materials Technology Group Holdings
Empiric Investments (One) Ltd
Farmcare Trading Limited
Forum Worldwide Holdings Ltd
General Alumina Holdings Ltd
Gosforth Funding 2014-1 PLC
Gosforth Holdings 2014-1 Ltd
Guildford No.1 PLC
Huawei Global Finance (UK) Ltd
International Game Technology PLC
JC Overseas Ltd
KMC Stirling Square Limited
Lightsource Radiate 2 Limited
Lingfield 2014 I PLC
Lion-Shoes Midco Limited
MAN UK Strategies Limited
MATW UK Holding LLP
MC Ocean Holdings Limited
Mastercard Europe Services Ltd
Melton Renewable Energy UK Ltd
Northstar Holding Limited
Northstar Investments Limited
Northstar Midco Limited
Oikia (UK) Limited
Pace Bidco Limited
Pace Topco Limited
Pall Mall 3 Limited
Primetals Technologies, Ltd
Punch Taverns Holdco (A) Ltd
Punch Taverns Intermediate Holdco (A)
RW Wentworth UK Limited
Rontec Roadside Retail Limited
SREP Holdings Ltd
SYND Holdco Limited
Salic (UK) Limited
Slate No.1 PLC
Slate No.2 PLC
Smith & Nephew ARTC Limited
Starbucks EMEA Holdings Ltd
Starbucks International (Holdings) Ltd
Structadene (LBG) Holdings Ltd
Structadene (LBG) Properties Ltd
Temese Funding 2 PLC
Thistle Investments (ERM) Ltd
Warwick Finance Residential Mortgages Number One

October-December 2014 [86]

AI Perform Holdings LLP
Arca Bidco Limited
Arca Holdco Limited
Arca Midco Limited
Arca Topco Limited
Azzurri Trading Limited
BG Netherlands Financing Unlimited
Babcock DSG Ltd
Baltic Sea Offshore Holdco Ltd
Bioenergy Infrastructure Ltd
Bridges Business Space LLP
CDW Finance Bidco Limited
CGN Europe Energy UK Holding Ltd
CLS Spring Gardens Limited
CRF Health Group Limited
Caledonian Rail Leasing Ltd
Cardinia Europe Limited
Carolia Tower Hotel Limited
Carolia Westminster Hotel Ltd
Cubico Sustainable Investments Holdings
Cubico Sustainable Investments Ltd
DHE Regional Limited
DTZ UK Bidco 2 Limited
Derwent London Angel Square Ltd
Derwent London Farringdon Ltd
Diamond Bidco Limited
Diamond Midco Limited
Diamond Topco Limited
Dress Holdco 4 Limited
Due West Investments Limited
ELQ Investors IX Ltd
Endeavour Acquisition UK Ltd
FPI (UK) 1 Limited
Gabelli Value Plus + Trust PLC
Great Ormond Street Hospital Children's Charity
Guy's and St Thomas' Charity
Hyperion Development UK Ltd
Informa US Holdings Limited
Ixellion Technologies Ltd
Kensington & Global Limited
Keybridge House LLP
Michael Kors (UK) Intermediate Ltd.
L & Q PRS Co Limited
LGPL Cornwall Limited
London Wall Capital Investments LLP
London Wall Investment Warehouse 01
Miracle Nova (UK) Limited
Mirion Technologies (Global), Ltd.
Mirion Technologies (HoldingRep), Ltd.
Mirion Technologies (HoldingSub1), Ltd.
Mirion Technologies (HoldingSub2), Ltd.
Motor 2015-1 PLC
Nintex Global Limited
Omega Leasing (No.10) Limited
Omnicom DDB Holdings Limited
Omnicom Network Holdings Ltd
PSPA Holdco Limited
PSPA Midco Limited
PSPA Topco Limited
Puente Holding Limited
Quest Diagnostics Holdings Ltd.
RI Income UK Holdings Limited
Retail Centres V (Sweden) Investment
River Island Holdings Limited
SCP Acquisition Bidco Limited
SCP Acquisition Topco Limited
State Grid Europe Development (2014) PLC
Superior Holdings Limited
TBWA EMEA Limited
Telereal (London Wall) Limited
Third Point RE (UK) Holdings Ltd
Tritax REIT Acquisition 16 Ltd
UK Green Investment Sheringham Shoal
Upfield Spreads UK Limited
VUR Holdings (UK) Limited
VUR Investment (UK) Limited
VUR Mezzanine I (UK) Limited
VUR Mezzanine II (UK) Limited
WBA Financial Limited
WBA Financial Services Limited
WBA UK Finance Limited
WBAD Holdings Limited
WIC (UK) Ltd
Westminster Topco Limited
Wework International Limited
Wisdom Profit (UK) Development Ltd

January 2015 [29]

Airbnb Payments UK Limited
BTGP-BSI Limited
Beaubien Finance Limited
Chemchina UK Limited
Dellmes GR Limited
Dress Holdco A Limited
Dress Holdco C Limited
European Legacy Holdings Ltd
Golden Charter Trust Limited
Kingfisher Holdings Limited
Liberty Global Broadband I Ltd
Liberty Living Investments Ltd
Lochside Asset Purchaser No.1 PLC
Marsh & McLennan Companies Acquisition
Miller 2015 Limited
Newday Funding 2015-1 PLC
Newday Funding Loan Note Issuer Ltd
Residential Mortgage Securities 28 PLC
Shaftesbury AV Investment Ltd
Shaftesbury AV Limited
Sureserve Group PLC
TFG Brands (London) Limited
VPC Specialty Lending Investments PLC
Victoria Investments Bidco Ltd
Victoria Investments Finco Ltd
Victoria Investments Midco Ltd
Wagamama Finance PLC
XTX Markets Limited
Zegona Communications PLC

February 2015 [29]

AAA UK Acquisition Co. Limited
AAA UK Holding Co. Limited
Aggregator of Loans Backed By Assets 2015-1
Amber Infrastructure Group Holdings
Big Bus Tours Group Holdings Ltd
Big Bus Tours Group Limited
Big Bus Tours Holdings 1 Ltd
Big Bus Tours Holdings 2 Ltd
Boeing European Holdings Ltd
Campaign Monitor Holdings (UK) Ltd
Corbiere Asset Investments Ltd
Cortina Race LLP
GWI UK Acquisition Co Ltd
GWI UK Holding Limited
HICP Holdings Limited
Hunt Amber London 1 Ltd
Hunt Amber London 2 Ltd
Livanova PLC
Macquarie Aerospace Finance UK Ltd
Macquarie Aerospace Holdings UK Ltd
Nexteer UK Holding Ltd.
Omnicom EMEA Holdings Limited
Patina Rail LLP
Ramchez GR Limited
SCDM Energy Limited
Socar Trading (UK) Limited
Trenport Property Holdings Ltd
Vertus NFL Limited
Victoria Investments Intermediate Holdco

March 2015 [37]

Accord Bidco Limited
Accord Topco Limited
Anchorage Ports LLP
Arcus Tivana Investor Vehicle 1 LLP
Arcus Tivana Investor Vehicle 2 LLP
Benton Finance Limited
CDCH Limited

CFL Auto Receivables Limited
CLH Pipeline System (CLH-PS) Ltd
Campaign Monitor (UK) Limited
Cerro Dominador UK, LLP
Closerstill Acquisitions Ltd
Closerstill Finance Limited
Closerstill Media Holdings Ltd
Discovery Finance Company Europe Ltd
Elios Energy Holdings Limited
Gosforth Funding 2015-1 PLC
Gosforth Holdings 2015-1 Ltd
Gresham Receivables (No.37) UK Ltd
Gresham Receivables (No.38) UK Ltd
Hathber GR Limited
Hubbell (UK) Gulfmex Limited
Lightsource BP Renewable Energy Investments
Newday Funding 2015-2 PLC
Noble Holding UK Limited
P & P Spearhead UK Holdings, Ltd
Petra Diamonds UK Treasury Ltd
Petra Diamonds US$ Treasury PLC
RDL Realisation PLC
RELX Overseas Holdings Limited
RMC Estates Co. LLP
Renbuff Investments Limited
Stage Shoreditch LLP
Synlab BondCo PLC
V Acquisition Limited
Victoria Asset Finance Limited
WBA Finance 1 Limited

April 2015 [30]

AEW UK REIT PLC
Bazalgette Equity Limited
Bazalgette Holdings Limited
Bazalgette Tunnel Limited
Bazalgette Ventures Limited
Blackrock UK A LLP
CD & R Firefly 2 Limited
CD & R Firefly 4 Limited
CD & R Firefly Holdco Limited
Digital River UK Holdings I Ltd
Digital River UK Holdings II Ltd
Elegant Hotels Group PLC
Empiric Investments (Four) Ltd
IO Investment 2 LLP
IO2 Propco LLP
Leadiant Biosciences Limited
Liberty Global Finance I (UK) Ltd
OHI UK Healthcare Properties Ltd
Quest Diagnostics Subsidiary Holdings Ltd.
Renewables Infrastructure Group (UK) Investments
SPX European Holding Limited
Softbank Group Capital Limited
Stage Shoreditch Residential Ltd
Stanlow Receivables Funding Ltd
State Street International Holdings UK
Take-Two Interactive Software UK Ltd
TransDigm UK Holdings PLC
Upfield Foods UK Limited
VIL Ltd
Warwick Finance Residential Mortgages Number Two

May 2015 [23]

Atos International IT Holdings Ltd
Atos UK Holdings Limited
Beta Centauri Limited
Betelgeuse Limited
Cars Alliance UK 2015 Limited
Castle Trust Finance Limited
E & A Property Investment Co Ltd
Foundry Bidco No.2 Limited
Foundry Holdco Limited
Foundry Midco 3 Limited
Foundry Topco No.2 Limited
Glyn Hopkin Holdings Limited
Ipek Investment Limited
Just Eat (Acquisitions) Holding Ltd
Just Eat Central Holdings Ltd
L-3 Global Holding UK Ltd
L-3 Technology & Services UK Ltd
Liberty Living Investments II Holdco 2
Mishcon de Reya LLP
Precise Mortgage Funding 2015-2B PLC
Principal Global Financial Services (Europe) II
Puretech Health PLC
Verisk UK Holdco Limited

June 2015 [33]

BBPF LLP
Babcock IP Management (Number Two)
CB-SDG Holdco Limited
CB-SDG Limited
CB-SDG Midco Limited
CB-SDG Topco Limited
CWG Newco Limited
Caledonia Thames Acquisitions Ltd
Caledonia Thames Group Limited
Caledonia Thames Holdings Ltd
Conning Holdings Limited
Daisy 2015 Holdco Limited
Daisy 2015 Topco Limited
ERM Emilion Limited
ERM Worldwide Group Limited
Frasers Hospitality UK Holdings Ltd
GCP (UK) Holdings Limited
GH Holdings 1 Limited
GH Holdings 2 Limited
GWW UK Holdings Ltd
Gardaworld Consulting (UK) Ltd
Lakeside Asset Backed Securitisation 1
Mercury UK Holdco Limited
RL Finance Bonds No. 3 PLC
SB Energy Holdings Limited
Synlab Holdco Limited
Synlab Limited
Synlab Unsecured BondCo PLC
Taste Bidco Limited
Taste Midco 2 Limited
URBN Holdings UK Limited
URBN International Operations Ltd
Viners Energy Limited

July 2015 [32]

Albion No.3 PLC
Anasuria Hibiscus UK Limited
Anthology Group Limited
BTG Pactual UK Holdco Limited
CDW International Holdings Ltd
Chime Finance Limited
Chime Group Holdings Limited
Concierge Holding Co Ltd
Cubico Holdings (UK) 2 Limited
Dukinfield PLC
E-Carat 6 PLC
Great Lakes Reinsurance (UK) SE
INEOS Offshore BCS Limited
LDC (Care Homes) Finco Limited
Liberty Living Investments II Ltd
Nimbus Acquisitions Holdings Ltd
Nimbus Acquisitions Midco 1 Ltd
Nimbus Acquisitions Midco Ltd
Ping Petroleum UK Limited
RG Engagement Group 5 Limited
RG Engagement Group Limited
Schroder Financial Holdings Ltd
Schroder Wealth Holdings Ltd
Selligent Holdings Limited
Suzaku Aviation One Limited
Syco Holdings Limited
Thrones 2015-1 PLC
Towd Point Mortgage Funding 2016 - Auburn 10
Truworths UK Holdco 1 Limited
UK Green Investment Gwynt y Mor Ltd
WBA Finance 2 Limited
West-Ward Holdings Limited

August 2015 [26]

Acquisition Company Finance Ltd
Beaubien UK Finance Limited
Bombardier UK Holding Limited
Brass No.5 PLC
CBRE Acquisition Company 2 Ltd
CBRE Acquisition Company 3 Ltd
DCC Energy Finance UK Limited
DTZ UK Newco Limited
Eucalyptus Energy Holdings Ltd
Eucalyptus Energy Limited
Fidelis Underwriting Limited
Genting Americas Holdings Ltd
Georgia Healthcare Group PLC
Gresham Receivables (No.39) UK Ltd
Interoute Finco Limited
Lightsource Pumbaa Limited
Lightsource Simba Limited
Lightsource Timon Limited
Mortar No.1 Limited
Pension Insurance Corporation Group
Petroceltic Holdings Limited
SIR Healthcare 2 Limited
SIR Umbrella Limited
Saturn UK Holdco Limited
Truworths UK Holdco 2 Limited
Voice Topco Limited

September 2015 [36]

Chime Group Limited
Chime Holdco Limited
Chime Midco Limited
Circle Anglia Social Housing 2 PLC
Cityfibre Limited
Concord Resources Limited
Darrowby No. 4 PLC
Discovery Lightning Investments Ltd
Enbridge Rampion UK Ltd
Enbridge UK Holdings Ltd
FC Skyfall TA Limited
FS JV Co Limited
FS Senior Co Limited
Garden Finance Limited
Garden Midco 1 Limited
Garden Midco 2 Limited
Hanover House Limited
IPC Information Systems UK Ltd
IPM Peacock Limited
Internetq Group Limited
Livn UK Holdco Limited
London Kensington Hotel Ltd

MMC Treasury Holdings (UK) Ltd
MacTaggart Heritable Limited
Omega Leasing (No.11) Limited
PA Consulting Group Limited
PA Consulting Management Services
Precise Mortgage Funding 2015-3R PLC
Snap Group Limited
TS Structured Finance Limited
Turbo Finance 6 PLC
UK Renewable Holdco 1 Limited
UK Renewable Holdco 2 Limited
UK Renewable Holdco 3 Limited
Unisys Europe Limited
Virtus IMH 2 Limited

October 2015 [35]

Acquisition Fine Art
Apple Bidco Limited
Barbados Enterprises PLC
Cleveland Clinic UK Holdings Ltd
Concordia Investment Holdings (UK)
Emerald Acquisition Limited
Equitix Capital Eurobond 4 Ltd
Equitix Infrastructure 4 Ltd
Fence Bidco Limited
Fence Topco Limited
Flavia Holdco Limited
Friary No.3 PLC
Great Beer Co Ltd
Gresham Receivables (No.40) UK Ltd
Horizon Bidco Limited
Horizon Debtco Limited
Horizon Groupco Limited
Horizon Holdco Limited
Horizon Midco Limited
Hostelworld Group PLC
International Schools Partnership
LYB Treasury Services Ltd.
MMC Holdings (UK) Limited
Mitsubishi Hitachi Power Systems Europe, Ltd.
Newday Funding 2016-1 PLC
Retirement Bridge Investments Ltd
Tolmar Holding Limited
Tombac No.2 PLC
Total E & P International K2 Ltd.
Total E & P International K3 Ltd.
Total E & P International Ltd.
Trinity Square 2015-1 PLC
Vertice Pharma UK Parent Ltd
Willis GS UK Holdings Limited
Willis GS UK Limited

November 2015 [27]

Almack Ltd
Bombardier Transportation (Global Holding) UK
Bombardier Transportation (Investment) UK
Dan Regents Place Finance Ltd
FFP Investment UK Ltd
Gosforth Funding 2016-1 PLC
International Nuclear Investment Ltd
James River Group Holdings UK Ltd
LGH Hotels Management Limited
Labcorp UK Holdings, Ltd.
Lightsource Pumpkin 4 Limited
Maref Topco Ltd
Marfrig Beef (UK) Limited
Marfrig Beef International Ltd
Mercury Acquisitions Limited
Montserrat Acquisitions Ltd
Queensgate Bow Opco Limited
Queensgate Bow UK Midco Ltd
Queensgate Bow UK Parent Ltd
Queensgate Bow UK Topco Ltd
Ribbon Bidco Limited
Ribbon Holdco Limited
Ribbon Mezzco Limited
Ribbon Midco Limited
Sensis Holding Limited
Truworths UK Holdco 3 Limited
Versum Materials UK Limited

December 2015 [39]

Axiata Investments (UK) Ltd
British American Tobacco Global Travel Retail
Cable & Wireless Communications Ltd
Cathexis UK Holdings Limited
Ceridian Global UK Holding Co Ltd
Covent Garden Group Holdings Ltd
D & P International Holdings (UK)
Dreof II Europe Holdings Ltd
EMT 2 Holdings Limited
EMT Holdings Limited
Element Materials Technology Group
Element Materials Technology Ltd
Endowment Investment Holdings Ltd
Global Reach Group Ltd
Griffon Funding Limited
Honeycomb Investment Trust PLC
ITW UK Finance Limited
JLIF Holdings (Barcelona Metro) Ltd
Le Creuset Holding Limited
Leggett & Platt UK Holdings LLP
Libra International Limited
Livn UK 2 Co Limited
Livn UK 3 Co Limited
Mercury Midco 1 Limited
Mercury Midco 2 Limited
Omnicom Finance Brazil Limited
Omnicom Latam Holdings Limited
Palace Holdco UK Limited
Palace Midco UK Limited
Places for People Ventures Ltd
Privilege Holdings Limited
Rochester Financing No.2 PLC
Sagittarius International Ltd
Silchester Capital Limited
Sojitz Global Finance PLC
Whitewell UK Investments 1 Ltd
Wyelands Holdings Limited
Zero Bypass Limited
Zeuss Childcare Limited

January 2016 [34]

AHK International LLP
AIG Holdings Europe Limited
Allianz Renewable Energy Partners VI
Allianz Renewable Energy Partners VIII
Ascential Financing Limited
Ascential PLC
Ascential Prefco Limited
Ash8 Group Holdings Limited
Ash8 Group Limited
BCI UK Holdings Limited
BGL Receivables Financing (1) Ltd
Brookfield BBP UK Holdings II Ltd
Brookfield BBP UK Holdings III Ltd
Docomo Digital Limited
FS Holdco Limited
HNVR Midco Limited
Homebase (UK & I) Holdings Ltd
Infrastructure Investments (A63) Holdings
Kinapse Bidco Limited
Kinapse Holdco Limited
Kinapse Midco Limited
Kinapse Topco Limited
Lancer Square Limited
Motorola Solutions UK Acquisition Co Ltd
Multiplex Global Limited
NEX Services Limited
Titanium UK Holdco 1 Limited
UIG Holdings (No 4) Ltd
UK Green Investment Lid Ltd
UK Group Finance Holdco Ltd
US Real Estate Holdings No.1 Ltd
Victoria Investments PIKco Ltd
WIG Holdings I Limited
WIG Holdings II Limited

February 2016 [33]

6-10 Cambridge Terrace Developments LLP
Avara Pharma Services Ltd
BMI Group Holdings UK Limited
Burbo Extension Holding Ltd
CMC Markets Holdings Limited
Control Risks Capital Limited
Digital London Limited
Dudgeon Holdings Ltd
Engelhart CTP Group (UK) Ltd
FDL Holdings Limited
Finsbury Square 2016-1 PLC
JLEAG Wind Holding Limited
JLEAG Wind Limited
Kirkbi Burbo Extension Holding (UK)
Lazari Finance Limited
Lazari Properties 1 Limited
Lazari Properties 2 Limited
Lazari Properties 3 Limited
Lazari Properties 5 Limited
London Wall Mortgage Capital PLC
MV Werften Holdings Limited
Malt Hill No.1 PLC
E D & F Man Capital Markets Treasury Management
Marks and Spencer (Bradford) Ltd
Molineux RMBS 2016-1 PLC
Offa No.1 PLC
Orsted Burbo Extension Holding Ltd
PKA Burbo Extension Holding (UK) Ltd
PSPA Finance Limited
Primetals Technologies Financial Services
Redrock Investment Limited
Solarwinds MSP Holdings Ltd
Towd Point Mortgage Funding 2016-Granite1

March 2016 [28]

Assembled Productions III UK Ltd
BPG Global Holdings UK Limited
Biocon Biologics Limited
Calypso Group UK Limited
Canary Finco Limited
Canary Holdco Limited
Colliers International EMEA Holdings
Constitution Bidco 2 Limited
Duncan Funding 2016-1 PLC
East Village London LLP
Ferrari Group Limited
GLIL Corporate Holdings Ltd
Gosforth Funding 2016-2 PLC
Gosforth Holdings 2016-2 Ltd
Hawk Newco Limited

Humber Gateway OFTO Holdings Ltd
Humber Gateway OFTO Limited
ISG PLC
Landesk Holdco UK Ltd
Marubeni Copper Holdings Ltd
Nextpower Radius Limited
C J O'Shea Group Limited
Onefinestay (Holdings) Limited
Regent's Place Holding Co Ltd
Securitisation of Consumer Agreements
WP R Holdco Limited
WP R Midco 1 Limited
WP R Midco 2 Limited

April 2016 [17]

Aviva Investors Realm Infrastructure No.5
Burford Investments Limited
Donnelley Financial Solutions Holdings UK
Envol Investments Limited
Envol Midco Limited
Fleet Bidco Limited
Fleet Midco Limited
Globaldrive Auto Receivables UK 2016-A
Grosvenor Europe Investments Ltd
Luxtail Limited
News Corp Investments II Ltd
Oncilla Mortgage Funding 2016-1 PLC
Perpetual Power (UK) Limited
Sainsbury's Intermediate Holdings
Stradawood Limited
Tottenham Hotspur Stadium Development
Tottenham Hotspur Stadium Ltd

May 2016 [23]

Calypso FX EUR Limited
Calypso FX USD Limited
Clarusone Sourcing Services LLP
Deltatre Group Limited
Deltatre Holdings Limited
Dukinfield II PLC
EGX Credit Liquidity Ltd
Feldspar 2016-1 PLC
Fleet Finco Limited
Fleet Midco I Limited
Fleet Midco II Limited
LIH Financing Limited
Livanova IP Limited
Mavenir Private Holdings I Ltd
Mavenir Private Holdings II Ltd
Project Lake Holdings Limited
Sarti Holdings (UK) Limited
Tesnik Holdings Limited
Titan Acquisition Holdco Ltd
Titan Acquisition Limited
Titan Financing Holdco Limited
Titan Financing Limited
Zero Bypass (Holdings) Limited

June 2016 [27]

Bedford Estates Bloomsbury Ltd
Blackrock UK (Alpha) Limited
Bumper 8 (UK) Finance PLC
Bupa Care Homes (Holdings) Ltd
CX Holdco Limited
Chiquita Finance Co Ltd
Danataugusta Propco1 Limited
Danataugusta Propco3 Limited
Dobbies Garden Centres Group Ltd
EFT Investments SE
Ecofin Global Utilities and Infrastructure Trust
G.I. Globinvestment Limited
GAM Systematic Holding Limited
HNVR Holdco Limited
HNVR Topco Limited
Hawksmoor Mortgages 2016-1 PLC
Iridium Midco Limited
Keller Investments LLP
Launcelot Investments (UK) Ltd
Martin's Family Holdings Ltd
Mastercard UK Holdco Limited
Newriver REIT PLC
Odeon Cinemas Group Limited
Pinsent Masons International LLP
SIR Hotels 1 Limited
TRU Taj Holdings 2 Limited
Woodside Energy Holdings (Senegal)

July 2016 [31]

111 Group Holdings Limited
Belmont Green Funding 1 Ltd
Belmont Green Funding 3 Ltd
Camelot UK Bidco Limited
Cascade Regional Holdings Ltd
Cranefield Limited
Daytona Midco 1 Limited
Dragonglass UK Holding Limited
EDF Energy Services Limited
Fiat Chrysler UK LLP
GM Global Treasury Centre Ltd
Gresham Receivables (No.45) UK Ltd
Gresham Receivables (No.46) UK Ltd
Koch Fertilizer International Ltd
Lazari Properties 7 Limited
MCD Investments Limited
MMC Middle East Holdings Ltd
Monaco Bidco Limited
Monaco Topco Limited
NH2 Limited
Orsted Race Bank (Holding) Ltd
Outsourcing UK Limited
PCL Asset Trustee Limited
PIL Investments LLP
PKA Teesrep Holding (UK) Ltd
Picture Holdco Limited
Race Bank Wind Farm (Holding) Ltd
Snacks International Development UK
UPP (Duncan House) Holdings Ltd
UPP (Duncan House) Limited
Union Lifestyle Holdings Ltd

August 2016 [15]

CBI UK Cayman Acquisition Ltd
CF Sparks Limited
Camelot UK Holdco Limited
Camelot UK Top Holdco Limited
Castile Acquisitions Ltd
Donnelley Financial Solutions Group UK
Ensono Opco Holdings Limited
Liberty GR Acquisition Co Ltd
Liberty GR Holding Co Ltd
MCD Global Franchising Limited
McKesson UK Finance IV Limited
New Topco Limited
Nexa Resources UK Limited
Olekit Investments Ltd
Sirius GR Limited

September 2016 [23]

Ardmore Group Limited
Ascot Underwriting Group Ltd
BL CW Holdings Limited
Big Box Midco UK Limited
Compart Systems Limited
Crops Holdings (UK) Limited
E-Carat 7 PLC
Equitix Orbital Holdings Ltd
Greencoat Solar Assets I Ltd
Hawksmoor Mortgages 2016-2 PLC
Hines Europe Limited
Hodson Holdings (Ashford) Ltd
ICAP Global Broking Finance Ltd
Inspired Education Holdings Ltd
Point Dume Holdings Limited
Qatar Airways Investments (UK) Ltd
Rock Rail East Anglia PLC
Ropemaker RB Holdings Limited
Symphony Bidco Limited
TKG-Storagemart Partners UK Ltd
Turbo Finance 7 PLC
VM Receivables Financing PLC
Willis Towers Watson UK Holdings Ltd

October 2016 [21]

Arches Holdings Limited
BL Ealing Limited
Bond Propco Limited
Castle Trust Treasury Limited
Consolidated Holdings Limited
Cushman & Wakefield UK USD Holdco
East Slope Residencies PLC
Hector Rail Holding UK Limited
Infrastructure Investments (Colorado)
Legal & General Homes Communities
Newday UK Limited
PTT International Trading London Ltd
Q Holdco Limited
Q Intermediate Holdco Limited
Smiths Group Finance EU Ltd
Smiths Group Finance US Ltd
TechnipFMC Holdings Limited
Thistle Investments (AMC) Ltd
Towd Point Mortgage Funding 2016-Granite2
Towd Point Mortgage Funding 2016-Granite3
XXIII Capital A Limited

November 2016 [53]

AI Mistral Holdco Limited
AI Mistral Limited
AI Mistral Parentco Limited
AI Mistral Topco Limited
Allied SX Ltd
Arcus A1 Investor Vehicle LLP
Aztech Advantage Ltd
BCP IV UK Fuel Holdings II Ltd
BCP IV UK Fuel Holdings IV Ltd
BCP IV UK Fuel Holdings V Ltd
BIG Legolas Holdings Limited
BIH Holdings Limited
BL HB Investments Limited
BL Retail Investments Limited
Bombardier Aerospace (Holdings) UK
Bounty Brands Holdings Limited
Broad Street Principal Investments UK
CGN Europe Energy Green Power Holding
CMI Canada Financing Ltd
Cboe Worldwide Holdings Ltd
Cone Investments UK Limited
Cubico Holdings (UK) 4 Limited
ELQ Omega UK Ltd
East Slope Residencies Student
Accommodation LLP
GS Funding Europe III Ltd
Galloper Holdco Limited

Hellen Holdings Limited
Hurricane Bidco Limited
Hurricane Cleanco Limited
Hurricane Noteco Limited
IPP Gas Holdings Limited
ITV Enterprises Limited
ITW UK Finance Beta Limited
Impact Healthcare REIT PLC
Lions Gate International Media Ltd
Newday BondCo PLC
OSW Co Holdings 1 Limited
OSW Co Holdings 2 Limited
OSW LP Holdco Limited
Omnicom Europe Subholdings Ltd
Ophir Holdings & Ventures Ltd
PSP Britannia Ltd
Quadgas Investments Bidco Ltd
SB Investment Advisers (UK) Ltd
Snap International I Limited
Snap International II Limited
Student Finance PLC
Towd Point Mortgage Funding 2016-Vantage1
Unlimited Marketing Group Ltd
Visa International Holdings Ltd
WEX Europe UK Limited
WMR Holdco Limited
WR Midco Limited

December 2016 [40]

Accor Hotelinvest UK Limited
Accor Hotelservices UK Limited
Burford Global Investments Ltd
Chrysaor E & P Finance Limited
Equitix MA 2 Capital Eurobond Ltd
FS Debtco Limited
FS Holdco 2 Limited
Finsbury Square 2017-1 PLC
GS Funding Europe V Limited
Genting Worldwide Services Ltd
Global Fashion Group Middle East Holdings (UK)
Global Fashion Group UK Finance Ltd
HCUK Auto Funding 2017-1 Ltd
ITW UK Finance Gamma Limited
LSEG (M) Financing Limited
LXI REIT PLC
Lion/Jenga Midco Limited
Marfrig NBM Holdings Limited
New Green Interim Holdco Ltd
Noble Holding Land Support Ltd
Omnicom EMEA Investments Ltd
Pyrenees Acquisitions Limited
QHG Holding LLP
QHG Investment LLP
QHG Trading LLP
Rampion Investco Limited
Residential Mortgage Securities 29 PLC
SSC Holdco (UK) Limited
SSC Intermediateco Limited
Shenda Investment UK Limited
Sixmoor Limited
Springer Nature One Limited
Springer Nature Two Limited
Sterling Midco Limited
Towd Point Mortgage Funding 2017 - Auburn 11
Trebuchet Investments (UK) Ltd
Tronox Sands UK Holdings Ltd
Tronox UK Holdings Limited
UK Green Investment Lyle Ltd
Vine Acquisitions Limited

January 2017 [21]

80 Charlotte Street Limited
CK William Midco 2 Limited
CK William Midco 3 Limited
CNH Industrial UK Limited
Cloudreach Acquisitions Ltd
Consolidated Developments Holdings
Enquest NNS Limited
Harding Midco Limited
Kiwara UK Limited
Legal & General Homes Communities (Crowthorne)
Patriot Topco Limited
Promontoria Gyle 2 Ltd
Promontoria Gyle Holding Ltd
Promontoria Gyle Holdings (2) Ltd
Recruit Global Treasury Services AUD Ltd
Recruit Global Treasury Services Ltd
Sky Holdco Limited
Stanlington No. 1 PLC
Tyman Financial Services Ltd
UPP (Hull) Holdings Limited
UPP (Hull) Limited

February 2017 [23]

Auria Solutions UK I Ltd.
E-Carat 8 PLC
Elios Energy Holdings 3 Ltd
European Fintyre Distribution Ltd
Fitzroy Property Limited
Global Ports Holding PLC
Henderson Diversified Income Trust PLC
Income Contingent Student Loans 1 (2002-2006)
Kili Topco Limited
Macquarie Infrastructure and Real Assets Core
Mavenir Private Finance Ltd
Orosi (UK) 2 Limited
PHP SB Limited
Phoenix Natural Gas PP Finance PLC
Promontoria Gyle Top Holding Ltd
Renewable Energy Income Partnership Holdings 1
SB Energy Three Holdings Ltd
SVF Holdings (UK) LLP
Sirius International UK Holdings Ltd
Sojitz Energy Development Ltd
Surgical Specialties Corporation Ltd
Vauxhall Square (Nominee 1) Ltd
Ventient Energy Limited

March 2017 [37]

APG (KE) Ltd.
BCP IV UK Fuel Holdings III Ltd
BGF Group PLC
Bridge Petroleum 3 Limited
Bridge Petroleum 4 Limited
CFC Group Limited
Connect Bidco Limited
Connect Midco Limited
Constantin Investment Limited
Cory Riverside Energy Finance Ltd
Cory Riverside Energy Holdings Ltd
European Financial Services Ltd
Frontier Finance PLC
Globaldrive Auto Receivables UK 2017 -A
Greenrock Bidco Limited
Greenrock Topco Limited
Harben Finance 2017-1 PLC
Infopro Digital Holding (UK) Ltd

LHC4 (UK) Limited
LXI Property Holdings 1 Ltd
LXI Property Holdings 2 Ltd
Leopard UK Kensington Propco Ltd
Neo (BC) UK Limited
Polyus Finance PLC
Precise Mortgage Funding 2017-1B PLC
Project Quill Holding Limited
Renewable Energy Income Partnership Holdings 2
Renewable Energy Income Partnership Holdings
Ripon Mortgages PLC
Sach 1 Ltd
Sach 2 Ltd
Tallwood Investments Ltd
Tronox UK Limited
WPP Fitzroy Square
WPP UK Germany Holdings
WTI Ferrybridge Limited
Westminster Acquisition Ltd

April 2017 [20]

Aberforth Split Level Income Trust PLC
Ardonagh Midco 3 PLC
Carestream Dental Technology Holdings 1
Carestream Dental Technology Holdings 2
Castell 2017-1 PLC
DIF Tamblin Limited
European Wind Investments Group Ltd
Friary No.4 PLC
Greif UK International Holding Ltd
Icebox Bidco Limited
Infrastructure Investments (Affinity)
Jupiter Emerging & Frontier Income Trust
Newday Funding 2017-1 PLC
Oat Hill No.1 PLC
Optimum Three Limited
Project Leopard Acquireco Ltd
Project Leopard Intermediateco Ltd
Project Leopard Topco Limited
SVF Investments (UK) Limited
Schroder Private Assets Holdings Ltd

May 2017 [31]

121222 Holdco Limited
121333 Limited
A-Gas Bidco Limited
A-Gas Group Limited
Aldea UK Holdco Limited
Annington Funding PLC
Barchester Finco 2017 UK Ltd
Black Star Holdings Limited
Building Energy Ltd
Dauphine Holdings (UK) Limited
Derwent London Oliver's Yard Ltd
Energean Oil & Gas PLC
Eversholt UK Rails (Holding) Ltd
Eversholt UK Rails Limited
FFI Holdings PLC
General Dynamics Swiss Financial Management
Greencoat Solar Assets II Ltd
IEP Infrastructure Holdco Ltd
Irobot UK Ltd.
Liquid Telecommunications Financing PLC
Liquid Telecommunications Investments
Office Group Holdings Limited
Omega Leasing (No. 12) Limited
Premier Oil Group Holdings Ltd
Residential Mortgage Securities 30 PLC

Rock Rail South Western (Holdings) 2
Rock Rail South Western PLC
Tiso Blackstar Holdings SE
Together Asset Backed Securitisation 1
Triplog Holdings Limited
WPP UK Torre

June 2017 [33]

Accorinvest UK BCT Limited
Agincourt (1) LLP
Aston Lark (Bidco) Limited
Aston Lark (Topco) Limited
Bavarian Sky UK 1 PLC
Brookfield Renewable UK Hydro Ltd
Building Energy 1 Holdings PLC
Canyon UK Americas Limited
Charter Mortgage Funding 2017-1 PLC
Cheetah Bidco Limited
Cheetah Holdco Limited
Cyan Auto Receivables Limited
EMR Capital RF II LLP
GFG UK 1 Limited
Goldman Sachs Funding International
Infrastructure Investments Trafalgar
Jester Bidco Limited
L.E.K. Consulting Group Ltd
L.E.K. International Group Ltd
LR Baker St Mezz Borrower Ltd
LR Baker St Mezz Holdco Ltd
LR Baker St Senior Holdco Ltd
LTG Treasury Limited
London & Regional (Baker Street) Ltd
Newco NHL UK (17) Limited
P2P BL-3 PLC
Punch Taverns (Chiltern) Ltd
RELX Finance Limited
Tiso Blackstar Group SE
Tower Bridge Funding No.1 PLC
Triple Point Social Housing REIT PLC
Werner European Holding Ltd
Werner US Holding Limited

July 2017 [22]

Betjeman Holdings JVCO Limited
Betjeman Holdings Limited
Betjeman Holdings Midco Ltd
Cedar Project Bidco Limited
Cedar Project Holdco Limited
Cedar Project Midco Limited
Chrysaor E & P Services Ltd
Comet Bidco Limited
ERPE Finco Limited
ERPE Topco Limited
Foxland 20FS (UK) Limited
Infrastructure Investments Betjeman
Jester Debtco Limited
Jester Midco Limited
Motor 2017-1 PLC
PE QIQ Holding Limited
Praesidiad Group Limited
Praesidiad Limited
Shine Acquisition Co Limited
Shine Holdco I Limited
Shine Holdco II Limited
Shine Holdco III Limited

August 2017 [11]

Auto ABS UK Loans 2017 PLC
Brass No.6 PLC
Comet Midco Limited
Kore Potash PLC
MF Bidco Limited
MF Intermediate Limited
MF Midco Limited
McKesson Global Sourcing UK Ltd
SBWW Investments Limited
Sensis Holding II Limited
Walney Extension Holdings Ltd

September 2017 [10]

Bakkavor Group PLC
ContourGlobal PLC
Lazari Financial Holdings Ltd
Lazari Investments Limited
M7 Real Estate Investment Holdings Holdco
MF Debtco Limited
Orbita Funding 2017-1 PLC
PE Pioneer Holding II Limited
Pearl Income Investments UK Ltd
SBWW Investments Asia Limited

October 2017 [8]

Aberdeen Standard European Logistics Income
Equitix Offshore 2 Limited
Equitix Offshore 3 Limited
Equitix Offshore 4 Limited
Equitix Offshore 5 Limited
MF Finco1 Limited
Selene Holdings Limited
Selene Midco Limited

November 2017

I-Logic Holdings Limited
I-Logic Technologies Bidco Ltd
Pearl Income Holdings UK Ltd
Pearl Income Investments II UK Ltd

December 2017

Galaxy Group Midco Limited
Selfridges Financing Limited

January 2018

SFP Holdings Limited

March 2018

Vivo Energy PLC

April 2018

Urban Exposure PLC

Company Profiles

1 & 4 & 7 Triton Limited
Incorporated: 11 December 2006
Net Worth: £164,440,032 *Total Assets:* £208,425,360
Registered Office: York House, 45 Seymour Street, London, W1H 7LX
Activities: Development of building projects
Parent: Regent's Place Holding Company Limited
Officers: Sarah Morrell Barzycki [1958] Director/Head of Finance; Timothy Charles Downes [1979] Director/Chartered Surveyor; Juliette Morgan [1979] Director/Asset Manager; Nigel Mark Webb [1963] Director/Chartered Surveyor

10 Brock Street Limited
Incorporated: 8 October 2010
Net Worth: £242,077,056 *Total Assets:* £466,966,272
Registered Office: York House, 45 Seymour Street, London, W1H 7LX
Activities: Development of building projects
Parent: Regent's Place Holding Company Limited
Officers: Sarah Morrell Barzycki [1958] Director; Paul Stuart Macey [1978] Director/Accountant; Jonathan Charles McNuff [1986] Director/Chartered Accountant; Charles John Middleton [1966] Director/Corporate Tax Executive; Timothy Andrew Roberts [1964] Director; Nigel Mark Webb [1963] Director

10 Gresham Street LLP
Incorporated: 27 July 2010
Net Worth: £124,205,000 *Total Assets:* £260,140,992
Registered Office: CBRE Global Investors Limited, One New Change, London, EC4M 9AF

10 Trinity Square Residences Limited
Incorporated: 10 May 2012
Net Worth Deficit: £114,126,400 *Total Assets:* £285,265,856
Registered Office: 5 Market Yard Mews, 194-204 Bermondsey Street, London, SE1 3TQ
Activities: Other business support service activities n.e.c.
Major Shareholder: Chanchai Ruayrungruang
Officers: Yi-Chun Lai [1966] Director [Taiwanese]; Woraphanit Ruayrungruang [1990] Director [Thai]

10 Triton Street Limited
Incorporated: 17 January 2012
Net Worth: £164,221,792 *Total Assets:* £167,356,464
Registered Office: York House, 45 Seymour Street, London, W1H 7LX
Activities: Development of building projects
Parent: Regent's Place Holding Company Limited
Officers: Sarah Morrell Barzycki [1958] Director/Head of Finance; Paul Stuart Macey [1978] Director/Accountant; Jonathan Charles McNuff [1986] Director/Chartered Accountant; Charles John Middleton [1966] Director/Corporate Tax Executive; Timothy Andrew Roberts [1964] Director/Chartered Surveyor; Nigel Mark Webb [1963] Director/Chartered Surveyor

111 Group Holdings Limited
Incorporated: 15 July 2016 *Employees:* 374
Net Worth: £21,943,000 *Total Assets:* £109,547,000
Registered Office: Warwick House, 25-27 Buckingham Palace Road, London, SW1W 0PP
Activities: Activities of head offices
Shareholders: Limerston Capital Spark Co-Investment LP; Railway Pension Investments Limited
Officers: Martim Avillez Caldeira [1977] Director [Portuguese]; Chris Gauld [1978] Director; Kevin John Lyon [1961] Director; Hamish Duncan Adam Osborne [1973] Director/Chief Financial Officer; James Paget [1967] Director [Swiss]

12 Smithfield General Partner Limited
Incorporated: 8 May 2007 *Employees:* 3
Net Worth: £75,240 *Total Assets:* £109,237,664
Registered Office: 7th Floor, Exchange House, 12 Exchange Square, London, EC2A 2NY
Activities: Other business support service activities n.e.c.
Parent: Railway Pension Investments Limited
Officers: Victoria Jill Bell [1972] Director/Accountant; Stuart Blackett [1975] Director/Financial Controller; Lisa Melanie Sunner [1969] Director/Company Secretary

121222 Holdco Limited
Incorporated: 24 May 2017 *Employees:* 1
Net Worth: £68,156,000 *Total Assets:* £208,571,008
Registered Office: c/o McCarthy Tetrault, 26th Floor, 125 Old Broad Street, London, EC2N 1AR
Activities: Wholesale trade of motor vehicle parts and accessories
Officers: Louis Juneau, Secretary; Andre Courville [1953] Director/Interim President and CEO of Uni-Select Inc [Canadian]; Neil Michael Croxson [1968] Director/Chief Financial Officer/Chartered Accountant; Peter Charles Sephton [1959] Director/Chief Executive Officer

121333 Limited
Incorporated: 24 May 2017
Net Worth: £70,477,000 *Total Assets:* £213,436,992
Registered Office: c/o McCarthy Tetrault, 26th Floor, 125 Old Broad Street, London, EC2N 1AR
Activities: Wholesale trade of motor vehicle parts and accessories
Parent: 121222 Holdco Limited
Officers: Louis Juneau, Secretary; Andre Courville [1953] Director/Interim President and CEO of Uni-Select Inc [Canadian]; Neil Michael Croxson [1968] Director/Chief Financial Officer/Chartered Accountant; Peter Charles Sephton [1959] Director/Chief Executive Officer

2 & 3 Triton Limited
Incorporated: 11 December 2006
Net Worth: £47,736,792 *Total Assets:* £158,380,000
Registered Office: 2 Triton Square, Regent's Place, London, NW1 3AN
Activities: Other letting and operating of own or leased real estate
Parent: Santander UK PLC
Officers: Andrew Roland Honey [1964] Director; Rachel Jane Morrison [1968] Director/Chartered Accountant; Nicholas Guy Roberts [1968] Director/Surveyor

20 Triton Street Limited
Incorporated: 17 January 2012
Net Worth: £370,804,256 *Total Assets:* £375,995,328
Registered Office: York House, 45 Seymour Street, London, W1H 7LX
Activities: Development of building projects
Parent: Regent's Place Holding Company Limited
Officers: Sarah Morrell Barzycki [1958] Director/Head of Finance; Paul Stuart Macey [1978] Director/Accountant; Jonathan Charles McNuff [1986] Director/Chartered Accountant; Charles John Middleton [1966] Director/Corporate Tax Executive; Timothy Andrew Roberts [1964] Director/Chartered Surveyor; Nigel Mark Webb [1963] Director/Chartered Surveyor

21CF Shine Holdings UK Limited
Incorporated: 17 January 2014
Net Worth: £217,282,000 *Total Assets:* £289,287,008
Registered Office: Shepherds Building Central, Charecroft Way, London, W14 0EE
Activities: Television programme production activities
Parent: Endemol Shine Group Holding UK Limited
Officers: Richard Robert Johnston [1967] Director; Peter Andrew Salmon [1956] Director/Chief Creative Officer; Sophie Henrietta Turner Laing [1960] Director

280 Bishopsgate Finance Limited
Incorporated: 12 July 2004
Net Worth Deficit: £75,313,000 *Total Assets:* £377,992,000
Registered Office: 250 Bishopsgate, London, EC2M 4AA
Activities: Other business support service activities n.e.c.
Shareholders: The Royal Bank of Scotland PLC; NatWest Markets PLC
Officers: Neil Thomson Boyes Miller [1965] Director/Bank Official

334 Ramsbury Oxford Limited
Incorporated: 26 October 2004
Previous: BF Propco (No.10) Limited
Net Worth: £269,401,632 *Total Assets:* £412,050,944
Registered Office: c/o Hackwood Secretaries Limited, One Silk Street, London, EC2Y 8HQ
Activities: Development of building projects
Officers: Lars Drangel, Secretary; Nils Ola Daniel Nilsson [1978] Director/Property Manager [Swedish]

338 Euston Road Limited
Incorporated: 6 January 1994
Net Worth: £133,496,272 *Total Assets:* £146,504,688
Registered Office: York House, 45 Seymour Street, London, W1H 7LX
Activities: Development of building projects
Parent: Regent's Place Holding Company Limited
Officers: Sarah Morrell Barzycki [1958] Director/Head of Finance; Timothy Andrew Roberts [1964] Director/Chartered Surveyor; Nigel Mark Webb [1963] Director/Chartered Surveyor

350 Euston Road Limited
Incorporated: 8 November 1993
Net Worth: £142,668,656 *Total Assets:* £150,800,496
Registered Office: York House, 45 Seymour Street, London, W1H 7LX
Activities: Development of building projects
Parent: Regent's Place Holding Company Limited
Officers: Paul Stuart Macey [1978] Director/Accountant; Jonathan Charles McNuff [1986] Director/Chartered Accountant; Charles John Middleton [1966] Director/Corporate Tax Executive; Timothy Andrew Roberts [1964] Director/Chartered Surveyor; Nigel Mark Webb [1963] Director/Chartered Surveyor

3i Assets LLP
Incorporated: 18 January 2012
Net Worth: £243,089,632 *Total Assets:* £243,089,632
Registered Office: 16 Palace Street, London, SW1E 5JD

3i Group PLC
Incorporated: 1 November 1973 *Employees:* 241
Net Worth: £7,024,000,000 *Total Assets:* £7,898,999,808
Registered Office: 16 Palace Street, London, SW1E 5JD
Activities: Financial intermediation not elsewhere classified
Officers: Kevin John Dunn, Secretary; Jonathan Paul Asquith [1956] Director; Caroline Janet Banszky [1953] Director; Simon Alexander Borrows [1959] Director; Stephen Wayne Daintith [1964] Director; Peter Grosch [1955] Director [German]; David Alexander McCall Hutchison [1960] Director [Canadian]; Coline Lucille McConville [1964] Director [Australian]; Simon Robert Thompson [1959] Director; Julia Susan Wilson [1967] Director/Finance Executive

3i Holdings PLC
Incorporated: 8 March 1991
Net Worth: £382,000,000 *Total Assets:* £697,000,000
Registered Office: 16 Palace Street, London, SW1E 5JD
Activities: Activities of head offices
Parent: 3i Group PLC
Officers: Jonathan Charles Murphy, Secretary; Kevin John Dunn [1963] Director/Solicitor; Julia Susan Wilson [1967] Director/Finance Executive

3i International Holdings
Incorporated: 19 May 1945
Net Worth: £131,113,000 *Total Assets:* £131,113,000
Registered Office: 16 Palace Street, London, SW1E 5JD
Activities: Activities of head offices
Parent: 3i Holdings PLC
Officers: Ian Cooper [1983] Director/Group Treasurer; Kevin John Dunn [1963] Director/Solicitor; Jonathan Charles Murphy [1960] Director/Solicitor; Helen Jane Price [1982] Director/Accountant; Alastair Philip Richardson [1969] Director/Solicitor

3i PLC
Incorporated: 21 July 1945 *Employees:* 159
Net Worth: £342,872,992 *Total Assets:* £676,505,984
Registered Office: 16 Palace Street, London, SW1E 5JD
Activities: Financial intermediation not elsewhere classified
Parent: 3i Holdings PLC
Officers: Jonathan Charles Murphy, Secretary; Kevin John Dunn [1963] Director/Solicitor; Julia Susan Wilson [1967] Director/Finance Executive

4 Howley Place Limited
Incorporated: 31 July 2007 *Employees:* 223
Net Worth: £34,789,212 *Total Assets:* £194,409,472
Registered Office: 58 Rochester Row, Westminster, London, SW1P 1JU
Activities: Hotels and similar accommodation
Parent: Globalgrange Limited
Officers: Harpal Singh Matharu, Secretary; Harpal Singh Matharu [1956] Director/Executive; Raj Singh Matharu [1958] Director/Executive; Tejinderpal Singh Matharu [1960] Director/Hotelier

4 Imprint USA Limited
Incorporated: 13 July 1994
Net Worth: £49,472,000 *Total Assets:* £175,503,008
Registered Office: 25 Southampton Buildings, London, WC2A 1AL
Activities: Activities of head offices
Parent: 4imprint UK Holdings Limited
Officers: Andrew James Scull, Secretary; Andrew James Scull [1956] Director; David John Emmott Seekings [1965] Director/Chartered Accountant

4 Ventures Limited
Incorporated: 8 November 2000
Net Worth: £144,200,000 *Total Assets:* £144,200,000
Registered Office: 124 Horseferry Road, London, SW1P 2TX
Activities: Television programming and broadcasting activities
Parent: Channel Four Television Corporation
Officers: Martin John Baker, Secretary; Jonathan Mark Allan [1974] Director; Martin John Baker [1960] Director; Dr Alexandra Rose Mahon [1973] Director/Chief Executive Officer; Sarah Rose [1973] Director

4imprint UK Holdings Limited
Incorporated: 12 April 2006
Net Worth: £21,269,000 *Total Assets:* £147,308,992
Registered Office: 25 Southampton Buildings, London, WC2A 1AL
Activities: Activities of head offices
Parent: 4imprint Group PLC
Officers: Andrew James Scull, Secretary; Andrew James Scull [1956] Director; David John Emmott Seekings [1965] Director/Chartered Accountant

6 Bevis Marks Limited
Incorporated: 1 July 2011
Net Worth: £100,117,744 *Total Assets:* £217,454,736
Registered Office: One Fleet Place, London, EC4M 7WS
Activities: Other letting and operating of own or leased real estate
Major Shareholder: H.E. Shaikh Khalid Bin Abdulaziz Al Tuwaijri
Officers: Danielle Noel Cotter [1974] Director/Senior Trust Officer Cititrust (Jersey) Limited [Irish]; Anthony Joseph Daly [1964] Director/Senior Relationship Manager Cititrust (Jersey) Limited; Robert Anthony Syvret [1968] Director

6-10 Cambridge Terrace Developments LLP
Incorporated: 2 February 2016
Net Worth: £80,954,632 *Total Assets:* £103,701,472
Registered Office: 35 Great St Helen's, London, EC3A 6AP

80 Charlotte Street Limited
Incorporated: 24 January 2017
Net Worth: £23,378,608 *Total Assets:* £246,540,480
Registered Office: 25 Savile Row, London, W1S 2ER
Activities: Other business support service activities n.e.c.
Parent: Derwent London PLC
Officers: David Andrew Lawler, Secretary; John David Burns [1944] Director; Nigel Quentin George [1963] Director; Simon Paul Silver [1960] Director; David Gary Silverman [1969] Director; Paul Malcolm Williams [1960] Director; Damian Mark Alan Wisniewski [1961] Director

A & L CF June (3) Limited
Incorporated: 10 February 1989
Net Worth: £7,426,957 *Total Assets:* £101,126,472
Registered Office: 2 Triton Square, Regent's Place, London, NW1 3AN
Activities: Financial leasing
Parent: Santander Asset Finance PLC
Officers: Stephen David Affleck [1979] Finance Director; Mr George Smith-Salmond Ashworth [1956] Managing Director; Anna Maria Konter [1967] Director [Dutch]

A & N Media Finance Services Limited
Incorporated: 8 February 1999 *Employees:* 73
Net Worth: £41,378,000 *Total Assets:* £709,387,008
Registered Office: Northcliffe House, 2 Derry Street, Kensington, London, W8 5TT
Activities: Other business support service activities n.e.c.
Parent: DMG Media Limited
Officers: Frances Louise Sallas, Secretary; James Justin Siderfin Welsh [1967] Director

A V Co 1 Limited
Incorporated: 20 June 2006
Net Worth: £137,934,000 *Total Assets:* £149,696,000
Registered Office: 13th Floor, 5 Aldermanbury Square, London, EC2V 7HR
Activities: Activities of other holding companies n.e.c.
Parent: ITW Global Investments LLC
Officers: Ryan Ronald Dale, Secretary; Giles Matthew Hudson [1972] Director/Chartered Accountant; Stephen James Rowell [1967] Director of International Corporate Finance; Maryann Spiegel [1964] Director/Attorney [American]

A-Gas Bidco Limited
Incorporated: 24 May 2017
Net Worth: £188,926,000 *Total Assets:* £381,399,008
Registered Office: 11th Floor, 200 Aldersgate Street, London, EC1A 4HD
Activities: Activities of other holding companies n.e.c.
Parent: A-Gas Group Limited
Officers: Andrew Ambrose [1962] Director/Manager [Australian]; Mattia Caprioli [1974] Director/Investment Executive [Italian]; Joerg Metzner [1985] Director/Investor [German]; Edouard Jean Charles Pillot [1977] Director/Investor [French]; Ian Victor Stewart Podmore [1973] Director/Manager; Richard Edward Marcel Stewart [1972] Director/Manager

A-Gas Group Limited
Incorporated: 26 May 2017 *Employees:* 474
Net Worth: £192,183,008 *Total Assets:* £440,728,000
Registered Office: 11th Floor, 200 Aldersgate Street, London, EC1A 4HD
Activities: Activities of other holding companies n.e.c.
Officers: Andrew Ambrose [1962] Director/Manager [Australian]; Joerg Metzner [1985] Director/Investor [German]; Edouard Jean Charles Pillot [1977] Director/Investor [French]; Ian Victor Stewart Podmore [1973] Director/Manager; Richard Edward Marcel Stewart [1972] Director/Manager

A.B.F.Holdings Limited
Incorporated: 22 April 1936 *Employees:* 139
Net Worth: £36,875,000 *Total Assets:* £548,924,992
Registered Office: Weston Centre, 10 Grosvenor Street, London, W1K 4QY
Activities: Activities of head offices
Parent: ABF Investments PLC
Officers: Rosalyn Sharon Schofield, Secretary; John George Bason [1957] Finance Director; Rosalyn Sharon Schofield [1956] Director/Solicitor; Andrew Arthur Smith [1972] Director/Chartered Accountant

A.G. Clothing Limited
Incorporated: 30 October 1968
Net Worth: £157,947,008 *Total Assets:* £158,147,008
Registered Office: Colegrave House, 70 Berners Street, London, W1T 3NL
Activities: Retail sale of clothing in specialised stores
Officers: Rebecca Rose Flaherty, Secretary; Richard Leeroy Burchill [1971] Director/Accountant; Richard Dedombal [1965] Director/Head of Tax; Michelle Jane Gammon [1977] Director/Solicitor; Gillian Anne Hague [1965] Director/Group Financial Controller; Sally Marion Wightman [1968] Director/Chartered Accountant

A2D Funding II PLC
Incorporated: 17 July 2014
Net Worth: £18,000 *Total Assets:* £149,524,992
Registered Office: Fifth Floor, 100 Wood Street, London, EC2V 7EX
Activities: Other business support service activities n.e.c.
Parent: The Law Debenture Intermediary Corporation P.L.C.
Officers: Mark Howard Filer [1967] Director

A2D Funding PLC
Incorporated: 7 August 2013
Net Worth: £20,000 *Total Assets:* £152,859,008
Registered Office: Fifth Floor, 100 Wood Street, London, EC2V 7EX
Activities: Other business support service activities n.e.c.
Parent: The Law Debenture Intermediary Corporation P.L.C.
Officers: Mark Howard Filer [1967] Director

A2dominion Developments Limited
Incorporated: 6 October 2005
Net Worth: £18,809,000 *Total Assets:* £412,836,000
Registered Office: The Point, 37 North Wharf Road, London, W2 1BD
Activities: Development of building projects
Parent: A2Dominion Homes Limited
Officers: Zoe Ollerearnshaw, Secretary; Peter James Braithwaite [1949] Director/Chartered Surveyor; Mark Gallagher [1950] Director/Retired; Nicholas Anthony Hutchings [1958] Executive Director; Darrell John Mercer [1955] Director/Chief Executive; Caroline Tolhurst [1961] Director/Company Secretary; Dean Stuart Tufts [1960] Finance Director; Anne Waterhouse [1975] Executive Director

A2dominion Residential Limited
Incorporated: 14 September 2004
Net Worth: £63,105,000 *Total Assets:* £309,292,000
Registered Office: The Point, 37 North Wharf Road, London, W2 1BD
Activities: Residents property management
Parent: A2Dominion Homes Limited
Officers: Zoe Ollerearnshaw, Secretary; David Coates [1965] Finance Director; Ian Douglas Cox [1957] Director; Sara Louise Dickinson [1968] Finance Director; Darrell John Mercer [1955] Director/CEO A2Dominion; Caroline Tiller [1956] Executive Director; Caroline Tolhurst [1961] Director/Company Secretary; Peter Llewellyn Walker [1956] Finance Director; Anne Waterhouse [1975] Executive Director

A2dominion Treasury Limited
Incorporated: 2 May 2008
Net Worth: £103,000 *Total Assets:* £303,657,984
Registered Office: The Point, 37 North Wharf Road, London, W2 1BD
Activities: Residents property management
Parent: A2Dominion Housing Group Limited
Officers: Zoe Ollerearnshaw, Secretary; Sara Louise Dickinson [1968] Finance Director; Martin John Huckerby [1953] Finance Director; Dean Stuart Tufts [1960] Finance Director; Peter Llewellyn Walker [1956] Finance Director

AAA UK Acquisition Co. Limited
Incorporated: 16 February 2015
Net Worth: £111,921,056 *Total Assets:* £113,211,576
Registered Office: 31st Floor, 20 Fenchurch Street, London, EC3M 3BY
Activities: Activities of other holding companies n.e.c.
Parent: AAA UK Holding Co. Limited
Officers: Iii Stroud, Secretary; Cary Jay Davis [1966] Managing Director [American]; Jitij Dwivedi [1984] Director/Vice President [Indian]; Michael Edward Martin [1956] Managing Director [American]; John Redett [1967] Managing Director [American]

AAA UK Holding Co. Limited
Incorporated: 16 February 2015
Net Worth: £111,357,768 *Total Assets:* £111,399,136
Registered Office: 31st Floor, 20 Fenchurch Street, London, EC3M 3BY
Activities: Activities of other holding companies n.e.c.
Officers: Iii Stroud, Secretary; Cary Jay Davis [1966] Managing Director [American]; Jitij Dwivedi [1984] Director/Vice President [Indian]; Michael Edward Martin [1956] Managing Director [American]; John Redett [1967] Managing Director [American]

Aamby Valley (UK) Limited
Incorporated: 9 July 2012
Net Worth: £526,408 *Total Assets:* £290,600,480
Registered Office: 6th Floor, 25 Farringdon Street, London, EC4A 4AB
Activities: Other service activities n.e.c.
Parent: Sahara Hospitality Operations LLP
Officers: Seemanto Roy [1977] Director [Indian]; Sushanto Roy [1974] Director [Macedonian]; Svvapna Roy [1949] Director [Macedonian]; Subrata Roy Sahara [1948] Director [Indian]; Om Prakash Srivastava [1955] Director [Indian]

AB Acquisitions FX Inter Limited
Incorporated: 18 May 2007
Net Worth: £240,170,000 *Total Assets:* £1,520,721,024
Registered Office: 4th Floor, Sedley Place, 361 Oxford Street, London, W1C 2JL
Activities: Other business support service activities n.e.c.
Parent: Superior Acquisitions Limited
Officers: Frank Standish, Company Secretary [Irish]; Aidan Gerard Clare [1966] Director [Irish]; Mark Francis Muller [1964] Director; Frank Standish [1963] Director/Company Secretary [Irish]

AB Agri Limited
Incorporated: 16 November 1923 *Employees:* 1,157
Net Worth: £132,850,000 *Total Assets:* £272,384,000
Registered Office: Weston Centre, 10 Grosvenor Street, London, W1K 4QY
Activities: Manufacture of prepared feeds for farm animals
Parent: A.B.F. Holdings Limited
Officers: Rosalyn Sharon Schofield, Secretary; Richard Charles Cloke [1961] Finance Director; Richard Graham Cooper [1958] Director; Alistair Graham Cross [1972] Director; Simon Mark Heath [1967] Managing Director; Alan Murphy [1963] Divisional Director; Jose Jorge Nobre [1961] Director [French]

AB Mauri (UK) Limited
Incorporated: 27 May 1987 *Employees:* 74
Net Worth Deficit: £30,173,000 *Total Assets:* £141,970,000
Registered Office: Weston Centre, 10 Grosvenor Street, London, W1K 4QY
Activities: Activities of head offices
Parent: ABF Investments PLC
Officers: Rosalyn Sharon Schofield, Secretary/Solicitor; Nigel John Fawcett [1974] Director/Chartered Management Accountant

Abbey Commercial Ltd
Incorporated: 9 July 2003 *Employees:* 2
Net Worth: £105,847,072 *Total Assets:* £259,263,952
Registered Office: 113 Brent Street, London, NW4 2DX
Activities: Renting and operating of Housing Association real estate
Parent: Bana One L1 Ltd
Officers: Barry Ackerman [1969] Director/Surveyor; Naomi Ackerman [1945] Director

Abbey Covered Bonds LLP
Incorporated: 8 April 2005
Net Worth Deficit: £260,112,992 *Total Assets:* £18,127,405,056
Registered Office: 2 Triton Square, Regent's Place, London, NW1 3AN

Abbey National Property Investments
Incorporated: 10 August 1989
Net Worth: £468,796,000 *Total Assets:* £500,529,216
Registered Office: 2 Triton Square, Regent's Place, London, NW1 3AN
Activities: Financial intermediation not elsewhere classified
Parent: Santander UK PLC
Officers: Andrew Roland Honey [1964] Director; Rachel Jane Morrison [1968] Director/Chartered Accountant

Abbey National Treasury Services Overseas Holdings
Incorporated: 19 December 1994
Net Worth: £361,306,656 *Total Assets:* £434,657,824
Registered Office: 2 Triton Square, Regent's Place, London, NW1 3AN
Activities: Financial intermediation not elsewhere classified
Parent: Santander Equity Investments Limited
Officers: Andrew Roland Honey [1964] Director; Rachel Jane Morrison [1968] Director/Chartered Accountant

Abbey National Treasury Services PLC
Incorporated: 24 January 1989
Net Worth: £3,881,999,872 *Total Assets:* £80,088,997,888
Registered Office: 2 Triton Square, Regent's Place, London, NW1 3AN
Activities: Financial intermediation not elsewhere classified
Parent: Santander UK Group Holdings PLC
Officers: Cheryl Samuels, Secretary; Patricia Halliday [1966] Director/Chief Risk Officer; Andrew Roland Honey [1964] Director; Timothy Simon Lloyd [1960] Director/Solicitor; Thomas Ranger [1977] Director; Antonio Roman [1967] Finance Director [Spanish]; Victoria Jane Wallis [1967] HR Director

Abbotstar Trading Ltd
Incorporated: 10 February 2006
Net Worth: £109,741,480 *Total Assets:* £109,755,680
Registered Office: 4th Floor, 1 Knightrider Court, London, EC4V 5BJ
Activities: Non-trading company
Parent: Raphe Investments Limited
Officers: Anna Christou [1970] Director/Administrator [Cypriot]

Abbott Mead Vickers Group Limited
Incorporated: 31 October 1977 *Employees:* 33
Net Worth: £259,046,448 *Total Assets:* £736,813,440
Registered Office: Bankside 3, 90-100 Southwark Street, London, SE1 0SW
Activities: Activities of head offices
Parent: Omnicom Europe Subholdings Limited
Officers: Sally Ann Bray, Secretary; John James Byrnes [1964] Finance Director; James Thomas Moser [1962] Director/Chairman, BBDO Europe [American]

ABC International Bank PLC
Incorporated: 3 December 1990 *Employees:* 245
Net Worth: £469,692,000 *Total Assets:* £2,955,578,112
Registered Office: 1-5 Moorgate, London, EC2R 6AB
Activities: Financial intermediation not elsewhere classified
Officers: David Thomas Holden, Secretary/Lawyer; Rajeev Santhiapillai Adrian [1968] Director/Banker; Dr Yousef Abdullah Al-Awadi [1948] Director/Consultant [Kuwaiti]; Abdullah Saud Abdulaziz Al-Humaidhi [1948] Director/Commercial Banker [Kuwaiti]; Dr Florence Hadi Eid [1967] Director/Economist [Lebanese]; Saddek Omar Ali Elkaber [1951] Director/Governor of The Central Bank of Libya [Libyan]; Paul Henry Jennings [1964] Director/Banker; Dr Khaled Said Ramadan Kawan [1956] Director/Banker [Libyan]; Angus Gillies MacLennan [1955] Director/Consultant; Andrew Frederick John Neden [1962] Director/Chartered Accountant

Abengoa Concessions Investments Limited
Incorporated: 17 December 2013
Net Worth: £619,280,000 *Total Assets:* £621,620,480
Registered Office: 26-28 Hammersmith Grove, London, W6 7BA
Activities: Production of electricity
Parent: Abengoa S.A.
Officers: Joaquin Fernandez de Pierola Marin [1973] Director/CEO Abengoa [Spanish]; Richard Anthony Lynn [1973] Director

Aberdeen Asset Investments Limited
Incorporated: 6 March 1964
Net Worth: £126,591,000 *Total Assets:* £151,239,008
Registered Office: Bow Bells House, Bread Street, London, EC4M 9HH
Activities: Activities of financial services holding companies
Parent: Aberdeen Asset Investment Group Limited
Officers: Lisa Anne Bowley [1972] Director/Head of Operational Risk; Stephen Christopher Alexander Docherty [1970] Director; Campbell David Fleming [1964] Director [Australian]; Andrew Arthur Laing [1952] Director; Katherine Lyn Malcolm [1971] Director; Gary Robert Marshall [1961] Director; Andrew McCaffery [1963] Director; Aron William Mitchell [1972] Director; Mandy Pike [1966] Director

Aberdeen Asset Management Life and Pensions Limited
Incorporated: 6 March 1998
Net Worth: £10,766,000 *Total Assets:* £1,617,616,000
Registered Office: Bow Bells House, 1 Bread Street, London, EC4M 9HH
Activities: Pension funding
Parent: Aberdeen Asset Management PLC
Officers: David John Paterson Hare [1961] Director; Aron William Mitchell [1972] Director; Otto Thoresen [1956] Director; Helen Margaret Webster [1971] Director

Aberdeen Infrastructure (No 2) LLP
Incorporated: 14 October 2008
Net Worth: £186,779,248 *Total Assets:* £186,786,640
Registered Office: Bow Bells House, 1 Bread Street, London, EC4M 9HH

Aberdeen Infrastructure (No.3) Limited
Incorporated: 27 June 2008
Net Worth: £301,969,184 *Total Assets:* £301,975,008
Registered Office: Bow Bells House, 1 Bread Street, London, EC4M 9HH
Activities: Activities of financial services holding companies
Shareholder: RHM Pension Trust Limited as Trustee of The RHM Pension Scheme
Officers: Karen Marie Hill [1977] Director/Senior Investment Manager; Martin Timothy Smith [1967] Director/Senior Investment Manager; Andrew Leslie Tennant [1958] Director/Senior Investment Manager; Ivan Hong-Yee Wong [1979] Director/Senior Investment Manager

Aberdeen Infrastructure II Limited
Incorporated: 12 August 2014
Net Worth: £33,649,212 *Total Assets:* £122,559,000
Registered Office: Bow Bells House, 1 Bread Street, London, EC4M 9HH
Activities: Financial intermediation not elsewhere classified
Shareholder: Stichting Depositary APG Infrastructure Pool 2012
Officers: Mohammed Sameer Amin [1973] Director/Head of Primary Investments; Ion Bruce Balfour [1963] Director/Investment Fund Manager; Gershon Daniel Cohen [1964] Director/Head of Infrastructure Funds; Ivan Hong-Yee Wong [1979] Director/Senior Specialist Manager

Aberdeen Infrastructure Limited
Incorporated: 12 August 2008
Net Worth: £297,761 *Total Assets:* £123,847,320
Registered Office: Bow Bells House, 1 Bread Street, London, EC4M 9HH
Activities: Financial intermediation not elsewhere classified
Shareholder: RHM Pension Trust Limited as Trustee of The RHM Pension Scheme
Officers: Karen Marie Hill [1977] Director/Senior Investment Manager; Martin Timothy Smith [1967] Director/Banker; Andrew Leslie Tennant [1958] Director/Banker; Ivan Hong-Yee Wong [1979] Director/Fund Manager

Aberdeen Investments Limited
Incorporated: 7 July 1993
Net Worth: £80,582,000 *Total Assets:* £137,438,000
Registered Office: Bow Bells House, 1 Bread Street, London, EC4M 9HH
Activities: Activities of financial services holding companies
Parent: Aberdeen Asset Management PLC
Officers: Malin Af Petersens [1967] Director [Swedish]; Andrew Arthur Laing [1952] Director; Aron William Mitchell [1972] Director

Aberdeen Japan Investment Trust PLC
Incorporated: 17 June 1998
Net Worth: £100,472,000 *Total Assets:* £112,038,000
Registered Office: Bow Bells House, 1 Bread Street, London, EC4M 9HH
Activities: Activities of investment trusts
Officers: Claire Marguerite Boyle [1968] Director; Karen Mary Brade [1965] Director [Irish]; Ralph Neil Gaskell [1948] Director; Kevin John Toussaint Pakenham [1947] Director/Investment Banker; Sir David Alexander Warren [1952] Director

Aberdeen New Dawn Investment Trust PLC
Incorporated: 2 May 1989
Net Worth: £311,816,000 *Total Assets:* £340,276,992
Registered Office: Bow Bells House, 1 Bread Street, London, EC4M 9HH
Activities: Activities of investment trusts
Officers: John Howard Lorimer [1953] Director [New Zealander]; Susan Rippingall [1966] Director; Marion Jane Sears [1962] Director; David James Buchanan Shearer [1959] Director; John Donald Black Workman [1952] Director; Hugh Young [1958] Director

Aberdeen New India Investment Trust PLC
Incorporated: 21 February 1994
Previous: New India Investment Trust PLC
Net Worth: £289,444,000 *Total Assets:* £289,847,008
Registered Office: Bow Bells House, 1 Bread Street, London, EC4M 9HH
Activities: Activities of investment trusts
Officers: Hasan Askari [1945] Director; Rachel Anne Beagles [1968] Director; Michael Hughes [1951] Director; Stephen Frank White [1955] Director

Aberdeen New Thai Investment Trust PLC
Incorporated: 1 December 1989
Net Worth: £117,168,000 *Total Assets:* £125,112,000
Registered Office: Bow Bells House, 1 Bread Street, London, EC4M 9HH
Activities: Activities of investment trusts
Officers: Clare Juliet Dobie [1957] Director; Sarah Juliet MacAulay [1962] Director; Sarah Elizabeth McCarthy [1974] Director; Andrew David Pomfret [1960] Director; Nicholas Michael Norman Smith [1951] Director

Aberdeen Sidecar LLP
Incorporated: 27 November 2013
Net Worth: £46,077,124 *Total Assets:* £139,247,008
Registered Office: Bow Bells House, 1 Bread Street, London, EC4M 9HH

Aberdeen Standard Asia Focus PLC
Incorporated: 20 September 1995
Previous: Aberdeen Asian Smaller Companies Investment Trust PLC
Net Worth: £433,705,984 *Total Assets:* £488,532,000
Registered Office: Bow Bells House, 1 Bread Street, London, EC4M 9HH
Activities: Activities of investment trusts
Officers: Charlotte Mary Black [1960] Director; Nigel Kenneth Cayzer [1954] Director; Haruko Fukuda OBE [1946] Director/Banker; Martin James Gilbert [1955] Director/Chief Executive; Debbie Jane Guthrie [1955] Director; Christopher Simon Maude [1944] Finance Director; Randal Alexander St John McDonnell [1967] Director; Philip Edward Yea [1954] Director; Hugh Young [1958] Director

Aberdeen Standard Equity Income Trust PLC
Incorporated: 24 September 1991
Previous: Standard Life Equity Income Trust PLC
Net Worth: £238,448,992 *Total Assets:* £270,012,992
Registered Office: Bow Bells House, 1 Bread Street, London, EC4M 9HH
Activities: Financial intermediation not elsewhere classified
Officers: Richard Ronald James Burns [1946] Director; Josephine Dixon [1959] Director; Caroline Margaret Hitch [1959] Director; Jeremy John Tigue [1959] Director; Mark Barry Ewart White [1955] Director

Aberdeen Standard European Logistics Income PLC
Incorporated: 25 October 2017
Net Worth: £185,619,008 *Total Assets:* £185,884,544
Registered Office: Bow Bells House, 1 Bread Street, London, EC4M 9HH
Activities: Activities of investment trusts
Parent: Aberdeen Asset Management PLC
Officers: Pascal Duval [1962] Director [French]; Caroline Gulliver [1965] Director; John Anthony Nicholas Heawood [1953] Director/Chartered Surveyor; Anthony Charles Roper [1960] Investment Director; Diane Wilde [1964] Director

Aberforth Split Level Income Trust PLC
Incorporated: 19 April 2017
Net Worth: £199,220,000 *Total Assets:* £248,230,000
Registered Office: Level 13, Broadgate Tower, 20 Primrose Street, London, EC2A 2EW
Activities: Activities of investment trusts
Officers: Graeme Bissett [1958] Director/Chartered Accountant; Jonathan Harry Cartwright [1953] Director; John Dominic Mortimer Fisher [1962] Director; Angus Charles Gordon Lennox [1964] Director; Graham Reid Menzies [1948] Director

ABF (No.1) Limited
Incorporated: 17 February 2003
Net Worth: £318,716,992 *Total Assets:* £319,444,000
Registered Office: Weston Centre, 10 Grosvenor Street, London, W1K 4QY
Activities: Other business support service activities n.e.c.
Parent: ABF Investments PLC
Officers: Rosalyn Sharon Schofield, Secretary/Solicitor; Rosalyn Sharon Schofield [1956] Director/Solicitor; Andrew Arthur Smith [1972] Director/Chartered Accountant

ABF Funding
Incorporated: 2 March 2005
Net Worth: £210,312,112 *Total Assets:* £213,490,672
Registered Office: Weston Centre, 10 Grosvenor Street, London, W1K 4QY
Activities: Other business support service activities n.e.c.
Parent: ABF Investments PLC
Officers: Rosalyn Sharon Schofield, Secretary/Solicitor; Rosalyn Sharon Schofield [1956] Director/Solicitor; Andrew Arthur Smith [1972] Director/Chartered Accountant

ABF Grain Products Limited
Incorporated: 30 December 1903 *Employees:* 5,983
Net Worth: £370,414,016 *Total Assets:* £690,345,024
Registered Office: Weston Centre, 10 Grosvenor Street, London, W1K 4QY
Activities: Manufacture of bread; manufacture of fresh pastry goods and cakes
Parent: Sunblest Bakeries Limited
Officers: Rosalyn Sharon Schofield, Secretary; David Stephen Barton [1965] Managing Director; Mark Fowle [1975] Director; Jonathan Howard Jenkins [1965] Managing Director; Victoria Lawrence [1980] Managing Director; Robin Anthony William Lee [1965] Managing Director; Ian Robert Mace [1966] Director/Accountant; Christopher John Mintern [1972] Director; Paul Simon Murphy [1965] Managing Director; Mark Andrew Ward [1969] Finance Director

ABF HK Finance Limited
Incorporated: 2 September 2011
Net Worth: £221,011,472 *Total Assets:* £221,011,472
Registered Office: Weston Centre, 10 Grosvenor Street, London, W1K 4QY
Activities: Other business support service activities n.e.c.
Parent: ABF Overseas Limited
Officers: Rosalyn Sharon Schofield, Secretary; Rosalyn Sharon Schofield [1956] Director/Solicitor; Andrew Arthur Smith [1972] Director/Chartered Accountant

ABF Investments PLC
Incorporated: 2 November 1935
Net Worth: £2,891,000,064 *Total Assets:* £3,022,000,128
Registered Office: Weston Centre, 10 Grosvenor Street, London, W1K 4QY
Activities: Activities of head offices
Parent: Associated British Foods PLC
Officers: Rosalyn Sharon Schofield, Secretary; John George Bason [1957] Finance Director; Andrew Arthur Smith [1972] Director/Chartered Accountant

ABF Overseas Limited
Incorporated: 5 February 1997
Net Worth: £2,792,600,064 *Total Assets:* £4,073,630,976
Registered Office: Weston Centre, 10 Grosvenor Street, London, W1K 4QY
Activities: Activities of head offices
Parent: ABF Investments PLC
Officers: Rosalyn Sharon Schofield, Secretary; John George Bason [1957] Finance Director; Rosalyn Sharon Schofield [1956] Director/Solicitor; Andrew Arthur Smith [1972] Director/Chartered Accountant

ABF US Holdings Limited
Incorporated: 20 December 2005
Previous: ABF Lux Limited
Net Worth: £996,041,024 *Total Assets:* £1,563,617,024
Registered Office: Weston Centre, 10 Grosvenor Street, London, W1K 4QY
Activities: Activities of head offices
Parent: ABF Overseas Limited
Officers: Rosalyn Sharon Schofield, Secretary; Rosalyn Sharon Schofield [1956] Director/Solicitor; Andrew Arthur Smith [1972] Director/Chartered Accountant

ABP Acquisitions UK Limited
Incorporated: 7 June 2006
Net Worth Deficit: £3,678,099,968 *Total Assets:* £3,150,000,128
Registered Office: 25 Bedford Street, London, WC2E 9ES
Activities: Activities of other holding companies n.e.c.
Parent: ABPA Holdings Limited
Officers: George Sebastian Matthew Bull [1960] Director/Chartered Accountant; Shaun Richard Kennedy [1979] Director/Group Treasurer [New Zealander]; Mr Henrik Lundgaard Pedersen [1974] Director/Chief Executive Officer [Danish]

ABP Bonds UK Limited
Incorporated: 24 July 2006
Net Worth: £781,600,000 *Total Assets:* £3,857,100,032
Registered Office: 25 Bedford Street, London, WC2E 9ES
Activities: Activities of other holding companies n.e.c.
Officers: George Sebastian Matthew Bull [1960] Director/Chartered Accountant; Shaun Richard Kennedy [1979] Director/Group Treasurer [New Zealander]; Mr Henrik Lundgaard Pedersen [1974] Director/Chief Executive Officer [Danish]

ABP Finance PLC
Incorporated: 14 November 2011
Net Worth: £11,300,000 *Total Assets:* £878,200,000
Registered Office: 25 Bedford Street, London, WC2E 9ES
Activities: Activities of other holding companies n.e.c.
Parent: ABPA Holdings Limited
Officers: Andrew Charles Garner, Secretary; George Sebastian Matthew Bull [1960] Director/Chartered Accountant; Shaun Richard Kennedy [1979] Director/Group Treasurer [New Zealander]; Mr Henrik Lundgaard Pedersen [1974] Director/Chief Executive Officer [Danish]

ABP Mezzanine Holdco UK Limited
Incorporated: 31 August 2006
Net Worth: £600,000 *Total Assets:* £489,700,000
Registered Office: 25 Bedford Street, London, WC2E 9ES
Activities: Financial management
Officers: George Sebastian Matthew Bull [1960] Director/Chartered Accountant; Shaun Richard Kennedy [1979] Director/Group Treasurer [New Zealander]; Mr Henrik Lundgaard Pedersen [1974] Director/Chief Executive Officer [Danish]

ABP Subholdings UK Limited
Incorporated: 7 June 2006
Net Worth: £974,800,000 *Total Assets:* £3,813,600,000
Registered Office: 25 Bedford Street, London, WC2E 9ES
Activities: Activities of head offices
Parent: ABP Bonds UK Limited
Officers: George Sebastian Matthew Bull [1960] Director/Chartered Accountant; Shaun Richard Kennedy [1979] Director/Group Treasurer [New Zealander]; Mr Henrik Lundgaard Pedersen [1974] Director/Chief Executive Officer [Danish]

ABPA Holdings Limited
Incorporated: 14 November 2011 *Employees:* 2,213
Net Worth Deficit: £948,800,000 *Total Assets:* £5,373,700,096
Registered Office: 25 Bedford Street, London, WC2E 9ES
Activities: Activities of other holding companies n.e.c.
Parent: ABP Subholdings UK Limited
Officers: James Alexander Bryce [1974] Director/Investor; George Sebastian Matthew Bull [1960] Director/Chartered Accountant; Philippe Anastase Busslinger [1975] Director [Swiss]; Philip Butcher [1985] Director/Principal [Canadian]; John Bernard Coghlan [1958] Director [Irish]; Hakim Drissi Kaitouni [1983] Director; Stewart Norman Hicks [1952] Director; Peter Francis Hofbauer [1960] Director/Investment Manager [Australian]; George Philip Roger Kay [1972] Director/Private Equity Investor [New Zealander]; Eric Philippe Marianne Machiels [1966] Managing Director [Belgian]; Helen Margaret Newell [1968] Director [Australian]; Dr Philip Michael Gerard Nolan [1953] Director/Chairman; Mr Henrik Lundgaard Pedersen [1974] Director/Chief Executive Officer [Danish]; Gregory Stuart Pestrak [1971] Director/Finance Executive; John Rishton [1958] Director; Dmitry Yashnikov [1989] Director/Investment Manager

Acacia Mining PLC
Incorporated: 12 January 2010 *Employees:* 2,748
Net Worth: £844,438,400 *Total Assets:* £1,356,600,320
Registered Office: 5th Floor, 1 Cavendish Place, London, W1G 0QF
Activities: Other mining and quarrying n.e.c.
Officers: Charles de Lancey Ritchie, Secretary; Stephen Charles Burrard-Lucas [1954] Director; Rachel June English [1962] Director; Andre Roger Falzon [1954] Director [Canadian]; Stephen Robin Galbraith [1971] Director/Business Executive; Peter Geleta [1963] Director; John Michael Kenyon [1949] Director [Canadian]

Academies Enterprise Trust
Incorporated: 19 June 2008 *Employees:* 6,380
Net Worth: £360,760,992 *Total Assets:* £486,832,992
Registered Office: 3rd Floor, 183 Eversholt Street, London, NW1 1BU
Activities: Primary education
Officers: Jack Boyer [1959] Director; Jude Chin [1956] Director/Consultant [Guyanese]; Christopher John Julian Drinkall [1964] Director/Chief Executive; Deborah Mary Eyre [1954] Director; Alison Jane Sargent Paines [1955] Director/Solicitor; Andrew Thraves [1965] Director of Education

Accantia Group Holdings
Incorporated: 28 October 2003
Net Worth: £198,474,000 *Total Assets:* £244,275,008
Registered Office: Unilever House, 100 Victoria Embankment, London, EC4Y 0DY
Activities: Non-trading company
Parent: Unilever UK Group Limited
Officers: James Oliver Earley, Secretary; Richard Clive Hazell, Secretary; Richard Clive Hazell [1966] Director/Solicitor; Amanda Louise King [1973] UK & Ireland Tax Director

Accenture (UK) Limited
Incorporated: 8 May 2003 *Employees:* 10,868
Net Worth: £1,883,145,984 *Total Assets:* £3,000,485,120
Registered Office: 30 Fenchurch Street, London, EC3M 3BD
Activities: Management consultancy activities other than financial management
Parent: Accenture PLC
Officers: Patrick Brian Francis Rowe, Secretary; Zahra Shiva Bahrololoumi [1975] Managing Director/Management Consultant; Oliver James Benzecry [1961] Managing Director; Daniel Kenneth Burton [1973] Finance Director; Emma Therese McGuigan [1971] Director/Technology Consultant; Patrick Brian Francis Rowe [1964] Director/Solicitor; Simon John Whitehouse [1960] Director/Management Consultant

Accor Hotelinvest UK Limited
Incorporated: 16 December 2016 *Employees:* 2
Net Worth: £21,896,180 *Total Assets:* £957,522,880
Registered Office: 10 Hammersmith Grove, London, W6 7AP
Activities: Activities of other holding companies n.e.c.
Shareholder: Accor SA
Officers: Cecile Marie Marguerite Verstraete, Secretary; Olivier Marie Pierre Daguzan [1976] Director [French]; Jan Hiljo Ozinga [1964] Director [Dutch]

Accor Hotelservices UK Limited
Incorporated: 2 December 2016
Net Worth: £5,750,000 *Total Assets:* £466,252,000
Registered Office: 10 Hammersmith Grove, London, W6 7AP
Activities: Hotels and similar accommodation
Parent: Accor (U.K.) Limited
Officers: Adrian John Whitehead, Secretary; Thomas Alexander Marie Dubaere [1965] Director [Belgian]; Karelle Marie Reine Jeanne Lamouche [1975] Director [French]; Ana Cristina Ragageles de Oliveira Frewen [1968] Director/SVP Operations (Franchise) [Portuguese]; Saro Seropyan [1981] Director/VP Finance [French]; Jean-Marc Francois Vendioux [1965] Director/Senior Vice President [French]

Accor UK Business & Leisure Hotels Limited
Incorporated: 30 June 1971 *Employees:* 1,719
Net Worth: £170,982,000 *Total Assets:* £224,406,000
Registered Office: 10 Hammersmith Grove, London, W6 7AP
Activities: Hotels and similar accommodation
Parent: Accor Hotelinvest UK Limited
Officers: Cecile Marie Marguerite Verstraete, Secretary; Olivier Marie Pierre Daguzan [1976] Director/Chief Operating Officer [French]; Etienne Michel Ghislain Bourel de La Ronciere [1975] Asset Management Director [French]; Alice Sophie Benedicte Neubert [1983] Finance Director [French]

Accor UK Economy Hotels Limited
Incorporated: 18 February 1976 *Employees:* 1,212
Net Worth: £147,760,000 *Total Assets:* £188,771,008
Registered Office: 10 Hammersmith Grove, London, W6 7AP
Activities: Hotels and similar accommodation
Parent: Accor Hotelinvest UK Limited
Officers: Cecile Marie Marguerite Verstraete, Secretary; Olivier Marie Pierre Daguzan [1976] Director/Chief Operating Officer [French]; Etienne Michel Ghislain Bourel de La Ronciere [1975] Asset Management Director [French]; Alice Sophie Benedicte Neubert [1983] Finance Director [French]

Accord Bidco Limited
Incorporated: 4 March 2015
Net Worth Deficit: £53,291,000 *Total Assets:* £257,920,992
Registered Office: Verde (c/o Oaktree Capital Management (UK) LLP), 10 Bressenden Place, London, SW1E 5DH
Activities: Activities of other holding companies n.e.c.
Parent: Accord Midco Limited
Officers: Charles Peter Bithell [1968] Director/Chief Financial Officer; Janet Elizabeth Entwistle [1961] Managing Director; Jean Rollier [1973] Managing Director; Jim Van Steenkiste [1978] Director/Investment Professional

Accord Topco Limited
Incorporated: 4 March 2015 *Employees:* 1,085
Net Worth Deficit: £44,652,000 *Total Assets:* £306,535,008
Registered Office: Verde (c/o Oaktree Capital Management (UK) LLP), 10 Bressenden Place, London, SW1E 5DH
Activities: Activities of other holding companies n.e.c.
Officers: Charles Peter Bithell [1968] Director/Chief Financial Officer; Janet Elizabeth Entwistle [1961] Managing Director; Jean Rollier [1973] Managing Director; Jim Van Steenkiste [1978] Director/Investment Professional

Accorinvest UK BCT Limited
Incorporated: 9 June 2017 *Employees:* 3
Net Worth: £1,258,000 *Total Assets:* £210,838,000
Registered Office: 10 Hammersmith Grove, London, W6 7AP
Activities: Other business support service activities n.e.c.
Parent: Accor Hotelinvest UK Limited
Officers: Cecile Marie Marguerite Verstraete, Secretary; Olivier Marie Pierre Daguzan [1976] Director [French]; Etienne Michel Ghislain Bourel de La Ronciere [1975] Asset Management Director [French]; Alice Sophie Benedicte Neubert [1983] Finance Director [French]

Ace European Holdings Limited
Incorporated: 15 March 2004
Net Worth: £1,501,926,016 *Total Assets:* £1,501,934,976
Registered Office: 100 Leadenhall Street, London, EC3A 3BP
Activities: Activities of financial services holding companies
Officers: David Michael Alan Furby [1963] Director; Mark Kent Hammond [1960] Director [American]; Ashley Craig Mullins [1976] Director/Lawyer [Australian]; Alexander Matthew Wenham Shaw [1964] Director

Acquisition Company Finance Limited
Incorporated: 14 August 2015
Net Worth Deficit: £436,186 *Total Assets:* £349,780,704
Registered Office: St Martin's Court, 10 Paternoster Row, London, EC4M 7HP
Activities: Other business support service activities n.e.c.
Parent: CBRE Holdings Limited
Officers: Duncan James Green [1962] Director; Christopher Rush Oster [1970] Director/Vice President Tax Planning; Elizabeth Cormack Thetford [1954] Legal and Compliance Executive Director; Pasha Zargarof [1973] Director/General Counsel [American]

Acquisition Fine Art
Incorporated: 27 October 2015
Net Worth: £346,102,208 *Total Assets:* £346,102,208
Registered Office: 29 Throgmorton Street, London, EC2N 2AT
Activities: Fund management activities
Officers: Claire Jacqueline Marie Gastaldi [1954] Director [French]

Acturis Group Limited
Incorporated: 9 June 2010 *Employees:* 523
Net Worth: £192,140,720 *Total Assets:* £216,196,288
Registered Office: Courtyard Suite, 100 Hatton Garden, London, EC1N 8NX
Activities: Activities of head offices
Shareholder: Summit Partners Europe Private Equity Fund L.P.
Officers: Scott Charles Collins [1965] Managing Director [American/British]; Theodore Sam Duchen [1966] Director; David McDonald [1962] Director; Han Sikkens [1978] Director/Investment Professional [Dutch]

Acturis International Limited
Incorporated: 9 June 2010
Net Worth: £6,146,441 *Total Assets:* £169,753,968
Registered Office: Courtyard Suite, 100 Hatton Garden, London, EC1N 8NX
Activities: Activities of head offices
Parent: Acturis Group Limited
Officers: Scott Charles Collins [1965] Managing Director [American/British]; Theodore Sam Duchen [1966] Director; David McDonald [1962] Director; Han Sikkens [1978] Director/Investment Professional [Dutch]

AD (Europe) Finance
Incorporated: 26 April 2002
Previous: Allied Domecq (Europe) Finance
Net Worth: £147,925,472 *Total Assets:* £147,925,488
Registered Office: Chivas House, 72 Chancellors Road, London, W6 9RS
Activities: Financial intermediation not elsewhere classified
Parent: AD Overseas (Europe) Limited
Officers: Stuart MacNab [1964] Director/Accountant; Vincent Turpin [1978] Director/Chief Financial Officer [French]

AD Atlantic Finance Limited
Incorporated: 30 April 2004
Previous: Allied Domecq Atlantic Finance Limited
Net Worth: £1,283,705,600 *Total Assets:* £1,283,705,600
Registered Office: Chivas House, 72 Chancellors Road, London, W6 9RS
Activities: Other business support service activities n.e.c.
Parent: Allied Domecq (Holdings) Limited
Officers: Stuart MacNab [1964] Director/Accountant; Catherine Louise Thompson [1971] Director/General Counsel [Australian]; Vincent Turpin [1978] Director/Chief Financial Officer [French]

AD European Investments Limited
Incorporated: 10 December 1992
Previous: Allied Domecq European Investments Limited
Net Worth: £135,690,768 *Total Assets:* £135,870,432
Registered Office: Chivas House, 72 Chancellors Road, London, W6 9RS
Activities: Administration of financial markets
Parent: ADIUK
Officers: Ailsa Mary Robertson Mapplebeck, Secretary; Stuart MacNab [1964] Director/Accountant; Vincent Turpin [1978] Director/Chief Financial Officer [French]

AD Fin Services Limited
Incorporated: 13 April 1992
Previous: Allied Domecq Financial Services Limited
Net Worth: £126,333,304 *Total Assets:* £126,333,304
Registered Office: Chivas House, 72 Chancellors Road, London, W6 9RS
Activities: Financial intermediation not elsewhere classified
Parent: Allied Domecq (Holdings) Limited
Officers: Jean-Christophe Coutures [1966] Director [French]; Stuart MacNab [1964] Director; Vincent Turpin [1978] Director/Chief Financial Officer [French]

AD INV Limited
Incorporated: 11 June 1957
Previous: Allied Domecq Investments Limited
Net Worth: £436,667,840 *Total Assets:* £436,667,840
Registered Office: Chivas House, 72 Chancellors Road, London, W6 9RS
Activities: Activities of head offices
Parent: Allied Domecq (Holdings) Limited
Officers: Ailsa Mary Robertson Mapplebeck, Secretary; Amanda Hamilton-Stanley [1968] Director/General Counsel; Stuart MacNab [1964] Director; Vincent Turpin [1978] Director/Chief Financial Officer [French]

AD Investment Holdings Limited
Incorporated: 30 April 2004
Previous: Allied Domecq Investment Holdings Limited
Net Worth: £1,945,149,184 *Total Assets:* £3,508,251,136
Registered Office: Chivas House, 72 Chancellors Road, London, W6 9RS
Activities: Other business support service activities n.e.c.
Parent: Allied Domecq Spirits & Wine Holdings Limited
Officers: Amanda Hamilton-Stanley [1968] Director/General Counsel; Stuart MacNab [1964] Director; Vincent Turpin [1978] Director/Chief Financial Officer [French]

AD Overseas (Europe) Limited
Incorporated: 15 December 1988
Previous: Allied Domecq Overseas (Europe) Limited
Net Worth: £5,153,252,352 *Total Assets:* £5,703,238,144
Registered Office: Chivas House, 72 Chancellors Road, London, W6 9RS
Activities: Activities of head offices
Parent: Allied Domecq (Holdings) Limited
Officers: Stuart MacNab [1964] Director/Accountant; Vincent Turpin [1978] Director/Chief Financial Officer [French]

AD Westport Limited
Incorporated: 30 April 2004
Previous: Allied Domecq Westport Limited
Net Worth: £551,344,704 *Total Assets:* £2,654,544,896
Registered Office: Chivas House, 72 Chancellors Road, London, W6 9RS
Activities: Other business support service activities n.e.c.
Parent: Pernod Ricard UK Group Limited
Officers: Ailsa Mary Robertson Mapplebeck, Secretary; Stuart MacNab [1964] Director/Accountant; Catherine Louise Thompson [1971] Director/General Counsel [Australian]; Vincent Turpin [1978] Director/Chief Financial Officer [French]

Adamant Investment Corporation Limited
Incorporated: 17 October 1927
Net Worth: £450,933,440 *Total Assets:* £463,083,424
Registered Office: York House, 45 Seymour Street, London, W1H 7LX
Activities: Development of building projects
Parent: BL Retail Holding Company Limited
Officers: Sarah Morrell Barzycki [1958] Director/Head of Finance; Timothy Andrew Roberts [1964] Director/Chartered Surveyor; Nigel Mark Webb [1963] Director/Chartered Surveyor

ADCG (UK) Limited
Incorporated: 18 February 2008 *Employees:* 278
Net Worth Deficit: £126,536,000 *Total Assets:* £392,136,000
Registered Office: 3 Bunhill Row, London, EC1Y 8YZ
Activities: Other business support service activities n.e.c.
Parent: The Government of Abu Dhabi
Officers: Humaid Matar Al Dhaheri [1978] Director [Emirati]; H.E. Saif Saeed Ahmed Saeed Ghobash [1982] Director General Abu Dhabi Tourism & Culture Authority [Emirati]

Addison Lee Financing Limited
Incorporated: 12 April 2013
Net Worth: £37,385,000 *Total Assets:* £406,199,008
Registered Office: The Point, 37 North Wharf Road, London, W2 1AF
Activities: Activities of other holding companies n.e.c.
Parent: Addison Lee Midco II Limited
Officers: Lee Gage, Secretary; Andrew Kenneth Boland [1969] Director/Accountant; Simon Gordon [1970] Director

Addison Lee Group Limited
Incorporated: 12 April 2013
Net Worth Deficit: £21,937,000 *Total Assets:* £337,360,000
Registered Office: The Point, 37 North Wharf Road, London, W2 1AF
Activities: Activities of other holding companies n.e.c.
Parent: Addison Lee Financing Ltd
Officers: Lee Gage, Secretary; Andrew Kenneth Boland [1969] Director/Accountant; Simon Gordon [1970] Director

Addison Lee Holdings Limited
Incorporated: 12 April 2013 *Employees:* 1,597
Net Worth Deficit: £18,364,000 *Total Assets:* £450,331,008
Registered Office: The Point, 37 North Wharf Road, London, W2 1AF
Activities: Activities of other holding companies n.e.c.
Parent: Carlyle Group LP
Officers: Lee Gage, Secretary; Andrew Kenneth Boland [1969] Director/Accountant; Andrew Richard Burgess [1964] Managing Director Investment Professional; Daryl Foster [1959] Managing Director; Simon Gordon [1970] Director/Chief Financial Officer; Liam Griffin [1973] Managing Director; Shaun Mercer [1980] Director/Financial Investment; Colin John Tenwick [1960] Director

Addison Lee Limited
Incorporated: 1 April 1975 *Employees:* 686
Net Worth: £80,460,000 *Total Assets:* £172,598,000
Registered Office: The Point, 37 North Wharf Road, London, W2 1AF
Activities: Taxi operation
Parent: Addison Lee Group Limited
Officers: Lee Gage, Secretary; Andrew Kenneth Boland [1969] Director/Accountant; Simon Gordon [1970] Director

Addison Lee Midco II Limited
Incorporated: 12 April 2013 *Employees:* 1,597
Net Worth: £42,997,000 *Total Assets:* £441,407,008
Registered Office: The Point, 37 North Wharf Road, London, W2 1AF
Activities: Activities of other holding companies n.e.c.
Parent: Addison Lee Midco I Ltd
Officers: Lee Gage, Secretary; Andrew Kenneth Boland [1969] Director/Accountant; Simon Gordon [1970] Director

Additional Securities Limited
Incorporated: 8 March 1937
Net Worth: £5,217,000 *Total Assets:* £488,889,984
Registered Office: Council Secretariat, One Lime Street, London, EC3M 7HA
Activities: Other activities auxiliary to insurance and pension funding
Officers: Andrew Stephen Gurney [1968] Director/Head, International Regulatory Affairs; Jamshaid Islam [1975] Director/Actuary; John David Parry [1963] Director/Accountant; Hayley Dana Spink [1970] Director/Deputy Head, Global Markets

Addleshaw Goddard LLP
Incorporated: 2 March 2006 *Employees:* 1,369
Net Worth: £104,145,000 *Total Assets:* £169,376,992
Registered Office: Milton Gate, 60 Chiswell Street, London, EC1Y 4AG
Officers: Justine Delroy [1973] Member; John Gerard Joyce [1963] Member; Michael Lowry [1970] Member; Malcolm Henry McPherson [1954] Member; Charles David St John Penney [1960] Member; Jonathan Mark Tattersall [1971] Member; William Granville Wastie [1970] Member; Neil Michael Addis [1971] LLP Member; Leona Shireen Ahmed [1968] LLP Member; David Jack Noble Anderson [1981] LLP Member; Emma Charlotte Armitage [1974] LLP Member; Caroline Kathreen MacDonald Armstrong [1974] LLP Member; Sarah Baillie [1976] LLP Member; Luke Zachary Baines [1977] LLP Member; Rona Bar-Isaac [1973] LLP Member; Paul Robert Barge [1970] LLP Member; Nicholas Anthony Mark Barlow [1970] LLP Member; Paul Robert Barnard [1981] LLP Member; Gerard Anthony Barnes [1971] LLP Member; Michael Felix Barnett [1963] LLP Member; Andrew Robert Bates [1979] LLP Member; George Adam Bennett [1961] LLP Member; Paul James Bentham [1964] LLP Member; Michael John Birchall [1967] LLP Member; Andrew Leslie Blower [1967] LLP Member; William James Boss [1968] LLP Member; Harold Brako [1970] LLP Member; Graham Michael Briggs [1959] LLP Member; Anna Bridgetta Brown [1966] LLP Member; Helena Anne Brown [1976] LLP Member; Rosanna Elizabeth Bryant [1975] LLP Member; Gerlando Butera [1958] LLP Member; Sally Anne Butt [1968] LLP Member; Oliver James Carruthers [1971] LLP Member; Christopher Cartwright [1973] LLP Member; Louisa Caswell [1971] LLP Member; Simon James Dawson Catto [1972] LLP Member; Will Chalk [1972] LLP Member; Jonathan Mark Cheney [1979] LLP Member; Richard Eric Clayton [1965] LLP Member; Euan Alastair Cluness [1978] LLP Member; Elizabeth Alison Collett [1979] LLP Member; Adrian Philip Collins [1966] LLP Member; Paul Martin Harcourt Concannon [1978] LLP Member; Timothy Cooper [1971] LLP Member; Simon Courie [1973] LLP Member; Julia Alison Court [1965] LLP Member; Alastair Lindsay Cowan [1975] LLP Member; Daniel Aster de Crecy Crawshaw [1973] LLP Member; Graham Cross [1976] LLP Member; Jonathan William Davey [1963] LLP Member; James Alexander Davison [1982] LLP Member; Michael Edward Davison [1976] LLP Member; Michelle de Kluyver [1967] LLP Member; Joan Gabrielle Devine [1966] LLP Member; Paul Dight [1976] LLP Member; Giles Henry Distin [1973] LLP Member; Patrick John Duffy [1968] LLP Member; Michael Francis Duggan [1971] LLP Member; Alex James Dumphy [1978] LLP Member; Yorke Joseph John Eaton [1976] LLP Member; Miles Jonathan Ede [1972] LLP Member; Sarah Nicola Egbu [1980] LLP Member; Garry John Elliott [1971] LLP Member; David Anthony Ellis [1970] LLP Member; Marnix Christiaan Elsenaar [1970] LLP Member; John Ath Emerton [1966] LLP Member; David Jonathan Engel [1957] LLP Member; Catherine Fearnhead [1981] LLP Member; Marc Field [1983] LLP Member; Lorna Helen Finlayson [1965] LLP Member; Michael Philip FitzGenerald [1964] LLP Member; Jonathan Fletcher Rogers [1976] LLP Member; Andrew James Fordham [1980] LLP Member; Rebecca Jane Garner [1976] LLP Member; Susan Mary Garrett [1967] LLP Member; Fiona Ghosh [1973] LLP Member; Benjamin Angus Finemore Gill [1978] LLP Member; Bill John Gilliam [1971] LLP Member; Alison Goldthorp [1965] LLP Member; Richard Andrew Goodfellow [1972] LLP Member; Amanda Claire Gray [1968] LLP Member; Andrew Green [1980] LLP Member; Martin Steven Griffiths [1983] LLP Member; Elaine Gwilt [1975] LLP Member; Mark Adrian Windsor Hallam [1973] LLP Member; Jamie Thomas Hamnett [1973] LLP Member; David Handy [1968] LLP Member; Peter Justin Hardy [1966] LLP Member; Sarah Harrop [1979] LLP Member; Roger Hart [1971] LLP Member; David Patrick Hartley [1964] LLP Member; Luke Alexander Harvey [1983] LLP Member; Michelle Helen Headrige [1972] LLP Member; Abigail Louise Healey [1979] LLP Member; Anna Heaton [1978] LLP Member; James Allister Herring [1978] LLP Member; Michael John Hinchliffe [1974] LLP Member; Iain Kenneth Richard Hindhaugh [1977] LLP Member; Paul Andrew Hirst [1973] LLP Member

Adecco UK Limited
Incorporated: 7 November 1957 *Employees:* 1,051
Net Worth: £38,572,000 *Total Assets:* £717,968,000
Registered Office: Millennium Bridge House, 2 Lambeth Hill, London, EC4V 4BG
Activities: Temporary employment agency activities
Parent: Olsten (UK) Holdings Limited
Officers: Rashida Atinuke Akinjobi, Secretary; Alexandra Helen Bishop [1974] Managing Director; Yann Serge Stephane Halka [1974] Director/Chief Financial Officer [French]; Gavin Kenneth Tagg [1972] Director; Federico Vione [1972] Director [Italian]

ADG Market Making LLP
Incorporated: 5 January 2006
Net Worth: £14,871,830 *Total Assets:* £292,496,480
Registered Office: 10 Chiswell Street, London, EC1Y 4UQ
Officers: Adam Philip Pasternak Wiseman [1971] Member; Nicholas Stephen Evans [1983] LLP Member; Paul Jang [1981] LLP Member; Jeremy Cunninghame Jauncey [1984] LLP Member; Selina Jenny Krespi [1986] LLP Member; Giles Alexander Macey [1976] LLP Member; Mark Martell [1982] LLP Member; Frederico Ribeiro [1985] LLP Member; Georgi Ivanov Stavrev [1988] LLP Member; Dmitri Zaporozhets [1989] LLP Member

ADIB (UK) Limited
Incorporated: 27 July 2010 *Employees:* 23
Net Worth: £37,964,144 *Total Assets:* £149,294,912
Registered Office: 9th Floor, 26-28 Hammersmith Grove, London, W6 7HA
Activities: Banks
Officers: Abdulla Zaid Mohamed Alhelali Al Shehhi [1969] Director/Banker [Emirati]; Brian Keith Belcher [1956] Director/Banker; Michael Robert Hanlon [1944] Director/Banking Consultancy; Keith George McLeod [1963] Director/Chief Financial Officer

ADIUK
Incorporated: 20 January 2005
Previous: Allied Domecq Investments UK
Net Worth: £2,578,682,880 *Total Assets:* £2,578,682,880
Registered Office: Chivas House, 72 Chancellors Road, London, W6 9RS
Activities: Other business support service activities n.e.c.
Parent: AD Overseas (Europe) Limited
Officers: Amanda Hamilton-Stanley [1968] Director/General Counsel; Stuart MacNab [1964] Director/Accountant; Vincent Turpin [1978] Director/Chief Financial Officer [French]

ADM Investor Services International Limited
Incorporated: 11 October 1990 *Employees:* 151
Net Worth: £80,002,192 *Total Assets:* £781,050,240
Registered Office: 4th Floor, Millennium Bridge House, 2 Lambeth Hill, London, EC4V 3TT
Activities: Financial intermediation not elsewhere classified
Parent: Archer Daniels Midland (UK) Limited
Officers: Diarmuid Conor O'Hegarty, Secretary; Marilyne Boulaie [1965] Director/EMEA CFO & Lead Controller ASM International Sarl [French]; Stuart Patrick Jackson [1969] Finance Director; Thomas Robert Kadlec [1957] Director/Senior Vice President [American]; Diarmuid Conor O'Hegarty [1961] Compliance Director [Irish]; Fabian James Dunbar Somerville-Cotton [1964] Managing Director

Admiral Taverns (780) Limited
Incorporated: 15 June 2006
Net Worth Deficit: £69,642,000 *Total Assets:* £106,379,000
Registered Office: 150 Aldersgate Street, London, EC1A 4EJ
Activities: Hotels and similar accommodation
Parent: Admiral Taverns (Max) Limited
Officers: Andrew Francis James Clifford [1970] Property Director; Kevin Roger Georgel [1970] Managing Director; Glenn Pearson [1970] Director/Accountant CFO

Admiral Taverns (Chester) Limited
Incorporated: 10 May 2000 *Employees:* 105
Net Worth: £26,378,000 *Total Assets:* £183,964,992
Registered Office: Milton Gate, 60 Chiswell Street, London, EC1Y 4AG
Activities: Management of real estate on a fee or contract basis
Parent: Admiral Taverns Bidco Limited
Officers: Andrew Francis James Clifford [1970] Property Director; Kevin Roger Georgel [1970] Managing Director; Glenn Pearson [1970] Director/Accountant CFO

Admiral Taverns Bidco Limited
Incorporated: 21 October 2009
Net Worth: £83,532,000 *Total Assets:* £174,655,008
Registered Office: Milton Gate, 60 Chiswell Street, London, EC1Y 4AG
Activities: Activities of head offices
Parent: Admiral Taverns Group Holdings Limited
Officers: Andrew Francis James Clifford [1970] Property Director; Kevin Roger Georgel [1970] Managing Director; Glenn Pearson [1970] Director/Accountant CFO

Admiral Taverns Limited
Incorporated: 28 April 2005
Net Worth: £122,842,000 *Total Assets:* £237,404,000
Registered Office: Milton Gate, 60 Chiswell Street, London, EC1Y 4AG
Activities: Licenced restaurants
Parent: Admiral Taverns Bidco Limited
Officers: Andrew Francis James Clifford [1970] Property Director; Kevin Roger Georgel [1970] Managing Director; Glenn Pearson [1970] Director/Accountant CFO

ADSW Investment Holdings Limited
Incorporated: 6 May 2004
Previous: Allied Domecq Spirits & Wine Investment Holdings Limited
Net Worth: £2,801,173,504 *Total Assets:* £3,476,164,352
Registered Office: Chivas House, 72 Chancellors Road, London, W6 9RS
Activities: Other business support service activities n.e.c.
Parent: Allied Domecq Investment Holdings Limited
Officers: Stuart MacNab [1964] Director/Accountant; Vincent Turpin [1978] Director/Chief Financial Officer [French]

Advanced Payment Solutions Limited
Incorporated: 29 October 2003 *Employees:* 116
Net Worth Deficit: £9,765,498 *Total Assets:* £288,976,928
Registered Office: 6th Floor, One London Wall, London, EC2Y 5EB
Activities: Other service activities n.e.c.
Officers: Robert Van Breda, Secretary; Donald Ross Dixon [1947] Director [American]; Alessandro Hatami [1962] Director/Business Executive; James Gilbert Jones [1948] Director/Investor [American]; Simon Timothy Talbot Knight [1964] Director; Mark Timothy John Sismey-Durrant [1959] Director; Richard Thomas Wagner [1964] Director/Banking [American]

Advantage Sales & Marketing Limited
Incorporated: 8 September 2014 *Employees:* 3,492
Net Worth: £105,548,000 *Total Assets:* £243,774,000
Registered Office: c/o Legalinx Limited, 1 Fetter Lane, London, EC4A 1BR
Activities: Other professional, scientific and technical activities n.e.c.
Officers: Tanya Lynn Domier [1965] Director/Chief Executive Officer [American]; Brian Gifford Stevens [1973] Director/Chief Financial Officer [American]

Advent Capital (Holdings) Ltd
Incorporated: 15 March 1995 *Employees:* 117
Net Worth: £104,644,416 *Total Assets:* £592,307,712
Registered Office: 2nd Floor, 2 Minster Court, London, EC3R 7BB
Activities: Other service activities n.e.c.
Officers: Neil Murdoch Ewing, Secretary; Trevor John Ambridge [1959] Director/Chief Financial Officer; Andrew Robert Creed [1983] Finance Director; Ian Malcolm Hewitt [1962] Risk and Compliance Director; Luke Robert Tanzer [1965] Director/Chief Executive Officer [British/Australian]

Advent Capital (No. 3) Limited
Incorporated: 5 August 2005
Net Worth Deficit: £2,830,188 *Total Assets:* £613,207,552
Registered Office: 2nd Floor, 2 Minster Court, London, EC3R 7BB
Activities: Non-life insurance
Parent: Advent Capital (Holdings) Ltd
Officers: Neil Murdoch Ewing, Secretary; Trevor John Ambridge [1959] Director/Finance Officer; Andrew Robert Creed [1983] Finance Director; Ian Malcolm Hewitt [1962] Director; Luke Robert Tanzer [1965] Director/Chief Executive [British/Australian]

AECOM Corporation Holdings (UK) Limited
Incorporated: 29 March 1995
Previous: URS Corporation Holdings (UK) Limited
Net Worth: £22,176,000 *Total Assets:* £148,936,000
Registered Office: St George's House, 5 St George's Road, Wimbledon, London, SW19 4DR
Activities: Activities of head offices
Parent: URS Corporation Group Limited
Officers: Bolaji Moruf Taiwo, Secretary; Cheryl Rosalind McCall [1974] Director; David John Price [1970] Director/Accountant

AECOM Holdings Limited
Incorporated: 1 April 1999
Net Worth: £126,924,000 *Total Assets:* £203,543,008
Registered Office: St George's House, 5 St George's Road, Wimbledon, London, SW19 4DR
Activities: Activities of head offices
Parent: AECOM Intercontinental Holdings UK Limited
Officers: Bolaji Moruf Taiwo, Secretary; Joanne Lucy Lang [1975] Director/Accountant; David John Price [1970] Director/Accountant

AECOM Limited
Incorporated: 6 September 1984 *Employees:* 4,094
Net Worth: £132,232,000 *Total Assets:* £340,448,992
Registered Office: St George's House, 5 St George's Road, Wimbledon, London, SW19 4DR
Activities: Engineering related scientific and technical consulting activities
Parent: AECOM International Holdings UK Limited
Officers: Bolaji Moruf Taiwo, Secretary; David Charles Webb Barwell [1965] Director; Andrew Noel Jones [1965] Director; Cheryl Rosalind McCall [1974] Director/Accountant; William Jan Charles Quarterman [1962] Director/Chief Operating Officer, UK and Ireland

Aegis Electric & Gas International Services Limited
Incorporated: 17 May 1996
Net Worth: £7,300,000 *Total Assets:* £938,700,032
Registered Office: 33 Gracechurch Street, London, EC3V 0BT
Activities: Non-life insurance
Officers: Thomas George Story Busher [1955] Director; David Patrick Croom Johnson [1963] Managing Director; Christopher David Forbes [1954] Director/Consultant; Dr Wesley William Von Shack [1944] Director/Chairman [American]

Aegis Finance
Incorporated: 15 January 2002
Net Worth: £386,265,984 *Total Assets:* £400,807,008
Registered Office: 10 Triton Street, Regent's Place, London, NW1 3BF
Activities: Activities of head offices
Parent: Dentsu Aegis Network Ltd
Officers: Andrew John Moberly, Secretary; Stuart Anthony Jarrold [1970] Director; Michael Parry [1961] Director/Accountant; Peter Pontidas [1961] Director/Treasury [Australian/Greek]; Nicholas Charles Priday [1974] Director

Aegis GPS Holdings Limited
Incorporated: 15 September 2008
Net Worth: £621,246,016 *Total Assets:* £753,484,992
Registered Office: 10 Triton Street, Regent's Place, London, NW1 3BF
Activities: Activities of head offices
Parent: Dentsu Aegis Network Ltd
Officers: Andrew John Moberly, Secretary; Stuart Anthony Jarrold [1970] Director; Michael Parry [1961] Director/Accountant; Peter Pontidas [1961] Director/Treasury [Australian/Greek]; Nicholas Charles Priday [1974] Director

Aegis Group Holdings Limited
Incorporated: 25 February 1987
Net Worth: £171,780,000 *Total Assets:* £2,997,874,944
Registered Office: 10 Triton Street, Regent's Place, London, NW1 3BF
Activities: Activities of head offices
Parent: Dentsu Aegis Network Ltd
Officers: Andrew John Moberly, Secretary; Stuart Anthony Jarrold [1970] Director; Michael Parry [1961] Director/Accountant; Peter Pontidas [1961] Director/Treasury [Australian/Greek]; Nicholas Charles Priday [1974] Director

Aegis Group Participations Limited
Incorporated: 15 August 2008
Net Worth: £413,700,000 *Total Assets:* £1,048,617,984
Registered Office: 10 Triton Street, Regent's Place, London, NW1 3BF
Activities: Activities of head offices
Parent: Aegis Triton Limited
Officers: Andrew John Moberly, Secretary; Stuart Anthony Jarrold [1970] Director; Michael Parry [1961] Director/Accountant; Peter Pontidas [1961] Director/Treasury [Australian/Greek]; Nicholas Charles Priday [1974] Director; David Mark Wein [1977] Director

Aegis International Limited
Incorporated: 27 October 1995
Net Worth: £636,792,000 *Total Assets:* £1,385,091,968
Registered Office: 10 Triton Street, Regent's Place, London, NW1 3BF
Activities: Activities of head offices
Parent: Aegis Group Participations Limited
Officers: Andrew John Moberly, Secretary; Stuart Anthony Jarrold [1970] Director; Michael Parry [1961] Director/Accountant; Peter Pontidas [1961] Director [Australian/Greek]; Nicholas Charles Priday [1974] Director; David Mark Wein [1977] Director

Aegis London Holdings Limited
Incorporated: 9 March 2012 *Employees:* 122
Net Worth: £90,200,000 *Total Assets:* £1,084,300,032
Registered Office: 33 Gracechurch Street, London, EC3V 0BT
Activities: Non-life insurance
Parent: Aegis Holding Inc.
Officers: Thomas George Story Busher [1955] Director; David Patrick Croom-Johnson [1963] Managing Director; Christopher David Forbes [1954] Director/Consultant; Wesley William Von Schack [1944] Director/Chairman [American]

Aegis Media Pacific Ltd
Incorporated: 2 December 2009
Net Worth Deficit: £2,033,000 *Total Assets:* £150,866,000
Registered Office: 10 Triton Street, Regent's Place, London, NW1 3BF
Activities: Activities of head offices
Parent: Dentsu Aegis Network Ltd
Officers: Andrew John Moberly, Secretary; Stuart Anthony Jarrold [1970] Director; Simon Glyndon Jones [1972] Director/Accountant; Peter Pontidas [1961] Director/Treasury [Australian/Greek]; Nicholas Charles Priday [1974] Director; Nicholas Waters [1968] Director; Simon Gregorevich Zinger [1970] Director/General Counsel [British/American/Canadian]

Aegis Triton Limited
Incorporated: 5 December 2012
Net Worth: £574,371,968 *Total Assets:* £1,415,796,992
Registered Office: 10 Triton Street, Regent's Place, London, NW1 3BF
Activities: Activities of head offices
Parent: Dentsu Aegis Network Ltd
Officers: Andrew John Moberly, Secretary; Stuart Anthony Jarrold [1970] Director; Michael Parry [1961] Director; Peter Pontidas [1961] Director [Australian/Greek]; Nicholas Charles Priday [1974] Director

Aegon Holdings (UK) Limited
Incorporated: 19 November 1990
Net Worth: £2,519,482,880 *Total Assets:* £2,519,556,096
Registered Office: Level 26, The Leadenhall Building, 122 Leadenhall Street, London, EC3V 4AB
Activities: Activities of head offices
Parent: Aegon Europe Holdings B.V
Officers: James Kenneth MacKenzie, Secretary; Adrian Thomas Grace [1963] Director/Business Manager; Matthew James Rider [1963] Director [American]

Aegon UK PLC
Incorporated: 1 December 1998
Net Worth: £2,639,399,936 *Total Assets:* £2,817,200,128
Registered Office: Level 26, The Leadenhall Building, 122 Leadenhall Street, London, EC3V 4AB
Activities: Activities of head offices
Parent: Aegon Holdings (UK) Limited
Officers: James Kenneth MacKenzie, Secretary; Mark Bloom [1964] Director [American]; David Martin Dalton-Brown [1959] Director; Adrian Mark Eastwood [1961] Director/Actuary; James Ewing [1970] Director/Chief Actuary; Adrian Thomas Grace [1963] Director/Business Manager; Simon James Gulliford [1958] Director; Stephen James McGee [1973] Director/Chief Financial Officer; Michael John Merrick [1960] Director; Caroline Frances Ramsay [1962] Director; Matthew James Rider [1963] Director [American]; Michael John Rogers [1964] Director

Aequor Investments Limited
Incorporated: 8 June 2011
Net Worth Deficit: £181,615 *Total Assets:* £2,494,335,744
Registered Office: 1 Churchill Place, London, E14 5HP
Activities: Financial intermediation not elsewhere classified
Parent: Barclays Bank PLC
Officers: Christopher Patrick Le Neve Foster [1981] Director/Banker; Vishal Shah [1984] Director/Banker; Patrick Brittain Voisey [1979] Director; Jonathan Michael Walthoe [1975] Director/Banker

Aether IOS Limited
Incorporated: 19 April 2010 *Employees:* 3
Net Worth: £6,232,653,312 *Total Assets:* £7,008,297,984
Registered Office: 5th Floor, Milton Gate, 60 Chiswell Street, London, EC1Y 4SA
Activities: Activities of financial services holding companies
Parent: Ice Europe Parent Limited
Officers: Elizabeth Miriam Holt, Secretary; Scott Anthony Hill [1967] Director [American]; Andrew James Surdykowski [1970] Director [American]; Stuart Glen Williams [1978] Director [South African]

Aetna Insurance Company Limited
Incorporated: 4 October 2006
Net Worth: £82,681,816 *Total Assets:* £239,318,032
Registered Office: 50 Cannon Street, London, EC4N 6JJ
Activities: Non-life insurance
Parent: Aetna Holdco (UK) Limited
Officers: Kevin Hughes, Secretary; Stephen Alexander Hartigan [1952] Director; Mark John Howe [1969] Director; Damian Lenihan [1968] Director; Andrew Frederick John Neden [1962] Director; Brian Paul O'Rourke [1963] Finance Director [Irish]

AEW UK REIT PLC
Incorporated: 1 April 2015
Net Worth: £146,034,000 *Total Assets:* £199,076,000
Registered Office: 6th Floor, 65 Gresham Street, London, EC2V 7NQ
Activities: Activities of real estate investment trusts
Officers: Mark Ashley Burton [1948] Director; Katrina Harriet Hart [1974] Director; James Balfour Hyslop [1945] Director; Bimaljit Singh Sandhu [1962] Director

Affinity Sutton Capital Markets PLC
Incorporated: 20 August 2008
Net Worth: £50,000 *Total Assets:* £500,574,016
Registered Office: Level 6, 6 More London Place, Tooley Street, London, SE1 2DA
Activities: Financial intermediation not elsewhere classified
Parent: Affinity Sutton Funding Limited
Officers: Louise Hyde, Secretary; Jack Bargholz [1966] Director of Financial Services [Danish]; Gareth Francis [1976] Treasury Director; Janice Murray [1959] Director of Financial Performance and Planning

Affinity Sutton Funding Limited
Incorporated: 11 October 2005
Net Worth: £37,000 *Total Assets:* £500,611,008
Registered Office: Level 6, 6 More London Place, Tooley Street, London, SE1 2DA
Activities: Financial intermediation not elsewhere classified
Officers: Louise Hyde, Secretary; Gareth Francis [1976] Treasury Director; Clare Miller [1962] Director/Chief Executive

Affordable Housing Finance PLC
Incorporated: 7 March 2013 *Employees:* 14
Net Worth: £6,092,000 *Total Assets:* £3,438,377,984
Registered Office: 4th Floor, 107 Cannon Street, London, EC4N 5AF
Activities: Financial intermediation not elsewhere classified
Parent: T.H.F.C. (Services) Limited
Officers: Colin John Burke, Secretary; Scott Lee Bottles [1956] Director [American]; Colin John Burke [1962] Director; Isabella Francesca Connell [1980] Director; Fenella Jane Edge [1963] Director; Keith Philip Exford [1954] Director; Peter Henry Impey [1952] Director; John Henry Parker [1949] Director; Gillian Caroline Sarah Payne [1963] Director; Ian Rex Peacock [1947] Director; William Richard Perry [1978] Director; Deborah Frances Shackleton [1952] Director; Shirley Diana Smith [1960] Director; John Piers Williamson [1961] Director

AGF Insurance Limited
Incorporated: 1 June 1960
Net Worth: £132,848,000 *Total Assets:* £270,728,992
Registered Office: 1 Alie Street, London, E1 8DE
Activities: Non-life insurance
Parent: Catalina Holdings UK Limited
Officers: Keith Andrew Lyon, Secretary; Timothy Michael Cox [1947] Independent Non-Executive Director; Christopher John Fleming [1973] Director/Chartered Accountant; Generald Sidney Haase [1976] Director/Insurance Executive [American]; Philip Michael Hernon [1958] Director/Chief Executive Officer; Richard Owen Hudson [1952] Director; Graeme John McAndrew [1968] Finance Director [Australian]; Steven John Richardson [1960] Client Director

Aggregator of Loans Backed By Assets 2015-1 PLC
Incorporated: 24 February 2015
Net Worth: £501,217 *Total Assets:* £223,713,136
Registered Office: 35 Great St Helen's, London, EC3A 6AP
Activities: Financial intermediation not elsewhere classified
Parent: Aggregator of Loans Backed By Assets 2015-1 Mortgage Holdings Limited
Officers: Susan Iris Abrahams [1957] Director

Aggregator Vehicle PLC
Incorporated: 8 August 2014
Net Worth Deficit: £3,557,000 *Total Assets:* £590,856,000
Registered Office: 3 More London Riverside, London, SE1 2AQ
Activities: Financial intermediation not elsewhere classified
Parent: Aggregator Holdco Limited
Officers: Amanda Elizabeth Woods, Secretary; Muhammad Ahmed Anwer [1984] Director/Accountant [Pakistani]; Giles James Frost [1962] Director; Michael John Gregory [1968] Director; Nicholas James MacKee [1976] Director/Solicitor

Agilisys Holdings Limited
Incorporated: 15 June 1999 *Employees:* 1,341
Net Worth: £66,774,000 *Total Assets:* £147,944,000
Registered Office: Third Floor, One Hammersmith Broadway, Hammersmith, London, W6 9DL
Activities: Other information technology service activities
Officers: Manoj Kumar Badale [1967] Director; Andrew Philip Alden Court [1963] Director/Chief Financial Officer; Thomas Waterworth Drury [1961] Director/Chairman; Andrew Philip Mindenhall [1970] Director; Charles Stuart Mindenhall [1971] Director; Ewan Peter Stradling [1971] Director

Agility Trains East (Holdings) Limited
Incorporated: 31 January 2012
Net Worth Deficit: £478,768,992 *Total Assets:* £941,915,008
Registered Office: 4th Floor, 4 Copthall Avenue, London, EC2R 7DA
Activities: Activities of other holding companies n.e.c.
Parent: Hitachi Rail Europe Limited
Officers: Nestor Augusto Castillo Borrero [1973] Director; Jacobus Marinus Commandeur [1960] Director [Dutch]; Yusuke Fukaya [1982] Director [Japanese]; Jane Aine Mee [1965] Director; Barbara Jane Moorhouse [1958] Director; Andrew Stephen Pearson [1964] Director

Agility Trains East Limited
Incorporated: 31 January 2012
Net Worth Deficit: £478,768,992 *Total Assets:* £941,915,008
Registered Office: 4th Floor, 4 Copthall Avenue, London, EC2R 7DA
Activities: Manufacture of railway locomotives and rolling stock
Parent: Agility Trains East Midco Limited
Officers: Nestor Augusto Castillo Borrero [1973] Director; Jacobus Marinus Commandeur [1960] Director [Dutch]; Yusuke Fukaya [1982] Director [Japanese]; Jane Aine Mee [1965] Director; Barbara Jane Moorhouse [1958] Director; Andrew Stephen Pearson [1964] Director

Agility Trains West (Holdings) Limited
Incorporated: 31 January 2012
Net Worth Deficit: £470,696,000 *Total Assets:* £1,782,455,040
Registered Office: 4th Floor, 4 Copthall Avenue, London, EC2R 7DA
Activities: Activities of other holding companies n.e.c.
Parent: Hitachi Rail Europe Limited
Officers: Yusuke Fukaya [1982] Director [Japanese]; Gregor Scott Jackson [1974] Director; Amanda Vanderneth Leness [1967] Director [American]; Jane Aine Mee [1965] Director; Anh Khoa Nguyen [1989] Director [British/Vietnamese]; Alistair Graham Ray [1974] Director; Mark Roy Swindell [1960] Director; Jeffrey Lance Woodard [1978] Director [British/American]

Agility Trains West Limited
Incorporated: 31 January 2012
Net Worth Deficit: £470,696,000 *Total Assets:* £1,782,455,040
Registered Office: 4th Floor, 4 Copthall Avenue, London, EC2R 7DA
Activities: Manufacture of railway locomotives and rolling stock
Parent: Agility Trains West (Midco) Limited
Officers: Yusuke Fukaya [1982] Director [Japanese]; Gregor Scott Jackson [1974] Director; Amanda Vanderneth Leness [1967] Director [American]; Jane Aine Mee [1965] Director; Anh Khoa Nguyen [1989] Director [British/Vietnamese]; Alistair Graham Ray [1974] Director; Mark Roy Swindell [1960] Director; Jeffrey Lance Woodard [1978] Director [British/American]

Agincourt (1) LLP
Incorporated: 16 June 2017
Net Worth: £287,202,944 *Total Assets:* £287,267,264
Registered Office: 12 Charles II Street, London, SW1Y 4QU

Agman Holdings Limited
Incorporated: 23 December 1999 *Employees:* 120
Net Worth Deficit: £86,692,304 *Total Assets:* £246,521,040
Registered Office: 3 London Bridge Street, London, SE1 9SG
Activities: Activities of other holding companies n.e.c.
Parent: E D & F Man Holdings Limited
Officers: Richard John Aldis Askew, Secretary; John Alan Coughtrie [1955] Corporate Development Director; Laurie Peter Adrian Foulds [1969] Director/Chief Financial Officer

Agman Investments Limited
Incorporated: 11 October 2000
Net Worth Deficit: £38,116,112 *Total Assets:* £280,990,560
Registered Office: 3 London Bridge Street, London, SE1 9SG
Activities: Non-trading company
Parent: Agman Holdings Limited
Officers: Gaynor Antigha Bassey, Secretary; John Alan Coughtrie [1955] Corporate Development Director; Laurie Peter Adrian Foulds [1969] Director/Chief Financial Officer

Agrichrome Limited
Incorporated: 9 March 1988
Net Worth Deficit: £2,130,000 *Total Assets:* £180,684,000
Registered Office: Caroline House, 55-57 High Holborn, London, WC1V 6DX
Activities: Non-trading company
Parent: Elementis Securities Limited
Officers: Laura Ann Maria Higgins, Secretary; Christopher John Gilbert [1973] Director; Ralph Rex Hewins [1963] Director; Laura Ann Maria Higgins [1977] Director/Company Secretary

AH UK Animal Health (PVT) Ltd
Incorporated: 4 February 1991 *Employees:* 1,199
Previous: Henry Schein UK Holdings Limited
Net Worth: £185,464,960 *Total Assets:* £348,898,784
Registered Office: 18 Stanhope Place, London, W2 2HH
Activities: Non-specialised wholesale trade
Parent: Henry Schein UK Finance Limited
Officers: Graham Michael Rhodes, Secretary; William Campbell Bright [1964] Director/Accountant; Russell Adrian Cooke [1965] Director; Mike Ellis [1959] Director; Graham Michael Rhodes [1962] Director; Timothy James Tattersfield [1971] Director

AHK International LLP
Incorporated: 20 January 2016
Net Worth: £106,268,976 *Total Assets:* £137,821,104
Registered Office: 1st Floor, Thavies Inn House, 3-4 Holborn Circus, London, EC1N 2HA
Officers: Abdul Haleem Kherallah [1964] Member; Judith Anne Kherallah [1961] Member

AHL Partners LLP
Incorporated: 11 December 2012
Net Worth: £295,463,680 *Total Assets:* £303,114,496
Registered Office: Riverbank House, 2 Swan Lane, London, EC4R 3AD
Officers: Antoine Hubert Joseph Marie Forterre [1983] Member; Matthew Walter Sargaison [1968] Member; Francis James Bovell Blackburn [1985] LLP Member; Giuliana Bordigoni [1978] LLP Member; Richard Bounds [1977] LLP Member; Thomas Royston Bowles [1980] LLP Member; Andrew Stewart Burrows [1978] LLP Member; Robert John Catterall [1968] LLP Member; Paul James Chambers [1980] LLP Member; Gary Collier [1970] LLP Member; Paul Adam Dackombe [1962] LLP Member; Rory James de Poulton Ferguson [1980] LLP Member; Thomas Erich Flury [1980] LLP Member; Dr Yoav Git [1973] LLP Member; Nicolas Mark Granger [1974] LLP Member; David John Greenaway [1969] LLP Member; Hinesh Dhiroo Kalian [1982] LLP Member; Mohan Russell Korgaonkar [1978] LLP Member; Dr Anthony William Ledford [1968] LLP Member; Slavi Marinov Marinov [1986] LLP Member; Andrea Mondelci [1977] LLP Member; Francois Stanislas Moreau [1981] LLP Member; James Julian Munro [1980] LLP Member; Alexander Law Nixon [1972] LLP Member; Dennis George Pilsworth [1966] LLP Member; Sandy Campbell Rattray [1969] LLP Member; Graham Scott Robertson [1969] LLP Member; Andre Rzym [1964] LLP Member; Emidio Sciulli [1985] LLP Member; Haris Skaliotis [1976] LLP Member; Kate Abigail Straker [1980] LLP Member; Richard Justin Turner Strutt [1977] LLP Member; Thomas Taylor [1985] LLP Member; Otto Anthonie Christoffel Van Hemert [1977] LLP Member; Timothy Wong [1967] LLP Member; Darrel Yawitch [1973] LLP Member

Ahli United Bank (UK) PLC
Incorporated: 27 April 1966 *Employees:* 115
Net Worth: £211,791,008 *Total Assets:* £2,021,229,312
Registered Office: 35 Portman Square, London, W1H 6LR
Activities: Banks
Officers: Neil Harnby, Secretary; Rashed Ismail Khalil Al Meer [1947] Director/Businessman [Bahraini]; Adnan Abdulmohsen Al-Marzouq [1958] Director [Kuwaiti]; Adel Mohamed Abdel Shafe El-Labban [1957] Director/Banker [Egyptian]; Keith Henry Gale [1960] Director/Deputy Group CEO-Risk, Legal & Compliance; David Howard Hodgkinson [1950] Director; Stephen James Hussey [1965] Director/Banker; James Thomas Jordan Steel [1960] Director; Sami Baha Eddine Tamim [1958] Director/Banker

Al Mistral Holdco Limited
Incorporated: 29 November 2016
Net Worth: £450,694,688 *Total Assets:* £450,705,568
Registered Office: 1st Floor, 63 Queen Victoria Street, London, EC4N 4UA
Activities: Activities of other holding companies n.e.c.
Parent: Al Mistral Parentco Limited
Officers: Elliot George Gow [1976] Director; Ian Vallance [1969] Director/Chartered Accountant

Al Mistral Limited
Incorporated: 29 November 2016
Net Worth: £443,879,200 *Total Assets:* £928,568,512
Registered Office: 1st Floor, 63 Queen Victoria Street, London, EC4N 4UA
Activities: Activities of other holding companies n.e.c.
Shareholders: Al Mistral Holdco Ltd; Al Mistral Holdco Limited
Officers: Elliot George Gow [1976] Director; Ian Vallance [1985] Director/Chartered Accountant

Al Mistral Parentco Limited
Incorporated: 29 November 2016
Net Worth: £450,694,688 *Total Assets:* £450,694,688
Registered Office: 1st Floor, 63 Queen Victoria Street, London, EC4N 4UA
Activities: Activities of other holding companies n.e.c.
Shareholders: Al Mistral Topco Ltd; Al Mistral Topco Limited
Officers: Elliot George Gow [1976] Director; Ian Vallance [1969] Director/Chartered Accountant

Al Mistral Topco Limited
Incorporated: 29 November 2016 *Employees:* 3,755
Net Worth: £456,620,224 *Total Assets:* £1,158,996,864
Registered Office: 1st Floor, 63 Queen Victoria Street, London, EC4N 4UA
Activities: Activities of other holding companies n.e.c.
Officers: James Generald Arthur Brocklebank [1970] Director; Hamdi Conger [1951] Director; Ian Ramsey Safwat El-Mokadem [1968] Director; Charalampos Kyriakopoulos [1977] Private Equity (Director) [Greek]; John Cook Pattullo [1952] Director; Graham Westgarth [1954] Director/Senior Executive

Al Perform Holdings LLP
Incorporated: 11 November 2014 *Employees:* 2,445
Net Worth Deficit: £143,307,008 *Total Assets:* £891,635,968
Registered Office: 6th Floor, Marble Arch House, 66 Seymour Street, London, W1H 5BT

AIB UK Loan Management Limited
Incorporated: 8 June 1988
Net Worth: £188,000,000 *Total Assets:* £1,732,000,000
Registered Office: AIB, St Helen's, 1 Undershaft, London, EC3A 8AB
Activities: Other business support service activities n.e.c.
Parent: AIB Holdings (U.K.) Limited
Officers: Iain Alexander Hamilton, Secretary; John Duff [1964] Director/Bank Manager [Irish]; Rachel Michelle Lawrence [1970] Director/Accountant; Michael Vivian Morris [1974] Director [Irish]; Donall O'Shea [1971] Director [Irish]

AIG Holdings Europe Limited
Incorporated: 28 January 2016
Net Worth: £4,096,194,048 *Total Assets:* £5,273,476,096
Registered Office: The AIG Building, 58 Fenchurch Street, London, EC3M 4AB
Activities: Other business support service activities n.e.c.
Parent: American International Group, Inc.
Officers: Kate Hillery, Secretary; Anthony Michael Baldwin [1969] Director/CEO UK & AEL/Commercial Underwriting; Martin Ronald Bowers [1945] Director/Insurance Broker; Fabrice Brossart [1972] Director/Chief Risk Officer [French]; Anthony Philip Hope [1947] Director; James Alan Lenton [1975] Director/Chief Financial Officer EMEA; Christopher David Seymour Newby [1973] Director/General Counsel; Philippe Zoetelief Tromp [1960] Director [French]; Adam Charles Winslow [1979] Director/CEO AIG Life/Consumer

AIG Life Limited
Incorporated: 11 September 2007 *Employees:* 249
Previous: Ageas Protect Limited
Net Worth: £327,640,992 *Total Assets:* £1,600,385,024
Registered Office: The AIG Building, 58 Fenchurch Street, London, EC3M 4AB
Activities: Life insurance
Parent: AIG Holdings Europe Limited
Officers: Kate Hillery, Secretary; Timothy Michael Heslin [1974] Director/Global Head of Risk Selection CoE, Life/Consumer [American]; Donald John MacLean [1980] Director/Chief Financial Officer; Laura Santori [1968] Independent Non-Executive Director [Italian]; Michael Norris Urmston [1949] Director; Adam Charles Winslow [1979] Director/Chief Operating Officer, EMEA

AIG Transaction Execution Limited
Incorporated: 27 October 2010
Net Worth: £1,553,000 *Total Assets:* £165,512,000
Registered Office: The AIG Building, 58 Fenchurch Street, London, EC3M 4AB
Activities: Other business support service activities n.e.c.
Parent: American International Group, Inc.
Officers: Kate Hillery, Secretary; Ola Bengtsson [1974] Director/EMEA Treasurer [Swedish]; Justin Jerome Walls Caulfield [1973] Director/Americas Treasurer AIG Property Casualty [American]; Alun Christopher Thomas [1968] Director/Head of Strategic Finance EMEA

Airbnb Payments UK Limited
Incorporated: 16 January 2015 *Employees:* 3
Net Worth: £7,569,920 *Total Assets:* £1,220,094,208
Registered Office: Suite 1, 3rd Floor, 11-12 St James's Square, London, SW1Y 4LB
Activities: Financial intermediation not elsewhere classified
Officers: Sharda Mehta [1970] Director/Attorney [American]; Hadi Moussa [1980] Director

Airport Group Investments Limited
Incorporated: 14 May 2007
Net Worth: £375,916,288 *Total Assets:* £429,530,720
Registered Office: 35 Great St Helen's, London, EC3A 6AP
Activities: Activities of financial services holding companies
Officers: Thiago Miguez Ramos Gouveia Silva [1973] Director [Portuguese]; David Mark Stanton [1969] Director; Michael Toms [1953] Director

Airwave Solutions Limited
Incorporated: 28 April 2000 *Employees:* 482
Net Worth: £85,851,000 *Total Assets:* £346,984,000
Registered Office: Nova South, 160 Victoria Street, London, SW1E 5LB
Activities: Other telecommunications activities
Parent: Guardian Digital Communications Limited
Officers: Joanne Bamber, Secretary; Vincent Kennedy [1972] Director [Irish]; Ian McCullagh [1963] Director/Business Executive [Irish]; Daniel George Pekofske [1976] Director/Corporate Vice President and Chief Accounting Officer [American]

Aitch Group Limited
Incorporated: 20 September 2011 *Employees:* 45
Net Worth: £61,313,620 *Total Assets:* £150,867,088
Registered Office: First Floor, Kirkdale House, Kirkdale Road, Leytonstone, London, E11 1HP
Activities: Development of building projects
Major Shareholder: Henry Thomas Smith
Officers: Chelsea Reynolds [1987] Director; Henry Thomas Smith [1962] Director/Investor; Christopher John Spires [1966] Finance Director

Akelius Residential Limited
Incorporated: 17 February 2012 *Employees:* 37
Net Worth: £327,894,336 *Total Assets:* £698,351,296
Registered Office: 10 Bloomsbury Way, London, WC1A 2SL
Activities: Management of real estate on a fee or contract basis
Officers: Tora Prickett, Secretary; Ralf Spann [1975] Director [German]; Andrew James Speller [1981] Director/Chartered Accountant; Leiv Inge Synnes [1970] Director [Swedish]

Akelius UK One Limited
Incorporated: 4 February 2014
Net Worth: £22,578,040 *Total Assets:* £121,488,040
Registered Office: 10 Bloomsbury Way, London, WC1A 2SL
Activities: Other letting and operating of own or leased real estate
Parent: Akelius Residential Limited
Officers: Tora Maria Prickett, Secretary; Ralf Spann [1975] Director [German]; Andrew James Speller [1981] Director/Chartered Accountant; Leiv Inge Synnes [1970] Director/Property [Swedish]

Aker Solutions Limited
Incorporated: 26 November 2003 *Employees:* 1,857
Previous: Aker Subsea Limited
Net Worth: £120,863,000 *Total Assets:* £346,300,000
Registered Office: Building 6, Chiswick Park, 566 Chiswick High Road, London, W4 5HR
Activities: Manufacture of other special-purpose machinery n.e.c.
Parent: Aker Solutions ASA
Officers: Kay Anderson [1970] Director of Legal; Stephanie Hoffmann [1971] Director/Head of Finance [German]; Sian Lloyd Rees [1960] Director/UK Country Manager & SVP CM EMEA

Al Rayan Bank PLC
Incorporated: 11 July 2002 *Employees:* 215
Net Worth: £128,762,000 *Total Assets:* £1,806,307,968
Registered Office: 44 Hans Crescent, London, SW1X 0LZ
Activities: Banks
Parent: Al Rayan (UK) Ltd
Officers: Mohammed Al Azam, Secretary; Ahmed Swaleh Abdisheikh [1971] Director/Chief Operating Officer [Kenyan]; Malcolm James Brookes [1955] Director; Sultan Ahmed Choudhury [1972] Director; Simon Alick Moore [1965] Director; Adel Mohammed Tayyeb Mustafawi [1967] Director/Group CEO [Qatari]; Richard Francis Sommers [1956] Director

Alba 2006-1 PLC
Incorporated: 17 March 2006
Net Worth: £71,000 *Total Assets:* £125,823,000
Registered Office: Fifth Floor, 100 Wood Street, London, EC2V 7EX
Activities: Other business support service activities n.e.c.
Parent: Oakwood Global Assets Limited
Officers: Mark Howard Filer [1967] Director

Alba 2006-2 PLC
Incorporated: 16 May 2006
Net Worth: £1,240,000 *Total Assets:* £178,004,992
Registered Office: Fifth Floor, 100 Wood Street, London, EC2V 7EX
Activities: Other business support service activities n.e.c.
Parent: Oakwood Global Assets Limited
Officers: Mark Howard Filer [1967] Director

Alba 2007-1 PLC
Incorporated: 13 October 2006
Net Worth Deficit: £1,685,000 *Total Assets:* £417,871,008
Registered Office: Fifth Floor, 100 Wood Street, London, EC2V 7EX
Activities: Other business support service activities n.e.c.
Parent: Oakwood Global Assets Limited
Officers: Mark Howard Filer [1967] Director

Alberto-Culver (Europe) Limited
Incorporated: 10 August 2009
Net Worth: £166,860,000 *Total Assets:* £166,860,000
Registered Office: Unilever House, 100 Victoria Embankment, London, EC4Y 0DY
Activities: Activities of head offices
Shareholders: Unilever US Investments Limited; Unilever N.V.
Officers: James Oliver Earley, Secretary; Richard Clive Hazell, Secretary; Richard Clive Hazell [1966] Director/Solicitor; Amanda Louise King [1973] UK & Ireland Tax Director

Alberto-Culver Group Limited
Incorporated: 14 October 1986
Net Worth: £165,828,000 *Total Assets:* £369,865,984
Registered Office: Unilever House, 100 Victoria Embankment, London, EC4Y 0DY
Activities: Activities of production holding companies
Parent: Alberto-Culver (Europe) Limited
Officers: James Oliver Earley, Secretary; Richard Clive Hazell, Secretary; Richard Clive Hazell [1966] Director/Solicitor; Amanda Louise King [1973] UK & Ireland Tax Director

Alberto-Culver UK Holdings Limited
Incorporated: 22 March 2012
Net Worth: £129,445,000 *Total Assets:* £129,455,000
Registered Office: Unilever House, 100 Victoria Embankment, London, EC4Y 0DY
Activities: Activities of head offices
Parent: Alberto-Culver UK Products Limited
Officers: James Oliver Earley, Secretary; Richard Clive Hazell, Secretary; Anna Jo Karen Elphick [1975] Director/Accountant; Richard Clive Hazell [1966] Director/Solicitor; Amanda Louise King [1973] UK & Ireland Tax Director

Alberto-Culver UK Products Limited
Incorporated: 11 December 2009
Net Worth: £368,076,000 *Total Assets:* £368,592,000
Registered Office: Unilever House, 100 Victoria Embankment, London, EC4Y 0DY
Activities: Activities of production holding companies
Parent: Alberto-Culver Group Limited
Officers: James Oliver Earley, Secretary; Richard Clive Hazell, Secretary; Richard Clive Hazell [1966] Director/Solicitor; Amanda Louise King [1973] UK & Ireland Tax Director

Albion No.3 PLC
Incorporated: 14 July 2015
Net Worth Deficit: £770,000 *Total Assets:* £183,232,000
Registered Office: 35 Great St Helen's, London, EC3A 6AP
Activities: Financial intermediation not elsewhere classified
Parent: Albion No.3 Holdings Limited
Officers: Helena Paivi Whitaker [1963] Director [Finnish]

Alcentra Limited
Incorporated: 12 August 1994 *Employees:* 88
Net Worth: £277,852,992 *Total Assets:* £343,567,008
Registered Office: 160 Queen Victoria Street, London, EC4V 4LA
Activities: Security and commodity contracts dealing activities
Parent: Alcentra Asset Management Limited
Officers: Daniel Steven Fabian, Secretary; Gregory Allan Brisk [1962] Director/Chief Operating Officer; Amir Eilon [1948] Director; Daniel Steven Fabian [1981] Director/Chief Financial Officer; David Forbes-Nixon [1964] Director/Banker; Mitchell Evan Harris [1955] Director [American]

Aldea UK Holdco Limited
Incorporated: 4 May 2017
Net Worth Deficit: £1,564,628 *Total Assets:* £140,161,440
Registered Office: 5 Broadgate, London, EC2M 2QS
Activities: Activities of other holding companies n.e.c.
Officers: Ilyas Ahmad [1971] Director/Finance; Bronte Louise Somes [1972] Director/Asset Management

Aldermanbury Investments Limited
Incorporated: 29 February 2000
Net Worth: £612,928,320 *Total Assets:* £2,164,326,400
Registered Office: 25 Bank Street, Canary Wharf, London, E14 5JP
Activities: Other business support service activities n.e.c.
Parent: J.P. Morgan Capital Financing Limited
Officers: Luiz Eduardo de Salvo [1975] Director [Italian]; Andrea de Zordo [1973] Director/Banker [Italian]; David Alexander Fellowes-Freeman [1976] Director; Clare Louise Johns [1976] Director; Kimberley Harden Taylor [1968] Director; Stephen Michael White [1973] Director/Legal Entity Controller

Aldwych Finance Limited
Incorporated: 2 April 2003
Net Worth: £153,456,000 *Total Assets:* £153,744,992
Registered Office: 80 Strand, London, WC2R 0RL
Activities: Activities of other holding companies n.e.c.
Parent: Pearson Overseas Holdings Limited
Officers: Stephen Andrew Jones, Secretary; Natalie Jane White, Secretary; Sally Kate Miranda Johnson [1973] Director; James Daniel Marshall [1960] Director/Chartered Accountant; Andrew John Midgley [1961] Director/Accountant

Algeco Global Finance PLC
Incorporated: 10 September 2012
Previous: Algeco Scotsman Global Finance PLC
Net Worth: £219,539,056 *Total Assets:* £1,802,126,208
Registered Office: Algeco Group, 12 Berkeley Street, London, W1J 8DT
Activities: Activities of head offices
Officers: James Howard O'Malley, Secretary; Gary May [1958] Director/Financial Consultant; James Howard O'Malley [1977] Director/Lawyer [American]; Sundip Thakrar [1965] Director/CFO, Algeco Europe

Alixpartners Ltd
Incorporated: 11 October 2002 *Employees:* 597
Net Worth: £63,911,000 *Total Assets:* £249,976,000
Registered Office: 6 New Street Square, London, EC4A 3BF
Activities: Management consultancy activities other than financial management
Shareholder: Jay Alix
Officers: Kathryn Louise Koorenny, Secretary; Stefano Aversa [1960] Managing Director-Business Unit Leader [Italian]; Lisa Landau Carnoy [1967] Director/Chief Financial Officer [American]; Stephen Michael Deedy [1959] Director/Chief Administrative Officer [American]; Kathryn Louise Koorenny [1962] Director/General Counsel [American]; Paul Matthew Thompson [1967] Director/Head of Operations, EMEA

The All England Lawn Tennis & Croquet Club Limited
Incorporated: 1 March 2011 *Employees:* 286
Net Worth: £273,643,008 *Total Assets:* £458,886,016
Registered Office: The All England Lawn Tennis Club, Church Road, Wimbledon, London, SW19 5AE
Activities: Activities of sport clubs
Officers: Sally Jane Ambrose [1969] Director/Buyer; Philip Graeme Howard Brook [1956] Director; Richard Michael Gradon [1959] Director; Timothy Henry Henman [1974] Director; Ian Leslie Hewitt [1947] Director; Alexandra Winifred Louise Innes [1978] Director/Investment Banking [British/Swedish]; Deborah Ann Jevans [1960] Director; Simon Alan Jones [1956] Director; Augustine Thomas Odonnell [1952] Director; Richard Timothy Stoakes [1959] Director; Ashley James Kenneth Tatum [1970] Director/Manager; The Honourable Henry Bruce Weatherill [1953] Director/Chartered Accountant

The All England Lawn Tennis Ground PLC
Incorporated: 23 June 1920
Net Worth: £396,248,992 *Total Assets:* £493,776,992
Registered Office: Church Road, Wimbledon, London, SW19 5AE
Activities: Operation of sports facilities
Parent: The All England Lawn Tennis & Croquet Club Limited
Officers: Philip Graeme Howard Brook [1956] Director; Lord Evan Mervyn Davies [1952] Director/Chairman; Richard Michael Gradon [1959] Director; Ian Leslie Hewitt [1947] Director; Alexandra Winnifred Louise Innes [1976] Director/Investment Banking [British/Swedish]; Simon Alan Jones [1956] Director; The Lord Augustine Thomas O'Donnell [1952] Director; David John Rawlinson [1953] Director/Chartered Accountant

All Saints Retail Limited
Incorporated: 25 October 2000 *Employees:* 3,224
Net Worth Deficit: £173,524,000 *Total Assets:* £122,146,000
Registered Office: Units C15-C17, Jack's Place, 6 Corbet Place, London, E1 6NN
Activities: Wholesale of clothing and footwear
Parent: Lion/Heaven UK II Limited
Officers: Peter James Wood, Secretary; Rory O'Connor [1966] Director/Investment Professional PE; Matthew Wilson [1986] Director/Investment Manager; Peter James Wood [1973] Director/Global CFO

All3media Finance Limited
Incorporated: 28 June 2006
Net Worth: £56,782,144 *Total Assets:* £231,122,992
Registered Office: Berkshire House, 168-173 High Holborn, London, WC1V 7AA
Activities: Other business support service activities n.e.c.
Parent: All3media Intermediate Limited
Officers: Angela McMullen, Secretary; Sara Kate Geater [1955] Director/Chief Operating Officer; Angela McMullen [1967] Director/Chartered Accountant; Victoria Jane Turton [1962] Director/Chief Executive Officer

All3media Limited
Incorporated: 1 June 2003 *Employees:* 54
Net Worth: £11,385,201 *Total Assets:* £128,633,720
Registered Office: Berkshire House, 168-173 High Holborn, London, WC1V 7AA
Activities: Television programme production activities
Parent: All3media Group Limited
Officers: Angela McMullen, Secretary; Sara Kate Geater [1955] Director/Chief Operating Officer; Angela McMullen [1967] Director/Chartered Accountant; Victoria Jane Turton [1962] Director/Chief Executive Officer

All3media USA Limited
Incorporated: 22 November 2012
Net Worth: £97,083,120 *Total Assets:* £146,994,176
Registered Office: Berkshire House, 168-173 High Holborn, London, WC1V 7AA
Activities: Television programme production activities
Parent: All3media Limited
Officers: Angela McMullen, Secretary; Sara Kate Geater [1955] Director/Chief Operating Officer; Angela McMullen [1967] Director/Chartered Accountant; Victoria Jane Turton [1962] Director/Chief Executive Officer

Allen & Ginter (UK) Limited
Incorporated: 21 December 1987
Net Worth: £1,090,668,032 *Total Assets:* £1,090,668,032
Registered Office: Globe House, 1 Water Street, London, WC2R 3LA
Activities: Activities of head offices
Parent: Weston Investment Company Limited
Officers: David Patrick Ian Booth [1974] Director/Group Chief Accountant; Noelle Colfer [1968] Director/Solicitor; Carola Wiegand [1966] Director/Global Commercial Tax Manager [German]

Allen & Overy LLP
Incorporated: 30 January 2004 *Employees:* 5,221
Net Worth: £449,500,000 *Total Assets:* £1,127,699,968
Registered Office: One Bishops Square, London, E1 6AD
Officers: Andrew Mark Ballheimer [1961] Member; Laetitia Julia Amandine Benard [1974] Member; Willem Michel Georges Clara Dejonghe [1961] Member; Denise Patricia Gibson [1979] Member; David Peter Lee [1966] Member; Daniel Joseph Shurman [1965] Member; Timaeus Magnus Stevens [1969] Member; James Abbott [1982] LLP Member; Frederiek Adams [1982] LLP Member; Dr Borries Ahrens [1971] LLP Member; Alexandre Ancel [1972] LLP Member; Christopher Hugh Andrew [1967] LLP Member; Guy Alexander Antrobus [1977] LLP Member; Matthew Appleton [1983] LLP Member; Dirk Frans Edmond Arts [1965] LLP Member; Nicolaus Ascherfeld [1971] LLP Member; Parya Renee Badie [1973] LLP Member; Alasdair MacLeod Balfour [1975] LLP Member; Peter Banks [1984] LLP Member; Matthias Gunter Baudisch [1969] LLP Member; Silvia Bauza Hernandez [1970] LLP Member; Antonio Francesco Bavasso [1971] LLP Member; Christian Marcel August Bayart [1971] LLP Member; Lorraine Bayliss [1974] LLP Member; Markulf Kurt Martin Behrendt [1974] LLP Member; Alexander Behrens [1975] LLP Member; Catherine Bell-Walker [1971] LLP Member; Duncan Bellamy [1977] LLP Member; David Michael Benton [1966] LLP Member; Driss Bererhi [1977] LLP Member; Fabian Beullekens [1972] LLP Member; Jonathan Edward Morgan Bevan [1967] LLP Member; Hendrik Jan Biemond [1969] LLP Member; Femke Josephine Bierman [1969] LLP Member; Diana Billik [1972] LLP Member; Trevor James Leslie Borthwick [1962] LLP Member; Lisa Marie Le Breton Botha [1970] LLP Member; Neil Alexander Bowden [1972] LLP Member; Philip Gideon Bowden [1969] LLP Member; Nicholas Bradbury [1980] LLP Member; Ellen Benedikta Maria Braun [1964] LLP Member; Jonathan Lugard Forrest Brayne [1955] LLP Member; Gottfried Breuninger [1958] LLP Member; David John Broadley [1970] LLP Member; Gregory Thornton Brown [1972] LLP Member; Richard Kimberley John Browne [1968] LLP Member; Jonathan Michael Brownson [1968] LLP Member; Katrina Mary Buckley [1969] LLP Member; Calum Donald Burnett [1968] LLP Member; James Oliver Simon Burton [1977] LLP Member; Dr Wolf Rainer Bussian [1977] LLP Member; Craig Hugh Byrne [1969] LLP Member; Lawson Caisley [1970] LLP Member; David John Campbell [1973] LLP Member; Meredith Campion [1962] LLP Member; Damian Patrick Carolan [1973] LLP Member; Jean-Dominique Casalta [1968] LLP Member; Marc Castagnede [1969] LLP Member; William Andrew Castle [1965] LLP Member; Javier Castresana [1979] LLP Member; Arnondo Moy Chakrabarti [1971] LLP Member; Lydia Challen [1971] LLP Member; Denis Chemla [1964] LLP Member; David Leith Christensen [1978] LLP Member; Andrew Joseph Campbell Clark [1955] LLP Member; Nicholas John Spencer Clark [1973] LLP Member; Joe Clinton [1978] LLP Member; Angela Helen Clist [1967] LLP Member; Paul Julian Wigg Cluley [1970] LLP Member; John Edward Coburn [1979] LLP Member; Timothy Clive Conduit [1973] LLP Member; Sheila Theresa Connell [1964] LLP Member; William Thomas Constance [1980] LLP Member; Neville Cordell [1970] LLP Member; Andrew Cork [1982] LLP Member; Pieternella Catharina Cramer de Jong [1970] LLP Member; Richard William Lionel Cranfield [1956] LLP Member; Timothy George Reginald Crocker [1972] LLP Member; Arnold Robert Jan Croiset Van Uchelen [1961] LLP Member; Annabelle Davina Croker [1980] LLP Member; Jeanette Cruz [1973] LLP Member; Sachin Dave [1973] LLP Member; Jean-Christophe David [1977] LLP Member; Katie Helen Davies [1974] LLP Member; Christiaan Jacob Cornelis de Brauw [1969] LLP Member; Richard Gert-Jan de Haan [1975] LLP Member; Caspar Nicolaas de Jong [1981] LLP Member; Wijnand Zeeger de Jongh [1976] LLP Member; Cornelis de Ru [1974] LLP Member; Yvo de Vries [1974] LLP Member; Inigo Del Val Torre [1975] LLP Member; Jason Andrew Denisenko [1970] LLP Member; Andrew Laurence Denny [1970] LLP Member; Sanjeev Rai Dhuna [1972] LLP Member; Hans Gustav Diekmann [1961] LLP Member; Karan Dinamani [1981] LLP Member; Anthony Gervase Drake-Brockman [1966] LLP Member; Michael Greig Duncan [1957] LLP Member; Rudy Dupont [1975] LLP Member; James Durham [1975] LLP Member

Alliance Automotive Procurement Limited
Incorporated: 2 December 2008 *Employees:* 9
Previous: GAU Supply Services Limited
Net Worth: £13,600,859 *Total Assets:* £262,744,832
Registered Office: 2nd Floor East, 90 Chancery Lane, London, WC2A 1EU
Activities: Wholesale trade of motor vehicle parts and accessories
Shareholder: Group Auto Union UK and Ireland Limited
Officers: John Frederick Coombes, Secretary/Director; John Frederick Coombes [1965] Director; Jean-Jacques Mathieu Lafont [1959] Director [Belgian]

Alliance Boots Holdings Limited
Incorporated: 31 May 2002
Net Worth: £7,608,000,000 *Total Assets:* £14,366,999,552
Registered Office: 4th Floor, Sedley Place, 361 Oxford Street, London, W1C 2JL
Activities: Activities of head offices
Parent: WBA Acquisitions UK Holdco 7 Limited
Officers: Frank Standish, Company Secretary [Irish]; Aidan Gerard Clare [1966] Director [Irish]; Mark Francis Muller [1964] Director; Frank Standish [1963] Director/Company Secretary [Irish]

Alliancebernstein Limited
Incorporated: 23 October 1990 *Employees:* 175
Net Worth: £140,904,912 *Total Assets:* £176,594,160
Registered Office: 50 Berkeley Street, London, W1J 8HA
Activities: Fund management activities
Shareholders: AllianceBernstein Holdings Limited; AllianceBernstein Preferred Limited
Officers: Leanne Heather Quinn, Secretary; Ian Christian Foster [1974] Director/International Head of FI Risk Operations; Joanna Clare Green [1971] Director/UK and European CFO; James William Hammond [1962] Director/CEO & Head of EMEA Client Group; David Roger Hutchins [1971] Director/Portfolio Manager; Lynn Mah [1972] Director/Head of EMEA Marketing [Canadian]; Mark Ivor Phelps [1959] Director

Allianz Europe Limited
Incorporated: 1 July 1981
Net Worth: £3,218,610,944 *Total Assets:* £3,241,573,632
Registered Office: 5th Floor, 6 St Andrew Street, London, EC4A 3AE
Activities: Activities of other holding companies n.e.c.
Officers: Johannes Christian Maria Zarnitz, Secretary; Cornelis Bunschoten [1957] Director [Dutch]; Johannes Christian Maria Zarnitz [1959] Director [German]

Allianz Renewable Energy Partners II Limited
Incorporated: 7 April 2009
Net Worth: £114,198,384 *Total Assets:* £252,027,536
Registered Office: Sion Hall, 56 Victoria Embankment, London, EC4Y 0DZ
Activities: Financial intermediation not elsewhere classified
Parent: Allianz SE
Officers: Robin Christian Jack-Kee, Secretary; Jurgen Gerke [1959] Director/Chief Executive Officer [German]; Marc Groves-Raines [1965] Director/Investment Fund Manager; Gordon James Johnston [1974] Director; Iain William McMorrine [1959] Director

Allianz Renewable Energy Partners IV Limited
Incorporated: 7 April 2009
Net Worth: £641,627,648 *Total Assets:* £1,233,590,912
Registered Office: Sion Hall, 56 Victoria Embankment, London, EC4Y 0DZ
Activities: Financial intermediation not elsewhere classified
Shareholders: Allianz Renewable Energy Partners V PLC; Allianz SE
Officers: Robin Christian Jack-Kee, Secretary; Jurgen Gerke [1959] Director/Chief Executive Officer [German]; Marc Groves-Raines [1965] Director/Investment Fund Manager; Gordon James Johnston [1974] Director; Iain William McMorrine [1959] Director

Allianz Renewable Energy Partners V PLC
Incorporated: 9 May 2007
Net Worth: £613,576,640 *Total Assets:* £615,602,752
Registered Office: Sion Hall, 56 Victoria Embankment, London, EC4Y 0DZ
Activities: Activities of open-ended investment companies
Parent: Allianz SE
Officers: Robin Christian Jack-Kee, Secretary; Jurgen Gerke [1959] Director/Chief Executive Officer [German]; Marc Groves Raines [1965] Director/Investment Fund Manager; Gordon James Johnston [1974] Director; Iain William McMorrine [1959] Director/Investment Fund Manager

Allianz Renewable Energy Partners VI Limited
Incorporated: 15 January 2016
Net Worth: £524,602,784 *Total Assets:* £532,901,472
Registered Office: Sion Hall, 56 Victoria Embankment, London, EC4Y 0DZ
Activities: Activities of open-ended investment companies
Shareholders: Allianz Renewable Energy Partners VIII Limited; Allianz SE
Officers: Robin Christian Jack-Kee, Secretary; Juergen Gerke [1959] Director [German]; James Marc Ralph Groves-Raines [1965] Director; Gordon James Johnston [1974] Director; Iain William McMorrine [1959] Director

Allianz Renewable Energy Partners VIII Limited
Incorporated: 14 January 2016
Net Worth: £198,855,088 *Total Assets:* £198,925,344
Registered Office: Sion Hall, 56 Victoria Embankment, London, EC4Y 0DZ
Activities: Financial intermediation not elsewhere classified
Parent: Allianz SE
Officers: Robin Christian Jack-Kee, Secretary; Jurgen Gerke [1959] Director [German]; James Marc Ralph Groves-Raines [1965] Director; Gordon James Johnston [1974] Director; Iain William McMorrine [1959] Director

Allianz Technology Trust PLC
Incorporated: 18 October 1995
Net Worth: £313,432,960 *Total Assets:* £314,789,312
Registered Office: 199 Bishopsgate, London, EC2M 3TY
Activities: Financial intermediation not elsewhere classified
Officers: Eleanor Emuss, Secretary; Kirsten June Salt, Secretary; Richard William Holway [1947] Director/Technology Analyst; Robert Charles Hubert Jeens [1953] Director/Chartered Accountant; Elisabeth Charlotte Scott [1962] Director; Humphrey Van Der Klugt [1953] Director

Allied Domecq (Holdings) Limited
Incorporated: 13 April 1961
Net Worth: £8,991,437,824 *Total Assets:* £12,382,331,904
Registered Office: Chivas House, 72 Chancellors Road, London, W6 9RS
Activities: Activities of head offices
Parent: Allied Domecq Limited
Officers: Ailsa Mary Robertson Mapplebeck, Secretary; Gilles Bogaert [1969] Deputy Manager Director Finance [French]; Amanda Hamilton-Stanley [1968] Director/Lawyer; Stuart MacNab [1964] Director/Accountant; Catherine Louise Thompson [1971] Director/General Counsel [Australian]; Vincent Turpin [1978] Director/Chief Financial Officer [French]

Allied Domecq Limited
Incorporated: 11 May 1999
Net Worth: £3,818,341,376 *Total Assets:* £7,146,972,160
Registered Office: Chivas House, 72 Chancellors Road, London, W6 9RS
Activities: Activities of head offices
Parent: Goal Acquisitions (Holdings) Limited
Officers: Ailsa Mary Robertson Mapplebeck, Secretary; Amanda Hamilton-Stanley [1968] Director/General Counsel; Stuart MacNab [1964] Director; Catherine Louise Thompson [1971] Director/General Counsel [Australian]; Vincent Turpin [1978] Director/Chief Financial Officer [French]

Allied Domecq Spirits & Wine Holdings Limited
Incorporated: 8 November 1993
Net Worth: £8,607,614,976 *Total Assets:* £8,618,527,744
Registered Office: Chivas House, 72 Chancellors Road, London, W6 9RS
Activities: Activities of head offices
Shareholders: Chivas Holdings IP Limited; Allied Domecq (Holdings) Limited
Officers: Ailsa Mary Robertson Mapplebeck, Secretary; Amanda Hamilton-Stanley [1968] Director/General Counsel; Stuart MacNab [1964] Director/Accountant; Catherine Louise Thompson [1971] Director/General Counsel [Australian]; Vincent Turpin [1978] Director/Chief Financial Officer [French]

Allied Domecq Spirits & Wine Limited
Incorporated: 25 September 1961
Net Worth: £1,680,000,000 *Total Assets:* £1,680,000,000
Registered Office: Chivas House, 72 Chancellors Road, London, W6 9RS
Activities: Other business support service activities n.e.c.
Parent: Chivas Brothers Limited
Officers: Ailsa Mary Robertson Mapplebeck, Secretary; Gordon William Buist [1964] Technical Director; Jean-Christophe Coutures [1966] Director [French]; Amanda Hamilton-Stanley [1968] Director/Legal Counsel; Stuart MacNab [1964] Director; Catherine Louise Thompson [1971] Director/General Counsel [Australian]; Vincent Turpin [1978] Director/Chief Financial Officer [French]

Allied SX Ltd
Incorporated: 2 November 2016
Net Worth: £1 *Total Assets:* £140,000,032
Registered Office: 71-75 Shelton Street, Covent Garden, London, WC2H 9JQ
Activities: Web portals
Major Shareholder: Edward James Fitzpatrick
Officers: Edward James Fitzpatrick [1967] Director

Allied World Capital (Europe) Limited
Incorporated: 19 April 2010
Net Worth Deficit: £149,116,000 *Total Assets:* £447,351,840
Registered Office: 19th Floor, 20 Fenchurch Street, London, EC3M 3BY
Activities: Other business support service activities n.e.c.
Parent: Fairfax Financial Holdings Limited
Officers: Scott Andrew Carmilani [1964] Director/Insurance Executive [American]; Wesley David Dupont [1968] Director/General Counsel [American]; Edward Joseph Moresco [1975] Director [American]

Almacantar (Centre Point) Limited
Incorporated: 15 September 2005
Net Worth: £134,527,472 *Total Assets:* £134,637,392
Registered Office: 3 Quebec Mews, London, W1H 7NX
Activities: Activities of other holding companies n.e.c.
Officers: Richard William Painter, Secretary; Matthew Filkin [1978] Director/Property Developer; Michael Richard Hussey [1965] Director/Property Developer; Jonathan Robert Stewart Paul [1967] Director

Almack Ltd
Incorporated: 26 November 2015 *Employees:* 1
Net Worth: £238,936,000 *Total Assets:* £242,607,008
Registered Office: 1st Floor, West End House, 11 Hills Place, London, W1F 7SE
Activities: Buying and selling of own real estate
Major Shareholder: Amancio Ortega Gaona
Officers: Roberto Cibeira Moreiras [1971] Director [Spanish]; Jose Arnau Sierra [1956] Director [Spanish]

Alopuc Limited
Incorporated: 21 May 2013
Net Worth: £120,879,720 *Total Assets:* £120,886,496
Registered Office: Room 790, Lloyd's, 1 Lime Street, London, EC3M 7DQ
Activities: Activities of head offices
Parent: Enstar Group Limited
Officers: Martha Blanche Waymark Bruce, Secretary; Siobhan Mary Hextall, Secretary; Richard de Winton Wilkin Harries [1965] Director; James Robert Francis Lee [1962] Director; Brendan Richard Anthony Merriman [1958] Director

Alpha Bank London Limited
Incorporated: 17 October 1922 *Employees:* 74
Net Worth: £59,501,000 *Total Assets:* £814,126,016
Registered Office: Capital House, 85 King William Street, London, EC4N 7BL
Activities: Banks
Parent: Alpha Bank A.E.
Officers: Claire Connor, Secretary; Mark Edward Austen [1949] Director; Ioannis Minas Emiris [1963] Director/Banker [Greek]; Spyros Nicolaos Filaretos [1958] Director/Banker [Greek]; William Lindsay MacKay [1962] Director/Banker; George Michalopoulos [1973] Director [Greek]; Richard Stanley Price [1961] Director; Martin John Waghorn [1953] Director/Banker

Alpha Offshore International Leasing Limited
Incorporated: 12 May 2010 *Employees:* 4
Net Worth: £5,154,051 *Total Assets:* £154,897,680
Registered Office: 95 Aldwych, London, WC2B 4JF
Activities: Other business support service activities n.e.c.
Officers: Kevin Klein, Secretary; Jonathan Paul Cross [1979] Director; Stephen Laurence Mooney [1983] Director [Irish]; Jan Van Bohemen [1964] Director [Dutch]

Alpha Partners Leasing Limited
Incorporated: 28 December 2000 *Employees:* 17
Net Worth: £479,929,952 *Total Assets:* £2,331,942,656
Registered Office: 62 Buckingham Gate, London, SW1E 6AT
Activities: Financial leasing
Shareholder: Rolls-Royce Overseas Holdings Limited
Officers: Rachel Johnson, Secretary; Mark Brady [1965] Director; Michael Brooks [1969] Director/Business Executive [American]; Marcus Paul Dix [1978] Director; Thomas Alan Ellman [1968] Director/Executive Vice President & CFO [American]; Mark Garrett [1969] Managing Director; Robert Clair Lyons [1964] Director/CFO Gatx Corp [American]

Alpha Plus Group Limited
Incorporated: 2 July 1947 *Employees:* 860
Net Worth: £39,920,000 *Total Assets:* £153,844,000
Registered Office: 50 Queen Anne Street, Marylebone, London, W1G 8HJ
Activities: Pre-primary education
Parent: Alpha Plus Holdings PLC
Officers: Julia Caroline Norton, Secretary; Graham George Able [1947] Director; Mark David Hanley-Browne [1961] Director; Richard Daniels Jones [1963] Director; Mark John Sample [1961] Director

Alpha Plus Holdings PLC
Incorporated: 17 April 2002 *Employees:* 939
Net Worth: £28,513,000 *Total Assets:* £211,120,992
Registered Office: 50 Queen Anne Street, Marylebone, London, W1G 8HJ
Activities: Activities of head offices
Officers: Julia Caroline Norton, Secretary; George Graham Able [1947] Director; Paul Dominic Brereton [1963] Director; Elizabeth Mary Francis [1958] Director; Mark David Hanley-Browne [1961] Director; Timothy Hugh Penzer Haynes [1955] Director; Richard Daniels Jones [1963] Director; Stafford Murray Lancaster [1968] Director; Rossella Proscia [1973] Director [Italian]; Sir John Henry Ritblat [1935] Director; Mark John Sample [1961] Director; Dame Rosalind Joy Savill [1951] Director; Jennifer Elaine Stephen [1950] Director; Colin Barry Wagman [1946] Director

Alpha Prema UK Limited
Incorporated: 4 November 2005
Net Worth Deficit: £7,728,283 *Total Assets:* £3,473,385,728
Registered Office: No 2 St James's Market, London, SW1Y 4AH
Activities: Activities of head offices
Parent: Delta 3 (UK) Limited
Officers: Richard Norman Baer [1957] Director/Chief Legal Officer [American]; Duncan Francis Llowarch [1968] Director/Accountant; Gregory Ben Maffei [1960] Director/President and Chief Executive Officer [American]; Albert Edwin Rosenthaler [1959] Director/Chief Corporate Development Officer [American]; Sacha Jane Woodward Hill [1969] Director/Lawyer

Alpha Shipping Finance Limited
Incorporated: 13 May 2014
Net Worth: £3,880 *Total Assets:* £496,321,568
Registered Office: c/o Wilmington Trust SP Services (London) Limited, Third Floor, 1 King's Arms Yard, London, EC2R 7AF
Activities: Other business support service activities n.e.c.
Parent: Alpha Shipping Holdco Limited
Officers: Daniel Jonathan Wynne [1970] Director

Alstom NL Service Provision Ltd
Incorporated: 1 September 1993
Net Worth: £844,000 *Total Assets:* £190,082,000
Registered Office: 8th Floor, The Place, 175 High Holborn, London, WC1V 7AA
Activities: Urban and suburban passenger railway transportation by underground, metro and similar systems
Parent: Alstom Transport UK (Holdings) Limited
Officers: Mary Joanne Chun Heath, Secretary; Nicholas Paul Crossfield [1965] Managing Director; Stuart James Robert MacLeod [1961] Finance Director; Piers Spencer Richard Wood [1965] Director

Alstom Transport UK (Holdings) Limited
Incorporated: 1 October 2013
Net Worth: £315,500,000 *Total Assets:* £591,600,000
Registered Office: 8th Floor, The Place, High Holborn, London, WC1V 7AA
Activities: Activities of head offices
Parent: Alstom Transport Holdings B.V.
Officers: Mary Joanne Chun Heath, Secretary; Nicholas Paul Crossfield [1965] Managing Director; Douglas Andrew Johnston [1981] Director/Lawyer; Stuart James Robert MacLeod [1961] Finance Director

Alstom Transport UK Limited
Incorporated: 26 March 2013 *Employees:* 2,284
Net Worth: £280,400,000 *Total Assets:* £449,700,000
Registered Office: The Place, 175 High Holborn, London, WC1V 7AA
Activities: Manufacture of railway locomotives and rolling stock
Parent: Alstom Transport UK (Holdings) Limited
Officers: Mary Joanne Chun Heath, Secretary; Nicholas Paul Crossfield [1965] Managing Director; Susan Ann Evans [1969] Managing Director; Michael David Lund Hulme [1966] Managing Director; Douglas Andrew Johnston [1981] Director/Lawyer; Stuart James Robert MacLeod [1961] Finance Director; Jonathan Kevin Willcock [1976] Managing Director; Piers Spencer Richard Wood [1965] Managing Director

Amalgamated Metal Corporation PLC
Incorporated: 7 December 1929 *Employees:* 631
Net Worth: £170,648,000 *Total Assets:* £370,615,008
Registered Office: 7th Floor, 55 Bishopsgate, London, EC2N 3AH
Activities: Wholesale of metals and metal ores
Parent: Amco Investments Limited
Officers: Hamish Michie, Secretary; Hamish Michie [1967] Director/Chartered Accountant; Giles Pruen Robbins [1960] Director/Engineer; Geoffrey Charles Leacroft Rowan [1950] Director/Chartered Accountant; David Stephen Sher [1983] Investment Director; Victor Herman Sher [1947] Director/Chartered Accountant

Amarin Corporation PLC
Incorporated: 1 March 1989 *Employees:* 227
Net Worth Deficit: £33,544,502 *Total Assets:* £118,798,544
Registered Office: One New Change, London, EC4M 9AF
Activities: Activities of head offices
Officers: Joseph Kennedy, Secretary; John Francis Thero, Secretary; Lars Ekman [1950] Director/Executive [Swedish]; Gerrit Jan Van Heek [1949] Director [American]; Patrick Joseph O'Sullivan [1941] Director/Pharma Business Consultant [Irish]; Kristine Peterson [1959] Director [American]; David Stack [1951] Director/President, CEO Pacira Pharmaceuticals Inc [American]; John Francis Thero [1960] Director/Business Manager [American]; Joseph S Zakrzewski [1962] Director [American]

Amazon UK Services Ltd.
Incorporated: 10 July 1996 *Employees:* 19,749
Previous: Amazon.co.uk Ltd.
Net Worth: £1,090,433,024 *Total Assets:* £1,930,919,040
Registered Office: 1 Principal Place, Worship Street, London, EC2A 2FA
Activities: Other business support service activities n.e.c.
Parent: Amazon.Com, Inc.
Officers: Phaedra Ann Andrews [1975] Finance Director [American]; Mark Anthony Hemming [1973] Director; John Bradford Stone [1971] Director [American]

Amazon Video Limited
Incorporated: 8 March 2008 *Employees:* 268
Previous: Amazon Instant Video Limited
Net Worth: £55,825,000 *Total Assets:* £214,974,000
Registered Office: 1 Principal Place, Worship Street, London, EC2A 2FA
Activities: Video distribution activities
Parent: Amazon.Com, Inc.
Officers: John Bradford Stone [1971] Director [American]; Darren Samuel Waterman [1978] Finance Director

Ambac Assurance UK Limited
Incorporated: 11 September 1996 *Employees:* 12
Net Worth: £266,284,992 *Total Assets:* £652,200,000
Registered Office: 2nd Floor, 21 Great Winchester Street, London, EC2N 2JA
Activities: Non-life insurance
Parent: Ambac Financial Group, Inc.
Officers: Miguel Antonio Sanchez, Secretary; David Peter Barranco [1970] Director/Senior Portfolio Risk Manager [American]; Hugh John Boyle [1971] Director [Irish]; Kenneth Harold Davies [1956] Director/Chartered Accountant; William Moray Newton Fall [1957] Director/Chairman; Anthony James McMahon [1952] Director/Retired; John Drapeau Tifft [1964] Director/Lawyer [American]; David Trick [1971] Director/Chief Financial Officer and Interim CEO [American]

Ambassador Square
Incorporated: 24 April 1996
Net Worth Deficit: £34,674,000 *Total Assets:* £209,503,008
Registered Office: Sea Containers House, 18 Upper Ground, London, SE1 9GL
Activities: Other business support service activities n.e.c.
Parent: WPP Group Holdings Limited
Officers: Charles Ward Van Der Welle [1959] Director of Treasury; Steve Richard Winters [1968] Director/Chartered Accountant

Amber Bidco Limited
Incorporated: 24 August 2006
Net Worth: £38,650,000 *Total Assets:* £150,803,008
Registered Office: Riverside Three, Albert Wharf, 22 Hester Road, London, SW11 4AN
Activities: Activities of head offices
Parent: Amber Midco Limited
Officers: David Brian Nelson [1951] Director/Head of Design; Matthew Alexander Streets [1962] Director

Amber Infrastructure Group Holdings Limited
Incorporated: 20 February 2015 *Employees:* 103
Net Worth: £129,624,000 *Total Assets:* £159,983,008
Registered Office: 3 More London Riverside, London, SE1 2AQ
Activities: Activities of other holding companies n.e.c.
Shareholder: Hunt Amber London 2 Ltd
Officers: Amanda Elizabeth Woods, Secretary; Hugh Luke Blaney [1963] Director/Investment Banker [Irish]; Giles James Frost [1962] Director; Michael John Gregory [1968] Director/Chartered Builder; James Christopher Hunt [1970] Director [American]; Marion Louis Hunt [1947] Director/Executive [American]; Daniel Charles Singer [1960] Director/Hunt Companies Executive Vice President [American]

AMC Networks International Broadcasting Limited
Incorporated: 8 April 1999
Previous: Zonemedia Broadcasting Limited
Net Worth: £109,140,000 *Total Assets:* £201,522,000
Registered Office: 111 Salusbury Road, London, NW6 6RG
Activities: Television programming and broadcasting activities
Parent: AMC Networks International Enterprises Limited
Officers: Rutger Andree Wiltens [1973] Director/General Counsel [Dutch]; Kevin William Dickie [1968] Director/SVP UK & MEA; Robert McDonald Stewart [1979] Director/Chief Financial Officer

AMC Networks International Zone Holdings Limited
Incorporated: 21 October 2013
Net Worth: £89,104,000 *Total Assets:* £344,959,008
Registered Office: 111 Salusbury Road, London, NW6 6RG
Activities: Television programme distribution activities
Parent: AMC UK Midco Limited
Officers: Antoon Willem Rutger Andree Wiltens, Secretary; Antoon Willem Rutger Andree Wiltens [1973] Director/General Counsel [Dutch]; Edward Arthur Carroll [1963] Director/Chief Operating Officer [American]; Jamie Gerard Gallagher [1958] Director/Executive Vice President [American]; Sean Stephen Sullivan [1967] Director/EVP & CFO [American]

Amco Investments Limited
Incorporated: 7 July 2003 *Employees:* 631
Net Worth: £170,784,000 *Total Assets:* £370,623,008
Registered Office: 55 Bishopsgate, London, EC2N 3AH
Activities: Activities of head offices
Shareholder: Victor Herman Sher
Officers: Hamish Michie, Secretary; Giles Pruen Robbins [1960] Director; Geoffrey Charles Leacroft Rowan [1950] Director/Chartered Accountant; David Stephen Sher [1983] Director; Victor Herman Sher [1947] Director/Chartered Accountant

Amcol (Holdings) Ltd.
Incorporated: 18 May 1965
Net Worth: £95,725,000 *Total Assets:* £110,531,000
Registered Office: Third Floor, The Broadgate Tower, Primrose Street, London, EC2A 2RS
Activities: Other service activities n.e.c.
Parent: Minerals Technologies, Inc
Officers: Matthew Eric Garth [1974] Director/Chief Financial Officer [American]; Jonathan Jones Hastings [1962] Director/Executive [American]

Amdipharm Mercury UK Limited
Incorporated: 6 August 2012
Net Worth: £198,726,080 *Total Assets:* £286,048,608
Registered Office: Capital House, 85 King William Street, London, EC4N 7BL
Activities: Other professional, scientific and technical activities n.e.c.
Parent: Amdipharm Mercury Holdco UK Limited
Officers: Robert Sully, Secretary; Adeel Ahmad [1973] Director/Chief Financial Officer [Canadian]; Graeme Neville Duncan [1973] Director/Chief Executive Officer; Vikram Laxman Kamath [1977] Director/Vice President Finance and Group Controller [Indian]

Amdocs (UK) Limited
Incorporated: 25 July 1995 *Employees:* 203
Net Worth: £184,600,912 *Total Assets:* £207,408,256
Registered Office: 3rd Floor, Chiswick Park, Building 4, 566 Chiswick High Road, London, W4 5YE
Activities: Information technology consultancy activities
Parent: Amdocs Limited
Officers: Sarit Galanos [1973] Director/Head of RAN, R&D [Israeli]; Aine Moran [1982] Director/Accountant [Irish]

American Express Group Services Limited
Incorporated: 6 June 2008 *Employees:* 235
Net Worth: £132,628,000 *Total Assets:* £143,676,992
Registered Office: Belgrave House, 76 Buckingham Palace Road, London, SW1W 9AX
Activities: Other business support service activities n.e.c.
Parent: American Express Company
Officers: David James Muddiman, Secretary; Colin Derek Allen [1972] Director/IT; Paraskevi Galani [1968] Director/Financial Services Executive [Greek]; Jonathan Anthony David Hipkin [1965] Director

American Express Holdings Limited
Incorporated: 25 June 2004
Net Worth: £257,648,992 *Total Assets:* £262,031,008
Registered Office: Belgrave House, 76 Buckingham Palace Road, London, SW1W 9AX
Activities: Activities of financial services holding companies
Parent: American Express Company
Officers: David James Muddiman, Secretary; David John Bailey [1968] Director/VP of Reporting & Accounting-EMEA & Japan; Rafael Francisco Marquez Garcia [1971] Director/SVP Card Services Western Europe and UK Country [Spanish]

American Express Payment Services Limited
Incorporated: 4 July 2007
Net Worth: £204,575,488 *Total Assets:* £1,776,193,664
Registered Office: Belgrave House, 76 Buckingham Palace Road, London, SW1W 9AX
Activities: Other business support service activities n.e.c.
Parent: American Express Company
Officers: David James Muddiman, Secretary; David John Bailey [1968] Director/Controller; Sujata Narain Bhatia [1973] Director; Maria Thelma de La Pena Lopez [1973] Director [Mexican]; Werner Heinrich Decker [1963] Director/Senior Vice President & General Manager [German]; Rafael Francisco Marquez Garcia [1971] Director/SVP Card Services Western Europe and UK Country [Spanish]; Alan David Holmes [1966] Director; Colin Gerard John Paul O'Flaherty [1978] Director [Irish]

American Express Services Europe Limited
Incorporated: 16 July 1984 *Employees:* 5,155
Net Worth: £669,292,992 *Total Assets:* £6,830,564,864
Registered Office: Belgrave House, 76 Buckingham Palace Road, London, SW1W 9AX
Activities: Other business support service activities n.e.c.
Parent: American Express Holdings Limited
Officers: David James Muddiman, Secretary; David John Bailey [1968] Director/Controller; Carlos Carriedo [1975] Director [Mexican]; Charlotte Anne Duerden [1970] Director; Daniel James Edelman [1978] Director; Rafael Francisco Marquez Garcia [1971] Director/SVP Card Services Western Europe and UK Country [Spanish]; Jill Elizabeth Grafflin [1963] Director/Vice President World Service UK [American]; David Paul Murray [1966] Director

Amesbury Holdings Limited
Incorporated: 10 March 2011 *Employees:* 2
Net Worth: £224,351,040 *Total Assets:* £242,070,816
Registered Office: 29 Queen Anne's Gate, London, SW1H 9BU
Activities: Activities of head offices
Officers: Carolyn Ann Gibson, Secretary; James Edward Brotherton [1969] Director/Chartered Accountant; Kevin Francis O'Connell [1960] Director/Accountant [Irish]

AMG Plymouth UK Holdings (1) Limited
Incorporated: 18 February 2010
Net Worth: £314,814,656 *Total Assets:* £319,957,088
Registered Office: Suite 1, 3rd Floor, 11-12 St James's Square, London, SW1Y 4LB
Activities: Activities of financial services holding companies
Parent: Affiliated Managers Group, Inc.
Officers: David Michael Billings [1962] Director [American]; Dean Aaron Maines [1970] Director [American]

Amore Group (Holdings) Limited
Incorporated: 24 June 2008
Previous: Craegmoor Group (No.4) Limited
Net Worth: £6,911,000 *Total Assets:* £394,257,984
Registered Office: Fifth Floor, 80 Hammersmith Road, London, W14 8UD
Activities: Activities of head offices
Parent: Craegmoor Group (No.3) Limited
Officers: David James Hall, Secretary; Nigel Myers [1966] Finance Director; Trevor Michael Torrington [1961] Director/Chief Executive

AMS Bidco Ltd
Incorporated: 23 October 2013
Net Worth: £30,394,000 *Total Assets:* £296,640,992
Registered Office: 7 Bishopsgate, London, EC2N 3AQ
Activities: Activities of other holding companies n.e.c.
Parent: AMS Midco Limited
Officers: Rosaleen Blair [1965] Director [Irish]; Vanessa Byrnes [1973] Director [Irish]; Matthew Rodger [1968] Director; Richard Keith Timmins [1960] Director

AMS Holdco Ltd
Incorporated: 19 November 2013 *Employees:* 3
Net Worth: £174,967,008 *Total Assets:* £174,967,008
Registered Office: 7 Bishopsgate, London, EC2N 3AQ
Activities: Activities of other holding companies n.e.c.
Shareholders: Auxey Bidco Ltd; Steven Klinsky
Officers: Rosaleen Blair [1965] Director [Irish]; Richard Keith Timmins [1960] Director; Sir David Allan Walker [1956] Director

AMS Midco Ltd
Incorporated: 19 November 2013 *Employees:* 3,386
Net Worth: £68,379,000 *Total Assets:* £397,456,000
Registered Office: 7 Bishopsgate, London, EC2N 3AQ
Activities: Activities of other holding companies n.e.c.
Parent: AMS Holdco Limited
Officers: Rosaleen Blair [1965] Director [Irish]; Richard Keith Timmins [1960] Director

AMT Mortgage Insurance Limited
Incorporated: 26 June 1991 *Employees:* 13
Previous: Genworth Financial Mortgage Insurance Limited
Net Worth: £70,964,744 *Total Assets:* £151,412,032
Registered Office: Exchequer Court, 33 St Mary Axe, London, EC3A 8AA
Activities: Non-life insurance
Parent: Amtrust Europe Limited
Officers: Richard Thomas Marino, Secretary; Jeremy Edward Cadle [1965] Director; Jan Eric Kvarnstrom [1948] Director/Self Employed [Swedish]; Angel Guillermo Mas Murcia [1968] Director [Spanish]; John Sinclair [1948] Director; Robin William Webster [1955] Director

Amtrust Corporate Member Limited
Incorporated: 25 August 1998 *Employees:* 309
Net Worth Deficit: £163,812,000 *Total Assets:* £1,119,700,992
Registered Office: Exchequer Court, 33 St Mary Axe, London, EC3A 8AA
Activities: Non-life insurance
Parent: Amtrust International Limited
Officers: Pauline Cockburn, Secretary; Jeremy Edward Cadle [1965] Director; Peter Dewey [1976] Director

AMV BBDO Investments Limited
Incorporated: 14 February 1983 *Employees:* 706
Net Worth: £115,997,816 *Total Assets:* £163,261,952
Registered Office: Bankside 3, 90-100 Southwark Street, London, SE1 0SW
Activities: Non-trading company
Parent: Abbott Mead Vickers Group Limited
Officers: Sally Ann Bray, Secretary; Suzanne Gilson [1976] Director/AMV Group CFO; James Thomas Moser [1962] Director/Chairman, BBDO Europe [American]

Amyn Hotels Limited
Incorporated: 4 September 1972 *Employees:* 996
Net Worth: £73,104,272 *Total Assets:* £165,033,328
Registered Office: Eighth Floor, 167 Fleet Street, London, EC4A 2EA
Activities: Hotels and similar accommodation
Major Shareholder: Alnur Madatali Dhanani
Officers: Nicola Coveney, Secretary; Nicola Coveney [1972] Director; Alnur Madatali Dhanani [1955] Director; Rahim Alnur Dhanani [1984] Director

Anasuria Hibiscus UK Limited
Incorporated: 21 July 2015
Net Worth: £77,918,672 *Total Assets:* £202,650,496
Registered Office: Cannon Place, 78 Cannon Street, London, EC4N 6AF
Activities: Other professional, scientific and technical activities n.e.c.
Officers: Kock Hooi Lim [1957] Director/Group General Counsel of Hibiscus Petroleum Berhad [Malaysian]; Mark John Paton [1959] Director/Chief Operating Officer, Hibiscus Petroleum Berhad [British/Australian]; Dr. Kenneth Gerard Pereira [1958] Director/MD of Hibiscus Petroleum Berhad [Malaysian]

Anchor Carehomes Limited
Incorporated: 22 November 2002 *Employees:* 1,211
Previous: Ideal Carehomes Limited
Net Worth: £3,525,760 *Total Assets:* £100,163,136
Registered Office: Suites A & B, The Heals Building, Torrington Place, London, WC1E 7HJ
Activities: Residential care activities for the elderly and disabled
Officers: Mary Keane, Secretary; Jane Rachel Ashcroft [1966] Director; Mark Curran [1959] Director; Mark Charles Greaves [1966] Director; Sarah Elizabeth Jones [1968] Director; Christopher David Munday [1959] Managing Director Housing Operations; Rona Nicholson [1957] Director of Governance and Compliance

Anchorage Ports LLP
Incorporated: 25 March 2015
Net Worth: £373,973,952 *Total Assets:* £374,000,000
Registered Office: Craven House, 16 Northumberland Avenue, London, WC2N 5AP

Angel Leasing Company Limited
Incorporated: 17 October 1995
Net Worth: £255,484,992 *Total Assets:* £737,321,984
Registered Office: 123 Victoria Street, London, SW1E 6DE
Activities: Renting and leasing of other machinery, equipment and tangible goods n.e.c.
Parent: The Great Rolling Stock Company Limited
Officers: Nesha Holas, Secretary; Mark Andrew Hicks [1967] Director/Chartered Mechanical Engineer; David Michael Jordan [1973] Director/Chief Operating Officer; Alan Edward Lowe [1968] Director/Chief Financial Officer; Kevin George Tribley [1963] Director

Angel Trains Group Limited
Incorporated: 1 August 1995
Net Worth: £804,486,976 *Total Assets:* £1,049,128,000
Registered Office: 123 Victoria Street, London, SW1E 6DE
Activities: Activities of head offices
Parent: Willow Rolling Stock UK Limited
Officers: Nesha Holas, Secretary; Jean-Bastien Auger [1978] Director/Investment Manager [Canadian]; Malcolm Brown [1967] Director/Asset Manager; Mark Andrew Hicks [1967] Director/Chartered Mechanical Engineer; David Michael Jordan [1973] Chief Operating Director; Alan Edward Lowe [1968] Director/Chief Financial Officer; Anthony Raymond Mercado [1951] Director/Consultant; Stuart Randall Paterson [1958] Director/Accountant; Adam James Petrie [1985] Investment Director [New Zealander]; Leonard Keith Porter [1952] Director; Thomas William McLardy Smith [1957] Director; Kevin George Tribley [1963] Director

Angel Trains Limited
Incorporated: 21 March 1994 *Employees:* 122
Net Worth: £333,800,000 *Total Assets:* £1,590,300,032
Registered Office: 123 Victoria Street, London, SW1E 6DE
Activities: Renting and leasing of other machinery, equipment and tangible goods n.e.c.
Officers: Nesha Holas, Secretary; Mark Andrew Hicks [1967] Director/Chartered Mechanical Engineer; David Michael Jordan [1973] Director/Chief Operating Officer; Alan Edward Lowe [1968] Director/Chief Financial Officer; Kevin George Tribley [1963] Director

Anglo American (London)
Incorporated: 11 March 2005 *Employees:* 3
Net Worth: £619,418,560 *Total Assets:* £619,418,560
Registered Office: 20 Carlton House Terrace, London, SW1Y 5AN
Activities: Other business support service activities n.e.c.
Parent: Anglo American Holdings Limited
Officers: Ceri Howells [1972] Director/Accountant; Elaine Klonarides [1976] Director/Company Secretary

Anglo American Capital PLC
Incorporated: 6 February 2003
Net Worth: £4,092,511,488 *Total Assets:* £24,489,158,656
Registered Office: 20 Carlton House Terrace, London, SW1Y 5AN
Activities: Other business support service activities n.e.c.
Parent: Anglo American PLC
Officers: Clare Elizabeth Davage [1970] Director/Chartered Secretary; Elaine Klonarides [1976] Director/Company Secretary; Alan Conway Macpherson [1970] Director/Group Head of Tax; Stephen Thomas Pearce [1964] Finance Director [Australian]; Richard Price [1963] Director/Group General Counsel & Company Secretary [Canadian]; Douglas Smailes [1959] Director; Matthew Thomas Samuel Walker [1981] Director/Chartered Accountant

Anglo American Diamond Holdings Limited
Incorporated: 23 March 2012 *Employees:* 3
Net Worth: £505,540,800 *Total Assets:* £3,719,691,520
Registered Office: 20 Carlton House Terrace, London, SW1Y 5AN
Activities: Activities of head offices
Parent: Anglo American Investments (UK) Limited
Officers: Ceri Howells [1972] Director/Accountant; Elaine Klonarides [1976] Director/Company Secretary

Anglo American Holdings Limited
Incorporated: 17 March 1999 *Employees:* 4
Net Worth: £4,871,492,096 *Total Assets:* £6,637,677,568
Registered Office: 20 Carlton House Terrace, London, SW1Y 5AN
Activities: Activities of head offices
Parent: Anglo American Prefco Limited
Officers: Alan Conway Macpherson [1970] Director/Group Head of Tax; Craig Wilson Miller [1973] Director/Group Finance Controller; Richard Price [1963] Director/Group General Counsel & Company Secretary [Canadian]; Douglas Smailes [1959] Director

Anglo American International Holdings Limited
Incorporated: 6 July 2005 *Employees:* 4
Net Worth: £7,083,143,680 *Total Assets:* £7,084,498,432
Registered Office: 20 Carlton House Terrace, London, SW1Y 5AN
Activities: Activities of head offices
Parent: Anglo American Investments (UK) Limited
Officers: Ceri Howells [1972] Director/Accountant; Elaine Klonarides [1976] Director/Company Secretary

Anglo American Investments (UK) Limited
Incorporated: 8 February 1989 *Employees:* 3
Net Worth: £13,193,284,608 *Total Assets:* £24,025,305,088
Registered Office: 20 Carlton House Terrace, London, SW1Y 5AN
Activities: Other business support service activities n.e.c.
Parent: Anglo American Services (UK) Ltd
Officers: Ceri Howells [1972] Director/Accountant; Elaine Klonarides [1976] Director/Company Secretary; William Kow Buabin Ward-Brew [1969] Director/Accountant

Anglo American Marketing Limited
Incorporated: 7 March 1946 *Employees:* 174
Net Worth: £200,042,176 *Total Assets:* £989,921,664
Registered Office: 20 Carlton House Terrace, London, SW1Y 5AN
Activities: Other business support service activities n.e.c.
Parent: Anglo American Investments (UK) Limited
Officers: Debra Drake [1969] Director [American]; Rodney Harold Elliott [1960] Director/General Manager [Australian]; Richard Price [1963] Director/Group General Counsel & Company Secretary [Canadian]; Alexander Schmitt [1972] Director [German]; Heike Truol [1970] Director/Group Head of Commercial Services [German]; Paul Ward [1975] Director; Peter Graeme Whitcutt [1965] Director [South African]; Deborah Mary Wilson [1964] Director/Head of Tax

Anglo American PLC
Incorporated: 14 May 1998 *Employees:* 69,000
Net Worth: £16,675,377,152 *Total Assets:* £39,605,837,824
Registered Office: 20 Carlton House Terrace, London, SW1Y 5AN
Activities: Other mining and quarrying n.e.c.
Officers: Clare Elizabeth Davage, Secretary; Elaine Klonarides, Secretary; Richard Price, Secretary; Ian Robert Ashby [1957] Director [Australian]; Stuart John Chambers [1956] Director; Mark Cutifani [1958] Director/Chief Executive [Australian]; Victoria Nolitha Fakude [1964] Director [South African]; Byron Elmer Grote [1948] Director; Anthony Martin O'Neill [1957] Director [Australian]; Stephen Thomas Pearce [1964] Finance Director [Australian]; Dr Mphu Keneiloe Ramatlapeng [1953] Director/Executive Vice-President HIV Aids [Mosotho]; James Edmund Rutherford [1959] Director; Anne Stevens [1948] Director [American]; Jack Edward Thompson [1950] Director [American]

Anglo American Prefco Limited
Incorporated: 17 March 1999
Net Worth: £1,235,872,640 *Total Assets:* £1,630,970,240
Registered Office: 20 Carlton House Terrace, London, SW1Y 5AN
Activities: Financial intermediation not elsewhere classified
Parent: Anglo American Holdings Limited
Officers: Roger William Henderson [1980] Director/Chartered Tax Adviser; Ceri Howells [1972] Director/Accountant; Elaine Klonarides [1976] Director/Company Secretary

Anglo American Services (UK) Ltd.
Incorporated: 13 September 1988 *Employees:* 326
Net Worth: £9,146,216,448 *Total Assets:* £14,008,655,872
Registered Office: 20 Carlton House Terrace, London, SW1Y 5AN
Activities: Other business support service activities n.e.c.
Parent: Anglo American PLC
Officers: Clare Elizabeth Davage [1970] Director/Chartered Secretary; Elaine Klonarides [1976] Director/Company Secretary; Stephen Thomas Pearce [1964] Finance Director [Australian]; Richard Price [1963] Director/Group General Counsel & Company Secretary [Canadian]; Douglas Smailes [1959] Director; Matthew Thomas Samuel Walker [1981] Director/Chartered Accountant; Timothy Deiniol Walker-Jones [1973] Director

Anglo Asian Mining PLC
Incorporated: 9 September 2004 *Employees:* 694
Net Worth: £64,296,044 *Total Assets:* £114,649,344
Registered Office: 7 Devonshire Square, Cutlers Gardens, London, EC2M 4YH
Activities: Other mining and quarrying n.e.c.
Officers: William Morgan, Secretary; Professor Andrew John Monhemius [1942] Director/Metallurgist; Richard Calvin Round [1958] Finance Director; John Henry Sununu [1939] Director/Consultant [American]; Mohammad Reza Vaziri [1953] Director/Chairman [American]; Khosrow Zamani [1943] Director [American]

Anglo Pacific Group PLC
Incorporated: 7 February 1967 *Employees:* 10
Net Worth: £218,936,992 *Total Assets:* £253,362,000
Registered Office: 1 Savile Row, London, W1S 3JR
Activities: Other mining and quarrying n.e.c.
Officers: Kevin Flynn, Secretary; David Stuart Archer [1956] Director/Chief Executive [Australian]; William Michael Blyth [1950] Director/Accountant; Vanessa Angela Dennett [1965] Director/Solicitor; Nicolas Patrick Henderson Meier [1949] Director/Retired; Robert Henry Stan [1953] Director [Canadian]; Julian Andre Treger [1962] Director

Anglo Platinum Marketing Limited
Incorporated: 16 October 2008 *Employees:* 19
Net Worth: £119,715,256 *Total Assets:* £662,708,096
Registered Office: 20 Carlton House Terrace, London, SW1Y 5AN
Activities: Other business support service activities n.e.c.
Parent: Anglo American Holdings Limited
Officers: Richard Todd Duffey [1973] Director/Accountant [Australian]; Christopher Ivan Griffith [1965] Director/Chief Executive Officer: Anglo American Platinum Limited [South African]; Hilton Clement Ingram [1970] Director; Craig Wilson Miller [1973] Director/Group Finance Controller; Benny Gustaff Clement Oeyen [1961] Director/Executive Head Market Development [Belgian]; Richard Price [1963] Director/Group General Counsel & Company Secretary [Canadian]; Alexander Schmitt [1972] Director [German]; Peter Graeme Whitcutt [1965] Director [South African]; Deborah Mary Wilson [1964] Director/Head of Tax

Anglo-Eastern Plantations PLC
Incorporated: 8 February 1985 *Employees:* 15,691
Net Worth: £290,088,128 *Total Assets:* £423,065,920
Registered Office: Floor 6, Quadrant House, 4 Thomas More Square, London, E1W 1YW
Activities: Activities of head offices
Officers: Jonathan Ngee Song Law [1966] Director/Lawyer [Malaysian]; Dato John Ewe Chuan Lim [1949] Director/Accountant [Malaysian]; Siew Kim Lim [1948] Director [Malaysian]; Tian Huat Lim [1954] Director/Accountant [Malaysian]

Angus Dundee Distillers PLC
Incorporated: 14 October 1950 *Employees:* 134
Net Worth: £141,472,272 *Total Assets:* £164,446,112
Registered Office: 20-21 Cato Street, London, W1H 5JQ
Activities: Wholesale of wine, beer, spirits and other alcoholic beverages
Shareholders: Tania Hillman; Aaron Nicholas Hillman
Officers: Jean Elizabeth Hillman, Secretary; Robert Fleming [1955] Distillery Director; Aaron Nicholas Hillman [1964] Director; Jean Elizabeth Hillman [1932] Director; Tania Hillman [1962] Director; Terence Michael Hillman [1933] Director; Michael Hubert Humphreys [1932] Director; Steven McNeil [1968] Director; Brian John Megson [1955] Director/Executive

Anmercosa Finance Limited
Incorporated: 8 October 1964 *Employees:* 3
Net Worth: £1,214,392,448 *Total Assets:* £1,215,576,704
Registered Office: 20 Carlton House Terrace, London, SW1Y 5AN
Activities: Activities of head offices
Parent: Anglo American Holdings Limited
Officers: Roger William Henderson [1980] Director/Chartered Tax Adviser; Ceri Howells [1972] Director/Accountant; Elaine Klonarides [1976] Director/Company Secretary

Annington Funding PLC
Incorporated: 11 May 2017
Net Worth: £4,023,000 *Total Assets:* £3,408,953,088
Registered Office: 1 James Street, London, W1U 1DR
Activities: Other business support service activities n.e.c.
Parent: Annington Homes Limited
Officers: Andrew Peter Chadd, Secretary; Andrew Peter Chadd [1964] Director/Chief Financial Officer; James Christian Hopkins [1959] Director/Chief Executive Officer; Nicholas Peter Vaughan [1962] Commercial Director

Annington Homes Limited
Incorporated: 29 July 1996
Net Worth: £2,041,921,024 *Total Assets:* £5,441,652,224
Registered Office: 1 James Street, London, W1U 1DR
Activities: Activities of other holding companies n.e.c.
Parent: Annington Limited
Officers: Andrew Peter Chadd, Secretary; Andrew Peter Chadd [1964] Director; James Christian Hopkins [1959] Director; Nicholas Peter Vaughan [1962] Director

Annington Limited
Incorporated: 29 October 2012 *Employees:* 38
Net Worth: £3,220,156,928 *Total Assets:* £7,285,855,232
Registered Office: 1 James Street, London, W1U 1DR
Activities: Activities of other holding companies n.e.c.
Officers: Andrew Peter Chadd, Secretary; Vivek Gopaldas Ahuja [1966] Director [Singaporean]; Andrew Peter Chadd [1964] Director; Fraser Scott Duncan [1960] Director; James Christian Hopkins [1959] Director; Justin Matthew King [1961] Director/Chairman; Baroness Helen Lawrie Liddell [1950] Director; Jonathan Ottley Short [1961] Director; Nicholas Peter Vaughan [1962] Director; Steven Keith Webber [1969] Financial Managing Director

Annington Property Limited
Incorporated: 29 July 1996
Net Worth: £5,488,902,144 *Total Assets:* £6,880,119,808
Registered Office: 1 James Street, London, W1U 1DR
Activities: Other letting and operating of own or leased real estate
Parent: Annington Subsidiary (Holdings) Limited
Officers: Andrew Peter Chadd, Secretary; Andrew Peter Chadd [1964] Director; James Christian Hopkins [1959] Director; Sally Elizabeth Parsons [1963] Director; Nicholas Peter Vaughan [1962] Director

Annington Rentals (Holdings) Limited
Incorporated: 28 July 1999
Net Worth Deficit: £85,869,000 *Total Assets:* £329,748,992
Registered Office: 1 James Street, London, W1U 1DR
Activities: Activities of other holding companies n.e.c.
Parent: Annington Limited
Officers: Andrew Peter Chadd, Secretary; Andrew Peter Chadd [1964] Director; James Christian Hopkins [1959] Director; Nicholas Peter Vaughan [1962] Director

Annington Rentals (No. 6) Limited
Incorporated: 9 May 2006
Net Worth: £54,947,112 *Total Assets:* £154,203,888
Registered Office: 1 James Street, London, W1U 1DR
Activities: Other letting and operating of own or leased real estate
Parent: Annington Rentals (Holdings) Limited
Officers: Andrew Peter Chadd, Secretary; Andrew Peter Chadd [1964] Director; James Christian Hopkins [1959] Director; Adrian Ronald James Needham [1957] Director; Nicholas Peter Vaughan [1962] Director

Annington Subsidiary Holdings Limited
Incorporated: 11 December 1997
Net Worth: £4,281,775,104 *Total Assets:* £4,281,799,936
Registered Office: 1 James Street, London, W1U 1DR
Activities: Activities of other holding companies n.e.c.
Parent: Annington Homes Limited
Officers: Andrew Peter Chadd, Secretary; Andrew Peter Chadd [1964] Director; James Christian Hopkins [1959] Director; Nicholas Peter Vaughan [1962] Director

Ansco Arena Limited
Incorporated: 9 January 2002 *Employees:* 195
Net Worth: £36,508,000 *Total Assets:* £330,484,000
Registered Office: The O2, Peninsula Square, London, SE10 0DX
Activities: Other amusement and recreation activities n.e.c.
Parent: Ansco UK Finance Co 2 Limited
Officers: Sarah Catherine McGuigan, Secretary; Gavin Neil Brind [1973] Finance Director; Alexander James Hill [1972] Director/President, AEG Europe; John Robert Langford [1971] Director/Chief Operating Officer [South African]; Sarah Catherine McGuigan [1974] Director/Chief Legal and Development Officer; Paul Reeve [1980] Director/Chief Finance Officer

Ansco Finance 2011 Limited
Incorporated: 10 June 2011 *Employees:* 198
Net Worth: £63,700,000 *Total Assets:* £379,688,000
Registered Office: The O2, Peninsula Square, London, SE10 0DX
Activities: Other business support service activities n.e.c.
Major Shareholder: Philip Fredrick Anschutz
Officers: Christopher Kangis, Secretary; Alistair Hardy Wood, Secretary; Gavin Neil Brind [1973] Finance Director; Alexander James Hill [1972] Director/President, AEG Europe; John Robert Langford [1971] Director/Chief Operating Officer [South African]; Sarah Catherine McGuigan [1974] Director/Chief Legal and Development Officer; Paul Reeve [1980] Director/Chief Finance Officer

Ansco UK Finance Co. 2 Ltd.
Incorporated: 8 February 2006
Net Worth: £196,835,008 *Total Assets:* £246,295,008
Registered Office: The O2, Peninsula Square, London, SE10 0DX
Activities: Other business support service activities n.e.c.
Parent: Ansco Finance 2011 Ltd
Officers: Christopher Kangis, Secretary; Alistair Hardy Wood, Secretary; Gavin Neil Brind [1973] Finance Director; Alexander James Hill [1972] Director/President, AEG Europe; John Robert Langford [1971] Director/Chief Operating Officer [South African]; Sarah Catherine McGuigan [1974] Director/Chief Legal and Development Officer; Paul Reeve [1980] Director/Chief Finance Officer

Ansell (U.K.) Limited
Incorporated: 2 November 1979 *Employees:* 3
Previous: Pacific Dunlop Holdings (Europe) Limited
Net Worth: £64,612,696 *Total Assets:* £171,663,248
Registered Office: 6th Floor, 60 Gracechurch Street, London, EC3V 0HR
Activities: Activities of head offices
Officers: Francois Henri Cmg Le Jeune D'Allegeershecque [1963] Director [Belgian]; Phillippe Henri Carlos Michel Maria Rommel [1973] Director [Belgian]; Peter Emiel Vosch [1968] Director [Belgian]

Antalis Group
Incorporated: 26 July 1919
Net Worth: £135,454,000 *Total Assets:* £135,456,000
Registered Office: 100 New Bridge Street, London, EC4V 6JA
Activities: Activities of head offices
Parent: Antalis Group (Holdings) Limited
Officers: David Hunter [1954] Director; Sebastien Marie Lefebvre [1975] Accounts and Administration Director [French]; Stephen Gerard McCue [1965] Financial Director

Antalis Group (Holdings) Limited
Incorporated: 15 September 1970
Net Worth: £162,994,448 *Total Assets:* £162,997,136
Registered Office: 100 New Bridge Street, London, EC4V 6JA
Activities: Activities of head offices
Parent: Antalis
Officers: David Hunter [1954] Director; Sebastien Marie Lefbvre [1975] Accounts and Administration Director [French]; Stephen Gerard McCue [1965] Financial Director

Antalis Holdings Limited
Incorporated: 2 December 1935
Net Worth: £124,466,000 *Total Assets:* £124,468,000
Registered Office: 100 New Bridge Street, London, EC4V 6JA
Activities: Activities of head offices
Parent: Antalis Group
Officers: David Hunter [1954] Director; Sebastien Marie Lefebvre [1975] Accounts and Administration Director [French]; Stephen Gerard McCue [1965] Financial Director

Antalis Limited
Incorporated: 22 December 1972 *Employees:* 1,081
Net Worth: £67,033,000 *Total Assets:* £247,910,000
Registered Office: 100 New Bridge Street, London, EC4V 6JA
Activities: Activities of head offices
Parent: Antalis Holdings Limited
Officers: Andrew John Powlesland Christian [1962] Marketing & Purchasing Director; David Hunter [1954] Director; Sebastien Marie Lefebvre [1975] Accounts and Administration Director [French]; Stephen Gerard McCue [1965] Financial Director; Bruce William Munro [1955] Sales Director

Antares Underwriting Limited
Incorporated: 6 July 2007
Net Worth Deficit: £57,502 *Total Assets:* £1,472,182,016
Registered Office: 21 Lime Street, London, EC3M 7HB
Activities: Non-life insurance
Parent: QIC Global Holdings Limited
Officers: James Michael Linsao, Secretary; Stephen David Redmond [1956] Director/Insurance; Richard Anthony Sutlow [1964] Director/Accountant

Antham 1 Limited
Incorporated: 25 October 2007
Total Assets: £241,783,008
Registered Office: One Coleman Street, London, EC2R 5AA
Activities: Renting and operating of Housing Association real estate
Parent: Legal and General Assurance Society Limited
Officers: Andrew Banks [1964] Finance Director; Jonathan James Malpas [1965] Director/Actuary

Anthology Group Limited
Incorporated: 9 July 2015 *Employees:* 29
Net Worth: £42,478,000 *Total Assets:* £201,248,992
Registered Office: 160-166 Borough High Street, London, SE1 1LB
Activities: Activities of head offices
Officers: Mark Davies Dickinson [1968] Managing Director; Nael Khatoun [1977] Director/Investment Professional [French]; Stefano Mazzoli [1980] Director/Investment Manager [Italian]

Antofagasta PLC
Incorporated: 7 April 1982 *Employees:* 5,410
Net Worth: £5,512,919,040 *Total Assets:* £10,704,105,472
Registered Office: Cleveland House, 33 King Street, St James's, London, SW1Y 6RJ
Activities: Other mining and quarrying n.e.c.
Officers: Julian Thomas Roddan Anderson, Secretary; Timothy Clive Baker [1952] Director [Canadian]; Jorge Arturo Bande Bruck [1952] Director [Chilean]; Vivianne Amelia Blanlot Soza [1955] Director/Economist [Chilean]; Francisca Castro Fones [1962] Director/Consultant [Chilean]; Juan Jose Hector Gabriel Claro [1950] Director/Business Executive [Chilean]; Manuel Lino Silva de Sousa Oliveira [1952] Director/Corporate Finance Adviser [Portuguese]; William Michael Hayes Vail [1945] Director/Private Investor [American]; Ramon Felipe Jara Araya [1953] Director/Lawyer [Chilean]; Andronico Mariano Luksic [1954] Business Director [Chilean]; Jean-Paul Luksic [1964] Director/Mining Executive [Chilean]; Gonzalo Menendez [1949] Director/Banker [Chilean]

Antofagasta Railway Company PLC
Incorporated: 27 November 1888 *Employees:* 917
Net Worth: £132,952,168 *Total Assets:* £337,045,568
Registered Office: Cleveland House, 33 King Street, St James's, London, SW1Y 6RJ
Activities: Passenger rail transport, interurban
Parent: Antofagasta PLC
Officers: Julian Thomas Roddan Anderson, Secretary; Ivan Dagoberto Arriagada [1963] Director/Mining Executive [Chilean]; Alfredo Felix Atucha Abad [1957] Director/Vice-President of Corporate Finance [Chilean]; Ana Maria Rabagliati Grunwald [1961] Director/Mining Executive [Chilean]; Francisco Veloso [1962] Director/Lawyer [Chilean]

ANV Corporate Name Limited
Incorporated: 23 September 2008
Net Worth Deficit: £34,610,228 *Total Assets:* £611,125,248
Registered Office: Exchequer Court, 33 St Mary Axe, London, EC3A 8AA
Activities: Non-life insurance
Parent: ANV Holdings (UK) Ltd.
Officers: Jeremy Edward Cadle [1965] Director/Lawyer; Peter Dewey [1976] Director

Anyslam Investments
Incorporated: 16 November 2000
Net Worth: £3,986,516,736 *Total Assets:* £3,986,516,736
Registered Office: Lakeside Drive, Park Royal, London, NW10 7HQ
Activities: Activities of head offices
Parent: Diageo US Holdings
Officers: James Matthew Crayden Edmunds [1974] Director/Solicitor; Kara Elizabeth Major [1977] Director [American]; Vinod Rao [1962] Director [Indian]; Prabhaharan Viswanathan [1972] Director [Australian]

Anyslam Limited
Incorporated: 24 October 1997
Net Worth: £822,190,976 *Total Assets:* £1,170,464,000
Registered Office: Lakeside Drive, Park Royal, London, NW10 7HQ
Activities: Activities of head offices
Parent: Diageo PLC
Officers: James Matthew Crayden Edmunds [1974] Director/Solicitor; Kara Elizabeth Major [1977] Director [American]; Vinod Rao [1962] Director [Indian]; Prabhaharan Viswanathan [1972] Director [Australian]

ANZ Europe Limited
Incorporated: 22 April 1987
Previous: ANZ Bank (Europe) Limited
Net Worth: £190,652,176 *Total Assets:* £221,103,808
Registered Office: 40 Bank Street, Canary Wharf, London, E14 5EJ
Activities: Activities auxiliary to financial intermediation n.e.c.
Parent: ANZ Funds Pty Ltd
Officers: Kelly-Ann Lesley McKinnis, Secretary; Diana Sarah Brightmore-Armour [1954] Director/Banker; John Dalrymple Callender [1950] Director; Nigel Christopher William Denby [1961] Director/Chief Risk Officer; David John Green [1966] Director/Banker [New Zealander]; Brenda Dianne Hebb Trenowden [1967] Director/Banker [Canadian/British]

Anzef Limited
Incorporated: 1 January 1934
Net Worth: £12,973,000 *Total Assets:* £163,244,000
Registered Office: 40 Bank Street, Canary Wharf, London, E14 5EJ
Activities: Financial intermediation not elsewhere classified
Parent: Minerva Holdings Limited
Officers: Kelly-Ann Lesley McKinnis, Secretary; Nigel Christopher William Denby [1961] Director/Chief Risk Officer; Brenda Dianne Hebb Trenowden [1967] Director/Bank Executive [Canadian/British]

AON Benfield Limited
Incorporated: 22 July 2008
Net Worth: £2,429,315,072 *Total Assets:* £2,485,278,976
Registered Office: The Aon Centre, The Leadenhall Building, 122 Leadenhall Street, London, EC3V 4AN
Activities: Activities of financial services holding companies
Parent: AON Delta UK Limited
Officers: Erica Margaret Hamnett [1979] Director/Accountant; Nicholas John Hardman [1966] Director/Chartered Accountant; Paul Arthur Hogwood [1949] Director/Company Secretary; Pelagia Katsaouni-Dodd [1979] Director/Chartered Accountant [Greek]

AON Delta UK Limited
Incorporated: 17 December 2013
Net Worth: £5,191,729,152 *Total Assets:* £5,196,163,072
Registered Office: The Aon Centre, The Leadenhall Building, 122 Leadenhall Street, London, EC3V 4AN
Activities: Activities of financial services holding companies
Parent: AON UK Holdings Intermediaries Limited
Officers: Erica Margaret Hamnett [1979] Director/Accountant; Paul Arthur Hogwood [1949] Director; Pelagia Katsaouni-Dodd [1979] Director/Chartered Accountant [Greek]

AON Global Holdings Limited
Incorporated: 16 September 2014 *Employees:* 7
Net Worth: £32,745,506,816 *Total Assets:* £36,046,557,184
Registered Office: The Aon Centre, The Leadenhall Building, 122 Leadenhall Street, London, EC3V 4AN
Activities: Activities of head offices
Officers: Domingo Garcia [1961] Director [American]; Paul Arthur Hogwood [1949] Director; Pelagia Katsaouni-Dodd [1979] Director/Chartered Accountant [Greek]

AON Global Operations PLC
Incorporated: 21 June 2012
Previous: AON Global Operations Limited
Net Worth: £551,570,048 *Total Assets:* £687,973,312
Registered Office: The Aon Centre, The Leadenhall Building, 122 Leadenhall Street, London, EC3V 4AN
Activities: Activities of financial services holding companies
Parent: AON Global Holdings Limited
Officers: Paul Arthur Hogwood, Secretary; Annabel Katherine Goddard Withington, Secretary; Alistair Patrick Boyd [1979] Director/Accountant; Pelagia Katsaouni-Dodd [1979] Director/Chartered Accountant [Greek]; Dominic Patrice Nicolas Mignon [1975] Director/Chartered Accountant; James Derrick Platt [1971] Director

AON Hewitt Limited
Incorporated: 18 March 2002 *Employees:* 1,966
Net Worth: £344,347,008 *Total Assets:* £486,351,008
Registered Office: The Aon Centre, The Leadenhall Building, 122 Leadenhall Street, London, EC3V 4AN
Activities: Management consultancy activities other than financial management
Parent: AON Benfield Limited
Officers: Michael Kenneth Clare [1965] Director; Andrew Darrell Cox [1965] Director/Actuary; David James Hardern [1974] Director/Actuary; Rachael Ingle [1966] Director/Actuary [Irish]; Stephen Dennis Philp [1977] Director

AON Overseas Holdings Limited
Incorporated: 27 July 2012
Net Worth: £1,640,804,864 *Total Assets:* £3,026,712,832
Registered Office: The Aon Centre, The Leadenhall Building, 122 Leadenhall Street, London, EC3V 4AN
Activities: Activities of financial services holding companies
Parent: AON Global Holdings Limited
Officers: Paul Arthur Hogwood [1949] Director/Company Secretary; Pelagia Katsaouni-Dodd [1979] Director/Chartered Accountant [Greek]; Gardner Mugashu [1973] Director/Chartered Accountant; Alexander Michael Vickers [1983] Director

AON PLC
Incorporated: 8 December 2011 *Employees:* 48,453
Net Worth: £3,471,939,840 *Total Assets:* £19,713,746,944
Registered Office: The Aon Centre, The Leadenhall Building, 122 Leadenhall Street, London, EC3V 4AN
Activities: Activities of head offices
Officers: Paul Arthur Hogwood, Secretary; Mary Moore Johnson, Secretary; Peter Michael Lieb, Secretary; Annabel Katherine Goddard Withington, Secretary; Jin-Yong Cai [1959] Director [Chinese]; Gregory Clarence Case [1962] Director/President and Chief Executive Officer [American]; Fulvio Conti [1947] Director/Chief Executive Officer; Cheryl Ann Francis [1954] Director/Consultant [American]; Lester Benjamin Knight [1958] Director/Partner [American]; John Michael Losh [1946] Director [American]; Robert Scheck Morrison [1942] Director [American]; Richard Bowman Myers [1942] Director/Chair of Department [American]; Richard Carlier Notebaert [1947] Director [American]; Gloria Santona Frazier [1950] Director/Executive VP General Counsel & Secretary [American]; Carolyn Yauyan Woo [1954] Director/President and Chief Executive Officer [American]

AON UK Group Limited
Incorporated: 26 June 1989
Net Worth: £2,161,000,960 *Total Assets:* £2,189,932,032
Registered Office: The Aon Centre, The Leadenhall Building, 122 Leadenhall Street, London, EC3V 4AN
Activities: Activities of financial services holding companies
Shareholders: AON US & International Holdings Limited; AON Global Holdings Limited
Officers: Erica Margaret Hamnett [1979] Director/Accountant; Paul Arthur Hogwood [1949] Director/Company Secretary; Pelagia Katsaouni-Dodd [1979] Director/Chartered Accountant [Greek]

AON UK Holdings Intermediaries Limited
Incorporated: 9 August 2001
Net Worth: £4,836,122,112 *Total Assets:* £5,389,986,816
Registered Office: The Aon Centre, The Leadenhall Building, 122 Leadenhall Street, London, EC3V 4AN
Activities: Activities of financial services holding companies
Parent: AON UK Group Limited
Officers: Erica Margaret Hamnett [1979] Director/Accountant; Paul Arthur Hogwood [1949] Director/Company Secretary; Pelagia Katsaouni-Dodd [1979] Director/Chartered Accountant [Greek]

AON UK Limited
Incorporated: 29 December 1925 *Employees:* 3,161
Net Worth: £1,220,152,064 *Total Assets:* £3,026,394,880
Registered Office: The Aon Centre, The Leadenhall Building, 122 Leadenhall Street, London, EC3V 4AN
Activities: Activities of insurance agents and brokers
Parent: AON Benfield Limited
Officers: Paul Arthur Hogwood, Secretary; Richard James Dudley [1970] Director/Reinsurance Broker; Nicholas Charles Frankland [1958] Director; Alison Margaret Halsey [1956] Director; Nicholas John Hardman [1966] Director/Chartered Accountant; Simon John Lewis Jeffreys [1952] Director/Chief Financial Officer; Matthew Paul Kimber [1968] Director/Chief Risk Officer; John James Nicholson [1953] Director; Julie Anne Page [1967] Director/Chief Executive Officer; Nathan Patrick Shanaghy [1974] Director/Chief Operating Officer; Anne Tracey Torry [1965] Director

AON US & International Holdings Limited
Incorporated: 5 June 2013
Net Worth: £6,909,276,672 *Total Assets:* £12,531,481,600
Registered Office: The Aon Centre, The Leadenhall Building, 122 Leadenhall Street, London, EC3V 4AN
Activities: Activities of financial services holding companies
Parent: AON PLC
Officers: Domingo Garcia [1961] Director/Global Tax Officer [American]; Paul Arthur Hogwood [1949] Director

Apache North Sea Limited
Incorporated: 11 December 2002
Net Worth: £1,529,397,888 *Total Assets:* £2,804,731,648
Registered Office: 27-28 Eastcastle Street, London, W1W 8DH
Activities: Extraction of crude petroleum
Officers: Grady Lee Ables [1961] Director/Businessman [American]; Jon Anthony Graham [1954] Director [American]; Jon William Sauer [1960] Director [American]

Apache UK Investment Limited
Incorporated: 29 March 2011
Net Worth: £248,461,248 *Total Assets:* £962,152,384
Registered Office: 27-28 Eastcastle Street, London, W1W 8DH
Activities: Other business support service activities n.e.c.
Officers: Rajesh Sharma, Secretary; Grady Lee Ables [1961] Director/Businessman [American]; Jon Anthony Graham [1954] Director [American]; Jon William Sauer [1960] Director [American]

APG (KE) Ltd.
Incorporated: 9 March 2017
Net Worth: £131,191,008 *Total Assets:* £131,418,272
Registered Office: Suite 1, 3rd Floor, 11-12 St James's Square, London, SW1Y 4LB
Activities: Activities of other holding companies n.e.c.
Parent: Prostar Asia-Pacific Energy Infrastructure Fund L.P.
Officers: David Barclay Noakes [1972] Director/Financier [Australian]; Steven John Bickerton [1967] Director [Australian]; Serge-Alexandre Lauper [1970] Director [Swiss]

Apollo Management International LLP
Incorporated: 15 November 2005 *Employees:* 123
Net Worth: £91,648,496 *Total Assets:* £167,545,984
Registered Office: 25 St George Street, London, W1S 1FS
Officers: Christopher Patrick Edward Buchanan [1979] LLP Member; Shaun Anthony Collins [1968] LLP Member; Kevin Edward Crowe Jr [1982] LLP Member; Philip Patrick Cuff [1982] LLP Member; Dominic Matthew Fry [1975] LLP Member; James Kim [1981] LLP Member; Gernot Wilhelm Friedrich Lohr [1969] LLP Member; Fabrice Nottin [1978] LLP Member; Bhavin Patel [1978] LLP Member; Michele Raba [1984] LLP Member; Robert Seminara [1962] LLP Member

Apple (UK) Limited
Incorporated: 14 October 1981 *Employees:* 374
Net Worth: £58,337,000 *Total Assets:* £133,259,000
Registered Office: 100 New Bridge Street, London, EC4V 6JA
Activities: Other information technology service activities
Parent: Apple Inc.
Officers: Michael Joseph Boyd [1974] Director/Businessman [American]; Peter Ronald Denwood [1963] Director/Lawyer [American]

Apple Bidco Limited
Incorporated: 13 October 2015 *Employees:* 216
Net Worth: £346,239,360 *Total Assets:* £925,400,576
Registered Office: 5th Floor, 6 St Andrew Street, London, EC4A 3AE
Activities: Activities of production holding companies
Officers: Guy Bentinck [1966] Director [Canadian]; John Campion [1963] Director [American]; Kazi Hasan [1977] Director/Energy Executive [American]; Quinn McLean [1979] Director/Portfolio Manager [Canadian]; Stephen Wallace [1956] Director/Secretary to The Governor General of Canada [Canadian]; Pieter Wernink [1967] Director/Finance [Dutch]

Apple Europe Limited
Incorporated: 20 February 2004 *Employees:* 870
Net Worth: £317,854,016 *Total Assets:* £478,473,984
Registered Office: 100 New Bridge Street, London, EC4V 6JA
Activities: Other business support service activities n.e.c.
Parent: Apple Inc.
Officers: Michael Joseph Boyd [1974] Director/Businessman [American]; Peter Ronald Denwood [1963] Director/Lawyer [American]

Apple Retail UK Limited
Incorporated: 16 December 2003 *Employees:* 4,911
Net Worth: £121,031,000 *Total Assets:* £312,116,000
Registered Office: 5th Floor, 6 St Andrew Street, London, EC4A 3AE
Activities: Other business support service activities n.e.c.
Parent: Apple Inc.
Officers: Michael Joseph Boyd [1974] Director/Businessman [American]; Peter Ronald Denwood [1963] Director/Lawyer [American]

APR Energy Holdings Limited
Incorporated: 15 December 2009 *Employees:* 3
Net Worth Deficit: £144,134,416 *Total Assets:* £896,947,712
Registered Office: 5th Floor, 6 St Andrew Street, London, EC4A 3AE
Activities: Production of electricity
Parent: APR Energy Limited
Officers: Benjamin John See, Secretary; Ronald Benson Crowell [1958] Director [American]; Charles Parker Ferry [1965] Director [American]; Benjamin John See [1980] Director [American]

APR Energy Limited
Incorporated: 30 October 2009 *Employees:* 216
Previous: APR Energy PLC
Net Worth: £313,080,704 *Total Assets:* £847,778,752
Registered Office: 5th Floor, 6 St Andrew Street, London, EC4A 3AE
Activities: Activities of other holding companies n.e.c.
Parent: Apple Bidco Limited
Officers: Guy Bentinck [1966] Director [Canadian]; John Campion [1963] Director [American]; Kazi Hasan [1977] Director/Energy Executive [American]; Quinn McLean [1979] Director/Portfolio Manager [Canadian]; Stephen Wallace [1956] Director/Secretary to The Governor General of Canada [Canadian]; Pieter Wernink [1967] Director/Finance [Dutch]

Aprilgrange Limited
Incorporated: 7 April 2003
Net Worth: £15,103,064 *Total Assets:* £447,809,088
Registered Office: 23-27 Alie Street, London, E1 8DS
Activities: Other business support service activities n.e.c.
Parent: The Travelers Companies, Inc.
Officers: John Matthew Abramson, Secretary; John Matthew Abramson [1961] Director/Solicitor; Michael John Gent [1964] Director/Chartered Accountant

APS Financial Limited
Incorporated: 15 December 2006 *Employees:* 2
Net Worth: £5,238,610 *Total Assets:* £251,991,120
Registered Office: 6th Floor, One London Wall, London, EC2Y 5EB
Activities: Other business support service activities n.e.c.
Parent: Advanced Payment Solutions Limited
Officers: David Edward Rodwell, Secretary; Lindsay Simon Burrett [1971] Director/Accountant; Robin Keith Dear [1957] Director; Simon Timothy Talbot Knight [1964] Director; David Edward Rodwell [1966] Director/Lawyer; Paul Schooley [1970] Director/Banker [American]; Richard Thomas Wagner [1964] Director/Banking [American]

Arbuthnot Banking Group PLC
Incorporated: 4 November 1985 *Employees:* 365
Net Worth: £236,375,008 *Total Assets:* £1,853,232,000
Registered Office: Arbuthnot House, 7 Wilson Street, London, EC2M 2SN
Activities: Financial intermediation not elsewhere classified
Shareholder: Flowidea Limited
Officers: Nicholas David de Burgh Jennings, Secretary; Sir Henry Angest [1940] Director; James Robert Cobb [1968] Director/Chartered Accountant; Ian Andrew Dewar [1957] Director/Chartered Accountant; Sir Christopher John Rome Meyer [1944] Director/Chairman of Press Complaints Commission; Andrew Alfred Salmon [1962] Director/Banker; Sir Alan Colin Drake Yarrow [1951] Director

Arbuthnot Latham & Co., Limited
Incorporated: 15 September 1964 *Employees:* 348
Net Worth: £132,937,000 *Total Assets:* £1,783,675,008
Registered Office: Arbuthnot House, 7 Wilson Street, London, EC2M 2SN
Activities: Financial intermediation not elsewhere classified
Parent: Arbuthnot Banking Group PLC
Officers: Nicholas David de Burgh Jennings, Secretary; Sir Henry Angest [1940] Director/Banker; James Robert Cobb [1968] Director/Chartered Accountant; Stephen John Fletcher [1961] Director/Banker; Stephen Peter Kelly [1971] Director/Chart Management Accountant; Angela Ann Knight [1950] Director; Paul Marrow [1952] Director/Banker; Sir Michael Charles Gerrard Peat [1949] Director/Accountant; Andrew Alfred Salmon [1962] Director/Banker

Arca Bidco Limited
Incorporated: 10 October 2014
Net Worth: £45,080,000 *Total Assets:* £284,056,992
Registered Office: 5th Floor, 6 St Andrew Street, London, EC4A 3AE
Activities: Activities of other holding companies n.e.c.
Parent: Arca Midco Limited
Officers: Robert John Gregor [1969] Director/Managing Partner - Investment Adviser [Australian]; Holt William John Hanna [1977] Director/Vice President - Investment Adviser; Steven Lowry [1972] Director/Partner - Investment Adviser; Jonathan Mark Pascoe [1967] Director/Chartered Accountant

Arca Holdco Limited
Incorporated: 10 October 2014
Net Worth: £26,007,000 *Total Assets:* £116,462,000
Registered Office: 5th Floor, 6 St Andrew Street, London, EC4A 3AE
Activities: Activities of other holding companies n.e.c.
Parent: Arca Topco Limited
Officers: Robert John Gregor [1969] Director/Managing Partner - Investment Adviser [Australian]; Holt William John Hanna [1977] Director/Vice President - Investment Adviser; Steven Lowry [1972] Director/Partner - Investment Adviser; Jonathan Mark Pascoe [1967] Director/Chartered Accountant

Arca Midco Limited
Incorporated: 10 November 2014 *Employees:* 518
Net Worth Deficit: £37,063,000 *Total Assets:* £237,848,000
Registered Office: 5th Floor, 6 St Andrew Street, London, EC4A 3AE
Activities: Activities of other holding companies n.e.c.
Parent: Arca Holdco Limited
Officers: Robert John Gregor [1969] Director/Managing Partner - Investment Adviser [Australian]; Holt William John Hanna [1977] Director/Vice President - Investment Adviser; Steven Lowry [1972] Director/Partner - Investment Adviser; Jonathan Mark Pascoe [1967] Director/Chartered Accountant

Arca Topco Limited
Incorporated: 10 October 2014 *Employees:* 518
Net Worth Deficit: £37,063,000 *Total Assets:* £237,848,000
Registered Office: 5th Floor, 6 St Andrew Street, London, EC4A 3AE
Activities: Activities of other holding companies n.e.c.
Parent: Basalt Infrastructure Partners LLP
Officers: Mike Andrew Bryan [1969] Director/Head of Infrastructure; Robert John Gregor [1969] Director/Managing Partner - Investment Adviser [Australian]; Holt William John Hanna [1977] Director/Vice President - Investment Adviser; Steven Lowry [1972] Director/Partner - Investment Adviser

Arcadia Group Limited
Incorporated: 27 February 1929 *Employees:* 23,424
Net Worth: £2,664,965,120 *Total Assets:* £3,708,280,064
Registered Office: Colegrave House, 70 Berners Street, London, W1T 3NL
Activities: Retail sale of clothing in specialised stores
Officers: Michelle Jane Gammon, Secretary; Richard Leeroy Burchill [1971] Director/Accountant; Siobhan Forey [1972] Director/Chief Operating Officer; Ian Michael Grabiner [1959] Director; Gillian Anne Hague [1965] Director/Group Financial Controller; Paul Stephen Price [1962] Director/CEO Topshop/Topman; David St John Shepherd [1963] Director/Chief Operating Officer

Arcadis LLP
Incorporated: 12 October 2011 *Employees:* 1,510
Previous: EC Harris LLP
Net Worth: £51,039,000 *Total Assets:* £160,904,000
Registered Office: Arcadis House, 34 York Way, London, N1 9AB
Officers: Steven James Bromhead [1972] Member; Anne Rosemary Clark [1964] Member; Mark Allan Cowlard [1969] Member; Benjamin Michael Adams [1970] LLP Member; Mahmoud Bakir Ahmad Alghita [1963] LLP Member; Keith Andrews [1959] LLP Member; Gary Lee Ashton [1971] LLP Member; Amir Ali Baharlou [1966] LLP Member; Tejinderpal Singh Bahia [1977] LLP Member; Andrew Barnes [1965] LLP Member; Andrew James Beard [1983] LLP Member; Ian Graeme Bell [1963] LLP Member; Nicholas Bellew [1979] LLP Member; Astrid Berkman [1971] LLP Member; Simon Bimpson [1974] LLP Member; Colin Stevenson Black [1972] LLP Member; Philip Howard Black [1964] LLP Member; Richard John Bonner [1969] LLP Member; Gregory Alexander Bradley [1976] LLP Member; Dr Jane Louise Brooke-Smith [1963] LLP Member; Alan Geoffrey Brookes [1961] LLP Member; James Lawrence Bryce [1982] LLP Member; Andrew James Bull [1972] LLP Member; Martin Lewis Canon [1957] LLP Member; Lee John Carroll [1979] LLP Member; Edel Louise Christie [1970] LLP Member; Richard John Clare [1953] LLP Member; Darren Ashley Clarke [1972] LLP Member; Mark Andrew Cleverly [1970] LLP Member; Gerard John Clohessy [1963] LLP Member; Adrian John Cole [1963] LLP Member; Jeffrey Collins [1964] LLP Member; Paul Anthony Collins [1960] LLP Member; Stephen John Collis [1971] LLP Member; Lee Cookson [1964] LLP Member; Timothy John Cooper [1968] LLP Member; Martyn Brian Court [1967] LLP Member; Robert Anthony Cox [1965] LLP Member; Andrew Robert Crawford [1966] LLP Member; Mark Crellin [1970] LLP Member; Matthew Nicolas Cutts [1966] LLP Member; Philip John Darby [1968] LLP Member; Andrew Michael Dawson [1968] LLP Member; Margot Annabel Day [2017] LLP Member; Mark Edward Dewhurst [1975] LLP Member; Steven Dixon [1979] LLP Member; Mark Paul Docherty [1972] LLP Member; Fiona Margaret Duncombe [1967] LLP Member; Leslie Ronald Dunn [1963] LLP Member; David John Edwards [1959] LLP Member; Gary Robert Empson [1968] LLP Member; Mark Owen Engelhardt [1972] LLP Member; Lucy Rachel Angharad England [1977] LLP Member; Vicky Ernst [1971] LLP Member; Marcus Kaye Fagent [1961] LLP Member; Antony Roger Faughnan [1966] LLP Member; Kerry Fleming [1970] LLP Member; Robert Forsyth [1969] LLP Member; Thomas Gallagher [1970] LLP Member; Kathryn Lucy Gardiner [1975] LLP Member; Patrick Dennis Geary [1967] LLP Member; Ian Picton George [1967] LLP Member; Ross Gissane [1982] LLP Member; Christian James Goldsmith [1977] LLP Member; John William Gordon [1973] LLP Member; John Howard Graham [1967] LLP Member; Catherine Frances Greaves [1977] LLP Member; William Edward Green [1962] LLP Member; Edward Brian Harris [1943] LLP Member; Lara Jennifer Hawkins [1970] LLP Member; Nigel Paul Hayward [1958] LLP Member; Nigel Herbert [1969] LLP Member; Graham Hill [1966] LLP Member; Richard Peter Hoare [1969] LLP Member; Keith Hobden [1970] LLP Member; Peter William Hogg [1969] LLP Member; Malcolm Paul Hope [1959] LLP Member; Matthew David Howell-Jones [1972] LLP Member; Philip Jeffrey Ince [1959] LLP Member; Stephen David James [1964] LLP Member; Gareth Edward Jones [1978] LLP Member; Leigh Jones [1976] LLP Member; Richard Alan Jones [1955] LLP Member; Ian Kennedy [1962] LLP Member; Daniel Keyes [1965] LLP Member; Shakir Imtiyazuddin Khaja [1971] LLP Member; Benjamin Michael Khan [1968] LLP Member; Matthew Gilliatt Kitching [1972] LLP Member; Gary Patrick Kitt [1965] LLP Member; James Alexander Knight [1973] LLP Member; Kostas Koultzis [1978] LLP Member; Mark Simon Langdale [1970] LLP Member; Dr Dominic Bruce Lascelles [1969] LLP Member; Kok Weng Lee [1956] LLP Member; Steven John Levin [1965] LLP Member; Aaron John Little [1972] LLP Member; Suzanne Rose Lloyd [1968] LLP Member; Peter Vincent Madden [1961] LLP Member; Irum Saeed Malik [1971] LLP Member

Arcadis UK (Holdings) Limited
Incorporated: 28 October 2005
Previous: EC Harris UK (Holdings) Limited
Net Worth: £68,520,000 *Total Assets:* £116,387,000
Registered Office: Arcadis House, 34 York Way, London, N1 9AB
Activities: Activities of head offices
Parent: Arcadis N.V.
Officers: Margot Annabel Day, Secretary; Fiona Margaret Duncombe, Secretary; Steven James Bromhead [1972] Director/LLP Member; Alan Geoffrey Brookes [1961] Director/Business Executive; Anne Rosemary Clark [1964] Director/Chief Finance Officer; Mark Allan Cowlard [1969] Risk and Operations Director; Peter Vincent Madden [1961] Director/Business Executive

Arch Insurance Company (Europe) Limited
Incorporated: 26 November 2003
Net Worth: £56,796,000 *Total Assets:* £679,980,992
Registered Office: 5th Floor, Plantation Place South, 60 Great Tower Street, London, EC3R 5AZ
Activities: Non-life insurance
Officers: Stephen Neil Bashford [1965] Director/Senior Vice President CUO Financial Lines; Nicholas Geoffrey Alastair Denniston [1955] Independent Non-Executive Director; Jason Allen Kittinger [1979] Finance Director [American/British]; Pasquale Leoni [1967] Director/Senior Vice President CUO Speciality [Italian]; Paul Martin [1964] Independent Non-Executive Director; Matthew Adam Shulman [1973] Director/President & Chief Executive Officer [American]; Patrick Desmond Storey [1958] Independent Non-Executive Director

Arch Syndicate Investments Ltd
Incorporated: 14 July 2008
Net Worth: £70,475,000 *Total Assets:* £528,316,000
Registered Office: 5th Floor, Plantation Place South, 60 Great Tower Street, London, EC3R 5AZ
Activities: Non-life insurance
Officers: Jason Allen Kittinger [1979] Finance Director [American/British]; Matthew Shulman [1973] Director [American]

Arches Holdings Limited
Incorporated: 10 October 2016
Net Worth: £2,442,450,176 *Total Assets:* £2,442,524,672
Registered Office: Cordy House, 91 Curtain Road, London, EC2A 3BS
Activities: Activities of other holding companies n.e.c.
Parent: McDonalds Corporation
Officers: Malcolm Wayne Hicks, Secretary; Thomas Joseph Dillon [1977] Director/Business Executive [American]; Malcolm Wayne Hicks [1963] Director/Business Executive [British/American]; Julian Crispin Hilton-Johnson [1964] Director/Business Executive

Arcus A1 Investor Vehicle LLP
Incorporated: 9 November 2016
Net Worth: £287,644,096 *Total Assets:* £311,387,360
Registered Office: 2nd Floor, 6 St Andrew Street, London, EC4A 3AE

Arcus Tivana Investor Vehicle 1 LLP
Incorporated: 23 March 2015
Net Worth: £441,222,400 *Total Assets:* £675,673,984
Registered Office: 2nd Floor, 6 St Andrew Street, London, EC4A 3AE

Arcus Tivana Investor Vehicle 2 LLP
Incorporated: 23 March 2015
Net Worth: £441,222,400 *Total Assets:* £675,675,712
Registered Office: 2nd Floor, 6 St Andrew Street, London, EC4A 3AE

Ardmore Construction Limited
Incorporated: 30 September 1974 *Employees:* 280
Net Worth: £16,325,198 *Total Assets:* £152,448,640
Registered Office: 6 Wharf Studios, 28 Wharf Road, London, N1 7GR
Activities: Construction of commercial buildings
Shareholders: Cormac James Byrne; Patrick Joseph Byrne
Officers: Celine Byrne, Secretary; Cormac James Byrne [1951] Director [Irish]; Marie Byrne [1952] Director [Irish]; Patrick Joseph Byrne [1955] Director [Irish]

Ardmore Group Limited
Incorporated: 16 September 2016 *Employees:* 315
Net Worth: £42,948,888 *Total Assets:* £190,794,784
Registered Office: 6 Wharf Studios, 28 Wharf Road, London, N1 7GR
Activities: Construction of commercial buildings
Major Shareholder: Cormac James Byrne
Officers: Cormac James Byrne [1951] Director [Irish]; Patrick Joseph Byrne [1955] Director [Irish]

Ardonagh Midco 3 PLC
Incorporated: 21 April 2017 *Employees:* 6,189
Net Worth: £156,267,008 *Total Assets:* £1,642,659,968
Registered Office: 55 Bishopsgate, London, EC2N 3AS
Activities: Activities of other holding companies n.e.c.
Parent: Ardonagh Midco 2 PLC
Officers: Dean Clarke, Secretary; Clive Bouch [1961] Director; Matthieu Yann Arnaud Boulanger [1975] Director/Investment Manager; Patrick Noel Butler [1960] Director [Irish]; Diane Cougill [1963] Director/Chief Finance Officer; Aurelio Cusaro [1985] Director; Christine Elaine Dandridge [1956] Director; Vahe Alex Dombalagian [1973] Director [American]; Scot French [1970] Director [American]; Feilim Mackle [1967] Director [Irish]; Matthew William Raino [1978] Director [American]; David Christopher Ross [1969] Director [Irish]; John Ivan Tiner [1957] Director

Area Estates Limited
Incorporated: 11 April 2003 *Employees:* 3
Net Worth: £783,764 *Total Assets:* £125,209,992
Registered Office: Ground Floor, 30 City Road, London, EC1Y 2AB
Activities: Buying and selling of own real estate
Parent: The William Pears Group of Companies Limited
Officers: William Frederick Bennett, Secretary; David Alan Pears [1968] Director; Mark Andrew Pears [1962] Director; Sir Trevor Steven Pears [1964] Director

Arena Leisure Limited
Incorporated: 27 August 1965
Net Worth: £227,502,336 *Total Assets:* £249,826,032
Registered Office: Millbank Tower, 21-24 Millbank, London, SW1P 4QP
Activities: Other business support service activities n.e.c.
Parent: Arena Racing Corporation Limited
Officers: Megan Joy Langridge, Secretary; Stephane Abraham Joseph Nahum [1975] Director/Private Equity [French]; James Adam Reuben [1986] Director/Investment; Kevin Stuart Robertson [1969] Director/Chief Financial Officer

Arena Leisure Racing Limited
Incorporated: 9 October 2006 *Employees:* 20
Net Worth: £69,730,032 *Total Assets:* £199,672,784
Registered Office: Millbank Tower, 21-24 Millbank, London, SW1P 4QP
Activities: Operation of sports facilities
Parent: Arena Leisure Limited
Officers: Megan Joy Langridge, Secretary; Stephane Abraham Joseph Nahum [1975] Director/Private Equity [French]; Kevin Stuart Robertson [1969] Director/Chief Financial Officer; Mark Spincer [1969] Director

Arena Racing Corporation Limited
Incorporated: 20 March 2012 *Employees:* 519
Net Worth Deficit: £73,355,000 *Total Assets:* £251,999,008
Registered Office: 4th Floor, Millbank Tower, 21-24 Millbank, London, SW1P 4QP
Activities: Other business support service activities n.e.c.
Officers: Megan Joy Langridge, Secretary; Martin John Cruddace [1964] Director/Solicitor; Stephane Abraham Joseph Nahum [1975] Director [French]; James Adam Reuben [1986] Director/Investment; Kevin Stuart Robertson [1969] Director/Chief Financial Officer; Eileen Marie Sawyer [1979] Director/Accountant; Mark Spincer [1969] Director; David Allan Thorpe [1949] Director

Argent Foods Limited
Incorporated: 19 November 2009 *Employees:* 1,511
Previous: Fletcher Bay Investment Company Limited
Net Worth: £9,077,000 *Total Assets:* £208,456,992
Registered Office: Level 5, 9 Hatton Street, London, NW8 8PL
Activities: Activities of head offices
Major Shareholder: David John Gray
Officers: Andrew John Barnes [1964] Director/Chartered Accountant; David John Gray [1959] Director; Andrew Stephen King [1949] Director; Dr Margaret Rose Mountford [1951] Director; John Oldcorn [1970] Director; Adam Lewis Olins [1959] Director; Penelope Jane Tomlinson [1968] Sales Director

Argenta Holdings Limited
Incorporated: 21 November 2003 *Employees:* 160
Previous: Argenta Holdings PLC
Net Worth: £58,675,000 *Total Assets:* £285,520,000
Registered Office: 5th Floor, 70 Gracechurch Street, London, EC3V 0XL
Activities: Activities of head offices
Parent: Hannover Ruck SE
Officers: Christopher John Rupert Fairs, Secretary; Graham Kevin Allen [1965] Finance Director; Sven Althoff [1969] Director [German]; Andrew John Annandale [1963] Director; Ian Michael Maguire [1965] Director/Insurance Underwriter; John Lindsay Pearce Whiter [1950] Director/Accountant

Argo (Alpha) Limited
Incorporated: 10 September 2009
Net Worth: £1,268,900 *Total Assets:* £182,182,592
Registered Office: 1 Fen Court, London, EC3M 5BN
Activities: Non-life insurance
Parent: Argo Underwriting Agency Ltd
Officers: Darren Argyle [1973] Director/Chartered Accountant; Dominic James Kirby [1970] Director

Argo (No. 604) Limited
Incorporated: 25 September 2001
Net Worth: £16,856,500 *Total Assets:* £690,510,528
Registered Office: 1 Fen Court, London, EC3M 5BN
Activities: Non-life insurance
Parent: Argo Underwriting Agency Ltd
Officers: Darren Argyle [1973] Director/Chartered Accountant; Dominic James Kirby [1970] Director

Argo (No. 703) Limited
Incorporated: 19 September 2002
Net Worth: £1,309,800 *Total Assets:* £165,595,296
Registered Office: 1 Fen Court, London, EC3M 5BN
Activities: Non-life insurance
Parent: Argo Underwriting Agency Ltd
Officers: Darren Argyle [1973] Director/Chartered Accountant; Dominic James Kirby [1970] Director

Argo International Holdings Limited
Incorporated: 25 March 2008
Net Worth: £176,468,992 *Total Assets:* £218,255,920
Registered Office: 1 Fen Court, London, EC3M 5BN
Activities: Activities of other holding companies n.e.c.
Parent: Argo RE
Officers: Craig Comeaux, Secretary; Darren Argyle [1973] Director/Chartered Accountant; Jay Stanley Bullock [1964] Director [American]; Dominic James Kirby [1970] Director

Argo Underwriting Agency Limited
Incorporated: 26 March 1999 *Employees:* 185
Net Worth: £51,200,000 *Total Assets:* £1,377,100,032
Registered Office: 1 Fen Court, London, EC3M 5BN
Activities: Activities of other holding companies n.e.c.
Parent: Argo International Holdings Ltd
Officers: Darren Argyle [1973] Director/Chartered Accountant; Jay Stanley Bullock [1964] Director [American]; Dominic James Kirby [1970] Director

Argus Media Limited
Incorporated: 10 June 1982 *Employees:* 426
Net Worth: £77,274,000 *Total Assets:* £168,795,008
Registered Office: Lacon House, 84 Theobald's Road, London, WC1X 8NL
Activities: Other publishing activities
Officers: Stuart John Ashman, Secretary/Publisher [Australian]; Stuart John Ashman [1965] Director/Accountant [Australian]; Mark Adrian Binks [1954] Director/Publisher; Matthew Prat Burkley [1971] Director/Chief Operating Officer [American]

Ariel Corporate Member Limited
Incorporated: 13 April 2007
Net Worth: £67,689,952 *Total Assets:* £637,393,216
Registered Office: 1 Fen Court, London, EC3M 5BN
Activities: Non-life insurance
Parent: Argo Underwriting Agency Limited
Officers: Darren Argyle [1973] Director/Chartered Accountant; Dominic James Kirby [1970] Director

Arig Capital Limited
Incorporated: 30 September 2010
Net Worth Deficit: £3,135,000 *Total Assets:* £225,170,000
Registered Office: c/o Callidus Secretaries Limited, 54 Fenchurch Street, London, EC3M 3JY
Activities: Other activities auxiliary to insurance and pension funding
Parent: Arab Insurance Group (B.S.C)
Officers: Michael Logan Glover [1958] Director; Kuttikatt Samuel Verghese [1960] Director [Indian]

Ark Corporate Member Limited
Incorporated: 2 February 2007
Net Worth: £19,427,100 *Total Assets:* £1,305,682,816
Registered Office: 30 Fenchurch Avenue, London, EC3M 5AD
Activities: Non-life insurance
Shareholders: Ian Eric Beaton; Nicholas Kershaw Bonnar
Officers: James David Masson, Secretary; Nicholas Kershaw Bonnar [1964] Director; Neil Christopher Brothers [1978] Director/Chief Risk Officer; Neil Martin Smith [1971] Director; Christopher Eric Watson [1950] Director [American]

Ark Schools
Incorporated: 26 April 2004 *Employees:* 2,971
Net Worth: £429,500,000 *Total Assets:* £485,255,008
Registered Office: 65 Kingsway, London, WC2B 6TD
Activities: Pre-primary education
Officers: Michael Sandall, Secretary; Christina Jean Alexandrou [1964] Director/Third Sector; Ron Eric Beller [1962] Director/Investor [American]; Lord Stanley Fink [1957] Director/Chartered Accountant; Joanna Avril Greenslade [1971] Director; Gerard Griffin [1968] Director/Fund Manager [British/American]; Lucy Lauris Heller [1959] Managing Director; Daniel Labbad [1972] Director/Chief Executive [Australian]; Paul Roderick Clucas Marshall [1959] Director/Fund Manager; Anthony Geraint Williams [1958] Director/Retired; Neil Timothy Wood [1965] Director

Arlington House Investments Limited
Incorporated: 8 January 1993 *Employees:* 24
Net Worth: £61,692,132 *Total Assets:* £243,493,280
Registered Office: 5 New Street Square, London, EC4A 3TW
Activities: Buying and selling of own real estate
Shareholders: The Bank of N.T Butterfield & Son Ltd; Mohammed Mahdi His Excellency Al Tajir
Officers: Amer Mohammed Mahdi Al Tajir [1961] Director/Businessman [Emirati]; Khalid Mohamed Mahdi Al Tajir [1958] Director/Businessman [Emirati]; Mohamed Sadiq Al Tajir [1941] Director/Businessman [Bahraini]; Mohammed Mahdi Al Tajir [1931] Director/Businessman [Emirati]

Arndale Properties Limited
Incorporated: 18 May 2003 *Employees:* 5
Net Worth: £122,851,000 *Total Assets:* £146,936,000
Registered Office: 2nd Floor, 14 St George Street, London, W1S 1FE
Activities: Other professional, scientific and technical activities n.e.c.
Parent: Trenport Property Holdings Limited
Officers: Christopher Derek Hall [1958] Director/Town Planner; Richard John Hall [1969] Director/Chartered Surveyor; Selwyn Heycock [1947] Director/Accountant; Philip Leslie Peters [1957] Director; Michael Seal [1948] Director/Chartered Accountant

Arrow Bidco Limited
Incorporated: 25 January 2010
Net Worth: £201,467,008 *Total Assets:* £201,467,008
Registered Office: Cassini House, 57 St James's Street, London, SW1A 1LD
Activities: Activities of other holding companies n.e.c.
Parent: Affiliated Managers Group, Inc
Officers: David Michael Billings [1962] Director/Financial/Asset Management [American]; John Erickson [1970] Director/Financial/Asset Management [American]; Adrian Charles Frost [1957] Director/Investment Manager; Dean Aaron Maines [1970] Director [American]; Mark James Murray [1969] Director

Arsenal (Emirates Stadium) Limited
Incorporated: 13 November 2000
Net Worth Deficit: £30,271,000 *Total Assets:* £428,489,984
Registered Office: Highbury House, 75 Drayton Park, London, N5 1BU
Activities: Other letting and operating of own or leased real estate
Parent: The Arsenal Football Club PLC
Officers: Stuart William Wisely, Secretary/Chartered Accountant; Kenneth John Friar [1934] Director; David Miles [1955] Director/Company Secretary

The Arsenal Football Club Public Limited Company
Incorporated: 26 April 1910 *Employees:* 717
Net Worth: £530,415,008 *Total Assets:* £1,011,310,016
Registered Office: Highbury House, 75 Drayton Park, London, N5 1BU
Activities: Activities of sport clubs
Parent: Arsenal (AFC Holdings) Limited
Officers: David Miles, Secretary; Richard Charles Lascelles Carr [1938] Director; Kenneth John Friar [1934] Director; Philip Charles Harris of Peckham [1942] Director; Sir John Chippendale Lindley Keswick [1940] Director/Banker; Enos Stanley Kroenke [1947] Director [American]; Josh Walton Kroenke [1980] Director/President of Sports Franchises [American]

Arsenal Holdings Limited
Incorporated: 11 July 2001 *Employees:* 733
Previous: Arsenal Holdings PLC
Net Worth: £419,916,000 *Total Assets:* £1,029,056,000
Registered Office: Highbury House, 75 Drayton Park, London, N5 1BU
Activities: Activities of sport clubs
Officers: David Miles, Secretary; Kenneth John Friar [1934] Director; Philip Charles Harris of Peckham [1942] Director; Sir John Chippendale Lindley Keswick [1940] Director/Banker; Enos Stanley Kroenke [1947] Director [American]; Josh Walton Kroenke [1980] Director/President of Sports Franchises [American]

Arsenal Securities PLC
Incorporated: 21 December 2005
Net Worth Deficit: £12,065,000 *Total Assets:* £361,136,000
Registered Office: Highbury House, 75 Drayton Park, London, N5 1BU
Activities: Financial intermediation not elsewhere classified
Parent: Arsenal Football Club PLC
Officers: Stuart William Wisely, Company Secretary; Susan Iris Abrahams [1957] Director; Kenneth John Friar [1934] Director; David Miles [1955] Director/Company Secretary; Paivi Helena Whitaker [1963] Director [Finnish]

Artemis Alpha Trust PLC
Incorporated: 22 January 1931
Net Worth: £161,720,000 *Total Assets:* £174,279,008
Registered Office: Artemis Investment Management LLP, Cassini House, 57-59 St James's Street, London, SW1A 1LD
Activities: Activities of investment trusts
Officers: John Anthony Cleeve Ayton [1961] Director; Blathnaid Bergin [1975] Director/Financial Controller [Irish]; Duncan William Allan Budge [1955] Director; James Robert Dominic Korner [1955] Director/Investment Manager

Artemis Investment Management LLP
Incorporated: 13 April 2010 *Employees:* 138
Net Worth: £105,750,000 *Total Assets:* £150,216,000
Registered Office: Cassini House, 57 St James's Street, London, SW1A 1LD
Officers: Stewart David Brown [1973] Member; Adrian Charles Frost [1957] Member; Jonathan Richard Loukes [1972] Member; Mark James Murray [1969] Member; Jasper Luke Berens [1970] LLP Member; Lesley Elaine Cairney [1969] LLP Member; Jacob Benjamin de Tusch-Lec [1974] LLP Member; John Edwin Dodd [1961] LLP Member; Simon Edelsten [1961] LLP Member; James Alexander Foster [1966] LLP Member; Andrew Philip Gray [1974] LLP Member; Peter Ross Leckie [1957] LLP Member; Edward Fergus Legget [1978] LLP Member; William John Littlewood [1965] LLP Member; Andrew Robert Marsh [1972] LLP Member; Alexandra McAndie [1977] LLP Member; Graeme Charles Mitchell [1966] LLP Member; Stephen Francis Moore [1974] LLP Member; Mark Richard Niznik [1967] LLP Member; Antony Mark Colin Page [1962] LLP Member; Johnathan Andrew Douglas Rigler [1980] LLP Member; Dr Peter Arnold Ernst-August Saacke [1970] LLP Member; Nicholas Thomas Woodhall Shenton [1980] LLP Member; Derek Colin Stuart [1968] LLP Member; Mark Robert John Tyndall [1958] LLP Member; Elaine Margaret Vincent [1967] LLP Member; William Thomas Warren [1971] LLP Member; Cormac John Weldon [1965] LLP Member; Lindsay James Whitelaw [1958] LLP Member; Philip John Wolstencroft [1963] LLP Member

Artesian Finance II PLC
Incorporated: 25 February 2003
Net Worth: £1,206,000 *Total Assets:* £771,998,016
Registered Office: 6th Floor, 65 Gresham Street, London, EC2V 7NQ
Activities: Other business support service activities n.e.c.
Parent: Link Trust Nominees No.1 Limited
Officers: Colin Arthur Benford [1962] Director

Artesian Finance III PLC
Incorporated: 15 November 2005
Net Worth: £196,000 *Total Assets:* £252,884,992
Registered Office: 6th Floor, 65 Gresham Street, London, EC2V 7NQ
Activities: Financial intermediation not elsewhere classified
Parent: Link Trust Nominees No.1 Limited
Officers: Colin Arthur Benford [1962] Director

Artesian Finance PLC
Incorporated: 7 February 2002
Net Worth: £1,342,000 *Total Assets:* £901,300,992
Registered Office: 6th Floor, 65 Gresham Street, London, EC2V 7NQ
Activities: Other business support service activities n.e.c.
Parent: Link Trust Nominees No. 1 Limited
Officers: Colin Arthur Benford [1962] Director

Arunvill Global Equity Trading Limited
Incorporated: 2 November 2012
Net Worth: £252,815,616 *Total Assets:* £374,113,760
Registered Office: Level 20, 125 Old Broad Street, London, EC2N 1AR
Activities: Security dealing on own account
Parent: AV Equity Trading Limited
Officers: Perry Christopher Wilson [1965] Director

Arup Group Limited
Incorporated: 4 May 1977 *Employees:* 13,841
Net Worth: £230,600,000 *Total Assets:* £916,700,032
Registered Office: 13 Fitzroy Street, London, W1T 4BQ
Activities: Activities of head offices
Parent: Ove Arup Partnership Trustees Limited
Officers: Martin James Ansley-Young, Secretary/Chartered Accountant; Peter Anthony Bailey [1960] Director/Principal [Australian]; Dr Alan James Belfield [1956] Director/Mechanical Engineer; Tristram George Allen Carfrae [1959] Director/Structural Engineer; Peter John Chamley [1956] Director/Geotechnical Engineer; Fiona Mary Cousins [1967] Director/Engineer [American]; Jerome Anthony Frost [1971] Director/Town Planner; Gregory Scott Hodkinson [1955] Director/Engineer [Australian]; Michael Ka-Yue Kwok [1962] Director/Engineer; Dervilla Mary Mitchell [1958] Director/Structural Engineer [Irish]; Genevieve Shore [1969] Director; Timothy John Stone [1951] Director; Matthew Stuart Tweedie [1971] Finance Director; Thomas John Fergal Whyte [1968] Director/Civil Engineer [Irish]

Arup Treasury Limited
Incorporated: 23 July 1990
Net Worth: £7,525,155 *Total Assets:* £178,856,848
Registered Office: 13 Fitzroy Street, London, W1T 4BQ
Activities: Financial management
Parent: Ove Arup Limited
Officers: Vanessa Jane Shakespeare, Secretary; Dr Alan James Belfield [1956] Director/Mechanical Engineer; Matthew Stuart Tweedie [1971] Director/Accountant

Ascend Overseas Limited
Incorporated: 4 November 2013
Net Worth Deficit: £33,796,064 *Total Assets:* £198,950,000
Registered Office: Suite 1, 3rd Floor, 11-12 St James's Square, London, SW1Y 4LB
Activities: Manufacture of lifting and handling equipment
Parent: KKR & Co. L.P.
Officers: Brandon Francis Brahm [1984] Director/Investment Professional [American]; William Joseph Janetschek Jnr [1962] Director/Chief Financial Officer [American]; Peter Max Stavros [1974] Director/Investment Professional [American]

Ascential Financing Limited
Incorporated: 6 January 2016
Net Worth: £246,700,000 *Total Assets:* £1,725,799,936
Registered Office: The Prow, 1 Wilder Walk, London, W1B 5AP
Activities: Financial intermediation not elsewhere classified
Parent: Ascential PLC
Officers: Shanny Looi, Secretary; Louise Meads, Secretary; Amanda Jane Gradden [1968] Director; Duncan Anthony Painter [1970] Director

Ascential Group Limited
Incorporated: 27 May 1947 *Employees:* 104
Previous: Top Right Group Limited
Net Worth: £871,400,000 *Total Assets:* £1,717,900,032
Registered Office: The Prow, 1 Wilder Walk, London, W1B 5AP
Activities: Activities of other holding companies n.e.c.
Parent: Ascential Financing Limited
Officers: Shanny Looi, Secretary; Louise Meads, Secretary; Amanda Jane Gradden [1968] Director; Duncan Anthony Painter [1970] Director

Ascential PLC
Incorporated: 4 January 2016 *Employees:* 1,777
Net Worth: £343,000,000 *Total Assets:* £987,400,000
Registered Office: The Prow, 1 Wilder Walk, London, W1B 5AP
Activities: Activities of head offices
Officers: Louise Meads, Secretary; Rita Ann Clifton [1958] Director; Scott Edward Forbes [1957] Director/Chairman [American/British]; Amanda Jane Gradden [1968] Director; Paul Scott Harrison [1964] Director/Chief Financial Officer; Gillian Dawn Celia Kent [1963] Director; Duncan Anthony Painter [1970] Director; Judith Vezmar [1956] Director [American]

Ascential Prefco Limited
Incorporated: 6 January 2016
Net Worth: £131,492,000 *Total Assets:* £135,478,000
Registered Office: The Prow, 1 Wilder Walk, London, W1B 5AP
Activities: Financial intermediation not elsewhere classified
Parent: Ascential Financing Limited
Officers: Shanny Looi, Secretary; Louise Meads, Secretary; Amanda Jane Gradden [1968] Director; Duncan Anthony Painter [1970] Director

Ascential UK Holdings Limited
Incorporated: 21 August 1954
Previous: EMAP Limited
Net Worth: £298,064,992 *Total Assets:* £321,156,000
Registered Office: c/o Ascential Group Limited, The Prow, 1 Wilder Walk, London, W1B 5AP
Activities: Activities of other holding companies n.e.c.
Parent: Ascential Group Limited
Officers: Shanny Looi, Company Secretary; Louise Meads, Secretary; Amanda Jane Gradden [1968] Director; Duncan Anthony Painter [1970] Director

Ascot Corporate Name Limited
Incorporated: 10 August 2001 *Employees:* 161
Net Worth Deficit: £11,149,000 *Total Assets:* £1,112,865,024
Registered Office: 20 Fenchurch Street, London, EC3M 3BY
Activities: Non-life insurance
Parent: Ascot Underwriting Group Limited
Officers: Elizabeth Helen Guyatt, Secretary; Helen Rachel Jones-Bak [1972] Director; Parth Patel [1978] Director/Actuary; Mark Charles Smith [1970] Director

Ascot Underwriting Group Limited
Incorporated: 5 September 2016 *Employees:* 206
Net Worth Deficit: £25,834,818 *Total Assets:* £1,255,400,192
Registered Office: 20 Fenchurch Street, London, EC3M 3BY
Activities: Non-life insurance
Parent: Minister of Finance, Canada
Officers: Elizabeth Helen Guyatt, Secretary; Andrew Lewis Brooks [1965] Director/CEO Ascot Underwriting Ltd; Katherine Hae-Eun Chung [1976] Director/Private Equity Investor [American]; Thomas Kalvik [1981] Director [Canadian]

Ash8 Group Holdings Limited
Incorporated: 19 January 2016 *Employees:* 132
Net Worth: £50,065,000 *Total Assets:* £171,883,008
Registered Office: Second Floor, 11 Pilgrim Street, London, EC4V 6RN
Activities: Other letting and operating of own or leased real estate
Parent: Ash8 UK Asset Co Limited
Officers: Sean Thomas McKeown [1970] Director [Australian]; George Nicholas Shweiry [1966] Director

Ash8 Group Limited
Incorporated: 19 January 2016 *Employees:* 5
Net Worth: £41,765,044 *Total Assets:* £108,211,080
Registered Office: Second Floor, 11 Pilgrim Street, London, EC4V 6RN
Activities: Other letting and operating of own or leased real estate
Parent: Ash8 Group Holdings Limited
Officers: Sean Thomas McKeown [1970] Director [Australian]; George Nicholas Shweiry [1966] Director

Laura Ashley Holdings PLC
Incorporated: 28 May 1971 *Employees:* 3,151
Net Worth: £36,400,000 *Total Assets:* £124,600,000
Registered Office: 27 Bagleys Lane, Fulham, London, SW6 2QA
Activities: Activities of head offices
Shareholder: Tan Sri Dr Khoo Kay Peng
Officers: Prajna Hegde, Secretary; Sean Thomas Anglim [1963] Finance Director [Irish]; Andrew Khoo Boo Yeow [1972] Director/Business Executive [Australian]; David Robert Cook [1965] Director; Kwan Cheong NG [1948] Director/Businessman [Malaysian]; Jane Margaret Rapley [1946] Director/Professor Emerita; Nyen Faat Wong [1957] Director [Malaysian]; Leon Yee [1976] Director [Singaporean]

Laura Ashley Limited
Incorporated: 31 March 1954 *Employees:* 2,810
Net Worth: £82,091,000 *Total Assets:* £184,608,000
Registered Office: 27 Bagleys Lane, Fulham, London, SW6 2QA
Activities: Retail sale of textiles in specialised stores
Parent: Laura Ashley Holdings PLC
Officers: Sagar Avinash Mavani, Secretary; Sean Thomas Anglim [1963] Director [Irish]; Nicos Kaloyirou [1961] Director; Kwan Cheong NG [1948] Director [Malaysian]

Ashmore Group PLC
Incorporated: 30 November 1998 *Employees:* 257
Net Worth: £759,200,000 *Total Assets:* £908,000,000
Registered Office: 61 Aldwych, London, WC2B 4AE
Activities: Activities of financial services holding companies
Officers: John Keith Taylor, Secretary; Clive Peter Adamson [1956] Director; David Jonathan Bennett [1962] Director; Jennifer Johan Bingham [1952] Director; Mark Langhorn Coombs [1960] Director; Dame Anne Fyfe Pringle [1955] Director/Diplomat; Tom Adam Shippey [1974] Finance Director

Ashmore Investment Management Limited
Incorporated: 3 April 1997
Net Worth: £52,221,000 *Total Assets:* £109,592,000
Registered Office: 61 Aldwych, London, WC2B 4AE
Activities: Fund management activities
Parent: Ashmore Investments (UK) Limited
Officers: John Keith Taylor, Secretary; Mark Langhorn Coombs [1960] Director/Banker; Tom Adam Shippey [1974] Finance Director

Ashmore Investments (UK) Limited
Incorporated: 4 April 1997
Net Worth: £114,714,000 *Total Assets:* £575,611,008
Registered Office: 61 Aldwych, London, WC2B 4AE
Activities: Activities of financial services holding companies
Parent: Ashmore Group PLC
Officers: John Keith Taylor, Secretary; Mark Langhorn Coombs [1960] Director/Banker; Thomas Adam Shippey [1974] Finance Director

Ashtead Financing Limited
Incorporated: 13 August 2008
Net Worth: £1,203,150,464 *Total Assets:* £1,940,051,584
Registered Office: 100 Cheapside, London, EC2V 6DT
Activities: Other business support service activities n.e.c.
Parent: Ashtead Holdings PLC
Officers: Eric Watkins, Secretary; Michael Richard Pratt [1964] Director/Accountant; Eric Watkins [1955] Director/Solicitor

Ashtead Group Public Limited Company
Incorporated: 11 April 1984 *Employees:* 15,621
Net Worth: £2,526,899,968 *Total Assets:* £6,743,000,064
Registered Office: 100 Cheapside, London, EC2V 6DT
Activities: Activities of other holding companies n.e.c.
Officers: Eric Watkins, Company Secretary Legal Counsel; Angus George Cockburn [1963] Director; Geoffrey Drabble [1959] Director; Tanya Dianne Fratto [1960] Director [American]; Brendan Christopher Horgan [1973] Director [American]; Michael Richard Pratt [1964] Director; Lucinda Jane Riches [1961] Director; Paul Ashton Walker [1957] Director

Ashtead Holdings Public Limited Company
Incorporated: 11 September 2003
Net Worth: £1,464,272,000 *Total Assets:* £1,810,540,032
Registered Office: 100 Cheapside, London, EC2V 6DT
Activities: Other business support service activities n.e.c.
Parent: Ashtead Group PLC
Officers: Eric Watkins, Company Secretary Legal Counsel; Geoffrey Drabble [1959] Director; Michael Richard Pratt [1964] Director

Ashtead Plant Hire Company Limited
Incorporated: 1 November 1947 *Employees:* 3,598
Net Worth: £161,812,000 *Total Assets:* £893,281,024
Registered Office: 100 Cheapside, London, EC2V 6DT
Activities: Renting and leasing of construction and civil engineering machinery and equipment
Parent: Ashtead Holdings PLC
Officers: Eric Watkins, Company Secretary Legal Counsel; Geoffrey Drabble [1959] Director; Philip John Parker [1979] Director; Michael Richard Pratt [1964] Director; Richard David Thomas [1979] Director

Ashurst LLP
Incorporated: 31 July 2007 *Employees:* 2,553
Net Worth: £268,311,008 *Total Assets:* £411,132,992
Registered Office: Broadwalk House, 5 Appold Street, London, EC2A 2HA
Officers: Karen Davies [1973] Member; Bernd Egbers [1974] Member; Paul Andrew Jenkins [1972] Member; Angela Margaret Mary Pearson [1966] Member; Sarah Ruth Sivyour [1974] Member; Benjamin James Cuthbert Tidswell [1965] Member; Robert James Aird [1980] LLP Member; Andres Alfonso [1978] LLP Member; Karim-Yann Alix [1981] LLP Member; Robert Lawrence Andrews [1967] LLP Member; Noam Ankri [1975] LLP Member; Umberto Antonelli [1975] LLP Member; Rafael Baena Zapatero [1975] LLP Member; Tamer Osama Alaaeldin Mahmoud Bahgat [1979] LLP Member; Kerion Ingley Ball [1976] LLP Member; Alexander Ballmann [1970] LLP Member; Christopher Bates [1977] LLP Member; Jose Christian Bertram [1972] LLP Member; Alexander James Walter Biles [1981] LLP Member; Matthew Charles Bool [1980] LLP Member; Giles Daniel Boothman [1967] LLP Member; Patrick William Boyle [1971] LLP Member; Philip Andrew Stuart Breden [1972] LLP Member; Simon Robert Ivor Bromwich [1966] LLP Member; Timothy Deakin Brookes [1959] LLP Member; Nicholas Stefen Bryans [1969] LLP Member; Ruth Marion Buchanan [1979] LLP Member; Simon Bullock [1981] LLP Member; Richard Michael Burns [1980] LLP Member; Euan Burrows [1970] LLP Member; Helen Claire Burton [1970] LLP Member; Dr Martin Bunning [1967] LLP Member; Cristina Calvo [1969] LLP Member; Tim Cant [1985] LLP Member; David Michael Capps [1963] LLP Member; Andrew Carter [1965] LLP Member; David Charles Carter [1969] LLP Member; Peter John Chalk [1968] LLP Member; Malcolm Charles [1970] LLP Member; Nicholas Nigel Cheshire [1972] LLP Member; James Coiley [1971] LLP Member; Martin Patrick Coleman [1965] LLP Member; James Henry Robin Collis [1970] LLP Member; Thomas Connor [1978] LLP Member; Alexander Roys Courteen Cox [1973] LLP Member; Thomas James Cummins [1981] LLP Member; Neil McLeod Cuninghame [1971] LLP Member; David Roger Davies [1962] LLP Member; Anna Delgado [1961] LLP Member; Anthony Generald Denholder [1969] LLP Member; Julia Helen Derrick [1981] LLP Member; Nicolas Matthias Georg Deuerling [1974] LLP Member; John Lee Doyle [1971] LLP Member; David Du Pont [1975] LLP Member; Thomas Alexander Courtney Duncan [1976] LLP Member; Lynn Noelle Dunne [1974] LLP Member; Mark Robert Edwards [1976] LLP Member; Mark Philip Elsey [1960] LLP Member; Nicholas Edward Taylor Elverston [1964] LLP Member; Pedro Ester Palacios [1978] LLP Member; Reinhard Eyring [1958] LLP Member; Ismael Fernandez Anton [1973] LLP Member; Jane Katharine Fissenden [1967] LLP Member; James Samuel Fletcher [1981] LLP Member; Angus Foley [1970] LLP Member; Marylyn Ru-Woei Foong [1984] LLP Member; Denis Fosselard [1968] LLP Member; David Futter [1977] LLP Member; Olga Galazoula [1980] LLP Member; Jonathan William Gale [1980] LLP Member; Pablo Garcia-Manzano [1973] LLP Member; Nicholas John George Gardner [1974] LLP Member; Christopher Georgiou [1967] LLP Member; Geoffrey Stuart Gishubl [1968] LLP Member; Elena Maria Giuffre [1972] LLP Member; Nicholas Simon Goddard [1976] LLP Member; Trevor Goode [1968] LLP Member; Jonathan Matthew Gordon [1967] LLP Member; Eduardo Gracia [1967] LLP Member; Jake Green [1981] LLP Member; Anne Grewlich [1977] LLP Member; Jonathan Andrew Haines [1972] LLP Member; Amanda Louise Hale [1966] LLP Member; Bruce John Hanton [1962] LLP Member; Alison Cheney Hardy [1975] LLP Member; Ruth Harris [1971] LLP Member; Michael Harrison [1968] LLP Member; Javier Hernandez Galante [1974] LLP Member; Laura Kar Ling Ho [1986] LLP Member; Nicholas Stephen Holmes [1965] LLP Member; Bernd Michael Holzhaeuser [1973] LLP Member; Nicola Jayne Hopkins [1976] LLP Member; Naomi Horton [1967] LLP Member; Hiroyuki Iwamura [1972] LLP Member; Hassan Javanshir [1967] LLP Member; Derwin John Hugh Jenkinson [1975] LLP Member; Anthony John Maurice Johnson [1978] LLP Member; David Andrew Owen Jones [1969] LLP Member; Melanie Jordan [1971] LLP Member

ASOS Intermediate Holdings Limited
Incorporated: 17 April 2013
Net Worth: £2,346,115,072 *Total Assets:* £2,346,115,072
Registered Office: Greater London House, Hampstead Road, London, NW1 7FB
Activities: Activities of other holding companies n.e.c.
Parent: ASOS PLC
Officers: Andrew Colin Magowan, Secretary; Nicholas Timothy Beighton [1968] Director; Andrew Colin Magowan [1974] Director/Company Secretary

ASOS PLC
Incorporated: 2 June 2000 *Employees:* 4,266
Net Worth: £438,800,000 *Total Assets:* £1,007,000,000
Registered Office: Greater London House, Hampstead Road, London, NW1 7FB
Activities: Activities of head offices
Officers: Andrew Magowan, Secretary; Nicholas Timothy Beighton [1968] Finance Director; Rita Ann Clifton [1958] Director; Adam Alexander Crozier [1964] Director; Ian Dyson [1962] Director/Accountant; Hilary Susan Riva [1957] Director; Nicholas John Robertson [1967] Director

Asos.Com Limited
Incorporated: 19 June 1998 *Employees:* 4,146
Net Worth: £471,086,016 *Total Assets:* £1,039,616,000
Registered Office: Greater London House, Hampstead Road, London, NW1 7FB
Activities: Retail sale via mail order houses or via Internet
Parent: ASOS Intermediate Holdings
Officers: Andrew Colin Magowan, Secretary; Nicholas Timothy Beighton [1968] Director; Andrew Colin Magowan [1974] Director/Company Secretary

Aspect Capital Limited
Incorporated: 12 January 1998 *Employees:* 132
Net Worth: £94,404,000 *Total Assets:* £157,919,008
Registered Office: 10 Portman Square, London, W1H 6AZ
Activities: Fund management activities
Major Shareholder: Anthony James Todd
Officers: Jonathan Greenwold, Secretary; Dr Kevin James Carter [1952] Director; Peter Gibbs [1958] Director; Jonathan Edward Stark Greenwold [1976] Director and Company Secretary; Kenneth Michael Edward Hope [1973] Director/Accountant; Martin Anthony Lueck [1961] Director [American]; Rosemary Jane Reynolds [1978] Director/Chief Commercial Officer; Anthony James Todd [1960] Director

Aspen (UK) Holdings Limited
Incorporated: 3 June 2003
Net Worth: £577,395,840 *Total Assets:* £601,392,832
Registered Office: 30 Fenchurch Street, London, EC3M 3BD
Activities: Non-life insurance
Parent: Aspen Insurance Holdings Limited
Officers: Helen Lipscomb, Secretary; Mike Cain [1972] Director/Lawyer; Scott Kenneth Kirk [1973] Director [Australian]; Charles Christopher O'Kane [1955] Director/Underwriter

Aspen European Holdings Limited
Incorporated: 12 August 2014
Net Worth: £1,038,195,840 *Total Assets:* £1,038,195,840
Registered Office: 30 Fenchurch Street, London, EC3M 3BD
Activities: Non-life insurance
Parent: Aspen Insurance Holdings Limited
Officers: Helen Lipscomb, Secretary; Mike Cain [1972] Director/Lawyer; Scott Kenneth Kirk [1973] Director/Group CFO [Australian]; Stuart Ian Riley [1964] Director

Aspen Insurance UK Limited
Incorporated: 16 September 1974
Net Worth: £644,434,496 *Total Assets:* £4,643,386,368
Registered Office: 30 Fenchurch Street, London, EC3M 3BD
Activities: Non-life insurance
Parent: Aspen European Holdings Limited
Officers: Helen Lipscomb, Secretary; Michael Roger Cain [1972] Director/Group General Counsel and CEO; Julian Michael Cusack [1950] Director/Accountant; Mark Ernest Dean [1962] Director/Chief Risk Officer; Gordon Roland Ireland [1953] Director/Accountant; Emil Issavi [1972] Director/Underwriter [American]; Timothy James Leggett [1952] Director/Chartered Accountant; Dr Karl Josef Mayr [1950] Director [German]; Peter David Webster [1951] Director

Aspen Managing Agency Limited
Incorporated: 21 December 2007
Net Worth Deficit: £35,878,000 *Total Assets:* £1,061,209,984
Registered Office: Plantation Place, 30 Fenchurch Street, London, EC3M 3BD
Activities: Non-life insurance
Parent: Aspen Insurance Holdings Limited
Officers: Helen Lipscomb, Secretary; Michael Roger Cain [1972] Director/Group General Counsel & CEO; Mark Ernest Dean [1962] Director/Chief Risk Officer; Karen Ann Green [1967] Director; Dr Karl Josef Mayr [1950] Director [German]; John William Joseph Roome [1960] Director; Peter David Webster [1951] Director

Aspen Underwriting Limited
Incorporated: 21 December 2007
Net Worth: £1,542,000 *Total Assets:* £1,099,101,056
Registered Office: Plantation Place, 30 Fenchurch Street, London, EC3M 3BD
Activities: Non-life insurance
Parent: Aspen Insurance Holdings Limited
Officers: Helen Lipscomb, Secretary; Stuart Ian Riley [1964] Director; Helen Rose [1966] Director/UK CFO

Aspers Group Limited
Incorporated: 15 October 2004 *Employees:* 2
Net Worth: £82,769,000 *Total Assets:* £129,103,000
Registered Office: 1 Hans Street, London, SW1X 0JD
Activities: Activities of head offices
Parent: Aspers UK Holdings Limited
Officers: John Damian Androcles Aspinall [1960] Director; Derek Louis Playford [1963] Director/Accountant

Assembled Productions III UK Limited
Incorporated: 17 March 2016 *Employees:* 1
Net Worth: £43,552 *Total Assets:* £112,739,160
Registered Office: 3 Queen Caroline Street, Hammersmith, London, W6 9PE
Activities: Motion picture production activities
Parent: The Walt Disney Company
Officers: Marsha Reed, Secretary; Nigel Anthony Cook [1967] Director/Executive; David Don Galluzzi [1974] Director/Chief Counsel [American]; Marsha Leigh Reed [1957] Director/Executive [American]

Associated British Foods PLC
Incorporated: 20 October 1934 *Employees:* 137,014
Net Worth: £9,210,999,808 *Total Assets:* £13,112,999,936
Registered Office: Weston Centre, 10 Grosvenor Street, London, W1K 4QY
Activities: Activities of head offices
Officers: Paul Andrew Lister, Secretary; Emma Susan Adamo [1963] Director [Canadian]; Graham Denis Allan [1955] Director [British/Australian]; John George Bason [1957] Finance Director; Linda Ruth Cairnie [1953] Director; Dr Wolfhart Gunnar Hauser [1949] Director [German]; Michael George Alexander McLintock [1961] Director; Richard Harry Reid [1956] Director/Chartered Accountant; George Garfield Weston [1964] Director [Canadian]

Associated British Ports Holdings Limited
Incorporated: 8 February 1982 *Employees:* 2
Net Worth: £2,475,699,968 *Total Assets:* £2,513,999,872
Registered Office: 25 Bedford Street, London, WC2E 9ES
Activities: Activities of head offices
Parent: ABP Acquisitions UK Limited
Officers: Andrew Charles Garner, Secretary; James Alexander Bryce [1974] Director/Investor; George Sebastian Matthew Bull [1960] Director/Chartered Accountant; Philippe Anastase Busslinger [1975] Director [Swiss]; Philip Butcher [1985] Director/Principal [Canadian]; John Bernard Coghlan [1958] Director [Irish]; Hakim Drissi Kaitouni [1983] Director; Stewart Norman Hicks [1952] Director; Peter Francis Hofbauer [1960] Director/Investment Manager [Australian]; George Philip Roger Kay [1972] Director/Private Equity Investor [New Zealander]; Eric Philippe Marianne Machiels [1966] Managing Director [Belgian]; Helen Margaret Newell [1968] Director [Australian]; Dr Philip Michael Gerard Nolan [1953] Director/Chairman; Mr Henrik Lundgaard Pedersen [1974] Director/Chief Executive Officer [Danish]; Gregory Stuart Pestrak [1971] Director/Finance Executive; John Rishton [1958] Director; Dmitry Yashnikov [1989] Director/Investment Manager

Associated Newspapers Limited
Incorporated: 1 April 1905 *Employees:* 1,785
Net Worth: £464,871,008 *Total Assets:* £649,889,024
Registered Office: Northcliffe House, 2 Derry Street, London, W8 5TT
Activities: Publishing of newspapers
Parent: DMG Media Limited
Officers: Frances Louise Sallas, Secretary; Kevin Joseph Beatty [1957] Director/Newspaper Management; The Fourth Viscount Rothermere [1967] Director/Chairman; James Justin Siderfin Welsh [1967] Director

Assured Guaranty (Europe) PLC
Incorporated: 8 June 1990
Previous: Assured Guaranty (Europe) Ltd.
Net Worth: £553,836,032 *Total Assets:* £1,318,460,032
Registered Office: 11th Floor, 6 Bevis Marks, London, EC3A 7BA
Activities: Non-life insurance
Officers: Ruth Cove, Secretary; Sandali Harvey, Secretary; Robert Adam Bailenson [1966] Director [American]; Charles Peter Barrington [1946] Director/Self Employed; Mark Batten [1957] Director; Dominic John Frederico [1953] Director/Insurance [American]; Simon William de Mussenden Leathes [1948] Director; Dominic James Brian Nathan [1966] Director; Nicholas James Proud [1963] Director

Aston Bidco Limited
Incorporated: 18 June 2014 *Employees:* 3
Net Worth Deficit: £35,086,360 *Total Assets:* £131,089,000
Registered Office: c/o XLN Telecom Ltd, First Floor, Millbank Tower, 21-24 Millbank, London, SW1P 4QP
Activities: Activities of head offices
Major Shareholder: Knud Erik Krey Nellemann
Officers: Panayiotis Koullas, Secretary; Neil Francis Conaghan [1971] Director; Christian Nelleman [1967] Director [Danish]

Aston Lark (Bidco) Limited
Incorporated: 15 June 2017 *Employees:* 6
Net Worth Deficit: £4,358,900 *Total Assets:* £173,620,800
Registered Office: 8th Floor, Ibex House, 42-47 Minories, London, EC3N 1DY
Activities: Non-life insurance
Parent: Aston Lark (Midco) Limited
Officers: Peter William Blanc [1970] Director; Carl Whitmore Brown [1966] Director; Timothy Mark Holland [1962] Director; Stephen John Starling Lark [1966] Director; Julian James Lawrence Masters [1973] Director/Investment Manager; David Torbet [1978] Director/Investment Manager

Aston Lark (Topco) Limited
Incorporated: 15 June 2017 *Employees:* 599
Net Worth Deficit: £6,591,271 *Total Assets:* £174,550,144
Registered Office: 8th Floor, Ibex House, 42-47 Minories, London, EC3N 1DY
Activities: Non-life insurance
Parent: Bowmark GP LLP
Officers: Peter William Blanc [1970] Director; Carl Whitmore Brown [1966] Director; Valerie Michelle Dias [1959] Director; Timothy Mark Holland [1962] Director/Accountant; Graham Robert Starling Lark [1959] Director; Stephen John Starling Lark [1966] Director; Julian James Lawrence Masters [1973] Director/Investment Manager; Nigel Mark Inches Robertson [1959] Director; Stuart Paul Rootham [1969] Director; David Torbet [1978] Director/Investment Manager

ATK Finance Limited
Incorporated: 15 December 2005
Net Worth: £28,575,544 *Total Assets:* £210,140,336
Registered Office: 12th Floor, Adelphi, 1-11 John Adam Street, London, WC2N 6HT
Activities: Other business support service activities n.e.c.
Parent: A.T. Kearney Holdings Limited
Officers: James Dyall, Secretary; Steve Bevan [1961] HR Director; James Dyall [1972] Finance Director; Christine Marianne Pauline Laurens [1970] Director/Chief Financial Officer [French]

Atlassian (Australia) Limited
Incorporated: 18 November 2013
Net Worth: £1,648,656,000 *Total Assets:* £1,648,656,000
Registered Office: c/o Herbert Smith Freehills LLP, Exchange House, Primrose Street, London, EC2A 2EG
Activities: Business and domestic software development
Parent: Atlassian (UK) Holdings Limited
Officers: Thomas Shrieve Kennedy, Secretary; Michael Canon-Brookes [1979] Director/CEO & Founder, Atlassian Corp Pty Ltd [Australian]; Scott Farquhar [1979] Director/CEO & Founder, Atlassian Corp Pty Ltd [Australian]; Thomas Shrieve Kennedy [1973] Director/Lawyer [American]; Jay Simons [1972] Director/President Atlassian Corp Pty Ltd [American]

Atlassian (UK) Limited
Incorporated: 15 November 2013
Net Worth: £2,779,006,464 *Total Assets:* £2,780,529,664
Registered Office: c/o Herbert Smith Freehills LLP, Exchange House, Primrose Street, London, EC2A 2EG
Activities: Business and domestic software development
Parent: Atlassian (UK) Holdings Limited
Officers: Thomas Shrieve Kennedy, Secretary; Michael Canon-Brookes [1979] Director/CEO & Founder, Atlassian Corp Pty Ltd [Australian]; Scott Farquhar [1979] Director/CEO & Founder, Atlassian Corp Pty Ltd [Australian]; Thomas Shrieve Kennedy [1973] Director/Lawyer [American]; Jay Simons [1972] Director/President, Atlassian Corp Pty Ltd [American]

Atlassian Corporation PLC
Incorporated: 14 November 2013 *Employees:* 2,425
Net Worth: £700,923,264 *Total Assets:* £1,903,520,512
Registered Office: c/o Herbert Smith Freehills LLP, Exchange House, Primrose Street, London, EC2A 2EG
Activities: Business and domestic software development
Officers: Thomas Shrieve Kennedy, Secretary; Shona Brown [1966] Director/Business Advisor [American]; Michael Canon-Brookes [1979] Director/CEO & Founder, Atlassian Corp Pty Ltd [Australian]; Scott Farquhar [1979] Director/CEO & Founder, Atlassian Corp Pty Ltd [Australian]; Heather Mirjahangir Fernandez [1975] Director/Business Executive [American]; Sasan Goodarzi [1968] Director/Intuit Executive [American]; Jay Parikh [1973] Director/VP of Infrastructure Engineering [American]; Enrique Salem [1965] Director CEO [American]; Steven Sordello [1969] Director/Chief Financial Officer [American]; Richard Wong [1969] Director/General Partner at Accel [American]

Atos International IT Holdings Limited
Incorporated: 26 May 2015
Net Worth: £131,104,808 *Total Assets:* £672,391,296
Registered Office: Second Floor, Mid City Place, 71 High Holborn, London, WC1V 6EA
Activities: Activities of head offices
Parent: Atos SE
Officers: James John Terrence Loughrey, Secretary; William James Donovan [1972] Director/Accountant [American]; Adrian Paul Gregory [1973] Director/CEO UK & Ireland

Atos International IT Limited
Incorporated: 23 April 1985
Net Worth: £655,201,024 *Total Assets:* £702,401,024
Registered Office: Second Floor, Mid City Place, 71 High Holborn, London, WC1V 6EA
Activities: Non-trading company
Shareholders: Atos IT Services UK Limited; Sema Investment UK Limited
Officers: James Terrence John Loughrey, Secretary/Lawyer; William James Donovan [1972] Director/Accountant [American]; Adrian Paul Gregory [1973] Director/CEO UK&I; James Terrence John Loughrey [1957] Director/Lawyer

Atos IT Services Limited
Incorporated: 16 January 1976
Net Worth: £801,062,976 *Total Assets:* £2,046,624,000
Registered Office: Second Floor, Mid City Place, 71 High Holborn, London, WC1V 6EA
Activities: Other business support service activities n.e.c.
Parent: Atos UK IT Limited
Officers: James Terrence John Loughrey, Secretary/Lawyer; William James Donovan [1972] Director/Accountant [American]; Adrian Paul Gregory [1973] Director/CEO UK&I; James Terrence John Loughrey [1957] Director/Lawyer

Atos IT Services UK Limited
Incorporated: 23 February 1976 *Employees:* 7,700
Net Worth: £1,771,198,976 *Total Assets:* £2,435,673,088
Registered Office: Second Floor, Mid City Place, 71 High Holborn, London, WC1V 6EA
Activities: Manufacture of computers and peripheral equipment
Parent: Atos IT Services Limited
Officers: James Terrence John Loughrey, Secretary/Lawyer; William James Donovan [1972] Director/Accountant [American]; Adrian Paul Gregory [1973] Director/CEO UK & Ireland; James Terrence John Loughrey [1957] Director/Lawyer

Atos UK Holdings Limited
Incorporated: 28 May 2015
Net Worth: £762,073,216 *Total Assets:* £762,073,216
Registered Office: Second Floor, Mid City Place, 71 High Holborn, London, WC1V 6EA
Activities: Activities of head offices
Parent: Atos UK IT Holdings Limited
Officers: James John Terrence Loughrey, Secretary; William James Donovan [1972] Director/Accountant [American]; Adrian Paul Gregory [1973] Director/CEO UK & Ireland

Atos UK IT Holdings Limited
Incorporated: 30 May 2002
Net Worth: £800,968,000 *Total Assets:* £1,556,670,976
Registered Office: Second Floor, Mid City Place, 71 High Holborn, London, WC1V 6EA
Activities: Activities of head offices
Parent: Atos SE
Officers: James Terrence John Loughrey, Secretary/Lawyer; William James Donovan [1972] Director/Accountant [American]; Adrian Paul Gregory [1973] Director/CEO UK & Ireland

Atos UK IT Limited
Incorporated: 12 March 1990
Net Worth: £877,448,000 *Total Assets:* £877,448,000
Registered Office: Second Floor, Mid City Place, 71 High Holborn, London, WC1V 6EA
Activities: Other information technology service activities
Parent: Atos UK IT Holdings Limited
Officers: James Terrence John Loughrey, Secretary/Lawyer; William James Donovan [1972] Director/Accountant [American]; Adrian Paul Gregory [1973] Director/CEO UK & Ireland; James Terrence John Loughrey [1957] Director/Lawyer

Atrato Issuer Holdco Limited
Incorporated: 19 August 2009
Net Worth: £289,490 *Total Assets:* £725,238,144
Registered Office: 35 Great St Helen's, London, EC3A 6AP
Activities: Non-trading company
Parent: Intertrust Corporate Services Limited
Officers: Daniel Marc Richard Jaffe [1975] Director

Atrium 100 Properties Limited
Incorporated: 2 August 2002
Net Worth: £173,568,000 *Total Assets:* £178,160,992
Registered Office: Weston Centre, 10 Grosvenor Street, London, W1K 4QY
Activities: Buying and selling of own real estate
Parent: A.B.F. Holdings Limited
Officers: Rosalyn Sharon Schofield, Secretary/Solicitor; Rosalyn Sharon Schofield [1956] Director/Solicitor; Andrew Arthur Smith [1972] Director/Chartered Accountant

Atrium 5 Limited
Incorporated: 11 October 1993
Net Worth: £14,451,307 *Total Assets:* £278,579,488
Registered Office: Room 790, Lloyds, 1 Lime Street, London, EC3M 7DQ
Activities: Non-life insurance
Parent: Atrium Underwriting Group Limited
Officers: Martha Blanche Waymark Bruce, Secretary; Richard de Winton Wilkin Harries [1965] Executive Director; James Robert Francis Lee [1962] Director/Chief Operating Officer; Brendan Richard Anthony Merriman [1958] Director

Auburn Securities 9 PLC
Incorporated: 4 December 2013
Net Worth: £28,000 *Total Assets:* £436,812,000
Registered Office: Third Floor, 1 Kings Arms Yard, London, EC2R 7AF
Activities: Other business support service activities n.e.c.
Parent: Auburn 4 Limited
Officers: Robert Sutton [1978] Director/Financial Services [American]; Daniel Jonathan Wynne [1970] Director

Auria Solutions UK I Ltd.
Incorporated: 14 February 2017 *Employees:* 514
Net Worth Deficit: £4,289,000 *Total Assets:* £132,468,000
Registered Office: One Fleet Place, London, EC4M 7WS
Activities: Manufacture of other parts and accessories for motor vehicles
Parent: Auria Solutions Ltd.
Officers: Marc Flegler [1967] Director [German]; Scott Allan Kehoe [1973] Director/Business Executive [American]; Brian Pour [1971] Director/Business Executive [American]; Maurice Robert Sessel [1961] Director [American]

Australian Gas Networks UK 2 Limited
Incorporated: 15 August 2014 *Employees:* 4
Net Worth: £1,337,176,960 *Total Assets:* £1,337,191,936
Registered Office: 3 More London Riverside, London, SE1 2AQ
Activities: Activities of investment trusts
Parent: Australian Gas Networks UK Limited
Officers: Loi Shun Chan [1962] Director [Chinese]; Graham Winston Edwards [1954] Director/Chief Executive; Guy Butterworth Ellis [1961] Director; Mark John Horsley [1959] Director/Chief Executive Officer; Andrew John Hunter [1958] Director; Hing Lam Kam [1946] Director [Chinese]; Jonathan Theodore Miller [1971] Director

Australian Gas Networks UK Limited
Incorporated: 22 May 2014
Net Worth: £1,063,832,128 *Total Assets:* £2,997,041,152
Registered Office: 3 More London Riverside, London, SE1 2AQ
Activities: Activities of financial services holding companies
Shareholders: CKH Gas Infrastructure Limited; CKI Gas Infrastructure Limited; PAH Gas Infrastructure Limited
Officers: Loi Shun Chan [1962] Director; Graham Winston Edwards [1954] Director/Chief Executive; Guy Butterworth Ellis [1961] Director; Mark John Horsley [1959] Director/Chief Executive Officer; Andrew John Hunter [1958] Director; Tzar Kuoi Victor Li [1964] Director [Chinese]; Jonathan Theodore Miller [1971] Director

Auto ABS UK Loans 2017 PLC
Incorporated: 8 August 2017
Net Worth: £1,015,720 *Total Assets:* £422,271,840
Registered Office: 35 Great St Helen's, London, EC3A 6AP
Activities: Financial intermediation not elsewhere classified
Parent: Auto ABS UK Loans 2017 Holdings Limited
Officers: Daniel Marc Richard Jaffe [1975] Managing Director

Auto ABS UK Loans PLC
Incorporated: 2 October 2012
Net Worth: £7,820,157 *Total Assets:* £1,221,537,280
Registered Office: 35 Great St Helen's, London, EC3A 6AP
Activities: Financial intermediation not elsewhere classified
Parent: Auto ABS UK Loans Holdings Limited
Officers: Daniel Marc Richard Jaffe [1975] Managing Director

Autovista Group Limited
Incorporated: 30 March 2006
Previous: Eurotaxglass's Limited
Net Worth: £211,315,280 *Total Assets:* £563,246,912
Registered Office: 5th Floor, Wellington House, 125 Strand, London, WC2R 0AP
Activities: Activities of other holding companies n.e.c.
Parent: Autovista Holdco UK Ltd
Officers: Giles Stuart Catron [1968] Director; Paul John Dunkley [1958] Director; Timothy B Flynn [1968] Director [British/American]; Carlos Jose Pla Fernandez [1976] Director [Spanish]; Lindsey Jill Roberts [1966] Director

Autovista Holdco UK Limited
Incorporated: 30 March 2006
Previous: Candle Holdco UK Limited
Net Worth Deficit: £66,867,840 *Total Assets:* £128,722,992
Registered Office: 5th Floor, Wellington House, 125 Strand, London, WC2R 0AP
Activities: Activities of other holding companies n.e.c.
Parent: Autovista Bidco Limited
Officers: Giles Stuart Catron [1968] Director; Paul John Dunkley [1958] Director; Timothy B Flynn [1968] Director [British/American]; Carlos Jose Pla Fernandez [1976] Director [Spanish]; Lindsey Jill Roberts [1966] Director

Autovista Limited
Incorporated: 30 March 2006
Previous: Candle Newco UK Limited
Net Worth: £193,373,008 *Total Assets:* £193,373,008
Registered Office: 5th Floor, Wellington House, 125 Strand, London, WC2R 0AP
Activities: Activities of other holding companies n.e.c.
Parent: Autovista Group Ltd
Officers: Giles Stuart Catron [1968] Director; John Stephen Evans [1961] Director; Lindsey Jill Roberts [1966] Director

AV Equity Trading Limited
Incorporated: 14 March 2012
Net Worth: £17,589,028 *Total Assets:* £1,008,718,976
Registered Office: Level 20, 125 Old Broad Street, London, EC2N 1AR
Activities: Security dealing on own account
Officers: Gary Brennan [1970] Director/Consultant [Irish]; Perry Christopher Wilson [1965] Director

Avanade Europe Holdings Ltd.
Incorporated: 15 September 2004 *Employees:* 36
Net Worth: £121,647,000 *Total Assets:* £128,089,000
Registered Office: 30 Cannon Street, London, EC4M 6XH
Activities: Information technology consultancy activities
Parent: Avanade International Corporation
Officers: Ruth Redman, Secretary; Kenneth Allen Guthrie [1965] Director/Chief Financial Officer [American]; Darren Hardman [1977] Director/Area President Europe; Brett Evan Lowry [1966] Director/Global Financial Controller [American]; Barry William Pettitt [1971] Finance Director

Avanade Europe Services Ltd.
Incorporated: 25 May 2004 *Employees:* 48
Net Worth: £210,962,000 *Total Assets:* £215,186,000
Registered Office: 30 Cannon Street, London, EC4M 6XH
Activities: Other information technology service activities
Parent: Avanade Europe Holdings Limited
Officers: Ruth Redman, Secretary; Kenneth Allen Guthrie [1965] Director/Chief Financial Officer [American]; Darren Hardman [1977] Director/Area President Europe; Brett Evan Lowry [1966] Director/Global Financial Controller [American]; Barry William Pettitt [1971] Finance Director

Avanti Communications Group PLC
Incorporated: 1 March 2007 *Employees:* 231
Net Worth: £101,258,328 *Total Assets:* £600,222,080
Registered Office: Cobham House, 20 Black Friars Lane, London, EC4V 6EB
Activities: Satellite telecommunications activities
Shareholder: Solus Alternative Asset Management
Officers: Natalie Mitchell, Secretary; Craig Chobor [1972] Director [American]; Nigel Adrian Dawson Fox [1962] Director; Alan Harper [1956] Director; Paul Robert Johnson [1952] Director/Chartered Accountant; Michael Leitner [1967] Director [American]; Richard Mastoloni [1964] Director [American]; Peter Andrew Reed [1979] Director [American]; John Slamecka [1964] Director [American]; Paul Steven Walsh [1955] Director; Kyle David Whitehill [1962] Director/Chief Executive

Avanti Communications Infrastructure Limited
Incorporated: 20 December 2004
Net Worth Deficit: £6,556,000 *Total Assets:* £263,243,008
Registered Office: Cobham House, 20 Black Friars Lane, London, EC4V 6EB
Activities: Management consultancy activities other than financial management
Parent: Avanti Communications Group PLC
Officers: Natalie Mitchell, Secretary; Nigel Adrian Dawson Fox [1962] Director/Accountant; Natalie Mitchell [1973] Director/Solicitor

Avanti Hylas 2 Limited
Incorporated: 11 November 2009
Net Worth Deficit: £122,436,400 *Total Assets:* £459,201,184
Registered Office: Cobham House, 20 Black Friars Lane, London, EC4V 6EB
Activities: Satellite telecommunications activities
Parent: Avanti Communications Group PLC
Officers: Natalie Mitchell, Secretary; Nigel Adrian Dawson Fox [1962] Director/Accountant; Natalie Mitchell [1973] Director/Solicitor

Avara Pharma Services Ltd
Incorporated: 23 February 2016 *Employees:* 1,098
Net Worth: £109,775,504 *Total Assets:* £319,280,512
Registered Office: 9a Burroughs Gardens, London, NW4 4AU
Activities: Activities of production holding companies
Major Shareholder: Leonard Levie
Officers: Leonard Maleson Levie [1955] Director [American]; Bertrand Christian Henri Talabart [1972] Investor/Non-Executive Director [French]

Avation PLC
Incorporated: 11 July 2006 *Employees:* 22
Net Worth: £175,820,096 *Total Assets:* £888,087,744
Registered Office: 5 Fleet Place, London, EC4M 7RD
Activities: Activities of head offices
Officers: Duncan Gerard Stephen Scott, Secretary; Robert Jeffries Chatfield [1964] Director [Australian]; Dr Stephen John Fisher [1964] Director [Australian]; Roderick Douglas Mahoney [1958] Director; Derek Sharples [1959] Director/President

Avaya UK Holdings Limited
Incorporated: 14 July 2000 *Employees:* 4
Net Worth: £152,661,264 *Total Assets:* £155,136,800
Registered Office: 25 Moorgate, London, EC2R 6AY
Activities: Non-trading company
Officers: Lee Hastings, Secretary; Ena Jennifer Hunter, Secretary; Lee Hastings [1975] Director/Accountant; Ena Jennifer Hunter [1976] Director/Solicitor/Corporate Counsel; Ioan Griffith MacRae [1973] Managing Director; Stephen John Wright [1974] Finance Director

Avenell Property PLC
Incorporated: 30 July 1999
Net Worth: £1,912,000 *Total Assets:* £112,519,000
Registered Office: Fifth Floor, 100 Wood Street, London, EC2V 7EX
Activities: Other business support service activities n.e.c.
Parent: Avenell Holdings Limited
Officers: Mark Howard Filer [1967] Director

Aviva Employment Services Limited
Incorporated: 19 November 1996 *Employees:* 15,861
Net Worth: £3,052,999,936 *Total Assets:* £3,860,999,936
Registered Office: St Helen's, 1 Undershaft, London, EC3P 3DQ
Activities: Other service activities n.e.c.
Parent: Aviva Central Services UK Limited
Officers: Arlene Cairns [1978] Director [British/Australian]; Angela Jane Darlington [1968] Director/Actuary; Alison Jane Gammon [1973] Director; Mr Ian Matthew Hughes [1979] Director; Andrew Guy Pooley [1973] Director; Lindsey Claire Rix [1980] Director; Marie Tracy Sigsworth [1966] Director; Sara Elizabeth Thompson [1965] Director; Benjamin Sheldon Turner [1968] Director/HR Professional

Aviva Europe SE
Incorporated: 4 October 2011
Net Worth: £203,796,032 *Total Assets:* £210,793,312
Registered Office: St Helen's, 1 Undershaft, London, EC3P 3DQ
Activities: Activities of financial services holding companies
Parent: Aviva Group Holdings Limited
Officers: Julian Charles Baddeley [1981] Member/Solicitor; David Elliot [1973] Member/Director; Chetan Singh [1976] Member/Director

Aviva Group Holdings Limited
Incorporated: 10 April 1981
Net Worth: £25,845,000,192 *Total Assets:* £34,008,000,512
Registered Office: St Helen's, 1 Undershaft, London, EC3P 3DQ
Activities: Activities of head offices
Parent: Aviva PLC
Officers: Angela Jane Darlington [1968] Director/Actuary; Sarah Maillet [1966] Director; Sir Adrian Alastair Montague [1948] Director/Solicitor; Martin John Muir [1967] Director/Group Chief Capital Officer; Thomas Dawson Stoddard [1966] Director [American]

Aviva International Holdings Limited
Incorporated: 19 October 1987
Net Worth: £352,000,000 *Total Assets:* £379,000,000
Registered Office: St Helens, 1 Undershaft, London, EC3P 3DQ
Activities: Activities of head offices
Parent: Aviva Group Holdings Limited
Officers: Julian Charles Baddeley [1981] Director/Solicitor; David Elliot [1973] Director; Mr Neil Harrison [1975] Director; Shamira Mohammed [1968] Director/Accountant; Chetan Singh [1976] Director

Aviva International Insurance Limited
Incorporated: 8 August 1885
Net Worth: £2,704,999,936 *Total Assets:* £56,064,999,424
Registered Office: St Helen's, 1 Undershaft, London, EC3P 3DQ
Activities: Non-life insurance
Parent: Aviva Group Holdings Limited
Officers: Judith Buttigieg [1969] Director/Chartered Accountant; Robert William Albert Howe [1949] Director; Paul Leonard Mylet [1974] Director; Thomas Dawson Stoddard [1966] Director [American]; Otto Thoresen [1956] Director; Nicholas David Williams [1955] Director; Derek John Wright [1954] Director

Aviva Investors Global Services Limited
Incorporated: 17 December 1973 *Employees:* 20
Net Worth: £245,876,992 *Total Assets:* £672,200,000
Registered Office: St Helen's, 1 Undershaft, London, EC3P 3DQ
Activities: Fund management activities
Parent: Aviva Investors Holdings Limited
Officers: David Clayton [1962] Director/Chartered Accountant; Susan Patricia Janet Ebenston [1959] Director/Chief Operating Officer; Euan George Munro [1970] Director/Actuary; Mark Richard Beavis Versey [1972] Director/Chief Investment Officer

Aviva Investors Holdings Limited
Incorporated: 11 August 1986
Net Worth: £1,095,800,064 *Total Assets:* £1,188,899,968
Registered Office: St Helen's, 1 Undershaft, London, EC3P 3DQ
Activities: Activities of financial services holding companies
Parent: Aviva Group Holdings Limited
Officers: David Clayton [1962] Director/Chartered Accountant; Michael David Thomas Craston [1958] Director/Business Manager; Patricia Anne Cross [1959] Director [Australian]; Sarah Louise Morris [1978] Director/Chief People Officer; Euan George Munro [1970] Director/Actuary; Jeffrey Michael Weingarten [1948] Director [American]; Anne Whitaker [1958] Director/Accountant; Mark Barry Ewart White [1955] Director

Aviva Investors Pensions Limited
Incorporated: 27 June 1972
Net Worth: £10,100,000 *Total Assets:* £1,276,999,936
Registered Office: St Helen's, 1 Undershaft, London, EC3P 3DQ
Activities: Life insurance
Parent: Aviva Investors Holdings Limited
Officers: David Clayton [1962] Director/Chartered Accountant; Nigel Robert Cosgrove [1976] Director; Michael David Thomas Craston [1958] Director/Business Manager; Christopher Adam Jones [1969] Director; Gregory Robert Neilson [1985] Director; Dr David Stephen Skinner [1969] Director/Chief Investment Officer

Aviva Investors Realm Infrastructure No.1 Limited
Incorporated: 19 March 2012
Net Worth Deficit: £36,892,160 *Total Assets:* £249,686,352
Registered Office: St Helen's, 1 Undershaft, London, EC3P 3DQ
Activities: Activities of financial services holding companies
Parent: Aviva Investors Infrastructure GP Limited
Officers: Ian Graham Berry [1972] Director/Finance; Sean Kent McLachlan [1970] Director/Finance; Nicholas Tebbutt [1984] Director/Chartered Accountant

Aviva Investors Realm Infrastructure No.5 Limited
Incorporated: 29 April 2016
Net Worth Deficit: £1,187,048 *Total Assets:* £198,292,272
Registered Office: St Helen's, 1 Undershaft, London, EC3P 3DQ
Activities: Fund management activities
Parent: Aviva Investors Infrastructure GP Limited
Officers: Ian Graham Berry [1972] Director/Finance; Sean Kent McLachlan [1970] Director/Finance; Nicholas Tebbutt [1984] Director/Chartered Accountant

Aviva Investors UK Fund Services Limited
Incorporated: 20 December 1985
Net Worth: £42,932,000 *Total Assets:* £132,788,000
Registered Office: St Helen's, 1 Undershaft, London, EC3P 3DQ
Activities: Financial intermediation not elsewhere classified
Parent: Aviva Investors Holdings Limited
Officers: Iain Keith Buckle [1968] Director; David Clayton [1962] Director/Chartered Accountant; Michael David Thomas Craston [1958] Director/Business Manager; Susan Patricia Janet Ebenston [1959] Director/Chief Operating Officer; Jeremy Hart Leadsom [1959] Director/Business Manager; Graeme John Hourston Miller [1968] Director; Dr David Stephen Skinner [1969] Director/Chief Investment Officer

Aviva PLC
Incorporated: 9 February 1990 *Employees:* 30,090
Net Worth: £17,899,999,232 *Total Assets:* £442,684,997,632
Registered Office: St Helen's, 1 Undershaft, London, EC3P 3DQ
Activities: Activities of head offices
Officers: Kirstine Ann Cooper, Secretary; Claudia Isobel Arney [1971] Independent Non-Executive Director; Glyn Barker [1953] Director; Andrew David Briggs [1966] Director; Patricia Anne Cross [1959] Director [Australian]; Michael John Hawker [1959] Director [Australian]; Michael Philip Mire [1948] Director; Sir Adrian Alastair Montague [1948] Director/Solicitor; Belen Romana Garcia [1965] Director [Spanish]; Thomas Dawson Stoddard [1966] Director [American]; Maurice Ewen Tulloch [1969] Director [Canadian]; Keith Williams [1956] Director

Awilco Drilling PLC
Incorporated: 30 December 2009 *Employees:* 141
Net Worth: £174,168,736 *Total Assets:* £250,017,328
Registered Office: 3rd Floor, 11-12 St James's Square, London, SW1Y 4LB
Activities: Support activities for petroleum and natural gas mining
Officers: Jon Oliver Sinclair Bryce [1968] Director/Chief Executive Officer; Henrik Fougner [1963] Director/Chief Operating Officer [Norwegian]; Daniel Allen Gold [1968] Director/Hedge Fund Manager [American]; John Nicol Simpson [1947] Director; Synne Syrrist [1972] Director and Consultant [Norwegian]; Sigurd Einar Thorvildsen [1965] Director/CEO Awilhelmsen Management AS [Norwegian]

Awin Ltd
Incorporated: 7 June 2000 *Employees:* 308
Previous: Digital Window Limited
Net Worth: £76,390,000 *Total Assets:* £173,036,000
Registered Office: 5th Floor, 2 Thomas More Square, London, E1W 1YN
Activities: Other information service activities n.e.c.
Officers: Kevin Mark Collett, Secretary; Peter John Loveday [1973] Director; Adam Benjamin Ross [1981] Director [Irish]; Mark Gary Walters [1969] Director

AWP Assistance UK Ltd
Incorporated: 29 March 1983 *Employees:* 546
Previous: Mondial Assistance (UK) Limited
Net Worth: £7,751,821 *Total Assets:* £104,735,600
Registered Office: P O Box 74005, 60 Gracechurch Street, London, EC3P 3DS
Activities: Activities auxiliary to financial intermediation n.e.c.
Parent: Allianz Worldwide Partners S.A.S
Officers: Neil James Travell, Secretary; Remi Henri Dominique Marie Grenier [1960] Director [French]; Antony Philip Dawson Lancaster [1942] Director; Lidia Barbara Luka-Lognone [1961] Director [French]; Willem Anton Snijders [1963] Director [Dutch]; Timothy David Tozer [1959] Director/Chief Executive; Michael David Webb [1960] Director

Axa Equity & Law Public Limited Company
Incorporated: 16 March 1987
Net Worth: £2,086,675,968 *Total Assets:* £2,087,686,016
Registered Office: 5 Old Broad Street, London, EC2N 1AD
Activities: Activities of financial services holding companies
Parent: Axa SA
Officers: Jeremy Peter Small, Secretary/Director; Amelie Marie Breitburd [1969] Director [French]; Jonathan Scott Wheway [1966] Director

Axa Insurance PLC
Incorporated: 15 May 1968
Net Worth: £2,037,629,056 *Total Assets:* £2,357,380,096
Registered Office: 5 Old Broad Street, London, EC2N 1AD
Activities: Activities of financial services holding companies
Parent: Guardian Royal Exchange Public Limited Company
Officers: Jeremy Peter Small, Secretary; Christopher Graham Bobby [1966] Director; Robin Dermer Pagden [1965] Director

Axa Insurance UK PLC
Incorporated: 27 October 1903
Net Worth: £3,086,000,128 *Total Assets:* £7,932,000,256
Registered Office: 5 Old Broad Street, London, EC2N 1AD
Activities: Non-life insurance
Parent: Axa Insurance PLC
Officers: Jeremy Peter Small, Secretary; Amelie Marie Breitburd [1969] Director [French]; Debra Jane Davies [1963] Director; Claudio Gienal [1974] Director [Swiss]; Peter Frank Hazell [1948] Director; Michael Richard Jackson [1962] Director; Mark Andrew Pain [1961] Director; Howard Michael Posner [1956] Director; Jonathan Paul Walker [1971] Director

Axa Investment Managers UK Limited
Incorporated: 19 June 1979
Net Worth: £89,089,512 *Total Assets:* £208,891,840
Registered Office: 7 Newgate Street, London, EC1A 7NX
Activities: Security and commodity contracts dealing activities
Parent: Axa Framlington Group Limited
Officers: Josephine Vanessa Tubbs, Secretary; Colin Martin Clark [1959] Director; Paul Dackombe [1962] Director; Hans-Christof Kutscher [1958] Director [German]; Philippe Pierre Paul Le Barrois D'Orgeval [1970] Director/Investment Manager [French]; Gilou Joseph Pinto [1969] Director [French]; Paolo Andrea Rossi [1966] Director [Italian]; John Stainsby [1961] Director

Axa Partners CLP UK Holdings Limited
Incorporated: 29 September 2003
Previous: Genworth Financial UK Holdings Limited
Net Worth: £397,551,008 *Total Assets:* £397,800,992
Registered Office: Building 6, Chiswick Park, 566 Chiswick High Road, London, W4 5HR
Activities: Activities of head offices
Parent: Axa Partners Holdings Limited
Officers: James Lawrence Rember, Secretary; Herve Ange Balzano [1968] Director [French]; Paul Charles Felix Caprez [1962] Director/Chief Risk Officer; Jeffrey Scott Whiteus [1957] Director [American]

Axa Partners Holdings Limited
Incorporated: 29 September 2003
Previous: Genworth Financial European Group Holdings Limited
Net Worth: £398,516,992 *Total Assets:* £398,516,992
Registered Office: Building 6, Chiswick Park, 566 Chiswick High Road, London, W4 5HR
Activities: Activities of head offices
Parent: Axa SA
Officers: James Lawrence Rember, Secretary; Paul Charles Felix Caprez [1962] Director/Chief Risk Officer; Jeffrey Scott Whiteus [1957] Director [American]

Axa PPP Healthcare Group Limited
Incorporated: 15 January 1996 *Employees:* 2,569
Previous: Axa PPP Healthcare Group PLC
Net Worth: £143,574,000 *Total Assets:* £209,379,008
Registered Office: 5 Old Broad Street, London, EC2N 1AD
Activities: Activities of financial services holding companies
Parent: Guardian Royal Exchange Public Limited Company
Officers: Jeremy Peter Small, Secretary; Fergus Alan Craig [1964] Director; Tracy Nicola Garrad [1970] Director; Mark Richardson Howes [1960] Director; Amber Wilkinson [1979] Director

Axa PPP Healthcare Limited
Incorporated: 15 January 1996
Net Worth: £377,400,000 *Total Assets:* £1,437,799,936
Registered Office: 5 Old Broad Street, London, EC2N 1AD
Activities: Non-life insurance
Parent: Axa Insurance UK PLC
Officers: Jeremy Peter Small, Secretary; Amelie Marie Breitburd [1969] Director [French]; Debra Jane Davies [1963] Director; Tracy Nicola Garrad [1970] Director; Claudio Gienal [1974] Director [Swiss]; Peter Frank Hazell [1948] Director; Michael Richard Jackson [1962] Director; Mark Andrew Pain [1961] Director; Howard Michael Posner [1956] Director; Amber Wilkinson [1979] Director

Axa Services Limited
Incorporated: 3 December 1947 *Employees:* 4,895
Net Worth: £3,532,000 *Total Assets:* £218,198,000
Registered Office: 5 Old Broad Street, London, EC2N 1AD
Activities: Other business support service activities n.e.c.
Parent: Guardian Royal Exchange Public Limited Company
Officers: Jeremy Peter Small, Secretary; Amelie Marie Breitburd [1969] Director [French]; Jonathan Paul Walker [1971] Director

Axa UK PLC
Incorporated: 10 June 1994
Net Worth: £3,903,000,064 *Total Assets:* £4,328,999,936
Registered Office: 5 Old Broad Street, London, EC2N 1AD
Activities: Activities of head offices
Shareholders: Axa SA; Axa Equity & Law Public Limited Company
Officers: Jeremy Peter Small, Secretary; Amelie Marie Breitburd [1969] Director [French]; Debra Jane Davies [1963] Director; Tracy Nicola Garrad [1970] Director; Claudio Gienal [1974] Director [Swiss]; Peter Frank Hazell [1948] Director; Michael Richard Jackson [1962] Director; Mark Andrew Pain [1961] Director; Antimo Perretta [1962] Director [Swiss]; Howard Michael Posner [1956] Director; Jonathan Scott Wheway [1966] Director

Axel Springer International Limited
Incorporated: 11 June 2014 *Employees:* 2
Net Worth: £253,034,368 *Total Assets:* £253,048,400
Registered Office: Blue Fin, 110 Southwark Street, London, SE1 0TA
Activities: Activities of other holding companies n.e.c.
Parent: Axel Springer SE
Officers: Patricia Meier Woster [1971] Director/General Manager [Swiss]; Heike Rust [1975] Director/Head of Finance [German]

Axelos Limited
Incorporated: 15 April 2013 *Employees:* 90
Net Worth: £99,732,528 *Total Assets:* £163,806,416
Registered Office: 30 Berners Street, London, W1T 3LR
Activities: Leasing of intellectual property and similar products, except copyright works
Shareholders: Capita Business Services Ltd; The Solicitor for The Affairs of Her Majesty's Treasury
Officers: Erika Bannerman [1971] Director; Mark Rutherford Basham [1966] Director; Richard Peter Gray [1975] Director/Chief Financial Officer; Matthew Richard Hunt [1983] Director; Richard John McCarthy [1958] Director; James Thomas Jordan Steel [1960] Director; Darren Christopher Tierney [1975] Director

Axia Finance PLC
Incorporated: 23 September 2008
Net Worth: £60,924 *Total Assets:* £223,002,048
Registered Office: Third Floor, 1 King's Arms Yard, London, EC2R 7AF
Activities: Other business support service activities n.e.c.
Parent: Wilmington Trust SP Services (London) Limited
Officers: Robert Sutton [1978] Director/Financial Services [American]; Daniel Jonathan Wynne [1970] Director

Axia III APC Limited
Incorporated: 29 July 2009
Net Worth: £52,523 *Total Assets:* £211,100,784
Registered Office: Third Floor, 1 King's Arms Yard, London, EC2R 7AF
Activities: Other business support service activities n.e.c.
Parent: Axia III Holdings Limited
Officers: Robert Sutton [1978] Director/Financial Services [American]; Daniel Jonathan Wynne [1970] Director

Axia III Finance PLC
Incorporated: 29 July 2009
Net Worth: £65,092 *Total Assets:* £209,728,976
Registered Office: Third Floor, 1 King's Arms Yard, London, EC2R 7AF
Activities: Other business support service activities n.e.c.
Parent: Axia III Holdings Limited
Officers: Robert Sutton [1978] Director/Financial Services [American]; Daniel Jonathan Wynne [1970] Director

Axiata Investments (UK) Limited
Incorporated: 14 December 2015
Net Worth Deficit: £43,457,112 *Total Assets:* £1,168,223,616
Registered Office: Suite 1, 3rd Floor, 11-12 St James's Square, London, SW1Y 4LB
Activities: Activities of open-ended investment companies
Officers: Annis Bin Sheikh Mohamed [1971] Director/Chief Corporate Development [Malaysian]; Vivek Sood [1964] Director/Group Chief Financial Officer [Indian]; Gim Boon Tan [1972] Director/General Counsel and Risk Officer [Malaysian]

Axis Bank UK Limited
Incorporated: 7 March 2011 *Employees:* 25
Net Worth: £60,782,432 *Total Assets:* £751,414,912
Registered Office: First Floor, 4 Chiswell Street, London, EC1Y 4UP
Activities: Banks
Parent: Axis Bank Limited
Officers: Kanchan Dasgupta, Secretary; Rajendra Dinkar Adsul [1959] Director/MD & CEO, Axis Bank UK Limited [Indian]; Kanchan Dasgupta [1962] Executive Director; Sanjeev Kumar Gupta [1961] Non-Executive Director - Axis Bank UK Ltd [Indian]; Cyril Anand Madireddi [1965] Director/CRO, Axis Bank Limited [Indian]; Diane Elizabeth Moore [1962] Director; Rajiv Anand Prattipati [1966] Executive Director, Axis Bank India [Indian]; Paul Kenneth Seward [1956] Director

Axis Corporate Capital UK Limited
Incorporated: 24 September 2013
Net Worth Deficit: £33,698,680 *Total Assets:* £631,026,752
Registered Office: Citypoint, 1 Ropemaker Street, London, EC2Y 9AW
Activities: Other activities auxiliary to insurance and pension funding
Parent: Axis Specialty UK Holdings Limited
Officers: Nicholas Bugler, Secretary; Tim Patrick Hennessy [1967] Director/Chief Executive Officer [Irish]; Sarah Jane Hills [1973] Director/VP Senior European Counsel

Axis Specialty Finance PLC
Incorporated: 3 January 2014
Net Worth: £312,618 *Total Assets:* £639,217,344
Registered Office: Citypoint, 1 Ropemaker Street, London, EC2Y 9AW
Activities: Other activities auxiliary to insurance and pension funding
Parent: Axis Capital Holdings Limited
Officers: Nicholas Bugler, Secretary; Tim Patrick Hennessy [1967] Director [Irish]; Sarah Jane Hills [1973] Director/VP Senior European Counsel

Aztech Advantage Ltd
Incorporated: 29 November 2016 *Employees:* 9
Net Worth Deficit: £1,379,394,944 *Total Assets:* £959,379,968
Registered Office: 7th Floor, 1 Minster Court, London, EC3R 7AA
Activities: Business and domestic software development
Parent: Azur Group Holdings Limited
Officers: Charles Jonathan Blackburn [1963] Director; Graham Andrew Elliott [1959] Director; Dan Peacock [1976] IT Director; Ian Pettifor [1960] Director/Accountant [Canadian]

Azzurri Group Limited
Incorporated: 3 July 2014 *Employees:* 6,466
Net Worth Deficit: £54,200,000 *Total Assets:* £361,200,000
Registered Office: 3rd Floor, Capital House, 25 Chapel Street, London, NW1 5DH
Activities: Non-trading company
Parent: BEV Nominees Limited
Officers: Lindsay Allan Dunsmuir, Secretary; Michael Norman Black [1968] Director; Lindsay Allan Dunsmuir [1967] Director; Stephen Holmes [1974] Director; Jason Scott McGibbon [1972] Director/Investment Professional; Kieran Pitcher [1970] Director; Harvey Smyth [1968] Director

Azzurri Midco 1 Limited
Incorporated: 3 July 2014
Net Worth: £26,330,000 *Total Assets:* £120,400,000
Registered Office: 3rd Floor, Capital House, 25 Chapel Street, London, NW1 5DH
Activities: Non-trading company
Parent: Azzurri Group Limited
Officers: Lindsay Allan Dunsmuir, Secretary; Lindsay Allan Dunsmuir [1967] Director; Stephen Holmes [1974] Director; Kieran Pitcher [1970] Director

Azzurri Restaurants Limited
Incorporated: 23 February 1993 *Employees:* 5,872
Previous: Gondola Restaurants Limited
Net Worth: £76,115,000 *Total Assets:* £196,214,000
Registered Office: 3rd Floor, Capital House, 25 Chapel Street, London, NW1 5DH
Activities: Licenced restaurants
Parent: Azzurri Central Limited
Officers: Lindsay Allan Dunsmuir, Secretary; Lindsay Allan Dunsmuir [1967] Director; Stephen Holmes [1974] Director

Azzurri Trading Limited
Incorporated: 19 November 2014 *Employees:* 14
Net Worth: £18,305,000 *Total Assets:* £279,788,000
Registered Office: 3rd Floor, Capital House, 25 Chapel Street, London, NW1 5DH
Activities: Activities of head offices
Parent: Azzurri Midco 2 Limited
Officers: Lindsay Allan Dunsmuir, Secretary; Lindsay Allan Dunsmuir [1967] Director; Stephen Holmes [1974] Director; Kieran Pitcher [1970] Director; Harvey Smyth [1968] Director

B.A.T (U.K. and Export) Limited
Incorporated: 24 May 1929 *Employees:* 36
Net Worth: £411,432,000 *Total Assets:* £527,912,992
Registered Office: Globe House, 1 Water Street, London, WC2R 3LA
Activities: Manufacture of tobacco products
Parent: British American Tobacco (Investments) Limited
Officers: Oliver James Martin, Secretary; Andrew James Barrett [1974] Director; David Patrick Ian Booth [1974] Director/Regional Finance Marketing Manager; Anthony Michael Hardy Cohn [1969] Director/Accountant; Mihovil James Dijanosic [1971] Director/General Management [Australian]; Andre Willem Joubert [1971] Director/Regional Head of Finance, EEMEA [South African]; Andres Santiago Lorenzo [1980] Director [Argentinian]; Stephan Matthiesen [1977] Director/Regional Head of Commercial Finance, ASPAC [German]; Markus Christian Rickheit [1968] Director [German]; Adin Trbonja [1969] Director/Assistant General Counsel, Commercial [American]

B.A.T Industries P.L.C.
Incorporated: 3 September 1928
Net Worth: £27,536,654,336 *Total Assets:* £32,012,267,520
Registered Office: Globe House, 4 Temple Place, London, WC2R 2PG
Activities: Activities of head offices
Parent: Weston (2009) Limited
Officers: Paul McCrory, Secretary; Andrew James Barrett [1974] Director/Group Financial Controller; Robert James Casey [1948] Director/Attorney [American]; Steven Glyn Dale [1967] Director/Tax Adviser; John Benedict Stevens [1959] Director/Tobacco Manufacturer

B.A.T Uzbekistan (Investments) Limited
Incorporated: 9 March 1994
Net Worth: £246,196,992 *Total Assets:* £246,196,992
Registered Office: Globe House, 1 Water Street, London, WC2R 3LA
Activities: Activities of head offices
Parent: British American Tobacco (Investments) Limited
Officers: Jonathan Michael Guttridge, Secretary; David Patrick Ian Booth [1974] Director/Group Chief Accountant; Robert James Casey [1948] Director/Attorney [American]; Anthony Michael Hardy Cohn [1969] Director/Accountant

B.A.T. China Limited
Incorporated: 6 March 1914 *Employees:* 29
Net Worth: £83,574,000 *Total Assets:* £143,436,992
Registered Office: Globe House, 1 Water Street, London, WC2R 3LA
Activities: Manufacture of tobacco products
Parent: British American Tobacco China Holdings Limited
Officers: Jessica Munday, Secretary; David Patrick Ian Booth [1974] Director/Group Chief Accountant; Robert James Casey [1948] Director/Attorney [American]; Noelle Colfer [1968] Director; Peter Garneau Henriques [1957] Director/Business Executive [Australian]; Hardeep Khangura [1972] Finance Director; Belinda Joy Ross [1966] Director/Regional General Counsel [New Zealander]

B.A.T. International Finance P.L.C.
Incorporated: 10 July 1972
Net Worth: £2,148,999,936 *Total Assets:* £46,015,000,576
Registered Office: Globe House, 4 Temple Place, London, WC2R 2PG
Activities: Financial intermediation not elsewhere classified
Parent: British American Tobacco P.L.C
Officers: Paul McCrory, Secretary; Andrew James Barrett [1974] Director/Group Finance Controller; Robert James Casey [1948] Director/Attorney [American]; Steven Glyn Dale [1967] Director/Tax Adviser; John Benedict Stevens [1959] Director/Tobacco Manufacturer; Neil Arthur Wadey [1964] Director/Treasurer

B.L.Holdings Limited
Incorporated: 4 November 1856
Net Worth: £1,192,749,824 *Total Assets:* £1,192,749,824
Registered Office: York House, 45 Seymour Street, London, W1H 7LX
Activities: Development of building projects
Parent: BL Residual Holding Company Limited
Officers: Sarah Morrell Barzycki [1958] Director/Head of Finance; Paul Stuart Macey [1978] Director/Accountant; Jonathan Charles McNuff [1986] Director/Chartered Accountant; Charles John Middleton [1966] Director/Corporate Tax Executive; Timothy Andrew Roberts [1964] Director/Chartered Surveyor; Nigel Mark Webb [1963] Director/Chartered Surveyor

Babcock (UK) Holdings Limited
Incorporated: 5 February 2007
Net Worth: £2,438,149,120 *Total Assets:* £4,726,946,816
Registered Office: 33 Wigmore Street, London, W1U 1QX
Activities: Activities of other holding companies n.e.c.
Parent: Babcock International Group PLC
Officers: Nicholas James William Borrett [1967] Director/Group Company Secretary and General Counsel; Franco Martinelli [1960] Director/Chartered Accountant; Iain Stuart Urquhart [1965] Director

Babcock Aviation Services (Holdings) Limited
Incorporated: 11 April 2014
Net Worth: £784,356,992 *Total Assets:* £1,442,179,968
Registered Office: 33 Wigmore Street, London, W1U 1QX
Activities: Activities of other holding companies n.e.c.
Shareholders: Babcock Holdings Limited; Babcock International Group PLC
Officers: Nicholas James William Borrett [1967] Director/Group Company Secretary and General Counsel; Ben Davey [1965] Director/Accountant; Franco Martinelli [1960] Director/Chartered Accountant; Iain Stuart Urquhart [1965] Director

Babcock Brazil Investments Limited
Incorporated: 19 September 2002
Net Worth: £72,716,000 *Total Assets:* £130,061,000
Registered Office: 33 Wigmore Street, London, W1U 1QX
Activities: Activities of other holding companies n.e.c.
Parent: Babcock Investments Limited
Officers: Nicholas James William Borrett [1967] Director/Group Company Secretary and General Counsel; Iain Stuart Urquhart [1965] Director

Babcock Communications Limited
Incorporated: 9 May 1996 *Employees:* 352
Net Worth: £65,404,000 *Total Assets:* £114,298,000
Registered Office: 33 Wigmore Street, London, W1U 1QX
Activities: Other telecommunications activities
Parent: Merlin Communications Group Limited
Officers: Dr Richard Daniel Drake [1973] Director/Engineer; Jonathan Hall [1962] Director; Matthew Jones [1983] Director/Accountant; Iain Stuart Urquhart [1965] Director; Samuel Michael White [1976] Director

Babcock Corporate Services Limited
Incorporated: 12 April 2002 *Employees:* 278
Net Worth: £212,791,008 *Total Assets:* £349,182,016
Registered Office: 33 Wigmore Street, London, W1U 1QX
Activities: Non-trading company
Parent: Vosper Thornycroft (UK) Limited
Officers: Ian Connell [1968] Director; Kevin William Goodman [1951] Director; Franco Martinelli [1960] Director/Chartered Accountant; William James Mason [1962] Managing Director; Simon William Parker [1962] Director/Group Chief Information Officer; Iain Stuart Urquhart [1965] Director

Babcock Critical Assets Holdings LLP
Incorporated: 5 July 2012
Net Worth: £243,492,000 *Total Assets:* £243,492,000
Registered Office: 33 Wigmore Street, London, W1U 1QX

Babcock Defence & Security Holdings LLP
Incorporated: 5 July 2012 *Employees:* 132
Net Worth: £997,302,016 *Total Assets:* £1,036,844,992
Registered Office: 33 Wigmore Street, London, W1U 1QX

Babcock DSG Ltd
Incorporated: 26 November 2014
Net Worth: £145,600,992 *Total Assets:* £239,002,000
Registered Office: 33 Wigmore Street, London, W1U 1QX
Activities: Defence activities
Officers: Nicholas James William Borrett [1967] Director/Group Company Secretary and General Counsel; Jonathan David Cohen [1974] Commercial Director; John Richard Davies [1963] Managing Director; James Mark Dixon [1962] Director; Mark David Lawton [1972] Finance Director; Robert Hartley Pemberton [1967] Director; Richard Hewitt Taylor [1961] Director/Accountant; Iain Stuart Urquhart [1965] Director

Babcock Education & Training Holdings LLP
Incorporated: 5 July 2012
Net Worth: £210,100,000 *Total Assets:* £217,600,992
Registered Office: 33 Wigmore Street, London, W1U 1QX

Babcock Group International Limited
Incorporated: 1 November 1990
Net Worth: £109,944,000 *Total Assets:* £142,884,992
Registered Office: 33 Wigmore Street, London, W1U 1QX
Activities: Other business support service activities n.e.c.
Parent: Babcock Southern Holdings Limited
Officers: Nicholas James William Borrett [1967] Director/Group Company Secretary and General Counsel; Franco Martinelli [1960] Director/Chartered Accountant; Iain Stuart Urquhart [1965] Director

Babcock Holdings Limited
Incorporated: 4 August 1994 *Employees:* 100
Net Worth: £4,357,054,976 *Total Assets:* £8,015,947,776
Registered Office: 33 Wigmore Street, London, W1U 1QX
Activities: Activities of other holding companies n.e.c.
Parent: Babcock (UK) Holdings Limited
Officers: Nicholas James William Borrett [1967] Director/Group Company Secretary and General Counsel; Franco Martinelli [1960] Director/Chartered Accountant; Iain Stuart Urquhart [1965] Director

Babcock Integrated Technology Limited
Incorporated: 7 October 2008 *Employees:* 767
Net Worth: £264,994,000 *Total Assets:* £471,657,984
Registered Office: 33 Wigmore Street, London, W1U 1QX
Activities: Other service activities n.e.c.
Parent: Babcock Marine Holdings (UK) Limited
Officers: Jonathan Hall [1962] Director; Derek Malcolm Jones [1971] Director; Matthew Jones [1983] Director/Accountant; Iain Stuart Urquhart [1965] Director

Babcock Integration LLP
Incorporated: 15 July 2010
Net Worth: £350,579,008 *Total Assets:* £352,720,000
Registered Office: 33 Wigmore Street, London, W1U 1QX

Babcock International Group PLC
Incorporated: 1 February 1989 *Employees:* 35,427
Net Worth: £2,892,900,096 *Total Assets:* £6,320,999,936
Registered Office: 33 Wigmore Street, London, W1U 1QX
Activities: Other engineering activities
Officers: Nicholas James William Borrett, Secretary; Archibald Anderson Bethel [1953] Director; John Richard Davies [1963] Managing Director; Lucy Rebecca Dimes [1966] Director/Company Executive; Ian Barnet Duncan [1961] Director/Accountant; Myles Peter Lee [1953] Director [Irish]; Professor Victoire Anne Marie de Margerie [1963] Director [French]; Franco Martinelli [1960] Director/Chartered Accountant; Sir David Bruce Omand [1947] Director/Self Employed; Jeff William Randall [1954] Director/Journalist; Michael John Turner [1948] Director; Kjersti Wiklund [1962] Director [Norwegian]

Babcock International Limited
Incorporated: 30 April 1900
Net Worth: £11,253,000 *Total Assets:* £470,164,000
Registered Office: 33 Wigmore Street, London, W1U 1QX
Activities: Activities of head offices
Parent: Babcock Holdings Limited
Officers: Nicholas James William Borrett [1967] Director/Group Company Secretary and General Counsel; Franco Martinelli [1960] Director/Chartered Accountant; Iain Stuart Urquhart [1965] Director

Babcock International Support Services Limited
Incorporated: 19 March 1997
Net Worth: £323,803,008 *Total Assets:* £369,835,008
Registered Office: 33 Wigmore Street, London, W1U 1QX
Activities: Activities of other holding companies n.e.c.
Parent: Vosper Thornycroft (UK) Limited
Officers: Roger Andrew Hardy [1966] Managing Director; Iain Stuart Urquhart [1965] Director

Babcock Investments (Number Eight) Limited
Incorporated: 18 June 1987
Net Worth: £802,147,968 *Total Assets:* £831,596,032
Registered Office: 33 Wigmore Street, London, W1U 1QX
Activities: Non-trading company
Parent: Babcock Management Limited
Officers: Nicholas James William Borrett [1967] Director/Group Company Secretary and General Counsel; Franco Martinelli [1960] Director/Chartered Accountant; Iain Stuart Urquhart [1965] Director

Babcock Investments (Number Four) Limited
Incorporated: 25 October 2004
Net Worth: £609,308,992 *Total Assets:* £620,320,000
Registered Office: 33 Wigmore Street, London, W1U 1QX
Activities: Activities of head offices
Parent: Babcock Holdings Limited
Officers: Nicholas James William Borrett [1967] Director/Group Company Secretary and General Counsel; Franco Martinelli [1960] Director/Chartered Accountant; Iain Stuart Urquhart [1965] Director

Babcock Investments (Number Three) Limited
Incorporated: 20 October 2004
Net Worth: £193,260,000 *Total Assets:* £204,003,008
Registered Office: 33 Wigmore Street, London, W1U 1QX
Activities: Activities of head offices
Parent: Babcock (UK) Holdings Limited
Officers: Nicholas James William Borrett [1967] Director/Group Company Secretary and General Counsel; Iain Stuart Urquhart [1965] Director

Babcock Investments Limited
Incorporated: 10 March 1920
Net Worth: £2,404,030,976 *Total Assets:* £2,647,686,912
Registered Office: 33 Wigmore Street, London, W1U 1QX
Activities: Non-trading company
Parent: Babcock Holdings Limited
Officers: Nicholas James William Borrett [1967] Director/Group Company Secretary and General Counsel; Franco Martinelli [1960] Director/Chartered Accountant; Iain Stuart Urquhart [1965] Director

Babcock IP Management (Number Two) Limited
Incorporated: 11 June 2015
Net Worth: £117,989,000 *Total Assets:* £173,144,000
Registered Office: 33 Wigmore Street, London, W1U 1QX
Activities: Other business support service activities n.e.c.
Parent: Babcock Integration LLP
Officers: Nicholas James William Borrett [1967] Director/Group Company Secretary and General Counsel; Jonathan Hall [1962] Director; Ian Jewell [1967] Director; Franco Martinelli [1960] Director; Iain Stuart Urquhart [1965] Director

Babcock Land Limited
Incorporated: 15 January 1998 *Employees:* 1,390
Net Worth: £86,542,000 *Total Assets:* £360,987,008
Registered Office: 33 Wigmore Street, London, W1U 1QX
Activities: Defence activities
Parent: Babcock Defence & Security Holdings LLP
Officers: Nicholas James William Borrett [1967] Director/Group Company Secretary and General Counsel; John Richard Davies [1963] Managing Director; James Mark Dixon [1962] Director; Jonathan Hall [1962] Director; Mark David Lawton [1972] Director/Accountant; Richard Hewitt Taylor [1961] Director/Accountant; Iain Stuart Urquhart [1965] Director

Babcock Management Limited
Incorporated: 9 February 1910
Net Worth: £1,679,224,960 *Total Assets:* £1,926,109,952
Registered Office: 33 Wigmore Street, London, W1U 1QX
Activities: Activities of other holding companies n.e.c.
Parent: Babcock Investments Limited
Officers: Nicholas James William Borrett [1967] Director/Group Company Secretary and General Counsel; Franco Martinelli [1960] Director/Chartered Accountant; Iain Stuart Urquhart [1965] Director

Babcock Marine & Technology Holdings Limited
Incorporated: 19 September 2002
Net Worth: £598,499,008 *Total Assets:* £598,502,016
Registered Office: 33 Wigmore Street, London, W1U 1QX
Activities: Activities of other holding companies n.e.c.
Parent: Babcock Investments (Number Four) Limited
Officers: Nicholas James William Borrett [1967] Director/Group Company Secretary and General Counsel; Franco Martinelli [1960] Director/Chartered Accountant; Iain Stuart Urquhart [1965] Director

Babcock Marine Holdings (UK) Limited
Incorporated: 20 October 2004
Net Worth: £122,912,000 *Total Assets:* £782,388,992
Registered Office: 33 Wigmore Street, London, W1U 1QX
Activities: Activities of head offices
Parent: Babcock Holdings Limited
Officers: Nicholas James William Borrett [1967] Director/Group Company Secretary and General Counsel; Franco Martinelli [1960] Director/Chartered Accountant; Iain Stuart Urquhart [1965] Director

Babcock Mission Critical Services Design and Completions Limited
Incorporated: 5 February 2004 *Employees:* 19
Previous: Bond Helicopters Europe Limited
Net Worth: £180,934,000 *Total Assets:* £207,899,008
Registered Office: 33 Wigmore Street, London, W1U 1QX
Activities: Activities of head offices
Parent: Bond Mission Critical Services PLC
Officers: Karen Veronica Hayzen-Smith [1970] Director; Luis Inigo Moreno Ventas [1976] Director/General Counsel [Spanish]; Alexandra Helen Pentecost [1957] Director; David Frank Plester [1964] Managing Director

Babcock Mission Critical Services Leasing Limited
Incorporated: 13 January 2003
Previous: International Aviation Leasing Limited
Net Worth: £156,907,008 *Total Assets:* £227,423,008
Registered Office: 33 Wigmore Street, London, W1U 1QX
Activities: Renting and leasing of other machinery, equipment and tangible goods n.e.c.
Parent: Babcock Mission Critical Services Design and Completions Limited
Officers: Alexandra Helen Pentecost [1957] Director; David Frank Plester [1964] Managing Director; Emilio Sanchez Vicente [1973] Director [Spanish]

Babcock Mission Critical Services Ltd
Incorporated: 28 March 2012 *Employees:* 34
Previous: Avincis Mission Critical Services Ltd
Net Worth: £310,833,984 *Total Assets:* £435,751,008
Registered Office: 33 Wigmore Street, London, W1U 1QX
Activities: Non-scheduled passenger air transport
Parent: Babcock Mission Critical Services Topco Ltd
Officers: Karen Veronica Hayzen-Smith [1970] Director; Steven Landrey [1969] Finance Director; Luis Inigo Moreno-Ventas [1976] Director/Company Secretary [Spanish]; Iain Stuart Urquhart [1965] Director

Babcock Mission Critical Services Topco Ltd
Incorporated: 20 December 2012
Previous: Avincis Mission Critical Services Topco Ltd
Net Worth: £186,928,992 *Total Assets:* £305,343,008
Registered Office: 33 Wigmore Street, London, W1U 1QX
Activities: Activities of other holding companies n.e.c.
Parent: Babcock Aviation Services (Holdings) Limited
Officers: Nicholas James William Borrett [1967] Director/Group Company Secretary and General Counsel; Karen Veronica Hayzen-Smith [1970] Director; Franco Martinelli [1960] Director/Chartered Accountant; Leonardo Tricarico [1942] Director/Board Member [Italian]; Iain Stuart Urquhart [1965] Director

Babcock Mission Critical Services UK Limited
Incorporated: 11 February 2011 *Employees:* 40
Previous: Bond Aviation Group Limited
Net Worth: £140,279,008 *Total Assets:* £546,681,984
Registered Office: 33 Wigmore Street, London, W1U 1QX
Activities: Activities of other holding companies n.e.c.
Parent: Bond Aviation Topco Limited
Officers: Karen Veronica Hayzen-Smith [1970] Director; Luis Inigo Moreno Ventas [1976] Director/General Counsel [Spanish]; David Frank Plester [1964] Managing Director

Babcock Overseas Investments Limited
Incorporated: 9 December 1991
Net Worth: £1,637,913,984 *Total Assets:* £2,537,028,096
Registered Office: 33 Wigmore Street, London, W1U 1QX
Activities: Other business support service activities n.e.c.
Parent: Babcock Holdings Limited
Officers: Nicholas James William Borrett [1967] Director/Group Company Secretary and General Counsel; Franco Martinelli [1960] Director/Chartered Accountant; Iain Stuart Urquhart [1965] Director

Babcock Rail Limited
Incorporated: 5 December 1994 *Employees:* 1,052
Net Worth: £84,643,000 *Total Assets:* £227,783,008
Registered Office: 33 Wigmore Street, London, W1U 1QX
Activities: Other service activities n.e.c.
Parent: Scimco Limited
Officers: Sally Fiona Brooks [1966] Finance Director; Pieter Esbach [1962] Director; Robert Forbes [1965] Commercial Director; Gerard Moy [1958] Director; Iain Stuart Urquhart [1965] Director

Babcock Services Group Limited
Incorporated: 6 March 2000
Net Worth: £137,959,008 *Total Assets:* £190,847,008
Registered Office: 33 Wigmore Street, London, W1U 1QX
Activities: Other business support service activities n.e.c.
Parent: Babcock Support Services (Investments) Limited
Officers: Simon Christopher Bowen [1960] Director; Kevin John Garvey [1967] Finance Director

Babcock Southern Holdings Limited
Incorporated: 22 May 1985
Net Worth: £680,326,976 *Total Assets:* £826,769,984
Registered Office: 33 Wigmore Street, London, W1U 1QX
Activities: Activities of other holding companies n.e.c.
Parent: Babcock Overseas Investments Limited
Officers: Nicholas James William Borrett [1967] Director/Group Company Secretary and General Counsel; Franco Martinelli [1960] Director/Chartered Accountant; Iain Stuart Urquhart [1965] Director

Babcock Support Services (Investments) Limited
Incorporated: 12 March 2002 *Employees:* 142
Net Worth: £541,734,976 *Total Assets:* £1,983,122,944
Registered Office: 33 Wigmore Street, London, W1U 1QX
Activities: Activities of head offices
Parent: Babcock Management Limited
Officers: Nicholas James William Borrett [1967] Director/Group Company Secretary and General Counsel; Franco Martinelli [1960] Director/Chartered Accountant; Iain Stuart Urquhart [1965] Director

Babcock Training Limited
Incorporated: 14 May 1993 *Employees:* 1,746
Net Worth: £95,674,000 *Total Assets:* £156,920,000
Registered Office: 33 Wigmore Street, London, W1U 1QX
Activities: Other business support service activities n.e.c.
Parent: Babcock Education & Training Holdings LLP
Officers: John Richard Davies [1963] Managing Director; Matthew Hayward [1966] Director; Richard Hewitt Taylor [1961] Director/Accountant; Iain Stuart Urquhart [1965] Director

Babcock UK Finance
Incorporated: 6 February 1908
Net Worth: £164,188,992 *Total Assets:* £166,624,000
Registered Office: 33 Wigmore Street, London, W1U 1QX
Activities: Non-trading company
Parent: Babcock Holdings Limited
Officers: Nicholas James William Borrett [1967] Director/Group Company Secretary and General Counsel; Iain Stuart Urquhart [1965] Director

Babcock US Investments Limited
Incorporated: 28 October 2010
Net Worth: £190,653,472 *Total Assets:* £217,003,424
Registered Office: 33 Wigmore Street, London, W1U 1QX
Activities: Activities of other holding companies n.e.c.
Parent: Babcock Overseas Investments Limited
Officers: Nicholas James William Borrett [1967] Director/Group Company Secretary and General Counsel; Iain Stuart Urquhart [1965] Director

Babcock2 Limited
Incorporated: 7 December 1994
Net Worth: £627,097,024 *Total Assets:* £627,622,016
Registered Office: 33 Wigmore Street, London, W1U 1QX
Activities: Non-trading company
Parent: Babcock Southern Holdings Limited
Officers: Nicholas James William Borrett [1967] Director/Group Company Secretary and General Counsel; Franco Martinelli [1960] Director/Chartered Accountant; Iain Stuart Urquhart [1965] Director

Badger Property Partners LLP
Incorporated: 21 May 2005
Net Worth: £42,759,092 *Total Assets:* £153,142,800
Registered Office: The Northern and Shell Building, 10 Lower Thames Street, London, EC3R 6EN
Officers: Richard Clive Desmond [1951] Member

BAE Systems PLC
Incorporated: 31 December 1979 *Employees:* 76
Net Worth: £4,741,000,192 *Total Assets:* £22,453,000,192
Registered Office: 6 Carlton Gardens, London, SW1Y 5AD
Activities: Manufacture of weapons and ammunition
Officers: David Stanley Parkes, Secretary; Revathi Advaithi [1967] Director [American]; Sir Roger Martyn Carr [1946] Director; Elizabeth Pauline Lucy Corley [1956] Director; Gerard Joseph Demuro [1955] Director [American]; Harriet Green [1961] Director/Chief Executive Officer; Christopher Montague Grigg [1959] Director; Peter John Lynas [1958] Financial Director; Paula Rosput Reynolds [1956] Director/Independent Business Advisor [American]; Nicholas Charles Rose [1957] Finance Director; Ian Paul Tyler [1960] Director; Charles Nicholas Woodburn [1971] Director

Baillie Gifford UK Growth Fund PLC
Incorporated: 28 January 1994
Previous: Schroder UK Growth Fund PLC
Net Worth: £312,252,000 *Total Assets:* £324,745,984
Registered Office: Grimaldi House, 28 St James's Square, London, SW1Y 4JH
Activities: Activities of investment trusts
Officers: Scott Cochrane [1971] Director/Solicitor; Carolan Dobson [1954] Director; Andrew James Hutton [1958] Director; James Ruary Drummond Neill [1959] Director; Ruary Neill [1959] Director; Andrew Thomas Karl Westenberger [1966] Finance Director

Baker & McKenzie LLP
Incorporated: 1 February 2005 *Employees:* 680
Net Worth: £186,843,008 *Total Assets:* £216,012,000
Registered Office: 100 New Bridge Street, London, EC4V 6JA
Officers: Alex Frederick Chadwick [1966] Member; Karen Guch [1972] Member; Samantha Jane Mobley [1967] Member; Edward Elcoat Poulton [1976] Member; Stephen Ashley Abraham [1973] LLP Member; Robert Elliot Adam [1974] LLP Member; David Allen [1978] LLP Member; Benjamin David Allgrove [1977] LLP Member; Philip Annett [1976] LLP Member; David Becker [1971] LLP Member; George Richard Gentry Blunt [1969] LLP Member; Michelle Louise Blunt [1974] LLP Member; Helen Bradley [1969] LLP Member; James Thomas Burdett [1967] LLP Member; Emily Radmila Carlisle [1976] LLP Member; Alison Kate Corby [1978] LLP Member; Matthew Logan Cox [1972] LLP Member; Ashley Roger Crossley [1971] LLP Member; Jannan Crozier [1980] LLP Member; Susannah Elaine Davies [1979] LLP Member; Matthew Paul Dening [1969] LLP Member; Ross Lindsay Denton [1961] LLP Member; Neil Martin Donoghue [1960] LLP Member; Michael Paul Doran [1963] LLP Member; David Walter Duncan [1979] LLP Member; Jessica Susannah Eden [1983] LLP Member; Jeremy Richard Edwards [1967] LLP Member; John Martin Evason [1968] LLP Member; Adam Benjamin Farlow [1972] LLP Member; Benjamin Oliver Farnell [1976] LLP Member; Marc Francis Fevre [1973] LLP Member; Timothy Edward Daniel Gee [1962] LLP Member; Luis Alfonso Gomez [1970] LLP Member; Sarah Christine Gregory [1966] LLP Member; Tristan James Grimmer [1980] LLP Member; David Ernest Hugh Halliday [1974] LLP Member; Michael Lawrence Hart [1959] LLP Member; Haden Leonard Henderson [1982] LLP Member; Michael John Edward Herington [1957] LLP Member; Joanna Teresa Hewitt [1976] LLP Member; Jane Elisabeth Hobson [1968] LLP Member; Gerard William Holder [1971] LLP Member; Jeanette Elizabeth Holland [1967] LLP Member; Stephen William Peter Holmes [1972] LLP Member; Kathleen Tracee Honeywood [1964] LLP Member; Melanie Jo Howard [1978] LLP Member; Ian William Jack [1964] LLP Member; David James Jamieson [1979] LLP Member; Keith Robert Jones [1970] LLP Member; Jukka Einar Karjalainen [1971] LLP Member; Monica Ruth Kurnatowska [1963] LLP Member; Jessica Leigh Le Gros [1975] LLP Member; John Christopher Leadley [1961] LLP Member; Jeremy Samuel Levy [1982] LLP Member; Michael Alexander Hulton Lewis [1977] LLP Member; Gordon Andrew Lochhead Low [1967] LLP Member; Ziaofei Lu [1978] LLP Member; Joanna Ludlam [1971] LLP Member; Hugh Jonathan Lyons [1971] LLP Member; Sunwinder Singh Mann [1975] LLP Member; Sebastien Emmanuel Hugh Marcelin-Rice [1975] LLP Member; Robert Stanley Mathews [1959] LLP Member; Susan Maureen McLean [1975] LLP Member; Bevis Mason Metcalfe [1980] LLP Member; Andrew Gist Moody [1975] LLP Member; Richard Paul Needham [1983] LLP Member; Nicola Jane Northway [1965] LLP Member; Geoffery James O'Dea [1974] LLP Member; Nicholas John Renny O'Donnell [1975] LLP Member; Patrick John O'Gara [1981] LLP Member; Nicholas George Carew O'Grady [1980] LLP Member; Jonathan Peter Peddie [1968] LLP Member; Beatriz Helen Pessoa de Araujo [1961] LLP Member; Simon Nicholas Porter [1967] LLP Member; Anthony Richard Poulton [1969] LLP Member; Stephen Christopher Martin Ratcliffe [1979] LLP Member; Paul Rawlinson [1962] LLP Member; Duncan Robert Reid-Thomas [1968] LLP Member; Jennifer Francoise Revis [1978] LLP Member; Carl Eliot Richards [1975] LLP Member; Francesca Anne Richmond [1981] LLP Member; Lynn Marie Rosell Rowley [1971] LLP Member; Justin John Salkeld [1964] LLP Member; Kim Louise Sartin [1979] LLP Member; Megan Schellinger [1978] LLP Member; David Stewart Scott [1979] LLP Member; Jonathan Michael Sharp [1979] LLP Member; Hiroshi John Sheraton [1973] LLP Member; Mark Andrew Simpson [1982] LLP Member; Arron Leigh Slocombe [1977] LLP Member; Harry Small [1957] LLP Member; James Hugh Wilkinson Smith [1975] LLP Member; Matthew Paul Smith [1983] LLP Member; Graham John Stuart [1965] LLP Member; Chantal Diana Curtois Thompson [1963] LLP Member; James Robert Thompson [1980] LLP Member; Charles McKenzie Thomson [1980] LLP Member; Nicholas Dudley Tostivin [1973] LLP Member; Stephen Michael Turner [1957] LLP Member

Baker Hughes Limited
Incorporated: 13 September 1978 *Employees:* 1,502
Net Worth Deficit: £270,556,000 *Total Assets:* £1,281,250,944
Registered Office: The Ark, 201 Talgarth Road, Hammersmith, London, W6 8BJ
Activities: Support activities for petroleum and natural gas mining
Officers: Lorraine Amanda Dunlop, Secretary; Paul Harding [1962] Manufacturing Director; Christopher Wyn Jones [1966] Director; Blair Alexander McLeish [1971] Director/Finance Manager; Oluwole Onabolu [1975] Director/Lawyer [Nigerian]

Ted Baker PLC
Incorporated: 23 June 1997 *Employees:* 3,462
Net Worth: £224,050,000 *Total Assets:* £449,164,000
Registered Office: The Ugly Brown Building, 6a St Pancras Way, London, NW1 0TB
Activities: Wholesale of clothing and footwear
Officers: Charles Francis Anderson, Secretary; Sharon Baylay [1968] Director; David Alan Bernstein [1943] Director; Andrew Richard Jennings [1948] Director; Raymond Stuart Kelvin [1955] Director; Lindsay Dennis Page [1958] Director; Jennifer Ellen Roebuck [1973] Director [British/American]; Ron Stewart [1947] Director

Bakethin Finance PLC
Incorporated: 16 March 2004
Net Worth: £2,211,000 *Total Assets:* £275,513,984
Registered Office: Third Floor, 1 King's Arms Yard, London, EC2R 7AF
Activities: Other business support service activities n.e.c.
Parent: Bakethin Holdings Limited
Officers: Christopher Ian Johns [1970] Director/Accountant; Robert Sutton [1978] Director/Financial Services [American]; Daniel Jonathan Wynne [1970] Director

Bakkavor (London) Limited
Incorporated: 20 July 2001
Net Worth: £1,051,043,968 *Total Assets:* £1,191,655,040
Registered Office: 5th Floor, Fitzroy Place, 8 Mortimer Street, London, W1T 3JJ
Activities: Activities of head offices
Parent: Bakkavor Finance (3) Limited
Officers: Simon Witham, Secretary; Agust Gudmundsson [1964] Director [Icelander]

Bakkavor Finance (1) Limited
Incorporated: 21 January 2011
Net Worth: £315,254,016 *Total Assets:* £315,254,016
Registered Office: 5th Floor, Fitzroy Place, 8 Mortimer Street, London, W1T 3JJ
Activities: Combined office administrative service activities
Parent: Bakkavor Holdings Limited
Officers: Simon Witham, Secretary; Edwin Peter Gates [1956] Director/Chief Financial Officer; Agust Gudmundsson [1964] Director [Icelander]

Bakkavor Finance (2) Limited
Incorporated: 21 January 2011 *Employees:* 19,593
Previous: Bakkavor Finance (2) PLC
Net Worth: £428,200,000 *Total Assets:* £1,233,699,968
Registered Office: 5th Floor, Fitzroy Place, 8 Mortimer Street, London, W1T 3JJ
Activities: Combined office administrative service activities
Parent: Bakkavor Finance (1) Limited
Officers: Simon Witham, Secretary; Edwin Peter Gates [1956] Director/Chief Financial Officer; Agust Gudmundsson [1964] Director [Icelander]

Bakkavor Finance (3) Limited
Incorporated: 21 January 2011
Net Worth: £458,068,000 *Total Assets:* £1,157,843,968
Registered Office: 5th Floor, Fitzroy Place, 8 Mortimer Street, London, W1T 3JJ
Activities: Combined office administrative service activities
Parent: Bakkavor Finance (2) PLC
Officers: Simon Witham, Secretary; Edwin Peter Gates [1956] Director/Chief Financial Officer; Agust Gudmundsson [1964] Director [Icelander]

Bakkavor Foods Limited
Incorporated: 7 July 1972 *Employees:* 16,445
Net Worth: £641,470,016 *Total Assets:* £1,055,966,016
Registered Office: 5th Floor, Fitzroy Place, 8 Mortimer Street, London, W1T 3JJ
Activities: Manufacture of prepared meals and dishes
Parent: Bakkavor Limited
Officers: Simon Witham, Secretary; Agust Gudmundsson [1964] Director [Icelander]

Bakkavor Group PLC
Incorporated: 28 September 2017 *Employees:* 19,593
Net Worth: £510,100,000 *Total Assets:* £1,233,100,032
Registered Office: 5th Floor, Fitzroy Place, 8 Mortimer Street, London, W1T 3JJ
Activities: Activities of head offices
Officers: Simon Witham, Secretary; Simon Paul Burke [1958] Director/Chartered Accountant [Irish]; Susan Michelle Clark [1964] Director; Patrick Cook [1985] Director [American]; Edwin Peter Gates [1956] Director/Chief Financial Officer; Agust Gudmundsson [1964] Director [Icelander]; Lydur Gudmundsson [1967] Director [Icelander]; Denis Michel Daniel Hennequin [1958] Director [French]; Todd Krasnow [1957] Director/Consultant [American]; Jane Ann Lodge [1955] Director

Bakkavor Holdings Limited
Incorporated: 17 April 2007
Previous: Bakkavor Group Limited
Net Worth: £309,620,992 *Total Assets:* £316,670,016
Registered Office: 5th Floor, Fitzroy Place, 8 Mortimer Street, London, W1T 3JJ
Activities: Activities of head offices
Shareholders: Agust Gudmundsson; Lydur Gudmundsson; Seth Andrew Klarman
Officers: Simon Witham, Secretary; Simon Paul Burke [1958] Director/Chartered Accountant [Irish]; Agust Gudmundsson [1964] Director [Icelander]; Lydur Gudmundsson [1967] Director [Icelander]; Denis Michel Daniel Hennequin [1958] Director [French]; Todd Krasnow [1957] Director/Consultant [American]

Bakkavor Invest Limited
Incorporated: 11 February 2004
Net Worth: £1,207,214,976 *Total Assets:* £1,212,955,008
Registered Office: 5th Floor, Fitzroy Place, 8 Mortimer Street, London, W1T 3JJ
Activities: Combined office administrative service activities
Shareholders: Bakkavor (London) Limited; Bakkavor Finance Limited
Officers: Simon Witham, Secretary; Agust Gudmundsson [1964] Director [Icelander]

Bakkavor Limited
Incorporated: 8 May 1986
Net Worth: £302,118,016 *Total Assets:* £313,177,984
Registered Office: 5th Floor, Fitzroy Place, 8 Mortimer Street, London, W1T 3JJ
Activities: Other business support service activities n.e.c.
Parent: Bakkavor Invest Limited
Officers: Simon Witham, Secretary; Agust Gudmundsson [1964] Director [Icelander]

Bal Global Finance (UK) Limited
Incorporated: 2 April 1990 *Employees:* 29
Net Worth: £100,180,000 *Total Assets:* £663,104,000
Registered Office: 2 King Edward Street, London, EC1A 1HQ
Activities: Financial leasing
Parent: Bank of America Corporation
Officers: Katherine Conklin Ashdown [1960] Director/Bank Officer [British/American]; John J Gould [1963] Director/Banker [American]; Clive William Rendell [1962] Director/Bank Officer

Balderton Aviation Holdings Limited
Incorporated: 7 September 2005
Net Worth: £4,038,656,000 *Total Assets:* £5,952,214,016
Registered Office: 3rd Floor, 105 Wigmore Street, London, W1U 1QY
Activities: Financial intermediation not elsewhere classified
Parent: BBA Aviation PLC
Officers: David John Mark Blizzard [1972] Director/Company Secretary/Barrister; Jennifer Chase [1978] Director/Chartered Accountant

Balfour Beatty Group Employment Limited
Incorporated: 29 November 2012 *Employees:* 14,173
Net Worth: £75,173,000 *Total Assets:* £260,028,992
Registered Office: 5 Churchill Place, Canary Wharf, London, E14 5HU
Activities: Human resources provision and management of human resources functions
Parent: Balfour Beatty Investment Holdings Limited
Officers: Philip James Harrison [1961] Director/Chartered Management Accountant; Jonathan Lagan [1975] Director/Group General Counsel, Head of Legal; Paul Anthony Raby [1963] Human Resources Director; Gavin Russell [1981] Director/Chartered Accountant; David Mark Smith [1970] Director/Chartered Accountant

Balfour Beatty Group Limited
Incorporated: 12 January 1909 *Employees:* 808
Net Worth: £71,000,000 *Total Assets:* £2,104,000,000
Registered Office: 5 Churchill Place, Canary Wharf, London, E14 5HU
Activities: Construction of commercial buildings
Parent: Balfour Beatty Investment Holdings Limited
Officers: Jonathan Lagan, Secretary; Dean John Banks [1971] Director; Philip James Harrison [1961] Director/Chartered Management Accountant; John Cooperwhite Moore [1959] Director; Leo Martin Quinn [1956] Director/Civil Engineer; Gavin Russell [1981] Director/Chartered Accountant; Stephen John Tarr [1959] Director

Balfour Beatty Infrastructure Investments Limited
Incorporated: 7 August 1948
Net Worth: £551,502,016 *Total Assets:* £809,683,968
Registered Office: 350 Euston Road, Regent's Place, London, NW1 3AX
Activities: Activities of head offices
Parent: Balfour Beatty PLC
Officers: Ion Francis Appuhamy [1964] Director; Gavin Russell [1981] Director/Chartered Accountant; Ian Kenneth Rylatt [1965] Director/Engineer; Adam Paul Walker [1986] Director/Accountant

Balfour Beatty Investment Holdings Limited
Incorporated: 29 January 1975
Net Worth: £1,153,069,056 *Total Assets:* £2,161,743,104
Registered Office: 5 Churchill Place, Canary Wharf, London, E14 5HU
Activities: Activities of head offices
Parent: Balfour Beatty PLC
Officers: Jonathan Lagan [1975] Director/Group General Counsel, Head of Legal; Gavin Russell [1981] Director/Chartered Accountant

Balfour Beatty Overseas Investments Limited
Incorporated: 29 January 1975
Net Worth: £1,129,403,008 *Total Assets:* £1,483,891,968
Registered Office: 5 Churchill Place, Canary Wharf, London, E14 5HU
Activities: Activities of head offices
Parent: Balfour Beatty Investment Holdings Limited
Officers: Jonathan Lagan [1975] Director/Group General Counsel, Head of Legal; Gavin Russell [1981] Director/Chartered Accountant

Balfour Beatty PLC
Incorporated: 31 May 1945 *Employees:* 20,940
Net Worth: £1,056,000,000 *Total Assets:* £4,877,000,192
Registered Office: 5 Churchill Place, Canary Wharf, London, E14 5HU
Activities: Activities of head offices
Officers: Jonathan Lagan, Secretary; David Ross Mercer, Secretary; Philip Stanley Aiken [1949] Director [Australian]; Stephen Robert Billingham [1958] Director; Stuart John Doughty [1943] Director/Chartered Civil Engineer; Anne Drinkwater [1956] Director; Iain George Thomas Ferguson [1955] Director; Philip James Harrison [1961] Director/Chartered Management Accountant; Michael Anthony Lucki [1956] Director [American]; Barbara Jane Moorhouse [1958] Director; Leo Martin Quinn [1956] Director/Civil Engineer

Ballymore Properties Limited
Incorporated: 20 May 1988 *Employees:* 8
Net Worth: £54,623,868 *Total Assets:* £327,999,424
Registered Office: 4th Floor, 161 Marsh Wall, London, E14 9SJ
Activities: Development of building projects
Shareholders: Ballymore Ltd; Ballymore Limited; Sean Mulryan
Officers: David Nicholas Pearson, Secretary; John Martin Mulryan [1982] Director [Irish]; Sean Mulryan [1954] Director [Irish]; David Nicholas Pearson [1968] Finance Director

Baltic Sea Offshore Holdco Limited
Incorporated: 5 December 2014
Net Worth: £43,552,008 *Total Assets:* £695,065,792
Registered Office: 18 St Swithin's Lane, London, EC4N 8AD
Activities: Activities of financial services holding companies
Parent: Baltic Sea Offshore Investment Limited
Officers: Markus Altenhoff [1962] Managing Director Investments [German]; Lutz Horstick [1974] Director/Department Head Securities and Loans [German]; Dennis Van Alphen [1968] Director [Dutch]; Cornelia Bernadette Maria Van Heijningen [1971] Director/Investment Manager [Dutch]

Bampton Property Group Limited (The)
Incorporated: 26 January 1960 *Employees:* 14
Net Worth: £93,668,960 *Total Assets:* £128,270,568
Registered Office: Freshwater House, 158-162 Shaftesbury Avenue, London, WC2H 8HR
Activities: Buying and selling of own real estate
Parent: Bampton Holdings Limited
Officers: Mark Roy Mason Jenner, Secretary; David Davis [1935] Director/Chartered Accountant; Benzion Schalom Eliezer Freshwater [1948] Director

Bana One Limited
Incorporated: 30 December 2010 *Employees:* 2
Net Worth: £186,852,992 *Total Assets:* £531,905,984
Registered Office: 113 Brent Street, London, NW4 2DX
Activities: Renting and operating of Housing Association real estate
Shareholders: Barry Ackerman; Naomi Ackerman
Officers: Barry Ackerman [1969] Director/Surveyor; Naomi Ackerman [1945] Director

Bank and Clients PLC
Incorporated: 28 May 1970 *Employees:* 51
Previous: Bank and Clients Limited
Net Worth: £10,109,000 *Total Assets:* £127,438,000
Registered Office: 30 King Street, London, EC2V 8EH
Activities: Banks
Shareholders: Pedro Errazuriz; Edouard Bridel
Officers: Georgina Mary Kingbsury, Secretary; Roger William Barlow [1954] Director/Chartered Accountant; Claire Marie Michel Bridel [1968] Director [French]; Edouard Bridel [1969] Director; William Francis Charnley [1960] Director/Solicitor; Nicole Coll [1976] Director/Accountant; Karen Elizabeth McCormick [1956] Director; Lord Thomas Dunlop Galloway de Roy de Blicquy Galbraith Strathclyde [1960] Director/Business Consultant; Anthony John Ward [1957] Director

Bank Leumi (U.K.) P.L.C.
Incorporated: 26 October 1959 *Employees:* 194
Net Worth: £207,596,992 *Total Assets:* £1,558,582,016
Registered Office: 20 Stratford Place, London, W1C 1BG
Activities: Banks
Parent: Bank Leumi Le Israel B.M
Officers: Robert S England, Secretary; Shmulik Arbel [1969] Director/Senior Management [Israeli]; Michael Jonathan Green [1947] Director/Banking Consultant; Gil Karni [1966] Director [Israeli]; Anthony Landes [1963] Director; Robert Michael Levy [1954] Director; William Michael Lindsay [1952] Director/Credit Officer Consultant; Yoel Mintz [1954] Director/Banker [Israeli]; Sasson Mordechay [1959] Director [Israeli]; Jean Margaret Stevenson [1953] Director; Adrian John Stirrup [1956] Director; Nicholas John Treble [1959] Director

Bank Mandiri (Europe) Limited
Incorporated: 22 June 1999 *Employees:* 12
Net Worth: £35,920,328 *Total Assets:* £111,691,728
Registered Office: 4 Thomas More Square, London, E1W 1YW
Activities: Banks
Parent: PT Bank Mandiri (Persero) Tbk
Officers: Ajaykumar Joshi, Secretary/Banker; Mahendra Siregar [1962] Director [Indonesian]; Inyoman Gede Suarja [1962] Director/Chief Executive [Indonesian]; Ita Tetralastwati [1970] Director/Banker [Indonesian]; John Kenrick Williams [1946] Director

Bank of Beirut (UK) Ltd
Incorporated: 30 March 2002 *Employees:* 58
Net Worth: £96,604,080 *Total Assets:* £520,774,112
Registered Office: 66 Cannon Street, London, EC4N 6AE
Activities: Banks
Officers: Sophoklis Argyrou [1973] Director [Cypriot]; Anthony John Bush [1952] Director/Retired; Fawaz Mohamad Hachem Naboulsi [1950] Director/Banker [Lebanese]; Martin John Osborne [1967] Director/Banker; Ramzi Nabil Saliba [1953] Director/Retired Banker [Lebanese]; Antoun Samia [1974] Director/Banker [Lebanese]; Salim Georges Sfeir [1944] Director/Banker [Lebanese]; Marcus John Sewell Trench [1944] Director/Self Employed Consultant

Bank of China (UK) Limited
Incorporated: 29 March 2007 *Employees:* 439
Net Worth: £307,054,016 *Total Assets:* £1,539,220,992
Registered Office: 1 Lothbury, London, EC2R 7DB
Activities: Banks
Officers: Qing Zhou, Secretary; Wenjian Fang [1970] Director/Chief Executive [Chinese]; Simon Charles Hardy [1955] Director; Dr Gerard Patrick Lyons [1961] Director; Li Ren [1969] Director/Banking [Chinese]; Wei Shi [1970] Director/Banker [Chinese]; Jonathan Spence [1960] Director/Fellow & Senior Bursar; Yu Sun [1973] Director/Banker [Chinese]; Stewart Henry Trussler [1963] Director/Chief Financial Officer

Bank of England Asset Purchase Facility Fund Limited
Incorporated: 30 January 2009
Total Assets: £605,167,026,176
Registered Office: 8 Lothbury, London, EC2R 7HH
Activities: Central banking
Officers: Victoria Mary Florence Cleland [1970] Director; Andrew George Haldane [1967] Director; Andrew Hauser [1970] Director

Bank of Ireland (UK) PLC
Incorporated: 17 September 2009 *Employees:* 715
Net Worth: £1,999,000,064 *Total Assets:* £26,235,000,832
Registered Office: Bow Bells House, 1 Bread Street, London, EC4M 9BE
Activities: Banks
Parent: The Governor and Company of The Bank of Ireland
Officers: John Duncan Baines [1962] Director; Ian David Buchanan [1964] Director; Daniel Laurence Collins [1959] Director/Banker [Irish]; Desmond Edward Crowley [1959] Director/Banker [Irish]; Neil Anthony Fuller [1966] Director/Chief Risk Officer; Mimi Kung [1965] Director [Chinese]; John Neil Maltby [1962] Director; Thomas McAreavey [1970] Director; Philip Wynford Moore [1960] Director; Jacqueline Dorothy Mary Noakes [1961] Director [Irish]; Robert Sharpe [1949] Director

Bank of London and The Middle East PLC
Incorporated: 7 August 2006 *Employees:* 112
Net Worth: £220,520,992 *Total Assets:* £1,025,888,000
Registered Office: Cannon Place, 78 Cannon Street, London, EC4N 6HL
Activities: Banks
Parent: BLME Holdings PLC
Officers: Peter Francis Bulkeley, Secretary; Adel Abdul Wahab Al-Majed [1958] Director [Kuwaiti]; Sheikh Abdullah Jaber Al-Ahmad Al-Sabah [1966] Director [Kuwaiti]; Giles Hullah Cunningham [1969] Director; Jabra Ghandour [1962] Director [Jordanian]; Joanne Hindle [1957] Director; Christopher Martin Power [1961] Director; Calum Thomson [1960] Director; David Gareth Williams [1960] Director; Michael Howard Williams [1950] Director

Bank of Montreal Capital Markets (Holdings) Limited
Incorporated: 25 June 1974 *Employees:* 132
Net Worth: £199,204,992 *Total Assets:* £1,756,530,048
Registered Office: 95 Queen Victoria Street, London, EC4V 4HG
Activities: Activities of financial services holding companies
Parent: Bank of Montreal
Officers: Paula Young, Secretary; Scott Joseph Matthews [1969] Director/Accountant [Australian]; Joan Z Mohammed [1961] Director/Chief Operating Officer [American]; William Kenneth Spinney Smith [1959] Director/Banker [British/Canadian]; Robert Andrew Yeung [1971] Managing Director

The Bank of New York Mellon (International) Limited
Incorporated: 9 August 1996 *Employees:* 39
Net Worth: £524,588,000 *Total Assets:* £10,117,220,352
Registered Office: 1 Canada Square, London, E14 5AL
Activities: Financial intermediation not elsewhere classified
Officers: Paola Bergamaschi Broyd [1961] Director [Italian]; Katherine Jane Damsell [1962] Director/Chief Executive; Kevin John Gregory [1957] Director; John William Jack [1966] Director/International CFO The Bank of New York Mellon; John Meikle Johnston [1960] Director and Trustee; Hani Kablawi [1968] Director [American]; Sophie Jane O'Connor [1970] Director; Joseph Gerard Patrick Wheatley [1960] Director/Head of European Investment Operations BNY Mellon [Irish]

Bank of Scotland Structured Asset Finance Limited
Incorporated: 21 July 1988
Net Worth: £58,785,000 *Total Assets:* £295,648,000
Registered Office: 25 Gresham Street, London, EC2V 7HN
Activities: Financial leasing
Parent: Bank of Scotland PLC
Officers: Alyson Elizabeth Mulholland, Secretary; Laura Frances Dorey [1978] Director; Colin Graham Dowsett [1964] Director/Chartered Accountant; Gerard Ashley Fox [1963] Director/Banker

Bank Saderat PLC
Incorporated: 3 August 1973 *Employees:* 22
Net Worth: £166,793,216 *Total Assets:* £199,185,312
Registered Office: 5 Lothbury, London, EC2R 7HD
Activities: Banks
Parent: Bank Saderat Iran
Officers: Michael Patrick Bailey, Secretary; Hamid Borhani [1952] Director/Banker [Iranian]; Dr David John Reid [1945] Director/Banker; Dr Hojatollah Saydi [1967] Director/Banker [Iranian]; Robert John Speedy [1947] Director/Banker

Bank Sepah International PLC
Incorporated: 29 March 2001 *Employees:* 34
Net Worth: £148,335,248 *Total Assets:* £319,288,064
Registered Office: 5-7 Eastcheap, London, EC3M 1JT
Activities: Banks
Parent: Bank Sepah Iran
Officers: Joseph Crowley, Secretary; Hadi Akhlaghi Feizasar [1966] Director/Banker [Iranian]; Robert Evan Stanley Angel [1947] Director/Banker; Ian Coleman [1960] Director/Banker; Mohammad Reza Fatemi [1955] Director/Banker [Iranian]; Mohammad Reza Khorsandi [1960] Director/Banker [Iranian]

The Bankers Investment Trust PLC
Incorporated: 13 April 1888
Net Worth: £1,077,563,008 *Total Assets:* £1,151,830,016
Registered Office: 201 Bishopsgate, London, EC2M 3AE
Activities: Activities of investment trusts
Officers: Julian Richard Chillingworth [1956] Director; Richard Norman Legh Huntingford [1956] Director; Susan Patricia Inglis [1964] Director/Corporate Financier; Richard William Killingbeck [1962] Managing Director; Isobel Nicol Sharp [1956] Director/Chartered Accountant

Barbados Enterprises PLC
Incorporated: 7 October 2015
Net Worth Deficit: £1,163,931 *Total Assets:* £451,490,016
Registered Office: 35 Great St Helen's, London, EC3A 6AP
Activities: Financial intermediation not elsewhere classified
Parent: Intertrust Corporate Services Limited
Officers: Susan Iris Abrahams [1957] Director

Barbican Corporate Member Limited
Incorporated: 16 October 2007
Net Worth Deficit: £48,300,000 *Total Assets:* £1,330,300,032
Registered Office: 33 Gracechurch Street, London, EC3V 0BT
Activities: Non-life insurance
Parent: Barbican Holdings (UK) Limited
Officers: Stephen John Britt, Secretary; Christopher William Haga [1967] Director/Portfolio Manager [American]; Mark John Harrington [1963] Director/Underwriter; David Edward Reeves [1955] Director/Chartered Accountant; Roy Harold Trice [1959] Director/Chief Operating Officer [American]; Michael David Weinberg [1964] Director/Fund Manager [American]

Barchester Finco 2017 UK Limited
Incorporated: 2 May 2017 *Employees:* 2
Net Worth Deficit: £1,509,000 *Total Assets:* £126,074,000
Registered Office: The Aspect, Finsbury Square, London, EC2A 1AS
Activities: Activities of other holding companies n.e.c.
Officers: Pete Calveley [1960] Director; Mark Antony Hazlewood [1966] Director

Barchester Healthcare Homes Limited
Incorporated: 1 September 1993 *Employees:* 15,329
Net Worth: £113,711,000 *Total Assets:* £1,033,468,032
Registered Office: 3rd Floor, The Aspect, Finsbury Square, London, EC2A 1AS
Activities: Other human health activities
Parent: Barchester Healthcare Limited
Officers: Michael Patrick O'Reilly, Secretary; Pete Calveley [1960] Director; Dr Dr Mark Antony Hazlewood [1966] Director; Michael Patrick O'Reilly [1960] Director

Barchester Healthcare Limited
Incorporated: 22 February 1993 *Employees:* 15,462
Net Worth: £122,502,000 *Total Assets:* £400,609,984
Registered Office: 3rd Floor, The Aspect, Finsbury Square, London, EC2A 1AS
Activities: Activities of head offices
Officers: Michael Patrick O'Reilly, Secretary; John Gerard Bateson [1963] Director [Irish]; Anthony Rhys Bourne [1953] Director; Keith Browne [1969] Director [Irish]; Pete Calveley [1960] Director; John Coleman [1952] Director; Dr Dr Mark Antony Hazlewood [1966] Director; Professor John Edward Hegarty [1949] Director [Irish]; Michael Patrick O'Reilly [1960] Director

Barclaycard Funding PLC
Incorporated: 13 August 1990
Net Worth: £248,000 *Total Assets:* £7,949,395,968
Registered Office: 1 Churchill Place, London, E14 5HP
Activities: Other business support service activities n.e.c.
Shareholders: Barclays Bank UK PLC; Structured Finance Management Limited
Officers: Rupert James Fowden [1964] Director/Banker; Adam Lishman [1981] Director/Banker

Barclays (Barley) Limited
Incorporated: 13 November 2000
Previous: Barley Investments Limited
Net Worth: £209,182,448 *Total Assets:* £786,381,824
Registered Office: 1 Churchill Place, London, E14 5HP
Activities: Financial intermediation not elsewhere classified
Parent: Barclays Term Funding Limited Liability Partnership
Officers: Vishal Shah [1984] Director/Banker; Jonathan Michael Walthoe [1975] Director/Banker

Barclays Aldersgate Investments Limited
Incorporated: 19 February 1988
Net Worth: £3,133,041,152 *Total Assets:* £5,976,604,160
Registered Office: 1 Churchill Place, London, E14 5HP
Activities: Financial intermediation not elsewhere classified
Parent: Barclays Bank PLC
Officers: Ben Ferry [1977] Director/Banker; Florian Huber [1978] Director/Banker [Austrian]; Edward James Sherwood [1984] Director/Banker; David Antony Simpson [1964] Director/Solicitor

Barclays Bank PLC
Incorporated: 4 October 1971
Net Worth: £65,733,001,216 *Total Assets:* £1,129,342,959,616
Registered Office: 1 Churchill Place, London, E14 5HP
Activities: Central banking
Parent: Barclays PLC
Officers: Jason Leslie Wright, Secretary; Peter James Bernard [1957] Director [American]; Steven John Ewart [1972] Director/Chief Financial Officer; Nigel Paul Higgins [1960] Director; Helen Keelan [1958] Director [Irish]; Maria Del Carmen Richter [1954] Director [American]; Jeremy Lloyd Scott [1955] Director; Timothy James Osborne Throsby [1966] Director/Banker [British/Australian]; Alexander Vincent Thursby [1960] Director; Helene Maria Vletter-Van Dort [1964] Director [Dutch]

Barclays Capital Asia Holdings Limited
Incorporated: 7 November 2005
Net Worth: £362,039,552 *Total Assets:* £362,039,552
Registered Office: 1 Churchill Place, London, E14 5HP
Activities: Activities of financial services holding companies
Parent: Barclays Bank PLC
Officers: Balwinder Singh Bagary [1969] Director/Accountant; Mahesh Beniwal [1971] Director/Accountant [Indian]; Hemal Sanghrajka [1976] Director/Accountant; David Spiteri [1973] Director/Accountant [Australian]

Barclays Capital Japan Securities Holdings Limited
Incorporated: 7 November 2005
Net Worth: £359,312,064 *Total Assets:* £359,312,064
Registered Office: 1 Churchill Place, London, E14 5HP
Activities: Activities of financial services holding companies
Parent: Barclays Capital Asia Holdings Limited
Officers: Balwinder Singh Bagary [1969] Director/Accountant; Mahesh Beniwal [1971] Director/Accountant [Indian]; Hemal Sanghrajka [1976] Director/Accountant; David Spiteri [1973] Director/Accountant [Australian]

Barclays Capital Securities Limited
Incorporated: 9 July 1985 *Employees:* 1
Net Worth: £1,209,123,968 *Total Assets:* £55,123,898,368
Registered Office: 1 Churchill Place, London, E14 5HP
Activities: Financial intermediation not elsewhere classified
Parent: Barclays Bank PLC
Officers: Michael St John Ashley [1954] Director; Timothy James Breedon [1958] Director; Stephen Brian Dainton [1967] Director/Banker; Steven John Ewart [1972] Director/Chief Financial Officer; Helen Keelan [1958] Director [Irish]

Barclays CCP Funding LLP
Incorporated: 26 October 2010
Net Worth: £7,667,714 *Total Assets:* £13,299,495,936
Registered Office: 1 Churchill Place, London, E14 5HP

Barclays Covered Bond Funding LLP
Incorporated: 29 September 2009
Total Assets: £3,006,658,048
Registered Office: 1 Churchill Place, London, E14 5HP

Barclays Covered Bonds Limited Liability Partnership
Incorporated: 23 October 2007
Net Worth: £79,369,000 *Total Assets:* £8,069,573,120
Registered Office: 1 Churchill Place, London, E14 5HP

Barclays Funds Investments Limited
Incorporated: 26 May 2000
Net Worth: £393,786,688 *Total Assets:* £396,382,496
Registered Office: 1 Churchill Place, London, E14 5HP
Activities: Financial intermediation not elsewhere classified
Parent: Barclays Bank PLC
Officers: Jonathan James Brown [1968] Director/Banker; Gavin John Chapman [1970] Director/Banker; Timothy John Hulbert [1972] Director/Marketer; Steven Alan Tait [1978] Director/Accountant

Barclays Investment Management Limited
Incorporated: 5 March 1986
Net Worth: £128,676,000 *Total Assets:* £160,731,008
Registered Office: 1 Churchill Place, London, E14 5HP
Activities: Financial intermediation not elsewhere classified
Parent: Barclays Bank PLC
Officers: Daniel Richard Fairclough [1977] Director/Banker; Hakki Miray Muminoglu [1965] Director/Banker

Barclays Long Island Limited
Incorporated: 3 October 2008
Net Worth: £160,448,688 *Total Assets:* £4,652,858,368
Registered Office: 1 Churchill Place, London, E14 5HP
Activities: Financial intermediation not elsewhere classified
Parent: Barclays Bank PLC
Officers: Benjamin Adam Gerrard-Jones [1986] Director/Banker; Christopher Patrick Le Neve Foster [1981] Director/Banker; David James Rothnie [1982] Director/Banker; Vishal Shah [1984] Director/Banker

Barclays Mercantile Business Finance Limited
Incorporated: 14 February 1967 *Employees:* 133
Net Worth: £116,400,000 *Total Assets:* £1,511,600,000
Registered Office: 1 Churchill Place, London, E14 5HP
Activities: Financial leasing
Parent: Barclays Bank PLC
Officers: Stephen Geoffrey Bolton [1962] Director/Banker; David Charles Hawkins [1967] Director/Banker; Vukkalam Rangaswami Praveen Kumar [1977] Director/Banker [Indian]; Angela Nicole Ottaway [1974] Director/Banker

Barclays PLC
Incorporated: 20 July 1896
Net Worth: £63,905,001,472 *Total Assets:* £1,133,247,987,712
Registered Office: 1 Churchill Place, London, E14 5HP
Activities: Central banking
Officers: Stephen Victor Shapiro, Secretary; Michael St John Ashley [1954] Director; Timothy James Breedon [1958] Director; Sir Ian Michael Cheshire [1959] Director; Mary Anne Citrino [1959] Director [American]; Mary Elizabeth Francis [1948] Director; Crawford Scott Gillies [1956] Director; Nigel Paul Higgins [1960] Director; Reuben Jeffery III [1953] Director [American]; Matthew John Lester [1963] Director/Accountant; John McFarlane [1947] Director [British/Australian]; Tushar Morzaria [1969] Finance Director; Dr Dambisa Felicia Moyo [1969] Director; Diane Lynn Schueneman [1952] Director [American]; James Edward Staley [1956] Director/Group Chief Executive [American]; Michael John Turner [1948] Director

Barclays Principal Investments Limited
Incorporated: 22 June 2012
Previous: Barclays Africa Group Holdings Limited
Net Worth: £810,480,000 *Total Assets:* £1,462,649,984
Registered Office: 1 Churchill Place, London, E14 5HP
Activities: Activities of financial services holding companies
Parent: Barclays PLC
Officers: Andrew David Challis [1974] Director/Banker; Gavin John Chapman [1970] Director/Banker; Kathryn McLeland [1971] Director/Group Treasurer [Australian]; Steven Matthew Poulter [1973] Director/Banker

Barclays Services Limited
Incorporated: 7 November 1983 *Employees:* 11,117
Previous: Barclays Capital Services Limited
Net Worth: £734,361,024 *Total Assets:* £6,021,302,784
Registered Office: 1 Churchill Place, London, E14 5HP
Activities: Other business support service activities n.e.c.
Parent: Barclays PLC
Officers: Lisa Margaret Norton, Secretary; Raheel Ahmed [1970] Director/Banker [Pakistani]; Stuart Baker [1973] Director/Chief Financial Officer; Alastair Blackwell [1970] Managing Director; Paul Herbert Compton [1964] Director/Banker [Australian]; Richard James Haworth [1973] Director/Banker; Diane Lynn Schueneman [1952] Director [American]

Barfair Limited
Incorporated: 24 April 1998
Net Worth: £1,102,109,952 *Total Assets:* £1,336,989,952
Registered Office: The Battleship Building, 179 Harrow Road, London, W2 6NB
Activities: Activities of other holding companies n.e.c.
Parent: Virgin Holdings Limited
Officers: Barry Alexander Ralph Gerrard, Secretary; Robert Pieter Blok [1976] Director/Lawyer; Amy Stirling [1969] Director; Ian Philip Woods [1974] Director/Solicitor

Barnsley SPV Three Limited
Incorporated: 7 September 2010
Net Worth Deficit: £1,253,000 *Total Assets:* £131,438,000
Registered Office: 5th Floor, 120 Aldersgate Street, London, EC1A 4JQ
Activities: Construction of commercial buildings
Parent: Barnsley Partnership for Learning Three Limited
Officers: Saeed Hasan Mian, Secretary; Robert Alistair Martin Gillespie [1990] Director/Financial Controller; Kirsty O'Brien [1982] Director/Operations Manager; Catherine Elizabeth Pantry [1982] Director/Chartered Accountant; Daniel Colin Ward [1982] BSFI Investment Director

Baronsmead Second Venture Trust PLC
Incorporated: 22 November 2000
Previous: Baronsmead VCT 3 PLC
Net Worth: £186,688,992 *Total Assets:* £188,139,008
Registered Office: 5 New Street Square, London, EC4A 3TW
Activities: Activities of investment trusts
Officers: John Davies [1946] Director/Retired Investment Manager; Malcolm Groat [1961] Director; Ian Jackson Orrock [1946] Director; John Anthony Victor Townsend [1948] Director/Investment Banker

Baronsmead Venture Trust PLC
Incorporated: 29 January 1998
Previous: Baronsmead VCT 2 PLC
Net Worth: £159,002,000 *Total Assets:* £160,714,000
Registered Office: 5 New Street Square, London, EC4A 3TW
Activities: Activities of investment trusts
Officers: Leslie Ian Gabb [1961] Director; Peter Anthony Lawrence [1948] Director; Valerie Margaret Marshall [1945] Director; Susannah Elizabeth McKean Nicklin [1969] Director

Barts Square First Limited
Incorporated: 24 June 2014
Net Worth: £41,627,424 *Total Assets:* £211,913,808
Registered Office: 5 Hanover Square, London, W1S 1HQ
Activities: Development of building projects
Parent: Barts Square Land One Limited
Officers: James Richard Moss, Secretary; Sarah Amy O'Reilly, Secretary; Generald Anthony Kaye [1958] Development Director; Timothy John Murphy [1959] Finance Director

BASF Metals Limited
Incorporated: 9 August 1982 *Employees:* 28
Net Worth: £83,046,784 *Total Assets:* £432,035,744
Registered Office: 21st Floor, 110 Bishopsgate, London, EC2N 4AY
Activities: Agents involved in the sale of fuels, ores, metals and industrial chemicals
Parent: BASF Catalysts UK Holdings Ltd
Officers: Helen Victoria Koerner, Secretary; Sik Yuen Katharine Boegenhold [1971] Director/Regional Controller; Richard John Carter [1962] Managing Director UK/Ireland; John Metcalf [1967] Director, Trading; Dr Vasileios Vergopoulos [1964] Director/Vice President Commercial & General Manager [Greek]

Bath Road Cheltenham Limited
Incorporated: 5 July 1999 *Employees:* 2
Net Worth: £7,842,209 *Total Assets:* £140,701,168
Registered Office: Hallswelle House, 1 Hallswelle Road, London, NW11 0DH
Activities: Other letting and operating of own or leased real estate
Officers: Dwora Feldman, Secretary/Director; Dwora Feldman [1937] Director; Heinrich Feldman [1935] Director

Batif Dollar Limited
Incorporated: 7 December 1923
Net Worth: £1,195,936,128 *Total Assets:* £3,229,317,888
Registered Office: Globe House, 1 Water Street, London, WC2R 3LA
Activities: Financial intermediation not elsewhere classified
Parent: B.A.T. International Finance P.L.C.
Officers: Noelle Colfer, Secretary; Andrew James Barrett [1974] Director/Group Finance Controller; Robert James Casey [1948] Director/Attorney [American]; Steven Glyn Dale [1967] Director/Tax Adviser; John Benedict Stevens [1959] Director/Tobacco Manufacturer; Neil Arthur Wadey [1964] Director/Treasurer

Batleys Properties Limited
Incorporated: 24 September 1920
Net Worth: £118,308,000 *Total Assets:* £285,641,984
Registered Office: 2 Abbey Road, London, NW10 7BW
Activities: Other letting and operating of own or leased real estate
Parent: Bestway UK Holdco Limited
Officers: Dawood Pervez, Secretary/Director; Zameer Mohammed Choudrey [1958] Director/Chartered Accountant; Dawood Pervez [1975] Director; Rizwan Pervez [1968] Director [British/Pakistani]; Mohammed Younus Sheikh [1946] Director

Bavarian Sky UK 1 PLC
Incorporated: 28 June 2017 *Employees:* 2
Net Worth Deficit: £293,452 *Total Assets:* £535,042,816
Registered Office: Third Floor, c/o Wilmington Trust SP Services (London) Limited, 1 King's Arms Yard, London, EC2R 7AF
Activities: Other business support service activities n.e.c.
Parent: Bavarian Sky UK Holdings Limited
Officers: Daniel Jonathan Wynne [1970] Director

Baxalta UK Investments Ltd.
Incorporated: 23 July 2002
Previous: Baxter Healthcare Pharmaceutical Limited
Net Worth Deficit: £88,212,856 *Total Assets:* £557,806,848
Registered Office: 1 Kingdom Street, London, W2 6BD
Activities: Wholesale of pharmaceutical goods
Parent: Takeda Pharmaceutical Company Limited
Officers: Damien Rodolphe Edmond Bailly [1966] Commercial Director [French]; Mark Gibbons [1984] Director/Accountant [South African]; Nicholas Hugh Meryon Insall [1982] Director/Accountant

Bayeast Property Co Limited
Incorporated: 26 August 1959
Net Worth: £233,956,080 *Total Assets:* £233,956,160
Registered Office: York House, 45 Seymour Street, London, W1H 7LX
Activities: Development of building projects
Parent: Union Property Corporation Limited
Officers: Sarah Morrell Barzycki [1958] Director/Head of Finance; Timothy Andrew Roberts [1964] Director/Chartered Surveyor; Nigel Mark Webb [1963] Director/Chartered Surveyor

Bazalgette Equity Limited
Incorporated: 21 April 2015
Net Worth: £485,000,000 *Total Assets:* £2,146,099,968
Registered Office: Cottons Centre, Cottons Lane, London, SE1 2QG
Activities: Construction of other civil engineering projects n.e.c.
Officers: Valmai Barclay, Secretary; Rukhi Johal, Secretary; Andrew Julian Frederick Cox [1967] Director/Fund Manager; Scott Roderick McGregor [1988] Director/Investment Professional [Canadian]; Joseph Eugene Philipsz [1967] Director/Investment Manager [Irish]; Alistair Graham Ray [1974] Director; Angela Louise Roshier [1975] Director/Partner and Head of Asset Management; Gavin Richard Tait [1970] Investment Director; Amanda Elizabeth Woods [1979] Investment Director

Bazalgette Holdings Limited
Incorporated: 21 April 2015 *Employees:* 179
Net Worth: £485,000,000 *Total Assets:* £2,146,099,968
Registered Office: Cottons Centre, Cottons Lane, London, SE1 2QG
Activities: Construction of other civil engineering projects n.e.c.
Parent: Bazalgette Ventures Limited
Officers: Valmai Barclay, Secretary; Rukhi Johal, Secretary; Andrew Julian Frederick Cox [1967] Director/Fund Manager; Scott Roderick McGregor [1988] Director/Investment Professional [Canadian]; Joseph Eugene Philipsz [1967] Director/Investment Manager [Irish]; Alistair Graham Ray [1974] Director; Angela Louise Roshier [1975] Director/Partner and Head of Asset Management; Gavin Richard Tait [1970] Investment Director; Amanda Elizabeth Woods [1979] Investment Director

Bazalgette Tunnel Limited
Incorporated: 21 April 2015
Net Worth: £485,000,000 *Total Assets:* £2,146,200,064
Registered Office: Cottons Centre, Cottons Lane, London, SE1 2QG
Activities: Construction of other civil engineering projects n.e.c.
Parent: Bazalgette Holdings Limited
Officers: Valmai Barclay, Secretary; Rukhi Johal, Secretary; Anne Elizabeth Baldock [1959] Director; Andrew Julian Frederick Cox [1967] Managing Director, Infrastructure; Mathew Robert Duncan [1962] Director/Chief Finance Officer; William John Holland-Kaye [1965] Director/Chief Executive; Andrew Harold Mitchell [1960] Director/Civil Engineer; Richard South Morse [1959] Director; Michael Colin Putnam [1960] Director; Michael James Queen [1961] Director; Alistair Graham Ray [1974] Director; Angela Louise Roshier [1975] Director/Partner and Head of Asset Management; Sir Neville Ian Simms [1944] Director/Chartered Civil Engineer; Alexander Mark Sneesby [1966] Director/Chief Operating Officer; Gavin Richard Tait [1970] Investment Director

Bazalgette Ventures Limited
Incorporated: 21 April 2015
Net Worth: £509,700,000 *Total Assets:* £1,224,099,968
Registered Office: Cottons Centre, Cottons Lane, London, SE1 2QG
Activities: Construction of other civil engineering projects n.e.c.
Parent: Bazalgette Equity Limited
Officers: Valmai Barclay, Secretary; Rukhi Johal, Secretary; Andrew Julian Frederick Cox [1967] Director/Fund Manager; Scott Roderick McGregor [1988] Director/Investment Professional [Canadian]; Joseph Eugene Philipsz [1967] Director/Investment Manager [Irish]; Alistair Graham Ray [1974] Director; Angela Louise Roshier [1975] Director/Partner and Head of Asset Management; Gavin Richard Tait [1970] Investment Director; Amanda Elizabeth Woods [1979] Investment Director

BB & R Limited
Incorporated: 28 June 2005 *Employees:* 270
Net Worth: £51,975,000 *Total Assets:* £254,874,000
Registered Office: 3 St James's Street, London, SW1A 1EG
Activities: Wholesale of wine, beer, spirits and other alcoholic beverages
Parent: Berry Bros. & Rudd Limited
Officers: Janet Ann Impey, Secretary; Christopher John Robinson [1969] Director; Elizabeth Margaret Rudd [1966] Director

BBA Aviation Finance
Incorporated: 1 November 2007 *Employees:* 2
Net Worth: £1,449,500,160 *Total Assets:* £1,449,742,848
Registered Office: 3rd Floor, 105 Wigmore Street, London, W1U 1QY
Activities: Financial intermediation not elsewhere classified
Parent: BBA Overseas Holdings Limited
Officers: David John Mark Blizzard [1972] Director/Company Secretary/Barrister; Jennifer Chase [1978] Director/Chartered Accountant; Daniel Vincent Marcinik [1964] Director/Accounting Finance [American]

BBA Aviation PLC
Incorporated: 10 August 1897 *Employees:* 6,745
Net Worth: £1,402,221,312 *Total Assets:* £2,954,776,320
Registered Office: 105 Wigmore Street, London, W1U 1QY
Activities: Service activities incidental to air transportation
Officers: David John Mark Blizzard, Secretary; Amee Chande [1974] Director; David Crook [1968] Director/Accountant; Wayne Edward Edmunds [1956] Director/CEO Invensys PLC [American]; Peter Graham Edwards [1956] Director/Industrial Consultant [American]; Charlotte Emma Tiffany Gilthorpe [1970] Director; Victoria Clare Jarman [1972] Director; Mark Robin Johnstone [1968] Director; Susan Saltzbart Kilsby [1958] Director [American]; Mr Stephen Anthony King [1960] Director; Sir Nigel Russell Rudd [1946] Director; Peter John Ventress [1960] Director

BBA Finance
Incorporated: 28 September 2000
Net Worth: £271,407,008 *Total Assets:* £272,423,008
Registered Office: 3rd Floor, 105 Wigmore Street, London, W1U 1QY
Activities: Financial intermediation not elsewhere classified
Parent: BBA Finance No. 4 Limited
Officers: David John Mark Blizzard [1972] Director/Company Secretary/Barrister; Jennifer Chase [1978] Director/Chartered Accountant

BBA Finance No. 4 Limited
Incorporated: 11 August 2003
Net Worth: £496,925,056 *Total Assets:* £496,925,056
Registered Office: 3rd Floor, 105 Wigmore Street, London, W1U 1QY
Activities: Financial intermediation not elsewhere classified
Parent: BBA Financial Services (UK) Limited
Officers: David John Mark Blizzard [1972] Director/Company Secretary/Barrister; Jennifer Chase [1978] Director/Chartered Accountant

BBA Finance No.1
Incorporated: 30 November 2001 *Employees:* 1
Net Worth: £700,131,968 *Total Assets:* £701,956,992
Registered Office: 3rd Floor, 105 Wigmore Street, London, W1U 1QY
Activities: Financial intermediation not elsewhere classified
Parent: BBA Overseas Holdings Limited
Officers: David John Mark Blizzard [1972] Director/Company Secretary/Barrister; Jennifer Chase [1978] Director/Chartered Accountant

BBA Holdings Limited
Incorporated: 29 March 1955 *Employees:* 5
Net Worth: £2,860,953,088 *Total Assets:* £3,541,129,984
Registered Office: 3rd Floor, 105 Wigmore Street, London, W1U 1QY
Activities: Financial intermediation not elsewhere classified
Parent: Balderton Aviation Holdings Limited
Officers: David John Mark Blizzard [1972] Director/Company Secretary/Barrister; Jennifer Chase [1978] Director/Chartered Accountant

BBA Overseas Holdings Limited
Incorporated: 12 August 1966 *Employees:* 4
Net Worth: £8,070,514,176 *Total Assets:* £9,264,089,088
Registered Office: 3rd Floor, 105 Wigmore Street, London, W1U 1QY
Activities: Activities of head offices
Parent: BBA Holdings Limited
Officers: David John Mark Blizzard [1972] Director/Company Secretary/Barrister; Jennifer Chase [1978] Director/Chartered Accountant

BBC Commercial Holdings Limited
Incorporated: 18 June 2002 *Employees:* 3,373
Net Worth: £465,300,000 *Total Assets:* £1,217,600,000
Registered Office: BC2 A5 Broadcast Centre, Media Village, 201 Wood Lane, London, W12 7TP
Activities: Activities of head offices
Officers: Anthony Corriette, Secretary; Anne Christine Bulford [1959] Director/Chartered Accountant; Timothy Douglas Davie [1967] Managing Director; Thomas Cyrus Fussell [1970] Finance Director; Lord Anthony William Hall [1951] Director-General; Sarah Jones [1961] Director/Solicitor; Mark Raymond Linsey [1961] Director; Dr Anna Celia Mallett [1974] Director/General Management; Dharmash Pravin Mistry [1970] Director/Investor & Advisor; Balraj Samra [1966] Director

BBC Studios Distribution Limited
Incorporated: 15 May 1979 *Employees:* 84
Previous: BBC Worldwide Limited
Net Worth: £333,900,000 *Total Assets:* £977,500,032
Registered Office: 1 Television Centre, 101 Wood Lane, London, W12 7FA
Activities: Television programme production activities
Parent: BBC Studios Limited
Officers: Anthony Corriette, Secretary; Timothy Douglas Davie [1967] Managing Director; Thomas Cyrus Fussell [1970] Finance Director

BBC Studios Limited
Incorporated: 18 June 2002
Previous: BBC Studios Group Limited
Net Worth: £166,860,000 *Total Assets:* £166,864,000
Registered Office: 1 Television Centre, 101 Wood Lane, London, W12 7FA
Activities: Activities of head offices
Parent: BBC Commercial Holdings Limited
Officers: Anthony Corriette, Secretary; Timothy Douglas Davie [1967] Managing Director; Thomas Cyrus Fussell [1970] Finance Director

BBDO EMEA Limited
Incorporated: 1 April 1985 *Employees:* 15
Net Worth: £146,402,704 *Total Assets:* £157,273,904
Registered Office: Bankside 3, 90-100 Southwark Street, London, SE1 0SW
Activities: Other business support service activities n.e.c.
Parent: BBDO European Holdings Limited
Officers: Sally Ann Bray, Secretary; John James Byrnes [1964] Finance Director; Helen Rosina Cavanagh [1971] Director/Solicitor

BBDO European Holdings Limited
Incorporated: 14 December 2000 *Employees:* 7
Net Worth: £336,524,576 *Total Assets:* £337,139,200
Registered Office: Bankside 3, 90-100 Southwark Street, London, SE1 0SW
Activities: Activities of head offices
Parent: Omnicom EMEA Holdings Limited
Officers: Sally Ann Bray, Secretary; John James Byrnes [1964] Finance Director; Helen Rosina Cavanagh [1971] Director/Solicitor

BBP Bandenia PLC
Incorporated: 28 January 2003 *Employees:* 350
Previous: Bandenia Banca Privada PLC
Net Worth: £764,533,248 *Total Assets:* £1,680,799,488
Registered Office: Holland House, Gherkin Piazza, 1-4 Bury Street, London, EC3A 5AW
Activities: Activities of financial services holding companies
Officers: Bulent Osman, Secretary; Massimiliano Arena [1970] Financial Director [Italian]; Fabio Pastore [1971] Executive Director and Group Chief Risk Officer [Italian]

BBPF LLP
Incorporated: 23 June 2015 *Employees:* 2
Net Worth: £109,589,240 *Total Assets:* £218,965,296
Registered Office: 350 Euston Road, Regents Place, London, NW1 3AX

BC Capital Management Services Limited
Incorporated: 28 April 2000 *Employees:* 337
Net Worth: £41,281,000 *Total Assets:* £151,590,000
Registered Office: Nova North, 11 Bressenden Place, London, SW1E 5BY
Activities: Activities of financial services holding companies
Officers: Paul Jay Dehadray, Secretary/General Counsel; Peter Anthony Cox [1964] Director/Chief Operating Officer; Paul Jay Dehadray [1974] Director/General Counsel

BCG UK1 Limited
Incorporated: 2 January 2001 *Employees:* 1,521
Net Worth: £122,459,848 *Total Assets:* £368,172,800
Registered Office: 20 Manchester Square, London, W1U 3PZ
Activities: Activities of head offices
Officers: Cecilia Helen Mary Biddle, Secretary; Mark Benedict Holden [1970] Director/Accountant; Mark Carroll Rosenthal [1966] Director/Executive Manager [American]

BCI UK Holdings Limited
Incorporated: 11 January 2016
Net Worth: £113,589,392 *Total Assets:* £239,008,048
Registered Office: Level 25, 1 Canada Square, London, E14 5AA
Activities: Activities of other holding companies n.e.c.
Parent: Brookfield Asset Management Inc
Officers: Edward Michael James Brogan [1983] Director/Solicitor; Ralf Niklas Rank [1977] Director/Managing Partner [Canadian/German]

BCP IV UK Fuel Holdings II Limited
Incorporated: 24 November 2016
Net Worth: £102,208,448 *Total Assets:* £204,174,208
Registered Office: Level 25, 1 Canada Square, London, E14 5AA
Activities: Activities of other holding companies n.e.c.
Officers: Edward Michael James Brogan [1983] Director/Solicitor; Andrew William Owens [1962] Director; Ralf Niklas Rank [1977] Director/Chief Investment Officer [Canadian/German]; Lorraine Ann Rienecker [1963] Managing Director; Adam John Traeger [1982] Director [Australian]

BCP IV UK Fuel Holdings III Limited
Incorporated: 16 March 2017 *Employees:* 793
Net Worth: £219,502,464 *Total Assets:* £2,137,484,160
Registered Office: Level 25, 1 Canada Square, London, E14 5AA
Activities: Activities of other holding companies n.e.c.
Parent: BCP IV UK Fuel Holdings II Limited
Officers: Edward Michael James Brogan [1983] Director/Solicitor; Andrew William Owens [1962] Director; Ralf Niklas Rank [1977] Director/Chief Investment Officer [Canadian/German]; Lorraine Ann Rienecker [1963] Managing Director; Adam John Traeger [1982] Director [Australian]

BCP IV UK Fuel Holdings IV Limited
Incorporated: 24 November 2016
Net Worth: £206,058,576 *Total Assets:* £370,521,120
Registered Office: Level 25, 1 Canada Square, London, E14 5AA
Activities: Activities of other holding companies n.e.c.
Parent: BCP IV UK Fuel Holdings III Limited
Officers: Edward Michael James Brogan [1983] Director/Solicitor; Andrew William Owens [1962] Director; Ralf Niklas Rank [1977] Director/Chief Investment Officer [Canadian/German]; Lorraine Ann Rienecker [1963] Managing Director; Adam John Traeger [1982] Director [Australian]

BCP IV UK Fuel Holdings V Limited
Incorporated: 28 November 2016 *Employees:* 4
Net Worth: £221,236,976 *Total Assets:* £429,251,424
Registered Office: Level 25, 1 Canada Square, London, E14 5AA
Activities: Activities of other holding companies n.e.c.
Parent: BCP IV UK Fuel Holdings IV Limited
Officers: Edward Michael James Brogan [1983] Director/Solicitor; Andrew William Owens [1962] Director; Ralf Niklas Rank [1977] Director/Chief Investment Officer [Canadian/German]; Lorraine Ann Rienecker [1963] Managing Director; Adam John Traeger [1982] Director [Australian]

BCS Prime Brokerage Limited
Incorporated: 20 April 2012 *Employees:* 187
Net Worth: £47,776,840 *Total Assets:* £554,758,528
Registered Office: 99 Bishopsgate, London, EC2M 3XD
Activities: Financial intermediation not elsewhere classified
Major Shareholder: Oleg Mikhasenko
Officers: Timothy Bevan [1976] Executive Director; Bradley Wayne Duke [1969] Director [French]; Edward Golosov [1973] Executive Director; Wendy Annette Langridge [1973] Director; Roman Lokhov [1976] Director [German]; Alexander Knyvett Romer-Lee [1953] Director

BDCG Holdings Limited
Incorporated: 28 August 2007 *Employees:* 47
Net Worth: £114,294,000 *Total Assets:* £147,023,008
Registered Office: Business Design Centre, 52 Upper Street, Islington, London, N1 0QH
Activities: Activities of head offices
Officers: Joseph Mullee, Secretary; Dominic Richard Albert Ismael Jones [1967] Director; Andrew Bernard Morris [1952] Director; Generald Edward Morris [1945] Director; Jack Anthony Morris [1956] Director; Paul Barry Morris [1951] Director; Philip Dennis Morris [1948] Director; Joseph Mullee [1978] Director

BDO LLP
Incorporated: 18 July 2003 *Employees:* 3,651
Net Worth: £144,400,000 *Total Assets:* £262,000,000
Registered Office: 55 Baker Street, London, W1U 7EU
Officers: Andrew Butterworth [1964] Member; Paul Mark Eagland [1965] Member; Simon Patrick Gallagher [1965] Member; Christopher John Grove [1964] Member; Scott William Knight [1970] Member; Gervase MacGregor [1959] Member; Jon Randall [1966] Member; Mark Andrew Sherfield [1962] Member; Wendy Michelle Walton [1969] Member; Matthew Robert White [1968] Member; Gurpal Singh Ahluwalia [1978] LLP Member; Ken Almand [1967] LLP Member; Dominic Earlstone Arnold [1969] LLP Member; Duncan Mark Ashman [1963] LLP Member; James Aston [1965] LLP Member; Sukhjinder Singh Aulak [1969] LLP Member; James Peter Austin [1968] LLP Member; Richard Douglas Austin [1969] LLP Member; Mark Andrew Ayres [1978] LLP Member; Paul Leslie Ayres [1966] LLP Member; Hasan Robert Simon Aziz [1960] LLP Member; Andrew Bailey [1963] LLP Member; Kerry Franchina Bailey [1967] LLP Member; John Leonard Barker [1954] LLP Member; Alex Barnes [1976] LLP Member; Stuart John Barnsdall [1961] LLP Member; Richard Barnwell [1979] LLP Member; Donald Edgar Bawtree [1958] LLP Member; Lorraine Maria Bay [1964] LLP Member; Simon John Baylis [1971] LLP Member; Martin Jeffrey Bell [1972] LLP Member; Christian Terence Bellairs [1975] LLP Member; Kyla Bellingall [1973] LLP Member; Lee Paul Bijoux [1978] LLP Member; Ian Anthony Bingham [1965] LLP Member; Andrea Bishop [1971] LLP Member; Mark Bomer [1964] LLP Member; Vanessa-Jayne Bradley [1974] LLP Member; David James Britton [1973] LLP Member; Simon Warren Brooker [1959] LLP Member; Daniel Brookes [1973] LLP Member; David Brookes [1969] LLP Member; Andrew James Buchanan [1965] LLP Member; Nicholas Roger Buckley [1964] LLP Member; Nigel Ferrier Burbidge [1957] LLP Member; Diane Ingrid Campbell [1964] LLP Member; Mark John Cardiff [1972] LLP Member; Michelle Ruth Carroll [1970] LLP Member; Nicholas Hallam Carter-Pegg [1964] LLP Member; Matthew James Chadwick [1963] LLP Member; Justin Michael Chait [1982] LLP Member; Richard Jonathan Citron [1952] LLP Member; Lisa Jane Clampin [1968] LLP Member; Paul Andrew Clark [1962] LLP Member; Ian Clayden [1973] LLP Member; Philip Damon Cliftlands [1975] LLP Member; Malcolm Cohen [1956] LLP Member; Stuart Charles Collins [1970] LLP Member; Kevin Richard Cook [1958] LLP Member; Ian Paul Cooper [1966] LLP Member; Michael Cooper [1960] LLP Member; Matthew John Copley [1970] LLP Member; Stephen Corrall [1965] LLP Member; Andrew Vaughan Cottle [1962] LLP Member; Philip James Cowan [1962] LLP Member; Gavin Crawford [1967] LLP Member; Shane Michael Crooks [1972] LLP Member; Kaley Dawn Crossthwaite [1972] LLP Member; Paul Andrew Daly [1973] LLP Member; Danny Nicolaas William Dartnaill [1976] LLP Member; Paul Richard Davies [1975] LLP Member; Fiona Louise Davis [1976] LLP Member; Stuart James Deacon [1971] LLP Member; Evangellos George Devetzis [1969] LLP Member; Daniel Isaac Dover [1953] LLP Member; Anna Heather Draper [1976] LLP Member; Gary Paul Drennan [1970] LLP Member; Edmund Hugh Dwan [1964] LLP Member; David Malcolm Eagle [1957] LLP Member; David Paul Eagles [1965] LLP Member; Mark Russell Andrew Edwards [1981] LLP Member; James Philip Egert [1971] LLP Member; Sarah Victoria Elms [1980] LLP Member; Graham Stewart Elsworth [1960] LLP Member; John Reginald Everingham [1958] LLP Member; Paul Timothy Falvey [1961] LLP Member; Richard John Faulkner [1960] LLP Member; James Patrick Gerard Fearon [1973] LLP Member; Paul Fenner [1969] LLP Member; Keith Ferguson [1960] LLP Member; Ryan Christopher Ewart Ferguson [1981] LLP Member; Timothy Hugh Ferris [1966] LLP Member; Russell Colin Field [1956] LLP Member; Tim David Sproston Foster [1971] LLP Member; Angela Louise Foyle [1963] LLP Member; Adam Richard Frais [1968] LLP Member; Julian Charles Hazelwood Frost [1968] LLP Member; Neil Anthony Robert Fung-On [1974] LLP Member; Ian Gardner [1971] LLP Member; Stuart Gerber [1965] LLP Member

Be Offices Limited
Incorporated: 5 August 2010 *Employees:* 147
Previous: Business Environment Holding Limited
Net Worth: £64,734,256 *Total Assets:* £166,703,312
Registered Office: 10 Queen Street Place, London, EC4R 1AG
Activities: Other business support service activities n.e.c.
Shareholders: David Gary Saul; Simon Michael Rusk
Officers: Andrew Marc Emden [1978] Director/Asset Manager; Nicolas Sean Gandy [1968] Director; Graham Anthony Hefferman [1972] Director; Andrew Issott [1980] Director/Online Marketing Manager; Alan Steven Jacobs [1962] Director; Jayson Jenkins [1965] Director/Chartered Accountant; Simon Michael Rusk [1966] Director; David Gary Saul [1964] Director; Nazia Siddiq [1981] HR Director; Andrew Lawrence Stewart [1961] Director

Beacon Rail Finance (Europe) Limited
Incorporated: 15 April 2013
Net Worth: £6,408,000 *Total Assets:* £865,273,024
Registered Office: Suite 1, 3rd Floor, 11-12 St James's Square, London, SW1Y 4LB
Activities: Renting and leasing of other machinery, equipment and tangible goods n.e.c.
Officers: Theodore Gaffney, Secretary; Michael Raymond Johnson, Secretary; Neil Ivor Bennett [1963] Director/Chief Operating Officer; Theodore James Gaffney [1964] Director/Management [American]; Robert Andrew Hardy [1974] Director/Banking; Richard John Thompson [1975] Director/Chief Investment Officer [American]

Bear Stearns Holdings Limited
Incorporated: 11 January 1989
Net Worth: £217,240,768 *Total Assets:* £217,240,768
Registered Office: 25 Bank Street, Canary Wharf, London, E14 5JP
Activities: Financial intermediation not elsewhere classified
Parent: Bear Stearns UK Holdings Limited
Officers: Mark Steven Allen [1970] Director/Accountant; James Anthony Paul Chatters [1979] Director/Accountant; John Richard Hobson [1973] Director/Accountant

Bear Stearns UK Holdings Limited
Incorporated: 16 August 2000
Net Worth: £259,102,320 *Total Assets:* £259,109,920
Registered Office: 25 Bank Street, Canary Wharf, London, E14 5JP
Activities: Non-trading company
Officers: Mark Steven Allen [1970] Director/Accountant; James Anthony Paul Chatters [1979] Director/Accountant; John Richard Hobson [1973] Director/Accountant

Beaubien Finance Limited
Incorporated: 7 January 2015
Net Worth: £6,380,800,000 *Total Assets:* £10,190,167,040
Registered Office: The Aon Centre, The Leadenhall Building, 122 Leadenhall Street, London, EC3V 4AN
Activities: Activities of other holding companies n.e.c.
Parent: Beaubien UK Finance Limited
Officers: Noel McNulty [1968] Director [Irish]; Denis Regrain [1968] Finance Director [French]

Beaubien UK Finance Limited
Incorporated: 4 August 2015
Net Worth: £5,804,099,584 *Total Assets:* £11,166,404,608
Registered Office: The Aon Centre, The Leadenhall Building, 122 Leadenhall Street, London, EC3V 4AN
Activities: Activities of other holding companies n.e.c.
Parent: AON Global Holdings Limited
Officers: Paul Arthur Hogwood [1949] Director; Gardner Mugashu [1973] Director/Chartered Accountant; Alexander Michael Vickers [1983] Director

Beaufort Dedicated No 2 Limited
Incorporated: 1 October 2001
Net Worth Deficit: £15,748,508 *Total Assets:* £320,003,968
Registered Office: Third Floor, One Minster Court, Mincing Lane, London, EC3R 7AA
Activities: Non-life insurance
Parent: MSP Underwriting Limited
Officers: Paul Simon O'Neill, Secretary; Derek Christopher Eales [1965] Director/Underwriter; Dr Arthur Hoffmann [1967] Director [German]

Beaufort Wind Limited
Incorporated: 26 March 2003
Net Worth Deficit: £86,904,000 *Total Assets:* £171,656,000
Registered Office: c/o Morton Fraser, St Martins House, 16 St Martin's-le-Grand, London, EC1A 4EN
Activities: Production of electricity
Parent: Zephyr Investments Limited
Officers: Katerina Brown [1973] Director/Accountant; David Huw Griffiths [1970] Director; Mark Richard Jones [1966] Director; Andrew William Lee [1957] Director/Energy Finance Professional; Mark Alan Walters [1979] Director/Asset Management

Beazley Furlonge Holdings Limited
Incorporated: 3 August 1993
Net Worth: £236,534,848 *Total Assets:* £240,979,280
Registered Office: Plantation Place South, 60 Great Tower Street, London, EC3R 5AD
Activities: Activities of head offices
Parent: Beazley Group Limited
Officers: Mark Simon Goodman [1963] Director; Christine Paula Oldridge [1966] Director [British/Canadian]

Beazley Group Limited
Incorporated: 3 October 2000
Net Worth: £337,099,808 *Total Assets:* £6,711,261,696
Registered Office: Plantation Place South, 60 Great Tower Street, London, EC3R 5AD
Activities: Life insurance
Parent: Beazley PLC
Officers: Mark Simon Goodman [1963] Director; Edward Joseph McGivney [1967] Director [Irish]; Christine Paula Oldridge [1966] Director [British/Canadian]

Beazley Management Limited
Incorporated: 15 January 2004
Net Worth: £14,000,000 *Total Assets:* £139,600,000
Registered Office: Plantation Place South, 60 Great Tower Street, London, EC3R 5AD
Activities: Non-life insurance
Parent: Beazley Furlonge Holdings Limited
Officers: Martin Lindsay Bride [1963] Finance Director [British/French]; David Andrew Horton [1962] Finance Director; Christine Paula Oldridge [1966] Director [British/Canadian]

Beazley Underwriting Limited
Incorporated: 18 September 2002
Net Worth: £34,500,940 *Total Assets:* £6,304,180,736
Registered Office: Plantation Place South, 60 Great Tower Street, London, EC3R 5AD
Activities: Non-life insurance
Shareholders: Beazley Furlonge Holdings Ltd; Beazley Furlonge Holdings Limited
Officers: Martin Lindsay Bride [1963] Director/Chief Financial Officer [British/French]; Christine Paula Oldridge [1966] Director [British/Canadian]

Bechtel Holdings Limited
Incorporated: 22 May 1991 *Employees:* 1,279
Net Worth Deficit: £238,664,992 *Total Assets:* £398,604,000
Registered Office: 11 Pilgrim Street, London, EC4V 6RN
Activities: Activities of construction holding companies
Officers: Martyn Nicholas Daw, Secretary; Nichola Jeanne Skinner, Secretary; Michael Cleveland Bailey [1958] Director/General Counsel [Canadian]; Catherine Hunt Ryan [1981] Financial Director [American]

Bechtel Limited
Incorporated: 28 March 1952 *Employees:* 743
Net Worth: £74,206,000 *Total Assets:* £151,756,992
Registered Office: 11 Pilgrim Street, London, EC4V 6RN
Activities: Construction of other civil engineering projects n.e.c.
Parent: Bechtel Holdings Limited
Officers: Martyn Nicholas Daw, Secretary; Nichola Jeanne Skinner, Secretary; Mark Ashwin [1965] Director/Manager; Michael Cleveland Bailey [1958] Director/General Manager [Canadian]; Sir David James Scott Cooksey [1940] Director/Businessman/Venture Capitalist; Martyn Nicholas Daw [1966] Director/General Counsel; Paul Humphrey Paterson Gibbs [1968] Director/Regional Manager; Catherine Hunt Ryan [1981] Finance Director [American]; Steven Christopher Kay [1973] Director/Operations Manager

Bedford Estates Bloomsbury Limited
Incorporated: 24 June 2016 *Employees:* 25
Net Worth: £158,037,728 *Total Assets:* £249,090,080
Registered Office: 29a Montague Street, London, WC1B 5BL
Activities: Other letting and operating of own or leased real estate
Shareholders: James Fitzroy Dean; Robert Bernard Waley-Cohen; Edmond Conolly Mahony; Charles William Cayzer
Officers: Kevin Leslie Shurrock, Secretary; Andrew Bedford [1962] Director/Bloodstock Auctioneer; Charles William Cayzer [1957] Director; Simon Richard Elmer [1964] Director/London Estate Steward; Paul Vere Lindon [1962] Director/Land Agent; Nigel Keith Ross [1951] Director/Property Developer; Lord James Edward Herbrand Russell [1975] Director/Investment Capitalist

Bedford Estates London Estates LLP
Incorporated: 1 March 2013 *Employees:* 25
Net Worth: £159,367,744 *Total Assets:* £250,849,664
Registered Office: 29a Montague Street, London, WC1B 5BL
Officers: The Honourable Charles William Cayzer [1957] Member; James Fitzroy Dean [1954] Member; Edmond Conolly Mahony [1960] Member; Robert Bernard Waley-Cohen [1948] Member

Beefeater Gin Limited
Incorporated: 28 January 2002
Net Worth: £730,520,384 *Total Assets:* £730,520,384
Registered Office: Chivas House, 72 Chancellors Road, London, W6 9RS
Activities: Activities of head offices
Parent: Optisure Limited
Officers: Stuart MacNab [1964] Director/Accountant; Vincent Turpin [1978] Director/Chief Financial Officer [French]

Bein IP Limited
Incorporated: 23 May 2014 *Employees:* 19
Net Worth: £1,266,830 *Total Assets:* £1,227,884,032
Registered Office: 25 Old Burlington Street, London, W1S 3AN
Activities: Television programme distribution activities
Parent: Bein IH Limited
Officers: Nasser Ghanim a Al Khelaifi [1973] Director/Chairman and CEO of beIN Media Group [Qatari]; Yousif Mohammed H a Al-Obaidli [1980] Director/Deputy CEO of beIN Media Group [Qatari]; Sophie Claude Lorraine Jordan [1966] Director [French]; Daniel James Markham [1973] Director; Tareq Darwish a M Zainal [1979] Director [Qatari]

Belgrave Square
Incorporated: 6 June 1996
Net Worth: £1,222,000 *Total Assets:* £186,160,992
Registered Office: Sea Containers House, 18 Upper Ground, London, SE1 9GL
Activities: Other business support service activities n.e.c.
Parent: WPP Group Holdings Limited
Officers: Charles Ward Van Der Welle [1959] Director/Group Treasurer; Steve Richard Winters [1968] Director/Chartered Accountant

Belmond Dollar Treasury Limited
Incorporated: 12 March 2014
Net Worth: £106,002,456 *Total Assets:* £254,479,024
Registered Office: Shackleton House, 4 Battle Bridge Lane, London, SE1 2HP
Activities: Financial management
Parent: Belmond Finance Services Limited
Officers: Martin O'Grady, Secretary; Abigail Jill Hunt [1974] Director/Solicitor; Martin O'Grady [1963] Director/VP & Chief Financial Officer

Belmond Finance Services Limited
Incorporated: 20 November 2013
Net Worth: £777,149,888 *Total Assets:* £808,343,744
Registered Office: Shackleton House, 4 Battle Bridge Lane, London, SE1 2HP
Activities: Travel agency activities
Parent: Belmond Interfin Limited
Officers: Abigail Jill Hunt [1974] Director/Solicitor; Martin O'Grady [1963] Director

Belmont Green Funding 1 Limited
Incorporated: 11 July 2016
Net Worth Deficit: £3,280,674 *Total Assets:* £100,781,344
Registered Office: 35 Great St Helen's, London, EC3A 6AP
Activities: Activities of mortgage finance companies
Parent: Belmont Green Funding 1 Holdings Limited
Officers: Adrian Scragg [1976] Director; Helena Paivi Whitaker [1963] Director/Chartered Secretary [Finnish]

Belmont Green Funding 3 Limited
Incorporated: 11 July 2016
Net Worth Deficit: £1,171,767 *Total Assets:* £126,401,728
Registered Office: 35 Great St Helen's, London, EC3A 6AP
Activities: Activities of mortgage finance companies
Parent: Belmont Green Funding 3 Holdings Limited
Officers: Adrian Scragg [1976] Director; Helena Paivi Whitaker [1963] Director/Chartered Secretary [Finnish]

The Belvedere Realty Investments Limited
Incorporated: 4 December 2000 *Employees:* 5
Net Worth: £123,291,912 *Total Assets:* £149,146,544
Registered Office: The Belvedere, 2 Back Lane, London, NW3 1HL
Activities: Other letting and operating of own or leased real estate
Officers: Ruth Mowlem, Secretary; Ruth Mowlem [1967] Director/Certified Chartered Accountant; Pamela Amanda Roditi [1953] Director/Art Historian; Spencer Nicholas Roditi [1945] Director/Investment Advisor; John Clive Viscount Mackintosh of Halifax [1958] Director/Chartered Accountant

Bendler Investments II Ltd
Incorporated: 7 May 1999 *Employees:* 4
Previous: Bendler Investment II Ltd
Net Worth: £433,313,984 *Total Assets:* £774,318,016
Registered Office: 21 Holborn Viaduct, London, EC1A 2DY
Activities: Other business support service activities n.e.c.
Parent: Pepsico, Inc.
Officers: Domenico Latronico [1969] Director/Team Leader [Italian]; Geoffrey Denis Luc Picrit [1978] Director/Finance Manager [Belgian]; Patrick Leonardus Cornelis Van Denzen [1971] Deputy Managing Director [Dutch]

Benesco Charity Limited
Incorporated: 18 February 1970
Net Worth: £220,600,352 *Total Assets:* £232,532,992
Registered Office: 150 Aldersgate Street, London, EC1A 4AB
Activities: Other social work activities without accommodation n.e.c.
Officers: Michael Morris Franks, Secretary; Jonathan Ragol-Levy [1954] Director/Bank Manager; Andrew Daniel Wolfson [1969] Director; David Wolfson [1968] Director/Queens Counsel; Lord David Wolfson of Sunningdale [1935] Director

Benton Finance Limited
Incorporated: 16 March 2015
Net Worth: £1,463,915,520 *Total Assets:* £2,185,212,672
Registered Office: The Aon Centre, The Leadenhall Building, 122 Leadenhall Street, London, EC3V 4AN
Activities: Activities of other holding companies n.e.c.
Parent: AON Overseas Holdings Limited
Officers: Noel McNulty [1968] Director [Irish]; Denis Regrain [1968] Finance Director [French]

The Berkeley Hotel Limited
Incorporated: 12 November 1998 *Employees:* 425
Net Worth: £56,224,000 *Total Assets:* £325,016,000
Registered Office: 41-43 Brook Street, Mayfair, London, W1K 4HJ
Activities: Hotels and similar accommodation
Parent: Selene Midco Limited
Officers: Fady Bakhos [1971] Director/Legal Counsel [French]; Liam Cunningham [1958] Director [Irish]

Berkley Estates London Limited
Incorporated: 11 December 1991 *Employees:* 34
Net Worth: £917,086 *Total Assets:* £668,023,168
Registered Office: 55 Baker Street, London, W1U 7EU
Activities: Development of building projects
Major Shareholder: Christopher George White
Officers: Cheryl Frances Moharm, Secretary; Thomas Richard Betts [1966] Director/Real Estate Finance; Mark Simon Kingston [1965] Director/Real Estate Professional; Cheryl Frances Moharm [1958] Director/Company Secretary; Steven Mark Pope [1965] Director/Chartered Surveyor; Simon Levick Garth Wilson [1974] Director/Accountant; Eddie Zakay [1950] Director; Sol Zakay [1952] Director

W. R. Berkley London Holdings, Limited
Incorporated: 3 February 2003
Net Worth: £129,274,000 *Total Assets:* £129,274,000
Registered Office: 14th Floor, 52 Lime Street, London, EC3M 7AF
Activities: Activities of head offices
Parent: W. R. Berkley Syndicate Holdings Limited
Officers: Ira Seth Lederman, Secretary [American]; William Robert Jr Berkley [1945] Director/Chairman & Chief Executive Officer [American]; William Robert Berkley Jr [1972] Director [American]; Ira Seth Lederman [1953] Director and Secretary [American]

Berkshire Hathaway International Insurance Limited
Incorporated: 26 July 1996 *Employees:* 21
Net Worth: £384,628,992 *Total Assets:* £1,995,023,744
Registered Office: 4th Floor, 8 Fenchurch Place, London, EC3M 4AJ
Activities: Non-life insurance
Officers: Howard Alexander Kaye, Secretary; Christopher John Colahan [1981] Director [Australian]; Andrew Michael D'Arcy [1983] Director [Irish]; Guy Edward Finney [1966] Director/Chartered Accountant; Robert Anthony Love [1971] Director/Chief Executive Officer; Stephen Andrew Michael [1961] Director/Certified Chartered Accountant; John Frederick Powell [1944] Director/Solicitor; Michael Martin Steel [1967] Director

Sanford C. Bernstein Limited
Incorporated: 20 April 1999 *Employees:* 158
Net Worth: £37,761,736 *Total Assets:* £604,549,184
Registered Office: 50 Berkeley Street, London, W1J 8SB
Activities: Security and commodity contracts dealing activities
Parent: AllianceBernstein Holding L.P.
Officers: Tobias Mathew Bayliss [1973] Director; Surendran Chellappah [1967] Director; Marie-Jose Elisabeth Freier de Amarins [1981] Director/Head of UK Sales and Product Manager [German]; Daniel Gordon [1970] Director/Head of International Trading; Denise Marie Keen [1970] Director/Head of Operations, Europe & Asia; Sebastian Henry Charles Lewis [1976] Director of European Research; John Richmond McConnell [1965] Senior VP/Managing Director of Institutional Sales; Dipak Mistry [1963] Director/Head of IT, Europe & Asia; Alexandra Paola Perricone [1965] Director/Talent Management & Recruitment [Italian]; Robert Pieter Van Brugge [1968] Director [Dutch]

Berrington UK
Incorporated: 28 March 1996
Net Worth: £875,406,976 *Total Assets:* £1,264,963,968
Registered Office: 13th Floor, 5 Aldermanbury Square, London, EC2V 7HR
Activities: Other business support service activities n.e.c.
Parent: ITW UK
Officers: Ryan Ronald Dale, Secretary; Giles Matthew Hudson [1972] Director/Chartered Accountant; Stephen James Rowell [1967] Director of International Corporate Finance

Berry Bros. & Rudd Limited
Incorporated: 24 June 2005 *Employees:* 378
Net Worth: £122,139,000 *Total Assets:* £307,287,008
Registered Office: 3 St James's Street, London, SW1A 1EG
Activities: Activities of head offices
Shareholders: John Randall Rudd; Richard Michael Moyse
Officers: Janet Ann Impey, Secretary; George Roderick D'Anyers Willis [1980] Creative Director; Emma Louise Fox [1968] Director; Richard Reid [1956] Director; Christopher John Robinson [1969] Director/Chief Financial Officer; Edward John Rudd [1971] Director/Accountant; Elizabeth Margaret Rudd [1966] Director; Matthew James Wright [1963] Director

Bertelsmann UK Limited
Incorporated: 12 April 1996
Net Worth: £1,075,581,056 *Total Assets:* £1,523,984,000
Registered Office: One Fleet Place, London, EC4M 7WS
Activities: Activities of head offices
Officers: Michael Beisheim [1964] Director/Diplom-Finanzwirt [German]; Mark William Gardiner [1961] Director; Robert Raymond Grant [1968] Director/Chartered Accountant

Besso Insurance Group Limited
Incorporated: 13 April 1994 *Employees:* 244
Net Worth: £9,259,669 *Total Assets:* £111,030,632
Registered Office: One Churchill Place, Canary Wharf, London, E14 5RD
Activities: Activities of head offices
Parent: Tower Bridge (One) Limited
Officers: David Jonathan Field, Secretary; Colin George Bird [1946] Director/Insurance Broker; Roderick Rudd Caxton-Spencer [1959] Director/Insurance Broker; Robert William Dowman [1973] Director/Insurance Broker; Howard Warner Green [1946] Director/Insurance Broker; Stephen Paul Greene [1948] Director; Samantha Jane Hovey [1970] Director/Chartered Accountant; Anthony Philip Hulse [1952] Director/Chartered Accountant; James Richard Lightbourne [1970] Director; Shaun David Lynn [1962] Director; Russell Brent Nichols [1966] Director/Insurance Broker; Robert Brian Stevens [1962] Director/Risk Officer; Sean Anthony Windeatt [1973] Director

Best Buy China UK, LLP
Incorporated: 6 May 2008
Net Worth: £623,003,008 *Total Assets:* £623,003,008
Registered Office: 100 New Bridge Street, London, EC4V 6JA

Best Buy Distributions Limited
Incorporated: 25 April 2008
Net Worth Deficit: £84,958,544 *Total Assets:* £262,927,024
Registered Office: 100 New Bridge Street, London, EC4V 6JA
Activities: Activities of head offices
Parent: Best Buy Co., Inc
Officers: Jodie Hagstrom Crist, Secretary; Todd Gregory Hartman, Secretary; Keith Nelsen [1963] Director/Business Executive [American]; Mathew Raymond Watson [1970] Director/VP Finance Controller [American]

Bestway (Holdings) Limited
Incorporated: 6 October 1978 *Employees:* 25,122
Net Worth: £1,319,102,976 *Total Assets:* £16,662,303,744
Registered Office: 2 Abbey Road, Park Royal, London, NW10 7BW
Activities: Non-specialised wholesale of food, beverages and tobacco
Parent: Bestway Group Limited
Officers: Rabiah Younus Sheikh, Secretary; Haider Zameer Choudrey [1987] Director/Chartered Accountant [British/Pakistani]; Zameer Mohammed Choudrey [1958] Director; Dawood Pervez [1975] Director/Solicitor; Sir Mohammed Anwar Pervez [1935] Director; Rizwan Pervez [1968] Director [British/Pakistani]; Mohammed Younus Sheikh [1946] Director

Bestway Northern Limited
Incorporated: 7 January 1992 *Employees:* 779
Net Worth: £188,051,008 *Total Assets:* £267,483,008
Registered Office: 2 Abbey Road, Park Royal, London, NW10 7BW
Activities: Non-specialised wholesale of food, beverages and tobacco
Parent: Bestway (Holdings) Limited
Officers: Dawood Pervez, Secretary/Solicitor; Zameer Mohammed Choudrey [1958] Director; Naser Janjua Khan [1970] Finance Director; Dawood Pervez [1975] Director/Solicitor; Sir Mohammed Anwar Pervez [1935] Director; Rizwan Pervez [1968] Director [British/Pakistani]; Mohammed Younus Sheikh [1946] Director

Bestway Securities Limited
Incorporated: 27 June 2014 *Employees:* 11,028
Net Worth: £280,896,000 *Total Assets:* £1,424,306,048
Registered Office: 2 Abbey Road, Park Royal, London, NW10 7BW
Activities: Activities of head offices
Parent: Bestway (Holdings) Limited
Officers: Rabiah Younus Sheikh, Secretary; Haider Zameer Choudrey [1987] Director/Chartered Accountant [British/Pakistani]; Zameer Mohammed Choudrey [1958] Director; Naser Janjua Khan [1970] Finance Director; Dawood Pervez [1975] Director; Rizwan Pervez [1968] Director [British/Pakistani]; Mohammed Younus Sheikh [1946] Managing Director

Bestway UK Holdco Limited
Incorporated: 27 June 2014
Net Worth: £185,079,008 *Total Assets:* £1,165,021,056
Registered Office: 2 Abbey Road, Park Royal, London, NW10 7BW
Activities: Activities of head offices
Parent: Bestway Securities Limited
Officers: Rabiah Younus Sheikh, Secretary; Haider Zameer Choudrey [1987] Director/Chartered Accountant [British/Pakistani]; Zameer Mohammed Choudrey [1958] Director; Naser Janjua Khan [1970] Finance Director; Dawood Pervez [1975] Director; Rizwan Pervez [1968] Director [British/Pakistani]; Mohammed Younus Sheikh [1946] Managing Director

Bestway Wholesale Limited
Incorporated: 11 April 1975 *Employees:* 3,706
Previous: Bestway Cash & Carry Limited
Net Worth: £88,162,000 *Total Assets:* £654,392,000
Registered Office: 2 Abbey Road, London, NW10 7BW
Activities: Non-specialised wholesale of food, beverages and tobacco
Parent: Bestway UK Holdco Limited
Officers: Dawood Pervez, Secretary/Solicitor; Zameer Mohammed Choudrey [1958] Director; Naser Janjua Khan [1970] Director/Chartered Accountant; Dawood Pervez [1975] Director/Solicitor; Rizwan Pervez [1968] Director [British/Pakistani]; Mohammed Younus Sheikh [1946] Director

Beta Centauri Limited
Incorporated: 22 May 2015 *Employees:* 2
Net Worth: £1,418,284,032 *Total Assets:* £2,525,975,040
Registered Office: Berkeley House, 304 Regents Park Road, London, N3 2JY
Activities: Buying and selling of own real estate
Officers: Paul Hallam, Secretary; Christopher Charles McGill [1960] Managing Director; William Kenneth Procter [1953] Director/Accountant

Beta Central Profits Limited
Incorporated: 29 June 2007 *Employees:* 7
Net Worth: £338,427,008 *Total Assets:* £339,535,008
Registered Office: 3 More London Riverside, London, SE1 2AQ
Activities: Activities of head offices
Parent: PAH Gas Infrastructure Limited
Officers: Loi Shun Chan [1962] Director [Chinese]; Guy Butterworth Ellis [1961] Director; Mark John Horsley [1959] Director/Chief Executive Officer; Jonathan Theodore Miller [1971] Director; Richard John Roberts [1964] Director/Chartered Accountant (Retired); Charles Chao Chung Tsai [1957] Director/General Manager [Canadian]; Chi Tin Wan [1950] Director [Australian]

Beta Holdings Limited
Incorporated: 3 March 2006
Net Worth: £2,063,040,000 *Total Assets:* £2,063,187,968
Registered Office: No 2 St James's Market, London, SW1Y 4AH
Activities: Activities of other holding companies n.e.c.
Parent: Alpha Prema UK Limited
Officers: Duncan Francis Llowarch [1968] Director/Accountant; Sacha Jane Woodward Hill [1969] Director/Lawyer

Betelgeuse Limited
Incorporated: 22 May 2015 *Employees:* 2
Net Worth: £1,418,284,032 *Total Assets:* £2,525,975,040
Registered Office: Berkeley House, 304 Regents Park Road, London, N3 2JY
Activities: Buying and selling of own real estate
Parent: Beta Centauri Limited
Officers: Paul Hallam, Secretary; Christopher Charles McGill [1960] Managing Director; William Kenneth Procter [1953] Director/Accountant

Betfair Group Limited
Incorporated: 31 January 2008
Previous: Betfair Group PLC
Net Worth: £1,094,590,976 *Total Assets:* £1,094,590,976
Registered Office: Waterfront, Hammersmith Embankment, Chancellors Road, access on Winslow Road, London, W6 9HP
Activities: Other information technology service activities
Parent: Paddy Power Betfair Public Limited Company
Officers: Pritti Patel, Secretary; Jeremy Peter Jackson [1975] Director; Edward Martin Traynor [1977] Director/General Counsel [Irish]

Betfair Limited
Incorporated: 28 May 2004 *Employees:* 521
Net Worth Deficit: £33,202,000 *Total Assets:* £337,767,008
Registered Office: Waterfront, Hammersmith Embankment, Chancellors Road, access on Winslow Road, London, W6 9HP
Activities: Gambling and betting activities
Parent: The Sporting Exchange Limited
Officers: Pritti Patel, Secretary; Recep Ozcan [1974] Director/Head of Legal; Philip Scott [1983] Director/Head of Commercial Finance

Betjeman Holdings JVCO Limited
Incorporated: 5 July 2017 *Employees:* 45
Net Worth: £180,800,000 *Total Assets:* £4,766,799,872
Registered Office: 5th Floor, Kings Place, 90 York Way, London, N1 9AG
Activities: Activities of other holding companies n.e.c.
Shareholders: Infrastructure Investments Betjeman Limited; Agincourt (1) LLP; Equitix HS1 Holdings 1 Limited
Officers: Lucy Ann Clark-Bodicoat, Secretary; Sion Laurence Jones [1974] Director; Amanda Vanderneth Leness [1967] Director [American]; Keith Lawrence Ludeman [1950] Director; Andrew Christopher Pitt [1959] Transport Director; Scott Springett [1968] Director/Asset Manager; Mark Richard Woodhams [1966] Director/Financier

Betjeman Holdings Limited
Incorporated: 5 July 2017 *Employees:* 45
Net Worth: £180,800,000 *Total Assets:* £4,766,799,872
Registered Office: 5th Floor, Kings Place, 90 York Way, London, N1 9AG
Activities: Activities of other holding companies n.e.c.
Parent: Betjeman Holdings Midco Limited
Officers: Lucy Ann Clarke-Bodicoat, Secretary; Sion Laurence Jones [1974] Director; Amanda Vanderneth Leness [1967] Director [American]; Keith Lawrence Ludeman [1950] Director; Andrew Christopher Pitt [1959] Transport Director; Scott Springett [1968] Director/Asset Manager; Mark Richard Woodhams [1966] Director/Financier

Betjeman Holdings Midco Limited
Incorporated: 5 July 2017
Net Worth: £330,000,000 *Total Assets:* £920,000,000
Registered Office: 5th Floor, Kings Place, 90 York Way, London, N1 9AG
Activities: Activities of other holding companies n.e.c.
Parent: Betjeman Holdings JVCO Limited
Officers: Lucy Ann Clarke-Bodicoat, Secretary; Sion Laurence Jones [1974] Director; Amanda Vanderneth Leness [1967] Director [American]; Keith Lawrence Ludeman [1950] Director; Andrew Christopher Pitt [1959] Transport Director; Scott Springett [1968] Director/Asset Manager; Mark Richard Woodhams [1966] Director/Financier

Better Properties Limited
Incorporated: 24 July 1987 *Employees:* 15
Net Worth: £56,085,832 *Total Assets:* £258,540,416
Registered Office: New Burlington House, 1075 Finchley Road, London, NW11 0PU
Activities: Buying and selling of own real estate
Parent: The Development and Property Holding Company Limited
Officers: Baila Rochel Englander, Secretary; Sarah Englander, Secretary; Joseph Leib Weiss, Secretary; Eliasz Englander [1932] Director; Sarah Englander [1932] Director; Shulem Zvi Englander [1960] Director; Hannah Zelda Weiss [1954] Director

Beverage Services Limited
Incorporated: 10 November 1986 *Employees:* 201
Net Worth: £128,776,136 *Total Assets:* £170,562,224
Registered Office: 1a Wimpole Street, London, W1G 0EA
Activities: Other business support service activities n.e.c.
Parent: Coca-Cola Holdings (United Kingdom) Limited
Officers: Ingrid Natalie Cope [1972] Director/Solicitor; Scott Edward Roche [1964] Finance Director [Canadian]; Ruben Christiaan Stephaan Rutten [1977] Finance Director [Belgian]; Margaret Ann Stewart [1972] HR Director [Irish]; Jonathan Mark Woods [1968] Director/Franchise Operations Manager

BF Properties (No.4) Ltd
Incorporated: 26 October 2004
Net Worth: £139,586,112 *Total Assets:* £520,585,440
Registered Office: York House, 45 Seymour Street, London, W1H 7LX
Activities: Development of building projects
Parent: BL Department Stores Holding Company Limited
Officers: Bryan Lewis [1967] Director/Chartered Surveyor; Timothy Andrew Roberts [1964] Director/Chartered Surveyor

BF Properties (No.5) Ltd
Incorporated: 26 October 2004
Net Worth: £354,748,800 *Total Assets:* £735,228,352
Registered Office: York House, 45 Seymour Street, London, W1H 7LX
Activities: Development of building projects
Parent: BF Properties (No 4) Limited
Officers: Bryan Lewis [1967] Director/Chartered Surveyor; Timothy Andrew Roberts [1964] Director/Chartered Surveyor

BG Atlantic Finance Limited
Incorporated: 13 March 2000
Net Worth: £1,334,979,072 *Total Assets:* £1,361,799,936
Registered Office: Shell Centre, London, SE1 7NA
Activities: Financial intermediation not elsewhere classified
Parent: BG North Sea Holdings Limited
Officers: David Nicholas Gardner [1978] Director/Oil Company Executive; Lindsey Jane Ritchie [1972] Director/Tax Advisor

BG Delta Limited
Incorporated: 19 September 1996
Net Worth: £1,043,341,312 *Total Assets:* £1,417,797,632
Registered Office: Shell Centre, London, SE1 7NA
Activities: Support activities for petroleum and natural gas mining
Parent: BG International Limited
Officers: Gasser Hanter [1968] Director/Engineer [Egyptian]; Nicholas Martin Humphrey [1972] Director/Oil Company Executive; Moira Tighe [1967] Director/Planning Manager, Exploration

BG Energy Capital PLC
Incorporated: 23 May 2001
Net Worth: £34,843,692 *Total Assets:* £7,090,577,920
Registered Office: Shell Centre, London, SE1 7NA
Activities: Other business support service activities n.e.c.
Parent: BG Energy Holdings Limited
Officers: Michael John Ashworth [1961] Director/Oil Company Executive; Frances Hinden [1968] Director/Oil Company Executive; Michael Harvey Pearman [1977] Director/Oil Company Executive; Kathryn Sheena Taylor [1968] Director/Funding and Investment Manager

BG Energy Holdings Limited
Incorporated: 28 April 1999
Net Worth: £13,381,035,008 *Total Assets:* £35,939,594,240
Registered Office: Shell Centre, London, SE1 7NA
Activities: Activities of head offices
Parent: BG Group Limited
Officers: Jeffrey Graham Connell [1973] Director/Oil Company Executive; Michael James Dawson [1980] Director/Assistant Treasurer; Frances Hinden [1968] Director/Oil Company Executive; Kate Jackson [1973] Director; Russell Leslie O'Brien [1974] Director/Oil Company Executive

BG Gas Marketing Ltd
Incorporated: 4 July 2001
Net Worth Deficit: £61,661,028 *Total Assets:* £267,350,816
Registered Office: Shell Centre, London, SE1 7NA
Activities: Sea and coastal freight water transport
Parent: BG LNG Investments Limited
Officers: Saheera Binti Ahmad [1976] Director/Oil Company Executive; Stefan Andrew Strausfeld-Perry [1985] Director/Oil Company Executive; Thomas Henry Summers [1978] Director LNG Supply & Commercial Operations

BG Gas Supply (UK) Limited
Incorporated: 8 June 1999
Net Worth Deficit: £296,793,472 *Total Assets:* £1,024,257,920
Registered Office: Shell Centre, London, SE1 7NA
Activities: Other business support service activities n.e.c.
Parent: BG UK Holdings Limited
Officers: Michael John Ashworth [1961] Director/Oil Company Executive

BG General Holdings Limited
Incorporated: 18 August 1999
Net Worth: £1,402,667,648 *Total Assets:* £1,413,924,992
Registered Office: Shell Centre, London, SE1 7NA
Activities: Activities of head offices
Parent: BG Overseas Holdings Limited
Officers: Gary James Archibald [1963] Director/Oil Company Executive; Philip Christopher Dalton [1972] Director/Assistant Treasurer; Grace Siew Hua Lim [1971] Director/Oil Company Executive [Malaysian]

BG Global Energy Limited
Incorporated: 25 November 1976
Net Worth: £802,401,984 *Total Assets:* £2,625,355,008
Registered Office: Shell Centre, London, SE1 7NA
Activities: Extraction of crude petroleum
Parent: BG LNG Trading, LLC
Officers: Saheera Binti Ahmad [1976] Director/Oil Company Executive; Marianne Wold Eide [1969] Director/Vice President [Norwegian]; Stephen James Hill [1969] Director/President - BG LNG Trading LLC; Jeroen Huijsmans [1972] Director/Oil Company Executive [Dutch]; Howard Edwin Jones [1978] Director/Oil Company Executive; Thomas Henry Summers [1978] Director LNG Supply & Commercial Operations

BG Great Britain Limited
Incorporated: 23 June 1967
Net Worth Deficit: £66,170,000 *Total Assets:* £119,328,000
Registered Office: Shell Centre, London, SE1 7NA
Activities: Extraction of crude petroleum
Parent: BG Energy Holdings Limited
Officers: Marianne Wold Eide [1969] Director/Vice President [Norwegian]; Howard Edwin Jones [1978] Director/Oil Company Executive; Shannon Lorraine Ouellette [1969] Director/Oil Company Executive [Canadian]

BG Group Limited
Incorporated: 30 December 1998
Previous: BG Group PLC
Net Worth: £6,747,923,968 *Total Assets:* £7,313,903,616
Registered Office: Shell Centre, London, SE1 7NA
Activities: Extraction of crude petroleum
Parent: Shell Petroleum N.V.
Officers: Michael John Ashworth [1961] Director/Oil Company Executive; Alan Daniel McLean [1966] Director/Oil Company Executive; Russell Leslie O'Brien [1974] Director/Oil Company Executive

BG International Limited
Incorporated: 30 March 1967 *Employees:* 122
Net Worth: £1,059,000,000 *Total Assets:* £5,517,000,192
Registered Office: Shell Centre, London, SE1 7NA
Activities: Extraction of crude petroleum
Parent: BG Energy Holdings Limited
Officers: Martinus Jacobus Ten Brink [1960] Director/Oil Company Executive [Dutch]; Simon Alan Constant-Glemas [1969] Director/Oil Company Executive; Nicholas Martin Humphrey [1972] Director/Oil Company Executive; Sinead Caitlin Lynch [1971] Director/Oil Company Executive [Irish]; Alan Daniel McLean [1966] Director/Oil Company Executive; Russell Leslie O'Brien [1974] Director/Oil Company Executive; Steven Robert Phimister [1969] Director/Oil Company Executive

BG Karachaganak Limited
Incorporated: 18 December 1996
Net Worth: £1,664,473,216 *Total Assets:* £2,151,838,720
Registered Office: Shell Centre, London, SE1 7NA
Activities: Extraction of crude petroleum
Parent: BG International Limited
Officers: Deepak Khosla [1970] Director/Chartered Accountant; Olivier Marie Charles Lazare [1960] Director/Oil Company Executive [French]; Manavala Kalyana Sundaram [1972] Director/Business Treasurer Trading and Supply [Indian]

BG LNG Investments Limited
Incorporated: 26 June 2009
Net Worth: £22,511,536 *Total Assets:* £179,831,584
Registered Office: Shell Centre, London, SE1 7NA
Activities: Extraction of natural gas
Parent: BG Energy Iberian Holdings S.L.
Officers: Saheera Binti Ahmad [1976] Director/Oil Company Executive; Thomas Henry Summers [1978] Director LNG Supply & Commercial Operations

BG Netherlands
Incorporated: 16 February 2006
Net Worth: £950,393,024 *Total Assets:* £955,337,024
Registered Office: Shell Centre, London, SE1 7NA
Activities: Other business support service activities n.e.c.
Parent: BG Gas Netherlands Holdings B.V.
Officers: Rodrigo Marcio Fraga [1970] Director/Oil Company Executive; David Nicholas Gardner [1978] Director/Oil Company Executive

BG Netherlands Financing Unlimited
Incorporated: 21 October 2014
Net Worth: £423,835,680 *Total Assets:* £425,758,080
Registered Office: Shell Centre, London, SE1 7NA
Activities: Other business support service activities n.e.c.
Parent: BG Gas Brazil Holdings B.V.
Officers: David Nicholas Gardner [1978] Director/Oil Company Executive; Michael Harvey Pearman [1977] Director/Oil Company Executive; David Andrew Warrilow [1969] Director/Chartered Accountant

BG North Sea Holdings Limited
Incorporated: 15 May 1989
Net Worth: £4,539,942,400 *Total Assets:* £4,567,176,192
Registered Office: Shell Centre, London, SE1 7NA
Activities: Extraction of crude petroleum
Parent: BG Energy Holdings Limited
Officers: Gary James Archibald [1963] Director/Oil Company Executive; Philip Christopher Dalton [1972] Director/Assistant Treasurer; Marianne Wold Eide [1969] Director/Oil Company Executive [Norwegian]; Howard Edwin Jones [1978] Director/Oil Company Executive; Shannon Lorraine Ouellette [1969] Director/Oil Company Executive [Canadian]

BG Overseas Holdings Limited
Incorporated: 22 December 1987
Net Worth: £10,120,612,864 *Total Assets:* £13,725,650,944
Registered Office: Shell Centre, London, SE1 7NA
Activities: Activities of head offices
Parent: BG UK Holdings Limited
Officers: David Nicholas Gardner [1978] Director/Oil Company Executive; Steven Robert Phimister [1969] Director/Oil Company Executive; Lindsey Jane Ritchie [1972] Director/Tax Advisor; Erica Jane Smart [1961] Director/Chief Developments Manager; David Andrew Warrilow [1969] Director/Chartered Accountant

BG Overseas Investments Limited
Incorporated: 1 December 1993
Net Worth: £760,928,000 *Total Assets:* £760,928,000
Registered Office: Shell Centre, London, SE1 7NA
Activities: Activities of head offices
Parent: BG Energy Holdings Limited
Officers: Gary James Archibald [1963] Director/Oil Company Executive; Grace Siew Hua Lim [1971] Director/Oil Company Executive [Malaysian]; David Andrew Warrilow [1969] Director/Chartered Accountant

BG Overseas Limited
Incorporated: 7 November 2013
Net Worth: £180,809,792 *Total Assets:* £181,099,808
Registered Office: Shell Centre, London, SE1 7NA
Activities: Support activities for petroleum and natural gas mining
Parent: BG Gas Netherlands Holdings B.V.
Officers: Gary James Archibald [1963] Director/Oil Company Executive; Philip Christopher Dalton [1972] Director/Assistant Treasurer; Grace Siew Hua Lim [1971] Director/Oil Company Executive [Malaysian]

BG Rosetta Limited
Incorporated: 11 August 2004
Net Worth: £226,922,480 *Total Assets:* £420,110,720
Registered Office: Shell Centre, London, SE1 7NA
Activities: Extraction of crude petroleum
Parent: BG Energy Holdings Limited
Officers: Gasser Hanter [1968] Director/Oil Company Executive [Egyptian]

BG Singapore Limited
Incorporated: 13 February 2001
Net Worth: £1,012,183,040 *Total Assets:* £1,014,964,992
Registered Office: Shell Centre, London, SE1 7NA
Activities: Activities of head offices
Parent: BG Gas Supply (UK) Limited
Officers: Gary James Archibald [1963] Director/Oil Company Executive; Grace Siew Hua Lim [1971] Director/Oil Company Executive [Malaysian]; David Andrew Warrilow [1969] Director/Chartered Accountant

BG Trinidad LNG Limited
Incorporated: 15 August 1994
Net Worth: £152,942,176 *Total Assets:* £179,470,160
Registered Office: Shell Centre, London, SE1 7NA
Activities: Extraction of crude petroleum
Parent: BG Energy Holdings Limited
Officers: Nicholas William Hermann Blaker [1975] Director/Tax Manager; Derek Hudson [1956] Director/VP

BG UK Holdings Limited
Incorporated: 29 September 1986
Net Worth: £6,160,477,696 *Total Assets:* £7,408,128,512
Registered Office: Shell Centre, London, SE1 7NA
Activities: Activities of head offices
Parent: BG Energy Holdings Limited
Officers: Gary James Archibald [1963] Director/Oil Company Executive; Grace Siew Hua Lim [1971] Director/Oil Company Executive [Malaysian]; Lindsey Jane Ritchie [1972] Director/Tax Advisor

BGC Global Limited
Incorporated: 27 July 2000
Net Worth: £532,061,696 *Total Assets:* £789,716,544
Registered Office: One Churchill Place, Canary Wharf, London, E14 5RD
Activities: Non-trading company
Officers: Robert Mark Snelling, Secretary; James Richard Lightbourne [1970] Director/General Counsel; Sean Anthony Windeatt [1973] Director/Chief Operating Officer

BGEO Group Limited
Incorporated: 14 October 2011 *Employees:* 10,038
Previous: BGEO Group PLC
Net Worth: £2,420,602,112 *Total Assets:* £15,168,668,672
Registered Office: 84 Brook Street, London, W1K 5EH
Activities: Activities of financial services holding companies
Parent: Bank of Georgia Group PLC
Officers: Archil Gachechiladze [1979] Director [Georgian]; Venera Suknidze [1979] Director [Georgian]

BGF Group PLC
Incorporated: 7 March 2017 *Employees:* 147
Net Worth: £1,319,411,968 *Total Assets:* £1,339,766,016
Registered Office: 13-15 York Buildings, London, WC2N 6JU
Activities: Fund management activities
Officers: David Robert Murray, Secretary; Alice Mary Cleoniki Avis [1962] Director; James Laurence Chew [1962] Director/Banker; Neil Anthony Johnson [1949] Director; Stuart Christopher Johnstone [1972] Director/Banker; Stephen Thomas Murphy [1956] Director; Diana Georgina Noble [1961] Director; Matthew Robert Reed [1975] Director [Australian]; Sir Anthony Nigel Russell Rudd [1946] Director; Kevin Charles Wall [1958] Director/Banker; Stephen Frank Welton [1961] Director; Adrian Patrick White [1967] Director/Banker

BGL Receivables Financing (1) Limited
Incorporated: 29 January 2016
Net Worth: £1,613 *Total Assets:* £362,109,184
Registered Office: Third Floor, c/o Wilmington Trust SP Services (London) Limited, 1 King's Arms Yard, London, EC2R 7AF
Activities: Other business support service activities n.e.c.
Parent: Wilmington Trust SP Services (London) Limited
Officers: Daniel Jonathan Wynne [1970] Director

BHF Group UK Limited
Incorporated: 30 October 2009
Previous: Kleinwort Benson Group Limited
Net Worth: £330,475,008 *Total Assets:* £352,742,016
Registered Office: One Silk Street, London, EC2Y 8HQ
Activities: Activities of head offices
Shareholder: Philippe Marie Francois Bernard Oddo
Officers: Serge Bunan [1964] Finance Director [French]; Jean Pierre Pinatton [1943] Director [French]

BHP Billiton (UK) Limited
Incorporated: 14 February 1994
Net Worth: £762,583,168 *Total Assets:* £795,286,080
Registered Office: Nova South, 160 Victoria Street, London, SW1E 5LB
Activities: Activities of head offices
Parent: BHP Billiton Group Limited
Officers: Ian Duncan Chisholm [1967] Director/VP Corporate Finance; Vandita Pant [1969] Director/Treasurer; Tzveta Ivanova Tchorbadjieva [1974] Director/Vice President, Acquisitions & Investments

BHP Billiton Group Limited
Incorporated: 6 January 1997
Net Worth: £4,129,966,592 *Total Assets:* £13,768,595,456
Registered Office: Nova South, 160 Victoria Street, London, SW1E 5LB
Activities: Activities of head offices
Parent: BHP Group PLC
Officers: Helen Ratsey, Secretary; Stewart Forster Cox [1968] Director [Australian]; Vandita Pant [1969] Director/Treasurer; Geofrey Peter Stapledon [1967] Director/Vice President Governance

BHP Billiton Holdings Limited
Incorporated: 6 January 1997
Net Worth: £4,482,136,064 *Total Assets:* £5,941,719,552
Registered Office: Nova South, 160 Victoria Street, London, SW1E 5LB
Activities: Activities of head offices
Parent: BHP Group PLC
Officers: Elisa Morniroli [1982] Director/Investor Relations, Vice President EMEA [Italian]; Geofrey Peter Stapledon [1967] Director/Vice President Governance; Tzveta Ivanova Tchorbadjieva [1974] Director/Vice President, Acquisitions & Investments

BHP Billiton Marketing UK Limited
Incorporated: 1 March 2013
Net Worth: £133,048,312 *Total Assets:* £133,068,704
Registered Office: Nova South, 160 Victoria Street, London, SW1E 5LB
Activities: Activities of other holding companies n.e.c.
Shareholder: BHP Billiton Holdings Limited
Officers: Victoria Jane Binns [1964] Director/Vice President, Marketing [Australian]; Stewart Forster Cox [1968] Director/Vice President Treasury Operations [Australian]; Hieronymus Cornelis Lambertus Lemmens [1972] Director/Regional Marketing Manager Coal, EMEA & Americas [Dutch]

BHP Billiton Petroleum Great Britain Limited
Incorporated: 30 June 1964 *Employees:* 6
Net Worth: £2,964,093,952 *Total Assets:* £3,031,198,464
Registered Office: Nova South, 160 Victoria Street, London, SW1E 5LB
Activities: Extraction of crude petroleum
Officers: Sarah Morgan, Secretary; Stewart Forster Cox [1968] Director/Vice President Treasury Operations [Australian]; Vincent Anthony Pereira [1955] Director/General Manager/Vice President [Trinidadian]; Marlon Ramotar Singh [1969] Director/Manager Treasury Operations

BHP Group PLC
Incorporated: 9 May 1996 *Employees:* 27,161
Previous: BHP Billiton PLC
Net Worth: £42,848,776,192 *Total Assets:* £86,321,102,848
Registered Office: Nova South, 160 Victoria Street, London, SW1E 5LB
Activities: Other mining and quarrying n.e.c.
Officers: Rachel Therese Agnew, Secretary; Geofrey Peter Stapledon, Secretary; Margaret Kay Taylor, Secretary; Terrence James Bowen [1966] Director [Australian]; Malcolm William Broomhead [1952] Director [Australian]; Anita Margaret Frew [1957] Director; Carolyn Judith Hewson [1955] Director [Australian]; Andrew Stewart MacKenzie [1956] Director/Chief Executive Officer; Kenneth Norman MacKenzie [1964] Director [Australian/Canadian]; Lindsay Philip Maxsted [1954] Director [Australian]; John Mogford [1953] Director; Baroness Shriti Vadera [1962] Director

Bifurcate Funding Limited
Incorporated: 3 February 2011
Net Worth: £64,853 *Total Assets:* £273,885,696
Registered Office: 6th Floor, 65 Gresham Street, London, EC2V 7NQ
Activities: Other business support service activities n.e.c.
Parent: Link Trust Nominees No.1 Limited
Officers: Sean Peter Martin [1965] Director

Big Box Midco UK Limited
Incorporated: 22 September 2016 *Employees:* 54
Net Worth: £33,547,804 *Total Assets:* £128,050,040
Registered Office: 5th Floor, 6 St Andrew Street, London, EC4A 3AE
Activities: Activities of other holding companies n.e.c.
Parent: TKG-Storagemart Partners UK Limited
Officers: Michael G Burnam [1953] Director/Chief Executive Officer [American]; E Stanley Kroenke [1947] Director/Real Estate [American]; R Otto Maly [1956] Director/Real Estate [American]

Big Bus Tours Group Holdings Limited
Incorporated: 11 February 2015 *Employees:* 1,863
Net Worth Deficit: £28,908,228 *Total Assets:* £391,107,872
Registered Office: 110 Buckingham Palace Road, London, SW1W 9SA
Activities: Activities of other holding companies n.e.c.
Shareholder: Merlin Entertainments Group Holdings Limited
Officers: Timothy Edward Easingwood [1977] Director; James Richard St John Lenane [1972] Director; Alexander de Muschamp Payne [1968] Director/Chief Executive Officer; Patrick William Mark Waterman [1959] Director; Sean Ernest Wilkins [1969] Director/Chief Financial Officer

Big Bus Tours Group Limited
Incorporated: 11 February 2015 *Employees:* 5
Net Worth Deficit: £18,726,520 *Total Assets:* £296,720,064
Registered Office: 110 Buckingham Palace Road, London, SW1W 9SA
Activities: Activities of other holding companies n.e.c.
Parent: Big Bus Tours Holdings 2 Limited
Officers: Timothy Edward Easingwood [1977] Director; James Richard St John Lenane [1972] Director; Alexander de Muschamp Payne [1968] Director/Chief Executive Officer; Patrick William Mark Waterman [1959] Director; Sean Ernest Wilkins [1969] Director/Chief Financial Officer

Big Bus Tours Holdings 1 Limited
Incorporated: 11 February 2015
Net Worth: £12,846,738 *Total Assets:* £218,801,664
Registered Office: 110 Buckingham Palace Road, London, SW1W 9SA
Activities: Activities of other holding companies n.e.c.
Parent: Big Bus Tours Group Holdings Limited
Officers: Timothy Edward Easingwood [1977] Director; James Richard St John Lenane [1972] Director; Alexander de Muschamp Payne [1968] Director/Chief Executive Officer; Patrick William Mark Waterman [1959] Director; Sean Ernest Wilkins [1969] Director/Chief Financial Officer

Big Bus Tours Holdings 2 Limited
Incorporated: 11 February 2015 *Employees:* 1,863
Net Worth Deficit: £47,575,712 *Total Assets:* £336,289,952
Registered Office: 110 Buckingham Palace Road, London, SW1W 9SA
Activities: Activities of other holding companies n.e.c.
Parent: Big Bus Tours Holdings 1 Limited
Officers: Timothy Edward Easingwood [1977] Director; James Richard St John Lenane [1972] Director; Alexander de Muschamp Payne [1968] Director/Chief Executive Officer; Patrick William Mark Waterman [1959] Director; Sean Ernest Wilkins [1969] Director/Chief Financial Officer

Big Bus Tours Limited
Incorporated: 10 February 2011 *Employees:* 43
Net Worth: £154,742,000 *Total Assets:* £301,372,000
Registered Office: 110 Buckingham Palace Road, London, SW1W 9SA
Activities: Other transportation support activities
Parent: Big Bus Tours Group Limited
Officers: Patrick William Mark Waterman [1959] Director; Sean Ernest Wilkins [1969] Director/Chief Financial Officer

BIG Legolas Holdings Limited
Incorporated: 9 November 2016
Net Worth Deficit: £27,649 *Total Assets:* £130,082,000
Registered Office: 3rd Floor, 86 Brook Street, London, W1K 5AY
Activities: Construction of utility projects for electricity and telecommunications
Parent: Bioenergy Infrastructure Finance Limited
Officers: Steven Wim Blase [1966] Director [Dutch]; Max David Charles Helmore [1984] Director/Fund Manager; Stephen Johnson [1960] Director; Robert Hamish McPherson [1976] Director; Ben Wright [1972] Director/Accountant

Big Society Capital Limited
Incorporated: 11 April 2011 *Employees:* 45
Net Worth: £484,424,992 *Total Assets:* £485,216,000
Registered Office: New Fetter Place, 8-10 New Fetter Lane, London, EC4A 1AZ
Activities: Fund management activities
Parent: The Big Society Trust
Officers: Alastair Ian Ballantyne, Secretary; Lesley-Anne Alexander [1959] Director; Kieron John Boyle [1980] Director/Chief Executive, Guy's and St Thomas' Charity; Paola Bergamaschi Broyd [1961] Director [Italian]; Sir Ronald Mourad Cohen [1945] Director; Fiona Mary Ellis [1954] Director/Consultant [Irish]; Stuart Peter John Foster [1973] Managing Director; Christina Margaret McComb [1956] Director; Sir Harvey Andrew McGrath [1952] Director; Clifford James Prior [1957] Director/Chief Executive Officer; Anne Katherine Wade [1972] Non-Executive Director/Trustee [American]; Danielle Jeanine Walker Palmour [1965] Director/Chief Executive Friends Provident Foundation [British/American]; Christopher Robert Wright [1962] Director/Chief Executive

The Big Society Trust
Incorporated: 20 April 2011 *Employees:* 51
Net Worth: £336,968,000 *Total Assets:* £531,660,992
Registered Office: New Fetter Place, 8-10 New Fetter Lane, London, EC4A 1AZ
Activities: Activities of other holding companies n.e.c.
Officers: Alastair Ian Ballantyne, Secretary; Robin Francis Budenberg [1959] Director/Corporate Adviser; Sir Stuart James Etherington [1955] Director/CEO of Charities' Representative Body; Joanna Lisette Fox [1970] Director/Civil Servant; Peter Holbrook [1971] Director/Chief Executive Social Enterprise UK; Stephen Lee Howard [1953] Director/Chief Executive/Lawyer [American/British]; Sir Harvey Andrew McGrath [1952] Director; Nicola Pollock [1955] Director/Charity Chief Executive; Dame Clare Tickell [1958] Director/Chief Executive Officer

BIH Holdings Limited
Incorporated: 28 November 2016
Net Worth: £17,572,878 *Total Assets:* £160,379,744
Registered Office: 3rd Floor, 86 Brook Street, London, W1K 5AY
Activities: Construction of utility projects for electricity and telecommunications
Parent: Bioenergy Infrastructure Finance Limited
Officers: Steven Wim Blase [1968] Director [Dutch]; Max David Charles Helmore [1984] Director/Fund Manager; Stephen Johnson [1960] Director; Robert Hamish McPherson [1976] Director; Ben Wright [1972] Director/Accountant

BIIF Bidco Limited
Incorporated: 23 September 2008
Net Worth Deficit: £427,416,992 *Total Assets:* £1,059,534,016
Registered Office: Cannon Place, 78 Cannon Street, London, EC4N 6AF
Activities: Other business support service activities n.e.c.
Parent: BIIF Parentco Limited
Officers: John Ivor Cavill [1972] Director; James Peter Dawes [1971] Director/Chief Financial Officer

BIIF Holdco III Limited
Incorporated: 27 September 2012
Net Worth: £12,557,041 *Total Assets:* £139,514,128
Registered Office: Cannon Place, 78 Cannon Street, London, EC4N 6AF
Activities: Other business support service activities n.e.c.
Parent: BIIF Bidco Limited
Officers: John Ivor Cavill [1972] Director; James Peter Dawes [1971] Director/Chief Financial Officer

BIIF Holdco Limited
Incorporated: 23 September 2008
Net Worth Deficit: £570,284,032 *Total Assets:* £2,403,419,904
Registered Office: Cannon Place, 78 Cannon Street, London, EC4N 6AF
Activities: Other business support service activities n.e.c.
Parent: BIIF GP Limited
Officers: John Ivor Cavill [1972] Director; James Peter Dawes [1971] Director/Chief Financial Officer

BIIF Issuerco Limited
Incorporated: 13 May 2008
Net Worth Deficit: £33,685,864 *Total Assets:* £648,602,944
Registered Office: Cannon Place, 78 Cannon Street, London, EC4N 6AF
Activities: Other business support service activities n.e.c.
Parent: BIIF Holdco Limited
Officers: John Ivor Cavill [1972] Director; James Peter Dawes [1971] Director/Chief Financial Officer

BIIF Parentco Limited
Incorporated: 23 September 2008
Net Worth: £10,191,204 *Total Assets:* £685,653,696
Registered Office: Cannon Place, 78 Cannon Street, London, EC4N 6AF
Activities: Other business support service activities n.e.c.
Parent: BIIF Issuerco Limited
Officers: John Ivor Cavill [1972] Director; James Peter Dawes [1971] Director/Chief Financial Officer

Biocon Biologics Limited
Incorporated: 2 March 2016 *Employees:* 547
Net Worth: £103,911,688 *Total Assets:* £352,694,368
Registered Office: 16 Great Queen Street, Covent Garden, London, WC2B 5AH
Activities: Activities of other holding companies n.e.c.
Officers: Kiran Mazumdar Shaw [1953] Director [Indian]; John McCallum Marshall Shaw [1949] Director; John Russell Fotheringham Walls [1944] Director

Bioenergy Infrastructure Limited
Incorporated: 24 October 2014 *Employees:* 7
Net Worth: £23,603,080 *Total Assets:* £385,801,664
Registered Office: 3rd Floor, 86 Brook Street, London, W1K 5AY
Activities: Construction of utility projects for electricity and telecommunications
Officers: Steven Wim Blase [1966] Director [Dutch]; Erez Gissin [1958] Director [Israeli]; Max David Charles Helmore [1984] Director/Fund Manager; Stephen Johnson [1960] Director; Andrew Matthews [1962] Director/Fund Manager; Robert Hamish McPherson [1976] Director; Ben Wright [1972] Director/Accountant

Biomed Central Limited
Incorporated: 8 December 1998 *Employees:* 210
Net Worth: £91,257,000 *Total Assets:* £129,479,000
Registered Office: The Campus, 4 Crinan Street, London, N1 9XW
Activities: Publishing of learned journals
Shareholders: Stefan von Holtzbrinck; Stampdew Limited
Officers: Gabrielle Mary Williams Hamer, Secretary; Steven Charles Inchcoombe [1964] Executive Director; Rachel Elizabeth Jacobs [1975] Director/Lawyer; Dr Ulrich Vest [1963] Director [German]; Gabrielle Mary Williams Hamer [1958] Director/Company Secretary

The Biotech Growth Trust PLC
Incorporated: 20 May 1997
Net Worth: £417,396,000 *Total Assets:* £446,073,984
Registered Office: One Wood Street, London, EC2V 7WS
Activities: Activities of investment trusts
Officers: Steven Andrew Ralph Bates [1957] Director/Investment Manager; Professor Dame Kay Elizabeth Davies [1951] Director/University Professor; Geoffrey Che-Chang Hsu [1974] Director/Investment Manager [American]; Andrew Neville Joy [1957] Director/Investment Manager; Julia Le Blan [1954] Director; David Lindsay Willetts [1956] Director/Chair of The Resolution Foundation

Birch Sites Limited
Incorporated: 19 October 2007
Net Worth Deficit: £99,318,000 *Total Assets:* £217,200,000
Registered Office: 1-3 Strand, London, WC2N 5EH
Activities: Development of building projects
Parent: National Grid Commercial Holdings Limited
Officers: Megan Barnes, Secretary; Rukshana Yousuf, Secretary; Richard Alden [1974] Director/Head of Commercial Property, Tax and Treasury; Philip Duncan Edwards [1970] Director/Chartered Surveyor; Prem Kumar Gabbi [1969] Director

Birchgree Limited
Incorporated: 4 June 1981
Net Worth: £1,407,769,984 *Total Assets:* £3,056,826,112
Registered Office: 3rd Floor, One New Change, London, EC4M 9AF
Activities: Activities of other holding companies n.e.c.
Parent: Ladbrokes Coral Group Limited
Officers: Stuart John Smith [1981] Director/Accountant; Charles Alexander Sutters [1980] Director

Bird & Bird LLP
Incorporated: 24 September 2008 *Employees:* 2,005
Net Worth: £96,320,256 *Total Assets:* £202,318,848
Registered Office: 12 New Fetter Lane, London, EC4A 1JP
Officers: Anna Katarina Ahlberg [1963] Member; Christopher Jeremy Richard Barrett [1962] Member; Christian Wolfgang Bartsch [1971] Member; Roger Michael Bickerstaff [1961] Member; Roger Howard Butterworth [1955] Member; Michael David Kerr [1960] Member; Massimiliano Mostardini [1966] Member; Patricia Mary Walsh [1963] Member; Dr Philip Mark Abell [1957] LLP Member; Maroun Abi-Nader [1977] LLP Member; Mikko Kalervo Ahonen [1981] LLP Member; Simon Peter Allport [1966] LLP Member; Michael Oliver Alt [1963] LLP Member; Hermenegildo Altozano Garcia-Figueras [1963] LLP Member; Jose Rivas Andres [1961] LLP Member; Generaldine-Marie Arbant [1974] LLP Member; Nicholas John Aries [1981] LLP Member; Maria Lourdes Ayala Munoz [1972] LLP Member; David Harvey Ayers [1961] LLP Member; Jonathan William Baker [1963] LLP Member; Raquel Ballesteros [1969] LLP Member; Julian Charles Balson [1979] LLP Member; Shane Leslie Barber [1965] LLP Member; Marion Barbier [1958] LLP Member; Dirk Manfred August Barcaba [1966] LLP Member; Vincenzo Baudille [1972] LLP Member; Jan Edvard Berg [1974] LLP Member; David Rowcroft Blnternationaliff [1979] LLP Member; Yves Marie Victor Bizollon [1957] LLP Member; Neil Stuart Peter Blundell [1963] LLP Member; Ruth Jane Boardman [1970] LLP Member; Swee Siang Boey [1970] LLP Member; Matthew James Bonass [1973] LLP Member; Willem Peter Bongaerts [1975] LLP Member; Guido Bormann [1975] LLP Member; Paul Dudley John Briggs [1964] LLP Member; Michael Paul Brown [1966] LLP Member; Peter Robert Brownlow [1966] LLP Member; Benedikt Burger [1969] LLP Member; Jan Byok [1961] LLP Member; Jan Osten Bystrom [1964] LLP Member; Dr Simone Cadeddu [1970] LLP Member; Roberto Paolo Giuseppe Maria Camilli [1966] LLP Member; Adam Carling [1976] LLP Member; Maria Mikaela Antonia Carlsson [1975] LLP Member; Man San Michelle Chan [1971] LLP Member; Ken Cheung [1968] LLP Member; Yu Jin Jonathan Choo [1977] LLP Member; Wen Kwan Chow [1973] LLP Member; Wing on Chui [1959] LLP Member; Ted Kai Tai Chwu [1975] LLP Member; Laurence Christiane Evelyne Clot [1969] LLP Member; Helen Conlan [1977] LLP Member; Edoardo Courir [1962] LLP Member; Dr Alexander Harald Dirk Csaki [1979] LLP Member; Andrew Richard Danson [1978] LLP Member; Sophia Jane Dawson [1970] LLP Member; David Scott Dederick [1962] LLP Member; Isidro Jose Del Moral Gonzalez [1963] LLP Member; Russell Jon Dellar [1968] LLP Member; Nathalie Odette Devernay [1980] LLP Member; Sophie Clemence Gustav Dingenen [1973] LLP Member; Dr Richard Wolfgang Robert Dissmann [1972] LLP Member; Dr Joachim Walter Alexander Duisberg [1965] LLP Member; Katia Marika Duncker [1971] LLP Member; Frederique Dupuis-Toubol [1959] LLP Member; Maxwell Bryan Duthie [1970] LLP Member; Richard John Eccles [1960] LLP Member; Ian Marcus Edwards [1977] LLP Member; Jalal El Ahdab [1973] LLP Member; Jonathan Kumar Emmanuel [1980] LLP Member; Jean-Jacques Parfait Essobme Moussio [1956] LLP Member; Isabel Cartwright Evans [1956] LLP Member; Sophie Jane Eyre [1970] LLP Member; Leo Fattorini [1974] LLP Member; Dr Stefano Febbi [1973] LLP Member; Anne Mechthilde Federle [1960] LLP Member; Dr Joseph Fesenmair [1964] LLP Member; Benjamine-Jeanne Fiedler [1964] LLP Member; Simon Paul Fielder [1970] LLP Member; James Matthew Fong [1975] LLP Member; James Matthew Fong [1975] LLP Member; Hamish Kenneth Barron Fraser [1964] LLP Member; Karen Elizabeth Friebe [1957] LLP Member; James David Froud [1977] LLP Member; Giovanni Galimberti [1971] LLP Member; Helen Elizabeth Gavin-Brown [1976] LLP Member; Marjolein Juricza Geus [1962] LLP Member; Craig Peter Giles [1980] LLP Member; Stefan Gottgetreu [1967] LLP Member; Philip Martin Graff [1965] LLP Member; Merav Stephanie Griguer [1977] LLP Member; Ewan James Grist [1979] LLP Member; Martin Vilhelm Von Haller Baggesen Groenbaek [1962] LLP Member; Andrew Gareth William Hallgarth [1971] LLP Member; Arto Sakari Halonen [1974] LLP Member; Anne-Cecile Pascale Claire Stephanie Hansson Lecoanet [1970] LLP Member; Jorn Felix Harbsmeier [1970] LLP Member; Jocelyn Oliver Hargrave [1974] LLP Member; Christian Harmsen [1968] LLP Member

BIS (Postal Services Act 2011) Company Limited
Incorporated: 8 February 2012
Net Worth: £494,351,008 *Total Assets:* £496,387,008
Registered Office: Masters House, 107 Hammersmith Road, London, W14 0QH
Activities: Activities of other holding companies n.e.c.
Parent: Department for Business, Energy & Industrial Strategy
Officers: David Roger Long [1969] Director/Public Servant; Niall Richard MacKenzie [1965] Director/Civil Servant; Jonathan Sell [1979] Director/Civil Servant

Bitstamp Limited
Incorporated: 25 July 2012 *Employees:* 1
Net Worth: £45,850,696 *Total Assets:* £1,462,374,528
Registered Office: 5 New Street Square, London, EC4A 3TW
Activities: Financial intermediation not elsewhere classified
Major Shareholder: Jungju Kim
Officers: Hendrik Ghys [1986] Director/Investment Executive [Belgian]; Jong Hyun Hong [1977] Director/Investment Executive [South Korean]; Nejc Kodric [1989] Director [Slovenian]

Biz Finance PLC
Incorporated: 18 February 2010
Net Worth Deficit: £82,785,952 *Total Assets:* £1,073,280,192
Registered Office: 6th Floor, 65 Gresham Street, London, EC2V 7NQ
Activities: Other business support service activities n.e.c.
Parent: Link Trust Nominees No.1 Limited
Officers: Sean Peter Martin [1965] Director

BL Bluebutton 2014 Limited
Incorporated: 20 May 2014
Net Worth: £1,050,303,488 *Total Assets:* £1,207,562,368
Registered Office: York House, 45 Seymour Street, London, W1H 7LX
Activities: Development of building projects
Parent: The British Land Company PLC
Officers: David Ian Lockyer [1969] Director/Chartered Surveyor; Paul Stuart Macey [1978] Director/Accountant; Jonathan Charles McNuff [1986] Director/Chartered Accountant; Charles John Middleton [1966] Director/Corporate Tax Executive; Timothy Andrew Roberts [1964] Director/Chartered Surveyor; Hursh Shah [1976] Director; Nigel Mark Webb [1963] Director/Chartered Surveyor

BL Chess Limited
Incorporated: 29 May 2013
Net Worth: £541,612,288 *Total Assets:* £666,869,440
Registered Office: York House, 45 Seymour Street, London, W1H 7LX
Activities: Development of building projects
Parent: BL Office (Non-City) Holding Company Limited
Officers: Sarah Morrell Barzycki [1958] Director/Head of Finance; David Ian Lockyer [1969] Director/Chartered Surveyor; Paul Stuart Macey [1978] Director/Accountant; Jonathan Charles McNuff [1986] Director/Chartered Accountant; Charles John Middleton [1966] Director/Corporate Tax Executive; Timothy Andrew Roberts [1964] Director/Chartered Surveyor; Nigel Mark Webb [1963] Director/Chartered Surveyor

BL City Offices Holding Company Limited
Incorporated: 17 November 2006
Net Worth: £930,006,528 *Total Assets:* £930,006,528
Registered Office: York House, 45 Seymour Street, London, W1H 7LX
Activities: Development of building projects
Parent: BL Office Holding Company Limited
Officers: Sarah Morrell Barzycki [1958] Director/Head of Finance; Paul Stuart Macey [1978] Director/Accountant; Jonathan Charles McNuff [1986] Director/Chartered Accountant; Charles John Middleton [1966] Director/Corporate Tax Executive; Timothy Andrew Roberts [1964] Director/Chartered Surveyor; Nigel Mark Webb [1963] Director/Chartered Surveyor

BL CW Holdings Limited
Incorporated: 28 September 2016
Net Worth Deficit: £22,307,796 *Total Assets:* £293,298,624
Registered Office: York House, 45 Seymour Street, London, W1H 7LX
Activities: Development of building projects
Parent: BL CW Upper Limited Partnership
Officers: Emma Jane Cariaga [1976] Development Director; Edward Cree [1969] Director; Bryan Lewis [1967] Director/Chartered Surveyor; Roger Nigel Madelin [1959] Director/Property Company Executive; Charles John Middleton [1966] Director/Corporate Tax Executive; Philip Tait [1978] Development Director

BL Department Stores Holding Company Limited
Incorporated: 17 November 2006
Net Worth: £155,151,536 *Total Assets:* £155,151,536
Registered Office: York House, 45 Seymour Street, London, W1H 7LX
Activities: Development of building projects
Parent: BL Retail Holding Company Limited
Officers: Sarah Morrell Barzycki [1958] Director/Head of Finance; Bryan Lewis [1967] Director/Chartered Surveyor; Paul Stuart Macey [1978] Director/Accountant; Jonathan Charles McNuff [1986] Director/Chartered Accountant; Charles John Middleton [1966] Director/Corporate Tax Executive; Timothy Andrew Roberts [1964] Director/Chartered Surveyor; Nigel Mark Webb [1963] Director/Chartered Surveyor

BL Ealing Limited
Incorporated: 17 October 2016
Net Worth: £13,315,706 *Total Assets:* £281,541,536
Registered Office: York House, 45 Seymour Street, London, W1H 7LX
Activities: Development of building projects
Parent: British Land in Town Retail Limited
Officers: Claire Ann Barber [1974] Director/Chartered Surveyor; Bryan Lewis [1967] Director/Chartered Surveyor; Jonathan Charles McNuff [1986] Director/Chartered Accountant; Charles John Middleton [1966] Director/Corporate Tax Executive; Nigel Mark Webb [1963] Director/Chartered Surveyor

BL HB Investments Limited
Incorporated: 3 November 2016
Net Worth: £31,858,832 *Total Assets:* £149,483,104
Registered Office: York House, 45 Seymour Street, London, W1H 7LX
Activities: Development of building projects
Parent: BL Retail Warehousing Holding Company Limited
Officers: Jonathan Charles McNuff [1986] Director/Head of Financial Reporting; Charles John Middleton [1966] Director/Group Financial Controller

BL HC PH LLP
Incorporated: 16 January 2006
Net Worth: £87,412,800 *Total Assets:* £142,766,368
Registered Office: York House, 45 Seymour Street, London, W1H 7LX

BL Intermediate Holding Company Limited
Incorporated: 10 November 2006
Net Worth: £15,475,297,280 *Total Assets:* £15,475,297,280
Registered Office: York House, 45 Seymour Street, London, W1H 7LX
Activities: Development of building projects
Shareholders: The British Land Company PLC; The British Land Company PLC
Officers: Sarah Morrell Barzycki [1958] Director/Head of Finance; Paul Stuart Macey [1978] Director/Accountant; Jonathan Charles McNuff [1986] Director/Chartered Accountant; Charles John Middleton [1966] Director/Corporate Tax Executive; Timothy Andrew Roberts [1964] Director/Chartered Surveyor; Nigel Mark Webb [1963] Director/Chartered Surveyor

BL Leisure and Industrial Holding Company Limited
Incorporated: 10 November 2006
Net Worth: £1,433,863,296 *Total Assets:* £1,433,863,296
Registered Office: York House, 45 Seymour Street, London, W1H 7LX
Activities: Development of building projects
Shareholders: BL Intermediate Holding Company Limited; BL Intermediate Holding Company Limited
Officers: Sarah Morrell Barzycki [1958] Director/Head of Finance; Bryan Lewis [1967] Director/Chartered Surveyor; Paul Stuart Macey [1978] Director/Accountant; Jonathan Charles McNuff [1986] Director/Chartered Accountant; Charles John Middleton [1966] Director/Corporate Tax Executive; Timothy Andrew Roberts [1964] Director/Chartered Surveyor; Nigel Mark Webb [1963] Director/Chartered Surveyor

BL Office (Non-City) Holding Company Limited
Incorporated: 17 November 2006
Net Worth: £1,460,423,296 *Total Assets:* £2,492,558,080
Registered Office: York House, 45 Seymour Street, London, W1H 7LX
Activities: Development of building projects
Parent: BL Office Holding Company Limited
Officers: Sarah Morrell Barzycki [1958] Director/Head of Finance; Paul Stuart Macey [1978] Director/Accountant; Jonathan Charles McNuff [1986] Director/Chartered Accountant; Charles John Middleton [1966] Director/Corporate Tax Executive; Timothy Andrew Roberts [1964] Director/Chartered Surveyor; Nigel Mark Webb [1963] Director/Chartered Surveyor

BL Office Holding Company Limited
Incorporated: 10 November 2006
Net Worth: £1,737,938,304 *Total Assets:* £1,737,938,304
Registered Office: York House, 45 Seymour Street, London, W1H 7LX
Activities: Development of building projects
Shareholders: BL Intermediate Holding Company Limited; BL Intermediate Holding Company Limited
Officers: Sarah Morrell Barzycki [1958] Director/Head of Finance; Paul Stuart Macey [1978] Director/Accountant; Jonathan Charles McNuff [1986] Director/Chartered Accountant; Charles John Middleton [1966] Director/Corporate Tax Executive; Timothy Andrew Roberts [1964] Director/Chartered Surveyor; Nigel Mark Webb [1963] Director/Chartered Surveyor

BL Piccadilly Residential Limited
Incorporated: 26 September 2013
Net Worth: £15,806,286 *Total Assets:* £315,688,608
Registered Office: York House, 45 Seymour Street, London, W1H 7LX
Activities: Development of building projects
Parent: BL Residual Holding Company Limited
Officers: Sarah Morrell Barzycki [1958] Director/Head of Finance; Paul Stuart Macey [1978] Director/Accountant; Jonathan Charles McNuff [1986] Director/Chartered Accountant; Charles John Middleton [1966] Director/Corporate Tax Executive; Timothy Andrew Roberts [1964] Director/Chartered Surveyor; James Fielding Taylor [1974] Director/Chartered Surveyor/Asset Manager; Nigel Mark Webb [1963] Director/Chartered Surveyor

BL Residual Holding Company Limited
Incorporated: 10 November 2006
Net Worth: £2,325,138,176 *Total Assets:* £2,325,138,176
Registered Office: York House, 45 Seymour Street, London, W1H 7LX
Activities: Development of building projects
Shareholders: BL Intermediate Holding Company Limited; BL Intermediate Holding Company Limited
Officers: Sarah Morrell Barzycki [1958] Director/Head of Finance; Paul Stuart Macey [1978] Director/Accountant; Jonathan Charles McNuff [1986] Director/Chartered Accountant; Charles John Middleton [1966] Director/Corporate Tax Executive; Timothy Andrew Roberts [1964] Director/Chartered Surveyor; Nigel Mark Webb [1963] Director/Chartered Surveyor

BL Retail Holding Company Limited
Incorporated: 10 November 2006
Net Worth: £9,026,970,624 *Total Assets:* £9,051,018,240
Registered Office: York House, 45 Seymour Street, London, W1H 7LX
Activities: Development of building projects
Parent: BL Intermediate Holding Company Limited
Officers: Sarah Morrell Barzycki [1958] Director/Head of Finance; Paul Stuart Macey [1978] Director/Accountant; Jonathan Charles McNuff [1986] Director/Chartered Accountant; Charles John Middleton [1966] Director/Corporate Tax Executive; Timothy Andrew Roberts [1964] Director/Chartered Surveyor; Nigel Mark Webb [1963] Director/Chartered Surveyor

BL Retail Investments Limited
Incorporated: 3 November 2016
Net Worth: £11,846,784 *Total Assets:* £261,227,280
Registered Office: York House, 45 Seymour Street, London, W1H 7LX
Activities: Development of building projects
Parent: BL Retail Warehousing Holding Company Limited
Officers: Jonathan Charles McNuff [1986] Director/Head of Financial Reporting; Charles John Middleton [1966] Director/Group Financial Controller

BL Retail Warehousing Holding Company Limited
Incorporated: 17 November 2006
Net Worth: £135,459,072 *Total Assets:* £1,209,484,160
Registered Office: York House, 45 Seymour Street, London, W1H 7LX
Activities: Development of building projects
Parent: BL Retail Holding Company Limited
Officers: Sarah Morrell Barzycki [1958] Director/Head of Finance; Paul Stuart Macey [1978] Director/Accountant; Jonathan Charles McNuff [1986] Director/Chartered Accountant; Charles John Middleton [1966] Director/Corporate Tax Executive; Timothy Andrew Roberts [1964] Director/Chartered Surveyor; Nigel Mark Webb [1963] Director/Chartered Surveyor

BL Sainsbury Superstores Limited
Incorporated: 26 February 2008
Net Worth: £341,400,000 *Total Assets:* £612,800,000
Registered Office: York House, 45 Seymour Street, London, W1H 7LX
Activities: Development of building projects
Shareholders: Linestair Limited; Sainsbury Property Investments Limited
Officers: Martyn Stephen Burke [1970] Director; Dean Clegg [1967] Director; Geraint Jamie Cowen [1972] Director; James Andrew Honeyman [1980] Director/Chartered Surveyor; James Michael Pinkstone [1987] Director/Corporate Finance Executive; Hursh Shah [1976] Director; James Watson [1988] Director/Investment Surveyor; David Clifford Wheeler [1984] Director

BL Superstores (Funding) Ltd
Incorporated: 7 December 2005
Net Worth: £81,259 *Total Assets:* £260,975,808
Registered Office: York House, 45 Seymour Street, London, W1H 7LX
Activities: Development of building projects
Parent: BLSSP Property Holdings Limited
Officers: Martyn Stephen Burke [1970] Director; Dean Clegg [1967] Director; Geraint Jamie Cowen [1972] Director; James Andrew Honeyman [1980] Director/Chartered Surveyor; James Michael Pinkstone [1987] Director/Corporate Finance Executive; Hursh Shah [1976] Director; James Watson [1988] Director/Investment Surveyor; David Clifford Wheeler [1984] Director

BL Superstores Finance PLC
Incorporated: 15 September 2005
Net Worth: £315,804 *Total Assets:* £261,046,432
Registered Office: York House, 45 Seymour Street, London, W1H 7LX
Activities: Development of building projects
Parent: BLSSP Property Holdings Limited
Officers: Martyn Stephen Burke [1970] Director; Dean Clegg [1967] Director; Geraint Jamie Cowen [1972] Director; James Andrew Honeyman [1980] Director/Chartered Surveyor; James Michael Pinkstone [1987] Director/Corporate Finance Executive; Hursh Shah [1976] Director; James Watson [1988] Director/Investment Surveyor; David Clifford Wheeler [1984] Director

BL Superstores Holding Company Limited
Incorporated: 17 November 2006
Net Worth: £497,491,808 *Total Assets:* £497,491,808
Registered Office: York House, 45 Seymour Street, London, W1H 7LX
Activities: Development of building projects
Parent: BL Retail Holding Company Limited
Officers: Sarah Morrell Barzycki [1958] Director/Head of Finance; Bryan Lewis [1967] Director/Chartered Surveyor; Paul Stuart Macey [1978] Director/Accountant; Jonathan Charles McNuff [1986] Director/Chartered Accountant; Charles John Middleton [1966] Director/Corporate Tax Executive; Timothy Andrew Roberts [1964] Director/Chartered Surveyor; Nigel Mark Webb [1963] Director/Chartered Surveyor

Black Horse Finance Holdings Limited
Incorporated: 6 October 1999
Net Worth: £174,000,000 *Total Assets:* £1,418,000,000
Registered Office: 25 Gresham Street, London, EC2V 7HN
Activities: Financial intermediation not elsewhere classified
Parent: Lloyds Bank Asset Finance Limited
Officers: David Dermot Hennessey, Secretary; Richard Andrew Jones [1972] Marketing Director; Timothy Robin Smith [1966] Director

Black Horse Group Limited
Incorporated: 3 May 1990
Net Worth: £523,559,008 *Total Assets:* £535,860,992
Registered Office: 25 Gresham Street, London, EC2V 7HN
Activities: Other business support service activities n.e.c.
Parent: Lloyds Bank Asset Finance Limited
Officers: David Dermot Hennessey, Secretary; Richard Andrew Jones [1972] Marketing Director; Timothy Robin Smith [1966] Director

Black Horse Limited
Incorporated: 1 June 1960 *Employees:* 411
Net Worth: £177,295,008 *Total Assets:* £5,286,018,048
Registered Office: 25 Gresham Street, London, EC2V 7HN
Activities: Financial intermediation not elsewhere classified
Parent: Black Horse Group Limited
Officers: David Dermot Hennessey, Secretary; Richard Andrew Jones [1972] Marketing Director; Raymond John Hildreth Milne [1959] Business Risk Director

Black Star Holdings Limited
Incorporated: 8 May 2017
Net Worth: £128,249,648 *Total Assets:* £130,029,448
Registered Office: 6 Broad Street Place, Broad Street, London, EC2M 7JH
Activities: Activities of other holding companies n.e.c.
Parent: Prudential Financial, Inc.
Officers: Gary Wayne Herbert [1968] Director [South African]; Norman Kelly [1968] Director/Actuary [Irish]

Blackmead Infrastructure Limited
Incorporated: 7 March 2014
Net Worth: £15,735,351 *Total Assets:* £222,214,144
Registered Office: The Shard, 32 London Bridge Street, London, SE1 9SG
Activities: Activities of head offices
Parent: Averon Park Limited
Officers: Gary Fraser [1971] Finance Director

Blackrock Advisors (UK) Limited
Incorporated: 18 March 1964 *Employees:* 7
Net Worth: £496,758,016 *Total Assets:* £554,667,008
Registered Office: 12 Throgmorton Avenue, London, EC2N 2DL
Activities: Financial intermediation not elsewhere classified
Parent: Blackrock Finance Europe Limited
Officers: Nicholas James Charrington [1952] Investment Director; Christian Clausen [1955] Director [Danish]; Rudolph Andrew Damm [1961] Director/Risk Management [American]; Eleanor Judith de Freitas [1974] Director/Company Executive; James Edward Fishwick [1960] Director/Company Executive; Rachel Lord [1965] Director/Chief Executive Officer; Stacey Mullin Outhwaite [1978] Director/Chief Operating Officer [American]; Patrick Michael Olson [1965] Director/Company Executive [Irish/American]; Colin Roy Thomson [1961] Managing Director, Finance; Margaret Anne Young [1954] Director

Blackrock Finco UK Ltd
Incorporated: 21 June 2006
Net Worth: £9,044,823,040 *Total Assets:* £12,214,462,464
Registered Office: 12 Throgmorton Avenue, London, EC2N 2DL
Activities: Financial intermediation not elsewhere classified
Parent: Blackrock, Inc.
Officers: Marc Comerchero [1972] Managing Director - Head of Controllers Group [American]; Colin Roy Thomson [1961] Managing Director Finance

Blackrock Frontiers Investment Trust PLC
Incorporated: 15 October 2010
Net Worth: £254,170,544 *Total Assets:* £267,097,248
Registered Office: 12 Throgmorton Avenue, London, EC2N 2DL
Activities: Activities of investment trusts
Officers: John Hyde Murray [1946] Investment Director [American]; Nicholas Andrew Pitts-Tucker [1951] Director/Banker; Audley William Twiston-Davies [1950] Director/Investment Fund Manager; Stephen Frank White [1955] Director; Sarmad Zok [1968] Director/Chief Executive Officer

Blackrock Fund Managers Limited
Incorporated: 20 March 1973
Net Worth: £61,879,000 *Total Assets:* £571,065,024
Registered Office: 12 Throgmorton Avenue, London, EC2N 2DL
Activities: Financial intermediation not elsewhere classified
Parent: Blackrock Investment Management (UK) Limited
Officers: Graham David Bamping [1957] Director; Martin Brian Cook [1964] Director; William Iain Cullen [1953] Director/Solicitor; Caron Lesley Ditchburn [1974] Director/Company Executive; Robert Aidan Roche Hayes [1962] Director/Company Executive; Adrian Michael Lawrence [1965] Director/Actuary; Louise Watkins [1978] Director; Margaret Theodora Zemek [1955] Director [American]

Blackrock Greater Europe Investment Trust PLC
Incorporated: 1 June 2004
Net Worth: £330,419,008 *Total Assets:* £338,467,008
Registered Office: 12 Throgmorton Avenue, London, EC2N 2DL
Activities: Activities of investment trusts
Officers: Peter Baxter [1960] Director; Davina Cordelia Curling [1964] Director; Eric Fenton Sanderson [1951] Director; Dr Paola Subacchi [1962] Director/Economist [Italian]

Blackrock Group Limited
Incorporated: 28 March 1969
Net Worth: £2,415,598,080 *Total Assets:* £3,321,967,104
Registered Office: 12 Throgmorton Avenue, London, EC2N 2DL
Activities: Activities of financial services holding companies
Parent: Blackrock Finco UK Ltd
Officers: Nicholas James Charrington [1952] Investment Director; Christian Clausen [1955] Director [Danish]; Rudolph Andrew Damm [1961] Director/Risk Management [American]; Eleanor Judith de Freitas [1974] Director/Company Executive; James Edward Fishwick [1960] Director/Company Executive; Rachel Lord [1965] Director/Chief Executive Officer; Stacey Mullin Outhwaite [1978] Director/Chief Operating Officer [American]; Patrick Michael Olson [1965] Director/Company Executive [Irish/American]; Colin Roy Thomson [1961] Managing Director, Finance; Margaret Anne Young [1954] Director

Blackrock Investment Management (UK) Limited
Incorporated: 16 May 1986 *Employees:* 3,049
Net Worth: £960,624,000 *Total Assets:* £2,208,962,048
Registered Office: 12 Throgmorton Avenue, London, EC2N 2DL
Activities: Financial intermediation not elsewhere classified
Parent: Blackrock Finance Europe Limited
Officers: Nicholas James Charrington [1952] Investment Director; Christian Clausen [1955] Director [Danish]; Rudolph Andrew Damm [1961] Director/Risk Management [American]; Eleanor Judith de Freitas [1974] Director/Company Executive; James Edward Fishwick [1960] Director/Company Executive; Rachel Lord [1965] Director/Chief Executive Officer; Stacey Mullin Outhwaite [1978] Director/Chief Operating Officer [American]; Patrick Michael Olson [1965] Director/Company Executive [Irish/American]; Colin Roy Thomson [1961] Managing Director, Finance; Margaret Anne Young [1954] Director

Blackrock Latin American Investment Trust PLC
Incorporated: 12 March 1990
Net Worth: £210,613,936 *Total Assets:* £229,985,680
Registered Office: 12 Throgmorton Avenue, London, EC2N 2DL
Activities: Activities of investment trusts
Officers: Craig McCowan Cleland [1963] Director; Carolan Dobson [1954] Director; Dr Mahrukh Doctor [1964] Director/Academic [German]; Antonio Monteiro de Castro [1945] Director/Chief Operating Officer [Portuguese/Brazilian]; Nigel John Webber [1953] Director; Laurence Andrew Whitehead [1944] Director/Academic

Blackrock Life Limited
Incorporated: 22 February 1988
Net Worth: £181,824,000 *Total Assets:* £111,044,689,920
Registered Office: 12 Throgmorton Avenue, London, EC2N 2DL
Activities: Other activities auxiliary to insurance and pension funding
Parent: Blackrock International Limited
Officers: Caroline Jane Barr [1967] Director; David Charles Meston Beattie [1974] Director/Chartered Accountant; Robert James Hall [1966] Director; Robert Aidan Roche Hayes [1962] Director/Company Executive; Adrian Michael Lawrence [1965] Director/Actuary; Barry O'Dwyer [1968] Director/Company Executive [Irish]; David Sims [1958] Director; Rebeccah Claire Tilston [1980] Director/Solicitor

Blackrock North American Income Trust PLC
Incorporated: 30 August 2012
Net Worth: £118,295,000 *Total Assets:* £122,209,000
Registered Office: 12 Throgmorton Avenue, London, EC2N 2DL
Activities: Activities of investment trusts
Officers: Christopher Casey [1955] Director; Andrew Robertson Irvine [1951] Director/Chartered Surveyor; Simon Edward Callum Miller [1952] Director; Alice Anne Ryder [1964] Director

Blackrock Throgmorton Trust PLC
Incorporated: 2 December 1957
Net Worth: £396,846,016 *Total Assets:* £406,383,008
Registered Office: 12 Throgmorton Avenue, London, EC2N 2DL
Activities: Activities of investment trusts
Officers: Simon Delaval Beart [1958] Director/Chartered Accountant; Loudon Ian Greenlees [1951] Director/Chartered Accountant; Jean Grace Kemmis-Matterson [1956] Director/Investment Manager; Andrew Pegge [1963] Director/Fund Manager; Christopher John Loraine Samuel [1958] Director

Blackrock UK (Alpha) Limited
Incorporated: 29 June 2016
Net Worth: £1,305,151,744 *Total Assets:* £6,528,287,744
Registered Office: 12 Throgmorton Avenue, London, EC2N 2DL
Activities: Activities of financial services holding companies
Parent: Blackrock, Inc.
Officers: Philippe Matsumoto [1971] Managing Director, Global Treasurer [French]; Alastair James Henry Peters [1982] Director

Blackrock UK 2 LLP
Incorporated: 28 December 2011
Net Worth: £2,496,546,048 *Total Assets:* £2,496,730,880
Registered Office: 12 Throgmorton Avenue, London, EC2N 2DL

Blackrock UK 3 LLP
Incorporated: 28 December 2011
Net Worth: £2,477,051,904 *Total Assets:* £2,477,234,432
Registered Office: 12 Throgmorton Avenue, London, EC2N 2DL

Blackrock UK 4 LLP
Incorporated: 28 December 2011
Net Worth: £3,643,668,992 *Total Assets:* £3,647,077,120
Registered Office: 12 Throgmorton Avenue, London, EC2N 2DL

Blackrock UK A LLP
Incorporated: 15 April 2015
Net Worth: £3,085,620,992 *Total Assets:* £3,085,823,232
Registered Office: 12 Throgmorton Avenue, London, EC2N 2DL

Blackrock UK Holdco Limited
Incorporated: 12 March 1981
Net Worth: £108,865,000 *Total Assets:* £138,075,008
Registered Office: 12 Throgmorton Avenue, London, EC2N 2DL
Activities: Financial intermediation not elsewhere classified
Parent: Blackrock Group Limited
Officers: Colin McDonald [1981] Director; Colin Roy Thomson [1961] Managing Director, Finance

Blackrock World Mining Trust PLC
Incorporated: 28 October 1993
Net Worth: £804,646,976 *Total Assets:* £911,721,984
Registered Office: 12 Throgmorton Avenue, London, EC2N 2DL
Activities: Activities of investment trusts
Officers: Colin Alexander Mason Buchan [1954] Director/Banker; David Watson Cheyne [1948] Director/Lawyer; Ian David Cockerill [1954] Director/Mining Executive; Russell Philip Edey [1942] Director/Merchant Banker; Jane Margaret Lewis [1963] Director [British/Australian]; Judith Mosely [1964] Director

The Blackstone Group International Partners LLP
Incorporated: 24 February 2010 *Employees:* 226
Net Worth: £203,427,264 *Total Assets:* £221,812,560
Registered Office: 40 Berkeley Square, London, W1J 5AL
Officers: Vijay Vithal Bharadia [1967] Member; Dr Gerard Martin Murphy [1955] Member; Michael Whitman [1972] Member; Syed Qasim Abbas [1976] LLP Member; Abhishek Agarwal [1982] LLP Member; Samir Kasrim Maximilien Amichi [1980] LLP Member; Lionel Yves Assant [1972] LLP Member; Geoffrey William James Bailhache [1980] LLP Member; Marc Bolland [1959] LLP Member; Sanja Cvetinovic [1985] LLP Member; Florent Alexis Raymond Pierre Danset [1983] LLP Member; Raphael Maurice Charles Vital de Botton [1979] LLP Member; Jean-Christophe Dubois [1968] LLP Member; Nadim El Gabbani [1981] LLP Member; Louis-Simon Ferland [1975] LLP Member; Vladimir Grlica [1971] LLP Member; Haide Hong [1984] LLP Member; Kalika Ashvini Jayasekera [1976] LLP Member; Pilar Alejandra Junco [1974] LLP Member; Lama Kanazeh [1981] LLP Member; Farhad Mawji Karim [1969] LLP Member; Gemma Nandita Kataky [1983] LLP Member; Chloe Kyprianou [1986] LLP Member; D Andrew Lax [1976] LLP Member; Johan Lilliehook [1982] LLP Member; Laurent Lucien Claude Machenaud [1979] LLP Member; David Shukry Mehenny [1973] LLP Member; Duco Merkens [1982] LLP Member; Olivier Franck Meyohas [1970] LLP Member; Daniel Alexander Peart [1977] LLP Member; Chad Rustan Pike [1971] LLP Member; Jurgen Pinker [1976] LLP Member; Robert Ramsauer [1979] LLP Member; Rafic Said [1974] LLP Member; Ruth Elizabeth Schodorf [1976] LLP Member; James Seppala [1979] LLP Member; Paolo Servado [1988] LLP Member; Mustafa Mohsin Siddiqui [1979] LLP Member; Tait Simpson [1981] LLP Member; Michael Joseph Slattery [1972] LLP Member; Michael Swank [1988] LLP Member; Andrea Valeri [1972] LLP Member; Panayot Kostadinov Vasilev [1976] LLP Member; Michael David Vrana [1980] LLP Member

Blaxmill (Ten) Limited
Incorporated: 3 November 2003
Net Worth Deficit: £58,209,128 *Total Assets:* £858,918,656
Registered Office: The Thomson Reuters Building, 30 South Colonnade, Canary Wharf, London, E14 5EP
Activities: Dormant company
Parent: Thomson Reuters Group Overseas Holdings UK Ltd
Officers: Carla O'Hanlon, Secretary; Timothy David Knowland [1980] Director/Solicitor; Peter Thorn [1963] Director/Accountant

BLD Property Holdings Limited
Incorporated: 20 October 1964
Net Worth: £319,718,624 *Total Assets:* £319,718,624
Registered Office: York House, 45 Seymour Street, London, W1H 7LX
Activities: Development of building projects
Parent: BL Davidson Limited
Officers: Sarah Morrell Barzycki [1958] Director/Head of Finance; Paul Stuart Macey [1978] Director/Accountant; Jonathan Charles McNuff [1986] Director/Chartered Accountant; Charles John Middleton [1966] Director/Corporate Tax Executive; Timothy Andrew Roberts [1964] Director/Chartered Surveyor; Nigel Mark Webb [1963] Director/Chartered Surveyor

Blind Veterans UK
Incorporated: 30 April 1923 *Employees:* 469
Net Worth: £146,814,000 *Total Assets:* £167,004,000
Registered Office: 12-14 Harcourt Street, London, W1H 4HD
Activities: Residential care activities for the elderly and disabled
Officers: Nicholas John Caplin, Secretary; David Buckley [1957] Director/Chartered Accountant; Christopher Cardwell [1952] Director; Barry Desmond Coupe [1951] Director; Minoo Sahni Court [1957] Director; Malcolm Cree CBE [1961] Director/Management Consultant; Guy Charles Davies [1966] Director/Investment Manager; Neelesh Heredia [1965] Director; Alan Peter Holderness [1964] Director; Liz Hunt [1961] Director; James Leavesley [1962] Director; Paul Luker [1951] Director/Retired; Mark William Poffley [1960] Director/Trustee; Nicola Pulford [1960] Director; Tim Seal [1965] Director/COO at Barchester Healthcare; David John Turner [1936] Director; Sarah Lucie Watson [1964] Director/Consultant Ophthalmic Surgeon; Colin Willamson [1956] Director/Communications Officer

BLME Holdings PLC
Incorporated: 24 April 2013 *Employees:* 119
Net Worth: £222,882,000 *Total Assets:* £1,027,534,016
Registered Office: Cannon Place, 78 Cannon Street, London, EC4N 6HL
Activities: Activities of financial services holding companies
Officers: Peter Francis Bulkeley, Secretary; Adel Abdul Wahab Al-Majed [1958] Director/Chairman and CEO [Kuwaiti]; Sheikh Abdullah Jaber Al-Ahmad Al-Sabah [1966] Director [Kuwaiti]; Giles Hullah Cunningham [1969] Director; Jabra Ghandour [1962] Director [Jordanian]; Joanne Hindle [1957] Director; Christopher Martin Power [1961] Director; Calum Thomson [1960] Director; David Gareth Williams [1960] Director; Michael Howard Williams [1950] Director

Bloomsbury Publishing PLC
Incorporated: 30 January 1986 *Employees:* 627
Net Worth: £139,563,008 *Total Assets:* £196,991,008
Registered Office: 50 Bedford Square, London, WC1B 3DP
Activities: Book publishing
Officers: Maya Margaret Abu-Deeb, Secretary; Jonathan Rennie Glasspool [1965] Director/Publisher; Steven Richard Hall [1956] Managing Director; Jill Louise Jones [1958] Director/Independent Publishing Consultant; Sir Richard Peter Lambert [1944] Director; John Nigel Newton [1955] Director/Publisher; Penelope Samantha Juliette Scott-Bayfield [1972] Finance Director; John Anthony Warren [1953] Director

BLSSP Property Holdings Limited
Incorporated: 3 November 2000
Net Worth: £88,586,960 *Total Assets:* £216,090,912
Registered Office: York House, 45 Seymour Street, London, W1H 7LX
Activities: Development of building projects
Parent: BL Sainsbury Superstores Limited
Officers: Martyn Stephen Burke [1970] Director; Dean Clegg [1967] Director; Geraint Jamie Cowen [1972] Director; James Andrew Honeyman [1980] Director/Chartered Surveyor; James Michael Pinkstone [1987] Director/Corporate Finance Executive; Hursh Shah [1976] Director; James Watson [1988] Director/Investment Surveyor; David Clifford Wheeler [1984] Director

Blue Finco Limited
Incorporated: 28 January 2014
Net Worth Deficit: £35,395,724 *Total Assets:* £640,165,376
Registered Office: 95 Queen Victoria Street, London, EC4V 4HG
Activities: Activities of financial services holding companies
Parent: Bank of Montreal
Officers: William Theodore Clarke, Secretary; Scott Joseph Matthews [1969] Director/Accountant [Australian]; Olaf Sheikh [1965] Director/Tax Accountant [Canadian]; William Kenneth Spinney Smith [1959] Director/Banker [British/Canadian]

Blue Manchester Limited
Incorporated: 15 October 2010 *Employees:* 311
Net Worth: £43,378,436 *Total Assets:* £111,008,600
Registered Office: 6th Floor, Charles House, 108-110 Finchley Road, London, NW3 5JJ
Activities: Hotels and similar accommodation
Parent: BM Manchester Limited
Officers: Christopher Christou [1961] Director/Solicitor; Loucas Louca [1978] Director [Greek/Cypriot]

Blue Transmission London Array Limited
Incorporated: 31 October 2012
Net Worth Deficit: £9,737,000 *Total Assets:* £463,172,000
Registered Office: Cannon Place, 78 Cannon Street, London, EC4N 6AF
Activities: Transmission of electricity
Parent: Blue Transmission London Array (Holdings) Limited
Officers: Matthew James Edwards [1985] Associate Director; Graham Farley [1949] Director; Matthew John Pitts [1970] Director/Project Financier; Gary Thornton [1965] Technical Director

Blue Transmission Sheringham Shoal Limited
Incorporated: 28 May 2012
Net Worth: £2,983,000 *Total Assets:* £199,590,000
Registered Office: Cannon Place, 78 Cannon Street, London, EC4N 6AF
Activities: Dormant company
Parent: Blue Transmission Sheringham Shoal (Holdings) Limited
Officers: Matthew James Edwards [1985] Associate Director; Graham Farley [1949] Director; Matthew John Pitts [1970] Director/Project Financier; Gary Thornton [1965] Technical Director

Blue Transmission Walney 1 Limited
Incorporated: 23 August 2010
Net Worth: £7,283,000 *Total Assets:* £113,530,000
Registered Office: Cannon Place, 78 Cannon Street, London, EC4N 6AF
Activities: Transmission of electricity
Parent: Blue Transmission Walney 1 (Holdings) Limited
Officers: Matthew James Edwards [1985] Associate Director; Graham Farley [1949] Director; Matthew John Pitts [1970] Director/Project Financier; Gary Thornton [1965] Technical Director

Blue Transmission Walney 2 Limited
Incorporated: 26 August 2011
Net Worth Deficit: £2,492,000 *Total Assets:* £125,943,000
Registered Office: Cannon Place, 78 Cannon Street, London, EC4N 6AF
Activities: Dormant company
Parent: Blue Transmission Walney 2 (Holdings) Limited
Officers: Matthew James Edwards [1985] Associate Director; Graham Farley [1949] Director; Matthew John Pitts [1970] Director/Project Financier; Gary Thornton [1965] Technical Director

Bluebay Asset Management (Services) Ltd
Incorporated: 11 October 1996
Net Worth: £173,259,008 *Total Assets:* £177,651,008
Registered Office: 77 Grosvenor Street, London, W1K 3JR
Activities: Fund management activities
Parent: Royal Bank of Canada
Officers: James Jackson Brace, Secretary; Stephen Rosenstjerne Krag [1959] Director; Luc Hector Therese Leclercq [1960] Director [Belgian]; James Neilson Pettigrew [1958] Director

Bluebay Asset Management LLP
Incorporated: 23 November 2011
Net Worth: £99,802,000 *Total Assets:* £127,369,000
Registered Office: 77 Grosvenor Street, London, W1K 3JR
Officers: James Jackson Brace [1970] Member; Andrew Chorley Archer [1969] LLP Member; Jean-Philippe Blua [1979] LLP Member; Paul Frederick Bromley [1974] LLP Member; Monique Brown [1968] LLP Member; Mark Charles David Dowding [1971] LLP Member; David James Gould Dowsett [1972] LLP Member; Erich Paul Gerth [1963] LLP Member; Justin James Oliver Jewell [1981] LLP Member; Polina Kurdyavko [1979] LLP Member; Luc Hector Therese Leclercq [1960] LLP Member; Russel Boyd Matthews [1973] LLP Member; Siu-Wai NG [1976] LLP Member; Michael Jonathan Reed [1967] LLP Member; Blair Maxwell Reid [1970] LLP Member; Raphael Robelin [1971] LLP Member; Craig Alan Tennier [1974] LLP Member; Stephen Thariyan [1966] LLP Member; Michael Timotheou [1986] LLP Member; Cenk Turkinan [1975] LLP Member; David Michael Willmoth-Riley [1965] LLP Member; Spencer Barry Woodward [1971] LLP Member

Bluebottle UK Limited
Incorporated: 26 March 1999
Net Worth: £1,110,940,032 *Total Assets:* £1,110,945,024
Registered Office: The Battleship Building, 179 Harrow Road, London, W2 6NB
Activities: Activities of other holding companies n.e.c.
Parent: Virgin Holdings Limited
Officers: Barry Alexander Ralph Gerrard, Secretary; Robert Pieter Blok [1976] Director/Lawyer; Ian Philip Woods [1974] Director/Solicitor

Bluebutton (5 Broadgate) UK Limited
Incorporated: 15 July 2010
Net Worth: £651,961,344 *Total Assets:* £968,969,664
Registered Office: 3 More London Riverside, London, SE1 2AQ
Activities: Development of building projects
Parent: CK Steel (UK) Limited
Officers: Edmond Wai Leung Ho [1959] Director; Generald Lai Chee Ma [1968] Director [Canadian]; Jonathan Theodore Miller [1971] Director; Eirene Yeung [1960] Director [Chinese]

Bluebutton Properties UK Limited
Incorporated: 14 September 2009
Net Worth: £4,975,967 *Total Assets:* £313,840,096
Registered Office: York House, 45 Seymour Street, London, W1H 7LX
Activities: Development of building projects
Shareholders: Minister of Finance; BL Bluebutton 2014 Limited
Officers: Norman Iain Cahoon [1979] Investment Director; Madeleine Elizabeth Cosgrave [1967] Director/Chartered Surveyor; Deepa Kewal Devani [1980] Director; David Ian Lockyer [1969] Director/Chartered Surveyor; Timothy Andrew Roberts [1964] Director/Chartered Surveyor; Hursh Shah [1976] Director

Blueco Limited
Incorporated: 9 May 1996
Net Worth: £595,422,016 *Total Assets:* £618,804,992
Registered Office: 100 Victoria Street, London, SW1E 5JL
Activities: Real estate agencies
Parent: Land Securities Portfolio Management Limited
Officers: Rosalind Charlotte Futter [1978] Director/Accountant

Bluecrest Capital Management (UK) LLP
Incorporated: 29 October 2009
Net Worth: £112,535,000 *Total Assets:* £130,618,000
Registered Office: Nova North, 11 Bressenden Place, London, SW1E 5BY
Officers: Paul Jay Dehadray [1974] Member; Simon William Ackroyd [1977] LLP Member; Jenna Rae Akgul [1976] LLP Member; Damien Aneja [1979] LLP Member; Mardoche Assor [1964] LLP Member; Roy Aviner [1984] LLP Member; David Bowen [1971] LLP Member; Mark Stephen Bradford [1984] LLP Member; Charles Stephen Buchan [1969] LLP Member; Nigel Chase [1977] LLP Member; Florent Chermat [1973] LLP Member; Charles Matthew Rhys Covill [1969] LLP Member; Peter Anthony Cox [1964] LLP Member; Franck Luc Deligny [1971] LLP Member; Romain Nicolas Denis [1986] LLP Member; David John Emery [1964] LLP Member; Steven Douglas Fage [1969] LLP Member; Paul Griffith [1961] LLP Member; Matthew James Haigh [1980] LLP Member; Philippe Haik [1971] LLP Member; Saad Hammoud [1975] LLP Member; Elisabeth Hinchley [1975] LLP Member; Daniel James Hiscox [1976] LLP Member; Alexander James Hough [1972] LLP Member; Robert Howard [1981] LLP Member; Christopher Jackson [1976] LLP Member; Dafydd Jones [1979] LLP Member; Catherine Mary Kerridge [1957] LLP Member; Marcel Kfoury [1977] LLP Member; Shakib Faisal Khan [1979] LLP Member; Simon Kingsbury [1980] LLP Member; Elizabeth Lander [1972] LLP Member; Paul Lawrence [1977] LLP Member; Christopher Loewe [1983] LLP Member; Vivek Luthra [1971] LLP Member; Irena Maravic [1973] LLP Member; Marguerite Marshall [1962] LLP Member; Benjamin Andrew Martin [1973] LLP Member; John Stuart McDonald [1975] LLP Member; Andrew Stewart McDougall [1966] LLP Member; Conleth Gerard McKeown [1977] LLP Member; Vineet Mehta [1983] LLP Member; Nick Moore [1970] LLP Member; Andrew Moss [1966] LLP Member; Jacob Niburg [1987] LLP Member; Melanie Niedermeier [1987] LLP Member; Hasan Ferit Orhon [1974] LLP Member; Nabil Ouajjane [1983] LLP Member; Adrian David Rates [1971] LLP Member; Michael Risely [1980] LLP Member; Samuel Joe Rosenberg [1988] LLP Member; Neil Russell [1980] LLP Member; Sarju Shah [1986] LLP Member; Edward Charles Shuttleworth [1977] LLP Member; Benjamin Souter [1976] LLP Member; Daniel Strauss Vasques [1981] LLP Member; Peter Thacker [1965] LLP Member; Sergei Vasilenko [1978] LLP Member; Richard Wade [1976] LLP Member; Ian Ferguson Walker [1986] LLP Member; John Frederick Reynell Wilson [1958] LLP Member; Marcin Tomasz Wiszniewski [1973] LLP Member; Luke Wyszynski [1976] LLP Member; Panayiotis Andrea Yiasoumi [1978] LLP Member

Bluefin Insurance Group Limited
Incorporated: 19 September 1996
Net Worth: £13,600,000 *Total Assets:* £100,800,000
Registered Office: 1 Tower Place West, Tower Place, London, EC3R 5BU
Activities: Activities of other holding companies n.e.c.
Parent: Marsh & McLennan Companies Inc
Officers: Dawn Jeanette Hodge, Secretary; Caroline Wendy Godwin [1962] Director/Accountant; James Michael Pickford [1978] Director/Accountant

Bluefin Insurance Services Limited
Incorporated: 13 May 1968 *Employees:* 1,439
Net Worth: £85,800,000 *Total Assets:* £155,800,000
Registered Office: 1 Tower Place West, Tower Place, London, EC3R 5BU
Activities: Non-life insurance
Parent: JELF Insurance Brokers Limited
Officers: Dawn Jeanette Hodges, Secretary; Jane Victoria Barker [1949] Director; Philip Andrew Barton [1962] Director/CEO (Insurance); Mark Christopher Chessher [1960] Director/Accountant; John Raymond Hirst [1952] Director

BM Manchester Limited
Incorporated: 23 September 2010
Net Worth: £47,908,436 *Total Assets:* £123,481,800
Registered Office: 6th Floor, Charles House, 108-110 Finchley Road, London, NW3 5JJ
Activities: Activities of head offices
Major Shareholder: Yiannakis Christodoulou
Officers: Christopher Christou [1961] Director/Solicitor; Loucas Louca [1978] Director [Greek/Cypriot]

BMA Investments Limited
Incorporated: 3 February 1992
Net Worth: £130,142,000 *Total Assets:* £134,632,992
Registered Office: Tavistock Square, London, WC1H 9JP
Activities: Non-trading company
Parent: British Medical Association
Officers: Ajay Obhrai, Secretary; Belinda Clare Phipps [1958] Director/Interim Chief Executive; Trevor Paul Pickersgill [1967] Director/Consultant Neurologist

BMCE Bank International PLC
Incorporated: 29 December 2004 *Employees:* 57
Net Worth: £77,889,000 *Total Assets:* £490,960,000
Registered Office: 26 Upper Brook Street, Mayfair, London, W1K 7QE
Activities: Financial intermediation not elsewhere classified
Parent: BMCE International (Holdings) PLC
Officers: Mohammed Afrine [1970] Director/Chief Executive Officer [Moroccan]; Mohammed Agoumi [1957] Director [French]; Houssam El Hak Morssi Barakat [1972] Director/Banker [Moroccan]; Brahim Benjelloun Touimi [1960] Director [Moroccan]; Richard Parry [1951] Director [British/American]; Ralph Cameron Snedden [1947] Director; David Suratgar [1938] Director

BMCE International (Holdings) PLC
Incorporated: 27 August 2004 *Employees:* 98
Net Worth: £152,772,000 *Total Assets:* £1,083,602,944
Registered Office: 26 Upper Brook Street, Mayfair, London, W1K 7QE
Activities: Other business support service activities n.e.c.
Shareholder: Othman Benjelloun
Officers: Mohammed Agoumi [1957] Director [French]; Othman Benjelloun [1932] Director/Chairman of BMCE Group [Moroccan]; Brahim Benjelloun Touimi [1960] Director [Moroccan]; Mohammed Bircharef [1962] Director/Chief Executive Officer [Moroccan]; David Suratgar [1938] Director/Banker

BMG Rights Management (UK) Limited
Incorporated: 23 September 2008 *Employees:* 165
Net Worth: £53,603,000 *Total Assets:* £675,192,000
Registered Office: 8th Floor, 5 Merchant Square, London, W2 1AS
Activities: Activities of head offices
Parent: Bertelsmann UK Limited
Officers: Jonathan Michael Baker [1979] Director; Dr Maximilian Dressendoerfer [1970] Director/Chief Financial Officer BMG Group [German]; Benjamin Jerome Katovsky [1981] Director; Hartwig Masuch [1954] Director/Publishing Management Assistant [German]; Alistair Mark Norbury [1966] Director; Paul Jonathan Wilson [1974] Director

BMI Group Holdings UK Limited
Incorporated: 3 February 2016 *Employees:* 11,091
Net Worth: £1,225,218,816 *Total Assets:* £3,141,145,856
Registered Office: 5th Floor, 20 Air Street, London, W1B 5AN
Activities: Activities of other holding companies n.e.c.
Major Shareholder: Charles Tappan Dowling
Officers: Thomas Joseph Anderson [1956] Director/Chief Operating Officer [American]; Susan Lynne Fornaro [1969] Director/General Counsel [Italian]; Jason Ivan Pollack [1970] Director/Attorney [American]; John Francis Rebele [1955] Director/Chief Financial Officer [American]; Dr Johannes Georg Schmidt-Schultes [1966] Director/Chief Financial Officer [German]

BMI Healthcare Holdings Limited
Incorporated: 13 March 2006
Previous: Pedalclip Limited
Net Worth Deficit: £243,151,008 *Total Assets:* £2,136,446,976
Registered Office: BMI Healthcare House, 3 Paris Garden, London, SE1 8ND
Activities: Other business support service activities n.e.c.
Parent: BMI Tenant 2 Limited
Officers: Henry Jonathan Davies [1968] Financial Director; Dr Karen Anita Prins [1961] Director/Chief Executive Officer [South African]; Michael Anthony Thomas [1976] Director/Chartered Accountant

BMI Healthcare Limited
Incorporated: 15 September 1987 *Employees:* 8,909
Net Worth: £1,126,692,992 *Total Assets:* £3,205,789,952
Registered Office: BMI Healthcare House, 3 Paris Garden, Southwark, London, SE1 8ND
Activities: Hospital activities
Parent: GHG Intermediate Holdings Limited
Officers: Henry Jonathan Davies [1968] Finance Director; Dr Karen Anita Prins [1961] Director/Chief Executive Officer [South African]

BMO AM Group (Holdings) Limited
Incorporated: 4 April 1989
Previous: F & C Group (Holdings) Limited
Net Worth: £374,479,008 *Total Assets:* £455,584,992
Registered Office: Exchange House, Primrose Street, London, EC2A 2NY
Activities: Activities of head offices
Parent: BMO Asset Management (Holdings) PLC
Officers: Rachel Danae Burgin, Secretary; Mandy Frances Mannix [1970] Director/Head of Client Management [New Zealander]; David Jonathan Sloper [1963] Director/Head, Product Management; Richard Adrian Watts [1972] Director/Chief Investment Officer

BMO AM Group (Management) Limited
Incorporated: 5 April 1989
Previous: F & C Group Management Limited
Net Worth: £308,820,000 *Total Assets:* £309,137,984
Registered Office: Exchange House, Primrose Street, London, EC2A 2NY
Activities: Activities of head offices
Parent: BMO AM Group (Holdings) Limited
Officers: Rachel Danae Burgin, Secretary; Mandy Frances Mannix [1970] Director/Head of Client Management [New Zealander]; David Jonathan Sloper [1963] Director/Head, Product Management; Richard Adrian Watts [1972] Director/Chief Investment Officer

BMO AM Holdings Limited
Incorporated: 3 March 1989
Previous: F & C Holdings Limited
Net Worth: £92,348,864 *Total Assets:* £176,805,888
Registered Office: Exchange House, Primrose Street, London, EC2A 2NY
Activities: Financial intermediation not elsewhere classified
Parent: BMO AM Group (Management) Limited
Officers: Rachel Danae Burgin, Secretary; Mandy Frances Mannix [1970] Director/Head of Client Management [New Zealander]; David Jonathan Sloper [1963] Director/Head, Product Management; Richard Adrian Watts [1972] Director/Chief Investment Officer

BMO AM Treasury Limited
Incorporated: 26 April 2002
Previous: F & C Treasury Limited
Net Worth Deficit: £18,710,000 *Total Assets:* £259,263,008
Registered Office: Exchange House, Primrose Street, London, EC2A 2NY
Activities: Non-trading company
Parent: BMO Asset Management (Holdings) PLC
Officers: Rachel Danae Burgin, Secretary; Mandy Frances Mannix [1970] Director/Head of Client Management [New Zealander]; David Jonathan Sloper [1963] Director/Head, Product Management; Richard Adrian Watts [1972] Director/Chief Investment Officer

BMO Asset Management Limited
Incorporated: 27 March 1953 *Employees:* 21
Previous: F & C Management Limited
Net Worth: £63,298,000 *Total Assets:* £107,828,000
Registered Office: Exchange House, Primrose Street, London, EC2A 2NY
Activities: Other business support service activities n.e.c.
Parent: BMO AM Holdings Limited
Officers: William Theodore Clarke, Secretary; Mandy Frances Mannix [1970] Director/Head of Client Management & Distribution EMEA [New Zealander]; Hugh Cameron Moir [1957] Director/Global Head of Operations and Business Technology; Richard Charles Wilson [1966] Investment Director; Stuart James Woodyatt [1968] Director/Head of Business Risk

BMO Capital and Income Investment Trust PLC
Incorporated: 17 July 1992
Previous: F & C Capital and Income Investment Trust PLC
Net Worth: £327,472,000 *Total Assets:* £347,862,016
Registered Office: 8th Floor, Exchange House, Primrose Street, London, EC2A 2NY
Activities: Financial intermediation not elsewhere classified
Officers: Steven Andrew Ralph Bates [1957] Director/Investment Manager; Sharon Brown [1968] Director; Clare Juliet Dobie [1957] Director; Jane Margaret Lewis [1963] Director [British/Australian]; Timothy Scholefield [1963] Director

BMO Capital Markets Limited
Incorporated: 9 May 1994 *Employees:* 100
Net Worth: £143,348,000 *Total Assets:* £1,682,835,968
Registered Office: 95 Queen Victoria Street, London, EC4V 4HG
Activities: Financial intermediation not elsewhere classified
Parent: Bank of Montreal Capital Markets (Holdings) Limited
Officers: Paula Young, Secretary; Kathleen Child-Villiers [1965] Director [American]; Jeffrey Edmund Couch [1969] Managing Director [Canadian]; Matthieu Pierre Albert Debost [1964] Managing Director [French]; Jonathan Stuart Graham Dunn [1973] Director/Finance Trader [Australian]; Rebecca Shelley Fuller [1970] Director/Lawyer; Kelsey Charles Gunderson [1970] Director [Canadian]; Ian Ramsay Henderson [1949] Director; Scott Joseph Matthews [1969] Director/Accountant [Australian]; William Kenneth Spinney Smith [1959] Director/Banker [British/Canadian]; Robert Andrew Yeung [1971] Managing Director

BMO Global Asset Management (Europe) Limited
Incorporated: 16 January 2014
Net Worth: £1,060,049,024 *Total Assets:* £1,060,049,024
Registered Office: 95 Queen Victoria Street, London, EC4V 4HG
Activities: Activities of financial services holding companies
Shareholders: Bank of Montreal; Blue Finco Limited
Officers: Paula Young, Secretary; William Kenneth Spinney Smith [1959] Director/Banker [British/Canadian]; Richard Charles Wilson [1966] Investment Director

BMO Global Smaller Companies PLC
Incorporated: 15 February 1889
Previous: F & C Global Smaller Companies PLC
Net Worth: £826,830,976 *Total Assets:* £880,344,000
Registered Office: Exchange House, Primrose Street, London, EC2A 2NY
Activities: Financial intermediation not elsewhere classified
Officers: Anja Maria Balfour [1963] Director; Josephine Dixon [1959] Director/Chartered Accountant; David Frederic Miles Stileman [1950] Director; John Anthony Victor Townsend [1948] Director/Investment Banker; Jane Elizabeth Tozer [1947] Director

BMO Real Estate Partners LLP
Incorporated: 27 June 2008 *Employees:* 67
Previous: F & C REIT Asset Management LLP
Net Worth: £164,671,008 *Total Assets:* £208,183,008
Registered Office: 7 Seymour Street, London, W1H 7JW

BNP Paribas Commodity Futures Limited
Incorporated: 2 June 1989 *Employees:* 13
Net Worth: £285,133,568 *Total Assets:* £4,430,562,816
Registered Office: 10 Harewood Avenue, London, NW1 6AA
Activities: Financial intermediation not elsewhere classified
Parent: BNP Paribas
Officers: Lisa Marvin, Secretary; Arne Groes [1966] Director/Global Co-Head of G10 Rates and PS&F [Danish]; Mr Serge Groff [1964] Director [Luxembourger]; Jean-Baptiste Jacques Emmanuel Valery Massignon [1964] Director/Group General Secretary [French]; Hadi Monceau [1976] Director/IT & Operations Manager [French]; Christopher Mark Penney [1965] Director/Chartered Accountant; Amanda Loraine Rajkumar [1972] Director/Head of HR; Kieron Alexander Smith [1977] Director; Ian Geoffrey Verrill [1966] Director/COO of Commodity Futures

BNP Paribas U.K. Holdings Limited
Incorporated: 6 March 1987
Net Worth: £1,239,032,960 *Total Assets:* £1,239,750,016
Registered Office: 10 Harewood Avenue, London, NW1 6AA
Activities: Financial intermediation not elsewhere classified
Parent: BNP Paribas
Officers: Lisa Marvin, Secretary; Marc Yves Carlos [1959] Director/Banker [French]; Stephane Chassard [1963] Director/Chief Risk Officer [French]; Patrick Colle [1959] Director/CEO of BNP Paribas Securities Services [French]; Francois Draveny [1964] Director [French]; Frederic Janbon [1963] Director/Banker [French]; Sophie Constance Chantal Javary [1959] Director/Banker [French]; Yannick Jung [1972] Director [French]; Laure Morsy [1964] Director/COO & Head of CIB BGL BNP Paribas [French]; Veronique Ormezzano [1961] Director/Head of Group Prudential Affairs [French]; Alain Papiasse [1955] Director/Banker [French]; Donald Paul Reynolds [1957] Director/Lawyer; Thierry Marie Maurice Varene [1952] Director/Global Head of CF CTE and Fig [French]; Anne Marie Odile Albertine Verstraeten [1954] Director/Banker [Belgian]

BNP Paribas UK Limited
Incorporated: 28 March 1980
Net Worth: £296,640,992 *Total Assets:* £312,344,000
Registered Office: 10 Harewood Avenue, London, NW1 6AA
Activities: Financial intermediation not elsewhere classified
Parent: Harewood Holdings Limited
Officers: Lisa Marvin, Secretary; Stephen Martin Middleton [1975] Director/Banker; Christopher Mark Penney [1965] Director/Chartered Accountant; Donald Paul Reynolds [1957] Director/Lawyer

BNP PUK Holding Limited
Incorporated: 17 June 1986
Net Worth: £275,828,000 *Total Assets:* £288,488,992
Registered Office: 10 Harewood Avenue, London, NW1 6AA
Activities: Activities of head offices
Parent: BNP Paribas
Officers: Francois Draveny [1964] Director [French]; Helen Louise Fletcher D'Arjuzon [1976] Director/Solicitor; Stephen Martin Middleton [1975] Director; Christopher Mark Penney [1965] Director/Chartered Accountant; Kara Lemont Sportelli [1963] Director/Head of Strategy & Risk Coordination [British/American]

BNY Mellon Fund Managers Limited
Incorporated: 11 March 1986
Net Worth: £28,793,000 *Total Assets:* £127,617,000
Registered Office: BNY Mellon Centre, 160 Queen Victoria Street, London, EC4V 4LA
Activities: Financial intermediation not elsewhere classified
Parent: BNY Mellon Investment Management EMEA Limited
Officers: Gregory Allan Brisk [1962] Director/COO BNY Mellon International Asset Management; Hilary Catherine Lopez [1971] Director/Head of Intermediary Sales; Jonathan Frank Lubran [1948] Executive Director of Institutional Business; Generald Dennis Rehn [1976] Director/Investment Management [American]

BNY Mellon International Asset Management (Holdings) Limited
Incorporated: 19 October 2012
Net Worth: £730,518,016 *Total Assets:* £730,529,024
Registered Office: 160 Queen Victoria Street, London, EC4V 4LA
Activities: Activities of other holding companies n.e.c.
Parent: BNY Mellon International Asset Management Group Limited
Officers: Gregory Allan Brisk [1962] Director/COO-BNY Mellon International; David John Peace [1962] Director/Chartered Accountant; Sandeep Singh Sumal [1971] Director/Senior Business Manager

BNY Mellon International Asset Management (Holdings) No. 1 Limited
Incorporated: 19 October 2012
Net Worth: £528,188,992 *Total Assets:* £1,053,241,024
Registered Office: 160 Queen Victoria Street, London, EC4V 4LA
Activities: Activities of other holding companies n.e.c.
Parent: BNY Mellon International Asset Management (Holdings) Limited
Officers: Gregory Allan Brisk [1962] Director/COO-BNY Mellon International; David John Peace [1962] Director/Chartered Accountant; Sandeep Singh Sumal [1971] Director/Senior Business Manager

BNY Mellon International Asset Management Group Limited
Incorporated: 20 April 1999
Net Worth: £1,491,307,008 *Total Assets:* £1,491,335,040
Registered Office: BNY Mellon Centre, 160 Queen Victoria Street, London, EC4V 4LA
Activities: Other business support service activities n.e.c.
Parent: BNY Mellon Investment Management Europe Holdings Limited
Officers: Gregory Allan Brisk [1962] Director; David John Peace [1962] Director/Chartered Accountant; Sandeep Singh Sumal [1971] Director/Senior Business Manager

BNY Mellon Investment Management (Europe) Limited
Incorporated: 28 November 2012
Net Worth: £290,555,008 *Total Assets:* £2,520,593,920
Registered Office: 160 Queen Victoria Street, London, EC4V 4LA
Activities: Activities of other holding companies n.e.c.
Officers: Gregory Allan Brisk [1962] Director/COO-BNY Mellon International; David John Peace [1962] Director/Chartered Accountant; Christoher David Rexworthy [1967] Director

BNY Mellon Investment Management EMEA Limited
Incorporated: 15 June 1973 *Employees:* 204
Net Worth: £181,904,000 *Total Assets:* £212,078,000
Registered Office: BNY Mellon Centre, 160 Queen Victoria Street, London, EC4V 4LA
Activities: Financial intermediation not elsewhere classified
Parent: BNY Mellon International Asset Management Group Limited
Officers: Gregory Allan Brisk [1962] Director/Global Head Risk and Compliance - Investment Management; Matthew John Oomen [1973] Director; Ann Lindsay Roughead [1962] Director; Geoffrey Charles Towers [1960] Director; David Michael Turnbull [1958] Director [New Zealander]

BNY Mellon Investment Management Seed Capital Limited
Incorporated: 20 November 2013
Net Worth: £133,139,032 *Total Assets:* £217,843,744
Registered Office: 160 Queen Victoria Street, London, EC4V 4LA
Activities: Activities of other holding companies n.e.c.
Officers: Gregory Allan Brisk [1962] Director/Global Head Risk and Compliance; Charles Patrick Dolan [1959] Director/Investment Strategist [American]; John William Jack [1966] Director/International CFO - The Bank of New York Mellon; David John Peace [1962] Director/Chartered Accountant

BOC Aviation (UK) Limited
Incorporated: 9 May 2014
Net Worth: £68,092,656 *Total Assets:* £329,803,392
Registered Office: c/o Cogency Global (UK) Limited, Unit 4CL, 6 Lloyds Avenue, London, EC3N 3AX
Activities: Other business support service activities n.e.c.
Officers: Aaron MacGregor [1978] Director/Senior Vice President, Airline Leasing & Sales; Jonathan James Edward Mahony [1967] Director/Businessman; Thim Fatt Phang [1956] Director/Businessman [Singaporean]; Steven Matthew Townend [1969] Director/Businessman

BOCI Global Commodities (UK) Limited
Incorporated: 6 July 2011 *Employees:* 12
Net Worth: £18,141,888 *Total Assets:* £370,902,336
Registered Office: 1 Lothbury, London, EC2R 7DB
Activities: Security and commodity contracts dealing activities
Parent: Bank of China International Holdings Limited
Officers: Siu Hong Fan [1976] Director/Investment Banker [Chinese]; Konstandinos Kakoulli [1958] Director/Compliance Officer; Tong Li [1970] Director [Chinese]; Zhongze Wang [1962] Director/Chief Financial Officer [Chinese]; Zhenlei Yao [1978] Director/Investment Banker

J.P. Boden & Co. Limited
Incorporated: 2 March 1992 *Employees:* 951
Net Worth: £60,390,972 *Total Assets:* £145,334,064
Registered Office: Boden House, 114-120 Victoria Road, London, NW10 6NY
Activities: Retail sale via mail order houses or via Internet
Parent: JP Boden (Holdings) Limited
Officers: Paul Simon O'Leary, Secretary; Francis Mark Binnington [1962] Marketing Director; John Peter Boden [1961] Director/Mail Order Proprietor; Jillian Alexandra Easterbrook [1971] Director; Julian Philip Granville [1967] Managing Director; Matthew Adam Hilgeman [1976] Product Director [American]; Paul Simon O'Leary [1967] Finance Director

Bodiam Hill Limited
Incorporated: 16 August 2007 *Employees:* 2
Net Worth: £145,778,000 *Total Assets:* £233,356,000
Registered Office: 2 King Edward Street, London, EC1A 1HQ
Activities: Financial intermediation not elsewhere classified
Parent: Bank of America Corporation
Officers: Andrew John Horton [1975] Director/Company Executive; Prashant Sood [1978] Director/Company Executive [Indian]

Boeing Commercial Aviation Services Europe Limited
Incorporated: 21 August 2012 *Employees:* 120
Net Worth: £152,684,864 *Total Assets:* £217,568,432
Registered Office: 25 Victoria Street, London, SW1H 0EX
Activities: Service activities incidental to air transportation
Parent: Boeing United Kingdom Limited
Officers: Simon Howard Jones, Secretary; Sir Michael Anthony Arthur [1950] Director/Businessman; John Norman Palmer [1962] Director; Daniella Dina Marie Turner [1957] Director/Operations; Christopher James Wolter [1965] Director [American]

Boeing Defence UK Limited
Incorporated: 13 December 1976 *Employees:* 1,182
Net Worth: £96,163,000 *Total Assets:* £229,212,000
Registered Office: 25 Victoria Street, London, SW1H 0EX
Activities: Defence activities
Parent: The Boeing Company
Officers: Simon Howard Jones, Secretary; Sir Michael Anthony Arthur [1950] Director/Businessman; Stephen John Burnell [1963] Managing Director UK Rotor Craft Support; Mark Griffiths [1981] Finance Director; Ross Harvey [1972] Supply Chain Director; Ian Niven McNeil [1966] Operations Director, BDUK Ltd; David John Pitchforth [1965] Director/Engineer; Richard Gerard Sikora [1963] Director/Business Strategy [American]; Nicholas Charles Whitney [1962] Sales and Marketing Director

Boeing European Holdings Limited
Incorporated: 27 February 2015
Net Worth: £1,001,453,696 *Total Assets:* £1,001,482,688
Registered Office: 25 Victoria Street, London, SW1H 0EX
Activities: Activities of other holding companies n.e.c.
Parent: The Boeing Company
Officers: Simon Howard Jones, Secretary; Sir Michael Anthony Arthur [1950] Director/Businessman; Natalie Rorem [1968] Tax Director [American]; Daniella Dina Marie Turner [1957] Director/Operations

Bombardier Aerospace (Holdings) UK Limited
Incorporated: 21 November 2016
Net Worth: £419,972,000 *Total Assets:* £419,972,000
Registered Office: Suite 1, 3rd Floor, 11-12 St James's Square, London, SW1Y 4LB
Activities: Activities of other holding companies n.e.c.
Officers: Colin Thompson, Secretary; Daniel Desjardins [1955] Director/Lawyer [Canadian]; Michael James Ryan [1959] Director [Irish]; Colin Thompson [1974] Director/Solicitor

Bombardier Transportation (Global Holding) UK Limited
Incorporated: 9 November 2015 *Employees:* 17
Net Worth: £4,174,704,384 *Total Assets:* £6,686,582,272
Registered Office: Two Pancras Square, King's Cross, London, N1C 4AG
Activities: Manufacture of railway locomotives and rolling stock
Parent: Bombardier Transportation (Investment) UK Limited
Officers: Lynn Suzanne West, Secretary; Matthew Byrne [1974] Director/Head of Global Services; Alexandre Decary [1978] Director, Private Equity, CDPQ [Canadian]; Daniel Desjardins [1955] Director/Senior Executive [Canadian]; Garry John Mowbray [1970] Director, Controlling; Lynn Suzanne West [1967] Director/Head of Contracts & Legal Affairs (UK)

Bombardier Transportation (Investment) UK Limited
Incorporated: 9 November 2015
Net Worth: £4,570,854,400 *Total Assets:* £4,793,449,472
Registered Office: Two Pancras Square, King's Cross, London, N1C 4AG
Activities: Manufacture of railway locomotives and rolling stock
Shareholders: Bombardier UK Holding Limited; Caisse de Depot et Placement du Quebec
Officers: Lynn Suzanne West, Secretary; Per Henrik Allmer [1965] Director/President WMA (Western Europe, Middle East and Africa) [Swedish]; Alexandre Decary [1978] Director, Private Equity, CDPQ [Canadian]; Daniel Desjardins [1955] Director/Senior Executive [Canadian]; Sophie Lussier [1972] Director/Vice President, Legal Affairs, Investment [Canadian]; Lynn Suzanne West [1967] Director/Head of Contracts & Legal Affairs and Company Secretary; Alessandro Zoratti [1971] Director/Finance Manager [Italian]

Bombardier UK Holding Limited
Incorporated: 19 August 2015
Net Worth: £3,270,234,368 *Total Assets:* £3,299,273,472
Registered Office: Two Pancras Square, King's Cross, London, N1C 4AG
Activities: Manufacture of railway locomotives and rolling stock
Officers: Lynn Suzanne West, Secretary; Per Henrik Allmer [1965] Director/President WMA (Western Europe, Middle East and Africa) [Swedish]; Daniel Desjardins [1955] Director/Senior Executive [Canadian]; Garry John Mowbray [1970] Director, Controlling

Bond Aviation Topco Limited
Incorporated: 17 April 2013
Net Worth: £98,535,000 *Total Assets:* £209,743,008
Registered Office: 33 Wigmore Street, London, W1U 1QX
Activities: Activities of head offices
Parent: Babcock Mission Critical Services Ltd
Officers: Karen Veronica Hayzen-Smith [1970] Director; Luis Francisco Inigo Moreno-Ventas [1976] Director/Lawyer [Spanish]

Bond Mission Critical Services PLC
Incorporated: 17 April 2013
Net Worth: £68,377,000 *Total Assets:* £401,480,992
Registered Office: 33 Wigmore Street, London, W1U 1QX
Activities: Activities of other holding companies n.e.c.
Parent: Babcock Mission Critical Services UK Limited
Officers: Karen Veronica Hayzen-Smith [1970] Director; Luis Francisco Inigo Moreno-Ventas [1976] Director/Lawyer [Spanish]

Bond Propco Limited
Incorporated: 28 October 2016 *Employees:* 3
Net Worth: £1 *Total Assets:* £105,550,000
Registered Office: c/o Skadden Arps Slate Meagher & Flom (UK) LLP, 40 Bank Street, London, E14 5DS
Activities: Residential care activities for the elderly and disabled
Parent: HCP UK Investments, Ltd
Officers: HE Weishi Allan [1964] Director/Merchant [Canadian]; Scott Brinker [1976] Director/Chief Investment Officer [American]; Adam Mabry [1984] Director/Senior Vice President - Corporate Transactions [American]; John Stasinos [1973] Director/Real Estate Private Equity [American]

Bonhams 1793 Limited
Incorporated: 21 November 2001 *Employees:* 338
Net Worth: £89,271,000 *Total Assets:* £115,112,000
Registered Office: Montpelier Galleries, Montpelier Street, London, SW7 1HH
Activities: Other service activities n.e.c.
Parent: Bonhams Holdings Ltd
Officers: Christopher David Watson, Secretary; Jonathan Andrew Baddeley [1952] Director/Valuer; Rupert Banner [1975] Director/Auctioneer; Malcolm John Barber [1951] Director; Simon Hamilton Cottle [1956] Director/Auctioneer; Jonathan Mark Fairhurst [1969] Director/Accountant; Matthew David Girling [1959] Director; Asaph Hyman [1973] Director/Valuer; James Edward Knight [1964] Director/Auctioneer; Caroline Oliphant [1957] Director/Auctioneer/Valuer; Colin David Sheaf [1952] Director/Auctioneer; Edward William Osborne Wilkinson [1969] Director/Valuer [American]; Leslie Wright [1949] Director/Auctioneer [American]

The Book Service Limited
Incorporated: 26 April 1948 *Employees:* 387
Net Worth Deficit: £3,353,628 *Total Assets:* £339,552,288
Registered Office: 20 Vauxhall Bridge Road, London, SW1V 2SA
Activities: Operation of warehousing and storage facilities for land transport activities
Parent: The Random House Group Limited
Officers: Sinead Mary Martin, Secretary; Mark William Gardiner [1961] Director; Thomas Daryl Weldon [1963] Director/Publisher

Boots Propco B Limited
Incorporated: 31 August 2007
Net Worth: £182,652,992 *Total Assets:* £215,360,992
Registered Office: 4th Floor, Sedley Place, 361 Oxford Street, London, W1C 2JL
Activities: Buying and selling of own real estate
Parent: Boots Properties Limited
Officers: Frank Standish, Secretary [Irish]; Aidan Gerard Clare [1966] Director [Irish]; Michael David Snape [1979] Director/Chief Financial Officer; Frank Standish [1963] Director/Company Secretary [Irish]

Borders & Southern Falkland Islands Limited
Incorporated: 18 October 2005
Net Worth Deficit: £134,949 *Total Assets:* £219,044,256
Registered Office: One Fleet Place, London, EC4M 7WS
Activities: Support activities for petroleum and natural gas mining
Parent: Borders & Southern Petroleum PLC
Officers: Peter William Fleming [1961] Director [New Zealander]; Dr Howard Obee [1959] Director

Borders & Southern Petroleum PLC
Incorporated: 8 June 2004 *Employees:* 5
Net Worth: £225,156,304 *Total Assets:* £225,633,152
Registered Office: One Fleet Place, London, EC4M 7WS
Activities: Extraction of crude petroleum
Officers: William John Walton Slack, Secretary; David Harry Williamson Dobson [1947] Director; Peter William Fleming [1961] Director [New Zealander]; Christopher Nigel Hurst Brown [1951] Director; Dr Howard Obee [1959] Director/Geologist

Borealis Infrastructure Europe (UK) Limited
Incorporated: 10 November 2003
Net Worth: £117,604,976 *Total Assets:* £117,617,152
Registered Office: 29th Floor, The Leadenhall Building, 122 Leadenhall Street, London, EC3V 4AB
Activities: Other business support service activities n.e.c.
Officers: John Anthony Guccione, Secretary; Ralph Adrian Berg [1972] Director; John Anthony Guccione [1972] Director/Solicitor [Canadian/Italian]

Boreas (Investment) Limited
Incorporated: 16 September 2013
Net Worth Deficit: £125,485,000 *Total Assets:* £647,022,016
Registered Office: 6th Floor, 65 Gresham Street, London, EC2V 7NQ
Activities: Financial intermediation not elsewhere classified
Parent: Boreas Holdco Limited
Officers: Melanie Julien, Secretary; Rana Ghorayeb [1973] Director/VP - Infrastructure [Canadian]; Emmanuel Jaclot [1978] Director [French]; Louis Marie St-Maurice [1958] Director/Vice-President, Caisse de Depot et Placement du Quebec [Canadian]

Boreas Holdco Limited
Incorporated: 17 September 2013
Net Worth Deficit: £125,542,000 *Total Assets:* £647,022,016
Registered Office: 6th Floor, 65 Gresham Street, London, EC2V 7NQ
Activities: Financial intermediation not elsewhere classified
Officers: Melanie Julien, Secretary; Rana Ghorayeb [1973] Director/VP - Infrastructure [Canadian]; Emmanuel Jaclot [1978] Director [French]; Louis Marie St-Maurice [1958] Director/Vice-President, Caisse de Depot et Placement du Quebec [Canadian]

The Boston Consulting Group UK LLP
Incorporated: 28 October 2010 *Employees:* 798
Net Worth: £25,118,904 *Total Assets:* £170,407,232
Registered Office: 20 Manchester Square, London, W1U 3PZ
Officers: Javier Anta Callersten [1975] LLP Member; Nicolas Aryana [1967] LLP Member; Jonathan Austin [1967] LLP Member; Justin Balcombe [1971] LLP Member; Nikolay Belkov [1981] LLP Member; Maurice Berns [1971] LLP Member; Julio Bezerra [1973] LLP Member; Christopher David Biggs [1979] LLP Member; Kiril Lubomirov Bliznakov [1977] LLP Member; Marcus Bokkerink [1965] LLP Member; Jeremy Richard Monckton Boote [1981] LLP Member; William James Martin Bruce [1965] LLP Member; Charmian Caines [1964] LLP Member; Hugo Canelas [1973] LLP Member; Paul Clark [1975] LLP Member; Karalee Close [1971] LLP Member; Frank Cordes [1976] LLP Member; Afonso de Lacerda Baiao Do Nascimento [1973] LLP Member; Ralf Dreischmeier [1965] LLP Member; Alla Dubrovina [1983] LLP Member; Eric Ellul [1959] LLP Member; Ofir Eyal [1975] LLP Member; Dominic Field [1968] LLP Member; Alastair Flanagan [1960] LLP Member; John Gooch [1970] LLP Member; Stuart Groves [1973] LLP Member; Denise Haylor [1964] LLP Member; Cristina Henrik [1976] LLP Member; Mark Benedict Holden [1970] LLP Member; Benjamin Horner [1973] LLP Member; David Hutchinson [1961] LLP Member; Fergus James Jarvis [1976] LLP Member; Pranay Jhunjhunwala [1981] LLP Member; Bernard Lequiller [1963] LLP Member; Jake Leslie Melville [1969] LLP Member; Mark Lubkeman [1962] LLP Member; Duncan Henry Martin [1968] LLP Member; Pierre Mercier [1969] LLP Member; Gaurav Nath [1979] LLP Member; Anne Nguyen [1975] LLP Member; Jesper Nielsen [1971] LLP Member; Pierre Paoli [1979] LLP Member; Shilpa Patel [1974] LLP Member; Jean-Paul Medard Petranca [1979] LLP Member; Stuart Quickenden [1972] LLP Member; Sukand Ramachandran [1971] LLP Member; Deepak Ravindran [1975] LLP Member; David Jeremy Rhodes [1958] LLP Member; Guillaume Ricome [1981] LLP Member; Patrick Roche [1978] LLP Member; Miguel-Angel Rodriguez-Sola [1966] LLP Member; Jacob Rosenzweig [1977] LLP Member; Aymen Saleh [1972] LLP Member; Antoon Schneider [1970] LLP Member; Ulrike Schwarz-Runer [1971] LLP Member; Eriola Shehu [1980] LLP Member; Nick South [1970] LLP Member; Bas Sudmeijer [1979] LLP Member; Johannes Thoms [1981] LLP Member; Elliot Daniel Vaughn [1975] LLP Member; Andrew Veitch [1978] LLP Member; Konrad Von Szczepanski [1963] LLP Member; Benjamin Wade [1981] LLP Member; Stuart Walker [1975] LLP Member; Ian Walsh [1975] LLP Member; Louis Watt [1981] LLP Member; Jon Webster [1973] LLP Member; Nadjia Yousif [1982] LLP Member

Bounty Brands Holdings Limited
Incorporated: 10 November 2016 *Employees:* 3,742
Net Worth: £69,634,008 *Total Assets:* £370,997,824
Registered Office: 73 Cornhill, London, EC3V 3QQ
Activities: Other business support service activities n.e.c.
Shareholders: James Bareham; Alison Callister
Officers: Stephen Owen, Secretary; Christopher Derek Bull [1960] Director; Nissim Ohayon [1972] Managing Director [Maltese]; Stefan Rabe [1972] Director [South African]; Peter Spinks [1980] Director/Accountant [South African]

Bouygues (U.K.) Limited
Incorporated: 4 November 1997 *Employees:* 1,298
Net Worth: £15,394,000 *Total Assets:* £386,499,008
Registered Office: Becket House, 1 Lambeth Palace Road, London, SE1 7EU
Activities: Development of building projects
Parent: Bouygues S.A.
Officers: Carole Ditty, Secretary; Robert Keith Bradley [1960] Director; Generald Farque [1964] Director/Engineer [French]; Nicolas Alexandre Pierre Guerin [1966] Property Development Director [French]; Jean-Luc Luc Midena [1969] Director/Chief Executive Officer [French]; Martin Schulz [1958] HR Director [South African]; Pierre Henri Skorochod [1962] Director [French]; Christopher James Stevens [1965] Director; Fabienne Paule Viala de Lisle [1962] Director/Chairman

Bowbell No. 1 PLC
Incorporated: 14 May 2010
Net Worth: £75,000 *Total Assets:* £1,157,815,040
Registered Office: 6th Floor, 65 Gresham Street, London, EC2V 7NQ
Activities: Other business support service activities n.e.c.
Parent: Bowbell No. 1 Holdings Limited
Officers: Sean Peter Martin [1965] Director

BP P.L.C.
Incorporated: 14 April 1909 *Employees:* 74,700
Net Worth: £71,494,631,424 *Total Assets:* £200,722,268,160
Registered Office: 1 St James's Square, London, SW1Y 4PD
Activities: Activities of head offices
Officers: Hannah Ashdown, Secretary; Jens Bertelsen, Secretary; Denise Dillon, Secretary; Nils Smedegaard Andersen [1958] Director [Danish]; Alan Boeckmann [1948] Director [American]; Frank Lee Bowman [1944] Director [American]; Dame Alison Jane Carnwath [1953] Director; Pamela Daley [1952] Director [American]; Ian Edward Lamert Davis [1951] Director; Professor Dame Ann Patricia Dowling [1952] Director/Professor of Engineering; Robert Warren Dudley [1955] Director [American]; Dr Brian Gilvary [1962] Director; Helge Lund [1962] Director [Norwegian]; Melody Boone Meyer [1957] Director [American]; Brendan Robert Nelson [1949] Director; Paula Rosput Reynolds [1956] Director [American]; Sir Robert John Sawers [1955] Director

BPG Global Holdings UK Limited
Incorporated: 21 March 2016
Net Worth: £155,534,272 *Total Assets:* £155,550,256
Registered Office: 7 Devonshire Square, London, EC2M 4YH
Activities: Activities of other holding companies n.e.c.
Major Shareholder: John Chan
Officers: Kwok Kit John Chan, Secretary; Kwok Kit John Chan [1977] Director/Business Manager [Hong Kong/Chinese]; David Deboer [1968] Director/Executive [American]; Shengyan Fan [1974] Director/Business Manager [Chinese]; Daniel Webber [1962] Director/Executive [American]

BPP Holdings Limited
Incorporated: 20 February 1976 *Employees:* 29
Net Worth: £187,031,008 *Total Assets:* £206,478,000
Registered Office: BPP House, Aldine Place, 142-144 Uxbridge Road, London, W12 8AA
Activities: Activities of head offices
Parent: Apollo UK Acquisition Company Limited
Officers: Gregory Cappelli [1967] Director [American]; Mary Folline Morris Cullen [1966] Director/Finance Executive [American]; Graham Stuart Mark Gaddes [1965] Director; Erin Kelly [1975] Director [American]; Richard John Simmons [1947] Director; Professor Timothy Stewart [1970] Director/Vice Chancellor; Marissa Vega [1972] Director/Higher Education Executive [American]

BPP Services Limited
Incorporated: 20 November 2006 *Employees:* 4
Net Worth Deficit: £68,618,000 *Total Assets:* £123,319,000
Registered Office: BPP House, Aldine Place, 142-144 Uxbridge Road, Shepherds Bush, London, W12 8AW
Activities: Other education n.e.c.
Parent: BPP Holdings Limited
Officers: Gary James Dart [1985] Director; Graham Stuart Mark Gaddes [1965] Director; Alison Carol Wells [1963] Director

Bracken Holdings Limited
Incorporated: 6 December 2007 *Employees:* 3
Net Worth: £118,728,128 *Total Assets:* £129,633,864
Registered Office: 6th Floor, 33 Holborn, London, EC1N 2HT
Activities: Activities of head offices
Parent: Octopus Investments Nominees Limited
Officers: Timothy Arthur [1962] Director/Chartered Accountant; Paul Stephen Latham [1956] Director; Keith James Willey [1962] Director

Braddell Limited
Incorporated: 24 December 1999 *Employees:* 5,727
Net Worth: £256,578,000 *Total Assets:* £340,278,016
Registered Office: Comfortdelgro House, 329 Edgware Road, Cricklewood, London, NW2 6JP
Activities: Repair and maintenance of other transport equipment n.e.c.
Parent: ComfortDelGro Corporation Limited
Officers: Ishai Eliezer Novick, Secretary; Juay Kiat Gan [1957] Director [Singaporean]; Jit Poh Lim [1939] Director [Singaporean]; Sean Poul O'Shea [1967] Director; Ban Seng Yang [1956] Director/Chief Executive [Singaporean]

Bradley Hall Holdings Limited
Incorporated: 14 September 2007
Net Worth: £225,863,648 *Total Assets:* £228,177,776
Registered Office: Peterborough Court, 133 Fleet Street, London, EC4A 2BB
Activities: Other business support service activities n.e.c.
Parent: GLQ Holdings (UK) Ltd
Officers: Thomas Kelly, Secretary; Clare Charlotte Richards, Secretary; Vikramjit Singh Chima [1973] Director/Accountant [Indian]; Piers Noel Ormiston Curle [1974] Director/Banker; William Thomas Gasson [1965] Director/Banker

Braehead Glasgow Limited
Incorporated: 23 June 1992
Net Worth: £119,800,000 *Total Assets:* £281,400,000
Registered Office: 40 Broadway, London, SW1H 0BT
Activities: Buying and selling of own real estate
Parent: Intu (SGS) Limited
Officers: Susan Marsden, Secretary; Martin Richard Breeden [1967] Director/Chartered Surveyor; David Andrew Fischel [1958] Director/Chartered Accountant; Colin Flinn [1969] Director; Hugh Michael Ford [1967] Director/General Corporate Counsel; Barbara Gibbes [1975] Director/Accountant; Kathryn Anne Grant [1973] Director/Chartered Surveyor; Trevor Pereira [1965] Director; Edward Matthew Giles Roberts [1963] Finance Director; Nick Round [1962] Director; Rebecca Mary Sarah Elizabeth Ryman [1975] Regional Director; Julian Nicholas Wilkinson [1963] Director/Chartered Surveyor

Braehead Park Investments Limited
Incorporated: 15 June 1992
Net Worth: £106,900,000 *Total Assets:* £277,400,000
Registered Office: 40 Broadway, London, SW1H 0BT
Activities: Buying and selling of own real estate
Parent: Intu (SGS) Limited
Officers: Susan Marsden, Secretary; Martin Richard Breeden [1967] Director/Chartered Surveyor; David Andrew Fischel [1958] Director/Chartered Accountant; Colin Flinn [1969] Director; Hugh Michael Ford [1967] Director/General Corporate Counsel; Barbara Gibbes [1975] Director/Accountant; Kathryn Anne Grant [1973] Director/Chartered Surveyor; Trevor Pereira [1965] Director; Edward Matthew Giles Roberts [1963] Finance Director; Nick Round [1962] Director; Rebecca Mary Sarah Elizabeth Ryman [1975] Regional Director; Julian Nicholas Wilkinson [1963] Director/Chartered Surveyor

Braemar Shipping Services PLC
Incorporated: 11 August 1988 *Employees:* 834
Net Worth: £93,659,000 *Total Assets:* £161,504,992
Registered Office: 1 Strand, Trafalgar Square, London, WC2N 5HR
Activities: Other transportation support activities
Officers: Peter Timothy James Mason, Secretary; Juergen Heinz Breuer [1965] Director/Businessman [German]; James Richard de Villeneuve Kidwell [1962] Director/Chief Executive; Stephen John Kunzer [1966] Director; David George Moorhouse [1947] Director; Lesley Susan Watkins [1959] Director

Brass No.3 PLC
Incorporated: 9 April 2013
Net Worth: £597,000 *Total Assets:* £348,886,016
Registered Office: Third Floor, Wilmington Trust SP Services (London) Limited, 1 King's Arms Yard, London, EC2R 7AF
Activities: Other business support service activities n.e.c.
Parent: Brass No.3 Mortgage Holdings Limited
Officers: Daniel Jonathan Wynne [1970] Director

Brass No.4 PLC
Incorporated: 19 August 2014
Net Worth Deficit: £2,027,000 *Total Assets:* £436,132,992
Registered Office: c/o Wilmington Trust SP Services (London) Limited, Third Floor, 1 King's Arms Yard, London, EC2R 7AF
Activities: Other business support service activities n.e.c.
Parent: Brass No.4 Mortgage Holdings Limited
Officers: Daniel Jonathan Wynne [1970] Director

Brass No.5 PLC
Incorporated: 11 August 2015
Net Worth: £1,158,000 *Total Assets:* £1,920,653,056
Registered Office: Third Floor, c/o Wilmington Trust SP Services (London) Limited, 1 King's Arms Yard, London, EC2R 7AF
Activities: Other business support service activities n.e.c.
Parent: Brass No.5 Mortgage Holdings Limited
Officers: Daniel Jonathan Wynne [1970] Director

Brass No.6 PLC
Incorporated: 15 August 2017
Net Worth Deficit: £480,000 *Total Assets:* £2,649,346,048
Registered Office: c/o Wilmington Trust SP Services (London) Limited, Third Floor, 1 Kings Arms Yard, London, EC2R 7AF
Activities: Other business support service activities n.e.c.
Parent: Brass No.6 Mortgage Holdings Limited
Officers: Daniel Jonathan Wynne [1970] Director

Breezeroad Limited
Incorporated: 18 March 2004 *Employees:* 484
Net Worth: £41,425,000 *Total Assets:* £380,140,000
Registered Office: c/o CMS Cameron McKenna LLP, 78 Cannon Street, London, EC4N 6AF
Activities: Hotels and similar accommodation
Shareholders: Qatar Investment Authority; HRH Prince Alwaleed Bin Talal Bin Abdulaziz Alsaud
Officers: Benjamin David Cadwell [1982] Director/Executive [American]; Ashley Fernandes [1968] Director [Indian]; Sean Piers Harrison [1971] Director/General Counsel; Kamal Rhazali [1979] Director/General Counsel [French]

Brent Co-Efficient Limited
Incorporated: 26 November 2007
Net Worth Deficit: £37,064,000 *Total Assets:* £134,298,000
Registered Office: 30 Park Street, London, SE1 9EQ
Activities: Renting and operating of Housing Association real estate
Officers: Kerry Andrew Tromanhauser, Secretary; Chyrel Ann Brown [1974] Housing Director; Sharon Pearce [1967] Managing Director; Simon William Vevers [1971] Commercial Director

Robert Brett & Sons Limited
Incorporated: 11 January 1928
Previous: Robert Brett & Sons,Limited
Net Worth: £125,737,000 *Total Assets:* £179,131,008
Registered Office: 150 Aldersgate Street, London, EC1A 4AB
Activities: Activities of head offices
Shareholders: James Robert Brett; Timothy William Brett; Harvey Marston Strange Barrett; Edward James Timothy Brett; William John Brett
Officers: John Gilbert, Secretary/Director; George William Bolsover [1950] Director; William John Brett [1965] Director; John Gilbert [1946] Director; Lindsay Poston [1953] Director; Hugh Anthony Shaw [1942] Director; Alan Henry Smith [1956] Director; Nicholas James Tarn [1965] Director

Brewin Dolphin Holdings PLC
Incorporated: 10 February 1992 *Employees:* 1,763
Net Worth: £269,240,992 *Total Assets:* £456,368,992
Registered Office: 12 Smithfield Street, London, EC1A 9BD
Activities: Activities of head offices
Officers: Tiffany Brill, Secretary; Ian Dewar [1957] Director; Michael John Kellard [1961] Director; Simon Edward Callum Miller [1952] Director; David Richardson Nicol [1955] Director; Simonetta Rigo [1970] Director [Italian]; Kathleen Mary Shailer [1963] Director; Caroline Helen Taylor [1962] Director; Paul Wilson [1951] Director

Brewin Dolphin Limited
Incorporated: 1 June 1987 *Employees:* 1,662
Net Worth: £217,688,000 *Total Assets:* £531,753,984
Registered Office: 12 Smithfield Street, London, EC1A 9BD
Activities: Financial intermediation not elsewhere classified
Parent: Brewin Dolphin Holdings PLC
Officers: Tiffany Brill, Secretary; Catherine Mullins, Secretary; Ian Dewar [1957] Director; Michael John Kellard [1961] Director; Simon Edward Callum Miller [1952] Director/Chairman; David Richardson Nicol [1955] Director/Chief Executive; Simonetta Rigo [1970] Director [Italian]; Kathleen Mary Shailer [1963] Director; Caroline Helen Taylor [1962] Director; Paul Wilson [1951] Director

Bridge Petroleum 3 Limited
Incorporated: 3 March 2017
Net Worth: £273,285,280 *Total Assets:* £277,386,336
Registered Office: Hill House, Little New Street, London, EC4A 3TR
Activities: Extraction of crude petroleum
Parent: Bridge Petroleum Limited
Officers: Guy de Speville, Secretary; Alexander Spring [1966] Director/Businessman; Dr Fazrie Wahid [1977] Director/Businessman [Malaysian]; David Williams [1961] Director/Businessman

Bridge Petroleum 4 Limited
Incorporated: 3 March 2017
Net Worth: £273,285,280 *Total Assets:* £275,281,760
Registered Office: Hill House, Little New Street, London, EC4A 3TR
Activities: Extraction of crude petroleum
Parent: Bridge Petroleum Limited
Officers: Guy de Speville, Secretary; Alexander Spring [1966] Director/Businessman; Dr Fazrie Wahid [1977] Director/Businessman [Malaysian]; David Williams [1961] Director/Businessman

Bridgepoint Funding III A Limited
Incorporated: 26 September 2011
Net Worth: £643,233 *Total Assets:* £115,978,200
Registered Office: 95 Wigmore Street, London, W1U 1FB
Activities: Financial intermediation not elsewhere classified
Parent: Bridgepoint Capital (Nominees) Limited
Officers: Rachel Clare Thompson, Secretary; Charles Stuart John Barter [1962] Director/Solicitor; Paul Richard Gunner [1973] Finance Director; Jonathan Raoul Hughes [1965] Director/Investment Banker

Bridges Business Space LLP
Incorporated: 17 December 2014
Net Worth: £66,158,844 *Total Assets:* £119,443,648
Registered Office: 38 Seymour Street, London, W1H 7BP

Bridging Trading LLP
Incorporated: 19 October 2010
Net Worth: £258,986,000 *Total Assets:* £259,024,000
Registered Office: 6th Floor, St Magnus House, 3 Lower Thames Street, London, EC3R 6HD

Brightsphere Investment Group PLC
Incorporated: 29 May 2014 *Employees:* 1,326
Previous: OM Asset Management PLC
Net Worth: £54,237,288 *Total Assets:* £1,124,143,104
Registered Office: c/o Brightsphere International Ltd, Millennium Bridge House, 2 Lambeth Hill, London, EC4V 4GG
Activities: Activities of financial services holding companies
Officers: Richard Jonathan Hart, Secretary; Mary Elizabeth Beams [1956] Director/Consultant [American]; Robert Chersi [1961] Director/Consultant [American]; Reginald Love [1982] Director/Partner [American]; John Paulson [1955] Director/President [American]; Barbara Trebbi [1966] Director/Retired [American]; Dr. Guang Yang [1963] Director/Managing Partner [American]

Brightsphere UK, Ltd.
Incorporated: 5 June 2014
Previous: Omam UK, Limited
Net Worth: £593,077,504 *Total Assets:* £1,621,716,608
Registered Office: c/o Brightsphere International Ltd, Millennium Bridge House, 2 Lambeth Hill, London, EC4V 4GG
Activities: Activities of financial services holding companies
Parent: OM Asset Management PLC
Officers: Richard Jonathan Hart, Secretary; Daniel Mahoney [1979] Director/Head of Finance [American]; Aidan Riordan [1972] Director/Head of Affiliate Management [American]

Bristol Water Group Limited
Incorporated: 15 June 2011 *Employees:* 554
Previous: CSE Water UK Limited
Net Worth: £227,700,000 *Total Assets:* £729,400,000
Registered Office: Suite 1, 3rd Floor, 11-12 St James's Square, London, SW1Y 4LB
Activities: Activities of other holding companies n.e.c.
Parent: Icon Infrastructure LLP
Officers: Colin Caldwell, Secretary; Indradoot Dhar [1982] Director/Investment Professional; Hajime Ichishi [1975] Director/Project Manager [Japanese]; Paul Richard Malan [1970] Director/Investment Professional

Brit Group Finance Limited
Incorporated: 3 April 2007
Net Worth: £2,417,092 *Total Assets:* £274,325,536
Registered Office: The Leadenhall Building, 122 Leadenhall Street, London, EC3V 4AB
Activities: Financial intermediation not elsewhere classified
Officers: Mark Andrew Allan [1981] Director/CFO/Insurance; Daniel Thomas Dixon [1970] Director/Head of Investments and Treasury; Antony Edward Usher [1965] Director/Accountant

Brit Insurance Holdings Limited
Incorporated: 30 October 1995
Net Worth: £605,976,640 *Total Assets:* £829,856,960
Registered Office: The Leadenhall Building, 122 Leadenhall Street, London, EC3V 4AB
Activities: Non-life insurance
Officers: Mark Andrew Allan [1981] Director/CFO/Insurance; Christopher Denton [1979] Director/Actuary/Head of Financial Strategy; Antony Edward Usher [1965] Director/Accountant

Brit Limited
Incorporated: 19 December 2013 *Employees:* 562
Net Worth: £805,458,560 *Total Assets:* £5,006,056,960
Registered Office: The Leadenhall Building, 122 Leadenhall Street, London, EC3V 4AB
Activities: Non-life insurance
Officers: Tim James Harmer, Secretary; Mark Andrew Allan [1981] Director/CFO/Insurance; Andrew Acheson Barnard [1955] Director/Insurance Professional [American]; Gordon Muir Campbell [1948] Director and Consultant [Canadian]; Jeremy Simon Ehrlich [1980] Director/Lawyer [Canadian]; Andrea Caroline Natascha Welsch [1977] Director; Matthew Dominic Wilson [1970] Director

Brit UW Limited
Incorporated: 27 June 1996
Net Worth: £92,203,392 *Total Assets:* £4,536,346,624
Registered Office: The Leadenhall Building, 122 Leadenhall Street, London, EC3V 4AB
Activities: Non-life insurance
Officers: Mark Andrew Allan [1981] Director/CFO/Insurance; Stuart Dawes [1973] Director/Head of Group Financial Performance; Christopher Denton [1979] Director/Actuary/Head of Financial Strategy; Antony Edward Usher [1965] Director/Accountant; Matthew Dominic Wilson [1970] Director/Underwriting Management

Britannia Steam Ship Insurance Association Limited (The)
Incorporated: 19 February 1876
Net Worth: £330,634,432 *Total Assets:* £1,227,281,664
Registered Office: Regis House, 45 King William Street, London, EC4R 9AN
Activities: Non-life insurance
Officers: James Andrew Young, Secretary; Andrew John Cutler [1966] Director/Lawyer; Anthony James Firmin [1953] Director/Chief Operating Officer; Paul Hunt [1950] Director; Shin-Chyi Lan [1976] Director/Vice President [Taiwanese]; Louis Martel [1965] Director/President [Canadian]; Bruce Thomas Nielsen [1962] Director [American]; Niall Joseph Nolan [1963] Finance Director [Irish]; Nigel John Palmer [1951] Director/Shipping Person; Jonathan Paul Rodgers [1965] Finance Director; Egied Octavius Ludovicus Verbeeck [1974] Director/General Counsel [Belgian]; James Walter FitzGenerald Warwick [1966] Managing Director; Yasushi Yamawaki [1948] Shipping Director [Japanese]

British Alcan Aluminium Limited
Incorporated: 25 February 1944
Previous: British Alcan Aluminium PLC
Net Worth: £143,260,992 *Total Assets:* £207,267,008
Registered Office: 6 St James's Square, London, SW1Y 4AD
Activities: Activities of head offices
Parent: Rio Tinto International Holdings Limited
Officers: Andrew William Hodges [1967] Director/Chartered Secretary; Denis Lhuissier [1971] Director/Chief Finance Officer RTLM [French]

British American Shared Services (GSD) Limited
Incorporated: 11 August 2004
Net Worth: £43,199,000 *Total Assets:* £166,020,992
Registered Office: Globe House, 1 Water Street, London, WC2R 3LA
Activities: Other information technology service activities
Parent: British American Global Shared Services Limited
Officers: Jonathan Michael Guttridge, Secretary; Jason Paul Allen [1969] Director/Group Head of Corporate Solutions, IT; Marina Fagundes Bellini [1973] Director/CIO & Group Head of Digital Transformation [Italian/Brazilian]; Mark Lindsay Burns [1965] Director/Accountant; Jean-Pierre Andre Cussac [1969] Director/Group Head of IT Enterprise Services [French]; Thomas Davey [1987] Director/Head of IT Finance

British American Tobacco (1998) Limited
Incorporated: 20 August 1997
Net Worth: £29,342,869,504 *Total Assets:* £32,152,942,592
Registered Office: Globe House, 4 Temple Place, London, WC2R 2PG
Activities: Activities of head offices
Parent: British American Tobacco P.L.C
Officers: Jessica Munday, Secretary; Jerome Bruce Abelman [1963] Director/Lawyer [American]; Alan Davy [1963] Group Operations Director; Giovanni Giordano [1965] HR Director [Italian/American]; John Benedict Stevens [1959] Director/Tobacco Manufacturer; Kingsley Wheaton [1973] Director/Company Executive

British American Tobacco (2009 Pca) Limited
Incorporated: 5 June 2009
Net Worth: £1,112,381,952 *Total Assets:* £1,112,381,952
Registered Office: Globe House, 4 Temple Place, London, WC2R 2PG
Activities: Activities of other holding companies n.e.c.
Parent: British American Tobacco International Holdings (UK) Limited
Officers: David Patrick Ian Booth [1974] Director/Group Chief Accountant; Noelle Colfer [1968] Director/Solicitor; Robert Fergus Heaton [1965] Director/Head of UK Tax

British American Tobacco (2009) Limited
Incorporated: 6 November 2009
Net Worth: £43,002,085,376 *Total Assets:* £63,439,478,784
Registered Office: Globe House, 4 Temple Place, London, WC2R 2PG
Activities: Activities of other holding companies n.e.c.
Parent: British American Tobacco (2012) Limited
Officers: Jerome Bruce Abelman [1963] Director/Lawyer [American]; Robert James Casey [1948] Director/Attorney [American]; Robert Fergus Heaton [1965] Director/Head of UK Tax; John Benedict Stevens [1959] Finance Director

British American Tobacco (2012) Limited
Incorporated: 1 November 2012
Net Worth: £75,728,437,248 *Total Assets:* £80,639,148,032
Registered Office: Globe House, 4 Temple Place, London, WC2R 2PG
Activities: Activities of head offices
Parent: British American Tobacco (1998) Limited
Officers: Jerome Bruce Abelman [1963] Director/Solicitor [American]; Robert James Casey [1948] Director/Attorney [American]; Nicandro Durante [1956] Director/Economist [Brazilian]; Robert Fergus Heaton [1965] Director/Head of UK Tax; John Benedict Stevens [1959] Director/Tobacco Manufacturer

British American Tobacco (AIT) Limited
Incorporated: 26 June 1968
Net Worth: £162,636,000 *Total Assets:* £163,287,008
Registered Office: Globe House, 1 Water Street, London, WC2R 3LA
Activities: Activities of head offices
Parent: B.A.T (U.K. and Export) Limited
Officers: David Patrick Ian Booth [1974] Director/Group Chief Accountant; Anthony Michael Hardy Cohn [1969] Director/Accountant; Noelle Colfer [1968] Director/Solicitor

British American Tobacco (Brands) Limited
Incorporated: 16 April 1998
Net Worth: £347,652,992 *Total Assets:* £773,982,016
Registered Office: Globe House, 4 Temple Place, London, WC2R 2PG
Activities: Activities of head offices
Parent: Batmark Limited
Officers: Jonathan Michael Guttridge, Secretary; David Patrick Ian Booth [1974] Director/Group Chief Accountant; Roger Anthony Carr Evans [1973] Director; Paul McCrory [1972] Director/Lawyer; Kingsley Wheaton [1973] Director/Chief Marketing Officer

British American Tobacco (GLP) Limited
Incorporated: 4 May 2007 *Employees:* 51
Net Worth: £173,363,488 *Total Assets:* £643,197,120
Registered Office: Globe House, 1 Water Street, London, WC2R 3LA
Activities: Wholesale of grain, unmanufactured tobacco, seeds and animal feeds
Parent: British American Tobacco International Holdings (UK) Limited
Officers: Jonathan Michael Guttridge, Secretary; John Stuart Alphin [1974] Director/Head of Leaf Sourcing [American]; Timothy James Bartle [1971] Director/Group Head of Operations Finance; Benjamin Daniel Guest [1973] Director/Leaf Business Development Manager; Paul Ogborn [1965] Director/Group Head of Leaf, Operations

British American Tobacco (Investments) Limited
Incorporated: 27 September 1902 *Employees:* 875
Net Worth: £1,031,849,984 *Total Assets:* £1,930,866,944
Registered Office: Globe House, 1 Water Street, London, WC2R 3LA
Activities: Activities of head offices
Parent: British-American Tobacco (Holdings) Limited
Officers: Noelle Colfer, Secretary; Jerome Bruce Abelman [1963] Director/Lawyer [American]; Steven Glyn Dale [1967] Director/Tax Adviser; Alan Davy [1963] Group Operations Director; Giovanni Giordano [1965] HR Director [Italian/American]; Dr David O'Reilly [1966] Director/Scientist; Naresh Kumar Sethi [1966] Business Development Director [Australian]; John Benedict Stevens [1959] Director/Tobacco Manufacturer; Kingsley Wheaton [1973] Director/Company Executive

British American Tobacco (NGP) Limited
Incorporated: 17 September 2013
Previous: Nicovations Limited
Net Worth: £634,000,000 *Total Assets:* £634,000,000
Registered Office: Globe House, 4 Temple Place, London, WC2R 2PG
Activities: Activities of head offices
Parent: British American Tobacco (1998) Limited
Officers: Jessica Munday, Secretary; Nicandro Durante [1956] Director/Economist [Brazilian/Italian]; David O'Reilly [1966] Director; John Benedict Stevens [1959] Finance Director

British American Tobacco China Holdings Limited
Incorporated: 10 March 1999
Net Worth: £102,995,000 *Total Assets:* £102,995,000
Registered Office: Globe House, 1 Water Street, London, WC2R 3LA
Activities: Activities of head offices
Parent: Weston Investment Company Limited
Officers: David Patrick Ian Booth [1974] Director/Group Chief Accountant; Robert James Casey [1948] Director/Attorney [American]; Carola Wiegand [1966] Director/Global Commercial Tax Manager [German]

British American Tobacco Global Travel Retail Limited
Incorporated: 11 December 2015 *Employees:* 127
Net Worth: £176,105,952 *Total Assets:* £236,178,800
Registered Office: Globe House, 1, Water Street, London, WC2R 3LA
Activities: Retail sale of tobacco products in specialised stores
Parent: British-American Tobacco (Holdings) Limited
Officers: Oliver James Martin, Secretary; Matthias Baltes [1972] Director/Head of Marketing Operations, Global Travel Retail [German]; Pablo Andres Banki [1982] Director [Hungarian]; Athanasios Trimis [1971] Director [Greek]

British American Tobacco International Holdings (UK) Limited
Incorporated: 30 November 1905
Net Worth: £1,324,366,976 *Total Assets:* £1,599,456,000
Registered Office: Globe House, 1 Water Street, London, WC2R 3LA
Activities: Activities of head offices
Parent: Weston Investment Company Limited
Officers: Oliver James Martin, Secretary; Robert James Casey [1948] Director/Attorney [American]; Alan Davy [1963] Group Operations Director; Robert Fergus Heaton [1965] Director/Head of UK Tax; John Benedict Stevens [1959] Director/Tobacco Manufacturer

British American Tobacco Italy Investments Limited
Incorporated: 12 February 2003
Net Worth Deficit: £302,671,008 *Total Assets:* £176,382,000
Registered Office: Globe House, 1 Water Street, London, WC2R 3LA
Activities: Activities of other holding companies n.e.c.
Parent: British American Tobacco International Holdings (UK) Limited
Officers: Oliver James Martin, Secretary; David Patrick Ian Booth [1974] Director/Group Chief Accountant; Robert James Casey [1948] Director/Attorney [American]; John Fry [1979] Director/Tax Manager; Robert Fergus Heaton [1965] Director/Head of UK Tax

British American Tobacco Italy Limited
Incorporated: 28 April 2003
Net Worth: £211,623,008 *Total Assets:* £661,716,992
Registered Office: Globe House, 1 Water Street, London, WC2R 3LA
Activities: Other professional, scientific and technical activities n.e.c.
Parent: British American Tobacco Italy Investments Limited
Officers: Oliver James Martin, Secretary; David Patrick Ian Booth [1974] Director/Group Chief Accountant; Robert James Casey [1948] Director/Attorney [American]; John Fry [1979] Director/Tax Manager; Robert Fergus Heaton [1965] Director/Head of UK Tax

British American Tobacco Malaysia (Investments) Limited
Incorporated: 1 February 1928
Net Worth: £434,211,008 *Total Assets:* £434,211,008
Registered Office: Globe House, 1 Water Street, London, WC2R 3LA
Activities: Activities of head offices
Parent: Weston Investment Company Limited
Officers: David Patrick Ian Booth [1974] Director/Group Chief Accountant; Robert James Casey [1948] Director/Attorney [American]; Carola Wiegand [1966] Director/Global Commercial Tax Manager [German]

British American Tobacco P.L.C.
Incorporated: 23 July 1997
Net Worth: £60,804,001,792 *Total Assets:* £141,037,993,984
Registered Office: Globe House, 4 Temple Place, London, WC2R 2PG
Activities: Activities of head offices
Officers: Paul McCrory, Secretary; Jack Bowles [1963] Director [French]; Richard George William Burrows [1946] Director/Chartered Accountant [Irish]; Nicandro Durante [1956] Director/Economist [Brazilian]; Dr Marion Helmes [1965] Director/Consultant [German]; Luc Jobin [1959] Director [Canadian]; Holly Keller Koeppel [1958] Director [American]; Savio Kwan [1948] Director; Susan Jane Mair [1956] Director; Evriviades Dimitri George Panayotopoulos [1951] Director; Kieran Charles Poynter [1950] Director; John Benedict Stevens [1959] Director/Tobacco Manufacturer

British American Tobacco Peru Holdings Limited
Incorporated: 15 January 2003
Net Worth: £177,632,000 *Total Assets:* £177,632,000
Registered Office: Globe House, 1 Water Street, London, WC2R 3LA
Activities: Activities of other holding companies n.e.c.
Parent: Weston Investment Company Limited
Officers: Sophie Louise Edmonds Kerr, Secretary; David Patrick Ian Booth [1974] Director/Group Chief Accountant; Robert James Casey [1948] Director/Attorney [American]; Anthony Michael Hardy Cohn [1969] Director/Accountant

British American Tobacco Western Europe Commercial Trading Limited
Incorporated: 11 August 2004 *Employees:* 224
Previous: British American Tobacco (Supply Chain WE) Limited
Net Worth: £159,278,864 *Total Assets:* £3,531,469,824
Registered Office: Globe House, 1 Water Street, London, WC2R 3LA
Activities: Manufacture of tobacco products
Parent: British-American Tobacco (Holdings) Limited
Officers: Oliver James Martin, Secretary; Stuart Damon Brazier [1971] Director/Regional Head of Finance - Western Europe; Tamas Csejtei [1976] Director [Hungarian]; Hikkaduwe Palliye Gurunnanselage Sandeep Nishan Drupath de Alwis [1967] Finance Director [Sri Lankan]; Jeroen Abraham Johannes Dees [1977] Director/Solicitor [Dutch]; Ivan Vicente Gomez Gamboa [1967] Director/Regional Head of Legal and External Affairs [Venezuelan]; Tadeu Luiz Marroco [1966] Regional Director, Western Europe [Brazilian]; Bernd Meyer [1966] Director/Regional Operations Manager, Western Europe [German]; Christiaan Sijtsma [1962] Director/Regional Marketing Manager ENA [Dutch]

British Arab Commercial Bank Public Limited Company
Incorporated: 23 March 1972
Net Worth: £216,832,992 *Total Assets:* £2,952,856,064
Registered Office: 8-10 Mansion House Place, London, EC4N 8BJ
Activities: Banks
Parent: Central Bank Libya
Officers: Patricia Jane Smith, Secretary; Ahmed Mohamed Aburkhis [1962] Director/Banker [Libyan]; Susannah Louise Aliker [1966] Director/Banker; Dr Kaled Ali Ahmed Kagigi [1966] Director/Banker [Libyan]; Abdalla Ramadan Naama [1951] Director/Banker [Libyan]; Faesal KH Ali Khalil Othman [1972] Director/Banker [Libyan]; Brahim Semid [1962] Director/Banker [Algerian]; Mohamed Shokri [1952] Director/Banker [Libyan]; Michael John Stevenson [1950] Director/Chartered Accountant; Mohamed Zine [1974] Director/Risk Management Chief Officer [Moroccan/Canadian]

British Heart Foundation
Incorporated: 28 July 1961 *Employees:* 3,824
Net Worth: £82,900,000 *Total Assets:* £430,300,000
Registered Office: Greater London House, 180 Hampstead Road, London, NW1 7AW
Activities: Other human health activities
Officers: Sam Paul Ryan, Secretary; Dr Sarah Catherine Clarke [1965] Director/Consultant Cardiologist; Professor Anna Felicja Dominiczak [1954] Director/Vice Principal and Head of College; Dr Robert James Campbell Easton [1963] Director; Lord Andrew Simon Feldman [1966] Director; Daryl Louise Fielding [1957] Director/CEO, Portfolio NED; Dr Douglas John Gurr [1964] Director/President; Timothy Jean-Paul Howe [1963] Director/Barrister; Professor John Peter Iredale [1960] Director/Physician and University Leader; Prof David Arthur Lomas [1962] Director/University Vice-Provost; Iain James MacKay [1961] Director/Accountant; Professor Sussan Nourshargh [1960] Director/Professor of Microvascular Pharmacology; Peter Sangster Phippen [1960] Director; Professor Liam Smeeth [1965] Director/Clinical Professor of Epidemiology; Professor Sir Kent Linton Woods [1948] Director/Emeritus Professor of Therapeutics

British Land (Joint Ventures) Limited
Incorporated: 28 February 2003
Net Worth: £352,564,992 *Total Assets:* £352,564,992
Registered Office: York House, 45 Seymour Street, London, W1H 7LX
Activities: Development of building projects
Parent: BL Residual Holding Company Limited
Officers: Sarah Morrell Barzycki [1958] Director/Head of Finance; Paul Stuart Macey [1978] Director/Accountant; Jonathan Charles McNuff [1986] Director/Chartered Accountant; Charles John Middleton [1966] Director/Corporate Tax Executive; Timothy Andrew Roberts [1964] Director/Chartered Surveyor; Nigel Mark Webb [1963] Director/Chartered Surveyor

British Land Acquisitions Limited
Incorporated: 26 May 2005
Net Worth: £1 *Total Assets:* £816,109,312
Registered Office: York House, 45 Seymour Street, London, W1H 7LX
Activities: Development of building projects
Parent: Glenway Limited
Officers: Bruce Michael James [1967] Director/Head of Secretariat; Jonathan Charles McNuff [1986] Director/Chartered Accountant; Charles John Middleton [1966] Director/Corporate Tax Executive

British Land Broadgate 2005 Limited
Incorporated: 1 December 2004
Net Worth: £168,114,944 *Total Assets:* £1,008,889,664
Registered Office: York House, 45 Seymour Street, London, W1H 7LX
Activities: Development of building projects
Parent: Bluebutton Properties UK Limited
Officers: David Ian Lockyer [1969] Director/Chartered Surveyor; Timothy Andrew Roberts [1964] Director/Chartered Surveyor; Hursh Shah [1976] Director

British Land Company Public Limited Company (The)
Incorporated: 26 February 1959 *Employees:* 265
Net Worth: £9,251,999,744 *Total Assets:* £13,180,000,256
Registered Office: York House, 45 Seymour Street, London, W1H 7LX
Activities: Development of building projects
Officers: Brona Rose McKeown, Secretary; Simon Geoffrey Carter [1975] Director/Chief Financial Officer; John Gildersleeve [1944] Director; Professor Lynn Faith Gladden [1961] Director/Professor; Christopher Montague Grigg [1959] Director/Chief Executive; Alastair James Hughes [1965] Director; William Nicholas Jackson [1963] Director; Nicholas Ian Macpherson [1959] Director; Charles Sheridan Alexander Maudsley [1964] Director; Preben Prebensen [1956] Director/Chief Executive; Timothy Andrew Roberts [1964] Director/Chartered Surveyor; Timothy Score [1960] Director/Chief Financial Officer; Laura Katharine Wade-Gery [1965] Executive Director; Rebecca Jane Worthington [1971] Director

British Land Department Stores Limited
Incorporated: 14 December 2004
Net Worth: £98,942,736 *Total Assets:* £484,833,472
Registered Office: York House, 45 Seymour Street, London, W1H 7LX
Activities: Development of building projects
Parent: BL Department Stores Holding Company Limited
Officers: Sarah Morrell Barzycki [1958] Director/Head of Finance; Bryan Lewis [1967] Director/Chartered Surveyor; Paul Stuart Macey [1978] Director/Accountant; Jonathan Charles McNuff [1986] Director/Chartered Accountant; Charles John Middleton [1966] Director/Corporate Tax Executive; Timothy Andrew Roberts [1964] Director/Chartered Surveyor; Nigel Mark Webb [1963] Director/Chartered Surveyor

British Land Fund Management Limited
Incorporated: 29 May 2002
Net Worth: £748,071,296 *Total Assets:* £1,146,279,296
Registered Office: York House, 45 Seymour Street, London, W1H 7LX
Activities: Development of building projects
Parent: British Land Acquisitions Limited
Officers: Benjamin Toby Grose [1969] Director/Chartered Surveyor; Timothy Andrew Roberts [1964] Director

British Land in Town Retail Limited
Incorporated: 21 February 1997
Net Worth Deficit: £34,726,584 *Total Assets:* £110,586,856
Registered Office: York House, 45 Seymour Street, London, W1H 7LX
Activities: Development of building projects
Parent: BL High Street and Shopping Centres Holding Company Limited
Officers: Sarah Morrell Barzycki [1958] Director/Head of Finance; Paul Stuart Macey [1978] Director/Accountant; Jonathan Charles McNuff [1986] Director/Chartered Accountant; Charles John Middleton [1966] Director/Corporate Tax Executive; Timothy Andrew Roberts [1964] Director/Chartered Surveyor; Nigel Mark Webb [1963] Director/Chartered Surveyor

British Land Industrial Limited
Incorporated: 1 December 1959
Net Worth: £775,281,088 *Total Assets:* £802,235,968
Registered Office: York House, 45 Seymour Street, London, W1H 7LX
Activities: Development of building projects
Parent: BL Leisure and Industrial Holding Company Limited
Officers: Sarah Morrell Barzycki [1958] Director/Head of Finance; Paul Stuart Macey [1978] Director/Accountant; Jonathan Charles McNuff [1986] Director/Chartered Accountant; Charles John Middleton [1966] Director/Corporate Tax Executive; Timothy Andrew Roberts [1964] Director/Chartered Surveyor; Nigel Mark Webb [1963] Director/Chartered Surveyor

British Land Leisure Limited
Incorporated: 26 August 2004
Net Worth: £253,242,720 *Total Assets:* £256,898,032
Registered Office: York House, 45 Seymour Street, London, W1H 7LX
Activities: Development of building projects
Parent: BL Leisure and Industrial Holding Company Limited
Officers: Jonathan Charles McNuff [1986] Director/Chartered Accountant; Charles John Middleton [1966] Director/Corporate Tax Executive

British Medical Association
Incorporated: 21 October 1874 *Employees:* 947
Net Worth: £102,872,000 *Total Assets:* £184,960,000
Registered Office: BMA House, British Medical Association, Tavistock Square, London, WC1H 9JP
Activities: Other professional, scientific and technical activities n.e.c.
Officers: Dr John William Chisholm [1950] Director/General Practitioner; Dr Helen Margaret Fidler [1962] Director/Doctor; Joan Harris Howard [1946] Director/Retired; Joseph Wharton Lippincott III [1951] Director/Publishing and Information Services Consultant [American]; Patrick Andrew Murphy [1963] Director/Accountant [American]; Dr Chaand Nagpaul [1961] Director/General Medical Practitioner; Dr Kevin O'Kane [1963] Director/Consultant Physician; Belinda Clare Phipps [1958] Director/Interim Chief Executive; Trevor Paul Pickersgill [1967] Director/Consultant Neurologist

The British Museum Trust Limited
Incorporated: 7 February 2011
Net Worth: £125,303,368 *Total Assets:* £125,357,528
Registered Office: The British Museum, Great Russell Street, London, WC1B 3DG
Activities: Museums activities
Officers: Professor Sir Barrington Windsor Cunliffe, Secretary; Professor Sir Barrington Windsor Cunliffe [1939] Director/Archaeologist; David Ronald Norgrove [1948] Director; Lord Charles David Powell [1941] Director/Legislator; John Robert Ryan [1949] Director/Portfolio Manager [American]

British Sugar (Overseas) Limited
Incorporated: 3 July 1989 *Employees:* 9
Net Worth: £336,324,992 *Total Assets:* £367,560,000
Registered Office: Weston Centre, 10 Grosvenor Street, London, W1K 4QY
Activities: Activities of head offices
Parent: A.B.F. Holdings Limited
Officers: Rosalyn Sharon Schofield, Secretary; Dr Mark Ian Carr [1962] Director/Chief Executive; Quintin Harvey Heath [1964] HR Director; Janet Catherine Ryan [1963] Finance Director

British Sugar PLC
Incorporated: 12 June 1936 *Employees:* 1,667
Net Worth: £255,700,000 *Total Assets:* £670,600,000
Registered Office: Weston Centre, 10 Grosvenor Street, London, W1K 4QY
Activities: Manufacture of sugar
Parent: ABF Investments PLC
Officers: Rosalyn Sharon Schofield, Secretary; Dr Mark Ian Carr [1962] Director/Chief Executive; Quintin Harvey Heath [1964] HR Director; Alexander Kitson Johnson [1974] Director/Global Financial Controller; Paul Robert Kenward [1973] Director; Janet Catherine Ryan [1963] Finance Director

British Telecommunications Public Limited Company
Incorporated: 1 April 1984 *Employees:* 106
Net Worth: £22,740,000,768 *Total Assets:* £56,277,999,616
Registered Office: 81 Newgate Street, London, EC1A 7AJ
Activities: Other telecommunications activities
Parent: BT Group Investments Limited
Officers: Heather Gwendolyn Brierley, Secretary; Aasa Ulrica Susanne Fearn [1973] Director/Civilekonom [Swedish]; Neil Richard Harris [1968] Director/Accountant; Simon Jonathan Lowth [1961] Executive Director

British United Provident Association Limited (The)
Incorporated: 3 April 1947 *Employees:* 62,989
Net Worth: £7,257,999,872 *Total Assets:* £15,057,699,840
Registered Office: 1 Angel Court, London, EC2R 7HJ
Activities: Other human health activities
Officers: Julian Philip Sanders, Secretary; Evelyn Brigid Bourke [1965] Director/Chief Financial Officer [Irish]; Roger William John Davis [1956] Director; Paul James Evans [1965] Director; Martin Joseph Houston [1957] Director; Joy Linton [1965] Director [Australian]; Nicholas Stephen Leland Lyons [1958] Director [Irish]; Matias Rodriguez Inciarte [1948] Director [Spanish]; Caroline Louise Silver [1962] Managing Director; Clare Eleanor Thompson [1954] Director; Professor John Edward Tooke [1949] Director; Janet Joslin Voute-Allen [1953] Director [Swiss/American]

British-American Tobacco (Holdings) Limited
Incorporated: 28 January 1932 *Employees:* 776
Net Worth: £25,273,372,672 *Total Assets:* £25,918,191,616
Registered Office: Globe House, 4 Temple Place, London, WC2R 2PG
Activities: Activities of head offices
Parent: B.A.T Industries P.L.C.
Officers: Noelle Colfer, Secretary; Jerome Bruce Abelman [1963] Director/Assistant General Counsel [American]; Marina Bellini [1973] Director [Italian/Brazilian]; Jack Bowles [1963] Director, Western Europe [French]; Luciano Comin [1969] Director [Italian/Argentinian]; Alan Davy [1963] Group Operations Director; Nicandro Durante [1956] Director/Economist [Brazilian]; Giovanni Giordano [1965] HR Director [Italian/American]; Hae in Kim [1974] Director [South Korean]; Paul Rutger Lageweg [1969] Director [Dutch]; Tadeu Luiz Marroco [1966] Business Development Director [Brazilian]; Guy Meldrum [1971] Director [New Zealander]; Dr David O'Reilly [1966] Director/Scientist; Ricardo Cesar de Almeida Oberlander [1963] Director/Statistician [Brazilian]; Naresh Kumar Sethi [1966] Group Business Development Director [Australian]; John Benedict Stevens [1959] Director/Tobacco Manufacturer; Johan Maurice Vandermeulen [1968] Regional Director, EEMEA [Belgian]; Kingsley Wheaton [1973] Director/Company Executive

Britned Development Limited
Incorporated: 12 July 2001
Net Worth: £403,505,696 *Total Assets:* £445,836,992
Registered Office: 1-3 Strand, London, WC2N 5EH
Activities: Transmission of electricity
Parent: National Grid Interconnector Holdings Limited
Officers: Megan Barnes, Secretary; Jonathan Butterworth [1962] Director; Guido Thomas Fricke [1967] Managing Director [German]; Alexander Adriaan Hartman [1954] Director/Manager [Dutch]; Nick Sides [1966] Director

Brixton (Axis Park) Limited
Incorporated: 18 April 2002
Net Worth: £18,616,000 *Total Assets:* £165,063,008
Registered Office: Cunard House, 15 Regent Street, London, SW1Y 4LR
Activities: Activities of head offices
Parent: Brixton Sub-Holdings Limited
Officers: Elizabeth Ann Blease, Secretary; Alan Michael Holland [1974] Director; Gareth John Osborn [1962] Director; Ann Octavia Peters [1969] Director; Andrew John Pilsworth [1974] Director; Simon Christian Pursey [1975] Director

Brixton (Metropolitan Park) 1 Limited
Incorporated: 28 May 2004
Net Worth: £67,702,000 *Total Assets:* £169,571,008
Registered Office: Cunard House, 15 Regent Street, London, SW1Y 4LR
Activities: Development of building projects
Parent: Brixton Limited
Officers: Elizabeth Ann Blease, Secretary; Alan Michael Holland [1974] Director; Gareth John Osborn [1962] Director; Ann Octavia Peters [1969] Director; Andrew John Pilsworth [1974] Director; Simon Christian Pursey [1975] Director

Brixton (Origin) Limited
Incorporated: 12 March 2004
Net Worth: £6,399,000 *Total Assets:* £121,964,000
Registered Office: Cunard House, 15 Regent Street, London, SW1Y 4LR
Activities: Development of building projects
Parent: Brixton Limited
Officers: Elizabeth Ann Blease, Secretary; Alan Michael Holland [1974] Director; Gareth John Osborn [1962] Director; Ann Octavia Peters [1969] Director; Andrew John Pilsworth [1974] Director; Simon Christian Pursey [1975] Director

Brixton Greenford Park Limited
Incorporated: 17 June 2004
Net Worth: £153,463,008 *Total Assets:* £247,908,992
Registered Office: Cunard House, 15 Regent Street, London, SW1Y 4LR
Activities: Development of building projects
Parent: Brixton Limited
Officers: Elizabeth Ann Blease, Secretary; Alan Michael Holland [1974] Director; Gareth John Osborn [1962] Director; Ann Octavia Peters [1969] Director; Andrew John Pilsworth [1974] Director; Simon Christian Pursey [1975] Director

Brixton Limited
Incorporated: 11 December 1924
Net Worth: £871,212,032 *Total Assets:* £914,547,008
Registered Office: Cunard House, 15 Regent Street, London, SW1Y 4LR
Activities: Development of building projects
Parent: Segro PLC
Officers: Elizabeth Ann Blease, Secretary; Soumen Das [1976] Director; Andrew Stephen Gulliford [1962] Director/Chartered Surveyor; Alan Michael Holland [1974] Director; Gareth John Osborn [1962] Director; Ann Octavia Peters [1969] Director; Andrew John Pilsworth [1974] Director; David John Rivers Sleath [1961] Director

Brixton Premier Park Limited
Incorporated: 17 June 2004
Net Worth: £175,160,992 *Total Assets:* £275,022,016
Registered Office: Cunard House, 15 Regent Street, London, SW1Y 4LR
Activities: Development of building projects
Parent: Brixton Limited
Officers: Elizabeth Ann Blease, Secretary; Alan Michael Holland [1974] Director; Gareth John Osborn [1962] Director; Ann Octavia Peters [1969] Director; Andrew John Pilsworth [1974] Director; Simon Christian Pursey [1975] Director

Broad Gain (UK) Limited
Incorporated: 3 September 2002 *Employees:* 1,695
Net Worth: £148,802,000 *Total Assets:* £236,256,000
Registered Office: 361-365 Chiswick High Road, London, W4 4HS
Activities: Activities of head offices
Parent: Boroughbridge Limited
Officers: Manju Malhotra, Secretary; Manju Malhotra [1972] Director; Dickson Poon [1956] Director; Daniela Francesca Rinaldi [1965] Director

Broad Street Principal Investments UK Ltd
Incorporated: 14 November 2016
Net Worth: £67,028,200 *Total Assets:* £330,222,464
Registered Office: Peterborough Court, 133 Fleet Street, London, EC4A 2BB
Activities: Financial intermediation not elsewhere classified
Parent: Goldman Sachs Group Holdings (U.K.) Limited
Officers: Thomas Kelly, Secretary; Penny Ann McSpadden [1968] Director/Banker [American/British]; Mark Desmond Charles Olivier [1974] Managing Director; Natalia Ross [1972] Director/Accountant [Polish]

Broadgate (Funding) 2005 Limited
Incorporated: 17 December 2004
Net Worth: £90,913 *Total Assets:* £1,583,732,480
Registered Office: York House, 45 Seymour Street, London, W1H 7LX
Activities: Development of building projects
Parent: Broadgate Property Holdings Limited
Officers: David Ian Lockyer [1969] Director/Chartered Surveyor; Timothy Andrew Roberts [1964] Director/Chartered Surveyor; Hursh Shah [1976] Director

Broadgate (PHC 11) 2005 Limited
Incorporated: 17 December 2004
Net Worth: £167,421,792 *Total Assets:* £436,293,856
Registered Office: York House, 45 Seymour Street, London, W1H 7LX
Activities: Development of building projects
Parent: Broadgate Property Holdings Limited
Officers: David Ian Lockyer [1969] Director/Chartered Surveyor; Timothy Andrew Roberts [1964] Director/Chartered Surveyor; Hursh Shah [1976] Director

Broadgate (PHC 14) Limited
Incorporated: 28 January 1999
Net Worth: £58,862,408 *Total Assets:* £161,597,040
Registered Office: York House, 45 Seymour Street, London, W1H 7LX
Activities: Development of building projects
Parent: Broadgate Property Holdings Limited
Officers: David Ian Lockyer [1969] Director/Chartered Surveyor; Timothy Andrew Roberts [1964] Director/Chartered Surveyor; Hursh Shah [1976] Director

Broadgate (PHC 15A) Limited
Incorporated: 28 January 1999
Net Worth: £44,117,320 *Total Assets:* £223,081,264
Registered Office: York House, 45 Seymour Street, London, W1H 7LX
Activities: Development of building projects
Parent: Broadgate Property Holdings Limited
Officers: David Ian Lockyer [1969] Director/Chartered Surveyor; Timothy Andrew Roberts [1964] Director/Chartered Surveyor; Hursh Shah [1976] Director

Broadgate (PHC 16) 2005 Limited
Incorporated: 17 December 2004
Net Worth: £123,058,008 *Total Assets:* £191,478,800
Registered Office: York House, 45 Seymour Street, London, W1H 7LX
Activities: Development of building projects
Parent: Broadgate Property Holdings
Officers: David Ian Lockyer [1969] Director/Chartered Surveyor; Timothy Andrew Roberts [1964] Director; Hursh Shah [1976] Director

Broadgate (PHC 2) Limited
Incorporated: 28 January 1999
Net Worth: £42,146,624 *Total Assets:* £212,060,016
Registered Office: York House, 45 Seymour Street, London, W1H 7LX
Activities: Development of building projects
Parent: Bluebutton Properties UK Limited
Officers: David Ian Lockyer [1969] Director/Chartered Surveyor; Timothy Andrew Roberts [1964] Director/Chartered Surveyor; Hursh Shah [1976] Director

Broadgate (PHC 3) Limited
Incorporated: 28 January 1999
Net Worth: £37,134,040 *Total Assets:* £339,584,832
Registered Office: York House, 45 Seymour Street, London, W1H 7LX
Activities: Development of building projects
Parent: Broadgate Property Holdings Limited
Officers: David Ian Lockyer [1969] Director/Chartered Surveyor; Timothy Andrew Roberts [1964] Director/Chartered Surveyor; Hursh Shah [1976] Director

Broadgate (PHC 5) 2005 Limited
Incorporated: 17 December 2004
Net Worth: £107,411,224 *Total Assets:* £205,735,184
Registered Office: York House, 45 Seymour Street, London, W1H 7LX
Activities: Development of building projects
Parent: Broadgate Property Holdings Limited
Officers: David Ian Lockyer [1969] Director/Chartered Surveyor; Timothy Andrew Roberts [1964] Director/Chartered Surveyor; Hursh Shah [1976] Director

Broadgate (PHC 6) 2005 Limited
Incorporated: 17 December 2004
Net Worth: £12,792,902 *Total Assets:* £210,261,824
Registered Office: York House, 45 Seymour Street, London, W1H 7LX
Activities: Development of building projects
Parent: Broadgate Property Holdings Limited
Officers: David Ian Lockyer [1969] Director/Chartered Surveyor; Timothy Andrew Roberts [1964] Director/Chartered Surveyor; Hursh Shah [1976] Director

Broadgate (PHC 7) Limited
Incorporated: 28 January 1999
Net Worth: £114,654,088 *Total Assets:* £346,756,768
Registered Office: York House, 45 Seymour Street, London, W1H 7LX
Activities: Development of building projects
Parent: Broadgate Property Holdings Limited
Officers: David Ian Lockyer [1969] Director/Chartered Surveyor; Timothy Andrew Roberts [1964] Director/Chartered Surveyor; Hursh Shah [1976] Director

Broadgate (PHC 8) 2008 Limited
Incorporated: 28 March 2008
Net Worth: £264,371,328 *Total Assets:* £523,813,408
Registered Office: York House, 45 Seymour Street, London, W1H 7LX
Activities: Development of building projects
Parent: Broadgate Property Holdings Limited
Officers: David Ian Lockyer [1969] Director/Chartered Surveyor; Timothy Andrew Roberts [1964] Director/Chartered Surveyor; Hursh Shah [1976] Director

Broadgate (PHC 9) Limited
Incorporated: 28 January 1999
Net Worth: £98,804,648 *Total Assets:* £240,521,392
Registered Office: York House, 45 Seymour Street, London, W1H 7LX
Activities: Development of building projects
Parent: Broadgate Property Holdings Limited
Officers: David Ian Lockyer [1969] Director/Chartered Surveyor; Timothy Andrew Roberts [1964] Director/Chartered Surveyor; Hursh Shah [1976] Director

Broadgate Financing PLC
Incorporated: 17 December 2004
Net Worth Deficit: £34,800,388 *Total Assets:* £1,783,904,768
Registered Office: York House, 45 Seymour Street, London, W1H 7LX
Activities: Development of building projects
Parent: Broadgate Property Holdings Limited
Officers: David Ian Lockyer [1969] Director/Chartered Surveyor; Timothy Andrew Roberts [1964] Director/Chartered Surveyor; Hursh Shah [1976] Director

Broadgate PHC 2010 Limited
Incorporated: 7 May 2010
Net Worth: £335,556,672 *Total Assets:* £561,745,664
Registered Office: York House, 45 Seymour Street, London, W1H 7LX
Activities: Development of building projects
Parent: Broadgate Property Holdings Limited
Officers: David Ian Lockyer [1969] Director/Chartered Surveyor; Timothy Andrew Roberts [1964] Director/Chartered Surveyor; Hursh Shah [1976] Director

Broadgate Property Holdings Limited
Incorporated: 3 February 1999
Net Worth: £108,444,624 *Total Assets:* £623,849,984
Registered Office: York House, 45 Seymour Street, London, W1H 7LX
Activities: Development of building projects
Parent: British Land Broadgate 2005 Limited
Officers: David Ian Lockyer [1969] Director/Chartered Surveyor; Timothy Andrew Roberts [1964] Director/Chartered Surveyor; Hursh Shah [1976] Director

Brokertec Investments
Incorporated: 12 June 2014
Net Worth: £553,263,744 *Total Assets:* £885,843,584
Registered Office: 2 Broadgate, London, EC2M 7UR
Activities: Activities of financial services holding companies
Parent: CME London Limited
Officers: Deborah Abrehart, Secretary; Allan Samuel Aldridge [1980] Director; Ranjit Paul [1983] Director

Brook Funding (No.1) Limited
Incorporated: 8 April 2011
Net Worth: £6,538 *Total Assets:* £203,195,456
Registered Office: 35 Great St Helen's, London, EC3A 6AP
Activities: Financial intermediation not elsewhere classified
Parent: Intertrust Corporate Services Limited
Officers: Helena Whtaker [1963] Director [Finnish]

Brooke Bond Assam Estates Limited
Incorporated: 24 March 1982
Net Worth: £841,475,008 *Total Assets:* £1,111,694,976
Registered Office: Unilever House, 100 Victoria Embankment, London, EC4Y 0DY
Activities: Activities of head offices
Parent: Brooke Bond Group Limited
Officers: James Oliver Earley, Secretary; Richard Clive Hazell, Secretary; Anna Jo Karen Elphick [1975] Director/Accountant; Richard Clive Hazell [1966] Director/Solicitor; Amanda Louise King [1973] UK & Ireland Tax Director

Brooke Bond South India Estates Limited
Incorporated: 2 March 1982
Net Worth: £3,211,131,904 *Total Assets:* £3,314,214,912
Registered Office: Unilever House, 100 Victoria Embankment, London, EC4Y 0DY
Activities: Activities of head offices
Parent: Unilever PLC
Officers: James Oliver Earley, Secretary; Richard Clive Hazell, Secretary; Anna Jo Karen Elphick [1975] Director/Accountant; Richard Clive Hazell [1966] Director/Solicitor; Amanda Louise King [1973] UK & Ireland Tax Director

Brookfield BBP UK Holdings II Limited
Incorporated: 12 January 2016
Net Worth: £227,535,104 *Total Assets:* £518,492,128
Registered Office: Level 25, 1 Canada Square, London, E14 5AA
Activities: Activities of other holding companies n.e.c.
Parent: BCI UK Holdings Limited
Officers: Edward Michael James Brogan [1983] Director/Solicitor; Ralf Niklas Rank [1977] Director/Managing Partner [Canadian/German]

Brookfield BBP UK Holdings III Limited
Incorporated: 12 January 2016
Net Worth: £516,496,832 *Total Assets:* £1,025,368,768
Registered Office: Level 25, 1 Canada Square, London, E14 5AA
Activities: Activities of other holding companies n.e.c.
Parent: Brookfield BBP UK Holdings II Limited
Officers: Edward Michael James Brogan [1983] Director/Solicitor; Ralf Niklas Rank [1977] Director/Managing Partner [Canadian/German]

Brookfield Global Corporate Investments Limited
Incorporated: 5 December 2013
Net Worth: £1,178,959,488 *Total Assets:* £1,178,971,904
Registered Office: Level 25, 1 Canada Square, London, E14 5AA
Activities: Activities of other holding companies n.e.c.
Parent: Brookfield Global Subinvestments Limited
Officers: Philippa Elder, Secretary; Danelle Fleur Campbell [1976] Finance Director [New Zealander]; Philippa Louise Elder [1976] Director/Lawyer; Connor David Teskey [1987] Director/Vice President [Canadian]

Brookfield Global Property Advisor Limited
Incorporated: 21 January 2013 *Employees:* 24
Net Worth: £121,906,944 *Total Assets:* £132,324,336
Registered Office: Level 25, 1 Canada Square, London, E14 5AA
Activities: Other service activities n.e.c.
Parent: Bhal Global Corporate Limited
Officers: Philippa Elder, Secretary; Philippa Louise Elder [1976] Director/Lawyer; James Bruce Flatt [1965] Director [Canadian]; Ralf Niklas Rank [1977] Director/Chief Investment Officer [Canadian/German]; Connor David Teskey [1987] Director/Senior Vice President, CIO [Canadian]

Brookfield Global Subinvestments Limited
Incorporated: 12 December 2013
Net Worth: £2,306,741,760 *Total Assets:* £2,496,358,144
Registered Office: Level 25, 1 Canada Square, London, E14 5AA
Activities: Activities of other holding companies n.e.c.
Parent: Bhal Global Corporate Limited
Officers: Philippa Elder, Secretary; Danelle Fleur Campbell [1976] Finance Director [New Zealander]; Philippa Louise Elder [1976] Director/Solicitor; Connor David Teskey [1987] Director/Vice President [Canadian]

Brookfield Renewable UK Hydro Limited
Incorporated: 2 June 2017
Net Worth: £250,000 *Total Assets:* £194,964,000
Registered Office: Level 25, 1 Canada Square, London, E14 5AA
Activities: Activities of other holding companies n.e.c.
Officers: Ruth Josephine Kent [1974] Director/Chief Financial Officer [Irish]; Thomas Joseph O'Brien [1968] Director/Chief Financial Officer [Irish]; Emmanuelle Rouchel [1974] Director/Lawyer [French]

Brooks MacDonald Group PLC
Incorporated: 22 March 2002 *Employees:* 490
Net Worth: £87,957,000 *Total Assets:* £125,531,000
Registered Office: 72 Welbeck Street, London, W1G 0AY
Activities: Activities of head offices
Officers: Simon Broomfield, Secretary; Caroline Mary Connellan [1973] Director/Chief Executive; Colin Robert Harris [1953] Director; Christopher John Knight [1946] Director/Consultant; John Frederick Linwood [1962] Director; Richard Stanley Price [1961] Director; Diane Seymour-Williams [1958] Investment Director; Andrew William Shepherd [1973] Director; David Stewart [1965] Director; Benjamin Lee Thorpe [1976] Director

Brown Shipley & Co. Limited
Incorporated: 8 September 1945 *Employees:* 327
Net Worth: £87,604,000 *Total Assets:* £784,942,976
Registered Office: Founders Court, Lothbury, London, EC2R 7HE
Activities: Banks
Parent: KBL European Private Bankers SA
Officers: James Ednie Brydie [1959] Director; Andrew Paul Curran [1963] Director; Nicholas John Harvey [1973] Director; Alan Mathewson [1970] Director; John Misselbrook [1950] Director; David Rough [1951] Director

Brown-Forman Beverages, Europe, Ltd
Incorporated: 22 December 2000 *Employees:* 77
Net Worth: £132,889,000 *Total Assets:* £143,020,992
Registered Office: 45 Mortimer Street, London, W1W 8HJ
Activities: Other business support service activities n.e.c.
Parent: Brown-Forman Corporation
Officers: Charles Edward Scholtz, Secretary/Attorney [American]; Michael Erb Carr Jr [1979] Director [American]; Michael Andrew Masick [1978] Director [American]; Charles Edward Scholtz [1960] Director/Attorney [American]; Jeremy James Shepherd [1974] Director [Canadian]

Brunel Residential Mortgage Securitisation No. 1 PLC
Incorporated: 5 September 2006
Net Worth: £706,000 *Total Assets:* £1,111,590,016
Registered Office: 6th Floor, 65 Gresham Street, London, EC2V 7NQ
Activities: Other business support service activities n.e.c.
Parent: Brunel Residential Mortgage Securitisation No. 1 Parent Limited
Officers: Colin Arthur Benford [1962] Director

Bruning Limited
Incorporated: 10 November 2003
Net Worth: £840,487,488 *Total Assets:* £843,220,864
Registered Office: 81 Newgate Street, London, EC1A 7AJ
Activities: Other business support service activities n.e.c.
Parent: BT Holdings Limited
Officers: Mark Philip Genikis [1961] Director/Accountant; Michael Joseph Mohun [1990] Director/Company Secretary Manager [Australian]; Christina Bridget Ryan [1960] Director/Company Secretary [Irish]

Brunner Investment Trust PLC (The)
Incorporated: 3 December 1927
Net Worth: £368,013,888 *Total Assets:* £419,014,432
Registered Office: 199 Bishopsgate, London, EC2M 3TY
Activities: Financial intermediation not elsewhere classified
Officers: Eleanor Emuss, Secretary; Kirsten June Salt, Secretary; Ian Edward Barlow [1951] Director/Chartered Accountant; Vivian Paul Bazalgette [1951] Director/Retired; Carolan Dobson [1954] Director; Peter Martin Maynard [1952] Director/Solicitor; James Edward Sharp [1967] Director

Bryan Cave Leighton Paisner LLP
Incorporated: 1 November 2005 *Employees:* 1,424
Previous: Berwin Leighton Paisner LLP
Net Worth: £89,064,000 *Total Assets:* £157,702,000
Registered Office: Adelaide House, London Bridge, London, EC4R 9HA
Officers: Adam Harold Dann [1966] Member; Neville Eisenberg [1962] Member; Robert Murray Robertson MacGregor [1960] Member; Lisa Jane Mayhew [1970] Member; Christopher John Adams [1955] LLP Member; Adriano Vito Amorese [1978] LLP Member; David George Anderson [1966] LLP Member; Michael Fenwick Anderson [1966] LLP Member; Daniyal Ahmad Ansari [1972] LLP Member; Kiran Arora [1978] LLP Member; Lesley Anne Avis [1959] LLP Member; Matthew Richard Baker [1976] LLP Member; Zahra Bardai [1978] LLP Member; Simon Harry Kenneth Barnett [1959] LLP Member; Craig Ashley Baylis [1957] LLP Member; Robert Bell [1959] LLP Member; Ian Benjamin [1978] LLP Member; John Emmanuel Bennett [1959] LLP Member; Celia Jayne Berg [1976] LLP Member; Nicole Bigby [1972] LLP Member; Kathrine Binedell [1971] LLP Member; Damian Paul Bloom [1973] LLP Member; Adam Bogdanor [1977] LLP Member; Elizabeth Kathleen Bradley Bradley [1976] LLP Member; Mark Russell Brailsford [1963] LLP Member; Carsten Bremer [1972] LLP Member; Katherine Jane Brimsted [1970] LLP Member; Chris Bryant [1978] LLP Member; George Robert Murray Burn [1968] LLP Member; Till Jonas Buschmann [1977] LLP Member; Georgina Cadieu [1978] LLP Member; Jason Paul Chamberlain [1970] LLP Member; Mukul Chawla [1961] LLP Member; Sunita Chawla [1974] LLP Member; Stephen Philip Clark [1961] LLP Member; Russell Christopher Clifford [1971] LLP Member; Alexandra Clough [1982] LLP Member; Louisa Cobbe [1984] LLP Member; Roger David Cohen [1959] LLP Member; Kirsty Corkum [1967] LLP Member; Alexander Justin Cornelius [1972] LLP Member; Edward John Crowther-Hunt Coulson [1980] LLP Member; Daniel Ernest Csefalvay [1976] LLP Member; Joby Davies [1970] LLP Member; Christopher Mark de Pury [1968] LLP Member; David Mark Dennison [1959] LLP Member; Nazir Hussein Dewji [1976] LLP Member; Christian Drage [1974] LLP Member; Shanan Dee Dunstan [1980] LLP Member; Robert Thomas Eldridge [1962] LLP Member; Thomas Duncan Eldridge [1971] LLP Member; Roland Bernd Fabian [1963] LLP Member; Sarah Fitzpatrick [1974] LLP Member; Damian James Fleming [1972] LLP Member; Prof Bernd Geier [1976] LLP Member; Oran Asher Gelb [1978] LLP Member; Oliver James David Glynn-Jones [1975] LLP Member; James Ieuam David Good [1971] LLP Member; Deborah Ann Greenwood [1972] LLP Member; Barry Jonathan Gross [1976] LLP Member; Antony Ian Grossman [1964] LLP Member; Claire Hagger [1967] LLP Member; Marc Cyrus Thomas Robert Hanson [1968] LLP Member; Richard Harbot [1976] LLP Member; Rebecca Harding Hill [1969] LLP Member; Andrew Hart [1975] LLP Member; Paul Edward Hauser [1954] LLP Member; Timothy Andrew Hellier [1958] LLP Member; Liana Louise Elizabeth Hewson [1977] LLP Member; Elizabeth Anne Hicks [1968] LLP Member; Andrew James Hockley [1976] LLP Member; Emma Howdle-Fuller [1971] LLP Member; Derek Hrydziuszko [1978] LLP Member; John Narbrough Hughes D'Aeth [1962] LLP Member; Eleanor Hunwicks [1972] LLP Member; Dr Norbert Impelmann [1960] LLP Member; Kate Louisa Ison [1982] LLP Member; Mary Elizabeth James [1978] LLP Member; Patrick Paul Johnson [1980] LLP Member; Benjamin David Seth Jones [1977] LLP Member; Philippe Alexis Kamarowsky [1976] LLP Member; Alexander Keepin [1973] LLP Member; Simon Kenley [1969] LLP Member; Roman Khodykin [1977] LLP Member; Tessa Karen Kimber [1967] LLP Member; James Peter Witherow Knox [1961] LLP Member; Peter John Bentley Knust [1979] LLP Member; Stephan Krampe [1975] LLP Member; Emma Jeanne Le Wita [1980] LLP Member; Benjamin Graham Lee [1972] LLP Member; Anthony James Lennox [1964] LLP Member; Mark Lewis [1954] LLP Member; Dylan Kenneth MacKenzie [1974] LLP Member; Akhil Markanday [1978] LLP Member; James Richard Marshall [1979] LLP Member; Robert Camillo Anthony Maynard [1962] LLP Member; William Gordon Alan McMillan [1984] LLP Member; Michael Neil Metliss [1982] LLP Member; Ruth Miller [1978] LLP Member; Wendy Josette Miller [1957] LLP Member

BT (International) Holdings Limited
Incorporated: 2 February 1988
Net Worth: £200,919,008 *Total Assets:* £373,079,008
Registered Office: 81 Newgate Street, London, EC1A 7AJ
Activities: Activities of other holding companies n.e.c.
Parent: BT Holdings Limited
Officers: Christina Bridget Ryan [1960] Director/Company Secretary [Irish]; Leslie Charles Winnister [1952] Director/Treasury Manager

BT European Investments Limited
Incorporated: 24 August 2001
Net Worth: £121,576,112 *Total Assets:* £426,212,128
Registered Office: 81 Newgate Street, London, EC1A 7AJ
Activities: Activities of other holding companies n.e.c.
Parent: British Telecommunications PLC
Officers: Mark Philip Genikis [1961] Director/Accountant; Michael Joseph Mohun [1990] Director/Company Secretary Manager [Australian]; Christina Bridget Ryan [1960] Director/Company Secretary [Irish]

BT Fifty-One
Incorporated: 20 August 1998
Net Worth: £1,115,573,504 *Total Assets:* £1,923,838,080
Registered Office: 81 Newgate Street, London, EC1A 7AJ
Activities: Activities of other holding companies n.e.c.
Parent: BT (International) Holdings Limited
Officers: Mark Philip Genikis [1961] Director/Accountant; Michael Joseph Mohun [1990] Director/Company Secretary Manager [Australian]; Christina Bridget Ryan [1960] Director/Company Secretary [Irish]

BT Fifty-Three Limited
Incorporated: 20 August 1998
Net Worth: £1,358,274,432 *Total Assets:* £1,363,487,104
Registered Office: 81 Newgate Street, London, EC1A 7AJ
Activities: Activities of other holding companies n.e.c.
Parent: BT Fifty-One
Officers: Mark Philip Genikis [1961] Director/Accountant; Michael Joseph Mohun [1990] Director/Company Secretary Manager [Australian]; Christina Bridget Ryan [1960] Director/Company Secretary [Irish]

BT Fleet Limited
Incorporated: 27 February 2002 *Employees:* 891
Net Worth: £768,940,032 *Total Assets:* £849,057,984
Registered Office: 81 Newgate Street, London, EC1A 7AJ
Activities: Maintenance and repair of motor vehicles
Parent: British Telecommunications PLC
Officers: Henry Joseph Sidney Brace [1976] Director/BT Executive; Nicholas Anthony Hale [1975] Managing Director; Christopher Paul Wides [1981] Finance Director

BT Global Services Limited
Incorporated: 3 August 1989
Net Worth: £33,576,000 *Total Assets:* £320,956,992
Registered Office: 81 Newgate Street, London, EC1A 7AJ
Activities: Other telecommunications activities
Parent: BT Sixty-Four Limited
Officers: Nicola Brenchley [1968] Director/Chartered Accountant; Christina Bridget Ryan [1960] Director/Company Secretary [Irish]

BT Group Investments Limited
Incorporated: 30 August 2001
Net Worth: £2,138,849,024 *Total Assets:* £18,603,681,792
Registered Office: 81 Newgate Street, London, EC1A 7AJ
Activities: Activities of head offices
Parent: BT Group PLC
Officers: Mark Philip Genikis [1961] Director/Accountant; Leslie Charles Winnister [1952] Director/Treasury Manager

BT Group PLC
Incorporated: 30 March 2001 *Employees:* 105,800
Net Worth: £10,304,000,000 *Total Assets:* £42,759,000,064
Registered Office: 81 Newgate Street, London, EC1A 7AJ
Activities: Other telecommunications activities
Officers: Rachel Canham, Secretary; Iain Cameron Conn [1962] Director; Jan Petrus Du Plessis [1954] Director [British/South African]; Timotheus Hottges [1962] Director/CEO Deutsche Telekom AG [German]; Isabel Frances Hudson [1959] Director; Michael James Inglis [1960] Director/Chartered Engineer; Philip Eric Rene Jansen [1967] Director; Matthew David Key [1963] Director; Simon Jonathan Lowth [1961] Executive Director; Nicholas Charles Rose [1957] Finance Director; Jasmine Mary Whitbread [1963] Director/Charity CEO [British/Swiss]

BT Holdings Limited
Incorporated: 3 February 1988
Net Worth: £8,830,042,112 *Total Assets:* £8,844,659,712
Registered Office: 81 Newgate Street, London, EC1A 7AJ
Activities: Activities of other holding companies n.e.c.
Parent: British Telecommunications PLC
Officers: Michael Joseph Mohun [1990] Director/Company Secretary Manager [Australian]; Christina Bridget Ryan [1960] Director/Company Secretary [Irish]; Leslie Charles Winnister [1952] Director/Treasury Manager

BT Limited
Incorporated: 2 February 1988 *Employees:* 313
Net Worth: £337,124,000 *Total Assets:* £487,292,000
Registered Office: 81 Newgate Street, London, EC1A 7AJ
Activities: Other telecommunications activities
Parent: BT Holdings Limited
Officers: Christina Bridget Ryan, Secretary [Irish]; Nicola Brenchley [1968] Director/Chartered Accountant; Christina Bridget Ryan [1960] Director/Company Secretary [Irish]

BT Sixty-Four Limited
Incorporated: 31 May 2000
Net Worth: £1,180,232,960 *Total Assets:* £1,180,393,984
Registered Office: 81 Newgate Street, London, EC1A 7AJ
Activities: Other business support service activities n.e.c.
Parent: BT Fifty-One
Officers: Michael Joseph Mohun [1990] Director/Company Secretary Manager [Australian]; Christina Bridget Ryan [1960] Director/Company Secretary [Irish]

BT SLE Euro Limited
Incorporated: 22 March 2011
Net Worth: £889,724,800 *Total Assets:* £1,341,618,816
Registered Office: 81 Newgate Street, London, EC1A 7AJ
Activities: Activities of other holding companies n.e.c.
Parent: British Telecommunications PLC
Officers: Mark Philip Genikis [1961] Director/Accountant; Michael Joseph Mohun [1990] Director/Company Secretary Manager [Australian]; Christina Bridget Ryan [1960] Director/Company Secretary [Irish]

BT SLE USD Limited
Incorporated: 22 March 2011
Net Worth: £3,143,582,720 *Total Assets:* £3,143,931,136
Registered Office: 81 Newgate Street, London, EC1A 7AJ
Activities: Activities of other holding companies n.e.c.
Parent: British Telecommunications PLC
Officers: Mark Philip Genikis [1961] Director/Accountant; Michael Joseph Mohun [1990] Director/Company Secretary Manager [Australian]; Christina Bridget Ryan [1960] Director/Company Secretary [Irish]

BTC Islands Limited
Incorporated: 17 October 2003
Net Worth: £276,275,008 *Total Assets:* £276,275,008
Registered Office: One Silk Street, London, EC2Y 8HQ
Activities: Activities of head offices
Officers: Bernadette Baynie, Secretary; Ahmed Al Khalifa [1969] Director [Bahraini]; Ian James Kelly [1965] Director/CEO of Sure [Australian]; Faisal Ismail Qamhiyah [1974] Director/CFO Batelco Group [Jordanian]

BTG International (Holdings) Limited
Incorporated: 12 June 2000
Net Worth: £475,636,992 *Total Assets:* £610,744,000
Registered Office: BTG PLC, 5 Fleet Place, London, EC4M 7RD
Activities: Other service activities n.e.c.
Parent: BTG PLC
Officers: Elaine Maureen Johnston, Secretary; Elaine Maureen Johnston [1976] Director/Lawyer [Irish]; Timothy John Martel [1975] Director/Accountant

BTG International Healthcare Limited
Incorporated: 16 May 2012
Net Worth: £302,921,120 *Total Assets:* £304,991,168
Registered Office: 5 Fleet Place, London, EC4M 7RD
Activities: Other service activities n.e.c.
Parent: BTG Management Services Limited
Officers: Elaine Maureen Johnston, Secretary; Elaine Maureen Johnston [1976] Director/Lawyer [Irish]; Timothy John Martel [1975] Director/Accountant

BTG International Limited
Incorporated: 14 November 1991 *Employees:* 6
Net Worth: £313,000,000 *Total Assets:* £372,600,000
Registered Office: 5 Fleet Place, London, EC4M 7RD
Activities: Other research and experimental development on natural sciences and engineering
Parent: BTG International (Holdings) Limited
Officers: Elaine Maureen Johnston, Secretary; Elaine Maureen Johnston [1976] Director/Lawyer [Irish]; Timothy John Martel [1975] Director/Accountant

BTG Management Services Limited
Incorporated: 12 January 1990 *Employees:* 50
Net Worth: £561,387,008 *Total Assets:* £1,019,619,968
Registered Office: 5 Fleet Place, London, EC4M 7RD
Activities: Activities of head offices
Parent: BTG International (Holdings) Limited
Officers: Elaine Maureen Johnston, Secretary; Elaine Maureen Johnston [1976] Director/Lawyer [Irish]; Timothy John Martel [1975] Director/Accountant

BTG Pactual UK Holdco Limited
Incorporated: 17 July 2015
Net Worth: £262,008,416 *Total Assets:* £262,024,000
Registered Office: Berkeley Square House, 4-19 Berkeley Square, London, W1J 6BR
Activities: Activities of other holding companies n.e.c.
Shareholders: Roberto Balls Sallouti; Guilherme Da Costa Paes; Antonio Carlos Canto Porto Filho; Renato Monteiro Dos Santos; Marcelo Kalim
Officers: Bruno Duque Horta Nogueira [1978] Director/Attorney-at-Law [Brazilian]; Steven Michael Jacobs [1969] Director/Financial Services Executive

BTG PLC
Incorporated: 12 December 1991 *Employees:* 1,512
Net Worth: £914,700,032 *Total Assets:* £1,164,600,064
Registered Office: 5 Fleet Place, London, EC4M 7RD
Activities: Other research and experimental development on natural sciences and engineering
Officers: Dr Paul Justin Mussenden, Secretary; Gregory Ackley Barrett [1953] Director [American]; Dr Susan Elizabeth Foden [1953] Director; Graham Charles Hetherington [1959] Director; Duncan Kennedy [1975] Director; Dame Pamela Louise Makin [1960] Director/Chief Executive; Ian Fraser Robert Much [1944] Director; William James O'Shea [1949] Director; Anne Thorburn [1960] Director; Garry Watts [1956] Director; Richard Leslie Martin Wohanka [1952] Director

BTGP-BSI Limited
Incorporated: 20 January 2015
Net Worth: £126,437,608 *Total Assets:* £351,137,152
Registered Office: Berkeley Square House, 4-19 Berkeley Square, London, W1J 6BR
Activities: Activities of other holding companies n.e.c.
Shareholders: Roberto Balls Sallouti; Antonio Carlos Canto Porto Filho; Guilherme Da Costa Paes; Renato Monteiro Dos Santos; Marcelo Kalim
Officers: Steven Michael Jacobs [1969] Director/Financial Services Executive

BTIG Limited
Incorporated: 22 October 2007 *Employees:* 45
Net Worth: £12,689,435 *Total Assets:* £125,385,592
Registered Office: 2nd Floor, Princes Court, 7 Princes Street, London, EC2R 8AQ
Activities: Financial intermediation not elsewhere classified
Shareholder: Steven Robert Starker
Officers: Richard Alan Jacklin [1969] Director/Head of International Equities [American]; David Richards [1963] Director/Chief Financial Officer; Christopher Charles Rollins [1978] Director/Chief Executive Officer [American]

Build King Construction Limited
Incorporated: 19 December 1978 *Employees:* 857
Previous: Kaden Construction Limited
Net Worth: £39,259,112 *Total Assets:* £228,167,264
Registered Office: Third Floor, The Broadgate Tower, 20 Primrose Street, London, EC2A 2RS
Activities: Construction of domestic buildings
Officers: Kin Man Book [1967] Director/Contracts Manager [Chinese]; Siu Lun Cheung [1950] Director/Chartered Engineer [Chinese]; Chi Ko Kwok [1956] Director [Chinese]; Man Wai Lee [1961] Director [Chinese]; Sing Pang Liu [1961] Director/Contracts Manager [Chinese]; Yau Chun Paul Lui [1961] Director [Chinese]; Hon Wa Kenneth Mok [1963] Director [Canadian]; Yiu Wing So [1974] Director [Chinese]; Wai Tim Tsui [1962] Director; Cheuk Hung Yiu [1965] Director [Chinese]

Building & Property (Holdings) Limited
Incorporated: 26 July 1996
Net Worth: £18,424,000 *Total Assets:* £162,330,000
Registered Office: Capital Tower, 91 Waterloo Road, London, SE1 8RT
Activities: Activities of other holding companies n.e.c.
Parent: InterserveFM (Holdings) Ltd
Officers: Stephanie Alison Pound, Secretary; Philip George Clark [1965] Business Development Director; John William Lambert [1966] HR Director; Lynn Christine Mawdsley [1959] Director/Deputy Chief Financial Officer

Building Energy 1 Holdings PLC
Incorporated: 2 June 2017 *Employees:* 107
Net Worth: £66,429,080 *Total Assets:* £317,840,352
Registered Office: 170 Piccadilly, London, W1J 9EJ
Activities: Activities of other holding companies n.e.c.
Shareholder: Fabrizio Zago
Officers: Stefano Macchi di Cellere, Secretary; Fabrizio Brocchieri [1969] Director [Italian]; Gianfilippo Cuneo [1942] Director [Italian]; Sergio D'Angelo [1977] Director [Italian]; Fabrizio Zago [1965] Director/CEO Building Energy SpA [Italian]

Building Energy Ltd
Incorporated: 19 May 2017 *Employees:* 7
Net Worth: £139,593,872 *Total Assets:* £169,609,104
Registered Office: 170 Piccadilly, London, W1J 9EJ
Activities: Activities of other holding companies n.e.c.
Parent: Building Energy 1 Holdings PLC
Officers: Stefano Macchi di Cellere, Secretary; Alessandro Azais Tatistscheff [1972] Director [Seychellois]; Gian Luca Bandini [1968] Director [Italian]; Alessandro Bragantini [1958] Director [Italian]; Fabrizio Brocchieri [1969] Director [Italian]; Gianfilippo Cuneo [1942] Director [Italian]; Sergio D'Angelo [1977] Director [Italian]; Fabrizio Zago [1965] Director/CEO Building Energy SpA [Italian]

Building Schools for The Future Investments LLP
Incorporated: 6 July 2006 *Employees:* 2
Net Worth: £15,586,000 *Total Assets:* £169,624,992
Registered Office: 3 More London Riverside, London, SE1 2AQ

H P Bulmer Limited
Incorporated: 27 June 1918
Net Worth: £120,968,000 *Total Assets:* £182,007,008
Registered Office: Elsley Court, 20-22 Great Titchfield Street, London, W1W 8BE
Activities: Manufacture of cider and other fruit wines
Parent: Scottish & Newcastle Limited
Officers: David Michael Forde [1968] Managing Director [Irish]; Lynsey Jane Nicoll [1980] Director/Lawyer; Radovan Sikorsky [1967] Finance Director [Slovak]; Kelly Taylor-Welsh [1978] Director/Head of UK Tax

Bumper 8 (UK) Finance PLC
Incorporated: 22 June 2016
Net Worth: £39,704 *Total Assets:* £610,081,792
Registered Office: 35 Great St Helen's, London, EC3A 6AP
Activities: Financial intermediation not elsewhere classified
Parent: Bumper 8 (UK) Finance Holdings Limited
Officers: Susan Iris Abrahams [1957] Director

Bunge Corporation Limited
Incorporated: 24 November 1995 *Employees:* 1
Net Worth: £1,197,400,192 *Total Assets:* £1,198,570,112
Registered Office: Room 113, 65 London Wall, London, EC2M 5TU
Activities: Activities of other holding companies n.e.c.
Parent: Bunge Limited
Officers: Walter Tregoning, Secretary; Edward Alan Elwig [1942] Director; David Gerard Kabbes [1962] Director [American]; Peter Charles Creighton Simeons [1953] Director/Chartered Accountant; Walter Tregoning [1936] Director/Chartered Secretary

Bunzl American Holdings (No.1) Limited
Incorporated: 25 October 1993
Net Worth: £1,974,408,576 *Total Assets:* £2,356,565,504
Registered Office: York House, 45 Seymour Street, London, W1H 7JT
Activities: Non-trading company
Parent: Henares Limited
Officers: Paul Nicholas Hussey, Secretary/Solicitor; Andrew James Ball [1963] Finance Director; Paul Nicholas Hussey [1959] Director/Solicitor; Brian Michael May [1964] Finance Director

Bunzl American Holdings (No.2) Limited
Incorporated: 15 November 2004
Net Worth: £786,044,032 *Total Assets:* £1,024,547,840
Registered Office: York House, 45 Seymour Street, London, W1H 7JT
Activities: Non-trading company
Parent: Yorse No. 3 Limited
Officers: Paul Nicholas Hussey, Secretary/Solicitor; Paul Nicholas Hussey [1959] Director/Solicitor; Daniel Joseph Lett [1969] Director/Attorney [American]; James McCool [1965] Director/Executive Vice President [American]

Bunzl Finance Public Limited Company
Incorporated: 30 October 1975
Net Worth: £241,900,000 *Total Assets:* £4,129,700,096
Registered Office: York House, 45 Seymour Street, London, W1H 7JT
Activities: Activities of head offices
Parent: Bunzl Public Limited Company
Officers: Paul Nicholas Hussey, Secretary; Andrew James Ball [1963] Finance Director; Damian George Bradley [1972] Director/Tax Manager; Timothy Richard Hayter [1961] Director/Group Treasurer; Paul Nicholas Hussey [1959] Director/Solicitor; Brian Michael May [1964] Finance Director

Bunzl Overseas Holdings (No. 2) Limited
Incorporated: 19 January 1987
Net Worth: £1,090,461,184 *Total Assets:* £2,024,051,584
Registered Office: York House, 45 Seymour Street, London, W1H 7JT
Activities: Non-trading company
Parent: Bunzl Public Limited Company
Officers: Paul Nicholas Hussey, Secretary/Solicitor; Andrew James Ball [1963] Finance Director; Paul Nicholas Hussey [1959] Director/Solicitor; Brian Michael May [1964] Finance Director

Bunzl Overseas Holdings (No. 3) Limited
Incorporated: 21 September 2012
Net Worth Deficit: £707,231 *Total Assets:* £353,134,912
Registered Office: York House, 45 Seymour Street, London, W1H 7JT
Activities: Non-trading company
Parent: Bunzl Overseas Holdings (No.2) Limited
Officers: Paul Nicholas Hussey, Secretary; Andrew James Ball [1963] Director; Paul Nicholas Hussey [1959] Director/Solicitor; Brian Michael May [1964] Finance Director

Bunzl Overseas Holdings Limited
Incorporated: 25 October 1993
Net Worth: £323,123,008 *Total Assets:* £468,146,784
Registered Office: York House, 45 Seymour Street, London, W1H 7JT
Activities: Non-trading company
Officers: Paul Nicholas Hussey, Secretary/Solicitor; Andrew James Ball [1963] Finance Director; Paul Nicholas Hussey [1959] Director/Solicitor; Brian Michael May [1964] Finance Director

Bunzl Public Limited Company
Incorporated: 22 January 1940
Net Worth: £1,448,600,064 *Total Assets:* £5,189,600,256
Registered Office: York House, 45 Seymour Street, London, W1H 7JT
Activities: Activities of head offices
Officers: Paul Nicholas Hussey, Secretary; Brian Michael May [1964] Finance Director; Vanda Murray [1960] Director; Stephan Ronald Nanninga [1957] Director [Dutch]; Lloyd Mark Pitchford [1971] Director; Philip Graham Rogerson [1945] Director; Eugenia Marie Ulasewicz [1953] Director [American]; Frank Andre Van Zanten [1967] Director [Dutch]

Bunzl Retail & Healthcare Supplies Limited
Incorporated: 13 June 1899 *Employees:* 1,216
Net Worth: £22,001,000 *Total Assets:* £238,888,992
Registered Office: York House, 45 Seymour Street, London, W1H 7JT
Activities: Non-specialised wholesale trade
Parent: Greenham Trading Limited
Officers: Paul Nicholas Hussey, Secretary; Helen Ruth Cockerham [1966] Director; Richard Ian Greenway [1970] Director/Accountant; George David Nicholas Tarratt [1975] Director/Accountant; Andrew James Tedbury [1964] Director; Christopher George Wakeman [1973] Managing Director; Lindsay Alexander Wilkie [1966] Finance Director

Bunzl UK Limited
Incorporated: 25 February 1994 *Employees:* 2,280
Net Worth: £45,058,000 *Total Assets:* £721,240,000
Registered Office: York House, 45 Seymour Street, London, W1H 7JT
Activities: Non-specialised wholesale trade
Parent: Lockhart Catering Equipment Limited
Officers: Paul Nicholas Hussey, Secretary/Solicitor; David Leslie Cousins [1966] Director; Laurence Walter Hill [1980] Finance Director; Matthew Ronald Johnson [1966] Director [Australian]; Richard Darragh Kelly [1959] Director/Accountant; Alastair Paul McLaughlin [1965] Director [Irish]; Steven Robert Norris [1979] Director/Accountant; Nik Rogers [1985] Director/Chartered Management Accountant; Dale Stokes [1978] Director; George David Nicholas Tarratt [1975] Director/Accountant; Andrew James Tedbury [1964] Director; Adam David Wright [1985] Director/Chartered Accountant

Bupa Care Homes (ANS) Limited
Incorporated: 18 November 1985 *Employees:* 2,758
Net Worth: £288,928,992 *Total Assets:* £508,508,992
Registered Office: 1 Angel Court, London, EC2R 7HJ
Activities: Other service activities n.e.c.
Parent: Bupa Care Homes (CFG) PLC
Officers: Neil Stephen Barker [1974] Director/Accountant; Joan Martina Elliott [1965] Finance Director; Michael Harrison [1974] Director; Rebecca Pearson [1976] Operations Director; Charles Austen Richardson [1972] Director

Bupa Care Homes (CFChomes) Limited
Incorporated: 4 April 1986 *Employees:* 1,780
Net Worth: £58,143,000 *Total Assets:* £167,564,992
Registered Office: 1 Angel Court, London, EC2R 7HJ
Activities: Other human health activities
Parent: Bupa Care Homes (ANS) Limited
Officers: Neil Stephen Barker [1974] Director/Accountant; Joan Martina Elliott [1965] Finance Director; Michael Harrison [1974] Director; Charles Austen Richardson [1972] Director

Bupa Care Homes (CFG) PLC
Incorporated: 6 December 1985
Net Worth: £48,793,000 *Total Assets:* £729,148,032
Registered Office: 1 Angel Court, London, EC2R 7HJ
Activities: Activities of head offices
Parent: Bupa Investments Overseas Limited
Officers: Julian Philip Sanders, Secretary; Neil Stephen Barker [1974] Director/Accountant; Joan Martina Elliott [1965] Finance Director; Michael Harrison [1974] Director; Charles Austen Richardson [1972] Director

Bupa Care Homes (Cfhcare) Limited
Incorporated: 19 August 1992 *Employees:* 3,449
Net Worth: £1,708,000 *Total Assets:* £400,664,000
Registered Office: 1 Angel Court, London, EC2R 7HJ
Activities: Other human health activities
Parent: Bupa Care Homes (ANS) Limited
Officers: Neil Stephen Barker [1974] Director/Accountant; Joan Martina Elliott [1965] Finance Director; Michael Harrison [1974] Director; Charles Austen Richardson [1972] Director

Bupa Care Homes (Holdings) Limited
Incorporated: 29 June 2016
Net Worth: £330,944,000 *Total Assets:* £501,759,008
Registered Office: 1 Angel Court, London, EC2R 7HJ
Activities: Activities of other holding companies n.e.c.
Parent: Bupa Finance PLC
Officers: Neil Stephen Barker [1974] Director/Accountant; Joan Martina Elliott [1965] Director; Charles Austen Richardson [1972] Director

Bupa Finance PLC.
Incorporated: 13 January 1993 *Employees:* 62,412
Net Worth: £6,796,400,128 *Total Assets:* £14,465,399,808
Registered Office: 1 Angel Court, London, EC2R 7HJ
Activities: Other business support service activities n.e.c.
Parent: The British United Provident Association Limited
Officers: Julian Philip Sanders, Secretary; Siobhan Kathleen Dolan [1970] Director/Chartered Accountant [Irish]; Gareth Morris Evans [1973] Director/Accountant; Joy Linton [1965] Director [Australian]; Gareth Huw Roberts [1978] Director

Bupa Global Holdings Limited
Incorporated: 31 August 2005
Previous: Bupa Investments Holdings Limited
Net Worth: £217,766,384 *Total Assets:* £217,828,624
Registered Office: 1 Angel Court, London, EC2R 7HJ
Activities: Activities of head offices
Parent: Bupa Investments Overseas Limited
Officers: Moses Dodo [1959] Director/General Manager [American]; Sheldon Robert Kenton [1969] Director; Taryn Leonie McHarg [1978] Director [Australian]

Bupa Insurance Limited
Incorporated: 27 March 2000 *Employees:* 48
Net Worth: £246,391,008 *Total Assets:* £2,076,237,056
Registered Office: 1 Angel Court, London, EC2R 7HJ
Activities: Non-life insurance
Parent: Bupa Finance PLC
Officers: Fiona Harris [1968] Director; Sheldon Robert Kenton [1969] Director; Maxwell Colin Ledlie [1966] Director/Actuary; Sophie Jane O'Connor [1970] Director; Alexander Philip Perry [1970] Director; Robin Ashley Phipps [1950] Director; David William Smith [1959] Director; Clare Eleanor Thompson [1954] Director

Bupa Insurance Services Limited
Incorporated: 23 August 1999 *Employees:* 3,208
Net Worth: £98,705,000 *Total Assets:* £396,067,008
Registered Office: 1 Angel Court, London, EC2R 7HJ
Activities: Other business support service activities n.e.c.
Parent: Bupa Finance PLC
Officers: Fiona Harris [1968] Director; Sheldon Robert Kenton [1969] Director; Maxwell Colin Ledlie [1966] Director/Actuary; Sophie Jane O'Connor [1970] Director; Alexander Philip Perry [1970] Director; Robin Ashley Phipps [1950] Director; David William Smith [1959] Director; Clare Eleanor Thompson [1954] Director

Bupa Investments Limited
Incorporated: 30 March 1967
Net Worth: £779,901,760 *Total Assets:* £1,824,108,032
Registered Office: 1 Angel Court, London, EC2R 7HJ
Activities: Other business support service activities n.e.c.
Parent: Bupa Finance PLC
Officers: Gareth Morris Evans [1973] Director/Accountant; Joy Linton [1965] Director [Australian]; Charles Austen Richardson [1972] Director; Gareth Huw Roberts [1978] Director

Bupa Investments Overseas Limited
Incorporated: 22 November 1994 *Employees:* 43
Net Worth: £4,458,274,816 *Total Assets:* £7,654,800,384
Registered Office: 1 Angel Court, London, EC2R 7HJ
Activities: Other business support service activities n.e.c.
Parent: Bupa Finance PLC
Officers: Gareth Morris Evans [1973] Director/Accountant; Stephanie Margaret Fielding [1971] Director [Australian]; Joy Linton [1965] Director [Australian]; Gareth Huw Roberts [1978] Director

Burberry Beauty Limited
Incorporated: 15 October 2012
Net Worth: £130,843,000 *Total Assets:* £130,843,000
Registered Office: Horseferry House, Horseferry Road, London, SW1P 2AW
Activities: Activities of financial services holding companies
Parent: Burberry Group PLC
Officers: Gemma Elizabeth Mary Parsons, Secretary; Ian Brimicombe [1963] Director; Nigel Philip Jones [1965] Director; Edward Charles Rash [1972] Director/Solicitor

Burberry Group PLC
Incorporated: 30 October 1997 *Employees:* 9,752
Net Worth: £1,420,499,968 *Total Assets:* £2,223,000,064
Registered Office: Horseferry House, Horseferry Road, London, SW1P 2AW
Activities: Activities of head offices
Officers: Gemma Elizabeth Mary Parsons, Secretary; Fabiola Raquel Arredondo [1966] Director [American]; Julie Brown [1962] Director; Ian Russell Carter [1961] Director; David Jeremy Darroch [1962] Director; Ronald Leroy Frasch [1948] Director [American]; Stephanie George [1956] Director [American]; Marco Gobbetti [1958] Director [Italian]; Matthew David Key [1963] Director/Accountant; Carolyn Julia McCall [1961] Director; Dr Gerard Martin Murphy [1955] Director [Irish]; Orna Nichionna [1956] Director [Irish]

Burberry Haymarket Limited
Incorporated: 15 August 2003
Net Worth: £457,592,000 *Total Assets:* £748,966,016
Registered Office: Horseferry House, Horseferry Road, London, SW1P 2AW
Activities: Activities of other holding companies n.e.c.
Parent: Burberry Group PLC
Officers: Gemma Elizabeth Mary Parsons, Secretary; Ian Brimicombe [1963] Director; Nigel Philip Jones [1965] Director; Edward Charles Rash [1972] Director/Solicitor

Burberry International Holdings Limited
Incorporated: 13 July 2001
Net Worth: £236,384,992 *Total Assets:* £265,968,000
Registered Office: Horseferry House, Horseferry Road, London, SW1P 2AW
Activities: Activities of other holding companies n.e.c.
Shareholders: Burberry Group PLC; Burberry Europe Holdings Limited
Officers: Gemma Elizabeth Mary Parsons, Secretary; Ian Brimicombe [1963] Director; Riad Djellas [1974] Director [French]; Nigel Philip Jones [1965] Director; Edward Charles Rash [1972] Director/Solicitor

Burberry Limited
Incorporated: 9 January 1920 *Employees:* 3,553
Net Worth: £377,188,992 *Total Assets:* £1,761,968,000
Registered Office: Horseferry House, Horseferry Road, London, SW1P 2AW
Activities: Manufacture of soft furnishings
Parent: Burberry (UK) Limited
Officers: Gemma Elizabeth Mary Parsons, Secretary; Ian Brimicombe [1963] Director; Julie Brown [1962] Director; Riad Djellas [1974] Director [French]; Edward Charles Rash [1972] Director/Solicitor

Burbo Extension Holding Ltd
Incorporated: 2 February 2016
Net Worth: £1,092,872,832 *Total Assets:* £1,092,881,664
Registered Office: 5 Howick Place, London, SW1P 1WG
Activities: Activities of other holding companies n.e.c.
Shareholder: Orsted Burbo Extension Holding Ltd
Officers: Nikolaj Birkwald [1988] Alternate Director of Kasper Trebbien [Danish]; Ulrik Pallisoe Bornoe [1981] Director [Danish]; Nadia D'Ippolito [1988] Alternate Director of Ulrik P. Bornoe [Italian]; Philip Henry de Villiers [1975] Alternate Director of Hugh A. Yendole; David Murray [1983] Director/Accountant [Irish]; Kasper Trebbien [1979] Senior Director [Danish]; Hugh Alistair Yendole [1968] Director

Burbo Extension Ltd
Incorporated: 7 July 2010
Previous: Dong Energy Burbo Extension (UK) Ltd
Net Worth: £1,196,089,088 *Total Assets:* £1,270,321,664
Registered Office: 5 Howick Place, London, SW1P 1WG
Activities: Other business support service activities n.e.c.
Parent: Burbo Extension Holding Ltd
Officers: Nikolaj Birkwald [1988] Alternate Director of Kasper Trebbien [Danish]; Ulrik Pallisoe Bornoe [1981] Director [Danish]; Nadia D'Ippolito [1988] Alternate Director of Ulrik P. Bornoe [Italian]; Philip Henry de Villiers [1975] Alternate Director of Hugh A. Yendole; David Murray [1983] Director/Accountant [Irish]; Kasper Trebbien [1979] Senior Director [Danish]; Hugh Alistair Yendole [1968] Director

Burford Capital Holdings (UK) Limited
Incorporated: 27 August 2010
Net Worth: £128,206,000 *Total Assets:* £224,224,000
Registered Office: 24 Cornhill, London, EC3V 3ND
Activities: Activities of head offices
Parent: Burford Capital Limited
Officers: Philipp Ferdinand Leibfried, Secretary; Craig Geoffrey Arnott [1966] Director/Barrister; Christopher Peter Bogart [1965] Director/CEO of Burford Group Limited [Canadian/American]; Ross David Clark [1968] Underwriting Director; Timothy James Dutton CBE QC [1957] Director/Barrister; Peter Edward Middleton [1934] Director/Chairman of Marsh & McLennan; Jonathan Todd Molot [1966] Director/Chief Investment Officer of Burford Group Limited [American]

Burford Capital PLC
Incorporated: 9 June 2014
Net Worth: £59,610,000 *Total Assets:* £429,369,984
Registered Office: 24 Cornhill, London, EC3V 3ND
Activities: Administration of financial markets
Parent: Burford Capital (UK) Limited
Officers: Philipp Ferdinand Leibfried, Secretary; Craig Geoffrey Arnott [1966] Director/Barrister; Philip Braverman [1957] Director [American]; Leslie Paster [1965] Director

Burford Global Investments Limited
Incorporated: 22 December 2016
Net Worth: £171,164,416 *Total Assets:* £171,358,736
Registered Office: 24 Cornhill, London, EC3V 3ND
Activities: Activities of head offices
Shareholder: Burford Capital PLC
Officers: Philipp Ferdinand Leibfried, Secretary; Craig Arnott [1966] Director; Philip Braverman [1957] Director [American]; Leslie Paster [1965] Director

Burford Investments Limited
Incorporated: 18 April 2016
Net Worth: £173,518,864 *Total Assets:* £173,872,112
Registered Office: 24 Cornhill, London, EC3V 3ND
Activities: Financial intermediation not elsewhere classified
Shareholder: Burford Capital PLC
Officers: Philipp Ferdinand Leibfried, Secretary; Craig Geoffrey Arnott [1966] Director/Barrister; Leslie Paster [1965] Director

Burlington Resources (Irish Sea) Limited
Incorporated: 22 September 1997
Net Worth: £172,968,000 *Total Assets:* £358,432,000
Registered Office: 20th Floor, 1 Angel Court, London, EC2R 7HJ
Activities: Extraction of crude petroleum
Parent: Burlington Resources (UK) Holdings Limited
Officers: David Grimshaw, Secretary; Terri Gay King [1961] Director/President, UK [American]; Russell Scott [1973] Director/Manager UK Finance; Katherine Susan Simpson [1961] Director/HSE Manager

Burlington Resources (UK) Holdings Limited
Incorporated: 21 October 1997
Net Worth: £157,346,000 *Total Assets:* £157,346,000
Registered Office: 20th Floor, 1 Angel Court, London, EC2R 7HJ
Activities: Other business support service activities n.e.c.
Parent: ConocoPhillips
Officers: David Grimshaw, Secretary; Terri Gay King [1969] Director/President, UK [American]; Russell Scott [1973] Director/Manager UK Finance; Katherine Susan Simpson [1961] Director/HSE Manager

Burlingtown LLP
Incorporated: 24 July 2006 *Employees:* 698
Net Worth: £682,908,864 *Total Assets:* £1,062,984,000
Registered Office: 3rd Floor, 25 Park Lane, London, W1K 1RA
Officers: Graziela Cutrale [1975] Member; Jose Luis Cutrale [1946] Member; Jose Luis Cutrale Jnr [1973] Member; Rosana Cutrale F [1950] Member

Burlingtown UK Limited
Incorporated: 12 November 2007 *Employees:* 9
Net Worth: £380,213,920 *Total Assets:* £480,930,016
Registered Office: 3rd Floor, 25 Park Lane, London, W1K 1RA
Activities: Wholesale of fruit and vegetable juices, mineral water and soft drinks
Shareholders: Jose Luis Cutrale; Rosana Cutrale
Officers: Philip John Warner, Secretary; Graziela Cutrale [1975] Director/Operations Manager [Italian]; Jose Luis Cutrale [1946] Director [Italian]; Jose Henrique Cutrale [1974] Director [Italian]; Rosana Cutrale F [1950] Director [Italian]; Jose Luis Cutrale Junior [1973] Director [Italian]

Burren Energy PLC
Incorporated: 14 January 1998
Net Worth: £120,596,608 *Total Assets:* £120,753,296
Registered Office: ENI House, 10 Ebury Bridge Road, London, SW1W 8PZ
Activities: Activities of other holding companies n.e.c.
Parent: ENI UK Holding PLC
Officers: Mila Trezza, Secretary; Gianluigi Ferrara [1959] Director [Italian]; Francesca Rinaldi [1978] Managing Director [Italian]; Mila Trezza [1975] Director/Solicitor [Italian]; Enrico Trovato [1974] Director [Italian]; Luca Vignati [1963] Director [Italian]

Business Design Centre Limited
Incorporated: 27 October 1981 *Employees:* 35
Net Worth: £107,895,000 *Total Assets:* £138,468,992
Registered Office: 52 Upper Street, London, N1 0QH
Activities: Letting and operating of conference and exhibition centres
Officers: Joseph Mullee, Secretary; Max Bull [1979] Director; Bradley John Cordes [1972] Venue Services Director; Dominic Richard Albert Ismael Jones [1967] Managing Director; Jack Anthony Morris [1956] Director; Joseph Mullee [1978] Director/Accountant; Kate Laura Simpson [1984] Marketing Director

Business Growth Fund Limited
Incorporated: 2 February 2011 *Employees:* 147
Previous: Business Growth Fund PLC
Net Worth: £1,228,308,992 *Total Assets:* £1,338,998,016
Registered Office: 13-15 York Buildings, London, WC2N 6JU
Activities: Activities of venture and development capital companies
Parent: BGF Group PLC
Officers: David Robert Murray, Secretary; Matthew Robert Reed [1975] Finance Director [Australian]; Stephen Frank Welton [1961] Director/Private Equity Manager

Business Mortgage Finance 6 PLC
Incorporated: 5 March 2007
Net Worth Deficit: £56,005,000 *Total Assets:* £184,736,992
Registered Office: 2nd Floor, Asticus Building, 21 Palmer Street, London, SW1H 0AD
Activities: Other business support service activities n.e.c.
Parent: BMF Holdings Limited
Officers: Coral Suzanne Bidel [1983] Director; Marc Speight [1985] Associate Director; Beejadhursingh Surnam [1970] Director

Busyexport Limited
Incorporated: 8 April 2002
Net Worth: £101,207,000 *Total Assets:* £101,354,000
Registered Office: Waterside House, 35 North Wharf Road, London, W2 1NW
Activities: Management of real estate on a fee or contract basis
Parent: Marks and Spencer PLC
Officers: Patricia Howell, Secretary; Steven John Bennett [1976] Director; Nicholas James Folland [1965] Director/Solicitor; Alistair James Willey [1976] Director/Accountant

BW Publishing Limited
Incorporated: 1 November 2011
Net Worth Deficit: £319,916,768 *Total Assets:* £796,069,056
Registered Office: 30 Golden Square, London, W1F 9LD
Activities: Sound recording and music publishing activities
Officers: Martin Neal Bandier [1941] Director/Business Executive [American]; Guy Robert Henderson [1960] Director/Business Executive; Steven Kober [1955] Director [American]; Guy Kimberly Moot [1965] Managing Director; Joseph Salvatore Puzio [1959] Director [American]

C & C Alpha Group Limited
Incorporated: 14 November 2002 *Employees:* 1,652
Net Worth Deficit: £48,803,308 *Total Assets:* £184,533,264
Registered Office: 23 Buckingham Gate, London, SW1E 6LB
Activities: Activities of head offices
Parent: JD Corporate and Trust Services SA
Officers: Satyabhama Pudaruth, Secretary/Compliance Officer [Mauritian]; Bhanu Choudhrie [1978] Director; Dhairya Choudhrie [1982] Director [Indian]; Sumant Kapur [1952] Director/Entrepreneur; Cherian Padinjarethalakal Thomas [1959] Director

C & C Bidco Limited
Incorporated: 28 November 2013 *Employees:* 2
Net Worth Deficit: £19,715,000 *Total Assets:* £126,634,000
Registered Office: 3rd Floor, Caparo House, 101-103 Baker Street, London, W1U 6EF
Activities: Activities of other holding companies n.e.c.
Parent: C & C Holdco Ltd
Officers: Nicholas Goodban, Secretary; Nicholas Goodban [1977] Finance Director; James Thorburn-Muirhead [1973] Director

C & C Properties UK Limited
Incorporated: 17 September 2001
Net Worth: £132,105,000 *Total Assets:* £132,105,000
Registered Office: 15 Grosvenor Street, London, W1K 4QZ
Activities: Activities of other holding companies n.e.c.
Parent: Capital & Counties Properties PLC
Officers: Leigh McCaveny, Secretary; Ruth Elizabeth Pavey, Secretary; Ian David Hawksworth [1965] Director/Chartered Surveyor; Situl Suryakant Jobanputra [1974] Director; Gary James Yardley [1965] Director/Chartered Surveyor

C & C Topco Limited
Incorporated: 28 November 2013 *Employees:* 9,814
Net Worth Deficit: £62,973,000 *Total Assets:* £133,836,000
Registered Office: 3rd Floor, Caparo House, 101-103 Baker Street, London, W1U 6EF
Activities: Activities of other holding companies n.e.c.
Officers: Nicholas Goodban, Secretary; Nicholas Goodban [1977] Finance Director; Malcolm Myer Miller [1955] Director; Craig Michael Rushton [1959] Director/Chief Executive Officer; James Thorburn-Muirhead [1973] Director

C.C. Licensing
Incorporated: 20 April 1988
Net Worth: £93,744,656 *Total Assets:* £407,750,432
Registered Office: 29 Great Smith Street, London, SW1P 3PS
Activities: Security dealing on own account
Officers: Joseph William Canon [1963] Director/Surveyor [Australian]; Nicola Ann Dymond [1966] Director/General Manager; Christopher Paul West [1978] Director/Chartered Surveyor

C.I. Property & Investments Limited
Incorporated: 30 December 1981
Net Worth: £144,314,000 *Total Assets:* £188,548,000
Registered Office: 8 King Street, St James's, London, SW1Y 6QT
Activities: Other letting and operating of own or leased real estate
Parent: Christie's International PLC
Officers: Adele Christine Falconer, Secretary; Timothy John Norman [1975] Director/Group Financial Controller; Rosalind Patient [1979] Director of Operations, UK; Annelies Emma Stevens [1978] Director/Solicitor

Cable & Wireless Communications Limited
Incorporated: 9 December 2015
Net Worth: £2,314,837,760 *Total Assets:* £6,591,843,840
Registered Office: Griffin House, 161 Hammersmith Road, London, W6 8BS
Activities: Activities of head offices
Parent: LGE Coral Holdco Limited
Officers: Leah Helena Pegg, Secretary; Leah Helena Pegg [1985] Director/Company Secretary; Matthew Edward Read [1977] Director/Treasurer

Cable & Wireless International HQ Limited
Incorporated: 1 September 2006 *Employees:* 12
Net Worth: £513,832,704 *Total Assets:* £2,610,723,840
Registered Office: Griffin House, 161 Hammersmith Road, London, W6 8BS
Activities: Other telecommunications activities
Parent: CWIGroup Limited
Officers: Leah Helena Pegg, Secretary; Leah Helena Pegg [1985] Director/Company Secretary; Matthew Edward Read [1977] Director/Treasurer

Cable & Wireless Limited
Incorporated: 8 April 1929
Net Worth: £3,895,576,064 *Total Assets:* £15,156,789,248
Registered Office: Griffin House, 161 Hammersmith Road, London, W6 8BS
Activities: Other telecommunications activities
Parent: Cable & Wireless Communications Limited
Officers: Leah Helena Pegg, Secretary; Leah Helena Pegg [1985] Director/Company Secretary; Matthew Edward Read [1977] Director/Treasurer

Cable and Wireless (West Indies) Limited
Incorporated: 9 January 1877 *Employees:* 10
Net Worth: £467,400,128 *Total Assets:* £911,741,952
Registered Office: Griffin House, 161 Hammersmith Road, London, W6 8BS
Activities: Other telecommunications activities
Parent: CWIGroup Limited
Officers: Leah Helena Pegg, Secretary; Leah Helena Pegg [1985] Director/Company Secretary; Matthew Edward Read [1977] Director/Treasurer

Cabot Place Holdings Limited
Incorporated: 15 January 1997 *Employees:* 3
Net Worth: £296,801,376 *Total Assets:* £437,870,112
Registered Office: 30th Floor, One Canary Wharf, London, E14 5AB
Activities: Renting and operating of Housing Association real estate
Parent: Canary Wharf Investments Limited
Officers: John Raymond Garwood, Secretary; A Peter Anderson II [1953] Director/Real Estate Executive [American]; George Iacobescu [1945] Director; Russell James John Lyons [1961] Director/Chartered Accountant

CACI Limited
Incorporated: 9 July 1982 *Employees:* 785
Net Worth: £89,371,424 *Total Assets:* £124,144,832
Registered Office: CACI House, Kensington Village, Avonmore Road, London, W14 8TS
Activities: Other software publishing
Officers: Steven Arthur Sadler, Secretary; Gregory Reese Bradford [1948] Director [American]; Manjeet Singh Khaira [1961] Director; Jack Phillip London [1937] Director [American]; Warren Randall Phillips [1941] Director [American]; Steven Arthur Sadler [1955] Director/Chief Finance Officer; Paul Winters [1953] Director

Cadogan Estates Limited
Incorporated: 22 March 1961 *Employees:* 63
Net Worth: £3,038,226,944 *Total Assets:* £5,780,406,784
Registered Office: 10 Duke of York Square, London, SW3 4LY
Activities: Other letting and operating of own or leased real estate
Parent: Cadogan Group Limited
Officers: Paul Morris Loutit, Secretary; Paul Morris Loutit [1968] Director/Chartered Accountant; Hugh Richard Seaborn [1962] Director/Chartered Surveyor

Cadogan Group Limited
Incorporated: 28 November 1994 *Employees:* 202
Net Worth: £4,585,126,912 *Total Assets:* £6,228,353,024
Registered Office: 10 Duke of York Square, London, SW3 4LY
Activities: Activities of head offices
Parent: Cadogan Settled Estates Limited
Officers: Paul Morris Loutit, Secretary; The Honourable James Henry Morys Bruce [1948] Director/Merchant Banker; Edward Charles Cadogan [1966] Director/Landowner; Charles Vincent Ellingworth [1957] Marketing Director; John David Gordon [1962] Director/Fund Manager; Francis William Salway [1957] Director/Surveyor; Hugh Richard Seaborn [1962] Director/Chartered Surveyor

Cadogan Holdings Limited
Incorporated: 22 June 1961
Net Worth: £264,051,008 *Total Assets:* £446,046,016
Registered Office: 10 Duke of York Square, London, SW3 4LY
Activities: Other letting and operating of own or leased real estate
Parent: Chelsea Land Limited
Officers: Paul Morris Loutit, Secretary; Paul Morris Loutit [1968] Director/Chartered Accountant; Hugh Richard Seaborn [1962] Director/Chartered Surveyor

Cadogan Settled Estates Limited
Incorporated: 5 January 1995 *Employees:* 108
Net Worth: £4,500,419,072 *Total Assets:* £6,875,872,768
Registered Office: 9 New Square, Lincoln's Inn, London, WC2A 3QN
Activities: Activities of head offices
Parent: Cadogan Settled Estates Shareholding Company Ltd
Officers: Julia Llewellyn Richards, Secretary; The Honourable James Henry Morys Bruce [1948] Director; Charles Vincent Ellingworth [1957] Director; John David Gordon [1962] Director/Fund Manager; Henry Merton Henderson [1952] Director/Investment; Alexandra Ahavni Sarkis [1957] Director/Solicitor

Caesars Entertainment UK Limited
Incorporated: 14 October 1993 *Employees:* 2
Previous: London Clubs International Limited
Net Worth: £50,790,000 *Total Assets:* £262,598,000
Registered Office: 55 Baker Street, London, W1U 8EW
Activities: Activities of head offices
Parent: CEOC LLC
Officers: Krishan Kaushal, Secretary; Eric Alan Hession [1974] Director/Senior Vice President of Finance [American]; Thomas Michael Jenkin [1955] Director/Global President of Destination Markets [American]; Alexis George Oswald [1981] Director; Michael Rothwell [1968] Finance Director

Caffe Nero Group Holdings Ltd
Incorporated: 15 September 2006 *Employees:* 6,003
Previous: Rome Pikco Limited
Net Worth Deficit: £320,272,992 *Total Assets:* £320,116,992
Registered Office: 9-15 Neal Street, London, WC2H 9QL
Activities: Activities of head offices
Parent: Rome PIK Holdco Ltd
Officers: Benedict James Price, Secretary; Dr Generald William Ford [1957] Director/Chairman & CEO [American]; Benedict James Price [1967] Finance Director

Caledonia Investments PLC
Incorporated: 8 December 1928 *Employees:* 52
Net Worth: £1,836,600,064 *Total Assets:* £1,872,099,968
Registered Office: Cayzer House, 30 Buckingham Gate, London, SW1E 6NN
Activities: Activities of investment trusts
Officers: Graeme Philip Denison, Secretary; Stuart John Bridges [1960] Director; The Honourable Charles William Cayzer [1957] Director; James Michael Beale Cayzer Colvin [1965] Director; Guy Bryce Davison [1957] Director; Charles Henry Gregson [1947] Director; Shonaid Christina Ross Jemmett-Page [1960] Director; David Coldwells Stewart [1960] Director; William Penfold Wyatt [1968] Director

Caledonia Thames Acquisitions Limited
Incorporated: 8 June 2015
Net Worth Deficit: £1,615,000 *Total Assets:* £102,120,000
Registered Office: 55 Bishopsgate, London, EC2N 3AS
Activities: Activities auxiliary to financial intermediation n.e.c.
Parent: Caledonia Thames Group Limited
Officers: Charles Edward Sparrow, Secretary; Thomas Gerard Sheridan [1953] Director; Charles Edward Sparrow [1963] Director

Caledonia Thames Group Limited
Incorporated: 8 June 2015 *Employees:* 248
Net Worth: £14,529,000 *Total Assets:* £159,567,008
Registered Office: 55 Bishopsgate, London, EC2N 3AS
Activities: Activities auxiliary to financial intermediation n.e.c.
Parent: Caledonia Thames Holdings Limited
Officers: Charles Edward Sparrow, Secretary; Thomas Gerard Sheridan [1953] Director; Charles Edward Sparrow [1963] Director

Caledonia Thames Holdings Limited
Incorporated: 8 June 2015
Net Worth: £96,462,000 *Total Assets:* £159,567,008
Registered Office: 55 Bishopsgate, London, EC2N 3AS
Activities: Activities of financial services holding companies
Parent: Caledonia Investments PLC
Officers: Charles Edward Sparrow, Secretary; Charles Hugh Edwards [1979] Director [Australian]; Duncan Edward Johnson [1970] Director; Dr Ian Bruce Owen [1953] Director; Thomas Gerard Sheridan [1953] Director; Charles Edward Sparrow [1963] Director

Caledonian Rail Leasing Limited
Incorporated: 8 December 2014
Net Worth Deficit: £23,696,684 *Total Assets:* £246,472,928
Registered Office: 99 Queen Victoria Street, London, EC4V 4EH
Activities: Financial leasing
Officers: Lee Lawrence Barnsley [1960] Director/Senior Vice President, Leasing; Lawrence James Butcher [1968] Managing Director, Leasing; Antony Edward Mitton [1967] Director/Senior Vice President, Leasing; Mark Jeremy Rutherford [1965] Director/Senior Vice President, Leasing; David Allen Ward [1956] Director/President/C.O.O, Leasing [American]

Calypso FX EUR Limited
Incorporated: 25 May 2016
Net Worth Deficit: £15,655,907 *Total Assets:* £103,703,904
Registered Office: 16 Great Queen Street, Covent Garden, London, WC2B 5AH
Activities: Other information service activities n.e.c.
Parent: Calypso Group UK Limited
Officers: Andrew Coll [1970] Director; Jonathan Doty Walsh [1975] Director [American]

Calypso FX USD Limited
Incorporated: 25 May 2016
Net Worth: £111,334,048 *Total Assets:* £111,346,320
Registered Office: 16 Great Queen Street, Covent Garden, London, WC2B 5AH
Activities: Other information service activities n.e.c.
Parent: Calypso FX EUR Limited
Officers: Andrew Coll [1970] Director; Jonathan Doty Walsh [1975] Director [American]

Calypso Group UK Limited
Incorporated: 15 March 2016
Net Worth: £385,125,344 *Total Assets:* £830,091,264
Registered Office: 16 Great Queen Street, Covent Garden, London, WC2B 5AH
Activities: Other information service activities n.e.c.
Parent: Calypso UK Midco Limited
Officers: Didier Bruno Bouillard [1964] Director [French]; Scott Charles Collins [1965] Director/Investment Professional [American]; Charles James FitzGenerald [1967] Director/Investment Professional [American]; Thomas Patrick Gavin [1972] Director [American]; David Benjamin Christophe Nicault [1979] Director [French]; Xavier Jean Robert [1971] Director/Partner [French]; Denis Francois Villafranca [1972] Director/Partner [French]

Cambian Education Services Limited
Incorporated: 6 September 2005 *Employees:* 4
Net Worth: £75,069,112 *Total Assets:* £141,435,424
Registered Office: 4th Floor, Waterfront, Manbre Wharf, Manbre Road, Hammersmith, London, W6 9RH
Activities: Activities of other holding companies n.e.c.
Officers: Catherine Apthorpe, Secretary; Anne Marie Carrie [1955] Director; Jeremy David Wiles [1962] Director

Cambian Group Holdings Limited
Incorporated: 7 March 2014 *Employees:* 128
Previous: Cambian Group Holdings I Limited
Net Worth: £315,624,064 *Total Assets:* £473,517,440
Registered Office: 4th Floor, Waterfront, Manbre Wharf, Manbre Road, Hammersmith, London, W6 9RH
Activities: Activities of head offices
Parent: Cambian Group PLC
Officers: Catherine Apthorpe, Secretary; Anne Marie Carrie [1955] Director; Jeremy David Wiles [1962] Director

Cambian Group Limited
Incorporated: 7 March 2014 *Employees:* 4,539
Previous: Cambian Group PLC
Net Worth: £311,428,992 *Total Assets:* £397,052,992
Registered Office: 4th Floor, Waterfront, Manbre Wharf, Manbre Road, Hammersmith, London, W6 9RH
Activities: Activities of head offices
Officers: Catherine Apthorpe, Secretary; Anne Marie Carrie [1955] Director; Jeremy David Wiles [1962] Director

Cambian Heritage I Limited
Incorporated: 10 June 2004
Net Worth: £110,211,408 *Total Assets:* £110,217,280
Registered Office: 4th Floor, Waterfront, Manbre Wharf, Manbre Road, Hammersmith, London, W6 9RH
Activities: Activities of other holding companies n.e.c.
Parent: Cambian Properties (U.K.) Limited
Officers: Catherine Apthorpe, Secretary; Anne Marie Carrie [1955] Director; Jeremy David Wiles [1962] Director

Cambian Heritage II Limited
Incorporated: 22 December 1999
Net Worth: £197,474,880 *Total Assets:* £199,812,304
Registered Office: 4th Floor, Waterfront, Manbre Wharf, Manbre Road, Hammersmith, London, W6 9RH
Activities: Other letting and operating of own or leased real estate
Parent: Cambian Heritage I Limited
Officers: Catherine Jane Apthorpe, Secretary; Anne Marie Carrie [1955] Director; Jeremy David Wiles [1962] Director

Cambian Properties (U.K.) Limited
Incorporated: 6 September 2005
Net Worth: £94,001,640 *Total Assets:* £178,375,632
Registered Office: 4th Floor, Waterfront, Manbre Wharf, Manbre Road, Hammersmith, London, W6 9RH
Activities: Activities of other holding companies n.e.c.
Officers: Catherine Apthorpe, Secretary; Anne Marie Carrie [1955] Director; Jeremy David Wiles [1962] Director

Camelot UK Bidco Limited
Incorporated: 7 July 2016 *Employees:* 10
Net Worth: £1,009,429,568 *Total Assets:* £2,271,803,392
Registered Office: Friars House, 160 Blackfriars Road, London, SE1 8EZ
Activities: Activities of other holding companies n.e.c.
Parent: Camelot UK Holdco Limited
Officers: Stephen Paul Hartman, Secretary; Stephen Paul Hartman [1969] Director/Solicitor; Andrew Graham Wright [1966] Director/International Controller

Camelot UK Holdco Limited
Incorporated: 5 August 2016
Net Worth: £1,261,008,384 *Total Assets:* £1,261,558,656
Registered Office: Friars House, 160 Blackfriars Road, London, SE1 8EZ
Activities: Activities of other holding companies n.e.c.
Parent: Camelot UK Top Holdco Limited
Officers: Stephen Paul Hartman, Secretary; Stephen Paul Hartman [1969] Director/Solicitor; Andrew Graham Wright [1966] Director/International Controller

Camelot UK Top Holdco Limited
Incorporated: 22 August 2016
Net Worth: £1,261,008,384 *Total Assets:* £1,261,558,528
Registered Office: Friars House, 160 Blackfriars Road, London, SE1 8EZ
Activities: Activities of other holding companies n.e.c.
Officers: Stephen Paul Hartman, Secretary; Stephen Paul Hartman [1969] Director/Solicitor; Andrew Graham Wright [1966] Director/International Controller

Cameron Flow Control Technology (UK) Limited
Incorporated: 29 January 2013 *Employees:* 486
Net Worth: £115,266,000 *Total Assets:* £258,540,000
Registered Office: 100 New Bridge Street, London, EC4V 6JA
Activities: Manufacture of other special-purpose machinery n.e.c.
Parent: Cameron Petroleum (UK) Limited
Officers: Mark Roman Higgins, Secretary; Gina Ann Karathanos, Secretary; Benjamin Robert Hayes [1975] Director/Chemical Engineer/Business Manager [Australian]; Mark Roman Higgins [1971] Director/Chartered Accountant; Michael John Smart [1963] Director/Business Executive

Cameron Petroleum (UK) Limited
Incorporated: 13 November 2002
Net Worth: £616,444,992 *Total Assets:* £616,990,976
Registered Office: 100 New Bridge Street, London, EC4V 6JA
Activities: Activities of other holding companies n.e.c.
Parent: Schlumberger Oilfield UK PLC
Officers: Mark Roman Higgins, Secretary; Gina Ann Karathanos, Secretary; Mark Roman Higgins [1971] Director/Chartered Accountant; Michael John Smart [1963] Director/Business Executive; Simon Smoker [1962] Director/Accountant

Campaign Monitor (UK) Limited
Incorporated: 3 March 2015
Net Worth: £220,288,144 *Total Assets:* £220,476,560
Registered Office: 4th Floor, New Penderel House, 283-288 High Holborn, London, WC1V 7HP
Activities: Other information technology service activities
Parent: Campaign Monitor Holdings (UK) Limited
Officers: Adam Berger [1963] Director [American]; David Greiner [1978] Director [Australian]; Nikitas Koutoupes [1964] Director [Greek]; Deven Parekh [1969] Director [American]; Benjamin Mark Richardson [1979] Director [Australian]

Campaign Monitor Holdings (UK) Limited
Incorporated: 18 February 2015 *Employees:* 356
Net Worth: £233,587,184 *Total Assets:* £444,028,416
Registered Office: 4th Floor, New Penderel House, 283-288 High Holborn, London, WC1V 7HP
Activities: Other information technology service activities
Officers: Jesal Shah, Secretary; Adam Berger [1963] Director [American]; David Greiner [1978] Director [Australian]; Nikitas Koutoupes [1964] Director [Greek]; Deven Parekh [1969] Director [American]; Benjamin Mark Richardson [1979] Director [Australian]; Boris Treskunov [1991] Director [American]

The Campden Charities Trustee
Incorporated: 5 April 2004 *Employees:* 14
Net Worth: £150,503,600 *Total Assets:* £151,531,120
Registered Office: 27a Pembridge Villas, London, W11 3EP
Activities: Educational support services
Officers: Christopher Stannard, Secretary; John Robert Atkinson [1954] Director/Campaign Organiser; David Charles John Banks [1958] Director/Commonwealth Secretariat; Samuel Berwick [1961] Director/Investment Manager; Dr Christopher Calman [1945] Director/General Practitioner; Gillean Weston Craig [1940] Director/Clergyman; Christopher Olga Davis [1946] Director/University Lecturer [American]; Timothy James Harvey-Samuel [1965] Director/Bursar; Daniel Hawkins [1976] Director/Digital Media Analyst; Susan Valerie Lockhart [1944] Director/Retired; Charles Patrick Ralph Sandys Manners [1963] Director/Retired; Frances Manthos [1966] Director; Julie Anne Mills [1957] Director/Councillor; Terry Jeff Myers [1965] Director/Computer Technician; Robert James Orr-Ewing [1953] Director/Surveyor; Marta Rodkina [1981] Director/Trustee; Richard Walker Arnott [1937] Director/Retired

CAN Holdings Limited
Incorporated: 20 July 1989 *Employees:* 649
Net Worth: £131,776,000 *Total Assets:* £147,444,000
Registered Office: St Bride's House, 10 Salisbury Square, London, EC4Y 8EH
Activities: Activities of head offices
Major Shareholder: Michael John Freeman
Officers: Adam Patrick Byrne [1964] Operations Director

Canaccord Genuity Limited
Incorporated: 30 November 1983 *Employees:* 223
Net Worth: £94,130,000 *Total Assets:* £543,500,032
Registered Office: 88 Wood Street, London, EC2V 7QR
Activities: Financial intermediation not elsewhere classified
Officers: Nicholas Russell, Secretary; Daniel Daviau [1964] Director [Canadian]; Alexis Marc Joel Louis de Rosnay [1967] Director/Chief Executive [French]; Terrence Allan Lyons [1949] Director [Canadian]; Donald Duncan MacFayden [1955] Commercial Director [Canadian]; Christopher William Courtenay Tregoning [1948] Director

Canada Square Investments Limited
Incorporated: 15 February 2013 *Employees:* 3
Net Worth: £252,764,992 *Total Assets:* £1,229,089,024
Registered Office: 33 Davies Street, London, W1K 4LR
Activities: Other letting and operating of own or leased real estate
Parent: Canada Square Holdings Limited
Officers: Walid Khaled Abu-Suud [1963] Director [Kuwaiti]; Sangeet Dhanani [1974] Director; Laraine Loh [1984] Director [Singaporean]

Canada Square Operations Limited
Incorporated: 9 December 1994 *Employees:* 35
Net Worth: £62,540,000 *Total Assets:* £229,907,008
Registered Office: Citigroup Centre, Canary Wharf, London, E14 5LB
Activities: Banks
Parent: Citigroup Inc
Officers: Simon James Cumming, Secretary; Jiten Vasantkumar Mistry [1978] Director/Analyst; David Ian Sharland [1959] Director

Canary Finco Limited
Incorporated: 15 March 2016
Net Worth: £113,310,504 *Total Assets:* £464,684,736
Registered Office: Acre House, 11-15 William Road, London, NW1 3ER
Activities: Other business support service activities n.e.c.
Parent: Canary Holdco Limited
Officers: Susan Gillian Boulton [1969] Director; John Eric Fountain-Johnston [1958] Director; Jose Maria Hurtado Carrasco [1972] Director [Spanish]

Canary Holdco Limited
Incorporated: 15 March 2016
Net Worth: £134,190,168 *Total Assets:* £134,190,168
Registered Office: Acre House, 11-15 William Road, London, NW1 3ER
Activities: Other business support service activities n.e.c.
Parent: Canary Topco Limited
Officers: Susan Gillian Boulton [1969] Director; John Eric Fountain-Johnston [1958] Director; Jose Maria Hurtado Carrasco [1972] Director [Spanish]

Canary Wharf (North Quay) Limited
Incorporated: 27 February 2008 *Employees:* 3
Net Worth: £66,270,172 *Total Assets:* £146,509,936
Registered Office: 1 Canada Square, London, E14 5AB
Activities: Construction of commercial buildings
Parent: Canary Wharf Investments (RSNQ) Limited
Officers: John Raymond Garwood, Secretary; A Peter Anderson-II [1953] Director/Real Estate Executive [American]; George Iacobescu [1945] Director; Russell James John Lyons [1961] Director/Chartered Accountant

Canary Wharf Contractors Limited
Incorporated: 24 February 1989 *Employees:* 377
Net Worth: £75,740,176 *Total Assets:* £1,185,198,848
Registered Office: One Canary Wharf, London, E14 5AB
Activities: Construction of commercial buildings
Parent: Canary Wharf Central Limited
Officers: John Raymond Garwood, Secretary; A Peter Anderson II [1953] Director/Real Estate Executive [American]; George Iacobescu [1945] Director; Russell James John Lyons [1961] Director/Chartered Accountant

Canary Wharf Developments Limited
Incorporated: 2 April 2007 *Employees:* 3
Net Worth: £259,399,552 *Total Assets:* £627,006,976
Registered Office: One Canary Wharf, London, E14 5AB
Activities: Development of building projects
Parent: Canary Wharf Holdings Limited
Officers: John Raymond Garwood, Secretary; A Peter Anderson II [1953] Director/Real Estate Executive [American]; George Iacobescu [1945] Director; Russell James John Lyons [1961] Director/Chartered Accountant

Canary Wharf Estate Limited
Incorporated: 17 October 1995 *Employees:* 3
Net Worth: £620,229,440 *Total Assets:* £620,297,728
Registered Office: Level 30, 1 Canary Wharf, London, E14 5AB
Activities: Other business support service activities n.e.c.
Parent: Canary Wharf Group PLC
Officers: John Raymond Garwood, Secretary; A Peter Anderson II [1953] Director/Real Estate Executive [American]; George Iacobescu [1945] Director; Russell James John Lyons [1961] Director/Chartered Accountant

Canary Wharf Finance II PLC
Incorporated: 16 February 2000 *Employees:* 6
Net Worth Deficit: £280,883,552 *Total Assets:* £1,623,979,776
Registered Office: 1 Canada Square, London, E14 5AB
Activities: Activities of head offices
Parent: Canary Wharf Finance Holdings Limited
Officers: John Raymond Garwood, Secretary; Khalifa Khalid Al-Thani [1990] Director [Qatari]; A Peter Anderson II [1953] Director/Real Estate Executive [American]; John Raymond Garwood [1958] Director/Company Secretary; George Iacobescu [1945] Director; Russell James John Lyons [1961] Director/Chartered Accountant; Zachary Bryan Vaughan [1977] Director [Canadian]

Canary Wharf Finance Leasing (BP1) Limited
Incorporated: 5 May 1988 *Employees:* 3
Net Worth: £314,547 *Total Assets:* £533,058,816
Registered Office: One Canary Wharf, London, E14 5AB
Activities: Financial intermediation not elsewhere classified
Parent: Canary Wharf Investments Limited
Officers: John Raymond Garwood, Secretary; A Peter Anderson II [1953] Managing Director - Finance [American]; George Iacobescu [1945] Director/Chairman and CEO; Russell James John Lyons [1961] Director/Chartered Accountant

Canary Wharf Group Investment Holdings PLC
Incorporated: 13 February 2004 *Employees:* 1,218
Previous: Songbird Estates PLC.
Net Worth: £4,165,700,096 *Total Assets:* £8,883,000,320
Registered Office: One Canary Wharf, London, E14 5AB
Activities: Other business support service activities n.e.c.
Shareholders: Brookfield Asset Management Inc; Qatar Investment Authority
Officers: John Raymond Garwood, Secretary; Mohamed Abdulrazzaq a Al-Hashmi [1988] Director [Qatari]; Jassim Abdulla Al-Thani [1983] Director [Qatari]; Khalifa Khalid Al-Thani [1990] Director [Qatari]; A Peter Anderson II [1953] Managing Director - Finance [American]; Jeffrey Miles Blidner [1948] Director/Executive [Canadian]; Navid Chamdia [1973] Director; Richard Byron Clark [1958] Director [American]; George Iacobescu [1945] Director; Brian William Kingston [1973] Director [Canadian]; Zachary Bryan Vaughan [1977] Director [Canadian]

Canary Wharf Group PLC
Incorporated: 30 March 2001 *Employees:* 5
Net Worth: £2,772,061,952 *Total Assets:* £3,555,894,016
Registered Office: One Canary Wharf, London, E14 5AB
Activities: Other business support service activities n.e.c.
Parent: CWG Newco Limited
Officers: John Raymond Garwood, Secretary; A Peter Anderson II [1953] Managing Director - Finance [American]; Richard David Stedman Archer [1964] Managing Director - Office; Clifford Thomas Bryant [1958] Managing Director, CWCL; Eugenio Caruso [1962] Director; Howard Dawber [1970] Director/Strategic Advisor; Ian Anthony Ferguson [1955] Managing Director, CWCL; John Raymond Garwood [1958] Director/Company Secretary; Philip Howard Gullett [1965] Director; Christopher John Henderson [1957] Managing Director and Chief Counsel; George Iacobescu [1945] Director/Chairman and CEO; Anthony James Sidney Jordan [1949] Managing Director - Development; Russell James John Lyons [1961] Managing Director and Chief Financial Officer; Camille Waxer [1956] Managing Director - Retail and Chief Administrative Officer

Canary Wharf Holdings (PB) Limited
Incorporated: 23 April 2013
Net Worth: £58,496,720 *Total Assets:* £138,263,120
Registered Office: One Canary Wharf, London, E14 5AB
Activities: Activities of other holding companies n.e.c.
Shareholders: Brookfield Property Partners LP; Qatar Investment Authority
Officers: John Raymond Garwood, Secretary; A Peter Anderson II [1953] Director/Real Estate Executive [American]; George Iacobescu [1945] Director; Russell James John Lyons [1961] Director

Canary Wharf Holdings Limited
Incorporated: 10 March 1993 *Employees:* 3
Net Worth: £1,395,909,248 *Total Assets:* £1,453,844,992
Registered Office: One Canary Wharf, London, E14 5AB
Activities: Activities of head offices
Parent: Canary Wharf Estate Limited
Officers: John Raymond Garwood, Secretary; A Peter Anderson II [1953] Director/Real Estate Executive [American]; George Iacobescu [1945] Director; Russell James John Lyons [1961] Director/Chartered Accountant

Canary Wharf Investments (BP4) Limited
Incorporated: 15 September 2011 *Employees:* 3
Net Worth: £54,693,452 *Total Assets:* £468,023,040
Registered Office: 30th Floor, One Canary Wharf, London, E14 5AB
Activities: Development of building projects
Parent: Canary Wharf (BP4) Limited
Officers: John Raymond Garwood, Secretary; A Peter Anderson II [1953] Director; George Iacobescu [1945] Director; Russell James John Lyons [1961] Director/Chartered Accountant

Canary Wharf Investments (DS8) Limited
Incorporated: 3 September 2002
Net Worth: £55,158,480 *Total Assets:* £101,142,640
Registered Office: 30th Floor, One Canada Square, London, E14 5AB
Activities: Buying and selling of own real estate
Parent: Canary Wharf Investment Holdings (DS8) Limited
Officers: John Raymond Garwood, Secretary; A Peter Anderson II [1953] Director/Real Estate Executive [American]; George Iacobescu [1945] Director; Russell James John Lyons [1961] Director/Chartered Accountant

Canary Wharf Investments (Three)
Incorporated: 28 December 1989 *Employees:* 3
Net Worth: £118,252,672 *Total Assets:* £118,623,608
Registered Office: One Canary Wharf, London, E14 5AB
Activities: Development of building projects
Parent: Canary Wharf Investments (Two) Limited
Officers: John Raymond Garwood, Secretary; A Peter Anderson II [1953] Director/Real Estate Executive [American]; George Iacobescu [1945] Director; Russell James John Lyons [1961] Director/Group Financial Controller

Canary Wharf Investments Limited
Incorporated: 1 May 1987 *Employees:* 3
Net Worth: £271,802,112 *Total Assets:* £284,075,776
Registered Office: One Canary Wharf, London, E14 5AB
Activities: Renting and operating of Housing Association real estate
Parent: Canary Wharf Holdings Limited
Officers: John Raymond Garwood, Secretary; A Peter Anderson II [1953] Director/Real Estate Executive [American]; George Iacobescu [1945] Director; Russell James John Lyons [1961] Director/Chartered Accountant

Canary Wharf Limited
Incorporated: 16 December 1985 *Employees:* 189
Net Worth: £1,171,652,352 *Total Assets:* £4,721,550,848
Registered Office: One Canary Wharf, London, E14 5AB
Activities: Development of building projects
Parent: Canary Wharf Central Limited
Officers: John Raymond Garwood, Secretary; A Peter Anderson II [1953] Director/Real Estate Executive [American]; George Iacobescu [1945] Director; Russell James John Lyons [1961] Director/Chartered Accountant

Canary Wharf Properties (Crossrail) Limited
Incorporated: 9 January 2008 *Employees:* 3
Net Worth: £155,833,792 *Total Assets:* £249,887,808
Registered Office: One Canary Wharf, London, E14 5AB
Activities: Construction of commercial buildings
Parent: Canary Wharf Investments (Crossrail) Limited
Officers: John Raymond Garwood, Secretary; A Peter Anderson II [1953] Director/Real Estate Executive [American]; George Iacobescu [1945] Director; Russell James John Lyons [1961] Director/Chartered Accountant

Canary Wharf Properties (FC2) Limited
Incorporated: 11 March 2005 *Employees:* 3
Net Worth: £181,467,584 *Total Assets:* £506,999,264
Registered Office: 30th Floor, One Canary Wharf, London, E14 5AB
Activities: Other business support service activities n.e.c.
Parent: Canary Wharf Funding (FC2/FC4) Limited
Officers: John Raymond Garwood, Secretary; A Peter Anderson II [1953] Director/Real Estate Executive [American]; George Iacobescu [1945] Director; Russell James John Lyons [1961] Director/Chartered Accountant

Canary Wharf Properties (FC4) Limited
Incorporated: 11 March 2005 *Employees:* 3
Net Worth: £177,924,608 *Total Assets:* £437,415,296
Registered Office: 30th Floor, One Canary Wharf, London, E14 5AB
Activities: Other business support service activities n.e.c.
Parent: Canary Wharf Funding (FC2/FC4)
Officers: John Raymond Garwood, Secretary; A Peter Anderson II [1953] Director/Real Estate Executive [American]; George Iacobescu [1945] Director; Russell James John Lyons [1961] Director/Chartered Accountant

Canary Wharf Properties (RT5) Limited
Incorporated: 9 January 2008 *Employees:* 3
Net Worth: £60,532,828 *Total Assets:* £127,083,304
Registered Office: One Canary Wharf, London, E14 5AB
Activities: Construction of commercial buildings
Parent: Canary Wharf Investments (RT5) Limited
Officers: John Raymond Garwood, Secretary; A Peter Anderson II [1953] Director/Real Estate Executive [American]; George Iacobescu [1945] Director; Russell James John Lyons [1961] Director/Chartered Accountant

Canary Wharf Properties (WF9) Limited
Incorporated: 21 November 2012 *Employees:* 3
Net Worth: £23,214,158 *Total Assets:* £148,581,264
Registered Office: One Canary Wharf, London, E14 5AB
Activities: Management of real estate on a fee or contract basis
Parent: Canary Wharf Investments Limited
Officers: John Raymond Garwood, Secretary; A Peter Anderson II [1953] Director; George Iacobescu [1945] Director; Russell James John Lyons [1961] Director

Canary Wharf Retail Funding Limited
Incorporated: 21 November 2012 *Employees:* 3
Net Worth: £24,983,400 *Total Assets:* £730,293,824
Registered Office: One Canary Wharf, London, E14 5AB
Activities: Non-trading company
Parent: Canary Wharf Investments Limited
Officers: John Raymond Garwood, Secretary; A Peter Anderson II [1953] Director; George Iacobescu [1945] Director; Russell James John Lyons [1961] Director

Cancer Research UK
Incorporated: 20 November 2001 *Employees:* 4,105
Net Worth: £409,200,000 *Total Assets:* £899,100,032
Registered Office: Angel Building, 407 St John Street, London, EC1V 4AD
Activities: Other human health activities
Officers: Niamh O'Sullivan, Secretary; Professor Sir Leszek Krzysztof Borysiewicz [1951] Director; Carolyn Jane Bradley [1964] Director/Independent Advisor; Catherine Ann Brown [1966] Group Strategy Director [British/New Zealander]; Peter Alan Chambre [1955] Director; Dr Adrian Mark Crellin [1954] Director/Consultant Clinical Oncologist; Tracy Anne de Groose [1968] Director/Media, Publishing & Advertising; Professor Dame Amanda Gay Fisher [1959] Director; Professor Stephen Townley Holgate [1947] Director/Clinical Professor; David Clive Lindsell [1947] Director; Andrew William Palmer [1953] Director; Professor Sir Bruce Anthony John Ponder [1944] Director/Senior Group Leader; Professor Sir Michael Adrian Richards [1951] Director/Retired

Canonical Group Limited
Incorporated: 6 April 2009 *Employees:* 443
Net Worth Deficit: £50,348,332 *Total Assets:* £264,696,960
Registered Office: 5th Floor, Blue Fin Building, 110 Southwark Street, London, SE1 0SU
Activities: Business and domestic software development
Parent: Canonical Holdings Limited
Officers: Katherine Ollerhead, Secretary; Neil Robert French [1964] Director/VP Operations

Canonsfield Estates Limited
Incorporated: 27 April 1971 *Employees:* 1
Net Worth: £121,676,968 *Total Assets:* £123,261,712
Registered Office: 11-15 Wigmore Street, London, W1A 2JZ
Activities: Activities of head offices
Parent: North Row Estates Limited
Officers: Carol Ann Stratton, Secretary; Jonathan Paul White [1951] Director

Cantor Fitzgerald Europe
Incorporated: 24 May 1990 *Employees:* 123
Net Worth: £31,427,120 *Total Assets:* £834,325,632
Registered Office: One Churchill Place, Canary Wharf, London, E14 5RB
Activities: Financial intermediation not elsewhere classified
Parent: Cantor Fitzgerald Services LLP
Officers: Robert Mark Snelling, Secretary; Russell Haley [1968] Director/Chief Financial Officer & Treasurer; Mark Elliot Kaplan [1960] Director/Chief Operating Officer [American]; James Richard Lightbourne [1970] Director/General Counsel; Diane Elizabeth Moore [1962] Director; Anthony James Simpson [1952] Director; Sofocles Sofocleous [1967] Director/Stockbroker

Cantor Fitzgerald Services LLP
Incorporated: 21 December 2011 *Employees:* 123
Net Worth: £30,998,112 *Total Assets:* £834,406,912
Registered Office: One Churchill Place, Canary Wharf, London, E14 5RD
Officers: Sofocles Sofocleous [1967] Member

Canyon UK Americas Limited
Incorporated: 23 June 2017
Net Worth: £460,016,864 *Total Assets:* £460,016,864
Registered Office: 5 Churchill Place, London, E14 5HU
Activities: Non-trading company
Parent: Canyon Holdings (Cayman), L.P.
Officers: Kevin Akeroyd [1968] Director [American]; Jacob Pearlstein [1964] Director [American]

Canyon UK Investments Ltd.
Incorporated: 29 May 2014
Previous: GTCR Canyon UK Investments Ltd
Net Worth Deficit: £9,958,474 *Total Assets:* £254,546,432
Registered Office: 5 Churchill Place, London, E14 5HU
Activities: Information technology consultancy activities
Parent: Cision Ltd
Officers: Kevin Akeroyd [1968] Director [American]; Jacob Pearlstein [1964] Director [American]

Caparo Holdings (US) Limited
Incorporated: 15 March 1988 *Employees:* 703
Net Worth: £83,166,336 *Total Assets:* £187,760,128
Registered Office: Caparo House, 103 Baker Street, London, W1U 6LN
Activities: Activities of head offices
Officers: David Patrick Dancaster [1956] Finance Director; The Lord Paul of Marylebone [1931] Director

Capco Group Treasury Limited
Incorporated: 12 December 2007
Net Worth: £246,588,000 *Total Assets:* £3,707,228,928
Registered Office: 15 Grosvenor Street, London, W1K 4QZ
Activities: Financial intermediation not elsewhere classified
Parent: Capital & Counties Properties PLC
Officers: Leigh McCaveny, Secretary; Ruth Elizabeth Pavey, Secretary; Ian David Hawksworth [1965] Director/Chartered Surveyor; Situl Suryakant Jobanputra [1974] Director; Terence David O'Beirne [1976] Director/Chartered Accountant [Irish]; Gary James Yardley [1965] Director/Chartered Surveyor

Capita Business Services Ltd
Incorporated: 26 September 1988 *Employees:* 13,592
Net Worth: £156,363,008 *Total Assets:* £1,579,714,048
Registered Office: 30 Berners Street, London, W1T 3LR
Activities: Information technology consultancy activities
Parent: Capita Holdings Limited
Officers: Christopher Francis Henry Baker [1955] Director; Erika Bannerman [1971] Director; Michael David Barnard [1973] Director; John James Hemming [1962] Director; David Colin Manuel [1969] Director; Robert David Tolfts [1962] Director; James D'Arcy Vincent [1966] Director

Capita Customer Management Limited
Incorporated: 2 November 1977 *Employees:* 11,639
Net Worth: £101,055,160 *Total Assets:* £207,211,248
Registered Office: 30 Berners Street, London, W1T 3LR
Activities: Data processing, hosting and related activities
Parent: Capita Holdings Limited
Officers: Michael David Barnard [1973] Director; Andrew John Bowman [1972] Director; Alexander Matthew Vallance [1968] Director

Capita Employee Benefits Limited
Incorporated: 20 May 1988 *Employees:* 1,484
Net Worth: £53,358,140 *Total Assets:* £103,912,152
Registered Office: 30 Berners Street, London, W1T 3LR
Activities: Pension funding
Parent: Capita Life & Pensions Regulated Services Limited
Officers: Christopher Charles Clements [1982] Director; Stuart Robert Heatley [1967] Director; Simon James Sherwood Mayall [1967] Director; Alexandra Mary Moffatt [1980] Director; Gareth Pickles [1967] Director; Peter Marcus Telford [1957] Director

Capita Holdings Limited
Incorporated: 13 December 2006
Net Worth: £166,140,992 *Total Assets:* £3,175,472,896
Registered Office: 30 Berners Street, London, W1T 3LR
Activities: Activities of head offices
Parent: Capita PLC
Officers: David Colin Manuel [1969] Director

Capita International Limited
Incorporated: 3 February 1992 *Employees:* 3
Net Worth Deficit: £19,484,168 *Total Assets:* £164,326,544
Registered Office: 30 Berners Street, London, W1T 3LR
Activities: Other business support service activities n.e.c.
Parent: Capita PLC
Officers: Michael David Barnard [1973] Director; Andrew John Bowman [1972] Director

Capita IT Services Holdings Limited
Incorporated: 20 November 2006
Net Worth: £89,974,304 *Total Assets:* £337,994,208
Registered Office: 30 Berners Street, London, W1T 3LR
Activities: Non-trading company
Parent: Capita Holdings Limited
Officers: Nicholas Siegfried Dale [1970] Director

Capita Justice & Secure Services Holdings Limited
Incorporated: 28 April 2003
Net Worth Deficit: £23,363,372 *Total Assets:* £186,609,360
Registered Office: 30 Berners Street, London, W1T 3LR
Activities: Activities of head offices
Parent: Capita Business Services Ltd
Officers: Christopher Francis Henry Baker [1955] Director; Stefan John Maynard [1972] Director

Capita Life & Pensions Regulated Services Limited
Incorporated: 20 September 1989 *Employees:* 4,177
Net Worth: £93,182,136 *Total Assets:* £241,236,640
Registered Office: 30 Berners Street, London, W1T 3LR
Activities: Financial intermediation not elsewhere classified
Parent: Capita PLC
Officers: Christopher Stuart Ashburn [1968] Director; Antony Paul Brown [1963] Director; James D'Arcy Vincent [1966] Director

Capita PLC
Incorporated: 8 December 1986 *Employees:* 69,459
Net Worth Deficit: £999,000,000 *Total Assets:* £4,421,199,872
Registered Office: 30 Berners Street, London, W1T 3LR
Activities: Other software publishing
Officers: Francesca Anne Todd, Secretary; Simon Patrick Butcher [1967] Director; John Harold Cresswell [1961] Director; Matthew Lester [1963] Director; Dr Jonathan James Muschamp Lewis [1961] Director; Baroness Lucy Jeanne Neville-Rolfe [1953] Director; Sir Ian Clifford Powell [1956] Director; Gillian Veronica Sheldon [1967] Director; Andrew John Williams [1967] Director

Capita Property and Infrastructure Holdings Limited
Incorporated: 13 September 1999
Net Worth: £107,786,000 *Total Assets:* £156,460,992
Registered Office: 30 Berners Street, London, W1T 3LR
Activities: Renting and operating of Housing Association real estate
Parent: Capita Holdings Limited
Officers: Christopher Stuart Ashburn [1968] Director

Capita Property and Infrastructure Limited
Incorporated: 12 May 1986 *Employees:* 2,144
Net Worth: £43,069,392 *Total Assets:* £106,589,376
Registered Office: 30 Berners Street, London, W1T 3LR
Activities: Other engineering activities
Parent: Capita Property and Infrastructure Holdings Limited
Officers: Natalie Garfield [1979] Director; Jonathan Mark Prew [1964] Director; Graham Michael Sant [1969] Director; David John Spencer [1970] Director; Oliver Leonard Wildgoose [1978] Director

Capita Resourcing Limited
Incorporated: 13 March 2000 *Employees:* 799
Net Worth: £54,229,204 *Total Assets:* £132,935,080
Registered Office: 30 Berners Street, London, W1T 3LR
Activities: Temporary employment agency activities
Parent: Capita Business Services Ltd
Officers: David Colin Manuel [1969] Director; Alexandra Mary Moffatt [1980] Director

Capita Secure Information Solutions Limited
Incorporated: 27 October 1981 *Employees:* 1,220
Net Worth: £4,821,045 *Total Assets:* £138,790,800
Registered Office: 30 Berners Street, London, W1T 3LR
Activities: Manufacture of telegraph and telephone apparatus and equipment
Parent: Capita Justice & Secure Services Holdings Limited
Officers: Christopher Francis Henry Baker [1955] Director; James Cowan [1974] Director; Stefan John Maynard [1972] Director

Capital & Counties Limited
Incorporated: 19 October 1933
Net Worth: £494,728,992 *Total Assets:* £495,000,000
Registered Office: 15 Grosvenor Street, London, W1K 4QZ
Activities: Activities of other holding companies n.e.c.
Parent: Capital & Counties Properties PLC
Officers: Leigh McCaveny, Secretary; Ruth Elizabeth Pavey, Secretary; Ian David Hawksworth [1965] Director/Chartered Surveyor; Situl Suryakant Jobanputra [1974] Director; Gary James Yardley [1965] Director/Chartered Surveyor

Capital & Counties Properties PLC
Incorporated: 3 February 2010 *Employees:* 171
Net Worth: £2,799,800,064 *Total Assets:* £3,961,200,128
Registered Office: 15 Grosvenor Street, London, W1K 4QZ
Activities: Activities of other holding companies n.e.c.
Officers: Leigh McCaveny, Secretary; Ruth Elizabeth Pavey, Secretary; Charlotte Jane Boyle [1971] Director; Graeme John Gordon [1963] Director [British/South African]; Ian David Hawksworth [1965] Director/Chartered Surveyor; Situl Suryakant Jobanputra [1974] Director; Jonathan Stewart Lane [1945] Director; John Gerard Murphy [1952] Director/Chartered Accountant; Henry Eric Staunton [1948] Director; Anthony Steains [1966] Director [Australian]; Andrew David Strang [1953] Director/Chartered Surveyor; Gary James Yardley [1965] Director/Chartered Surveyor

Capital & Regional Holdings Limited
Incorporated: 22 December 2005
Net Worth: £80,000,000 *Total Assets:* £123,891,560
Registered Office: 22 Chapter Street, London, SW1P 4NP
Activities: Development of building projects
Parent: Capital & Regional PLC
Officers: Stuart Andrew Wetherly, Secretary; Lawrence Francis Hutchings [1966] Director/Chartered Surveyor; James Maltby Ryman [1972] Director/Chartered Surveyor; Stuart Andrew Wetherly [1977] Director/Chartered Accountant

Capital & Regional PLC
Incorporated: 13 November 1978 *Employees:* 238
Net Worth: £481,400,000 *Total Assets:* £1,007,900,032
Registered Office: 22 Chapter Street, London, SW1P 4NP
Activities: Buying and selling of own real estate
Officers: Stuart Andrew Wetherly, Secretary; Antony John Hales [1948] Director; Wessel Johannes Hamman [1972] Director/Fund Manager; Lawrence Francis Hutchings [1966] Director/Chartered Surveyor; Ian Stephen Krieger [1952] Director/Chartered Accountant; Louis Norval [1956] Director/Businessman [Australian]; Hugh Yelverton Scott-Barrett [1958] Director; Diane Laura Whyte [1959] Director

Capital Hill Hotels Group Europe Limited
Incorporated: 28 May 1996 *Employees:* 367
Net Worth: £1,019,000 *Total Assets:* £103,211,000
Registered Office: 50 Berners Street, London, W1T 3NG
Activities: Hotels and similar accommodation
Parent: Capital Hill Hotels Limited
Officers: Sheikh Jassim Bin Hamad Bin Jassim Al-Thani [1982] Director [Qatari]; Fady Bakhos [1971] Director/Lawyer [Lebanese]; Karin Cooper [1969] Director/Architect [German]; Zaki El Guiziri [1957] Director [Egyptian]

Capital Hill Hotels Group London Limited
Incorporated: 7 November 1997 *Employees:* 367
Net Worth: £13,648,000 *Total Assets:* £121,616,000
Registered Office: 50 Berners Street, London, W1T 3NG
Activities: Hotels and similar accommodation
Parent: Capital Hill Hotels Group Europe Limited
Officers: Sheikh Jassim Bin Hamad Bin Jassim Al-Thani [1982] Director [Qatari]; Fady Bakhos [1971] Director/Lawyer [Lebanese]; Karin Cooper [1969] Director/Architect [German]; Zaki El Guziri [1957] Director [Egyptian]

Capital Hill Hotels Limited
Incorporated: 23 September 2011 *Employees:* 367
Net Worth: £72,510,000 *Total Assets:* £195,903,008
Registered Office: 50 Berners Street, London, W1T 3NG
Activities: Activities of other holding companies n.e.c.
Officers: Sheikh Jassim Bin Hamad Bin Jassim Al-Thani [1982] Director [Qatari]; Fady Bakhos [1971] Director/Lawyer [Lebanese]; Karin Cooper [1969] Director/Architect [German]; Zaki Nasser Zaki El Guiziri [1957] Director [Egyptian]

Car Giant Limited
Incorporated: 3 January 1979 *Employees:* 808
Net Worth: £243,431,008 *Total Assets:* £439,583,008
Registered Office: 44 Hythe Road, London, NW10 6RS
Activities: Sale of used cars and light motor vehicles
Major Shareholder: Geoffrey Michael Warren
Officers: John Anthony Forsdyke [1964] Purchasing Director; Michael Eugene Holahan [1971] Finance Director; Antonio Manuel Rocha Mendes [1964] Managing Director [Portuguese]

Cardinia Europe Limited
Incorporated: 31 October 2014
Previous: Omnicom DDB Investments Limited
Net Worth: £568,850,048 *Total Assets:* £568,850,048
Registered Office: Bankside 3, 90-100 Southwark Street, London, SE1 0SW
Activities: Activities of head offices
Parent: Omnicom EMEA Holdings Limited
Officers: Sally-Ann Bray, Secretary; Stephen Christopher Nigel Medhurst [1960] Director; Anthony Peter Phipkin [1957] Director/Accountant

Cardnet Merchant Services Limited
Incorporated: 19 September 1962
Net Worth: £28,000,000 *Total Assets:* £335,000,000
Registered Office: 25 Gresham Street, London, EC2V 7HN
Activities: Other business support service activities n.e.c.
Shareholder: Lloyds Banking Group PLC
Officers: Alyson Elizabeth Mulholland, Secretary; Gregory David Gould [1969] Director; Tony Nash [1965] Managing Director; Philip Stunt [1963] Director/SVP and CIO International

Care Homes 1 Limited
Incorporated: 6 April 2006
Net Worth: £11,220,242 *Total Assets:* £126,376,504
Registered Office: 250 Bishopsgate, London, EC2M 4AA
Activities: Financial intermediation not elsewhere classified
Parent: Care Homes Holdings Limited
Officers: Stephen Paul Nixon [1970] Director/Bank Official; Keith Damian Pereira [1978] Director/Bank Official; Luke Esrom Roberts [1979] Director/Bank Official [Irish]

Care Homes 2 Limited
Incorporated: 6 April 2006
Net Worth: £40,781,780 *Total Assets:* £341,372,960
Registered Office: 250 Bishopsgate, London, EC2M 4AA
Activities: Financial intermediation not elsewhere classified
Parent: Care Homes Holdings Limited
Officers: Stephen Paul Nixon [1970] Director/Bank Official; Keith Damian Pereira [1978] Director/Bank Official; Luke Esrom Roberts [1979] Director/Bank Official [Irish]

Care Homes 3 Limited
Incorporated: 5 April 2006
Net Worth: £59,210,596 *Total Assets:* £304,854,976
Registered Office: 250 Bishopsgate, London, EC2M 4AA
Activities: Financial intermediation not elsewhere classified
Parent: Care Homes Holdings Limited
Officers: Stephen Paul Nixon [1970] Director/Bank Official; Keith Damian Pereira [1978] Director/Bank Official; Luke Esrom Roberts [1979] Director/Bank Official [Irish]

Carestream Dental Technology Holdings 1 Limited
Incorporated: 3 April 2017 *Employees:* 1,135
Net Worth: £214,190,688 *Total Assets:* £770,097,920
Registered Office: Cleveland House, 33 King Street, London, SW1Y 6RJ
Activities: Activities of head offices
Major Shareholder: Donald J. Gogel
Officers: Derek Louis Strum, Secretary; Jane Louise Guinn [1959] Director/VP Global Customer Care; Anne Kinson [1974] Director/EMEA Controller [French]; Derek Louis Strum [1978] Director/Private Equity Partner [American]

Carestream Dental Technology Holdings 2 Limited
Incorporated: 3 April 2017 *Employees:* 2
Net Worth: £135,224,288 *Total Assets:* £240,825,504
Registered Office: Cleveland House, 33 King Street, London, SW1Y 6RJ
Activities: Activities of head offices
Parent: Carestream Dental Technology Holdings 1 Limited
Officers: Derek Louis Strum, Secretary; Jane Louise Guinn [1959] Director/VP Global Customer Care; Anne Kinson [1974] Director/EMEA Controller [French]; Derek Louis Strum [1978] Director/Private Equity Partner [American]

Carlton Communications Limited
Incorporated: 11 January 1939
Net Worth: £2,239,200,000 *Total Assets:* £2,558,000,128
Registered Office: 2 Waterhouse Square, 140 Holborn, London, EC1N 2AE
Activities: Activities of head offices
Parent: ITV PLC
Officers: Sharjeel Suleman [1976] Director/Chartered Accountant; Helen Jane Tautz [1963] Director/Company Secretary

Carnival Film & Television Limited
Incorporated: 3 November 1978 *Employees:* 22
Net Worth: £67,863,000 *Total Assets:* £156,852,000
Registered Office: 1 Central St Giles, St Giles High Street, London, WC2H 8NU
Activities: Television programme production activities
Parent: NBCUniversal International Limited
Officers: Alison Mansfield, Company Secretary; Sarah Felicity Cooper [1963] Director/COO, International Television Production; Gareth Neame [1967] Director; Paul Joseph Randle [1975] Director/Solicitor; Jeffrey Leigh Wachtel [1953] Director/President, NBCU International Studios [American]

Carolia Tower Hotel Limited
Incorporated: 28 November 2014 *Employees:* 168
Net Worth: £12,564,000 *Total Assets:* £293,547,008
Registered Office: 14 Chester Terrace, London, NW1 4ND
Activities: Hotels and similar accommodation
Parent: Cranefield Limited
Officers: Jitendra Patel, Secretary; Gulshan Bhatia [1933] Managing Director; Nimet Esmail [1958] Operations Director; Shelina Jetha [1961] Marketing Director

Carolia Westminster Hotel Limited
Incorporated: 27 November 2014 *Employees:* 99
Net Worth Deficit: £8,473,000 *Total Assets:* £164,868,992
Registered Office: Hill House, 1 Little New Street, London, EC4A 3TR
Activities: Hotels and similar accommodation
Officers: Kelly Adair, Secretary; Ashley Simon Krais [1962] Director

Carphone Warehouse Europe Limited
Incorporated: 13 March 2008
Net Worth: £153,608,000 *Total Assets:* £852,049,024
Registered Office: 1 Portal Way, London, W3 6RS
Activities: Activities of head offices
Parent: Dixons Carphone Holdings Limited
Officers: Catherine Springett, Secretary; Alistair Gibson [1975] Director; Leon Smith [1976] Director/Chartered Accountant

The Carphone Warehouse Limited
Incorporated: 26 June 1987 *Employees:* 8,301
Net Worth: £1,142,599,936 *Total Assets:* £1,865,100,032
Registered Office: 1 Portal Way, London, W3 6RS
Activities: Retail sale of mobile telephones
Parent: Carphone Warehouse Europe Limited
Officers: Catherine Springett, Secretary; Stephen Lawrence Ager [1959] Director; Antreas Athanassopoulos [1966] Director/Chief Customer Officer [Greek]; Jonathan Peter Mason [1964] Finance Director; Alan Joseph Clayton Ritchie [1958] Managing Director, Retail and Operations

Carrington Power Limited
Incorporated: 21 March 2003
Net Worth: £38,706,000 *Total Assets:* £650,667,008
Registered Office: Tricor Suite, 4th Floor, 50 Mark Lane, London, EC3R 7QR
Activities: Production of electricity
Parent: ESBII UK Limited
Officers: John Healy, Secretary; Senan Colleran [1969] Director [Irish]; Mark Fogarty [1973] Director/Accountant [Irish]; John Healy [1959] Director/Risk Manager [Irish]; John Redmond [1955] Director/ESB Secretary [Irish]

Carros Sensors Topco Limited
Incorporated: 31 March 2014 *Employees:* 1,292
Previous: Innovista Sensors Topco Ltd
Net Worth: £84,643,104 *Total Assets:* £223,031,504
Registered Office: 35 Great St Helen's, London, EC3A 6AP
Activities: Activities of other holding companies n.e.c.
Officers: Christopher Marc Afors [1979] Director/Private Equity Professional [Swedish]; Emmanuel Babeau [1967] Director/Deputy CEO for Finance and Legal [French]; Vladimir Albert Georges Lasocki [1973] Director/Private Equity Professional [French]; Augustin Laurent-Bellue [1979] Director/VP M&A Schneider Electric [French]; Colm Paul O'Sullivan [1967] Director/Private Equity Investor [Irish]; Eric Pilaud [1957] Director/President and CEO [French]; Laurent Rivoire [1967] Director/Partner in Private Equity Firm [French]; Jonathan Nicolas Zafrani [1977] Director/Investment Professional [French]; Andrew Zimmermann [1971] Director/EMEA Assistant Controller

Cars Alliance UK 2015 Limited
Incorporated: 1 May 2015
Net Worth Deficit: £7,757 *Total Assets:* £1,912,724,096
Registered Office: 35 Great St Helen's, London, EC3A 6AP
Activities: Non-trading company
Parent: Intertrust Corporate Services Limited
Officers: Daniel Marc Richard Jaffe [1975] Managing Director

Cascade Regional Holdings Limited
Incorporated: 18 July 2016 *Employees:* 5
Net Worth: £1,111,316,096 *Total Assets:* £2,583,450,880
Registered Office: 1 Tower Place West, Tower Place, London, EC3R 5BU
Activities: Activities of other holding companies n.e.c.
Parent: Marsh & McLennan Companies, Inc.
Officers: Claire Margaret Valentine, Secretary; Justin Bruce Broad [1968] Director/Treasurer; Jean-Paul D'Offay [1972] Director/Chartered Accountant; Karen Anne Farrell [1956] Director/Assistant Treasurer [American]; Ian Richard Hadley [1964] Director/Treasurer

Casper UK Bidco Limited
Incorporated: 28 August 2014
Net Worth: £455,655,648 *Total Assets:* £785,103,552
Registered Office: 125 Old Broad Street, London, EC2N 1AR
Activities: Activities of other holding companies n.e.c.
Parent: DTZ Worldwide Limited
Officers: John Forrester [1962] Director/Chief Executive EMEA; Sunita Kaushal [1973] Director/General Counsel & Company Secretary; Duncan John Palmer [1965] Director/Global Chief Financial Officer; Brett David Soloway [1968] Director/Global General Counsel [American]

Cast Limited
Incorporated: 5 June 1989
Net Worth: £2,039,469,056 *Total Assets:* £2,039,469,056
Registered Office: 6th Floor, 322 High Holborn, London, WC1V 7PB
Activities: Non-trading company
Parent: Airgare Limited
Officers: William Flexon [1963] Director/Chartered Accountant [American]; Christopher Michael Hix [1962] Director/Chief Financial Officer [American]; Mark Paul Lehman [1967] Director/Solicitor [American]; Sarah Elizabeth McIntyre [1984] Director; Daniel Alexis Pryor [1968] Director [American]; Eileen Annabelle Raperport [1951] Director/Pensions Co-ordinator; Guy Rostron [1960] Director/Chartered Accountant

Castell 2017-1 PLC
Incorporated: 4 April 2017
Net Worth Deficit: £22,427 *Total Assets:* £239,197,824
Registered Office: 35 Great St Helen's, London, EC3A 6AP
Activities: Other business support service activities n.e.c.
Parent: Castell 2017-1 Holdings Limited
Officers: Helena Paivi Whitaker [1963] Director [Finnish]

Castile Acquisitions Ltd
Incorporated: 11 August 2016
Net Worth: £47,170,252 *Total Assets:* £169,663,904
Registered Office: Peterborough Court, 133 Fleet Street, London, EC4A 2BB
Activities: Financial intermediation not elsewhere classified
Shareholders: ELQ Investors II Ltd; ELQ Investors II Ltd
Officers: Thomas Kelly, Secretary; Ana Estrada Lopez [1981] Director/Economist [Spanish]; Mark Desmond Charles Olivier [1974] Managing Director; Jeremy Alan Wiltshire [1981] Director/Banker

Castle Lane Securities Limited
Incorporated: 5 February 1937 *Employees:* 3
Net Worth: £140,683,856 *Total Assets:* £177,702,000
Registered Office: Ground Floor, 30 City Road, London, EC1Y 2AB
Activities: Renting and operating of Housing Association real estate
Parent: The William Pears Group of Companies Limited
Officers: William Frederick Bennett, Secretary; David Alan Pears, Secretary; David Alan Pears [1968] Director; Mark Andrew Pears [1962] Director; Sir Trevor Steven Pears [1964] Director

Castle Trust Capital PLC
Incorporated: 29 November 2010 *Employees:* 229
Net Worth: £64,816,000 *Total Assets:* £835,164,032
Registered Office: 10 Norwich Street, London, EC4A 1BD
Activities: Activities of mortgage finance companies
Officers: Andrew MacDonald, Secretary; Martin Paul Bischoff [1968] Director; Jonathan James Cox [1980] Director; Lord John Selwyn Deben [1939] Director; Andrew Spencer Doman [1951] Director [British/Australian]; Patrick Nigel Christopher Gale [1960] Independent Director; Timothy John Hanford [1964] Director/Investor; Richard Alexander McGregor Ramsay [1949] Director

Castle Trust Direct PLC
Incorporated: 19 May 2014
Net Worth: £500,000 *Total Assets:* £722,684,032
Registered Office: 10 Norwich Street, London, EC4A 1BD
Activities: Financial intermediation not elsewhere classified
Parent: Castle Trust Capital PLC
Officers: Andrew MacDonald, Secretary; Martin Paul Bischoff [1968] Director; Richard Alexander McGregor Ramsay [1949] Director

Castle Trust Finance Limited
Incorporated: 18 May 2015
Net Worth: £6,807,000 *Total Assets:* £147,420,992
Registered Office: 10 Norwich Street, London, EC4A 1BD
Activities: Financial intermediation not elsewhere classified
Parent: Castle Trust Capital PLC
Officers: Andrew MacDonald, Secretary; Martin Paul Bischoff [1968] Director; Richard Alexander McGregor Ramsay [1949] Director

Castle Trust Treasury Limited
Incorporated: 31 October 2016
Net Worth: £976,000 *Total Assets:* £723,344,000
Registered Office: 10 Norwich Street, London, EC4A 1BD
Activities: Financial intermediation not elsewhere classified
Parent: Castle Trust Capital PLC
Officers: Andrew MacDonald, Secretary; Martin Paul Bischoff [1968] Director; Richard Alexander McGregor Ramsay [1949] Director

Casual Dining Bidco Limited
Incorporated: 7 December 2006 *Employees:* 7,522
Previous: Tragus Bidco Limited
Net Worth: £11,900,000 *Total Assets:* £414,800,000
Registered Office: 1st Floor, 163 Eversholt Street, London, NW1 1BU
Activities: Licenced restaurants
Officers: Giles Matthew Oliver David, Secretary; Giles Matthew Oliver David [1967] Director/Accountant; Stephen Richards [1967] Director; Anthony Martin Robinson [1962] Director

Casual Dining Group Limited
Incorporated: 22 August 2014 *Employees:* 7,526
Net Worth Deficit: £96,200,000 *Total Assets:* £502,500,000
Registered Office: 163 Eversholt Street, London, NW1 1BU
Activities: Activities of head offices
Officers: Giles Matthew Oliver David, Secretary; Alexander Edward St Clair Clark [1984] Director/Investor [British/Canadian]; Philip Patrick Cuff [1982] Director; Giles Matthew Oliver David [1967] Director/Accountant; Alexandra Ahrens Jung [1970] Portfolio Manager, Director [American]; Anthony John Land [1981] Director; Stephen Richards [1967] Director

Casual Dining Limited
Incorporated: 9 January 2002 *Employees:* 469
Previous: Tragus Holdings Limited
Net Worth Deficit: £6,052,000 *Total Assets:* £145,763,008
Registered Office: 1st Floor, 163 Eversholt Street, London, NW1 1BU
Activities: Activities of head offices
Parent: Casual Dining Restaurants Group Limited
Officers: Giles Matthew Oliver David, Secretary; Giles Matthew Oliver David [1967] Director/Accountant; Stephen Richards [1967] Director

Catalina Echo Limited
Incorporated: 18 November 2010 *Employees:* 24
Net Worth: £83,398,360 *Total Assets:* £235,451,536
Registered Office: 1 Alie Street, London, E1 8DE
Activities: Activities of financial services holding companies
Officers: Keith Andrew Lyon, Secretary; Milton Dean Dwonczyk [1958] Director/Actuary [Australian]; Christopher Mark Fagan [1962] Director/Businessman; Christopher John Fleming [1973] Director/Chartered Accountant

Catalina Holdings UK Limited
Incorporated: 2 March 1999 *Employees:* 56
Net Worth: £210,836,912 *Total Assets:* £1,175,658,752
Registered Office: 1 Alie Street, London, E1 8DE
Activities: Activities of financial services holding companies
Officers: Keith Lyon, Secretary; Christopher John Fleming [1973] Director/Accountant; Generald Sidney Haase [1976] Director/Insurance Executive [American]; Philip Michael Hernon [1958] Director/SVP Operations; Graeme John McAndrew [1968] Finance Director [Australian]

Catalyst Finance Limited
Incorporated: 12 September 2001
Total Assets: £216,312,000
Registered Office: Ealing Gateway, 26-30 Uxbridge Road, Ealing, London, W5 2AU
Activities: Financial intermediation not elsewhere classified
Parent: Catalyst Housing Limited
Officers: Sophie Atkinson, Secretary; Rachael Dennis [1966] Finance Director; Ian Jeffrey McDermott [1962] Director

Cater Allen Limited
Incorporated: 30 September 1943 *Employees:* 80
Net Worth: £433,889,984 *Total Assets:* £5,046,842,880
Registered Office: 2 Triton Square, Regent's Place, London, NW1 3AN
Activities: Banks
Parent: Santander Private Banking UK Limited
Officers: Susan Mary Allen [1966] Director/Banker [Irish]; Annemarie Verna Florence Durbin [1963] Director [British/New Zealander]; Patricia Halliday [1966] Director/Chief Risk Officer; Antonio Roman [1967] Director/Banker [Spanish]

Cathedral Capital (1998) Limited
Incorporated: 11 July 1997
Net Worth: £3,034,275 *Total Assets:* £381,147,264
Registered Office: 20 Fenchurch Street, London, EC3M 3BY
Activities: Other activities auxiliary to insurance and pension funding
Parent: Cathedral Capital Holdings Limited
Officers: Marjorie Eva Lynn, Secretary; Adam Clive Beardon [1965] Director; Christopher John Whittle [1967] Director

Cathedral Capital Holdings Limited
Incorporated: 16 May 1997 *Employees:* 76
Net Worth: £34,194,352 *Total Assets:* £476,714,880
Registered Office: 20 Fenchurch Street, London, EC3M 3BY
Activities: Activities of insurance agents and brokers
Parent: Cathedral Capital Limited
Officers: Marjorie Eva Lynn, Secretary; Christopher John Whittle [1967] Director; Emma Louise Woolley [1979] Director

Cathedral Capital Limited
Incorporated: 5 October 2006
Net Worth: £139,736,784 *Total Assets:* £139,736,784
Registered Office: 20 Fenchurch Street, London, EC3M 3BY
Activities: Activities of financial services holding companies
Parent: Lancashire Holdings Limited
Officers: Marjorie Eva Lynn, Secretary; Christopher John Whittle [1967] Director; Emma Louise Woolley [1979] Director

Cathexis UK Holdings Limited
Incorporated: 8 December 2015 *Employees:* 2,659
Net Worth: £32,500,000 *Total Assets:* £655,900,032
Registered Office: Suite 1, 3rd Floor, 11-12 St James's Square, London, SW1Y 4LB
Activities: Activities of construction holding companies
Officers: William Bruce Harrison [1986] Director/Chief Executive Officer [American]; Frances McLeod Jandjel [1967] Director/Accountant [American]; Marshall Travis White [1958] Director/Attorney [American]

Catlin (North American) Holdings Ltd
Incorporated: 13 September 2005
Net Worth: £536,880,768 *Total Assets:* £956,544,576
Registered Office: 20 Gracechurch Street, London, EC3V 0BG
Activities: Activities of head offices
Parent: Axa SA
Officers: Marie Louise Rees, Secretary; Paul Richard Bradbrook [1976] Director/Insurance Executive; Clynton Jacobus Luttig [1973] Director; Juliet Phillips [1972] Director/Chartered Accountant

Catlin Finance (UK) Ltd.
Incorporated: 7 January 2005
Net Worth: £25,125,600 *Total Assets:* £396,145,696
Registered Office: 20 Gracechurch Street, London, EC3V 0BG
Activities: Other business support service activities n.e.c.
Parent: Axa SA
Officers: Marie Louise Rees, Secretary; Paul Richard Bradbrook [1976] Director/Insurance Executive; Clynton Jacobus Luttig [1973] Director; Juliet Phillips [1972] Director/Chartered Accountant

Catlin Holdings Limited
Incorporated: 12 September 1986
Net Worth: £43,311,368 *Total Assets:* £131,135,720
Registered Office: 20 Gracechurch Street, London, EC3V 0BG
Activities: Activities of head offices
Parent: Catlin Holdings (UK) Limited
Officers: Marie Louise Rees, Secretary; Paul Richard Bradbrook [1976] Director/Insurance Executive; Clynton Jacobus Luttig [1973] Director; Juliet Phillips [1972] Director/Chartered Accountant

Catlin Insurance Company (UK) Holdings Ltd.
Incorporated: 10 January 2005
Net Worth: £158,785,504 *Total Assets:* £158,785,696
Registered Office: 20 Gracechurch Street, London, EC3V 0BG
Activities: Activities of head offices
Shareholders: Axa SA; Catlin Finance (UK) Ltd.
Officers: Marie Louise Rees, Secretary; Paul Richard Bradbrook [1976] Director/Insurance Executive; Clynton Jacobus Luttig [1973] Director; Juliet Phillips [1972] Director/Chartered Accountant

Catlin Syndicate 6112 Limited
Incorporated: 22 November 2011
Total Assets: £118,770,000
Registered Office: 20 Gracechurch Street, London, EC3V 0BG
Activities: Non-life insurance
Parent: Catlin Holdings Limited
Officers: Marie Louise Rees, Secretary; Paul Richard Bradbrook [1976] Director/Insurance Executive; Richard Paul Greensmith [1975] Director; Robert David Littlemore [1968] Director/Chief Executive, London Reinsurance

Catlin Syndicate Limited
Incorporated: 15 September 1994
Net Worth Deficit: £94,775,456 *Total Assets:* £8,039,814,144
Registered Office: 20 Gracechurch Street, London, EC3V 0BG
Activities: Non-life insurance
Parent: Catlin (North American) Holdings Ltd
Officers: Marie Louise Rees, Secretary; Paul Richard Bradbrook [1976] Director/Insurance Executive; Richard Paul Greensmith [1975] Director; Robert David Littlemore [1968] Director/Chief Executive, London Reinsurance

Cavendish Fluor Partnership Limited
Incorporated: 7 April 2014 *Employees:* 2,442
Net Worth: £13,940,000 *Total Assets:* £155,970,000
Registered Office: 33 Wigmore Street, London, W1U 1QX
Activities: Activities of head offices
Parent: Cavendish Nuclear Limited
Officers: Simon Christopher Bowen [1960] Director; Kenneth Malcolm Douglas [1970] Director/Chartered Accountant; Kevin John Garvey [1967] Finance Director; Susan Jee [1955] Director/Chartered Accountant; Peter Michael Knollmeyer [1960] Director [American]; J Gregory Meyer [1950] Director [American]; Dr Dr Andrew Spurr [1953] Director

The Cavendish Hotel (London) Limited
Incorporated: 6 September 2006 *Employees:* 87
Net Worth: £1,309,000 *Total Assets:* £116,209,000
Registered Office: Third Floor, The Broadgate Tower, 20 Primrose Street, London, EC2A 2RS
Activities: Hotels and similar accommodation
Officers: Marie-Isabelle Aw [1966] Finance Director [French]; Eric Julien Adrien Fombonne [1960] Director/RGM France and Belgium [French]; Kian Tiong Alfred Ong [1963] Managing Director [Singaporean]

Cavendish Nuclear Limited
Incorporated: 18 April 2000 *Employees:* 1,205
Net Worth: £120,944,000 *Total Assets:* £281,270,016
Registered Office: 33 Wigmore Street, London, W1U 1QX
Activities: Other business support service activities n.e.c.
Parent: Babcock Services Group Limited
Officers: Simon Christopher Bowen [1960] Director; Kevin John Garvey [1967] Finance Director; Iain Stuart Urquhart [1965] Director

The Cayzer Trust Company Limited
Incorporated: 8 December 2003 *Employees:* 5
Net Worth: £291,360,864 *Total Assets:* £292,804,768
Registered Office: Cayzer House, 30 Buckingham Gate, London, SW1E 6NN
Activities: Activities of other holding companies n.e.c.
Shareholder: Dominic Vaughan Gibbs
Officers: Sonia Claire Barry, Secretary; The Honourable Charles William Cayzer [1957] Director; James Michael Beale Cayzer-Colvin [1965] Director; James Patrick Lamert Davis [1946] Director/Solicitor; Dominic Vaughan Gibbs [1966] Director; The Hon Elizabeth Gilmour [1946] Director; Roseanna Neville Leslie [1972] Director/Self Employed; William Penfold Wyatt [1968] Director

CB & I UK Limited
Incorporated: 14 May 2002 *Employees:* 245
Net Worth: £183,695,008 *Total Assets:* £228,016,992
Registered Office: 40 Eastbourne Terrace, London, W2 6LG
Activities: Construction of other civil engineering projects n.e.c.
Parent: McDermott International Inc.
Officers: Jason Kitts, Secretary; Frazer Grenville Budd [1965] Director of Operations; Ashok Joshi [1959] Director/Solicitor [Indian]; Tareq Kawash [1968] Director/Senior Vice President [American]; Timothy Moran [1955] Finance Director; Lynn Ann Sheach [1971] Director, Finance and Accounting

CB-SDG Holdco Limited
Incorporated: 25 June 2015
Net Worth Deficit: £11,521,000 *Total Assets:* £152,903,008
Registered Office: Commodity Quay, St Katharine Docks, London, E1W 1AZ
Activities: Non-trading company
Parent: CB-SDG Topco Limited
Officers: David Michael Howson [1970] Director; Steven Keith Mitchell [1976] Director

CB-SDG Limited
Incorporated: 12 June 2015
Net Worth: £152,651,008 *Total Assets:* £304,323,008
Registered Office: Commodity Quay, St Katharine Docks, London, E1W 1AZ
Activities: Non-trading company
Parent: CB-SDG Midco Limited
Officers: Ryan Carroll [1975] Director [American]; Michael Choe [1972] Director [American]; David Michael Howson [1970] Director; Steven Keith Mitchell [1976] Director

CB-SDG Midco Limited
Incorporated: 16 June 2015 *Employees:* 433
Net Worth: £76,419,000 *Total Assets:* £245,136,000
Registered Office: Commodity Quay, St Katharine Docks, London, E1W 1AZ
Activities: Non-trading company
Parent: CB-SDG Holdco Limited
Officers: David Michael Howson [1970] Director; Steven Keith Mitchell [1976] Director

CB-SDG Topco Limited
Incorporated: 16 June 2015 *Employees:* 433
Net Worth Deficit: £77,389,000 *Total Assets:* £245,208,992
Registered Office: Commodity Quay, St Katharine Docks, London, E1W 1AZ
Activities: Non-trading company
Parent: CB-SDG Jersey Limited
Officers: Ryan Carroll [1975] Director [American]; Michael Choe [1972] Director [American]; Ken Desgarrenes [1970] Director [American]; David Michael Howson [1970] Director; Steven Keith Mitchell [1976] Director; Pedro Vaz [1983] Director/Senior Vice President [American]

CB/TCC Global Holdings Limited
Incorporated: 19 October 2006 *Employees:* 5
Net Worth: £1,537,160,960 *Total Assets:* £1,537,160,960
Registered Office: St Martin's Court, 10 Paternoster Row, London, EC4M 7HP
Activities: Real estate agencies
Parent: CBRE Group, Inc.
Officers: Elizabeth Cormack Thetford, Secretary; Dara Ann Bazzano [1968] Director/Chief Accounting Officer [American]; Duncan James Green [1962] Managing Director; Marcus George Smith [1969] Director Corporate Development; Elizabeth Cormack Thetford [1954] Director/Legal and Compliance; Pasha Zargarof [1973] Director/General Counsel [American]

CBI UK Cayman Acquisition Limited
Incorporated: 26 August 2016
Net Worth: £213,427,632 *Total Assets:* £213,430,480
Registered Office: 40 Eastbourne Terrace, London, W2 6LG
Activities: Other service activities n.e.c.
Parent: McDermott International Inc.
Officers: Jason Kitts, Secretary; Ashok Joshi [1959] Director/Solicitor [Indian]; Tareq Kawash [1968] Director/Senior Vice President [American]; Timothy Moran [1955] Finance Director

Cboe Worldwide Holdings Limited
Incorporated: 9 November 2016
Net Worth: £69,459,632 *Total Assets:* £152,806,800
Registered Office: 5th Floor, The Monument Building, 11 Monument Street, London, EC3R 8AF
Activities: Activities of head offices
Parent: Cboe Global Markets, Inc.
Officers: Antonio Amelia, Secretary; Mark Simon Hemsley [1962] Director; Edward Thomas Tilly [1963] Director/Chairman/President/CEO - Cboe Global [American]

CBRE Acquisition Company 2 Limited
Incorporated: 14 August 2015
Net Worth: £191,767,920 *Total Assets:* £191,792,784
Registered Office: St Martin's Court, 10 Paternoster Row, London, EC4M 7HP
Activities: Other business support service activities n.e.c.
Shareholders: CBRE Holdings Limited; CBRE UK Acquisition Company Limited
Officers: Duncan James Green [1962] Director; Christopher Rush Oster [1970] Director/Vice President Tax Planning; Elizabeth Cormack Thetford [1954] Legal and Compliance Executive Director; Pasha Zargarof [1973] Director/General Counsel [American]

CBRE Acquisition Company 3 Limited
Incorporated: 14 August 2015
Net Worth: £191,914,816 *Total Assets:* £191,939,696
Registered Office: St Martin's Court, 10 Paternoster Row, London, EC4M 7HP
Activities: Other business support service activities n.e.c.
Shareholders: CBRE Holdings Limited; CBRE UK Acquisition Company Limited
Officers: Duncan James Green [1962] Director; Christopher Rush Oster [1970] Director/Vice President Tax Planning; Elizabeth Cormack Thetford [1954] Legal and Compliance Executive Director; Pasha Zargarof [1973] Director/General Counsel [American]

CBRE Finance Europe LLP
Incorporated: 28 November 2003
Net Worth: £917,908,288 *Total Assets:* £917,908,288
Registered Office: St Martins Court, 10 Paternoster Row, London, EC4M 7HP

CBRE Global Investors Europe Holdings Limited
Incorporated: 6 December 2004
Net Worth Deficit: £28,306,576 *Total Assets:* £274,260,480
Registered Office: Third Floor, One New Change, London, EC4M 9AF
Activities: Management of real estate on a fee or contract basis
Parent: CBRE Limited
Officers: Jiri Lhotak [1971] Director [Czech]; Jeremy James Plummer [1959] Director/Fund Manager

CBRE GWS Limited
Incorporated: 2 June 1960 *Employees:* 2,407
Previous: Johnson Controls Limited
Net Worth: £57,282,000 *Total Assets:* £238,648,000
Registered Office: 61 Southwark Street, London, SE1 0HL
Activities: Combined facilities support activities
Shareholders: CBRE Acquisition Company 3 Limited; CBRE Acquisition Company 2 Limited
Officers: Ian David Entwisle [1963] Director; Claire Louisa Lloyd [1976] Director; Paul James Saville-King [1969] Director; Marcus Howell Williams [1954] Senior Commercial Director

CBRE Holdings Limited
Incorporated: 14 March 2013
Net Worth: £319,632,384 *Total Assets:* £1,247,320,320
Registered Office: St Martin's Court, 10 Paternoster Row, London, EC4M 7HP
Activities: Other business support service activities n.e.c.
Parent: CBRE Group, Inc.
Officers: Duncan James Green [1962] Director/Chief Finance Officer - EMEA; Christopher Rush Oster [1970] Director/Vice President Tax Planning; Elizabeth Cormack Thetford [1954] Director; Pasha Zargarof [1973] Director/General Counsel [American]

CBRE Limited
Incorporated: 27 March 1998 *Employees:* 2,391
Net Worth: £403,408,000 *Total Assets:* £773,142,016
Registered Office: St Martin's Court, 10 Paternoster Row, London, EC4M 7HP
Activities: Development of building projects
Officers: Alex Constantinos Naftis, Secretary; Dara Ann Bazzano [1968] Director/Chief Accounting Officer [American]; Ciaran Edward Bird [1971] Director; Duncan James Green [1962] Managing Director; David Mercado [1976] Finance Director; Martin David Samworth [1960] Director/Chartered Surveyor; Pasha Zargarof [1973] Director/General Counsel [American]

CBRE Managed Services Limited
Incorporated: 13 March 1984 *Employees:* 5,446
Previous: Norland Managed Services Limited
Net Worth: £154,864,000 *Total Assets:* £441,544,000
Registered Office: 61 Southwark Street, London, SE1 0HL
Activities: Other business support service activities n.e.c.
Parent: Norland Enablement Limited
Officers: John Edward Joseph Dunstan [1976] Director; Ian David Entwisle [1963] Managing Director; Duncan James Green [1962] Director; Kevin Stuart Lynn [1969] Director; Guy Robert Phillips [1969] Director; Paul James Saville-King [1969] Director; Anthony Smith [1963] Director

CBRE UK Acquisition Company Limited
Incorporated: 25 October 2013
Net Worth: £326,491,840 *Total Assets:* £329,545,440
Registered Office: St Martin's Court, 10 Paternoster Row, London, EC4M 7HP
Activities: Other business support service activities n.e.c.
Parent: CBRE Holdings Limited
Officers: Duncan James Green [1962] Director; Christopher Rush Oster [1970] Director/Vice President Tax Planning; Elizabeth Cormack Thetford [1954] Legal and Compliance Director; Pasha Zargarof [1973] Director/General Counsel [American]

CD & R Firefly 2 Limited
Incorporated: 17 April 2015
Net Worth: £89,037,000 *Total Assets:* £172,466,000
Registered Office: Cleveland House, 33 King Street, London, SW1Y 6RJ
Activities: Activities of head offices
Parent: CD & R Firefly Holdco Limited
Officers: Marco Luigi Kurt Herbst, Secretary; Marco Luigi Kurt Herbst [1972] Director/Private Equity Partner [Italian]; Gregory Lai [1979] Director/Private Equity Partner [French]

CD & R Firefly 4 Limited
Incorporated: 17 April 2015 *Employees:* 81
Net Worth: £5,277,000 *Total Assets:* £759,217,984
Registered Office: Cleveland House, 33 King Street, London, SW1Y 6RJ
Activities: Activities of head offices
Parent: CD & R Firefly 3 Limited
Officers: Marco Luigi Kurt Herbst, Secretary; William Bahlsen Bannister [1967] Director/Chief Executive Officer; Marco Luigi Kurt Herbst [1972] Director/Private Equity Partner [Italian]; Gregory Lai [1979] Director/Private Equity Partner [French]; Simon Lane [1963] Director/Accountant

CD & R Firefly Holdco Limited
Incorporated: 17 April 2015 *Employees:* 81
Net Worth: £5,449,000 *Total Assets:* £759,217,984
Registered Office: Cleveland House, 33 King Street, London, SW1Y 6RJ
Activities: Activities of head offices
Officers: Marco Luigi Kurt Herbst, Secretary; Marco Luigi Kurt Herbst [1972] Director/Private Equity Partner [Italian]; Gregory Lai [1979] Director/Private Equity Partner [French]

CDC Group PLC
Incorporated: 8 December 1999 *Employees:* 245
Net Worth: £5,053,499,904 *Total Assets:* £5,084,700,160
Registered Office: 123 Victoria Street, London, SW1E 6DE
Activities: Activities of venture and development capital companies
Parent: Department for International Development
Officers: Jane Earl, Secretary; Andrew Folorunsho Alli [1967] Director [Nigerian]; Dolika Banda [1962] Director [Zambian]; Wim Borgdorff [1960] Director/Senior Advisor [Dutch]; Valentine Chitalu [1964] Director/Accountant/Entrepreneur [Zambian]; Samuel Fankhauser [1964] Director; Michele Caroline Giddens [1965] Investment Director; Clive Robert MacTavish [1970] Director; Keki Minoo Mistry [1954] Director/Chartered Accountant [Indian]; Nicholas Peter O'Donohoe [1957] Director; Laurie Jean Spengler [1962] Director [American]; Graham Lloyd Wrigley [1962] Director

CDCH Limited
Incorporated: 4 March 2015
Net Worth: £129,286,128 *Total Assets:* £180,078,896
Registered Office: c/o Ion, 3rd Floor, One New Change, London, EC4M 9AF
Activities: Activities of head offices
Parent: Bessel RE S.A R.L.
Officers: Ashley Woods, Secretary; Conor Gerard Clinch [1979] Director/Accountant [Irish]; Andrea Pignataro [1970] Director/Executive [Italian]; Ashley Graham Woods [1973] Director/Solicitor

CDW Finance Bidco Limited
Incorporated: 29 October 2014
Net Worth: £52,121,392 *Total Assets:* £286,459,040
Registered Office: 10 Fleet Place, London, EC4M 7RB
Activities: Information technology consultancy activities
Officers: Christina Marie Corley [1968] Director [American]; Neil Barry Fairfield [1975] Director/Financial Controller; Daniel Andrew Laws [1977] Managing Director; James Prior [1973] Finance Director

CDW International Holdings Limited
Incorporated: 13 July 2015
Net Worth: £215,501,136 *Total Assets:* £361,466,592
Registered Office: 10 Fleet Place, London, EC4M 7RB
Activities: Other information service activities n.e.c.
Officers: Christina Marie Corley [1968] Director [American]; Robert Joseph Welyki [1964] Director [American]

CDW Limited
Incorporated: 31 January 1990 *Employees:* 1,086
Previous: Kelway Limited
Net Worth: £118,498,424 *Total Assets:* £326,784,192
Registered Office: 10 Fleet Place, London, EC4M 7RB
Activities: Other information service activities n.e.c.
Officers: David Chapman [1973] Sales Director; Christine Marie Corley [1968] Director [American]; Neil Barry Fairfield [1975] Director/Financial Controller; Daniel Andrew Laws [1977] Managing Director; James Prior [1973] Finance Director

CE Acquisition 1 Limited
Incorporated: 9 November 2004
Net Worth: £386,428,992 *Total Assets:* £4,373,700,096
Registered Office: 3rd Floor, One New Change, London, EC4M 9AF
Activities: Activities of head offices
Parent: Ladbrokes Betting & Gaming Limited
Officers: Stuart John Smith [1981] Director/Accountant; Charles Alexander Sutters [1980] Director

Cedar Project Bidco Limited
Incorporated: 18 July 2017 *Employees:* 5
Net Worth Deficit: £1,060,674 *Total Assets:* £280,545,824
Registered Office: 14 St George Street, London, W1S 1FE
Activities: Other business support service activities n.e.c.
Parent: Cedar Project Midco Limited
Officers: Roberta Battaglia [1983] Director/Investment Professional [Italian]; Mark John Crosbie [1959] Director; Margaret Hill [1956] Director; Nicolas Eric Marfe Mallet [1980] Director [French]; Andrew John Murrell [1969] Director

Cedar Project Holdco Limited
Incorporated: 18 July 2017 *Employees:* 1,211
Net Worth Deficit: £3,225,746 *Total Assets:* £319,058,560
Registered Office: 14 St George Street, London, W1S 1FE
Activities: Other business support service activities n.e.c.
Officers: Roberta Battaglia [1983] Director/Investment Professional [Italian]; Mark John Crosbie [1959] Director; Margaret Hill [1956] Director; Nicolas Eric Marfe Mallet [1980] Director [French]; Andrew John Murrell [1969] Director; Christopher John Spanoudakis [1965] Director

Cedar Project Midco Limited
Incorporated: 18 July 2017 *Employees:* 5
Net Worth: £2,986,088 *Total Assets:* £181,277,136
Registered Office: 14 St George Street, London, W1S 1FE
Activities: Other business support service activities n.e.c.
Parent: Cedar Project Holdco Limited
Officers: Roberta Battaglia [1983] Director/Investment Professional [Italian]; Mark John Crosbie [1959] Director; Margaret Hill [1956] Director; Nicolas Eric Marfe Mallet [1980] Director [French]; Andrew John Murrell [1969] Director

CELF Advisors LLP
Incorporated: 11 August 2010 *Employees:* 22
Net Worth: £254,792,992 *Total Assets:* £316,320,992
Registered Office: 1 St James's Market, London, SW1Y 4AH
Officers: Colin John Atkins [1968] Member; Matthew Christian Cottrell [1972] LLP Member; Martin Glavin [1980] LLP Member; Merrill Graham Goulding [1982] LLP Member; Ian Barrie Jackson [1973] LLP Member; Szymon Jaroszewski [1979] LLP Member; Adnan Mokhtar Khalef [1986] LLP Member; Stuart MacKenzie [1979] LLP Member; Louis Reynolds [1977] LLP Member; Christian Schmitz [1975] LLP Member; Tajinder Singh Sidhu [1977] LLP Member

Cello Health PLC
Incorporated: 5 May 2004 *Employees:* 978
Previous: Cello Group PLC
Net Worth: £82,873,000 *Total Assets:* £145,608,000
Registered Office: Queens House, 8-9 Queen Street, London, EC4N 1SP
Activities: Activities of head offices
Officers: Andrew Robert Brown, Secretary; Mark Bentley [1970] Director/Chartered Accountant; Stephen Martin Highley [1960] Director/Chief Operating Officer; Chris Jones [1995] Director; Joanna Susan Lecouilliard [1963] Director; Michele Luzi [1956] Director [Italian]; Julia Ralston [1957] Director [New Zealander]; Mark Scott [1965] Director; Clifford Peter Tompsett [1957] Director

Centaur Media PLC
Incorporated: 30 October 2003 *Employees:* 515
Net Worth: £84,900,000 *Total Assets:* £113,700,000
Registered Office: Wells Point, 79 Wells Street, London, W1T 3QN
Activities: Activities of head offices
Officers: Helen Frances Silver, Secretary; Robert William Boyle [1948] Director; Christopher William Eccleshare [1955] Director/Chairman & CEO, Clear Channel International; Neil Anthony Johnson [1949] Director; Colin Robert Jones [1960] Director; Rebecca Sylvie Miskin [1965] Director/Media Executive; Swagatam Mukerji [1961] Director/Chief Financial Officer; Andria Louise Vidler [1966] Director

Central Asia Metals PLC
Incorporated: 9 September 2005 *Employees:* 465
Net Worth: £337,017,984 *Total Assets:* £604,878,016
Registered Office: Masters House, 107 Hammersmith Road, London, W14 0QH
Activities: Activities of head offices
Officers: Anthony George Hunter, Secretary; Robert Maitland Cathery [1944] Director/Retired; Nicholas Royston Clarke [1952] Director/Engineer; Roger Owen Davey [1945] Director; Gavin Ronald Ferrar [1969] Business Development Director; Christopher Nigel Hurst-Brown [1951] Director; Nigel Francis Robinson [1960] Director/Chartered Accountant; David John Swan [1955] CFO/Director [Australian]; Nurlan Zhakupov [1978] Director/Banker [Kazakh]

Central Equity Limited
Incorporated: 24 January 2001
Net Worth: £110,659,040 *Total Assets:* £261,877,744
Registered Office: Level 1, 93 Knightsbridge, London, SW1X 7RB
Officers: Eddie Kutner, Secretary; Geoffrey Mark Otto, Secretary; John William Bourke [1947] Director [Australian]; Eddie Kutner [1947] Director [Australian]; Dennis John Wilson [1947] Director [Australian]

Central London Commercial Estates Limited
Incorporated: 20 April 1960
Net Worth: £104,676,040 *Total Assets:* £105,457,264
Registered Office: 25 Savile Row, London, W1S 2ER
Activities: Buying and selling of own real estate
Parent: Derwent Valley Limited
Officers: David Andrew Lawler, Secretary; John David Burns [1944] Director; Nigel Quentin George [1963] Director; Simon Paul Silver [1950] Director; David Gary Silverman [1969] Director; Paul Malcolm Williams [1960] Director/Surveyor; Damian Mark Alan Wisniewski [1961] Director

Centremanor Limited
Incorporated: 25 April 1975
Net Worth: £883,217,984 *Total Assets:* £1,202,200,960
Registered Office: 158-162 Shaftesbury Avenue, London, WC2H 8HR
Activities: Development of building projects
Officers: Mark Roy Mason Jenner, Secretary; David Davis [1935] Director/Chartered Accountant; Benzion Schalom Eliezer Freshwater [1948] Director

Centro Asset Management Limited
Incorporated: 13 May 1999 *Employees:* 4
Net Worth: £170,636,016 *Total Assets:* £179,540,464
Registered Office: Second Floor, York House, 74-82 Queen Victoria Street, London, EC4N 4SJ
Activities: Other letting and operating of own or leased real estate
Parent: Centro Holdings (UK) Limited
Officers: Michel Charles Dessolain, Secretary; Michel Charles Dessolain [1955] Director/Chief Strategy and Innovation Officer [French]; Thomas Oliver Jackson [1981] Director; Jacob Cornelius Warmolt Lunsingh Tonckens [1962] Director/Chief Financial Officer [Dutch/American]; Andrea Alessandro Orlandi [1971] Managing Director [Italian]; Vanisha Ashok Thakrar [1987] Director/Real Estate; Rudolf Vogelaar [1960] Group Director of Tax [Dutch]

Centro Europe Limited
Incorporated: 16 December 1986 *Employees:* 7
Net Worth: £131,560,392 *Total Assets:* £131,916,208
Registered Office: Second Floor, York House, 74-82 Queen Victoria Street, London, EC4N 4SJ
Activities: Non-trading company
Parent: Centro Asset Management Ltd
Officers: Olivier Jean-Marie Paul Coutin, Secretary; Olivier Jean-Marie Paul Coutin [1962] Group Director of Operations [French]; Michel Charles Dessolain [1955] Director/Chief Strategy and Innovation Officer [French]; Thomas Oliver Jackson [1981] Director; Jacob Cornelius Warmolt Lunsingh Tonckens [1962] Director/Chief Financial Officer [Dutch/American]; Andrea Alessandro Orlandi [1971] Managing Director [Italian]; Vanisha Ashok Thakrar [1987] Director/Real Estate; Rudolf Vogelaar [1960] Group Director of Tax [Dutch]

Centro Holdings (UK) Limited
Incorporated: 13 May 1999 *Employees:* 4
Net Worth: £849,036,864 *Total Assets:* £1,867,877,760
Registered Office: Second Floor, York House, 74-82 Queen Victoria Street, London, EC4N 4SJ
Activities: Activities of head offices
Officers: Michel Charles Dessolain, Secretary; Michel Charles Dessolain [1955] Director/Chief Strategy and Innovation Officer [French]; Thomas Oliver Jackson [1981] Director; Jacob Cornelius Warmolt Lunsingh Tonckens [1962] Director/Chief Financial Officer [Dutch/American]; Andrea Alessandro Orlandi [1971] Managing Director [Italian]; Vanisha Ashok Thakrar [1987] Director/Real Estate; Rudolf Vogelaar [1960] Group Director of Tax [Dutch]

Centurycomm Limited
Incorporated: 16 June 1997 *Employees:* 275
Net Worth: £212,690,000 *Total Assets:* £231,010,000
Registered Office: 5 Fleet Place, London, EC4M 7RD
Activities: Reproduction of computer media
Parent: Stradbrook Holdings Limited
Officers: Mark Louis Francis, Secretary; Alan John Byrne [1962] Director/Consultant; Mark Louis Francis [1973] Director; Mark John Renshaw [1975] Director

CenturyLink Communications Europe Limited
Incorporated: 4 March 1999 *Employees:* 134
Previous: Level 3 Communications Europe Limited
Net Worth Deficit: £44,494,468 *Total Assets:* £144,563,152
Registered Office: 7th Floor, 10 Fleet Place, London, EC4M 7RB
Activities: Other telecommunications activities
Parent: CenturyLink Inc
Officers: Michael Charles Reinke [1975] Director/Senior Vice President Finance EMEA [American]; Nicholas Alexander Spence [1962] Director/VP Managing Corporate Counsel

CenturyLink Communications UK Limited
Incorporated: 25 April 1990 *Employees:* 858
Previous: Level 3 Communications UK Limited
Net Worth: £190,244,992 *Total Assets:* £389,547,008
Registered Office: 7th Floor, 10 Fleet Place, London, EC4M 7RB
Activities: Other telecommunications activities
Parent: Level 3 EMEA Holdings Limited
Officers: Michael Charles Reinke [1975] Director/Senior Vice President - Finance EMEA [American]; Dougald MacDonald Robinson [1956] Director/Attorney; Nicholas Alexander Spence [1962] Director/General Counsel

CenturyLink EMEA Holdings Limited
Incorporated: 8 October 1999
Previous: Level 3 EMEA Holdings Limited
Net Worth Deficit: £369,204,992 *Total Assets:* £311,319,008
Registered Office: 7th Floor, 10 Fleet Place, London, EC4M 7RB
Activities: Wired telecommunications activities
Parent: CenturyLink Inc
Officers: Dougald MacDonald Robinson [1956] Senior Director, Regulatory Affairs; Nicholas Alexander Spence [1962] Director/VP Managing Corporate Counsel

CenturyLink Impsat Holdings I Limited
Incorporated: 17 January 2007
Previous: GC Impsat Holdings I Limited
Net Worth Deficit: £143,397,984 *Total Assets:* £212,247,184
Registered Office: 7th Floor, 10 Fleet Place, London, EC4M 7RB
Activities: Activities of head offices
Parent: CenturyLink Inc
Officers: Nicholas Alexander Spence, Secretary; Hector Roberto Alonso [1957] Managing Director [Argentinian]; Qamar Ul Arfeen Qadeer [1965] Director/Tax Specialist; Nicholas Alexander Spence [1962] Director/General Counsel

CenturyLink Impsat Holdings II Limited
Incorporated: 17 January 2007
Previous: GC Impsat Holdings II Limited
Net Worth: £283,958,432 *Total Assets:* £411,103,264
Registered Office: 7th Floor, 10 Fleet Place, London, EC4M 7RB
Activities: Activities of head offices
Parent: GC Impsat Holdings I Limited
Officers: Nicholas Alexander Spence, Secretary; Hector Roberto Alonso [1957] Managing Director [Argentinian]; Qamar Ul Arfeen Qadeer [1965] Director; Nicholas Alexander Spence [1962] Director/General Counsel

Ceridian Global UK Holding Company Limited
Incorporated: 4 December 2015 *Employees:* 3
Net Worth: £333,924,768 *Total Assets:* £859,831,232
Registered Office: Level 37, 25 Canada Square, London, E14 5LQ
Activities: Activities of head offices
Officers: Nicholas David Cucci [1961] Director/Finance [American]; Arthur Gitajn [1952] Director/Chief Executive Officer [American]; William Everett McDonald [1965] Director/Legal Executive [American]

Cerner Limited
Incorporated: 6 July 1990 *Employees:* 479
Net Worth: £90,644,664 *Total Assets:* £103,180,280
Registered Office: The Point, 37 North Wharf Road, Paddington, London, W2 1AF
Activities: Other information technology service activities
Officers: Randy Sims, Secretary; Emil Edward Peters [1973] Director/Businessman [American]; Distie Profit [1979] Director/Businesswoman [American/British]; Randy Sims [1960] Director/Businessman [American]

Cerro Dominador UK, LLP
Incorporated: 24 March 2015
Net Worth: £431,590,720 *Total Assets:* £937,003,072
Registered Office: 35 Great St Helen's, London, EC3A 6AP

CEVA Group PLC
Incorporated: 9 August 2006 *Employees:* 42,265
Net Worth Deficit: £1,100,464,640 *Total Assets:* £2,627,032,576
Registered Office: Suite 1, 3rd Floor, 11-12 St James's Square, London, SW1Y 4LB
Activities: Activities of head offices
Parent: CEVA Logistics AG
Officers: Leigh Martin Pomlett [1956] Executive Director; Xavier Urbain [1957] Director [French]; Dawn Amanda Wetherall [1962] Director/Chief Compliance Officer

CF Sparks Limited
Incorporated: 9 August 2016 *Employees:* 2
Net Worth: £17,211,024 *Total Assets:* £158,341,936
Registered Office: 7 Clarges Street, London, W1J 8AE
Activities: Buying and selling of own real estate
Parent: Fortress Investment Group LLC
Officers: Nicholas Paul Fegan [1974] Director/Solicitor; Christopher Carl Linkas [1969] Director/Investment Professional [American]

CFC Group Limited
Incorporated: 13 March 2017 *Employees:* 279
Net Worth: £97,914,000 *Total Assets:* £267,292,992
Registered Office: 85 Gracechurch Street, London, EC3V 0AA
Activities: Activities of other holding companies n.e.c.
Parent: Vitruvian Partners LLP
Officers: Philip Peter Clinton Gregory [1955] Director/Accountant; Michael Benjamin Grist [1974] Director; David Charles Anthony Walsh [1969] Director

CFL Auto Receivables Limited
Incorporated: 12 March 2015
Net Worth: £11,983,137 *Total Assets:* £968,964,480
Registered Office: Third Floor, 1 King's Arms Yard, London, EC2R 7AF
Activities: Other business support service activities n.e.c.
Parent: Wilmington Trust SP Services (London) Limited
Officers: Daniel Jonathan Wynne [1970] Director

CGI Corporate Holdings Limited
Incorporated: 27 October 2003
Previous: Logicacmg Corporate Holdings Limited
Net Worth: £1,253,924,992 *Total Assets:* £1,254,360,064
Registered Office: 14th Floor, 20 Fenchurch Street, London, EC3M 3BY
Activities: Activities of other holding companies n.e.c.
Parent: Logica Limited
Officers: Sarah Landry Maltais, Secretary; Francois Boulanger [1965] Director/Executive Vice-President & Chief Financial Officer [Canadian]; Tara McGeehan [1967] Director/Businesswoman; Faris Mehdi Kadhim Mohammed [1961] Director/Vice President Finance UK, CGI

CGI Eurofin UK Limited
Incorporated: 23 November 2010 *Employees:* 3
Previous: Logica Eurofin UK Limited
Net Worth: £730,742,080 *Total Assets:* £760,523,328
Registered Office: 14th Floor, 20 Fenchurch Street, London, EC3M 3BY
Activities: Non-trading company
Parent: Logica Limited
Officers: Sarah Landry Maltais, Secretary; Francois Boulanger [1965] Director/Executive Vice-President & Chief Financial Officer [Canadian]; Tara McGeehan [1967] Director/Businesswoman; Faris Mehdi Kadhim Mohammed [1961] Director/Vice President Finance UK, CGI

CGI Finance (UK) Limited
Incorporated: 10 September 2012 *Employees:* 3
Net Worth: £74,786,000 *Total Assets:* £134,748,992
Registered Office: 14th Floor, 20 Fenchurch Street, London, EC3M 3BY
Activities: Non-trading company
Parent: Logica Limited
Officers: Sarah Landry Maltais, Secretary; Francois Boulanger [1965] Director/Executive Vice-President & Chief Financial Officer [Canadian]; Tara McGeehan [1967] Director/Businesswoman; Faris Mehdi Kadhim Mohammed [1961] Director/Vice President Finance UK CGI

CGI Finance Holdco Two Limited
Incorporated: 14 September 2012 *Employees:* 3
Net Worth: £493,419,008 *Total Assets:* £493,419,008
Registered Office: 14th Floor, 20 Fenchurch Street, London, EC3M 3BY
Activities: Activities of other holding companies n.e.c.
Parent: CGI Nordic Holdings Limited
Officers: Sarah Landry Maltais, Secretary; Francois Boulanger [1965] Director/Executive Vice-President & Chief Financial Officer [Canadian]; Tara McGeehan [1967] Director/Businesswoman; Faris Mehdi Kadhim Mohammed [1961] Director/Vice President Finance UK, CGI

CGI Group Holdings Europe Limited
Incorporated: 10 December 1996 *Employees:* 3
Net Worth: £1,539,256,960 *Total Assets:* £2,697,449,984
Registered Office: 14th Floor, 20 Fenchurch Street, London, EC3M 3BY
Activities: Activities of other holding companies n.e.c.
Parent: CGI Inc.
Officers: Sarah Landry Maltais, Secretary; Francois Boulanger [1965] Director/Executive Vice-President & Chief Financial Officer [Canadian]; Tara McGeehan [1967] Director/Businesswoman; Faris Mehdi Kadhim Mohammed [1961] Director/Vice President Finance UK, CGI

CGI IT UK Limited
Incorporated: 13 February 1969 *Employees:* 6,226
Net Worth: £994,596,992 *Total Assets:* £1,335,243,008
Registered Office: 14th Floor, 20 Fenchurch Street, London, EC3M 3BY
Activities: Information technology consultancy activities
Parent: CGI Group Holdings Europe Limited
Officers: Sarah Landry Maltais, Secretary; Francois Boulanger [1965] Director/Executive Vice-President & Chief Financial Officer [Canadian]; Tara McGeehan [1967] Director/Businesswoman; Faris Mehdi Kadhim Mohammed [1961] Director/Vice President Finance UK, CGI; Neil Geoffrey Timms [1967] Director/Businessman

CGI Nordic Holdings Limited
Incorporated: 18 August 2011 *Employees:* 3
Previous: Logica Cosec Limited
Net Worth: £960,323,008 *Total Assets:* £960,323,008
Registered Office: 14th Floor, 20 Fenchurch Street, London, EC3M 3BY
Activities: Activities of other holding companies n.e.c.
Parent: CGI Nordic Investments Limited
Officers: Sarah Landry Maltais, Secretary; Francois Boulanger [1965] Director/Executive Vice-President & Chief Financial Officer [Canadian]; Tara McGeehan [1967] Director/Businesswoman; Faris Mehdi Kadhim Mohammed [1961] Director/Vice President, Finance UK, CGI

CGI Nordic Investments Limited
Incorporated: 10 May 2005 *Employees:* 3
Previous: WM-Data Ltd
Net Worth: £989,406,016 *Total Assets:* £989,649,984
Registered Office: 14th Floor, 20 Fenchurch Street, London, EC3M 3BY
Activities: Activities of other holding companies n.e.c.
Parent: CGI Corporate Holdings Limited
Officers: Sarah Landry Maltais, Secretary; Francois Boulanger [1965] Director/Executive Vice-President & Chief Financial Officer [Canadian]; Tara McGeehan [1967] Director/Businesswoman; Faris Mehdi Kadhim Mohammed [1961] Director/Vice President Finance UK, CGI

CGIS Group (No. 3) Limited
Incorporated: 4 December 2002 *Employees:* 3
Net Worth: £39,857,000 *Total Assets:* £118,034,000
Registered Office: 10 Upper Berkeley Street, London, W1H 7PE
Activities: Buying and selling of own real estate
Shareholders: Terence Shelby Cole; Mark Neil Steinberg; Steven Ross Collins
Officers: Terence Shelby Cole [1932] Director; Steven Ross Collins [1952] Director; Mark Neil Steinberg [1959] Director

CGN Europe Energy Green Power Holding Limited
Incorporated: 22 November 2016
Net Worth Deficit: £5,769,097 *Total Assets:* £215,406,816
Registered Office: First Floor, St Martin's House, 3 Priory Court, Pilgrim Street, London, EC4V 6DE
Activities: Production of electricity
Parent: State-Owned Assets Supervision and Administration Commission of The State Council (SASAC)
Officers: Xiangsheng Li [1972] Finance Director [Chinese]; You Li [1962] Business Development Director CGNEE [Chinese]; Yuguang Liu [1964] Deputy Managing Director CGNEE [Chinese]; Yuhua Xiao [1972] Engineering and O&M Director CGNEE [Chinese]

CGN Europe Energy UK Holding Limited
Incorporated: 12 November 2014 *Employees:* 2
Net Worth: £12,016,000 *Total Assets:* £142,559,008
Registered Office: First Floor, St Martin's House, 3 Priory Court, Pilgrim Street, London, EC4V 6DE
Activities: Production of electricity
Officers: Xiangsheng Li [1972] Financial Director [Chinese]; You Li [1962] Investment Director [Chinese]; Yuguang Liu [1964] Deputy Managing Director [Chinese]; Wei Lu [1962] Managing Director [Chinese]; Yuhua Xiao [1972] Construction and O&M Director [Chinese]

Chambertin (Holdings) Limited
Incorporated: 3 May 2013 *Employees:* 3,416
Net Worth Deficit: £140,347,008 *Total Assets:* £614,148,992
Registered Office: Southbank Central, 30 Stamford Street, London, SE1 9LQ
Activities: Activities of head offices
Parent: Camelia Bidco Limited
Officers: Michael Stoddard, Secretary; Gavin Leigh [1972] Commercial Director; Phillip David Rowland [1971] Director; Wayne Andrew Story [1961] Director

Chambertin Acquisition Limited
Incorporated: 3 May 2013
Net Worth Deficit: £35,508,000 *Total Assets:* £320,928,000
Registered Office: Southbank Central, 30 Stamford Street, London, SE1 9LQ
Activities: Activities of head offices
Parent: Chambertin Midco Limited
Officers: Michael Stoddard, Secretary; Phillip David Rowland [1971] Director; Wayne Andrew Story [1961] Director

Chambertin Finance Limited
Incorporated: 3 May 2013 *Employees:* 2
Net Worth Deficit: £13,551,000 *Total Assets:* £341,884,000
Registered Office: Southbank Central, 30 Stamford Street, London, SE1 9LQ
Activities: Activities of head offices
Parent: Chambertin (Holdings) Limited
Officers: Michael Stoddard, Secretary; Phillip David Rowland [1971] Director; Wayne Andrew Story [1961] Director

Chambertin Midco Limited
Incorporated: 3 May 2013
Net Worth: £227,000 *Total Assets:* £341,305,984
Registered Office: Southbank Central, 30 Stamford Street, London, SE1 9LQ
Activities: Activities of head offices
Parent: Chambertin Finance Limited
Officers: Michael Stoddard, Secretary; Phillip David Rowland [1971] Director; Wayne Andrew Story [1961] Director

Chanel Limited
Incorporated: 6 February 1925 *Employees:* 20,197
Net Worth: £2,818,455,808 *Total Assets:* £6,879,171,584
Registered Office: 5 Barlow Place, London, W1J 6DG
Activities: Wholesale of clothing and footwear
Officers: Paul Stuart Gaff, Secretary; Paul Alain Abecassis [1950] Director/Banker [Swiss]; Philippe Bernard Blondiaux [1965] Director/Chief Financial Officer [French]; Richard Maurice Collasse [1953] Director/President [French]; John Stephen Galantic [1961] Director/President [American/Swiss]; Bertrand Henry Gros [1950] Director/Lawyer [Swiss]; Suzanne Elizabeth Heywood [1969] Managing Director; Baroness Martha Lane Fox [1973] Director/Entrepreneur; Olivier Nicolay [1957] Director [French]; Bruno Andre Jean Pavlovsky [1962] Director/President [French]; Vincent Graham Shaw [1958] Director/President

Channel 5 Broadcasting Limited
Incorporated: 17 January 1996 *Employees:* 224
Net Worth: £4,649,909,248 *Total Assets:* £4,793,490,944
Registered Office: Fieldfisher LLP, Riverbank House, 2 Swan Lane, London, EC4R 3TT
Activities: Television programme production activities
Parent: Viacom Camden Lock Limited
Officers: James Robert Currell [1971] Director/Finance; Paul Dunthorne [1967] Director/COO and SVP; David Gerard Lynn [1968] Managing Director [Irish]

Chapelcrest Investments Limited
Incorporated: 22 September 2009
Net Worth: £214,915,120 *Total Assets:* £214,915,120
Registered Office: 1 Churchill Place, London, E14 5HP
Activities: Financial intermediation not elsewhere classified
Parent: Barclays Bank PLC
Officers: Carl Thomas Senior [1978] Director/Banker; Vishal Shah [1984] Director/Banker; Patrick Brittain Voisey [1979] Director; Jonathan Michael Walthoe [1975] Director/Banker

Chapelfield LP Limited
Incorporated: 13 October 2000
Net Worth: £122,571,000 *Total Assets:* £305,652,000
Registered Office: 40 Broadway, London, SW1H 0BT
Activities: Activities of other holding companies n.e.c.
Parent: intu Chapelfield Limited
Officers: Susan Marsden, Secretary; Hugh Michael Ford [1967] Director/General Corporate Counsel; Barbara Gibbes [1975] Director/Accountant; Edward Matthew Giles Roberts [1963] Finance Director

Charcoal Midco 2 Limited
Incorporated: 14 September 2006
Net Worth Deficit: £826,000 *Total Assets:* £122,849,000
Registered Office: Cavendish House, 18 Cavendish Square, London, W1G 0PJ
Activities: Non-trading company
Parent: Secure Income REIT PLC
Officers: Sandra Louise Gumm, Secretary [Australian]; Philip Michael Brown [1960] Investment Director; Timothy James Evans [1969] Director/Chartered Surveyor; Sandra Louise Gumm [1966] Director/Chartered Accountant [Australian]; Nicholas Mark Leslau [1959] Director/Chartered Surveyor

Charity Projects
Incorporated: 5 April 1984 *Employees:* 295
Net Worth: £116,885,000 *Total Assets:* £256,515,008
Registered Office: Hanover House, 14 Hanover Square, London, W1S 1HP
Activities: Other social work activities without accommodation n.e.c.
Officers: Vincent Seth Collins, Secretary; Suzi Aplin [1967] Director/Television Producer; Dr Susan Elizabeth Black [1962] Director/Professor of Computer Science; William Henry Rymer Cayton [1950] Director/Government Advisor; Richard Whalley Anthony Curtis [1956] Director/Script Writer; Timothy Douglas Davie [1967] Director/Chief Executive BBC Worldwide; Michael Ross Harris [1955] Director/Business Consultant; Tristia Adele Harrison [1973] Director Executive; Colin Margetson Howes [1956] Director/Solicitor; Saul Charles Klein [1970] Director; Rupert Oliver Henry Morley [1965] Director; Tessy Ojo [1971] Director; Alexandra Ami Reid [1980] Deputy Director; Jr Shropshire [1971] Director/Lawyer; Theodosia Sowa [1957] Director

Charles Street Conduit Asset Backed Securitisation 1 Limited
Incorporated: 19 July 2007
Net Worth: £100 *Total Assets:* £1,123,976,704
Registered Office: 6th Floor, 65 Gresham Street, London, EC2V 7NQ
Activities: Other business support service activities n.e.c.
Parent: Link Trust Nominees No.1 Limited
Officers: Colin Arthur Benford [1962] Director

Charter Central Finance Limited
Incorporated: 19 December 1952
Net Worth: £496,040,992 *Total Assets:* £2,799,216,896
Registered Office: 6th Floor, 322 High Holborn, London, WC1V 7PB
Activities: Banks
Parent: Cast Limited
Officers: William Flexon [1963] Director/Chartered Accountant [American]; Christopher Michael Hix [1962] Director/Chief Financial Officer [American]; Mark Paul Lehman [1967] Director/Solicitor [American]; Daniel Alexis Pryor [1968] Director [American]; Eileen Annabelle Raperport [1951] Director/Pensions Co-ordinator; Guy Rostron [1960] Director/Chartered Accountant

Charter Consolidated Holdings Limited
Incorporated: 8 October 2008
Net Worth: £1,172,989,056 *Total Assets:* £1,470,809,984
Registered Office: 6th Floor, 322 High Holborn, London, WC1V 7PB
Activities: Non-trading company
Parent: Colfax Corporation
Officers: William Flexon [1963] Director/Chartered Accountant [American]; Mark Paul Lehman [1967] Director/Solicitor [American]; Eileen Annabelle Raperport [1951] Director/Pensions Co-ordinator; Guy Rostron [1960] Director/Chartered Accountant

Charter Consolidated Limited
Incorporated: 18 December 1964
Net Worth: £625,216,000 *Total Assets:* £692,246,016
Registered Office: 6th Floor, 322 High Holborn, London, WC1V 7PB
Activities: Activities of head offices
Parent: Charter Limited
Officers: William Flexon [1963] Director/Chartered Accountant [American]; Mark Paul Lehman [1967] Director/Solicitor [American]; Eileen Annabelle Raperport [1951] Director/Pensions Co-ordinator; Guy Rostron [1960] Director/Chartered Accountant

Charter Limited
Incorporated: 1 March 1993
Net Worth: £1,876,259,968 *Total Assets:* £1,905,538,944
Registered Office: 6th Floor, 322 High Holborn, London, WC1V 7PB
Activities: Activities of head offices
Parent: Charter Consolidated Holdings Limited
Officers: Ian Halliday Brander [1961] Director; William Flexon [1963] Director/Chartered Accountant [American]; Mark Paul Lehman [1967] Director/Solicitor [American]; Eileen Annabelle Raperport [1951] Director/Pensions Co-ordinator; Guy Rostron [1960] Director/Chartered Accountant

Charter Mortgage Funding 2017-1 PLC
Incorporated: 12 June 2017
Net Worth: £526,000 *Total Assets:* £292,532,992
Registered Office: 35 Great St Helen's, London, EC3A 6AP
Activities: Financial intermediation not elsewhere classified
Parent: Charter Mortgage Holdings 2017-1 Limited
Officers: Daniel Marc Richard Jaffe [1975] Director

Chaucer Capital Investments Limited
Incorporated: 24 December 1996
Previous: Hayward Brick Stuchbery Holdings Limited
Net Worth: £233,311,008 *Total Assets:* £233,311,008
Registered Office: Plantation Place, 30 Fenchurch Street, London, EC3M 3AD
Activities: Activities of other holding companies n.e.c.
Parent: Chaucer Holdings Limited
Officers: Richard Nicholas Barnett, Secretary; Robert John Callan [1968] Director/Chartered Accountant; David Stephen Saker [1977] Director/Accountant; Daniel John Willis [1973] Director/Accountant

Chaucer Corporate Capital (No. 3) Limited
Incorporated: 11 August 2004
Net Worth: £142,340,000 *Total Assets:* £2,955,379,968
Registered Office: Plantation Place, 30 Fenchurch Street, London, EC3M 3AD
Activities: Other activities auxiliary to insurance and pension funding
Parent: Chaucer Holdings Limited
Officers: Richard Nicholas Barnett, Secretary; Robert John Callan [1968] Director/Chartered Accountant; David Stephen Saker [1977] Director/Accountant; Daniel John Willis [1973] Director/Accountant

Chaucer Holdings Limited
Incorporated: 25 August 1993
Net Worth: £227,560,992 *Total Assets:* £280,480,992
Registered Office: Plantation Place, 30 Fenchurch Street, London, EC3M 3AD
Activities: Activities of other holding companies n.e.c.
Parent: The Hanover Insurance International Holdings Limited
Officers: Richard Nicholas Barnett, Secretary; Robert John Callan [1968] Director/Chartered Accountant; John Fowle [1969] Director/Underwriter; Dr Huiqiang Zuo [1965] Director/Reinsurer [Chinese]

Cheetah Bidco Limited
Incorporated: 14 June 2017
Net Worth: £316,780,992 *Total Assets:* £319,846,016
Registered Office: 35 Great St Helen's, London, EC3A 6AP
Activities: Other service activities n.e.c.
Parent: Cheetah Holdco Limited
Officers: Charles Richard Green [1970] Director/Chartered Surveyor; Matthew Allan Green [1982] Director/Accountant; Gemma Nandita Kataky [1983] Director; Andrew Lax [1976] Director [Canadian]; James Robert Lock [1976] Director; Oliver Andrew Edward Olsen [1973] Director; James Christopher Seppala [1979] Director; Michael David Vrana [1980] Director [American]

Cheetah Holdco Limited
Incorporated: 22 June 2017 *Employees:* 253
Net Worth: £182,842,000 *Total Assets:* £623,660,992
Registered Office: 35 Great St Helen's, London, EC3A 6AP
Activities: Other service activities n.e.c.
Officers: Charles Richard Green [1970] Director/Chartered Surveyor; Matthew Allan Green [1982] Director/Accountant; Andrew Lax [1976] Director [Canadian]; James Robert Lock [1976] Director; Oliver Andrew Edward Olsen [1973] Director; James Christopher Seppala [1979] Director; Michael David Vrana [1980] Director [American]

Chel (Shares) LLP
Incorporated: 16 August 2010 *Employees:* 29
Net Worth: £90,720,000 *Total Assets:* £321,064,000
Registered Office: 10 Upper Berkeley Street, London, W1H 7PE
Officers: Terence Shelby Cole [1932] Member; Steven Ross Collins [1952] Member; Andrew John Pettit [1968] Member; Mark Neil Steinberg [1959] Member

Chello Zone Holdings Limited
Incorporated: 18 November 2004
Net Worth: £103,772,000 *Total Assets:* £111,612,000
Registered Office: 111 Salusbury Road, London, NW6 6RG
Activities: Television programming and broadcasting activities
Parent: AMC Networks International Zone Holdings Limited
Officers: Rutger Andree Wiltens [1973] Director/General Counsel [Dutch]; Kevin William Dickie [1968] Director/SVP UK & MEA; Robert McDonald Stewart [1979] Director/CFO AMCNI Zone

Chelsea FC PLC
Incorporated: 3 September 1990 *Employees:* 756
Net Worth: £392,623,008 *Total Assets:* £755,345,984
Registered Office: Stamford Bridge, Fulham Road, London, SW6 1HS
Activities: Activities of head offices
Parent: Fordstam Limited
Officers: James Christian Generald Bonington, Secretary; Bruce Michael Buck [1946] Director/Attorney [American]; Marina Granovskaia [1975] Director/Executive Assistant [Canadian]; Jonathan Guy Laurence [1961] Director/Chief Executive Officer; Eugene Tenenbaum [1964] Director/Financier [Canadian]

Chelsea Football Club Limited
Incorporated: 26 November 1985 *Employees:* 341
Net Worth Deficit: £632,611,968 *Total Assets:* £382,318,016
Registered Office: Stamford Bridge Ground, Fulham Road, London, SW6 1HS
Activities: Activities of sport clubs
Parent: Fordstam Limited
Officers: James Christian Generald Bonington, Secretary; David Barnard [1952] Director/Club Secretary; Bruce Michael Buck [1946] Director/Attorney [American]; Marina Granovskaia [1975] Director/Executive Assistant [Canadian]; Jonathan Guy Laurence [1961] Director/Chief Executive Officer; Eugene Tenenbaum [1964] Director/Financier [Canadian]

Chelsea Harbour Estates Limited
Incorporated: 3 November 1999 *Employees:* 17
Net Worth: £100,179,000 *Total Assets:* £320,928,992
Registered Office: 319 Harbour Yard, Chelsea Harbour, London, SW10 0XD
Activities: Activities of other holding companies n.e.c.
Shareholders: Chel (No. 3) Ltd; Chel (No.3) Limited
Officers: Terence Shelby Cole [1932] Director; Steven Ross Collins [1952] Director; Andrew John Pettit [1968] Director/Lawyer; Mark Neil Steinberg [1959] Director

Chelsea Harbour Limited
Incorporated: 6 December 1950
Net Worth: £171,843,008 *Total Assets:* £289,268,000
Registered Office: 319 Harbour Yard, Chelsea Harbour, London, SW10 0XD
Activities: Other letting and operating of own or leased real estate
Parent: Chelsea Harbour Estates Limited
Officers: Terence Shelby Cole [1932] Director; Steven Ross Collins [1952] Director; Mark Neil Steinberg [1959] Director

Chelsea Land Limited
Incorporated: 26 May 1961
Net Worth: £140,944,992 *Total Assets:* £140,944,992
Registered Office: 10 Duke of York Square, London, SW3 4LY
Activities: Activities of head offices
Parent: Cadogan Group Limited
Officers: Paul Morris Loutit, Secretary; Paul Morris Loutit [1968] Director/Chartered Accountant; Hugh Richard Seaborn [1962] Director/Chartered Surveyor

Chelwood Trading & Investment Company Limited
Incorporated: 26 January 1911
Net Worth: £387,059,008 *Total Assets:* £387,374,016
Registered Office: Globe House, 1 Water Street, London, WC2R 3LA
Activities: Activities of head offices
Parent: Allen & Ginter (UK) Limited
Officers: David Patrick Ian Booth [1974] Director/Group Chief Accountant; Robert James Casey [1948] Director/Attorney [American]; Robert Fergus Heaton [1965] Director/Head of UK Tax; Carola Wiegand [1966] Director/Global Commercial Tax Manager [German]

Chemchina UK Limited
Incorporated: 13 January 2015 *Employees:* 10
Net Worth: £28,886,468 *Total Assets:* £130,738,240
Registered Office: 7 Curzon Street, London, W1J 5HG
Activities: Other business support service activities n.e.c.
Parent: State-Owned Assets Supervision and Administration Commission of The State Council
Officers: Qinghui Liu [1964] Director; Dazhuang Wang [1962] Director [Chinese]; Hong Wu [1975] Managing Director [Chinese]; Hong Zhu [1966] Director

Cheniere Marketing International LLP
Incorporated: 12 December 2013 *Employees:* 56
Net Worth: £423,535,424 *Total Assets:* £597,477,568
Registered Office: Wing 4, Fifth Floor, Berkeley Square House, Berkeley Square, London, W1J 6BY

Chepstow Blue PLC
Incorporated: 23 April 2009
Net Worth: £21,000 *Total Assets:* £1,300,295,936
Registered Office: 35 Great St Helen's, London, EC3A 6AP
Activities: Financial intermediation not elsewhere classified
Parent: Chepstow Blue Holdings Limited
Officers: Daniel Marc Richard Jaffe [1975] Director

Leonard Cheshire Disability
Incorporated: 3 August 1955 *Employees:* 4,201
Net Worth: £128,229,000 *Total Assets:* £155,668,000
Registered Office: 66 South Lambeth Road, London, SW8 1RL
Activities: Other human health activities
Officers: Susan Ruth Irene Lightman, Secretary; Dr Sylvia Josephine Anie [1964] Director; Richard John Brooman [1955] Director; Martin Stuart Davidson [1955] Director; Sally Margaret Davis [1953] Director; Dr Stephen Charles Duckworth [1960] Director; Dr Elizabeth Zaidee Haywood [1955] Director; Vidar Paul Hjardeng [1962] Director/Consultant; Dr Colin Moffat Hunter [1958] Director/Medical Doctor; Ranald Stanley Mair [1950] Director/Retired; David Richard Pugh [1961] Director/Chief Finance Officer; Catriona Rayner [1953] Director

Chesterfield Properties Limited
Incorporated: 19 November 1945 *Employees:* 1
Net Worth: £257,445,584 *Total Assets:* £264,465,888
Registered Office: 180 Great Portland Street, London, W1W 5QZ
Activities: Development of building projects
Parent: Quintain (Holdings) Limited
Officers: Frances Victoria Heazell, Secretary; Angus Alexander Dodd [1967] Senior Managing Director; Michael Ben Jenkins [1972] Director [British/Australian]; James Michael Edward Saunders [1966] Director

Chesterlodge Limited
Incorporated: 5 February 1982 *Employees:* 117
Net Worth: £368,040,384 *Total Assets:* £426,804,288
Registered Office: Chelsea Cloisters, Sloane Avenue, London, SW3 3DW
Activities: Activities of head offices
Major Shareholder: Christopher John Moran
Officers: Christopher John Moran [1948] Director/Financier

Chevron Energy Limited
Incorporated: 30 November 2004 *Employees:* 1,020
Net Worth: £994,463,232 *Total Assets:* £1,023,069,824
Registered Office: 1 Westferry Circus, Canary Wharf, London, E14 4HA
Activities: Other business support service activities n.e.c.
Parent: Chevron Captain Company LLC
Officers: Brigitte Zaza, Secretary; Nahid Ali [1968] Director/Finance Manager; John Gregor Cameron [1964] Director/General Manager; Mark Andrew Knights [1978] Director/Finance Manager; Greta Gill Lydecker [1957] Managing Director [American]; Michael James John Williams [1966] Director/General Counsel; Stewart William Wright [1961] Director/Country Manager UK

Chevron North Sea Limited
Incorporated: 20 February 1981
Net Worth: £1,152,600,064 *Total Assets:* £2,568,000,000
Registered Office: 9 Cavendish Square, London, W1G 9DF
Activities: Extraction of crude petroleum
Parent: Chevron Products UK Limited
Officers: Brigitte Zaza, Secretary; Tearle William Thomas Harlan [1972] Director/Legal Manager [American]; Greta Gill Lydecker [1957] Managing Director [American]; Anthony Robert McGarva [1965] Director/Business Service Manager; Alan Stewart Pitts [1966] Director/General Manager, UK Operated Assets; Michael Robert Thompson [1977] Finance Director [American]

Chevron Products UK Limited
Incorporated: 20 July 1998 *Employees:* 339
Net Worth: £883,097,024 *Total Assets:* £1,063,958,016
Registered Office: 1 Westferry Circus, Canary Wharf, London, E14 4HA
Activities: Wholesale of other fuels and related products
Parent: Chevron Energy Limited
Officers: Brigitte Zaza, Secretary; Nahid Ali [1968] Director/Finance Manager; John Gregor Cameron [1964] Director/General Manager; Gary George Cole [1969] Director/Manager; Mark Andrew Knights [1978] Director/Finance Manager; Marina Lyon [1961] Director/Business Development Executive [British/Russian]; Michael James John Williams [1966] Director/General Counsel; Stewart William Wright [1961] Director/Country Manager UK

Childcare Vouchers Limited
Incorporated: 6 September 1989 *Employees:* 67
Net Worth: £12,901,000 *Total Assets:* £160,538,000
Registered Office: 50 Vauxhall Bridge Road, London, SW1V 2RS
Activities: Other business support service activities n.e.c.
Parent: Edenred (UK Group) Limited
Officers: Patrick Marc Jean Langlois, Secretary; Arnaud Marie Gildas Erulin [1970] Director/Chief Operating Officer [French]; Patrick Marc Jean Langlois [1969] Managing Director [French]; Olivier Soula [1981] Finance Director [French]; Johann Fabrice Martin Vaucanson [1973] Managing Director [French]

The Children's Investment Fund Foundation (UK)
Incorporated: 8 February 2002 *Employees:* 80
Net Worth: £3,974,105,600 *Total Assets:* £4,433,676,288
Registered Office: 7 Clifford Street, London, W1S 2FT
Activities: Other education n.e.c.
Officers: Jamie Anne Cooper Hohn [1965] Non Profit Director [American]; Benjamin James Goldsmith [1980] Director/Investment Manager; Christopher Anthony Hohn [1966] Director/Fund Manager; Masroor Taale Siddiqui [1971] Director [American]; Graeme Stewart Sutherland Sweeney [1952] Director

Chilean Northern Mines Limited
Incorporated: 25 August 1910
Net Worth: £18,092,464 *Total Assets:* £405,213,536
Registered Office: Cleveland House, 33 King Street, St James's, London, SW1Y 6RJ
Activities: Activities of head offices
Officers: Julian Thomas Roddan Anderson, Secretary; Alfredo Felix Atucha Abad [1957] Director/Vice-President of Corporate Finance [Chilean]; Francisco Javier Veloso Barraza [1962] Director/Lawyer [Chilean]; Andrew Mark Lindsay [1962] Mining Executive/Director London Office

Chime Communications Limited
Incorporated: 29 January 1986 *Employees:* 45
Previous: Chime Communications PLC
Net Worth: £223,323,008 *Total Assets:* £298,358,016
Registered Office: 62 Buckingham Gate, London, SW1E 6AJ
Activities: Activities of head offices
Parent: Chime Finance Limited
Officers: Thomas George Tolliss, Secretary; Stephanie Brimacombe [1983] Director/Group MD; Adrian Michael Coleman [1963] Director/Advertising Consultant; David Crowther [1975] Director/Finance; Joanne Marie Parker [1966] Director/Marketing Executive; Matthew James Vandrau [1969] Director

Chime Finance Limited
Incorporated: 24 July 2015 *Employees:* 3
Net Worth: £276,392,000 *Total Assets:* £543,316,992
Registered Office: P O Box 70693, 62 Buckingham Gate, London, SW1P 9ZP
Activities: Activities of head offices
Parent: Chime Group Limited
Officers: Thomas George Tolliss, Secretary; Adrian Michael Coleman [1963] Director/Advertising Consultant; David Crowther [1975] Director/Finance; Matthew James Vandrau [1969] Director

Chime Group Holdings Limited
Incorporated: 24 July 2015 *Employees:* 2,488
Net Worth: £140,391,008 *Total Assets:* £585,772,032
Registered Office: 62 Buckingham Gate, London, SW1E 6AJ
Activities: Other reservation service activities n.e.c.
Shareholders: PM VII S.A.R.L.; WPP Beans Limited
Officers: Thomas George Tolliss, Secretary; Adrian Michael Coleman [1963] Director/Advertising Consultant; John Carl Hahn [1958] Director [British/American]; Lindsay Pattison [1973] Director; Christopher James Satterthwaite [1956] Director; Roderik August Schlosser [1980] Director [Dutch]; Andrew Adams Tisdale [1961] Director [American]; Matthew James Vandrau [1969] Director; Paul Steven Walsh [1955] Director; Mr Steve Richard Winters [1968] Director/Chartered Accountant

Chime Group Limited
Incorporated: 16 September 2015 *Employees:* 2,488
Net Worth: £142,727,008 *Total Assets:* £583,385,984
Registered Office: P O Box 70693, 62 Buckingham Gate, London, SW1P 9ZP
Activities: Activities of head offices
Parent: Chime Midco Limited
Officers: Thomas George Tolliss, Secretary; Adrian Michael Coleman [1963] Director/Advertising Consultant; David Crowther [1975] Director/Finance; Joanne Marie Parker [1966] Director/Marketing Executive; Matthew James Vandrau [1969] Director

Chime Holdco Limited
Incorporated: 16 September 2015
Net Worth: £302,155,008 *Total Assets:* £302,156,000
Registered Office: P O Box 70693, 62 Buckingham Gate, London, SW1P 9ZP
Activities: Non-trading company
Parent: Chime Group Holdings Limited
Officers: Thomas George Tolliss, Secretary; David Crowther [1975] Director/Finance; Roderik August Schlosser [1980] Director [Dutch]; Andrew Adams Tisdale [1961] Director [American]

Chime Midco Limited
Incorporated: 16 September 2015
Net Worth: £298,807,008 *Total Assets:* £298,808,000
Registered Office: P O Box 70693, 62 Buckingham Gate, London, SW1P 9ZP
Activities: Other reservation service activities n.e.c.
Parent: Chime Holdco Limited
Officers: Thomas George Tolliss, Secretary; David Crowther [1975] Director/Finance; Roderik August Schlosser [1980] Director [Dutch]; Andrew Adams Tisdale [1961] Director [American]

China Construction Bank (London) Limited
Incorporated: 17 December 2007 *Employees:* 102
Net Worth: £378,322,944 *Total Assets:* £1,220,489,088
Registered Office: 111 Old Broad Street, London, EC2N 1AP
Activities: Financial intermediation not elsewhere classified
Officers: Elizabeth Susan Corrin, Secretary; Shounian Cao [1968] Director/Banker [Chinese]; Brian Ronald Cook [1943] Director/Retired Investment Banker; Stephen Martin Fish [1946] Director/Retired; Yang Lu [1975] Director/Banker [Chinese]; Dr Darren John Sherman [1961] Director/Banker; Aimin Yang [1965] Director/Banker [Chinese]

China Merchants Securities (UK) Limited
Incorporated: 25 October 2013 *Employees:* 14
Net Worth: £15,849,783 *Total Assets:* £232,548,272
Registered Office: 3rd Floor, 50 Bank Street, London, E14 5NT
Activities: Security and commodity contracts dealing activities
Officers: Cheung Hung Chan [1976] Director/Head of Global Commodities Business Management [Chinese]; Bin Ling [1985] Executive Director, Compliance Officer [Chinese]; Fan Yang [1972] Director/Banker [Chinese]; Wei Zhang [1981] Director/Accountant

China Navigation Company Limited (The)
Incorporated: 31 January 1872
Net Worth: £320,016,992 *Total Assets:* £328,622,016
Registered Office: Swire House, 59 Buckingham Gate, London, SW1E 6AJ
Activities: Activities of other holding companies n.e.c.
Parent: John Swire & Sons Limited
Officers: David Charles Morris, Secretary; Barnaby Nicholas Swire [1964] Director; Samuel Compton Swire [1980] Director; James Hugh Woodrow [1967] Managing Director

China RE UK Limited
Incorporated: 28 September 2011
Net Worth Deficit: £29,852,308 *Total Assets:* £322,030,016
Registered Office: No 1 Minster Court, London, EC3R 7AA
Activities: Non-life reinsurance
Officers: Kun Huang [1975] Director [Chinese]; Huiqiang Zuo [1965] Director/Deputy General Manager of China P&C RE Ltd [Chinese]

Chiquita Finance Company Limited
Incorporated: 1 June 2016
Net Worth: £174,182,176 *Total Assets:* £174,886,960
Registered Office: 3rd Floor, 25 Park Lane, London, W1K 1RA
Activities: Other credit granting n.e.c.
Parent: Chiquita Holdings Limited
Officers: Oliver Abraham Cartade [1976] Director/Banker; Philip John Warner [1963] Director/Chartered Accountant

Chiquita Holdings Limited
Incorporated: 14 August 2014 *Employees:* 22,348
Net Worth: £569,743,168 *Total Assets:* £1,760,657,024
Registered Office: 3rd Floor, 25 Park Lane, London, W1K 1RA
Activities: Activities of agricultural holding companies
Shareholders: Jose Luis Cutrale; Joseph Yacoub Safra
Officers: Ailton Generaldo Bernardo [1955] Director/Banker [Brazilian]; Oliver Abraham Cartade [1976] Director/Banker; Graziela Cutrale [1975] Director [Brazilian]; Jose Henrique Cutrale [1974] Director [Italian]; Jose Luis Cutrale [1946] Director [Italian]; Jose Luis Cutrale Junior [1973] Director [Italian]; Michael Seth Rubinoff [1962] Director/Investor/Advisor [American]; Jacob Joseph Safra [1975] Director/Banker [Greek]

Chivas Atlantic Holdings Limited
Incorporated: 27 September 2006
Net Worth: £2,686,401,536 *Total Assets:* £3,319,808,768
Registered Office: Chivas House, 72 Chancellors Road, London, W6 9RS
Activities: Activities of head offices
Officers: Stuart MacNab [1964] Director/Chartered Accountant; Vincent Turpin [1978] Director/Chief Financial Officer [French]

Chivas Brothers (Holdings) Limited
Incorporated: 9 July 2001
Net Worth: £831,619,968 *Total Assets:* £3,864,496,128
Registered Office: Chivas House, 72 Chancellors Road, London, W6 9RS
Activities: Activities of head offices
Officers: Ailsa Mary Robertson Mapplebeck, Secretary; Jean-Christophe Coutures [1966] Director [French]; Eric Laborde [1962] Director/Chief Executive Officer [French]; Stuart MacNab [1964] Director; Catherine Louise Thompson [1971] Director/General Counsel [Australian]; Vincent Turpin [1978] Director/Chief Financial Officer [French]

Choicezone Limited
Incorporated: 27 September 2007
Net Worth: £85,847,000 *Total Assets:* £262,394,000
Registered Office: 14 Chester Terrace, London, NW1 4ND
Activities: Other letting and operating of own or leased real estate
Officers: Jitendra Patel, Secretary; Gulshan Bhatia [1933] Director; Nimet Esmail [1958] Marketing Director; Shelina Jetha [1961] Marketing Director

Jimmy Choo (Holdings) Limited
Incorporated: 1 September 2014
Net Worth: £350,764,992 *Total Assets:* £896,396,992
Registered Office: 10 Howick Place, London, SW1P 1GW
Activities: Activities of other holding companies n.e.c.
Parent: Jimmy Choo Group Limited
Officers: Hannah Lucy Victoria Merritt, Secretary; Pierre Robert Denis [1964] Director [French]; Simon William Kemmett [1970] Director

Jimmy Choo Group Limited
Incorporated: 1 September 2014 *Employees:* 2
Previous: Jimmy Choo Group PLC
Net Worth: £686,868,992 *Total Assets:* £702,265,024
Registered Office: 10 Howick Place, London, SW1P 1GW
Activities: Activities of other holding companies n.e.c.
Parent: Michael Kors Holdings Limited
Officers: Hannah Lucy Victoria Merritt, Secretary; Pierre Robert Denis [1964] Director [French]; Thomas J Edwards Jr [1964] Director [American]; John Debus Idol [1958] Director [American]; Simon William Kemmett [1970] Director

J. Choo Limited
Incorporated: 15 April 1996 *Employees:* 244
Net Worth: £314,852,000 *Total Assets:* £472,080,992
Registered Office: 10 Howick Place, London, SW1P 1GW
Activities: Wholesale of clothing and footwear
Parent: Jimmy Choo (Holdings) Limited
Officers: Hannah Lucy Victoria Merritt, Secretary/Solicitor; Pierre Robert Denis [1964] Director [French]; Simon William Kemmett [1970] Director

Choo Luxury Finance Limited
Incorporated: 6 May 2011
Net Worth Deficit: £158,570,000 *Total Assets:* £613,603,968
Registered Office: 10 Howick Place, London, SW1P 1GW
Activities: Activities of other holding companies n.e.c.
Parent: Jimmy Choo (Holdings) UK Limited
Officers: Hannah Merritt, Secretary; Pierre Robert Denis [1964] Director [French]; Simon William Kemmett [1970] Director

Choo Luxury Holdings Limited
Incorporated: 6 May 2011
Net Worth: £507,777,984 *Total Assets:* £514,512,000
Registered Office: 10 Howick Place, London, SW1P 1GW
Activities: Activities of other holding companies n.e.c.
Parent: Jimmy Choo (Holdings) Limited
Officers: Hannah Merritt, Secretary; Pierre Robert Denis [1964] Director [French]; Simon William Kemmett [1970] Director

Christie Manson & Woods Limited
Incorporated: 10 August 1973 *Employees:* 718
Net Worth: £111,274,000 *Total Assets:* £730,792,000
Registered Office: 8 King Street, St James's, London, SW1Y 6QT
Activities: Activities of other holding companies n.e.c.
Parent: Christie's International PLC
Officers: Adele Christine Falconer, Secretary; Stephen John Brooks [1965] Director/Deputy Chief Executive Officer; Sophie Jane Carter [1969] Director/Solicitor; Juha Pekka Pylkkanen [1963] Director/Auctioneer

Christie's International PLC
Incorporated: 8 May 1972
Net Worth: £215,690,000 *Total Assets:* £314,270,016
Registered Office: 8 King Street, St James's, London, SW1Y 6QT
Activities: Activities of other holding companies n.e.c.
Officers: Sophie Jane Carter, Secretary; Stephen John Brooks [1965] Director/Deputy Chief Executive Officer; Guillaume Cerutti [1966] Director/Chief Executive Officer [French]; Francois Philippe Curiel [1948] Director & Jewellery Specialist and Auctioneer [French]; Jean-Francois Edmond Robert Palus [1961] Managing Director [French]; Francois Henri Joseph Pinault [1936] Director [French]; Juha Pekka Pylkkanen [1963] Director/Auctioneer; Stephanie Renault [1973] Director/Finance Controller [French]; Heloise Temple-Boyer [1978] Investment Director [French]

Christie's Private Sales Limited
Incorporated: 19 April 2002
Net Worth: £48,961,000 *Total Assets:* £186,428,992
Registered Office: 8 King Street, St James's, London, SW1Y 6QT
Activities: Agents specialised in the sale of other particular products
Parent: Christie's Private Sales Holdings Limited
Officers: Adele Christine Falconer, Secretary; Karen Cole [1964] Senior Director, Client Operations & Accounting; Tina Law [1977] Director/Global Head of Private Sale Service Centre

Chrysaor E & P Finance Limited
Incorporated: 22 December 2016
Total Assets: £1,200,201,088
Registered Office: Brettenham House, Lancaster Place, London, WC2E 7EN
Activities: Extraction of crude petroleum
Parent: Chrysaor E & P Limited
Officers: Howard Ralph Landes, Secretary; Philip Andrew Kirk [1966] Director; Andrew Jon Osborne [1969] Director

Chrysaor E & P Services Limited
Incorporated: 19 July 2017 *Employees:* 149
Net Worth Deficit: £3,507,000 *Total Assets:* £249,932,000
Registered Office: Brettenham House, Lancaster Place, London, WC2E 7EN
Activities: Extraction of crude petroleum
Parent: Chrysaor E & P Limited
Officers: Howard Ralph Landes, Secretary; Philip Andrew Kirk [1966] Director/Chief Executive Officer; Andrew Jon Osborne [1969] Director/Chief Financial Officer

Chrysaor Limited
Incorporated: 6 November 2007 *Employees:* 6
Net Worth: £40,351,000 *Total Assets:* £3,390,341,888
Registered Office: Brettenham House, Lancaster Place, London, WC2E 7EN
Activities: Extraction of crude petroleum
Parent: Chrysaor E & P Limited
Officers: Howard Ralph Landes, Secretary; Philip Andrew Kirk [1966] Director; Andrew Jon Osborne [1969] Director/Chief Finance Officer

Chrysaor North Sea Limited
Incorporated: 24 July 1969
Previous: BG International (CNS) Limited
Net Worth: £62,300,000 *Total Assets:* £481,476,992
Registered Office: Brettenham House, Lancaster Place, London, WC2E 7EN
Activities: Extraction of crude petroleum
Parent: Chrysaor E & P Limited
Officers: Howard Ralph Landes, Secretary; Philip Andrew Kirk [1966] Director/Chief Executive Officer; Andrew Jon Osborne [1969] Director/Chief Financial Officer

Chubb Capital I Limited
Incorporated: 8 September 1995
Previous: Ace Capital Limited
Net Worth: £211,094,000 *Total Assets:* £1,877,490,944
Registered Office: 100 Leadenhall Street, London, EC3A 3BP
Activities: Non-life insurance
Parent: Chubb Market Company Limited
Officers: Mark Kent Hammond [1960] Director [American]; Ashley Craig Mullins [1976] Director/Lawyer [Australian]; Alexander Matthew Wenham Shaw [1964] Director

Chubb Capital Ltd
Incorporated: 18 January 2010
Net Worth: £109,623,000 *Total Assets:* £303,180,992
Registered Office: 100 Leadenhall Street, London, EC3A 3BP
Activities: Non-life insurance
Officers: Mark Kent Hammond [1960] Director [American]; Ashley Craig Mullins [1976] Director/Lawyer [Australian]; Alexander Matthew Wenham Shaw [1964] Director

Chubb Capital V Limited
Incorporated: 15 July 1994
Previous: Ace Capital V Limited
Net Worth: £131,002,000 *Total Assets:* £136,230,000
Registered Office: 100 Leadenhall Street, London, EC3A 3BP
Activities: Non-life insurance
Officers: Mark Kent Hammond [1960] Director [American]; Ashley Craig Mullins [1976] Director/Lawyer [Australian]; Alexander Matthew Wenham Shaw [1964] Director

Chubb Market Company Limited
Incorporated: 14 July 1998
Previous: Ace Global Markets Limited
Net Worth: £198,306,000 *Total Assets:* £473,139,008
Registered Office: 100 Leadenhall Street, London, EC3A 3BP
Activities: Activities of financial services holding companies
Parent: Chubb Limited
Officers: Mark Kent Hammond [1960] Director [American]; Ashley Craig Mullins [1976] Director/Lawyer [Australian]; Alexander Matthew Wenham Shaw [1964] Director

Chubb Services UK Limited
Incorporated: 24 July 1980 *Employees:* 1,426
Previous: Ace Ina Services U.K. Limited
Net Worth: £47,415,000 *Total Assets:* £288,137,984
Registered Office: 100 Leadenhall Street, London, EC3A 3BP
Activities: Other business support service activities n.e.c.
Officers: David Michael Alan Furby [1963] Director; Mark Kent Hammond [1960] Director [American]; Ashley Craig Mullins [1976] Director/Lawyer [Australian]; David Peter Robinson [1967] Director/UK & Ireland Regional President

Chugai Pharma Europe Limited
Incorporated: 22 December 1997 *Employees:* 120
Previous: Chugai Pharma Marketing Ltd.
Net Worth: £197,716,832 *Total Assets:* £210,165,520
Registered Office: Mulliner House, Flanders Road, Turnham Green, London, W4 1NN
Activities: Activities of head offices
Parent: Chugai Pharmaceutical Co, Ltd
Officers: Grigorios Karamperis, Secretary; John Leslie Seaton Halls [1950] Director; Dr Yasushi Ito [1956] Director [Japanese]; Koichi Nishikawa [1960] Director [Japanese]; Hisanori Takanashi [1959] Director [Japanese]

CIB Properties Limited
Incorporated: 22 May 1985
Net Worth: £227,291,008 *Total Assets:* £364,287,008
Registered Office: Citigroup Centre, Canary Wharf, London, E14 5LB
Activities: Development of building projects
Parent: Citigroup Global Markets Europe Finance Limited
Officers: Simon James Cumming, Secretary; John Reginald Killey [1955] Director/Banker; David Ian Sharland [1959] Director/Chartered Accountant; Jeremy David Robert Smith [1964] Director of Corporate Estate

CIBC World Markets PLC
Incorporated: 21 July 1992 *Employees:* 13
Net Worth: £396,520,032 *Total Assets:* £555,850,944
Registered Office: 150 Cheapside, London, EC2V 6ET
Activities: Banks
Officers: Meghan Purves, Secretary; Paul David Atkinson [1967] Director/Bank Officer; Marshall Charles Bailey [1966] Director; David Buckley [1962] Director; Donald Christopher Bryce Climo [1962] Executive Director [Canadian]; Wayne Lee [1974] Managing Director, Head, Europe & Asia Pacific [Canadian]

Cigna Chestnut Holdings, Ltd
Incorporated: 21 October 2013 *Employees:* 5
Net Worth: £2,378,025,728 *Total Assets:* £2,424,423,424
Registered Office: 13th Floor, 5 Aldermanbury Square, London, EC2V 7HR
Activities: Activities of financial services holding companies
Parent: Cigna Walnut Holdings Limited
Officers: Christine Butler, Secretary; Franklin Clark Barlow [1954] Accounting Director [American]; Terence James Dillon [1972] Accounting Senior Director [American]; Irene Pope Gentile [1960] Tax Senior Director [American]; Joanne Ruth Hart [1961] Director/Treasury Manager [American]; Craig Bryce Nicholls [1972] Director/Treasurer [New Zealander]; David Sawyer Scheibe [1964] Treasury Senior Director [American]

Cigna Walnut Holdings, Ltd.
Incorporated: 10 April 2014
Net Worth: £1,967,457,664 *Total Assets:* £2,519,239,168
Registered Office: 13th Floor, 5 Aldermanbury Square, London, EC2V 7HR
Activities: Activities of financial services holding companies
Parent: Cigna APAC Holdings Limited (Bermuda)
Officers: Christine Butler, Secretary; Franklin Clark Barlow [1954] Accounting Director [American]; Terence James Dillon [1972] Accounting Senior Director [American]; Irene Pope Gentile [1960] Tax Senior Director [American]; Joanne Ruth Hart [1961] Director/Treasury Manager [American]; Craig Bryce Nicholls [1972] Director/Treasurer [New Zealander]; David Sawyer Scheibe [1964] Treasury Senior Director [American]

CII Holdco Ltd
Incorporated: 23 October 2013
Net Worth: £23,058,484 *Total Assets:* £115,541,824
Registered Office: c/o Watson Farley & Williams LLP, 15 Appold Street, London, EC2A 2HB
Activities: Activities of other holding companies n.e.c.
Officers: Torsten Lodberg Smed [1970] Director/Senior Partner [Danish]; Soren Toftgaard [1976] Director/Associate Partner [Danish]

Circadian Limited
Incorporated: 6 October 1999
Net Worth Deficit: £14,850,971 *Total Assets:* £343,647,264
Registered Office: Hutchison House, 5 Hester Road, Battersea, London, SW11 4AN
Activities: Development of building projects
Parent: Circadian (CH) Limited
Officers: Eirene Yeung, Secretary; Justin Kwok Hung Chiu [1950] Director [Canadian]; Wai Kam Raymond Chow [1947] Director; Hing Lam Kam [1946] Director [Chinese]; Raymond Tam [1954] Director of Finance

Circle Anglia Social Housing 2 PLC
Incorporated: 16 September 2015
Net Worth: £50,000 *Total Assets:* £152,120,000
Registered Office: Level 6, 6 More London Place, London, SE1 2DA
Activities: Activities of financial services holding companies
Officers: Louise Hyde, Secretary; Jack Bargholz [1966] Director of Financial Services [Danish]; Gareth Francis [1976] Treasury Director; Janice Murray [1959] Director of Financial Planning and Performance

Circle Anglia Social Housing PLC
Incorporated: 13 September 2007
Net Worth: £50,000 *Total Assets:* £668,187,008
Registered Office: Level 6, 6 More London Place, London, SE1 2DA
Activities: Activities of financial services holding companies
Officers: Louise Hyde, Secretary; Jack Bargholz [1966] Director of Financial Services [Danish]; Gareth Francis [1976] Treasury Director; Janice Murray [1959] Director of Financial Performance and Planning

Citadel Enterprise Europe Limited
Incorporated: 12 November 1998 *Employees:* 240
Previous: Citadel Investment Group (Europe) Limited
Net Worth: £34,319,000 *Total Assets:* £214,428,992
Registered Office: 120 London Wall, London, EC2Y 5ET
Activities: Other business support service activities n.e.c.
Major Shareholder: Kenneth Cordele Griffin
Officers: Generald Albert Beeson [1972] Director/Investments [American]; Shawn Francis Fagan [1969] Director/Attorney [American]

Citadel Europe LLP
Incorporated: 20 October 2008
Net Worth: £186,647,008 *Total Assets:* £186,844,000
Registered Office: 16th Floor, Moor House, 120 London Wall, London, EC2Y 5ET
Officers: Benjamin Amsellem [1978] Member; Andrew Charles Bound [1972] Member; Tio Chaharbaghi [1987] Member; Jonas Benjamin Diedrich [1983] Member; Nico Paul Dil [1981] Member; Hossam Elsokari [1977] Member; Stefan Peter Ivar Ericsson [1972] Member; Christopher David Foster [1978] Member; Joseph Francis Jenkins [1988] Member; George Dennis Klavdianos [1976] Member; Andrew David Quessy [1967] Member; Sean Joseph Salji [1979] Member; Nicholas Edward Wilson [1984] Member

Citadel Securities (Europe) Limited
Incorporated: 25 May 2005
Net Worth: £329,710,848 *Total Assets:* £1,577,947,520
Registered Office: 120 London Wall, London, EC2Y 5ET
Activities: Security dealing on own account
Major Shareholder: Kenneth Cordele Griffin
Officers: Steven William Atkinson [1970] Director/Chief Operating Officer; Matthew Lee Culek [1979] Director [American]; Richard Pike [1967] Director [Irish]; Anthony Ronald Walker [1966] Director; Mark Wright [1966] Director/Risk Officer

Citibank Investments Limited
Incorporated: 3 May 1985
Net Worth: £202,000,000 *Total Assets:* £294,000,000
Registered Office: Citigroup Centre, Canary Wharf, London, E14 5LB
Activities: Activities of head offices
Parent: Citigroup Inc.
Officers: Simon James Cumming, Secretary; Bradley Jay Gans [1960] Director/General Counsel [American]; Peter McCarthy [1957] Director/Chief Administrative Officer, EMEA; David Ian Sharland [1959] Director/Chartered Accountant

Citifinancial Europe Limited
Incorporated: 23 June 1978
Previous: Citifinancial Europe PLC
Net Worth: £42,221,000 *Total Assets:* £107,788,000
Registered Office: Citigroup Centre, Canary Wharf, London, E14 5LB
Activities: Financial intermediation not elsewhere classified
Parent: Citigroup Inc.
Officers: Simon James Cumming, Secretary; Jiten Vasantkumar Mistry [1978] Director/Analyst; David Ian Sharland [1959] Director/Chartered Accountant

Citigroup Capital UK Limited
Incorporated: 16 December 1998
Net Worth: £196,375,008 *Total Assets:* £222,632,992
Registered Office: Citigroup Centre, Canary Wharf, London, E14 5LB
Activities: Activities auxiliary to financial intermediation n.e.c.
Officers: Simon James Cumming, Secretary; Tim Nevard Hassard [1981] Director [American]; Jiten Vasantkumar Mistry [1978] Director/Analyst; Robert Keith Pinniger [1971] Director/Banker [American]

Citigroup Global Markets Europe Finance Limited
Incorporated: 9 December 2003
Net Worth: £237,305,840 *Total Assets:* £237,482,176
Registered Office: Citigroup Centre, Canary Wharf, London, E14 5LB
Activities: Activities of head offices
Parent: Citigroup Inc
Officers: Jill Denise Robson, Secretary; Bradley Jay Gans [1960] Director/General Counsel [American]; David Ian Sharland [1959] Director/Chartered Accountant

Citigroup Global Markets Limited
Incorporated: 21 October 1983 *Employees:* 3,519
Net Worth: £12,195,511,296 *Total Assets:* £287,517,671,424
Registered Office: Citigroup Centre, Canary Wharf, London, E14 5LB
Activities: Security and commodity contracts dealing activities
Parent: Citigroup Inc.
Officers: Jill Denise Robson, Secretary; Cyrus Ardalan [1950] Director/Ex Banker; Leonardo Arduini [1963] Director/EMEA Head of Markets & Securities Services [Italian]; James David Kempster Bardrick [1962] Director/Co Head Corporate & Investment Banking for EMEA; Malcolm Phillip Basing [1956] Director; James Charles Cowles [1955] Director/Head of Markets EMEA; Richard Frank Goulding [1959] Director/Self Employed [Irish]; Peter McCarthy [1957] Director/Chief Administrative Officer EMEA; Diana Taylor [1955] Managing Director [American]

Citigroup Participation Luxembourg Limited
Incorporated: 26 November 2001 *Employees:* 2
Net Worth: £1,009,599,808 *Total Assets:* £1,010,713,792
Registered Office: Citigroup Centre, Canary Wharf, London, E14 5LB
Activities: Financial intermediation not elsewhere classified
Parent: Citigroup International Luxembourg Limited
Officers: Jill Denise Robson, Secretary; Alberta Brusi [1968] Director/Citi Country Officer [Italian]; Anne Emmanuelle David [1965] Director/Accountant [French]

City and Country Properties Limited
Incorporated: 14 July 1959 *Employees:* 28
Net Worth: £217,727,584 *Total Assets:* £316,945,536
Registered Office: Freshwater House, 158-162 Shaftesbury Avenue, London, WC2H 8HR
Activities: Buying and selling of own real estate
Shareholder: Daejan (UK) Limited
Officers: Mark Roy Mason Jenner, Secretary; David Davis [1935] Director/Chartered Accountant; Benzion Schalom Eliezer Freshwater [1948] Director

City Football Group Limited
Incorporated: 10 January 2013 *Employees:* 812
Net Worth: £855,667,968 *Total Assets:* £1,308,027,008
Registered Office: 14th Floor, Regent's Place, 10 Brock Street, London, NW1 3FG
Activities: Activities of other holding companies n.e.c.
Parent: Abu Dhabi United Group for Development & Investment
Officers: Simon Richard Cliff, Secretary; Abdulla Al Khouri [1974] Director/Government Employee [Emirati]; Mohamed Mubarak Al Mazrouei [1977] Director/Civil Servant [Emirati]; Khaldoon Khalifa Al Mubarak [1976] Director/Chairman [Emirati]; Martin Lee Edelman [1941] Director/Strategic Advisor [American]; Alberto Galassi [1964] Director/Chief Executive [Italian]; Ruigang Li [1969] Director/Businessman [Chinese]; John Theodore MacBeath [1956] Director; Simon Pearce [1971] Director

The City of London Investment Trust PLC
Incorporated: 26 September 1891
Net Worth: £1,520,996,992 *Total Assets:* £1,652,814,976
Registered Office: 201 Bishopsgate, London, EC2M 3AE
Activities: Activities of investment trusts
Officers: Simon Charles Barratt [1959] Director/General Counsel; Robert Edward Holmes [1969] Director/Finance [American]; Martin William Howard Morgan [1950] Director/Chief Executive; Philip John Remnant [1954] Director/CD; Samantha Anne Wren [1966] Director

City of London Real Property Company Limited (The)
Incorporated: 11 April 1864
Net Worth: £1,065,611,008 *Total Assets:* £1,090,621,952
Registered Office: 100 Victoria Street, London, SW1E 5JL
Activities: Development of building projects
Parent: LS London Holdings One Limited
Officers: Timothy John Ashby [1962] Director/Solicitor; Robert Montague Noel [1964] Director/Chartered Surveyor

Cityfibre Holdings Limited
Incorporated: 11 January 2011
Net Worth: £11,344,000 *Total Assets:* £106,221,000
Registered Office: 15 Bedford Street, London, WC2E 9HE
Activities: Other telecommunications activities
Parent: Cityfibre Infrastructure Holdings PLC
Officers: Christopher Gawn, Secretary; Mark Grahame Collins [1968] Director; Terence Alan Hart [1965] Director; William Gregory Mesch [1960] Director [Irish/American]

Cityfibre Infrastructure Holdings Limited
Incorporated: 13 November 2013 *Employees:* 189
Previous: Cityfibre Infrastructure Holdings PLC
Net Worth: £287,689,984 *Total Assets:* £384,441,984
Registered Office: 15 Bedford Street, London, WC2E 9HE
Activities: Other telecommunications activities
Parent: Connect Infrastructure Bidco Limited
Officers: Christopher Gawn, Secretary; Mark Grahame Collins [1968] Director; Terence Alan Hart [1965] Director; William Gregory Mesch [1960] Director [Irish/American]

Cityfibre Limited
Incorporated: 2 September 2015
Net Worth: £59,286,000 *Total Assets:* £182,655,008
Registered Office: 15 Bedford Street, London, WC2E 9HE
Activities: Other telecommunications activities
Parent: Cityfibre Networks Limited
Officers: Christopher Leslie Gawn, Secretary; Mark Grahame Collins [1968] Director; Terence Alan Hart [1965] Director; William Gregory Mesch [1960] Director [Irish/American]

Citywide Trading (UK) Limited
Incorporated: 15 May 2008
Net Worth: £87,494 *Total Assets:* £188,416,976
Registered Office: Dalton House, 60 Windsor Avenue, Wimbledon, London, SW19 2RR
Activities: Wholesale of wood, construction materials and sanitary equipment
Major Shareholder: Diane Patricia Sanger
Officers: Diane Patricia Sanger [1960] Director

Civica Group Limited
Incorporated: 18 November 2003 *Employees:* 4
Net Worth: £112,259,000 *Total Assets:* £177,324,992
Registered Office: Southbank Central, 30 Stamford Street, London, SE1 9LQ
Activities: Other information technology service activities
Parent: Cornwall Bidco Limited
Officers: Michael Stoddard, Secretary/Director; Gavin Leigh [1972] Commercial Director; Phillip David Rowland [1971] Director; Michael Stoddard [1957] Director; Wayne Andrew Story [1961] Director

Civica Holdings Limited
Incorporated: 13 May 1987 *Employees:* 5
Net Worth: £60,011,000 *Total Assets:* £122,956,000
Registered Office: Southbank Central, 30 Stamford Street, London, SE1 9LQ
Activities: Activities of head offices
Parent: Civica Group Limited
Officers: Michael Stoddard, Secretary/Accountant; Gavin Leigh [1972] Commercial Director; Phillip David Rowland [1971] Director; Michael Stoddard [1957] Director/Accountant; Wayne Andrew Story [1961] Director

Civica UK Limited
Incorporated: 14 April 1982 *Employees:* 2,242
Net Worth: £114,084,000 *Total Assets:* £372,212,000
Registered Office: Southbank Central, 30 Stamford Street, London, SE1 9LQ
Activities: Other information technology service activities
Parent: Civica Holdings Limited
Officers: Michael Stoddard, Secretary/Director; Gary David Bell [1965] Director; Simon Richard Downing [1965] Director; Jeffrey Hewitt [1971] Director; John William Hood [1968] Director; Anthony William Hughes [1969] Director; Gavin Leigh [1972] Commercial Director; William James Loughrey [1961] Director; David Philip Roots [1957] Director; Phillip David Rowland [1971] Director; Michael Stoddard [1957] Director/Accountant; Wayne Andrew Story [1961] Director; Stephen Mark Thorn [1969] Director

CK William Midco 2 Limited
Incorporated: 3 January 2017
Net Worth: £765,129,088 *Total Assets:* £765,137,536
Registered Office: c/o Norose Company Secretarial Service Ltd, 3 More London Riverside, London, SE1 2AQ
Activities: Other business support service activities n.e.c.
Parent: CKI Gas Infrastructure Limited
Officers: Graham Winston Edwards [1954] Director/Chief Executive; Guy Butterworth Ellis [1961] Director; Mark John Horsley [1959] Director/Chief Executive Officer; Andrew John Hunter [1958] Director; Edmond Tak Chuen IP [1952] Director [Chinese]; Hing Lam Kam [1946] Director [Chinese]; Jonathan Theodore Miller [1971] Director

CK William Midco 3 Limited
Incorporated: 3 January 2017
Net Worth: £382,560,352 *Total Assets:* £382,568,768
Registered Office: c/o Norose Company Secretarial Service Ltd, 3 More London Riverside, London, SE1 2AQ
Activities: Other business support service activities n.e.c.
Parent: PAH Gas Infrastructure Limited
Officers: Loi Shun Chan [1962] Director [Chinese]; Guy Butterworth Ellis [1961] Director; Mark John Horsley [1959] Director/Chief Executive Officer; Jonathan Theodore Miller [1971] Director; Richard John Roberts [1964] Director/Chartered Accountant (Retired); Charles Chao Chung Tsai [1957] Director [Canadian]; Chi Tin Wan [1950] Director [Australian]

CKH Gas Infrastructure Limited
Incorporated: 22 May 2014
Net Worth: £283,921,984 *Total Assets:* £398,563,008
Registered Office: 3 More London Riverside, London, SE1 2AQ
Activities: Other business support service activities n.e.c.
Officers: Guy Butterworth Ellis [1961] Director; Mark John Horsley [1959] Director/Chief Executive Officer; Hing Lam Kam [1946] Director [Chinese]; Tzar Kuoi Victor Li [1964] Director [Chinese]; Jonathan Theodore Miller [1971] Director

CKI Gas Infrastructure Limited
Incorporated: 9 April 2014 *Employees:* 7
Net Worth: £1,408,802,944 *Total Assets:* £2,657,058,048
Registered Office: 3 More London Riverside, London, SE1 2AQ
Activities: Activities of other holding companies n.e.c.
Officers: Graham Winston Edwards [1954] Director/Chief Executive; Guy Butterworth Ellis [1961] Director; Mark John Horsley [1959] Director/Chief Executive Officer; Andrew John Hunter [1958] Director; Tak Chuen Edmond IP [1952] Director [Chinese]; Hing Lam Kam [1946] Director [Chinese]; Jonathan Theodore Miller [1971] Director

CKI Number 1 Limited
Incorporated: 15 June 2010
Net Worth: £862,156,992 *Total Assets:* £884,486,016
Registered Office: Newington House, 237 Southwark Bridge Road, London, SE1 6NP
Activities: Activities of head offices
Parent: Newington House
Officers: Andrew Charles Pace, Secretary; Andrew John Hunter [1958] Director; Edmond Tak Chuen IP [1952] Director [Chinese]; Hing Lam Kam [1946] Director [Chinese]; Duncan Nicholas MacRae [1970] Director; Basil Scarsella [1955] Director [Australian]

CKI Number 2 Limited
Incorporated: 14 June 2010
Net Worth: £941,014,016 *Total Assets:* £941,014,016
Registered Office: Newington House, 237 Southwark Bridge Road, London, SE1 6NP
Activities: Activities of head offices
Parent: CKI Number 3 Limited
Officers: Andrew Charles Pace, Secretary; Andrew John Hunter [1958] Director; Edmond Tak Chuen IP [1952] Director [Chinese]; Hing Lam Kam [1946] Director [Chinese]; Duncan Nicholas MacRae [1970] Director; Basil Scarsella [1955] Director [Australian]

CKI Number 3 Limited
Incorporated: 11 June 2010
Net Worth: £710,249,024 *Total Assets:* £1,036,926,016
Registered Office: Newington House, 237 Southwark Bridge Road, London, SE1 6NP
Activities: Activities of head offices
Officers: Andrew Charles Pace, Secretary; Andrew John Hunter [1958] Director; Edmond Tak Chuen IP [1952] Director [Chinese]; Hing Lam Kam [1946] Director [Chinese]; Duncan Nicholas MacRae [1970] Director; Basil Scarsella [1955] Director [Australian]

CL Intermediate (UK) Limited
Incorporated: 19 September 2012
Net Worth: £440,240,480 *Total Assets:* £890,522,560
Registered Office: 60 Fenchurch Street, London, EC3M 4AD
Activities: Activities of other holding companies n.e.c.
Officers: Jonathan Sutton, Secretary; Domenick C. di Cicco [1963] Director [American]; Henry Clay Lyons [1963] Director/Finance [American]; Meera Odedra [1960] Finance Director; Stewart Craig Steel [1961] Director; Jonathan Sutton [1969] Finance Director

Claranet Group Limited
Incorporated: 20 July 2000 *Employees:* 1,841
Net Worth: £6,300,000 *Total Assets:* £373,600,000
Registered Office: 21 Southampton Row, London, WC1B 5HA
Activities: Other information technology service activities
Officers: Michel Robert, Secretary; Guillaume Jacques David Benhamou [1981] Director [French]; Nigel Robert Fairhurst [1963] Director/Chartered Accountant; Charles Nasser [1969] Director; Michel Francois Robert [1965] Director/MD [French]

Claranet Limited
Incorporated: 30 January 1996 *Employees:* 499
Net Worth: £67,300,000 *Total Assets:* £128,200,000
Registered Office: 21 Southampton Row, London, WC1B 5HA
Activities: Other information technology service activities
Officers: Michel Robert, Secretary; Nigel Robert Fairhurst [1963] Director; Charles Nasser [1969] Director; Michel Francois Robert [1965] Managing Director [French]

Claridge's Hotel Holdings Limited
Incorporated: 12 November 1998
Net Worth Deficit: £598,000 *Total Assets:* £419,864,000
Registered Office: 41-43 Brook Street, Mayfair, London, W1K 4HJ
Activities: Activities of head offices
Parent: MHG Senior Borrower Limited
Officers: Ziyad Clot [1977] Director/General Counsel [French]; Liam Cunningham [1958] Director [Irish]; Michele Faissola [1968] Director [Italian]

Claridge's Hotel Limited
Incorporated: 28 May 1889 *Employees:* 535
Net Worth: £229,380,992 *Total Assets:* £271,292,992
Registered Office: 41-43 Brook Street, Mayfair, London, W1K 4HJ
Activities: Hotels and similar accommodation
Parent: Claridge's Hotel Holdings Limited
Officers: Liam Cunningham [1958] Director [Irish]; Michele Faissola [1968] Director [Italian]; Marc Socker [1976] Director

Clarion Acquisition Limited
Incorporated: 12 February 2008
Net Worth: £7,095,000 *Total Assets:* £191,635,008
Registered Office: Bedford House, 69-79 Fulham High Street, London, SW6 3JW
Activities: Activities of head offices
Parent: Clarion UK Midco Limited
Officers: Richard Johnson [1963] Director; Simon Reed Kimble [1963] Director; Russell Stephen Wilcox [1971] Director

Clarion Events Limited
Incorporated: 1 June 1948 *Employees:* 258
Net Worth: £20,395,000 *Total Assets:* £462,028,992
Registered Office: Bedford House, Fulham High Street, London, SW6 3JW
Activities: Activities of exhibition and fair organisers
Officers: Monica Pahwa, Secretary; Lisa Amanda Hannant [1970] Director; Richard Johnson [1963] Director; Simon Reed Kimble [1963] Director; Russell Stephen Wilcox [1971] Director

Clarion Treasury Limited
Incorporated: 1 March 2007
Previous: Circle Anglia Treasury Limited
Net Worth: £177,000 *Total Assets:* £3,435,504,128
Registered Office: Level 6, More London Place, Tooley Street, London, SE1 2DA
Activities: Financial management
Officers: Louise Hyde, Secretary; Tania Alexandra Teofana Beatrice Brisby [1962] Director; Mark Hattersley [1966] Director/Chief Financial Officer; Kwok Chung Liu [1973] Director/Treasurer; Aruna Anand Mehta [1962] Director/Banker; Clare Miller [1962] Director/Chief Executive; Maxim Lewis Sinclair [1958] Director

Clarion UK Holdco Limited
Incorporated: 12 February 2008
Net Worth: £105,135,000 *Total Assets:* £105,135,000
Registered Office: Bedford House, 69-79 Fulham High Street, London, SW6 3JW
Activities: Activities of head offices
Parent: Clarion UK Topco Limited
Officers: Richard Johnson [1963] Director; Simon Reed Kimble [1963] Director; Russell Stephen Wilcox [1971] Director

Clarion UK Midco Limited
Incorporated: 12 February 2008
Net Worth: £111,555,000 *Total Assets:* £136,423,008
Registered Office: Bedford House, 69-79 Fulham High Street, London, SW6 3JW
Activities: Activities of head offices
Parent: Clarion UK Holdco Limited
Officers: Richard Johnson [1963] Director; Simon Reed Kimble [1963] Director; Russell Stephen Wilcox [1971] Director

Clarion UK Topco Limited
Incorporated: 12 February 2008
Net Worth Deficit: £28,655,000 *Total Assets:* £105,558,000
Registered Office: Bedford House, 69-79 Fulham High Street, London, SW6 3JW
Activities: Activities of head offices
Parent: PSPA Limited
Officers: Richard Johnson [1963] Director; Simon Reed Kimble [1963] Director; Russell Stephen Wilcox [1971] Director

T Clarke Public Limited Company
Incorporated: 23 December 1911 *Employees:* 1,348
Net Worth: £16,400,000 *Total Assets:* £144,900,000
Registered Office: 45 Moorfields, London, EC2Y 9AE
Activities: Electrical installation
Officers: David James Lanchester, Secretary; Michael Crowder [1964] Director/Electrical Engineer; Louise Dier [1959] Director; Mark Lawrence [1967] Director/Electrical Engineer; Peter John Maskell [1957] Director; Iain Colquhoun McCusker [1952] Director/Accountant; Trevor John Mitchell [1960] Director/Accountant; Michael Timothy Robson [1960] Director/Chartered Accountant

Clarkson PLC
Incorporated: 12 November 1974 *Employees:* 1,435
Net Worth: £419,700,000 *Total Assets:* £585,299,968
Registered Office: Commodity Quay, St Katharine Docks, London, E1W 1BF
Activities: Activities of head offices
Officers: Rachel Louise Spencer, Secretary; Peter Anker [1957] Director/Shipbroker [Norwegian]; Peter George Backhouse [1951] Director; Andrew Leigh Case [1966] Director/Shipbroker; Marie-Louise Clayton [1960] Director; James Hughes-Hallett [1949] Director; Timothy John Miller [1957] Director; Birger Nergaard [1951] Director [Norwegian]; William Gennydd Thomas [1959] Director; Jeffrey David Woyda [1962] Director

Clarusone Sourcing Services LLP
Incorporated: 16 May 2016
Net Worth: £252,344,688 *Total Assets:* £255,661,328
Registered Office: TMF Corporate Administration Services Limited, 5th Floor, 6 St Andrew Street, London, EC4A 3AE

Classboss Limited
Incorporated: 8 September 1997
Net Worth: £1,146,635,008 *Total Assets:* £1,146,635,008
Registered Office: The Battleship Building, 179 Harrow Road, London, W2 6NB
Activities: Activities of other holding companies n.e.c.
Parent: Virgin UK Holdings Limited
Officers: Barry Alexander Ralph Gerrard, Secretary; Robert Pieter Blok [1976] Director/Lawyer; Amy Stirling [1969] Director; Ian Philip Woods [1974] Director/Solicitor

Clavis Securities PLC
Incorporated: 11 April 2006
Net Worth: £2,668,000 *Total Assets:* £209,260,992
Registered Office: 35 Great St Helens, London, EC3A 6AP
Activities: Financial intermediation not elsewhere classified
Parent: Intertrust Corporate Services Limited
Officers: Paivi Helena Whitaker [1963] Director/Chartered Secretary [Finnish]

CLDN UK Limited
Incorporated: 23 May 2014 *Employees:* 1
Net Worth: £135,481,536 *Total Assets:* £149,799,936
Registered Office: 2nd Floor, 130 Shaftesbury Avenue, London, W1D 5EU
Activities: Agents involved in the sale of a variety of goods
Officers: Benjamin David Dove-Seymour [1977] Director; Patricia Ann Grout [1945] Director/Administrative Assistant

Clear Channel Holdings Limited
Incorporated: 18 May 1998
Net Worth: £108,356,000 *Total Assets:* £696,900,992
Registered Office: 33 Golden Square, London, W1F 9JT
Activities: Advertising agencies
Parent: Clear Channel International Holdings B.V.
Officers: Adam Tow, Secretary; Christopher William Eccleshare [1955] Director/Chief Executive Officer; Michael Peter Saunter [1969] Director/Chief Financial Officer; Adam Paul Raymond Tow [1967] Director/General Counsel

Clear Channel International Limited
Incorporated: 6 January 1936 *Employees:* 112
Net Worth: £641,977,984 *Total Assets:* £884,860,032
Registered Office: 33 Golden Square, London, W1F 9JT
Activities: Advertising agencies
Parent: Clear Channel Holdings Limited
Officers: Adam Tow, Secretary; Christopher William Eccleshare [1955] Director/Chief Executive Officer; Michael Peter Saunter [1969] Director/Chief Financial Officer; Adam Paul Raymond Tow [1967] Director/General Counsel

Clear Channel Overseas Limited
Incorporated: 3 August 1979
Net Worth: £193,200,000 *Total Assets:* £318,904,992
Registered Office: 33 Golden Square, London, W1F 9JT
Activities: Advertising agencies
Parent: Clear Channel International Limited
Officers: Adam Tow, Secretary; Christopher William Eccleshare [1955] Director/Chief Executive Officer; Michael Peter Saunter [1969] Director/Chief Financial Officer; Adam Paul Raymond Tow [1967] Director/General Counsel

Clear Channel UK Limited
Incorporated: 24 March 1969 *Employees:* 626
Net Worth: £130,680,000 *Total Assets:* £226,330,000
Registered Office: 33 Golden Square, London, W1F 9JT
Activities: Advertising agencies
Parent: Clear Channel International Limited
Officers: Byron Kee Chye Hoo, Secretary; Justin Malcolm Brian Cochrane [1972] Director of Finance; Byron Kee Chye Hoo [1970] Director/Chief Financial Officer; Chris Pelekanou [1964] Commercial Director; Michael Peter Saunter [1969] Director; Mark Webb [1962] Director

Clearmoon Commercial Ltd
Incorporated: 24 January 2006
Net Worth: £109,741,800 *Total Assets:* £109,754,976
Registered Office: 4th Floor, 1 Knightrider Court, London, EC4V 5BJ
Activities: Activities of other holding companies n.e.c.
Officers: Colin Richard Walker [1951] Director/Businessman

Clearstone Holdings (International) Ltd
Incorporated: 4 May 2011
Net Worth: £1,189,163,904 *Total Assets:* £2,436,870,400
Registered Office: 21 Holborn Viaduct, London, EC1A 2DY
Activities: Technical testing and analysis
Parent: Labcorp UK Holdings, Ltd.
Officers: Sandra Dillard Van Der Vaart, Secretary; Floyd Samuel Eberts III [1959] Director/President [American]; Glenn Andrew Eisenberg [1961] Director/Chief Financial Officer [American]; Robert Stewart Pringle [1964] Director

CLEF Holdings Limited
Incorporated: 2 April 2007
Net Worth Deficit: £90,386,400 *Total Assets:* £3,385,960,192
Registered Office: Third Floor, 1 King's Arms Yard, London, EC2R 7AF
Activities: Other business support service activities n.e.c.
Parent: Wilmington Trust SP Services (London) Limited
Officers: Daniel Jonathan Wynne [1970] Director

Cleveland Clinic UK Holdings Ltd
Incorporated: 7 October 2015 *Employees:* 3
Net Worth: £124,986,000 *Total Assets:* £404,692,000
Registered Office: Suite 1, 3rd Floor, 11-12 St James's Square, London, SW1Y 4LB
Activities: Activities of other holding companies n.e.c.
Officers: Dr Brian Donley [1963] Director/CEO of CCL Ltd [American]; Steven Glass [1966] Director/CFO and Treasurer [American]; William Peacock [1959] Director/Chief of Operations [American]; David Rowan [1953] Director/Chief Legal Officer [American]

CLH Pipeline System (CLH-PS) Ltd
Incorporated: 18 March 2015 *Employees:* 259
Net Worth: £93,821,904 *Total Assets:* £149,832,480
Registered Office: 69 Wilson Street, London, EC2A 2BB
Activities: Transport via pipeline
Parent: CLH International UK Limited
Officers: Marie Elizabeth Edwards, Secretary; Juan Rafael Bonilla Abascal [1959] Director/Chairman [Spanish]; Andrew Marco Brown [1963] Director; Ignacio Jose Casajus Lopez [1976] Director/Chief Executive Officer [Spanish]; Clive William Condie [1960] Director; Stephen David Land [1969] Director/Engineer

Clifford Chance International LLP
Incorporated: 17 December 2007 *Employees:* 180
Net Worth: £103,080,344 *Total Assets:* £136,927,872
Registered Office: 10 Upper Bank Street, London, E14 5JJ
Officers: David Harkness [1963] Member; Christopher Courtenay Perrin [1956] Member; Terence Foo [1973] LLP Member; Maggie Hoi Yan Lo [1976] LLP Member; Glen Yun Ma [1978] LLP Member; Jiahua NI [1980] LLP Member; Jean Puay Jin Thio [1974] LLP Member; Tim Yanfeng Wang [1974] LLP Member; Ying Zhang White [1970] LLP Member

Clifford Chance LLP
Incorporated: 1 November 2006 *Employees:* 6,008
Net Worth: £246,000,000 *Total Assets:* £1,220,000,000
Registered Office: 10 Upper Bank Street, London, E14 5JJ
Officers: David Harkness [1963] Member; Matthew Robert Layton [1961] Member; Christopher Courtenay Perrin [1956] Member; Julian Anthony Acratopulo [1970] LLP Member; Charles James Adams [1968] LLP Member; Howard Bryan Adler [1960] LLP Member; Jutta Aichele [1961] LLP Member; Pieter Matthijs Alexander [1963] LLP Member; Jaime Rafael Almenar Belenguer [1972] LLP Member; Luis Antonio Alonso [1979] LLP Member; Javier Amantegui [1965] LLP Member; Thierry Dominique Pierre Arachtingi [1967] LLP Member; Lee Av Askenazi [1976] LLP Member; Maria Yolanda Azanza [1972] LLP Member; Samir Azzouzi Maanan [1979] LLP Member; Gianluca Giuseppe Bacchiocchi [1971] LLP Member; Carmen Nadia Badea [1972] LLP Member; Mircea Daniel Badea [1975] LLP Member; Alexander Bafi [1965] LLP Member; Marcin Bartnicki [1977] LLP Member; Christopher John Bates [1956] LLP Member; Michael David Bates [1967] LLP Member; Thomas Baudesson [1959] LLP Member; Spencer Aaron Baylin [1969] LLP Member; Lori Ann Bean [1969] LLP Member; Hans Bernard Wim Beerlage [1972] LLP Member; Stefan Behrens [1962] LLP Member; Marc Benzler [1968] LLP Member; Marie-Emmanuelle Berard [1975] LLP Member; Jeffrey Daniel Berman [1958] LLP Member; Joshua Glen Berman [1970] LLP Member; Jay Lawrence Bernstein [1959] LLP Member; Marc Besen [1971] LLP Member; Roger Simon Melliship Best [1955] LLP Member; Patrick Curt Biagosch [1965] LLP Member; David John Bickerton [1964] LLP Member; Charles-Henri Boeringer [1976] LLP Member; Fabian Bohm [1974] LLP Member; James Benjamin Bole [1979] LLP Member; Lucio Bonavitacola [1972] LLP Member; Francois-Robert Alban Guy Bonteil [1963] LLP Member; Gary David Boss [1966] LLP Member; James Roy Boswell [1977] LLP Member; Josef Brinkhaus [1960] LLP Member; Generald David Brinton [1960] LLP Member; Gary Alan Brooks [1968] LLP Member; Cedric Burford [1970] LLP Member; Clare Burgess [1979] LLP Member; Jeff Edward Butler [1969] LLP Member; James Sebastian Butters [1967] LLP Member; Jose Antonio Cainzos [1960] LLP Member; Gareth Richard Camp [1977] LLP Member; Simonetta Candela [1968] LLP Member; Anthony Mathias Candido [1969] LLP Member; Aline Virginie Cardin [1968] LLP Member; Andrew John Carnegie [1962] LLP Member; Paul Athol Carrington [1980] LLP Member; Adrian David Cartwright [1966] LLP Member; Helen Louise Carty [1972] LLP Member; Richard Stephen Catalano [1965] LLP Member; Claudio Fulvio Franco Cerabolini [1975] LLP Member; Jane Christina Cheong Tung Sing [1973] LLP Member; Per Benjamin Chilstrom [1975] LLP Member; Marcin Cieminski [1977] LLP Member; Julia Margaret Clarke [1962] LLP Member; Timothy Raymond Cleary [1978] LLP Member; Leonard Irving William Cleland [1968] LLP Member; Katherine Ann Coates [1959] LLP Member; Andrew Jervis Nicholas Coats [1964] LLP Member; Charles Richard Allan Cochrane [1969] LLP Member; Adrian Leon Cohen [1963] LLP Member; Evan Jay Cohen [1963] LLP Member; Fabrice Cohen [1970] LLP Member; Ness Maurice Cohen [1971] LLP Member; Xavier Comaills [1970] LLP Member; Carlos Manuel Conceicao [1964] LLP Member; Clifford Cone [1980] LLP Member; Lee Dennis Coney [1972] LLP Member; Jeremy Adrian Connick [1963] LLP Member; John William Connolly III [1960] LLP Member; Alexander Lee Cook [1970] LLP Member; Catherine Stacey Cook [1970] LLP Member; Timothy Cornell [1970] LLP Member; Joseph Cosentino [1970] LLP Member; Franck Coudert [1974] LLP Member; Alexandre Couturier [1977] LLP Member; Andrew James Crook [1975] LLP Member; Gregory George Crookes [1969] LLP Member; Michael Desmond Crossan [1970] LLP Member; Robert Thomas Ferguson Crothers [1975] LLP Member; Simon David Crown [1973] LLP Member; Jose Manuel Cuenca [1970] LLP Member; Mark Andrew Currell [1973] LLP Member; Stephen Marc Curtis [1968] LLP Member; Lounia Zoe Czupper [1973] LLP Member; Thibaud D'Ales [1976] LLP Member; Henri D'Ursel [1972] LLP Member; Peter Carl Dahlen [1976] LLP Member; Michael Dakin [1973] LLP Member; Reinhard Dammann [1959] LLP Member

Clifford Chance London Limited
Incorporated: 23 May 1997 *Employees:* 1,721
Net Worth Deficit: £141,723,008 *Total Assets:* £174,024,992
Registered Office: 10 Upper Bank Street, London, E14 5JJ
Activities: Other business support service activities n.e.c.
Parent: Mithras Limited
Officers: Michael David Bates [1967] Director/Solicitor; Helen Louise Carty [1972] Director/Solicitor; David Harkness [1963] Director/Solicitor; Clare Elizabeth Hoxey [1974] Director/Solicitor; Matthew Robert Layton [1961] Director/Solicitor; Emma Louise Matebalavu [1975] Director/Solicitor; Christopher Courtenay Perrin [1956] Director/Solicitor; Malcolm John Sweeting [1957] Director/Solicitor

Cliffrange Limited
Incorporated: 2 December 1985
Net Worth: £230,272,992 *Total Assets:* £679,932,992
Registered Office: 33 Holborn, London, EC1N 2HT
Activities: Financial intermediation not elsewhere classified
Parent: Home Retail Group (UK) Limited
Officers: Timothy Fallowfield, Secretary; Claire Louise Catlin [1980] Director

Close Asset Management Holdings Limited
Incorporated: 19 May 1999 *Employees:* 647
Net Worth: £59,753,000 *Total Assets:* £152,844,000
Registered Office: 10 Crown Place, London, EC2A 4FT
Activities: Activities of head offices
Parent: Close Brothers Holdings Limited
Officers: Jessica Abigail Lewis, Secretary; Martin Andrew [1963] Director; Preben Prebensen [1956] Director/Chairman; Iain Paul Wallace [1969] Director

Close Brothers Finance PLC
Incorporated: 14 November 2001
Net Worth: £12,502 *Total Assets:* £660,564,928
Registered Office: 10 Crown Place, London, EC2A 4FT
Activities: Financial intermediation not elsewhere classified
Parent: Close Brothers Limited
Officers: John Edward Hudspith, Secretary; Theovinder Chatha [1980] Finance Director; Malcolm Paul Hook [1960] Director; Adrian John Sainsbury [1968] Director/Banker

Close Brothers Group PLC
Incorporated: 3 June 1953
Net Worth: £1,349,500,032 *Total Assets:* £10,251,799,552
Registered Office: 10 Crown Place, London, EC2A 4FT
Activities: Activities of head offices
Officers: Robert George Alexander Dunn, Secretary; Michael Nicholas Biggs [1952] Director; Oliver Roebling Panton Corbett [1965] Director/Chartered Accountant; Peter Bernard Duffy [1966] Director; Geoffrey Michael Thomas Howe [1949] Director; Margaret Lesley Jones [1954] Director; Elizabeth Anne Lee [1961] Director/Solicitor; Bridget Ann MacAskill [1948] Director; Michael Bartlett Morgan [1965] Director; Preben Prebensen [1956] Director/Chief Executive

Close Brothers Holdings Limited
Incorporated: 1 May 2008
Net Worth: £419,371,008 *Total Assets:* £652,102,976
Registered Office: 10 Crown Place, London, EC2A 4FT
Activities: Activities of head offices
Parent: Close Brothers Group PLC
Officers: Theovinder Chatha [1980] Finance Director; Elizabeth Anne Lee [1961] Director/Solicitor

Close Brothers Limited
Incorporated: 9 February 1924 *Employees:* 63
Net Worth: £1,117,299,968 *Total Assets:* £9,396,200,448
Registered Office: 10 Crown Place, London, EC2A 4FT
Activities: Financial intermediation not elsewhere classified
Parent: Close Brothers Holdings Limited
Officers: John Hudspith, Secretary; Michael Nicholas Biggs [1952] Director; Oliver Roebling Panton Corbett [1965] Director/Chartered Accountant; Peter Bernard Duffy [1966] Director; Geoffrey Michael Thomas Howe [1949] Director; Margaret Lesley Jones [1954] Director; Elizabeth Anne Lee [1961] Director/Solicitor; Bridget Ann MacAskill [1948] Director; Michael Bartlett Morgan [1965] Director; Preben Prebensen [1956] Director/Chief Executive; Adrian John Sainsbury [1968] Director/Banker

Close Invoice Finance Limited
Incorporated: 24 July 1968 *Employees:* 165
Net Worth: £7,473,548 *Total Assets:* £564,080,896
Registered Office: 10 Crown Place, London, EC2A 4FT
Activities: Financial intermediation not elsewhere classified
Parent: Close Brothers Limited
Officers: Jacqueline Mary Brown [1969] Director/Chief Operating Officer; Ciaran Gerard McAreavey [1968] Director/Banker; Adrian John Sainsbury [1968] Director/Banker; Megduth Sooknah [1976] Finance Director; Ian Michael Steward [1961] Director; David Peter Thomson [1963] Director

Close PF Funding I Limited
Incorporated: 5 January 2010
Net Worth: £31,909 *Total Assets:* £415,344,288
Registered Office: Level 37, 25 Canada Square, London, E14 5LQ
Activities: Other business support service activities n.e.c.
Parent: CSC Corporate Services (UK) Limited
Officers: John Paul Nowacki [1979] Director

Closerstill Acquisitions Limited
Incorporated: 2 March 2015 *Employees:* 199
Net Worth Deficit: £19,840,140 *Total Assets:* £147,109,424
Registered Office: Exhibition House, Addison Bridge Place, London, W14 8XP
Activities: Other business support service activities n.e.c.
Parent: Closerstill Finance Limited
Officers: Suzanne King, Secretary; Suzanne Jane King [1963] Director; Philip James Nelson [1964] Director; Phil William Soar [1947] Director; Michael James Westcott [1966] Director

Closerstill Finance Limited
Incorporated: 2 March 2015 *Employees:* 5
Net Worth Deficit: £33,690,744 *Total Assets:* £115,940,112
Registered Office: Exhibition House, Addison Bridge Place, London, W14 8XP
Activities: Other business support service activities n.e.c.
Parent: Closerstill Group Limited
Officers: Suzanne King, Secretary; Suzanne Jane King [1963] Director; Philip James Nelson [1964] Director; Phil William Soar [1947] Director; Michael James Westcott [1966] Director

Closerstill Media Holdings Limited
Incorporated: 2 March 2015 *Employees:* 199
Previous: Closerstill Group Limited
Net Worth Deficit: £54,108,056 *Total Assets:* £147,109,504
Registered Office: Exhibition House, Addison Bridge Place, London, W14 8XP
Activities: Other business support service activities n.e.c.
Officers: Suzanne King, Secretary; Suzanne Jane King [1963] Director; Alexia Maycock [1974] Marketing Director; Phil Nelson [1964] Director/Business Executive; David John Packford [1961] Director; Phil Soar [1947] Director/Businessman; Michael James Westcott [1966] Director/Businessman

Clothworkers' Foundation (The)
Incorporated: 18 July 1977
Net Worth: £198,246,448 *Total Assets:* £202,635,632
Registered Office: Clothworkers' Hall, Dunster Court, Mincing Lane, London, EC3R 7AH
Activities: Activities of other membership organisations n.e.c.
Officers: Jocelyn Stuart-Grumbar, Secretary; Andrew Charles Blessley [1951] Director/Retired; Dr Carolyn Jane Boulter [1945] Director/Retired; John Ashley Coombe-Tennant [1957] Director; Joanna Louise Sayer Dodd [1962] Director/PR Consultant; Melville Ellis Vernon Haggard [1949] Director/Corporate Financier; Nick Horne [1960] Director/Hotel Proprietor; Michael William Jarvis [1951] Director/Chartered Accountant; Anne Elizabeth Luttman-Johnson [1962] Director/Client Support Manager; Alexander John Nelson [1961] Director/Transport; Susanna Priestley O'Leary [1967] Director/Solicitor; Sir Jonathan Francis Portal [1953] Director/Accountant; Dr Lucy Elisabeth Rawson [1964] Director/GP; Hanif Virji [1963] Director/Consultant; John Wake [1953] Director/Investment Banker

Cloudreach Acquisitions Limited
Incorporated: 30 January 2017 *Employees:* 274
Net Worth: £71,688,000 *Total Assets:* £108,571,000
Registered Office: 3rd Floor, Saffron House, Kirby Street, London, EC1N 8TS
Activities: Activities of other holding companies n.e.c.
Officers: Ruth Orpwood, Secretary; Matthew Millar Gordon [1974] Director/Chief Financial Officer; Aaron Michael Painter [1981] Director/Chief Executive Officer [American]

CLS Holdings PLC
Incorporated: 14 May 1992 *Employees:* 190
Net Worth: £1,026,499,968 *Total Assets:* £2,157,400,064
Registered Office: 16 Tinworth Street, London, SE11 5AL
Activities: Activities of head offices
Officers: David Francis Fuller, Secretary; Malcolm Charles Cooper [1959] Group Tax & Treasury Director; Elizabeth Frida Edwards [1957] Director/Chartered Surveyor; Christopher Patrick Jarvis [1955] Director/Chartered Surveyor; Erik Henry Klotz [1944] Director/Executive Vice Chairman [Swedish]; Bengt Filip Mortstedt [1948] Director [Swedish]; Sten Ake Mortstedt [1940] Director [Swedish]; Anna Linnea Kristina Seeley [1971] Director [Swedish]; Lennart Arne Sten [1959] Director [Swedish]; John Howard Whiteley [1958] Director/Chief Financial Officer; Fredrik Jonas Widlund [1968] Director/Chief Executive Officer [Swedish]

CLS One Limited
Incorporated: 28 October 1998
Net Worth: £149,846,256 *Total Assets:* £150,046,208
Registered Office: 16 Tinworth Street, London, SE11 5AL
Activities: Activities of other holding companies n.e.c.
Parent: CLS Holdings PLC
Officers: David Francis Fuller, Secretary; Erik Henry Klotz [1944] Director/Executive Vice Chairman [Swedish]; Alain Gustave Paul Millet [1968] Director/Group Treasurer [French]; John Howard Whiteley [1958] Director/Chief Financial Officer; Fredrik Jonas Widlund [1968] Director [Swedish]; Simon Laborda Wigzell [1968] Director

CLS Spring Gardens Limited
Incorporated: 4 December 2014
Net Worth: £49,863,180 *Total Assets:* £164,513,184
Registered Office: 16 Tinworth Street, London, SE11 5AL
Activities: Other letting and operating of own or leased real estate
Parent: CLS Holdings PLC
Officers: David Francis Fuller, Secretary; Erik Henry Klotz [1944] Director [Swedish]; Alain Gustave Paul Millet [1968] Director [French]; John Howard Whiteley [1958] Director; Fredrik Jonas Widlund [1968] Director [Swedish]; Simon Laborda Wigzell [1968] Director

CLS UK Intermediate Holdings Ltd.
Incorporated: 19 June 1997 *Employees:* 45
Net Worth: £254,386,000 *Total Assets:* £259,032,992
Registered Office: Exchange Tower, 1 Harbour Exchange Square, London, E14 9GE
Activities: Other business support service activities n.e.c.
Officers: Michael Preston, Secretary; Javid Canteenwala [1970] Director/Group Financial Controller; John Francis Hagon [1966] Director/Banker; Michael David Lawrence [1979] Managing Director, Global CAO, Foreign Exchange; Gilbert Marcel Lichter [1951] Director [Luxembourger]; William Nicholas Stenning [1969] Director

CLS UK Properties PLC
Incorporated: 29 June 2012 *Employees:* 5
Net Worth: £80,902,120 *Total Assets:* £152,427,376
Registered Office: 16 Tinworth Street, London, SE11 5AL
Activities: Dormant company
Parent: CLS Holdings PLC
Officers: David Francis Fuller, Secretary; Erik Henry Klotz [1944] Director/Executive Vice Chairman [Swedish]; Alain Gustave Paul Millet [1968] Director/Group Treasurer [French]; John Howard Whiteley [1958] Director/Chief Financial Officer; Fredrik Jonas Widlund [1968] Director [Swedish]; Simon Laborda Wigzell [1968] Director

CLSA (UK)
Incorporated: 19 April 1971 *Employees:* 50
Net Worth: £20,665,000 *Total Assets:* £347,772,992
Registered Office: 12th Floor, Moor House, 120 London Wall, London, EC2Y 5ET
Activities: Security and commodity contracts dealing activities
Officers: Simon Cowen [1962] Director/Chief Operating Officer; Alan Damian Dwerryhouse [1966] Director/Executive; Christopher Charles Hipkins [1950] Director/Stockbroker Retired; Donald William Lennox Skinner [1962] Director/Stockbroker Group COO; Jonathan David Slone [1962] Director [American]; Richard Paul Ziegler [1971] Director

Clyde & Co LLP
Incorporated: 5 March 2007 *Employees:* 3,378
Net Worth: £197,326,000 *Total Assets:* £451,137,984
Registered Office: The St Botolph Building, 138 Houndsditch, London, EC3A 7AR
Officers: Dean Carrigan [1966] Member; Elizabeth Jane Jenkins [1959] Member; Michael Knoerzer [1962] Member; Simon Nicholas Konsta [1964] Member; Andrew Christopher Nicholas [1970] Member; Andrew James Preston [1968] Member; Emma-Jayne Ager [1978] LLP Member; Leslie Susan Ahari [1963] LLP Member; Anthony Michael Albertini [1965] LLP Member; Barbara Maria Almeida [1973] LLP Member; David Amentas [1975] LLP Member; Elizabeth Jane Andrewartha [1952] LLP Member; Toni Ashby [1977] LLP Member; Kathryn Courtney Ashton [1971] LLP Member; Nicholas Charles Austin [1973] LLP Member; Lee Richard Bacon [1975] LLP Member; Sina Bahadoran [1975] LLP Member; Joseph Anselm Bailey III [1975] LLP Member; Austin Paul Barham [1967] LLP Member; Philip Michael Bass [1956] LLP Member; Duncan Bachelor [1977] LLP Member; Nicholas Charles Stuart Bathurst [1968] LLP Member; Tony Alan Walter Baumgartner [1971] LLP Member; Alison Katherine Beanum [1977] LLP Member; David Peter Bennet [1965] LLP Member; Neil Beresford [1977] LLP Member; Scott Fain Bertschi [1967] LLP Member; Andrew Lloyd Bicknell [1961] LLP Member; Mark Alexander Bisset [1966] LLP Member; Andrew David Blair [1962] LLP Member; Jason Colin Romaine Bleasdale [1968] LLP Member; Helen Cathrine Bourne [1971] LLP Member; Eileen King Bower [1964] LLP Member; Henry Thompson Dalgety Boyle [1967] LLP Member; Gemma Kirsten Brannigan [1981] LLP Member; Clive Stewart Brett [1959] LLP Member; Nigel Geoffrey Brook [1956] LLP Member; Anthony George Asquith Brown [1965] LLP Member; David William Brown [1957] LLP Member; Jonathan Brown [1976] LLP Member; Stephen Browning [1963] LLP Member; Christopher John Burdett [1966] LLP Member; James Andrew Burns [1967] LLP Member; Clinton Earl Cameron [1965] LLP Member; Steven Michael Canon [1976] LLP Member; Christopher Carlsen [1957] LLP Member; Kate Emily Carmichael [1978] LLP Member; Owen Bernard Carragher Jr [1963] LLP Member; Maylis Casati-Ollier [1953] LLP Member; William Joseph Casey [1958] LLP Member; Fergal Austin Cathie [1968] LLP Member; Anthony Cawley [1973] LLP Member; Bruce Daniel Celebrezze [1954] LLP Member; Maria Teresa Cetta [1960] LLP Member; Nigel Cedric Benjamin Chapman [1953] LLP Member; Conte Carmelo Cicala [1968] LLP Member; Conte Carmelo Cicala [1968] LLP Member; Anne Sarah Clover [1958] LLP Member; Robert Collins [1975] LLP Member; Andrew Constable [1972] LLP Member; Louis-Philippe Emmanuel Constant [1978] LLP Member; Enrique Navarro Contreras [1971] LLP Member; Keith Mark Conway [1960] LLP Member; Laura Anne Cooke [1966] LLP Member; James Edward Cooper [1972] LLP Member; Amelia Costa [1983] LLP Member; Ralph Pelham Thornton Cox [1964] LLP Member; Timothy Michael Crockford [1981] LLP Member; Michelle Louise Crorie [1978] LLP Member; Elizabeth Cubitt [1970] LLP Member; Simon Leonard James Culhane [1963] LLP Member; David Frederick Cutter [1967] LLP Member; Joan Nancy D'Ambrosio [1966] LLP Member; James Dadge [1973] LLP Member; Nadia Darwazeh [1974] LLP Member; Nathalie David [1969] LLP Member; Barry Davis [1955] LLP Member; Ricardo de Abreu Lewandowski [1980] LLP Member; William John Deeprose [1982] LLP Member; Jo-Anne Suzanne Demers [1958] LLP Member; Eric Diamantis [1968] LLP Member; Paul Michael Dillon [1964] LLP Member; Christopher William Duffy [1957] LLP Member; Katherine Elizabeth Duffy [1981] LLP Member; Angus Neil Duncan [1974] LLP Member; Michelle Maree Dunne [1969] LLP Member; Karen Patricia Earl [1962] LLP Member; John Paul Eastlake [1968] LLP Member; Ivor Edwards [1970] LLP Member; Jonathan Masterman Edwards [1961] LLP Member; Richard Peter Elks [1980] LLP Member; Jeffrey John Ellis [1953] LLP Member; Nicholas Brent Elwell-Sutton [1971] LLP Member; Robert David Girard Emblem [1965] LLP Member; Frederick Jay Fein [1964] LLP Member; Ignacio Figuerol Roncal [1970] LLP Member; Robert Fisher [1956] LLP Member; Angela Dawn Flaherty [1986] LLP Member; John David Flaherty [1968] LLP Member; Andrew Foster [1972] LLP Member

Clydesdale Financial Services Limited
Incorporated: 23 February 1994
Net Worth: £148,368,992 *Total Assets:* £4,045,036,032
Registered Office: 1 Churchill Place, London, E14 5HP
Activities: Banks
Parent: Carnegie Holdings Limited
Officers: Konrad Xavier Kelling [1975] Director [New Zealander]; Sarah-Jayne O'Donovan [1970] Director/Banker; Christopher Mark Wood [1970] Managing Director

CMC Markets Holdings Limited
Incorporated: 1 February 2016
Net Worth: £727,993,984 *Total Assets:* £728,499,456
Registered Office: 133 Houndsditch, London, EC3A 7BX
Activities: Financial intermediation not elsewhere classified
Parent: CMC Markets PLC
Officers: Jonathan Bradshaw, Secretary; Peter Andrew Cruddas [1953] Director/Chief Executive Officer; David John Fineberg [1979] Group Director of Trading; Grant Jeffrey Foley [1972] Director/Chief Financial Officer

CMC Markets PLC
Incorporated: 3 June 2004 *Employees:* 592
Net Worth: £220,030,000 *Total Assets:* £329,871,008
Registered Office: 133 Houndsditch, London, EC3A 7BX
Activities: Financial intermediation not elsewhere classified
Officers: Jonathan Bradshaw, Secretary; Peter Andrew Cruddas [1953] Managing Director; David John Fineberg [1979] Group Director of Trading; Grant Jeffrey Foley [1972] Group Director of Finance and Risk; Sarah Lucy Ing [1966] Director; James Stuart Richards [1957] Director/Solicitor; Clare Leslie Salmon [1963] Director; Paul Philip Wainscott [1951] Director

CMC Markets UK Holdings Limited
Incorporated: 6 September 2005 *Employees:* 3
Net Worth: £71,710,752 *Total Assets:* £164,719,088
Registered Office: 133 Houndsditch, London, EC3A 7BX
Activities: Financial intermediation not elsewhere classified
Parent: CMC Markets Holdings Limited
Officers: Jonathan Bradshaw, Secretary; Peter Andrew Cruddas [1953] Director; David John Fineberg [1979] Group Director of Trading; Grant Jeffrey Foley [1972] Group Director of Finance and Risk

CMC Markets UK PLC
Incorporated: 1 December 1989 *Employees:* 392
Net Worth: £234,920,000 *Total Assets:* £315,727,008
Registered Office: 133 Houndsditch, London, EC3A 7BX
Activities: Financial intermediation not elsewhere classified
Parent: CMC Markets UK Holdings Limited
Officers: Jonathan Bradshaw, Secretary; Peter Andrew Cruddas [1953] Director; David John Fineberg [1979] Group Director of Trading; Grant Jeffrey Foley [1972] Group Director of Finance and Risk

CMI Canada Financing Ltd
Incorporated: 8 November 2016
Net Worth: £717,343,872 *Total Assets:* £717,343,872
Registered Office: 3rd Floor, 10 Eastbourne Terrace, Paddington, London, W2 6LG
Activities: Other professional, scientific and technical activities n.e.c.
Parent: Cummins, Inc
Officers: Joseph Morgan Rigler, Secretary; Alouis Ngoshi [1974] Regional Treasury Director - EMEA [Zimbabwean]; Joseph Morgan Rigler [1980] Director/Corporate Counsel/Solicitor; Edward David Smith [1976] Director/Chartered Accountant

CMS Cameron McKenna Nabarro Olswang LLP
Incorporated: 2 December 2004 *Employees:* 376
Previous: CMS Cameron McKenna LLP
Net Worth: £140,267,008 *Total Assets:* £339,129,984
Registered Office: Cannon Place, 78 Cannon Street, London, EC4N 6AF
Officers: Stephen Samuel Alexander Millar [1972] Member; Susan Penelope Warne [1955] Member; David Graeme Abel [1982] LLP Member; Sian Elizabeth Margaret Aitken [1979] LLP Member; Judith Elizabeth Aldersey-Williams [1963] LLP Member; Jennifer Mary Allan [1980] LLP Member; Valerie Louise Allan [1973] LLP Member; Philip Anderson [1978] LLP Member; Phillip Spencer Ashley [1976] LLP Member; Fraser James Derwin Askham [1972] LLP Member; Mark Aaron Atkinson [1968] LLP Member; Sally Jane Badham [1967] LLP Member; Richard James Bamforth [1966] LLP Member; Andrew Edward Sturrock Banton [1967] LLP Member; Marcus Robert William Barclay [1961] LLP Member; Joel Anthony Barry [1970] LLP Member; Susan Caroline Barty [1959] LLP Member; Adrian Bell [1979] LLP Member; Jennifer Ann Bell [1967] LLP Member; Matthew John Bennett [1971] LLP Member; Mark Hugh David Bertram [1966] LLP Member; Andrew Brian Besser [1962] LLP Member; Steven Michael Billingham [1980] LLP Member; Paul Andrew Blackmore [1969] LLP Member; Candice Blackwood [1962] LLP Member; Nicholas Matthew Blair [1979] LLP Member; Tamsin Blow [1983] LLP Member; Stuart Haddow Blythe [1964] LLP Member; Christopher Graham Bowes [1972] LLP Member; Elisabeth Anne Bremner [1972] LLP Member; Colin Victor Brett [1977] LLP Member; Melissa Brett [1975] LLP Member; David Bridge [1979] LLP Member; Monica Brij [1974] LLP Member; Jason Chalmers Brooks [1975] LLP Member; Martin Duncan Milner Brown [1973] LLP Member; Richard Brown [1968] LLP Member; Graeme Murray Bruce [1969] LLP Member; David James Anthony Bunker [1975] LLP Member; Anna Burchner [1976] LLP Member; Zoe Michele Burge [1976] LLP Member; Emma Burnett [1972] LLP Member; Nicholas James Burt [1975] LLP Member; Aidan George Campbell [1973] LLP Member; William Murley Carr [1967] LLP Member; Paul Barry Carter [1966] LLP Member; Dr Ciaran Carvalho [1961] LLP Member; Michael John Cavers [1979] LLP Member; Christopher Roberts Chambers [1977] LLP Member; Graham Neil Chase [1964] LLP Member; Anne Chitan [1974] LLP Member; Karen Clarke [1975] LLP Member; Graeme Matheson Clubley [1978] LLP Member; Hugo Coetzee [1969] LLP Member; Nicholas John Collins [1962] LLP Member; Wendy Margaret Colquhoun [1963] LLP Member; Rachel Cooper [1971] LLP Member; Steven Thomas Corney [1968] LLP Member; Peter Coyne [1975] LLP Member; Darren Alexander Craig [1976] LLP Member; Alan Ian Clark Crawford [1977] LLP Member; Anna Crew [1980] LLP Member; Nicholas Hedley Crosbie [1978] LLP Member; David John Crossley [1979] LLP Member; Matthew Daniel Culver [1975] LLP Member; John Robert Cumpson [1967] LLP Member; Maxine Eleanor Cupitt [1961] LLP Member; Richard Charles Currier [1973] LLP Member; Hannah Ruth Curtis [1981] LLP Member; Jonathan Charles Dames [1973] LLP Member; Samantha Dames [1974] LLP Member; Ashley Damiral [1976] LLP Member; Tom Dane [1977] LLP Member; David William Davidson [1966] LLP Member; David Christopher Day [1964] LLP Member; Dr Kuruneruge Samitha Sujith de Silva [1973] LLP Member; Michael Francis Delaney [1975] LLP Member; Karen Denny [1967] LLP Member; Alexander Denslow [1972] LLP Member; Mark Jonathan Devereux [1956] LLP Member; William James Dibble [1973] LLP Member; Patrick Joseph Donegan [1976] LLP Member; Carl Dray [1960] LLP Member; Danielle Drummond - Brassington [1977] LLP Member; Dominic David Dryden [1974] LLP Member; Kristy Elizabeth Duane [1975] LLP Member; Katherine Duffield [1978] LLP Member; Philip Duffield [1978] LLP Member; Paul Hamilton Edmondson [1970] LLP Member; John Trafford Theodore Enser [1964] LLP Member; Martin David Evans [1964] LLP Member; Aaron Fairhurst [1977] LLP Member; Anthony Leonard Rupert Fincham [1955] LLP Member; John Jeffrey Finnemore [1980] LLP Member; Glen Thomas Flannery [1976] LLP Member; Edward John Foss [1966] LLP Member; Frank Alexander Fowlie [1976] LLP Member; Martin Patrick Fox [1966] LLP Member; Shona McNae Frame [1969] LLP Member; Marc Russell Franks [1965] LLP Member

CMS Distribution Limited
Incorporated: 27 January 1988 *Employees:* 196
Net Worth: £19,849,656 *Total Assets:* £121,463,128
Registered Office: 2nd Floor, 15 Worship Street, London, EC2A 2DT
Activities: Other business support service activities n.e.c.
Major Shareholder: Frank Joseph Salmon
Officers: Tom Burke, Secretary [Irish]; Tom Burke [1973] Finance Director [Irish]; Onofrios Constantinou [1967] Director/Sales Manager; Nicholas Simon Preston [1969] Director; Paul Nicholas Roughley [1954] Director; Frank Joseph Salmon [1965] Director [Irish]

CNA Europe Holdings Limited
Incorporated: 6 March 1998
Net Worth: £101,722,000 *Total Assets:* £101,722,000
Registered Office: 20 Fenchurch Street, London, EC3M 3BY
Activities: Non-life insurance
Shareholders: Continental Casualty Company; The Continental Insurance Company
Officers: James Michael Anderson [1972] Director [American]; David John Brosnan [1962] Director/Insurance Executive [American]; Anna Maria Louisa Andrea D'Hulster [1964] Director [Belgian]; Phillip John Hamer [1976] Director; Carl Anthony Kearney [1972] Director/Chief Actuarial and Risk Officer [Irish]; Jalil Ur Rehman [1964] Director; David John Stevens [1963] Director/Chief Finance Officer; Heather Irene Thomas [1952] Director; Robert Thomson [1955] Director; Anthony David Williams [1974] Director [Australian]; Douglas Merle Worman [1967] Director [American]

CNA Insurance Company Limited
Incorporated: 8 February 1864 *Employees:* 102
Net Worth: £404,191,008 *Total Assets:* £1,139,515,008
Registered Office: 20 Fenchurch Street, London, EC3M 3BY
Activities: Non-life insurance
Parent: CNA Europe Holdings Limited
Officers: James Michael Anderson [1972] Director [American]; David John Brosnan [1962] Director/Insurance Executive [American]; Anna Maria Louisa Andrea D'Hulster [1964] Director/Secretary General, The Geneva Association [Belgian]; Phillip John Hamer [1976] Director; Carl Anthony Kearney [1972] Director/Chief Actuary [Irish]; Jalil Ur Rehman [1964] Director; David John Stevens [1963] Director/Chief Finance Officer; Heather Irene Thomas [1952] Director; Robert Thomson [1955] Director; Anthony David Williams [1974] Director [Australian]; Douglas Merle Worman [1967] Director [American]

CNH Industrial UK Limited
Incorporated: 6 January 2017
Net Worth: £905,592,448 *Total Assets:* £908,967,360
Registered Office: 25 St James's Street, London, SW1A 1HA
Activities: Financial intermediation not elsewhere classified
Parent: CNH Industrial NV
Officers: Simon Marc McCarthy, Secretary; Paul Jeff Hunter [1956] Director; Simon Marc McCarthy [1971] Director/Solicitor [British/Australian]

CNR International (U.K.) Developments Limited
Incorporated: 19 August 1971
Net Worth: £54,571,000 *Total Assets:* £264,780,000
Registered Office: c/o Pinsent Masons LLP, 30 Crown Place, London, EC2A 4ES
Activities: Extraction of crude petroleum
Parent: CNR International (U.K.) Limited
Officers: David Stewart Ogilvie, Secretary; Barry Duncan [1966] Finance Director; Stephen Wilson Laut [1957] Director/Corporate Executive [Canadian]; Timothy Shawn McKay [1961] Director/Executive [Canadian]; David Stewart Ogilvie [1966] Director/Lawyer; David Benjamin Whitehouse [1967] Director/Engineer

CNR International (U.K.) Investments Limited
Incorporated: 6 January 1977
Net Worth: £202,100,000 *Total Assets:* £202,100,000
Registered Office: c/o Pinsent Masons LLP, 30 Crown Place, London, EC2A 4ES
Activities: Extraction of crude petroleum
Parent: Canadian Natural Resources Limited
Officers: David Stewart Ogilvie, Secretary; Barry Duncan [1966] Finance Director; Stephen Wilson Laut [1957] Director/Corporate Executive [Canadian]; Timothy Shawn McKay [1961] Director/Executive [Canadian]; David Stewart Ogilvie [1966] Director/Lawyer; David Benjamin Whitehouse [1967] Director/Engineer

CNR International (U.K.) Limited
Incorporated: 17 July 1964 *Employees:* 326
Net Worth: £65,440,000 *Total Assets:* £1,058,984,000
Registered Office: c/o Pinsent Masons LLP, 30 Crown Place, London, EC2A 4ES
Activities: Extraction of crude petroleum
Parent: CNR International (U.K.) Investments Limited
Officers: David Stewart Ogilvie, Secretary; Barry Duncan [1966] Finance Director; Stephen Wilson Laut [1957] Director/Corporate Executive [Canadian]; Timothy Shawn McKay [1961] Director/Executive [Canadian]; David Stewart Ogilvie [1966] Director/Lawyer; David Benjamin Whitehouse [1967] Director/Engineer

Coach Stores Limited
Incorporated: 15 April 2010 *Employees:* 258
Net Worth: £2,804,486,912 *Total Assets:* £2,835,601,920
Registered Office: 2 Cavendish Square, London, W1G 0PU
Activities: Retail sale of clothing in specialised stores
Parent: Coach, Inc
Officers: David Edward Howard [1975] Director/Lawyer [American]; Leonard Todd Kahn [1963] Director [American]

Cobalt Data Centres Limited
Incorporated: 14 December 2005
Net Worth: £1,090,300 *Total Assets:* £212,815,536
Registered Office: Emperor's Gate, 114a Cromwell Road, London, SW7 4AG
Activities: Development of building projects
Parent: Safedove Limited
Officers: Piet James Pulford, Secretary/Director; Guy Norman Marsden [1957] Director; Piet James Pulford [1954] Director

Coca-Cola Holdings (United Kingdom) Limited
Incorporated: 19 May 1983 *Employees:* 6
Net Worth: £155,702,784 *Total Assets:* £157,000,608
Registered Office: 1a Wimpole Street, London, W1G 0EA
Activities: Activities of head offices
Parent: The Coca-Cola Company
Officers: Ingrid Natalie Cope [1972] Director/Solicitor; Scott Edward Roche [1964] Finance Director [Canadian]; Ruben Christiaan Stephaan Rutten [1977] Finance Director [Belgian]; Margaret Ann Stewart [1972] HR Director [Irish]; Jonathan Mark Woods [1968] Director/Franchise Operations Manager

COFCO Holdings 1 Limited
Incorporated: 1 June 2011
Net Worth: £251,000 *Total Assets:* £822,089,984
Registered Office: 6th Floor, 65 Gresham Street, London, EC2V 7NQ
Activities: Other business support service activities n.e.c.
Parent: Link Trust Nominees No.1 Limited
Officers: Carl Steven Baldry [1966] Director

Cofunds Limited
Incorporated: 5 April 2000
Net Worth: £111,082,000 *Total Assets:* £176,955,008
Registered Office: Level 43, The Leadenhall Building, 122 Leadenhall Street, London, EC3V 4AB
Activities: Financial intermediation not elsewhere classified
Parent: Aegon UK PLC
Officers: James Kenneth MacKenzie, Secretary; Mark Bloom [1964] Director [American]; David Martin Dalton-Brown [1959] Director; James Ewing [1970] Director; Adrian Thomas Grace [1963] Director; David Geoffrey Hobbs [1969] Director; Stephen James McGee [1973] Director; Caroline Frances Ramsay [1962] Director; Michael John Rogers [1964] Director

Cognizant Worldwide Limited
Incorporated: 18 March 2010 *Employees:* 5,156
Previous: Cognizant Technology Solutions UK Limited
Net Worth: £403,724,992 *Total Assets:* £1,109,720,064
Registered Office: 1 Kingdom Street, Paddington Central, London, W2 6BD
Activities: Information technology consultancy activities
Parent: Cognizant Holdings UK Limited
Officers: Richard Simpson, Secretary; Karen Anne McLoughlin [1964] Director [American]; Harry Harold Demas [1975] Director/Attorney [American]; Sanjiv Gossain [1965] Director; James Suk-Won Yu [1968] Director [American]; Simon Francis White [1976] Director/Lawyer

Cola Holdings Limited
Incorporated: 30 October 1979 *Employees:* 619
Net Worth Deficit: £25,790,000 *Total Assets:* £324,363,008
Registered Office: Flat 1, 1-2 Coach and Horses Yard, London, W1S 2EH
Activities: Hotels and similar accommodation
Major Shareholder: Bakir Ali Cola
Officers: Azad Bakir Ali Cola, Secretary/Director; Azad Bakir Ali Cola [1979] Director

Colart International Holdings Limited
Incorporated: 29 October 1998 *Employees:* 125
Net Worth: £40,053,000 *Total Assets:* £101,276,000
Registered Office: The Studio Building, 21 Evesham Street, London, W11 4AJ
Activities: Non-specialised wholesale trade
Parent: Colart Group Holdings Ltd
Officers: Mark Barratt [1961] Director/Chief Operations Officer; Jane Marie Beeston [1966] Group HR Director; Gail Moira Pasquier [1965] Director/Chief Commercial Officer; Toby Russell [1971] Director/Chief Technology Officer; Jonathan Paul William Spight [1968] Director/Chief Financial Officer; Adrianus Hendrikus Maria Van Schie [1967] Director/Chief Executive Officer [Dutch]

Colas Rail Limited
Incorporated: 28 November 1994 *Employees:* 1,316
Net Worth: £5,903,000 *Total Assets:* £156,060,000
Registered Office: Dacre House, 19 Dacre Street, London, SW1H 0DJ
Activities: Construction of railways and underground railways
Parent: Colas Rail Holdings Limited
Officers: James Joseph Quinnell, Secretary; Jean-Pierre Bertrand [1962] Director [French]; Francis Grass [1970] Director/Chief Executive Officer [French]; Gregory Oriol [1974] Director/Chief Financial Officer [French]

Colfax UK Finance Ltd
Incorporated: 7 September 2011
Net Worth: £796,528,704 *Total Assets:* £1,531,834,880
Registered Office: 6th Floor, 322 High Holborn, London, WC1V 7PB
Activities: Activities of head offices
Parent: Colfax Corporation
Officers: William Flexon [1963] Director/Chartered Accountant [American]; Mark Paul Lehman [1967] Director/Solicitor [American]; Dominic Albert Daniel Morgan [1975] Tax Director; Eileen Annabelle Raperport [1951] Director/Pensions Co-ordinator; Guy Rostron [1960] Director/Chartered Accountant

Colfax UK Holdings Ltd
Incorporated: 7 September 2011
Net Worth: £1,702,696,832 *Total Assets:* £2,358,837,760
Registered Office: 6th Floor, 322 High Holborn, London, WC1V 7PB
Activities: Activities of head offices
Parent: Colfax UK Finance Ltd
Officers: Christopher Michael Hix [1962] Director/Chief Financial Officer [American]; Mark Paul Lehman [1967] Director/Solicitor [American]; Sarah Elizabeth McIntyre [1984] Director; Eileen Annabelle Raperport [1951] Director/Pensions Co-ordinator; Guy Rostron [1960] Director/Chartered Accountant

Colgems Productions Limited
Incorporated: 21 January 1983 *Employees:* 3
Net Worth: £18,420,900 *Total Assets:* £230,024,672
Registered Office: Sony Pictures, Europe House, 25 Golden Square, London, W1F 9LU
Activities: Motion picture distribution activities
Parent: Columbia Pictures Corporation Limited
Officers: Darren Nigel Hopgood, Secretary; Darren Nigel Hopgood [1977] Director/Chartered Accountant; Daxesh Mehta [1967] Director/Chartered Accountant; Angel Orengo [1968] Director/Sales [American]

Colliers International EMEA Holdings Limited
Incorporated: 9 March 2016
Net Worth: £262,247,504 *Total Assets:* £330,942,272
Registered Office: 50 George Street, London, W1U 7GA
Activities: Real estate agencies
Parent: Colliers International Group Inc
Officers: Davoud Reza Amel-Azizpour [1979] Director/Accountant; Richard Alexander Bruce [1974] Operations Director; David Colin Jones [1981] Director/Accountant

Collin Estates Limited
Incorporated: 6 February 1939 *Employees:* 4
Net Worth: £203,677,744 *Total Assets:* £204,352,480
Registered Office: 33 Cavendish Square, London, W1G 0PW
Activities: Buying and selling of own real estate
Parent: Great Portland Estates PLC
Officers: Desna Lee Martin, Secretary; Toby Augustine Courtauld [1968] Director; Steven Richard Mew [1968] Director; Nicholas James Sanderson [1973] Director/Accountant; Andrew Nicholas Howard White [1970] Director

Collins Stewart Former Holdings Limited
Incorporated: 1 March 2012
Net Worth Deficit: £1,501,958 *Total Assets:* £143,963,040
Registered Office: 88 Wood Street, London, EC2V 7QR
Activities: Activities of other holding companies n.e.c.
Officers: Christopher William Courtenay Tregoning [1948] Director

Collinson Finance Limited
Incorporated: 30 September 2014
Net Worth: £6,164,345 *Total Assets:* £192,612,960
Registered Office: Cutlers Exchange, 123 Houndsditch, London, EC3A 7BU
Activities: Financial management
Parent: Collinson International Limited
Officers: Mark Richard Hampton, Secretary; Colin Robert Evans [1947] Director; Mark Richard Hampton [1964] Finance Director

Collinson International Limited
Incorporated: 28 January 1991 *Employees:* 1,899
Previous: The Collinson Group Limited
Net Worth: £40,443,000 *Total Assets:* £371,536,000
Registered Office: Cutlers Exchange, 123 Houndsditch, London, EC3A 7BU
Activities: Activities of head offices
Parent: The Collinson Group Limited
Officers: Mark Richard Hampton, Secretary; Mignon Louise Buckingham [1965] Director; Christopher James Evans [1975] Marketing Director; Colin Robert Evans [1947] Director/Management Consultant; David Evans [1976] Director; Denise Margaret Evans [1949] Director; Mark Richard Hampton [1964] Finance Director; Stephen John Pinches [1957] Marketing Director

Colt Technology Services
Incorporated: 15 December 1989 *Employees:* 743
Net Worth Deficit: £199,154,000 *Total Assets:* £581,110,976
Registered Office: Colt House, 20 Great Eastern Street, London, EC2A 3EH
Activities: Other telecommunications activities
Officers: Esmee Alicen Devi Chengapen, Secretary; Gary Stephen Carr [1964] Director/Group Financial Controller; Carl James Grivner [1953] Director [American]; Tommaso Panico [1974] Director [Italian]; Richard Martin Tilbrook [1977] Director/Lawyer

Colt Technology Services Europe Limited
Incorporated: 28 June 1996
Net Worth Deficit: £1,211,886,080 *Total Assets:* £621,708,160
Registered Office: Colt House, 20 Great Eastern Street, London, EC2A 3EH
Activities: Other telecommunications activities
Officers: Esmee Alicen Devi Chengapen, Secretary; Gary Stephen Carr [1964] Finance Director; Alessandro Galtieri [1972] Director/Lawyer [Italian]; Caroline Emma Griffin Pain [1964] Director/Lawyer; Richard Martin Tilbrook [1977] Director/Lawyer

Colt Technology Services Group Limited
Incorporated: 2 August 1996 *Employees:* 6
Net Worth: £1,185,673,344 *Total Assets:* £1,890,084,224
Registered Office: Colt House, 20 Great Eastern Street, London, EC2A 3EH
Activities: Other telecommunications activities
Officers: Esmee Alicen Devi Chengapen, Secretary; Gary Stephen Carr [1964] Director/Group Financial Controller; Hugo Martin Eales [1967] Director; Alessandro Galtieri [1972] Director/Lawyer [Italian]; Caroline Emma Griffin Pain [1964] Director/Lawyer; Carl James Grivner [1953] Director [American]

Colt Telecom Finance Euro
Incorporated: 22 April 2002
Net Worth: £451,802,240 *Total Assets:* £825,897,152
Registered Office: Colt House, 20 Great Eastern Street, London, EC2A 3EH
Activities: Other telecommunications activities
Officers: Esmee Alicen Devi Chengapen, Secretary; Gary Stephen Carr [1964] Director/Group Financial Controller; Esmee Alicen Devi Chengapen [1970] Director/Company Secretary; Caroline Emma Griffin Pain [1964] Director/Lawyer

Colt Telecom Finance Switzerland
Incorporated: 22 April 2002
Net Worth: £3,056,928 *Total Assets:* £176,216,768
Registered Office: Colt House, 20 Great Eastern Street, London, EC2A 3EH
Activities: Other telecommunications activities
Officers: Esmee Alicen Devi Chengapen, Secretary; Gary Stephen Carr [1964] Director/Group Financial Controller; Esmee Alicen Devi Chengapen [1970] Director/Company Secretary; Caroline Emma Griffin Pain [1964] Director/Lawyer

Colt Telecom Holdings Limited
Incorporated: 6 December 1999
Net Worth: £479,508,064 *Total Assets:* £479,659,552
Registered Office: Colt House, 20 Great Eastern Street, London, EC2A 3EH
Activities: Other telecommunications activities
Officers: Esmee Alicen Devi Chengapen, Secretary; Gary Stephen Carr [1964] Director/Group Financial Controller; Caroline Emma Griffin Pain [1964] Director/Lawyer

Columbia Pictures Corporation Limited
Incorporated: 17 September 1929 *Employees:* 332
Net Worth: £294,760,992 *Total Assets:* £1,254,567,936
Registered Office: Sony Pictures, Europe House, 25 Golden Square, London, W1F 9LU
Activities: Motion picture distribution activities
Parent: Sony Corporate Services Europe Limited
Officers: Darren Nigel Hopgood, Secretary; Dr Wayne Fernley Garvie [1963] Director/Chief Creative Officer; Ian Michael George [1962] Managing Director, Theatrical; Darren Nigel Hopgood [1977] Director/Chartered Accountant; Jacqueline Louise Marshall [1976] Director/Legal Executive; Rhona Anne O'Shea [1972] Director/Labour Relations Executive [Irish]; John Rossiter [1971] Director/TV Executive; Mark Young [1975] Director/TV Executive

Comet Bidco Limited
Incorporated: 14 July 2017 *Employees:* 881
Net Worth: £124,614,000 *Total Assets:* £746,640,000
Registered Office: Bedford House, 69-79 Fulham High Street, London, SW6 3JW
Activities: Other service activities n.e.c.
Officers: Lionel Yves Assant [1972] Director [French]; Haide Hong [1984] Director; Simon Reed Kimble [1963] Director; Russell Stephen Wilcox [1971] Director

Comet Midco Limited
Incorporated: 8 August 2017 *Employees:* 881
Net Worth: £124,614,000 *Total Assets:* £746,640,000
Registered Office: Bedford House, 69-79 Fulham High Street, London, SW6 3JW
Activities: Activities of other holding companies n.e.c.
Officers: Lionel Yves Assant [1972] Director [French]; Haide Hong [1984] Director; Simon Reed Kimble [1963] Director; Russell Stephen Wilcox [1971] Director

Commercial Acceptances Limited
Incorporated: 14 April 1983 *Employees:* 22
Net Worth: £10,335,325 *Total Assets:* £420,788,192
Registered Office: 100 George Street, London, W1U 8NU
Activities: Financial intermediation not elsewhere classified
Parent: Close Brothers Limited
Officers: Lawrence Barry Brown [1961] Director/Manager; Daniel Ashley Hertz [1965] Director/Property Finance; Richard Anthony Murkin [1966] Director; Francis David Pennal [1959] Managing Director; Nicholas Oliver Potter [1979] Director/Merchant Banker

Commerzbank Finance Limited
Incorporated: 30 June 1955
Net Worth: £425,801,984 *Total Assets:* £3,614,480,896
Registered Office: 30 Gresham Street, London, EC2V 7PG
Activities: Banks
Parent: Commerzbank AG (London Branch)
Officers: James Cameron Wall, Secretary; John Patrick Benson [1968] Director/Solicitor; Anthony David Levy [1966] Director/Chartered Accountant; Ian Robert Smith [1971] Director/Chartered Accountant

Communications Networking Services (UK)
Incorporated: 29 July 1993
Net Worth: £93,958,000 *Total Assets:* £273,144,992
Registered Office: 81 Newgate Street, London, EC1A 7AJ
Activities: Other telecommunications activities
Parent: BT Holdings Limited
Officers: Mark Philip Genikis [1961] Director/Accountant; David Lawrence Lee [1957] Director/BT Executive [American]

Community Finance Company 1 PLC
Incorporated: 3 December 2010
Net Worth: £264,000 *Total Assets:* £822,089,984
Registered Office: 6th Floor, 65 Gresham Street, London, EC2V 7NQ
Activities: Financial intermediation not elsewhere classified
Parent: COFCO Holdings 1 Limited
Officers: Carl Steven Baldry [1966] Director

Compart Systems Limited
Incorporated: 9 September 2016
Net Worth: £58,796,524 *Total Assets:* £177,897,568
Registered Office: 100 New Bridge Street, London, EC4V 6JA
Activities: Activities of other holding companies n.e.c.
Officers: Ian Michael Stuart Downie [1949] Director/Finance Officer; Eva Monica Kalawski [1955] Director [American]; Mary Ann Sigler [1954] Director [American]

Computer Patent Annuities International Limited
Incorporated: 13 June 2000 *Employees:* 1,895
Net Worth: £11,147,000 *Total Assets:* £413,412,000
Registered Office: 1st Floor, 55 King William Street, London, EC4R 9AD
Activities: Activities of head offices
Officers: Dawn Heaney Kirkbride Logan Keeffe, Secretary; Ben Gujral [1974] Director/Chief Financial Officer; Toni Nijm [1977] Director/Chief Technology Officer [Swedish]; Simon Linley Webster [1969] Business Operations Director

Concierge Holding Company Limited
Incorporated: 29 July 2015 *Employees:* 2
Net Worth: £113,441,152 *Total Assets:* £117,286,992
Registered Office: 10 Hammersmith Grove, London, W6 7AP
Activities: Other service activities n.e.c.
Parent: Accor S.A.
Officers: David Amsellem [1978] Director/Chairman [French]; Nicolas David Jean Eugene Guernier [1973] Director [French]; Olivier Andre Georges Thibault Larigaldie [1975] Director [French]; Amir Nahai [1978] Commercial Director [American]; Thibault Marie Laurent Viort [1972] Director [French]

Concord Resources Limited
Incorporated: 22 September 2015 *Employees:* 43
Net Worth: £120,474,600 *Total Assets:* £943,126,272
Registered Office: 27 Old Gloucester Street, London, WC1N 3AX
Activities: Agents involved in the sale of fuels, ores, metals and industrial chemicals
Officers: Dwight Anderson [1967] Director/Investment Manager [American]; Stephen Branton-Speak [1964] Director; Nathan Ebeling [1973] Director/Finance [American]; Mark Hansen [1983] Director; Jason Kellman [1977] Director/Chief Investment Officer [American]; Sir Graeme Cameron Maxwell Lamb [1953] Director/Consultant; John Nagulendran [1977] Director/Portfolio Manager [Singaporean]; Marwan Shakarchi [1961] Director/Chairman of MKS (Switzerland) SA [Swiss]

Concordia Investment Holdings (UK) Limited
Incorporated: 13 October 2015
Net Worth Deficit: £1,041,202,752 *Total Assets:* £593,745,536
Registered Office: Capital House, King William Street, London, EC4N 7BL
Activities: Other human health activities
Officers: Robert Sully, Secretary; Adeel Ahmad [1973] Director/VP Finance [Canadian]; Graeme Neville Duncan [1973] Director/Chief Executive Officer; Vikram Laxman Kamath [1977] Director/Vice President Finance and Group Controller [Indian]

Conde Nast International Limited
Incorporated: 25 July 2005 *Employees:* 2,008
Net Worth: £223,599,008 *Total Assets:* £472,932,000
Registered Office: The Adelphi, 1-11 John Adam Street, London, WC2N 6HT
Activities: Other publishing activities
Officers: Sabine Livine Vandenbroucke, Secretary; Nicholas David Coleridge [1957] Managing Director; Giampaolo Grandi [1940] Director [Italian]; Jonathan Edward Newhouse [1952] Director/Chairman [American]

Conde Nast Publications Limited (The)
Incorporated: 28 December 1927 *Employees:* 610
Net Worth: £41,965,000 *Total Assets:* £105,794,000
Registered Office: Vogue House, Hanover Square, London, W1S 1JU
Activities: Other publishing activities
Officers: Sabine Livine Vandenbroucke, Secretary; Nicholas David Coleridge [1957] Editorial Director; Shelagh Crofts [1956] Director/Advertising; Edward Enninful [1972] Director/Editor, Vogue; Dylan Jones [1960] Director/Editor; Simon Nicholas Gresham Jones [1975] Director/Chief Digital Officer; Jonathan Edward Newhouse [1952] Director/Company President [American]; Albert Nathaniel Read [1970] Director/General Manager; Sabine Livine Vandenbroucke [1971] Director/Chief Operating Officer [Belgian]

Conduent Business Process Solutions Limited
Incorporated: 27 June 2000 *Employees:* 285
Previous: ACS Business Process Solutions Limited
Net Worth: £126,749,000 *Total Assets:* £142,926,000
Registered Office: 9th Floor, 1 Angel Court, London, EC2R 7HJ
Activities: Data processing, hosting and related activities
Officers: James Michael Peffer, Secretary; Srikanth Iyengar [1974] Director/Chief Executive Officer Europe; James Michael Peffer [1961] Director/Attorney [American]

Conduit Insurance Holdings Limited
Incorporated: 18 December 1981
Net Worth: £195,100,000 *Total Assets:* £249,200,000
Registered Office: 40 Broadway, London, SW1H 0BT
Activities: Activities of other holding companies n.e.c.
Parent: Intu Properties PLC
Officers: Susan Marsden, Secretary; David Andrew Fischel [1958] Director/Chartered Accountant; Gary Richard Hoskins [1971] Director/Chartered Accountant

Cone Investments UK Limited
Incorporated: 17 November 2016 *Employees:* 322
Net Worth: £200,829,680 *Total Assets:* £431,731,264
Registered Office: Warwick Court, Paternoster Square, London, EC4M 7DX
Activities: Other business support service activities n.e.c.
Officers: Paul Nigel Burrow [1973] Director/Accountant; Thomas Spencer Patrick [1972] Director/Solicitor; Giuseppe Prestia [1975] Director/Investment Manager [Italian]

Conegate Developments Limited
Incorporated: 8 September 1978
Previous: Conegate Limited
Net Worth: £188,351,840 *Total Assets:* £360,082,240
Registered Office: Ramillies House, 1-2 Ramillies Street, London, W1F 7LN
Activities: Development of building projects
Shareholder: Rosequake Developments Holdings Limited
Officers: Cheryl Sullivan, Secretary; Clive Sullivan [1946] Director/Management Consultant; David Sullivan [1949] Director

The Congregation of The Daughters of The Cross of Liege
Incorporated: 15 January 1998 *Employees:* 2,354
Net Worth: £176,203,008 *Total Assets:* £181,168,000
Registered Office: Provincialate, 29 Tite Street, Chelsea, London, SW3 4JX
Activities: Hospital activities
Officers: Sister Josephine Anne Clemence [1938] Director/Religious Sister; Sister Veronica Hagen [1941] Director/Religious Sister; Anne Kelly [1948] Director/Religious Sister [Irish]; Sister Mary Catherine McGinn [1942] Director [Irish]; Sister Maureen O'Brien [1939] Director/Retired; Sister Kathleen O'Reilly [1946] Director/Retired [Irish]

The Connaught Hotel Limited
Incorporated: 12 November 1998 *Employees:* 442
Net Worth: £8,024,000 *Total Assets:* £176,734,000
Registered Office: 41-43 Brook Street, Mayfair, London, W1K 4HJ
Activities: Hotels and similar accommodation
Parent: Selene Midco Limited
Officers: Fady Bakhos [1971] Director/Legal Counsel [French]; Liam Cunningham [1958] Director [Irish]

Connect Bidco Limited
Incorporated: 13 March 2017 *Employees:* 6
Net Worth: £152,556,992 *Total Assets:* £257,380,000
Registered Office: 85 Gracechurch Street, London, EC3V 0AA
Activities: Activities of other holding companies n.e.c.
Parent: Connect Midco II Limited
Officers: Michael Benjamin Grist [1974] Director; David Charles Anthony Walsh [1969] Director

Connect M1-A1 Holdings Limited
Incorporated: 22 May 1995
Net Worth: £46,209,000 *Total Assets:* £112,769,000
Registered Office: 6th Floor, 350 Euston Road, Regents Place, London, NW1 3AX
Activities: Construction of roads and motorways
Shareholders: M1A1 Yorkshire Limited; Infrastructure Investments Holdings Limited
Officers: Patrick McCarthy, Secretary; David William Bowler [1945] Director; Ross Driver [1981] Director/Investment Executive, Infrastructure; Matthew James Edwards [1985] Associate Director; Clement David Baptiste Leverd [1986] Director/Investment Executive [French]; Mark Philip Mageean [1973] Director; Adam Paul Walker [1986] Director/Accountant

Connect M1-A1 Limited
Incorporated: 7 December 1994
Net Worth: £46,209,000 *Total Assets:* £113,886,000
Registered Office: 6th Floor, 350 Euston Road, Regents Place, London, NW1 3AX
Activities: Construction of roads and motorways
Parent: Connect M1-A1 Holdings Limited
Officers: Patrick McCarthy, Secretary; David William Bowler [1945] Director; Ross Driver [1981] Director; Matthew James Edwards [1985] Associate Director; Clement David Baptiste Leverd [1986] Director/Investment Executive [French]; Mark Philip Mageean [1973] Director; Adam Paul Walker [1986] Director/Accountant

Connect M77/GSO Holdings Limited
Incorporated: 10 March 2003
Net Worth Deficit: £29,127,000 *Total Assets:* £143,916,992
Registered Office: 6th Floor, 350 Euston Road, Regents Place, London, NW1 3AX
Activities: Activities of head offices
Parent: Balfour Beatty Infrastructure Investments Limited
Officers: Patrick McCarthy, Secretary; David Graham Blanchard [1967] Director; David William Bowler [1945] Director; Matthew James Edwards [1985] Associate Director; Mark Philip Mageean [1973] Director

Connect M77/GSO PLC
Incorporated: 14 March 2003
Net Worth Deficit: £29,127,000 *Total Assets:* £143,916,992
Registered Office: 6th Floor, 350 Euston Road, Regents Place, London, NW1 3AX
Activities: Construction of roads and motorways
Parent: Connect M77/GSO Holdings Limited
Officers: Patrick McCarthy, Secretary; David Graham Blanchard [1967] Director; David William Bowler [1945] Director; Matthew James Edwards [1985] Associate Director; Mark Philip Mageean [1973] Director

Connect Midco Limited
Incorporated: 13 March 2017 *Employees:* 2
Net Worth: £154,148,000 *Total Assets:* £159,948,000
Registered Office: 85 Gracechurch Street, London, EC3V 0AA
Activities: Activities of other holding companies n.e.c.
Parent: Connect Topco Limited
Officers: Michael Benjamin Grist [1974] Director; David Charles Anthony Walsh [1969] Director

Conning Holdings Limited
Incorporated: 10 June 2015
Net Worth: £321,410,816 *Total Assets:* £322,362,560
Registered Office: 24 Monument Street, London, EC3R 8AJ
Activities: Activities of financial services holding companies
Officers: Vi Smalley, Secretary; John Frederick Boneparth [1949] Director [American]; Jr Bradford [1967] Director/Chief Executive Officer [American]; Meryl Deborah Hartzband [1954] Director [American]; Ronald P Joelson [1958] Director/Chief Investment Officer [American]; David Paul Marks [1947] Director [American]; Jason Alan Rotman [1972] Director/Financial Services [American]; David Paul Sun [1963] Director/Financial Services [American]; Tzung-Han Tsai [1976] Director/Senior Executive Vice President [Chinese]

ConocoPhillips (U.K.) Limited
Incorporated: 20 October 1953 *Employees:* 1,056
Net Worth: £828,300,032 *Total Assets:* £11,660,699,648
Registered Office: 20th Floor, 1 Angel Court, London, EC2R 7HJ
Activities: Extraction of crude petroleum
Parent: COP Holdings Limited
Officers: David Grimshaw, Secretary; Birger Balteskard [1962] Director/Manager, Global LNG Market and London Office [Norwegian]; Terri Gay King [1961] Director/President, UK [American]; Russell Scott [1973] Director/Manager UK Finance; Katherine Susan Simpson [1961] Director/HSE Manager

ConocoPhillips (U.K.) Sigma Limited
Incorporated: 2 November 2011
Net Worth: £1,553,620,992 *Total Assets:* £3,841,976,064
Registered Office: 20th Floor, 1 Angel Court, London, EC2R 7HJ
Activities: Extraction of crude petroleum
Parent: ConocoPhillips (U.K.) Limited
Officers: Joseph Anthony Farrell, Secretary; David Grimshaw, Secretary; Terri Gay King [1961] Director/President, UK [American]; Russell Scott [1973] Director/Manager UK Finance; Katherine Susan Simpson [1961] Director/HSE Manager

ConocoPhillips (U.K.) Theta Limited
Incorporated: 15 April 1980
Net Worth: £205,532,992 *Total Assets:* £303,548,000
Registered Office: 20th Floor, 1 Angel Court, London, EC2R 7HJ
Activities: Extraction of crude petroleum
Parent: ConocoPhillips (U.K.) Sigma Limited
Officers: David Grimshaw, Secretary; Terri Gay King [1961] Director/President, UK [American]; Russell Scott [1973] Director/Manager UK Finance; Katherine Susan Simpson [1961] Director/HSE Manager

ConocoPhillips (U.K.) Zeta Limited
Incorporated: 6 December 1983
Net Worth: £273,900,992 *Total Assets:* £273,900,992
Registered Office: 20th Floor, 1 Angel Court, London, EC2R 7HJ
Activities: Activities of head offices
Parent: ConocoPhillips (U.K.) Limited
Officers: David Grimshaw, Secretary; Terri Gay King [1961] Director/President, UK [American]; Russell Scott [1973] Director/Manager UK Finance; Katherine Susan Simpson [1961] Director/HSE Manager

ConocoPhillips Holdings Limited
Incorporated: 4 September 1998 *Employees:* 1,056
Net Worth: £1,221,699,968 *Total Assets:* £12,829,800,448
Registered Office: 20th Floor, 1 Angel Court, London, EC2R 7HJ
Activities: Activities of head offices
Parent: ConocoPhillips
Officers: David Grimshaw, Secretary; Birger Balteskard [1962] Director/Manager, Global LNG Market and London Office [Norwegian]; Terri Gay King [1961] Director/President, UK [American]; Russell Scott [1973] Director/Manager UK Finance; Katherine Susan Simpson [1961] Director/HSE Manager

ConocoPhillips Petroleum Company U.K. Limited
Incorporated: 20 February 1964
Net Worth: £342,132,992 *Total Assets:* £1,209,287,936
Registered Office: 20th Floor, 1 Angel Court, London, EC2R 7HJ
Activities: Extraction of crude petroleum
Parent: ConocoPhillips Holdings Limited
Officers: David Grimshaw, Secretary; Birger Balteskard [1962] Director/Manager, Global LNG Market and London Office [Norwegian]; Terri Gay King [1961] Director/President, UK [American]; Russell Scott [1973] Director/Manager UK Finance; Katherine Susan Simpson [1961] Director/HSE Manager

ConocoPhillips Treasury Limited
Incorporated: 26 May 1998
Net Worth: £83,413,000 *Total Assets:* £5,049,383,936
Registered Office: 20th Floor, 1 Angel Court, London, EC2R 7HJ
Activities: Banks
Parent: ConocoPhillips (U.K.) Limited
Officers: David Grimshaw, Secretary; Alastair James Blain [1967] Director/UK Tax Manager; Catherine Jane Duthie [1972] Director/Manager, Corporate Accounting; Russell Scott [1973] Director/Manager Corporate Accounting

Consolidated Developments Holdings Limited
Incorporated: 13 January 2017
Net Worth: £1 *Total Assets:* £294,449,536
Registered Office: 3rd Floor, 114a Cromwell Road, London, SW7 4AG
Activities: Other business support service activities n.e.c.
Parent: St Giles Obligor Limited
Officers: Laurence Grant Kirschel [1962] Director

Consolidated Developments Limited
Incorporated: 2 March 1994
Net Worth: £203,433,824 *Total Assets:* £386,464,288
Registered Office: 3rd Floor, 114a Cromwell Road, London, SW7 4AG
Activities: Development of building projects
Parent: Consolidated Developments Holdings Limited
Officers: Laurence Grant Kirschel [1962] Director

Consolidated Holdings Limited
Incorporated: 18 October 2016
Net Worth: £220,999,888 *Total Assets:* £232,203,568
Registered Office: 3rd Floor, 114a Cromwell Road, London, SW7 4AG
Activities: Activities of other holding companies n.e.c.
Major Shareholder: Laurence Grant Kirschel
Officers: Laurence Grant Kirschel [1962] Director

Consolidated Insurance Group Limited
Incorporated: 10 December 1984
Net Worth: £286,825,984 *Total Assets:* £286,825,984
Registered Office: Building 6, Chiswick Park, 566 Chiswick High Road, London, W4 5HR
Activities: Activities of head offices
Parent: Financial Assurance Company Limited
Officers: James Lawrence Rember, Secretary; Paul Charles Felix Caprez [1962] Director; Jeffrey Scott Whiteus [1957] Director/Chief Financial Officer [American]

Consort Healthcare (Birmingham) Funding PLC
Incorporated: 16 August 2005
Net Worth: £50,000 *Total Assets:* £748,032,000
Registered Office: 6th Floor, 350 Euston Road, Regents Place, London, NW1 3AX
Activities: Hospital activities
Parent: Consort Healthcare (Birmingham) Holdings Limited
Officers: David Graham Blanchard [1967] Investment Director; Andrew Brian Deacon [1980] Portfolio Director; Lynn Gladwell [1966] Director/Solicitor; Elena Giorgiana Wegener [1975] Director

Consort Healthcare (Birmingham) Holdings Limited
Incorporated: 16 August 2005
Net Worth: £29,245,000 *Total Assets:* £782,716,032
Registered Office: 6th Floor, 350 Euston Road, Regents Place, London, NW1 3AX
Activities: Activities of other holding companies n.e.c.
Shareholders: Infrastructure Investments Trafalgar Limited; Infrared Infrastructure Yield Holdings Limited; BBPF LLP
Officers: David Graham Blanchard [1967] Investment Director; Andrew Brian Deacon [1980] Portfolio Director; Lynn Gladwell [1966] Director/Solicitor; Elena Giorgiana Wegener [1975] Director

Consort Healthcare (Birmingham) Limited
Incorporated: 16 August 2005
Net Worth: £29,195,000 *Total Assets:* £782,716,032
Registered Office: 6th Floor, 350 Euston Road, Regents Place, London, NW1 3AX
Activities: Hospital activities
Parent: Consort Healthcare (Birmingham) Holdings Limited
Officers: David Graham Blanchard [1967] Investment Director; Andrew Brian Deacon [1980] Portfolio Director; Lynn Gladwell [1966] Director/Solicitor; Elena Giorgiana Wegener [1975] Director

Constantin Investment Limited
Incorporated: 20 March 2017
Net Worth: £640,116,352 *Total Assets:* £1,999,371,264
Registered Office: c/o Partners Group UK Ltd, 14th Floor, Heron Tower, 110 Bishopsgate, London, EC2N 4AY
Activities: Other service activities n.e.c.
Shareholders: Partners Group Management (Scots) LLP; PSP Investments Holding Europe Ltd
Officers: Melissa Gabrielle Bourgeois [1983] Director; Christopher Raoul Auguste Mauss [1982] Director/Investment Manager [French]; Cihat Tolga Sengel [1982] Director/Fund Manager

Constellation Barclay UK Limited
Incorporated: 5 December 2013
Net Worth: £205,516,368 *Total Assets:* £207,200,800
Registered Office: Lynton House, 7-12 Tavistock Square, London, WC1H 9LT
Activities: Hotels and similar accommodation
Officers: Zaki Nasser Zaki El-Guiziri, Secretary; Jassim Bin Hamad Bin Jassim Bin Jaber Al-Thani [1982] Director [Qatari]; Fady Jan Bakhos [1971] Director/Legal Advisor [Lebanese]

Constitution Bidco 2 Limited
Incorporated: 24 March 2016
Net Worth Deficit: £2,540,000 *Total Assets:* £117,131,000
Registered Office: 1 Shortlands, London, W6 8DR
Activities: Other accommodation
Parent: Onefinestay (Holdings) Limited
Officers: Adrian John Whitehead, Secretary; Sven Louis Boinet [1953] Director [French]

ContourGlobal PLC
Incorporated: 26 September 2017 *Employees:* 1,873
Net Worth: £434,651,616 *Total Assets:* £3,277,815,552
Registered Office: 6th Floor, 15 Berkeley Street, London, W1J 8DY
Activities: Activities of other holding companies n.e.c.
Officers: Kerry Anne Watson, Secretary; Joseph Courtney Brandt [1964] Director/President & CEO [American]; Linda Ruth Cairnie [1953] Director; Daniel Camus [1952] Director [French/Canadian]; Dr Alan Raymond Gillespie [1950] Director; Craig Allen Huff [1964] Director [American]; Alejandro Santo Domingo [1977] Director [Colombian/American]; Ronald Frank Traechsel [1959] Director [Swiss]; Gregg Zeitlin [1967] Director [American]

Control Risks Capital Limited
Incorporated: 3 February 2016 *Employees:* 3
Net Worth: £71,709,000 *Total Assets:* £120,452,000
Registered Office: Cottons Centre, Cottons Lane, London, SE1 2QG
Activities: Private security activities
Officers: Sally Kathleen McNair Scott, Secretary; Stuart John Bridges [1960] Finance Director; Richard John Fenning [1962] Director; Sally Kathleen McNair Scott [1972] Director/Lawyer

Control Risks Group Holdings Limited
Incorporated: 3 March 1981 *Employees:* 10
Net Worth: £30,790,664 *Total Assets:* £152,832,832
Registered Office: Cottons Centre, Cottons Lane, London, SE1 2QG
Activities: Other business support service activities n.e.c.
Parent: Control Risks Capital Limited
Officers: Sally Kathleen McNair Scott, Secretary; Stuart John Bridges [1960] Finance Director; Richard John Fenning [1962] Director/Consultant; Sally Kathleen McNair Scott [1972] Director/Lawyer

Convoys Properties Limited
Incorporated: 20 January 2005
Net Worth Deficit: £4,628,900 *Total Assets:* £124,282,808
Registered Office: Hutchison House, 5 Hester Road, Battersea, London, SW11 4AN
Activities: Development of building projects
Officers: Eirene Yeung, Secretary; Justin Kwok Hung Chiu [1950] Director [Canadian]; Raymond Wai Kam Chow [1947] Director; Hing Lam Kam [1946] Director [Chinese]; Raymond Tam [1954] Director of Finance

The Conygar Investment Company PLC
Incorporated: 22 September 2003 *Employees:* 7
Net Worth: £135,790,000 *Total Assets:* £136,874,000
Registered Office: Fourth Floor, 110 Wigmore Street, London, W1U 3RW
Activities: Buying and selling of own real estate
Officers: Ross Hillier McCaskill, Secretary; Nigel Jonathan Hamway [1956] Director/Banker; Frederick Nicholas Gruffudd Jones [1980] Director; Ross Hillier McCaskill [1979] Director/Chartered Accountant; Christopher James David Ware [1985] Director/Chartered Surveyor; Robert Thomas Ernest Ware [1959] Director/Chartered Accountant; Michael Derek Wigley [1939] Director

Thomas Cook Group PLC
Incorporated: 8 February 2007 *Employees:* 21,263
Net Worth: £291,000,000 *Total Assets:* £6,568,999,936
Registered Office: 3rd Floor, South Building, 200 Aldersgate, London, EC1A 4HD
Activities: Activities of head offices
Officers: Alice Marsden, Secretary; Dawn Elizabeth Airey [1960] Director/TV Executive; Emre Berkin [1961] Director/Consultant [Turkish]; Sten Daugaard [1957] Director [Danish]; Paul Russell Edgecliffe-Johnson [1972] Director; Peter Fankhauser [1960] Director [Swiss]; Lesley Mary Samuel Knox [1953] Director/Businesswoman; Francois Louis Virginie Meysman [1952] Director [Belgian]; Jurgen Schreiber [1962] Director [German]; Martine Verluyten [1951] Director [Belgian]

COP Holdings Limited
Incorporated: 1 October 2002
Net Worth: £474,897,984 *Total Assets:* £474,897,984
Registered Office: 20th Floor, 1 Angel Court, London, EC2R 7HJ
Activities: Other business support service activities n.e.c.
Parent: ConocoPhillips Holdings Limited
Officers: David Grimshaw, Secretary; Birger Balteskard [1962] Director/Manager, Global LNG Market and London Office [Norwegian]; Terri Gay King [1961] Director [American]; Russell Scott [1973] Director/Manager UK Finance; Katherine Susan Simpson [1961] Director/HSE Manager

Coppid Farming Enterprises LLP
Incorporated: 16 December 2011 *Employees:* 14
Net Worth: £118,358,648 *Total Assets:* £124,322,400
Registered Office: 31 Hill Street, London, W1J 5LS
Officers: Dominic Peter Corti Emmerson [1973] Member; The Right Honourable Francis Stephen Phillimore [1944] Member; The Right Honourable Nathalie Berthe Louise Phillimore [1949] Member; Hon. Tristan Anthony Stephen Phillimore [1977] Member; Hon John Hugo Trenchard Russell [1950] Member; Timothy James Alexander Wilson [1958] Member

Coral (Holdings) Limited
Incorporated: 1 January 1963
Net Worth: £361,332,000 *Total Assets:* £361,332,000
Registered Office: 3rd Floor, One New Change, London, EC4M 9AF
Activities: Non-trading company
Parent: Coral Group Trading Limited
Officers: Stuart John Smith [1981] Director/Accountant; Charles Alexander Sutters [1980] Director

Coral Eurobet Holdings Limited
Incorporated: 16 July 2002
Net Worth: £3,630,162,944 *Total Assets:* £3,634,161,920
Registered Office: 3rd Floor, One New Change, London, EC4M 9AF
Activities: Activities of head offices
Parent: Coral Limited
Officers: Stuart John Smith [1981] Director/Accountant; Charles Alexander Sutters [1980] Director

Coral Eurobet Limited
Incorporated: 24 September 2004
Net Worth: £53,723,000 *Total Assets:* £209,348,000
Registered Office: 3rd Floor, One New Change, London, EC4M 9AF
Activities: Activities of head offices
Parent: Coral Eurobet Holdings Limited
Officers: Stuart John Smith [1981] Director/Accountant; Charles Alexander Sutters [1980] Director

Coral Group Limited
Incorporated: 9 November 2004
Previous: CE Acquisition 2 Limited
Net Worth: £2,661,957,888 *Total Assets:* £5,180,214,784
Registered Office: 3rd Floor, One New Change, London, EC4M 9AF
Activities: Activities of head offices
Parent: CE Acquisition 1 Limited
Officers: Stuart John Smith [1981] Director/Accountant; Charles Alexander Sutters [1980] Director

Coral Group Trading Limited
Incorporated: 27 November 1998 *Employees:* 32
Net Worth: £656,492,992 *Total Assets:* £764,088,000
Registered Office: 3rd Floor, One New Change, London, EC4M 9AF
Activities: Activities of head offices
Parent: Coral Limited
Officers: Stuart John Smith [1981] Director/Accountant; Charles Alexander Sutters [1980] Director

Coral Limited
Incorporated: 24 September 2004
Previous: CE Finance 3 Limited
Net Worth: £3,466,928,128 *Total Assets:* £3,794,546,944
Registered Office: 3rd Floor, One New Change, London, EC4M 9AF
Activities: Activities of head offices
Parent: Coral Group Limited
Officers: Stuart John Smith [1981] Director/Accountant; Charles Alexander Sutters [1980] Director

Coral Racing Limited
Incorporated: 7 December 1954 *Employees:* 8,758
Net Worth: £237,512,000 *Total Assets:* £1,241,900,032
Registered Office: 3rd Floor, One New Change, London, EC4M 9AF
Activities: Gambling and betting activities
Parent: Coral (Holdings) Limited
Officers: Paul Bowtell [1968] Director; Mark Russel Chambers [1972] Director/Accountant; John David Kerr [1959] Director; Robert Matthew Wood [1980] Director/Accountant

Coralglade Limited
Incorporated: 7 June 2001 *Employees:* 4
Net Worth: £136,625,728 *Total Assets:* £295,748,736
Registered Office: 73 Cornhill, London, EC3V 3QQ
Activities: Activities of head offices
Officers: Anne Benjamin, Secretary; William Richard Collins [1946] Director; Stephane Abraham Joseph Nahum [1975] Director [French]; Eileen Marie Sawyer [1979] Director/Accountant; Malcolm Robin Turner [1935] Director

Corbiere Asset Investments Ltd
Incorporated: 9 February 2015
Net Worth: £1,028,000 *Total Assets:* £213,904,000
Registered Office: 25 Gresham Street, London, EC2V 7HN
Activities: Financial intermediation not elsewhere classified
Parent: Lloyds Bank Financial Services (Holdings) Limited
Officers: Alyson Elizabeth Mulholland, Secretary; Mark Bradshaw [1969] Director; Gavin Stuart Parker [1968] Director; Richard Douglas Shrimpton [1970] Director

Cordiant Communications Group Limited
Incorporated: 11 July 1977
Net Worth: £110,223,000 *Total Assets:* £110,223,000
Registered Office: Sea Containers House, 18 Upper Ground, London, SE1 9GL
Activities: Advertising agencies
Parent: WPP Dutch Holdings Limited
Officers: Charles Ward Van Der Welle [1959] Director of Treasury; Steve Richard Winters [1968] Director/Chartered Accountant

Core Laboratories Interests One Limited
Incorporated: 31 March 2011
Net Worth: £375,232,800 *Total Assets:* £623,090,368
Registered Office: 5th Floor, 6 St Andrew Street, London, EC4A 3AE
Activities: Financial management
Officers: George Bruce [1958] Director/General Manager; Jacqueline Watson [1970] Director/Financial Controller

Core Laboratories Interests Two Limited
Incorporated: 31 March 2011
Net Worth: £457,601,952 *Total Assets:* £609,115,136
Registered Office: 5th Floor, 6 St Andrew Street, London, EC4A 3AE
Activities: Financial management
Parent: Core Laboratories Interests One Limited
Officers: George Bruce [1958] Director/General Manager; Jacqueline Watson [1970] Director/Financial Controller

Corfe Hill Limited
Incorporated: 17 December 2007 *Employees:* 2
Net Worth: £105,356,000 *Total Assets:* £105,617,000
Registered Office: 2 King Edward Street, London, EC1A 1HQ
Activities: Financial intermediation not elsewhere classified
Parent: Bank of America Corporation
Officers: David Sean McNulty [1957] Director/Company Executive; Emma Louisa Scott [1971] Director/Company Executive

Cornwall Bidco Limited
Incorporated: 4 March 2008
Net Worth Deficit: £103,549,000 *Total Assets:* £249,374,000
Registered Office: Southbank Central, 30 Stamford Street, London, SE1 9LQ
Activities: Activities of head offices
Parent: Cornwall Midco Limited
Officers: Michael Stoddard, Secretary; Phillip David Rowland [1971] Director; Wayne Andrew Story [1961] Director

Cornwall Midco Limited
Incorporated: 4 March 2008 *Employees:* 2
Net Worth Deficit: £120,299,000 *Total Assets:* £118,452,000
Registered Office: Southbank Central, 30 Stamford Street, London, SE1 9LQ
Activities: Activities of head offices
Parent: Cornwall Topco Limited
Officers: Michael Stoddard, Secretary; Phillip David Rowland [1971] Director; Wayne Andrew Story [1961] Director

Corob Consolidated Limited
Incorporated: 6 March 1984 *Employees:* 12
Net Worth: £52,161,664 *Total Assets:* £107,223,784
Registered Office: 62 Grosvenor Street, London, W1K 3JF
Activities: Activities of other holding companies n.e.c.
Officers: Simon Neil Bentley, Secretary; Felix Cook [1946] Director/Teacher; Alison Lavinia Corob [1959] Director; Laura Elaine Corob [1953] Director; Tricia a Corob [1951] Director; Joseph Vilmos Hajnal [1958] Director/Physicist

Coroin Limited
Incorporated: 2 April 2004 *Employees:* 1,481
Net Worth: £255,091,008 *Total Assets:* £765,742,016
Registered Office: 41-43 Brook Street, Mayfair, London, W1K 4HJ
Activities: Activities of head offices
Major Shareholder: His Highness Sheikh Hamad Bin Khalifa Al Thani
Officers: Sheikha Lulwah Bint Hamad Al-Thani [1984] Director [Qatari]; Michele Faissola [1968] Director [Italian]

Corsair Mint III Limited
Incorporated: 25 June 2012 *Employees:* 1,151
Net Worth Deficit: £18,509,000 *Total Assets:* £267,107,008
Registered Office: c/o Buzzacott LLP, 130 Wood Street, London, EC2V 6DL
Activities: Other service activities n.e.c.
Officers: Paul Michael Cabral [1974] Director/Chief Financial Officer [American]; Paul Michael Cabral [1974] Director/Chief Financial Officer [American]; Dharma Teja Ignacio Jayanti [1968] Director/Private Equity Investor

Cortina Race LLP
Incorporated: 3 February 2015 *Employees:* 2,501
Net Worth: £25,336,428 *Total Assets:* £109,470,600
Registered Office: 21 Palmer Street, London, SW1H 0AD

Corus Group Limited
Incorporated: 16 July 1999 *Employees:* 1
Net Worth Deficit: £1,094,000,000 *Total Assets:* £434,000,000
Registered Office: 30 Millbank, London, SW1P 4WY
Activities: Activities of head offices
Parent: Tata Steel UK Holdings Limited
Officers: Sharone Vanessa Gidwani, Secretary; Helen Lochhead Matheson Avontuur [1964] Director, Legal; Narendra Kumar Misra [1956] Director [Indian]

Corus International (Overseas Holdings) Limited
Incorporated: 4 September 1991
Net Worth: £477,220,000 *Total Assets:* £477,591,008
Registered Office: 30 Millbank, London, SW1P 4WY
Activities: Activities of head offices
Parent: Corus Group Limited
Officers: Lajwanti Rupani, Secretary; Sharone Vanessa Gidwani [1971] Director/Solicitor/Secretary; Colin Lloyd Harvey [1967] Director/Chartered Accountant

Corus International Limited
Incorporated: 16 January 1963
Net Worth: £302,564,992 *Total Assets:* £349,176,000
Registered Office: 30 Millbank, London, SW1P 4WY
Activities: Activities of head offices
Parent: Tata Steel UK Limited
Officers: Lajwanti Rupani, Secretary; Sharone Vanessa Gidwani [1971] Director/Solicitor/Secretary; Colin Lloyd Harvey [1967] Director/Chartered Accountant

Cory Environmental Holdings Limited
Incorporated: 10 February 2005 *Employees:* 32
Net Worth: £328,028,992 *Total Assets:* £331,579,008
Registered Office: 2 Coldbath Square, London, EC1R 5HL
Activities: Activities of head offices
Parent: Viking Consortium Acquisition Limited
Officers: Tess Bridgman, Secretary; Benjamin James Butler [1981] Director; Andrew Robert Pike [1975] Director; Charles Nicholas Pollard [1958] Director; Julian William Walker [1973] Director/Chief Operating Officer

Cory Riverside (Holdings) Ltd
Incorporated: 15 February 2008 *Employees:* 258
Net Worth Deficit: £36,344,000 *Total Assets:* £609,470,976
Registered Office: 2 Coldbath Square, London, EC1R 5HL
Activities: Activities of head offices
Shareholders: Cory Riverside Energy Holdings Limited; Cory Riverside (Holdings) Limited
Officers: Tess Bridgman, Secretary; Benjamin James Butler [1981] Director; Andrew Robert Pike [1975] Director; Charles Nicholas Pollard [1958] Director; Julian William Walker [1973] Director/Chief Operating Officer

Cory Riverside Energy Finance Limited
Incorporated: 7 March 2017
Net Worth: £170,628,992 *Total Assets:* £331,468,000
Registered Office: 2 Coldbath Square, London, EC1R 5HL
Activities: Activities of head offices
Parent: Cory Environmental Holdings Limited
Officers: Tess Mary Bridgman, Secretary; Benjamin James Butler [1981] Director; Andrew Robert Pike [1975] Director; Charles Nicholas Pollard [1958] Director; Julian William Walker [1973] Director/Chief Operating Officer

Cory Riverside Energy Holdings Limited
Incorporated: 8 March 2017
Net Worth: £164,415,008 *Total Assets:* £302,660,992
Registered Office: 2 Coldbath Square, London, EC1R 5HL
Activities: Activities of head offices
Parent: Cory Riverside Energy Finance Limited
Officers: Tess Mary Bridgman, Secretary; Benjamin James Butler [1981] Director; Andrew Robert Pike [1975] Director; Charles Nicholas Pollard [1958] Director; Julian William Walker [1973] Director/Chief Operating Officer

Cosmo Oil (U.K.) Limited
Incorporated: 12 July 1991 *Employees:* 3
Previous: Cosmo Oil (U.K.) PLC
Net Worth: £3,862,515 *Total Assets:* £101,203,544
Registered Office: 4th Floor, 100 Fenchurch Street, London, EC3M 5JD
Activities: Wholesale of petroleum and petroleum products
Parent: Cosmo Energy Holdings Co.Ltd
Officers: Yusuke Onuma, Secretary; Shigeru Yamada [1965] Director [Japanese]; Tatsuya Yano [1971] Director/Office Worker [Japanese]

G. Costa (Holdings) Limited
Incorporated: 7 December 1998
Net Worth: £3,220,777 *Total Assets:* £107,624,904
Registered Office: Weston Centre, 10 Grosvenor Street, London, W1K 4QY
Activities: Activities of head offices
Parent: AB World Foods (Holdings) Limited
Officers: Rosalyn Sharon Schofield, Secretary/Solicitor; Stephen Henderson [1971] Finance Director; Andrew James Mayhew [1970] Managing Director; Paul Michael Wildman [1958] Supply Director

Cote Group (Bidco) Limited
Incorporated: 23 August 2013
Net Worth Deficit: £9,613,000 *Total Assets:* £104,286,000
Registered Office: 2nd Floor, 61 Berners Street, London, W1T 3NJ
Activities: Activities of head offices
Parent: Cote Group (Financing) Limited
Officers: Kristina Zienko, Secretary; Alexander Rupert Gauvain Scrimgeour [1971] Director; Strahan Leonard Arthur Wilson [1975] Director

Cote Group (Financing) Limited
Incorporated: 23 August 2013
Net Worth Deficit: £12,674,000 *Total Assets:* £113,900,000
Registered Office: 2nd Floor, 61 Berners Street, London, W1T 3NJ
Activities: Activities of head offices
Parent: Cote Restaurants Group Holdings Limited
Officers: Kristina Zienko, Secretary; Alexander Rupert Gauvain Scrimgeour [1971] Director; Strahan Leonard Arthur Wilson [1975] Director

Cote Restaurants Group Holdings Limited
Incorporated: 21 August 2013
Net Worth: £9,114,000 *Total Assets:* £134,610,000
Registered Office: 2nd Floor, 61 Berners Street, London, W1T 3NJ
Activities: Activities of head offices
Parent: Taste Bidco Limited
Officers: Kristina Zienko, Secretary; Alexander Rupert Gauvain Scrimgeour [1971] Director; Strahan Leonard Arthur Wilson [1975] Director

Council for World Mission (UK)
Incorporated: 9 May 2003 *Employees:* 2
Net Worth: £173,242,688 *Total Assets:* £175,721,152
Registered Office: 10 Queen Street Place, London, EC4R 1BE
Activities: Activities of religious organisations
Officers: Jennifer Joy Flett [1960] Director/Chartered Accountant [New Zealander]; Victor Wan Chi Hsu [1950] Director/Church Administrator [Taiwanese]; Reverend Mukondeleli Edward Ramulondi [1955] Director/Pastor [South African]; Rose Althea Wedderburn [1964] Director/Administrative Manager [Jamaican]; Reverend Thomas Jeffrey Williams [1948] Director/Retired; Dr Elizabeth John Zachariah [1952] Director/Medical Doctor [Indian]

Coutts & Company
Incorporated: 24 June 1892 *Employees:* 1,694
Net Worth: £1,147,691,008 *Total Assets:* £31,217,485,824
Registered Office: 440 Strand, London, WC2R 0QS
Activities: Central banking
Parent: National Westminster Bank PLC
Officers: Ralph Antoine Ricks, Secretary; Marie Claire Baird [1973] Director/Bank Official [Irish]; Francesca Barnes [1958] Director/Bank Official; Mark Joseph Lund [1957] Director/Bank Official; Linda Hamilton Urquhart [1959] Director/Bank Official; William Arthur Waldegrave [1946] Director/Provost of Eton College

Coutts Finance Co.
Incorporated: 14 June 1967
Net Worth: £84,472,000 *Total Assets:* £1,517,250,944
Registered Office: 440 Strand, London, WC2R 0QS
Activities: Financial leasing
Parent: Coutts & Company
Officers: Annabelle Katy Arber, Secretary; James Antony Clarry [1974] Director/Bank Official; Stuart William Newey [1964] Director/Bank Official; Dylan Lee Williams [1973] Managing Director, North and Ireland

Cove Energy Limited
Incorporated: 15 December 2003 *Employees:* 1
Net Worth Deficit: £142,170,512 *Total Assets:* £369,359,040
Registered Office: 4 More London Riverside, London, SE1 2AU
Activities: Extraction of crude petroleum
Parent: The Ministry of Finance
Officers: Mana Rojpibulstit [1959] Director/Senior Vice President, Petroleum Engineering [Thai]; Direk Wangudomsuk [1966] Director/Vice President [Thai]

Covent Garden Group Holdings Limited
Incorporated: 2 December 2015
Net Worth: £130,500,000 *Total Assets:* £2,566,700,032
Registered Office: 15 Grosvenor Street, London, W1K 4QZ
Activities: Activities of other holding companies n.e.c.
Parent: Capco Covent Garden Limited
Officers: Leigh McCaveny, Secretary; Ruth Elizabeth Pavey, Secretary; Thomas Glenn Attree [1975] Director/Chartered Accountant; Ian David Hawksworth [1965] Director/Chartered Surveyor; Situl Suryakant Jobanputra [1974] Director; Michelle Veronica Athena McGrath [1983] Director/Head of Investor Relations; Gary James Yardley [1965] Director/Chartered Surveyor

CP Co 3 Limited
Incorporated: 7 September 2012
Net Worth: £14,837,780 *Total Assets:* £183,760,976
Registered Office: 5th Floor, 6 St Andrew Street, London, EC4A 3AE
Activities: Other letting and operating of own or leased real estate
Parent: CP Co Borrower Limited
Officers: Nita Ramesh Savjani [1980] Director; Hugh Edward Francis Sayer [1963] Director/Chartered Surveyor

CP Co 7 Limited
Incorporated: 7 September 2012
Net Worth: £26,588,588 *Total Assets:* £194,292,048
Registered Office: 5th Floor, 6 St Andrew Street, London, EC4A 3AE
Activities: Other letting and operating of own or leased real estate
Parent: CP Co Borrower Limited
Officers: Nita Ramesh Savjani [1980] Director; Hugh Edward Francis Sayer [1963] Director/Chartered Surveyor

CP Co Borrower Limited
Incorporated: 7 September 2012
Net Worth Deficit: £22,663,944 *Total Assets:* £341,170,176
Registered Office: 5th Floor, 6 St Andrew Street, London, EC4A 3AE
Activities: Other letting and operating of own or leased real estate
Officers: Nita Ramesh Savjani [1980] Director; Hugh Edward Francis Sayer [1963] Director/Chartered Surveyor

CP Global Trading LLP
Incorporated: 12 April 2013
Net Worth: £9,197,740 *Total Assets:* £150,842,192
Registered Office: Unit 702, Salisbury House, London Wall, London, EC2M 5QQ

CPA Global Management Services Ltd
Incorporated: 5 October 2000 *Employees:* 95
Net Worth: £53,291,512 *Total Assets:* £191,424,784
Registered Office: 1st Floor, 55 King William Street, London, EC4R 9AD
Activities: Activities of head offices
Parent: Computer Patent Annuities International Limited
Officers: Dawn Heaney Kirkbride Logan Keeffe, Secretary; Ben Gujral [1974] Director/Chief Financial Officer; Toni Nijm [1977] Director/Chief Technology Officer [Swedish]; Simon Linley Webster [1969] Business Operations Director

CPB Residential Finance Limited
Incorporated: 3 May 2013
Net Worth: £46,000 *Total Assets:* £189,780,000
Registered Office: 3rd Floor, 9 Berkeley Street, London, W1J 8DW
Activities: Other credit granting n.e.c.
Officers: Iorweth Antcliff [1976] Director; Andrew John Blenkinsop [1961] Director; Sally Margaret Doyle-Linden [1959] Finance Director; William Nicholson [1989] Director/Private Equity; Sigvard Oscar Henrik Von Reis [1985] Director/Investment Manager [Swedish]

Craegmoor Group (No.3) Limited
Incorporated: 24 June 2008
Net Worth Deficit: £86,771,000 *Total Assets:* £243,035,008
Registered Office: Fifth Floor, 80 Hammersmith Road, London, W14 8UD
Activities: Activities of head offices
Parent: Craegmoor Group (No.2) Limited
Officers: David James Hall, Secretary; Nigel Myers [1966] Finance Director; Trevor Michael Torrington [1961] Director/Chief Executive

Craegmoor Group (No.5) Limited
Incorporated: 24 April 2001
Net Worth: £109,252,000 *Total Assets:* £109,253,000
Registered Office: Fifth Floor, 80 Hammersmith Road, London, W14 8UD
Activities: Other human health activities
Parent: Craegmoor Group (No.3) Limited
Officers: David James Hall, Secretary; Nigel Myers [1966] Finance Director; Trevor Michael Torrington [1961] Director/Chief Executive

Craegmoor Group (No.6) Limited
Incorporated: 6 June 2001
Net Worth: £174,516,000 *Total Assets:* £200,202,000
Registered Office: Fifth Floor, 80 Hammersmith Road, London, W14 8UD
Activities: Activities of head offices
Parent: Craegmoor Group (No.5) Limited
Officers: David James Hall, Secretary; Nigel Myers [1966] Finance Director; Trevor Michael Torrington [1961] Director/Chief Executive

Craegmoor Group Limited
Incorporated: 22 May 2008
Net Worth: £272,700,000 *Total Assets:* £335,324,992
Registered Office: Fifth Floor, 80 Hammersmith Road, London, W14 8UD
Activities: Activities of head offices
Parent: Priory Group No.3 Limited
Officers: David James Hall, Secretary; Nigel Myers [1966] Finance Director; Trevor Michael Torrington [1961] Director/Chief Executive

Craegmoor Limited
Incorporated: 9 June 1993
Net Worth: £69,132,000 *Total Assets:* £608,579,968
Registered Office: Fifth Floor, 80 Hammersmith Road, London, W14 8UD
Activities: Activities of head offices
Parent: Craegmoor Group (No.6) Limited
Officers: David James Hall, Secretary; Nigel Myers [1966] Finance Director; Trevor Michael Torrington [1961] Director/Chief Executive

Cranefield Limited
Incorporated: 13 July 2016
Net Worth Deficit: £8,425,000 *Total Assets:* £277,384,000
Registered Office: 14 Chester Terrace, London, NW1 4ND
Activities: Hotels and similar accommodation
Shareholders: Tower Hill Holdings Limited; Prestmade Ltd
Officers: Jitendra Patel, Secretary; Gulshan Bhatia [1933] Director; Nimet Esmail [1958] Operations Director; Shelina Jetha [1961] Marketing Director

The Cranemere Group Limited
Incorporated: 21 December 2012
Net Worth: £303,566,592 *Total Assets:* £414,117,184
Registered Office: 53 Davies Street, London, W1K 5JH
Activities: Other business support service activities n.e.c.
Officers: Lucie Barakova, Secretary; Mulham Al Jarf [1970] Director/Chief Investment Officer [Omani]; Paul Antony Bishop [1975] Director/Investor; Esteban Coppel [1992] Director [Mexican]; Jose German Coppel Garcia [1986] Director [Mexican]; Guy Jacques Marie Ernest de Selliers de Moranville [1952] Director [Belgian]; Jennifer Susan Duvalier [1969] Director; Raed Abdulla Mohammed Fakhri [1970] Director/Vice President, Investments [Bahraini]; Marcos Jose Jorge Leon [1986] Director/CEO Henla SA [Dominican]; Stephen Craig Lindner Jnr [1978] Director/Investments, Insurance [American]; Vincent Alexis Mai [1940] Director/Chairman and CEO [American]; Stephen James Moseley [1964] Director/Investor [American/British]; Jack McCune Nelson [1956] Director/Investment Professional [American]; G Jeffrey Records Jnr [1959] Director/Banking Executive [American]; Sir David Generald Scholey [1935] Director/Senior Adviser, UBS Investment Bank; Aykut Umit Taftali [1962] Director/Banking/Investments [Turkish]; Jochen Zeitz [1963] Director/Business Executive, Entrepreneur & Philanthropist [German]; Jeffrey Dunston Zients [1966] Director/President [American]

Crawford & Company EMEA/A-P Holdings Limited
Incorporated: 27 January 2009
Net Worth Deficit: £70,629,000 *Total Assets:* £101,390,000
Registered Office: 70 Mark Lane, London, EC3R 7NQ
Activities: Other activities auxiliary to insurance and pension funding
Parent: Crawford & Company International, Inc
Officers: Stephen David Pearsall, Secretary; Joseph Odilo Blanco [1970] Director/Attorney [American]; Stephen David Pearsall [1968] Director; Kieran Lawrence Rigby [1964] Director/Chief Executive Officer [Irish]; William Bruce Swain [1963] Director [American]

Crawford & Company Risk Services Investments Limited
Incorporated: 21 September 1993
Net Worth: £33,673,000 *Total Assets:* £113,856,000
Registered Office: 70 Mark Lane, London, EC3R 7NQ
Activities: Other activities auxiliary to insurance and pension funding
Parent: Crawford & Company Adjusters Limited
Officers: Stephen Pearsall, Secretary; Clive Geoffrey Nicholls [1958] Director/Chief Executive Officer; Stephen Pearsrall [1968] Finance Director

Creation Communications Limited
Incorporated: 10 November 2005
Net Worth: £185,068,992 *Total Assets:* £185,195,008
Registered Office: 3 Grosvenor Gardens, London, SW1W 0BD
Activities: Non-trading company
Parent: CMGRP Holdings Limited
Officers: Louise Bean, Secretary; Anthony George Alexandrou [1953] Director/SVP Global Tax [American]; Derek John Coleman [1955] Director/Solicitor; Warren Spencer Kay [1971] Director/Accountant

Creative Education Trust
Incorporated: 28 April 2011 *Employees:* 1,298
Previous: Creative Education Academies Trust
Net Worth: £135,436,992 *Total Assets:* £161,703,008
Registered Office: 7 Sicilian Avenue, London, WC1A 2QR
Activities: Primary education
Officers: Nicholas Stephen Brann, Secretary; David John Lane Freer Anderson [1956] Director/Banker; Sasha Sakunthala Bhavan [1959] Director/Architect; Nicholas James Douglas Bull [1952] Director/Banker; Simon Richard Frank Figgis [1955] Director; Karen Brenda Forster [1986] Director/Investment Professional; Diana Judith Generald [1968] Director/Chief Executive; Mary Josephine Groom [1954] Director/Solicitor; Marc Lowis Aron Jordan [1955] Director/Corporate Executive; Dr William Boys Richardson [1956] Director/Trades Union General Secretary; Peter Ewart Walls [1954] Director

Credit Suisse (UK) Limited
Incorporated: 11 April 1986 *Employees:* 264
Net Worth: £237,844,000 *Total Assets:* £3,334,735,872
Registered Office: Credit Suisse Private Banking, Compliance Dept, 16th Floor, Five Cabot Square, London, E14 4QR
Activities: Financial intermediation not elsewhere classified
Parent: Credit Suisse Group AG
Officers: Paul Edward Hare, Secretary; Wilhelm Christian Berchem [1965] Managing Director [German]; Michael Adrian Bussey [1959] Director; Maureen Anne Erasmus [1960] Director; Jason Pierpoint Forrester [1969] Director/Banker; Ian Michael Hale [1966] Director/Chief Risk Officer; Alexandra Brigid Kinney [1958] Director [Irish]; Simon David Politzer [1972] Director/Banker; Maura Sullivan [1966] Managing Director

Credit Suisse Asset Management (UK) Holding Limited
Incorporated: 6 April 1995
Net Worth: £163,730,000 *Total Assets:* £168,392,992
Registered Office: One Cabot Square, London, E14 4QJ
Activities: Financial intermediation not elsewhere classified
Parent: Credit Suisse Group AG
Officers: Paul Edward Hare, Secretary; Timothy Charles Bradshaw [1978] Director/Investment Manager; Tracy Cherrington [1968] Director/Chief Operating Officer; Stephen Foster [1959] Director/Banker; Maura Sullivan [1966] Managing Director

Credit Suisse Asset Management Limited
Incorporated: 21 December 1982 *Employees:* 57
Net Worth: £140,652,992 *Total Assets:* £307,521,984
Registered Office: One Cabot Square, London, E14 4QJ
Activities: Financial intermediation not elsewhere classified
Parent: Credit Suisse Asset Management (UK) Holding Limited
Officers: Paul Edward Hare, Secretary; Tracy Cherrington [1968] Director/Chief Operating Officer; Stephen Foster [1959] Director/Banker; Angela Dawn Henderson [1968] Director; Robert Lister [1960] Director/Banker; Michael Joseph Murphy [1973] Director/Banker; Maura Sullivan [1966] Managing Director

Credit Suisse International
Incorporated: 9 May 1990
Net Worth: £16,017,957,888 *Total Assets:* £177,752,440,832
Registered Office: One Cabot Square, London, E14 4QJ
Activities: Banks
Parent: Credit Suisse Group AG
Officers: Paul Edward Hare, Secretary; John Devine [1958] Director; Michael Anthony Diiorio [1973] Director/Banker [American]; Noreen Doyle [1949] Director [Irish]; Robert Duncan Endersby [1959] Director; Andreas Peter Gottschling [1967] Director [German]; Alison Margaret Halsey [1956] Director; Christopher Gerard Bryan Horne [1964] Director/Banker; Paul Robert Ingram [1963] Director/Chief Risk Officer; Nicola Suzanne Kane [1966] Managing Director; David Richard Mathers [1965] Director/Banker; Jonathan Jackson Moore [1979] Managing Director; Caroline Mary Waddington [1969] Director/Chartered Accountant

Credit Suisse Investment Holdings (UK)
Incorporated: 6 April 1995
Net Worth: £5,305,640,960 *Total Assets:* £6,927,594,496
Registered Office: One Cabot Square, London, E14 4QJ
Activities: Activities of head offices
Parent: Credit Suisse Investments (UK)
Officers: Paul Edward Hare, Secretary; Paul Edward Hare [1960] Director/Company Secretary; Christopher Gerard Bryan Horne [1964] Director/Banker; Julian Ralph Houghton [1971] Director/EMEA Treasurer; Caroline Mary Waddington [1969] Director

Credit Suisse Investments (UK)
Incorporated: 17 June 1998
Net Worth: £5,241,536,512 *Total Assets:* £9,725,370,368
Registered Office: One Cabot Square, London, E14 4QJ
Activities: Activities of head offices
Parent: Credit Suisse Group AG
Officers: Paul Edward Hare, Secretary; Paul Edward Hare [1960] Director/Company Secretary; Christopher Gerard Bryan Horne [1964] Director/Banker; Julian Ralph Houghton [1971] Director/EMEA Treasurer; Caroline Mary Waddington [1969] Director

Credit Suisse Securities (Europe) Limited
Incorporated: 9 November 1966
Net Worth: £5,502,743,552 *Total Assets:* £88,207,794,176
Registered Office: One Cabot Square, London, E14 4QJ
Activities: Financial intermediation not elsewhere classified
Parent: Credit Suisse Investment Holdings (UK)
Officers: Paul Edward Hare, Secretary; John Devine [1958] Director; Michael Anthony Diiorio [1973] Director/Banker [American]; Noreen Doyle [1949] Director [Irish]; Robert Duncan Endersby [1959] Director; Andreas Peter Gottschling [1967] Director [German]; Alison Margaret Halsey [1956] Director; Christopher Gerard Bryan Horne [1964] Director/Banker; Paul Robert Ingram [1963] Director/Chief Risk Officer; Nicola Suzanne Kane [1966] Managing Director; David Richard Mathers [1965] Director/Banker; Jonathan Jackson Moore [1979] Managing Director; Caroline Mary Waddington [1969] Director/Chartered Accountant

Creditex Holdco Limited
Incorporated: 11 April 2008 *Employees:* 4
Net Worth: £363,413,312 *Total Assets:* £363,413,312
Registered Office: Milton Gate, 60 Chiswell Street, London, EC1Y 4SA
Activities: Activities of financial services holding companies
Parent: Intercontinental Exchange Holdings, Inc.
Officers: Elizabeth Miriam Holt, Secretary; Scott Anthony Hill [1967] Director/Chief Finance Officer [American]; Duncan Ellis Moyle [1979] Director/Derivatives Broker; Andrew James Surdykowski [1970] Director [American]

CRF Health Group Limited
Incorporated: 3 December 2014 *Employees:* 597
Net Worth Deficit: £27,484,854 *Total Assets:* £349,517,120
Registered Office: Ground Floor, Waterfront Building, Manbre Road, London, W6 9RH
Activities: Research and experimental development on biotechnology
Parent: Buccaneer Bidco Limited
Officers: Michael Nolte [1969] Director [American]

The Francis Crick Institute Limited
Incorporated: 23 April 2009 *Employees:* 1,294
Net Worth: £605,673,984 *Total Assets:* £632,203,008
Registered Office: 1 Midland Road, London, NW1 1AT
Activities: Other service activities n.e.c.
Officers: Joseph Daniel Fitz, Secretary; Kate Elizabeth Bingham [1965] Director/Managing Partner; Lord Edmund John Philip Browne [1948] Director/Businessman; Professor Margaret Jane Dallman [1957] Director/Principal, Faculty of Natural Sciences; Isabelle Marie Ealet [1963] Director/Retired [French]; Dr Jeremy Farrar [1961] Director of The Wellcome Trust; Dr Iain Walter Foulkes [1971] Executive Director CRUK/CEO CRT; Dr Brian Gilvary [1962] Director/Group CFO; Professor Sir Robert Ian Lechler [1951] Director/University Professor; Professor Henrietta Miriam Ottoline Leyser Day [1965] Director and Professor of Plant Development; Prof David Arthur Lomas [1962] Director/Vice Provost Health, UCL; Dr Menelas Nicolas Pangalos [1967] Director/Scientist; Fiona Mary Watt [1956] Director/Executive Chair, Medical Research Council

Crops Holdings (UK) Limited
Incorporated: 30 September 2016 *Employees:* 1,047
Net Worth: £65,555,456 *Total Assets:* £204,028,496
Registered Office: Investcorp House, 48 Grosvenor Street, London, W1K 3HW
Activities: Activities of other holding companies n.e.c.
Officers: Andrea Jayne Davis [1965] Managing Director/Banker; Grahame Ivey [1958] Director/Chartered Accountant

Crosby Worldwide Limited
Incorporated: 4 October 2013
Net Worth: £357,417,760 *Total Assets:* £357,417,760
Registered Office: Suite 1, 3rd Floor, 11-12 St James's Square, London, SW1Y 4LB
Activities: Non-trading company
Parent: Ascend Overseas Limited
Officers: Brandon Francis Brahm [1984] Director/Investment Professional [American]; Peter Max Stavros [1974] Director/Investment Professional [American]

Crossrail Limited
Incorporated: 8 May 2001 *Employees:* 499
Net Worth: £8,720,600,064 *Total Assets:* £11,418,099,712
Registered Office: 5 Endeavour Square, Stratford, London, E20 1JN
Activities: Construction of railways and underground railways
Parent: Transport Trading Limited
Officers: Susan Margaret Beadles, Secretary; Phil Gaffney [1947] Director; David Charles Hendry [1957] Director/Chief Finance Officer; Robert Archie Jennings [1955] Director/Consultant; Anne Marie McMeel [1954] Director/Business Advisor and Non-Executive; Anthony Jan Michael Meggs [1952] Director; Dr Olawale Nelson Ogunshakin [1960] Director/Civil Engineer; Andrew Christopher Pitt [1959] Rail Director; Wyvill Richard Nicolls Raynsford [1945] Director/Consultant; Christopher Michael Sexton [1955] Director/Deputy CEO; Mark Wild [1965] Director/CEO, Crossrail Limited

Crown Financial & Merchant Bank PLC
Incorporated: 19 October 2007
Net Worth: £87,877,744 *Total Assets:* £529,517,760
Registered Office: 3rd Floor, 70 Gracechurch Street, London, EC3V 0HR
Activities: Other credit granting n.e.c.
Officers: Gasan Mamedov [1962] Director/Businessman [Turkish]; Dr Mariia Vengrinovych [1961] Director/Consultant [Ukrainian]

CTRL Section 1 Finance PLC
Incorporated: 18 August 2003
Net Worth: £6,711,000 *Total Assets:* £1,363,539,968
Registered Office: 33 Horseferry Road, London, SW1P 4DR
Activities: Financial intermediation not elsewhere classified
Parent: Secretary of State for Transport
Officers: Malcolm Lowe, Secretary; Mark Filer [1997] Director; Malcolm Lowe [1965] Director/Civil Servant; Helene Walden [1970] Director/Civil Servant

Cubcall Limited
Incorporated: 10 June 1976 *Employees:* 12
Net Worth: £78,887,144 *Total Assets:* £259,131,696
Registered Office: Taylor Wessing LLP, 5 New Street Square, London, EC4A 3TW
Activities: Other letting and operating of own or leased real estate
Parent: Arlington House Investments Limited
Officers: Amer Mohammed Mahdi Al Tajir [1961] Director/Businessman [Emirati]; Khalid Mohamed Mahdi Al Tajir [1958] Director/Businessman [Emirati]; Mohamed Sadiq Al Tajir [1941] Director/Businessman [Bahraini]; Mohammed Mahdi Al Tajir [1931] Director/Businessman [Emirati]

Cubico Holdings (UK) 2 Limited
Incorporated: 29 July 2015
Net Worth: £20,577,000 *Total Assets:* £153,710,000
Registered Office: 110 Floor, 15 Bishopsgate, London, EC2N 4AY
Activities: Activities of production holding companies
Parent: Cubico Holdings (UK) Limited
Officers: Stephen Lewis Harmon Packwood [1981] Director; Alberto Ramos [1962] Director; David Swindin [1968] Director

Cubico Holdings (UK) 4 Limited
Incorporated: 23 November 2016
Net Worth: £43,417,000 *Total Assets:* £181,750,000
Registered Office: Floor 15, 110 Bishopsgate, London, EC2N 4AY
Activities: Activities of other holding companies n.e.c.
Parent: Cubico Holdings (UK) 3 Limited
Officers: Stephen Lewis Harmon Packwood [1981] Director; Alberto Ramos [1962] Director; David Swindin [1968] Director/Head of EMEA

Cubico Sustainable Investments Holdings Limited
Incorporated: 13 October 2014
Net Worth: £363,502,464 *Total Assets:* £363,536,576
Registered Office: Floor 15, 110 Bishopsgate, London, EC2N 4AY
Activities: Production of electricity
Shareholder: The Canadian Federal Government
Officers: Olga Maria Garcia Gonzalez, Secretary; Alberto Ramos [1962] Director; Stephen Riley [1961] Director; David Swindin [1968] Director

Cubico Sustainable Investments Limited
Incorporated: 14 October 2014 *Employees:* 83
Net Worth: £448,049,248 *Total Assets:* £1,240,590,464
Registered Office: Floor 15, 110 Bishopsgate, London, EC2N 4AY
Activities: Production of electricity
Parent: Cubico Sustainable Investments Holdings Limited
Officers: Olga Maria Garcia Gonzalez, Secretary; Alberto Ramos [1962] Director; Stephen Riley [1961] Director; David Swindin [1968] Director

Cummins EMEA Holdings Limited
Incorporated: 31 October 2011
Net Worth: £3,296,727,040 *Total Assets:* £5,645,561,856
Registered Office: 3rd Floor, 10 Eastbourne Terrace, Paddington, London, W2 6LG
Activities: Activities of other holding companies n.e.c.
Parent: Cummins Inc.
Officers: Paul Jonathan Fertleman, Secretary; John McCormack Barrowman [1952] Director/Engineer; Paul Jonathan Fertleman [1971] Director/Lawyer; Antonio Leitao [1964] Director [French]; Desmond Joseph McMenamin [1978] Director/Manager; Amanda Jane Robinson [1964] Director; Alexey Ustinov [1970] Managing Director [Russian]

Cummins Ltd.
Incorporated: 7 November 1956 *Employees:* 3,883
Net Worth: £559,731,008 *Total Assets:* £1,313,540,992
Registered Office: 3rd Floor, 10 Eastbourne Terrace, Paddington, London, W2 6LG
Activities: Manufacture of engines and turbines, except aircraft, vehicle and cycle engines
Parent: Cummins Generator Technologies Limited
Officers: Paul Jonathan Fertleman, Secretary; John McCormack Barrowman [1952] Director/Engineer; Paul Jonathan Fertleman [1971] Director/Senior Lawyer; Antonio Leitao [1964] Director [French]; Mark O'Connor [1966] Director; Edward David Smith [1976] Director/Chartered Accountant; Alexey Ustinov [1970] Managing Director [Russian]

Cummins PGI Holdings Ltd
Incorporated: 22 November 2012
Net Worth: £424,168,000 *Total Assets:* £460,811,008
Registered Office: 3rd Floor, 10 Eastbourne Terrace, Paddington, London, W2 6LG
Activities: Activities of other holding companies n.e.c.
Parent: Cummins EMEA Holdings Limited
Officers: Joseph Morgan Rigler, Secretary; Antonio Leitao [1964] Director [French]; Alouis Ngoshi [1974] Regional Treasury Director [Zimbabwean]; Joseph Morgan Rigler [1980] Director/Lawyer; Amanda Jane Robinson [1964] Director

Cummins Power Generation Limited
Incorporated: 30 January 1932 *Employees:* 383
Net Worth Deficit: £2,158,000 *Total Assets:* £122,393,000
Registered Office: 3rd Floor, 10 Eastbourne Terrace, Paddington, London, W2 6LG
Activities: Machining
Parent: Cummins PGI Holdings Ltd
Officers: Joseph Morgan Rigler, Secretary; John McCormack Barrowman [1952] Director; Ignacio Gonzalez Garcia de Quevedo [1971] Director [Spanish]; Casimiro Antonio Vieira Leitao [1964] Director/Vice President [French]; Joseph Morgan Rigler [1980] Director/Lawyer; Edward David Smith [1976] Director/Chartered Accountant

Marie Curie
Incorporated: 3 May 1952 *Employees:* 4,317
Previous: Marie Curie Cancer Care
Net Worth: £103,204,000 *Total Assets:* £134,504,000
Registered Office: 89 Albert Embankment, London, SE1 7TP
Activities: Other information service activities n.e.c.
Officers: Elizabeth Jane Silver, Secretary; Manvinder Singh Banga [1954] Senior Independent Director [Indian]; Timothy James Breedon [1958] Director; Dr Rachel Elizabeth Mary Burman [1965] Director/Medical Hospital Consultant; Steve Trevor Carson [1967] Director; Charles William John Compton [1950] Director; Richard David Flint [1968] Director; Ruth Holt [1965] Director/Chief Nurse; Patricia Lesley Lee [1962] Director/Chief Executive Officer; Christopher Martin [1959] Director/Chairman; Dame Barbara Monroe [1951] Director; Linda Hamilton Urquhart [1959] Director; Helen Weir [1962] Director

Currencies Direct Holdings Limited
Incorporated: 9 October 2007 *Employees:* 433
Net Worth: £36,760,000 *Total Assets:* £251,304,992
Registered Office: 1 Canary Wharf, London, E14 5AA
Activities: Financial intermediation not elsewhere classified
Officers: Jonathan Matthew Beddell [1978] Director; Neil Cooper [1967] Director; Keith Nigel Hatton [1958] Director/Chief Executive Officer; Leonidas Markides [1971] Director

Cushman & Wakefield Debenham Tie Leung Limited
Incorporated: 16 October 1992 *Employees:* 1,131
Previous: DTZ Debenham Tie Leung Limited
Net Worth Deficit: £52,012,000 *Total Assets:* £324,272,992
Registered Office: 125 Old Broad Street, London, EC2N 1AR
Activities: Real estate agencies
Parent: DTZ Europe Limited
Officers: Sunita Kaushal, Secretary; Manuel Uria Fernandez [1968] Director [Spanish]; John Forrester [1962] Director/Chartered Surveyor; Sunita Kaushal [1973] Director/General Counsel & Company Secretary, EMEA; Parimal Raojibhai Patel [1965] Director; George Roberts [1969] Director/Head of UK & Ireland; Colin Joseph Tennant Wilson [1966] Director/Chartered Surveyor

Cushman & Wakefield UK USD Holdco Limited
Incorporated: 27 October 2016
Net Worth: £478,010,080 *Total Assets:* £478,010,080
Registered Office: 125 Old Broad Street, London, EC2N 1AR
Activities: Activities of other holding companies n.e.c.
Parent: DTZ Worldwide Limited
Officers: John Forrester [1962] Director/Chief Executive, EMEA P8; Sunita Kaushal [1973] Director/General Counsel & Company Secretary P6; Duncan John Palmer [1965] Director/Global Chief Financial Officer; Brett David Soloway [1968] Director/Global General Counsel [American]

CW Lending II Limited
Incorporated: 16 February 2000
Net Worth: £5,591,271 *Total Assets:* £1,639,175,168
Registered Office: 1 Canada Square, London, E14 5AB
Activities: Credit granting by non-deposit taking finance houses and other specialist consumer credit grantors
Parent: Canary Wharf Finance Holdings Limited
Officers: John Raymond Garwood, Secretary; A Peter Anderson II [1953] Director/Real Estate Executive [American]; George Iacobescu [1945] Director; Russell James John Lyons [1961] Director/Chartered Accountant

CW Properties DS7B Limited
Incorporated: 24 September 1997 *Employees:* 3
Net Worth: £189,618 *Total Assets:* £103,216,496
Registered Office: 30th Floor, One Canary Wharf, London, E14 5AB
Activities: Renting and operating of Housing Association real estate
Parent: Canary Wharf Investments Limited
Officers: John Raymond Garwood, Secretary; A Peter Anderson II [1953] Director/Real Estate Executive [American]; George Iacobescu [1945] Director; Russell James John Lyons [1961] Director/Chartered Accountant

CWBC Finance (BP1) Limited
Incorporated: 6 December 2002 *Employees:* 3
Net Worth Deficit: £160,670,448 *Total Assets:* £573,174,016
Registered Office: Canary Wharf Group, 30th Floor, 1 Canada Square, London, E14 5AB
Activities: Financial intermediation not elsewhere classified
Parent: Canary Wharf Investments Limited
Officers: John Raymond Garwood, Secretary; A Peter Anderson II [1953] Director/Real Estate Executive [American]; George Iacobescu [1945] Director; Russell James John Lyons [1961] Director/Chartered Accountant

CWBC Finance Two (BP1) Limited
Incorporated: 1 July 2013 *Employees:* 3
Net Worth: £104,749 *Total Assets:* £692,275,328
Registered Office: 30th Floor, One Canary Wharf, London, E14 5AB
Activities: Financial intermediation not elsewhere classified
Parent: CWBC Finance (BP1) Limited
Officers: John Raymond Garwood, Secretary; A Peter Anderson II [1953] Director [American]; George Iacobescu [1945] Director; Russell James John Lyons [1961] Director

CWBC Properties (BP1) Limited
Incorporated: 6 December 2002 *Employees:* 3
Net Worth: £102,117,744 *Total Assets:* £1,476,261,760
Registered Office: Canary Wharf Group PLC, 30th Floor, 1 Canada Square, London, E14 5AB
Activities: Non-trading company
Parent: CWCB Holdings Limited
Officers: John Raymond Garwood, Secretary; A Peter Anderson II [1953] Director/Real Estate Executive [American]; George Iacobescu [1945] Director; Russell James John Lyons [1961] Director/Chartered Accountant

CWCB Finance II Limited
Incorporated: 22 July 1998 *Employees:* 3
Net Worth: £1 *Total Assets:* £2,632,645,376
Registered Office: 30th Floor, One Canary Wharf, London, E14 5AB
Activities: Non-trading company
Parent: Canary Wharf Central Limited
Officers: John Raymond Garwood, Secretary; A Peter Anderson II [1953] Director/Real Estate Executive [American]; George Iacobescu [1945] Director; Russell James John Lyons [1961] Director/Chartered Accountant

CWCB Finance Leasing (DS7B) Limited
Incorporated: 22 February 1995
Net Worth: £151,063 *Total Assets:* £102,088,496
Registered Office: One Canary Wharf, London, E14 5AB
Activities: Financial leasing
Parent: Canary Wharf Investments Limited
Officers: John Raymond Garwood, Secretary; A Peter Anderson II [1953] Managing Director - Finance [American]; George Iacobescu [1945] Director/Chairman and CEO; Russell James John Lyons [1961] Director/Chartered Accountant

CWCB Investments (Rt2) Limited
Incorporated: 15 October 1997 *Employees:* 3
Net Worth: £124,503,776 *Total Assets:* £300,461,376
Registered Office: 30th Floor, One Canary Wharf, London, E14 5AB
Activities: Activities of head offices
Parent: CWCB Holdings Limited
Officers: John Raymond Garwood, Secretary; A Peter Anderson II [1953] Director/Real Estate Executive [American]; George Iacobescu [1945] Director; Russell James John Lyons [1961] Director/Chartered Accountant

CWCB Leasing (DS6) Limited
Incorporated: 2 March 2000 *Employees:* 3
Net Worth: £1 *Total Assets:* £152,836,288
Registered Office: 30th Floor, One Canary Wharf, London, E14 5AB
Activities: Non-trading company
Parent: CWCB Holdings Limited
Officers: John Raymond Garwood, Secretary; A Peter Anderson II [1953] Director/Real Estate Executive [American]; George Iacobescu [1945] Director; Russell James John Lyons [1961] Director/Chartered Accountant

CWCB Properties (DS6) Limited
Incorporated: 2 March 2000 *Employees:* 3
Net Worth: £91,790,128 *Total Assets:* £412,080,288
Registered Office: 30th Floor, One Canary Wharf, London, E14 5AB
Activities: Renting and operating of Housing Association real estate
Parent: CWCB Holdings Limited
Officers: John Raymond Garwood, Secretary; A Peter Anderson II [1953] Director/Real Estate Executive [American]; George Iacobescu [1945] Director; Russell James John Lyons [1961] Director/Chartered Accountant

CWCB Properties (DS7) Limited
Incorporated: 27 April 2005 *Employees:* 3
Net Worth: £77,361,136 *Total Assets:* £883,276,928
Registered Office: One Canary Wharf, London, E14 5AB
Activities: Other business support service activities n.e.c.
Shareholders: Canary Wharf Investments Limited; Canary Wharf Holdings Limited
Officers: John Raymond Garwood, Secretary; A Peter Anderson II [1953] Director/Real Estate Executive [American]; George Iacobescu [1945] Director; Russell James John Lyons [1961] Director/Chartered Accountant

CWE SPV HCO Limited
Incorporated: 7 November 1995 *Employees:* 3
Net Worth: £32,036,252 *Total Assets:* £164,957,472
Registered Office: 30th Floor, One Canary Wharf, London, E14 5AB
Activities: Other business support service activities n.e.c.
Parent: CWE SPV Super HCO Limited
Officers: John Raymond Garwood, Secretary; A Peter Anderson II [1953] Director/Real Estate Executive [American]; George Iacobescu [1945] Director; Russell James John Lyons [1961] Director/Chartered Accountant

CWG (Wood Wharf Two) Limited
Incorporated: 21 July 2010 *Employees:* 3
Net Worth: £89,988,424 *Total Assets:* £443,313,344
Registered Office: One Canary Wharf, London, E14 5AB
Activities: Development of building projects
Parent: CWG (Wood Wharf) Holdings Limited
Officers: John Raymond Garwood, Secretary; Peter a Anderson II [1953] Director [American]; George Iacobescu [1945] Director; Russell James John Lyons [1961] Director

CWG Newco Limited
Incorporated: 10 June 2015 *Employees:* 2
Net Worth: £4,079,304,448 *Total Assets:* £4,079,311,616
Registered Office: 30th Floor, One Canary Wharf, London, E14 5AB
Activities: Activities of construction holding companies
Shareholders: Canary Wharf Group Investment Holdings PLC; Songbird Finance Limited
Officers: John Raymond Garwood, Secretary; Khalifa Khalid Al-Thani [1990] Director [Qatari]; Kevin O'Donnell McCrain [1979] Director/Senior Vice President [American]

CWIGroup Limited
Incorporated: 12 May 1995
Net Worth: £789,223,360 *Total Assets:* £847,876,992
Registered Office: Griffin House, 161 Hammersmith Road, London, W6 8BS
Activities: Activities of head offices
Parent: Sable Holding Limited
Officers: Leah Helena Pegg, Secretary; Leah Helena Pegg [1985] Director/Company Secretary; Matthew Edward Read [1977] Director/Treasurer

CX Holdco Limited
Incorporated: 2 June 2016 *Employees:* 2,094
Net Worth Deficit: £15,808,000 *Total Assets:* £170,819,008
Registered Office: 2nd Floor, Asticus Building, 21 Palmer Street, London, SW1H 0AD
Activities: Residential nursing care facilities
Officers: Liam Stuart Goddard [1982] Director/Venture Capital; Adrian Leslie Jeffery [1977] Director/Private Equity; Ian Stephen Venter [1970] Director/Private Equity

Cyan Auto Receivables Limited
Incorporated: 8 June 2017
Net Worth: £406 *Total Assets:* £266,576,944
Registered Office: 35 Great St Helen's, London, EC3A 6AP
Activities: Financial intermediation not elsewhere classified
Parent: Cyan Auto Receivables Holdings Limited
Officers: Susan Iris Abrahams [1957] Director

Cynergy Bank Limited
Incorporated: 9 April 2003 *Employees:* 248
Previous: Bank of Cyprus UK Limited
Net Worth: £112,718,000 *Total Assets:* £1,877,117,952
Registered Office: 27-31 Charlotte Street, London, W1T 1RP
Activities: Banks
Parent: Cynergy Capital Limited
Officers: Paul Jordan, Secretary; Pradip Khodidas Dhamecha [1958] Director; Nicholas Gerard Fahy [1967] Director/Chief Executive Officer [Irish]; David Green [1956] Director/Banker; Euan Graeme Hamilton [1961] Director/Consultant; Francesca Margaret Hampton [1970] Director/Chief Financial Officer; Philip Haldane Nunnerley [1946] Director/Retired Banker; Kim Louise Rebecchi [1966] Director; Balbinder Singh Sohal [1975] Director; Jean Stevenson [1953] Director/Chartered Accountant

Czarnikow Group Limited
Incorporated: 2 October 1991 *Employees:* 188
Net Worth: £47,292,808 *Total Assets:* £332,222,624
Registered Office: Paternoster House, 65 St Paul's Churchyard, London, EC4M 8AB
Activities: Activities of other holding companies n.e.c.
Parent: C. Czarnikow Limited
Officers: Robin Cave [1964] Director; Adam William Ian Leetham [1969] Director/Sugar Trader; Julian Norman Cyril Randles [1970] Director/Accountant; William James Rook [1967] Director/Sugar Trader; Jonathan Gareth Williams [1962] Director

C. Czarnikow Limited
Incorporated: 18 June 1996 *Employees:* 188
Net Worth: £48,834,888 *Total Assets:* £332,236,864
Registered Office: Paternoster House, 65 St Paul's Churchyard, London, EC4M 8AB
Activities: Activities of other holding companies n.e.c.
Shareholder: British Sugar PLC
Officers: Matthew James Spencer Booth [1971] Director/Banking; Robin Cave [1964] Director/CEO Czarnikow Group; Richard Iain Morrison [1961] Business Performance Director; Julian Norman Cyril Randles [1970] Director; William James Rook [1967] Director/Sugar Trader; Daniel Edward West [1976] Director/Businessman; Paul Michael Weston [1980] Director/Solicitor [British/Australian]

D & P International Holdings (UK) Limited
Incorporated: 2 December 2015 *Employees:* 663
Net Worth Deficit: £14,604,000 *Total Assets:* £126,703,000
Registered Office: 7 Albemarle Street, London, W1S 4HQ
Activities: Activities of financial services holding companies
Parent: Deerfield UK Holdings Limited
Officers: Edward S Foreman [1969] Director/Attorney [American]; Patrick Michael Puzzuoli [1970] Director/Chief Financial Officer [American]

D B Investments (GB) Limited
Incorporated: 4 July 1989
Net Worth: £1,485,731,968 *Total Assets:* £2,023,958,016
Registered Office: Winchester House, 1 Great Winchester Street, London, EC2N 2DB
Activities: Activities of other holding companies n.e.c.
Parent: Deutsche Bank Aktiengesellschaft
Officers: Joanne Louise Bagshaw, Secretary; Scott Jamieson Dobbie [1939] Director/Stockbroker; Philip Haldane Nunnerley [1946] Director/Banker; Benjamin Jon Pallas [1976] Director/Banker

D-Clear Europe Limited
Incorporated: 29 October 2007 *Employees:* 904
Net Worth: £35,896,648 *Total Assets:* £186,273,856
Registered Office: St Helens, 1 Undershaft, London, EC3A 8EE
Activities: Activities of head offices
Officers: Claudia Giunta, Secretary; Khalifa Hassan Al Daboos [1967] Director [Emirati]; Ahmad Abdulkarim Mohd Julfar [1961] Director/Engineer [Emirati]; Abdulla Abdulrahman Qassem [1963] Director [Emirati]

DAC Beachcroft LLP
Incorporated: 16 February 2006 *Employees:* 2,296
Net Worth: £67,954,000 *Total Assets:* £156,846,000
Registered Office: 25 Walbrook, London, EC4N 8AF
Officers: Virginia Eve Clegg [1965] Member; Benjamin James Vaughan Daniels [1971] Member; David Egerton Pollitt [1965] Member; Udara Ranasinghe [1974] Member; Khurram Shamsee [1975] Member; David Weatherburn [1962] Member; Ruth Winterbottom [1964] Member; William Henry Allison [1966] LLP Member; Hans Victor Edward Frederick Allnutt [1980] LLP Member; Jose Maria Alvarez-Cienfuegos Fernandez [1980] LLP Member; Thomas Cooper Baker [1972] LLP Member; David Laurence Bear [1963] LLP Member; Charles Bending [1971] LLP Member; John Michael Charles Blackburne [1956] LLP Member; Henry Louis Michael Bothamley [1957] LLP Member; Andrew Peter Boulton [1969] LLP Member; Deborah Ann Bradley [1962] LLP Member; John Francis Bramhall [1961] LLP Member; Lisa Broderick [1970] LLP Member; Jonathan Brogden [1972] LLP Member; Graham Charles Brothwood [1961] LLP Member; Nathan James Butcher [1967] LLP Member; John Marcus Campbell [1964] LLP Member; Nicholas John Chronias [1969] LLP Member; Darragh James Colville [1969] LLP Member; Thomas George Corrigan [1961] LLP Member; Matthew Edward Darling [1964] LLP Member; Paul Anthony Davison [1969] LLP Member; Ashley Robert Dewar [1970] LLP Member; John Stuart Henry Dunlop [1973] LLP Member; Campbell James Dye [1967] LLP Member; Helen Louise Faulkner [1967] LLP Member; Nicholas Charles Gibbon [1964] LLP Member; Fiona Mary Ann Gill [1966] LLP Member; Jonathan Goodman [1964] LLP Member; Duncan Mark Greenwood [1965] LLP Member; James Stephen Harrison [1977] LLP Member; Richard Ian Highley [1963] LLP Member; Patrick Allan Hill [1970] LLP Member; Stephen John Hocking [1970] LLP Member; Wendy Hopkins [1969] LLP Member; Clare Hughes-Williams [1966] LLP Member; Warren Robert Kemp [1975] LLP Member; Mark Andrew Richard Kendall [1971] LLP Member; Alison Mary Key [1971] LLP Member; Nicholas William Knapman [1965] LLP Member; David Richard William Knapp [1960] LLP Member; Robert James Lee [1959] LLP Member; Paul Robert Leighton [1962] LLP Member; Gemma Leonard [1981] LLP Member; Jan Matthew Levinson [1968] LLP Member; Alex Richard Lock [1968] LLP Member; John Parker Maillie [1964] LLP Member; Andrew Christopher Michael Marsh [1962] LLP Member; Sara Elizabeth May [1964] LLP Member; Ian Frederick McConkey [1966] LLP Member; Matthew John Alexander McGrath [1963] LLP Member; Anthony John Menzies [1968] LLP Member; Julian Lawrence Nicholas Miller [1961] LLP Member; Nigel Gregson Montgomery [1960] LLP Member; James Sinclair Benedict Morris [1965] LLP Member; Paul Calvert Murray [1955] LLP Member; Philip James Murrin [1971] LLP Member; Mark Hastings Neville [1969] LLP Member; Richard John Ottley [1966] LLP Member; Andrew John Cunningham Parker [1959] LLP Member; Michael Peter David Peeters [1963] LLP Member; Jose Maria Pimentel Pardo [1978] LLP Member; Daniel Seth Preddy [1974] LLP Member; James Derek Reed [1976] LLP Member; Gary Rice [1963] LLP Member; Stephen Rhodri Richards [1970] LLP Member; Mark Trevanion Roach [1977] LLP Member; Sally Jane Roff [1966] LLP Member; Mathew David Rutter [1969] LLP Member; Timothy Michael Ryan [1976] LLP Member; Rodney Searl [1966] LLP Member; Danielle Singer [1969] LLP Member; Tania Caroline Sless [1961] LLP Member; Corinne Dawn Slingo [1971] LLP Member; Christopher James Fraser Stanwell [1972] LLP Member; Paul Taylor [1965] LLP Member; Sakis Jonathan Tombolis [1972] LLP Member; Antony Crispin Tomlinson [1958] LLP Member; Lucinda Mary Walsh [1959] LLP Member; Thomas Alexander Watkinson [1975] LLP Member; Suzanne Wharton [1970] LLP Member; Christopher John Wilkes [1959] LLP Member; John Benedict Alan Williams [1968] LLP Member; Nicholas Michael Young [1965] LLP Member; Sally Elizabeth Yuill [1964] LLP Member

Daejan (UK) Limited
Incorporated: 23 April 2001
Net Worth: £431,747,584 *Total Assets:* £495,504,352
Registered Office: 158-162 Shaftesbury Avenue, London, WC2H 8HR
Activities: Renting and operating of Housing Association real estate
Parent: Daejan Holdings PLC
Officers: Mark Roy Mason Jenner, Secretary; David Davis [1935] Director; Benzion Schalom Eliezer Freshwater [1948] Director; Solomon Israel Freshwater [1950] Director

Daejan (US) Limited
Incorporated: 24 April 2001
Net Worth: £98,570,968 *Total Assets:* £110,447,024
Registered Office: Freshwater House, 158-162 Shaftesbury Avenue, London, WC2H 8HR
Activities: Renting and operating of Housing Association real estate
Parent: Daejan Holdings PLC
Officers: Mark Roy Mason Jenner, Secretary; David Davis [1935] Director; Benzion Schalom Eliezer Freshwater [1948] Director; Solomon Israel Freshwater [1950] Director

Daejan Holdings PLC
Incorporated: 18 September 1935
Net Worth: £1,812,902,016 *Total Assets:* £2,535,004,928
Registered Office: 158-162 Shaftesbury Avenue, London, WC2H 8HR
Activities: Buying and selling of own real estate
Officers: Mark Roy Mason Jenner, Secretary; Solomon Benjamin Benaim [1955] Director/Chartered Accountant; David Davis [1935] Director/Chartered Accountant; Alexander Mordechai Freshwater [1971] Director [American]; Benzion Schalom Eliezer Freshwater [1948] Director; Chaim Benzion Freshwater [1972] Director/Lecturer; Raphael Elozer Freshwater [1969] Director/Lecturer; Solomon Israel Freshwater [1950] Director; Sander Srulowitz [1952] Director/Attorney [American]

Daejan Investments (Grove Hall) Limited
Incorporated: 26 June 1959
Net Worth: £167,603,136 *Total Assets:* £204,019,360
Registered Office: Freshwater House, 158-162 Shaftesbury Avenue, London, WC2H 8HR
Activities: Buying and selling of own real estate
Parent: Daejan (UK) Limited
Officers: Mark Roy Mason Jenner, Secretary; David Davis [1935] Director/Chartered Accountant; Benzion Schalom Eliezer Freshwater [1948] Director

Daejan Investments Limited
Incorporated: 2 June 1959
Net Worth: £232,340,656 *Total Assets:* £376,934,688
Registered Office: 158-162 Shaftesbury Avenue, London, WC2H 8HR
Activities: Buying and selling of own real estate
Parent: Daejan (UK) Limited
Officers: Mark Roy Mason Jenner, Secretary; David Davis [1935] Director/Chartered Accountant; Benzion Schalom Eliezer Freshwater [1948] Director

Daejan Properties Limited
Incorporated: 2 June 1959 *Employees:* 29
Net Worth: £342,773,600 *Total Assets:* £614,441,280
Registered Office: Freshwater House, 158-162 Shafesbury Avenue, London, WC2H 8HR
Activities: Buying and selling of own real estate
Parent: Daejan Traders Limited
Officers: Mark Roy Mason Jenner, Secretary; David Davis [1935] Director/Chartered Accountant; Benzion Schalom Eliezer Freshwater [1948] Director

Daejan Traders Limited
Incorporated: 24 April 2001
Net Worth: £177,228,656 *Total Assets:* £273,240,448
Registered Office: 158-162 Shaftesbury Avenue, London, WC2H 8HR
Activities: Buying and selling of own real estate
Parent: Daejan Holdings PLC
Officers: Mark Roy Mason Jenner, Secretary; David Davis [1935] Director; Benzion Schalom Eliezer Freshwater [1948] Director; Solomon Israel Freshwater [1950] Director

Dagger Holdings Limited
Incorporated: 23 August 2006
Net Worth Deficit: £39,500,000 *Total Assets:* £144,759,008
Registered Office: 55 Baker Street, London, W1U 8EW
Activities: Activities of head offices
Parent: Het International 2 B.V.
Officers: Eric Alan Hession [1974] Director/Executive Vice President, Chief Financial Officer [American]

Daily Mail and General Holdings Limited
Incorporated: 20 January 1983 *Employees:* 41
Net Worth: £481,980,992 *Total Assets:* £2,745,842,944
Registered Office: Northcliffe House, 2 Derry Street, Kensington, London, W8 5TT
Activities: Activities of head offices
Parent: Daily Mail and General Trust PLC
Officers: Frances Louise Sallas, Secretary; Timothy Guy Collier [1963] Director; William Richard Flint [1969] Director/Accountant; Frances Louise Sallas [1977] Director/Company Secretary; Adam Bjorn Webster [1973] Director/Accountant

Daily Mail and General Investments Limited
Incorporated: 4 May 1988 *Employees:* 3
Previous: Daily Mail and General Investments PLC
Net Worth: £732,833,984 *Total Assets:* £753,390,976
Registered Office: Northcliffe House, 2 Derry Street, Kensington, London, W8 5TT
Activities: Activities of head offices
Parent: Daily Mail and General Holdings Limited
Officers: Frances Louise Sallas, Secretary; William Richard Flint [1969] Director/Accountant; Frances Louise Sallas [1977] Director/Company Secretary

Daily Mail and General Trust P L C
Incorporated: 27 September 1922 *Employees:* 8,301
Net Worth: £908,200,000 *Total Assets:* £2,048,199,936
Registered Office: Northcliffe House, 2 Derry Street, Kensington, London, W8 5TT
Activities: Activities of head offices
Officers: Frances Louise Sallas, Secretary; Kevin Joseph Beatty [1957] Director/Newspaper Manager; Timothy Guy Collier [1963] Director; The Honourable Lady Annabel Therese Keswick [1942] Director; Andrew Herbert Lane [1957] Director/Solicitor; Francois Leo Morin [1963] Director [Canadian]; David Howard Nelson [1963] Director/Accountant; Kevin Allen Huw Parry [1962] Director; Jayaprakasa Rangaswami [1957] Director/Scientist [Indian]; Jo Anne Heidi Roizen [1958] Director [American]; The Fourth Viscount Rothermere [1967] Director/Chairman; Dominique Trempont [1954] Director [Belgian]; Paul Adam Zwillenberg [1967] Director/CEO - Media and Publishing [British/American]

Daily Mail International Limited
Incorporated: 28 November 1985
Net Worth: £191,846,400 *Total Assets:* £327,368,736
Registered Office: Northcliffe House, 2 Derry Street, Kensington, London, W8 5TT
Activities: Financial intermediation not elsewhere classified
Parent: Daily Mail and General Holdings Limited
Officers: Frances Louise Sallas, Secretary; William Richard Flint [1969] Director/Accountant; Frances Louise Sallas [1977] Director/Company Secretary

Daisy 2015 Holdco Limited
Incorporated: 10 June 2015 *Employees:* 274
Net Worth Deficit: £18,989,264 *Total Assets:* £110,507,632
Registered Office: 1 Carter Lane, London, EC4V 5ER
Activities: Wholesale of clothing and footwear
Parent: Daisy 2015 Midco Limited
Officers: Mark Piasecki [1980] Director/Principal, Silverfleet Capital Partners LLP; Gareth Ridgwell Whiley [1967] Director/Partner

Daisy 2015 Topco Limited
Incorporated: 10 June 2015 *Employees:* 274
Net Worth Deficit: £21,999,190 *Total Assets:* £110,776,936
Registered Office: 1 Carter Lane, London, EC4V 5ER
Activities: Wholesale of clothing and footwear
Officers: Louise Bechmann [1962] Director [Danish]; Roger Clive Best [1952] Director; Sune Bjerregaard [1968] Director/Chief Executive Officer [Danish]; Mark Piasecki [1980] Director/Principal, Silverfleet Capital Partners LLP; Gareth Ridgwell Whiley [1967] Director/Partner

Daiwa Capital Markets Europe Limited
Incorporated: 25 March 1980 *Employees:* 365
Net Worth: £481,476,000 *Total Assets:* £11,171,809,280
Registered Office: 5 King William Street, London, EC4N 7AX
Activities: Financial intermediation not elsewhere classified
Parent: Daiwa Securities Group Inc.
Officers: Roger Champness Massey, Secretary; Junichi Arihara [1964] Director [Japanese]; Peter Richard Goshawk [1959] Director; Hiroki Ikeda [1966] Director [Japanese]; Keith Meekins [1963] Director/Investment Banking; Keiko Tashiro [1963] Director [Japanese]; Andrew Douglas Van Den Aardweg [1954] Director/Chartered Accountant [South African/British]; Shiko Yanagisawa [1964] Director/Chairman [Japanese]; Yuzo Yonemoto [1964] Director/Chief Operating Officer [Japanese]

Dan Regents Place Finance Limited
Incorporated: 3 November 2015
Net Worth: £160,822,000 *Total Assets:* £161,483,008
Registered Office: 10 Triton Street, Regent's Place, London, NW1 3BF
Activities: Activities of head offices
Parent: Aegis International Limited
Officers: Andrew John Moberly, Secretary; Stuart Anthony Jarrold [1970] Director; Peter Pontidas [1961] Director [Australian/Greek]; Nicholas Charles Priday [1974] Director

Dana Petroleum (BvUK) Limited
Incorporated: 21 March 1997
Net Worth: £86,929,000 *Total Assets:* £146,280,992
Registered Office: 5th Floor, 6 St Andrew Street, London, EC4A 3AE
Activities: Extraction of crude petroleum
Parent: Dana Petroleum Limited
Officers: Laura Anne Hutchison [1980] Director; Yongwoo Kang [1966] Director [South Korean]; Jungwoo Seo [1972] Director [South Korean]; Bert Eiko Van Dalen [1973] Director [Dutch]

Dana Petroleum (E & P) Limited
Incorporated: 12 September 1988 *Employees:* 34
Net Worth: £309,537,984 *Total Assets:* £1,956,797,952
Registered Office: 5th Floor, 6 St Andrew Street, London, EC4A 3AE
Activities: Extraction of crude petroleum
Parent: Dana Petroleum Limited
Officers: Laura Anne Hutchison [1980] Director; Yongwoo Kang [1966] Director [South Korean]; Jungwoo Seo [1972] Director [South Korean]; Bert Eiko Van Dalen [1973] Director [Dutch]

Dana Petroleum Limited
Incorporated: 23 October 1997 *Employees:* 241
Net Worth: £1,003,153,984 *Total Assets:* £2,566,415,104
Registered Office: 5th Floor, 6 St Andrew Street, London, EC4A 3AE
Activities: Other business support service activities n.e.c.
Parent: South Korean Government/Ministry of Trade, Industry and Energy
Officers: Andrew Stephen Begg, Secretary; Ohkyeu Baek [1962] Director [South Korean]; Dr Robert David Elliot [1950] Independent Non-Executive Director; Laura Anne Hutchison [1980] Director; Yongwoo Kang [1996] Director [South Korean]; Byungjin Kim [1966] Director [South Korean]; Byunghyun Moon [1968] Director [South Korean]; Yongjoon Park [1968] Director [South Korean]; Jungwoo Seo [1972] Director [South Korean]; Bert Eiko Van Dalen [1973] Director [Dutch]

Danataugusta Propco1 Limited
Incorporated: 14 June 2016
Net Worth: £63,226,000 *Total Assets:* £244,316,992
Registered Office: Fourth Floor, 22-23 Old Burlington Street, London, W1S 2JJ
Activities: Other letting and operating of own or leased real estate
Parent: Danataugusta Bidco Limited
Officers: Debbie Mary Harding, Secretary; Andrew James Mark Lewis Bracey [1967] Director/Partner at Midlothian Capital Partners; David Henry Barnaby Burgess [1971] Director/Partner at Hattington Investment Partners LLP; Aiden Charles Barwick Clegg [1966] Director/Partner at Midlothian Capital Partners; Neil Allen Currie [1965] Director/Partner at Midlothian Capital Partners; Elizabeth Sharon Glass [1971] Director/Chief Financial Officer; Frederick Matthew Goltz [1971] Director/Partner at Hattington Investment Partners LLP [American/Irish]; Graeme McKinlay Jenkins [1975] Director/Chief Executive

Danataugusta Propco3 Limited
Incorporated: 14 June 2016
Net Worth: £156,984,000 *Total Assets:* £243,531,008
Registered Office: Fourth Floor, 22-23 Old Burlington Street, London, W1S 2JJ
Activities: Other letting and operating of own or leased real estate
Parent: Danataugusta Propco2 Limited
Officers: Debbie Mary Harding, Secretary; Andrew James Mark Lewis Bracey [1967] Director/Partner at Midlothian Capital Partners; David Henry Barnaby Burgess [1971] Director/Partner at Hattington Investment Partners LLP; Aiden Charles Barwick Clegg [1966] Director/Partner at Midlothian Capital Partners; Neil Allen Currie [1965] Director/Partner at Midlothian Capital Partners; Elizabeth Sharon Glass [1971] Director/Chief Financial Officer; Frederick Matthew Goltz [1971] Director/Partner at Hattington Investment Partners LLP [American/Irish]; Graeme McKinlay Jenkins [1975] Director/Chief Executive Officer

Danone Financing UK Limited
Incorporated: 9 December 2013
Net Worth: £8,765,310 *Total Assets:* £730,302,784
Registered Office: 100 New Bridge Street, London, EC4V 6JA
Activities: Activities of head offices
Parent: Danone SA
Officers: Paul Leslie Avis [1974] Director/Accountant; Irene Boj [1972] Financial Director [Spanish]; Sudip Dasgupta [1964] Finance Director [Indian]

Danone Holdings (UK)
Incorporated: 10 May 1988
Net Worth: £4,639,638,016 *Total Assets:* £5,112,710,144
Registered Office: 100 New Bridge Street, London, EC4V 6JA
Activities: Activities of head offices
Parent: Danone SA
Officers: Paul Leslie Avis [1974] Director/Accountant; Christophe Didier Bombled [1960] Director [French]; Sudip Dasgupta [1964] Finance Director [Indian]

Darrowby No. 3 PLC
Incorporated: 9 July 2013
Net Worth: £243,000 *Total Assets:* £186,372,000
Registered Office: 35 Great St Helen's, London, EC3A 6AP
Activities: Financial intermediation not elsewhere classified
Parent: Darrowby 3 Holdings Limited
Officers: Anthony James Chapman [1974] Director/Building Society Treasurer; Daniel Marc Richard Jaffe [1975] Director

Darrowby No. 4 PLC
Incorporated: 21 September 2015
Net Worth: £106,000 *Total Assets:* £264,507,008
Registered Office: 35 Great St Helen's, London, EC3A 6AP
Activities: Financial intermediation not elsewhere classified
Parent: Darrowby 4 Holdings Limited
Officers: Anthony James Chapman [1974] Director/Building Society Treasurer; Daniel Marc Richard Jaffe [1975] Director

Das Europe Limited
Incorporated: 24 December 1979 *Employees:* 18
Net Worth: £621,487,168 *Total Assets:* £655,641,984
Registered Office: Bankside 3, 90-100 Southwark Street, London, SE1 0SW
Activities: Other business support service activities n.e.c.
Parent: Diversified Agency Services Limited
Officers: Sally Ann Bray, Secretary; John Martin William Betts [1971] Director/Legal Counsel; John Henry Wardle [1967] Director/Chartered Accountant; Sally Ann Williams [1962] Development Director

Dashwood House Limited
Incorporated: 21 June 1990
Net Worth: £136,688,000 *Total Assets:* £171,760,992
Registered Office: 100 Victoria Street, London, SW1E 5JL
Activities: Development of building projects
Parent: LS London Holdings One Limited
Officers: Elizabeth Miles [1977] Director/Solicitor

Daunus Limited
Incorporated: 3 June 2003
Net Worth Deficit: £235,984,992 *Total Assets:* £551,070,976
Registered Office: 35 Great St Helen's, London, EC3A 6AP
Activities: Financial intermediation not elsewhere classified
Parent: Intertrust Management Limited
Officers: Daniel Marc Richard Jaffe [1975] Director

Dauphine Holdings (UK) Limited
Incorporated: 8 May 2017 *Employees:* 389
Net Worth: £101,522,528 *Total Assets:* £243,208,864
Registered Office: Investcorp House, 48 Grosvenor Street, London, W1K 3HW
Activities: Activities of other holding companies n.e.c.
Officers: Andrea Jayne Davis [1965] Managing Director; Grahame Ivey [1958] Director/Chartered Accountant

Henry Davies (Holborn) Limited
Incorporated: 22 November 1951
Net Worth: £114,040,808 *Total Assets:* £136,755,296
Registered Office: Freshwater House, 158-162 Shaftesbury Avenue, London, WC2H 8HR
Activities: Buying and selling of own real estate
Parent: Norman Sinclair (Properties) Limited
Officers: Mark Roy Mason Jenner, Secretary; Benzion Schalom Eliezer Freshwater [1948] Director; Leib Stempel [1935] Director

Dayshape Limited
Incorporated: 10 September 1997
Net Worth: £120,608,624 *Total Assets:* £120,826,464
Registered Office: First Floor, 3 More London Riverside, London, SE1 2RE
Activities: Other human health activities
Officers: Julian Mark Anthony Griffiths [1972] Director; Kevin Leslie Jones [1966] Trust Director; Oliver Pemberton Giles Parker [1967] Trust Director; James Anthony Wetherall [1973] Director

Daytona Midco 1 Limited
Incorporated: 27 July 2016 *Employees:* 62
Net Worth: £6,337,000 *Total Assets:* £202,711,008
Registered Office: 10 Norwich Street, London, EC4A 1BD
Activities: Activities of other holding companies n.e.c.
Shareholder: Charme Capital Partners Limited
Officers: Eric Peter de Cavaignac [1970] Director/Founder and Managing Partner, deCAR Partners, LLC [American]; Martyn Thomas Evans [1988] Director/Investment Manager; Christopher Joseph Lister Fielding [1981] Director; David Randall Winn [1969] Alternate Director for Eric de Cavaignac [American]

DB Group Services (UK) Limited
Incorporated: 4 July 1995 *Employees:* 7,472
Total Assets: £2,371,000,064
Registered Office: 23 Great Winchester Street, London, EC2P 2AX
Activities: Other business support service activities n.e.c.
Parent: DB UK Holdings Limited
Officers: Joanne Louise Bagshaw, Secretary; Andrew William Bartlett, Secretary; David Hards [1956] Director/Accountant; Tiina Le-Seong Lee [1968] Director/Banker; Benjamin Jon Pallas [1976] Director/Banker; Steven George Ward [1962] HR Director

DB UK Bank Limited
Incorporated: 30 June 1936 *Employees:* 47
Net Worth: £564,688,000 *Total Assets:* £1,816,420,992
Registered Office: 23 Great Winchester Street, London, EC2P 2AX
Activities: Financial intermediation not elsewhere classified
Parent: Deutsche Holdings Limited
Officers: Joanne Louise Bagshaw, Secretary; Scott Jamieson Dobbie [1939] Director/Stockbroker; Michael Morley [1957] Director; Arjun Vivek Nagarkatti [1980] Director/Banker [Indian]; Philip Haldane Nunnerley [1946] Director/Banker; Benjamin Jon Pallas [1976] Director/Banker; John Terence Saunders [1967] Director/Banker

DB UK Holdings Limited
Incorporated: 15 October 1998
Net Worth: £486,605,184 *Total Assets:* £673,542,592
Registered Office: 23 Great Winchester Street, London, EC2P 2AX
Activities: Activities of other holding companies n.e.c.
Parent: Deutsche Holdings No.3 Limited
Officers: Philip James Davis, Secretary; Nicholas Kristian James Calvert [1970] Director/Banker; Benjamin Jon Pallas [1976] Director/Banker

DCC Energy Finance UK Limited
Incorporated: 24 August 2015
Net Worth: £403,950,400 *Total Assets:* £417,610,272
Registered Office: Hill House, 1 Little New Street, London, EC4A 3TR
Activities: Activities of other holding companies n.e.c.
Parent: DCC Energy UK Limited
Officers: Gerard Whyte, Secretary; Michael Victor Alden [1949] Director; Anthony Francis Levy [1957] Director; Fergal John O'Dwyer [1960] Director [Irish]

DCC Holdings (UK) Limited
Incorporated: 15 July 1993
Net Worth: £265,271,440 *Total Assets:* £799,668,608
Registered Office: Hill House, 1 Little New Street, London, EC4A 3TR
Activities: Activities of other holding companies n.e.c.
Parent: DCC Limited
Officers: Gerard Whyte, Secretary/Chartered Accountant [Irish]; Michael Victor Alden [1949] Director; Anthony Francis Levy [1957] Director; Fergal John O'Dwyer [1960] Director/Chartered Accountant [Irish]

DCC Limited
Incorporated: 24 March 2003
Net Worth: £444,366,240 *Total Assets:* £1,083,148,544
Registered Office: Hill House, 1 Little New Street, London, EC4A 3TR
Activities: Activities of other holding companies n.e.c.
Parent: DCC Public Limited Company
Officers: Gerard Whyte, Secretary; Michael Victor Alden [1949] Director; Anthony Francis Levy [1957] Director; Fergal John O'Dwyer [1960] Director/Chartered Accountant [Irish]

DCC Technology Limited
Incorporated: 30 April 1986
Previous: DCC Technology UK Limited
Net Worth: £186,074,448 *Total Assets:* £278,057,056
Registered Office: Hill House, 1 Little New Street, London, EC4A 3TR
Activities: Activities of other holding companies n.e.c.
Parent: DCC Limited
Officers: Gerard Whyte, Secretary [Irish]; Paul William Bryan [1969] Director; Timothy David Griffin [1967] Director; Gerard Patrick O'Keeffe [1964] Director [Irish]

DCC Treasury 2014 Limited
Incorporated: 5 February 2014
Net Worth Deficit: £15,146,207 *Total Assets:* £970,175,488
Registered Office: Hill House, 1 Little New Street, London, EC4A 3TR
Activities: Financial management
Parent: DCC Limited
Officers: Gerard Whyte, Secretary; Michael Victor Alden [1949] Director; Anthony Francis Levy [1957] Director; Fergal John O'Dwyer [1960] Director [Irish]

DDB UK Investments Limited
Incorporated: 1 October 2013 *Employees:* 680
Net Worth: £11,138,071 *Total Assets:* £229,576,656
Registered Office: Bankside 3, 90-100 Southwark Street, London, SE1 0SW
Activities: Activities of head offices
Parent: DDB Europe Limited
Officers: Sally-Ann Bray, Secretary; Michael Gregory Barlow [1975] Director/Chief Financial Officer [American]; Dominic Mark Nagy [1972] Director/Solicitor

De Beers Jewellers Limited
Incorporated: 30 November 2000 *Employees:* 101
Previous: De Beers Diamond Jewellers Limited
Net Worth: £70,823,592 *Total Assets:* £105,679,792
Registered Office: 45 Old Bond Street, London, W1S 4QT
Activities: Activities of head offices
Shareholders: Anglo American Diamond Holdings Limited; Riverbank Investments Limited
Officers: Francois Louis Michel Delage [1965] Director/Chief Executive Officer [French]; Richard Graham Giles [1977] Director/Chartered Accountant; Stephen Christopher Lussier [1957] Director

De Beers UK Limited
Incorporated: 10 September 1986 *Employees:* 224
Net Worth: £829,214,912 *Total Assets:* £934,226,816
Registered Office: 20 Carlton House Terrace, London, SW1Y 5AN
Activities: Other business support service activities n.e.c.
Parent: Anglo American Diamond Holdings Limited
Officers: Nicholas Martin Byers [1962] Director/Senior Manager, Administration; Jeanine Catherine Frankish [1980] Director/Senior Finance Manager; David Spencer Fricker [1966] Director/Head of Business Development; Esther Oberbeck [1961] Director/De Beers Group Strategy Manager [Italian]; Faried Sallie [1969] Director/Head of Technology, Technology & Innovation [South African]; Jonathan David Harrison Savage [1965] Director/Senior Vice President

De Facto 1341 Limited
Incorporated: 10 March 2006
Net Worth: £189,435,008 *Total Assets:* £190,927,008
Registered Office: Ground Floor, 107 Power Road, Chiswick, London, W4 5PY
Activities: Activities of head offices
Parent: Marken Services Limited
Officers: Doaa Abdel Fathallah [1970] Director/Lawyer [American]; Andrew Scott Gravatt [1962] Director/Accountant; Joseph Mozzali [1970] Director/VP of Finance [American]; Wesley Potter Wheeler [1956] Director [American]

Dealogic (Holdings) Limited
Incorporated: 22 August 2001
Net Worth: £311,071,072 *Total Assets:* £311,071,072
Registered Office: 3rd Floor, One New Change, London, EC4M 9AF
Activities: Activities of head offices
Parent: Diamond Bidco Limited
Officers: Neil Murray Griffin, Secretary; Jonathan Osborne Drulard [1971] Managing Director [American]; Thomas Aquinas Fleming [1958] Director/Executive [American]; Kunal Gullapalli [1984] Director/Manager [American]; Toby Haddon [1967] Director/Manager

Debenhams Group Holdings Limited
Incorporated: 1 September 1997
Net Worth: £143,200,000 *Total Assets:* £1,141,100,032
Registered Office: 10 Brock Street, Regent's Place, London, NW1 3FG
Activities: Activities of head offices
Officers: Paul Rex Eardley, Secretary; Sergio Rodriguez Bucher [1963] Director [Spanish]; Rachel Claire Elizabeth Osborne [1965] Director/Chief Financial Officer

Debenhams PLC
Incorporated: 10 May 2005 *Employees:* 25,663
Net Worth: £489,400,000 *Total Assets:* £1,967,900,032
Registered Office: 10 Brock Street, Regent's Place, London, NW1 3FG
Activities: Activities of head offices
Officers: Paul Rex Eardley, Secretary; David Adams [1954] Director; Terence Duddy [1956] Director; Stephen John Ingham [1962] Director; Nicola Kinnaird [1964] Director; Lisa Myers [1967] Director [American]; Rachel Claire Elizabeth Osborne [1965] Director/Chief Financial Officer

Debenhams Properties Limited
Incorporated: 30 September 1938
Net Worth: £47,747,000 *Total Assets:* £909,686,016
Registered Office: 10 Brock Street, Regent's Place, London, NW1 3FG
Activities: Development of building projects
Parent: Debenhams Group Holdings Limited
Officers: Paul Rex Eardley, Secretary; Rachel Claire Elizabeth Osborne [1965] Director/Chief Financial Officer

Debenhams Retail PLC
Incorporated: 28 January 1905 *Employees:* 23,727
Net Worth: £1,270,099,968 *Total Assets:* £2,868,999,936
Registered Office: 10 Brock Street, Regent's Place, London, NW1 3FG
Activities: Retail sale of clothing in specialised stores
Parent: Debenhams Group Holdings Limited
Officers: Paul Rex Eardley, Secretary; Sergio Rodriguez Bucher [1963] Director [Spanish]; Rachel Claire Elizabeth Osborne [1965] Director/Chief Financial Officer

Debussy DTC PLC
Incorporated: 25 January 2013
Net Worth: £21,647 *Total Assets:* £264,278,832
Registered Office: 6th Floor, 65 Gresham Street, London, EC2V 7NQ
Activities: Financial intermediation not elsewhere classified
Parent: Link Trust Nominees No.1 Limited
Officers: Colin Arthur Benford [1962] Director

Deco 11 - UK Conduit 3 P.L.C.
Incorporated: 7 November 2006
Net Worth Deficit: £126,148,368 *Total Assets:* £144,981,360
Registered Office: Suite 2, 3rd Floor, 11-12 St James's Square, London, SW1Y 4LB
Activities: Other business support service activities n.e.c.
Parent: Deco 11-UK Conduit 3 Holding Limited
Officers: Sunil Masson, Secretary; Graham Derek Edward Cox [1953] Director; Graham John Hodgkin [1966] Director

Deco 8 - UK Conduit 2 PLC
Incorporated: 16 March 2006
Net Worth Deficit: £208,565,520 *Total Assets:* £233,217,856
Registered Office: Suite 2, 3rd Floor, 11-12 St James's Square, London, SW1Y 4LB
Activities: Other business support service activities n.e.c.
Parent: Deco 8-UK Conduit 2 Holding Limited
Officers: Sunil Masson, Secretary; Graham Derek Edward Cox [1953] Director; Graham John Hodgkin [1966] Director

DEKA Energy Associates Limited
Incorporated: 4 February 2014 *Employees:* 101
Net Worth: £53,981,268 *Total Assets:* £224,066,144
Registered Office: 35 Great St Helen's, London, EC3A 6AP
Activities: Activities of other holding companies n.e.c.
Parent: Equitix Rory Limited
Officers: Achal Prakash Bhuwania [1979] Director; Sion Laurence Jones [1974] Director; Michael Patrick Gerrard Scott [1968] Managing Director

DEKA Energy Enterprises Limited
Incorporated: 4 February 2014
Net Worth: £37,804,224 *Total Assets:* £187,691,888
Registered Office: 35 Great St Helen's, London, EC3A 6AP
Activities: Activities of other holding companies n.e.c.
Parent: DEKA Energy Associates Limited
Officers: Michael Patrick Gerrard Scott [1968] Managing Director

Delamare Cards Funding 1 Limited
Incorporated: 11 January 2013
Net Worth: £5,000 *Total Assets:* £2,437,082,112
Registered Office: 2nd Floor, Asticus Building, 21 Palmer Street, London, SW1H 0AD
Activities: Other business support service activities n.e.c.
Parent: Delamare Cards Holdco Limited
Officers: Marc Speight [1985] Associate Director; Beejadhursingh Mahen Surnam [1970] Director; Christopher Michael Warnes [1977] Director

Delamare Cards MTN Issuer PLC
Incorporated: 22 July 2008
Net Worth: £109,000 *Total Assets:* £2,363,154,944
Registered Office: 2nd Floor, Asticus Building, 21 Palmer Street, London, SW1H 0AD
Activities: Other business support service activities n.e.c.
Parent: Delamare Cards Holdco Limited
Officers: Marc Speight [1985] Associate Director; Beejadhursingh Mahen Surnam [1970] Director; Christopher Michael Warnes [1977] Director

Delamare Finance PLC
Incorporated: 10 March 2004
Net Worth Deficit: £13,398,876 *Total Assets:* £613,328,768
Registered Office: 35 Great St Helens, London, EC3A 6AP
Activities: Financial intermediation not elsewhere classified
Parent: Delamare Group Holdings Limited
Officers: Daniel Marc Richard Jaffe [1975] Director

Delamare Group Holdings Limited
Incorporated: 12 March 2004
Net Worth Deficit: £13,398,828 *Total Assets:* £613,328,768
Registered Office: 35 Great St Helen's, London, EC3A 6AP
Activities: Non-trading company
Parent: Intertrust Corporate Services Limited
Officers: Daniel Marc Richard Jaffe [1975] Director

Delfont Mackintosh Theatres Limited
Incorporated: 5 July 1990 *Employees:* 570
Net Worth: £117,908,944 *Total Assets:* £202,895,536
Registered Office: 1 Bedford Square, London, WC1B 3RB
Activities: Artistic creation
Officers: Richard Trevor Knibb, Secretary; Nicholas David Allott [1954] Director/Theatrical Producer; Alan Arthur Finch [1965] Director; Richard Arthur Johnston [1955] Director/Chief Executive; Sir Cameron Anthony Mackintosh [1946] Director/Theatrical Producer

Dellmes GR Limited
Incorporated: 2 January 2015 *Employees:* 2
Net Worth: £441,107,488 *Total Assets:* £937,774,336
Registered Office: Berkeley House, 304 Regents Park Road, London, N3 2JY
Activities: Buying and selling of own real estate
Parent: Ramchez GR Limited
Officers: Paul Hallam, Secretary; Christopher Charles McGill [1960] Managing Director; William Kenneth Procter [1953] Director/Accountant

Deloitte Global Services Holdings Limited
Incorporated: 11 May 2010 *Employees:* 1,096
Net Worth Deficit: £36,515,784 *Total Assets:* £286,040,320
Registered Office: Hill House, 1 Little New Street, London, EC4A 3TR
Activities: Other business support service activities n.e.c.
Officers: Francisco Celma [1963] Director/Economist/Auditor [Spanish]; Cesar Tecsen Cheng Vargas [1958] Director/Partner [Peruvian/Colombian]; Enrico Ciai [1957] Director/Partner of Deloitte & Touche S.P.A [Italian]; Adrian Duncan Crampton [1959] Director/Chartered Accountant [German]; David John Ogilvie Cruickshank [1959] Director/Chartered Accountant; Omar Fahoum [1959] Director/CEO - Deloitte & Touche M.E [Jordanian]; Michael John Fucci [1958] Director/Management Consultant [American]; Yoriko Goto [1958] Director/Certified Public Accountant [Japanese]; Robert Trevor Hillard [1968] Director/Professional Services [Australian]; Twalizidanga Mlondolozi Mgcinisihlalo Jordan [1976] Director/Business Partner [South African]; Frederic Rene Moulin [1963] Director/Audit Partner [French]; Ramesh Prathivadi Bhayankara [1955] Director/Chartered Accountant [Indian]; Punit Renjen [1961] Director/Management Consultant [American]; Duncan Lamont Sinclair [1966] Director/Chairman [Canadian]; Philip Wing Chung Tsai [1959] Director/Accountant; Philip Ewe Jin Yuen [1963] Director/Public Accountant [Malaysian]

Deloitte Global Services Limited
Incorporated: 11 May 2010 *Employees:* 1,096
Net Worth Deficit: £126,283,760 *Total Assets:* £263,217,952
Registered Office: Hill House, 1 Little New Street, London, EC4A 3TR
Activities: Other business support service activities n.e.c.
Parent: Deloitte Global Services Holdings Limited
Officers: Francisco Celma [1963] Director/Economist/Auditor [Spanish]; Cesar Tecsen Cheng Vargas [1958] Director/Partner [Peruvian/Colombian]; Enrico Ciai [1957] Director/Partner of Deloitte & Touche S.P.A [Italian]; Adrian Duncan Crampton [1959] Director/Chartered Accountant [German]; David John Ogilvie Cruickshank [1959] Director/Chartered Accountant; Omar Fahoum [1959] Director/CEO - Deloitte & Touche M.E [Jordanian]; Michael John Fucci [1958] Director/Management Consultant [American]; Yoriko Goto [1958] Director/Certified Public Accountant [Japanese]; Robert Trevor Hillard [1968] Director/Professional Services [Australian]; Twalizidanga Mlondolozi Mgcinisihlalo Jordan [1976] Director/Business Partner [South African]; Frederic Rene Moulin [1963] Director/Audit Partner [French]; Ramesh Prathivadi Bhayankara [1955] Director/Chartered Accountant [Indian]; Punit Renjen [1961] Director/Management Consultant [American]; Duncan Lamont Sinclair [1966] Director/Chairman [Canadian]; Philip Wing Chung Tsai [1959] Director/Accountant; Philip Ewe Jin Yuen [1963] Director/Public Accountant [Malaysian]

Deloitte MCS Limited
Incorporated: 31 January 1997 *Employees:* 3,734
Net Worth: £64,444,000 *Total Assets:* £305,003,008
Registered Office: Hill House, 1 Little New Street, London, EC4A 3TR
Activities: Accounting and auditing activities
Parent: D & T Consulting Holdings Limited
Officers: Glyn Bunting [1962] Director/Chartered Accountant; Stephen Griggs [1964] Director/Chartered Accountant; Paul Anthony Robinson [1964] Director/Executive

Delta 3 (UK) Limited
Incorporated: 3 November 2006
Net Worth: £4,323,503,616 *Total Assets:* £7,626,900,992
Registered Office: No 2 St James's Market, London, SW1Y 4AH
Activities: Activities of head offices
Parent: Liberty GR Acquisition Company Limited
Officers: Duncan Francis Llowarch [1968] Director/Accountant; Sacha Jane Woodward Hill [1969] Director/Lawyer

Deltatre Group Limited
Incorporated: 24 May 2016 *Employees:* 7
Net Worth: £98,268,464 *Total Assets:* £101,373,424
Registered Office: Media House, 3 Palmerston Road, London, SW19 1PG
Activities: Management consultancy activities other than financial management
Parent: Deltatre Midco 2 Limited
Officers: Tony Crispino [1966] Director/Investment Professional [American]; Andrea Marini [1986] Director/Manager [Italian]; George Pyne [1965] Director/Investment Professional [American]; Giampiero Rinaudo [1959] Director [Italian]; Jeffrey Roth [1985] Director/Investment Professional [American]

Deltatre Holdings Limited
Incorporated: 10 May 2016
Net Worth: £86,548,848 *Total Assets:* £136,043,680
Registered Office: Media House, 3 Palmerston Road, London, SW19 1PG
Activities: Activities of other holding companies n.e.c.
Major Shareholder: George Pyne
Officers: Tony Crispino [1966] Director/Investment Professional [American]; Ronald Walton Downey [1961] Director [New Zealander]; Andrea Marini [1986] Director/Manager [Italian]; George Pyne [1965] Director/Investment Professional [American]; Giampiero Rinaudo [1959] Director [Italian]; Jeffrey Roth [1985] Director/Investment Professional [American]

J. & J. Denholm Limited
Incorporated: 28 May 1969 *Employees:* 1,000
Net Worth: £118,077,000 *Total Assets:* £172,316,000
Registered Office: 8th Floor, The Aspect, 12 Finsbury Square, London, EC2A 1AS
Activities: Activities of head offices
Officers: Gregory Albert Hanson, Secretary; John Stephen Denholm [1956] Director/Chartered Accountant; Robert Keith Denholm [1965] Director/Company Executive; The Rt Hon Lord Michael Bruce Forsyth [1954] Director/Banker; Gregory Albert Hanson [1961] Director/Group Company Secretary; Jan Marceli Kopernicki [1948] Director; Benjamin Donald Robert MacLehose [1981] Director; Alexander David MacLellan [1959] Director; Simon Luke Preston [1980] Director

Dentons UK and Middle East LLP
Incorporated: 1 September 2006 *Employees:* 1,026
Previous: Dentons UKMEA LLP
Net Worth: £65,620,000 *Total Assets:* £129,053,000
Registered Office: One Fleet Place, London, EC4M 7WS
Officers: David Lawrence Cohen [1969] Member; Jeremy Leonard Cohen [1967] Member; David Anthony Collins [1965] Member; Lucille Sunalini de Silva [1968] Member; Matthew Lawrence Wilton Hanslip Ward [1965] Member; Paul Pascal Edward Holland [1966] Member; Susan Mary Kelly [1970] Member; Michael Bruce Livingston [1958] Member; Richard James William Macklin [1962] Member; Jayne Elizabeth Schnider [1970] Member; Kenneth David Shand [1958] Member; Scott Jerome Singer [1971] Member; Madeleine Anne Smallwood [1962] Member; Teresa Clare Stothard [1965] Member; Elizabeth Jane Tout [1958] Member; Euan Robert Wilson [1970] Member; Darren Acres [1982] LLP Member; Akinbayo Oladimeji Akinbode [1971] LLP Member; Dali Rahmatalla Al Habboub [1958] LLP Member; Daren Peter Allen [1965] LLP Member; Virginia Katherine Elizabeth Allen [1979] LLP Member; Russell Joseph Altendorff [1982] LLP Member; Celyn James Edward Armstrong [1974] LLP Member; Claire Armstrong [1975] LLP Member; Stephen John Ashworth [1963] LLP Member; Qasim Ali Aslam [1972] LLP Member; Catherine Gillian Mary Astruc [1970] LLP Member; Richard Edgar Charles Barham [1964] LLP Member; Yusuf Ahmed Battiwala [1981] LLP Member; Sarah Jane Elizabeth Beeby [1980] LLP Member; Danielle Ann Beggs [1960] LLP Member; Miriam Best [1967] LLP Member; Catherine Mary Bingham [1962] LLP Member; Alistair Alexander Richard Black [1977] LLP Member; Iain Hugh Black [1973] LLP Member; Tessa Rachel Blank [1982] LLP Member; Douglas John Blyth [1976] LLP Member; Daniel Scott Bodle [1978] LLP Member; Helen Anne Bowdren [1979] LLP Member; Alison Helen Bryce [1974] LLP Member; Sadaf Shahid Buchanan [1975] LLP Member; Richard George Budge [1960] LLP Member; Daniel James David Burge [1966] LLP Member; Richard Francis Caird [1958] LLP Member; Allan Steven Cairns [1980] LLP Member; Joanna Mary Campbell-Smith [1969] LLP Member; Jonathan Brian Cantor [1970] LLP Member; Ryan Holman Carthew [1975] LLP Member; Nicholas Edward Chandler [1962] LLP Member; Candice Chapman [1973] LLP Member; Mark James Cheney [1974] LLP Member; Helen Mary Cleaveland [1958] LLP Member; Nikolas Karl Colbridge [1972] LLP Member; Christopher John Colclough [1979] LLP Member; Simon William Colledge [1963] LLP Member; Timothy Simon Constable [1968] LLP Member; Anna Louise Copeman [1983] LLP Member; Alex Patrick Coulter [1975] LLP Member; Peter Charles Cox [1956] LLP Member; Amanda Crawford Jones [1968] LLP Member; David Andrew Cruickshank [1972] LLP Member; James Anthony Dallas [1955] LLP Member; Ian Christopher Dalley [1972] LLP Member; Lorraine Helen Davis [1969] LLP Member; Michael John Dean [1960] LLP Member; Deepa Deb [1975] LLP Member; William Elmer Doonan [1955] LLP Member; Graham Humphrey Douglas [1973] LLP Member; Rupert John Dowdell [1973] LLP Member; Gillian Stevenson Downie [1961] LLP Member; Sarah Jane Dyke [2009] LLP Member; Barry Edgar [1979] LLP Member; Timothy James Edward [1963] LLP Member; Simon Gairdner Elliott [1981] LLP Member; Simon Paul Etchells [1962] LLP Member; Felicity Clare Ewing [1974] LLP Member; James Edward Keith Fairbairn [1959] LLP Member; Martin Gerard John Fanning [1975] LLP Member; Isaac Felberbaum [1947] LLP Member; Andrew Figgins [1970] LLP Member; Stuart Thomas Fitzsimmons [1980] LLP Member; Campbell Alexander James Forsyth [1971] LLP Member; William Fowler [1968] LLP Member; Ian David Fox [1976] LLP Member; Celia Gardiner [1962] LLP Member; Jonathan Henri Garforth [1983] LLP Member; Andrian John Giles [1967] LLP Member; Virginia Glastonbury [1957] LLP Member; Christopher Graf [1982] LLP Member; Alexis Irene Graham [1980] LLP Member; Nicholas Roger Selwoode Graham [1968] LLP Member; Roland Hugh Gray [1971] LLP Member; Gurbinder Singh Grewal [1980] LLP Member; Neil Robert Griffiths [1959] LLP Member; Malcolm John Gunnyeon [1978] LLP Member; Gareth Jonathan Hale [1981] LLP Member; Cameron Edward Half [1975] LLP Member; Mark Russell Hamilton [1963] LLP Member; Paul Sydney Haniford [1955] LLP Member

Dentsu Aegis London Limited
Incorporated: 15 August 1985 *Employees:* 2,228
Previous: Dentsu Aegis UK Limited
Net Worth Deficit: £25,218,000 *Total Assets:* £1,074,704,000
Registered Office: 10 Triton Street, Regents Place, London, NW1 3BF
Activities: Advertising agencies
Parent: Aegis Finance
Officers: Andrew John Moberly, Secretary; Robert Patrick Baldwin [1975] Director/Accountant; Matthew Platts [1971] Commercial Director; Peter Pontidas [1961] Director [Australian/Greek]; Nicholas Paul Thomas [1962] Director

Dentsu Aegis Network Ltd.
Incorporated: 5 December 1978 *Employees:* 37,077
Net Worth: £1,065,800,000 *Total Assets:* £12,277,799,936
Registered Office: 10 Triton Street, Regent's Place, London, NW1 3BF
Activities: Activities of head offices
Parent: Dentsu Inc.
Officers: Andrew John Moberly, Secretary; Timothy Paul Andree [1961] Director/Senior Vice President, Dentsu Inc [American]; Takaki Hibino [1959] Director [Japanese]; Nicholas Charles Priday [1974] Director; Shun Sakurai [1953] Director [Japanese]; Valerie Anne Scoular [1955] HR Director; Jun Shibata [1961] Director [Japanese]; Arinobu Soga [1965] Director [Japanese]; Nobuyuki Tohya [1959] Director [Japanese]; Toshihiro Yamamoto [1958] Director [Japanese]

Derwent Central Cross Limited
Incorporated: 20 July 2010
Net Worth: £146,239,472 *Total Assets:* £350,491,808
Registered Office: 25 Savile Row, London, W1S 2ER
Activities: Development of building projects
Parent: Derwent London PLC
Officers: David Andrew Lawler, Secretary; John David Burns [1944] Director; Nigel Quentin George [1963] Director; Simon Paul Silver [1950] Director; David Gary Silverman [1969] Director; Paul Malcolm Williams [1960] Director/Surveyor; Damian Mark Alan Wisniewski [1961] Director

Derwent London Angel Square Limited
Incorporated: 10 November 2014
Net Worth: £16,877,614 *Total Assets:* £102,433,216
Registered Office: 25 Savile Row, London, W1S 2ER
Activities: Buying and selling of own real estate
Parent: Derwent London PLC
Officers: David Andrew Lawler, Secretary; John David Burns [1944] Director; Nigel Quentin George [1963] Director; Simon Paul Silver [1950] Director; David Gary Silverman [1969] Director; Paul Malcolm Williams [1960] Director; Damian Mark Alan Wisniewski [1961] Director

Derwent London Farringdon Limited
Incorporated: 13 November 2014
Net Worth: £29,835,782 *Total Assets:* £143,530,624
Registered Office: 25 Savile Row, London, W1S 2ER
Activities: Buying and selling of own real estate
Parent: Derwent London PLC
Officers: David Andrew Lawler, Secretary; John David Burns [1944] Director; Nigel Quentin George [1963] Director; Simon Paul Silver [1950] Director; David Gary Silverman [1969] Director; Paul Malcolm Williams [1960] Director; Damian Mark Alan Wisniewski [1961] Director

Derwent London Oliver's Yard Limited
Incorporated: 17 May 2017
Net Worth: £32,220,586 *Total Assets:* £157,612,816
Registered Office: 25 Savile Row, London, W1S 2ER
Activities: Development of building projects
Parent: Derwent London PLC
Officers: David Andrew Lawler, Secretary; John David Burns [1944] Director; Nigel Quentin George [1963] Director; Simon Paul Silver [1950] Director; David Gary Silverman [1969] Director; Paul Malcolm Williams [1960] Director; Damian Mark Alan Wisniewski [1961] Director

Derwent London Page Street Limited
Incorporated: 23 February 2011
Net Worth: £29,851,488 *Total Assets:* £124,268,920
Registered Office: 25 Savile Row, London, W1S 2ER
Activities: Buying and selling of own real estate
Parent: Derwent London PLC
Officers: David Andrew Lawler, Secretary; John David Burns [1944] Director; Nigel Quentin George [1963] Director; Simon Paul Silver [1950] Director; David Gary Silverman [1969] Director; Paul Malcolm Williams [1960] Director/Surveyor; Damian Mark Alan Wisniewski [1961] Director

Derwent London PLC
Incorporated: 25 May 1984 *Employees:* 105
Net Worth: £4,128,300,032 *Total Assets:* £5,038,099,968
Registered Office: 25 Savile Row, London, W1S 2ER
Activities: Development of building projects
Officers: David Andrew Lawler, Secretary; Claudia Isobel Arney [1971] Director; Lucinda Margaret Bell [1964] Director; John David Burns [1944] Director; Richard David Charles Dakin [1963] Director; Simon William Fraser [1963] Director; Nigel Quentin George [1963] Director/Surveyor; Helen Christine Gordon [1959] Director; Hon. Robert Anthony Rayne [1949] Director; Simon Paul Silver [1950] Director; David Gary Silverman [1969] Director; Priscilla Deborah Snowball [1958] Director/Chairman and CEO Advertising; Paul Malcolm Williams [1960] Director/Surveyor; Damian Mark Alan Wisniewski [1961] Director; Stephen Gareth Young [1955] Director/Chartered Management Accountant

Derwent Valley Central Limited
Incorporated: 11 April 1925
Net Worth: £1,028,846,528 *Total Assets:* £1,044,385,536
Registered Office: 25 Savile Row, London, W1S 2ER
Activities: Buying and selling of own real estate
Parent: Derwent London PLC
Officers: David Andrew Lawler, Secretary; John David Burns [1944] Director; Nigel Quentin George [1963] Director/Surveyor; Simon Paul Silver [1950] Director; David Gary Silverman [1969] Director; Paul Malcolm Williams [1960] Director/Surveyor; Damian Mark Alan Wisniewski [1961] Director

Derwent Valley Finance Limited
Incorporated: 15 November 2005
Net Worth Deficit: £15,047,070 *Total Assets:* £839,914,176
Registered Office: 25 Savile Row, London, W1S 2ER
Activities: Financial intermediation not elsewhere classified
Parent: LMS Finance Limited
Officers: David Andrew Lawler, Secretary; John David Burns [1944] Director; Nigel Quentin George [1963] Director; Simon Paul Silver [1950] Director; David Gary Silverman [1969] Director; Paul Malcolm Williams [1960] Director/Surveyor; Damian Mark Alan Wisniewski [1961] Director

Derwent Valley Limited
Incorporated: 13 November 1947
Net Worth: £1,753,456,640 *Total Assets:* £1,906,819,328
Registered Office: 25 Savile Row, London, W1S 2ER
Activities: Activities of other holding companies n.e.c.
Parent: LMS Finance Limited
Officers: David Andrew Lawler, Secretary; John David Burns [1944] Director; Nigel Quentin George [1963] Director; Simon Paul Silver [1950] Director; David Gary Silverman [1969] Director; Paul Malcolm Williams [1960] Director/Surveyor; Damian Mark Alan Wisniewski [1961] Director

Derwent Valley London Limited
Incorporated: 31 March 1928
Net Worth: £456,388,512 *Total Assets:* £650,484,096
Registered Office: 25 Savile Row, London, W1S 2ER
Activities: Buying and selling of own real estate
Parent: Derwent London PLC
Officers: David Andrew Lawler, Secretary; John David Burns [1944] Director; Nigel Quentin George [1963] Director/Surveyor; Simon Paul Silver [1950] Director; David Gary Silverman [1969] Director; Paul Malcolm Williams [1960] Director/Surveyor; Damian Mark Alan Wisniewski [1961] Director

Derwent Valley Property Developments Limited
Incorporated: 17 July 1987
Net Worth: £360,544,512 *Total Assets:* £412,683,616
Registered Office: 25 Savile Row, London, W1S 2ER
Activities: Buying and selling of own real estate
Parent: Derwent London PLC
Officers: David Andrew Lawler, Secretary; John David Burns [1944] Director; Nigel Quentin George [1963] Director/Surveyor; Simon Paul Silver [1950] Director; David Gary Silverman [1969] Director; Paul Malcolm Williams [1960] Director/Surveyor; Damian Mark Alan Wisniewski [1961] Director

Derwent Valley Property Investments Limited
Incorporated: 13 February 1985
Net Worth: £166,147,984 *Total Assets:* £167,599,120
Registered Office: 25 Savile Row, London, W1S 2ER
Activities: Buying and selling of own real estate
Parent: Derwent London PLC
Officers: David Andrew Lawler, Secretary; John David Burns [1944] Director; Nigel Quentin George [1963] Director/Surveyor; Simon Paul Silver [1950] Director; David Gary Silverman [1969] Director; Paul Malcolm Williams [1960] Director/Surveyor; Damian Mark Alan Wisniewski [1961] Director

Deutsche Alternative Asset Management (UK) Limited
Incorporated: 8 March 1990 *Employees:* 60
Net Worth: £86,976,000 *Total Assets:* £239,092,992
Registered Office: Winchester House, 1 Great Winchester Street, London, EC2N 2DB
Activities: Development of building projects
Parent: Deutsche Bank Aktiengesellschaft
Officers: Andrew William Bartlett, Secretary; Hamish MacPhail Massie MacKenzie [1969] Director/Investment Banker; Gianluca Muzzi [1970] Director/Investment Manager [Italian]; Stephen James Thomas Shaw [1957] Director [Australian]

Deutsche Holdings Limited
Incorporated: 14 October 2005
Net Worth: £1,306,314,496 *Total Assets:* £1,308,632,320
Registered Office: Winchester House, 1 Great Winchester Street, London, EC2N 2DB
Activities: Activities of other holding companies n.e.c.
Parent: DB Investments (GB) Limited
Officers: Philip Davis, Secretary; Benjamin Jon Pallas [1976] Director/Banker

Deutsche Holdings No.2 Limited
Incorporated: 23 November 2006
Net Worth: £140,726,752 *Total Assets:* £1,100,027,776
Registered Office: Winchester House, 1 Great Winchester Street, London, EC2N 2DB
Activities: Financial intermediation not elsewhere classified
Parent: Deutsche Bank Aktiengesellschaft
Officers: Philip Davis, Secretary; Benjamin Jon Pallas [1976] Director/Banker; Christopher Charles Snailham [1976] Director/Accountant

Deutsche Holdings No.3 Limited
Incorporated: 23 November 2006
Net Worth: £293,794,496 *Total Assets:* £1,619,823,360
Registered Office: Winchester House, 1 Great Winchester Street, London, EC2N 2DB
Activities: Financial intermediation not elsewhere classified
Parent: Deutsche Holdings No.2 Limited
Officers: Philip Davis, Secretary; Benjamin Jon Pallas [1976] Director/Banker; Christopher Charles Snailham [1976] Director/Accountant

Deutsche Holdings No.4 Limited
Incorporated: 17 July 2007
Net Worth: £112,679,504 *Total Assets:* £127,315,248
Registered Office: Winchester House, 1 Great Winchester Street, London, EC2N 2DB
Activities: Financial intermediation not elsewhere classified
Parent: Deutsche Bank Aktiengesellschaft
Officers: Andrew William Bartlett, Secretary; Paul Anderson [1973] Director/Banker; Dr Blandine Marie-Jeanne Benedicte Denise Walker [1977] Director/Chief Operating Officer

Deutsche Morgan Grenfell Group Public Limited Company
Incorporated: 24 November 1971
Net Worth: £825,048,576 *Total Assets:* £831,026,880
Registered Office: 23 Great Winchester Street, London, EC2P 2AX
Activities: Activities of other holding companies n.e.c.
Parent: Deutsche Holdings No.3 Limited
Officers: Andrew William Bartlett, Secretary; Andrew William Bartlett [1964] Director/Company Secretary; Benjamin Jon Pallas [1976] Director/Banker; Christopher Charles Snailham [1976] Director/Accountant

Deva Financing PLC
Incorporated: 8 September 2008
Net Worth: £48,000 *Total Assets:* £3,379,876,096
Registered Office: 35 Great St Helen's, London, EC3A 6AP
Activities: Financial intermediation not elsewhere classified
Parent: Deva Financing Holdings Limited
Officers: Daniel Marc Richard Jaffe [1975] Director

Device Finance Collections Limited
Incorporated: 9 September 2013
Net Worth: £3,188 *Total Assets:* £345,774,304
Registered Office: 5th Floor, 6 St Andrew Street, London, EC4A 3AE
Activities: Other business support service activities n.e.c.
Parent: TMF Trustee Limited
Officers: Andrew Wallace [1971] Director/DCS, UK, Management

DHCM Holdco Limited
Incorporated: 15 August 2008 *Employees:* 28
Net Worth Deficit: £123,879,000 *Total Assets:* £233,235,008
Registered Office: 45 Pall Mall, London, SW1Y 5JG
Activities: Activities of financial services holding companies
Shareholder: Richard Peter Hanson
Officers: Benjamin Martin Dooley [1983] Director; Richard Peter Hanson [1956] Director; Graeme Dominic Stening [1964] Director

DHE Regional Limited
Incorporated: 25 November 2014
Previous: DDB Holding Europe Limited
Net Worth: £269,594,176 *Total Assets:* £273,427,552
Registered Office: Bankside 3, 90-100 Southwark Street, London, SE1 0SW
Activities: Activities of head offices
Parent: Omnicom DDB Holdings Limited
Officers: Sally-Ann Bray, Secretary; Michael Gregory Barlow [1975] Director/Chief Financial Officer [American]; Dominic Mark Nagy [1972] Director/Solicitor

Diageo DV Limited
Incorporated: 9 June 1880
Net Worth: £116,594,000 *Total Assets:* £150,331,008
Registered Office: Lakeside Drive, Park Royal, London, NW10 7HQ
Activities: Activities of venture and development capital companies
Parent: Grand Metropolitan Limited
Officers: Elizabeth Anna Brown [1980] Business Development Director; Tanya Maria Clarke [1974] Director/General Manager [Irish]; Cristina Diezhandino [1966] Managing Director [Spanish]; James Matthew Crayden Edmunds [1974] Director/Solicitor; Ian Anthony Hockney [1975] Director/Accountant; Gabor Kovacs [1980] Director [Hungarian]; Kara Elizabeth Major [1977] Director [American]; Sylvia Condon Saller [1957] Director/Chief Marketing Officer [American]

Diageo Eire Finance & Co
Incorporated: 16 February 2004
Net Worth: £1,771,538,944 *Total Assets:* £2,092,270,720
Registered Office: Lakeside Drive, Park Royal, London, NW10 7HQ
Activities: Other business support service activities n.e.c.
Parent: Diageo Investment Holdings Limited
Officers: James Matthew Crayden Edmunds [1974] Director/Solicitor; Kara Elizabeth Major [1977] Director [American]; Vinod Rao [1962] Director [Indian]; Prabhaharan Viswanathan [1972] Director [Australian]

Diageo Finance PLC
Incorporated: 23 April 1926
Net Worth: £5,500,000,256 *Total Assets:* £41,414,000,640
Registered Office: Lakeside Drive, Park Royal, London, NW10 7HQ
Activities: Other business support service activities n.e.c.
Parent: Diageo PLC
Officers: James Matthew Crayden Edmunds, Secretary; James Matthew Crayden Edmunds [1974] Director/Solicitor; Kara Elizabeth Major [1977] Director [American]; Monika Pais [1973] Director [Hungarian]; Vinod Rao [1962] Director [Indian]; Prabhaharan Viswanathan [1972] Director [Australian]

Diageo Finance US Limited
Incorporated: 14 July 2000
Net Worth: £113,588,000 *Total Assets:* £1,691,309,056
Registered Office: Lakeside Drive, Park Royal, London, NW10 7HQ
Activities: Other business support service activities n.e.c.
Parent: UDV (SJ) Limited
Officers: James Matthew Crayden Edmunds [1974] Director/Solicitor; Kara Elizabeth Major [1977] Director [American]; Vinod Rao [1962] Director [Indian]; Prabhaharan Viswanathan [1972] Director [Australian]

Diageo Financing Turkey Limited
Incorporated: 23 August 2012
Net Worth: £316,836,992 *Total Assets:* £316,836,992
Registered Office: Lakeside Drive, Park Royal, London, NW10 7HQ
Activities: Other business support service activities n.e.c.
Parent: UDV (SJ) Limited
Officers: James Matthew Crayden Edmunds [1974] Director/Solicitor; Kara Elizabeth Major [1977] Director [American]; Vinod Rao [1962] Director [Indian]; Prabhaharan Viswanathan [1972] Director [Australian]

Diageo Great Britain Limited
Incorporated: 5 May 1952 *Employees:* 1,238
Net Worth: £2,988,000,000 *Total Assets:* £3,436,999,936
Registered Office: Lakeside Drive, Park Royal, London, NW10 7HQ
Activities: Distilling, rectifying and blending of spirits
Parent: Grand Metropolitan Limited
Officers: Gavin Paul Crickmore [1958] Director/Chartered Accountant; James Matthew Crayden Edmunds [1974] Director/Solicitor; Sharon Lynnette Fennessy [1967] Director/Group Treasurer [Irish]; Kerryn Louise Haynes [1970] Director/Accountant; David Heginbottom [1970] Director/Group Treasurer; Hina Patel [1979] Director/Company Secretary Senior Assistant; Gabor Zeisler [1973] Director/General Manager [Hungarian]

Diageo Holdings Limited
Incorporated: 24 August 1998
Net Worth: £13,392,000,000 *Total Assets:* £27,000,000,512
Registered Office: Lakeside Drive, Park Royal, London, NW10 7HQ
Activities: Activities of head offices
Parent: Diageo PLC
Officers: James Matthew Crayden Edmunds [1974] Director/Solicitor; Hina Patel [1979] Director/Company Secretary Senior Assistant; Vinod Rao [1962] Director [Indian]; Prabhaharan Viswanathan [1972] Director [Australian]

Diageo Investment Holdings Limited
Incorporated: 2 March 1990
Net Worth: £17,308,037,120 *Total Assets:* £20,069,316,608
Registered Office: Lakeside Drive, Park Royal, London, NW10 7HQ
Activities: Non-trading company
Parent: UDV (SJ) Limited
Officers: James Matthew Crayden Edmunds [1974] Director/Solicitor; Kara Elizabeth Major [1977] Director [American]; Vinod Rao [1962] Director [Indian]; Prabhaharan Viswanathan [1972] Director [Australian]

Diageo Overseas Holdings Limited
Incorporated: 27 March 1997
Net Worth: £1,343,374,976 *Total Assets:* £2,283,339,008
Registered Office: Lakeside Drive, Park Royal, London, NW10 7HQ
Activities: Non-trading company
Shareholders: Diageo Investment Holdings Limited; Diageo US Holdings
Officers: James Matthew Crayden Edmunds [1974] Director/Solicitor; Kara Elizabeth Major [1977] Director [American]; Vinod Rao [1962] Director [Indian]; Prabhaharan Viswanathan [1972] Director [Australian]

Diageo PLC
Incorporated: 21 October 1886 *Employees:* 29,917
Net Worth: £9,948,000,256 *Total Assets:* £29,714,999,296
Registered Office: Lakeside Drive, Park Royal, London, NW10 7HQ
Activities: Activities of head offices
Officers: Siobhan Teresa Moriarty-Macdonnell, Secretary; Lord Evan Mervyn Davies [1952] Director; Francisco Javier Ferran Larraz [1956] Director [Spanish]; Kwon Ping Ho [1952] Director [Singaporean]; Susan Saltzbart Kilsby [1958] Director [American]; Lady Nicola Sharon Mendelsohn [1971] Director; Ivan Manuel Menezes [1959] Director/Chief Executive; Kathryn Ann Mikells [1965] Director/Chief Financial Officer [American]; Alan James Harris Stewart [1960] Director

Diageo Treasury Australia LLP
Incorporated: 19 March 2012
Net Worth: £263,008,000 *Total Assets:* £263,008,000
Registered Office: Lakeside Drive, Park Royal, London, NW10 7HQ

Diageo UK Turkey Holdings Limited
Incorporated: 15 March 2013
Net Worth: £462,461,024 *Total Assets:* £747,438,208
Registered Office: Lakeside Drive, Park Royal, London, NW10 7HQ
Activities: Activities of distribution holding companies
Officers: James Matthew Crayden Edmunds [1974] Director/Solicitor; Kara Elizabeth Major [1977] Director [American]; Vinod Rao [1962] Director [Indian]; Prabhaharan Viswanathan [1972] Director [Australian]

Diageo UK Turkey Limited
Incorporated: 18 March 2013
Net Worth: £773,823,872 *Total Assets:* £1,133,721,216
Registered Office: Lakeside Drive, Park Royal, London, NW10 7HQ
Activities: Activities of financial services holding companies
Parent: Diageo UK Turkey Holdings Limited
Officers: James Matthew Crayden Edmunds [1974] Director/Solicitor; Kara Elizabeth Major [1977] Director [American]; Vinod Rao [1962] Director [Indian]; Prabhaharan Viswanathan [1972] Director [Australian]

Diageo US Holdings
Incorporated: 3 July 2001
Net Worth: £8,981,520,384 *Total Assets:* £9,411,539,968
Registered Office: Lakeside Drive, Park Royal, London, NW10 7HQ
Activities: Financial intermediation not elsewhere classified
Parent: Diageo US Investments
Officers: James Matthew Crayden Edmunds [1974] Director/Solicitor; Claire-Louise Jordan [1972] Director/Global Head of Tax; Darryl Malcolm Francis Leese [1959] Finance Director; Kara Elizabeth Major [1977] Director [American]

Diageo US Investments
Incorporated: 4 January 2006
Net Worth: £8,563,607,040 *Total Assets:* £8,586,552,832
Registered Office: Lakeside Drive, Park Royal, London, NW10 7HQ
Activities: Other business support service activities n.e.c.
Shareholders: Diageo Investment Holdings Limited; Diageo Investment Holdings Limited
Officers: James Matthew Crayden Edmunds [1974] Director/Solicitor; Kara Elizabeth Major [1977] Director [American]; Vinod Rao [1962] Director [Indian]; Prabhaharan Viswanathan [1972] Director [Australian]

Dialight PLC
Incorporated: 28 March 1990
Net Worth: £75,800,000 *Total Assets:* £106,000,000
Registered Office: Leaf C, Level 36, Tower 42, 25 Old Broad Street, London, EC2N 1HQ
Activities: Manufacture of electronic components
Officers: Ronan Michael Sheehy, Secretary; Stephen Clive Bird [1960] Director; David Wayland Blood [1959] Director; Wayne Edmunds [1956] Director [American]; Steve Paul Good [1961] Director; Gaelle Hotelier [1972] Director [French]; Fariyal Khanbabi [1967] Finance Director; Martin Lee Rapp [1960] Director [American]; David Jeremy Thomas [1954] Director

Dialog Semiconductor (UK) Limited
Incorporated: 20 May 1985 *Employees:* 366
Net Worth: £285,773,600 *Total Assets:* £490,619,808
Registered Office: Tower Bridge House, St Katherine's Way, London, E1W 1AA
Activities: Other engineering activities
Parent: Dialog Semiconductor PLC
Officers: Timothy Richard Black Anderson, Secretary; Jalal Bagherli [1956] Director/Chief Executive Officer; Vivek Bhan [1974] Director/Senior Vice President [American]; Wissam Georges Jabre [1969] Director/Chief Financial Officer [American]; Colin Sturt [1969] Director/Legal Executive

Dialog Semiconductor PLC
Incorporated: 5 February 1998 *Employees:* 1,907
Net Worth: £974,463,552 *Total Assets:* £1,144,589,184
Registered Office: Tower Bridge House, St Katharine's Way, London, E1W 1AA
Activities: Activities of head offices
Officers: Timothy Richard Black Anderson, Secretary/Solicitor; Jalal Bagherli [1956] Director/Chief Executive Officer; Richard Beyer [1948] Director/Consultant/Advisor [American]; Alan Campbell [1958] Director/Retired (Chief Financial Officer) [American]; Michael Canon [1952] Director [American]; Mary Chan [1962] Director [American]; Aidan John Hughes [1960] Director; Nicholas Simon Jeffery [1968] Director; Eamonn O'Hare [1963] Director

Diamond Bank (UK) PLC
Incorporated: 13 June 2007
Net Worth: £33,621,412 *Total Assets:* £255,525,328
Registered Office: 36-38 Leadenhall Street, London, EC3A 1AT
Activities: Banks
Parent: Diamond Bank PLC
Officers: John Barr Stevenson Connell, Secretary; Uzoma Chukwumaeze Dozie [1969] Director/Banker; Christopher Stuart Duncan [1948] Director/Retired Banker; Peter Horton [1966] Director/Banker; Carey Anthony Pennington Leonard [1954] Director/Banker; Garry Andrew Marsh [1955] Director/Banker; Chizoma Joy Okoli [1968] Director/Banker [Nigerian]

Diamond Bidco Limited
Incorporated: 28 October 2014
Net Worth: £317,850,944 *Total Assets:* £574,081,088
Registered Office: c/o Dealogic, 3rd Floor, One New Change, London, EC4M 9AF
Activities: Activities of other holding companies n.e.c.
Parent: Diamond Midco Limited
Officers: Neil Murray Griffin, Secretary; Thomas Aquinas Fleming [1958] Director/Business Executive [American]; Ashley Graham Woods [1973] Director/Lawyer

Diamond Generating Europe Limited
Incorporated: 13 September 2012 *Employees:* 79
Net Worth: £324,728,256 *Total Assets:* £354,196,256
Registered Office: Mid City Place, 71 High Holborn, London, WC1V 6BA
Activities: Production of electricity
Parent: Mitsubishi Corporation
Officers: Tetsuya Aiba [1960] Director/General Manager [Japanese]; Isao Kano [1960] Director [Japanese]; Yutaka Kashiwagi [1964] Director [Japanese]; Yasuo Ohashi [1974] Director [Japanese]; Keiichi Suzuki [1969] Director/Chief Executive [Japanese]

Diamond Midco Limited
Incorporated: 28 October 2014
Net Worth: £320,673,920 *Total Assets:* £553,668,608
Registered Office: c/o Dealogic, 3rd Floor, One New Change, London, EC4M 9AF
Activities: Activities of other holding companies n.e.c.
Parent: Diamond Topco Limited
Officers: Neil Murray Griffin, Secretary; Thomas Aquinas Fleming [1958] Director/Business Executive [American]; Ashley Graham Woods [1973] Director/Lawyer

Diamond Offshore Drilling (UK) Limited.
Incorporated: 25 November 1992 *Employees:* 46
Net Worth: £201,989,568 *Total Assets:* £217,183,936
Registered Office: One Fleet Place, London, EC4M 7WS
Activities: Extraction of crude petroleum
Parent: Diamond Offshore Enterprises Limited
Officers: George Creighton Cole Henderson [1959] Director; David Lynn Roland [1961] Director/Business Manager [American]; Dominic Antony Savarino [1970] Director/Vice President and Chief Tax Officer [American]

Diamond Offshore Enterprises Limited
Incorporated: 11 November 2008
Net Worth: £142,706,368 *Total Assets:* £142,771,600
Registered Office: One Fleet Place, London, EC4M 7WS
Activities: Other business support service activities n.e.c.
Parent: Diamond Offshore Drilling Inc.
Officers: George Creighton Cole Henderson [1959] Director/Manager; David Lynn Roland [1961] Director/Business Manager [American]; Dominic Antony Savarino [1970] Director/Vice President and Chief Tax Officer [American]

Diamond Offshore Limited
Incorporated: 2 December 1968
Net Worth: £2,888,270,336 *Total Assets:* £2,892,802,304
Registered Office: One Fleet Place, London, EC4M 7WS
Activities: Extraction of crude petroleum
Parent: Diamond Offshore Drilling Inc
Officers: George Creighton Cole Henderson [1959] Director; David Lynn Roland [1961] Director/Business Manager [American]; Dominic Antony Savarino [1970] Director/Vice President and Chief Tax Officer [American]

Diamond Rig Investments Limited
Incorporated: 12 December 2008
Net Worth: £221,588,592 *Total Assets:* £251,072,608
Registered Office: One Fleet Place, London, EC4M 7WS
Activities: Other business support service activities n.e.c.
Parent: Diamond Offshore Drilling Inc.
Officers: George Creighton Cole Henderson [1959] Director/Manager; David Lynn Roland [1961] Director/Business Manager [American]; Dominic Antony Savarino [1970] Director/Vice President and Chief Tax Officer [American]

Diamond Topco Limited
Incorporated: 27 October 2014 *Employees:* 828
Net Worth: £272,945,248 *Total Assets:* £592,360,832
Registered Office: c/o Dealogic, 3rd Floor, One New Change, London, EC4M 9AF
Activities: Activities of other holding companies n.e.c.
Officers: Ashley Graham Woods, Secretary; Thomas Aquinas Fleming [1958] Director/Business Executive [American]; Edward Alexander Triplett [1981] Director [American]; Ashley Graham Woods [1973] Director/Lawyer

Diamond Transmission Corporation Limited
Incorporated: 11 April 2013 *Employees:* 17
Net Worth: £262,481,824 *Total Assets:* £265,720,400
Registered Office: Mid City Place, 71 High Holborn, London, WC1V 6BA
Activities: Transmission of electricity
Parent: Mitsubishi Corporation
Officers: Kazuyoshi Kawakami [1969] Director [Japanese]; Keitaro Kono [1971] Director [Japanese]; Masanobu Muramiya [1978] Director [Japanese]; Kenichi Takahashi [1975] Director [Japanese]; Yasushi Umemura [1974] Director [Japanese]

DIF Infra 3 UK Limited
Incorporated: 15 May 2012
Net Worth: £25,895,912 *Total Assets:* £157,554,192
Registered Office: 1st Floor, 94-96 Wigmore Street, London, W1U 3RF
Activities: Fund management activities
Officers: Andrew Derek Freeman [1978] Director/Investment Manager; Christopher John Mansfield [1963] Director/Fund Manager; Paul William Nash [1967] Director

DIF Tamblin Limited
Incorporated: 19 April 2017
Net Worth: £199,982,912 *Total Assets:* £199,993,920
Registered Office: 94-96 Wigmore Street, London, W1U 3RF
Activities: Activities of other holding companies n.e.c.
Shareholder: DIF Infra 4 UK Limited
Officers: Andrew Derek Freeman [1978] Director/Investment Manager; Paul William Nash [1967] Director/Investment Manager; Angela Louise Roshier [1975] Director/Asset Manager

Digital Appliance Controls (UK) Limited
Incorporated: 4 June 1990
Net Worth: £205,712,000 *Total Assets:* £205,712,000
Registered Office: Accurist House, 44 Baker Street, London, W1U 7AL
Activities: Activities of head offices
Parent: Emerson Electric Co.
Officers: Martin Benedict Fernandez, Secretary; Bente Bulow Bundgaard-Antoine [1972] Director/Accountant [Danish]; Martin Benedict Fernandez [1959] Director/Treasury Manager; Derek Shaw [1955] Tax Director

Digital London Limited
Incorporated: 2 February 2016
Net Worth Deficit: £7,681,000 *Total Assets:* £382,056,000
Registered Office: Level 7, 40 Gracechurch Street, London, EC3V 0BT
Activities: Other business support service activities n.e.c.
Parent: Digital Realty Trust, Inc
Officers: Robert Andrew Coupland [1970] Managing Director EMEA; Jeannie Lee [1976] Director/Vice President [American]

Digital River UK Holdings I Ltd
Incorporated: 2 April 2015
Net Worth: £212,288,736 *Total Assets:* £212,294,240
Registered Office: 125 Wood Street, London, EC2V 7AW
Activities: Activities of other holding companies n.e.c.
Parent: Digital River, Inc.
Officers: Kristopher Thomas Schmidt [1965] Director/Vice President of HR and General Counsel [American]

Digital River UK Holdings II Ltd
Incorporated: 2 April 2015
Net Worth: £240,318,688 *Total Assets:* £240,324,416
Registered Office: 125 Wood Street, London, EC2V 7AW
Activities: Activities of financial services holding companies
Parent: Digital River UK Holdings I Ltd
Officers: Kristopher Thomas Schmidt [1965] Director/Vice President of HR and General Counsel [American]

Dinosaur Merchant Bank Limited
Incorporated: 26 November 2003 *Employees:* 38
Net Worth: £17,067,824 *Total Assets:* £852,285,120
Registered Office: 48-54 Moorgate, London, EC2R 6EJ
Activities: Financial intermediation not elsewhere classified
Officers: Ivy Choo, Secretary; Venisha Racquel Frith, Secretary; Marinette Rosales Abanilla [1960] Director/Investment Banker [American]; Paul Emanuel Becker [1964] Director/Financial Services; Jonathan Michael Bloch [1952] Director [South African]; Glenn Grossman [1949] Director/Investment Banker [American]

Diploma Holdings PLC
Incorporated: 1 May 1931 *Employees:* 14
Net Worth: £129,587,000 *Total Assets:* £173,316,992
Registered Office: 12 Charterhouse Square, London, EC1M 6AX
Activities: Activities of head offices
Parent: Diploma PLC
Officers: Anthony James Gallagher, Secretary; Nigel Peter Lingwood [1959] Director/Chartered Accountant; John Edward Nicholas [1956] Director

Diploma PLC
Incorporated: 24 December 1999 *Employees:* 1,765
Net Worth: £291,200,000 *Total Assets:* £404,400,000
Registered Office: 12 Charterhouse Square, London, EC1M 6AX
Activities: Activities of head offices
Officers: Anthony James Gallagher, Secretary; Nigel Peter Lingwood [1959] Director/Chartered Accountant; John Edward Nicholas [1956] Director; Charles Max Packshaw [1952] Director; Andrew Patrick Smith [1960] Director; Jonathan David Thomson [1972] Director; Anne Thorburn [1960] Director

Discovery Communications Europe Limited
Incorporated: 10 February 2004 *Employees:* 221
Net Worth: £505,044,000 *Total Assets:* £1,510,935,040
Registered Office: Discovery House, Building 2, Chiswick Park, 566 Chiswick High Road, London, W4 5YB
Activities: Television programme production activities
Parent: DNI Europe Holdings Limited
Officers: James Richard Cooke [1980] Director/SVP - Chief of Staff EMEA; Hester Jane Wheeley [1969] Director

Discovery Finance Company Europe Limited
Incorporated: 10 March 2015
Net Worth: £26,693,072 *Total Assets:* £133,961,240
Registered Office: 3 More London Riverside, London, SE1 2AQ
Activities: Activities of head offices
Parent: Discovery Limited
Officers: Richard Farber [1971] Director [South African]; Ian Leonard Slonim [1970] Director

Discovery Group Europe Limited
Incorporated: 29 January 2004 *Employees:* 3
Net Worth: £671,824,704 *Total Assets:* £756,391,936
Registered Office: 3 More London Riverside, London, SE1 2AQ
Activities: Activities of head offices
Parent: Discovery Limited
Officers: Richard Farber [1971] Director [South African]; Adrian Gore [1964] Director/Chief Executive Officer [South African]; Monty Isidore Hilkowitz [1940] Director [Israeli]; Shaun Matisonn [1972] Director/Actuary [South African]

Discovery Holdings Europe Limited
Incorporated: 12 September 2006
Net Worth: £539,574,976 *Total Assets:* £665,985,024
Registered Office: 3 More London Riverside, London, SE1 2AQ
Activities: Non-life insurance
Officers: Gabrielle Miranda Dinah Mocatta, Secretary; Dr Wolf Siegfried Becke [1947] Director [German]; Nicholas Michael Caplan [1959] Director; Lord Sebastian Newbold Coe [1956] Director; Andrew Michael Crossley [1956] Director/Chief Financial Officer; Sir Andrew William Foster [1944] Director; Adrian Gore [1964] Director/Actuary [South African]; Rosemary Hilary [1955] Director; Monty Isidore Hilkowitz [1940] Director [Israeli]; Neville Stanley Koopowitz [1964] Director/Chief Executive Officer Pru Health [South African]; Alastair David Lyons [1953] Independent Non-Executive Director; Herschel Philip Mayers [1960] Director/Chief Executive Officer [South African]; Nicola Joanne McCabe [1969] Independent Non-Executive Director; Ayanda Ntsaluba [1960] Director [South African]; Stephen John Sarjant [1960] Director; Joanne Mary Shaw [1963] Independent Non-Executive Director

Discovery Lightning Investments Ltd
Incorporated: 18 September 2015
Net Worth: £118,642,952 *Total Assets:* £135,875,184
Registered Office: Building 2, Chiswick Park, 566 Chiswick High Road, London, W4 5YB
Activities: Motion picture production activities
Parent: Discovery Communications, Inc.
Officers: James T'sung Jen Gibbons [1969] Director/EVP General Manager UK & ANZ, Commercial Development EMEA [Malaysian]; Roanne LEA Weekes [1978] Director [Australian]

Discovery Networks International Holdings Limited
Incorporated: 2 July 2007
Net Worth: £283,268,992 *Total Assets:* £303,777,984
Registered Office: Discovery House, Building 2, Chiswick Park, 566 Chiswick High Road, London, W4 5YB
Activities: Television programme production activities
Parent: Discovery, Inc.
Officers: Roanne LEA Weekes [1978] Director/SVP DNI Controller [Australian]; Hester Jane Wheeley [1969] Director/SVP Legal

Walt Disney Company Limited (The)
Incorporated: 8 March 1954 *Employees:* 1,640
Net Worth: £1,436,157,952 *Total Assets:* £3,651,851,008
Registered Office: 3 Queen Caroline Street, Hammersmith, London, W6 9PE
Activities: Artistic creation
Parent: Wedco EMEA Ventures Limited
Officers: Zelda Hansson, Secretary; Simon Unsworth Bailey [1966] Director/Chartered Accountant; Alexandra Clare Minton Haines [1967] Director/Lawyer; Zelda Hansson [1976] Director/Finance Executive; Peter Lloyd Wiley [1968] Director/Lawyer

Disney Magic Company Limited
Incorporated: 17 June 1998
Net Worth: £122,895,984 *Total Assets:* £123,432,248
Registered Office: 3 Queen Caroline Street, Hammersmith, London, W6 9PE
Activities: Other business support service activities n.e.c.
Parent: The Walt Disney Company
Officers: Nigel Anthony Cook, Secretary; Nigel Anthony Cook [1967] Director/Accountant; Marsha Leigh Reed [1957] Director/Executive [American]

Diversified Agency Services Limited
Incorporated: 6 February 1989
Net Worth: £103,662,344 *Total Assets:* £508,600,960
Registered Office: Bankside 3, 90-100 Southwark Street, London, SE1 0SW
Activities: Activities of head offices
Parent: Cardinia Europe Limited
Officers: Sally Ann Bray, Secretary; John Martin William Betts [1971] Director/Legal Counsel; John Henry Wardle [1967] Director/Chartered Accountant; Sally Ann Williams [1962] Development Director

Divisional Finance UK Limited
Incorporated: 10 March 2005
Net Worth: £12,963,367 *Total Assets:* £418,187,584
Registered Office: Hill House, 1 Little New Street, London, EC4A 3TR
Activities: Activities of other holding companies n.e.c.
Parent: DCC Holdings (UK) Limited
Officers: Gerard Whyte, Secretary; Michael Victor Alden [1949] Director; Orla Mary Cooper [1975] Director/Chartered Secretary [Irish]; Anthony Francis Levy [1957] Director

DIVX Express Limited
Incorporated: 17 June 1996
Net Worth: £402,408,000 *Total Assets:* £439,371,008
Registered Office: 5 Howick Place, London, SW1P 1WG
Activities: Activities of head offices
Parent: UBMG Limited
Officers: Carl Sheldon Adrian [1972] Director/Accountant

Dixons Carphone Holdings Limited
Incorporated: 30 November 2011 *Employees:* 108
Previous: New CPW Limited
Net Worth: £1,496,189,056 *Total Assets:* £2,149,748,992
Registered Office: 1 Portal Way, London, W3 6RS
Activities: Activities of other holding companies n.e.c.
Parent: Dixons Carphone PLC
Officers: Catherine Springett, Secretary; Alistair Gibson [1975] Director; Leon Smith [1976] Director/Chartered Accountant

Dixons Carphone PLC
Incorporated: 15 December 2009 *Employees:* 43,760
Net Worth: £3,196,000,000 *Total Assets:* £7,296,000,000
Registered Office: 1 Portal Way, London, W3 6RS
Activities: Other business support service activities n.e.c.
Officers: Nigel Paterson, Secretary; Alexander David Baldock [1970] Director; Eileen Burbidge [1971] Director; Antonio Denunzio [1960] Director; Andrea Gisle Joosen [1964] Director [Swedish]; Ian Paul Livingston [1964] Director; Jonathan Peter Mason [1964] Finance Director; Fiona Catherine McBain [1961] Director; John Gerard Murphy [1952] Director

Dixons Retail Group Limited
Incorporated: 24 September 1999
Previous: Dixons Retail Group PLC
Net Worth: £1,159,000,064 *Total Assets:* £1,782,000,000
Registered Office: 1 Portal Way, London, W3 6RS
Activities: Activities of head offices
Parent: Dixons Carphone Holdings Limited
Officers: Catherine Springett, Secretary; Alistair Gibson [1975] Director; Leon Smith [1976] Director/Chartered Accountant

DLA Piper International LLP
Incorporated: 22 August 2003 *Employees:* 5,120
Net Worth: £418,800,000 *Total Assets:* £690,200,000
Registered Office: 160 Aldersgate Street, London, EC1A 4HT
Officers: Bertold Bar-Bouyssiere [1963] Member; Dr Generald Michael Dee Bean [1960] Member; Andrew David Darwin [1959] Member; Jonathan Magnor Hayes [1963] Member; Simon Robert Levine [1965] Member; Samantha Jane O'Brien [1969] Member; Claudine Agnes Vartian [1968] Member; Jonathan Paul Watkins [1970] Member; Joris Valentijn Willems [1975] Member; Colin John Wilson [1970] Member; Niccolo Abriani [1966] LLP Member; Jakub Adam [1972] LLP Member; Eddie Byunghyo Ahn [1981] LLP Member; Orson Alcocer Rodriguez [1974] LLP Member; Francesco Maria Aleandri [1965] LLP Member; Paul Robert Allen [1976] LLP Member; Benjamin Aller [1968] LLP Member; Kirstie Anne Allerton [1977] LLP Member; Matteo Almini [1973] LLP Member; David Rexford Kofi Addae Ampaw [1978] LLP Member; Chiara Anceschi [1975] LLP Member; Jeremy Edward Needham Andrews [1974] LLP Member; Alberto Angeloni [1976] LLP Member; Danius Gerardus Arends [1975] LLP Member; Fabrice Armand [1968] LLP Member; Robert William Henry Arnison [1974] LLP Member; Christopher Stephen Xavier Arnold [1983] LLP Member; Vinita Arora [1975] LLP Member; Marco Arteaga [1961] LLP Member; Colin Ian Ashford [1969] LLP Member; Stephen Atkinson [1968] LLP Member; Christophe Bachelet [1972] LLP Member; Gunne Bahr [1967] LLP Member; Christopher Baird [1976] LLP Member; Gitanjali Bajaj [1981] LLP Member; Onno Johannes Bakker [1968] LLP Member; Radu Balas [1978] LLP Member; Andrzej Balicki [1977] LLP Member; Nicholas Alan Bamford [1969] LLP Member; George Barboutis [1973] LLP Member; Toby James Barker [1971] LLP Member; Martin Joseph Bartlam [1964] LLP Member; Howard John Leonard Bassford [1972] LLP Member; Leo Batalov [1971] LLP Member; Andrew Batterton [1976] LLP Member; David Christian Bauer [1975] LLP Member; Joseph Bauerschmidt [1959] LLP Member; Miguel Baz Baz [1965] LLP Member; Mark Peter Beardwood [1962] LLP Member; David Beech [1983] LLP Member; Astrid Beemster [1982] LLP Member; Okko Hendrik Behrends [1965] LLP Member; Claire Margaret Bell [1977] LLP Member; Sarah Jane Bell [1974] LLP Member; Daphne Berdina Richarda Bens [1973] LLP Member; Raphael Bera [1977] LLP Member; James Derek Berg [1972] LLP Member; Pierre Berger [1978] LLP Member; Florian Biesalski [1979] LLP Member; Petra Billing [1969] LLP Member; Robert Ludo James Bishop [1970] LLP Member; Stephen Guy Blacksell [1961] LLP Member; Dr Kai Bodenstedt [1972] LLP Member; Helene Bogaard [1971] LLP Member; Richard Brian Joseph Bonnar [1962] LLP Member; Gabor Borbely [1977] LLP Member; Bernd Borgmann [1969] LLP Member; Alessandro Boso Caretta [1969] LLP Member; Stephen Paul Bottley [1972] LLP Member; Michael Bowen [1956] LLP Member; Neil David Bowker [1968] LLP Member; Iain William Bowler [1963] LLP Member; Alexander Brabant [1964] LLP Member; Peter George Bradshaw [1978] LLP Member; Ian Patrick Brierley [1962] LLP Member; Lee David Brierley [1964] LLP Member; Peter Brook [1972] LLP Member; Jeremy Frazer Brooks [1956] LLP Member; Benjamin Brown [1976] LLP Member; Alin Buftea [1976] LLP Member; Keith Bullen [1982] LLP Member; Christopher Frederick Burden [1968] LLP Member; Mark Henry Burger [1962] LLP Member; Mark Leonard Burgess [1969] LLP Member; Daljit Singh Burrha [1975] LLP Member; Trevor Butcher [1960] LLP Member; Dirk Caestecker [1962] LLP Member; Ugo Domenico Calo [1973] LLP Member; Duncan Clive Calow [1970] LLP Member; Tamara Jane Calvert [1973] LLP Member; John Charles Campion [1964] LLP Member; Antonio Carino [1977] LLP Member; Andrew James Carter [1979] LLP Member; Lawrence Carter [1969] LLP Member; David Carthy [1971] LLP Member; Germana Cassar [1966] LLP Member; Rick Catanzariti [1965] LLP Member; Natalie Caton [1977] LLP Member; Filippo Cecchetti [1979] LLP Member; Dr Philipp Cepl [1973] LLP Member

DLA Piper UK LLP
Incorporated: 4 May 2004 *Employees:* 2,331
Net Worth: £151,300,000 *Total Assets:* £375,000,000
Registered Office: 160 Aldersgate Street, London, EC1A 4HT
Officers: Andrew David Darwin [1959] Member; Jonathan Magnor Hayes [1963] Member; Simon Robert Levine [1965] Member; Jonathan Paul Watkins [1970] Member; Colin John Wilson [1970] Member; Benjamin Aller [1968] LLP Member; Kirstie Anne Allerton [1977] LLP Member; David Rexford Kofi Addae Ampaw [1978] LLP Member; Jeremy Edward Needham Andrews [1974] LLP Member; Fabrice Armand [1968] LLP Member; Robert William Henry Arnison [1974] LLP Member; Christopher Stephen Xavier Arnold [1983] LLP Member; Vinita Arora [1975] LLP Member; Marco Arteaga [1961] LLP Member; Colin Ian Ashford [1969] LLP Member; Stephen Atkinson [1968] LLP Member; Gunne Bahr [1967] LLP Member; Christopher Baird [1976] LLP Member; Nicholas Alan Bamford [1969] LLP Member; Toby James Barker [1971] LLP Member; Martin Joseph Bartlam [1964] LLP Member; Howard John Leonard Bassford [1972] LLP Member; Andrew Batterton [1976] LLP Member; Mark Peter Beardwood [1962] LLP Member; David Beech [1983] LLP Member; Okko Hendrik Behrends [1965] LLP Member; Claire Margaret Bell [1977] LLP Member; Sarah Jane Bell [1974] LLP Member; Raphael Bera [1977] LLP Member; Florian Biesalski [1979] LLP Member; Petra Billing [1969] LLP Member; Robert Ludo James Bishop [1970] LLP Member; Stephen Guy Blacksell [1961] LLP Member; Dr Kai Bodenstedt [1972] LLP Member; Richard Brian Joseph Bonnar [1962] LLP Member; Bernd Borgmann [1969] LLP Member; Stephen Paul Bottley [1972] LLP Member; Neil David Bowker [1968] LLP Member; Iain William Bowler [1963] LLP Member; Alexander Todd Brabant [1964] LLP Member; Ian Patrick Brierley [1962] LLP Member; Lee David Brierley [1964] LLP Member; Peter Brook [1972] LLP Member; Jeremy Frazer Brooks [1956] LLP Member; Benjamin Brown [1976] LLP Member; Christopher Frederick Burden [1968] LLP Member; Mark Leonard Burgess [1969] LLP Member; Daljit Singh Burrha [1975] LLP Member; Duncan Clive Calow [1970] LLP Member; Tamara Jane Calvert [1973] LLP Member; John Charles Campion [1964] LLP Member; Andrew James Carter [1979] LLP Member; Dr Philipp Cepl [1973] LLP Member; Kate Helen Cervantes-Knox [1975] LLP Member; Alan Chalmers [1967] LLP Member; Christopher Chan [1982] LLP Member; Simon Charbit [1973] LLP Member; Mark Chivers [1977] LLP Member; Philip Brendan Chong [1966] LLP Member; Linos Dimitrios Choo [1974] LLP Member; Matthew James Christmas [1973] LLP Member; David Peter Church [1950] LLP Member; Michael Cieslarczyk [1971] LLP Member; Andrew Keith Clarke [1970] LLP Member; John Tristan Cloke [1979] LLP Member; Alastair Clough [1973] LLP Member; Roger Graeme Collier [1963] LLP Member; Fanny Combourieu [1972] LLP Member; Michael Alan Conradi [1972] LLP Member; Charles Edward Cook [1970] LLP Member; Simon Timothy Cookson [1959] LLP Member; Joel Cooper [1984] LLP Member; Liam Anthony Paul Cowell [1970] LLP Member; Philip Crump [1972] LLP Member; Alan James Cunningham [1971] LLP Member; James David Paton Curle [1971] LLP Member; Philippe Danesi [1971] LLP Member; Mike-Josef Danielewsky [1972] LLP Member; Andrew Stewart Davies [1979] LLP Member; Andrew Davies [1966] LLP Member; Timothy Squire Dawson [1969] LLP Member; Anthony Day [1979] LLP Member; Sarah Jane Day [1965] LLP Member; Sonia de Kondserovsky [1969] LLP Member; Cendrine Delivre [1974] LLP Member; Mark Andrew James Dewar [1962] LLP Member; Thomas Dick [1979] LLP Member; Paul Dineen [1977] LLP Member; Karine Disdier-Mikus [1971] LLP Member; Ian Stuart Doig [1964] LLP Member; James Huw Dolphin [1966] LLP Member; Jean-Pierre Gray Douglas-Henry [1968] LLP Member; Nigel Jonathan Drew [1957] LLP Member; Dr Jan Joachim Dreyer [1968] LLP Member; Alistair David Drummond [1970] LLP Member; Gurpreet Singh Duhra [1979] LLP Member; Matthew Duncombe [1975] LLP Member; Mark James Dwyer [1972] LLP Member; Andrew Simon Dyson [1972] LLP Member; Jonathan Eatough [1968] LLP Member

DLG Acquisitions Limited
Incorporated: 2 May 2014 *Employees:* 2,443
Net Worth: £34,492,000 *Total Assets:* £855,846,016
Registered Office: Berkshire House, 168-173 High Holborn, London, WC1V 7AA
Activities: Activities of head offices
Shareholders: Discovery, Inc; Liberty Global PLC
Officers: Ellis Justin Wolfe, Secretary; Bruce Loren Campbell [1967] Director/Chief Development Officer [American]; Simon James Christopher Freer [1976] Director/Investment; Marc Jeffery Graboff [1956] Director/President - Global BLA PLD & Studios [American]; Alyson Jackson [1972] Director; Robert McKay Leighton [1955] Director/Television Executive [American]; Bruce Michael Mann [1955] Director/MD Programming Liberty Global [American]

DLG Financing 1 Limited
Incorporated: 8 August 2014
Net Worth: £5,604,871 *Total Assets:* £283,967,424
Registered Office: Berkshire House, 168-173 High Holborn, London, WC1V 7AA
Activities: Other business support service activities n.e.c.
Parent: DLG Acquisitions Limited
Officers: Daniel Oliver Brook [1984] Director/Accountant; Bruce Loren Campbell [1967] Director [American]; Simon James Christopher Freer [1976] Director/Investment; Angela McMullen [1967] Director/Chartered Accountant; Roanne LEA Weekes [1978] Director/Accountant [Australian]; Ellis Justin Wolfe [1972] Director/Solicitor

DLG Financing 2 Limited
Incorporated: 8 August 2014
Net Worth Deficit: £28,862,960 *Total Assets:* £256,346,816
Registered Office: Berkshire House, 168-173 High Holborn, London, WC1V 7AA
Activities: Other business support service activities n.e.c.
Officers: Daniel Oliver Brook [1984] Director/Accountant; Bruce Loren Campbell [1967] Director [American]; Simon James Christopher Freer [1976] Director/Investment; Angela McMullen [1967] Director/Chartered Accountant; Roanne LEA Weekes [1978] Director/Accountant [Australian]; Ellis Justin Wolfe [1972] Director/Solicitor

DLJ Group
Incorporated: 12 March 1990
Net Worth: £1,982,177,792 *Total Assets:* £1,985,705,216
Registered Office: One Cabot Square, London, E14 4QJ
Activities: Activities of head offices
Parent: DLJ UK Holding
Officers: Paul Edward Hare, Secretary; Lawrence Bruce Fletcher [1968] Director/Head of Structured Credit Solutions; Paul Edward Hare [1960] Director/Company Secretary; Ahmed Bassam Kubba [1968] Director/Chief Operating Officer

DLJ International Group Limited
Incorporated: 18 July 1997
Net Worth: £1,883,977,216 *Total Assets:* £2,283,652,608
Registered Office: One Cabot Square, London, E14 4QJ
Activities: Activities of head offices
Parent: DLJ UK Investment Holdings Limited
Officers: Paul Edward Hare, Secretary; Lawrence Bruce Fletcher [1968] Director/Head of Structured Credit Solutions; Paul Edward Hare [1960] Director/Company Secretary; Ahmed Bassam Kubba [1968] Director/Chief Operating Officer

DLJ UK Holding
Incorporated: 18 July 1997
Net Worth: £2,014,685,440 *Total Assets:* £4,377,460,224
Registered Office: One Cabot Square, London, E14 4QJ
Activities: Activities of head offices
Parent: DLJ International Group Limited
Officers: Paul Edward Hare, Secretary; Lawrence Bruce Fletcher [1968] Director/Head of Structured Credit Solutions; Paul Edward Hare [1960] Director/Company Secretary; Ahmed Bassam Kubba [1968] Director/Chief Operating Officer

DLJ UK Investment Holdings Limited
Incorporated: 19 August 1997
Net Worth: £99,806,216 *Total Assets:* £3,448,834,304
Registered Office: One Cabot Square, London, E14 4QJ
Activities: Activities of head offices
Parent: Credit Suisse Group AG
Officers: Paul Edward Hare, Secretary; Lawrence Bruce Fletcher [1968] Director/Head of Structured Credit Solutions; Paul Edward Hare [1960] Director/Company Secretary; Ahmed Bassam Kubba [1968] Director/Chief Operating Officer

DMEP Holdco Limited
Incorporated: 24 October 2011
Net Worth Deficit: £1,027,440 *Total Assets:* £115,396,448
Registered Office: 6 St Andrew Street, London, EC4A 3AE
Activities: Other business support service activities n.e.c.
Shareholders: Hellenic Petroleum SA; Bridge Opportunity Limited
Officers: Ioannis Doratis [1969] Director/Accountant [Cypriot]; Kenneth Howard Prince-Wright [1956] Director

DMG Atlantic Limited
Incorporated: 29 August 2002
Net Worth: £1,083,770,624 *Total Assets:* £1,176,072,064
Registered Office: Northcliffe House, 2 Derry Street, London, W8 5TT
Activities: Activities of head offices
Parent: DMGB Limited
Officers: Frances Louise Sallas, Secretary; William Richard Flint [1969] Director/Accountant

DMG Charles Limited
Incorporated: 4 May 2001
Net Worth: £612,408,576 *Total Assets:* £613,156,096
Registered Office: Northcliffe House, 2 Derry Street, London, W8 5TT
Activities: Activities of head offices
Parent: DMG Investment Holdings Limited
Officers: Frances Louise Sallas, Secretary; William Richard Flint [1969] Director/Chartered Accountant; Frances Louise Sallas [1977] Director/Company Secretary

DMG Information Limited
Incorporated: 4 February 1999
Net Worth: £32,444,246 *Total Assets:* £121,054,208
Registered Office: c/o Daily Mail & General Trust PLC, Northcliffe House, 2 Derry Street, London, W8 5TT
Activities: Non-trading company
Parent: DMGB Limited
Officers: Frances Louise Sallas, Secretary; William Richard Flint [1969] Director/Accountant

DMG Investment Holdings Limited
Incorporated: 14 October 1996 *Employees:* 2
Net Worth: £598,624,896 *Total Assets:* £598,732,992
Registered Office: Northcliffe House, 2 Derry Street, London, W8 5TT
Activities: Activities of head offices
Parent: DMGB Limited
Officers: Frances Louise Sallas, Secretary; William Richard Flint [1969] Director/Accountant; Frances Louise Sallas [1977] Director/Company Secretary

DMG Loanco Limited
Incorporated: 14 November 1995
Net Worth: £95,035,000 *Total Assets:* £251,888,000
Registered Office: Northcliffe House, 2 Derry Street, Kensington, London, W8 5TT
Activities: Non-trading company
Parent: DMGB Limited
Officers: Frances Louise Sallas, Secretary; William Richard Flint [1969] Director/Accountant

DMG Media Limited
Incorporated: 3 April 2006
Net Worth: £567,651,008 *Total Assets:* £652,225,984
Registered Office: Northcliffe House, 2 Derry Street, London, W8 5TT
Activities: Non-trading company
Parent: Daily Mail and General Holdings Limited
Officers: Frances Louise Sallas, Secretary; Kevin Joseph Beatty [1957] Director/Newspaper Management; James Justin Siderfin Welsh [1967] Director

DMGB Limited
Incorporated: 29 August 2002 *Employees:* 2
Net Worth: £2,207,194,624 *Total Assets:* £2,717,094,656
Registered Office: Northcliffe House, 2 Derry Street, London, W8 5TT
Activities: Activities of head offices
Parent: Daily Mail and General Trust PLC
Officers: Frances Louise Sallas, Secretary; William Richard Flint [1969] Director/Accountant

DMGV Limited
Incorporated: 26 May 2006
Previous: DMG Media Investments Limited
Net Worth: £181,020,000 *Total Assets:* £181,328,000
Registered Office: Northcliffe House, 2 Derry Street, London, W8 5TT
Activities: Activities of head offices
Parent: Daily Mail and General Holdings Limited
Officers: Frances Louise Sallas, Secretary; Kevin Joseph Beatty [1957] Director/Newspaper Management; Manuel Lopo de Carvalho [1984] Director/CEO DMG Ventures [Portuguese]; Frances Louise Sallas [1977] Director/Company Secretary

DMGZ Limited
Incorporated: 17 January 1933
Previous: Northcliffe Media Holdings Limited
Net Worth: £171,325,984 *Total Assets:* £390,674,464
Registered Office: Northcliffe House, 2 Derry Street, Kensington, London, W8 5TT
Activities: Activities of head offices
Parent: DMGB Limited
Officers: Frances Louise Sallas, Secretary; Timothy Guy Collier [1963] Director; William Richard Flint [1969] Director/Accountant

DNB (UK) Limited
Incorporated: 27 March 1997 *Employees:* 5
Net Worth: £1,251,015,040 *Total Assets:* £4,793,042,944
Registered Office: 8th Floor, The Walbrook Building, 25 Walbrook, London, EC4N 8AF
Activities: Banks
Parent: DNB ASA
Officers: Vidar Andersen [1972] Director/Banker [Norwegian]; Jan Fredrik Skjeltorp [1972] Director [Norwegian]; Christopher William Courtenay Tregoning [1948] Director/Banker; Terje Turnes [1963] Director & CEO [Norwegian]

DNI Europe Holdings Limited
Incorporated: 10 May 2011
Net Worth: £931,248,128 *Total Assets:* £1,052,553,344
Registered Office: Discovery House, Building 2, Chiswick Park, 566 Chiswick High Road, London, W4 5YB
Activities: Activities of other holding companies n.e.c.
Parent: DNI Foreign Holdings Limited
Officers: Peter David Walesby [1980] Director/VP Content - Sports Rights FP&A; Roanne LEA Weekes [1978] Director/SVP, DNI Controller [Australian]

DNI Foreign Holdings Limited
Incorporated: 6 August 2013
Net Worth: £566,003,968 *Total Assets:* £1,433,177,216
Registered Office: Building 2, Chiswick Park, 566 Chiswick High Road, London, W4 5YB
Activities: Activities of other holding companies n.e.c.
Parent: DNI Global LLP
Officers: Roanne LEA Weekes [1978] Director/VP DNI Controller [Australian]; Hester Jane Wheeley [1969] Director/SVP Head of Legal EMEA

Dobbies Garden Centres Group Limited
Incorporated: 14 June 2016
Net Worth: £13,619,000 *Total Assets:* £292,004,000
Registered Office: Fourth Floor, 22-23 Old Burlington Street, London, W1S 2JJ
Activities: Activities of other holding companies n.e.c.
Officers: Debbie Mary Harding, Secretary; Andrew James Mark Lewis Bracey [1967] Director/Partner at Midlothian Capital Partners; David Henry Barnaby Burgess [1971] Director/Partner at Hattington Investment Partners LLP; Aiden Charles Barwick Clegg [1966] Director/Partner at Midlothian Capital Partners; Neil Allen Currie [1965] Director/Partner at Midlothian Capital Partners; Elizabeth Sharon Glass [1971] Director/Chief Financial Officer; Frederick Matthew Goltz [1971] Director/Partner at Hattington Investment Partners LLP [American/Irish]; Graeme McKinlay Jenkins [1975] Director/Chief Executive

Docklands Aviation Group Limited
Incorporated: 18 July 2006 *Employees:* 3
Net Worth: £214,494,000 *Total Assets:* £1,060,457,984
Registered Office: City Aviation House, London City Airport, Royal Docks, London, E16 2PB
Activities: Scheduled passenger air transport
Officers: Wilma Mary Allan [1962] Director/Chief Financial Officer; Robert Gary Sinclair [1966] Director/Chief Executive [New Zealander]

Docklands Light Railway Limited
Incorporated: 4 September 1986 *Employees:* 49
Net Worth: £1,900,000 *Total Assets:* £1,465,100,032
Registered Office: 55 Broadway, London, SW1H 0BD
Activities: Urban and suburban passenger railway transportation by underground, metro and similar systems
Parent: Transport Trading Limited
Officers: Howard Ernest Carter, Secretary; Jill Louise Collis [1968] Director of HSE; Patrick Doig [1982] Director/Planning & Reporting Controller; Jonathan Fox [1964] Director; Gareth William Powell [1976] Director of Strategy & Service Development

Docomo Digital Limited
Incorporated: 26 January 2016 *Employees:* 695
Net Worth: £101,763,352 *Total Assets:* £506,635,616
Registered Office: 5th Floor, 10 Dominion Street, London, EC2M 2EF
Activities: Wireless telecommunications activities
Parent: NTT Docomo, Inc
Officers: Mauro Del Rio [1964] Director [Italian]; Carlo Giuseppe Frigato [1963] Director/CFO Docomo Digital [Italian]; Hideto Motohashi [1968] Director [Japanese]; Hiroyuki Sato [1967] Director/Chief Executive Officer [Japanese]; Katsuyuki Takagi [1964] Director [Japanese]

The Doctors Laboratory Limited
Incorporated: 3 December 1987 *Employees:* 449
Net Worth: £111,836,000 *Total Assets:* £335,769,984
Registered Office: The Halo Building, 1 Mabledon Place, London, WC1H 9AX
Activities: Other human health activities
Parent: Sonic Healthcare Holding Company
Officers: Paul Joseph Alexander, Secretary; Thomas George Timothy Amies, Secretary; Thomas George Timothy Amies [1971] Finance Director; David Anthony Byrne [1959] Director; Dr Colin Stephen Goldschmidt [1954] Managing Director [Australian]; Timothy Herriman [1977] Director; Dr Lisa Levett [1972] Director; John Robert Matthews [1972] Director; Dr Raymond Prudo-Chlebosz [1944] Director/Medical Practitioner [Canadian]; Annette Joan Wilkinson [1957] Sales Director [Canadian]; Christopher David Wilks [1958] Finance Director [Australian]

Dollar Financial U.K. Limited
Incorporated: 26 January 1999 *Employees:* 2
Net Worth: £242,720,992 *Total Assets:* £572,625,984
Registered Office: 6 Bevis Marks, London, EC3A 7BA
Activities: Activities of head offices
Officers: Scott Aaron Cohen [1971] Director/Business Executive [American]

Dollar Financial UK Holding Ltd
Incorporated: 11 November 2013
Net Worth: £149,279,008 *Total Assets:* £149,279,008
Registered Office: 6 Bevis Marks, London, EC3A 7BA
Activities: Activities of financial services holding companies
Shareholders: Dollar Financial U.K. Limited; Sterling UK Holdco Limited
Officers: Scott Aaron Cohen [1971] Director/Business Executive [American]

Dolphin Drilling Limited
Incorporated: 13 July 1971 *Employees:* 45
Net Worth: £80,184,776 *Total Assets:* £180,943,040
Registered Office: 2nd Floor, 64-65 Vincent Square, London, SW1P 2NU
Activities: Support activities for petroleum and natural gas mining
Shareholders: Dolphin Drilling Operations Limited; Dolphin Drilling ASA
Officers: James David Lomax, Secretary; Ivar Brandvold [1956] Director [Norwegian]; James David Lomax [1955] Director/Contracts Manager; Hjalmar Krogseth Moe [1971] Director [Norwegian]

Domestic & General Acquisitions 1 Limited
Incorporated: 17 August 2007
Net Worth Deficit: £102,427,776 *Total Assets:* £285,609,664
Registered Office: Swan Court, 11 Worple Road, Wimbledon, London, SW19 4JS
Activities: Activities of head offices
Officers: Thomas Edward Hinton [1979] Director

Domestic & General Insurance PLC
Incorporated: 30 August 1950 *Employees:* 378
Net Worth: £90,053,000 *Total Assets:* £476,196,992
Registered Office: Swan Court, 11 Worple Road, Wimbledon, London, SW19 4JS
Activities: Non-life insurance
Parent: Domestic & General Group Limited
Officers: Mark John Jenkins, Secretary; Thomas Edward Hinton [1979] Director; Ian Mason [1962] Director/Chief Executive Officer; Barbara Jane Merry [1957] Director; David Tyler [1953] Director

Domestic & General Services Limited
Incorporated: 13 December 1985
Net Worth: £276,032,000 *Total Assets:* £732,024,000
Registered Office: Swan Court, 11 Worple Road, Wimbledon, London, SW19 4JS
Activities: Non-life insurance
Parent: Domestic & General Acquisitions 1 Limited
Officers: Thomas Edward Hinton [1979] Director; Ian Mason [1962] Director/Chief Executive

Donnelley Financial Solutions Group UK Limited
Incorporated: 19 August 2016
Net Worth: £111,754,936 *Total Assets:* £111,754,936
Registered Office: 3rd Floor, 88 Wood Street, London, EC2V 7AJ
Activities: Activities of other holding companies n.e.c.
Officers: Alexander James Levinger, Secretary; Tuan Jin Aw [1976] Director [Malaysian]; Jeremy Charles Hall [1965] Director

Donnelley Financial Solutions Holdings UK Limited
Incorporated: 1 April 2016
Net Worth: £108,875,488 *Total Assets:* £131,138,792
Registered Office: 3rd Floor, 88 Wood Street, London, EC2V 7AJ
Activities: Data processing, hosting and related activities
Officers: Alexander James Levinger, Secretary; Tuan Jin Aw [1976] Director [Malaysian]; Jeremy Charles Hall [1965] Director/Accountant

Donvand Limited
Incorporated: 23 May 1975 *Employees:* 402
Net Worth: £23,570,160 *Total Assets:* £338,311,712
Registered Office: 27 Goswell Road, London, EC1M 7GT
Activities: Other service activities n.e.c.
Parent: GTA Holdco Limited
Officers: Darren James Anniss [1977] Director; Martin Charles Jones [1973] Director; Alistair Rodger [1969] Director; Richard Stuart Wheatley [1967] Director

Dorchester Group Limited
Incorporated: 11 June 1984 *Employees:* 3,041
Net Worth: £1,139,012,992 *Total Assets:* £2,217,145,088
Registered Office: 3 Tilney Street, London, W1K 1BJ
Activities: Activities of head offices
Shareholder: Ministry of Finance of Brunei Darussalam
Officers: Azmi Abdul Rahman Ibrahim [1978] Director [Bruneian]; Dr Mohd Amin Liew Abdullah [1962] Director [Bruneian]; Sofian MD Jani [1971] Director [Bruneian]

Dorchester Hotel Limited
Incorporated: 13 October 1975 *Employees:* 776
Net Worth: £384,999,008 *Total Assets:* £558,947,968
Registered Office: The Dorchester Hotel, 53 Park Lane, London, W1A 2HJ
Activities: Hotels and similar accommodation
Parent: Dorchester Group Limited
Officers: Azmi Abdul Rahman Ibrahim [1978] Director [Bruneian]; Sofian MD Jani [1971] Director [Bruneian]

Dorney Issuer Holdco Limited
Incorporated: 25 September 2012
Net Worth: £261,412 *Total Assets:* £548,355,264
Registered Office: 35 Great St Helen's, London, EC3A 6AP
Activities: Non-trading company
Parent: Intertrust Corporate Services Limited
Officers: Daniel Marc Richard Jaffe [1975] Director

Dornoch Limited
Incorporated: 4 August 1995
Net Worth: £234,983,008 *Total Assets:* £776,259,008
Registered Office: 20 Gracechurch Street, London, EC3V 0BG
Activities: Non-life insurance
Parent: XL London Market Group Ltd
Officers: Marie Louise Rees, Secretary; Paul Richard Bradbrook [1976] Finance Director; Neil Donald Robertson [1968] Director/Insurance Executive

Dorrington Investment P L C
Incorporated: 10 August 1959
Net Worth: £22,248,608 *Total Assets:* £277,083,776
Registered Office: 16 Hans Road, London, SW3 1RT
Activities: Buying and selling of own real estate
Parent: Dorrington PLC
Officers: Manfred Stanley Gorvy [1938] Director/Chartered Accountant; Dr Sean Gorvy [1963] Director/Executive; John Patrick Kennedy [1957] Director/Group Financial Controller [Irish]; Alan Jay Leibowitz [1952] Director/Chartered Surveyor; Trevor Moross [1948] Director/Chartered Surveyor; Duncan James Salvesen [1957] Director/Chartered Surveyor

Dorrington London Flats Limited
Incorporated: 19 January 1938
Net Worth: £36,769,016 *Total Assets:* £125,003,632
Registered Office: 16 Hans Road, London, SW3 1RT
Activities: Other letting and operating of own or leased real estate
Parent: Dorrington Investment PLC
Officers: Francesco Cirillo [1963] Director/Chartered Surveyor [Italian]; Manfred Stanley Gorvy [1938] Director/Chartered Accountant; John Patrick Kennedy [1957] Director/Accountant [Irish]; Alan Jay Leibowitz [1952] Director/Surveyor; Trevor Moross [1948] Director/Chartered Surveyor; Duncan James Salvesen [1957] Director/Chartered Surveyor; Bruce Thompson [1964] Director/Investment Surveyor; Peter Yeates [1969] Director

Dorrington PLC
Incorporated: 29 July 1987 *Employees:* 25
Net Worth: £511,852,992 *Total Assets:* £930,150,016
Registered Office: 16 Hans Road, London, SW3 1RT
Activities: Buying and selling of own real estate
Parent: Tamoa Limited
Officers: Andrew Richard Giblin [1978] Director/Financial Analyst; Manfred Stanley Gorvy [1938] Director/Chartered Accountant; Dr Sean Gorvy [1963] Director/Executive; Robert Harris [1962] Director/Chartered Surveyor; John Patrick Kennedy [1957] Director/Accountant [Irish]; Alan Jay Leibowitz [1952] Director/Surveyor; Trevor Moross [1948] Director/Chartered Surveyor; Duncan James Salvesen [1957] Director/Chartered Surveyor; Bruce Oliver Thompson [1964] Director/Chartered Surveyor

Dorrington Properties PLC
Incorporated: 7 August 1987 *Employees:* 11
Net Worth: £70,418,904 *Total Assets:* £197,053,888
Registered Office: 16 Hans Road, London, SW3 1RT
Activities: Buying and selling of own real estate
Parent: Dorrington PLC
Officers: Andrew Richard Giblin [1978] Director/Financial Analyst; Manfred Stanley Gorvy [1938] Director/Chartered Accountant; Dr Sean Gorvy [1963] Director/Executive; Robert Harris [1962] Director/Chartered Surveyor; John Patrick Kennedy [1957] Director/Group Financial Controller [Irish]; Alan Jay Leibowitz [1952] Director/Chartered Surveyor; Trevor Moross [1948] Director/Chartered Surveyor; Bruce Oliver Thompson [1964] Director/Chartered Surveyor

Doubleplay I Limited
Incorporated: 10 July 2013 *Employees:* 936
Net Worth Deficit: £35,457,000 *Total Assets:* £323,665,984
Registered Office: 7th Floor, Lacon House, 84 Theobald's Road, London, WC1X 8NL
Activities: Non-trading company
Officers: Anthony John Booker [1970] Financial Director; Rupa Pravin Patel [1975] Director/Lawyer; Leon Taviansky [1970] Director/Chief Operating & Financial Officer

Doubleplay II Limited
Incorporated: 10 July 2013
Net Worth: £327,212,000 *Total Assets:* £328,696,000
Registered Office: 7th Floor, Lacon House, 84 Theobald's Road, London, WC1X 8NL
Activities: Activities of other holding companies n.e.c.
Parent: Doubleplay I Limited
Officers: Anthony John Booker [1970] Finance Director; Rupa Pravin Patel [1975] Director/Lawyer; Leon Taviansky [1970] Director/Chief Operating & Financial Officer

Doubleplay III Limited
Incorporated: 10 July 2013
Net Worth: £430,744,000 *Total Assets:* £500,127,008
Registered Office: 7th Floor, Lacon House, 84 Theobald's Road, London, WC1X 8NL
Activities: Activities of other holding companies n.e.c.
Parent: Exterion Media Holdings Limited
Officers: Anthony John Booker [1970] Finance Director; Rupa Pravin Patel [1975] Director/Lawyer; Leon Taviansky [1970] Director/Chief Operating & Financial Officer

Doughty Hanson & Co Managers Limited
Incorporated: 27 January 1995 *Employees:* 28
Net Worth: £166,880,000 *Total Assets:* £347,649,984
Registered Office: 45 Pall Mall, London, SW1Y 5JG
Activities: Fund management activities
Parent: DHCM Holdco Limited
Officers: Benjamin Martin Dooley [1983] Director; Richard Peter Hanson [1956] Director; Graeme Dominic Stening [1964] Director

Dow Jones Business Interactive (U.K.), Limited
Incorporated: 11 December 2006
Net Worth: £75,364,000 *Total Assets:* £250,481,280
Registered Office: 7th Floor, The News Building, 1 London Bridge Street, London, SE1 9GF
Activities: Other business support service activities n.e.c.
Parent: DJBI, LLC
Officers: Keysha Zalika McNeil, Secretary; Azmina Allaudin Airi [1976] Finance Director; Eric Steven Mandrackie [1970] Finance Director [American]

Doyle London Hotels Limited
Incorporated: 5 October 1976 *Employees:* 215
Net Worth: £99,056,000 *Total Assets:* £148,151,008
Registered Office: 47 Welbeck Street, London, W1G 8DN
Activities: Hotels and similar accommodation
Parent: Doyle Hotels Holdings (UK) Limited
Officers: Seamus Daly, Secretary; Seamus Daly [1953] Director/Company Secretary [Irish]; Bernadette Gallagher [1959] Director [Irish]; Patrick King [1970] Director/Chief Executive Officer [Irish]; Justin Radcliffe [1970] Director/Financial Controller

Dragonglass UK Holding Limited
Incorporated: 1 July 2016 *Employees:* 116
Net Worth: £39,055,008 *Total Assets:* £110,354,352
Registered Office: 2nd Floor, One Eagle Place, St James's, London, SW1Y 6AF
Activities: Hotels and similar accommodation
Parent: Dragonglass Bidco Ltd
Officers: Sarah Broughton [1976] Director/Accountant; Nicholas Mark Chadwick [1981] Director/Chartered Accountant; Thomas Mark Tolley [1978] Director/Solicitor

Dreof II Europe Holdings Limited
Incorporated: 2 December 2015
Net Worth: £110,105,672 *Total Assets:* £158,526,176
Registered Office: Siguler Guff UK LLP, 4th Floor, Brookfield House, 44 Davies Street, London, W1K 5JA
Activities: Activities of other holding companies n.e.c.
Officers: David George Boal [1958] Managing Director; Jun Isoda [1981] Principal, Director of Accounting [American]; Sandip Kakar [1971] Director/Managing Counsel [American]; Jarrad Krulick [1980] Principal, Director of Tax [American]

Dress Holdco 4 Limited
Incorporated: 22 December 2014
Net Worth: £115,013,000 *Total Assets:* £239,168,000
Registered Office: 55 Kimber Road, London, SW18 4NX
Activities: Retail sale of clothing in specialised stores
Parent: Dress Holdco C Limited
Officers: Stuart Andrew Baird [1965] Retail Director [South African]; Benjamin Lawrence Maximilian Barnett [1979] Director; Lee Eric Harlow [1971] Director; Catherine Ann Lambert [1965] Director/Chief Financial Officer; Alexander Douglas Murray [1957] Director; Bongiwe Ntuli [1977] Director [South African]; Anthony Edward Thunstrom [1970] Director [South African]

Dress Holdco A Limited
Incorporated: 8 January 2015
Net Worth: £259,374,000 *Total Assets:* £260,760,000
Registered Office: 55 Kimber Road, London, SW18 4NX
Activities: Retail sale of clothing in specialised stores
Parent: The Foschini Group Limited
Officers: Stuart Andrew Baird [1965] Retail Director [South African]; Alexander Douglas Murray [1957] Director; Bongiwe Ntuli [1977] Director [South African]; Anthony Edward Thunstrom [1970] Director [South African]

Dress Holdco C Limited
Incorporated: 8 January 2015
Net Worth: £135,436,000 *Total Assets:* £203,584,992
Registered Office: 55 Kimber Road, London, SW18 4NX
Activities: Retail sale of clothing in specialised stores
Parent: TFG Brands (London) Limited
Officers: Stuart Andrew Baird [1965] Retail Director [South African]; Benjamin Lawrence Maximilian Barnett [1979] Director; Lee Eric Harlow [1971] Director; Catherine Ann Lambert [1965] Director/Chief Financial Officer; Alexander Douglas Murray [1957] Director; Bongiwe Ntuli [1977] Director [South African]; Anthony Edward Thunstrom [1970] Director [South African]

Drift Properties Limited
Incorporated: 6 December 1961
Net Worth: £257,391,696 *Total Assets:* £336,155,424
Registered Office: 5 New Street Square, London, EC4A 3TW
Activities: Buying and selling of own real estate
Parent: Park Tower Investments Limited
Officers: Amer Mohammed Mahdi Al Tajir [1961] Director [Emirati]; Khalid Mohamed Mahdi Al Tajir [1958] Director/Businessman [Emirati]; Mohamed Sadiq Al Tajir [1941] Director/Businessman [Bahraini]; Mohammed Mahdi Al Tajir [1931] Director/Businessman [Emirati]

Drillgreat Limited
Incorporated: 26 June 2007 *Employees:* 2,737
Net Worth: £257,103,008 *Total Assets:* £400,352,992
Registered Office: Notting Dale Village, 1 Nicholas Road, London, W11 4AN
Activities: Activities of other holding companies n.e.c.
Major Shareholder: Peter Simon
Officers: Bridget Sophie Green, Secretary; Paul Christopher Allen [1964] Finance Director [Irish]; Elaine Jacqueline Deste [1963] Director/Accountant; Vinod Kumar Dhawan [1951] Director [Indian]; Peter Simon [1949] Director [Irish]

Drilton Limited
Incorporated: 20 July 1992 *Employees:* 3,878
Net Worth: £217,361,184 *Total Assets:* £477,515,872
Registered Office: Hiview House, Highgate Road, London, NW5 1TN
Activities: Activities of construction holding companies
Officers: John Patrick Murphy, Secretary; Alastair Gibson Kerr [1950] Director; Deborah Lodge [1968] Director/Business Consultant; Clare Patricia Mara [1975] Director/Self Employed [Irish]; Bernard Joseph Murphy [1945] Director [Irish]; James Alexander Murphy [1984] Director/Contracts Manager [Irish]; Dr Karina Duarte Corware Murphy [1984] Director/Safety Surveillance & Risk Management Lead; Kathleen Murphy [1949] Director/Business Consultant [Irish]

DSG Card Handling Services Limited
Incorporated: 22 March 2001
Net Worth: £226,460,992 *Total Assets:* £343,423,008
Registered Office: 1 Portal Way, London, W3 6RS
Activities: Banks
Parent: DSG Retail Limited
Officers: Catherine Springett, Secretary; Alistair Gibson [1975] Director; Leon Smith [1976] Director/Chartered Accountant

DSG European Investments Limited
Incorporated: 9 December 1999
Net Worth Deficit: £93,995,000 *Total Assets:* £344,328,000
Registered Office: 1 Portal Way, London, W3 6RS
Activities: Other business support service activities n.e.c.
Parent: DSG Overseas Investments Limited
Officers: Catherine Springett, Secretary; Alistair Gibson [1975] Director; Leon Smith [1976] Director/Chartered Accountant

DSG International Holdings Limited
Incorporated: 2 December 1999
Net Worth: £1,635,971,968 *Total Assets:* £1,805,773,952
Registered Office: 1 Portal Way, London, W3 6RS
Activities: Activities of head offices
Parent: Dixons Retail Group Limited
Officers: Catherine Springett, Secretary; Alistair Gibson [1975] Director; Leon Smith [1976] Director/Chartered Accountant

DSG Overseas Investments Limited
Incorporated: 27 July 1992
Net Worth Deficit: £48,349,000 *Total Assets:* £572,396,992
Registered Office: 1 Portal Way, London, W3 6RS
Activities: Activities of head offices
Parent: DSG International Holdings Limited
Officers: Catherine Springett, Secretary; Alistair Gibson [1975] Director; Leon Smith [1976] Director/Chartered Accountant

DSG Retail Limited
Incorporated: 28 February 1952 *Employees:* 20,623
Net Worth: £772,899,968 *Total Assets:* £2,681,499,904
Registered Office: 1 Portal Way, London, W3 6RS
Activities: Retail sale of electrical household appliances in specialised stores
Parent: DSG International Holdings Limited
Officers: Catherine Springett, Secretary; Stephen Lawrence Ager [1959] Director; Antreas Athanassopoulos [1966] Director/Chief Customer Officer [Greek]; Jonathan Peter Mason [1964] Finance Director; Alan Joseph Clayton Ritchie [1958] Managing Director, Retail and Operations

DTEK Finance PLC
Incorporated: 27 February 2013
Net Worth Deficit: £52,992,088 *Total Assets:* £958,607,936
Registered Office: Fifth Floor, 25 Park Lane, London, W1K 1RA
Activities: Activities of other holding companies n.e.c.
Major Shareholder: Rinat Akhmetov
Officers: Paul John Cooper, Secretary; Johan Frans Jozef Maria Bastin [1952] Director [Dutch]; Maksym Viktorovych Timchenko [1975] Director [Ukrainian]

DTEK Investments Limited
Incorporated: 27 February 2013
Net Worth: £633,123,136 *Total Assets:* £899,817,728
Registered Office: Fifth Floor, 25 Park Lane, London, W1K 1RA
Activities: Activities of other holding companies n.e.c.
Parent: DTEK Finance PLC
Officers: Johan Frans Jozef Maria Bastin [1952] Director [Dutch]; Maksym Viktorovych Timchenko [1975] Director [Ukrainian]

DTZ UK Bidco 2 Limited
Incorporated: 27 October 2014
Net Worth: £10,976,124 *Total Assets:* £185,642,080
Registered Office: 125 Old Broad Street, London, EC2N 1AR
Activities: Activities of other holding companies n.e.c.
Parent: DTZ Worldwide Limited
Officers: John Forrester [1962] Director/Chief Executive, EMEA; Sunita Kaushal [1973] Director/General Counsel & Company Secretary; Duncan Palmer [1965] Director/Global Chief Financial Officer [British/American]; Brett David Soloway [1968] Director/Global General Counsel [American]

DTZ UK Bidco Limited
Incorporated: 15 August 2014
Net Worth: £542,440,320 *Total Assets:* £542,468,928
Registered Office: 125 Old Broad Street, London, EC2N 1AR
Activities: Activities of other holding companies n.e.c.
Parent: DTZ UK Holdco Limited
Officers: John Forrester [1962] Director/Chief Executive EMEA; Sunita Kaushal [1973] Director/General Counsel & Company Secretary; Duncan John Palmer [1965] Director/Global Chief Financial Officer; Brett David Soloway [1968] Director/Global General Counsel [American]

DTZ UK Guarantor Limited
Incorporated: 22 August 2014
Net Worth: £1,391,324,032 *Total Assets:* £1,395,609,088
Registered Office: 125 Old Broad Street, London, EC2N 1AR
Activities: Activities of other holding companies n.e.c.
Shareholders: Cushman & Wakefield PLC; Cushman & Wakefield Limited
Officers: John Forrester [1962] Director/Chief Executive; William Joseph Knightly [1979] Director/Finance Executive [American]; Duncan John Palmer [1965] Director/Global Chief Financial Officer; Brett David Soloway [1968] Director/Global General Counsel [American]

DTZ UK Holdco Limited
Incorporated: 15 August 2014
Net Worth: £685,532,864 *Total Assets:* £716,638,528
Registered Office: 125 Old Broad Street, London, EC2N 1AR
Activities: Activities of other holding companies n.e.c.
Parent: DTZ Worldwide Limited
Officers: John Forrester [1962] Director/Chief Executive EMEA; Sunita Kaushal [1973] Director/General Counsel & Company Secretary; Duncan Palmer [1965] Director/Global Chief Financial Officer [British/American]; Brett David Soloway [1968] Director/Global General Counsel [American]

DTZ UK Newco Limited
Incorporated: 18 August 2015
Net Worth: £4,443,775 *Total Assets:* £959,593,280
Registered Office: 125 Old Broad Street, London, EC2N 1AR
Activities: Activities of other holding companies n.e.c.
Parent: DTZ Worldwide Limited
Officers: John Forrester [1962] Director/Chief Executive EMEA; Sunita Kaushal [1973] Director/General Counsel & Company Secretary; Duncan Palmer [1965] Director/Global Chief Financial Officer [British/American]; Brett David Soloway [1968] Director/Global General Counsel [American]

Dudgeon Holdings Ltd
Incorporated: 24 February 2016
Net Worth: £188,361,104 *Total Assets:* £284,827,424
Registered Office: One Kingdom Street, London, W2 6BD
Activities: Activities of head offices
Shareholders: Equinor New Energy Limited; Masdar Offshore Wind UK Limited
Officers: Lina Balbuckaite, Secretary; Bader Al Lamki [1975] Director, Masdar Clean Energy [Emirati]; Mohammad Alramahi [1971] Director, Asset Management and Technical Services [American]; Federico Fassio [1983] Director/Manager [Italian]; Stian Florenaes [1968] Director/Vice President Finance and Control [Norwegian]; Trine Ingebjorg Ulla [1961] Director/Manager BD [Norwegian]; Qi Peng [1979] Managing Director [Chinese]; Rune Ronvik [1958] Director/Project Manager [Norwegian]; Ding Yuankui [1974] Director/Vice President [Chinese]; Tim Tianwei Zhang [1963] Director/Corporate Management [American]

Dudgeon Offshore Wind Limited
Incorporated: 17 April 2002
Net Worth: £165,356,992 *Total Assets:* £1,469,698,944
Registered Office: One Kingdom Street, London, W2 6BD
Activities: Production of electricity
Parent: Dudgeon Holdings II Limited
Officers: Lina Balbuckaite, Secretary; Bader Saeed Mohammedd Salem Al Lamki [1975] Director, Masdar Clean Energy [Emirati]; Mohammad Alramahi [1971] Director, Asset Management and Technical Services [American]; Federico Fassio [1983] Director [Italian]; Stian Florenaes [1968] Director/Vice President Finance and Control [Norwegian]; Trine Ingebjorg Ulla [1961] Director/Manager BD [Norwegian]; Qi Peng [1979] Managing Director [Chinese]; Rune Ronvik [1958] Director/Project Manager [Norwegian]; Ding Yuankui [1974] Director/Vice President [Chinese]; Tim Tianwei Zhang [1963] Director/Corporate Management [American]

Due West Investments Limited
Incorporated: 12 December 2014
Net Worth: £2,576,000 *Total Assets:* £159,738,000
Registered Office: 70 Grosvenor Street, London, W1K 3JP
Activities: Buying and selling of own real estate
Parent: Grosvenor Properties
Officers: Derek John Lewis, Secretary; Keith John Bailey [1979] Director/Chartered Surveyor; Roger Frederick Crawford Blundell [1962] Finance Director; Anna Clare Bond [1981] Director/Chartered Surveyor; Douglas Nigel Crichton [1976] Director/Chartered Surveyor; Simon Geoffrey Harding-Roots [1968] Director; Chantal Antonia Henderson [1975] Director/Accountant; Nigel Auriol Hughes [1957] Director/Chartered Surveyor; Richard Alexander Jefferies [1963] Operations Director; Craig David McWilliam [1972] Director/Chartered Surveyor; Paul Francis O'Grady [1985] Director/Chartered Surveyor; Amelia Mary Staveley [1986] Director/Chartered Surveyor

Dukinfield II PLC
Incorporated: 12 May 2016
Net Worth Deficit: £2,557,815 *Total Assets:* £299,349,536
Registered Office: 35 Great St Helen's, London, EC3A 6AP
Activities: Financial intermediation not elsewhere classified
Parent: Dukinfield II Holdings Limited
Officers: Susan Iris Abrahams [1957] Director

Dukinfield PLC
Incorporated: 8 July 2015
Net Worth: £14,970 *Total Assets:* £371,998,656
Registered Office: 35 Great St Helen's, London, EC3A 6AP
Activities: Financial intermediation not elsewhere classified
Parent: Dukinfield Holdings Limited
Officers: Susan Iris Abrahams [1957] Director; Clifford Pearce [1970] Director

Dunbar Assets PLC
Incorporated: 20 November 1969 *Employees:* 5
Net Worth: £130,630,000 *Total Assets:* £132,355,000
Registered Office: 70 Mark Lane, London, EC3R 7NQ
Activities: Credit granting by non-deposit taking finance houses and other specialist consumer credit grantors
Shareholders: Dunbar Assets Ireland; Dunbar Assets Ireland Unlimited Company
Officers: Simon Royston Barnes [1963] Director/Manager; Oscar Manuel Carrillo [1966] Director; Neil Andrew Freshwater [1969] Director

Duncan Funding 2015-1 PLC
Incorporated: 19 December 2013
Net Worth Deficit: £256,000 *Total Assets:* £1,678,760,960
Registered Office: 35 Great St Helen's, London, EC3A 6AP
Activities: Financial intermediation not elsewhere classified
Parent: Duncan Holdings 2015-1 Limited
Officers: Daniel Marc Richard Jaffe [1975] Managing Director

Duncan Funding 2016-1 PLC
Incorporated: 30 March 2016
Net Worth Deficit: £91,000 *Total Assets:* £2,878,428,928
Registered Office: 35 Great St Helen's, London, EC3A 6AP
Activities: Financial intermediation not elsewhere classified
Parent: Duncan Holdings 2016-1 Limited
Officers: Daniel Marc Richard Jaffe [1975] Managing Director

The Dunhill Medical Trust
Incorporated: 16 December 2010 *Employees:* 5
Net Worth: £139,923,328 *Total Assets:* £151,119,184
Registered Office: 5th Floor, 6 New Bridge Street, London, EC4V 6AB
Activities: Other human health activities
Officers: Michael Charles Bellamy [1945] Director/Retired; Professor Deborah Kay Dunn-Walters [1963] Director/University Lecturer; Kay Glendinning [1935] Director; Anne Claire Keatinge [1958] Director; Professor Thomas Burton Loram Kirkwood [1951] Director/Professor of Biogerontology; Professor Peter Reginald Lansley [1946] Director/Professor of Construction Management; James Lorigan [1979] Director/Senior Management, NHS; Professor James McEwen [1940] Director/Emeritus Professor of Public Health; Alison Jean Petch [1950] Director; John Anthony Ransford [1948] Director/Retired Local Government Officer; Keith Anthony Shepherd [1960] Director/Institutional Investment Professional (Retired)

Dunhill Tobacco of London Limited
Incorporated: 13 October 1993
Net Worth: £139,300,000 *Total Assets:* £139,982,000
Registered Office: Globe House, 4 Temple Place, London, WC2R 2PG
Activities: Other business support service activities n.e.c.
Parent: British American Tobacco (Brands) Limited
Officers: Jonathan Michael Guttridge, Secretary; David Patrick Ian Booth [1974] Director/Group Chief Accountant; Roger Anthony Carr Evans [1973] Director; Paul McCrory [1972] Director/Lawyer

Dunnhumby Limited
Incorporated: 24 May 1989 *Employees:* 1,835
Net Worth: £205,080,992 *Total Assets:* £336,665,984
Registered Office: 184 Shepherds Bush Road, London, W6 7NL
Activities: Management consultancy activities other than financial management
Parent: Tesco Holdings Limited
Officers: Sarah Anne McCarthy, Secretary; Guillaume Bacuvier [1973] Director/Chief Executive Officer [French]; Rosemary Joanne Wilson [1975] Director/Chief Financial Officer

Dunwilco (1783) Limited
Incorporated: 18 December 2012
Net Worth: £84,884,000 *Total Assets:* £890,947,008
Registered Office: c/o CMS Cameron McKenna LLP, 78 Cannon Street, London, EC4N 6AF
Activities: Hotels and similar accommodation
Parent: Dunwilco (1847) Limited
Officers: Benjamin David Cadwell [1982] Director/Executive [American]; Ashley Fernandes [1968] Director [Indian]; Sean Piers Harrison [1971] Director/General Counsel; Kamal Rhazali [1979] Director/General Counsel [French]

Dunwilco (1784) Limited
Incorporated: 18 December 2012
Net Worth: £83,662,000 *Total Assets:* £891,054,016
Registered Office: c/o CMS Cameron McKenna LLP, 78 Cannon Street, London, EC4N 6AF
Activities: Hotels and similar accommodation
Parent: Dunwilco (1783) Limited
Officers: Benjamin David Cadwell [1982] Director/Executive [American]; Ashley Fernandes [1968] Director [Indian]; Sean Piers Harrison [1971] Director/General Counsel; Kamal Rhazali [1979] Director/General Counsel [French]

Dunwilco (1847) Limited
Incorporated: 19 August 2014
Net Worth: £83,388,000 *Total Assets:* £1,026,764,032
Registered Office: c/o CMS Cameron McKenna LLP, 78 Cannon Street, London, EC4N 6AF
Activities: Hotels and similar accommodation
Parent: Breezeroad Limited
Officers: Benjamin David Cadwell [1982] Director/Executive [American]; Ashley Fernandes [1968] Director [Indian]; Sean Piers Harrison [1971] Director/General Counsel; Kamal Rhazali [1979] Director/General Counsel [French]

DVB Transport Finance Limited
Incorporated: 25 June 1998 *Employees:* 4
Net Worth: £58,204,640 *Total Assets:* £914,629,120
Registered Office: 6th Floor, Park House, 16-18 Finsbury Circus, London, EC2M 7EB
Activities: Other credit granting n.e.c.
Officers: James Gordon Peter Webb, Secretary; David Rhys Goring-Thomas [1965] Director/Banker; Guido Schmitz [1966] Director/Banker [German]; Eelco Jan Jacob Van de Stadt [1965] Director/Banker [Dutch]

DWS Alternatives Global Limited
Incorporated: 26 October 2005 *Employees:* 50
Previous: Deutsche Alternative Asset Management (Global) Limited
Net Worth: £205,611,008 *Total Assets:* £313,280,992
Registered Office: Winchester House, 1 Great Winchester Street, London, EC2N 2DB
Activities: Financial intermediation not elsewhere classified
Parent: Deutsche Bank Aktiengesellschaft
Officers: Andrew William Bartlett, Secretary; Hamish MacPhail Massie MacKenzie [1969] Director/Investment Banker; Gianluca Muzzi [1970] Director/Investment Manager [Italian]; Stephen James Thomas Shaw [1957] Director [Australian]

DWS Group Services UK Limited
Incorporated: 28 August 1985 *Employees:* 58
Previous: Deutsche Asset Management Group Limited
Net Worth: £50,016,000 *Total Assets:* £215,908,000
Registered Office: Winchester House, 1 Great Winchester Street, London, EC2N 2DB
Activities: Financial intermediation not elsewhere classified
Parent: Deutsche Bank Aktiengesellschaft
Officers: Andrew William Bartlett, Secretary; Sarah Mei-Yun Johns [1985] Director/Banker; Andrew Levy [1978] Director; Maria Ryan Dalton [1968] Director/Banker [Irish]

Dynamic Estates Limited
Incorporated: 3 November 2008 *Employees:* 12
Net Worth: £76,462,552 *Total Assets:* £172,042,912
Registered Office: 219 Baker Street, London, NW1 6XE
Activities: Other letting and operating of own or leased real estate
Parent: Farmont Baker Street Limited
Officers: Massimiliano Dall'osso [1965] Director [Italian]

E & A Property Investment Company Limited
Incorporated: 15 May 2015
Net Worth: £21,532,000 *Total Assets:* £169,096,992
Registered Office: 33 Ely Place, London, EC1N 6TD
Activities: Other letting and operating of own or leased real estate
Parent: Estates & Agency Holdings Limited
Officers: Echo Chong, Secretary; John Stuart Ian Rosefield [1944] Director; Stephen Michael Rosefield [1952] Director/Solicitor

E D F Trading Limited
Incorporated: 7 April 1999 *Employees:* 465
Net Worth: £2,720,459,008 *Total Assets:* £12,557,363,200
Registered Office: 3rd Floor, Cardinal Place, 80 Victoria Street, London, SW1E 5JL
Activities: Trade of electricity
Parent: EDF SA
Officers: Robert William Quick, Secretary; Marc Benayoun [1966] Director/Senior Executive VP Gas & Italy [French]; Bruno Bensasson [1972] Director/Group Senior Ex VP Renewable Energies [French]; Xavier Girre [1969] Director/Group CFO [French]; Robert Guyler [1966] Director/Chief Financial Officer; Marianne Laigneau [1964] Director General Affairs [French]; Sabine Le Gac [1975] Director/General Counsel Supply Optimisation & Trading [French]; Stanislas Hugues Patrick Marie Foulques Martin [1968] Director/Chief Risk Officer [French]; Laurent Jean-Lionel Reber [1967] Director/Executive Vice President, Operations Centre [French]; John Hunter Rittenhouse [1958] Director/Chief Executive; Stephanie Roger-Selwan [1966] Director/CFO Direction Commerce-EDF SAA [French]; Magali Fabienne Renee Viandier [1968] Director/Head of Group and Corporate Accounting [French]

E-Act
Incorporated: 6 March 2008 *Employees:* 2,264
Net Worth: £136,016,992 *Total Assets:* £177,783,008
Registered Office: Unit 9.2.1 The Leathermarket, 11-13 Weston Street, London, SE1 3ER
Activities: Other education n.e.c.
Officers: Harriet Jane Rushton, Secretary; Hugo Sean Alleyne [1971] Director/Internal Auditor; Pamela Mary Coles [1961] Director/Company Secretary; Gurpreet Singh Dehal [1967] Director; Angus John Steedman Hislop [1946] Director; Theresa Keating [1964] Director/Accountant; Nadeem Maqsood Kiyani [1970] Director; Brian Peter Leon Lightman [1955] Director; David Moran [1971] Director/Chief Executive; Dr Cameron Samuel Benjamin Pyke [1971] Director; Jean Anne Scott [1950] Director/Education Consultant; John Michael Wemms [1940] Director; Professor Bryan Gordon Winchester [1941] Director/Retired Lecturer

E-Carat 6 PLC
Incorporated: 21 July 2015
Net Worth: £14,110 *Total Assets:* £174,593,264
Registered Office: 35 Great St Helen's, London, EC3A 6AP
Activities: Financial intermediation not elsewhere classified
Parent: E-Carat 6 Holdings Limited
Officers: Daniel Marc Richard Jaffe [1975] Director

E-Carat 7 PLC
Incorporated: 9 September 2016
Net Worth: £13,468 *Total Assets:* £341,596,864
Registered Office: 35 Great St Helen's, London, EC3A 6AP
Activities: Financial intermediation not elsewhere classified
Parent: E-Carat 7 Holdings Limited
Officers: Daniel Marc Richard Jaffe [1975] Director

E-Carat 8 PLC
Incorporated: 9 February 2017
Net Worth: £13,148 *Total Assets:* £389,287,488
Registered Office: 35 Great St Helen's, London, EC3A 6AP
Activities: Financial intermediation not elsewhere classified
Parent: E-Carat 8 Holdings Limited
Officers: Daniel Marc Richard Jaffe [1975] Director

E-Rewards Bidco Limited
Incorporated: 14 October 2009
Net Worth: £138,418,320 *Total Assets:* £138,483,088
Registered Office: Ground Floor, 160 Queen Victoria Street, London, EC4V 4BF
Activities: Market research and public opinion polling
Parent: Research Now Group, Inc.
Officers: Samuel Scott Anderson [1978] Director/Global Controller [American]; Gary Selden Laben [1964] Director/Business Executive [American]; Jeremy Paul Summerfield [1977] Director/Business Executive

E. F. Oil and Gas Limited
Incorporated: 5 September 1997
Net Worth: £96,943,000 *Total Assets:* £439,857,984
Registered Office: 18th Floor, 10 Upper Bank Street, London, E14 5BF
Activities: Extraction of crude petroleum
Parent: Elf Exploration UK Limited
Officers: Bryan Wilson, Secretary; Karen Dyrskjot Boesen [1971] Director/Chief Financial Officer [Danish]; Pierre Xavier Gilbert Cuisnier [1962] CGA Director [French]; Jean-Luc Guiziou [1961] Director/Engineer [French]; Mariam Aissata Francoise Kane-Garcia [1977] Business Development Director [French]

Eagle 3 Limited
Incorporated: 14 October 2005
Net Worth: £242,365,184 *Total Assets:* £289,106,272
Registered Office: 2nd Floor, Exchequer Court, 33 St Mary Axe, London, EC3A 8AA
Activities: Activities of head offices
Parent: ERM Group Limited
Officers: Roy Antony Burrows, Secretary; Simon Paul Crowe [1967] Director/Chief Financial Officer; Mark Robert Pearson [1967] Director

Eagle 4 Limited
Incorporated: 14 October 2005
Net Worth: £620,931,200 *Total Assets:* £1,120,092,288
Registered Office: 2nd Floor, Exchequer Court, 33 St Mary Axe, London, EC3A 8AA
Activities: Activities of head offices
Parent: Eagle 3 Limited
Officers: Roy Antony Burrows, Secretary; Simon Paul Crowe [1967] Director/Chief Financial Officer; Keryn Lee James [1968] Director [Australian]; Mark Robert Pearson [1967] Director

Eagle Financial and Leasing Services (UK) Limited
Incorporated: 16 July 1990
Net Worth: £230,000 *Total Assets:* £1,380,973,952
Registered Office: 1 Churchill Place, London, E14 5HP
Activities: Financial intermediation not elsewhere classified
Parent: Barclays Bank PLC
Officers: Mark Francis Beastall [1978] Director/Accountant; Mahesh Beniwal [1971] Director/Accountant [Indian]; Sven Pongs [1975] Director/Banker [German]; Christopher Simon White [1978] Director/Banker

Earls Court Partnership Limited
Incorporated: 31 January 2014
Net Worth: £826,534,976 *Total Assets:* £896,339,968
Registered Office: 15 Grosvenor Street, London, W1K 4QZ
Activities: Development of building projects
Shareholders: Capital & Counties Properties PLC; TTL Earls Court Properties Limited
Officers: Leigh McCaveny, Secretary; Ruth Elizabeth Pavey, Secretary; William Jonathan Cornelius [1967] Director/Chartered Surveyor; Ian David Hawksworth [1965] Director/Chartered Surveyor; Situl Suryakant Jobanputra [1974] Director; Terence David O'Beirne [1976] Director/Chartered Accountant [Irish]; Gary James Yardley [1965] Director/Chartered Surveyor; Kenneth John Youngman [1956] Finance Director

East Anglia One Limited
Incorporated: 6 September 2010
Net Worth: £36,600,000 *Total Assets:* £649,299,968
Registered Office: 3rd Floor, 1 Tudor Street, London, EC4Y 0AH
Activities: Production of electricity
Parent: ScottishPower Renewables (UK) Limited
Officers: Andrew Philip, Secretary; Heather Chalmers White [1964] Director/Accountant; Jonathan Thomas Kirkwood Cole [1977] Offshore Managing Director; Charles Jordan [1975] Project Director

East End Homes Limited
Incorporated: 21 August 2002 *Employees:* 113
Net Worth: £69,671,000 *Total Assets:* £168,460,992
Registered Office: 3 Resolution Plaza, Spitalfields, London, E1 6PS
Activities: Renting and operating of Housing Association real estate
Officers: Stuart George Veysey, Secretary; Susan Patricia Blunden [1956] Director/Retired; Helen Goody [1960] Director/Tenant Representative; Margaret Frances Higgins [1955] Director/Retired Registrar; Carol Mary Hinvest [1966] Director/Local Government Officer; John Hedley Kettlewell [1949] Director/Accountant; Emdadul Haque Jahangir Mannan [1979] Director/Accountant; Maureen McEleney [1961] Director/Consultant; Kevin John Moore [1967] Director; Cllr John Pierce [1981] Director/Manager [Irish]; MoTIn Uz-Zaman [1969] Director/Lecturer; Kevin Brian Whittle [1952] Director/Retired; Marek Andrzej Wiluszynski [1957] Director/Consultant

East Finance PLC
Incorporated: 9 March 2012
Net Worth: £13,000 *Total Assets:* £252,320,000
Registered Office: 29-35 West Ham Lane, Stratford, London, E15 4PH
Activities: Financial intermediation not elsewhere classified
Parent: London & Quadrant Housing Trust
Officers: Henry Arthur Potter, Secretary; Edward Paul Farnsworth [1982] Director of Business Planning & Development; Martin Stuart Watts [1977] Director of Treasury - London & Quadrant HT

East Slope Residencies PLC
Incorporated: 18 October 2016
Net Worth: £50,000 *Total Assets:* £196,904,000
Registered Office: 350 Euston Road, Regent's Place, London, NW1 3AX
Activities: Activities of other holding companies n.e.c.
Parent: Balfour Beatty Infrastructure Projects Investments Limited
Officers: Saiema Ibrahim, Secretary; David Graham Blanchard [1967] Director; Christopher John Funnell [1966] Director; Richard Allan Spencer [1959] Director

East Slope Residencies Student Accommodation LLP
Incorporated: 17 November 2016
Net Worth: £5,050,628 *Total Assets:* £207,660,400
Registered Office: 350 Euston Road, Regent's Place, London, NW1 3AX

East Village London LLP
Incorporated: 23 March 2016 *Employees:* 83
Net Worth: £801,736,000 *Total Assets:* £1,312,467,968
Registered Office: 6th Floor, Lansdowne House, Berkeley Square, London, W1J 6ER

Eastern & Oriental PLC
Incorporated: 2 May 1913 *Employees:* 8
Previous: Eastern & Oriental Property (UK) PLC
Net Worth Deficit: £5,272,665 *Total Assets:* £103,218,912
Registered Office: 13th Floor, Landmark House, Hammersmith Bridge Road, London, W6 9DP
Activities: Activities of other holding companies n.e.c.
Officers: Meng Chow Kok [1959] Finance Director [Malaysian]; Tuck Cheong Kok [1955] Director [Malaysian]; Dato Ka Hon Tham [1953] Director [Malaysian]

Eastern Power Networks PLC
Incorporated: 1 April 1989
Net Worth: £1,350,099,968 *Total Assets:* £4,975,200,256
Registered Office: Newington House, 237 Southwark Bridge Road, London, SE1 6NP
Activities: Distribution of electricity
Parent: UK Power Networks Holdings Limited
Officers: Andrew Charles Pace, Secretary; Kee Ham Chan [1963] Director/Chief Financial Officer; Loi Shun Chan [1962] Director [Chinese]; Hok Shan Chong [1948] Director [Chinese]; Christopher John David Clarke [1950] Director/Solicitor; Andrew John Hunter [1958] Director; Paul Robert Jeffery [1955] Director; Hing Lam Kam [1946] Director [Chinese]; Duncan Nicholas MacRae [1970] Director; Neil Douglas McGee [1951] Director [Australian]; Mei Fan Ngan [1965] Director [Chinese]; Basil Scarsella [1955] Director [Australian]; Charles Chao Chung Tsai [1957] Director and Chief Executive Officer [Canadian]; Chi Tin Wan [1950] Director [Australian]

Eastlink Lanker PLC
Incorporated: 30 October 1992 *Employees:* 315
Net Worth: £74,028,688 *Total Assets:* £282,955,488
Registered Office: Palladium House, 1-4 Argyll Street, London, W1F 7LD
Activities: Non-specialised wholesale trade
Shareholders: Mark Shabad; Gregory Schtulberg
Officers: Denis Korotkov-Koganovich, Secretary; Michelle Minhduc Gilligan [1971] Director/Legal Counsel [Australian]; Denis Korotkov-Koganovich [1977] Director/Financial Officer

Eaton Square Limited
Incorporated: 6 December 1995
Net Worth: £3,304,596,992 *Total Assets:* £3,304,667,904
Registered Office: Sea Containers House, 18 Upper Ground, London, SE1 9GL
Activities: Non-trading company
Parent: Readysquare Limited
Officers: Charles Ward Van Der Welle [1959] Director/Group Treasurer; Steve Richard Winters [1968] Director/Chartered Accountant

Eaton Square Properties Limited
Incorporated: 22 August 1946
Net Worth: £503,236,000 *Total Assets:* £610,966,976
Registered Office: 70 Grosvenor Street, London, W1K 3JP
Activities: Buying and selling of own real estate
Parent: Grosvenor Limited
Officers: Derek John Lewis, Secretary; Keith John Bailey [1979] Director/Chartered Surveyor; Roger Frederick Crawford Blundell [1962] Finance Director; Anna Clare Bond [1981] Director/Chartered Surveyor; Douglas Nigel Crichton [1976] Director/Chartered Surveyor; Simon Geoffrey Harding-Roots [1968] Director; Chantal Antonia Henderson [1975] Director/Accountant; Nigel Auriol Hughes [1957] Director/Chartered Surveyor; Richard Alexander Jefferies [1963] Operations Director; Craig David McWilliam [1972] Director/Chartered Surveyor; Paul Francis O'Grady [1985] Director/Chartered Surveyor; Amelia Mary Staveley [1986] Director/Chartered Surveyor

Eaton Towers Limited
Incorporated: 1 August 2011 *Employees:* 193
Net Worth: £272,912,320 *Total Assets:* £686,630,400
Registered Office: 3rd Floor, 22-25 Eastcastle Street, London, W1W 8DF
Activities: Activities of head offices
Officers: Craig Alexander James Morris, Secretary; Alfred Ngalaah Chuphi [1961] Director/Private Equity Investor [Kenyan]; Martin Diaz Plata [1967] Director/Investment Analyst; James Scott Eisenstein [1958] Director/Communications Executive [American]; Eduardo Gutierrez Ibanez [1967] Director/Corporate Partner [Spanish]; Taimoor Yahya Labib [1975] Managing Director [Egyptian]; Terence Edward Rhodes [1955] Director; Christian Philip Skaanild [1974] Director/Investment Manager [Danish]

Ebay KTA (UK) Ltd
Incorporated: 31 January 2001
Net Worth: £1,450,881,664 *Total Assets:* £1,450,932,352
Registered Office: 5 New Street Square, London, EC4A 3TW
Activities: Other business support service activities n.e.c.
Parent: Ebay Inc.
Officers: Alec Patrick Latimer [1971] Director/Lawyer

Ebiquity PLC
Incorporated: 4 April 2000 *Employees:* 932
Net Worth: £51,942,000 *Total Assets:* £113,012,000
Registered Office: Citypoint, One Ropemaker Street, London, EC2Y 9AW
Activities: Activities of head offices
Officers: Mark John Sanford, Secretary; Thomas Simon Alexander [1959] Director; Julie Margaret Baddeley [1951] Director; Michael Karg [1971] Director; Alan Philip Stephen Newman [1957] Director/Chief Financial and Operating Officer; Richard Stephen Nichols [1965] Director; Robert Stanley Lawrence Woodward [1959] Director/Chairman

EBS Dealing Resources International Limited
Incorporated: 10 December 1991 *Employees:* 148
Net Worth: £39,310,000 *Total Assets:* £127,190,000
Registered Office: 2 Broadgate, London, EC2M 7UR
Activities: Activities auxiliary to financial intermediation n.e.c.
Parent: EBS No. 2 Limited
Officers: Deborah Anne Abrehart, Secretary; Timothy Michael Cartledge [1970] Director; Jason Todd Cohen [1972] Director [American]; Eliran Glazer [1971] Director [Israeli]; Seth Johnson [1968] Director; Jeffrey William Ward [1966] Director [American]

EBS Group Limited
Incorporated: 30 July 1991 *Employees:* 6
Net Worth: £218,939,008 *Total Assets:* £372,206,016
Registered Office: 2 Broadgate, London, EC2M 7UR
Activities: Activities of financial services holding companies
Parent: NEX Markets Limited
Officers: Deborah Anne Abrehart, Secretary; Timothy Michael Cartledge [1970] Director; Eliran Glazer [1971] Director [Israeli]; Seth Johnson [1968] Director; Jeffrey William Ward [1966] Director [American]

EBS Investments
Incorporated: 12 June 2014
Net Worth: £271,654,240 *Total Assets:* £343,033,696
Registered Office: 2 Broadgate, London, EC2M 7UR
Activities: Activities of financial services holding companies
Parent: CME London Limited
Officers: Deborah Abrehart, Secretary; Allan Samuel Aldridge [1980] Director; Ranjit Paul [1983] Director

EC Finance PLC
Incorporated: 17 March 2010
Net Worth: £60,382 *Total Assets:* £309,141,056
Registered Office: 5th Floor, 6 St Andrew Street, London, EC4A 3AE
Activities: Other business support service activities n.e.c.
Parent: TMF Trustee Limited
Officers: Stephen William Spencer Norton [1959] Finance Director

Eclectic Capital Limited
Incorporated: 27 June 2013
Net Worth: £112,768,016 *Total Assets:* £112,840,168
Registered Office: 2nd Floor, Berkeley Square House, Berkeley Square, London, W1J 6BD
Activities: Retail sale in commercial art galleries
Officers: Nika Kirpichenko [1969] Director [Russian]

Eclipse Film Partners No. 26 LLP
Incorporated: 9 December 2005
Net Worth: £218,904,528 *Total Assets:* £218,908,176
Registered Office: 27-28 Eastcastle Street, London, W1W 8DH
Officers: Paul Richard Daniel [1960] LLP Member; Stephen Trevor Din [1964] LLP Member; Michael John Thornton Dudley [1957] LLP Member; John Edward Inglis [1961] LLP Member; Richard Douglas Johnson [1963] LLP Member; James Hedley Paget [1967] LLP Member; David Anthony Robins [1949] LLP Member; Tariq Shaikh [1969] LLP Member; Stephen Arthur West [1959] LLP Member; Thomas Henry Wiggin [1969] LLP Member

Ecofin Global Utilities and Infrastructure Trust PLC
Incorporated: 27 June 2016
Net Worth: £132,070,000 *Total Assets:* £142,244,992
Registered Office: 10 Harewood Avenue, London, NW1 6AA
Activities: Activities of investment trusts
Officers: Malcolm Robert King [1957] Director; Iain Archibald McLaren [1951] Director; Martin Andre Bernard Negre [1946] Director [French]; David Robert Simpson [1957] Director

ECOM Agrotrade Holdings Limited
Incorporated: 14 May 2014 *Employees:* 635
Net Worth: £121,646,704 *Total Assets:* £449,119,392
Registered Office: 10th Floor, 55 Old Broad Street, London, EC2M 1RX
Activities: Wholesale of coffee, tea, cocoa and spices
Parent: Ecom Agroindustrial Corp Limited
Officers: Imogen Chopra, Secretary; Andrew David Falconer [1967] Managing Director Asia Pacific Coffee; Alain Philippe Poncelet [1968] Director [Belgian]; Nicolas de Wasseige [1969] Director/Cocoa Trader [Belgian]

ECOM Agrotrade Limited
Incorporated: 4 June 1998 *Employees:* 53
Net Worth: £119,692,656 *Total Assets:* £354,628,992
Registered Office: 10th Floor, 55 Old Broad Street, London, EC2M 1RX
Activities: Wholesale of coffee, tea, cocoa and spices
Parent: ECOM Agrotrade Holdings Limited
Officers: Imogen Chopra, Secretary; Andrew David Falconer [1967] Managing Director Asia Pacific Coffee; Simon Hodge [1973] Director; Alain Philippe Poncelet [1968] Director [Belgian]; Nicolas de Wasseige [1969] Director/Cocoa Trader [Belgian]

The Economist Group (US Holdings) Limited
Incorporated: 11 December 2008
Net Worth: £147,566,464 *Total Assets:* £309,729,376
Registered Office: The Adelphi, 1-11 John Adam Street, London, WC2N 6HT
Activities: Activities of other holding companies n.e.c.
Parent: The Economist Newspaper Group Incorporated
Officers: Oscar Kolya Meisen Grut, Secretary [Danish]; Cecelia Chahal Block [1966] Director [American]; Oscar Kolya Meisen Grut [1969] Director/Solicitor [Danish]; John Thomas Hunt [1972] Director/Accountant [American]; Shane Paul Naughton [1967] Director/Accountant [Irish]; Vinay Shah [1968] Director/Certified Public Accountant [American]

The Economist Intelligence Unit Limited
Incorporated: 19 October 1983 *Employees:* 141
Net Worth: £11,015,000 *Total Assets:* £117,545,000
Registered Office: The Adelphi, 1-11 John Adam Street, London, WC2N 6HT
Activities: Book publishing
Parent: The Economist Newspaper (Holdings) Limited
Officers: Anna MacDonald Samuelsson, Secretary; Robin Lysander Bew [1970] Director/Economist; John Arthur Bowler [1957] Director/Economist; Shane Paul Naughton [1967] Director/Accountant [Irish]; Alasdair Martin Ross [1958] Director/Consultant; Christopher John Stibbs [1963] Director/Chartered Accountant

Economist Newspaper Limited (The)
Incorporated: 14 January 1929 *Employees:* 1,493
Net Worth Deficit: £90,789,000 *Total Assets:* £248,560,992
Registered Office: The Adelphi, 1-11 John Adam Street, London, WC2N 6HT
Activities: Book publishing
Shareholder: Exor N.V.
Officers: Oscar Kolya Meisen Grut, Secretary [Danish]; Lord Paul Clive Deighton [1956] Director; John Elkann [1976] Director/Industrialist [Italian]; Eli Emanuel Goldstein [1985] Director [American]; Suzanne Elizabeth Heywood [1969] Director; Dr Alexander Karp [1967] Director [American]; Philip Stephan Arnold Mallinckrodt [1962] Director/Banker [British/German]; Susan Minton Beddoes [1967] Director/Journalist; Christopher John Stibbs [1963] Director/Chartered Accountant

The Economist Overseas (Holdings) Limited
Incorporated: 14 July 1987
Net Worth: £109,260,904 *Total Assets:* £109,260,904
Registered Office: The Adelphi, 1-11 John Adam Street, London, WC2N 6HT
Activities: Activities of head offices
Shareholders: The Economist Newspaper (Holdings) Limited; The Economist Intelligence Unit Limited
Officers: Oscar Kolya Meisen Grut, Secretary [Danish]; Oscar Kolya Meisen Grut [1969] Director/Solicitor [Danish]; Shane Paul Naughton [1967] Director/Accountant [Irish]; Christopher John Stibbs [1963] Director/Chartered Accountant

ED Broking Group Limited
Incorporated: 14 May 2010
Previous: Cooper Gay Swett & Crawford Limited
Net Worth: £57,200,796 *Total Assets:* £177,487,536
Registered Office: 52 Leadenhall Street, London, EC3A 2EB
Activities: Non-life insurance
Parent: EC3 Union Holdings Limited
Officers: Stephen Patrick Hearn [1966] Director; James Richard Lightbourne [1970] Director; Neil Phillip Perry [1970] Director; Robert Brian Stevens [1962] Director; Andrew David Wallin [1977] Group Commercial Director; John Lindsay Pearce Whiter [1950] Director

ED Broking Holdings (London) Limited
Incorporated: 1 January 1971
Previous: ED Broking (Holdings) Limited
Net Worth: £137,727,008 *Total Assets:* £210,126,000
Registered Office: 52 Leadenhall Street, London, EC3A 2EB
Activities: Non-life insurance
Parent: ED Broking Group Limited
Officers: Stephen Patrick Hearn [1966] Director; Neil Phillip Perry [1970] Director/Chief Financial Officer; Andrew David Wallin [1977] Director

Eddystone Finance Holdings Limited
Incorporated: 29 December 2005
Net Worth Deficit: £31,677,976 *Total Assets:* £721,154,048
Registered Office: 35 Great St Helen's, London, EC3A 6AP
Activities: Non-trading company
Parent: Intertrust Corporate Services Limited
Officers: Daniel Marc Richard Jaffe [1975] Director

Edenred (UK Group) Limited
Incorporated: 4 November 1954 *Employees:* 150
Net Worth: £76,545,000 *Total Assets:* £276,148,992
Registered Office: 50 Vauxhall Bridge Road, London, SW1V 2RS
Activities: Other business support service activities n.e.c.
Parent: Edenred SA
Officers: Patrick Marc Jean Langlois, Secretary; Arnaud Marie Gildas Erulin [1970] Director/Chief Operating Officer [French]; Patrick Marc Jean Langlois [1969] Managing Director [French]; Oliver Jacques Henri Raguis [1971] Director [French]; Olivier Soula [1981] Finance Director [French]; Johann Fabrice Martin Vaucanson [1973] Managing Director [French]

EDF Development Company Limited
Incorporated: 23 April 2007
Net Worth: £296,929,984 *Total Assets:* £398,390,016
Registered Office: 90 Whitfield Street, London, W1T 4EZ
Activities: Production of electricity
Officers: Julia Pyke, Secretary; Humphrey Alan Edward Cadoux-Hudson [1960] Director/MD New Nuclear Build; Patrick Pruvot [1959] Director [French]

EDF Energy (Cottam Power) Limited
Incorporated: 19 September 2000
Net Worth Deficit: £336,392,992 *Total Assets:* £138,663,008
Registered Office: 90 Whitfield Street, London, W1T 4EZ
Activities: Production of electricity
Parent: EDF Energy (Energy Branch) PLC
Officers: Matthew Sykes [1962] Director/Chief Nuclear Officer; David Tomblin [1976] Director/Accountant

EDF Energy (Energy Branch) Limited
Incorporated: 5 December 1989 *Employees:* 478
Previous: EDF Energy (Energy Branch) PLC
Net Worth: £66,598,000 *Total Assets:* £304,444,992
Registered Office: 90 Whitfield Street, London, W1T 4EZ
Activities: Production of electricity
Parent: EDF Energy PLC
Officers: Charles Hugo Lidbetter, Secretary; Matthew Sykes [1962] Director/Chief Nuclear Officer; David Tomblin [1976] Director/Accountant

EDF Energy (Thermal Generation) Limited
Incorporated: 9 August 2001
Previous: EDF Energy (West Burton Power) Limited
Net Worth Deficit: £457,420,992 *Total Assets:* £730,721,984
Registered Office: 90 Whitfield Street, London, W1T 4EZ
Activities: Production of electricity
Parent: EDF Energy (Energy Branch) Limited
Officers: Charles Hugo Lidbetter, Secretary; Christopher Andrew Bebbington [1975] Director; Martin Cheetham [1971] Director; Brian Cowell [1961] Director; Andrew Charles Powell [1981] Director; Matilda Jane Spencer [1986] Director; Matthew Sykes [1962] Director/Chief Nuclear Officer; David Tomblin [1976] Director/Accountant; Paul Anthony Winkle [1966] Director

EDF Energy (UK) Limited
Incorporated: 14 June 1991
Net Worth: £10,954,706,944 *Total Assets:* £17,011,545,088
Registered Office: 90 Whitfield Street, London, W1T 4EZ
Activities: Activities of head offices
Officers: Guido Santi, Secretary; Mrs Marie-Christine Aulagnon [1963] Director [French]; Ariel Heman Fefer [1970] Director [French]; Robert Guyler [1966] Director/Accountant; Simone Rossi [1968] Director/Chief Financial Officer [Italian]

EDF Energy Customers Limited
Incorporated: 8 March 1988 *Employees:* 4,947
Previous: EDF Energy Customers PLC
Net Worth: £18,800,000 *Total Assets:* £2,673,600,000
Registered Office: 90 Whitfield Street, London, W1T 4EZ
Activities: Distribution of electricity
Parent: EDF Energy PLC
Officers: Joe Souto, Secretary; Beatrice Bigois [1969] Director [French]; Dawn Fortune [1979] Director; Richard Tudor Hughes [1973] Director; Katherine Rebecca Jacob [1977] Director; Mr James Nicholas Poole [1967] Director

EDF Energy Group Holdings Limited
Incorporated: 9 October 1996
Previous: EDF Energy Group Holdings PLC
Net Worth: £2,655,899,904 *Total Assets:* £2,655,899,904
Registered Office: 90 Whitfield Street, London, W1T 4EZ
Activities: Activities of head offices
Parent: EDF Energy Holdings Limited
Officers: Joe Souto, Secretary; Robert Guyler [1966] Director/Accountant; Simone Rossi [1968] Director/Chief Financial Officer [Italian]

EDF Energy Holdings Limited
Incorporated: 10 June 2009 *Employees:* 12,946
Net Worth: £13,921,999,872 *Total Assets:* £33,383,999,488
Registered Office: 90 Whitfield Street, London, W1T 4EZ
Activities: Activities of head offices
Parent: EDF Energy (UK) Limited
Officers: Guido Santi, Secretary; Christophe Carval [1960] Director [French]; Xavier Rene Louise Girre [1969] Director [French]; Robert Guyler [1966] Director/Accountant; Veronique Lacour [1964] Director [French]; Henri Joseph Clement Lafontaine [1957] Director [French]; Jean-Bernard Levy [1955] Director [French]; Colin Stephen Matthews [1956] Director; Dominique Christophe Miniere [1958] Director [French]; Simone Rossi [1968] Director/Chief Financial Officer [Italian]; Pierre Christian Todorov [1958] Director [French]; Xavier Bernard Yves Ursat [1966] Director [French]

EDF Energy Lake Limited
Incorporated: 2 September 2014
Net Worth: £6,895,000,064 *Total Assets:* £6,896,000,000
Registered Office: 90 Whitfield Street, London, W1T 4EZ
Activities: Activities of head offices
Parent: EDF Energy Holdings Limited
Officers: Guido Santi, Secretary; Robert Guyler [1966] Director/Accountant; Jean-Marc Lefeuvre [1970] Director [French]; Simone Rossi [1968] Director/Chief Financial Officer [Italian]

EDF Energy Limited
Incorporated: 1 April 1989 *Employees:* 996
Previous: EDF Energy PLC
Net Worth: £1,837,100,032 *Total Assets:* £5,056,000,000
Registered Office: 90 Whitfield Street, London, W1T 4EZ
Activities: Production of electricity
Parent: EDF Energy Holdings Limited
Officers: Joe Souto, Secretary; Robert Guyler [1966] Director/Accountant; Simone Rossi [1968] Director/Chief Financial Officer [Italian]

EDF Energy Services Limited
Incorporated: 12 July 2016 *Employees:* 4
Net Worth: £100,446,000 *Total Assets:* £137,666,000
Registered Office: 90 Whitfield Street, London, W1T 4EZ
Activities: Other service activities n.e.c.
Shareholders: EDF Energy Customers Limited; EDF Energy Customers PLC
Officers: Joe Souto, Secretary; Beatrice Bigois [1969] Director [French]; Fabien Bremont [1978] Director [French]; Robert Guyler [1966] Director/Accountant; Sylvie Jehanno [1969] Director [French]; Simone Rossi [1968] Director/Chief Financial Officer [Italian]; Jean-Charles Samy [1963] Director [French]

Edgbaston RMBS 2010-1 PLC
Incorporated: 9 November 2009
Net Worth: £20,000 *Total Assets:* £1,968,989,056
Registered Office: 35 Great St Helen's, London, EC3A 6AP
Activities: Financial intermediation not elsewhere classified
Parent: Edgbaston RMBS Holdings Limited
Officers: Daniel Marc Richard Jaffe [1975] Managing Director

Edgen Murray Europe Limited
Incorporated: 20 January 1976 *Employees:* 266
Net Worth: £84,607,000 *Total Assets:* £152,426,000
Registered Office: Vintners Place, Upper Thames Street, London, EC4V 3BJ
Activities: Wholesale of metals and metal ores
Parent: Pipe Acquisition Limited
Officers: Susan Jayne Holmes, Secretary; Anthony Alan Brown [1973] Director/Vice President - Europe & Africa; Craig Douglas Doel [1967] Director [New Zealander]; Ordella Rebello [1978] Director/Chartered Accountant [Indian]

Ediston Property Investment Company PLC
Incorporated: 17 June 2014
Net Worth: £145,816,000 *Total Assets:* £203,707,008
Registered Office: Level 13, Broadgate Tower, 20 Primrose Street, London, EC2A 2EW
Activities: Activities of real estate investment trusts
Officers: Robert Archibald [1959] Director; Robert John Westwater Dick [1955] Director; William Anthony Hill [1960] Director; Colin James Marshall Skinner [1961] Director/Fund Management

EDM Business Services Holdings Limited
Incorporated: 3 June 2011 *Employees:* 951
Net Worth Deficit: £111,165,000 *Total Assets:* £103,821,000
Registered Office: Queens House, 8-9 Queen Street, London, EC4N 1SP
Activities: Activities of other holding companies n.e.c.
Shareholder: Lloyds Development Capital (Holdings) Limited
Officers: Alistair Charles Wragg, Secretary; David Lindsay [1956] Director/Chief Financial Officer; John Fraser Grant Willox [1967] Director/Chief Executive Officer

The Education Endowment Foundation
Incorporated: 1 April 2011 *Employees:* 23
Net Worth: £87,283,936 *Total Assets:* £108,149,400
Registered Office: 5th Floor, Millbank Tower, 21-24 Millbank, London, SW1P 4QP
Activities: Educational support services
Officers: Naomi Helen Eisenstadt [1950] Director/Trustee; Louis Goodman Elson [1962] Director/Finance [American]; Sir Peter Oliver Gershon [1947] Director/Company Chairman; David John Hall [1947] Director/Chairman; Lucy Lauris Heller [1959] Director/Chief Executive; Sir Peter Lampl [1947] Director; Dr Lee Elliot Major [1968] Research Director; Nathaniel Lester Sloane [1953] Director/Investor [American]; Hanneke Smits [1966] Director/Chief Executive Officer [Dutch]

EFG Private Bank Limited
Incorporated: 25 November 1988 *Employees:* 383
Net Worth: £134,355,008 *Total Assets:* £2,728,581,120
Registered Office: Leconfield House, Curzon Street, London, W1J 5JB
Activities: Banks
Parent: EFG International AG
Officers: Amanda Evans, Secretary; Anthony Edmund Cooke-Yarborough [1956] Director/Banker; Michael Norland Higgin [1949] Director/Chartered Accountant; Jennifer Elizabeth Mathias [1974] Director; Dimitrios Politis [1971] Director/Chief Financial Officer [Greek]; Piergiorgio Pradelli [1967] Director/Banker [Italian]; John Reed [1959] Director; Andrew Warwick Simmonds [1956] Director; Richard Anthony Aubrey Thomas [1967] Director/Banker

EFL Futures Limited
Incorporated: 14 September 1984
Net Worth: £9,454,191 *Total Assets:* £193,832,064
Registered Office: One Carter Lane, London, EC4V 5AN
Activities: Activities auxiliary to financial intermediation n.e.c.
Parent: Skandinaviska Enskilda Ltd
Officers: Bengt Kristian Eriksson, Secretary; Maj-Britt Krejcir [1968] Director [Swedish]; Tony Racanelli [1955] Director/Chief Operating Officer [American]; Simon Taylor [1980] Director/Banker

EFT International Investments Holdings Limited
Incorporated: 1 November 2010 *Employees:* 2
Net Worth: £259,818,192 *Total Assets:* £343,732,320
Registered Office: Ground Floor, Bury House, 31 Bury Street, London, EC3A 5AR
Activities: Other business support service activities n.e.c.
Parent: EFT Investments SE
Officers: Ivan Jennings, Secretary; Zoran Ivkovic [1961] Director [Serbian]; Ivan Jennings [1976] Director/Chartered Accountant; Dr James Gregor David Nye [1961] Director/Vice-Chairman EFT Group

EFT Investments SE
Incorporated: 3 June 2016 *Employees:* 867
Net Worth: £225,428,864 *Total Assets:* £626,471,680
Registered Office: Ground Floor, Bury House, 31 Bury Street, London, EC3A 5AR
Activities: Other business support service activities n.e.c.
Shareholders: Zoran Ivkovic; Milos Hamovic
Officers: Zoran Ivkovic [1961] Member [Serbian]; Ivan Jennings [1976] Member; Dr James Gregor David Nye [1961] Member

EGX Credit Liquidity Ltd
Incorporated: 12 May 2016
Previous: Thawer Credit Liquidity Co Ltd
Net Worth: £60,156,284 *Total Assets:* £133,670,704
Registered Office: 71-75 Shelton Street, Covent Garden, London, WC2H 9JQ
Activities: Security dealing on own account
Parent: Thawer Fund Management LLC
Officers: Abraham Cohen [1972] Director/Investor [South African]; Rahim Thawer [1977] Director/Hedge Fund Manager [American]; Peter Wasserman [1965] Director/Fund Manager [American]

EI Ventures Limited
Incorporated: 18 July 2006 *Employees:* 2
Net Worth Deficit: £126,400,000 *Total Assets:* £1,760,199,936
Registered Office: 35 Great St Helen's, London, EC3A 6AP
Activities: Activities of other holding companies n.e.c.
Officers: Alwyn Whitford, Secretary; Mohamed Adel El Gazzar [1979] Managing Director; Ronald Schweizer [1972] Director/Chief Financial Officer [American]

EII (Ventures) Limited
Incorporated: 25 July 2006
Previous: Euromoney Institutional Investor (Ventures) Limited
Net Worth: £157,607,008 *Total Assets:* £230,260,832
Registered Office: 8 Bouverie Street, London, EC4Y 8AX
Activities: Activities of head offices
Parent: Euromoney Institutional Investor PLC
Officers: Tim Jonathan Bratton [1972] Director/General Counsel; Sarah Joanne Cooke [1975] Director; Andrew David Himsley [1980] Director

EIS Group Public Limited Company
Incorporated: 7 April 1899 *Employees:* 2
Net Worth: £139,959,008 *Total Assets:* £155,248,000
Registered Office: c/o Smiths Group PLC, 4th Floor, 11-12 St James's Square, London, SW1Y 4LB
Activities: Activities of head offices
Parent: Smiths Group PLC
Officers: Fiona Margaret Gillespie, Secretary; George James Montague [1964] Director/Group Financial Controller [American]; Melanie Jane Rowlands [1968] Director/Solicitor

Elbon Holdings (1) Limited
Incorporated: 21 September 2005
Net Worth: £96,934,416 *Total Assets:* £121,041,304
Registered Office: Cannon Place, 78 Cannon Street, London, EC4N 6AF
Activities: Activities of head offices
Parent: PFI Senior Funding Limited
Officers: John Ivor Cavill [1972] Director; Jonathan Peter Doberman [1977] Director/Financial Controller

Elbon Holdings (2) Limited
Incorporated: 26 September 2005
Net Worth: £84,650,520 *Total Assets:* £135,216,176
Registered Office: Cannon Place, 78 Cannon Street, London, EC4N 6AF
Activities: Activities of head offices
Parent: BIIF Bidco Limited
Officers: John Ivor Cavill [1972] Director; Jonathan Peter Doberman [1977] Director/Financial Controller

Elbon Holdings (3) Limited
Incorporated: 23 September 2005
Net Worth: £35,965,000 *Total Assets:* £377,729,984
Registered Office: Cannon Place, 78 Cannon Street, London, EC4N 6AF
Activities: Activities of head offices
Parent: BIIF Issuerco Limited
Officers: John Ivor Cavill [1972] Director; Jonathan Peter Doberman [1977] Director/Financial Controller

Electra Investments Limited
Incorporated: 11 December 1885
Net Worth Deficit: £2,159,000 *Total Assets:* £234,050,000
Registered Office: First Floor, 50 Grosvenor Hill, London, W1K 3QT
Activities: Other business support service activities n.e.c.
Parent: Electra Private Equity PLC
Officers: Neil Anthony Johnson [1949] Director; Gavin Maxwell Manson [1966] Director/Chief Financial Officer

Electra Private Equity PLC
Incorporated: 15 July 1935 *Employees:* 7
Net Worth: £758,000,000 *Total Assets:* £793,000,000
Registered Office: First Floor, 50 Grosvenor Hill, London, W1K 3QT
Activities: Activities of investment trusts
Officers: Edward John Michael Bramson [1951] Director/Investor; Paul Andrew Goodson [1963] Director; Neil Anthony Johnson [1949] Director; David George Lis [1950] Director; Gavin Maxwell Manson [1966] Director/Chief Financial Officer; Linda Wilding [1959] Director

Electricinvest Acquisitions Limited
Incorporated: 18 July 2006
Net Worth: £415,200,000 *Total Assets:* £1,351,200,000
Registered Office: 35 Great St Helen's, London, EC3A 6AP
Activities: Activities of other holding companies n.e.c.
Parent: Electricinvest Holding Company Limited
Officers: Alwyn Whitford, Secretary; Mohamed Adel El Gazzar [1979] Managing Director; Ronald Schweizer [1972] Director/Chief Financial Officer [American]

Electricinvest Holding Company Limited
Incorporated: 18 July 2006
Net Worth: £356,000,000 *Total Assets:* £850,800,000
Registered Office: 35 Great St Helen's, London, EC3A 6AP
Activities: Activities of other holding companies n.e.c.
Parent: El Ventures Limited
Officers: Alwyn Whitford, Secretary; Mohamed Adel El Gazzar [1979] Managing Director; Ronald Schweizer [1972] Director/Chief Financial Officer [American]

Electricity First Limited
Incorporated: 23 April 2010
Net Worth: £35,272,000 *Total Assets:* £190,930,000
Registered Office: 3 More London Riverside, London, SE1 2AQ
Activities: Activities of financial services holding companies
Officers: Loi Shun Chan [1962] Director [Chinese]; Mark John Horsley [1959] Director/Chief Executive Officer; Andrew John Hunter [1958] Director; Tak Chuen Edmond IP [1952] Director [Chinese]; Hing Lam Kam [1946] Director [Chinese]; Charles Chao Chung Tsai [1957] Director/General Manager [Canadian]; Chi Tin Wan [1950] Director [Australian]

Electrocomponents Public Limited Company
Incorporated: 22 January 1960 *Employees:* 5,868
Net Worth: £482,500,000 *Total Assets:* £1,107,399,936
Registered Office: Fifth Floor, Two Pancras Square, London, N1C 4AG
Activities: Activities of head offices
Officers: Ian Peter Haslegrave, Secretary; Bertrand Bodson [1975] Director/Chief Digital Officer [Belgian]; Louisa Sachiko Burdett [1968] Finance Director; David John Egan [1967] Finance Director [British/Australian]; Karen Guerra [1956] Director; Peter Michael Johnson [1947] Director; John Cook Pattullo [1952] Director; Simon Charles Conrad Pryce [1961] Director/Group Chief Executive; Lindsley Ruth [1970] Director [American]

Electrocomponents U.K. Limited
Incorporated: 5 July 1982
Net Worth: £538,339,968 *Total Assets:* £711,860,992
Registered Office: Fifth Floor, Two Pancras Square, London, N1C 4AG
Activities: Activities of head offices
Shareholders: RS Components Limited; Electrocomponents PLC
Officers: Ian Peter Haslegrave, Secretary; David John Egan [1967] Finance Director [British/Australian]; Vanessa Elizabeth Gough [1967] Director/Group Financial Controller; Lindsley Ruth [1970] Director [American]

Electrocomponents US Finance Limited
Incorporated: 15 March 2001
Net Worth: £246,205,632 *Total Assets:* £251,275,008
Registered Office: Fifth Floor, Two Pancras Square, London, N1C 4AG
Activities: Other business support service activities n.e.c.
Parent: Electrocomponents U.K. Limited
Officers: Ian Peter Haslegrave, Secretary; Vanessa Elizabeth Gough [1967] Director/Group Financial Controller; Ian Peter Haslegrave [1968] Director/Solicitor

Elegant Hotels Group PLC
Incorporated: 10 April 2015 *Employees:* 1,041
Net Worth: £79,667,632 *Total Assets:* £143,341,792
Registered Office: 10 Norwich Street, London, EC4A 1BD
Activities: Other business support service activities n.e.c.
Officers: Shauna Kissoon, Secretary; Steven John Baldwin [1968] Director/Investment Banker; Sunil Chatrani [1967] Director/Chief Executive Officer [Barbadian]; Luke Oliver Johnson [1962] Director/Entrepreneur; Simon Michael Cross Sherwood [1960] Director; Jeffrey Philip Singleton [1975] Director/Chief Financial Officer

Element Materials Technology Group Holdings CC1 Limited
Incorporated: 22 July 2014
Net Worth: £61,507,800 *Total Assets:* £232,769,120
Registered Office: 10 Lower Grosvenor Place, London, SW1W 0EN
Activities: Activities of other holding companies n.e.c.
Parent: Element Materials Technology Group Holdings Limited
Officers: Matthew Alexander White, Secretary; Charles Arthur Noall [1959] Director; Joseph Daniel Wetz [1976] Director

Element Materials Technology Group Holdings CC2 Limited
Incorporated: 22 July 2014
Net Worth: £259,532,320 *Total Assets:* £316,226,336
Registered Office: 10 Lower Grosvenor Place, London, SW1W 0EN
Activities: Activities of other holding companies n.e.c.
Parent: Element Materials Technology Group Holdings CC1 Limited
Officers: Matthew Alexander White, Secretary; Charles Arthur Noall [1959] Director; Joseph Daniel Wetz [1976] Director

Element Materials Technology Group Holdings Limited
Incorporated: 22 July 2014
Net Worth: £110,008,368 *Total Assets:* £110,008,368
Registered Office: 10 Lower Grosvenor Place, London, SW1W 0EN
Activities: Activities of other holding companies n.e.c.
Parent: EMT 2 Holdings Limited
Officers: Matthew Alexander White, Secretary; Charles Arthur Noall [1959] Director; Joseph Daniel Wetz [1976] Director

Element Materials Technology Group Limited
Incorporated: 14 December 2015 *Employees:* 4,003
Net Worth Deficit: £114,850,880 *Total Assets:* £2,053,285,248
Registered Office: 5 Fleet Place, London, EC4M 7RD
Activities: Activities of other holding companies n.e.c.
Parent: BEV Nominees Limited
Officers: Christopher John Busby [1972] Director; Raoul Hughes [1965] Director; Allan Leslie Leighton [1953] Director; Charles Arthur Noall [1959] Director; Joseph Daniel Wetz [1976] Director

Element Materials Technology Holding UK Ltd
Incorporated: 15 November 1985 *Employees:* 44
Net Worth: £40,917,692 *Total Assets:* £147,136,368
Registered Office: 10 Lower Grosvenor Place, London, SW1W 0EN
Activities: Activities of head offices
Parent: Element Materials Technology Group Holdings CC2 Limited
Officers: Neil Conway MacLennan, Secretary; Charles Arthur Noall [1959] Director; Joseph Daniel Wetz [1976] Director; Matthew Alexander White [1967] Director

Element Materials Technology Limited
Incorporated: 14 December 2015 *Employees:* 4,003
Net Worth: £580,847,936 *Total Assets:* £2,053,361,920
Registered Office: 10 Lower Grosvenor Place, London, SW1W 0EN
Activities: Activities of other holding companies n.e.c.
Parent: EMT Finance 2 Limited
Officers: Charles Arthur Noall [1959] Director; Joseph Daniel Wetz [1976] Director

Elementis Holdings Limited
Incorporated: 8 May 1908 *Employees:* 67
Net Worth: £1,048,600,000 *Total Assets:* £1,562,000,000
Registered Office: Caroline House, 55-57 High Holborn, London, WC1V 6DX
Activities: Activities of head offices
Parent: Elementis Group Limited
Officers: Laura Ann Maria Higgins, Secretary; Christopher John Gilbert [1973] Director; Ralph Rex Hewins [1963] Director; Laura Ann Maria Higgins [1977] Director/Chartered Secretary

Elementis PLC
Incorporated: 7 January 1997 *Employees:* 1,417
Net Worth: £509,799,648 *Total Assets:* £972,488,384
Registered Office: Caroline House, 55-57 High Holborn, London, WC1V 6DX
Activities: Activities of head offices
Officers: Laura Ann Maria Higgins, Secretary; Sandra Lynne Boss [1967] Director [British/American]; Dorothee Anna Deuring [1968] Director [Austrian]; Andrew James Duff [1959] Director; Stephen Paul Good [1961] Director; Ralph Rex Hewins [1963] Director; Anne Philomena Hyland [1960] Director; Nicholas Robin Salmon [1952] Director; Lynn Paul Waterman [1964] Director [American]

Elementis Securities Limited
Incorporated: 16 January 1958
Net Worth Deficit: £5,874,000 *Total Assets:* £526,135,008
Registered Office: Caroline House, 55-57 High Holborn, London, WC1V 6DX
Activities: Other business support service activities n.e.c.
Parent: Elementis Overseas Investments Limited
Officers: Laura Ann Maria Higgins, Secretary; Christopher John Gilbert [1973] Director; Ralph Rex Hewins [1963] Director; Laura Ann Maria Higgins [1977] Director/Company Secretary

Elementis UK Limited
Incorporated: 13 April 1960
Net Worth: £173,200,000 *Total Assets:* £302,100,000
Registered Office: Caroline House, 55-57 High Holborn, London, WC1V 6DX
Activities: Wholesale of chemical products
Shareholders: Elementis Holdings Limited; Elementis London Limited
Officers: Laura Ann Maria Higgins, Secretary; Christopher John Gilbert [1973] Director; Ralph Rex Hewins [1963] Director; Laura Ann Maria Higgins [1977] Director/Company Secretary

Elementis US Limited
Incorporated: 26 March 2012
Net Worth: £244,838,512 *Total Assets:* £246,078,128
Registered Office: Caroline House, 55-57 High Holborn, London, WC1V 6DX
Activities: Non-trading company
Parent: Elementis Overseas Investments Limited
Officers: Laura Ann Maria Higgins, Secretary; Christopher John Gilbert [1973] Director; Ralph Rex Hewins [1963] Director; Laura Ann Maria Higgins [1977] Director/Company Secretary

Elephant and Castle LLP
Incorporated: 26 November 2013
Net Worth: £62,914,676 *Total Assets:* £104,916,360
Registered Office: 6th Floor, Lansdowne House, Berkeley Square, London, W1J 6ER

Elexon Limited
Incorporated: 4 June 1999 *Employees:* 150
Total Assets: £197,979,008
Registered Office: 4th Floor, 350 Euston Road, London, NW1 3AW
Activities: Other business support service activities n.e.c.
Parent: National Grid Electricity Transmission PLC
Officers: Nicholas Brown, Secretary; Mark Lindsay Bygraves [1965] Director/Chief Executive; Clare Duffy [1973] Director; Michael John Stanley Gibbons [1948] Director; Anne Elizabeth Heal [1962] Director; David James Rigney [1963] Director; Sara Lyn Vaughan [1964] Director

Elf Petroleum UK Limited
Incorporated: 10 December 1976
Net Worth: £848,974,016 *Total Assets:* £850,377,984
Registered Office: 18th Floor, 10 Upper Bank Street, Canary Wharf, London, E14 5BF
Activities: Activities of head offices
Parent: Total Holdings UK Limited
Officers: Bryan Wilson, Secretary; Karen Dyrskjot Boesen [1971] Director/Chief Financial Officer [Danish]; Michael Simon Borrell [1962] Director; Jean-Luc Guiziou [1961] Director/Engineer [French]

Elios Energy Holdings 3 Limited
Incorporated: 23 February 2017 *Employees:* 3
Net Worth: £294,288,992 *Total Assets:* £297,017,984
Registered Office: 6th Floor, 33 Holborn, London, EC1N 2HT
Activities: Production of electricity
Parent: Elios Energy Holdings Limited
Officers: Jonathan Charles Nigel Digges [1970] Director; Paul Stephen Latham [1956] Director; Matthew George Setchell [1977] Director

Elios Energy Holdings Limited
Incorporated: 3 March 2015 *Employees:* 3
Net Worth: £318,985,984 *Total Assets:* £318,988,992
Registered Office: 6th Floor, 33 Holborn, London, EC1N 2HT
Activities: Production of electricity
Parent: Fern Energy Holdings Limited
Officers: Jonathan Charles Nigel Digges [1970] Director; Paul Stephen Latham [1956] Director; Matthew George Setchell [1977] Director/Investment Manager

Elios Renewable Energy Limited
Incorporated: 19 January 2010 *Employees:* 3
Previous: Lightsource Renewable Energy Limited
Net Worth Deficit: £7,492,000 *Total Assets:* £225,274,000
Registered Office: 6th Floor, 33 Holborn, London, EC1N 2HT
Activities: Production of electricity
Parent: Elios Energy Holdings 3 Limited
Officers: Jonathan Charles Nigel Digges [1970] Director; Paul Stephen Latham [1956] Director; Matthew George Setchell [1977] Director/Investment Manager

Elite Gemstones Properties Limited
Incorporated: 22 November 2013 *Employees:* 249
Previous: London Wall Outsourcing Investments Limited
Net Worth: £354,891,008 *Total Assets:* £2,570,065,920
Registered Office: c/o Legalinx Limited, One Fetter Lane, London, EC4A 1BR
Activities: Management of real estate on a fee or contract basis
Parent: Elite UK Commercial Limited
Officers: Mow Chow Hoon [1967] Executive Director [Singaporean]

Ellerman Investments Limited
Incorporated: 13 September 1984 *Employees:* 6
Net Worth: £710,137,984 *Total Assets:* £821,326,976
Registered Office: 2nd Floor, 14 St George Street, London, W1S 1FE
Activities: Activities of head offices
Officers: Aidan Stuart Barclay [1956] Director; Howard Myles Barclay [1959] Director/Financier; Richard Julian Robert Faber [1974] Director/Corporate Financier; Nicholas John Hopper [1954] Director/Chartered Certified Accountant; Philip Leslie Peters [1957] Director and Banker; Michael Seal [1948] Director/Chartered Accountant

Elm Trading Limited
Incorporated: 3 December 2012
Net Worth: £208,129,376 *Total Assets:* £284,190,304
Registered Office: 6th Floor, 338 Euston Road, London, NW1 3BG
Activities: Activities of head offices
Officers: Stephen Richards Daniels [1980] Director; Edward William Mole [1983] Director/Accountant; Benjamin Alexander Philips [1983] Director; Roger Skeldon [1979] Director/Accountant

ELQ Holdings (UK) Ltd
Incorporated: 25 October 2007
Net Worth: £771,083,392 *Total Assets:* £2,553,020,672
Registered Office: Peterborough Court, 133 Fleet Street, London, EC4A 2BB
Activities: Financial intermediation not elsewhere classified
Parent: The Goldman Sachs Group, Inc.
Officers: Thomas Kelly, Secretary; Clare Charlotte Richards, Secretary; Richard Michael Thomas [1974] Director/Accountant; Jeremy Alan Wiltshire [1981] Director/Banker

ELQ Investors II Ltd
Incorporated: 19 September 2007
Net Worth: £637,761,664 *Total Assets:* £1,957,196,160
Registered Office: Peterborough Court, 133 Fleet Street, London, EC4A 2BB
Activities: Financial intermediation not elsewhere classified
Parent: ELQ Investors IX Ltd
Officers: Thomas Kelly, Secretary; Clare Charlotte Richards, Secretary; Beat Mathias Cabiallavetta [1979] Director/Finance [Swiss]; Tavis Colm Peter Cannell [1978] Director/Banker [Canadian]; William Thomas Gasson [1965] Director/Banker; Nishi Somaiya Grose [1980] Director/Banker; Michael Holmes [1973] Director/Accountant; Jeremy Alan Wiltshire [1981] Director/Banker

ELQ Investors IX Ltd
Incorporated: 3 November 2014
Net Worth: £591,273,536 *Total Assets:* £591,273,536
Registered Office: Peterborough Court, 133 Fleet Street, London, EC4A 2BB
Activities: Financial intermediation not elsewhere classified
Parent: ELQ Holdings (UK) Ltd
Officers: Thomas Kelly, Secretary; Richard Michael Thomas [1974] Director/Accountant; Jeremy Alan Wiltshire [1981] Director/Banker

ELQ Investors VI Ltd
Incorporated: 16 April 2013
Net Worth: £272,085,984 *Total Assets:* £1,176,619,904
Registered Office: Peterborough Court, 133 Fleet Street, London, EC4A 2BB
Activities: Financial intermediation not elsewhere classified
Parent: ELQ Holdings (UK) Ltd
Officers: Thomas Kelly, Secretary; Clare Charlotte Richards, Secretary; Tavis Colm Peter Cannell [1978] Director/Banker [Canadian]; Richard Michael Thomas [1974] Director/Accountant; Jeremy Alan Wiltshire [1981] Director/Banker

ELQ Investors VII Ltd
Incorporated: 15 May 2014
Net Worth: £308,104,704 *Total Assets:* £308,706,080
Registered Office: Peterborough Court, 133 Fleet Street, London, EC4A 2BB
Activities: Financial intermediation not elsewhere classified
Parent: ELQ Holdings (UK) Ltd
Officers: Thomas Kelly, Secretary; Clare Charlotte Richards, Secretary; Tavis Colm Peter Cannell [1978] Director/Banker [Canadian]; Vikramjit Singh Chima [1973] Director/Accountant [Indian]; Piers Noel Ormiston Curle [1974] Director/Banker; William Thomas Gasson [1965] Director/Banker; Jeremy Alan Wiltshire [1981] Director/Banker

ELQ Investors VIII Ltd
Incorporated: 19 August 2014
Net Worth: £318,716,320 *Total Assets:* £1,508,769,408
Registered Office: Peterborough Court, 133 Fleet Street, London, EC4A 2BB
Activities: Financial intermediation not elsewhere classified
Parent: Goldman Sachs Group Holdings (U.K.) Limited
Officers: Thomas Kelly, Secretary; Clare Charlotte Richards, Secretary; Beat Mathias Cabiallavetta [1979] Director/Banker [Swiss]; Tavis Colm Peter Cannell [1978] Director/Banker [Canadian]; Piers Noel Ormiston Curle [1974] Director/Banker; William Thomas Gasson [1965] Director/Banker; Nishi Somaiya Grose [1980] Director/Banker; Michael Holmes [1973] Director/Accountant; Jeremy Alan Wiltshire [1981] Director/Banker

ELQ Investors, Ltd
Incorporated: 13 May 2003
Net Worth: £286,081,824 *Total Assets:* £1,058,372,096
Registered Office: Peterborough Court, 133 Fleet Street, London, EC4A 2BB
Activities: Financial intermediation not elsewhere classified
Parent: The Goldman Sachs Group, Inc.
Officers: Thomas Kelly, Secretary; Clare Charlotte Richards, Secretary; Oliver John Bingham [1977] Director/Chartered Accountant; William Thomas Gasson [1965] Director/Banker; Michael Holmes [1973] Director/Accountant; Jeremy Alan Wiltshire [1981] Director/Banker

ELQ Omega UK Ltd
Incorporated: 24 November 2016
Net Worth: £110,744,832 *Total Assets:* £110,744,832
Registered Office: Peterborough Court, 133 Fleet Street, London, EC4A 2BB
Activities: Financial intermediation not elsewhere classified
Parent: ELQ Investors II Ltd
Officers: Clare Charlotte Richards, Secretary; Heather Louise Mulahasani [1978] Director/Banker; Henrik Ohlsen [1984] Director [Swedish]; Mark Desmond Charles Olivier [1974] Managing Director; Richard James Spencer [1974] Director

Ember Overseas Holdings Limited
Incorporated: 26 October 2007
Net Worth: £203,330,000 *Total Assets:* £203,330,000
Registered Office: 6th Floor, 322 High Holborn, London, WC1V 7PB
Activities: Non-trading company
Parent: Colfax Corporation
Officers: William Flexon [1963] Director/Chartered Accountant [American]; Mark Paul Lehman [1967] Director/Solicitor [American]; Eileen Annabelle Raperport [1951] Director/Pensions Co-ordinator; Guy Rostron [1960] Director/Chartered Accountant

Emerald 2 Limited
Incorporated: 4 March 2011 *Employees:* 4,336
Net Worth: £52,282,448 *Total Assets:* £1,147,504,384
Registered Office: 2nd Floor, Exchequer Court, 33 St Mary Axe, London, EC3A 8AA
Activities: Activities of head offices
Parent: ERM Worldwide Limited
Officers: Roy Antony Burrows, Secretary; Simon Paul Crowe [1967] Director/Chief Financial Officer; Keryn Lee James [1968] Director [Australian]; Mark Robert Pearson [1967] Director

Emerald 3 Limited
Incorporated: 29 December 2010
Net Worth: £431,167,008 *Total Assets:* £589,701,120
Registered Office: 2nd Floor, Exchequer Court, 33 St Mary Axe, London, EC3A 8AA
Activities: Activities of head offices
Parent: Emerald 2 Limited
Officers: Roy Antony Burrows, Secretary; Simon Paul Crowe [1967] Director/Chief Financial Officer; Keryn Lee James [1968] Director [Australian]; Mark Robert Pearson [1967] Director

Emerald Acquisition Limited
Incorporated: 5 October 2015
Net Worth: £125,318,368 *Total Assets:* £125,318,368
Registered Office: Rex House, 10 Regent Street, London, SW1Y 4PE
Activities: Activities of other holding companies n.e.c.
Officers: Milton Berlinski [1956] Director/Managing Partner, Reverence Capital Management [American]; Todd Crockett [1970] Director/Private Equity Investor [American]; Roger Kafker [1962] Managing Director of TA Associates Management, LP [American]; Arthur Lev [1961] Director [American]; Michelle Renae Seitz [1965] Director/Chief Executive [American]

Emerson Electric U.K. Limited
Incorporated: 30 July 1965 *Employees:* 40
Net Worth: £46,962,000 *Total Assets:* £246,712,000
Registered Office: 2nd Floor, Accurist House, 44 Baker Street, London, W1U 7AL
Activities: Other manufacturing n.e.c.
Parent: Emerson Holding Company Limited
Officers: Lynne Blakey Beutlich [1963] Director/Chartered Tax Adviser; Bente Bulow Bundgaard-Antoine [1972] Director/Accountant [Danish]; Martin Benedict Fernandez [1959] Director/Treasury Manager; Derek Shaw [1955] Tax Director

Emerson Holding Company Limited
Incorporated: 10 February 1984
Net Worth: £68,966,000 *Total Assets:* £145,986,000
Registered Office: 2nd Floor, Accurist House, 44 Baker Street, London, W1U 7AL
Activities: Activities of head offices
Parent: Digital Appliance Controls (UK) Limited
Officers: Bente Bulow Bundgaard-Antoine [1972] Director/Accountant [Danish]; Martin Benedict Fernandez [1959] Director/Treasury Manager; David Joseph Rabe [1959] Director/Business Executive [American]; Derek Shaw [1955] Tax Director

Emerson USD Finance Company Limited
Incorporated: 20 June 2011
Net Worth: £149,411,296 *Total Assets:* £1,740,362,240
Registered Office: 2nd Floor, Accurist House, 44 Baker Street, London, W1U 7AL
Activities: Activities of head offices
Parent: Emerson Electric Co.
Officers: Lynne Blakey Beutlich [1963] Director/Chartered Tax Adviser; Bente Bulow Bundgaard-Antoine [1972] Director/Accountant [Danish]; Martin Benedict Fernandez [1959] Director/Treasury Manager; Derek Shaw [1955] Tax Director; James Henry Thomasson [1967] Director/Treasurer [American]

EMF-UK 2008-1 PLC
Incorporated: 15 February 2008
Net Worth: £5,881,000 *Total Assets:* £176,348,992
Registered Office: Third Floor, 1 King's Arms Yard, London, EC2R 7AF
Activities: Other business support service activities n.e.c.
Parent: EMF-UK 2008-1 Parent Limited
Officers: Robert Sutton [1978] Director/Financial Services [American]; Daniel Jonathan Wynne [1970] Director

EMGH Limited
Incorporated: 14 December 2009
Net Worth: £87,816,880 *Total Assets:* £129,781,536
Registered Office: Vintners' Place, Upper Thames Street, London, EC4V 3BJ
Activities: Activities of head offices
Parent: Edgen Murray Corporation
Officers: Ordella Rebello, Secretary; Craig Douglas Doel [1967] Managing Director [New Zealander]; Ordella Rebello [1978] Director/Chartered Accountant [Indian]

EMI Group (Newco) Limited
Incorporated: 6 October 2011
Net Worth: £80,728,000 *Total Assets:* £1,670,873,984
Registered Office: 4 Pancras Square, London, N1C 4AG
Activities: Activities of other holding companies n.e.c.
Parent: EMI Group Worldwide Holdings Limited
Officers: Abolanle Abioye, Secretary; Simon Lloyd Carmel [1973] Director/Solicitor; Paramjit Jassal [1963] Director/Chief Financial Officer - Finance Operations; Boyd Johnston Muir [1959] Director/EVP & CFO

EMI Group Finance Limited
Incorporated: 22 May 1964
Net Worth: £567,284,992 *Total Assets:* £5,670,162,944
Registered Office: 4 Pancras Square, London, N1C 4AG
Activities: Financial intermediation not elsewhere classified
Parent: EMI Group Limited
Officers: Abolanle Abioye, Secretary; Adam Martin Barker [1968] Director/Lawyer; Simon Lloyd Carmel [1973] Director/Solicitor; Boyd Johnston Muir [1959] Director/EVP & CFO; David Richard James Sharpe [1967] Director/Chief Operating Officer [Irish]

EMI Group Global Limited
Incorporated: 28 January 2011
Net Worth: £633,587,200 *Total Assets:* £635,157,440
Registered Office: Citigroup Centre, 25 Canada Square, London, E14 5LB
Activities: Activities of other holding companies n.e.c.
Parent: Citigroup Inc
Officers: Jill Denise Robson, Secretary; Charles Barclay Proctor Beauchamp [1969] Director/Solicitor; David Ian Sharland [1959] Director/Chartered Accountant

EMI Group International Holdings Limited
Incorporated: 4 January 1979
Net Worth: £127,127,000 *Total Assets:* £430,889,984
Registered Office: 4 Pancras Square, London, N1C 4AG
Activities: Artistic creation
Parent: EMI Group Worldwide
Officers: Abolanle Abioye, Secretary; Simon Lloyd Carmel [1973] Director/Solicitor; Paramjit Jassal [1963] Director/Chief Financial Officer - Finance Operations; Boyd Johnston Muir [1959] Director/EVP & CFO

EMI Group Limited
Incorporated: 29 March 1928
Net Worth: £1,609,900,032 *Total Assets:* £1,650,844,032
Registered Office: 4 Pancras Square, London, N1C 4AG
Activities: Activities of head offices
Parent: EMI Group (Newco) Limited
Officers: Abolanle Abioye, Secretary; Simon Lloyd Carmel [1973] Director/Solicitor; Paramjit Jassal [1963] Director/Chief Financial Officer - Finance Operations; Boyd Johnston Muir [1959] Director/EVP & CFO

EMI Group Worldwide
Incorporated: 13 February 1996
Net Worth: £1,372,279,040 *Total Assets:* £2,121,426,944
Registered Office: 4 Pancras Square, London, N1C 4AG
Activities: Activities of head offices
Parent: Virgin Music Group
Officers: Abolanle Abioye, Secretary; Simon Lloyd Carmel [1973] Director/Solicitor; Paramjit Jassal [1963] Director/Chief Financial Officer - Finance Operations; Boyd Johnston Muir [1959] Director/EVP & CFO

EMI Group Worldwide Holdings Limited
Incorporated: 25 April 2007
Net Worth: £1,203,079,936 *Total Assets:* £1,764,120,064
Registered Office: 4 Pancras Square, London, N1C 4AG
Activities: Activities of head offices
Parent: Vivendi S.A
Officers: Abolanle Abioye, Secretary; Simon Lloyd Carmel [1973] Director/Solicitor; Paramjit Jassal [1963] Director/Chief Financial Officer - Finance Operations; Boyd Johnston Muir [1959] Director/EVP & CFO; David Richard James Sharpe [1967] Director [Irish]

EMI Music Publishing Finance (UK) Limited
Incorporated: 22 October 2007 *Employees:* 72
Net Worth: £111,914,000 *Total Assets:* £1,066,124,992
Registered Office: 30 Golden Square, London, W1F 9LD
Activities: Book publishing
Parent: BW Publishing Limited
Officers: Martin Neal Bandier [1941] Director/Business Executive [American]; Guy Robert Henderson [1960] Director/Business Executive; Guy Kimberly Moot [1965] Managing Director; Joseph Salvatore Puzio [1959] Director [American]

EMI Music Publishing Limited
Incorporated: 4 December 1957 *Employees:* 72
Net Worth: £291,946,400 *Total Assets:* £676,472,320
Registered Office: 30 Golden Square, London, W1F 9LD
Activities: Book publishing
Parent: EMI Music Publishing Finance (UK) Limited
Officers: Martin Neal Bandier [1941] Director/Business Executive [American]; Guy Robert Henderson [1960] Director/Business Executive; Guy Kimberly Moot [1965] Managing Director; Joseph Salvatore Puzio [1959] Director [American]

EMI Songs Limited
Incorporated: 22 March 1966
Net Worth: £153,676,080 *Total Assets:* £153,923,536
Registered Office: 30 Golden Square, London, W1F 9LD
Activities: Book publishing
Parent: EMI Music Publishing Finance (UK) Limited
Officers: Martin Neal Bandier [1941] Director/Business Executive [American]; Guy Robert Henderson [1960] Director/Business Executive; Guy Kimberly Moot [1965] Managing Director; Joseph Salvatore Puzio [1959] Director [American]

EMP Exploration (Kangean) Limited
Incorporated: 17 March 1966
Net Worth: £54,793,008 *Total Assets:* £199,706,896
Registered Office: 5th Floor, 6 St Andrew Street, London, EC4A 3AE
Activities: Extraction of crude petroleum
Officers: Riri Hosniari Harahap, Secretary/VP Legal [Indonesian]; Imam Pria Agustino [1964] Director/Entrepreneur [Indonesian]; Syailendra Surmansyah Bakrie [1980] Director [Indonesian]; Minoru Kuniyasu [1958] Director/Executive Officer [Japanese]; Takehiko Sato [1966] Director/Chief Representative, London Representative Office [Japanese]

Emperador Holdings (GB) Ltd
Incorporated: 19 June 2014
Net Worth: £141,996,560 *Total Assets:* £142,009,056
Registered Office: Suite 1, 3rd Floor, 11-12 St James's Square, London, SW1Y 4LB
Activities: Other business support service activities n.e.c.
Parent: Emperador International Ltd
Officers: Bryan Harold Donaghey [1961] Director; Michael Robert William Sloan [1978] Director/Chief Financial Officer; Andrew Chongbuan Tan [1949] Director [Filipino]

Empiric Investments (Four) Limited
Incorporated: 15 April 2015
Net Worth: £23,302,150 *Total Assets:* £268,000,608
Registered Office: 6th Floor, Swan House, 17-19 Stratford Place, London, W1C 1BQ
Activities: Other letting and operating of own or leased real estate
Parent: Empiric Investment Holdings (Four) Limited
Officers: Timothy Laurence Attlee [1961] Director; Lynne Fennah [1963] Director/Chief Financial Officer

Empiric Investments (One) Limited
Incorporated: 28 August 2014
Net Worth: £19,123,726 *Total Assets:* £134,220,960
Registered Office: 6th Floor, Swan House, 17-19 Stratford Place, London, W1C 1BQ
Activities: Other letting and operating of own or leased real estate
Parent: Empiric Student Property PLC
Officers: Timothy Laurence Attlee [1961] Director; Lynne Fennah [1963] Director/Chief Financial Officer

Empiric Student Property PLC
Incorporated: 11 February 2014 *Employees:* 138
Net Worth: £629,257,984 *Total Assets:* £972,993,984
Registered Office: 6th Floor, Swan House, 17-19 Stratford Place, London, W1C 1BQ
Activities: Other letting and operating of own or leased real estate
Officers: Charles Stephen Withycombe Alston [1962] Director; Timothy Laurence Attlee [1961] Director; Stuart Robert Hartley Beevor [1957] Director/Chartered Surveyor; Lynne Fennah [1963] Director/Chief Financial Officer; Mark Andrew Pain [1961] Director; Aubyn James Sugden Prower [1955] Director/Chartered Accountant

EMR Capital RF II LLP
Incorporated: 2 June 2017
Net Worth: £120,142,736 *Total Assets:* £122,688,216
Registered Office: Suite 1, 3rd Floor, 11-12 St James's Square, London, SW1Y 4LB

EMT 2 Holdings Limited
Incorporated: 8 December 2015
Net Worth: £81,657,952 *Total Assets:* £782,225,472
Registered Office: 10 Lower Grosvenor Place, London, SW1W 0EN
Activities: Activities of other holding companies n.e.c.
Parent: Element Materials Technology Limited
Officers: Charles Arthur Noall [1959] Director; Joseph Daniel Wetz [1976] Director; Matthew Alexander White [1967] Director

EMT Holdings Limited
Incorporated: 14 December 2015
Net Worth: £394,804,864 *Total Assets:* £647,828,736
Registered Office: 5 Fleet Place, London, EC4M 7RD
Activities: Activities of other holding companies n.e.c.
Parent: Element Materials Technology Group Limited
Officers: Christopher John Busby [1972] Director; Raoul Hughes [1965] Director

Enbridge Rampion UK Ltd
Incorporated: 28 September 2015
Net Worth: £293,642,432 *Total Assets:* £316,585,952
Registered Office: One Fleet Place, London, EC4M 7WS
Activities: Activities of other holding companies n.e.c.
Parent: Enbridge UK Holdings Ltd
Officers: Andrew Clive Buglass [1966] Director/Consultant; Vincent Guy Julier [1966] Director; Ian Robert McFeely [1961] Director/Executive Vice President [Canadian]

Enbridge UK Holdings Ltd
Incorporated: 28 September 2015
Net Worth: £321,783,936 *Total Assets:* £323,476,352
Registered Office: One Fleet Place, London, EC4M 7WS
Activities: Activities of other holding companies n.e.c.
Parent: Enbridge Inc.
Officers: Andrew Clive Buglass [1966] Director/Consultant; Vincent Guy Julier [1966] Director; Ian Robert McFeely [1961] Director/Executive Vice President [Canadian]

Encore Oil Limited
Incorporated: 5 March 1997
Net Worth: £224,663,520 *Total Assets:* £225,123,472
Registered Office: 23 Lower Belgrave Street, London, SW1W 0NR
Activities: Extraction of crude petroleum
Parent: Premier Oil Holdings Limited
Officers: Daniel Alexander Rose, Secretary; Robert Andrew Allan [1959] Director/Geologist; Anthony Richard Charles Durrant [1958] Director/Oil Industry Executive; Andrew George Gibb [1968] Director/Solicitor; Richard Andrew Rose [1972] Finance Director

Endeavour Acquisition UK Limited
Incorporated: 20 November 2014 *Employees:* 565
Net Worth: £96,161,208 *Total Assets:* £231,079,472
Registered Office: 3rd Floor, Enterprise House, Cargo Works, 1-2 Hatfields, London, SE1 9PG
Activities: Activities of other holding companies n.e.c.
Shareholders: Thomas Barnds; Robert Palumbo
Officers: Peter Yeung, Secretary; Thomas Barnds [1968] Director [American]; Mark Antony Duffell [1962] Director [American]; Dean Jacobson [1977] Director/Investor [American]; Jason Michael Klein [1973] Director/Investor [American]

The Endeavour Company Holdings Limited
Incorporated: 19 May 2000 *Employees:* 12
Net Worth: £137,776,000 *Total Assets:* £220,228,000
Registered Office: 33 Ely Place, London, EC1N 6TD
Activities: Activities of head offices
Officers: Echo Chong, Secretary; John Stuart Ian Rosefield [1944] Director; Stephen Michael Rosefield [1952] Director/Solicitor

Endeavour Energy UK Limited
Incorporated: 30 January 2004 *Employees:* 5
Net Worth Deficit: £855,653,632 *Total Assets:* £224,295,600
Registered Office: 24th Floor, 20 Fenchurch Street, London, EC3M 3BY
Activities: Extraction of crude petroleum
Officers: Gary Clyde Hanna [1958] Director/Oil and Gas Executive [American]; James John Lachance [1965] Director/Consultant [American]; Joseph Lewis McInnis [1975] Director/Analyst [Canadian]; Steven Pully [1960] Director/Consultant [American]; George Frederick Sandison [1956] Director/Consultant [American]; Catherine L. Stubbs [1966] Director/President, Chief Financial Officer [American]

Endeavour Resources Limited
Incorporated: 21 March 2001 *Employees:* 2
Net Worth: £1,076,494,976 *Total Assets:* £1,077,647,104
Registered Office: 8th & 9th Floors, 1 St Martin's-le-Grand, London, EC1A 4AS
Activities: Activities of head offices
Parent: Mitsui & Co., Ltd.
Officers: Taichi Nagino, Secretary; Eiichi Ueno, Secretary; Taichi Nagino [1967] Director [Japanese]; Eiichi Ueno [1965] Director [Japanese]

Endell Properties Limited
Incorporated: 22 November 2007
Net Worth Deficit: £419,846,976 *Total Assets:* £1,801,531,776
Registered Office: Freshwater House, 158-162 Shaftesbury Avenue, London, WC2H 8HR
Activities: Buying and selling of own real estate
Parent: Daejan Holdings PLC
Officers: Mark Roy Mason Jenner, Secretary; Benzion Schalom Eliezer Freshwater [1948] Director; Solomon Israel Freshwater [1950] Director

Endemol Shine Group Holding UK Limited
Incorporated: 9 October 2007 *Employees:* 46
Previous: Endemol Group Limited
Net Worth: £38,082,000 *Total Assets:* £462,212,992
Registered Office: Central Legal Department, Shepherds Building, Endemol Shine UK, Charecroft Way, London, W14 0EE
Activities: Television programme production activities
Officers: John Russell Parsons, Secretary/Director of Legal Affairs; Richard Robert Johnston [1967] Joint Managing Director; Peter Andrew Salmon [1956] Director/Chief Creative Officer; Sophie Henrietta Turner Laing [1960] Director

Endemol Shine UK Limited
Incorporated: 19 January 1983 *Employees:* 185
Previous: Endemol UK Limited
Net Worth: £100,425,000 *Total Assets:* £254,548,000
Registered Office: Central Legal Department, Shepherds Building, Endemol Shine UK, Charecroft Way, London, W14 0EE
Activities: Television programme production activities
Parent: Endemol UK Holding Limited
Officers: John Russell Parsons, Secretary; Lucinda Hannah Michelle Hicks [1979] Director/Media Management; Richard Robert Johnston [1967] Finance Director; Derek O'Gara [1965] Finance Director [Irish]; Sophie Henrietta Turner Laing [1960] Director

Endowment Investment Holdings Limited
Incorporated: 11 December 2015
Net Worth: £199,571,264 *Total Assets:* £216,078,656
Registered Office: 16 Palace Street, London, SW1E 5JD
Activities: Activities of financial services holding companies
Officers: Adam Benedykt [1981] Director; Oliver James Dunn [1986] Director/Accountant; Rohan Maxwell [1977] Director

Endurance Corporate Capital Limited
Incorporated: 2 April 2007
Previous: Montpelier Capital Limited
Net Worth: £71,760,000 *Total Assets:* £844,979,968
Registered Office: 2 Minster Court, Mincing Lane, London, EC3R 7BB
Activities: Non-life insurance
Parent: Endurance Holdings Limited
Officers: Daniel Simeon Lurie, Secretary; Graham Peter Evans [1967] Director/Insurance Executive; Richard John Ronald Housley [1967] Director/Insurance Executive; Philip Anthony Rooke [1969] Director/Accountant

Endurance Worldwide Holdings Limited
Incorporated: 10 April 2002
Net Worth: £377,828,800 *Total Assets:* £377,993,760
Registered Office: 1st Floor, 2 Minster Court, Mincing Lane, London, EC3R 7BB
Activities: Other activities auxiliary to insurance and pension funding
Officers: Daniel Simeon Lurie, Secretary/Attorney; Graham Peter Evans [1967] Director/Insurance Executive; Richard John Ronald Housley [1967] Director/Insurance Executive; Philip Anthony Rooke [1969] Director/Chief Financial Officer

Endurance Worldwide Insurance Limited
Incorporated: 10 April 2002 *Employees:* 60
Net Worth: £371,824,000 *Total Assets:* £1,015,262,016
Registered Office: 1st Floor, 2 Minster Court, Mincing Lane, London, EC3R 7BB
Activities: Non-life insurance
Parent: Endurance Holdings Limited
Officers: Marcus Stephen Iestyn Llewellyn Bonnell, Secretary; Graham Peter Evans [1967] Director/Insurance Executive; Michael Graham Furgueson [1962] Independent Non-Executive Director [American]; Christopher Brian Gallagher [1973] Director; James Andrew Giordano [1952] Director [American]; Richard John Ronald Housley [1967] Director/Insurance Executive; John Andrew Kuhn [1964] Director/Insurance Executive [American]; Takashi Kurumisawa [1973] Director/Chief Operations Officer [Japanese]; Philip Anthony Rooke [1969] Director/Chief Financial Officer; Ian Michael Winchester [1946] Director

Energean Oil & Gas PLC
Incorporated: 8 May 2017 *Employees:* 386
Net Worth: £47,638,264 *Total Assets:* £347,033,664
Registered Office: Accurist House, 44 Baker Street, London, W1U 7AL
Activities: Extraction of crude petroleum
Officers: Michelle Churchward, Secretary; Andrew Donald Bartlett [1957] Director; Panagiotis Benos [1979] Director [Greek]; David Whalen Bonanno [1981] Director [American]; Simon John Newton Heale [1953] Director; Ohad Marani [1955] Director [Israeli]; Robert William Peck [1959] Director [Canadian]; Matthaios Rigas [1967] Director/Businessman [Greek]; Karen Simon [1959] Director [American]; Efstathios Topouzoglou [1956] Director/Businessman [Greek]

Energy Power Resources Limited
Incorporated: 15 January 1997 *Employees:* 24
Net Worth: £76,231,000 *Total Assets:* £112,098,000
Registered Office: 6th Floor, 33 Holborn, London, EC1N 2HT
Activities: Activities of head offices
Parent: EPR Renewable Energy Limited
Officers: Paul Stephen Latham [1956] Director; Matthew George Setchell [1977] Director/Investment Manager; Edwin John Wilkinson [1965] Director/CEO/Accountant

Engelhart CTP Group (UK) Limited
Incorporated: 4 February 2016
Net Worth: £530,625,088 *Total Assets:* £646,261,760
Registered Office: Berkeley Square House, 4-19 Berkeley Square, London, W1J 6BR
Activities: Activities of other holding companies n.e.c.
Shareholders: Roberto Balls Sallouti; Guilherme Da Costa Paes; Antonio Carlos Canto Porto Filho; Renato Monteiro Dos Santos; Marcelo Kalim
Officers: Ricardo Alves Ferreira Froes [1970] Director [Brazilian]; John Huw Gwili Jenkins [1958] Director/Investment Professional

Engelhart CTP Holding (UK) Limited
Incorporated: 25 June 2013
Previous: BTG Pactual Commodities Holding (UK) Limited
Net Worth: £528,226,464 *Total Assets:* £703,991,040
Registered Office: Berkeley Square House, 4-19 Berkeley Square, London, W1J 6BR
Activities: Activities of other holding companies n.e.c.
Parent: Engelhart CTP Group (UK) Limited
Officers: Ricardo Alves Ferreira Froes [1970] Director [Brazilian]; Alexis Gontow Maron [1974] Director/Head of Tax [Brazilian]

Engine Acquisition Limited
Incorporated: 10 June 2014 *Employees:* 834
Net Worth: £3,497,000 *Total Assets:* £110,072,000
Registered Office: 60 Great Portland Street, London, W1W 7RT
Activities: Activities of head offices
Officers: Collin Roy Abert [1985] Director/Private Equity [American]; Paul Jason Caine [1964] Director [American]; Lawrence Jeffrey Diamond [1963] Director/Chief Financial Officer [American]

The Engine Group Limited
Incorporated: 14 January 2004 *Employees:* 3
Net Worth Deficit: £28,816,000 *Total Assets:* £109,472,000
Registered Office: 60 Great Portland Street, London, W1W 7RT
Activities: Public relations and communications activities
Parent: Engine Acquisition Limited
Officers: Mary Louise Cole, Secretary; Collin Roy Abert [1985] Director/Private Equity [American]; Paul Jason Caine [1964] Director [American]; Lawrence Jeffrey Diamond [1963] Director/Chief Financial Officer [American]; James Nicholas Peter Moffatt [1975] Director

Engine Partners UK LLP
Incorporated: 22 June 2011
Net Worth: £151,150,000 *Total Assets:* £178,080,992
Registered Office: 60 Great Portland Street, London, W1W 7RT
Officers: Mary Louise Cole [1969] Member; Simon Edward Peck [1972] Member; Nicholas Jonah Barron [1975] LLP Member; Daniella Bertolone [1980] LLP Member; George Bruxner [1974] LLP Member; Alastair Stewart Leslie Cole [1976] LLP Member; Francine Cory [1972] LLP Member; John Harold Crowther [1965] LLP Member; Nicholas John Denton [1955] LLP Member; Robert Donlan [1967] LLP Member; Elisa Generaldine Edmonds [1971] LLP Member; Matthew Thomas Edwards [1973] LLP Member; Peter John Hamer Edwards [1966] LLP Member; William Eyre Faithfull [1975] LLP Member; Barnaby Marshall Fry [1974] LLP Member; Anne Susan Jane Gallimore [1973] LLP Member; Thomas Stewart Robert Gladstone [1978] LLP Member; James Goldhill [1975] LLP Member; Aaron Luke Goldring [1976] LLP Member; Reginald Nicholas Rolls Hoare [1961] LLP Member; Johan Bengt Hogsander [1970] LLP Member; Julian Hough [1961] LLP Member; Katie Hunt [1974] LLP Member; Andrew Gavin Jaques [1965] LLP Member; Leon Charles Michael Jaume [1955] LLP Member; Paul Johnson [1970] LLP Member; Jonathan Jones [1973] LLP Member; Pauline Mary Jones [1971] LLP Member; Olenka Lawrensen [1982] LLP Member; Sally Lipsius [1960] LLP Member; Eliot Michael Liss [1975] LLP Member; Emma Marsland [1970] LLP Member; Karen Lorraine McDonald [1961] LLP Member; James Nicholas Peter Moffatt [1975] LLP Member; Joanna Claire Moore [1964] LLP Member; Gemma Louise Moroney [1980] LLP Member; Martin Nieri [1971] LLP Member; Derek Roy Palmer [1964] LLP Member; Lisa Parfitt [1979] LLP Member; Nicolas James Parnell [1983] LLP Member; Harriet Playford [1966] LLP Member; Ian David Pocock [1975] LLP Member; Mark Paul Redwood-Sayce [1971] LLP Member; Emma Robertson [1977] LLP Member; Joshua Robinson [1976] LLP Member; Simon William Robinson [1965] LLP Member; Daniel Rowe [1973] LLP Member; Andrew Smith [1974] LLP Member; Damon Statt [1976] LLP Member; Carsten Thode [1974] LLP Member; Timothy James Watson [1970] LLP Member; Victoria Wilkinson [1977] LLP Member; Matthew Willifer [1972] LLP Member; Natalie Winford [1977] LLP Member; David Wood [1964] LLP Member

ENI AEP Limited
Incorporated: 5 December 1935
Net Worth: £110,805,000 *Total Assets:* £170,364,992
Registered Office: ENI House, 10 Ebury Bridge Road, London, SW1W 8PZ
Activities: Extraction of crude petroleum
Parent: ENI UK Limited
Officers: Mila Trezza, Secretary; Gianluigi Ferrara [1959] Director [Italian]; Francesca Rinaldi [1978] Managing Director [Italian]; Mila Trezza [1975] Director/Solicitor [Italian]

ENI Australia Limited
Incorporated: 13 August 1971 *Employees:* 131
Net Worth: £136,839,920 *Total Assets:* £209,467,424
Registered Office: ENI House, 10 Ebury Bridge Road, London, SW1W 8PZ
Activities: Extraction of crude petroleum
Officers: Mila Trezza, Secretary; Ernest Frank Oliver Delfos [1963] Director [Australian]; Gianluigi Ferrara [1959] Director [Italian]; Franco Polo [1957] Director [Italian]; Francesca Rinaldi [1978] Managing Director [Italian]

ENI Elgin/Franklin Limited
Incorporated: 18 May 1999
Net Worth: £230,207,008 *Total Assets:* £673,075,008
Registered Office: ENI House, 10 Ebury Bridge Road, London, SW1W 8PZ
Activities: Extraction of crude petroleum
Parent: ENI UK Limited
Officers: Mila Trezza, Secretary; Gianluigi Ferrara [1959] Director [Italian]; Francesca Rinaldi [1978] Managing Director [Italian]; Mila Trezza [1975] Director/Solicitor [Italian]

ENI Investments PLC
Incorporated: 12 December 2000
Net Worth: £4,212,311,040 *Total Assets:* £4,212,641,792
Registered Office: ENI House, 10 Ebury Bridge Road, London, SW1W 8PZ
Activities: Activities of other holding companies n.e.c.
Parent: ENI S.P.A
Officers: Mila Trezza, Secretary; Gianluigi Ferrara [1959] Director [Italian]; Francesca Rinaldi [1978] Managing Director [Italian]; Mila Trezza [1975] Director/Solicitor [Italian]

ENI JPDA 03-13 Limited
Incorporated: 19 November 1991
Net Worth: £71,751,408 *Total Assets:* £182,843,696
Registered Office: ENI House, 10 Ebury Bridge Road, London, SW1W 8PZ
Activities: Extraction of natural gas
Officers: Mila Trezza, Secretary; Ernest Frank Oliver Delfos [1963] Director [Australian]; Gianluigi Ferrara [1959] Director [Italian]; Franco Polo [1957] Director [Italian]; Francesca Rinaldi [1978] Managing Director [Italian]

ENI Lasmo PLC
Incorporated: 23 April 1971
Net Worth: £2,984,803,840 *Total Assets:* £3,297,575,936
Registered Office: ENI House, 10 Ebury Bridge Road, London, SW1W 8PZ
Activities: Extraction of crude petroleum
Parent: ENI Investments PLC
Officers: Mila Trezza, Secretary; Gianluigi Ferrara [1959] Director [Italian]; Francesca Rinaldi [1978] Managing Director [Italian]; Carlo Vito Russo [1959] Director [Italian]; Lazzaro Vassallo [1962] Director [Italian]

ENI Oil Algeria Limited
Incorporated: 5 July 1988
Net Worth: £564,936,512 *Total Assets:* £683,906,048
Registered Office: ENI House, 10 Ebury Bridge Road, London, SW1W 8PZ
Activities: Extraction of crude petroleum
Parent: ENI Lasmo PLC
Officers: Mila Trezza, Secretary; Mario Bello [1965] Director [Italian]; Gianluigi Ferrara [1959] Director [Italian]; Francesca Rinaldi [1978] Managing Director [Italian]; Mila Trezza [1975] Director/Solicitor [Italian]; Eva Natalia Turteltaub [1964] Director [Italian]

ENI Pakistan Limited
Incorporated: 13 November 1918 *Employees:* 408
Net Worth: £69,261,768 *Total Assets:* £183,039,552
Registered Office: ENI House, 10 Ebury Bridge Road, London, SW1W 8PZ
Activities: Extraction of crude petroleum
Parent: ENI ULX Limited
Officers: Mila Trezza, Secretary; Gianluigi Ferrara [1959] Director [Italian]; Angelo Ligrone [1962] Director [Italian]; Francesca Rinaldi [1978] Managing Director [Italian]; Luca Vignati [1963] Director [Italian]

ENI UK Holding PLC
Incorporated: 15 November 2007
Net Worth: £1,328,044,416 *Total Assets:* £1,328,149,120
Registered Office: ENI House, 10 Ebury Bridge Road, London, SW1W 8PZ
Activities: Activities of other holding companies n.e.c.
Parent: ENI Lasmo PLC
Officers: Mila Trezza, Secretary; Gianluigi Ferrara [1959] Director [Italian]; Francesca Rinaldi [1978] Managing Director [Italian]; Mila Trezza [1975] Director/Solicitor [Italian]

ENI UK Limited
Incorporated: 29 October 1965 *Employees:* 183
Net Worth: £427,968,000 *Total Assets:* £1,128,280,960
Registered Office: ENI House, 10 Ebury Bridge Road, London, SW1W 8PZ
Activities: Extraction of crude petroleum
Officers: Mila Trezza, Secretary; Gianluigi Ferrara [1959] Director [Italian]; Francesca Rinaldi [1978] Managing Director [Italian]; Carlo Vito Russo [1959] Director [Italian]; Rosalyn Stallard [1961] Director

ENI ULT Limited
Incorporated: 3 May 1935
Net Worth: £794,432,384 *Total Assets:* £794,444,416
Registered Office: ENI House, 10 Ebury Bridge Road, London, SW1W 8PZ
Activities: Activities of other holding companies n.e.c.
Parent: ENI Lasmo PLC
Officers: Mila Trezza, Secretary; Gianluigi Ferrara [1959] Director [Italian]; Francesca Rinaldi [1978] Managing Director [Italian]; Alberto Tonna [1962] Director [Italian]

ENI ULX Limited
Incorporated: 29 July 1968 *Employees:* 1
Net Worth: £557,563,072 *Total Assets:* £1,015,713,728
Registered Office: ENI House, 10 Ebury Bridge Road, London, SW1W 8PZ
Activities: Extraction of crude petroleum
Parent: ENI ULT Limited
Officers: Mila Trezza, Secretary; Gianluigi Ferrara [1959] Director [Italian]; Francesca Rinaldi [1978] Managing Director [Italian]; Alberto Tonna [1962] Director [Italian]

Enovert Management Limited
Incorporated: 12 December 1996 *Employees:* 129
Previous: Cory Environmental Management Limited
Net Worth: £18,283,000 *Total Assets:* £105,769,000
Registered Office: 20 Old Broad Street, London, EC2N 1DP
Activities: Activities of head offices
Parent: Trebuchet Investments (UK) Limited
Officers: Thomas Peter Alcock, Secretary; Brad Scott Huntington [1959] Director/Insurance Professional [Canadian]; Doreen Pauline Elizabeth Richards [1948] Director/Accountant; Steven Michael Ryland [1967] Director/Insurance Professional; John Caldicott Williams [1958] Director/Insurance Professional

Enquest Britain Limited
Incorporated: 8 September 1998 *Employees:* 328
Net Worth: £438,284,896 *Total Assets:* £2,441,362,432
Registered Office: 5th Floor, Cunard House, 15 Regent Street, London, SW1Y 4LR
Activities: Extraction of crude petroleum
Parent: Enquest PLC
Officers: Kathryn Anna Christ, Secretary; Glenn Andrew Corr [1970] Director; Neill Michael Hamilton [1966] Director; Paul Euan Massie [1982] Director; Stefan John Ricketts [1967] Director

Enquest ENS Limited
Incorporated: 29 October 2007
Net Worth: £50,907,768 *Total Assets:* £311,715,488
Registered Office: 5th Floor, Cunard House, 15 Regent Street, London, SW1Y 4LR
Activities: Extraction of crude petroleum
Parent: Enquest Britain Limited
Officers: Kathryn Anna Christ, Secretary; Glenn Andrew Corr [1970] Director; Neill Michael Hamilton [1966] Director; Paul Euan Massie [1982] Director; Stefan John Ricketts [1967] Director

Enquest Global Limited
Incorporated: 10 April 2013
Net Worth: £55,009,584 *Total Assets:* £126,513,840
Registered Office: c/o Enquest PLC, 5th Floor, Cunard House, 15 Regent Street, London, SW1Y 4LR
Activities: Extraction of crude petroleum
Parent: Enquest PLC
Officers: Kathryn Anna Christ, Secretary; Faysal Essam Hamza [1963] Director [Saudi Arabian]; Stefan John Ricketts [1967] Director; Daniel Gama Rodrigues [1982] Director [Portuguese]

Enquest Heather Leasing Limited
Incorporated: 15 November 2011
Net Worth: £118,021,160 *Total Assets:* £119,805,256
Registered Office: 5th Floor, Cunard House, 15 Regent Street, London, SW1Y 4LR
Activities: Extraction of crude petroleum
Parent: Enquest Heather Limited
Officers: Kathryn Anna Christ, Secretary; Glenn Andrew Corr [1970] Director; Neill Michael Hamilton [1966] Director; Paul Euan Massie [1982] Director; Stefan John Ricketts [1967] Director

Enquest Heather Limited
Incorporated: 21 September 1992 *Employees:* 2
Net Worth: £574,498,176 *Total Assets:* £3,623,812,096
Registered Office: 5th Floor, Cunard House, 15 Regent Street, London, SW1Y 4LR
Activities: Extraction of crude petroleum
Parent: Enquest Britain Limited
Officers: Kathryn Anna Christ, Secretary; Glenn Andrew Corr [1970] Director; Neill Michael Hamilton [1966] Director; Paul Euan Massie [1982] Director; Stefan John Ricketts [1967] Director

Enquest NNS Limited
Incorporated: 19 January 2017
Net Worth: £1,156,942 *Total Assets:* £155,212,752
Registered Office: Cunard House, 15 Regent Street, London, SW1Y 4LR
Activities: Extraction of crude petroleum
Parent: Enquest NNS Holdings Limited
Officers: Kathryn Anna Christ, Secretary; Glenn Andrew Corr [1970] Director; Neill Michael Hamilton [1966] Director; Paul Euan Massie [1982] Director; Stefan John Ricketts [1967] Director

Enquest PLC
Incorporated: 29 January 2010 *Employees:* 506
Net Worth: £573,157,056 *Total Assets:* £3,795,458,304
Registered Office: 5th Floor, Cunard House, 15 Regent Street, London, SW1Y 4LR
Activities: Extraction of crude petroleum
Officers: Stefan John Ricketts, Secretary; Amjad Adnan Bseisu [1963] Director [British/Bahrani]; Laurie Lee Fitch [1970] Director [American]; Philip Malcolm Holland [1954] Director; Carl David Hughes [1962] Director; Helmut Langanger [1950] Director [Austrian]; John Fyfe Lennox [1956] Director; Jonathan Anthony Robert Swinney [1966] Director; John Martin Winterman [1956] Director

ENRC Finance Limited
Incorporated: 12 January 2007
Net Worth: £3,090,306,560 *Total Assets:* £6,643,820,032
Registered Office: 5th Floor, 6 St Andrew Street, London, EC4A 3AE
Activities: Activities of other holding companies n.e.c.
Parent: Eurasian Natural Resources Corporation Limited
Officers: Dmitry Melnikov [1981] Director/Chief Legal Officer, Erg [Russian]; Satzhan Temirgaliyev [1975] Director/Group Chief Financial Officer [Kazakh]; Felix Jeff Vulis [1955] Director [American]

Enrichment Holdings Ltd.
Incorporated: 2 October 2007
Net Worth: £543,401,024 *Total Assets:* £543,422,016
Registered Office: 1 Victoria Street, London, SW1H 0ET
Activities: Activities of other holding companies n.e.c.
Parent: Secretary of State for Business, Energy and Industrial Strategy
Officers: Justin Christopher John Manson [1960] Director/Deputy Chief Executive; Richard Henry Charles Nourse [1964] Director/Civil Servant

Enrichment Investments Limited
Incorporated: 25 May 2001
Net Worth: £446,264,000 *Total Assets:* £446,264,000
Registered Office: 1 Victoria Street, London, SW1H 0ET
Activities: Activities of other holding companies n.e.c.
Parent: Enrichment Holdings Limited
Officers: Justin Christopher John Manson [1960] Director/Deputy Chief Executive; Richard Henry Charles Nourse [1964] Director/Civil Servant

Ensco Deepwater Drilling Limited
Incorporated: 10 May 2013
Net Worth Deficit: £426,470,912 *Total Assets:* £608,295,616
Registered Office: 7 Albemarle Street, London, W1S 4HQ
Activities: Support activities for petroleum and natural gas mining
Parent: Ensco PLC
Officers: Jonathan Paul Cross, Secretary; Jonathan Paul Cross [1979] Director/Chartered Tax Adviser; Julian Richard Hall [1963] Director/Businessman; Stephen Laurence Mooney [1983] Director/Businessman [Irish]

Ensco Finance Limited
Incorporated: 8 December 2009
Net Worth: £243,765,232 *Total Assets:* £243,765,232
Registered Office: 7 Albemarle Street, London, W1S 4HQ
Activities: Support activities for petroleum and natural gas mining
Parent: Ensco Worldwide Investments Limited
Officers: Julian Richard Hall, Secretary; Jonathan Baksht [1975] Director/Businessman [American]; Stephen Joseph Brady [1959] Director/Businessman [American]; Stephen Laurence Mooney [1983] Director/Businessman [Irish]

Ensco Holdco Limited
Incorporated: 15 July 2009
Net Worth: £6,274,615,296 *Total Assets:* £6,377,086,464
Registered Office: 7 Albemarle Street, London, W1S 4HQ
Activities: Activities of head offices
Parent: Ensco Universal Limited
Officers: Stephen Mooney, Secretary; Johannes Bernardus Wilhelmus Gerardus Maria Van Bohemen, Secretary; Jonathan Baksht [1975] Director/Businessman [American]; Stephen Joseph Brady [1959] Director/Businessman [American]; Patrick Carey Lowe [1958] Director/Businessman [American]

Ensco Offshore U.K. Limited
Incorporated: 2 November 1993 *Employees:* 13
Net Worth: £77,205,024 *Total Assets:* £126,134,648
Registered Office: 7 Albemarle Street, London, W1S 4HQ
Activities: Support activities for petroleum and natural gas mining
Parent: Ensco PLC
Officers: Julian Richard Hall, Secretary; Stephen Laurence Mooney, Secretary [Irish]; Derek Andrew Sangster, Secretary; Johannes Bernardus Wilhelmus Gerardus Maria Van Bohemen, Secretary; Julian Richard Hall [1963] Director/Businessman; Stephen Laurence Mooney [1983] Director/Businessman [Irish]; Derek Andrew Sangster [1959] Director/Businessman

Ensco PLC
Incorporated: 18 September 2009 *Employees:* 4,438
Net Worth: £3,348,678,144 *Total Assets:* £7,659,516,928
Registered Office: 3rd Floor, 6 Chesterfield Gardens, London, W1J 5BQ
Activities: Support activities for petroleum and natural gas mining
Officers: Michael Terence McGuinty, Secretary; Davor Vukadin, Secretary; James Roderick Clark [1950] Director President and COO of Baker Hughes Inc [American]; Roxanne Decyk [1952] Director Executive VP President of Global [American]; Mary Francis CBE [1948] Director Senior Civil Servant; Charles Christopher Gaut [1956] Director/Chairman and CEO of Forum Energy Technologies Inc [American]; Jack Golden [1948] Director/Managing Partner of Edgewater Energy LLC [American]; Generald Wayne Haddock [1947] Director/Private Investor [American]; Francis Samuel Kalman [1947] Director Executive VP [American]; Keith Owen Rattie [1954] Director Chairman, President & CEO [American]; Paul Edward Rowsey III [1954] Director/CEO of Compatriot Capital Inc [American]; Carl Geoffrey Trowell [1969] Director/Chief Executive Officer and President; Phil Wedemeyer [1949] Director [American]

Ensco U.K. Limited
Incorporated: 1 October 2002
Net Worth: £80,308,808 *Total Assets:* £129,047,224
Registered Office: 7 Albemarle Street, London, W1S 4HQ
Activities: Support activities for petroleum and natural gas mining
Parent: Ensco PLC
Officers: Julian Richard Hall, Secretary; Stephen Laurence Mooney, Secretary [Irish]; Derek Andrew Sangster, Secretary; Johannes Bernardus Wilhelmus Gerardus Maria Van Bohemen, Secretary; Julian Richard Hall [1963] Director/Businessman; Stephen Laurence Mooney [1983] Director/Businessman [Irish]; Derek Andrew Sangster [1959] Director/Businessman

Ensco Universal Limited
Incorporated: 8 December 2009
Net Worth: £6,246,243,840 *Total Assets:* £9,130,490,880
Registered Office: 7 Albemarle Street, London, W1S 4HQ
Activities: Support activities for petroleum and natural gas mining
Parent: Ensco PLC
Officers: Stephen Laurence Mooney, Secretary [Irish]; Jonathan Baksht [1975] Director/Businessman [American]; Stephen Joseph Brady [1959] Director/Businessman [American]; Patrick Carey Lowe [1958] Director/Businessman [American]; Stephen Laurence Mooney [1983] Director/Businessman [Irish]

Ensco Worldwide Investments Limited
Incorporated: 8 December 2009
Net Worth: £2,201,021,952 *Total Assets:* £2,370,854,912
Registered Office: 7 Albemarle Street, London, W1S 4HQ
Activities: Support activities for petroleum and natural gas mining
Parent: Ensco Holdco Limited
Officers: Julian Richard Hall, Secretary; Stephen Laurence Mooney, Secretary [Irish]; Stephen Joseph Brady [1959] Director/Businessman [American]; Julian Richard Hall [1963] Director/Businessman; Stephen Laurence Mooney [1983] Director/Businessman [Irish]

Ensono Opco Holdings Limited
Incorporated: 2 August 2016 *Employees:* 278
Net Worth: £67,019,000 *Total Assets:* £116,985,000
Registered Office: c/o Bryan Cave Leighton Paisner LLP, Adelaide House, London Bridge, London, EC4R 9HA
Activities: Activities of other holding companies n.e.c.
Officers: Peter John Bazil [1972] Director [American]; Norman Smagley [1958] Director/Chief Financial Officer [American]

Enterprise Oil Limited
Incorporated: 26 November 1982
Net Worth: £1,785,600,000 *Total Assets:* £5,823,799,808
Registered Office: 8 York Road, London, SE1 7NA
Activities: Extraction of crude petroleum
Parent: Shell U.K. Limited
Officers: Gary James Archibald [1963] Director/Oil Company Executive; Marianne Wold Eide [1969] Director/Oil Company Executive [Norwegian]; Howard Edwin Jones [1978] Director/Oil Company Executive; Shannon Lorraine Ouellette [1969] Director/Oil Company Executive [Canadian]

Enterprise Oil Middle East Limited
Incorporated: 30 September 1991
Net Worth: £992,833,024 *Total Assets:* £1,374,418,944
Registered Office: 8 York Road, London, SE1 7NA
Activities: Extraction of crude petroleum
Parent: Enterprise Oil Limited
Officers: Marianne Wold Eide [1969] Director/Oil Company Executive [Norwegian]; Howard Edwin Jones [1978] Director/Oil Company Executive; Shannon Lorraine Ouellette [1969] Director/Oil Company Executive [Canadian]

Enterprise Oil U.K. Limited
Incorporated: 26 August 1988
Net Worth: £27,314,000 *Total Assets:* £168,672,992
Registered Office: 8 York Road, London, SE1 7NA
Activities: Extraction of crude petroleum
Parent: Enterprise Oil Limited
Officers: Marianne Wold Eide [1969] Director/Oil Company Executive [Norwegian]; Howard Edwin Jones [1978] Director/Oil Company Executive; Shannon Lorraine Ouellette [1969] Director/Oil Company Executive [Canadian]

Entertainment One UK Holdings Limited
Incorporated: 5 June 2007
Net Worth: £74,966,000 *Total Assets:* £579,206,016
Registered Office: 45 Warren Street, London, W1T 6AG
Activities: Activities of head offices
Parent: Entertainment One Ltd.
Officers: Nicholas John Murray Gawne [1977] Director/Chief Operating Officer, eOne Family; Edward David Parry [1971] Director of Group Finance

Entertainment One UK Limited
Incorporated: 14 November 1994 *Employees:* 183
Net Worth: £206,204,000 *Total Assets:* £348,175,008
Registered Office: 45 Warren Street, London, W1T 6AG
Activities: Motion picture production activities
Parent: Entertainment One UK Holdings Limited
Officers: Nicholas John Murray Gawne [1977] Director; Alexander Douglas Hamilton [1966] Director; Nelson Hao-Cheng Kuo-Lee [1967] Director/COO & EVP, Global Film Group [Canadian]; Edward David Parry [1971] Director of Group Finance; Kezia Maria Siobhan Williams [1980] Managing Director, UK, Film

Envol Investments Limited
Incorporated: 21 April 2016
Net Worth: £359,828,800 *Total Assets:* £682,898,688
Registered Office: 6th Floor, 65 Gresham Street, London, EC2V 7NQ
Activities: Activities of other holding companies n.e.c.
Parent: Envol Midco Limited
Officers: Matthew Giles Barker [1985] Director/Partner, 3i Infrastructure; Tom Joeri Bellekens [1978] Director/Chief Executive Officer [Belgian]; Benoit Biebuyck [1972] Director/Manager [Belgian]; Harold Marie Jean-Loup D'Hauteville [1976] Investment Director [French]; Walter Manara [1980] Investment Director [Italian]; Celine Marie Maronne [1987] Director [French]; Aparna Narain [1985] Director; Bernardo Sottomayor [1978] Director/Partner, 3i Infrastructure [Portuguese]

Envol Midco Limited
Incorporated: 21 April 2016 *Employees:* 8
Net Worth: £31,385,488 *Total Assets:* £349,720,608
Registered Office: 6th Floor, 65 Gresham Street, London, EC2V 7NQ
Activities: Activities of other holding companies n.e.c.
Officers: Matthew Giles Barker [1985] Director/Partner, 3i Infrastructure; Tom Joeri Bellekens [1978] Director/Chief Executive Officer [Belgian]; Benoit Biebuyck [1972] Director/Manager [Belgian]; Harold Marie Jean-Loup D'Hauteville [1976] Investment Director [French]; Walter Manara [1980] Investment Director [Italian]; Celine Marie Maronne [1987] Director [French]; Aparna Narain [1985] Director; Bernardo Sottomayor [1978] Director/Partner, 3i Infrastructure [Portuguese]

EP Langage Limited
Incorporated: 10 November 1997 *Employees:* 54
Previous: Centrica Langage Limited
Net Worth: £30,317,000 *Total Assets:* £197,620,992
Registered Office: Berger House, 36-38 Berkeley Square, London, W1J 5AE
Activities: Production of electricity
Parent: EP UK Investments Ltd
Officers: John Marcus Nettelton, Secretary; Tarloke Singh Bains [1968] Director/Chartered Accountant; Pavel Horsky [1973] Director/Chief Financial Officer [Czech]; Victoria Rose Pearson [1985] Director; Jan Springl [1978] Director [Czech]; Marek Spurny [1974] Director/Head of Legal Counsel [Czech]; Antonia Charlotte Stockton [1988] Director

EP SHB Limited
Incorporated: 2 January 1991 *Employees:* 77
Previous: Centrica SHB Limited
Net Worth: £57,118,000 *Total Assets:* £176,960,992
Registered Office: Berger House, 36-38 Berkeley Square, London, W1J 5AE
Activities: Production of electricity
Parent: EP UK Investments Ltd
Officers: John Marcus Nettelton, Secretary; Tarloke Singh Bains [1968] Director/Chartered Accountant; Pavel Horsky [1973] Director/Chief Financial Officer [Czech]; Victoria Rose Pearson [1985] Director; Jan Springl [1978] Director [Czech]; Marek Spurny [1974] Director/Head of Legal Counsel [Czech]; Antonia Charlotte Stockton [1988] Director

Epic (No. 1) Limited
Incorporated: 27 June 2014 *Employees:* 4
Net Worth: £141,012,000 *Total Assets:* £198,796,000
Registered Office: Level 13, Broadgate Tower, 20 Primrose Street, London, EC2A 2EW
Activities: Activities of real estate investment trusts
Parent: Ediston Property Investment Company PLC
Officers: Robert Archibald [1959] Director; Robert John Westwater Dick [1955] Director; William Anthony Hill [1960] Director/Chartered Surveyor; Colin James Marshall Skinner [1961] Director/Fund Management

Epihiro PLC
Incorporated: 10 March 2009
Net Worth: £17,415 *Total Assets:* £1,631,506,432
Registered Office: Third Floor, 1 King's Arms Yard, London, EC2R 7AF
Activities: Other business support service activities n.e.c.
Parent: Epihiro Holdings Limited
Officers: Robert Sutton [1978] Director/Financial Services [American]; Daniel Jonathan Wynne [1970] Director

Eponymousco Limited
Incorporated: 29 April 1994
Net Worth: £240,966,624 *Total Assets:* £519,028,768
Registered Office: 11 Grosvenor Place, London, SW1X 7HH
Activities: Activities of head offices
Parent: Petropavlovsk PLC
Officers: Amanda Whalley, Secretary; Natalia Buynova [1976] Director/Group Head of Corporate Reporting [Russian]; Alexei Maslovsky [1979] Director [Russian]; Dr Alfiya Samokhvalova [1967] Director/Deputy Chief Executive Strategic Development; Anna Karolina Subczynska-Samberger [1978] Director/Lawyer

Equifax EUA Limited
Incorporated: 26 February 2010
Net Worth: £65,695,000 *Total Assets:* £231,827,008
Registered Office: Capital House, 25 Chapel Street, London, NW1 5DS
Activities: Other business support service activities n.e.c.
Parent: Equifax Inc
Officers: Suzanne Helen Brown [1978] Finance Director; Patricio Remon [1971] Director [Spanish]

Equinix (UK) Limited
Incorporated: 18 November 1998 *Employees:* 276
Net Worth: £221,342,000 *Total Assets:* £729,064,000
Registered Office: Masters House, 107 Hammersmith Road, London, W14 0QH
Activities: Other business support service activities n.e.c.
Parent: Equinix, Inc.
Officers: Russell Alan Poole [1969] Director/General Manager; Eric Charles Schwartz [1966] Director [American]

Equinor New Energy Limited
Incorporated: 19 February 2009
Previous: Statoil Wind Limited
Net Worth: £737,713,984 *Total Assets:* £740,041,984
Registered Office: 1 Kingdom Street, London, W2 6BD
Activities: Activities of head offices
Parent: Wind Power AS
Officers: Anthony Joseph Saul, Secretary; Halfdan Brustad [1960] Director/Vice President [Norwegian]; Stephen Martin Bull [1972] Director/Senior Vice President; Beate Myking [1966] Director/SVP New Energy Operations [Norwegian]; Joyce Wong [1965] Director/Advisor Finance

Equinor UK Limited
Incorporated: 10 November 1976 *Employees:* 317
Previous: Statoil (U.K.) Limited
Net Worth: £1,659,360,000 *Total Assets:* £3,237,627,904
Registered Office: 1 Kingdom Street, London, W2 6BD
Activities: Extraction of natural gas
Parent: Equinor ASA
Officers: Anthony Joseph Saul, Secretary; Robert Stephen Adams [1969] Director/Vice President - Finance and Control; Hedda Felin [1978] Director/SVP DPI UK [Norwegian]; Helge Haugane [1978] Director/VP Finance and Control [Norwegian]; Jenny Elizabeth Morris [1975] Director/Exploration Manager UKCS; Beate Myking [1966] Director/SVP NES Operations [Norwegian]; Uno Holm Rognli [1959] Project Director [Norwegian]; Svein Skeie [1967] Director [Norwegian]

Equion Energia Limited
Incorporated: 5 June 1959 *Employees:* 315
Net Worth: £319,242,496 *Total Assets:* £445,565,440
Registered Office: Suite 1, 3rd Floor, 11-12 St James's Square, London, SW1Y 4LB
Activities: Extraction of crude petroleum
Shareholders: Ecopetrol S.A; Talisman Colombia Holdco Limited
Officers: Luis Antonio Garcia Sanchez [1960] Director/Lawyer - Economist [Spanish]; Hector Manosalva Rojas [1962] Director [Colombian]; Evandro Correa Nacul [1956] Director [Brazilian]; Alberto Vargas Penalosa [1958] Director/Corporate Control & Reporting Manager [Colombian]; Camilo Ernesto Vela Villota [1969] Director/D&P Legal Manager [Colombian]

Equitas Holdings Limited
Incorporated: 5 December 1995 *Employees:* 1
Net Worth: £83,000,000 *Total Assets:* £4,502,000,128
Registered Office: 4th Floor, 8 Fenchurch Place, London, EC3M 4AJ
Activities: Activities of head offices
Officers: William Patrick Robertson, Secretary; Jane Victoria Barker [1949] Director/Chartered Accountant; Glenn Edward Brace [1961] Director/Lawyer [American]; Michael Eunan McLarnon Deeny [1944] Director/Company Chairman; Jeremy Wilfrid Heap [1961] Director/Chartered Accountant; John David Parry [1963] Director/Chartered Accountant; Sir Adam Nicholas Ridley [1942] Director; David Endon Stuart Shipley [1955] Director; Richard Brett Spooner [1946] Director

Equitas Limited
Incorporated: 11 March 1996
Net Worth: £41,000,000 *Total Assets:* £4,470,000,128
Registered Office: 4th Floor, 8 Fenchurch Place, London, EC3M 4AJ
Activities: Non-life reinsurance
Parent: Equitas Reinsurance Limited
Officers: William Patrick Robertson, Secretary; Jane Victoria Barker [1949] Director/Chartered Accountant; Glenn Edward Brace [1961] Director/Lawyer [American]; Michael Eunan McLarnon Deeny [1944] Director/Company Chairman; Jeremy Wilfrid Heap [1961] Director/Chartered Accountant; John David Parry [1963] Director/Chartered Accountant; Sir Adam Nicholas Ridley [1942] Director; David Endon Stuart Shipley [1955] Director; Richard Brett Spooner [1946] Director

Equitas Reinsurance Limited
Incorporated: 5 December 1995
Net Worth: £46,000,000 *Total Assets:* £4,464,999,936
Registered Office: 4th Floor, 8 Fenchurch Place, London, EC3M 4AJ
Activities: Non-life reinsurance
Parent: Equitas Insurance Limited
Officers: William Patrick Robertson, Secretary; Jane Victoria Barker [1949] Director/Chartered Accountant; Glenn Edward Brace [1961] Director/Lawyer [American]; Michael Eunan McLarnon Deeny [1944] Director/Company Chairman; Jeremy Wilfrid Heap [1961] Director/Chartered Accountant; John David Parry [1963] Director/Chartered Accountant; Sir Adam Nicholas Ridley [1942] Director; David Endon Stuart Shipley [1955] Director; Richard Brett Spooner [1946] Director

Equitix Capital Eurobond 2 Limited
Incorporated: 24 November 2010
Net Worth: £145,846,000 *Total Assets:* £612,945,024
Registered Office: 10-11 Charterhouse Square, London, EC1M 6EH
Activities: Activities of head offices
Parent: Equitis Holdings Ltd
Officers: Hugh Barnabas Crossley [1973] Director; Geoffrey Allan Jackson [1954] Director; Jonathan Charles Smith [1980] Director

Equitix Capital Eurobond 3 Limited
Incorporated: 5 March 2013
Net Worth Deficit: £4,713,000 *Total Assets:* £629,918,976
Registered Office: 10-11 Charterhouse Square, London, EC1M 6EH
Activities: Financial intermediation not elsewhere classified
Parent: Equitix Holdings Limited
Officers: Hugh Barnabas Crossley [1973] Director; Geoffrey Allan Jackson [1954] Director; Sion Laurence Jones [1974] Director; Jonathan Charles Smith [1980] Director

Equitix Capital Eurobond 4 Limited
Incorporated: 12 October 2015
Net Worth Deficit: £5,069,000 *Total Assets:* £555,246,016
Registered Office: Welken House, 10-11 Charterhouse Square, London, EC1M 6EH
Activities: Other business support service activities n.e.c.
Officers: Hugh Barnabas Crossley [1973] Director; Geoffrey Allan Jackson [1954] Director; Jonathan Charles Smith [1980] Director

Equitix Capital Eurobond Limited
Incorporated: 4 November 2008
Net Worth: £21,100,000 *Total Assets:* £204,604,992
Registered Office: 10-11 Charterhouse Square, London, EC1M 6EH
Activities: Financial intermediation not elsewhere classified
Parent: Equitix Holdings Ltd
Officers: Hugh Barnabas Crossley, Secretary; Hugh Barnabas Crossley [1973] Director; Geoffrey Allan Jackson [1954] Director; Jonathan Charles Smith [1980] Director

Equitix Healthcare 2 Limited
Incorporated: 11 May 2011
Net Worth: £92,758,000 *Total Assets:* £278,769,984
Registered Office: 10-11 Charterhouse Square, London, EC1M 6EH
Activities: Activities of head offices
Parent: Equitix Capital Eurobond 2 Ltd
Officers: Hugh Barnabas Crossley [1973] Director; Geoffrey Allan Jackson [1954] Director; Jonathan Charles Smith [1980] Director

Equitix Healthcare Limited
Incorporated: 17 September 2007
Net Worth: £70,615,000 *Total Assets:* £131,300,000
Registered Office: 10-11 Charterhouse Square, London, EC1M 6EH
Activities: Activities of other holding companies n.e.c.
Parent: Equitix Capital Eurobond Ltd
Officers: Jonathan Charles Smith, Secretary; Hugh Barnabas Crossley [1973] Director; Geoffrey Allan Jackson [1954] Director; Jonathan Charles Smith [1980] Director

Equitix Highways 2 Limited
Incorporated: 24 November 2010
Net Worth Deficit: £1,573,000 *Total Assets:* £124,025,000
Registered Office: 10-11 Charterhouse Square, London, EC1M 6EH
Activities: Activities of head offices
Parent: Equitix Capital Eurobond 2 Ltd
Officers: Hugh Barnabas Crossley [1973] Director; Geoffrey Allan Jackson [1954] Director; Sion Laurence Jones [1974] Director; Jonathan Charles Smith [1980] Director

Equitix Infrastructure 3 Limited
Incorporated: 18 November 2013
Net Worth: £69,893,000 *Total Assets:* £403,036,000
Registered Office: Welken House, 10-11 Charterhouse Square, London, EC1M 6EH
Activities: Financial intermediation not elsewhere classified
Parent: Equitix Capital Eurobond 3 Limited
Officers: Hugh Barnabas Crossley [1973] Director; Geoffrey Allan Jackson [1954] Director; Sion Laurence Jones [1974] Director; Jonathan Charles Smith [1980] Director

Equitix Infrastructure 4 Limited
Incorporated: 14 October 2015
Net Worth: £12,027,000 *Total Assets:* £519,571,008
Registered Office: Welken House, 10-11 Charterhouse Square, London, EC1M 6EH
Activities: Activities of financial services holding companies
Officers: Hugh Barnabas Crossley [1973] Director; Geoffrey Allan Jackson [1954] Director; Jonathan Charles Smith [1980] Director

Equitix MA 2 Capital Eurobond Limited
Incorporated: 16 December 2016
Net Worth Deficit: £1,902,000 *Total Assets:* £100,230,000
Registered Office: Welken House, 10-11 Charterhouse Square, London, EC1M 6EH
Activities: Activities of other holding companies n.e.c.
Parent: Equitix Holdings Ltd
Officers: Hugh Barnabas Crossley [1973] Director; Geoffrey Allan Jackson [1954] Director; Jonathan Charles Smith [1980] Director

Equitix Offshore 2 Limited
Incorporated: 20 October 2017
Net Worth: £57,735,000 *Total Assets:* £134,352,000
Registered Office: 5th Floor, 120 Aldersgate Street, London, EC1A 4JQ
Activities: Activities of production holding companies
Shareholders: Equitix MA 1 LP; Equitix Fund IV LP
Officers: Hugh Barnabas Crossley [1973] Director; Adam Charles Peel Irwin [1987] Director; Pablo Saavedra [1978] Director [Spanish]

Equitix Offshore 3 Limited
Incorporated: 20 October 2017
Net Worth: £92,316,000 *Total Assets:* £213,960,000
Registered Office: 5th Floor, 120 Aldersgate Street, London, EC1A 4JQ
Activities: Activities of production holding companies
Shareholders: Equitix Fund IV LP; Offshore Wind Investments Group Limited
Officers: Hugh Barnabas Crossley, Secretary; Hugh Barnabas Crossley [1973] Director; Robert John Fradley [1973] Director; Pablo Saavedra [1978] Director [Spanish]

Equitix Offshore 4 Limited
Incorporated: 20 October 2017
Net Worth: £92,316,000 *Total Assets:* £213,960,000
Registered Office: 5th Floor, 120 Aldersgate Street, London, EC1A 4JQ
Activities: Activities of production holding companies
Shareholders: Equitix Fund IV LP; Offshore Wind Investments Group Limited
Officers: Hugh Barnabas Crossley [1973] Director; Robert John Fradley [1973] Director; Pablo Saavedra [1978] Director [Spanish]

Equitix Offshore 5 Limited
Incorporated: 20 October 2017
Net Worth: £89,932,000 *Total Assets:* £566,507,008
Registered Office: 5th Floor, 120 Aldersgate Street, London, EC1A 4JQ
Activities: Activities of production holding companies
Shareholders: Equitix Fund IV LP; Offshore Wind Investments Group Limited
Officers: Hugh Barnabas Crossley [1973] Director; Robert John Fradley [1973] Director; Pablo Saavedra [1978] Director [Spanish]

Equitix Orbital Holdings Limited
Incorporated: 23 September 2016
Net Worth: £1,875,000 *Total Assets:* £179,810,000
Registered Office: Welken House, 10-11 Charterhouse Square, London, EC1M 6EH
Activities: Activities of construction holding companies
Parent: Equitix Infrastructure 4 Limited
Officers: Hugh Barnabas Crossley [1973] Director; Geoffrey Allan Jackson [1954] Director; Jonathan Charles Smith [1980] Director

Equity Release Funding (No.1) PLC
Incorporated: 20 September 2000
Net Worth: £33,000 *Total Assets:* £321,140,992
Registered Office: Third Floor, 1 King's Arms Yard, London, EC2R 7AF
Activities: Other business support service activities n.e.c.
Parent: Equity Release Holdings Limited
Officers: Robert Sutton [1978] Director/Financial Services [American]; Daniel Jonathan Wynne [1970] Director

Equity Release Funding (No.2) PLC
Incorporated: 11 April 2002
Net Worth: £41,000 *Total Assets:* £465,556,992
Registered Office: Third Floor, 1 King's Arms Yard, London, EC2R 7AF
Activities: Other business support service activities n.e.c.
Parent: Equity Release Holdings Limited
Officers: Robert Sutton [1978] Director/Financial Services [American]; Daniel Jonathan Wynne [1970] Director

Equity Release Funding (No.3) PLC
Incorporated: 18 March 2003
Net Worth: £51,000 *Total Assets:* £649,414,016
Registered Office: Third Floor, 1 King's Arms Yard, London, EC2R 7AF
Activities: Other business support service activities n.e.c.
Parent: Equity Release Holdings Limited
Officers: Robert Sutton [1978] Director/Financial Services [American]; Daniel Jonathan Wynne [1970] Director

Equity Release Funding (No.4) PLC
Incorporated: 5 December 2003
Net Worth: £53,000 *Total Assets:* £736,700,992
Registered Office: Third Floor, 1 King's Arms Yard, London, EC2R 7AF
Activities: Other business support service activities n.e.c.
Officers: Robert Sutton [1978] Director/Financial Kingdom [American]; Daniel Jonathan Wynne [1970] Director

Equity Release Funding (No.5) PLC
Incorporated: 30 June 2005
Net Worth: £38,000 *Total Assets:* £554,608,000
Registered Office: Third Floor, 1 King's Arms Yard, London, EC2R 7AF
Activities: Other business support service activities n.e.c.
Parent: Equity Release Holdings (No. 5) Limited
Officers: Robert Sutton [1978] Director/Financial Services [American]; Daniel Jonathan Wynne [1970] Director

Equity Release Holdings (No. 5) Limited
Incorporated: 27 June 2005
Net Worth: £25,000 *Total Assets:* £554,595,008
Registered Office: Third Floor, 1 King's Arms Yard, London, EC2R 7AF
Activities: Other business support service activities n.e.c.
Officers: Robert Sutton [1978] Director/Financial Services [American]; Daniel Jonathan Wynne [1970] Director

Equity Release Holdings Limited
Incorporated: 21 August 2000
Net Worth: £86,000 *Total Assets:* £1,436,112,000
Registered Office: Third Floor, 1 King's Arms Yard, London, EC2R 7AF
Activities: Other business support service activities n.e.c.
Shareholders: Angela Icolaro; Wilmington Trust SP Services (London) Limited
Officers: Robert Sutton [1978] Director/Financial Services [American]; Daniel Jonathan Wynne [1970] Director

ERM Emilion Limited
Incorporated: 10 June 2015
Net Worth Deficit: £14,087,817 *Total Assets:* £791,106,432
Registered Office: 2nd Floor, Exchequer Court, 33 St Mary Axe, London, EC3A 8AA
Activities: Activities of head offices
Parent: ERM Worldwide Group Limited
Officers: Roy Burrows, Secretary; John George Alexander [1961] Director; Simon Paul Crowe [1967] Director/Chief Financial Officer; Keryn Lee James [1968] Director [Australian]; David James McArthur [1964] Director

ERM Worldwide Group Limited
Incorporated: 10 June 2015 *Employees:* 4,403
Net Worth Deficit: £267,658,512 *Total Assets:* £1,651,917,440
Registered Office: 2nd Floor, Exchequer Court, St Mary Axe, London, EC3A 8AA
Activities: Activities of head offices
Officers: Roy Burrows, Secretary; John George Alexander [1961] Director; Simon Paul Crowe [1967] Director/Chief Financial Officer; Shawn Doherty [1964] Director [American]; Keryn Lee James [1968] Director [Australian]; David James McArthur [1964] Director; John Mogford [1953] Director; Jonathan Mussellwhite [1967] Director/Private Equity Executive; Peter James Teti [1967] Director/Senior Vice President Private Equity and Relationship Investment [Canadian]

Ernst & Young (Asia-Pacific) Services Limited
Incorporated: 29 April 2010
Total Assets: £312,475,456
Registered Office: 6 More London Place, London, SE1 2DA
Activities: Accounting and auditing activities
Parent: EYGS LLP
Officers: Andy Yiu Leung Cheung [1959] Director/Partner in Accounting Firm [Canadian]; Herman de Ruijter [1961] Director/Partner in Accounting Firm [Dutch]; David Nelson Holtze [1958] Director/Partner in Accounting Firm [American]; Louis Peter Pagnutti [1958] Director/Partner in Accounting Firm [Canadian]; Patrick Douglas Winter [1964] Director/Partner in Accounting Firm [Australian]

Ernst & Young (EMEIA) Services Limited
Incorporated: 6 June 2008
Total Assets: £958,624,448
Registered Office: 6 More London Place, London, SE1 2DA
Activities: Accounting and auditing activities
Parent: EYGS LLP
Officers: Herve Labaude, Secretary; Andrew James Baldwin [1966] Director/Partner in Accounting Firm; Dr Oliver Graf [1962] Director [German]; David Nelson Holtze [1958] Director/Partner in Accounting Firm [American]; Herve Labaude [1957] Director/Lawyer [French]; Louis Peter Pagnutti [1958] Director/Partner in Accounting Firm [Canadian]

Ernst & Young Accountants LLP
Incorporated: 14 March 2008 *Employees:* 2,743
Total Assets: £163,074,656
Registered Office: 6 More London Place, London, SE1 2DA

Ernst & Young LLP
Incorporated: 6 April 2001 *Employees:* 14,501
Net Worth: £284,000,000 *Total Assets:* £1,138,000,000
Registered Office: 1 More London Place, London, SE1 2AF
Officers: Lisa Gwen Cameron [1968] Member; Lynn Stacey Rattigan [1965] Member; Stephen Andrew Varley [1968] Member; Richard John Abbey [1970] LLP Member; John Philip Abbot [1962] LLP Member; Lynda Julia Abel [1974] LLP Member; James Alexander Abery [1965] LLP Member; Shaun Nicholas Abueita [1978] LLP Member; Richard John Julian Addison [1961] LLP Member; Robin William Aitchison [1957] LLP Member; Michael-John Albert [1967] LLP Member; Charles Philip Alexander [1971] LLP Member; Omar Ali [1977] LLP Member; Syed Muhammed Faizul Ali [1976] LLP Member; Mark Anthony Allcroft [1974] LLP Member; Sophie Elizabeth Allen [1978] LLP Member; Peter Ames [1972] LLP Member; Alasdair Graeme Neil Anderson [1982] LLP Member; Gareth Anderson [1971] LLP Member; Jonathan Edward Leslie Anderson [1966] LLP Member; Anna Anthony [1977] LLP Member; Peter Geoffrey Arnold [1978] LLP Member; Caroline Elizabeth Artis [1962] LLP Member; Ross Alexander Ashbourn [1978] LLP Member; Lisa Ashe [1968] LLP Member; Simon Atherton [1967] LLP Member; Robert Charles Bradley Atkinson [1973] LLP Member; Sunny Aurora [1981] LLP Member; Jolyon Austin [1964] LLP Member; Christine Aymard-Fairclough [1965] LLP Member; Nicholas Bacon [1963] LLP Member; Ian Jonathan Jordan Baggs [1966] LLP Member; Andrew Vivian Bailey [1970] LLP Member; David Francis Baker [1971] LLP Member; Richard John Baker [1966] LLP Member; Paul Bakstad [1977] LLP Member; Andrew James Baldwin [1966] LLP Member; Hywel William Ball [1962] LLP Member; Kathryn Anne Bamford [1970] LLP Member; Stephen James Banks [1966] LLP Member; Mirco Manlio Giacomo Adelchi Bardella [1959] LLP Member; David Michael Barker [1960] LLP Member; Fiona Claire Barnett [1968] LLP Member; Kathryn Lucy Barrow [1971] LLP Member; Matthew James Bartell [1972] LLP Member; James Andrew Bates [1973] LLP Member; Richard Michael Battersby [1970] LLP Member; Graham Ashley Beal [1963] LLP Member; Daniel Sheridan Beard [1982] LLP Member; David John Bearman [1967] LLP Member; Kerstin Beaumont [1973] LLP Member; David Ralph Bedford [1961] LLP Member; Ian Scott Beer [1974] LLP Member; Jon Bell [1974] LLP Member; Steven David Bell [1965] LLP Member; Alexandra Justine Belton [1970] LLP Member; Gregory Ben [1975] LLP Member; Charles Comyns William Berkeley [1971] LLP Member; Jean-Benoit Berty [1966] LLP Member; James Anthony Beszant [1980] LLP Member; Sanjay Bhandari [1968] LLP Member; Gagan Bhatnagar [1968] LLP Member; Rajesh Jayantilal Bhundia [1974] LLP Member; William Thomas Binns [1973] LLP Member; Alexander Mark Birkin [1975] LLP Member; Dr Mona Bitar [1972] LLP Member; Andrew David Black [1979] LLP Member; Amanda Jane Blackhall O'Sullivan [1973] LLP Member; Jon George Blackie [1971] LLP Member; Niall Munro Blacklaw [1964] LLP Member; Andrew Robert Blackmore [1978] LLP Member; Matthew Edward Blaker [1972] LLP Member; Alan Bloom [1955] LLP Member; Rodney Hunten Bonnard [1974] LLP Member; Marc Paul Bourde [1966] LLP Member; Jonathan Bourne [1960] LLP Member; Tracey Ann Bowen Lowe [1964] LLP Member; Christopher Stephen Bowles [1960] LLP Member; Mark Edward Boyle [1977] LLP Member; Martin Kim Bradley [1968] LLP Member; Charles Linton Brayne [1969] LLP Member; Adam James Brocklesby [1981] LLP Member; Andrew Robert Brogan [1966] LLP Member; Karina Elizabeth Brookes [1971] LLP Member; Julian William Howard Broughton [1975] LLP Member; Chris Brown [1968] LLP Member; Colin Macpherson Brown [1971] LLP Member; Dean William Robert Brown [1969] LLP Member; Iain Brown [1966] LLP Member; Lloyd David Brown [1964] LLP Member; Richard Brown [1971] LLP Member; Richard Simon Brown [1966] LLP Member; Paul Adrian Browne [1970] LLP Member; Robert William James Bruce [1978] LLP Member; Gillian Bryant [1962] LLP Member; Laurence George Buchanan [1976] LLP Member; Francesco Buffone [1964] LLP Member; Marc Edward Bunch [1973] LLP Member; Karl-Fredrik Burger [1976] LLP Member; Naomi Burger [1975] LLP Member

Ernst & Young Nederland LLP
Incorporated: 14 March 2008 *Employees:* 3,965
Net Worth: £106,680,328 *Total Assets:* £409,903,776
Registered Office: 6 More London Place, London, SE1 2DA

Eros International Limited
Incorporated: 11 May 1989 *Employees:* 14
Net Worth: £5,961,594 *Total Assets:* £162,765,424
Registered Office: Unit 23 Sovereign Park, Coronation Road, Park Royal, London, NW10 7QP
Activities: Television programme production activities
Parent: Eros Network Limited
Officers: Nidhi Agarwal [1982] Director; Dilip Chudasama [1961] Director

ERPE Finco Limited
Incorporated: 3 July 2017
Net Worth: £8,492,834 *Total Assets:* £347,744,864
Registered Office: Praesidiad, 8th Floor, The Gridiron Building, One Pancras Square, London, N1C 4AG
Activities: Activities of other holding companies n.e.c.
Parent: ERPE Topco Limited
Officers: Jane Elizabeth Douglas [1982] Director/Lawyer [Australian]; Paul Clifford Skertchly [1962] Director

ERPE Topco Limited
Incorporated: 3 July 2017 *Employees:* 1,239
Net Worth Deficit: £21,727,620 *Total Assets:* £787,892,480
Registered Office: Praesidiad, 8th Floor, The Gridiron Building, One Pancras Square, London, N1C 4AG
Activities: Activities of other holding companies n.e.c.
Officers: Andrew Richard Burgess [1964] Director/Investment Professional; Fraser Scott Robson [1980] Director/Investment Professional; Paul Clifford Skertchly [1962] Director; Andrew John Stevens [1956] Director

ERS Corporate Member Limited
Incorporated: 26 October 1994
Net Worth: £53,509,000 *Total Assets:* £682,003,008
Registered Office: 52-54 Leadenhall Street, London, EC3A 2BJ
Activities: Non-life insurance
Parent: ERS Insurance Group Limited
Officers: David Charles Turner, Secretary; Ian David Parker [1965] Director/Chief Executive; Katharine Anne Wade [1973] Director/Chartered Accountant

ERS DGB Limited
Incorporated: 17 December 2012 *Employees:* 682
Net Worth: £105,227,000 *Total Assets:* £702,006,976
Registered Office: 52-54 Leadenhall Street, London, EC3A 2BJ
Activities: Activities of financial services holding companies
Officers: David Charles Turner, Secretary; Jeffrey Wayne Greenberg [1951] Director [American]; Kunal Gujadhur [1985] Director/Finance; Robert Power Gullett [1945] Director/Retired [American]; Patrick Henry O'Sullivan [1949] Director [Irish]; Ian David Parker [1965] Director; Christopher Eric Watson [1950] Director [American]

Esab Holdings Limited
Incorporated: 17 December 1982 *Employees:* 27
Net Worth: £273,316,992 *Total Assets:* £886,091,008
Registered Office: 6th Floor, 322 High Holborn, London, WC1V 7PB
Activities: Activities of head offices
Parent: Cast Limited
Officers: Kevin Francis Atkins [1957] Director; William Flexon [1963] Director/Chartered Accountant [American]; Christopher Michael Hix [1962] Director/Chief Financial Officer [American]; Mark Paul Lehman [1967] Director/Solicitor [American]; Daniel Alexis Pryor [1968] Director [American]

ESB Asset Development UK Limited
Incorporated: 5 June 2009
Net Worth: £96,673,000 *Total Assets:* £207,644,992
Registered Office: Tricor Suite, 4th Floor, 50 Mark Lane, London, EC3R 7QR
Activities: Production of electricity
Parent: ESB Group (UK) Limited
Officers: Brendan Corcoran, Secretary; Jim Caplis [1972] Director/Accountant [Irish]; John Healy [1959] Director/Risk Manager [Irish]; David McNamara [1962] Director/Engineer [Irish]; John Redmond [1955] Director/ESB Secretary [Irish]

ESB Group (UK) Limited
Incorporated: 20 March 2001
Previous: Marchwood Power Development Limited
Net Worth: £140,039,008 *Total Assets:* £165,744,000
Registered Office: Tricor Suite, 4th Floor, 50 Mark Lane, London, EC3R 7QR
Activities: Production of electricity
Parent: The Government of Ireland
Officers: Brendan Corcoran, Secretary; Senan Colleran [1969] Director [Irish]; Mark Fogarty [1973] Director/Accountant [Irish]; John Healy [1959] Director/Risk Manager [Irish]; Caitriona Kinsman [1970] Director/General Manager [Irish]; John Redmond [1955] Director/ESB Secretary [Irish]

ESBII UK Limited
Incorporated: 8 August 2000
Net Worth: £92,956,000 *Total Assets:* £324,580,992
Registered Office: Tricor Suite, 4th Floor, 50 Mark Lane, London, EC3R 7QR
Activities: Activities of other holding companies n.e.c.
Parent: ESB Group (UK) Limited
Officers: Brendan Corcoran, Secretary; Jim Caplis [1972] Director/Accountant [Irish]; John Healy [1959] Director/Risk Manager [Irish]; Siobhan McAdam [1981] Director [Irish]; Michael O'Mahony [1957] Director/Engineer [Irish]; John Redmond [1955] Director/ESB Secretary [Irish]

Eskmuir Properties Limited
Incorporated: 18 June 1990 *Employees:* 7
Net Worth: £145,504,992 *Total Assets:* £264,882,000
Registered Office: 8 Queen Anne Street, London, W1G 9LD
Activities: Other letting and operating of own or leased real estate
Shareholders: Christopher Mark William Aitken; Simon Webley; Nicholas John Treble
Officers: James Arthur Harding, Secretary; Richard John Millard Collier [1945] Director/Business Consultant; James Arthur Harding [1972] Director/Chartered Accountant; Paul Andrew Hodgson [1968] Director/Chartered Surveyor; Christopher Maurice Laing [1948] Director; David Eric Laing [1945] Director/Architect; John Martin Kirby Laing [1942] Director; Nicholas John Treble [1959] Director

Eskmuir Securities Limited
Incorporated: 22 February 2011
Net Worth: £19,544,000 *Total Assets:* £116,250,000
Registered Office: 8 Queen Anne Street, London, W1G 9LD
Activities: Other letting and operating of own or leased real estate
Parent: Eskmuir Properties Ltd
Officers: James Arthur Harding, Secretary; Richard John Millard Collier [1945] Director/Solicitor; James Arthur Harding [1972] Director/Chartered Accountant; Paul Andrew Hodgson [1968] Director/Chartered Surveyor; Christopher Maurice Laing [1948] Director; David Eric Laing [1945] Director/Architect; John Martin Kirby Laing [1942] Director; Nicholas John Treble [1959] Director

Eskom Holdings SOC Limited
Incorporated: 19 October 2006
Net Worth: £6,653,372,928 *Total Assets:* £28,049,713,152
Registered Office: Rooms 625-627, 50 Broadway, London, SW1H 0RG
Officers: Johannes Malesela Phukubje, Secretary; Chwayita Mabude [1969] Director [South African]

Esporta Health & Fitness Limited
Incorporated: 7 December 1994
Net Worth: £18,780,000 *Total Assets:* £280,932,000
Registered Office: 100 Aldersgate Street, London, EC1A 4LX
Activities: Fitness facilities
Parent: Esporta Non Racquets Limited
Officers: James Archibald, Secretary; Matthew William Bucknall [1960] Director; David Anthony Rowland Carter [1970] Finance Director; Robert Barclay Cook [1966] UK Managing Director; Johanna Ruth Hartley [1975] Director

Essar Energy Limited
Incorporated: 18 December 2009 *Employees:* 1,975
Net Worth Deficit: £587,056,320 *Total Assets:* £5,280,370,176
Registered Office: 2nd Floor, Lansdowne House, 57 Berkeley Square, London, W1J 6ER
Activities: Activities of head offices
Shareholders: John Stephen Riches; Richard Edward Douglas; William Edward John Walmsey; Stanley Alan Milgate; Tamara Diane Corbin
Officers: Sushil Kumar Baid [1966] Director [Indian]; Uday Kumar Gujadhur [1955] Director [Mauritian]; Jason Paul Harel [1971] Director/Lawyer [Mauritian]

Esselco Estates Limited
Incorporated: 23 October 2013 *Employees:* 2
Net Worth: £51,904,000 *Total Assets:* £120,163,000
Registered Office: 22 Manchester Square, London, W1U 3PT
Activities: Other business support service activities n.e.c.
Parent: Esselco Group Limited
Officers: Christodoulos Mouskoundi, Secretary; Charles Samuel Dorfman [1983] Director; Lloyd Marshall Dorfman [1952] Director

Esselco Group Limited
Incorporated: 20 December 2013 *Employees:* 9
Previous: Esselco (2014) Limited
Net Worth: £208,080,000 *Total Assets:* £237,924,000
Registered Office: 22 Manchester Square, London, W1U 3PT
Activities: Other business support service activities n.e.c.
Parent: Esselco Limited
Officers: Christodoulos Mouskoundi, Secretary; Charles Samuel Dorfman [1983] Director; Lloyd Marshall Dorfman [1952] Director

Estates & Agency Holdings Limited
Incorporated: 29 May 1957 *Employees:* 12
Net Worth: £165,512,000 *Total Assets:* £247,903,008
Registered Office: 33 Ely Place, London, EC1N 6TD
Activities: Other letting and operating of own or leased real estate
Parent: The Endeavour Trust Limited
Officers: Echo Chong, Secretary; John Stuart Ian Rosefield [1944] Director; Stephen Michael Rosefield [1952] Director/Solicitor; James Winstanley [1963] Director/Accountant

Esterline Technologies Europe Limited
Incorporated: 9 January 2009 *Employees:* 3
Net Worth: £941,493,568 *Total Assets:* £941,664,512
Registered Office: 5 New Street Square, London, EC4A 3TW
Activities: Activities of head offices
Parent: Esterline Technologies Limited
Officers: Stephen Nolan [1969] Director [American]; Curtis Carl Reusser [1960] Director/President and Chief Executive Officer [American]; Albert Scott Yost [1965] Director/Group Vice President [American]

Esterline Technologies Global Limited
Incorporated: 17 April 2014 *Employees:* 2
Net Worth: £243,469,152 *Total Assets:* £287,315,648
Registered Office: 5 New Street Square, London, EC4A 3TW
Activities: Activities of head offices
Officers: Stephen Nolan [1969] Director [American]; Albert Scott Yost [1965] Director/Group Vice President [American]

Esterline Technologies Holdings Limited
Incorporated: 8 June 2004 *Employees:* 3
Net Worth: £1,061,193,984 *Total Assets:* £1,063,425,216
Registered Office: 5 New Street Square, London, EC4A 3TW
Activities: Activities of head offices
Officers: Stephen Nolan [1969] Director [American]; Curtis Carl Reusser [1960] Director/President and Chief Executive Officer [American]; Albert Scott Yost [1965] Director/Group Vice President [American]

Esterline Technologies Limited
Incorporated: 7 September 1999 *Employees:* 3
Net Worth: £897,778,560 *Total Assets:* £897,778,560
Registered Office: 5 New Street Square, London, EC4A 3TW
Activities: Activities of head offices
Parent: TA Mfg Limited
Officers: Stephen Nolan [1969] Director [American]; Curtis Carl Reusser [1960] Director/President and Chief Executive Officer [American]; Albert Scott Yost [1965] Director/Group Vice President [American]

Estia Mortgage Finance II PLC
Incorporated: 25 May 2007
Net Worth: £40,880 *Total Assets:* £539,654,080
Registered Office: Third Floor, 1 King's Arms Yard, London, EC2R 7AF
Activities: Other business support service activities n.e.c.
Parent: Wilmington Trust SP Services (London) Limited
Officers: Daniel Jonathan Wynne [1970] Director

Eucalyptus Energy Holdings Limited
Incorporated: 24 August 2015 *Employees:* 3
Net Worth: £151,598,000 *Total Assets:* £151,603,008
Registered Office: 6th Floor, 33 Holborn, London, EC1N 2HT
Activities: Activities of head offices
Parent: Fern Trading Limited
Officers: Jonathan Charles Nigel Digges [1970] Director; Paul Stephen Latham [1956] Director; Matthew George Setchell [1977] Director/Investment Manager

Eucalyptus Energy Limited
Incorporated: 26 August 2015 *Employees:* 3
Net Worth: £148,204,992 *Total Assets:* £152,976,992
Registered Office: 6th Floor, 33 Holborn, London, EC1N 2HT
Activities: Activities of head offices
Parent: Eucalyptus Energy Holdings Limited
Officers: Jonathan Charles Nigel Digges [1970] Director; Paul Stephen Latham [1956] Director; Matthew George Setchell [1977] Director/Investment Manager

Eunetworks Fiber UK Limited
Incorporated: 22 July 2003 *Employees:* 112
Net Worth: £46,943,520 *Total Assets:* £142,258,368
Registered Office: 15 Worship Street, London, EC2A 2DT
Activities: Other telecommunications activities
Parent: Eunetworks Group Limited
Officers: Richard Henry Taylor, Secretary; Brady Reid Rafuse [1963] Director/Chief Executive Officer; Richard Henry Taylor [1973] Director/General Counsel

Eurasia Finance Management Limited
Incorporated: 19 October 2012
Net Worth: £177,538 *Total Assets:* £113,828,280
Registered Office: 3 London Bridge Street, London, SE1 9SG
Activities: Financial intermediation not elsewhere classified
Parent: E D & F Man Ukraine Investments B.V.
Officers: Jonathan Laurence Hugh [1970] Financial Director

Eurasian Natural Resources Corporation Limited
Incorporated: 8 December 2006
Net Worth: £3,164,871,680 *Total Assets:* £3,585,147,136
Registered Office: 5th Floor, 6 St Andrew Street, London, EC4A 3AE
Activities: Mining of iron ores
Shareholder: Committee of The State Property and Privatization of The Ministry of Finance of The Republic of Kazakhstan
Officers: Felix Jeff Vulis [1955] Director [American]

Euroclear Limited
Incorporated: 7 July 1972 *Employees:* 3,924
Previous: Euroclear PLC
Net Worth: £3,217,063,168 *Total Assets:* £19,288,576,000
Registered Office: 33 Cannon Street, London, EC4M 5SB
Activities: Financial intermediation not elsewhere classified
Officers: Marc Antoine Autheman [1954] Director/Independent Financial Adviser [French]; Nils-Fredrik Nyblaeus [1951] Director/Banker [Swedish]

Euroclear UK & Ireland Limited
Incorporated: 8 December 1993
Net Worth: £103,086,856 *Total Assets:* £116,665,424
Registered Office: 33 Cannon Street, London, EC4M 5SB
Activities: Activities of financial services holding companies
Officers: Jennifer Clare Parker, Secretary; Tom Challenor [1955] Independent Director; Sue Concannon [1955] Director; Yves Dupuy [1967] Director/Group CIO [French]; Robert Charles Anthony Hingley [1960] Director; Peter Sucaet [1959] Director/Head of Strategy & Corporate Planning [Belgian]; Philippe Tromp [1960] Independent Non-Executive Director [French]; John Trundle [1957] Director/Chief Executive Officer

Eurohome UK Mortgages 2007 - 1 PLC
Incorporated: 11 September 2006
Net Worth: £201,194 *Total Assets:* £170,231,984
Registered Office: 35 Great St Helen's, London, EC3A 6AP
Activities: Financial intermediation not elsewhere classified
Parent: Eurohome Mortgages Holdings Company Limited
Officers: Paivi Helena Whitaker [1963] Director/Chartered Secretary [Finnish]

Eurohome UK Mortgages 2007-2 PLC
Incorporated: 16 May 2007
Net Worth: £170,887 *Total Assets:* £235,976,720
Registered Office: 35 Great St Helen's, London, EC3A 6AP
Activities: Financial intermediation not elsewhere classified
Parent: Eurohome Mortgages Holdings Company Limited
Officers: Paivi Helena Whitaker [1963] Director/Chartered Secretary [Finnish]

Euromoney Canada Limited
Incorporated: 30 December 1985 *Employees:* 4
Net Worth: £495,031,968 *Total Assets:* £577,207,040
Registered Office: 8 Bouverie Street, London, EC4Y 8AX
Activities: Activities of head offices
Parent: Euromoney Institutional Investor PLC
Officers: Tim Jonathan Bratton [1972] Director/General Counsel; Sarah Joanne Cooke [1975] Director; Andrew David Himsley [1980] Director

Euromoney Charles Limited
Incorporated: 3 October 2000 *Employees:* 2
Net Worth: £246,377,120 *Total Assets:* £246,377,120
Registered Office: 8 Bouverie Street, London, EC4Y 8AX
Activities: Activities of head offices
Parent: Euromoney Canada Limited
Officers: Tim Jonathan Bratton [1972] Director/General Counsel; Sarah Joanne Cooke [1975] Director

Euromoney Consortium 2 Limited
Incorporated: 8 July 1999 *Employees:* 2
Net Worth: £163,812,432 *Total Assets:* £163,837,984
Registered Office: 8 Bouverie Street, London, EC4Y 8AX
Activities: Activities of head offices
Parent: EII (Ventures) Limited
Officers: Tim Jonathan Bratton [1972] Director/General Counsel; Sarah Joanne Cooke [1975] Director

Euromoney Consortium Limited
Incorporated: 3 October 2000 *Employees:* 2
Net Worth: £165,408,336 *Total Assets:* £361,844,416
Registered Office: 8 Bouverie Street, London, EC4Y 8AX
Activities: Activities of head offices
Parent: Euromoney Charles Limited
Officers: Tim Jonathan Bratton [1972] Director/General Counsel; Sarah Joanne Cooke [1975] Director

Euromoney Institutional Investor PLC
Incorporated: 22 May 1969 *Employees:* 1,992
Net Worth: £493,616,992 *Total Assets:* £781,281,984
Registered Office: 8 Bouverie Street, London, EC4Y 8AX
Activities: Publishing of consumer and business journals and periodicals
Officers: Tim Bratton, Secretary; Janice Babiak [1958] Director; Kevin Joseph Beatty [1957] Director; Timothy Guy Collier [1963] Director; Colin Day [1955] Director; Tristan Patrick Alan Hillgarth [1949] Director; Imogen Joss [1962] Director; Wendy Monica Pallot [1965] Director; Andrew Rashbass [1965] Director; Lorna Mona Tilbian [1957] Director; Philippe Leslie Van de Walle [1956] Director [French]

Euromoney Trading Limited
Incorporated: 14 September 2006 *Employees:* 608
Net Worth: £101,418,000 *Total Assets:* £202,932,000
Registered Office: 8 Bouverie Street, London, EC4Y 8AX
Activities: Activities of head offices
Parent: Euromoney Consortium 2 Limited
Officers: Tim Jonathan Bratton [1972] Director/General Counsel; Rosalind Irving [1970] Managing Director; John Graham Orchard [1969] Director/Publisher

Europe Arab Bank PLC
Incorporated: 27 September 2005 *Employees:* 131
Net Worth: £243,574,736 *Total Assets:* £2,913,797,888
Registered Office: 13-15 Moorgate, London, EC2R 6AD
Activities: Banks
Officers: Andrew David Wilson, Secretary; Quentin Roger Aylward [1946] Director; Haytham Kamhiya [1969] Director/Chief Executive Officer [Jordanian]; Achim Paul Helmuth Klueber [1957] Managing Director Corp & Institutional Banking [German]; Edward Julian Egerton Leigh [1950] Director/Member of Parliament; Eric Jacques Modave [1966] Director/Chief Operating Officer [Belgian]; Nemeh Elias Sabbagh [1951] Director/Chief Executive Officer; Ghassan Tarazi [1964] Director/Chief Financial Officer Head of Internal Audit

European Express Enterprises Limited
Incorporated: 14 September 2005 *Employees:* 1
Net Worth: £184,082,768 *Total Assets:* £253,755,520
Registered Office: 3 Chiswick Park, London, W4 5YA
Activities: Other business support service activities n.e.c.
Officers: Amalia Rodriguez Cosmen, Secretary; Felipe Cosmen Menendez Castenedo [1973] Director [Spanish]; Amalia Rodriguez Cosmen [1971] Director [Spanish]

European Ferries Limited
Incorporated: 12 June 1935 *Employees:* 2
Net Worth: £106,183,032 *Total Assets:* £106,183,032
Registered Office: 16 Palace Street, London, SW1E 5JQ
Activities: Activities of head offices
Parent: Partkestrel Limited
Officers: Mohammad Alhashimy, Secretary; Rashed Ali Hassan Abdulla Al Qahtani Al Qahtani [1971] Director/SVP & MD Europe & Russia [Emirati]; Sarmad Mehmood Qureshi [1970] Director/Chartered Accountant

European Financial Services Limited
Incorporated: 2 March 2017
Net Worth: £145,444,064 *Total Assets:* £155,894,064
Registered Office: 20 Hanover Square, Mayfair, London, W1S 1JY
Activities: Activities of financial services holding companies
Shareholders: Gabriel Anastassiades; Aaron Katsman
Officers: Gabriel Anastassiades [1966] Director/Chairman of The Board [Cypriot]; Aaron Katsman [1970] Director/Member of The Board [Israeli]

European Fintyre Distribution Limited
Incorporated: 16 February 2017
Net Worth: £90,737,856 *Total Assets:* £615,039,424
Registered Office: 6th Floor, Heron House, 15 Adams Street, London, WC2N 6RJ
Activities: Activities of other holding companies n.e.c.
Officers: Giovanni Camera [1983] Director [Italian]; Mauro Pessi [1967] Director [Italian]; Ivano Sessa [1977] Director [Italian]; Dr Michael Franz Siefke [1967] Managing Director [German]; Paolo Massimilano Maria Vismara [1985] Director/Vice President [Italian]

European Investments Solar Holdings Limited
Incorporated: 3 January 2013
Net Worth: £36,429,000 *Total Assets:* £176,799,008
Registered Office: 12 Charles II Street, London, SW1Y 4QU
Activities: Other specialised construction activities n.e.c.
Shareholders: The Renewables Infrastructure Group (UK) Investments Limited; The Renewables Infrastructure Group (UK) Investments Limited
Officers: Emily Mendes, Secretary; Richard Crawford [1963] Director; Jonathan Mark Entract [1972] Investment Director; Philip Roger Perkins George [1971] Portfolio Director; Christopher Paul Gill [1957] Director/Merchant Banker

European Legacy Holdings Limited
Incorporated: 8 January 2015
Net Worth: £153,478,336 *Total Assets:* £153,510,000
Registered Office: 1 Maple Place, London, W1T 4BB
Activities: Activities of financial services holding companies
Officers: Claus Henrik Stenbaek [1961] Managing Director [Danish]; Sasha Van de Water [1968] Managing Director [Dutch]

European Policy Exchange Limited
Incorporated: 19 September 2003 *Employees:* 4
Net Worth: £19,623,268 *Total Assets:* £195,889,216
Registered Office: Amadeus House, 27b Floral Street, Covent Garden, London, WC2E 9DP
Activities: Activities auxiliary to financial intermediation n.e.c.
Officers: Till Heimlich, Secretary; Till Heimlich [1978] Director [German]; Klaus Henke [1969] Director [German]; Sebastian Siebert [1977] Director [German]

European Wind Investments Group Limited
Incorporated: 19 April 2017
Net Worth: £31,649,000 *Total Assets:* £131,152,000
Registered Office: 12 Charles II Street, London, SW1Y 4QU
Activities: Financial intermediation not elsewhere classified
Parent: The Renewables Infrastructure Group (UK) Investments Limited
Officers: Emily Mendes, Secretary; William Richard Crawford [1963] Investment Director; Jonathan Mark Entract [1972] Investment Director; Philip Roger Perkins George [1971] Portfolio Director; Christopher Paul Gill [1957] Director/Merchant Banker

Eurosail 2006-1 PLC
Incorporated: 13 February 2006
Net Worth: £3,047,000 *Total Assets:* £146,992,000
Registered Office: Third Floor, 1 King's Arms Yard, London, EC2R 7AF
Activities: Other business support service activities n.e.c.
Parent: Eurosail 2006-1 Parent Limited
Officers: Daniel Jonathan Wynne [1970] Director

Eurosail 2006-2BL PLC
Incorporated: 30 March 2006
Net Worth: £5,554,000 *Total Assets:* £223,304,000
Registered Office: Third Floor, 1 King's Arms Yard, London, EC2R 7AF
Activities: Other business support service activities n.e.c.
Parent: Eurosail 2006-2 Parent Limited
Officers: Daniel Jonathan Wynne [1970] Director

Eurosail 2006-3NC PLC
Incorporated: 5 September 2006
Net Worth Deficit: £1,204,000 *Total Assets:* £146,248,000
Registered Office: Third Floor, 1 King's Arms Yard, London, EC2R 7AF
Activities: Other business support service activities n.e.c.
Parent: Eurosail 2006-3NC Parent Limited
Officers: Daniel Jonathan Wynne [1970] Director

Eurosail 2006-4NP PLC
Incorporated: 5 September 2006 *Employees:* 4
Net Worth: £1,930,000 *Total Assets:* £231,500,992
Registered Office: Third Floor, 1 King's Arms Yard, London, EC2R 7AF
Activities: Other business support service activities n.e.c.
Parent: Eurosail 2006-4NP Parent Limited
Officers: Daniel Jonathan Wynne [1970] Director

Eurosail Prime-UK 2007-A PLC
Incorporated: 13 September 2007
Net Worth: £1,835,000 *Total Assets:* £117,366,000
Registered Office: Third Floor, 1 King's Arms Yard, London, EC2R 7AF
Activities: Other business support service activities n.e.c.
Parent: Eurosail Prime-UK 2007-A Parent Limited
Officers: Robert Sutton [1978] Director/Financial Services [American]; Daniel Jonathan Wynne [1970] Director

Eurosail-UK 2007-1NC PLC
Incorporated: 15 November 2006
Net Worth: £1,564,000 *Total Assets:* £288,403,008
Registered Office: Third Floor, 1 King's Arms Yard, London, EC2R 7AF
Activities: Other business support service activities n.e.c.
Parent: Eurosail-UK 2007-1NC Parent Limited
Officers: Daniel Jonathan Wynne [1970] Director

Eurosail-UK 2007-2NP PLC
Incorporated: 29 December 2006
Net Worth: £5,934,000 *Total Assets:* £262,463,008
Registered Office: Third Floor, 1 King's Arms Yard, London, EC2R 7AF
Activities: Other business support service activities n.e.c.
Parent: Eurosail-UK 2007-2NP Parent Limited
Officers: Daniel Jonathan Wynne [1970] Director

Eurosail-UK 2007-3BL PLC
Incorporated: 8 May 2007
Net Worth: £12,265,000 *Total Assets:* £246,550,000
Registered Office: Third Floor, 1 King's Arms Yard, London, EC2R 7AF
Activities: Other business support service activities n.e.c.
Parent: Eurosail-UK 2007-3BL Parent Limited
Officers: Daniel Jonathan Wynne [1970] Director

Eurosail-UK 2007-4BL PLC
Incorporated: 29 May 2007
Net Worth: £14,205,000 *Total Assets:* £319,808,992
Registered Office: Third Floor, 1 King's Arms Yard, London, EC2R 7AF
Activities: Other business support service activities n.e.c.
Parent: Eurosail-UK 2007-4BL Parent Limited
Officers: Daniel Jonathan Wynne [1970] Director

Eurosail-UK 2007-5NP PLC
Incorporated: 2 October 2007
Net Worth: £5,055,000 *Total Assets:* £261,942,000
Registered Office: Third Floor, 1 King's Arms Yard, London, EC2R 7AF
Activities: Other business support service activities n.e.c.
Parent: Eurosail-UK 2007-5NP Parent Limited
Officers: Robert Sutton [1978] Director/Financial Services [American]; Daniel Jonathan Wynne [1970] Director

Eurosail-UK 2007-6NC PLC
Incorporated: 8 October 2007
Net Worth: £4,259,000 *Total Assets:* £169,180,992
Registered Office: Third Floor, 1 King's Arms Yard, London, EC2R 7AF
Activities: Other business support service activities n.e.c.
Parent: Eurosail-UK 2007-6NC Parent Limited
Officers: Robert Sutton [1978] Director/Financial Services [American]; Daniel Jonathan Wynne [1970] Director

Eurostar International Limited
Incorporated: 22 January 1990 *Employees:* 1,481
Net Worth: £520,300,000 *Total Assets:* £1,166,099,968
Registered Office: Times House, Bravingtons Walk, London, N1 9AW
Activities: Passenger rail transport, interurban
Shareholders: Patina Rail LLP; Gouvernement de la Republique Francaise
Officers: Gareth Williams, Secretary; Patrick Pierre Bastien [1964] Director Asset Management [French]; James Cheesewright [1962] Director; Hon. Denis Willie Joseph Coderre [1963] Director/Special Advisor, Strategy & International Development [Canadian]; Michael David Cooper [1963] Director; Antoine Dominique Olivier Rene de Rocquigny Du Fayel [1970] Director Finances, Strategy, Legal Affairs [French]; Odile Francoise Fagot [1959] Director/Finance Transformation Officer [French]; Susanne Johanne Given [1964] Director/Chairman [Danish]; Jean-Baptiste Paul Marie Guenot [1973] Director/Head of Corporate Development [French]; Denis Michel Daniel Hennequin [1958] Director/Chief Executive Officer [French]; Clare Margaret Hollingsworth [1960] Director; Renaud Hubert Pierre Lorand [1969] Director/General Manager [Belgian]; Heidi Mottram [1965] Director/Chief Executive Officer; Rachel Picard [1966] Director/Chief Executive Officer [French]; Laurent Etienne Trevisani [1963] Director Finance & Development [French]

Euston Tower Limited
Incorporated: 11 December 2006
Net Worth: £284,065,472 *Total Assets:* £285,184,928
Registered Office: York House, 45 Seymour Street, London, W1H 7LX
Activities: Development of building projects
Parent: Regent's Place Holding Company Limited
Officers: Sarah Morrell Barzycki [1958] Director/Head of Finance; Timothy Andrew Roberts [1964] Director/Chartered Surveyor; Nigel Mark Webb [1963] Director/Chartered Surveyor

Evergreen Marine (UK) Limited
Incorporated: 2 November 1979 *Employees:* 602
Net Worth: £29,847,172 *Total Assets:* £1,162,165,888
Registered Office: Evergreen House, 160 Euston Road, London, NW1 2DX
Activities: Sea and coastal freight water transport
Officers: Chih-Ho Tsai, Secretary; Kuo-Cheng Chang [1960] Director [Taiwanese]; Maurice Storey [1943] Director/Honorary Chairman; Chih-Ho Tsai [1963] Director/Chairman [Taiwanese]

Eversheds Sutherland (International) LLP
Incorporated: 5 March 2003 *Employees:* 3,175
Previous: Eversheds LLP
Net Worth: £166,292,000 *Total Assets:* £285,665,984
Registered Office: One Wood Street, London, EC2V 7WS
Officers: Lisa Louise Barge [1975] Member; Michael Frederick Clavell-Bate [1966] Member; Keith Froud [1970] Member; Jeremy Paul Goodwin [1973] Member; Ian John Basil Gray [1966] Member; Lee Ranson [1964] Member; Pamela Mary Thompson [1956] Member; Frank Achilles [1971] LLP Member; Iftkhar Ahmed [1966] LLP Member; Carl Henry Allen [1981] LLP Member; Matthew James Allen [1971] LLP Member; Stuart Daniel Andrews [1966] LLP Member; Helen Jane Annable [1974] LLP Member; Gareth John Ashfield [1977] LLP Member; Mark Stephen Aspinall [1962] LLP Member; Deborah Attali [1974] LLP Member; Gurjit Singh Atwal [1971] LLP Member; George Bacon [1970] LLP Member; Francois Richard Barker [1964] LLP Member; Ian Kenneth Barker [1969] LLP Member; Paula Barrett [1969] LLP Member; Nicholas Michael Bartlett [1972] LLP Member; Richard John Bachelor [1978] LLP Member; David James Batham [1970] LLP Member; Mark Heric Beardmore [1971] LLP Member; Paul Fergus Beausang [1972] LLP Member; Martin Wolfgang Bechtold [1957] LLP Member; Nicola Jane Bennison [1967] LLP Member; Rupert William Timothy Bent [1972] LLP Member; David John Beswick [1963] LLP Member; Thomas James Birchall [1977] LLP Member; Louise Elizabeth Bland [1975] LLP Member; Nicholas Charles Blane [1965] LLP Member; Wijnand Michael Blom [1974] LLP Member; Daniel Blum [1975] LLP Member; Matthijs Alexander Bolkenstein [1978] LLP Member; Kevin Charles Booth [1960] LLP Member; Franck Bourgeois [1967] LLP Member; Jean Pascal Dominique Boutin [1967] LLP Member; Jonathan Bowley [1971] LLP Member; David James Boyd [1968] LLP Member; Gregory Michael Brandman [1970] LLP Member; Thomas Michael Bray [1976] LLP Member; Alison Fiona Brearey [1962] LLP Member; Thomas Robert Bridgord [1968] LLP Member; Nicola Emma Brookes [1982] LLP Member; Simon David Brooks [1967] LLP Member; Rachel Mary Broquard [1975] LLP Member; Julian Marshall Brown [1967] LLP Member; Nancy Joanne Brown [1965] LLP Member; Carsten Brueninghaus [1962] LLP Member; Mark John Brunton [1964] LLP Member; Michael Andrew John Buchanan [1973] LLP Member; Michael Gregory Buckley [1977] LLP Member; Susan Buckworth [1962] LLP Member; Andrew James Burns [1975] LLP Member; Michael Anthony Burns [1968] LLP Member; Christopher Neal Busby [1972] LLP Member; Neville Paul Byford [1966] LLP Member; Joanne Louise Canning [1975] LLP Member; Claire Elizabrth Carroll [1971] LLP Member; Paul John Castle [1977] LLP Member; Simon Mark Chamberlain [1970] LLP Member; Michel Chatelin [1965] LLP Member; Mark Andrew Chester [1969] LLP Member; Naeema Atta Choudry [1968] LLP Member; Simon Charles Cloke [1980] LLP Member; Stephen John Collings [1961] LLP Member; Kathryn Mair Cook [1966] LLP Member; Nigel Edward Cooke [1981] LLP Member; Paul Edward Coppin [1965] LLP Member; Gaetan Cordier [1977] LLP Member; Paul Christopher Brian Cotton [1968] LLP Member; Jonathan Martin Cox-Brown [1974] LLP Member; James Alistair Cree [1976] LLP Member; Simon Paul Crossley [1966] LLP Member; Mark John Davenport [1972] LLP Member; Anthony George Davies [1972] LLP Member; Ian Hudson Davies [1960] LLP Member; Michelle Thomas Davies [1966] LLP Member; Patrick Michael Davis [1979] LLP Member; Frederique de La Chapelle [1971] LLP Member; Viviane de Moreau D'Andoy [1971] LLP Member; Bruce Robert Dear [1964] LLP Member; Gary Delderfield [1970] LLP Member; Mark Anthony Dennison [1979] LLP Member; Vincent Aurelien Rene Denoyelle [1976] LLP Member; William George Ryan Densham [1975] LLP Member; Catherine Detalle [1979] LLP Member; Dawn Dickson [1976] LLP Member; Stefan Andreas Diemer [1972] LLP Member; Alexander Robert Doughty [1957] LLP Member; Jonathan Douglas [1967] LLP Member; Stephen Dunseath [1970] LLP Member; Paul Nicholas Symon Dutton [1965] LLP Member; Stuart Lloyd Earle [1979] LLP Member; Natalie Rose Edwards [1976] LLP Member; Catherine Jane Eley [1972] LLP Member; Audrey Frances Elliott [1969] LLP Member; Kevin Elliott [1969] LLP Member

Eversholt Funding PLC
Incorporated: 29 July 2010
Net Worth Deficit: £143,684,000 *Total Assets:* £1,995,033,984
Registered Office: 210 Pentonville Road, London, N1 9JY
Activities: Other business support service activities n.e.c.
Parent: Eversholt Finance Holdings Limited
Officers: Michelle Sharma, Secretary; Andrew James Course [1966] Director/Chief Operating Officer and Chartered Engineer; Mary Bridget Kenny [1965] Director; Andrea Justine Wesson [1969] Director/Chartered Accountant

Eversholt Rail Leasing Limited
Incorporated: 5 June 1992
Previous: European Rail Finance (GB) Limited
Net Worth: £79,588,000 *Total Assets:* £2,518,537,984
Registered Office: 210 Pentonville Road, London, N1 9JY
Activities: Financial leasing
Parent: Eversholt UK Rails (Holding) Limited
Officers: Michelle Sharma, Secretary; Andrew James Course [1966] Director/Chief Operating Officer and Chartered Engineer; Mary Bridget Kenny [1965] Director/Accountant; Andrea Justine Wesson [1969] Director/Chartered Accountant

Eversholt Rail Limited
Incorporated: 6 July 2009 *Employees:* 110
Previous: Eversholt Rail (UK) Limited
Net Worth: £125,062,000 *Total Assets:* £2,725,143,040
Registered Office: 210 Pentonville Road, London, N1 9JY
Activities: Other service activities incidental to land transportation, n.e.c.
Parent: Eversholt Rail Leasing Limited
Officers: Michelle Sharma, Secretary; Andrew James Course [1966] Director/Chief Operating Officer and Chartered Engineer; Mary Bridget Kenny [1965] Director/Accountant; Andrea Justine Wesson [1969] Director/Chartered Accountant

Eversholt UK Rails (Holding) Limited
Incorporated: 22 May 2017
Net Worth: £764,470,016 *Total Assets:* £1,107,275,008
Registered Office: 210 Pentonville Road, London, N1 9JY
Activities: Other business support service activities n.e.c.
Parent: Eversholt UK Rail Limited
Officers: Michelle Sharma, Secretary; Andrew James Course [1966] Director; Mary Bridget Kenny [1966] Director; Andrea Justine Wesson [1969] Director

Eversholt UK Rails Limited
Incorporated: 19 May 2017
Net Worth: £764,619,008 *Total Assets:* £1,105,244,032
Registered Office: 210 Pentonville Road, London, N1 9JY
Activities: Other business support service activities n.e.c.
Officers: Michelle Sharma, Secretary; Loi Shun Chan [1962] Director [Chinese]; Andrew John Hunter [1958] Director; Hing Lam Kam [1946] Director [Chinese]; Mary Bridget Kenny [1965] Director; Keith Lawrence Ludeman [1950] Director; Duncan Nicholas MacRae [1970] Director; Wai Che Wendy Tong Barnes [1960] Director

EVRAZ North America PLC
Incorporated: 28 November 2012 *Employees:* 3,395
Net Worth: £982,433,920 *Total Assets:* £2,222,204,928
Registered Office: Suite 1, 3rd Floor, 11-12 St James's Square, London, SW1Y 4LB
Activities: Activities of other holding companies n.e.c.
Parent: EVRAZ PLC
Officers: Alexander Vasiliev [1981] Director Business Coordination & Administration Evaluation [Russian]; Conrad Winkler [1966] Director/President CEO Evraz Inc North America Canada [American]

EVRAZ PLC
Incorporated: 23 September 2011 *Employees:* 76,020
Net Worth: £1,343,879,424 *Total Assets:* £7,819,209,216
Registered Office: 5th Floor, 6 St Andrew Street, London, EC4A 3AE
Activities: Manufacture of basic iron and steel and of ferro-alloys
Officers: Alexander Abramov [1959] Director [Russian]; Laurie Hamilton Argo [1972] Director [American]; Alexander Frolov [1964] Director/Business Executive [Russian]; Karl Gruber [1952] Director/Mechanical Engineer [Austrian]; Deborah Jane Gudgeon [1960] Director/Chartered Accountant; Alexander Izosimov [1964] Director [Russian]; Sir Michael Peat [1949] Director/Chartered Accountant; Eugene Shvidler [1964] Director/Manager [British/American]; Eugene Tenenbaum [1964] Director/Finance [Canadian]

Exane Limited
Incorporated: 6 June 1994 *Employees:* 221
Net Worth: £62,967,640 *Total Assets:* £231,505,600
Registered Office: One Hanover Street, London, W1S 1YZ
Activities: Financial intermediation not elsewhere classified
Parent: Exane SA
Officers: Laurence Philip Adams [1956] Director; Benoit Francois Catherine [1967] Director/Chief Financial Officer [French]; Nicolas Chanut [1959] Director/Chief Executive Officer [French]; Ben Leo Spruntulis [1979] Director/Head of Research

Exelvia Company
Incorporated: 10 July 1996
Net Worth: £125,474,000 *Total Assets:* £125,474,000
Registered Office: 6th Floor, 322 High Holborn, London, WC1V 7PB
Activities: Financial intermediation not elsewhere classified
Parent: Colfax Corporation
Officers: William Flexon [1963] Director/Chartered Accountant [American]; Mark Paul Lehman [1967] Director/Solicitor [American]; Daniel Alexis Pryor [1968] Director [American]; Eileen Annabelle Raperport [1951] Director/Pensions Co-ordinator; Guy Rostron [1960] Director/Chartered Accountant

Exova 2014 Limited
Incorporated: 10 October 2008
Net Worth: £265,100,000 *Total Assets:* £386,700,000
Registered Office: 10 Lower Grosvenor Place, London, SW1W 0EN
Activities: Activities of other holding companies n.e.c.
Parent: Exova Group Limited
Officers: Neil Conway MacLennan, Secretary; Joseph Daniel Wetz [1976] Director; William Thomas Edward Winter [1976] Finance Director

Exova Group Limited
Incorporated: 21 February 2014 *Employees:* 5
Previous: Exova Group PLC
Net Worth: £203,800,000 *Total Assets:* £234,300,000
Registered Office: 10 Lower Grosvenor Place, London, SW1W 0EN
Activities: Other professional, scientific and technical activities n.e.c.
Parent: Greenrock Bidco Limited
Officers: Neil Conway MacLennan, Secretary; Charles Arthur Noall [1959] Director; Joseph Daniel Wetz [1976] Director

Exova Treasury Limited
Incorporated: 15 August 2008
Previous: Exova Limited
Net Worth: £206,300,000 *Total Assets:* £456,400,000
Registered Office: 10 Lower Grosvenor Place, London, SW1W 0EN
Activities: Activities of head offices
Parent: Exova 2014 Limited
Officers: Neil Conway MacLennan, Secretary; Joseph Daniel Wetz [1976] Director; William Thomas Edward Winter [1976] Finance Director

Expedia.Com Limited
Incorporated: 23 September 1999 *Employees:* 1,434
Net Worth: £204,475,616 *Total Assets:* £469,166,080
Registered Office: Angel Building, 407 St John Street, London, EC1V 4EX
Activities: Other business support service activities n.e.c.
Parent: Expedia Group, Inc.
Officers: Robert John Dzielak [1971] Director/Business Executive [American]; Frances Josephine Erskine [1969] Director/Business Executive [American]; Alan Pickerill [1966] Director/Business Executive [American]; Lance Allen Soliday [1972] Director/Business Executive [American]

Experis Limited
Incorporated: 23 March 1987 *Employees:* 340
Net Worth: £68,715,000 *Total Assets:* £171,770,000
Registered Office: Second Floor, 6 New Bridge Street, London, EC4V 6AB
Activities: Temporary employment agency activities
Officers: Mark Anthony Cahill [1958] Director; Mark Joseph Donnelly [1968] Finance Director; Damian Paul Whitham [1967] Commercial Director

Express Newspapers
Incorporated: 2 October 1915 *Employees:* 501
Net Worth: £379,043,008 *Total Assets:* £526,648,000
Registered Office: One Canary Wharf, London, E14 5AP
Activities: Publishing of newspapers
Parent: TM Media Holdings Limited
Officers: Simon Richard Fox [1961] Director/Chief Executive; Simon Jeremy Ian Fuller [1977] Director/Chartered Accountant; Vijay Lakhman Vaghela [1966] Director/Accountant

Exterion Holdings (UK) Limited
Incorporated: 22 August 2007
Net Worth: £178,118,000 *Total Assets:* £178,120,000
Registered Office: 7th Floor, Lacon House, 84 Theobald's Road, London, WC1X 8NL
Activities: Activities of other holding companies n.e.c.
Parent: Doubleplay III Limited
Officers: Anthony John Booker [1970] Director/Consultant; Rupa Pravin Patel [1975] Director/General Counsel

Exterion Media (UK) Limited
Incorporated: 26 October 1993 *Employees:* 384
Net Worth: £89,182,000 *Total Assets:* £169,055,008
Registered Office: 7th Floor, Lacon House, 84 Theobald's Road, London, WC1X 8NL
Activities: Advertising agencies
Officers: Anthony John Booker [1970] Finance Director; Jason Richard Cotterell [1968] Director/Chief Strategy Officer; Rupa Pravin Patel [1975] Director/Lawyer; Leon Taviansky [1970] Director/Chief Operating & Financial Officer

Extraclick Limited
Incorporated: 3 October 2002
Net Worth: £707,744,960 *Total Assets:* £707,752,704
Registered Office: 81 Newgate Street, London, EC1A 7AJ
Activities: Activities of other holding companies n.e.c.
Parent: BT Sixty-Four Limited
Officers: Michael Joseph Mohun [1990] Director/Company Secretary Manager [Australian]; Christina Bridget Ryan [1960] Director/Company Secretary [Irish]

EY Global Services Limited
Incorporated: 17 June 2005
Total Assets: £1,015,152,704
Registered Office: 6 More London Place, London, SE1 2DA
Activities: Accounting and auditing activities
Parent: EYGS LLP
Officers: Sukanta Kumar Dutt [1958] Director/Partner in Accounting Firm [Malaysian]; David Nelson Holtze [1958] Director/Partner in Accounting Firm [American]; Srinivasa Rao Velliyur Nott [1969] Director/Partner in Accounting Firm [Indian]; Louis Peter Pagnutti [1958] Director [Canadian]; Lawrence Thomas Phelan [1962] Director [American]

EYGS LLP
Incorporated: 27 November 2001 *Employees:* 145
Total Assets: £2,327,863,808
Registered Office: 6 More London Place, London, SE1 2DA
Officers: Carmine di Sibio [1963] Member; David Nelson Holtze [1958] Member; Louis Peter Pagnutti [1958] Member

F & C Investment Trust PLC
Incorporated: 15 March 1879
Previous: Foreign & Colonial Investment Trust PLC
Net Worth: £3,668,023,040 *Total Assets:* £3,970,356,992
Registered Office: Exchange House, Primrose Street, London, EC2A 2NY
Activities: Financial intermediation not elsewhere classified
Officers: Sarah Fiona Arkle [1956] Director; Sir Roger Bridgland Bone [1944] Director/President Boeing United Kingdom Limited; Francesca Eva Ecsery [1963] Director; Simon John Fraser [1959] Director/Senior Advisor; Jeffrey Lindsay Hewitt [1947] Director; Beatrice Hannah Millicent Hollond [1960] Director; Edward Stephen Knapp [1983] Director; Nicholas David Moakes [1964] Director/Investment Manager

F & G UK Underwriters Limited
Incorporated: 12 September 1995
Net Worth: £22,310,608 *Total Assets:* £312,447,424
Registered Office: 23-27 Alie Street, London, E1 8DS
Activities: Other business support service activities n.e.c.
Parent: The Travelers Companies, Inc.
Officers: John Matthew Abramson, Secretary; John Matthew Abramson [1961] Director/Solicitor; Michael John Gent [1964] Director/Chartered Accountant

Facebook UK Ltd
Incorporated: 1 August 2007 *Employees:* 1,290
Net Worth: £200,488,224 *Total Assets:* £568,161,024
Registered Office: 10 Brock Street, Regent's Place, London, NW1 3FG
Activities: Advertising agencies
Parent: Facebook, Inc.
Officers: David William Kling [1972] Director/Lawyer [American]; Susan Jennifer Simone Taylor [1968] Director [Canadian]

Factset Europe Limited
Incorporated: 23 April 1999 *Employees:* 444
Net Worth: £101,257,000 *Total Assets:* £114,113,000
Registered Office: Broadgate Quarter, 1 Snowden Street, London, EC2A 2DQ
Activities: Other information service activities n.e.c.
Officers: Rachel Rebecca Stern, Secretary/General Counsel FactSet Research; Andrew Carl Burton [1973] VP, Director - International Human Resources; Mark Anthony Dell'isola [1958] Director/VP, Tax Planning & Compliance [American]; Helen Shan [1967] CFO/Director [American]

Factset UK Limited
Incorporated: 4 January 2005 *Employees:* 17
Previous: Factset Holdings UK Limited
Net Worth: £160,058,752 *Total Assets:* £196,191,344
Registered Office: Broadgate Quarter, 1 Snowden Street, London, EC2A 2DQ
Activities: Activities of head offices
Officers: Rachel Rebecca Stern, Secretary; Andrew Carl Burton [1973] International Human Resources Director; Frederick Philip Snow [1964] Director [American]

Fair Isaac Software Holdings Limited
Incorporated: 19 November 1992 *Employees:* 4
Net Worth: £276,764,192 *Total Assets:* £281,556,352
Registered Office: 5th Floor, Cottons Centre, Hays Lane, London, SE1 2QP
Activities: Activities of other holding companies n.e.c.
Parent: Fair Isaac UK International Holdings Ltd.
Officers: Mark Russell Scadina, Secretary/General Counsel [American]; Richard Shawn Deal [1967] Director/Business Executive [American]; Michael Joseph Pung [1963] Director/Finance Executive [American]; Dean George Sanderson [1964] Finance Director; Mark Russell Scadina [1969] Director/General Counsel [American]

Fair Isaac UK Group Limited
Incorporated: 13 April 2004 *Employees:* 4
Net Worth: £111,306,000 *Total Assets:* £220,262,000
Registered Office: 5th Floor, Cottons Centre, Hays Lane, London, SE1 2QP
Activities: Activities of other holding companies n.e.c.
Parent: Fair Isaac Corporation
Officers: Mark Russell Scadina, Secretary/General Counsel [American]; Richard Shawn Deal [1967] Director/Business Executive [American]; Michael Joseph Pung [1963] Director/Finance Executive [American]; Dean George Sanderson [1964] Finance Director; Mark Russell Scadina [1969] Director/General Counsel [American]

Fair Isaac UK International Holdings Ltd.
Incorporated: 28 July 1988 *Employees:* 4
Previous: Fair Isaac Africa Ltd.
Net Worth: £220,120,384 *Total Assets:* £220,240,928
Registered Office: 5th Floor, Cottons Centre, Hays Lane, London, SE1 2QP
Activities: Information technology consultancy activities
Parent: Fair Isaac UK Group Limited
Officers: Mark Russell Scadina, Secretary/General Counsel [American]; Richard S. Deal [1967] Director/Business Executive [American]; Michael Joseph Pung [1963] Director/Finance Executive [American]; Dean George Sanderson [1964] Finance Senior Director; Mark Russell Scadina [1969] Director/Senior Vice President General Counsel [American]

Fairhold Finance Limited
Incorporated: 19 July 2005 *Employees:* 2
Net Worth: £63,707,232 *Total Assets:* £1,342,543,104
Registered Office: Berkeley House, 304 Regents Park Road, London, N3 2JY
Activities: Buying and selling of own real estate
Officers: Paul Hallam, Secretary; Christopher Charles McGill [1960] Managing Director; William Kenneth Procter [1953] Director/Accountant

Fairhold Homes (No.2) Limited
Incorporated: 17 June 1997 *Employees:* 2
Net Worth: £64,151,040 *Total Assets:* £164,189,712
Registered Office: Berkeley House, 304 Regents Park Road, London, N3 2JY
Activities: Buying and selling of own real estate
Parent: Fairhold Finance Limited
Officers: Paul Hallam, Secretary; Christopher Charles McGill [1960] Managing Director; William Kenneth Procter [1953] Director/Accountant

Fairhold Homes (No.6) Limited
Incorporated: 19 January 1999 *Employees:* 2
Net Worth: £41,243,432 *Total Assets:* £139,234,192
Registered Office: Berkeley House, 304 Regents Park Road, London, N3 2JY
Activities: Buying and selling of own real estate
Parent: Fairhold Finance Ltd
Officers: Paul Hallam, Secretary; Christopher Charles McGill [1960] Managing Director; William Kenneth Procter [1953] Director/Accountant

Fairhold Homes (No.7) Limited
Incorporated: 19 January 1999 *Employees:* 2
Net Worth: £31,693,516 *Total Assets:* £108,357,104
Registered Office: Berkeley House, 304 Regents Park Road, London, N3 2JY
Activities: Buying and selling of own real estate
Parent: Fairhold Finance Ltd
Officers: Paul Hallam, Secretary; Christopher Charles McGill [1960] Managing Director; William Kenneth Procter [1953] Director

Fairhold Homes (No.9) Limited
Incorporated: 19 January 1999 *Employees:* 2
Net Worth: £46,501,496 *Total Assets:* £145,416,416
Registered Office: Berkeley House, 304 Regents Park Road, London, N3 2JY
Activities: Buying and selling of own real estate
Parent: Fairhold Finance Ltd
Officers: Paul Hallam, Secretary; Christopher Charles McGill [1960] Managing Director; William Kenneth Procter [1953] Director/Accountant

Fairhold Homes Investment (No.16) AL Limited
Incorporated: 17 April 2008
Net Worth: £2,727,551 *Total Assets:* £160,106,496
Registered Office: Berkeley House, 304 Regents Park Road, London, N3 2JY
Activities: Buying and selling of own real estate
Officers: Paul Hallam, Secretary; Christopher Charles McGill [1960] Managing Director; William Kenneth Procter [1953] Director/Accountant

Fairhold Homes Limited
Incorporated: 7 November 1990 *Employees:* 2
Net Worth: £58,644,532 *Total Assets:* £144,352,960
Registered Office: Berkeley House, 304 Regents Park Road, London, N3 2JY
Activities: Buying and selling of own real estate
Parent: Fairhold Finance Limited
Officers: Paul Hallam, Secretary; Christopher Charles McGill [1960] Managing Director; William Kenneth Procter [1953] Director/Accountant

Fairhold Services Limited
Incorporated: 25 May 2007 *Employees:* 164
Net Worth: £49,454,380 *Total Assets:* £349,458,400
Registered Office: Berkeley House, 304 Regents Park Road, London, N3 2JY
Activities: Management of real estate on a fee or contract basis
Officers: Paul Hallam, Secretary; Michael John Gaston [1959] Managing Director; William Kenneth Procter [1953] Director/Accountant

Faist Limited
Incorporated: 5 December 1986 *Employees:* 4,264
Net Worth: £108,264,368 *Total Assets:* £320,560,864
Registered Office: 2nd Floor, Whitehall House, 41 Whitehall, London, SW1A 2BY
Activities: Other professional, scientific and technical activities n.e.c.
Major Shareholder: Gianfranco Natali
Officers: Richard Alexander Nava [1972] Director

Falck Renewables Wind Limited
Incorporated: 1 August 2002 *Employees:* 32
Net Worth: £194,966,000 *Total Assets:* £241,327,008
Registered Office: 7-10 Beaumont Mews, London, W1G 6EB
Activities: Other professional, scientific and technical activities n.e.c.
Parent: Falck Renewables SpA
Officers: Patrick Paul Adam [1958] Director/Falck Renewables Spa Planning and Control [Belgian]; Richard Stewart Dibley [1972] Managing Director; William Scott Gilbert [1975] Director/Head of Engineering and Construction; David Picton-Turbervill [1964] Director

Fall Ridge Partners LLP
Incorporated: 21 November 2012
Net Worth: £2,127,437,056 *Total Assets:* £2,357,430,016
Registered Office: The Shard, 32 London Bridge Street, London, SE1 9SG

Fantfoot Limited
Incorporated: 8 July 2005 *Employees:* 4
Net Worth: £274,672,768 *Total Assets:* £454,420,832
Registered Office: 8 Bouverie Street, London, EC4Y 8AX
Activities: Activities of head offices
Parent: Euromoney Institutional Investor PLC
Officers: Tim Jonathan Bratton [1972] Director/General Counsel; Sarah Joanne Cooke [1975] Director; Andrew David Himsley [1980] Director

Faraday Capital Limited
Incorporated: 24 October 1994
Net Worth: £36,033,000 *Total Assets:* £1,255,332,992
Registered Office: Corn Exchange, 55 Mark Lane, London, EC3R 7NE
Activities: Other activities auxiliary to insurance and pension funding
Parent: Faraday Holdings Limited
Officers: Elisabeth Anne Richardson, Secretary; Andrew Michael D'Arcy [1983] Director [Irish]; Kevin James Harker [1972] Director/Accountant; Stephen Andrew Michael [1961] Director

Farfetch UK Limited
Incorporated: 16 October 2007 *Employees:* 367
Net Worth Deficit: £126,650,000 *Total Assets:* £459,999,008
Registered Office: The Bower, 211 Old Street, London, EC1V 9NR
Activities: Retail sale via mail order houses or via Internet
Officers: Elliot Gilbert Jordan [1975] Director/Chief Financial Officer [Irish]; Jose Manuel Ferreira Neves [1974] Director/Business Executive [Portuguese]; Andrew George Robb [1976] Director/Chief Operations Officer

Farmcare Trading Limited
Incorporated: 29 July 2014 *Employees:* 103
Net Worth: £223,006,000 *Total Assets:* £232,788,000
Registered Office: Gibbs Building, 215 Euston Road, London, NW1 2BE
Activities: Mixed farming
Parent: Gower Place Investments Limited
Officers: Carolyn Kloet, Secretary; Robert Anthony Argyle [1974] Finance Director; Elaina Tatem Elzinga [1984] Director/Investment Manager; Peter John Pereira Gray [1963] Managing Director Investments; Richard Quinn [1979] Director/Head of Farms

Farmont Baker Street Limited
Incorporated: 16 May 2005 *Employees:* 12
Net Worth: £105,783,648 *Total Assets:* £177,823,728
Registered Office: 219 Baker Street, London, NW1 6XE
Activities: Development of building projects
Officers: Massimiliano Dall'osso [1965] Director [Italian]

Faroe Petroleum (U.K.) Limited
Incorporated: 28 July 2003
Net Worth Deficit: £92,230,000 *Total Assets:* £107,885,000
Registered Office: 30 Crown Place, London, EC2A 4ES
Activities: Extraction of crude petroleum
Parent: Faroe Petroleum PLC
Officers: Julian Galloway Money Riddick, Secretary; Bjorn Kenneth Dale [1974] Managing Director [Norwegian]; Christopher Thomas Hyde Spencer [1966] Commercial Director; Nicholas John Paul Whiteley [1975] Director/Geoscientist

Faroe Petroleum PLC
Incorporated: 19 December 2002 *Employees:* 80
Net Worth: £226,002,000 *Total Assets:* £743,065,984
Registered Office: 30 Crown Place, London, EC2A 4ES
Activities: Extraction of crude petroleum
Parent: DNO ASA
Officers: Julian Galloway Money Riddick, Secretary/Administrator; Bjorn Kenneth Dale [1974] Managing Director [Norwegian]; Orjan Gjerde [1969] Director/Manager [Norwegian]

FBN Bank (UK) Limited
Incorporated: 12 June 2002 *Employees:* 171
Net Worth: £164,916,368 *Total Assets:* £2,717,581,056
Registered Office: 28 Finsbury Circus, London, EC2M 7DT
Activities: Banks
Officers: Barry Taleghany, Secretary; Dr Adesola Kazeem Adeduntan [1969] Director/Banker [Nigerian]; Oluwatosin Adewuyi [1972] Director/Banker [Nigerian]; Samuel Oladipupo Aiyere [1965] Director/Banking; Katrina Irene Matilda Arnold [1958] Director; Paul Antoon Ludwina Cardoen [1965] Director [Belgian]; Oye Hassan-Odukale [1956] Managing Director, Leadway Assurance Co Ltd [Nigerian]; Dr Oyindasola Oluremi Oni [1961] Director/Banker [Nigerian]; Geoffrey Scott Russell [1958] Director; Ibrahim Dahiru Waziri [1958] Non-Executive Director, Banking [Nigerian]

FC Skyfall Bidco Ltd
Incorporated: 17 June 2014
Net Worth: £155,339,808 *Total Assets:* £852,417,344
Registered Office: Level 37, 25 Canada Square, London, E14 5LQ
Activities: Activities of other holding companies n.e.c.
Parent: FC Skyfall Intermediate Holdco 3 Limited
Officers: Brian Scott Beckwith [1969] Director [American]; Scott Brown [1969] Director/Senior Vice President [American]; David Russ [1972] Director/Senior Vice President [American]

FC Skyfall TA Limited
Incorporated: 3 September 2015 *Employees:* 1
Net Worth: £82,603,864 *Total Assets:* £102,684,560
Registered Office: Level 37, 25 Canada Square, London, E14 5LQ
Activities: Activities of other holding companies n.e.c.
Officers: Chaitanya Bhupendra Patel [1954] Director; David Andrew Smith [1974] Director

FC Skyfall Upper Midco Ltd
Incorporated: 17 June 2014 *Employees:* 13,712
Net Worth: £181,048,992 *Total Assets:* £536,985,984
Registered Office: Level 37, 25 Canada Square, London, E14 5LQ
Activities: Activities of other holding companies n.e.c.
Officers: Brian Scott Beckwith [1969] Director [American]; Scott Brown [1969] Director/Senior Vice President [American]; David Russ [1972] Director/Senior Vice President [American]; David Andrew Smith [1974] Director

FDL Holdings Limited
Incorporated: 9 February 2016 *Employees:* 238
Net Worth: £57,656,536 *Total Assets:* £109,666,792
Registered Office: Metropolitan Wharf, 70 Wapping Wall, London, E1W 3SS
Activities: Activities of head offices
Major Shareholder: Laurence E Hirsch
Officers: Guy Neville Humphry-Baker, Secretary; Stewart Antony Baseley [1958] Director; Jeff Hull [1966] Director [American]; Mac Mardi [1960] Director; Michael Robert Nicolais [1957] Director/President [American]; Charles Calvert Thomas [1982] Director/Vice President [American]

Feldspar 2016-1 PLC
Incorporated: 11 May 2016
Net Worth: £16,053 *Total Assets:* £630,382,080
Registered Office: 35 Great St Helen's, London, EC3A 6AP
Activities: Financial intermediation not elsewhere classified
Parent: Feldspar 2016-1 Mortgage Holdings Limited
Officers: Daniel Marc Richard Jaffe [1975] Director

Fence Bidco Limited
Incorporated: 26 October 2015 *Employees:* 3
Net Worth Deficit: £11,262,000 *Total Assets:* £158,350,000
Registered Office: 5 Fleet Place, London, EC4M 7RD
Activities: Financial management
Parent: Fence Holdco Limited
Officers: Mark Louis Francis, Secretary; Alan John Byrne [1962] Director; Mark Louis Francis [1973] Director; Richard Lawrence Segal [1963] Director

Fence Topco Limited
Incorporated: 26 October 2015 *Employees:* 291
Net Worth Deficit: £15,190,000 *Total Assets:* £169,283,008
Registered Office: 5 Fleet Place, London, EC4M 7RD
Activities: Financial management
Parent: Exponent Private Equity LLP
Officers: Mark Louis Francis, Secretary; Oliver Bradley Bower [1976] Director/Partner; Alan John Byrne [1962] Director; Mark Louis Francis [1973] Director; James Richard St John Lenane [1972] Director/Senior Partner; Mark John Renshaw [1975] Director; Richard Lawrence Segal [1963] Director

Fern Renewable Energy Limited
Incorporated: 29 April 2014 *Employees:* 3
Net Worth: £42,375,000 *Total Assets:* £102,386,000
Registered Office: 6th Floor, 33 Holborn, London, EC1N 2HT
Activities: Other business support service activities n.e.c.
Parent: Fern Energy Limited
Officers: Samuel Goss [1977] Investment Director; David Hastings [1966] Director; Paul Stephen Latham [1956] Director

Fern Trading Limited
Incorporated: 6 December 2007 *Employees:* 331
Net Worth: £1,415,040,000 *Total Assets:* £2,303,143,936
Registered Office: 6th Floor, 33 Holborn, London, EC1N 2HT
Activities: Activities of head offices
Parent: Octopus Investments Nominees Limited
Officers: Peter George Barlow [1953] Director; Paul Stephen Latham [1956] Director; Keith James Willey [1962] Director

Ferrari Group Limited
Incorporated: 9 March 2016 *Employees:* 962
Net Worth: £27,135,032 *Total Assets:* £110,162,824
Registered Office: 43 Grosvenor Street, London, W1K 3HL
Activities: Activities of other holding companies n.e.c.
Shareholders: Marco Deiana; Corrado Deiana
Officers: Corrado Deiana [1976] Director/Entrepreneur [Italian]; Marco Deiana [1970] Director/Entrepreneur [Italian]; Alessandro Scala [1974] Director [Italian]; Alessandro Nicolo' Ugo [1980] Director/Consultant [Italian]

Ferrexpo Finance PLC
Incorporated: 29 September 2003 *Employees:* 715
Net Worth: £1,167,608 *Total Assets:* £639,993,216
Registered Office: 55 St James's Street, London, SW1A 1LA
Activities: Financial management
Parent: Ferrexpo PLC
Officers: Brian McLelland, Secretary; Christopher Mawe [1962] Director; Ingrid McMahon [1976] Director/Investor Relations

Ferrexpo PLC
Incorporated: 22 April 2005 *Employees:* 9,063
Net Worth: £449,041,056 *Total Assets:* £920,370,624
Registered Office: 55 St Jame's Street, London, SW1A 1LA
Activities: Mining of iron ores
Officers: Brian McLelland, Secretary; Stephen Charles Burrard-Lucas [1954] Director; Raffaele Giuseppe Salvatore Genovese [1962] Director [Swiss]; Vitali Lisovenko [1972] Director [Ukrainian]; Christopher Mawe [1962] Director; Lambertus Jozef Gertruda Nacken [1949] Director/Mining Consultant [Dutch]; Mary Reilly [1953] Director; Kostyantyn Zhevago [1974] Director [Ukrainian]

Ferrovial Agroman (UK) Limited
Incorporated: 12 April 2006 *Employees:* 455
Net Worth: £7,157,000 *Total Assets:* £109,373,000
Registered Office: 10th Floor, BSI Building, 389 Chiswick High Road, London, W4 4AL
Activities: Construction of roads and motorways
Parent: Ferrovial Agroman Limited
Officers: Andres Blanco Diez [1971] Finance Director [Spanish]; Ignacio Clopes Estela [1965] Director/Engineer [Spanish]; Mario Mostoles Nieto [1975] Managing Director [Spanish]; Miguel Angel Sagaz Quesada [1968] International Legal Director [Spanish]

Ferrovial Agroman Limited
Incorporated: 1 October 2012 *Employees:* 1,372
Net Worth: £27,144,000 *Total Assets:* £128,450,000
Registered Office: 10th Floor, BSI Building, 389 Chiswick High Road, London, W4 4AL
Activities: Construction of roads and motorways
Parent: Ferrovial Agroman International PLC
Officers: Andres Blanco Diez [1971] Finance Director [Spanish]; Ignacio Clopes Estela [1965] Managing Director [Spanish]; Miguel Angel Sagaz Quesada [1968] International Legal Director [Spanish]

FET Global Holdings Limited
Incorporated: 24 October 2006
Net Worth: £139,963,008 *Total Assets:* £195,666,000
Registered Office: 150 Minories, London, EC3N 1LS
Activities: Activities of other holding companies n.e.c.
Parent: Forum Worldwide Holdings Limited
Officers: John Cornel Ivascu, Secretary; Tylar Kipp Schmitt [1973] Director [American]; David Lyle Williams Jr [1969] Director/Senior Vice President - Operations [American]

Fevertree Drinks PLC
Incorporated: 22 February 2013 *Employees:* 51
Net Worth: £130,084,008 *Total Assets:* £171,789,328
Registered Office: Kildare House, 3 Dorset Rise, London, EC4Y 8EN
Activities: Activities of head offices
Officers: Andrew Branchflower [1979] Finance Director; Domenico John de Lorenzo [1964] Director [Italian]; Kevin John Havelock [1957] Director; Coline Lucille McConville [1964] Director [Australian]; Jeff Popkin [1964] Director [American]; Charles Timothy Rolls [1957] Director of Drinks Company; Timothy Daniel Gray Warrillow [1975] Director/Marketing

FFI Holdings PLC
Incorporated: 30 May 2017 *Employees:* 127
Net Worth: £47,727,908 *Total Assets:* £129,362,168
Registered Office: 15 Conduit Street, London, W1S 2XJ
Activities: Risk and damage evaluation
Shareholders: Steven Arthur Ransohoff; 7Side Nominees Limited
Officers: Stephen Argent [1957] Director; Julian Antony Bartlett [1964] Director; Simon Henry Ingram [1969] Director; Antony Mitchell [1965] Director/Chief Operating Officer; Steven Arthur Ransohoff [1958] Director/Chief Executive Officer [American]; James Dominic Terlizzi [1964] Director [American]

FFP Investment UK Ltd
Incorporated: 27 November 2015
Net Worth: £103,199,184 *Total Assets:* £217,436,064
Registered Office: 2 Duke Street, London, W1U 3EH
Activities: Activities of investment trusts
Parent: FFP
Officers: Frederic Banzet [1958] Director [French]; Sebastien Louis Philippe Coquard [1975] Director/Head of Investments [French]; Bertrand Marcel Henri Marie Finet [1965] Director/Deputy Chief Executive Officer [French]; Bernard Georges Gault [1958] Director [French]; Edouard Andre Gerard Peugeot [1984] Investment Director [French]; Robert Peugeot [1950] Director/Chief Executive Officer [French]; Christian Simon Schlumberger [1949] Director [French]

FGIC UK Limited
Incorporated: 30 January 2004
Net Worth: £68,917,000 *Total Assets:* £145,016,000
Registered Office: Tower Bridge House, St Katharine's Way, London, E1W 1DD
Activities: Credit granting by non-deposit taking finance houses and other specialist consumer credit grantors
Officers: Sarah Elizabeth Ouarbya, Secretary; Derek Marshall Donnelly [1970] Director [American]; Nicholas Anthony Jones [1952] Director/Retired; Philip Charles Sullivan [1955] Director; Timothy Sean Travers [1961] Director/CEO, FGIC UK Ltd & Snr MD [American]; Amedeo Edward Turi III [1958] Director/Senior VP & General Counsel, FGIC [American]

FHH No.1 Limited
Incorporated: 3 December 2003
Net Worth: £224,200,992 *Total Assets:* £224,200,992
Registered Office: Level 20, 25 Canada Square, London, E14 5LQ
Activities: Activities of head offices
Parent: IP Karugamo Holdings (UK) Limited
Officers: Sarah Jane Gregory, Secretary; David George Alcock [1965] Director; Andrew Wilson Garner [1962] Director; Thomas Joseph O'Brien [1968] Director [Irish]; Simon David Pinnell [1964] Director/Accountant

FIA Foundation
Incorporated: 18 May 2001 *Employees:* 14
Previous: FIA Foundation for The Automobile and Society
Net Worth: £364,008,384 *Total Assets:* £370,140,768
Registered Office: 60 Trafalgar Square, London, WC2N 5DS
Activities: Non-trading company
Officers: Earl Wesley Jarrett, Secretary; Jose Abed [1945] Director/President, Omdai ASN Mexico [Mexican]; Marilena Amoni [1954] Director/Retired [American]; Martin David Angle [1950] Director; Nicholas Wesson Craw [1936] Director/President and CEO, ACCUS, FIA Inc [American]; Brian Gibbons [1950] Director/CEO, NZAA [New Zealander]; Alan James Gow [1955] Director/Chairman, Motor Sports Association UK [Australian]; Earl Wesley Jarrett [1960] Director/Accountant/General Manager, JAA [Jamaican]; Werner Kraus [1942] Director/Honorary President, OEAMTC [Austrian]; Augusto Lagman [1939] Director/CEO of AA Philippines [Filipino]; Miquel Nadal [1964] Director/Consultant [Spanish]; Lord George Islay MacNeill Robertson of Port Ellen [1946] Director/Member of UK House of Lords; Graham Kenneth Robert Stoker [1952] Director/Barrister; Jean Todt [1946] Director/President, FIA [French]; Kenneth David Woodier [1952] Director/Retired; Choo Kheng Yeoh [1962] Director/Actress and UN Goodwill Ambassador [Malaysian]

FIA UK Funding Limited
Incorporated: 21 June 2012
Net Worth: £2,917,145,344 *Total Assets:* £2,917,246,464
Registered Office: 2 King Edward Street, London, EC1A 1HQ
Activities: Other business support service activities n.e.c.
Parent: Bank of America Corporation
Officers: Jonathan Howard Redvers Lee [1966] Director/Company Executive; Trevor Caleb Martin [1960] Director/Company Executive

Fiat Chrysler UK LLP
Incorporated: 28 July 2016
Net Worth: £3,636,994,048 *Total Assets:* £3,637,008,640
Registered Office: 25 St James' Street, London, SW1A 1HA

Fiberweb Limited
Incorporated: 22 January 2006
Net Worth: £113,408,000 *Total Assets:* £113,488,000
Registered Office: 35 Great St Helen's, London, EC3A 6AP
Activities: Manufacture of non-wovens and articles made from non-wovens, except apparel
Parent: PGI Acquisition Limited
Officers: Jason Kent Greene [1970] Director/General Counsel [American]; Mark William Miles [1971] Director [American]

Fidelis Underwriting Limited
Incorporated: 28 August 2015
Net Worth: £120,772,920 *Total Assets:* £352,085,216
Registered Office: 34th Floor, The Leadenhall Building, 122 Leadenhall Street, London, EC3V 4AB
Activities: Non-life insurance
Officers: Patricia Roufca, Secretary; Daniel David Burrows [1969] Director/UK CEO Fidelis; Adrian John Reginald Collins [1954] Director/Chairman; Christopher Alan Hawkins [1965] Director/Portfolio Manager; Sharon Julia Ingham [1979] Director/UK CFO; Michael Justin Pearson [1969] Director; Michael Howard Tripp [1955] Director

Fidessa Group Holdings Limited
Incorporated: 6 August 1996 *Employees:* 1,728
Previous: Fidessa Group Holdings PLC
Net Worth: £166,744,992 *Total Assets:* £313,540,992
Registered Office: c/o Ion, 3rd Floor, One New Change, London, EC4M 9AF
Activities: Activities of head offices
Parent: Ion Investment Group Limited
Officers: Anil Manilal Shah, Secretary; Conor Gerard Clinch [1979] Director [Irish]; Ashley Graham Woods [1973] Director/Lawyer

FIL Holdings (UK) Limited
Incorporated: 30 October 2008 *Employees:* 2,697
Net Worth: £281,276,992 *Total Assets:* £798,444,992
Registered Office: 25 Cannon Street, London, EC4M 5TA
Activities: Activities of financial services holding companies
Officers: Peter John Horrell [1968] Director; Kristina Isherwood [1968] Director; Anthony Stephen Lanser [1968] Director/Chief Operating Officer; Dr Dr Teresa Robson-Capps [1955] Director; Dominic Michael Joseph Rossi [1963] Director; Bruce Weatherill [1953] Director; David Avery Weymouth [1955] Director

FIL Investment Management Limited
Incorporated: 20 February 1989 *Employees:* 2,686
Net Worth: £53,689,000 *Total Assets:* £325,124,992
Registered Office: 25 Cannon Street, London, EC4M 5TA
Activities: Fund management activities
Officers: Matthew Alan Heath [1966] Director/Lawyer; Robert Musgrove [1967] Director/Company Secretary; Robert Musgrove [1967] Director/Company Secretary; Sally Rowena Nelson [1964] Director; Christopher Robert Pirnie [1978] Director/Company Secretary

Finance for Higher Education Limited
Incorporated: 7 November 1997
Net Worth Deficit: £74,207,000 *Total Assets:* £111,980,000
Registered Office: 6th Floor, 65 Gresham Street, London, EC2V 7NQ
Activities: Other business support service activities n.e.c.
Parent: The Higher Education Securitised Investments Series (Holdings) Limited
Officers: Sean Peter Martin [1965] Director

Finance for Residential Social Housing PLC
Incorporated: 15 January 1997
Net Worth: £2,793,000 *Total Assets:* £803,032,000
Registered Office: 6th Floor, 65 Gresham Street, London, EC2V 7NQ
Activities: Other business support service activities n.e.c.
Parent: Finance for Residential Social Housing (Holdings) Limited
Officers: Sean Peter Martin [1965] Director

Finance Holdings Limited
Incorporated: 7 October 2005 *Employees:* 5
Net Worth Deficit: £96,340,000 *Total Assets:* £117,486,000
Registered Office: 8-12 York Gate, London, NW1 4QG
Activities: Activities of head offices
Parent: Rubicon Partners Industries LLP
Officers: Jonathan Charles Richardson, Secretary/Director; Joseph Boucher [1983] Director/Chartered Accountant; Andrew Olaf Fischer [1964] Director [German]; Ian Fisher [1950] Director; Alan Thomas Fletcher [1934] Director; Jonathan Charles Richardson [1960] Director

The Financial Conduct Authority
Incorporated: 7 June 1985 *Employees:* 3,561
Net Worth Deficit: £87,300,000 *Total Assets:* £436,200,000
Registered Office: 12 Endeavour Square, London, E20 1JN
Activities: Investigation activities
Officers: Simon Marshall Pearce, Secretary; Dr Andrew Bailey [1959] Central Bank Director; Catherine Annick Caroline Bradley [1959] Director/Banker [French]; Professor Amelia Fletcher [1966] Director/Economist; Baroness Sarah Elizabeth Mary Hogg [1946] Director; Ruth Maria Kelly [1968] Director; Jane Christine Platt [1957] Director/Civil Servant; Charles David Randell [1958] Director/Chairman; Nicholas Charles Stace [1971] Director; Samuel Richard Woods [1973] Director/Deputy Governor of The PRA; Christopher Woolard [1972] Director

Financial Models Corporation Limited
Incorporated: 29 December 1989
Net Worth: £3,529,000 *Total Assets:* £370,591,008
Registered Office: 1 St Martins-le-Grand, London, EC1A 4AS
Activities: Other service activities n.e.c.
Parent: SS & C Technologies Holdings, Inc.
Officers: Normand Augustine Boulanger [1962] Director/Executive [American]; Patrick John Louis Pedonti [1951] Director/Executive [American]

Financial Ombudsman Service Limited
Incorporated: 26 February 1999 *Employees:* 3,016
Net Worth: £229,731,008 *Total Assets:* £284,353,984
Registered Office: Exchange Tower, Harbour Exchange Square, London, E14 9SR
Activities: Activities of other membership organisations n.e.c.
Officers: Julia Cavanagh, Secretary; Gerard Dominic Connell [1958] Director/Chief Finance Officer; Alan Dominique Jenkins [1952] Director/Lawyer; Sir Nicholas Lionel John Montagu [1944] Director; Sienne Nina Veit [1968] Director, Online Product; Baroness Diana Warwick [1945] Director/Peer; Jennifer Watson [1964] Non-Executive Director

Financial Services Compensation Scheme Limited
Incorporated: 3 March 2000 *Employees:* 191
Total Assets: £5,067,403,776
Registered Office: 10th Floor, Beaufort House, 15 St Botolph Street, London, EC3A 7QU
Activities: Other business support service activities n.e.c.
Officers: Mark Lindsay Thomas, Secretary; Mark Keith Adams [1966] Director/Chartered Accountant; Marshall Charles Bailey [1966] Director/Banker; James Alexander Barber [1967] Director/Chief Operating Officer; Steven Martin Cooper [1970] Director/Banking and Payments; Marian Glen [1960] Director; Aleksander Jozef Kuczynski [1965] Director/Solicitor; Charles McKenna [1954] Director/Solicitor; Mark Frost Neale [1957] Director/Chief Executive; Patrick John Neville [1960] Director/Chartered Accountant; Helen Mary Parker [1965] Director/Charity Leader; Kathryn Ann Sherratt [1971] Director/Chief Financial Officer

Financial Times Group Limited
Incorporated: 18 May 1966
Net Worth: £378,208,992 *Total Assets:* £403,223,008
Registered Office: Number One, Southwark Bridge, London, SE1 9HL
Activities: Activities of other holding companies n.e.c.
Officers: Alison Mary Fortescue, Secretary; Franklin Lionel Barber [1955] Director/Editor; James Douglas Lund [1972] Director/Management Accountant; Hirotomo Nomura [1957] Director [Japanese]; Kathleen Mary O'Riordan [1971] Director/Chief Production & Information Officer; John Joseph Ridding [1965] Director

Financial Times Limited (The)
Incorporated: 26 January 1928 *Employees:* 1,291
Net Worth: £88,216,000 *Total Assets:* £252,068,000
Registered Office: Number One, Southwark Bridge, London, SE1 9HL
Activities: Publishing of newspapers
Parent: Financial Times Group Limited
Officers: Alison Mary Fortescue, Secretary; Franklin Lionel Barber [1955] Director/Editor; James Douglas Lund [1972] Director/Management Accountant; Hirotomo Nomura [1957] Director [Japanese]; Kathleen Mary O'Riordan [1971] Director/Chief Production & Information Officer; John Joseph Ridding [1965] Director

Finantia UK Limited
Incorporated: 24 September 1993 *Employees:* 8
Previous: Finantia Securities Limited
Net Worth: £99,888,512 *Total Assets:* £502,953,664
Registered Office: 11 Austin Friars, London, EC2N 2HG
Activities: Security dealing on own account
Shareholder: Antonio Manuel Afonso Guerreiro
Officers: Maria Luisa Falcao Libano Monteiro Antas [1955] Director/Banker [Portuguese]; Antonio Manuel Afonso Guerreiro [1952] Director/Banker [Portuguese]; David Guerreiro [1980] Director/Banking [Portuguese]; Michael John Hamilton [1939] Director/Banker; David Harrison Pfeiffer [1958] Director [British/American]

Finastra Global Limited
Incorporated: 1 November 2011 *Employees:* 206
Previous: Misys Global Limited
Net Worth Deficit: £185,067,856 *Total Assets:* £256,901,760
Registered Office: Four Kingdom Street, Paddington, London, W2 6BD
Activities: Other software publishing
Officers: Simon Peter Dowler [1965] Director/General Counsel; Janet Ruth Hughes [1968] Finance Director; Christian Jehle [1975] Director [German]; Thomas Edward Kilroy [1970] Director/Chief of Staff; Timo Schloesser [1970] Director/Solicitor [German]

Finastra Group Holdings Limited
Incorporated: 29 March 1978
Previous: Misys Limited
Net Worth: £544,968,704 *Total Assets:* £1,149,005,056
Registered Office: Four Kingdom Street, Paddington, London, W2 6BD
Activities: Other software publishing
Parent: Misys International Limited
Officers: Simon Peter Dowler [1965] Director/General Counsel; Janet Ruth Hughes [1968] Finance Director; Christian Jehle [1975] Director [German]; Thomas Edward Kilroy [1970] Director/Chief of Staff; Timo Schloesser [1970] Director/Solicitor [German]

Finastra Holdings Limited
Incorporated: 24 March 1966
Previous: MIBS Holdings Limited
Net Worth: £298,203,360 *Total Assets:* £353,934,336
Registered Office: Four Kingdom Street, Paddington, London, W2 6BD
Activities: Non-trading company
Parent: Finastra Group Holdings Limited
Officers: Simon Peter Dowler [1965] Director/General Counsel; Janet Ruth Hughes [1968] Finance Director; Christian Jehle [1975] Director [German]; Thomas Edward Kilroy [1970] Director/Chief of Staff; Timo Schloesser [1970] Director/Solicitor [German]

Finastra International Limited
Incorporated: 2 February 1970 *Employees:* 444
Previous: Misys International Banking Systems Limited
Net Worth: £99,449,000 *Total Assets:* £406,431,008
Registered Office: Four Kingdom Street, Paddington, London, W2 6BD
Activities: Other software publishing
Parent: Finastra Holdings Limited
Officers: Simon Peter Dowler [1965] Director/General Counsel; Janet Ruth Hughes [1968] Finance Director; Christian Jehle [1975] Director [German]; Thomas Edward Kilroy [1970] Director/Chief of Staff; Timo Schloesser [1970] Director/Solicitor [German]

Finastra UK Limited
Incorporated: 17 August 1984 *Employees:* 145
Previous: Kapiti Limited
Net Worth: £402,136,992 *Total Assets:* £456,341,312
Registered Office: Four Kingdom Street, Paddington, London, W2 6BD
Activities: Other software publishing
Parent: Finastra Holdings Limited
Officers: Simon Peter Dowler [1965] Director/General Counsel; Janet Ruth Hughes [1968] Finance Director; Christian Jehle [1975] Director [German]; Thomas Edward Kilroy [1970] Director/Chief of Staff; Timo Schloesser [1970] Director/Solicitor [German]

Finco Omaha Ltd
Incorporated: 30 May 2014
Net Worth: £1,195,200,512 *Total Assets:* £4,367,323,648
Registered Office: 35 Great St Helen's, London, EC3A 6AP
Activities: Activities of other holding companies n.e.c.
Parent: The Blackstone Group, L.P.
Officers: Nathan Andrew Rogers [1964] Director [American]; Jamey Susan Seely [1971] Director/Executive Vice President [American]; Marc Gregory Swanson [1969] Director/Vice President, Global Tax [American]

Finlay Extracts & Ingredients UK Limited
Incorporated: 21 December 2007 *Employees:* 49
Previous: Finlay Extracts Limited
Net Worth: £67,087,048 *Total Assets:* £199,493,232
Registered Office: Swire House, 59 Buckingham Gate, London, SW1E 6AJ
Activities: Tea processing
Parent: James Finlay Limited
Officers: David Charles Morris, Secretary; Guy Rufus Chambers [1970] Managing Director; Mark Anthony Lawson [1967] Trading Director-Tea; Julian Michael Rutherford [1971] Director/Accountant; Generald Owain Williams [1958] Director/Engineer; Neil Robert Willsher [1962] Managing Director

Finlay Group Limited
Incorporated: 14 December 2001
Net Worth: £203,356,000 *Total Assets:* £278,329,984
Registered Office: Swire House, 59 Buckingham Gate, London, SW1E 6AJ
Activities: Activities of head offices
Parent: John Swire & Sons Limited
Officers: David Charles Morris, Secretary; Philippe Anthony Wynne de Gentile-Williams [1964] Director; Barnaby Nicholas Swire [1964] Director

Finsbury Square 2016-1 PLC
Incorporated: 10 February 2016
Net Worth: £22,000 *Total Assets:* £176,378,000
Registered Office: 35 Great St Helen's, London, EC3A 6AP
Activities: Financial intermediation not elsewhere classified
Parent: Finsbury Square 2016-1 Parent Limited
Officers: Daniel Marc Richard Jaffe [1975] Director

Finsbury Square 2017-1 PLC
Incorporated: 8 December 2016
Net Worth: £31,000 *Total Assets:* £444,004,992
Registered Office: 35 Great St Helen's, London, EC3A 6AP
Activities: Activities of mortgage finance companies
Parent: Finsbury Square 2017-1 Parent Limited
Officers: Daniel Marc Richard Jaffe [1975] Director

Fintry 3 Limited
Incorporated: 5 July 2004
Net Worth: £17,947,000 *Total Assets:* £110,966,000
Registered Office: Bedford House, 69-79 Fulham High Street, London, SW6 3JW
Activities: Activities of head offices
Parent: Clarion Events Group Limited
Officers: Richard Johnson [1963] Director; Simon Reed Kimble [1963] Director; Russell Stephen Wilcox [1971] Director

Finventures UK Limited
Incorporated: 23 August 2001
Net Worth Deficit: £62,090,008 *Total Assets:* £363,097,440
Registered Office: 1 Basinghall Avenue, London, EC2V 5DD
Activities: Financial intermediation not elsewhere classified
Parent: Standard Chartered I H Limited
Officers: Paul Stuart Chambers [1967] Director/Chartered Accountant; Simon William Gardiner [1975] Director; Ivo Laurence Philipps [1967] Director

Firestone Diamonds PLC
Incorporated: 24 June 1998 *Employees:* 214
Net Worth: £59,836,596 *Total Assets:* £148,522,432
Registered Office: The Triangle, 5-17 Hammersmith Grove, London, W6 0LG
Activities: Other mining and quarrying n.e.c.
Officers: Paul Bosma [1967] Director [South African]; Raffaele Lucio Giuseppe Salvatore Genovese [1962] Director/Investment Manager [Swiss/South African/Italian]; Keith Brian Johnson [1961] Director/Self Employed; Nicolas Patrick Henderson Meier [1949] Director; Kenric Charles Owen [1950] Director/Mining Engineer [South African]; Paul Andrew Sobie [1961] Director/Geologist [Canadian]; Kenneth Niall Young [1960] Director/Geologist

Firmdale Holdings Limited
Incorporated: 27 January 2003 *Employees:* 1,636
Net Worth: £450,700,992 *Total Assets:* £891,068,992
Registered Office: 21 Golden Square, London, W1F 9JN
Activities: Other business support service activities n.e.c.
Shareholder: Timothy John Reginald Kemp
Officers: Malcolm Thomas Soden, Secretary; Claude Markus Aberle [1954] Director/Lawyer [Swiss]; Christopher Kelso Bedford Brotchie [1946] Director; John Paul Gray [1944] Director/Solicitor; Timothy John Reginald Kemp [1946] Director/Hotelier

Firmdale Hotels PLC
Incorporated: 1 October 1981 *Employees:* 217
Net Worth: £174,632,000 *Total Assets:* £202,732,992
Registered Office: 21 Golden Square, London, W1F 9JN
Activities: Hotels and similar accommodation
Parent: Firmdale Holdings Limited
Officers: Malcolm Thomas Soden, Secretary; Rolando Cheles [1954] Construction Director [Italian]; Howard Michael Field [1944] Director/Hotel Business Advisor; Anna Elizabeth Jackson [1973] Director [Australian]; Judith Kit Kemp [1950] Director; Timothy John Reginald Kemp [1946] Director/Hotelier; Craig Andrew Markham [1961] Director/Hotel Executive [Australian]; Mark Rupert Read [1967] Director; Malcolm Thomas Soden [1960] Director/Company Secretary

Firmdale Property Investments Limited
Incorporated: 7 April 2003 *Employees:* 397
Net Worth: £31,373,000 *Total Assets:* £165,288,000
Registered Office: 21 Golden Square, London, W1F 9JN
Activities: Other business support service activities n.e.c.
Parent: Firmdale West End Limited
Officers: Malcolm Thomas Soden, Secretary; Judith Kit Kemp [1950] Director; Timothy John Reginald Kemp [1946] Director/Hotelier

Firmus Energy (Distribution) Limited
Incorporated: 24 February 2005 *Employees:* 101
Net Worth: £13,710,799 *Total Assets:* £141,770,624
Registered Office: 35 Great St Helen's, London, EC3A 6AP
Activities: Distribution of gaseous fuels through mains
Parent: DEKA Energy Enterprises Limited
Officers: Norman McKeown, Secretary; Michael O'Sullivan [1955] Director/Management Consultant [Irish]; Angela Reavey [1964] Director/Chartered Accountant; Michael Patrick Gerrard Scott [1968] Director

Firoka (Kings Cross) Limited
Incorporated: 2 February 1990 *Employees:* 216
Net Worth: £141,521,104 *Total Assets:* £221,164,800
Registered Office: 1 Kings Cross Road, London, WC1X 9HX
Activities: Hotels and similar accommodation
Major Shareholder: Firoz Alibhai Kassam
Officers: Anne Lowry, Secretary; Feroza Firoz Kassam [1989] Director; Firoz Alibhai Kassam [1955] Director; Anne Lowry [1962] Director; Ashwini Dayal Tawakley [1956] Director/Accountant

First Corporate Consultants Ltd
Incorporated: 20 August 1987 *Employees:* 601
Net Worth: £96,261,000 *Total Assets:* £342,036,000
Registered Office: Level 8, 71 Queen Victoria Street, London, EC4V 4AY
Activities: Other business support service activities n.e.c.
Major Shareholder: Terence Charles Mordaunt
Officers: Ian David Sharper, Secretary; Christopher Charles Tite, Secretary; Jonathan Charles Mordaunt [1978] Director; Terence Charles Mordaunt [1947] Director; Sir David Charles Ord [1948] Director

First Corporate Shipping Limited
Incorporated: 24 September 1990 *Employees:* 599
Net Worth: £183,335,008 *Total Assets:* £331,729,984
Registered Office: Level 8, 71 Queen Victoria Street, London, EC4V 4AY
Activities: Other service activities n.e.c.
Parent: The City Council of Bristol
Officers: Martin Alexander Skelton, Secretary; Christopher Charles Tite, Secretary; John Bernard Alexander [1941] Director/Merchant Banker; David Alfred John Brown [1965] Director of Operations; Councillor Christopher Davies [1944] Director/Elected City Councillor; Jonathan Charles Mordaunt [1978] Director of Engineering; Terence Charles Mordaunt [1947] Director; Andrew Charles Ord [1977] Commercial Director; Sir David Charles Ord [1948] Director; Jonathan Nicholas Ord [1983] Director; Ian David Sharper [1974] Director/Accountant; Martin Alexander Skelton [1948] Director; Jeremy Hugh Stanford [1959] Director/Haven Master; Christopher Charles Tite [1959] Director/Solicitor

First Hydro Company
Incorporated: 17 November 1989 *Employees:* 167
Net Worth: £444,110,016 *Total Assets:* £491,545,984
Registered Office: Level 20, 25 Canada Square, London, E14 5LQ
Activities: Production of electricity
Parent: First Hydro Holdings Company
Officers: Sarah Jane Gregory, Secretary; David George Alcock [1965] Director; Andrew Wilson Garner [1962] Director/Accountant; Thomas Joseph O'Brien [1968] Director [Irish]; Simon David Pinnell [1964] Director/Accountant

First Hydro Finance PLC
Incorporated: 31 July 1995
Net Worth: £142,000 *Total Assets:* £415,268,000
Registered Office: Level 20, 25 Canada Square, London, E14 5LQ
Activities: Activities of head offices
Parent: First Hydro Holdings Company
Officers: Sarah Jane Gregory, Secretary; David George Alcock [1965] Director; Andrew Wilson Garner [1962] Director; Thomas Joseph O'Brien [1968] Director [Irish]; Simon David Pinnell [1964] Director/Accountant

First Hydro Holdings Company
Incorporated: 15 December 1995 *Employees:* 167
Net Worth: £20,905,000 *Total Assets:* £484,804,000
Registered Office: Level 20, 25 Canada Square, London, E14 5LQ
Activities: Activities of head offices
Parent: FHH No. 1 Limited
Officers: Sarah Jane Gregory, Secretary; David George Alcock [1965] Director; Andrew Wilson Garner [1962] Director; Thomas Joseph O'Brien [1968] Director [Irish]; Simon David Pinnell [1964] Director/Accountant

First Olsen (Holdings) Limited
Incorporated: 3 December 2007
Net Worth: £200,387,008 *Total Assets:* £200,520,000
Registered Office: 2nd Floor, 64-65 Vincent Square, London, SW1P 2NU
Activities: Activities of head offices
Parent: Bonheur ASA
Officers: Jeremy Dowler, Secretary; Richard Olav AA [1966] Director [Norwegian]; Jeremy Dowler [1948] Director; Anette Sofie Olsen [1956] Director/Ship Owner [Norwegian]; Thomas Fredrik Olsen [1929] Director/Ship Owner [Norwegian]; Thomas Fredrik Olsen Junior [1959] Director/Ship Owner [Norwegian]

First Property Group PLC
Incorporated: 12 September 1994 *Employees:* 49
Net Worth: £46,735,000 *Total Assets:* £184,080,000
Registered Office: 32 St James's Street, London, SW1A 1HD
Activities: Management of real estate on a fee or contract basis
Officers: George Richard Wingfield Digby, Secretary; Benyamin Naeem Habib [1965] Director; Alasdair James Dougall Locke [1953] Director; Peter Geoffrey Moon [1949] Director; George Richard Wingfield Digby [1955] Director

First Rail Holdings Limited
Incorporated: 15 June 2004 *Employees:* 91
Net Worth: £104,781,000 *Total Assets:* £118,814,000
Registered Office: 4th Floor, Capital House, 25 Chapel Street, London, NW1 5DH
Activities: Activities of head offices
Parent: FirstGroup PLC
Officers: Barbara Mary Salter, Secretary; Clive Burrows [1958] Director; Nicholas Keith Chevis [1964] Director; Hugh Patrick Clancy [1964] Director; Kevin Gardner [1960] Director; Stephen Montgomery [1962] Director

First State Investment Services (UK) Limited
Incorporated: 11 January 2000 *Employees:* 358
Net Worth: £24,868,000 *Total Assets:* £120,554,000
Registered Office: Finsbury Circus House, 15 Finsbury Circus, London, EC2M 7EB
Activities: Financial intermediation not elsewhere classified
Parent: First State Investments (UK Holdings) Limited
Officers: Rebecca Sarah Sheppard, Secretary; Paul Thomas Griffiths [1967] Director/Chief Investment Officer, Fixed Income; Cyril Francis Johnson [1958] Director; Wai-Choo Kubitscheck [1959] Independent Director; Christian Richard Spencer Turpin [1972] Managing Director EMEA; Richard Carleton Wastcoat [1961] Director [American]

First State Investments (UK) Limited
Incorporated: 12 September 1988
Net Worth: £10,827,000 *Total Assets:* £209,244,000
Registered Office: Finsbury Circus House, 15 Finsbury Circus, London, EC2M 7EB
Activities: Financial intermediation not elsewhere classified
Parent: Colonial First State Investment Managers (UK) Limited
Officers: Rebecca Sarah Sheppard, Secretary; Adrian Hilderly [1964] Director/Head of Risk and Compliance; Cyril Francis Johnson [1958] Director; Wai-Choo Kubitscheck [1959] Independent Director; Christian Richard Spencer Turpin [1972] Regional Managing Director EMEA; Richard Carleton Wastcoat [1961] Director [American]

Firstbus (North) Limited
Incorporated: 10 October 1996
Net Worth: £139,876,992 *Total Assets:* £139,876,992
Registered Office: 8th Floor, The Point, 37 North Wharf Road, London, W2 1AF
Activities: Activities of head offices
Parent: FirstGroup PLC
Officers: Michael Hampson, Secretary; David Brian Alexander [1965] Regional Managing Director; James Thomas Bowen [1974] Director/Chartered Accountant; Nicholas Keith Chevis [1964] Director; Giles Robin Fearnley [1954] Director; Matthew Gregory [1970] Director/Chief Financial Officer

Firstbus Investments Limited
Incorporated: 15 December 1987
Net Worth: £532,312,000 *Total Assets:* £836,089,984
Registered Office: 8th Floor, The Point, 37 North Wharf Road, London, W2 1AF
Activities: Activities of head offices
Parent: FirstGroup PLC
Officers: Michael Hampson, Secretary; Nicholas Keith Chevis [1964] Director; Duncan McLellan Collie [1966] Director/Accountant; William Alexander Forbes [1970] Director/Chartered Accountant; Matthew Gregory [1970] Director/Chief Financial Officer

Firstclear Limited
Incorporated: 15 June 2000
Net Worth: £5,146,000 *Total Assets:* £196,068,992
Registered Office: 4th Floor, Imperial House, 15 Kingsway, London, WC2B 6UN
Activities: Other business support service activities n.e.c.
Parent: Kindred Services Limited
Officers: Gavin Hughes Hayward [1964] Director; Albin Jean Marie Harold Turquet de Beauregard [1978] Director [French]

FirstGroup Canadian Finance Limited
Incorporated: 30 December 1997
Net Worth: £109,928,568 *Total Assets:* £109,928,568
Registered Office: 8th Floor, The Point, 37 North Wharf Road, London, W2 1AF
Activities: Non-trading company
Parent: FirstGroup PLC
Officers: Michael Hampson, Secretary; Duncan McLellan Collie [1966] Director/Accountant; William Alexander Forbes [1970] Director/Chartered Accountant; Matthew Gregory [1970] Director/Chief Financial Officer

FirstGroup Holdings Limited
Incorporated: 18 June 1986 *Employees:* 171
Net Worth: £62,659,000 *Total Assets:* £380,044,992
Registered Office: 8th Floor, The Point, 37 North Wharf Road, London, W2 1AF
Activities: Activities of head offices
Parent: FirstGroup PLC
Officers: Michael Hampson, Secretary; Nicholas Keith Chevis [1964] Director; Duncan McLellan Collie [1966] Director/Accountant; Matthew Gregory [1970] Director/Chief Financial Officer

Firstplus Financial Group Limited
Incorporated: 10 February 1997
Previous: Firstplus Financial Group PLC
Net Worth: £58,285,000 *Total Assets:* £123,882,000
Registered Office: 1 Churchill Place, London, E14 5HP
Activities: Financial intermediation not elsewhere classified
Parent: Barclays Bank UK PLC
Officers: Anne-Marie Coulson [1984] Director/Banker; Mark Maconachie [1973] Director/Accountant; Mark Newbery [1980] Director/Banker

FIS UK Holdings Limited
Incorporated: 17 June 2005
Previous: Sungard UK Holdings Limited
Net Worth: £187,145,552 *Total Assets:* £354,972,832
Registered Office: 25 Canada Square, London, E14 5LQ
Activities: Activities of other holding companies n.e.c.
Parent: Metavante Technologies Limited
Officers: Howard Wallis, Secretary; Marc Mayo [1954] Director/Attorney [American]; Kathleen Teresa Thompson [1965] Director/Certified Public Accountant [American]

Fisher Island Limited
Incorporated: 28 February 2006 *Employees:* 29
Net Worth Deficit: £94,462,000 *Total Assets:* £257,087,008
Registered Office: Tower Bridge House, St Katharine's Way, London, E1W 1DD
Activities: Activities of other holding companies n.e.c.
Officers: Robin Paul Graetz [1984] Director [Swiss]; Daria Nikolaevna Mirovaia [1981] Director [Swiss]

Fitch Ratings Ltd
Incorporated: 3 June 1977 *Employees:* 1,867
Net Worth: £718,795,008 *Total Assets:* £986,675,008
Registered Office: 30 North Colonnade, London, E14 5GN
Activities: Financial intermediation not elsewhere classified
Officers: Bruce Alexander Legorburu, Secretary; Sanjeev Handa [1961] Director/Consultant [Indian]; Ian Charles Linnell [1967] Managing Director; Dominique Netter [1951] Director [French]; David Lawrence Samuel [1964] Director/Chartered Accountant

Fitch Solutions Group Limited
Incorporated: 26 November 2013 *Employees:* 217
Previous: Fitch Information Services Limited
Net Worth Deficit: £23,729,140 *Total Assets:* £143,330,720
Registered Office: 30 North Colonnade, London, E14 5GN
Activities: Financial intermediation not elsewhere classified
Officers: Jonathan Prosser, Secretary; Julian Peter Acquari [1963] Managing Director; Peter Anthony Evans [1960] Director/Chartered Accountant; David Lawrence Samuel [1964] Director/Accountant

Fitzroy Property Limited
Incorporated: 10 February 2017
Net Worth: £15,019,647 *Total Assets:* £208,244,576
Registered Office: 13 Fitzroy Street, London, W1T 4BQ
Activities: Non-trading company
Parent: Ove Arup Limited
Officers: Vanessa Jane Shakespeare, Secretary; Dr Alan James Belfield [1956] Director/Mechanical Engineer; Matthew Stuart Tweedie [1971] Finance Director

Flavia Holdco Limited
Incorporated: 20 October 2015 *Employees:* 1
Net Worth: £357,414,368 *Total Assets:* £357,539,904
Registered Office: 60 Cannon Street, London, EC4N 6NP
Activities: Activities of other holding companies n.e.c.
Officers: Casper Antonius Berendsen [1975] Director [Dutch]; Rory Alexander Ivor Neeson [1981] Director; Heinz-Peter Ross [1965] Director [German]

Flectat Limited
Incorporated: 22 June 1995
Net Worth Deficit: £109,717,512 *Total Assets:* £1,921,375,488
Registered Office: Gallery 9, 1 Lime Street, London, EC3M 7HA
Activities: Non-life insurance
Parent: Canopius Holdings UK Limited
Officers: Mariana Daoud- O'Connell, Secretary; Michael Patrick Duffy [1964] Director; Nigel Sinclair Meyer [1967] Director; Michael Clive Watson [1954] Director

Fleet Bidco Limited
Incorporated: 20 April 2016 *Employees:* 3
Net Worth Deficit: £67,320,000 *Total Assets:* £748,424,000
Registered Office: Lacon House, 84 Theobald's Road, London, WC1X 8NL
Activities: Other publishing activities
Parent: Fleet Midco II Limited
Officers: Stuart John Ashman, Secretary; Stuart John Ashman [1965] Company Secretary/Director [Australian]; Matthew Prat Burkley [1971] Director/Chief Operating Officer [American]

Fleet Finco Limited
Incorporated: 26 May 2016 *Employees:* 860
Net Worth Deficit: £44,097,000 *Total Assets:* £1,099,036,032
Registered Office: Lacon House, 84 Theobald's Road, London, WC1X 8NL
Activities: Other publishing activities
Parent: Fleet Topco Limited
Officers: Stuart John Ashman, Secretary; Stuart John Ashman [1965] Company Secretary/Director [Australian]; Matthew Prat Burkley [1971] Director/Chief Operating Officer [American]

Fleet Midco I Limited
Incorporated: 26 May 2016
Net Worth: £4,705,000 *Total Assets:* £795,054,016
Registered Office: Lacon House, 84 Theobald's Road, London, WC1X 8NL
Activities: Other publishing activities
Parent: Fleet Midco Limited
Officers: Stuart John Ashman, Secretary; Stuart John Ashman [1965] Company Secretary/Director [Australian]; Matthew Prat Burkley [1971] Director/Chief Operating Officer [American]

Fleet Midco II Limited
Incorporated: 26 May 2016
Net Worth Deficit: £19,082,000 *Total Assets:* £771,267,008
Registered Office: Lacon House, 84 Theobald's Road, London, WC1X 8NL
Activities: Other publishing activities
Parent: Fleet Midco I Limited
Officers: Stuart John Ashman, Secretary; Stuart John Ashman [1965] Company Secretary/Director [Australian]; Matthew Prat Burkley [1971] Director/Chief Operating Officer [American]

Fleet Midco Limited
Incorporated: 20 April 2016
Net Worth: £4,705,000 *Total Assets:* £795,054,016
Registered Office: Lacon House, 84 Theobald's Road, London, WC1X 8NL
Activities: Other publishing activities
Parent: Fleet Finco Limited
Officers: Stuart John Ashman, Secretary; Stuart John Ashman [1965] Company Secretary/Director [Australian]; Matthew Prat Burkley [1971] Director/Chief Operating Officer [American]

Fleet Trade & Transport Limited
Incorporated: 10 April 1989
Net Worth: £188,058,736 *Total Assets:* £205,062,480
Registered Office: Peterborough Court, 133 Fleet Street, London, EC4A 2BB
Activities: Sea and coastal freight water transport
Parent: Goldman Sachs Group UK Limited
Officers: Jolie Anita Norris, Secretary; Beverly Lisa O'Toole, Secretary; Luke Duncan Craig Taylor [1975] Director/Operations Manager; Richard Michael Thomas [1974] Director/Accountant

Flemings Hotel Mayfair Ltd
Incorporated: 23 November 2012 *Employees:* 102
Net Worth: £2,364,609 *Total Assets:* £123,590,456
Registered Office: 7-12 Half Moon Street, London, W1J 7BH
Activities: Hotels and similar accommodation
Officers: Sudha Gulhati, Secretary; Satinder Kishore Gulhati [1944] Director/Hotelier; Shagun Kishor Gulhati [1981] Director/Hotelier

Fletcher Bay Group Limited
Incorporated: 6 November 2009 *Employees:* 1,512
Net Worth: £9,634,000 *Total Assets:* £216,684,992
Registered Office: Level 5, 9 Hatton Street, London, NW8 8PL
Activities: Activities of head offices
Major Shareholder: David John Gray
Officers: David John Gray [1959] Director

Flint Nominees Limited
Incorporated: 9 December 1991
Net Worth: £52,346,220 *Total Assets:* £152,085,344
Registered Office: Suite 1, 3rd Floor, 11-12 St James's Square, London, SW1Y 4LB
Activities: Activities of other holding companies n.e.c.
Parent: FMS Wertmanagement Aor
Officers: David Kenneth Duggins [1955] Director/Chartered Accountant; Paul Stephen Flannery [1968] Director [Irish]

Flodrive Holdings Limited
Incorporated: 10 February 1992 *Employees:* 8
Net Worth: £40,021,180 *Total Assets:* £142,803,728
Registered Office: 68 Grafton Way, London, W1T 5DS
Activities: Development of building projects
Shareholder: Anthony Menashi Khalastchi
Officers: Peter Salim David Khalastchi, Secretary/Director; Anthony Menashi Khalastchi [1961] Director; Frank Khalastchi [1933] Director; Peter Salim David Khalastchi [1963] Director

Folgate Estates Limited
Incorporated: 23 November 1938
Net Worth: £170,183,824 *Total Assets:* £188,258,720
Registered Office: Hiview House, Highgate Road, London, NW5 1TN
Activities: Other letting and operating of own or leased real estate
Parent: Folgates Holdings Limited
Officers: John Patrick Murphy, Secretary; Paul Brosnahan [1951] Director [Irish]; Deborah Lodge [1968] Director/Business Consultant; Clare Patricia Mara [1975] Director/Self Employed [Irish]; Bernard Joseph Murphy [1945] Director [Irish]; James Alexander Murphy [1984] Director/Contracts Manager [Irish]; Dr Karina Duarte Corware Murphy [1984] Director/Safety Surveillance and Risk Management Lead; Kathleen Murphy [1949] Director/Business Consultant [Irish]; Andrew Luis Wilson [1954] Chartered Surveyor/Director

Folgate Holdings Limited
Incorporated: 20 July 1992
Net Worth: £206,289,056 *Total Assets:* £229,219,760
Registered Office: Hiview House, Highgate Road, London, NW5 1TN
Activities: Activities of other holding companies n.e.c.
Officers: John Patrick Murphy, Secretary; Deborah Lodge [1968] Director/Business Consultant; Clare Patricia Mara [1975] Director/Self Employed [Irish]; Bernard Joseph Murphy [1945] Director [Irish]; James Alexander Murphy [1984] Director/Contracts Manager [Irish]; Dr Karina Duarte Corware Murphy [1984] Director/Safety Surveillance & Risk Management Lead; Kathleen Murphy [1949] Director/Business Consultant [Irish]; Andrew Luis Wilson [1954] Chartered Surveyor Director

Folio London Limited
Incorporated: 9 February 2007
Previous: Notting Hill Market Rent Limited
Net Worth: £126,496,000 *Total Assets:* £288,177,984
Registered Office: Bruce Kenrick House, 2 Killick Street, London, N1 9FL
Activities: Other letting and operating of own or leased real estate
Officers: Andrew James Nankivell, Secretary; Andrew Jude Belton [1958] Executive Director [Irish]; Elizabeth Margaret McCallum [1949] Retired - Former Director of Lettings; Paul Christopher Phillips [1955] Finance Director; John Alexander Stephen [1947] Director/Accountant; Mark Vaughan [1970] Director

Food Investments Limited
Incorporated: 21 January 1942
Net Worth: £36,972,000 *Total Assets:* £475,087,008
Registered Office: Weston Centre, 10 Grosvenor Street, London, W1K 4QY
Activities: Grain milling
Parent: ABF Investments PLC
Officers: Rosalyn Sharon Schofield, Secretary; Jonathan Howard Jenkins [1965] Managing Director; Robin Anthony William Lee [1965] Managing Director; Mark Andrew Ward [1969] Finance Director

The Football Association Premier League Limited
Incorporated: 27 May 1992 *Employees:* 153
Net Worth Deficit: £116,108,000 *Total Assets:* £2,690,025,984
Registered Office: 30 Gloucester Place, London, W1U 8PL
Activities: Other sports activities
Officers: Kevin Mark Plumb, Secretary; Claudia Isobel Arney [1971] Director; Kevin Stanley Beeston [1962] Director; Richard James Masters [1966] Director/Interim Chief Executive

Fordstam Limited
Incorporated: 2 June 2003 *Employees:* 842
Net Worth Deficit: £733,825,984 *Total Assets:* £712,243,968
Registered Office: Stamford Bridge, Fulham Road, London, SW6 1HS
Activities: Activities of head offices
Major Shareholder: Roman Abramovich
Officers: Paul Heagren, Secretary/Accountant; Eugene Tenenbaum [1964] Director/Financier [Canadian]

Foresight Solar (UK Holdco) Limited
Incorporated: 25 June 2013
Net Worth: £4,354,071 *Total Assets:* £657,509,248
Registered Office: The Shard, 32 London Bridge Street, London, SE1 9SG
Activities: Non-trading company
Parent: Foresight Solar Fund Limited
Officers: Ricardo Silva Santos de Cima Pineiro [1981] Director [Portuguese]

Foresight VCT PLC
Incorporated: 19 August 1997
Net Worth: £140,428,992 *Total Assets:* £140,848,992
Registered Office: The Shard, 32 London Bridge Street, London, SE1 9SG
Activities: Fund management activities
Officers: John Howard Gregory [1948] Director; Jocelin Montague St John Harris [1945] Director; Gordon James Humphries [1961] Investment Director; Margaret Littlejohns [1959] Director

Forex Capital Markets Limited
Incorporated: 15 September 2000 *Employees:* 48
Net Worth: £65,676,264 *Total Assets:* £294,042,016
Registered Office: Fourth Floor, 20 Gresham Street, London, EC2V 7JE
Activities: Security and commodity contracts dealing activities
Officers: Idowu Akanbi, Secretary; Juan Miguel Cafe [1981] Director/Chief Operating Officer [American]; Brendan Callan [1978] Director/Corporate Executive [American]; David Elon King [1945] Director; Edwin Philip Alfred Manning [1958] Director; Lorenzo Naldini [1962] Director/Broker [Italian]

Formpart (HPL) Limited
Incorporated: 7 February 1958
Net Worth: £103,435,000 *Total Assets:* £103,435,000
Registered Office: Grand Buildings, 1-3 Strand, London, WC2N 5JR
Activities: Other business support service activities n.e.c.
Parent: RELX (Holdings) Limited
Officers: Alan William McCulloch [1966] Director/Chartered Secretary; Henry Adam Udow [1957] Director/Chief Legal Officer

Formula One World Championship Limited
Incorporated: 7 March 2001
Net Worth: £408,238,912 *Total Assets:* £718,209,024
Registered Office: No 2 St James's Market, London, SW1Y 4AH
Activities: Television programming and broadcasting activities
Parent: Alpha Prema UK Limited
Officers: Duncan Francis Llowarch [1968] Director/Accountant; Sacha Jane Woodward Hill [1969] Director/Lawyer

Rocco Forte & Family (London) Limited
Incorporated: 26 March 2003 *Employees:* 212
Net Worth: £29,810,000 *Total Assets:* £107,404,000
Registered Office: 70 Jermyn Street, London, SW1Y 6NY
Activities: Hotels and similar accommodation
Parent: Rocco Forte & Family (Luxury Hotels) Limited
Officers: Rocco Giovanni Forte [1945] Director; Maurizio Saccani [1950] Director [Italian]

Rocco Forte & Family (Luxury Hotels) Limited
Incorporated: 10 April 2002
Net Worth: £60,544,000 *Total Assets:* £108,852,000
Registered Office: 70 Jermyn Street, London, SW1Y 6NY
Activities: Other business support service activities n.e.c.
Parent: Rocco Forte Hotels Limited
Officers: Rachel Louise Ellen [1978] Director; Rocco Giovanni Forte [1945] Director

Rocco Forte Hotels Limited
Incorporated: 14 November 1996 *Employees:* 2,166
Previous: Rocco Forte & Family Limited
Net Worth: £151,167,008 *Total Assets:* £486,287,008
Registered Office: 70 Jermyn Street, London, SW1Y 6NY
Activities: Hotels and similar accommodation
Shareholder: The Hon Sir Rocco Giovanni Forte
Officers: Giancarla Maria Gerarda Alen-Buckley [1959] Director; Rachel Louise Ellen [1978] Director; Aliai Giovanna Maria Forte [1965] Director; Rocco Giovanni Forte [1945] Director; Marco Lucchini [1968] Investment Director [Italian]; Roberto G Mendoza [1945] Director/Finance [American]; Karim Naffah [1963] Director; David Howard Nelson [1963] Director/Chartered Accountant; Michele Norsa [1948] Director/Executive [Italian]; Olga Marie Louise Anna Polizzi di Sorrentino [1946] Director; John Leigh Walker-Haworth [1944] Director

Fortune Oil Limited
Incorporated: 2 October 1987 *Employees:* 49
Previous: Fortune Oil PLC
Net Worth: £506,491,008 *Total Assets:* £832,443,008
Registered Office: 4th Floor, Nova South, 160 Victoria Street, London, SW1E 5LB
Activities: Support activities for petroleum and natural gas mining
Major Shareholder: Tat Jung Daniel Chiu
Officers: Elizabeth Essex, Secretary; Tat Jung Daniel Chiu [1960] Director [Chinese]; Ching Li [1958] Director [Chinese]; Ian Roper Taylor [1956] Director

Forum Worldwide Holdings Limited
Incorporated: 30 September 2014
Net Worth Deficit: £42,736,336 *Total Assets:* £197,505,168
Registered Office: 150 Minories, London, EC3N 1LS
Activities: Activities of other holding companies n.e.c.
Officers: John Cornel Ivascu, Secretary; Tylar Kipp Schmitt [1973] Director [American]; David Lyle Williams Jr [1969] Director/Senior Vice President - Operations [American]

Foseco Holding Limited
Incorporated: 6 June 2001
Net Worth: £267,048,000 *Total Assets:* £369,887,008
Registered Office: 165 Fleet Street, London, EC4A 2AE
Activities: Activities of other holding companies n.e.c.
Parent: Foseco Limited
Officers: Jennifer Smith, Secretary; Henry James Knowles [1969] Director/General Counsel and Company Secretary; Ian James Lawson [1968] Director/Accountant; Simon Christopher Upcott [1958] Director/Group Taxation Manager

Foseco Limited
Incorporated: 5 April 2005
Net Worth: £96,188,000 *Total Assets:* £151,562,000
Registered Office: 165 Fleet Street, London, EC4A 2AE
Activities: Activities of other holding companies n.e.c.
Parent: Vesuvius Overseas Limited
Officers: Jennifer Smith, Secretary; Henry James Knowles [1969] Director/General Counsel and Company Secretary; Ian James Lawson [1968] Director/Accountant; Simon Christopher Upcott [1958] Director/Group Taxation Manager

Fosse Funding (No.1) Limited
Incorporated: 5 September 2006
Net Worth Deficit: £4,290,000 *Total Assets:* £622,299,008
Registered Office: c/o Structured Finance Management Limited, 35 Great St Helens, London, EC3A 6AP
Activities: Banks
Parent: Fosse (Master Issuer) Holdings Limited
Officers: Thomas Ranger [1977] Director

Fosse Master Issuer PLC
Incorporated: 5 September 2006
Net Worth Deficit: £1,462,000 *Total Assets:* £648,595,968
Registered Office: c/o Structured Finance Management Limited, 35 Great St Helens, London, EC3A 6AP
Activities: Banks
Parent: Fosse (Master Issuer) Holdings Limited
Officers: Thomas Ranger [1977] Director

Foster + Partners Group Limited
Incorporated: 24 October 2006 *Employees:* 1,266
Net Worth: £62,910,000 *Total Assets:* £288,990,016
Registered Office: Riverside Three, Albert Wharf, 22 Hester Road, London, SW11 4AN
Activities: Activities of other holding companies n.e.c.
Officers: Lord Norman Foster of Thames Bank Om [1935] Director/Architect; Victor Frederick Ganzi [1947] Director/Executive [American]; Stuart John Miners [1977] Director/Investment Professional; David Brian Nelson [1951] Director/Architect; Matthew Alexander Streets [1962] Director

Foster + Partners Limited
Incorporated: 21 June 1982 *Employees:* 1,075
Net Worth: £24,639,000 *Total Assets:* £128,467,000
Registered Office: Riverside Three, Albert Wharf, 22 Hester Road, London, SW11 4AN
Activities: Architectural activities
Parent: Foster Holdings Limited
Officers: Professor Stefan Behling [1962] Director/Architect [German/American]; Grant Ashley Brooker [1961] Director/Architect; Nigel Dancey [1964] Director/Architect; Spencer Thomas de Grey [1944] Director/Architect; Gerard Evenden [1964] Director/Architect; Lord Norman Foster of Thames Bank Om [1935] Director/Architect; Luke Kamuela Fox [1969] Director/Architect [Australian]; David Brian Nelson [1951] Director/Architect; Matthew Alexander Streets [1962] Director; David Summerfield [1965] Director/Architect

The Foundation for Social Entrepreneurs
Incorporated: 15 March 2001 *Employees:* 61
Net Worth: £149,991,728 *Total Assets:* £152,688,976
Registered Office: 123 Whitecross Street, London, EC1Y 8JJ
Activities: Other service activities n.e.c.
Officers: Raymond Vinh Khu Tran, Secretary; Rachel Elizabeth Ferrier Barton [1975] Managing Director; Stephen Kwasi Bediako [1980] Director; Gwenda Lynne Berry [1953] Director/Academic; Susan Charteris [1950] Director/Strategy Advisor and Leadership Coach; Timothy James Neil Davies-Pugh [1966] Director/Management Consultant; Nicholas James Farhi [1979] Director/Strategy Consultant; Anne Margaret Glover [1954] Director/Venture Capitalist; Edward James Lawson [1976] Director/Wealth Manager; Amma Mensah [1989] Director; Professor Nicholas Petford [1961] Director/University Vice Chancellor; Elizabeth Ellen Sideris [1953] Director/Trustee; Krishna Kumar Vishnubhotla [1964] Director/Chartered Accountant

The Foundry Bidco No.2 Limited
Incorporated: 18 May 2015
Net Worth Deficit: £24,223,000 *Total Assets:* £177,700,000
Registered Office: 5 Golden Square, London, W1F 9HT
Activities: Activities of other holding companies n.e.c.
Parent: The Foundry Midco 3 Limited
Officers: Martin David Franks [1974] Director/Chief Executive Officer; Craig Hilton Rodgerson [1964] Director

The Foundry Holdco Limited
Incorporated: 18 May 2015
Net Worth Deficit: £2,694,000 *Total Assets:* £200,596,992
Registered Office: 5 Golden Square, London, W1F 9HT
Activities: Activities of other holding companies n.e.c.
Parent: The Foundry Topco No.2 Limited
Officers: Martin David Franks [1974] Director/Chief Financial Officer; Craig Hilton Rodgerson [1964] Director

The Foundry Midco 3 Limited
Incorporated: 18 May 2015
Net Worth: £940,000 *Total Assets:* £200,200,000
Registered Office: 5 Golden Square, London, W1F 9HT
Activities: Activities of other holding companies n.e.c.
Parent: The Foundry Holdco Limited
Officers: Martin David Franks [1974] Director/Chief Financial Officer; Craig Hilton Rodgerson [1964] Director

The Foundry Topco No.2 Limited
Incorporated: 18 May 2015 *Employees:* 276
Net Worth Deficit: £52,695,000 *Total Assets:* £236,972,000
Registered Office: 5 Golden Square, London, W1F 9HT
Activities: Activities of other holding companies n.e.c.
Officers: Jonathan Philip Boyes [1977] Director; Martin David Franks [1974] Director/Chief Financial Officer; Nicholas James Humphries [1967] Director; Dr Alexandra Rose Mahon [1973] Director/Chief Executive Officer; Craig Hilton Rodgerson [1964] Director; Karen Slatford [1956] Director

Fox Healthcare Acquisitions Limited
Incorporated: 29 January 2008
Net Worth: £33,142,000 *Total Assets:* £216,858,000
Registered Office: 3 Dorset Rise, London, EC4Y 8EN
Activities: Activities of head offices
Parent: Fox Healthcare Holdco 2 Limited
Officers: Daniel Francis Toner, Secretary; Justinian Joseph Ash [1965] Director/Chief Executive Officer; Peter James Corfield [1971] Director/Chief Commercial Officer; Jitesh Himatlal Sodha [1968] Director/Chief Financial Officer; Daniel Francis Toner [1968] Director/Solicitor

Fox Healthcare Holdco 2 Limited
Incorporated: 6 March 2008
Net Worth: £123,428,000 *Total Assets:* £124,576,000
Registered Office: 3 Dorset Rise, London, EC4Y 8EN
Activities: Activities of other holding companies n.e.c.
Parent: Spire Healthcare Holdings 3 Limited
Officers: Daniel Francis Toner, Secretary; Justinian Joseph Ash [1965] Director/Chief Executive Officer; Peter James Corfield [1971] Director/Chief Commercial Officer; Jitesh Himatlal Sodha [1968] Director/Chief Financial Officer; Daniel Francis Toner [1968] Director/Solicitor

Fox Investments Limited
Incorporated: 7 July 2000 *Employees:* 187
Net Worth: £68,680,408 *Total Assets:* £110,564,472
Registered Office: 1 Mercer Street, London, WC2H 9QJ
Activities: Security dealing on own account
Major Shareholder: Iain Henry Abrahams
Officers: Iain Henry Abrahams [1959] Director

Fox Networks Group (UK) Limited
Incorporated: 24 June 2002 *Employees:* 226
Previous: Fox International Channels (UK) Limited
Net Worth: £38,001,608 *Total Assets:* £170,126,816
Registered Office: Third Floor, 10 Hammersmith Grove, Hammersmith, London, W6 7AP
Activities: Television programming and broadcasting activities
Parent: Twenty-First Century Fox, Inc.
Officers: Terry William Downing [1965] Director/CFO Europe and Africa; Diego Fernando Londono [1970] Executive Director [Colombian]; Jan Koeppen [1970] Executive Director [Dutch]; Colin Robert McLeod [1967] Director; Namrata Patel [1983] Director/CFO & VP

Foxland 20FS (UK) Limited
Incorporated: 10 July 2017
Net Worth Deficit: £15,357,726 *Total Assets:* £411,830,464
Registered Office: Suite 1, 3rd Floor, 11-12 St James's Square, London, SW1Y 4LB
Activities: Other business support service activities n.e.c.
Officers: Wai Hong Stephen Chung [1963] Director/Senior Vice President [Chinese]; Man Wai NG [1965] Director [Chinese]

Foxtons Group PLC
Incorporated: 18 December 2009 *Employees:* 1,170
Net Worth: £140,922,000 *Total Assets:* £177,220,000
Registered Office: Building One, Chiswick Park, 566 Chiswick High Road, London, W4 5BE
Activities: Activities of head offices
Officers: Mark Ian James Berry, Secretary; Ian Edward Barlow [1951] Director; Mark Ian James Berry [1973] Director/Chief Financial Officer; Nicholas John Budden [1968] Director/Chief Executive; Sheena Mary MacKay [1961] Director; Garry Watts [1956] Director

Foxtons Intermediate Holdings Limited
Incorporated: 14 March 2007
Net Worth: £163,864,992 *Total Assets:* £186,956,000
Registered Office: Building One, Chiswick Park, 566 Chiswick High Road, London, W4 5BE
Activities: Activities of head offices
Parent: Foxtons Group PLC
Officers: James Vincent McDonald, Secretary; Mark Ian James Berry [1973] Director; Nicholas John Budden [1968] Director/Chief Operating Officer

FPI (UK) 1 Limited
Incorporated: 19 December 2014
Net Worth: £237,829,168 *Total Assets:* £239,892,064
Registered Office: c/o Legalinx Limited, One Fetter Lane, London, EC4A 1BR
Activities: Buying and selling of own real estate
Officers: Joao Nuno Dos Santos Silva Madeira de Andrade [1972] Director [Portuguese]; Andre Maria Pires Marques Gomes de Sousa [1977] Director [Portuguese]

Frasers Hospitality UK Holdings Limited
Incorporated: 5 June 2015 *Employees:* 2,324
Net Worth: £59,531,000 *Total Assets:* £459,904,000
Registered Office: 3rd Floor, 95 Cromwell Road, London, SW7 4DL
Activities: Other letting and operating of own or leased real estate
Shareholders: Charoen Sirivadhanabhakdi; Khunying Wanna Sirivadhanabhakdi
Officers: Diana Ndirwa, Secretary; Gustaaf Franciscus Joseph Bakker [1961] Director/Chief Executive Officer [Dutch]; Peng Sum Choe [1960] Chief Executive Officer/Director [Singaporean]; Alan Yew Kuen Tang [1966] Director/Chief Operating Officer [Singaporean]

Frasers Property (UK) Limited
Incorporated: 23 March 2005 *Employees:* 23
Net Worth: £79,592,000 *Total Assets:* £118,165,000
Registered Office: 95 Cromwell Road, London, SW7 4DL
Activities: Development of building projects
Parent: Frasers Centrepoint Limited
Officers: Seng Khoon NG, Secretary; Khong Shoong Chia [1971] Director/Chief Financial Officer [Singaporean]; Ilaria Jane Del Beato [1966] Director/Chief Executive; Panote Sirivadhanabhakdi [1977] Director/Group Chief Executive Officer [Thai]

Freepoint Commodities Enterprises Ltd.
Incorporated: 9 September 2011 *Employees:* 39
Net Worth: £45,325,464 *Total Assets:* £132,784,632
Registered Office: 62 Buckingham Gate, London, SW1E 6AJ
Activities: Other business support service activities n.e.c.
Officers: Robert Joel Feilbogen [1968] Director/Chief Operating Officer [American]; Daniel Marc Hecht [1974] Director/Attorney [American]; Giuseppe Marcello Minichiello [1970] Director/Controller; Michael Walter [1965] Director [German]

Freepoint Commodities Europe LLP
Incorporated: 9 September 2011
Net Worth: £54,224,488 *Total Assets:* £295,441,984
Registered Office: 62 Buckingham Gate, London, SW1E 6AJ

Freepoint Commodities Holdings Ltd
Incorporated: 9 September 2011 *Employees:* 75
Net Worth: £48,070,228 *Total Assets:* £304,436,096
Registered Office: 62 Buckingham Gate, London, SW1E 6AJ
Activities: Other business support service activities n.e.c.
Officers: Robert Joel Feilbogen [1968] Director/Chief Operating Officer [American]; Daniel Marc Hecht [1974] Director/Attorney [American]; Giuseppe Marcello Minichiello [1970] Director/Controller

Freightliner Heavy Haul Limited
Incorporated: 25 August 1999 *Employees:* 555
Net Worth: £48,704,000 *Total Assets:* £145,808,992
Registered Office: 3rd Floor, 90 Whitfield Street, Fitzrovia, London, W1T 4EZ
Activities: Freight rail transport
Parent: Management Consortium Bid Limited
Officers: Geraint Rhys Harries, Secretary; Adam Lewis Cunliffe [1972] Managing Director; Gary Richards Long [1961] Director [American]; Charles Noble [1977] Director; Timothy Michael Shakerley [1972] Director

Freightliner Limited
Incorporated: 20 October 1995 *Employees:* 1,184
Net Worth: £90,502,000 *Total Assets:* £231,786,000
Registered Office: 3rd Floor, 90 Whitfield Street, Fitzrovia, London, W1T 4EZ
Activities: Freight rail transport
Parent: Management Consortium Bid Limited
Officers: Geraint Rhys Harries, Secretary; Adam Lewis Cunliffe [1972] Managing Director; Gary Richards Long [1961] Director [American]; Charles Noble [1977] Director; Timothy Michael Shakerley [1972] Director

Fremantlemedia Group Limited
Incorporated: 25 May 1939 *Employees:* 69
Net Worth: £201,639,008 *Total Assets:* £367,287,008
Registered Office: 1 Stephen Street, London, W1T 1AL
Activities: Activities of head offices
Officers: Ernitia Ferguson, Secretary; Andrew Bott [1968] Director/Chief Financial Officer; Nicola Louise Gray [1965] Director/HR Professional; Jacqueline Frances Moreton [1965] Director; Andrea Scrosati [1972] Director/Chief Operating Officer [Italian]

Fremantlemedia Limited
Incorporated: 16 June 1933 *Employees:* 617
Net Worth: £136,392,000 *Total Assets:* £385,035,008
Registered Office: 1 Stephen Street, London, W1T 1AL
Activities: Television programme production activities
Parent: Fremantlemedia Group Limited
Officers: Ernitia Ferguson, Secretary; Andrew Bott [1968] Director/Chief Financial Officer; Nicola Louise Gray [1965] Director/HR Professional; Jacqueline Frances Moreton [1965] Director; Andrea Scrosati [1972] Director/Chief Operating Officer [Italian]

Frenchgate Interchange Limited
Incorporated: 5 July 2006
Net Worth Deficit: £21,313,138 *Total Assets:* £157,288,384
Registered Office: 3rd Floor, 26-28 Great Portland Street, London, W1W 8QT
Activities: Buying and selling of own real estate
Shareholders: Patrick McKillen; ColFrenchgate Holding SARL; Garvagh Investments Ltd
Officers: Padraig Anthony Drayne [1962] Director [Irish]; Shane McCrory [1980] Director/Accountant [Irish]; Patrick Gerard McKillen [1955] Director [Irish]

Freshfields Bruckhaus Deringer LLP
Incorporated: 13 February 2008 *Employees:* 4,542
Net Worth Deficit: £495,000,000 *Total Assets:* £1,125,600,000
Registered Office: 65 Fleet Street, London, EC4Y 1HS
Officers: Edward Charles Braham [1961] Member; Dr Stephan Rolf Eilers [1959] Member; Colin Percival Hargreaves [1963] Member; James McGill Aitken [1973] LLP Member; David Charles Aitman [1956] LLP Member; Jose Armando Jimenez Albarran [1969] LLP Member; Franz Johann Aleith [1964] LLP Member; Peter Philip Allen [1974] LLP Member; Andrew Christopher Austin [1975] LLP Member; Mark Timothy Austin [1974] LLP Member; Rafique Gabriel Bachour [1974] LLP Member; Kenneth Baird [1964] LLP Member; Catherine Mary Balmond [1975] LLP Member; Nicolas Barberis [1976] LLP Member; Christopher Barratt [1966] LLP Member; Moritz Johannes Engelbert Becker [1979] LLP Member; Ryan Patrick Beckwith [1977] LLP Member; Guy Benda [1967] LLP Member; Stephane Benouville [1966] LLP Member; Thomas Markus Benzing [1976] LLP Member; Marius Benedikt Berenbrok [1959] LLP Member; Helmut Adolf Bergmann [1961] LLP Member; Jennifer Bethlehem [1965] LLP Member; Klaus Jakob Beucher [1961] LLP Member; David Sebastian Beutel [1978] LLP Member; John Alexander Blain [1969] LLP Member; Simone Eliane Bono [1973] LLP Member; Heiner Braun [1967] LLP Member; Jan Brinkmann [1967] LLP Member; Michael Antonius Broeders [1975] LLP Member; David Andrew Brooks [1976] LLP Member; Onno Willem Brouwer [1954] LLP Member; Matthew Richard Bruce [1978] LLP Member; Helen Hermione Buchanan [1973] LLP Member; Thomas Bucker [1963] LLP Member; Bertram Johannes Burtscher [1966] LLP Member; Karin Buzanich-Sommeregger [1980] LLP Member; Roderick Johannes Carlton [1965] LLP Member; Alex Peter Carver [1969] LLP Member; Alastair John Chapman [1976] LLP Member; Dr Patrick Cichy [1973] LLP Member; Murray John Clayson [1961] LLP Member; Peter Thomas Clements [1979] LLP Member; Johannes Conradi [1962] LLP Member; Stephanie Noerie Corbiere [1980] LLP Member; Andrew James Craig [1973] LLP Member; Pascal Rene Anselme Cuche [1970] LLP Member; Vincent Daniel-Mayeur [1976] LLP Member; Debashis Das [1984] LLP Member; John Graham Davies [1956] LLP Member; Christopher Lyle Davis [1966] LLP Member; Michele Therese Davis [1977] LLP Member; Paul Edmund Marcus Davison [1975] LLP Member; Martina de Lind Van Wijngaarden [1970] LLP Member; Carlos Alfonso de Marcos Gonzalez-Irun [1977] LLP Member; Dr Stephan Denk [1971] LLP Member; Shawn Der Kinderen [1973] LLP Member; Jochen Dieselhorst [1966] LLP Member; Dr Natascha Doll [1975] LLP Member; Alexander Doorman [1977] LLP Member; Dr Rene Doring [1974] LLP Member; Boris Richard Dzida [1969] LLP Member; Jochen Ellrott [1970] LLP Member; Dr Timo Elsner [1975] LLP Member; Bruce Embley [1971] LLP Member; Andreas Fabritius [1957] LLP Member; Thijs Peter Flokstra [1973] LLP Member; Raquel Florez Escobar [1970] LLP Member; David Franco Gongora [1972] LLP Member; Nicholas George French [1968] LLP Member; Nicholas John Frey [1980] LLP Member; Igancio Gabilondo Egana [1968] LLP Member; Adam Jonathan Gallagher [1973] LLP Member; Laurent Jose Henri Francois Garzaniti [1966] LLP Member; Katrin Gassner [1977] LLP Member; Jill Gatehouse [1977] LLP Member; Christoph Leonhard Heinrich Gustav Ludwig Gleske [1968] LLP Member; Alexander Michael Glos [1974] LLP Member; Neil Anthony Golding [1964] LLP Member; Natasha Rachel Good [1968] LLP Member; Yann Gozal [1973] LLP Member; Alice Mary Sebright Greenwell [1978] LLP Member; Fabrice Jean Bruno Grillo [1972] LLP Member; Konrad Franz Michael Maria Groller [1975] LLP Member; Paul Nicholas Gunther [1980] LLP Member; Julia Haas [1979] LLP Member; Axel Marie Victor Haelterman [1960] LLP Member; Andrew Franklin Hagan [1980] LLP Member; Michael Haidinger [1960] LLP Member; Peter Gordon Lyndon Hall [1965] LLP Member; Andrew Russell Hart [1962] LLP Member; Richard Timothy Michael Hart [1980] LLP Member; Kai Hasselbach [1970] LLP Member; Charles Forbes Raymond Hayes [1978] LLP Member; Kathleen Mary Healy [1971] LLP Member; Dawn Margaret Heath [1975] LLP Member; Friedrich Heilmann [1959] LLP Member; Robin Helmke [1976] LLP Member; Johann Wessel Heukamp [1972] LLP Member; Stephen Anthony Hewes [1969] LLP Member

Fresnillo PLC
Incorporated: 15 August 2007 *Employees:* 4,898
Net Worth: £2,268,436,992 *Total Assets:* £3,569,088,512
Registered Office: 2nd Floor, 21 Upper Brook Street, London, W1K 7PY
Activities: Mining of other non-ferrous metal ores
Officers: Alejandro Bailleres [1960] Director [Mexican]; Alberto Bailleres Gonzalez [1931] Director [Mexican]; Juan Bordes Aznar [1947] Director [Mexican]; Arturo Fernandez [1953] Director [Mexican]; Barbara Garza Laguera Gonda [1959] Director/Businesswoman [Mexican]; Charles Richard Jacobs [1967] Director/Lawyer [Irish]; Georgina Yamilet Kessel Martinez [1950] Director/Economist [Mexican]; Jaime Lomelin Guillen [1935] Director [Mexican]; Dame Judith MacGregor [1952] Director/Diplomat; Fernando Benjamin Ruiz Sahagun [1943] Director/Tax Consultant [Mexican]; Victor Alberto Tiburcio Celorio [1951] Director/Accountant [Mexican]

Freston Ventures Investments LLP
Incorporated: 8 November 2010 *Employees:* 9
Net Worth: £183,433,216 *Total Assets:* £193,018,112
Registered Office: 146 Freston Road, London, W10 6TR
Officers: Robert Patrick Kelvin Clarkson [1965] Member; Lady Celia Anne Dunstone [1979] Member; Sir Charles William Dunstone [1964] Member; John Haden Eckbert [1967] Member; John Gildersleeve [1944] Member; Andrew John Harrison [1970] Member; Timothy Simon Morris [1964] Member; Roger William Taylor [1964] Member; Peter Morton [1953] LLP Member

Friary Court Investments Limited
Incorporated: 8 February 2010 *Employees:* 959
Net Worth: £21,844,000 *Total Assets:* £132,979,000
Registered Office: Friary Court, 65 Crutched Friars, London, EC3N 2AE
Activities: Activities of other holding companies n.e.c.
Officers: Robert Nicholas Hutton, Secretary; Marcus Robin Bowman [1954] Director/Solicitor; Christopher Andrew Cardona [1959] Director/Solicitor; Giles Wilfred Conor Kavanagh [1959] Director/Solicitors; Craig Ashley Neame [1971] Director/Solicitor; Maximilian Marek Wieliczko [1961] Director/Solicitor

Friary Intermediate Limited
Incorporated: 26 March 2002
Net Worth: £300,470,016 *Total Assets:* £663,510,976
Registered Office: The Walbrook Building, 25 Walbrook, London, EC4N 8AW
Activities: Non-life reinsurance
Parent: HLG Holdings Limited
Officers: Alistair Charles Peel, Secretary; Michael Peter Rea [1966] Director; Carol Richmond [1963] Director; Charles Douglas Scott [1973] Director

Friary No.2 PLC
Incorporated: 16 April 2014
Net Worth Deficit: £995,000 *Total Assets:* £268,963,008
Registered Office: 35 Great St Helen's, London, EC3A 6AP
Activities: Financial intermediation not elsewhere classified
Parent: Friary No.2 Mortgages Holdings Limited
Officers: Helena Paivi Whitaker [1963] Director/Chartered Secretary [Finnish]

Friary No.3 PLC
Incorporated: 14 October 2015
Net Worth: £711,000 *Total Assets:* £348,408,992
Registered Office: 35 Great St Helen's, London, EC3A 6AP
Activities: Financial intermediation not elsewhere classified
Parent: Friary No.3 Mortgages Holdings Limited
Officers: Helena Paivi Whitaker [1963] Director/Chartered Secretary [Finnish]

Friary No.4 PLC
Incorporated: 12 April 2017
Net Worth: £1,132,000 *Total Assets:* £509,367,008
Registered Office: 11th Floor, 200 Aldersgate Street, London, EC1A 4HD
Activities: Activities of mortgage finance companies
Parent: Friary No.4 Mortgages Holdings Limited
Officers: Charles Michael Leahy [1975] Director

Frontier Agriculture Limited
Incorporated: 16 November 2004 *Employees:* 1,054
Net Worth: £245,432,992 *Total Assets:* £477,916,000
Registered Office: Associated British Foods PLC, Group Secretarial Department, Weston Centre, 10 Grosvenor Street, London, W1K 4QY
Activities: Support activities for crop production
Shareholders: A.B.F. Holdings Limited; Cargill PLC
Officers: Rosalyn Sharon Schofield, Secretary/Solicitor; Kenneth Mark Aitchison [1960] Director/Business Unit Leader; Oscar Casanova Ruiz [1973] Director [Spanish]; Richard Charles Cloke [1961] Finance Director; Roger Michael Janson [1962] Director/Vice President, Cargill Agricultural Supply Chain [Dutch]; Zsolt Kocza [1971] Managing Director, Grains, Cargill Agricultural Supply Chain [Hungarian]; Diana Caroline MacDuff [1973] Director/Chartered Accountant; Jose Jorge Nobre [1961] Director [French]; David Jonathan Douglas Yiend [1951] Director

Frontier Finance PLC
Incorporated: 3 March 2017
Net Worth: £50,000 *Total Assets:* £163,600,000
Registered Office: 155 Moorgate, London, EC2M 6XB
Activities: Non-trading company
Parent: Mace Limited
Officers: Carolyn Pate, Secretary; Stephen Gerard Pycroft [1958] Director/Chairman; Mark Peter Reynolds [1963] Director

FS Debtco Limited
Incorporated: 2 December 2016
Net Worth: £10,268,564 *Total Assets:* £195,203,872
Registered Office: c/o Foresight Group LLP, The Shard, 32 London Bridge Street, London, SE1 9SG
Activities: Activities of head offices
Parent: FS Holdco 2 Limited
Officers: Ricardo Silva Santos de Cima Pineiro [1981] Director/Investment Manager [Portuguese]

FS Holdco 2 Limited
Incorporated: 1 December 2016
Net Worth: £10,456,009 *Total Assets:* £131,274,024
Registered Office: c/o Foresight Group LLP, The Shard, 32 London Bridge Street, London, SE1 9SG
Activities: Activities of head offices
Parent: Foresight Solar (UK Holdco) Limited
Officers: Ricardo Silva Santos de Cima Pineiro [1981] Director/Investment Manager [Portuguese]

FS Holdco Limited
Incorporated: 11 January 2016
Net Worth: £53,328,856 *Total Assets:* £596,767,680
Registered Office: c/o Foresight Group LLP, The Shard, 32 London Bridge Street, London, SE1 9SG
Activities: Activities of head offices
Parent: Foresight Solar (UK Holdco) Limited
Officers: Ricardo Silva Santos de Cima Pineiro [1981] Director/Investment Manager [Portuguese]

FS JV Co Limited
Incorporated: 24 September 2015 *Employees:* 835
Net Worth: £2,392,000 *Total Assets:* £185,018,000
Registered Office: 54 Portland Place, London, W1B 1DY
Activities: Other business support service activities n.e.c.
Shareholders: Fico Holding (UK) Limited; S Hotels and Resorts (UK) Limited
Officers: Naris Cheyklin [1961] Director/Business Executive [Thai]; Dirk Andre L de Cuyper [1965] Director [Belgian]; Sanjay Kumar Singh [1961] Director/Business Executive [Indian]; Krit Srichawla [1976] Director/Business Executive [Thai]

FS Senior Co Limited
Incorporated: 24 September 2015 *Employees:* 951
Net Worth: £11,513,000 *Total Assets:* £194,787,008
Registered Office: 54 Portland Place, London, W1B 1DY
Activities: Other business support service activities n.e.c.
Parent: FS Mid Co Limited
Officers: Naris Cheyklin [1961] Director/Business Executive [Thai]; Dirk Andre L de Cuyper [1965] Director [Belgian]; Sanjay Kumar Singh [1961] Director/Business Executive [Indian]; Krit Srichawla [1976] Director/Business Executive [Thai]

FTI Consulting LLP
Incorporated: 20 February 2012 *Employees:* 705
Net Worth: £207,847,008 *Total Assets:* £238,742,000
Registered Office: 200 Aldersgate, Aldersgate Street, London, EC1A 4HD
Officers: Ben Atwell [1972] LLP Member; Giles Barrie [1966] LLP Member; Leslie Alan Benson [1963] LLP Member; Edward Berry [1981] LLP Member; Mark Bezant [1962] LLP Member; Adam David Bradley [1970] LLP Member; Benjamin David Brewerton [1968] LLP Member; Edward Walter Rollet Bridges [1967] LLP Member; Jonathon Brill [1966] LLP Member; Bruno Campana [1982] LLP Member; Christopher Clark [1965] LLP Member; Simon Paul Conway [1967] LLP Member; Caroline Das-Monfrais [1977] LLP Member; Stephen Day [1978] LLP Member; Alex Deane [1979] LLP Member; Matthew Dixon [1981] LLP Member; Neil Doyle [1972] LLP Member; Toni Adele Dyson [1962] LLP Member; Craig Earnshaw [1975] LLP Member; David Eastwood [1960] LLP Member; Richard James Dominic Edwards [1970] LLP Member; John Ellison [1953] LLP Member; Alastair Farr [1968] LLP Member; Julian Glass [1973] LLP Member; Lisa Goldstone [1971] LLP Member; Iain Graham [1976] LLP Member; Simon Granger [1975] LLP Member; Chad Griffin [1972] LLP Member; Greg Harman [1968] LLP Member; Paul Henninger [1975] LLP Member; Kevin Hewitt [1965] LLP Member; John Nicholas Hourigan [1968] LLP Member; Mark Hunt [1960] LLP Member; Paul Nigel John Inglis [1969] LLP Member; Andrew Johnson [1974] LLP Member; Aris Karcanias [1983] LLP Member; Andrew David Kennell [1968] LLP Member; Rustom Kharegat [1962] LLP Member; Simon Kirkhope [1971] LLP Member; Dido Laurimore [1973] LLP Member; Andrew Lorenz [1955] LLP Member; Ian William Mackie [1970] LLP Member; Alwin Magimay [1969] LLP Member; John Paul Maloney [1965] LLP Member; Aneesh Maloo [1976] LLP Member; Jason Mann [1970] LLP Member; Alaric Marsden [1973] LLP Member; Noel Matthews [1978] LLP Member; Maria Meloria Meschi [1963] LLP Member; James Meville-Ross [1972] LLP Member; Ant Moore [1974] LLP Member; David Morris [1975] LLP Member; Richard Mountain [1966] LLP Member; Rory William O'Brien [1964] LLP Member; Charles Palmer [1971] LLP Member; Alpesh Patel [1970] LLP Member; Julia Phillips [1958] LLP Member; Michael Anthony Pilgrem [1966] LLP Member; Andrew Pimlott [1979] LLP Member; Brett David Pollard [1974] LLP Member; David Quantrill [1967] LLP Member; Christopher Ruell [1972] LLP Member; Deborah Mary Scott [1974] LLP Member; Rajesh Kumar Sennik [1966] LLP Member; Manish Shah [1966] LLP Member; Ruth Elizabeth Steedman [1966] LLP Member; Brian Stuart [1967] LLP Member; Richard Sunderland [1969] LLP Member; Euan Sutherland [1977] LLP Member; Ian Thompson [1975] LLP Member; Richard Turner [1972] LLP Member; Navin Waghe [1977] LLP Member; David Ross Waller [1962] LLP Member; John Charles Waples [1960] LLP Member; Nigel John Webb [1966] LLP Member; Fergus Mark Campbell Wheeler [1969] LLP Member; Chris Williams [1972] LLP Member; Charmaine Wong [1976] LLP Member; Andrew Wynn [1977] LLP Member; Almira Zejnilagic [1979] LLP Member

FTSE Global Debt Capital Markets Limited
Incorporated: 23 November 2012
Previous: FTSE TMX Global Debt Capital Markets Limited
Net Worth: £130,962,000 *Total Assets:* £136,558,000
Registered Office: 10 Paternoster Square, London, EC4M 7LS
Activities: Activities auxiliary to financial intermediation n.e.c.
Parent: FTSE International Limited
Officers: Teresa Joanne Elizabeth Hogan, Secretary; Mohammad Reza Ghassemieh [1959] Director [Iranian]; Jonathan Raymond Horton [1957] Marketing Director; Waqas Samad [1969] Director/Chief Executive

FTSE International Limited
Incorporated: 25 September 1995 *Employees:* 185
Net Worth: £258,808,992 *Total Assets:* £480,563,008
Registered Office: 10 Paternoster Square, London, EC4M 7LS
Activities: Other information service activities n.e.c.
Parent: London Stock Exchange Group Holdings Limited
Officers: Teresa Joanne Elizabeth Hogan, Secretary; Nicolas Rene Pierre Bertrand [1971] Director/Head of Equity Markets and IDEM [French]; John Ehnes [1951] Director/Chief Executive [American]; Mohammad Reza Ghassemieh [1959] Director [Iranian]; Denzil Manistre Benedict Jenkins [1967] Director/Head of UK Compliance & Group Regulatory Policy; Waqas Samad [1969] Director/Chief Executive; Catherine Anne Thomas [1968] Director/Solicitor

Fujitsu EMEA PLC
Incorporated: 2 February 1988 *Employees:* 2
Net Worth: £14,938,000 *Total Assets:* £122,880,000
Registered Office: 22 Baker Street, London, W1U 3BW
Activities: Financial intermediation not elsewhere classified
Parent: Fujitsu Limited
Officers: Takanobu Oda, Secretary; Takanobu Oda [1974] Director [Japanese]; Toshiaki Okada [1965] Director/Corporate Treasurer [Japanese]

Fujitsu Services Holdings PLC
Incorporated: 22 November 1915 *Employees:* 11,446
Net Worth: £704,400,000 *Total Assets:* £1,402,700,032
Registered Office: 22 Baker Street, London, W1U 3BW
Activities: Other software publishing
Parent: Fujitsu Limited
Officers: Rachel Heulwen Hitching, Secretary; Duncan Andrew Tait [1966] Director; Hidehiro Tsukano [1958] Director [Japanese]

Fujitsu Services Limited
Incorporated: 13 December 1907 *Employees:* 8,391
Net Worth: £659,800,000 *Total Assets:* £1,267,299,968
Registered Office: 22 Baker Street, London, W1U 3BW
Activities: Other software publishing
Parent: Fujitsu Services Holdings PLC
Officers: Rachel Heulwen Hitching, Secretary; Roberto Adriano Putland [1971] Director/Lawyer; Duncan Andrew Tait [1966] Director

Fuller Smith & Turner PLC
Incorporated: 22 August 1929 *Employees:* 4,913
Net Worth: £338,800,000 *Total Assets:* £677,299,968
Registered Office: Griffin Brewery, Chiswick Lane South, Chiswick, London, W4 2QB
Activities: Hotels and similar accommodation
Officers: Severine Pascale Bequin, Secretary; Simon Ray Dodd [1974] Director; John Michael Dunsmore [1959] Director; Simon Emeny [1965] Group Managing Director; Sir James Henry Fleetwood Fuller [1970] Director; Richard Hamilton Fleetwood Fuller [1960] Sales & Personnel Director; Juliette Natasha Stacey [1970] Director; Jonathon David Swaine [1971] Director; Peter Stuart Swinburn [1953] Director [British/American]; Michael John Turner [1951] Director/Chairman

Funding Circle Holdings PLC
Incorporated: 13 January 2010 *Employees:* 719
Previous: Funding Circle Holdings Limited
Net Worth: £153,400,000 *Total Assets:* £167,900,000
Registered Office: 71 Queen Victoria Street, London, EC4V 4AY
Activities: Other business support service activities n.e.c.
Officers: Lucy Vernall, Secretary; John Eric Daniels [1951] Director; Samir Desai [1983] Director/Financial Services Professional; Sean Robert Glithero [1973] Director/Accountant; Geeta Gopalan [1964] Director; Catherine Jane Keers [1965] Director; Andrew Digby Learoyd [1961] Director; Dr Hendrik Willem Nelis [1964] Director/Venture Capitalist [Dutch]; Neil Rimer [1963] Director [Swiss]; Robert King Steel [1951] Director [American]; Edward James Wray [1968] Director

Fundsmith Emerging Equities Trust PLC
Incorporated: 31 October 2013
Net Worth: £310,672,992 *Total Assets:* £312,295,008
Registered Office: 33 Cavendish Square, London, W1G 0PW
Activities: Activities of investment trusts
Officers: David Martin Bralsford [1948] Director/Chartered Accountant; Rachel de Gruchy [1965] Director; David Roger William Potter [1944] Director; John Strathmore Spencer [1944] Director/Chartered Accountant

G.H. Financials Limited
Incorporated: 4 January 1993 *Employees:* 63
Net Worth: £48,672,256 *Total Assets:* £261,379,952
Registered Office: 4th Floor, 29 Ludgate Hill, London, EC4M 7JR
Activities: Security and commodity contracts dealing activities
Officers: Marino Luchmun, Secretary; Mark Scott Ibbotson [1967] Director/Chairman; Robert Michael Levy [1954] Director; Mark Phelps [1973] Director/Chief Executive

G.I. Globinvestment Limited
Incorporated: 8 June 2016 *Employees:* 1
Net Worth: £103,763,424 *Total Assets:* £117,459,888
Registered Office: 22a St James's Square, London, SW1Y 4JH
Activities: Management consultancy activities other than financial management
Parent: Withers Trust Corporation Limited
Officers: Marco Nuzzo [1977] Director/Manager [Italian]

G4S Care and Justice Services (UK) Limited
Incorporated: 11 October 1944 *Employees:* 4,353
Net Worth: £76,437,000 *Total Assets:* £204,506,000
Registered Office: Southside, 105 Victoria Street, London, SW1E 6QT
Activities: Justice and judicial activities
Parent: G4S Regional Management (UK & I) Limited
Officers: Vaishali Jagdish Patel, Secretary; Julian Mark Hartley [1961] Finance Director; Graham Austen Levinsohn [1962] Director; Gawie Murray Nienaber [1957] Director/Lawyer

G4S Corporate Services Limited
Incorporated: 15 October 2010 *Employees:* 124
Net Worth: £1,404,834,048 *Total Assets:* £3,667,202,048
Registered Office: 5th Floor, Southside, 105 Victoria Street, London, SW1E 6QT
Activities: Activities of head offices
Parent: G4S PLC
Officers: Vaishali Jagdish Patel, Secretary; Celine Arlette Virginie Barroche [1974] Director/Solicitor [French]; Soren Lundsberg-Nielsen [1951] Director [Danish]; Timothy Peter Weller [1963] Director

G4S Facilities Management (UK) Limited
Incorporated: 14 March 1997 *Employees:* 5,061
Net Worth Deficit: £9,704,000 *Total Assets:* £107,704,000
Registered Office: Southside, 105 Victoria Street, London, SW1E 6QT
Activities: Other business support service activities n.e.c.
Parent: G4S Regional Management (UK & I) Limited
Officers: Vaishali Jagdish Patel, Secretary; Philip Charles Dove [1974] Director/Chief Operating Officer - FM; Julian Mark Hartley [1961] Director/Accountant; Ian David Ridgley [1961] Director; Phillip James Thorne [1961] Director

G4S Finance Limited
Incorporated: 5 October 2005
Net Worth: £300,100,000 *Total Assets:* £3,293,779,968
Registered Office: 5th Floor, Southside, 105 Victoria Street, London, SW1E 6QT
Activities: Activities of other holding companies n.e.c.
Parent: G4S PLC
Officers: Vaishali Jagdish Patel, Secretary; Celine Arlette Virginie Barroche [1974] Director/Solicitor [French]; Soren Lundsberg-Nielsen [1951] Director/General Counsel [Danish]; Gareth Nigel Christopher Roberts [1962] Director/Treasurer; Timothy Peter Weller [1963] Director

G4S International Finance PLC
Incorporated: 14 May 2010
Net Worth Deficit: £21,000,000 *Total Assets:* £2,175,000,064
Registered Office: 5th Floor, Southside, 105 Victoria Street, London, SW1E 6QT
Activities: Activities of other holding companies n.e.c.
Parent: G4S PLC
Officers: Vaishali Jagdish Patel, Secretary; Celine Arlette Virginie Barroche [1974] Director/Solicitor [French]; Soren Lundsberg-Nielsen [1951] Director/Group General Counsel [Danish]; Timothy Peter Weller [1963] Director

G4S International Holdings Limited
Incorporated: 10 May 2005
Net Worth: £2,181,541,120 *Total Assets:* £2,716,150,016
Registered Office: 5th Floor, Southside, 105 Victoria Street, London, SW1E 6QT
Activities: Activities of other holding companies n.e.c.
Parent: G4S Corporate Services Limited
Officers: Vaishali Jagdish Patel, Secretary; Celine Arlette Virginie Barroche [1974] Director/Solicitor [French]; Soren Lundsberg Nielsen [1951] Director [Danish]; Timothy Peter Weller [1963] Director

G4S Investment London Limited
Incorporated: 12 October 2011
Net Worth: £1,609,021,952 *Total Assets:* £1,613,858,944
Registered Office: 5th Floor, Southside, 105 Victoria Street, London, SW1E 6QT
Activities: Activities of other holding companies n.e.c.
Shareholders: G4S International Holdings Limited; G4S UK Holdings Limited
Officers: Vaishali Jagdish Patel, Secretary; Celine Arlette Virginie Barroche [1974] Director/Solicitor [French]; Soren Lundsberg-Nielsen [1951] Director/General Counsel [Danish]; Timothy Peter Weller [1963] Director

G4S PLC
Incorporated: 11 December 2003 *Employees:* 573,671
Net Worth: £850,000,000 *Total Assets:* £5,421,000,192
Registered Office: 5th Floor, Southside, 105 Victoria Street, London, SW1E 6QT
Activities: Private security activities
Officers: Celine Arlette Virginie Barroche, Secretary; Ashley Martin Almanza [1963] Director [Irish]; John Patrick Connolly [1950] Director; John Patrick Daly [1956] Director [Irish]; Elisabeth Fleuriot [1956] Director [French]; Winnie Kin Wah Fok [1956] Director; Steven Lewis Mogford [1956] Director; John Ramsay [1957] Director; Paul David Spence [1959] Director [American]; Barbara Rose Milian Thoralfsson [1959] Director [American]; Timothy Peter Weller [1963] Director/Chief Financial Officer

G4S Regional Management (UK & I) Limited
Incorporated: 23 April 1996 *Employees:* 243
Net Worth: £375,179,008 *Total Assets:* £608,891,008
Registered Office: Southside, 105 Victoria Street, London, SW1E 6QT
Activities: Activities of head offices
Parent: G4S UK Holding Limited
Officers: Vaishali Jagdish Patel, Secretary; Julian Mark Hartley [1961] Finance Director; Graham Austen Levinsohn [1962] Director; Gawie Murray Nienaber [1957] Director/Lawyer

G4S UK Holdings Limited
Incorporated: 13 December 1999
Net Worth: £670,102,976 *Total Assets:* £1,047,446,016
Registered Office: 5th Floor, Southside, 105 Victoria Street, London, SW1E 6QT
Activities: Activities of other holding companies n.e.c.
Parent: G4S Corporate Services Limited
Officers: Vaishali Patel, Secretary; Julian Mark Hartley [1961] Finance Director; Graham Austen Levinsohn [1962] Director; Gawie Murray Nienaber [1957] Director/Lawyer

G4S US Holdings Limited
Incorporated: 27 June 2007
Net Worth: £595,644,032 *Total Assets:* £1,056,648,000
Registered Office: 5th Floor, Southside, 105 Victoria Street, London, SW1E 6QT
Activities: Activities of other holding companies n.e.c.
Parent: G4S Corporate Services Limited
Officers: Vaishali Jagdish Patel, Secretary; Celine Arlette Virginie Barroche [1974] Director/Solicitor [French]; Soren Lundsberg Nielsen [1951] Director [Danish]; Timothy Peter Weller [1963] Director

G4S US Investments Limited
Incorporated: 24 July 2008
Net Worth Deficit: £14,378,248 *Total Assets:* £144,669,728
Registered Office: 5th Floor, Southside, 105 Victoria Street, London, SW1E 6QT
Activities: Activities of other holding companies n.e.c.
Parent: G4S Holding One Inc
Officers: Vaishali Jagdish Patel, Secretary; Celine Arlette Virginie Barroche [1974] Director/Solicitor [French]; Soren Lundsberg Nielsen [1951] Director [Danish]; Timothy Peter Weller [1963] Director

GA HC REIT II CH U.K. Senior Housing Portfolio Limited
Incorporated: 24 July 2001
Net Worth: £88,709,000 *Total Assets:* £320,859,008
Registered Office: 2nd Floor, Asticus Building, 21 Palmer Street, London, SW1H 0AD
Activities: Residential nursing care facilities
Parent: GA HC REIT II UK Acquisition SH Limited
Officers: Jonathan David Farkas [1980] Managing Director [American]; Trevor Kincaid Ross [1977] Director [American]; Richard Stephen Welch [1970] Director [American]

Gabelli Value Plus + Trust PLC
Incorporated: 18 December 2014
Net Worth: £129,437,000 *Total Assets:* £131,696,000
Registered Office: 64 St James's Street, London, SW1A 1NF
Activities: Activities of investment trusts
Officers: Rudolf Bohli [1969] Director/Chief Executive Officer [Swiss]; Jonathan Richard Davie [1946] Director; Richard Andrew Fitzalan Howard [1953] Director; Christopher Harwood Bernard Mills [1952] Director; Katarzyna Maria Robinski [1962] Director/Finance

Gabriel International Assets Limited
Incorporated: 26 October 2006
Net Worth: £238,327,376 *Total Assets:* £456,810,016
Registered Office: 39a Welbeck Street, London, W1G 8DH
Activities: Other letting and operating of own or leased real estate
Officers: Revital Gabriel, Secretary; Philip Gabriel [1961] Director/Property Investor; Revital Gabriel [1973] Director/Solicitor

Gabriel International Holdings Limited
Incorporated: 26 October 2006
Net Worth: £238,313,728 *Total Assets:* £456,810,144
Registered Office: 39a Welbeck Street, London, W1G 8DH
Activities: Activities of head offices
Shareholders: Philip Gabriel; Revital Gabriel
Officers: Revital Gabriel, Secretary; Philip Gabriel [1961] Director; Revital Gabriel [1973] Director/Solicitor

Gabriel International Limited
Incorporated: 7 December 2001
Net Worth: £183,938,544 *Total Assets:* £350,121,952
Registered Office: 39a Welbeck Street, London, W1G 8DH
Activities: Other letting and operating of own or leased real estate
Shareholders: Philip Gabriel; Revital Gabriel
Officers: Revital Gabriel, Secretary; Philip Gabriel [1961] Director/Property Investor; Revital Gabriel [1973] Director/Solicitor

GAI Indemnity, Ltd.
Incorporated: 27 September 2007 *Employees:* 180
Net Worth Deficit: £2,224,000 *Total Assets:* £223,340,000
Registered Office: c/o Neon Underwriting Limited, 20 Gracechurch Street, London, EC3V 0BG
Activities: Non-life insurance
Officers: Larysa Alla Dlaboha, Secretary; Ian James Harman [1985] Director; David John Witzgall [1959] Director/Insurance Executive [American]

Gain Capital Holdings Ltd
Incorporated: 12 September 1988 *Employees:* 6
Previous: City Index (Holdings) Limited
Net Worth: £120,672,000 *Total Assets:* £136,943,008
Registered Office: Park House, 16 Finsbury Circus, London, EC2M 7EB
Activities: Activities of other holding companies n.e.c.
Parent: Gain Capital Holdings, Inc
Officers: Michael Peter Lear [1968] Director/Chief Information Officer; Timothy Francis O'Sullivan [1964] Director/Risk Manager Gain Capital Group [American]; Samantha Michelle Roady [1969] Director/Chief Marketing Officer [American]; Diego Andres Rotsztain [1970] Director/Executive/Attorney [American]

Galaxy Group Midco Limited
Incorporated: 14 December 2017
Net Worth: £89,760,000 *Total Assets:* £389,920,000
Registered Office: c/o Amp Capital, Level 4, Berkeley Square House, Berkeley Square, London, W1J 6BX
Activities: Activities of other holding companies n.e.c.
Officers: Manish Aggarwal [1972] Investment Director; Niamh Ann McBreen [1971] Investment Director [Irish]; Kate Solway [1979] Director/Fund Controller

Arthur J. Gallagher (UK) Limited
Incorporated: 9 December 1974
Net Worth: £98,516,000 *Total Assets:* £831,446,976
Registered Office: The Walbrook Building, 25 Walbrook, London, EC4N 8AW
Activities: Non-life insurance
Parent: Gallagher Holdings (UK) Limited
Officers: Alistair Charles Peel, Secretary; James Drummond-Smith [1960] Director; Philip Leighton Hanson [1977] Director/Chartered Accountant; Elisabeth Ibeson [1966] Director; Lady Louise Alexandra Virginia Patten [1954] Director; Carol Richmond [1963] Director/Chief Risk and Compliance Officer; Charles Douglas Scott [1973] Director; John Thompson [1964] Director; Julian Eric Ledward Wallers [1959] Director

Gallagher Holdings (UK) Limited
Incorporated: 13 September 2006
Net Worth: £796,689,984 *Total Assets:* £870,972,992
Registered Office: The Walbrook Building, 25 Walbrook, London, EC4N 8AW
Activities: Activities of head offices
Parent: Arthur J. Gallagher Holdings (UK) Limited
Officers: Alistair Charles Peel, Secretary; Michael Peter Rea [1966] Director; Carol Richmond [1963] Director; Charles Douglas Scott [1973] Director

Arthur J. Gallagher Holdings (UK) Limited
Incorporated: 28 April 2008
Net Worth: £262,626,000 *Total Assets:* £752,902,976
Registered Office: The Walbrook Building, 25 Walbrook, London, EC4N 8AW
Activities: Non-life insurance
Parent: Arthur J. Gallagher & Co
Officers: Alistair Charles Peel, Secretary; David John Coldman [1947] Director; James Drummond-Smith [1960] Director; Thomas Joseph Gallagher [1958] Director [American]; Simon Anthony Green [1963] Director; Susan Carol Langley [1963] Director; Simon Matson [1971] Director; Trevor Philip Newbery [1950] Director; Lady Louise Alexandra Virginia Patten [1954] Director; Ian Graham Story [1963] Director

Galloper Holdco Limited
Incorporated: 22 November 2016
Net Worth Deficit: £14,315 *Total Assets:* £169,036,480
Registered Office: 18 St Swithin's Lane, London, EC4N 8AD
Activities: Activities of other holding companies n.e.c.
Parent: OSW Co Holdings 2 Limited
Officers: Dominic Tan, Secretary; Richard Abel [1970] Director/Investment Banking; Stephen Alan John Deeley [1980] Director/Investment Manager; Mark Jonathan Dooley [1962] Director/Investment Banker [Australian]; Erin Kate Eisenberg [1978] Director [American]; Tom Kelly [1989] Director/Investment Manager [Irish]; Gordon Ian Winston Parsons [1967] Director/Accountant; Roberto Purcaro [1978] Senior Managing Director [Italian]; David Paul Tilstone [1969] Director/Banker

Gam (U.K.) Limited
Incorporated: 16 September 1982 *Employees:* 427
Net Worth: £127,006,000 *Total Assets:* £432,663,008
Registered Office: 8 Finsbury Circus, London, EC2M 7GB
Activities: Activities of financial services holding companies
Officers: Cynthia Mike-Eze, Secretary; Howard Roland Jones [1969] Director; Darren Edward Nicholls [1965] Director; William Harold Norris [1967] Director [Irish]

GAM Systematic Holding Limited
Incorporated: 16 June 2016 *Employees:* 59
Net Worth: £11,328,000 *Total Assets:* £292,132,992
Registered Office: 8 Finsbury Circus, London, EC2M 7GB
Activities: Fund management activities
Parent: Gam UK Limited
Officers: Cynthia Mike-Eze, Secretary; Daniel Hawksley [1975] Director; Anthony Michael Lawler [1973] Director; Fraser Robert McIntyre [1969] Director; Darren Edward Nicholls [1965] Director

Gamesys Limited
Incorporated: 28 July 2000 *Employees:* 1,044
Net Worth: £207,569,520 *Total Assets:* £334,330,944
Registered Office: 4th Floor, 10 Piccadilly, London, W1J 0DD
Activities: Ready-made interactive leisure and entertainment software development
Parent: Gamesys (Holdings) Ltd
Officers: Michael John Robert Mee, Secretary; Lee Daniel Fenton [1970] Director; Philip Jarlath Graham [1973] Director/Chief Technical Officer; Noel Hayden [1970] Director/Businessman; Michael John Robert Mee [1971] Finance Director; Robeson Mandela Reeves [1983] Director/Chief Executive Officer

Gamma Communications PLC
Incorporated: 17 March 2014 *Employees:* 845
Net Worth: £98,800,000 *Total Assets:* £141,200,000
Registered Office: 5 Fleet Place, London, EC4M 7RD
Activities: Other information technology service activities
Officers: Malcolm Charles Goddard, Secretary; Andrew Scott James Belshaw [1974] Finance Director; Alan Bertram Gibbins [1949] Director; Richard Last [1957] Director; Martin Robert Edward LEA [1957] Director; Andrew Jonathan Stone [1970] Director; Andrew George Taylor [1968] Director; Long Peng Wu [1953] Director [Singaporean]

GAP (UK Holdings) Limited
Incorporated: 25 February 1999 *Employees:* 14
Net Worth: £134,865,120 *Total Assets:* £246,929,248
Registered Office: 2nd Floor, Nation House, 103 Wigmore Street, London, W1U 1QS
Activities: Activities of head offices
Parent: The Gap, Inc.
Officers: Lisa Deborah Mertens, Secretary [American]; Edward James Gardiner [1983] Director/Business Executive; Nicola Margaret Groom [1965] Director/Business Executive; Lisa Deborah Mertens [1965] Director/Business Executive [American]

Garban Group Holdings Limited
Incorporated: 21 July 1998
Net Worth: £330,480,000 *Total Assets:* £341,184,992
Registered Office: Floor 2, 155 Bishopsgate, London, EC2M 3TQ
Activities: Activities of financial services holding companies
Parent: ICAP Global Broking Holdings Limited
Officers: Paul James Ashley [1978] Finance Director; Richard Cordeschi [1967] Director/Chartered Secretary

Garban-Intercapital (2001) Limited
Incorporated: 9 February 2001
Net Worth: £188,096,992 *Total Assets:* £188,096,992
Registered Office: Floor 2, 155 Bishopsgate, London, EC2M 3TQ
Activities: Activities of financial services holding companies
Parent: ICAP America Investments Limited
Officers: Paul James Ashley [1978] Finance Director; Richard Cordeschi [1967] Director/Chartered Secretary

Garban-Intercapital US Investments (Holdings) Limited
Incorporated: 9 February 2001
Net Worth: £184,584,992 *Total Assets:* £184,587,008
Registered Office: Floor 2, 155 Bishopsgate, London, EC2M 3TQ
Activities: Dormant company
Parent: Garban-Intercapital (2001) Limited
Officers: Paul James Ashley [1978] Finance Director; Richard Cordeschi [1967] Director/Chartered Secretary

Garban-Intercapital US Investments (No 1) Limited
Incorporated: 12 February 2001
Net Worth: £184,587,008 *Total Assets:* £184,587,008
Registered Office: Floor 2, 155 Bishopsgate, London, EC2M 3TQ
Activities: Dormant company
Parent: Garban-Intercapital US Investments (Holdings) Limited
Officers: Paul James Ashley [1978] Finance Director; Richard Cordeschi [1967] Director/Chartered Secretary

Gardaworld Consulting (UK) Limited
Incorporated: 9 June 2015 *Employees:* 2
Net Worth: £3,996,917 *Total Assets:* £109,235,168
Registered Office: The St Botolph Building, 138 Houndsditch, London, EC3A 7AR
Activities: Activities of other holding companies n.e.c.
Officers: Pierre-Hubert Seguin, Secretary; Patrick Prince [1962] Director/Chief Financial Officer, CPA [Canadian]; Pierre-Hubert Seguin [1970] Director/Attorney [Canadian]

Garden Finance Limited
Incorporated: 4 September 2015
Net Worth: £15,103,560 *Total Assets:* £512,707,808
Registered Office: 10 Bressenden Place, London, SW1E 5DN
Activities: Activities of other holding companies n.e.c.
Parent: Garden Midco 1 Limited
Officers: Ruairidh Gregor Cameron [1975] Finance Director; Kully Janjuah [1968] Director/Company Secretary; Alan Middleton [1966] Director

Garden Midco 1 Limited
Incorporated: 3 September 2015
Net Worth: £15,676,975 *Total Assets:* £361,164,608
Registered Office: 10 Bressenden Place, London, SW1E 5DN
Activities: Activities of other holding companies n.e.c.
Parent: PA Consulting Group Limited
Officers: Ruairidh Gregor Cameron [1975] Finance Director; Kully Janjuah [1968] Director/Company Secretary; Alan Middleton [1966] Director

Garden Midco 2 Limited
Incorporated: 4 September 2015
Net Worth: £26,375,778 *Total Assets:* £512,697,888
Registered Office: 10 Bressenden Place, London, SW1E 5DN
Activities: Activities of other holding companies n.e.c.
Parent: Garden Finance Limited
Officers: Ruairidh Gregor Cameron [1975] Finance Director; Kully Janjuah [1968] Director/Company Secretary; Alan Middleton [1966] Director

Gartmore Investment Management Limited
Incorporated: 7 May 1969
Net Worth: £111,717,000 *Total Assets:* £115,358,000
Registered Office: 201 Bishopsgate, London, EC2M 3AE
Activities: Activities of head offices
Parent: Henderson Global Investors Asset Management
Officers: Alexander John Ayres [1980] Director/Accountant; Rhiannon Willow Chaudhuri [1978] Director/Accountant

Gatehouse Bank PLC
Incorporated: 25 May 2007 *Employees:* 44
Net Worth: £127,461,648 *Total Assets:* £280,526,240
Registered Office: 14 Grosvenor Street, London, W1K 4PS
Activities: Banks
Shareholder: Kuwait Investment Authority Acting on behalf of The Government of Kuwait
Officers: Mohammed Abdul Mohaimin Chowdhury, Secretary; Abdulaziz Saud Albader [1958] Director [Kuwaiti]; Fahed Faisal Boodai [1973] Director/Chairman [Kuwaiti]; Andrew Robert Gray [1963] Director; Generald Arthur Gregory [1955] Director; Charles William Haresnape [1958] Director; Danesh Paul Mahadeva [1983] Director/Chief Financial Officer; Stephen Paul Smith [1953] Director

Gates Acquisitions Limited
Incorporated: 22 July 2010
Net Worth: £164,992,720 *Total Assets:* £498,964,960
Registered Office: 35 Great St Helen's, London, EC3A 6AP
Activities: Activities of head offices
Parent: Finco Omaha Limited
Officers: Nathan Andrew Rogers [1964] Director [American]; Jamey Susan Seely [1971] Director/Executive Vice President [American]; Marc Gregory Swanson [1969] Director/Vice President, Global Tax [American]

Gates European Holdings Limited
Incorporated: 27 April 2006
Net Worth: £381,532,608 *Total Assets:* £381,603,200
Registered Office: 35 Great St Helen's, London, EC3A 6AP
Activities: Activities of head offices
Parent: Finco Omaha Limited
Officers: Nathan Andrew Rogers [1964] Director [American]; Jamey Susan Seely [1971] Director/Executive Vice President [American]; Marc Gregory Swanson [1969] Director/Vice President, Global Tax [American]

Gates Finance Limited
Incorporated: 19 June 2003
Net Worth: £332,592,192 *Total Assets:* £1,553,783,680
Registered Office: 35 Great St Helen's, London, EC3A 6AP
Activities: Activities of head offices
Parent: Gates Worldwide Limited
Officers: Nathan Andrew Rogers [1964] Director [American]; Jamey Susan Seely [1971] Director/Executive Vice President [American]; Marc Gregory Swanson [1969] Director/Vice President, Global Tax [American]

Gates Holdings Limited
Incorporated: 21 February 2001
Net Worth: £190,399,456 *Total Assets:* £268,790,144
Registered Office: 35 Great St Helen's, London, EC3A 6AP
Activities: Activities of head offices
Parent: Gates Finance Limited
Officers: Nathan Andrew Rogers [1964] Director [American]; Jamey Susan Seely [1971] Director/Executive Vice President [American]; Marc Gregory Swanson [1969] Director/Vice President, Global Tax [American]

Gates Worldwide Limited
Incorporated: 2 February 1925 *Employees:* 3
Net Worth: £484,704,448 *Total Assets:* £485,624,480
Registered Office: 35 Great St Helen's, London, EC3A 6AP
Activities: Activities of head offices
Parent: Gates Acquisitions Limited
Officers: Nathan Andrew Rogers [1964] Director [American]; Jamey Susan Seely [1971] Director/Executive Vice President [American]; Marc Gregory Swanson [1969] Director/Vice President, Global Tax [American]

Gazeley Blue UK Limited
Incorporated: 3 May 2013 *Employees:* 3
Previous: BSREP Logistics UK Limited
Net Worth: £161,840,000 *Total Assets:* £274,312,000
Registered Office: 6th Floor, 99 Bishopsgate, London, EC2M 3XD
Activities: Activities of other holding companies n.e.c.
Officers: Nicholas Robert Cook [1977] Director/Chief Executive Officer; Shane Roger Kelly [1969] Director/Chief Financial Officer; Rachel Ann Walker [1980] Director/General Counsel

Gazeley Holdings UK Limited
Incorporated: 23 May 2008 *Employees:* 1
Net Worth: £13,739,768 *Total Assets:* £236,044,848
Registered Office: 6th Floor, 99 Bishopsgate, London, EC2M 3XD
Activities: Activities of other holding companies n.e.c.
Officers: Patrick John McGillycuddy [1952] Director [Irish]

Gazeley Limited
Incorporated: 28 November 1988 *Employees:* 30
Net Worth: £194,491,232 *Total Assets:* £248,722,288
Registered Office: 6th Floor, 99 Bishopsgate, London, EC2M 3XD
Activities: Development of building projects
Parent: Gazeley Holdings (UK) Limited
Officers: Shane Roger Kelly, Secretary; Nicholas Robert Cook [1977] Director-Property Development; Shane Roger Kelly [1969] Director/Chartered Accountant; Patrick John McGillycuddy [1952] Director/CEO of Gazeley [Irish]

Gazeley UK Limited
Incorporated: 30 April 1987 *Employees:* 3
Net Worth: £172,414,336 *Total Assets:* £282,299,392
Registered Office: 6th Floor, 99 Bishopsgate, London, EC2M 3XD
Activities: Development of building projects
Parent: Gazeley Limited
Officers: Shane Roger Kelly, Secretary; Shane Roger Kelly [1969] Director/Chartered Accountant; Bruce Alistair Topley [1970] Development Director; Alexander Christopher Verbeek [1972] Director

Gazprom Global LNG Limited
Incorporated: 22 August 2008 *Employees:* 26
Net Worth: £14,857,778 *Total Assets:* £131,593,192
Registered Office: 20 Triton Street, London, NW1 3BF
Activities: Other business support service activities n.e.c.
Parent: Gazprom Marketing & Trading Limited
Officers: Andrey Mikhalev [1961] Director/Chief Corporate & Financial Officer [Russian]

Gazprom Marketing & Trading Limited
Incorporated: 6 May 1999 *Employees:* 828
Net Worth: £876,291,008 *Total Assets:* £3,240,242,944
Registered Office: 20 Triton Street, London, NW1 3BF
Activities: Trade of electricity
Shareholder: The Russian Federation Represented By The Federal Agency for State Property Management
Officers: Andrey Mikhalev [1961] Director/Chief Corporate & Financial Officer [Russian]; Lavrenty Pilyagin [1968] Deputy Managing Director [Russian]

Gazprom Marketing & Trading Retail Limited
Incorporated: 11 January 2000 *Employees:* 296
Net Worth: £13,233,000 *Total Assets:* £405,369,984
Registered Office: 20 Triton Street, London, NW1 3BF
Activities: Distribution of electricity
Parent: Gazprom Marketing & Trading Limited
Officers: Evgeny Gribov [1974] Director [Russian]; Dmitry Kotulskiy [1978] Director/Deputy Head of Department [Russian]; Igor Iosifovich Lipskii [1966] Director/Deputy Head of Department [Russian]; Kurt Bligaard Pedersen [1959] Director [Danish]

GB Railfreight Limited
Incorporated: 4 February 1999 *Employees:* 653
Net Worth: £45,243,000 *Total Assets:* £145,156,000
Registered Office: 55 Old Broad Street, London, EC2M 1RX
Activities: Freight rail transport
Parent: Hector Rail Holding UK Limited
Officers: Karl Peter Goulding-Davis [1971] Director; John Geoffrey Smith [1961] Director

GB Social Housing PLC
Incorporated: 22 February 2010
Net Worth: £561,491 *Total Assets:* £300,839,968
Registered Office: 35 Great St Helen's, London, EC3A 6AP
Activities: Credit granting by non-deposit taking finance houses and other specialist consumer credit grantors
Officers: Michael Leslie Jones [1948] Director/Corporate Finance Adviser; Sir Duncan Michael [1937] Director; Gerhard Oberholzer [1963] Director/Asset Manager; John Pilkington [1949] Director/Management Consultant

GBG International Holding Company Limited
Incorporated: 18 December 2013 *Employees:* 53
Net Worth: £1,104,418,944 *Total Assets:* £1,332,350,976
Registered Office: 242-246 Marylebone Road, London, NW1 6JQ
Activities: Activities of head offices
Officers: Richard Nixon Darling [1953] Director [American]; Dr Dow Peter Famulak [1960] Director [Canadian]; Ronald Ventricelli [1959] Director/Chief Financial Officer [American]

GBT Travel Services UK Limited
Incorporated: 13 November 2013 *Employees:* 923
Net Worth: £60,193,208 *Total Assets:* £290,376,448
Registered Office: 5 Churchill Place, Canary Wharf, London, E14 5HU
Activities: Travel agency activities
Officers: Sheena Varma, Secretary; Eric J. Bock [1965] Director/Chief Legal Officer and Corporate Secretary [American]; Philippe Marie Charles Chereque [1951] Director/Chief Commercial & Technology Officer [French]; Jason Matthew Geall [1976] Director/Vice President/General Manager UK; John Christopher Gibson [1964] Director, Tax; Joanna Sutherland MacLeod [1967] Director/Senior Vice President, Global Service Delivery

GC Campden Hill LLP
Incorporated: 11 December 2009
Net Worth: £190,903,296 *Total Assets:* £240,168,080
Registered Office: The Pavilion, 118 Southwark Street, London, SE1 0SW

GCM Global Energy PLC
Incorporated: 26 September 2007 *Employees:* 136
Net Worth: £55,269,304 *Total Assets:* £229,834,272
Registered Office: Second Floor, 11 Pilgrim Street, London, EC4V 6RN
Activities: Activities of head offices
Shareholders: Said Gutseriev; Mikail Gutseriev
Officers: Regina Dubrovskaya [1966] Finance Director; Maxim Kalyuzhny [1974] Director/Legal Consultant; Anton Aleksandrovich Zhuchenko [1975] Director

GCP (UK) Holdings Limited
Incorporated: 3 June 2015
Net Worth: £224,877,824 *Total Assets:* £387,252,384
Registered Office: 100 New Bridge Street, London, EC4V 6JA
Activities: Activities of head offices
Parent: GCP Applied Technologies Inc.
Officers: Elizabeth Ann Cowell [1958] Director/Business Executive [American]; Andrew Julian Kelly [1964] Business Director/General Manager; Alexander Holger Emil Nielsen [1966] Director/Company Lawyer [German]; Upkar Ricky Singh Tatla [1976] Director/Business Executive

Kurt Geiger Limited
Incorporated: 10 December 1969 *Employees:* 2,143
Net Worth: £128,720,000 *Total Assets:* £205,622,000
Registered Office: 24 Britton Street, London, EC1M 5UA
Activities: Retail sale of footwear in specialised stores
Officers: Dale Nicholas Christilaw, Finance Director; Dale Nicholas Christilaw [1970] Finance Director; Neil Charles Clifford [1967] Director/Retail Executive; Rebecca Elizabeth Alden Farrar Hockley [1971] Director/Retail Executive

Gemfields Limited
Incorporated: 14 May 2004 *Employees:* 2,191
Previous: Gemfields PLC
Net Worth: £174,265,584 *Total Assets:* £341,119,904
Registered Office: 1 New Burlington Place, London, W1S 2HR
Activities: Other mining and quarrying n.e.c.
Officers: Toby Edward George Hewitt, Secretary; Adrian Banks [1978] Product Director [South African/British]; Brian Patrick Gilbertson [1943] Director/Chairman; Sean Thomas Gilbertson [1972] Director/Chief Executive Officer [South African/British]; David John Lovett [1982] Director/Chief Financial Officer; David John Lovett [1982] Director/Chief Financial Officer; Kartikeya Parikshya [1964] Director [Indian]; Chandana Venkata Suresh [1960] Director of Operations [Indian]

Genel Energy Miran Bina Bawi Limited
Incorporated: 19 December 2011
Net Worth Deficit: £177,718,608 *Total Assets:* £593,602,496
Registered Office: Fifth Floor, 36 Broadway, London, SW1H 0BH
Activities: Activities of other holding companies n.e.c.
Parent: Genel Energy PLC
Officers: Chandni Karania, Secretary; William George Higgs [1964] Director; Esa Tapani Ikaheimonen [1963] Director/Chief Financial Officer [Finnish]; Kemal Pars Kutay [1959] Director/Head of Governance & Public Affairs [Turkish]

General Alumina Holdings Limited
Incorporated: 29 September 2014
Net Worth Deficit: £5,104,890 *Total Assets:* £120,839,944
Registered Office: 33 Cavendish Square, London, W1G 0PW
Activities: Activities of other holding companies n.e.c.
Officers: Chee Ying Lim, Secretary; Jeffrey Mark Alam [1958] Director; Timothy Martin Eyre [1969] Director; William James Randall [1974] Director [Australian]

General Dynamics European Finance Limited
Incorporated: 13 December 2013 *Employees:* 1
Net Worth: £133,144,760 *Total Assets:* £652,667,840
Registered Office: 21 Holborn Viaduct, London, EC1A 2DY
Activities: Activities of other holding companies n.e.c.
Parent: General Dynamics Global Holdings Limited
Officers: Kyle J. McNamara, Secretary; David Herbert Fogg [1955] Director/Executive [American]; Gregory Stratis Gallopoulos [1959] Director/Attorney [American]; Steven Edward Rowbotham [1957] Director/Executive

General Dynamics Global Holdings Limited
Incorporated: 18 November 2013 *Employees:* 3
Net Worth: £4,220,357,376 *Total Assets:* £4,261,932,800
Registered Office: 21 Holborn Viaduct, London, EC1A 2DY
Activities: Activities of head offices
Parent: General Dynamics Corporation
Officers: Kyle J. McNamara, Secretary; Jason Wright Aiken [1972] Director [American]; Gregory Stratis Gallopoulos [1959] Director/Attorney [American]; Steven Edward Rowbotham [1957] Director/Executive

General Dynamics Swiss Financial Management Limited
Incorporated: 24 May 2017
Net Worth: £802,184,640 *Total Assets:* £1,203,788,288
Registered Office: 21 Holborn Viaduct, London, EC1A 2DY
Activities: Other business support service activities n.e.c.
Parent: General Dynamics Global Holdings Limited
Officers: Kyle J. McNamara, Secretary; Jason Wright Aiken [1972] Director/Executive [American]; David Herbert Fogg [1955] Director/Executive [American]

General Dynamics United Kingdom Limited
Incorporated: 7 May 1985 *Employees:* 1,027
Net Worth: £278,599,008 *Total Assets:* £597,075,008
Registered Office: 21 Holborn Viaduct, London, EC1A 2DY
Activities: Defence activities
Parent: General Dynamics Limited
Officers: Zara Nina Mitchell, Secretary; Jason Monahan, Secretary; Sir Andrew Thomas Cahn [1951] Director; Lord Peter Keith Levene of Portsoken [1941] Director; Christopher Marzilli [1959] Director [American]; Gary Lee Whited [1960] Director/President [American]

General Healthcare Group Limited
Incorporated: 4 July 2000
Net Worth: £400,172,992 *Total Assets:* £418,748,000
Registered Office: BMI Healthcare House, 3 Paris Garden, London, SE1 8ND
Activities: Activities of head offices
Parent: Pedalclip Limited
Officers: Henry Jonathan Davies [1968] Finance Director; Dr Karen Anita Prins [1961] Director/Chief Executive Officer [South African]; Neil Jonathan Robson [1969] Director/Chartered Accountant; Michael Anthony Thomas [1976] Director/Chartered Accountant

General Healthcare Holding Partnership LLP
Incorporated: 5 May 2006
Net Worth: £540,470,144 *Total Assets:* £540,470,144
Registered Office: BMI Healthcare House, 3 Paris Garden, London, SE1 8ND

General Healthcare Holdings (2) Limited
Incorporated: 4 July 2000
Net Worth: £764,275,008 *Total Assets:* £1,853,044,992
Registered Office: BMI Healthcare House, 3 Paris Garden, Southwark, London, SE1 8ND
Activities: Activities of other holding companies n.e.c.
Parent: General Healthcare Group Limited
Officers: Henry Jonathan Davies [1968] Finance Director; Dr Karen Anita Prins [1961] Director/Chief Executive Officer [South African]; Michael Anthony Thomas [1976] Director/Chartered Accountant

General Healthcare Holdings (3) Limited
Incorporated: 25 August 2000
Net Worth: £505,999,008 *Total Assets:* £804,883,008
Registered Office: BMI Healthcare House, 3 Paris Garden, Southwark, London, SE1 8ND
Activities: Activities of other holding companies n.e.c.
Parent: General Healthcare Holdings (2) Limited
Officers: Henry Jonathan Davies [1968] Finance Director; Dr Karen Anita Prins [1961] Director/Chief Executive Officer [South African]

General Healthcare Holdings (4) Limited
Incorporated: 4 July 2000
Net Worth: £34,098,000 *Total Assets:* £793,024,000
Registered Office: BMI Healthcare House, 3 Paris Garden, London, SE1 8ND
Activities: Activities of other holding companies n.e.c.
Parent: GHG Intermediate Holdings Limited
Officers: Henry Jonathan Davies [1968] Finance Director; Dr Karen Anita Prins [1961] Director/Chief Executive Officer [South African]

General Healthcare Mixer Partnership LLP
Incorporated: 5 May 2006 *Employees:* 7,547
Net Worth: £203,586,000 *Total Assets:* £772,556,032
Registered Office: BMI Healthcare House, 3 Paris Garden, Southwark, London, SE1 8ND

General Motors Europe Limited
Incorporated: 9 March 2011 *Employees:* 19
Net Worth Deficit: £213,100,000 *Total Assets:* £340,200,000
Registered Office: 100 New Bridge Street, London, EC4V 6JA
Activities: Other business support service activities n.e.c.
Parent: General Motors Company
Officers: Vikas Khare [1971] Director/Chartered Accountant; Gustavo Quintaes Vello [1973] Financial Director [Brazilian]

GenFinance II PLC
Incorporated: 5 October 2009
Net Worth: £83,000 *Total Assets:* £257,730,000
Registered Office: Bruce Kenrick House, Killick Street, London, N1 9FL
Activities: Other business support service activities n.e.c.
Officers: Andrew Nankivell, Secretary; Andrew Jude Belton [1958] Executive Director [Irish]; Carl Francis Byrne [1978] Director; Kate Davies [1956] Director; John Hughes [1962] Executive Director [Irish]; Bruce Robert Mew [1954] Director/Accountant; Paul Christopher Phillips [1955] Executive Director; Jeremy Hugh Stibbe [1963] Executive Director; Vipulchandra Biharilal Thacker [1965] Executive Director; Mark Vaughan [1970] Executive Director

Genome Research Limited
Incorporated: 20 August 1992 *Employees:* 1,070
Net Worth: £55,555,000 *Total Assets:* £212,844,992
Registered Office: Gibbs Building, 215 Euston Road, London, NW1 2BE
Activities: Research and experimental development on biotechnology
Officers: Henry Parkinson, Secretary; Professor Dame Kay Elizabeth Davies [1951] Director/Dr Lee's Professor of Anatomy Associate Head; Professor Rolf Dieter Heuer [1948] Director General of CERN [German]; Sir James Cuthbert Smith [1954] Director of Science; The Rt Hon Lord David Lindsay Willetts [1956] Director/House of Lords

Genting Americas Holdings Limited
Incorporated: 5 August 2015
Net Worth: £204,730,448 *Total Assets:* £204,783,152
Registered Office: Suite 1, 3rd Floor, 11-12 St James's Square, London, SW1Y 4LB
Activities: Activities of other holding companies n.e.c.
Officers: Declan Thomas Kenny [1961] Director/Certified Accountant; Poy Yong Koh [1956] Director/Chief Financial Officer [Malaysian]; Dato' Sri Choong Yan Lee [1961] Director/President/Chief Operating Officer [Malaysian]

Genting Worldwide Services Limited
Incorporated: 15 December 2016
Net Worth: £813,056,000 *Total Assets:* £819,277,888
Registered Office: Suite 1, 3rd Floor, 11-12 St James's Square, London, SW1Y 4LB
Activities: Other credit granting n.e.c.
Officers: James Axelby [1972] Director; Poy Yong Koh [1956] Director/Chief Financial Officer [Malaysian]; Dato' Sri Choong Yan Lee [1961] Director/President & Chief Operating Officer [Malaysian]

Georgia Healthcare Group PLC
Incorporated: 27 August 2015 *Employees:* 13,894
Net Worth: £138,630,000 *Total Assets:* £334,708,992
Registered Office: 84 Brook Street, London, W1K 5EH
Activities: Activities of head offices
Officers: Dr Michael George Anderson [1951] Director/Consultant Physician; Fabian Stephan Blank [1974] Director/Investor & Advisor [German]; Timothy James Elsigood [1954] Director; Nikoloz Gamkrelidze [1979] Director/Chief Executive Officer [Georgian]; Irakli Gilauri [1976] Director/Chairman [Georgian]; William Huyett [1955] Director [American]; David Fielding Morrison [1952] Director; Ingeborg Dydbal Oie [1983] Director/Chief Financial Officer [Norwegian]; Jacques Blaise Richier [1955] Director

GESB PLC
Incorporated: 1 January 1994
Net Worth: £239,017 *Total Assets:* £105,860,096
Registered Office: Third Floor, 1 King's Arms Yard, London, EC2R 7AF
Activities: Other business support service activities n.e.c.
Parent: Royal Exchange Trust Company Limited
Officers: Robert Sutton [1978] Director/Financial Services [American]; Daniel Jonathan Wynne [1970] Director

Get Living London EV N01 Limited
Incorporated: 17 July 2013
Net Worth: £49,959,000 *Total Assets:* £157,888,000
Registered Office: 6th Floor, Lansdowne House, Berkeley Square, London, W1J 6ER
Activities: Other letting and operating of own or leased real estate
Parent: Get Living London EV Holdco Limited
Officers: Abdulla Al-Ajail [1979] Director [Qatari]; Jeremy Martin Holmes [1960] Director/Chief Development Officer, Qatari Diar UK Limited; Stafford Murray Lancaster [1968] Director; James William Jeremy Ritblat [1967] Director; Gawain Sydney Edward Smart [1970] Director/Head of Legal [Canadian]; Mabel Tan [1974] Director of Asset Management

Get Living London EV N07 Limited
Incorporated: 17 July 2013
Net Worth: £41,195,000 *Total Assets:* £128,541,000
Registered Office: 6th Floor, Lansdowne House, Berkeley Square, London, W1J 6ER
Activities: Other letting and operating of own or leased real estate
Parent: Get Living London EV Holdco Limited
Officers: Abdulla Al-Ajail [1979] Director [Qatari]; Jeremy Martin Holmes [1960] Director/Chief Development Officer, Qatari Diar UK Limited; Stafford Murray Lancaster [1968] Director; James William Jeremy Ritblat [1967] Director; Gawain Sydney Edward Smart [1970] Director/Head of Legal [Canadian]

Get Living London EV2 Holdco Limited
Incorporated: 17 July 2013
Total Assets: £193,824,992
Registered Office: 6th Floor, Lansdowne House, Berkeley Square, London, W1J 6ER
Activities: Activities of other holding companies n.e.c.
Parent: Get Living London EV1 Holdco Limited
Officers: Abdulla Al-Ajail [1979] Director [Qatari]; Jeremy Martin Holmes [1960] Director/Chief Development Officer, Qatari Diar UK Limited; Stafford Murray Lancaster [1968] Director; James William Jeremy Ritblat [1967] Director; Gawain Sydney Edward Smart [1970] Director/Head of Legal [Canadian]; Mabel Tan [1974] Director of Asset Management

GF Financial Markets (UK) Limited
Incorporated: 2 February 1976 *Employees:* 38
Net Worth: £25,848,576 *Total Assets:* £284,516,544
Registered Office: 1 Broadgate, London, EC2M 2QS
Activities: Financial intermediation not elsewhere classified
Officers: Adrian Paul Penney, Secretary; Jiu Chang [1974] Director/Risk Management [Chinese]; Robert Smith Leighton [1941] Director/Banker; Boya Liu [1978] Director/GF Futures Hong Kong CEO and Business Development [Chinese]; Adrian Paul Penney [1965] Director/Chief Financial Officer; Shaohui Shi [1967] Managing Director; Guiping Zhao [1964] Director/Chairperson of GF Futures Co., Limited [Chinese]

GFG UK 1 Limited
Incorporated: 14 June 2017
Net Worth: £213,153,136 *Total Assets:* £213,191,680
Registered Office: The Space, 120 Regent Street, London, W1B 5FE
Activities: Activities of other holding companies n.e.c.
Officers: Yana Valletta, Secretary; Nils Chrestin [1980] Director/Group Chief Financial Officer [German]; Yana Valletta [1978] Director/General Counsel [Italian]

GFI EMEA Holdings Limited
Incorporated: 7 February 2013
Net Worth: £311,043,520 *Total Assets:* £474,752,384
Registered Office: 1 Snowden Street, London, EC2A 2DQ
Activities: Activities of financial services holding companies
Officers: Robert Mark Snelling, Secretary; Darryl Anthony Denyssen [1973] Director; Julian Simon Johns Swain [1966] Managing Director

GFI Holdings Limited
Incorporated: 14 July 1997 *Employees:* 310
Net Worth: £711,611,584 *Total Assets:* £1,024,769,600
Registered Office: 1 Snowden Street, London, EC2A 2DQ
Activities: Activities of financial services holding companies
Parent: GFI EMEA Holdings Limited
Officers: Robert Mark Snelling, Secretary; Prashant Kumar Chandrakant Naik [1971] Finance Director; Julian Simon Johns Swain [1966] Managing Director; Sean Anthony Windeatt [1973] Director/Chief Operating Officer

GFI Markets Limited
Incorporated: 19 January 2010 *Employees:* 13
Net Worth: £258,980,288 *Total Assets:* £258,980,288
Registered Office: 1 Snowden Street, London, EC2A 2DQ
Activities: Activities of financial services holding companies
Parent: GFI Holdings Limited
Officers: Robert Mark Snelling, Secretary; Darryl Anthony Denyssen [1973] Director; John Dudley Fishburn [1946] Independent Director; Marc Victor Samy Souffir [1972] Managing Director [French]; Julian Simon Johns Swain [1966] Managing Director Head of London

GFI Securities Limited
Incorporated: 14 July 1997 *Employees:* 171
Net Worth: £90,562,904 *Total Assets:* £268,811,136
Registered Office: 1 Snowden Street, London, EC2A 2DQ
Activities: Financial intermediation not elsewhere classified
Parent: GFI Markets Limited
Officers: Robert Mark Snelling, Secretary; Prashant Kumar Chandrakant Naik [1971] Finance Director; Marc Victor Samy Souffir [1972] Managing Director [French]; Julian Simon Johns Swain [1966] Managing Director

GFS Renewable Energy Limited
Incorporated: 22 August 2011 *Employees:* 4
Net Worth: £92,985,000 *Total Assets:* £224,136,000
Registered Office: c/o Hackwood Secretaries Limited, One Silk Street, London, EC2Y 8HQ
Activities: Activities of other holding companies n.e.c.
Shareholder: Development Bank of Japan Inc.
Officers: Akira Hirano [1971] Director, Electrical Engineer [Japanese]; Shingo Kanatani [1976] Director/Banker [Japanese]; Takeo Kitamura [1976] Director/Employee in a Financial Institution [Japanese]; Ken Matsuda [1973] Director/General Manager [Japanese]

GGR Capital Limited
Incorporated: 4 October 2006
Net Worth: £20,250,056 *Total Assets:* £747,928,000
Registered Office: One Fleet Place, London, EC4M 7WS
Activities: Other business support service activities n.e.c.
Major Shareholder: Elizabeth Walton Snyder
Officers: Colin Robert Ormiston, Secretary; Michael Thomas Enright [1964] Director [American]; Charles Bradford Jones [1952] Director/Businessman [American]; Colin Robert Ormiston [1961] Director/Accountant

GH Holdings 1 Limited
Incorporated: 8 June 2015 *Employees:* 942
Net Worth: £88,376,000 *Total Assets:* £174,251,008
Registered Office: 4th Floor, 159 St John Street, London, EC1V 4QJ
Activities: Activities of other holding companies n.e.c.
Officers: Srikanth Balachandran [1961] Director [Indian]; Sonal Kapasi [1971] Director [Indian]; Shravin Bharti Mittal [1987] Director; Sharan Pasricha [1980] Director

GH Holdings 2 Limited
Incorporated: 8 June 2015 *Employees:* 3
Net Worth: £65,337,000 *Total Assets:* £161,795,008
Registered Office: 4th Floor, 159 St John Street, London, EC1V 4QJ
Activities: Activities of other holding companies n.e.c.
Parent: GH Holdings 1 Limited
Officers: Srikanth Balachandran [1961] Director [Indian]; Sonal Kapasi [1971] Director [Indian]; Shravin Bharti Mittal [1987] Director; Sharan Pasricha [1980] Director

Ghana International Bank Public Limited Company
Incorporated: 13 November 1997 *Employees:* 80
Net Worth: £139,959,824 *Total Assets:* £781,577,984
Registered Office: 1st Floor, Regina House, 67 Cheapside, London, EC2V 6AZ
Activities: Banks
Parent: Bank of Ghana
Officers: Beatrice Mettle Nunoo, Secretary; Dr Ernest Kwamina Yedu Addison [1963] Director/Economist [Ghanaian]; Jude Kofi Arthur [1955] Director/Banker [Ghanaian]; Lord Paul Boateng [1951] Director/Barrister; Hamish Cameron Galbraith Marr [1962] Director/Banker; Dr John Kofi Mensah [1961] Director/Banker [Ghanaian]; Dr John Ofori - Tenkorang [1965] Director/Electrical Engineer [Ghanaian]; Dr Maxwell Opoku Afari [1970] Director/Economist [Ghanaian]; Raymond Jacob Bakary Sambou [1963] Director/Banker

GHG 1 (Hospital Operations) Limited
Incorporated: 18 April 2006 *Employees:* 7
Net Worth Deficit: £299,740,000 *Total Assets:* £644,283,008
Registered Office: BMI Healthcare House, 3 Paris Garden, Southwark, London, SE1 8ND
Activities: Activities of other holding companies n.e.c.
Parent: General Healthcare Mixer Partnership LLP
Officers: Melanie Sandra Fernandes Da Costa [1972] Director of Strategy & Health Policy [South African]; Travis Charles Dewing [1973] Director/Chief Information Officer [South African]; Dr Steven Lewis Dyson [1973] Director/Investor Professional (Partner at Apax Partners); Dr Richard Harold Friedland [1961] Director/Doctor Executive [South African]; Keith Norman Gibson [1970] Director [South African]; Gary William Hughes [1962] Director/Private Equity Executive; Leonard Kevin Chandran Sebastian [1969] Lawyer and Director [Swiss]; Christoffel Smith [1967] Director/Finance; Peter Warrener [1961] Director of Human Resources [South African]

GHG Intermediate Holdings Limited
Incorporated: 3 May 2001
Net Worth: £1,091,346,048 *Total Assets:* £1,103,768,064
Registered Office: BMI Healthcare House, 3 Paris Garden, London, SE1 8ND
Activities: Activities of other holding companies n.e.c.
Parent: General Healthcare Holdings (2) Limited
Officers: Henry Jonathan Davies [1968] Finance Director; Dr Karen Anita Prins [1961] Director/Chief Executive Officer [South African]; Michael Anthony Thomas [1976] Director/Chartered Accountant

Giltbrook Retail Park Nottingham Limited
Incorporated: 2 June 2005
Net Worth: £132,131,704 *Total Assets:* £139,503,408
Registered Office: York House, 45 Seymour Street, London, W1H 7LX
Activities: Development of building projects
Parent: BL Retail Warehousing Holding Company Limited
Officers: Sarah Morrell Barzycki [1958] Director/Head of Finance; Paul Stuart Macey [1978] Director/Accountant; Jonathan Charles McNuff [1986] Director/Chartered Accountant; Charles John Middleton [1966] Director/Corporate Tax Executive; Timothy Andrew Roberts [1964] Director/Chartered Surveyor; Nigel Mark Webb [1963] Director/Chartered Surveyor

GIP II (Vista) Holdco 1, Limited
Incorporated: 7 March 2014
Net Worth: £46,898,740 *Total Assets:* £212,228,240
Registered Office: 5th Floor, 6 St Andrew Street, London, EC4A 3AE
Activities: Activities of other holding companies n.e.c.
Officers: Andrew Harvey Gillespie-Smith [1967] Director/Principal; Michael John McGhee [1956] Director/Partner

The Girls' Day School Trust
Incorporated: 26 June 1872 *Employees:* 3,273
Net Worth: £458,070,016 *Total Assets:* £541,883,008
Registered Office: 10 Bressenden Place, London, SW1E 5DH
Activities: Pre-primary education
Major Shareholder: Juliet Claire Humphries
Officers: Kathryn Ruth Davis [1964] Director; Rita Dhut [1972] Director/Investment Professional; Maria Vladimirovna Gordon [1974] Director; Richard John Harris [1952] Director/Chartered Accountant; Anne Mary Hockaday [1962] Director/Editor; Juliet Claire Humphries [1961] Director/Consultant; Fraser Stewart Montgomery [1970] Commercial Director; Peter Geoffrey Oliver [1978] Managing Director; Professor Judith Ann Simons [1945] Director; Anne Victoria Tuck [1953] Director; Helen Mary Williams [1950] Director

GLA Land and Property Limited
Incorporated: 16 January 2012
Net Worth: £255,228,000 *Total Assets:* £700,180,992
Registered Office: 55 Broadway, London, SW1H 0BD
Activities: Other letting and operating of own or leased real estate
Parent: Greater London Authority Holdings Limited
Officers: Howard Ernest Carter, Secretary; David John Bellamy [1975] Director/Chief of Staff; Martin David Clarke [1955] Director/Accountant; David Simon Lunts [1957] Director/Local Government Officer; James Stewart Murray [1983] Director/Deputy Mayor; Simon Powell [1972] Project Director

Glen Scotia Distillery Company Limited
Incorporated: 19 July 2013 *Employees:* 3
Net Worth: £73,773,000 *Total Assets:* £154,226,000
Registered Office: 30 Broadwick Street, London, W1F 8JB
Activities: Distilling, rectifying and blending of spirits
Parent: Loch Lomond Distillery Company Limited
Officers: Colin Matthews [1965] Director; Richard Miles [1966] Director; Nicholas Rose [1957] Director

Glen Water (Holdings) Limited
Incorporated: 21 November 2005
Net Worth Deficit: £34,597,000 *Total Assets:* £120,197,000
Registered Office: 210 Pentonville Road, London, N1 9JY
Activities: Activities of head offices
Shareholders: Veolia Water Outsourcing Limited; Portfolio Solutions (Northern Ireland) Limited
Officers: Elaine Margaret Aitken, Secretary; Colin John Anderson [1963] Director/General Counsel; David Robert Hardingham [1974] Commercial Director; Nigel John Paterson [1957] Director/Civil Engineer; Sinead Isobel Patton [1975] Director/Chief Financial and Commercial Officer Ireland [Irish]

Glen Water Limited
Incorporated: 21 November 2005
Net Worth Deficit: £34,597,000 *Total Assets:* £120,197,000
Registered Office: 210 Pentonville Road, London, N1 9JY
Activities: Remediation activities and other waste management services
Parent: Glen Water (Holdings) Limited
Officers: Elaine Margaret Aitken, Secretary; Colin John Anderson [1963] Director/General Counsel; David Robert Hardingham [1974] Commercial Director; Nigel John Paterson [1957] Director/Civil Engineer; Sinead Isobel Patton [1975] Director/Chief Financial and Commercial Officer Ireland [Irish]

Glencore Commodities Ltd
Incorporated: 3 February 1984
Net Worth: £249,760,080 *Total Assets:* £1,204,430,976
Registered Office: 50 Berkeley Street, London, W1J 8HD
Activities: Security and commodity contracts dealing activities
Parent: Glencore UK Ltd
Officers: Nicholas James Reid, Secretary; Alexander Frank Beard [1967] Director/Oil Trader; Warren Michael Blount [1973] Director/Chief Financial Officer [South African]

Glencore Energy UK Ltd.
Incorporated: 23 September 2002 *Employees:* 404
Net Worth: £209,028,768 *Total Assets:* £8,398,569,472
Registered Office: 50 Berkeley Street, London, W1J 8HD
Activities: Security and commodity contracts dealing activities
Parent: Glencore UK Ltd
Officers: Nicholas James Reid, Secretary; Alexander Frank Beard [1967] Director/Oil Trader; Warren Michael Blount [1973] Director/Chief Financial Officer [South African]; Louise Jayne Bullen [1979] Director/Operations Manager

Glencore UK Ltd.
Incorporated: 20 May 1974 *Employees:* 363
Net Worth: £102,655,336 *Total Assets:* £196,032,752
Registered Office: 50 Berkeley Street, London, W1J 8HD
Activities: Security and commodity contracts dealing activities
Parent: Glencore PLC
Officers: Nicholas James Reid, Secretary; Alexander Frank Beard [1967] Director/Oil Trader; Warren Michael Blount [1973] Director/Chief Financial Officer [South African]; Louise Jayne Bullen [1979] Director/Operations Manager

GLH Hotels Holdings Limited
Incorporated: 11 October 2002 *Employees:* 1,690
Net Worth: £130,022,000 *Total Assets:* £685,366,976
Registered Office: 110 Central Street, London, EC1V 8AJ
Activities: Management consultancy activities other than financial management
Shareholder: Leng Chan Quek
Officers: Susan Lim Geok Mui, Secretary; Neil Gallagher [1973] Director/Chief Executive Officer; Kah Meng Ho [1966] Executive Director [Malaysian]; Susan Lim Geok Mui [1963] Director/Group Company Secretary [Singaporean]

GLH Hotels Limited
Incorporated: 25 February 1932 *Employees:* 1,690
Net Worth: £514,119,008 *Total Assets:* £772,536,000
Registered Office: 110 Central Street, London, EC1V 8AJ
Activities: Activities of head offices
Shareholder: GLH Hotels Holdings Limited
Officers: Susan Lim Geok Mui, Secretary; Neil Gallagher [1973] Director/Chief Executive Officer; Kah Meng Ho [1966] Executive Director [Malaysian]; Leng Hai Kwek [1953] Director/President CEO [Singaporean]; Hong Cheong Tang [1955] Group Managing Director [Malaysian]

GLIL Corporate Holdings Limited
Incorporated: 7 March 2016
Net Worth: £120,813,840 *Total Assets:* £209,760,592
Registered Office: 2nd Floor, 169 Union Street, London, SE1 0LL
Activities: Activities of financial services holding companies
Parent: GLIL Infrastructure LLP
Officers: Patrick George Dowdall [1975] Director; Daniel Frank Hobson [1979] Director/Local Government Officer; Christopher Paul Rule [1979] Director/Chief Investment Officer

Global Aerospace Underwriting Managers Limited
Incorporated: 14 June 1990 *Employees:* 340
Net Worth: £33,606,000 *Total Assets:* £119,051,000
Registered Office: Fitzwilliam House, 10 St Mary Axe, London, EC3A 8EQ
Activities: Non-life insurance
Shareholders: Munchener Ruckversicherungs-Gesellschaft Aktiengesellschaft in Munchen; Northern States Agency
Officers: Nicolas Brown [1961] Director; Guy Edward Finney [1966] Finance Director; Claus-Ulrich Kroll [1976] Director [German]; Robert Anthony Love [1971] Director/Chief Executive Officer; Stephen Andrew Michael [1961] Director/Chartered Accountant; Simone Osterlein [1969] Director/Underwriter [German]; Alan Michael Edric Tasker [1956] Director

Global Fashion Group Middle East Holdings (UK) Limited
Incorporated: 7 December 2016
Net Worth: £273,515,456 *Total Assets:* £309,625,440
Registered Office: The Space, 120 Regent Street, London, W1B 5FE
Activities: Activities of other holding companies n.e.c.
Shareholders: Kinnevik AB; Rocket Internet SE
Officers: Nils Chrestin [1980] Director/Group Chief Financial Officer [German]; Yana Valletta [1978] Director/Group General Counsel [Italian]

Global Fashion Group UK Finance Limited
Incorporated: 7 December 2016
Net Worth Deficit: £9,993,724 *Total Assets:* £125,245,648
Registered Office: The Space, 120 Regent Street, London, W1B 5FE
Activities: Activities of other holding companies n.e.c.
Shareholders: Kinnevik AB; Rocket Internet SE
Officers: Nils Chrestin [1980] Director/Group Chief Financial Officer [German]; Yana Valletta [1978] Director/Group General Counsel [Italian]

Global Media & Entertainment Limited
Incorporated: 18 May 2007 *Employees:* 1,323
Previous: This Is Global Limited
Net Worth Deficit: £344,452,992 *Total Assets:* £594,673,984
Registered Office: 30 Leicester Square, London, WC2H 7LA
Activities: Activities of head offices
Officers: Ruth Patricia Daniels, Secretary; Charles Lamb Allen [1957] Director; Michael Gordon [1962] Commercial Director; Ian Lawrence Hanson [1964] Director; Will Harding [1969] Group Strategy Director; Stephen Gabriel Miron [1965] Director/Chief Executive Officer; Richard Francis Jackson Park [1948] Director; Darren David Singer [1969] Director/Accountant; Ashley Daniel Tabor [1977] Director/Founder and Executive President

Global Ports Holding PLC
Incorporated: 20 February 2017 *Employees:* 635
Net Worth: £124,734,320 *Total Assets:* £545,603,968
Registered Office: 3rd Floor, 34 Brook Street, London, W1K 5DN
Activities: Activities of head offices
Officers: Alison Mary Chilcott, Secretary; Jerome Bernard Jean Auguste Bayle [1948] Director [French]; Aysegul Bensel [1963] Director/Vice Chairman [Turkish]; Thierry Edmond Deau [1969] Director [French]; Ercan Nuri Ergul [1968] Director [Turkish]; Mehmet Kutman [1960] Director/Chairman [Turkish]; Thomas Josef Maier [1958] Director/EBRD Board Member [German]; Lord Peter Benjamin Mandelson [1953] Director

Global Prime Partners Ltd
Incorporated: 14 July 2009 *Employees:* 54
Net Worth: £25,096,376 *Total Assets:* £2,247,709,184
Registered Office: 101 Wigmore Street, London, W1U 1QU
Activities: Financial intermediation not elsewhere classified
Shareholders: Amit Jayanti Unalkat; Julian Parker; Daniel Bunner
Officers: Rajvinder Kaur Somal, Secretary; Clive Atkinson [1962] Director/Chief Financial Officer; Daniel Stuart Bunner [1976] Director/Banking; Sean Robert Capstick [1966] Director/Head of Prime Brokerage; Julian Parker [1970] Director/Finance; Markus Hardy Ruetimann [1958] Director [British/Swiss]; Amit Jayanti Unalkat [1975] Director

Global Radio Acquisitions Limited
Incorporated: 5 November 2007
Net Worth Deficit: £252,670,000 *Total Assets:* £256,482,000
Registered Office: 30 Leicester Square, London, WC2H 7LA
Activities: Activities of head offices
Parent: Global Media & Entertainment Limited
Officers: Ruth Patricia Daniels, Secretary; Charles Lamb Allen [1957] Director; Stephen Gabriel Miron [1965] Director/Chief Executive Officer; Richard Francis Jackson Park [1948] Director; Darren David Singer [1969] Director/Accountant

Global Radio Holdings Limited
Incorporated: 25 September 2000
Net Worth: £274,574,016 *Total Assets:* £407,246,016
Registered Office: 30 Leicester Square, London, WC2H 7LA
Activities: Radio broadcasting
Shareholders: Global Media & Entertainment Limited; Global Radio Acquisitions Limited
Officers: Ruth Patricia Daniels, Secretary; Charles Lamb Allen [1957] Director; Michael Gordon [1962] Commercial Director; Will Harding [1969] Group Strategy Director; Stephen Gabriel Miron [1965] Director/Chief Executive Officer; Richard Francis Jackson Park [1948] Director; Darren David Singer [1969] Director/Accountant

Global Radio Limited
Incorporated: 22 November 1967
Net Worth: £208,623,008 *Total Assets:* £208,648,000
Registered Office: 30 Leicester Square, London, WC2H 7LA
Activities: Radio broadcasting
Parent: Global Radio Holdings Limited
Officers: Ruth Patricia Daniels, Secretary; Charles Lamb Allen [1957] Director; Stephen Gabriel Miron [1965] Director/Chief Executive Officer; Richard Francis Jackson Park [1948] Director; Darren David Singer [1969] Director/Accountant

Global Radio Services Limited
Incorporated: 27 December 1996 *Employees:* 1,255
Net Worth: £62,212,000 *Total Assets:* £154,532,000
Registered Office: 30 Leicester Square, London, WC2H 7LA
Activities: Other business support service activities n.e.c.
Parent: GWR Group Limited
Officers: Ruth Patricia Daniels, Secretary; Charles Lamb Allen [1957] Director; Michael Gordon [1962] Commercial Director; Stephen Gabriel Miron [1965] Director/Chief Executive Officer; Richard Francis Jackson Park [1948] Director; Darren David Singer [1969] Director/Accountant

Global Reach Group Ltd
Incorporated: 8 December 2015 *Employees:* 176
Net Worth: £2,694,000 *Total Assets:* £216,135,008
Registered Office: Woolgate Exchange, 25 Basinghall Street, London, EC2V 5HA
Activities: Activities of financial services holding companies
Officers: David Alistair Campbell [1958] Director; Edward Muirhead Fraser [1985] Investment Director; Nicholas Fullerton [1981] Director; John David Harper [1972] Investment Director; Martyn John Hindley [1962] Finance Director; Camilla Jane Richardson [1972] Director/Compliance Officer; David James Stevens [1966] Director

Global Reach Partners Limited
Incorporated: 21 December 2001 *Employees:* 141
Net Worth: £6,891,000 *Total Assets:* £114,260,000
Registered Office: Woolgate Exchange, 25 Basinghall Street, London, EC2V 5HA
Activities: Financial intermediation not elsewhere classified
Parent: Project Galaxy Bidco Limited
Officers: Nicholas Fullerton [1981] Director; Martyn John Hindley [1962] Finance Director; Camilla Jane Richardson [1972] Director/Compliance Officer; David James Stevens [1966] Director

Global Starnet Limited
Incorporated: 10 March 2006 *Employees:* 159
Net Worth: £79,509,776 *Total Assets:* £284,477,760
Registered Office: c/o Waterstone Company Secretaries Ltd, Third Floor, 5 St Bride Street, London, EC4A 4AS
Activities: Other service activities n.e.c.
Major Shareholder: Francesco Corallo
Officers: Rudolf Theodoor Anna Baetsen [1966] Director [Dutch]

Global Switch Estates 1 Limited
Incorporated: 10 April 2003
Net Worth: £131,091,000 *Total Assets:* £465,592,000
Registered Office: 4th Floor, Millbank Tower, 21-24 Millbank, London, SW1P 4QP
Activities: Other business support service activities n.e.c.
Parent: Global Switch Limited
Officers: Megan Joy Langridge, Secretary; John Anthony Corcoran [1958] Director [Australian]; John Weir Stevenson [1958] Managing Director

Global Switch Estates 2 Limited
Incorporated: 10 April 2003
Net Worth: £485,832,992 *Total Assets:* £1,442,770,048
Registered Office: 4th Floor, Millbank Tower, 21-24 Millbank, London, SW1P 4QP
Activities: Other business support service activities n.e.c.
Parent: Global Switch Limited
Officers: Megan Joy Langridge, Secretary; John Anthony Corcoran [1958] Director [Australian]; John Weir Stevenson [1958] Managing Director

Global Switch Limited
Incorporated: 4 May 2007 *Employees:* 66
Net Worth: £4,494,000 *Total Assets:* £300,907,008
Registered Office: 4th Floor, Millbank Tower, 21-24 Millbank, London, SW1P 4QP
Activities: Other business support service activities n.e.c.
Officers: Anne Benjamin, Secretary; John Anthony Corcoran [1958] Director [Australian]; David Colin Doyle [1966] Director/Chartered Accountant [Australian]

Global World-Check
Incorporated: 8 February 2007
Net Worth: £326,098,048 *Total Assets:* £326,098,048
Registered Office: The Thomson Reuters Building, 30 South Colonnade, Canary Wharf, London, E14 5EP
Activities: Dormant company
Parent: Global World-Check Holdings Limited
Officers: Carla O'Hanlon, Secretary; Timothy David Knowland [1980] Director/Solicitor; Peter Thorn [1963] Director/Accountant

Globaldata PLC
Incorporated: 9 February 2000 *Employees:* 2,404
Previous: Progressive Digital Media Group PLC
Net Worth: £83,991,000 *Total Assets:* £214,491,008
Registered Office: John Carpenter House, John Carpenter Street, London, EC4Y 0AN
Activities: Activities of head offices
Major Shareholder: Michael Thomas Danson
Officers: Graham Charles Lilley, Secretary; Annette Marie Barnes [1968] Director; Bernard Anthony Cragg [1954] Director/Chartered Accountant; Michael Thomas Danson [1962] Director; Andrew David Day [1968] Director; Peter Martin Harkness [1949] Director/Publisher; Murray John Legg [1957] Director/Chartered Accountant; Graham Charles Lilley [1983] Director

Globaldrive Auto Receivables UK 2016-A PLC
Incorporated: 11 April 2016
Net Worth: £403,220 *Total Assets:* £353,116,032
Registered Office: c/o Wilmington Trust SP Services (London) Limited, Third Floor, 1 King's Arms Yard, London, EC2R 7AF
Activities: Other business support service activities n.e.c.
Parent: Wilmington Trust SP Services (London) Limited
Officers: Daniel Jonathan Wynne [1970] Director

Globaldrive Auto Receivables UK 2017 -A PLC
Incorporated: 2 March 2017
Net Worth Deficit: £30,145 *Total Assets:* £387,080,512
Registered Office: c/o Wilmington Trust SP Services (London) Limited, Third Floor, 1 King's Arms Yard, London, EC2R 7AF
Activities: Other business support service activities n.e.c.
Parent: Wilmington Trust SP Services (London) Limited
Officers: Daniel Jonathan Wynne [1970] Director

Globalgrange Limited
Incorporated: 20 June 1980 *Employees:* 1,536
Net Worth: £921,190,016 *Total Assets:* £1,316,551,040
Registered Office: 58 Rochester Row, Westminster, London, SW1P 1JU
Activities: Hotels and similar accommodation
Parent: New Grange Holdings 3 Limited
Officers: Harpal Singh Matharu, Secretary; Harpal Singh Matharu [1956] Director/Executive; Raj Singh Matharu [1958] Director/Executive; Tejinderpal Singh Matharu [1960] Director/Hotelier

GM Global Treasury Centre Limited
Incorporated: 7 July 2016
Net Worth: £515,593,792 *Total Assets:* £4,004,572,416
Registered Office: 100 New Bridge Street, London, EC4V 6JA
Activities: Other business support service activities n.e.c.
Parent: General Motors Company
Officers: Vikas Khare [1971] Director; Samuil Petrov Markov [1974] Director; Duoyi Zhan [1978] Director/Finance Executive [Chinese]

GMR Capital Limited
Incorporated: 5 February 1993 *Employees:* 299
Net Worth: £301,895,008 *Total Assets:* £592,974,016
Registered Office: Acre House, 11-15 William Road, London, NW1 3ER
Activities: Activities of head offices
Shareholders: Ian Isaac Rosenblatt; Marc Sulman Zilkha; Gail Ronson; Alan Irving Goldman
Officers: Ian Samuel George Pogue, Secretary/Accountant [Irish]; Lisa Debra Althasen [1968] Marketing Director; Alan Irving Goldman [1943] Director; Ian Samuel George Pogue [1958] Director/Accountant [Irish]; Dame Gail Ronson [1946] Director/Personal Assistant; Generald Maurice Ronson [1939] Director; Nicole Julia Ronson-Allalouf [1972] Managing Director Nicron Productions

GMS Estates Limited
Incorporated: 15 December 1925 *Employees:* 20
Net Worth: £633,779,712 *Total Assets:* £703,354,624
Registered Office: 32 Great James Street, London, WC1N 3HB
Activities: Buying and selling of own real estate
Officers: Bernadette Helen Griffin, Secretary; Jamieson Oliver Andrews [1957] Director/Chartered Surveyor; Adrian Charles Buckmaster [1949] Director/Engineer; Adam Charles Gibbon [1965] Director/Surveyor; Thomas Geoffrey Jacomb Gibbon [1963] Director/Chartered Surveyor; Anna Katharine Greenacre [1963] Director/Art Consultant; Richard Towry Lewis [1952] Director/Engineer; Thomson Henry Charles Mitchell [1978] Director/Landscape Contractor; Andrew James Moore [1965] Director; Andrew John Rogers [1945] Director/Chartered Surveyor; Jason Noel Smith [1973] Director/Chartered Surveyor; Nicholas John Willett Tavener [1949] Director/Solicitor; Thomas Henry Tavener [1980] Director/Farmer

GNI (UK) Limited
Incorporated: 17 June 1993
Previous: BGE (UK) Limited
Net Worth: £127,765,000 *Total Assets:* £372,643,008
Registered Office: 5th Floor, 6 St Andrew Street, London, EC4A 3AE
Activities: Transport via pipeline
Officers: William Gerard O'Riordan, Secretary; James Beazley Burchill [1967] Director/Head of Asset Operations [Irish]; Richard William Jemmett [1959] Director; Andrew McCrea [1954] Director/Independent Consultant; Denis Patrick O'Sullivan [1973] Director/Engineer [Irish]

Goal Acquisitions (Holdings) Limited
Incorporated: 11 April 2005
Net Worth: £6,359,830,016 *Total Assets:* £12,403,410,944
Registered Office: Chivas House, 72 Chancellors Road, London, W6 9RS
Activities: Activities of head offices
Officers: Ailsa Mary Robertson Mapplebeck, Secretary; Gilles Bogaert [1969] Director [French]; Jean-Christophe Coutures [1966] Director [French]; Amanda Hamilton-Stanley [1968] Director/General Counsel; Stuart MacNab [1964] Director/Accountant; Catherine Louise Thompson [1971] Director/General Counsel [Australian]; Vincent Turpin [1978] Director/Chief Financial Officer [French]

Gold Quay Assets Limited
Incorporated: 16 January 2014
Net Worth: £9,001,610 *Total Assets:* £154,710,608
Registered Office: 6th Floor, Charles House, 108-110 Finchley Road, London, NW3 5JJ
Activities: Activities of other holding companies n.e.c.
Parent: Yianis Holdings Limited
Officers: Yiannakis Theophani Christodoulou [1965] Director; Lambros Hadjiioannou [1978] Director

The Golden Charter Trust Limited
Incorporated: 16 January 2015 *Employees:* 10
Net Worth: £731,049,024 *Total Assets:* £1,021,179,008
Registered Office: Suite 1, 3rd Floor, 11-12 St James's Square, London, SW1Y 4LB
Activities: Funeral and related activities
Shareholders: Paul Robert Stevenson; Geraldine Elizabeth Gammell; Iain Douglas Collins Webster; Ian Blackford
Officers: Ian Murray Barnett [1947] Director; Ian Blackford [1961] Director; Gordon Haig Brough [1959] Director/Lawyer; Generaldine Elizabeth Gammell [1955] Director/Chartered Accountant; Gareth Adrian Howlett [1958] Director/Investment Manager; David Paul Kidd [1960] Director/Independent Pension Trustee; Paul Robert Stevenson [1963] Funeral Director; Iain Douglas Collins Webster [1960] Director/Chartered Accountant

Goldman Sachs Asset Management International
Incorporated: 27 February 1990
Net Worth: £249,183,360 *Total Assets:* £372,600,896
Registered Office: Peterborough Court, 133 Fleet Street, London, EC4A 2BB
Activities: Banks
Parent: Goldman Sachs Group UK Limited
Officers: Ville Harju, Secretary; Carolyne Jane Hodkin, Secretary; Daniel Jackson, Secretary; David Plutzer, Secretary; Ellen Randy Porges, Secretary; Lisa Anne Donnelly [1969] Director; Michael Holmes [1973] Director/Accountant; Glenn Raymond Thorpe [1971] Director/Chartered Accountant [Australian]; Katherine Uniacke [1961] Director [American]; Andrew Francis Wilson [1962] Director/Co-Head of GSAM EMEA [New Zealander]; Carinne Sophie Withey [1972] Director

Goldman Sachs Funding International Limited
Incorporated: 21 June 2017
Net Worth: £93,196,352 *Total Assets:* £1,098,740,352
Registered Office: Peterborough Court, 133 Fleet Street, London, EC4A 2BB
Activities: Activities of financial services holding companies
Parent: Goldman Sachs Group UK Limited
Officers: Daniel Matthew John Parker, Secretary; Teodoro Moscoso [1971] Director; Kenneth Grant Purtell [1970] Director/Accountant [American]; Ganesh Ramani [1970] Director [Indian]

Goldman Sachs Group Holdings (U.K.) Limited
Incorporated: 7 May 1999
Net Worth: £490,526,560 *Total Assets:* £1,012,618,432
Registered Office: Peterborough Court, 133 Fleet Street, London, EC4A 2BB
Activities: Other business support service activities n.e.c.
Parent: Goldman Sachs Group UK Limited
Officers: Steven Michael Bunson, Secretary; Carolyne Jane Hodkin, Secretary; Beverly Lisa O'Toole, Secretary; Piers Noel Ormiston Curle [1974] Director/Banker; Graham Philip Shaw [1964] Director; Richard Michael Thomas [1974] Director/Accountant

Goldman Sachs Group U.K. Finance Limited
Incorporated: 17 June 2008
Net Worth: £50,577,320 *Total Assets:* £386,361,280
Registered Office: Peterborough Court, 133 Fleet Street, London, EC4A 2BB
Activities: Financial intermediation not elsewhere classified
Parent: Goldman Sachs Group Holdings (U.K.) Limited
Officers: Thomas Kelly, Secretary; Clare Charlotte Richards, Secretary; Oliver John Bingham [1977] Director/Chartered Accountant; Balvir Dhesi [1979] Director/Banker; William Thomas Gasson [1965] Director/Banker; Richard Michael Thomas [1974] Director/Accountant; Charles Alexander Thorogood [1984] Director/Investment Banker

Goldman Sachs Group UK Limited
Incorporated: 20 August 2013
Net Worth: £24,274,843,648 *Total Assets:* £44,642,377,728
Registered Office: Peterborough Court, 133 Fleet Street, London, EC4A 2BB
Activities: Other business support service activities n.e.c.
Parent: The Goldman Sachs Group, Inc.
Officers: Carolyne Jane Hodkin, Secretary; David Michael Bicarregui [1975] Director; Petra Lorna Monteiro [1970] Director/Chartered Accountant; Richard John Taylor [1972] Director/Investment Banker

Goldman Sachs International
Incorporated: 2 June 1988 *Employees:* 4,688
Net Worth: £23,011,760,128 *Total Assets:* £682,632,085,504
Registered Office: Peterborough Court, 133 Fleet Street, London, EC4A 2BB
Activities: Financial intermediation not elsewhere classified
Parent: Goldman Sachs Group UK Limited
Officers: Andrew John Bagley, Secretary; Richard Mark Buckingham, Secretary; Eoghainn Leith Calder, Secretary; Jonathan Lloyd Cheatle, Secretary; Matthew Brian Flett, Secretary; Jeremy Philip Herman, Secretary; Carolyne Jane Hodkin, Secretary; Andreas Koernlein, Secretary; Daniel Matthew John Parker, Secretary; Clare Charlotte Richards, Secretary; Faryar Shirzad, Secretary; Kyle Robert Williams, Secretary; Sally Ann Boyle [1961] Director/Solicitor; Jose Manuel Durao Barroso [1956] Director [Portuguese]; Richard John Gnodde [1960] Director/Investment Banker [Irish]; Lord Anthony Stephen Grabiner [1945] Director/Barrister; Nigel Harman [1959] Director/Chartered Accountant; Dermot William McDonogh [1964] Director/Banker [Irish]; Therese Lynn Miller [1951] Director/Lawyer [British/American]; Esta Eiger Stecher [1957] Director [American]; Marius Otto Winkelman [1946] Director [Dutch]

Goldman Sachs International Bank
Incorporated: 12 July 1973 *Employees:* 6
Net Worth: £2,202,161,664 *Total Assets:* £39,522,959,360
Registered Office: Peterborough Court, 133 Fleet Street, London, EC4A 2BB
Activities: Banks
Parent: Goldman Sachs Group UK Limited
Officers: Richard Mark Buckingham, Secretary; Timothy James Grayson, Secretary; Jeremy Philip Herman, Secretary; Carolyne Jane Hodkin, Secretary; Clare Charlotte Richards, Secretary; Faryar Shirzad, Secretary; Kyle Robert Williams, Secretary; David Michael Bicarregui [1975] Director/Treasurer; Lord Anthony Stephen Grabiner [1945] Director/Barrister; Nigel Harman [1959] Director/Chartered Accountant; Dermot William McDonogh [1964] Director/Banker [Irish]; Therese Lynn Miller [1951] Director/Lawyer [British/American]; Esta Eiger Stecher [1957] Director [American]; David Daniel Wildermuth [1964] Director/Risk Manager [American]

Goldman Sachs International Investments Limited
Incorporated: 22 November 2013
Net Worth: £1,363,080,576 *Total Assets:* £1,363,080,576
Registered Office: Peterborough Court, 133 Fleet Street, London, EC4A 2BB
Activities: Financial intermediation not elsewhere classified
Parent: The Goldman Sachs Group, Inc.
Officers: Carolyne Jane Hodkin, Secretary; Vikramjit Singh Chima [1973] Director/Accountant [Indian]; Graham Philip Shaw [1964] Director

Goldman Sachs Property Management
Incorporated: 16 October 1989
Net Worth: £210,578,000 *Total Assets:* £441,571,008
Registered Office: Peterborough Court, 133 Fleet Street, London, EC4A 2BB
Activities: Development of building projects
Parent: Goldman Sachs International Service Entities Holdings Limited
Officers: Carolyne Jane Hodkin, Secretary; Tulika SEN, Secretary; Vikramjit Singh Chima [1973] Director/Accountant [Indian]; Orla Dunne [1965] Director/Technology Management [Irish]; Mike Christopher Taylor [1971] Director/Chartered Surveyor; Gavin Anthony Wills [1965] Director/Accountant

Goodenough College
Incorporated: 28 March 1930 *Employees:* 88
Net Worth: £157,191,008 *Total Assets:* £199,046,000
Registered Office: London House, Mecklenburgh Square, London, WC1N 2AB
Activities: Other accommodation
Officers: Richard Michael Barker, Secretary; Alexander John Dyke Acland [1973] Director/Executive Search Consultant; David Charles Brooks Wilson [1944] Director; Andrew Lawson Brown [1966] Director/Advocate; Corey Joseph Cook [1971] Director/Investment Management; Hugh Barnabas Crossley [1973] Director/Chief Investment Officer; James Alexander Douglas [1962] Director/Partner; Fiona Kirk [1958] Managing Director; Charles Gavin McGregor [1951] Director/Retired [Australian]; Martin Juergen Schwab [1974] Director/Investment Professional [German]; Eric Frank Tracey [1948] Director/Accountant [New Zealander]; Graham Norman Charles Ward [1952] Director/Commissioner

Google Payment Limited
Incorporated: 11 August 2006
Net Worth: £32,527,464 *Total Assets:* £521,829,504
Registered Office: 5 New Street Square, London, EC4A 3TW
Activities: Financial intermediation not elsewhere classified
Parent: Alphabet, Inc.
Officers: Madeleine Clare Babey [1972] Director/Head of Retail Partnerships, Google Play; Amitesh Bhushan [1976] Director/Payments Compliance Risk Manager [American]; Ioanna Lykidi [1977] Director/Regional Controller [Greek]; Mounir Mouawad [1982] Director/Head of EMEA Product Operations, Consumer Payments [Lebanese]; Lewis Allen Segall [1959] Director/Attorney [American]

Google UK Limited
Incorporated: 20 April 2000 *Employees:* 3,280
Net Worth: £390,167,200 *Total Assets:* £1,050,065,728
Registered Office: Belgrave House, 76 Buckingham Palace Road, London, SW1W 9TQ
Activities: Other business support service activities n.e.c.
Parent: Alphabet, Inc.
Officers: Amitesh Bhushan [1976] Director/Payments Compliance Risk Manager [American]; Paul Terence Manicle [1975] Director/Regional Controller [Irish]; Kenneth Hohee Yi [1970] Director/Attorney [American]

Gorkana Group Holdings Limited
Incorporated: 25 June 2010
Net Worth: £75,961,984 *Total Assets:* £126,666,696
Registered Office: 5 Churchill Place, London, E14 5HU
Activities: Activities of head offices
Shareholders: Cision Ltd; Discovery Group Holdings Limited
Officers: Kevin Akeroyd [1968] Director [American]; Jacob Pearlstein [1964] Director/Chief Financial Officer [American]; Abraham Smith [1969] Director/President [American]

Gosforth Funding 2014-1 PLC
Incorporated: 9 July 2014
Net Worth: £66,000 *Total Assets:* £880,702,016
Registered Office: Fifth Floor, 100 Wood Street, London, EC2V 7EX
Activities: Other business support service activities n.e.c.
Parent: Gosforth Holdings 2014-1 Limited
Officers: Adrian Paul Sargent [1972] Director/Accountant/Treasurer

Gosforth Funding 2015-1 PLC
Incorporated: 23 March 2015
Net Worth: £60,000 *Total Assets:* £1,032,249,984
Registered Office: Fifth Floor, 100 Wood Street, London, EC2V 7EX
Activities: Other business support service activities n.e.c.
Parent: Gosforth Holdings 2015-1 Limited
Officers: Adrian Paul Sargent [1972] Director/Accountant/Treasurer

Gosforth Funding 2016-1 PLC
Incorporated: 6 November 2015
Net Worth Deficit: £2,279,000 *Total Assets:* £1,309,976,064
Registered Office: Fifth Floor, 100 Wood Street, London, EC2V 7EX
Activities: Other business support service activities n.e.c.
Parent: Gosforth Holdings 2016-1 Limited
Officers: Adrian Paul Sargent [1972] Director/Accountant/Treasurer

Gosforth Funding 2016-2 PLC
Incorporated: 15 March 2016
Net Worth Deficit: £81,000 *Total Assets:* £804,118,016
Registered Office: Fifth Floor, 100 Wood Street, London, EC2V 7EX
Activities: Other business support service activities n.e.c.
Parent: Gosforth Holdings 2016-2 Limited
Officers: Adrian Paul Sargent [1972] Director/Accountant/Treasurer

Gosforth Holdings 2014-1 Limited
Incorporated: 9 July 2014
Net Worth: £14,000 *Total Assets:* £917,940,992
Registered Office: Fifth Floor, 100 Wood Street, London, EC2V 7EX
Activities: Other business support service activities n.e.c.
Parent: The Law Debenture Intermediary Corporation P.L.C.
Officers: Adrian Paul Sargent [1972] Director/Accountant/Treasurer

Gosforth Holdings 2015-1 Limited
Incorporated: 11 March 2015
Net Worth: £22,000 *Total Assets:* £1,043,129,984
Registered Office: Fifth Floor, 100 Wood Street, London, EC2V 7EX
Activities: Other business support service activities n.e.c.
Parent: The Law Debenture Intermediary Corporation P.L.C.
Officers: Adrian Paul Sargent [1972] Director/Accountant/Treasurer

Gosforth Holdings 2016-2 Limited
Incorporated: 15 March 2016
Net Worth Deficit: £132,000 *Total Assets:* £853,489,024
Registered Office: Fifth Floor, 100 Wood Street, London, EC2V 7EX
Activities: Other business support service activities n.e.c.
Parent: The Law Debenture Intermediary Corporation P.L.C.
Officers: Adrian Paul Sargent [1972] Director/Accountant/Treasurer

Gosling Foundation Limited (The)
Incorporated: 5 March 1985
Net Worth: £113,581,160 *Total Assets:* £117,223,544
Registered Office: 21 Bryanston Street, Marble Arch, London, W1H 7PR
Activities: Other social work activities without accommodation n.e.c.
Shareholders: Hon Capt Adam Peter Gosling; Hon Vice Admiral Sir Frederick Donald Gosling
Officers: Anne Yusof, Secretary; Peter Leonard Caplan [1954] Director; Adam Peter Gosling [1963] Director; Frederick Donald Gosling [1929] Director

Gower Place Investments Limited
Incorporated: 2 July 2013
Net Worth: £567,885,696 *Total Assets:* £578,492,224
Registered Office: Gibbs Building, 215 Euston Road, London, NW1 2BE
Activities: Other service activities n.e.c.
Parent: The Wellcome Trust Limited, as Trustee of The Wellcome Trust
Officers: Carolyn Kloet, Secretary; Elaina Tatem Elzinga [1984] Director/Investment Principal; Peter John Pereira Gray [1963] Director/Managing Partner; Nicholas David Moakes [1964] Director/Managing Partner; Lisha Nagin Patel [1980] Director/Head of Direct Transactions

Gowling WLG (UK) LLP
Incorporated: 7 April 2003 *Employees:* 1,157
Previous: Wragge Lawrence Graham & Co LLP
Net Worth: £59,555,000 *Total Assets:* £119,517,000
Registered Office: 4 More London Riverside, London, SE1 2AU
Officers: David Fennell [1969] Member; Andrew Witts [1962] Member; Robert Thomas Adam [1965] LLP Member; Bernardine Mary Adkins [1963] LLP Member; Patrick Charles Arben [1971] LLP Member; Sharon Ayres [1968] LLP Member; Gareth Baker [1977] LLP Member; Philip James Baker [1973] LLP Member; Kirsty Ann Barnes [1971] LLP Member; David Raymond Barron [1964] LLP Member; Richard Bate [1966] LLP Member; Richard Vaughan Beckingsale [1975] LLP Member; Gordon Francis Bell [1964] LLP Member; Susan Lynn Bennett [1961] LLP Member; Celine Bey [1971] LLP Member; Richard John Black [1967] LLP Member; Valerie Blandeau-Fossat [1971] LLP Member; Charles Richard William Bond [1968] LLP Member; Robert Breedon [1965] LLP Member; David Ernest Brennan [1979] LLP Member; Christopher George Brierley [1962] LLP Member; Alexandra Susan Brodie [1973] LLP Member; Jonathan Michael Raphael Brufal de Melgarejo [1971] LLP Member; John Richard Burns [1965] LLP Member; Paul Thomas Carberry [1973] LLP Member; Rabinder Singh Chaggar [1960] LLP Member; Clive David Chalkley [1975] LLP Member; Charles Jonathan Chamberlain [1966] LLP Member; Martin Edward Chitty [1961] LLP Member; Giles Clifford [1963] LLP Member; Philip Gregory Clissitt [1964] LLP Member; Jason Paul Coates [1970] LLP Member; John Coldham [1980] LLP Member; Thomas Patrick Edward Colreavy [1975] LLP Member; John Peter Cooper [1970] LLP Member; Michael Darowski [1977] LLP Member; Frederic Rene Roland Dereux [1967] LLP Member; Patrick Charles Duxbury [1968] LLP Member; Mathew Adam East [1975] LLP Member; Jeffrey Graham Elway [1960] LLP Member; Helen Shirley Emmerson [1977] LLP Member; Zoe Elsie Fatchen [1975] LLP Member; Paul Feathers [1971] LLP Member; Jane Fielding [1967] LLP Member; Manuela Regina Finger [1974] LLP Member; Victoria Jane Fowler [1973] LLP Member; Sarah Louise Galvin [1977] LLP Member; Elizabeth Gane [1975] LLP Member; Ian Jason Gordon [1971] LLP Member; Davinia Dorothy Gransbury [1968] LLP Member; Paul Stuart Green [1972] LLP Member; Richard David Green [1969] LLP Member; Daniel John Gwilliam [1974] LLP Member; Gordon David Harris [1959] LLP Member; Matthew James Harvey [1964] LLP Member; Nicholas Roy Heather [1961] LLP Member; Julian Richard Henwood [1962] LLP Member; Samantha Claire Holland [1974] LLP Member; Christopher Huzzard Hunt [1967] LLP Member; Paul Maurice Inman [1966] LLP Member; Christine Marie Jackson [1959] LLP Member; Sheena Rohini Jacob [1965] LLP Member; Nisha Jassal [1972] LLP Member; Alex Simon James Jay [1980] LLP Member; Jasvir Kaur Jootla [1972] LLP Member; Barbara Jouffa [1979] LLP Member; Sunil Shantilal Kakkad [1959] LLP Member; Luke Robert Charles Kempton [1964] LLP Member; Stephen Charles Kenny [1961] LLP Member; Myles Patrick Kiely [1962] LLP Member; Jacqueline Knox [1967] LLP Member; Michael Robert Anthony Lacey [1963] LLP Member; Richard Martin Lee [1966] LLP Member; Jonathan David Lent [1978] LLP Member; Felicity Jane Lindsay [1976] LLP Member; Andrew Chrstopher John Litchfield [1970] LLP Member; Jonathan Edwin Lloyd [1962] LLP Member; David Lowe [1971] LLP Member; Simon Lowe [1961] LLP Member; Michael John Luckman [1960] LLP Member; Ian James Mason [1964] LLP Member; Hugh Patrick Guerin Maule [1965] LLP Member; Thomas Mayer [1967] LLP Member; Lee Patrick McBride [1964] LLP Member; Sally Ann Mewies [1963] LLP Member; Richard John Miles [1965] LLP Member; Jeremy Steven Millington [1964] LLP Member; Ashley Fraser Lewis Mitchell [1970] LLP Member; Joseph David Morris [1978] LLP Member; Duncan Murth Luke Murphy [1972] LLP Member; Michael Brian Murphy [1961] LLP Member; Lee Nuttall [1966] LLP Member; Michael Gerard O'Shea [1962] LLP Member; Emmanuel Paillard [1969] LLP Member; Julian Charles Pallett [1958] LLP Member; Antoine Pampouille [1977] LLP Member; Reena Patel [1971] LLP Member; Jerome Patenotte [1969] LLP Member; Carole Elizabeth Peet [1958] LLP Member

GPS (Great Britain) Limited
Incorporated: 8 July 1988 *Employees:* 3,323
Net Worth: £40,451,000 *Total Assets:* £105,428,000
Registered Office: 2nd Floor, Nation House, 103 Wigmore Street, London, W1U 1QS
Activities: Retail sale of clothing in specialised stores
Parent: GAP (UK Holdings) Limited
Officers: Lisa Deborah Mertens, Secretary [American]; Mark Abrahams [1958] Director/Business Executive [American]; Deborah Edwards [1964] Director/Business Executive; Delaram Mireskandari [1969] Director/Business Executive

Gracechurch Bellyard Limited
Incorporated: 11 August 1997 *Employees:* 63
Net Worth: £19,301,794 *Total Assets:* £114,060,368
Registered Office: 2nd Floor, 21-22 Great Castle Street, London, W1G 0HZ
Activities: Hotels and similar accommodation
Shareholder: Dorothy Joanne Bahna
Officers: Mark Kronick, Secretary; Jonathan D Horowitz [1962] Director/Attorney [American]; Mark Kronick [1964] Director/Finance [American]; Allen Lorne Stevens [1943] Director/Executive [American]

Gracechurch Card Programme Funding PLC
Incorporated: 3 October 2008
Net Worth: £40,000 *Total Assets:* £7,949,421,056
Registered Office: 1 Churchill Place, London, E14 5HP
Activities: Other business support service activities n.e.c.
Parent: Gracechurch Card (Holdings) Limited
Officers: Paivi Helena Whitaker [1963] Director/Head of Operations [Finnish]

Graff Diamonds International Limited
Incorporated: 13 December 1973 *Employees:* 584
Net Worth: £608,662,912 *Total Assets:* £830,131,840
Registered Office: 29 Albemarle Street, London, W1S 4JA
Activities: Wholesale of watches and jewellery
Officers: Nicholas Paine, Secretary; Francois Xavier Graff [1963] Director/Jeweller; Nicholas Paine [1960] Director

Graff Diamonds Limited
Incorporated: 23 December 1960 *Employees:* 197
Net Worth: £502,146,880 *Total Assets:* £699,510,336
Registered Office: 29 Albemarle Street, London, W1S 4JA
Activities: Manufacture of jewellery and related articles
Parent: Graff Diamonds International Limited
Officers: Bryan Bamberger, Secretary; Elliott Harry Marc Graff [1973] Director/Buyer; Francois Xavier Graff [1963] Director/Jeweller; Raymond Graff [1947] Director/Production Manager

Grainmarket Properties Limited
Incorporated: 5 May 1995 *Employees:* 6
Net Worth: £58,528,572 *Total Assets:* £120,736,744
Registered Office: Bridewell Gate, 9 Bridewell Place, London, EC4V 6AW
Activities: Other letting and operating of own or leased real estate
Major Shareholder: Mark Jason Crader
Officers: Peter John Hart, Secretary/Property Manager; Mark Jason Crader [1962] Director; Elizabeth Susanna Morriss [1964] Director/Accountant

Granada Group Limited
Incorporated: 11 July 1934
Net Worth: £2,163,000,064 *Total Assets:* £2,180,000,000
Registered Office: 2 Waterhouse Square, 140 Holborn, London, EC1N 2AE
Activities: Non-trading company
Parent: Granada Limited
Officers: David Richard Osborn [1968] Human Resources Director; Sharjeel Suleman [1976] Director/Chartered Accountant; Helen Jane Tautz [1963] Director/Company Secretary

Granada Limited
Incorporated: 3 April 2000
Net Worth: £1,059,000,000 *Total Assets:* £2,142,000,000
Registered Office: 2 Waterhouse Square, 140 Holborn, London, EC1N 2AE
Activities: Non-trading company
Parent: ITV Services Limited
Officers: Sharjeel Suleman [1976] Director/Chartered Accountant; Helen Jane Tautz [1963] Director/Company Secretary

Granada Media Limited
Incorporated: 26 September 1995
Net Worth: £2,663,000,064 *Total Assets:* £2,820,999,936
Registered Office: 2 Waterhouse Square, 140 Holborn, London, EC1N 2AE
Activities: Non-trading company
Parent: Granada Group Limited
Officers: Sharjeel Suleman [1976] Director/Chartered Accountant; Helen Jane Tautz [1963] Director/Company Secretary

Granada Television Overseas Limited
Incorporated: 21 August 1962
Net Worth: £211,452,992 *Total Assets:* £211,452,992
Registered Office: 2 Waterhouse Square, 140 Holborn, London, EC1N 2AE
Activities: Non-trading company
Shareholders: ITV Studios Limited; Campania Limited
Officers: Maxine Louise Gardner [1968] Director/Accountant; David Philip McGraynor [1972] Finance Director [Irish]

Granada UK Rental and Retail Limited
Incorporated: 22 August 1930
Net Worth: £135,276,000 *Total Assets:* £148,840,992
Registered Office: 2 Waterhouse Square, 140 Holborn, London, EC1N 2AE
Activities: Non-trading company
Parent: Granada Media Limited
Officers: Eleanor Kate Irving [1966] Director/Company Secretary; Helen Jane Tautz [1963] Director/Company Secretary

Grand Metropolitan Capital Company Limited
Incorporated: 16 September 1996
Net Worth: £3,007,181,056 *Total Assets:* £3,007,181,056
Registered Office: Lakeside Drive, Park Royal, London, NW10 7HQ
Activities: Activities of head offices
Parent: Grand Metropolitan Limited
Officers: James Matthew Crayden Edmunds [1974] Director/Solicitor; Kara Elizabeth Major [1977] Director [American]; Vinod Rao [1962] Director [Indian]; Prabhaharan Viswanathan [1972] Director [Australian]

Grand Metropolitan Estates Limited
Incorporated: 12 June 1941
Net Worth: £173,132,000 *Total Assets:* £444,339,008
Registered Office: Lakeside Drive, Park Royal, London, NW10 7HQ
Activities: Buying and selling of own real estate
Parent: Grand Metropolitan Limited
Officers: James Matthew Crayden Edmunds [1974] Director/Solicitor; Gabor Kovacs [1980] Director [Hungarian]; Kara Elizabeth Major [1977] Director [American]; Richelle Therese Twomey [1975] Director/Manager [Irish]

Grand Metropolitan International Holdings Limited
Incorporated: 21 January 1970
Net Worth: £14,529,507,328 *Total Assets:* £14,670,177,280
Registered Office: Lakeside Drive, Park Royal, London, NW10 7HQ
Activities: Activities of head offices
Parent: Grand Metropolitan Limited
Officers: James Matthew Crayden Edmunds [1974] Director/Solicitor; Gabor Kovacs [1980] Director [Hungarian]; Kara Elizabeth Major [1977] Director [American]

Grand Metropolitan Limited
Incorporated: 6 September 1934
Net Worth: £41,380,999,168 *Total Assets:* £44,032,999,424
Registered Office: Lakeside Drive, Park Royal, London, NW10 7HQ
Activities: Activities of head offices
Parent: Diageo Holdings Limited
Officers: James Matthew Crayden Edmunds [1974] Director/Solicitor; Gabor Kovacs [1980] Director [Hungarian]; Hina Patel [1979] Director/Company Secretary Senior Assistant

Grange (Prescot Street) Limited
Incorporated: 15 March 2005 *Employees:* 271
Net Worth: £171,200,224 *Total Assets:* £217,765,552
Registered Office: 58 Rochester Row, Westminster, London, SW1P 1JU
Activities: Hotels and similar accommodation
Parent: Sectormatch Limited
Officers: Harpal Singh Matharu, Secretary; Harpal Singh Matharu [1956] Director/Executive; Raj Singh Matharu [1958] Director/Hotelier; Tejinderpal Singh Matharu [1960] Director/Executive

Grant Thornton UK LLP
Incorporated: 24 April 2004 *Employees:* 4,597
Net Worth Deficit: £34,578,000 *Total Assets:* £295,001,984
Registered Office: 30 Finsbury Square, London, EC2A 1AG
Officers: Norman Michael Armstrong [1968] Member; Simon Bruce Bevan [1959] Member; Mark Richard Byers [1959] Member; Kathleen Louise Campbell-Williams [1965] Member; Helen Julia Dale [1980] Member; David John Dunckley [1973] Member; Malcolm Antony Gomersall [1966] Member; Robert Hannah [1968] Member; Wendy Elizabeth Hart [1967] Member; Sarah Elizabeth Howard [1965] Member; Nigel Morrison [1963] Member; David Paul Munton [1973] Member; Nicholas Scott Page [1969] Member; Jonathan Charles Riley [1963] Member; Philip James Secrett [1972] Member; Roopa Aitken [1970] LLP Member; Senthil Nathan Alagar [1974] LLP Member; Susan Christina Almond [1959] LLP Member; Nicholas David Andrews [1958] LLP Member; David Paul Ascott [1960] LLP Member; Venkatesha Balakrishnan [1967] LLP Member; Fiona Baldwin [1970] LLP Member; Neil Barrell [1970] LLP Member; Philip John Barrett [1963] LLP Member; Jennifer Bachelor [1975] LLP Member; Darren Michael Bear [1976] LLP Member; Monique Beaulieu [1970] LLP Member; Sarah Carolynne Bell [1978] LLP Member; Adrian James Bennett [1973] LLP Member; Robert Miles Benson [1978] LLP Member; Eddie John Best [1973] LLP Member; Mark Edward Bishop [1982] LLP Member; Andrew Stuart Boak [1973] LLP Member; Paul Francis Brice [1964] LLP Member; Elizabeth Ann Brion [1963] LLP Member; Stuart Cunningham Brodie [1974] LLP Member; Owen Brookman [1967] LLP Member; James Robert Brown [1967] LLP Member; Andrew Marc Burman [1978] LLP Member; Michael John Burt [1963] LLP Member; Perry Burton [1971] LLP Member; Sergio Fernando Moreira Cardoso [1979] LLP Member; Hazel Ann Carpenter [1971] LLP Member; Robert Caven [1961] LLP Member; Thomas James Chadwick [1978] LLP Member; Anuj Jayantilal Chande [1959] LLP Member; Andrew Ian Charters [1982] LLP Member; Vishal Chopra [1980] LLP Member; Philip Crooks [1959] LLP Member; Sean Kenneth Croston [1965] LLP Member; James Richard Fisher Cruttenden [1964] LLP Member; Alan James Dale [1967] LLP Member; William Howell Wyndham Davies [1966] LLP Member; Peter Michael Dawson [1970] LLP Member; Hugh Dickson [1964] LLP Member; Paul David Dossett [1965] LLP Member; Martin John Drummond [1974] LLP Member; Rebecca Clare Eagle [1979] LLP Member; Karl John Eddy [1963] LLP Member; Alex Ellerton [1974] LLP Member; Rachel Engwell [1978] LLP Member; Clive John Fathers [1967] LLP Member; Paul Flatley [1963] LLP Member; Ewen Archibald Fleming [1960] LLP Member; Nicolas Kelsham Foster-Taylor [1968] LLP Member; Michael Neil Frankish [1975] LLP Member; Tomas Andrew Freyman [1975] LLP Member; Chiristopher James Newton Frostwick [1960] LLP Member; Kevin Alexander Gale [1963] LLP Member; Peter John Gamson [1973] LLP Member; John Paul William Garbutt [1967] LLP Member; Martin Gardner [1972] LLP Member; Nicholas Frank Gillott [1977] LLP Member; Richard Goldsack [1977] LLP Member; Jake Edward Andrew Green [1975] LLP Member; Trefor Owen Griffith [1975] LLP Member; Philip Grindley [1965] LLP Member; Daniel Paul Hartland [1974] LLP Member; Terry John Heatley [1983] LLP Member; Andrew Heffron [1966] LLP Member; Kevin John Hellard [1967] LLP Member; Mark Henshaw [1964] LLP Member; Phillippa Jane Hill [1974] LLP Member; David Arthur Hillan [1971] LLP Member; Keith Hinds [1959] LLP Member; Paul Richard Houghton [1970] LLP Member; Andrew Howie [1970] LLP Member; Elizabeth Anne Hughes [1973] LLP Member; Alexander Samuel Hyde [1973] LLP Member; David Anthony Ingram [1962] LLP Member; Alexander Simon Khaloi [1968] LLP Member; Susan Knight [1973] LLP Member; Neil Aaron Knights [1972] LLP Member; Sandeep Kumar [1963] LLP Member; Francesca Clare Lagerberg [1964] LLP Member; Martin Reade Lambert [1964] LLP Member; Christine Mary Laverty [1961] LLP Member; Michael Thomas Leeds [1982] LLP Member; Steven Leith [1978] LLP Member

Grantchester Holdings Limited
Incorporated: 18 July 2000 *Employees:* 2
Net Worth: £108,910,000 *Total Assets:* £267,011,008
Registered Office: Kings Place, 90 York Way, London, N1 9GE
Activities: Activities of head offices
Parent: Hammerson PLC
Officers: Andrew John Berger-North [1961] Director/Chartered Surveyor; Peter William Beaumont Cole [1959] Director/Chartered Surveyor

Grantchester Limited
Incorporated: 5 April 1990 *Employees:* 2
Net Worth: £155,598,000 *Total Assets:* £156,024,992
Registered Office: Kings Place, 90 York Way, London, N1 9GE
Activities: Development of building projects
Parent: Grantchester Holdings Limited
Officers: Andrew John Berger-North [1961] Director/Chartered Surveyor; Peter William Beaumont Cole [1959] Director/Chartered Surveyor

The Great Beer Company Limited
Incorporated: 20 October 2015 *Employees:* 1
Net Worth: £143,059,504 *Total Assets:* £165,237,680
Registered Office: Suite 31, Second Floor, 107 Cheapside, London, EC2V 6DN
Activities: Activities of production holding companies
Shareholder: Eugene Kashper
Officers: Nicholas Henderson-Stewart [1974] Director/Administrator; Igor Kim [1969] Deputy General Director [Russian]; Maxim Sedunov [1969] Director/Businessman [Russian]; Natalia Tretyakova [1974] Managing Director [Russian]

Great Hall Mortgages No.1 PLC
Incorporated: 28 September 2006
Net Worth Deficit: £29,378,000 *Total Assets:* £1,052,625,984
Registered Office: Fifth Floor, 100 Wood Street, London, EC2V 7EX
Activities: Other business support service activities n.e.c.
Parent: The Law Debenture Intermediary Corporation P.L.C.
Officers: Mark Howard Filer [1967] Director

Great Lakes Reinsurance (UK) SE
Incorporated: 28 July 2015
Net Worth: £329,439,008 *Total Assets:* £5,518,255,104
Registered Office: Plantation Place, 30 Fenchurch Street, London, EC3M 3AJ
Activities: Non-life insurance
Officers: Timothy Joseph Carroll [1955] Member/Director [Irish]; Claus-Ulrich Kroll [1976] Member/Non-Executive Director [German]; Anthony John Medniuk [1948] Member/Non-Executive Director; Dr Stefan Pasternak [1974] Member/Chief Financial Officer [German]; Nigel Hugh Hamilton Smith [1949] Member/Retired Ex Partner KPMG; Dr Achim Karl-Heinz Stegner [1968] Member/Director [German]

Great Ormond Street Hospital Children's Charity
Incorporated: 3 December 2014 *Employees:* 252
Net Worth: £342,054,016 *Total Assets:* £439,535,008
Registered Office: 4th Floor, 40 Bernard Street, London, WC1N 1LE
Activities: Other human health activities
Officers: Ian Chivers, Secretary; Jennifer Bethlehem [1965] Director/Lawyer; Nina Stephanie Bibby [1965] Marketing Director; Nicky Bishop [1960] Director/Fundraising Consultant; John Patrick Connolly [1950] Director; Margaret Ewing [1955] Director; Kaela Deanne Fenn-Smith [1969] Director [Canadian]; Professor Stephen Townley Holgate [1947] Director/Professor; Sandeep Shashikant Katwala [1960] Director/Lawyer; Michael Timothy Marrinan [1954] Director/Doctor [Irish]; Mark Peter Sartori [1969] Director

Great Portland Estates P L C
Incorporated: 30 December 1957
Net Worth: £2,366,899,968 *Total Assets:* £3,120,000,000
Registered Office: 33 Cavendish Square, London, W1G 0PW
Activities: Development of building projects
Officers: Desna Lee Martin, Secretary; Wendy Becker [1965] Director; Toby Augustine Courtauld [1968] Director; Nick Hampton [1967] Director; Richard Stephen Mully [1961] Director; Charles Edward Laurence Philipps [1959] Director/Chief Executive Officer; Alison Marie Rose-Slade [1969] Director; Nicholas James Sanderson [1973] Director/Accountant

The Great Rolling Stock Company Limited
Incorporated: 1 August 1995
Net Worth: £173,900,992 *Total Assets:* £2,251,412,992
Registered Office: 123 Victoria Street, London, SW1E 6DE
Activities: Renting and leasing of other machinery, equipment and tangible goods n.e.c.
Parent: Angel Trains Group Limited
Officers: Nesha Holas, Secretary; Mark Andrew Hicks [1967] Director/Chartered Mechanical Engineer; David Michael Jordan [1973] Director/Chief Operating Officer; Alan Edward Lowe [1968] Director/Chief Financial Officer; Kevin George Tribley [1963] Director/Chief Executive Officer

Greater Gabbard OFTO Holdings Limited
Incorporated: 15 August 2012
Net Worth: £16,035,000 *Total Assets:* £346,494,016
Registered Office: Welken House, Charterhouse Square, London, EC1M 6EH
Activities: Activities of head offices
Shareholders: Equitix Fund IV LP; Equitix Fund II LP
Officers: Kirti Ratilal Shah, Secretary; Rebecca Collins [1971] Development Director; Robert Alistair Martin Gillespie [1990] Director/Financial Controller; Richard Daniel Knight [1974] Director; Nathan John Wakefield [1974] Director

Greater Gabbard OFTO PLC
Incorporated: 15 August 2012
Net Worth: £16,035,000 *Total Assets:* £346,494,016
Registered Office: 5th Floor, 120 Aldersgate Street, London, EC1A 4JQ
Activities: Transmission of electricity
Shareholders: Equitix Fund 4 LP; Equitix Fund II LP
Officers: Kirti Ratilal Shah, Secretary; Rebecca Collins [1971] Development Director; Robert Alistair Martin Gillespie [1990] Director/Financial Controller; Richard Daniel Knight [1974] Director; Nathan John Wakefield [1974] Director

Greater London Authority Holdings Limited
Incorporated: 25 January 2012
Net Worth: £255,228,000 *Total Assets:* £700,180,992
Registered Office: 55 Broadway, London, SW1H 0BD
Activities: Other letting and operating of own or leased real estate
Parent: Greater London Authority
Officers: Howard Ernest Carter, Secretary; David John Bellamy [1975] Director/Chief of Staff; Martin David Clarke [1955] Director/Accountant; David Simon Lunts [1957] Director/Local Government Officer

Green Bidco Limited
Incorporated: 27 March 2012
Net Worth: £5,553,000 *Total Assets:* £553,352,000
Registered Office: 5th Floor, 6 St Andrew Street, London, EC4A 3AE
Activities: Activities of head offices
Parent: Green Midco Limited
Officers: Andrew Harvey Gillespie-Smith [1967] Director/Principal; Michael John McGhee [1956] Director/Partner

Green Midco Limited
Incorporated: 28 March 2012
Net Worth: £47,827,000 *Total Assets:* £387,833,984
Registered Office: 5th Floor, 6 St Andrew Street, London, EC4A 3AE
Activities: Activities of head offices
Officers: Andrew Harvey Gillespie-Smith [1967] Director/Principal; Michael John McGhee [1956] Director/Partner

Green Park Reading No. 1 LLP
Incorporated: 9 November 2011
Net Worth: £177,920,752 *Total Assets:* £626,145,344
Registered Office: Asticus Building, 21 Palmer Street, London, SW1H 0AD

Greencoat Solar Assets I Limited
Incorporated: 13 September 2016
Net Worth Deficit: £5,152,490 *Total Assets:* £298,301,216
Registered Office: 27-28 Eastcastle Street, London, W1W 8DH
Activities: Activities of other holding companies n.e.c.
Parent: Greencoat Solar I LP
Officers: Laurence Jon Fumagalli [1972] Director; Lee Shamai Moscovitch [1976] Director/Investment Manager; Richard Charles Henry Nourse [1964] Director

Greencoat Solar Assets II Limited
Incorporated: 18 May 2017
Net Worth Deficit: £3,964,825 *Total Assets:* £121,079,816
Registered Office: 5 Old Bailey, London, EC4M 7BA
Activities: Activities of other holding companies n.e.c.
Parent: Greencoat Solar II LP
Officers: Laurence Jon Fumagalli [1972] Director/Investment Manager; Lee Shamai Moscovitch [1976] Director/Investment Manager; Richard Charles Henry Nourse [1964] Director/Investment Manager

Greencoat UK Wind Holdco Limited
Incorporated: 14 January 2013
Net Worth: £738,860,992 *Total Assets:* £1,412,962,944
Registered Office: 27-28 Eastcastle Street, London, W1W 8DH
Activities: Activities of other holding companies n.e.c.
Parent: Greencoat UK Wind PLC
Officers: Laurence Jon Fumagalli [1972] Director/Investment Manager; Stephen Bernard Lilley [1968] Director/Investment Manager

Greencoat UK Wind PLC
Incorporated: 4 December 2012
Net Worth: £1,144,039,936 *Total Assets:* £1,413,127,936
Registered Office: 27-28 Eastcastle Street, London, W1W 8DH
Activities: Other business support service activities n.e.c.
Officers: Daniel Bradford Badger [1946] Director/M&A Advisory; Timothy Charles William Ingram [1947] Director/Chairman; Shonaid Christina Ross Jemmett-Page [1960] Director; Martin Patrick McAdam [1961] Director [Irish]; William Francis Sebastian Rickett [1953] Director

Greene King Finance Parent Limited
Incorporated: 23 December 2004
Net Worth: £18,000 *Total Assets:* £1,519,115,008
Registered Office: Fifth Floor, 100 Wood Street, London, EC2V 7EX
Activities: Other business support service activities n.e.c.
Parent: The Law Debenture Intermediary Corporation P.L.C.
Officers: Mark Howard Filer [1967] Director

Greene King Finance PLC
Incorporated: 14 January 2005
Net Worth: £44,000 *Total Assets:* £1,519,115,008
Registered Office: Fifth Floor, 100 Wood Street, London, EC2V 7EX
Activities: Other business support service activities n.e.c.
Parent: Greene King Finance Parent Limited
Officers: Mark Howard Filer [1967] Director

Greenergy Fuels Holdings Limited
Incorporated: 19 July 2010 *Employees:* 793
Net Worth: £221,972,000 *Total Assets:* £1,870,023,040
Registered Office: 198 High Holborn, London, WC1V 7BD
Activities: Other business support service activities n.e.c.
Parent: BCP IV UK Fuel Holdings V Limited
Officers: Richard William Clifton, Secretary; Paul Trevor Bateson [1960] Director/Chief Operations Officer; Christopher John Brookhouse [1965] Director/Head of Infrastructure; Robert James Day [1959] Director; Tamara Gail Earley [1968] Director/Manager; Caroline Sarah Lumbard [1972] Sales Director; Christopher Paul O'Callaghan [1961] Director [Irish]; Andrew William Owens [1962] Director; Adam John Traeger [1982] Director [Australian]

Greenergy Fuels Limited
Incorporated: 24 August 2000
Net Worth: £98,499,000 *Total Assets:* £1,647,969,024
Registered Office: 198 High Holborn, London, WC1V 7BD
Activities: Wholesale of other fuels and related products
Parent: Greenergy International Limited
Officers: Richard William Clifton, Secretary; Paul Trevor Bateson [1960] Director/Chief Operations Officer; Caroline Sarah Lumbard [1972] Director; Andrew William Owens [1962] Director; Adam John Traeger [1982] Director [Australian]

Greenergy International Limited
Incorporated: 16 April 1993 *Employees:* 223
Net Worth: £135,943,008 *Total Assets:* £370,756,992
Registered Office: 198 High Holborn, London, WC1V 7BD
Activities: Other business support service activities n.e.c.
Parent: Greenergy Fuels Holdings Limited
Officers: Richard William Clifton, Secretary; Paul Trevor Bateson [1960] Director; Christopher John Brookhouse [1965] Director; Tamara Gail Earley [1968] Director; Caroline Sarah Lumbard [1972] Director; Andrew William Owens [1962] Director; Adam John Traeger [1982] Director [Australian]

Greenham Trading Limited
Incorporated: 6 March 1961
Net Worth: £461,567,008 *Total Assets:* £799,017,024
Registered Office: York House, 45 Seymour Street, London, W1H 7JT
Activities: Non-trading company
Parent: Bunzl Public Limited Company
Officers: Paul Nicholas Hussey, Secretary; Andrew James Ball [1963] Finance Director; Paul Nicholas Hussey [1959] Director/Solicitor; Brian Michael May [1964] Finance Director

Greenland (United Kingdom) Investment Limited
Incorporated: 13 February 2014 *Employees:* 36
Net Worth Deficit: £123,461,432 *Total Assets:* £291,287,040
Registered Office: 11th Floor, City Tower, 40 Basinghall Street, London, EC2V 5DE
Activities: Development of building projects
Officers: Taotao Song [1972] Managing Director [Chinese]

Greenland Hertsmere (London) Limited
Incorporated: 31 March 2014 *Employees:* 1
Net Worth Deficit: £13,471,250 *Total Assets:* £180,215,008
Registered Office: 11th Floor, City Tower, 40 Basinghall Street, London, EC2V 5DE
Activities: Development of building projects
Parent: Greenland (United Kingdom) Investment Limited
Officers: Taotao Song [1972] Managing Director [Chinese]

Greenland Ram (London) Limited
Incorporated: 31 March 2014 *Employees:* 2
Net Worth Deficit: £72,975,152 *Total Assets:* £286,207,872
Registered Office: 11th Floor, City Tower, 40 Basinghall Street, London, EC2V 5DE
Activities: Development of building projects
Parent: Greenland (United Kingdom) Investment Limited
Officers: Taotao Song [1972] Managing Director [Chinese]

Greenrock Bidco Limited
Incorporated: 31 March 2017
Net Worth: £351,500,000 *Total Assets:* £636,700,032
Registered Office: 10 Lower Grosvenor Place, London, SW1W 0EN
Activities: Activities of other holding companies n.e.c.
Shareholders: Greenrock Topco Limited; Greenrock Midco Limited
Officers: Charles Arthur Noall [1959] Director; Joseph Daniel Wetz [1976] Director

Greenrock Topco Limited
Incorporated: 31 March 2017
Net Worth: £146,944,720 *Total Assets:* £197,712,176
Registered Office: 10 Lower Grosvenor Place, London, SW1W 0EN
Activities: Activities of other holding companies n.e.c.
Parent: EMT 2 Holdings Limited
Officers: Charles Arthur Noall [1959] Director; Joseph Daniel Wetz [1976] Director

Greenway Infrastructure Capital PLC
Incorporated: 13 October 2006
Net Worth Deficit: £5,095,688 *Total Assets:* £152,689,392
Registered Office: 5th Floor, 6 St Andrew Street, London, EC4A 3AE
Activities: Other business support service activities n.e.c.
Parent: Greenway Infrastructure Captal Holdings Limited
Officers: Stephen William Spencer Norton [1959] Finance Director

Greenwich BSF SPV Limited
Incorporated: 20 October 2009
Net Worth Deficit: £25,719,000 *Total Assets:* £111,013,000
Registered Office: 120 Aldersgate Street, London, EC1A 4JQ
Activities: General public administration activities
Parent: Greenwich BSF Holdco Limited
Officers: George Bodgan Bucur, Secretary; Robert Alistair Martin Gillespie [1990] Director/Financial Controller; David John Harding [1980] Director/Chartered Accountant; Philip Arthur Would [1971] Director/Asset Management

Greif UK International Holding Ltd
Incorporated: 28 April 2017
Net Worth: £235,908,288 *Total Assets:* £235,953,968
Registered Office: 35 Great St Helen's, London, EC3A 6AP
Activities: Manufacture of steel drums and similar containers
Officers: Barbara Jean Arthur [1960] Director [American]; Dennis Hoffman [1968] Director/Attorney [American]; David Christopher Lloyd [1969] Director [American]

Gresham Receivables (No. 15) UK Limited
Incorporated: 15 November 2006
Net Worth: £1,029 *Total Assets:* £140,219,600
Registered Office: Third Floor, 1 King's Arms Yard, London, EC2R 7AF
Activities: Other business support service activities n.e.c.
Parent: Wilmington Trust SP Services (London) Limited
Officers: Robert Sutton [1978] Director/Financial Services [American]; Daniel Jonathan Wynne [1970] Director

Gresham Receivables (No. 19) UK Limited
Incorporated: 22 August 2007
Net Worth: £1,029 *Total Assets:* £159,275,472
Registered Office: Third Floor, 1 King's Arms Yard, London, EC2R 7AF
Activities: Other business support service activities n.e.c.
Parent: Wilmington Trust SP Services (London) Limited
Officers: Robert Sutton [1978] Director/Financial Services [American]; Daniel Jonathan Wynne [1970] Director

Gresham Receivables (No. 26) UK Limited
Incorporated: 5 January 2010
Net Worth: £1,029 *Total Assets:* £421,650,592
Registered Office: Third Floor, 1 King's Arms Yard, London, EC2R 7AF
Activities: Other business support service activities n.e.c.
Parent: Wilmington Trust SP Services (London) Limited
Officers: Robert Sutton [1978] Director/Financial Services [American]; Daniel Jonathan Wynne [1970] Director

Gresham Receivables (No. 30) UK Limited
Incorporated: 16 June 2011
Net Worth: £1,029 *Total Assets:* £102,889,752
Registered Office: Third Floor, 1 Kings Arms Yard, London, EC2R 7AF
Activities: Other business support service activities n.e.c.
Parent: Wilmington Trust SP Services (London) Limited
Officers: Daniel Jonathan Wynne [1970] Director

Gresham Receivables (No. 31) UK Limited
Incorporated: 16 June 2011
Net Worth: £1,029 *Total Assets:* £292,653,344
Registered Office: Third Floor, 1 Kings Arms Yard, London, EC2R 7AF
Activities: Other business support service activities n.e.c.
Parent: Wilmington Trust SP Services (London) Limited
Officers: Daniel Jonathan Wynne [1970] Director

Gresham Receivables (No. 32) UK Limited
Incorporated: 11 October 2011
Net Worth: £1,029 *Total Assets:* £245,321,952
Registered Office: c/o Wilmington Trust SP Services (London) Limited, Third Floor, 1 King's Arms Yard, London, EC2R 7AF
Activities: Other business support service activities n.e.c.
Parent: Wilmington Trust SP Services (London) Limited
Officers: Daniel Jonathan Wynne [1970] Director

Gresham Receivables (No. 33) UK Limited
Incorporated: 12 October 2011
Net Worth: £1,029 *Total Assets:* £189,987,152
Registered Office: c/o Wilmington Trust SP Services (London) Limited, Third Floor, 1 King's Arms Yard, London, EC2R 7AF
Activities: Other business support service activities n.e.c.
Parent: Wilmington Trust SP Services (London) Limited
Officers: Daniel Jonathan Wynne [1970] Director

Gresham Receivables (No. 34) UK Limited
Incorporated: 12 October 2011
Net Worth: £1,029 *Total Assets:* £386,315,296
Registered Office: c/o Wilmington Trust SP Services (London) Limited, Third Floor, 1 King's Arms Yard, London, EC2R 7AF
Activities: Other business support service activities n.e.c.
Parent: Wilmington Trust SP Services (London) Limited
Officers: Daniel Jonathan Wynne [1970] Director

Gresham Receivables (No.11) UK Limited
Incorporated: 22 February 2006
Net Worth: £1,029 *Total Assets:* £211,310,544
Registered Office: Third Floor, 1 King's Arms Yard, London, EC2R 7AF
Activities: Other business support service activities n.e.c.
Parent: Wilmington Trust SP Services (London) Limited
Officers: Robert Sutton [1978] Director/Financial Services [American]; Daniel Jonathan Wynne [1970] Director

Gresham Receivables (No.16) UK Limited
Incorporated: 8 February 2007
Net Worth: £1,029 *Total Assets:* £159,470,352
Registered Office: Third Floor, 1 King's Arms Yard, London, EC2R 7AF
Activities: Other business support service activities n.e.c.
Parent: Wilmington Trust SP Services (London) Limited
Officers: Robert Sutton [1978] Director/Financial Services [American]; Daniel Jonathan Wynne [1970] Director

Gresham Receivables (No.27) UK Limited
Incorporated: 12 October 2010
Net Worth: £1,029 *Total Assets:* £292,197,536
Registered Office: Third Floor, 1 King's Arms Yard, London, EC2R 7AF
Activities: Other business support service activities n.e.c.
Parent: Wilmington Trust SP Services (London) Limited
Officers: Daniel Jonathan Wynne [1970] Director

Gresham Receivables (No.36) UK Limited
Incorporated: 18 April 2013
Net Worth: £1,029 *Total Assets:* £594,585,344
Registered Office: Third Floor, 1 Kings Arms Yard, London, EC2R 7AF
Activities: Other business support service activities n.e.c.
Parent: Wilmington Trust SP Services (London) Limited
Officers: Robert Sutton [1978] Director/Financial Services [American]; Daniel Jonathan Wynne [1970] Director

Gresham Receivables (No.37) UK Limited
Incorporated: 24 March 2015
Net Worth: £1,029 *Total Assets:* £158,132,608
Registered Office: c/o Wilmington Trust SP Services (London) Limited, Third Floor, 1 King's Arms Yard, London, EC2R 7AF
Activities: Other business support service activities n.e.c.
Parent: Wilmington Trust SP Services (London) Limited
Officers: Daniel Jonathan Wynne [1970] Director

Gresham Receivables (No.38) UK Limited
Incorporated: 24 March 2015
Net Worth: £1,029 *Total Assets:* £150,916,368
Registered Office: c/o Wilmington Trust SP Services (London) Limited, Third Floor, 1 King's Arms Yard, London, EC2R 7AF
Activities: Other business support service activities n.e.c.
Parent: Wilmington Trust SP Services (London) Limited
Officers: Daniel Jonathan Wynne [1970] Director

Gresham Receivables (No.39) UK Limited
Incorporated: 27 August 2015
Net Worth: £1,029 *Total Assets:* £133,372,992
Registered Office: Third Floor, 1 King's Arm Yard, London, EC2R 7AF
Activities: Other business support service activities n.e.c.
Parent: Wilmington Trust SP Services (London) Limited
Officers: Robert Sutton [1978] Director/Financial Services [American]; Daniel Jonathan Wynne [1970] Director

Gresham Receivables (No.40) UK Limited
Incorporated: 5 October 2015
Net Worth: £1,029 *Total Assets:* £443,018,336
Registered Office: c/o Wilmington Trust SP Services (London) Limited, Third Floor, 1 King's Arms Yard, London, EC2R 7AF
Activities: Other business support service activities n.e.c.
Parent: Wilmington Trust SP Services (London) Limited
Officers: Daniel Jonathan Wynne [1970] Director

Gresham Receivables (No.45) UK Limited
Incorporated: 4 July 2016
Net Worth: £964 *Total Assets:* £119,433,736
Registered Office: Third Floor, c/o Wilmington Trust SP Services (London) Limited, 1 King's Arms Yard, London, EC2R 7AF
Activities: Other business support service activities n.e.c.
Parent: Wilmington Trust SP Services (London) Limited
Officers: Daniel Jonathan Wynne [1970] Director

Gresham Receivables (No.46) UK Limited
Incorporated: 4 July 2016
Net Worth: £1,353 *Total Assets:* £428,380,736
Registered Office: Third Floor, c/o Wilmington Trust SP Services (London) Limited, 1 King's Arms Yard, London, EC2R 7AF
Activities: Other business support service activities n.e.c.
Parent: Wilmington Trust SP Services (London) Limited
Officers: Daniel Jonathan Wynne [1970] Director

Grey Communications Group Limited
Incorporated: 29 February 1984 *Employees:* 27
Net Worth: £70,469,000 *Total Assets:* £109,474,000
Registered Office: The Johnson Building, 77 Hatton Garden, London, EC1N 8JS
Activities: Activities of head offices
Parent: Grey Global Group (UK) Limited
Officers: John Anthony Grudzina [1953] Director [American]; Eduardo Maruri [1966] Director [Ecuadorean]; Ian David Wood [1964] Director/CFO - EMEA

The Griffin Insurance Association Limited
Incorporated: 22 May 1987
Net Worth: £91,594,352 *Total Assets:* £126,896,792
Registered Office: Regis House, 45 King William Street, London, EC4R 9AN
Activities: Non-life insurance
Officers: Susan Nicola Parramore, Secretary; Hugh Anthony Armytage [1955] Director/Insurance Broker; William David Bloomer [1969] Director/Lawyer; Andrew Somerville Cross [1957] Director/Insurance; Maryse Therese Hazell [1966] Director/Insurance Broker; Duncan Alexander James McKechnie [1958] Director/Accountant; Samantha Jane Peat [1972] Director/Insurance; Anthony Peter Phillips [1958] Director/Accountant and Insurance Broker; Simon Charles Guy Scriven [1958] Director/Insurance; Chetan Kantilal Shah [1966] Director; Andrew John Sindall [1957] Finance Director; John Crispin Speers [1946] Director/Insurance; Mark Rhoderick Wylie Warren [1967] Director/Insurance

Griffon Funding Limited
Incorporated: 14 December 2015
Net Worth: £4,235 *Total Assets:* £1,161,046,656
Registered Office: 35 Great St Helen's, London, EC3A 6AP
Activities: Non-trading company
Parent: Intertrust Corporate Services Limited
Officers: Paivi Helena Whitaker [1963] Director [Finnish]

Grifonas Finance No.1 PLC
Incorporated: 15 December 2005
Net Worth: £11,165,839 *Total Assets:* £424,332,320
Registered Office: Third Floor, 1 King's Arms Yard, London, EC2R 7AF
Activities: Other business support service activities n.e.c.
Parent: Grifonas Holdings Limited
Officers: Daniel Jonathan Wynne [1970] Director

Grifonas Holdings Limited
Incorporated: 26 May 2006
Net Worth: £11,149,520 *Total Assets:* £424,316,000
Registered Office: Third Floor, 1 King's Arms Yard, London, EC2R 7AF
Activities: Other business support service activities n.e.c.
Parent: Wilmington Trust SP Services (London) Limited
Officers: Daniel Jonathan Wynne [1970] Director

Grosvenor Americas Holdings Limited
Incorporated: 5 November 2013
Net Worth: £544,336,000 *Total Assets:* £544,366,976
Registered Office: 70 Grosvenor Street, London, W1K 3JP
Activities: Activities of head offices
Parent: Grosvenor Overseas Holdings Limited
Officers: Judith Patricia Ball, Secretary; Timothy Leslie Budden [1966] Director/Chartered Accountant; Christopher James Jukes [1978] Director/Accountant; Richard Allan Jeffrey Marshall [1964] Director/Accountant; Stephen Jeremy Moore [1960] Director/Chartered Accountant; Mark Robin Preston [1968] Director/Chartered Surveyor; Nicholas Richard Scarles [1962] Director/Chartered Accountant; Peter Sean Vernon [1959] Director/Surveyor

Grosvenor Continental Europe Holdings Limited
Incorporated: 13 June 2001
Net Worth: £628,899,200 *Total Assets:* £715,541,120
Registered Office: 70 Grosvenor Street, London, W1K 3JP
Activities: Activities of head offices
Parent: Grosvenor Overseas Holdings Limited
Officers: Judith Patricia Ball, Secretary; Timothy Leslie Budden [1966] Director/Chartered Accountant; Christopher James Jukes [1978] Director/Accountant; Richard Allan Jeffrey Marshall [1964] Director/Accountant; Stephen Jeremy Moore [1960] Director/Chartered Accountant; Mark Robin Preston [1968] Director/Chartered Surveyor; Nicholas Richard Scarles [1962] Director/Chartered Accountant; Peter Sean Vernon [1959] Director/Surveyor

Grosvenor Estate Holdings
Incorporated: 9 February 1979 *Employees:* 60
Net Worth: £1,721,280,000 *Total Assets:* £2,115,403,008
Registered Office: 70 Grosvenor Street, London, W1K 3JP
Activities: Activities of head offices
Parent: Grosvenor Group Limited
Officers: Judith Patricia Ball, Secretary; Timothy Leslie Budden [1966] Director/Chartered Accountant; Christopher James Jukes [1978] Director/Accountant; Richard Allan Jeffrey Marshall [1964] Director/Accountant; Stephen Jeremy Moore [1960] Director/Chartered Accountant; Mark Robin Preston [1968] Director/Chartered Surveyor; Nicholas Richard Scarles [1962] Director/Chartered Accountant; Peter Sean Vernon [1959] Director/Surveyor

Grosvenor Europe Investments Limited
Incorporated: 26 April 2016
Net Worth: £148,374,304 *Total Assets:* £173,923,728
Registered Office: 70 Grosvenor Street, London, W1K 3JP
Activities: Other business support service activities n.e.c.
Parent: Grosvenor Europe Limited
Officers: Lisa Sorrell, Secretary; Robert Richard Davis [1967] Finance Director; Sara Elizabeth Lucas [1965] Director; Richard Brian Mallett [1967] Director/Chartered Accountant; James Gilles Raynor [1973] Director/Chief Executive Officer

Grosvenor Europe Limited
Incorporated: 21 August 2000 *Employees:* 13
Previous: Grosvenor Fund Management Limited
Net Worth: £141,295,008 *Total Assets:* £221,304,992
Registered Office: 70 Grosvenor Street, London, W1K 3JP
Activities: Activities of head offices
Parent: Grosvenor Estate Holdings
Officers: Lisa Sorrell, Secretary; Patricia Abril [1968] Director/Franchisee [Spanish]; Robert Richard Davis [1967] Finance Director; Jonathan Lawrence Lane [1958] Director/Banker; Sara Elizabeth Lucas [1965] Director; Olivier Bernard Robert Vincent Piani [1954] Director/Chief Executive Officer [French]; Mark Robin Preston [1968] Director/Chartered Surveyor; James Gilles Raynor [1973] Director/Fund Manager; Nicholas Richard Scarles [1962] Director/Chartered Accountant

Grosvenor Group Limited
Incorporated: 3 July 1996 *Employees:* 748
Net Worth: £4,888,399,872 *Total Assets:* £6,730,200,064
Registered Office: 70 Grosvenor Street, London, W1K 3JP
Activities: Activities of head offices
Shareholders: Dame Fiona Claire Reynolds; Mark Robin Preston; Francis Alexander Scott; Jeremy Henry Moore Newsum; Michael George Alexander McLintock; William Bruce Kendall
Officers: Suzanne McConnell, Secretary; Sir Philip Graham Dilley [1955] Director/Engineer; Michael George Alexander McLintock [1961] Director; Christopher Dale Pratt [1956] Director; Mark Robin Preston [1968] Director/Chartered Surveyor; Dame Fiona Claire Reynolds [1958] Director/Trustee; Nicholas Richard Scarles [1962] Director/Chartered Accountant; Domenico Siniscalco [1954] Managing Director [Italian]; Peter Sean Vernon [1959] Director/Surveyor

Grosvenor Limited
Incorporated: 24 November 1993 *Employees:* 457
Net Worth: £2,484,300,032 *Total Assets:* £3,708,600,064
Registered Office: 70 Grosvenor Street, London, W1K 3JP
Activities: Activities of head offices
Parent: Grosvenor Estate Holdings
Officers: Derek John Lewis, Secretary; Dawn Elizabeth Airey [1960] Director; Roger Frederick Crawford Blundell [1962] Finance Director; Simon Geoffrey Harding-Roots [1968] Director; Stephen Augustus Lovegrove [1966] Director/Civil Servant; Craig David McWilliam [1972] Director/Chartered Surveyor; Jorge Emanuel Mendonca [1963] Director; Graham Fenwick Pimlott [1949] Director; Heather Victoria Rabbatts [1955] Director; Nicholas Richard Scarles [1962] Director/Chartered Accountant; Peter Sean Vernon [1959] Director/Surveyor

Grosvenor Overseas Holdings Limited
Incorporated: 6 April 1994
Net Worth: £1,413,028,992 *Total Assets:* £1,414,027,008
Registered Office: 70 Grosvenor Street, London, W1K 3JP
Activities: Activities of head offices
Parent: Grosvenor Estate Holdings
Officers: Judith Patricia Ball, Secretary; Timothy Leslie Budden [1966] Director/Chartered Accountant; Christopher James Jukes [1978] Director/Accountant; Richard Allan Jeffrey Marshall [1964] Director/Accountant; Stephen Jeremy Moore [1960] Director/Chartered Accountant; Mark Robin Preston [1968] Director/Chartered Surveyor; Nicholas Richard Scarles [1962] Director/Chartered Accountant; Peter Sean Vernon [1959] Director/Surveyor

Grosvenor Properties
Incorporated: 12 December 1969
Net Worth: £709,193,984 *Total Assets:* £927,049,024
Registered Office: 70 Grosvenor Street, London, W1K 3JP
Activities: Buying and selling of own real estate
Parent: Grosvenor Limited
Officers: Derek John Lewis, Secretary; Keith John Bailey [1979] Director/Chartered Surveyor; Roger Frederick Crawford Blundell [1962] Finance Director; Anna Clare Bond [1981] Director/Chartered Surveyor; Douglas Nigel Crichton [1976] Director/Chartered Surveyor; Simon Geoffrey Harding-Roots [1968] Director; Chantal Antonia Henderson [1975] Director/Accountant; Nigel Auriol Hughes [1957] Director/Chartered Surveyor; Richard Alexander Jefferies [1963] Operations Director; Craig David McWilliam [1972] Director/Chartered Surveyor; Paul Francis O'Grady [1985] Director/Chartered Surveyor; Amelia Mary Staveley [1986] Director/Chartered Surveyor

Grosvenor UK Finance PLC
Incorporated: 12 January 2001
Net Worth: £5,924,000 *Total Assets:* £210,688,000
Registered Office: 70 Grosvenor Street, London, W1K 3JP
Activities: Other business support service activities n.e.c.
Parent: Grosvenor Limited
Officers: Derek John Lewis, Secretary; Roger Frederick Crawford Blundell [1962] Finance Director; Craig David McWilliam [1972] Director/Chartered Surveyor; Graham Fenwick Pimlott [1949] Director; Heather Victoria Rabbatts [1955] Director

Grosvenor West End Properties
Incorporated: 16 June 1969
Net Worth: £1,352,673,024 *Total Assets:* £1,635,565,952
Registered Office: 70 Grosvenor Street, London, W1K 3JP
Activities: Buying and selling of own real estate
Parent: Grosvenor Limited
Officers: Derek John Lewis, Secretary; Keith John Bailey [1979] Director/Chartered Surveyor; Roger Frederick Crawford Blundell [1962] Finance Director; Anna Clare Bond [1981] Director/Chartered Surveyor; Douglas Nigel Crichton [1976] Director/Chartered Surveyor; Simon Geoffrey Harding-Roots [1968] Director; Chantal Antonia Henderson [1975] Director/Accountant; Nigel Auriol Hughes [1957] Director/Chartered Surveyor; Richard Alexander Jefferies [1963] Operations Director; Craig David McWilliam [1972] Director/Chartered Surveyor; Paul Francis O'Grady [1985] Director/Chartered Surveyor; Amelia Mary Staveley [1986] Director/Chartered Surveyor

Ground Rents Income Fund PLC
Incorporated: 23 April 2012 *Employees:* 3
Net Worth: £113,155,936 *Total Assets:* £134,971,632
Registered Office: 72 Welbeck Street, London, W1G 0AY
Activities: Activities of investment trusts
Officers: William Martin Robinson, Secretary; Paul Anthony Craig [1970] Director; Robert Malcolm Naish [1953] Director/Chartered Surveyors; Simon Paul Wombwell [1961] Director

Group Miki Holdings Limited
Incorporated: 13 September 1972 *Employees:* 1,523
Previous: GM Communications Limited
Net Worth: £86,428,352 *Total Assets:* £198,067,696
Registered Office: Vintners Place, 68 Upper Thames Street, London, EC4V 3BJ
Activities: Activities of other holding companies n.e.c.
Parent: H.I.S. Co., Ltd
Officers: Ingrid Cawood, Secretary; Tetsunori Dambara [1963] Managing Director [Japanese]; Osamu Hanazaki [1970] Director [Japanese]; Tomoshi Kobayashi [1963] Director [Japanese]; Masayuki Oda [1966] Director [Japanese]

GroupBT Limited
Incorporated: 12 March 2001
Net Worth: £326,585,088 *Total Assets:* £730,985,792
Registered Office: 81 Newgate Street, London, EC1A 7AJ
Activities: Undifferentiated goods-producing activities of private households for own use
Shareholders: British Telecommunications PLC; BT Sixty-Four Limited
Officers: Mark Philip Genikis [1961] Director/Accountant; Leslie Charles Winnister [1952] Director/Treasury Manager

GS Finco Limited
Incorporated: 22 December 2003
Net Worth: £13,992,143 *Total Assets:* £270,194,976
Registered Office: 4th Floor, Millbank Tower, 21-24 Millbank, London, SW1P 4QP
Activities: Development of building projects
Officers: Stephane Abraham Joseph Nahum [1975] Director/Private Equity [French]; Malcolm Robin Turner [1935] Director

GS Funding Europe
Incorporated: 8 December 2004
Net Worth: £1,469,965,056 *Total Assets:* £3,915,727,104
Registered Office: Peterborough Court, 133 Fleet Street, London, EC4A 2BB
Activities: Financial intermediation not elsewhere classified
Parent: GS Funding Europe VI Ltd
Officers: Thomas Kelly, Secretary; Clare Charlotte Richards, Secretary; Oliver John Bingham [1977] Director/Chartered Accountant; Vikramjit Singh Chima [1973] Director/Accountant [Indian]; William Thomas Gasson [1965] Director/Banker; Stephen Blackwood Scobie [1963] Director/Banker

GS Funding Europe III Ltd
Incorporated: 22 November 2016
Net Worth: £2,731,717,120 *Total Assets:* £9,989,707,776
Registered Office: Peterborough Court, 133 Fleet Street, London, EC4A 2BB
Activities: Financial intermediation not elsewhere classified
Parent: The Goldman Sachs Group, Inc.
Officers: Thomas Kelly, Secretary; Clare Charlotte Richards, Secretary; Oliver John Bingham [1977] Director/Chartered Accountant; Vikramjit Singh Chima [1973] Director/Accountant [Indian]; William Thomas Gasson [1965] Director/Banker

GS Funding Europe V Limited
Incorporated: 13 December 2016
Net Worth: £8,017,375,232 *Total Assets:* £8,021,595,136
Registered Office: Peterborough Court, 133 Fleet Street, London, EC4A 2BB
Activities: Financial intermediation not elsewhere classified
Parent: GS Funding Europe
Officers: Thomas Kelly, Secretary; Clare Charlotte Richards, Secretary; Oliver John Bingham [1977] Director/Chartered Accountant; Vikramjit Singh Chima [1973] Director/Accountant [Indian]; William Thomas Gasson [1965] Director/Banker

GS Sapphire Investment Limited
Incorporated: 24 November 2010
Previous: Kew Green Holdings Limited
Net Worth: £428,602,624 *Total Assets:* £456,725,408
Registered Office: Peterborough Court, 133 Fleet Street, London, EC4A 2BB
Activities: Financial intermediation not elsewhere classified
Parent: GS Sapphire Holding Limited
Officers: Thomas Kelly, Secretary; Clare Charlotte Richards, Secretary; Vikramjit Singh Chima [1973] Director/Accountant [Indian]; Piers Noel Ormiston Curle [1974] Director/Banker; William Thomas Gasson [1965] Director/Banker

GTA Holdco Limited
Incorporated: 18 February 2011 *Employees:* 3
Net Worth: £207,778,016 *Total Assets:* £290,944,480
Registered Office: 27 Goswell Road, London, EC1M 7GT
Activities: Non-trading company
Parent: Kuoni Holdings Limited
Officers: Darren James Anniss [1977] Director; Martin Charles Jones [1973] Director; Andrew John Tempest [1962] Director

Guaranty Trust Bank (UK) Limited
Incorporated: 17 October 2006 *Employees:* 74
Net Worth: £32,463,592 *Total Assets:* £467,793,856
Registered Office: 62 Margaret Street, London, W1W 8TF
Activities: Banks
Parent: Guaranty Trust Bank PLC
Officers: Olusegun Agbaje [1964] Director/Banking [Nigerian]; Gbenga Temitope Alade [1962] Director/Banker [Canadian]; Ademola Ayodeji Odeyemi [1970] Director/Banking [Nigerian]; Stuart Victor Orton [1964] Director/Banker; Christopher David Taylor [1946] Director/Consultant; Robert John Wild [1948] Director

Guardian Digital Communications Limited
Incorporated: 7 March 2007
Net Worth: £563,625,984 *Total Assets:* £563,625,984
Registered Office: Nova South, 160 Victoria Street, London, SW1E 5LB
Activities: Activities of head offices
Parent: Motorola Solutions UK Acquisition Company Limited
Officers: Joanne Bamber, Secretary; Vincent Kennedy [1972] Director [Irish]; Ian McCullagh [1963] Director/Business Executive [Irish]; Daniel George Pekofske [1976] Director/Corporate Vice President and Chief Accounting Officer [American]

Guardian Media Group PLC
Incorporated: 9 August 1907 *Employees:* 1,475
Net Worth: £971,800,000 *Total Assets:* £1,056,099,968
Registered Office: P O Box 68164, Kings Place, 90 York Way, London, N1P 2AP
Activities: Publishing of newspapers
Parent: The Scott Trust Limited
Officers: Stephen John Godsell, Secretary; Neil Anthony Berkett [1955] Director [New Zealander]; Jennifer Susan Duvalier [1969] Director/Business Executive; Yasmin Jetha [1952] Director; Richard James Kerr [1974] Director; Nigel Donald Morris [1958] Director; John Paton [1957] Director; David Skipwith Pemsel [1968] Director; Baroness Gail Ruth Rebuck [1952] Director; Katharine Sophie Viner [1971] Director/Journalist; Coram Williams [1974] Director/Chief Financial Officer

Guardian News & Media Limited
Incorporated: 14 June 1967 *Employees:* 1,333
Net Worth: £23,831,000 *Total Assets:* £165,096,992
Registered Office: P O Box 68164, Kings Place, 90 York Way, London, N1P 2AP
Activities: Publishing of newspapers
Parent: Guardian News & Media (Holdings) Limited
Officers: James Iain Bishop [1976] Director; Richard James Kerr [1974] Director; David Skipwith Pemsel [1968] Director; Katharine Sophie Viner [1971] Director/Journalist

Guardian Royal Exchange Public Limited Company
Incorporated: 1 June 1984 *Employees:* 9,092
Net Worth: £3,252,000,000 *Total Assets:* £11,036,999,680
Registered Office: 5 Old Broad Street, London, EC2N 1AD
Activities: Activities of financial services holding companies
Parent: Axa UK PLC
Officers: Jeremy Peter Small, Secretary; Christopher Graham Bobby [1966] Director; Amelie Marie Breitburd [1969] Director [French]; Robin Dermer Pagden [1965] Director

Guildford No.1 PLC
Incorporated: 19 August 2014
Net Worth Deficit: £1,278,000 *Total Assets:* £480,937,984
Registered Office: Third Floor, c/o Wilmington Trust SP Services (London) Limited, 1 King's Arms Yard, London, EC2R 7AF
Activities: Other business support service activities n.e.c.
Parent: Guildford No.1 Holdings Limited
Officers: Daniel Jonathan Wynne [1970] Director

Guildhall Asset Purchasing Company (No.11) UK Limited
Incorporated: 26 August 2010
Net Worth Deficit: £25,531,000 *Total Assets:* £177,166,000
Registered Office: Third Floor, 1 King's Arms Yard, London, EC2R 7AF
Activities: Other business support service activities n.e.c.
Parent: Wilmington Trust SP Services (London) Limited
Officers: Robert Sutton [1978] Director/Financial Services [American]; Daniel Jonathan Wynne [1970] Director

Guinness Limited
Incorporated: 16 August 1952
Net Worth: £1,196,669,056 *Total Assets:* £1,198,080,000
Registered Office: Lakeside Drive, Park Royal, London, NW10 7HQ
Activities: Manufacture of malt
Parent: Diageo PLC
Officers: James Matthew Crayden Edmunds [1974] Director/Solicitor; Gabor Kovacs [1980] Director [Hungarian]; Kara Elizabeth Major [1977] Director [American]; Richelle Therese Twomey [1975] Director/Manager [Irish]

Guinness Overseas Limited
Incorporated: 24 October 1963
Net Worth: £389,612,992 *Total Assets:* £389,788,000
Registered Office: Lakeside Drive, Park Royal, London, NW10 7HQ
Activities: Other business support service activities n.e.c.
Parent: Diageo Overseas Holdings Limited
Officers: James Matthew Crayden Edmunds [1974] Director/Solicitor; Gabor Kovacs [1980] Director [Hungarian]; Kara Elizabeth Major [1977] Director [American]; Vinod Rao [1962] Director [Indian]

Gulf International Bank (UK) Limited
Incorporated: 22 August 1975 *Employees:* 67
Net Worth: £252,198,384 *Total Assets:* £5,470,513,664
Registered Office: One Knightsbridge, London, SW1X 7XS
Activities: Banks
Parent: Gulf International Bank BSC
Officers: Abdullah Al Zamil [1965] Director [Saudi Arabian]; Abdulaziz Abdulrahman Al-Helaissi [1966] Director/Chief Executive [Saudi Arabian]; Turki Ibrahim Mohammed Almalik [1977] Director [Saudi Arabian]; Katherine Lucy Garrett-Cox [1967] Director/Chief Executive Officer; Osamah Mohammed Shaker [1965] Director/CEO of GIB Capital [Saudi Arabian]; Andrew Francis Sykes [1957] Director; John Emanuel Xefos [1954] Director/Consultant [American]

Gulf Marine Services PLC
Incorporated: 24 January 2014 *Employees:* 490
Net Worth: £316,920,512 *Total Assets:* £652,228,992
Registered Office: 6th Floor, 65 Gresham Street, London, EC2V 7NQ
Activities: Other manufacturing n.e.c.
Officers: John Davies Brown, Secretary; Duncan Stewart Anderson [1963] Director/Chief Executive Officer; William Richard Anderson [1953] Director/Chief Financial Officer [American]; Simon George Batey [1953] Director/Chartered Accountant; Dr Shona MacFarlane Grant [1961] Independent Non-Executive Director; Simon John Newton Heale [1953] Director

Gulfmark North Sea Limited
Incorporated: 26 June 1991 *Employees:* 4
Net Worth: £126,938,000 *Total Assets:* £127,062,000
Registered Office: c/o Peachey & Co LLP, 95 Aldwych, London, WC2B 4JF
Activities: Sea and coastal freight water transport
Officers: Ewan McIntosh Geddes, Secretary; Quintin Venable Kneen [1965] Director/Chief Financial Officer [American]; Ewan McIntosh Geddes [1969] Director/Manager; Steven Ronald Wilson [1965] Director

Gulfmark UK Ltd
Incorporated: 21 September 1990 *Employees:* 29
Net Worth: £125,654,000 *Total Assets:* £139,647,008
Registered Office: c/o Peachey & Co LLP, 95 Aldwych, London, WC2B 4JF
Activities: Sea and coastal freight water transport
Parent: Gulfmark North Sea Ltd
Officers: Ewan McIntosh Geddes, Secretary; Ewan McIntosh Geddes [1969] Director/Manager; Quintin Venable Kneen [1965] Director [American]; Steven Ronald Wilson [1965] Director

Gunfleet Sands Holding Ltd
Incorporated: 23 June 2011
Net Worth: £305,755,872 *Total Assets:* £305,772,960
Registered Office: 5 Howick Place, London, SW1P 1WG
Activities: Activities of production holding companies
Shareholders: Orsted Power (Gunfleet Sands) Limited; MC GFS Investment Company Limited
Officers: Philip Henry de Villiers [1975] Director/Asset Manager; Mairi Dudley [1988] Director; Akira Hirano [1971] Director/Electrical Engineer [Japanese]; Ken Matsuda [1973] Director/General Manager [Japanese]; David Murray [1983] Director/Accountant [Irish]

Gunfleet Sands Limited
Incorporated: 16 June 2000
Net Worth: £169,012,416 *Total Assets:* £192,744,208
Registered Office: 5 Howick Place, London, SW1P 1WG
Activities: Production of electricity
Parent: Gunfleet Sands Holding Ltd
Officers: Philip Henry de Villiers [1975] Director/Asset Manager; Mairi Dudley [1988] Director; Akira Hirano [1971] Director/Electrical Engineer [Japanese]; Ken Matsuda [1973] Director/General Manager [Japanese]; David Murray [1983] Director/Accountant [Irish]

Gunwharf Quays Limited
Incorporated: 21 August 2000
Net Worth: £565,371,008 *Total Assets:* £576,248,000
Registered Office: 100 Victoria Street, London, SW1E 5JL
Activities: Non-trading company
Parent: Land Securities Portfolio Management Limited
Officers: Elizabeth Miles [1977] Director/Solicitor

The Guthrie Corporation Limited
Incorporated: 12 March 1965
Net Worth: £476,771,008 *Total Assets:* £586,305,024
Registered Office: 3rd Floor, 105 Wigmore Street, London, W1U 1QY
Activities: Activities of head offices
Parent: BBA Holdings Limited
Officers: David John Mark Blizzard [1972] Director/Company Secretary/Barrister; Jennifer Chase [1978] Director/Chartered Accountant

Guthrie Overseas Investments Limited
Incorporated: 18 March 1910
Net Worth: £478,911,008 *Total Assets:* £509,856,000
Registered Office: 3rd Floor, 105 Wigmore Street, London, W1U 1QY
Activities: Activities of head offices
Parent: The Guthrie Corporation Limited
Officers: David John Mark Blizzard [1972] Director/Company Secretary/Barrister; Jennifer Chase [1978] Director/Chartered Accountant

Guy's and St Thomas' Charity
Incorporated: 4 December 2014 *Employees:* 33
Net Worth: £771,640,000 *Total Assets:* £883,937,024
Registered Office: 9 King's Head Yard, London, SE1 1NA
Activities: Other human health activities
Officers: Hazel Ann Peck, Secretary; Helen Ruth Bailey [1961] Director/Management Consultant; Dr David Geoffrey Colin-Thome [1943] Director/Healthcare Consultant; Tom Joy [1972] Investment Director; Sir Ronald James Kerr [1950] Director/Health Service Manager/Advisor; Oluwole Olatunde Kolade [1966] Director/Finance; Yasemin Saltuk Lamy [1979] Director/Investor; Barbara Jane Moorhouse [1958] Director; Duncan James Milne Selbie [1962] Director/Civil Servant; Sally Jennifer Joan Tennant [1955] Director/Banker

GWI UK Acquisition Company Limited
Incorporated: 19 February 2015 *Employees:* 6
Net Worth: £274,740,992 *Total Assets:* £550,174,016
Registered Office: 3rd Floor, 90 Whitfield Street, Fitzrovia, London, W1T 4EZ
Activities: Activities of other holding companies n.e.c.
Parent: GWI UK Holding Limited
Officers: Geraint Rhys Harries, Secretary; David Adolphus Brown II [1959] Director/Chief Operating Officer [American]; Timothy Joseph Gallagher [1962] Director/Chief Financial Officer [American]; John Hellmann [1970] Director/Business Executive [American]; Gary Richards Long [1961] Director [American]; Charles Noble [1977] Director; Ian Charles Strachan [1943] Director/Retired [British/American]; Matthew Walsh [1974] Director/Rail Finance [American]

GWI UK Holding Limited
Incorporated: 19 February 2015 *Employees:* 3
Net Worth: £149,015,008 *Total Assets:* £290,752,000
Registered Office: 3rd Floor, 90 Whitfield Street, Fitzrovia, London, W1T 4EZ
Activities: Activities of other holding companies n.e.c.
Parent: Genesee & Wyoming Inc.
Officers: Geraint Rhys Harries, Secretary; Gary Richards Long [1961] Director [American]; Charles Noble [1977] Director; Thomas Savage [1979] Director/Rail Finance [American]

GWR Group Limited
Incorporated: 12 February 1962
Net Worth: £114,711,000 *Total Assets:* £114,711,000
Registered Office: 30 Leicester Square, London, WC2H 7LA
Activities: Radio broadcasting
Parent: Global Radio Limited
Officers: Ruth Patricia Daniels, Secretary; Stephen Gabriel Miron [1965] Director/Chief Executive Officer; Richard Francis Jackson Park [1948] Director; Darren David Singer [1969] Director/Accountant

GWW UK Holdings Ltd
Incorporated: 15 June 2015
Net Worth: £174,900,640 *Total Assets:* £320,046,048
Registered Office: c/o TMF Group, 5th Floor, 6 St Andrew Street, London, EC4A 3AE
Activities: Activities of other holding companies n.e.c.
Parent: W.W. Grainger, Inc.
Officers: Fred James Costello Jr [1960] Director/Executive [American]; Horace Vincent Draa III [1956] Director/Executive [American]; Thomas Bernard Okray [1962] Director/Executive [American]

Gwynt y Mor OFTO Holdings Limited
Incorporated: 29 November 2013
Net Worth Deficit: £22,416,000 *Total Assets:* £357,168,992
Registered Office: 6th Floor, 350 Euston Road, London, NW1 3AX
Activities: Transmission of electricity
Shareholders: Equitix Transmission 2 Limited; Balfour Beatty OFTO Holdings Limited
Officers: Rosamond Holden, Secretary; Rebecca Collins [1971] Development Director; Simon Rooke [1967] Director; Nathan John Wakefield [1974] Director; Brian Roland Walker [1955] Director

Gwynt y Mor OFTO PLC
Incorporated: 29 November 2013
Net Worth Deficit: £22,416,000 *Total Assets:* £357,168,992
Registered Office: 6th Floor, 350 Euston Road, London, NW1 3AX
Activities: Transmission of electricity
Parent: Gwynt y Mor OFTO Holdings Limited
Officers: Rosamond Holden, Secretary; Rebecca Collins [1971] Development Director; Simon Rooke [1967] Director; Nathan John Wakefield [1974] Director; Brian Roland Walker [1955] Director

Gyrus Group Limited
Incorporated: 6 August 1996
Net Worth: £573,893,952 *Total Assets:* £576,972,224
Registered Office: 100 New Bridge Street, London, EC4V 6JA
Activities: Manufacture of medical and dental instruments and supplies
Parent: Olympus Finance UK Limited
Officers: Yasutoshi Fujiwara [1971] Director/Business Executive [Japanese]; Yasuo Takeuchi [1957] Director/Chief Finance Officer [Japanese]

H.A. Funding Limited
Incorporated: 26 July 1996
Net Worth: £166,411 *Total Assets:* £155,181,392
Registered Office: 6th Floor, 65 Gresham Street, London, EC2V 7NQ
Activities: Other business support service activities n.e.c.
Parent: Royal Exchange Trust Company Limited
Officers: Sean Peter Martin [1965] Director

Habib Allied Holding Limited
Incorporated: 15 November 2000 *Employees:* 140
Previous: Habib Allied Holding PLC
Net Worth: £73,901,000 *Total Assets:* £672,569,024
Registered Office: 9 Portman Street, London, W1H 6DZ
Activities: Activities of financial services holding companies
Parent: Habib Bank Limited
Officers: Hamid Masud Qazi, Secretary/Banker; Muhammad Aurangzeb [1964] Director/Banker [Dutch]; David John Blatchford [1954] Director/Retired Banker; Syed Abbas Hasan [1960] Director/Banker [Pakistani]; Rayomond Kotwal [1960] Director/Banker [Pakistani]; Faisal Noorali Lalani [1963] Director/Banker [Pakistani/Dutch]; Tahir Hassan Qureshi [1961] Director/Banker [Pakistani]

Habib Bank Zurich PLC
Incorporated: 28 January 2014 *Employees:* 136
Previous: Habib AG Zurich UK PLC
Net Worth: £67,739,792 *Total Assets:* £604,948,096
Registered Office: Habib House, 42 Moorgate, London, EC2R 6JJ
Activities: Banks
Officers: Rajat Garg [1963] Director/Regional CEO [Singaporean]; Generald Arthur Gregory [1955] Director; Muhammad Habib [1959] Director/Banker [Swiss]; Anjum Zahoor Iqbal [1952] Director/Banker; Carey Anthony Pennington Leonard [1954] Director Banking; Satyajeet Roy [1967] Director/Chief Executive Officer

Hachette UK (Holdings) Limited
Incorporated: 26 January 1999 *Employees:* 1
Net Worth: £277,065,280 *Total Assets:* £356,115,840
Registered Office: Carmelite House, 50 Victoria Embankment, London, EC4Y 0DZ
Activities: Other publishing activities
Officers: Pierre de Cacqueray, Secretary; Fabrice Bakhouche [1974] Director/Chief Financial Officer [French]; Pierre de Cacqueray [1963] Director/Financial Controller [French]; Arnaud Nourry [1961] Director/Chief Executive Officer Hachette [French]; David Richard Shelley [1976] Director/Group Chief Executive

Hachette UK Limited
Incorporated: 15 May 1986 *Employees:* 195
Net Worth: £198,295,264 *Total Assets:* £318,445,280
Registered Office: Carmelite House, 50 Victoria Embankment, London, EC4Y 0DZ
Activities: Book publishing
Parent: Hachette UK (Holdings) Limited
Officers: Pierre de Cacqueray, Secretary; Pierre de Cacqueray [1963] Finance Director [French]; James Hodder-Williams [1964] Director/Book Publisher; Richard David Kitson [1977] Director/Publishing; Hilary Murray Hill [1965] Director; Arnaud Nourry [1961] Director/CEO [French]; David Richard Shelley [1976] Director/Group Chief Executive; Elisabeth Jane Tribe [1965] Director/Publisher

Hadley Shipping Group Limited
Incorporated: 16 May 2011 *Employees:* 8
Net Worth: £70,311,112 *Total Assets:* £162,737,472
Registered Office: Fourth Floor, 117-119 Houndsditch, London, EC3A 7BT
Activities: Activities of head offices
Parent: Warwick & Esplen Limited
Officers: Robert Amyon John Templeman Chaffey [1975] Director/Chartered Accountant; Sunit Das [1971] Director/Vessel Management; John Stephen Denholm [1956] Director/Chartered Accountant; Paul George Mersham Lewis [1976] Director/Property; Peter Bruce Morton [1948] Director; James Walter FitzGenerald Warwick [1966] Director

Hakkasan Limited
Incorporated: 5 January 1998 *Employees:* 3,110
Net Worth: £49,656,144 *Total Assets:* £239,011,792
Registered Office: 3rd Floor, Elsley House, 24-30 Great Titchfield Street, London, W1W 8BF
Activities: Licenced restaurants
Officers: Martin Edelman [1941] Director/Lawyer [American]; Rami Fathi Elwan [1975] Financial Director [Jordanian]; Matthew John Hurn [1972] Director/Chief Financial Officer; Marwan Naim Nijmeh [1977] Director/Lawyer [Jordanian]

Halcrow Holdings Limited
Incorporated: 27 October 1982 *Employees:* 3,739
Net Worth Deficit: £259,388,000 *Total Assets:* £175,463,008
Registered Office: Elms House, 43 Brook Green, London, W6 7EF
Activities: Activities of head offices
Parent: CH2M Hill Europe Limited
Officers: Mr Tejender Singh Chaudhary, Secretary; Mr Samuel James Hannis [1978] Human Resources Director; Brian R Shelton [1961] Director [American]

Halcyon Finance Limited
Incorporated: 13 April 1984
Net Worth: £24,539,000 *Total Assets:* £745,393,984
Registered Office: 3 Sheldon Square, Paddington, London, W2 6PX
Activities: Other business support service activities n.e.c.
Parent: Kingfisher Holdings Limited
Officers: Paul Moore, Secretary; Jean-Noel Hughes Roger Groleau [1974] Director [French]; Paul Anthony Moore [1970] Director/Company Secretary

Halifax Leasing (September) Limited
Incorporated: 25 November 1996
Net Worth: £139,871,008 *Total Assets:* £234,614,000
Registered Office: 25 Gresham Street, London, EC2V 7HN
Activities: Financial leasing
Parent: Bank of Scotland Structured Asset Finance Limited
Officers: Alyson Elizabeth Mulholland, Secretary; Colin Graham Dowsett [1964] Director/Chartered Accountant; John Robert Turner [1964] Director

Halliburton Global Holdings Limited
Incorporated: 28 November 2013
Net Worth: £63,737,000 *Total Assets:* £340,324,000
Registered Office: c/o Halliburton, Building 4, Chiswick Park, 566 Chiswick High Road, London, W4 5YE
Activities: Activities of other holding companies n.e.c.
Parent: Halliburton Company
Officers: Scot Clifton, Secretary; Helga Cotgove [1967] Director Corporate Development [Norwegian]; David Alexander Johnston [1971] Director/UK F & A Manager; Colin Reid [1977] Director/Europe Manager Halliburton Completion Tools; Martin Robert White [1973] Director/Vice President

Halliburton Manufacturing and Services Limited
Incorporated: 18 September 1958 *Employees:* 1,384
Net Worth: £222,811,008 *Total Assets:* £759,612,992
Registered Office: c/o Halliburton, Building 4, Chiswick Park, 566 Chiswick High Road, London, W4 5YE
Activities: Support activities for petroleum and natural gas mining
Parent: Halliburton Holdings (No 3)
Officers: Scot Clifton, Secretary; Margulan Abzalov [1975] Director/Senior Country Manager, Cementing, Europe [Kazakh]; Michael Gerard Burns [1968] Director/Business Development Manager; Scot Clifton [1966] Director/Contract Specialist; Archibald Robert Forster [1960] Director/Plant Manager; David Alexander Johnston [1971] Director/Chartered Accountant; Nathan Guy Mery [1982] Director/Area Manager [American]; Colin Reid [1977] Director/Europe Manager Halliburton Completion Tools; Martin Robert White [1973] Director/Vice President

Ham Yard Investment Limited
Incorporated: 4 July 2003 *Employees:* 358
Net Worth: £111,199,000 *Total Assets:* £258,308,000
Registered Office: 21 Golden Square, London, W1F 9JN
Activities: Hotels and similar accommodation
Parent: HY Hotels Limited
Officers: Malcolm Thomas Soden, Secretary; Judith Kit Kemp [1950] Director; Timothy John Reginald Kemp [1946] Director

J O Hambro Capital Management Holdings Limited
Incorporated: 13 June 2011 *Employees:* 7
Net Worth: £211,684,992 *Total Assets:* £212,330,000
Registered Office: Level 3, 1 St James's Market, London, SW1Y 4AH
Activities: Activities of financial services holding companies
Parent: Pendal UK Limited
Officers: Joanne Marjorie Hawkins, Secretary; Mark Purnell, Secretary; Sally Clare Collier [1959] Director [Australian]; James Kingsman Evans [1952] Director [Australian]; Mr Andrew James Fay [1965] Director [Australian]; Emilio Gonzalez [1964] Director [Australian]; James Daryl Hambro [1949] Director/Investment Management; Christopher Mark Jones [1960] Director [American]; Kathryn Ann Matthews [1959] Director; Deborah Ruth Page [1959] Director [Australian]

J O Hambro Capital Management Limited
Incorporated: 9 October 1987 *Employees:* 142
Net Worth: £110,600,000 *Total Assets:* £188,600,000
Registered Office: Level 3, 1 St James's Market, London, SW1Y 4AH
Activities: Financial intermediation not elsewhere classified
Parent: J O Hambro Capital Management Holdings Limited
Officers: Mark Purnell, Secretary; Emilio Gonzalez [1964] Director [Australian]; Stephen Donald Lynn [1969] Director/Certified Chartered Accountant; Brian Vincent Wright [1962] Director/Chartered Accountant [Australian]

Paul Hamlyn Foundation
Incorporated: 12 February 2004 *Employees:* 35
Net Worth: £755,089,984 *Total Assets:* £778,419,968
Registered Office: 5-11 Leeke Street, London, WC1X 9HY
Activities: Activities of head offices
Officers: Lucinda Palfreyman, Secretary; Timothy Brian Bunting [1963] Director/Venture Capitalist; Lord Anthony William Hall [1951] Director General, BBC; Jane Sarah Hamlyn [1958] Director/Artist; Michael Paul Frederick Hamlyn [1955] Director; Charles Richard Leadbeater [1959] Director/Consultant; James Peter Boyce Lingwood [1959] Director/Arts Promoter; Dr Janet Dorothea McKenley-Simpson [1955] Director/Consultant; Sir Anthony Michael Vaughan Salz [1950] Director/Solicitor; Claire Lois Whitaker [1963] Director; Tom Wylie [1945] Director

Hammerson (60 Threadneedle Street) Limited
Incorporated: 4 August 2008 *Employees:* 2
Net Worth: £112,342,000 *Total Assets:* £112,342,000
Registered Office: Kings Place, 90 York Way, London, N1 9GE
Activities: Development of building projects
Parent: Hammerson UK Properties PLC
Officers: Peter William Beaumont Cole [1959] Director/Chartered Surveyor; Andrew John Berger-North [1961] Director/Chartered Surveyor

Hammerson (Brent Cross) Limited
Incorporated: 29 May 1997
Net Worth: £251,068,992 *Total Assets:* £384,833,984
Registered Office: Kings Place, 90 York Way, London, N1 9GE
Activities: Development of building projects
Parent: Hammerson UK Properties PLC
Officers: Warren Stuart Austin [1966] Director/Chartered Accountant; Andrew John Berger-North [1961] Director/Chartered Surveyor; Mark Richard Bourgeois [1968] Managing Director UK and Ireland; Peter William Beaumont Cole [1959] Director/Chartered Surveyor; Richard Geoffrey Shaw [1973] Director/Accountant

Hammerson (Bristol Investments) Limited
Incorporated: 4 August 2008 *Employees:* 3
Net Worth: £264,640,992 *Total Assets:* £327,256,992
Registered Office: Kings Place, 90 York Way, London, N1 9GE
Activities: Development of building projects
Parent: Hammerson UK Properties PLC
Officers: Warren Stuart Austin [1966] Director/Chartered Accountant; Nicholas Timon Drakesmith [1965] Director/Chief Financial Officer; Richard Geoffrey Shaw [1973] Director/Accountant

Hammerson (Leeds Investments) Limited
Incorporated: 21 September 2001
Net Worth: £117,563,000 *Total Assets:* £259,208,000
Registered Office: Kings Place, 90 York Way, London, N1 9GE
Activities: Development of building projects
Parent: Hammerson UK Properties PLC
Officers: Warren Stuart Austin [1966] Director/Chartered Accountant; Andrew John Berger-North [1961] Director/Chartered Surveyor; Mark Richard Bourgeois [1968] Managing Director UK and Ireland; Peter William Beaumont Cole [1959] Director/Chartered Surveyor; Richard Geoffrey Shaw [1973] Director/Accountant

Hammerson (Leicester) Limited.
Incorporated: 1 February 2002 *Employees:* 2
Net Worth: £200,034,000 *Total Assets:* £238,427,008
Registered Office: Kings Place, 90 York Way, London, N1 9GE
Activities: Development of building projects
Parent: Highcross Leicester Limited Partnership
Officers: Nicholas Timon Drakesmith [1965] Director/Chief Financial Officer; Richard Geoffrey Shaw [1973] Director/Accountant

Hammerson (Merthyr) Limited
Incorporated: 4 August 2008
Net Worth: £78,268,000 *Total Assets:* £127,404,000
Registered Office: Kings Place, 90 York Way, London, N1 9GE
Activities: Development of building projects
Parent: Hammerson UK Properties PLC
Officers: Warren Stuart Austin [1966] Director/Chartered Accountant; Andrew John Berger-North [1961] Director/Chartered Surveyor; Peter William Beaumont Cole [1959] Director/Chartered Surveyor; Richard Geoffrey Shaw [1973] Director/Accountant

Hammerson (Rugby) Limited
Incorporated: 15 November 2001
Net Worth: £66,514,000 *Total Assets:* £128,691,000
Registered Office: Kings Place, 90 York Way, London, N1 9GE
Activities: Development of building projects
Parent: Hammerson UK Properties PLC
Officers: Warren Stuart Austin [1966] Director/Chartered Accountant; Andrew John Berger-North [1961] Director/Chartered Surveyor; Peter William Beaumont Cole [1959] Director/Chartered Surveyor; Richard Geoffrey Shaw [1973] Director/Accountant

Hammerson (Value Retail Investments) Limited
Incorporated: 23 July 2008
Net Worth: £173,282,000 *Total Assets:* £405,153,984
Registered Office: Kings Place, 90 York Way, London, N1 9GE
Activities: Development of building projects
Parent: Hammerson UK Properties PLC
Officers: Andrew John Berger-North [1961] Director/Chartered Surveyor; Peter William Beaumont Cole [1959] Director; Nicholas Timon Drakesmith [1965] Director/Chief Financial Officer

Hammerson Bull Ring Limited
Incorporated: 10 May 2005
Net Worth: £138,483,008 *Total Assets:* £189,732,992
Registered Office: Kings Place, 90 York Way, London, N1 9GE
Activities: Development of building projects
Parent: Hammerson UK Properties PLC
Officers: Warren Stuart Austin [1966] Director/Chartered Accountant; Nicholas Timon Drakesmith [1965] Director/Chief Financial Officer

Hammerson International Holdings Limited
Incorporated: 27 July 1960
Net Worth: £3,144,632,064 *Total Assets:* £4,325,985,792
Registered Office: Kings Place, 90 York Way, London, N1 9GE
Activities: Activities of head offices
Parent: Hammerson PLC
Officers: David John Atkins [1966] Director/Surveyor; Mark Richard Bourgeois [1968] Managing Director UK and Ireland; Peter William Beaumont Cole [1959] Director/Chartered Surveyor; Nicholas Timon Drakesmith [1965] Director/Chief Financial Officer

Hammerson Oracle Investments Limited
Incorporated: 9 December 1996
Net Worth: £26,999,000 *Total Assets:* £120,632,000
Registered Office: Kings Place, 90 York Way, London, N1 9GE
Activities: Development of building projects
Parent: Hammerson UK Properties PLC
Officers: Nicholas Timon Drakesmith [1965] Director/Chief Financial Officer; Richard Geoffrey Shaw [1973] Director/Accountant

Hammerson PLC
Incorporated: 17 April 1940 *Employees:* 789
Net Worth: £6,023,499,776 *Total Assets:* £9,875,699,712
Registered Office: Kings Place, 90 York Way, London, N1 9GE
Activities: Development of building projects
Officers: Rachel Sarah Booth, Secretary; David John Atkins [1966] Director/Surveyor; Pierre Bruno Charles Bouchut [1955] Director/Chief Financial Officer [French]; Gwyneth Victoria Burr [1963] Retail Director; Nicholas Timon Drakesmith [1965] Director/Chief Financial Officer; Andrew James Formica [1971] Director [British/Australian]; Judith Mary Gibbons [1957] Director/Venture Partner; David Alan Tyler [1953] Director; Carol Ann Welch [1970] Managing Director

Hammerson UK Properties PLC
Incorporated: 15 March 1935
Net Worth: £1,559,463,040 *Total Assets:* £3,248,049,920
Registered Office: Kings Place, 90 York Way, London, N1 9GE
Activities: Development of building projects
Parent: Hammerson International Holdings Limited
Officers: David John Atkins [1966] Director/Chartered Surveyor; Andrew John Berger-North [1961] Director/Chartered Surveyor; Rachel Sarah Booth [1966] Director/General Counsel and Company Secretary; Mark Richard Bourgeois [1968] Managing Director UK and Ireland; Peter William Beaumont Cole [1959] Director/Chartered Surveyor; Nicholas Timon Drakesmith [1965] Director/Chief Financial Officer

Hampshire Trust Bank PLC
Incorporated: 28 April 1977 *Employees:* 122
Previous: Hampshire Trust PLC
Net Worth: £115,640,000 *Total Assets:* £742,259,968
Registered Office: 55 Bishopsgate, London, EC2N 3AS
Activities: Banks
Parent: Hoggant Limited
Officers: Audrey Morrison, Secretary; Timothy Mark Blackwell [1969] Director; James Robert Drummond Smith [1960] Director; Robert David East [1960] Director; Astrid Cecile Helene Grey [1964] Director [French/Swedish]; Richard Stanley Price [1961] Director; Robert Sharpe [1949] Director; Dominic James Haviland Slade [1971] Director/Venture Capitalist; Matthew Peter Vincent Wyles [1958] Director

Hampshire Waste Services Limited
Incorporated: 5 September 1990 *Employees:* 4
Net Worth Deficit: £10,271,000 *Total Assets:* £141,144,992
Registered Office: 210 Pentonville Road, London, N1 9JY
Activities: Collection of non-hazardous waste
Parent: Veolia ES Aurora Limited
Officers: Benjamin Peter Lambert, Secretary; Christophe Bellynck [1961] Director [French]; Neil Vincent Gallagher [1963] Finance Director; David Andrew Gerrard [1964] Executive Director; Benjamin Slater [1971] Regional Director

Hanover & Oxford Property Limited
Incorporated: 11 October 2013
Net Worth: £42,714,824 *Total Assets:* £111,581,608
Registered Office: Unit A, 10 Fashion Street, London, E1 6PX
Activities: Buying and selling of own real estate
Major Shareholder: Anders Holch Povlsen
Officers: Soren From, Secretary; Soren From [1961] Director [Danish]; Anders Holch Povlsen [1972] Director [Danish]

Hanover Acceptances Limited
Incorporated: 31 July 1972 *Employees:* 40
Net Worth: £660,550,976 *Total Assets:* £1,049,590,016
Registered Office: 16 Hans Road, London, SW3 1RT
Activities: Activities of head offices
Officers: Lydia Ruth Gorvy [1942] Director/Executive; Manfred Stanley Gorvy [1938] Director/Chartered Accountant; Dr Sean Gorvy [1963] Director/Executive; Dr Juergen Grossmann [1952] Director [German]; Alan Jay Leibowitz [1952] Director/Surveyor; Trevor Moross [1948] Director/Chartered Surveyor; Christopher Julian Sheridan [1943] Director/Banker; Edward Ian Walker Arnott [1939] Director/Solicitor

Hanover House Limited
Incorporated: 24 September 2015
Net Worth: £97,624,568 *Total Assets:* £180,947,376
Registered Office: Unit A, 10 Fashion Street, London, E1 6PX
Activities: Buying and selling of own real estate
Major Shareholder: Anders Holch Povlsen
Officers: Soren From [1961] Director [Danish]; Anders Holch Povlsen [1972] Director [Danish]

The Hanover Insurance International Holdings Limited
Incorporated: 17 April 2011
Net Worth: £132,009,488 *Total Assets:* £359,455,456
Registered Office: 4th Floor, Plantation Place, 30 Fenchurch Street, London, EC3M 3AD
Activities: Activities of other holding companies n.e.c.
Officers: Richard Nicholas Barnett, Secretary; Robert John Callan [1968] Director/Chartered Accountant; John Fowle [1969] Director/Underwriter; Dr Huiqiang Zuo [1965] Director/Reinsurer [Chinese]

Hansa Trust PLC
Incorporated: 23 December 1912
Net Worth: £323,100,992 *Total Assets:* £324,108,000
Registered Office: 50 Curzon Street, London, W1J 7UW
Activities: Activities of investment trusts
Officers: Jonathan Richard Davie [1946] Director; Robert Alexander Hammond Chambers [1942] Director; Raymond Benedict Bartholomew Michael Oxford [1952] Director; William Henry Salomon [1957] Director/Banker; Professor Geoffrey Edward Wood [1945] Director/Professor of Economics

Hansteen Holdings PLC
Incorporated: 27 October 2005 *Employees:* 79
Net Worth: £557,500,032 *Total Assets:* £910,000,000
Registered Office: 1st Floor, Pegasus House, 37-43 Sackville Street, London, W1S 3DL
Activities: Activities of head offices
Officers: Jim Clarke [1960] Director; Melvyn John Egglenton [1957] Director; Morgan Lewis Jones [1957] Director; Richard Phillip Lowes [1954] Director; David Rough [1951] Director; Ian Richard Watson [1960] Director

Hansteen Property Investments Limited
Incorporated: 13 December 2005
Net Worth: £176,055,808 *Total Assets:* £183,161,696
Registered Office: 1st Floor, Pegasus House, 37-43 Sackville Street, London, W1S 3DL
Activities: Other letting and operating of own or leased real estate
Parent: Hansteen Holdings PLC
Officers: Derek Kevin Heathwood [1972] Director; Morgan Lewis Jones [1957] Director; Sarah Jane Lindsay [1972] Director/Property Executive; Richard Phillip Lowes [1954] Director/Accountant; Janine Anne McDonald [1964] Director/Accountant; Ian Richard Watson [1960] Director

Happybadge Projects Limited
Incorporated: 20 May 1993 *Employees:* 33
Net Worth: £122,252,296 *Total Assets:* £278,820,672
Registered Office: Edelman House, 1238 High Road, Whetstone, London, N20 0LH
Activities: Development of building projects
Parent: Legacy Properties (UK) Limited
Officers: Alan Lawrence Banes, Secretary/Solicitor; Angela Susan Davies, Secretary; Benjamin James Bourne [1989] Property Director; Robert Anthony Bourne [1950] Director; Angela Susan Davies [1959] Director/Property Manager; Leslie Robert Hardie [1957] Director/Property Manager

Harben Finance 2017-1 PLC
Incorporated: 17 March 2017
Net Worth: £14,120 *Total Assets:* £1,886,124,672
Registered Office: 35 Great St Helen's, London, EC3A 6AP
Activities: Activities of mortgage finance companies
Parent: Harben Finance 2017-1 Holdings Limited
Officers: Susan Iris Abrahams [1957] Director

Harbour Funding PLC
Incorporated: 13 August 2003
Net Worth: £12,500 *Total Assets:* £208,878,320
Registered Office: 4th Floor, 107 Cannon Street, London, EC4N 5AF
Activities: Financial intermediation not elsewhere classified
Parent: T.H.F.C. (Services) Limited
Officers: Colin John Burke [1962] Director/Company Secretary; Fenella Jane Edge [1963] Director/Treasurer; John Piers Williamson [1961] Director/Chief Executive

Hard Rock International Limited
Incorporated: 17 October 1977
Net Worth: £88,112,000 *Total Assets:* £114,406,000
Registered Office: Cannon Place, 78 Cannon Street, London, EC4N 6AF
Activities: Licenced restaurants
Parent: Seminole Hard Rock UK Limited
Officers: Brian Learned Alexander [1971] Director/Attorney [American]; David Stuart Pellow [1976] Director/Area Vice President

Harding Midco Limited
Incorporated: 13 January 2017 *Employees:* 95
Net Worth Deficit: £2,522,000 *Total Assets:* £111,287,000
Registered Office: Holden House, 57 Rathbone Place, London, W1T 1JU
Activities: Other business support service activities n.e.c.
Shareholders: Eric Robert Newnham; Mayfair Equity Partners Nominees Limited
Officers: Frank Bryant [1962] Director; James Copley [1972] Director; Grant Murray [1964] Director/Chief Financial Officer; Eric Robert Newnham [1959] Director

Hardy Underwriting Group Limited
Incorporated: 24 June 1996 *Employees:* 10
Previous: Hardy Underwriting Group PLC
Net Worth: £84,952,000 *Total Assets:* £742,731,008
Registered Office: 20 Fenchurch Street, London, EC3M 3BY
Activities: Other activities auxiliary to insurance and pension funding
Parent: Hardy Underwriting Bermuda Limited
Officers: David John Brosnan [1962] Director/Chief Executive [American]; David John Stevens [1963] Director/Chief Financial Officer

Hardy Underwriting Limited
Incorporated: 21 October 1994
Net Worth: £36,313,000 *Total Assets:* £692,849,984
Registered Office: 20 Fenchurch Street, London, EC3M 3BY
Activities: Non-life insurance
Parent: Hardy Underwriting Group PLC
Officers: David John Brosnan [1962] Director/Chief Executive Officer [American]; David John Stevens [1963] Director/Chief Financial Officer

Harewood Helena 2 Limited
Incorporated: 21 May 2008
Net Worth: £99,531,568 *Total Assets:* £111,071,424
Registered Office: 5 Aldermanbury Square, London, EC2V 7BP
Activities: Financial intermediation not elsewhere classified
Parent: BNP Paribas SA
Officers: Ingrid Furtado, Secretary; Iain Heeps [1970] Director/Chief Operating Officer BNP Paribas IP UK Limited; Patrick Perez [1958] Director/Chief Operating Officer [French]

Harewood Holdings Limited
Incorporated: 15 September 2006
Net Worth: £217,504,992 *Total Assets:* £287,736,992
Registered Office: 10 Harewood Avenue, London, NW1 6AA
Activities: Financial intermediation not elsewhere classified
Parent: BNP Paribas
Officers: Stephen Martin Middleton [1975] Director/Banker; Christopher Mark Penney [1965] Director/Chartered Accountant; Donald Paul Reynolds [1957] Director/Lawyer

HarperCollins (UK)
Incorporated: 5 May 1989
Net Worth Deficit: £327,704,992 *Total Assets:* £748,902,976
Registered Office: 1 London Bridge Street, London, SE1 9GF
Activities: Activities of head offices
Officers: Simon Dowson-Collins, Secretary; Janet Ann Gervasio [1959] Director/Senior VP Finance [American]; Brian Murray [1966] Director/President & CEO [American]; Charles George Mariner Redmayne [1966] Director/Chief Executive - Harpercollins UK

Harrods (UK) Limited
Incorporated: 25 February 1985 *Employees:* 2
Net Worth: £1,698,000,000 *Total Assets:* £1,698,200,064
Registered Office: 87-135 Brompton Road, Knightsbridge, London, SW1X 7XL
Activities: Activities of head offices
Parent: Harrods Holdings Limited
Officers: Daniel Jonathan Webster, Secretary; James Philip Healy [1966] Director/Retail Executive; Michael Ashley Ward [1956] Managing Director

Harrods Commercial Property Limited
Incorporated: 18 November 2011
Net Worth: £74,400,000 *Total Assets:* £127,200,000
Registered Office: 87-135 Brompton Road, Knightsbridge, London, SW1X 7XL
Activities: Other letting and operating of own or leased real estate
Parent: QH Partners Limited
Officers: Daniel Jonathan Webster, Secretary; Michael Ashley Ward [1956] Managing Director; Daniel Jonathan Webster [1970] Director/Group General Counsel

Harrods Corporate Management Limited
Incorporated: 5 April 2012
Net Worth: £24,000,000 *Total Assets:* £491,600,000
Registered Office: 87-135 Brompton Road, Knightsbridge, London, SW1X 7XL
Activities: Activities of head offices
Parent: Harrods Holdings Limited
Officers: Daniel Jonathan Webster, Secretary; Michael Ashley Ward [1956] Managing Director; Daniel Jonathan Webster [1970] Director/Group General Counsel

Harrods Group (Holding) Limited
Incorporated: 7 November 2006 *Employees:* 4,595
Net Worth: £118,000,000 *Total Assets:* £2,073,299,968
Registered Office: 87-135 Brompton Road, Knightsbridge, London, SW1X 7XL
Activities: Activities of head offices
Parent: Qatar Investment Authority
Officers: Daniel Jonathan Webster, Secretary; Hussain Ali a A Al-Abdulla [1957] Director/State Minister [Qatari]; Mansoor Ebrahim SI Al-Mahmoud [1974] Director/CEO of QIA [Qatari]; Hamad Bin Jassim Bin Jaber Al-Thani [1959] Director/State Minister [Qatari]; Sarah Jane Brown [1963] Charity Director & Writer; Michael Ashley Ward [1956] Managing Director

Harrods Holdings Limited
Incorporated: 14 September 1984
Net Worth: £460,700,000 *Total Assets:* £1,330,499,968
Registered Office: 87-135 Brompton Road, Knightsbridge, London, SW1X 7XL
Activities: Activities of head offices
Shareholders: QH Partners Limited; QH Participations Limited
Officers: Daniel Jonathan Webster, Secretary; Michael Ashley Ward [1956] Managing Director; Daniel Jonathan Webster [1970] Director/Group General Counsel

Harrods Limited
Incorporated: 20 November 1889 *Employees:* 3,924
Net Worth: £1,995,600,000 *Total Assets:* £2,630,700,032
Registered Office: 87-135 Brompton Road, London, SW1X 7XL
Activities: Other retail sale in non-specialised stores
Parent: Harrods (UK) Limited
Officers: Daniel Jonathan Webster, Secretary; Hussain Ali a A Al-Abdulla [1957] Director/State Minister [Qatari]; Mansoor Ebrahim SI Al-Mahmoud [1974] Director/CEO of QIA [Qatari]; Hamad Bin Jassim Bin Jaber Al-Thani [1959] Director/State Minister [Qatari]; Rajiv Lochan Assanand [1957] Director/Retail Executive; James Philip Healy [1966] Director/Retail Executive; Michael Ashley Ward [1956] Managing Director

Harrods Property Limited
Incorporated: 1 November 2006
Net Worth: £512,139,008 *Total Assets:* £512,872,000
Registered Office: 87-135 Brompton Road, London, SW1X 7XL
Activities: Other letting and operating of own or leased real estate
Parent: Harrods Limited
Officers: Daniel Jonathan Webster, Secretary; Michael Ashley Ward [1956] Managing Director; Daniel Jonathan Webster [1970] Director/Group General Counsel

Hartree Partners Power & Gas Company (UK) Limited
Incorporated: 19 October 2001 *Employees:* 12
Previous: Hess Energy Power & Gas Company (UK) Limited
Net Worth: £14,671,308 *Total Assets:* £203,917,984
Registered Office: 2nd Floor, Cardinal Place, 100 Victoria Street, London, SW1E 5JL
Activities: Other professional, scientific and technical activities n.e.c.
Officers: Paul Martin Garske [1968] Director/Trader [Australian]; Stephen Michael Hendel [1951] Director [American]; Jonathan Hugh O'Neill [1957] Director/Oil Trading; Stephen Michael Semlitz [1953] Director [American]; Heiko Voelker [1962] Director/Oil Trader [German]

Harvey Nichols and Company Limited
Incorporated: 1 December 1983 *Employees:* 687
Net Worth: £72,119,000 *Total Assets:* £195,892,000
Registered Office: 361-365 Chiswick High Road, London, W4 4HS
Activities: Other retail sale in non-specialised stores
Parent: Harvey Nichols Group Limited
Officers: Manju Malhotra, Secretary; Manju Malhotra [1972] Director; Dickson Poon [1956] Director; Pearson Poon [1994] Director; Daniela Francesca Rinaldi [1965] Director; Barry Tallintire [1962] Group Property and Facilities Director

Harvey Nichols Group Limited
Incorporated: 22 January 1902
Net Worth: £37,610,000 *Total Assets:* £120,159,000
Registered Office: 361-365 Chiswick High Road, London, W4 4HS
Activities: Activities of head offices
Parent: Broad Gain (UK) Limited
Officers: Manju Malhotra, Secretary; Manju Malhotra [1972] Director; Dickson Poon [1956] Director; Daniela Francesca Rinaldi [1965] Director

Harwood Capital Management Limited
Incorporated: 13 June 2011 *Employees:* 44
Net Worth: £124,840,720 *Total Assets:* £150,366,464
Registered Office: 6 Stratton Street, Mayfair, London, W1J 8LD
Activities: Financial intermediation not elsewhere classified
Major Shareholder: Christopher Harwood Bernard Mills
Officers: Jeremy James Brade [1961] Director/Fund Manager; Sidney Cabessa [1943] Director/Senior Advisor [French]; Alan Richard Durrant [1972] Director; John Colin Keith [1944] Director; Charles Patrick Harwood Mills [1988] Director/Property Management; Christopher Harwood Bernard Mills [1952] Director/Investment Manager; Lynne Theresa Mills [1958] Director; Jonathan Whittingham [1975] Director

Hathber GR Limited
Incorporated: 25 March 2015 *Employees:* 2
Net Worth: £167,281,072 *Total Assets:* £452,034,880
Registered Office: Berkeley House, 304 Regents Park Road, London, N3 2JY
Activities: Buying and selling of own real estate
Parent: Renbuff Investments Limited
Officers: Paul Hallam, Secretary; Christopher Charles McGill [1960] Managing Director; William Kenneth Procter [1953] Director/Accountant

Hatton Garden Properties Limited
Incorporated: 21 July 2006
Net Worth: £86,977,744 *Total Assets:* £302,539,488
Registered Office: Floor 6, Quadrant House, 4 Thomas More Square, London, E1W 1YW
Activities: Other business support service activities n.e.c.
Parent: Structadene (LBG) Properties Limited
Officers: David Alan Pearlman, Secretary; Michael Robert Goldberger [1956] Director; Gulam Mohamed Patel [1948] Director/Chartered Accountant; David Alan Pearlman [1945] Director; Howard Alan Pearlman [1975] Director/Property Management

Haut Investments Limited
Incorporated: 1 March 2013 *Employees:* 873
Net Worth: £320,705,984 *Total Assets:* £967,409,024
Registered Office: One Coleman Street, London, EC2R 5AA
Activities: Other business support service activities n.e.c.
Parent: Legal & General Capital Investments Limited
Officers: Matteo Charles Colombo [1980] Director/Investor; Geoffrey Julian Timms [1960] Director/Group General Counsel

Havana Holdings (UK) Limited
Incorporated: 19 February 1998 *Employees:* 56
Net Worth: £10,822,000 *Total Assets:* £172,412,992
Registered Office: 30 Portman Square, London, W1A 4ZX
Activities: Hotels and similar accommodation
Parent: Stellar Hotels S.A.
Officers: Karin Cooper, Secretary; Sheikh Jassim Bin Hamad Al Thani [1982] Director/Chairman [Qatari]; Fady Bakhos [1971] Director/Lawyer [Lebanese]; Michael Anthony Cairns [1940] Director; Karin Cooper [1969] Director/Architect [German]; Zaki Nasser Zaki El Guiziri [1957] Director [Egyptian]

Haven Funding PLC
Incorporated: 14 December 1995
Net Worth: £12,500 *Total Assets:* £258,643,488
Registered Office: 4th Floor, 107 Cannon Street, London, EC4N 5AF
Activities: Financial intermediation not elsewhere classified
Parent: Haven Fundings (Holdings) Limited
Officers: Colin John Burke [1962] Director/Finance Manager; Fenella Jane Edge [1963] Director/Treasurer; John Piers Williamson [1961] Director

Havin Bank Ltd
Incorporated: 3 October 1972 *Employees:* 18
Net Worth: £22,101,356 *Total Assets:* £172,801,360
Registered Office: 4th Floor, South Quay Building, 189 Marsh Wall, London, E14 9SH
Activities: Banks
Officers: Shirish Amratlal Shah, Secretary; Guillermo Gil Gomez [1969] Director [Cuban]; Roy Luis Recio-Carbajal [1984] Director [Cuban]; Maikel Rico-Trujillo [1977] Director [Cuban]; Gustavo Renan Roca Sanchez [1940] Director/Chairman [Cuban]; Shirish Amratlal Shah [1959] Director; Lord David Maxim Triesman [1943] Director

Hawk Newco Limited
Incorporated: 30 March 2016
Net Worth: £51,266,000 *Total Assets:* £187,156,000
Registered Office: 30 Crown Place, London, EC2A 4ES
Activities: Other business support service activities n.e.c.
Parent: Hawk Finco Limited
Officers: Neil Austin Johnson [1969] Director; Stewart Andrew Alan Mitchell [1966] Director

Hawkins Funding Limited
Incorporated: 10 October 2002
Net Worth: £32,391,120 *Total Assets:* £6,178,557,440
Registered Office: 1 Churchill Place, London, E14 5HP
Activities: Financial intermediation not elsewhere classified
Parent: Barclays Bank PLC
Officers: Christopher Patrick Le Neve Foster [1981] Director/Banker; Carl Thomas Senior [1978] Director/Banker; Vishal Shah [1984] Director/Banker; Patrick Brittain Voisey [1979] Director

Hawksmoor Mortgages 2016-1 PLC
Incorporated: 7 June 2016
Net Worth: £31,628 *Total Assets:* £2,008,933,376
Registered Office: 35 Great St Helen's, London, EC3A 6AP
Activities: Financial intermediation not elsewhere classified
Parent: Hawksmoor Mortgages 2016-1 Holdings Limited
Officers: Daniel Marc Richard Jaffe [1975] Director

Hawksmoor Mortgages 2016-2 PLC
Incorporated: 15 September 2016
Net Worth: £27,034 *Total Assets:* £1,016,599,744
Registered Office: 35 Great St Helen's, London, EC3A 6AP
Activities: Financial intermediation not elsewhere classified
Parent: Hawksmoor Mortgages 2016-2 Holdings Limited
Officers: Daniel Marc Richard Jaffe [1975] Director

Hawthorn Asset Co Limited
Incorporated: 26 September 2006
Net Worth: £7,000 *Total Assets:* £644,088,000
Registered Office: Third Floor, 1 King's Arms Yard, London, EC2R 7AF
Activities: Other business support service activities n.e.c.
Parent: Wilmington Trust SP Services (London) Limited
Officers: Robert Sutton [1978] Director/Financial Services [American]; Daniel Jonathan Wynne [1970] Director

Hayabusa Limited
Incorporated: 25 October 2013
Net Worth: £42,959,000 *Total Assets:* £123,756,000
Registered Office: Level 20, 25 Canada Square, London, E14 5LQ
Activities: Activities of head offices
Shareholders: Hayabusa Holdings Limited; Equitix Hayabus 3 Limited
Officers: Sarah Jane Gregory, Secretary; Fabio D'Alonzo [1976] Director [Italian]; Matteo Maino [1965] Director [Italian]; Simon David Pinnell [1964] Director/Accountant; Daniel Marinus Maria Vermeer [1981] Director [Dutch]

Haymarket Capital Ventures LLP
Incorporated: 2 June 2008
Net Worth: £173,875,600 *Total Assets:* £177,007,600
Registered Office: 71-75 Shelton Street, Covent Garden, London, WC2H 9JQ

Hays International Holdings Limited
Incorporated: 13 October 2005
Net Worth: £308,609,984 *Total Assets:* £492,432,992
Registered Office: 250 Euston Road, London, NW1 2AF
Activities: Activities of other holding companies n.e.c.
Parent: Hays PLC
Officers: Alistair Richard Cox [1961] Director; Douglas George Evans [1962] Director/Solicitor; Ian David Pratt [1965] Director/Deputy Group Financial Controller; Paul Venables [1961] Director; Christopher John Winters [1972] Director/Deputy Company Secretary

Hays PLC
Incorporated: 28 July 1987 *Employees:* 10,978
Net Worth: £700,499,968 *Total Assets:* £1,508,700,032
Registered Office: 250 Euston Road, London, NW1 2AF
Activities: Activities of head offices
Officers: Douglas George Evans, Secretary; Alistair Richard Cox [1961] Director; Torsten Gunter Kreindl [1963] Director [German]; Andrew David Martin [1960] Director; Susan Elizabeth Murray [1957] Director; Mary Teresa Rainey [1955] Director; Paul Venables [1961] Director; John Peter Williams [1953] Director

Hays Specialist Recruitment Limited
Incorporated: 25 March 1970 *Employees:* 2,818
Net Worth: £71,567,000 *Total Assets:* £321,428,992
Registered Office: 250 Euston Road, London, NW1 2AF
Activities: Temporary employment agency activities
Parent: Hays Specialist Recruitment (Holdings) Limited
Officers: Alistair Richard Cox [1961] Director; Douglas George Evans [1962] Director/Solicitor; John Harrington [1962] Director; Paul Venables [1961] Director; Simon Winfield [1969] Director

HBL Bank UK Limited
Incorporated: 29 April 1983 *Employees:* 140
Previous: Habibsons Bank Limited
Net Worth: £74,012,000 *Total Assets:* £672,680,000
Registered Office: 9 Portman Street, London, W1H 6DZ
Activities: Banks
Parent: Habib Allied Holding Limited
Officers: Hamid Masud Qazi, Secretary; Arif Mahmood Ali [1960] Director/Banker; Michael David Bendon [1939] Director/Retired Bank Manager; David John Blatchford [1954] Director/Banker; John Nicholas Cotton [1941] Director/Consultant; Syed Abbas Hasan [1960] Director/Banker [Pakistani]; Rayomond Kotwal [1960] Director/Banker [Pakistani]; Faisal Noorali Lalani [1963] Director/Banker [Dutch/Pakistani]

HBOS Financial Services Limited
Incorporated: 17 February 1997
Net Worth: £453,799,008 *Total Assets:* £464,252,000
Registered Office: 33 Old Broad Street, London, EC2N 1HZ
Activities: Activities of head offices
Parent: Scottish Widows Financial Services Holdings
Officers: Christina Ann Hankin, Secretary; Sean William Lowther [1960] Director; Gregory Miles Norton [1968] Director; Ian Henry Price [1965] Director

HBOS Insurance & Investment Group Limited
Incorporated: 1 May 1996
Net Worth: £64,700,000 *Total Assets:* £200,300,000
Registered Office: 33 Old Broad Street, London, EC2N 1HZ
Activities: Activities of head offices
Parent: Lloyds Bank PLC
Officers: Alyson Elizabeth Mulholland, Secretary; Paul Jacques Sylvain Astruc [1966] Director; Israel Santos Perez [1972] Director [Spanish]

HCA Global Capital LLP
Incorporated: 19 January 2012
Net Worth: £111,365,480 *Total Assets:* £111,401,520
Registered Office: 242 Marylebone Road, London, NW1 6JL

HCA International Holdings Limited
Incorporated: 25 March 1969
Net Worth: £48,293,000 *Total Assets:* £258,515,008
Registered Office: 242 Marylebone Road, London, NW1 6JL
Activities: Activities of head offices
Parent: HCA UK Services Limited
Officers: Catherine Mary Jane Vickery, Secretary; John Mozart Franck [1962] Director/Attorney [American]; Jeremy Randal Midkiff [1979] Director [American]; Michael Thomas Neeb [1962] Director/Accountant; Teresa Finch Pritchard [1960] Director [American]; John Michael Reay [1961] Director; Catherine Mary Jane Vickery [1975] Director/Solicitor

HCA International Limited
Incorporated: 10 February 1995 *Employees:* 3,362
Net Worth: £584,822,016 *Total Assets:* £1,373,726,976
Registered Office: 242 Marylebone Road, London, NW1 6JL
Activities: Hospital activities
Parent: HCA International Holdings Limited
Officers: Catherine Mary Jane Vickery, Secretary; Michael Thomas Neeb [1962] Director/Chief Executive; Teresa Finch Pritchard [1960] Director [American]; John Michael Reay [1961] Director; Catherine Mary Jane Vickery [1975] Director/Solicitor

HCA Swiss Capital 1 LLP
Incorporated: 22 April 2013
Net Worth: £482,216,992 *Total Assets:* £482,504,000
Registered Office: 242 Marylebone Road, London, NW1 6JL

HCA UK Capital Limited
Incorporated: 28 May 2003
Net Worth: £388,152,000 *Total Assets:* £421,072,000
Registered Office: 242 Marylebone Road, London, NW1 6JL
Activities: Activities of head offices
Parent: HCA UK Holdings Limited
Officers: Catherine Mary Jane Vickery, Secretary; Jeremy Randal Midkiff [1979] Director [American]; Michael Thomas Neeb [1962] Director/Chief Executive; Teresa Finch Pritchard [1960] Director [American]; John Michael Reay [1961] Director; Catherine Mary Jane Vickery [1975] Director/Solicitor

HCA UK Holdings Limited
Incorporated: 2 July 1996
Net Worth: £22,447,000 *Total Assets:* £514,615,008
Registered Office: 242 Marylebone Road, London, NW1 6JL
Activities: Other business support service activities n.e.c.
Parent: HCA Healthcare, Inc.
Officers: Catherine Mary Jane Vickery, Secretary; Jeremy Randal Midkiff [1979] Director [American]; Michael Thomas Neeb [1962] Director/Chief Executive; Teresa Finch Pritchard [1960] Director [American]; John Michael Reay [1961] Director; Catherine Mary Jane Vickery [1975] Director/Solicitor

HCA UK Services Limited
Incorporated: 21 March 2002
Net Worth: £187,408,992 *Total Assets:* £196,370,000
Registered Office: 242 Marylebone Road, London, NW1 6JL
Activities: Hospital activities
Parent: HCA UK Holdings Limited
Officers: Catherine Mary Jane Vickery, Secretary; Jeremy Randal Midkiff [1979] Director [American]; Michael Thomas Neeb [1962] Director/Chief Executive Officer; Teresa Finch Pritchard [1960] Director [American]; John Michael Reay [1961] Director; Catherine Mary Jane Vickery [1975] Director/Solicitor

HCC International Insurance Company PLC
Incorporated: 22 July 1981 *Employees:* 183
Net Worth: £486,801,824 *Total Assets:* £1,400,646,272
Registered Office: 1 Aldgate, London, EC3N 1RE
Activities: Non-life insurance
Parent: Pepys Holdings Limited
Officers: David Feldman, Secretary; Jenna Louise Holliday, Secretary; Nicholas John Walkett, Secretary/Accountant; Simon Button [1965] Director/Chief Underwriting Officer; Barry John Cook [1960] Director/CEO Insurance Group; Thibaud Jacques Gerard Hervy [1974] Director/Insurance Executive [French]; Nicholas Ian Hutton Penman [1966] Director/COO Insurance Company; Hideyuki Ishii [1971] Director [Japanese]; Katherine Lee Letsinger [1962] Director/Chief Financial Officer; Nicholas Carl Marsh [1955] Director; Hans-Dieter Rohlf [1950] Director [German]; Craig Anthony Scarr [1962] Director/Auditor; Graham Richard Austen White [1968] Director/Chief Risk Officer and Chief Actuary

HCUK Auto Funding 2017-1 Ltd
Incorporated: 14 December 2016
Net Worth: £1,939 *Total Assets:* £219,543,664
Registered Office: 35 Great St Helen's, London, EC3A 6AP
Activities: Financial intermediation not elsewhere classified
Parent: Intertrust Corporate Services Limited
Officers: Susan Iris Abrahams [1957] Director

The Health Foundation
Incorporated: 14 April 1983 *Employees:* 135
Net Worth: £1,008,790,016 *Total Assets:* £1,048,235,008
Registered Office: 90 Long Acre, London, WC2E 9RA
Activities: Other human health activities
Officers: Sir David Nigel Dalton [1961] Director/Chief Executive of NHS Foundation Trust; Eric Allan Gregory [1957] Director/Independent Adviser; Loraine Hawkins [1957] Director/Expert Adviser; Martyn Hole [1959] Director/Investment Manager; Dr Ruth Mary Hussey [1956] Director/Public Health Consultant; Branwen Jeffreys [1965] Director/Journalist; Bridget Fiona McIntyre [1961] Director; Sharmila Nebhrajani [1966] Director/Holds Several Posts; Melloney Marina Caroline Poole [1948] Director/Solicitor; Professor Rosalind Louise Smyth [1958] Director/Professor in Child Health; Sir Hugh Henderson Taylor [1950] Director/Chair of NHS Trust; David Zahn [1970] Director/Investment Manager [British/American]

Hectagon Assets Limited
Incorporated: 16 January 2014
Net Worth: £69,764,000 *Total Assets:* £326,477,504
Registered Office: 6th Floor, Charles House, 108-110 Finchley Road, London, NW3 5JJ
Activities: Development of building projects
Parent: Gold Quay Assets Limited
Officers: Yiannakis Theophani Christodoulou [1965] Director; Lambros Hadjiioannou [1978] Director

Hector Rail Holding UK Limited
Incorporated: 11 October 2016
Net Worth: £116,654,000 *Total Assets:* £118,748,000
Registered Office: 3rd Floor, 55 Old Broad Street, London, EC2M 1RX
Activities: Activities of other holding companies n.e.c.
Officers: Kurt Aake Haakansson [1950] Non-Executive Director [Swedish]; Alexander Hedderich [1965] Non-Executive Director [German]; Masoud Homayoun [1980] Non-Executive Director [Swedish]; Timothy Andrew Robinson [1973] Non-Executive Director; Anna Viktoria Sundell [1981] Non-Executive Director [Swedish]

Heineken (Orange) 1 Limited
Incorporated: 21 September 2007
Net Worth: £1,439,259,008 *Total Assets:* £6,764,737,024
Registered Office: Elsley Court, 20-22 Great Titchfield Street, London, W1W 8BE
Activities: Other business support service activities n.e.c.
Parent: Heineken (Orange) 2 Limited
Officers: David Michael Forde [1968] Managing Director [Irish]; Sean Michael Paterson [1982] Director/Accountant; Radovan Sikorsky [1967] Finance Director [Slovak]; Kelly Taylor-Welsh [1978] Director/Head of UK Tax

Heineken (Orange) 2 Limited
Incorporated: 10 September 2007
Net Worth: £2,722,736,896 *Total Assets:* £3,709,016,320
Registered Office: Elsley Court, 20-22 Great Titchfield Street, London, W1W 8BE
Activities: Other business support service activities n.e.c.
Parent: Heineken N.V.
Officers: David Michael Forde [1968] Managing Director [Irish]; Sean Michael Paterson [1982] Director/Accountant; Radovan Sikorsky [1967] Finance Director [Slovak]; Kelly Taylor-Welsh [1978] Director/Head of UK Tax

Heineken (Orange) 3 Limited
Incorporated: 16 January 2008
Net Worth Deficit: £488,239,488 *Total Assets:* £2,182,822,400
Registered Office: Elsley Court, 20-22 Great Titchfield Street, London, W1W 8BE
Activities: Other business support service activities n.e.c.
Parent: Heineken (Orange) 1 Limited
Officers: David Michael Forde [1968] Managing Director [Irish]; Sean Michael Paterson [1982] Director/Accountant; Radovan Sikorsky [1967] Finance Director [Slovak]; Kelly Taylor-Welsh [1978] Director/Head of UK Tax

H.J. Heinz Company Limited
Incorporated: 28 November 2012 *Employees:* 2
Net Worth: £1,100,690,944 *Total Assets:* £2,435,106,048
Registered Office: The Shard, 32 London Bridge Street, London, SE1 9SG
Activities: Wholesale of other food, including fish, crustaceans and molluscs
Parent: The Kraft Heinz Company
Officers: Victoria Louise White, Secretary; Christine Page [1962] Director; Adam Rathbone [1968] Director

H.J. Heinz Finance UK PLC
Incorporated: 15 September 1999 *Employees:* 2
Net Worth: £1,967,000 *Total Assets:* £132,950,000
Registered Office: The Shard, 32 London Bridge Street, London, SE1 9SG
Activities: Other business support service activities n.e.c.
Parent: Carlton Bridge Ltd
Officers: Victoria Louise White, Secretary; Christine Page [1962] Director/VP Controller Europe; Adam Rathbone [1968] Tax Director

H.J. Heinz Foods UK Limited
Incorporated: 7 December 2012 *Employees:* 405
Net Worth: £93,000,000 *Total Assets:* £458,700,000
Registered Office: The Shard, 32 London Bridge Street, London, SE1 9SG
Activities: Wholesale of other food, including fish, crustaceans and molluscs
Parent: HP Foods Ltd
Officers: Victoria Louise White, Secretary; Elias Diaz [1973] Managing Director [Spanish]; Rafael de Oliveira Oliveira [1974] UK&I Managing Director and European Zone President; Walter Paganucci [1988] Finance Director [Brazilian]; Christine Page [1962] Director; James Pollard [1981] Director/Chief Finance Officer

H.J. Heinz Manufacturing UK Limited
Incorporated: 1 June 1917 *Employees:* 981
Net Worth: £1,452,099,968 *Total Assets:* £1,670,899,968
Registered Office: The Shard, 32 London Bridge Street, London, SE1 9SG
Activities: Manufacture of other food products n.e.c.
Parent: HJ Heinz Company Limited
Officers: Victoria Louise White, Secretary; Julien Karma Favre [1981] Finance Director [Swiss]; Stuart Lawson [1964] Director; Christine Page [1962] Director/VP Controller Europe

Helical PLC
Incorporated: 3 July 1919 *Employees:* 36
Previous: Helical Bar PLC
Net Worth: £533,894,016 *Total Assets:* £1,024,110,976
Registered Office: 5 Hanover Square, London, W1S 1HQ
Activities: Development of building projects
Officers: James Richard Moss, Secretary; Matthew Charles Bonning Snook [1968] Director/Chartered Surveyor; Susan Vivien Clayton [1957] Director/Chartered Surveyor; Richard Robert Cotton [1956] Director; Richard John Grant [1954] Director/Chartered Accountant; Generald Anthony Kaye [1958] Director/Chief Executive; Joseph Julian Lister [1971] Director/Chartered Accountant; Timothy John Murphy [1959] Finance Director; Michael Kane O'Donnell [1967] Director/Consultant [Irish]; Michael Eric Slade [1946] Director/Chairman

Helios Underwriting PLC
Incorporated: 1 August 2006 *Employees:* 6
Net Worth: £21,010,000 *Total Assets:* £117,920,000
Registered Office: 5th Floor, 40 Gracechurch Street, London, EC3V 0BT
Activities: Non-life insurance
Shareholder: Will Roseff
Officers: Martha Blanche Waymark Bruce, Secretary; Andrew Hildred Christie [1956] Director; Mr Harold Michael Clunie Cunningham [1947] Director/Stockbroker; Jeremy Richard Holt Evans [1958] Director/Lloyd's Agent; Edward William Fitzalan Howard [1956] Director; Nigel John Hanbury [1957] Director; Arthur Roger Manners [1959] Director/Chartered Accountant

Helix Acquisition Limited
Incorporated: 3 November 2010 *Employees:* 45
Net Worth: £192,000,000 *Total Assets:* £3,352,600,064
Registered Office: 5th Floor, Kings Place, 90 York Way, London, N1 9AG
Activities: Activities of other holding companies n.e.c.
Parent: Helix Bufferco Limited
Officers: Lucy Ann Clarke-Bodicoat, Secretary; John Hamilton Ainsworth Curley [1954] Director; Sion Laurence Jones [1974] Director; Amanda Vanderneth Leness [1967] Director [American]; Keith Lawrence Ludeman [1950] Director; Andrew Christopher Pitt [1959] Transport Director; Scott Springett [1968] Director/Asset Manager; Mark Richard Woodhams [1966] Director/Financier

Helix Bufferco Limited
Incorporated: 3 November 2010
Total Assets: £1,050,400,000
Registered Office: 5th Floor, Kings Place, 90 York Way, London, N1 9AG
Activities: Activities of other holding companies n.e.c.
Parent: Helix Midco Limited
Officers: Lucy Ann Clarke-Bodicoat, Secretary; John Hamilton Ainsworth Curley [1954] Director; Sion Laurence Jones [1974] Director; Amanda Vanderneth Leness [1967] Director [American]; Keith Lawrence Ludeman [1950] Director; Andrew Christopher Pitt [1959] Transport Director; Scott Springett [1968] Director/Asset Manager; Mark Richard Woodhams [1966] Director/Financier

Helix Midco Limited
Incorporated: 3 November 2010
Total Assets: £1,050,400,000
Registered Office: 5th Floor, Kings Place, 90 York Way, London, N1 9AG
Activities: Activities of other holding companies n.e.c.
Parent: Betjeman Holdings Limited
Officers: Lucy Ann Clarke-Bodicoat, Secretary; John Hamilton Ainsworth Curley [1954] Director; Sion Laurence Jones [1975] Director; Amanda Vanderneth Leness [1967] Director [American]; Keith Lawrence Ludeman [1950] Director; Andrew Christopher Pitt [1959] Transport Director; Scott Springett [1968] Director/Asset Manager; Mark Richard Woodhams [1966] Director/Financier

Hellen Holdings Limited
Incorporated: 24 November 2016 *Employees:* 29
Net Worth: £193,049,056 *Total Assets:* £4,127,237,120
Registered Office: 35 Great St Helen's, London, EC3A 6AP
Activities: Activities of other holding companies n.e.c.
Major Shareholder: Paul Elliott Singer
Officers: Melissa Gabrielle Bourgeois [1983] Director/Chartered Secretary; Stefano Cocirio [1984] Director/Financial Analyst [Italian]; Jonas Ulrik Rydell [1972] Director/Investment Manager [Swedish]

Hellenic Petroleum Finance PLC
Incorporated: 2 November 2005
Net Worth: £19,550,472 *Total Assets:* £723,469,440
Registered Office: 5th Floor, 6 St Andrew Street, London, EC4A 3AE
Activities: Other business support service activities n.e.c.
Parent: Hellenic Petroleum S.A
Officers: Robertos Karahannas [1967] Director/Group General Manager [Cypriot]; Kenneth Howard Prince-Wright [1956] Director; Nita Ramesh Savjani [1980] Director; Andreas Shiamishis [1966] Director [Greek]

Henares Limited
Incorporated: 2 October 2007
Net Worth: £272,403,872 *Total Assets:* £272,633,312
Registered Office: York House, 45 Seymour Street, London, W1H 7JT
Activities: Non-trading company
Parent: Bunzl Public Limited Company
Officers: Paul Nicholas Hussey, Secretary; Andrew James Ball [1963] Finance Director; Paul Nicholas Hussey [1959] Director/Solicitor; Brian Michael May [1964] Finance Director

Henderson Administration Limited
Incorporated: 26 July 1934 *Employees:* 831
Net Worth: £226,996,992 *Total Assets:* £1,448,064,000
Registered Office: 201 Bishopsgate, London, EC2M 3AE
Activities: Activities of head offices
Parent: Henderson Global Investors (Holdings) Limited
Officers: Rhiannon Willow Chaudhuri [1978] Director/Accountant; Roger Martin James Thompson [1967] Director

Henderson Asset Management Limited
Incorporated: 3 May 2000
Net Worth: £124,636,000 *Total Assets:* £126,787,000
Registered Office: 201 Bishopsgate, London, EC2M 3AE
Activities: Activities of head offices
Parent: Henderson Alternative Investment Advisor Limited
Officers: Rhiannon Willow Chaudhuri [1978] Director/Accountant; Anna Nicole Kurzon [1978] Director/Chartered Accountant

Henderson Diversified Income Trust PLC
Incorporated: 23 February 2017
Net Worth: £165,799,008 *Total Assets:* £203,546,000
Registered Office: 201 Bishopsgate, London, EC2M 3AE
Activities: Activities of investment trusts
Parent: DM Company Services (London) Limited
Officers: Denise Hadgill [1961] Director; Rupert Angus Macpherson [1966] Director; Lord Stewart Wood [1968] Director/Politician; Ian Wright [1956] Director

Henderson European Focus Trust PLC
Incorporated: 20 January 1947
Net Worth: £293,790,016 *Total Assets:* £345,360,992
Registered Office: 201 Bishopsgate, London, EC2M 3AE
Activities: Activities of investment trusts
Officers: Robert Archibald [1959] Director/Corporate Financier; Alexander Michael Comba [1953] Director; Rodney John Dennis [1952] Director; Alain Dromer [1954] Director [French]; Eliza Jane Dungworth [1967] Director/Chartered Accountant

Henderson Eurotrust PLC
Incorporated: 28 May 1992
Net Worth: £264,116,000 *Total Assets:* £264,792,992
Registered Office: 201 Bishopsgate, London, EC2M 3AE
Activities: Activities of investment trusts
Officers: Rutger Koopmans [1958] Director/Entrepreneur [Dutch]; David Wayne Marsh [1952] Director; Nicola Thomas Ralston [1955] Director; Ekaterina Thomson [1970] Director/Independent Financial and Business Development

Henderson Global Investors (Holdings) Limited
Incorporated: 9 May 1983
Net Worth: £383,849,984 *Total Assets:* £1,103,132,032
Registered Office: 201 Bishopsgate, London, EC2M 3AE
Activities: Activities of head offices
Parent: HGI Group Limited
Officers: Anna Nicole Kurzon [1978] Director/Chartered Accountant; Roger Martin James Thompson [1967] Director

Henderson Global Investors Asset Management Limited
Incorporated: 31 March 1988
Net Worth: £3,166,000 *Total Assets:* £164,206,000
Registered Office: 201 Bishopsgate, London, EC2M 3AE
Activities: Banks
Parent: Henderson Global Investors (Holdings) Limited
Officers: Anna Nicole Kurzon [1978] Director/Chartered Kingdom; Roger Martin James Thompson [1967] Director

Henderson Global Investors Limited
Incorporated: 17 May 1967 *Employees:* 6
Net Worth: £268,540,992 *Total Assets:* £355,976,000
Registered Office: 201 Bishopsgate, London, EC2M 3AE
Activities: Security and commodity contracts dealing activities
Parent: Henderson Global Investors Holdings Limited
Officers: Brennan Allen Hughes [1976] Director [American]; Roger Martin James Thompson [1967] Director

Henderson Group Holdings Asset Management Limited
Incorporated: 27 September 2012
Net Worth: £1,403,885,056 *Total Assets:* £1,403,885,056
Registered Office: 201 Bishopsgate, London, EC2M 3AE
Activities: Activities of financial services holding companies
Parent: Henderson Group PLC
Officers: Angela Charlotte Seymour-Jackson [1966] Director; Roger Martin James Thompson [1967] Director; Richard Weil [1963] Director/Chief Executive [American]

Henderson High Income Trust PLC
Incorporated: 13 September 1989
Net Worth: £257,243,008 *Total Assets:* £314,220,000
Registered Office: 201 Bishopsgate, London, EC2M 3AE
Activities: Activities of investment trusts
Officers: Zoe King [1973] Director; Margaret Littlejohns [1959] Director; Anthony John Raymond Newhouse [1947] Director/Solicitor; Jeremy Peter Rigg [1966] Director/Independent Investment Consultant; Jonathan Charles Silver [1957] Director; Janet Sheila Walker [1953] Finance Director

Henderson Holdings Group Limited
Incorporated: 6 November 2008
Net Worth: £607,166,976 *Total Assets:* £920,793,024
Registered Office: 201 Bishopsgate, London, EC2M 3AE
Activities: Non-trading company
Parent: HGI Asset Management Group Limited
Officers: Anna Nicole Kurzon [1978] Director/Chartered Accountant; Roger Martin James Thompson [1967] Director

Henderson Holdings Limited
Incorporated: 13 October 1978
Net Worth: £103,665,000 *Total Assets:* £103,665,000
Registered Office: 201 Bishopsgate, London, EC2M 3AE
Activities: Activities of head offices
Parent: Henderson Global Investors (Holdings) Limited
Officers: Anna Nicole Kurzon [1978] Director/Chartered Accountant

Henderson International Income Trust PLC
Incorporated: 2 March 2011
Net Worth: £296,748,000 *Total Assets:* £303,836,000
Registered Office: 201 Bishopsgate, London, EC2M 3AE
Activities: Activities of investment trusts
Officers: William Duncan Eason [1950] Director; Richard John Hills [1955] Director; Simon John Lewis Jeffreys [1952] Director; Aidan Charles Lisser [1959] Director; Katarzyna Maria Robinski [1962] Director

Henderson Investment Funds Limited
Incorporated: 17 January 1992
Net Worth: £101,691,000 *Total Assets:* £313,404,992
Registered Office: 201 Bishopsgate, London, EC2M 3AE
Activities: Financial intermediation not elsewhere classified
Parent: Henderson Global Investors (Holdings) Limited
Officers: Rhiannon Willow Chaudhuri [1978] Director/Accountant; Alexander Arthur Crooke [1969] Director; Havilland James de Sausmarez [1958] Director; John Graham Foggin [1964] Director; Georgina Louise Fogo [1973] Director; Simon Hillenbrand [1967] Director; Roger Martin James Thompson [1967] Director

The Henderson Smaller Companies Investment Trust PLC
Incorporated: 16 December 1887
Net Worth: £782,067,968 *Total Assets:* £856,572,032
Registered Office: 201 Bishopsgate, London, EC2M 3AE
Activities: Activities of investment trusts
Officers: James Michael Beale Cayzer-Colvin [1965] Director; Penelope Anne Freer [1960] Director; Beatrice Hannah Millicent Hollond [1960] Director; David John Lamb [1987] Director/Actuary; Alexandra Jane Mackesy [1962] Director; Victoria Louise Sant [1977] Director/Senior Adviser

H & M Hennes & Mauritz UK Limited
Incorporated: 6 February 1979 *Employees:* 7,357
Net Worth: £156,360,704 *Total Assets:* £422,466,624
Registered Office: 1st Floor, 25 Argyll Street, London, W1F 7TS
Activities: Retail sale of clothing in specialised stores
Officers: Antonietta Galli [1963] Director/Country Manager [Canadian]; Nairn Paterson [1980] Director/Country Controller UK & Ireland; Karl-Johan Erling Goran Persson [1975] Director/Chief Executive [Swedish]; Jyrki Peter Tervonen [1966] Director/Accountant [Swedish]

Henwick Ventures Ltd
Incorporated: 14 March 2006
Net Worth: £109,740,752 *Total Assets:* £109,753,608
Registered Office: 4th Floor, 1 Knightrider Court, London, EC4V 5BJ
Activities: Activities of other holding companies n.e.c.
Officers: Christian Dayer [1980] Director/Businessman [Swiss]

Herald Investment Trust PLC
Incorporated: 10 December 1993
Net Worth: £966,649,984 *Total Assets:* £969,092,992
Registered Office: 10-11 Charterhouse Square, London, EC1M 6EE
Activities: Activities of investment trusts
Officers: Thomas Joseph Black [1959] Director; Charles Julian Cazalet [1947] Director; Stephanie Mary Eastment [1960] Director; Ian Simon MacGregor Russell [1953] Director; Karl Stephen Sternberg [1969] Director/Investment Manager; James Robert Will [1955] Director

Herbert Smith Freehills Global LLP
Incorporated: 6 June 2012 *Employees:* 4,110
Net Worth: £239,000,000 *Total Assets:* £700,200,000
Registered Office: Exchange House, Primrose Street, London, EC2A 2EG
Officers: Kenneth Alexander Adams [1966] Member; Nigel Jonathan Farr [1962] Member; Anthony Colin Joyner [1963] Member; Jay Leary [1975] Member; Nicolas Martin Martinez de Lecea [1967] Member; Rebecca Jane Maslen-Stannage [1969] Member; Gregory James Mulley [1967] Member; James Edwin Palmer [1963] Member; Mark John Rigotti [1964] Member; Donald Martin Rowlands [1970] Member; Alan Thomas Watts [1966] Member; Nicola Marie Yeomans [1978] Member; Nico Abel [1972] LLP Member; Bryony Kate Adams [1976] LLP Member; Alexander Robert Winston Aitken [1974] LLP Member; Dina Mireille Albagli [1962] LLP Member; Christina Joy Amis [1980] LLP Member; Greig John Anderson [1980] LLP Member; Karen Elizabeth Anderson [1958] LLP Member; Toby Richard Thomas Anderson [1969] LLP Member; John Peirce Angus [1958] LLP Member; Paul Zoltan Apathy [1978] LLP Member; William Francis Arrenberg [1976] LLP Member; Heidi Adeola Asten [1978] LLP Member; Raji Azzam [1975] LLP Member; Michael John Back [1957] LLP Member; Damien Joseph Bailey [1970] LLP Member; Brigette Ann Baillie [1966] LLP Member; James Edward Hugo Baily [1972] LLP Member; Nicholas Pasquale Alan Baker [1980] LLP Member; Scott Sonny Balber [1969] LLP Member; Dinesh Dayal Banani [1976] LLP Member; Mark Philip Bardell [1976] LLP Member; Edward Francis Desmond Baring [1972] LLP Member; Stuart John Barrymore [1959] LLP Member; Miles Martin Bastick [1967] LLP Member; Soenke Becker [1971] LLP Member; Peter John Behmke [1977] LLP Member; Steven Mark Bell [1980] LLP Member; Thomas Bethel [1980] LLP Member; Jason Lawrence Betts [1975] LLP Member; Robert John Bileckij [1978] LLP Member; Susan Elisabeth Black [1964] LLP Member; Andrew John Blacoe [1978] LLP Member; Neil Robert Blake [1980] LLP Member; Christopher Thomas Crampton Blue [1966] LLP Member; Laure Bonin [1976] LLP Member; Matthew John Donald Bonye [1969] LLP Member; Andrew John Booth [1966] LLP Member; Amal Hafida Bouchenaki [1972] LLP Member; Frederic Bouvet [1970] LLP Member; Nina Bowyer [1976] LLP Member; Stephane Brabant [1956] LLP Member; Paul Branston [1977] LLP Member; William Eric Breeze [1975] LLP Member; Sophie Anne Sylvia Brezin [1966] LLP Member; Peter Kevin Briggs [1960] LLP Member; Timothy Roy Briggs [1971] LLP Member; Alison Marie Brown [1968] LLP Member; Samantha Elizabeth Brown [1978] LLP Member; Priscilla Amber Bryans [1969] LLP Member; Natalie Bryce [1973] LLP Member; Matthew Darren Bull [1974] LLP Member; Christopher Anthony Bushell [1978] LLP Member; Peter Gerard Butler [1971] LLP Member; Peter Mark Butler [1952] LLP Member; Damien John Byrne Hill [1967] LLP Member; Joanna Samira Caen [1983] LLP Member; Katherine Lucinda Cahill [1976] LLP Member; Rachel Mary Campbell [1976] LLP Member; Andrew Michael John Canon [1973] LLP Member; Nicholas Edward Carney [1980] LLP Member; Robert Adam Carr [1981] LLP Member; Philip Maitland Carrington [1958] LLP Member; Liza Windel Carver [1962] LLP Member; Hannah Estelle Cassidy [1982] LLP Member; Melanie Jayne Cave [1975] LLP Member; Simon Travis Chadney [1971] LLP Member; Pariyanuj Jinny Chaimungkalanont [1976] LLP Member; Malika Chandrasegaran [1984] LLP Member; Simon James Chapman [1980] LLP Member; Elizabeth Anne Charlesworth [1982] LLP Member; Paul Sven Chases [1977] LLP Member; Siu Lun Chau [1964] LLP Member; Adrian Hui-Jin Cheng [1968] LLP Member; Frederic Marie Gonzague Chevallier [1979] LLP Member; Leon Chung [1976] LLP Member; Simon Jonathan Bailey Clarke [1970] LLP Member; Nicholas Langley Clayton [1985] LLP Member; Mark Russell Clifton [1964] LLP Member; David John Clinch [1971] LLP Member; Adrian John Clough [1963] LLP Member; Andrew Barry Clyne [1969] LLP Member; Scott Russell Cochrane [1971] LLP Member; Susannah Miriam Cogman [1977] LLP Member; Michael Gerard Coonan [1955] LLP Member; Glynn Brian Cooper [1979] LLP Member; Julian Mark Copeman [1967] LLP Member; John George Joseph Corrie [1979] LLP Member; Melita Cottrell [1972] LLP Member

Herbert Smith Freehills LLP
Incorporated: 14 January 2005 *Employees:* 401
Net Worth: £109,100,000 *Total Assets:* £529,800,000
Registered Office: Exchange House, Primrose Street, London, EC2A 2EG
Officers: Nigel Jonathan Farr [1962] Member; Gregory James Mulley [1967] Member; James Edwin Palmer [1963] Member; Donald Martin Rowlands [1970] Member; Alan Thomas Watts [1966] Member; Nico Abel [1972] LLP Member; Dina Mireille Albagli [1962] LLP Member; Christina Joy Amis [1980] LLP Member; Greig John Anderson [1980] LLP Member; Karen Elizabeth Anderson [1958] LLP Member; William Francis Arrenberg [1976] LLP Member; Brigette Ann Baillie [1966] LLP Member; James Edward Hugo Baily [1972] LLP Member; Dinesh Dayal Banani [1976] LLP Member; Mark Philip Bardell [1976] LLP Member; Edward Francis Desmond Baring [1972] LLP Member; Soenke Becker [1971] LLP Member; Thomas Bethel [1980] LLP Member; Susan Elisabeth Black [1964] LLP Member; Andrew John Blacoe [1978] LLP Member; Neil Robert Blake [1980] LLP Member; Matthew John Donald Bonye [1969] LLP Member; Frederic Bouvet [1970] LLP Member; Nina Bowyer [1976] LLP Member; Stephane Robert Auguste Brabant [1956] LLP Member; William Eric Breeze [1975] LLP Member; Timothy Roy Briggs [1971] LLP Member; Alison Marie Brown [1968] LLP Member; Samantha Elizabeth Brown [1978] LLP Member; Christopher Anthony Bushell [1978] LLP Member; Damien John Byrne Hill [1967] LLP Member; Andrew Michael John Canon [1973] LLP Member; Robert Adam Carr [1981] LLP Member; Philip Maitland Carrington [1958] LLP Member; Simon Travis Chadney [1971] LLP Member; Paul Sven Chases [1977] LLP Member; Siu Lun Chau [1964] LLP Member; Simon Jonathan Bailey Clarke [1970] LLP Member; Nicholas Langley Clayton [1985] LLP Member; Adrian John Clough [1963] LLP Member; Scott Russell Cochrane [1971] LLP Member; Susannah Miriam Cogman [1977] LLP Member; Julian Mark Copeman [1967] LLP Member; John George Joseph Corrie [1979] LLP Member; David Peter James Coulling [1979] LLP Member; Ian James Cox [1963] LLP Member; Heather Louise Culshaw [1977] LLP Member; Clive Leonard George Cunningham [1964] LLP Member; Lawrance Norman Alexander Currie [1971] LLP Member; Reza Dadbakhsh [1981] LLP Member; Steven James Dalton [1974] LLP Member; Gavin Sinclair Davies [1967] LLP Member; Louis de Longeaux [1968] LLP Member; Anthony David Robert Dempster [1962] LLP Member; Kim Erskine Dietzel [1974] LLP Member; Saman Nishanath Dissanayake [1979] LLP Member; Alice Victoria Dockar [1978] LLP Member; James Nicholas Peter Doe [1974] LLP Member; Nicholas Paul Downing [1961] LLP Member; Barend Rudolph Du Plessis [1970] LLP Member; Clement Benoit Dupoirier [1978] LLP Member; Henry James Benedict Edwards [1982] LLP Member; Paul Daniel Ellerman [1968] LLP Member; James Thomas Hugh Farrell [1966] LLP Member; Eric Jean Fiszelson [1974] LLP Member; Ian Roderick Fletcher [1957] LLP Member; Michael James Chalmers Flockhart [1981] LLP Member; Richard John Forsdyke [1968] LLP Member; Kyriakos Fountoukakos [1970] LLP Member; Peter John Frost [1960] LLP Member; Jeremy Paul Garson [1972] LLP Member; Amy Kehi Geddes [1973] LLP Member; Heather Gething [1958] LLP Member; David Andrew Gilmore [1974] LLP Member; Silke Yael Muter Goldberg [1974] LLP Member; Shona Mary Grey [1980] LLP Member; Dr Dirk Walter Hamann [1963] LLP Member; Vincent Georges Marie Hatton [1975] LLP Member; Timothy John Healey [1978] LLP Member; Barnaby John Hinnigan [1979] LLP Member; Paula Hodges [1965] LLP Member; Gary Hommel [1968] LLP Member; Catherine Jane Howard [1975] LLP Member; Charles Bernard Paul Howarth [1967] LLP Member; Daniel Thomas Hudson [1977] LLP Member; Laura Slocombe Hulett [1983] LLP Member; Christopher James Hunt [1979] LLP Member; Mark Andrew Ife [1975] LLP Member; Jake Matthew Michael Forrest Jackaman [1964] LLP Member; Elizabeth Jane Bewick Jackson [1971] LLP Member; John Hywel Jenkins [1979] LLP Member; Mark James Alexander Jephcott [1972] LLP Member; Matthew Brian Job [1972] LLP Member; Adam Martin Johnson [1965] LLP Member; Natasha Kate Johnson [1980] LLP Member; Antoine Juaristi [1960] LLP Member; Martin David Kavanagh [1972] LLP Member; Alexander Kay [1972] LLP Member; Hans Thomas Kessler [1966] LLP Member; Emma Elizabeth Kratochvilova [1973] LLP Member

Hermes Fund Managers Limited
Incorporated: 3 September 1982 *Employees:* 377
Net Worth: £50,864,000 *Total Assets:* £154,072,000
Registered Office: Sixth Floor, 150 Cheapside, London, EC2V 6ET
Activities: Financial intermediation not elsewhere classified
Shareholders: Federated Holdings (UK) II Limited; Britel Fund Trustees Limited
Officers: Susan Jane Cane, Secretary; Gordon Joseph Ceresino [1957] Director/Investment Professional [American]; Deborah Ann Cunningham [1959] Director/Investment Professional [American]; Thomas Robert Donahue [1958] Director/Investment Professional [American]; John Basil Fisher [1956] Director/Investment Professional [American]; Sally Ann James [1949] Director; Jane Lambesis [1961] Director/Investment Professional [American]; Denis McAuley III [1946] Director/Investment Professional [American]; William McClory [1950] Trustee Director; Saker Anwar Nusseibeh [1961] Director/Head of Investments; Harriet Anne Steel [1965] Director; David Coldwells Stewart [1960] Director; David Kenneth Watson [1959] Director; Theodore William Zierden III [1960] Director/Investment Professional [American]

Heron Corporation
Incorporated: 25 November 1964 *Employees:* 13
Net Worth: £275,382,016 *Total Assets:* £514,127,008
Registered Office: Heron House, 4 Bentinck Street, London, W1U 2EF
Activities: Activities of head offices
Parent: Heron International Holdings
Officers: James Eric Manning, Secretary; Generald Maurice Ronson [1939] Director; Joseph Thomas Sutton [1961] Director/Chartered Accountant [Irish]

Heron International Holdings
Incorporated: 1 October 1965 *Employees:* 38
Net Worth: £417,252,000 *Total Assets:* £542,595,008
Registered Office: Heron House, 4 Bentinck Street, London, W1U 2EF
Activities: Activities of head offices
Officers: James Eric Manning, Secretary; Generald Maurice Ronson [1939] Director; Joseph Thomas Sutton [1961] Director/Chartered Accountant [Irish]

Heron Property Corporation Limited
Incorporated: 25 March 1980
Net Worth: £318,073,984 *Total Assets:* £459,950,016
Registered Office: Heron House, 4 Bentinck Street, London, W1U 2EF
Activities: Activities of head offices
Parent: Heron Corporation
Officers: James Eric Manning, Secretary; Generald Maurice Ronson [1939] Director; Joseph Thomas Sutton [1961] Director/Chartered Accountant [Irish]

Heron Quays Investments (RT3) Limited
Incorporated: 27 April 2005 *Employees:* 3
Net Worth: £156,692,384 *Total Assets:* £262,956,432
Registered Office: One Canary Wharf, London, E14 5AB
Activities: Other business support service activities n.e.c.
Parent: Canary Wharf Investments Limited
Officers: John Raymond Garwood, Secretary; A Peter Anderson II [1953] Director/Real Estate Executive [American]; George Iacobescu [1945] Director; Russell James John Lyons [1961] Director/Chartered Accountant

Heron Treasury Services Limited
Incorporated: 11 November 1987
Net Worth: £133,412,904 *Total Assets:* £172,657,856
Registered Office: Heron House, 4 Bentinck Street, London, W1U 2EF
Activities: Other business support service activities n.e.c.
Parent: Heron Property Corporation Limited
Officers: James Eric Manning, Secretary; Generald Maurice Ronson [1939] Director; Joseph Thomas Sutton [1961] Director/Chartered Accountant [Irish]

Hess Finance
Incorporated: 22 August 2000
Net Worth: £760,014,336 *Total Assets:* £760,014,336
Registered Office: One Fleet Place, London, EC4M 7WS
Activities: Extraction of crude petroleum
Officers: Michael James Chadwick [1972] Director/Oil Company Executive; Mark Grinfeld [1978] Director/Oil Company Executive [American]

Hess Limited
Incorporated: 1 June 1964
Net Worth: £439,575,968 *Total Assets:* £488,840,864
Registered Office: One Fleet Place, London, EC4M 7WS
Activities: Extraction of crude petroleum
Parent: Hess NWE Holdings
Officers: Michael James Chadwick [1972] Director/Oil Company Executive; Virgil William Cleveland [1965] Director/Oil Company Executive [American]; Martin George Edwards [1960] Director/Oil Company Executive; Mark Grinfeld [1978] Director/Oil Company Executive [American]

Hess Malaysia and Thailand Limited
Incorporated: 7 September 2012
Net Worth Deficit: £212,194,768 *Total Assets:* £939,230,272
Registered Office: One Fleet Place, London, EC4M 7WS
Activities: Extraction of crude petroleum
Parent: Hess Corporation
Officers: Michael James Chadwick [1972] Director/Oil Company Executive; Mark Grinfeld [1978] Director/Oil Company Executive [American]; Zhiyong Zhao [1962] Director/Oil Company Executive [Chinese]

Hess NWE Holdings
Incorporated: 21 November 2000
Net Worth: £136,118,848 *Total Assets:* £516,650,592
Registered Office: One Fleet Place, London, EC4M 7WS
Activities: Activities of other holding companies n.e.c.
Parent: Hess Corporation
Officers: Michael James Chadwick [1972] Director/Oil Company Executive; Mark Grinfeld [1978] Director/Oil Company Executive [American]

Hestok Limited
Incorporated: 29 January 2008
Net Worth: £13,062,993 *Total Assets:* £104,373,024
Registered Office: 78 Fairgate House, New Oxford Street, London, WC1A 1HB
Activities: Development of building projects
Parent: Stapilay Limited
Officers: Irina Lukovnikova, Secretary; Nikolay Kasradze [1984] Director/Project Development [Russian]

Heven Limited
Incorporated: 16 January 2007 *Employees:* 71
Net Worth: £19,218,020 *Total Assets:* £142,915,040
Registered Office: 15 Regent Street, London, SW1Y 4LR
Activities: Buying and selling of own real estate
Major Shareholder: Jonathan Hunt
Officers: Lois Jane Hunt, Secretary; Matthew Cornish Gresham [1976] COO/Director; Jonathan Michael Hunt [1953] Director/Estate Agent; Lois Jane Hunt [1955] Director

HgCapital Trust PLC
Incorporated: 31 October 1980
Net Worth: £721,024,000 *Total Assets:* £722,788,992
Registered Office: 2 More London Riverside, London, SE1 2AP
Activities: Financial intermediation not elsewhere classified
Officers: Richard John Brooman [1955] Director/Chartered Accountant; Peter William Dunscombe [1949] Director; Roger Philip Mountford [1948] Director; James Mark Nelson Strang [1971] Director; Guy Richard Wakeley [1970] Director; Anne Edmond West [1950] Director/Retired

HGHL Holdings Ltd
Incorporated: 21 November 2012
Net Worth: £49,846,092 *Total Assets:* £133,546,920
Registered Office: 4th Floor, 16 Charles II Street, London, SW1Y 4QU
Activities: Other business support service activities n.e.c.
Officers: Sandra Agnes Georgeson, Secretary; Sandra Agnes Georgeson [1967] Director/Chartered Secretary; Camille Antoine Nehme [1969] Director [French]

HGI Asset Management Group Limited
Incorporated: 27 September 2012
Net Worth: £847,187,968 *Total Assets:* £847,400,000
Registered Office: 201 Bishopsgate, London, EC2M 3AE
Activities: Activities of financial services holding companies
Parent: Henderson Group Holdings Asset Management Limited
Officers: Roger Martin James Thompson [1967] Director

HGI Group Limited
Incorporated: 10 November 1986 *Employees:* 3
Net Worth: £982,099,968 *Total Assets:* £1,884,700,032
Registered Office: 201 Bishopsgate, London, EC2M 3AE
Activities: Banks
Parent: Henderson Holdings Group Limited
Officers: Anna Nicole Kurzon [1978] Director/Chartered Accountant; Roger Martin James Thompson [1967] Director

HGPE FRWL Holdco Limited
Incorporated: 27 November 2013
Net Worth: £112,645,600 *Total Assets:* £286,798,304
Registered Office: Arnold Hill & Co LLP, Craven House, 16 Northumberland Avenue, London, WC2N 5AP
Activities: Activities of head offices
Parent: Britel Fund Trustees Limited
Officers: Emma Lewis [1979] Director/Investment Manager; Perry Denis Noble [1960] Director/Solicitor; Robert Boyd Pierre Wall [1979] Director/Investment Manager

HHT PLC
Incorporated: 17 February 2014
Net Worth: £50,000 *Total Assets:* £156,792,992
Registered Office: 169 Union Street, London, SE1 0LL
Activities: Other letting and operating of own or leased real estate
Parent: HH No. 1 Limited
Officers: Christopher Paul Rule [1979] Director/Chief Investment Officer; John Richard Tomlinson [1960] Investment Director

HICP Holdings Limited
Incorporated: 19 February 2015
Net Worth: £26,917,000 *Total Assets:* £285,406,016
Registered Office: 35 Great St Helen's, London, EC3A 6AP
Activities: Hotels and similar accommodation
Major Shareholder: Stephen Andrew Feinberg
Officers: Raoul Rene Hofland [1967] Director [Dutch]; Gerardus Johannes Schipper [1965] Managing Director [Dutch]

HIG Finance Limited
Incorporated: 7 October 2013
Net Worth: £4,843,824 *Total Assets:* £357,382,720
Registered Office: One Creechurch Place, London, EC3A 5AF
Activities: Non-life insurance
Parent: HIG Finance 2 Limited
Officers: Andrew John Moore, Secretary; William David Bloomer [1969] Director/Solicitor; Mark Skimming Craig [1972] Director/Finance; David Philip Howden [1963] Director

High Speed Rail Finance (1) PLC
Incorporated: 3 January 2013
Net Worth: £100,000 *Total Assets:* £911,600,000
Registered Office: 5th Floor, Kings Place, 90 York Way, London, N1 9AG
Activities: Other business support service activities n.e.c.
Parent: Helix Acquisition Limited
Officers: Lucy Ann Clarke-Bodicoat, Secretary; John Hamilton Ainsworth Curley [1954] Director; Sion Laurence Jones [1974] Director; Amanda Vanderneth Leness [1967] Director [American]; Keith Lawrence Ludeman [1950] Director; Andrew Christopher Pitt [1959] Transport Director; Scott Springett [1968] Director/Asset Manager; Mark Richard Woodhams [1966] Director/Financier

High Speed Rail Finance PLC
Incorporated: 30 August 2012
Net Worth: £100,000 *Total Assets:* £938,000,000
Registered Office: 5th Floor, Kings Place, 90 York Way, London, N1 9AG
Activities: Other business support service activities n.e.c.
Parent: Helix Acquisition Limited
Officers: Lucy Ann Clarke-Bodicoat, Secretary; John Hamilton Ainsworth Curley [1954] Director; Sion Laurence Jones [1974] Director; Amanda Vanderneth Leness [1967] Director [American]; Keith Lawrence Ludeman [1950] Director; Andrew Christopher Pitt [1959] Transport Director; Scott Springett [1968] Director/Asset Manager; Mark Richard Woodhams [1966] Director/Financier

Highdorn Co. Limited
Incorporated: 21 April 1958 *Employees:* 38
Net Worth: £175,200,000 *Total Assets:* £247,083,008
Registered Office: Freshwater House, 158-162 Shaftesbury Avenue, London, WC2H 8HR
Activities: Buying and selling of own real estate
Shareholders: Benzion Schalom Eliezer Freshwater; Solomon Israel Freshwater
Officers: Mark Roy Mason Jenner, Secretary; Benzion Schalom Eliezer Freshwater [1948] Director; Solomon Israel Freshwater [1950] Director; Leib Stempel [1935] Director

Hikma Acquisitions (UK) Limited
Incorporated: 29 August 2006
Net Worth: £2,125,140,864 *Total Assets:* £2,125,187,968
Registered Office: 1 New Burlington Place, London, W1S 2HR
Activities: Activities of other holding companies n.e.c.
Parent: Hikma Pharmaceuticals PLC
Officers: Peter Alexander Speirs, Secretary; Gurpal Singh Atwal [1964] Director/Tax Consultant; Peter Alexander Speirs [1979] Director/Company Secretary

Hikma Holdings (UK) Limited
Incorporated: 30 August 2006
Net Worth: £1,670,635,264 *Total Assets:* £1,670,646,784
Registered Office: 1 New Burlington Place, London, W1S 2HR
Activities: Activities of other holding companies n.e.c.
Parent: Hikma Acquisitions (UK) Limited
Officers: Peter Alexander Speirs, Secretary; Gurpal Singh Atwal [1964] Director/Tax Consultant; Peter Alexander Speirs [1979] Director/Company Secretary

Hikma Pharmaceuticals Public Limited Company
Incorporated: 8 September 2005 *Employees:* 8,521
Net Worth: £1,099,012,736 *Total Assets:* £2,459,349,504
Registered Office: 1 New Burlington Place, London, W1S 2HR
Activities: Manufacture of basic pharmaceutical products
Officers: Peter Alexander Speirs, Secretary; Ali Mohammed Al Husry [1935] Director [Jordanian]; Patrick Noel Butler [1960] Director [Irish]; John Julius Castellani [1951] Director [American]; Mazen Samih Darwazah [1958] Director [Jordanian]; Said Samih Darwazah [1957] Director/Chief Executive Officer [Jordanian]; Jochen Gann [1964] Finance Director [German]; Mary Regina Henderson [1950] Director [American]; Dr Pamela Josephine Kirby [1953] Director; Sigurdur Oli Olafsson [1968] Director/Chief Executive Officer [Icelander]; Robert Mark Pickering [1959] Director/Investment Banker and Financial Consultant

Hikma UK Limited
Incorporated: 3 July 2005
Previous: Hikma Ventures Limited
Net Worth: £1,511,870,464 *Total Assets:* £1,696,593,792
Registered Office: 1 New Burlington Place, London, W1S 2HR
Activities: Manufacture of basic pharmaceutical products
Parent: Hikma Holdings (UK) Limited
Officers: Peter Alexander Speirs, Secretary; Gurpal Singh Atwal [1964] Director/Tax Consultant; Peter Alexander Speirs [1979] Director/Company Secretary

William Hill Holdings Limited
Incorporated: 24 December 1998
Net Worth: £40,167,000 *Total Assets:* £2,575,843,072
Registered Office: 1 Bedford Avenue, London, WC1B 3AU
Activities: Gambling and betting activities
Officers: Balbir Kelly-Bisla, Secretary; Ruth Catherine Prior [1967] Director/Chief Financial Officer; Harry Andrew Willits [1964] Director/Group General Counsel

William Hill Investments Limited
Incorporated: 25 February 1999
Net Worth: £27,609,000 *Total Assets:* £3,502,823,936
Registered Office: 1 Bedford Avenue, London, WC1B 3AU
Activities: Gambling and betting activities
Officers: Balbir Kelly-Bisla, Secretary; Claire Margaret Pape [1974] Director/Deputy CFO; Ruth Catherine Prior [1967] Director/Chief Financial Officer

Will Hill Limited
Incorporated: 6 October 1997
Net Worth: £807,827,968 *Total Assets:* £3,276,499,968
Registered Office: 1 Bedford Avenue, London, WC1B 3AU
Activities: Gambling and betting activities
Shareholders: William Hill Investments Limited; Baseflame Limited
Officers: Balbir Kelly-Bisla, Secretary; Claire Margaret Pape [1974] Director/Deputy CFO; Ruth Catherine Prior [1967] Director/Chief Financial Officer

William Hill Organization Limited
Incorporated: 26 July 1933 *Employees:* 14,128
Net Worth Deficit: £126,400,000 *Total Assets:* £3,592,499,968
Registered Office: 1 Bedford Avenue, London, WC1B 3AU
Activities: Gambling and betting activities
Officers: Balbir Kelly-Bisla, Secretary; Philip Hedley Bowcock [1968] Director/Chief Financial Officer; Balbir Kelly-Bisla [1974] Director/Company Secretary; Claire Margaret Pape [1974] Director/Deputy CFO; Ruth Catherine Prior [1967] Director/Chief Financial Officer

William Hill PLC
Incorporated: 8 May 2001 *Employees:* 16,436
Net Worth: £1,062,700,032 *Total Assets:* £2,361,999,872
Registered Office: 1 Bedford Avenue, London, WC1B 3AU
Activities: Gambling and betting activities
Officers: Balbir Kelly-Bisla, Secretary; Philip Hedley Bowcock [1968] Director/Chief Financial Officer; Mark Brooker [1971] Director; Roger William Devlin [1957] Director; Georgina Harvey [1964] Director; David Soutar Lowden [1957] Director; Ruth Catherine Prior [1967] Director/Chief Financial Officer; Robin James Terrell [1970] Director; Gordon Alexander Wilson [1966] Director

Hinduja Automotive Limited
Incorporated: 27 September 1919 *Employees:* 19,601
Net Worth: £465,388,000 *Total Assets:* £3,992,753,920
Registered Office: 13th Floor, New Zealand House, 80 Haymarket, London, SW1Y 4TE
Activities: Activities of head offices
Officers: Abhijit Mukhopadhyay, Secretary/Lawyer; Jose Maria Alapont [1950] Director [Spanish]; Dheeraj Gopichand Hinduja [1971] Director; Gopichand Parmanand Hinduja [1940] Director/Chairman; Venkatesan Venkataraman [1956] Director/Corporate Executive

Hindwain Limited
Incorporated: 5 December 1977
Net Worth: £18,172,000 *Total Assets:* £143,228,000
Registered Office: 3rd Floor, One New Change, London, EC4M 9AF
Activities: Other business support service activities n.e.c.
Parent: Ladbroke (Rentals) Limited
Officers: Stuart John Smith [1981] Director/Accountant; Charles Alexander Sutters [1980] Director

Hines Europe Limited
Incorporated: 30 September 2016 *Employees:* 298
Net Worth: £67,139,432 *Total Assets:* £114,340,144
Registered Office: 5 Welbeck Street, London, W1G 9YQ
Activities: Activities of head offices
Shareholder: Jeffrey C. Hines
Officers: David Scott Braaten [1960] Director/CFO/COO [American]; Lars Steffen Werner Huber [1971] CEO/Senior Managing Director [German]; Elaine Murphy Rizzo [1970] Managing Director [American/Irish]

Hirecorp Limited
Incorporated: 6 June 2003
Net Worth Deficit: £25,206,000 *Total Assets:* £198,891,008
Registered Office: 5 Howick Place, London, SW1P 1WG
Activities: Other business support service activities n.e.c.
Parent: UBM Holdings Limited
Officers: Rupert John Joseph Hopley [1969] Director/Solicitor

Hiscox Dedicated Corporate Member Limited.
Incorporated: 30 September 1993
Net Worth: £196,764,992 *Total Assets:* £4,182,275,072
Registered Office: 1 Great St Helens, London, EC3A 6HX
Activities: Non-life insurance
Parent: Hiscox PLC
Officers: Bethany Francesca Emma Hunt, Secretary; Robert Simon Childs [1951] Director/Underwriter; Hamayou Akbar Hussain [1972] Director; Bronislaw Edmund Masojada [1961] Director/Chief Executive; Thomas David Shewry [1974] Finance Director

Hiscox Holdings Limited
Incorporated: 8 December 1987
Net Worth: £121,778,000 *Total Assets:* £310,040,992
Registered Office: 1 Great St Helens, London, EC3A 6HX
Activities: Activities of head offices
Parent: Hiscox PLC
Officers: Bethany Francesca Emma Hunt, Secretary; Hamayou Akbar Hussain [1972] Director; Bronislaw Edmund Masojada [1961] Director; Richard Colin Watson [1963] Director

Hiscox Insurance Company Limited
Incorporated: 17 May 1901
Net Worth: £243,440,992 *Total Assets:* £1,366,727,040
Registered Office: 1 Great St Helens, London, EC3A 6HX
Activities: Non-life insurance
Parent: Hiscox Insurance Holdings Limited
Officers: Keith Michael Hubber, Secretary; Bethany Francesca Emma Hunt, Secretary; Robert Simon Childs [1951] Director/Underwriter; Helen Louise Heslop [1969] Director; Hamayou Akbar Hussain [1972] Director; Henry Charles Vaughan Keeling [1955] Director; Colin Denis Keogh [1953] Director; Joanne Riddick Musselle [1970] Director; Christian Leth Nielsen [1975] Director [Danish]; Benjamin Adam Walter [1974] Director [American]

Hiscox PLC
Incorporated: 20 July 1993
Net Worth: £253,660,992 *Total Assets:* £851,043,968
Registered Office: 1 Great St Helens, London, EC3A 6HX
Activities: Non-life insurance
Parent: Hiscox Ltd
Officers: Keith Michael Hubber, Secretary; Bethany Francesca Emma Hunt, Secretary; Hamayou Akbar Hussain [1972] Director; Bronislaw Edmund Masojada [1961] Director; Richard Colin Watson [1963] Director

Hiscox Underwriting Group Services Limited
Incorporated: 9 January 2001 *Employees:* 1,186
Net Worth: £39,601,000 *Total Assets:* £390,224,992
Registered Office: 1 Great St Helens, London, EC3A 6HX
Activities: Activities of business and employers membership organisations
Parent: Hiscox PLC
Officers: Keith Michael Hubber, Secretary; Bethany Francesca Emma Hunt, Secretary; Amanda Victoria Brown [1968] Director; Hamayou Akbar Hussain [1972] Director; Bronislaw Edmund Masojada [1961] Director; Richard Colin Watson [1963] Director

Hiscox Underwriting Ltd
Incorporated: 17 April 1989
Net Worth: £23,500,000 *Total Assets:* £254,584,000
Registered Office: 1 Great St Helens, London, EC3A 6HX
Activities: Non-life insurance
Parent: Hiscox Holdings Limited
Officers: Lori-Lee Hall, Secretary; Juan de Castro Paredes [1976] Director/Chief Operating Officer [Spanish]; Christian Leth Nielsen [1975] Director [Danish]; Adam Rushin [1968] Director/Operations Manager

Hitachi Rail Europe Limited
Incorporated: 20 October 2005 *Employees:* 1,949
Net Worth: £946,937,024 *Total Assets:* £2,075,116,032
Registered Office: 40 Holborn Viaduct, London, EC1N 2PB
Activities: Passenger rail transport, interurban
Parent: Hitachi, Ltd.
Officers: Jane Aine Mee, Secretary; Yoshio Araki [1960] Director/Chief Strategy Officer [Japanese]; Karen Boswell [1963] Managing Director; Ryoichi Hirayanagi [1959] Director/Deputy Chief Finance Officer [Japanese]; Maurizio Manfellotto [1952] Director/Chief Operations Officer [Italian]

The Robert Hitchins Group Limited
Incorporated: 28 December 1960 *Employees:* 54
Net Worth: £114,949,872 *Total Assets:* £225,528,000
Registered Office: St Brides House, 10 Salisbury Square, London, EC4Y 8EH
Activities: Development of building projects
Major Shareholder: Carl Hermann Konrad Friedlaender
Officers: Jonathan James Stewart Dunley, Secretary; Jonathan James Stewart Dunley [1970] Director; David Anthony Furst [1950] Director/Chartered Accountant; Jeremy Charles Hitchins [1954] Director; Jonathan Richard Hitchins [1950] Director; Stephen Robert Hitchins [1947] Director

HKEX Investment (UK) Limited
Incorporated: 22 May 2012
Net Worth: £570,725,184 *Total Assets:* £1,764,817,792
Registered Office: 10 Finsbury Square, London, EC2A 1AJ
Activities: Activities of other holding companies n.e.c.
Parent: HKEX International Limited
Officers: Marcos Castro, Secretary; Matthew James Chamberlain [1982] Director; Adrian John Winston Farnham [1965] Director; Romnesh Lamba [1963] Director [Chinese]

HLG Holdings Limited
Incorporated: 5 May 2005
Net Worth: £432,702,016 *Total Assets:* £438,038,016
Registered Office: The Walbrook Building, 25 Walbrook, London, EC4N 8AW
Activities: Non-life insurance
Parent: Gallagher Holdings (UK) Limited
Officers: Alistair Charles Peel, Secretary; Matthew William Pike [1964] Director

HM Treasury UK Sovereign Sukuk PLC
Incorporated: 21 May 2014
Net Worth: £65,000 *Total Assets:* £200,842,000
Registered Office: 27 Old Gloucester Street, London, WC1N 3AX
Activities: Activities of other holding companies n.e.c.
Parent: Her Majesty's Treasury
Officers: George Francis Martin, Secretary; James Robert Neilson [1969] Director/Solicitor [British/Australian]; Mario Thomas Pisani [1978] Director/Civil Servant

HNVR Holdco Limited
Incorporated: 8 June 2016 *Employees:* 6,905
Net Worth: £1,060,222,016 *Total Assets:* £3,398,304,256
Registered Office: 27 Goswell Road, London, EC1M 7GT
Activities: Activities of other holding companies n.e.c.
Parent: HNVR Midco Limited
Officers: Joanne Ellen Grant, Secretary; Darren James Anniss [1977] Finance Director; Christopher James Good [1979] Director/Private Equity Principal; Hafiz Lalani [1979] Director/Private Equity Principal [Canadian]; Richard Stuart Wheatley [1967] Director

HNVR Midco Limited
Incorporated: 18 January 2016 *Employees:* 6,905
Net Worth: £61,183,464 *Total Assets:* £3,371,208,704
Registered Office: 27 Goswell Road, London, EC1M 7GT
Activities: Activities of other holding companies n.e.c.
Parent: HNVR Topco Limited
Officers: Joanne Ellen Grant, Secretary; Darren James Anniss [1977] Finance Director; Christopher James Good [1979] Director; Hafiz Lalani [1979] Director [Canadian]; Richard Stuart Wheatley [1967] Director

HNVR Topco Limited
Incorporated: 1 June 2016 *Employees:* 6,905
Net Worth Deficit: £139,847,920 *Total Assets:* £3,376,453,120
Registered Office: 27 Goswell Road, London, EC1M 7GT
Activities: Activities of other holding companies n.e.c.
Parent: HBG Limited
Officers: Joanne Ellen Grant, Secretary; Darren James Anniss [1977] Finance Director; Christopher James Good [1979] Director/Private Equity Principal; Hafiz Lalani [1979] Director/Private Equity Principal [Canadian]; Richard Stuart Wheatley [1967] Director

C. Hoare & Co.
Incorporated: 5 July 1929 *Employees:* 381
Net Worth: £352,456,992 *Total Assets:* £4,573,112,832
Registered Office: 37 Fleet Street, London, EC4P 4DQ
Activities: Banks
Officers: Katie Jane White, Secretary; Steven Martin Cooper [1970] Director/Banker; Alexander Richard Quintin Hoare [1973] Director/Banker; Alexander Simon Hoare [1962] Director/Banker; Arabella Saxon Hoare [1968] Director/Banker; Simon Merrik Hoare [1967] Director/Banker; Venetia Elizabeth Hoare [1965] Director/Banker; Nicholas Ian Macpherson [1959] Director; Andrew James McIntyre [1956] Director/Chartered Accountant; Dame Susan Ilene Rice [1946] Director; Johanna Elizabeth Martin Waterous [1957] Senior Independent Director [Canadian/Irish]

Hochschild Mining Holdings Limited
Incorporated: 11 April 2006
Net Worth: £1,274,356,352 *Total Assets:* £1,292,860,544
Registered Office: 17 Cavendish Square, London, W1G 0PH
Activities: Mining of other non-ferrous metal ores
Parent: Hochschild Mining PLC
Officers: Rajish Dev Bhasin, Secretary; Ramon Barua Costa [1972] Director [Peruvian]; Ignacio Jose Bustamante Romero [1971] Director [Peruvian]

Hochschild Mining PLC
Incorporated: 11 April 2006
Net Worth: £551,044,096 *Total Assets:* £1,131,694,208
Registered Office: 17 Cavendish Square, London, W1G 0PH
Activities: Mining of other non-ferrous metal ores
Officers: Rajish Dev Bhasin, Secretary; Dr Graham John Birch [1960] Director/Farming; Jorge Born [1962] Director/Businessman [Belgian/Argentinian]; Ignacio Jose Bustamante Romero [1971] Director [Peruvian]; Eduardo Hochschild [1963] Director/Businessman [Peruvian]; Eileen Ann Kamerick [1958] Independent Director and Adjunct Professor of Law [American]; Michael Ian Rawlinson [1969] Director/Investment Banker; Dionisio Romero Paoletti [1965] Director/Businessman [Peruvian/Italian]; Emani Sanjay Sarma [1968] Director/Professor of Mechanical Engineering [American]

Hodson Holdings (Ashford) Limited
Incorporated: 22 September 2016
Net Worth: £247,712 *Total Assets:* £104,535,480
Registered Office: Office Suite 9, 55 Park Lane, London, W1K 1NA
Activities: Construction of domestic buildings
Major Shareholder: Alan Derek Hodson
Officers: Rama Manian, Secretary; Alan Derek Hodson [1952] Director; Thomas Steven Hodson [1981] Director

Hoebridge LLP
Incorporated: 19 May 2009
Net Worth: £657,378,816 *Total Assets:* £657,385,792
Registered Office: Suite 1, 3rd Floor, 11-12 St James's Square, London, SW1Y 4LB

Hogan Lovells International LLP
Incorporated: 2 November 2006 *Employees:* 3,308
Net Worth: £314,152,000 *Total Assets:* £585,950,976
Registered Office: Atlantic House, Holborn Viaduct, London, EC1A 2FG
Officers: Leopold Von Gerlach [1967] Member; Benjamin Charles Ivan Higson [1973] Member; Karen Elizabeth Hughes [1964] Member; Stephen Joseph Immelt [1951] Member; Adrian John Walker [1967] Member; Rahail Ali [1966] LLP Member; John Robert Allison [1968] LLP Member; Penelope Catherine Angell [1970] LLP Member; Francesca Angeloni [1970] LLP Member; Lutz Klaus Angerer [1961] LLP Member; Ernesto Apuzzo [1971] LLP Member; Thomas William Astle [1980] LLP Member; Fulvia Astolfi [1963] LLP Member; Nicholas Mark Atkins [1961] LLP Member; Patrick Olivier Marc Ayad [1973] LLP Member; Ludovic Babin [1968] LLP Member; Jonathan Baird [1968] LLP Member; Katherine Emma Banks [1969] LLP Member; Joseph Bahlsen Bannister [1962] LLP Member; Sohail Rasheed Barkatali [1969] LLP Member; Lars Hermann Benger [1974] LLP Member; Stephen David Bennett [1970] LLP Member; Marco Berliri [1969] LLP Member; Shalini Bhuchar [1976] LLP Member; Sabine Bironneau Loy [1970] LLP Member; Klaas Adriaan Jan Bisschop [1968] LLP Member; Anskje Katlen Bloecker [1970] LLP Member; Charles Bogle [1970] LLP Member; Roland Bomhard [1960] LLP Member; Sabrina Borocci [1973] LLP Member; Andreas Bothe [1962] LLP Member; Edward Christopher Bowyer [1972] LLP Member; Tim Oliver Brandi [1965] LLP Member; Sven Brandt [1964] LLP Member; Thomas William Brassington [1974] LLP Member; Charles Robert Nicholas Brasted [1980] LLP Member; Susan Vivien Bright [1965] LLP Member; Whiston Peter Bristow [1977] LLP Member; Jeremy Derek Scott Brittenden [1966] LLP Member; Ina Ulrike Brock [1969] LLP Member; Daniel Charles Brook [1977] LLP Member; Edward Quentin Fitzwilliam Brown [1980] LLP Member; Paul James Brown [1977] LLP Member; Philip George Lees Brown [1966] LLP Member; Francois Brunet [1964] LLP Member; Steven Donald Bryan [1963] LLP Member; Duncan Ian Buchanan [1965] LLP Member; Matthew John Bullen [1979] LLP Member; Johannes Buntjer [1967] LLP Member; Markus Burgstaller [1975] LLP Member; Bruno Cantier [1969] LLP Member; Andrew Peter de Vic Carey [1962] LLP Member; Lourdes Catrain [1966] LLP Member; Oliver Luke Chamberlain [1974] LLP Member; Owen Chan [1970] LLP Member; Charles Nicholas Cheffings [1960] LLP Member; Jonathan Chertkow [1977] LLP Member; Filippo Andrea Chiaves [1971] LLP Member; Emma Jane Clarke [1973] LLP Member; Andrew John Condliffe [1971] LLP Member; John Connell [1979] LLP Member; Manon Henriette Regine Nancy Yvette Cordewener [1966] LLP Member; Christelle Coslin [1981] LLP Member; Matthew John Cottis [1962] LLP Member; Angus William Coulter [1974] LLP Member; Julian Craughan [1975] LLP Member; Alice Theresa Valder Curran [1967] LLP Member; Michael Durham Davison [1964] LLP Member; Marie Aimee Jacqueline Alphonsine de Dampierre [1964] LLP Member; Anita de Jong [1959] LLP Member; Victor de Vlaam [1972] LLP Member; Dirk Debald [1974] LLP Member; Daniel Dehghanian [1976] LLP Member; Federico Del Monte [1969] LLP Member; Cecile Derycke [1978] LLP Member; Michael Dettmeier [1970] LLP Member; Sylvain Generald Dhennin [1978] LLP Member; Natale Christian di Mauro [1975] LLP Member; Richard Paul Diffenthal [1980] LLP Member; Dennis Dillon [1959] LLP Member; Angela Margaret Dimsdale Gill [1948] LLP Member; Mathew James Ditchburn [1973] LLP Member; Christopher John Dobby [1972] LLP Member; Ingmar Doerr [1976] LLP Member; Xavier Doumen [1977] LLP Member; Aline Regine Simone Renee Doussin [1982] LLP Member; Roberta Catherine Claire Deschamps Downey [1967] LLP Member; James Dudley Doyle [1975] LLP Member; Yvonne Draheim [1970] LLP Member; Dr Thomas Duenchheim [1966] LLP Member; Leah Rosamond Dunlop [1959] LLP Member; Cecile Marie Clothilde Dupoux [1971] LLP Member; Claire Louise Dutch [1972] LLP Member; Tanja Eisenblaetter [1971] LLP Member; Nicola Jane Evans [1970] LLP Member; Tobias Faber [1978] LLP Member; Martin Fahndrich [1965] LLP Member; Andreas Johannes Nikolaus Von Falck [1966] LLP Member; Matthew Felwick [1976] LLP Member; Vincent Fidelle [1979] LLP Member

Hoggant Limited
Incorporated: 23 September 2013 *Employees:* 122
Net Worth: £118,549,000 *Total Assets:* £745,190,016
Registered Office: 21 Palmer Street, London, SW1H 0AD
Activities: Activities of financial services holding companies
Parent: Alchemy Special Opportunites LLP
Officers: Alexander Leicester [1979] Director/Investment Manager; Dominic James Haviland Slade [1971] Director/Venture Capitalist; Nicholas Toby Westcott [1978] Director

Holbud Group Limited
Incorporated: 22 October 2013 *Employees:* 39
Net Worth: £111,981,360 *Total Assets:* £334,627,552
Registered Office: 66 Leman Street, London, E1 8EU
Activities: Activities of other holding companies n.e.c.
Officers: Bimal Dharamvir Sabarwal, Secretary; Mahmood Gulamhusein Khaku [1941] Director/Manager; Hasnain Roshanali Merali [1967] Director/Commodity Trader; Shaukat Akberali Merali [1960] Director/Manager; David George Rowe [1941] Director

Holbud Limited
Incorporated: 6 September 1977 *Employees:* 25
Net Worth: £84,601,664 *Total Assets:* £291,019,808
Registered Office: 66 Leman Street, London, E1 8EU
Activities: Wholesale of grain, unmanufactured tobacco, seeds and animal feeds
Parent: Holbud Group Limited
Officers: Bimal Dharamvir Sabarwal, Secretary; Mahmood Gulamhusein Khaku [1941] Director/Manager; Gulamali Masumali Merali [1977] Director/Chartered Accountant; Hasnain Roshanali Merali [1967] Director/Commodity Trader; Shaukat Akberali Merali [1960] Director/Manager; David George Rowe [1941] Director/Accountant

Holidaybreak Limited
Incorporated: 14 October 1988 *Employees:* 2,804
Net Worth: £199,700,000 *Total Assets:* £522,100,000
Registered Office: 3rd Floor, 30 Millbank, London, SW1P 4DU
Activities: Activities of head offices
Parent: Prometheon Holdings (UK) Limited
Officers: Navneet Bali [1956] Director; Dinesh Goel [1978] Director [Indian]; Ajay Ajit Peter Kerkar [1963] Director [Indian]; Shyam Maheshwari [1976] Director [Indian]; Ajit Paramparambath Menon [1957] Director; Andreas Rizal Vourloumis [1974] Alternate Director [Indonesian]

Holmes Funding Limited
Incorporated: 28 April 2000
Net Worth Deficit: £36,440,000 *Total Assets:* £1,711,021,952
Registered Office: 2 Triton Square, Regent's Place, London, NW1 3AN
Activities: Financial intermediation not elsewhere classified
Parent: Holmes Holdings Limited
Officers: Rachel Jane Morrison [1968] Director/Chartered Accountant; Daniel Jonathan Wynne [1970] Director

Holmes Master Issuer PLC
Incorporated: 3 October 2006
Net Worth: £533,000 *Total Assets:* £1,794,055,040
Registered Office: 2 Triton Square, Regent's Place, London, NW1 3AN
Activities: Financial intermediation not elsewhere classified
Parent: Holmes Holdings Limited
Officers: Rachel Jane Morrison [1968] Director/Chartered Accountant; Daniel Jonathan Wynne [1970] Director

Homebase (UK & I) Holdings Limited
Incorporated: 11 January 2016 *Employees:* 2
Previous: Bunnings (UK & I) Holdings Limited
Net Worth: £441,014,016 *Total Assets:* £738,116,992
Registered Office: 80 New Bond Street, London, W1S 1SB
Activities: Activities of other holding companies n.e.c.
Parent: Ark UK Holdings Limited
Officers: Inca Lockhart-Ross, Secretary; Andrew Charles Coleman [1974] Director/Chief Financial Officer; Henry William Foster [1979] Director; Damian Garry McGloughlin [1969] Director/Chief Executive; Paul Patrick McGowan [1962] Director [Irish]; Steven Richard Pell [1983] Director

Homer Newco Limited
Incorporated: 7 December 2009 *Employees:* 95
Net Worth: £83,662,256 *Total Assets:* £284,965,952
Registered Office: 93 Dollis Road, Finchley, London, N3 1RE
Activities: Other business support service activities n.e.c.
Shareholders: Jonathan Owen; Paul McGrath
Officers: Paul McGrath [1971] Director; Jonathan Owen [1971] Director; Armand Chimmaya Perera [1969] Director/Consultant [Sri Lankan]

Honeycomb Investment Trust PLC
Incorporated: 2 December 2015
Net Worth: £304,759,008 *Total Assets:* £397,782,016
Registered Office: 6th Floor, 65 Gresham Street, London, EC2V 7NQ
Activities: Other credit granting n.e.c.
Officers: James Coyle [1956] Director; Robert Sharpe [1949] Director; Ravi Takhar [1965] Director

Honours (Holdings) Limited
Incorporated: 28 January 1999
Net Worth Deficit: £41,677,000 *Total Assets:* £144,787,008
Registered Office: Third Floor, 1 King's Arms Yard, London, EC2R 7AF
Activities: Other business support service activities n.e.c.
Parent: Wilmington Trust SP Services (London) Limited
Officers: Daniel Jonathan Wynne [1970] Director

Glyn Hopkin Holdings Limited
Incorporated: 15 May 2015 *Employees:* 823
Net Worth: £27,826,000 *Total Assets:* £136,939,008
Registered Office: 10 Queen Street Place, London, EC4R 1AG
Activities: Other business support service activities n.e.c.
Major Shareholder: Glyn Kenneth Hopkin
Officers: Michael Anthony Salida, Secretary; Jonathan Robert Beveridge [1970] Director; Fraser Cohen [1969] Managing Director; Sally Anne Germain [1966] Brand Director; Stuart James Hodson [1975] Director; David Anthony Hopkin [1964] Director; Glyn Kenneth Hopkin [1961] Director/Chairman; Hady Habib Laba [1970] Finance Director; Dean David Quy [1976] Director/Sales Manager; Michael Anthony Salida [1951] Director/Solicitor; Paul Dominic Sozzi [1962] Director

Glyn Hopkin Limited
Incorporated: 16 October 1992 *Employees:* 823
Net Worth: £21,364,000 *Total Assets:* £121,245,000
Registered Office: 10 Queen Street Place, London, EC4R 1AG
Activities: Sale of new cars and light motor vehicles
Parent: Glyn Hopkin Holdings Limited
Officers: Michael Anthony Salida, Secretary; Jonathan Robert Beveridge [1959] Director; Fraser Cohen [1969] Managing Director; Sally Anne Germain [1966] Brand Director; Stuart James Hodson [1975] Brand Director; David Anthony Hopkin [1964] Director; Glyn Kenneth Hopkin [1961] Director/Chairman; Hady Habib Laba [1970] Finance Director; Dean David Quy [1976] Brand Director; Michael Anthony Salida [1951] Director/Solicitor; Paul Dominic Sozzi [1962] After Sales Director

Horizon Bidco Limited
Incorporated: 5 October 2015 *Employees:* 10
Net Worth: £8,510,000 *Total Assets:* £603,552,000
Registered Office: 10 Back Hill, London, EC1R 5EN
Activities: Management consultancy activities other than financial management
Parent: Horizon Midco Limited
Officers: Alan Robert Burns [1973] Director; Jody Matthew Robertson Ford [1975] Director; Claudette Anne Robinson [1970] Director/Accountant [South African]

Horizon Debtco Limited
Incorporated: 5 October 2015
Net Worth Deficit: £18,928,000 *Total Assets:* £230,171,008
Registered Office: 10 Back Hill, London, EC1R 5EN
Activities: Activities of other holding companies n.e.c.
Parent: Horizon Holdco Limited
Officers: Alan Robert Burns [1973] Director; Jody Matthew Robertson Ford [1975] Director

Horizon Groupco Limited
Incorporated: 5 October 2015
Net Worth: £3,062,000 *Total Assets:* £230,488,000
Registered Office: 10 Back Hill, London, EC1R 5EN
Activities: Activities of other holding companies n.e.c.
Parent: Horizon Debtco Limited
Officers: Alan Robert Burns [1973] Director; Jody Matthew Robertson Ford [1975] Director

Horizon Holdco Limited
Incorporated: 5 October 2015 *Employees:* 1,361
Net Worth Deficit: £132,343,000 *Total Assets:* £457,500,992
Registered Office: 10 Back Hill, London, EC1R 5EN
Activities: Activities of head offices
Shareholder: Exponent Private Equity Partners III, L.P.
Officers: Alan Robert Burns [1973] Director; Simon Russell Davidson [1977] Director/Private Equity Executive; Jody Matthew Robertson Ford [1975] Director; Douglas Stuart McCallum [1966] Director; David Hugh McGovern [1985] Director/Financier [Irish]; Thomas Sweet-Escott [1957] Director/Private Equity Executive

Horizon Midco Limited
Incorporated: 5 October 2015 *Employees:* 1,361
Net Worth Deficit: £110,093,000 *Total Assets:* £457,556,992
Registered Office: 10 Back Hill, London, EC1R 5EN
Activities: Activities of other holding companies n.e.c.
Parent: Horizon Groupco Limited
Officers: Alan Robert Burns [1973] Director; Jody Matthew Robertson Ford [1975] Director

Horizon RE Limited
Incorporated: 7 December 2005 *Employees:* 198
Net Worth: £82,759,792 *Total Assets:* £312,594,336
Registered Office: c/o Waterstone Company Secretaries Ltd, Third Floor, 5 St Bride Street, London, EC4A 4AS
Activities: Non-trading company
Major Shareholder: Francesco Corallo
Officers: Rudolf Theodoor Anna Baetsen [1966] Director [Dutch]

Hostelworld Group PLC
Incorporated: 9 October 2015 *Employees:* 254
Net Worth: £128,880,024 *Total Assets:* £138,240,656
Registered Office: High Holborn House, 52-54 High Holborn, London, WC1V 6RL
Activities: Activities of other holding companies n.e.c.
Officers: John Duggan, Secretary; Michael Edward Cawley [1954] Director [Irish]; Tj Kelly [1974] Director/Chartered Accountant [Irish]; Andrew McCue [1974] Director [Irish]; Eimear Moloney [1970] Director/Chartered Accountant [Irish]; Gary Magnus Morrison [1967] Director/Chief Executive Officer

Hotel (PL Property) Holdco Limited
Incorporated: 3 October 2008 *Employees:* 2
Net Worth: £100 *Total Assets:* £170,295,840
Registered Office: Floor 6, Quadrant House, 4 Thomas More Square, London, E1W 1YW
Activities: Other business support service activities n.e.c.
Parent: London & Regional Group Investments Limited
Officers: Richard John Livingstone [1964] Director

Hotel (PL Property) Holding Limited
Incorporated: 29 November 2001 *Employees:* 2
Previous: Hotel (PL Property) Limited
Net Worth: £387,380,000 *Total Assets:* £547,171,008
Registered Office: Floor 6, Quadrant House, 4 Thomas More Square, London, E1W 1YW
Activities: Development of building projects
Parent: Hotel (PL Property) Holdco Limited
Officers: Richard John Livingstone [1964] Director; Leonard Kevin Sebastian [1969] Group Managing and Legal Director [Swiss]

Houlihan Lokey Capital (Holdings) Limited
Incorporated: 1 August 2007
Net Worth: £113,234,248 *Total Assets:* £143,973,808
Registered Office: 83 Pall Mall, London, SW1Y 5ES
Activities: Activities of financial services holding companies
Parent: Houlihan Lokey, Inc.
Officers: John Andrew Cowan, Secretary; James Lindsey Alley [1966] Director/Chief Financial Officer [American]; John Andrew Cowan [1966] Director/Lawyer; David Abraham Preiser [1957] Director/Investment Banker [American]

House of Fraser (UK & Ireland) Acquisitions Limited
Incorporated: 27 April 2006
Previous: Highland Acquisitions Limited
Net Worth Deficit: £1,700,000 *Total Assets:* £528,400,000
Registered Office: 27 Baker Street, London, W1U 8AH
Activities: Activities of head offices
Parent: House of Fraser (UK & Ireland) Ltd
Officers: Peter Geoffrey Hearsey, Secretary; Fei-Er Cheng [1982] Director [Chinese]; Peter Geoffrey Hearsey [1965] Executive Director; Yong Shen [1972] Director; Alex Patrick Williamson [1974] Director

Housing Association Funding PLC
Incorporated: 3 May 1996
Net Worth: £208,513 *Total Assets:* £116,543,848
Registered Office: 6th Floor, 65 Gresham Street, London, EC2V 7NQ
Activities: Other business support service activities n.e.c.
Parent: H.A. Funding Limited
Officers: Sean Peter Martin [1965] Director

Howard de Walden Estates Holdings Limited
Incorporated: 28 November 2007 *Employees:* 134
Net Worth: £3,360,012,032 *Total Assets:* £4,556,026,880
Registered Office: 23 Queen Anne Street, London, W1G 9DL
Activities: Activities of other holding companies n.e.c.
Shareholders: Maurice Nicholas Beech Thompson; Steven John Baldwin; Mark Jonathan Musgrave
Officers: Peter Griffith, Secretary; The Honourable Camilla Anne Bronwen Acloque [1947] Director/Housewife; Simon William de Mouchet Baynham [1956] Director/Chartered Surveyor; The Honourable Blanche Susan Fionudbhar Buchan [1937] Director/Housewife; Marc Edward Charles Gilbard [1962] Director; Sir Christopher Kingston Howes [1942] Director; Andrew James Hynard [1960] Director; Ajay Kumar Kakkar [1964] Director/Professor; Mark Kildea [1965] Finance Director; The Right Honourable Mary Hazel Caridwen Lady Howard de Walden [1935] Director/Housewife; Elizabeth Ann Peace [1952] Director; Sir William Henry Proby [1949] Director; Toby Richard Shannon [1957] Director/Chartered Accountant; The Honourable Jessica Jane Vronwy White [1941] Director/Farmer

Howard de Walden Estates Limited
Incorporated: 15 November 1963 *Employees:* 134
Net Worth: £3,150,929,920 *Total Assets:* £4,521,849,856
Registered Office: 23 Queen Anne Street, London, W1G 9DL
Activities: Other letting and operating of own or leased real estate
Parent: Howard de Walden Estates Holdings Limited
Officers: Peter Griffith, Secretary; The Honourable Camilla Anne Bronwen Acloque [1947] Director/Housewife; Simon William de Mouchet Baynham [1956] Director/Chartered Surveyor; Susan Buchan [1937] Director/Housewife; The Lady Howard de Walden [1935] Director/Housewife; Marc Edward Charles Gilbard [1962] Director; Sir Christopher Kingston Howes [1942] Director; Andrew James Hynard [1960] Director; Ajay Kumar Kakkar [1964] Director/Professor; Mark Kildea [1965] Finance Director; Elizabeth Ann Peace [1952] Director; Sir William Henry Proby [1949] Director; Toby Richard Shannon [1957] Director/Chartered Accountant; The Honourable Jessica Jane Vronwy White [1941] Director/Farmer

Howard Investments Limited
Incorporated: 9 March 1999
Net Worth: £705,897,024 *Total Assets:* £706,067,008
Registered Office: Weston Centre, 10 Grosvenor Street, London, W1K 4QY
Activities: Financial intermediation not elsewhere classified
Parent: Wittington Investments Limited
Officers: Amanda Geday, Secretary; Anna Catrina Hobhouse [1962] Director; George Garfield Weston [1964] Director [Canadian]; Guy Howard Weston [1960] Director

Howden Broking Group Limited
Incorporated: 16 May 2007 *Employees:* 15
Net Worth: £705,756,992 *Total Assets:* £1,088,606,976
Registered Office: One Creechurch Place, London, EC3A 5AF
Activities: Non-life insurance
Parent: Hyperion Development UK Limited
Officers: Andrew John Moore, Secretary; Jose Manuel Gonzalez Perez [1973] Director/Insurance Broker [Spanish]; Louise Fenella Reina [1967] Director/Chief of Staff; Rebecca Briony Scott [1979] Director/Accountant

Howden Group Limited
Incorporated: 7 September 1949 *Employees:* 97
Net Worth: £139,672,000 *Total Assets:* £157,644,000
Registered Office: 6th Floor, 322 High Holborn, London, WC1V 7PB
Activities: Activities of head offices
Parent: Howden Holdings Limited
Officers: Fionnuala Mary Barrie [1962] Global HR Director; Ian Halliday Brander [1961] Director; William Flexon [1963] Director/Chartered Accountant [American]; Alastair Irvine [1981] Director; Mark Paul Lehman [1967] Director/Solicitor [American]; Daniel Alexis Pryor [1968] Director [American]; Elias Zabaneh [1960] Director [Spanish]

Howden Holdings Limited
Incorporated: 24 July 2002 *Employees:* 10
Net Worth: £238,592,000 *Total Assets:* £349,372,992
Registered Office: 6th Floor, 322 High Holborn, London, WC1V 7PB
Activities: Activities of head offices
Parent: Cast Limited
Officers: Fionnuala Mary Barrie [1962] Global HR Director; Ian Halliday Brander [1961] Director; William Flexon [1963] Director/Chartered Accountant [American]; Alastair Irvine [1981] Director; Allan Jan Foremann Kristensen [1965] Director [Danish]; Mark Paul Lehman [1967] Director/Solicitor [American]; Daniel Alexis Pryor [1968] Director [American]; Elias Zabaneh [1960] Director [Spanish]

Howden Joinery Corporate Services Limited
Incorporated: 4 November 1983 *Employees:* 53
Net Worth Deficit: £172,719,008 *Total Assets:* £519,907,008
Registered Office: 40 Portman Square, London, W1H 6LT
Activities: Other business support service activities n.e.c.
Parent: Howden Joinery Holdings Limited
Officers: Forbes McNaughton, Secretary; Gareth Hopkins [1957] HR Director; Theresa Keating [1964] Finance Director; Mark Philip William Robson [1958] Director/Chief Financial Officer

Howden Joinery Group PLC
Incorporated: 7 May 1987 *Employees:* 9,044
Net Worth: £454,200,000 *Total Assets:* £808,499,968
Registered Office: 40 Portman Square, London, W1H 6LT
Activities: Activities of head offices
Officers: Forbes McNaughton, Secretary; Mark Allen [1959] Director; Karen Margaret Caddick [1969] Group Human Resources Director; Andrew Graham Cripps [1957] Director; Geoffrey Drabble [1959] Director; Tiffany Anne Hall [1964] Marketing Director; William Andrew Livingston [1967] Director/Chief Executive Officer; Richard John Pennycook [1964] Director; Mark Philip William Robson [1958] Director/Chief Financial Officer; Debra Jayne White [1962] Director

Howden Joinery Holdings Limited
Incorporated: 19 February 1997
Net Worth: £5,493,000 *Total Assets:* £689,209,024
Registered Office: 40 Portman Square, London, W1H 6LT
Activities: Activities of other holding companies n.e.c.
Parent: Howden Joinery Group PLC
Officers: Forbes McNaughton, Secretary; Theresa Keating [1964] Director/Group Financial Controller; William Andrew Livingston [1967] Director/Chief Executive Officer; Mark Philip William Robson [1958] Director/Chief Financial Officer

Howden Joinery Limited
Incorporated: 15 December 1953 *Employees:* 7,054
Net Worth: £313,142,016 *Total Assets:* £1,548,800,000
Registered Office: 40 Portman Square, London, W1H 6LT
Activities: Retail of furniture, lighting, and similar (not musical instruments or scores) in specialised store
Parent: Howden Joinery Holdings Limited
Officers: Forbes McNaughton, Secretary; Kevin Richard Barrett [1970] Group Development Director; Clive Cockburn [1967] Director/Chief Information Officer; Robert Raymond Fenwick [1959] Director; Andrew Ian Gault [1975] E Commerce Director; Gareth Hopkins [1957] HR Director; Theresa Keating [1964] Director/Group Financial Controller; William Andrew Livingston [1967] Director/Chief Executive Officer; Mark Philip William Robson [1958] Director/Chief Financial Officer; Andrew Witts [1960] Sales Director

Howden UK Group Limited
Incorporated: 1 June 1962 *Employees:* 452
Previous: R K Harrison Group Limited
Net Worth: £134,988,992 *Total Assets:* £239,256,000
Registered Office: One Creechurch Place, London, EC3A 5AF
Activities: Non-life insurance
Parent: Howden Broking Group Limited
Officers: Andrew John Moore, Secretary; John Duncan Irvine Bennett [1963] Director/Insurance Broker; John Charles Birkmire [1954] Director/Accountant; Christopher Peter Richard Evans [1965] Director/Insurance Broker; Eliot James Powell [1971] Director/Insurance Broker; Serge Robert Thieriet [1972] Director/Chief Financial Officer [French]

HP Foods Limited
Incorporated: 5 May 1988
Net Worth: £5,901,000 *Total Assets:* £1,363,459,968
Registered Office: The Shard, 32 London Bridge Street, London, SE1 9SG
Activities: Wholesale of other food, including fish, crustaceans and molluscs
Parent: H.J. Heinz Company Ltd
Officers: Victoria Louise White, Secretary; Julien Karma Favre [1981] Finance Director [Swiss]; Christine Page [1962] Director/Vice President Controller; Adam Rathbone [1968] Director/Tax Manager

HPI UK Holding Ltd.
Incorporated: 20 October 2005 *Employees:* 506
Net Worth Deficit: £28,427,000 *Total Assets:* £151,700,992
Registered Office: 7 Albemarle Street, London, W1S 4HQ
Activities: Hotels and similar accommodation
Officers: Bradley Dean Hornbacher, Secretary; Patrick M Gaffney [1955] Director/Financial Executive [American]; Karl Daniel Heininger [1961] Director/Executive Vice President [American]; Daniel Sedlmayer [1967] Director/Executive [German]; Peter Voit [1962] Director/Executive [German]

HQCB Investments Limited
Incorporated: 15 January 2002 *Employees:* 3
Net Worth: £14,007,083 *Total Assets:* £1,153,777,024
Registered Office: 30th Floor, 1 Canada Square, London, E14 5AB
Activities: Development of building projects
Parent: HQCB Properties (HQ5 (2)) Limited
Officers: John Raymond Garwood, Secretary; A Peter Anderson II [1953] Director/Real Estate Executive [American]; George Iacobescu [1945] Director; Russell James John Lyons [1961] Director/Chartered Accountant

HQCB Properties (HQ5 (2)) Limited
Incorporated: 3 September 2002
Net Worth: £10,797,727 *Total Assets:* £1,143,172,992
Registered Office: 30th Floor, One Canada Square, London, E14 5AB
Activities: Buying and selling of own real estate
Parent: CWCB Holdings Limited
Officers: John Raymond Garwood, Secretary; A Peter Anderson II [1953] Director/Real Estate Executive [American]; George Iacobescu [1945] Director; Russell James John Lyons [1961] Director/Chartered Accountant

HS1 Limited
Incorporated: 2 April 1998 *Employees:* 45
Net Worth: £1,400,300,032 *Total Assets:* £4,560,699,904
Registered Office: 5th Floor, Kings Place, 90 York Way, London, N1 9AG
Activities: Other urban, suburban or metropolitan passenger land transport (not underground, metro or similar)
Parent: Helix Acquisition Limited
Officers: Lucy Ann Clarke-Bodicoat, Secretary; John Hamilton Ainsworth Curley [1954] Director; Sion Laurence Jones [1974] Director; Amanda Vanderneth Leness [1967] Director [American]; Keith Lawrence Ludeman [1950] Director; Andrew Christopher Pitt [1959] Transport Director; Scott Springett [1968] Director/Asset Manager; Mark Richard Woodhams [1966] Director/Financier

HSB Engineering Insurance Limited
Incorporated: 16 June 1989 *Employees:* 679
Net Worth: £122,378,000 *Total Assets:* £304,249,984
Registered Office: New London House, 6 London Street, London, EC3R 7LP
Activities: Non-life insurance
Parent: Munchener Ruckversicherungs-Gesellschaft Aktiengesellschaft in Munchen
Officers: Kelli Close-Smith, Secretary; Jeffrey Niven Herdman [1953] Director/Chairman; Stephen David Arthur Morris [1962] Director/Chief Underwriting Officer; Anya Marjorie O'Reilly [1974] Finance Director; Jeffrey Charles O'Shaughnessy [1971] Director/Chief Underwriting Officer [American]; Peter Richter [1972] Director/Head of Corporate Finance [German]; Craig Anthony Scarr [1962] Director/Chair of the Audit Committee; Stephen David Worrall [1976] Director/Chartered Accountant

HSBC (BGF) Investments Limited
Incorporated: 13 September 2004
Net Worth Deficit: £2,609,077 *Total Assets:* £304,295,328
Registered Office: 8 Canada Square, London, E14 5HQ
Activities: Financial intermediation not elsewhere classified
Parent: HSBC Bank PLC
Officers: Jonathan Beater, Secretary; James Laurence Chew [1962] Director/Banker; James Cundy [1978] Director/Banker; Leslie Curtis [1979] Director/Chartered Accountant; Tom Wood [1981] Director/Banker

HSBC Asia Holdings (UK) Limited
Incorporated: 19 October 2001
Net Worth: £19,901,364,224 *Total Assets:* £24,768,167,936
Registered Office: 8 Canada Square, London, E14 5HQ
Activities: Activities of financial services holding companies
Parent: HSBC Finance (Netherlands)
Officers: Gavin Andrew Francis [1965] Director/Accountant; Richard John Hennity [1970] Director/Lawyer; Iain Francis MacKinnon [1957] Director/Accountant

HSBC Asia Holdings B.V.
Incorporated: 1 October 2013
Net Worth: £46,225,965,056 *Total Assets:* £51,143,344,128
Registered Office: 8 Canada Square, London, E14 5HQ
Officers: Gavin Andrew Francis [1965] Director/Accountant; Richard John Hennity [1970] Director/Lawyer; Iain Francis MacKinnon [1957] Director/Accountant

HSBC Asia Pacific Holdings (UK) Limited
Incorporated: 10 May 1973
Net Worth: £2,591,173,120 *Total Assets:* £2,591,429,888
Registered Office: 8 Canada Square, London, E14 5HQ
Activities: Activities of financial services holding companies
Parent: HSBC Asia Holdings (UK) Limited
Officers: Kathleen Chieh Huey Gan [1975] Director/Chief Financial Officer Asia Pacific [Singaporean]; Daniel Gareth Hankinson [1978] Director; Richard John Hennity [1970] Director/Lawyer; Iain Francis MacKinnon [1957] Director/Accountant

HSBC Asset Finance (UK) Limited
Incorporated: 31 March 1928
Net Worth: £133,500,000 *Total Assets:* £8,576,399,872
Registered Office: 8 Canada Square, London, E14 5HQ
Activities: Financial intermediation not elsewhere classified
Parent: HSBC Bank PLC
Officers: Molly Ranger, Secretary; Crispin Robert John Irvin [1978] Director/Chief Financial Officer; Simon Einar Long [1974] Director/Banker; Gareth Owen Conway [1966] Director/Investment Banking; Jaya Subramaniyan [1962] Director/Accountant [Malaysian]; Okechukwu Uwakwe [1969] Director [Irish]

HSBC Bank PLC
Incorporated: 1 July 1880 *Employees:* 45,342
Net Worth: £43,462,000,640 *Total Assets:* £818,867,994,624
Registered Office: 8 Canada Square, London, E14 5HQ
Activities: Banks
Parent: HSBC UK Holdings Limited
Officers: Loren Wulfsohn, Secretary; James Alasdair Emmett [1971] Director/Chief Executive; Jacques Fleurant [1967] Director/Chief Financial Officer [Canadian]; Dame Mary Elizabeth Marsh [1946] Director; Stephen Paul O'Connor [1961] Director; Yukiko Omura [1955] Director [Japanese]; Dr Eric Wolfgang Strutz [1964] Non-Employee Non-Executive Director [German]; John Francis Trueman [1943] Director; Andrew Merlay Wright [1960] Director

HSBC Equipment Finance (UK) Limited
Incorporated: 24 June 1980
Net Worth: £136,451,008 *Total Assets:* £3,480,096,000
Registered Office: 8 Canada Square, London, E14 5HQ
Activities: Financial intermediation not elsewhere classified
Parent: HSBC UK Bank PLC
Officers: Molly Ranger, Secretary; Bryan Bulford [1956] Director/Head of Credit and Risk; Mark Harris [1962] Director/Bank Official; Gayle Helen Lacey [1979] Director/Service; Robert Ian McElroy [1980] Director/Banker; Sanjay Sankaran Nair [1968] Director/Accountant [Indian]

HSBC Finance (Netherlands)
Incorporated: 5 May 1993
Net Worth: £7,175,449,088 *Total Assets:* £23,077,050,368
Registered Office: 8 Canada Square, London, E14 5HQ
Activities: Activities of financial services holding companies
Parent: HSBC Holdings PLC
Officers: Larissa Wilson, Secretary; Gavin Andrew Francis [1965] Director/Accountant; Richard John Hennity [1970] Director/Lawyer; Iain Francis MacKinnon [1957] Director/Accountant

HSBC Global Asset Management (UK) Limited
Incorporated: 31 May 1985 *Employees:* 374
Net Worth: £133,542,000 *Total Assets:* £289,171,008
Registered Office: 8 Canada Square, London, E14 5HQ
Activities: Fund management activities
Parent: HSBC Global Asset Management Limited
Officers: Danielle Pass, Secretary; Christopher Spencer Cheetham [1955] Director/Chief Executive Officer; Andrew Simon Clark [1969] Director; Anthony Charles Corfield [1965] Director/Chief Operating Officer; Peter George Patrick Dew [1945] Director; Philip James Francis Glaze [1964] Director/Chief Investment Officer; Joanna Mary Munro [1962] Director/Global Head of Fiduciary Governance; Timothy James Palmer [1954] Director; Jennifer Rosalind Paterson [1953] Director

HSBC Global Asset Management Limited
Incorporated: 19 February 1982 *Employees:* 152
Net Worth: £376,249,984 *Total Assets:* £760,737,024
Registered Office: 8 Canada Square, London, E14 5HQ
Activities: Activities of financial services holding companies
Parent: HSBC Holdings PLC
Officers: Danielle Pass, Secretary; Sridhar Chandrasekharan [1970] Director/Chief Executive [Indian]; Christopher Spencer Cheetham [1955] Director/Global Chief Investment Office; Christophe Raoul Fernand de Backer [1962] Director [French]; George Andrew Efthimiou [1963] Director/Chief Operating Officer; Stephen Colin Moss [1967] Director/Chief of Staff; Charlie Nunn [1971] Director; Jennifer Rosalind Paterson [1953] Director; Antonio Simoes [1975] Director; John Francis Trueman [1943] Director

HSBC Global Services (China) Holdings Limited
Incorporated: 23 November 2001
Previous: HSBC Canada Holdings (UK) Limited
Net Worth: £1,645,356,672 *Total Assets:* £1,645,356,672
Registered Office: 8 Canada Square, London, E14 5HQ
Activities: Activities of financial services holding companies
Parent: HSBC Overseas Holdings (UK) Limited
Officers: Romana Lewis, Secretary; Gavin Andrew Francis [1965] Director/Accountant; Richard John Hennity [1970] Director/Lawyer; Iain Francis MacKinnon [1957] Director/Accountant

HSBC Global Services Limited
Incorporated: 29 November 2005 *Employees:* 32
Net Worth: £259,742,304 *Total Assets:* £541,986,048
Registered Office: 8 Canada Square, London, E14 5HQ
Activities: Activities of head offices
Parent: HSBC Holdings PLC
Officers: Rhys Williams, Secretary; Maria Andrea Colin [1970] Director/Chief Financial Officer [American]; Michael Stewart Henley [1960] Director/Banker; Richard John Hennity [1970] Director/Lawyer; Helen Ruth Horgan [1965] Director; Iain Francis MacKinnon [1957] Director/Accountant; Menasey Marc Moses [1957] Director/Accountant

HSBC Holdings PLC
Incorporated: 1 January 1959 *Employees:* 44,788
Net Worth: £135,573,291,008 *Total Assets:* £1,797,029,101,568
Registered Office: 8 Canada Square, London, E14 5HQ
Activities: Activities of head offices
Officers: Benedict John Spurway Mathews, Secretary; Kathleen Louise Casey [1966] Director/Consultant [American]; Laura May Lung Cha [1949] Director [Chinese]; Monsieur Henri Reni Marie Augustin de La Croix de Castries [1954] Director [French]; Sir Jonathan Douglas Evans [1958] Director; John Michael Flint [1968] Director/Chief Executive Officer; Irene Yun Lien Lee [1953] Director/Chairman, Hysan Development Company Limited [Chinese]; Dr. Jose Antonio Meade Kuribrena [1969] Independent Non-Executive Director [Mexican]; Heidi Miller [1953] Director [American]; Menasey Marc Moses [1957] Director/Accountant; David Thomas Nish [1960] Director; Ewen James Stevenson [1966] Director/Group Chief Financial Officer; Jonathan Richard Symonds [1959] Director/Chartered Accountant; Jackson Peter Tai [1950] Non-Employee Non-Executive Director [American]; Mark Edward Tucker [1957] Director/Group Chairman; Pauline Francoise Marie Van Der Meer Mohr [1960] Director [Dutch]

HSBC Investment Bank Holdings Limited
Incorporated: 22 December 1995
Previous: HSBC Investment Bank Holdings PLC
Net Worth: £559,254,848 *Total Assets:* £1,048,858,816
Registered Office: 8 Canada Square, London, E14 5HQ
Activities: Activities of financial services holding companies
Parent: HSBC Bank PLC
Officers: Felipe Chagas Villasuso Lago, Secretary; Richard Martin Blackburn [1965] Director/Risk Management; Edward James Jenkins [1974] Director/Chief Risk Officer; Jonathan Peter Marlow [1968] Director/Banker; Peter John Reid [1962] Director/Accountant

HSBC Latin America B.V.
Incorporated: 1 October 2013
Net Worth: £877,253,696 *Total Assets:* £877,330,560
Registered Office: 8-14 Canada Square, London, E14 5HQ
Officers: Gavin Andrew Francis [1965] Director/Accountant; Richard John Hennity [1970] Director/Lawyer; Iain Francis MacKinnon [1957] Director/Accountant

HSBC Latin America Holdings (UK) Limited
Incorporated: 24 January 1980
Net Worth: £3,936,082,176 *Total Assets:* £4,751,256,576
Registered Office: 8 Canada Square, London, E14 5HQ
Activities: Activities of head offices
Parent: HSBC Holdings PLC
Officers: Marcial Lujan, Secretary; Edgar David Ancona [1952] Director/Retired Chief Financial Officer [American]; Maria Andrea Colin [1970] Director [American]; Nicholas Bernard Frank Fishwick [1958] Director; Iain Francis MacKinnon [1957] Director; Paulo Cezar Torre Maia [1958] Director [Brazilian]; Graham Alexander McIsaac [1951] Director/Chartered Accountant [Canadian]; Brian Robertson [1954] Director/Banker; Martin David Spurling [1966] Director

HSBC Life (UK) Limited
Incorporated: 8 May 1906
Net Worth: £152,410,000 *Total Assets:* £1,498,814,976
Registered Office: 8 Canada Square, London, E14 5HQ
Activities: Life insurance
Parent: HSBC Bank PLC
Officers: Andrew Douglas Van Den Aardweg [1954] Director/Chartered Accountant [South African/British]; Michael John Bolton [1950] Director/Actuary; Douglas Angus Clow [1968] Director/Accountant; Nigel John Cooke [1955] Director/Actuary; Margot Cronin [1963] Non-Employee Non-Executive Director [Irish]; Neil Richard Davies [1968] Director/Actuary; Mark Erden Hussein [1966] Director/Head of Insurance and Investments; Tracy Amanda Pearce [1973] Director; Paul Kenneth Seward [1956] Director/General Manager

HSBC Overseas Holdings (UK) Limited
Incorporated: 4 August 1982
Net Worth: £19,798,693,888 *Total Assets:* £31,377,111,040
Registered Office: 8 Canada Square, London, E14 5HQ
Activities: Activities of financial services holding companies
Parent: HSBC Holdings PLC
Officers: Romana Lewis, Secretary; Gavin Andrew Francis [1965] Director/Accountant; Richard John Hennity [1970] Director/Lawyer; Iain Francis MacKinnon [1957] Director/Accountant

HSBC Private Bank (UK) Limited
Incorporated: 17 September 1951 *Employees:* 293
Net Worth: £614,067,968 *Total Assets:* £6,404,240,896
Registered Office: 8 Canada Square, London, E14 5HQ
Activities: Banks
Parent: HSBC UK Bank PLC
Officers: Jesujuwonlo Williams, Secretary; Charles Boulton [1971] Director/Chief Executive Officer; James Coyle [1956] Director; David William Lister [1958] Director; David Stewart [1965] Director; John Francis Trueman [1943] Director

HSBC Securities (Japan) Limited
Incorporated: 7 March 1986 *Employees:* 184
Net Worth: £166,014,192 *Total Assets:* £14,962,477,056
Registered Office: 8 Canada Square, London, E14 5HQ
Activities: Financial intermediation not elsewhere classified
Parent: HSBC Asia Pacific Holdings (UK) Limited
Officers: Amar Darira [1949] Managing Director [American]; Matthew Gold [1976] Director [Australian]; Olivier Pacton [1962] Managing Director [French]; Antony John Shaw [1973] Director [Australian]; Robert Ian Wall [1978] Director Global Banking Financial Institutions Group [Canadian]

HSBC Specialist Investments Limited
Incorporated: 30 March 1998
Net Worth: £55,282,000 *Total Assets:* £198,632,992
Registered Office: 8 Canada Square, London, E14 5HQ
Activities: Financial intermediation not elsewhere classified
Parent: HSBC Investment Bank Holdings Limited
Officers: Jennafer Te Brake, Secretary; Crispin Robert John Irvin [1978] Director/Chief Financial Officer; Jonathan Peter Marlow [1968] Director/Banker; James Wilkinson [1977] Director/Banker

HSBC Trust Company (UK) Limited
Incorporated: 7 December 1909
Net Worth: £46,155,000 *Total Assets:* £182,564,992
Registered Office: 8 Canada Square, London, E14 5HQ
Activities: Financial intermediation not elsewhere classified
Parent: HSBC UK Bank PLC
Officers: Larissa Wilson, Secretary; David John Coke [1958] Director/Bank Manager; James Coyle [1956] Director; Deborah Ann Morse [1967] Director/Head of Wealth Operations; Paul Michael Spencer [1970] Director/Banking

HSIL Investments Limited
Incorporated: 2 May 2002
Net Worth: £84,001,000 *Total Assets:* £137,914,000
Registered Office: 8 Canada Square, London, E14 5HQ
Activities: Activities of financial services holding companies
Parent: HSBC Property Funds (Holding) Limited
Officers: Jennafer Te Brake, Secretary; Crispin Robert John Irvin [1978] Director/Chief Financial Officer; Jonathan Peter Marlow [1968] Director/Banker; James Wilkinson [1977] Director/Banker

Huawei Global Finance (UK) Limited
Incorporated: 19 September 2014 *Employees:* 196
Net Worth: £25,724,170 *Total Assets:* £4,441,466,880
Registered Office: 99 Bishopsgate, London, EC2M 3XD
Activities: Other business support service activities n.e.c.
Officers: Adam James Page, Secretary; Jichao Lin [1977] Director/Legal Counsel [Chinese]; Guo Wei [1973] Director [Australian]; Guolin Yuan [1973] Director [Chinese]

Hubbell (UK) Gulfmex Limited
Incorporated: 2 March 2015
Net Worth: £496,339,808 *Total Assets:* £496,363,552
Registered Office: Cannon Place, 78 Cannon Street, London, EC4N 6AF
Activities: Other professional, scientific and technical activities n.e.c.
Parent: Hubbell Incorporated
Officers: Jonathan Griffith Toby Balmer [1958] Director/Comptroller/Finance; An-Ping Hsieh [1960] Director/Senior VP, General Counsel and Secretary [American]; Maria Ricciardone Lee [1975] Director/Vice President, Treasurer and Investor Relations [American]

Hubbell Holdings Europe Limited
Incorporated: 14 May 2013
Net Worth: £137,494,000 *Total Assets:* £227,494,000
Registered Office: Cannon Place, 78 Cannon Street, London, EC4N 6AF
Activities: Activities of head offices
Parent: Hubbell Incorporated
Officers: Jonathan Griffith Toby Balmer [1958] Director/Comptroller/Finance; An-Ping Hsieh [1960] Director/Senior VP, General Counsel and Secretary [American]; Maria Ricciardone Lee [1975] Director/VP - Treasurer & Investor Relations [American]; Rodd Richard Ruland [1957] Director/Group President, Construction and Energy [American]; Markus Schneider [1967] Director of Finance [Swiss]; Darrin Sylvanus Wegman [1967] Director/Group President, Commercial and Industrial [American]

Hull Esteem Consortium PSP Limited
Incorporated: 9 December 2009
Net Worth Deficit: £365,781 *Total Assets:* £118,459,232
Registered Office: Cannon Place, 78 Cannon Street, London, EC4N 6AF
Activities: Other business support service activities n.e.c.
Shareholders: Cobalt Project Investments (Hull-Sewell) Limited; Cobalt Project Investments (Hull BSF) Limited; Cobalt Project Investments (Hull) Limited
Officers: John Stephen Gordon [1962] Director; Peter Kenneth Johnstone [1965] Director; David Adrian Leedham [1967] Director/Accountant

Humber Gateway OFTO Holdings Limited
Incorporated: 9 March 2016
Net Worth Deficit: £2,687,000 *Total Assets:* £180,614,000
Registered Office: Balfour Beatty Investments Limited, 6th Floor, 350 Euston Road, London, NW1 3AX
Activities: Transmission of electricity
Parent: Equitix Infrastructure 4 Limited
Officers: Rosamond Holden, Secretary; Rebecca Collins [1971] Development Director; John Sinclair [1962] Director; Nathan John Wakefield [1974] Director; Brian Roland Walker [1955] Director

Humber Gateway OFTO Limited
Incorporated: 9 March 2016
Net Worth Deficit: £2,687,000 *Total Assets:* £180,614,000
Registered Office: Balfour Beatty Investments Limited, 6th Floor, 350 Euston Road, London, NW1 3AX
Activities: Transmission of electricity
Shareholders: Humber Gateway OFTO Holdings Limited; Humber Gateway OFTO Holdings Limited
Officers: Rosamond Holden, Secretary; Rebecca Collins [1971] Development Director; John Sinclair [1962] Director; Nathan John Wakefield [1974] Director; Brian Roland Walker [1955] Director

Hunt Amber London 1 Ltd
Incorporated: 24 February 2015
Net Worth: £118,915,448 *Total Assets:* £118,923,536
Registered Office: Suite 1, 3rd Floor, 11-12 St James's Square, London, SW1Y 4LB
Activities: Activities of head offices
Major Shareholder: Woodley Larkin Hunt
Officers: James Christopher Hunt [1970] Director [American]; Daniel Charles Singer [1960] Director/Executive [American]

Hunt Amber London 2 Ltd
Incorporated: 24 February 2015
Net Worth: £32,161,894 *Total Assets:* £120,805,328
Registered Office: Suite 1, 3rd Floor, 11-12 St James's Square, London, SW1Y 4LB
Activities: Activities of head offices
Parent: Hunt Amber London 1 Ltd
Officers: James Christopher Hunt [1970] Director [American]; Daniel Charles Singer [1960] Director/Executive [American]

Hunter Up 1 Limited
Incorporated: 12 July 2005
Net Worth Deficit: £71,969,376 *Total Assets:* £235,827,264
Registered Office: 35 Great St Helen's, London, EC3A 6AP
Activities: Other business support service activities n.e.c.
Parent: Intertrust Corporate Services Limited
Officers: Susan Iris Abrahams [1957] Director; Jane Alison Stammers [1963] Director

Hunting Energy Holdings Limited
Incorporated: 1 February 1974
Net Worth: £480,680,128 *Total Assets:* £481,165,184
Registered Office: 5 Hanover Square, London, W1S 1HQ
Activities: Activities of head offices
Parent: Hunting PLC
Officers: Ben Willey, Secretary; Mark Edwin Jarvis [1966] Director/Group Financial Controller; Arthur James Johnson [1960] Director/Chief Executive [American]; Dean Mitchell [1961] Director/Accountant; Peter Rose [1958] Finance Director; Dr Ben Willey [1973] Director/Company Secretary

Hunting Knightsbridge Holdings Limited
Incorporated: 1 June 1978
Net Worth: £74,338,328 *Total Assets:* £458,136,640
Registered Office: 5 Hanover Square, London, W1S 1HQ
Activities: Other business support service activities n.e.c.
Parent: Hunting Oil Holdings Limited
Officers: Ben Willey, Secretary; Christopher Paul Berris [1979] Director/Group Treasurer; Cormac John Peter Gilmore [1959] Director/Accountant [Irish]; Mark Edwin Jarvis [1966] Director/Group Financial Controller; Arthur James Johnson [1960] Director/Chief Executive [American]; Peter Rose [1958] Finance Director

Hunting Oil Holdings Limited
Incorporated: 23 March 1973
Net Worth: £197,497,184 *Total Assets:* £198,666,864
Registered Office: 5 Hanover Square, London, W1S 1HQ
Activities: Activities of head offices
Parent: Hunting PLC
Officers: Ben Willey, Secretary; Mark Edwin Jarvis [1966] Director/Group Financial Controller; Arthur James Johnson [1960] Director/Chief Executive [American]; Peter Rose [1958] Director/Accountant; Dr Ben Willey [1973] Director/Company Secretary

Hunting PLC
Incorporated: 13 March 1970 *Employees:* 2,384
Net Worth: £777,952,000 *Total Assets:* £912,563,264
Registered Office: 5 Hanover Square, London, W1S 1HQ
Activities: Activities of head offices
Officers: David Benjamin Willey, Secretary; Annell Russell Bay [1955] Director [American]; Ellen Carol Chesney [1962] Director [American]; John Frederick Glick [1952] Director/Chairman [American]; Richard Hugh Hunting [1946] Director; Arthur James Johnson [1960] Director/Chief Executive [American]; Keith Geddes Lough [1959] Director; Peter Rose [1958] Director/Accountant

Huntsworth Holdings Limited
Incorporated: 18 October 2005 *Employees:* 2
Net Worth: £43,352,160 *Total Assets:* £198,031,232
Registered Office: 8th Floor, Holborn Gate, 26 Southampton Buildings, London, WC2A 1AN
Activities: Activities of head offices
Parent: Huntsworth PLC
Officers: Martin Morrow [1967] Director/Chartered Accountant; Paul Anthony Taaffe [1961] Director/Chief Executive [American]

Huntsworth PLC
Incorporated: 6 June 1983 *Employees:* 1,560
Net Worth: £157,400,992 *Total Assets:* £280,356,992
Registered Office: 8th Floor, Holborn Gate, 26 Southampton Buildings, London, WC2A 1AN
Activities: Activities of head offices
Officers: Martin Morrow, Secretary; Patricia Marusia Billingham [1952] Director; Andrew Kenneth Boland [1969] Director; Nicola Joy Dulieu [1963] Director; Neil Garth Jones [1966] Director/Chief Financial Officer; David Soutar Lowden [1957] Director; Derek Mapp [1950] Director; Elizabeth McKee Anderson [1957] Director [American]; Paul Anthony Taaffe [1961] Director/Chief Executive [American]

Hurricane Bidco Limited
Incorporated: 7 November 2016
Net Worth: £229,351,168 *Total Assets:* £362,300,128
Registered Office: 401 Westbourne Studios, 242 Acklam Road, London, W10 5JJ
Activities: Activities of financial services holding companies
Parent: Hurricane Cleanco Limited
Officers: Juan Sebastien Farrarons [1976] Director [French]; George Vahak Karibian [1964] Director/Entrepreneur - Management

Hurricane Cleanco Limited
Incorporated: 7 November 2016 *Employees:* 252
Net Worth: £162,449,520 *Total Assets:* £298,314,912
Registered Office: 401 Westbourne Studios, 242 Acklam Road, London, W10 5JJ
Activities: Activities of financial services holding companies
Parent: Hurricane Noteco Limited
Officers: Juan Sebastien Farrarons [1976] Director [French]; George Vahak Karibian [1964] Director/Entrepreneur - Management

Hurricane Noteco Limited
Incorporated: 7 November 2016 *Employees:* 252
Net Worth: £162,428,864 *Total Assets:* £298,236,384
Registered Office: 401 Westbourne Studios, 242 Acklam Road, London, W10 5JJ
Activities: Activities of financial services holding companies
Parent: Typhoon Bidco Limited
Officers: Juan Sebastien Farrarons [1976] Director [French]; George Vahak Karibian [1964] Director/Entrepreneur - Management

Hutchison Whampoa Finance UK PLC
Incorporated: 7 November 2006
Net Worth Deficit: £206,934 *Total Assets:* £402,392,480
Registered Office: Hutchison House, 5 Hester Road, Battersea, London, SW11 4AN
Activities: Other business support service activities n.e.c.
Officers: Edith Shih, Secretary; Dominic Kai Ming Lai [1953] Director; Neil Douglas McGee [1951] Director [Australian]; Christian Nicolas Roger Salbaing [1950] Director [French]; Frank John Sixt [1951] Director [Canadian]; Robin Cheng Khoong Sng [1940] Director [Singaporean]

Hydrasun Group Acquisitions Ltd
Incorporated: 21 January 2013
Net Worth Deficit: £33,637,000 *Total Assets:* £151,675,008
Registered Office: 48 Grosvenor Street, London, W1K 3HW
Activities: Support activities for petroleum and natural gas mining
Parent: Hydrasun Group Investments Ltd
Officers: Gary John Doherty, Secretary; Sunil Bhilotra [1971] Investment Director [Canadian]; Gary John Doherty [1970] Director; Robert Sommerville Drumond [1955] Director

Hydrasun Group Finance Ltd
Incorporated: 21 January 2013 *Employees:* 2
Net Worth Deficit: £81,740,000 *Total Assets:* £100,178,000
Registered Office: 48 Grosvenor Street, London, W1K 3HW
Activities: Support activities for petroleum and natural gas mining
Parent: Hydrasun Group Holdings Ltd
Officers: Gary John Doherty, Secretary; Gary John Doherty [1970] Director; Robert Sommerville Drummond [1955] Director

Hydrasun Group Holdings Ltd
Incorporated: 21 January 2013 *Employees:* 412
Net Worth Deficit: £88,810,000 *Total Assets:* £139,722,000
Registered Office: 48 Grosvenor Street, London, W1K 3HW
Activities: Support activities for petroleum and natural gas mining
Officers: Gary John Doherty, Secretary; Sunil Bhilotra [1971] Investment Director [Canadian]; Brian Norman Dickie [1955] Director; Gary John Doherty [1970] Director; Robert Sommerville Drummond [1955] Director

Hyperion Development UK Limited
Incorporated: 10 December 2014 *Employees:* 2
Net Worth: £30,571,996 *Total Assets:* £703,024,448
Registered Office: One Creechurch Place, London, EC3A 5AF
Activities: Non-life insurance
Parent: HIG Finance 2 Limited
Officers: Andrew John Moore, Secretary; Mark Skimming Craig [1972] Director/Finance; David Philip Howden [1963] Director/Insurance Broker

Hyperion Insurance Group Limited
Incorporated: 9 June 1994 *Employees:* 3,794
Net Worth Deficit: £125,177,000 *Total Assets:* £1,388,800,000
Registered Office: One Creechurch Place, London, EC3A 5AF
Activities: Non-life insurance
Officers: Andrew John Moore, Secretary; John Daniel Bernstein [1961] Director; Clement Burns Booth [1954] Director; Andrew Dominic John Bucke Collins [1956] Director/Insurance Broker; David Charles Hodgson [1956] Director/Private Equity Investor [American]; Richard David Houghton [1965] Director; David Philip Howden [1963] Director/Insurance Broker; Signe Michel [1981] Director/Senior Associate [German]; Luis Munoz-Rojas Entrecanales [1964] Director/Insurance Executive; Thomas Mark Stephen [1957] Director

I-Environment Investments Limited
Incorporated: 31 March 2011 *Employees:* 8
Net Worth: £90,873,640 *Total Assets:* £161,582,352
Registered Office: The Broadgate Tower, 20 Primrose Street, London, EC2A 2EW
Activities: Other professional, scientific and technical activities n.e.c.
Shareholders: Itochu Corporation; Itochu Europe PLC
Officers: Eiichiro Higashiyama [1970] Director [Japanese]; Toshio Hoshino [1967] Director [Japanese]; Hajime Ichishi [1975] Director [Japanese]; Yasuhiro Imazawa [1964] Director [Japanese]; Hiroyuki Kodera [1976] Director [Japanese]; Yuji Suzuki [1970] Managing Director [Japanese]

I-Logic Holdings Limited
Incorporated: 17 November 2017 *Employees:* 2,025
Net Worth: £315,760,960 *Total Assets:* £1,188,963,456
Registered Office: c/o Ion, 3rd Floor, One New Change, London, EC4M 9AF
Activities: Business and domestic software development
Parent: Ion Investment Group Limited
Officers: Ashley Woods, Secretary; Conor Gerard Clinch [1979] Director/Accountant [Irish]; Campbell Robert Dyer [1973] Director [American]; Thomas Aquinas Fleming [1958] Director [American]; Luke Flemmer [1971] Director [American]; Andrea Pignataro [1970] Director [Italian]; Anna Randall Tye [1981] Director [American]; Ashley Graham Woods [1973] Director/Solicitor

I-Logic Technologies Bidco Limited
Incorporated: 14 November 2017 *Employees:* 802
Net Worth: £577,896,960 *Total Assets:* £1,188,963,456
Registered Office: c/o Ion, 3rd Floor, One New Change, London, EC4M 9AF
Activities: Business and domestic software development
Parent: Ion Investment Group Limited
Officers: Ashley Woods, Secretary; Conor Gerard Clinch [1979] Director/Accountant [Irish]; Ashley Graham Woods [1973] Director/Solicitor

I2 Bidco Limited
Incorporated: 26 April 2007
Net Worth Deficit: £84,060,608 *Total Assets:* £193,781,888
Registered Office: Cannon Place, 78 Cannon Street, London, EC4N 6AF
Activities: Activities of head offices
Parent: I2 Holdco Limited
Officers: John Ivor Cavill [1972] Director; James Peter Dawes [1971] Director/Chief Financial Officer

I2 Holdco 2 Limited
Incorporated: 8 May 2007
Net Worth: £4,303,124 *Total Assets:* £177,586,976
Registered Office: Cannon Place, 78 Cannon Street, London, EC4N 6AF
Activities: Activities of head offices
Parent: BIIF Bidco Limited
Officers: John Ivor Cavill [1972] Director; James Peter Dawes [1971] Director/Chief Financial Officer

I2 Holdco Limited
Incorporated: 26 April 2007
Net Worth: £1,396 *Total Assets:* £196,745,360
Registered Office: Cannon Place, 78 Cannon Street, London, EC4N 6AF
Activities: Activities of head offices
Parent: I2 Holdco 2 Limited
Officers: John Ivor Cavill [1972] Director; James Peter Dawes [1971] Director/Chief Financial Officer

IAG UK Holdings Limited
Incorporated: 28 November 2006 *Employees:* 3
Net Worth: £399,432,224 *Total Assets:* £407,060,896
Registered Office: c/o Hackwood Secretaries Limited, One Silk Street, London, EC2Y 8HQ
Activities: Non-trading company
Officers: Nicholas Barrie Hawkins [1967] Director/Chief Financial Officer [Australian]; Michael Anthony Sampson [1951] Director/Chartered Accountant; Leonard Francis West [1951] Director/Chartered Accountant

IBC (Ten) Limited
Incorporated: 31 August 1984 *Employees:* 4
Net Worth: £122,524,000 *Total Assets:* £123,641,000
Registered Office: 5 Howick Place, London, SW1P 1WG
Activities: Other business support service activities n.e.c.
Parent: Informa Group PLC
Officers: Rupert John Joseph Hopley, Secretary; Simon Robert Bane [1971] Director/Solicitor; Rupert John Joseph Hopley [1969] Director/Solicitor; Nicholas Michael Perkins [1969] Tax Director; Gareth Richard Wright [1972] Director/Accountant [Australian]

IBC Fourteen Limited
Incorporated: 27 October 1995 *Employees:* 4
Net Worth: £471,599,008 *Total Assets:* £472,457,984
Registered Office: 5 Howick Place, London, SW1P 1WG
Activities: Activities of head offices
Parent: Informa Holdings Limited
Officers: Rupert John Joseph Hopley, Secretary; Simon Robert Bane [1971] Director/Solicitor; Rupert John Joseph Hopley [1969] Director/Solicitor; Nicholas Michael Perkins [1969] Tax Director; Gareth Richard Wright [1972] Director/Accountant [Australian]

IBM Global Asset Management Limited
Incorporated: 17 May 2013
Net Worth: £103,059,424 *Total Assets:* £1,550,872,192
Registered Office: 76 Upper Ground, South Bank, London, SE1 9PZ
Activities: Financial intermediation not elsewhere classified
Parent: International Business Machines Corporation
Officers: Hayden James Gunton Reeve, Secretary; Timothy John Martin Clements [1970] Director; Edward Thomas Cook [1975] Director; Joanne Louise Stanton [1972] Director

IBM Global Financing UK Company
Incorporated: 27 December 2001
Net Worth: £699,078,016 *Total Assets:* £699,363,008
Registered Office: 76 Upper Ground, London, SE1 9PZ
Activities: Activities of head offices
Parent: International Business Machines Corporation
Officers: Hayden James Gunton Reeve, Secretary; Timothy John Martin Clements [1970] Director; Edward Thomas Cook [1975] Director; Joanne Louise Stanton [1972] Director

IBM North Region Holdings
Incorporated: 24 May 2001 *Employees:* 3
Net Worth: £536,609,664 *Total Assets:* £3,164,149,248
Registered Office: 76 Upper Ground, London, SE1 9PZ
Activities: Activities of head offices
Parent: International Business Machines Corporation
Officers: Ian Duncan Ferguson, Secretary; Timothy Daren Matthew Eagle [1972] Director/Business Executive; William Anthony Kelleher [1963] Director/IBM Executive; Flavio Sciutti [1961] Director/Finance Executive [Italian]

ICAP America Investments Limited
Incorporated: 18 February 2003
Net Worth: £183,367,008 *Total Assets:* £188,094,000
Registered Office: Floor 2, 155 Bishopsgate, London, EC2M 3TQ
Activities: Activities of financial services holding companies
Parent: ICAP Global Broking Holdings Limited
Officers: Paul James Ashley [1978] Finance Director; Richard Cordeschi [1967] Director/Chartered Secretary

ICAP Global Broking Finance Limited
Incorporated: 16 September 2016
Net Worth: £327,472,320 *Total Assets:* £331,522,176
Registered Office: Floor 2, 155 Bishopsgate, London, EC2M 3TQ
Activities: Activities of financial services holding companies
Parent: ICAP Global Broking Holdings Limited
Officers: Paul James Ashley [1978] Finance Director; Richard Cordeschi [1967] Director/Chartered Secretary

ICAP Global Broking Holdings Limited
Incorporated: 11 June 2014
Net Worth: £1,099,486,976 *Total Assets:* £2,928,928,000
Registered Office: Floor 2, 155 Bishopsgate, London, EC2M 3TQ
Activities: Activities of financial services holding companies
Parent: TP ICAP PLC
Officers: Philip Price [1965] Director/Group General Counsel; Robin James Stewart [1967] Director

ICAP Global Broking Investments
Incorporated: 12 June 2014
Net Worth: £60,088,120 *Total Assets:* £370,399,200
Registered Office: Floor 2, 155 Bishopsgate, London, EC2M 3TQ
Activities: Activities of financial services holding companies
Parent: Tullett Prebon Investment Holdings Limited
Officers: Paul James Ashley [1978] Finance Director; Richard Cordeschi [1967] Director/Chartered Secretary

ICAP Holdings (UK) Limited
Incorporated: 15 February 2008
Net Worth: £223,316,992 *Total Assets:* £247,348,000
Registered Office: Floor 2, 155 Bishopsgate, London, EC2M 3TQ
Activities: Activities of financial services holding companies
Parent: ICAP Securities Limited
Officers: Paul James Ashley [1978] Finance Director; Jack Scard-Morgan [1962] Director/Chief Operating Officer

ICAP Holdings Limited
Incorporated: 10 September 2008
Net Worth: £497,791,008 *Total Assets:* £502,540,992
Registered Office: Floor 2, 155 Bishopsgate, London, EC2M 3TQ
Activities: Activities of financial services holding companies
Parent: ICAP Global Broking Holdings Limited
Officers: Paul James Ashley [1978] Finance Director; Richard Cordeschi [1967] Director/Chartered Secretary

ICAP Management Services Limited
Incorporated: 6 November 1987 *Employees:* 349
Net Worth: £48,775,000 *Total Assets:* £190,948,992
Registered Office: Floor 2, 155 Bishopsgate, London, EC2M 3TQ
Activities: Activities of head offices
Parent: ICAP Holdings Limited
Officers: Philip Price [1965] Director/Group General Counsel; Jack Scard-Morgan [1962] Director; Robin James Stewart [1967] Director

ICAP Securities Limited
Incorporated: 27 October 1951 *Employees:* 83
Net Worth: £351,040,992 *Total Assets:* £3,245,105,920
Registered Office: Floor 2, 155 Bishopsgate, London, EC2M 3TQ
Activities: Security and commodity contracts dealing activities
Parent: ICAP Global Broking Holdings Limited
Officers: Nicolas Noel Andre Breteau [1968] Director [French]; Jack Scard-Morgan [1962] Director/Chief Operating Officer; Garry Hunter Stewart [1970] Director/Stockbroker; Frederik Vogels [1964] Director [Dutch]

ICAP WCLK Limited
Incorporated: 2 October 1984 *Employees:* 11
Net Worth: £8,961,000 *Total Assets:* £118,228,000
Registered Office: Floor 2, 155 Bishopsgate, London, EC2M 3TQ
Activities: Security and commodity contracts dealing activities
Parent: ICAP Holdings (UK) Limited
Officers: Jack Scard-Morgan [1962] Director/Chief Operating Officer; Frederik Vogels [1964] Director [Dutch]

ICBC (London) PLC
Incorporated: 3 October 2002 *Employees:* 151
Net Worth: £300,112,992 *Total Assets:* £1,831,441,792
Registered Office: 81 King William Street, London, EC4N 7BG
Activities: Banks
Parent: Industrial and Commercial Bank of China Limited
Officers: John Kerr, Secretary; Alan Gemes [1956] Director/Management Consultant; Ruixiang Han [1963] Director/Banker [Chinese]; Dr. Hao Hu [1962] Director/Banker [Chinese]; John Kerr [1948] Director/Banker; Qingsheng Lin [1968] Director/Banker [Chinese]; David Newton [1955] Director/Chartered Accountant; Shuyi Yuan [1966] Director/Banker [Chinese]

ICBC Standard Bank PLC
Incorporated: 11 May 1987
Previous: Standard Bank PLC
Net Worth: £913,774,656 *Total Assets:* £16,998,289,408
Registered Office: 20 Gresham Street, London, EC2V 7JE
Activities: Banks
Shareholder: Standard Bank London Holdings Limited
Officers: Robert James Otterson, Secretary; Isabella Derizans Da Costa Mendes [1969] Director/Banker [Portuguese]; Judith Elizabeth Eden [1964] Director; Andrew Hall [1965] Director/Banker; Ruixiang Han [1963] Director/Banker [Chinese]; Binliang Jin [1972] Director/Banker [Chinese]; Barend Johannes Kruger [1959] Director/Banker [South African]; Andrew Warwick Simmonds [1956] Director/Banker; Marc Martin Van Der Spuy [1966] Director/Chief Executive; Hailu Wang [1977] Director/Banker [Chinese]; Lubin Wang [1973] Director/Banker [Chinese]; Dr Shoujiang Wang [1973] Director/Banker [Chinese]; Wenbin Wang [1975] Director/Banker [Chinese]; Ruwan Upendra Weerasekera [1966] Director

ICE Asia Holdings Limited
Incorporated: 16 October 2013
Net Worth: £119,342,512 *Total Assets:* £119,354,816
Registered Office: 5th Floor, Milton Gate, 60 Chiswell Street, London, EC1Y 4SA
Activities: Activities of financial services holding companies
Parent: Aether IOS Limited
Officers: Elizabeth Miriam Holt, Secretary; Scott Anthony Hill [1967] Director [American]; Andrew James Surdykowski [1970] Director [American]; Stuart Glen Williams [1978] Director [South African]

Ice Clear Europe Limited
Incorporated: 19 April 2007 *Employees:* 77
Net Worth: £472,626,112 *Total Assets:* £18,150,565,888
Registered Office: Milton Gate, 60 Chiswell Street, London, EC1Y 4SA
Activities: Administration of financial markets
Parent: Intercontinentalexchange Holdings
Officers: Kelly Anne Millar, Secretary; Roger Nigel Barton [1954] Director/Consultant; Ann Cairns [1957] Director; Scott Anthony Hill [1967] Director/Chief Finance Officer [American]; Finbarr Patrick Hutcheson [1969] Director [Irish]; Lynn Alexandra Johansen [1959] Director/Lawyer; Andrew John Mack [1961] Director; Peter Harrison Nicholls [1946] Director; James Philip Repard [1956] Director; Jeffrey Craig Sprecher [1955] Director [American]; Ronald K Tanemura [1963] Director/Consultant [American]

Ice Europe Parent Limited
Incorporated: 25 June 2010
Net Worth: £3,998,384,640 *Total Assets:* £6,344,938,496
Registered Office: 5th Floor, Milton Gate, 60 Chiswell Street, London, EC1Y 4SA
Activities: Activities of financial services holding companies
Parent: Ice Europe Partners LP
Officers: Elizabeth Miriam Holt, Secretary; Scott Anthony Hill [1967] Director [American]; Andrew James Surdykowski [1970] Director [American]; Stuart Glen Williams [1978] Director [South African]

ICE Overseas Limited
Incorporated: 1 July 2011 *Employees:* 4
Net Worth: £386,698,624 *Total Assets:* £386,730,048
Registered Office: 5th Floor, Milton Gate, 60 Chiswell Street, London, EC1Y 4SA
Activities: Activities auxiliary to financial intermediation n.e.c.
Parent: Aether IOS Limited
Officers: Elizabeth Miriam Holt, Secretary; Scott Anthony Hill [1967] Director [American]; Andrew James Surdykowski [1970] Director [American]; Stuart Glen Williams [1978] Director [South African]

Icebox Bidco Limited
Incorporated: 18 April 2017
Net Worth: £271,923,392 *Total Assets:* £271,952,160
Registered Office: c/o Alter Domus (UK) Limited, 18 St Swithin's Lane, London, EC4N 8AD
Activities: Activities of other holding companies n.e.c.
Officers: Paul Richard Armstrong [1973] Director/Solicitor; Matthew Leonard Molton [1983] Director/Chartered Accountant

ICF Debt Pool LLP
Incorporated: 10 September 2009
Net Worth Deficit: £15,959,701 *Total Assets:* £261,841,776
Registered Office: c/o PIDG Ltd, 10th Floor, 6 Bevis Marks, London, EC3A 7BA

ICG Carbon Funding Limited
Incorporated: 3 December 2013
Net Worth: £48,900,336 *Total Assets:* £191,791,760
Registered Office: Juxon House, 100 St Paul's Churchyard, London, EC4M 8BU
Activities: Financial intermediation not elsewhere classified
Parent: Intermediate Capital Group PLC
Officers: Benoit Laurent Pierre Durteste [1968] Director/Banker [French]; Philip Henry Keller [1965] Director/Accountant

ICG Enterprise Trust PLC
Incorporated: 29 June 1981
Previous: Graphite Enterprise Trust PLC
Net Worth: £664,323,008 *Total Assets:* £665,286,016
Registered Office: Juxon House, 100 St Paul's Churchyard, London, EC4M 8BU
Activities: Activities of investment trusts
Officers: Alastair Charles Bruce [1963] Director; Sandra Pajarola [1963] Director [Swiss]; Andrew David Pomfret [1960] Director/Accountant; Lucinda Jane Riches [1961] Director; Jeremy John Tigue [1959] Director/Fund Manager

ICG FMC Limited
Incorporated: 26 May 2010 *Employees:* 160
Net Worth Deficit: £57,800,000 *Total Assets:* £188,100,000
Registered Office: Juxon House, 100 St Paul's Churchyard, London, EC4M 8BU
Activities: Activities of head offices
Parent: Intermediate Capital Group PLC
Officers: Benoit Laurent Pierre Durteste [1968] Director/Banker [French]; Philip Henry Keller [1965] Finance Director

ICG Global Investment UK Limited
Incorporated: 25 May 2011
Net Worth: £1,048,268,992 *Total Assets:* £1,048,268,992
Registered Office: Juxon House, 100 St Paul's Churchyard, London, EC4M 8BU
Activities: Financial intermediation not elsewhere classified
Parent: Intermediate Capital Group PLC
Officers: Benoit Laurent Pierre Durteste [1968] Director/Banker [French]; Philip Henry Keller [1965] Director/Accountant

ICG-Longbow Senior Debt Investments No. 1 LLP
Incorporated: 5 February 2014
Net Worth: £394,217,632 *Total Assets:* £394,285,056
Registered Office: 42 Wigmore Street, London, W1U 2RY

ICICI Bank UK PLC
Incorporated: 11 February 2003 *Employees:* 178
Net Worth: £381,676,576 *Total Assets:* £2,925,615,616
Registered Office: One Thomas More Square, London, E1W 1YN
Activities: Building societies
Officers: Aarti Sharma, Secretary; Sandeep Batra [1966] Director [Indian]; John Warwick Burbidge [1958] Director; Vijay Kumar Chandok [1968] Director/Banker [Indian]; Sir Alan Stanley Collins [1948] Director; Loknath Mishra [1969] Director/MD & CEO [Indian]; Robert Huw Morgan [1960] Director

ICP Capital Limited
Incorporated: 17 June 2005
Net Worth: £2,026,000 *Total Assets:* £333,624,992
Registered Office: Unit A21 Jacks Place, Corbet Place, London, E1 6NN
Activities: Non-life insurance
Parent: ICP Holdings Ltd
Officers: Andrew Staley Fox, Secretary; Sir Nicholas Hickman Ponsonby Bacon [1953] Director/Self Employed; Lord Jonathan Peter Marland of Odstock [1956] Director; Robin Crispin William Odey [1959] Director/Chief Investment Officer; Timothy Shenton [1954] Director/Chartered Accountant

ICP Holdings Limited
Incorporated: 2 August 2006
Net Worth: £10,065,000 *Total Assets:* £341,024,992
Registered Office: Unit A21 Jacks Place, 6 Corbet Place, London, E1 6NN
Activities: Life insurance
Officers: Andrew Staley Fox, Secretary; Sir Nicholas Hickman Ponsonsby Bacon [1953] Director; Lord Jonathan Peter Marland of Odstock [1956] Director; Robin Crispin William Odey [1959] Director/Investment Manager; Timothy Shenton [1954] Director/Chartered Accountant

IDCO Overseas Holdings Limited
Incorporated: 13 December 2002
Net Worth: £177,144,992 *Total Assets:* £177,159,008
Registered Office: Milton Gate, 60 Chiswell Street, London, EC1Y 4SA
Activities: Activities of other holding companies n.e.c.
Parent: IDCO Worldwide Holdings Limited
Officers: Elizabeth Miriam Holt, Secretary; Scott Anthony Hill [1967] Director [American]; Timothy Taihibou Michael Frederic Noble [1966] Director; Andrew James Surdykowski [1970] Director [American]; Stuart Glen Williams [1978] Director [South African]

IDCO Worldwide Holdings Limited
Incorporated: 13 December 2002 *Employees:* 5
Net Worth: £166,934,000 *Total Assets:* £166,948,000
Registered Office: Milton Gate, 60 Chiswell Street, London, EC1Y 4SA
Activities: Activities of other holding companies n.e.c.
Parent: Interactive Data Luxembourg Management S.A.R.L
Officers: Elizabeth Miriam Holt, Secretary; Scott Anthony Hill [1967] Director [American]; Timothy Taihibou Michael Frederic Noble [1966] Director; Andrew James Surdykowski [1970] Director [American]; Stuart Glen Williams [1978] Director [South African]

Idex UK Investment Ltd
Incorporated: 25 May 2011
Net Worth: £8,231,235 *Total Assets:* £165,039,488
Registered Office: 100 New Bridge Street, London, EC4V 6JA
Activities: Activities of head offices
Parent: Idex Corporation
Officers: Lisa Michelle Anderson, Secretary; Brian Patrick Hanigan, Secretary; Lisa Michelle Anderson [1976] Director/Attorney [American]; Denise Rene Perry Cade [1962] Director/Business Executive [American]; William Kevin Grogan [1978] Director/Business Executive [American]; Neil Thompson [1965] Director/Business Executive

Idex UK Ltd.
Incorporated: 16 September 2008
Net Worth: £32,924,068 *Total Assets:* £111,252,568
Registered Office: 100 New Bridge Street, London, EC4V 6JA
Activities: Financial intermediation not elsewhere classified
Parent: Idex Corporation
Officers: Lisa Michelle Anderson, Secretary; Brian Patrick Hanigan, Secretary; Lisa Michelle Anderson [1976] Director/Attorney [American]; Denise Rene Perry Cade [1962] Director/Business Executive [American]

IDR Finance UK II Limited
Incorporated: 21 March 2012
Net Worth: £568,535 *Total Assets:* £109,176,384
Registered Office: Camelford House, 89 Albert Embankment, London, SE1 7TP
Activities: Fund management activities
Officers: Selina Lee Burdell [1969] Director; Adrian Richard Cloake [1975] Director

IEP Infrastructure Holdco Limited
Incorporated: 25 May 2017
Net Worth Deficit: £1,325,299 *Total Assets:* £123,751,448
Registered Office: 15 Golden Square, London, W1F 9JG
Activities: Activities of other holding companies n.e.c.
Parent: IEP Infrastructure Topco Limited
Officers: Sarah Cruickshank, Secretary; Jennifer Wright, Secretary; Roberto Castiglioni [1976] Investment Director [Italian]; Sebastian James Speight [1967] Director

IFG UK Holdings Limited
Incorporated: 19 December 2006
Net Worth: £99,841,000 *Total Assets:* £100,124,000
Registered Office: 1 Gresham Street, London, EC2V 7BX
Activities: Other professional, scientific and technical activities n.e.c.
Parent: IFG Group PLC
Officers: Richard Andrew Beale [1955] Compliance Director; Kathryn Elizabeth Purves [1973] Director/Chief Executive

IG Communications Limited
Incorporated: 1 April 1986 *Employees:* 2
Net Worth: £52,107,000 *Total Assets:* £337,876,992
Registered Office: 8th Floor, Holborn Gate, 26 Southampton Buildings, London, WC2A 1AN
Activities: Activities of head offices
Parent: Huntsworth Holdings Limited
Officers: Martin Morrow [1967] Director/Chartered Accountant; Paul Anthony Taaffe [1961] Director/Chief Executive [American]

IG Finance
Incorporated: 23 January 2004
Net Worth: £150,916,576 *Total Assets:* £150,916,576
Registered Office: Cannon Bridge House, 25 Dowgate Hill, London, EC4R 2YA
Activities: Other business support service activities n.e.c.
Parent: IG Group Limited
Officers: Tony Lee, Secretary; Paul Richard Mainwaring [1963] Director; Bridget Elizabeth Messer [1979] Director [British/Australian]; Jonathan Mark Noble [1976] Director

IG Finance Three
Incorporated: 26 November 2004
Net Worth: £179,236,992 *Total Assets:* £180,648,992
Registered Office: Cannon Bridge House, 25 Dowgate Hill, London, EC4R 2YA
Activities: Financial intermediation not elsewhere classified
Parent: IG Finance Two
Officers: Tony Lee, Secretary; Paul Richard Mainwaring [1963] Director; Bridget Elizabeth Messer [1979] Director [British/Australian]; Jonathan Mark Noble [1976] Director

IG Finance Two
Incorporated: 25 May 2004
Net Worth: £157,706,544 *Total Assets:* £157,706,544
Registered Office: Cannon Bridge House, 25 Dowgate Hill, London, EC4R 2YA
Activities: Financial intermediation not elsewhere classified
Parent: IG Finance
Officers: Tony Lee, Secretary; Paul Richard Mainwaring [1963] Director; Bridget Elizabeth Messer [1979] Director [British/Australian]; Jonathan Mark Noble [1976] Director

IG Group Holdings PLC
Incorporated: 25 February 2003 *Employees:* 1,597
Net Worth: £842,099,968 *Total Assets:* £1,061,100,032
Registered Office: Cannon Bridge House, 25 Dowgate Hill, London, EC4R 2YA
Activities: Activities of financial services holding companies
Officers: Tony Lee, Secretary; Samantha Jane Duncan [1964] Director; June Yee Felix [1956] Director [American]; Andrew James Green [1955] Director; Sally-Ann Hibberd [1965] Director; Stephen Guy Hill [1960] Director; Malcolm John Le May [1958] Director; Paul Richard Mainwaring [1963] Director; Jonathan Paul Moulds [1965] Director; James Allen Newman [1964] Director

IG Group Limited
Incorporated: 1 June 2000
Net Worth: £313,800,000 *Total Assets:* £314,800,000
Registered Office: Cannon Bridge House, 25 Dowgate Hill, London, EC4R 2YA
Activities: Activities of head offices
Parent: IG Group Holdings PLC
Officers: Tony Lee, Secretary; Paul Richard Mainwaring [1963] Director; Bridget Elizabeth Messer [1979] Director [British/Australian]; Jonathan Mark Noble [1976] Director

IG Index Limited
Incorporated: 18 November 1974 *Employees:* 765
Net Worth: £126,700,000 *Total Assets:* £191,400,000
Registered Office: Cannon Bridge House, 25 Dowgate Hill, London, EC4R 2YA
Activities: Financial intermediation not elsewhere classified
Parent: Market Data Limited
Officers: Tony Lee, Secretary; June Yee Felix [1956] Director [American]; Paul Richard Mainwaring [1963] Director; Bridget Elizabeth Messer [1979] Director [British/Australian]; Jonathan Mark Noble [1976] Director

IG Markets Limited
Incorporated: 1 June 2000 *Employees:* 174
Net Worth: £410,200,000 *Total Assets:* £712,600,000
Registered Office: Cannon Bridge House, 25 Dowgate Hill, London, EC4R 2YA
Activities: Other business support service activities n.e.c.
Parent: Market Data Limited
Officers: Tony Lee, Secretary; June Yee Felix [1956] Director [American]; Paul Richard Mainwaring [1963] Director; Bridget Elizabeth Messer [1979] Director [British/Australian]; Jonathan Mark Noble [1976] Director

IGas Energy PLC
Incorporated: 1 December 2003 *Employees:* 160
Net Worth: £181,600,992 *Total Assets:* £254,926,000
Registered Office: 7 Down Street, London, W1J 7AJ
Activities: Extraction of crude petroleum
Officers: Stephen David Bowler [1973] Director/Chief Executive Officer; Anthony Philip Jackson [1959] Director; Cuthbert John McDowell [1956] Director; Robert Michael McTighe [1953] Director; Kumar Tushar [1978] Director [Indian]

IHS Markit Group Holdings Limited
Incorporated: 9 May 2007
Previous: Markit Group Holdings Limited
Net Worth: £7,037,642,240 *Total Assets:* £10,650,873,856
Registered Office: 4th Floor, Ropemaker Place, 25 Ropemaker Street, London, EC2Y 9LY
Activities: Financial intermediation not elsewhere classified
Parent: IHS Markit Ltd
Officers: Christopher Guy McLoughlin [1978] Director/Solicitor; Kathryn Ann Owen [1976] Accounting Executive Director

IIR Exhibitions Limited
Incorporated: 28 September 1994 *Employees:* 64
Net Worth: £267,376,000 *Total Assets:* £295,873,984
Registered Office: 5 Howick Place, London, SW1P 1WG
Activities: Other service activities n.e.c.
Parent: IIR Management Limited
Officers: Rupert John Joseph Hopley, Secretary; Simon Robert Bane [1971] Director/Solicitor; Simon Robert Bane [1971] Director/Solicitor; Rupert John Joseph Hopley [1969] Director/Solicitor; Nicholas Michael Perkins [1969] Tax Director; Gareth Richard Wright [1972] Director/Accountant [Australian]

IIR Management Limited
Incorporated: 26 April 1994 *Employees:* 4
Net Worth: £255,863,008 *Total Assets:* £257,799,008
Registered Office: 5 Howick Place, London, SW1P 1WG
Activities: Activities of head offices
Parent: IBC Fourteen Limited
Officers: Rupert John Joseph Hopley, Secretary; Simon Robert Bane [1971] Director/Solicitor; Rupert John Joseph Hopley [1969] Director/Solicitor; Nicholas Michael Perkins [1969] Tax Director; Gareth Richard Wright [1972] Director/Accountant [Australian]

Imagination Industries Ltd
Incorporated: 28 April 2009 *Employees:* 1,277
Previous: Ovo Group Ltd
Net Worth: £3,379,000 *Total Assets:* £268,537,984
Registered Office: 140-142 Kensington Church Street, London, W8 4BN
Activities: Activities of head offices
Major Shareholder: Stephen James Fitzpatrick
Officers: Vincent Francis Casey [1983] Director; Stephen Fitzpatrick [1977] Director

IMG Media Limited
Incorporated: 12 June 2002 *Employees:* 801
Net Worth: £44,988,284 *Total Assets:* £251,994,256
Registered Office: Building 6, Chiswick Park, 566 Chiswick High Road, London, W4 5HR
Activities: Television programme production activities
Officers: John Cooper, Secretary; John Thomas Cooper [1966] Director [American]; Duncan Edward Fay [1963] Finance Director; Ioris Francini [1973] Director/Executive Vice President - Head of Worldwide Sales [Italian]; Graham Richard Fry [1953] Director

Immediate Media Company Limited
Incorporated: 16 May 2011 *Employees:* 3
Net Worth Deficit: £21,289,000 *Total Assets:* £121,460,000
Registered Office: Vineyard House, 44 Brook Green, Hammersmith, London, W6 7BT
Activities: Other publishing activities
Parent: Vancouver Topco Limited
Officers: Katherine Conlon, Secretary; Thomas Pierre Bureau [1968] Director/C.E.O; Kevin Donald Langford [1964] Director/Accountant; Martin Weiss [1967] Managing Director [German]; Philipp Welte [1962] Director [German]

Impact Healthcare REIT PLC
Incorporated: 7 November 2016
Net Worth: £193,450,000 *Total Assets:* £196,383,008
Registered Office: 7th Floor, 9 Berkeley Street, London, W1J 8DW
Activities: Activities of real estate investment trusts
Officers: Rupert George Maxwell Lothian Barclay [1957] Director; Rosemary Jane Cecilia Boot [1962] Director; Paul Anthony Craig [1970] Director/Fund Manager; Philip Charles Leonard Hall [1954] Director

Impax Environmental Markets PLC
Incorporated: 7 January 2002
Net Worth: £506,907,008 *Total Assets:* £537,734,016
Registered Office: Mermaid House, 2 Puddle Dock, London, EC4V 3DB
Activities: Activities of investment trusts
Officers: Victoria Katherine Hastings [1966] Director; Aine Mary Kelly [1960] Director/Independent Impact Consultant [Irish]; Julia Le Blan [1954] Director; William Francis Sebastian Rickett [1953] Director; John Philip Henry Schomberg Scott [1952] Director

Imperial London Hotels Group Limited
Incorporated: 14 December 2010 *Employees:* 1,117
Net Worth: £233,966,352 *Total Assets:* £260,678,272
Registered Office: c/o Directors Office, Imperial Hotel, 61-66 Russell Square, London, WC1B 5BB
Activities: Activities of head offices
Shareholders: Hugh Richard Walduck; Stephen Howard Walduck
Officers: Alexander Harold Edward Peter Walduck [1971] Director/Accountant; Hugh Richard Walduck [1941] Director/Hotelier; Jason Alexander George Walduck [1970] Director/Hotelier; Nicholas Stanley Richard David Walduck [1972] Director/Hotelier; Stephen Howard Walduck [1947] Director/Hotelier; Katharine Tanya Waller [1970] Director/Hotelier; Candida Stephanie Walton [1976] Director/Hotelier

Imperial London Hotels Limited (The)
Incorporated: 10 October 1946 *Employees:* 1,104
Net Worth: £213,017,136 *Total Assets:* £238,855,712
Registered Office: The Imperial Hotel, Russell Square, Holborn, London, WC1B 5BB
Activities: Hotels and similar accommodation
Parent: Imperial London Hotels Group Ltd
Officers: Alexander Harold Edward Peter Walduck [1971] Director; Hugh Richard Walduck [1941] Director/Hotelier; Jason Alexander George Walduck [1970] Director; Nicholas Stanley Richard David Walduck [1972] Director; Stephen Howard Walduck [1947] Director/Hotelier; Katharine Tanya Waller [1970] Director; Candida Stephanie Walton [1976] Director

Inchcape Corporate Services Limited
Incorporated: 1 December 1975
Net Worth: £256,390,000 *Total Assets:* £256,512,992
Registered Office: 22A St James's Square, London, SW1Y 5LP
Activities: Activities of head offices
Parent: Inchcape International Holdings Limited
Officers: Tamsin Waterhouse, Secretary; Michael Jonathan Bowers [1967] Director; Jonathan Hartley Greenwood [1971] Director; Anton Clive Jeary [1957] Director/Company Secretary; Bertrand Mallet [1972] Director [French]; Dr Kathryn Isabel Mecklenburgh [1973] Director; Tamsin Waterhouse [1973] Director; Martin Peter Wheatley [1959] Property Director

Inchcape Finance PLC
Incorporated: 6 August 1987 *Employees:* 5
Net Worth: £117,400,000 *Total Assets:* £1,770,499,968
Registered Office: 22a St James's Square, London, SW1Y 5LP
Activities: Financial intermediation not elsewhere classified
Parent: Inchcape PLC
Officers: Michael Jonathan Bowers [1967] Director; Jonathan Hartley Greenwood [1971] Director; Bertrand Mallet [1972] Director [French]; Dr Kathryn Isabel Mecklenburgh [1973] Director; Tamsin Waterhouse [1973] Director

Inchcape International Holdings Limited
Incorporated: 12 June 1998 *Employees:* 7
Net Worth: £1,334,321,024 *Total Assets:* £2,070,939,008
Registered Office: 22a St James's Square, London, SW1Y 5LP
Activities: Activities of head offices
Parent: Inchcape PLC
Officers: Michael Jonathan Bowers [1967] Director; Jonathan Hartley Greenwood [1971] Director; Anton Clive Jeary [1957] Director; Bertrand Mallet [1972] Director [French]; Dr Kathryn Isabel Mecklenburgh [1973] Director; Tamsin Waterhouse [1973] Director; Martin Peter Wheatley [1959] Director

Inchcape PLC
Incorporated: 15 August 1958 *Employees:* 16,789
Net Worth: £1,434,200,064 *Total Assets:* £4,876,199,936
Registered Office: 22a St James's Square, London, SW1Y 5LP
Activities: Activities of head offices
Officers: Tamsin Waterhouse, Secretary; Stefan Bomhard [1967] Director [German]; Jeremy Martin Buhlmann [1959] Director; Rachel Clare Empey [1976] Director; Richard David Howes [1969] Director; Jane Sarah May Kingston [1957] Director; John Langston [1949] Director; Coline Lucille McConville [1964] Director [Australian]; Nigel Hargreaves Northridge [1956] Director; Nigel MacRae Stein [1955] Director; Till Bernhard Vestring [1964] Director [German]

Inchcape Shipping Services Holdings Limited
Incorporated: 1 December 2003 *Employees:* 3,660
Net Worth: £182,090,016 *Total Assets:* £674,154,688
Registered Office: 8th Floor, 60 Fenchurch Street, London, EC3M 4AD
Activities: Sea and coastal freight water transport
Parent: Inchcape Shipping Services World Limited
Officers: Beenadevi Mahabeer, Secretary; Kenneth Henriks [1966] Director/Chief Financial Officer [Danish]; Frank Georg Opsahl Olsen [1979] Director/Chief Operating Officer [Norwegian]

INCJ SJ Investment Limited
Incorporated: 2 March 2012
Net Worth: £215,079,904 *Total Assets:* £215,121,136
Registered Office: Hays Galleria, 1 Hays Lane, London, SE1 2RD
Activities: Activities of head offices
Parent: Ministry of Finance Japan
Officers: Peter Niklai [1973] Director [Hungarian]; Ikumori Osuka [1988] Director [Japanese]; Tetsuro Toyoda [1962] Director/Private Equity Fund Manager [Japanese]

Income Contingent Student Loans 1 (2002-2006) PLC
Incorporated: 1 February 2017
Net Worth Deficit: £13,146,779 *Total Assets:* £2,056,414,976
Registered Office: 35 Great St Helen's, London, EC3A 6AP
Activities: Financial intermediation not elsewhere classified
Parent: Income Contingent Student Loans 1 (2002-2006) Holdings Limited
Officers: Susan Iris Abrahams [1957] Director

Independent Clinical Services Limited
Incorporated: 18 May 2003 *Employees:* 247
Net Worth: £135,154,000 *Total Assets:* £209,484,000
Registered Office: Caledonia House, 223 Pentonville Road, London, N1 9NG
Activities: Other activities of employment placement agencies
Parent: ICS Healthcare Services Limited
Officers: Thomas Christopher Richards, Secretary; Richard Paul Thomas Macmillan [1970] Director; Thomas Christopher Richards [1977] Director

India Infrastructure Finance Company (UK) Limited
Incorporated: 7 February 2008 *Employees:* 3
Net Worth: £92,209,344 *Total Assets:* £1,724,697,088
Registered Office: Third Floor, 72 King William Street, London, EC4N 7HR
Activities: Credit granting by non-deposit taking finance houses and other specialist consumer credit grantors
Parent: The Government of The Republic of India
Officers: Sanjiv Chadha [1963] Director [Indian]; Naresh Goyal [1971] Managing Director [Indian]; Pankaj Jain [1965] Director/Government Service [Indian]; Manoj Kumar Ladwa [1973] Director/Legal Professional

Indigo Bidco Limited
Incorporated: 6 May 2014 *Employees:* 2
Net Worth Deficit: £75,287,000 *Total Assets:* £362,772,992
Registered Office: Caledonia House, 223 Pentonville Road, London, N1 9NG
Activities: Activities of head offices
Parent: Indigo Cleanco Limited
Officers: Thomas Christopher Richards, Secretary; Gordon Andrew Holmes [1969] Director [Irish]; Richard Paul Thomas Macmillan [1970] Director; Edouard Andre Gerard Peugeot [1984] Director [French]; Thomas Christopher Richards [1977] Director

Indigo Cleanco Limited
Incorporated: 29 May 2014
Net Worth: £1,525,000 *Total Assets:* £171,831,008
Registered Office: Caledonia House, 223 Pentonville Road, London, N1 9NG
Activities: Activities of other holding companies n.e.c.
Parent: Indigo Intermediate Limited
Officers: Thomas Christopher Richards, Secretary; Gordon Andrew Holmes [1969] Director [Irish]; Richard Paul Thomas Macmillan [1970] Director; Edouard Andre Gerard Peugeot [1984] Director [French]; Thomas Christopher Richards [1977] Director

Indigo Intermediate Limited
Incorporated: 29 May 2014
Net Worth: £324,000 *Total Assets:* £171,832,000
Registered Office: Caledonia House, 223 Pentonville Road, London, N1 9NG
Activities: Activities of other holding companies n.e.c.
Parent: Indigo Parent Limited
Officers: Thomas Christopher Richards, Secretary; Gordon Andrew Holmes [1969] Director [Irish]; Richard Paul Thomas Macmillan [1970] Director; Edouard Andre Gerard Peugeot [1984] Director [French]; Thomas Christopher Richards [1977] Director

Indigo Parent Limited
Incorporated: 29 May 2014 *Employees:* 1,528
Net Worth: £25,157,000 *Total Assets:* £450,963,008
Registered Office: Caledonia House, 223 Pentonville Road, London, N1 9NG
Activities: Activities of other holding companies n.e.c.
Shareholder: Indigo Manco Limited
Officers: Thomas Christopher Richards, Secretary; Nicholas Sanders Discombe [1962] Director; Gordon Andrew Holmes [1969] Director [Irish]; Richard Paul Thomas Macmillan [1970] Director; Edouard Andre Gerard Peugeot [1984] Director [French]; Paul Richard Martin Pindar [1959] Director; Thomas Christopher Richards [1977] Director

INEOS E & P (UK) Limited
Incorporated: 18 February 2002
Previous: Dong E & P (UK) Limited
Net Worth: £80,954,000 *Total Assets:* £340,828,992
Registered Office: Anchor House, 15-19 Britten Street, London, SW3 3TY
Activities: Extraction of crude petroleum
Parent: INEOS UK E & P Holdings Limited
Officers: Gemma McLucas, Secretary; Cordelia Pace, Secretary; David Nicholas Brooks [1966] Director; Mads Weng Gade [1978] Commercial Director; Andrew James Pizzey [1970] Director/Accountant; Douglas Stewart Scott [1969] Drilling and Decommissioning Director; Martin Alfred Stephenson [1953] Director/Geologist

INEOS Offshore BCS Limited
Incorporated: 15 July 2015
Net Worth Deficit: £114,507,000 *Total Assets:* £477,012,000
Registered Office: Anchor House, 15-19 Britten Street, London, SW3 3TY
Activities: Extraction of natural gas
Parent: INEOS Upstream Holdings Limited
Officers: Gemma Louise McLucas, Secretary; Cordelia Alexis Loveday Pace, Secretary; David Nicholas Brooks [1966] Director; Mads Weng Gade [1978] Commercial Director; Andrew James Pizzey [1970] Finance Director; Douglas Stewart Scott [1969] Drilling and Decommissioning Director; Martin Alfred Stephenson [1953] Director/Geologist

INEOS UK SNS Limited
Incorporated: 17 August 1971
Previous: DEA UK SNS Limited
Net Worth Deficit: £203,036,992 *Total Assets:* £434,639,008
Registered Office: Anchor House, 15-19 Britten Street, London, SW3 3TY
Activities: Extraction of natural gas
Parent: INEOS UK E & P Holdings Limited
Officers: Gemma Louise McLucas, Secretary; Cordelia Alexis Loveday Pace, Secretary; David Nicholas Brooks [1966] Director; Mads Weng Gade [1978] Commercial Director; Andrew James Pizzey [1970] Director/Accountant; Douglas Stewart Scott [1969] Drilling and Decommissioning Director; Martin Alfred Stephenson [1953] Director/Geologist

Infopro Digital Holding (UK) Limited
Incorporated: 20 March 2017
Net Worth: £44,361,536 *Total Assets:* £118,319,840
Registered Office: Haymarket House, 28-29 Haymarket, London, SW1Y 4RX
Activities: Activities of other holding companies n.e.c.
Officers: Christophe Czajka [1964] Director [French]

Informa Finance UK Limited
Incorporated: 14 November 2013 *Employees:* 4
Net Worth: £347,374,016 *Total Assets:* £351,220,992
Registered Office: 5 Howick Place, London, SW1P 1WG
Activities: Financial management
Parent: Informa PLC
Officers: Rupert John Joseph Hopley, Secretary; Simon Robert Bane [1971] Director/Solicitor; Rupert John Joseph Hopley [1969] Director/Solicitor; Nicholas Michael Perkins [1969] Tax Director; Gareth Richard Wright [1972] Director/Accountant [Australian]

Informa Finance USA Limited
Incorporated: 14 March 2014
Net Worth: £808,513,408 *Total Assets:* £818,830,016
Registered Office: 5 Howick Place, London, SW1P 1WG
Activities: Financial management
Parent: Informa PLC
Officers: Rupert John Joseph Hopley, Secretary; Simon Robert Bane [1971] Director/Solicitor; Nicholas Michael Perkins [1969] Tax Director; Gareth Richard Wright [1972] Director/Accountant [Australian]

Informa Group Holdings Limited
Incorporated: 24 June 2009 *Employees:* 5
Net Worth: £2,856,047,104 *Total Assets:* £5,655,541,760
Registered Office: 5 Howick Place, London, SW1P 1WG
Activities: Other business support service activities n.e.c.
Parent: Informa PLC
Officers: Rupert John Joseph Hopley, Secretary; Simon Robert Bane [1971] Director/Solicitor; Stephen Andrew Carter [1964] Director/Chief Executive; Rupert John Joseph Hopley [1969] Director/Solicitor; Nicholas Michael Perkins [1969] Tax Director; Gareth Richard Wright [1972] Director/Accountant [Australian]

Informa Group Limited
Incorporated: 6 September 1995 *Employees:* 98
Previous: Informa Group PLC
Net Worth: £1,316,400,000 *Total Assets:* £1,880,099,968
Registered Office: 5 Howick Place, London, SW1P 1WG
Activities: Activities of head offices
Parent: Informa Group Holdings Ltd
Officers: Rupert John Joseph Hopley, Secretary; Simon Robert Bane [1971] Director/Solicitor; Stephen Andrew Carter [1964] Director/Chief Executive; Glyn William Fullelove [1961] Director/Chartered Accountant; Rupert John Joseph Hopley [1969] Director/Solicitor; Nicholas Michael Perkins [1969] Tax Director; Gareth Richard Wright [1972] Director/Accountant [Australian]

Informa PLC
Incorporated: 24 January 2014 *Employees:* 7,539
Net Worth: £2,219,399,936 *Total Assets:* £4,892,100,096
Registered Office: 5 Howick Place, London, SW1P 1WG
Activities: Activities of head offices
Officers: Rupert John Joseph Hopley, Secretary; Gareth Richard Bullock [1953] Director; Stephen Andrew Carter [1964] Director/Chief Executive; Stephen James Davidson [1955] Director; David Jenkin Steward Flaschen [1955] Director [American]; Gregory Hugh Lock [1947] Director; Derek Mapp [1950] Director; Mary McDowell [1964] Director [American]; Helen Owers [1963] Director; John Rishton [1958] Director; Cindy Helen Rose [1965] Director; David Zhe Wei [1970] Director/Chairman [Hong Kong]; Gareth Richard Wright [1972] Director/Accountant [Australian]

Informa Telecoms & Media Limited
Incorporated: 14 October 1970 *Employees:* 317
Net Worth Deficit: £43,636,000 *Total Assets:* £209,708,000
Registered Office: 5 Howick Place, London, SW1P 1WG
Activities: Book publishing
Parent: Informa Group PLC
Officers: Rupert John Joseph Hopley, Secretary; Simon Robert Bane [1971] Director/Solicitor; Rupert John Joseph Hopley [1969] Director/Solicitor; Nicholas Michael Perkins [1969] Tax Director; Gareth Richard Wright [1972] Director/Accountant [Australian]

Informa UK Limited
Incorporated: 21 September 1972 *Employees:* 1,783
Net Worth: £548,553,024 *Total Assets:* £929,913,984
Registered Office: 5 Howick Place, London, SW1P 1WG
Activities: Book publishing
Parent: Informa Holdings Limnited
Officers: Rupert John Joseph Hopley, Secretary; Simon Robert Bane [1971] Director/Solicitor; Stephen Andrew Carter [1964] Director/Chief Executive; Rupert John Joseph Hopley [1969] Director/Solicitor; Nicholas Michael Perkins [1969] Tax Director; Gareth Richard Wright [1972] Director/Accountant [Australian]

Informa US Holdings Limited
Incorporated: 19 November 2014 *Employees:* 2
Net Worth: £172,836,992 *Total Assets:* £1,509,158,016
Registered Office: 5 Howick Place, London, SW1P 1WG
Activities: Non-trading company
Parent: Informa Group PLC
Officers: Nicholas Michael Perkins [1969] Tax Director; Gareth Richard Wright [1972] Director/Accountant [Australian]

Infrared Infrastructure Yield Holdings Limited
Incorporated: 18 June 2012
Net Worth: £122,315,000 *Total Assets:* £435,332,000
Registered Office: 12 Charles II Street, London, SW1Y 4QU
Activities: Other business support service activities n.e.c.
Parent: Infrared Infrastructure Yield General Partner Limited
Officers: Emily Mendes, Secretary; Christopher Paul Gill [1957] Director/Merchant Banker; Keith William Pickard [1968] Portfolio Director; Werner Marc Friedrich Von Guionneau [1957] Director/Banker [German]

Infrastructure Investments (A63) Holdings Limited
Incorporated: 6 January 2016
Net Worth: £75,690,304 *Total Assets:* £126,093,936
Registered Office: 12 Charles II Street, London, SW1Y 4QU
Activities: Financial intermediation not elsewhere classified
Parent: Infrastructure Investments Holdings Limited
Officers: Emily Mendes, Secretary; Keith William Pickard [1968] Portfolio Director; Caroline Louise Pitcher [1991] Director/Accountant; Harry Edward Charles Seekings [1973] Director/Financier

Infrastructure Investments (Affinity) Limited
Incorporated: 18 April 2017
Net Worth: £189,915,040 *Total Assets:* £240,562,304
Registered Office: 12 Charles II Street, London, SW1Y 4QU
Activities: Activities of financial services holding companies
Shareholders: Infrastructure Investments General Partner Limited; Infrastructure Investments Holdings Limited
Officers: Emily Mendes, Secretary; Keith William Pickard [1968] Portfolio Director; Caroline Louise Pitcher [1991] Director/Accountant; Harry Edward Charles Seekings [1973] Director/Financier

Infrastructure Investments (Colorado) Limited
Incorporated: 4 October 2016
Net Worth: £109,769,696 *Total Assets:* £143,421,536
Registered Office: 12 Charles II Street, London, SW1Y 4QU
Activities: Activities of financial services holding companies
Parent: Infrastructure Investments Holdings Limited
Officers: Emily Mendes, Secretary; Keith William Pickard [1968] Portfolio Director; Caroline Louise Pitcher [1991] Director/Accountant; Harry Edward Charles Seekings [1973] Director/Financier

Infrastructure Investments Betjeman Limited
Incorporated: 3 July 2017
Net Worth: £128,959,440 *Total Assets:* £128,959,440
Registered Office: 12 Charles II Street, London, SW1Y 4QU
Activities: Financial intermediation not elsewhere classified
Shareholders: Infrastructure Investments Betjeman (Holdco) Limited; Waterloo Place (2) GP LLP
Officers: Emily Mendes, Secretary; Keith William Pickard [1968] Portfolio Director; Caroline Louise Pitcher [1991] Director/Accountant; Harry Edward Charles Seekings [1973] Director/Financier

Infrastructure Investments Holdings Limited
Incorporated: 4 April 2008
Net Worth: £560,302,976 *Total Assets:* £838,348,992
Registered Office: 12 Charles II Street, London, SW1Y 4QU
Activities: Other business support service activities n.e.c.
Parent: Infrastructure Investments Trafalgar Limited
Officers: Emily Mendes, Secretary; Christopher Paul Gill [1957] Director/Merchant Banker; Keith William Pickard [1968] Director/Accountant; Caroline Louise Pitcher [1991] Director/Accountant; Harry Edward Charles Seekings [1973] Director/Financier

Infrastructure Investments Trafalgar Limited
Incorporated: 29 June 2017
Net Worth: £913,464,000 *Total Assets:* £913,590,016
Registered Office: 12 Charles II Street, London, SW1Y 4QU
Activities: Financial intermediation not elsewhere classified
Parent: Infrastructure Investments General Partner Limited
Officers: Emily Mendes, Secretary; Christopher Paul Gill [1957] Director/Merchant Banker; Keith William Pickard [1968] Portfolio Director; Caroline Louise Pitcher [1991] Director/Accountant; Harry Edward Charles Seekings [1973] Director/Financier

Infund LLP
Incorporated: 13 June 2003
Net Worth: £1,541,800,576 *Total Assets:* £1,572,931,456
Registered Office: 4th Floor, Clerks Well House, 20 Britton Street, London, EC1M 5UA
Officers: Hector Juan Jose Garcia [1951] Member

ING Services Limited
Incorporated: 1 January 1973
Net Worth: £6,402,000 *Total Assets:* £491,972,992
Registered Office: 8-10 Moorgate, London, EC2R 6DA
Activities: Human resources provision and management of human resources functions
Parent: ING Intermediate Holdings Limited
Officers: Adrian Neil Marsh, Secretary; Greg John Richardson [1971] Director/UK Head of Internal Controls and Regulatory Report; Ronald Visser [1972] Director/Head of Human Resources [Dutch]

Ingenious Media Holdings Limited
Incorporated: 5 March 2008 *Employees:* 201
Previous: Ingenious Media Holdings PLC
Net Worth: £55,246,000 *Total Assets:* £939,628,032
Registered Office: 15 Golden Square, London, W1F 9JG
Activities: Activities of other holding companies n.e.c.
Major Shareholder: Patrick Anthony McKenna
Officers: Sarah Cruickshank, Secretary; Jennifer Wright, Secretary; Neil Andrew Forster [1970] Finance Director; Patrick Anthony McKenna [1956] Director; Duncan Murray Reid [1958] Director; Peter Michael Shawyer [1950] Director

Ingenious Media Limited
Incorporated: 2 June 1998 *Employees:* 201
Net Worth Deficit: £6,564,000 *Total Assets:* £124,513,000
Registered Office: 15 Golden Square, London, W1F 9JG
Activities: Other business support service activities n.e.c.
Parent: Ingenious Media Holdings PLC
Officers: Sarah Cruickshank, Secretary; Jennifer Wright, Secretary; Neil Andrew Forster [1970] Finance Director; Patrick Anthony McKenna [1956] Director; Duncan Murray Reid [1958] Director

Inmarsat Finance PLC
Incorporated: 13 October 2003
Net Worth: £1,506,364 *Total Assets:* £1,062,212,864
Registered Office: 99 City Road, London, EC1Y 1AX
Activities: Satellite telecommunications activities
Parent: Inmarsat Group Limited
Officers: Alison Claire Horrocks, Secretary/Director; Antony Jeffrey Bates [1956] Director; Alison Claire Horrocks [1962] Director; Rupert Edward Pearce [1964] Director/Lawyer

Inmarsat Global Limited
Incorporated: 24 November 1998 *Employees:* 766
Net Worth: £2,425,285,632 *Total Assets:* £5,042,091,520
Registered Office: 99 City Road, London, EC1Y 1AX
Activities: Other telecommunications activities
Shareholders: Inmarsat New Ventures Limited; Inmarsat Ventures Limited
Officers: Alison Claire Horrocks, Secretary; Antony Jeffrey Bates [1956] Director; Alison Claire Horrocks [1962] Director/Company Secretary; Rupert Edward Pearce [1964] Director/Lawyer

Inmarsat Group Limited
Incorporated: 3 September 2003 *Employees:* 1,852
Net Worth: £1,083,659,904 *Total Assets:* £3,553,908,736
Registered Office: 99 City Road, London, EC1Y 1AX
Activities: Activities of head offices
Parent: Inmarsat Holdings Limited
Officers: Alison Claire Horrocks, Secretary/Director; Antony Jeffrey Bates [1956] Director; Alison Claire Horrocks [1962] Director/Company Secretary; Rupert Edward Pearce [1964] Director/Lawyer; Andrew John Sukawaty [1955] Director/Executive [American]

Inmarsat Holdings Limited
Incorporated: 1 October 2003
Net Worth: £750,207,168 *Total Assets:* £756,007,552
Registered Office: 99 City Road, London, EC1Y 1AX
Activities: Satellite telecommunications activities
Parent: Inmarsat PLC
Officers: Alison Claire Horrocks, Secretary/Director; Antony Jeffrey Bates [1956] Director; Alison Claire Horrocks [1962] Director/Company Secretary; Rupert Edward Pearce [1964] Director; Andrew John Sukawaty [1955] Director/Executive [American]

Inmarsat Investments Limited
Incorporated: 3 September 2003 *Employees:* 1,852
Net Worth: £1,144,030,080 *Total Assets:* £3,773,860,608
Registered Office: 99 City Road, London, EC1Y 1AX
Activities: Activities of head offices
Parent: Inmarsat Group Limited
Officers: Alison Claire Horrocks, Secretary/Director; Antony Jeffrey Bates [1956] Director; Alison Claire Horrocks [1962] Director; Rupert Edward Pearce [1964] Director/Lawyer; Andrew John Sukawaty [1955] Director [American]

Inmarsat PLC
Incorporated: 3 September 2003 *Employees:* 1,854
Net Worth: £945,160,064 *Total Assets:* £3,735,969,792
Registered Office: 99 City Road, London, EC1Y 1AX
Activities: Activities of head offices
Officers: Alison Claire Horrocks, Secretary/Director; Antony Jeffrey Bates [1956] Director; Simon Tristan Bax [1959] Director; Sir Bryan Victor Carsberg [1939] Director/Accountant; Tracy Jayne Clarke [1967] Director; Warren Alan Finegold [1957] Director; Robert Kehler [1952] Director [American]; Philippa McCrostie [1957] Director; Janice Obuchowski [1951] Director [American]; Rupert Edward Pearce [1964] Director/Lawyer; Dr Abraham Peled [1945] Director [American]; Robert Arnold Ruijter [1951] Director [Dutch]; Andrew John Sukawaty [1955] Director/Executive [American]; Dr Hamadoun Toure [1953] Director [Malian]

Inmarsat Solutions Limited
Incorporated: 2 March 2007
Net Worth Deficit: £28,355,440 *Total Assets:* £393,781,344
Registered Office: 99 City Road, London, EC1Y 1AX
Activities: Activities of head offices
Parent: Inmarsat Finance III Limited
Officers: Alison Claire Horrocks, Company Secretary; Alison Claire Horrocks [1962] Director/Company Secretary; Rupert Edward Pearce [1964] Director

Inn on BW (UK) Limited
Incorporated: 13 May 2014 *Employees:* 28
Net Worth: £49,740,620 *Total Assets:* £122,157,744
Registered Office: 8 Sackville Street, London, W1S 3DG
Activities: Hotels and similar accommodation
Officers: Marc John Haslam [1975] Director/Chartered Surveyor; Wendy Jane Patterson [1969] Director/Chartered Accountant; Paul Dennis Perris [1973] Director/Chartered Secretary; Paul Justin Windsor [1957] Director/Chartered Accountant

Inn on the Park (London) Limited
Incorporated: 30 October 1984 *Employees:* 365
Net Worth: £16,792,000 *Total Assets:* £114,185,000
Registered Office: 8 Sackville Street, London, W1S 3DG
Activities: Hotels and similar accommodation
Officers: Marc John Haslam [1975] Director/Chartered Surveyor; Bruno Chibuzo Obasi [1973] Director/Chartered Accountant; Wendy Jane Patterson [1969] Director/Chartered Accountant; Paul Dennis Perris [1973] Director/Chartered Secretary; Paul Justin Windsor [1957] Director/Chartered Accountant

Innocent Limited
Incorporated: 2 June 2000 *Employees:* 295
Net Worth: £49,300,000 *Total Assets:* £121,799,000
Registered Office: 342 Ladbroke Grove, London, W10 5BU
Activities: Manufacture of fruit and vegetable juice
Parent: Fresh Trading Limited
Officers: James Lewis Davenport, Secretary; James Lewis Davenport [1973] Director and Company Secretary; Douglas Ross Lamont [1973] Director; Scott Edward Roche [1964] Director [Canadian]

Inpex Angola Block 14 Ltd.
Incorporated: 25 June 2012
Net Worth: £199,278,960 *Total Assets:* £199,425,456
Registered Office: 2nd Floor, Park House, 16-18 Finsbury Circus, London, EC2M 7EB
Activities: Extraction of crude petroleum
Parent: Inpex Corporation
Officers: Takashi Hara [1966] Director [Japanese]; Keiji Nagase [1970] Director [Japanese]; Yutaka Shimura [1969] Director [Japanese]; Toshiaki Takimoto [1961] Director [Japanese]

Inremco 26 Limited
Incorporated: 6 December 1983 *Employees:* 10
Net Worth: £137,203,632 *Total Assets:* £187,550,368
Registered Office: Hallswelle House, 1 Hallswelle Road, London, NW11 0DH
Activities: Activities of other holding companies n.e.c.
Officers: Dwora Feldman, Secretary; Dwora Feldman [1937] Director; Heinrich Feldman [1935] Director

Insight Group Limited
Incorporated: 29 June 1898 *Employees:* 421
Net Worth: £34,901,844 *Total Assets:* £121,857,896
Registered Office: 14 Grosvenor Place, London, SW1X 7HH
Activities: Activities of head offices
Major Shareholder: Victoria Tollman O'Hana
Officers: Derek Ivol David Howie, Secretary; Benjamin Robin Hall [1971] Director; Derek Ivol David Howie [1965] Director/Chartered Accountant

Insight Investment Management (Global) Limited
Incorporated: 19 November 1964
Net Worth: £326,620,000 *Total Assets:* £352,744,992
Registered Office: 160 Queen Victoria Street, London, EC4V 4LA
Activities: Security and commodity contracts dealing activities
Parent: Insight Investment Management Limited
Officers: Eric Edward Anstee [1951] Director; Gregory Allan Brisk [1962] Director/Investment Management; Jonathan Edward Francis Eliot [1966] Director/Chief Risk Officer; Andrew Brian Giles [1962] Director; Adrian Grey [1964] Director/Asset Management; Mitchell Evan Harris [1955] Director [American]; Sir Brian Gammell Ivory [1949] Director; Atul Manek [1962] Director; Abdallah Habib Nauphal [1960] Director/Chief Investment Officer [American]; Angus Sutherland Hamish Woolhouse [1963] Director/Global Head of Distribution

Insight Investment Management Limited
Incorporated: 16 March 1987 *Employees:* 523
Net Worth: £103,563,000 *Total Assets:* £308,249,984
Registered Office: 160 Queen Victoria Street, London, EC4V 4LA
Activities: Activities of other holding companies n.e.c.
Parent: BNY Mellon International Asset Management Group Limited
Officers: Eric Edward Anstee [1951] Director; Gregory Allan Brisk [1962] Director/Investment Management; Jonathan Edward Francis Eliot [1966] Director/Chief Risk Officer; Andrew Brian Giles [1962] Director; Adrian Grey [1964] Director/Asset Management; Mitchell Evan Harris [1955] Director [American]; Sir Brian Gammell Ivory [1949] Director; Atul Manek [1962] Director; Abdallah Habib Nauphal [1960] Director/Chief Investment Officer [American]; Angus Sutherland Hamish Woolhouse [1963] Director/Global Head of Distribution

Inspired Education Holdings Limited
Incorporated: 23 September 2016 *Employees:* 3,729
Net Worth: £274,032,288 *Total Assets:* £629,913,088
Registered Office: Meadows House, 20-22 Queen Street, London, W1J 5PR
Activities: Other business support service activities n.e.c.
Officers: David Goulden Brickell [1975] Director; Nadim Marwan Nsouli [1969] Director; Christopher Graham Parkin [1973] Director/Investor; Dr Stephen Spurr [1953] Director

Instant Cash Loans Limited
Incorporated: 7 February 1992 *Employees:* 1,353
Net Worth: £63,619,000 *Total Assets:* £200,831,008
Registered Office: 6 Bevis Marks, London, EC3A 7BA
Activities: Credit granting by non-deposit taking finance houses and other specialist consumer credit grantors
Parent: Aurajoki Holdings UK Limited
Officers: Jonathan Ashley [1966] Director [American]; Alpesh Kumar Patel [1973] Director; Justin Staadecker [1968] Director

Instinet Europe Limited
Incorporated: 22 May 1985
Net Worth: £95,834,000 *Total Assets:* £771,105,024
Registered Office: 1 Angel Lane, London, EC4R 3AB
Activities: Security and commodity contracts dealing activities
Parent: Instinet International Limited
Officers: Michelle Sylvia Rodrigues, Secretary; Yasuo Kashiwagi [1962] Director/Banker [Japanese]; Jonathan Wayne Lewis [1967] Director/Chartered Accountant; Richard William Parsons [1975] Director/Financial Services; Jeremy Bernard Soames [1952] Director

Instinet Global Services Limited
Incorporated: 22 October 1990 *Employees:* 144
Net Worth: £26,765,000 *Total Assets:* £331,760,000
Registered Office: 1 Angel Lane, London, EC4R 3AB
Activities: Other business support service activities n.e.c.
Parent: Instinet International Limited
Officers: Michelle Sylvia Rodrigues, Secretary; Richard William Parsons [1975] Director/Financial Services; Michelle Sylvia Rodrigues [1974] Director/Solicitor

Instinet International Limited
Incorporated: 12 June 1979
Net Worth: £160,372,000 *Total Assets:* £166,624,992
Registered Office: 1 Angel Lane, London, EC4R 3AB
Activities: Activities of head offices
Parent: Nomura Holdings Inc.
Officers: Michelle Sylvia Rodrigues, Secretary; Yasuo Kashiwagi [1962] Director/Banker [Japanese]; Jonathan Wayne Lewis [1967] Director/Chartered Accountant; Jeremy Bernard Soames [1952] Director

Institute of Cancer Research: Royal Cancer Hospital (The)
Incorporated: 4 June 1954 *Employees:* 1,143
Net Worth: £342,503,008 *Total Assets:* £396,222,016
Registered Office: 123 Old Brompton Road, London, SW7 3RP
Activities: Other research and experimental development on natural sciences and engineering
Officers: Dr Charmaine Helen Griffiths, Secretary; Professor Jeffrey Colin Bamber [1950] Director/Scientist; William Murray Burns [1947] Director; Mandy Donald [1972] Director; Dr Iain Walter Foulkes [1971] Director/Charity Research Administrator; Charles Slade Henry Geffen [1959] Director; Jane Elizabeth Hamilton [1955] Director; Jeremy Grahame Hill [1958] Solicitor and Director; Professor Clare Margaret Isacke [1957] Director/Research Scientist; Luke Oliver Johnson [1962] Director/Restaurateur; Professor Nicholas Jones [1950] Director; Professor Timothy Stanley Maughan [1954] Director/Professor of Clinical Oncology; David James Philip McBay [1993] Director/Student; Karl Munslow Ong [1980] Director/Chief Operating Officer; Dr Brendan Richard O'Neill [1948] Director; Caroline Ann Palmer [1958] Director/Chief Executive Royal Marsden; Dr Paul Workman [1952] Director/Chief Executive

Instron International Limited
Incorporated: 19 July 1978
Net Worth: £116,790,000 *Total Assets:* £116,844,000
Registered Office: 13th Floor, 5 Aldermanbury Square, London, EC2V 7HR
Activities: Other service activities n.e.c.
Parent: Instron Holdings Limited
Officers: Ryan Ronald Dale, Secretary; Giles Matthew Hudson [1972] Director/Chartered Accountant; Stephen James Rowell [1967] Director of International Corporate Finance

Intact Limited
Incorporated: 17 November 1995
Net Worth: £309,332,992 *Total Assets:* £309,339,008
Registered Office: Sea Containers House, 18 Upper Ground, London, SE1 9GL
Activities: Other business support service activities n.e.c.
Parent: WPP LN Limited
Officers: Charles Ward Van Der Welle [1959] Director of Treasury; Steve Richard Winters [1968] Director/Chartered Accountant

Integrafin Holdings PLC
Incorporated: 24 January 2014 *Employees:* 451
Previous: Integrafin Holdings Limited
Net Worth: £102,526,000 *Total Assets:* £12,129,095,680
Registered Office: 29 Clement's Lane, London, EC4N 7AE
Activities: Activities of other holding companies n.e.c.
Officers: David Johnson, Secretary; Caroline Janet Banszky [1953] Director; Victoria Cochrane [1956] Director/Lawyer; Neil Jonathan Holden [1959] Director; Michael Howard [1958] Director [British/Australian]; Christopher Iain Craddock Munro [1949] Director; Alexander Scott [1970] Director/Chief Financial Officer; Ian Anthony Taylor [1964] Director

Integral UK Limited
Incorporated: 8 December 2004 *Employees:* 3,124
Net Worth: £10,020,000 *Total Assets:* £160,264,000
Registered Office: 30 Warwick Street, London, W1B 5NH
Activities: Plumbing, heat and air-conditioning installation
Parent: Integral UK Holdings Limited
Officers: Bryan Glastonbury [1953] Director; Yashdeep Kapila [1967] Director/Chief Operating Officer; Andrew John Osborn [1965] Director/Accountant

Integralife UK Limited
Incorporated: 26 March 1964
Net Worth: £20,887,000 *Total Assets:* £10,780,856,320
Registered Office: 29 Clement's Lane, London, EC4N 7AE
Activities: Life insurance
Parent: Integrated Financial Arrangements Ltd
Officers: David Johnson, Secretary; Neil Jonathan Holden [1959] Director; John Lyle McKenzie [1951] Director/Actuary; Alexander Scott [1970] Director/Chief Financial Officer; Ian Anthony Taylor [1964] Director

Integro Insurance Brokers Holdings Limited
Incorporated: 16 June 2000
Net Worth: £37,976,000 *Total Assets:* £183,511,008
Registered Office: 71 Fenchurch Street, London, EC3M 4BS
Activities: Activities of insurance agents and brokers
Officers: Peter John Burton, Secretary; Andrew Edward Behrends [1971] Director/Accountant [American]; Adam John Cockburn [1972] Director/Compliance Officer

Integro Insurance Brokers Limited
Incorporated: 11 August 1994 *Employees:* 539
Net Worth: £38,776,000 *Total Assets:* £152,787,008
Registered Office: 71 Fenchurch Street, London, EC3M 4BS
Activities: Activities of insurance agents and brokers
Parent: Integro Insurance Brokers Holdings Ltd
Officers: Peter John Burton, Secretary; David Mathew Abraham [1970] Director/Insurance Broker; Andrew Edward Behrends [1971] Director/Accountant [American]; Neil Martin Clayton [1966] Director/Insurance Broker; Adam John Cockburn [1972] Director/Compliance Officer; Jason Hugh Collins [1968] Director/Insurance Broker; Peter Colin Frank Haynes [1954] Director; Robert Alan Pybus [1962] Director/Insurance Broker; Christopher Michael Spratt [1945] Director/Insurance Broker

Intelligent Processing Solutions Limited
Incorporated: 5 June 2000 *Employees:* 1,525
Net Worth: £41,206,000 *Total Assets:* £223,436,000
Registered Office: 1st Floor, Building 6, Chiswick Park, 566 Chiswick High Road, London, W4 5HR
Activities: Financial intermediation not elsewhere classified
Parent: Unisys Limited
Officers: Gwyn Reeves, Secretary; Michael Robinson, Secretary; Catherine Elizabeth Caldwell [1967] Director/Bank Official; Josephine Elizabeth Clapham [1968] Managing Director; Irene Rudge Graham [1967] Director; David Alexander Grant [1965] Risk Director; James Charles McLay Martin [1961] Director; Matthew Roy Piercy [1961] Director/Chartered Accountant; Mehran Radfar [1959] Director/VP Enterprise Solutions

Intelsat Global Sales & Marketing Ltd.
Incorporated: 30 October 2000 *Employees:* 49
Net Worth Deficit: £11,330,982 *Total Assets:* £994,452,992
Registered Office: 100 New Bridge Street, London, EC4V 6JA
Activities: Satellite telecommunications activities
Parent: Intelsat S.A.
Officers: Adriano David Ros, Secretary; Jean-Philippe Gillet [1965] Director/Business Executive [French]; Rhys Owen Morgan [1970] Director/Business Executive; Kurt Charles Riegelman [1963] Director/Sales Executive [American]; Adriano David Ros [1978] Director/Attorney

Intelsat UK Financial Services Ltd.
Incorporated: 26 September 2005
Net Worth: £779,707,136 *Total Assets:* £784,788,032
Registered Office: 100 New Bridge Street, London, EC4V 6JA
Activities: Other business support service activities n.e.c.
Parent: Intelsat Global Sales & Marketing Ltd.
Officers: Adriano David Ros, Secretary; Jean-Philippe Gillet [1965] Director/Business Executive [French]; Rhys Owen Morgan [1970] Director/Business Executive; Kurt Charles Riegelman [1963] Director/Sales Executive [American]; Adriano David Ros [1978] Director/Attorney

Interactive Brokers (U.K.) Limited
Incorporated: 28 March 2000 *Employees:* 31
Net Worth: £89,616,000 *Total Assets:* £428,656,000
Registered Office: Level 20, Heron Tower, 110 Bishopsgate, London, EC2N 4AY
Activities: Security and commodity contracts dealing activities
Officers: Paul Brody, Secretary; Paul Jonathan Brody [1960] Director [American]; Jonathan Chait [1961] Director [American]; Earl Harold Nemser [1947] Director [American]; Generald Perez [1963] Managing Director [American]; Thomas Peterffy [1944] Director/Chairman [American]; William George Sirett [1980] Director/Operations

Intercapital Limited
Incorporated: 24 May 1979
Net Worth: £873,889,024 *Total Assets:* £931,644,992
Registered Office: 2 Broadgate, London, EC2M 7UR
Activities: Activities of head offices
Parent: NEX International Limited
Officers: Deborah Anne Abrehart, Secretary; Deborah Anne Abrehart [1957] Director/Chartered Secretary; David Charles Ireland [1969] Director

Interconnector (UK) Limited
Incorporated: 14 November 1994 *Employees:* 68
Net Worth: £60,287,000 *Total Assets:* £264,088,992
Registered Office: 10 Furnival Street, London, EC4A 1AB
Activities: Transport via pipeline
Shareholder: Fluxys UK Limited
Officers: Mary Conor Matthew Simmons, Secretary; Arno Bux [1967] Director/Chief Commercial Officer [Belgian]; Steven Daniel de Ranter [1986] Director/Chief Commercial Officer [Belgian]; Ben de Waele [1979] Director Installations and Grid [Belgian]; Matteo Tanteri [1982] Director/Head of International Assets Portfolio Management [Italian]; Stephen John Turner [1971] Director/Chief Operations Officer; Rafael Van Elst [1968] Director Installations & Grid [Belgian]; Erik Jean Corneel Vennekens [1978] Director/Acquisition Implementation Manager [Belgian]

Intercontinentalexchange Holdings
Incorporated: 3 May 2002 *Employees:* 3
Net Worth: £5,056,394,752 *Total Assets:* £5,069,827,584
Registered Office: Milton Gate, 60 Chiswell Street, London, EC1Y 4SA
Activities: Activities of financial services holding companies
Parent: Exchange Participations Limited
Officers: Elizabeth Miriam Holt, Secretary; Scott Anthony Hill [1967] Director/Chief Finance Officer [American]; Andrew James Surdykowski [1970] Director [American]; Stuart Glen Williams [1978] Director [South African]

Intergen Holdings (UK) Limited
Incorporated: 21 March 2007
Net Worth: £427,457,632 *Total Assets:* £699,899,584
Registered Office: 30 Crown Place, Earl Street, London, EC2A 4ES
Activities: Activities of head offices
Officers: Timothy John Menzie [1965] Director/Chief Executive Officer [American]; Michael Jon Novelli [1968] Director/General Manager [American]

Intergen Projects (UK) Limited
Incorporated: 22 March 2007
Net Worth: £479,368,992 *Total Assets:* £684,550,976
Registered Office: 30 Crown Place, Earl Street, London, EC2A 4ES
Activities: Other business support service activities n.e.c.
Parent: Intergen Holdings (UK) Limited
Officers: Christopher James Elder [1976] Director/General Manager, UK; Lisa MacKay [1977] Commercial Director UKNL; Paul Teague [1972] Finance Director

Interior Services Group (UK Holdings) Limited
Incorporated: 23 May 2002 *Employees:* 82
Net Worth: £26,606,000 *Total Assets:* £150,950,000
Registered Office: Aldgate House, 33 Aldgate High Street, London, EC3N 1AG
Activities: Activities of head offices
Parent: ISG Central Services Limited
Officers: Nicholas James Heard, Secretary; Paul Martin Cossell [1965] Commercial Director; Mark Stockton [1964] Director/Accountant

Intermediate Capital Group PLC
Incorporated: 23 March 1988 *Employees:* 290
Net Worth: £1,317,600,000 *Total Assets:* £6,306,400,256
Registered Office: Juxon House, 100 St Paul's Churchyard, London, EC4M 8BU
Activities: Financial intermediation not elsewhere classified
Officers: Andrew Gareth Lewis, Secretary; Benoit Laurent Pierre Durteste [1968] Director/Banker [French]; Virginia Anne Holmes [1960] Director; Philip Henry Keller [1965] Director/Accountant; Michael Nelligan [1954] Director; Kevin Allen Huw Parry [1962] Director/Accountant; Kathryn Elizabeth Purves [1973] Director/Chief Risk Officer for Life Assurance; Amy Lee Schioldager [1962] Director/Strategic Advisor [American]; Andrew Francis Sykes [1957] Director; Stephen Welton [1961] Director

Intermediate Capital Managers Limited
Incorporated: 12 December 1988 *Employees:* 27
Net Worth: £247,604,992 *Total Assets:* £251,123,008
Registered Office: Juxon House, 100 St Paul's Churchyard, London, EC4M 8BU
Activities: Security and commodity contracts dealing activities
Parent: ICG FMC Limited
Officers: Benoit Laurent Pierre Durteste [1968] Director/Banker [French]; Philip Henry Keller [1965] Director/Accountant

International Bible Students Association
Incorporated: 30 June 1914
Net Worth: £121,771,128 *Total Assets:* £136,628,640
Registered Office: IBSA House, The Ridgeway, London, NW7 1RN
Activities: Activities of religious organisations
Officers: Ivor Darby [1971] Director/Minister of Religion; Jonathan Manley [1981] Director/Administrator; Stephen Papps [1959] Director/Minister of Religion; Karl William Snaith [1961] Director/Minister; Stephen Charles Hale Symonds [1971] Director/Minister of Religion

International Biotechnology Trust PLC
Incorporated: 31 January 1994
Net Worth: £262,472,992 *Total Assets:* £263,216,992
Registered Office: 10 Harewood Avenue, London, NW1 6AA
Activities: Activities of investment trusts
Officers: John Christopher Aston [1954] Director; Dr Veronique Anne Bouchet [1959] Director [British/French]; Caroline Gulliver [1965] Director; James Horsburgh [1955] Director

International Entertainment Finance Limited
Incorporated: 11 November 2013
Previous: ATG Finance Limited
Net Worth: £236,128,992 *Total Assets:* £236,472,000
Registered Office: 28 St George Street, London, W1S 2FA
Activities: Performing arts
Parent: International Entertainment Midco Ltd
Officers: Mark Ralph Delano Cornell [1966] Director; Robert Sudo [1976] Director [German]; Shanmae Teo [1976] Director; Andrew Adams Tisdale [1961] Managing Director [American]

International Entertainment Holdings Limited
Incorporated: 11 November 2013 *Employees:* 4,399
Previous: International Entertainment Group Holdings Limited
Net Worth: £102,715,000 *Total Assets:* £794,190,016
Registered Office: 28 St George Street, London, W1S 2FA
Activities: Performing arts
Officers: Anthony Frank Elliott Ball [1955] Director/Chairman; Mark Ralph Delano Cornell [1966] Director; Sinisa Krnic [1973] Director; David Bernard Leigh [1971] Director; Robert Sudo [1976] Director [German]; Shanmae Teo [1976] Director; Andrew Adams Tisdale [1961] Managing Director [American]

International Entertainment Investments Limited
Incorporated: 11 November 2013
Previous: ATEG Limited
Net Worth Deficit: £56,124,000 *Total Assets:* £468,416,000
Registered Office: 28 St George Street, London, W1S 2FA
Activities: Support activities to performing arts
Parent: International Entertainment Finance Ltd
Officers: Mark Ralph Delano Cornell [1966] Director; Robert Sudo [1976] Director [German]; Shanmae Teo [1976] Director; Andrew Adams Tisdale [1961] Managing Director [American]

International Entertainment Midco Limited
Incorporated: 11 November 2013
Previous: ATG Midco Limited
Net Worth: £155,360,000 *Total Assets:* £236,128,992
Registered Office: 28 St George Street, London, W1S 2FA
Activities: Performing arts
Parent: International Entertainment Group Holdings Ltd
Officers: Mark Ralph Delano Cornell [1966] Director; Robert Sudo [1976] Director [German]; Shanmae Teo [1976] Director; Andrew Adams Tisdale [1961] Managing Director [American]

International Finance Facility for Immunisation Company
Incorporated: 26 June 2006
Net Worth: £786,491,904 *Total Assets:* £2,637,988,608
Registered Office: 2 Lambs Passage, London, EC1Y 8BB
Activities: Other service activities n.e.c.
Officers: Cyrus Ardalan [1950] Director/Retired; Bertrand de Mazieres [1957] Director General - Finance [French]; Fatimatou Zahra Diop [1957] Director/Vice President of Afrivac [Senegalese]; Marcus Fedder [1959] Director [German]; Doris Aida D Lourdes Herrera Pol [1958] Director [Dominican]; Helge Weiner-Trapness [1963] Director/Partner-Finance [Swedish]

International Game Technology PLC
Incorporated: 11 July 2014
Net Worth: £1,455,426,048 *Total Assets:* £11,004,070,912
Registered Office: 2nd Floor, Marble Arch House, 66 Seymour Street, London, W1H 5BT
Activities: Activities of head offices
Officers: Pierfrancesco Boccia, Secretary; Paget Leonard Alves III [1954] Director [American]; Professor Alberto Dessy [1953] Director/Chartered Accountant [Italian]; Marco Drago [1946] Director/Chairman [Italian]; Patti Sarles Hart [1956] Director/CEO/Chairman [American]; James Francis McCann [1951] Director/Chairman and Chief Executive Officer [American]; Professor Heather Jane McGregor [1962] Director; Lorenzo Pellicioli [1951] Director/Chief Executive Officer [Italian]; Vincent Louis Sadusky [1965] Director/President/CEO [American]; Marco Sala [1959] Director/Chief Executive [Italian]; Gianmario Tondato Da Ruos [1960] Director/Chief Executive Officer [Italian]

International General Insurance Company (UK) Limited
Incorporated: 5 April 2009 *Employees:* 44
Net Worth: £57,395,380 *Total Assets:* £273,796,096
Registered Office: Forum House, 15-18 Lime Street, London, EC3M 7AN
Activities: Non-life insurance
Shareholder: Wasef Jabsheh
Officers: Rawan Alsulaiman, Secretary; Christopher Norman Clark [1958] Director; William Graham Hensman [1960] Managing Director, North Star Underwriting Ltd; Walid Wasef Jabsheh [1976] Director [Canadian]; Wasef Salim Jabsheh [1943] Director/CEO, International General Insurance Holdings Ltd [Jordanian]; David Elon King [1945] Director; Andreas Costas Loucaides [1952] Director/Chief Executive; Charles Louis Colin Manchester [1961] Director/Chairman, Manchester Underwriting Management; Paul Martin [1964] Director; Clifford Edward Murphy [1959] Director/Head of Finance; Pervez Rizvi [1961] Director/Group Chief Finance Officer [Indian]

International Hoteliers (UK) Limited
Incorporated: 11 February 1983
Net Worth: £124,176,000 *Total Assets:* £125,541,000
Registered Office: 30 Portman Square, London, W1A 4ZX
Activities: Hotels and similar accommodation
Parent: Primeairo
Officers: Karin Cooper, Secretary; Sheikh Jassim Bin Hamad Al Thani [1982] Director/Chairman [Qatari]; Fady Bakhos [1971] Director/Architect [Lebanese]; Michael Anthony Cairns [1940] Director; Karin Cooper [1969] Director/Architect [German]; Zaki Nasser Zaki El Guiziri [1957] Director [Egyptian]

International Nuclear Investment Limited
Incorporated: 30 November 2015
Net Worth: £294,395,552 *Total Assets:* £1,723,886,080
Registered Office: First Floor, Stratton House, 5 Stratton Street, Mayfair, London, W1J 8LA
Activities: Other service activities n.e.c.
Parent: State-Owned Assets Supervision and Administration Commission of The State Council
Officers: Dongshan Zheng [1962] Director [Chinese]

International Power (Fawkes)
Incorporated: 27 November 2003
Net Worth: £259,240,624 *Total Assets:* £745,605,184
Registered Office: Level 20, 25 Canada Square, London, E14 5LQ
Activities: Activities of head offices
Parent: National Power International Holdings
Officers: Sarah Jane Gregory, Secretary; David George Alcock [1965] Director; Sarah Frances Fleure Mingham [1977] Director; Simon David Pinnell [1964] Director

International Power (Genco) Limited
Incorporated: 15 December 2003
Net Worth: £76,536,672 *Total Assets:* £240,790,752
Registered Office: Level 20, 25 Canada Square, London, E14 5LQ
Activities: Non-trading company
Parent: International Power Consolidated Holdings Limited
Officers: Sarah Jane Gregory, Secretary; David George Alcock [1965] Director; Sarah Frances Fleure Mingham [1977] Director; Simon David Pinnell [1964] Director/Accountant

International Power (Zebra) Limited
Incorporated: 25 November 2010
Net Worth: £6,955,534,848 *Total Assets:* £7,682,992,640
Registered Office: Level 20, 25 Canada Square, London, E14 5LQ
Activities: Activities of head offices
Parent: International Power Ltd.
Officers: Sarah Jane Gregory, Secretary; David George Alcock [1965] Director; Sarah Frances Fleure Mingham [1977] Director; Simon David Pinnell [1964] Director

International Power Australia Holdings (1) Limited
Incorporated: 6 June 2003
Net Worth: £91,427,120 *Total Assets:* £109,345,056
Registered Office: Level 20, 25 Canada Square, London, E14 5LQ
Activities: Activities of head offices
Parent: International Power Ausralia Holdings Limited
Officers: Sarah Jane Gregory, Secretary; Lawrence Kim, Secretary; Augustin Marie Luc Honorat [1977] Director/Chief Executive Officer [French]; Masao Omura [1959] Director [Japanese]

International Power Australia Holdings Limited
Incorporated: 6 June 2003
Net Worth: £240,671,856 *Total Assets:* £240,671,856
Registered Office: Level 20, 25 Canada Square, London, E14 5LQ
Activities: Activities of head offices
Parent: International Power Ltd.
Officers: Sarah Jane Gregory, Secretary; Lawrence Kim, Secretary; Augustin Marie Luc Honorat [1977] Director/Chief Executive Officer [French]; Masao Omura [1959] Director [Japanese]

International Power Consolidated Holdings Limited
Incorporated: 2 August 2006
Net Worth: £2,513,168,640 *Total Assets:* £4,005,031,168
Registered Office: Level 20, 25 Canary Wharf, London, E14 5LQ
Activities: Activities of head offices
Parent: International Power Ltd.
Officers: Sarah Jane Gregory, Secretary; David George Alcock [1965] Director; Sarah Frances Fleure Mingham [1977] Director; Simon David Pinnell [1964] Director

International Power Holdings Limited
Incorporated: 3 April 2000
Net Worth: £743,276,352 *Total Assets:* £743,276,352
Registered Office: Level 20, 25 Canary Wharf, London, E14 5LQ
Activities: Activities of head offices
Parent: International Power Consolidated Holdings Limited
Officers: Sarah Jane Gregory, Secretary; David George Alcock [1965] Director; Sarah Frances Fleure Mingham [1977] Director; Simon David Pinnell [1964] Director/Accountant

International Power Ltd.
Incorporated: 1 April 1989 *Employees:* 255
Net Worth: £6,297,706,496 *Total Assets:* £7,463,030,272
Registered Office: Level 20, 25 Canada Square, London, E14 5LQ
Activities: Production of electricity
Parent: Engie S.A.
Officers: Pieter Marie Gustaaf Moens, Secretary; Sarah Jane Gregory [1965] Director/General Counsel; Sarah Frances Fleure Mingham [1977] Director; Wilfrid John Petrie [1965] Director; Simon David Pinnell [1964] Director/Accountant

International Power Luxembourg Finance Limited
Incorporated: 22 October 2003
Net Worth: £452,843,808 *Total Assets:* £488,660,576
Registered Office: Level 20, 25 Canada Square, London, E14 5LQ
Activities: Activities of head offices
Parent: International Power Luxembourg Holdings Limited
Officers: Sarah Jane Gregory, Secretary; David George Alcock [1965] Director; Sarah Frances Fleure Mingham [1977] Director; Simon David Pinnell [1964] Director

International Publishing Corporation Limited
Incorporated: 31 December 1962
Net Worth: £312,148,000 *Total Assets:* £312,148,000
Registered Office: 6th Floor, 60 Gracechurch Street, London, EC3V 0HR
Activities: Activities of other holding companies n.e.c.
Parent: IPC Magazines (UK) Limited
Officers: Joseph Henry Ceryanec [1961] Director [American]; John Stanley Zieser [1959] Director [American]

International Schools Partnership Limited
Incorporated: 9 October 2015
Net Worth Deficit: £4,598,898 *Total Assets:* £211,641,856
Registered Office: 101 Wigmore Street, London, W1U 1QU
Activities: Educational support services
Parent: Permotio International Learning SARL
Officers: Paul David Brett [1950] Director; Steven David Russell Brown [1968] Director/Accountant; Andrew David Deakin [1973] Director; Darren Mee [1965] Director; Charles David Robinson [1961] Director; Ryan James Robson [1970] Director

International Trade and Exhibitions Overseas Limited
Incorporated: 6 May 1994 *Employees:* 1
Net Worth: £32,946,396 *Total Assets:* £123,048,816
Registered Office: 2 Kingdom Street, London, W2 6JG
Activities: Other business support service activities n.e.c.
Parent: ITE Enterprises Limited
Officers: Andrew Beach [1975] Director/Chief Financial Officer; William David Hudson [1963] Director/Chartered Accountant; Desmond William James McEwan [1980] Director/Accountant

International Transport Intermediaries Club Limited
Incorporated: 18 June 1992
Net Worth: £28,601,750 *Total Assets:* £148,480,784
Registered Office: 90 Fenchurch Street, London, EC3M 4ST
Activities: Non-life insurance
Officers: Kieran Patrick Halpenny, Secretary; Robert MacNair Bishop [1957] Director; Christoph Doehle [1965] Director [German]; Timothy Martin Evans [1964] Director; Eduardo Fernandez Davila [1957] Director [Spanish]; Peter Douglas French [1949] Director; Scott Michael Jones [1959] Director [American]; Timothy Taylor Jones [1955] Director; Allan Stuart Munro [1957] Director; Lars Goran Safverstrom [1952] Director [Swedish]; Ugo Salerno [1953] Director [Italian]; Michael Shakesheff [1975] Director; Jeffrey David Woyda [1962] Director

Internetq Group Limited
Incorporated: 28 September 2015 *Employees:* 149
Net Worth: £23,932,636 *Total Assets:* £135,561,648
Registered Office: 14 Old Queen Street, London, SW1H 9HP
Activities: Other information service activities n.e.c.
Shareholder: Panagiotis Dimitropoulos
Officers: Veronica Julia Nocetti, Secretary; David George Calder [1965] Director/Partner; Panagiotis Dimitropoulos [1970] Director/Company Executive [Greek]; Veronica Julia Nocetti [1969] Director [Greek]

Interoute Communications Holdings Limited
Incorporated: 9 October 2003
Net Worth: £576,428,160 *Total Assets:* £1,238,397,184
Registered Office: 31st Floor, 25 Canary Wharf, London, E14 5LQ
Activities: Other telecommunications activities
Parent: GTT Holdings Limited
Officers: Jessica Anne Kaman [1974] Director/Vice President of Finance and Treasurer [American]; Christopher Turing McKee [1968] Director/General Counsel [American]; Michael Thomas Sicoli [1970] Managing Director [American]

Interoute Communications Limited
Incorporated: 28 June 2002 *Employees:* 231
Net Worth: £229,872,592 *Total Assets:* £1,594,560,768
Registered Office: 31st Floor, 25 Canary Wharf, London, E14 5LQ
Activities: Other telecommunications activities
Parent: Interoute Communications Holdings Ltd
Officers: Jessica Anne Kaman [1974] Director/Vice President of Finance and Treasurer [American]; Christopher Turing McKee [1968] Director/General Counsel [American]; Michael Thomas Sicoli [1970] Managing Director [American]

Interoute Finco Limited
Incorporated: 11 August 2015
Previous: Interoute Finco PLC
Net Worth: £292,231 *Total Assets:* £573,395,392
Registered Office: 31st Floor, 25 Canary Wharf, London, E14 5LQ
Activities: Other credit granting n.e.c.
Parent: Interoute Communications Holdings Ltd
Officers: Jessica Anne Kaman [1974] Director/Vice President of Finance and Treasurer [American]; Christopher Turing McKee [1968] Director/General Counsel [American]; Michael Thomas Sicoli [1970] Managing Director [American]

Interoute Managed Services UK Limited
Incorporated: 22 March 2013 *Employees:* 376
Previous: Easynet Global Services Limited
Net Worth: £39,345,000 *Total Assets:* £156,608,000
Registered Office: 31st Floor, 25 Canada Square, London, E14 5LQ
Activities: Wired telecommunications activities
Parent: MDNX Group Holdings Limited
Officers: Jessica Anne Kaman [1974] Director/Vice President of Finance and Treasurer [American]; Christopher Turing McKee [1968] Director/General Counsel [American]; Michael Thomas Sicoli [1970] Managing Director [American]

Interpayment Services Limited
Incorporated: 27 November 1987
Net Worth: £28,689,000 *Total Assets:* £163,666,000
Registered Office: 4th Floor, Kings Place, 90 York Way, London, N1 9AG
Activities: Other service activities n.e.c.
Parent: Travelex Global and Financial Services Limited
Officers: Victoria Benis-Lonsdale, Secretary; James Edward Sullivan Birch [1964] Director/General Counsel; Anthony Francis D'Souza [1971] Director

Interpublic Limited
Incorporated: 29 December 1965 *Employees:* 28
Net Worth: £63,619,000 *Total Assets:* £245,632,992
Registered Office: 3 Grosvenor Gardens, London, SW1W 0BD
Activities: Activities of head offices
Officers: Louise Bean, Secretary; Derek John Coleman [1955] Director/Solicitor; Warren Spencer Kay [1971] Director/Accountant; Alessandro Francesco Nisita [1969] Director/VP Assistant Treasurer [Italian]

Interserve (Defence) Ltd
Incorporated: 18 January 1991 *Employees:* 1,425
Net Worth: £72,758,000 *Total Assets:* £154,714,000
Registered Office: Capital Tower, 91 Waterloo Road, London, SE1 8RT
Activities: Combined facilities support activities
Parent: InterserveFM Ltd
Officers: Stephanie Alison Pound, Secretary; Kevin Alan Dobbs [1973] Commercial Director; Nicholas John Goodridge [1970] Finance Director; Lynn Christine Mawdsley [1959] Director/Deputy Chief Financial Officer; Brian Talbot [1968] Director

Interserve (Facilities Management) Ltd
Incorporated: 23 September 1996 *Employees:* 13,328
Net Worth: £66,956,000 *Total Assets:* £303,823,008
Registered Office: Capital Tower, 91 Waterloo Road, London, SE1 8RT
Activities: Combined facilities support activities
Parent: InterserveFM Ltd
Officers: Stephanie Alison Pound, Secretary; Aidan Patrick Bell [1972] Managing Director [Irish]; Martin Sean Burholt [1968] Managing Director; Philip George Clark [1965] Business Development Director; Jeffrey Paul Flanagan [1960] Managing Director; John William Lambert [1966] HR Director; Lynn Christine Mawdsley [1959] Director/Deputy Chief Financial Officer; Brian Talbot [1968] Director

Interserve FS (UK) Limited
Incorporated: 19 December 1988 *Employees:* 9,863
Net Worth: £21,438,000 *Total Assets:* £104,651,000
Registered Office: Capital Tower, 91 Waterloo Road, London, SE1 8RT
Activities: Activities of households as employers of domestic personnel
Parent: InterserveFM Ltd
Officers: Stephanie Alison Pound, Secretary; Aidan Patrick Bell [1972] Managing Director [Irish]; Martin Sean Burholt [1968] Managing Director; Philip George Clark [1965] Business Development Director; Jeffrey Paul Flanagan [1960] Managing Director; John William Lambert [1966] HR Director; Lynn Christine Mawdsley [1959] Director/Deputy Chief Financial Officer

Interservefm (Holdings) Ltd
Incorporated: 19 December 2000
Net Worth: £152,406,000 *Total Assets:* £207,708,992
Registered Office: Capital Tower, 91 Waterloo Road, London, SE1 8RT
Activities: Activities of other holding companies n.e.c.
Parent: How Group Limited
Officers: Stephanie Alison Pound, Secretary; Philip George Clark [1965] Business Development Director; John William Lambert [1966] HR Director; Lynn Christine Mawdsley [1959] Director/Deputy Chief Financial Officer

Interservefm Ltd
Incorporated: 21 May 1993 *Employees:* 908
Net Worth Deficit: £75,788,000 *Total Assets:* £363,403,008
Registered Office: Capital Tower, 91 Waterloo Road, London, SE1 8RT
Activities: Activities of head offices
Parent: Building & Property (Holdings) Limited
Officers: Stephanie Alison Pound, Secretary; Philip George Clark [1965] Business Development Director; John William Lambert [1966] HR Director; Lynn Christine Mawdsley [1959] Director/Deputy Chief Financial Officer

Intertek Group PLC
Incorporated: 9 August 2001 *Employees:* 43,306
Net Worth: £709,699,968 *Total Assets:* £2,052,400,000
Registered Office: 33 Cavendish Square, London, W1G 0PS
Activities: Activities of head offices
Officers: Fiona Maria Evans, Secretary; Graham Denis Allan [1955] Director [British/Australian]; Gurnek Singh Bains [1957] Director; Andre Pierre Joseph Lacroix [1960] Director [French]; Pamela Louise Makin [1960] Director/Chief Executive Officer; Andrew David Martin [1960] Director; Ross McCluskey [1980] Director; Sir David Edward Reid [1947] Director/Chairman; Gillian Ann Rider [1954] Director; Jean-Michel Gerard Valette [1960] Director [American]; Lena Cooper Wilson [1964] Director/Chief Executive Officer

INTL FCStone Ltd
Incorporated: 9 November 2005 *Employees:* 271
Net Worth: £187,680,592 *Total Assets:* £4,185,970,944
Registered Office: First Floor, Moor House, 120 London Wall, London, EC2Y 5ET
Activities: Security and commodity contracts dealing activities
Parent: INTL Netherlands B.V.
Officers: Catherine Osayande Odigie, Secretary; Stephen Richard Bailey [1956] Director/Accounts; Lindsay James McNeile [1948] Director; Sean Michael O'Connor [1962] Director [American]; Philip Andrew Smith [1972] Director/Finance; Malcolm Wilde [1950] Director

Intu (SGS) Finance PLC
Incorporated: 8 January 2013
Net Worth: £17,424 *Total Assets:* £1,157,463,552
Registered Office: 35 Great St Helen's, London, EC3A 6AP
Activities: Financial intermediation not elsewhere classified
Parent: Intertrust Corporate Services Limited
Officers: Susan Iris Abrahams [1957] Director

Intu (SGS) Finco Limited
Incorporated: 10 January 2013
Total Assets: £2,133,100,032
Registered Office: 40 Broadway, London, SW1H 0BT
Activities: Activities of head offices
Parent: Intu (SGS) Limited
Officers: Susan Marsden, Secretary; David Andrew Fischel [1958] Director/Chartered Accountant; Hugh Michael Ford [1967] Director/General Corporate Counsel; Barbara Gibbes [1975] Director/Accountant; Edward Matthew Giles Roberts [1963] Finance Director

Intu (SGS) Holdco Limited
Incorporated: 10 January 2013
Net Worth: £643,200,000 *Total Assets:* £3,188,699,904
Registered Office: 40 Broadway, London, SW1H 0BT
Activities: Activities of other holding companies n.e.c.
Parent: Intu (SGS) Topco Limited
Officers: Susan Marsden, Secretary; David Andrew Fischel [1958] Director/Chartered Accountant; Hugh Michael Ford [1967] Director/General Corporate Counsel; Barbara Gibbes [1975] Director/Accountant; Edward Matthew Giles Roberts [1963] Finance Director

Intu Debenture PLC
Incorporated: 28 July 2006
Net Worth Deficit: £16,000,000 *Total Assets:* £680,700,032
Registered Office: 40 Broadway, London, SW1H 0BT
Activities: Activities of head offices
Parent: Intu Properties PLC
Officers: Susan Marsden, Secretary; David Andrew Fischel [1958] Director/Chartered Accountant; Barbara Gibbes [1975] Director/Accountant; Trevor Pereira [1965] Director; Edward Matthew Giles Roberts [1963] Finance Director

Intu Eldon Square Limited
Incorporated: 8 July 2005
Net Worth: £130,400,000 *Total Assets:* £253,800,000
Registered Office: 40 Broadway, London, SW1H 0BT
Activities: Other letting and operating of own or leased real estate
Parent: Intu Debenture PLC
Officers: Susan Marsden, Secretary; Martin Richard Breeden [1967] Director/Chartered Surveyor; David Andrew Fischel [1958] Director/Chartered Accountant; Colin Flinn [1969] Director; Barbara Gibbes [1975] Director/Accountant; Kathryn Anne Grant [1973] Director/Chartered Surveyor; Trevor Pereira [1965] Director; Edward Matthew Giles Roberts [1963] Finance Director; Nick Round [1962] Director; Rebecca Mary Sarah Elizabeth Ryman [1975] Regional Director; Julian Nicholas Wilkinson [1963] Director/Chartered Surveyor

Intu Finance MH Limited
Incorporated: 16 January 2013
Net Worth: £17,200,000 *Total Assets:* £772,600,000
Registered Office: 40 Broadway, London, SW1H 0BT
Activities: Activities of head offices
Parent: Liberty International Holdings Limited
Officers: Susan Marsden, Secretary; David Andrew Fischel [1958] Director/Chartered Accountant; Hugh Michael Ford [1967] Director/General Corporate Counsel; Barbara Gibbes [1975] Director/Accountant; Trevor Pereira [1965] Director; Edward Matthew Giles Roberts [1963] Finance Director

Intu Investments Limited
Incorporated: 17 December 1993
Net Worth: £1,022,499,968 *Total Assets:* £1,035,299,968
Registered Office: 40 Broadway, London, SW1H 0BT
Activities: Other letting and operating of own or leased real estate
Parent: intu Shopping Centres PLC
Officers: Susan Marsden, Secretary; Martin Richard Breeden [1967] Director/Chartered Surveyor; David Andrew Fischel [1958] Director/Chartered Accountant; Colin Flinn [1969] Director; Hugh Michael Ford [1967] Director/General Corporate Counsel; Barbara Gibbes [1975] Director/Accountant; Kathryn Anne Grant [1973] Director/Chartered Surveyor; Trevor Pereira [1965] Director; Edward Matthew Giles Roberts [1963] Finance Director; Nick Round [1962] Director; Rebecca Mary Sarah Elizabeth Ryman [1975] Regional Director; Julian Nicholas Wilkinson [1963] Director/Chartered Surveyor

Intu Lakeside Limited
Incorporated: 19 January 2001
Net Worth: £591,900,032 *Total Assets:* £1,685,600,000
Registered Office: 40 Broadway, London, SW1H 0BT
Activities: Other letting and operating of own or leased real estate
Parent: Intu (SGS) Limited
Officers: Susan Marsden, Secretary; Martin Richard Breeden [1967] Director/Chartered Surveyor; David Andrew Fischel [1958] Director/Chartered Accountant; Colin Flinn [1969] Director; Hugh Michael Ford [1967] Director/General Corporate Counsel; Barbara Gibbes [1975] Director/Accountant; Kathryn Anne Grant [1973] Director/Chartered Surveyor; Trevor Pereira [1965] Director; Edward Matthew Giles Roberts [1963] Finance Director; Nick Round [1962] Director; Rebecca Mary Sarah Elizabeth Ryman [1975] Regional Director; Julian Nicholas Wilkinson [1963] Director/Chartered Surveyor

Intu Metrocentre Finance PLC
Incorporated: 24 September 2013
Net Worth: £17,308 *Total Assets:* £484,724,288
Registered Office: 35 Great St Helen's, London, EC3A 6AP
Activities: Financial intermediation not elsewhere classified
Parent: Intertrust Corporate Services Limited
Officers: Susan Iris Abrahams [1957] Director

Intu Metrocentre Limited
Incorporated: 1 August 2000
Net Worth Deficit: £159,400,000 *Total Assets:* £290,600,000
Registered Office: 40 Broadway, London, SW1H 0BT
Activities: Other letting and operating of own or leased real estate
Parent: intu Shopping Centres PLC
Officers: Susan Marsden, Secretary; David Andrew Fischel [1958] Director/Chartered Accountant; Edward Matthew Giles Roberts [1963] Finance Director

Intu Milton Keynes Limited
Incorporated: 6 July 2012
Previous: Intu Midsummer Limited
Net Worth: £56,300,000 *Total Assets:* £286,700,000
Registered Office: 40 Broadway, London, SW1H 0BT
Activities: Other letting and operating of own or leased real estate
Parent: intu Shopping Centres PLC
Officers: Susan Marsden, Secretary; Martin Richard Breeden [1967] Director/Chartered Surveyor; David Andrew Fischel [1958] Director/Chartered Accountant; Colin Flinn [1969] Director; Hugh Michael Ford [1967] Director/General Corporate Counsel; Barbara Gibbes [1975] Director/Accountant; Kathryn Anne Grant [1973] Director/Chartered Surveyor; Trevor Pereira [1965] Director; Edward Matthew Giles Roberts [1963] Finance Director; Nick Round [1962] Director; Rebecca Mary Sarah Elizabeth Ryman [1975] Regional Director; Julian Nicholas Wilkinson [1963] Director/Chartered Surveyor

Intu Potteries Limited
Incorporated: 24 April 2002
Net Worth: £11,600,000 *Total Assets:* £133,900,000
Registered Office: 40 Broadway, London, SW1H 0BT
Activities: Activities of other holding companies n.e.c.
Parent: Intu Debenture PLC
Officers: Susan Marsden, Secretary; David Andrew Fischel [1958] Director/Chartered Accountant; Barbara Gibbes [1975] Director/Accountant; Trevor Pereira [1965] Director; Edward Matthew Giles Roberts [1963] Finance Director

Intu Properties Investments Limited
Incorporated: 25 July 1996
Net Worth: £111,700,000 *Total Assets:* £140,000,000
Registered Office: 40 Broadway, London, SW1H 0BT
Activities: Activities of other holding companies n.e.c.
Parent: Intu (SGS) Limited
Officers: Susan Marsden, Secretary; David Andrew Fischel [1958] Director/Chartered Accountant; Hugh Michael Ford [1967] Director/General Corporate Counsel; Barbara Gibbes [1975] Director/Accountant; Trevor Pereira [1965] Director; Edward Matthew Giles Roberts [1963] Finance Director

Intu Properties PLC
Incorporated: 14 December 1998 *Employees:* 2,603
Net Worth: £5,074,999,808 *Total Assets:* £10,794,500,096
Registered Office: 40 Broadway, London, SW1H 0BT
Activities: Activities of real estate investment trusts
Officers: Susan Marsden, Secretary; Rakhi Goss-Custard [1974] Director [American]; Adele Helen Anderson [1965] Director; Michael Ian Burke [1956] Director; David Andrew Fischel [1958] Director/Chartered Accountant; Edward Matthew Giles Roberts [1963] Finance Director; John Strachan [1951] Director; Steven Keith Underwood [1974] Director; John Whittaker [1942] Director

Intu Shopping Centres PLC
Incorporated: 26 January 1994
Net Worth: £1,203,399,936 *Total Assets:* £2,409,600,000
Registered Office: 40 Broadway, London, SW1H 0BT
Activities: Other letting and operating of own or leased real estate
Parent: Intu Properties PLC
Officers: Susan Marsden, Secretary; David Andrew Fischel [1958] Director/Chartered Accountant; Hugh Michael Ford [1967] Director/General Corporate Counsel; Barbara Gibbes [1975] Director/Accountant; Trevor Pereira [1965] Director; Edward Matthew Giles Roberts [1963] Finance Director

Intu The Hayes Limited
Incorporated: 19 January 2001
Net Worth Deficit: £27,100,000 *Total Assets:* £359,200,000
Registered Office: 40 Broadway, London, SW1H 0BT
Activities: Other letting and operating of own or leased real estate
Parent: intu Shopping Centres PLC
Officers: Susan Marsden, Secretary; Hugh Michael Ford [1967] Director/General Corporate Counsel; Barbara Gibbes [1975] Director/Accountant; Trevor Pereira [1965] Director

Intu Trafford Centre Group (UK) Limited
Incorporated: 8 June 2004
Net Worth: £227,066,000 *Total Assets:* £886,937,024
Registered Office: 40 Broadway, London, SW1H 0BT
Activities: Activities of other holding companies n.e.c.
Parent: Intu Trafford Centre Group Limited
Officers: Susan Marsden, Secretary; David Andrew Fischel [1958] Director/Chartered Accountant; Barbara Gibbes [1975] Director/Accountant; Edward Matthew Giles Roberts [1963] Finance Director

Intu Watford Limited
Incorporated: 11 March 2005
Net Worth: £40,700,000 *Total Assets:* £339,300,000
Registered Office: 40 Broadway, London, SW1H 0BT
Activities: Other letting and operating of own or leased real estate
Parent: Intu (SGS) Limited
Officers: Susan Marsden, Secretary; Martin Richard Breeden [1967] Director/Chartered Surveyor; David Andrew Fischel [1958] Director/Chartered Accountant; Colin Flinn [1969] Director; Hugh Michael Ford [1967] Director/General Corporate Counsel; Barbara Gibbes [1975] Director/Accountant; Kathryn Anne Grant [1973] Director/Chartered Surveyor; Trevor Pereira [1965] Director; Edward Matthew Giles Roberts [1963] Finance Director; Nick Round [1962] Director; Rebecca Mary Sarah Elizabeth Ryman [1975] Regional Director; Julian Nicholas Wilkinson [1963] Director/Chartered Surveyor

Investcorp Credit Management EU Limited
Incorporated: 15 December 2005
Previous: 3i Debt Management Investments Limited
Net Worth: £130,993,000 *Total Assets:* £275,499,008
Registered Office: Investcorp House, 48 Grosvenor Street, London, W1K 3HW
Activities: Security and commodity contracts dealing activities
Officers: Jonathan Adam Lay, Secretary; Jeremy Ranjan Ghose [1962] Executive Director; Peter Goody [1969] Director/Fund Management; Daniel Jose Lopez-Cruz [1965] Director/Banker [Spanish]

Investec 1 Limited
Incorporated: 10 January 1912
Net Worth: £1,244,720,000 *Total Assets:* £2,365,828,096
Registered Office: 30 Gresham Street, London, EC2V 7QP
Activities: Activities of financial services holding companies
Parent: Investec PLC
Officers: David Miller, Secretary; Bernard Kantor [1949] Director/Banker [Irish]; Stephen Koseff [1951] Director/Banker [South African]; Kevin Patrick McKenna [1966] Director/Chief Operating Officer of Investec Bank PLC [Irish]; David Michael Van Der Walt [1964] Director/Banker [South African]

Investec Asset Management Limited
Incorporated: 10 July 1986 *Employees:* 409
Net Worth: £102,004,000 *Total Assets:* £276,782,016
Registered Office: Woolgate Exchange, 25 Basinghall Street, London, EC2V 5HA
Activities: Fund management activities
Parent: Investec 1 Limited
Officers: Adrian Brettell Dyke, Secretary; Hendrik Jacobus Du Toit [1961] Investment Director; Domenico Ferrini [1968] Director/Chief Executive Officer [South African]; Lord Howard Emerson Flight [1948] Director; John Conrad Green [1965] Director/Investment Manager [South African]; Hugh Sidney Herman [1940] Director [South African]; Bernard Kantor [1949] Director [Irish]; Ian Robert Kantor [1946] Director [Dutch]; Stephen Koseff [1951] Director [South African]; Kim Mary McFarland [1964] Operations Director; Richard Berry Saunders [1951] Director; Khumo Lesego Shuenyane [1970] Director/Chartered Accountant [South African]; Bradley Tapnack [1947] Director/Banker [South African]; Fani Titi [1962] Director [South African]

Investec Bank PLC
Incorporated: 20 December 1950
Net Worth: £2,012,226,944 *Total Assets:* £20,100,284,416
Registered Office: 30 Gresham Street, London, EC2V 7QP
Activities: Banks
Parent: Investec 1 Limited
Officers: David Miller, Secretary; Zarina Bibi Mahomed Bassa [1964] Director/Businesswoman [South African]; David Friedland [1953] Director/Retired [South African]; Haruko Fukuda OBE [1946] Director/Investment Banker; Ruth Leas [1972] Director/Risk Management - Banking; Sheikh Mansurah Tal-At Mannings [1963] Director; Kevin Patrick McKenna [1966] Director/Chief Operating Officer of Investec Bank PLC [Irish]; Brian David Stevenson [1953] Senior Independent Director; Fani Titi [1962] Director/Investment Banker [South African]; David Michael Van Der Walt [1964] Director/Banker [South African]; Lesley Susan Watkins [1959] Director; James Kieran Colum Whelan [1963] Director/Banker [Irish]; Ian Robert Wohlman [1954] Director/Manager

Investec Group (UK) Limited
Incorporated: 2 February 1988
Previous: Investec Group (UK) PLC
Net Worth: £443,451,008 *Total Assets:* £518,907,008
Registered Office: 30 Gresham Street, London, EC2V 7QP
Activities: Non-trading company
Officers: David Miller, Secretary; Catherine Elizabeth Dyson [1976] Director/Chartered Accountant; Brian Mark Johnson [1974] Director/Accountant; Bernard Kantor [1949] Director/Banker [Irish]; Stephen Koseff [1951] Director/Banker [South African]; Kevin Patrick McKenna [1966] Director/Chief Operating Officer of Investec Bank PLC [Irish]

Investec Holding Company Limited
Incorporated: 9 November 2000
Net Worth: £303,216,000 *Total Assets:* £303,216,000
Registered Office: 30 Gresham Street, London, EC2V 7QP
Activities: Activities of financial services holding companies
Parent: Investec PLC
Officers: David Miller, Secretary; Bernard Kantor [1949] Director/Banker [Irish]; Stephen Koseff [1951] Director/Banker [South African]; David Michael Van Der Walt [1964] Director/Banker [South African]

Investec Investments (UK) Limited
Incorporated: 24 April 1925
Net Worth: £265,092,992 *Total Assets:* £531,236,000
Registered Office: 30 Gresham Street, London, EC2V 7QP
Activities: Non-trading company
Parent: Investec Bank PLC
Officers: David Miller, Secretary; Catherine Elizabeth Dyson [1976] Director/Chartered Accountant; Brian Mark Johnson [1974] Director/Accountant; Kevin Patrick McKenna [1966] Director/Chief Operating Officer of Investec Bank PLC [Irish]; David Michael Van Der Walt [1964] Director/Banker [South African]; Ian Robert Wohlman [1954] Director

Investec PLC
Incorporated: 17 September 1998
Net Worth: £2,324,951,040 *Total Assets:* £20,611,751,936
Registered Office: 30 Gresham Street, London, EC2V 7QP
Activities: Activities of financial services holding companies
Officers: David Miller, Secretary; Zarina Bibi Mahomed Bassa [1964] Director/Businesswoman [South African]; Laurel Charmaine Bowden [1965] Director; Glynn Robert Burger [1956] Director/Banker [South African]; Cheryl Carolus [1958] Director/Businesswoman [South African]; Peregrine Kenneth Oughton Crosthwaite [1949] Director/Stockbroker; Hendrik Jacobus Du Toit [1961] Investment Director [South African]; David Friedland [1953] Director/Retired [South African]; Philip Alan Hourquebie [1953] Director; Charles Richard Jacobs [1967] Director/Partner - Linklaters [Irish]; Bernard Kantor [1949] Director/Banker [Irish]; Ian Robert Kantor [1946] Director/Banker [Dutch]; Stephen Koseff [1951] Director/Banker [South African]; Lord George Mark Malloch-Brown [1953] Director; Kim Mary McFarland [1964] Operations Director; Khumo Lesego Shuenyane [1970] Consultant and Director [South African]; Fani Titi [1962] Director/Investment Banker [South African]

Investec Wealth & Investment Limited
Incorporated: 13 April 1987 *Employees:* 1,233
Net Worth: £198,607,008 *Total Assets:* £513,784,992
Registered Office: 30 Gresham Street, London, EC2V 7QN
Activities: Financial intermediation not elsewhere classified
Parent: Rensburg Sheppards PLC
Officers: Steven Robert Kilday, Secretary; Elizabeth Margaret Catchpole [1965] Director/Accountant; Stephen Maclaurin Elliott [1954] Director/Banker [South African]; Louise Drummond Hall [1966] Director/Investment Manager; Iain William Hooley [1972] Director/Secretary; Robert Lister [1960] Director; Murray Allan MacKay [1963] Director/Investment Manager; Dr Timothy May [1952] Director; Judith Edna Price [1957] Director; Mike Rigby [1969] Director/Compliance Officer; Andrew Paul Rydon [1967] Director/Chief Technology Officer; Tomas Haydn Street [1964] Director; Catherine Helen Thorpe [1965] Director/Solicitor; Nicola Jane Warren [1965] Director; Jonathan Peter Wragg [1967] Director

Investors in Private Capital Limited
Incorporated: 12 August 2004 *Employees:* 23
Net Worth: £159,439,008 *Total Assets:* £504,670,016
Registered Office: 73 Cornhill, London, EC3V 3QQ
Activities: Other business support service activities n.e.c.
Officers: Anne Benjamin, Secretary; Stephane Abraham Joseph Nahum [1975] Director/Private Equity [French]; James Adam Reuben [1986] Director/Investment; Eileen Marie Sawyer [1979] Director/Accountant; Malcolm Robin Turner [1935] Director

IO Investment 2 LLP
Incorporated: 24 April 2015
Net Worth: £61,291,064 *Total Assets:* £128,207,992
Registered Office: 9-10 Carlos Place, London, W1K 3AT

IO2 Propco LLP
Incorporated: 24 April 2015
Net Worth: £61,306,288 *Total Assets:* £128,206,944
Registered Office: 9-10 Carlos Place, London, W1K 3AT

IOCL Exploration and Production Oman Limited
Incorporated: 13 August 1962
Previous: Shell Exploration and Production Oman Limited
Net Worth: £174,533,472 *Total Assets:* £317,222,272
Registered Office: 3rd Floor, 5 Lloyds Avenue, London, EC3N 3AE
Activities: Wholesale of other fuels and related products
Parent: IOCL Singapore Pte. Ltd.
Officers: Lakshmi Narasimha Sastri Dhulipala [1960] Executive Director (International Trade) [Indian]; Om Parkash [1961] Executive Director (Business Development Finance) [Indian]; Debashis Roy [1959] Executive Director (Exploration & Production) [Indian]

IP Fibre Devices (UK) Limited
Incorporated: 14 November 1994
Net Worth: £778,931,712 *Total Assets:* £960,196,736
Registered Office: 1 Vincent Square, London, SW1P 2PN
Activities: Activities of other holding companies n.e.c.
Officers: Timothy Peter Verghese Mammen, Secretary/Accountant; Dr Valentin Pavlovich Gapontsev [1939] Director/Scientist [Russian]; Dr Eugeni Scherbakov [1947] Director/Scientist [Russian]

IP Group PLC
Incorporated: 24 April 2001 *Employees:* 115
Net Worth: £1,504,499,968 *Total Assets:* £1,660,499,968
Registered Office: The Walbrook Building, 25 Walbrook, London, EC4N 8AF
Activities: Activities of venture and development capital companies
Officers: Angela Leach, Secretary/Lawyer; Alan John Aubrey [1961] Director; David Graham Baynes [1964] Director; Professor David Knox Houston Begg [1950] Director; Jonathan Brooks [1956] Director; Heejae Richard Chae [1969] Director [American]; Sir Douglas Jardine Flint [1955] Director/Banker; Greg Smith [1978] Director/Accountant; Dr Elaine Sullivan [1961] Director; Michael Charles Nettleton Townend [1962] Director

IP Karugamo Holdings (UK) Limited
Incorporated: 2 May 2014
Net Worth: £761,561,984 *Total Assets:* £877,011,968
Registered Office: Level 20, 25 Canada Square, London, E14 5LQ
Activities: Activities of head offices
Parent: International Power Consolidated Holdings Limited
Officers: Sarah Jane Gregory, Secretary; David George Alcock [1965] Director; Sarah Frances Fleure Mingham [1977] Director; Simon David Pinnell [1964] Director/Accountant

IP2IPO Innovations Limited
Incorporated: 2 October 1986 *Employees:* 68
Previous: Imperial Innovations Limited
Net Worth Deficit: £36,965,720 *Total Assets:* £444,518,400
Registered Office: Top Floor, The Walbrook Building, 25 Walbrook, London, EC4N 8AF
Activities: Other professional, scientific and technical activities n.e.c.
Parent: Touchstone Innovations PLC
Officers: Alan John Aubrey [1961] Director; David Graham Baynes [1964] Director; Gregory Simon Smith [1978] Director; Michael Charles Nettleton Townend [1962] Director

IP2IPO Limited
Incorporated: 18 September 2000 *Employees:* 71
Net Worth: £242,643,008 *Total Assets:* £853,177,024
Registered Office: The Walbrook Building, 25 Walbrook, London, EC4N 8AF
Activities: Management consultancy activities other than financial management
Parent: IP Group PLC
Officers: Alan John Aubrey [1961] Director; David Graham Baynes [1964] Financial Director; Greg Simon Smith [1978] Director/Accountant; Michael Charles Nettleton Townend [1962] Director

IPC Information Systems UK Limited
Incorporated: 2 September 2015
Net Worth: £10,314,380 *Total Assets:* £177,269,616
Registered Office: Tower House, 67-73 Worship Street, London, EC2A 2DZ
Activities: Activities of head offices
Officers: Linda Marie Pennington-Benton, Secretary; Damian Joseph Peter Hart [1963] Director/Accountant

Ipek Investment Limited
Incorporated: 26 May 2015
Net Worth: £423,557,184 *Total Assets:* £423,582,240
Registered Office: 99 Gray's Inn Road, London, WC1X 8TY
Activities: Activities of investment trusts
Officers: Hamdi Akin Ipek [1963] Director [Turkish]

IPG Holdings (UK) Limited
Incorporated: 28 February 1989 *Employees:* 4,742
Net Worth: £55,872,000 *Total Assets:* £1,080,169,984
Registered Office: 3 Grosvenor Gardens, London, SW1W 0BD
Activities: Activities of head offices
Parent: IPG Europe Limited
Officers: Louise Bean, Secretary; William Francis Cleary [1963] Senior Director, Finance [American]; Derek John Coleman [1955] Director/Solicitor; Warren Spencer Kay [1971] Director/Accountant

IPGL (Holdings) Limited
Incorporated: 30 May 2014 *Employees:* 200
Net Worth: £1,039,827,968 *Total Assets:* £1,175,111,936
Registered Office: IPGL Limited, 3rd Floor, 39 Sloane Street, Knightsbridge, London, SW1X 9LP
Activities: Activities of other holding companies n.e.c.
Shareholders: Michael Alan Spencer; Lady Lorraine Geraldine Spencer; David Jeremy Courtenay-Stamp
Officers: Bibi Rahima Ally, Secretary; David Jeremy Courtenay-Stamp [1962] Director/Solicitor; David Gelber [1947] Director [Canadian]; Michael Alan Spencer [1955] Director

IPGL Limited
Incorporated: 16 April 1986 *Employees:* 15
Net Worth: £107,582,000 *Total Assets:* £609,936,000
Registered Office: 3rd Floor, 39 Sloane Street, Knightsbridge, London, SW1X 9LP
Activities: Activities of other holding companies n.e.c.
Parent: IPGL (Holdings) Limited
Officers: Bibi Rahima Ally, Secretary; David Jeremy Courtenay-Stamp [1962] Director/Solicitor; David Gelber [1947] Director [Canadian]; Michael Alan Spencer [1955] Director/Chairman

IPM Energy Trading Limited
Incorporated: 23 January 1990
Net Worth Deficit: £1,033,000 *Total Assets:* £393,924,000
Registered Office: Level 20, 25 Canada Square, London, E14 5LQ
Activities: Production of electricity
Parent: IP Karugamo Holdings (UK) Limited
Officers: Sarah Jane Gregory, Secretary; Simon Huw Bateman [1966] Director; Andrew Wilson Garner [1962] Director/Accountant; Charlotte McGuinness [1973] Director

IPM Holdings (UK) Limited
Incorporated: 2 May 2014
Net Worth: £158,311,008 *Total Assets:* £173,415,008
Registered Office: Level 20, 25 Canada Square, London, E14 5LQ
Activities: Activities of head offices
Parent: IP Karugamo Holdings (UK) Limited
Officers: Sarah Jane Gregory, Secretary; David George Alcock [1965] Director; Isao Kajimura [1969] Director [Japanese]; Isao Kajimura [1969] Alternate Director [Japanese]; Hiromu Kayamori [1972] Director [Japanese]; Wilfrid John Petrie [1965] Director; Simon David Pinnell [1964] Director/Accountant

IPM Peacock Limited
Incorporated: 22 September 2015
Net Worth: £659,534,784 *Total Assets:* £660,259,136
Registered Office: Level 20, 25 Canada Square, London, E14 5LQ
Activities: Non-trading company
Parent: Normanclose 2 LLP
Officers: Sarah Jane Gregory, Secretary; David George Alcock [1965] Director; Hiromu Kayamori [1972] Director [Japanese]; Sarah Frances Fleure Mingham [1977] Director; Simon David Pinnell [1964] Director

IPP Bond Limited
Incorporated: 2 August 2007
Net Worth: £3,879,331 *Total Assets:* £1,424,407,808
Registered Office: 3 More London Riverside, London, SE1 2AQ
Activities: Activities of head offices
Parent: IPP Holdings 1 Limited
Officers: Amanda Elizabeth Woods, Secretary; Muhammad Ahmed Anwer [1984] Director/Accountant [Pakistani]; Giles James Frost [1962] Director/Investment Banker; Michael John Gregory [1968] Director/Chartered Builder

IPP Gas Holdings Limited
Incorporated: 11 November 2016
Net Worth: £234,239,616 *Total Assets:* £276,008,256
Registered Office: 3 More London Riverside, London, SE1 2AQ
Activities: Activities of other holding companies n.e.c.
Parent: IPP Bond Limited
Officers: Amanda Elizabeth Woods, Secretary; Giles James Frost [1962] Director/Solicitor; Michael John Gregory [1968] Director/Chartered Builder; Gavin Richard Tait [1970] Director

Ipsos EMEA Holdings Ltd
Incorporated: 16 December 2003
Net Worth: £83,202,000 *Total Assets:* £315,311,008
Registered Office: 3 Thomas More Square, London, E1W 1YW
Activities: Market research and public opinion polling
Parent: Ipsos SA
Officers: Rupert Van Hullen, Secretary; Brian Gosschalk [1955] Director; John Roger Haworth [1961] Director; Laurence Stoclet [1965] Director [French]; Didier Michel Truchot [1946] Director [French]

IQVIA Holdings (UK) Ltd.
Incorporated: 22 October 1980
Previous: IMS Holdings (U.K.) Limited
Net Worth: £174,068,000 *Total Assets:* £229,368,992
Registered Office: 210 Pentonville Road, London, N1 9JY
Activities: Activities of head offices
Parent: IQVIA Solutions HQ Ltd.
Officers: Alistair Roland Grenfell [1973] Director/Executive Manager; Pavan Hayer [1968] Finance Director

IQVIA Solutions Finance UK I Ltd.
Incorporated: 6 November 2013
Previous: IMS Health Finance UK I Limited
Net Worth: £219,271,200 *Total Assets:* £219,706,352
Registered Office: 210 Pentonville Road, London, N1 9JY
Activities: Activities of other holding companies n.e.c.
Parent: IQVIA Holdings Inc.
Officers: James Grant Berkshire [1973] Director/Vice President, Business Management; Alistair Roland Grenfell [1973] Director/Executive Manager; Pavan Hayer [1968] Finance Director

IQVIA Solutions Finance UK II Ltd.
Incorporated: 6 November 2013
Previous: IMS Health Finance UK II Ltd
Net Worth: £181,862,304 *Total Assets:* £181,862,304
Registered Office: 210 Pentonville Road, London, N1 9JY
Activities: Activities of other holding companies n.e.c.
Parent: IQVIA Solutions Global Holdings UK Ltd.
Officers: James Grant Berkshire [1973] Director/Vice President, Business Management; Alistair Roland Grenfell [1973] Director/Executive Manager; Pavan Hayer [1968] Finance Director

IQVIA Solutions Finance UK V Ltd.
Incorporated: 6 November 2013
Previous: IMS Health Finance UK V Ltd
Net Worth: £96,360,976 *Total Assets:* £286,200,960
Registered Office: 210 Pentonville Road, London, N1 9JY
Activities: Activities of other holding companies n.e.c.
Parent: IQVIA Holdings Inc.
Officers: James Grant Berkshire [1973] Director/Vice President, Business Management; Alistair Roland Grenfell [1973] Director/Executive Manager; Pavan Hayer [1968] Finance Director

IQVIA Solutions Global Holdings UK Ltd.
Incorporated: 27 October 2008
Previous: IMS Health Global Holdings UK Limited
Net Worth: £180,810,000 *Total Assets:* £181,260,000
Registered Office: 210 Pentonville Road, London, N1 9JY
Activities: Activities of other holding companies n.e.c.
Parent: IQVIA Holdings (UK) Ltd.
Officers: James Grant Berkshire [1973] Director/Vice President Business Management; Pavan Hayer [1968] Finance Director

IQVIA Solutions HQ Ltd.
Incorporated: 12 August 1998 *Employees:* 143
Previous: IMS Health HQ Limited
Net Worth: £134,560,992 *Total Assets:* £216,478,000
Registered Office: 210 Pentonville Road, London, N1 9JY
Activities: Activities of head offices
Parent: IMS Health Group Limited
Officers: James Grant Berkshire [1973] Director/Vice President Business Management; Alistair Roland Grenfell [1973] Director/Executive Manager

IQVIA Solutions UK Limited
Incorporated: 5 August 1959 *Employees:* 205
Previous: IMS Health Limited
Net Worth: £39,088,000 *Total Assets:* £325,131,008
Registered Office: 210 Pentonville Road, London, N1 9JY
Activities: Advertising agencies
Parent: Pharmadeals Limited
Officers: Alistair Roland Grenfell [1973] Director/Executive Manager; Imran Mecci [1977] Director/Accountant; Timothy Peter Sheppard [1971] Director/General Manager

Iranian Oil Company (U.K.) Limited
Incorporated: 4 August 1971 *Employees:* 2
Net Worth Deficit: £145,467,008 *Total Assets:* £172,479,008
Registered Office: 6th Floor, NIOC House, 4 Victoria Street, London, SW1H 0NE
Activities: Extraction of natural gas
Parent: F.C.M Limited
Officers: Jafar Damanpak, Secretary; Jafar Damanpak [1975] Managing Director [Iranian]

Irida PLC
Incorporated: 20 October 2009 *Employees:* 3
Net Worth Deficit: £24,401,008 *Total Assets:* £413,628,384
Registered Office: Third Floor, 1 King's Arms Yard, London, EC2R 7AF
Activities: Other business support service activities n.e.c.
Parent: Irida Holdings Limited
Officers: Robert Sutton [1978] Director/Financial Services [American]; Daniel Jonathan Wynne [1970] Director

Iridium Midco Limited
Incorporated: 20 June 2016 *Employees:* 154
Net Worth Deficit: £19,840,000 *Total Assets:* £105,888,000
Registered Office: Allan House, 10 John Princes Street, London, W1G 0JW
Activities: Television programme distribution activities
Parent: Iridium Topco Limited
Officers: Richard Verity, Secretary; Simon Cox [1962] Director; Richard Alexander Buchan Smith [1969] Director

Irobot UK Ltd.
Incorporated: 23 May 2017 *Employees:* 2
Net Worth: £82,216,992 *Total Assets:* £131,196,800
Registered Office: 111 Buckingham Palace Road, London, SW1W 0SR
Activities: Other professional, scientific and technical activities n.e.c.
Parent: Irobot Corporation
Officers: Glen Daniel Weinstein, Secretary; Jean Jacques Blanc [1965] Director/Vice President and General Manager EMEA [French]; Glen Daniel Weinstein [1970] Director/Attorney [American]; Karian Sauha Wong [1976] Director [American]

Iron Mountain (UK) PLC
Incorporated: 11 February 1980 *Employees:* 316
Previous: Iron Mountain (UK) Limited
Net Worth: £216,896,000 *Total Assets:* £846,876,992
Registered Office: Ground Floor, 4 More London Riverside, London, SE1 2AU
Activities: Operation of warehousing and storage facilities for land transport activities
Parent: Iron Mountain Europe (Group) Limited
Officers: Simon Patrick Moynihan, Secretary; Simon Paul Golesworthy [1968] Finance Director; Patrick John Keddy [1954] Director; Charlotte Helen Marshall [1970] Managing Director

Iron Mountain Europe (Group) Limited
Incorporated: 20 July 2006
Net Worth: £716,454,016 *Total Assets:* £1,066,531,008
Registered Office: Ground Floor, 4 More London Riverside, London, SE1 2AU
Activities: Activities of other holding companies n.e.c.
Parent: Iron Mountain Incorporated
Officers: Simon Patrick Moynihan, Secretary; Simon Paul Golesworthy [1968] Finance Director; Patrick John Keddy [1954] Director; Charlotte Helen Marshall [1970] Director

Iron Mountain Europe Limited
Incorporated: 25 November 1988 *Employees:* 138
Previous: Iron Mountain Europe PLC
Net Worth: £218,430,000 *Total Assets:* £226,174,000
Registered Office: Ground Floor, 4 More London Riverside, London, SE1 2AU
Activities: Activities of head offices
Parent: Iron Mountain Europe (Group) Limited
Officers: Simon Patrick Moynihan, Secretary; Simon Paul Golesworthy [1968] Finance Director; Patrick John Keddy [1954] Director; Charlotte Helen Marshall [1970] Director

ISG Central Services Limited
Incorporated: 2 December 1994 *Employees:* 41
Previous: ISG Central Services PLC
Net Worth: £71,947,000 *Total Assets:* £117,498,000
Registered Office: Aldgate House, 33 Aldgate High Street, London, EC3N 1AG
Activities: Activities of head offices
Parent: ISG PLC
Officers: Nicholas James Heard, Secretary; Matthew Charles James Blowers [1973] Director; Paul Martin Cossell [1965] Director; Jane Louise Falconer [1965] Director; Richard John Hubbard [1968] Director; Gordon Patrick Kew [1965] Director; Mark Stockton [1964] Director/Accountant; Paul Charles Weaver [1964] Director

ISG Construction Limited
Incorporated: 26 February 1948 *Employees:* 703
Net Worth: £16,947,000 *Total Assets:* £159,767,008
Registered Office: Aldgate House, 33 Aldgate High Street, London, EC3N 1AG
Activities: Construction of commercial buildings
Parent: ISG Construction Holdings Limited
Officers: Nicholas James Heard, Secretary; Paul Martin Cossell [1965] Director; Richard John Hubbard [1968] Director; Robert Samuel Martin [1961] Director; Andrew McLinden [1965] Director; Mark Stockton [1964] Director/Accountant

ISG Fit Out Limited
Incorporated: 7 July 2009 *Employees:* 494
Net Worth: £10,161,000 *Total Assets:* £146,807,008
Registered Office: Aldgate House, 33 Aldgate High Street, London, EC3N 1AG
Activities: Construction of commercial buildings
Parent: ISG UK Fit Out Limited
Officers: Nicholas James Heard, Secretary; Daniel John Blakeston [1967] Director/Engineer; Paul Martin Cossell [1965] Commercial Director; Richard John Hubbard [1968] Director; Mark Stockton [1964] Director/Accountant

ISG PLC
Incorporated: 23 March 2016 *Employees:* 2,659
Net Worth: £101,300,000 *Total Assets:* £654,600,000
Registered Office: Aldgate House, 33 Aldgate High Street, London, EC3N 1AG
Activities: Activities of other holding companies n.e.c.
Parent: Cathexis UK Holdings Limited
Officers: Nicholas James Heard, Secretary; Matthew Charles James Blowers [1973] Director; Paul Martin Cossell [1965] Director; Jane Louise Falconer [1965] Director; Joshua Dannenberg Friedman [1979] Director [American]; William Bruce Harrison [1986] Director/Chief Executive Officer [American]; Richard John Hubbard [1968] Director; Gordon Patrick Kew [1965] Director; Jonathan Daniel Moy [1983] Director [American]; Mark Stockton [1964] Director/Accountant; Paul Charles Weaver [1964] Director

Island Gas Limited
Incorporated: 12 November 2003
Net Worth Deficit: £8,661,000 *Total Assets:* £380,665,984
Registered Office: 7 Down Street, London, W1J 7AJ
Activities: Extraction of crude petroleum
Parent: IGas Energy PLC
Officers: John Malcolm Blaymires [1957] Director; Stephen David Bowler [1973] Director; Julian Lester Tedder [1969] Director/Chief Financial Officer

ISS Group Holdings Limited
Incorporated: 15 October 1998 *Employees:* 2
Net Worth: £114,482,864 *Total Assets:* £253,964,576
Registered Office: 8th Floor, 60 Fenchurch Street, London, EC3M 4AD
Activities: Sea and coastal freight water transport
Parent: Inchcape Shipping Services Holdings Limited
Officers: Beenadevi Mahabeer, Secretary; Kenneth Henriks [1966] Director/Chief Financial Officer [Danish]; Frank Georg Opsahl Olsen [1979] Director/Chief Operating Officer [Norwegian]

Istithmar P & O Estates (UK) Limited
Incorporated: 25 January 2007
Net Worth Deficit: £3,737,389 *Total Assets:* £141,541,984
Registered Office: 16 Palace Street, London, SW1E 5JQ
Activities: Activities of head offices
Parent: The Government of Dubai
Officers: Junaid Muhammad Rahimullah Muhammad [1968] Director/Chief Financial Officer [Pakistani]; Khwaja Kamran Shah [1977] Director/Financial Controller [Pakistani]

Itau BBA International PLC
Incorporated: 1 November 2010 *Employees:* 337
Net Worth: £856,989,248 *Total Assets:* £5,941,576,192
Registered Office: Level 20, The Broadgate Tower, 20 Primrose Street, London, EC2A 2EW
Activities: Banks
Officers: Teresa Paiva de Abreu Trigo de Negreiros, Secretary; Carlos Fernando Rossi Constantini [1974] Director [Brazilian]; Caio Ibrahim David [1968] Director [Brazilian]; Joao Marcos Pequeno de Biase [1967] Director [Brazilian]; Jean-Marc Robert Nogueira Baptista Etlin [1962] Director [Brazilian]; Gay Evans [1954] Director; Paulo Jorge Lopes [1971] Director [Portuguese]; Renato Lulia Jacob [1974] Director [Brazilian]; Milton Maluhy Filho [1976] Director [Brazilian]; Robert Mark Pickering [1959] Director

ITE Group PLC
Incorporated: 28 June 1985 *Employees:* 1,408
Net Worth: £301,035,008 *Total Assets:* £669,209,984
Registered Office: 2 Kingdom Street, London, W2 6JG
Activities: Activities of head offices
Officers: Sharon Baylay [1968] Director; Andrew Beach [1975] Director; Richard Last [1957] Director; Stephen Ronald Puckett [1961] Director; Mark Samuel Shashoua [1970] Director

ITE Holdings Limited
Incorporated: 28 July 2009
Net Worth: £432,000 *Total Assets:* £142,483,008
Registered Office: 2 Kingdom Street, London, W2 6JG
Activities: Activities of head offices
Parent: ITE Group PLC
Officers: Andrew Beach [1975] Director/Chief Financial Officer; William David Hudson [1963] Director/Chartered Accountant; Desmond William James McEwan [1980] Director

Itochu Europe PLC
Incorporated: 9 February 1987 *Employees:* 74
Net Worth: £63,995,000 *Total Assets:* £334,200,992
Registered Office: The Broadgate Tower, 20 Primrose Street, London, EC2A 2EW
Activities: Other service activities n.e.c.
Parent: Itochu Corporation
Officers: Susumu Aoyama, Secretary; Yasuhiro Imazawa [1964] Director [Japanese]; Hiroaki Shiokawa [1967] Director [Japanese]; Hiroyuki Tsubai [1960] Director/Chief Executive Officer [Japanese]; Mitsuru Umino [1966] Director [Japanese]

Itochu Fibre Limited
Incorporated: 13 April 2012 *Employees:* 11
Net Worth: £302,074,112 *Total Assets:* £779,686,400
Registered Office: The Broadgate Tower, 20 Primrose Street, London, EC2A 2EW
Activities: Wholesale of chemical products
Shareholders: Itochu Europe PLC; Itochu Corporation
Officers: Jin Asada [1971] Director/Chief Executive Officer [Japanese]; Tetsuji Kawakami [1964] Director [Japanese]; Satoshi Miyake [1961] Director [Japanese]; Masataka Tomishima [1973] Director/Chief Administrative Officer [Japanese]

Itochu Treasury Centre Europe PLC
Incorporated: 16 September 2008 *Employees:* 3
Net Worth: £134,204,000 *Total Assets:* £1,431,687,936
Registered Office: 20 Primrose Street, London, EC2A 2EW
Activities: Financial intermediation not elsewhere classified
Parent: Itochu Corporation
Officers: Yasuhiro Imazawa, Secretary; Naoki Hattori [1973] Director [Japanese]; Yasuhiro Imazawa [1964] Managing Director [Japanese]; Koichi Nitta [1964] Director/Deputy General Manager [Japanese]; Yoshiyuki Ochiai [1972] Director/General Manager [Japanese]

ITV Broadcasting Limited
Incorporated: 11 June 1969 *Employees:* 1,171
Net Worth: £452,872,000 *Total Assets:* £838,264,000
Registered Office: 2 Waterhouse Square, Holborn, London, EC1N 2AE
Activities: Television programme production activities
Parent: Granada Media Limited
Officers: Julian Stanley Ashworth [1970] Director [British/Canadian]; Sarah Louise Clarke [1975] Director; Kevin Anthony Lygo [1957] Director; Rosemary Newell [1963] Director of Programme Strategy; Rufus Radcliffe [1972] Director; Mark Norman Smith [1968] Director; Christopher Joseph Swords [1969] Managing Director; Edward Kelly Williams [1967] Director

ITV Consumer Limited
Incorporated: 6 June 1994 *Employees:* 161
Net Worth: £120,124,000 *Total Assets:* £236,518,000
Registered Office: 2 Waterhouse Square, Holborn, London, EC1N 2AE
Activities: Activities of head offices
Parent: Granada Media Limited
Officers: Ann Elizabeth Cook [1964] Director; Christopher Joseph Swords [1969] Director of Operations and Strategy; William Edward Oliver Van Rest [1971] Director

ITV Digital Channels Limited
Incorporated: 13 September 1995
Net Worth: £158,911,008 *Total Assets:* £176,362,000
Registered Office: 2 Waterhouse Square, 140 Holborn, London, EC1N 2AE
Activities: Television programme production activities
Parent: ITV Broadcasting Limited
Officers: Kevin Anthony Lygo [1957] Director; Christopher Joseph Swords [1969] Director of Operations and Strategy

ITV Enterprises Limited
Incorporated: 24 November 2016
Net Worth: £12,781,000 *Total Assets:* £336,728,000
Registered Office: 2 Waterhouse Square, 140 Holborn, London, EC1N 2AE
Activities: Non-trading company
Parent: ITV Studios Limited
Officers: Sharjeel Suleman [1976] Director/Chartered Accountant; Helen Jane Tautz [1963] Director/Company Secretary

ITV Global Entertainment Limited
Incorporated: 9 December 1987 *Employees:* 84
Net Worth: £69,748,000 *Total Assets:* £255,998,000
Registered Office: 2 Waterhouse Square, 140 Holborn, London, EC1N 2AE
Activities: Television programme production activities
Parent: Carlton Content Holdings Limited
Officers: Ruth Ann Berry [1979] Director; Maria Panayiotis Kyriacou [1969] Director; David Philip McGraynor [1972] Finance Director [Irish]; Duncan Thurston Russell Walker [1970] Finance Director

ITV Holdings Limited
Incorporated: 13 February 2001
Net Worth: £2,680,105,984 *Total Assets:* £4,177,444,096
Registered Office: 2 Waterhouse Square, 140 Holborn, London, EC1N 2AE
Activities: Non-trading company
Parent: Carlton Communications Limited
Officers: Sharjeel Suleman [1976] Director/Chartered Accountant; Helen Jane Tautz [1963] Director/Company Secretary

ITV PLC
Incorporated: 18 November 2003 *Employees:* 6,055
Net Worth: £685,000,000 *Total Assets:* £3,351,000,064
Registered Office: 2 Waterhouse Square, 140 Holborn, London, EC1N 2AE
Activities: Other business support service activities n.e.c.
Officers: Kyla Lynne Anthea Mullins, Secretary; Salman Amin [1959] Director [American]; Sir Peter Lytton Bazalgette [1953] Director; Edward Henry Bonham Carter [1960] Director; Margaret Ewing [1955] Director/Chartered Accountant; Roger Conant Faxon [1948] Director [American]; Mary Elaine Harris [1966] Director; Christopher John Kennedy [1964] Director; Anna Olive Magdelene Manz [1973] Director; Dame Carolyn Julia McCall [1961] Director; Duncan Anthony Painter [1970] Director

ITV Rights Limited
Incorporated: 30 June 2008
Net Worth: £236,944,000 *Total Assets:* £521,532,992
Registered Office: 2 Waterhouse Square, 140 Holborn, London, EC1N 2AE
Activities: Non-trading company
Parent: Granada Media Limited
Officers: Eleanor Kate Irving [1966] Director/Company Secretary; Christopher Joseph Swords [1969] Director of Operations and Strategy; Helen Jane Tautz [1963] Director/Company Secretary

ITV Services Limited
Incorporated: 12 April 1928 *Employees:* 822
Net Worth: £1,298,809,984 *Total Assets:* £2,437,592,064
Registered Office: 2 Waterhouse Square, 140 Holborn, London, EC1N 2AE
Activities: Other business support service activities n.e.c.
Parent: ITV Holdings Limited
Officers: Julian Stanley Ashworth [1970] Director [British/Canadian]; Julian Christopher Bellamy [1970] Director; Kevin Anthony Lygo [1957] Director; Paul Joseph Moore [1962] Director; Kyla Lynne Anthea Mullins [1966] Director/Lawyer; David Richard Osborn [1968] Human Resources Director; Rufus Radcliffe [1972] Director; Mark Norman Smith [1968] Director; Edward Kelly Williams [1967] Director

ITV Studios Limited
Incorporated: 26 September 1995 *Employees:* 1,268
Net Worth: £510,864,000 *Total Assets:* £1,042,483,008
Registered Office: 2 Waterhouse Square, Holborn, London, EC1N 2AE
Activities: Television programme production activities
Parent: Granada Media Limited
Officers: Julian Stanley Ashworth [1970] Director [British/Canadian]; Julian Christopher Bellamy [1970] Director; Darren Campbell [1970] Director [Australian]; Maria Panayiotis Kyriacou [1969] Director; David Philip McGraynor [1972] Finance Director [Irish]; Denise O'Donoghue [1955] Director

ITV2 Limited
Incorporated: 30 November 1984
Net Worth: £136,492,992 *Total Assets:* £295,028,000
Registered Office: 2 Waterhouse Square, 140 Holborn, London, EC1N 2AE
Activities: Television programme production activities
Parent: ITV Broadcasting Limited
Officers: Kevin Anthony Lygo [1957] Director; Christopher Joseph Swords [1969] Director of Operations and Strategy

ITW CS (UK) Ltd
Incorporated: 11 November 2009
Net Worth: £263,068,000 *Total Assets:* £263,220,992
Registered Office: 13th Floor, 5 Aldermanbury Square, London, EC2V 7HR
Activities: Other business support service activities n.e.c.
Parent: ITW Limited
Officers: Ryan Ronald Dale, Secretary; Giles Matthew Hudson [1972] Director/Chartered Accountant; Stephen James Rowell [1967] Director of International Corporate Finance

ITW Holdings UK
Incorporated: 15 November 1996
Net Worth: £328,264,000 *Total Assets:* £330,011,008
Registered Office: 13th Floor, 5 Aldermanbury Square, London, EC2V 7HR
Activities: Non-trading company
Parent: ITW Gamma SARL
Officers: Ryan Ronald Dale, Secretary; Giles Matthew Hudson [1972] Director/Chartered Accountant; Stephen James Rowell [1967] Director of International Corporate Finance

ITW UK
Incorporated: 4 September 1998
Net Worth: £889,217,984 *Total Assets:* £930,108,992
Registered Office: 13th Floor, 5 Aldermanbury Square, London, EC2V 7HR
Activities: Activities of head offices
Parent: ITW Group France (Luxembourg) S.A.R.L.
Officers: Ryan Ronald Dale, Secretary; Benoit Amiot [1966] Director/Country Controller [French]; Giles Matthew Hudson [1972] Director/Chartered Accountant; Stephen James Rowell [1967] Director of International Corporate Finance; Maryann Spiegel [1964] Director/Attorney [American]

ITW UK Finance Beta Limited
Incorporated: 18 November 2016
Total Assets: £1,419,807,232
Registered Office: 13th Floor, 5 Aldermanbury Square, London, EC2V 7HR
Activities: Other service activities n.e.c.
Parent: ITW UK Finance Limited
Officers: Ryan Ronald Dale, Secretary; Giles Matthew Hudson [1972] Director/Chartered Accountant; Stephen James Rowell [1967] Director of International Corporate Finance

ITW UK Finance Gamma Limited
Incorporated: 2 December 2016
Net Worth: £1,422,917,632 *Total Assets:* £1,435,109,504
Registered Office: 13th Floor, 5 Aldermanbury Square, London, EC2V 7HR
Activities: Other service activities n.e.c.
Parent: ITW UK Finance Beta Limited
Officers: Ryan Ronald Dale, Secretary; Giles Matthew Hudson [1972] Director/Chartered Accountant; Stephen James Rowell [1967] Director of International Corporate Finance

ITW UK Finance Limited
Incorporated: 4 December 2015
Net Worth: £613,647,680 *Total Assets:* £1,816,972,800
Registered Office: 13th Floor, 5 Aldermanbury Square, London, EC2V 7HR
Activities: Other business support service activities n.e.c.
Officers: Ryan Ronald Dale, Secretary; Giles Matthew Hudson [1972] Director/Chartered Accountant; Stephen James Rowell [1967] Director of International Corporate Finance

ITWP Acquisitions Limited
Incorporated: 14 January 2011 *Employees:* 1,400
Net Worth: £125,919,000 *Total Assets:* £230,632,000
Registered Office: Ealing Cross, 85 Uxbridge Road, Ealing, London, W5 5TH
Activities: Activities of head offices
Officers: Richard Philip Bernstein [1962] Director Chartered Accountant; Pierre Camagne [1983] Director/Chief Financial Officer [French]; Frederic de Mevius [1958] Director [Belgian]; Richard Henry Grogan [1953] Director [American/French]; George Alexander Bryson Kynoch [1946] Director/Management Consultant; Frederic-Charles Petit [1970] Director [French]

Ivy Bidco Limited
Incorporated: 16 April 2009
Net Worth: £886,099,968 *Total Assets:* £913,500,032
Registered Office: 5th Floor, 6 St Andrew Street, London, EC4A 3AE
Activities: Activities of head offices
Parent: Gatwick Airport Limited
Officers: Andrew Harvey Gillespie Smith [1967] Director; John Benedict McCarthy [1958] Director/Global Head of Infrastructure [Australian]; Michael John McGhee [1956] Director; William Alan Woodburn [1951] Director [American]

Ivy Holdco Limited
Incorporated: 18 January 2011 *Employees:* 3,231
Net Worth: £191,000,000 *Total Assets:* £3,392,699,904
Registered Office: 5th Floor, 6 St Andrew Street, London, EC4A 3AE
Activities: Activities of other holding companies n.e.c.
Parent: Ivy Midco Limited
Officers: Andrew Harvey Gillespie Smith [1967] Director; John Benedict McCarthy [1958] Director/Global Head of Infrastructure [Australian]; Michael John McGhee [1956] Director; William Alan Woodburn [1951] Director [American]

Ivy Midco Limited
Incorporated: 1 May 2009 *Employees:* 3,231
Net Worth Deficit: £358,100,000 *Total Assets:* £3,444,499,968
Registered Office: 5th Floor, 6 St Andrew Street, London, EC4A 3AE
Activities: Other business support service activities n.e.c.
Officers: Andrew Harvey Gillespie Smith [1967] Director; John Benedict McCarthy [1958] Director/Global Head of Infrastructure [Australian]; Michael John McGhee [1956] Director; William Alan Woodburn [1951] Director [American]

IW Group Services (UK) Limited
Incorporated: 7 October 1992 *Employees:* 826
Previous: Regus Management (UK) Limited
Net Worth: £776,000 *Total Assets:* £151,212,992
Registered Office: 1 Burwood Place, London, W2 2UT
Activities: Other business support service activities n.e.c.
Parent: IWG PLC
Officers: Peter David Edward Gibson [1973] Director/Accountant; Richard Morris [1975] Director

Ixellion Technologies Ltd
Incorporated: 21 November 2014 *Employees:* 1
Net Worth: £903,984,256 *Total Assets:* £907,070,592
Registered Office: No 1 Royal Exchange, London, EC3V 3DG
Activities: Manufacture of electrical and electronic equipment for motor vehicles and their engines
Shareholder: Ixellion OU
Officers: Dr Antonio Sedino [1975] Director [Italian]

Jac Travel Group (Holdings) Limited
Incorporated: 17 June 2014 *Employees:* 570
Net Worth: £90,587,000 *Total Assets:* £201,336,000
Registered Office: 8 Holmes Road, Kentish Town, London, NW5 3AB
Activities: Other service activities n.e.c.
Parent: Webbeds Limited
Officers: Shelley Lynne Earhart Beasley [1969] Director/Manager [American]; John Guscic [1964] Director [Australian]; Nigel Peter Horne [1969] Director; Christopher Colin Montgomery [1972] Finance Director; Stuart Edward Nassos [1968] Director/Chief Operating Officer [British/American]; Marco Torrente [1975] Finance Director [Italian]

James River Group Holdings UK Limited
Incorporated: 4 November 2015
Net Worth: £433,645,184 *Total Assets:* £433,645,568
Registered Office: c/o Bryan Cave Leighton Paisner LLP, Adelaide House, London Bridge, London, EC4R 9HA
Activities: Activities of other holding companies n.e.c.
Parent: James River Group Holdings, Ltd
Officers: Carol Osborne, Secretary; Kevin Copeland [1971] Director/SVP Finance & Chief Investment Officer [Canadian]; Sarah Doran [1973] Director [American]; Robert Myron [1968] Director [American/Bermudian]

Jane Street Europe Limited
Incorporated: 11 August 2006 *Employees:* 142
Net Worth: £340,241,504 *Total Assets:* £2,662,740,992
Registered Office: Floor 30, 20 Fenchurch Street, London, EC3M 3BY
Activities: Security dealing on own account
Officers: Dominique Olivia Lawrie, Secretary; Robert Anthony Granieri [1972] Director/Manager [American]

Jane Street Financial Limited
Incorporated: 13 April 2007 *Employees:* 154
Net Worth: £212,376,752 *Total Assets:* £1,553,337,472
Registered Office: Floor 30, 20 Fenchurch Street, London, EC3M 3BY
Activities: Security dealing on own account
Officers: Dominique Olivia Lawrie, Secretary; Richard Stockton Emmet [1971] Managing Director [American]; David Michael Galkowski [1986] Director/Chief Executive Officer [American]; Robert Anthony Granieri [1972] Director/Manager [American]; David Michael House [1989] Director/Head of Trading Systems; Tien-Fu Liu [1978] Managing Director [American]; John Steven MacKenzie [1977] Director/Lawyer

Jardine Lloyd Thompson Group PLC
Incorporated: 18 November 1982 *Employees:* 10,575
Net Worth: £377,793,984 *Total Assets:* £2,708,623,872
Registered Office: The St Botolph Building, 138 Houndsditch, London, EC3A 7AW
Activities: Activities of head offices
Officers: Darren Lennark, Secretary; Dominic James Burke [1958] Director/Chief Executive; Annette Elizabeth Court [1962] Director; Andrew Didham [1956] Director; Mark Frederick Grayson Drummond Brady [1957] Director/Insurance Broker; Geoffrey Michael Thomas Howe [1949] Director; Adam Phillip Charles Keswick [1973] Director; Richard Henry Meddings [1958] Director; Lynne Margaret Peacock [1953] Director; Charles Arthur Rozes [1967] Finance Director [British/American]; Lord James Meyer Sassoon [1955] Director; Nicholas Charles Walsh [1950] Director

Jasper Acquisition Holdings Limited
Incorporated: 1 February 2007 *Employees:* 3
Net Worth: £325,552,000 *Total Assets:* £541,630,976
Registered Office: 29 Queen Anne's Gate, London, SW1H 9BU
Activities: Activities of head offices
Parent: Tyman PLC
Officers: Carolyn Ann Gibson, Secretary; James Edward Brotherton [1969] Director/Chartered Accountant; Louis Leslie Alexander Eperjesi [1962] Director [British/Canadian]; Kevin Francis O'Connell [1960] Director/Accountant [Irish]

Jasper Acquisition Limited
Incorporated: 19 April 2007 *Employees:* 3
Net Worth: £161,897,552 *Total Assets:* £167,443,312
Registered Office: 29 Queen Anne's Gate, London, SW1H 9BU
Activities: Financial intermediation not elsewhere classified
Parent: Amesbury Holdings Limited
Officers: Carolyn Ann Gibson, Secretary; James Edward Brotherton [1969] Director/Chartered Accountant; Louis Leslie Alexander Eperjesi [1962] Director [British/Canadian]; Kevin Francis O'Connell [1960] Director/Accountant [Irish]

JC No. 3 (UK) Limited
Incorporated: 7 November 1988
Net Worth: £101,562,832 *Total Assets:* £101,566,048
Registered Office: Room 403, Intershore Suites, Dowgate Hill House, 14-16 Dowgate Hill, London, EC4R 2SU
Activities: Activities of financial services holding companies
Parent: Chinese Estates Holdings Limited
Officers: Sze Wan Chan [1978] Director [Chinese]; Kwong Wai Lam [1955] Director/Group Financial Controller [Chinese]

JC Overseas Ltd
Incorporated: 19 August 2014
Net Worth: £503,267,008 *Total Assets:* £506,699,008
Registered Office: 2nd Floor, Mitre House, 44-46 Fleet Street, London, EC4Y 1BN
Activities: Other business support service activities n.e.c.
Officers: Pedro Pablo Barragan [1978] Director/General Counsel [Mexican]; Angel Ignacio Abarrategui Diez [1955] Executive General Director [Spanish]; Salvador Rizo Lopez [1977] Director/Financial Operational Controller EMEA & APAC [Irish]

Jeco 2 Ltd
Incorporated: 22 February 2010 *Employees:* 6
Net Worth: £163,026,736 *Total Assets:* £341,908,704
Registered Office: Mid City Place, 71 High Holborn, London, WC1V 6BA
Activities: Other service activities n.e.c.
Shareholders: Mitsubishi Corporation; JXTG Holdings Inc.
Officers: Kota Abe [1973] Director [Japanese]; Yukiko Ariga [1963] Director [Japanese]; Nobuharu Masaki [1967] Director [Japanese]; Junya Nagase [1963] Director/General Manager [Japanese]; Shigetoshi Nakamura [1968] Director/Deputy General Manager [Japanese]; Kazufumi Yano [1963] Director/General Manager [Japanese]

Jefferies International Limited
Incorporated: 16 January 1986 *Employees:* 805
Net Worth: £501,023,008 *Total Assets:* £7,499,702,784
Registered Office: Vintners Place, 68 Upper Thames Street, London, EC4V 3BJ
Activities: Financial intermediation not elsewhere classified
Parent: Jefferies Financial Group Inc.
Officers: Andrew Peter Coe, Secretary; Timothy Edward Cronin [1954] Director [American]; Alan Bertram Gibbins [1949] Director; Jacob Katz [1952] Director [American]; Joel Michael Maryles [1959] Director [American]; Huw Martin Tucker [1962] Director/Chief Financial Officer (CFO); Nicholas Mark Williams [1956] Director

Jester Bidco Limited
Incorporated: 20 June 2017
Net Worth Deficit: £3,292,382 *Total Assets:* £166,330,496
Registered Office: The Adelphi, 1-11 John Adam Street, London, WC2N 6HT
Activities: Activities of other holding companies n.e.c.
Parent: Jester Midco Limited
Officers: David Joseph Barry [1963] Chartered Surveyor/Director [Irish]; Giles Thomas Bradley Derry [1971] Director; Robert Adrian Palles-Clark [1964] Chartered Surveyor/Director

Jester Debtco Limited
Incorporated: 31 July 2017
Net Worth: £3 *Total Assets:* £120,460,664
Registered Office: The Adelphi, 1-11 John Adam Street, London, WC2N 6HT
Activities: Activities of other holding companies n.e.c.
Parent: Jester Topco Limited
Officers: David Joseph Barry [1963] Chartered Surveyor/Director [Irish]; Giles Thomas Bradley Derry [1971] Director

Jester Midco Limited
Incorporated: 31 July 2017
Net Worth: £1 *Total Assets:* £120,460,664
Registered Office: The Adelphi, 1-11 John Adam Street, London, WC2N 6HT
Activities: Activities of other holding companies n.e.c.
Parent: Jester Debtco Limited
Officers: David Joseph Barry [1963] Chartered Surveyor/Director [Irish]; Giles Thomas Bradley Derry [1971] Director

Jewish Care
Incorporated: 30 November 1989 *Employees:* 20
Net Worth: £123,631,000 *Total Assets:* £153,118,000
Registered Office: Amelie House, Maurice and Vivienne Wohl Campus, 221 Golders Green Road, London, NW11 9DQ
Activities: Residential care activities for the elderly and disabled
Officers: Jonathan Simon West, Secretary; Rachel Anticoni [1968] Director/NHS Manager; Julia Ruth Bekhor [1960] Director; Linda Bogod [1964] Director; Michael Harris Brodtman [1960] Director/Chartered Surveyor; Adam David Dawson [1975] Director/Barrister; Graham Henry Edwards [1964] Director/Company Chairman; Simon Friend [1960] Director/Accountant; Harold Gittelmon [1962] Director; Gayle Klein [1972] Director; Douglas Henry Krikler [1965] Director/Banker; Steven David Lewis [1963] Director/Chartered Surveyor; Lord Ian Livingston [1964] Director; Nicola Caren Loftus [1971] Director/Housewife; Dr Dean Jason Noimark [1976] Director/Consultant Geriatrician; Stuart Grant Roden [1963] Director; Arnold Wagner OBE [1949] Director; Matthew Simon Weiner [1970] Director

JIB Group Holdings Limited
Incorporated: 8 August 1994
Net Worth: £256,208,000 *Total Assets:* £437,011,008
Registered Office: The St Botolph Building, 138 Houndsditch, London, EC3A 7AW
Activities: Activities of head offices
Parent: JIB Group Limited
Officers: Dean Andrew Byrne [1964] Director; Christopher Lewis Rayner [1978] Director

JIB Group Limited
Incorporated: 31 October 1988
Net Worth: £136,906,000 *Total Assets:* £1,309,075,968
Registered Office: The St Botolph Building, 138 Houndsditch, London, EC3A 7AW
Activities: Activities of head offices
Parent: Jardine Lloyd Thompson Group PLC
Officers: Dean Andrew Byrne [1964] Director; Michael Peter Methley [1965] Director/Chief Operating Officer; Christopher Lewis Rayner [1978] Director

JIB Overseas Holdings Limited
Incorporated: 8 August 1994
Net Worth: £153,700,992 *Total Assets:* £317,294,016
Registered Office: The St Botolph Building, 138 Houndsditch, London, EC3A 7AW
Activities: Activities of head offices
Parent: JIB Group Holdings Limited
Officers: Dean Andrew Byrne [1964] Director; Christopher Lewis Rayner [1978] Director

JIB UK Holdings Limited
Incorporated: 8 August 1994
Net Worth: £196,311,008 *Total Assets:* £497,720,992
Registered Office: The St Botolph Building, 138 Houndsditch, London, EC3A 7AW
Activities: Activities of head offices
Parent: JIB Group Holdings Limited
Officers: Dean Andrew Byrne [1964] Director; Christopher Lewis Rayner [1978] Director

JKX Oil & Gas PLC
Incorporated: 27 April 1995 *Employees:* 527
Net Worth: £105,915,360 *Total Assets:* £171,476,480
Registered Office: 6 Cavendish Square, London, W1G 0PD
Activities: Activities of head offices
Officers: Julian Paul Hicks, Secretary; Michael Bakunenko [1979] Director [American]; Christian Bukovics [1951] Director [Austrian]; Adrian John Geoffrey Coates [1958] Director; Hans Jochum Horn [1948] Director/Business Executive [Norwegian]; Andrey Shtyrba [1972] Director/Business Executive [Russian]

JLEAG Wind Holding Limited
Incorporated: 3 February 2016
Net Worth Deficit: £18,941,000 *Total Assets:* £206,254,000
Registered Office: 1 Kingsway, London, WC2B 6AN
Activities: Activities of other holding companies n.e.c.
Parent: John Laing Environmental Assets Group (UK) Limited
Officers: Christopher Holmes [1976] Director/Investment Manager; Muxin Ma [1975] Director/Chartered Financial Analyst [Chinese]; Christopher James Tanner [1972] Investment Director

JLEAG Wind Limited
Incorporated: 3 February 2016
Net Worth Deficit: £18,965,000 *Total Assets:* £206,254,000
Registered Office: 1 Kingsway, London, WC2B 6AN
Activities: Activities of other holding companies n.e.c.
Parent: JLEAG Wind Holding Limited
Officers: Christopher Holmes [1976] Director/Investment Manager; Muxin Ma [1975] Director/Chartered Financial Analyst [Chinese]; Christopher James Tanner [1972] Investment Director

JLIF Holdings (Barcelona Metro) Limited
Incorporated: 14 December 2015
Net Worth: £34,596,000 *Total Assets:* £129,598,000
Registered Office: 1 Kingsway, London, WC2B 6AN
Activities: Activities of other holding companies n.e.c.
Parent: JLIF (GP) Limited
Officers: Carl Harvey Dix [1966] Operations Director; Jamie Pritchard [1971] Director/Investment Manager

JLIF Investments Limited
Incorporated: 20 March 2013 *Employees:* 4
Net Worth: £77,348,000 *Total Assets:* £294,927,008
Registered Office: 1 Kingsway, London, WC2B 6AN
Activities: Activities of head offices
Parent: JLIF (GP) Limited
Officers: Carl Harvey Dix [1966] Operations Director; David Michael Hardy [1957] Director/Chartered Accountant; Jamie Pritchard [1971] Director/Investment Manager

JLL 2002
Incorporated: 26 January 1996
Net Worth: £134,414,928 *Total Assets:* £134,414,928
Registered Office: 30 Warwick Street, London, W1B 5NH
Activities: Real estate agencies
Parent: Jones Lang Lasalle Europe Limited
Officers: Nicolas Guillaume Taylor, Secretary; Richard Henry Webster, Secretary; Richard William Bloxam [1971] Director/Chartered Surveyor; Christopher Mackintosh Ireland [1957] Director/Chartered Surveyor

JLT Benefit Solutions Limited
Incorporated: 6 April 1988 *Employees:* 1,191
Net Worth: £67,731,000 *Total Assets:* £148,500,000
Registered Office: The St Botolph Building, 138 Houndsditch, London, EC3A 7AW
Activities: Other activities auxiliary to insurance and pension funding
Parent: JLT EB Holdings Limited
Officers: Eamonn Michael Flanagan [1963] Director; Patrick Nigel Christopher Gale [1960] Director; David Lyndon Jones [1956] Director; Mark Anthony McNulty [1972] Managing Director [Irish]; Tony O'Dwyer [1970] Director [Irish]; Malcolm Terence Reynolds [1967] Director; Steven Paul Robinson [1962] Director/Actuary; Balamurugan Viswanathan [1972] Director [Indian]

JLT EB Holdings Limited
Incorporated: 18 April 1911 *Employees:* 6
Net Worth: £139,210,000 *Total Assets:* £222,424,992
Registered Office: The St Botolph Building, 138 Houndsditch, London, EC3A 7AW
Activities: Other business support service activities n.e.c.
Parent: JLT UK Investment Holdings Limited
Officers: Teresa Dawn Beach [1971] Director/Chief Operating Officer; Eamonn Michael Flanagan [1963] Director; Patrick Nigel Christopher Gale [1960] Director; David Lyndon Jones [1956] Director; Tony O'Dwyer [1970] Director [Irish]; Balamurugan Viswanathan [1972] Director [Indian]

JLT Insurance Group Holdings Limited
Incorporated: 20 November 1996
Net Worth: £274,424,000 *Total Assets:* £477,795,008
Registered Office: The St Botolph Building, 138 Houndsditch, London, EC3A 7AW
Activities: Non-life insurance
Parent: JIB UK Holdings Limited
Officers: Phillip Eric Goodings [1959] Finance Director; Christopher Lewis Rayner [1978] Director

JLT Management Services Limited
Incorporated: 31 January 1984 *Employees:* 476
Net Worth: £44,889,000 *Total Assets:* £542,601,024
Registered Office: The St Botolph Building, 138 Houndsditch, London, EC3A 7AW
Activities: Activities of head offices
Parent: JIB UK Holdings Limited
Officers: Graham John Hurrell [1963] Finance Director; Michael Peter Methley [1965] Director/Chief Operating Officer; Balamurugan Viswanathan [1972] Director [Indian]

JLT Reinsurance Brokers Limited
Incorporated: 1 August 2005 *Employees:* 324
Net Worth: £66,965,000 *Total Assets:* £297,419,008
Registered Office: The St Botolph Building, 138 Houndsditch, London, EC3A 7AW
Activities: Non-life insurance
Parent: JLT Insurance Group Holdings Ltd
Officers: Jacqueline Ann Aggett [1962] Director; Eamonn Michael Flanagan [1963] Director; Keith Andrew Harrison [1967] Director/Insurance Broker; Ross Charles Howard [1953] Director/Broker; Nicholas James Moss [1966] Director; John Todd Young [1957] Director

JLT Specialty Limited
Incorporated: 30 December 1980 *Employees:* 1,382
Net Worth: £138,982,000 *Total Assets:* £649,588,992
Registered Office: The St Botolph Building, 138 Houndsditch, London, EC3A 7AW
Activities: Non-life insurance
Parent: JLT Insurance Group Holdings Ltd
Officers: Adrian Brian Girling [1955] Director/Insurance Broker; Phillip Eric Goodings [1959] Finance Director; Paul Keith Knowles [1968] Director/Insurance Broker; Gavin Russell Cameron Munnoch [1952] Director; Adrian Jeremy Walker [1956] Director; Nicholas Toby Williams-Walker [1968] Director; Mark Andrew Wood [1963] Director

JLT UK Investment Holdings Limited
Incorporated: 27 March 2000 *Employees:* 2
Net Worth: £76,373,000 *Total Assets:* £139,474,000
Registered Office: The St Botolph Building, 138 Houndsditch, London, EC3A 7AW
Activities: Activities of head offices
Parent: JIB UK Holdings Limited
Officers: Thomas McDonald [1980] Director/Accountant; Tony O'Dwyer [1970] Director [Irish]

Jockey Club Racecourses (Holdings) Limited
Incorporated: 26 May 1964 *Employees:* 564
Net Worth: £80,900,000 *Total Assets:* £287,300,000
Registered Office: 75 High Holborn, London, WC1V 6LS
Activities: Activities of head offices
Officers: John Baker [1968] Director; Simon Louis Bazalgette [1962] Director; Scott Bowers [1981] Director; Linda Jane Bowles [1966] Director; Paul Richard Fisher [1965] Director; William Angus Gittus [1966] Director; Christopher Thomas James Manners [1965] Director; Richard John Norris [1980] Group Racing Director; Ian Robert Renton [1958] Director; Amy Louise Starkey [1981] Director; Nevin John Truesdale [1974] Finance Director; Stephen Henry Wallis [1957] Managing Director; Dickon White [1971] Director; Philip David White [1975] Director

Jockey Club Racecourses Limited
Incorporated: 17 March 1994 *Employees:* 544
Net Worth: £83,100,000 *Total Assets:* £287,300,000
Registered Office: 75 High Holborn, London, WC1V 6LS
Activities: Operation of sports facilities
Parent: Jockey Club Racecourses (Holdings) Ltd
Officers: John Baker [1968] Director; Simon Louis Bazalgette [1962] Director; Scott Bowers [1981] Director; Linda Jane Bowles [1966] Director; David Michael Dommett [1966] IT Director; Paul Richard Fisher [1965] Director; William Angus Gittus [1966] Director; Christopher Thomas James Manners [1965] Director; Richard John Norris [1980] Group Racing Director; Ian Robert Renton [1958] Director; Amy Louise Starkey [1981] Director; Nevin John Truesdale [1974] Finance Director; Stephen Henry Wallis [1957] Managing Director; Dickon White [1971] Director; Philip David White [1975] Director/Regional General Manager

Johnson & Johnson Swiss Finance Company Limited
Incorporated: 17 March 1999
Net Worth: £16,535,060,480 *Total Assets:* £16,535,329,792
Registered Office: c/o Hackwood Secretaries Limited, 1 Silk Street, London, EC2Y 8HQ
Activities: Financial intermediation not elsewhere classified
Officers: David Geelan [1969] Director [Irish]; Gerard Anthony Greaney [1958] Director [Irish]; Hugh Murphy [1978] Director [Irish]; Brendan O'Leary [1959] Director [Irish]; Barry John O'Sullivan [1966] Director [Irish]; Lorcan Travers [1973] Director [Irish]

Johnson Matthey (CM) Limited
Incorporated: 7 January 1994
Net Worth: £199,772,000 *Total Assets:* £329,774,016
Registered Office: 5th Floor, 25 Farringdon Street, London, EC4A 4AB
Activities: Other business support service activities n.e.c.
Parent: Johnson Matthey PLC
Officers: Simon Farrant, Secretary; Simon Farrant [1961] Director/Solicitor; Andrew Holford [1970] Director

Johnson Matthey Investments Limited
Incorporated: 10 March 1971
Net Worth: £1,701,452,032 *Total Assets:* £2,440,176,128
Registered Office: 5th Floor, 25 Farringdon Street, London, EC4A 4AB
Activities: Activities of other holding companies n.e.c.
Parent: Matthey Holdings Limited
Officers: Simon Farrant, Secretary; Simon Farrant [1961] Director/Solicitor; Andrew Holford [1970] Director; Julian Charles Edward Tasker [1975] Director/Treasurer

Johnson Matthey PLC
Incorporated: 11 April 1891 *Employees:* 12,319
Net Worth: £2,377,999,872 *Total Assets:* £4,817,999,872
Registered Office: 5th Floor, 25 Farringdon Street, London, EC4A 4AB
Activities: Manufacture of other chemical products n.e.c.
Officers: Simon Farrant, Secretary; Odile Desforges [1950] Director [French]; Alan Murray Ferguson [1958] Director; Dr Jane Veronica Griffiths [1955] Director; Robert James MacLeod [1964] Director; Anna Olive Magdelene Manz [1973] Director; Christopher John Mottershead [1955] Director/University Vice Principal; John Edward O'Higgins [1964] Director [Irish]; Patrick Webster Thomas [1957] Director; John Francis Walker [1960] Director [American]

Johnson Matthey Precious Metals Limited
Incorporated: 28 October 1998
Net Worth: £273,052,160 *Total Assets:* £283,208,896
Registered Office: 5th Floor, 25 Farringdon Street, London, EC4A 4AB
Activities: Precious metals production
Parent: Johnson Matthey PLC
Officers: Simon Farrant, Secretary; Mark Bedford [1961] Director; Simon Farrant [1961] Director/Solicitor; Andrew Holford [1970] Director

Jones Lang Lasalle Capital Investments, Limited
Incorporated: 14 December 2005
Net Worth: £554,935,552 *Total Assets:* £1,207,898,240
Registered Office: 30 Warwick Street, London, W1B 5NH
Activities: Real estate agencies
Parent: Jones Lang Lasalle Incorporated
Officers: Nicolas Guillaume Taylor, Secretary; Richard Henry Webster, Secretary; Richard William Bloxam [1971] Director/Chartered Surveyor; Guy John Grainger [1967] Director/Chartered Surveyor; Maria Dimitrova Grigorova [1970] Director [Belgian/Bulgarian]; Christopher Mackintosh Ireland [1957] Director/Chartered Surveyor; James Steven Jasionowski [1959] Director/Corporate Manager [American]

Jones Lang Lasalle Dorchester Ltd
Incorporated: 4 April 2011
Net Worth: £126,279,392 *Total Assets:* £128,121,680
Registered Office: 30 Warwick Street, London, W1B 5NH
Activities: Management of real estate on a fee or contract basis
Parent: Jones Lang Lasalle Capital Investments, Limited
Officers: Nicolas Guillaume Taylor, Secretary; Richard Henry Webster, Secretary; Richard William Bloxam [1971] Director/Chartered Surveyor; Christopher Mackintosh Ireland [1957] Director/Chartered Surveyor; James Steven Jasionowski [1959] Director/Accountant [American]

Jones Lang Lasalle Europe Limited
Incorporated: 5 November 1999
Net Worth: £111,936,592 *Total Assets:* £479,134,848
Registered Office: 30 Warwick Street, London, W1B 5NH
Activities: Real estate agencies
Parent: Jones Lang Lasalle Incorporated
Officers: Nicolas Guillaume Taylor, Secretary; Richard Henry Webster, Secretary; Guy John Grainger [1967] Director/Chartered Surveyor; Maria Dimitrova Grigorova [1970] Director [Belgian/Bulgarian]; James Scott Lyon [1964] Director/Chartered Accountant

Jones Lang Lasalle European Holdings Limited
Incorporated: 14 November 1973
Net Worth: £226,617,200 *Total Assets:* £307,476,576
Registered Office: 30 Warwick Street, London, W1B 5NH
Activities: Real estate agencies
Parent: Jones Lang Lasalle Limited
Officers: Nicolas Guillaume Taylor, Secretary; Richard Henry Webster, Secretary; Richard Charles Batten [1954] Director/Chartered Surveyor; Richard William Bloxam [1971] Director/Chartered Surveyor; Guy John Grainger [1967] Director/Chartered Surveyor; Maria Dimitrova Grigorova [1970] Director [Belgian/Bulgarian]

Jones Lang Lasalle Limited
Incorporated: 25 October 1974 *Employees:* 2,853
Net Worth: £271,811,008 *Total Assets:* £554,233,024
Registered Office: 30 Warwick Street, London, W1B 5NH
Activities: Real estate agencies
Parent: Jones Lang Lasalle Europe Limited
Officers: Nicolas Guillaume Taylor, Secretary; Geraint Richard Thomas, Secretary; Richard Henry Webster, Secretary; Richard Charles Batten [1954] Director/Chartered Surveyor; James Edward Gregory [1975] Director/Chartered Accountant; Maria Dimitrova Grigorova [1970] Director [Belgian/Bulgarian]; Richard Howling [1979] Director/Accountant; Alasdair Neacal MacKillop Humphrey [1963] Director/Chartered Surveyor; Christopher Mackintosh Ireland [1957] Director/Chartered Surveyor; Christopher Lane MacFarlane [1965] Director/Chartered Surveyor; Andrew Michael Renshaw [1964] Director/Chartered Surveyor; Thomas Mark Wynne Burton Smith [1963] Director/Chartered Surveyor

Jordan International Bank PLC
Incorporated: 4 May 1984 *Employees:* 43
Net Worth: £83,148,000 *Total Assets:* £393,107,008
Registered Office: Almack House, King Street, London, SW1Y 6QW
Activities: Banks
Officers: Justine Magdalen Goldberg, Secretary; James Anthony Story, Secretary; Hani Abdulkader Abdallah Al-Qadi [1962] Director/Banker [Jordanian]; Samer Abdulkadir Al-Qadi [1966] Director/Banker [Jordanian]; Ammar Bashir Ali Al-Safadi [1967] Director/Banker [Jordanian]; Rakan Al-Tarawneh [1975] Director/Banker [Jordanian]; Adel Ibrahim Assad [1967] Director/Banker [Jordanian]; Nabil Subhi Ahmed Hamadeh [1950] Director/Banker; Ian Lunn Schmiegelow [1943] Director/Banker; Riyad Ali Ahmad Taweel [1971] Director/Banker [Jordanian]; Mark Alexander Williams [1968] Director/Chief Financial Officer

JPMorgan American Investment Trust PLC
Incorporated: 18 June 1881
Net Worth: £980,430,016 *Total Assets:* £1,086,210,048
Registered Office: 60 Victoria Embankment, London, EC4Y 0JP
Activities: Financial intermediation not elsewhere classified
Officers: Simon William Bragg [1964] Director; Dr Kevin Carter [1952] Director; Sir Alan Collins [1948] Director; Nadia Manzoor [1986] Director/Solicitor; Robert Edwin Talbut [1960] Director

JPMorgan Asian Investment Trust PLC
Incorporated: 22 May 1997
Net Worth: £353,167,008 *Total Assets:* £354,265,984
Registered Office: 60 Victoria Embankment, London, EC4Y 0JP
Activities: Financial intermediation not elsewhere classified
Officers: June Aitken [1960] Director; Dean Robert Buckley [1960] Director; Bronwyn Nanette Curtis [1948] Director [British/Australian]; Peter Geoffrey Moon [1949] Director/Investment Manager; Sir Charles Richard Vernon Stagg [1955] Director

JPMorgan Asset Management (UK) Limited
Incorporated: 27 February 1974 *Employees:* 1,478
Net Worth: £700,380,032 *Total Assets:* £995,660,032
Registered Office: 25 Bank Street, Canary Wharf, London, E14 5JP
Activities: Financial intermediation not elsewhere classified
Parent: JPMorgan Asset Management Holdings (UK) Limited
Officers: Bethany Marie Burrow, Secretary; Victoria Katherine Hastings [1966] Director; Stephen Edward Pond [1979] Director [British/American]; Arthur Mark Ruston Smith [1964] Director; Patrick MacDonald Thomson [1967] Director/Business Head; Daniel Watkins [1975] Director

JPMorgan Asset Management Holdings (UK) Limited
Incorporated: 8 February 1988
Net Worth: £931,689,984 *Total Assets:* £936,790,016
Registered Office: 25 Bank Street, Canary Wharf, London, E14 5JP
Activities: Financial intermediation not elsewhere classified
Parent: JPMorgan Asset Management International Limited
Officers: Bethany Marie Burrow, Secretary; Stephen Edward Pond [1979] Director [British/American]; Daniel Watkins [1975] Director

JPMorgan Asset Management International Limited
Incorporated: 5 April 2001
Net Worth: £698,505,984 *Total Assets:* £698,505,984
Registered Office: 25 Bank Street, Canary Wharf, London, E14 5JP
Activities: Other business support service activities n.e.c.
Officers: Bethany Marie Burrow, Secretary; Victoria Katherine Hastings [1966] Director; Stephen Edward Pond [1979] Director [British/American]; Arthur Mark Ruston Smith [1964] Director; Patrick MacDonald Thomson [1967] Director/Business Head; Daniel Watkins [1975] Director

JPMorgan Chinese Investment Trust PLC
Incorporated: 10 September 1993
Net Worth: £225,962,000 *Total Assets:* £250,552,000
Registered Office: 60 Victoria Embankment, London, EC4Y 0JP
Activities: Financial intermediation not elsewhere classified
Officers: David Rowley Graham [1955] Director; Alexandra Jane Mackesy [1962] Director; John Misselbrook [1950] Director; Oscar Sai Hung Wong [1955] Director/Investment Manager [Hong Kong]

JPMorgan Claverhouse Investment Trust PLC
Incorporated: 22 March 1963
Net Worth: £428,497,984 *Total Assets:* £494,184,992
Registered Office: 60 Victoria Embankment, London, EC4Y 0JP
Activities: Financial intermediation not elsewhere classified
Officers: David Faviell Fletcher [1954] Director/Chartered Accountant; Jill Miranda May [1961] Director; Andrew Lang Sutch [1952] Director/Lawyer; Jane Tufnell [1964] Director/Investment Professional; Humphrey Van Der Klugt [1953] Director

JPMorgan Elect PLC
Incorporated: 16 September 1999
Net Worth: £354,124,000 *Total Assets:* £354,339,008
Registered Office: 60 Victoria Embankment, London, EC4Y 0JP
Activities: Activities of investment trusts
Officers: Rupert Dickinson [1973] Director; Alan Charles Hodson [1962] Director; James Peyton Robinson [1953] Director/Investment Advisor; Carla Rosaline Stent [1971] Director/Accountant; Karl Sternberg [1969] Director

JPMorgan Emerging Markets Investment Trust PLC
Incorporated: 10 June 1991
Net Worth: £1,196,855,040 *Total Assets:* £1,199,570,048
Registered Office: 60 Victoria Embankment, London, EC4Y 0JP
Activities: Financial intermediation not elsewhere classified
Officers: Sarah Fiona Arkle [1956] Director/Investment Professional; Richard George Laing [1954] Director & Consultant; Aidan Charles Lisser [1959] Marketing Director; James Ruary Drummond Neill [1959] Director/Trustee; Andrew Page [1958] Director/Chartered Accountant

JPMorgan European Investment Trust PLC
Incorporated: 15 March 1929
Net Worth: £426,136,992 *Total Assets:* £483,779,008
Registered Office: 60 Victoria Embankment, London, EC4Y 0JP
Activities: Financial intermediation not elsewhere classified
Officers: Countess Jutta Grevinde Af Rosenborg [1958] Director [Danish]; Josephine Dixon [1959] Director/Chartered Accountant; Stephen Robert Goldman [1951] Director/Investment Management (Retired); Stephen Michael Russell [1964] Non-Executive Director

JPMorgan European Smaller Companies Trust PLC
Incorporated: 10 October 1989
Net Worth: £702,174,976 *Total Assets:* £798,044,992
Registered Office: 60 Victoria Embankment, London, EC4Y 0JP
Activities: Activities of investment trusts
Officers: Carolan Dobson [1954] Director; Ashok Kumar Gupta [1954] Director; Nicholas Michael Norman Smith [1951] Director; Marc Christiaan Van Gelder [1961] Director [Dutch]; Stephen Frank White [1955] Director/Investment Manager

JPMorgan Global Emerging Markets Income Trust PLC
Incorporated: 4 June 2010
Net Worth: £399,513,984 *Total Assets:* £431,252,000
Registered Office: 60 Victoria Embankment, London, EC4Y 0JP
Activities: Activities of investment trusts
Officers: Mark James Timothy Edwards [1957] Director; Sarah Katrinka Fromson [1959] Director; Caroline Gulliver [1965] Director; Richard Edwin Winwood Robinson [1958] Investment Director

JPMorgan Global Growth & Income PLC
Incorporated: 21 April 1887
Previous: JPMorgan Overseas Investment Trust PLC
Net Worth: £410,790,016 *Total Assets:* £444,516,992
Registered Office: 60 Victoria Embankment, London, EC4Y 0JP
Activities: Financial intermediation not elsewhere classified
Officers: Jonathan Hugh David Carey [1950] Director; Gay Collins [1963] Director/Executive Chairman MFP Communications; Tristan Patrick Alan Hillgarth [1949] Director; Nigel David Wightman [1953] Director

JPMorgan Indian Investment Trust PLC
Incorporated: 29 March 1994
Net Worth: £770,145,024 *Total Assets:* £770,302,976
Registered Office: 60 Victoria Embankment, London, EC4Y 0JP
Activities: Financial intermediation not elsewhere classified
Officers: Richard Ronald James Burns [1946] Director; Jasper Rayner Augusto Judd [1960] Director/Chartered Accountant; Rosemary Jane Morgan [1954] Director/Investment Professional; Nimisha Aonbalol Patel [1955] Director/Solicitor; Hugh Sanderman [1951] Director

JPMorgan Japan Smaller Companies Trust PLC
Incorporated: 26 January 2000
Net Worth: £263,350,000 *Total Assets:* £290,960,992
Registered Office: 60 Victoria Embankment, London, EC4Y 0JP
Activities: Activities of investment trusts
Officers: Debbie Jane Guthrie [1955] Director; Alexa Hamilton Henderson [1961] Director; Christopher Yuuichiro Nakajima [1960] Director/Advisor [Japanese]; Robert Niels White [1952] Director/Investment Manager

JPMorgan Japanese Investment Trust PLC
Incorporated: 2 August 1927
Net Worth: £678,838,016 *Total Assets:* £778,545,984
Registered Office: 60 Victoria Embankment, London, EC4Y 0JP
Activities: Activities of investment trusts
Officers: Stephen Cohen [1956] Director; Sir Stephen John Gomersall [1948] Director; Sally Helen Hunt MacDonald [1964] Director/Fund Manager; Dr George Olcott [1955] Director; Christopher John Loraine Samuel [1958] Director

JPMorgan Life Limited
Incorporated: 10 October 1996
Net Worth: £72,028,000 *Total Assets:* £2,164,753,920
Registered Office: 25 Bank Street, Canary Wharf, London, E14 5JP
Activities: Life insurance
Parent: JPMorgan Asset Management Holdings (UK) Limited
Officers: Bethany Marie Burrow, Secretary; Paul Farrell [1972] Managing Director; Nigel Barry Masters [1952] Director; Stephen Edward Pond [1979] Director [British/American]; Daniel Watkins [1975] Director; Alan Keith Whalley [1956] Director

JPMorgan Mid Cap Investment Trust PLC
Incorporated: 28 March 1972
Net Worth: £314,129,984 *Total Assets:* £343,873,984
Registered Office: 60 Victoria Embankment, London, EC4Y 0JP
Activities: Financial intermediation not elsewhere classified
Officers: John Martin Evans [1957] Director; Richard Simon Gubbins [1957] Director/Lawyer; Michael Hughes [1951] Director/Retired Investment Manager; Richard Norman Legh Huntingford [1956] Director; Margaret Littlejohns [1959] Director; Margaret Payn [1960] Director [British/Australian]

JPMorgan Russian Securities PLC
Incorporated: 18 October 2002
Net Worth: £303,188,992 *Total Assets:* £303,319,008
Registered Office: 60 Victoria Embankment, London, EC4Y 0JP
Activities: Financial intermediation not elsewhere classified
Officers: Alexander Easton [1965] Director; Robert Charles Hubert Jeens [1953] Director; George Nianias [1955] Director; Gillian Nott [1945] Director; Tamara Sakovska [1977] Director/Partner

JPMorgan Smaller Companies Investment Trust PLC
Incorporated: 26 June 1990
Net Worth: £227,108,000 *Total Assets:* £253,543,008
Registered Office: 60 Victoria Embankment, London, EC4Y 0JP
Activities: Financial intermediation not elsewhere classified
Officers: Susanna Frances Davies [1959] Director/Partner Corporate Finance; Andrew Michael Impey [1961] Director [British/Canadian]; Michael Francis Quicke [1956] Director; Andrew Stephen Robson [1958] Director/Corporate Financier; Alice Anne Ryder [1964] Director/Partner, Investment Consultancy

JPMorgan US Smaller Companies Investment Trust PLC
Incorporated: 30 July 1955
Net Worth: £166,687,008 *Total Assets:* £181,596,992
Registered Office: 60 Victoria Embankment, London, EC4Y 0JP
Activities: Financial intermediation not elsewhere classified
Officers: Christopher John Galleymore [1948] Director; Julia Le Blan [1954] Director; Christopher Metcalfe [1960] Director; Dominic Mark Neary [1969] Director; David Thomas McLeod Ross [1949] Director; Davina Jane Walter [1954] Director; Dr Shefaly Maya Yogendra [1971] Director

JS Information Systems Limited
Incorporated: 1 February 2001
Net Worth: £101,112,000 *Total Assets:* £118,649,000
Registered Office: 33 Holborn, London, EC1N 2HT
Activities: Other information technology service activities
Parent: J Sainsbury PLC
Officers: Timothy Fallowfield, Secretary; Timothy Fallowfield [1963] Director/Solicitor; Richard Philip Newsome [1960] Digital & Technology Director

Jump Trading International Limited
Incorporated: 24 October 2006 *Employees:* 94
Net Worth: £80,844,896 *Total Assets:* £137,980,528
Registered Office: 11th Floor, One London Wall, London, EC2Y 5EA
Activities: Security dealing on own account
Shareholders: Paul Gurinas; William Disomma
Officers: Peter Carl Deaner [1972] Director of Business Development; Rupert Alexander Hugh Godber [1977] Director; Colleen Hickey [1979] Director/Treasurer/CF1 [American]; Marcelena Holmes [1982] Director/Compliance Manager [American]

Jupiter Acquisitions (Holdings) Limited
Incorporated: 25 March 2011
Net Worth: £28,000 *Total Assets:* £100,654,000
Registered Office: Morton Fraser LLP, St Martin's-le-Grand, London, EC1A 4EN
Activities: Activities of other holding companies n.e.c.
Parent: Infinis Wind Holdings Limited
Officers: Katerina Brown [1973] Director/Accountant; David Huw Griffiths [1970] Director; Scott Leitch MacKenzie [1969] Director

Jupiter Asset Management Group Limited
Incorporated: 9 March 2007
Net Worth: £676,848,000 *Total Assets:* £677,843,008
Registered Office: The Zig Zag Building, 70 Victoria Street, London, SW1E 6SQ
Activities: Financial intermediation not elsewhere classified
Parent: Jupiter Fund Management Group Limited
Officers: Simon Andrew Rowson [1972] Director/Legal Counsel; Alex James Sargent [1968] Director/Head of Finance; Jasveer Singh [1973] Director

Jupiter Asset Management Limited
Incorporated: 11 July 1986 *Employees:* 489
Net Worth: £198,800,000 *Total Assets:* £329,800,000
Registered Office: The Zig Zag Building, 70 Victoria Street, London, SW1E 6SQ
Activities: Financial intermediation not elsewhere classified
Parent: Jupiter Investment Management Group Limited
Officers: Jasveer Singh, Secretary; Katharine Grace Dryer [1972] Director/Deputy Chief Investment Officer; Robert Vernon Parker [1965] Director; Stephen Brian Pearson [1963] Director/Fund Manager; Jasveer Singh [1973] Director

Jupiter Emerging & Frontier Income Trust PLC
Incorporated: 4 April 2017
Net Worth: £91,473,000 *Total Assets:* £103,387,000
Registered Office: The Zig Zag Building, 70 Victoria Street, London, SW1E 6SQ
Activities: Activities of investment trusts
Parent: Jupiter Unit Trust Managers Limited
Officers: Mark William Dampier [1956] Director; Audrey Janette McNair [1960] Director; Nicholas David Moakes [1964] Director; John Philip Henry Schomberg Scott [1952] Director

Jupiter European Opportunities Trust PLC
Incorporated: 16 August 2000
Net Worth: £873,195,008 *Total Assets:* £948,438,976
Registered Office: The Zig Zag Building, 70 Victoria Street, London, SW1E 6SQ
Activities: Activities of investment trusts
Officers: Philip Edward Fraser Best [1960] Director/Fund Manager; Virginia Anne Holmes [1960] Director; Norman Stewart Hughson Lamont [1942] Director; Andrew Lang Sutch [1952] Director/Solicitor; John David Arnold Wallinger [1940] Consultant and Director

Jupiter Fund Management Group Limited
Incorporated: 13 March 2007
Net Worth: £297,000,000 *Total Assets:* £297,000,000
Registered Office: The Zig Zag Building, 70 Victoria Street, London, SW1E 6SQ
Activities: Financial intermediation not elsewhere classified
Parent: Jupiter Fund Management PLC
Officers: Simon Andrew Rowson [1972] Director/Legal Counsel; Alex James Sargent [1968] Director/Head of Finance; Jasveer Singh [1973] Director

Jupiter Fund Management PLC
Incorporated: 9 March 2007 *Employees:* 504
Net Worth: £640,300,032 *Total Assets:* £890,200,000
Registered Office: The Zig Zag Building, 70 Victoria Street, London, SW1E 6SQ
Activities: Financial intermediation not elsewhere classified
Officers: Jasveer Singh, Secretary; Elisabeth Patricia Airey [1959] Director; Jonathon Roderick Alan Bond [1963] Director; Edward Henry Bonham Carter [1960] Director/Investment Manager; Andrew James Formica [1971] Director/Chief Executive Officer [British/Australian]; Charlotte Claire Jones [1968] Director; Bridget Ann MacAskill [1948] Director [British/American]; Karl Stephen Sternberg [1969] Director; Polly Ann Williams [1965] Director; Roger Philip Yates [1957] Director

Jupiter Hotels Limited
Incorporated: 3 March 2011 *Employees:* 929
Net Worth: £61,538,000 *Total Assets:* £144,003,008
Registered Office: 54 Portland Place, London, W1B 1DY
Activities: Other business support service activities n.e.c.
Parent: Jupiter Hotels Midco Limited
Officers: Naris Cheyklin [1961] Director/Business Executive [Thai]; Dirk Andre L de Cuyper [1965] Director [Belgian]; Shane Harris [1958] Director [Irish]; Andrew Edward Pring [1962] Director/Company Executive; Sanjay Kumar Singh [1961] Director/Business Executive [Indian]; Krit Srichawla [1976] Director/Business Executive [Thai]; Gavin Stephen Taylor [1974] Director/Chartered Accountant

Jupiter Properties 2011 UK Limited
Incorporated: 7 January 2011 *Employees:* 2
Net Worth: £149,340,000 *Total Assets:* £166,739,008
Registered Office: 6th Floor, Lansdowne House, Berkeley Square, London, W1J 6ER
Activities: Activities of other holding companies n.e.c.
Officers: Paul Jonathan Goswell [1964] Director; Alexander Wilson Lamont [1978] Director; John Manwaring Robertson [1951] Director/Partner

Jupiter Unit Trust Managers Limited
Incorporated: 11 April 1986
Net Worth: £61,600,000 *Total Assets:* £205,200,000
Registered Office: The Zig Zag Building, 70 Victoria Street, London, SW1E 6SQ
Activities: Financial intermediation not elsewhere classified
Parent: Jupiter Asset Management Limited
Officers: Rupert John Conyngham Corfield [1966] Director; Paula Marion Moore [1963] Director; Nicholas John Ring [1965] Director; Jasveer Singh [1973] Director

Jupiter US Smaller Companies PLC
Incorporated: 15 January 1993
Net Worth: £163,339,008 *Total Assets:* £171,474,000
Registered Office: The Zig Zag Building, 70 Victoria Street, London, SW1E 6SQ
Activities: Activities of investment trusts
Officers: Norman McLeod Bachop [1946] Director/Investment Manager; Malcolm Peter Speight Barton [1937] Director/Investment Banker; Lisa Clare Booth [1967] Director; Gordon David Grender [1944] Director/Investment Manager; Clive Anthony Parritt [1943] Director/Chartered Accountant

Jurys Inns (UK) Limited
Incorporated: 24 January 2007
Net Worth Deficit: £170,684,000 *Total Assets:* £151,672,992
Registered Office: 35 Great St Helen's, London, EC3A 6AP
Activities: Hotels and similar accommodation
Officers: Nima Abrishamchian [1982] Director; Daniel Marc Richard Jaffe [1975] Director; Liia Nou [1965] Director/Chief Financial Officer [Swedish]; Carl Jacob Rasin [1980] Alternate Director [Swedish]; Soren Jonas Torner [1971] Director [Swedish]

Just Eat (Acquisitions) Holding Limited
Incorporated: 5 May 2015
Net Worth: £400,210,304 *Total Assets:* £400,210,304
Registered Office: Masters House, 107 Hammersmith Road, London, W14 0QH
Activities: Activities of other holding companies n.e.c.
Parent: Just Eat Central Holdings Limited
Officers: Anthony George Hunter, Secretary; Paul Scott Harrison [1964] Director/Accountant; James Alan Sporle [1976] Director/Solicitor

Just Eat Central Holdings Limited
Incorporated: 7 May 2015
Net Worth: £297,600,000 *Total Assets:* £297,600,000
Registered Office: Masters House, 107 Hammersmith Road, London, W14 0QH
Activities: Activities of other holding companies n.e.c.
Parent: Just Eat PLC
Officers: Anthony George Hunter, Secretary; Paul Scott Harrison [1964] Director/Accountant; James Alan Sporle [1976] Director/Solicitor

Just Eat Holding Limited
Incorporated: 28 April 2005 *Employees:* 456
Net Worth: £419,500,000 *Total Assets:* £629,600,000
Registered Office: Masters House, 107 Hammersmith Road, London, W14 0QH
Activities: Web portals
Parent: Just Eat PLC
Officers: Anthony George Hunter, Secretary; Graham John Corfield [1969] Managing Director UK; Paul Scott Harrison [1964] Director/Accountant; James Alan Sporle [1976] Director/Solicitor

Just Eat PLC
Incorporated: 30 June 2009 *Employees:* 2,116
Net Worth: £718,499,968 *Total Assets:* £1,014,700,032
Registered Office: Masters House, 107 Hammersmith Road, London, W14 0QH
Activities: Web portals
Officers: Anthony George Hunter, Secretary; Gwyn Burr [1963] Director; Juan Diego Oliva Camacho [1974] Director [Spanish]; Frederic Maria Coorevits [1970] Director [Belgian]; Alistair Richard Cox [1961] Director; Roisin Jane Catherine Donnelly [1961] Marketing Director; Peter Bernard Duffy [1966] Director; Mike Evans [1961] Director; Andrew John Griffith [1971] Director; Paul Scott Harrison [1964] Director/Accountant; Helen Alison Weir [1962] Director

Just Eat.co.uk Ltd
Incorporated: 4 February 2003 *Employees:* 415
Net Worth: £126,400,000 *Total Assets:* £222,700,000
Registered Office: Masters House, 107 Hammersmith Road, London, W14 0QH
Activities: Web portals
Parent: Just Eat Holding Limited
Officers: Anthony George Hunter, Secretary; Graham John Corfield [1969] Director/Accountant; Paul Scott Harrison [1964] Director/Accountant; James Alan Sporle [1976] Director/Solicitor

Justerini & Brooks,Limited
Incorporated: 22 December 1900 *Employees:* 51
Net Worth: £1,399,778,048 *Total Assets:* £1,432,017,024
Registered Office: 61 St James's Street, London, SW1A 1LZ
Activities: Distilling, rectifying and blending of spirits
Parent: Diageo Great Britain Limited
Officers: Gavin Paul Crickmore [1958] Director/Chartered Accountant; James Matthew Crayden Edmunds [1974] Director/Solicitor; Sharon Lynnette Fennessy [1967] Director/Group Treasurer [Irish]; David Heginbottom [1970] Director/Group Treasurer; Aniko Mahler [1976] Director/Head of Statutory Compliance [Hungarian]; Kara Elizabeth Major [1977] Director [American]; Edward Martin Peachey [1973] Commercial Financial Director

Juturna (European Loan Conduit No. 16) PLC
Incorporated: 19 May 2003
Net Worth Deficit: £99,004,432 *Total Assets:* £785,574,016
Registered Office: 35 Great St Helen's, London, EC3A 6AP
Activities: Financial intermediation not elsewhere classified
Parent: Intertrust Corporate Services Limited
Officers: Susan Iris Abrahams [1957] Director

JX Nippon Exploration and Production (U.K.) Limited
Incorporated: 2 December 1996 *Employees:* 25
Net Worth: £732,848,192 *Total Assets:* £2,139,213,568
Registered Office: 6th Floor, Saddlers' House, 44 Gutter Lane, Cheapside, London, EC2V 6BR
Activities: Extraction of crude petroleum
Parent: JXTG Holdings, Inc
Officers: Laurence Frederick Fry, Secretary; Naoyoshi Kaneko [1963] Director/Manager [Japanese]; Akira Tanaka [1958] Director [Japanese]; Hisao Tatsumi [1957] Director [Japanese]; Jeremy Hugh Valentine [1962] Director/Manager; Tetsuo Yamada [1960] Director [Japanese]

K Line Bulk Shipping (UK) Limited
Incorporated: 11 July 2003 *Employees:* 15
Net Worth: £31,976,972 *Total Assets:* £332,273,856
Registered Office: 200 Aldersgate Street, London, EC1A 4HD
Activities: Sea and coastal freight water transport
Officers: Yadoonandan Beeraj Ramlalsing, Secretary; Akira Misaki [1960] Director/Shipping Executive [Japanese]

K Line LNG Shipping (UK) Limited
Incorporated: 8 February 2005 *Employees:* 36
Net Worth: £61,518,328 *Total Assets:* £133,127,656
Registered Office: 200 Aldersgate Street, London, EC1A 4HD
Activities: Sea and coastal freight water transport
Officers: Yadoonandan Beeraj Ramlalsing, Secretary; Derek Bain [1970] Director/Shipping Executive; Hiromichi Kato [1968] Director/Shipping Executive [Japanese]; Jitsuo Narita [1969] Director and General Manager [Japanese]

Kajima Europe Limited
Incorporated: 1 July 2008 *Employees:* 299
Net Worth: £121,179,000 *Total Assets:* £267,948,992
Registered Office: 55 Baker Street, London, W1U 8EW
Activities: Development of building projects
Officers: Hiroshi Takei, Secretary; Hiroto Ichiki [1962] Director/Real Estate Developer [Japanese]; Masanori Iwasaki [1959] Director/General Manager [Japanese]; Hiroyoshi Koizumi [1949] Director [Japanese]; Keisuke Koshijima [1956] Director/Executive Officer [Japanese]; Hiroshi Takei [1965] Director/Chief Financial Officer [Japanese]; Mitsuyoshi Tamura [1959] Director/Employee [Japanese]; Ken Uchida [1956] Director/General Manager [Japanese]; Teruaki Yamaguchi [1946] Director/Company Executive Officer [Japanese]

Kantar Media UK Ltd
Incorporated: 25 April 1933 *Employees:* 362
Net Worth: £28,696,338 *Total Assets:* £118,646,456
Registered Office: 222 Gray's Inn Road, London, WC1X 8HB
Activities: Advertising agencies
Shareholders: J. Walter Thompson U.K. Holdings Limited; Mortimer Square Limited
Officers: Giles Harvey Roberts Richardson, Secretary; Andrew James Brown [1963] Director; Giles Harvey Roberts Richardson [1974] Director

Kantar UK Limited
Incorporated: 28 June 1995 *Employees:* 1,642
Previous: TNS UK Limited
Net Worth: £100,426,000 *Total Assets:* £258,600,992
Registered Office: TNS House, Westgate, London, W5 1UA
Activities: Other service activities n.e.c.
Parent: Millward Brown UK Limited
Officers: Ian Christopher Dunkley [1967] Director; William James Hyde Galgey [1975] Director; Timothy Russell Kidd [1961] Managing Director; Kelly Rebecca Smith [1965] Director/Accountant; Charles Ward Van Der Welle [1959] Director of Treasury; Steve Richard Winters [1968] Director/Chartered Accountant

Karta II PLC
Incorporated: 22 July 2011
Net Worth: £34,236 *Total Assets:* £358,730,176
Registered Office: Third Floor, 1 King's Arms Yard, London, EC2R 7AF
Activities: Other business support service activities n.e.c.
Parent: Karta II Holdings Limited
Officers: Daniel Jonathan Wynne [1970] Director

KAS No.2 Limited
Incorporated: 14 December 2004 *Employees:* 214
Net Worth: £43,372,832 *Total Assets:* £124,022,112
Registered Office: 144-146 Kings Cross Road, London, WC1X 9DU
Activities: Activities of head offices
Shareholder: Seacastle Limited
Officers: Alykhan Kassam, Secretary; Navroz Nurmohamed Darvesh Bandali [1949] Director/Consultant [Canadian]; Alykhan Kassam [1972] Director; Karim Shiraz Kassam [1974] Director

Kas No.8 Limited
Incorporated: 6 December 2012 *Employees:* 244
Net Worth: £100,158,808 *Total Assets:* £301,302,464
Registered Office: 144-146 King's Cross Road, London, WC1X 9DU
Activities: Activities of head offices
Shareholder: Seacastle Limited
Officers: Alykhan Kassam, Secretary; Navroz Nurmohamed Darvesh Bandali [1949] Director [Canadian]; Alykhan Kassam [1972] Director; Karim Kassam [1974] Director

Kaspersky Lab UK Limited
Incorporated: 22 October 1998 *Employees:* 126
Net Worth: £141,504,448 *Total Assets:* £492,121,664
Registered Office: New Bridge Street House, 30-34 New Bridge Street, London, EC4V 6BJ
Activities: Information technology consultancy activities
Parent: Kaspersky Labs Limited
Officers: Svetlana Ivanova, Secretary; Svetlana Ivanova [1971] Director [Russian/British]; Eugeny Kaspersky [1965] Director [Russian]

Kaspersky Labs Limited
Incorporated: 10 July 2001 *Employees:* 3,976
Net Worth: £39,254,468 *Total Assets:* £620,440,448
Registered Office: New Bridge Street House, 30-34 New Bridge Street, London, EC4V 6BJ
Activities: Information technology consultancy activities
Major Shareholder: Eugeny Kaspersky
Officers: Svetlana Ivanova, Secretary; Daniil Borshchev [1975] Director [Russian]; Alexei de Monderik [1965] Director [Russian]; Eugeny Kaspersky [1965] Director [Russian]; Andrey Tikhonov [1966] Director [Russian]

Katanalotika PLC
Incorporated: 10 October 2008
Net Worth Deficit: £137,189,200 *Total Assets:* £1,299,683,840
Registered Office: Third Floor, 1 King's Arms Yard, London, EC2R 7AF
Activities: Other business support service activities n.e.c.
Parent: Katanalotika Holdings Limited
Officers: Robert Sutton [1978] Director/Financial Services [American]; Daniel Jonathan Wynne [1970] Director

KAZ Minerals Aktogay Finance Limited
Incorporated: 18 March 2011
Net Worth Deficit: £213,182,672 *Total Assets:* £905,461,376
Registered Office: 6th Floor, Cardinal Place, 100 Victoria Street, London, SW1E 5JL
Activities: Other business support service activities n.e.c.
Parent: KAZ Minerals Aktogay BV
Officers: Susanna Freeman, Secretary; John Paul Simeon Hadfield [1975] Director/Deputy CFO; Andrew John Paton [1961] Director/Group Treasurer [New Zealander]; Andrew Southam [1977] Director/Chartered Accountant

KAZ Minerals Aktogay Project Finance Limited
Incorporated: 9 November 2012
Net Worth: £586,390,656 *Total Assets:* £593,343,872
Registered Office: 6th Floor, Cardinal Place, 100 Victoria Street, London, SW1E 5JL
Activities: Other business support service activities n.e.c.
Parent: KAZ Minerals Aktogay Finance Limited
Officers: Susanna Freeman, Secretary; John Paul Simeon Hadfield [1975] Director/Deputy CFO; Andrew John Paton [1961] Director/Group Treasurer [New Zealander]; Andrew Southam [1977] Director/Chartered Accountant

KAZ Minerals Copper Finance Limited
Incorporated: 17 August 2010
Net Worth: £2,754,049,024 *Total Assets:* £2,754,049,024
Registered Office: 6th Floor, Cardinal Place, 100 Victoria Street, London, SW1E 5JL
Activities: Other business support service activities n.e.c.
Parent: Vostoktsvetmet LLC
Officers: Susanna Freeman, Secretary; John Paul Simeon Hadfield [1975] Director/Deputy CFO; Andrew John Paton [1961] Director/Group Treasurer [New Zealander]; Andrew Southam [1977] Director/Chartered Accountant

KAZ Minerals Finance PLC
Incorporated: 8 January 2008
Net Worth: £280,979,296 *Total Assets:* £5,248,210,944
Registered Office: 6th Floor, Cardinal Place, 100 Victoria Street, London, SW1E 5JL
Activities: Other business support service activities n.e.c.
Parent: KAZ Minerals PLC
Officers: Susanna Freeman, Secretary; John Paul Simeon Hadfield [1975] Director/Deputy CFO; Andrew John Paton [1961] Director/Group Treasurer [New Zealander]; Andrew Southam [1977] Director/Chartered Accountant

KAZ Minerals Investments Limited
Incorporated: 24 July 2007
Net Worth: £2,986,064,128 *Total Assets:* £7,212,806,144
Registered Office: 6th Floor, Cardinal Place, 100 Victoria Street, London, SW1E 5JL
Activities: Activities of head offices
Parent: KAZ Minerals PLC
Officers: Susanna Freeman, Secretary; John Paul Simeon Hadfield [1975] Director/Deputy CFO; Andrew Southam [1977] Director/Chartered Accountant; Christopher John Sweeney [1973] Director/Chartered Accountant

KAZ Minerals PLC
Incorporated: 15 July 2004 *Employees:* 13,003
Net Worth: £722,270,592 *Total Assets:* £4,081,010,432
Registered Office: 6th Floor, Cardinal Place, 100 Victoria Street, London, SW1E 5JL
Activities: Wholesale of metals and metal ores
Officers: Susanna Freeman, Secretary; Lynda Anne Armstrong [1950] Director; Alison Baker [1971] Director; Vladimir Sergeivich Kim [1960] Director/Chairman [Kazakh]; Michael David Lynch-Bell [1953] Director; John Fraser MacKenzie [1968] Director/Mining Executive [South African]; Oleg Novachuk [1971] Director [Kazakh]; Andrew Southam [1977] Director/Chartered Accountant; Charles Hugh Easton Watson [1954] Director/Executive

KAZ Minerals Projects Finance Limited
Incorporated: 30 September 2010
Net Worth: £896,969,088 *Total Assets:* £913,193,344
Registered Office: 6th Floor, Cardinal Place, 100 Victoria Street, London, SW1E 5JL
Activities: Other business support service activities n.e.c.
Parent: KAZ Minerals Bozshakol B.V.
Officers: Susanna Freeman, Secretary; John Paul Simeon Hadfield [1975] Director/Deputy CFO; Andrew John Paton [1961] Director/Group Treasurer [New Zealander]; Andrew Southam [1977] Director/Chartered Accountant

KAZ Minerals Sales Limited
Incorporated: 24 July 2007
Net Worth: £107,721,280 *Total Assets:* £331,450,080
Registered Office: 6th Floor, Cardinal Place, 100 Victoria Street, London, SW1E 5JL
Activities: Wholesale of metals and metal ores
Parent: KAZ Minerals PLC
Officers: Susanna Freeman, Secretary; John Paul Simeon Hadfield [1975] Director/Deputy CFO; Andrew Southam [1977] Director/Chartered Accountant; Christopher John Sweeney [1973] Director/Chartered Accountant

Kazphosphate Limited
Incorporated: 23 November 2006 *Employees:* 6,028
Net Worth: £168,822,256 *Total Assets:* £347,144,288
Registered Office: 3rd Floor, Fairgate House, 78 New Oxford Street, London, WC1A 1HB
Activities: Activities of other holding companies n.e.c.
Officers: Steven Harry Landes [1960] Director/Accountant; Yerzhan Kuanisheviq Nurgozhayev [1976] Director/Finance Manager [Kazakh]

KCG Europe Limited
Incorporated: 16 September 1998 *Employees:* 128
Net Worth: £42,855,936 *Total Assets:* £877,106,496
Registered Office: 1st Floor, 55 Bishopsgate, London, EC2N 3AS
Activities: Security and commodity contracts dealing activities
Parent: Virtu Financial, Inc.
Officers: Des Carbery [1974] Director [Irish]; David Furlong [1976] Director [Irish]; Christopher Paul Ham [1964] Director/Business Owner; John Michael Morgan Holland [1963] Director; James McQuillan [1981] Director [Irish]

Kddi Europe Limited
Incorporated: 21 July 1989 *Employees:* 148
Net Worth: £33,598,000 *Total Assets:* £173,164,992
Registered Office: Hill House, 1 Little New Street, London, EC4A 3TR
Activities: Other telecommunications activities
Parent: Kddi Corporation
Officers: Shane Gallen, Secretary; Hiroyuki Aota [1963] Director [Japanese]; Ken Sakai [1964] Managing Director [Japanese]; Yasuhiko Shiozaki [1960] Director [Japanese]

A.T. Kearney Holdings Limited
Incorporated: 16 November 2005 *Employees:* 3,546
Net Worth Deficit: £6,459,551 *Total Assets:* £520,147,648
Registered Office: 12th Floor, Adelphi, 1-11 John Adam Street, London, WC2N 6HT
Activities: Activities of other holding companies n.e.c.
Officers: Affan Arain, Secretary; Marcia Beitle [1963] Director/Management Consultant [American]; Axel Freyberg [1969] Director/Consultant [German]; Robert John Haas [1962] Director/Management Consultant [American]; Masahiro Kishida [1961] Director/Management Consultant [Japanese]; Alexander Yin Hwa Liu [1958] Director [American]; Thomas Rings [1963] Director/Consultant [German]; James Henry Singer [1963] Director/Management Consultant [American]; Jerome Simon Souied [1971] Director/Management Consultant [French]; Daniel George Starta [1960] Director/Management Consultant [American]; Patrick Van Den Bossche [1968] Director/Management Consultant [American/Belgian]; Mauricio Zuazua Elizondo [1975] Director/Management Consultant [Mexican]

Keele Residential Funding PLC
Incorporated: 13 September 1999 *Employees:* 2
Net Worth: £119,995,192 *Total Assets:* £409,898,176
Registered Office: Third Floor, 1 King's Arms Yard, London, EC2R 7AF
Activities: Other business support service activities n.e.c.
Officers: Eileen Marie Hughes [1966] Director/Head of Structured Products UK [American]; Daniel Jonathan Wynne [1970] Director

Kellas Holdco Limited
Incorporated: 20 May 2014
Previous: Cats Holdco Limited
Net Worth: £165,471,008 *Total Assets:* £537,846,976
Registered Office: 14 St George Street, London, W1S 1FE
Activities: Activities of other holding companies n.e.c.
Parent: Cats Topco Limited
Officers: Mark John Crosbie [1959] Director/Investment Manager; Guillaume Jacques Robert Friedel [1982] Director/Investment Manager [French]; Stephane Julien Ifker [1973] Director/Investment Manager [French]

Kellas Midstream Limited
Incorporated: 20 May 2014 *Employees:* 8
Previous: Cats Management Limited
Net Worth: £117,078,000 *Total Assets:* £911,534,976
Registered Office: 14 St George Street, London, W1S 1FE
Activities: Other business support service activities n.e.c.
Parent: Cats Parentco Limited
Officers: Guy Robert Maurice Appleton [1972] Finance Director; Christopher Martin Cox [1961] Director/Chairman; Mark John Crosbie [1959] Director/Investment Manager; Guillaume Jacques Robert Friedel [1982] Director/Investment Manager [French]; Andrew David Hessell [1965] Managing Director; Stephane Julien Ifker [1973] Director/Investment Manager [French]

Kellas Topco Limited
Incorporated: 20 May 2014 *Employees:* 8
Previous: Cats Topco Limited
Net Worth: £121,005,000 *Total Assets:* £913,841,024
Registered Office: 14 St George Street, London, W1S 1FE
Activities: Activities of other holding companies n.e.c.
Officers: Mark John Crosbie [1959] Director/Investment Manager; Guillaume Jacques Robert Friedel [1982] Director/Investment Manager [French]; Stephane Julien Ifker [1973] Director/Investment Manager [French]

Kellen Acquisitions Limited
Incorporated: 16 February 2005
Net Worth: £14,619,000 *Total Assets:* £256,438,000
Registered Office: c/o Hackwood Secretaries, One Silk Street, London, EC2Y 8HQ
Activities: Activities of head offices
Parent: Kellen Investments Limited
Officers: Kailash Chada, Secretary; Ivan Robert Bell [1968] Director; Kailash Chada [1971] Director/Chartered Accountant; Philip Bernard Holder [1948] Director/Trust and Estate Practitioner, Solicitor; Anne-Noelle Le Gal [1983] Director [French]; William Francis Michael McKinstry [1965] Director; Rachel Amelia Ockelford Drew [1976] Investment Director [Irish/New Zealander]; Valeria Rosati [1975] Director [Italian]

Kellen Investments Limited
Incorporated: 16 February 2005
Net Worth: £81,026,000 *Total Assets:* £126,200,000
Registered Office: c/o Hackwood Secretaries, One Silk Street, London, EC2Y 8HQ
Activities: Activities of head offices
Parent: Lionrai Investments No 2 Limited
Officers: Kailash Chada, Secretary; Ivan Robert Bell [1968] Director; Kailash Chada [1971] Director/Chartered Accountant; Philip Bernard Holder [1948] Director/Trust and Estate Practitioner, Solicitor; Anne-Noelle Le Gal [1983] Director [French]; William Francis Michael McKinstry [1965] Director; Rachel Amelia Ockelford Drew [1976] Investment Director [Irish/New Zealander]; Valeria Rosati [1975] Director [Italian]

Keller Group PLC
Incorporated: 13 November 1989 *Employees:* 10,534
Net Worth: £468,400,000 *Total Assets:* £1,384,999,936
Registered Office: 5th Floor, 1 Sheldon Square, London, W2 6TT
Activities: Activities of head offices
Officers: Kerry Anne Abigail Porritt, Secretary; Paula Bell [1967] Director; Peter John Hill [1952] Director; James William George Hind [1964] Director; Eva Lindqvist [1958] Director [Swedish]; Maximillian Alain Philip Michaelis [1966] Director; Dr Vegesna Ranganadha Raju [1961] Director [Singaporean]; Kate Harriet Alexandra Rock [1968] Director; Michael James Speakman [1964] Director; Nancy R Tuor Moore [1948] Director [American]; Paul Nigel Withers [1956] Director

Keller Holdings Limited
Incorporated: 8 May 1990 *Employees:* 4
Net Worth: £392,578,688 *Total Assets:* £798,325,376
Registered Office: 5th Floor, 1 Sheldon Square, London, W2 6TT
Activities: Activities of other holding companies n.e.c.
Parent: Keller Group PLC
Officers: Kerry Anne Abigail Porritt, Secretary; Mark Hooper [1967] Director/Group Financial Controller; Kennith John Oakley [1962] Director/Head of Tax; Kerry Anne Abigail Porritt [1970] Director/Group Company Secretary

Keller Investments LLP
Incorporated: 14 June 2016
Net Worth: £296,062,880 *Total Assets:* £296,062,880
Registered Office: 5th Floor, 1 Sheldon Square, London, W2 6TT

Kenmin (HP) Limited
Incorporated: 10 June 2009
Previous: Minerva (Holland Park) Limited
Net Worth: £24,359,248 *Total Assets:* £102,574,864
Registered Office: 3rd Floor, 3 St James's Square, London, SW1Y 4JU
Activities: Development of building projects
Parent: SM Kenmin Limited
Officers: Pranav Goel [1975] Director [Indian]; Shravin Bharti Mittal [1987] Director

The Kennedy Trust for Rheumatology Research
Incorporated: 13 October 1969 *Employees:* 2
Net Worth: £269,467,008 *Total Assets:* £311,222,016
Registered Office: Boundary House, 91 Charterhouse Street, London, EC1M 6HR
Activities: Other research and experimental development on natural sciences and engineering
Officers: Margaret Susan Preston, Secretary/Accountant; Edmund James Aldous Buckley [1978] Director; Prof Andrew Paul Cope [1961] Director/University Professor; Mark Stefano Dighero [1964] Director/Retired; Margaret Flynn Frost [1961] Director/Fund Manager [American/British]; Professor John Stanley Hill Gaston [1952] Director/Professor of Rheumatology; Professor Stephen Townley Holgate [1947] Director/Professor; Rodney Maxwell Hornstein [1940] Director; Jennifer Johnson [1948] Director; David Ronald George Paterson [1947] Former Investment Director; Victoria Louise White [1978] Director/Counsel; Sir Gregory Paul Winter [1951] Director

Kenon Limited
Incorporated: 7 February 2013
Net Worth: £75,215,648 *Total Assets:* £139,547,232
Registered Office: 17-18 Old Bond Street, London, W1S 4PT
Activities: Activities of other holding companies n.e.c.
Shareholders: Patrizio Bertelli; Miuccia Prada Bianchi
Officers: Lanfranco Fabio Lania [1966] Director/Manager [Italian]

Kensington & Global Limited
Incorporated: 24 December 2014
Net Worth: £172,570,512 *Total Assets:* £175,701,584
Registered Office: 71-75 Shelton Street, Covent Garden, London, WC2H 9JQ
Activities: Activities of other holding companies n.e.c.
Officers: Itzel Cesar de Blanco [1958] Corporate Director [Panamanian]

Kensington Close Hotel Limited
Incorporated: 23 July 2002 *Employees:* 318
Net Worth: £11,963,000 *Total Assets:* £138,818,000
Registered Office: Flat 1, 1-2 Coach and Horses Yard, London, W1S 2EH
Activities: Hotels and similar accommodation
Parent: Cola Holdings Limited
Officers: Azad Bakir Ali Cola, Secretary/Director; Azad Bakir Ali Cola [1979] Director

Kensington Mortgage Securities PLC
Incorporated: 10 January 2007
Net Worth: £30,000 *Total Assets:* £304,827,008
Registered Office: 6th Floor, 65 Gresham Street, London, EC2V 7NQ
Activities: Credit granting by non-deposit taking finance houses and other specialist consumer credit grantors
Parent: KMS Securitisation Limited
Officers: Sean Peter Martin [1965] Director

Kexim Bank (UK) Limited
Incorporated: 3 March 1992 *Employees:* 11
Net Worth: £33,161,120 *Total Assets:* £316,801,824
Registered Office: 3rd Floor, Moorgate Hall, 155 Moorgate, London, EC2M 6XB
Activities: Banks
Parent: The Export Import Bank of Korea
Officers: Chris Peter Edwards [1956] Director; Christopher Paul Julian Fitzgibbon [1956] Director; DOO Wha Jung [1967] Director [South Korean]; Hojun Kim [1966] Managing Director [South Korean]; Jae Rak Lee [1972] Director [South Korean]; Chun Il Lim [1972] Director [South Korean]

Keybridge House LLP
Incorporated: 4 November 2014
Net Worth: £61,811,000 *Total Assets:* £204,074,000
Registered Office: 140 Aldersgate Street, London, EC1A 4HY

KG Group Holdings Limited
Incorporated: 12 February 2008
Net Worth: £27,036,000 *Total Assets:* £130,610,000
Registered Office: 24 Britton Street, London, EC1M 5UA
Activities: Retail sale of footwear in specialised stores
Officers: Dale Nicholas Christilaw, Finance Director; Dale Nicholas Christilaw [1970] Finance Director; Neil Charles Clifford [1967] Director/Chief Executive Officer; Rebecca Elizabeth Alden Farrar-Hockley [1971] Director/Head of Buying

Khodorkovsky Foundation
Incorporated: 8 December 2003
Net Worth: £397,968,352 *Total Assets:* £399,837,536
Registered Office: c/o Tulloch & Co, 4 Hill Street, London, W1J 5NE
Activities: Other social work activities without accommodation n.e.c.
Officers: Denise Ann Forsdick, Secretary; Rupert Mark Caldecott [1953] Director/Investment Manager; Anton Veniahinovich Drel [1968] Director [Russian]; Boris Georgievich Saltykov [1940] Director/Science & Technology Manager [Russian]; Anthony David Smith [1938] Director/Retired; Alastair Robert Clifford Tulloch [1955] Director/Solicitor

Khoo Teck Puat UK Foundation
Incorporated: 8 June 2011
Net Worth: £67,133,632 *Total Assets:* £136,156,224
Registered Office: 5 Fleet Place, London, EC4M 7RD
Activities: Other service activities n.e.c.
Officers: Jennifer Khoo Carmichael [1956] Director [Singaporean]; Elizabeth Khoo [1959] Director [Singaporean]; Eric Kim Hai Khoo [1965] Director [Singaporean]; Mavis Bee Geok Khoo [1946] Director [Singaporean]

Cath Kidston Acquisitions Limited
Incorporated: 5 March 2010 *Employees:* 1
Net Worth: £42,022,000 *Total Assets:* £141,278,000
Registered Office: 2nd Floor, Frestonia, 125 Freston Road, London, W10 6TH
Activities: Activities of other holding companies n.e.c.
Parent: Cath Kidston Mezzco Limited
Officers: Kenneth Albolote [1970] Director [American]; William Winship Flanz [1944] Director [American]; Melinda Paraie [1962] Director [American]

Cath Kidston Group Limited
Incorporated: 5 March 2010 *Employees:* 827
Net Worth Deficit: £86,692,000 *Total Assets:* £152,238,000
Registered Office: 2nd Floor, Frestonia, 125-135 Freston Road, London, W10 6TH
Activities: Other retail sale of new goods in specialised stores (not commercial art galleries and opticians)
Major Shareholder: Jean Eric Salata Rothleder
Officers: Kenneth Albolote [1970] Private Equity Managing Director [American]; William Winship Flanz [1944] Director [American]; Kosmas Kalliarekos [1965] Managing Director [American]; Melinda Paraie [1962] Director [American]; Martha Wikstrom [1956] Non-Executive Board Director [American]; Shuting You [1985] Director/Investment Professional [Hong Kong]

Kili Topco Limited
Incorporated: 21 February 2017 *Employees:* 312
Net Worth Deficit: £8,929,694 *Total Assets:* £107,722,920
Registered Office: 1-3 Heathmans Road, London, SW6 4TJ
Activities: Other business support service activities n.e.c.
Officers: Philip Rudolph Botha [1970] Director; Antonio Gulino [1978] Director [Italian]; Andrew Mainwaring [1971] Director/Investment Management; Peter David Manning [1955] Director; Fabrizia Rizzi [1986] Assistant Director [Italian]

Kin and Carta Marketing Services Limited
Incorporated: 25 February 2013
Previous: St Ives Marketing Services Limited
Net Worth: £38,791,552 *Total Assets:* £121,201,872
Registered Office: 1 Tudor Street, London, EC4Y 0AH
Activities: Activities of head offices
Parent: St Ives PLC
Officers: Daniel Fattal, Secretary; Paul Bradley Gray [1961] Director; J Schwan [1975] Director [American]

Kin and Carta PLC
Incorporated: 23 March 1981 *Employees:* 3,352
Previous: St Ives PLC
Net Worth: £81,363,000 *Total Assets:* £191,692,992
Registered Office: One Tudor Street, London, EC4Y 0AH
Activities: Activities of head offices
Officers: Daniel Fattal, Secretary; David Bell [1943] Director [American]; Michael Guy Butterworth [1961] Finance Director; Paul Bradley Gray [1961] Director; Nigel David Pocklington [1971] Director; J Schwan [1975] Director [American]; Helen Claire Stevenson [1960] Director; Richard Nathan Stillwell [1949] Director

Kinapse Bidco Limited
Incorporated: 22 January 2016
Net Worth Deficit: £37,786,000 *Total Assets:* £111,062,000
Registered Office: 27-37 St Georges Road, London, SW19 4EU
Activities: Other professional, scientific and technical activities n.e.c.
Parent: Kinapse Midco Limited
Officers: Stuart James Donald [1969] Director/Head of Operational Services; Matthew Brendan Joseph McLoughlin [1972] Director [Irish]

Kinapse Holdco Limited
Incorporated: 22 January 2016 *Employees:* 2
Net Worth: £917,000 *Total Assets:* £117,114,000
Registered Office: 27-37 St Georges Road, London, SW19 4EU
Activities: Other professional, scientific and technical activities n.e.c.
Parent: Kinapse Topco Limited
Officers: Stuart James Donald [1969] Director/Head of Operational Services; Matthew Brendan Joseph McLoughlin [1972] Director [Irish]

Kinapse Midco Limited
Incorporated: 22 January 2016
Net Worth: £689,000 *Total Assets:* £116,916,000
Registered Office: 27-37 St Georges Road, London, SW19 4EU
Activities: Other professional, scientific and technical activities n.e.c.
Parent: Kinapse Holdco Limited
Officers: Stuart James Donald [1969] Director/Head of Operational Services; Matthew Brendan Joseph McLoughlin [1972] Director [Irish]

Kinapse Topco Limited
Incorporated: 22 January 2016 *Employees:* 676
Net Worth Deficit: £47,795,000 *Total Assets:* £110,639,000
Registered Office: 27-37 St Georges Road, London, SW19 4EU
Activities: Other professional, scientific and technical activities n.e.c.
Parent: Syneos Health, Inc.
Officers: Stuart James Donald [1969] Director/Head of Operational Services; Matthew Brendan Joseph McLoughlin [1972] Director [Irish]

King & Shaxson Limited
Incorporated: 26 January 1966 *Employees:* 68
Net Worth: £11,440,191 *Total Assets:* £1,341,111,040
Registered Office: 6th Floor, Candlewick House, 120 Cannon Street, London, EC4N 6AS
Activities: Financial intermediation not elsewhere classified
Officers: Miranda Lauraine Telfer, Secretary; Martin Vaughan Carey [1961] Director; Marc Vincent Dodd [1967] Managing Director; Jared James Inkster [1983] Director and Company Secretary [Canadian]; Gavin John Martin [1972] Managing Director; Miranda Lauraine Telfer [1968] Finance Director; David Ian Robert Wileman [1956] Director/Stockbroker

Kingfisher France Limited
Incorporated: 9 May 2001 *Employees:* 3
Net Worth: £3,168,740,096 *Total Assets:* £3,224,738,048
Registered Office: 3 Sheldon Square, Paddington, London, W2 6PX
Activities: Other business support service activities n.e.c.
Parent: Sheldon Holdings Limited
Officers: Paul Moore, Secretary; Jean-Noel Hughes Roger Groleau [1974] Director [French]; Paul Anthony Moore [1970] Director/Company Secretary

Kingfisher Holdings Limited
Incorporated: 23 January 2015
Net Worth: £3,956,220,928 *Total Assets:* £6,848,625,152
Registered Office: 3 Sheldon Square, Paddington, London, W2 6PX
Activities: Activities of other holding companies n.e.c.
Parent: Kingfisher PLC
Officers: Paul Moore, Secretary; Jean-Noel Hughes Roger Groleau [1974] Director [French]; Paul Anthony Moore [1970] Director/Company Secretary; Julian James Lawrence Smith [1965] Director

Kingfisher Information Technology Services (UK) Limited
Incorporated: 1 May 1986 *Employees:* 457
Net Worth: £238,982,000 *Total Assets:* £435,916,992
Registered Office: 3 Sheldon Square, Paddington, London, W2 6PX
Activities: Other information technology service activities
Officers: Paul Moore, Secretary; Eric Bosmans [1968] Director/Accountant [Belgian]; Anthony David Godwin [1956] Director; David Anthony Roger Haycocks [1962] Director; Neil Anthony Jones [1965] Director/Business Manager; David Richard Palmer [1970] Director; Garry Kenneth Porter [1979] Director/Chartered Accountant; Steven Barry Willett [1959] Director/CEO UK Trade; Andrew Wolfe [1972] Director

Kingfisher International Holdings Limited
Incorporated: 15 November 1990
Net Worth: £1,317,372,032 *Total Assets:* £3,768,948,992
Registered Office: 3 Sheldon Square, Paddington, London, W2 6PX
Activities: Activities of head offices
Parent: Zeus Land Investments Limited
Officers: Paul Moore, Secretary; Jean-Noel Hughes Roger Groleau [1974] Director [French]; Paul Anthony Moore [1970] Director/Company Secretary

Kingfisher PLC
Incorporated: 16 September 1982 *Employees:* 78
Net Worth: £6,748,000,256 *Total Assets:* £10,346,999,808
Registered Office: 3 Sheldon Square, Paddington, London, W2 6PX
Activities: Activities of head offices
Officers: Paul Moore, Secretary; Claudia Arney [1971] Director; Pascal Cagni [1961] Director [French]; Jeffrey Carr [1961] Director; Clare Moira Chapman [1960] Director; Andrew Cosslett [1955] Director; Anders Dahlvig [1957] Director [Swedish]; Sophie Gasperment [1964] Director [French]; Rakhi Goss-Custard [1974] Director [American]; Veronique Laury [1965] Director [French]; Mark Donald Seligman [1956] Director; Karen Witts [1963] Finance Director

Kingfisher UK Limited
Incorporated: 9 January 2008
Net Worth: £152,648,992 *Total Assets:* £152,871,008
Registered Office: 3 Sheldon Square, Paddington, London, W2 6PX
Activities: Other business support service activities n.e.c.
Officers: Paul Moore, Secretary; Jean-Noel Hughes Roger Groleau [1974] Director [French]; Paul Anthony Moore [1970] Director/Company Secretary

Kirkbi Burbo Extension Holding (UK) Limited
Incorporated: 3 February 2016
Net Worth: £356,864,672 *Total Assets:* £362,230,560
Registered Office: 5th Floor, 6 St Andrew Street, London, EC4A 3AE
Activities: Other business support service activities n.e.c.
Shareholder: Kjeld Kirk Kristiansen
Officers: Kasper Bech Trebbien [1979] Senior Director, Kirkbi A/S [Danish]; Sidsel Marie Kristensen [1975] Director/Vice President, Head of Legal Kirkbi A/S [Danish]; Thomas Lau Schleicher [1973] Director/Chief Investment Officer, Kirkbi A/S [Danish]

Kirkglade Limited
Incorporated: 5 June 2001 *Employees:* 4
Net Worth: £136,625,632 *Total Assets:* £295,748,640
Registered Office: 73 Cornhill, London, EC3V 3QQ
Activities: Renting and operating of Housing Association real estate
Parent: Coralglade Limited
Officers: Anne Benjamin, Secretary; William Richard Collins [1946] Director; Stephane Abraham Joseph Nahum [1975] Director [French]; Eileen Marie Sawyer [1979] Director/Accountant; Malcolm Robin Turner [1935] Director

Kiwara UK Limited
Incorporated: 17 January 2017
Net Worth: £1,966,319,872 *Total Assets:* £1,966,322,304
Registered Office: 4th Floor, The Charlotte Building, 17 Gresse Street, London, W1T 1QL
Activities: Other service activities n.e.c.
Officers: Geoffrey Clive Newall [1950] Director/President; Sarah Elizabeth Highton Robertson [1970] Director/Company Secretary; Anthony David Silvestro [1973] Director/Group Manager, Tax [Italian]

KMC Stirling Square Limited
Incorporated: 15 September 2014
Net Worth Deficit: £14,663,000 *Total Assets:* £167,152,000
Registered Office: 35 Great St Helen's, London, EC3A 6AP
Activities: Non-trading company
Parent: KMC Mayfair Holdco Limited
Officers: Daniel Marc Richard Jaffe [1975] Director

Knight Dragon Developments Limited
Incorporated: 12 July 2001 *Employees:* 71
Net Worth Deficit: £3,801,559 *Total Assets:* £200,678,384
Registered Office: Level 9, 6 Mitre Passage, Greenwich Peninsula, London, SE10 0ER
Activities: Development of building projects
Parent: Knight Dragon Investments Limited
Officers: Karl Daniel Heininger [1961] Director/Executive Vice President and Chief Legal Officer [American]; Sammy Sean Lee [1958] Director [Chinese]; Richard Paul Margree [1965] Director/Lawyer; Robert Thomas Jonathan Rann [1964] Director/Chartered Accountant; Kerri Leigh Sibson [1975] Sales & Marketing Director; Patrick on Yip Tsang [1971] Director/Merchant [Chinese]

Knight Dragon Investments Limited
Incorporated: 30 April 2007
Net Worth: £60,820,448 *Total Assets:* £896,361,664
Registered Office: Level 9, 6 Mitre Passage, Greenwich Peninsula, London, SE10 0ER
Activities: Development of building projects
Officers: Penelope Ann Hylton Elliott [1955] Director/Solicitor; Karl Daniel Heininger [1961] Director/Executive Vice President and Chief Legal Officer [American]; Sammy Sean Lee [1958] Director [Chinese]; Richard Paul Margree [1965] Director/Lawyer; Robert Thomas Jonathan Rann [1964] Director/Chartered Accountant; Patrick on Yip Tsang [1971] Director/Merchant [Chinese]; Peter Voit [1962] Director/Hotel Expert [German]

Knight Frank LLP
Incorporated: 3 November 2003 *Employees:* 4,726
Net Worth: £259,564,992 *Total Assets:* £399,896,000
Registered Office: 55 Baker Street, London, W1U 8AN
Officers: Christopher John Bell [1964] Member; Stephen James Clifton [1967] Member; Kevin David Coppel [1964] Member; John Edward Diggins [1959] Member; Alistair Charles Elliott [1962] Member; Lord Andrew Arthur George Hay [1959] Member; Roderick Charles Abram [1980] LLP Member; James Francis Charles Ackerley [1985] LLP Member; Robert Brian Adams [1972] LLP Member; Nicholas Samuel Alderman [1980] LLP Member; Stuart Jon Andrews [1981] LLP Member; Matthew Armstrong [1970] LLP Member; Timothy Peter Atherton [1985] LLP Member; Simon Austin [1974] LLP Member; Christopher Bailey [1969] LLP Member; Liam John Bailey [1972] LLP Member; Stuart Bailey [1970] LLP Member; Mark Michael Bamber [1977] LLP Member; Thomas Charles Banwell [1983] LLP Member; Charles Richard Barke [1977] LLP Member; Simon Paul Barker [1962] LLP Member; Anthony Barnard [1964] LLP Member; Giles Peter Barrett [1979] LLP Member; Thomas Peto Barrow [1965] LLP Member; James Harry Barton [1985] LLP Member; Mark Andrew Batty [1982] LLP Member; Elizabeth Jane Baugh [1972] LLP Member; Oliver Patrick Beales [1980] LLP Member; William Beardmore-Gray [1966] LLP Member; Nicolas Alan Bell [1967] LLP Member; Natalie Anne Berthiaud [1984] LLP Member; Peter John Bevan [1976] LLP Member; Simon Peter Biddulph [1979] LLP Member; Thomas Anthony Bill [1972] LLP Member; Charles Binks [1964] LLP Member; Alastair John Richard Bird [1980] LLP Member; Alastair John Richard Bird [1980] LLP Member; Richard Frank Booth [1977] LLP Member; Michael Hugh Richard Bowden [1978] LLP Member; Peter Bowden [1957] LLP Member; Matthew Bowen [1978] LLP Member; Benjamin Bjorn Bowles [1979] LLP Member; Gillian Mary Bowman [1961] LLP Member; Nathaniel Paul Bracegirdle [1980] LLP Member; Joshua Simon Braid [1984] LLP Member; George Philip Todhunter Bramley [1982] LLP Member; Jonathan Michael Bramwell [1971] LLP Member; Nicholas Edward Braybrook [1973] LLP Member; Neil Brookes [1979] LLP Member; Michael Edward Brownsdon [1977] LLP Member; Simon Gregory James Burgoyne [1980] LLP Member; Adam Stuart Burlison [1975] LLP Member; Adam Peter Burney [1984] LLP Member; David William Burns [1977] LLP Member; Andrew Russell Burt [1982] LLP Member; Elizabeth Rachel Burton [1978] LLP Member; Edmund Richard Duyland Bush [1985] LLP Member; Rebecca Louise Bussey [1976] LLP Member; Karen Judith Callahan [1971] LLP Member; Martin Stephen Camps [1967] LLP Member; Rachel Candelaria [1980] LLP Member; Simon Stuart Capaldi [1975] LLP Member; Riccardo Antonio Carrelli [1981] LLP Member; Timothy Ian Carter [1967] LLP Member; Cleo Michelle Cassell [1972] LLP Member; Sally Elizabeth Chacatte [1964] LLP Member; Adam Chapman [1983] LLP Member; David Richard Charlton [1981] LLP Member; Nicholas David Charles Chivers [1975] LLP Member; Raul Cimesa [1973] LLP Member; George Edward Laurence Clarendon [1976] LLP Member; James John Clarke [1979] LLP Member; Edward Robert Hamilton Clarkson [1973] LLP Member; Richard James Claxton [1970] LLP Member; Anthony John Clay [1959] LLP Member; James Cleland [1972] LLP Member; James Owen Clements [1985] LLP Member; Emma Venetia Cleugh [1968] LLP Member; Alastair James Coates [1977] LLP Member; Paul Cockerham [1965] LLP Member; Nicholas Fraser Codling [1978] LLP Member; Kieren Cole [1976] LLP Member; Stuart James Cole [1968] LLP Member; Annabelle Fawn Catherine Pearl Coliadis [1989] LLP Member; Samuel John Cookman [1974] LLP Member; Keith Donal Cooney [1964] LLP Member; Joanne Marie Corney [1964] LLP Member; Giles Alexander Coward [1974] LLP Member; Douglas John Cranston [1981] LLP Member; James Alastair Seton Crawford [1964] LLP Member; Christian Crawfurd [1981] LLP Member; Kathryn Mary Cripps [1984] LLP Member; Matthew Frederick Philip Cripps [1958] LLP Member; Nicholas Frederick Cripps [1985] LLP Member; Michael Leslie Crowe [1977] LLP Member; James Nicholas Culley [1980] LLP Member; Edward Wentworth Cunningham [1963] LLP Member; Neil Angus Cunningham [1971] LLP Member; Anna Czaban [1983] LLP Member

Knighton Estates Limited
Incorporated: 23 March 1943
Net Worth: £737,012,416 *Total Assets:* £764,434,432
Registered Office: 33 Cavendish Square, London, W1G 0PW
Activities: Buying and selling of own real estate
Parent: Great Portland Estates PLC
Officers: Desna Lee Martin, Secretary; Toby Augustine Courtauld [1968] Director; Steven Richard Mew [1968] Director; Nicholas James Sanderson [1973] Director/Accountant; Andrew Nicholas Howard White [1970] Director

Knightsbridge Asset Management Limited
Incorporated: 19 January 1995
Net Worth: £234,496,992 *Total Assets:* £234,496,992
Registered Office: The Zig Zag Building, 70 Victoria Street, London, SW1E 6SQ
Activities: Activities of other holding companies n.e.c.
Parent: Jupiter Asset Management Group Limited
Officers: Simon Andrew Rowson [1972] Director/Legal Counsel; Alex James Sargent [1968] Director/Head of Finance; Jasveer Singh [1973] Director

Kobalt Music Group Limited
Incorporated: 21 June 2000 *Employees:* 376
Net Worth: £21,109,528 *Total Assets:* £209,967,936
Registered Office: The River Building, 1 Cousin Lane, London, EC4R 3TE
Activities: Activities of head offices
Officers: Thomas Sansone, Secretary; Willard Bengt Anders Ahdritz [1964] Director [Swedish]; Timothy Brian Bunting [1963] Director; Johan Ekelund [1960] Managing Director [Swedish]; James Piers Fitzherbert-Brockholes [1973] Director; Shamit Grover [1982] Director [Indian]; Neeraj Lal Khemlani [1970] Director [American]; William Maris [1975] Director [American]; Anders Johan Palm [1960] Director [Swedish]; Alex Vukajlovic [1974] Director [Swiss]

Koch Commodities Europe Limited
Incorporated: 25 March 2009
Net Worth: £12,906,540 *Total Assets:* £439,546,880
Registered Office: 4th Floor, 20 Gresham Street, London, EC2V 7JE
Activities: Security and commodity contracts dealing activities
Officers: Daniel Simon Eld [1977] Director/Business Executive; Frances Louise Evans [1969] Director/Business Executive; Rodger Emerson Lindwall [1964] Director/Business Executive [American]; Clifford Alan Woodard [1955] Director/Accounting Executive [American]

Koch Fertilizer International Limited
Incorporated: 7 July 2016 *Employees:* 20
Net Worth: £71,770,112 *Total Assets:* £434,382,752
Registered Office: 4th Floor, 20 Gresham Street, London, EC2V 7JE
Activities: Wholesale of other intermediate products
Officers: Maxime Henri Thibaud Hugo Austruy, Secretary; Maxime Henri Thibaud Hugo Austruy [1984] Director/Business Executive [French]; Matt Dane Claassen [1984] Director/Business Executive [American]

Koch Industries International Limited
Incorporated: 9 May 1988 *Employees:* 82
Net Worth: £133,692,400 *Total Assets:* £396,620,416
Registered Office: 100 New Bridge Street, London, EC4V 6JA
Activities: Security and commodity contracts dealing activities
Officers: Daniel Simon Eld [1977] Director/Business Executive; Michael Rutger Prins [1971] Director/Accountant [Dutch]

Koch Metals Trading Limited
Incorporated: 19 February 1997
Net Worth: £127,545,040 *Total Assets:* £381,076,448
Registered Office: 4th Floor, 20 Gresham Street, London, EC2V 7JE
Activities: Financial intermediation not elsewhere classified
Parent: Koch Industries International Limited
Officers: Daniel Simon Eld [1977] Director/Business Executive; Michael Rutger Prins [1971] Director/Accountant [Dutch]

Kookmin Bank International Limited
Incorporated: 26 June 1991 *Employees:* 17
Net Worth: £56,551,248 *Total Assets:* £343,546,016
Registered Office: 6th Floor, Princes Court, 7 Princes Street, London, EC2R 8AQ
Activities: Banks
Parent: Kookmin Bank Co Ltd
Officers: Meb Khatri, Secretary; Chae-Oak Jun [1969] Director/Banker [South Korean]

Kore Potash PLC
Incorporated: 25 August 2017 *Employees:* 172
Net Worth: £111,996,264 *Total Assets:* £114,374,544
Registered Office: 25 Moorgate, London, EC2R 6AY
Activities: Mining of chemical and fertilizer minerals
Officers: Henko Vos, Secretary; David Andrew Hathorn [1962] Director [South African]; Timothy Keating [1974] Director [South African]; Leonard Vun Chee Math [1981] Director/Chief Financial Officer and Company Secretary [Australian]; Jose Antonio Merino [1982] Director [Chilean]; David George Netherway [1952] Director [Australian]; Stuart Bradley Sampson [1966] Director [Australian]; Jonathan Alfred Grey Trollip [1958] Director [Australian]

Korn Ferry GH1 Limited
Incorporated: 1 May 2013
Net Worth: £87,252,144 *Total Assets:* £283,652,096
Registered Office: Ryder Court, 14 Ryder Street, London, SW1Y 6QB
Activities: Activities of other holding companies n.e.c.
Officers: Anthony Goodes, Secretary; Sonamara Marie-Amelie Jeffreys [1966] Managing Director and Head of Financial Services; Robert Paul Rozek [1960] Director/Chief Financial Officer [American]; Julian Christopher Slater [1955] Director/Vice President of Finance

Korn Ferry Global Holdings (UK) Limited
Incorporated: 1 May 2013
Net Worth: £365,074,016 *Total Assets:* £384,886,944
Registered Office: Ryder Court, 14 Ryder Street, London, SW1Y 6QB
Activities: Activities of other holding companies n.e.c.
Officers: Anthony Goodes, Secretary; Sonamara Marie-Amelie Jeffreys [1966] Managing Director and Head of Financial Services; Robert Paul Rozek [1960] Director/Chief Financial Officer [American]; Julian Christopher Slater [1955] Director/Vice President of Finance

Michael Kors (UK) Holdings Limited
Incorporated: 5 June 2014
Net Worth Deficit: £439,975,584 *Total Assets:* £1,180,764,672
Registered Office: 33 Kingsway, London, WC2B 6UF
Activities: Activities of head offices
Parent: Capri Holdings Limited
Officers: Claire Harries Ogle, Secretary; Nicolas Jacques Francois Marie Crespin [1967] Director/Finance Executive [French]; David Michael Provenzano [1979] Director [American]; Cedric Dominique Alain Wilmotte [1975] Director/Employee/Executive [French]

Michael Kors (UK) Intermediate Ltd.
Incorporated: 12 November 2014
Net Worth: £1,945,752,320 *Total Assets:* £1,945,752,320
Registered Office: 33 Kingsway, London, WC2B 6UF
Activities: Activities of head offices
Parent: Capri Holdings Limited
Officers: Alexandra Simmerson, Secretary; Boris Djordjevic [1969] Director/Business Executive [American]; David Michael Provenzano [1979] Director [American]; Cedric Dominique Alain Wilmotte [1975] Director/Business Executive [French]

KPMG LLP
Incorporated: 22 February 2002 *Employees:* 14,559
Net Worth: £225,000,000 *Total Assets:* £1,542,000,000
Registered Office: 15 Canada Square, London, E14 5GL
Officers: Jeremy Daniel Barton [1963] Member; Philip Michael Davidson [1964] Member; Bill Michael [1968] Member; Sarah Kate Gilchrist Willows [1967] Member; Philip George Abram [1970] LLP Member; Marc Abrams [1974] LLP Member; Stephen John Absolom [1973] LLP Member; Giles Franklin Walton Adams [1963] LLP Member; Ross MacKean Agnew [1977] LLP Member; Simon Albrighton [1975] LLP Member; Iain James Alexander [1964] LLP Member; Melissa Allen [1969] LLP Member; Michael John Allen [1975] LLP Member; Mark Stuart Andrews [1975] LLP Member; Richard John Andrews [1976] LLP Member; Claire Mary Angell [1980] LLP Member; Sarah Marie Anthony [1981] LLP Member; Graham Paul Armitage [1968] LLP Member; Rees Aronson [1967] LLP Member; Grant Philip Ashbrook [1981] LLP Member; David Harvey Ashworth [1965] LLP Member; Tudor Tsun Wei Aw [1964] LLP Member; Jawahar Bomi Ayrton [1970] LLP Member; Andrew Bailey [1975] LLP Member; Mark Robert Baillache [1967] LLP Member; Edward William Baker [1968] LLP Member; Lorraine Elizabeth Ball [1970] LLP Member; Stephen Ball [1958] LLP Member; Steven Balmer [1965] LLP Member; Iain Robert Bannatyne [1969] LLP Member; Moray William Barber [1974] LLP Member; Rebecca Elizabeth Barford [1982] LLP Member; Bethan Mair Barham [1973] LLP Member; Annette Louise Barker [1973] LLP Member; Christopher Barnes [1978] LLP Member; Edward Neil Barnicoat [1970] LLP Member; Michael Francis Barradell [1970] LLP Member; Anna Louise Barrell [1978] LLP Member; Robert Oliver Bass [1974] LLP Member; Joanne Catherine Bateson [1979] LLP Member; Mandeep Singh Baura [1980] LLP Member; Robert Michael Arthur Baxter [1978] LLP Member; Emma Jodie Baylis [1974] LLP Member; Ian Beaumont [1966] LLP Member; Nathan Benjamin Beaver [1978] LLP Member; Peter Justin Beckett [1962] LLP Member; Bedria Bedri [1970] LLP Member; Glynn Michael Bellamy [1973] LLP Member; John Charles Quentin Bennett [1974] LLP Member; Neil Howard Berry [1971] LLP Member; Jonathan Bingham [1975] LLP Member; Punam Birly [1963] LLP Member; John Steven Blacker [1974] LLP Member; Timothy Blake [1969] LLP Member; Robert Bolton [1960] LLP Member; Ian Keith Bone [1965] LLP Member; Susan Philippa Bonney [1962] LLP Member; James Thomas Boon [1977] LLP Member; Ian James Borley [1965] LLP Member; Eleanor Catherine Rose Bosley [1977] LLP Member; Andrew John Bostock [1974] LLP Member; Caroline Bott [1979] LLP Member; Charlotte Natalia Bottomley [1984] LLP Member; Jonathan Mark Boyers [1967] LLP Member; Andrew Peter Boyle [1979] LLP Member; Edward George Boyle [1972] LLP Member; Miles Arthur Bradbury [1977] LLP Member; Andrew John Bradshaw [1980] LLP Member; Emma Louise Branch [1971] LLP Member; Aidan Joseph Brennan [1965] LLP Member; Robert John Brent [1969] LLP Member; Magdalene Sarah Brereton [1970] LLP Member; Karen Sarah Briggs [1963] LLP Member; Mark Douglas Britnell [1966] LLP Member; Richard Derek Broadbelt [1970] LLP Member; Ian James Brokenshire [1966] LLP Member; Philip Dudley Anthony Brook [1966] LLP Member; Amanda Brown [1968] LLP Member; Bernard Joseph Brown [1965] LLP Member; Huw James William Newman Brown [1978] LLP Member; Jonathan David Brown [1976] LLP Member; Thomas James Brown [1963] LLP Member; William David Brown [1962] LLP Member; Robert Browne [1971] LLP Member; Stephen Bryans [1960] LLP Member; Peter James Bull [1970] LLP Member; Stuart Burdass [1966] LLP Member; Andrew James Sebastian Burn [1974] LLP Member; Catherine Burnet [1970] LLP Member; Marc Burrows [1974] LLP Member; Timothy Alexander Butchart [1977] LLP Member; Ferdia Byrne [1969] LLP Member; David Bywater [1967] LLP Member; John David Cain [1964] LLP Member; Nathan Alan Cain [1976] LLP Member; Brent Warrick Cairney [1978] LLP Member; Jonathan Robert Calvert-Davies [1968] LLP Member; David Keith Campbell [1973] LLP Member; Andrew Colin Campbell Orde [1969] LLP Member; Richard John Care [1970] LLP Member

KPMG UK Limited
Incorporated: 12 June 1998 *Employees:* 13,587
Net Worth: £24,244,000 *Total Assets:* £171,638,000
Registered Office: 15 Canary Wharf, London, E14 5GL
Activities: Human resources provision and management of human resources functions
Parent: KPMG Holdings Limited
Officers: Joanne Dean, Secretary; Edward Neil Barnicoat [1970] Director/Solicitor; Paul Long [1961] Director; Sarah Kate Gilchrist Willows [1967] Director/Chartered Accountant

KRF Holdings Limited
Incorporated: 13 September 1999 *Employees:* 2
Net Worth: £119,995,192 *Total Assets:* £409,898,176
Registered Office: Third Floor, 1 King's Arms Yard, London, EC2R 7AF
Activities: Other business support service activities n.e.c.
Shareholders: Derek John Miller; Glenda Katherine Helena Miller; Mark Barnish
Officers: Eileen Marie Hughes [1966] Director/Head of Structured Products UK [American]; Daniel Jonathan Wynne [1970] Director

Kufpec UK Limited
Incorporated: 14 May 2010
Net Worth Deficit: £47,285,228 *Total Assets:* £1,140,575,104
Registered Office: 5th Floor, 6 St Andrew Street, London, EC4A 3AE
Activities: Extraction of crude petroleum
Parent: Kuwait Petroleum Company
Officers: Ahmad Al-Eidan [1966] Director [Kuwaiti]; Khaled Abdullah Hassan Abdullah Al-Qaoud [1960] Director/Engineer [Kuwaiti]; Nawaf Saud Nasir Al-Sabah [1971] Director [Kuwaiti]

Kuoni Holdings Limited
Incorporated: 26 October 1998 *Employees:* 1,602
Previous: Kuoni Holdings PLC
Net Worth Deficit: £323,451,168 *Total Assets:* £386,754,880
Registered Office: 27 Goswell Road, London, EC1M 7GT
Activities: Tour operator activities
Parent: Trina Group Limited
Officers: Darren James Anniss [1977] Director; Martin Charles Jones [1973] Director; Andrew John Tempest [1962] Director

Kusuma Trust UK
Incorporated: 19 November 2008 *Employees:* 5
Net Worth: £369,829,312 *Total Assets:* £370,414,688
Registered Office: 5th Floor, 55 New Oxford Street, London, WC1A 1BS
Activities: Other business support service activities n.e.c.
Officers: Andrew Richard Arthurson, Secretary; Anurag Dikshit [1971] Director; Nitin Dass Jain [1975] Director; Soma Pujari [1976] Director/Founder & Advisor

Kypris Acquisitions Ltd
Incorporated: 20 December 2005
Net Worth: £178,023,360 *Total Assets:* £946,319,424
Registered Office: Peterborough Court, 133 Fleet Street, London, EC4A 2BB
Activities: Financial intermediation not elsewhere classified
Parent: ELQ Investors, Ltd
Officers: Thomas Kelly, Secretary; Clare Charlotte Richards, Secretary; Oliver John Bingham [1977] Director/Chartered Accountant; Vikramjit Singh Chima [1973] Director/Accountant [Indian]; William Thomas Gasson [1965] Director/Banker

L & Q New Homes Limited
Incorporated: 10 July 2003
Net Worth: £550,000,000 *Total Assets:* £913,772,032
Registered Office: 29-35 West Ham Lane, London, E15 4PH
Activities: Buying and selling of own real estate
Officers: Emuoborohwo Siakpere, Secretary; Waqar Ahmed [1967] Finance Director; Fiona Carswell [1968] Group Director Development & Sales [Irish]; Edward Paul Farnsworth [1982] Director/Head of Business Planning & Development Finance; Craig David Luttman [1975] Director; Janet Lynne Mackey [1959] Development Director; Stuart Whitehill Miller [1961] Director; Andrew Peter Rowland [1959] Development Director; Victoria Elizabeth Savage [1965] Regional Managing Director

L & Q PRS Co Limited
Incorporated: 4 November 2014
Net Worth: £124,697,000 *Total Assets:* £607,241,024
Registered Office: 29-35 West Ham Lane, London, E15 4PH
Activities: Other letting and operating of own or leased real estate
Parent: London & Quadrant Housing Trust
Officers: Emuoborohwo Siakpere, Secretary; Lukman Ahmed [1976] Director/Property Portfolio Manager; Waqar Ahmed [1967] Director; Diane Linda Hart [1965] Group Director Neighbourhoods; Martin Stuart Watts [1977] Director of Treasury

L'Oreal (U.K.) Limited
Incorporated: 24 December 1932 *Employees:* 4,846
Net Worth: £220,012,000 *Total Assets:* £561,248,000
Registered Office: 255 Hammersmith Road, London, W6 8AZ
Activities: Wholesale of perfume and cosmetics
Officers: Mark Andrew Chesson, Secretary; Stephan Jean Paul Marie Bezy [1963] Director [French]; Yannick Chalme [1958] Director/Group General Counsel [French]; Vianney Marie Hugues Derville [1967] Director [French]; Vismay Sharma [1971] Managing Director [Indian]; Geoffrey Christopher Skingsley [1958] Director/Chairman

L-3 Communications Limited
Incorporated: 3 May 2006 *Employees:* 2
Net Worth: £1,130,516,992 *Total Assets:* £1,130,516,992
Registered Office: 100 New Bridge Street, London, EC4V 6JA
Activities: Activities of other holding companies n.e.c.
Parent: L3 Technologies, Inc.
Officers: Dan Yaakov Azmon [1963] Director/Business Executive [American]; Ronald Cook [1953] Director/Vice President

L-3 Global Holding UK Ltd
Incorporated: 14 May 2015
Net Worth: £1,118,017,280 *Total Assets:* £1,772,999,296
Registered Office: 100 New Bridge Street, London, EC4V 6JA
Activities: Activities of other holding companies n.e.c.
Parent: L-3 Communications Limited
Officers: Ronald Cook [1953] Director; Ronald Mark Mandler [1971] Director [American]; David Reilly [1965] Director [American]

L-3 Technology & Services UK Ltd
Incorporated: 14 May 2015 *Employees:* 3
Net Worth: £141,165,376 *Total Assets:* £175,921,952
Registered Office: 100 New Bridge Street, London, EC4V 6JA
Activities: Financial management
Parent: L-3 Communications Limited
Officers: Dan Yaakov Azmon [1963] Director [American]; Ronald Cook [1953] Director; Ronald M Mandler [1971] Director [American]

L.E.K. Consulting Group Limited
Incorporated: 16 June 2017 *Employees:* 1,211
Net Worth Deficit: £49,845,896 *Total Assets:* £141,356,288
Registered Office: 160 Victoria Street, London, SW1E 5LB
Activities: Other service activities n.e.c.
Parent: L.E.K. Consulting Nominees Limited
Officers: Eileen Clare Coveney [1960] Director/Management Consultant [American]; Reiji Fujii [1975] Director/Strategy Consultant [Japanese]; Johnny Clayton Heskett [1969] Director/Management Consultant [American]; Nicholas Holder [1965] Director/Management Consultant [Australian]; Stuart Edward Jackson [1961] Director/Management Consultant [American]; Alan Lewis [1975] Director/Strategy Consultant [Irish/American]; Robert Norman Rourke [1968] Director [American]; Jonathan Nigel Edward Sparey [1957] Director/Management Consultant; Lawrence Matthew Verge [1959] Director/Management Consultant [Canadian]; Jonathan David Weber [1972] Director/Strategy Consultant [American]

L.E.K. International Group Limited
Incorporated: 16 June 2017 *Employees:* 1,211
Net Worth Deficit: £73,099,744 *Total Assets:* £141,356,288
Registered Office: 160 Victoria Street, London, SW1E 5LB
Activities: Other service activities n.e.c.
Parent: L.E.K. Consulting Group Limited
Officers: Johnny Clayton Heskett [1969] Director/Management Consultant [American]; Lawrence Matthew Verge [1959] Director/Management Consultant [Canadian]

L3 Commercial Training Solutions Limited
Incorporated: 12 May 2006 *Employees:* 274
Previous: L-3 Communications Link Simulation and Training UK Limited
Net Worth: £469,456,000 *Total Assets:* £655,654,016
Registered Office: 100 New Bridge Street, London, EC4V 6JA
Activities: Manufacture of air and spacecraft and related machinery
Parent: L-3 Global Holding UK Ltd
Officers: Craig Timothy Collins [1972] Director/Business Executive [American]; Ronald Cook [1953] Director/Vice President; Alan Edward Crawford [1982] Director/Business Executive [Australian]; Ashton Dallsingh [1967] Director/Business Executive [Irish]; Todd Winston Gautier [1963] Director/Business Executive [American]; Robin George Glover-Faure [1965] Director/Business Executive; Matthew Steven Weingast [1965] Director/Business Executive/Corporate Attorney [American]

L51N Limited
Incorporated: 14 January 2009 *Employees:* 644
Net Worth: £338,700,000 *Total Assets:* £1,375,600,000
Registered Office: Chelsea House, West Gate, London, W5 1DR
Activities: Activities of head offices
Officers: Benjamin Joseph Lewis [1967] Director; Clive Robert Lewis [1956] Director; Julian Harley Lewis [1954] Director; Michael Henry Rosehill [1960] Director/Chartered Accountant [Irish]

La Perla Global Management (UK) Limited
Incorporated: 14 January 2010 *Employees:* 1,616
Net Worth Deficit: £40,574,660 *Total Assets:* £170,024,048
Registered Office: 23 Savile Row, London, W1S 2ET
Activities: Other amusement and recreation activities n.e.c.
Officers: Paolo Barbieri [1962] Director [Italian]; Pascal Perrier [1964] Director [French]; Tareq Shabib [1970] Director [Jordanian]; Paolo Angelo Marco Vannucchi [1963] Director [Italian]

Labcorp UK Holdings, Ltd.
Incorporated: 11 November 2015
Net Worth: £2,146,314,240 *Total Assets:* £2,146,331,648
Registered Office: 21 Holborn Viaduct, London, EC1A 2DY
Activities: Activities of head offices
Parent: Laboratory Corporation of America Holdings
Officers: Sandra Dillard Van Der Vaart, Secretary; Floyd Samuel Eberts III [1959] Director/Chief Legal Officer [American]; Glenn Andrew Eisenberg [1961] Director/Chief Financial Officer [American]; Robert Stewart Pringle [1964] Director

Labuan RE Underwriting Limited
Incorporated: 24 October 2006
Net Worth: £1,506,668 *Total Assets:* £133,380,520
Registered Office: 5th Floor, 40 Gracechurch Street, London, EC3V 0BT
Activities: Non-life insurance
Officers: Sharkawi Bin Alis [1947] Director [Malaysian]; Johana Era Binti Zainudin [1971] Director [Malaysian]

Ladbroke & Co., Limited
Incorporated: 5 October 1921
Net Worth: £1,715,635,968 *Total Assets:* £2,293,805,056
Registered Office: 3rd Floor, One New Change, London, EC4M 9AF
Activities: Activities of other holding companies n.e.c.
Parent: Ladbrokes Investments Holdings Limited
Officers: Stuart John Smith [1981] Director/Accountant; Charles Alexander Sutters [1980] Director

Ladbroke Group
Incorporated: 14 May 1999
Net Worth: £211,304,000 *Total Assets:* £211,304,000
Registered Office: 3rd Floor, One New Change, London, EC4M 9AF
Activities: Activities of other holding companies n.e.c.
Parent: Ladbrokes Investments Holdings Limited
Officers: Stuart John Smith [1981] Director/Accountant; Charles Alexander Sutters [1980] Director

Ladbroke US Investments Limited
Incorporated: 11 December 1958
Net Worth: £1,223,257,984 *Total Assets:* £1,223,794,048
Registered Office: 3rd Floor, One New Change, London, EC4M 9AF
Activities: Activities of other holding companies n.e.c.
Parent: Ladbrokes Investments Holdings Limited
Officers: Stuart John Smith [1981] Director/Accountant; Charles Alexander Sutters [1980] Director

Ladbrokes Betting & Gaming Limited
Incorporated: 1 October 1963 *Employees:* 10,882
Net Worth: £813,980,992 *Total Assets:* £1,889,208,064
Registered Office: 3rd Floor, One New Change, London, EC4M 9AF
Activities: Gambling and betting activities
Parent: Birchgree Limited
Officers: Sian Amanda Hoskin, Secretary; Fiona Lorraine Perez, Secretary; John Paul Maurice Bowtell [1968] Director/Accountant; Mark Russel Chambers [1972] Director/Accountant; John David Kerr [1959] Director; Robert Matthew Wood [1980] Director/Accountant

Ladbrokes Coral Group Limited
Incorporated: 16 May 1956 *Employees:* 24,117
Previous: Ladbrokes Coral Group PLC
Net Worth: £1,274,000,000 *Total Assets:* £3,096,800,000
Registered Office: 3rd Floor, One New Change, London, EC4M 9AF
Activities: Gambling and betting activities
Parent: GVC Holdings (UK) Limited
Officers: Robert Hoskin, Secretary; Kenneth Jack Alexander [1969] Director/Chief Executive Officer; John Paul Maurice Bowtell [1968] Director/Accountant; Adam Robert Arthur Lewis [1969] Director/Chief Marketing Officer

Ladbrokes Group Finance PLC
Incorporated: 14 June 1979
Net Worth: £657,688,000 *Total Assets:* £5,485,705,216
Registered Office: 3rd Floor, One New Change, London, EC4M 9AF
Activities: Other business support service activities n.e.c.
Parent: GVC Holdings (UK) Limited
Officers: Kenneth Jack Alexander [1969] Director/Chief Executive Officer; John Paul Maurice Bowtell [1968] Director/Accountant; Stuart John Smith [1981] Director/Accountant; Charles Alexander Sutters [1980] Director

Ladbrokes Investments Holdings Limited
Incorporated: 24 March 1875
Net Worth: £2,855,657,984 *Total Assets:* £3,490,473,984
Registered Office: 3rd Floor, One New Change, London, EC4M 9AF
Activities: Activities of other holding companies n.e.c.
Shareholders: Birchgree Limited; Ladbrokes Group Holdings Limited
Officers: Stuart John Smith [1981] Director/Accountant; Charles Alexander Sutters [1980] Director

John Laing Environmental Assets Group (UK) Limited
Incorporated: 22 January 2014 *Employees:* 3
Net Worth: £159,568,000 *Total Assets:* £437,097,984
Registered Office: 1 Kingsway, London, WC2B 6AN
Activities: Activities of other holding companies n.e.c.
Parent: John Laing Environmental Assets Group Limited
Officers: David Michael Hardy [1957] Director/Chartered Accountant; Christopher Holmes [1976] Director/Investment Manager; Christopher James Tanner [1972] Investment Director

John Laing Group PLC
Incorporated: 23 October 2006 *Employees:* 160
Previous: John Laing Group Limited
Net Worth: £1,123,900,032 *Total Assets:* £1,357,100,032
Registered Office: 1 Kingsway, London, WC2B 6AN
Activities: Activities of head offices
Officers: Clare Underwood, Secretary; Andrea Abt [1960] Portfolio Director [German]; Dr Jeremy John Beeton [1953] Director; Olivier Brousse [1965] Director [French]; Nicholas Toby Hiscock [1960] Director/Chartered Accountant; Patrick Francis John O'Donnell Bourke [1957] Director; David Rough [1951] Director; William Meredith Samuel [1952] Director; Anne Katherine Wade [1972] Director [American]

John Laing Holdco Limited
Incorporated: 14 September 2006 *Employees:* 2
Previous: Henderson Infrastructure Holdco Limited
Net Worth: £1,053,600,000 *Total Assets:* £1,053,600,000
Registered Office: 1 Kingsway, London, WC2B 6AN
Activities: Activities of head offices
Parent: John Laing Group PLC
Officers: Stuart Martin Colvin [1972] Director/Chartered Accountant; Patrick Francis John O'Donnell Bourke [1957] Director

John Laing Infrastructure Limited
Incorporated: 22 March 2002
Net Worth: £148,548,000 *Total Assets:* £153,028,992
Registered Office: 1 Kingsway, London, WC2B 6AN
Activities: Construction of roads and motorways
Parent: John Laing Investments Limited
Officers: Stuart Martin Colvin [1972] Director/Chartered Accountant; Clare Underwood [1972] Director/Accountant

John Laing Investments Limited
Incorporated: 7 November 1963
Net Worth: £1,015,000,000 *Total Assets:* £1,363,699,968
Registered Office: 1 Kingsway, London, WC2B 6AN
Activities: Activities of head offices
Parent: John Laing Limited
Officers: Stuart Martin Colvin [1972] Director/Chartered Accountant; Patrick Francis John O'Donnell Bourke [1957] Director; Clare Underwood [1972] Director/Accountant

John Laing Investments Overseas Holdings Limited
Incorporated: 2 February 2011
Net Worth: £177,744,896 *Total Assets:* £177,937,104
Registered Office: 1 Kingsway, London, WC2B 6AN
Activities: Activities of head offices
Parent: John Laing Investments Limited
Officers: Stuart Martin Colvin [1972] Director/Chartered Accountant; Michael Christopher Dixon [1963] Director/Corporate Treasurer

John Laing Limited
Incorporated: 23 December 1977 *Employees:* 9
Previous: John Laing Public Limited Company
Net Worth: £1,051,699,968 *Total Assets:* £1,106,400,000
Registered Office: 1 Kingsway, London, WC2B 6AN
Activities: Activities of head offices
Parent: John Laing Holdco Limited
Officers: Olivier Brousse [1965] Director [French]; Stuart Martin Colvin [1972] Director/Chartered Accountant; Patrick Francis John O'Donnell Bourke [1957] Director; Clare Underwood [1972] Director/Accountant

John Laing Social Infrastructure Limited
Incorporated: 4 June 1998
Net Worth: £130,620,000 *Total Assets:* £132,219,000
Registered Office: 1 Kingsway, London, WC2B 6AN
Activities: Financial intermediation not elsewhere classified
Parent: John Laing Investments Limited
Officers: Stuart Martin Colvin [1972] Director/Chartered Accountant; Clare Underwood [1972] Director/Accountant

Laird (Finance) Limited
Incorporated: 28 November 2005
Net Worth: £112,845,000 *Total Assets:* £117,504,000
Registered Office: 100 Pall Mall, London, SW1Y 5NQ
Activities: Activities of head offices
Parent: Laird Asia Holdings Limited
Officers: Kevin Jeremy Dangerfield [1967] Director

Laird Asia Holdings Limited
Incorporated: 2 December 2009
Net Worth: £284,280,992 *Total Assets:* £284,280,992
Registered Office: 100 Pall Mall, London, SW1Y 5NQ
Activities: Activities of head offices
Shareholders: Laird Holdings Limited; Laird Overseas Holdings Limited
Officers: Kevin Jeremy Dangerfield [1967] Director

Laird Limited
Incorporated: 4 January 1898 *Employees:* 10,132
Previous: Laird PLC
Net Worth: £569,900,032 *Total Assets:* £1,119,500,032
Registered Office: 100 Pall Mall, London, SW1Y 5NQ
Activities: Activities of head offices
Parent: Al Ladder Limited
Officers: Kevin Jeremy Dangerfield [1967] Director; Anthony James Quinlan [1965] Director/Chief Financial Officer

Laird Overseas Holdings Limited
Incorporated: 2 March 2007
Net Worth: £877,224,000 *Total Assets:* £877,224,000
Registered Office: 100 Pall Mall, London, SW1Y 5NQ
Activities: Activities of head offices
Parent: Laird Limited
Officers: Kevin Jeremy Dangerfield [1967] Director

Lake Acquisitions Limited
Incorporated: 5 June 2008
Net Worth: £8,176,999,936 *Total Assets:* £8,182,000,128
Registered Office: 90 Whitfield Street, London, W1T 4EZ
Activities: Activities of head offices
Parent: EDF Energy Lake Limited
Officers: Guido Santi, Secretary; Humphrey Alan Edward Cadoux-Hudson [1960] Director/Accountant; Marie-Sylvie Laura Frederique Collet [1964] Director [Belgian]; Robert Guyler [1966] Director/Accountant; Richard Hookway [1961] Director; Lisa Ann Katherine Minns [1975] Director [Irish]; Jean-Michel Quilichini [1966] Director/Chief of Nuclear Operations EDF DPN [French]; Simone Rossi [1968] Director/Chief Financial Officer [Italian]

Lakenorth Limited
Incorporated: 2 September 2005
Net Worth: £56,987,760 *Total Assets:* £164,390,944
Registered Office: 7th Floor, Portman House, 2 Portman Street, London, W1H 6DU
Activities: Other letting and operating of own or leased real estate
Officers: Joshua Lawrence, Secretary; Richard James Cotton [1971] Director/Chartered Surveyor

Lakeside Asset Backed Securitisation 1 Limited
Incorporated: 1 June 2015
Net Worth: £1 *Total Assets:* £235,501,472
Registered Office: 6th Floor, 65 Gresham Street, London, EC2V 7NQ
Activities: Other business support service activities n.e.c.
Parent: Link Trust Nominees No.1 Limited
Officers: Colin Arthur Benford [1962] Director

Lakeside MWS Limited Liability Partnership
Incorporated: 23 June 2010
Net Worth: £544,158,976 *Total Assets:* £544,158,976
Registered Office: Lakeside Drive, Park Royal, London, NW10 7HQ

Lanark Funding Limited
Incorporated: 5 July 2007
Net Worth: £96,000 *Total Assets:* £4,714,863,104
Registered Office: Suite 2, 3rd Floor, 11-12 St James's Square, London, SW1Y 4LB
Activities: Financial intermediation not elsewhere classified
Parent: Lanark Holdings Limited
Officers: Sunil Masson, Secretary; Julius Manuel Bozzino [1970] Director; Sunil Masson [1971] Director; David Rudge [1970] Director; Miles Beamish Storey [1964] Director/Treasurer

Lanark Master Issuer PLC
Incorporated: 5 July 2007
Net Worth Deficit: £973,000 *Total Assets:* £4,600,932,864
Registered Office: Suite 2, 3rd Floor, 11-12 St James's Square, London, SW1Y 4LB
Activities: Financial intermediation not elsewhere classified
Parent: Lanark Funding Limited
Officers: Sunil Masson, Secretary; Julius Manuel Bozzino [1970] Director; Sunil Masson [1971] Director; David Rudge [1970] Director; Miles Beamish Storey [1964] Director/Treasurer

Lancashire Insurance Company (UK) Limited
Incorporated: 17 March 2006
Net Worth: £132,730,696 *Total Assets:* £565,273,088
Registered Office: Level 29, 20 Fenchurch Street, London, EC3M 3BY
Activities: Non-life insurance
Parent: Lancashire Insurance Holdings (UK) Limited
Officers: Michael Sean Connor, Secretary/Solicitor; Adrian Colosso [1957] Consultant-Non-Executive Director; Michael Sean Connor [1966] Director/General Counsel; Paul Gregory [1978] Director/Chief Executive Officer; Samantha Jane Hoe-Richardson [1971] Director/Head of Environment & Sustainable Development; David George Horne [1951] Director; Hayley Johnston [1971] Director/Chief Underwriting Officer; Steven David Smart [1962] Director/Chief Executive Officer Claimcert Ltd; Russell Worsley [1960] Director; Stephen Daniel Yeo [1978] Director/Group Head of Claims

Lancashire Insurance Holdings (UK) Limited
Incorporated: 11 April 2006
Net Worth: £145,692,416 *Total Assets:* £145,699,936
Registered Office: Level 29, 20 Fenchurch Street, London, EC3M 3BY
Activities: Other activities auxiliary to insurance and pension funding
Parent: Lancashire Holdings Limited
Officers: Michael David Bambury, Secretary; Michael Sean Connor [1966] Director/General Counsel; Robert William Kennedy [1972] Director/Financial Controller; Russell Worsley [1960] Director/Insurance

The Lancaster Landmark Hotel Company Limited
Incorporated: 1 July 1993 *Employees:* 308
Net Worth: £128,456,000 *Total Assets:* £256,484,992
Registered Office: Lancaster London, Lancaster Terrace, London, W2 2TY
Activities: Hotels and similar accommodation
Major Shareholder: Jatuporn Sihanatkathakul
Officers: Mohamed Hassan Gemei [1943] Director/Hotel Manager [Egyptian]; Brian Darko Hladnik [1952] Director/Hotel Manager; Jatuporn Sihanatkathakul [1941] Director/Hotel Owner [Thai]; Thiti Sihanatkathakul [1975] Director [Thai]; Tosaporn Sihanatkathakul [1983] Director/Hotelier [Thai]

Lancer Square Limited
Incorporated: 19 January 2016
Net Worth: £86,820,520 *Total Assets:* £112,717,840
Registered Office: Floor 6, Quadrant House, 4 Thomas More Square, London, E1W 1YW
Activities: Other service activities n.e.c.
Officers: Khoon Jay Kevin Kuok [1968] Director [Malaysian]; Chee Meng Lim [1972] Director [Malaysian]; Chin Sean Lim [1981] Director [Malaysian]; Shiak Ling Lim [1971] Director [Malaysian]

Land Securities (Finance) Limited
Incorporated: 16 January 1961
Net Worth: £651,782,016 *Total Assets:* £8,340,336,128
Registered Office: 100 Victoria Street, London, SW1E 5JL
Activities: Other business support service activities n.e.c.
Parent: Land Securities PLC
Officers: Marc Peter Cadwaladr [1972] Director/Chartered Accountant; Alastair Michael Deutsch [1983] Commercial Director; Julie Louise Fountain [1984] Director/Chartered Accountant [New Zealander]; Rosalind Charlotte Futter [1978] Director/Accountant; Martin Frederick Greenslade [1965] Finance Director; Martin Reay Wood [1960] Director/Treasurer; Martin Richard Worthington [1978] Director/Accountant

Land Securities (Hotels) Limited
Incorporated: 10 January 2007
Net Worth: £509,659,008 *Total Assets:* £513,580,000
Registered Office: 100 Victoria Street, London, SW1E 5JL
Activities: Other letting and operating of own or leased real estate
Parent: Land Securities Portfolio Management Limited
Officers: Elizabeth Miles [1977] Director/Solicitor

Land Securities Buchanan Street Developments Limited
Incorporated: 21 February 2007
Net Worth: £91,734,000 *Total Assets:* £112,608,000
Registered Office: 100 Victoria Street, London, SW1E 5JL
Activities: Other letting and operating of own or leased real estate
Parent: Ravenseft Properties Limited
Officers: Elizabeth Miles [1977] Director/Solicitor

Land Securities Capital Markets PLC
Incorporated: 30 July 2004
Net Worth: £631,000 *Total Assets:* £4,581,364,224
Registered Office: 100 Victoria Street, London, SW1E 5JL
Activities: Solicitors
Parent: Land Securities PLC
Officers: Elizabeth Miles, Secretary; Timothy John Ashby [1962] Director/Solicitor; Marc Peter Cadwaladr [1972] Director/Chartered Accountant; Rosalind Charlotte Futter [1978] Director/Accountant; Martin Frederick Greenslade [1965] Finance Director; David John Heaford [1978] Finance Director; Martin Reay Wood [1960] Director/Treasurer; Martin Richard Worthington [1978] Director/Accountant

Land Securities Group PLC
Incorporated: 7 February 2002 *Employees:* 570
Net Worth: £10,492,000,256 *Total Assets:* £14,469,000,192
Registered Office: 100 Victoria Street, London, SW1E 5JL
Activities: Activities of real estate investment trusts
Officers: Timothy John Ashby, Secretary; Christopher John Bartram [1949] Director; Edward Henry Bonham Carter [1960] Director; Nicholas Theodore Cadbury [1966] Finance Director; Madeleine Elizabeth Cosgrave [1967] Managing Director; Martin Frederick Greenslade [1965] Finance Director; Cressida Mary Hogg [1969] Director; Robert Montague Noel [1964] Director/Chartered Surveyor; Colette O'Shea [1968] Director/Chartered Surveyor; Simon Dan Palley [1957] Director/Investment Adviser; Stacey Rauch [1958] Director [American]

Land Securities Management Limited
Incorporated: 13 December 2007
Net Worth: £215,796,992 *Total Assets:* £217,275,008
Registered Office: 100 Victoria Street, London, SW1E 5JL
Activities: Other business support service activities n.e.c.
Parent: Land Securities Property Holdings Limited
Officers: Elizabeth Miles [1977] Director/Solicitor

Land Securities P L C
Incorporated: 1 July 1955
Net Worth: £5,397,801,984 *Total Assets:* £7,710,180,864
Registered Office: 100 Victoria Street, London, SW1E 5JL
Activities: Development of building projects
Parent: Land Securities Intermediate Limited
Officers: Marc Peter Cadwaladr [1972] Director/Chartered Accountant; Rosalind Charlotte Futter [1978] Director/Accountant; Martin Frederick Greenslade [1965] Finance Director; David John Heaford [1978] Finance Director; Robert Montague Noel [1964] Director/Chartered Surveyor; Martin Reay Wood [1960] Director/Treasurer

Land Securities Portfolio Management Limited
Incorporated: 28 February 2000
Net Worth: £2,004,462,976 *Total Assets:* £4,374,756,864
Registered Office: 100 Victoria Street, London, SW1E 5JL
Activities: Activities of other holding companies n.e.c.
Parent: Land Securities PLC
Officers: Elizabeth Miles [1977] Director/Solicitor

Land Securities Properties Limited
Incorporated: 5 September 1969
Net Worth: £73,222,000 *Total Assets:* £2,973,893,888
Registered Office: 100 Victoria Street, London, SW1E 5JL
Activities: Management of real estate on a fee or contract basis
Parent: Land Securities Property Holdings Limited
Officers: Timothy John Ashby [1962] Director/Solicitor; Martin Frederick Greenslade [1965] Finance Director; Elizabeth Miles [1977] Director/Solicitor; Robert Montague Noel [1964] Director/Chartered Surveyor

Land Securities Property Holdings Limited
Incorporated: 16 March 2004
Net Worth: £1,712,578,944 *Total Assets:* £1,720,057,984
Registered Office: 100 Victoria Street, London, SW1E 5JL
Activities: Activities of other holding companies n.e.c.
Parent: Land Securities Group PLC
Officers: Marc Peter Cadwaladr [1972] Director/Chartered Accountant; Martin Frederick Greenslade [1965] Finance Director; Robert Montague Noel [1964] Director/Chartered Surveyor; Scott Cameron Parsons [1969] Property Director; Martin Richard Worthington [1978] Director/Accountant

Land Securities Trinity Limited
Incorporated: 18 July 2007
Net Worth: £394,112,992 *Total Assets:* £577,961,984
Registered Office: 100 Victoria Street, London, SW1E 5JL
Activities: Other business support service activities n.e.c.
Parent: Land Securities Portfolio Management Limited
Officers: Andrew Stephen Dudley [1965] Director/Project Manager

Landesk Holdco UK Ltd
Incorporated: 8 March 2016
Net Worth: £14,088,353 *Total Assets:* £108,552,472
Registered Office: 5 New Street Square, London, EC4A 3TW
Activities: Other business support service activities n.e.c.
Officers: Brian Elmer Agle [1962] Director/Accountant [American]; Andrzej Baldin [1956] Director/Vice President, Sales EMEA

Landmark Hotel London Limited
Incorporated: 12 June 2008 *Employees:* 480
Net Worth: £31,828,000 *Total Assets:* £202,462,000
Registered Office: Lancaster London, Lancaster Terrace, London, W2 2TY
Activities: Hotels and similar accommodation
Major Shareholder: Jatuporn Sihanatkathakul
Officers: Mohamed Hassan Gemei [1943] Director/Hotel Manager [Egyptian]; Brian Darko Hladnik [1952] Director/Hotel Manager; Jatuporn Sihanatkathakul [1941] Director/Hotel Owner [Thai]; Thiti Sihanatkathakul [1975] Director [Thai]; Tosaporn Sihanatkathakul [1983] Director/Hotelier [Thai]

Landmark Mortgage Securities No.2 PLC
Incorporated: 10 January 2007
Net Worth: £5,867,194 *Total Assets:* £159,127,568
Registered Office: 35 Great St Helens, London, EC3A 6AP
Activities: Financial intermediation not elsewhere classified
Parent: Landmark Mortgage Securities No.2 Holdings Limited
Officers: Daniel Marc Richard Jaffe [1975] Director

Landmark Mortgage Securities No.3 PLC
Incorporated: 11 July 2007
Net Worth Deficit: £1,406,118 *Total Assets:* £205,514,208
Registered Office: 35 Great St Helens, London, EC3A 6AP
Activities: Financial intermediation not elsewhere classified
Parent: Landmark Mortgage Securities No.3 Holdings Ltd
Officers: Daniel Marc Richard Jaffe [1975] Director

Lanesborough Management Limited
Incorporated: 15 December 1989 *Employees:* 308
Net Worth: £117,063,056 *Total Assets:* £266,096,480
Registered Office: 5th Floor, 6 St Andrew Street, London, EC4A 3AE
Activities: Renting and operating of Housing Association real estate
Parent: Government of The Emirate of Abu Dhabi
Officers: Salem Khamis Saeed Khamis Aldarmaki [1983] Director [Emirati]; Sultan Ali Ahmed Hamad Aldhaheri [1984] Director [Emirati]; Khaled Mohamed Abul Husain Alkhajeh [1974] Director [Emirati]; Khalifa Abdulla Bhutti Obaid Alshamsi [1989] Director [Emirati]

Lanespace Limited
Incorporated: 1 May 2002
Net Worth: £109,302,160 *Total Assets:* £245,840,576
Registered Office: 5th Floor, Leconfield House, Curzon Street, London, W1J 5JA
Activities: Activities of head offices
Officers: Robert Tchenguiz [1960] Director; Malcolm Robin Turner [1935] Director/Chartered Surveyor

Langton Funding (No.1) Limited
Incorporated: 20 November 2007
Net Worth Deficit: £17,318,000 *Total Assets:* £2,385,041,920
Registered Office: 35 Great St Helens, London, EC3A 6AP
Activities: Financial intermediation not elsewhere classified
Parent: Langton Securities Holdings Limited
Officers: Thomas Ranger [1977] Director

Langton Securities (2008-1) PLC.
Incorporated: 20 November 2007
Net Worth: £1,277,000 *Total Assets:* £1,417,760,000
Registered Office: 35 Great St Helen's, London, EC3A 6AP
Activities: Financial intermediation not elsewhere classified
Parent: Langton Securities Holdings Limited
Officers: Thomas Ranger [1977] Director

Langton Securities (2010-1) PLC
Incorporated: 20 September 2010
Net Worth: £117,000 *Total Assets:* £1,022,577,984
Registered Office: 35 Great St Helen's, London, EC3A 6AP
Activities: Financial intermediation not elsewhere classified
Parent: Langton Securities Holdings Limited
Officers: Clifford Pearce [1970] Director; Thomas Ranger [1977] Director

The Lankellychase Foundation
Incorporated: 9 December 2004 *Employees:* 13
Net Worth: £144,396,736 *Total Assets:* £148,635,408
Registered Office: Greenworks, Dog and Duck Yard, Princeton Street, London, WC1R 4BH
Activities: Other social work activities without accommodation n.e.c.
Officers: Oliver James Bachelor [1956] Charity Director; Hilary Andrea Berg [1962] Director/Communications Consultant; Morag Helen Burnett [1968] Director/Consultant; Jacob Hayman [1982] Director/Consultant; Marion Janner [1959] Charity Director; Jane Isobel Millar [1953] Director/University Professor; Darren Jamie Murinas [1972] Director/Filmmaker Blogger Agent for Systems Change; Myron Edwards Rogers [1952] Director/Management Consultant and Author [American]; Simon George Tucker [1972] Director/Independent Consultant; Robin John Tuddenham [1968] Director of Communities and Service Support

Lannraig Funding Limited
Incorporated: 23 June 2011
Net Worth: £36,000 *Total Assets:* £918,337,984
Registered Office: 35 Great St Helen's, London, EC3A 6AP
Activities: Non-trading company
Parent: Lannraig Holdings Limited
Officers: Miles Beamish Storey [1964] Director/Banker Treasurer

Lannraig Master Issuer PLC
Incorporated: 29 November 2010
Net Worth: £41,000 *Total Assets:* £904,920,000
Registered Office: 35 Great St Helen's, London, EC3A 6AP
Activities: Financial intermediation not elsewhere classified
Parent: Lannraig Holdings Limited
Officers: Miles Beamish Storey [1964] Director/Banker Treasurer

Lanterndew Limited
Incorporated: 20 May 2004
Net Worth: £149,500,848 *Total Assets:* £353,883,360
Registered Office: Cannon Place, 78 Cannon Street, London, EC4N 6AF
Activities: Other business support service activities n.e.c.
Parent: BIIF Bidco Limited
Officers: John Ivor Cavill [1972] Director; James Peter Dawes [1971] Director/Chief Financial Officer

Lapsent Limited
Incorporated: 9 November 1988 *Employees:* 365
Net Worth Deficit: £24,104,000 *Total Assets:* £137,910,000
Registered Office: 8 Sackville Street, London, W1S 3DG
Activities: Non-trading company
Officers: Marc John Haslam [1975] Director/Chartered Surveyor; Wendy Jane Patterson [1969] Director/Chartered Accountant; Paul Dennis Perris [1973] Director/Chartered Secretary; Paul Justin Windsor [1957] Director/Chartered Accountant

Larch (Nursing Homes) Holdco Ltd
Incorporated: 3 October 2008 *Employees:* 1
Net Worth Deficit: £332,236,704 *Total Assets:* £122,488,504
Registered Office: Floor 6, Quadrant House, 4 Thomas More Square, London, E1W 1YW
Activities: Other business support service activities n.e.c.
Parent: London & Regional Group Investments Limited
Officers: Leonard Kevin Sebastian [1969] Group Managing and Legal Director [Swiss]

Larch (Nursing Homes) Ltd
Incorporated: 6 January 2004 *Employees:* 1
Net Worth Deficit: £117,787,360 *Total Assets:* £425,367,584
Registered Office: 30 Finsbury Square, London, EC2A 1AG
Activities: Other business support service activities n.e.c.
Parent: Larch (Nursing Homes) Holdco Ltd
Officers: Stuart David Maddison, Secretary; Mark Calvert [1961] Director; Stuart David Maddison [1963] Director/Chartered Accountant

Larch Funding (UK) Ltd
Incorporated: 23 April 2004 *Employees:* 1
Net Worth Deficit: £7,470,649 *Total Assets:* £205,470,720
Registered Office: 30 Finsbury Square, London, EC2A 1AG
Activities: Other business support service activities n.e.c.
Officers: Stuart David Maddison, Secretary; Mark Calvert [1961] Director; Stuart David Maddison [1963] Director/Chartered Accountant

Larch Life No.1 (UK) Ltd
Incorporated: 27 May 2004
Net Worth Deficit: £64,454,700 *Total Assets:* £145,305,568
Registered Office: 30 Finsbury Square, London, EC2A 1AG
Activities: Renting and operating of Housing Association real estate
Officers: Stuart David Maddison, Secretary; Mark Andrew Calvert [1961] Managing Director; Stuart David Maddison [1963] Director/Chartered Accountant

Largenta Limited
Incorporated: 16 March 2010
Net Worth: £409,771,008 *Total Assets:* £409,771,008
Registered Office: 1 The Village Offices, Ariel Way, London, W12 7GF
Activities: Activities of head offices
Parent: YOOX Net A Porter Group SpA
Officers: Angelica Longanesi Cattani, Secretary; Federico Marchetti [1969] Director/Chief Executive Officer of YOOX [Italian]

Laser Hotels One Limited
Incorporated: 2 August 2006
Previous: MREF Hotels One Limited
Net Worth Deficit: £41,163,000 *Total Assets:* £373,488,992
Registered Office: 17 Dominion Street, London, EC2M 2EF
Activities: Activities of head offices
Officers: Vincent Vernier, Secretary; Michael Gallagher [1978] Finance Director [Irish]; Timothy Selwyn Jones [1985] Director/Asset Manager; Vincent Frederic Marc Vernier [1978] Director Portfolio Management [French]

Laser Tradeco Limited
Incorporated: 11 August 2006 *Employees:* 765
Previous: MREF Tradeco Limited
Net Worth Deficit: £109,802,000 *Total Assets:* £183,639,008
Registered Office: 60 Welbeck Street, London, W1G 9XB
Activities: Hotels and similar accommodation
Officers: Christos Dimitriadis [1971] Director [Greek]

Lattice Group Limited
Incorporated: 29 December 1999
Previous: Lattice Group PLC
Net Worth: £2,809,999,872 *Total Assets:* £2,956,000,000
Registered Office: 1-3 Strand, London, WC2N 5EH
Activities: Activities of head offices
Parent: National Grid Holdings One PLC
Officers: Megan Barnes, Secretary; Andrew Jonathan Agg [1969] Director/Accountant; Jonathan Paul Clay [1975] Director; Simon Warren Grant [1979] Director; Harriet Hill [1967] Director/Solicitor; Stuart Calvin Humphreys [1963] Director/Chartered Accountant; Andrew Kenneth Mead [1971] Director/Accountant; David Anthony Preston [1971] Director/Treasurer; Christopher John Waters [1967] Director/Accountant

Estee Lauder Cosmetics Limited
Incorporated: 16 May 1960 *Employees:* 9,723
Net Worth: £503,360,992 *Total Assets:* £789,843,008
Registered Office: One Fitzroy, 6 Mortimer Street, London, W1T 3JJ
Activities: Wholesale of perfume and cosmetics
Parent: Estee Lauder UK Holdings Limited
Officers: Steffi Kipperman Bogart, Secretary; Raniero de Stasio, Secretary; Edward Robert Hughes, Secretary; Sara Ellen Moss, Secretary [American]; Charles Edward Reese, Secretary; Spencer Gary Smul, Assistant Secretary; Agnieszka Trzesicka, Secretary; Agata Wieczorek, Secretary; Alison Claire Day [1971] Finance Director; Marc Cedric Yann Prouve [1960] Director/Business Executive [French]; Tracey Thomas Travis [1962] Director/Executive Vice President and CFO [American]; Philippe Michel Warnery [1970] Director/Corporate General Manager [French]

Laudico Limited
Incorporated: 15 April 2003 *Employees:* 1
Net Worth: £1,376,928 *Total Assets:* £321,017,408
Registered Office: 5th Floor, Leconfield House, Curzon Street, London, W1J 5JA
Activities: Activities of head offices
Officers: Robert Tchenguiz [1960] Director

Launcelot Investments (UK) Limited
Incorporated: 10 June 2016
Net Worth: £124,037,632 *Total Assets:* £144,271,248
Registered Office: 17 Clifford Street, London, W1S 3RQ
Activities: Buying and selling of own real estate
Major Shareholder: Nic Hugh Byrom
Officers: Emma Louise Bowman [1984] Director; James Charles Christopher Byrom [1986] Director; Nicholas Hugh Byrom [1953] Director; Cyril John Edwards [1950] Director/Retired; Matthew Simon Thorley [1984] Director

Lavenham Underwriting Limited
Incorporated: 15 August 2002
Net Worth Deficit: £78,715,000 *Total Assets:* £233,280,000
Registered Office: c/o Neon Underwriting Limited, 20 Gracechurch Street, London, EC3V 0BG
Activities: Non-life insurance
Parent: Neon Holdings (U.K.) Limited
Officers: Larysa Alla Dlaboha, Secretary; Ian James Harman [1985] Director/Head of Finance; David John Witzgall [1959] Director [American]

Law Debenture Corporation PLC (The)
Incorporated: 12 December 1889 *Employees:* 120
Net Worth: £748,257,984 *Total Assets:* £884,427,008
Registered Office: Fifth Floor, 100 Wood Street, London, EC2V 7EX
Activities: Financial intermediation not elsewhere classified
Officers: Timothy Nicholas Bond [1962] Director/Investment Manager; Mark George Orlando Bridgeman [1968] Director/Investment Manager; Robert Charles Anthony Hingley [1960] Director/Financial Adviser; Denis Jackson [1966] Director; The Hon. Robert John Laing [1953] Director; Katie Elizabeth Thorpe [1979] Director

Lawn Tennis Association Limited
Incorporated: 3 December 2010 *Employees:* 275
Net Worth: £139,656,992 *Total Assets:* £151,703,008
Registered Office: The National Tennis Centre, 100 Priory Lane, Roehampton, London, SW15 5JQ
Activities: Other sports activities
Officers: Stephen James Farrow, Secretary; Rachel Mary Baillache [1969] Director/Partner (KPMG); Sara Philippa Bennison [1967] Chief Marketing Officer and Non-Executive Director; Martin Francis Corrie [1954] Director/Chartered Accountant; Lord Evan Mervyn Davies [1952] Director/Chairman; Craig Martin Haworth [1964] Managing Director; Clare Margaret Hollingsworth [1960] Director; Scott Anthony Lloyd [1975] Director/Chief Executive; Nicola Dawn Maskens [1954] Research Director; Sandra Anne Procter [1951] Director/Sports Centre Manager; David John Rawlinson [1953] Director/Chartered Accountant; Simon Naunton Steele [1971] Finance Director; Sir David Whitlock Tanner [1947] Director

Lazard & Co., Holdings Limited
Incorporated: 6 December 1999
Net Worth: £94,488,000 *Total Assets:* £246,362,000
Registered Office: 50 Stratton Street, London, W1J 8LL
Activities: Activities of financial services holding companies
Officers: Robert Jamieson Farrer-Brown, Secretary; Robert Jamieson Farrer-Brown [1968] Director/General Counsel; Archibald John Norman [1954] Director/Company Chairman; Jeffrey Allen Rosen [1952] Director/Investment Banker [American]; Robert James Rountree [1959] Director/Chartered Accountant; William John Rucker [1963] Director/Merchant Banker; Nicholas Roland Shott [1951] Director/Merchant Banker

Lazard & Co., Limited
Incorporated: 30 December 1919
Net Worth: £91,454,000 *Total Assets:* £134,359,008
Registered Office: 50 Stratton Street, London, W1J 8LL
Activities: Financial intermediation not elsewhere classified
Parent: Lazard & Co., Holdings Limited
Officers: Robert Jamieson Farrer-Brown, Secretary; Robert Jamieson Farrer-Brown [1968] Director/General Counsel; Archibald John Norman [1954] Director/Company Chairman; Jeffrey Allen Rosen [1952] Director/Investment Banker [American]; Robert James Rountree [1959] Director/Chartered Accountant; William John Rucker [1963] Director/Merchant Banker; Nicholas Roland Shott [1951] Director/Merchant Banker

Lazard Asset Management (UK) Holdings Limited
Incorporated: 26 July 2002 *Employees:* 137
Net Worth: £38,886,672 *Total Assets:* £131,322,200
Registered Office: 50 Stratton Street, London, W1J 8LL
Activities: Activities of head offices
Parent: Lazard Ltd
Officers: Tim Russell, Secretary; John Reinsberg [1956] Director [American]; Jeremy Marshall Taylor [1973] Director

Lazari Finance Limited
Incorporated: 1 February 2016 *Employees:* 1
Net Worth: £702,017,216 *Total Assets:* £705,782,528
Registered Office: Accurist House, 44 Baker Street, London, W1U 7BR
Activities: Activities of mortgage finance companies
Parent: Lazari Financial Holdings Limited
Officers: Maritsa Lazari [1943] Director

Lazari Financial Holdings Limited
Incorporated: 6 September 2017 *Employees:* 1
Net Worth: £702,000,896 *Total Assets:* £705,792,512
Registered Office: Accurist House, 44 Baker Street, London, W1U 7BR
Activities: Activities of other holding companies n.e.c.
Major Shareholder: Maritsa Lazari
Officers: Maritsa Lazari [1943] Director

Lazari Investments Limited
Incorporated: 6 September 2017 *Employees:* 70
Net Worth: £1,064,261,696 *Total Assets:* £3,032,346,112
Registered Office: Accurist House, 44 Baker Street, London, W1U 7BR
Activities: Activities of other holding companies n.e.c.
Shareholders: Andrie Lazari; Leonidas Lazari; Nicholas Lazari
Officers: Nicholas Lazari, Secretary; Andrie Lazari [1977] Director; Leonidas Lazari [1967] Director; Nicholas Lazari [1971] Director

Lazari Properties 1 Limited
Incorporated: 1 February 2016
Net Worth: £453,291,584 *Total Assets:* £1,438,514,816
Registered Office: Accurist House, 44 Baker Street, London, W1U 7BR
Activities: Other letting and operating of own or leased real estate
Parent: Lazari Investments Limited
Officers: Nicholas Lazari, Secretary; Andrie Lazari [1977] Director; Leonidas Lazari [1967] Director; Nicholas Lazari [1971] Director

Lazari Properties 2 Limited
Incorporated: 1 February 2016
Net Worth: £158,820,768 *Total Assets:* £496,940,512
Registered Office: Accurist House, 44 Baker Street, London, W1U 7BR
Activities: Other letting and operating of own or leased real estate
Parent: Lazari Investments Limited
Officers: Nicholas Lazari, Secretary; Andrie Lazari [1977] Director; Leonidas Lazari [1967] Director; Nicholas Lazari [1971] Director

Lazari Properties 3 Limited
Incorporated: 1 February 2016
Net Worth: £206,535,696 *Total Assets:* £613,906,816
Registered Office: Accurist House, 44 Baker Street, London, W1U 7BR
Activities: Other letting and operating of own or leased real estate
Parent: Lazari Investments Limited
Officers: Nicholas Lazari, Secretary; Andrie Lazari [1977] Director; Leonidas Lazari [1967] Director; Nicholas Lazari [1971] Director

Lazari Properties 5 Limited
Incorporated: 1 February 2016
Net Worth: £44,708,668 *Total Assets:* £121,035,280
Registered Office: Accurist House, 44 Baker Street, London, W1U 7BR
Activities: Other letting and operating of own or leased real estate
Parent: Lazari Investments Limited
Officers: Nicholas Lazari, Secretary; Andrie Lazari [1977] Director; Leonidas Lazari [1967] Director; Nicholas Lazari [1971] Director

Lazari Properties 7 Limited
Incorporated: 14 July 2016
Net Worth: £98,159,928 *Total Assets:* £289,747,488
Registered Office: Accurist House, 44 Baker Street, London, W1U 7BR
Activities: Other letting and operating of own or leased real estate
Parent: Lazari Investments Limited
Officers: Nicholas Lazari, Secretary; Andrie Lazari [1977] Director; Leonidas Lazari [1967] Director; Nicholas Lazari [1971] Director

LBG Capital Holdings Limited
Incorporated: 10 October 2007
Net Worth: £115,332,000 *Total Assets:* £646,334,016
Registered Office: 25 Gresham Street, London, EC2V 7HN
Activities: Activities of financial services holding companies
Parent: Lloyds Banking Group PLC
Officers: Alyson Elizabeth Mulholland, Secretary; Alan Toby Rougier [1967] Director; Vishal Dilip Savadia [1981] Director; Richard Douglas Shrimpton [1970] Director/Banker

LCH Group Holdings Limited
Incorporated: 24 April 2003 *Employees:* 861
Previous: LCH.Clearnet Group Limited
Net Worth: £951,368,832 *Total Assets:* £612,180,426,752
Registered Office: Aldgate House, 33 Aldgate High Street, London, EC3N 1EA
Activities: Activities of head offices
Parent: London Stock Exchange (C) Limited
Officers: Simon Tutton, Secretary; Marshall Charles Bailey [1966] Director/Banker; Ronaldus Johannes Berndsen [1965] Director/Professor [Dutch]; Jill M Considine [1944] Director/Retired [American]; Chris Francis Corrado [1959] Director [American]; Jonathan Edward Cossey [1971] Director/Banker; Jonathan Desler [1973] Director/Banker; Dr Leonard Hubertus Hoogduin [1956] Director/Banker [Dutch]; James Andrew Hudis [1956] Director/Retired [American]; Ashok Krishnan [1970] Director/Banker; Dominique Le Masson [1959] Director/Senior Coordinator European Market Infrastructures [French]; Daniel Maguire [1976] Director/Senior Executive; Puneet Malhi [1969] Director/Banker; Shona Milne [1957] Director/Retired; David Adam Schwimmer [1969] Director [American]; David Porter Warren [1954] Director/Chief Financial Officer [American]

LCH Limited
Incorporated: 22 February 1888 *Employees:* 641
Previous: LCH.Clearnet Limited
Net Worth: £588,209,600 *Total Assets:* £359,171,260,416
Registered Office: Aldgate House, 33 Aldgate High Street, London, EC3N 1EA
Activities: Other business support service activities n.e.c.
Parent: LCH.Clearnet Group Limited
Officers: Simon Tutton, Secretary; Laurence Philip Adams [1956] Director; Ronaldus Johannes Berndsen [1965] Director/Professor [Dutch]; Dr Leonard Hubertus Hoogduin [1956] Director/Banker [Dutch]; Matthew Jerman [1968] Director/Banker; Daniel Maguire [1976] Director/Senior Executive; Dennis McLaughlin [1963] Director/Chief Risk Officer [Irish]; Shona Milne [1957] Director/Retired; Susan O'Flynn [1976] Director/Banker [Irish]; Mr Martin Pluves [1973] Director/Chief Executive; Nikhil Rathi [1979] Director/Chief Executive; Graham Wright [1959] Director

LCI Helicopters (UK) Limited
Incorporated: 18 December 2013
Net Worth: £36,299,600 *Total Assets:* £391,545,664
Registered Office: 13-14 Hobart Place, London, SW1W 0HH
Activities: Activities of head offices
Officers: Jaspal Jandu [1974] Director; Derek Crispin George Maunder [1949] Director

LCR Finance PLC
Incorporated: 31 July 1998
Net Worth: £50,000 *Total Assets:* £2,763,379,968
Registered Office: 33 Horseferry Road, London, SW1P 4DR
Activities: Financial intermediation not elsewhere classified
Parent: Secretary of State for Transport
Officers: Malcolm Lowe, Secretary; Malcolm Lowe [1965] Director/Civil Servant; Helene Walden [1970] Director/Civil Servant

LDC (Care Homes) Finco Limited
Incorporated: 25 July 2015
Net Worth: £39,926 *Total Assets:* £104,226,664
Registered Office: Fifth Floor, 100 Wood Street, London, EC2V 7EX
Activities: Other business support service activities n.e.c.
Shareholder: Victor Khosla
Officers: Mark Howard Filer [1967] Director

LDC (Managers) Limited
Incorporated: 25 April 1990 *Employees:* 93
Net Worth: £4,758,000 *Total Assets:* £188,614,000
Registered Office: One Vine Street, London, W1J 0AH
Activities: Other business support service activities n.e.c.
Parent: Lloyds Development Capital (Holdings) Limited
Officers: David Dermot Hennessey, Secretary; Mark George Culmer [1962] Finance Director; Andrew John Cumming [1954] Director; Martin John Draper [1964] Director; Christopher Richard Hurley [1974] Director; Hugh Alexander McKay [1960] Director; Alan Toby Rougier [1967] Director

Le Creuset Holding Limited
Incorporated: 3 December 2015 *Employees:* 3,358
Net Worth: £399,033,184 *Total Assets:* £494,433,216
Registered Office: 22 Grosvenor Gardens, London, SW1W 0DH
Activities: Activities of distribution holding companies
Officers: Luc Marie Arthur Torre' [1956] Director [Belgian]; Paul Johannes Van Zuydam [1938] Director

Leadenhall Securities Corporation Limited
Incorporated: 10 July 1935
Net Worth: £229,472,000 *Total Assets:* £1,049,675,008
Registered Office: 1 London Wall Place, London, EC2Y 5AU
Activities: Financial intermediation not elsewhere classified
Parent: Schroder Investment Company Limited
Officers: Tim McCann [1973] Director/Group Head of Tax; Wayne Mepham [1973] Director/Head of Principal Reporting; Graham Staples [1961] Director/Chartered Secretary; Nicholas Michael Taylor [1968] Director

Leadiant Biosciences Limited
Incorporated: 15 April 2015 *Employees:* 15
Net Worth: £106,717,424 *Total Assets:* £112,069,976
Registered Office: 21 Holborn Viaduct, London, EC1A 2DY
Activities: Wholesale of pharmaceutical goods
Officers: Marco Maria Brughera [1955] Director [Italian]; Michael Ford [1946] Director/Chairman; Antonio Manuel Maia Devesa Gama Da Silva [1963] Director [Portuguese]

Lear Corporation (UK) Limited
Incorporated: 14 May 1993 *Employees:* 1,522
Net Worth: £89,442,000 *Total Assets:* £301,100,992
Registered Office: c/o TMF Corporate Administration Services Limited, 5th Floor, 6 St Andrew Street, London, EC4A 3AE
Activities: Manufacture of bodies (coachwork) for motor vehicles (except caravans)
Parent: Lear Corporation UK Holdings Limited
Officers: Martin Henningsen [1967] Director/Associate General Counsel [German]; Robert Chalders Hooper [1953] Director/Chartered Accountant

Leathbond Limited
Incorporated: 4 March 1983 *Employees:* 164
Net Worth: £510,574,016 *Total Assets:* £1,706,120,960
Registered Office: c/o Michael Simkins LLP, Lynton House, 7-12 Tavistock Square, London, WC1H 9LT
Activities: Buying and selling of own real estate
Officers: David Dibsdall, Secretary; Anthony Michael Chandris [1987] Director; Dimitri John Chandris [1984] Director; Anthony Tomazos [1968] Director

Lebara Limited
Incorporated: 25 September 2001 *Employees:* 201
Net Worth: £178,709,904 *Total Assets:* £341,635,360
Registered Office: 7th Floor, Import Building, 2 Clove Crescent, London, E14 2BE
Activities: Other telecommunications activities
Shareholders: Raphael Ilya Auerbach; Suzanei Lynne Archer
Officers: Paul Van Straaten, Secretary; Richard Wolfgang Henry Schaefer [1971] Director/Chief Financial Officer; Patrick Albert Wild [1960] Senior Managing Director [Swiss]

Leconport Estates
Incorporated: 30 May 2000 *Employees:* 18
Net Worth: £125,000,000 *Total Assets:* £129,300,000
Registered Office: Sixth Floor, 150 Cheapside, London, EC2V 6ET
Activities: Other letting and operating of own or leased real estate
Shareholders: Britel Fund Trustees Limited; Caduceus Estates Limited
Officers: Christian Ross St. John Judd [1979] Director/Chartered Accountant [Irish]; Matthew James Torode [1984] Director/Accountant; Kirsty Ann-Marie Wilman [1980] Director/Chartered Accountant

Legal & General (Unit Trust Managers) Limited
Incorporated: 28 April 1971
Net Worth: £81,300,000 *Total Assets:* £328,400,000
Registered Office: One Coleman Street, London, EC2R 5AA
Activities: Activities of unit trusts
Parent: Legal & General Investment Management (Holdings) Limited
Officers: Andrew John Cyril Craven [1978] Finance Director; Simon Andrew Hynes [1968] Director; Helena Louise Morrissey [1966] Director/Head of Personal Investing; Honor Julia Eli Solomon [1978] Director; Lee William Toms [1965] Director; Dr Ali Reza Toutounchi [1958] Director/Investment Manager; Mark Joseph Zinkula [1967] Director/Investment Manager [American]

Legal & General Capital Investments Limited
Incorporated: 4 March 2013
Net Worth: £696,558,976 *Total Assets:* £928,761,984
Registered Office: One Coleman Street, London, EC2R 5AA
Activities: Activities of financial services holding companies
Parent: Legal & General Group PLC
Officers: Stephen Paul Halliwell [1969] Director/Chief Financial Officer; Kerrigan William Procter [1969] Director/Investment Manager; Geoffrey Julian Timms [1960] Director/Group General Counsel; Dr Nigel David Wilson [1956] Director

Legal & General Finance PLC
Incorporated: 24 January 1989
Net Worth: £5,400,000 *Total Assets:* £2,106,899,968
Registered Office: One Coleman Street, London, EC2R 5AA
Activities: Financial management
Parent: Legal & General Group PLC
Officers: Martin John Brookes [1962] Director of Investment Strategy; Stuart Jeffrey Davies [1971] Executive Director; Garvan O'Neill [1966] Director [Irish]; Francis Bernard Turley [1961] Director/Treasurer

Legal & General Group PLC
Incorporated: 27 February 1979 *Employees:* 7,570
Net Worth: £7,842,999,808 *Total Assets:* £505,877,004,288
Registered Office: One Coleman Street, London, EC2R 5AA
Activities: Activities of financial services holding companies
Officers: Geoffrey Timms, Secretary; Henrietta Caroline Baldock [1971] Director; Philip Arthur John Broadley [1961] Director; Stuart Jeffrey Davies [1971] Executive Director; Sir John Oliver Frank Kingman [1969] Director; Lesley Mary Samuel Knox [1953] Director [South African]; Melville George Lewis [1960] Director [Canadian]; Kerrigan William Procter [1969] Director/Investment Manager; Toby Emil Strauss [1959] Director; Julia Susan Wilson [1967] Director; Dr Nigel David Wilson [1956] Director; Mark Joseph Zinkula [1967] Director/Investment Manager [American]

Legal & General Homes Communities (Crowthorne) Limited
Incorporated: 13 January 2017
Net Worth: £111,370,032 *Total Assets:* £115,905,120
Registered Office: One Coleman Street, London, EC2R 5AA
Activities: Other specialised construction activities n.e.c.
Parent: Legal & General Homes Communities Limited
Officers: John Allan [1960] Director/Chartered Surveyor; Andrew John Dicker [1974] Technical Director; Christopher Alan Swordy [1972] Commercial Director

Legal & General Homes Communities Limited
Incorporated: 25 October 2016
Net Worth: £134,000,000 *Total Assets:* £134,239,456
Registered Office: One Coleman Street, London, EC2R 5AA
Activities: Development of building projects
Parent: Legal & General Homes Holdings Limited
Officers: John Allan [1960] Director/Chartered Surveyor; Andrew John Dicker [1974] Technical Director; James Robert Lidgate [1978] Director of Housing; Christopher Alan Swordy [1972] Commercial Director

Legal & General Insurance Holdings Limited
Incorporated: 17 September 1991
Net Worth: £1,972,800,000 *Total Assets:* £1,973,299,968
Registered Office: One Coleman Street, London, EC2R 5AA
Activities: Activities of financial services holding companies
Parent: Legal & General Insurance Holdings No. 2 Limited
Officers: Simon Jonathan Burke [1963] Director; Garvan O'Neill [1966] Director [Irish]; Dr Nigel David Wilson [1956] Director

Legal & General Insurance Holdings No.2 Limited
Incorporated: 15 February 2007
Net Worth: £8,114,400,256 *Total Assets:* £8,114,500,096
Registered Office: One Coleman Street, London, EC2R 5AA
Activities: Activities of financial services holding companies
Parent: Legal & General Group PLC
Officers: Simon Jonathan Burke [1963] Director; Garvan O'Neill [1966] Director [Irish]; Dr Nigel David Wilson [1956] Director

Legal & General Insurance Limited
Incorporated: 19 November 1946
Net Worth: £267,184,992 *Total Assets:* £646,302,976
Registered Office: One Coleman Street, London, EC2R 5AA
Activities: Non-life insurance
Parent: Legal and General Assurance Society Limited
Officers: Cheryl Margaret Agius [1971] Director/CEO, Legal & General Insurance [Irish]; Henrietta Caroline Baldock [1971] Director; Simon Pollack [1971] Director/Actuary; Christopher James Wren-Kirkham [1970] Director/Actuary

Legal & General International (Holdings) Limited
Incorporated: 28 June 1994
Net Worth: £166,216,992 *Total Assets:* £167,016,000
Registered Office: One Coleman Street, London, EC2R 5AA
Activities: Activities of financial services holding companies
Parent: Legal and General Assurance Society Limited
Officers: Simon Jonathan Burke [1963] Director; Garvan O'Neill [1966] Director [Irish]

Legal & General International Limited
Incorporated: 8 October 1979
Net Worth: £268,500,000 *Total Assets:* £269,700,000
Registered Office: One Coleman Street, London, EC2R 5AA
Activities: Activities of financial services holding companies
Parent: Legal & General International (Holdings) Limited
Officers: Simon Jonathan Burke [1963] Director; Garvan O'Neill [1966] Director [Irish]

Legal & General Investment Management (Holdings) Limited
Incorporated: 11 October 2001 *Employees:* 1,232
Net Worth: £613,800,000 *Total Assets:* £958,400,000
Registered Office: One Coleman Street, London, EC2R 5AA
Activities: Activities of financial services holding companies
Parent: Legal & General Group PLC
Officers: Simon William Fraser [1963] Director/Viticulturalist; Kathleen Moira Gallagher [1958] Director [American]; Sir John Oliver Frank Kingman [1969] Director; Richard Lee [1976] Director; Dr Nigel David Wilson [1956] Director; Mark Joseph Zinkula [1967] Director/Investment Manager [American]

Legal & General Investment Management Limited
Incorporated: 21 January 1987
Net Worth: £159,500,000 *Total Assets:* £191,000,000
Registered Office: One Coleman Street, London, EC2R 5AA
Activities: Fund management activities
Parent: Legal & General Investment Management (Holdings) Limited
Officers: Sarah Frances Elizabeth Aitken [1964] Director; Anton Norman Karl Eser [1974] Director/Investment Manager [German]; Michael Jacob Marks [1966] Director/Chief Operating Officer; Chad Rakvin [1971] Director [American]; Colin John Reedie [1968] Director/Co-Head Global Fixed Income; John William Roe [1979] Director/Head of Multi-Asset Funds; Sacha Sadan [1970] Director; Emiel Van Den Heiligenberg [1968] Director/Head of Asset Allocation [Dutch]; Mark Joseph Zinkula [1967] Director/Investment Manager [American]

Legal & General Overseas Holdings Limited
Incorporated: 12 September 1979
Net Worth: £243,200,000 *Total Assets:* £298,400,000
Registered Office: One Coleman Street, London, EC2R 5AA
Activities: Activities of financial services holding companies
Parent: Legal & General International Limited
Officers: Simon Jonathan Burke [1963] Director; Garvan O'Neill [1966] Director [Irish]

Legal & General Overseas Operations Limited
Incorporated: 26 August 1999
Net Worth: £291,800,000 *Total Assets:* £1,006,400,000
Registered Office: One Coleman Street, London, EC2R 5AA
Activities: Activities of financial services holding companies
Parent: Legal & General Group PLC
Officers: Simon Jonathan Burke [1963] Director; Garvan O'Neill [1966] Director [Irish]

Legal & General Pensions Limited
Incorporated: 14 September 2006
Total Assets: £2,300,456,960
Registered Office: One Coleman Street, London, EC2R 5AA
Activities: Non-life reinsurance
Parent: Legal and General Assurance Society Limited
Officers: Andrew Banks [1964] Director/Accountant; Michael Donald Barrie [1967] Director/Chartered Surveyor; Jonathan James Malpas [1965] Director/Actuary

Legal & General RE Holdings Limited
Incorporated: 29 July 2013
Net Worth: £223,900,000 *Total Assets:* £223,900,000
Registered Office: One Coleman Street, London, EC2R 5AA
Activities: Activities of financial services holding companies
Parent: Legal & General Group PLC
Officers: Bryan Robert Blunt [1978] Director/Actuary; Richard Lee [1976] Director; Kerrigan William Procter [1969] Director/Investment Manager

Legal & General Resources Limited
Incorporated: 11 January 1989 *Employees:* 6,471
Net Worth Deficit: £313,926,016 *Total Assets:* £1,210,182,016
Registered Office: One Coleman Street, London, EC2R 5AA
Activities: Activities of head offices
Parent: Legal & General Group PLC
Officers: Emma Miller Byron [1980] Managing Director, Retail Retirement Income; Emma Hardaker-Jones [1973] Group HR Director; Susan Margaret Hunter [1969] Finance Director; Grace Elanor Stevens [1977] Director/Chief Tax Officer

Legal and General Assurance (Pensions Management) Limited
Incorporated: 26 March 1971
Net Worth: £387,000,000 *Total Assets:* £315,446,099,968
Registered Office: One Coleman Street, London, EC2R 5AA
Activities: Life insurance
Parent: Legal & General Investment Management (Holdings) Limited
Officers: Sarah Frances Elizabeth Aitken [1964] Director; Laura Jane Brown [1979] Director; Justin Christian Browne [1970] Director/Actuary; Simon William Fraser [1963] Director; Richard Lee [1976] Director; Pauline Plunkett [1982] Director/Head of Group Client Team [Irish]; Michael Walsh [1978] Director

Legal and General Assurance Society Limited
Incorporated: 1 April 1920
Net Worth: £5,872,999,936 *Total Assets:* £141,413,007,360
Registered Office: One Coleman Street, London, EC2R 5AA
Activities: Life insurance
Parent: Legal & General Insurance Holdings Limited
Officers: Henrietta Caroline Baldock [1971] Non-Executive Director Chairman; Stuart Jeffrey Davies [1971] Executive Director; Christian Wilhelm Tore Dinesen [1961] Director/Management Consultant [Danish]; Catherine Laura Mason [1976] Director/CEO Legal & General Retirement Institutional; Kevin Murphy [1951] Director [Irish]; Dr Nigel David Wilson [1956] Director

Leggett & Platt UK Holdings LLP
Incorporated: 3 December 2015
Net Worth: £1,418,586,752 *Total Assets:* £1,418,586,880
Registered Office: Second Floor, 77 Kingsway, London, WC2B 6SR

LEH Global Ltd
Incorporated: 12 November 2013
Net Worth: £975,088,192 *Total Assets:* £978,256,256
Registered Office: 4 Harley Street, London, W1G 9PB
Activities: Activities of other holding companies n.e.c.
Major Shareholder: Muhammad Ali Qureshi
Officers: Dr Muhammad Ali Qureshi [1970] Director

Lendlease (Elephant & Castle) Limited
Incorporated: 19 March 2010
Previous: Lend Lease (Elephant & Castle) Limited
Net Worth: £28,268,000 *Total Assets:* £266,116,000
Registered Office: 20 Triton Street, Regent's Place, London, NW1 3BF
Activities: Development of building projects
Parent: Lendlease Europe Limited
Officers: John David Clark [1970] Director/EGMF Finance, Construction; Justin Davies [1976] Director/Head of Development Operations [Australian]; Jonathan Michael Emery [1966] Managing Director of Property, Europe; Kristy Sheridan Lansdown [1977] Project Director; Georgina Jane Scott [1975] Director/EGM Finance

Lendlease Construction (Europe) Limited
Incorporated: 7 April 1949 *Employees:* 638
Previous: Lend Lease Construction (EMEA) Limited
Net Worth: £136,567,008 *Total Assets:* £311,507,008
Registered Office: 20 Triton Street, Regent's Place, London, NW1 3BF
Activities: Construction of commercial buildings
Parent: Lendlease Construction Holdings (Europe) Limited
Officers: Alan John Bates [1970] Director/Executive General Manager; Mark Boor [1965] Director/Chartered Surveyor; Jonathan Michael Emery [1966] Managing Director of Property, Europe; Simon William Gorski [1969] Director/Executive General Manager; Daniel Labbad [1972] Director/Chief Executive Officer [Australian]; Peter Dominic Leonard [1964] Commercial Director; Thomas Lachlan MacKellar [1982] Director/Chief Financial Officer [Australian]; Neil Christopher Martin [1967] Director/MD Construction Lend Lease EMEA; Mark John Packer [1965] Director/Solicitor; Claire Marianne Pettett [1975] Director/Chartered Accountant; Victoria Elizabeth Quinlan [1976] Operations Director [Australian]; Lisa White [1966] Director/Europe and Group Head of Performance

Lendlease Construction Holdings (Europe) Limited
Incorporated: 11 July 1928
Previous: Lend Lease Construction Holdings (EMEA) Limited
Net Worth: £159,926,000 *Total Assets:* £231,532,000
Registered Office: 20 Triton Street, Regent's Place, London, NW1 3BF
Activities: Activities of head offices
Parent: Lendlease Europe Holdings Limited
Officers: Mark John Packer, Secretary; Alan John Bates [1970] Director/Executive General Manager; Peter Dominic Leonard [1964] Commercial Director; Neil Christopher Martin [1967] Director/MD Construction Lend Lease EMEA; Claire Marianne Pettett [1975] Director/Chartered Accountant

Lendlease Europe Finance PLC
Incorporated: 17 March 2000
Previous: Lend Lease Europe Finance PLC
Net Worth: £14,043,000 *Total Assets:* £483,627,008
Registered Office: 20 Triton Street, Regent's Place, London, NW1 3BF
Activities: Financial intermediation not elsewhere classified
Parent: Lendlease Europe Holdings Limited
Officers: Mark John Packer, Secretary; Yvonne Kostopoulos [1973] Director/Financial Controller [Australian]; Thomas Lachlan MacKellar [1982] Director/Chief Financial Officer [Australian]; Victoria Elizabeth Quinlan [1976] Director/Chief Financial Officer, EMEA [Australian]

Lendlease Europe Holdings Limited
Incorporated: 25 March 1991 *Employees:* 1,250
Previous: Lend Lease Europe Holdings Limited
Net Worth: £158,608,992 *Total Assets:* £1,142,829,952
Registered Office: 20 Triton Street, Regent's Place, London, NW1 3BF
Activities: Activities of construction holding companies
Shareholders: Lendlease Europe Finance PLC; Lendlease International Pty Limited
Officers: Joanna Moriarty, Secretary; Daniel Labbad [1972] Director/Group Chief Operating Officer and CEO, EMEA [Australian]; Thomas Lachlan MacKellar [1982] Director/Chief Financial Officer [Australian]; Neil Christopher Martin [1967] Director/Solicitor; Mark John Packer [1965] Director/Solicitor; Kirsten Lisa White [1970] Director/Head of Tax, Europe [Australian]

Lendlease Europe Limited
Incorporated: 9 May 1996 *Employees:* 177
Previous: Lend Lease Europe Limited
Net Worth: £15,291,000 *Total Assets:* £190,400,000
Registered Office: 20 Triton Street, Regent's Place, London, NW1 3BF
Activities: Buying and selling of own real estate
Parent: Lendlease Europe Holdings Limited
Officers: Joanna Moriarty, Secretary; Yvonne Kostopoulos [1973] Director/Financial Controller [Australian]; Thomas Lachlan MacKellar [1982] Director/Chief Financial Officer [Australian]; Mark John Packer [1965] Director/Solicitor

Lendlease Residential (CG) Limited
Incorporated: 10 April 1986
Previous: Lendlease Residential (CG) PLC
Net Worth: £79,719,000 *Total Assets:* £373,705,984
Registered Office: 20 Triton Street, Regent's Place, London, NW1 3BF
Activities: Activities of head offices
Parent: Lendlease Residential Group (Europe) Limited
Officers: Mark John Packer, Secretary; John David Clark [1970] Director/Chartered Accountant; Justin Davies [1976] Director/Head of Development Operations [Australian]; Jonathan Michael Emery [1966] Director/Head of Property; Georgina Jane Scott [1975] Director/Commercial Manager

Lenlyn Holdings Limited
Incorporated: 20 October 1993 *Employees:* 1,684
Previous: Lenlyn Holdings PLC
Net Worth: £80,239,000 *Total Assets:* £486,863,008
Registered Office: 19-21 Shaftesbury Avenue, London, W1D 7ED
Activities: Activities of head offices
Officers: James Michael Alexander Vallance, Secretary; Professor Russel George Griggs [1948] Director; Peter Richard Ibbetson [1956] Director; Aleem Hassanali Tejani [1985] Director/Head of Special Projects; Firozali Gulamali Tejani [1944] Director; Hassanali Gulamali Tejani [1957] Director; Nizarali Gulamali Tejani [1946] Director; Rahim Zulfikarally Tejani [1977] Director/Private Landlord; Rehanah Tejani [1985] Director/Marketing; Zulfikarally Gulamali Tejani [1943] Director

J. Leon & Company Limited
Incorporated: 7 February 1929 *Employees:* 11
Net Worth: £216,542,096 *Total Assets:* £224,655,776
Registered Office: 32 Hampstead High Street, London, NW3 1JQ
Activities: Buying and selling of own real estate
Shareholders: Tania Liliana Slowe; Michael Abraham Leon Slowe
Officers: Dominique Howe, Secretary; Alexander Percy Church [1975] Director; John Edward Eades [1951] Director/Chartered Surveyor; Joanne Shenton [1971] Finance Director; Jonathan Leon Slowe [1969] Director; Tania Liliana Slowe [1962] Director; Vincent Robert Smith [1958] Director; Patrick William Walker [1962] Director

Leopard UK Kensington Propco Limited
Incorporated: 9 March 2017
Net Worth Deficit: £401,000 *Total Assets:* £119,797,000
Registered Office: 18 Culford Gardens, London, SW3 2ST
Activities: Activities of other holding companies n.e.c.
Parent: Leopard UK Kensington JV Limited
Officers: Derrick Beare [1961] Director/Property Executive; Ari Jason Boyd [1977] Finance Director; David Tugendhaft [1978] Director/Property Executive

John Lewis Partnership PLC
Incorporated: 23 April 1929 *Employees:* 84,500
Net Worth: £2,312,199,936 *Total Assets:* £6,251,200,000
Registered Office: 171 Victoria Street, London, SW1E 5NN
Activities: Activities of head offices
Parent: John Lewis Partnership Trust Limited
Officers: Peter Simpson, Secretary; Robert Collins [1970] Managing Director; Steve Mark Gardiner [1967] Director/Branch Manager; David Hay [1966] Director/Service Experience Manager; Tracey Anne Killen [1961] Director; Oliver Stephen Killinger [1991] Director/Change Manager, Business Transformation; Patrick Lewis [1965] Director; Andrew David Martin [1960] Director; Sir Andrew Charles Mayfield [1966] Director; Paula Margaret Nickolds [1973] Director/Retail Buyer; Nicola Ann Spurgeon [1967] Director/Programme Manager; Laura Katharine Wade-Gery [1965] Director; Keith Williams [1956] Director; Rebecca Faith Wollam [1987] Director/Regional Manager

John Lewis PLC
Incorporated: 20 September 1928 *Employees:* 84,500
Net Worth: £2,308,000,000 *Total Assets:* £6,281,399,808
Registered Office: 171 Victoria Street, London, SW1E 5NN
Activities: Other retail sale in non-specialised stores
Parent: John Lewis Partnership PLC
Officers: Peter Simpson, Secretary; Tracey Anne Killen [1961] Director; John Patrick Lewis [1965] Director/Retailer; Sir Andrew Charles Mayfield [1966] Director; Berangere Andree Mireille Michel [1973] Director [French]; Paula Margaret Nickolds [1973] Director/Retail Buyer

John Lewis Properties PLC
Incorporated: 22 July 1935
Net Worth: £977,000,000 *Total Assets:* £1,049,000,000
Registered Office: 171 Victoria Street, London, SW1E 5NN
Activities: Buying and selling of own real estate
Parent: John Lewis PLC
Officers: Peter Simpson, Secretary; John Patrick Lewis [1965] Finance Director; Sir Andrew Charles Mayfield [1966] Director/Chairman

Lewis Trust Group Limited
Incorporated: 23 April 1963 *Employees:* 17
Net Worth: £401,713,728 *Total Assets:* £688,754,624
Registered Office: Chelsea House, West Gate, London, W5 1DR
Activities: Activities of head offices
Parent: L51N Limited
Officers: Benjamin Joseph Lewis [1967] Director; Bernard Lewis [1926] Director; Leonard Richard Lewis [1954] Director; Simon Gabriel Lewis [1962] Director; Michael Henry Rosehill [1960] Director/Chartered Accountant [Irish]

Lewis Trust Holdings Limited
Incorporated: 12 October 2012
Net Worth: £107,727,000 *Total Assets:* £518,577,984
Registered Office: Chelsea House, West Gate, London, W5 1DR
Activities: Activities of other holding companies n.e.c.
Parent: L51N Limited
Officers: Benjamin Joseph Lewis [1967] Director; Clive Robert Lewis [1956] Director; Julian Harley Lewis [1954] Director; Michael Henry Rosehill [1960] Director [Irish]

Lex Autolease Limited
Incorporated: 12 January 1973 *Employees:* 1,234
Net Worth: £361,692,000 *Total Assets:* £5,612,012,032
Registered Office: 25 Gresham Street, London, EC2V 7HN
Activities: Renting and leasing of cars and light motor vehicles
Parent: ACL Autolease Holdings Limited
Officers: David Dermot Hennessey, Secretary; Andrew John Hartley [1969] Director; Carol Ann Parkes [1966] Finance Director

Lexadon Limited
Incorporated: 22 January 1980 *Employees:* 9
Net Worth: £112,009,936 *Total Assets:* £251,702,176
Registered Office: Unit 3 The Viaduct Business Centre, 364a Coldharbour Lane, Brixton, London, SW9 8PL
Activities: Buying and selling of own real estate
Shareholders: Jerrard Michael Knight; Janet Anne Knight
Officers: Jerrard Michael Knight, Secretary; Janet Anne Knight [1957] Director/Secretary; Jerrard Michael Knight [1956] Director/Property Developer

Lexton Investments Limited
Incorporated: 2 October 1987 *Employees:* 14
Net Worth: £104,260,144 *Total Assets:* £160,345,488
Registered Office: New Burlington House, 1075 Finchley Road, London, NW11 0PU
Activities: Buying and selling of own real estate
Officers: Maurice Freund, Secretary [Belgian]; Marcus Landau [1951] Director; Beila Low [1931] Director; Elieser Low [1962] Director

LGH Hotels Management Limited
Incorporated: 6 November 2015 *Employees:* 1,960
Previous: Lapithus Hotels Management UK Limited
Net Worth: £115,344,000 *Total Assets:* £691,736,000
Registered Office: 10 Queen Street Place, London, EC4R 1AG
Activities: Hotels and similar accommodation
Officers: David Mark Andrew Beveridge [1959] Director; Gideon Efrati [1956] Director [Israeli]; Simon Michael Teasdale [1965] Director

LGPL Cornwall Limited
Incorporated: 28 November 2014
Net Worth: £1 *Total Assets:* £109,756,152
Registered Office: One Coleman Street, London, EC2R 5AA
Activities: Non-trading company
Parent: Legal & General Pensions Limited
Officers: Gordon Clark Aitchison [1964] Director; Andrew Banks [1964] Director

LHA London Ltd
Incorporated: 5 November 1940 *Employees:* 72
Net Worth: £212,614,432 *Total Assets:* £214,467,536
Registered Office: 11 Belgrave Road, London, SW1V 1RB
Activities: Other accommodation
Officers: Anthony Roy Perkins, Secretary; Emma Elizabeth Beardmore [1976] Director/Planning Consultant; Kay Buxton [1966] Director/Chief Executive; Giles Byford [1978] Director/Banker; Alison Craze [1950] Director/Retired; Petra Green [1967] Marketing Director; Linda Holford [1950] Director/Retired; Susan Catherine Johnson [1958] Director/Architect; Alec Derek McTavish [1948] Director/Retired; June Antoinette O'Sullivan [1959] Director/Chief Executive [Irish]; David Malcolm Robertson [1942] Director/Chartered Engineer; Alexandra Jane Whiston-Dew [1982] Director/Solicitor

LHC4 (UK) Limited
Incorporated: 2 March 2017
Net Worth: £1,673,309,056 *Total Assets:* £3,056,537,344
Registered Office: 2 Fitzroy Place, 8 Mortimer Street, London, W1T 3JJ
Activities: Activities of other holding companies n.e.c.
Officers: Blake Christopher Kleinman [1976] Director [American]; Johannes Korp [1984] Director [Austrian]; Christopher Paul Reid [1977] Director; Leonora Olivia Saurel de Sola [1977] Director [Spanish]

Liberty Commodities Limited
Incorporated: 10 April 1997 *Employees:* 30
Net Worth: £75,230,792 *Total Assets:* £304,431,328
Registered Office: No 7 Hertford Street, London, W1J 7RH
Activities: Wholesale of metals and metal ores
Major Shareholder: Sanjeev Gupta
Officers: Surinder Jolly, Secretary; Sanjeev Gupta [1971] Director

Liberty Corporate Capital (Two) Ltd
Incorporated: 25 June 2008
Previous: Ironshore Corporate Capital Ltd.
Net Worth Deficit: £5,304,000 *Total Assets:* £1,371,415,040
Registered Office: Level 3, 8 Fenchurch Place, London, EC3M 4AJ
Activities: Non-life insurance
Parent: Ironshore International Ltd
Officers: Angela Ocrah, Secretary; Bruce Kevin Campbell [1977] Director/Head of Investments & Finance Risks [Irish]; Nigel James Davenport [1975] Director/General Counsel

Liberty Corporate Capital Limited
Incorporated: 22 November 1994
Net Worth: £849,005,696 *Total Assets:* £5,554,416,640
Registered Office: 20 Fenchurch Street, London, EC3M 3AW
Activities: Non-life insurance
Officers: Angela Aso Ocrah, Secretary; Bruce Kevin Campbell [1977] Director [Irish]; Nigel James Davenport [1975] Director; Keith Nicholson [1949] Director

Liberty Global Broadband I Limited
Incorporated: 9 January 2015
Net Worth: £22,867,226,624 *Total Assets:* £23,129,763,840
Registered Office: Griffin House, 161 Hammersmith Road, London, W6 8BS
Activities: Activities of head offices
Parent: Liberty Global PLC
Officers: Bryan Hambleton Hall, Secretary; Andrew James Cole [1966] Director/CEO, Asurion Europe; Miranda Theresa Claire Curtis [1955] Director/Retired; John William Dick [1938] Director/Private Investor [Canadian]; Michael Thomas Fries [1963] Director/President & CEO [American]; Paul Alan Gould [1945] Managing Director, Allen & Company [American]; Richard Roy Green [1937] Director/Retired [American]; Bryan Hambleton Hall [1962] Director/Lawyer [American]; John Carl Malone [1941] Director/Chairman [American]; David Ellis Rapley [1941] Director/Retired [American]; Larry Romrell [1939] Director/Retired [American]; Jc Sparkman [1932] Director/Retired [American]; J David Wargo [1953] Director/President, Wargo & Company [American]

Liberty Global Europe 2 Limited
Incorporated: 29 January 2013
Previous: Liberty Global Europe 2 Limited Limited
Net Worth: £8,686,254,080 *Total Assets:* £14,027,634,688
Registered Office: Griffin House, 161 Hammersmith Road, London, W6 8BS
Activities: Activities of head offices
Parent: Liberty Global PLC
Officers: Charles Henry Rowland Bracken [1966] Finance Director; Jeremy Lewis Evans [1965] Director/Lawyer; Bryan Hambleton Hall [1962] Director/General Counsel [American]

Liberty Global Finance I (UK) Limited
Incorporated: 14 April 2015
Net Worth: £642,412,160 *Total Assets:* £642,418,304
Registered Office: Griffin House, 161 Hammersmith Road, London, W6 8BS
Activities: Activities of head offices
Parent: Liberty Global PLC
Officers: Charles Henry Rowland Bracken [1966] Director/Chief Financial Officer; Jeremy Lewis Evans [1965] Director/Lawyer

Liberty Global Incorporated Limited
Incorporated: 4 February 2013
Net Worth: £212,273,776 *Total Assets:* £1,592,778,624
Registered Office: Griffin House, 161 Hammersmith Road, London, W6 8BS
Activities: Activities of head offices
Parent: Liberty Global PLC
Officers: Charles Henry Rowland Bracken [1966] Finance Director; Jeremy Lewis Evans [1965] Director/Lawyer; Bryan Hambleton Hall [1962] Director/General Counsel [American]

Liberty Global PLC
Incorporated: 29 January 2013 *Employees:* 28,000
Net Worth: £4,963,995,136 *Total Assets:* £41,762,631,680
Registered Office: Griffin House, 161 Hammersmith Road, London, W6 8BS
Activities: Activities of head offices
Officers: Bryan Hambleton Hall, Secretary; Andrew James Cole [1966] Director/CEO, Asurion Europe; Miranda Theresa Claire Curtis [1955] Director/Retired; John William Dick [1938] Director/Private Investor [Canadian]; Michael Thomas Fries [1963] Director/President & CEO [American]; Paul Alan Gould [1945] Managing Director [American]; Richard Roy Green [1937] Director/Retired [American]; John Carl Malone [1941] Director/Chairman [American]; David Ellis Rapley [1941] Director/Retired [American]; Larry Romrell [1939] Director/Retired [American]; Jc Sparkman [1932] Director/Retired [American]; J David Wargo [1953] Director/President of Wargo & Company [American]

Liberty GR Acquisition Company Limited
Incorporated: 26 August 2016
Net Worth: £4,260,072,960 *Total Assets:* £4,260,072,960
Registered Office: No 2 St James's Market, London, SW1Y 4AH
Activities: Activities of other holding companies n.e.c.
Parent: Liberty GR Holding Company Limited
Officers: Richard Baer [1957] Director/Chief Legal Officer [American]; Timothy Paul Lenneman [1964] Director/Senior Vice President [American]; Duncan Francis Llowarch [1968] Director/Accountant; Gregory Maffei [1960] Director/President and Chief Executive [American]; Craig Edward Troyer [1969] Director/Vice President Deputy General Counsel Assistant Secretary; Sacha Jane Woodward Hill [1969] Director/Lawyer

Liberty GR Holding Company Limited
Incorporated: 26 August 2016
Net Worth: £3,425,234,688 *Total Assets:* £4,260,072,960
Registered Office: No 2 St James's Market, London, SW1Y 4AH
Activities: Activities of other holding companies n.e.c.
Parent: Liberty Media Corporation
Officers: Richard Baer [1957] Director/Chief Legal Officer [American]; Timothy Paul Lenneman [1964] Director/Senior Vice President [American]; Duncan Francis Llowarch [1968] Director/Accountant; Gregory Maffei [1960] Director/President and Chief Executive [American]; Craig Edward Troyer [1969] Director/Vice President; Sacha Jane Woodward Hill [1969] Director/Lawyer

Liberty International Financial Services Limited
Incorporated: 17 May 1924
Net Worth: £171,600,000 *Total Assets:* £314,200,000
Registered Office: 40 Broadway, London, SW1H 0BT
Activities: Activities of head offices
Parent: Liberty International Holdings Limited
Officers: Susan Marsden, Secretary; David Andrew Fischel [1958] Director/Chartered Accountant; Barbara Gibbes [1975] Director/Accountant; Trevor Pereira [1965] Director; Edward Matthew Giles Roberts [1963] Finance Director

Liberty International Group Treasury Limited
Incorporated: 1 October 1985
Net Worth: £53,200,000 *Total Assets:* £3,034,299,904
Registered Office: 40 Broadway, London, SW1H 0BT
Activities: Financial intermediation not elsewhere classified
Parent: Liberty International Holdings Limited
Officers: Susan Marsden, Secretary; David Andrew Fischel [1958] Director/Chartered Accountant; Hugh Michael Ford [1967] Director/General Corporate Counsel; Barbara Gibbes [1975] Director/Accountant; Trevor Pereira [1965] Director; Edward Matthew Giles Roberts [1963] Finance Director

Liberty International Holdings Limited
Incorporated: 24 June 1980
Net Worth: £801,400,000 *Total Assets:* £998,899,968
Registered Office: 40 Broadway, London, SW1H 0BT
Activities: Activities of other holding companies n.e.c.
Shareholders: TAI Investments Limited; Conduit Insurance Holdings Limited; Intu Properties PLC
Officers: Susan Marsden, Secretary; David Andrew Fischel [1958] Director/Chartered Accountant; Hugh Michael Ford [1967] Director/General Corporate Counsel; Trevor Pereira [1965] Director; Edward Matthew Giles Roberts [1963] Finance Director

Liberty Living Investments II Holdco 2 Limited
Incorporated: 5 May 2015
Net Worth: £210,775,008 *Total Assets:* £210,779,008
Registered Office: Fifth Floor, Peninsular House, 30-36 Monument Street, London, EC3R 8NB
Activities: Activities of other holding companies n.e.c.
Parent: Liberty Living Investments II Limited
Officers: Rachel Heslehurst, Secretary; Maximilian Boerries Peter Biagosch [1972] Director [German]; Thomas Oliver Jackson [1981] Director/Portfolio Manager; Paul Meyrick Mullins [1973] Director

Liberty Living Investments II Limited
Incorporated: 10 July 2015
Net Worth: £234,731,008 *Total Assets:* £234,742,000
Registered Office: Fifth Floor, Peninsular House, 30-36 Monument Street, London, EC3R 8NB
Activities: Activities of other holding companies n.e.c.
Officers: Rachel Heslehurst, Secretary; Maximilian Boerries Peter Biagosch [1972] Director [German]; Thomas Oliver Jackson [1981] Director/Portfolio Manager; Paul Meyrick Mullins [1973] Director

Liberty Living Investments Limited
Incorporated: 6 January 2015
Net Worth: £138,539,008 *Total Assets:* £166,920,992
Registered Office: Fifth Floor, Peninsular House, 30-36 Monument Street, London, EC3R 8NB
Activities: Activities of other holding companies n.e.c.
Parent: Liberty Living (HE) Holdings Limited
Officers: Rachel Heslehurst, Secretary; Maximilian Boerries Peter Biagosch [1972] Director [German]; Thomas Oliver Jackson [1981] Director/Portfolio Manager; Paul Meyrick Mullins [1973] Director

Liberty Managing Agency Limited
Incorporated: 20 December 1994 *Employees:* 354
Net Worth: £99,014,688 *Total Assets:* £224,357,808
Registered Office: 20 Fenchurch Street, London, EC3M 3AW
Activities: Non-life insurance
Parent: Liberty UK and Europe Holdings Limited
Officers: Nigel James Davenport [1975] Director; Christopher Douglas Hanks [1950] Director/Insurance Professional; Philip Hobbs [1978] Director; Matthew Moore [1974] Director/Underwriter; Keith Nicholson [1949] Director; Dr Richard David George Reid [1952] Director/Academic

Liberty Plaza (London) Limited
Incorporated: 18 August 2011 *Employees:* 14
Previous: SC Leman Street Limited
Net Worth: £113,836,000 *Total Assets:* £188,347,008
Registered Office: Fifth Floor, Peninsular House, 30-36 Monument Street, London, EC3R 8NB
Activities: Other letting and operating of own or leased real estate
Parent: Liberty Living Investments II Holdco Limited
Officers: Rachel Heslehurst, Secretary; Maximilian Boerries Peter Biagosch [1972] Director [German]; Thomas Oliver Jackson [1981] Director/Portfolio Manager; Paul Meyrick Mullins [1973] Director

Liberty Theta Limited
Incorporated: 15 October 2013
Net Worth: £53,115,000 *Total Assets:* £118,897,000
Registered Office: 210-220 Regent Street, Mayfair, London, W1B 5AH
Activities: Other business support service activities n.e.c.
Parent: Liberty Zeta Limited
Officers: Abdul Wahab Saud Albabtain [1945] Director [Saudi Arabian]; Marco Anatriello [1981] Director/Partner [Italian]; Marco Capello [1960] Director/Partner [Italian]; Sarah Jane Halsall [1968] Director; Adil Mehboob-Khan [1964] Director/Business Executive; Emilio di Spiezio Sardo [1977] Director [Italian]; Robert Unsworth [1973] Finance Director

Liberty UK and Europe Holdings Limited
Incorporated: 30 October 2009
Net Worth: £2,794,016,768 *Total Assets:* £3,627,690,496
Registered Office: 20 Fenchurch Street, London, EC3M 3AW
Activities: Non-trading company
Officers: Siena Blake Byass Colegrave, Secretary; Maria Mercedes Castillo Vano [1979] Director/Solicitor [Spanish]; Siena Byass Blake Colegrave [1983] Director/Lawyer [American/British]; Nigel James Davenport [1975] Director/Solicitor; James Clifford Reeves [1976] Director; Lara Maria Alexandra Sojka [1977] Director/Accountant

Liberty Zeta Limited
Incorporated: 15 October 2013 *Employees:* 570
Net Worth: £126,596,000 *Total Assets:* £240,586,000
Registered Office: 16 Berkeley Street, London, W1J 8DZ
Activities: Other business support service activities n.e.c.
Shareholder: Bluegem II GP LP
Officers: Abdul Wahab Saud Albabtain [1945] Director [Saudi Arabian]; Marco Anatriello [1981] Director/Partner [Italian]; Marco Capello [1960] Director/Partner [Italian]; Enrico Letta [1966] Director [Italian]; Adil Mehboob-Khan [1964] Director/Business Executive; Massimo Saracchi [1957] Director/Business Executive [Italian]; Emilio di Spiezio Sardo [1977] Director [Italian]; Robert Unsworth [1973] Finance Director

Libra International Limited
Incorporated: 1 December 2015 *Employees:* 1
Net Worth: £341,997,088 *Total Assets:* £1,624,870,784
Registered Office: First Floor, Stratton House, 5 Stratton Street, Mayfair, London, W1J 8LA
Activities: Other service activities n.e.c.
Parent: International Nuclear Investment Limited
Officers: Dongshan Zheng [1962] Director [Chinese]

Lifeways Finance Limited
Incorporated: 27 June 2007 *Employees:* 9,839
Net Worth: £154,125,952 *Total Assets:* £309,086,816
Registered Office: 56 Southwark Bridge Road, London, SE1 0AS
Activities: Activities of head offices
Parent: Listrac Bidco Limited
Officers: Matthew Stevens [1969] Director; Justin Antony James Tydeman [1970] Director

Lightsource BP Renewable Energy Investments Limited
Incorporated: 17 March 2015 *Employees:* 283
Previous: Lightsource Renewable Energy Investments Limited
Net Worth: £83,783,000 *Total Assets:* £569,163,008
Registered Office: Level 7, 33 Holborn, London, EC1N 2HU
Activities: Production of electricity
Shareholders: BP Alternative Energy Investments Limited; Nicholas Thomson Boyle
Officers: Randal John Clifton Barker, Secretary; David Thomas Anderson [1964] Director/Oil Company Executive; Kareen Boutonnat [1970] Managing Director [French]; Nicholas Thomson Boyle [1966] Director; Paul McCartie [1976] Finance Director; Michael James Roney [1954] Director [British/American]; David Windle [1967] Director

Lightsource Pumbaa Limited
Incorporated: 27 August 2015
Net Worth Deficit: £21,376,896 *Total Assets:* £127,031,608
Registered Office: 7th Floor, 33 Holborn, London, EC1N 2HU
Activities: Production of electricity
Parent: Lightsource Timon Limited
Officers: Kareen Boutonnat [1970] Director [French]; Ian David Hardie [1978] Director/Finance Manager; Paul McCartie [1976] Finance Director

Lightsource Pumpkin 4 Limited
Incorporated: 9 November 2015
Net Worth: £13,828,922 *Total Assets:* £171,909,584
Registered Office: 7th Floor, 33 Holborn, London, EC1N 2HU
Activities: Production of electricity
Parent: Lightsource Pumpkin 3 Limited
Officers: Kareen Boutonnat [1970] Director [French]; Patrick Jude O'Kane [1970] Director; Stephane Christophe Tetot [1981] Director/Financier [French]

Lightsource Radiate 2 Limited
Incorporated: 9 July 2014 *Employees:* 2
Net Worth Deficit: £6,180,766 *Total Assets:* £241,353,520
Registered Office: 7th Floor, 33 Holborn, London, EC1N 2HT
Activities: Production of electricity
Parent: Lightsource Radiate 1 Limited
Officers: Adele Ara [1981] Director [Italian]; Paul McCartie [1976] Finance Director

Lightsource Simba Limited
Incorporated: 4 August 2015
Net Worth Deficit: £1,326,018 *Total Assets:* £127,723,552
Registered Office: 7th Floor, 33 Holborn, London, EC1N 2HU
Activities: Production of electricity
Parent: Lightsource Asset Holdings Limited
Officers: Ian David Hardie [1978] Director/Finance Manager; Paul McCartie [1976] Finance Director

Lightsource Timon Limited
Incorporated: 24 August 2015
Net Worth Deficit: £21,382,332 *Total Assets:* £127,031,288
Registered Office: 7th Floor, 33 Holborn, London, EC1N 2HU
Activities: Production of electricity
Parent: Lightsource Nala Limited
Officers: Kareen Boutonnat [1970] Director [French]; Ian David Hardie [1978] Director/Finance Manager; Paul McCartie [1976] Finance Director

LIH Financing Limited
Incorporated: 19 May 2016
Net Worth Deficit: £7,656,000 *Total Assets:* £155,128,992
Registered Office: 140 London Wall, London, EC2Y 5DN
Activities: Activities of other holding companies n.e.c.
Parent: The Bank of N.T. Butterfield & Son Limited
Officers: Aaron Jon Burns, Secretary; Adam Dakin [1962] Director; Graham Henry Edwards [1964] Director/Chief Executive Officer; Russell Charles Gurnhill [1970] Director; Michael Akiva Hackenbroch [1973] Director; Graeme Richard William Hunter [1963] Director; James Leslie Stone [1974] Land Director

LIH UK Topco Limited
Incorporated: 18 September 2006 *Employees:* 2,474
Net Worth: £17,201,524 *Total Assets:* £397,861,728
Registered Office: The St Botolph Building, 138 Houndsditch, London, EC3A 7AG
Activities: Activities of head offices
Officers: Sarah Jeffs, Secretary; Henry Bond [1965] Director [American]; Christopher Mark Arthur Brown [1965] Director; William Humphrey III [1965] Director/Attorney [American]; Andrew Laurence Monkhouse [1966] Director/Chief Financial Officer; Neil Keith Nimmo [1961] Director

Lime Street (Funding) Limited
Incorporated: 19 June 2002
Net Worth: £152,163,008 *Total Assets:* £152,163,008
Registered Office: 25 Gresham Street, London, EC2V 7HN
Activities: Other business support service activities n.e.c.
Parent: Lloyds Bank Subsidiaries Limited
Officers: Alyson Elizabeth Mulholland, Secretary; Allen Eric Appen [1961] Director [American]; Prasad Nagnath Pitale [1971] Director

Limited Life Assets Issuance PLC
Incorporated: 24 March 2011
Net Worth: £18,441 *Total Assets:* £121,844,256
Registered Office: Third Floor, 1 King's Arms Yard, London, EC2R 7AF
Activities: Other business support service activities n.e.c.
Parent: Wilmington Trust SP Services (London) Limited
Officers: Daniel Jonathan Wynne [1970] Director

Limited Life Assets Master Limited
Incorporated: 8 March 2011
Net Worth: £155,586,496 *Total Assets:* £277,453,184
Registered Office: 1 Jermyn Street, London, SW1Y 4UH
Activities: Other business support service activities n.e.c.
Officers: Timothy Edward Church [1955] Director; Alan William Morgan [1951] Director/Investor/Advisor to Financial Services Businesses

Limited Life Assets Services Limited
Incorporated: 9 March 2011
Net Worth: £107,658,312 *Total Assets:* £194,991,216
Registered Office: 1 Jermyn Street, London, SW1Y 4UH
Activities: Other business support service activities n.e.c.
Parent: Limited Life Assets Master Limited
Officers: Timothy Edward Church [1955] Director; Alan William Morgan [1951] Director/Investor/Advisor to Financial Services Businesses

Linestair Limited
Incorporated: 16 December 2005
Net Worth: £381,071,968 *Total Assets:* £473,866,144
Registered Office: York House, 45 Seymour Street, London, W1H 7LX
Activities: Development of building projects
Parent: The British Land Company PLC
Officers: Sarah Morrell Barzycki [1958] Director/Head of Finance; James Andrew Honeyman [1980] Director/Chartered Surveyor; Paul Stuart Macey [1978] Director/Accountant; Jonathan Charles McNuff [1986] Director/Chartered Accountant; Charles John Middleton [1966] Director/Corporate Tax Executive; James Michael Pinkstone [1987] Director/Corporate Finance Executive; Timothy Andrew Roberts [1964] Director/Chartered Surveyor; James Watson [1988] Director/Investment Surveyor; Nigel Mark Webb [1963] Director/Chartered Surveyor

Lingfield 2014 I PLC
Incorporated: 11 September 2014
Net Worth: £19,000 *Total Assets:* £3,214,054,912
Registered Office: 35 Great St Helens, London, EC3A 6AP
Activities: Financial intermediation not elsewhere classified
Parent: Lingfield 2014 I Holdings Limited
Officers: Daniel Marc Richard Jaffe [1975] Director

Link Fund Solutions Limited
Incorporated: 21 November 1973
Previous: Capita Financial Managers Limited
Net Worth: £22,209,728 *Total Assets:* £326,603,488
Registered Office: 6th Floor, 65 Gresham Street, London, EC2V 7NQ
Activities: Financial intermediation not elsewhere classified
Shareholders: Link Market Services (EMEA) Limited; Link Financial Group Limited
Officers: Christopher Addenbrooke [1962] Director; Nigel Stephen Boyling [1956] Director; Benjamin Hammond [1978] Director; Karl Joseph Midl [1974] Director; Peter Hugh Smith [1969] Director; Antony John Stuart [1952] Director

Linklaters Business Services
Incorporated: 30 July 1959 *Employees:* 2,033
Net Worth: £158,235,008 *Total Assets:* £221,436,000
Registered Office: One Silk Street, London, EC2Y 8HQ
Activities: Other business support service activities n.e.c.
Parent: Linklaters Business Services Holdings
Officers: Raymond Martin Cohen, Secretary/Solicitor; Raymond Martin Cohen [1961] Director/Solicitor; Peter David Hickman [1963] Director; Charles Richard Jacobs [1967] Director/Solicitor [Irish]; Christine Mary Lynch [1961] Director of Human Resources; Gideon David Moore [1963] Director/Solicitor

Linklaters LLP
Incorporated: 27 February 2007 *Employees:* 4,677
Net Worth: £561,000,000 *Total Assets:* £1,038,499,968
Registered Office: One Silk Street, London, EC2Y 8HQ
Officers: Charles Richard Jacobs [1967] Member; Gideon David Moore [1963] Member; Cyril Abtan [1973] LLP Member; Christian Ahlborn [1963] LLP Member; William Aitken-Davies [1981] LLP Member; Tom Alabaster [1979] LLP Member; Edward Philip Aldred [1979] LLP Member; Ian Andrews [1965] LLP Member; Bertrand Andriani [1961] LLP Member; Markus Appel [1974] LLP Member; Francois April [1970] LLP Member; Andrea Arosio [1969] LLP Member; David Maurice Avery-Gee [1974] LLP Member; David Ballegeer [1971] LLP Member; Christa Jane Band [1963] LLP Member; Sebastian Barling [1983] LLP Member; Rachel Barrett [1983] LLP Member; Stuart Barnaby Bedford [1967] LLP Member; Alexandra Flora Beidas [1978] LLP Member; Bruce Bell [1972] LLP Member; Rupert Bellinghausen [1966] LLP Member; Michael John Bennett [1965] LLP Member; Sebastian Benz [1966] LLP Member; Peter Ednyfed Bevan [1972] LLP Member; Michael Bienenfeld [1973] LLP Member; Patrik Bjorklund [1980] LLP Member; Matthew James Edward Bland [1975] LLP Member; Jean Pierre Simon Blumberg [1957] LLP Member; Mark Terence Blyth [1965] LLP Member; Cyril Boussion [1979] LLP Member; Christopher Boycott [1985] LLP Member; Simon Branigan [1974] LLP Member; Mark Andrew Brown [1966] LLP Member; Andrew Bruce [1970] LLP Member; William Donald McLean Buckley [1965] LLP Member; Anthony Bugg [1956] LLP Member; Mark Crispin Burgess-Smith [1963] LLP Member; Robert David Burt [1972] LLP Member; Richard John Bussell [1966] LLP Member; Ian David Callaghan [1983] LLP Member; Susana Cao Miranda [1977] LLP Member; Marco Carbonare [1973] LLP Member; Ben Thomas Carroll [1980] LLP Member; Thomas Kennedy Cassels [1969] LLP Member; Edward Chan [1970] LLP Member; Edouard Chapellier [1977] LLP Member; Alexandros Chatzinerantzis [1971] LLP Member; Euan Ellis Cole Clarke [1971] LLP Member; Owen Harvey Clay [1967] LLP Member; Richard Andrew Coar [1978] LLP Member; Arnaud Coibion [1975] LLP Member; Aedamar Ita Comiskey [1967] LLP Member; Rory John Conway [1980] LLP Member; Daniel Cousens [1971] LLP Member; John Percy Crozier [1964] LLP Member; Richard James Cumbley [1972] LLP Member; Julian Edward Lacy Cunningham Day [1973] LLP Member; Sebastian Daub [1972] LLP Member; Julian Edward Joseph Davies [1962] LLP Member; Jan Willem de Boer [1964] LLP Member; Arnaud de La Cotardiere [1965] LLP Member; Fabrice de La Morandiere [1965] LLP Member; Jonathan Mark de Lance-Holmes [1962] LLP Member; Aymar de Mauleon [1961] LLP Member; Pauline Debre [1978] LLP Member; Andreas Dehio [1980] LLP Member; Veronique Delaittre [1971] LLP Member; Bruno Derieux [1973] LLP Member; Etienne Dessy [1974] LLP Member; Matthew Devey [1976] LLP Member; Marly Didizian [1971] LLP Member; Ilia Ditiatev [1981] LLP Member; Kurt Dittrich [1967] LLP Member; Julia Dixon [1984] LLP Member; Neil Dixon [1980] LLP Member; Patrice Doat [1969] LLP Member; Satindar Dogra [1971] LLP Member; James Armstrong Douglas [1968] LLP Member; Ralph Drebes [1971] LLP Member; Mark Drury [1981] LLP Member; Benjamin Dulieu [1973] LLP Member; Pierre Duprey [1967] LLP Member; Janusz Dzianachowski [1980] LLP Member; Harry Shadwell Eddis [1971] LLP Member; Oliver William Albert Edwards [1978] LLP Member; Thomas Elkins [1980] LLP Member; Harriet Rose Ellis [1979] LLP Member; Jan Endler [1963] LLP Member; Timo Engelhardt [1973] LLP Member; Carlton Peter Evans [1963] LLP Member; Jasper Adie Ashley Evans [1963] LLP Member; Iain William Fenn [1966] LLP Member; Adam Michael John Fogarty [1978] LLP Member; Nemone Franks [1974] LLP Member; Adam Freeman [1970] LLP Member; Jessamy Gallagher [1973] LLP Member; Rosalind Clare Winifred Gallagher [1975] LLP Member; Alain Jean Louis Philippe Garnier [1963] LLP Member; Daniel Gendron [1977] LLP Member; Jeremy Benjamin Gewirtz [1965] LLP Member

Lion-Shoes Midco Limited
Incorporated: 30 July 2014 *Employees:* 1,964
Net Worth Deficit: £60,004,484 *Total Assets:* £422,659,136
Registered Office: 21 Grosvenor Place, London, SW1X 7HF
Activities: Activities of financial services holding companies
Officers: Simon David Brown [1960] Director; Augusto Cosulich [1991] Director/Investment Manager [Italian]; Richard Sean Lewis [1967] Director/Company Secretary

Lion/Heaven UK II Limited
Incorporated: 28 April 2011
Net Worth Deficit: £5,120,000 *Total Assets:* £214,896,000
Registered Office: Units C15-C17, Jack's Place, 6 Corbet Place, London, E1 6NN
Activities: Activities of other holding companies n.e.c.
Parent: Lion/Heaven UK Limited
Officers: Rory O'Connor [1966] Director/Investment Professional PE; Matthew Wilson [1986] Director/Investment Manager; Peter James Wood [1973] Director/Global CFO

Lion/Heaven UK Limited
Incorporated: 27 April 2011 *Employees:* 3,225
Net Worth Deficit: £160,536,000 *Total Assets:* £135,630,000
Registered Office: Units C15-C17, Jack's Place, 6 Corbet Place, London, E1 6NN
Activities: Activities of other holding companies n.e.c.
Officers: Richard Sean Lewis [1967] Director/Compliance Officer; Rory O'Connor [1966] Director/Investment Professional PE; Matthew Wilson [1986] Director/Investment Manager; Peter James Wood [1973] Director/Global CFO

Lion/Jenga Midco Limited
Incorporated: 13 December 2016 *Employees:* 3,002
Net Worth: £62,368,000 *Total Assets:* £180,247,008
Registered Office: 21 Grosvenor Place, London, SW1X 7HF
Activities: Activities of other holding companies n.e.c.
Officers: James Cocker [1982] Director/Investment Manager; Helena Duey Malchione [1990] Director/Investment Manager [American]; Matthew Wilson [1986] Director/Investment Manager

Lionrai Investments No.1 Limited
Incorporated: 16 July 2013 *Employees:* 164
Net Worth: £130,544,000 *Total Assets:* £912,745,984
Registered Office: c/o Hackwood Secretaries Limited, One Silk Street, London, EC2Y 8HQ
Activities: Activities of head offices
Shareholder: RBS Pension Trustee Limited
Officers: Ivan Robert Bell [1968] Director; Kailash Chada [1971] Director/Chartered Accountant; Peter Vincent Dixon [1960] Director; Philip Bernard Holder [1948] Director/Trust and Estate Practitioner, Solicitor; Anne-Noelle Noelle Le Gal [1983] Director [French]; William Francis Michael McKinstry [1965] Director/Accountant; Rachel Amelia Ockelford Drew [1976] Investment Director [New Zealander]; Valeria Rosati [1975] Director/Fund Manager [Italian]

Lionrai Investments No.2 Limited
Incorporated: 16 July 2013
Net Worth: £134,263,008 *Total Assets:* £332,015,008
Registered Office: c/o Hackwood Secretaries Limited, One Silk Street, London, EC2Y 8HQ
Activities: Activities of head offices
Parent: Lionrai Investments No. 1 Limited
Officers: Ivan Robert Bell [1968] Director; Kailash Chada [1971] Director/Chartered Accountant; Philip Bernard Holder [1948] Director/Trust and Estate Practitioner, Solicitor; Anne-Noelle Noelle Le Gal [1983] Director [French]; William Francis Michael McKinstry [1965] Director/Accountant; Rachel Amelia Ockelford Drew [1976] Investment Director [New Zealander]; Valeria Rosati [1975] Director/Fund Manager [Italian]

Lions Gate International Media Limited
Incorporated: 18 November 2016
Net Worth: £82,207,312 *Total Assets:* £103,299,856
Registered Office: 5th Floor, 45 Mortimer Street, London, W1W 8HJ
Activities: Motion picture distribution activities
Parent: Lions Gate Entertainment Corp
Officers: Zygmunt Jan Kamasa [1969] Director/CEO Lionsgate Films UK & Europe; Nicola Jane Pearcey [1978] Director/President UK & EMEA Strategy & Operations; Christian Robert Perala [1980] Director/Senior Vice President [American]; Wendy Leigh Reeds [1963] Director/EVP, International Sales [American]

Liquid Telecommunications Financing PLC
Incorporated: 8 May 2017
Net Worth: £36,583,008 *Total Assets:* £600,374,848
Registered Office: 9th Floor, 6 New Street Square, London, EC4A 3BF
Activities: Activities of other holding companies n.e.c.
Officers: Helen Kathryn Marsh, Secretary; Strive Masiyiwa [1961] Director [Zimbabwean]; Hardwork Njodzi Pemhiwa [1968] Director [Zimbabwean]; Nicholas Trevor Rudnick [1970] Director [German]

Liquid Telecommunications Investments Limited
Incorporated: 9 May 2017
Net Worth: £196,135,072 *Total Assets:* £196,159,392
Registered Office: 9th Floor, 6 New Street Square, London, EC4A 3BF
Activities: Activities of other holding companies n.e.c.
Parent: Liquid Telecommunications Financing PLC
Officers: Helen Kathryn Marsh, Secretary; Nicholas Trevor Rudnick [1970] Director [German]

Listrac Bidco Limited
Incorporated: 26 April 2012
Net Worth Deficit: £375,302,912 *Total Assets:* £103,717,488
Registered Office: 29th Floor, The Leadenhall Building, 122 Leadenhall Street, London, EC3V 4AB
Activities: Activities of head offices
Parent: Listrac Midco Limited
Officers: Matt Baird [1973] Director; James Frankish [1982] Director/Investment Professional; Paul Marriner [1967] Director; Matthew Stevens [1969] Director; Justin Antony James Tydeman [1970] Director

Listrac Finance Limited
Incorporated: 25 April 2012 *Employees:* 5
Net Worth Deficit: £140,870,544 *Total Assets:* £162,387,424
Registered Office: 29th Floor, The Leadenhall Building, 122 Leadenhall Street, London, EC3V 4AB
Activities: Activities of head offices
Officers: Matt Baird [1973] Director; James Frankish [1982] Director/Investment Professional; Paul Marriner [1967] Director; Matthew Stevens [1969] Director; Justin Antony James Tydeman [1970] Director

Listrac Midco Limited
Incorporated: 26 April 2012
Net Worth Deficit: £134,176,624 *Total Assets:* £172,901,600
Registered Office: 29th Floor, The Leadenhall Building, 122 Leadenhall Street, London, EC3V 4AB
Activities: Activities of head offices
Parent: Listrac Intermediate Holdings Limited
Officers: Matt Baird [1973] Director; James Frankish [1982] Director/Investment Professional; Paul Marriner [1967] Director; Matthew Stevens [1969] Director; Justin Antony James Tydeman [1970] Director

Littonace HMF Limited
Incorporated: 20 July 2005 *Employees:* 2
Net Worth: £28,047,904 *Total Assets:* £458,935,744
Registered Office: Berkeley House, Regents Park Road, London, N3 2JY
Activities: Buying and selling of own real estate
Parent: Fairhold Finance Limited
Officers: Paul Hallam, Secretary; Christopher Charles McGill [1960] Managing Director; William Kenneth Procter [1953] Director/Accountant

Livanova IP Limited
Incorporated: 23 May 2016
Net Worth: £8,319,854 *Total Assets:* £272,070,016
Registered Office: 20 Eastbourne Terrace, London, W2 6LG
Activities: Non-trading company
Officers: Alexander Hans-Josef Neumann [1969] Director/Lawyer [German]; Carl Oorts [1968] Finance Director [Belgian]

Livanova PLC
Incorporated: 20 February 2015 *Employees:* 4,500
Net Worth: £1,368,818,816 *Total Assets:* £1,868,007,552
Registered Office: 20 Eastbourne Terrace, London, W2 6LG
Activities: Manufacture of irradiation, electromedical and electrotherapeutic equipment
Officers: Catherine Moroz, Secretary; Francesco Bianchi [1956] Director [Italian]; William Kozy [1952] Director [American]; Damien McDonald [1965] Director/Chief Executive Officer [Australian]; Daniel Jeffrey Moore [1961] Director/Chief Executive Officer [American]; Hugh Morrison [1946] Director/Chairman [American]; Alfred Novak [1948] Director [American]; Sharon O'Kane [1967] Director and Scientific Advisor; Arthur Rosenthal [1946] Director [American]; Andrea Lynn Saia [1957] Director [American]

Live Nation (Music) UK Limited
Incorporated: 1 August 1989 *Employees:* 260
Net Worth Deficit: £23,006,024 *Total Assets:* £102,734,032
Registered Office: 2nd Floor, Regent Arcade House, 19-25 Argyll Street, London, W1F 7TS
Activities: Performing arts
Parent: Midland Concert Promotions Group Limited
Officers: Selina Holliday Emeny, Secretary; Melvin John Benn [1955] Director/Promoter; Stuart Robert Douglas [1967] Director/Accountant; Niall Alphonsus Dunphy [1973] Director; Selina Holliday Emeny [1968] Director/Solicitor

Live Nation Limited
Incorporated: 12 July 1999
Net Worth: £85,635,904 *Total Assets:* £156,889,136
Registered Office: 2nd Floor, Regent Arcade House, 19-25 Argyll Street, London, W1F 7TS
Activities: Activities of head offices
Parent: Live Nation Entertainment, Inc.
Officers: Selina Holliday Emeny, Secretary; Stuart Robert Douglas [1967] Director; Niall Alphonsus Dunphy [1973] Director; Selina Holliday Emeny [1968] Director/Solicitor; Alan Brian Ridgeway [1966] Director

Livn UK 2 Co Limited
Incorporated: 16 December 2015
Net Worth: £109,793,496 *Total Assets:* £109,799,216
Registered Office: 20 Eastbourne Terrace, London, W2 6LG
Activities: Non-trading company
Parent: Livanova PLC
Officers: Alexander Hans-Josef Neumann [1969] Director/Lawyer [German]; Carl Oorts [1968] Finance Director [Belgian]

Livn UK 3 Co Limited
Incorporated: 17 December 2015
Net Worth: £214,923,824 *Total Assets:* £214,929,328
Registered Office: 20 Eastbourne Terrace, London, W2 6LG
Activities: Non-trading company
Parent: Livanova PLC
Officers: Alexander Hans-Josef Neumann [1969] Director/Lawyer [German]; Carl Oorts [1968] Finance Director [Belgian]

Livn UK Holdco Limited
Incorporated: 21 September 2015
Net Worth: £230,235,312 *Total Assets:* £230,488,480
Registered Office: 20 Eastbourne Terrace, London, W2 6LG
Activities: Activities of other holding companies n.e.c.
Shareholders: Livn UK 2 Co Limited; Livanova PLC
Officers: Alexander Hans-Josef Neumann [1969] Director/Lawyer [German]; Carl Oorts [1968] Finance Director [Belgian]

Lloyd's Register Foundation
Incorporated: 11 January 2012 *Employees:* 7,489
Net Worth: £701,411,968 *Total Assets:* £1,222,445,056
Registered Office: 71 Fenchurch Street, London, EC3M 4BS
Activities: Activities of other holding companies n.e.c.
Officers: Michelle Davies, Secretary; Thomas Thune Anderson [1955] Director/Chairman [Danish]; Sir Brian Geoffrey Bender [1949] Director; Ronald Andrew Henderson [1946] Director; Rosemary Elizabeth Scudamore Martin [1960] Director; Carol Frances Sergeant [1952] Director; Andreas Sohmen-Pao [1971] Director/Chairman [Austrian]; Lambros Cleanthis Varnavides [1949] Director/Bank Official

Lloyd's Register Group Limited
Incorporated: 2 July 2012 *Employees:* 6,809
Net Worth: £532,371,008 *Total Assets:* £997,294,976
Registered Office: 71 Fenchurch Street, London, EC3M 4BS
Activities: Activities of other holding companies n.e.c.
Parent: Lloyd's Register Foundation
Officers: Michelle Davies, Secretary; Thomas Thune Andersen [1955] Director/Chairman [Danish]; William Ellis Armstrong [1957] Director; Christopher Geoffrey Finlayson [1956] Director/Petroleum Engineer; Caroline Bradshaw Firstbrook [1960] Director; Mark Vickers Kelsey [1960] Director; Michael Fotis Lykiardopulo [1961] Director [Greek]; Ishbel Jean Stewart Macpherson [1960] Director; Alastair Stewart Marsh [1961] Director/Accountant; Mary Elizabeth Waldner [1969] Finance Director

Lloyd's Register Group Services Limited
Incorporated: 30 March 2007 *Employees:* 526
Net Worth: £495,000 *Total Assets:* £698,243,968
Registered Office: 71 Fenchurch Street, London, EC3M 4BS
Activities: Other business support service activities n.e.c.
Parent: Lloyd's Register Group Limited
Officers: Tracey Anne Bigmore, Secretary; Andrew Punter [1970] Director/Accountant; Mary Elizabeth Waldner [1969] Finance Director; Andrew James Williams [1976] Director

Lloyd's Register Inspection Limited
Incorporated: 26 June 1975 *Employees:* 42
Net Worth Deficit: £41,546,000 *Total Assets:* £128,296,000
Registered Office: 71 Fenchurch Street, London, EC3M 4BS
Activities: Other business support service activities n.e.c.
Parent: Lloyd's Register Group Limited
Officers: Tracey Anne Bigmore, Secretary; David James Mitchell [1961] Director/Accountant; James Ian Pinder [1977] Director; Andrew James Williams [1976] Director

Lloyds Bank Asset Finance Limited
Incorporated: 20 November 1958
Net Worth: £998,000,000 *Total Assets:* £4,846,000,128
Registered Office: 25 Gresham Street, London, EC2V 7HN
Activities: Financial intermediation not elsewhere classified
Parent: Lloyds Bank PLC
Officers: David Dermot Hennessey, Secretary; Bertil Derrick Bos [1974] Director [Dutch]; Richard Andrew Jones [1972] Marketing Director

Lloyds Bank Corporate Asset Finance (No. 1) Limited
Incorporated: 21 July 2003
Net Worth Deficit: £44,199,000 *Total Assets:* £135,082,000
Registered Office: 25 Gresham Street, London, EC2V 7HN
Activities: Other business support service activities n.e.c.
Parent: Lloyds Bank Corporate Markets PLC
Officers: Alyson Elizabeth Mulholland, Secretary; Colin Graham Dowsett [1964] Director/Chartered Accountant

Lloyds Bank Corporate Asset Finance (No. 4) Limited
Incorporated: 21 July 2003
Net Worth Deficit: £5,594,000 *Total Assets:* £157,175,008
Registered Office: 25 Gresham Street, London, EC2V 7HN
Activities: Other business support service activities n.e.c.
Parent: Lloyds Bank Leasing Limited
Officers: Alyson Elizabeth Mulholland, Secretary; Colin Graham Dowsett [1964] Director/Chartered Accountant

Lloyds Bank Covered Bonds LLP
Incorporated: 12 September 2008
Net Worth: £33,645,000 *Total Assets:* £18,900,615,168
Registered Office: 35 Great St Helen's, London, EC3A 6AP

Lloyds Bank Equipment Leasing (No. 1) Limited
Incorporated: 3 September 2001
Net Worth: £5,469,000 *Total Assets:* £244,838,000
Registered Office: 25 Gresham Street, London, EC2V 7HN
Activities: Other business support service activities n.e.c.
Parent: Lloyds Bank Leasing Limited
Officers: Alyson Elizabeth Mulholland, Secretary; Laura Frances Dorey [1978] Director; Colin Graham Dowsett [1964] Director/Chartered Accountant

Lloyds Bank Equipment Leasing (No. 7) Limited
Incorporated: 16 May 2002
Net Worth Deficit: £13,267,000 *Total Assets:* £198,743,008
Registered Office: 25 Gresham Street, London, EC2V 7HN
Activities: Other business support service activities n.e.c.
Parent: Lloyds Bank Leasing Limited
Officers: Alyson Elizabeth Mulholland, Secretary; Laura Frances Dorey [1978] Director; Colin Graham Dowsett [1964] Director/Chartered Accountant; Gerard Ashley Fox [1963] Director/Banker

Lloyds Bank Financial Services (Holdings) Limited
Incorporated: 2 November 1978
Net Worth: £109,417,000 *Total Assets:* £3,344,986,112
Registered Office: 25 Gresham Street, London, EC2V 7HN
Activities: Activities of head offices
Parent: Lloyds Bank PLC
Officers: Alyson Elizabeth Mulholland, Secretary; Allen Eric Appen [1961] Director [American]; Prasad Nagnath Pitale [1971] Director

Lloyds Bank General Insurance Limited
Incorporated: 9 March 1925
Net Worth: £450,320,000 *Total Assets:* £1,021,953,024
Registered Office: 25 Gresham Street, London, EC2V 7HN
Activities: Non-life insurance
Parent: Lloyds Bank General Insurance Holdings Limited
Officers: Joanne Margaret Jolly, Secretary; Andrea Margaret Blance [1964] Director; Kate Cheetham [1963] Director/Group General Counsel; Mark George Culmer [1962] Finance Director; Jane Elizabeth Mary Curtis [1960] Director; Michael Harris [1965] Director; John Francis Hylands [1951] Director; Antonio Lorenzo [1966] Director [Spanish]; Christopher John George Moulder [1958] Director; Sophie Jane O'Connor [1970] Director; Dr Jakob Pfaudler [1972] Community Banking Director [Austrian]; Nicholas Edward Tucker Prettejohn [1960] Director

Lloyds Bank General Leasing (No. 3) Limited
Incorporated: 8 June 2004
Net Worth Deficit: £5,598,000 *Total Assets:* £109,409,000
Registered Office: 25 Gresham Street, London, EC2V 7HN
Activities: Other business support service activities n.e.c.
Parent: Lloyds Bank Leasing Limited
Officers: Alyson Elizabeth Mulholland, Secretary; Laura Frances Dorey [1978] Director; Colin Graham Dowsett [1964] Director/Chartered Accountant; Gerard Ashley Fox [1963] Director/Banker

Lloyds Bank Hill Samuel Holding Company Limited
Incorporated: 1 January 1920
Net Worth: £296,064,992 *Total Assets:* £328,404,992
Registered Office: 25 Gresham Street, London, EC2V 7HN
Activities: Activities of head offices
Parent: Lloyds Bank PLC
Officers: Paul Gittins, Secretary; David Ralph Chalk [1958] Director; David John Joyce [1961] Director/Accountant

Lloyds Bank Insurance Services Limited
Incorporated: 16 December 1969
Net Worth: £89,845,000 *Total Assets:* £262,320,992
Registered Office: 25 Gresham Street, London, EC2V 7HN
Activities: Non-life insurance
Parent: Lloyds Bank General Insurance Holdings Limited
Officers: Natalie Clarice Gracey, Secretary; James Christopher Steuart Hillman [1969] Director; Jacqueline Leiper [1972] Director; Craig James Thornton [1972] Director

Lloyds Bank Leasing Limited
Incorporated: 15 March 1971
Net Worth: £33,113,000 *Total Assets:* £283,139,008
Registered Office: 25 Gresham Street, London, EC2V 7HN
Activities: Other business support service activities n.e.c.
Parent: Lloyds Bank PLC
Officers: Alyson Elizabeth Mulholland, Secretary; Laura Frances Dorey [1978] Director; Colin Graham Dowsett [1964] Director/Chartered Accountant; Gerard Ashley Fox [1963] Director/Banker

Lloyds Bank Pension ABCS (No 1) LLP
Incorporated: 12 November 2009
Net Worth: £4,756,259,840 *Total Assets:* £4,756,259,840
Registered Office: 25 Gresham Street, London, EC2V 7HN

Lloyds Bank Pension ABCS (No 2) LLP
Incorporated: 12 November 2009
Net Worth: £755,296,000 *Total Assets:* £755,296,000
Registered Office: 25 Gresham Street, London, EC2V 7HN

Lloyds Bank PLC
Incorporated: 20 April 1865 *Employees:* 73,438
Net Worth: £50,815,000,576 *Total Assets:* £823,029,989,376
Registered Office: 25 Gresham Street, London, EC2V 7HN
Activities: Banks
Parent: Lloyds Banking Group PLC
Officers: Malcolm James Wood, Secretary; Sarah Elise Bentley [1971] Director; Lord Norman Roy Blackwell [1952] Director; Juan Colombas Calafat [1962] Director [Spanish]; Mark George Culmer [1962] Finance Director; Alan Peter Dickinson [1950] Director; Anita Margaret Frew [1957] Director; Brendan Edward Gilligan [1956] Director [Irish]; Simon Peter Henry [1961] Director; Nigel Grant Hinshelwood [1966] Director; Antonio Mota de Sousa Horta-Osorio [1964] Director [Portuguese]; Lord James Roger Crompton Lupton [1955] Director; Amanda Felicity MacKenzie [1963] Director; Nicholas Edward Tucker Prettejohn [1960] Director; Stuart William Sinclair [1953] Director; Sara Vivienne Weller [1961] Director

Lloyds Bank Subsidiaries Limited
Incorporated: 26 July 1911
Net Worth: £2,955,000,064 *Total Assets:* £2,963,000,064
Registered Office: 25 Gresham Street, London, EC2V 7HN
Activities: Activities of head offices
Parent: Lloyds Bank PLC
Officers: Paul Gittins, Secretary; Philip Robert Grant [1966] Director; David John Joyce [1961] Director/Accountant

Lloyds Development Capital (Holdings) Limited
Incorporated: 11 April 1973
Net Worth: £661,132,032 *Total Assets:* £1,972,082,944
Registered Office: One Vine Street, London, W1J 0AH
Activities: Other business support service activities n.e.c.
Parent: LBG Equity Investments Limited
Officers: David Dermot Hennessey, Secretary; Mark George Culmer [1962] Finance Director; Martin John Draper [1964] Director; Christopher Richard Hurley [1974] Director; Alan Toby Rougier [1967] Director

Lloyds General Leasing Limited
Incorporated: 11 July 1990
Net Worth: £6,124,000 *Total Assets:* £108,056,000
Registered Office: 25 Gresham Street, London, EC2V 7HN
Activities: Other business support service activities n.e.c.
Parent: Lloyds Bank Leasing Limited
Officers: Alyson Elizabeth Mulholland, Secretary; Colin Graham Dowsett [1964] Director/Chartered Accountant; Gerard Ashley Fox [1963] Director/Banker

Lloyds UDT Limited
Incorporated: 6 October 1926
Net Worth: £14,088,000 *Total Assets:* £815,451,008
Registered Office: 25 Gresham Street, London, EC2V 7HN
Activities: Financial intermediation not elsewhere classified
Parent: Black Horse Finance Holdings Limited
Officers: David Dermot Hennessey, Secretary

LME Clear Limited
Incorporated: 21 April 2011 *Employees:* 45
Net Worth: £175,609,024 *Total Assets:* £16,732,098,560
Registered Office: 10 Finsbury Square, London, EC2A 1AJ
Activities: Administration of financial markets
Parent: HKEX Investment (UK) Limited
Officers: Marcos Castro, Secretary; Roland Paul Chai [1972] Director; Matthew James Chamberlain [1982] Director; Adrian John Winston Farnham [1965] Director; Marye Louise Humphery [1959] Director; Romnesh Lamba [1963] Director [Chinese]; Marco Andrea Strimer [1961] Director [Swiss]; Antony John Stuart [1952] Director; Richard John Thornhill [1954] Director; Kin Wah Stephen Yiu [1960] Director

LMS (City Road) Limited
Incorporated: 1 December 2005
Net Worth: £174,225,472 *Total Assets:* £345,816,256
Registered Office: 25 Savile Row, London, W1S 2ER
Activities: Buying and selling of own real estate
Parent: Derwent Valley Limited
Officers: David Andrew Lawler, Secretary; John David Burns [1944] Director; Nigel Quentin George [1963] Director/Surveyor; Simon Paul Silver [1950] Director; David Gary Silverman [1969] Director; Paul Malcolm Williams [1960] Director/Surveyor; Damian Mark Alan Wisniewski [1961] Director

LMS Capital Group Limited
Incorporated: 29 December 2005
Net Worth: £134,910,112 *Total Assets:* £140,141,744
Registered Office: Two London Bridge, London, SE1 9RA
Activities: Activities of financial services holding companies
Parent: LMS Capital PLC
Officers: Nicholas Robert Friedlos [1957] Director; Hon. Robert Anthony Rayne [1949] Director

LMS Capital Holdings Limited
Incorporated: 7 March 2000
Net Worth: £94,701,992 *Total Assets:* £158,597,616
Registered Office: Two London Bridge, London, SE1 9RA
Activities: Activities of financial services holding companies
Parent: LMS Capital PLC
Officers: Nicholas Robert Friedlos [1957] Director; Hon. Robert Anthony Rayne [1949] Director

LMS Capital PLC
Incorporated: 17 March 2006 *Employees:* 6
Net Worth: £64,488,000 *Total Assets:* £144,528,000
Registered Office: Two London Bridge, London, SE1 9RA
Activities: Financial intermediation not elsewhere classified
Officers: Roderic Aidan Birkett [1961] Director; Dr Martin Peter Knight [1949] Director; Neil Joseph Lerner [1947] Director/Chartered Accountant; The Hon Robert Anthony Rayne [1949] Director

LMS Finance Limited
Incorporated: 15 November 2005
Net Worth: £1,230,005,376 *Total Assets:* £1,825,535,744
Registered Office: 25 Savile Row, London, W1S 2ER
Activities: Financial intermediation not elsewhere classified
Parent: London Merchant Securities Limited
Officers: David Andrew Lawler, Secretary; John David Burns [1944] Director; Nigel Quentin George [1963] Director; Simon Paul Silver [1950] Director; Paul Malcolm Williams [1960] Director/Surveyor; Damian Mark Alan Wisniewski [1961] Director

LMS Offices Limited
Incorporated: 9 December 2004
Net Worth: £510,369,472 *Total Assets:* £516,957,312
Registered Office: 25 Savile Row, London, W1S 2ER
Activities: Buying and selling of own real estate
Parent: Derwent Valley Limited
Officers: David Andrew Lawler, Secretary; John David Burns [1944] Director; Nigel Quentin George [1963] Director; Simon Paul Silver [1950] Director; David Gary Silverman [1969] Director; Paul Malcolm Williams [1960] Director/Surveyor; Damian Mark Alan Wisniewski [1961] Director

LN-Gaiety Holdings Limited
Incorporated: 30 December 2004 *Employees:* 630
Net Worth: £39,169,912 *Total Assets:* £175,027,744
Registered Office: 2nd Floor, Regent Arcade House, 19-25 Argyll Street, London, W1F 7TS
Activities: Activities of head offices
Parent: Live Nation (Music) UK Limited
Officers: Selina Holliday Emeny, Secretary; Caroline Elizabeth Desmond [1961] Director [Irish]; Denis James Desmond [1953] Director [Irish]; Zachary Alexander Desmond [1986] Director/Concert Promoter [Irish]; Stuart Robert Douglas [1967] Director/Vice President Finance; Niall Alphonsus Dunphy [1973] Director; Selina Holliday Emeny [1968] Director/Solicitor

Local Trust
Incorporated: 3 November 2011
Net Worth: £142,814,000 *Total Assets:* £174,896,992
Registered Office: CAN Mezzanine, 7-14 Great Dover Street, Borough, London, SE1 4YR
Activities: Other social work activities without accommodation n.e.c.
Officers: Matt Leach, Secretary; Sahil Khan [1983] Director/Head of Community Investment; Benjamin Yat Meng Lee [1972] Director; Jeannette Ann Lichner [1957] Director/Senior Adviser [British/American]; Karen Louise Mellanby [1970] Executive Director; Peter Ensell Mills [1965] Consulting Director; Nicola Pollock [1955] Director/Charity Chief Executive; John Kevin Sugrue [1950] Director; Robert Charles Thust [1978] Director/Self-Employed Consultant; David Timothy Warner [1963] Director/Social Change and Philanthropy Consultant; Dr John David Whitton [1971] Director/Scientist; Richard Simon Wilson [1976] Director

Loch Lomond Distillers Limited
Incorporated: 12 September 2013 *Employees:* 217
Net Worth: £30,660,000 *Total Assets:* £217,186,000
Registered Office: 30 Broadwick Street, London, W1F 8JB
Activities: Distilling, rectifying and blending of spirits
Parent: Glen Scotia Distillery Company Limited
Officers: Colin Matthews [1965] Director; Richard Miles [1966] Director; Nicholas Rose [1957] Director

Loch Lomond Distillery Company Limited
Incorporated: 19 July 2013 *Employees:* 3
Net Worth Deficit: £35,812,000 *Total Assets:* £154,226,000
Registered Office: 30 Broadwick Street, London, W1F 8JB
Activities: Distilling, rectifying and blending of spirits
Parent: The Littlemill Distillery Company Limited
Officers: Colin Matthews [1965] Director; Richard Miles [1966] Director; Nicholas Rose [1957] Director

Loch Lomond Holdings 1 Limited
Incorporated: 19 July 2013 *Employees:* 217
Net Worth Deficit: £83,520,000 *Total Assets:* £217,984,992
Registered Office: 30 Broadwick Street, London, W1F 8JB
Activities: Activities of production holding companies
Officers: Richard Loxton Campin [1961] Director/Investment Executive; Bruce Charles Davidson [1956] Director; Christopher Michael Graham [1959] Director/Investment Executive; Colin Matthews [1965] Director; Richard Miles [1966] Director; Nicholas Rose [1957] Director; Mark Steven Taylor [1978] Director/Investment Executive; William Burnfield White [1961] Operations Director

Lochside Asset Purchaser No.1 PLC
Incorporated: 16 January 2015
Net Worth: £3,065,000 *Total Assets:* £409,990,016
Registered Office: 35 Great St Helen's, London, EC3A 6AP
Activities: Financial intermediation not elsewhere classified
Parent: Lochside Asset Purchaser No.1 Holdings Limited
Officers: Daniel Marc Richard Jaffe [1975] Director

Lockton Companies LLP
Incorporated: 12 March 2010
Net Worth: £90,529,016 *Total Assets:* £254,708,208
Registered Office: The St Botolph Building, 138 Houndsditch, London, EC3A 7AG
Officers: Stephen Douglas Ambidge [1958] LLP Member; Edward Alexander Gifford Aspinall [1969] LLP Member; Martin Edward Bailey [1956] LLP Member; Calum MacDonald Bannerman [1966] LLP Member; Calvin Barnes [1974] LLP Member; Ian Prendergast Blackadder [1963] LLP Member; Brian John Daniel Boehmer [1976] LLP Member; Alexander Boswell [1968] LLP Member; Miles Barrington Charles Bourne [1978] LLP Member; Margaret Lorraine Boyle [1963] LLP Member; Stephen James Bracey [1966] LLP Member; Christopher Mark Arthur Brown [1965] LLP Member; Francis Stephen Burridge [1957] LLP Member; Ian Nicholas Canham [1964] LLP Member; George Herbert Carrington [1953] LLP Member; Samuel Thomas Budgen Clark [1975] LLP Member; Julie Dawn Coates [1966] LLP Member; Dominic Adam Ashley Coleman [1962] LLP Member; Simon Richard Coleman [1961] LLP Member; Irineo Combarro Lopez [1976] LLP Member; Ian John Cooper [1970] LLP Member; Paul James Cooper [1969] LLP Member; Andrew John Cornish [1958] LLP Member; Kevin John Culliney [1965] LLP Member; Stephen Patrick Davey [1977] LLP Member; Matthew Thomas John Davies [1970] LLP Member; Debbie Day [1970] LLP Member; Gary William Doran [1977] LLP Member; Henry Owen Dyson [1982] LLP Member; Gary Ennis [1963] LLP Member; Michael Andrew Farrell [1974] LLP Member; Simon Edward Fenn [1960] LLP Member; Rachel Sarah Gilliam [1973] LLP Member; Paul Michael Goudime Levkovitsch [1965] LLP Member; Robbie John Foster Graham [1966] LLP Member; David Charles Hair [1965] LLP Member; Roland Walter Haiser [1967] LLP Member; Peter Newman Hall [1970] LLP Member; Tony Peter Hardy [1961] LLP Member; Ian Charles Michael Harrison [1963] LLP Member; Kevin Charles Harte [1964] LLP Member; Colin Graham Hasler [1965] LLP Member; David Richard Hayhow [1972] LLP Member; Ever-Jan Jouke Hentenaar [1967] LLP Member; Allison Paige Hollern [1977] LLP Member; Sarah Jane Horler [1975] LLP Member; Peter George Stewart Hornsby [1959] LLP Member; Paul Vincent Jack [1960] LLP Member; Colin Johnson [1964] LLP Member; Michael Robert LEA [1969] LLP Member; Neville John Charles Miles [1960] LLP Member; Carla Jane Moffett [1974] LLP Member; Andrew Laurence Monkhouse [1966] LLP Member; Carl Nicholas Moore [1974] LLP Member; James Edward Moss [1967] LLP Member; Andrew Clark Nicholson [1960] LLP Member; Neil Keith Nimmo [1961] LLP Member; Andrew William Norris [1955] LLP Member; Richard James O'Keefe [1968] LLP Member; Richard Charles Clarke Lee Owen [1966] LLP Member; Anthony James Place [1969] LLP Member; James Dudley Pryke [1977] LLP Member; Alistair James Christopher Rivers [1964] LLP Member; Mark Peter Rose [1979] LLP Member; Blake Kenneth Spice Roseveare [1975] LLP Member; Steven David Rust [1969] LLP Member; Simon Christopher Scholfield [1967] LLP Member; Larry Karl Spurgeon [1962] LLP Member; Christopher James Tagg [1972] LLP Member; Betton Craig Warburton-Smith [1969] LLP Member; Benjamin Austen Warman [1980] LLP Member; Mark John Matthew Waterkeyn [1957] LLP Member; Adam Bannatyne Watson [1971] LLP Member; Christopher Charles Wetherell [1978] LLP Member; Russell Gerard Winter [1963] LLP Member; Vincent Edward Wood [1963] LLP Member; Graham Daniel Wynes [1976] LLP Member

Lockfold Communications Limited
Incorporated: 20 November 1967
Net Worth: £140,888,144 *Total Assets:* £178,831,904
Registered Office: 22 Chancery Lane, London, WC2A 1LS
Activities: Activities of head offices
Parent: Sableknight Limited
Officers: Thomas Morton West, Secretary; Robin Shedden Broadhurst [1946] Director/Chartered Surveyor; Desmond Roger Wingate Harrison [1933] Director; Rosemary Frances Norris [1961] Director

Lockton International Holdings Limited
Incorporated: 16 August 2006
Net Worth: £100,961,880 *Total Assets:* £252,444,704
Registered Office: The St Botolphs Building, 138 Houndsditch, London, EC3A 7AG
Activities: Activities of head offices
Parent: LIH UK Topco Limited
Officers: Sarah Anne Jeffs, Secretary; Henry Bond [1965] Director [American]; Christopher Mark Arthur Brown [1965] Director; David John Gee [1947] Director; William Humphrey III [1965] Director/General Counsel [American]; David Marshall Lockton [1953] Director [American]; Ronald Lockton [1966] Director [American]; John Lumelleau [1951] Director [American]; Neil Keith Nimmo [1961] Director

Lockton International Limited
Incorporated: 5 September 1990
Net Worth: £163,008,160 *Total Assets:* £178,931,104
Registered Office: The St Botolph Building, 138 Houndsditch, London, EC3A 7AG
Activities: Activities of head offices
Parent: Lockton International Holdings Limited
Officers: Sarah Jeffs, Secretary; Simon Richard Coleman [1961] Director; Neil Keith Nimmo [1961] Director

Logica Limited
Incorporated: 27 April 1982
Net Worth: £2,016,694,016 *Total Assets:* £2,069,613,056
Registered Office: 14th Floor, 20 Fenchurch Street, London, EC3M 3BY
Activities: Activities of other holding companies n.e.c.
Parent: CGI Group Holdings Europe Limited
Officers: Sarah Landry Maltais, Secretary; Francois Boulanger [1965] Director/Executive Vice-President & Chief Financial Officer [Canadian]; Tara McGeehan [1967] Director/Businesswoman; Faris Mehdi Kadhim Mohammed [1961] Director/Vice President Finance UK, CGI

Lok'n Store Limited
Incorporated: 25 February 1994 *Employees:* 128
Net Worth: £73,523,368 *Total Assets:* £134,286,240
Registered Office: One Fleet Place, London, EC4M 7WS
Activities: Other service activities n.e.c.
Parent: Loknstore Group PLC
Officers: Raymond Alan Davies [1957] Director/Chartered Accountant; Richard John Holmes [1960] Marketing Director; Andrew Jacobs [1959] Director/Stockbroker; Neil James John Newman-Shepherd [1976] Director; Simon Griffith Thomas [1959] Director

Lombard Business Leasing Limited
Incorporated: 1 November 2001
Net Worth: £10,699,000 *Total Assets:* £1,016,168,000
Registered Office: 280 Bishopsgate, London, EC2M 4RB
Activities: Financial intermediation not elsewhere classified
Parent: Lombard North Central PLC
Officers: David Generald Harris [1969] Director/Bank Official; Ian John Isaac [1963] Director/Head of Asset Finance Portfolio; Alan David Parry [1967] Director/Bank Official; Joseph Alexander Pattara [1973] Director/Bank Official

Lombard North Central Public Limited Company
Incorporated: 19 February 1938 *Employees:* 560
Net Worth: £393,000,000 *Total Assets:* £9,217,000,448
Registered Office: 280 Bishopsgate, London, EC2M 4RB
Activities: Financial intermediation not elsewhere classified
Parent: National Westminster Bank PLC
Officers: Christopher William Green [1972] Director/Bank Official; Ian John Isaac [1963] Director/Head of Asset Finance Portfolio; Alan David Parry [1967] Director/Bank Official; Joseph Alexander Pattara [1973] Director/Bank Official

Lombard Technology Services Limited
Incorporated: 22 July 1986 *Employees:* 74
Net Worth: £9,856,000 *Total Assets:* £266,254,000
Registered Office: 280 Bishopsgate, London, EC2M 4RB
Activities: Wholesale of computers, computer peripheral equipment and software
Parent: Lombard North Central PLC
Officers: Stuart Gregory Clark [1968] Director/Bank Official; Ian John Isaac [1963] Director/Head of Asset Finance Portfolio; Joseph Alexander Pattara [1973] Director/Bank Official

London & Associated Properties PLC
Incorporated: 25 June 1938 *Employees:* 237
Net Worth: £45,854,000 *Total Assets:* £144,791,008
Registered Office: 24 Bruton Place, London, W1J 6NE
Activities: Buying and selling of own real estate
Officers: Jonathan Mintz, Secretary; Howard David Goldring [1950] Director/Global Investment Strategist; John Alexander Heller [1966] Executive Director; Sir Michael Aron Heller [1936] Director/Chairman Chartered Accountant; Jonathan Mintz [1969] Finance Director; Clive Anthony Parritt [1943] Director/Chartered Accountant; Robin Priest [1958] Managing Director

London & Birmingham Hotels Limited
Incorporated: 11 March 2014
Net Worth: £436,500,000 *Total Assets:* £436,500,000
Registered Office: 3 Park Place, St James's, London, SW1A 1LP
Activities: Activities of other holding companies n.e.c.
Parent: Tonstate Metropole Hotels Limited
Officers: Rachel Elizabeth Robertson [1961] Director

London & Continental Railways Limited
Incorporated: 8 September 1994 *Employees:* 42
Net Worth: £346,233,984 *Total Assets:* £414,127,008
Registered Office: 4th Floor, One Kemble Street, London, WC2B 4AN
Activities: Buying and selling of own real estate
Parent: Secretary of State for Transport
Officers: Peter Hawthorne, Secretary; Timothy Claude Garnham [1956] Development Director; Peter Hawthorne [1966] Director/Accountant; David Joy [1954] Director/Town Planner; Alexander Lloyd Reeves [1974] Director; Nichola Jane Wilden [1960] Director

London & Regional (Baker Street) Holdings Limited
Incorporated: 8 April 2002 *Employees:* 3
Previous: London & Regional (Baker Street) Limited
Net Worth: £513,462,016 *Total Assets:* £518,684,992
Registered Office: Floor 6, Quadrant House, 4 Thomas More Square, London, E1W 1YW
Activities: Management of real estate on a fee or contract basis
Parent: London & Regional Group Investments Limited
Officers: Richard John Livingstone [1964] Director; Leonard Kevin Chandran Sebastian [1969] Group Managing and Legal Director [Swiss]

London & Regional (Baker Street) Limited
Incorporated: 23 June 2017 *Employees:* 1
Net Worth: £565,828,992 *Total Assets:* £941,305,024
Registered Office: Floor 6, Quadrant House, 4 Thomas More Square, London, E1W 1YW
Activities: Other business support service activities n.e.c.
Parent: LR Baker St Senior Holdco Limited
Officers: Leonard Kevin Sebastian [1969] Group Managing and Legal Director [Swiss]

London & Regional (Empire) Limited
Incorporated: 2 September 2002
Net Worth: £47,428,728 *Total Assets:* £133,285,672
Registered Office: Floor 6, Quadrant House, 4 Thomas More Square, London, E1W 1YW
Activities: Other business support service activities n.e.c.
Parent: London & Regional Group Securitisation No.2 Limited
Officers: Leonard Kevin Sebastian [1969] Group Managing and Legal Director [Swiss]

London & Regional (HC Properties) Limited
Incorporated: 20 April 2006 *Employees:* 2
Net Worth: £101,557,632 *Total Assets:* £340,204,832
Registered Office: Floor 6, Quadrant House, 4 Thomas More Square, London, E1W 1YW
Activities: Other business support service activities n.e.c.
Parent: London & Regional (Health Clubs) Limited
Officers: Richard John Livingstone [1964] Director

London & Regional (St. Georges Court) Limited
Incorporated: 17 April 1997 *Employees:* 1
Net Worth: £87,434,480 *Total Assets:* £228,207,872
Registered Office: Floor 6, Quadrant House, 4 Thomas More Square, London, E1W 1YW
Activities: Other business support service activities n.e.c.
Parent: LR Skipton and Bloomsbury Ltd
Officers: Leonard Kevin Sebastian [1969] Group Managing and Legal Director [Swiss]; Leonard Kevin Chandran Sebastian [1969] Group Managing and Legal Director [Swiss]

London & Regional Dormant Holdings Limited
Incorporated: 3 September 2002 *Employees:* 2
Net Worth: £1,070,253 *Total Assets:* £369,081,696
Registered Office: Floor 6, Quadrant House, 4 Thomas More Square, London, E1W 1YW
Activities: Other business support service activities n.e.c.
Parent: London & Regional Group Holdings Limited
Officers: Richard John Livingstone [1964] Director; Leonard Kevin Sebastian [1969] Group Managing and Legal Director [Swiss]

London & Regional Group Holdings Limited
Incorporated: 4 September 2002 *Employees:* 2,744
Net Worth: £1,820,000,000 *Total Assets:* £4,872,999,936
Registered Office: Floor 6, Quadrant House, 4 Thomas More Square, London, E1W 1YW
Activities: Development of building projects
Parent: Loopsign No.2 Limited
Officers: Ian Malcolm Livingstone [1962] Director; Richard John Livingstone [1964] Director; Leonard Kevin Sebastian [1969] Group Managing and Legal Director [Swiss]

London & Regional Group Investments Limited
Incorporated: 22 September 2008 *Employees:* 2
Net Worth: £447,789,376 *Total Assets:* £447,792,000
Registered Office: Floor 6, Quadrant House, 4 Thomas More Square, London, E1W 1YW
Activities: Other business support service activities n.e.c.
Parent: London & Regional Group Holdings Limited
Officers: Richard John Livingstone [1964] Director; Leonard Kevin Sebastian [1969] Group Managing and Legal Director [Swiss]

London & Regional Group Securitisation No.1 Limited
Incorporated: 22 September 2008 *Employees:* 3
Net Worth: £156,911,824 *Total Assets:* £156,911,824
Registered Office: Floor 6, Quadrant House, 4 Thomas More Square, London, E1W 1YW
Activities: Other business support service activities n.e.c.
Parent: London & Regional Group Holdings Limited
Officers: Richard John Livingstone [1964] Director; Leonard Kevin Chandran Sebastian [1969] Group Managing and Legal Director [Swiss]

London & Regional Group Trading No.3 Limited
Incorporated: 23 September 2008 *Employees:* 2
Net Worth: £68,115,856 *Total Assets:* £277,039,296
Registered Office: Floor 6, Quadrant House, 4 Thomas More Square, London, E1W 1YW
Activities: Other business support service activities n.e.c.
Shareholders: London & Regional Group Trading No.2 Limited; London & Regional Group Holdings Limited
Officers: Richard John Livingstone [1964] Director; Leonard Kevin Sebastian [1969] Group Managing and Legal Director [Swiss]

London & Regional Hotel Finance Limited
Incorporated: 3 July 2002 *Employees:* 2
Net Worth Deficit: £142,267,008 *Total Assets:* £115,264,000
Registered Office: Floor 6, Quadrant House, 4 Thomas More Square, London, E1W 1YW
Activities: Buying and selling of own real estate
Parent: London and Regional Group Finance Limited
Officers: Richard John Livingstone [1964] Director

London & Regional Overseas Limited
Incorporated: 28 April 1999
Net Worth: £148,512,896 *Total Assets:* £391,469,312
Registered Office: Floor 6, Quadrant House, 4 Thomas More Square, London, E1W 1YW
Activities: Non-trading company
Parent: London & Regional Group Holdings Limited
Officers: Leonard Kevin Sebastian [1969] Group Managing and Legal Director [Swiss]

London & Regional Portfolio Finance Limited
Incorporated: 2 June 2006
Net Worth: £1,628,703 *Total Assets:* £107,706,032
Registered Office: Floor 6, Quadrant House, 4 Thomas More Square, London, E1W 1YW
Activities: Other business support service activities n.e.c.
Officers: Leonard Kevin Chandran Sebastian [1969] Group Managing and Legal Director [Swiss]

London & Regional Trading Holdings Limited
Incorporated: 4 September 2002 *Employees:* 2
Net Worth: £414,016,576 *Total Assets:* £414,024,064
Registered Office: Floor 6, Quadrant House, 4 Thomas More Square, London, E1W 1YW
Activities: Other business support service activities n.e.c.
Shareholders: London & Regional Guarantee Company Limited; London & Regional Group Holdings Limited
Officers: Richard John Livingstone [1964] Director; Leonard Kevin Sebastian [1969] Group Managing and Legal Director [Swiss]

London and City Group Holdings Limited
Incorporated: 11 December 2004 *Employees:* 29
Net Worth: £112,525,664 *Total Assets:* £280,388,736
Registered Office: 1 Maltings Place, 169 Tower Bridge Road, London, SE1 3JB
Activities: Activities of other holding companies n.e.c.
Major Shareholder: Graham Harris
Officers: Christine Robson, Secretary; Graham Harris [1946] Director/Property Developer

The London and Overseas Insurance Company Limited
Incorporated: 25 April 1893
Net Worth Deficit: £570,070,528 *Total Assets:* £104,422,296
Registered Office: Hays Galleria, 1 Hays Lane, London, SE1 2RD
Activities: Non-life insurance
Parent: OIC Run-Off Limited
Officers: Dan Yoram Schwarzmann, Secretary; Paul Anthony Brereton Evans [1951] Director/Chartered Accountant; Dan Yoram Schwarzmann [1963] Director/Chartered Accountant

London and Regional Group Finance Limited
Incorporated: 29 October 2001 *Employees:* 2
Net Worth: £129,041,776 *Total Assets:* £679,730,624
Registered Office: Floor 6, Quadrant House, 4 Thomas More Square, London, E1W 1YW
Activities: Other business support service activities n.e.c.
Parent: London & Regional Group Holdings Limited
Officers: Leonard Kevin Chandran Sebastian [1969] Group Managing and Legal Director [Swiss]

London and Regional Properties Limited
Incorporated: 17 March 1994 *Employees:* 48
Net Worth: £53,957,008 *Total Assets:* £1,403,138,560
Registered Office: Floor 6, Quadrant House, 4 Thomas More Square, London, E1W 1YW
Activities: Management of real estate on a fee or contract basis
Parent: London & Regional Group Holdings Limited
Officers: Ian Malcolm Livingstone [1962] Director; Richard John Livingstone [1964] Director; Leonard Kevin Sebastian [1969] Group Managing and Legal Director [Swiss]

London Bus Services Limited
Incorporated: 24 January 2000
Net Worth: £1,000,000 *Total Assets:* £524,000,000
Registered Office: 55 Broadway, London, SW1H 0BD
Activities: Other passenger land transport
Parent: Transport Trading Limited
Officers: Howard Ernest Carter, Secretary; Patrick Doig [1982] Director/Planning & Reporting Controller; Geoffrey William Hobbs [1967] Director/Economist; Claire Mann [1973] Director of Bus Operations; Gareth William Powell [1976] Director of Strategy; David John Wylie [1974] Director/Chief Procurement Officer

London City Airport Limited
Incorporated: 22 November 1985 *Employees:* 555
Net Worth: £149,975,008 *Total Assets:* £188,496,000
Registered Office: London City Airport, City Aviation House, Royal Docks, London, E16 2PB
Activities: Scheduled passenger air transport
Officers: Wilma Mary Allan [1962] Director/Chief Financial Officer; Robert Gary Sinclair [1966] Director/Chief Executive [New Zealander]

London Clubs Management Limited
Incorporated: 5 August 1992 *Employees:* 61
Net Worth: £178,458,000 *Total Assets:* £396,465,984
Registered Office: 55 Baker Street, London, W1U 8EW
Activities: Activities of head offices
Parent: London Clubs Holding Limited
Officers: Krishan Kaushal, Secretary; Thomas Michael Jenkin [1955] Director/Global President of Destination Markets [American]; Alexis George Oswald [1981] Director; Michael Rothwell [1968] Director/Chartered Accountant

London Diocesan Fund (The)
Incorporated: 29 June 1918 *Employees:* 89
Net Worth: £451,500,000 *Total Assets:* £481,300,000
Registered Office: London Diocesan House, 36 Causton Street, London, SW1P 4AU
Activities: Activities of religious organisations
Officers: Richard Gough, Secretary; Elizabeth Adekunle [1977] Director/Archdeacon of Hackney; Jonathan Mark Richard Baker [1966] Director/Clerk in Holy Orders; Enid Monica Barron [1945] Director/Civil Servant (Retired); Michael John Bithell [1967] Director/Accountant; Revd Judith Elizabeth Blackburn [1958] Director/Member of a Religious Community; Peter Alan Broadbent [1952] Director/Bishop; Deborah Ruth Buggs [1972] Director/Accountant; Revd Edmund Alwyn James Cargill Thompson [1972] Director/Minister of Religion; John Ronald Dolling [1943] Director/Government Service; Howard Arthur Evans [1945] Director/Secretary General Trade Association; Duncan Jamie Green [1952] Director/Archdeacon; John Edward Inskipp Hawkins [1963] Director/Archdeacon of Hampstead; Revd Graham Alexander Wells Hunter [1978] Director/Minister of Religion; David Berkeley Hurst [1940] Director/Economist; David John Ison [1954] Director/Clerk in Holy Orders; Alison Jane Joyce [1959] Director/Anglican Parish Priest; Rosemary Jane Lain-Priestley [1967] Director/Priest; Amanda McIntyre [1964] Charity Director; The Venerable Luke Jonathan Miller [1966] Director/Archdeacon of London; Reverend Leslie Alan Moses [1949] Director/Clergy; Sarah Elisabeth Mullally [1962] Director/Holy Orders; Josile Wenus Alexandra Munro [1963] Director/Local Court Officer; James Patrick Normand [1954] Director/Chartered Accountant; Brian William O'Donoghue [1969] Director/Church Manager; Dr Phillip Rice [1949] Director/Self Employed; David Westlake Richards [1969] Director/School Business Manager; Dr Judith Frances Richardson [1948] Director/Retired; Clive Richard Scowen [1958] Director/Barrister; Revd Christopher Matthew Smith [1967] Director/Priest; Christina Titilayo Sosanya [1949] Director/Public Administrator [Nigerian]; Sarah Louise Tett [1971] Director/Housewife-Voluntary Worker; Jeremy Alec Thomas [1960] Director/Author; The Right Reverend Richard Charles Thorpe [1965] Director/Bishop of Islington; Graham Stuart Tomlin [1958] Director/Bishop of Kensington; Dr Christopher Roy Mason Ward [1947] Director/Retired; The Venerable Stephan John Welch [1950] Director/Archdeacon; The Right Reverend Robert James Wickham [1972] Director/Clerk in Holy Orders, Bishop of Edmonton; Inigo Rodney Milman Woolf [1946] Director/Bank Manager

London Forfaiting Company Limited
Incorporated: 22 June 1983 *Employees:* 38
Net Worth: £56,726,496 *Total Assets:* £196,454,640
Registered Office: 11 Ironmonger Lane, London, EC2V 8EY
Activities: Financial intermediation not elsewhere classified
Parent: Fimbank PLC
Officers: William Ramzan, Secretary; Majed ESSA Ahmed Al-Ajeel [1953] Director/Banker [Kuwaiti]; Mohamed Fekih Ahmed [1949] Director/Banker [Tunisian]; Robert James Frost [1965] Director/Banker [Australian]; Dr John Carmel Grech [1948] Director/Banker [Maltese]

London Gateway Port Limited
Incorporated: 17 December 2001 *Employees:* 485
Net Worth Deficit: £222,764,992 *Total Assets:* £1,164,696,064
Registered Office: 16 Palace Street, London, SW1E 5JQ
Activities: Service activities incidental to water transportation
Parent: London Gateway Port Holdings Limited
Officers: Mohammad Alhashimy, Secretary; Rashed Ali Hassan Abdulla Al Qahtani Al Qahtani [1971] Director/SVP & MD Europe & Russia [Emirati]; Mantraraj Dipak Budhdev [1986] Director/Solicitor; Francis Christopher Lewis [1954] Managing Director; Nicholas Paul Loader [1962] Finance Director; Alan Shaoul [1971] Business Development Director; Dirk Van Den Bosch [1958] Commercial Director [Belgian]; Robert Barclay Woods [1946] Director

London International Exhibition Centre Holdings PLC
Incorporated: 27 July 1998
Net Worth: £132,635,000 *Total Assets:* £132,635,000
Registered Office: 3 Bunhill Row, London, EC1Y 8YZ
Activities: Activities of head offices
Parent: ADCG (UK) Limited
Officers: Simon Price, Secretary; Humaid Matar Al Dhaheri [1978] Director [Emirati]; Dr. Omniyat Mohammed Jasim Al Hajeri [1974] Director Abu Dhabi Health Authority [Emirati]; Salah Saleh Salem Al Jaeedi [1963] Director/Chief Financial Officer [Emirati]; Ali Murshed Ali Murshed Al Marar [1971] Director/Senior Vice President Administration Al Hosn Gas [Emirati]; Hareb Mubarak Abdulla Mohammed Al Muhairi [1977] Director/SVP Corporate & International Affairs [Emirati]; Mohamed Najem Mohamed Al Qubaisi [1974] Director/Vice Chairman Abu Dhabi Global Market [Emirati]; Dr. Yousef Al Shaibi Khamis Al Sheryani [1975] Director/Consultant - DG Office Abu Dhabi Education Council [Emirati]; H.E. Saif Saeed Ahmed Saeed Ghobash [1982] Director General Abu Dhabi Tourism & Culture Authority [Emirati]; Michael James Henderson [1967] Director; Lord Thomas Jeremy King [1933] Director; Kevin Leslie Murphy [1953] Director; Steven John Norris [1945] Director

London International Exhibition Centre PLC
Incorporated: 30 October 1997 *Employees:* 197
Net Worth: £126,792,000 *Total Assets:* £322,095,008
Registered Office: 3 Bunhill Row, London, EC1Y 8YZ
Activities: Other business support service activities n.e.c.
Parent: London International Exhibition Centre Holdings PLC
Officers: Simon Price, Secretary; Humaid Matar Al Dhaheri [1978] Director [Emirati]; Dr. Omniyat Mohammed Jasim Al Hajeri [1974] Director Abu Dhabi Health Authority [Emirati]; Salah Saleh Salem Al Jaeedi [1963] Director/Chief Financial Officer [Emirati]; Ali Murshed Ali Murshed Al Marar [1971] Director/Senior Vice President - Administration Al Hosn Gas [Emirati]; Hareb Mubarak Abdulla Mohammed Al Muhairi [1977] Director/SVP Corporate & International Affairs [Emirati]; Mohamed Najem Mohamed Al Qubaisi [1974] Director/Vice Chairman Abu Dhabi Global Market [Emirati]; Dr. Yousef Al Shaibi Khamis Al Sheryani [1975] Director/Consultant - DG Office Abu Dhabi Education Council [Emirati]; H.E. Saif Saeed Ahmed Saeed Ghobash [1982] Director General Abu Dhabi Tourism & Culture Authority [Emirati]; Michael James Henderson [1967] Director; Lord Thomas Jeremy King [1933] Director; Kevin Leslie Murphy [1953] Deputy CEO & Commercial Director; Steven John Norris [1945] Director

London Kensington Hotel Limited
Incorporated: 3 September 2015 *Employees:* 69
Net Worth: £715,944 *Total Assets:* £131,277,344
Registered Office: 144-146 Kings Cross Road, London, WC1X 9DU
Activities: Hotels and similar accommodation
Parent: Kas No.12 Limited
Officers: Alykhan Kassam, Secretary; Navroz Nurmohamed Darvesh Bandali [1949] Director [Canadian]; Alykhan Kassam [1972] Director; Karim Shiraz Kassam [1974] Director

London Leasehold Flats Limited
Incorporated: 18 October 2005
Net Worth: £28,484,686 *Total Assets:* £110,577,192
Registered Office: 70 Grosvenor Street, London, W1K 3JP
Activities: Other letting and operating of own or leased real estate
Parent: Grosvenor Limited
Officers: Derek John Lewis, Secretary; Keith John Bailey [1979] Director/Chartered Surveyor; Roger Frederick Crawford Blundell [1962] Finance Director; Anna Clare Bond [1981] Director/Chartered Surveyor; Douglas Nigel Crichton [1976] Director/Chartered Surveyor; Simon Geoffrey Harding-Roots [1968] Director; Chantal Antonia Henderson [1975] Director/Accountant; Nigel Auriol Hughes [1957] Director/Chartered Surveyor; Richard Alexander Jefferies [1963] Operations Director; Craig David McWilliam [1972] Director/Chartered Surveyor; Paul Francis O'Grady [1985] Director/Chartered Surveyor; Amelia Mary Staveley [1986] Director/Chartered Surveyor

London Merchant Securities Limited
Incorporated: 12 March 1873
Net Worth: £1,470,011,904 *Total Assets:* £1,766,908,160
Registered Office: 25 Savile Row, London, W1S 2ER
Activities: Activities of other holding companies n.e.c.
Parent: Derwent London PLC
Officers: David Andrew Lawler, Secretary; John David Burns [1944] Director; Nigel Quentin George [1963] Director; Simon Paul Silver [1950] Director; David Gary Silverman [1969] Director; Paul Malcolm Williams [1960] Director/Surveyor; Damian Mark Alan Wisniewski [1961] Director

The London Metal Exchange
Incorporated: 6 May 1987 *Employees:* 476
Net Worth: £155,682,352 *Total Assets:* £195,007,264
Registered Office: 10 Finsbury Square, London, EC2A 1AJ
Activities: Security and commodity contracts dealing activities
Parent: LME Holdings Limited
Officers: Marcos Castro, Secretary; Sir Brian Geoffrey Bender [1949] Director/Retired/Portfolio; Laura May-Lung Cha [1949] Director [Chinese]; Matthew James Chamberlain [1982] Director; David Graham [1958] Director; Romnesh Lamba [1963] Director [Chinese]; Charles Xiaojia Li [1961] Director [Chinese]; Antony John Stuart [1952] Director; Dr Herta Von Stiegel [1957] Director; Kin Wah Stephen Yiu [1960] Director

London Metropolitan University
Incorporated: 11 March 1970 *Employees:* 1,017
Net Worth: £151,224,000 *Total Assets:* £279,728,000
Registered Office: London Metropolitan University, 166-220 Holloway Road, London, N7 8DB
Activities: First-degree level higher education
Officers: Christopher Ince, Secretary; Mark Russell Anderson [1961] Director; Rolande Jane Anderson [1955] Non-Executive Director, Genesis Housing; Rosemary Ann Benson [1969] Director/University Administrator; Timothy James Cochrane [1975] Director/Consultant; Patricia Anne Trow Croasdell [1980] Director/Civil Servant; Professor Lynn Dobbs [1957] Director/Vice-Chancellor; Margaret Ann Farragher [1973] Director of Education, CCEA; Renarta Kelly Guy [1979] HR Director; Harini Iyengar [1973] Director/Barrister; Anders Krohn [1992] Director/CEO (Aula Education Ltd) [Danish]; Catherine Emily McCabe [1966] Director/CEO, Proximity Insight; Michael Murphy [1954] Director/Business Consultant; Mohamediini Muse [1994] Director/Sabbatical Officer; Cecile Monique Tschirhart [1967] Director/University Manager [French]; Dr Shefaly Maya Yogendra [1971] Board Director and Strategy Consultant

London Power Networks PLC
Incorporated: 15 February 2000
Net Worth: £1,069,699,968 *Total Assets:* £3,695,699,968
Registered Office: Newington House, 237 Southwark Bridge Road, London, SE1 6NP
Activities: Distribution of electricity
Parent: UK Power Networks Holdings Limited
Officers: Andrew Charles Pace, Secretary; Kee Ham Chan [1963] Director/Chief Financial Officer; Loi Shun Chan [1962] Director [Chinese]; Hok Shan Chong [1948] Director [Chinese]; Christopher John David Clarke [1950] Director/Solicitor; Andrew John Hunter [1958] Director; Paul Robert Jeffery [1955] Director; Hing Lam Kam [1946] Director [Chinese]; Duncan Nicholas MacRae [1970] Director; Neil Douglas McGee [1951] Director [Australian]; Mei Fan Ngan [1965] Director [Chinese]; Basil Scarsella [1955] Director [Australian]; Charles Chao Chung Tsai [1957] Director and Chief Executive Officer [Canadian]; Chi Tin Wan [1950] Director [Australian]

London School of Economics & Political Science
Incorporated: 18 June 1901 *Employees:* 2,289
Net Worth: £510,023,008 *Total Assets:* £838,145,984
Registered Office: LSE, Houghton Street, London, WC2A 2AE
Activities: First-degree level higher education
Officers: Louise Clare Nadal, Secretary; Alastair John Dacosta [1964] Director/Solicitor; Chukwuzulum Elumogo [1996] Director/Student; John Charles Hughes [1961] Director/Consultant; William Nigel Hugill [1958] Director; Professor Simona Iammarino [1965] Director/Academic [Italian]; Professor Emily Meg Jackson [1966] Director/Academic; Susan Elene Liautaud [1962] Director/Consultant [French/American]; Akash Mehta [1994] Director/Student [Indian]; Roger Philip Mountford [1948] Director/Merchant Banker; Ali Nikpay [1970] Director/Lawyer; Dame Shirley Anne Pearce [1954] Director; Professor Terhi Rantanen [1953] Director/Academic [Finnish/British]; Dr Nemat Talaat Shafik [1962] Director; Lady Mechthild Elisabeth Talma Stheeman [1964] Director/Banking [German/British]; Alexander Voorhoeve [1975] Director/University Teacher and Researcher [Dutch/American]

London South Bank University
Incorporated: 12 August 1970 *Employees:* 1,387
Net Worth: £110,289,000 *Total Assets:* £287,739,008
Registered Office: 103 Borough Road, London, SE1 0AA
Activities: First-degree level higher education
Officers: James David Stevenson, Secretary; Stephen John Balmont [1960] Director/Pension Trustee; Shachi Blakemore [1975] Director/Chartered Accountant; Duncan Brown [1962] Director/Chartered Accountant; Jeremy Ewart Cope [1951] Director; Michael Andrew Cutbill [1962] Director/Business Consultant; Douglas Denham-St-Pinnock [1959] Director/Financier; Prof Peter Fidler [1947] Director/Retired University Vice Chancellor; Nelly Kibirige [1981] Director; Professor Hilary McCallion [1957] Director/Retired Nurse; Kevin David McGrath [1963] Director/Chartered Surveyor; Dr Mee Ling NG [1952] Director/Retired; Jenny Owen [1961] Director/University Lecturer; Jeremy Arthur Parr [1962] Director/Lawyer; Prof David Andrew Phoenix [1966] Director/Vice Chancellor; Tony Roberts [1967] Director/Head of Technical Support Services; Nazene Hassan Smout [1992] Director/Student [Dutch]

London Southend Airport Company Limited
Incorporated: 17 December 1993 *Employees:* 307
Net Worth Deficit: £26,726,296 *Total Assets:* £131,213,856
Registered Office: Third Floor, 15 Stratford Place, London, W1C 1BE
Activities: Scheduled passenger air transport
Parent: Stobart Aviation Limited
Officers: Warwick Brady [1964] Director; Ricky Martyn Jackson [1969] Finance Director; Glyn Jones [1958] Director/Chief Executive Officer

London Stock Exchange (C) Limited
Incorporated: 9 February 2012
Net Worth Deficit: £40,848,664 *Total Assets:* £645,733,184
Registered Office: London Stock Exchange (C) Limited, 10 Paternoster Square, London, EC4M 7LS
Activities: Non-trading company
Parent: London Stock Exchange Group PLC
Officers: Teresa Joanne Elizabeth Hogan, Secretary; Lisa Margaret Condron [1967] Director/Company Secretary; Mark Freedman [1968] Director/Accountant; Catherine Anne Thomas [1968] Director/Lawyer

London Stock Exchange Group Holdings (Italy) Limited
Incorporated: 20 January 2009
Net Worth: £1,173,566,080 *Total Assets:* £1,690,054,400
Registered Office: 10 Paternoster Square, London, EC4M 7LS
Activities: Non-trading company
Parent: London Stock Exchange Group PLC
Officers: Lisa Margaret Condron, Company Secretary; Raffaele Carlo Jerusalmi [1961] CEO Borsa Italiana & Director of Capital Markets [Italian]; David Porter Warren [1954] Director/Chief Financial Officer [American]

London Stock Exchange Group Holdings Limited
Incorporated: 20 January 2009
Net Worth: £27,381,000 *Total Assets:* £490,449,984
Registered Office: 10 Paternoster Square, London, EC4M 7LS
Activities: Non-trading company
Parent: London Stock Exchange Group PLC
Officers: Teresa Joanne Elizabeth Hogan, Secretary; Lisa Margaret Condron [1967] Director/Company Secretary; Mark Freedman [1968] Director/Accountant; Catherine Anne Thomas [1968] Director/Solicitor

London Stock Exchange Group PLC
Incorporated: 18 February 2005 *Employees:* 4,741
Net Worth: £3,227,000,064 *Total Assets:* £741,979,979,776
Registered Office: 10 Paternoster Square, London, EC4M 7LS
Activities: Activities of head offices
Officers: Lisa Margaret Condron, Secretary; Jacques Aigrain [1954] Director [French/Swiss]; Marshall Charles Bailey [1966] Director/Banker; Donald Hood Brydon [1945] Director; Professor Kathleen Derose [1960] Director/Professor [American]; Paul Heiden [1957] Director; Raffaele Carlo Jerusalmi [1961] CEO Borsa Italiana & Director of Capital Markets [Italian]; Stephen Paul O'Connor [1961] Director/Banker; Valerie Rahmani [1957] Director; Donald Austin Robert [1959] Director/Chairman; David Adam Schwimmer [1969] Director/Chief Executive Officer [American]; Andrea Sironi [1964] Director [Italian]; Ruth Wandhofer [1976] Director/Consultant, NED [German]; David Porter Warren [1954] Director/Chief Financial Officer [American]

London Stock Exchange PLC
Incorporated: 19 November 1986 *Employees:* 432
Net Worth: £420,900,000 *Total Assets:* £704,899,968
Registered Office: 10 Paternoster Square, London, EC4M 7LS
Activities: Administration of financial markets
Parent: London Stock Exchange Group PLC
Officers: Lisa Margaret Condron, Secretary; Baroness Sharon Margaret Bowles [1953] Director/Consultant on European Affairs; Donald Hood Brydon [1945] Director; Sherry Leigh Coutu [1964] Director [Canadian]; Paul Heiden [1957] Director; Mark Gerard Hoban [1964] Director/Member of Parliament; Denzil Manistre Benedict Jenkins [1967] Director/Head of UK Compliance & Group Regulatory Policy; Stephen Paul O'Connor [1961] Director/Banker; Nikhil Rathi [1979] Director/Chief Executive; David Porter Warren [1954] Director/Chief Financial Officer [American]

London Town Group of Companies Holdings Limited
Incorporated: 13 May 2010 *Employees:* 167
Net Worth: £102,884,872 *Total Assets:* £212,605,552
Registered Office: 8-14 Talbot Square, London, W2 1TS
Activities: Activities of head offices
Officers: Koolesh Dhiru Shah [1956] Director

London Town Group of Companies Limited
Incorporated: 8 August 1984 *Employees:* 167
Net Worth: £111,480,576 *Total Assets:* £212,601,248
Registered Office: 8-14 Talbot Square, London, W2 1TS
Activities: Activities of head offices
Officers: Koolesh Dhiru Shah, Secretary/Hotelier; Koolesh Dhiru Shah [1956] Director/Businessman; Dr Nikhil Koolesh Shah [1984] Director/Geophysicist

London Trocadero (2015) LLP
Incorporated: 5 December 2006
Previous: Slough Shopping Centre LLP
Net Worth: £7,829,797 *Total Assets:* £923,785,408
Registered Office: 16 Babmaes Street, London, SW1Y 6HD

London Underground Limited
Incorporated: 29 March 1985
Net Worth: £1,958,800,000 *Total Assets:* £20,205,099,008
Registered Office: 55 Broadway, London, SW1H 0BD
Activities: Urban and suburban passenger railway transportation by underground, metro and similar systems
Parent: Transport Trading Limited
Officers: Howard Ernest Carter, Secretary; Tanya Louise Coff [1962] Finance Director; Jill Louise Collis [1968] Director of Health Safety & Environment; Nigel Graham Holness [1966] Director; David Emrys Hughes [1970] Director of Strategy & Network Development; Andrew Martin Pollins [1967] Director

London Wall Capital Investments LLP
Incorporated: 21 October 2014
Net Worth: £192,928,096 *Total Assets:* £1,099,951,488
Registered Office: 6th Floor, 65 Gresham Street, London, EC2V 7NQ

London Wall Investment Warehouse 01 Limited
Incorporated: 22 October 2014
Net Worth Deficit: £61,000 *Total Assets:* £383,393,984
Registered Office: Fifth Floor, 100 Wood Street, London, EC2V 7EX
Activities: Other business support service activities n.e.c.
Parent: London Wall Capital Investment LLP
Officers: Mark Howard Filer [1967] Director

London Wall Mortgage Capital PLC
Incorporated: 11 February 2016
Net Worth: £62,000 *Total Assets:* £537,627,008
Registered Office: Fifth Floor, 100 Wood Street, London, EC2V 7EX
Activities: Other business support service activities n.e.c.
Parent: London Wall Mortgage Capital Holdings Limited
Officers: Mark Howard Filer [1967] Director

London Wall Outsourcing Freeholds Limited
Incorporated: 25 November 2013 *Employees:* 6
Net Worth: £192,588,992 *Total Assets:* £1,152,864,000
Registered Office: 140 London Wall, London, EC2Y 5DN
Activities: Management of real estate on a fee or contract basis
Parent: Telereal Investment Properties Limited
Officers: Aaron Jon Burns, Secretary; Adam Dakin [1962] Director; Graham Henry Edwards [1964] Director/Chief Executive Officer; Russell Charles Gurnhill [1970] Director; Michael Akiva Hackenbroch [1973] Director; Graeme Richard William Hunter [1963] Director

London Wall Outsourcing Limited
Incorporated: 28 November 2008 *Employees:* 241
Net Worth: £1,070,596,992 *Total Assets:* £1,964,824,960
Registered Office: 5th Floor, 140 London Wall, London, EC2Y 5DN
Activities: Activities of head offices
Officers: Aaron Jon Burns, Secretary; Adam Dakin [1962] Director; Graham Henry Edwards [1964] Director/Chief Executive Officer; Russell Charles Gurnhill [1970] Director; Michael Akiva Hackenbroch [1973] Director; Graeme Richard William Hunter [1963] Director

Londonmetric Property PLC
Incorporated: 13 January 2010 *Employees:* 31
Net Worth: £1,149,489,024 *Total Assets:* £1,826,616,064
Registered Office: 1 Curzon Street, London, W1J 5HB
Activities: Buying and selling of own real estate
Officers: Jadzia Zofia Duzniak, Secretary; Suzanne Lee Avery [1968] Director/Corporate Finance Advisor; Valentine Tristram Beresford [1965] Investment Director; James Fitzroy Dean [1954] Director; Robert Turner Fowlds [1961] Director; Andrew Marc Jones [1968] Director/Chartered Surveyor; William Andrew Livingston [1967] Director/Chief Executive Officer, Screwfix; Martin Francis McGann [1961] Director/Chartered Accountant; Alexander Gerard Pelmore [1953] Director; Mark Andrew Stirling [1963] Director/Chartered Surveyor; Lionel Patrick Vaughan [1947] Director; Philip Mark Watson [1948] Director; Rosalyn Susan Wilton [1952] Director

Londonmetric Retail Distribution I Limited
Incorporated: 10 May 2013
Net Worth: £238,266,912 *Total Assets:* £370,769,760
Registered Office: First Floor, 1 Curzon Street, London, W1J 5HB
Activities: Other letting and operating of own or leased real estate
Parent: Londonmetric Property PLC
Officers: Jadzia Zofia Duzniak, Secretary; Valentine Tristram Beresford [1965] Investment Director; Andrew Marc Jones [1968] Director/Chartered Surveyor; Martin Francis McGann [1961] Director/Chartered Accountant; Mark Andrew Stirling [1963] Director/Chartered Surveyor

Londonmetric Saturn Limited
Incorporated: 19 December 2012
Net Worth: £84,713,120 *Total Assets:* £138,567,088
Registered Office: 1 Curzon Street, London, W1J 5HB
Activities: Other letting and operating of own or leased real estate
Parent: Londonmetric Property PLC
Officers: Jadzia Zofia Duzniak, Secretary; Valentine Tristram Beresford [1965] Investment Director; Andrew Marc Jones [1968] Director/Chartered Surveyor; Martin Francis McGann [1961] Director/Accountant; Mark Andrew Stirling [1963] Director/Chartered Surveyor

Long Island Assets Limited
Incorporated: 24 November 2010
Net Worth: £3,731,258,880 *Total Assets:* £3,746,043,904
Registered Office: 1 Churchill Place, London, E14 5HP
Activities: Financial intermediation not elsewhere classified
Parent: Barclays Long Island Limited
Officers: Benjamin Adam Gerrard-Jones [1986] Director/Banker; Christopher Patrick Le Neve Foster [1981] Director/Banker; David James Rothnie [1982] Director/Banker; Vishal Shah [1984] Director/Banker

Longman Group (Overseas Holdings) Limited
Incorporated: 19 April 1961
Net Worth: £556,691,968 *Total Assets:* £608,614,016
Registered Office: 80 Strand, London, WC2R 0RL
Activities: Activities of head offices
Parent: Pearson Education Holdings Limited
Officers: Natalie Jane White, Secretary; Graeme Stuart Baldwin [1975] Director/Solicitor; Suzanne Margaret Brennan [1969] Director; Donna Elizabeth Houston [1965] Director/Chartered Accountant

Longmartin Properties Limited
Incorporated: 19 November 2004
Net Worth: £278,888,992 *Total Assets:* £466,899,008
Registered Office: 22 Ganton Street, Carnaby, London, W1F 7FD
Activities: Development of building projects
Shareholders: The Mercers' Company; Shaftesbury PLC
Officers: Penelope Ruth Thomas, Secretary; Brian Bickell [1954] Director/Chartered Accountant; Michael Alan Jones [1954] Director/Retired/Part-Time Consultant; Frederick William Scarborough [1949] Director/Chartered Surveyor; Arthur Jervoise Trafford Scott [1984] Director; Thomas James Chisnell Welton [1961] Director/Chartered Surveyor

Longstone Finance PLC
Incorporated: 29 December 2005
Net Worth Deficit: £42,174,124 *Total Assets:* £723,367,168
Registered Office: 35 Great St Helen's, London, EC3A 6AP
Activities: Financial intermediation not elsewhere classified
Parent: Longstone Finance Holdings Limited
Officers: Daniel Marc Richard Jaffe [1975] Director

Lonmin Public Limited Company
Incorporated: 13 May 1909 *Employees:* 24,060
Net Worth: £497,097,248 *Total Assets:* £866,473,152
Registered Office: 5th Floor, Connaught House, 1-3 Mount Street, London, W1K 3NB
Activities: Activities of head offices
Officers: Seema Kamboj, Secretary; Brian Richard Beamish [1956] Director [South African]; Kennedy Gcinumuzi Bungane [1974] Director [South African]; Gillian Amanda Fairfield [1971] Director/Lawyer; Jonathan Charles Alexander Leslie [1950] Director; Bennetor Magara [1967] Director [Zimbabwean]; Barend Johannes Van Der Merwe [1975] Director/Chartered Accountant [South African]; Varda Shine [1963] Director

Lonrho Africa (Holdings) Limited
Incorporated: 23 December 1970 *Employees:* 16
Net Worth Deficit: £193,418,032 *Total Assets:* £102,728,032
Registered Office: 10th Floor, 26-28 Hammersmith Grove, London, W6 7HA
Activities: Activities of head offices
Parent: Lonrho Holdings Limited
Officers: Nicholas Peter Taylor [1984] Director/Chief Investment Officer; Ashleigh Jane Woolf [1986] Director/Lawyer

Lonrho Holdings Limited
Incorporated: 24 April 2013 *Employees:* 779
Net Worth: £133,282,616 *Total Assets:* £233,548,880
Registered Office: 10th Floor, 26-28 Hammersmith Grove, London, W6 7HA
Activities: Activities of head offices
Shareholders: Rainer-Marc Frey; Thomas Max Schmidheiny
Officers: Ashleigh Jane Woolf, Secretary; Christopher Michael Chambers [1961] Director/Chairman; Rainer-Marc Frey [1963] Director [Swiss]; Dr Johannes Fritz [1954] Director/Head of Family Office [German]; Dieter Spalti [1961] Director [Swiss]

Lonrho Limited
Incorporated: 31 March 1993
Net Worth: £153,518,448 *Total Assets:* £153,518,448
Registered Office: 10th Floor, 26-28 Hammersmith Grove, London, W6 7HA
Activities: Activities of agricultural holding companies
Parent: Lonrho Holdings Limited
Officers: Christopher Michael Chambers [1961] Director; Rainer Marc Frey [1963] Director [Swiss]; Bruno Sidler [1957] Director [Swiss]; Dieter Paul Spalti [1961] Director [Swiss]; Ashleigh Jane Woolf [1986] Director/Solicitor

Loopsign No.2 Limited
Incorporated: 22 September 2008
Net Worth: £720,650,944 *Total Assets:* £720,650,944
Registered Office: Floor 6, Quadrant House, 4 Thomas More Square, London, E1W 1YW
Activities: Other business support service activities n.e.c.
Parent: Loopsign Limited
Officers: Richard John Livingstone [1964] Director; Leonard Kevin Sebastian [1969] Group Managing and Legal Director [Swiss]

Lotus Group Ltd
Incorporated: 3 May 1983 *Employees:* 450
Net Worth: £123,231,624 *Total Assets:* £221,102,176
Registered Office: Sandpiper House, 37-39 Queen Elizabeth Street, London, SE1 2BT
Activities: Activities of head offices
Major Shareholder: Peter Anthony Stephens
Officers: Christine Burrowes, Secretary; Christine Burrowes [1948] Director; John Christopher Phelps [1949] Director; George Ross [1952] Director; Peter Anthony Stephens [1950] Director

Louisville Securities Limited
Incorporated: 25 January 1995
Net Worth: £24,008,570,880 *Total Assets:* £34,172,938,240
Registered Office: Globe House, 4 Temple Place, London, WC2R 2PG
Activities: Activities of head offices
Parent: B.A.T Industries P.L.C.
Officers: Jonathan Michael Guttridge, Secretary; James Andrew Barrett [1974] Director; Robert James Casey [1948] Director/Attorney [American]; Steven Glyn Dale [1967] Director/Tax Adviser; John Benedict Stevens [1959] Director/Tobacco Manufacturer

Lovell Partnerships Limited
Incorporated: 22 May 1989 *Employees:* 985
Net Worth: £130,807,000 *Total Assets:* £331,323,008
Registered Office: Kent House, 14-17 Market Place, London, W1W 8AJ
Activities: Construction of commercial buildings
Parent: Morgan Sindall Group PLC
Officers: Clare Sheridan, Secretary; Steven Mark Breslin [1976] Finance Director; Steve Coleby [1973] Managing Director; Stephen Paul Crummett [1965] Finance Director; Justine Samantha Elliott [1975] Sales Director; David Edward Gough [1972] Commercial Director; John Christopher Leary [1960] Commercial Director; John Christopher Morgan [1955] Director

Low Carbon Contracts Company Ltd
Incorporated: 18 December 2013 *Employees:* 59
Total Assets: £16,010,862,592
Registered Office: Fleetbank House, 2-6 Salisbury Square, London, EC4Y 8JX
Activities: Other professional, scientific and technical activities n.e.c.
Parent: Secretary of State for Business, Energy and Industrial Strategy
Officers: Claire Anne Williams, Secretary; Anne Elizabeth Baldock [1959] Director; Anthony Oliver Bickerstaff [1964] Finance Director; Katherine Sara Collyer [1978] Director/Civil Servant; Catherine Gan [1971] Director/Chief Finance Officer - Accountant; James Anthony Keohane [1949] Director; David Roger Long [1969] Director/Civil Servant; Neil McDermott [1964] Director; Christopher John Murray [1956] Director; Dr Simon James Orebi Gann [1950] Director and Senior Advisor

Lowland Investment Company P L C
Incorporated: 20 September 1960
Net Worth: £439,896,000 *Total Assets:* £480,911,008
Registered Office: 201 Bishopsgate, London, EC2M 3AE
Activities: Activities of investment trusts
Officers: Duncan William Allan Budge [1955] Director; Dr Kevin Carter [1952] Director; Susan Gaynor Coley [1958] Director; Robert Sinclair Robertson [1951] Director; Karl Stephen Sternberg [1969] Director

LR (Baker St) Limited
Incorporated: 26 January 2005
Net Worth: £178,679,760 *Total Assets:* £179,504,432
Registered Office: Floor 6, Quadrant House, 4 Thomas More Square, London, E1W 1YW
Activities: Other business support service activities n.e.c.
Parent: LR Office Developments Limited
Officers: Leonard Kevin Sebastian [1969] Group Managing and Legal Director [Swiss]

LR (City Road) Ltd
Incorporated: 20 January 2014
Net Worth: £29,152,906 *Total Assets:* £128,679,616
Registered Office: Floor 6, Quadrant House, 4 Thomas More Square, London, E1W 1YW
Activities: Other business support service activities n.e.c.
Parent: London & Regional Group Investments Limited
Officers: Leonard Kevin Chandran Sebastian [1969] Group Managing and Legal Director [Swiss]

LR Baker St Mezz Borrower Limited
Incorporated: 22 June 2017 *Employees:* 1
Net Worth: £589,833,024 *Total Assets:* £709,154,688
Registered Office: Floor 6, Quadrant House, 4 Thomas More Square, London, E1W 1YW
Activities: Other business support service activities n.e.c.
Parent: LR Baker St Mezz Holdco Limited
Officers: Leonard Kevin Sebastian [1969] Group Managing and Legal Director [Swiss]

LR Baker St Mezz Holdco Limited
Incorporated: 22 June 2017
Net Worth: £144,614,944 *Total Assets:* £589,860,032
Registered Office: Floor 6, Quadrant House, 4 Thomas More Square, London, E1W 1YW
Activities: Other business support service activities n.e.c.
Parent: London & Regional (Baker Street) Holdings Limited
Officers: Leonard Kevin Sebastian [1969] Group Managing and Legal Director [Swiss]

LR Baker St Senior Holdco Limited
Incorporated: 23 June 2017
Net Worth: £589,865,536 *Total Assets:* £915,821,888
Registered Office: Floor 6, Quadrant House, 4 Thomas More Square, London, E1W 1YW
Activities: Other business support service activities n.e.c.
Parent: LR Baker St Mezz Borrower Limited
Officers: Leonard Kevin Sebastian [1969] Group Managing and Legal Director [Swiss]

LR Office Developments Limited
Incorporated: 2 September 2002 *Employees:* 2
Net Worth Deficit: £221,072,992 *Total Assets:* £371,424,000
Registered Office: Floor 6, Quadrant House, 4 Thomas More Square, London, E1W 1YW
Activities: Other business support service activities n.e.c.
Parent: London and Regional Group Finance Limited
Officers: Richard John Livingstone [1964] Director

LR Skipton House Limited
Incorporated: 17 August 2001
Net Worth: £80,255,416 *Total Assets:* £164,367,824
Registered Office: Floor 6, Quadrant House, 4 Thomas More Square, London, E1W 1YW
Activities: Buying and selling of own real estate
Parent: LR Skipton and Bloomsbury Ltd
Officers: Leonard Kevin Chandran Sebastian [1969] Group Managing and Legal Director [Swiss]

LS (Finchley Road) Limited
Incorporated: 17 March 2003
Net Worth: £146,184,992 *Total Assets:* £181,532,992
Registered Office: 100 Victoria Street, London, SW1E 5JL
Activities: Non-trading company
Parent: Land Securities Portfolio Management Limited
Officers: Elizabeth Miles [1977] Director/Solicitor

LS 1 New Street Square Limited
Incorporated: 29 August 2012
Net Worth: £259,603,008 *Total Assets:* £344,327,008
Registered Office: 100 Victoria Street, London, SW1E 5JL
Activities: Development of building projects
Parent: The City of London Real Property Company Limited
Officers: Elizabeth Miles [1977] Director/Solicitor

LS 62 Buckingham Gate Limited
Incorporated: 13 October 2004
Previous: LS Selborne House Limited
Net Worth: £398,792,992 *Total Assets:* £424,100,000
Registered Office: 100 Victoria Street, London, SW1E 5JL
Activities: Development of building projects
Parent: LS London Holdings One Limited
Officers: Elizabeth Miles [1977] Director/Solicitor

LS Ashdown Limited
Incorporated: 22 February 2001
Net Worth: £249,936,000 *Total Assets:* £315,142,016
Registered Office: 100 Victoria Street, London, SW1E 5JL
Activities: Other letting and operating of own or leased real estate
Parent: LS London Holdings One Limited
Officers: Elizabeth Miles [1977] Director/Solicitor

LS Buchanan Limited
Incorporated: 20 October 1988
Net Worth: £193,398,000 *Total Assets:* £274,824,000
Registered Office: 100 Victoria Street, London, SW1E 5JL
Activities: Renting and operating of Housing Association real estate
Parent: Land Securities Portfolio Management Limited
Officers: Elizabeth Miles [1977] Director/Solicitor

LS Cardiff Limited
Incorporated: 15 February 2001
Net Worth: £218,770,000 *Total Assets:* £327,521,984
Registered Office: 100 Victoria Street, London, SW1E 5JL
Activities: Other letting and operating of own or leased real estate
Parent: LS Cardiff (Holdings) Limited
Officers: Elizabeth Miles [1977] Director/Solicitor

LS Cardinal Limited
Incorporated: 15 October 2010
Net Worth: £856,644,992 *Total Assets:* £1,128,208,000
Registered Office: 100 Victoria Street, London, SW1E 5JL
Activities: Management of real estate on a fee or contract basis
Parent: LS London Holdings One Limited
Officers: Elizabeth Miles [1977] Director/Solicitor

LS City & West End Limited
Incorporated: 13 October 2004
Net Worth: £183,228,992 *Total Assets:* £188,348,000
Registered Office: 100 Victoria Street, London, SW1E 5JL
Activities: Development of building projects
Parent: LS London Holdings One Limited
Officers: Elizabeth Miles [1977] Director/Solicitor

LS Harbour Exchange Option Limited
Incorporated: 21 November 2007
Net Worth: £66,087,000 *Total Assets:* £108,122,000
Registered Office: 100 Victoria Street, London, SW1E 5JL
Activities: Development of building projects
Parent: LS London Holdings One Limited
Officers: Elizabeth Miles [1977] Director/Solicitor

LS Hill House Limited
Incorporated: 20 February 2001
Net Worth: £119,422,000 *Total Assets:* £120,818,000
Registered Office: 100 Victoria Street, London, SW1E 5JL
Activities: Other letting and operating of own or leased real estate
Parent: LS London Holdings One Limited
Officers: Elizabeth Miles [1977] Director/Solicitor

LS Lewisham Limited
Incorporated: 24 March 1988
Net Worth: £125,813,000 *Total Assets:* £129,509,000
Registered Office: 100 Victoria Street, London, SW1E 5JL
Activities: Development of building projects
Parent: Land Securities Portfolio Management Limited
Officers: Elizabeth Miles [1977] Director/Solicitor

LS London Holdings One Limited
Incorporated: 13 December 2007
Net Worth: £3,122,627,072 *Total Assets:* £3,392,847,104
Registered Office: 100 Victoria Street, London, SW1E 5JL
Activities: Other business support service activities n.e.c.
Parent: Land Securities PLC
Officers: Martin Richard Worthington [1978] Director/Accountant

LS Ludgate (No.1) Limited
Incorporated: 13 June 2011
Net Worth: £191,778,000 *Total Assets:* £253,495,008
Registered Office: 100 Victoria Street, London, SW1E 5JL
Activities: Non-trading company
Parent: The City of London Real Property Company Limited
Officers: Elizabeth Miles [1977] Director/Solicitor

LS Ludgate (No.2) Limited
Incorporated: 13 June 2011
Net Worth: £188,374,000 *Total Assets:* £281,847,008
Registered Office: 100 Victoria Street, London, SW1E 5JL
Activities: Non-trading company
Parent: The City of London Real Property Company Limited
Officers: Elizabeth Miles [1977] Director/Solicitor

LS Mirage Limited
Incorporated: 6 February 2012
Net Worth: £460,494,016 *Total Assets:* £559,720,000
Registered Office: 100 Victoria Street, London, SW1E 5JL
Activities: Other letting and operating of own or leased real estate
Parent: Land Securities Portfolio Management Limited
Officers: Elizabeth Miles [1977] Director/Solicitor

LS One New Change Limited
Incorporated: 22 February 2001
Net Worth: £503,796,992 *Total Assets:* £667,859,008
Registered Office: 100 Victoria Street, London, SW1E 5JL
Activities: Other letting and operating of own or leased real estate
Parent: LS London Holdings One Limited
Officers: Elizabeth Miles [1977] Director/Solicitor

LS Property Finance Company Limited
Incorporated: 25 June 2004
Net Worth: £22,684,000 *Total Assets:* £4,837,088,256
Registered Office: 100 Victoria Street, London, SW1E 5JL
Activities: Other business support service activities n.e.c.
Parent: Land Securities PLC
Officers: Marc Peter Cadwaladr [1972] Director/Chartered Accountant; Alastair Michael Deutsch [1983] Commercial Director; Julie Louise Fountain [1984] Director/Chartered Accountant [New Zealander]; Rosalind Charlotte Futter [1978] Director/Accountant; James Stephen Gillard [1977] Director/Treasurer; Martin Frederick Greenslade [1965] Finance Director; Martin Reay Wood [1960] Director/Treasurer; Martin Richard Worthington [1978] Director/Accountant

LS QAM Limited
Incorporated: 12 October 2000
Previous: Land Securities Reserve A Limited
Net Worth: £280,464,992 *Total Assets:* £500,934,016
Registered Office: 100 Victoria Street, London, SW1E 5JL
Activities: Non-trading company
Parent: LS London Holdings One Limited
Officers: Elizabeth Miles [1977] Director/Solicitor

LS Retail Warehouses Limited
Incorporated: 13 October 2004
Net Worth: £175,040,000 *Total Assets:* £178,248,000
Registered Office: 100 Victoria Street, London, SW1E 5JL
Activities: Development of building projects
Parent: Ravenside Investments Limited
Officers: Elizabeth Miles [1977] Director/Solicitor

LS Shepherds Bush Limited
Incorporated: 17 February 1986
Previous: Tops Shop Centres Limited
Net Worth: £110,194,000 *Total Assets:* £112,435,000
Registered Office: 100 Victoria Street, London, SW1E 5JL
Activities: Development of building projects
Parent: Land Securities Portfolio Management Limited
Officers: Elizabeth Miles [1977] Director/Solicitor

LS Victoria Circle Lp1 Limited
Incorporated: 7 October 2011
Net Worth Deficit: £646,000 *Total Assets:* £163,964,992
Registered Office: 100 Victoria Street, London, SW1E 5JL
Activities: Other business support service activities n.e.c.
Parent: LC25 Limited
Officers: Marcus Campbell Geddes [1975] Director/Chartered Surveyor; Elizabeth Miles [1977] Director/Solicitor

LS Victoria Circle Lp2 Limited
Incorporated: 7 October 2011
Net Worth Deficit: £646,000 *Total Assets:* £163,964,992
Registered Office: 100 Victoria Street, London, SW1E 5JL
Activities: Other business support service activities n.e.c.
Parent: LC25 Limited
Officers: Marcus Campbell Geddes [1975] Director/Chartered Surveyor; Elizabeth Miles [1977] Director/Solicitor

LS Victoria Properties Limited
Incorporated: 13 December 2007
Net Worth: £953,203,008 *Total Assets:* £963,771,008
Registered Office: 100 Victoria Street, London, SW1E 5JL
Activities: Other business support service activities n.e.c.
Parent: LS London Holdings One Limited
Officers: Elizabeth Miles [1977] Director/Solicitor

LS White Rose Limited
Incorporated: 14 November 2007
Previous: 20 Gillingham Street Limited
Net Worth: £343,312,000 *Total Assets:* £458,056,000
Registered Office: 100 Victoria Street, London, SW1E 5JL
Activities: Non-trading company
Parent: Land Securities Portfolio Management Limited
Officers: Elizabeth Miles [1977] Director/Solicitor

LS Zig Zag Limited
Incorporated: 28 March 2013
Net Worth: £213,368,992 *Total Assets:* £384,790,016
Registered Office: 100 Victoria Street, London, SW1E 5JL
Activities: Other letting and operating of own or leased real estate
Parent: LS London Holdings One Limited
Officers: Elizabeth Miles [1977] Director/Solicitor

LSEG (M) Financing Limited
Incorporated: 19 December 2016
Net Worth: £85,403,648 *Total Assets:* £312,862,720
Registered Office: 10 Paternoster Square, London, EC4M 7LS
Activities: Non-trading company
Parent: LSEGH (Luxembourg) Limited
Officers: Teresa Joanne Elizabeth Hogan, Secretary; Lisa Margaret Condron [1967] Director/Solicitor; Mark Freedman [1968] Director/Accountant; Catherine Anne Thomas [1968] Director/Solicitor

LSEG Business Services Limited
Incorporated: 4 April 2014
Net Worth: £16,826,800 *Total Assets:* £218,517,408
Registered Office: 10 Paternoster Square, London, EC4M 7LS
Activities: Other information technology service activities
Parent: London Stock Exchange Group (Services) Limited
Officers: Teresa Joanne Elizabeth Hogan, Secretary; Lisa Margaret Condron [1967] Director/Company Secretary; Chris Francis Corrado [1959] Director [American]; Ann Giacobbe Neidenbach [1962] Director/Chief Information Officer [American]; Catherine Anne Thomas [1968] Director/Solicitor; David Porter Warren [1954] Director/Chief Financial Officer [American]

LTG International Limited
Incorporated: 20 December 1993 *Employees:* 8
Net Worth: £41,919,444 *Total Assets:* £224,694,928
Registered Office: Chelsea House, West Gate, London, W5 1DR
Activities: Financial intermediation not elsewhere classified
Parent: Lewis Trust Group Limited
Officers: Clive Robert Lewis [1956] Director; Julian Harley Lewis [1954] Director; Michael Henry Rosehill [1960] Director/Chartered Accountant [Irish]

LTG Treasury Limited
Incorporated: 16 June 2017
Net Worth: £664,672,000 *Total Assets:* £664,675,072
Registered Office: Chelsea House, West Gate, London, W5 1DR
Activities: Financial management
Officers: Clive Robert Lewis [1956] Director; Michael Henry Rosehill [1960] Director/Chartered Accountant [Irish]

Ludgate Funding PLC
Incorporated: 28 September 2006
Net Worth: £16,000 *Total Assets:* £611,078,016
Registered Office: 6th Floor, 65 Gresham Street, London, EC2V 7NQ
Activities: Financial intermediation not elsewhere classified
Parent: Ludgate Funding Holdings Limited
Officers: Carl Steven Baldry [1966] Director; Sean Peter Martin [1965] Director

Ludgate Northumberland Holdings Limited
Incorporated: 20 January 2005 *Employees:* 147
Net Worth: £111,162,968 *Total Assets:* £169,693,456
Registered Office: Heywards, 2nd Floor, 21-22 Great Castle Street, London, W1G 0HZ
Activities: Renting and operating of Housing Association real estate
Shareholder: Dorothy Joanne Bahna
Officers: Mark Kronick, Secretary; Jonathan D Horowitz [1962] Director/Attorney [American]; Mark Kronick [1964] Director/Finance [American]; Allen Lorne Stevens [1943] Director/Executive [American]

Luminus Finance Limited
Incorporated: 27 November 2007
Net Worth Deficit: £11,915,000 *Total Assets:* £230,976,000
Registered Office: 80 Cheapside, London, EC2V 6EE
Activities: Financial intermediation not elsewhere classified
Officers: Christopher Paul Martin, Secretary; Matthew John Cooper [1977] Tax and Treasury Director; David Nigel Finney [1964] Managing Director; Michael Leslie Forrest [1955] Director of Studies in an Independent School; Andrew Winstanley [1978] Finance Director

Luminus Group Limited
Incorporated: 30 May 2003 *Employees:* 243
Net Worth: £165,146,000 *Total Assets:* £471,321,984
Registered Office: 80 Cheapside, London, EC2V 6EE
Activities: Development of building projects
Officers: Christopher Paul Martin, Secretary; Reverend Kevin Robin Burdett [1947] Director/Reverend; Patrick Laurence Egan [1957] Director; David Nigel Finney [1964] Managing Director; Michael Leslie Forrest [1955] Director of Studies in an Independent School; Lynette Lackey [1961] Director; Rita Elaine Mathews [1946] Director/District Councillor/Retired Accountant; Cecilia Mary Tredget [1959] Managing Director

Lur Berri International Limited
Incorporated: 1 December 2004
Previous: Lur Berri UK Limited
Net Worth: £156,156,272 *Total Assets:* £156,197,440
Registered Office: c/o Browne Jacobson LLP, 6 Bevis Marks, London, EC3A 7BA
Activities: Processing and preserving of fish, crustaceans and molluscs
Officers: Stephan David Gaude [1970] Director [French]; Olivier Gemin [1958] Director [French]; Frederic Jean Hiale-Guilhamou [1971] Director [French]; Mr Bertrand Massein [1978] Director/Farmer [French]; Sauveur Urrutiaguer [1959] Director [French]

Luxtail Limited
Incorporated: 15 April 2016
Net Worth Deficit: £1,154,184 *Total Assets:* £156,941,264
Registered Office: 35 Albemarle Street, London, W1S 4JD
Activities: Activities of other holding companies n.e.c.
Major Shareholder: Graeme Walter Briggs
Officers: Matthew Martin Farrell [1989] Director; Jonathon Ian Lee McLuskie [1990] Director

LW Theatres Group Limited
Incorporated: 8 May 2000 *Employees:* 210
Previous: Really Useful Theatres Group Limited
Net Worth: £64,686,000 *Total Assets:* £245,442,000
Registered Office: 65 Drury Lane, London, WC2B 5SP
Activities: Operation of arts facilities
Parent: Really Useful Theatres Entertainment Limited
Officers: Darren Peter Atkins [1974] Operations Director; Daniel James Freeman [1976] Finance Director; Rebecca Kane Burton [1975] Managing Director; Mark Gregory Wordsworth [1959] Director

LW Theatres Holdings Limited
Incorporated: 9 July 2009 *Employees:* 454
Previous: Really Useful Investments Limited
Net Worth: £57,420,000 *Total Assets:* £184,374,000
Registered Office: 65 Drury Lane, London, WC2B 5SP
Activities: Activities of head offices
Major Shareholder: Andrew Lloyd Webber
Officers: Daniel James Freeman [1976] Finance Director; Rebecca Kane Burton [1975] Managing Director; Lord Andrew Lloyd Webber [1948] Director/Composer; Lady Madeleine Astrid Lloyd Webber [1962] Director; Mark Gregory Wordsworth [1959] Director

LXI Property Holdings 1 Limited
Incorporated: 2 March 2017
Net Worth: £194,094,432 *Total Assets:* £327,915,328
Registered Office: Mermaid House, 2 Puddle Dock, London, EC4V 3DB
Activities: Activities of real estate investment trusts
Parent: LXI REIT PLC
Officers: Jamie Nigel Beale [1983] Director; Stephen Arthur Hubbard [1952] Director; Simon Lee [1976] Director

LXI Property Holdings 2 Limited
Incorporated: 31 March 2017
Net Worth: £130,019,912 *Total Assets:* £143,816,928
Registered Office: Mermaid House, 2 Puddle Dock, London, EC4V 3DB
Activities: Buying and selling of own real estate
Parent: LXI Property Holdings 1 Limited
Officers: Jamie Nigel Beale [1983] Director; Simon Lee [1976] Director

LXI REIT PLC
Incorporated: 21 December 2016
Net Worth: £211,980,992 *Total Assets:* £310,739,008
Registered Office: Mermaid House, 2 Puddle Dock, London, EC4V 3DB
Activities: Activities of real estate investment trusts
Officers: John Liberty Cartwright [1953] Director; Jeannette Elaine Etherden [1960] Director; Stephen Arthur Hubbard [1952] Director; Colin Deverell Smith [1947] Director

Ly Holding Limited
Incorporated: 12 June 2014 *Employees:* 2,336
Net Worth: £37,125,304 *Total Assets:* £129,641,072
Registered Office: 843 Finchley Road, London, NW11 8NA
Activities: Other business support service activities n.e.c.
Officers: Quang Anh Duy Ly [1987] Director/Business Executive [American]

LYB Treasury Services Ltd.
Incorporated: 2 October 2015
Net Worth: £1,301,030,400 *Total Assets:* £1,301,045,376
Registered Office: 1 Vine Street, London, W1J 0AH
Activities: Financial intermediation not elsewhere classified
Parent: Lyondellbasell Industries N.V.
Officers: Muhammad Adil Qureshi [1986] Director, Corporate Finance Manager; Frank Gerardus Maria Antonius Van ES [1959] Director, Financial Risk Management [Dutch]

Lycamobile UK Limited
Incorporated: 11 August 2006 *Employees:* 65
Net Worth: £18,996,000 *Total Assets:* £175,298,000
Registered Office: 3rd Floor, Walbrook Building, 195 Marsh Wall, London, E14 9SG
Activities: Other telecommunications activities
Major Shareholder: Allirajah Subaskaran
Officers: Aiadurai Sivasamy Premananthan [1963] Director/Businessman; Allirajah Subaskaran [1972] Director/Businessman

Lynwood Retail UK Limited
Incorporated: 17 June 2011 *Employees:* 3,313
Previous: Waterstones Holdings Limited
Net Worth Deficit: £12,157,000 *Total Assets:* £219,124,992
Registered Office: 4 Hill Street, London, W1J 5NE
Activities: Activities of other holding companies n.e.c.
Shareholders: Nikolai Mamut; Marina Groenberg
Officers: Alastair Robert Clifford Tulloch, Secretary; Rebecca David [1966] Director [Cypriot]; Marina Groenberg [1972] Director [Swiss]; Margarita Maksimenkova [1981] Director [Russian]

M & G Group Limited
Incorporated: 24 July 1959 *Employees:* 1,919
Net Worth: £748,876,032 *Total Assets:* £1,720,452,992
Registered Office: Laurence Pountney Hill, London, EC4R 0HH
Activities: Financial intermediation not elsewhere classified
Parent: M & G Prudential Limited
Officers: Sharna Ludlow, Secretary; Margaret Mary Ammon [1967] Director/Chief Risk Officer; Clare Jane Bousfield [1968] Director/Chief Executive Officer Insurance; Michael Jonathan Evans [1961] Director/Actuary; John William Foley [1956] Director; Beatrice Hannah Millicent Hollond [1960] Director; Colin Denis Keogh [1953] Director

M & G Investment Management Limited
Incorporated: 5 August 1968
Net Worth: £97,889,000 *Total Assets:* £139,242,000
Registered Office: Laurence Pountney Hill, London, EC4R 0HH
Activities: Security and commodity contracts dealing activities
Parent: M & G Limited
Officers: Margaret Mary Ammon [1967] Director/Risk Officer; Gary Nicholas Cotton [1969] Director/Business Manager; Neil Michael Donnelly [1972] Director/Compliance Officer [Irish]; John William Foley [1956] Director; Graham David Mason [1962] Director [South African]; Simon Humphrey Westland Pilcher [1966] Director of Fixed Income

M & G Limited
Incorporated: 4 April 1972 *Employees:* 1,583
Net Worth: £433,336,992 *Total Assets:* £839,422,016
Registered Office: Laurence Pountney Hill, London, EC4R 0HH
Activities: Activities of head offices
Parent: M & G Group Limited
Officers: David Gareth Jones [1966] HR Director; Nicholas Robert McMorran [1974] Finance Director

M & G. Securities Limited
Incorporated: 12 November 1906
Net Worth: £170,423,008 *Total Assets:* £729,380,992
Registered Office: Laurence Pountney Hill, London, EC4R 0HH
Activities: Financial intermediation not elsewhere classified
Parent: M & G Limited
Officers: Tara Christina Nelson, Secretary; Margaret Mary Ammon [1967] Director/Risk Officer; Gary Nicholas Cotton [1969] Director/Business Manager; Carolan Dobson [1954] Director; Neil Michael Donnelly [1972] Director/Compliance Officer [Irish]; Philip Robert Jelfs [1976] Product Director; Michelle Anne McGrade [1960] Director; Laurence John Mumford [1966] Director

M I Investment Holding Limited
Incorporated: 20 May 2005 *Employees:* 889
Net Worth: £69,791,000 *Total Assets:* £143,740,992
Registered Office: 2nd Floor, Bride House, 20 Bride Lane, London, EC4Y 8JP
Activities: Activities of head offices
Officers: Claire Elspeth Satow, Secretary; Alexander Sebastian Berry [1981] Director/Investor; William Alexander Berry [1978] Director/Investor; Claire Elspeth Satow [1958] Director/Accountant

M7 Real Estate Investment Holdings Holdco Ltd
Incorporated: 7 September 2017
Net Worth: £5,825,949 *Total Assets:* £129,836,336
Registered Office: 10 Queen Street Place, London, EC4R 1AG
Activities: Activities of real estate investment trusts
Parent: M7 Multi-Let REIT PLC
Officers: Christopher John Croft Sharland [1964] Director; Richard Martin Hamilton Croft Sharland [1969] Director/Chief Executive Officer; David Charles Ebbrell [1975] Director; Teresa Laura Harriet Gilchrist [1971] Director; Andrew Jenkins [1955] Director; Thomas Joseph Pearman [1979] Director and General Counsel; David John Simmonds [1969] Director/Chief Financial Officer; Jack Stuart Thoms [1972] Director/Surveyor

M7 Real Estate Ltd
Incorporated: 18 July 2013 *Employees:* 205
Net Worth: £44,700,000 *Total Assets:* £193,203,008
Registered Office: 10 Queen Street Place, London, EC4R 1AG
Activities: Other business support service activities n.e.c.
Officers: John Croft-Sharland [1964] Director; Richard Martin Hamlton Croft-Sharland [1969] Director/Businessman; David Charles Ebbrell [1975] Director; Anthony Peter David Edgley [1956] Non-Executive Director Chairman; Teresa Laura Harriet Gilchrist [1971] Director/Real Estate Investment Management; Andrew Jenkins [1955] Director; Chak Cheong Roger Lee [1962] Director/Engineer [Chinese]; John Julian Murnaghan [1977] Director/Surveyor [Irish]; Thomas Joseph Pearman [1979] Director/Businessman; David John Simmonds [1969] Director; Jack Stuart Thoms [1972] Director/Surveyor; Chi Wah Terrence Tsang [1975] Director/Investment Manager [Chinese]

Mabanaft Limited
Incorporated: 19 August 1994 *Employees:* 53
Net Worth: £42,760,000 *Total Assets:* £132,602,000
Registered Office: 5th Floor, Portland House, Cardinal Place, London, SW1E 5RS
Activities: Wholesale of other fuels and related products
Parent: Mabanaft UK Holding Limited
Officers: Eoin Michael Dilworth, Secretary; Martin Cook [1982] Director; Eoin Michael Dilworth [1973] Finance Director; Mark Robert Wayne [1969] Director/Businessman

Mabel Bidco Limited
Incorporated: 8 March 2011
Net Worth: £17,466,000 *Total Assets:* £251,844,992
Registered Office: 76 Wardour Street, London, W1F 0UR
Activities: Activities of other holding companies n.e.c.
Parent: Mabel Mezzco Limited
Officers: John Wilfred Rooney, Secretary; Kirk Dyson Davis [1971] Director; Andrew McCue [1974] Director [Irish]; Nicholas Charles Fraser Taylor [1974] Director; Emma Margaret Woods [1968] Director

Mabel Mezzco Limited
Incorporated: 8 March 2011 *Employees:* 5,719
Net Worth Deficit: £6,949,000 *Total Assets:* £279,979,008
Registered Office: 76 Wardour Street, London, W1F 0UR
Activities: Activities of other holding companies n.e.c.
Parent: Mabel Midco Limited
Officers: John Wilfred Rooney, Secretary; Kirk Dyson Davis [1971] Director; Andrew McCue [1974] Director [Irish]; Nicholas Charles Fraser Taylor [1974] Director; Emma Margaret Woods [1968] Director

Mabel Midco Limited
Incorporated: 8 March 2011 *Employees:* 6
Net Worth Deficit: £7,755,000 *Total Assets:* £133,375,000
Registered Office: 76 Wardour Street, London, W1F 0UR
Activities: Activities of other holding companies n.e.c.
Parent: Mabel Topco Limited
Officers: John Wildfred Rooney, Secretary; Kirk Dyson Davis [1971] Director; Andrew McCue [1974] Director [Irish]; Nicholas Charles Fraser Taylor [1974] Director; Emma Margaret Woods [1968] Director

Mabel Topco Limited
Incorporated: 8 March 2011 *Employees:* 5,719
Net Worth Deficit: £147,684,992 *Total Assets:* £280,056,992
Registered Office: 76 Wardour Street, London, W1F 0UR
Activities: Activities of other holding companies n.e.c.
Parent: TRG (Holdings) Limited
Officers: John Wilfred Rooney, Secretary; Kirk Dyson Davis [1971] Director; Allan Leighton [1953] Director/Chairman; Andrew McCue [1974] Director [Irish]; Nicholas Charles Fraser Taylor [1974] Director; Emma Margaret Woods [1968] Director

Mace Finance Limited
Incorporated: 4 May 2012 *Employees:* 4,741
Net Worth: £87,115,000 *Total Assets:* £989,419,008
Registered Office: 155 Moorgate, London, EC2M 6XB
Activities: Activities of construction holding companies
Officers: Carolyn Pate, Secretary; Mark Castle [1965] Director; David Richard Grover [1963] Director; Jonathan Mark Holmes [1961] Director; Dennis Vincent Hone [1958] Finance Director; Stephen Paul Jeffery [1965] Technical Director; Clare Anne Lewis [1968] Director; Gareth Mark Lewis [1962] Director; Jason David Millett [1965] Director; Lee James Penlington [1970] Commercial Director; Stephen Gerard Pycroft [1958] Director; Mark Peter Reynolds [1963] Director; Mandy Jane Willis [1970] Director/Tax Consultant

Mace Limited
Incorporated: 2 August 1989 *Employees:* 4,731
Net Worth: £62,308,000 *Total Assets:* £944,235,008
Registered Office: 155 Moorgate, London, EC2M 6XB
Activities: Development of building projects
Parent: Mace Group Limited
Officers: Carolyn Pate, Secretary; Mark Castle [1965] Director; Amy Elizabeth Chapman [1973] Director/Solicitor; David Richard Grover [1963] Director/Project Manager; Jonathan Mark Holmes [1961] Director/Construction Manager; Dennis Vincent Hone [1958] Finance Director; Stephen Paul Jeffery [1965] Technical Director; Gareth Mark Lewis [1962] Director/Project Manager; Jason David Millett [1965] Director/Project Management; Lee James Penlington [1970] Director; Stephen Gerard Pycroft [1958] Director/Project Manager; Mark Peter Reynolds [1963] Director/Project Manager; Mandy Jane Willis [1970] Director/Tax Consultant; Ian Martin Wylie [1940] Director/Construction Manager

MacFarlanes LLP
Incorporated: 28 January 2008 *Employees:* 585
Net Worth: £103,077,000 *Total Assets:* £132,864,000
Registered Office: 20 Cursitor Street, London, EC4A 1LT
Officers: Julian Francis Howard [1961] Member; Charles David Zelenka Martin [1961] Member; Peter William Abbott [1980] LLP Member; Jessica Helen Adam [1979] LLP Member; Alexander Rudolph Amos [1978] LLP Member; Jonathan David Arr [1983] LLP Member; Jatinder Bains [1977] LLP Member; Mark Baldwin [1963] LLP Member; Nicholas Edward Barclay [1975] LLP Member; Piers David Barclay [1972] LLP Member; Nicholas Andrew Barnes [1982] LLP Member; Camilla Clare Barry [1968] LLP Member; Andrew John Barton [1972] LLP Member; Neill Francis Kenneth Blundell [1970] LLP Member; Robert Samuel Boyle [1966] LLP Member; Clare Bruce Breeze [1970] LLP Member; Samuel Tempest Brooks [1982] LLP Member; Anthony Thomas Burnett-Scott [1965] LLP Member; Richard Edward Burrows [1980] LLP Member; Harry Robert Murray Coghill [1978] LLP Member; Robert Ivan Collard [1969] LLP Member; Andrew Jonathan Conder [1961] LLP Member; Howard James Corney [1974] LLP Member; Oliver Henry Court [1977] LLP Member; Damien Adrian Crossley [1978] LLP Member; Dominic Francis Cunliffe [1969] LLP Member; Angus Robert Dawson [1977] LLP Member; John Robert Stuart Dodsworth [1967] LLP Member; Barry Sean Donnelly [1962] LLP Member; Stephen Robert Drewitt [1970] LLP Member; Alexander James Edmondson [1980] LLP Member; Paul Martin Ellison [1981] LLP Member; Cameron Andrew Firth [1975] LLP Member; Richard Michael Fletcher [1980] LLP Member; Lora Claire Froud [1981] LLP Member; Norman Graham Gibb [1973] LLP Member; Christopher David Henry Good [1981] LLP Member; Charles Nicholas Cockerell Gothard [1972] LLP Member; Alexander James Stephen Green [1981] LLP Member; David Ashley Greenbank [1963] LLP Member; Nicholas John Samuel Harries [1971] LLP Member; William Thomas Hedges [1984] LLP Member; Justin Mark Arnold Hope [1980] LLP Member; Lois Evelyn Horne [1980] LLP Member; Kirstie Hutchinson [1971] LLP Member; Generald Victor Kelly [1968] LLP Member; Michelle Mary Kirschner [1978] LLP Member; Daniel Lavender [1969] LLP Member; Michael Daniel Sean Lavin [1967] LLP Member; Christopher Charles Lawrence [1972] LLP Member; Charles Alexander Lloyd [1964] LLP Member; Christopher Richard Henri Lyon-Dalberg-Acton [1977] LLP Member; Iain Halliwell Mackie [1967] LLP Member; John Daniel Keir Marriott [1980] LLP Member; Ian Christopher Martin [1966] LLP Member; Andrew Jonathan Mather [1975] LLP Member; Matthew James McCahearty [1977] LLP Member; James Howard McCredie [1981] LLP Member; Charles Harry Meek [1959] LLP Member; Jeremy Charles Moncrieff [1981] LLP Member; Colin James Morgan [1968] LLP Member; Isobel Mary Morton [1983] LLP Member; Ian Bertram Nisse [1956] LLP Member; Simon Nicholas Nurney [1966] LLP Member; Thomas Richard Pedder [1968] LLP Member; Andrew Elliot Perkins [1976] LLP Member; Simon Christopher Perry [1970] LLP Member; Steven Neil Pitchford [1964] LLP Member; James Nicholas Popperwell [1975] LLP Member; Luke Powell [1972] LLP Member; Sebastian James Prichard Jones [1973] LLP Member; Edward Nicholas Reed [1970] LLP Member; Ceinwen Ruth Rees [1982] LLP Member; Hayley Jane Robinson [1976] LLP Member; Stephen Charles Robinson [1968] LLP Member; Gideon Simon Sanitt [1976] LLP Member; Jennifer Michelle Smithson [1974] LLP Member; William Frederick Sykes [1977] LLP Member; Thomas Knyvett Usher [1968] LLP Member; Malcolm John Walton [1972] LLP Member; John Ralph Tristan Ward [1966] LLP Member; Sarah Louise Ward [1977] LLP Member; Douglas Wass [1975] LLP Member

Cameron Mackintosh Limited
Incorporated: 15 April 1980 *Employees:* 783
Net Worth: £208,628,352 *Total Assets:* £339,015,136
Registered Office: 1 Bedford Square, London, WC1B 3RB
Activities: Artistic creation
Officers: Richard Trevor Knibb, Secretary; Nicholas David Allott [1954] Director/Theatrical Producer; Alan Arthur Finch [1965] Director; Richard Arthur Johnston [1955] Director; Richard Trevor Knibb [1961] Director/Chief Financial Officer; Sir Cameron Anthony Mackintosh [1946] Director/Theatrical Producer; Robert Frederick Strang Noble [1965] Director

Macmillan Cancer Support
Incorporated: 30 June 1989 *Employees:* 1,715
Net Worth: £65,586,000 *Total Assets:* £283,772,000
Registered Office: 89 Albert Embankment, London, SE1 7UQ
Activities: Hospital activities
Officers: Elspeth Cox, Secretary; Dr Jagjit Singh Ahluwalia [1962] Director/Consultant Neonatologist; Iain Charles Andrew Cornish [1960] Director; Jane Frances Cummings [1961] Director/Chief Nursing Officer; Andrew James Duff [1959] Director; Professor Timothy George Eisen [1963] Director/Professor of Medical Oncology; Susan Carol Langley [1963] Director/Chairman; Feilim Mackle [1967] UK Sales and Service Director [Irish]; Richard Andrew Murley [1957] Director; Una Noelle O'Brien [1957] Director/Retired; Julia Charlotte Palca [1956] Director/Solicitor; Toby Emil Strauss [1959] Director

Macquarie (UK) Group Services Limited
Incorporated: 20 June 2007
Net Worth: £399,302,144 *Total Assets:* £1,062,174,720
Registered Office: Ropemaker Place, 28 Ropemaker Street, London, EC2Y 9HD
Activities: Other business support service activities n.e.c.
Officers: Helen Louise Everitt, Secretary; Warrick Booth [1964] Director/Banker [New Zealander]; Kathryn Elizabeth Burgess [1970] Director/Accountant [Australian]; Abigail Louise Nottingham [1978] Director/Chartered Accountant; Robert Michael Alan Thompson [1971] Director/Banker

Macquarie Aerospace Finance UK Limited
Incorporated: 25 February 2015
Net Worth: £227,682,336 *Total Assets:* £1,974,771,200
Registered Office: Ropemaker Place, 28 Ropemaker Street, London, EC2Y 9HD
Activities: Renting and leasing of air passenger transport equipment
Parent: Macquarie Aerospace Holdings UK Limited
Officers: Helen Louise Everitt, Secretary; Stephen Wesley Cook [1960] Director [Australian]; Timothy Sebastian Durham [1962] Director; Gregg MacAlister Walker [1967] Director

Macquarie Aerospace Holdings UK Limited
Incorporated: 25 February 2015
Net Worth: £141,738,240 *Total Assets:* £411,140,000
Registered Office: Ropemaker Place, 28 Ropemaker Street, London, EC2Y 9HD
Activities: Activities of other holding companies n.e.c.
Parent: Macquarie Airfinance Holdings Limited
Officers: Helen Louise Everitt, Secretary; Timothy Sebastian Durham [1962] Director; Liam James Kavanagh [1968] Director; Gregg MacAlister Walker [1967] Director

Macquarie Bank International Limited
Incorporated: 11 July 2007 *Employees:* 12
Net Worth: £207,712,000 *Total Assets:* £1,199,666,048
Registered Office: Ropemaker Place, 28 Ropemaker Street, London, EC2Y 9HD
Activities: Financial intermediation not elsewhere classified
Parent: Macquarie Holdings (UK) No.1 Limited
Officers: Helen Louise Everitt, Secretary; George Francis Onslow Alford [1948] Director/Banker; David Victor Fass [1963] Director/Banker [American]; Paul Christian Plewman [1972] Director/Banker [Irish]; Timothy Cardwell Wade [1959] Director [Australian]; Andrew Christopher Williams [1952] Director

Macquarie Capital (Europe) Limited
Incorporated: 28 January 1999
Net Worth: £208,650,672 *Total Assets:* £1,094,912,128
Registered Office: Ropemaker Place, 28 Ropemaker Street, London, EC2Y 9HD
Activities: Financial intermediation not elsewhere classified
Officers: Helen Louise Everitt, Secretary; George Francis Onslow Alford [1948] Director/Banker; Kathryn Elizabeth Burgess [1970] Director/Accountant [Australian]; David Victor Fass [1963] Director/Banker [American]; Paul Christian Plewman [1972] Director/Banker [Irish]; Daniel Chor Choy Wong [1975] Director/Banker [Australian]

Macquarie Commodities (UK) Limited
Incorporated: 14 October 2004
Net Worth: £215,918,848 *Total Assets:* £1,118,053,376
Registered Office: Ropemaker Place, 28 Ropemaker Street, London, EC2Y 9HD
Activities: Factoring
Parent: Macquarie Commodities Factoring Holdings (UK) Limited
Officers: Helen Louise Everitt, Secretary; Iain Douglas Hamilton Lappin-Smith [1965] Director/Banker; Shane McCarthy [1972] Finance Director [Irish]; Paul Christian Plewman [1972] Director/Banker [Irish]

Macquarie Commodities Factoring Holdings (UK) Limited
Incorporated: 30 March 2009
Net Worth: £220,722,384 *Total Assets:* £221,276,720
Registered Office: Ropemaker Place, 28 Ropemaker Street, London, EC2Y 9HD
Activities: Other business support service activities n.e.c.
Parent: Macquarie Commodities Finance (UK) Limited
Officers: Helen Louise Everitt, Secretary; Carmel Maree Ferguson [1973] Director/Banker [Australian]; Shane McCarthy [1972] Finance Director [Irish]; Paul Christian Plewman [1972] Director/Banker [Irish]

Macquarie Commodities Finance (UK) Limited
Incorporated: 14 October 2004
Net Worth: £222,009,568 *Total Assets:* £501,151,776
Registered Office: Ropemaker Place, 28 Ropemaker Street, London, EC2Y 9HD
Activities: Activities of other holding companies n.e.c.
Officers: Helen Louise Everitt, Secretary; Carmel Maree Ferguson [1973] Director/Banker [Australian]; Paul Christian Plewman [1972] Director/Banker [Irish]; Robert Michael Alan Thompson [1971] Director

Macquarie Euro Limited
Incorporated: 21 July 2011
Net Worth: £190,533,120 *Total Assets:* £1,139,362,688
Registered Office: Ropemaker Place, 28 Ropemaker Street, London, EC2Y 9HD
Activities: Financial intermediation not elsewhere classified
Parent: Macquarie European Investment Holdings Limited
Officers: Helen Louise Everitt, Secretary; Adam Frederick Lilley [1979] Director/Chartered Accountant; Sharand Maharaj [1984] Director; Robert Michael Alan Thompson [1971] Director

Macquarie European Investment Holdings Limited
Incorporated: 8 March 2007
Net Worth: £287,022,944 *Total Assets:* £706,162,048
Registered Office: Ropemaker Place, 28 Ropemaker Street, London, EC2Y 9HD
Activities: Activities of other holding companies n.e.c.
Parent: Macquarie Principal Finance UK Limited
Officers: Helen Louise Everitt, Secretary; Kathryn Elizabeth Burgess [1970] Director/Accountant [Australian]; Hamish Alexander Jones [1980] Director/Finance [Irish]; Adam Frederick Lilley [1979] Director/Chartered Accountant

Macquarie European Rail Limited
Incorporated: 15 October 2012
Net Worth: £85,603,944 *Total Assets:* £190,833,952
Registered Office: Ropemaker Place, 28 Ropemaker Street, London, EC2Y 9HD
Activities: Financial leasing
Parent: Macquarie Asset Finance Holdings Limited
Officers: Helen Louise Everitt, Secretary; Timothy Sebastian Durham [1962] Director; Michael Sims [1986] Director/Banker [Australian]; Jonathan Richard William Watkinson [1976] Director [Australian]

Macquarie Factoring (UK) Limited
Incorporated: 30 March 2009
Net Worth: £203,704,128 *Total Assets:* £353,697,632
Registered Office: Ropemaker Place, 28 Ropemaker Street, London, EC2Y 9HD
Activities: Factoring
Parent: Macquarie Commodities (UK) Limited
Officers: Helen Louise Everitt, Secretary; Marc Daniel Hari [1971] Director [Swiss]; Iain Douglas Hamilton Lappin-Smith [1965] Director/Banker; Shane McCarthy [1972] Finance Director [Irish]; Paul Christian Plewman [1972] Director/Banker [Irish]

Macquarie Group Investments (UK) No.2 Limited
Incorporated: 12 November 2010
Net Worth: £681,139,200 *Total Assets:* £681,241,984
Registered Office: Ropemaker Place, 28 Ropemaker Street, London, EC2Y 9HD
Activities: Financial intermediation not elsewhere classified
Shareholder: Macquarie Group Investments (UK) No.1 Limited
Officers: Helen Louise Everitt, Secretary; Kathryn Elizabeth Burgess [1970] Director/Accountant [Australian]; Abigail Louise Nottingham [1978] Director/Chartered Accountant; Robert Michael Alan Thompson [1971] Director/Banker

Macquarie Holdings (UK) No.1 Limited
Incorporated: 11 July 2007
Net Worth: £200,000,000 *Total Assets:* £200,000,000
Registered Office: Ropemaker Place, 28 Ropemaker Street, London, EC2Y 9HD
Activities: Activities of head offices
Officers: Helen Louise Everitt, Secretary; Kathryn Elizabeth Burgess [1970] Director/Accountant [Australian]; David Victor Fass [1963] Director/Banker [American]; Paul Christian Plewman [1972] Director/Banker [Irish]

Macquarie Infrastructure and Real Assets Core Limited
Incorporated: 27 February 2017
Net Worth: £55,169 *Total Assets:* £196,680,848
Registered Office: Ropemaker Place, 28 Ropemaker Street, London, EC2Y 9HD
Activities: Non-trading company
Parent: Macquarie Infrastructure and Real Assets Investments Limited
Officers: Danielle Shoemark, Secretary; Mark Kevin Cruikshank [1977] Director [Australian]; James Christopher Dyckhoff [1977] Director; Leigh Peter Harrison [1976] Director [Australian]; Philip Hogan [1973] Director

Macquarie Infrastructure and Real Assets Investments Limited
Incorporated: 10 October 2012
Net Worth: £50,978,136 *Total Assets:* £259,832,144
Registered Office: Ropemaker Place, 28 Ropemaker Street, London, EC2Y 9HD
Activities: Non-trading company
Parent: Macquarie (UK) Group Services Limited
Officers: Danielle Cherie Shoemark, Secretary; Mark Kevin Cruikshank [1977] Director [Australian]; James Christopher Dyckhoff [1977] Director; Leigh Peter Harrison [1976] Director/Banker [Australian]; Philip Hogan [1973] Director

Macquarie International Holdings Limited
Incorporated: 14 December 2000
Net Worth: £132,938,024 *Total Assets:* £501,500,736
Registered Office: Ropemaker Place, 28 Ropemaker Street, London, EC2Y 9HD
Activities: Activities of head offices
Parent: Macquarie Internationale Investments Limited
Officers: Helen Louise Everitt, Secretary; Holly Coleman [1974] Director/Chartered Accountant [Australian]; Abigail Louise Nottingham [1978] Director/Chartered Accountant; Robert Michael Alan Thompson [1971] Director/Banker

Macquarie Internationale Investments Limited
Incorporated: 7 November 2003
Net Worth: £160,070,496 *Total Assets:* £196,987,936
Registered Office: Ropemaker Place, 28 Ropemaker Street, London, EC2Y 9HD
Activities: Activities of head offices
Parent: Macquarie (UK) Group Services Limited
Officers: Helen Louise Everitt, Secretary; Kathryn Elizabeth Burgess [1970] Director/Accountant [Australian]; Abigail Louise Nottingham [1978] Director/Chartered Accountant; Robert Michael Alan Thompson [1971] Director/Banker

Macquarie Investments (UK) Limited
Incorporated: 9 November 2000
Net Worth: £382,547,584 *Total Assets:* £1,020,599,360
Registered Office: Ropemaker Place, 28 Ropemaker Street, London, EC2Y 9HD
Activities: Financial intermediation not elsewhere classified
Officers: Helen Louise Everitt, Secretary; Gourang Agrawal [1977] Director/Banker; Bernard Donnelly [1970] Director/Banker [Irish]; Robert Michael Alan Thompson [1971] Director

Macquarie Lending & Investment Partners LLP
Incorporated: 23 March 2011
Net Worth: £1,586,061,440 *Total Assets:* £1,590,259,840
Registered Office: Ropemaker Place, 28 Ropemaker Street, London, EC2Y 9HD

Macquarie Meters 3 (UK) Limited
Incorporated: 31 August 2010
Net Worth: £63,873,000 *Total Assets:* £1,023,539,968
Registered Office: Ropemaker Place, 28 Ropemaker Street, London, EC2Y 9HD
Activities: Financial leasing
Officers: Helen Louise Everitt, Secretary; Julian David Blair Liddy [1979] Director/Banker [Australian]; Stuart Mackie [1984] Associate Director, Asset Finance [Australian]; Luigi Tricarico [1970] Director/Banker [Australian]

Macquarie UK Passenger Leasing Limited
Incorporated: 16 May 2005
Net Worth: £12,254,000 *Total Assets:* £271,819,008
Registered Office: Ropemaker Place, 28 Ropemaker Street, London, EC2Y 9HD
Activities: Other business support service activities n.e.c.
Parent: Macquarie Asset Finance Holdings Limited
Officers: Helen Louise Everitt, Secretary; Stephen Wesley Cook [1960] Director [Australian]; Timothy Sebastian Durham [1962] Director; Michael Sims [1986] Director/Banker [Australian]; David John Weightman [1971] Director [Australian]

Macsco 22 Limited
Incorporated: 6 May 2010 *Employees:* 203
Net Worth: £42,783,000 *Total Assets:* £329,846,016
Registered Office: Moor House, 120 London Wall, London, EC2Y 5ET
Activities: Security and commodity contracts dealing activities
Officers: Sunil Dhall, Secretary; Richard Mark Brewster [1956] Director; James Martin Britton [1956] Managing Director; Alexander Corfield Key Carter [1971] Director/Stockbroker; Darren Carter [1966] Director/Banker; Andrew Charles Chapman [1961] Managing Director; Sunil Dhall [1974] Director/Chief Operating Officer; Steven Harvey Fine [1966] Director/Financial Services; Charles Gerard Peirs Hall [1968] Director/Stockbroker; Simon Hayes [1970] Director/Stockbroker; Edward Robeson Horton [1970] Managing Director, Sales; Iain Fraser Morgan [1971] Director/Market Maker; Neil Alan Utley [1962] Director

MacTaggart Heritable Limited
Incorporated: 3 September 2015 *Employees:* 14
Net Worth: £153,338,000 *Total Assets:* £219,180,992
Registered Office: 2 Babmaes Street, London, SW1Y 6HD
Activities: Buying and selling of own real estate
Shareholder: Philip Auld MacTaggart
Officers: William John Cane, Secretary; Peter Nelson Armstrong [1955] Director/Property; Rupert James Clarke [1958] Director/Banker; Hugh James Freund [1945] Director/Lawyer; William Karl David Laxton [1983] Director/Real Estate Private Equity; Sir John Auld MacTaggart [1951] Director/Chartered Surveyor; Philip Auld MacTaggart [1956] Director; Ivaylo Volodiev Ninov [1985] Director/Real Estate & Finance [Bulgarian]; John Harald Orneberg [1963] Director/Fund Manager [Swedish]; Robert Henry Haldane Peto [1950] Director/Chartered Surveyor

Maestro (Holdings 1) Limited
Incorporated: 20 December 2010
Net Worth: £9,237,000 *Total Assets:* £134,235,008
Registered Office: St Martin's House, 16 St Martins-le-Grand, London, EC1A 4EN
Activities: Activities of other holding companies n.e.c.
Parent: Infinis Wind Holdings Limited
Officers: Katerina Brown [1973] Director/Accountant; David Huw Griffiths [1970] Director; Scott Leitch MacKenzie [1969] Director

Maestro (Holdings 2) Limited
Incorporated: 20 December 2010
Net Worth Deficit: £11,595,000 *Total Assets:* £115,230,000
Registered Office: c/o Morton Fraser LLP, St Martins House, 16 St Martins-le-Grand, London, EC1A 4EN
Activities: Activities of other holding companies n.e.c.
Parent: Maestro (Holdings 1) Limited
Officers: Katerina Brown [1973] Director/Accountant; David Huw Griffiths [1970] Director; Scott Leitch MacKenzie [1969] Director

Magical Cruise Company, Limited
Incorporated: 6 February 1996
Net Worth: £1,312,439,552 *Total Assets:* £1,863,322,240
Registered Office: 3 Queen Caroline Street, Hammersmith, London, W6 9PE
Activities: Sea and coastal passenger water transport
Parent: Wedco Global Ventures LLP
Officers: Rebecca Suzanne Campbell [1961] Director/Business Executive [American]; Jr Diercksen [1968] Director/Business Executive [American]; Tasia Marie Filippatos [1972] Director/Business Executive [American]; Matthew David Grossman [1971] Director/Business Executive [American]; Steven Larry Konstanz [1958] Director/Business Executive [British/American]; Egbert Leonardus Swets [1965] Director/Business Executive [Dutch]; Jeffrey Norman Vahle [1963] Director/Business Executive [American]

Maintel Holdings PLC
Incorporated: 2 April 1996 *Employees:* 652
Net Worth: £27,063,000 *Total Assets:* £114,285,000
Registered Office: 160 Blackfriars Road, London, SE1 8EZ
Activities: Activities of head offices
Officers: William Drysdale Todd, Secretary/Accountant; John David Sebastian Booth [1958] Director; Edward Buxton [1961] Director; Stuart David Legg [1972] Sales Director; Angus John McCaffery [1966] Director; Dr Annette Patricia Nabavi [1952] Director; Kevin Stevens [1965] Director; Nicholas James Taylor [1966] Director; Mark Vincent Townsend [1963] Finance Director

Majedie Asset Management Limited
Incorporated: 24 May 2002 *Employees:* 58
Net Worth: £52,060,284 *Total Assets:* £125,762,688
Registered Office: 10 Old Bailey, London, EC4M 7NG
Activities: Security and commodity contracts dealing activities
Officers: John William Marshall Barlow [1964] Director/Fund Manager; James Sebastian Duppa de Uphaugh [1966] Director/Investment Manager; Christopher Field [1964] Director/Investment Manager; Robert Harris [1971] Director/Investment Manager; Christopher Andrew Simmons [1977] Director/Investment Manager

Majedie Investments PLC
Incorporated: 28 April 1910 *Employees:* 3
Net Worth: £178,626,000 *Total Assets:* £200,248,000
Registered Office: 1 Kings Arms Yard, London, EC2R 7AF
Activities: Activities of investment trusts
Officers: John William Marshall Barlow [1964] Director/Manager; Paul David Gadd [1965] Director/Solicitor; Robert David Charles Henderson [1948] Director; Jane Margaret Lewis [1963] Director [British/Australian]

Majority Kingdom Investment Limited
Incorporated: 17 October 2013
Net Worth: £298,464,768 *Total Assets:* £421,737,280
Registered Office: Level 37, 25 Canada Square, London, E14 5LQ
Activities: Activities of head offices
Parent: Primount LLP
Officers: Gina Anne Beredo [1974] Director/Attorney [American]; Raymond Leland Cushing [1954] Director/Treasurer [American]; Kathleen M Kennedy [1971] Assistant Director of Tax [American]

Mako Global Derivatives Partnership LLP
Incorporated: 22 January 2004 *Employees:* 7
Net Worth: £10,483,784 *Total Assets:* £498,951,168
Registered Office: 1 Snowden Street, London, EC2A 2DQ
Officers: Ashley Ball [1970] LLP Member; Paulius Chmieliauskas [1985] LLP Member; James Cole [1967] LLP Member; Jean Fouquet [1983] LLP Member; Michael Hugh Humphrey [1978] LLP Member; Paul Elliot John [1972] LLP Member; Richard Kirk [1982] LLP Member; Richards Robinson [1975] LLP Member; Graham Francis Windett [1983] LLP Member

Malmaison and Hotel du Vin Property Holdings Limited
Incorporated: 7 November 2006
Net Worth: £105,559,000 *Total Assets:* £545,097,984
Registered Office: 3rd Floor, 95 Cromwell Road, London, SW7 4DL
Activities: Other letting and operating of own or leased real estate
Parent: Malmaison Hotel du Vin Holdings Limited
Officers: Gustaaf Franciscus Joseph Bakker [1961] Director/Chief Executive [Dutch]; Peng Sum Choe [1960] Director [Singaporean]

Malmaison Hotel du Vin Brand Services Limited
Incorporated: 26 March 2014 *Employees:* 127
Net Worth: £2,400,000 *Total Assets:* £241,928,000
Registered Office: 3rd Floor, 95 Cromwell Road, London, SW7 4DL
Activities: Hotels and similar accommodation
Parent: Malmaison Hotel du Vin Holdings Limited
Officers: Gustaaf Franciscus Joseph Bakker [1961] Director/Chief Executive [Dutch]; Peng Sum Choe [1960] Director [Singaporean]

Malmaison Hotel du Vin Holdings Limited
Incorporated: 1 February 2000
Net Worth: £258,036,000 *Total Assets:* £288,036,000
Registered Office: 3rd Floor, 95 Cromwell Road, London, SW7 4DL
Activities: Activities of other holding companies n.e.c.
Parent: MHDV Holdings (UK) Limited
Officers: Gustaaf Franciscus Joseph Bakker [1961] Director/Chief Executive [Dutch]; Peng Sum Choe [1960] Director [Singaporean]

Malt Hill No.1 PLC
Incorporated: 24 February 2016
Net Worth: £37,311 *Total Assets:* £179,566,752
Registered Office: 35 Great St Helen's, London, EC3A 6AP
Activities: Financial intermediation not elsewhere classified
Parent: Malt Hill No.1 Holdings Limited
Officers: Paivi Helena Whitaker [1963] Director [Finnish]

E D & F Man Capital Markets Limited
Incorporated: 30 December 1976 *Employees:* 185
Net Worth: £119,953,296 *Total Assets:* £652,302,080
Registered Office: 3 London Bridge Street, London, SE1 9SG
Activities: Security and commodity contracts dealing activities
Parent: E D & F Man Holdings Limited
Officers: Gaynor Antigha Bassey, Secretary; Stephen Elton Hawksworth [1967] Director/Trader; Jacqueline Cecilia Kilgour [1963] Director; Ross George Reason [1961] Director; Christopher John Robert Smith [1958] Managing Director

E D & F Man Capital Markets Treasury Management PLC
Incorporated: 1 February 2016
Net Worth: £18,544,992 *Total Assets:* £125,916,544
Registered Office: 3 London Bridge Street, London, SE1 9SG
Activities: Activities auxiliary to financial intermediation n.e.c.
Parent: E D & F Man Holdings Limited
Officers: Richard John Aldis Askew, Secretary; Michael Gerard Broom [1957] Director/Accountant [New Zealander]; Laurie Peter Adrian Foulds [1969] Director/Chief Financial Officer; Paul Parness [1965] Group Tax Director; Deborah Elizabeth Singleton [1964] Director/Senior Treasurer; Terry Paul Moore Stroud [1963] Director/Global CFO - Capital Markets

MAN Group Holdings Limited
Incorporated: 11 February 1992 *Employees:* 5
Net Worth: £537,736,000 *Total Assets:* £594,125,504
Registered Office: Riverbank House, 2 Swan Lane, London, EC4R 3AD
Activities: Activities of head offices
Parent: MAN Group UK Limited
Officers: Elizabeth Anne Woods, Secretary; Fiona Jane Conway Blakemore [1974] Director; Tania Inge Maria Cruickshank [1977] Director/Legal Counsel; Michelle Robyn Grew [1968] Director/Compliance; Mark Daniel Jones [1980] Director; George Edmund Richard Wood [1966] Director/Manager

MAN Group PLC
Incorporated: 8 August 2012
Net Worth: £1,716,000,000 *Total Assets:* £2,976,999,936
Registered Office: Riverbank House, 2 Swan Lane, London, EC4R 3AD
Activities: Activities of head offices
Officers: Rachel Rowson, Secretary; Dame Katharine Mary Barker [1957] Director; Richard David Antony Berliand [1962] Director; Zoe Cruz [1955] Director [American]; John Michael Cryan [1960] Director; Stephen Luke Ellis [1963] Director; David Andrew Horton [1962] Director; Mark Daniel Jones [1980] Director; Matthew John Lester [1963] Director/Chief Finance Officer; Ian Paul Livingston [1964] Director; Debasish Satya Sanyal [1965] Director/Executive Vice President, Strategy and Regions, BP; Jonathan Edward Hugh Sorrell [1977] Director

MAN Group UK Limited
Incorporated: 23 June 2006 *Employees:* 4
Net Worth: £3,133,334,272 *Total Assets:* £3,134,629,888
Registered Office: Riverbank House, 2 Swan Lane, London, EC4R 3AD
Activities: Other business support service activities n.e.c.
Parent: MAN Investments Finance Limited
Officers: Elizabeth Anne Woods, Secretary; Fiona Jane Conway Blakemore [1974] Director; Tania Inge Maria Cruickshank [1977] Director/Legal Counsel; Mark Daniel Jones [1980] Director; George Edmund Richard Wood [1966] Director/Manager

E D & F Man Holdings Limited
Incorporated: 14 January 2000 *Employees:* 7,124
Net Worth: £595,428,160 *Total Assets:* £13,064,151,040
Registered Office: 3 London Bridge Street, London, SE1 9SG
Activities: Activities of head offices
Officers: Richard John Aldis Askew, Secretary; Mark Haynes Daniell [1955] Director; Laurie Peter Adrian Foulds [1969] Finance Director; Dr Wolfgang Helmut Heer [1956] Director [German]; Thomas Kolbl [1962] Director [German]; Rafael Muguiro Sartorius [1957] Director [Spanish]; Ross George Reason [1961] Director; Niels Vesterdal [1953] Director/Sugar Trader [Danish]

MAN Investments Finance Limited
Incorporated: 31 January 2006 *Employees:* 3
Net Worth: £2,747,108,096 *Total Assets:* £4,433,313,792
Registered Office: Riverbank House, 2 Swan Lane, London, EC4R 3AD
Activities: Other business support service activities n.e.c.
Parent: MAN Strategic Holdings Limited
Officers: Elizabeth Anne Woods, Secretary; Fiona Jane Conway Blakemore [1974] Director; Mark Daniel Jones [1980] Director; Michael Alexander Kasper [1982] Director [American]; George Edmund Richard Wood [1966] Director/Manager

MAN Investments Holdings Limited
Incorporated: 23 September 1988 *Employees:* 4
Net Worth: £165,829,600 *Total Assets:* £165,920,128
Registered Office: Riverbank House, 2 Swan Lane, London, EC4R 3AD
Activities: Other business support service activities n.e.c.
Parent: MAN Group UK Limited
Officers: Elizabeth Anne Woods, Secretary; Fiona Jane Conway Blakemore [1974] Director; Tania Inge Maria Cruickshank [1977] Director/Legal Counsel; Mark Daniel Jones [1980] Director; George Edmund Richard Wood [1966] Director/Manager

MAN Investments Limited
Incorporated: 27 January 1987 *Employees:* 127
Net Worth: £140,653,104 *Total Assets:* £183,859,888
Registered Office: Riverbank House, 2 Swan Lane, London, EC4R 3AD
Activities: Other business support service activities n.e.c.
Parent: MAN Investments Holdings Limited
Officers: Elizabeth Anne Woods, Secretary; Tania Inge Maria Cruickshank [1977] Director/Legal Counsel; Stephen Luke Ellis [1963] Director/Investment Manager; Michelle Robyn Grew [1968] Director/Compliance; Mark Daniel Jones [1980] Director; Deborah Claire Kester [1978] Director/Head of HR; Rachel Hannah Thomas [1974] Director/Legal Counsel

E D & F Man Limited
Incorporated: 11 December 1973 *Employees:* 517
Net Worth Deficit: £160,295,936 *Total Assets:* £135,442,768
Registered Office: Riverbank House, 2 Swan Lane, London, EC4R 3AD
Activities: Activities of head offices
Parent: MAN Group UK Limited
Officers: Elizabeth Anne Woods, Secretary; Fiona Jane Conway Blakemore [1974] Director; Tania Inge Maria Cruickshank [1977] Director/Legal Counsel; Geoffrey David Galbraith [1975] Director; George Edmund Richard Wood [1966] Director/Manager

MAN Mash Limited
Incorporated: 10 December 1992 *Employees:* 8
Net Worth: £215,501,248 *Total Assets:* £384,989,824
Registered Office: Riverbank House, 2 Swan Lane, London, EC4R 3AD
Activities: Activities of head offices
Parent: MAN Investments Holdings Limited
Officers: Elizabeth Anne Woods, Secretary; Fiona Jane Conway Blakemore [1974] Director; Mark Daniel Jones [1980] Director; Michael Alexander Kasper [1982] Director [American]; Benedict Malcolm Tibbalds [1973] Director/Investment Manager; George Edmund Richard Wood [1966] Director/Manager

MAN Strategic Holdings Limited
Incorporated: 22 April 1994 *Employees:* 7
Net Worth: £2,796,710,912 *Total Assets:* £2,796,930,048
Registered Office: Riverbank House, 2 Swan Lane, London, EC4R 3AD
Activities: Activities of head offices
Parent: MAN Group PLC
Officers: Elizabeth Anne Woods, Secretary; Fiona Jane Conway Blakemore [1974] Director; Stephen Luke Ellis [1963] Director; Michelle Robyn Grew [1968] Director/Compliance; Mark Daniel Jones [1980] Director; Jonathan Edward Hugh Sorrell [1977] Director; George Edmund Richard Wood [1966] Director/Manager

E D & F Man Sugar Limited
Incorporated: 8 December 1950 *Employees:* 126
Net Worth: £29,153,120 *Total Assets:* £544,923,776
Registered Office: 3 London Bridge Street, London, SE1 9SG
Activities: Agents specialised in the sale of other particular products
Parent: Agman Holdings Limited
Officers: Gaynor Antigha Bassey, Secretary; Mario Andres Galindo Garcia [1978] Director/Sugar Trader - Raw Sugar; Joseph Noel Kenny [1969] Director/Head of Sugar Business Unit [Irish]; Arthur Constant Stephane Rivoire [1979] Trading Director [French]; Johanna Louise Sutcliff [1970] Director

E D & F Man Treasury Management PLC
Incorporated: 21 January 2000
Net Worth: £154,662,560 *Total Assets:* £1,853,746,048
Registered Office: 3 London Bridge Street, London, SE1 9SG
Activities: Other business support service activities n.e.c.
Parent: E D & F Man Holdings Limited
Officers: Richard John Aldis Askew, Secretary; Michael Gerard Broom [1957] Director/Accountant [New Zealander]; Laurie Peter Adrian Foulds [1969] Director/Chief Financial Officer; Paul Parness [1965] Tax Director; Deborah Elizabeth Singleton [1964] Director/Senior Treasurer

MAN UK Strategies Limited
Incorporated: 21 August 2014
Net Worth: £31,662,272 *Total Assets:* £182,472,704
Registered Office: Riverbank House, 2 Swan Lane, London, EC4R 3AD
Activities: Other business support service activities n.e.c.
Parent: MAN Group Holdings Limited
Officers: Elizabeth Anne Woods, Secretary; Fiona Jane Conway Blakemore [1974] Director; Tania Inge Maria Cruickshank [1977] Director/Solicitor; George Edmund Richard Wood [1966] Director/Manager

Managed Pension Funds Limited
Incorporated: 15 July 2002
Net Worth: £15,048,000 *Total Assets:* £37,302,767,616
Registered Office: 20 Churchill Place, Canary Wharf, London, E14 5HJ
Activities: Pension funding
Parent: State Street Corporation
Officers: Vathoulla Sullivan, Secretary; Griffiths Ian Ashley Armfield [1956] Director; Alex Joseph Castle [1968] Director/Head of EMEA Operations; Scott Victor Sanderson [1971] Director/Chartered Accountant; William Derek Russell Street [1968] Director/Head of Investments, EMEA; Nigel David Wightman [1953] Director

Management Consortium Bid Limited
Incorporated: 11 August 1994 *Employees:* 65
Net Worth: £23,079,000 *Total Assets:* £182,166,000
Registered Office: 3rd Floor, 90 Whitfield Street, Fitzrovia, London, W1T 4EZ
Activities: Freight rail transport
Parent: Freightliner Acquisitions Limited
Officers: Geraint Rhys Harries, Secretary; Adam Lewis Cunliffe [1972] Managing Director; Gary Richards Long [1961] Director [American]; Charles Noble [1977] Director; Timothy Michael Shakerley [1972] Director

Mandarin Oriental Hyde Park (Investment) Limited
Incorporated: 25 October 1996
Net Worth: £100,187,000 *Total Assets:* £105,221,000
Registered Office: 3 Lombard Street, London, EC3V 9AQ
Activities: Hotels and similar accommodation
Parent: Mandarin Oriental International Limited
Officers: Craig Alan Beattie [1976] Director/Chief Financial Officer; Lesley Amanda Hyndman [1963] Director/Hotelier; Alexander Nicholas Kwok Wing Li [1986] Director; Philippe Alexandre Protto [1975] Regional Director of Finance [French]

Mandarin Oriental Hyde Park Limited
Incorporated: 29 March 2007
Net Worth: £78,505,000 *Total Assets:* £280,643,008
Registered Office: 3 Lombard Street, London, EC3V 9AQ
Activities: Hotels and similar accommodation
Parent: Mandarin Oriental London Limited
Officers: Craig Alan Beattie [1976] Director/Chief Financial Officer; Lesley Amanda Hyndman [1963] Director/Hotelier; Alexander Nicholas Kwok Wing Li [1986] Director; Philippe Alexandre Protto [1975] Regional Director of Finance [French]

Alexander Mann Group Limited
Incorporated: 8 May 1998 *Employees:* 3,386
Net Worth: £79,534,000 *Total Assets:* £208,446,000
Registered Office: 7 Bishopsgate, London, EC2N 3AQ
Activities: Activities of head offices
Parent: Newincco 781 Limited
Officers: Rosaleen Blair [1965] Managing Director [Irish]; Vanessa Ann Marie Byrnes [1973] Director of Client Delivery [Irish]; Matthew Rodger [1968] Client Services Director; Richard Keith Timmins [1960] Director

Alexander Mann Solutions Limited
Incorporated: 12 November 1986 *Employees:* 1,171
Net Worth: £55,970,000 *Total Assets:* £180,336,992
Registered Office: 7 Bishopsgate, London, EC2N 3AQ
Activities: Human resources provision and management of human resources functions
Parent: Alexander Mann Group Limited
Officers: Rosaleen Blair [1965] Director [Irish]; Vanessa Ann Marie Byrnes [1973] Director of Client Delivery [Irish]; Matthew Rodger [1968] Client Services Director; Richard Keith Timmins [1960] Director

Mansard Mortgages 2006-1 PLC
Incorporated: 3 August 2006
Net Worth: £3,889,049 *Total Assets:* £120,133,064
Registered Office: 35 Great St Helen's, London, EC3A 6AP
Activities: Financial intermediation not elsewhere classified
Parent: Mansard Mortgages 2006-1 Parent Limited
Officers: Susan Iris Abrahams [1957] Director

Mansard Mortgages 2007-2 PLC
Incorporated: 31 August 2007
Net Worth Deficit: £6,442,208 *Total Assets:* £303,262,912
Registered Office: Suite 2, 3rd Floor, 11-12 St James's Square, London, SW1Y 4LB
Activities: Financial intermediation not elsewhere classified
Officers: Sunil Masson, Secretary; Julius Manuel Bozzino [1970] Director; Sunil Masson [1971] Director; David Rudge [1970] Director

MAP Capital Limited
Incorporated: 4 May 2000
Net Worth: £15,891,000 *Total Assets:* £109,810,000
Registered Office: Fitzwilliam House, 10 St Mary Axe, London, EC3A 8EN
Activities: Non-life insurance
Officers: Paul Langridge, Secretary; Andrew Swift Foote [1968] Director/Investment Manager [American]; Aidan Kong [1965] Director/Underwriter; David Endon Stuart Shipley [1955] Director; Christopher James Smelt [1974] Director/Underwriter; Richard Kevin Trubshaw [1964] Director/Underwriter; Andrew John Westmore [1962] Director/Underwriter

Marathon Oil West of Shetlands Limited
Incorporated: 6 November 2000
Net Worth: £32,758,152 *Total Assets:* £254,471,648
Registered Office: 91 Wimpole Street, London, W1G 0EF
Activities: Extraction of crude petroleum
Officers: Jessel Nazir Shah-Gair, Secretary; Alistair Buchan [1965] Director/Non Operated Assets Manager; James Andrew Edens [1965] Director/Regional Vice President; Helga Fergus Sandison [1979] Director/UK Finance & Accounting Manager

Marble Arch Hotel (London) Limited
Incorporated: 28 November 2001 *Employees:* 220
Previous: Thistle Marble Arch Limited
Net Worth: £191,536,992 *Total Assets:* £200,411,008
Registered Office: 110 Central Street, London, EC1V 8AJ
Activities: Hotels and similar accommodation
Shareholder: GLH Hotels Limited
Officers: Susan Lim Geok Mui, Secretary; Neil Gallagher [1973] Director/Chief Financial Officer; Peter Michael Herbert [1980] Director/Chief Financial Officer; Kah Meng Ho [1966] Executive Director [Malaysian]

Marble Arch Residential Securitisation No. 4 PLC
Incorporated: 16 May 2006
Net Worth: £9,975,000 *Total Assets:* £271,896,992
Registered Office: Third Floor, 1 King's Arms Yard, London, EC2R 7AF
Activities: Other business support service activities n.e.c.
Parent: Marble Arch Residential Securitisation No. 4 Parent Limited
Officers: Robert Sutton [1978] Director/Financial Services [American]; Daniel Jonathan Wynne [1970] Director

Maref Topco Ltd
Incorporated: 27 November 2015 *Employees:* 351
Net Worth: £192,556,992 *Total Assets:* £267,028,992
Registered Office: Moorfield Group, 10 Grosvenor Street, London, W1K 4QB
Activities: Activities of other holding companies n.e.c.
Officers: Nicholas William John Edwards [1973] Director; Charles John Ferguson-Davie [1978] Director; Marc Edward Charles Gilbard [1962] Director

Marex Financial
Incorporated: 4 November 2005 *Employees:* 314
Previous: Marex Financial Limited
Net Worth: £134,705,344 *Total Assets:* £603,389,888
Registered Office: 155 Bishopsgate, London, EC2M 3TQ
Activities: Financial intermediation not elsewhere classified
Parent: Marex Spectron Group Limited
Officers: Scott Linsley, Secretary; Richard John Reid [1975] Director/Risk Officer; Paolo Roberto Tonucci [1968] Director/Accountant; Simon James Van Den Born [1967] Director [Dutch]; Robin Stewart Watts [1974] Director

Marex Spectron Group Limited
Incorporated: 4 November 2005 *Employees:* 509
Net Worth: £270,313,600 *Total Assets:* £787,351,936
Registered Office: 155 Bishopsgate, London, EC2M 3TQ
Activities: Financial intermediation not elsewhere classified
Officers: Scott Linsley, Secretary; John Hunter Baldwin [1967] Director [American]; Vittorio Pignatti-Morano Campori [1957] Director [Italian]; Joseph Charles Cohen [1967] Director; Lord Stanley Fink [1957] Director; Daniel Arthur Hallgarten [1961] Director HGT Management; Jeremy Michael Isaacs [1964] Director/Partner, JRJ Group; Peter Kadas [1962] Director/Principal [Canadian]; Ian Theo Lowitt [1964] Director [American]; Roger Benjamin Nagioff [1964] Director/Partner, JRJ Group; Henry David Penrose Richards [1984] Director/Investment Analysis & Execution; Carla Rosaline Stent [1971] Director; Paolo Roberto Tonucci [1968] Director/Accountant; Simon James Van Den Born [1967] Director [Dutch]

Marfrig Beef (UK) Limited
Incorporated: 20 November 2015
Previous: Keystone Foods (UK) Limited
Net Worth: £240,628,192 *Total Assets:* £461,645,952
Registered Office: 35 Great St Helen's, London, EC3A 6AP
Activities: Other service activities n.e.c.
Officers: Melissa Gabrielle Bourgeois [1983] Director; Marcos Antonio Molina Dos Santos [1970] Director/Entrepreneur [Brazilian]; Jose Eduardo de Oliveira Miron [1963] Director/Accountant [Brazilian]

Marfrig Beef International Limited
Incorporated: 20 November 2015
Previous: Keystone Foods International Limited
Net Worth: £373,473,376 *Total Assets:* £373,517,472
Registered Office: 35 Great St Helen's, London, EC3A 6AP
Activities: Other service activities n.e.c.
Officers: Melissa Gabrielle Bourgeois [1983] Director; Marcos Antonio Molina Dos Santos [1970] Director/Entrepreneur [Brazilian]; Jose Eduardo de Oliveira Miron [1963] Director/Accountant [Brazilian]

Marfrig NBM Holdings Limited
Incorporated: 15 December 2016
Net Worth: £40,688,688 *Total Assets:* £452,466,304
Registered Office: 35 Great St Helen's, London, EC3A 6AP
Activities: Activities of production holding companies
Shareholders: Marfrig Beef (UK) Limited; Marfrig Beef International Limited
Officers: Melissa Gabrielle Bourgeois [1983] Director; Marcos Antonio Molina Dos Santos [1970] Director/Entrepreneur [Brazilian]; Jose Eduardo de Oliveira Miron [1963] Director/Accountant [Brazilian]

Margolis and Ridley Limited
Incorporated: 26 April 1954
Net Worth: £2,095,000 *Total Assets:* £100,000,000
Registered Office: 3rd Floor, One New Change, London, EC4M 9AF
Activities: Activities of other holding companies n.e.c.
Parent: Ladbrokes Betting & Gaming Limited
Officers: Ross Martin Sandbach [1977] Finance Director; Charles Alexander Sutters [1980] Director

Maritime Drilling Holdings Limited
Incorporated: 30 November 2012 *Employees:* 780
Net Worth: £47,080,016 *Total Assets:* £412,209,312
Registered Office: Suite 1, 3rd Floor, 11-12 St James's Square, London, SW1Y 4LB
Activities: Non-trading company
Major Shareholder: Oswaldo Jesus Cisneros Fajardo
Officers: Gonzalo Fernandez Tinoco [1962] Director/Business Manager [Venezuelan]

Markel Capital Holdings Limited
Incorporated: 13 October 2008
Net Worth: £1,019,357,952 *Total Assets:* £1,028,029,632
Registered Office: 20 Fenchurch Street, London, EC3M 3AZ
Activities: Activities of head offices
Parent: Markel International Holdings Limited
Officers: Andrew John Bailey, Secretary; Andrew John Davies [1966] Finance Director; Nicholas James Stephen Line [1972] Director/Chief Actuary; Ian Marshall [1947] Director; Ralph Cameron Snedden [1947] Director/Chartered Accountant; William David Stovin [1961] Director; Richard Reeves Whitt [1964] Director/Chief Financial Officer [American]

Markel Capital Limited
Incorporated: 17 October 1995
Net Worth: £468,215,520 *Total Assets:* £2,269,119,744
Registered Office: 20 Fenchurch Street, London, EC3M 3AZ
Activities: Non-life insurance
Parent: Markel Capital Holdings Limited
Officers: Andrew John Bailey, Secretary; Andrew John Davies [1966] Finance Director; Nicholas James Stephen Line [1972] Director/Chief Actuary; William David Stovin [1961] Director; Richard Reeves Whitt [1964] Director/Controller Treasurer [American]

Markel International Insurance Company Limited
Incorporated: 20 November 1969 *Employees:* 15
Net Worth: £393,994,912 *Total Assets:* £1,588,570,368
Registered Office: 20 Fenchurch Street, London, EC3M 3AZ
Activities: Non-life insurance
Parent: Markel Capital Holdings Limited
Officers: Andrew John Bailey, Secretary; Andrew John Davies [1966] Finance Director; Paul Holt Jenks [1954] Director/Insurance Underwriter; Nicholas James Stephen Line [1972] Director/Chief Actuary; Hugh Avery John Maltby [1964] Director; Ian Marshall [1947] Director; Hannah Elizabeth Purves [1973] Claims Director; Ralph Cameron Snedden [1947] Director/Chartered Accountant; John William James Spencer [1957] Director; William David Stovin [1961] Director; Anne Whitaker [1958] Director; Simon Wilson [1978] Director

Marken Limited
Incorporated: 13 March 1980 *Employees:* 286
Net Worth: £154,599,008 *Total Assets:* £231,155,008
Registered Office: Ground Floor, 107 Power Road, Chiswick, London, W4 5PY
Activities: Other transportation support activities
Parent: De Facto 1341 Limited
Officers: Doaa Abdel Fathallah [1970] Director/Lawyer [American]; Andrew Scott Gravatt [1962] Director/Accountant; Joseph Mozzali [1970] Director/VP of Finance [American]; Wesley Potter Wheeler [1956] Director [American]

Marken Services Limited
Incorporated: 14 February 2013
Net Worth Deficit: £1,260,422 *Total Assets:* £204,914,848
Registered Office: Ground Floor, 107 Power Road, Chiswick, London, W4 5PY
Activities: Activities of other holding companies n.e.c.
Parent: Maze 3 Limited
Officers: Doaa Abdel Fathallah [1970] Director/Lawyer [American]; Andrew Scott Gravatt [1962] Director/Accountant; Joseph Mozzali [1970] Director/VP of Finance [American]; Wesley Potter Wheeler [1956] Director [American]

Market Data Limited
Incorporated: 21 January 2004
Net Worth: £381,300,992 *Total Assets:* £806,152,000
Registered Office: Cannon Bridge House, 25 Dowgate Hill, London, EC4R 2YA
Activities: Other business support service activities n.e.c.
Parent: IG Group Limited
Officers: Tony Lee, Secretary; Paul Richard Mainwaring [1963] Director; Bridget Elizabeth Messer [1979] Director [British/Australian]; Jonathan Mark Noble [1976] Director

Markit Group Limited
Incorporated: 22 March 2001 *Employees:* 881
Net Worth: £859,987,648 *Total Assets:* £7,994,546,176
Registered Office: 4th Floor, Ropemaker Place, 25 Ropemaker Street, London, EC2Y 9LY
Activities: Financial intermediation not elsewhere classified
Parent: IHS Markit Group Holdings Limited
Officers: Christopher Guy McLoughlin [1978] Director/Solicitor; Kathryn Ann Owen [1976] Accounting Executive Director

Markitserv Holdings Limited
Incorporated: 6 May 2009
Net Worth: £179,320,208 *Total Assets:* £184,435,552
Registered Office: 4th Floor, Ropemaker Place, 25 Ropemaker Street, London, EC2Y 9LY
Activities: Financial intermediation not elsewhere classified
Parent: IHS Markit Group Holdings Limited
Officers: Stefano Pietro Davide Maestri [1973] Director/MD; Kirston Gareth Winters [1978] Director/MD

Marks & Spencer Simply Foods Limited
Incorporated: 22 April 2003
Net Worth: £108,341,000 *Total Assets:* £522,369,984
Registered Office: Waterside House, 35 North Wharf Road, London, W2 1NW
Activities: Management of real estate on a fee or contract basis
Parent: Marks and Spencer PLC
Officers: Patricia Howell, Secretary; Steven John Bennett [1976] Director; Nicholas James Folland [1965] Director/Solicitor; Alistair James Willey [1976] Director/Accountant

Marks and Spencer (Bradford) Limited
Incorporated: 18 February 2016
Net Worth: £3,245,000 *Total Assets:* £111,417,000
Registered Office: Waterside House, 35 North Wharf Road, London, W2 1NW
Activities: Management of real estate on a fee or contract basis
Parent: Marks and Spencer PLC
Officers: Nicholas James Folland, Secretary; Steven John Bennett [1976] Director; Nicholas James Folland [1965] Director/Solicitor; Alistair James Willey [1976] Director/Accountant

Marks and Spencer Group P.L.C.
Incorporated: 23 July 2001 *Employees:* 84,621
Net Worth: £2,956,699,904 *Total Assets:* £7,552,699,904
Registered Office: Waterside House, 35 North Wharf Road, London, W2 1NW
Activities: Other retail sale in non-specialised stores
Officers: Nicholas James Folland, Secretary; Katie Bickerstaffe [1967] Director; Alison Jane Brittain [1965] Director; Andrew Raymond Fisher [1969] Director; Andrew Nigel Halford [1959] Director; Justin King [1961] Director; Pip McCrostie [1957] Director [New Zealander]; Archibald John Norman [1954] Director/Chairman; Stephen Joseph Rowe [1967] Director; Humphrey Stewart Morgan Singer [1965] Director/Accountant

Marks and Spencer Guernsey Investments Limited Liability Partnership
Incorporated: 17 September 2009
Net Worth: £228,972,080 *Total Assets:* £229,047,536
Registered Office: Waterside House, 35 North Wharf Road, London, W2 1NW

Marks and Spencer International Holdings Limited
Incorporated: 28 May 1991
Net Worth: £642,651,008 *Total Assets:* £691,219,008
Registered Office: Waterside House, 35 North Wharf Road, London, W2 1NW
Activities: Activities of head offices
Parent: Marks and Spencer PLC
Officers: Patricia Howell, Secretary; Nicholas James Folland [1965] Director/Solicitor; Andrew Scott Holmes [1975] Director; Humphrey Stewart Morgan Singer [1965] Director

Marks and Spencer Investments
Incorporated: 17 September 2003
Net Worth: £159,832,000 *Total Assets:* £160,011,008
Registered Office: Waterside House, 35 North Wharf Road, London, W2 1NW
Activities: Financial intermediation not elsewhere classified
Parent: Marks and Spencer (Nederland) B.V.
Officers: Patricia Howell, Secretary; Nicholas James Folland [1965] Director/Solicitor; Joanna Marageret Hawkes [1961] Director; Patricia Howell [1972] Director/Solicitor

Marks and Spencer P.L.C.
Incorporated: 17 June 1926 *Employees:* 84,621
Net Worth: £5,512,500,224 *Total Assets:* £10,109,400,064
Registered Office: Waterside House, 35 North Wharf Road, London, W2 1NW
Activities: Other retail sale in non-specialised stores
Parent: Marks and Spencer Group PLC
Officers: Nicholas James Folland, Secretary; Nicholas James Folland [1965] Director/Solicitor; Stephen Joseph Rowe [1967] Director; Humphrey Stewart Morgan Singer [1965] Director

Marlbray Limited
Incorporated: 28 May 2003
Net Worth Deficit: £24,906,000 *Total Assets:* £228,660,992
Registered Office: 2nd Floor, County Hall, Riverside Building, Belvedere Road, London, SE1 7GP
Activities: Hotels and similar accommodation
Officers: Inbar Zilberman, Secretary; Victoria Ebbon [1979] Director/Regional Financial Controller; Greg Hegarty [1977] Director/Chief Commercial Officer

Marsh & McLennan Companies Acquisition Limited
Incorporated: 27 January 2015
Net Worth: £364,779,296 *Total Assets:* £365,533,696
Registered Office: 1 Tower Place West, Tower Place, London, EC3R 5BU
Activities: Activities of other holding companies n.e.c.
Parent: Marsh & McLennan Companies Acquisition Funding Limited
Officers: Claire Margaret Valentine, Secretary; Mark Christopher Chessher [1960] Director/Accountant; Joseph Christopher Grogan [1956] Director/Insurance Broker [Irish]

Marsh & McLennan Companies UK Limited
Incorporated: 5 May 1995
Net Worth: £2,199,015,680 *Total Assets:* £2,214,318,592
Registered Office: 1 Tower Place West, Tower Place, London, EC3R 5BU
Activities: Activities of head offices
Parent: MMC Holdings (UK) Limited
Officers: Wendy Patricia Marsh, Secretary; Mark Christopher Chessher [1960] Director/Accountant; Fiona Stewart Dunsire [1966] Director/Actuary; Ferdinand Gerhard Jahnel [1965] Director/Treasurer [American]; Christopher John Lay [1961] Director/Insurance Broker; David Nicholas Williams [1971] Director/Accountant

Marsh Corporate Services Limited
Incorporated: 24 July 1947
Net Worth: £84,400,000 *Total Assets:* £185,100,000
Registered Office: 1 Tower Place West, Tower Place, London, EC3R 5BU
Activities: Other business support service activities n.e.c.
Parent: Sedgwick Group Limited
Officers: Wendy Patricia Marsh, Secretary; David James Bruce [1966] Director/Chief Operating Officer; Aileen Johanna Croft [1962] Director [Irish]

Marsh Limited
Incorporated: 11 July 1980
Net Worth: £1,392,300,032 *Total Assets:* £2,699,399,936
Registered Office: 1 Tower Place West, Tower Place, London, EC3R 5BU
Activities: Activities of insurance agents and brokers
Parent: MMC UK Group Limited
Officers: Claire Margaret Valentine, Secretary; Jane Victoria Barker [1949] Director; Philip Andrew Barton [1962] Director/CEO (Insurance); Mark Christopher Chessher [1960] Director/Accountant; Thomas Colraine [1958] Director/Accountant; John Raymond Hirst [1952] Director; Ailsa Jane King [1965] Director/Chief Client Officer; Christopher John Lay [1961] Director/Insurance Broker; Paul Edward Moody [1967] Director/CEO, UK Specialties; James Harwood Nash [1965] Director/Reinsurance Broker; Roy Ian White [1958] Director/Insurance Broker

Marsh Services Limited
Incorporated: 5 May 1995 *Employees:* 3,754
Net Worth Deficit: £101,100,000 *Total Assets:* £853,000,000
Registered Office: 1 Tower Place West, Tower Place, London, EC3R 5BU
Activities: Other business support service activities n.e.c.
Parent: MMC UK Group Limited
Officers: Wendy Patricia Marsh, Secretary; Aileen Johanna Croft [1962] Director [Irish]; Katherine Jane Hamilton [1968] Director/Head of International HR; Andrew Christopher Herring [1963] Director/Insurance Broker; Roy Ian White [1958] Director/Insurance Broker

Marsh Treasury Services Limited
Incorporated: 14 April 1960
Net Worth: £83,400,000 *Total Assets:* £252,600,000
Registered Office: 1 Tower Place West, Tower Place, London, EC3R 5BU
Activities: Financial intermediation not elsewhere classified
Parent: Sedgwick Group Limited
Officers: Wendy Patricia Marsh, Secretary; Justin Bruce Broad [1968] Director/Treasurer; Caroline Wendy Godwin [1962] Director/Accountant; Ian Richard Hadley [1964] Director/Treasurer; Ferdinand Gerhard Jahnel [1965] Director/Treasurer [American]

Marston Properties Holdings Limited
Incorporated: 15 March 2000 *Employees:* 36
Net Worth: £137,974,384 *Total Assets:* £174,338,784
Registered Office: 1 Mills Yard, Fulham, London, SW6 3AQ
Activities: Activities of head offices
Shareholders: Nicola Jane Marston; Caroline Louise Marston; Michael Jonathon Daniels
Officers: Noreen Samya Tapp, Secretary; Michael Jonathon Daniels [1952] Director/Solicitor; Caroline Louise Marston [1962] Managing Director Designer; John James Shepherd Marston [1935] Civil Engineer/Director; David Arthur Thomas Robinson [1946] Director/Business Adviser; Noreen Samya Tapp [1972] Director/Accountant; David Mark Tonge [1958] Director

Marston Properties Limited
Incorporated: 2 March 1938 *Employees:* 31
Net Worth: £128,458,168 *Total Assets:* £168,913,168
Registered Office: 1 Mills Yard, Fulham, London, SW6 3AQ
Activities: Other letting and operating of own or leased real estate
Parent: Marston Properties Holdings Limited
Officers: Noreen Samya Tapp, Secretary; Caroline Louise Marston [1962] Director/Interior Designer; John James Shepherd Marston [1935] Director/Civil Engineer; Noreen Samya Tapp [1972] Director/Accountant

Marston's Issuer PLC
Incorporated: 21 May 2004
Net Worth: £100,000 *Total Assets:* £1,059,299,968
Registered Office: Third Floor, 1 King's Arms Yard, London, EC2R 7AF
Activities: Other business support service activities n.e.c.
Parent: Marston's Issuer Parent Limited
Officers: Robert Sutton [1978] Director/Financial Services [American]; Daniel Jonathan Wynne [1970] Director

Martin Pecheur Sterling Investments Limited
Incorporated: 19 November 2012
Net Worth: £272,225,984 *Total Assets:* £275,713,984
Registered Office: 3 Sheldon Square, Paddington, London, W2 6PX
Activities: Other business support service activities n.e.c.
Parent: Sheldon Holdings Limited
Officers: Paul Moore, Secretary; Jean-Noel Hughes Roger Groleau [1974] Director [French]; Paul Anthony Moore [1970] Director/Company Secretary

Martin's Family Holdings Ltd
Incorporated: 24 June 2016 *Employees:* 23
Net Worth: £222,634,400 *Total Assets:* £332,118,144
Registered Office: 6th Floor, 25 Farringdon Street, London, EC4A 4AB
Activities: Activities of other holding companies n.e.c.
Shareholders: Rex Daniel Newman; Emma Catherine Carlton-Smith; Beth Christian Gilbey; Thomas Henry Martin
Officers: Emma Catherine Carlton-Smith [1967] Director; Beth Christian Gilbey [1971] Director; Thomas Henry Martin [1966] Director; Rex Daniel Newman [1957] Director/Lawyer; Paul William Nicholson [1957] Director

Martin's Properties Holdings Limited
Incorporated: 17 July 1963 *Employees:* 23
Previous: Radnor Walk Investments Limited
Net Worth: £221,085,200 *Total Assets:* £330,562,336
Registered Office: 6th Floor, 25 Farringdon Street, London, EC4A 4AB
Activities: Development of building projects
Parent: Martin's Family Holdings Ltd
Officers: Richard Charles Bourne [1979] Property Director; Emma Catherine Carlton-Smith [1967] Director/Designer; Michael Richard Hussey [1965] Director/Chief Executive; Thomas Henry Martin [1966] Director/Surveyor; Jane Moriarty [1964] Director/Chartered Accountant [Irish]; Rex Daniel Newman [1957] Director/Lawyer; Balbinder Singh Tattar [1964] Finance Director

Marubeni Copper Holdings Limited
Incorporated: 8 March 2016 *Employees:* 9
Net Worth: £987,485,376 *Total Assets:* £987,988,736
Registered Office: 95 Gresham Street, London, EC2V 7AB
Activities: Other mining and quarrying n.e.c.
Parent: Marubeni LP Holding B.V.
Officers: Hajime Ichiki [1956] Director [Japanese]; Shuichi Kamizono [1965] Director [Japanese]; Daisuke Tsuchiya [1967] Director [Japanese]

Marubeni Europe PLC
Incorporated: 11 February 1985 *Employees:* 167
Net Worth: £213,564,160 *Total Assets:* £339,178,240
Registered Office: 95 Gresham Street, London, EC2V 7AB
Activities: Non-specialised wholesale trade
Parent: Marubeni Corporation
Officers: Michael Hammill, Secretary; Tomohiko Hirano [1963] Director [Japanese]; Mutsumi Ishizuki [1958] Managing Director [Japanese]; Jun Kakizoe [1963] Director [Japanese]; Shuichi Kamizono [1965] Director [Japanese]; Takeshi Motoyama [1962] Director [Japanese]

Marubeni Finance Europe PLC
Incorporated: 9 March 2012 *Employees:* 3
Net Worth: £238,385,680 *Total Assets:* £1,211,043,328
Registered Office: 95 Gresham Street, London, EC2V 7AB
Activities: Financial intermediation not elsewhere classified
Parent: Marubeni Corporation
Officers: Michael Hammill, Secretary; Shuichi Kamizono [1965] Director [Japanese]; Hiroaki Kawai [1979] Director [Japanese]; Masahiko Tanigaki [1967] Director [Japanese]; Daisuke Yamasaki [1974] Director [Japanese]

Marubeni North Sea Limited
Incorporated: 5 May 2004 *Employees:* 11
Net Worth: £257,730,000 *Total Assets:* £938,316,288
Registered Office: 1st Floor, Burdett House, 15-16 Buckingham Street, London, WC2N 6DU
Activities: Extraction of crude petroleum
Officers: Takeo Morita, Secretary; Mutsumi Ishizuki [1958] Director/Chief Executive [Japanese]; Takeo Morita [1967] Director [Japanese]; Akihiko Sagara [1961] Director/Chief Operating Officer [Japanese]; Satoshi Shijima [1972] Director/General Manager [Japanese]; Isao Suzuki [1964] Director [Japanese]

Marubeni Oil & Gas (U.K.) Limited
Incorporated: 9 March 2000
Net Worth: £605,302,784 *Total Assets:* £1,095,623,040
Registered Office: 1st Floor, Burdett House, 15-16 Buckingham Street, London, WC2N 6DU
Activities: Extraction of crude petroleum
Parent: Marubeni North Sea Limited
Officers: Takeo Morita, Secretary; Takeo Morita [1967] Director [Japanese]; Gary Nienow [1963] Director/Employee; Isao Suzuki [1964] Director [Japanese]

The Mary Street Estate Limited
Incorporated: 27 November 1894
Net Worth: £210,524,400 *Total Assets:* £213,343,136
Registered Office: York House, 45 Seymour Street, London, W1H 7LX
Activities: Development of building projects
Shareholders: BLD Property Holdings Limited; BLD Property Holdings Limited
Officers: Sarah Morrell Barzycki [1958] Director/Head of Finance; Bryan Lewis [1967] Director/Chartered Surveyor; Paul Stuart Macey [1978] Director/Accountant; Jonathan Charles McNuff [1986] Director/Chartered Accountant; Charles John Middleton [1966] Director/Corporate Tax Executive; Timothy Andrew Roberts [1964] Director/Chartered Surveyor; Nigel Mark Webb [1963] Director/Chartered Surveyor

Masdar Energy UK Limited
Incorporated: 6 May 2009
Net Worth: £10,109,404 *Total Assets:* £357,498,400
Registered Office: 35 Great St Helen's, London, EC3A 6AP
Activities: Other business support service activities n.e.c.
Parent: Government of Abu Dhabi
Officers: Wenda Adriaanse [1971] Director [Dutch]; Mahmoud Ahmed Mahmoud Ahmed Alhosani [1983] Director [Emirati]; Niall Patrick Hannigan [1966] Director [Irish]

Masdar Offshore Wind UK Limited
Incorporated: 25 June 2014
Net Worth: £18,206,138 *Total Assets:* £172,735,680
Registered Office: 35 Great St Helen's, London, EC3A 6AP
Activities: Activities of other holding companies n.e.c.
Parent: Government of Abu Dhabi
Officers: Wenda Adriaanse [1971] Director [Dutch]; Mahmoud Ahmed Mahmoud Ahmed Alhosani [1983] Director [Emirati]; Niall Patrick Hannigan [1966] Director/Chief Financial Officer [Irish]

Mastcraft Limited
Incorporated: 5 September 1984 *Employees:* 18
Net Worth: £17,165,846 *Total Assets:* £138,994,880
Registered Office: 30 Poland Street, London, W1F 8QS
Activities: Other business support service activities n.e.c.
Shareholders: Joginder Pal Sanger; Sunity Sanger
Officers: Dr Joginder Pal Sanger, Secretary [Indian]; Girish Sanger [1976] Director; Dr Joginder Pal Sanger [1942] Director [Indian]; Reema Sanger [1973] Director; Sunity Sanger [1950] Director

Mastercard Europe Services Limited
Incorporated: 9 September 2014
Net Worth: £1,576,565,760 *Total Assets:* £1,621,655,424
Registered Office: 10 Upper Bank Street, Canary Wharf, London, E14 5NP
Activities: Technical testing and analysis
Parent: Mastercard Incorporated
Officers: John McLaren, Secretary; Mark David Ashley Barnett [1967] Director/Business Executive; Timothy Gerard Berger [1963] Director/Business Executive [American]; Justin Stuart Goddard [1971] Director/Business Executive

Mastercard Payment Gateway Services Group Limited
Incorporated: 5 March 1996
Previous: Datacash Group Limited
Net Worth: £829,267,968 *Total Assets:* £829,390,976
Registered Office: 19th Floor, 10 Upper Bank Street, London, E14 5NP
Activities: Data processing, hosting and related activities
Parent: Mastercard Incorporated
Officers: Hemal Parekh, Secretary; Keith Robert Douglas [1969] Director [Irish]; Tine Christiane Fincioen [1980] Director [Belgian]; Sandra Monica Simoes de Matos [1977] Director [Portuguese]

Mastercard Payment Gateway Services Limited
Incorporated: 5 September 1997 *Employees:* 145
Previous: Datacash Ltd.
Net Worth: £126,841,000 *Total Assets:* £187,836,000
Registered Office: 19th Floor, 10 Upper Bank Street, London, E14 5NP
Activities: Other information technology service activities
Parent: Mastercard Payment Gateway Services Group Limited
Officers: Keith Robert Douglas [1969] Director [Irish]; Tine Christiane Fincioen [1980] Director [Belgian]; Sandra Monica Simoes de Matos [1977] Director [Portuguese]

Mastercard UK Holdco Limited
Incorporated: 28 June 2016
Net Worth: £718,254,016 *Total Assets:* £875,022,976
Registered Office: 19th Floor, 10 Upper Bank Street, London, E14 5NP
Activities: Activities of other holding companies n.e.c.
Parent: Mastercard Payment Gateway Services Group Limited
Officers: Jackie Panayi, Secretary; Ajay Banga [1959] Director/President & Chief Executive Officer [American]; Mark David Ashley Barnett [1967] Director/Division President; Timothy Gerard Berger [1963] Director/Accountant [American]; Martina Hund-Mejean [1960] Director/Chief Financial Officer [American]; Maximiliano Mamondez [1971] Director/CFO Europe Mastercard; Tim Murphy [1967] Director/General Counsel [American]

Mastercard/Europay U.K. Limited
Incorporated: 27 June 1989
Net Worth: £7,890,328,576 *Total Assets:* £8,975,220,736
Registered Office: 19th Floor, 10 Upper Bank Street, London, E14 5NP
Activities: Activities of head offices
Parent: Mastercard Incorporated
Officers: John Spencer McLaren, Secretary; Timothy Gerard Berger [1963] Director/Finance [American]; Paul Devin Corr [1980] Director [American]; Justin Stuart Goddard [1971] Director; Alfred Kamanja Kibe [1974] Director [American]

Match.Com Europe Limited
Incorporated: 7 June 2011 *Employees:* 6
Net Worth: £412,253,152 *Total Assets:* £602,343,104
Registered Office: c/o Skadden, 40 Bank Street, Canary Wharf, London, E14 5DS
Activities: Other information technology service activities
Parent: Match.Com Foreign Holdings III Limited
Officers: Philip Douglas Eigenmann [1970] Director/Accountant [American]; Jared Franklin Sine [1979] Director/General Counsel [American]

Match.Com Foreign Holdings Limited
Incorporated: 17 June 2013
Net Worth: £580,900,480 *Total Assets:* £879,188,736
Registered Office: c/o Skadden, 40 Bank Street, Canary Wharf, London, E14 5DS
Activities: Other information technology service activities
Parent: Match Group, Inc.
Officers: Philip Douglas Eigenmann [1970] Director/Accountant [American]; Jared Franklin Sine [1979] Director/General Counsel [American]

Matthey Finance Limited
Incorporated: 29 May 1935
Net Worth: £208,236,992 *Total Assets:* £208,238,000
Registered Office: 5th Floor, 25 Farringdon Street, London, EC4A 4AB
Activities: Activities of other holding companies n.e.c.
Parent: Matthey Holdings Limited
Officers: Simon Farrant, Secretary; Simon Farrant [1961] Director/Solicitor; Andrew Holford [1970] Director; Julian Charles Edward Tasker [1975] Director/Treasurer

Matthey Holdings Limited
Incorporated: 24 November 1995
Net Worth: £1,091,308,032 *Total Assets:* £1,580,434,048
Registered Office: 5th Floor, 25 Farringdon Street, London, EC4A 4AB
Activities: Other business support service activities n.e.c.
Parent: Johnson Matthey PLC
Officers: Simon Farrant, Secretary; Simon Farrant [1961] Director/Solicitor; Andrew Holford [1970] Director; Julian Charles Edward Tasker [1975] Director/Treasurer

MATW UK Holding LLP
Incorporated: 10 September 2014
Net Worth: £78,284,520 *Total Assets:* £154,924,304
Registered Office: Second Floor, Angel House, 338-346 Goswell Road, London, EC1V 7LQ

Maurice Investments Limited
Incorporated: 30 January 1997 *Employees:* 8
Net Worth: £15,646,146 *Total Assets:* £122,935,592
Registered Office: 7 Cadbury Close, Whetstone, London, N20 9BD
Activities: Buying and selling of own real estate
Major Shareholder: Mark Wogman
Officers: Mark Wogman, Secretary/Estate Agent; Laura de Friend [1982] Director; Gavin Jamie Wogman [1978] Director; Katie Alexis Wogman [1980] Director; Mark Wogman [1952] Director/Estate Agent; Susan Anne Wogman [1954] Director

Maven Investment Partners Ltd
Incorporated: 1 February 2011 *Employees:* 14
Previous: Maven Trading Ltd
Net Worth: £47,191,884 *Total Assets:* £483,179,360
Registered Office: 6 Bevis Marks, London, EC3A 7BA
Activities: Security dealing on own account
Parent: Maven Securities Holding Limited
Officers: Benjamin Nur Huda [1979] Director [Australian]; Ivan Koedjikov [1981] Director [Bulgarian]; Ian Mark Toon [1974] Director

Mavenir Private Finance Ltd
Incorporated: 21 February 2017 *Employees:* 2,158
Net Worth: £381,774,304 *Total Assets:* £1,123,801,472
Registered Office: 11th Floor, 200 Aldersgate Street, London, EC1A 4HD
Activities: Wireless telecommunications activities
Officers: Roy Luria, Secretary; Frank Baker [1972] Director/Partner [American]; Peter Berger [1950] Director/Partner [American]; Jeffrey Hendren [1959] Director/Partner [American]; Walter Wei-Min Loh [1971] Director [American]

Mavenir Private Holdings I Ltd
Incorporated: 3 May 2016
Net Worth: £573,469,248 *Total Assets:* £573,469,248
Registered Office: 11th Floor, 200 Aldersgate Street, London, EC1A 4HD
Activities: Activities of other holding companies n.e.c.
Parent: Mavenir Private Finance Ltd
Officers: Roy Luria, Secretary; Frank Baker [1972] Director/Partner [American]; Peter Elliott Berger [1950] Director/Partner [American]; Jeffrey Hendren [1959] Director/Partner [American]; Walter Wei-Min Loh [1971] Director [American]

Mavenir Private Holdings II Ltd
Incorporated: 3 May 2016
Net Worth: £549,784,192 *Total Assets:* £780,737,600
Registered Office: 11th Floor, 200 Aldersgate Street, London, EC1A 4HD
Activities: Activities of other holding companies n.e.c.
Parent: Mavenir Private Holdings I Ltd
Officers: Roy Shimon Luria, Secretary; Frank Baker [1972] Director/Partner [American]; Peter Elliott Berger [1950] Director/Partner [American]; Ronald Jay de Lange [1958] Director/Partner [American]; Hubert Xavier Marie Dominique Dubosc de Pesquidoux [1965] Director/Partner [French]; Merle Lee Gilmore Jr [1948] Director/Partner [American]; Jeffrey Hendren [1959] Director/Partner [American]; Michael Hulslander [1985] Director [American]; Pardeep Kohli [1965] Director [American]; Walter Loh [1971] Director/Chief Financial Officer [American]; Roderick Kirkland Randall [1959] Director/Partner [American]; Theodore H Schell [1944] Director/Partner [American]

Max Credit Investment Limited
Incorporated: 16 June 2008
Net Worth Deficit: £6,864,047 *Total Assets:* £156,131,056
Registered Office: Suite 1, 3rd Floor, 11-12 St James's Square, London, SW1Y 4LB
Activities: Other business support service activities n.e.c.
Officers: Karl Konradsson [1972] Director/Specialist, Asset Management [Icelander]

Max Recovery Limited
Incorporated: 12 December 2003 *Employees:* 8
Net Worth: £189,319,840 *Total Assets:* £250,420,304
Registered Office: 25 Bank Street, Canary Wharf, London, E14 5JP
Activities: Financial intermediation not elsewhere classified
Officers: Matthew Paul Melling [1971] Director; Michael Grant Norris [1961] Executive Director

Maxus Communications (UK) Limited
Incorporated: 11 December 1991 *Employees:* 339
Net Worth: £47,753,000 *Total Assets:* £186,423,008
Registered Office: Sea Containers, 18 Upper Ground, London, SE1 9ET
Activities: Advertising agencies
Parent: BJK & E Holdings Limited
Officers: Anna Hickey [1976] Director; Shil Patel [1977] Director

Maxwell Asset Management Ltd
Incorporated: 21 May 2007 *Employees:* 3
Net Worth: £14,513,091 *Total Assets:* £112,269,376
Registered Office: 88-90 Hatton Garden, Holborn, London, EC1N 8PG
Activities: Management consultancy activities other than financial management
Parent: Menostar Holdings Limited
Officers: Tatiana Soumilova, Secretary; Dmitry Petrovich Kirpichenko [1969] Director/Businessman [Russian]

Maybourne Hotels Limited
Incorporated: 12 November 1998 *Employees:* 79
Net Worth: £796,000 *Total Assets:* £117,095,000
Registered Office: 41-43 Brook Street, Mayfair, London, W1K 4HJ
Activities: Activities of head offices
Parent: Selene Midco Limited
Officers: Fady Bakhos [1971] Director/Legal Counsel [French]; Liam Cunningham [1958] Director [Irish]

Mayfair Charities Limited
Incorporated: 28 February 1968
Net Worth: £97,777,000 *Total Assets:* £124,514,000
Registered Office: Freshwater House, 158-162 Shaftesbury Avenue, London, WC2H 8HR
Activities: Other social work activities without accommodation n.e.c.
Officers: Mark Roy Mason Jenner, Secretary; David Davis [1935] Director/Chartered Accountant; Richard Fischer [1937] Director/Lecturer Rtd; Benzion Schalom Eliezer Freshwater [1948] Director; Solomon Israel Freshwater [1950] Director

MBC Europe Limited
Incorporated: 25 March 2014 *Employees:* 1
Net Worth: £188,956,576 *Total Assets:* £189,214,880
Registered Office: 95 Gresham Street, London, EC2V 7AB
Activities: Activities of production holding companies
Officers: Yoshito Ishihara [1973] Director [Japanese]

MC GFS Investment Company Limited
Incorporated: 22 August 2011
Net Worth: £91,915,000 *Total Assets:* £223,534,000
Registered Office: 68 Lombard Street, London, EC3V 9LJ
Activities: Trade of electricity
Parent: MC GFS Holding Company Limited
Officers: Akira Hirano [1971] Director, Electrical Engineer [Japanese]; Takeo Kitamura [1976] Director/Employee in a Financial Institution [Japanese]; Ken Matsuda [1973] Director/General Manager [Japanese]

MC GIP-UK Ltd.
Incorporated: 17 June 2013 *Employees:* 3
Net Worth: £159,446,000 *Total Assets:* £171,764,784
Registered Office: Mid City Place, 71 High Holborn, London, WC1V 6BA
Activities: Activities of financial services holding companies
Parent: Mitsubishi Corporation
Officers: Toshiya Aoki [1972] Director [Japanese]; Yusuke Shioya [1988] Director/Assistant Manager [Japanese]

MC Ocean Holdings Limited
Incorporated: 5 September 2014 *Employees:* 1
Net Worth: £817,190,464 *Total Assets:* £822,750,784
Registered Office: Mid City Place, 71 High Holborn, London, WC1V 6BA
Activities: Activities of other holding companies n.e.c.
Parent: Mitsubishi Corporation
Officers: Yukio Takahashi [1965] Director/General Manager [Japanese]

MC Resource Development Ltd.
Incorporated: 6 May 2011
Net Worth: £1,447,004,032 *Total Assets:* £1,447,123,456
Registered Office: Mid City Place, 71 High Holborn, London, WC1V 6BA
Activities: Support activities for other mining and quarrying
Parent: Mitsubishi Corporation
Officers: Daisuke Hirata [1973] Director/Deputy General Manager [Japanese]; Hiroyuki Miura [1981] Director [Japanese]; Hideyuki Takemura [1972] Director [Japanese]

MCD Europe Limited
Incorporated: 13 August 2004
Net Worth: £17,254,903,808 *Total Assets:* £25,501,835,264
Registered Office: Cordy House, 91 Curtain Road, London, EC2A 3BS
Activities: Activities of other holding companies n.e.c.
Parent: McDonald's Corporation
Officers: Malcolm Wayne Hicks, Secretary; Thomas Joseph Dillon [1977] Director/Business Executive [American]; Malcolm Wayne Hicks [1963] Director; Julian Crispin Hilton-Johnson [1964] Director

MCD Global Franchising Limited
Incorporated: 16 August 2016 *Employees:* 119
Net Worth: £11,269,220,352 *Total Assets:* £14,030,362,624
Registered Office: Cordy House, 91 Curtain Road, Shoreditch, London, EC2A 3BS
Activities: Activities of other holding companies n.e.c.
Parent: McDonalds Corporation
Officers: Malcolm Wayne Hicks, Secretary; Thomas Joseph Dillon [1977] Director/Business Executive [American]; Malcolm Wayne Hicks [1963] Director [British/American]; Julian Crispin Hilton-Johnson [1964] Director/Business Executive

MCD Investments Limited
Incorporated: 27 July 2016
Net Worth: £4,784,112,128 *Total Assets:* £7,135,839,232
Registered Office: Cordy House, 91 Curtain Road, Shoreditch, London, EC2A 3BS
Activities: Activities of head offices
Shareholders: MCD Europe Limited; MCDI Holdings Limited
Officers: Malcolm Wayne Hicks, Secretary; Thomas Joseph Dillon [1977] Director/Business Executive [American]; Malcolm Wayne Hicks [1963] Director/Business Executive [British/American]; Julian Crispin Hilton-Johnson [1964] Director

McDonald's Real Estate Company No.1 Limited
Incorporated: 12 June 2002
Net Worth: £423,985,984 *Total Assets:* £488,444,992
Registered Office: 11-59 High Road, East Finchley, London, N2 8AW
Activities: Other business support service activities n.e.c.
Parent: MCD Europe Limited
Officers: Christine Marie Dekker, Secretary; Paul James Pomroy [1973] Director; Henry William Trickey [1968] Director/Development & IT Officer

McDonald's Real Estate LLP
Incorporated: 11 October 2002
Net Worth: £109,269,000 *Total Assets:* £743,952,000
Registered Office: 11-59 High Road, East Finchley, London, N2 8AW

McDonald's Restaurants Limited
Incorporated: 18 February 1971 *Employees:* 35,878
Net Worth: £1,351,876,992 *Total Assets:* £1,605,803,008
Registered Office: 11-59 High Road, East Finchley, London, N2 8AW
Activities: Unlicenced restaurants and cafes
Parent: McDonald's Real Estate LLP
Officers: Christine Marie Dekker, Secretary; Jason Clark [1970] Director/Chief Operations Officer; Joseph Matthew Erlinger [1973] Director/Business Executive [American]; John Park [1976] Director/Chartered Accountant; Paul James Pomroy [1973] Director; Henry William Trickey [1968] Director/Chartered Secretary

McGraw-Hill Education (UK) Limited
Incorporated: 13 March 2012 *Employees:* 116
Net Worth: £81,700,000 *Total Assets:* £146,300,000
Registered Office: 8th Floor, Regent's Place, 338 Euston Road, London, NW1 3BH
Activities: Other publishing activities
Parent: McGraw-Hill Global Education UK Holdco II Limited
Officers: Deborah Flanagan [1956] Director/Tax Attorney [American]; Christopher Phillip Knight [1969] Director/Chartered Certified Accountant; Ian Edward White [1972] Director/Finance

McKechnie Aerospace (Europe) Ltd
Incorporated: 20 April 2007
Net Worth: £488,873,408 *Total Assets:* £494,852,640
Registered Office: Suite 1, 3rd Floor, 11-12 St James's Square, London, SW1Y 4LB
Activities: Non-trading company
Parent: TransDigm Group Inc
Officers: Jonathan David Crandall [1977] Director [American]; Sarah Louise Wynne [1973] Director

McKesson Global Procurement & Sourcing Limited
Incorporated: 2 October 2013 *Employees:* 13
Net Worth: £2,736,779,520 *Total Assets:* £3,192,374,272
Registered Office: TMF Corporate Administration Services Limited, 5th Floor, 6 St Andrew Street, London, EC4A 3AE
Activities: Wholesale of pharmaceutical goods
Officers: Stanton McComb [1970] Director/President, McKesson Medical-Surgical [American]; Jack Thomas Stephens III [1975] Director/Health Care [American]; Gareth Bryn Thomas [1964] Director/Chief Legal Counsel, Global Procurement & Sourcing

McKesson Global Sourcing UK Limited
Incorporated: 1 August 2017 *Employees:* 5
Net Worth: £16,817,168 *Total Assets:* £110,886,528
Registered Office: TMF Corporate Administration Services Limited, 5th Floor, 6 St Andrew Street, London, EC4A 3AE
Activities: Wholesale of pharmaceutical goods
Officers: Andrew Keith Birken [1964] Director/SVP, Global Sourcing-Medical [American]; Jack Thomas Stephens III [1975] Director/Health Care [American]; Gareth Bryn Thomas [1964] Director/Chief Legal Counsel, Global Procurement & Sourcing

McKesson UK Finance I Limited
Incorporated: 2 October 2013
Net Worth: £8,120,014,848 *Total Assets:* £11,790,977,024
Registered Office: TMF Corporate Administration Services Limited, 5th Floor, 6 St Andrew Street, London, EC4A 3AE
Activities: Activities of head offices
Parent: McKesson US Finance Corporation
Officers: Francois Bodereau [1968] Director/VP Finance, Global Procurement & Sourcing; John Thomas Herlihy [1978] Finance Director [Irish]; Adrian Francis Kelly [1982] Finance Director [Irish]

McKesson UK Finance II Limited
Incorporated: 2 October 2013
Net Worth: £567,256,832 *Total Assets:* £1,228,445,312
Registered Office: TMF Corporate Administration Services Limited, 5th Floor, 6 St Andrew Street, London, EC4A 3AE
Activities: Activities of head offices
Parent: McKesson UK Finance I Limited
Officers: Francois Bodereau [1968] Director/VP Finance, Global Procurement & Sourcing; John Thomas Herlihy [1978] Finance Director [Irish]; Adrian Francis Kelly [1982] Finance Director [Irish]

McKesson UK Finance IV Limited
Incorporated: 22 August 2016
Net Worth: £299,823,488 *Total Assets:* £299,837,376
Registered Office: TMF Corporate Administration Services Limited, 5th Floor, 6 St Andrew Street, London, EC4A 3AE
Activities: Activities of head offices
Parent: McKesson UK Finance I Limited
Officers: Francois Bodereau [1968] Director/VP Finance, Global Procurement & Sourcing; John Thomas Herlihy [1978] Finance Director [Irish]; Adrian Francis Kelly [1982] Finance Director [Irish]

McLaren Construction Group PLC
Incorporated: 7 March 2005 *Employees:* 691
Net Worth: £29,096,900 *Total Assets:* £217,452,480
Registered Office: 3rd Floor, East Leconfield House, Curzon Street, London, W1J 5JA
Activities: Activities of construction holding companies
Major Shareholder: Kevin Robert Taylor
Officers: Philip James Pringle [1963] Managing Director; Kevin Robert Taylor [1966] Director

MCX Dunlin (UK) Limited
Incorporated: 12 December 2007 *Employees:* 6
Net Worth Deficit: £58,289,000 *Total Assets:* £544,252,032
Registered Office: Mid City Place, 71 High Holborn, London, WC1V 6BA
Activities: Extraction of crude petroleum
Parent: Mitsubishi Corporation
Officers: Fumio Ichishima, Secretary; Isao Kano [1960] Director/Company Executive [Japanese]; Michio Kawamata [1962] Director/General Manager [Japanese]; Takeshi Matsushita [1971] Director/General Manager [Japanese]; Jiro Mukai [1964] Director/Deputy General Manager [Japanese]; Jun Nishizawa [1961] Director/Senior Vice President [Japanese]

MCX Osprey (UK) Limited
Incorporated: 12 December 2007 *Employees:* 6
Net Worth Deficit: £24,752,000 *Total Assets:* £142,362,000
Registered Office: Mid City Place, 71 High Holborn, London, WC1V 6BA
Activities: Extraction of crude petroleum
Parent: Mitsubishi Corporation
Officers: Fumio Ichishima, Secretary; Isao Kano [1960] Director/Company Executive [Japanese]; Michio Kawamata [1962] Director/General Manager [Japanese]; Takeshi Matsushita [1971] Director/General Manager [Japanese]; Jiro Mukai [1964] Director/Deputy General Manager [Japanese]; Jun Nishizawa [1961] Director/Senior Vice President [Japanese]

MDU Investments Limited
Incorporated: 6 December 1996
Net Worth: £98,774,000 *Total Assets:* £1,342,523,008
Registered Office: One Canada Square, London, E14 5GS
Activities: Other business support service activities n.e.c.
Parent: The Medical Defence Union Limited
Officers: Nicholas John Bowman, Secretary; Chika Aghadiuno [1969] Director; Stella Beaumont [1957] Director; William Robert John Dinning [1959] Director/Head of Investment Strategy; Nicholas Andrew Dungay [1961] Marketing and Sales Director; Dr Paul Goldsmith [1970] Director; Ian David Hutchinson [1954] Director/Accountant; Dr Matthew Thomas Wilton Lee [1971] Professional Services Director; Jeremy Hardwick Riley [1960] Director; Paul Riordan Eva [1958] Director/Consultant Opthalmologist; Professor Sunil Shaunak [1958] Director; Owen Charles Ellis Sparrow [1951] Director/Consultant Neurosurgeon; Dr Christine Margaret Tomkins [1955] Director/Chief Executive Officer; Dr Simon Wilfred Watkin [1960] Director/Medical Doctor; Anthony Richard Wright [1971] Director/Actuary

Meadowhall Centre (1999) Limited
Incorporated: 23 May 1988
Net Worth: £847,637,184 *Total Assets:* £847,686,464
Registered Office: York House, 45 Seymour Street, London, W1H 7LX
Activities: Development of building projects
Shareholders: Meadowhall Centre Limited; Meadowhall Centre Limited
Officers: Claire Ann Barber [1974] Director/Chartered Surveyor; Sarah Morrell Barzycki [1958] Director/Head of Finance; Paul Stuart Macey [1978] Director/Accountant; Jonathan Charles McNuff [1986] Director/Chartered Accountant; Charles John Middleton [1966] Director/Corporate Tax Executive; Timothy Andrew Roberts [1964] Director/Chartered Surveyor

Meadowhall Finance PLC
Incorporated: 2 November 2006
Net Worth Deficit: £12,273,812 *Total Assets:* £652,292,736
Registered Office: York House, 45 Seymour Street, London, W1H 7LX
Activities: Development of building projects
Officers: Claire Ann Barber [1974] Director/Chartered Surveyor; Paul Case [1967] Director; Jayesh Patel [1980] Director/Real Estate Investment Manager [Canadian]; Hursh Shah [1976] Director; Egil Strysse [1964] Director [Norwegian]

Meadowhall Shopping Centre Limited
Incorporated: 24 August 2001
Net Worth: £673,267,648 *Total Assets:* £1,026,838,656
Registered Office: York House, 45 Seymour Street, London, W1H 7LX
Activities: Development of building projects
Shareholders: Meadowhall Shopping Centre Property Holdings Limited; Meadowhall Shopping Centre Property Holdings Limited
Officers: Claire Ann Barber [1974] Director/Chartered Surveyor; Paul Case [1967] Director; Jayesh Patel [1980] Director/Real Estate Investment Manager [Canadian]; Hursh Shah [1976] Director; Egil Strysse [1964] Director [Norwegian]

Meadowhall Shopping Centre Property Holdings Limited
Incorporated: 24 August 2001
Net Worth: £609,100,736 *Total Assets:* £609,113,216
Registered Office: York House, 45 Seymour Street, London, W1H 7LX
Activities: Development of building projects
Shareholders: MSC Property Intermediate Holdings Limited; MSC Property Intermediate Holdings Limited
Officers: Claire Ann Barber [1974] Director/Chartered Surveyor; Paul Case [1967] Director; Jayesh Patel [1980] Director/Real Estate Investment Manager [Canadian]; Hursh Shah [1976] Director; Egil Strysse [1964] Director [Norwegian]

Mediacom UK Limited
Incorporated: 6 February 1975 *Employees:* 954
Net Worth: £106,794,000 *Total Assets:* £540,497,984
Registered Office: 124 Theobalds Road, London, WC1X 8RX
Activities: Advertising agencies
Parent: Mediacom Group Limited
Officers: Stephen David Allan [1963] Director; Joshua Wilfred Krichefski [1975] Managing Director; Nicholas Alexander Lawson [1965] Director/Chief Executive Officer; Peter Wade [1964] Director

Mediaedge:cia (UK) Holdings Limited
Incorporated: 17 February 1992
Net Worth: £1,105,000 *Total Assets:* £140,019,008
Registered Office: Sea Containers, 18 Upper Ground, London, SE1 9ET
Activities: Activities of head offices
Parent: Mediaedge:cia Worldwide Limited
Officers: Paul Hutchison [1975] Director/Chief Operations Officer; Shil Patel [1977] Director

Medical Centre Holdings Limited
Incorporated: 1 December 1993
Net Worth: £104,015,704 *Total Assets:* £253,825,792
Registered Office: 54 Weymouth Street, London, W1G 6NU
Activities: Activities of other holding companies n.e.c.
Parent: Hobden Capital Limited
Officers: Clodagh Woodall, Secretary; Nigel Kevin Ford [1967] Director; Christopher Martin Hobden [1949] Director; David James Shannon [1966] Director/Chartered Surveyor

The Medical Defence Union Limited
Incorporated: 23 October 1885 *Employees:* 461
Net Worth: £284,931,008 *Total Assets:* £1,575,585,024
Registered Office: One Canada Square, London, E14 5GS
Activities: Other business support service activities n.e.c.
Officers: Nicholas John Bowman, Secretary; Chika Aghadiuno [1969] Director; Stella Beaumont [1957] Director; William Robert John Dinning [1959] Director/Head of Investment Strategy; Nicholas Andrew Dungay [1961] Marketing and Sales Director; Dr Paul Goldsmith [1970] Director; Ian David Hutchinson [1954] Director/Accountant; Dr Matthew Thomas Wilton Lee [1971] Professional Services Director; Jeremy Hardwick Riley [1960] Director; Paul Riordan Eva [1958] Director/Consultant Opthalmologist; Professor Sunil Shaunak [1958] Director; Owen Charles Ellis Sparrow [1951] Director/Consultant Neurosurgeon; Dr Christine Margaret Tomkins [1955] Director/Chief Executive Officer; Dr Simon Wilfred Watkin [1960] Director/Medical Doctor; Anthony Richard Wright [1971] Director/Actuary

The Medical Protection Society Limited
Incorporated: 31 March 1892 *Employees:* 944
Net Worth: £1,960,706,944 *Total Assets:* £3,107,610,880
Registered Office: Level 19, The Shard, 32 London Bridge Street, London, SE1 9SG
Activities: Activities of professional membership organisations
Officers: David Wheeler, Secretary; Dr Richard Brennan [1954] Director/Medical Doctor [Irish]; Dr Fiona Elizabeth Cornish [1960] Director/Doctor; Ian Eardley [1958] Director/Surgeon; Patrick Bruce Forbes [1951] Director/Consultant Obstetrician & Gynaecologist; Simon James Kayll [1963] Finance Director; Howard Roger Kew [1960] Finance Director; Professor Kay-Tee Khaw-Fawcett [1950] Director/University Professor; Dr James McLenachan [1957] Director/Doctor; Simon Mark Pashby [1958] Director/Chartered Accountant; Dr Alexander William Scott [1956] Director/Doctor; Sally Jane Scutt [1956] Director/Trade Association Official; Dr Graham Douglas Stokes [1962] Director/Dentist; Martin Nicholas Caleb Thomas [1963] Director; Michael Norris Urmston [1949] Director; Tom Weitzman [1959] Director/Barrister; Professor Callum Cormack Youngson [1958] Director/Dentist

Mediclinic International PLC
Incorporated: 20 December 2012 *Employees:* 31,504
Previous: Al Noor Hospitals Group PLC
Net Worth: £3,286,000,128 *Total Assets:* £6,343,000,064
Registered Office: 6th Floor, 65 Gresham Street, London, EC2V 7NQ
Activities: Hospital activities
Officers: Dr Muhadditha Al Hashimi [1966] Director [Emirati]; Jan Jonathan Durand [1966] Director/Chief Executive Officer [South African]; James Alan Grieve [1952] Director/Chartered Accountant; Dr Felicity Ann Hope Harvey [1956] Director; Dr Edwin de La Harpe Hertzog [1949] Director/Businessman [South African]; Seamus Declan Keating [1963] Director/Accountant [Irish]; Daniel Petrus Meintjes [1956] Director [South African]; Petrus Jurgens Myburgh [1975] Executive Director [South African]; Dr Anja Klara Oswald [1968] Director [Swiss]; Trevor David Petersen [1955] Director/Chartered Accountant [South African]; Desmond Kent Smith [1947] Director/Actuary [South African]; Petrus Johannes Uys [1962] Alternate Director [South African]; Dr Carel Aron Van Der Merwe [1962] Director/Chief Executive Officer [South African]

MEIF II CP Holdings 1 Limited
Incorporated: 1 March 2007 *Employees:* 1,239
Net Worth Deficit: £13,637,000 *Total Assets:* £235,586,000
Registered Office: 18 St Swithin's Lane, London, EC4N 8AD
Activities: Activities of head offices
Officers: Philip Hogan [1973] Director; Gordon Ian Winston Parsons [1967] Director/Accountant; William David George Price [1984] Director/Finance Professional

MEIF II CP Holdings 3 Limited
Incorporated: 1 March 2007
Net Worth: £50,042,000 *Total Assets:* £214,474,000
Registered Office: Saffron Court, 14b St Cross Street, London, EC1N 8XA
Activities: Activities of head offices
Parent: MEIF II CP Holdings 2 Limited
Officers: Norifumi Kawakami [1965] Director [Japanese]; Hiroyasu Matsui [1965] Director [Japanese]; Koichi Nishikawa [1964] Director [Japanese]; Kenichi Sasaki [1967] Director [Japanese]; Jonathan Paul Scott [1961] Director/Accountant

MEIF II CP SPV 2 Limited
Incorporated: 27 March 2012
Net Worth: £197,000,992 *Total Assets:* £426,132,000
Registered Office: Saffron Court, 14b St Cross Street, London, EC1N 8XA
Activities: Activities of head offices
Parent: MEIF II CP Holdings 3 Limited
Officers: Hiroyasu Matsui [1965] Director [Japanese]; Jonathan Paul Scott [1961] Director/Accountant

Meininger Hotels Limited
Incorporated: 14 February 2014 *Employees:* 2
Net Worth: £114,767,000 *Total Assets:* £115,179,000
Registered Office: 3rd Floor, 30 Millbank, London, SW1P 4DU
Activities: Activities of head offices
Parent: Holidaybreak Limited
Officers: Navneet Bali [1956] Director; Clare Joanne Gates [1971] HR Director; Michael Friedrich Gies [1959] Director/Chief Financial Officer [German]; Abhishek Goenka [1979] Director/General Manager [Indian]; Ajay Ajit Peter Kerkar [1963] Director [Indian]; Timothy William May [1960] Director; Ajit Paramparambath Menon [1957] Director; Hannes Spanring [1969] Director [Austrian]; Theodoros Christakis Theodorou [1972] Director/Chief Commercial Officer

Melli Bank PLC
Incorporated: 1 February 2001 *Employees:* 46
Net Worth: £241,791,312 *Total Assets:* £322,174,400
Registered Office: 98a Kensington High Street, London, W8 4SG
Activities: Banks
Parent: Government of The Islamic Republic of Iran
Officers: Abdolreza Zand, Secretary; Gholamhassan Asgharzadeh Zaferani [1949] Director/Banker [Iranian]; Bahman Ataii [1952] Director/Banker [Iranian]; Roy England [1945] Director/Banker; Mohammad Reza Hosein Zadeh [1964] Director/Banker [Iranian]; Gholamreza Panahi [1968] Director/Banker [Iranian]; John Michael Thompson [1944] Director/Accountant; Abdolreza Zand [1959] Director/Banking [Iranian]

Melton Renewable Energy UK Limited
Incorporated: 29 August 2014 *Employees:* 254
Previous: Melton Renewable Energy UK PLC
Net Worth Deficit: £22,289,000 *Total Assets:* £277,388,000
Registered Office: 6th Floor, 33 Holborn, London, EC1N 2HT
Activities: Trade of electricity
Parent: Eucalyptus Energy Limited
Officers: Dr Michael John Bullard [1966] Director; Paul Stephen Latham [1956] Director; Matthew George Setchell [1977] Director/Investment Manager; Edwin John Wilkinson [1965] Director

Menzies Distribution Limited
Incorporated: 15 June 1979 *Employees:* 2,902
Net Worth: £132,500,000 *Total Assets:* £437,800,000
Registered Office: Unit E, Twelvetrees Business Park, Twelvetrees Crescent, London, E3 3JG
Activities: Wholesale of other intermediate products
Parent: Endless Newco 2 Limited
Officers: Paul Raymond Patrick McCourt [1975] Finance Director; Gregory John Michael [1967] Director

MEPC (1946) Limited
Incorporated: 1 October 1946
Net Worth: £257,600,000 *Total Assets:* £261,100,000
Registered Office: Sixth Floor, 150 Cheapside, London, EC2V 6ET
Activities: Renting and operating of Housing Association real estate
Parent: Leconport Estates
Officers: Christian Ross St. John Judd [1979] Director/Chartered Accountant [Irish]; Matthew James Torode [1984] Director; Kirsty Ann-Marie Wilman [1980] Director/Chartered Accountant

The Mercantile Investment Trust PLC
Incorporated: 8 December 1884
Net Worth: £2,019,592,960 *Total Assets:* £2,210,979,072
Registered Office: 60 Victoria Embankment, London, EC4Y 0JP
Activities: Financial intermediation not elsewhere classified
Officers: Angus Charles Gordon Lennox [1964] Director/Executive Chairman; Heather Anne Hopkins [1973] Managing Director [Canadian]; Helen James [1970] Managing Director; Graham John Kitchen [1967] Director; Harry Michael Charles Morley [1965] Director; Jeremy John Tigue [1959] Director/Fund Manager

Mercantile Leasing Company (No.132) Limited
Incorporated: 8 February 1994
Net Worth: £2,660,000 *Total Assets:* £2,178,737,920
Registered Office: 1 Churchill Place, London, E14 5HP
Activities: Financial leasing
Parent: Barclays Bank PLC
Officers: Mark Francis Beastall [1978] Director/Accountant; Rohit Chaku [1980] Director/Trader [American]; Enver Khairov [1972] Director/Banker; Christopher Simon White [1978] Director/Banker

Mercer Africa Limited
Incorporated: 19 June 2014
Net Worth: £161,800,000 *Total Assets:* £305,000,000
Registered Office: 1 Tower Place West, Tower Place, London, EC3R 5BU
Activities: Non-trading company
Parent: Marsh & McLennan Companies Inc.
Officers: Sallie Ellis, Secretary; David John Anderson [1968] Director/CEO/President [Australian]; Jean-Paul D'Offay [1972] Director/Chartered Accountant; William Simon O'Regan [1959] Director/President - North America Region; David Nicholas Williams [1971] Director/Accountant

Mercer Limited
Incorporated: 10 July 1970 *Employees:* 2,393
Net Worth: £798,700,032 *Total Assets:* £1,096,000,000
Registered Office: 1 Tower Place West, Tower Place, London, EC3R 5BU
Activities: Other business support service activities n.e.c.
Parent: MMC UK Group Limited
Officers: Sallie Ellis, Secretary; Jane Victoria Barker [1949] Director; Fiona Stewart Dunsire [1966] Director/Actuary; Catrina Holme [1970] Director/Lawyer; Dr Siobhan Elise Martin [1967] HR Director; William Simon O'Regan [1959] Director; David Nicholas Williams [1971] Director/Accountant

Merchant Retail Group Limited
Incorporated: 6 December 1979
Net Worth: £63,009,000 *Total Assets:* £104,989,000
Registered Office: Hutchinson House, 5 Hester Road, Battersea, London, SW11 4AN
Activities: Activities of head offices
Parent: A.S. Watson (P & C UK) Ltd
Officers: Edith Shih, Secretary; Claire Nicole Dines [1972] Finance Director; Dr Alan John Heaton [1962] Director; Dominic Kai Ming Lai [1953] Director [Canadian]; Gillian Greig Smith [1966] Finance Director

Merchants Trust PLC (The)
Incorporated: 16 February 1889
Net Worth: £619,451,264 *Total Assets:* £734,629,632
Registered Office: 199 Bishopsgate, London, EC2M 3TY
Activities: Financial intermediation not elsewhere classified
Officers: Eleanor Emuss, Secretary; Kirsten June Salt, Secretary; Nicholas Timon Drakesmith [1965] Director; Simon John Fraser [1959] Director; Mary Ann Sieghart [1961] Director/Journalist; Sybella Jane Stanley [1961] Director; Paul Tennant Yates [1957] Director

Mercia No.1 PLC
Incorporated: 3 October 2012
Net Worth: £18,000 *Total Assets:* £1,165,888,000
Registered Office: 35 Great St Helen's, London, EC3A 6AP
Activities: Financial intermediation not elsewhere classified
Parent: Mercia No.1 Holdings Limited
Officers: Helena Paivi Whitaker [1963] Director [Finnish]

Mercury Acquisitions Limited
Incorporated: 18 November 2015
Net Worth: £108,411,000 *Total Assets:* £251,474,000
Registered Office: 24 Britton Street, London, EC1M 5UA
Activities: Retail sale of leather goods in specialised stores
Officers: Dale Nicholas Christilaw [1970] Finance Director; Neil Charles Clifford [1967] Director/Retail Executive; Rebecca Elizabeth Alden Farrar-Hockley [1971] Director/Retail Executive

Mercury Holding Limited
Incorporated: 7 March 2014
Net Worth: £966,594,688 *Total Assets:* £966,606,336
Registered Office: Tricor Suite, 4th Floor, 50 Mark Lane, London, EC3R 7QR
Activities: Activities of head offices
Parent: OCI N.V.
Officers: Hassan Hossam Hassan Badrawi [1976] Director [Egyptian]; Kevin Charles Struve [1966] Director/Executive [American]

Mercury Midco 1 Limited
Incorporated: 16 December 2015 *Employees:* 2,339
Net Worth Deficit: £20,689,000 *Total Assets:* £326,497,984
Registered Office: 24 Britton Street, London, EC1M 5UA
Activities: Retail sale of leather goods in specialised stores
Officers: Dale Nicholas Christilaw [1970] Finance Director; Neil Charles Clifford [1967] Director/Retail Executive; Rebecca Elizabeth Alden Farrar-Hockley [1971] Director/Retail Executive

Mercury Midco 2 Limited
Incorporated: 16 December 2015
Net Worth Deficit: £5,829,000 *Total Assets:* £136,006,000
Registered Office: 24 Britton Street, London, EC1M 5UA
Activities: Retail sale of leather goods in specialised stores
Officers: Dale Nicholas Christilaw [1970] Finance Director; Neil Charles Clifford [1967] Director/Retail Executive; Rebecca Elizabeth Alden Farrar-Hockley [1971] Director/Retail Executive

Mercury Pharma Group Limited
Incorporated: 23 December 1988
Net Worth: £126,976,456 *Total Assets:* £202,432,240
Registered Office: Capital House, 85 King William Street, London, EC4N 7BL
Activities: Manufacture of basic pharmaceutical products
Parent: Concordia Investment Holdings (UK) Limited
Officers: Robert Sully, Secretary; Adeel Ahmad [1973] Director/Vice-President, Finance [Canadian]; Graeme Neville Duncan [1973] Director/Chief Executive Officer; Vikram Laxman Kamath [1977] Director/Vice President Finance and Group Controller [Indian]

Mercury UK Holdco Limited
Incorporated: 15 June 2015 *Employees:* 3,265
Net Worth: £3,072,712,448 *Total Assets:* £12,177,212,416
Registered Office: 111 Buckingham Palace Road, London, SW1W 0SR
Activities: Activities of financial services holding companies
Officers: Christopher John Coombe [1958] Director/Finance Professional; Emanuele Cuccio [1982] Director/Investment Professional [Italian]; Christophe Patrick Marie Victor Jacobs Van Merlen [1978] Director [Belgian]; Giacomo Massetti [1988] Director/Investment Professional [Italian]; Giles Edward Reaney [1981] Director/Finance Professional; Nick Simon Rose [1980] Director; Jill Isobel Whittaker [1960] Director/Investment Professional

Mergermarket Bidco Limited
Incorporated: 22 October 2013
Net Worth: £441,892,992 *Total Assets:* £930,537,024
Registered Office: 10 Queen Street Place, London, EC4R 1BE
Activities: Activities of other holding companies n.e.c.
Parent: Mergermarket Midco 2 Limited
Officers: Jonathan Frederick Gomer [1968] Director; Hamilton Ian Matthews [1971] Director

Mergermarket Limited
Incorporated: 18 November 1999 *Employees:* 389
Net Worth: £78,033,000 *Total Assets:* £153,466,000
Registered Office: 10 Queen Street Place, London, EC4R 1BE
Activities: Other publishing activities
Parent: Mergermarket Bidco Limited
Officers: Jonathan Frederick Gomer [1968] Director; Hamilton Matthews [1971] Director

Mergermarket Midco 1 Limited
Incorporated: 22 October 2013
Net Worth: £294,920,992 *Total Assets:* £473,171,008
Registered Office: 10 Queen Street Place, London, EC4R 1BE
Activities: Activities of other holding companies n.e.c.
Parent: Mergermarket Topco Limited
Officers: Jonathan Frederick Gomer [1968] Director; Hamilton Ian Matthews [1971] Director

Mergermarket Midco 2 Limited
Incorporated: 22 October 2013 *Employees:* 1,486
Net Worth Deficit: £41,698,000 *Total Assets:* £565,339,008
Registered Office: 10 Queen Street Place, London, EC4R 1BE
Activities: Activities of other holding companies n.e.c.
Parent: Mergermarket Midco 1 Limited
Officers: Jonathan Frederick Gomer [1968] Director; Hamilton Ian Matthews [1971] Director

Mergermarket Topco Limited
Incorporated: 16 December 2013 *Employees:* 1,486
Net Worth Deficit: £210,014,000 *Total Assets:* £575,283,008
Registered Office: 10 Queen Street Place, London, EC4R 1BE
Activities: Activities of other holding companies n.e.c.
Officers: Jonathan Frederick Gomer [1968] Director; Stylianos Ilia [1981] Director/Investment Executive [Cypriot]; Hamilton Ian Matthews [1971] Director; Christopher Paul Reid [1977] Director/Investment Professional; Nikos Stathopoulos [1969] Director [Greek]

Merrill Lynch (Camberley) Limited
Incorporated: 6 April 2005 *Employees:* 2
Net Worth: £121,465,000 *Total Assets:* £125,357,000
Registered Office: 2 King Edward Street, London, EC1A 1HQ
Activities: Financial intermediation not elsewhere classified
Parent: Bank of America Corporation
Officers: Ian Thomas Crowe [1961] Director/Company Executive; Nicholas Maxwell Scrimshaw [1968] Director/Company Executive

Merrill Lynch Europe Limited
Incorporated: 23 March 1929 *Employees:* 2
Net Worth: £23,658,000 *Total Assets:* £111,040,000
Registered Office: 2 King Edward Street, London, EC1A 1HQ
Activities: Financial intermediation not elsewhere classified
Parent: MLEIH Funding
Officers: Jonathan Howard Redvers Lee [1966] Director/Company Executive; Trevor Caleb Martin [1960] Director/Company Executive

Merrill Lynch International
Incorporated: 2 November 1988 *Employees:* 1,996
Net Worth: £26,374,260,736 *Total Assets:* £280,847,286,272
Registered Office: 2 King Edward Street, London, EC1A 1HQ
Activities: Financial intermediation not elsewhere classified
Parent: ML UK Capital Holdings Limited
Officers: Julien Yves Bahurel [1974] Director/Company Executive [French]; Dr Susan Schmidt Bies [1947] Director [American]; Martin Butler [1963] Director/Company Executive; Pierre Jacques Philippe de Weck [1950] Director [Swiss]; Claire Aimie Clara Ighodaro [1953] Director; Richard John Keys [1951] Director; Bernard Amponsah Mensah [1968] Director/Company Executive; Rosemary Prudence Thorne [1952] Director

Merrill Lynch UK Finance
Incorporated: 5 December 2002 *Employees:* 2
Net Worth: £1,358,679,040 *Total Assets:* £1,358,928,000
Registered Office: 2 King Edward Street, London, EC1A 1HQ
Activities: Financial intermediation not elsewhere classified
Parent: Bank of America Corporation
Officers: Trevor Caleb Martin [1960] Director/Company Executive; Philip John Wood [1979] Director/Manager - Finance Business Support - Capital Markets

Mesoblast UK Limited
Incorporated: 7 April 2011
Net Worth: £151,043,808 *Total Assets:* £153,025,392
Registered Office: 5 New Street Square, London, EC4A 3TW
Activities: Non-trading company
Parent: Mesoblast Limited
Officers: Silviu Itescu [1957] Director/Chief Executive Officer [Australian]; Michael Anthony Sampson [1951] Director/Chartered Accountant; Leonard Francis West [1951] Director/Chartered Accountant

Metallon Corporation Limited
Incorporated: 23 April 2007
Net Worth: £274,953 *Total Assets:* £110,404,520
Registered Office: Suite 31, Second Floor, 107 Cheapside, London, EC2V 6DN
Activities: Activities of head offices
Major Shareholder: Mzilikazi Godfrey Khumalo
Officers: Raymond Sifiso Ndlovu Dabengwa [1958] Director [South African]; Mzilikazi Godfrey Khumalo [1955] Director [South African]; Andile Joy Reve [1962] Director [South African]; Dr Tomaz Augusto Salomao [1954] Director/Visiting Research Fellow [Mozambican]; Tulani Sikwila [1979] Finance Director [Zimbabwean]; Ibrahima Sory Tall [1977] Director/Civil Engineer [Guinean]

Metals Exploration PLC
Incorporated: 8 April 2004 *Employees:* 676
Net Worth: £107,975,400 *Total Assets:* £191,138,832
Registered Office: 200 Strand, London, WC2R 1DJ
Activities: Other mining and quarrying n.e.c.
Shareholder: Nicholas Anthony Christopher Candy
Officers: Darren Patrick Bowden [1969] Director [Australian]; Andrew Dean Stancliffe [1977] Director; Guy Redvers Walker [1969] Director [New Zealander]

Metdist Limited
Incorporated: 26 February 1970 *Employees:* 14
Net Worth: £189,480,944 *Total Assets:* £250,398,688
Registered Office: One Fleet Place, London, EC4M 7WS
Activities: Non-specialised wholesale trade
Major Shareholder: The Honourable Mr Apurv Bagri
Officers: Apurv Bagri [1959] Director/Business Executive [Indian]; Lady Usha Bagri [1939] Director [Indian]; Christakis Klerides [1951] Director/Chartered Accountant [Cypriot]; Viktor Papadopoulos [1953] Director/Businessman [Cypriot]; Phidias Pilides [1951] Director/Chartered Accountant [Cypriot]; Uday Singhi [1952] Director/Executive [Indian]

Meteogroup Limited
Incorporated: 21 November 1991 *Employees:* 7
Net Worth: £38,410,436 *Total Assets:* £111,165,504
Registered Office: PA Newscentre, 292 Vauxhall Bridge Road, London, SW1V 1AE
Activities: Activities of head offices
Officers: Mario Cesari [1967] Director [Swiss]; Ben James Leonard Kelly [1982] Director/Solicitor; Roger McMahon [1957] Director

Methane Services Limited
Incorporated: 9 October 1962
Net Worth: £141,294,224 *Total Assets:* £1,795,226,112
Registered Office: Shell Centre, London, SE1 7NA
Activities: Sea and coastal freight water transport
Parent: BG Energy Holdings Limited
Officers: Osler D'Costa [1977] Director/Oil Company Executive; Anthony Richard Dickins [1963] Director/Oil Company Executive; Michael Paul Lockey [1964] Director/Oil Company Executive; Stefan Andrew Strausfeld-Perry [1985] Director/Oil Company Executive

Methodist Independent Schools Trust
Incorporated: 26 May 2011 *Employees:* 2,349
Net Worth: £79,705,000 *Total Assets:* £124,512,000
Registered Office: Methodist Church House, 25 Marylebone Road, London, NW1 5JR
Activities: Educational support services
Officers: John Martin Weaving, Secretary; Steven Abbott [1956] Director/Retired RAF/Independent Consultant; Rev John Charles Allanson Barrett [1943] Director/Minister; Nicholas Brian Buckland OBE [1951] Non-Executive Chair and Director; Revd Stephen John Burgess [1949] Director/Methodist Minister; Elizabeth Elaine Cleland [1944] Director/Personal Development Consultant; Lorna Joan Cocking [1941] Director/Vice Chancellor; Barbara Mary Easton [1959] Director of Education; Margaret Joan Faulkner [1946] Director/Retired; Veronica Lesley Knight [1954] Director/Circuit Judge; Keith William Norman [1953] Director/Education Consultant; Dr Neil Tunnicliffe [1964] Director/Sports Consultant

Metinvest Capital UK Limited
Incorporated: 21 November 2013 *Employees:* 1
Net Worth: £151,294,848 *Total Assets:* £211,210,656
Registered Office: 3rd Floor, 11-12 St James's Square, London, SW1Y 4LB
Activities: Financial intermediation not elsewhere classified
Parent: Metinvest Investments Limited
Officers: Oleksandr Lyubarev [1980] Director/Head of Corporate Finance [Ukrainian]

Metinvest Investments Limited
Incorporated: 21 November 2013
Net Worth Deficit: £5,850,972 *Total Assets:* £209,282,384
Registered Office: 3rd Floor, 11-12 St James's Square, London, SW1Y 4LB
Activities: Financial intermediation not elsewhere classified
Major Shareholder: Rinat Akhmetov
Officers: Oleksandr Lyubarev [1980] Director/Head of Corporate Finance [Ukrainian]

Metric Property Investments Limited
Incorporated: 1 March 2010
Previous: Metric Property Investments PLC
Net Worth: £170,275,536 *Total Assets:* £170,276,832
Registered Office: 1 Curzon Street, London, W1J 5HB
Activities: Buying and selling of own real estate
Parent: Londonmetric Property PLC
Officers: Jadzia Zofia Duzniak, Secretary; Valentine Tristram Beresford [1965] Director; Andrew Marc Jones [1968] Director; Martin Francis McGann [1961] Director/Accountant; Mark Andrew Stirling [1963] Director

Metro Bank PLC
Incorporated: 6 November 2007 *Employees:* 2,831
Net Worth: £1,095,889,024 *Total Assets:* £16,355,354,624
Registered Office: One Southampton Row, London, WC1B 5HA
Activities: Banks
Officers: David Thomas Arden, Secretary; David Thomas Arden [1969] Director; Stuart David Murray Bernau [1951] Director; Catherine Ann Brown [1966] Director [British/New Zealander]; Keith Arthur Carby [1946] Director; Craig Francis Donaldson [1971] Managing Director; Roger Farah [1953] Director [American]; Howard Emerson Flight [1948] Director; Alastair Roy Geoffrey Gunn [1950] Director; Vernon William Hill [1945] Director [American]; Harry Eugene Lockhart [1949] Director [American]; Anna Monique Melis [1966] Managing Director [Swedish]; Sir Michael John Snyder [1950] Director/Chartered Accountant; Pavandeep Paul Thandi [1966] Director

Metroline Limited
Incorporated: 11 June 1993 *Employees:* 5,569
Net Worth: £215,120,000 *Total Assets:* £294,353,984
Registered Office: Comfortdelgro House, 329 Edgware Road, Cricklewood, London, NW2 6JP
Activities: Other urban, suburban or metropolitan passenger land transport (not underground, metro or similar)
Parent: Braddell Limited
Officers: Ishai Eliezer Novick, Secretary; Juay Kiat Gan [1957] Director [Singaporean]; Jit Poh Lim [1939] Director [Singaporean]; Sean Poul O'Shea [1967] Director; Ban Seng Yang [1956] Director/Chief Executive [Singaporean]

Metroline Travel Limited
Incorporated: 14 December 1988 *Employees:* 4,087
Net Worth: £121,430,000 *Total Assets:* £220,036,000
Registered Office: Comfortdelgro House, 329 Edgware Road, Cricklewood, London, NW2 6JP
Activities: Other urban, suburban or metropolitan passenger land transport (not underground, metro or similar)
Parent: Metroline Limited
Officers: Ishai Eliezer Novick, Secretary; Ian Geoffrey Foster [1960] Director; Sean Poul O'Shea [1967] Director

Metropolitan Properties Co. (F.G.C.) Limited
Incorporated: 13 December 1965 *Employees:* 8
Net Worth: £125,208,608 *Total Assets:* £230,389,968
Registered Office: Freshwater House, 158-162 Shaftesbury Avenue, London, WC2H 8HR
Activities: Buying and selling of own real estate
Parent: Metropolitan Properties Company Limited
Officers: Mark Roy Mason Jenner, Secretary; David Davis [1935] Director/Chartered Accountant; Benzion Schalom Eliezer Freshwater [1948] Director

Metropolitan Properties Company Limited
Incorporated: 23 February 1895 *Employees:* 37
Net Worth: £545,944,000 *Total Assets:* £721,740,992
Registered Office: Freshwater House, 158-162 Shaftesbury Avenue, London, WC2H 8HR
Activities: Buying and selling of own real estate
Parent: Freshwater Family Holdings Limited
Officers: Mark Roy Mason Jenner, Secretary; David Davis [1935] Director/Chartered Accountant; Benzion Schalom Eliezer Freshwater [1948] Director

Meurice Limited
Incorporated: 30 January 1997
Net Worth: £12,928,973 *Total Assets:* £120,557,688
Registered Office: 3 Tilney Street, London, W1K 1BJ
Activities: Hotels and similar accommodation
Parent: Dorchester Group Limited
Officers: Azmi Abdul Rahman Ibrahim [1978] Director [Bruneian]; Sofian MD Jani [1971] Director [Bruneian]

Mezqual Limited
Incorporated: 13 January 2014 *Employees:* 167
Net Worth: £89,644,760 *Total Assets:* £227,753,104
Registered Office: 5th Floor, 6 St Andrew Street, London, EC4A 3AE
Activities: Activities of other holding companies n.e.c.
Officers: Emilio Alvarez Mezquiriz [1957] Director/Business Executive [Spanish]; Juan Carlos Alvarez Mezquiriz [1956] Director/Business Executive [Spanish]; Maria Elvira Alvarez Mezquiriz [1960] Director/Business Executive [Spanish]; Marta Maria Alvarez Mezquiriz [1966] Director/Business Executive [Spanish]; Pablo Manuel Alvarez Mezquiriz [1954] Director/Business Executive [Spanish]; Stephen William Spencer Norton [1959] Director

MF Bidco Limited
Incorporated: 24 August 2017
Net Worth: £608,075,776 *Total Assets:* £975,293,824
Registered Office: Matchesfashion, The Shard, 32 London Bridge Street, London, SE1 9SG
Activities: Non-trading company
Parent: MF Intermediate Limited
Officers: Gabriele Cipparrone [1975] Director [Italian]; Fiona Louise Greiner [1966] Director; Ulric Jerome [1978] Director [French]; Vidur Narain [1989] Director

MF Debtco Limited
Incorporated: 15 September 2017
Net Worth: £612,337,920 *Total Assets:* £711,783,040
Registered Office: Matchesfashion, The Shard, 32 London Bridge Street, London, SE1 9SG
Activities: Non-trading company
Parent: MF Midco Limited
Officers: Gabriele Cipparrone [1975] Director [Italian]; Vidur Narain [1989] Director

MF Finco1 Limited
Incorporated: 11 October 2017
Net Worth: £46,038,664 *Total Assets:* £150,000,000
Registered Office: Matchesfashion, The Shard, 32 London Bridge Street, London, SE1 9SG
Activities: Non-trading company
Parent: MF Bidco Limited
Officers: Gabriele Cipparrone [1975] Director [Italian]; Vidur Narain [1989] Director

MF Intermediate Limited
Incorporated: 24 August 2017 *Employees:* 614
Net Worth: £601,590,912 *Total Assets:* £946,333,376
Registered Office: Matchesfashion, The Shard, 32 London Bridge Street, London, SE1 9SG
Activities: Non-trading company
Parent: MF Debtco Limited
Officers: Gabriele Cipparrone [1975] Director [Italian]; Vidur Narain [1989] Director

MF Midco Limited
Incorporated: 24 August 2017 *Employees:* 614
Net Worth: £490,137,536 *Total Assets:* £963,459,008
Registered Office: Matchesfashion, The Shard, 32 London Bridge Street, London, SE1 9SG
Activities: Non-trading company
Officers: Gabriele Cipparrone [1975] Director [Italian]; Vidur Narain [1989] Director

MF White Television City Limited
Incorporated: 24 May 2012
Net Worth: £270,412,256 *Total Assets:* £270,412,448
Registered Office: 7th Floor, Berger House, 38 Berkeley Square, London, W1J 5AE
Activities: Other business support service activities n.e.c.
Parent: Mitsui Fudosan (U.K.) Ltd.
Officers: Hiroshi Hisada [1971] Director [Japanese]; Eiichiro Onozawa [1963] Director [Japanese]

MGL2 Limited
Incorporated: 2 May 2007 *Employees:* 245
Net Worth: £80,903,000 *Total Assets:* £1,018,627,968
Registered Office: One Canary Wharf, London, E14 5AP
Activities: Activities of head offices
Parent: Reach Publishing Group Limited
Officers: Simon Richard Fox [1961] Director/Chief Executive; Simon Jeremy Ian Fuller [1977] Director/Chartered Accountant; Vijay Lakhman Vaghela [1966] Director/Accountant

MGM Advantage Holdings Limited
Incorporated: 7 February 2013 *Employees:* 101
Net Worth: £120,701,000 *Total Assets:* £2,701,523,968
Registered Office: 6th Floor, 110 Cannon Street, London, EC4N 6EU
Activities: Activities of financial services holding companies
Officers: Abayomi Kehinde Akisanya, Secretary; Douglas Allan Brown [1971] Director; John Robert Cusins [1972] Director/Finance; Robert Craig Fazzini-Jones [1975] Director/Chief Executive Officer; Nathan Moss [1955] Director; Derek Nigel Donald Netherton [1945] Director/Chairman; Sir William Henry Proby [1949] Director

MGN Limited
Incorporated: 2 January 1991 *Employees:* 676
Net Worth: £840,246,016 *Total Assets:* £862,868,992
Registered Office: One Canary Wharf, London, E14 5AP
Activities: Printing of newspapers
Parent: MGL2 Limited
Officers: Simon Richard Fox [1961] Director/Chief Executive; Simon Jeremy Ian Fuller [1977] Director/Chartered Accountant; Vijay Lakhman Vaghela [1966] Director/Accountant

MHDV Holdings (UK) Limited
Incorporated: 29 November 2012
Net Worth: £548,000 *Total Assets:* £114,223,000
Registered Office: 3rd Floor, 95 Cromwell Road, London, SW7 4DL
Activities: Activities of other holding companies n.e.c.
Parent: Frasers Hospitality UK Holdings Limited
Officers: Gustaaf Franciscus Joseph Bakker [1961] Director/Chief Executive [Dutch]; Peng Sum Choe [1960] Director [Singaporean]

MHG Senior Borrower Limited
Incorporated: 30 November 2012
Net Worth: £188,531,008 *Total Assets:* £452,097,984
Registered Office: 41-43 Brook Street, Mayfair, London, W1K 4HJ
Activities: Activities of other holding companies n.e.c.
Parent: MHG Senior Holdco Limited
Officers: Liam Cunningham [1958] Director [Irish]; Marc Socker [1976] Director; Mark Vose [1966] Director

Midasplayer.Com Ltd.
Incorporated: 13 September 2002 *Employees:* 448
Net Worth: £127,639,960 *Total Assets:* £189,846,208
Registered Office: The Ampersand Building, 178 Wardour Street, London, W1F 8FY
Activities: Other information technology service activities
Parent: Activision Blizzard, Inc.
Officers: Marius Joseph McKeon [1954] Director [Maltese]; Humam Sakhnini [1968] Director/Chief Financial & Strategy Officer [American]

Midcorp Limited
Incorporated: 18 June 1957
Net Worth: £160,922,000 *Total Assets:* £160,922,000
Registered Office: 8 Canada Square, London, E14 5HQ
Activities: Activities of financial services holding companies
Officers: Romana Lewis, Secretary; Philip Antony Alvey [1974] Director/Accountant; Christopher Peter Davies [1962] Director; Rajiv Kumar Gopaul [1968] Director/Accountant; Peter John Reid [1962] Director/Accountant

Miki Travel Limited
Incorporated: 25 July 1980 *Employees:* 412
Net Worth: £45,758,024 *Total Assets:* £143,779,952
Registered Office: Vintners Place, 68 Upper Thames Street, London, EC4V 3BJ
Activities: Travel agency activities
Shareholders: Group Miki Holdings Limited; His Co., Ltd
Officers: Ingrid Cawood, Secretary; Ingrid Cawood [1974] Finance Director; Fuk Wai Lau [1956] Director; Adam Lotinga [1955] Director/Hotel Division Manager; Hirohiko Saito [1968] Director [Japanese]; Shingo Togami [1971] Director [Japanese]

Millennium Capital Management Ltd.
Incorporated: 26 March 2002 *Employees:* 241
Net Worth: £26,348,000 *Total Assets:* £156,736,000
Registered Office: 50 Berkeley Street, London, W1J 8HD
Activities: Financial intermediation not elsewhere classified
Major Shareholder: Israel Alexander Englander
Officers: Milos Naumovic, Secretary; Mark Israel Meskin [1967] Managing Director; Yannis Vasatis [1957] Senior Managing Director [Greek]; Robert Westling [1965] Managing Director [American]

Millennium Capital Partners LLP
Incorporated: 21 April 2005 *Employees:* 110
Net Worth: £59,997,000 *Total Assets:* £136,392,000
Registered Office: 50 Berkeley Street, London, W1J 8HD
Officers: John Frederick Anderson [1965] LLP Member; Andres Ricardo Anker [1973] LLP Member; James Oliver Chapman [1967] LLP Member; Gregory Tracy Alexander Knight [1967] LLP Member; Diego Megia Zunzarren [1969] LLP Member; Niels-Nicolas Patrick Pecriaux [1985] LLP Member; Hendrikus Augustus Petermeijer [1967] LLP Member; Adam Keith Sutton [1974] LLP Member; James Stuart Michael Watson [1979] LLP Member; Linus James Wright [1970] LLP Member

Miller 2015 Limited
Incorporated: 13 January 2015
Net Worth: £181,323,008 *Total Assets:* £276,464,992
Registered Office: 51 Lime Street, London, EC3M 7DQ
Activities: Activities of other holding companies n.e.c.
Parent: Willis Group Limited
Officers: Peter James Carter [1970] Director; Andrew Krasner [1975] Director/Corporate Finance [American]; David Maelor Thomas [1961] Director/Insurance Broker

Miller Freeman Worldwide Limited
Incorporated: 7 September 1983
Net Worth: £118,830,000 *Total Assets:* £128,476,000
Registered Office: 5 Howick Place, London, SW1P 1WG
Activities: Other business support service activities n.e.c.
Parent: UBMG Holdings
Officers: Rupert John Joseph Hopley [1969] Director/Solicitor

Miller Insurance Services LLP
Incorporated: 12 February 2002 *Employees:* 423
Net Worth: £138,502,000 *Total Assets:* £657,651,008
Registered Office: 70 Mark Lane, London, EC3R 7NQ
Officers: Edward Richard Graham Clarke [1956] Member; Gregory Eugene Mary Collins [1958] Member; Martin John Davison [1964] Member; Kenneth Scott MacDonald [1962] Member; Andrew Charles Bettis [1974] LLP Member; Mark Carver [1973] LLP Member; Andrew Nicholas Challacombe [1965] LLP Member; Gary James Clark [1966] LLP Member; Nigel Christopher St John Cross [1969] LLP Member; Stephen Paul Daniels [1961] LLP Member; Peter John Dixon [1964] LLP Member; Anthony Dryden [1969] LLP Member; John Clifford Eltham [1961] LLP Member; Nicholas Fearon [1968] LLP Member; Stephen Michael Peter Finch [1957] LLP Member; Andrew Kenneth Ford [1968] LLP Member; Arnaud Froideval [1975] LLP Member; Jonathan David Fussell [1963] LLP Member; Alexander Carlisle Gray [1967] LLP Member; Pierre Henri Dominique Yves Guntzberger [1978] LLP Member; James Michael Hands [1975] LLP Member; Martin Alexander Henderson [1982] LLP Member; Neil John Higgins [1969] LLP Member; Johanna Roseanne Holiday [1968] LLP Member; Thomas Hamilton Holmes [1975] LLP Member; Charles Lane [1966] LLP Member; Andrew Henry Benedict Miller [1958] LLP Member; Douglas Robert Milne [1959] LLP Member; David Philip Neilson [1961] LLP Member; Timothy William Norman [1971] LLP Member; Michael Peter Papworth [1963] LLP Member; Mark Nicholas Popple [1960] LLP Member; Timothy John Press [1969] LLP Member; Paul Watson Ray [1967] LLP Member; Timothy James Regan [1967] LLP Member; Jonathan Michael Walker Sale [1962] LLP Member; Julian Mark Sawyer [1961] LLP Member; Richard Gregg Scurrell [1978] LLP Member; Jason Michael Sidgwick [1970] LLP Member; Benjamin Robert Speers [1975] LLP Member; Robert Tarr [1968] LLP Member; Alexander Thomas Edward Vincent [1968] LLP Member; Philip John Wheeler [1977] LLP Member

Millward Brown No.2337 Limited
Incorporated: 26 February 2003
Previous: WPP No.2337 Limited
Net Worth: £524,694,016 *Total Assets:* £524,694,016
Registered Office: Sea Containers House, 18 Upper Ground, London, SE1 9GL
Activities: Other business support service activities n.e.c.
Parent: WPP LN Limited
Officers: Charles Ward Van Der Welle [1959] Director/Group Treasurer; Steve Richard Winters [1968] Director/Chartered Accountant

Milton Magna Limited
Incorporated: 23 August 2012 *Employees:* 2
Net Worth: £53,299,644 *Total Assets:* £183,753,344
Registered Office: Acre House, 11-15 William Road, London, NW1 3ER
Activities: Security dealing on own account
Officers: Hamish MacGregor Ogston [1948] Director

Mindshare Media UK Limited
Incorporated: 20 August 1997 *Employees:* 807
Net Worth: £32,393,000 *Total Assets:* £288,172,000
Registered Office: Central St Giles, 1 St Giles High Street, London, WC2H 8AR
Activities: Advertising agencies
Parent: WPP Toronto Limited
Officers: Colin Barlow [1968] Finance Director; Dawn Louise Dickie [1961] Director/Treasurer; Tony Gaymer [1976] Director/Chief Financial Officer; Helen McRae [1971] Director/Chief Executive Officer [Australian]; Nicholas James Morris [1969] Director/Global CFO

Minerva Corporation Limited
Incorporated: 12 October 1987 *Employees:* 2
Net Worth Deficit: £150,915,584 *Total Assets:* £136,396,592
Registered Office: 40 Queen Anne Street, London, W1G 9EL
Activities: Activities of head offices
Parent: Minerva Limited
Officers: Michael George Cohen [1963] Director/Chartered Accountant; Paul Jonathan Goswell [1964] Director; Alexander Wilson Lamont [1978] Director; James Anthony Piper [1983] Managing Director, Real Estate Investment

Minerva Limited
Incorporated: 27 September 1991
Net Worth: £95,539,232 *Total Assets:* £104,863,456
Registered Office: 40 Queen Anne Street, London, W1G 9EL
Activities: Activities of head offices
Parent: Jupiter Properties 2011 UK Limited
Officers: Paul Jonathan Goswell [1964] Director; Alexander Wilson Lamont [1978] Director; John Manwaring Robertson [1951] Director/Partner; Colin Barry Wagman [1946] Director/Chartered Accountant

Minmetals (U.K) Limited
Incorporated: 25 March 1985 *Employees:* 16
Net Worth: £26,830,068 *Total Assets:* £191,641,648
Registered Office: 5a Praed Street, London, W2 1NJ
Activities: Wholesale of metals and metal ores
Officers: Jing Xiang Yuan, Secretary; Liangmin Gu [1963] Deputy Managing Director [Chinese]; Han Sun [1981] Deputy Managing Director [Chinese]; Jin Wang [1963] Managing Director [Chinese]

Minova Insurance Holdings Limited
Incorporated: 29 April 1980 *Employees:* 465
Net Worth Deficit: £42,323,000 *Total Assets:* £106,488,000
Registered Office: One America Square, London, EC3N 2LS
Activities: Activities of head offices
Officers: Shaun Kevin Bryant, Secretary; Nicholas James Edward Cook [1970] Director/Insurance Broker; Dr Dane Jonathan Douetil [1960] Director; Christopher John Hopton [1955] Director/Management Consultant; Jonathan Dennis Kelly [1964] Director [American]; Andrew Neil McMellin [1966] Director; James Morley [1949] Director; Paul John Vincent [1966] Finance Director; Ian Waterston [1967] Director/Insurance Broker

MIPL Group Limited
Incorporated: 3 February 2011 *Employees:* 181
Net Worth: £467,892,960 *Total Assets:* £569,194,560
Registered Office: Fifth Floor, 10 Gresham Street, London, EC2V 7JD
Activities: Non-trading company
Officers: Jason Menegakis, Secretary; Elizabeth Anne Desmond [1961] Director [American]; Clive Ashley Gillmore [1960] Director; Hamish Owen Parker [1959] Director; Warren David Shirvell [1967] Director/Chief Operating Officer; David George Tilles [1952] Director/Chairman

MIPL Holdings Limited
Incorporated: 7 February 2011 *Employees:* 181
Net Worth: £468,277,472 *Total Assets:* £569,579,008
Registered Office: Fifth Floor, 10 Gresham Street, London, EC2V 7JD
Activities: Non-trading company
Officers: Jason Menegakis, Secretary; Elizabeth Anne Desmond [1960] Director [American]; Clive Ashley Gillmore [1960] Director; Hamish Owen Parker [1959] Director; Warren David Shirvell [1967] Director/Chief Operating Officer; David George Tilles [1952] Director/Chairman

Miracle Nova (UK) Limited
Incorporated: 29 December 2014
Net Worth Deficit: £28,368 *Total Assets:* £451,574,016
Registered Office: Fosun, 2 Thomas More Square, London, E1W 1YN
Activities: Activities of other holding companies n.e.c.
Officers: Qiyu Chen [1972] Director/Executive [Chinese]; Zhuo Chen [1982] Director [Chinese]; Fulin Liang [1977] Director [Chinese]

Mirion Technologies (Global), Ltd.
Incorporated: 7 November 2014
Net Worth: £51,955,288 *Total Assets:* £495,010,784
Registered Office: Warwick Court, Paternoster Square, London, EC4M 7DX
Activities: Other business support service activities n.e.c.
Officers: Irina Marsovna Watson, Secretary; James Francis Charles Cocks [1971] Director; Pierre Marie Alain de Sarrau [1982] Director/Investment Manager [French]; Christopher Laurence Warren [1975] Director/Partner

Mirion Technologies (HoldingRep), Ltd.
Incorporated: 6 November 2014
Net Worth: £520,577,024 *Total Assets:* £520,683,744
Registered Office: Warwick Court, Paternoster Square, London, EC4M 7DX
Activities: Other business support service activities n.e.c.
Officers: Irina Marsovna Watson, Secretary; James Francis Charles Cocks [1971] Director; Pierre Marie Alain de Sarrau [1982] Director/Investment Manager [French]

Mirion Technologies (HoldingSub1), Ltd.
Incorporated: 6 November 2014
Net Worth: £1,658,219 *Total Assets:* £538,679,296
Registered Office: Warwick Court, Paternoster Square, London, EC4M 7DX
Activities: Other business support service activities n.e.c.
Officers: Irina Marsovna Watson, Secretary; James Simon Edward Arnell [1969] Director/Investment Banker; James Francis Charles Cocks [1971] Director; Pierre Marie Alain de Sarrau [1982] Director/Investment Manager [French]; Christopher Laurence Warren [1975] Director/Partner

Mirion Technologies (HoldingSub2), Ltd.
Incorporated: 6 November 2014
Net Worth Deficit: £97,401,584 *Total Assets:* £432,825,920
Registered Office: Warwick Court, Paternoster Square, London, EC4M 7DX
Activities: Other business support service activities n.e.c.
Officers: Irina Marsovna Watson, Secretary; James Francis Charles Cocks [1971] Director; Pierre Marie Alain de Sarrau [1982] Director/Investment Manager [French]

Mishcon de Reya LLP
Incorporated: 18 May 2015 *Employees:* 666
Net Worth: £66,234,000 *Total Assets:* £122,107,000
Registered Office: Africa House, 70 Kingsway, London, WC2B 6AH
Officers: Nicholas Mark Davis [1961] Member; Charalambos Georgiou [1961] Member; Kevin John Gold [1961] Member; James Lewis Libson [1966] Member; Joel Julius Adler [1952] LLP Member; Shasitah Akhtar [1973] LLP Member; Leslie Brian Allen [1961] LLP Member; Michael Charles Armstrong [1968] LLP Member; Rajendran Selvakumar Bartlett [1963] LLP Member; Jonathan Richard Berman [1961] LLP Member; Raymond David Black [1952] LLP Member; Joanna Caroline Blackburn [1969] LLP Member; Steven Allan Bostock [1981] LLP Member; Susan Elizabeth Breen [1959] LLP Member; Nicola Yvanna Bridge [1973] LLP Member; Sally Louise Britton [1974] LLP Member; Claire Louise Broadbelt [1974] LLP Member; Jarret Bevan Brown [1959] LLP Member; Samuel Ross Bryson [1969] LLP Member; Malcolm Gregory Campbell [1970] LLP Member; Sonia Campbell [1974] LLP Member; Simon Marc Chadowitz [1982] LLP Member; Laura Jane Chandler [1980] LLP Member; Lewis Theodore Cohen [1973] LLP Member; David Brennan Cummings [1977] LLP Member; Karel Daele [1972] LLP Member; David Martin Davies [1956] LLP Member; Danny Joseph Davis [1964] LLP Member; Mark Jonathan Davis [1959] LLP Member; Sandra Sharon Davis [1956] LLP Member; Vanessa Ann Dewhurst [1967] LLP Member; Stephen Francis Diosi [1976] LLP Member; Nicholas Ian Doffman [1961] LLP Member; Elizabeth Jane Ellen [1982] LLP Member; John William Arthur England [1972] LLP Member; Adam James Epstein [1965] LLP Member; Timothy Andrew Field [1965] LLP Member; Philip Bernard Freedman [1947] LLP Member; Susan Marion Freeman [1953] LLP Member; Kathryn Garbett [1963] LLP Member; Richard Darryl Gerstein [1958] LLP Member; Benjamin Giaretta [1974] LLP Member; Andrew Francis Goldstone [1965] LLP Member; Daniel Brian Greenaway [1977] LLP Member; Martyn Charles Hann [1962] LLP Member; Simon Thomas Hart [1977] LLP Member; Robert Edward Hartley [1972] LLP Member; Rowena Kirsten Sonia Heather Herdman-Smith [1964] LLP Member; Jeremy Milton Hertzog [1971] LLP Member; Sarah Marion Houghton [1980] LLP Member; Stephen Hughes [1970] LLP Member; Edward Christopher Hughes-Power [1983] LLP Member; Simon Leigh Hunter [1966] LLP Member; Chhavie Kapoor [1976] LLP Member; Kirpal Kaur [1963] LLP Member; Sarah Margaret Keeble [1964] LLP Member; Mark Reginald Keenan [1966] LLP Member; Mohammed Jaffer Khamisa QC [1962] LLP Member; Susannah Kintish [1983] LLP Member; Joanna Kate Lampert [1973] LLP Member; Richard James Leedham [1966] LLP Member; Jonathan Charles Legg [1976] LLP Member; David Uri Leibowitz [1960] LLP Member; Melissa Marie Brigitte Lesson [1974] LLP Member; Mark Alexander Levine [1974] LLP Member; Daniel Joseph Levy [1972] LLP Member; Daniel Lipman [1969] LLP Member; David Brodie Lister [1961] LLP Member; Emma Mary MacIntyre [1969] LLP Member; Kevin Edward Francis McCarthy [1970] LLP Member; Stuart Charles McMaster [1971] LLP Member; Nadim Mahomed Meer [1973] LLP Member; Abul Kassim Meghjee [1972] LLP Member; Gary Paul Miller [1954] LLP Member; Jennifer Ann Millins [1979] LLP Member; Nicholas Minkoff [1971] LLP Member; Anthony Morton-Hooper [1954] LLP Member; Elliot David Moss [1970] LLP Member; Robert Paul Murray [1963] LLP Member; Daniel Avram Naftalin [1971] LLP Member; Larry Graeme Nathan [1962] LLP Member; Paul Gerard Noble [1967] LLP Member; Nicholas John Nocton [1970] LLP Member; Filippo Noseda [1970] LLP Member; Michael Nouril [1970] LLP Member; James Robert Oldnall [1978] LLP Member; Maria Patsalos [1980] LLP Member; Ian Stuart Paul [1961] LLP Member; Victoria Sarah Pigott [1978] LLP Member; Hugo John Alexander Plowman [1977] LLP Member; Dean Russell Poster [1965] LLP Member; Genevieve Quierin [1974] LLP Member; Kamal Jyoti Ayesha Rahman [1965] LLP Member; Barbara Reeves [1962] LLP Member; Gary Richards [1955] LLP Member; Joanne Elisabeth Rickards [1963] LLP Member; Andrew Rimmington [1969] LLP Member; Anita Rivera [1965] LLP Member; Adam Daniel Rose [1966] LLP Member; David Rose [1969] LLP Member

The Mission Marketing Group Public Limited Company
Incorporated: 7 March 2006 *Employees:* 1,015
Net Worth: £79,645,000 *Total Assets:* £133,134,000
Registered Office: 36 Percy Street, London, W1T 2DH
Activities: Advertising agencies
Officers: Peter David Campbell Fitzwilliam, Secretary; Dylan Bogg [1969] Director; James Spencer Clifton [1972] Managing Director; Robert Andrew Day [1965] Director/Designer; Peter David Campbell Fitzwilliam [1960] Director/Chartered Accountant; Julian Christopher Hanson-Smith [1962] Director/Business Consultant; Giles Derek Lee [1970] Director/Accountant; David William Morgan [1947] Director/Advertising Agent; Susan Maire Mullen [1961] Managing Director; Andrew John Nash [1957] Director; Michael Jack Rose [1976] Director; Fiona Shepherd [1965] Director

Misys International Limited
Incorporated: 13 March 2012
Previous: Magic Bidco Limited
Net Worth Deficit: £886,413,056 *Total Assets:* £1,395,958,784
Registered Office: Four Kingdom Street, Paddington, London, W2 6BD
Activities: Other software publishing
Officers: Robert Hugh Binns [1968] Director; Simon Peter Dowler [1965] Director/General Counsel; Janet Ruth Hughes [1968] Finance Director; Christian Jehle [1975] Director [German]; Thomas Edward Kilroy [1970] Director/Chief of Staff; Timo Schloesser [1970] Director/Solicitor [German]

Mithras Leasing (No.1) Ltd
Incorporated: 2 December 2005
Net Worth: £5,956,375 *Total Assets:* £186,901,072
Registered Office: 99 Queen Victoria Street, London, EC4V 4EH
Activities: Financial leasing
Officers: Lee Lawrence Barnsley [1960] Director/Banker; Lawrence James Butcher [1968] Director/Banker; Antony Edward Mitton [1967] Director/Chartered Accountant; Mark Jeremy Rutherford [1965] Director/Banker; David Allen Ward [1956] Director/Banker [American]

Mithras Leasing (No.4) Limited
Incorporated: 3 March 1989
Previous: Lloyds (Nimrod) Machinery Finance Limited
Net Worth: £11,780,037 *Total Assets:* £162,723,392
Registered Office: 99 Queen Victoria Street, London, EC4V 4EH
Activities: Financial leasing
Officers: Lee Lawrence Barnsley [1960] Director; Lawrence James Butcher [1968] Director; Antony Edward Mitton [1967] Director; Mark Jeremy Rutherford [1965] Director; David Allen Ward [1956] Director [American]

Mitie Holdings Limited
Incorporated: 17 August 2006
Previous: Mitie Treasury Services Limited
Net Worth: £260,076,992 *Total Assets:* £480,476,992
Registered Office: Level 12, The Shard, 32 London Bridge Street, London, SE1 9SG
Activities: Non-trading company
Parent: Mitie Treasury Management Limited
Officers: Gillian Bonthron [1977] Director/Accountant; Peter John Goddard Dickinson [1962] Director; David Michael Forbes [1976] Director/Group Treasurer; Matthew Idle [1968] Director

Mitie Limited
Incorporated: 13 June 1994 *Employees:* 876
Previous: Mitie Facilities Services Limited
Net Worth: £278,449,984 *Total Assets:* £499,351,008
Registered Office: Level 12, The Shard, 32 London Bridge Street, London, SE1 9SG
Activities: Other business support service activities n.e.c.
Parent: Mitie Holdings Limited
Officers: Peter John Goddard Dickinson [1962] Director; Matthew Idle [1968] Director

Mitie Security Holdings Limited
Incorporated: 17 August 2006
Net Worth: £116,617,000 *Total Assets:* £116,945,000
Registered Office: Level 12, The Shard, 32 London Bridge Street, London, SE1 9SG
Activities: Activities of other holding companies n.e.c.
Parent: Mitie Limited
Officers: Peter John Goddard Dickinson [1962] Director; Matthew Idle [1968] Director

Mitie Technical Facilities Management Holdings Limited
Incorporated: 3 December 2009
Net Worth: £101,790,000 *Total Assets:* £220,376,992
Registered Office: Level 12, The Shard, 32 London Bridge Street, London, SE1 9SG
Activities: Activities of other holding companies n.e.c.
Parent: Mitie Treasury Management Limited
Officers: Peter John Goddard Dickinson [1962] Director; Matthew Idle [1968] Director

Mitie Technical Facilities Management Limited
Incorporated: 24 May 1967 *Employees:* 4,250
Net Worth Deficit: £3,442,000 *Total Assets:* £288,719,008
Registered Office: Level 12, The Shard, 32 London Bridge Street, London, SE1 9SG
Activities: Other service activities n.e.c.
Parent: Mitie Technical Facilities Management Holdings Limited
Officers: Peter John Goddard Dickinson [1962] Director; Matthew Idle [1968] Director

Mitie Treasury Management Limited
Incorporated: 19 August 2010
Net Worth: £618,612,992 *Total Assets:* £1,201,356,032
Registered Office: Level 12, The Shard, 32 London Bridge Street, London, SE1 9SG
Activities: Other service activities n.e.c.
Parent: Mitie Group PLC
Officers: Gillian Bonthron [1977] Director/Accountant; Peter John Goddard Dickinson [1962] Director; David Michael Forbes [1976] Director/Group Treasurer; Matthew Idle [1968] Director

Mitsubishi Corporation Finance PLC
Incorporated: 20 November 1984
Net Worth: £280,979,296 *Total Assets:* £3,181,845,504
Registered Office: 8F Mid City Place, 71 High Holborn, London, WC1V 6BA
Activities: Financial intermediation not elsewhere classified
Parent: Mitsubishi Corporation
Officers: Guy Usher, Secretary; Isao Kano [1960] Director [Japanese]; Hiroko Niwa [1966] Managing Director & CEO [Japanese]; Makoto Okawara [1963] Director [Japanese]

Mitsubishi Corporation International (Europe) PLC
Incorporated: 26 January 1988 *Employees:* 164
Net Worth: £168,931,008 *Total Assets:* £604,982,016
Registered Office: Mid City Place, 71 High Holborn, London, WC1V 6BA
Activities: Agents involved in the sale of a variety of goods
Parent: Mitsubishi Corporation
Officers: Hiroyuki Hayakawa, Secretary; Andrew John Fraser [1950] Director/Senior Adviser; Isao Kano [1960] Managing Director [Japanese]; Yoshinori Katayama [1962] Director/Senior Vice President [Japanese]; Kazuyoshi Kawakami [1969] Director/Chief Financial Officer [Japanese]; Takeshi Matsushita [1971] Director/General Manager [Japanese]; Junya Nagase [1963] Director/General Manager [Japanese]; Koichi Ninomiya [1968] Alternate Director [Japanese]; Martin Joel Pratt [1972] Director/Chief Operating Officer; Julie Rogers [1968] Director/General Manager; Norio Suzuki [1965] Director/Regional Head of Gib Div [Japanese]; Gary Neil Williams [1961] Director/General Manager

Mitsubishi Estate Europe Limited
Incorporated: 26 November 2009
Net Worth: £362,445,632 *Total Assets:* £362,456,256
Registered Office: Cannon Place, 78 Cannon Street, London, EC4N 6AF
Activities: Activities of head offices
Parent: Mitsubishi Estate Company Limited
Officers: Shinichi Kagitomi [1970] Director/Office Worker [Japanese]; Yuichiro Shioda [1967] Director [Japanese]

Mitsubishi Estate London Limited
Incorporated: 24 October 1989 *Employees:* 13
Net Worth: £802,006,016 *Total Assets:* £1,269,094,016
Registered Office: Cannon Place, 78 Cannon Street, London, EC4N 6AF
Activities: Buying and selling of own real estate
Parent: Mitsubishi Estate Europe Limited
Officers: Yuko Koibuchi, Secretary; Shinichi Kagitomi [1970] Director/Office Worker [Japanese]; Yuichiro Shioda [1967] Director [Japanese]

Mitsubishi Hitachi Power Systems Europe, Ltd.
Incorporated: 1 October 2015 *Employees:* 191
Net Worth: £384,883,008 *Total Assets:* £446,872,992
Registered Office: The Point, 37 North Wharf Road, London, W2 1AF
Activities: Repair of machinery
Shareholders: Mitsubishi Heavy Industries, Ltd.; Hitachi, Ltd.
Officers: Robert Edward Evans, Secretary; Yasuo Fujitani [1955] Director [Japanese]; Satoshi Honda [1964] Director [Japanese]; Takeo Nakamura [1978] Director [Japanese]; Yoshihiro Shiraiwa [1956] Director [Japanese]; Taiji Yoshida [1957] Director [Japanese]

Mitsui & Co. Europe PLC
Incorporated: 9 December 1987 *Employees:* 293
Net Worth: £113,113,000 *Total Assets:* £478,259,008
Registered Office: 8th and 9th Floors, 1 St Martin's-le-Grand, London, EC1A 4AS
Activities: Non-specialised wholesale trade
Parent: Mitsui & Co., Ltd.
Officers: Masafumi Suehiro, Secretary; Yasushi Anzai [1961] Director [Japanese]; Yasuyuki Fujitani [1958] Managing Director [Japanese]; Naotaka Hayashi [1963] Director [Japanese]; Haruhisa Iida [1960] Director [Japanese]; Satoshi Kurimoto [1963] Director [Japanese]; Makoto Tanaka [1967] Director [Japanese]

Mitsui & Co. Financial Services (Europe) PLC
Incorporated: 27 March 2012 *Employees:* 5
Net Worth: £31,023,700 *Total Assets:* £1,086,739,072
Registered Office: 8th and 9th Floors, 1 St Martin's-le-Grand, London, EC1A 4AS
Activities: Financial intermediation not elsewhere classified
Parent: Mitsui & Co. Ltd.
Officers: Yoshimitsu Gushiken [1962] Director/Office Worker [Japanese]; Tetsu Itabashi [1962] Director [Japanese]; Hiroshi Matsuzaki [1968] Director [Japanese]; Makoto Tanaka [1967] Director [Japanese]

Mitsui Bussan Commodities Ltd
Incorporated: 15 March 2002 *Employees:* 125
Previous: Mitsui & Co. Commodity Risk Management Limited
Net Worth: £121,853,936 *Total Assets:* £564,504,384
Registered Office: 6th Floor, 1 St Martin's-le-Grand, London, EC1A 4BB
Activities: Security and commodity contracts dealing activities
Parent: Mitsui & Co., Ltd
Officers: Ryutaro Takeuchi, Secretary; Martin Abbott [1960] Director; Stuart Alexander Aitken [1974] Director; Peter Douglas Allan [1962] Director; Tsuguo Kato [1963] Director [Japanese]; Fusaaki Matsumoto [1963] Director [Japanese]; Sho Miichi [1974] Director [Japanese]; Takeshi Okada [1969] Chief Executive Director [Japanese]; Ryutaro Takeuchi [1971] Director [Japanese]

Mitsui E & P Mozambique Area 1 Limited
Incorporated: 20 November 2007 *Employees:* 8
Net Worth: £236,164,112 *Total Assets:* £251,497,792
Registered Office: 8th and 9th Floors, 1 St Martin's-le-Grand, London, EC1A 4AS
Activities: Extraction of natural gas
Shareholders: Mitsui & Co. Ltd.; Japan Oil, Gas and Metals National Corporation
Officers: Takashi Masuda [1959] Director [Japanese]; Kei Matsuoka [1977] Director [Japanese]; Motoyasu Nozaki [1960] Managing Director [Japanese]; Takashi Tomita [1973] Director [Japanese]; Eiichi Ueno [1965] Director [Japanese]

Mitsui E & P UK Limited
Incorporated: 31 May 2011 *Employees:* 12
Net Worth: £297,075,520 *Total Assets:* £433,462,016
Registered Office: 8th and 9th Floors, 1 St Martin's-le-Grand, London, EC1A 4AS
Activities: Extraction of crude petroleum
Parent: Mitsui & Co. Ltd.
Officers: Yasutomo Fujii [1958] Director [Japanese]; Naoki Ishii [1967] Director [Japanese]; Osamu Kobayashi [1971] Director [Japanese]; Haruaki Moritani [1978] Director [Japanese]; Takayuki Ogawa [1972] Director/Deputy General Manager [Japanese]; Kenichiro Yamaguchi [1968] Director/SVP & DOO [Japanese]

Mitsui Fudosan (U.K.) Ltd.
Incorporated: 17 January 1990 *Employees:* 15
Net Worth: £794,696,896 *Total Assets:* £1,809,905,280
Registered Office: 7th Floor, Berger House, 38 Berkeley Square, London, W1J 5AE
Activities: Other business support service activities n.e.c.
Parent: Mitsui Fudosan Company Limited
Officers: Yutaka Kawamura [1963] Director/Managing Officer, General Manager of International Department [Japanese]; Eiichiro Onozawa [1963] Director [Japanese]; Takashi Yamamoto [1959] Director/Executive Managing Officer [Japanese]

Mitsui Sumitomo Insurance Company (Europe), Limited
Incorporated: 28 July 1972 *Employees:* 36
Net Worth: £111,191,000 *Total Assets:* £265,940,000
Registered Office: 25 Fenchurch Avenue, London, EC3M 5AD
Activities: Non-life insurance
Parent: MS & AD Insurance Group Holdings, Inc.
Officers: Fumika Yamamoto, Secretary; Robin John Leaver Adam [1971] Director; Jean Hellewell [1955] Director/Insurance Consultant; Akihiko Ikeno [1966] Director [Japanese]; Yasuo Inoue [1979] Director [Japanese]; Johan Garth Slabbert [1970] Director [South African]; Andrew Edward Slater [1969] Finance Director

Mixhold Investments Limited
Incorporated: 12 April 2002
Net Worth: £3,911,467,008 *Total Assets:* £4,207,941,888
Registered Office: Unilever House, 100 Victoria Embankment, London, EC4Y 0DY
Activities: Other business support service activities n.e.c.
Parent: Unilever US Investments Limited
Officers: James Oliver Earley, Secretary; Richard Clive Hazell, Secretary; Anna Jo Karen Elphick [1975] Director/Accountant; Richard Clive Hazell [1966] Director/Solicitor; Amanda Louise King [1973] UK & Ireland Tax Director

Mizkan Euro Holdings Limited
Incorporated: 1 February 2012 *Employees:* 503
Net Worth: £119,535,000 *Total Assets:* £140,286,000
Registered Office: 2nd Floor, Building 10, Chiswick Park, 566 Chiswick High Road, Chiswick, London, W4 5XS
Activities: Activities of other holding companies n.e.c.
Parent: Nakano Asset Global Ltd.
Officers: Kosuke Matsushima, Secretary; Kazuhide Nakano [1950] Director [Japanese]; Miwa Nakano [1951] Director [Japanese]; Seiko Nakano [1979] Director [Japanese]; Yuko Nakano [1976] Director [Japanese]

Mizkan Euro Ltd.
Incorporated: 1 May 2012 *Employees:* 472
Net Worth: £16,578,000 *Total Assets:* £140,630,000
Registered Office: 2nd Floor, Building 10, Chiswick Park, 566 Chiswick High Road, Chiswick, London, W4 5XS
Activities: Manufacture of condiments and seasonings
Parent: Mizkan Euro Holdings Limited
Officers: Kosuke Matsushima, Secretary; Hironobu Asai [1973] Director [Japanese]; Tomoyo Hikosaka [1968] Director [Japanese]; Ichizo Kobayashi [1953] Director [Japanese]; Hiroshi Sasaoka [1974] Director [Japanese]

Mizuho International PLC
Incorporated: 14 March 1975 *Employees:* 498
Net Worth: £761,600,000 *Total Assets:* £15,517,299,712
Registered Office: Mizuho House, 30 Old Bailey, London, EC4M 7AU
Activities: Banks
Parent: Mizuho Securities Co., Ltd.
Officers: Brian Douglas Lanaghan, Secretary/Solicitor; Suneel Bakhshi [1958] Director/Chief Executive; Maureen Anne Erasmus [1960] Director/Financial Strategist; Kenji Fujii [1956] Director/Banker [Japanese]; Hideyuki Kawashima [1961] Director/Banker [Japanese]; Masahiko Mochizuki [1960] Director/Banker [Japanese]; Hiroshi Nagamine [1964] Director [Japanese]; Christopher David Newell [1960] Director; Thierry Jean-Philippe Sciard [1956] Director/Managing Principal [French]; Robert John Tallentire [1968] Executive Director; David Avery Weymouth [1955] Director

ML Invest Holdings
Incorporated: 13 November 1997 *Employees:* 5
Net Worth: £85,395,000 *Total Assets:* £117,222,000
Registered Office: 2 King Edward Street, London, EC1A 1HQ
Activities: Financial intermediation not elsewhere classified
Parent: Bank of America Corporation
Officers: Jonathan Howard Redvers Lee [1966] Director/Company Executive; Trevor Caleb Martin [1960] Director/Company Executive

ML UK Capital Holdings Limited
Incorporated: 20 November 2003 *Employees:* 5
Previous: ML UK Capital Holdings
Net Worth: £23,047,815,168 *Total Assets:* £28,004,702,208
Registered Office: 2 King Edward Street, London, EC1A 1HQ
Activities: Financial intermediation not elsewhere classified
Parent: Bank of America Corporation
Officers: Martin Butler [1963] Director/Company Executive; Bernard Amponsah Mensah [1968] Director/Company Executive; Peter Stuart O'Flynn [1969] Director/Company Executive; Jennifer Mary Taylor [1968] Director [Irish]

MLEIH Funding
Incorporated: 4 December 2007 *Employees:* 2
Net Worth: £707,238,080 *Total Assets:* £944,490,496
Registered Office: 2 King Edward Street, London, EC1A 1HQ
Activities: Financial intermediation not elsewhere classified
Parent: Bank of America Corporation
Officers: Jonathan Howard Redvers Lee [1966] Director/Company Executive; Trevor Caleb Martin [1960] Director/Company Executive

MMC Holdings (UK) Limited
Incorporated: 19 October 2015
Net Worth: £7,611,899,904 *Total Assets:* £7,612,199,936
Registered Office: 1 Tower Place West, Tower Place, London, EC3R 5BU
Activities: Activities of head offices
Parent: MMC Treasury Holdings (UK) Limited
Officers: Wendy Patricia Marsh, Secretary; Justin Bruce Broad [1968] Director/Treasurer; Jean-Paul D'Offay [1972] Director/Chartered Accountant

MMC International Limited
Incorporated: 22 January 1999
Net Worth: £1,780,524,928 *Total Assets:* £1,781,133,568
Registered Office: 1 Tower Place West, Tower Place, London, EC3R 5BU
Activities: Activities of other holding companies n.e.c.
Parent: Marsh & McLennan Companies UK Limited
Officers: Claire Margaret Valentine, Secretary; Justin Bruce Broad [1968] Director/Treasurer; Christopher John Lay [1961] Director/Insurance Broker; David Nicholas Williams [1971] Director/Accountant

MMC International Treasury Centre Limited
Incorporated: 7 August 2006
Net Worth: £49,296,312 *Total Assets:* £2,824,343,808
Registered Office: 1 Tower Place West, Tower Place, London, EC3R 5BU
Activities: Financial intermediation not elsewhere classified
Parent: MMC UK Group Limited
Officers: Wendy Patricia Marsh, Secretary; Caroline Wendy Godwin [1962] Director/Accountant; Ian Richard Hadley [1964] Director/Treasurer; Ferdinand Gerhard Jahnel [1965] Director/Treasurer [American]

MMC Middle East Holdings Limited
Incorporated: 27 July 2016
Net Worth: £248,050,960 *Total Assets:* £248,050,960
Registered Office: 1 Tower Place West, Tower Place, London, EC3R 5BU
Activities: Activities of other holding companies n.e.c.
Parent: Cascade Regional Holdings Limited
Officers: Claire Margaret Valentine, Secretary; Justin Bruce Broad [1968] Director/Treasurer; Jean-Paul D'Offay [1972] Director/Chartered Accountant; Karen Anne Farrell [1956] Director/Assistant Treasurer [American]; Ian Richard Hadley [1964] Director/Treasurer

MMC Treasury Holdings (UK) Limited
Incorporated: 21 September 2015
Net Worth: £4,670,101,504 *Total Assets:* £7,964,472,320
Registered Office: 1 Tower Place West, Tower Place, London, EC3R 5BU
Activities: Activities of head offices
Parent: Marsh & McLennan Companies, Inc.
Officers: Wendy Patricia Marsh, Secretary; Justin Bruce Broad [1968] Director/Treasurer; Karen Anne Farrell [1956] Director/Assistant Treasurer [American]; Caroline Wendy Godwin [1962] Director/Accountant; Ian Richard Hadley [1964] Director/Treasurer

MMC UK Group Limited
Incorporated: 28 January 1999
Net Worth: £1,357,682,944 *Total Assets:* £1,955,831,040
Registered Office: 1 Tower Place West, Tower Place, London, EC3R 5BU
Activities: Activities of other holding companies n.e.c.
Parent: MMC International Limited
Officers: Claire Margaret Valentine, Secretary; Justin Bruce Broad [1968] Director/Treasurer; Christopher John Lay [1961] Director/Insurance Broker; David Nicholas Williams [1971] Director/Accountant

MMS UK Holdings Limited
Incorporated: 2 December 2003
Net Worth: £610,302,016 *Total Assets:* £1,207,149,952
Registered Office: 1st Floor, 2 Television Centre, 101 Wood Lane, London, W12 7FR
Activities: Advertising agencies
Parent: Publicis Groupe S.A
Officers: Joanne Munis, Secretary; Jean-Michel Michel Etienne [1951] Director/Chief Finance Officer [French]; Keith Edward Widdowson [1967] Director

Mobius Life Holdings Limited
Incorporated: 5 June 2013 *Employees:* 33
Net Worth Deficit: £1,762,000 *Total Assets:* £11,614,446,592
Registered Office: 7th Floor, 20 Gresham Street, London, EC2V 7JE
Activities: Activities of other holding companies n.e.c.
Parent: Souter FT Limited
Officers: Louisa Elizabeth Voss, Secretary; John Douglas Berthinussen [1980] Director/Investment Manager; Michael Christophers [1942] Director/Actuary; Jonathan Edward Derry-Evans [1957] Director; Martin Andrew Griffiths [1966] Director; Andrew James MacFie [1956] Director; Sean Steve Pereira [1976] Finance Director; Alwyn Jacobus Smit [1961] Director [South African]; Adrian Philip Swales [1967] Director; Christopher Bruce Trebilcock [1974] Director [British/Australian]

Mobius Life Limited
Incorporated: 21 September 1995
Net Worth: £7,525,000 *Total Assets:* £11,614,778,368
Registered Office: 7th Floor, 20 Gresham Street, London, EC2V 7JE
Activities: Life insurance
Parent: Mobius Life Group Limited
Officers: Louisa Elizabeth Voss, Secretary; Mark Goodale [1955] Director; John Simon Bertie Smith [1964] Director; Adrian Philip Swales [1967] Director/Actuary

Mobius Wind Holdings Limited
Incorporated: 25 November 2009
Previous: Mobuis Wind Holdings Limited
Net Worth: £82,006,000 *Total Assets:* £428,632,000
Registered Office: c/o Morton Fraser LLP, St Martin's House, 16 St Martin's-le-Grand, London, EC1A 4EN
Activities: Activities of other holding companies n.e.c.
Shareholders: Ventient Energy Limited; Infinis Energy Holdings Limited
Officers: Katerina Brown [1973] Director/Accountant; David Huw Griffiths [1970] Director; Mark Richard Jones [1966] Director; Andrew William Lee [1957] Director/Energy Finance Professional; Mark Alan Walters [1979] Director/Chartered Accountant

Modernelite Limited
Incorporated: 23 November 2001
Net Worth: £187,400,960 *Total Assets:* £240,596,832
Registered Office: c/o Ion, 3rd Floor, One New Change, London, EC4M 9AF
Activities: Other business support service activities n.e.c.
Parent: Ion Investment Group Limited
Officers: Ashley Graham Woods, Secretary; Conor Gerard Clinch [1979] Director/Accountant [Irish]; Ashley Graham Woods [1973] Director/Solicitor

G. Modiano Limited
Incorporated: 24 February 1966 *Employees:* 392
Net Worth: £134,223,008 *Total Assets:* £176,384,000
Registered Office: Broad Street House, 55 Old Broad Street, London, EC2M 1RX
Activities: Preparation and spinning of textile fibres
Major Shareholder: Michael Modiano
Officers: Russell Thomas Parsons, Secretary; Emir Avigdor [1965] Director/Wool Trader; William Frederick Costin [1952] Director/Wool Trader; John Eastwood Dallas [1942] Director; Laurence Simon Modiano [1965] Director/Wool Trader [Italian]; Michael Modiano [1968] Managing Director [Italian]; Russell Thomas Parsons [1960] Director/Accountant

Molineux RMBS 2016-1 PLC
Incorporated: 17 February 2016
Net Worth: £29,000 *Total Assets:* £2,322,417,920
Registered Office: 35 Great St Helen's, London, EC3A 6AP
Activities: Financial intermediation not elsewhere classified
Parent: Molineux RMBS Holdings Limited
Officers: Daniel Marc Richard Jaffe [1975] Managing Director

Moly-Cop UK Holdings Limited
Incorporated: 29 October 2010
Previous: Onesteel UK Holdings Limited
Net Worth: £438,244,800 *Total Assets:* £668,905,152
Registered Office: 100 New Bridge Street, London, EC4V 6JA
Activities: Activities of head offices
Officers: Lance Joseph Dawber [1976] Director/Business Executive [Australian]; Christopher Alan Harrison [1955] Director/Consultant; Glenn Allan Miller [1963] Director/Business Executive [American]

Monaco Bidco Limited
Incorporated: 26 July 2016 *Employees:* 5
Net Worth Deficit: £17,978,000 *Total Assets:* £129,028,000
Registered Office: 25 Farringdon Street, London, EC4A 4AF
Activities: Other service activities n.e.c.
Parent: Monaco Midco Limited
Officers: Angela Tracy Baumfield [1962] Director; Joseph James Hanly [1971] Director [Irish]; Frederick Anthony Stratford [1963] Director; Mark Llewellyn Williams [1978] Director/Investment Partner

Monaco Topco Limited
Incorporated: 25 July 2016 *Employees:* 567
Net Worth Deficit: £13,826,000 *Total Assets:* £175,892,992
Registered Office: 25 Farringdon Street, London, EC4A 4AF
Activities: Other service activities n.e.c.
Officers: Henry Miles Arundel [1987] Director/Private Equity; Angela Tracy Baumfield [1962] Director; Richard James Boardman [1966] Director; Joseph James Hanly [1971] Director [Irish]; Gary Wade Spellins [1957] Director/Chairman; Frederick Anthony Stratford [1963] Director; Mark Llewellyn Williams [1978] Director/Investment Partner

Mondrian Investment Partners Limited
Incorporated: 21 August 1990 *Employees:* 150
Net Worth: £40,984,060 *Total Assets:* £135,975,648
Registered Office: Fifth Floor, 10 Gresham Street, London, EC2V 7JD
Activities: Financial management
Parent: MIPL Group Limited
Officers: Jason Menegakis, Secretary; Elizabeth Anne Desmond [1961] Director [American]; John Emberson [1958] Director; Clive Ashley Gillmore [1960] Director; Jane Sylvia Orr [1960] Director; Hamish Owen Parker [1959] Director; Warren David Shirvell [1967] Director/Chief Operating Officer; David George Tilles [1952] Director/Chairman

Monecor (London) Limited
Incorporated: 16 June 1965 *Employees:* 133
Net Worth: £12,837,000 *Total Assets:* £145,507,008
Registered Office: One Broadgate, London, EC2M 2QS
Activities: Financial intermediation not elsewhere classified
Officers: Philip Adler [1959] Director; Simon Russell Bird [1965] Director; Nicholas David James Iggulden [1985] Director; Roger Benjamin Nagioff [1964] Director; Peter Michael Sugarman [1960] Director; John Michael Richford Wilson [1959] Director

Monex Europe Limited
Incorporated: 30 November 2006 *Employees:* 141
Net Worth: £36,888,288 *Total Assets:* £274,497,568
Registered Office: 3rd Floor, 1 Bartholomew Lane, London, EC2N 2AX
Activities: Financial intermediation not elsewhere classified
Shareholders: Monex Europe Holdings Limited; Schneider Foreign Exchange Limited
Officers: Neil David Burns [1963] Operations Director; Nicholas Peter Edgeley [1961] Managing Director; Shelton Lanning Fray [1972] Director; Maria Magdalena Gonzalez [1978] Director/Group Liaison Officer [Mexican]; Hector Pio Lagos Donde [1959] Director [Mexican]; Jorge Hierro Molina [1959] Deputy General Director of Operations and Finance [Mexican]; Mauricio Naranjo Gonzalez [1967] Director [Mexican]; Moises Tiktin Nickin Tiktin [1958] General Director of Private Banking and Markets [Mexican]; William Patrick Tracey [1976] Marketing Sales Director

Monks Investment Trust Public Limited Company (The)
Incorporated: 6 February 1929
Net Worth: £1,656,534,016 *Total Assets:* £1,762,496,000
Registered Office: Computershare Investor Services PLC, Moor House, 120 London Wall, London, EC2Y 5ET
Activities: Activities of investment trusts
Officers: Belinda Jane Carew-Jones [1958] Director; James Gordon Dickson Ferguson [1947] Director; Edward Mortimer Harley [1960] Director; Douglas Christopher Patrick McDougall [1944] Director/Retired Investment Manager; Professor Sir Nigel Richard Shadblt [1956] Director/College Principal; Karl Stephen Sternberg [1969] Director; Jeremy John Tigue [1959] Director

Monopro Limited
Incorporated: 10 May 1962 *Employees:* 12
Net Worth: £122,073,072 *Total Assets:* £158,728,016
Registered Office: 4 Carlos Place, Mayfair, London, W1K 3AW
Activities: Other letting and operating of own or leased real estate
Officers: Elie Basil Victor Dangoor, Secretary; David Alan Dangoor [1948] Director; Elie Basil Victor Dangoor [1959] Company Secretary/Director; Michael Arthur Jonathan Dangoor [1951] Director

Monsoon Accessorize Limited
Incorporated: 22 February 1973 *Employees:* 1,667
Net Worth: £13,166,000 *Total Assets:* £411,822,016
Registered Office: 1 Nicholas Road, London, W11 4AN
Activities: Retail sale of clothing in specialised stores
Parent: Monsoon Holdings Limited
Officers: Bridget Sophie Green, Secretary; Paul Christopher Allen [1964] Finance Director [Irish]; Elaine Jacqueline Deste [1963] Director/Accountant; Peter Simon [1949] Director [Irish]

Monsoon Holdings (No.1) Limited
Incorporated: 25 February 1991 *Employees:* 3
Previous: Monsoon Limited
Net Worth: £244,770,480 *Total Assets:* £248,830,336
Registered Office: 1 Nicholas Road, London, W11 4AN
Activities: Activities of other holding companies n.e.c.
Parent: Drillgreat Limited
Officers: Bridget Sophie Green, Secretary; Paul Christopher Allen [1964] Finance Director [Irish]; Elaine Jacqueline Deste [1963] Director/Accountant; Vinod Kumar Dhawan [1951] Director [Indian]; Peter Simon [1949] Director [Irish]

Montserrat Acquisitions Ltd
Incorporated: 11 November 2015
Net Worth: £86,286,824 *Total Assets:* £280,834,720
Registered Office: Peterborough Court, 133 Fleet Street, London, EC4A 2BB
Activities: Financial intermediation not elsewhere classified
Parent: ELQ Investors II Ltd
Officers: Thomas Kelly, Secretary; Ana Estrada Lopez [1981] Director/Economist [Spanish]; Mark Desmond Charles Olivier [1974] Managing Director; Jeremy Alan Wiltshire [1981] Director/Banker

Monument Containers Limited
Incorporated: 4 February 2004
Net Worth: £86,657,000 *Total Assets:* £128,887,000
Registered Office: Swire House, 59 Buckingham Gate, London, SW1E 6AJ
Activities: Other business support service activities n.e.c.
Parent: Swire Oilfield Services (Holdings) Limited
Officers: David Charles Morris, Secretary; Michael King [1970] Director; Martin Humphrey Shaw [1972] Director/Chartered Accountant; Manfred Vonlanthen [1970] Director [Swiss]

Moody's Analytics UK Limited
Incorporated: 26 March 1999 *Employees:* 442
Net Worth: £85,225,000 *Total Assets:* £276,720,000
Registered Office: One Canary Wharf, London, E14 5FA
Activities: Other information service activities n.e.c.
Parent: Moody's Holdings Limited
Officers: David de Cliffe Aldrich-Blake [1964] Director/Solicitor; Isabel Maria Gomez Vidal [1971] Managing Director, EMEA Sales [Spanish]; Robert David King [1974] Director

Moody's Group (Holdings) Unlimited
Incorporated: 14 March 2012
Previous: Moody's Group (Holdings) Limited
Net Worth: £2,223,988,224 *Total Assets:* £3,251,386,112
Registered Office: One Canary Wharf, London, E14 5FA
Activities: Activities of other holding companies n.e.c.
Parent: Moody's Corporation
Officers: Timothy John Crawford Herring [1969] Managing Director; Laura Jacqueline Thomas [1969] Director

Moody's Group Finance Limited
Incorporated: 13 March 2012
Net Worth: £453,675,008 *Total Assets:* £453,686,560
Registered Office: One Canary Wharf, London, E14 5FA
Activities: Other information service activities n.e.c.
Parent: Moody's International (UK) Limited
Officers: Timothy John Crawford Herring [1969] Director/Accountant

Moody's Group UK Ltd
Incorporated: 28 September 2007
Net Worth: £2,611,268,096 *Total Assets:* £2,690,549,760
Registered Office: One Canary Wharf, London, E14 5FA
Activities: Other information service activities n.e.c.
Parent: Moody's International (UK) Limited
Officers: Timothy John Crawford Herring [1969] Director/Senior Vice President; Laura Jacqueline Thomas [1969] Director

Moody's International (UK) Limited
Incorporated: 20 March 2012
Net Worth: £3,229,540,096 *Total Assets:* £5,928,298,496
Registered Office: One Canary Wharf, London, E14 5FA
Activities: Other information service activities n.e.c.
Parent: Moody's Group (Holdings) Unlimited
Officers: Timothy John Crawford Herring [1969] Director/Accountant; Laura Jacqueline Thomas [1969] Director

Moody's Investors Service Limited
Incorporated: 25 September 1985 *Employees:* 548
Net Worth: £127,342,000 *Total Assets:* £227,268,992
Registered Office: One Canary Wharf, London, E14 5FA
Activities: Other information service activities n.e.c.
Parent: Moody's Shared Services UK Limited
Officers: Robert Fauber [1970] Managing Director [American]; Rudolf Wolfgang Ferscha [1961] Director [Austrian]; Monica Merli [1964] Managing Director [Italian]; Roderick Marie Stella Maris Munsters [1963] Director [Dutch]; Jan Pethick [1947] Director; Nigel Phipps [1959] Director; Michael Lawrence West [1968] Managing Director

Moorgate Funding 2014-1 PLC
Incorporated: 7 March 2014
Net Worth Deficit: £2,453,000 *Total Assets:* £385,007,008
Registered Office: Fifth Floor, 100 Wood Street, London, EC2V 7EX
Activities: Other business support service activities n.e.c.
Parent: The Law Debenture Intermediary Corporation P.L.C.
Officers: Mark Howard Filer [1967] Director

Christopher Moran Holdings Limited
Incorporated: 18 May 1972
Net Worth: £57,168,000 *Total Assets:* £114,635,184
Registered Office: Chelsea Cloisters, Sloane Avenue, London, SW3 3DW
Activities: Other letting and operating of own or leased real estate
Officers: Charles John William Moran [1989] Director; Christopher John Moran [1948] Director/Financier; Jamie Christopher George Moran [1988] Director; Colin James Reilly [1979] Director/Chartered Accountant [Irish]

J.P. Morgan Capital Financing Limited
Incorporated: 26 August 1988
Net Worth: £940,415,360 *Total Assets:* £942,744,768
Registered Office: 25 Bank Street, Canary Wharf, London, E14 5JP
Activities: Financial intermediation not elsewhere classified
Officers: Mark Steven Allen [1970] Director/Accountant; Christoph Benkert [1971] Director/Banker [German]; John Richard Hobson [1973] Director/Accountant

J.P. Morgan Capital Holdings Limited
Incorporated: 1 November 1999 *Employees:* 4,348
Net Worth: £37,025,992,704 *Total Assets:* £482,353,741,824
Registered Office: 25 Bank Street, Canary Wharf, London, E14 5JP
Activities: Activities of other holding companies n.e.c.
Officers: Kevin Bryan Curtis, Secretary; Dale Thomas Braithwait [1977] Director; Jesus Hernan Cristerna Bautista [1965] Managing Director [Spanish]; Jeannette Smits Van Oyen [1976] Managing Director [Dutch]; Deborah Ann Toennies [1966] Director [American]

J.P. Morgan Chase International Financing Limited
Incorporated: 12 September 2000
Net Worth: £380,367,424 *Total Assets:* £380,692,288
Registered Office: 25 Bank Street, Canary Wharf, London, E14 5JP
Activities: Financial intermediation not elsewhere classified
Parent: J.P. Morgan Capital Financing Limited
Officers: Mark Steven Allen [1970] Director/Accountant; James Anthony Paul Chatters [1979] Director/Accountant; John Richard Hobson [1973] Director/Accountant

J.P. Morgan Europe Limited
Incorporated: 18 September 1968 *Employees:* 916
Net Worth: £2,836,306,688 *Total Assets:* £10,488,334,336
Registered Office: 25 Bank Street, Canary Wharf, London, E14 5JP
Activities: Other business support service activities n.e.c.
Parent: J.P. Morgan Securities PLC
Officers: Hina Patel, Secretary; Ann Teresa Doherty [1965] Director; Mark Stephen Garvin [1952] Director/Banker [Irish]; Matthew Paul Melling [1971] Director; Viswas Raghavan [1966] Director/Investment Banker [Indian]

J.P. Morgan Limited
Incorporated: 6 June 1930 *Employees:* 326
Net Worth: £1,404,339,072 *Total Assets:* £1,451,663,232
Registered Office: 25 Bank Street, Canary Wharf, London, E14 5JP
Activities: Banks
Parent: J.P. Morgan Capital Holdings Limited
Officers: Andrew John Alonzo Cox [1965] Director/Credit Executive; Jesus Hernan Cristerna Bautista [1965] Managing Director [Spanish]; Ronald Debate [1950] Director/Banker [American]; Matthew Paul Melling [1971] Director; Kristian Orssten [1962] Managing Director

J.P. Morgan Markets Limited
Incorporated: 16 October 1981
Net Worth: £2,908,004,608 *Total Assets:* £3,067,082,496
Registered Office: 25 Bank Street, Canary Wharf, London, E14 5JP
Activities: Financial intermediation not elsewhere classified
Parent: J.P. Morgan Financial Investments Limited
Officers: Andrew John Alonzo Cox [1965] Director/Credit Executive; Matthew Paul Melling [1971] Director; Ryan O'Grady [1975] Director

J.P. Morgan Securities PLC
Incorporated: 30 April 1992 *Employees:* 1,959
Net Worth: £30,135,394,304 *Total Assets:* £450,722,070,528
Registered Office: 25 Bank Street, Canary Wharf, London, E14 5JP
Activities: Banks
Parent: J.P. Morgan Capital Holdings Limited
Officers: Abimbola Adesanya, Secretary; Clive Peter Adamson [1956] Director; Sir Winfried Franz Wilhelm Bischoff [1941] Director/Banking; Andrew John Alonzo Cox [1965] Director/Credit Executive; Mark Stephen Garvin [1952] Director/Banker [Irish]; Laban Phelps Jackson [1942] Director/Chairman Clear Creek Properties Inc [American]; Julia Meazzo [1969] Director/EMEA HR Executive; Scott David Moeller [1954] Director/Professor; Jane Elizabeth Moran [1962] Director [American]; Daniel Eduardo Pinto [1962] Director [Argentinian]; Viswas Raghavan [1966] Director/Investment Banker [Indian]; Monique Susan Shivanandan [1963] Director [American]; Jason Edwin Sippel [1969] Managing Director

Morgan Sindall Construction & Infrastructure Ltd
Incorporated: 20 August 2001 *Employees:* 3,328
Previous: Morgan Sindall Construction & Infrastructure Limited
Net Worth: £247,456,000 *Total Assets:* £675,254,016
Registered Office: Kent House, 14-17 Market Place, London, W1W 8AJ
Activities: Construction of commercial buildings
Parent: Morgan Sindall Holdings Limited
Officers: Clare Sheridan, Company Secretary; Patrick Denis Boyle [1968] Managing Director; Stephen Paul Crummett [1965] Finance Director; Joseph John Ledwidge [1970] Finance Director; John Christopher Morgan [1955] Director; Simon Craven Smith [1970] Managing Director

Morgan Sindall Group PLC
Incorporated: 20 July 1953
Net Worth: £316,600,000 *Total Assets:* £1,252,800,000
Registered Office: Kent House, 14-17 Market Place, London, W1W 8AJ
Activities: Development of building projects
Officers: Clare Sheridan, Secretary; Malcolm Charles Cooper [1959] Director/Accountant; Stephen Paul Crummett [1965] Finance Director; Michael Alan Findlay [1968] Director; Tracey Killen [1961] Director of Personnel; David Soutar Lowden [1957] Director; John Christopher Morgan [1955] Director

Morgan Stanley & Co. International PLC
Incorporated: 28 October 1986 *Employees:* 327
Net Worth: £14,032,392,192 *Total Assets:* £347,541,995,520
Registered Office: Legal Department, 25 Cabot Square, Canary Wharf, London, E14 4QA
Activities: Security and commodity contracts dealing activities
Officers: Guy Matthew Clayton, Secretary; Jonathan Watson Haile, Secretary; Jonathan William Bloomer [1954] Director; David Oliver Canon [1955] Director; Terri Lynn Duhon [1972] Director [American]; Lee Guy [1964] Director/Risk Officer; Dr Jakob Horder [1969] Director/Banker [Danish/British]; Arun Kohli [1969] Director/Chief Operations Officer [Indian]; Kim Maree Lazaroo [1969] Director/Accountant [Australian]; Mary Catherine Phibbs [1957] Director; David Andrew Russell [1966] Director/Banker; Noreen Philomena Whyte [1972] Director/Mortgage Operations Manager; Clare Eleanor Woodman [1967] Director/Banker

Morgan Stanley Alpha Investments LLP
Incorporated: 17 June 2003
Net Worth: £1,000,000 *Total Assets:* £209,626,000
Registered Office: 20 Bank Street, Canary Wharf, London, E14 4AD

Morgan Stanley Bank International Limited
Incorporated: 23 February 1999 *Employees:* 81
Net Worth: £654,675,968 *Total Assets:* £5,321,350,144
Registered Office: 25 Cabot Square, London, E14 4QA
Activities: Banks
Shareholders: Morgan Stanley Investments (UK); Morgan Stanley Investments (UK)
Officers: Guy Matthew Clayton, Secretary; Jonathan Watson Haile, Secretary; Jonathan William Bloomer [1954] Director; David Oliver Canon [1955] Director; Mandy Jennifer Defilippo [1975] Managing Director; Terri Lynn Duhon [1972] Director [American]; Lee Guy [1964] Director/Risk Officer; Dr Jakob Horder [1969] Director/Banker [Danish/British]; Arun Kohli [1969] Director/Chief Operations Officer [Indian]; Kim Maree Lazaroo [1969] Director/Accountant [Australian]; Mary Catherine Phibbs [1957] Director; Noreen Philomena Whyte [1972] Director/Mortgage Operations Manager

Morgan Stanley Corporate Trader
Incorporated: 12 November 2004
Net Worth: £141,793,296 *Total Assets:* £142,304,688
Registered Office: 20 Bank Street, Canary Wharf, London, E14 4AD
Activities: Financial intermediation not elsewhere classified
Officers: Jonathan Watson Haile, Secretary; Sandra Gail Walters, Secretary; Stewart Edward Bayfield [1976] Director/Investment Banker; Bryn Mansell Lewis Young [1976] Director/Banker

Morgan Stanley Employment Services UK Limited
Incorporated: 8 March 2004 *Employees:* 1,962
Previous: Morgan Stanley Bramley Investments Limited
Net Worth: £5,532,957 *Total Assets:* £746,849,728
Registered Office: 20 Bank Street, Canary Wharf, London, E14 4AD
Activities: Financial intermediation not elsewhere classified
Parent: Morgan Stanley Group (Europe)
Officers: Paul Eugene Bartlett, Secretary; Jonathan Watson Haile, Secretary; Leigh Bainbridge [1967] Executive Director; Susan Elizabeth Watts [1959] Managing Director

Morgan Stanley Gamma Investments
Incorporated: 13 June 2003
Net Worth: £28,283,000 *Total Assets:* £238,896,992
Registered Office: 20 Bank Street, Canary Wharf, London, E14 4AD
Activities: Financial intermediation not elsewhere classified
Parent: Morgan Stanley Beta Investments Limited
Officers: Paul Eugene Bartlett, Secretary; Emily Theriault Laino [1977] Director/Investment Banker [American]; Scott Iain Merry [1967] Director/Tax Advisor; Charles Alexander Villar [1970] Finance Director

Morgan Stanley Group (Europe)
Incorporated: 2 February 1988
Net Worth: £252,871,264 *Total Assets:* £254,409,264
Registered Office: 20 Bank Street, Canary Wharf, London, E14 4AD
Activities: Activities of head offices
Officers: Jonathan Watson Haile, Secretary; Leigh Bainbridge [1967] Executive Director; Kim Maree Lazaroo [1969] Director/Accountant [Australian]; Susan Elizabeth Watts [1959] Managing Director

Morgan Stanley International Limited
Incorporated: 18 June 1998
Net Worth: £10,476,190,720 *Total Assets:* £34,516,549,632
Registered Office: 25 Cabot Square, London, E14 4QA
Activities: Activities of head offices
Officers: Guy Matthew Clayton, Secretary; Jonathan Watson Haile, Secretary; Jonathan William Bloomer [1954] Director; David Oliver Canon [1955] Director; Terri Lynn Duhon [1972] Director [American]; Lee Guy [1964] Director/Risk Officer; Dr Jakob Horder [1969] Director/Banker [Danish/British]; Arun Kohli [1969] Director/Chief Operations Officer [Indian]; Kim Maree Lazaroo [1969] Director/Accountant [Australian]; Mary Catherine Phibbs [1957] Director; David Andrew Russell [1966] Director/Banker; Noreen Philomena Whyte [1972] Director/Mortgage Operations Manager; Clare Eleanor Woodman [1967] Director/Banker

Morgan Stanley Investment Management Limited
Incorporated: 22 January 1986 *Employees:* 40
Net Worth: £242,338,848 *Total Assets:* £428,167,840
Registered Office: Legal Department, 25 Cabot Square, Canary Wharf, London, E14 4QA
Activities: Fund management activities
Parent: Morgan Stanley Investments (UK)
Officers: Paul Eugene Bartlett, Secretary; Terri Lynn Duhon [1972] Director [American]; Fiona Cameron Kelly [1967] Director/Operations Manager; Richard Andrew Lockwood [1963] Director/Asset Manager; Ruairi O'Healai [1971] Director/Risk Manager [Irish]; Dominic Paul Price [1967] Director/Banker [Irish]

Morgan Stanley Investments (UK)
Incorporated: 30 October 2008
Net Worth: £12,722,503,680 *Total Assets:* £35,662,630,912
Registered Office: 20 Bank Street, Canary Wharf, London, E14 4AD
Activities: Activities of head offices
Parent: Morgan Stanley UK Group
Officers: Paul Eugene Bartlett, Secretary; Jonathan Watson Haile, Secretary; Leigh Bainbridge [1967] Executive Director; Kim Maree Lazaroo [1969] Director/Accountant [Australian]; Susan Elizabeth Watts [1959] Managing Director; Victoria Worster [1972] Director/Chartered Accountant

Morgan Stanley Langton Limited
Incorporated: 28 February 2006
Net Worth Deficit: £1,098,704,256 *Total Assets:* £4,237,922,816
Registered Office: 20 Bank Street, Canary Wharf, London, E14 4AD
Activities: Financial intermediation not elsewhere classified
Parent: Morgan Stanley & Co. International PLC
Officers: Jonathan Watson Haile, Secretary; Sandra Gail Walters, Secretary; Stewart Edward Bayfield [1976] Director/Investment Banker; Scott Iain Merry [1967] Director/Tax Adviser; Bryn Mansell Lewis Young [1976] Director/Banker

Morgan Stanley Longcross Limited
Incorporated: 28 February 2006
Net Worth: £38,908,992 *Total Assets:* £262,255,616
Registered Office: 20 Bank Street, Canary Wharf, London, E14 4AD
Activities: Financial intermediation not elsewhere classified
Parent: Morgan Stanley & Co. International PLC
Officers: Jonathan Watson Haile, Secretary; Sandra Gail Walters, Secretary; Stewart Edward Bayfield [1976] Director/Investment Banker; Scott Iain Merry [1967] Director/Tax Adviser; Bryn Mansell Lewis Young [1976] Director/Banker

Morgan Stanley Mallard Investments Limited
Incorporated: 17 October 2000
Net Worth Deficit: £79,458,624 *Total Assets:* £2,963,236,608
Registered Office: 20 Bank Street, Canary Wharf, London, E14 4AD
Activities: Activities of head offices
Parent: Morgan Stanley Montgomerie Investments Limited
Officers: Paul Eugene Bartlett, Secretary; Sandra Gail Walters, Secretary; Emily Theriault Laino [1977] Director/Investment Banker [American]; Scott Iain Merry [1967] Director/Tax Adviser

Morgan Stanley Montgomerie Investments Limited
Incorporated: 17 October 2000
Net Worth Deficit: £65,928,944 *Total Assets:* £477,116,256
Registered Office: 20 Bank Street, Canary Wharf, London, E14 4AD
Activities: Activities of head offices
Parent: Morgan Stanley Turnberry Limited
Officers: Paul Eugene Bartlett, Secretary; Sandra Gail Walters, Secretary; Emily Theriault Laino [1977] Director/Investment Banker [American]; Scott Iain Merry [1967] Director/Tax Adviser

Morgan Stanley Swallow Limited
Incorporated: 7 October 2005
Net Worth Deficit: £100,383,000 *Total Assets:* £1,207,240,960
Registered Office: 20 Bank Street, Canary Wharf, London, E14 4AD
Activities: Financial intermediation not elsewhere classified
Officers: Paul Eugene Bartlett, Secretary; Jonathan Watson Haile, Secretary; Yee Wah Goddard [1973] Director/Tax Adviser [Australian]; Scott Iain Merry [1967] Director/Tax Adviser; Susan Elizabeth Watts [1959] Managing Director

Morgan Stanley UK Group
Incorporated: 13 October 1976
Net Worth: £36,439,172 *Total Assets:* £561,694,144
Registered Office: Legal Department, 25 Cabot Square, Canary Wharf, London, E14 4QA
Activities: Financial intermediation not elsewhere classified
Parent: Morgan Stanley International Limited
Officers: Paul Eugene Bartlett, Secretary; Jonathan Watson Haile, Secretary; Jonathan David Bendall [1971] Director/Banker; Anthony Philip Mullineaux [1967] Director/Accountant; Susan Elizabeth Watts [1959] Managing Director

Morgan Stanley UK Limited
Incorporated: 8 September 2000 *Employees:* 3,173
Net Worth: £28,637,288 *Total Assets:* £1,178,667,392
Registered Office: Legal Dept, 5th Floor, 25 Cabot Square, Canary Wharf, London, E14 4QA
Activities: Other business support service activities n.e.c.
Parent: Morgan Stanley UK Group
Officers: Paul Eugene Bartlett, Secretary; Jonathan Watson Haile, Secretary; Jonathan David Bendall [1971] Director/Banker; David Timothy Harding [1966] Director/Accountant; Fiona Cameron Kelly [1967] Director/Operations Manager; Anthony Philip Mullineaux [1967] Director/Accountant; Susan Elizabeth Watts [1959] Managing Director

David Morris International Limited
Incorporated: 12 July 1991 *Employees:* 50
Net Worth: £66,317,792 *Total Assets:* £101,921,632
Registered Office: 180 New Bond Street, London, W1S 4RL
Activities: Manufacture of jewellery and related articles
Shareholder: Jeremy Lee Morris
Officers: Wayne Donald Pond, Secretary; Ali Mohammed Alobaidli [1967] Director [Qatari]; Jeremy Lee Morris [1961] Director/Jeweller; Wayne Donald Pond [1969] Director/Accountant; Scott Samuel Strachan [1970] Director/Chartered Accountant

Mortar No.1 Limited
Incorporated: 10 August 2015
Net Worth: £2,000 *Total Assets:* £142,548,000
Registered Office: 35 Great St Helens, London, EC3A 6AP
Activities: Non-trading company
Parent: Intertrust Corporate Services Limited
Officers: Paivi Helena Whitaker [1963] Director [Finnish]

Mortgage Funding 2008-1 PLC
Incorporated: 15 February 2008 *Employees:* 4
Net Worth: £10,481,000 *Total Assets:* £444,988,992
Registered Office: Third Floor, 1 King's Arms Yard, London, EC2R 7AF
Activities: Other business support service activities n.e.c.
Parent: Mortgage Funding 2008-1 Parent Limited
Officers: Robert Sutton [1978] Director/Financial Services [American]; Daniel Jonathan Wynne [1970] Director

Motability Operations Group PLC
Incorporated: 20 March 2008 *Employees:* 890
Net Worth: £2,553,900,032 *Total Assets:* £8,308,700,160
Registered Office: City Gate House, 22 Southwark Bridge Road, London, SE1 9HB
Activities: Renting and leasing of cars and light motor vehicles
Shareholder: Lloyds Bank PLC
Officers: Joanne Caroline Pentland, Secretary; Lisa Jane Bartrip [1971] Director; Michael Keith Betts [1962] Director; Steve Bolton [1962] Director/Co-Head of Asset Finance; Martin Richard Dodd [1970] Director; Matthew John Hamilton-James [1974] Director/Accountant; Alison Jane Hastings [1965] Director/Consultant; Joseph Hennessy [1942] Director/Consultant; Michael Roger William Hordley [1979] Director/Banking; Neil Anthony Johnson [1949] Director; Peter Edmund Lord [1958] Director/Senior Manager, Asset Finance; Daniel Meredith-Jones [1971] Director; Simon Minty [1968] Director/Trainer and Consultant; Stephen Rothwell O'Brien [1957] Director; Barry John O'Byrne [1975] Director/Chief Operating Officer [Irish]; Ruth Elizabeth Owen [1960] Director/CEO of Whizz-Kidz; Ruth Catherine Prior [1967] Director/Chief Financial Officer; David Miles Smith [1961] Finance Director; Neill Peter Thomas [1964] Director/Company Advisor; John Paul Thwaite [1971] Director/Banker

Motability Operations Limited
Incorporated: 16 June 1978 *Employees:* 890
Net Worth: £1,675,000,064 *Total Assets:* £7,522,599,936
Registered Office: City Gate House, 22 Southwark Bridge Road, London, SE1 9HB
Activities: Financial leasing
Parent: Motability Operations Group PLC
Officers: Julie Rose McManus, Secretary; Michael Keith Betts [1962] Director; Ian Michael Roy Goswell [1959] Director; Matthew John Hamilton-James [1974] Director/Accountant; Joanne Caroline Pentland [1959] Director/Chartered Secretary; Ashley Graham Sylvester [1964] Director

The Motability Tenth Anniversary Trust
Incorporated: 16 March 1989
Net Worth: £192,018,000 *Total Assets:* £219,122,000
Registered Office: 66 Lincoln's Inn Fields, London, WC2A 3LH
Activities: Other business support service activities n.e.c.
Officers: Anne-Marie Piper, Secretary; Sir Generald Acher [1945] Director/Chartered Accountant; Christopher John Scott Brearley [1943] Director; David Peter Pritchard [1944] Director/Banker; Lord Jeffrey Maurice Sterling of Plaistow [1934] Director

Motor 2015-1 PLC
Incorporated: 11 December 2014
Net Worth Deficit: £426,405 *Total Assets:* £178,130,752
Registered Office: 35 Great St Helen's, London, EC3A 6AP
Activities: Financial intermediation not elsewhere classified
Parent: Motor 2015-1 Holdings Limited
Officers: Paivi Helena Whitaker [1963] Director [Finnish]

Motor 2017-1 PLC
Incorporated: 12 July 2017
Net Worth Deficit: £1,556,463 *Total Assets:* £619,067,840
Registered Office: 35 Great St Helen's, London, EC3A 6AP
Activities: Financial intermediation not elsewhere classified
Parent: Motor 2017-1 Holdings Limited
Officers: Paivi Helena Whitaker [1963] Director [Finnish]

Motor Oil Finance PLC
Incorporated: 2 May 2014
Net Worth: £134,337 *Total Assets:* £304,020,864
Registered Office: c/o Avin (London) Limited, Second Floor, 26 Grosvenor Gardens, London, SW1W 0GT
Activities: Financial intermediation not elsewhere classified
Officers: Alan Dennis Blyghton, Secretary; Alan Dennis Blyghton [1952] Director/Shipbroker; Pavlina Tavridaki [1968] Director/Investment Adviser [Greek]; Petros Tzanetakis [1955] Deputy Managing Director [Greek]

Motorola Solutions Finance EMEA Limited
Incorporated: 18 August 2005
Net Worth: £243,750,640 *Total Assets:* £867,403,328
Registered Office: Nova South, 160 Victoria Street, London, SW1E 5LB
Activities: Other business support service activities n.e.c.
Parent: Motorola Solutions International Holding Limited
Officers: Joanne Louise Bamber, Secretary; Daniel George Pekofske [1976] Director/CPA Vice President Finance Assistant Treasurer [American]; Akash Raj [1977] Director/Finance Executive [American]; Tetyana Vasylevska [1972] Director/Finance Manager

Motorola Solutions International Holding Limited
Incorporated: 20 September 2012
Net Worth: £428,423,296 *Total Assets:* £448,356,288
Registered Office: Nova South, 160 Victoria Street, London, SW1E 5LB
Activities: Other business support service activities n.e.c.
Parent: Motorola Solutions Holding S.A R.L.
Officers: Joanne Bamber, Secretary; Daniel George Pekofske [1976] Director/Corporate Vice President and Chief Accounting Officer [American]; Akash Raj [1977] Director/Finance Executive [American]

Motorola Solutions UK Acquisition Company Limited
Incorporated: 18 January 2016
Net Worth: £291,419,840 *Total Assets:* £595,780,992
Registered Office: Nova South, 160 Victoria Street, London, SW1E 5LB
Activities: Activities of other holding companies n.e.c.
Parent: Motorola Solutions U.S. Holdco One, Inc.
Officers: Joanne Bamber, Secretary; Daniel George Pekofske [1976] Director/Corporate Vice President and Chief Accounting Officer [American]; Akash Raj [1977] Director/Finance Executive [American]

Motorola Solutions UK Limited
Incorporated: 2 August 1967 *Employees:* 384
Net Worth: £233,700,000 *Total Assets:* £366,800,000
Registered Office: Nova South, 160 Victoria Street, London, SW1E 5LB
Activities: Wholesale of electronic and telecommunications equipment and parts
Parent: Motorola Solutions Finance EMEA Limited
Officers: Joanne Louise Bamber, Secretary; Philip Ashley Jefferson [1975] Sales Director; Ian McCullagh [1963] Director/Vice President Finance EMEA [Irish]; Daniel George Pekofske [1976] Director/Corporate Vice President and Chief Accounting Officer [American]; Akash Raj [1977] Director/Finance Executive [American]; Simon Ross Smith [1981] Finance Director

Mount Anvil Group Limited
Incorporated: 5 April 2002 *Employees:* 205
Net Worth: £61,274,000 *Total Assets:* £119,105,000
Registered Office: 140 Aldersgate Street, London, EC1A 4HY
Activities: Development of building projects
Major Shareholder: Cornelius Killian Hurley
Officers: Ewan Thomas Anderson, Secretary; Ewan Thomas Anderson [1966] Finance Director; Jon Richard Hall [1973] Sales Director; Cornelius Killian Hurley [1958] Director [Irish]; Darragh Richard Joseph Hurley [1987] Investment Director [Irish]; Kieran Hurley [1944] Director [Irish]

Mount Anvil Limited
Incorporated: 13 April 1992 *Employees:* 205
Net Worth: £10,738,000 *Total Assets:* £137,276,992
Registered Office: 140 Aldersgate Street, London, EC1A 4HY
Activities: Construction of domestic buildings
Parent: Mount Anvil (Old Co) Limited
Officers: Ewan Thomas Anderson, Secretary; Ewan Thomas Anderson [1966] Finance Director; Jon Richard Hall [1973] Sales Director; Cornelius Killian Hurley [1958] Director [Irish]; Darragh Richard Joseph Hurley [1987] Investment Director [Irish]

Mount Anvil New Holdings Limited
Incorporated: 31 March 2010 *Employees:* 205
Net Worth: £63,745,000 *Total Assets:* £119,508,000
Registered Office: 140 Aldersgate Street, London, EC1A 4HY
Activities: Development of building projects
Parent: Mount Anvil Group Limited
Officers: Ewan Thomas Anderson, Secretary; Ewan Thomas Anderson [1966] Finance Director; Jon Richard Hall [1973] Sales Director; Cornelius Killian Hurley [1958] Director [Irish]; Darragh Richard Joseph Hurley [1987] Investment Director [Irish]; John Manwaring Robertson [1951] Director/Fund Manager; William Gowanloch Westbrook [1976] Director/Fund Manager

Mountain Warehouse International Limited
Incorporated: 11 October 2013 *Employees:* 1,571
Net Worth: £19,561,000 *Total Assets:* £148,916,000
Registered Office: 5 Eccleston Street, London, SW1W 9LX
Activities: Activities of other holding companies n.e.c.
Major Shareholder: Mark Robert Neale
Officers: Richard Allen, Secretary; Shantelle Augier [1976] Director; Edward Lynch [1986] Director; Mark Robert Neale [1967] Director; Simon David Neale [1972] Director; Keith Pacey [1949] Director/Chairman; Marcus David Ward [1971] Finance Director; Carl Edmund Wormald [1969] Director

Mountsfield Park Finance Limited
Incorporated: 14 December 2011
Net Worth: £21,297,000 *Total Assets:* £136,804,000
Registered Office: Weston Centre, 10 Grosvenor Street, London, W1K 4QY
Activities: Financial intermediation not elsewhere classified
Parent: ABF Investments PLC
Officers: Rosalyn Sharon Schofield, Secretary; Rosalyn Sharon Schofield [1956] Director/Solicitor; Andrew Arthur Smith [1972] Director/Chartered Accountant

Mountview Estates PLC
Incorporated: 21 May 1937 *Employees:* 28
Net Worth: £354,462,016 *Total Assets:* £413,702,016
Registered Office: Mountview House, 151 High Street, Southgate, London, N14 6EW
Activities: Buying and selling of own real estate
Officers: Maria Magdalena Bray, Secretary [Polish]; Maria Magdalena Bray [1961] Director/Certified Accountant [Polish]; Mhairi Lindsay Jarvis [1974] Director/Chartered Surveyor; Duncan Morrall Sinclair [1947] Director/Chartered Accountant; Anthony Christopher John Solway [1959] Director; Dr Andrew Raymond Williams [1976] Director/Doctor; Anthony Wiseman Powell [1951] Director/Chartered Accountant

Moussaieff Jewellers Limited
Incorporated: 11 March 1963 *Employees:* 36
Net Worth: £294,561,728 *Total Assets:* £363,709,760
Registered Office: P O Box 7010, 2nd Floor, 38 Warren Street, London, W1A 2EA
Activities: Wholesale of household goods (other than musical instruments) n.e.c
Major Shareholder: Alisa Moussaieff
Officers: Rohit Gupta, Secretary; Rohit Gupta [1964] Director; Alisa Moussaieff [1929] Director [Israeli]

MP Granite Ltd
Incorporated: 31 May 2012
Net Worth: £80,236,992 *Total Assets:* £172,681,760
Registered Office: 30 Golden Square, London, W1F 9LD
Activities: Sound recording and music publishing activities
Officers: Francis Crimmins, Secretary; Martin Neal Bandier [1941] Director/Business Executive [American]; Guy Robert Henderson [1960] Director/Business Executive; Guy Kimberly Moot [1965] Managing Director; Joseph Salvatore Puzio [1959] Director [American]

MPG Finco Limited
Incorporated: 2 December 2010
Net Worth Deficit: £102,022 *Total Assets:* £181,406,880
Registered Office: Asticus Building, 21 Palmer Street, London, SW1H 0AD
Activities: Other professional, scientific and technical activities n.e.c.
Officers: Jason Christopher Bingham [1978] Director; Simon David Austin Davies [1976] Director; Gemma Nandita Kataky [1983] Director; Panayot Kostadinov Vasilev [1976] Director [French]; Christopher Michael Warnes [1977] Director

Mphasis UK Limited
Incorporated: 14 May 1999 *Employees:* 193
Net Worth: £129,824,176 *Total Assets:* £138,376,544
Registered Office: 88 Wood Street, London, EC2V 7RS
Activities: Other information technology service activities
Officers: Gurpreet Singh Grewal [1964] Director; Vilas Kanyal [1967] Director/Corporate Executive [Indian]; Subramanian Narayan [1978] Director [Indian]

MPI (London) Limited
Incorporated: 1 April 1992 *Employees:* 7
Net Worth: £2,252,603,904 *Total Assets:* £2,856,695,040
Registered Office: Level 19, The Shard, 32 London Bridge Street, London, SE1 9SG
Activities: Activities of investment trusts
Parent: The Medical Protection Society Limited
Officers: David Wheeler, Secretary; Patrick Bruce Forbes [1951] Director/Consultant Obstetrician & Gynaecologist; Simon James Kayll [1963] Finance Director; Howard Roger Kew [1960] Finance Director; Professor Kay-Tee Khaw-Fawcett [1950] Director/University Professor; Simon Mark Pashby [1958] Director/Chartered Accountant; Dr Alexander William Scott [1956] Director; Martin Nicholas Caleb Thomas [1963] Director; Michael Norris Urmston [1949] Director

MPS Group International Limited
Incorporated: 21 May 1997
Net Worth: £95,695,000 *Total Assets:* £177,271,008
Registered Office: Millennium Bridge House, 2 Lambeth Hill, London, EC4V 4BG
Activities: Activities of head offices
Parent: Olsten (UK) Holdings Limited
Officers: Rashida Atinuke Akinjobi, Secretary; Alexandra Helen Bishop [1974] Director; Yann Serge Stephane Halka [1974] Director/Chief Financial Officer [French]; Gavin Kenneth Tagg [1972] Director

MS Amlin Corporate Member Limited
Incorporated: 19 September 1994 *Employees:* 1,156
Previous: Amlin Corporate Member Limited
Net Worth Deficit: £182,200,000 *Total Assets:* £5,426,899,968
Registered Office: The Leadenhall Building, 122 Leadenhall Street, London, EC3V 4AG
Activities: Non-life insurance
Parent: Amlin Corporate Services Limited
Officers: Frances Moule, Secretary; Thomas Cowley Clementi [1979] Director/Insurance Manager; Philip James Green [1967] Director/Chief Financial Officer; James Le Tall Illingworth [1961] Insurance Director

MS Amlin Corporate Services Limited
Incorporated: 1 August 1988 *Employees:* 1,156
Previous: Amlin Corporate Services Limited
Net Worth: £50,056,000 *Total Assets:* £678,390,976
Registered Office: The Leadenhall Building, 122 Leadenhall Street, London, EC3V 4AG
Activities: Activities of head offices
Parent: Amlin PLC
Officers: Frances Moule, Secretary; James Le Tall Illingworth [1961] Director; Vivian Leinster [1969] Director/Chief People Officer; Martyn Brian Rodden [1976] Insurance Director; Julian Nicholas Scofield [1975] Director/Chartered Accountant; Simon Paul Smith [1969] Director/Group Chief Operations Officer

MS Amlin PLC
Incorporated: 17 September 1993 *Employees:* 15
Previous: Amlin PLC
Net Worth: £2,075,500,032 *Total Assets:* £2,699,699,968
Registered Office: The Leadenhall Building, 122 Leadenhall Street, London, EC3V 4AG
Activities: Non-life insurance
Officers: Esther Felton, Secretary; Robin John Leaver Adam [1971] Director; Martin Albers [1960] Director [Swiss]; Simon Charles Waldegrave Beale [1961] Director/Lloyd's Underwriter; Philip James Calnan [1954] Director; Kenichi Fukuhara [1960] Director [Japanese]; James Le Tall Illingworth [1961] Director; Shinichi Imayoshi [1964] Director/General Manager [Japanese]; Shonaid Christina Ross Jemmett-Page [1960] Director; Hironori Morimoto [1966] Director [Japanese]; Oliver Lars Edwin Peterken [1956] Director; Kiyotaka Shuto [1963] Director [Japanese]; John Alexander Worth [1963] Director/Chief Financial Officer

MS Amlin Underwriting Limited
Incorporated: 29 November 1988
Previous: Amlin Underwriting Limited
Net Worth: £47,826,000 *Total Assets:* £109,857,000
Registered Office: The Leadenhall Building, 122 Leadenhall Street, London, EC3V 4AG
Activities: Non-life insurance
Parent: Amlin Underwriting Limited
Officers: Frances Moule, Secretary; Simon Charles Waldegrave Beale [1961] Director/Lloyds Underwriter; Gilles Alex Maxime Bonvarlet [1964] Director [French]; Philip James Calnan [1954] Director; Thomas Cowley Clementi [1979] Director/Insurance Manager; Mark Richard Clements [1968] Director; James Andrew Collinson [1967] Director; Philip James Green [1967] Director/Chief Financial Officer; John Giles Holland [1976] Director [Maltese]; Martyn Brian Rodden [1976] Insurance Director; Miles Jeremy Taffs [1965] Director; Derek Thornton [1949] Director; Philip John Wooldridge [1972] Director/Underwriter

MSC Property Intermediate Holdings Limited
Incorporated: 24 August 2001
Net Worth: £887,042,688 *Total Assets:* £1,941,668,096
Registered Office: York House, 45 Seymour Street, London, W1H 7LX
Activities: Development of building projects
Shareholders: The British Land Company PLC; NBIM Victoria GP Limited
Officers: Claire Ann Barber [1974] Director/Chartered Surveyor; Paul Case [1967] Director; Jayesh Patel [1980] Director/Real Estate Investment Manager [Canadian]; Hursh Shah [1976] Director; Egil Strysse [1964] Director [Norwegian]

MSCI Limited
Incorporated: 26 April 2000 *Employees:* 178
Net Worth: £152,114,176 *Total Assets:* £354,198,240
Registered Office: Ninth Floor, Ten Bishops Square, London, E1 6EG
Activities: Other publishing activities
Parent: MSCI UK Holdings Limited
Officers: Stuart Harvey Doole [1968] Managing Director-Research; Terry Edward Foster [1976] Director/Global Operations Manager; Sebastien Robert Lieblich [1977] Managing Director-Global Head of Equity Solutions [Swiss]; Carroll Douglas Baer Pettit [1964] Managing Director and COO; Jonathan Michael Procter [1967] Director/Financial Controller

MSCI UK Holdings Limited
Incorporated: 13 August 2012
Net Worth: £19,663,000 *Total Assets:* £174,812,000
Registered Office: Ninth Floor, 10 Bishops Square, London, E1 6EG
Activities: Activities of other holding companies n.e.c.
Parent: MSCI Scot 2 LP
Officers: Terry Edward Foster [1976] Director/Global Operations Manager; Christopher Michael Harte [1981] Director/Legal Counsel; Sebastien Robert Lieblich [1977] Global Head of Equity Solutions-Managing Director [Swiss]; Jamie Cinnamon Pawliczek [1969] Director/Legal Counsel [American]; Carroll Douglas Baer Pettit [1964] Managing Director, Chief Operations Officer; Jonathan Michael Procter [1967] Director/Financial Controller; Laurent Jean-Marie Henri Seyer [1965] Director/Chief Operating and Chief Client Officer, Coverage [French]

MSI Corporate Capital Limited
Incorporated: 7 January 2000 *Employees:* 46
Net Worth Deficit: £11,758,000 *Total Assets:* £703,907,968
Registered Office: The Leadenhall Building, 122 Leadenhall Street, London, EC3V 4AG
Activities: Non-life insurance
Parent: Mitsui Sumitomo Insurance (London Management) Limited
Officers: Frances Moule, Secretary; Martin Thomas Burke [1976] Director/Actuary [Irish]; Shinichi Imayoshi [1964] Director/General Manager [Japanese]

MT Property Investments LLP
Incorporated: 15 June 2009
Net Worth: £99,631,000 *Total Assets:* £169,778,000
Registered Office: 1 London Wall Place, London, EC2Y 5AU

MUFG Securities EMEA PLC
Incorporated: 11 February 1983 *Employees:* 629
Previous: Mitsubishi UFJ Securities International PLC
Net Worth: £1,531,992,064 *Total Assets:* £57,118,375,936
Registered Office: Ropemaker Place, 25 Ropemaker Street, London, EC2Y 9AJ
Activities: Security dealing on own account
Parent: Mitsubishi UFJ Financial Group, Inc.
Officers: Richard Michael House, Secretary; Catherine Mary Brett [1965] Managing Director; William Moray Newton Fall [1957] Director/Banker; Stephen Andrew Jack [1958] Director/Banker; David John King [1968] Director/Chartered Accountant; Masahiro Kuwahara [1962] Director/Finance [Japanese]; Christopher David Barnes Kyle [1965] Director/Accountant; Diane Elizabeth Moore [1962] Director/Banker; Gordon James Sangster [1952] Director; Yasutaka Suehiro [1962] Director/Banker [Japanese]; Masamichi Yasuda [1960] Director/Banker [Japanese]

Muirgold Limited
Incorporated: 29 September 1977 *Employees:* 188
Net Worth: £23,497,000 *Total Assets:* £222,958,000
Registered Office: 14 Chester Terrace, London, NW1 4ND
Activities: Hotels and similar accommodation
Parent: Prestmade Limited
Officers: Jitendra Patel, Secretary; Gulshan Bhatia [1933] Director; Nimet Esmail [1958] Sales Director; Shelina Jetha [1961] Marketing Director

Multiplex Construction Europe Holding Limited
Incorporated: 31 July 2003
Previous: Brookfield Multiplex Construction Europe Holding Limited
Net Worth: £97,329,928 *Total Assets:* £186,554,672
Registered Office: Second Floor, 99 Bishopsgate, London, EC2M 3XD
Activities: Activities of construction holding companies
Parent: Multiplex Europe Limited
Officers: Benjamin Keenan, Secretary; Ashley Thomas Edward Muldoon [1971] Director/Construction Management [Australian/British]

Multiplex Construction Europe Limited
Incorporated: 19 July 1999 *Employees:* 1,023
Previous: Brookfield Multiplex Construction Europe Limited
Net Worth: £125,936,000 *Total Assets:* £526,220,992
Registered Office: Second Floor, 99 Bishopsgate, London, EC2M 3XD
Activities: Other specialised construction activities n.e.c.
Parent: Multiplex Construction Europe Holding Limited
Officers: Thomas Marke, Secretary; George Assimakopoulos [1964] Director/Project Manager; John Charles Ballantyne [1961] Director, Construction; Benjamin Francis Keenan [1975] Director/Lawyer [Australian]; Paul Maguire [1968] Director; Ashley Thomas Edward Muldoon [1971] Director/Construction Management [Australian/British]; Andrew Michael Ridley-Barker [1968] Director

Multiplex Europe Limited
Incorporated: 13 October 2010
Previous: Brookfield Multiplex Europe Limited
Net Worth: £98,094,944 *Total Assets:* £188,801,088
Registered Office: Second Floor, 99 Bishopsgate, London, EC2M 3XD
Activities: Activities of construction holding companies
Parent: Multiplex Global Limited
Officers: Benjamin Francis Keenan, Secretary; Ashley Thomas Edward Muldoon [1971] Director/Construction Management [Australian/British]

Multiplex Global Limited
Incorporated: 12 January 2016
Net Worth: £718,418,048 *Total Assets:* £1,327,984,896
Registered Office: Second Floor, 99 Bishopsgate, London, EC2M 3XD
Activities: Activities of construction holding companies
Parent: Brookfield BBP UK Holdings III Limited
Officers: Benjamin Francis Keenan, Secretary; Margaret Ann Redwin, Secretary; John Flecker [1967] Director [Australian]; Derek Edward Gorgi [1978] Director/Accountant [Canadian]; Ashley Thomas Edward Muldoon [1971] Director/Construction Management [Australian/British]

Munich RE Capital Limited
Incorporated: 21 October 1996
Net Worth: £70,493,000 *Total Assets:* £1,084,914,048
Registered Office: St Helens, 1 Undershaft, London, EC3A 8EE
Activities: Non-life insurance
Parent: Munich RE Specialty Group Limited
Officers: Timur Coskun, Secretary; Thomas Eduard Artmann [1962] Director [German]; Grigoriy Guelfand [1974] Director/Group Financial Controller [Australian]; Dominick James Rolls Hoare [1963] Director/Chief Underwriting Officer; John Curt Wilkinson [1964] Director

Murderme Limited
Incorporated: 20 April 2000 *Employees:* 2
Net Worth: £15,275,273 *Total Assets:* £189,014,832
Registered Office: Eighth Floor, 6 New Street Square, New Fetter Lane, London, EC4A 3AQ
Activities: Other business support service activities n.e.c.
Major Shareholder: Damien Steven Hirst
Officers: Damien Steven Hirst [1965] Director/Contemporary Artist

J. Murphy & Sons Limited
Incorporated: 28 February 1951 *Employees:* 3,878
Net Worth: £218,627,360 *Total Assets:* £478,782,048
Registered Office: Hiview House, Highgate Road, London, NW5 1TN
Activities: Construction of other civil engineering projects n.e.c.
Parent: Drilton Limited
Officers: John Patrick Murphy, Secretary; Peter Stuart Anderson [1966] Director/Chartered Civil Engineer; David Anthony Burke [1965] Finance Director [Irish]; David Huw Davies [1956] Director/Chief Financial Officer; Stephen Hollingshead [1956] Director; Alastair Gibson Kerr [1950] Director; Deborah Lodge [1968] Director/Business Consultant; Clare Patricia Mara [1975] Director/Self Employed [Irish]; Bernard Joseph Murphy [1945] Director [Irish]; James Alexander Murphy [1984] Director/Consultant [Irish]; John Paul Murphy [1979] Director [Irish]; Dr Karina Duarte Corware Murphy [1984] Director/Safety Surveillance & Risk Management Lead; Kathleen Murphy [1949] Director/Business Consultant [Irish]; Michael Rodney Toms [1953] Director/Economist

Muse Developments Limited
Incorporated: 20 May 1992 *Employees:* 71
Net Worth: £72,873,000 *Total Assets:* £182,604,992
Registered Office: Kent House, 14-17 Market Place, London, W1W 8AJ
Activities: Other service activities n.e.c.
Parent: Morgan Sindall Group PLC
Officers: Clare Sheridan, Secretary; Matthew Ellis Crompton [1961] Director/Chartered Surveyor; Stephen Paul Crummett [1965] Finance Director; Nigel John Howard Franklin [1956] Director/Chartered Surveyor; David Hoyle [1961] Financial Director; John Christopher Morgan [1955] Director; Sarah Anne Shankland [1965] Director/Solicitor

Music Sales Group Limited
Incorporated: 28 July 1966 *Employees:* 325
Net Worth: £39,225,952 *Total Assets:* £101,640,912
Registered Office: 14-15 Berners Street, London, W1T 3LJ
Activities: Book publishing
Shareholder: Mildred Berta Wise
Officers: Nicholas John Marcus Kemp, Secretary; Christopher Mark Butler [1963] Director; Claude Duvivier [1948] Managing Director [French]; Ian Nigel Gilroy [1963] Director/Solicitor; David Holley [1965] Director; David Barry Rockberger [1946] Director/Solicitor; James Thomas Chadwick Rushton [1956] Director; Marcus Daniel Wise [1977] Director; Mildred Berta Wise [1938] Director [Swiss]; Robert Wise [1934] Director/Publisher [American]; Tomas Wise [1971] Director/Internet Operations [British/American]

MV Werften Holdings Limited
Incorporated: 24 February 2016
Net Worth: £275,793,952 *Total Assets:* £546,103,040
Registered Office: c/o Hackwood Secretaries Limited, One Silk Street, London, EC2Y 8HQ
Activities: Activities of other holding companies n.e.c.
Shareholders: First Names Trust Company (Isle of Man) Limited; Golden Hope Limited
Officers: Colin Fook Yew Au [1949] Director/Advisor [Malaysian]; Christian Albert Bockler [1969] Director/Economist [German]; Joachim Hagemann [1943] Director/Chairman of The Supervisory Board of Lloyd Werft Bremerhaven AG [German]; Kok Thay Lim [1951] Director/Chairman and Chief Executive Officer of Genting Hong Kong Limited [Malaysian]

Mycitydeal Limited
Incorporated: 23 December 2009 *Employees:* 267
Net Worth: £36,623,000 *Total Assets:* £110,278,000
Registered Office: Floors 11-12, Aldgate Tower, 2 Leman Street, London, E1 8FA
Activities: Other business support service activities n.e.c.
Parent: Groupon, Inc
Officers: Rachel George [1982] Director of Treasury; Damien Matthew Schmitz [1977] Director [American]; Jonathan Wilson [1976] Director

MYI UK Holdings (No.1) Limited
Incorporated: 12 August 2011 *Employees:* 1,268
Net Worth: £50,131,900 *Total Assets:* £294,833,152
Registered Office: Suite 1, 3rd Floor, 11-12 St James's Square, London, SW1Y 4LB
Activities: Activities of other holding companies n.e.c.
Parent: McLarens Global Limited
Officers: Liz Tubb, Secretary; Gary Brown [1966] Director/Insurance [American]; Ross Glenn Landsbaum [1962] Director [American]

N.B.S.A. Limited
Incorporated: 21 November 1935
Net Worth: £19,718,272 *Total Assets:* £446,610,400
Registered Office: 1st Floor, Millennium Bridge House, 2 Lambeth Hill, London, EC4V 4GG
Activities: Activities of financial services holding companies
Officers: David Sidgwick, Secretary; Glen Duncan Corbett [1967] Director/Lawyer; Kevin Charles Ryder [1962] Director Investment Banking Nedbank [South African]; David Sidgwick [1972] Director/Chief Operating Officer

Nadezhda Limited
Incorporated: 2 June 2014 *Employees:* 1,291
Net Worth: £1,775,008,000 *Total Assets:* £3,487,471,104
Registered Office: 35 Great St Helen's, London, EC3A 6AP
Activities: Activities of other holding companies n.e.c.
Shareholders: Victor Batrachenko; Stanislav Batrachenko
Officers: Anna Batrachenko [1992] Director [Ukrainian]; Viktor Batrachenko [1960] Director/Entrepreneur [Ukrainian]

Nakano Asset Global Ltd.
Incorporated: 30 November 2001 *Employees:* 9
Net Worth: £2,448,319,744 *Total Assets:* £2,459,655,424
Registered Office: 2nd Floor, Building 10, Chiswick Park, 566 Chiswick High Road, Chiswick, London, W4 5XS
Activities: Activities of head offices
Major Shareholder: Kazuhide Nakano
Officers: Hiroshi Sasaoka, Secretary; Kazuhide Nakano [1950] Director [Japanese]; Miwa Nakano [1951] Director [Japanese]; Seiko Nakano [1979] Director [Japanese]; Yuko Nakano [1976] Director [Japanese]

Nameco (No.808) Limited
Incorporated: 20 August 2003 *Employees:* 11
Net Worth: £15,758,000 *Total Assets:* £268,418,000
Registered Office: 1 Aldgate, London, EC3N 1RE
Activities: Non-life insurance
Parent: HCC Intermediate Holdings Inc.
Officers: Jenna Louise Holliday, Secretary; David Robert Feldman [1974] Director/Lloyd's Agent; Nicholas Ian Hutton-Penman [1966] Director/Insurer Accountant; Katherine Lee Letsinger [1962] Director/Chief Financial Officer

Nando's Chickenland Limited
Incorporated: 5 February 1991 *Employees:* 14,793
Net Worth: £189,826,000 *Total Assets:* £613,513,984
Registered Office: St Marys House, 42 Vicarage Crescent, London, SW11 3LD
Activities: Licenced restaurants
Parent: Nando's Finance Limited
Officers: James Dominic Fowler [1967] Finance Director; Michael Gardner [1965] Property Director [Irish]; Robert Papps [1973] Director/Chief Executive Officer

Nando's Finance Limited
Incorporated: 6 April 2005
Net Worth: £81,922,000 *Total Assets:* £653,094,976
Registered Office: St Mary's House, 42 Vicarage Crescent, London, SW11 3LD
Activities: Activities of head offices
Parent: Nando's Group Limited
Officers: James Dominic Fowler [1967] Finance Director; Robert Papps [1973] Director/Chief Executive Officer

Nando's Group Holdings Limited
Incorporated: 12 December 2007 *Employees:* 19,506
Net Worth: £2,409,000 *Total Assets:* £1,245,709,056
Registered Office: St Marys House, 42 Vicarage Crescent, London, SW11 3LD
Activities: Activities of head offices
Officers: Robert Adrian Graham 't Hooft [1968] Director [Dutch]; Charles Francis Luyckx [1969] Director [Italian]

Nando's Group Limited
Incorporated: 11 March 2008
Net Worth: £73,795,000 *Total Assets:* £389,044,000
Registered Office: St Marys House, 42 Vicarage Crescent, London, SW11 3LD
Activities: Activities of head offices
Parent: Nando's Group Holdings Limited
Officers: Robert Adrian Graham 't Hooft [1968] Director [Dutch]; Charles Francis Luyckx [1969] Director [Italian]

Nando's Limited
Incorporated: 4 August 2010 *Employees:* 28
Net Worth Deficit: £59,063,000 *Total Assets:* £121,780,000
Registered Office: St Mary's House, 42 Vicarage Crescent, London, SW11 3LD
Activities: Licenced restaurants
Parent: Nando's Group Holdings Limited
Officers: Andrew Patrick Lynch [1956] Director/CEO of Nando's Group; Jane Margaret O'Riordan [1964] Director; Luke Logan Tait [1973] Director

Harvey Nash Group Limited
Incorporated: 13 February 1997 *Employees:* 2,518
Previous: Harvey Nash Group PLC
Net Worth: £60,655,000 *Total Assets:* £234,156,992
Registered Office: 110 Bishopsgate, London, EC2N 4AY
Activities: Other service activities n.e.c.
Shareholder: Alexander Maria Paiusco
Officers: Mark Jonathan Garratt, Secretary; Albert George Hector Ellis [1964] Director; Mark Jonathan Garratt [1965] Director; Adrian Paul Gunn [1965] Non-Executive Director; Simon Mark Wassall [1962] Director

Natgrid One Limited
Incorporated: 28 July 2005
Net Worth Deficit: £366,459,008 *Total Assets:* £1,286,078,976
Registered Office: 1-3 Strand, London, WC2N 5EH
Activities: Other business support service activities n.e.c.
Parent: National Grid (US) Partner 1 Limited
Officers: Megan Barnes, Secretary; Jonathan Paul Clay [1975] Director; Simon Warren Grant [1979] Director; Andrew Kenneth Mead [1971] Director/Accountant; David Anthony Preston [1971] Director/Treasurer; Christopher John Waters [1967] Director/Accountant

NatgridTW1 Limited
Incorporated: 25 March 2011
Net Worth: £3,614,525,696 *Total Assets:* £3,642,069,248
Registered Office: 1-3 Strand, London, WC2N 5EH
Activities: Other business support service activities n.e.c.
Parent: National Grid (US) Holdings Limited
Officers: Megan Barnes, Secretary; Jonathan Paul Clay [1975] Director; Simon Warren Grant [1979] Director; Andrew Kenneth Mead [1971] Director/Accountant; David Anthony Preston [1971] Director/Treasurer; Christopher John Waters [1967] Director/Accountant

National Australia Finance (Vessel Leasing No.5) Limited
Incorporated: 4 July 2007
Net Worth: £8,404,168 *Total Assets:* £106,231,072
Registered Office: 88 Wood Street, London, EC2V 7QQ
Activities: Financial leasing
Parent: National Australia Finance (Europe Holdings) Limited
Officers: Bernadette Lewis, Secretary; Rolfe Alan Cameron Lakin [1961] Director/Banker; Mona Melin Wong [1962] Director/Accountant [British/Australian]

National Bank of Egypt (UK) Limited
Incorporated: 28 August 1992 *Employees:* 72
Net Worth: £149,856,448 *Total Assets:* £1,471,021,440
Registered Office: 11 Waterloo Place, London, SW1Y 4AU
Activities: Banks
Parent: The Central Bank of Egypt
Officers: Mahmoud Montaser Ibrahim El-Sayed Al Asfar [1955] Director/Deputy Chairman National Bank of Egypt [Egyptian]; Dr Ziad Ahmed Bahaa El Din [1964] Director/Independent Legal Advisor [Egyptian]; Nicholas Charles Beecroft [1960] Director/Bank Official; Dalia Abdallah Mohamed El Baz [1973] Director [Egyptian]; Mokhtar Abdel Gawad El Shennawy [1948] Deputy Managing Director [Egyptian]; Doctor Farouk Abdel Baki El-Okdah [1946] Director/Chairman [Egyptian]; Yasser Adel Ibrahim [1968] Chief Executive Office and Managing Director [German]; Hisham Ahmed Okasha [1968] Director/Chairman of NBE Cairo [Egyptian/British]; David Somers [1948] Director

National Bank of Kuwait (International) PLC
Incorporated: 9 December 1992 *Employees:* 142
Net Worth: £226,454,992 *Total Assets:* £2,278,753,280
Registered Office: 13 George Street, London, W1U 3QJ
Activities: Banks
Officers: Stephen George Byrne, Secretary; Dagmar Moravkova, Secretary; Shaikhah Khaled Ali Al Bahar [1954] Director/Banker [Kuwaiti]; Hamad Abdul Aziz Al Sagar [1934] Director [Kuwaiti]; Isam Jassim Al Sager [1955] Director/Banker [Kuwaiti]; Ghassan Ahmad Saoud Al-Khaled [1949] Director/Merchant [Kuwaiti]; Nasser Musaed Al-Sayer [1947] Director [Kuwaiti]; Fawzi Adnan Dajani [1953] Director/Banker; Hamish Cameron Galbraith Marr [1962] Director/Banker; Georges Richani [1959] Director/Banker; Andrew Simon Richardson [1960] Director/Banker; Lesley Jane Titcomb [1961] Director/Regulator

National Car Parks Limited
Incorporated: 3 January 1931 *Employees:* 1,154
Net Worth: £210,138,000 *Total Assets:* £847,369,984
Registered Office: Saffron Court, 14b St Cross Street, London, EC1N 8XA
Activities: Other service activities incidental to land transportation, n.e.c.
Parent: National Parking Corporation Limited
Officers: Aaron Campbell, Secretary; Norifumi Kawakami [1965] Director [Japanese]; Hiroyasu Matsui [1965] Director [Japanese]; Hideyuki Nagahiro [1966] Director/Banker [Japanese]; Koichi Nishikawa [1964] Director [Japanese]; Kenichi Sasaki [1967] Director [Japanese]; Jonathan Paul Scott [1961] Director/Accountant; Chihiro Shima [1973] Director [Japanese]

National Grid (US) Holdings Limited
Incorporated: 18 July 1991
Net Worth: £8,878,922,752 *Total Assets:* £13,182,314,496
Registered Office: 1-3 Strand, London, WC2N 5EH
Activities: Other business support service activities n.e.c.
Parent: National Grid PLC
Officers: Megan Barnes, Secretary; Andrew Jonathan Agg [1969] Director/Accountant; Kylee Marie Dickie [1981] Director [New Zealander]; Simon Warren Grant [1979] Director; Stuart Calvin Humphreys [1963] Director/Chartered Accountant; Alexandra Morton Lewis [1972] Director/Chartered Accountant; Andrew Kenneth Mead [1971] Director/Accountant; David Anthony Preston [1971] Director/Treasurer; Christopher John Waters [1967] Director/Accountant

National Grid (US) Investments 2 Limited
Incorporated: 3 June 1999
Net Worth: £2,394,771,968 *Total Assets:* £2,397,646,080
Registered Office: 1-3 Strand, London, WC2N 5EH
Activities: Other business support service activities n.e.c.
Parent: National Grid (US) Partner 1 Limited
Officers: Megan Barnes, Secretary; Jonathan Paul Clay [1975] Director; Simon Warren Grant [1979] Director; Andrew Kenneth Mead [1971] Director/Accountant; David Anthony Preston [1971] Director/Treasurer; Christopher John Waters [1967] Director/Accountant

National Grid (US) Investments 4 Limited
Incorporated: 22 October 1999
Net Worth: £5,807,913,984 *Total Assets:* £14,143,995,904
Registered Office: 1-3 Strand, London, WC2N 5EH
Activities: Other business support service activities n.e.c.
Parent: National Grid (US) Holdings Limited
Officers: Megan Barnes, Secretary; Jonathan Paul Clay [1975] Director; Simon Warren Grant [1979] Director; Stuart Calvin Humphreys [1963] Director/Chartered Accountant; Andrew Kenneth Mead [1971] Director/Accountant; David Anthony Preston [1971] Director/Treasurer; Christopher John Waters [1967] Director/Accountant

National Grid (US) Partner 1 Limited
Incorporated: 31 October 2001
Net Worth: £11,221,173,248 *Total Assets:* £11,225,111,552
Registered Office: 1-3 Strand, London, WC2N 5EH
Activities: Other business support service activities n.e.c.
Parent: National Grid (US) Investments 4 Limited
Officers: Megan Barnes, Secretary; Jonathan Paul Clay [1975] Director; Simon Warren Grant [1979] Director; Andrew Kenneth Mead [1971] Director/Accountant; David Anthony Preston [1971] Director/Treasurer; Christopher John Waters [1967] Director/Accountant

National Grid Commercial Holdings Limited
Incorporated: 28 July 2000 *Employees:* 289
Net Worth: £799,000,000 *Total Assets:* £874,000,000
Registered Office: 1-3 Strand, London, WC2N 5EH
Activities: Activities of head offices
Parent: Lattice Group PLC
Officers: Megan Barnes, Secretary; Andrew Jonathan Agg [1969] Director/Accountant; Kylee Marie Dickie [1981] Director [New Zealander]; Simon Warren Grant [1979] Director; Andrew Kenneth Mead [1971] Director/Accountant; David Anthony Preston [1971] Director/Treasurer; Deborah Jane Waller [1975] Director/Solicitor [British/New Zealander]; Christopher John Waters [1967] Director/Accountant

National Grid Electricity Transmission PLC
Incorporated: 1 April 1989 *Employees:* 3,703
Net Worth: £3,473,999,872 *Total Assets:* £14,156,000,256
Registered Office: 1-3 Strand, London, WC2N 5EH
Activities: Transmission of electricity
Parent: National Grid Holdings Limited
Officers: Derek John Goodban, Secretary; Lawrence Hagan, Secretary; Dr Catherine Elisabeth Dorcas Bell [1951] Director; Christopher Paul Bennett [1971] Director; Dr Clive Harry Elphick [1956] Director; Alan Peter Foster [1971] Director/Accountant; Alexandra Morton Lewis [1972] Director/Chartered Accountant; Lucy Nicola Shaw [1969] Director; Fintan Charles Slye [1970] Director [Irish]; David Richard John Wright [1967] Director

National Grid Gas Holdings Limited
Incorporated: 27 November 1998
Net Worth: £4,017,999,872 *Total Assets:* £7,464,999,936
Registered Office: 1-3 Strand, London, WC2N 5EH
Activities: Activities of head offices
Parent: Lattice Group PLC
Officers: Megan Barnes, Secretary; Lawrence Hagan, Secretary; Alan Peter Foster [1971] Director/Accountant; Alexandra Morton Lewis [1972] Director/Chartered Accountant; Lucy Nicola Shaw [1969] Director

National Grid Gas PLC
Incorporated: 1 April 1986 *Employees:* 1,992
Net Worth: £4,501,000,192 *Total Assets:* £11,230,000,128
Registered Office: 1-3 Strand, London, WC2N 5EH
Activities: Manufacture of gas
Parent: National Grid Gas Holdings Limited
Officers: Derek John Goodban, Secretary; Lawrence Hagan, Secretary; Dr Catherine Elisabeth Dorcas Bell [1951] Director; Christopher Paul Bennett [1971] Director; Dr Clive Harry Elphick [1956] Director; Alan Peter Foster [1971] Director/Accountant; Alexandra Morton Lewis [1972] Director/Chartered Accountant; Lucy Nicola Shaw [1969] Director; Philip Graham Sheppard [1964] Director of SO Operations; Fintan Charles Slye [1970] Director [Irish]

National Grid Grain LNG Limited
Incorporated: 18 June 2002 *Employees:* 150
Net Worth: £570,211,008 *Total Assets:* £870,526,016
Registered Office: 1-3 Strand, London, WC2N 5EH
Activities: Extraction of crude petroleum
Parent: Lattice Group PLC
Officers: Megan Barnes, Secretary; Lawrence Hagan, Secretary; Jonathan Butterworth [1962] Director; Simon Ross Culkin [1972] Director; Nick Hooper [1975] Director; Stuart Calvin Humphreys [1963] Director/Chartered Accountant

National Grid Holdings Limited
Incorporated: 31 August 1995
Net Worth: £6,233,999,872 *Total Assets:* £15,676,999,680
Registered Office: 1-3 Strand, London, WC2N 5EH
Activities: Other business support service activities n.e.c.
Parent: National Grid Holdings One PLC
Officers: Megan Barnes, Secretary; Andrew Jonathan Agg [1969] Director/Accountant; Simon Warren Grant [1979] Director; Stuart Calvin Humphreys [1963] Director/Chartered Accountant; Alexandra Morton Lewis [1972] Director/Chartered Accountant; Andrew Kenneth Mead [1971] Director/Accountant; Christopher John Waters [1967] Director/Accountant

National Grid Holdings One PLC
Incorporated: 1 April 1989
Net Worth: £4,425,999,872 *Total Assets:* £19,753,000,960
Registered Office: 1-3 Strand, London, WC2N 5EH
Activities: Activities of head offices
Parent: National Grid PLC
Officers: Megan Barnes, Secretary; Andrew Jonathan Agg [1969] Director/Accountant; Simon Warren Grant [1979] Director; Stuart Calvin Humphreys [1963] Director/Chartered Accountant; Alexandra Morton Lewis [1972] Director/Chartered Accountant; Andrew Kenneth Mead [1971] Director/Accountant; John Mark Pettigrew [1968] Director; Christopher John Waters [1967] Director/Accountant

National Grid Interconnector Holdings Limited
Incorporated: 6 August 2012 *Employees:* 11
Net Worth: £251,372,992 *Total Assets:* £666,958,016
Registered Office: 1-3 Strand, London, WC2N 5EH
Activities: Activities of other holding companies n.e.c.
Parent: National Grid Holdings One PLC
Officers: Megan Barnes, Secretary; Lawrence Hagan, Secretary; Jonathan Butterworth [1962] Director; Nick Hooper [1975] Director; Zachary John Richardson [1971] Director; Nick Sides [1966] Director; Aarti Singhal [1977] Director

National Grid Interconnectors Limited
Incorporated: 12 June 1997 *Employees:* 53
Net Worth: £341,734,016 *Total Assets:* £403,448,992
Registered Office: 1-3 Strand, London, WC2N 5EH
Activities: Transmission of electricity
Parent: National Grid Holdings One PLC
Officers: Megan Barnes, Secretary; Lawrence Hagan, Secretary; Jonathan Butterworth [1962] Director; Nick Hooper [1975] Director; Nick Sides [1966] Director; Aarti Singhal [1977] Director

National Grid International Limited
Incorporated: 5 September 1990
Net Worth: £40,723,000 *Total Assets:* £259,355,008
Registered Office: 1-3 Strand, London, WC2N 5EH
Activities: Activities of head offices
Parent: National Grid Holdings Limited
Officers: Megan Barnes, Secretary; Kylee Marie Dickie [1981] Director [New Zealander]; Simon Warren Grant [1979] Director; Andrew Kenneth Mead [1971] Director/Accountant; David Anthony Preston [1971] Director/Treasurer; Christopher John Waters [1967] Director/Accountant

National Grid Metering Limited
Incorporated: 2 February 1999 *Employees:* 301
Net Worth: £118,112,000 *Total Assets:* £145,119,008
Registered Office: 1-3 Strand, London, WC2N 5EH
Activities: Trade of gas through mains
Parent: National Grid Gas PLC
Officers: Megan Barnes, Secretary; Lawrence Hagan, Secretary; Jonathan Charles Fenn [1962] Director; Nick Hooper [1975] Director; Stuart Calvin Humphreys [1963] Director/Chartered Accountant; Maxine Yvette Long [1969] Director; Daniel Francis Westerman [1978] Director

National Grid PLC
Incorporated: 11 July 2000 *Employees:* 23,023
Net Worth: £18,831,998,976 *Total Assets:* £58,787,000,320
Registered Office: 1-3 Strand, London, WC2N 5EH
Activities: Activities of head offices
Officers: Alison Barbara Kay, Secretary; Andrew Jonathan Agg [1969] Director/Accountant; Nora Mead Brownell [1947] Director [American]; Jonathan Donald Sherlock Dawson [1952] Director; Therese Marie Esperdy [1960] Director [American]; Sir Peter Oliver Gershon [1947] Director; Dr Paul Golby [1951] Director; Amanda Jo Mesler [1963] Director [American]; John Mark Pettigrew [1968] Director; Dean Lamont Seavers [1960] Director [American]; Lucy Nicola Shaw [1969] Director; Earsel Lloyd Shipp [1957] Director [American]; Mark David Williamson [1957] Director

National Grid Property Holdings Limited
Incorporated: 24 June 1999 *Employees:* 42
Net Worth: £14,946,000 *Total Assets:* £325,055,008
Registered Office: 1-3 Strand, London, WC2N 5EH
Activities: Development of building projects
Parent: National Grid Commercial Holdings Limited
Officers: Megan Barnes, Secretary; Rukshana Yousuf, Secretary; Richard Alden [1974] Director/Head of Commercial Property, Tax and Treasury; Philip Duncan Edwards [1970] Director/Chartered Surveyor; Prem Kumar Gabbi [1969] Director

National Grid Seventeen Limited
Incorporated: 23 July 2002
Net Worth: £2,640,244,992 *Total Assets:* £2,869,391,104
Registered Office: 1-3 Strand, London, WC2N 5EH
Activities: Other business support service activities n.e.c.
Parent: National Grid Holdings Limited
Officers: Megan Barnes, Secretary; Kylee Marie Dickie [1981] Director [New Zealander]; Andrew Kenneth Mead [1971] Director/Accountant; David Anthony Preston [1971] Director/Treasurer; Christopher John Waters [1967] Director/Accountant

National Grid Thirty Five Limited
Incorporated: 12 November 2004
Previous: NGT Luxembourg One Limited
Net Worth: £6,183,735,808 *Total Assets:* £6,412,739,072
Registered Office: 1-3 Strand, London, WC2N 5EH
Activities: Activities of head offices
Parent: National Grid Holdings One PLC
Officers: Megan Barnes, Secretary; Kylee Marie Dickie [1981] Director [New Zealander]; Simon Warren Grant [1979] Director; Andrew Kenneth Mead [1971] Director/Accountant; David Anthony Preston [1971] Director/Treasurer; Christopher John Waters [1967] Director/Accountant

National Grid Twelve Limited
Incorporated: 18 January 2002
Net Worth: £4,209,197,824 *Total Assets:* £5,425,227,776
Registered Office: 1-3 Strand, London, WC2N 5EH
Activities: Other business support service activities n.e.c.
Parent: National Grid (US) Investments 4 Limited
Officers: Megan Barnes, Secretary; Jonathan Paul Clay [1975] Director; Simon Warren Grant [1979] Director; Andrew Kenneth Mead [1971] Director/Accountant; David Anthony Preston [1971] Director/Treasurer; Christopher John Waters [1967] Director/Accountant

National Grid Twenty Seven Limited
Incorporated: 27 January 2012
Net Worth: £83,530,000 *Total Assets:* £614,417,984
Registered Office: 1-3 Strand, London, WC2N 5EH
Activities: Other business support service activities n.e.c.
Parent: National Grid Property Holdings Limited
Officers: Megan Barnes, Secretary; Rukshana Yousuf, Secretary; Richard Alden [1974] Director/Head of Commercial Property, Tax and Treasury; Philip Duncan Edwards [1970] Director/Chartered Surveyor; Prem Kumar Gabbi [1969] Director

National Grid Twenty Three Limited
Incorporated: 24 August 2009
Net Worth: £4,282,979,584 *Total Assets:* £5,707,447,808
Registered Office: 1-3 Strand, London, WC2N 5EH
Activities: Other business support service activities n.e.c.
Parent: National Grid (US) Partner 1 Limited
Officers: Megan Barnes, Secretary; Kylee Marie Dickie [1981] Director [New Zealander]; Simon Warren Grant [1979] Director; Andrew Kenneth Mead [1971] Director/Accountant; David Anthony Preston [1971] Director/Treasurer; Christopher John Waters [1967] Director/Accountant

National Grid Twenty-Five Limited
Incorporated: 21 June 2010
Net Worth: £1,486,115,584 *Total Assets:* £1,497,356,416
Registered Office: 1-3 Strand, London, WC2N 5EH
Activities: Non-trading company
Parent: National Grid (US) Holdings Limited
Officers: Megan Barnes, Secretary; Kylee Marie Dickie [1981] Director [New Zealander]; Simon Warren Grant [1979] Director; Andrew Kenneth Mead [1971] Director/Accountant; David Anthony Preston [1971] Director/Treasurer; Christopher John Waters [1967] Director/Accountant

National Grid William Limited
Incorporated: 21 June 2010
Net Worth: £106,165,000 *Total Assets:* £106,176,000
Registered Office: 1-3 Strand, London, WC2N 5EH
Activities: Non-trading company
Parent: National Grid Property Holdings Limited
Officers: Megan Barnes, Secretary; Rukshana Yousuf, Secretary; Richard Alden [1974] Director/Head of Commercial Property; Philip Duncan Edwards [1970] Director/Chartered Surveyor; Prem Kumar Gabbi [1969] Director; Michael John Westcott [1962] Group HR Director

National Magazine Company Limited (The)
Incorporated: 29 November 1910 *Employees:* 968
Net Worth Deficit: £3,118,000 *Total Assets:* £148,028,000
Registered Office: 30 Panton Street, London, SW1Y 4AJ
Activities: Publishing of consumer and business journals and periodicals
Officers: Aimee Leonora Nisbet, Secretary; Frank Anthony Bennack [1933] Director/President [American]; Claire Jacqueline Blunt [1967] Director/Chief Operating Officer/Chief Financial Officer; Debi Chirichella [1963] Director/Chief Financial Officer [American]; Michael Clinton [1953] Director/Media Executive [American]; Simon Peter Barry Horne [1963] Director/Chartered Accountant; Gilbert Charles Maurer [1928] Director [American]; James David Wildman [1966] Director/President and CEO; Troy William Young [1967] Director/President [Canadian]

National Power International Holdings
Incorporated: 25 November 1992
Net Worth: £1,077,886,336 *Total Assets:* £1,461,725,568
Registered Office: Level 20, 25 Canary Wharf, London, E14 5LQ
Activities: Activities of head offices
Parent: International Power Consolidated Holdings Limited
Officers: Sarah Jane Gregory, Secretary; David George Alcock [1965] Director; Sarah Frances Fleure Mingham [1977] Director; Simon David Pinnell [1964] Director/Accountant

National Westminster Bank Public Limited Company
Incorporated: 18 March 1968
Net Worth: £16,286,000,128 *Total Assets:* £340,843,003,904
Registered Office: 250 Bishopsgate, London, EC2M 4AA
Activities: Activities auxiliary to financial intermediation n.e.c.
Officers: Aileen Norma Taylor, Secretary; Francesca Barnes [1958] Director; Graham John Beale [1958] Director; Ian Donald Cormack [1947] Director; Howard John Davies [1951] Director; Alison Davis [1961] Director [American]; Patrick Gerard Flynn [1960] Director/Bank Official [Irish]; Morten Nicolai Friis [1953] Director [Norwegian]; Robert Andrew Joseph Gillespie [1955] Director/Bank Official; Yasmin Jetha [1952] Director; Ross Maxwell McEwan [1957] Director/Bank Official [New Zealander]; Katie Murray [1969] Director/Bank Official; Baroness Sheila Valerie Noakes [1949] Director; Michael John Rogers [1964] Director; Alison Marie Rose-Slade [1969] Director/Bank Official; Mark Donald Seligman [1956] Director; Lena Cooper Wilson [1964] Director

NatWest Covered Bonds Limited Liability Partnership
Incorporated: 22 October 2009
Previous: RBS Covered Bonds Limited Liability Partnership
Net Worth: £1,020,924,992 *Total Assets:* £7,456,384,000
Registered Office: 1 Princes Street, London, EC2R 8BP

Nautical Petroleum Limited
Incorporated: 28 January 2002
Net Worth: £55,272,000 *Total Assets:* £971,502,976
Registered Office: 4th Floor, Wellington House, 125 The Strand, London, WC2R 0AP
Activities: Extraction of crude petroleum
Parent: Capricorn Energy Limited
Officers: Duncan Wood, Secretary; Brita Holstad [1966] Director [Norwegian]; Paul Joseph Mayland [1968] Director; James Donald Smith [1977] Director; Simon John Thomson [1965] Director

Navigator Gas Invest Limited
Incorporated: 25 May 2010
Net Worth: £28,841,984 *Total Assets:* £103,760,824
Registered Office: 150 Aldersgate Street, London, EC1A 4AB
Activities: Activities of other holding companies n.e.c.
Parent: Navigator Holdings Ltd
Officers: Niall Joseph Nolan [1963] Director/Accountant [Irish]

Navigators Corporate Underwriters Limited
Incorporated: 4 September 1996
Net Worth: £73,081,000 *Total Assets:* £853,934,016
Registered Office: Floors 7-8, 6 Bevis Marks, London, EC3A 7BA
Activities: Non-life insurance
Parent: Navigators Holdings (UK) Limited
Officers: Carl Lee Bach III [1975] Managing Director [American]; Colin Douglas Sprott [1969] Director

Navona Issuer Holdco Limited
Incorporated: 30 November 2010
Net Worth: £588,071 *Total Assets:* £702,495,488
Registered Office: 35 Great St Helen's, London, EC3A 6AP
Activities: Non-trading company
Parent: Intertrust Corporate Services Limited
Officers: Daniel Marc Richard Jaffe [1975] Director

Naxos Investments Limited
Incorporated: 24 March 2005
Net Worth: £18,808,134 *Total Assets:* £1,021,158,784
Registered Office: 1 Churchill Place, London, E14 5HP
Activities: Financial intermediation not elsewhere classified
Parent: Barclays Bank PLC
Officers: Carl Thomas Senior [1978] Director/Banker; Vishal Shah [1984] Director/Banker; Patrick Brittain Voisey [1979] Director; Jonathan Michael Walthoe [1975] Director/Banker

Nbcuniversal International Limited
Incorporated: 12 April 2002 *Employees:* 292
Net Worth: £67,588,000 *Total Assets:* £110,231,000
Registered Office: 1 Central St Giles, St Giles High Street, London, WC2H 8NU
Activities: Activities of head offices
Parent: Comcast Corporation
Officers: Alison Mansfield, Secretary; Jason Jon Beesley [1976] Director/SVP, CFO NBCUniversal International [American]; Duncan John Timothy Bratchell [1958] Director/Chartered Accountant; Oliver Canning [1970] Director/Solicitor; Tracy Lockhart [1970] Director/SVP & Group Financial Controller International; Kevin Michael MacLellan [1967] Director/Chairman, NBCUniversal International [American]

NBG Finance (Dollar) PLC
Incorporated: 20 February 2008 *Employees:* 3
Net Worth: £257,748,384 *Total Assets:* £260,890,496
Registered Office: 75 King William Street, London, EC4N 7BE
Activities: Financial intermediation not elsewhere classified
Parent: National Bank of Greece S.A.
Officers: Owolewa Abiodun Daramola, Secretary; George Aggelides [1974] Director/Banking [Cypriot]; Owolewa Abiodun Daramola [1974] Director/Banking; John Harry North [1935] Director

NC Shine Acquisition Ltd.
Incorporated: 29 March 2011
Net Worth: £386,897,984 *Total Assets:* £386,897,984
Registered Office: Shepherds Building Central, Charecroft Way, London, W14 0EE
Activities: Television programme production activities
Parent: 21CF Shine Holdings UK Ltd
Officers: Richard Robert Johnston [1967] Director; Peter Andrew Salmon [1956] Director/Chief Creative Officer; Sophie Henrietta Turner Laing [1960] Director

NCR Limited
Incorporated: 8 November 1895 *Employees:* 1,274
Net Worth: £183,887,008 *Total Assets:* £260,072,000
Registered Office: 9th Floor, 5 Merchant Square, London, W2 1BQ
Activities: Other information technology service activities
Parent: NCR UK Group Limited
Officers: Caroline Amanda Kee, Secretary; John Boudreau [1963] Director [American]; Caroline Amanda Kee [1966] Director/Solicitor [Irish]; Geoffrey Robert Smith [1962] EMEA Labour and Employee Relations Director

NCR UK Group Limited
Incorporated: 25 June 1996 *Employees:* 3
Net Worth: £171,330,000 *Total Assets:* £184,904,000
Registered Office: 9th Floor, 5 Merchant Square, London, W2 1BQ
Activities: Other business support service activities n.e.c.
Parent: NCR Corporation
Officers: Caroline Amanda Kee, Secretary; John Boudreau [1963] Director [American]; Caroline Amanda Kee [1966] Director [Irish]; Geoffrey Robert Smith [1962] EMEA Labour and Employee Relations Director

Nectar Loyalty Limited
Incorporated: 30 May 2001 *Employees:* 164
Previous: Aimia Coalition Loyalty UK Limited
Net Worth Deficit: £1,401,000 *Total Assets:* £248,076,000
Registered Office: 6th Floor, 80 Strand, London, WC2R 0NN
Activities: Other professional, scientific and technical activities n.e.c.
Parent: Nectar EMEA Limited
Officers: Timothy Fallowfield, Secretary; Duncan John Cooper [1979] Director/Chartered Accountant; Nicolas Paul Michael Angelo Mills-Hicks [1971] Director/Chartered Accountant; James Moir [1976] Director

Nemo Link Limited
Incorporated: 6 August 2012
Previous: National Grid Nemo Link Limited
Net Worth: £162,820,560 *Total Assets:* £486,769,856
Registered Office: 1-3 Strand, London, WC2N 5EH
Activities: Construction of utility projects for electricity and telecommunications
Shareholders: National Grid Interconnector Holdings Limited; Elia System Operator NV/SA
Officers: Megan Barnes, Secretary; Lawrence Hagan, Secretary; Markus Josef Berger [1963] Director [Belgian]; Jonathan Butterworth [1962] Director; Patrick Francis de Leener [1965] Director [Belgian]; Nick Hooper [1975] Director; Nick Sides [1966] Director; Ilse Tant [1973] Director [Belgian]

Neo (BC) UK Limited
Incorporated: 13 March 2017 *Employees:* 1,328
Net Worth: £92,293,072 *Total Assets:* £611,671,424
Registered Office: 6th Floor, Heron House, 15 Adams Street, London, WC2N 6RJ
Activities: Activities of other holding companies n.e.c.
Officers: Giovanni Camera [1983] Director [Italian]; Ivano Sessa [1977] Director [Italian]

Neon Capital Limited
Incorporated: 12 July 2002 *Employees:* 214
Previous: Marketform Group Limited
Net Worth: £16,705,000 *Total Assets:* £513,561,984
Registered Office: 5th Floor, 20 Gracechurch Street, London, EC3V 0BG
Activities: Activities of head offices
Officers: Alastair George Clark-Mckay, Secretary; Ronald James Brichler [1955] Director/Insurance Professional [American]; Joseph Evans Consolino [1966] Director [American]; Donald Dumford Larson [1951] Director/Insurance Executive [American]; Vito Charles Peraino [1956] Director/Insurance Executive [American]; Martin Robert Davidson Reith [1965] Director; David John Witzgall [1959] Director/Insurance Executive [American]

Neptune E & P UKCS Limited
Incorporated: 9 June 1997 *Employees:* 107
Previous: Neptune E & P UK Ltd
Net Worth: £423,073,984 *Total Assets:* £810,516,992
Registered Office: Nova North, 11 Bressenden Place, London, SW1E 5BY
Activities: Extraction of crude petroleum
Parent: Neptune Energy Group Holdings Limited
Officers: Katharine Edwina Louise Ash, Secretary/Solicitor; James Lynn House [1961] Director/Chief Executive Officer Neptune Energy International [American]; Peter David Anderson Jones [1971] Managing Director; Harald Knoebl [1969] Director/General Secretary [German]; William Samuel Hugh Laidlaw [1956] Director/Chairman Neptune Energy Group; Armand Jean Margrete Lumens [1968] Director/Chief Financial Officer [Dutch]

Nero Holdings Limited
Incorporated: 5 December 1996 *Employees:* 5,262
Net Worth: £241,898,000 *Total Assets:* £330,273,984
Registered Office: 9-15 Neal Street, London, WC2H 9QL
Activities: Unlicenced restaurants and cafes
Parent: Italian Coffee Holdings Ltd
Officers: James Stewart, Secretary; Dr Generald William Ford [1957] Director/Businessman [American]; Glyn Maurice House [1966] Director; Benedict James Price [1967] Director/Accountant

Nesta
Incorporated: 15 July 2011 *Employees:* 193
Net Worth: £445,188,000 *Total Assets:* £461,948,000
Registered Office: 58 Victoria Embankment, London, EC4Y 0DS
Activities: Research and experimental development on social sciences and humanities
Officers: Delores Francesca Rajkumari Mohan, Secretary; Judith Mary Gibbons [1957] Non-Executive Chair, Director and Trustee; Sir John Gieve [1950] Director; Imran Khan [1985] Director/Senior Manager; Professor Anthony William Lilley [1970] Director; Simon John Linnett [1954] Director/Banker; Jonathan Piers Daniel Linney [1971] Director; David James Pitt-Watson [1956] Director; Natalie Patricia Tydeman [1971] Director/Private Equity Investor; Moira Wallace [1961] Director/Provost, Oriel College; Edward James Wray [1968] Director/Entrepreneur and Angel Investor

The Net-a-Porter Group Limited
Incorporated: 5 August 1999 *Employees:* 1,821
Net Worth: £333,108,000 *Total Assets:* £624,489,024
Registered Office: 1 The Village Offices, Westfield, Ariel Way, London, W12 7GF
Activities: Retail sale via mail order houses or via Internet
Parent: Largenta Limited
Officers: Angelica Longanesi Cattani, Secretary; Alison Loehnis [1970] Director/President - The Net-A-Porter Group [American]; Federico Marchetti [1969] Director/Chief Executive Officer of YOOX [Italian]

Network Rail (High Speed) Limited
Incorporated: 9 May 2002 *Employees:* 7
Net Worth: £88,229,000 *Total Assets:* £104,460,000
Registered Office: 1 Eversholt Street, London, NW1 2DN
Activities: Passenger rail transport, interurban
Parent: Network Rail Infrastructure Limited
Officers: Katie Elizabeth Frost [1982] Director; John Halsall [1966] Director; Duncan Thomas Rimmer [1972] Director; Jon Stephen Shaw [1972] Director; Rupert Justin Houlihan Walker [1968] Director/Head of High Speed Rail Development; Jeremy William Westlake [1965] Director/Chief Finance Officer

Network Rail Infrastructure Finance PLC
Incorporated: 31 March 2004
Net Worth: £1,000,000 *Total Assets:* £27,595,999,232
Registered Office: 1 Eversholt Street, London, NW1 2DN
Activities: Financial intermediation not elsewhere classified
Parent: Intertrust Corporate Services Limited
Officers: Paul Daniel Marshall [1979] Director/Accountant; Clifford Pearce [1970] Director; Helena Paivi Whitaker [1963] Director [Finnish]

Network Rail Infrastructure Limited
Incorporated: 28 February 1994 *Employees:* 39,370
Net Worth: £6,566,000,128 *Total Assets:* £67,720,998,912
Registered Office: 1 Eversholt Street, London, NW1 2DN
Activities: Development of building projects
Parent: Network Rail Holdco Limited
Officers: Stuart Malcolm Kelly, Secretary; Robert William Brighouse [1957] Director/Civil Engineer; Richard Howard Brown [1953] Director; Sharon Emma Flood [1965] Director; Christopher Leslie Gibb [1963] Director/Railwayman; Andrew Haines [1964] Director; Sir Peter Gerard Hendy [1953] Director; Drusilla Maizey [1957] Director; David Michael Noyes [1962] Director; Michael Colin Putnam [1960] Director; Bridget Clare Rosewell [1951] Director/Economist; Jeremy William Westlake [1965] Director/Chief Finance Officer

Network Rail Limited
Incorporated: 22 March 2002 *Employees:* 39,370
Net Worth: £6,774,000,128 *Total Assets:* £68,860,002,304
Registered Office: 1 Eversholt Street, London, NW1 2DN
Activities: Passenger rail transport, interurban
Officers: Stuart Malcolm Kelly, Secretary; Robert William Brighouse [1957] Director/Civil Engineer; Richard Howard Brown [1953] Director; Sharon Emma Flood [1965] Director; Christopher Leslie Gibb [1963] Director/Railwayman; Andrew Haines [1964] Director; Sir Peter Gerard Hendy [1953] Director; Drusilla Maizey [1957] Director; David Michael Noyes [1962] Director; Michael Colin Putnam [1960] Director; Bridget Clare Rosewell [1951] Director/Economist; Jeremy William Westlake [1965] Director/Chief Finance Officer

Neuberger Berman Europe Limited
Incorporated: 25 May 2005 *Employees:* 186
Net Worth: £73,514,640 *Total Assets:* £163,933,056
Registered Office: 4th Floor, Lansdowne House, 57 Berkeley Square, London, W1J 6ER
Activities: Financial intermediation not elsewhere classified
Parent: NBEH Limited
Officers: Joseph Vincent Amato [1962] Director/Banker [American]; Michelle Simone Green [1967] Director/Solicitor; James Charles Frazer Harvey [1970] Director/Finance; Dirk Van Lomwel [1964] Director/Banker [Dutch]; Heather Phyl Zuckerman [1971] Director/Administrative Officer [American]

New England Paint Company Limited
Incorporated: 22 August 2000
Net Worth: £121,772,000 *Total Assets:* £121,772,000
Registered Office: 3 Sheldon Square, Paddington, London, W2 6PX
Activities: Non-trading company
Shareholder: Sheldon Holdings Limited
Officers: Paul Moore, Secretary; Jean-Noel Hughes Roger Groleau [1974] Director [French]; Paul Anthony Moore [1970] Director/Company Secretary

New Green Interim Holdco Limited
Incorporated: 29 December 2016
Net Worth: £1,697,738 *Total Assets:* £529,785,312
Registered Office: 18 St Swithin's Lane, London, EC4N 8AD
Activities: Activities of other holding companies n.e.c.
Parent: UK Green Investment Rampion Limited
Officers: Dominic Tan, Secretary; Richard Abel [1970] Director/Investment Banker; Stephen Alan John Deeley [1980] Director/Investment Manager; Mark Jonathan Dooley [1962] Director/Investment Banker [Australian]; Erin Kate Eisenberg [1978] Director [American]; Tom Kelly [1989] Director/Investment Manager [Irish]; Gordon Ian Winston Parsons [1967] Director/Accountant; Roberto Purcaro [1978] Senior Managing Director [Italian]; David Paul Tilstone [1969] Director/Investment Banker

New Printing House Square Limited
Incorporated: 4 June 1992
Net Worth: £69,359,184 *Total Assets:* £143,443,120
Registered Office: 16 Tinworth Street, London, SE11 5AL
Activities: Other letting and operating of own or leased real estate
Officers: David Francis Fuller, Secretary; Erik Henry Klotz [1944] Director/Executive Vice Chairman [Swedish]; Alain Gustave Paul Millet [1968] Director/Group Treasurer [French]; John Howard Whiteley [1958] Director/Chief Financial Officer; Fredrik Jonas Widlund [1968] Director [Swedish]; Simon Laborda Wigzell [1968] Director

New River Company Limited (The)
Incorporated: 1 July 1905
Net Worth: £417,653,056 *Total Assets:* £453,612,928
Registered Office: 25 Savile Row, London, W1S 2ER
Activities: Buying and selling of own real estate
Parent: Derwent Valley Limited
Officers: David Andrew Lawler, Secretary; John David Burns [1944] Director; Nigel Quentin George [1963] Director; Simon Paul Silver [1950] Director; David Gary Silverman [1969] Director; Paul Malcolm Williams [1960] Director/Surveyor; Damian Mark Alan Wisniewski [1961] Director

New Star Asset Management Group Limited
Incorporated: 10 January 2007
Net Worth: £60,151,000 *Total Assets:* £150,724,000
Registered Office: 201 Bishopsgate, London, EC2M 3AE
Activities: Non-trading company
Parent: Henderson Global Investors Asset Management Limited
Officers: Rhiannon Willow Chaudhuri [1978] Director/Accountant; Anna Nicole Kurzon [1978] Director/Chartered Accountant

New Topco Limited
Incorporated: 12 August 2016 *Employees:* 2,458
Net Worth Deficit: £17,711,000 *Total Assets:* £142,792,000
Registered Office: c/o Intermediate Capital Group PLC, Juxon House, 100 St Paul's Churchyard, London, EC4M 8BU
Activities: Activities of head offices
Officers: Max Anthony Mitchell [1975] Senior Managing Director

New Ventures II (UK) Limited
Incorporated: 8 March 2012 *Employees:* 2
Net Worth: £199,367,136 *Total Assets:* £199,789,264
Registered Office: Hays Galleria, 1 Hays Lane, London, SE1 2RD
Activities: Activities of other holding companies n.e.c.
Parent: RPM NVUK Limited
Officers: Hilde Maria Eleonora de Backer [1969] Director [Belgian]; Richard Murray Hill [1960] Director

Newco NHL UK (17) Limited
Incorporated: 29 June 2017 *Employees:* 154
Net Worth Deficit: £105,938,672 *Total Assets:* £156,904,544
Registered Office: 4th Floor, 159 St John Street, London, EC1V 4QJ
Activities: Other business support service activities n.e.c.
Parent: Norlake Hospitality Limited
Officers: Srikanth Balachandran [1961] Director [Indian]; Sonal Kapasi [1971] Director [Indian]; Shravin Bharti Mittal [1987] Director; Sharan Pasricha [1980] Director

Newday BondCo PLC
Incorporated: 7 November 2016
Net Worth: £100,000 *Total Assets:* £435,500,000
Registered Office: 7 Handyside Street, London, N1C 4DA
Activities: Activities of other holding companies n.e.c.
Parent: Newday Group UK Limited
Officers: Stephen Rowland, Secretary; James Bernard Corcoran [1954] Director; Paul Nigel Sheriff [1969] Director

Newday Funding 2015-1 PLC
Incorporated: 13 January 2015
Net Worth: £20,000 *Total Assets:* £283,228,992
Registered Office: 35 Great St Helen's, London, EC3A 6AP
Activities: Financial intermediation not elsewhere classified
Parent: Newday Funding Securitisation Holdings Limited
Officers: Paivi Helena Whitaker [1963] Director [Finnish]

Newday Funding 2015-2 PLC
Incorporated: 19 March 2015
Net Worth: £15,000 *Total Assets:* £282,388,992
Registered Office: 35 Great St Helen's, London, EC3A 6AP
Activities: Financial intermediation not elsewhere classified
Parent: Newday Funding Securitisation Holdings Limited
Officers: Paivi Helena Whitaker [1963] Director [Finnish]

Newday Funding 2016-1 PLC
Incorporated: 16 October 2015
Net Worth: £30,000 *Total Assets:* £248,188,000
Registered Office: 35 Great St Helen's, London, EC3A 6AP
Activities: Financial intermediation not elsewhere classified
Parent: Newday Funding Securitisation Holdings Limited
Officers: Paivi Helena Whitaker [1963] Director [Finnish]

Newday Funding 2017-1 PLC
Incorporated: 28 April 2017
Net Worth: £18,000 *Total Assets:* £244,504,000
Registered Office: 35 Great St Helen's, London, EC3A 6AP
Activities: Financial intermediation not elsewhere classified
Parent: Newday Funding Securitisation Holdings Ltd
Officers: Paivi Helena Whitaker [1963] Director [Finnish]

Newday Funding Loan Note Issuer Ltd
Incorporated: 9 January 2015
Net Worth: £12,000 *Total Assets:* £1,256,936,960
Registered Office: 35 Great St Helen's, London, EC3A 6AP
Activities: Non-trading company
Officers: Paivi Helena Whitaker [1963] Director [Finnish]

Newday Funding Transferor Ltd
Incorporated: 7 September 2012
Previous: Newday Funding Ltd
Net Worth: £14,284,000 *Total Assets:* £1,476,162,944
Registered Office: 7 Handyside Street, London, N1C 4DA
Activities: Other business support service activities n.e.c.
Officers: Stephen Rowland, Secretary; James Bernard Corcoran [1954] Director/Chief Executive Officer; Paul Nigel Sheriff [1969] Director/Chief Financial Officer

Newday Partnership Funding 2015-1 PLC
Incorporated: 29 May 2014
Net Worth: £16,000 *Total Assets:* £244,454,000
Registered Office: 35 Great St Helen's, London, EC3A 6AP
Activities: Financial intermediation not elsewhere classified
Parent: Newday Partnership Securitisation Holdings Limited
Officers: Paivi Helena Whitaker [1963] Director [Finnish]

Newday Partnership Loan Note Issuer Ltd
Incorporated: 5 February 2014
Net Worth: £12,000 *Total Assets:* £789,769,024
Registered Office: 35 Great St Helen's, London, EC3A 6AP
Activities: Non-trading company
Officers: Paivi Helena Whitaker [1963] Director [Finnish]

Newday Partnership Transferor PLC
Incorporated: 14 December 2012
Net Worth: £89,963,000 *Total Assets:* £995,265,024
Registered Office: 7 Handyside Street, London, N1C 4DA
Activities: Other business support service activities n.e.c.
Officers: Stephen Rowland, Secretary; James Bernard Corcoran [1954] Director/Chief Executive Officer; Paul Nigel Sheriff [1969] Director/Chief Financial Officer

Newday UK Limited
Incorporated: 21 October 2016
Net Worth Deficit: £31,400,000 *Total Assets:* £919,100,032
Registered Office: 7 Handyside Street, London, N1C 4DA
Activities: Activities of other holding companies n.e.c.
Parent: Newday Group UK Limited
Officers: Stephen Rowland, Secretary; James Bernard Corcoran [1954] Director; Paul Nigel Sheriff [1969] Director

Newfound Bay Limited
Incorporated: 18 February 2005
Net Worth: £4,429,725,184 *Total Assets:* £4,430,040,064
Registered Office: 2 King Edward Street, London, EC1A 1HQ
Activities: Financial intermediation not elsewhere classified
Parent: Bank of America Corporation
Officers: Jonathan Howard Redvers Lee [1966] Director/Company Executive; David Alan Spring [1970] Director/Trader [British/Australian]

Newgate Funding PLC
Incorporated: 17 February 2006
Net Worth: £25,000 *Total Assets:* £1,494,880,000
Registered Office: 6th Floor, 65 Gresham Street, London, EC2V 7NQ
Activities: Financial intermediation not elsewhere classified
Parent: Newgate Funding Holdings Limited
Officers: Carl Steven Baldry [1966] Director; Sean Peter Martin [1965] Director

Newline Corporate Name Limited
Incorporated: 11 July 1996
Net Worth: £276,528,000 *Total Assets:* £863,665,024
Registered Office: Corn Exchange, 55 Mark Lane, London, EC3R 7NE
Activities: Non-life insurance
Parent: Newline Holdings UK Limited
Officers: Henry James Louis Withinshaw, Secretary; Jan Christiansen [1957] Director/Insurance [Danish]; Robert Bernhard Kastner [1968] Director/Insurance; Michael Gerard Wacek [1956] Director/Insurance [American]; Henry James Louis Withinshaw [1966] Director

Newline Insurance Company Limited
Incorporated: 5 April 2002
Net Worth: £29,121,000 *Total Assets:* £177,358,000
Registered Office: Corn Exchange, 55 Mark Lane, London, EC3R 7NE
Activities: Non-life insurance
Parent: Newline Holdings UK Limited
Officers: Henry James Louis Withinshaw, Secretary; Jan Christiansen [1957] Director/Insurance [Danish]; Neil David Duncan [1976] Director/Chief Risk Officer and Chief Actuary; Sonny Kapur [1960] Director/Chief Financial Officer; Robert Bernhard Kastner [1968] Director; Carl Anthony Overy [1968] Director; Matthew Scales [1954] Director; John William James Spencer [1957] Director/Insurance; Michael Gerard Wacek [1956] Director/Insurance [American]; Henry James Louis Withinshaw [1966] Director

Newport Holdings Limited
Incorporated: 7 September 1993
Net Worth: £69,747,864 *Total Assets:* £173,277,792
Registered Office: Floor 6, Quadrant House, 4 Thomas More Square, London, E1W 1YW
Activities: Renting and operating of Housing Association real estate
Parent: Mintglade Limited
Officers: Michael Robert Goldberger, Secretary; Howard Alan Pearlman, Secretary; Michael Robert Goldberger [1956] Director; David Alan Pearlman [1945] Director; Howard Alan Pearlman [1975] Director/Property Management

Newriver REIT PLC
Incorporated: 8 June 2016 *Employees:* 56
Net Worth: £892,380,032 *Total Assets:* £1,390,360,960
Registered Office: 16 New Burlington Place, London, W1S 2HX
Activities: Buying and selling of own real estate
Officers: Robert John Marcus, Secretary; Kay Elizabeth Chaldecott [1962] Director/Chartered Surveyor; Mark Anthony Philip Davies [1974] Director/Chartered Accountant; Baroness Margaret Anne Ford [1957] Director; Allan Stevenson Robert Lockhart [1965] Director/Chartered Surveyor; David Alfred Stevenson Lockhart [1943] Director; Alastair Miller [1958] Director/Chartered Accountant; Colin Rutherford [1959] Director

News Corp Holdings UK & Ireland
Incorporated: 27 February 2003
Net Worth: £699,219,008 *Total Assets:* £699,219,008
Registered Office: 1 London Bridge Street, London, SE1 9GF
Activities: Activities of head offices
Parent: News Corp Investments UK & Ireland
Officers: Rebekah Mary Brooks [1968] Director/Chief Executive Officer; Michael Charles Gill [1963] Director/Accountant; Christopher Charles Stoddart Longcroft [1971] Managing Director Operations

News Corp Investments II Limited
Incorporated: 28 April 2016
Net Worth: £1,100,397,696 *Total Assets:* £1,100,397,696
Registered Office: The News Building, 1 London Bridge Street, London, SE1 9GF
Activities: Other business support service activities n.e.c.
Officers: Michael Charles Gill [1963] Director/Accountant; Christopher Charles Stoddart Longcroft [1971] Director/Chief Financial Officer

News Corp Investments UK & Ireland
Incorporated: 13 July 1979
Net Worth Deficit: £221,820,992 *Total Assets:* £470,968,992
Registered Office: 1 London Bridge Street, London, SE1 9GF
Activities: Activities of head offices
Parent: News Corporation
Officers: Rebekah Mary Brooks [1968] Director/Chief Executive Officer; Michael Charles Gill [1963] Director/Accountant; Christopher Charles Stoddart Longcroft [1971] Director/Chief Financial Officer

News Corp UK & Ireland Limited
Incorporated: 28 July 1904
Net Worth: £816,907,008 *Total Assets:* £1,985,889,024
Registered Office: 1 London Bridge Street, London, SE1 9GF
Activities: Publishing of newspapers
Parent: News Corp Holdings UK & Ireland
Officers: Rebekah Mary Brooks [1968] Director/Chief Executive Officer; David William Dinsmore [1968] Director/Chief Operating Officer; Christopher Charles Stoddart Longcroft [1971] Director/Chief Financial Officer

News Group Newspapers Limited
Incorporated: 30 December 1960 *Employees:* 590
Net Worth: £548,932,992 *Total Assets:* £857,824,000
Registered Office: 1 London Bridge Street, London, SE1 9GF
Activities: Publishing of newspapers
Parent: News Corp UK & Ireland Limited
Officers: Rebekah Mary Brooks [1968] Director/Chief Executive Officer; David William Dinsmore [1968] Director/Chief Operating Officer; Christopher Charles Stoddart Longcroft [1971] Director/Chief Financial Officer

News UK & Ireland Limited
Incorporated: 7 March 1985 *Employees:* 1,100
Net Worth: £143,840,000 *Total Assets:* £389,009,984
Registered Office: 1 London Bridge Street, London, SE1 9GF
Activities: Other business support service activities n.e.c.
Parent: News Corp UK & Ireland Limited
Officers: David William Dinsmore [1968] Director/Chief Operating Officer; Christopher Charles Stoddart Longcroft [1971] Director/Chief Financial Officer

Newsprinters (Broxbourne) Limited
Incorporated: 14 September 2004 *Employees:* 167
Net Worth Deficit: £163,756,992 *Total Assets:* £171,608,992
Registered Office: 1 London Bridge Street, London, SE1 9GF
Activities: Non-trading company
Parent: News Printers Assets Limited
Officers: David William Dinsmore [1968] Director/Chief Operating Officer; Christopher Charles Stoddart Longcroft [1971] Managing Director Operations

Newton Investment Management Limited
Incorporated: 6 June 1978 *Employees:* 292
Net Worth: £357,648,992 *Total Assets:* £417,651,008
Registered Office: BNY Mellon Centre, 160 Queen Victoria Street, London, EC4V 4LA
Activities: Fund management activities
Parent: Newton Management Limited
Officers: Isabella Iona Alison Partridge, Secretary; Gregory Allan Brisk [1962] Director; Dr Kevin James Carter [1952] Director; Curtis William Custard [1969] Director/Chief Investment Officer [American]; Andrew Terence Downs [1963] Director/Chartered Accountant; Mitchell Evan Harris [1955] Director/Banking/Finance [American/British]; Henrietta Jowitt [1959] Director/Investment; Susan Margaret Noble [1957] Director/Investment; Hanneke Smits [1966] Director [Dutch]

Newton Management Limited
Incorporated: 2 December 1992
Net Worth: £282,134,016 *Total Assets:* £308,958,016
Registered Office: BNY Mellon Centre, 160 Queen Victoria Street, London, EC4V 4LA
Activities: Fund management activities
Parent: BNY Mellon International Asset Management Group Limited
Officers: Isabella Iona Alison Partridge, Secretary; Gregory Allan Brisk [1962] Director; Andrew Terence Downs [1963] Director/Chartered Accountant; Hanneke Smits [1966] Director [Dutch]

NEX Group Holdings Limited
Incorporated: 10 September 2008 *Employees:* 1,946
Previous: NEX Group Holdings PLC
Net Worth: £338,000,000 *Total Assets:* £2,054,000,000
Registered Office: 2 Broadgate, London, EC2M 7UR
Activities: Activities of head offices
Parent: NEX International Limited
Officers: Deborah Anne Abrehart, Secretary; Deborah Anne Abrehart [1957] Director/Chartered Secretary; Allan Samuel Aldridge [1980] Director; David Alexander Williamson [1980] Director; Samantha Anne Wren [1966] Director

NEX International Limited
Incorporated: 3 August 1998
Previous: NEX International PLC
Net Worth: £1,500,000,000 *Total Assets:* £2,103,000,064
Registered Office: 2 Broadgate, London, EC2M 7UR
Activities: Activities of head offices
Parent: NEX Group Limited
Officers: Deborah Anne Abrehart, Secretary; David Alexander Williamson [1980] Director; Samantha Anne Wren [1966] Director

NEX Markets Limited
Incorporated: 10 June 2014
Previous: ICAP Electronic Markets Limited
Net Worth: £1,728,083,968 *Total Assets:* £1,857,302,016
Registered Office: 2 Broadgate, London, EC2M 7UR
Activities: Activities of financial services holding companies
Parent: NEX Group Holdings Limited
Officers: Deborah Abrehart, Secretary; Jason Todd Cohen [1972] Director [American]; Eliran Glazer [1971] Director [Israeli]; Seth Johnson [1968] Director

NEX Optimisation Limited
Incorporated: 11 June 2014
Previous: ICAP Post Trade Holdings Limited
Net Worth: £503,228,992 *Total Assets:* £574,574,016
Registered Office: 2 Broadgate, London, EC2M 7UR
Activities: Activities of financial services holding companies
Parent: NEX Group Holdings Limited
Officers: Deborah Abrehart, Secretary; David Charles Ireland [1969] Director; Kenneth Michael Pigaga [1954] Director [American]

NEX Services Limited
Incorporated: 5 January 2016 *Employees:* 208
Net Worth Deficit: £17,266,000 *Total Assets:* £173,660,000
Registered Office: 2 Broadgate, London, EC2M 7UR
Activities: Activities of head offices
Parent: NEX Group Holdings Limited
Officers: Deborah Anne Abrehart, Secretary; Deborah Anne Abrehart [1957] Director/Chartered Secretary; Lorraine Emma Barclay [1966] Director; Samantha Anne Wren [1966] Director

Nexa Resources UK Limited
Incorporated: 2 August 2016
Previous: Milpo UK Limited
Net Worth Deficit: £6,363,484 *Total Assets:* £154,760,176
Registered Office: 100 New Bridge Street, London, EC4V 6JA
Activities: Wholesale of metals and metal ores
Officers: Jones Aparecido Belther [1968] Mining Director [Brazilian]; Claudia Patricia Torres Beltran [1979] Director/Business Executive [Peruvian]; Mario Antonio Bertoncini [1968] Director [Brazilian]; John Anthony King [1951] Director; Luciana Rodrigues Da Motta Pires [1980] Director/Tax Manager [Brazilian]; Ricardo Moraes Galvao Porto [1973] Logistics and Supply Chain Director [Brazilian]; Susy Magaly Bardales Rojas [1970] Director/General Counsel [Peruvian]; Jacqueline Flor Torres Villar [1975] Director/Accountant [Peruvian]

Next Fifteen Communications Group PLC
Incorporated: 12 August 1981 *Employees:* 1,777
Net Worth: £76,964,000 *Total Assets:* £195,330,000
Registered Office: 75 Bermondsey Street, London, SE1 3XF
Activities: Public relations and communications activities
Officers: Nicholas Lee Morrison, Secretary; Timothy John Bruce Dyson [1960] Director/Public Relations Executive; Richard Anthony Eyre [1954] Director; Peter Jonathan Harris [1962] Director; Penelope Anne Ladkin-Brand [1977] Director; Genevieve Helen Shore [1969] Director

Nexteer UK Holding Ltd.
Incorporated: 5 February 2015
Net Worth: £765,819,840 *Total Assets:* £765,838,976
Registered Office: 100 New Bridge Street, London, EC4V 6JA
Activities: Activities of other holding companies n.e.c.
Parent: The State Council of The People's Republic of China
Officers: Yi Fan [1966] Director/Business Executive [Chinese]; William Generald Quigley III [1961] Director/Business Executive [American]

Nextenergy Solar Holdings Limited
Incorporated: 24 March 2014
Net Worth: £191,858,368 *Total Assets:* £359,341,024
Registered Office: 5th Floor, North Side, 7-10 Chandos Street, Cavendish Square, London, W1G 9DQ
Activities: Activities of other holding companies n.e.c.
Parent: Nextenergy Solar Fund Ltd
Officers: Aldo Beolchini [1974] Director/Consultant [Italian]; Michael Fritz Herbert Bonte Friedheim [1966] Director [German]; Ross Grier [1985] Director; Abid Kazim [1964] Director

Nextpower Radius Limited
Incorporated: 16 March 2016
Net Worth: £4,387,634 *Total Assets:* £103,606,280
Registered Office: 5th Floor, North Side, 7-10 Chandos Street, Cavendish Square, London, W1G 9DQ
Activities: Activities of other holding companies n.e.c.
Parent: Nextenergy Solar Holdings IV Limited
Officers: Aldo Beolchini [1974] Director/Consultant [Italian]; Michael Fritz Herbert Bonte Friedheim [1966] Director [German]

NGC Europe Limited
Incorporated: 24 February 2010
Net Worth: £137,026,000 *Total Assets:* £230,372,992
Registered Office: Third Floor, 10 Hammersmith Grove, Hammersmith, London, W6 7AP
Activities: Television programming and broadcasting activities
Parent: NGC UK Holdings Company Limited
Officers: Terry William Downing [1965] Director/CFO Europe and Africa; Diego Fernando Londono [1970] Executive Director [Colombian]; Jan Koeppen [1970] Executive Director [Dutch]; Colin Robert McLeod [1967] Director; Namrata Patel [1983] Director/CFO & VP

NGC UK Holdings Company Limited
Incorporated: 10 December 2007
Net Worth: £71,645,000 *Total Assets:* £175,928,000
Registered Office: Third Floor, 10 Hammersmith Grove, Hammersmith, London, W6 7AP
Activities: Television programme production activities
Parent: Twenty-First Century Fox, Inc.
Officers: Terry William Downing [1965] Director/CFO Europe and Africa; Jan Koeppen [1970] Director/President of FNG Europe & Africa [Dutch]; Diego Fernando Londono [1970] Director/COO Fox Europe & Africa [Colombian]; Colin Robert McLeod [1967] Director; Namrata Patel [1983] Director/CFO & VP

NGG Finance PLC
Incorporated: 21 May 2001
Net Worth: £655,544,000 *Total Assets:* £2,887,589,888
Registered Office: 1-3 Strand, London, WC2N 5EH
Activities: Other business support service activities n.e.c.
Parent: National Grid PLC
Officers: Megan Barnes, Secretary; Andrew Jonathan Agg [1969] Director/Accountant; Simon Warren Grant [1979] Director; Stuart Calvin Humphreys [1963] Director/Chartered Accountant; Alexandra Morton Lewis [1972] Director/Chartered Accountant; Andrew Kenneth Mead [1971] Director/Accountant

NH2 Limited
Incorporated: 25 July 2016
Net Worth: £121,306,992 *Total Assets:* £121,306,992
Registered Office: 9th Floor, 107 Cheapside, London, EC2V 6DN
Activities: Engineering related scientific and technical consulting activities
Major Shareholder: Titus Johannes Weinheimer
Officers: Bruce Barnet [1945] Director/Chairman Nanoholdings [American]; Justin Hall-Tipping [1956] Director; Hemang Jadavji Shah [1975] Director [Indian]; Titus Johannes Weinheimer [1965] Director/General Counsel [German]

NHS Property Services Limited
Incorporated: 20 December 2011 *Employees:* 3,938
Net Worth: £3,674,454,016 *Total Assets:* £4,613,486,080
Registered Office: 99 Gresham Street, London, EC2V 7NG
Activities: Management of real estate on a fee or contract basis
Parent: Secretary of State for Health
Officers: Rita Chudasama, Secretary; Ian David Ellis [1955] Director/Chartered Surveyor; David Roy Godden [1958] Director; Elaine Ruth Hewitt [1964] Director/Chief Executive Officer; Jane Anne Kennedy [1963] Director; Benjamin Michael Patrick Masterson [1964] Director/Senior Civil Servant; Julian Alexander Pearce [1968] Director/Accountant; Martin Leonard Steele [1961] Director/C.O.O; Michael John Strong [1947] Director/Chartered Surveyor; Dr Martin Stephen West [1965] Director/Consultant; John Philip Westwood [1970] Director/Chartered Surveyor

Nicoventures Holdings Limited
Incorporated: 4 December 2012 *Employees:* 50
Net Worth: £426,686,016 *Total Assets:* £443,483,008
Registered Office: Globe House, 1 Water Street, London, WC2R 3LA
Activities: Activities of head offices
Parent: British American Tobacco (NGP) Limited
Officers: Jessica Munday, Secretary; Frederico Pinto Monteiro [1966] Marketing Director [Brazilian]; David O'Reilly [1966] Director; Pablo Daniel Sconfianza [1977] Director [Italian]; Marina Trani [1965] Director/Head of Research and Development [Italian]

Nimbus Acquisitions Holdings Limited
Incorporated: 6 July 2015 *Employees:* 491
Net Worth Deficit: £55,216,000 *Total Assets:* £172,004,000
Registered Office: 90 Long Acre, Covent Garden, London, WC2E 9RA
Activities: Activities of other holding companies n.e.c.
Officers: Ross Devor [1984] Director [American]; Stuart Mark Goldblatt [1979] Director/Chief Financial Officer; Steven Harper [1958] Director [American]; Benjamin William Hood [1973] Director; Jeff Horing [1974] Director [American]; Stephen Paul Rowley [1958] Director/Executive

Nimbus Acquisitions Midco 1 Limited
Incorporated: 10 July 2015 *Employees:* 480
Net Worth: £6,507,000 *Total Assets:* £171,996,000
Registered Office: 90 Long Acre, Covent Garden, London, WC2E 9RA
Activities: Activities of other holding companies n.e.c.
Parent: Nimbus Aquisitions Midco Limited
Officers: Stuart Mark Goldblatt [1979] Director/Chief Financial Officer; Benjamin William Hood [1973] Director

Nimbus Acquisitions Midco Limited
Incorporated: 7 July 2015 *Employees:* 2
Net Worth: £38,218,000 *Total Assets:* £121,169,000
Registered Office: 90 Long Acre, Covent Garden, London, WC2E 9RA
Activities: Activities of other holding companies n.e.c.
Parent: Nimbus Acquisitions Holdings Limited
Officers: Stuart Mark Goldblatt [1979] Director/Chief Financial Officer; Benjamin William Hood [1973] Director

Nine United Properties UK Ltd
Incorporated: 29 March 2004 *Employees:* 8
Previous: Bestseller United (UK) Limited
Net Worth: £120,579,912 *Total Assets:* £125,140,520
Registered Office: 16 Queen Annes Gate, London, SW1H 9AA
Activities: Other retail sale not in stores, stalls or markets
Major Shareholder: Troels Holch Povlsen
Officers: Troels Holch Povlsen [1949] Director [Danish]

Nintex Global Limited
Incorporated: 13 October 2014 *Employees:* 427
Net Worth: £62,162,800 *Total Assets:* £167,022,144
Registered Office: Suite 1, 3rd Floor, 11-12 St James's Square, London, SW1Y 4LB
Activities: Business and domestic software development
Parent: Tau NX Ltd
Officers: Justin Richard John Avery, Secretary; Jeffrey Allan Christianson, Secretary; Laurens Albada [1971] Director/Operating Partner [Trinidadian]; Robert Charles Hausmann [1963] Director/Independent Consultant [American]; Eric Johnson [1976] Director [American]; David Murphy [1962] Director/Senior Operating Partner [American]; Carl Minoo Press [1984] Director/Investor [American]; Hudson Day Smith [1977] Director/Partner [American]; Harry Davis Taylor [1974] Director/Private Equity [American]

Nintex UK Limited
Incorporated: 4 May 2012 *Employees:* 48
Net Worth: £33,044,784 *Total Assets:* £113,899,128
Registered Office: 16 Great Queen Street, Covent Garden, London, WC2B 5AH
Activities: Business and domestic software development
Parent: Nintex Global Limited
Officers: Laurens Albada [1971] Director/Operating Partner [Trinidadian]; Robert Charles Hausmann [1963] Director/Independent Consultant [American]; Eric Johnson [1976] Director/Executive [American]; David Murphy [1962] Director/Partner [American]; Carl Minoo Press [1984] Director/Principal [American]; Hudson Day Smith [1977] Director/Partner [American]; Harry Davis Taylor [1974] Director/Private Equity [American]

Nixes Six PLC
Incorporated: 25 July 2013 *Employees:* 2
Net Worth Deficit: £10,785,857 *Total Assets:* £1,387,321,088
Registered Office: Third Floor, c/o Wilmington Trust SP Services (London) Limited, 1 Kings Arms Yard, London, EC2R 7AF
Activities: Other business support service activities n.e.c.
Parent: Wilmington Trust SP Services (London) Limited
Officers: Daniel Jonathan Wynne [1970] Director

NM Money Holdings Limited
Incorporated: 25 June 2012 *Employees:* 1,470
Previous: Corsair Mint Limited
Net Worth Deficit: £21,023,000 *Total Assets:* £295,284,992
Registered Office: c/o Buzzacott LLP, 130 Wood Street, London, EC2V 6DL
Activities: Other service activities n.e.c.
Parent: Corsair Mint II Limited
Officers: Paul Michael Cabral [1974] Director/Chief Financial Officer [American]; Paul Michael Cabral [1974] Director/Chief Financial Officer [American]; Lord Evan Mervyn Davies [1952] Director/Banker; Dharma Teja Ignacio Jayanti [1968] Director/Private Equity Investor; Peter Denis McNamara [1951] Director

NMC Health PLC
Incorporated: 20 July 2011
Net Worth: £562,588,352 *Total Assets:* £562,635,008
Registered Office: Level 1, Devonshire House, One Mayfair Place, Mayfair, London, W1J 8AJ
Activities: Hospital activities
Officers: Simon Andrew Watkins, Secretary; Dr Ayesha Mohd Abdulla Yasin Abdullah [1966] Managing Director [Emirati]; Khaleefa Butti Omair Yousif Almuhairi [1979] Director [Emirati]; Abdulrahman Sadiq Salim Basaddiq [1948] Director/Chartered Accountant [Kenyan]; Jonathon Galton Bomford [1948] Director; Hani Buttikhi [1984] Director; Salma Ali Said Bin Hareb Almheiri [1965] Director [Emirati]; Prasanth Manghat [1974] Director/Chief Finance Officer [Indian]; Patrick James Meade [1960] Director; Bavaguthu Raghuram Shetty [1942] CEO and Managing Director [Indian]; Henry John Mark Tompkins [1940] Director

NNB Generation Company (HPC) Limited
Incorporated: 17 June 2009
Previous: NNB Generation Company Limited
Net Worth: £4,448,099,840 *Total Assets:* £5,010,699,776
Registered Office: 90 Whitfield Street, London, W1T 4EZ
Activities: Production of electricity
Parent: NNB Holding Company (HPC) Limited
Officers: Claire Rachel Gooding, Secretary; Catherine Sylvie Back [1967] Director [French]; Humphrey Alan Edward Cadoux-Hudson [1960] Director; Nigel Francis Cann [1964] Director; Dr Yigang Cao [1972] Director [Chinese]; Stuart Crooks [1965] Director; Mark Stephen Hartley [1972] Director; Andrew David Hugh Matthews [1958] Director; Dr Fiona McMillan [1952] Director/Consultant; Patrick Pruvot [1959] Director [French]; Richard Arthur Savage [1963] Director; Bin Shangguan [1965] Director [Chinese]; Dr Michael William Weightman [1949] Director; Huang Xiangchou [1974] Director [Chinese]; Xiaohui Zeng [1974] Director [Chinese]; Dongshan Zheng [1962] Director [Chinese]

NNB Holding Company (HPC) Limited
Incorporated: 17 June 2009
Previous: NNB Holding Company Limited
Net Worth: £4,542,014,976 *Total Assets:* £4,542,014,976
Registered Office: 90 Whitfield Street, London, W1T 4EZ
Activities: Activities of head offices
Shareholders: Sagittarius International Limited; NNB Top Company HPC (A) Ltd
Officers: Guido Santi, Secretary; Mrs Marie-Christine Aulagnon [1963] Director [French]; Humphrey Alan Edward Cadoux-Hudson [1960] Director; Christophe Carval [1960] Director [French]; Stuart Crooks [1965] Director; Tat Man Lau [1951] Director; Simone Rossi [1968] Director/Chief Financial Officer [Italian]; Pierre Christian Todorov [1958] Director [French]; Xavier Bernard Yves Ursat [1966] Director [French]; Yuan Xu [1962] Director [Chinese]; Liming Yu [1962] Director [Chinese]; Dongshan Zheng [1962] Director [Chinese]

No Ordinary Designer Label Limited
Incorporated: 8 June 1990 *Employees:* 2,075
Net Worth: £188,571,008 *Total Assets:* £396,052,000
Registered Office: The Ugly Brown Building, 6a St Pancras Way, London, NW1 0TB
Activities: Wholesale of clothing and footwear
Parent: Ted Baker PLC
Officers: Charles Francis Anderson [1970] Director; Matthew Ashby [1967] Special Projects Director; Donald Elliot Browne [1955] Director; Phil Clark [1973] Director; Richard Green [1962] Director; Raymond Stuart Kelvin [1955] Director; Craig Edward MacKinnon Smith [1970] Director of Communications; Lindsay Dennis Page [1958] Finance Director; Rebecca Louise Rodden [1973] Director [Australian]; Leon Shepherd [1966] Director; Victoria Singleton [1977] Director

Nobel Oil E & P (UK) Limited
Incorporated: 9 January 2014 *Employees:* 12
Net Worth: £84,012,176 *Total Assets:* £137,818,176
Registered Office: 48 Dover Street, London, W1S 4FF
Activities: Extraction of crude petroleum
Major Shareholder: Nasib Jabbar Oglu Hasanov
Officers: Lawrence Elliott Bates [1965] Director [American]; Matthew James Bryza [1964] Director/Consultant and Academic [American]; Yusif Jabbarov [1981] Director [Azerbaijani]; Francis Stephen Sommer [1959] Director/Engineer [American]

Nobel Oil Services (UK) Limited
Incorporated: 25 June 2014 *Employees:* 475
Net Worth: £184,727,952 *Total Assets:* £401,217,728
Registered Office: 10-18 Union Street, London, SE1 1SZ
Activities: Activities of other holding companies n.e.c.
Major Shareholder: Nasib Jabbar Oglu Hasanov
Officers: Eamon Joseph Gorman [1954] Director/Engineer; Gustaf Tage Nobel [1950] Director/Business Consultant [Swedish]; Vugar Samadli [1981] Director/Chief Executive Officer [Azerbaijani]

Noble Clean Fuels Limited
Incorporated: 5 February 2009 *Employees:* 15
Net Worth Deficit: £66,662,648 *Total Assets:* £256,477,360
Registered Office: 33 Cavendish Square, London, W1G 0PW
Activities: Non-specialised wholesale trade
Officers: Chee Ying Lim, Secretary; Jeffrey Mark Alam [1958] Director; Paul Alan Jackaman [1972] Director

Noble Corporation PLC
Incorporated: 10 January 2013 *Employees:* 3
Net Worth: £669,159,424 *Total Assets:* £4,427,305,984
Registered Office: Second Floor, 10 Brook Street, London, W1S 1BG
Activities: Extraction of crude petroleum
Officers: William Turcotte, Secretary; Julie Edwards [1959] Director [American]; Scott Josey [1957] Director/Chairman, CEO & President [American]; Jon Marshall [1951] Director [American]; Mary Ricciardello [1955] Director [American]; Julie Johnson Robertson [1956] Director/Chairman, CEO and President [American]

Noble Europe Limited
Incorporated: 20 September 1991 *Employees:* 59
Net Worth Deficit: £21,294,948 *Total Assets:* £899,918,720
Registered Office: 33 Cavendish Square, London, W1G 0PW
Activities: Other professional, scientific and technical activities n.e.c.
Officers: Chee Ying Lim, Secretary; Jeffrey Mark Alam [1958] Director; Timothy Martin Eyre [1969] Director

Noble Holding Land Support Limited
Incorporated: 21 December 2016
Net Worth: £2,274,144,256 *Total Assets:* £2,274,169,088
Registered Office: Second Floor, 10 Brook Street, London, W1S 1BG
Activities: Extraction of crude petroleum
Shareholder: Noble Corporation PLC
Officers: Matthew Brodie, Secretary; Matthew John Brodie [1974] Director/Regional Manager; Richard Chaplin [1966] Director; Alan Middleton [1967] Director

Noble Holding UK Limited
Incorporated: 25 March 2015
Net Worth: £1,033,990,080 *Total Assets:* £1,034,073,792
Registered Office: Second Floor, 10 Brook Street, London, W1S 1BG
Activities: Support activities for petroleum and natural gas mining
Parent: Noble Corporation PLC
Officers: Matthew John Brodie, Secretary; Matthew John Brodie [1974] Director/Regional Manager; Richard Chaplin [1966] Director/Barrister; Alan Middleton [1967] Director

Noble Resources UK Holdings Limited
Incorporated: 24 June 2011
Net Worth: £88,976,896 *Total Assets:* £997,345,600
Registered Office: 33 Cavendish Square, London, W1G 0PW
Activities: Activities of other holding companies n.e.c.
Officers: Chee Ying Lim, Secretary; Jeffrey Mark Alam [1958] Director; Timothy Eyre [1969] Director

Noble Resources UK Limited
Incorporated: 4 February 2009 *Employees:* 5
Net Worth Deficit: £139,434,944 *Total Assets:* £101,881,472
Registered Office: 33 Cavendish Square, London, W1G 0PW
Activities: Non-specialised wholesale trade
Officers: Chee Ying Lim, Secretary; Jeffrey Mark Alam [1958] Director; Timothy Eyre [1969] Director

Noerr LLP
Incorporated: 8 October 2009 *Employees:* 995
Net Worth: £114,430,696 *Total Assets:* £143,096,640
Registered Office: Level 40, Tower 42, 25 Old Broad Street, London, EC2N 1HQ
Officers: Dr Torsten Fett [1971] Member; Dr Alexander Tibor Mihaly Ritvay [1964] Member; Dr Holger Alfes [1970] LLP Member; Dr Peter Klaus Adalbert Bachmann [1965] LLP Member; Dr Fabian Badtke [1977] LLP Member; Gregor Barbers [1967] LLP Member; Dr Florian Becker [1972] LLP Member; Dr Tom Beckerhoff [1969] LLP Member; Dr Alexander Michael Birnstiel [1967] LLP Member; Felix Blobel [1973] LLP Member; Dr Stefan Blum [1973] LLP Member; Sebastian Bock [1968] LLP Member; Dr Tobias Bosch [1967] LLP Member; Dr Michael Brellochs [1976] LLP Member; Christoph Brenzinger [1969] LLP Member; Dr Peter Brautigam [1964] LLP Member; Dr Andreas Butz [1970] LLP Member; Dr Tobias Burgers [1962] LLP Member; Dr Kolja Dorrscheidt [1974] LLP Member; Holger Heinz Ebersberger [1977] LLP Member; Georg Sylvester Edelmann [1965] LLP Member; Christof Federwisch [1972] LLP Member; Dr Tibor Fedke [1975] LLP Member; Dr Roland Sebastian Fischer [1977] LLP Member; Dr Astrid Adelheid Suriana Frense [1962] LLP Member; Dr Martin Tobias Frevert [1968] LLP Member; Jens Gehlich [1969] LLP Member; Dr Alexander Johannes Dietrich Goepfert [1956] LLP Member; Dr Sophia Habbe [1980] LLP Member; Dr Martin Haisch [1973] LLP Member; Tillmann Georg Hecht [1960] LLP Member; Dr Carsten Heinz [1972] LLP Member; Dr Thomas Josef Heitzer [1971] LLP Member; Kai-Michael Hingst [1965] LLP Member; Dr Alexander Richard Hirsch [1970] LLP Member; Dr Thomas Hoffmann [1964] LLP Member; Alexander Israel [1978] LLP Member; Dr Alexander Jaenecke [1974] LLP Member; Dr Arun Kapoor [1976] LLP Member; Dr Cornelia Kermel [1961] LLP Member; Hans Christian Kirchner [1964] LLP Member; Dr Martin Kleinschmitt [1960] LLP Member; Prof Dr Thomas Klindt [1966] LLP Member; Dr Till Kosche [1973] LLP Member; Prof Dr Johannes Kreile [1958] LLP Member; Dr Jens Kunz [1974] LLP Member; Dr Lars Kutzner [1974] LLP Member; Dr Volker Land [1967] LLP Member; Dr Dirk Lentfer [1968] LLP Member; Dr Sascha Leske [1974] LLP Member; Prof Dr Alexander Liegl [1958] LLP Member; Dr Jens Liese [1974] LLP Member; Dr Heidi Mahr [1969] LLP Member; Dr Anke Meier [1973] LLP Member; Dr Karsten Metzlaff [1959] LLP Member; Michael Molitoris [1959] LLP Member; Dr Patrick Muckl [1978] LLP Member; Dr Ralph Nack [1973] LLP Member; Andreas Naujoks [1975] LLP Member; Bjorn Paulsen [1973] LLP Member; Prof Dr Christian Carl Wilhelm Pleister [1968] LLP Member; Annette Pospich [1979] LLP Member; Dr Mansur Pour Rafsendjani [1964] LLP Member; Dr Hans Joachim Radau [1963] LLP Member; Marlies Raschke [1976] LLP Member; Dr Karl Rauser [1959] LLP Member; Dr Generald Josef Reger [1970] LLP Member; Dr Michael Gerhard Reiling [1974] LLP Member; Dr Thorsten Reinhard [1970] LLP Member; Dr Daniel Ruecker [1975] LLP Member; Santiago Ruiz de Vargas Thiel [1966] LLP Member; Dr Baerbel Sachs [1975] LLP Member; Dr Ralph Schilha [1978] LLP Member; Dr Hans Christoph Max Wilhelm Schimmelpfennig [1957] LLP Member; Oliver Schliesser [1969] LLP Member; Dr Holger Schmitz [1962] LLP Member; Dr Georg Christoph Schneider [1966] LLP Member; Dr Karl Christoph Schotte [1961] LLP Member; Prof Dr Joachim Schrey [1962] LLP Member; Dr Stephan Schulz [1975] LLP Member; Dr Thomas Joachim Heinrich Schulz [1963] LLP Member; Dr Maurice Seche [1975] LLP Member; Dr Oliver Siegfried Sieg [1965] LLP Member; Silvia Sparfeld [1962] LLP Member; Dr Christoph Spiering [1968] LLP Member; Dr Albin Strobl [1974] LLP Member; Matthias Stupp-Johnston [1971] LLP Member; Dr Thomas Thalhofer [1979] LLP Member; Dr Wolfram Albert Christian Ivo Caspar Theiss [1960] LLP Member; Dr Ingo Theusinger [1973] LLP Member; Dr Marco Tucci [1973] LLP Member; Christine Volohonsky [1970] LLP Member; Meike Von Levetzow [1976] LLP Member; Dr Nikolai Warneke [1977] LLP Member; Dr Stefan Weise [1959] LLP Member; Dr Alexander Dominik Lothar Wendel [1964] LLP Member; Dr Kathrin Westermann [1968] LLP Member; Dr Laurenz Wieneke [1966] LLP Member

Nomura Bank International PLC.
Incorporated: 22 January 1986
Net Worth: £367,242,304 *Total Assets:* £5,967,992,320
Registered Office: 1 Angel Lane, London, EC4R 3AB
Activities: Banks
Parent: Nomura Europe Holdings PLC
Officers: Christopher Colin Barlow, Secretary; Neeta Avnash Kaur Atkar [1965] Director/Banker; Jonathan Britton [1954] Finance Director; David Godfrey [1950] Director; Jonathan Wayne Lewis [1967] Director/Chartered Accountant; Lewis John O'Donald [1965] Director/Banker; John Gerard Mary Tierney [1972] Director/Accountant [Irish]

Nomura Capital Markets Limited
Incorporated: 15 June 2007
Net Worth: £927,841,408 *Total Assets:* £1,212,168,192
Registered Office: 1 Angel Lane, London, EC4R 3AB
Activities: Financial intermediation not elsewhere classified
Parent: Nomura Holdings, Inc. (formerly The Nomura Securities Co., Ltd.)
Officers: Christopher Colin Barlow, Secretary; Darren Burnett [1976] Director/Accountant

Nomura Europe Holdings PLC
Incorporated: 24 March 1998
Net Worth: £3,766,327,552 *Total Assets:* £6,571,153,920
Registered Office: 1 Angel Lane, London, EC4R 3AB
Activities: Activities of financial services holding companies
Parent: Nomura Holdings, Inc. (formerly The Nomura Securities Co., Ltd.)
Officers: Christopher Colin Barlow, Secretary; Neeta Avnash Kaur Atkar [1965] Director/Banker; Anna Maria Josephine Cavanagh Bentley [1960] Director; Jonathan Britton [1954] Finance Director; David Godfrey [1950] Director; Yasuo Kashiwagi [1962] Director/Banker [Japanese]; Jonathan Wayne Lewis [1967] Director/Chartered Accountant; Hisato Miyashita [1958] Director [Japanese]; Rosemary Carol Murray [1965] Director; Lewis John O'Donald [1965] Director/Banker; John Gerard Mary Tierney [1972] Director/Accountant [Irish]

Nomura European Investment Limited
Incorporated: 11 June 1996
Net Worth: £274,439,008 *Total Assets:* £1,376,929,024
Registered Office: 1 Angel Lane, London, EC4R 3AB
Activities: Financial intermediation not elsewhere classified
Parent: Nomura Holdings, Inc. (formerly The Nomura Securities Co., Ltd.)
Officers: Christopher Colin Barlow, Secretary; Daisy Alice Le Vay [1979] Director/Solicitor; John Gerard Mary Tierney [1972] Director/Accountant [Irish]; Russell John Watson [1969] Director/Chartered Accountant; Tina Margaret Whitehouse [1971] Director/Banker

Nomura International PLC
Incorporated: 12 March 1981
Net Worth: £3,879,656,192 *Total Assets:* £203,614,633,984
Registered Office: 1 Angel Lane, London, EC4R 3AB
Activities: Financial intermediation not elsewhere classified
Parent: Nomura Europe Holdings PLC
Officers: Christopher Colin Barlow, Secretary; Neeta Avnash Kaur Atkar [1965] Director/Banker; Anna Maria Josephine Cavanagh Bentley [1960] Director; Jonathan Britton [1954] Finance Director; David Godfrey [1950] Director; Yasuo Kashiwagi [1962] Director/Banker [Japanese]; Jonathan Wayne Lewis [1967] Director/Chartered Accountant; Hisato Miyashita [1958] Director [Japanese]; Rosemary Carol Murray [1965] Director; Lewis John O'Donald [1965] Director/Banker; John Gerard Mary Tierney [1972] Director/Accountant [Irish]

Nomura Properties PLC
Incorporated: 3 June 1986
Net Worth: £11,201,641 *Total Assets:* £133,219,384
Registered Office: 1 Angel Lane, London, EC4R 3AB
Activities: Other letting and operating of own or leased real estate
Parent: Nomura European Investment Limited
Officers: Christopher Colin Barlow, Secretary; Anthony Gerard Bartle [1955] Director/Real Estate & Services Manager; Stephen Andrew Fuggle [1979] Director/Accountant

Nord Anglia Education (UK) Holdings PLC
Incorporated: 13 May 2008
Net Worth: £301,445,568 *Total Assets:* £1,089,372,288
Registered Office: St Clements House, 27-28 Clements Lane, London, EC4N 7AE
Activities: Activities of head offices
Officers: Jodie Leanne Coutts, Secretary; Inderjit Dehal [1968] Director/Education Management; Andrew Fitzmaurice [1960] Director; Mark Andrew Orrow-Whiting [1969] Director; Antonius Jacobus Cornelis Van Vilsteren [1970] Director/Chief Financial Officer [Dutch]

Nord Anglia Education Limited
Incorporated: 27 March 1987 *Employees:* 30
Net Worth: £499,484,000 *Total Assets:* £808,990,016
Registered Office: St Clements House, 27-28 Clements Lane, London, EC4N 7AE
Activities: Activities of head offices
Parent: Nord Anglia Education (UK) Holdings PLC
Officers: Inderjit Dehal [1968] Director/Education Management; Andrew Fitzmaurice [1960] Director/Chief Executive; Mark Andrew Orrow-Whiting [1969] Director; Antonius Jacobus Cornelis Van Vilsteren [1970] Director/Chief Financial Officer [Dutch]

Nordic Entertainment Group UK Limited
Incorporated: 9 March 1988 *Employees:* 156
Previous: Modern Times Group MTG Limited
Net Worth: £353,453,920 *Total Assets:* £648,895,360
Registered Office: Chiswick Green, 610 Chiswick High Road, London, W4 5RU
Activities: Television programming and broadcasting activities
Parent: Nordic Entertainment Group AB
Officers: Adrian Howard Dicker [1974] Director and Company Secretary; Matthew Rufus Hooper [1970] Director/Head of Corporate Communications; Anders Ytrup Jensen [1969] Director [Swedish]; Kevin Edward White [1974] Director

Nordson London Limited
Incorporated: 14 December 2010 *Employees:* 2
Net Worth: £77,694,312 *Total Assets:* £100,139,728
Registered Office: Level 37, 25 Canada Square, London, E14 5LQ
Activities: Activities of head offices
Parent: Majority Kingdom Investment Limited
Officers: Raymond Leland Cushing [1954] Director/Treasurer [American]; Kathleen M Kennedy [1971] Assistant Director of Tax [American]

Norlake Hospitality Limited
Incorporated: 18 May 2012 *Employees:* 225
Net Worth: £193,276,864 *Total Assets:* £569,768,896
Registered Office: 53-54 Grosvenor Street, London, W1K 3HU
Activities: Other business support service activities n.e.c.
Officers: Srikanth Balachandran [1961] Director [Indian]; Sonal Kapasi [1971] Director [Indian]; Nyna Mittal [1960] Director/Investor; Shravin Bharti Mittal [1987] Director; Sharan Pasricha [1980] Director

Norland Holdings Ltd
Incorporated: 14 February 2005 *Employees:* 5,446
Net Worth: £165,682,000 *Total Assets:* £443,864,000
Registered Office: 61 Southwark Street, London, SE1 0HL
Activities: Activities of head offices
Shareholders: CBRE Holdings Limited; CBRE UK Acquisition Company Limited
Officers: Duncan James Green, Secretary; Ian David Entwisle [1963] Director; Duncan James Green [1962] Finance Director

Normanclose 2 LLP
Incorporated: 22 October 2004
Net Worth: £1,311,547,904 *Total Assets:* £1,311,547,904
Registered Office: Level 20, 25 Canada Square, London, E14 5LQ

Normanglade 4 LLP
Incorporated: 12 October 2004
Net Worth: £234,965,120 *Total Assets:* £533,096,672
Registered Office: Level 20, 25 Canada Square, London, E14 5LQ

Norsea Pipeline Limited
Incorporated: 27 November 1972
Net Worth: £42,578,000 *Total Assets:* £194,191,008
Registered Office: 20th Floor, 1 Angel Court, London, EC2R 7HJ
Activities: Mineral oil refining
Parent: Norpipe Terminal Holdco Limited
Officers: David Grimshaw, Secretary; Ove Andre Ardal [1967] Director/Commercial Manager [Norwegian]; Jan-Arne Johansen [1969] Director/General Manager [Norwegian]; Dag Oeyvind Sanner [1963] Director/General Manager Partner Operated Assets, Commercial; Mark John Seger [1967] Asset Director; Joachim Kleiberg Strom [1982] Director/Asset Lead [Norwegian]; Tor Bustrak Tangvald [1958] Director/Technical & License Manager [Norwegian]

North Atlantic Smaller Companies Investment Trust PLC
Incorporated: 18 January 1973
Net Worth: £499,423,008 *Total Assets:* £503,508,000
Registered Office: 6 Stratton Street, London, W1J 8LD
Activities: Activities of investment trusts
Officers: Greville Patrick Charles Howard [1941] Director/Peer of The Realm; George Walter Loewenbaum [1944] Director/Investor [American]; Christopher Harwood Bernard Mills [1952] Director/Investment Manager; The Hon Peregrine David Euan Malcolm Moncreiffe [1951] Director; Sir Hereward Charles Wake [1952] Semi-Retired Farmer and Director

North Colonnade Limited
Incorporated: 2 May 2007 *Employees:* 4
Net Worth: £61,186,200 *Total Assets:* £289,416,768
Registered Office: 30 North Colonnade, Canary Wharf, London, E14 5GP
Activities: Development of building projects
Major Shareholder: Marc Ladreit de Lacharriere
Officers: Jean-Philippe Laval, Secretary; James Michael Asher [1949] Director/Business Executive [American]; Bernard de Lattre [1948] Managing Director-London-EMEA [French]; Robert Francois Manuel Gimenez [1954] Director [French]

North Row Estates Limited
Incorporated: 3 November 2000
Net Worth: £1,111,382 *Total Assets:* £121,680,792
Registered Office: 11-15 Wigmore Street, London, W1A 2JZ
Activities: Other business support service activities n.e.c.
Parent: North Row Holdings Limited
Officers: Carol Ann Stratton, Secretary; Paul Baron Bray [1965] Director/Chartered Accountant; Jonathan Paul White [1951] Director

Northern & Shell Enterprises Limited
Incorporated: 20 January 1995 *Employees:* 2
Previous: Northern & Shell Television Group Limited
Net Worth: £125,745,000 *Total Assets:* £126,314,000
Registered Office: The Northern & Shell Building, 10 Lower Thames Street, London, EC3R 6EN
Activities: Artistic creation
Parent: Northern & Shell Broadcasting (CI) Limited
Officers: Robert Sanderson, Secretary; Martin Stephen Ellice [1957] Group Joint Managing Director; Robert Sanderson [1960] Group Joint Managing Director

Northern & Shell PLC
Incorporated: 4 October 2000 *Employees:* 692
Previous: Northern & Shell Limited
Net Worth: £338,659,008 *Total Assets:* £427,102,016
Registered Office: The Northern & Shell Building, 10 Lower Thames Street, London, EC3R 6EN
Activities: Activities of head offices
Officers: Robert Sanderson, Secretary; Richard Clive Desmond [1951] Director/Publisher & Broadcaster; Martin Stephen Ellice [1957] Group Joint Managing Director; Richard John Martin [1971] Commercial Director; Digby Rancombe [1976] Finance Director; Robert Sanderson [1960] Group Joint Managing Director

Northern & Shell Properties Limited
Incorporated: 9 November 2000 *Employees:* 3
Net Worth: £349,561,984 *Total Assets:* £477,919,008
Registered Office: The Northern and Shell Building, 10 Lower Thames Street, London, EC3R 6EN
Activities: Activities of head offices
Parent: Northern & Shell PLC
Officers: Robert Sanderson, Secretary; Richard Clive Desmond [1951] Director/Publisher & Broadcaster; Martin Stephen Ellice [1957] Group Joint Managing Director; Robert Sanderson [1960] Group Joint Managing Director

Northern Trust Holdings Limited
Incorporated: 11 June 2003
Net Worth: £272,273,440 *Total Assets:* £339,387,392
Registered Office: 50 Bank Street, London, E14 5NT
Activities: Financial intermediation not elsewhere classified
Parent: Northern Trust Corporation
Officers: Matthew Wright, Secretary; David Wicks [1964] Director

Northern Trust Management Services Limited
Incorporated: 11 June 2003 *Employees:* 1,529
Net Worth: £325,791,968 *Total Assets:* £407,932,512
Registered Office: 50 Bank Street, London, E14 5NT
Activities: Financial intermediation not elsewhere classified
Parent: Northern Trust Corporation
Officers: Matthew Wright, Secretary; John Ronald Davie [1971] Director/Bank Officer; Mark David Lacey [1973] Director/Bank Officer

Northrop Grumman Global Holdings Limited
Incorporated: 21 July 1999 *Employees:* 14
Previous: Northrop Grumman Europe Holdings Limited
Net Worth: £173,915,008 *Total Assets:* £313,907,008
Registered Office: 2nd Floor, Clareville House, 26-27 Oxendon Street, London, SW1Y 4EL
Activities: Activities of head offices
Parent: Northrop Grumman International Holdings B.V.
Officers: Susie Lee Choung, Secretary; Roger Campbell Wiltshire, Secretary; Robert Brian Gray [1968] Director Tax Accounting [American]; Steven David Spiegel [1964] Director and Assistant Treasurer [American]; Roger Campbell Wiltshire [1967] Legal Director

Northstar Holding Limited
Incorporated: 2 July 2014
Net Worth: £103,032,000 *Total Assets:* £104,162,000
Registered Office: Stirling Square, 7 Carlton Gardens, London, SW1Y 5AD
Activities: Financial intermediation not elsewhere classified
Parent: Northstar Midco Limited
Officers: Michael Edward Hall [1963] Director; John Miller Heiton [1976] Director/Chief Executive Officer; Andrew John Leeser [1958] Director/Accountant [British/German]

Northstar Investments Limited
Incorporated: 2 July 2014
Net Worth: £59,135,000 *Total Assets:* £217,340,992
Registered Office: Stirling Square, 7 Carlton Gardens, London, SW1Y 5AD
Activities: Financial intermediation not elsewhere classified
Parent: Northstar Holding Limited
Officers: Michael Edward Hall [1963] Director; John Miller Heiton [1976] Director

Northstar Midco Limited
Incorporated: 2 July 2014 *Employees:* 169
Net Worth Deficit: £118,483,000 *Total Assets:* £122,020,000
Registered Office: Stirling Square, 7 Carlton Gardens, London, SW1Y 5AD
Activities: Financial intermediation not elsewhere classified
Officers: Michael Edward Hall [1963] Director; John Miller Heiton [1976] Director/Chief Executive Officer

Northwharf Investments Limited
Incorporated: 14 September 2004
Net Worth: £196,899,008 *Total Assets:* £589,313,984
Registered Office: 1 Churchill Place, London, E14 5HP
Activities: Financial intermediation not elsewhere classified
Parent: Cpia Scotland Executives 2009 Limited Partnership
Officers: Gavin John Chapman [1970] Director/Banker; James Campbell Ferrier [1977] Director/Banker; Jiten Mistry [1982] Director/Banker; Steven Alan Tait [1978] Director/Accountant

Norton Rose Fulbright LLP
Incorporated: 30 May 2007 *Employees:* 2,143
Net Worth: £177,422,000 *Total Assets:* £368,057,984
Registered Office: 3 More London Riverside, London, SE1 2AQ
Officers: Farmida Bi [1967] Member; Anne Louise Higginbottom [1958] Member; Martin David Keith Scott [1959] Member; Nicholas Adams [1968] LLP Member; Christophe Asselineau [1963] LLP Member; Dimitrios Assimakis [1970] LLP Member; Klaus Fabian Bader [1973] LLP Member; Alan Bainbridge [1972] LLP Member; Jonathan Frank Ball [1969] LLP Member; Eva-Maria Barbosa [1972] LLP Member; Davide Barzilai [1970] LLP Member; Duncan Peter Hector Bachelor [1973] LLP Member; James Graham Dingwall Bateson [1961] LLP Member; Alison Jane Baxter [1967] LLP Member; Arnaud Belisaire [1973] LLP Member; Mark Joseph Berry [1964] LLP Member; Nicholas Peter Berry [1981] LLP Member; Heiko Bertelmann [1978] LLP Member; Victoria Jane Birch [1977] LLP Member; Onil Biswas [1966] LLP Member; Michael William Black [1969] LLP Member; Saskia Blokland [1976] LLP Member; Andreas Boerner [1962] LLP Member; Nadine Damaris Bourgeois [1980] LLP Member; John Patrick Bernard Bourke [1968] LLP Member; Giles Brand [1964] LLP Member; Stephane Braun [1976] LLP Member; Daphne Nathalie Broerse [1976] LLP Member; Christopher Earlstone Brown [1958] LLP Member; Lesley Ann Browning [1967] LLP Member; Andrew James Buisson [1973] LLP Member; Cecilia Buresti [1966] LLP Member; Jean-Pascal Bus [1967] LLP Member; Janet Butterworth [1964] LLP Member; Richard John Calnan [1952] LLP Member; Alexander Cappel [1979] LLP Member; Milana Chamberlain [1963] LLP Member; Simon Timothy Chamberlain [1953] LLP Member; Ioannis Yianni Cheilas [1972] LLP Member; Nicholas John Clayson [1976] LLP Member; Antoine Marie Gaston D'Istria Colonna [1962] LLP Member; Anthony James Corsi [1973] LLP Member; Sarah Janice Coucher [1966] LLP Member; Ruth Elizabeth Cowley [1975] LLP Member; Mark Craggs [1981] LLP Member; Berend Jan Hendrik Crans [1952] LLP Member; Roberto Guido Ugo Cristofolini [1958] LLP Member; Richard Crosby [1971] LLP Member; Sarah Mary Cullen [1973] LLP Member; Christian Dargham [1971] LLP Member; Valerie Elen Mary Davies [1952] LLP Member; Benedicte Odette Anne Marie Denis-Brabant [1970] LLP Member; Nigel Robert Dickinson [1977] LLP Member; Manfred Dietrich [1971] LLP Member; Susan Gillian Dingwall [1960] LLP Member; Christopher Michael Down [1976] LLP Member; David James Dunnett [1972] LLP Member; Tino Duttine [1974] LLP Member; Jan Duyvensz [1977] LLP Member; Huw Nigel Evans [1965] LLP Member; Marcus James Julius Evans [1972] LLP Member; Christine Ezcutari [1964] LLP Member; Patrick Farrell [1957] LLP Member; Stefan Feuerriegel [1975] LLP Member; Duncan Field [1970] LLP Member; Matthew Gary Findley [1976] LLP Member; Christian Flippitsch [1968] LLP Member; Ffion Griffudd Flockhart [1981] LLP Member; Peter Christopher Ford [1962] LLP Member; Sven Forster [1979] LLP Member; Patrick William Foss [1963] LLP Member; Matthew Foster [1983] LLP Member; Ian John Fox [1968] LLP Member; Daniel Simon Franks [1978] LLP Member; Sebastian Frech [1979] LLP Member; Tomas Vilhelm Gardfors [1969] LLP Member; Imogen Garner [1979] LLP Member; Michelle George [1963] LLP Member; Emma Giddings [1973] LLP Member; Ian David Giles [1974] LLP Member; Benedikt Gillessen [1970] LLP Member; Michael David Godden [1975] LLP Member; Charez Golvala [1966] LLP Member; Radford Goodman [1971] LLP Member; Madhavi Gosavi [1970] LLP Member; Nicholas Edmund Grandage [1966] LLP Member; Christopher Michael Grieves [1971] LLP Member; Paul Thomas Griffin [1969] LLP Member; Raquel Guevara [1975] LLP Member; Robert Andrew Haken [1976] LLP Member; Cllr Glenn Anthony Hall [1968] LLP Member; Peter Michael Hall [1962] LLP Member; Philippe Jean Claude Hameau [1960] LLP Member; Marc Richard Gerard Hamilton [1965] LLP Member; Egbert Hannema [1961] LLP Member; Matthew James Hardwick [1974] LLP Member; David Harris [1979] LLP Member; Andrew Paul Stephen Hart [1964] LLP Member; Simon Richard Hartley [1964] LLP Member; David John Hawkins [1972] LLP Member

Norwegian Compass Ltd
Incorporated: 17 September 2013
Net Worth: £133,001,688 *Total Assets:* £133,051,584
Registered Office: The St Botolph Building, 138 Houndsditch, London, EC3A 7AR
Activities: Sea and coastal passenger water transport
Parent: Norwegian Cruise Line Holdings Ltd.
Officers: Francisco Jose Del Rio [1954] Director/Chief Executive Officer [American]; Daniel Seth Farkas [1968] Director/Businessman [American]

Norwegian Sextant Ltd
Incorporated: 17 September 2013
Net Worth: £259,103,344 *Total Assets:* £259,151,472
Registered Office: The St Botolph Building, 138 Houndsditch, London, EC3A 7AR
Activities: Sea and coastal passenger water transport
Parent: Norwegian Cruise Line Holdings Ltd.
Officers: Francisco Jose Del Rio [1954] Director/Chief Executive Officer [American]; Daniel Seth Farkas [1968] Director/Businessman [American]

Nostrum Oil & Gas PLC
Incorporated: 3 October 2013 *Employees:* 977
Net Worth: £504,371,360 *Total Assets:* £1,706,296,064
Registered Office: 9th Floor, 20 Eastbourne Terrace, London, W2 6LG
Activities: Extraction of crude petroleum
Officers: Thomas Hartnett, Secretary; Simon Byrne [1967] Director/Chief Executive Office at Steppe Capital Pte Ltd; Michael John Calvey [1967] Director/Investment Advisor [American]; Martin Cocker [1959] Director; BT Codrington [1960] Director; Atul Gupta [1959] Director Essar Capital; Pankaj Jain [1967] Alternate Director [Indian]; Kai-Uwe Kessel [1961] Director [German]; Mark Martin [1969] Director; Ralph Tavakolian Morgan [1968] Director/Partner [American]; Thomas Donald Richardson [1981] Director/Financier; Kaat Van Hecke [1971] Director/Engineer [Belgian]

Novae Corporate Underwriting Limited
Incorporated: 7 April 1995
Net Worth: £62,700,000 *Total Assets:* £2,585,100,032
Registered Office: 21 Lombard Street, London, EC3V 9AH
Activities: Financial intermediation not elsewhere classified
Parent: Novae Holdings Limited
Officers: Matthew Kailey Fosh [1962] Director; Mark Austen John Gregory [1959] Director; Fintan Mullarkey [1974] Director [Irish]

Novae Group Limited
Incorporated: 12 January 2006
Previous: Novae Group PLC
Net Worth: £263,120,000 *Total Assets:* £268,199,008
Registered Office: 21 Lombard Street, London, EC3V 9AH
Activities: Activities of head offices
Parent: Axis Speciality UK Holdings Limited
Officers: Matthew Kailey Fosh [1957] Director; Mark Austen John Gregory [1959] Director; Timothy Hennessy [1967] Director [Irish]; Alistair Mark Robson [1964] Director

NRG Victory Holdings Limited
Incorporated: 26 March 1987
Net Worth: £197,764,992 *Total Assets:* £197,782,000
Registered Office: 4th Floor, 8 Fenchurch Place, London, EC3M 4AJ
Activities: Activities of head offices
Officers: Colleen Martin, Company Secretary; Vijay Anantray Mavani [1962] Director/Insurance Executive; Stephen Andrew Michael [1961] Director/Insurance Executive; Andrew Wilson [1967] Director/Insurance Executive

NRG Victory Reinsurance Limited
Incorporated: 29 July 1919
Net Worth: £192,276,992 *Total Assets:* £367,152,000
Registered Office: 4th Floor, 8 Fenchurch Place, London, EC3M 4AJ
Activities: Non-life insurance
Officers: Colleen Martin, Company Secretary; Karen Lesley Amos [1959] Director; Christopher Peter Hare [1947] Director; Vijay Anantray Mavani [1962] Director/Insurance Executive; Brian Gerard Snover [1962] Director/Senior Vice President and Legal Counsel [American]; Andrew Wilson [1967] Director/Insurance Executive

NSC Europe Limited
Incorporated: 7 October 2002
Net Worth: £765,131,008 *Total Assets:* £903,430,976
Registered Office: 13th Floor, 5 Aldermanbury Square, London, EC2V 7HR
Activities: Activities of head offices
Parent: CS (Australasia) SARL
Officers: Ryan Ronald Dale, Secretary; Giles Matthew Hudson [1972] Director/Chartered Accountant; Stephen James Rowell [1967] Director of International Corporate Finance

NTT Data EMEA Ltd.
Incorporated: 16 March 2012
Net Worth: £255,596,608 *Total Assets:* £453,437,152
Registered Office: 3rd Floor, 2 Royal Exchange, London, EC3V 3DG
Activities: Other information service activities n.e.c.
Parent: NTT Data Corporation
Officers: Koji Ito [1962] Snr Vice President Director, Global Bus NTT Data Corp [Japanese]; Swen Rehders [1961] NTT Data EMEA Director and Deputy CEO [German]; Manabu Tanaka [1968] Director/IT Consultant [Japanese]; Ken Tsuchihashi [1963] Director/Executive Manager Global Business Sector [Japanese]; Benito Vazquez Blanco [1964] Executive Director and CEO NTT Data EMEA [Spanish]

NTT Europe Ltd.
Incorporated: 20 October 1988 *Employees:* 606
Net Worth: £40,972,000 *Total Assets:* £157,788,992
Registered Office: 1 King William Street, London, EC4N 7AR
Activities: Wholesale of electronic and telecommunications equipment and parts
Officers: Makoto Shimizu, Secretary; Clive Hamilton [1967] Director/Chief Commercial Officer; Hiroyuki Nishioka [1967] Director [Japanese]; Tomoyuki Sakae [1973] Director [Japanese]; Takashi Yamaguchi [1970] Director [Japanese]

Nugent Shopping Park Limited
Incorporated: 12 March 2007
Net Worth: £109,119,872 *Total Assets:* £110,924,584
Registered Office: York House, 45 Seymour Street, London, W1H 7LX
Activities: Development of building projects
Parent: BL Leisure and Industrial Holding Company Limited
Officers: Sarah Morrell Barzycki [1958] Director/Head of Finance; Timothy Andrew Roberts [1964] Director/Chartered Surveyor; Nigel Mark Webb [1963] Director/Chartered Surveyor

Numis Corporation PLC
Incorporated: 24 April 1989 *Employees:* 273
Net Worth: £143,136,000 *Total Assets:* £541,248,000
Registered Office: 10 Paternoster Square, London, EC4M 7LT
Activities: Activities of head offices
Officers: Andrew Mark Holloway, Secretary; Alan Thomas Carruthers [1962] Director; Alexander Burnell Ham [1982] Director; Andrew Mark Holloway [1979] Director; Caterine Beris James [1954] Director/Head of Investor Relations; Ross James Mitchinson [1978] Director; Luke Savage [1961] Director; Robert Hiles Sutton [1954] Lawyer/Director

Numis Securities Limited
Incorporated: 11 August 1988 *Employees:* 258
Net Worth: £121,314,368 *Total Assets:* £537,101,120
Registered Office: 10 Paternoster Square, London, EC4M 7LT
Activities: Financial intermediation not elsewhere classified
Parent: Numis Corporation PLC
Officers: Andrew Mark Holloway, Secretary; Marcus Jeremy Chorley [1961] Director; Gemma Lucy Cook [1978] HR Director; Alexander Burnell Ham [1982] Managing Director - Corporate Broking; Andrew Mark Holloway [1979] Director; Michael James Lee [1978] Director; Ross James Mitchinson [1978] Director Equity Sales; Rene Obregon [1974] Director [American]; Timothy Blair Valmas [1971] Director; Will Wallis [1969] Director/Analyst

Nuveen FCACO Limited
Incorporated: 16 July 2013
Previous: TH RE FCACO Limited
Net Worth: £110,020,432 *Total Assets:* £113,090,352
Registered Office: 201 Bishopsgate, London, EC2M 3BN
Activities: Activities of financial services holding companies
Parent: Nuveen Real Estate Limited
Officers: Raymond John Adderley [1977] Director/Investment Management; Mark Griffiths [1968] Director/Head of Property Systems and Operations; Michael Hugh Neal [1971] Director/Chartered Surveyor; Michael John Lawson Sales [1964] Director; Colin Paul Throssell [1976] Director/Accountant

Nuveen Real Estate Limited
Incorporated: 11 June 2013
Previous: TIAA Henderson Real Estate Limited
Net Worth: £218,210,224 *Total Assets:* £219,097,312
Registered Office: 201 Bishopsgate, London, EC2M 3BN
Activities: Activities of financial services holding companies
Parent: TIAA International Holdings 3 Limited
Officers: Timothy Horrocks [1965] Director; Michael Hugh Neal [1971] Director/Chartered Surveyor; Christopher Stephen Reilly [1967] Director [Irish]; Michael John Lawson Sales [1964] Director/Fund Manager; Colin Paul Throssell [1976] Director/Accountant

Nuveen Real Estate Management Limited
Incorporated: 4 June 1987 *Employees:* 64
Previous: Henderson Real Estate Asset Management Limited
Net Worth: £89,925,928 *Total Assets:* £115,361,584
Registered Office: 9th Floor, 201 Bishopsgate, London, EC2M 3BN
Activities: Fund management activities
Parent: Nuveen FCACO Limited
Officers: Raymond John Adderley [1977] Director/Investment Management; Mark Griffiths [1968] Director of IT and Operations; Michael Hugh Neal [1971] Director/Chartered Surveyor; Michael John Lawson Sales [1964] Director/Fund Manager; Colin Paul Throssell [1976] Director/Accountant

NYK International PLC
Incorporated: 27 November 1985 *Employees:* 5
Net Worth: £33,439,440 *Total Assets:* £214,367,872
Registered Office: 25 Canary Wharf, London, E14 5LQ
Activities: Activities of financial services holding companies
Parent: NYK Group Europe Limited
Officers: Yuta Watanabe, Secretary; Keiji Kubota [1964] Director [Japanese]; Katsuya Nakano [1962] Director [Japanese]; Takashi Yamamoto [1966] Director [Japanese]; Tomotaka Yamauchi [1981] Director [Japanese]

NYK Investments Limited
Incorporated: 25 November 1992
Net Worth: £36,545,632 *Total Assets:* £494,075,616
Registered Office: 16 Tinworth Street, London, SE11 5AL
Activities: Financial intermediation not elsewhere classified
Parent: CLS Holdings PLC
Officers: David Francis Fuller, Secretary; Erik Henry Klotz [1944] Director/Executive Vice Chairman [Swedish]; Alain Gustave Paul Millet [1968] Director/Group Treasurer [French]; John Howard Whiteley [1958] Director/Chief Financial Officer; Fredrik Jonas Widlund [1968] Director [Swedish]; Simon Laborda Wigzell [1968] Director

NYOP Education (Aberdeen) Limited
Incorporated: 27 April 2007
Net Worth: £21,989,536 *Total Assets:* £149,156,384
Registered Office: Office 7, 35-37 Ludgate Hill, London, EC4M 7JN
Activities: Educational support services
Parent: NYOP Education (Aberdeen) Holdings Ltd
Officers: Alan James Steen, Secretary; David George Conlon [1978] Director/Finance; Alastair William Nicol [1965] Director; Gabriel Oke [1986] Director/Credit Risk Manager; Kenneth Montgomery Simpson [1959] Director/Chief Executive; Alan James Steen [1957] Director/Civil Engineer

Nyraff Limited
Incorporated: 3 April 1986 *Employees:* 13
Net Worth: £62,885,088 *Total Assets:* £107,023,584
Registered Office: 2 Madrid Road, London, SW13 9PD
Activities: Other letting and operating of own or leased real estate
Shareholders: Nyree Sima Tanielian; Raffi Berge Tanielian
Officers: Hourig Mercedes Tanielian, Secretary; Agop Tanielian [1947] Director; Hourig Mercedes Tanielian [1952] Director/Housewife; Nyree Sima Tanielian [1980] Director; Raffi Berge Tanielian [1975] Director

NYSE Holdings UK Limited
Incorporated: 2 October 2007 *Employees:* 3
Net Worth: £109,515,096 *Total Assets:* £109,811,720
Registered Office: Milton Gate, 60 Chiswell Street, London, EC1Y 4SA
Activities: Activities of financial services holding companies
Parent: Intercontinentalexchange Holdings
Officers: Elizabeth Miriam Holt, Secretary; Scott Anthony Hill [1967] Director [American]; Andrew James Surdykowski [1970] Director [American]; Stuart Glen Williams [1978] Director [South African]

O & H (NBS) Limited
Incorporated: 8 March 2005 *Employees:* 4
Net Worth: £109,192,968 *Total Assets:* £189,986,464
Registered Office: 2 Mill Street, London, W1S 2AT
Activities: Buying and selling of own real estate
Parent: O & H Limited
Officers: Peter Dee-Shapland [1964] Director; Alan Gabbay [1984] Director; Dr David Selim Gabbay [1944] Director; Eli Allen Shahmoon [1966] Director

O & H Capital Limited
Incorporated: 9 December 1998
Net Worth: £79,865,816 *Total Assets:* £113,653,016
Registered Office: 2 Mill Street, London, W1S 2AT
Activities: Development of building projects
Parent: O & H Holdings Limited
Officers: Caroline Hanouka, Secretary; Alan Gabbay [1984] Director; Dr David Selim Gabbay [1944] Director; Joyce Gabbay [1950] Director/Housewife; Eli Allen Shahmoon [1966] Director; Lily Shahmoon [1942] Director/Housewife; Ronnie Aaron Shahmoon [1970] Director

O & H Holdings Limited
Incorporated: 24 February 2006 *Employees:* 38
Net Worth: £1,043,401,024 *Total Assets:* £1,454,804,992
Registered Office: 2 Mill Street, London, W1S 2AT
Activities: Buying and selling of own real estate
Officers: Caroline Hanouka, Secretary; Alan Gabbay [1984] Director; Dr David Selim Gabbay [1944] Director; Joyce Gabbay [1950] Director; Eli Allen Shahmoon [1966] Director/Property Manager; Lily Shahmoon [1942] Director; Ronnie Aaron Shahmoon [1970] Director/Property Manager

O & H Properties Limited
Incorporated: 22 June 1982 *Employees:* 33
Net Worth: £52,292,668 *Total Assets:* £246,090,224
Registered Office: 2 Mill Street, London, W1S 2AT
Activities: Development of building projects
Parent: O & H Holdings No.2 Limited
Officers: Caroline Hanouka, Secretary; Alison Virginia Allen [1962] Director/Surveyor; Peter Dee Shapland [1964] Director/Surveyor; Alan Gabbay [1984] Director; Dr David Selim Gabbay [1944] Director; Caroline Hanouka [1979] Director/Solicitor; David Warren Lyons [1963] Director/Chartered Surveyor; Eli Allen Shahmoon [1966] Director/Property Manager; Lily Shahmoon [1942] Director; Ronnie Aaron Shahmoon [1970] Director

O & H Q7 Limited
Incorporated: 3 November 2004
Net Worth: £79,160,280 *Total Assets:* £132,492,352
Registered Office: 2 Mill Street, London, W1S 2AT
Activities: Development of building projects
Parent: O & H Capital Limited
Officers: Caroline Hanouka, Secretary; Alison Virginia Allen [1962] Director/Surveyor; Peter Dee-Shapland [1964] Director; Alan Gabbay [1984] Director; Dr David Selim Gabbay [1944] Director; Caroline Hanouka [1979] Director/Solicitor; David Warren Lyons [1963] Director/Chartered Surveyor; Eli Allen Shahmoon [1966] Director/Property Manager; Ronnie Aaron Shahmoon [1970] Director

C J O'Shea Group Limited
Incorporated: 3 March 2016 *Employees:* 154
Net Worth: £104,804,736 *Total Assets:* £148,816,352
Registered Office: Unit 1 Granard Business Centre, Bunns Lane, London, NW7 2DZ
Activities: Buying and selling of own real estate
Shareholders: Coscomp Limited; Ocosco Limited
Officers: James McMillan, Secretary; Rory Anthony O'Connor [1959] Director [Irish]; Anne O'Shea [1936] Director [Irish]; Crohan John O'Shea [1938] Director [Irish]

Oak No.1 PLC
Incorporated: 13 December 2013
Net Worth: £2,405,000 *Total Assets:* £131,839,000
Registered Office: 35 Great St Helen's, London, EC3A 6AP
Activities: Financial intermediation not elsewhere classified
Parent: Oak No.1 Mortgage Holdings Limited
Officers: Paivi Helena Whitaker [1963] Director [Finnish]

Oaknorth Bank PLC
Incorporated: 3 July 2013 *Employees:* 62
Previous: Oaknorth Bank Limited
Net Worth: £253,828,992 *Total Assets:* £770,944,000
Registered Office: 3rd Floor, 57 Broadwick Street, Soho, London, W1F 9QS
Activities: Banks
Officers: Nicola Peters, Secretary; Cristina Alba Ochoa [1973] Director/Chief Financial Officer [Spanish]; Cyrus Ardalan [1950] Director; Gagan Banga [1975] Director [Indian]; Edward Barry Berk [1973] Director/Professor; Robert Michael Burgess [1965] Director; Rishi Khosla [1975] Director; Ajit Kumar Mittal [1959] Director [Indian]; Navtej Singh Nandra [1966] Director [American]; Graham Leslie Olive [1965] Director/Deputy Chief Executive Officer; Joel Jack Perlman Azout [1974] Director

Oaktree Capital Management (UK) LLP
Incorporated: 15 April 2011 *Employees:* 93
Net Worth: £137,648,000 *Total Assets:* £149,300,000
Registered Office: Verde, 10 Bressenden Place, London, SW1E 5DH
Officers: Mario Adario [1978] LLP Member; Federico Alvarez-Demalde [1981] LLP Member; Fiona Anderson [1973] LLP Member; Guillaume Philippe Gerry Bayol [1982] LLP Member; Barry Alan Broomberg [1970] LLP Member; Fraser Brown [1980] LLP Member; Samuele Cappelletti [1980] LLP Member; Jeffrey Kevin Chalmers [1985] LLP Member; Jay Daryanani [1980] LLP Member; Antonin de Margerie [1975] LLP Member; Alison Endemano [1970] LLP Member; Naina Ghelani [1960] LLP Member; Katherine Mara Gitelson [1972] LLP Member; Francesco Giuliani [1972] LLP Member; Martin David Graham [1978] LLP Member; Jesse Huff [1974] LLP Member; Mark Hulbert [1964] LLP Member; Thomas Andrew Jaggers [1977] LLP Member; Madelaine Jones [1975] LLP Member; Dominic John Cameron Keenan [1974] LLP Member; Karim Michael Khairallah [1972] LLP Member; Nael Khatoun [1977] LLP Member; Caleb Samuel Kramer [1969] LLP Member; Aman Kumar [1980] LLP Member; Stefano Mazzoli [1980] LLP Member; Matthew McCabe [1973] LLP Member; Andrew Murray [1969] LLP Member; Vuk Nikcevic [1975] LLP Member; Frederick Richard McPhie Powles [1981] LLP Member; Peter Preisler [1965] LLP Member; Sanjay Rathod [1976] LLP Member; Jean Rollier [1973] LLP Member; Robert John Charles Self [1978] LLP Member; Anthony Shackleton [1979] LLP Member; Savan-Himatlal Himatlal Shah [1978] LLP Member; David Claude Snelgrove [1980] LLP Member; Gerlinde Thompson [1975] LLP Member; Jim Van Steenkiste [1978] LLP Member; Pablo Velez Calvo [1974] LLP Member; Richard Young [1986] LLP Member

Oakwood Global Assets Limited
Incorporated: 19 May 2005
Net Worth Deficit: £495,000 *Total Assets:* £795,537,024
Registered Office: Fifth Floor, 100 Wood Street, London, EC2V 7EX
Activities: Other business support service activities n.e.c.
Parent: The Law Debenture Intermediary Corporation P.L.C.
Officers: Mark Howard Filer [1967] Director

Oasis Charitable Trust
Incorporated: 18 May 1993 *Employees:* 30
Net Worth: £597,465,984 *Total Assets:* £815,022,976
Registered Office: 1 Kennington Road, London, SE1 7QP
Activities: Primary education
Officers: Dave Joseph Parr, Secretary; David Francis Bright [1981] Director/Solicitor; Mark Francis McAllister [1958] Director/CEO (Oil Company); Graham John Mungeam [1936] Director/Retired; Nicholas William Salisbury [1956] Director/Consultant; Janice Ann Smith [1960] Director/Solicitor; Philip John Warland [1945] Director/Head of Public Policy

Oasis Community Learning
Incorporated: 18 March 2005 *Employees:* 4,621
Net Worth: £361,839,008 *Total Assets:* £439,065,984
Registered Office: 75 Westminster Bridge Road, London, SE1 7HS
Activities: Primary education
Officers: John Barneby, Secretary; Nicholas John Bent [1971] Director/Consultant; Andrew Richard Blundell [1947] Director/Retired; Craig Anthony Dean [1975] Director/Chief Executive; Keith Dennis [1943] Director; Kathleen Ann Holt [1947] Director; Anthony Walrond Lowman [1947] Director/Heating Engineer; Graham John Mungeam [1936] Director/Retired; Nita Rogers [1954] Director/Consultant; Andrew Keith John Simmonds [1952] Director/Chartered Accountant; John Lindsay Pearce Whiter [1950] Director/Chartered Accountant

Oat Hill No.1 PLC
Incorporated: 11 April 2017
Net Worth: £15,741 *Total Assets:* £445,222,272
Registered Office: 35 Great St Helen's, London, EC3A 6AP
Activities: Financial intermediation not elsewhere classified
Parent: Oat Hill No.1 Holdings Limited
Officers: Paivi Helena Whitaker [1963] Director [Finnish]

Oath (UK) Limited
Incorporated: 7 November 1997
Previous: AOL (UK) Limited
Net Worth: £61,108,000 *Total Assets:* £138,679,008
Registered Office: Midcity Place, 71 High Holborn, London, WC1V 6DA
Activities: Other publishing activities
Officers: Maria Louise Samuels, Secretary; Stuart Alan Flint [1975] Director/Business Executive; Anna Maria Watkins [1974] Director/Business Executive

The Ocean Marine Insurance Company Limited
Incorporated: 31 July 1888
Net Worth: £115,000,000 *Total Assets:* £501,000,000
Registered Office: St Helen's, 1 Undershaft, London, EC3P 3DQ
Activities: Non-life insurance
Parent: Aviva Insurance Limited
Officers: Thomas James Latter [1977] Director/Accountant; Andrew James Morrish [1968] Director; Robert Ian Leyman Townend [1967] Director/Insurance Company Official

Oceaneering International Services Limited
Incorporated: 6 September 1971 *Employees:* 2,071
Net Worth: £238,418,000 *Total Assets:* £297,031,008
Registered Office: 100 New Bridge Street, London, EC4V 6JA
Activities: Other service activities n.e.c.
Parent: Oceaneering International, Inc.
Officers: Hilary Frisbie, Secretary; Steven Cowie [1967] Director/Vice President and Country Manager - UK; Clyde Winston Hewlett [1954] Director/Chief Operating Officer [American]; Martin James McDonald [1964] Director/Senior Vice President

OCHL (Globe) Limited
Incorporated: 5 July 2012
Net Worth Deficit: £4,717,000 *Total Assets:* £108,212,000
Registered Office: Stirling Square, 7 Carlton Gardens, London, SW1Y 5AD
Activities: Financial intermediation not elsewhere classified
Parent: Northstar Investments Limited
Officers: John Miller Heiton [1976] Director

Octagon Assets Limited
Incorporated: 9 November 1999
Net Worth: £162,389,504 *Total Assets:* £188,632,448
Registered Office: 6th Floor, Charles House, 108-110 Finchley Road, London, NW3 5JJ
Activities: Development of building projects
Parent: Yianis Holdings Limited
Officers: Yiannakis Theophani Christodoulou [1965] Director; Christopher Christou [1961] Director/Solicitor; Lambros Hadjiioannou [1978] Director

Octagon Overseas Limited
Incorporated: 13 October 2003
Net Worth: £102,782,872 *Total Assets:* £161,707,136
Registered Office: 6th Floor, Charles House, 108-110 Finchley Road, London, NW3 5JJ
Activities: Activities of head offices
Parent: Yianis Met Limited
Officers: Yiannakis Theophani Christodoulou [1965] Director; Lambros Hadjiioannou [1978] Director

Octopus AIM VCT PLC
Incorporated: 8 December 1997
Net Worth: £127,070,000 *Total Assets:* £128,033,000
Registered Office: 6th Floor, 33 Holborn, London, EC1N 2HT
Activities: Financial intermediation not elsewhere classified
Officers: Suzanna Eloise Lauren Waterhouse, Secretary; Stephen John Hazell-Smith [1954] Director/Investment Manager; Joanne Parfrey [1972] Director; Neal Ransome [1960] Director; Roger John Smith [1939] Director

Octopus Apollo VCT PLC
Incorporated: 7 June 2006
Net Worth: £130,377,000 *Total Assets:* £132,324,000
Registered Office: 6th Floor, 33 Holborn, London, EC1N 2HT
Activities: Financial intermediation not elsewhere classified
Officers: Parisha Kanani, Secretary; Alexander Robert Hambro [1962] Director; James Otter [1957] Director; Christopher John Powles [1963] Director; William Murray Black Steele [1948] Director

Octopus Capital Limited
Incorporated: 19 April 2000 *Employees:* 1,516
Net Worth: £176,114,000 *Total Assets:* £438,481,984
Registered Office: 6th Floor, 33 Holborn, London, EC1N 2HT
Activities: Security and commodity contracts dealing activities
Officers: Parisha Kanani, Secretary; John Julian Browett [1963] Director; Matthew Jonathan Cooper [1966] Director [American]; Robert Alan Devey [1968] Director; Christopher Robert Hulatt [1976] Director/Fund Manager; Simon Andrew Rogerson [1974] Director/Fund Manager

Octopus Titan VCT PLC
Incorporated: 12 October 2007
Net Worth: £432,703,008 *Total Assets:* £477,111,008
Registered Office: 6th Floor, 33 Holborn, London, EC1N 2HT
Activities: Financial intermediation not elsewhere classified
Officers: Parisha Kanani, Secretary; Matthew Jonathan Cooper [1966] Director [American]; Mark Ledlie Hawkesworth [1950] Director; John Randolph Hustler [1946] Director/Venture Capitalist; Thomas William Leader [1964] Director; Jane Margaret O'Riordan [1964] Director

Ocubis Financing Limited
Incorporated: 27 July 2011
Net Worth: £1,002,249 *Total Assets:* £176,886,752
Registered Office: 15 Regent Street, London, SW1Y 4LR
Activities: Real estate agencies
Major Shareholder: Jonathan Hunt
Officers: Matthew Cornish Gresham [1976] Director/Operations Manager; Emma Jane Hunt [1981] Director; Jonathan Michael Hunt [1953] Director

Ocubis Limited
Incorporated: 16 October 2000 *Employees:* 52
Net Worth: £27,100,098 *Total Assets:* £111,199,664
Registered Office: 15 Regent Street, London, SW1Y 4LR
Activities: Other letting and operating of own or leased real estate
Shareholders: Heven Holdings Limited; Jonathan Michael Hunt
Officers: Emma Hunt, Secretary; Matthew Cornish Gresham [1976] Director; Jonathan Michael Hunt [1953] Director

Odeon and UCI Cinemas Holdings Limited
Incorporated: 19 March 2007
Net Worth: £373,200,000 *Total Assets:* £1,076,899,968
Registered Office: St Albans House, 57-59 Haymarket, London, SW1Y 4QX
Activities: Activities of head offices
Parent: Odeon Cinemas Group Limited
Officers: Christopher Thomas, Secretary; Andrew Stephen Alker [1966] Director/Accountant; Adam Madline Aron [1954] Director/Executive (Chief Executive Officer & President) [American]; Jan Bernhardsson [1962] Director [Swedish]; Mark Alan McDonald [1958] Director/Executive (EVP, Development) [American]; Craig Ramsey [1951] Director/Executive Vice President & CFO [American]; Gary Suter [1958] Director/Senior Vice President M&A International [American]; Mark Jonathan Way [1971] Director/Chartered Accountant

Odeon Cinemas Group Limited
Incorporated: 22 June 2016
Net Worth: £876,800,000 *Total Assets:* £880,899,968
Registered Office: 57-59 St Albans House, Haymarket, London, SW1Y 4QX
Activities: Activities of head offices
Parent: AMC Lux Finance II SARL
Officers: Kevin Connor, Secretary; Andrew Stephen Alker [1966] Director/Accountant; Adam Aron [1954] Director/Chief Executive Officer and President [American]; Jan Bernhardsson [1962] Director [Swedish]; Mark Alan McDonald [1958] Director/Executive Vice President, Development [American]; Craig Ramsey [1951] Director/Executive Vice President and Chief Financial Officer [American]; Gary Suter [1958] Director/Senior VP M&A and International Development [American]; Mark Jonathan Way [1971] Managing Director

Odeon Cinemas Holdings Limited
Incorporated: 16 November 1999 *Employees:* 1
Net Worth Deficit: £268,713,984 *Total Assets:* £382,784,992
Registered Office: St Albans House, 57-59 Haymarket, London, SW1Y 4QX
Activities: Activities of head offices
Shareholders: Odeon and UCI Cinemas Holdings Limited; Odeon and UCI Cinemas Group Limited
Officers: Christopher Thomas, Secretary; Andrew Stephen Alker [1966] Director/Accountant; Mark Jonathan Way [1971] Director/Chartered Accountant; Neil James Williams [1971] Director/Accountant

Odeon Cinemas Limited
Incorporated: 10 October 1984 *Employees:* 3,176
Net Worth: £185,127,008 *Total Assets:* £389,348,000
Registered Office: St Albans House, 57-59 Haymarket, London, SW1Y 4QX
Activities: Motion picture distribution activities
Parent: Odeon Cinemas Holdings Limited
Officers: Christopher Thomas, Secretary; Andrew Stephen Alker [1966] Director/Accountant; Jan Bernhardsson [1962] Director [Swedish]; Duncan Reynolds [1962] Managing Director; Mark Jonathan Way [1971] Director/Chartered Accountant; Carol Ann Welch [1970] Managing Director; Neil James Williams [1971] Director/Accountant

ODH Investments Limited
Incorporated: 4 June 2013
Net Worth: £10,538,931 *Total Assets:* £542,241,984
Registered Office: 21b Groombridge Road, London, E9 7DP
Activities: Financial management
Officers: Carolina Luque Frances [1983] Director/Consultant [Spanish]; Ramon Rullo Amoros [1964] Director/Businessman [Spanish]

Offa No.1 PLC
Incorporated: 5 February 2016
Net Worth: £15,000 *Total Assets:* £347,432,992
Registered Office: 35 Great St Helen's, London, EC3A 6AP
Activities: Financial intermediation not elsewhere classified
Parent: Offa No.1 Holdings Limited
Officers: Helena Paivi Whitaker [1963] Director [Finnish]

The Office Group Holdings Limited
Incorporated: 12 May 2017
Net Worth: £263,000,000 *Total Assets:* £263,000,000
Registered Office: The Smiths Building, 179 Great Portland Street, London, W1W 5PL
Activities: Other business support service activities n.e.c.
Parent: TOG UK Pledgeco Ltd
Officers: Charles Richard Green [1970] Director; Matthew Allan Green [1982] Director/Accountant; Gemma Nandita Kataky [1983] Director; Oliver Andrew Edward Olsen [1973] Director

The Office Group Midco Limited
Incorporated: 24 August 2010 *Employees:* 241
Previous: Esselco Office Limited
Net Worth: £92,990,000 *Total Assets:* £394,288,000
Registered Office: The Smiths Building, 179 Great Portland Street, London, W1W 5PL
Activities: Other business support service activities n.e.c.
Parent: The Office Group Holdings Limited
Officers: Charles Richard Green [1970] Director/Chartered Surveyor; Matthew Allan Green [1982] Director/Accountant; Gemma Nandita Kataky [1983] Director; Oliver Andrew Edward Olsen [1973] Director

The Office Group Properties Limited
Incorporated: 24 August 2010
Previous: Esselco Office Properties Limited
Net Worth: £65,096,000 *Total Assets:* £323,596,992
Registered Office: The Smiths Building, 179 Great Portland Street, London, W1W 5PL
Activities: Other business support service activities n.e.c.
Parent: The Office Group Midco Limited
Officers: Charles Richard Green [1970] Director/Chartered Surveyor; Matthew Allan Green [1982] Director/Accountant; Gemma Nandita Kataky [1983] Director; Oliver Andrew Edward Olsen [1973] Director

Office Holdings Limited
Incorporated: 25 October 1983 *Employees:* 2,895
Net Worth: £144,178,000 *Total Assets:* £195,231,008
Registered Office: Classic House, Martha's Buildings, 180 Old Street, London, EC1V 9BP
Activities: Retail sale of footwear in specialised stores
Parent: Truworths UK Holdco 1 Limited
Officers: Michael Samuel Mark [1952] Director/Chief Executive Officer [South African]; Lorenzo Giovanni Moretti [1970] Director/Chief Executive Officer; David Brian Pfaff [1965] Director [South African]; Kerry-Lee Anne Van Der Merwe [1976] Director

Office Retail Limited
Incorporated: 18 November 2010 *Employees:* 4
Net Worth Deficit: £25,687,000 *Total Assets:* £132,731,000
Registered Office: Classic House, Martha's Buildings, 180 Old Street, London, EC1V 9BP
Activities: Retail sale of footwear in specialised stores
Parent: Truworths UK Holdco 1 Limited
Officers: Michael Samuel Mark [1952] Director/Chief Executive Officer [South African]; Lorenzo Giovanni Moretti [1970] Director/Chief Executive Officer; David Brian Pfaff [1965] Director [South African]; Kerry-Lee Anne Van Der Merwe [1976] Director

Ofto Superholdco Limited
Incorporated: 24 January 2011
Net Worth Deficit: £46,000 *Total Assets:* £326,990,016
Registered Office: 3 More London Riverside, London, SE1 2AQ
Activities: Activities of head offices
Parent: IPP Bond Limited
Officers: Amanda Elizabeth Woods, Secretary; Muhammad Ahmed Anwer [1984] Director/Accountant [Pakistani]; Simon Fennell [1980] Director/Chartered Accountant; Giles James Frost [1962] Director/Solicitor; Michael John Gregory [1968] Director/Chartered Builder

Ogilvy & Mather Group (Holdings) Limited
Incorporated: 30 October 1895
Net Worth: £247,991,008 *Total Assets:* £450,340,000
Registered Office: Sea Containers, 18 Upper Ground, London, SE1 9RQ
Activities: Advertising agencies
Parent: Ambassador Square
Officers: Ralph Clementson [1961] Director; John William Cornwell [1972] Director; Michael Frohlich [1972] Director; Paul Simon O'Donnell [1962] Director/Advertising Executive; Steve Richard Winters [1968] Director/Chartered Accountant

OHI UK Healthcare Properties Ltd
Incorporated: 8 April 2015 *Employees:* 3
Net Worth: £134,815,232 *Total Assets:* £295,727,776
Registered Office: Tower 42, 25 Old Broad Street, London, EC2N 1HQ
Activities: Activities of other holding companies n.e.c.
Officers: Daniel J Booth, Secretary; Daniel J Booth [1963] Director/Chief Operating Officer [American]; Michael Daniel Ritz [1968] Director/Chief Accounting Officer [American]; Robert O Stephenson [1963] Director/Chief Financial Officer [American]

OIC Run-Off Limited
Incorporated: 30 April 1931
Net Worth Deficit: £349,612,064 *Total Assets:* £410,925,408
Registered Office: Hays Galleria, 1 Hays Lane, London, SE1 2RD
Activities: Non-life insurance
Parent: Nationale-Nederlanden Overseas Finance and Investment Company
Officers: Dan Yoram Schwarzmann, Secretary; Paul Anthony Brereton Evans [1951] Director/Chartered Accountant; Dan Yoram Schwarzmann [1963] Director/Chartered Accountant

Oikia (UK) Limited
Incorporated: 29 September 2014 *Employees:* 109
Net Worth: £2,443,937 *Total Assets:* £123,657,744
Registered Office: 5 Fleet Place, London, EC4M 7RD
Activities: Activities of other holding companies n.e.c.
Major Shareholder: Rinaldo Invernizzi
Officers: Paola Invernizzi [1967] Director [Swiss]; Michele Carlo Felice Milani [1968] Director [Italian]

Old Hall Street Properties Limited
Incorporated: 12 November 1992 *Employees:* 5
Net Worth: £120,633,000 *Total Assets:* £135,034,000
Registered Office: 2nd Floor, 14 St George Street, London, W1S 1FE
Activities: Buying and selling of own real estate
Parent: Trenport Property Holdings Limited
Officers: Christopher Derek Hall [1958] Director/Town Planner; Richard John Hall [1969] Director/Chartered Surveyor; Selwyn Heycock [1947] Director/Accountant; Philip Leslie Peters [1957] Director; Michael Seal [1948] Director/Chartered Accountant

Old Mutual Business Services Limited
Incorporated: 12 August 1998 *Employees:* 150
Net Worth: £32,200,000 *Total Assets:* £120,147,000
Registered Office: 5th Floor, Millennium Bridge House, 2 Lambeth Hill, London, EC4V 4GG
Activities: Activities of head offices
Parent: Old Mutual Limited
Officers: Paul Forsythe, Secretary; Colin Robert Campbell [1971] Director/Solicitor; Paul Forsythe [1976] Director/Company Secretary; Michael Generald Ilsley [1961] Director [South African]; Cornelius Christiaan Thiart [1969] Director/Auditor [South African]

Old Mutual Financial Services (UK) Limited
Incorporated: 28 October 1997
Net Worth: £207,808,992 *Total Assets:* £207,808,992
Registered Office: Millennium Bridge House, 2 Lambeth Hill, London, EC4V 4GG
Activities: Other business support service activities n.e.c.
Parent: Skandia UK Limited
Officers: Duncan John Lane Eardley [1967] Director/Lawyer; Kevin Stephen Lee-Crossett [1960] Director/Lawyer [American]; Mark Oscar Satchel [1969] Director/Chartered Accountant [British/South African]

Old Oak Holdings Limited
Incorporated: 4 October 2004 *Employees:* 26
Net Worth: £360,407,584 *Total Assets:* £396,797,184
Registered Office: 7th Floor, 90 Long Acre, London, WC2E 9RA
Activities: Activities of financial services holding companies
Major Shareholder: Martin Brian Hughes
Officers: Martin James McKay, Secretary/Accountant; Martin Brian Hughes [1961] Director/Bank Analyst; Michael Norman Colin Kerr-Dineen [1952] Director; Sir George Ross Mathewson [1940] Director; John McFarlane [1947] Director

Olekit Investments Ltd
Incorporated: 1 August 2016
Net Worth: £135,003 *Total Assets:* £185,385,536
Registered Office: 1 Kings Avenue, London, N21 3NA
Activities: Other credit granting n.e.c.
Major Shareholder: Christina Palala
Officers: Bernadette Skordi [1982] Director [Cypriot]

Fred. Olsen Cruise Lines Limited
Incorporated: 12 December 1991 *Employees:* 1,888
Net Worth: £31,099,000 *Total Assets:* £124,028,000
Registered Office: 2nd Floor, 64-65 Vincent Square, London, SW1P 2NU
Activities: Sea and coastal passenger water transport
Parent: First Olsen (Holdings) Limited
Officers: Jeremy Dowler, Secretary; Jeremy Dowler [1948] Director; Anette Sofie Olsen [1956] Director/Ship-Owner [Norwegian]; Thomas Fredrik Olsen Junior [1959] Director/Shipowner [Norwegian]; Michael Howard Rodwell [1959] Director/Accountant

Fred. Olsen Renewables Limited
Incorporated: 12 December 1991 *Employees:* 9
Net Worth: £79,695,000 *Total Assets:* £518,380,992
Registered Office: 2nd Floor, 64-65 Vincent Square, London, SW1P 2NU
Activities: Activities of head offices
Parent: Bonheur ASA
Officers: Hannah Louisa Acquokoh, Secretary; Hannah Louisa Acquokoh [1981] Director/Chief Group Controller; David Charles Brunt [1963] Director CEO; Christian Ruth [1962] Director/Chief Financial Officer [Norwegian]; Gareth Mark Swales [1976] Commercial Director

Fred. Olsen Wind Holdings Limited
Incorporated: 28 April 2008
Net Worth Deficit: £34,635,000 *Total Assets:* £251,660,992
Registered Office: 2nd Floor, 64-65 Vincent Square, London, SW1P 2NU
Activities: Activities of head offices
Parent: Fred. Olsen Wind Limited
Officers: Hannah Louisa Acquokoh, Secretary; Jasbir Singh Bains [1966] Group Commercial Director; Anders Knut Falkfjell [1968] Director/Operations Manager [Norwegian]; Christian Ruth [1962] Director/Chief Financial Officer [Norwegian]; Christopher David Sweetman [1975] Director/Chartered Accountant

Fred. Olsen Wind Limited
Incorporated: 28 April 2008
Net Worth Deficit: £29,974,000 *Total Assets:* £402,726,016
Registered Office: 2nd Floor, 64-65 Vincent Square, London, SW1P 2NU
Activities: Activities of head offices
Shareholders: Fred. Olsen Renewables Limited; The Renewables Infrastructure Group (UK) Investments Limited
Officers: David Charles Brunt, Secretary; David Charles Brunt [1963] Director CEO; William Richard Crawford [1963] Investment Director; Philip Roger Perkins George [1971] Portfolio Director; Sofie Eleanor Lilla Jebsen [1986] Director/Project Manager [Norwegian]

Olsten (U.K.) Holdings Limited
Incorporated: 11 October 1990
Net Worth: £91,059,000 *Total Assets:* £536,075,008
Registered Office: Millennium Bridge House, 2 Lambeth Hill, London, EC4V 4BG
Activities: Activities of head offices
Shareholders: Adecco Group AG; Adecco International Holding B.V.
Officers: Rashida Atinuke Akinjobi, Secretary; Alexandra Helen Bishop [1974] Director; Yann Serge Stephane Halka [1974] Director/Chief Financial Officer [French]; Gavin Kenneth Tagg [1972] Director

Olympus Finance UK Limited
Incorporated: 19 February 2010
Net Worth: £343,155,936 *Total Assets:* £343,194,016
Registered Office: 100 New Bridge Street, London, EC4V 6JA
Activities: Other business support service activities n.e.c.
Parent: Olympus Corporation
Officers: Yasutoshi Fujiwara [1971] Director/Business Executive [Japanese]; Yasuo Takeuchi [1957] Director/Senior Executive Managing Officer [Japanese]

OM Group (UK) Limited
Incorporated: 26 June 1998
Net Worth: £397,051,008 *Total Assets:* £424,896,000
Registered Office: 5th Floor, Millennium Bridge House, 2 Lambeth Hill, London, EC4V 4GG
Activities: Activities of head offices
Parent: Old Mutual Limited
Officers: Paul Forsythe, Secretary; Paul Forsythe [1976] Director/Company Secretary; Michael Generald Ilsley [1961] Director [South African]; Cornelius Christiaan Thiart [1969] Director/Auditor [South African]

OM Residual UK Limited
Incorporated: 26 June 1998 *Employees:* 65,395
Previous: OM Residual UK PLC
Net Worth: £8,128,000,000 *Total Assets:* £181,832,007,680
Registered Office: 5th Floor, Millennium Bridge House, 2 Lambeth Hill, London, EC4V 4GG
Activities: Activities of head offices
Parent: Old Mutual Limited
Officers: Paul Forsythe, Secretary; Michael Arnold [1947] Director/Actuary; Danuta Gray [1958] Director; Michael Generald Ilsley [1961] Director [South African]; John Robert Lister [1958] Director; Trevor Andrew Manuel [1956] Director [South African]; Roger Michael James Marshall [1948] Director/Chartered Accountant; Cornelius Christiaan Thiart [1969] Director/Auditor [South African]; Casparus Gerhardus Troskie [1963] Director [South African]

OM Zimbabwe Holdco Limited
Incorporated: 20 December 2012
Net Worth: £89,852,000 *Total Assets:* £119,726,000
Registered Office: 5th Floor, 6 St Andrew Street, London, EC4A 3AE
Activities: Activities of financial services holding companies
Parent: Old Mutal Limited
Officers: Colin Robert Campbell [1971] Director/Solicitor; Robert Harold Coxon [1960] Director/Head of Tax [Australian]; Wayne Mark Fuller [1967] Director/Senior International Tax Manager [South African]

OMD EMEA Limited
Incorporated: 23 October 2000 *Employees:* 366
Previous: OMD International Limited
Net Worth: £23,282,482 *Total Assets:* £207,590,304
Registered Office: Bankside 3, 90-100 Southwark Street, London, SE1 0SW
Activities: Advertising agencies
Parent: Omnicom Media Group Europe Limited
Officers: Sally Ann Bray, Secretary; David Geraint Thomas Jeremiah [1987] Director/Chartered Accountant; Guy Marks [1980] Director/CEO OMD EMEA

OMD Group Limited
Incorporated: 1 December 1986 *Employees:* 699
Net Worth: £34,667,596 *Total Assets:* £283,872,096
Registered Office: Bankside 3, 90-100 Southwark Street, London, SE1 0SW
Activities: Other business support service activities n.e.c.
Parent: Omnicom Media Group UK Limited
Officers: Sally Ann Bray, Secretary; Ronald James Bell [1972] Finance Director; Daniel John Clays [1974] Managing Director

Omega Leasing (No. 12) Limited
Incorporated: 18 May 2017 *Employees:* 2
Net Worth: £74,112,728 *Total Assets:* £394,210,336
Registered Office: 62 Buckingham Gate, London, SW1E 6AT
Activities: Financial leasing
Parent: Alpha Leasing (No.12) Limited
Officers: Rachel Johnson, Secretary; Mark Brady [1965] Director; Mark Garrett [1969] Director

Omega Leasing (No.10) Limited
Incorporated: 18 November 2014 *Employees:* 2
Net Worth: £25,334,000 *Total Assets:* £132,679,752
Registered Office: 62 Buckingham Gate, London, SW1E 6AT
Activities: Financial leasing
Parent: Alpha Leasing (No.10) Limited
Officers: Rachel Johnson, Secretary; Mark Brady [1965] Director; Mark Garrett [1969] Director

Omega Leasing (No.11) Limited
Incorporated: 30 September 2015 *Employees:* 2
Net Worth: £24,742,954 *Total Assets:* £129,311,648
Registered Office: 62 Buckingham Gate, London, SW1E 6AT
Activities: Financial leasing
Parent: Alpha Leasing (No.11) Limited
Officers: Rachel Johnson, Secretary; Mark Brady [1965] Director; Mark Garrett [1969] Director

Omega Leasing (No.9) Limited
Incorporated: 17 May 2012 *Employees:* 2
Net Worth: £52,713,680 *Total Assets:* £304,946,144
Registered Office: 62 Buckingham Gate, London, SW1E 6AT
Activities: Financial leasing
Parent: Alpha Leasing (No.9) Limited
Officers: Rachel Johnson, Secretary; Mark Brady [1965] Director; Mark Garrett [1969] Director

OMFS (GGP) Limited
Incorporated: 12 May 1986
Net Worth: £570,348,992 *Total Assets:* £758,268,032
Registered Office: Millennium Bridge House, 2 Lambeth Hill, London, EC4V 4GG
Activities: Other business support service activities n.e.c.
Parent: Skandia UK Limited
Officers: Duncan John Lane Eardley [1967] Director/Lawyer; Kevin Stephen Lee-Crossett [1960] Director/Lawyer [American]; Mark Oscar Satchel [1969] Director/Chartered Accountant [British/South African]

Omnicom DDB Holdings Limited
Incorporated: 31 October 2014
Net Worth: £570,677,056 *Total Assets:* £571,212,288
Registered Office: Bankside 3, 90-100 Southwark Street, London, SE1 0SW
Activities: Activities of head offices
Parent: Cardinia Europe Limited
Officers: Sally-Ann Bray, Secretary; Michael Gregory Barlow [1975] Director/Chief Financial Officer [American]; Dominic Mark Nagy [1972] Director/Solicitor

Omnicom EMEA Holdings Limited
Incorporated: 26 February 2015
Net Worth: £932,409,984 *Total Assets:* £1,077,181,696
Registered Office: Bankside 3, 90-100 Southwark Street, London, SE1 0SW
Activities: Activities of head offices
Shareholders: Omnicom International Finance; Omnicom EMEA Investments Limited; Omnicom Europe Limited
Officers: Sally-Ann Bray, Secretary; Stephen Christopher Nigel Medhurst [1960] Director; Anthony Peter Phipkin [1957] Director/Accountant

Omnicom EMEA Investments Limited
Incorporated: 22 December 2016
Net Worth: £775,176,704 *Total Assets:* £775,176,896
Registered Office: Bankside 3, 90-100 Southwark Street, London, SE1 0SW
Activities: Activities of other holding companies n.e.c.
Parent: Omnicom Regional Investments Limited
Officers: Sally-Ann Bray, Secretary; Stephen Christopher Nigel Medhurst [1960] Director; Anthony Peter Phipkin [1957] Director/Accountant

Omnicom Europe Limited
Incorporated: 1 July 2003 *Employees:* 1
Net Worth: £1,726,701,824 *Total Assets:* £2,455,342,848
Registered Office: Bankside 3, 90-100 Southwark Street, London, SE1 0SW
Activities: Activities of head offices
Parent: Omnicom Group Inc
Officers: Sally Ann Bray, Secretary; Philip Angelastro [1964] Director/Exec Vice President & CFO of Omnicom Group Inc [American]; Nicolas Paul Claude Bordas [1960] Director [French]; Colin Andrew Gottlieb [1961] Managing Director; Peter William Mead [1940] Director/Chairman of Omnicom Europe Ltd; Stephen Christopher Nigel Medhurst [1960] Director; James Thomas Moser [1962] Director/Chairman, BBDO Europe [American]; Pietro Giuseppe Tramontin [1942] Director/CEO DDB Europe [Dutch]; Sally Ann Williams [1962] Development Director

Omnicom Europe Subholdings Limited
Incorporated: 10 November 2016
Net Worth: £1,640,310,656 *Total Assets:* £1,640,310,656
Registered Office: Bankside 3, 90-100 Southwark Street, London, SE1 0SW
Activities: Activities of other holding companies n.e.c.
Parent: Omnicom Group Inc
Officers: Sally-Ann Bray, Secretary; Stephen Christopher Nigel Medhurst [1960] Director; Anthony Peter Phipkin [1957] Director/Accountant

Omnicom Finance Brazil Limited
Incorporated: 11 December 2015
Net Worth: £347,362,752 *Total Assets:* £357,046,112
Registered Office: Bankside 3, 90-100 Southwark Street, London, SE1 0SW
Activities: Other business support service activities n.e.c.
Parent: Omnicom Finance Holdings PLC
Officers: Sally-Ann Bray, Secretary; Stephen Christopher Nigel Medhurst [1960] Director; Anthony Peter Phipkin [1957] Director/Accountant

Omnicom Finance Limited
Incorporated: 3 August 1972 *Employees:* 19
Previous: Omnicom Finance PLC
Net Worth: £444,365,856 *Total Assets:* £1,754,459,008
Registered Office: Bankside 3, 90-100 Southwark Street, London, SE1 0SW
Activities: Other business support service activities n.e.c.
Parent: Omnicom Management Europe
Officers: Sally Ann Bray, Secretary; Stephen Christopher Nigel Medhurst [1960] Director; Anthony Peter Phipkin [1957] Director/Accountant; Jeffrey Stewart Rodd [1967] Director/Treasurer

Omnicom Holdings Limited
Incorporated: 24 June 2003
Net Worth: £278,497,856 *Total Assets:* £279,608,960
Registered Office: Bankside 3, 90-100 Southwark Street, London, SE1 0SW
Activities: Activities of head offices
Parent: Omnicom Europe Subholdings Limited
Officers: Sally Ann Bray, Secretary; Stephen Christopher Nigel Medhurst [1960] Director; Anthony Peter Phipkin [1957] Director/Accountant; Denis Jean Marie Streiff [1963] Director [French]

Omnicom Latam Holdings Limited
Incorporated: 11 December 2015
Net Worth: £139,399,184 *Total Assets:* £225,021,744
Registered Office: Bankside 3, 90-100 Southwark Street, London, SE1 0SW
Activities: Activities of head offices
Parent: Omnicom EMEA Holdings Limited
Officers: Sally-Ann Bray, Secretary; Michael Gregory Barlow [1975] Director/Chief Financial Officer [American]; Dominic Mark Nagy [1972] Director/Solicitor

Omnicom Management Europe
Incorporated: 19 November 2004 *Employees:* 48
Net Worth: £588,843,008 *Total Assets:* £804,806,272
Registered Office: Bankside 3, 90-100 Southwark Street, London, SE1 0SW
Activities: Activities of head offices
Parent: Omnicom Europe Limited
Officers: Sally Ann Bray, Secretary; David Julian Barry [1974] Tax Director; Sally Ann Bray [1960] Director/Company Secretary; Sarah Jayne Carter [1978] Director/Chartered Accountant; Jose Manuel Feijoo Villoldo [1971] EMEA Tax Director [Spanish]; Stephen Christopher Nigel Medhurst [1960] Director; Russell James Moore [1971] Group Director, SAS International; Anthony Peter Phipkin [1957] Director/Accountant; Stuart Young [1960] Director/Executive Vice President - Real Estate

Omnicom Media Group Europe Limited
Incorporated: 8 September 1982 *Employees:* 155
Net Worth: £26,165,076 *Total Assets:* £258,506,032
Registered Office: Bankside 3, 90-100 Southwark Street, London, SE1 0SW
Activities: Other business support service activities n.e.c.
Parent: Omnicom EMEA Holdings Limited
Officers: Sally Ann Bray, Secretary; Juliet Andrea Jane Ashley [1972] Director/General Counsel; Colin Andrew Gottlieb [1961] Managing Director; Peter Poelzlbauer [1958] Director/CFO Europe [Austrian]

Omnicom Media Group UK Limited
Incorporated: 3 May 2002 *Employees:* 1,385
Net Worth: £62,387,956 *Total Assets:* £593,902,848
Registered Office: Bankside 3, 90-100 Southwark Street, London, SE1 0SW
Activities: Advertising agencies
Parent: Omnicom Media Group Europe Limited
Officers: Sally Ann Bray, Secretary; Philippa Anne Brown [1966] Director/CEO, Media Company; Martin Telling [1966] Director/Chartered Accountant

Omnicom Network Holdings Limited
Incorporated: 31 October 2014
Net Worth: £210,117,792 *Total Assets:* £210,119,296
Registered Office: Bankside 3, 90-100 Southwark Street, London, SE1 0SW
Activities: Activities of head offices
Parent: Omnicom EMEA Holdings Limited
Officers: Sally-Ann Bray, Secretary; Stephen Christopher Nigel Medhurst [1960] Director; Anthony Peter Phipkin [1957] Director/Accountant

OMV Supply & Trading Limited
Incorporated: 2 April 1991 *Employees:* 34
Net Worth: £38,021,092 *Total Assets:* £697,013,184
Registered Office: 10 Bressenden Place, London, SW1E 5DH
Activities: Agents involved in the sale of fuels, ores, metals and industrial chemicals
Parent: OMV Aktiengesellschaft
Officers: Adil Malik, Secretary; Oliver Dillenz [1970] Director/Divisional Chief Financial Officer [Austrian]; Clifford Evans [1959] Managing Director; Vladimir Langhamer [1980] Trading Director [Czech]; Manfred Leitner [1960] Director/Exec Vice President Downstream [Austrian]; Adil Malik [1981] Finance Director; Andreas Schwingshackl [1966] Director/Senior VP - Optimisation & Trading [Italian]

Oncilla Mortgage Funding 2016-1 PLC
Incorporated: 21 April 2016
Net Worth: £3,275,320 *Total Assets:* £222,107,280
Registered Office: 35 Great St Helen's, London, EC3A 6AP
Activities: Financial intermediation not elsewhere classified
Parent: Oncilla Mortgage Funding 2016-1 Holdings Limited
Officers: Paivi Helena Whitaker [1963] Director [Finnish]

One Fleet Realty Ltd
Incorporated: 9 July 2013
Net Worth: £66,248,116 *Total Assets:* £114,065,960
Registered Office: Tavistock House North, Tavistock Square, London, WC1H 9HR
Activities: Other letting and operating of own or leased real estate
Parent: TAK Realty UK, Ltd.
Officers: Jun Fukada [1967] Director [Japanese]; Masaatsu Ohga [1948] Director [Japanese]; Kuniyasu Shimizu [1955] Director [Japanese]; Akihiro Tachibana [1965] Director [Japanese]; Simon Williams [1955] Director

Onefinestay (Holdings) Limited
Incorporated: 24 March 2016
Net Worth: £1 *Total Assets:* £150,174,048
Registered Office: 1 Shortlands, London, W6 8DR
Activities: Other accommodation
Parent: Accor (U.K.) Limited
Officers: Edouard Peers de Nieuwburgh, Secretary; Adrian John Whitehead [1964] Director

Onesubsea Investments UK Limited
Incorporated: 6 March 2013
Net Worth: £259,374,032 *Total Assets:* £474,073,376
Registered Office: 100 New Bridge Street, London, EC4V 6JA
Activities: Activities of other holding companies n.e.c.
Parent: Schlumberger Oilfield UK PLC
Officers: Gina Ann Karathanos, Secretary; Simon Smoker, Secretary; Simon Walter McCloud [1965] Director/Business Executive; Simon Smoker [1962] Director/Accountant

Onesubsea UK Limited
Incorporated: 7 November 1945 *Employees:* 1,121
Net Worth: £195,636,368 *Total Assets:* £443,526,816
Registered Office: 100 New Bridge Street, London, EC4V 6JA
Activities: Manufacture of other special-purpose machinery n.e.c.
Parent: Schlumberger Limited
Officers: Gina Ann Karathanos, Secretary; Simon Smoker, Secretary; Simon Walter McCloud [1965] Director/Business Executive; Simon Smoker [1962] Director/Accountant

Ontic Engineering & Manufacturing UK Limited
Incorporated: 25 September 2008 *Employees:* 167
Net Worth: £45,208,356 *Total Assets:* £150,695,568
Registered Office: 3rd Floor, 105 Wigmore Street, London, W1U 1QY
Activities: Manufacture of air and spacecraft and related machinery
Parent: The Guthrie Corporation Limited
Officers: Gareth Hall [1972] Director/Chartered Accountant; Matthew Lewis Pritchard [1978] Site Director; Michael Edward Waters [1958] Director/Chief Engineer

Onyx Germany (1) Ltd
Incorporated: 6 October 2005 *Employees:* 1
Previous: Hansteen Germany Limited
Net Worth: £80,608,560 *Total Assets:* £168,472,240
Registered Office: 3rd Floor, The Monument Building, Monument Street, London, EC3R 8AF
Activities: Other letting and operating of own or leased real estate
Officers: Kiril Dimov Petrov [1984] Director [Bulgarian]; Jack Stuart Thoms [1972] Director/Surveyor; Panayot Kostadinov Vasilev [1976] Managing Director [French]

Onyx Germany (2) Ltd
Incorporated: 19 March 2007
Previous: Hansteen Germany (2) Limited
Net Worth: £72,749,368 *Total Assets:* £129,501,704
Registered Office: 3rd Floor, The Monument Building, 11 Monument Street, London, EC3R 8AF
Activities: Other letting and operating of own or leased real estate
Officers: Kiril Dimov Petrov [1984] Director [Bulgarian]; Jack Stuart Thoms [1972] Director/Surveyor; Panayot Kostadinov Vasilev [1976] Managing Director [French]

Openbet Technologies Limited
Incorporated: 1 October 2008 *Employees:* 671
Net Worth Deficit: £104,327,000 *Total Assets:* £135,924,000
Registered Office: Fourth Floor, Building 9, Chiswick Park, 566 Chiswick High Road, London, W4 5XT
Activities: Business and domestic software development
Parent: OB Acquisition Limited
Officers: Michael Alan Quartieri, Secretary [American]; Jordan Ellis Levin [1976] Director/Chief Executive Officer [American]; Michael Alan Quartieri [1968] Director/Chief Financial Officer [American]

Opet International Limited
Incorporated: 6 February 1996 *Employees:* 11
Net Worth: £18,616,402 *Total Assets:* £245,744,000
Registered Office: 4th Floor, 180 Piccadilly, London, W1J 9ER
Activities: Other service activities n.e.c.
Parent: Opet Trade BV
Officers: Taner Kose, Secretary; Taner Kose [1964] Director/General Manager; Ufuk Ozturk [1971] Director

Ophir Energy PLC
Incorporated: 18 February 2004 *Employees:* 283
Net Worth: £1,060,967,616 *Total Assets:* £1,448,106,880
Registered Office: Level 4, 123 Victoria Street, London, SW1E 6DE
Activities: Extraction of crude petroleum
Officers: Philip Laing, Secretary; Dr Carol Bell [1958] Director; Alan Booth [1958] Director; Adel Chaouch [1968] Director [American]; David Charles Davies [1955] Director; Vivien Murray Gibney [1946] Director/Barrister; Anthony John Rouse [1956] Director Finance; William George Schrader [1958] Director/Consultant [American]; Dr Carl Trowell [1969] Director

Ophir Holdings & Ventures Limited
Incorporated: 8 November 2016
Net Worth: £457,936,064 *Total Assets:* £462,155,936
Registered Office: Level 4, 123 Victoria Street, London, SW1E 6DE
Activities: Extraction of crude petroleum
Parent: Ophir Holdings & Services (UK) Limited
Officers: Philip Laing, Secretary; Euphemia Milligan Gilbert [1960] Director; Anthony John Mulgrove [1964] Director; Dr Oliver Francis Quinn [1978] Director; Anthony John Rouse [1956] Director

Ophir Thailand (E & P) Limited
Incorporated: 22 February 2005 *Employees:* 22
Previous: Salamander Energy (E & P) Limited
Net Worth: £97,397,072 *Total Assets:* £346,719,328
Registered Office: Level 4, 123 Victoria Street, London, SW1E 6DE
Activities: Extraction of crude petroleum
Parent: Salamander Energy Group Limited
Officers: Lucy Rhiannon Morris, Secretary; Anthony John Mulgrove [1964] Director; Dr Oliver Francis Quinn [1978] Director; Anthony John Rouse [1956] Director

Opodo Limited
Incorporated: 8 August 2000 *Employees:* 154
Net Worth: £282,475,040 *Total Assets:* £808,578,048
Registered Office: 26-28 Hammersmith Grove, London, W6 7BA
Activities: Travel agency activities
Parent: Edreams Odigeo SA
Officers: Dana Philip Dunne [1963] Director; David Elizaga [1973] Director/Chief Financial Officer [Spanish]

Optimum Three Limited
Incorporated: 24 April 2017
Net Worth Deficit: £368,731 *Total Assets:* £115,703,760
Registered Office: 35 Great St Helen's, London, EC3A 6AP
Activities: Financial intermediation not elsewhere classified
Parent: Intertrust Corporate Services Limited
Officers: Helena Paivi Whitaker [1963] Director [Finnish]

Orange Brand Services Limited
Incorporated: 10 June 1988 *Employees:* 208
Net Worth: £3,602,309,120 *Total Assets:* £3,663,056,128
Registered Office: 3 More London Riverside, London, SE1 2AQ
Activities: Other telecommunications activities
Parent: Orange S.A.
Officers: Ibiyemi Solanke, Secretary; Martin John Crossley [1965] Director/International Telecoms Manager; Mickael Jean Faure [1976] Brand Strategy and Performance Director [French]; Gillian Mary Miles [1966] HR and Operations Director; Christophe Marie Pascal Henri Naulleau [1960] Director [French]; Jean-Francois Rodriguez [1971] Director [French]; Christine Walser-Sacau [1963] Director [French]

Orange Participations UK Limited
Incorporated: 8 July 1998 *Employees:* 1
Previous: Orange Spain, Limited
Net Worth: £9,189,509,120 *Total Assets:* £9,191,870,464
Registered Office: 3 More London Riverside, London, SE1 2AQ
Activities: Other telecommunications activities
Parent: Orange SA
Officers: Ibiyemi Ibidapo Ifederu, Secretary; Rachel Deborah Marks [1970] Director/Solicitor; Olivia Jacqueline Esther Andrea Signoret [1982] Director/Project Manager [French]; Johan Van Den Cruijce [1968] Director/Head of Legal and Corporate Affairs [Belgian]

Oranje-Nassau Energie Resources Limited
Incorporated: 20 March 1998
Previous: Sterling Resources (UK) Ltd.
Net Worth: £189,624,000 *Total Assets:* £249,782,000
Registered Office: Fifth Floor, 100 Wood Street, London, EC2V 7EX
Activities: Extraction of crude petroleum
Major Shareholder: Martialis Quirinus Henricus Van Poecke
Officers: Alexander Ferdinand Diederik Berger [1966] Director [Dutch]; Christiaan Hendrick de Ruyter Van Steveninck [1971] Director [Dutch]

Orbita Funding 2017-1 PLC
Incorporated: 4 September 2017
Net Worth: £30,159 *Total Assets:* £204,474,736
Registered Office: 35 Great St Helen's, London, EC3A 6AP
Activities: Other business support service activities n.e.c.
Parent: Orbita Holdings Limited
Officers: Paivi Helena Whitaker [1963] Director [Finnish]

Orbital Shopping Park Swindon Limited
Incorporated: 23 June 2005
Net Worth: £88,279,224 *Total Assets:* £106,377,408
Registered Office: York House, 45 Seymour Street, London, W1H 7LX
Activities: Development of building projects
Parent: BL Retail Warehousing Holding Company Limited
Officers: Sarah Morrell Barzycki [1958] Director/Head of Finance; Paul Stuart Macey [1978] Director/Accountant; Jonathan Charles McNuff [1986] Director/Chartered Accountant; Charles John Middleton [1966] Director/Corporate Tax Executive; Timothy Andrew Roberts [1964] Director/Chartered Surveyor; Nigel Mark Webb [1963] Director/Chartered Surveyor

Orchard Street UK Prime Property GP Limited
Incorporated: 17 December 2013
Net Worth: £2,187 *Total Assets:* £194,395,808
Registered Office: 16 New Burlington Place, London, W1S 2HX
Activities: Other letting and operating of own or leased real estate
Officers: Philip John Gadsden [1962] Director/Chartered Surveyor; John Philip Humberstone [1964] Director; David Robert Lee [1960] Director/Partner; Reginald John Barnabas Rowe [1976] Director/Chartered Surveyor

Origin Finance Limited
Incorporated: 12 November 2007
Net Worth: £42,000 *Total Assets:* £121,264,000
Registered Office: St Richard's House, 110 Eversholt Street, London, NW1 1BS
Activities: Renting and operating of Housing Association real estate
Parent: Origin Housing Limited
Officers: Zhonghua Gloria Yang, Secretary; Carol Ann Carter [1960] Director/Chief Executive of Origin Housing; Neil Bryden McCall [1958] Director/Chairman

Origin Invest Limited
Incorporated: 1 December 2009
Net Worth: £150,000,000 *Total Assets:* £150,511,520
Registered Office: Floor 2, Berkeley Square House, Berkeley Square, Mayfair, London, W1J 6BD
Activities: Construction of other civil engineering projects n.e.c.
Major Shareholder: Vincent Julius Lewis
Officers: Vincent Julius Lewis [1966] Director/Chief Operations Officer

Ormonde Energy Limited
Incorporated: 21 August 2003 *Employees:* 4
Net Worth: £266,592,000 *Total Assets:* £299,820,000
Registered Office: First Floor, 1 Tudor Street, London, EC4Y 0AH
Activities: Production of electricity
Parent: Vattenfall Wind Power Ltd
Officers: Bo Erik Fredrik Lundeborg [1978] Director [Swedish]; Klemens Millonig [1970] Director [Austrian]; Katarina Anna Maria Romberg [1979] Director/Investment Manager [Swedish]; Christian Sommer [1979] Director [Swedish]

Orosi (UK) 2 Limited
Incorporated: 8 February 2017
Net Worth: £53,947,280 *Total Assets:* £221,709,584
Registered Office: c/o Langham Estate Management, 9a Margaret Street, London, W1W 8RJ
Activities: Activities of other holding companies n.e.c.
Parent: Orosi Holdings (Singapore) Pte. Ltd
Officers: Philip James Hardie [1943] Director/Civil Engineer

Orsted Burbo (UK) Limited
Incorporated: 21 December 2000
Previous: Dong Energy Burbo (UK) Limited
Net Worth: £72,979,360 *Total Assets:* £108,847,736
Registered Office: 5 Howick Place, London, SW1P 1WG
Activities: Other business support service activities n.e.c.
Parent: Orsted A/S
Officers: Philip Henry de Villiers [1975] Director; David Murray [1983] Director/Accountant [Irish]; Hugh Alistair Yendole [1968] Director

Orsted Burbo Extension Holding Ltd
Incorporated: 2 February 2016
Net Worth: £576,895,296 *Total Assets:* £587,620,672
Registered Office: 5 Howick Place, London, SW1P 1WG
Activities: Activities of other holding companies n.e.c.
Parent: Orsted Power (UK) Limited
Officers: David Murray [1983] Director/Accountant [Irish]; Hugh Alistair Yendole [1968] Director

Orsted Lincs (UK) Ltd
Incorporated: 15 June 2011
Previous: Dong Energy Lincs (UK) Ltd
Net Worth: £135,295,280 *Total Assets:* £249,480,352
Registered Office: 5 Howick Place, London, SW1P 1WG
Activities: Other business support service activities n.e.c.
Parent: Orsted A/S
Officers: Philip Henry de Villiers [1975] Director/Asset Manager; Mairi Dudley [1988] Director; Kasper Holst Skyttegaard-Nielsen [1979] Director [Danish]

Orsted London Array II Limited
Incorporated: 4 July 2008
Previous: Dong Energy London Array II Limited
Net Worth: £152,743,504 *Total Assets:* £487,599,840
Registered Office: 5 Howick Place, London, SW1P 1WG
Activities: Other business support service activities n.e.c.
Parent: Orsted Power (UK) Limited
Officers: Philip Henry de Villiers [1975] Director/Asset Manager

Orsted London Array Limited
Incorporated: 22 September 1999
Previous: Dong Energy London Array Limited
Net Worth: £80,714,848 *Total Assets:* £101,779,464
Registered Office: 5 Howick Place, London, SW1P 1WG
Activities: Production of electricity
Shareholders: Orsted A/S; Orsted Power (UK) Limited
Officers: Philip Henry de Villiers [1975] Director/Asset Manager

Orsted Power (Gunfleet Sands) Ltd
Incorporated: 23 June 2011
Previous: Dong Energy Power (Gunfleet Sands) Ltd
Net Worth: £231,720,976 *Total Assets:* £277,132,864
Registered Office: 5 Howick Place, London, SW1P 1WG
Activities: Other business support service activities n.e.c.
Parent: Orsted Power (UK) Limited
Officers: Philip Henry de Villiers [1975] Director; David Murray [1983] Director/Accountant [Irish]

Orsted Power (UK) Limited
Incorporated: 4 December 2003 *Employees:* 637
Previous: Dong Energy Power (UK) Limited
Net Worth: £840,230,016 *Total Assets:* £2,526,134,272
Registered Office: 5 Howick Place, London, SW1P 1WG
Activities: Production of electricity
Parent: Orsted A/S
Officers: Hanne Legardt Blume Levy, Secretary; Rasmus Errboe [1979] Director/Lawyer [Danish]; Benjamin John Sykes [1965] Director/UK Country Manager; Matthew Reginald Wright [1965] Managing Director

Orsted Race Bank (Holding) Limited
Incorporated: 11 July 2016
Net Worth: £8,679,141 *Total Assets:* £790,390,464
Registered Office: 5 Howick Place, London, SW1P 1WG
Activities: Production of electricity
Parent: Orsted Power (UK) Limited
Officers: Philip Henry de Villiers [1975] Director/Asset Manager; Mairi Dudley [1988] Director; Benjamin John Sykes [1965] Director/UK Country Manager

Orsted Sales (UK) Limited
Incorporated: 18 July 1989 *Employees:* 121
Previous: Dong Energy Sales (UK) Limited
Net Worth: £27,458,000 *Total Assets:* £174,792,992
Registered Office: 5 Howick Place, London, SW1P 1WG
Activities: Trade of gas through mains
Parent: Orsted S & D (UK) Limited
Officers: Allan Bodskov Andersen [1972] Director/Senior Vice President, Finance DCS & Treasury Risk Management [Danish]; Paul Etienne Baan [1964] Director [Dutch]; Lars Brinch Danielsen [1978] Director [Danish]; Rick Hitchcock [1976] UK Operations Director; Morten Hultberg Buchgreitz [1967] Director/Executive Vice President [Danish]; David Ashley Phillips [1976] Sales & Marketing Director

Orsted West of Duddon Sands (UK) Limited
Incorporated: 5 February 2008
Previous: Dong Energy West of Duddon Sands (UK) Limited
Net Worth: £287,490,720 *Total Assets:* £614,502,464
Registered Office: 5 Howick Place, London, SW1P 1WG
Activities: Production of electricity
Parent: Orsted Power (UK) Limited
Officers: Philip Henry de Villiers [1975] Director; David Murray [1983] Director/Accountant [Irish]; Hugh Alistair Yendole [1968] Director

Orsted Westermost Rough Limited
Incorporated: 19 February 2014
Previous: Dong Energy Westermost Rough Limited
Net Worth: £125,675,952 *Total Assets:* £291,576,960
Registered Office: 5 Howick Place, London, SW1P 1WG
Activities: Other business support service activities n.e.c.
Parent: Orsted Power (UK) Limited
Officers: Philip Henry de Villiers [1975] Director/Asset Manager; Mairi Dudley [1988] Director; Kasper Holst Skyttegaard-Nielsen [1979] Director [Danish]

Osaka Gas UK, Ltd.
Incorporated: 28 April 2010 *Employees:* 11
Net Worth: £244,137,760 *Total Assets:* £263,109,536
Registered Office: 1st Floor, Carrington House, 126-130 Regent Street, London, W1B 5SE
Activities: Activities of other holding companies n.e.c.
Parent: Osaka Gas Co., Ltd
Officers: Naoshi Kishida [1969] Director [Japanese]; Ryosuke Kobayashi [1973] Director [Japanese]; Ryuichi Nishida [1965] Director [Japanese]; Kenji Oida [1964] Director [Japanese]; Yo Otsuka [1972] Director [Japanese]

Osnaburgh Street Limited
Incorporated: 25 July 2006
Net Worth: £266,725,968 *Total Assets:* £266,898,016
Registered Office: York House, 45 Seymour Street, London, W1H 7LX
Activities: Development of building projects
Shareholders: Regent's Place Holding Company Limited; Regent's Place Holding Company Limited
Officers: Sarah Morrell Barzycki [1958] Director/Head of Finance; Timothy Andrew Roberts [1964] Director/Chartered Surveyor; Nigel Mark Webb [1963] Director/Chartered Surveyor

OSW Co Holdings 1 Limited
Incorporated: 22 November 2016
Net Worth: £1,772,579 *Total Assets:* £531,573,408
Registered Office: 18 St Swithin's Lane, London, EC4N 8AD
Activities: Activities of other holding companies n.e.c.
Parent: New Green Interim Holdco Limited
Officers: Dominic Tan, Secretary; Richard Abel [1970] Director/Investment Banking; Stephen Alan John Deeley [1980] Director/Investment Manager; Mark Jonathan Dooley [1962] Director/Investment Banker [Australian]; Erin Kate Eisenberg [1978] Director [American]; Tom Kelly [1989] Director/Investment Manager [Irish]; Gordon Ian Winston Parsons [1967] Director/Accountant; Roberto Purcaro [1978] Senior Managing Director [Italian]; David Paul Tilstone [1969] Director/Banker

OSW Co Holdings 2 Limited
Incorporated: 22 November 2016
Net Worth Deficit: £3,532,273 *Total Assets:* £850,518,336
Registered Office: 18 St Swithin's Lane, London, EC4N 8AD
Activities: Activities of other holding companies n.e.c.
Parent: OSW Co Holdings 1 Limited
Officers: Dominic Tan, Secretary; Richard Abel [1970] Director/Investment Banker; Stephen Alan John Deeley [1980] Director/Investment Manager; Mark Jonathan Dooley [1962] Director/Investment Banker [Australian]; Erin Kate Eisenberg [1978] Director [American]; Tom Kelly [1989] Director/Investment Manager [Irish]; Gordon Ian Winston Parsons [1967] Director/Accountant; Roberto Purcaro [1978] Senior Managing Director [Italian]; David Paul Tilstone [1969] Director/Investment Banker

OSW LP Holdco Limited
Incorporated: 22 November 2016
Net Worth Deficit: £6,766,813 *Total Assets:* £154,769,680
Registered Office: 18 St Swithin's Lane, London, EC4N 8AD
Activities: Activities of other holding companies n.e.c.
Parent: OSW Co Holdings 2 Limited
Officers: Dominic Tan, Secretary; Richard Abel [1970] Director/Investment Banking; Stephen Alan John Deeley [1980] Director/Investment Manager; Mark Jonathan Dooley [1962] Director/Investment Banker [Australian]; Erin Kate Eisenberg [1978] Director [American]; Tom Kelly [1989] Director/Investment Manager [Irish]; Gordon Ian Winston Parsons [1967] Director/Accountant; Roberto Purcaro [1978] Senior Managing Director [Italian]; David Paul Tilstone [1969] Director/Banker

OTE PLC
Incorporated: 17 December 1999 *Employees:* 1
Net Worth: £29,341,904 *Total Assets:* £1,656,523,392
Registered Office: Third Floor, 1 King's Arms Yard, London, EC2R 7AF
Activities: Other business support service activities n.e.c.
Officers: Eileen Marie Hughes [1966] Director/Head of Structured Products UK [American]; Panos Kaliabetsos [1964] Director/Group Treasurer [Greek]; Charalambos Mazarakis [1964] Director/OTE S.A. Group Chief Financial Officer (CFO) [Greek]; Anastasios Tzoulas [1966] Director/Chief Financial Officer Romania [Greek]; Daniel Jonathan Wynne [1970] Director

Otis Investments Limited
Incorporated: 28 June 1900
Net Worth: £112,117,000 *Total Assets:* £158,804,992
Registered Office: Ground Floor, Chiswick Park Building 5, 566 Chiswick High Road, London, W4 5YF
Activities: Non-trading company
Parent: United Technologies Holdings Limited
Officers: Rene Bisson [1971] Managing Director [American]; Robert William Sadler [1967] Director/Solicitor; Maxime Yao [1977] Director

Otis Limited
Incorporated: 3 May 1917 *Employees:* 1,486
Net Worth: £445,223,008 *Total Assets:* £603,323,008
Registered Office: Ground Floor, Chiswick Park Building 5, 566 Chiswick High Road, London, W4 5YF
Activities: Manufacture of lifting and handling equipment
Parent: Otis UK Holding Limited
Officers: Michele Batty [1982] Executive Director; Rene Bisson [1971] Managing Director [American]; Ales Korotvicka [1978] Service Director [Czech]; Bertrand Rotagnon [1981] Director [French]; Robert William Sadler [1967] Director/Solicitor; Dorje Soley [1975] New Equipment Director; Maxime Yao [1977] Director

Otis UK Holding Limited
Incorporated: 18 April 2006
Net Worth: £235,964,992 *Total Assets:* £235,964,992
Registered Office: Ground Floor, Building 5, Chiswick Park, 566 Chiswick High Road, London, W4 5YF
Activities: Non-trading company
Officers: Rene Bisson [1971] Managing Director [American]; Robert William Sadler [1967] Director/Solicitor; Maxime Yao [1977] Director

OTPPB Investments (U.K.) Limited
Incorporated: 7 June 2004
Net Worth: £117,496,040 *Total Assets:* £117,528,312
Registered Office: c/o Hackwood Secretaries Limited, One Silk Street, London, EC2Y 8HQ
Activities: Non-trading company
Officers: Jeffrey Michael Davis, Secretary; Jeffrey Michael Davis [1970] Director/Lawyer [Canadian]; Charles Thomazi [1963] Managing Director [Canadian]

Otter Ports I Limited
Incorporated: 2 March 2011
Net Worth: £104,956 *Total Assets:* £497,233,024
Registered Office: 8th Floor, 10 Bressenden Place, London, SW1E 5DH
Activities: Activities of head offices
Parent: Otter Ports Holdings Limited
Officers: Pamela Smyth, Secretary; Simon Daniel Beer [1980] Director/Asset Manager; Diana Callebaut [1980] Director/Investments [Australian]; Richard Wing-Eng Chang [1971] Director/Investment Professional [British/Australian]; Patrick Charbonneau [1978] Managing Director [Canadian]; Simon George Davy [1970] Director/Investment Manager; Stephen Kynaston [1978] Director/Investment Manager; Patrick Samson [1971] Director [Canadian]; Lord Robert Smith [1944] Managing Director

Otter Ports II Limited
Incorporated: 2 March 2011
Net Worth Deficit: £18,240 *Total Assets:* £497,069,792
Registered Office: 8th Floor, 10 Bressenden Place, London, SW1E 5DH
Activities: Activities of head offices
Parent: Otter Ports I Limited
Officers: Pamela Smyth, Secretary; Simon Daniel Beer [1980] Director/Asset Manager; Diana Callebaut [1980] Director/Investments [Australian]; Richard Wing-Eng Chang [1971] Director/Investment Professional [British/Australian]; Patrick Charbonneau [1978] Managing Director [Canadian]; Simon George Davy [1970] Director/Investment Manager; Stephen Kynaston [1978] Director/Investment Manager; Patrick Samson [1971] Director [Canadian]; Lord Robert Smith [1944] Managing Director

Otter Ports Limited
Incorporated: 2 March 2011
Net Worth Deficit: £16,198,655 *Total Assets:* £752,239,744
Registered Office: 8th Floor, 10 Bressenden Place, London, SW1E 5DH
Activities: Activities of head offices
Parent: Otter Ports II Limited
Officers: Pamela Smyth, Secretary; Simon Daniel Beer [1980] Director/Asset Manager; Diana Callebaut [1980] Director/Investments [Australian]; Richard Wing-Eng Chang [1971] Director/Investment Professional [British/Australian]; Patrick Charbonneau [1978] Managing Director [Canadian]; Simon George Davy [1970] Director/Investment Manager; Stephen Kynaston [1978] Director/Investment Manager; Patrick Samson [1971] Director [Canadian]; Lord Robert Smith [1944] Managing Director

Outsourcing UK Limited
Incorporated: 15 July 2016 *Employees:* 1,405
Net Worth: £26,975,000 *Total Assets:* £119,970,000
Registered Office: Floor 9, Peninsular House, 30-36 Monument Street, London, EC3R 8LJ
Activities: Activities of other holding companies n.e.c.
Parent: Outsourcing Inc.
Officers: Timothy John Francis Collins, Secretary; Charles Edward Bruin [1971] Director; Masaki Motegi [1978] Director [Japanese]; Yuya Ono [1977] Director [Japanese]; Kazuhiko Suzuki [1969] Director [Japanese]; Nicholas Sean Tubbs [1967] Director

Oval (2041) Limited
Incorporated: 23 May 2005
Net Worth Deficit: £642,574,976 *Total Assets:* £212,232,992
Registered Office: Saffron Court, 14b St Cross Street, London, EC1N 8XA
Activities: Activities of head offices
Parent: Oval (2042) Limited
Officers: Aaron Campbell, Secretary; Hiroyasu Matsui [1965] Director [Japanese]; Jonathan Paul Scott [1961] Director/Accountant

Ove Arup & Partners Hong Kong Limited
Incorporated: 28 March 1978 *Employees:* 2,115
Net Worth: £14,920,000 *Total Assets:* £108,145,000
Registered Office: 13 Fitzroy Street, London, W1T 4BQ
Activities: Engineering related scientific and technical consulting activities
Parent: Arup Group Limited
Officers: Vanessa Jane Shakespeare, Secretary; Ka Yue Michael Kwok [1962] Director/Structural Engineer; Wai Tong Wilfred Lau [1955] Director/Transportation Engineer [Canadian]; Yuk Nin Andy Lee [1967] Director/Engineer; Lup Moon Lui [1952] Director/Civil/Structural Engineer; Timothy Kai-Cheung Suen [1956] Director/Civil Engineer; Matthew Stuart Tweedie [1971] Finance Director; Thomas John Fergal Whyte [1968] Director/Engineer [Irish]; Cheuk Fai Peter Wong [1974] Legal Director [Australian]; Kwok-On Yeung [1954] Director/Mechanical Engineer

Ove Arup & Partners International Limited
Incorporated: 18 April 1969 *Employees:* 5,408
Net Worth: £108,900,000 *Total Assets:* £410,400,000
Registered Office: 13 Fitzroy Street, London, W1T 4BQ
Activities: Engineering related scientific and technical consulting activities
Parent: Ove Arup Holdings Limited
Officers: Vanessa Jane Shakespeare, Secretary; Dr Alan James Belfield [1956] Director/Mechanical Engineer; Jerome Anthony Frost [1971] Director/Town Planner; Geoffrey Nevil Hunt [1961] Director/Chartered Structural Engineer; Patricia Marion Johnstone [1964] Director/Structural Engineer; Anthony Frederick Lovell [1968] Director/Consulting Engineer; Dervilla Mary Mitchell [1958] Director/Structural Engineer [Irish]; Matthew Stuart Tweedie [1971] Finance Director

Overbury PLC
Incorporated: 8 February 1965 *Employees:* 636
Net Worth: £73,342,000 *Total Assets:* £224,016,000
Registered Office: Kent House, 14-17 Market Place, London, W1W 8AJ
Activities: Construction of commercial buildings
Parent: Morgan Sindall Group PLC
Officers: Clare Sheridan, Secretary; John Baker [1965] Director; Robert Henry Banister [1959] Team Managing Director; Christopher Stephen Booth [1963] Director; Andrew Boyle [1962] Director; Paul Brazier [1962] Director/Quantity Surveyor; Stephen Paul Crummett [1965] Finance Director; Peter Knight [1964] Divisional Director; John Christopher Morgan [1955] Director; Andrew Paton [1960] Director; Neil Skelding [1971] Finance Director; Andrew David Wood [1968] Managing Director

H.R.Owen PLC
Incorporated: 15 September 1983 *Employees:* 553
Net Worth: £27,654,000 *Total Assets:* £144,499,008
Registered Office: Melton Court, Old Brompton Road, London, SW7 3TD
Activities: Sale of new cars and light motor vehicles
Officers: Denise Grimston, Secretary; Graham Christopher William Beegan [1979] Director [Irish]; Veh Ken Choo [1973] Director [Malaysian]; Jeffrey Edmund Couch [1969] Director [Canadian]; Mehmet Dalman [1958] Director; Mokhzani Mahathir [1961] Director [Malaysian]; Robin Tan [1974] Director [Malaysian]; U-Peng Tan [1992] Director [Malaysian]

Oxhauth Limited
Incorporated: 3 August 2001
Net Worth: £44,370,528 *Total Assets:* £450,840,192
Registered Office: Suite 100, 25 Upper Brook Street, London, W1K 7QD
Activities: Other business support service activities n.e.c.
Officers: Matthew John Allen [1972] Director/Company Secretary; Janet Treacy Pierce [1977] Director

P & O Dover (Holdings) Limited
Incorporated: 9 January 1998 *Employees:* 3
Net Worth: £242,619,629,568 *Total Assets:* £677,548,326,912
Registered Office: 16 Palace Street, London, SW1E 5JQ
Activities: Non-trading company
Parent: The Peninsular and Oriental Steam Navigation Company
Officers: Mohammad Alhashimy, Secretary; Rashed Ali Hassan Abdulla Al Qahtani Al Qahtani [1971] Director/SVP & MD Europe & Russia [Emirati]; Mohammad Alhashimy [1985] Director/Corporate Governance & Company Secretariat Manager [Emirati]; Sarmad Mehmood Qureshi [1970] Director/Chartered Accountant

P & O Overseas Holdings Limited
Incorporated: 4 September 1954 *Employees:* 2
Net Worth: £4,545,644,032 *Total Assets:* £99,695,878,144
Registered Office: 16 Palace Street, London, SW1E 5JQ
Activities: Non-trading company
Parent: Partkestrel Limited
Officers: Mohammad Alhashimy, Secretary; Rashed Ali Hassan Abdulla Al Qahtani Al Qahtani [1971] Director/SVP & MD Europe & Russia [Emirati]; Sarmad Mehmood Qureshi [1970] Director/Chartered Accountant

P & O Properties International Limited
Incorporated: 28 February 1973 *Employees:* 2
Net Worth: £191,032,432 *Total Assets:* £408,416,160
Registered Office: 16 Palace Street, London, SW1E 5JQ
Activities: Other service activities n.e.c.
Parent: The Peninsular and Oriental Steam Navigation Company
Officers: Mohammad Alhashimy, Secretary; Rashed Ali Hassan Abdulla Al Qahtani Al Qahtani [1971] Director/SVP & MD Europe & Russia [Emirati]; Sarmad Mehmood Qureshi [1970] Director/Chartered Accountant

P & O Property Accounts Limited
Incorporated: 28 March 1967 *Employees:* 2
Net Worth: £56,699,844 *Total Assets:* £196,275,808
Registered Office: 16 Palace Street, London, SW1E 5JQ
Activities: Banks
Parent: P & O Property Holdings Limited
Officers: Junaid Muhammad Rahimullah Muhammad [1968] Director/Chief Financial Officer [Pakistani]; Khwaja Kamran Shah [1977] Director/Financial Controller [Pakistani]

P & O Property Holdings Limited
Incorporated: 1 December 1933
Net Worth: £121,687,000 *Total Assets:* £125,312,000
Registered Office: 16 Palace Street, London, SW1E 5JQ
Activities: Renting and operating of Housing Association real estate
Parent: Istithmar P & O Estates (UK) Limited
Officers: Junaid Muhammad Rahimullah Muhammad [1968] Director/Chief Financial Officer [Pakistani]; Khwaja Kamran Shah [1977] Director/Financial Controller [Pakistani]

P & P Spearhead UK Holdings, Ltd
Incorporated: 20 March 2015 *Employees:* 1,744
Net Worth: £139,513,184 *Total Assets:* £399,981,184
Registered Office: Suite 1, 3rd Floor, 11-12 St James's Square, London, SW1Y 4LB
Activities: Activities of agricultural holding companies
Officers: John Christopher Atkin [1953] Director; David James Buckeridge [1960] Director/Private Equity Investor; Thomas Michael Curtis Green [1966] Farmer Director; Justin Wesley Kern [1981] Director/Finance Investment [American]; William Dexter Paine III [1960] Director/Private Equity Investor [American]; Tomasz Jacek Zdziebkowski [1962] Director [Polish]

P1 Reversions Limited
Incorporated: 24 January 2007 *Employees:* 1
Net Worth: £981,000 *Total Assets:* £124,364,000
Registered Office: DMS Governance (UK) Limited, Suite 402, 52 Brook Street, London, W1K 5DS
Activities: Other professional, scientific and technical activities n.e.c.
Parent: XYQ Cayman Ltd
Officers: Gavin Devitt [1979] Director [Irish]; Matthew John Northover [1971] Investor Director; John Nicholas Spinney [1965] Investor Director [American]

P2P BL-3 PLC
Incorporated: 7 June 2017
Net Worth: £827,481 *Total Assets:* £164,493,504
Registered Office: Suite 2, 3rd Floor, 11-12 St James's Square, London, SW1Y 4LB
Activities: Other credit granting n.e.c.
Officers: Sunil Masson, Secretary; Julius Manuel Bozzino [1970] Director; Sunil Masson [1971] Director; David Rudge [1970] Director

P2P Global Investments PLC
Incorporated: 6 December 2013
Net Worth: £789,855,040 *Total Assets:* £1,427,292,672
Registered Office: 6th Floor, 65 Gresham Street, London, EC2V 7NQ
Activities: Activities of investment trusts
Officers: Doctor Mahnaz Akbary-Safa [1964] Banker/Managing Director; Michael John Cassidy [1947] Director; Stuart Cruickshank [1954] Director; David Fisher [1958] Director; Simon John King [1964] Director

PA Consulting Group Limited
Incorporated: 3 September 2015 *Employees:* 2,645
Net Worth Deficit: £105,126,000 *Total Assets:* £687,870,016
Registered Office: 10 Bressenden Place, London, SW1E 5DN
Activities: Activities of head offices
Officers: Marcus Agius [1946] Director; John George Alexander [1961] Director; Andrew Richard Burgess [1964] Partner, Managing Director; Kully Janjuah [1968] Director/Company Secretary; Alan Middleton [1966] Director; Fraser Scott Robson [1980] Director

PA Consulting Holdings Limited
Incorporated: 11 October 2012 *Employees:* 1
Previous: PA Consulting Group Limited
Net Worth: £12,903,481 *Total Assets:* £110,613,072
Registered Office: 10 Bressenden Place, London, SW1E 5DN
Activities: Activities of head offices
Parent: PA Consulting Management Services Limited
Officers: Kully Janjuah, Secretary; Marcus Ambrose Paul Agius [1946] Director; John George Alexander [1961] Director; Ruairidh Gregor Cameron [1975] Finance Director; Anita Chandraker [1961] Director/Consultant; Andrew Maitland Hooke [1962] Director; Adam Justin Hughes [1969] Director/Senior Partner; Kully Janjuah [1968] Director/Company Secretary; Hamish Maule [1972] Director/Head of Operations; Alan Middleton [1966] Director; Jo Scarlet [1971] Director/Chief Marketing Officer; Conrad James Andrew Thompson [1966] Director/Management Consultant; Kenneth John Toombs [1961] Director/Consultant [American]

PA Consulting Management Services Limited
Incorporated: 4 September 2015 *Employees:* 2
Net Worth: £76,929,288 *Total Assets:* £661,130,496
Registered Office: 10 Bressenden Place, London, SW1E 5DN
Activities: Activities of other holding companies n.e.c.
Parent: Garden Midco 2 Limited
Officers: Ruairidh Gregor Cameron [1975] Finance Director; Kully Janjuah [1968] Director/Company Secretary; Alan Middleton [1966] Director

PA Consulting Services Limited
Incorporated: 3 July 1946 *Employees:* 49
Net Worth: £92,601,000 *Total Assets:* £200,071,008
Registered Office: 10 Bressenden Place, London, SW1E 5DN
Activities: Management consultancy activities other than financial management
Parent: PA Holdings Limited
Officers: James William Greenfield, Secretary; Charles Roland Barrett [1969] Director/Head of Group Legal; Ruairidh Gregor Cameron [1975] Finance Director; Kully Janjuah [1968] Director; Alan Middleton [1966] Director; David Martin Vickerstaffe [1971] Director/Tax Manager

PA Group Holdings Limited
Incorporated: 11 July 2012 *Employees:* 3
Previous: Genghis Midco Limited
Net Worth: £125,667,000 *Total Assets:* £139,315,008
Registered Office: 15th Floor, 6 Bevis Marks, Bury Court, London, EC3A 7BA
Activities: Wholesale trade of motor vehicle parts and accessories
Parent: PA Topco Limited
Officers: Louis Juneau, Secretary; Andre Courville [1953] Director [Canadian]; Neil Michael Croxson [1968] Director/Chief Financial Officer; Peter Charles Sephton [1959] Director

PA Group Limited
Incorporated: 6 November 1868 *Employees:* 839
Net Worth: £90,617,000 *Total Assets:* £110,545,000
Registered Office: PA Newscentre, 292 Vauxhall Bridge Road, London, SW1V 1AE
Activities: Other service activities n.e.c.
Officers: Louise Irwin, Secretary; Generaldine Ruth Pratt Allinson [1966] Director; Rebekah Mary Brooks [1968] Director/Chief Executive Officer; Andrew John Dowsett [1966] Director/Chief Operating Officer; Dominic Joseph Fitzpatrick [1966] Managing Director [Irish]; Simon Richard Fox [1961] Director/Chief Executive Officer; Murdoch MacLennan [1949] Director/Chief Executive of Telegraph Media Group; Clive Paul Marshall [1958] Director/Chief Executive, PA Group; Anthony Gerard Watson [1955] Managing Director of The Press Association

PA Group Treasury Services Limited
Incorporated: 30 January 1986
Net Worth: £119,827,824 *Total Assets:* £510,671,392
Registered Office: 10 Bressenden Place, London, SW1E 5DN
Activities: Other business support service activities n.e.c.
Parent: PA Overseas Holdings Limited
Officers: James William Greenfield, Secretary; Ruairidh Gregor Cameron [1975] Finance Director; Kully Janjuah [1968] Director; Alan Middleton [1966] Director

PA Holdings Limited
Incorporated: 24 March 1988 *Employees:* 1,872
Net Worth: £124,917,984 *Total Assets:* £285,297,184
Registered Office: 10 Bressenden Place, London, SW1E 5DN
Activities: Activities of head offices
Parent: PACG2 Limited
Officers: James William Greenfield, Secretary; Charles Roland Barrett [1969] Director/Head of Group Legal; Ruairidh Gregor Cameron [1975] Finance Director; Kully Janjuah [1968] Director; Alan Middleton [1966] Director/Senior Partner

PA International Consulting Group Limited
Incorporated: 19 July 1965
Net Worth: £150,498,352 *Total Assets:* £150,501,104
Registered Office: 10 Bressenden Place, London, SW1E 5DN
Activities: Activities of head offices
Parent: PA Holdings Limited
Officers: James William Greenfield, Secretary; Ruairidh Gregor Cameron [1975] Finance Director; Kully Janjuah [1968] Director; Alan Middleton [1966] Director/Chief Executive Officer

PA Netherlands Treasury Services Limited
Incorporated: 21 April 2006
Net Worth: £118,208,968 *Total Assets:* £118,376,616
Registered Office: 10 Bressenden Place, London, SW1E 5DN
Activities: Other business support service activities n.e.c.
Parent: PA Overseas Holdings Limited
Officers: James William Greenfield, Secretary; Ruairidh Gregor Cameron [1975] Finance Director; Kully Janjuah [1968] Director

PA Overseas Holdings Limited
Incorporated: 24 August 1988
Net Worth: £137,778,112 *Total Assets:* £145,051,168
Registered Office: 10 Bressenden Place, London, SW1E 5DN
Activities: Activities of head offices
Parent: PA International Consulting Group Limited
Officers: James William Greenfield, Secretary; Ruairidh Gregor Cameron [1975] Finance Director; Kully Janjuah [1968] Director

PA Topco Limited
Incorporated: 10 July 2012
Previous: Genghis Topco Limited
Net Worth: £153,802,000 *Total Assets:* £153,832,992
Registered Office: 15th Floor, 6 Bevis Marks, Bury Court, London, EC3A 7BA
Activities: Wholesale trade of motor vehicle parts and accessories
Officers: Louis Juneau, Secretary; Andre Courville [1953] Director [Canadian]; Neil Michael Croxson [1968] Director/Chief Financial Officer; Peter Charles Sephton [1959] Director

Pace Bidco Limited
Incorporated: 11 September 2014
Net Worth: £5,293,566 *Total Assets:* £160,434,400
Registered Office: Welken House, 10-11 Charterhouse Square, London, EC1M 6EH
Activities: Fund management activities
Parent: Pace Topco Limited
Officers: Reade Eugene Griffith [1965] Director; Sven Edvard Krogius [1965] Director/Lawyer [American/Irish]

Pace Topco Limited
Incorporated: 11 September 2014 *Employees:* 99
Net Worth: £55,555,092 *Total Assets:* £246,798,272
Registered Office: Welken House, 10-11 Charterhouse Square, London, EC1M 6EH
Activities: Activities of financial services holding companies
Officers: Reade Eugene Griffith [1965] Director; Sven Edvard Krogius [1965] Director/Lawyer [American/Irish]

PACG2 Limited
Incorporated: 4 April 2008
Net Worth: £7,591,182 *Total Assets:* £210,219,568
Registered Office: 10 Bressenden Place, London, SW1E 5DN
Activities: Activities of head offices
Parent: PA Consulting Holdings Limited
Officers: Kully Janjuah, Secretary/Director; Charles Roland Barrett [1969] Director/Head of Group Legal; Ruairidh Gregor Cameron [1975] Finance Director; Kully Janjuah [1968] Director/Company Secretary; Alan Middleton [1966] Director

Pacific Horizon Investment Trust PLC
Incorporated: 1 February 1989
Net Worth: £204,880,000 *Total Assets:* £225,630,000
Registered Office: Computershare Investor Services Moor House, 120 London Wall, London, EC2Y 5ET
Activities: Activities of investment trusts
Officers: Edward George Creasy [1955] Director; Angela Claire Lane [1962] Director/Chartered Accountant; Rupert Angus Macpherson [1966] Director; Jean Grace Kemmis Matterson [1956] Director/Investment Manager; Richard Frank Studwell [1967] Director/Writer

Pacific Life RE Holdings Limited
Incorporated: 2 June 2008 *Employees:* 270
Net Worth: £388,191,008 *Total Assets:* £1,961,270,016
Registered Office: Tower Bridge House, St Katharine's Way, London, E1W 1BA
Activities: Activities of head offices
Officers: Joanna Magdalena Blazey, Secretary; Clare Jane Bousfield [1968] Director; Gary Luther Falde [1958] Director [American]; Duncan Leigh Hayward [1964] Director; David Ralph Howell [1967] Director; John Robert Lister [1958] Director; Simon Christopher John Machell [1963] Director; Stephen John Payne [1961] Director; George Rupert Hird Scott [1968] Director; Toby Emil Strauss [1959] Director

Pacific Life RE Limited
Incorporated: 29 October 1964 *Employees:* 68
Net Worth: £430,056,000 *Total Assets:* £1,913,273,984
Registered Office: Tower Bridge House, St Katharine's Way, London, E1W 1BA
Activities: Life reinsurance
Parent: Pacific Life RE Services Limited
Officers: Joanna Magdalena Blazey, Secretary; Clare Jane Bousfield [1968] Director; Gary Falde [1958] Director/Vice President [American]; Duncan Leigh Hayward [1964] Director/Accountant; David Ralph Howell [1967] Director/Actuary; John Robert Lister [1958] Director; Simon Christopher John Machell [1963] Director; Stephen John Payne [1961] Director; George Rupert Hird Scott [1968] Director/Lawyer; Toby Emil Strauss [1959] Director

Pacific Life RE Services Limited
Incorporated: 8 July 1987 *Employees:* 172
Net Worth: £474,235,008 *Total Assets:* £514,976,000
Registered Office: Tower Bridge House, St Katharine's Way, London, E1W 1BA
Activities: Other activities auxiliary to insurance and pension funding
Parent: Pacific Life RE Holdings Limited
Officers: Joanna Magdalena Blazey, Secretary; Clare Jane Bousfield [1968] Director; Gary Falde [1958] Director/Vice President [American]; Duncan Leigh Hayward [1964] Director/Accountant; David Ralph Howell [1967] Director; John Robert Lister [1958] Director; Simon Christopher John Machell [1963] Director; Stephen John Payne [1961] Director; George Rupert Hird Scott [1968] Director/Solicitor; Toby Emil Strauss [1959] Director

Pacific Quay Finance PLC
Incorporated: 30 April 2004
Net Worth Deficit: £16,542,394 *Total Assets:* £124,023,088
Registered Office: 35 Great St Helen's, London, EC3A 6AP
Activities: Financial intermediation not elsewhere classified
Parent: Pacific Quay Holdings Limited
Officers: Susan Iris Abrahams [1957] Director

Pacific Quay Holdings Limited
Incorporated: 9 July 2004
Net Worth Deficit: £16,554,895 *Total Assets:* £124,010,584
Registered Office: 35 Great St Helen's, London, EC3A 6AP
Activities: Financial intermediation not elsewhere classified
Parent: Intertrust Corporate Services Limited
Officers: Susan Iris Abrahams [1957] Director

PAH Gas Infrastructure Limited
Incorporated: 9 April 2014 *Employees:* 7
Net Worth: £758,542,976 *Total Assets:* £1,558,784,000
Registered Office: 3 More London Riverside, London, SE1 2AQ
Activities: Activities of head offices
Officers: Loi Shun Chan [1962] Director [Chinese]; Guy Butterworth Ellis [1961] Director; Mark John Horsley [1959] Director/Chief Executive Officer; Jonathan Theodore Miller [1971] Director; Richard John Roberts [1964] Director/Chartered Accountant (Retired); Charles Chao Chung Tsai [1957] Director and Chief Executive Officer [Canadian]; Chi Tin Wan [1950] Director and Chief Executive Officer [Australian]

Palace Capital PLC
Incorporated: 14 January 2005
Net Worth: £163,587,008 *Total Assets:* £167,254,000
Registered Office: Lower Ground Floor, One George Yard, London, EC3V 9DF
Activities: Other letting and operating of own or leased real estate
Officers: David Malcolm Kaye, Secretary; Stanley Harold Davis [1938] Director; Anthony Charles Dove [1945] Director; Stephen John Silvester [1981] Director; Ronald Neil Sinclair [1943] Director; Richard Paul Starr [1974] Director; Kim David Spencer Taylor-Smith [1957] Director; Mickola Rosemary Wilson [1955] Director

Palace Holdco UK Limited
Incorporated: 2 December 2015 *Employees:* 196
Net Worth: £66,555,000 *Total Assets:* £206,224,000
Registered Office: Selhurst Park Stadium, Holmesdale Road, London, SE25 6PU
Activities: Activities of sport clubs
Officers: Sean O'Loughlin, Secretary; David Scott Blitzer [1969] Director [American]; Joshua Jordan Harris [1964] Director [American]; Stephen Parish [1965] Director/Business Executive

Palace Midco UK Limited
Incorporated: 2 December 2015 *Employees:* 5
Net Worth: £94,312,000 *Total Assets:* £107,725,000
Registered Office: Selhurst Park Stadium, Holmesdale Road, London, SE25 6PU
Activities: Activities of sport clubs
Parent: Palace Holdco UK Limited
Officers: Sean O'Loughlin, Secretary; David Scott Blitzer [1969] Director [American]; Stephen John Browett [1959] Director/Business Executive; Joshua Jordan Harris [1964] Director [American]; Jeremy John Hosking [1958] Director/Business Executive; Stephen Parish [1965] Director/Business Executive

Pall Mall 3 Limited
Incorporated: 3 September 2014
Net Worth: £65,720,056 *Total Assets:* £155,333,520
Registered Office: New Burlington House, 1075 Finchley Road, London, NW11 0PU
Activities: Other letting and operating of own or leased real estate
Parent: Pall Mall 2 Limited
Officers: Miriam Kraus [1942] Director; Zeev Meir Kraus [1980] Director

Pall Mall and Woodcote Park Clubhouses Limited
Incorporated: 31 May 1979 *Employees:* 580
Net Worth: £72,259,000 *Total Assets:* £125,341,000
Registered Office: Royal Automobile Club, 89-91 Pall Mall, London, SW1Y 5HS
Activities: Activities of other membership organisations n.e.c.
Officers: Miles William Ellis Wade, Secretary; Benjamin Piers Cussons [1966] Director, Wholesaler; Christopher Ellis Moyle [1946] Director/Retired; Miles William Ellis Wade [1958] Director/Chief Executive

Pall Mall Investments (London) Limited
Incorporated: 12 June 1985 *Employees:* 24
Net Worth: £110,131,280 *Total Assets:* £269,763,552
Registered Office: New Burlington House, 1075 Finchley Road, London, NW11 0PU
Activities: Other letting and operating of own or leased real estate
Major Shareholder: Mathias Kraus
Officers: Miriam Kraus, Secretary; Miriam Kraus [1942] Director; Zeev Meir Kraus [1980] Director

Palmbest Limited
Incorporated: 16 October 1990
Net Worth: £107,327,000 *Total Assets:* £147,404,000
Registered Office: 2 Abbey Road, Park Royal, London, NW10 7BW
Activities: Buying and selling of own real estate
Parent: Bestway UK Holdco Limited
Officers: Dawood Pervez, Secretary/Director/Solicitor; Zameer Mohammed Choudrey [1958] Director; Dawood Pervez [1975] Director/Solicitor; Rizwan Pervez [1968] Director [British/Pakistani]; Mohammed Younus Sheikh [1946] Director

Pam Acquisitionco Limited
Incorporated: 11 February 2008
Net Worth: £399,750,016 *Total Assets:* £892,049,024
Registered Office: 75B Verde, 10 Bressenden Place, London, SW1E 5DH
Activities: Retail sale in non-specialised stores with food, beverages or tobacco predominating
Parent: Pam Subco Limited
Officers: Clive Schlee, Secretary; Clive Edward Benedict Schlee [1959] Director

Pam Group Limited
Incorporated: 21 December 2007
Net Worth Deficit: £300,300,000 *Total Assets:* £531,600,000
Registered Office: 75B Verde, 10 Bressenden Place, London, SW1E 5DH
Activities: Activities of head offices
Parent: Jab (Acquisition) Ltd
Officers: Konrad Meyer, Secretary; Lambertus Johannes Hermanus Becht [1956] Director [Dutch]; Olivier Goudet [1964] Director/Business Executive [French]; Dr Gerd Peter Harf [1946] Director/Chairman [German]; Manuel Martinez [1969] Director; Konrad Meyer [1980] Director/Member [German]; Clive Edward Benedict Schlee [1959] Director

Pan African Resources PLC
Incorporated: 25 February 2000 *Employees:* 3,678
Net Worth: £115,703,744 *Total Assets:* £265,342,112
Registered Office: Suite 31, Second Floor, 107 Cheapside, London, EC2V 6DN
Activities: Other mining and quarrying n.e.c.
Officers: Hester Helena Hickey [1953] Director of Companies & Governance Consultant [South African]; Jacobus Albertus Johannes Loots [1978] Director/Chartered Accountant [South African]; Gideon Petrus Louw [1962] Financial Director [South African]; Thabo Mosololi [1969] Director [South African]; Rowan Murray Smith [1964] Director [South African]; Keith Cousens Spencer [1949] Mining Engineer Director [South African]

Pandora Jewellery UK Limited
Incorporated: 23 July 2008 *Employees:* 535
Net Worth: £91,168,000 *Total Assets:* £170,668,992
Registered Office: 33 George Street, London, W1U 3BH
Activities: Wholesale of watches and jewellery
Parent: Pandora A/S
Officers: Nicholas Golding, Secretary; David Allen [1969] Director/President of Pandora EMEA [Australian]; Anders Boyer [1970] Director/Chief Financial Officer [Danish]; Kirstin Mary de Klerk [1984] Finance Director [British/South African]; Peter Ring [1977] Director/Lawyer [Danish]; Kate Walsh [1981] Managing Director

Pangaea Funding 1 PLC
Incorporated: 5 June 2014
Net Worth: £36,519 *Total Assets:* £213,079,200
Registered Office: 35 Great St Helen's, London, EC3A 6AP
Activities: Financial intermediation not elsewhere classified
Parent: Intertrust Corporate Services Limited
Officers: Daniel Marc Richard Jaffe [1975] Director

Paragon Group Limited
Incorporated: 13 October 2004 *Employees:* 5,674
Net Worth: £79,600,560 *Total Assets:* £404,930,528
Registered Office: Lower Ground Floor, Park House, 16-18 Finsbury Circus, London, EC2M 7EB
Activities: Data processing, hosting and related activities
Shareholders: Investment (Paragon) Limited; Patrick James Crean
Officers: Richard Joseph Cahill, Secretary; Patrick James Crean [1963] Director [Irish]; Nelson Loane [1942] Director [Irish]; Laurent Thierry Salmon [1963] Finance Director [French]; Sean Aongus Shine [1963] Director/Chief Operating Officer [Irish]

Paramount British Pictures Limited
Incorporated: 19 April 1916
Net Worth: £27,088,000 *Total Assets:* £529,103,008
Registered Office: 17-29 Hawley Crescent, London, NW1 8TT
Activities: Motion picture production activities
Parent: Viacom Camden Lock Limited
Officers: Paul Dunthorne [1967] Director/Chief Operating Officer; Johnny Nareshdat Kanhai [1960] Director/Vice President [Dutch]

Paramount Pictures International Limited
Incorporated: 31 October 1997 *Employees:* 105
Net Worth: £529,472,992 *Total Assets:* £1,692,887,680
Registered Office: Building 5, Chiswick Park, 566 Chiswick High Road, London, W4 5YF
Activities: Other business support service activities n.e.c.
Parent: Viacom Interactive Limited
Officers: Lisa Elaine Kramer [1965] Director/Film Distribution Executive [American]; Charlie McAuley [1959] Director/Film Distribution Executive; Robert William Mosley [1967] Director/Human Resources; Brigit Rathouse [1968] Director/Lawyer; Cameron Saunders [1973] Director/Executive Vice President

Park Tower Investments Limited
Incorporated: 16 December 1992 *Employees:* 221
Net Worth: £195,665,296 *Total Assets:* £423,218,784
Registered Office: 5 New Street Square, London, EC4A 3TW
Activities: Financial intermediation not elsewhere classified
Major Shareholder: Mohammed Mahdi His Excellency Al Tajir
Officers: Amer Mohammed Mahdi Al Tajir [1961] Director [Emirati]; Khalid Mohamed Mahdi Al Tajir [1958] Director/Businessman [Emirati]; Mohamed Sadiq Al Tajir [1941] Director/Businessman [Bahraini]; Mohammed Mahdi Al Tajir [1931] Director/Businessman [Emirati]

Parkcare Homes (No.2) Limited
Incorporated: 18 May 2000 *Employees:* 2,145
Net Worth: £79,169,000 *Total Assets:* £350,968,000
Registered Office: Fifth Floor, 80 Hammersmith Road, London, W14 8UD
Activities: Other human health activities
Parent: Craegmoor Care (Holdings) Limited
Officers: David James Hall, Secretary; Nigel Myers [1966] Finance Director; Trevor Michael Torrington [1961] Director/Chief Executive

Partnership Assurance Group Limited
Incorporated: 26 February 2013
Previous: Partnership Assurance Group PLC
Net Worth: £658,401,984 *Total Assets:* £711,953,984
Registered Office: 5th Floor, 110 Bishopsgate, London, EC2N 4AY
Activities: Other activities auxiliary to insurance and pension funding
Parent: Just Group PLC
Officers: Simon Andrew O'Hara, Secretary; Paul Bishop [1954] Director; Ian Donald Cormack [1947] Corporate Director; Dr Christopher Shaw Gibson Smith [1945] Director/Chairman; David Louis Richardson [1972] Director/Chief Financial Officer [Irish]; Clare Spottiswoode [1953] Director; Paul James Turner [1971] Director

Partnership Group Holdings Limited
Incorporated: 27 May 2005
Net Worth: £179,640,992 *Total Assets:* £179,640,992
Registered Office: 5th Floor, 110 Bishopsgate, London, EC2N 4AY
Activities: Activities of head offices
Parent: Partnership Holdings Limited
Officers: Simon Andrew O'Hara, Secretary; Rodney Malcolm Cook [1957] Director/Chief Executive; David Louis Richardson [1972] Director/Deputy Group CEO and MD UK Corporate Business [Irish]

Partnership Holdings Limited
Incorporated: 4 June 2008
Net Worth: £315,001,984 *Total Assets:* £315,001,984
Registered Office: 5th Floor, 110 Bishopsgate, London, EC2N 4AY
Activities: Activities of head offices
Parent: Partnership Assurance Group Limited
Officers: Simon Andrew O'Hara, Secretary; Paul Bishop [1954] Director; Rodney Malcolm Cook [1957] Director/Chief Executive; David Louis Richardson [1972] Director/Chief Financial Officer [Irish]

Partnership Life Assurance Company Limited
Incorporated: 26 May 2005
Net Worth: £549,641,024 *Total Assets:* £8,944,087,040
Registered Office: 5th Floor, 110 Bishopsgate, London, EC2N 4AY
Activities: Life insurance
Parent: Partnership Group Holdings Limited
Officers: Simon Andrew O'Hara, Secretary; Paul Bishop [1954] Director; Rodney Malcolm Cook [1957] Director; Ian Donald Cormack [1947] Director; Michael John Deakin [1953] Director; Dr Christopher Shaw Gibson-Smith [1945] Director/Company Chairman; Andrew Stephen Melcher [1949] Director; Keith Nicholson [1949] Director; Nicholas Hugh Poyntz-Wright [1963] Director; David Louis Richardson [1972] Director/Chief Financial Officer [Irish]; Clare Spottiswoode [1953] Director; Paul James Turner [1971] Director

Partnerships in Care Investments 1 Limited
Incorporated: 14 September 2011
Net Worth Deficit: £39,441,000 *Total Assets:* £708,550,016
Registered Office: Fifth Floor, 80 Hammersmith Road, London, W14 8UD
Activities: Hospital activities
Parent: Partnerships in Care UK 2 Limited
Officers: David James Hall, Secretary; Nigel Myers [1966] Finance Director; Trevor Michael Torrington [1961] Director/Chief Executive

Partnerships in Care Limited
Incorporated: 21 June 1991 *Employees:* 3,758
Net Worth: £75,378,000 *Total Assets:* £112,737,000
Registered Office: Fifth Floor, 80 Hammersmith Road, London, W14 8UD
Activities: Hospital activities
Parent: Partnerships in Care Management Ltd
Officers: David James Hall, Secretary; Nigel Myers [1966] Finance Director; Trevor Michael Torrington [1961] Director/Chief Executive

Partnerships in Care Property 1 Limited
Incorporated: 24 March 2005
Net Worth Deficit: £310,841,984 *Total Assets:* £449,929,984
Registered Office: Fifth Floor, 80 Hammersmith Road, London, W14 8UD
Activities: Other business support service activities n.e.c.
Parent: Partnerships in Care Property Holding Company Ltd
Officers: David James Hall, Secretary; Nigel Myers [1966] Finance Director; Trevor Michael Torrington [1961] Director/Chief Executive

Parvus Asset Management Limited
Incorporated: 2 April 2004 *Employees:* 5
Net Worth: £192,884,400 *Total Assets:* £218,240,144
Registered Office: 7 Clifford Street, London, W1S 2FT
Activities: Security and commodity contracts dealing activities
Major Shareholder: Edoardo Mercadante
Officers: Mads Eg Gensmann, Secretary; Edoardo Mercadante [1967] Director/Investment Manager [Italian]; Rahul Nath Moodgal [1971] Director/Investor Relations

Passaic Issuer Holdco Limited
Incorporated: 12 May 2010
Net Worth: £806,107 *Total Assets:* £1,090,515,712
Registered Office: 35 Great St Helen's, London, EC3A 6AP
Activities: Non-trading company
Parent: Intertrust Corporate Services Limited
Officers: Daniel Marc Richard Jaffe [1975] Director

Patina Rail LLP
Incorporated: 20 February 2015
Net Worth: £535,121,856 *Total Assets:* £535,208,320
Registered Office: 6th Floor, 65 Gresham Street, London, EC2V 7NQ

Patriot Topco Limited
Incorporated: 25 January 2017 *Employees:* 119
Net Worth Deficit: £5,177,015 *Total Assets:* £133,635,600
Registered Office: 3rd Floor, Audrey House, 16-20 Ely Place, London, EC1N 6SN
Activities: Activities of other holding companies n.e.c.
Shareholders: Frances Teresa Windheuser Duthie McLeod; Tobias John Windheuser Duthie; Gregory James Mason
Officers: Tobias John Windheuser Duthie [1968] Director/Forensic and Legal Advice; Philip Allan Gore-Randall [1952] Director; Mark Murray Ligertwood [1972] Director; Gregory Malkin Mason [1970] Director/Computer Technician [American]; Frances Teresa Windheuser Duthie McLeod [1965] Director/Forensic and Legal Advice

Paysafe Financial Services Limited
Incorporated: 5 July 2002 *Employees:* 37
Previous: Optimal Payments Limited
Net Worth: £46,084,564 *Total Assets:* £442,009,120
Registered Office: Floor 27, 25 Canada Square, London, E14 5LQ
Activities: Activities auxiliary to financial intermediation n.e.c.
Parent: Paysafe Group Limited
Officers: Elaine Quine, Secretary; Mohammed Fayyaz Ansari [1970] Director/Financial Controller; Miroslav Bojilov [1974] Director/General Manager [Bulgarian]; Daniel Jay Chazonoff [1963] Director/Chief Operating Officer [Canadian]; Andrea Maria Dunlop [1970] Director/Head of Innovation; Mark Aidan Jeffrey [1958] Director; Lorenzo Pellegrino [1974] Director [Italian]; Elliott Mark Wiseman [1974] Director/Solicitor

Paysafe Holdings UK Limited
Incorporated: 22 May 1996 *Employees:* 15
Previous: Netinvest Limited
Net Worth: £499,817,024 *Total Assets:* £1,631,395,328
Registered Office: Floor 27, 25 Canada Square, London, E14 5LQ
Activities: Other business support service activities n.e.c.
Parent: Paysafe Group Limited
Officers: Paul James Brooking [1976] Director/Chartered Accountant; Elliott Mark Wiseman [1974] Director/Solicitor

Paysafe Processing Limited
Incorporated: 22 May 1996 *Employees:* 41
Previous: Netbanx Limited
Net Worth: £16,064,417 *Total Assets:* £168,041,024
Registered Office: Floor 27, Canada Square, London, E14 5LQ
Activities: Other business support service activities n.e.c.
Parent: Paysafe Holdings UK Limited
Officers: Paul James Brooking [1976] Director/Chartered Accountant; Andrea Maria Dunlop [1970] Director/Head of Innovation; Shaun Lavelle [1973] Director; Elliott Mark Wiseman [1974] Director/Solicitor

PCF Group PLC
Incorporated: 18 October 1993 *Employees:* 67
Previous: Private & Commercial Finance Group PLC
Net Worth: £42,551,000 *Total Assets:* £286,470,016
Registered Office: Pinners Hall, 105-108 Old Broad Street, London, EC2N 1ER
Activities: Activities of financial services holding companies
Officers: Robert John Murray, Secretary; Mark Finlay Brown [1963] Director/Stockbroker; David Richard Bull [1971] Finance Director; Timothy Alan Franklin [1961] Director; Christine Anne Higgins [1959] Director; Scott David Maybury [1961] Director/Accountant [Australian]; David John Morgan [1957] Director/Banker; Robert John Murray [1960] Director/Banker; David Titmuss [1963] Director

PCL Asset Trustee Limited
Incorporated: 11 July 2016
Net Worth: £1,000 *Total Assets:* £1,048,204,992
Registered Office: Third Floor, c/o Wilmington Trust SP Services (London) Limited, 1 King's Arms Yard, London, EC2R 7AF
Activities: Other business support service activities n.e.c.
Parent: Wilmington Trust SP Services (London) Limited
Officers: Eileen Marie Hughes [1966] Director/Head of Structured Products UK [American]; Daniel Jonathan Wynne [1970] Director

PCL Funding I Limited
Incorporated: 5 May 2011
Net Worth: £2,000 *Total Assets:* £496,924,992
Registered Office: Third Floor, 1 King's Arms Yard, London, EC2R 7AF
Activities: Other business support service activities n.e.c.
Parent: Wilmington Trust SP Services (London) Limited
Officers: Daniel Jonathan Wynne [1970] Director

PE Pioneer Holding II Limited
Incorporated: 12 September 2017 *Employees:* 1,028
Net Worth: £436,070,016 *Total Assets:* £755,217,984
Registered Office: 100 New Bridge Street, London, EC4V 6JA
Activities: Activities of other holding companies n.e.c.
Officers: Eva Monica Kalawski, Secretary; Ian Michael Stuart Downie [1949] Director/Executive; Eva Monica Kalawski [1955] Director/Executive [American]; Mary Ann Sigler [1954] Director/Executive [American]

PE QIQ Holding Limited
Incorporated: 14 July 2017 *Employees:* 1,510
Net Worth Deficit: £20,904,700 *Total Assets:* £275,857,536
Registered Office: 100 New Bridge Street, London, EC4V 6JA
Activities: Activities of other holding companies n.e.c.
Officers: Eva Monica Kalawski, Secretary; Ian Michael Stuart Downie [1949] Director/Executive; Eva Monica Kalawski [1955] Director/Executive [American]; Mary Ann Sigler [1954] Director/Executive [American]

Peabody Capital No 2 PLC
Incorporated: 19 November 2013
Net Worth: £50,000 *Total Assets:* £364,937,984
Registered Office: Minster Court, 45 Westminster Bridge Road, London, SE1 7JB
Activities: Activities of venture and development capital companies
Officers: Sarah Cameron, Secretary; Susan Laura Hickey [1963] Director; The Lord Robert Walter Kerslake [1955] Director/Member of The House of Lords; Ian Peters [1958] Director; Brendan Patrick Sarsfield [1960] Director/Chief Executive

Peabody Capital PLC
Incorporated: 17 January 2011
Net Worth: £50,000 *Total Assets:* £207,799,008
Registered Office: Minster Court, 45 Westminster Bridge Road, London, SE1 7JB
Activities: Financial intermediation not elsewhere classified
Officers: Sarah Cameron, Secretary; Susan Laura Hickey [1963] Executive Director Finance [New Zealander]; The Lord Robert Walter Kerslake [1955] Director/Member of House of Lords; Ian Peters [1958] Director; Brendan Patrick Sarsfield [1960] Director/Chief Executive

Pearl Group Holdings (No. 1) Limited
Incorporated: 10 March 1998
Net Worth: £3,083,800,064 *Total Assets:* £3,104,300,032
Registered Office: Juxon House, 100 St Pauls Churchyard, London, EC4M 8BU
Activities: Other business support service activities n.e.c.
Parent: Impala Holdings Limited
Officers: James McConville [1956] Finance Director; Rakesh Kishore Thakrar [1975] Director/Financial Controller; Simon Charles True [1968] Director/Actuary

Pearl Income Holdings UK Limited
Incorporated: 15 November 2017 *Employees:* 53
Net Worth Deficit: £19,141,208 *Total Assets:* £2,429,190,912
Registered Office: 6th Floor, 99 Bishopsgate, London, EC2M 3XD
Activities: Activities of other holding companies n.e.c.
Officers: Haidee Charise Klein [1980] Director

Pearl Income Investments II UK Limited
Incorporated: 15 November 2017 *Employees:* 1
Net Worth Deficit: £1,263,861 *Total Assets:* £180,432,720
Registered Office: 6th Floor, 99 Bishopsgate, London, EC2M 3XD
Activities: Activities of other holding companies n.e.c.
Officers: Brian Patrick McEnery [1984] Director [Irish]

Pearl Income Investments UK Limited
Incorporated: 29 September 2017 *Employees:* 1
Net Worth Deficit: £11,290,741 *Total Assets:* £1,557,207,808
Registered Office: 6th Floor, 99 Bishopsgate, London, EC2M 3XD
Activities: Activities of other holding companies n.e.c.
Officers: Haidee Charise Klein [1980] Director

William Pears Group Investments Limited
Incorporated: 9 April 2013 *Employees:* 3
Net Worth: £382,984,384 *Total Assets:* £806,517,376
Registered Office: Ground Floor, 30 City Road, London, EC1Y 2AB
Activities: Activities of other holding companies n.e.c.
Parent: William Pears Group Limited
Officers: William Frederick Bennett, Secretary; David Alan Pears [1968] Director; Mark Andrew Pears [1962] Director; Sir Trevor Steven Pears [1964] Director

William Pears Group Limited
Incorporated: 5 April 2013 *Employees:* 134
Net Worth: £1,009,988,992 *Total Assets:* £1,404,701,056
Registered Office: Ground Floor, 30 City Road, London, EC1Y 2AB
Activities: Activities of other holding companies n.e.c.
Shareholders: Barry Michael Howard Shaw; Mark Andrew Pears; Michael Terence Baker; The Bank of N T Butterfield & Son Limited
Officers: William Frederick Bennett, Secretary; David Alan Pears [1968] Director; Mark Andrew Pears [1962] Director; Sir Trevor Steven Pears [1964] Director

William Pears Group of Companies Limited (The)
Incorporated: 27 October 1955 *Employees:* 46
Net Worth: £8,353,401 *Total Assets:* £466,644,384
Registered Office: Ground Floor, 30 City Road, London, EC1Y 2AB
Activities: Activities of head offices
Parent: William Pears Group Investments Limited
Officers: William Frederick Bennett, Secretary; David Alan Pears, Secretary/Director; David Alan Pears [1968] Director; Mark Andrew Pears [1962] Director; Sir Trevor Steven Pears [1964] Director

Pearson Australia Finance Unlimited
Incorporated: 29 September 2005
Net Worth: £101,326,000 *Total Assets:* £101,672,000
Registered Office: 80 Strand, London, WC2R 0RL
Activities: Activities of other holding companies n.e.c.
Parent: Pearson Strand Finance Limited
Officers: Stephen Andrew Jones, Secretary; Natalie Jane White, Secretary; Sally Kate Miranda Johnson [1973] Director; James Daniel Marshall [1960] Director/Chartered Accountant; Andrew John Midgley [1961] Director/Accountant

Pearson Dollar Finance PLC
Incorporated: 23 April 2004
Net Worth: £1,369,445,632 *Total Assets:* £1,375,620,352
Registered Office: 80 Strand, London, WC2R 0RL
Activities: Activities of other holding companies n.e.c.
Parent: Pearson PLC
Officers: Stephen Andrew Jones, Secretary; Natalie Jane White, Secretary; Sally Kate Miranda Johnson [1973] Director; James John Tod Kelly [1980] Director; Andrew John Midgley [1961] Director/Accountant

Pearson Dollar Finance Two Limited
Incorporated: 18 February 2008
Previous: Pearson Dollar Finance Two PLC
Net Worth: £2,745,728,256 *Total Assets:* £5,098,252,800
Registered Office: 80 Strand, London, WC2R 0RL
Activities: Activities of other holding companies n.e.c.
Parent: Pearson Overseas Holdings Limited
Officers: Stephen Andrew Jones, Secretary; Natalie Jane White, Secretary; Sally Kate Miranda Johnson [1973] Director; James John Tod Kelly [1980] Director; Andrew John Midgley [1961] Director/Accountant

Pearson Education Holdings Limited
Incorporated: 2 January 1926
Net Worth: £822,419,968 *Total Assets:* £822,945,984
Registered Office: 80 Strand, London, WC2R 0RL
Activities: Activities of head offices
Parent: Pearson PLC
Officers: Natalie Jane White, Secretary; Graeme Stuart Baldwin [1975] Director/Solicitor; Suzanne Margaret Brennan [1969] Director; Donna Elizabeth Houston [1965] Director/Chartered Accountant

Pearson Education Investments Limited
Incorporated: 14 March 2013
Net Worth: £636,475,712 *Total Assets:* £3,297,648,384
Registered Office: 80 Strand, London, WC2R 0RL
Activities: Activities of other holding companies n.e.c.
Parent: Pearson Overseas Holdings Limited
Officers: Stephen Jones, Secretary; Natalie White, Secretary; Sally Kate Miranda Johnson [1973] Director; James Daniel Marshall [1960] Director/Chartered Accountant; Andrew John Midgley [1961] Director/Accountant

Pearson Education Limited
Incorporated: 3 March 1966 *Employees:* 2,114
Net Worth: £195,815,008 *Total Assets:* £644,780,992
Registered Office: 80 Strand, London, WC2R 0RL
Activities: Book publishing
Parent: Pearson Education Holdings Limited
Officers: Natalie Jane White, Secretary; Suzanne Margaret Brennan [1969] Director; Kenneth Roderick Bristow [1958] Director/President UK and Core; Sally Ann Sheila Dicketts [1955] Director/Chief Executive - Activate Learning; Sharon Ellen Hague [1970] Qualification Development and Assessment Director; John Laramy [1971] Director; Sir David Melville [1944] Director/University Vice Chancellor; Richard Ralph Price [1944] Director/Retired; Cindy Purnamattie Rampersaud [1966] Director; Derek James Richardson [1974] Director; Valerie Malvia May Todd [1962] Director; Dr Margaret Melrose Wilson [1957] Director/Headteacher

Pearson Funding Five PLC
Incorporated: 27 February 2013
Net Worth: £423,944,992 *Total Assets:* £1,407,681,024
Registered Office: 80 Strand, London, WC2R 0RL
Activities: Activities of other holding companies n.e.c.
Parent: Pearson PLC
Officers: Stephen Andrew Jones, Secretary; Natalie White, Secretary; Sally Kate Miranda Johnson [1973] Director; James John Tod Kelly [1980] Director; Andrew John Midgley [1961] Director

Pearson Funding Four PLC
Incorporated: 29 February 2012
Net Worth: £118,617,000 *Total Assets:* £206,896,000
Registered Office: 80 Strand, London, WC2R 0RL
Activities: Activities of other holding companies n.e.c.
Parent: Pearson PLC
Officers: Stephen Andrew Jones, Secretary; Natalie Jane White, Secretary; Sally Kate Miranda Johnson [1973] Director; James John Tod Kelly [1980] Director; Andrew John Midgley [1961] Director

Pearson International Finance Limited
Incorporated: 26 April 1990
Net Worth: £162,056,000 *Total Assets:* £162,056,000
Registered Office: 80 Strand, London, WC2R 0RL
Activities: Activities of other holding companies n.e.c.
Parent: Pearson PLC
Officers: Stephen Andrew Jones, Secretary; Natalie Jane White, Secretary; Sally Kate Miranda Johnson [1973] Director; James Daniel Marshall [1960] Director/Chartered Accountant; Andrew John Midgley [1961] Director/Accountant

Pearson Loan Finance Unlimited
Incorporated: 3 June 2004
Net Worth: £697,129,024 *Total Assets:* £697,345,984
Registered Office: 80 Strand, London, WC2R 0RL
Activities: Activities of other holding companies n.e.c.
Parent: Pearson Overseas Holdings Limited
Officers: Stephen Andrew Jones, Secretary; Natalie Jane White, Secretary; Sally Kate Miranda Johnson [1973] Director; James Daniel Marshall [1960] Director/Chartered Accountant; Andrew John Midgley [1961] Director/Accountant

Pearson Management Services Limited
Incorporated: 30 December 1907 *Employees:* 476
Net Worth Deficit: £53,913,000 *Total Assets:* £502,767,008
Registered Office: 80 Strand, London, WC2R 0RL
Activities: Activities of other holding companies n.e.c.
Parent: Pearson PLC
Officers: Stephen Andrew Jones, Secretary; Natalie Jane White, Secretary; Sally Kate Miranda Johnson [1973] Director; Stephen Andrew Jones [1966] Director/Company Secretary; Coram Williams [1974] Finance Director

Pearson Overseas Holdings Limited
Incorporated: 1 November 1916
Net Worth: £1,803,476,992 *Total Assets:* £4,661,514,240
Registered Office: 80 Strand, London, WC2R 0RL
Activities: Activities of other holding companies n.e.c.
Parent: Pearson PLC
Officers: Stephen Andrew Jones, Secretary; Natalie Jane White, Secretary; Sally Kate Miranda Johnson [1973] Director; James Daniel Marshall [1960] Director/Chartered Accountant; Andrew John Midgley [1961] Director/Accountant

Pearson PLC
Incorporated: 12 August 1897 *Employees:* 30,339
Net Worth: £4,012,999,936 *Total Assets:* £7,888,000,000
Registered Office: 80 Strand, London, WC2R 0RL
Activities: Other publishing activities
Officers: Stephen Andrew Jones, Secretary; Elizabeth Pauline Lucy Corley [1956] Director/Chief Executive Officer; Dr Vivienne Cox [1959] Chairman & Non-Executive Director; John Joseph Fallon [1962] Director; Salim Joshua Lewis [1962] Director/Financier [American]; Linda Koch Lorimer [1952] Director/Administrator, Higher Education [American]; Michael Mark Lynton [1960] Director [American]; Timothy Score [1960] Director; Sidney Taurel [1949] Director [American]; Lincoln Anthony Wallen [1960] Director; Coram Williams [1974] Finance Director

Pearson PRH Holdings Limited
Incorporated: 7 June 2013
Net Worth: £702,483,968 *Total Assets:* £703,046,016
Registered Office: 80 Strand, London, WC2R 0RL
Activities: Activities of other holding companies n.e.c.
Parent: Pearson Overseas Holdings Limited
Officers: Stephen Jones, Secretary; Natalie White, Secretary; Sally Kate Miranda Johnson [1973] Director; Soren Kroon [1974] Director [Danish]; James Daniel Marshall [1960] Director/Chartered Accountant; Andrew John Midgley [1961] Director/Accountant

Pearson Services Limited
Incorporated: 29 November 1977
Net Worth: £474,996,992 *Total Assets:* £578,584,000
Registered Office: 80 Strand, London, WC2R 0RL
Activities: Activities of other holding companies n.e.c.
Parent: Pearson PLC
Officers: Stephen Andrew Jones, Secretary; Natalie Jane White, Secretary; Andrew John Midgley [1961] Director/Accountant; Coram Williams [1974] Finance Director

Pearson Shared Services Limited
Incorporated: 20 December 2002 *Employees:* 316
Net Worth: £45,740,000 *Total Assets:* £190,968,000
Registered Office: 80 Strand, London, WC2R 0RL
Activities: Other business support service activities n.e.c.
Parent: Pearson PLC
Officers: Stephen Andrew Jones, Secretary; Natalie Jane White, Secretary; Rachel Maria Coulson [1975] Director/Finance Professional; Donna Elizabeth Houston [1965] Director/Chartered Accountant; Andrew Siclari [1963] Finance Director [American]; Benjamin John Stagg [1975] Director/Accountant

Peel Hunt LLP
Incorporated: 11 August 2010 *Employees:* 201
Net Worth: £42,140,000 *Total Assets:* £329,436,000
Registered Office: Moor House, 120 London Wall, London, EC2Y 5ET
Officers: Sunil Dhall [1974] Member; Steven Harvey Fine [1966] Member; Ross Allister [1985] LLP Member; Caroline Andrew [1969] LLP Member; Toma Arpino [1985] LLP Member; Maria de Fatima Badini [1963] LLP Member; Hayden Ballard [1984] LLP Member; Christopher Bamberry [1970] LLP Member; Jonathan Banks [1977] LLP Member; Nicholas Batram [1968] LLP Member; Charles James Batten [1958] LLP Member; Thomas Scott Beattie [1968] LLP Member; William Beausire [1962] LLP Member; Michael Bell [1980] LLP Member; Indranil Bhattacharyya [1976] LLP Member; Deborah Louise Brewster [1975] LLP Member; James Martin Britton [1956] LLP Member; Andrew Buchanan [1971] LLP Member; James Carswell [1986] LLP Member; Alexander Corfield Key Carter [1971] LLP Member; Darren Carter [1966] LLP Member; Henry Carver [1980] LLP Member; Andrew Charles Chapman [1961] LLP Member; Jeremy Clement [1960] LLP Member; Dominic Convey [1976] LLP Member; James Cooper [1975] LLP Member; Richard Crichton [1977] LLP Member; Samuel Croft [1986] LLP Member; Nicholas Cullen [1983] LLP Member; David Curran [1981] LLP Member; Andreas Degroot-Vanembden [1968] LLP Member; Christian Dench [1972] LLP Member; Stuart Duncan [1973] LLP Member; Ian Dunton [1970] LLP Member; Robert Ellis [1965] LLP Member; Andrew Ells [1985] LLP Member; Dean Eynon [1969] LLP Member; Stuart Michael Galvin [1961] LLP Member; Dominic Gauld [1990] LLP Member; Jon Gerty [1976] LLP Member; John Gilbert [1982] LLP Member; Christopher Golden [1979] LLP Member; Colin Goodey [1969] LLP Member; Carl Andrew Gough [1966] LLP Member; Charles Gerard Peirs Hall [1968] LLP Member; Stephen Hall [1962] LLP Member; Ben Hammond [1984] LLP Member; Adrian John Haxby [1958] LLP Member; Simon Hayes [1970] LLP Member; Lisa Hennessy [1977] LLP Member; James Hipkiss [1978] LLP Member; Christopher Holmes [1977] LLP Member; Matthew Honour [1974] LLP Member; Edward Robeson Horton [1970] LLP Member; Capel Robert Powell Irwin [1967] LLP Member; Harold David Douglas Jack [1966] LLP Member; Gavin Jago [1977] LLP Member; Rory James-Duff [1978] LLP Member; Damindu Vijayapani Jayaweera [1978] LLP Member; Ivor Jones [1964] LLP Member; Justin Charles Jones [1966] LLP Member; Adam Kellard [1982] LLP Member; David Kent [1967] LLP Member; Patrick George Prior King [1965] LLP Member; David Kininmonth [1961] LLP Member; Edward Knight [1976] LLP Member; Stephen David Knight [1972] LLP Member; Roger Mark Uvedale Lambert [1959] LLP Member; Anthony Leatham [1977] LLP Member; Clyde Lewis [1969] LLP Member; Hywel Llewellyn [1978] LLP Member; Peter John Mallin-Jones [1974] LLP Member; Jose Martinez [1965] LLP Member; John Ronald Maxwell MacDonald [1965] LLP Member; Kurt John Mayer [1960] LLP Member; Sean McPherson [1988] LLP Member; Aaqib Rafiq Mirza [1973] LLP Member; Alkesh Mistry [1984] LLP Member; Iain Fraser Morgan [1971] LLP Member; Malcolm Morgan [1964] LLP Member; Nazya Nawaz [1981] LLP Member; Harry Nicholas [1976] LLP Member; Michael Nicholson [1983] LLP Member; Andrew Nussey [1970] LLP Member; Nick Pettman [1974] LLP Member; Henry Philips [1963] LLP Member; Jonathan Pritchard [1971] LLP Member; Alastair Frame Rae [1970] LLP Member; Matthew Reali [1969] LLP Member; Will Regis [1968] LLP Member; Werner Riding [1979] LLP Member; Todd Row [1986] LLP Member; Dominic Rutter [1983] LLP Member; Matthew Saperia [1979] LLP Member; Andrew Shepherd-Barron [1959] LLP Member; George Albert Luke Simpson [1974] LLP Member; Graham Myles Smith [1979] LLP Member; James Steel [1971] LLP Member; John Stevenson [1971] LLP Member; Karen Stevenson [1960] LLP Member

Peer Group PLC
Incorporated: 25 June 1976 *Employees:* 24
Net Worth: £113,598,912 *Total Assets:* £221,015,984
Registered Office: The Peer Suite, The Hop Exchange, 24 Southwark Street, London, SE1 1TY
Activities: Other letting and operating of own or leased real estate
Shareholders: Susan Alice Birrane; Amanda Phyllis Birrane; Bridget Kathleen Birrane; Brendan Murphy
Officers: Michael David Breeze, Secretary; Lis Birrane [1957] Property Director; Susan Alice Birrane [1939] Director; Amanda Phylis Birrane-Rule [1964] Marketing Director; Michael David Breeze [1952] Director/Solicitor; Howard James Dawson [1960] Director/Chartered Surveyor; Jonathan Simon Dean [1965] Property Director

Pelham Capital Investments Ltd
Incorporated: 23 December 2010 *Employees:* 3
Net Worth: £426,151,168 *Total Assets:* £512,441,696
Registered Office: 9th Floor, 25 Smithson Plaza, St James's Street, London, SW1A 1HA
Activities: Fund management activities
Major Shareholder: Ross James Turner
Officers: Hamant Lad, Secretary; Ross James Turner [1977] Director/Fund Manager

Pelican Point Power Limited
Incorporated: 3 March 1994 *Employees:* 28
Net Worth: £111,415,848 *Total Assets:* £284,506,816
Registered Office: Level 20, 25 Canada Square, London, E14 5LQ
Activities: Activities of head offices
Parent: International Power Australia Funding (2)
Officers: Sarah Jane Gregory, Secretary; Wayne Gregory Kevern, Secretary; Lawrence Kim, Secretary; Augustin Marie Luc Honorat [1977] Director/Chief Executive Officer [French]; Masao Omura [1959] Director [Japanese]

Penarth Master Issuer PLC
Incorporated: 10 June 2008
Net Worth Deficit: £22,000 *Total Assets:* £4,092,088,064
Registered Office: 35 Great St Helen's, London, EC3A 6AP
Activities: Financial intermediation not elsewhere classified
Shareholder: Intertrust Nominees Limited
Officers: Paivi Helena Whitaker [1963] Director [Finnish]

Pendal UK Limited
Incorporated: 15 June 2011
Previous: BTIM UK Limited
Net Worth: £170,347,008 *Total Assets:* £211,656,992
Registered Office: Level 3, 1 St James's Market, London, SW1Y 4AH
Activities: Activities of financial services holding companies
Parent: Pendal Group Limited
Officers: Joanne Marjorie Hawkins, Secretary; Mark Purnell, Secretary; Emilio Gonzalez [1964] Director [Australian]; Cameron Williamson [1970] Director [Australian]

Penguin Books Limited
Incorporated: 15 October 1965 *Employees:* 535
Net Worth: £120,545,000 *Total Assets:* £214,134,000
Registered Office: 20 Vauxhall Bridge Road, London, SW1V 2SA
Activities: Book publishing
Parent: Penguin Random House Limited
Officers: Sinead Mary Martin, Secretary; Markus Franz-Joseph Dohle [1968] Director/Chief Executive Officer [German]; Mark William Gardiner [1961] Finance Director; Robert Angus Waddington [1970] Sales Director; Thomas Daryl Weldon [1963] Director/Publisher

Penguin Random House Limited
Incorporated: 5 September 1962
Net Worth: £432,064,992 *Total Assets:* £960,153,984
Registered Office: 80 Strand, London, WC2R 0RL
Activities: Book publishing
Parent: Bertelsmann UK Limited
Officers: Sinead Mary Martin, Secretary; Markus Franz-Joseph Dohle [1968] Director/Chief Executive Officer [German]; John Joseph Fallon [1962] Director/Publisher; Dr Thomas Andreas Gotz [1971] Director/General Counsel [German]; Bernd Hirsch [1970] Finance Director [German]; James Johnston [1963] Finance Director [American]; Thomas Hermann Rabe [1965] Director/Chief Executive Officer [German]; Gail Rebuck [1952] Director/Publisher; Coram Williams [1974] Director/Chief Financial Officer

Pension Insurance Corporation Group Limited
Incorporated: 19 August 2015 *Employees:* 169
Net Worth: £2,083,000,064 *Total Assets:* £37,405,999,104
Registered Office: 14 Cornhill, London, EC3V 3ND
Activities: Other activities auxiliary to insurance and pension funding
Shareholder: Reinet Investments S.C.A.
Officers: Louise Jane Inward, Secretary; Jonathan Robert Aisbitt [1957] Director; Tracy Marie Blackwell [1967] Director [Irish]; Stuart King [1959] Director; Arno Kitts [1963] Director; Josua Malherbe [1955] Director/Businessman [South African/Australian]; Roger Michael James Marshall [1948] Director; Jerome Mourgue D'Algue [1970] Director [French]; Peter William James Rutland [1979] Director; Thomas Mark Stephen [1957] Director/Chartered Accountant; Frederik Wilhelm Van Zyl [1965] Director/Actuary [South African]

Pension Insurance Corporation PLC
Incorporated: 13 February 2006 *Employees:* 14
Net Worth: £2,076,000,000 *Total Assets:* £37,387,001,856
Registered Office: 14 Cornhill, London, EC3V 3ND
Activities: Other activities auxiliary to insurance and pension funding
Parent: Pension Holding Company (UK) 3 Limited
Officers: Louise Inward, Secretary; Jonathan Robert Aisbitt [1957] Director; Tracy Marie Blackwell [1967] Director [Irish]; Stuart King [1959] Director; Arno Kitts [1963] Director; Roger Michael James Marshall [1948] Director; Eloy Urbain Paul Ghislain Michotte [1948] Director [Belgian]; Jerome Mourgue D'Algue [1970] Director [French]; Peter William James Rutland [1979] Director; Stephen John Sarjant [1960] Director; Robert Peter Sewell [1964] Finance Director; Thomas Mark Stephen [1957] Director/Chartered Accountant; Frederik Wilhelm Van Zyl [1965] Director/Actuary [South African]

Pentland Group PLC
Incorporated: 27 February 1964 *Employees:* 32,290
Net Worth: £915,200,000 *Total Assets:* £2,229,199,872
Registered Office: 8 Manchester Square, London, W1U 3PH
Activities: Activities of head offices
Shareholder: Robert Stephen Rubin
Officers: Timothy Edward Cullen, Secretary; Timothy John Hockings [1962] Director/Accountant; John Dennis Morgan [1953] Director; Alison Jayne Mosheim [1967] Director; Barry Allan Mosheim [1967] Director; Andrew Keith Rubin [1965] Director/Corporate Executive; Angela Sophia Rubin [1937] Director; Carolyn Louise Rubin [1960] Director; Robert Stephen Rubin OBE [1937] Director/Company Chairman

Pepsico Holdings
Incorporated: 9 September 1980 *Employees:* 4
Net Worth: £422,095,008 *Total Assets:* £479,164,992
Registered Office: Building 4, Chiswick Park, 566 Chiswick High Road, London, W4 5YE
Activities: Other service activities n.e.c.
Parent: Pepsico Inc
Officers: Andrew John MacLeod, Secretary; Joanne Kerry Averiss [1963] Director/VP Law; Victoria Elizabeth Evans [1970] Director/Legal VP; Andrew John MacLeod [1962] Director/Solicitor; Claire Ellen Stone [1969] Finance Director

Pepsico International Limited
Incorporated: 9 October 1980 *Employees:* 693
Net Worth: £48,018,000 *Total Assets:* £124,306,000
Registered Office: Building 4, Chiswick Park, 566 Chiswick High Road, London, W4 5YE
Activities: Other service activities n.e.c.
Parent: Walkers Snacks Limited
Officers: Andrew John MacLeod, Secretary; Joanne Kerry Averiss [1963] Director/VP Law; Andrew John MacLeod [1962] Director/Solicitor; Claire Ellen Stone [1969] Finance Director; Andrew Williams [1960] Director/General Manager

Percy Village Limited
Incorporated: 13 March 2002
Net Worth: £73,111,992 *Total Assets:* £111,998,152
Registered Office: Floor 6, Quadrant House, 4 Thomas More Square, London, E1W 1YW
Activities: Development of building projects
Parent: Structadene (LBG) Properties Limited
Officers: Michael Robert Goldberger, Secretary/Director; Michael Robert Goldberger [1956] Director; David Alan Pearlman [1945] Director; Howard Alan Pearlman [1975] Director/Property Management

Perenco CUU Long Limited
Incorporated: 22 April 2003 *Employees:* 37
Net Worth: £200,233,072 *Total Assets:* £323,560,544
Registered Office: 8 Hanover Square, London, W1S 1HQ
Activities: Extraction of natural gas
Parent: Perenco Overseas Holdings Limited
Officers: Averil Eager, Secretary; Gilles Marie Philippe D'Argouges [1981] Director/General Manager [French]; Averil Eager [1959] Director/Secretary [Irish]; Jonathan Brian Parr [1971] Director/Lawyer; Timothy Mark Sandford [1976] Director/Lawyer

Perenco Oil and Gas Colombia Limited
Incorporated: 7 February 1984 *Employees:* 77
Net Worth: £178,089,056 *Total Assets:* £207,525,376
Registered Office: 8 Hanover Square, London, W1S 1HQ
Activities: Other business support service activities n.e.c.
Officers: Averil Eager, Secretary; Emmanuel Marie Patrick Colombel [1973] Director/Accountant [French]; Averil Eager [1959] Director/Secretary [Irish]; Jonathan Brian Parr [1971] Director/Solicitor

Perenco Overseas Holdings Limited
Incorporated: 4 February 2011 *Employees:* 37
Net Worth: £526,782,944 *Total Assets:* £988,140,736
Registered Office: 8 Hanover Square, London, W1S 1HQ
Activities: Activities of head offices
Officers: Timothy Mark Sandford, Secretary; Nicholas James Fallows [1967] Director/Deputy CFO; Timothy Mark Sandford [1976] Director/Solicitor

Perenco Rang Dong Limited
Incorporated: 19 February 1999
Net Worth: £120,350,384 *Total Assets:* £183,365,792
Registered Office: 8 Hanover Square, London, W1S 1HQ
Activities: Extraction of crude petroleum
Parent: Perenco Overseas Holdings Limited
Officers: Averil Eager, Secretary; Gilles Marie Philippe D'Argouges [1981] Director/General Manager [French]; Averil Eager [1959] Director/Secretary [Irish]; Jonathan Brian Parr [1971] Director/Lawyer; Timothy Mark Sandford [1976] Director/Lawyer

Perenco UK Limited
Incorporated: 30 January 2003 *Employees:* 757
Net Worth: £23,375,000 *Total Assets:* £1,670,051,968
Registered Office: 8 Hanover Square, London, W1S 1HQ
Activities: Activities of head offices
Officers: Jonathan Day, Secretary; Emmanuel Marie Patrick Colombel [1973] Director/Chief Financial Officer [French]; Laurent Combe [1968] Director/Engineer [French]; Franck Roland Michel Dy [1966] Director/Operations Manager [French]; Mark Hughes [1991] Director/Instrument Technician; Brian James [1957] Director/General Manager; Arnaud Loic Marie Le Blanc [1972] Director/Finance Manager [French]; Jonathan Brian Parr [1971] Director/Lawyer; Michael Richardson [1961] Director/Corporate QHSE Manager

Performing Right Society,Limited
Incorporated: 6 March 1914 *Employees:* 632
Net Worth Deficit: £68,406,000 *Total Assets:* £385,148,000
Registered Office: 2 Pancras Square, London, N1C 4AG
Activities: Artistic creation
Officers: Deborah Ann Stones, Secretary; Jacqueline Gay Alway [1966] Director; Dr Simon John Anderson [1967] Director; Robert John Ashcroft [1956] Director; Barry Ian Blue [1950] Director/Songwriter; Charles William Booth [1957] Director/Publisher; Christopher Mark Butler [1963] Director; Simon Darlow [1960] Director/Composer; Stephen James Davidson [1955] Director; James Paxton McMillan Duguid [1974] Director/Songwriter and Musician; Nigel Robert Elderton [1956] Director/Music Publisher; Michelle Andrea Escoffery-Ojo [1974] Director/Songwriter; Nicholas Lynedoch Graham [1945] Director; Edward Gregson [1945] Director/Composer; Stuart Alexander Hornall [1947] Director/Music Publisher; Richard Malcolm King [1963] Managing Director; Stephen Alec Levine [1958] Director/Composer and Producer; Dru Masters [1965] Director/Composer; John Berchmans Minch [1957] Director/Publisher; Mitch Murray [1940] Director/Songwriter; Roberto Bruno Neri [1973] Director; Julian Francis Kandahar Nott [1960] Director/Composer; Simon Howard Platz [1957] Director/Publisher; Mark Poole [1962] Director; John Simmonds [1962] Director; Joanne Sian Smith [1968] Director

The Perfume Shop Limited
Incorporated: 23 March 1992 *Employees:* 2,226
Net Worth: £19,820,000 *Total Assets:* £180,992,000
Registered Office: Hutchison House, 5 Hester Road, Battersea, London, SW11 4AN
Activities: Retail sale of cosmetic and toilet articles in specialised stores
Parent: The Perfume Shop Holdings Limited
Officers: Edith Shih, Secretary; Claire Nicole Dines [1972] Finance Director; Michelle Karen Fellows [1968] Training Director; Dr Alan John Heaton [1962] Director; Dominic Kai Ming Lai [1953] Director [Canadian]; Christian Nicolas Roger Salbaing [1950] Director [French]; Gillian Greig Smith [1966] Finance Director

Permanent Funding (No.2) Limited
Incorporated: 17 May 2002
Net Worth: £2,268,000 *Total Assets:* £5,143,396,864
Registered Office: 35 Great St Helen's, London, EC3A 6AP
Activities: Financial intermediation not elsewhere classified
Parent: Permanent Holdings Limited
Officers: Daniel Marc Richard Jaffe [1975] Director

Permanent Master Issuer PLC
Incorporated: 1 September 2006
Net Worth Deficit: £1,454,000 *Total Assets:* £5,215,036,928
Registered Office: 35 Great St Helens, London, EC3A 6AP
Activities: Financial intermediation not elsewhere classified
Parent: Permanent Holdings Limited
Officers: Daniel Marc Richard Jaffe [1975] Director

Permasteelisa (UK) Limited
Incorporated: 18 September 1989 *Employees:* 103
Net Worth: £234,879 *Total Assets:* £158,510,128
Registered Office: 2nd Floor, 1 Old Jewry, London, EC2R 8DN
Activities: Other specialised construction activities n.e.c.
Parent: Lixil Group Corporation
Officers: Andrea de Vito [1965] Director/Group Chief Financial Officer [Italian]; Gordon Andrew Earle [1964] Director/General Manager; Klaus Ernst Lother [1966] Director [German]

Pernod Ricard UK Limited
Incorporated: 10 December 1984 *Employees:* 252
Net Worth: £490,279,008 *Total Assets:* £576,435,968
Registered Office: Building 12, Chiswick Park, 566 Chiswick High Road, London, W4 5AN
Activities: Wholesale of wine, beer, spirits and other alcoholic beverages
Parent: Chivas Investments Limited
Officers: Gilles Pierre Francis Bogaert [1969] Managing Director [French]; Thomas Yves Marie D'Aboville [1980] Finance Director [French]; David Anthony Haworth [1962] Managing Director; Stuart MacNab [1964] Director/Accountant; Anne-Louise Varroquier [1980] Director/General Counsel [French]

Perpetual Power (UK) Limited
Incorporated: 19 April 2016
Net Worth Deficit: £27,430,906 *Total Assets:* £336,728,224
Registered Office: c/o Quintas Energy UK Ltd, Suite C, 3rd Floor, 3 Harbour Exchange Square, London, E14 9GE
Activities: Production of electricity
Parent: Perpetual Power (UK) Holdings Limited
Officers: Liam James Kavanagh [1977] Director; Andrew Paul Williams [1964] Director

Fred Perry (Holdings) Limited
Incorporated: 17 October 1995 *Employees:* 433
Net Worth: £158,128,000 *Total Assets:* £172,592,000
Registered Office: 37 Mount Pleasant, Clerkenwell, London, WC1X 0AA
Activities: Activities of head offices
Officers: John Thomas Stephen Flynn [1950] Director/Chairman; Richard Martin Gilmore [1970] Director; Katsuyuki Tanabe [1945] Director [Japanese]; Keiji Tanabe [1976] Director [Japanese]

Fred Perry Limited
Incorporated: 17 October 1995 *Employees:* 340
Net Worth: £122,301,000 *Total Assets:* £137,563,008
Registered Office: 37 Mount Pleasant, Clerkenwell, London, WC1X 0AA
Activities: Manufacture of other wearing apparel and accessories n.e.c.
Parent: Fred Perry (Holdings) Limited
Officers: John Thomas Stephen Flynn [1950] Director/Chairman; Rosario Irene Gallen [1969] Finance Director [Irish]; Richard Martin Gilmore [1970] Director; Katsuyuki Tanabe [1945] Director [Japanese]; Keiji Tanabe [1976] Director [Japanese]

Persia International Bank PLC
Incorporated: 16 May 2001 *Employees:* 44
Net Worth: £87,581,968 *Total Assets:* £164,217,744
Registered Office: 6 Lothbury, London, EC2R 7HH
Activities: Banks
Shareholders: Bank Mellat; Bank Tejarat
Officers: Peter James Cathcart, Secretary; Rassoul Ajdari [1966] Director/Banker [Iranian]; Mohammad Bigdeli [1966] Executive Director [Iranian]; Reza Dolatabadi [1967] Managing Director [Iranian]; Mohammad Reza Meskarian [1951] Director/Commercial Banker [Iranian]; Mohammed Nasrollahi [1952] Director/Banker [Iranian]; Farrokh Shahmir [1955] Director/Chartered Accountant

Petra Diamonds UK Treasury Limited
Incorporated: 31 March 2015 *Employees:* 2
Net Worth: £198,694,752 *Total Assets:* £198,697,792
Registered Office: c/o Memery Crystal LLP, 165 Fleet Street, London, EC4A 2DY
Activities: Financial intermediation not elsewhere classified
Shareholders: Petra Diamonds US$ Treasury PLC; Petra Diamonds US$ Treasury PLC
Officers: Jacques Breytenbach [1972] Director/Chief Financial Officer [South African]; Alexander Gordon Kelso Hamilton [1945] Director

Petra Diamonds US$ Treasury PLC
Incorporated: 31 March 2015
Net Worth Deficit: £56,167,232 *Total Assets:* £452,656,192
Registered Office: c/o Memery Crystal LLP, 165 Fleet Street, London, EC4A 2DY
Activities: Financial intermediation not elsewhere classified
Shareholders: Petra Diamonds Limited; Petra Diamonds Limited
Officers: Jacques Breytenbach [1972] Director/Chief Financial Officer [South African]; Alexander Gordon Kelso Hamilton [1945] Director

Petroceltic Holdings Limited
Incorporated: 12 August 2015 *Employees:* 57
Net Worth: £126,919,424 *Total Assets:* £260,352,672
Registered Office: 5th Floor, 10 Finsbury Square, London, EC2A 1AF
Activities: Activities of other holding companies n.e.c.
Officers: Peter Wilson, Secretary; Denis Ischenko [1970] Director; Angelo Radostinov Moskov [1967] Director

Petroceltic Resources Limited
Incorporated: 10 June 1996 *Employees:* 1
Previous: Petroceltic Resources PLC
Net Worth Deficit: £156,923,248 *Total Assets:* £109,813,696
Registered Office: 5th Floor, 10 Finsbury Square, London, EC2A 1AF
Activities: Extraction of crude petroleum
Parent: Petroceltic Holdings Limited
Officers: Peter Wilson, Secretary; Denis Ischenko [1970] Director; Angelo Radostinov Moskov [1967] Director

Petrochina International (London) Co., Limited
Incorporated: 8 April 2002 *Employees:* 15
Net Worth: £831,600,000 *Total Assets:* £1,470,448,128
Registered Office: The Adelphi, 1-11 John Adam Street, London, WC2N 6HT
Activities: Other business support service activities n.e.c.
Parent: Petrochina Company Limited
Officers: Yizhou Luo, Secretary; Yizhou Luo [1977] Director [Chinese]; Yong Zhao [1967] Director/Vice-President [Chinese]

Petrofac (Malaysia-PM 304) Limited
Incorporated: 13 August 1997 *Employees:* 288
Net Worth Deficit: £25,803,880 *Total Assets:* £717,077,376
Registered Office: 117 Jermyn Street, London, SW1Y 6HH
Activities: Extraction of crude petroleum
Parent: Petrofac Limited
Officers: Jeanne-Marie Marie de Larrazabal [1955] Director/Lawyer; Nigel Hooker [1971] Director; Robert John Jewkes [1955] Director/Engineer

Petroineos Europe Limited
Incorporated: 10 December 2004 *Employees:* 21
Net Worth: £673,004,672 *Total Assets:* £674,768,064
Registered Office: The Adelphi, 1-11 John Adam Street, London, WC2N 6HT
Activities: Manufacture of other inorganic basic chemicals
Parent: Petrochina International (London) Company Limited
Officers: Franck Francois Demay [1959] Director [French]; Gerard Stephen Hepburn [1979] Director; Dai Kai [1972] Director [Chinese]; Yizhou Luo [1977] Director [Chinese]; Gong Wang [1977] Director [Chinese]

Petroineos Fuels Limited
Incorporated: 28 August 2009
Net Worth: £209,921,024 *Total Assets:* £511,922,112
Registered Office: The Adelphi, 1-11 John Adam Street, London, WC2N 6HT
Activities: Wholesale of other fuels and related products
Parent: Petrochina International (London) Co., Limited
Officers: Daniel John Brain [1975] Director/Commercial Manager; Yizhou Luo [1977] Director [Chinese]; Russell Edward Mann [1966] Director

Petronas Energy Trading Limited
Incorporated: 18 April 1997 *Employees:* 82
Net Worth: £45,753,000 *Total Assets:* £610,454,016
Registered Office: 9th Floor, One New Ludgate, 60 Ludgate Hill, London, EC4M 7AW
Activities: Trade of gas through mains
Parent: Minister of Finance of Malaysia (Incorporated)
Officers: Nailesh Kantilal Rambhai, Secretary; Ahmad Adly Alias [1969] Director [Malaysian]; Mohamed Fasluddeen Bin Abdul Hadi [1974] Director [Malaysian]; Nasmiza Binti Ismail [1965] Director [Malaysian]; Ezhar Yazid Bin Mat Jaafar [1965] Director/Head of Global Marketing [Malaysian]

Petropavlovsk Mining Treasury UK Limited
Incorporated: 18 May 2009
Previous: Peter Hambro Mining Treasury UK Limited
Net Worth Deficit: £569,384,064 *Total Assets:* £596,645,632
Registered Office: 11 Grosvenor Place, London, SW1X 7HH
Activities: Other business support service activities n.e.c.
Parent: Petropavlovsk PLC
Officers: Amanda Whalley, Secretary; Natalia Buynova [1976] Director/Group Head of Corporate Reporting [Russian]; Dr Alfiya Samokhvalova [1967] Director/Group Head of External Communications; Anna Karolina Subczynska-Samberger [1978] Director/Lawyer

Petropavlovsk PLC
Incorporated: 20 December 2001 *Employees:* 8,519
Net Worth: £429,897,568 *Total Assets:* £1,092,428,288
Registered Office: 11 Grosvenor Place, Belgravia, London, SW1X 7HH
Activities: Other mining and quarrying n.e.c.
Officers: Amanda Whalley, Secretary; James William Cameron Jr [1947] Director [American]; Damien Hackett [1947] Director; Robert John Garton Jenkins [1953] Director/Chartered Accountant; Harry James Rodolph Kenyon-Slaney [1961] Director; Sir Roderic Michael John Lyne [1948] Consultant and Director; Dr Pavel Maslovskiy [1956] Director [Russian]; Bektas Mukazhanov [1983] Managing Director [Kazakh]

PFI Infrastructure Finance Limited
Incorporated: 2 April 2004
Net Worth: £79,671,672 *Total Assets:* £190,701,936
Registered Office: Cannon Place, 78 Cannon Street, London, EC4N 6AF
Activities: Other business support service activities n.e.c.
Parent: I2 Bidco Limited
Officers: John Ivor Cavill [1972] Director; Jonathan Peter Doberman [1977] Director/Financial Controller

PFI Senior Funding Limited
Incorporated: 10 January 2001
Net Worth: £243,919,008 *Total Assets:* £751,164,992
Registered Office: Cannon Place, 78 Cannon Street, London, EC4N 6AF
Activities: Other business support service activities n.e.c.
Parent: Elbon Holdings (3) Limited
Officers: John Ivor Cavill [1972] Director; James Peter Dawes [1971] Director/Chief Financial Officer

PG (April) Limited
Incorporated: 19 April 2007 *Employees:* 7
Net Worth: £356,228,992 *Total Assets:* £357,452,000
Registered Office: 3 More London Riverside, London, SE1 2AQ
Activities: Activities of open-ended investment companies
Parent: CKI Gas Infrastructure Limited
Officers: Graham Winston Edwards [1954] Director/Chief Executive; Guy Butterworth Ellis [1961] Director; Mark John Horsley [1959] Director/Chief Executive Officer; Andrew John Hunter [1958] Director; Tak Chuen Edmond IP [1952] Director/Deputy Chairman [Chinese]; Hing Lam Kam [1946] Director [Chinese]; Jonathan Theodore Miller [1971] Director

PG Media Services Limited
Incorporated: 30 January 1968
Net Worth: £115,016,000 *Total Assets:* £351,304,000
Registered Office: 1st Floor, 2 Television Centre, 101 Wood Lane, London, W12 7FR
Activities: Advertising agencies
Parent: MMS UK Holdings Limited
Officers: Joanne Munis, Secretary; Gerard Paul Boyle [1971] Director/Chief Executive Officer - APAC & EMEA; Guillaume Jean Daniel Herbette [1966] Director/Chief Executive Officer [French]; Arco Nobels [1970] Director [Dutch]

PGI Acquisition Limited
Incorporated: 13 September 2013
Net Worth: £221,285,760 *Total Assets:* £221,287,296
Registered Office: 35 Great St Helen's, London, EC3A 6AP
Activities: Manufacture of non-wovens and articles made from non-wovens, except apparel
Parent: Berry Plastics Group Inc
Officers: Jason Kent Greene [1970] Director/General Counsel [American]; Mark William Miles [1971] Director [American]

PGIM Financial Limited
Incorporated: 20 September 1971 *Employees:* 157
Previous: Pramerica Financial Limited
Net Worth: £96,536,528 *Total Assets:* £356,924,960
Registered Office: Grand Buildings, 1-3 Strand, Trafalgar Square, London, WC2N 5HR
Activities: Activities of financial services holding companies
Parent: Prudential Financial Inc
Officers: Mark Generald Fresson, Secretary; Philip Mathew Barrett [1968] Director/Private Equity Fund Manager; Donald John Campbell [1963] Director; Heather Carol Day [1975] Director/Chief Operating Officer; Andrew Charles Louis Dyson [1964] Managing Director; Marie Louise Fioramonti [1961] Director/Int. Finance Div MD [American]; Mark Generald Fresson [1965] Finance Director; Richard Greenwood [1961] Director/Investment Manager [American]; Elizabeth Ann Samson [1968] Director/Investment Manager [American]; Steven Saperstein [1961] Director/Investment Manager [American]

PGIM Limited
Incorporated: 14 July 1999 *Employees:* 2
Previous: Pramerica Investment Management Limited
Net Worth: £48,279,480 *Total Assets:* £298,342,080
Registered Office: Grand Buildings, 1-3 Strand, Trafalgar Square, London, WC2N 5HR
Activities: Financial intermediation not elsewhere classified
Parent: PGIM Financial Limited
Officers: Mark Generald Fresson, Secretary; Raimondo Amabile [1969] Director/Investment Manager [Italian]; Philip Mathew Barrett [1968] Director/Private Equity Fund Manager; Jonathan Paul Butler [1971] Director/Investment Manager; Mathew Royal Crowther [1977] Director/Investment Manager [Australian]; Heather Carol Day [1975] Director/Chief Operating Officer; Mark Generald Fresson [1965] Finance Director; Richard Greenwood [1961] Director/Investment Manager [American]; Andrew John Macland [1970] Director/Investment Manager; Elizabeth Ann Samson [1968] Director/Investment Manager [American]; Steven Saperstein [1961] Director/Investment Manager [American]

Pharm Research Associates (UK) Limited
Incorporated: 9 September 1996 *Employees:* 1,041
Net Worth: £199,888,768 *Total Assets:* £419,205,120
Registered Office: Cannon Place, 78 Cannon Street, London, EC4N 6AF
Activities: Data processing, hosting and related activities
Parent: PRA Health Sciences, Inc.
Officers: Christopher John Gray [1963] Director/VP-Operations Finance, EAPA; Colin Shannon [1959] Director/President & Chief Executive Officer

Pharmadeals Limited
Incorporated: 26 February 2002
Net Worth: £248,970,000 *Total Assets:* £259,192,992
Registered Office: 210 Pentonville Road, London, N1 9JY
Activities: Activities of other holding companies n.e.c.
Parent: IQVIA Solutions Finance UK V Ltd.
Officers: Alistair Roland Grenfell [1973] Director/Executive Manager; Pavan Hayer [1968] Finance Director

PHD Media Limited
Incorporated: 19 September 1989 *Employees:* 370
Net Worth: £15,191,773 *Total Assets:* £206,538,624
Registered Office: The Telephone Exchange, 5 North Crescent, Chenies Street, London, WC1E 7PH
Activities: Advertising agencies
Parent: Omnicom Media Group UK Limited
Officers: Sally Ann Bray, Chartered Secretary; Verica Djurdjevic [1975] Director; Damien Glackin [1975] Finance Director

PhillipCapital UK Ltd
Incorporated: 19 October 1993 *Employees:* 68
Previous: King & Shaxson Capital Limited
Net Worth: £14,769,176 *Total Assets:* £1,342,800,128
Registered Office: 6th Floor, Candlewick House, 120 Cannon Street, London, EC4N 6AS
Activities: Administration of financial markets
Major Shareholder: Hua Min Lim
Officers: Miranda Lauraine Telfer, Secretary; Hua Min Lim [1946] Director/Group Chairman [Singaporean]; Linus Wen Sheong Lim [1975] Sales Director [Singaporean]; Cheng Han Tan [1981] Director [Singaporean]; Miranda Lauraine Telfer [1968] Finance Director; David Ian Robert Wileman [1956] Director/Chief Executive

Phillips 66 CS Limited
Incorporated: 16 April 1993
Net Worth: £141,577,200 *Total Assets:* £152,253,152
Registered Office: 7th Floor, 200-202 Aldersgate Street, London, EC1A 4HD
Activities: Operation of warehousing and storage facilities for water transport activities
Parent: Phillips 66 UK Funding Limited
Officers: Sarah Gennings, Secretary; Anna Janaszek, Secretary; Ruth Maretta White, Secretary; Kimberly Diane Head [1969] Director/Global Trading Lead [American]; Neal Andrew Holland [1965] Director/Manager, Accounting; Leslie Leroy Jenkins [1968] Director/Manager, Finance [American]; Gary Stuart Taylor [1964] Director/Senior Tax Advisor

Phillips 66 Limited
Incorporated: 10 February 1954 *Employees:* 1,018
Net Worth: £2,563,827,456 *Total Assets:* £3,900,176,384
Registered Office: 7th Floor, 200-202 Aldersgate Street, London, EC1A 4HD
Activities: Mineral oil refining
Parent: Phillips 66 UK Holdings Limited
Officers: Sarah Gennings, Secretary; Anna Janaszek, Secretary; Elaine Marie Price, Secretary; Ruth Maretta White, Secretary; Darren James Cunningham [1964] Director/Operations Manager; Kimberly Diane Head [1969] Director/Global Trading Lead [American]; Leslie Leroy Jenkins [1968] Director/Manager, Finance [American]; Robert Edwin Sherwell [1975] Director/Maintenance Execution Superintendent; Gary Stuart Taylor [1964] Director/Senior Tax Advisor; Mary Elizabeth Wolf [1972] Managing Director UK and Ireland Marketing [American]

Phillips 66 Treasury Limited
Incorporated: 21 November 2011
Net Worth: £35,792,832 *Total Assets:* £1,036,897,856
Registered Office: 7th Floor, 200-202 Aldersgate Street, London, EC1A 4HD
Activities: Financial intermediation not elsewhere classified
Parent: Phillips 66 Limited
Officers: Sarah Gennings, Secretary; Anna Janaszek, Secretary; Ruth Maretta White, Secretary; Neal Andrew Holland [1965] Director/Manager, Commercial & Corporate Accounting Europe; Leslie Leroy Jenkins [1968] Director/Manager, Finance [American]; Gary Stuart Taylor [1964] Director/Senior Tax Advisor

Phillips 66 UK Funding Limited
Incorporated: 25 November 2011
Net Worth: £116,351,120 *Total Assets:* £143,127,504
Registered Office: 7th Floor, 200-202 Aldersgate Street, London, EC1A 4HD
Activities: Other activities auxiliary to insurance and pension funding
Parent: Phillips 66 Limited
Officers: Sarah Gennings, Secretary; Anna Janaszek, Secretary; Ruth Maretta White, Secretary; Darren James Cunningham [1964] Director/Operations Manager; Kimberly Diane Head [1969] Director/Global Trading Lead [American]; Neal Andrew Holland [1965] Director/Manager, Commercial & Corporate Accounting Europe; Leslie Leroy Jenkins [1968] Director/Manager, Finance [American]; Gary Stuart Taylor [1964] Director/Senior Tax Advisor

Phillips 66 UK Holdings Limited
Incorporated: 21 November 2011
Net Worth: £1,706,667,136 *Total Assets:* £2,641,619,968
Registered Office: 7th Floor, 200-202 Aldersgate Street, London, EC1A 4HD
Activities: Activities of head offices
Parent: Phillips 66 International Investments Ltd.
Officers: Sarah Gennings, Secretary; Anna Janaszek, Secretary; Ruth Maretta White, Secretary; Darren James Cunningham [1964] Director/Operations Manager; Kimberly Diane Head [1969] Director/Global Trading Lead [American]; Leslie Leroy Jenkins [1968] Director/Manager, Finance [American]; Robert Edwin Sherwell [1975] Director/Maintenance Execution Superintendent; Gary Stuart Taylor [1964] Director/Senior Tax Advisor; Mary Elizabeth Wolf [1972] Managing Director UK and Ireland Marketing [American]

Phoenix Distribution Holdings Limited
Incorporated: 17 December 2007 *Employees:* 119
Net Worth: £468,200,000 *Total Assets:* £1,039,100,032
Registered Office: c/o Hackwood Secretaries, One Silk Street, London, EC2Y 8HQ
Activities: Activities of head offices
Parent: Phoenix Energy Holdings Limited
Officers: Kailash Chada, Secretary; Ivan Robert Bell [1968] Director; Kailash Chada [1971] Director/Chartered Accountant; Philip Bernard Holder [1948] Director/Trust and Estate Practitioner, Solicitor; Anne-Noelle Le Gal [1983] Director [French]; William Francis Michael McKinstry [1965] Director; Rachel Amelia Ockelford Drew [1976] Investment Director [Irish/New Zealander]; Valeria Rosati [1975] Director/Fund Manager [Italian]

Phoenix Energy Holdings Limited
Incorporated: 4 January 2001
Net Worth: £88,538,000 *Total Assets:* £237,426,000
Registered Office: c/o Hackwood Secretaries, One Silk Street, London, EC2Y 8HQ
Activities: Activities of head offices
Parent: Kellen Acquisitions Limited
Officers: Kailash Chada, Secretary; Ivan Robert Bell [1968] Director; Kailash Chada [1971] Director/Chartered Accountant; Peter Vincent Dixon [1960] Director; Philip Bernard Holder [1948] Director/Trust and Estate Practitioner, Solicitor; Anne-Noelle Le Gal [1983] Director [French]; William Francis Michael McKinstry [1965] Director; Rachel Amelia Ockelford Drew [1976] Investment Director [Irish/New Zealander]; Valeria Rosati [1975] Director/Fund Manager [Italian]

Phoenix Global Resources PLC
Incorporated: 25 March 2004 *Employees:* 102
Previous: Andes Energia PLC
Net Worth: £212,786,448 *Total Assets:* £500,506,976
Registered Office: 6th Floor, King's House, 10 Haymarket, London, SW1Y 4BP
Activities: Extraction of crude petroleum
Officers: Nigel John Duxbury, Secretary/Finance; Javier Francisco Alvarez [1972] Director [Argentinian]; John William Sharp Bentley [1948] Director; Kevin Thomas Dennehy [1958] Director [American]; Timothy William Harrington [1958] Director [American]; Ricardo Nicolas Mallo Huergo [1969] Director [Argentinian]; David Clifford Jackson [1948] Director; Daniel Jaeggi [1960] Director [Swiss]; Sir Michael Derek Vaughan Rake [1948] Director; Anuj Kumar Sharma [1973] Director [American]; Garrett Douglas Soden [1974] Director/Natural Resources Executive [American]

Phoenix Natural Gas PP Finance PLC
Incorporated: 23 February 2017
Net Worth: £17,000 *Total Assets:* £282,944,992
Registered Office: c/o Hackwood Secretaries Limited, One Silk Street, London, EC2Y 8HQ
Activities: Activities auxiliary to financial intermediation n.e.c.
Parent: Phoenix Distribution Holdings Limited
Officers: Kailash Chada, Secretary; Ivan Robert Bell [1968] Director; Kailash Chada [1971] Director/Chartered Accountant; Philip Bernard Holder [1948] Director/Trust and Estate Practitioner, Solicitor; Anne-Noelle Noelle Le Gal [1983] Director [French]; William Francis Michael McKinstry [1965] Director/Accountant; Rachel Amelia Ockelford Drew [1976] Investment Director [Irish/New Zealander]; Valeria Rosati [1975] Director/Fund Manager [Italian]

The Phone House Holdings (UK) Limited
Incorporated: 6 November 1998 *Employees:* 2
Net Worth: £237,540,992 *Total Assets:* £247,812,000
Registered Office: 1 Portal Way, London, W3 6RS
Activities: Retail sale of mobile telephones
Parent: Carphone Warehouse Europe Limited
Officers: Catherine Springett, Secretary; Alistair Gibson [1975] Director; Leon Smith [1976] Director/Chartered Accountant

Phonographic Performance Limited
Incorporated: 12 May 1934 *Employees:* 317
Net Worth Deficit: £7,109,000 *Total Assets:* £163,624,992
Registered Office: 1 Upper James Street, London, W1F 9DE
Activities: Sound recording and music publishing activities
Officers: David James Edward Harmsworth, Secretary; Roger Colin Armstrong [1948] Managing Director [Irish]; Roxanne de Bastion [1986] Director/Singer Songwriter; Robin Michael Firman [1947] Director/Musician; Julian French [1967] Director/Business Affairs [British/American]; Robert Alexander Gruschke [1969] Director/VP Global Collective Rights [Dutch]; Nicholas Bruce Hartley [1960] Director; Crispin MacMichael Sandys Hunt [1968] Director/Composer/Record Producer; Mark Colbert Kelly [1961] Director/Musician [Irish]; Peter John Leathem [1965] Director/Solicitor; James Heneage Radice [1961] Senior Director; Adrian Sear [1954] Commercial Director; John Frank Smith [1950] Director/TU General Secretary; Michael Anthony Smith [1959] Director/Lawyer; Christopher Robert Smith of Finsbury [1951] Director; Peter Stack [1959] Director; David Richard Stopps [1948] Director/Artist Manager; Horace Trubridge [1957] Director/Trade Union Official

Photobox Holdco Alpha Limited
Incorporated: 26 May 2011
Net Worth: £376,071,008 *Total Assets:* £380,443,008
Registered Office: 10 Back Hill, London, EC1R 5EN
Activities: Activities of other holding companies n.e.c.
Parent: Horizon Bidco Limited
Officers: Alan Robert Burns [1973] Director/Chartered Accountant; Jody Matthew Robertson Ford [1975] Director

Photobox Holdco Beta Limited
Incorporated: 26 May 2011
Net Worth: £338,212,000 *Total Assets:* £482,839,008
Registered Office: 10 Back Hill, London, EC1R 5EN
Activities: Activities of other holding companies n.e.c.
Parent: Photobox Holdco Alpha Limited
Officers: Alan Robert Burns [1973] Director/Chartered Accountant; Jody Matthew Robertson Ford [1975] Director

PHP Glen Spean Limited
Incorporated: 15 February 2001 *Employees:* 3
Net Worth: £46,520,048 *Total Assets:* £167,723,712
Registered Office: 5th Floor, Greener House, 66-68 Haymarket, London, SW1Y 4RF
Activities: Other letting and operating of own or leased real estate
Parent: PHP Medical Properties Limited
Officers: David Christopher Austin [1970] Director/Chartered Surveyor; Richard Howell [1965] Director/Accountant; Harry Abraham Hyman [1956] Director/Chartered Accountant

PHP Investments No.2 Limited
Incorporated: 26 May 2011
Net Worth: £19,209,584 *Total Assets:* £170,074,384
Registered Office: 5th Floor, Greener House, 66-68 Haymarket, London, SW1Y 4RF
Activities: Renting and operating of Housing Association real estate
Parent: PHP Healthcare Investments (Holdings) Limited
Officers: David Christopher Austin [1970] Director/Chartered Surveyor; Richard Howell [1965] Director/Chartered Accountant; Harry Abraham Hyman [1956] Director/Chartered Accountant

PHP Primary Properties Limited
Incorporated: 7 April 2005
Net Worth: £68,675,000 *Total Assets:* £207,092,016
Registered Office: 5th Floor, Greener House, 66-68 Haymarket, London, SW1Y 4RF
Activities: Other letting and operating of own or leased real estate
Parent: PHP Primary Properties (Haymarket) Limited
Officers: David Christopher Austin [1970] Director/Chartered Surveyor; Richard Howell [1965] Director/Accountant; Harry Abraham Hyman [1956] Director/Chartered Accountant

PHP SB Limited
Incorporated: 9 February 2017 *Employees:* 2
Net Worth: £15,924,218 *Total Assets:* £144,948,960
Registered Office: 5th Floor, Greener House, 66-68 Haymarket, London, SW1Y 4RF
Activities: Financial intermediation not elsewhere classified
Parent: Primary Health Properties PLC
Officers: Richard Howell [1965] Director/Accountant; Harry Abraham Hyman [1956] Director

PIAS Holding (UK) Limited
Incorporated: 29 June 1998 *Employees:* 140
Net Worth Deficit: £12,083,000 *Total Assets:* £220,131,008
Registered Office: 1 Bevington Path, London, SE1 3PW
Activities: Artistic creation
Officers: Nicholas Bruce Hartley, Secretary; Kenneth Bruno Gates [1963] Director; Nicholas Bruce Hartley [1960] Director; Michel Joseph Lambot [1960] Director [Belgian]

Pic Holdings Limited
Incorporated: 13 February 2006
Previous: Pension Holding Company (UK) 3 Limited
Net Worth: £1,059,849,984 *Total Assets:* £1,059,910,016
Registered Office: 14 Cornhill, London, EC3V 3ND
Activities: Other activities auxiliary to insurance and pension funding
Parent: Pension Insurance Corporation Group Limited
Officers: Tracy Marie Blackwell [1967] Director [Irish]; Louise Jane Inward [1966] Director/Barrister; Robert Peter Sewell [1964] Finance Director

Pictet Asset Management Limited
Incorporated: 21 August 1995 *Employees:* 369
Net Worth: £81,107,624 *Total Assets:* £255,614,496
Registered Office: Level 11, Moor House, 120 London Wall, London, EC2Y 5ET
Activities: Financial intermediation not elsewhere classified
Shareholder: Pictet (London) Limited
Officers: Nian Lala, Secretary; Richard James Heelis [1962] Director/Chief Investment Officer - Equities; Niall Michael Quinn [1971] Director/Head of Institutional [Irish]; Laurent Anastase Ramzy Ramsey [1970] Director/Head of Distribution [Swiss]

Picture Holdco Limited
Incorporated: 26 July 2016 *Employees:* 290
Net Worth: £190,683,008 *Total Assets:* £508,604,000
Registered Office: 4th Floor, 18 St Swithin's Lane, London, EC4N 8AD
Activities: Activities of financial services holding companies
Officers: Paul William Martin Golding [1965] Director; Luis Moner Parra [1981] Director [Spanish]; Spencer Alexander Wells [1973] Director/Accountant

PIL Investments LLP
Incorporated: 14 July 2016
Net Worth: £202,056,976 *Total Assets:* £285,891,136
Registered Office: 80 Pall Mall, London, SW1Y 5ES

Pillar City PLC
Incorporated: 11 October 2000
Net Worth Deficit: £30,014,920 *Total Assets:* £328,173,952
Registered Office: York House, 45 Seymour Street, London, W1H 7LX
Activities: Development of building projects
Parent: Pillar Property Group Limited
Officers: Benjamin Toby Grose [1969] Director/Chartered Surveyor; Jonathan Charles McNuff [1986] Director/Chartered Accountant; Charles John Middleton [1966] Director/Corporate Tax Executive

Pillar Denton Limited
Incorporated: 24 October 1994
Net Worth: £98,420,432 *Total Assets:* £101,191,728
Registered Office: York House, 45 Seymour Street, London, W1H 7LX
Activities: Development of building projects
Parent: Pillar Property Group Limited
Officers: Sarah Morrell Barzycki [1958] Director/Head of Finance; Benjamin Toby Grose [1969] Director/Chartered Surveyor; Timothy Andrew Roberts [1964] Director/Chartered Surveyor; Nigel Mark Webb [1963] Director/Chartered Surveyor

Pillar Property Group Limited
Incorporated: 24 December 1990
Net Worth: £721,413,376 *Total Assets:* £723,151,808
Registered Office: York House, 45 Seymour Street, London, W1H 7LX
Activities: Development of building projects
Parent: British Land Fund Management Limited
Officers: Benjamin Toby Grose [1969] Director/Chartered Surveyor; Jonathan Charles McNuff [1986] Director/Chartered Accountant; Charles John Middleton [1966] Director/Corporate Tax Executive

PIMCO Europe Ltd
Incorporated: 24 April 1991 *Employees:* 277
Net Worth: £171,672,992 *Total Assets:* £248,174,000
Registered Office: 11 Baker Street, London, W1U 3AH
Activities: Fund management activities
Parent: Allianz SE
Officers: Thomas Edmund Rice, Secretary/Lawyer; Michael Cecil Alexander Amey [1970] Managing Director; Lisa Arnold [1962] Director; Ryan Patrick Blute [1975] Director [American]; Craig Allen Dawson [1968] Director [American]; David Carl Flattum [1964] Managing Director, General Counsel [American]; Robert Anastassis Kyprianou [1953] Director; Laurent Luccioni [1971] Director/Portfolio Manager [French]; John Charles Maney [1959] Director/Chief Financial Officer [American]; Emmanuel Roman [1963] Director/Chief Executive [French]

Ping Petroleum UK Limited
Incorporated: 22 July 2015
Net Worth: £89,066,704 *Total Assets:* £237,891,680
Registered Office: Cannon Place, 78 Cannon Street, London, EC4N 6AF
Activities: Other professional, scientific and technical activities n.e.c.
Officers: Paul a Baltensperger [1957] Director [American]; David Roy Phillips [1949] Director/Chairman [American]; Ning Zhang [1975] Director/CEO of Ping Petroleum Limited [American]

Pinnacle Resources Limited
Incorporated: 21 December 2000 *Employees:* 4
Net Worth: £1,009,306,304 *Total Assets:* £1,009,340,992
Registered Office: Mid City Place, 71 High Holborn, London, WC1V 6BA
Activities: Activities of other holding companies n.e.c.
Parent: Mitsubishi Corporation
Officers: Takeshi Matsushita [1971] Director/General Manager [Japanese]; Michihiko Okabe [1968] Director [Japanese]; Masaru Saito [1964] Director [Japanese]; Yuichi Sakaguchi [1973] Director/Deputy General Manager [Japanese]

Pinsent Masons International LLP
Incorporated: 1 June 2016 *Employees:* 2,525
Net Worth: £223,163,008 *Total Assets:* £332,936,000
Registered Office: 30 Crown Place, London, EC2A 4ES
Officers: Charlotte Anne Beckett [1962] Member; John Cleland [1964] Member; Joanne Elizabeth Ellis [1970] Member; Richard Edward Foley [1962] Member; Rainer Kreifels [1964] Member; Alastair John MacKinnon Morrison [1962] Member; David Ian Rennick [1962] Member; Catherine Workman [1968] Member; Dennis Joseph Agnew [1974] LLP Member; Amir Ali Ahmad [1974] LLP Member; Mohammad Hammad Akhtar [1974] LLP Member; Ewan Grant Alexander [1966] LLP Member; Michael Iain Allan [1971] LLP Member; Shirley Jean Allen [1975] LLP Member; Graham James Alty [1971] LLP Member; Anthony David Anderson [1967] LLP Member; Sadie Andrew [1975] LLP Member; Bernard Eng Kiat Ang [1966] LLP Member; Stephan Appt [1973] LLP Member; Timothy John Armsby [1973] LLP Member; Anthony Isaac Arrow [1973] LLP Member; Idoya Maria Arteagabeitia Gonzalez [1971] LLP Member; Tobin Massey Charles Ashby [1972] LLP Member; Stacey Bairner [1981] LLP Member; Mark Edward Baker [1976] LLP Member; Matthew Charles Baker [1971] LLP Member; Dr Volker Frank Balda [1969] LLP Member; Jennifer Anne Ballantyne [1967] LLP Member; Junaid Banoobhai [1977] LLP Member; Andrew Stephen Barber [1977] LLP Member; Claire Allison Barclay [1973] LLP Member; David Christopher Barker [1969] LLP Member; Stuart John Barr [1974] LLP Member; Thomas Peter Edward Barton [1979] LLP Member; Michael John Battye [1963] LLP Member; Dr Kurt Alexander Maximilian Bayer [1970] LLP Member; Dr Torsten Bergau [1969] LLP Member; Nicholas John Berry [1959] LLP Member; Thomas David Bicknell [1982] LLP Member; Phillip Stuart Birchall [1979] LLP Member; Ian Michael Birdsey [1976] LLP Member; Martin Kent Bishop [1968] LLP Member; Andrew James Black [1970] LLP Member; Neil Thomas Black [1974] LLP Member; Peter William Blackmore [1956] LLP Member; Charles James Blamire-Brown [1983] LLP Member; Nigel Gwyn Blundell [1965] LLP Member; Kevin William Boa [1971] LLP Member; Russell Stuart Booker [1957] LLP Member; Alistair George Booth [1966] LLP Member; Allistair Paul Booth [1964] LLP Member; Deborah Susan Bould [1970] LLP Member; Anne Catharine Bowden [1972] LLP Member; Gabrielle Dawn Bowen [1974] LLP Member; Samuel James Boyling [1976] LLP Member; Hannah Louise Brader [1978] LLP Member; Anthony Richard Bradley [1972] LLP Member; Nicholas Stanley Bradley [1960] LLP Member; Christopher Mark Breen [1977] LLP Member; Angelique Claire Bret [1972] LLP Member; Kevin David Bridges [1973] LLP Member; Jonathan Brocklehurst [1968] LLP Member; Nicholas Alexander Brown [1971] LLP Member; Stephen Victor Brown [1957] LLP Member; Maria Paloma Bru Arce [1973] LLP Member; John Robert Bruce [1980] LLP Member; Puay Siang Wu Peichan BU [1975] LLP Member; Charles Robert Buchanan [1967] LLP Member; Elizabeth Christina Mary Budd [1966] LLP Member; William Alistair Calvert [1979] LLP Member; James Watson Cameron [1979] LLP Member; Laura Elaine Cameron [1969] LLP Member; Gregory James Campbell [1956] LLP Member; Nicholas Charles Carlin [1981] LLP Member; Andreas Michael Carney [1974] LLP Member; Alan McLeod Cassels [1975] LLP Member; Inmaculada Castello Bernabeu [1979] LLP Member; Rosalie Madeleine Chadwick [1977] LLP Member; Helena Hsi-Chia Chen [1971] LLP Member; Kenneth Kee Ho Chong [1965] LLP Member; Dr Peter Roman Christ [1975] LLP Member; Wai Fun Chu [1976] LLP Member; Peter Mark Clayton [1970] LLP Member; Matthew John Clayton-Stead [1981] LLP Member; Jonathan David Coley [1969] LLP Member; Jonathan Collier [1970] LLP Member; Robert Jason Alexi Collins [1970] LLP Member; Stacey Collins [1977] LLP Member; Simon Nicholas Colvin [1971] LLP Member; Robert Craig Connal [1954] LLP Member; Paul Anthony Connolly [1976] LLP Member; Iain Richard Connor [1972] LLP Member; Vincent Connor [1964] LLP Member; Alan Russell Cook [1969] LLP Member; Helen Elizabeth Corden [1975] LLP Member; Philip Corfield-Smith [1978] LLP Member; James Shearer Cormack [1968] LLP Member; Steven James Cottee [1972] LLP Member; Bruce Craig [1965] LLP Member; Matthew Edward Croagh [1972] LLP Member

Pinsent Masons LLP
Incorporated: 18 December 2007 *Employees:* 189
Net Worth: £208,868,000 *Total Assets:* £314,792,000
Registered Office: 30 Crown Place, London, EC2A 4ES
Officers: John Cleland [1964] Member; Richard Edward Foley [1962] Member; Dennis Joseph Agnew [1974] LLP Member; Mohammad Hammad Akhtar [1974] LLP Member; Ewan Grant Alexander [1966] LLP Member; Michael Iain Allan [1971] LLP Member; Shirley Jean Allen [1975] LLP Member; Graham James Alty [1971] LLP Member; Anthony David Dominic Anderson [1953] LLP Member; Sadie Andrew [1975] LLP Member; Stephan Appt [1973] LLP Member; Anthony Isaac Arrow [1973] LLP Member; Idoya Arteagabeitia Gonzalez [1971] LLP Member; Tobin Massey Charles Ashby [1972] LLP Member; Stacey Bairner [1981] LLP Member; Mark Edward Baker [1976] LLP Member; Matthew Charles Baker [1971] LLP Member; Dr Volker Frank Balda [1969] LLP Member; Jennifer Anne Ballantyne [1967] LLP Member; Andrew Stephen Barber [1977] LLP Member; David Christopher Barker [1969] LLP Member; Stuart John Barr [1974] LLP Member; Thomas Peter Edward Barton [1979] LLP Member; Michael John Battye [1963] LLP Member; Dr Kurt Alexander Maximilian Bayer [1970] LLP Member; Dr Torsten Bergau [1969] LLP Member; Nicholas John Berry [1959] LLP Member; Phillip Stuart Birchall [1979] LLP Member; Ian Michael Birdsey [1976] LLP Member; Martin Kent Bishop [1968] LLP Member; Andrew James Black [1970] LLP Member; Neil Thomas Black [1974] LLP Member; Charles James Blamire-Brown [1983] LLP Member; Nigel Gwyn Blundell [1965] LLP Member; Kevin William Boa [1971] LLP Member; Russell Stuart Booker [1957] LLP Member; Alistair George Booth [1966] LLP Member; Allistair Paul Booth [1964] LLP Member; Deborah Susan Bould [1970] LLP Member; Anne Catharine Bowden [1972] LLP Member; Gabrielle Dawn Bowen [1974] LLP Member; Hannah Louise Brader [1978] LLP Member; Anthony Richard Bradley [1972] LLP Member; Nicholas Stanley Bradley [1960] LLP Member; Christopher Mark Breen [1977] LLP Member; Angelique Claire Bret [1972] LLP Member; Kevin David Bridges [1973] LLP Member; Jonathan Brocklehurst [1968] LLP Member; Stephen Victor Brown [1957] LLP Member; Maria Paloma Bru Arce [1973] LLP Member; John Robert Bruce [1980] LLP Member; Charles Robert Buchanan [1967] LLP Member; Elizabeth Christina Mary Budd [1966] LLP Member; William Alistair Calvert [1979] LLP Member; James Watson Cameron [1979] LLP Member; Laura Elaine Cameron [1969] LLP Member; Gregory James Campbell [1956] LLP Member; Nicholas Charles Carlin [1981] LLP Member; Andreas Michael Carney [1974] LLP Member; Alan McLeod Cassels [1975] LLP Member; Inmaculada Castello Bernabeu [1979] LLP Member; Rosalie Madeleine Chadwick [1977] LLP Member; Dr Peter Roman Christ [1975] LLP Member; Matthew John Clayton-Stead [1981] LLP Member; Jonathan David Coley [1969] LLP Member; Robert Jason Alexi Collins [1970] LLP Member; Stacey Collins [1977] LLP Member; Simon Nicholas Colvin [1971] LLP Member; Robert Craig Connal [1954] LLP Member; Paul Anthony Connolly [1976] LLP Member; Iain Richard Connor [1972] LLP Member; Alan Russell Cook [1969] LLP Member; Helen Elizabeth Corden [1975] LLP Member; James Shearer Cormack [1968] LLP Member; Steven James Cottee [1972] LLP Member; Bruce Craig [1965] LLP Member; Matthew Edward Croagh [1972] LLP Member; James Crookes [1969] LLP Member; Siobhan Generaldine Cross [1962] LLP Member; Richard Daffern [1969] LLP Member; Katharine Margaret Davies [1957] LLP Member; Lawrence Michael Davies [1959] LLP Member; Alan Peter Davis [1967] LLP Member; Gregg Davison [1971] LLP Member; Zoe Siobhan de Courcy Arbiser [1980] LLP Member; Matthew de Ferrars [1975] LLP Member; Andrew Nigel Denton [1963] LLP Member; Kevin Alexander Devanny [1970] LLP Member; Martin Gerard Devine [1977] LLP Member; Didar Singh Dhillon [1975] LLP Member; Alan Lindsay Diamond [1971] LLP Member; Julian Diaz-Rainey [1971] LLP Member; Gayle Elizabeth Ditchburn [1977] LLP Member; David Michael Doogan [1976] LLP Member; Pablo Dorronsoro Martin [1975] LLP Member; Catherine Mary Drew [1982] LLP Member; Yvonne Louise Dunn [1972] LLP Member; Adrian Daniel Eakin [1970] LLP Member; Claire Louise Edwards [1973] LLP Member; Dr Martin Eimer [1975] LLP Member

PIP Infrastructure Investments (No 6) Limited
Incorporated: 9 May 2012
Previous: Aberdeen Infrastructure Investments (No 6) Limited
Net Worth: £300,682 *Total Assets:* £202,841,984
Registered Office: Cannon Place, Cannon Street, London, EC4N 6AF
Activities: Financial intermediation not elsewhere classified
Parent: PIP Infrastructure Managers Limited
Officers: Paula Burgess [1975] Director/Manager; Nicholas Tommy Cole [1978] Director/Manager; Edward Arthur Wilson [1965] Director/Manager

Pipesafe Limited
Incorporated: 15 April 1999
Net Worth: £119,688,336 *Total Assets:* £242,335,328
Registered Office: 5th Floor, Leconfield House, Curzon Street, London, W1J 5JA
Activities: Other letting and operating of own or leased real estate
Parent: Holaw (581) Limited
Officers: Nicole Martin [1963] Director/Lawyer; Stephane Abraham Joseph Nahum [1975] Director/Investment Advisor [French]; Robert Tchenguiz [1960] Director; Malcolm Robin Turner [1935] Director/Chartered Surveyor

Pips Asset Investments Limited
Incorporated: 14 May 2012
Net Worth: £10,762,000 *Total Assets:* £1,668,941,952
Registered Office: 25 Gresham Street, London, EC2V 7HN
Activities: Financial intermediation not elsewhere classified
Parent: Lloyds Bank Financial Services (Holdings) Limited
Officers: Alyson Elizabeth Mulholland, Secretary; Mark Bradshaw [1969] Director; Gavin Stuart Parker [1968] Director; Richard Douglas Shrimpton [1970] Director

Pisti 2010-1 PLC
Incorporated: 29 January 2010
Net Worth: £38,699 *Total Assets:* £517,854,656
Registered Office: Third Floor, 1 King's Arms Yard, London, EC2R 7AF
Activities: Other business support service activities n.e.c.
Parent: Pisti Holdings Limited
Officers: Robert Sutton [1978] Director/Financial Services [American]; Daniel Jonathan Wynne [1970] Director

Pitch International LLP
Incorporated: 14 September 2004 *Employees:* 56
Net Worth: £68,286,480 *Total Assets:* £247,011,232
Registered Office: 17 Brewhouse Lane, Putney Wharf, London, SW15 2JX
Officers: Philip Nigel Hope Kealy [1955] Member; Paul McGrath [1971] Member; Jonathan Owen [1971] Member; Trevor James East [1950] LLP Member; Jonathan Youell [1972] LLP Member

PKA Burbo Extension Holding (UK) Limited
Incorporated: 3 February 2016
Net Worth: £75,487,976 *Total Assets:* £353,897,568
Registered Office: 5th Floor, 6 St Andrew Street, London, EC4A 3AE
Activities: Other business support service activities n.e.c.
Officers: Ulrik Pallisoe Bornoe [1981] Director/Senior Investment Manager [Danish]; Nadia D'Ippolito [1988] Director/Asset Manager [Italian]; Stephen William Spencer Norton [1959] Finance Director; Andrew Wallace [1971] Director/DCS, UK, Management

PKA Teesrep Holding (UK) Limited
Incorporated: 5 July 2016 *Employees:* 1
Net Worth: £75,671,992 *Total Assets:* £106,046,328
Registered Office: 5th Floor, 6 St Andrew Street, London, EC4A 3AE
Activities: Other business support service activities n.e.c.
Officers: Kasper Hansen [1978] Director/Investment Manager [Danish]; Stephen William Spencer Norton [1959] Finance Director; Andrew Wallace [1971] Director/DCS, UK, Management

PL Hotel Limited
Incorporated: 25 August 2004
Net Worth: £74,720,232 *Total Assets:* £179,250,240
Registered Office: 8 Sackville Street, London, W1S 3DG
Activities: Hotels and similar accommodation
Officers: Marc John Haslam [1975] Director/Chartered Surveyor; Bruno Chibuzo Obasi [1973] Director/Chartered Accountant; Wendy Jane Patterson [1969] Director/Chartered Accountant; Paul Dennis Perris [1973] Director/Chartered Secretary; Paul Justin Windsor [1957] Director/Chartered Accountant

Places for People Developments Limited
Incorporated: 9 October 2000
Net Worth: £155,616,992 *Total Assets:* £179,003,008
Registered Office: 80 Cheapside, London, EC2V 6EE
Activities: Development of building projects
Parent: Places for People Ventures Limited
Officers: Christopher Paul Martin, Secretary; David Cowans [1957] Director/Group Chief Executive; Colin Kenneth Rae [1964] Director; Andrew Winstanley [1978] Director

Places for People Group Limited
Incorporated: 20 May 1999 *Employees:* 6,041
Net Worth: £506,200,000 *Total Assets:* £5,197,100,032
Registered Office: 80 Cheapside, London, EC2V 6EE
Activities: Activities of head offices
Officers: Christopher Paul Martin, Secretary; Michael Harris Brodtman [1960] Director/Chartered Surveyor; Adam Anthony Cleal [1956] Director; David Cowans [1957] Director/Group Chief Executive; Patrick Laurence Egan [1957] Group Director, Affordable Homes; Nigel Peter Hopkins [1958] Director; Amjad Mazhar Hussain [1958] Director; Graham John Kitchen [1967] Director; Lynette Lackey [1961] Director/Chartered Accountant; Jonathan Simon Lloyd [1956] Director; Mary Valerie Linda Parsons [1969] Director; Christopher Robin Leslie Phillips [1950] Director; Colin Kenneth Rae [1964] Group Development Director; Graham John Waddell [1957] Director; Andrew Winstanley [1978] Director

Places for People Ventures Limited
Incorporated: 21 December 2015
Net Worth: £182,364,000 *Total Assets:* £186,551,008
Registered Office: 80 Cheapside, London, EC2V 6EE
Activities: Activities of head offices
Officers: Christopher Paul Martin, Secretary; David Cowans [1957] Director; Cecily Diana Davis [1967] Director/Solicitor; Amjad Mazhar Hussain [1958] Director; Lynette Lackey [1961] Director; Jonathan Simon Lloyd [1956] Director; Mary Valerie Linda Parsons [1969] Director; Christopher Robin Leslie Phillips [1950] Director; Colin Kenneth Rae [1964] Group Development Director; Andrew Winstanley [1978] Director

PLJ Chelsea Limited
Incorporated: 27 February 2014
Net Worth: £2,891,011 *Total Assets:* £170,220,656
Registered Office: 10 Old Burlington Street, London, W1S 3AG
Activities: Buying and selling of own real estate
Parent: PLJ Holdco UK Ltd
Officers: Judah Bendayan [1961] Director [Canadian]; David Philip Berman [1961] Director; Jonathan Richard Elkington [1978] Director; Andrew Charles Williams [1964] Director/Chief Executive Officer

Thomas Pocklington Trust
Incorporated: 9 February 2005 *Employees:* 102
Previous: Thomas Pocklington Trust Limited
Net Worth: £167,916,992 *Total Assets:* £173,430,000
Registered Office: Tavistock House South, Tavistock Square, London, WC1H 9LG
Activities: Other human health activities
Officers: Alastair Balfour Chapman [1948] Director/Chartered Surveyor; Marsha Chantol de Cordova [1976] Director/Member of Parliament; Graham Arthur Findlay [1967] Director; Philip James Longworth [1960] Director/Chief Executive; Jenny Susan Pearce [1951] Director/Retired Chief Executive; Rodney Stanley Powell [1948] Director/Chartered Surveyor; John Anthony Thompson [1951] Director/Retired; Matthew William Wadsworth [1974] Director/Musician; Mervyn John Williamson [1963] Director/Chartered Accountant

Point Dume Holdings Limited
Incorporated: 20 September 2016
Net Worth Deficit: £824,324 *Total Assets:* £130,020,280
Registered Office: 5th Floor, 70 Gracechurch Street, London, EC3V 0XL
Activities: Other business support service activities n.e.c.
Officers: James Anthony MacKay [1969] Director; Alexander Patrick Nyren [1980] Director [American]; Benjamin Robert Robbins [1984] Director [American]

Polar Capital Global Financials Trust PLC
Incorporated: 17 May 2013
Net Worth: £280,984,000 *Total Assets:* £296,440,000
Registered Office: 16 Palace Street, London, SW1E 5JD
Activities: Activities of investment trusts
Officers: Joanne Lesley Elliott [1962] Director; Katrina Harriet Hart [1974] Director; Robert Kyprianou [1953] Director

Polar Capital Global Healthcare Trust PLC
Incorporated: 12 May 2010
Previous: Polar Capital Global Healthcare Growth and Income Trust PLC
Net Worth: £296,263,008 *Total Assets:* £335,188,000
Registered Office: 16 Palace Street, London, SW1E 5JD
Activities: Activities of investment trusts
Officers: Lisa Arnold [1962] Director; Anthony David Brampton [1957] Director; Neal John Ransome [1960] Director; James Peyton Robinson [1953] Director

Polar Capital Holdings PLC.
Incorporated: 15 June 2001 *Employees:* 120
Net Worth: £87,668,000 *Total Assets:* £128,914,000
Registered Office: 16 Palace Street, London, SW1E 5JD
Activities: Activities of financial services holding companies
Officers: Neil Philip Taylor, Secretary; Brian Jonathan David Ashford-Russell [1959] Director; Thomas Hugh Bartlam [1947] Director; James Michael Beale Cayzer Colvin [1965] Director; Alexa Jane Coates [1970] Director; John Bradbury Mansell [1959] Director/Accountant; Quintin Rupert Salter Price [1961] Director; Winifred Robbins [1956] Director; Gavin Mark Rochussen [1959] Director/Chief Executive

Polar Capital Technology Trust PLC
Incorporated: 15 July 1996
Net Worth: £1,551,611,008 *Total Assets:* £1,604,515,968
Registered Office: 16 Palace Street, London, SW1E 5JD
Activities: Activities of investment trusts
Officers: Sarah Catherine Bates [1959] Director/Consultant; Timothy Paul Cruttenden [1968] Director/Chief Executive; Maria Charlotta Ginman [1965] Director [Finnish]; Peter John Hames [1961] Director/Fund Manager Retired; Charles John Roberson Park [1966] Director/Investment Manager; Stephen Frank White [1955] Director

Polyus Finance PLC
Incorporated: 28 March 2017
Net Worth: £2,026,365 *Total Assets:* £1,568,725,376
Registered Office: 5th Floor, 6 St Andrew Street, London, EC4A 3AE
Activities: Other service activities n.e.c.
Officers: Antonios Antoniou [1958] Director; Alexandra Maria Beckwith [1983] Director; Sergei Igorevich Nossoff [1977] Executive Director

Pontegadea UK Ltd
Incorporated: 6 September 2013 *Employees:* 5
Net Worth: £1,778,950,016 *Total Assets:* £1,895,106,944
Registered Office: 1st Floor, West End House, 11 Hills Place, London, W1F 7SE
Activities: Buying and selling of own real estate
Major Shareholder: Amancio Ortega Gaona
Officers: Jose Arnau Sierra [1956] Director [Spanish]

Pontoon Europe Limited
Incorporated: 7 July 1997 *Employees:* 360
Previous: Hy-Phen.Com Limited
Net Worth: £43,086,000 *Total Assets:* £537,817,024
Registered Office: Millennium Bridge House, 2 Lambeth Hill, London, EC4V 4BG
Activities: Other activities of employment placement agencies
Parent: Spring Group Limited
Officers: Rashida Atinuke Akinjobi, Secretary; Alexandra Helen Bishop [1974] Director; Yann Serge Stephane Halka [1974] Director/Chief Financial Officer [French]; Gavin Kenneth Tagg [1972] Director

Pontsarn Investments Limited
Incorporated: 10 September 1958 *Employees:* 4
Net Worth: £1,257,903,232 *Total Assets:* £1,370,111,872
Registered Office: 33 Cavendish Square, London, W1G 0PW
Activities: Buying and selling of own real estate
Parent: Great Portland Estates PLC
Officers: Desna Lee Martin, Secretary; Toby Augustine Courtauld [1968] Director; Steven Richard Mew [1968] Director; Nicholas James Sanderson [1973] Director/Accountant; Andrew Nicholas Howard White [1970] Director

Pool Reinsurance Company Limited
Incorporated: 8 March 1993 *Employees:* 26
Net Worth: £5,801,413,120 *Total Assets:* £6,717,011,968
Registered Office: Hanover House, 14 Hanover Square, London, W1S 1HP
Activities: Non-life reinsurance
Officers: Rhodri David Cruwys, Secretary; Sir Brian Geoffrey Bender [1949] Director/Retired Civil Servant; Peter John Box [1952] Director [British/Australian]; Alan John Brown [1954] Director; Denise Nichola Jagger [1958] Director/Solicitor; Stephen Lewis [1968] Director; Bronislaw Edmund Masojada [1961] Director; Barbara Jane Merry [1957] Director; Geoffrey Martin Riddell [1956] Director; Andrew Graham Skirton [1963] Director/Investor; Maurice Ewen Tulloch [1969] Director [Canadian]

Poplar HARCA Capital PLC
Incorporated: 4 April 2013
Net Worth: £50,000 *Total Assets:* £139,500,992
Registered Office: 167a East India Dock Road, London, E14 0EA
Activities: Activities of other holding companies n.e.c.
Parent: Poplar Housing and Regeneration Community Association Limited
Officers: Jonathan Christopher Spearing, Secretary; Paul Martin Brickell [1957] Executive Director; Stephen Edwin Arthur Stride [1958] Director/Chief Executive

Portman Investments (Baker Street) Limited
Incorporated: 27 May 1964
Net Worth: £144,225,856 *Total Assets:* £180,434,128
Registered Office: 25 Savile Row, London, W1S 2ER
Activities: Buying and selling of own real estate
Parent: Derwent Valley Limited
Officers: David Andrew Lawler, Secretary; John David Burns [1944] Director; Oliver Barry Kemp Fenn-Smith [1965] Director/Chartered Surveyor; The Viscount Edward James Wingfield Lifford [1949] Director; Mark Peter Southern [1959] Director; Paul Malcolm Williams [1960] Director; Damian Mark Alan Wisniewski [1961] Director

Portman Square US Holdings Limited
Incorporated: 13 November 2006
Net Worth: £189,414,496 *Total Assets:* £1,007,092,608
Registered Office: 10 Triton Street, Regent's Place, London, NW1 3BF
Activities: Activities of head offices
Parent: Aegis GPS Holdings Limited
Officers: Andrew John Moberly, Secretary; Simon Glyndon Jones [1972] Director/Accountant; Nicholas Charles Priday [1974] Director; David Mark Wein [1975] Director; Simon Gregorevich Zinger [1970] Director/General Counsel [British/American/Canadian]

Portobar Capital Limited
Incorporated: 11 April 2006 *Employees:* 2
Net Worth: £139,524,864 *Total Assets:* £139,587,040
Registered Office: 21 Holborn Viaduct, London, EC1A 2DY
Activities: Activities of open-ended investment companies
Parent: A.P. Moller-Maersk A/S
Officers: Willem Adriaan Lagaay [1967] Director [Dutch]; Maria de Los Angeles Reyes Barranquero [1962] Director [Spanish]

Portswood Investments Limited
Incorporated: 19 November 2012
Net Worth: £1,637,953,024 *Total Assets:* £1,660,224,000
Registered Office: 3 Sheldon Square, Padington, London, W2 6PX
Activities: Other business support service activities n.e.c.
Parent: Kingfisher International Holdings Limited
Officers: Paul Moore, Secretary; Jean-Noel Hughes Roger Groleau [1974] Director [French]; Paul Anthony Moore [1970] Director/Company Secretary

Post Office Limited
Incorporated: 13 August 1987 *Employees:* 5,020
Net Worth: £203,000,000 *Total Assets:* £1,480,999,936
Registered Office: Finsbury Dials, 20 Finsbury Street, London, EC2Y 9AQ
Activities: Postal activities under universal service obligation
Parent: Secretary of State for Business, Energy and Industrial Strategy
Officers: Jane Elizabeth MacLeod, Secretary; Alisdair Charles John Cameron [1965] Director/Chief Financial Officer; Tom Knut Glenn Cooper [1962] Director; Timothy Alan Franklin [1961] Director; Shirine Khoury-Haq [1971] Director; Kenneth Stanely McCall [1957] Director; Timothy Charles Parker [1955] Director/Chairman; Carla Rosaline Stent [1971] Director; The Reverend Paula Anne Vennells [1959] Director

Power Leisure Bookmakers Limited
Incorporated: 10 August 1999 *Employees:* 3,066
Net Worth: £61,465,680 *Total Assets:* £855,336,512
Registered Office: Waterfront, Hammersmith Embankment, Chancellors Road, London, W6 9HP
Activities: Gambling and betting activities
Parent: Paddy Power Betfair PLC
Officers: Pritti Patel, Secretary; Mark Irwin [1971] Director [Irish]; Daniel Taylor [1980] Managing Director; Edward Martin Traynor [1977] Director/General Counsel [Irish]

PP Oil & Gas (Indonesia-Jabung) Limited
Incorporated: 17 May 1996
Net Worth: £91,716,240 *Total Assets:* £187,739,824
Registered Office: 1 Fleet Place, London, EC4M 7WS
Activities: Extraction of crude petroleum
Officers: Gong Bencai [1966] Director/Management/President [Chinese]; Emi Suhardi Bin Mohd Fadzil [1966] Director/Head, Upstream Risk & Assurance, Finance & Risk [Malaysian]; Yu Guoyi [1966] Director/General Manager [Chinese]; Mohd Nazlee Bin Rasol [1974] Director/President, PC Muriah Ltd [Malaysian]

PR Goal 3 Limited
Incorporated: 26 August 2005
Net Worth: £737,426,304 *Total Assets:* £737,426,304
Registered Office: Chivas House, 72 Chancellors Road, London, W6 9RS
Activities: Activities of head offices
Parent: Goal Acquisitions (Holdings) Limited
Officers: Amanda Hamilton-Stanley [1968] Director/General Counsel; Stuart MacNab [1964] Director/Accountant; Vincent Turpin [1978] Director/Chief Financial Officer [French]

PRA Corporate Capital Limited
Incorporated: 24 September 2013
Net Worth Deficit: £15,118,687 *Total Assets:* £171,761,376
Registered Office: 5th Floor, 70 Gracechurch Street, London, EC3V 0XL
Activities: Other activities auxiliary to insurance and pension funding
Parent: PRACCL Limited
Officers: Howard Harley Friedman [1958] Director/Chief Underwriting Officer and Actuary [American]; Edward Lewis Rand Jr [1966] Director/Accountant [American]

PRACCL Limited
Incorporated: 24 September 2013
Net Worth Deficit: £18,622,876 *Total Assets:* £171,567,600
Registered Office: 5th Floor, 70 Gracechurch Street, London, EC3V 0XL
Activities: Activities of other holding companies n.e.c.
Officers: Howard Harley Friedman [1958] Director/Chief Underwriting Officer and Actuary [American]; Edward Lewis Rand Jr [1966] Director/Chief Financial Officer [American]

Praesidiad Group Limited
Incorporated: 3 July 2017 *Employees:* 1,239
Net Worth Deficit: £21,731,160 *Total Assets:* £787,892,480
Registered Office: Praesidiad, 8th Floor, The Gridiron Building, One Pancras Square, London, N1C 4AG
Activities: Activities of other holding companies n.e.c.
Parent: ERPE Finco Limited
Officers: Paul Clifford Skertchly [1962] Director; Andrew John Stevens [1956] Director

Praesidiad Limited
Incorporated: 3 July 2017 *Employees:* 4
Net Worth: £14,357,490 *Total Assets:* £577,007,552
Registered Office: Praesidiad, 8th Floor, The Gridiron Building, One Pancras Square, London, N1C 4AG
Activities: Activities of other holding companies n.e.c.
Parent: Praesidiad Group Limited
Officers: Jane Elizabeth Douglas [1982] Director/Lawyer [Australian]; Paul Clifford Skertchly [1962] Director

Praxis I Finance PLC
Incorporated: 24 February 2009
Net Worth: £40,009 *Total Assets:* £222,494,512
Registered Office: Third Floor, 1 King's Arms Yard, London, EC2R 7AF
Activities: Other business support service activities n.e.c.
Parent: Wilmington Trust SP Services (London) Limited
Officers: Robert Sutton [1978] Director/Financial Services [American]; Daniel Jonathan Wynne [1970] Director

Praxis II APC Limited
Incorporated: 14 July 2009
Net Worth: £32,118 *Total Assets:* £331,909,920
Registered Office: Third Floor, 1 King's Arms Yard, London, EC2R 7AF
Activities: Other business support service activities n.e.c.
Parent: Praxis II Holdings Limited
Officers: Robert Sutton [1978] Director/Financial Services [American]; Daniel Jonathan Wynne [1970] Director

Praxis II Finance PLC
Incorporated: 14 July 2009
Net Worth: £17,290 *Total Assets:* £329,855,680
Registered Office: Third Floor, 1 King's Arms Yard, London, EC2R 7AF
Activities: Other business support service activities n.e.c.
Parent: Praxis II Holdings Limited
Officers: Robert Sutton [1978] Director/Financial Services [American]; Daniel Jonathan Wynne [1970] Director

Precis (1789) Limited
Incorporated: 23 July 1999
Net Worth: £244,795,008 *Total Assets:* £250,468,992
Registered Office: Globe House, 4 Temple Place, London, WC2R 2PG
Activities: Activities of head offices
Parent: Weston Investment Company Limited
Officers: Robert James Casey [1948] Director/Attorney [American]; Noelle Colfer [1968] Director/Solicitor; Naresh Kumar Sethi [1966] Business Development Director [Australian]; Carola Wiegand [1966] Director/Global Commercial Tax Manager [German]

Precis (1814) Limited
Incorporated: 2 September 1999
Net Worth: £761,192,000 *Total Assets:* £1,267,864,960
Registered Office: Globe House, 4 Temple Place, London, WC2R 2PG
Activities: Activities of head offices
Parent: Weston Investment Company Limited
Officers: Sophie Louise Edmonds Kerr, Secretary; Andrew James Barrett [1974] Director; Robert James Casey [1948] Director/Attorney [American]; Naresh Kumar Sethi [1966] Business Development Director [Australian]; Neil Arthur Wadey [1964] Director/Treasurer; Carola Wiegand [1966] Director/Global Commercial Tax Manager [German]

Precise Mortgage Funding 2015-2B PLC
Incorporated: 12 May 2015
Net Worth: £14,668 *Total Assets:* £148,449,120
Registered Office: 35 Great St Helen's, London, EC3A 6AP
Activities: Financial intermediation not elsewhere classified
Parent: Precise Mortgage Holdings 2015-2B Limited
Officers: Daniel Marc Richard Jaffe [1975] Director

Precise Mortgage Funding 2015-3R PLC
Incorporated: 9 September 2015
Net Worth: £13,000 *Total Assets:* £383,940,992
Registered Office: 35 Great St Helen's, London, EC3A 6AP
Activities: Financial intermediation not elsewhere classified
Parent: Precise Mortgage Holdings 2015-3R Limited
Officers: Daniel Marc Richard Jaffe [1975] Director

Precise Mortgage Funding 2017-1B PLC
Incorporated: 13 March 2017
Net Worth: £12,987 *Total Assets:* £320,159,136
Registered Office: 35 Great St Helen's, London, EC3A 6AP
Activities: Financial intermediation not elsewhere classified
Parent: Precise Mortgage Holdings 2017-1B Limited
Officers: Daniel Marc Richard Jaffe [1975] Director

Premier Lotteries Investments UK Limited
Incorporated: 25 March 2010 *Employees:* 963
Net Worth Deficit: £136,900,000 *Total Assets:* £815,200,000
Registered Office: 10 Portman Square, London, W1H 6AZ
Activities: Activities of head offices
Officers: John Edward Michael Dillon [1963] Legal Director and Company Secretary; Ilya Kachko [1979] Director/Portfolio Manager [Canadian]; Andrew Jonathan Mark Taylor [1961] Director/Private Equity Investor

Premier Oil E & P UK EU Limited
Incorporated: 11 March 1994
Previous: E.On E & P UK EU Limited
Net Worth: £9,152,000 *Total Assets:* £192,364,000
Registered Office: 23 Lower Belgrave Street, London, SW1W 0NR
Activities: Extraction of crude petroleum
Parent: Premier Oil E & P UK Limited
Officers: Daniel Alexander Rose, Secretary; Robert Andrew Allan [1959] Director; Anthony Richard Charles Durrant [1958] Director; Julie Elizabeth Forsyth [1969] Director/Solicitor; Andrew George Gibb [1968] Director/Solicitor; Dean Geoffrey Griffin [1969] Director/Geologist; Richard Andrew Rose [1972] Director; Paul David Williams [1963] Director/Oil Industry Executive

Premier Oil E & P UK Limited
Incorporated: 2 November 1992
Previous: E.On E & P UK Limited
Net Worth: £511,035,616 *Total Assets:* £1,021,145,600
Registered Office: 23 Lower Belgrave Street, London, SW1W 0NR
Activities: Extraction of crude petroleum
Parent: Premier Oil E & P Holdings Limited
Officers: Daniel Alexander Rose, Secretary; Robert Andrew Allan [1959] Director; Anthony Richard Charles Durrant [1958] Director; Julie Elizabeth Forsyth [1969] Director/Solicitor; Andrew George Gibb [1968] Director/Solicitor; Dean Geoffrey Griffin [1969] Director/Geologist; Richard Andrew Rose [1972] Director; Paul David Williams [1963] Director/Oil Industry Executive

Premier Oil Exploration and Production Limited
Incorporated: 11 July 2012 *Employees:* 1
Net Worth: £2,910,424 *Total Assets:* £479,706,976
Registered Office: 23 Lower Belgrave Street, London, SW1W 0NR
Activities: Extraction of crude petroleum
Parent: Premier Oil Holdings Limited
Officers: Daniel Alexander Rose, Secretary; Robert Andrew Allan [1959] Director/Geologist; Anthony Richard Charles Durrant [1958] Director/Oil Industry Executive; Andrew George Gibb [1968] Director/Solicitor; Richard Andrew Rose [1972] Finance Director

Premier Oil Group Holdings Limited
Incorporated: 23 May 2017
Net Worth: £454,201,248 *Total Assets:* £454,201,248
Registered Office: 23 Lower Belgrave Street, London, SW1W 0NR
Activities: Activities of head offices
Parent: Premier Oil PLC
Officers: Daniel Alexander Rose, Secretary; Robert Andrew Allan [1959] Director/Geologist; Anthony Richard Charles Durrant [1958] Director/Oil Industry Executive; Andrew George Gibb [1968] Director/Solicitor; Richard Andrew Rose [1959] Director

Premier Oil Holdings Limited
Incorporated: 29 December 1998
Net Worth Deficit: £226,555,696 *Total Assets:* £1,218,181,760
Registered Office: 23 Lower Belgrave Street, London, SW1W 0NR
Activities: Support activities for petroleum and natural gas mining
Parent: Premier Oil Group Limited
Officers: Daniel Alexander Rose, Secretary; Robert Andrew Allan [1959] Director/Geologist; Anthony Richard Charles Durrant [1958] Director/Oil Industry Executive; Andrew George Gibb [1968] Director/Solicitor; Richard Andrew Rose [1972] Finance Director

Premier Place Finance Limited
Incorporated: 12 July 2004
Net Worth Deficit: £85,886,000 *Total Assets:* £239,100,992
Registered Office: 5th Floor, 6 St Andrew Street, London, EC4A 3AE
Activities: Other business support service activities n.e.c.
Parent: Premier Place Propco Limited
Officers: Nita Ramesh Savjani [1980] Director; Guido Dietrik Seleski [1972] Director/Consultant [Dutch]

Premiertel PLC
Incorporated: 15 April 2003
Net Worth: £341,783 *Total Assets:* £271,939,808
Registered Office: 35 Great St Helen's, London, EC3A 6AP
Activities: Financial intermediation not elsewhere classified
Parent: Intertrust Corporate Services Limited
Officers: Daniel Marc Richard Jaffe [1975] Director

Prepaid Financial Services Limited
Incorporated: 8 August 2007 *Employees:* 48
Net Worth: £8,323,511 *Total Assets:* £260,460,720
Registered Office: Fifth Floor, Langham House, 302-308 Regent Street, London, W1B 3AT
Activities: Other credit granting n.e.c.
Parent: Prepaid Financial Services (Ireland) Ltd
Officers: Valerie Willis, Secretary [Zimbabwean]; Lee James Britton [1968] Director; Noel Gerard Moran [1969] Director [Irish]; Oren Haim Rose [1970] Director [Israeli]; Valerie Willis [1975] Director [Zimbabwean]

Prepaid Services Company Limited
Incorporated: 30 March 2006 *Employees:* 6
Net Worth: £11,918,971 *Total Assets:* £215,474,144
Registered Office: Floor 27, 25 Canary Wharf, London, E14 5LQ
Activities: Other business support service activities n.e.c.
Parent: Paysafecard.Com Wertkarten GmbH
Officers: Elaine Quine, Secretary; Paul James Brooking [1976] Director/Chartered Accountant; Daniel Jay Chazonoff [1963] Director/Chief Operating Officer [Canadian]; Mark Aidan Jeffrey [1958] Director; Udo Mueller [1975] Director [Austrian]; Maximilian Von Both [1979] Director/Vice President Compliance [German]; Elliott Mark Wiseman [1974] Director/Solicitor

Prepay Technologies Limited
Incorporated: 5 June 2000 *Employees:* 159
Net Worth: £13,467,968 *Total Assets:* £332,164,544
Registered Office: Floor 6, 3 Sheldon Square, London, W2 6HY
Activities: Other business support service activities n.e.c.
Shareholders: Edenred (UK Group) Limited; Mastercard Europe SA; Edenred SA
Officers: Julian Alastair Brand, Secretary; Raymond Cantrille Brash [1965] Managing Director; Andrew James Buckley [1965] Director; Garry Michael Comley [1959] Director; Eimear Bernice Creaven [1978] Director [Irish]; Marc Francois Andre Divay [1981] Director [French]; Elie Marie Gregoire Du Pre de Saint Maur [1976] Director [French]; Paul-Henri Marie Motel [1972] Director/Chief Financial Officer [French]

Press Acquisitions Limited
Incorporated: 8 April 2004 *Employees:* 1,131
Net Worth: £3,800,000 *Total Assets:* £271,500,000
Registered Office: 2nd Floor, 14 St George Street, London, W1S 1FE
Activities: Activities of head offices
Officers: Aidan Stuart Barclay [1956] Director; Howard Myles Barclay [1959] Financier Director; Rigel Kent Mowatt [1948] Director/Chartered Accountant; Philip Leslie Peters [1957] Company Banking Director; Michael Seal [1948] Director/Chartered Accountant

Prestbury Investment Holdings Limited
Incorporated: 4 May 2000 *Employees:* 16
Net Worth: £86,241,000 *Total Assets:* £104,603,000
Registered Office: Cavendish House, 18 Cavendish Square, London, W1G 0PJ
Activities: Management of real estate on a fee or contract basis
Shareholders: Nicholas Mark Leslau; Nigel William Wray
Officers: Sandra Louise Gumm, Secretary [Australian]; Sandra Louise Gumm [1966] Director/Chartered Accountant [Australian]; Nicholas Mark Leslau [1959] Director/Chartered Surveyor; Nigel William Wray [1948] Director

Prestmade Limited
Incorporated: 13 May 1998 *Employees:* 404
Net Worth: £40,680,000 *Total Assets:* £562,833,024
Registered Office: 14 Chester Terrace, London, NW1 4ND
Activities: Other letting and operating of own or leased real estate
Major Shareholder: Gulshan Bhatia
Officers: Shelina Jetha, Secretary; Jitendra Patel, Secretary; Gulshan Bhatia [1933] Director; Nimet Esmail [1958] Sales Director; Shelina Jetha [1961] Marketing Director

Pret A Manger (Europe) Limited
Incorporated: 10 October 1984 *Employees:* 8,581
Net Worth: £450,323,008 *Total Assets:* £543,872,000
Registered Office: 75B Verde, 10 Bressenden Place, London, SW1E 5DH
Activities: Retail sale in non-specialised stores with food, beverages or tobacco predominating
Parent: Pam Acquisitionco Limited
Officers: Clive Edward Benedict Schlee, Secretary; Clare Patricia Clough [1980] Food and Coffee Director; Clive Edward Benedict Schlee [1959] Director; Andrea Wareham [1972] Director of People

Priceline. Com International Limited
Incorporated: 11 July 2005
Net Worth: £10,276,704,256 *Total Assets:* £10,280,983,552
Registered Office: 100 New Bridge Street, London, EC4V 6JA
Activities: Travel agency activities
Parent: Priceline.Com Holdco U.K. Limited
Officers: Anthony Joseph Cali Jnr [1972] Director/Finance-SVP, Corporate Controller [American]; David Ian Goulden [1959] Director [American]

Priceline.Com Holdco U.K. Limited
Incorporated: 16 August 2004
Net Worth: £304,650,560 *Total Assets:* £306,015,616
Registered Office: 100 New Bridge Street, London, EC4V 6JA
Activities: Activities of head offices
Parent: Booking Holdings Inc.
Officers: Eduardo Nils Tarto Andrade [1969] Director/Attorney [American]; Anthony Joseph Cali Jnr [1972] Director/Finance-SVP, Corporate Controller [American]

Pricewaterhousecoopers LLP
Incorporated: 9 December 2002 *Employees:* 22,601
Net Worth: £310,000,000 *Total Assets:* £1,662,000,000
Registered Office: 1 Embankment Place, London, WC2N 6RH
Officers: Kevin James Burrowes [1962] Member; Kevin James David Ellis [1963] Member; Warwick Ean Hunt [1962] Member; Richard Pierre Abadie [1966] LLP Member; Amit Abhyankar [1973] LLP Member; Mark Addley [1980] LLP Member; Simon Piers Ager [1973] LLP Member; Steve Aherne [1974] LLP Member; Joanna Ahlstrom [1975] LLP Member; Arif Mahtab Ahmad [1975] LLP Member; Matthew Alabaster [1974] LLP Member; Bron Alexander [1980] LLP Member; Iain Andrew Alexander [1976] LLP Member; Shamshad Ali [1970] LLP Member; David Paul Allen [1979] LLP Member; David Allen [1963] LLP Member; Tim Allen [1977] LLP Member; Timothy James Allen [1963] LLP Member; Stella Claire Amiss [1971] LLP Member; Marco Amitrano [1969] LLP Member; Heather Clare Ancient [1965] LLP Member; David Christian Andersen [1969] LLP Member; David Anderson [1967] LLP Member; Hamish Anderson [1974] LLP Member; Iain Blair Anderson [1973] LLP Member; Mark Richard Anderson [1972] LLP Member; James John Andrews [1984] LLP Member; Jonathan Stuart Christian Andrews [1966] LLP Member; James Arden-Davis [1964] LLP Member; Mohammed Armoghan [1966] LLP Member; David Martin Armstrong [1966] LLP Member; Stephen Martin Arnold [1978] LLP Member; Damien Ashford [1977] LLP Member; Brian Andrew Ashmead-Siers [1977] LLP Member; Nicholas James Dale Atkin [1967] LLP Member; Frederick Paul Atkinson [1961] LLP Member; Paul James Atkinson [1978] LLP Member; Ranjit Singh Auluk [1968] LLP Member; Hugh Glynn Austen-Brown [1977] LLP Member; Thomas Hedley Ayerst [1973] LLP Member; Shazia Azim [1970] LLP Member; Glen Howard Babcock [1971] LLP Member; Lynne Roberta Baber [1982] LLP Member; Richard Jonathan Bailes [1975] LLP Member; Isabelle Anne Jamesina Bailey [1978] LLP Member; Michael Bailey [1967] LLP Member; Scott Bailey [1972] LLP Member; John Kenneth Baker [1959] LLP Member; Robert George Banham [1975] LLP Member; John-Paul Barker [1973] LLP Member; Paul Andrew Barkus [1964] LLP Member; Matthew Barling [1966] LLP Member; Colin Adrian Bates [1975] LLP Member; Leigh Bates [1975] LLP Member; Stephen Paul Batt [1970] LLP Member; Mark Edward Batten [1972] LLP Member; Ian Robert Baxter [1965] LLP Member; David Andrew Beer [1974] LLP Member; Andrew Nicholas Bell [1965] LLP Member; Daniel Bell [1972] LLP Member; Joanna Bello [1971] LLP Member; Marc Paul Henri Bena [1971] LLP Member; David Bendall [1971] LLP Member; Ian Benson [1976] LLP Member; Ermelinda Beqiraj [1977] LLP Member; Dr Oliver Bernath [1963] LLP Member; Scott Berryman [1975] LLP Member; Alexander Jonathan Bertolotti [1970] LLP Member; David Sean Bettesworth [1969] LLP Member; Caroline Bevan [1973] LLP Member; James William Edward Bichard [1973] LLP Member; Neil Thomas Bindoff [1968] LLP Member; Mark Binney [1971] LLP Member; Claire Elizabeth Blackburn [1979] LLP Member; Justin Douglas Blackburn [1975] LLP Member; Rosemary Katherine Blackham [1967] LLP Member; Anna Louise Blackman [1979] LLP Member; Steven Robert Raymond Blackmore [1977] LLP Member; Martin Blanche [1973] LLP Member; Philip Bloomfield [1963] LLP Member; Georgie Robert Blyth [1980] LLP Member; Nicholas William Edward Boden [1962] LLP Member; Mark Neil Bolton [1971] LLP Member; Philippa Louise Booth [1974] LLP Member; Christopher John Boreham [1971] LLP Member; Nicholas Andrew Bouch [1974] LLP Member; Andrew Paul Boucher [1963] LLP Member; Robert Mark Boulding [1978] LLP Member; Jonathan Mark Boulton [1974] LLP Member; Charles Edward Beck Bowman [1961] LLP Member; Christopher John Stanley Box [1972] LLP Member; Steven Brian Boyd [1973] LLP Member; Giovanni Giorgio Bracco [1966] LLP Member; Simon Bradford [1979] LLP Member; Sally Ann Bradley [1963] LLP Member; Roger Thomas Braybrooks [1969] LLP Member; Alison Breadon [1974] LLP Member; Robert John Bridson [1966] LLP Member; Gregory Diarmid Briggs [1969] LLP Member; Andrew Broad [1971] LLP Member

Pricewaterhousecoopers Services Limited
Incorporated: 29 June 1962 *Employees:* 15,911
Net Worth: £75,727,000 *Total Assets:* £580,878,016
Registered Office: 1 Embankment Place, London, WC2N 6RH
Activities: Other business support service activities n.e.c.
Parent: PWC Holdings (UK) Limited
Officers: Philip Patterson, Secretary; Jonathan Stuart Christian Andrews [1966] Director; Kevin James Burrowes [1962] Director; Margaret Rose Cole [1961] Director/Solicitor; Andrew Julian Bailye Cope [1964] Director/Chartered Accountant; Kevin James David Ellis [1963] Director/Accountant; Laura Hinton [1972] Director; Warwick Ean Hunt [1962] Director/Accountant [New Zealander]; Dan Yoram Schwarzmann [1963] Director/Chartered Accountant

Primark Stores Limited
Incorporated: 30 April 1948 *Employees:* 35,781
Net Worth: £593,049,984 *Total Assets:* £1,969,549,952
Registered Office: Weston Centre, 10 Grosvenor Street, London, W1K 4QY
Activities: Retail sale of clothing in specialised stores
Parent: ABF Investments PLC
Officers: Rosalyn Sharon Schofield, Secretary; John George Bason [1957] Finance Director; Simon Summerfield Gibbs [1969] Director; Bernard John Michael Mansfield [1954] Sales Director [Irish]

Primary Health Investment Properties Limited
Incorporated: 8 March 1994 *Employees:* 3
Net Worth: £69,008,880 *Total Assets:* £315,049,824
Registered Office: 5th Floor, Greener House, 66-68 Haymarket, London, SW1Y 4RF
Activities: Other letting and operating of own or leased real estate
Parent: Primary Health Properties PLC
Officers: David Christopher Austin [1970] Director/Chartered Surveyor; Richard Howell [1965] Director/Chartered Accountant; Harry Abraham Hyman [1956] Director/Chartered Accountant

Primary Health Properties PLC
Incorporated: 16 March 1995
Net Worth: £788,000,000 *Total Assets:* £1,514,000,000
Registered Office: 5th Floor, Greener House, 66-68 Haymarket, London, SW1Y 4RF
Activities: Other letting and operating of own or leased real estate
Officers: Peter William Beaumont Cole [1959] Director/Chartered Surveyor; Richard Howell [1965] Director/Chartered Accountant; Harry Abraham Hyman [1956] Director/Chartered Accountant; Dr Stephen Wallace Kell [1971] Director/Medical Doctor; Generaldine Ann Kennell [1968] Director; Ian Stephen Krieger [1952] Director/Chartered Accountant; Steven Jonathan Owen [1957] Director/Chartered Accountant; Nick Wiles [1961] Director

Primary Medical Property Investments Limited
Incorporated: 9 October 1956
Net Worth: £57,162,120 *Total Assets:* £115,803,672
Registered Office: 6th Floor, 33 Holborn, London, EC1N 2HT
Activities: Development of building projects
Parent: Medicx Properties IX Limited
Officers: Mark Andrew Woodall [1962] Director

Primeairo Limited
Incorporated: 26 November 1987
Net Worth: £107,006,000 *Total Assets:* £107,006,000
Registered Office: 30 Portman Square, London, W1A 4ZX
Activities: Hotels and similar accommodation
Parent: Havana Holding UK Ltd
Officers: Karin Cooper, Secretary; Jassim Bin Hamad Al Thani [1982] Director/Chairman [Qatari]; Fady Bakhos [1971] Director/Lawyer [Lebanese]; Michael Anthony Cairns [1940] Director; Karin Cooper [1969] Director/Architect [German]; Zaki Nasser Zaki El Guiziri [1957] Director [Egyptian]

Primepanel Limited
Incorporated: 23 April 2002
Net Worth Deficit: £18,487,000 *Total Assets:* £215,256,992
Registered Office: Saffron Court, 14b St Cross Street, London, EC1N 8XA
Activities: Non-trading company
Parent: PIHL (2003) Limited
Officers: Aaron Campbell, Secretary; Hiroyasu Matsui [1965] Director [Japanese]; Jonathan Paul Scott [1961] Director/Accountant

Primetals Technologies Financial Services Limited
Incorporated: 8 February 2016 *Employees:* 5
Net Worth: £32,095,988 *Total Assets:* £294,796,768
Registered Office: Building No 11, Chiswick Park, 566 Chiswick High Road, London, W4 5YA
Activities: Other service activities n.e.c.
Parent: Primetals Technologies Limited
Officers: Paul Wallace, Secretary; Jeremy Didier Hamon [1986] Director/Head of Group Treasury [French]; Yuichi Yokota [1971] Director/Businessman [Japanese]; Miljenko Solje [1973] Director/Head of Group Finance [Croatian]

Primetals Technologies, Limited
Incorporated: 31 July 2014 *Employees:* 353
Net Worth: £400,374,016 *Total Assets:* £565,897,024
Registered Office: Building 11, Chiswick Park, 566 Chiswick High Road, London, W4 5YA
Activities: Engineering design activities for industrial process and production
Shareholders: Mitsubishi Heavy Industries, Ltd.; Siemens Aktiengesellschaft
Officers: Paul Wallace, Secretary; Etsuro Hirai [1959] Director [Japanese]; Satoru Iijima [1960] Director/CEO and Chairman [Japanese]; Peter Walter Schraut [1964] Director [German]; Yasukuni Yamasaki [1949] Director/Business Executive [Japanese]

Primount LLP
Incorporated: 15 October 2013
Net Worth: £425,954,336 *Total Assets:* £429,203,392
Registered Office: Level 37, 25 Canada Square, London, E14 5LQ

Principal Financial Services I (UK) LLP
Incorporated: 10 July 2012
Net Worth: £1,841,471,744 *Total Assets:* £1,841,471,744
Registered Office: 1 Wood Street, London, EC2V 7JB

Principal Financial Services II (UK) Ltd
Incorporated: 10 July 2012
Net Worth: £922,041,792 *Total Assets:* £924,107,648
Registered Office: 1 Wood Street, London, EC2V 7JB
Activities: Activities of financial services holding companies
Parent: Principal Financial Services I (UK) LLP
Officers: Timothy Mark Dunbar [1957] Corporate Director [American]; Paul McConomy [1968] Director/Business Executive; Karen Elizabeth Shaff [1954] Director/Lawyer [American]

Principal Financial Services III (UK) Ltd
Incorporated: 12 July 2012
Net Worth: £977,335,040 *Total Assets:* £977,335,360
Registered Office: 1 Wood Street, London, EC2V 7JB
Activities: Activities of financial services holding companies
Parent: Principal Financial Services II (UK)
Officers: Timothy Mark Dunbar [1957] Director/Corporate Officer [American]; Paul McConomy [1968] Director/Business Executive; Karen Elizabeth Shaff [1954] Director/Lawyer [American]

Principal Financial Services IV (UK) LLP
Incorporated: 29 November 2012
Net Worth: £992,834,816 *Total Assets:* £992,834,816
Registered Office: 1 Wood Street, London, EC2V 7JB

Principal Financial Services Latin America Ltd
Incorporated: 10 July 2012
Net Worth: £918,830,720 *Total Assets:* £918,830,720
Registered Office: 1 Wood Street, London, EC2V 7JB
Activities: Activities of financial services holding companies
Parent: Principal Financial Services III (UK) Ltd
Officers: Timothy Mark Dunbar [1957] Corporate Director [American]; Paul McConomy [1968] Director/Business Executive; Karen Elizabeth Shaff [1954] Director/Lawyer [American]

Principal Financial Services V (UK) Ltd
Incorporated: 30 November 2012
Net Worth: £1,041,240,192 *Total Assets:* £1,126,968,064
Registered Office: 1 Wood Street, London, EC2V 7JB
Activities: Other activities auxiliary to insurance and pension funding
Parent: Principal Financial Services IV (UK) LLP
Officers: Timothy Mark Dunbar [1957] Director/Corporate Officer [American]; Paul McConomy [1968] Director/Business Executive; Karen Elizabeth Shaff [1954] Director/Lawyer [American]

Principal Global Financial Services (Europe) II Ltd
Incorporated: 5 May 2015
Net Worth: £180,886,752 *Total Assets:* £185,976,512
Registered Office: c/o Principal Global Investors (Europe) Ltd, 1 Wood Street, London, EC2V 7JB
Activities: Activities of head offices
Parent: Principal Financial Group Inc
Officers: Timothy Mark Dunbar [1957] Director/Corporate Officer [American]; Paul McConomy [1968] Director/Business Executive; Karen Elizabeth Shaff [1954] Director/Corporate Officer [American]

Principal International Latin America Ltd
Incorporated: 10 July 2012
Net Worth: £919,632,448 *Total Assets:* £919,632,448
Registered Office: 1 Wood Street, London, EC2V 7JB
Activities: Activities of financial services holding companies
Parent: Principal Financial Services Latin America Ltd
Officers: Timothy Mark Dunbar [1957] Corporate Director [American]; Paul McConomy [1968] Director/Business Executive; Karen Elizabeth Shaff [1954] Director/Lawyer [American]

Principal International South America I Ltd
Incorporated: 10 July 2012
Net Worth: £589,181,888 *Total Assets:* £589,181,888
Registered Office: 1 Wood Street, London, EC2V 7JB
Activities: Activities of financial services holding companies
Parent: Principal International Latin America Ltd
Officers: Timothy Mark Dunbar [1957] Director/Corporate Officer [American]; Paul McConomy [1968] Director/Business Executive; Karen Elizabeth Shaff [1954] Director/Lawyer [American]

Principal International South America II Ltd
Incorporated: 10 July 2012
Net Worth: £476,603,584 *Total Assets:* £476,603,584
Registered Office: 1 Wood Street, London, EC2V 7JB
Activities: Activities of financial services holding companies
Parent: Principal International South America I Ltd
Officers: Karen Arlene Pearston, Secretary; Timothy Mark Dunbar [1957] Corporate Director [American]; Paul McConomy [1968] Director/Business Executive; Karen Elizabeth Shaff [1954] Director/Lawyer [American]

Priority Pass Limited
Incorporated: 3 July 1992 *Employees:* 97
Net Worth: £62,265,736 *Total Assets:* £151,347,904
Registered Office: Cutlers Exchange, 123 Houndsditch, London, EC3A 7BU
Activities: Activities of other membership organisations n.e.c.
Parent: Priority Pass (UK Holdings) Limited
Officers: Mark Richard Hampton, Secretary; Susan Burns [1954] Director; Colin Robert Evans [1947] Director/Management Consultant; Mark Richard Hampton [1964] Finance Director; Stephen John Pinches [1957] Director/Marketing

Priory Education Services Limited
Incorporated: 11 May 2007 *Employees:* 2,073
Net Worth: £2,585,000 *Total Assets:* £133,549,000
Registered Office: Fifth Floor, 80 Hammersmith Road, London, W14 8UD
Activities: General secondary education
Parent: Priory Group No.3 Limited
Officers: David James Hall, Secretary; Nigel Myers [1966] Finance Director; Trevor Michael Torrington [1961] Director/Chief Executive Officer

Priory Finance Property LLP
Incorporated: 14 October 2005
Net Worth Deficit: £138,963,008 *Total Assets:* £526,184,000
Registered Office: Fifth Floor, 80 Hammersmith Road, London, W14 8UD

Priory Group Limited
Incorporated: 8 May 2002
Net Worth: £65,038,000 *Total Assets:* £135,636,992
Registered Office: Fifth Floor, 80 Hammersmith Road, London, W14 8UD
Activities: Activities of head offices
Parent: Priory Healthcare Finance Company Limited
Officers: David James Hall, Secretary; David James Hall [1962] Director/Company Lawyer

Priory Group No. 1 Limited
Incorporated: 30 December 2010
Net Worth: £1,087,497,984 *Total Assets:* £1,087,517,952
Registered Office: Fifth Floor, 80 Hammersmith Road, London, W14 8UD
Activities: Activities of other holding companies n.e.c.
Parent: Whitewell UK Investments 1 Limited
Officers: David James Hall, Secretary; Nigel Myers [1966] Finance Director; Trevor Michael Torrington [1961] Director/Chief Executive

Priory Group No. 3 Limited
Incorporated: 31 December 2010
Previous: Priory Group No. 3 PLC
Net Worth: £977,884,992 *Total Assets:* £1,231,181,056
Registered Office: Fifth Floor, 80 Hammersmith Road, London, W14 8UD
Activities: Activities of other holding companies n.e.c.
Parent: Priory Group No.2 Limited
Officers: David James Hall, Secretary; Nigel Myers [1966] Finance Director; Trevor Michael Torrington [1961] Director/Chief Executive

Priory Group UK 1 Limited
Incorporated: 27 May 2014 *Employees:* 20,707
Previous: Partnerships in Care UK 1 Limited
Net Worth: £542,416,000 *Total Assets:* £1,970,803,968
Registered Office: Fifth Floor, 80 Hammersmith Road, London, W14 8UD
Activities: Hospital activities
Officers: David James Hall, Secretary; Christopher Lee Howard [1966] Director [American]; Nigel Myers [1966] Director; Debra Kay Osteen [1955] Director/Chief Executive [American]; Trevor Michael Torrington [1961] Director

Priory Group UK 2 Limited
Incorporated: 28 May 2014
Previous: Partnerships in Care UK 2 Limited
Net Worth: £472,814,016 *Total Assets:* £747,990,976
Registered Office: Fifth Floor, 80 Hammersmith Road, London, W14 8UD
Activities: Hospital activities
Parent: Whitewell UK Holding Company 1
Officers: David James Hall, Secretary; Christopher Lee Howard [1966] Director [American]; Nigel Myers [1966] Director; Debra Kay Osteen [1955] Director/Chief Executive [American]; Trevor Michael Torrington [1961] Director

Priory Securitisation Holdings Limited
Incorporated: 10 June 2003
Net Worth: £173,380,992 *Total Assets:* £178,936,000
Registered Office: Fifth Floor, 80 Hammersmith Road, London, W14 8UD
Activities: Activities of head offices
Parent: Priory Group Limited
Officers: David James Hall, Secretary; David James Hall [1962] Director

Priory Securitisation Limited
Incorporated: 27 April 2000
Net Worth: £398,179,008 *Total Assets:* £455,556,992
Registered Office: Fifth Floor, 80 Hammersmith Road, London, W14 8UD
Activities: Non-trading company
Parent: Priory Securitisation Holdings Ltd
Officers: David James Hall, Secretary; David James Hall [1962] Director/Company Lawyer

Private Oil Holdings Oman Limited
Incorporated: 19 July 1937
Net Worth: £43,866,600 *Total Assets:* £1,157,691,904
Registered Office: 8 York Road, London, SE1 7NA
Activities: Wholesale of other fuels and related products
Parent: The Shell Petroleum Company Limited
Officers: Murat Kamil Vanlioglu, Secretary; Walid Abdul Hady Hamad [1979] Director/Oil Company Executive [Dutch]; Fernando Barata Alves [1957] Director/Oil Company Executive [Portuguese]; Christopher Mark Breeze [1963] Director/Oil Company Executive; Karim Chaouche [1968] Director/Vice-President Country Delegate Qatar & Oman [French]; Dr Antonio Jose Costa Silva [1952] Director [Portuguese]; Jennifer Debrauwer [1976] Director/Finance Manager [Dutch]; Sami Monir Amin Iskander [1965] Director/Oil Company Executive [French]; Elias Kassis [1965] Director/Vice President North Africa [French]; Yves Jean Henri Le Bail [1957] Director/Total Country Chair in Oman [French]; Stephane Michel [1973] Director/President [French]; Mohammed Khalid Sardar [1965] Director/NOV Asset Manager; Gerhardhus Johannes Maria Schotman [1961] Director/Vice President Joint Venture Excellence [Dutch]

Privilege Holdings Limited
Incorporated: 16 December 2015 *Employees:* 24
Net Worth: £8,449,000 *Total Assets:* £357,695,008
Registered Office: 4th Floor, 36 Spital Square, London, E1 6DY
Activities: Activities of head offices
Shareholder: Craig Reeves
Officers: Graham Philip May, Secretary; Philip Neil Gerrard [1961] Director/Businessman; Deborah Ann Hardy [1970] Director/Businesswoman; David Peter Head [1953] Director/Businessman

Privilege Project Finance Limited
Incorporated: 16 November 2001 *Employees:* 17
Previous: Eastern Counties Finance Limited
Net Worth: £7,049,000 *Total Assets:* £356,260,000
Registered Office: 4th Floor, 36 Spital Square, London, E1 6DY
Activities: Credit granting by non-deposit taking finance houses and other specialist consumer credit grantors
Shareholder: Craig Reeves
Officers: Graham Philip May, Secretary; Philip Neil Gerrard [1961] Director/Businessman; Deborah Ann Hardy [1970] Director; David Peter Head [1953] Director; Andrew Michael Vernau [1979] Director/Accountant

Progressive Global Energy Kurdistan Limited
Incorporated: 8 November 2012
Net Worth: £243,000,000 *Total Assets:* £322,000,000
Registered Office: 1st Floor, 75 King William Street, London, EC4N 7BE
Activities: Temporary employment agency activities
Parent: SThree UK Holdings Limited
Officers: Sarah Anderson [1977] Director/Company Secretary

Project Lake Holdings Limited
Incorporated: 5 May 2016
Net Worth: £158,305,856 *Total Assets:* £359,741,696
Registered Office: 35 Great St Helen's, London, EC3A 6AP
Activities: Activities of other holding companies n.e.c.
Officers: Melissa Gabrielle Bourgeois [1983] Director; Michelle O'Flaherty [1973] Director; John David Owens [1971] Director/SVP Finance and Operations International [Irish]

Project Leopard Acquireco Limited
Incorporated: 13 April 2017 *Employees:* 4
Net Worth: £169,430,400 *Total Assets:* £1,122,965,120
Registered Office: 3rd Floor, 11-12 St James's Square, London, SW1Y 4LB
Activities: Activities of other holding companies n.e.c.
Parent: Project Leopard Intermediateco Limited
Officers: Paul John Cooper [1957] Director/Chartered Accountant; Andrew Martins Almeida [1987] Director [American]; Marina Ronen [1982] Director/Manager - Corporate & Private Clients; Kenneth Virnig II [1984] Director [American]

Project Leopard Intermediateco Limited
Incorporated: 13 April 2017 *Employees:* 4
Net Worth: £175,369,168 *Total Assets:* £175,374,528
Registered Office: 3rd Floor, 11-12 St James's Square, London, SW1Y 4LB
Activities: Activities of other holding companies n.e.c.
Parent: Project Leopard Topco Limited
Officers: Paul John Cooper [1957] Director/Chartered Accountant; Andrew Martins Almeida [1987] Director [American]; Marina Ronen [1982] Director/Manager - Corporate & Private Clients; Kenneth Virnig II [1984] Director [American]

Project Leopard Topco Limited
Incorporated: 13 April 2017
Net Worth: £228,740,992 *Total Assets:* £228,740,992
Registered Office: 3rd Floor, 11-12 St James's Square, London, SW1Y 4LB
Activities: Activities of other holding companies n.e.c.
Officers: Paul John Cooper [1957] Director/Chartered Accountant; Andrew Martins Almeida [1987] Director [American]; Marina Ronen [1982] Director/Manager - Corporate & Private Clients; Kenneth Virnig II [1984] Director [American]

Project Quill Holding Limited
Incorporated: 6 March 2017
Net Worth Deficit: £22,515,800 *Total Assets:* £275,825,504
Registered Office: 100 New Bridge Street, London, EC4V 6JA
Activities: Activities of other holding companies n.e.c.
Officers: Eva Monica Kalawski, Secretary; Ian Michael Stuart Downie [1949] Director/Finance Executive; Eva Monica Kalawski [1955] Director/Executive [American]; Mary Ann Sigler [1954] Director/Executive [American]

Prometheon Enterprise Limited
Incorporated: 24 November 2011 *Employees:* 3,016
Net Worth Deficit: £62,000,000 *Total Assets:* £750,300,032
Registered Office: 6th Floor, 30 Millbank, London, SW1P 4EE
Activities: Travel agency activities
Officers: Anthony Bruton Meyrick Good [1933] Director; Peter Ajit Ajay Kerkar [1963] Director [Indian]

Prometheon Holdings (UK) Limited
Incorporated: 30 June 2011 *Employees:* 2,804
Net Worth: £186,500,000 *Total Assets:* £510,200,000
Registered Office: 6th Floor, 30 Millbank, London, SW1P 4EE
Activities: Travel agency activities
Parent: Prometheon Enterprise Limited
Officers: Peter Ajit Ajay Kerkar [1963] Director [Indian]; Ajit Paramparambath Menon [1957] Strategy Director; Pesi Savak Patel [1952] Director [Indian]

Promontoria Gyle 2 Ltd
Incorporated: 13 January 2017
Net Worth: £56,140,624 *Total Assets:* £188,713,904
Registered Office: 35 Great St Helen's, London, EC3A 6AP
Activities: Other business support service activities n.e.c.
Parent: Promontoria Gyle Holdings (2) Ltd
Officers: Melissa Gabrielle Bourgeois [1983] Director/Chartered Secretary; Raoul Rene Hofland [1967] Director [Dutch]; Amy Nicole Lejune [1977] Director/Accountant [American]; Michelle O'Flaherty [1973] Director; Gerardus Johannes Schipper [1965] Managing Director [Dutch]

Promontoria Gyle Holding Ltd
Incorporated: 13 January 2017
Net Worth: £56,033,804 *Total Assets:* £189,608,512
Registered Office: 35 Great St Helen's, London, EC3A 6AP
Activities: Activities of other holding companies n.e.c.
Officers: Melissa Gabrielle Bourgeois [1983] Director/Chartered Secretary; Raoul Rene Hofland [1967] Director [Dutch]; Amy Nicole Lejune [1977] Director/Accountant [American]; Michelle O'Flaherty [1973] Director; Gerardus Johannes Schipper [1965] Managing Director [Dutch]

Promontoria Gyle Holdings (2) Ltd
Incorporated: 13 January 2017
Net Worth: £56,146,220 *Total Assets:* £189,705,072
Registered Office: 35 Great St Helen's, London, EC3A 6AP
Activities: Activities of other holding companies n.e.c.
Parent: Promontoria Gyle Holding Ltd
Officers: Melissa Gabrielle Bourgeois [1983] Director/Chartered Secretary; Raoul Rene Hofland [1967] Director [Dutch]; Amy Nicole Lejune [1977] Director/Accountant [American]; Michelle O'Flaherty [1973] Director; Gerardus Johannes Schipper [1965] Managing Director [Dutch]

Promontoria Gyle Top Holding Ltd
Incorporated: 15 February 2017
Net Worth: £55,991,692 *Total Assets:* £189,574,912
Registered Office: 35 Great St Helen's, London, EC3A 6AP
Activities: Activities of other holding companies n.e.c.
Officers: Melissa Gabrielle Bourgeois [1983] Director/Chartered Secretary; Raoul Rene Hofland [1967] Director [Dutch]; Amy Nicole Lejune [1977] Director/Accountant [American]; Michelle O'Flaherty [1973] Director; Gerardus Johannes Schipper [1965] Managing Director [Dutch]

Prophaven Limited
Incorporated: 1 September 1988
Net Worth: £89,466,000 *Total Assets:* £118,849,000
Registered Office: Sea Containers House, 18 Upper Ground, London, SE1 9GL
Activities: Activities of head offices
Parent: Thistleclub Limited
Officers: Charles Ward Van Der Welle [1959] Director of Treasury; Steve Richard Winters [1968] Director/Chartered Accountant

Proserv Operations Limited
Incorporated: 12 April 2007
Net Worth Deficit: £24,363,000 *Total Assets:* £231,134,000
Registered Office: Suite 1, 3rd Floor, 11-12 St James's Square, London, SW1Y 4LB
Activities: Activities of other holding companies n.e.c.
Parent: Proserv Holdings Limited
Officers: Davis Marc Larssen, Secretary; Stephen Robert Cox [1977] Director; David John Raphael Currie [1955] Director/Chief Executive Officer; Davis Marc Larssen [1971] Director/Chief Financial Officer

Proxima GR Properties Limited
Incorporated: 23 August 1999 *Employees:* 2
Net Worth: £1,802,633,984 *Total Assets:* £2,330,184,960
Registered Office: Berkeley House, 304 Regents Park Road, London, N3 2JY
Activities: Buying and selling of own real estate
Parent: Betelgeuse Limited
Officers: Paul Hallam, Secretary; Christopher Charles McGill [1960] Managing Director; William Kenneth Procter [1953] Director/Accountant

PRS for Music Limited
Incorporated: 29 September 1997 *Employees:* 632
Net Worth Deficit: £61,653,000 *Total Assets:* £153,044,992
Registered Office: 2 Pancras Square, London, N1C 4AG
Activities: Other business support service activities n.e.c.
Parent: Performing Right Society Ltd
Officers: Deborah Ann Stones, Secretary; Jacqueline Gay Alway [1966] Director; Robert John Ashcroft [1956] Director; Charles William Booth [1957] Director/Publisher; Christopher Mark Butler [1963] Director; Stephen John Cooke [1959] Director; Simon Darlow [1960] Director/Composer; Stephen James Davidson [1955] Director; Nigel Robert Elderton [1956] Director; Edward Gregson [1945] Director/Composer; Stephen Alec Levine [1958] Director/Composer and Producer; John Berchmans Minch [1957] Director/Publisher; Julian Francis Kandahar Nott [1960] Director/Composer; Mark Poole [1962] Director; Thomas Christoforos Toumazis [1961] Director

Prudential (US Holdco 1) Limited
Incorporated: 1 March 2006
Net Worth: £4,040,727,040 *Total Assets:* £4,807,709,184
Registered Office: c/o Prudential PLC, Laurence Pountney Hill, London, EC4R 0HH
Activities: Activities of financial services holding companies
Parent: Prudential Public Limited Company
Officers: Kieran Joseph Devlin [1966] Director/Tax Adviser [Irish]; David Charles Martin [1956] Director/Accountant; Darren Wayne Sheppard [1970] Director/Chief Operating Officer

The Prudential Assurance Company Limited
Incorporated: 1 June 1881
Net Worth: £15,610,999,808 *Total Assets:* £198,531,006,464
Registered Office: Laurence Pountney Hill, London, EC4R 0HH
Activities: Life reinsurance
Parent: M & G Prudential Limited
Officers: Jennifer Anne Owens, Secretary; Clive Peter Adamson [1956] Director; Richard Bennison [1958] Independent Non-Executive Director; Clare Jane Bousfield [1968] Director/Chief Executive Officer Insurance; Joanne Dawson [1962] Director; Michael Jonathan Evans [1961] Director/Actuary; Mark Thomas Fitzpatrick [1968] Director/Chief Financial Officer [Irish]; John William Foley [1956] Director; Dr Ian Bruce Owen [1953] Director; Paul Spencer [1950] Director

Prudential Capital Holding Company Limited
Incorporated: 10 March 2006
Net Worth: £17,555,000 *Total Assets:* £1,720,482,944
Registered Office: Laurence Pountney Hill, London, EC4R 0HH
Activities: Activities of financial services holding companies
Parent: Prudential Public Limited Company
Officers: Jonathan Mark Brewis Daniels [1963] Director/Banker; David William King [1962] Finance Director; Raymond Paul Newby [1971] Director/Chief Financial Officer; Elisabeth Wenusch [1960] Director/Banker [Austrian]

Prudential Capital Public Limited Company
Incorporated: 4 November 1988 *Employees:* 31
Net Worth: £28,100,000 *Total Assets:* £4,136,003,072
Registered Office: Laurence Pountney Hill, London, EC4R 0HH
Activities: Financial intermediation not elsewhere classified
Parent: Prudential Capital Holding Company Limited
Officers: Jonathan Mark Brewis Daniels [1963] Director/Banker; Katherine Jones [1981] Director; David William King [1962] Finance Director; Raymond Paul Newby [1971] Director/Chief Financial Officer; Elisabeth Wenusch [1960] Director/Banker [Austrian]

Prudential Corporation Holdings Limited
Incorporated: 11 December 1978
Net Worth: £2,578,726,912 *Total Assets:* £3,821,992,960
Registered Office: Laurence Pountney Hill, London, EC4R 0HH
Activities: Activities of other holding companies n.e.c.
Parent: Prudential Holdings Limited
Officers: Kieran Joseph Devlin [1966] Director/Tax Adviser [Irish]; Katherine Jones [1981] Director; David Charles Martin [1956] Director/Accountant

Prudential Financial Services Limited
Incorporated: 1 August 1986
Net Worth Deficit: £122,218,000 *Total Assets:* £107,153,000
Registered Office: Laurence Pountney Hill, London, EC4R 0HH
Activities: Activities of financial services holding companies
Parent: M & G Prudential Limited
Officers: Clare Jane Bousfield [1968] Director/Chief Executive Officer, Insurance

Prudential Group Holdings Limited
Incorporated: 31 March 1965
Net Worth Deficit: £41,714,000 *Total Assets:* £637,800,000
Registered Office: Laurence Pountney Hill, London, EC4R 0HH
Activities: Activities of other holding companies n.e.c.
Parent: Prudential Public Limited Company
Officers: Kieran Joseph Devlin [1966] Director/Tax Adviser [Irish]; David Charles Martin [1956] Director/Accountant

Prudential Pensions Limited
Incorporated: 26 October 1970
Net Worth: £74,750,000 *Total Assets:* £12,351,028,224
Registered Office: Laurence Pountney Hill, London, EC4R 0HH
Activities: Life reinsurance
Parent: The Prudential Assurance Company Limited
Officers: Clare Jane Bousfield [1968] Director; Paul Spencer [1950] Director

Prudential Public Limited Company
Incorporated: 1 November 1978 *Employees:* 27,151
Net Worth: £16,087,000,064 *Total Assets:* £493,940,998,144
Registered Office: Laurence Pountney Hill, London, EC4R 0HH
Activities: Activities of head offices
Officers: Alan Fraser Porter, Secretary; Sir Howard John Davies [1951] Director; Michael Irving Falcon [1962] Director [American]; Mark Thomas Fitzpatrick [1968] Director/Group Chief Financial Officer [Irish]; John William Foley [1956] Director; David John Alexander Law [1960] Director; Paul Victor Falzon Sant Manduca [1951] Director; Kaikhushru Shiavax Nargolwala [1950] Director [Singaporean]; Nicolaos Andreas Nicandrou [1965] Director; Anthony John Liddell Nightingale [1947] Director and Businessman; Philip John Remnant [1954] Director; Alice Davey Schroeder [1956] Director/Investor [American]; Lord Jonathan Adair Turner [1955] Director; Stuart James Turner [1969] Director; Thomas Ros Watjen [1954] Director [American]; Michael Andrew Wells [1960] Director/President and Chief Executive Officer [American]; Jane Fields Wicker-Miurin [1958] Director

Prudential Services Limited
Incorporated: 4 November 1988 *Employees:* 945
Net Worth: £34,607,000 *Total Assets:* £239,867,008
Registered Office: Laurence Pountney Hill, London, EC4R 0HH
Activities: Other business support service activities n.e.c.
Parent: Prudential Group Holdings Limited
Officers: Katherine Jones [1981] Director; Alan Fraser Porter [1963] Director; Timothy Miles Rolfe [1971] Group HR Director

Prutec Limited
Incorporated: 18 July 1980
Net Worth: £569,921,216 *Total Assets:* £1,066,272,000
Registered Office: Laurence Pountney Hill, London, EC4R 0HH
Activities: Financial intermediation not elsewhere classified
Parent: The Prudential Assurance Company Limited
Officers: Jonathan Mark Brewis Daniels [1963] Director/Insurance Company Executive; David William King [1962] Finance Director

PSP Britannia Ltd
Incorporated: 10 November 2016
Net Worth: £335,726,208 *Total Assets:* £1,186,223,744
Registered Office: 8th Floor, 10 Bressenden Place, London, SW1E 5DH
Activities: Activities of other holding companies n.e.c.
Parent: PSP Investments Holding Europe Ltd
Officers: Nicola Noel, Secretary; Michael John Adams [1984] Finance Director; Melanie Bernier [1975] Director/Lawyer [Canadian]; Marie-Claude Cardin [1964] Director [Canadian]; Patrick Charbonneau [1978] Director/Business Executive [Canadian]; Neil Cunningham [1959] Director [Canadian]; Oliver Miles Christian Duff [1969] Director/Business Executive; Stephane Jalbert [1972] Director/Business Executive [Canadian]; Przemyslaw Obloj [1977] Director/Private Equity Executive [British/Polish]

PSPA Finance Limited
Incorporated: 25 February 2016
Net Worth: £37,301,000 *Total Assets:* £135,199,008
Registered Office: Bedford House, 69-79 Fulham High Street, London, SW6 3JW
Activities: Activities of exhibition and fair organisers
Parent: PSPA Midco Limited
Officers: Richard Johnson [1963] Director; Russell Stephen Wilcox [1971] Director

PSPA Holdco Limited
Incorporated: 17 December 2014
Net Worth: £135,119,008 *Total Assets:* £141,144,992
Registered Office: Bedford House, Fulham High Street, London, SW6 3JW
Activities: Activities of exhibition and fair organisers
Parent: PSPA Finance Limited
Officers: Richard Johnson [1963] Director; Russell Stephen Wilcox [1971] Director/Executive Manager

PSPA Midco Limited
Incorporated: 30 December 2014
Net Worth: £82,567,000 *Total Assets:* £143,224,992
Registered Office: Bedford House, Fulham High Street, London, SW6 3JW
Activities: Activities of exhibition and fair organisers
Parent: PSPA Topco Limited
Officers: Richard Johnson [1963] Director; Russell Stephen Wilcox [1971] Director/Executive Manager

PSPA Topco Limited
Incorporated: 30 December 2014 *Employees:* 844
Net Worth Deficit: £12,318,000 *Total Assets:* £526,369,984
Registered Office: Bedford House, Fulham High Street, London, SW6 3JW
Activities: Activities of exhibition and fair organisers
Parent: PSPA Luxco S A R L
Officers: Richard Johnson [1963] Director; Simon Reed Kimble [1963] Director; Russell Stephen Wilcox [1971] Director

Psygnosis Limited
Incorporated: 21 January 1972
Net Worth: £104,205,272 *Total Assets:* £108,104,952
Registered Office: 10 Great Marlborough Street, London, W1F 7LP
Activities: Other business support service activities n.e.c.
Parent: Sony Interactive Entertainment Europe Limited
Officers: Marian Toole, Secretary; Michael Stuart Denny [1964] Director/VP SCE WWS Europe; Simon Gerrard Rutter [1967] Director/EVP Marketing and Sales; James George Ryan [1959] Director

PTT International Trading London Ltd
Incorporated: 24 October 2016 *Employees:* 8
Net Worth: £8,176,513 *Total Assets:* £100,062,504
Registered Office: Suite 7, 5th Floor, Berkeley Square House, Berkeley Square, London, W1J 6BU
Activities: Wholesale of petroleum and petroleum products
Parent: Ministry of Finance
Officers: Kritch Chairuangyoth [1974] Director/State Enterprise Employee [Thai]; Disathat Panyarachun [1964] Director/State Enterprise Employee [Thai]; Donnaya Senanarong [1965] Director/State Enterprise Employee [Thai]; Pattaraporn Vorasaph [1969] Director/Senior Government Officer [Thai]

PTTEP SP Limited
Incorporated: 31 May 1995
Net Worth: £102,019,616 *Total Assets:* £288,041,408
Registered Office: 4 More London Riverside, London, SE1 2AU
Activities: Extraction of crude petroleum
Parent: The Ministry of Finance
Officers: Anutra Bunnag [1963] VP attached to Finance Division and Managing Director [Thai]; Tawee Limsoontorn [1964] Director [Thai]

Public Power Corporation Finance PLC
Incorporated: 21 January 2009
Net Worth: £69,264 *Total Assets:* £439,496,064
Registered Office: 3 More London Riverside, London, SE1 2AQ
Activities: Distribution of electricity
Shareholder: Hellenic Republic (The Greek State)
Officers: Anargiros Economou [1960] Director [Greek]; Anna Kamileri [1958] Director [Greek]; Alexandra Konida [1968] Director [Greek]; Emmanouil Panagiotakis [1948] Chairman of The Board of Directors and CEO of PPC [Greek]; Lazaros Stathakis [1950] Director/Chemical Engineer [Greek]

Publicis Media Limited
Incorporated: 2 July 2001 *Employees:* 74
Previous: Zenith Optimedia Group Limited
Net Worth: £6,366,000 *Total Assets:* £123,208,000
Registered Office: 1st Floor, 2 Television Centre, 101 Wood Lane, London, W12 7FR
Activities: Advertising agencies
Parent: MMS UK Holdings Limited
Officers: Joanne Munis, Secretary; Stephen David King [1959] Director; Adrian Carl Sayliss [1960] Director/Chief Financial Officer

Puente Holding Limited
Incorporated: 19 December 2014 *Employees:* 311
Net Worth: £31,714,688 *Total Assets:* £125,933,896
Registered Office: Hill House, 1 Little New Street, London, EC4A 3TR
Activities: Activities of other holding companies n.e.c.
Major Shareholder: Federico Tomasevich
Officers: Gonzalo Miguel Spinedi [1981] Director [Argentinian]; Federico Tomasevich [1976] Director [Argentinian]; Marcos Ernst Wentzel [1976] Director [Argentinian]

Pulford Trading Limited
Incorporated: 7 January 2013 *Employees:* 3
Net Worth: £169,764,000 *Total Assets:* £171,779,008
Registered Office: 6th Floor, St Magnus House, 3 Lower Thames Street, London, EC3R 6HD
Activities: Development of building projects
Officers: Thomas Edward Mullard, Secretary; Paul Younger, Secretary; Pierre Alexis Clarke [1972] Director/Accountant; Dennis William Patrick Hallahane [1944] Director; Peter Roscrow [1963] Director

Punch Partnerships (PTL) Limited
Incorporated: 17 February 1998
Net Worth: £529,036,992 *Total Assets:* £1,999,080,960
Registered Office: Elsley Court, 20-22 Great Titchfield Street, London, W1W 8BE
Activities: Public houses and bars
Parent: Punch Taverns Holdings Limited
Officers: David Forde [1968] Director [Irish]; Christopher John Moore [1970] Director; Lawson John Wembridge Mountstevens [1968] Director; David James Tannahill [1977] Director

Punch Taverns (Chiltern) Limited
Incorporated: 28 June 2017
Net Worth Deficit: £488,000 *Total Assets:* £265,568,000
Registered Office: Elsley Court, 20-22 Great Titchfield Street, London, W1W 8BE
Activities: Activities of other holding companies n.e.c.
Parent: Heineken UK Limited
Officers: David Forde [1968] Director [Irish]; Christopher John Moore [1970] Director; Lawson John Wembridge Mountstevens [1968] Director; David James Tannahill [1977] Director

Punch Taverns Holdco (A) Limited
Incorporated: 24 September 2014
Net Worth: £242,174,000 *Total Assets:* £242,174,000
Registered Office: Elsley Court, 20-22 Great Titchfield Street, London, W1W 8BE
Activities: Non-trading company
Parent: Punch Taverns (Chiltern) Limited
Officers: David Forde [1968] Director [Irish]; Christopher John Moore [1970] Director; Lawson John Wembridge Mountstevens [1968] Director; David James Tannahill [1977] Director

Punch Taverns Holdings Limited
Incorporated: 26 January 1998
Net Worth: £132,036,000 *Total Assets:* £373,036,000
Registered Office: Elsley Court, 20-22 Great Titchfield Street, London, W1W 8BE
Activities: Non-trading company
Parent: Punch Taverns Intermediate Holdco (A) Limited
Officers: David Forde [1968] Director [Irish]; Christopher John Moore [1970] Director; Lawson John Wembridge Mountstevens [1968] Director; David James Tannahill [1977] Director

Punch Taverns Intermediate Holdco (A) Limited
Incorporated: 25 September 2014
Net Worth: £242,174,000 *Total Assets:* £242,174,000
Registered Office: Elsley Court, 20-22 Great Titchfield Street, London, W1W 8BE
Activities: Non-trading company
Parent: Punch Taverns Holdco (A) Limited
Officers: David Forde [1968] Director [Irish]; Christopher John Moore [1970] Director; Lawson John Wembridge Mountstevens [1968] Director; David James Tannahill [1977] Director

Punjab National Bank (International) Limited
Incorporated: 13 April 2006 *Employees:* 140
Net Worth: £162,511,984 *Total Assets:* £914,431,360
Registered Office: 1 Moorgate, London, EC2R 6JH
Activities: Central banking
Parent: Punjab National Bank
Officers: Camilla Shaw, Secretary; Sundeep Bhandari [1965] Director; Antanu Das [1960] Director/Chief Executive [Indian]; Shri Sunil Mehta [1959] Managing Director & CEO PNB (India) [Indian]; Muddoor Sadananda Nayak [1952] Executive Director; Ashwini Vats [1963] Director/General Manager IBD PNB India [Indian]

Punter Southall Group Limited
Incorporated: 26 October 2000 *Employees:* 996
Net Worth: £1,943,945 *Total Assets:* £108,744,800
Registered Office: 11 Strand, London, WC2N 5HR
Activities: Activities of head offices
Shareholder: PSG Trustees Limited
Officers: Ian Eric Nash, Secretary; Clive Christopher Roger Bannister [1958] Director; Sandra Mary Curtis [1952] Director; Mandy Donald [1972] Director; Gareth James Knight [1978] Director; Kenneth John McKelvey [1956] Director/Consulting Actuary; Jonathan Dominic Punter [1957] Director/Actuary; James Anthony Angus Samuels [1950] Managing Director; Lukas Van Der Walt [1960] Director [South African]

Puretech Health PLC
Incorporated: 8 May 2015 *Employees:* 138
Net Worth: £161,432,768 *Total Assets:* £369,228,640
Registered Office: 5th Floor, 6 St Andrew Street, London, EC4A 3AE
Activities: Research and experimental development on biotechnology
Officers: Stephen Muniz, Secretary; Joichi Ito [1966] Director [Japanese]; Dr Raju Kucherlapati [1943] Director [American]; Dr. John Lamattina [1950] Director [American]; Dr Robert Langer [1948] Director [American]; Stephen Muniz [1970] Director/EVP, Legal, Finance and Operations [American]; Dame Marjorie Morris Scardino [1947] Director [American]; Dr. Bennett Michael Shapiro [1939] Director [American]; Christopher Viehbacher [1960] Director [Canadian]; Daphne Zohar [1970] Director/CEO - Puretech [American]

Pyrenees Acquisitions Limited
Incorporated: 1 December 2016
Net Worth: £63,589,956 *Total Assets:* £265,519,440
Registered Office: Peterborough Court, 133 Fleet Street, London, EC4A 2BB
Activities: Financial intermediation not elsewhere classified
Parent: ELQ Investors II Ltd
Officers: Thomas Kelly, Secretary; Ana Estrada Lopez [1981] Director/Economist [Spanish]; Farbod Nia [1982] Director/Banker; Mark Desmond Charles Olivier [1974] Managing Director; Jeremy Alan Wiltshire [1981] Director/Banker

PZ Cussons Beauty LLP
Incorporated: 28 April 2011 *Employees:* 79
Net Worth: £179,776,992 *Total Assets:* £234,435,008
Registered Office: 14 Upper St Martin's Lane, Covent Garden, London, WC2H 9FB
Officers: Andrew Bowie [1966] Member; Gemma Gilbert [1981] Member; Simon Paul Plant [1969] Member; Marie Angela Newell [1978] LLP Member

Q Holdco Limited
Incorporated: 10 October 2016 *Employees:* 3,082
Net Worth: £160,094,896 *Total Assets:* £425,344,576
Registered Office: 35 Great St Helen's, London, EC3A 6AP
Activities: Activities of other holding companies n.e.c.
Officers: Thomas Hook [1962] Director [American]; Nikhil Patel [1985] Associate Director [American]; William Purslow [1951] Director/Advisor [American]; Richard Relyea [1976] Managing Director [American]; Saied Tousi [1958] Director [American]; Shlomo Yamai [1952] Director [Israeli]

Q Intermediate Holdco Limited
Incorporated: 10 October 2016
Net Worth: £180,994,960 *Total Assets:* £180,994,960
Registered Office: 35 Great St Helen's, London, EC3A 6AP
Activities: Activities of other holding companies n.e.c.
Parent: Q Holdco Limited
Officers: Cary Glay [1968] Director/CEO, EVP/CFO, Q Holding Company [American]; Thomas Hook [1962] Director [American]; Peter Wilson [1981] Director

Qatar Airways Investments (UK) Ltd
Incorporated: 28 September 2016
Net Worth: £737,846,208 *Total Assets:* £750,490,432
Registered Office: 3rd Floor, 5 Lloyd's Avenue, London, EC3N 3AE
Activities: Activities of other holding companies n.e.c.
Parent: Qatar Airways Q.C.S.C.
Officers: Daniel Hong Man Ho [1961] Director/Chief Financial Officer; Michael Craig Lawrence [1985] Director/Accountant; Andrzej Waclaw Radomski [1972] Sales Director

QBE Corporate Limited
Incorporated: 18 October 1995
Net Worth: £8,921,000 *Total Assets:* £5,393,604,096
Registered Office: Plantation Place, 30 Fenchurch Street, London, EC3M 3BD
Activities: Non-life insurance
Parent: QBE Holdings (EO) Limited
Officers: Alexandra Jane Smith, Secretary; Ian David Beckerson [1967] Director; Richard Vaughan Pryce [1959] Director/Chief Executive Officer; Nigel Joseph Douty Terry [1970] Director/Chartered Accountant; David James Winkett [1969] Director/Chartered Accountant

QBE European Operations PLC
Incorporated: 29 August 1991
Net Worth: £2,813,360,128 *Total Assets:* £4,151,699,968
Registered Office: Plantation Place, 30 Fenchurch Street, London, EC3M 3BD
Activities: Activities of head offices
Parent: QBE Insurance Holdings Pty Limited
Officers: Alexandra Jane Smith, Secretary; Timothy Charles William Ingram [1947] Director; Richard Vaughan Pryce [1959] Director/Chief Executive Officer; Nigel Joseph Douty Terry [1970] Director/Chartered Accountant; David James Winkett [1969] Director/Chartered Accountant

QBE Holdings (EO) Limited
Incorporated: 9 October 2008
Net Worth: £2,945,650,944 *Total Assets:* £3,181,549,056
Registered Office: Plantation Place, 30 Fenchurch Street, London, EC3M 3BD
Activities: Activities of head offices
Parent: QBE European Operations PLC
Officers: Alexandra Jane Smith, Secretary; Ian David Beckerson [1967] Director; Richard Vaughan Pryce [1959] Director/Chief Executive Officer; Robert Charles Stone [1975] Director; Nigel Joseph Douty Terry [1970] Director/Chartered Accountant; David James Winkett [1969] Director/Chartered Accountant

QBE Management Services (UK) Limited
Incorporated: 31 January 1996 *Employees:* 1,689
Net Worth: £33,038,000 *Total Assets:* £155,267,008
Registered Office: Plantation Place, 30 Fenchurch Street, London, EC3M 3BD
Activities: Activities of head offices
Parent: QBE European Operations PLC
Officers: Alexandra Jane Smith, Secretary; Joe Gordon [1962] Operations Director [Irish]; Richard Vaughan Pryce [1959] Director/Chief Executive Officer; Nigel Joseph Douty Terry [1970] Director/Chartered Accountant; David James Winkett [1969] Director/Chartered Accountant

QBE RE (Europe) Limited
Incorporated: 17 July 1978 *Employees:* 87
Net Worth: £610,556,672 *Total Assets:* £1,946,952,832
Registered Office: Plantation Place, 30 Fenchurch Street, London, EC3M 3BD
Activities: Non-life insurance
Parent: QBE Holdings (EO) Limited
Officers: Alexandra Jane Smith, Secretary; Timothy Charles William Ingram [1947] Director; Malcolm Graham McCaig [1955] Director; Richard Vaughan Pryce [1959] Director/Chief Executive Officer; Nigel Joseph Douty Terry [1970] Director/Chartered Accountant; David James Winkett [1969] Director/Chartered Accountant

QBE UK Limited
Incorporated: 14 October 1983 *Employees:* 223
Previous: QBE Insurance (Europe) Limited
Net Worth: £1,403,533,952 *Total Assets:* £5,711,200,768
Registered Office: Plantation Place, 30 Fenchurch Street, London, EC3M 3BD
Activities: Non-life insurance
Parent: QBE Holdings (EO) Limited
Officers: Alexandra Jane Smith, Secretary; Wai-Fong Au [1956] Director; Timothy Charles William Ingram [1947] Director; Malcolm Graham McCaig [1955] Director; Colin Raymond O'Farrell [1964] Director/Chief Underwriting Officer; Richard Vaughan Pryce [1959] Director/Chief Executive Officer; Stuart William Sinclair [1953] Director; Nigel Joseph Douty Terry [1970] Director/Chartered Accountant; David James Winkett [1969] Director/Chartered Accountant

QDD Athletes Village UK Limited
Incorporated: 24 January 2011 *Employees:* 83
Net Worth: £430,775,008 *Total Assets:* £1,312,434,944
Registered Office: 6th Floor, Lansdowne House, Berkeley Square, London, W1J 6ER
Activities: Activities of other holding companies n.e.c.
Parent: East Village London LLP
Officers: Abdulla Al-Ajail [1979] Director [Qatari]; Jeremy Martin Holmes [1960] Director/Chief Development Officer, Qatari Diar UK Limited; Sir John Henry Ritblat [1935] Director; Gawain Sydney Edward Smart [1970] Director/Head of Legal [Canadian]

QH Participations Limited
Incorporated: 21 February 2008
Net Worth: £307,024,992 *Total Assets:* £1,249,634,944
Registered Office: 87-135 Brompton Road, Knightsbridge, London, SW1X 7XL
Activities: Activities of head offices
Parent: Harrods Group (Holding) Limited
Officers: Daniel Jonathan Webster, Secretary; Michael Ashley Ward [1956] Managing Director; Daniel Jonathan Webster [1970] Director/Group General Counsel

QH Partners Limited
Incorporated: 10 October 2006
Net Worth: £290,137,984 *Total Assets:* £555,601,984
Registered Office: 87-135 Brompton Road, Knightsbridge, London, SW1X 7XL
Activities: Activities of head offices
Parent: QH Participations Limited
Officers: Daniel Jonathan Webster, Secretary; Michael Ashley Ward [1956] Managing Director; Daniel Jonathan Webster [1970] Director/Group General Counsel

QHG Holding LLP
Incorporated: 5 December 2016
Net Worth Deficit: £174,484,368 *Total Assets:* £9,363,457,024
Registered Office: 50 Berkeley Street, London, W1J 8HD

QHG Investment LLP
Incorporated: 5 December 2016
Net Worth: £1,047,962 *Total Assets:* £9,611,516,928
Registered Office: 50 Berkeley Street, London, W1J 8HD

QHG Trading LLP
Incorporated: 5 December 2016
Net Worth Deficit: £177,040,240 *Total Assets:* £2,946,301,952
Registered Office: 50 Berkeley Street, London, W1J 8HD

QHotels Holdings Limited
Incorporated: 11 January 2013
Net Worth: £138,276,000 *Total Assets:* £138,276,000
Registered Office: 4th Floor, 20 Balderton Street, London, W1K 6TL
Activities: Activities of head offices
Officers: Manish Mansukhlal Gudka [1970] Director; Gareth Jones [1973] Director/Chartered Accountant

QHotels Services Limited
Incorporated: 3 March 2003 *Employees:* 174
Net Worth: £2,361,000 *Total Assets:* £210,163,008
Registered Office: 20 Balderton Street, London, W1K 6TL
Activities: Activities of head offices
Officers: Manish Mansukhlal Gudka [1970] Director; Gareth Jones [1973] Director/Chartered Accountant

QIB (UK) PLC
Incorporated: 4 February 2003 *Employees:* 37
Net Worth: £60,100,740 *Total Assets:* £529,767,552
Registered Office: 43 Grosvenor Street, London, W1K 3HL
Activities: Banks
Officers: Gareth Howells, Secretary; Bassel Gamaleldin Mohamed Aly [1966] Director/Banker [Egyptian]; Gourang Hemani [1969] Director/Chartered Accountant [Indian]; Gareth Howells [1973] Director/Chief Risk Officer; Marianne Laing Ismail [1952] Director/Financial Consultant; Rakesh Sanghvi [1964] Director/Banker [Indian]; Duncan Steele-Bodger [1962] Director/Banker; David Victor Thomas [1949] Director/Banker

Quadgas Investments Bidco Limited
Incorporated: 18 November 2016
Net Worth: £3,184,787,968 *Total Assets:* £3,735,307,008
Registered Office: c/o Alter Domus (UK) Limited, 18 St Swithin's Lane, London, EC4N 8AD
Activities: Activities of other holding companies n.e.c.
Parent: Macquarie Infrastructure and Real Assets (Europe) Limited
Officers: Abdulla Al-Ansari [1988] Director/Investment Manager [Qatari]; Nicholas John Axam [1979] Director/Infrastructure Investment Manager [Australian]; Mark William Braithwaite [1965] Director; Eduard Benjamin Fidler [1977] Director [Canadian]; Michael John Gregory [1968] Director; Howard Charles Higgins [1953] Director; Deven Arvind Karnik [1967] Director; Jaroslava Korpancova [1974] Director [Czech]; Emma Lewis [1979] Director/Principal Infrastructure; Mark William Mathieson [1966] Director; Perry Denis Noble [1960] Director; Hua Su [1990] Director/Investment [Chinese]; David Jinlin Xie [1978] Director [American]

Quadrant Construction Services Limited
Incorporated: 25 June 2003
Net Worth Deficit: £7,702,000 *Total Assets:* £396,022,016
Registered Office: 29-35 West Ham Lane, London, E15 4PH
Activities: Development of building projects
Officers: Emuoborohwo Siakpere, Secretary; Waqar Ahmed [1967] Finance Director; Fiona Carswell [1968] Group Director Development & Sales [Irish]; Edward Paul Farnsworth [1982] Director/Head of Business Planning & Development Finance; Craig David Luttman [1975] Director; Janet Lynne Mackey [1959] Development Director; Stuart Whitehill Miller [1961] Development Director; Andrew Peter Rowland [1959] Development Director; Victoria Elizabeth Savage [1965] Regional Managing Director

Quantoil Limited
Incorporated: 14 February 1995
Net Worth: £624,697,536 *Total Assets:* £625,209,472
Registered Office: 5th Floor, 6 St Andrew Street, London, EC4A 3AE
Activities: Other service activities n.e.c.
Parent: Core Laboratories Interests Two Limited
Officers: George Bruce [1958] Director/General Manager; Jacqueline Watson [1970] Director/Financial Controller

Quarto Publishing PLC
Incorporated: 1 April 1976 *Employees:* 251
Net Worth: £18,244,000 *Total Assets:* £112,034,000
Registered Office: 6 Blundell Street, London, N7 9BH
Activities: Book publishing
Parent: Quarto Group Inc
Officers: Dr Michael Peter Clarke, Secretary; Chuk Kin Lau [1952] Director; Michael Mousley [1953] Director

Queensgate Bow Opco Limited
Incorporated: 11 November 2015 *Employees:* 201
Net Worth: £17,403,000 *Total Assets:* £385,856,000
Registered Office: 8 Hill Street, London, W1J 5NG
Activities: Other letting and operating of own or leased real estate
Parent: Queensgate Bow UK Holdco Limited
Officers: Jonathan James Millet [1982] Director; Jueane Thiessen [1974] Director/Accountant

Queensgate Bow Propco Limited
Incorporated: 21 June 1950
Previous: London LRG Hotel Limited
Net Worth: £343,795,008 *Total Assets:* £356,014,016
Registered Office: 8 Hill Street, London, W1J 5NG
Activities: Other service activities n.e.c.
Parent: Queensgate Bow UK Holdco Limited
Officers: Jueane Thiessen, Secretary; Jonathan James Millet [1980] Director; Jueane Thiessen [1974] Director/Accountant

Queensgate Bow UK Midco Limited
Incorporated: 11 November 2015
Net Worth: £59,562,000 *Total Assets:* £123,355,000
Registered Office: 8 Hill Street, London, W1J 5NG
Activities: Other letting and operating of own or leased real estate
Parent: Queensgate Bow UK Topco Limited
Officers: Jonathan James Millet [1980] Director; Jueane Thiessen [1974] Director/Accountant

Queensgate Bow UK Parent Limited
Incorporated: 10 November 2015 *Employees:* 201
Net Worth: £59,498,000 *Total Assets:* £377,615,008
Registered Office: 8 Hill Street, London, W1J 5NG
Activities: Other letting and operating of own or leased real estate
Officers: Jonathan James Millet [1980] Director; Jueane Thiessen [1974] Director/Accountant

Queensgate Bow UK Topco Limited
Incorporated: 10 November 2015 *Employees:* 201
Net Worth: £59,521,000 *Total Assets:* £377,627,008
Registered Office: 8 Hill Street, London, W1J 5NG
Activities: Other letting and operating of own or leased real estate
Parent: Queensgate Bow UK Parent Limited
Officers: Jonathan James Millet [1980] Director; Jueane Thiessen [1974] Director/Accountant

Quest Diagnostics Holdings Ltd.
Incorporated: 3 December 2014 *Employees:* 2
Net Worth: £151,031,024 *Total Assets:* £151,055,216
Registered Office: 1st Floor, 48 Chancery Lane, London, WC2A 1JF
Activities: Activities of other holding companies n.e.c.
Parent: Quest Diagnostics Incorporated
Officers: William Joseph O'Shaughnessy, Secretary; Stephen Andrew Calamari [1954] Director/Vice President, Tax [American]; Sandip R. Patel [1974] Director/Vice President and Treasurer [American]

Quest Diagnostics Subsidiary Holdings Ltd.
Incorporated: 27 April 2015 *Employees:* 2
Net Worth: £118,494,960 *Total Assets:* £121,754,760
Registered Office: 1st Floor, 48 Chancery Lane, London, WC2A 1JF
Activities: Activities of other holding companies n.e.c.
Parent: Quest Diagnostics Holdings Limited
Officers: William Joseph O'Shaughnessy, Secretary; Stephen Andrew Calamari [1954] Director/Vice President, Tax [American]; Sandip R. Patel [1974] Director/Vice President and Treasurer [American]

Questor Properties Ltd
Incorporated: 7 January 1998
Net Worth: £55,799,052 *Total Assets:* £103,543,440
Registered Office: Saxonbury House, High Street Wanstead, London, E11 1QQ
Activities: Buying and selling of own real estate
Major Shareholder: Marcus Stephen Jays
Officers: Karen Jays, Secretary; Marcus Stephen Jays [1968] Director/Property Investor

Quilter Cheviot Holdings Limited
Incorporated: 17 October 2012
Net Worth: £208,314,000 *Total Assets:* £208,314,000
Registered Office: One Kingsway, London, WC2B 6AN
Activities: Activities of financial services holding companies
Parent: Old Mutual Wealth Holdings Limited
Officers: Mark Ian MacLeod [1967] Director/Accountant; Andrew Iain McGlone [1971] Director/Investment Manager; Mark Oscar Satchel [1969] Director [British/South African]

Quilter Cheviot Limited
Incorporated: 18 June 1985 *Employees:* 539
Net Worth: £116,531,000 *Total Assets:* £224,292,992
Registered Office: One Kingsway, London, WC2B 6AN
Activities: Financial intermediation not elsewhere classified
Parent: Quilter Cheviot Holdings Limited
Officers: Ian Michael Buckley [1950] Director; Rosemary Harris [1958] Director; Mark Ian MacLeod [1967] Director/Accountant; Andrew Iain McGlone [1971] Director/Investment Manager; Mark Oscar Satchel [1969] Director [British/South African]; Philip George Tew [1957] Director

Quilter Investors Limited
Incorporated: 4 June 2001
Previous: Old Mutual Investment Management Limited
Net Worth: £57,337,000 *Total Assets:* £244,436,992
Registered Office: Millennium Bridge House, 2 Lambeth Hill, London, EC4V 4AJ
Activities: Other business support service activities n.e.c.
Parent: Quilter PLC
Officers: Jonathan Michael Little [1964] Director; Paul Robert Simpson [1958] Director; Catherine Lucy Turner [1963] Director

Quilter PLC
Incorporated: 19 October 2007
Previous: Quilter Limited
Net Worth: £2,257,298,944 *Total Assets:* £2,437,400,064
Registered Office: Millennium Bridge House, 2 Lambeth Hill, London, EC4V 4AJ
Activities: Activities of head offices
Officers: Patrick Anthony Gonsalves, Secretary; Paul William Feeney [1963] Director; Rosemary Harris [1958] Director; Glyn Parry Jones [1952] Director; Dr Suresh Parbhoo Kana [1955] Director [South African]; Moira Kilcoyne [1961] Director [American]; Jonathan Michael Little [1964] Director; Ruth Markland [1953] Director; Paul Stephen Matthews [1960] Director; George McGrimmon Reid [1965] Director; Timothy James William Tookey [1962] Director; Catherine Lucy Turner [1963] Director

Quintain Limited
Incorporated: 3 March 1992
Previous: Quintain PLC
Net Worth: £569,100,032 *Total Assets:* £1,040,300,032
Registered Office: 180 Great Portland Street, London, W1W 5QZ
Activities: Development of building projects
Major Shareholder: John Patrick Grayken
Officers: Frances Victoria Heazell, Secretary; Olivier Vincent Daniel Brahin [1966] Director/President, Europe [French]; Angus Alexander Dodd [1967] Senior Managing Director; Jerome Foulon [1974] Director [Canadian/French]; John Ryan Herbert [1956] Director [American]; George Evagelos Kountouris [1954] Director [Greek]; Donald John Quintin [1972] Director [American]; James Hendry Riddell [1979] Director/Fund Manager; James Michael Edward Saunders [1966] Director

QVC UK
Incorporated: 6 April 1993 *Employees:* 1,863
Previous: QVC
Net Worth: £143,228,992 *Total Assets:* £226,948,000
Registered Office: Building 8, Chiswick Park, 566 Chiswick High Road, London, W4 5XU
Activities: Retail sale via mail order houses or via Internet
Parent: QVC Britain
Officers: Lawrence Ronald Hayes, Secretary/Director [American]; Lawrence Ronald Hayes [1960] Director [American]; Robert William Muller [1970] Director [American]; Aidan James O'Meara [1962] Director/President International [Irish]

QVC UK Holdings Limited
Incorporated: 30 September 2008 *Employees:* 4
Net Worth: £867,019,008 *Total Assets:* £1,291,952,000
Registered Office: Building 8, Chiswick Park, 566 Chiswick High Road, London, W4 5XU
Activities: Activities of head offices
Parent: Liberty Interative Corporation
Officers: Lawrence Ronald Hayes, Secretary/Director [American]; Lawrence Ronald Hayes [1960] Director [American]; Robert William Muller [1970] Director [American]; Aidan James O'Meara [1962] Director/President International [Irish]

QW Rail Leasing Limited
Incorporated: 11 June 2007
Net Worth Deficit: £18,608,000 *Total Assets:* £302,383,008
Registered Office: 99 Queen Victoria Street, London, EC4V 4EH
Activities: Financial leasing
Shareholders: National Australia Finance (Infrastructure Leasing No.2) Limited; SMBC Leasing (UK) Limited
Officers: Bernadette Lewis, Secretary; Lawrence James Butcher [1968] Director/Banker; Rolfe Alan Cameron Lakin [1961] Director/Bank Executive; Antony Edward Mitton [1967] Director/Chartered Accountant; Mark Jeremy Rutherford [1965] Director/Banker; David Allen Ward [1956] Director [American]; Mona Melin Wong [1962] Director/Accountant [British/Australian]

Qwest Communications International Ltd.
Incorporated: 21 November 1997
Net Worth: £105,055,216 *Total Assets:* £112,951,032
Registered Office: 10 Fleet Place, London, EC4M 7RB
Activities: Other telecommunications activities
Parent: CenturyLink Inc.
Officers: Lyle James Hippen [1967] Director/Vice-President - Finance [American]; Michael Charles Reinke [1975] Director/Senior Vice President EMEA [American]

R & F One (UK) Limited
Incorporated: 26 September 2013 *Employees:* 20
Previous: Wanda One (UK) Limited
Net Worth Deficit: £107,391,120 *Total Assets:* £335,727,808
Registered Office: 3rd & 5th Floor, Sky Gardens Nine Elms, 153 Wandsworth Road, London, SW8 2GB
Activities: Development of building projects
Shareholders: Sze Lim Li; Li Zhang
Officers: Sze Lim Li [1957] Director [Chinese]; Ning Xia [1978] Director/Architect [Chinese]

R & Q Capital No. 6 Limited
Incorporated: 4 November 2009
Previous: Prosight Specialty (ECUCM) Limited
Net Worth: £6,926,000 *Total Assets:* £159,264,992
Registered Office: 71 Fenchurch Street, London, EC3M 4BS
Activities: Other business support service activities n.e.c.
Parent: Randall & Quilter II Holdings Limited
Officers: Michael Logan Glover [1958] Director; Mark Andrew Langridge [1963] Director; Kenneth Edward Randall [1948] Director

R.B. Bishopsgate Investments Limited
Incorporated: 3 May 1994 *Employees:* 3
Net Worth: £539,897,024 *Total Assets:* £1,228,057,984
Registered Office: 33 Davies Street, London, W1K 4LR
Activities: Other letting and operating of own or leased real estate
Parent: Canada Square Investments Limited
Officers: Walid Khaled Abu-Suud [1963] Director [Kuwaiti]; Sangeet Dhanani [1974] Director; Laraine Loh [1984] Director [Singaporean]

R.E.A. Holdings PLC
Incorporated: 27 September 1960 *Employees:* 10,026
Net Worth: £188,085,072 *Total Assets:* £469,868,608
Registered Office: First Floor, 32-36 Great Portland Street, London, W1W 8QX
Activities: Other business support service activities n.e.c.
Officers: David John Blackett [1950] Director; Irene Chia [1941] Director [Singaporean]; Carol Elizabeth Gysin [1957] Director/Company Secretary; John Clifton Oakley [1948] Director; Richard Michael Robinow [1945] Director; Rizal Satar [1957] Director [Indonesian]; Michael Anthony St Clair-George [1942] Director

Rabai Power Holdings Limited
Incorporated: 30 May 2008
Net Worth: £48,213,848 *Total Assets:* £123,984,224
Registered Office: 30 King Street, London, EC2V 8EH
Activities: Activities of head offices
Shareholders: Mitsui Engineering and Shipbuilding Co Ltd; Aldwych Rabai Holdings Limited
Officers: Neil Allen Hopkins, Finance Director; Carl Peter Andersen [1963] Director/Department Manager [Danish]; Henrik Frosig [1960] Investment Director [Danish]; Neil Allen Hopkins [1964] Finance Director

Race Bank Wind Farm (Holding) Limited
Incorporated: 11 July 2016
Net Worth: £170,320,192 *Total Assets:* £170,586,480
Registered Office: 5 Howick Place, London, SW1P 1WG
Activities: Production of electricity
Shareholders: Firebolt RB Holdings Limited; Orsted Race Bank (Holding) Limited
Officers: Philip Henry de Villiers [1975] Director/Asset Manager; Mairi Dudley [1988] Director; Erin Kate Eisenberg [1978] Finance Director [American]; Christoph Friedrich Mertens [1969] Director/CEO Summit Renewable Power Europe GmbH [German]; David Murray [1983] Director/Accountant [Irish]; Benjamin John Sykes [1965] Director/UK Country Manager; David Paul Tilstone [1969] Director; Anthony James Wort [1977] Director/Banker

Race Bank Wind Farm Limited
Incorporated: 16 January 2004
Previous: Dong Energy RB (UK) Limited
Net Worth: £258,788,768 *Total Assets:* £1,909,658,112
Registered Office: 5 Howick Place, London, SW1P 1WG
Activities: Production of electricity
Parent: Race Bank Wind Farm (Holding) Limited
Officers: Philip Henry de Villiers [1975] Director/Asset Manager; Mairi Dudley [1988] Director; Erin Kate Eisenberg [1978] Finance Director [American]; Christoph Friedrich Mertens [1969] Director/CEO Summit Renewable Power Europe GmbH [German]; David Murray [1983] Director/Accountant [Irish]; Benjamin John Sykes [1965] Director/UK Country Manager; David Paul Tilstone [1969] Director; Anthony James Wort [1977] Director/Banker

Radianz Limited
Incorporated: 3 February 2000
Net Worth: £327,208,000 *Total Assets:* £327,771,008
Registered Office: 81 Newgate Street, London, EC1A 7AJ
Activities: Activities of head offices
Parent: British Telecommunications PLC
Officers: Michael Joseph Mohun [1990] Director/Company Secretary Manager [Australian]; Christina Bridget Ryan [1960] Director/Company Secretary [Irish]

Rail for London Limited
Incorporated: 13 October 2006 *Employees:* 331
Net Worth Deficit: £12,600,000 *Total Assets:* £2,221,100,032
Registered Office: 55 Broadway, London, SW1H 0BD
Activities: Passenger rail transport, interurban
Parent: Transport Trading Limited
Officers: Howard Ernest Carter, Secretary/General Counsel; Jill Louise Collis [1968] Director of Health Safety & Environment; Patrick Doig [1982] Director/Planning & Reporting Controller; Jonathan Fox [1964] Director; Gareth William Powell [1976] Director

Rail Settlement Plan Limited
Incorporated: 12 June 1995
Net Worth: £621,000 *Total Assets:* £264,544,000
Registered Office: Part Second Floor, 200-202 Aldersgate Street, London, EC1A 4HD
Activities: Passenger rail transport, interurban
Officers: Peter Charles Dyer [1961] Director/Accountant; Adam Charles Robert Golton [1965] Director/Senior Business Executive; Timothy Brendan Kavanagh [1968] Finance Director; Ian McLaren [1968] Finance Director; Ola Ogun [1972] Finance Director; Paul Jonathan Plummer [1965] Director; Jonathan Luke Roberts [1978] Finance Director; Robert William Taylor [1976] Finance Director; Mark Edward Whitehouse [1979] Director/Chartered Accountant

Ralph US Holdings
Incorporated: 13 August 2007
Net Worth: £726,482,240 *Total Assets:* £848,661,376
Registered Office: Northcliffe House, 2 Derry Street, London, W8 5TT
Activities: Activities of head offices
Parent: DMG Atlantic Limited
Officers: Frances Louise Sallas, Secretary; William Richard Flint [1969] Director/Chartered Accountant

Ramchez GR Limited
Incorporated: 13 February 2015 *Employees:* 2
Net Worth: £441,106,592 *Total Assets:* £937,773,440
Registered Office: Berkeley House, 304 Regents Park Road, London, N3 2JY
Activities: Buying and selling of own real estate
Officers: Paul Hallam, Secretary; Christopher Charles McGill [1960] Managing Director; William Kenneth Procter [1953] Director/Accountant

Rampion Investco Limited
Incorporated: 1 December 2016
Net Worth Deficit: £14,406,431 *Total Assets:* £354,662,336
Registered Office: 18 St Swithin's Lane, London, EC4N 8AD
Activities: Activities of other holding companies n.e.c.
Parent: Rampion Holdco Limited
Officers: Dominic Tan, Secretary; Richard Abel [1970] Director/Investment Banking; Stephen Alan John Deeley [1980] Director/Investment Manager; Mark Jonathan Dooley [1962] Director/Investment Banker [Australian]; Erin Kate Eisenberg [1978] Director [American]; Tom Kelly [1989] Director/Investment Manager [Irish]; Gordon Ian Winston Parsons [1967] Director/Accountant; Roberto Purcaro [1978] Senior Managing Director [Italian]; David Paul Tilstone [1969] Director/Banker

Ramsay Health Care (UK) Limited
Incorporated: 5 January 2007 *Employees:* 15
Net Worth: £311,208,992 *Total Assets:* £607,214,976
Registered Office: Tower 42 Level 18, 25 Old Broad Street, London, EC2N 1HQ
Activities: Activities of head offices
Officers: Mehdi Erfan, Secretary; John Dennis Charles O'Grady, Secretary; Andrew Watkin Jones [1974] Director/Chief Executive; Craig Ralph McNally [1961] Director/Management Executive [Australian]; Hiten Mehta [1961] Director/Public Officer

Ramsay Health Care UK Operations Limited
Incorporated: 8 December 1980 *Employees:* 5,930
Net Worth: £69,836,000 *Total Assets:* £342,732,992
Registered Office: Tower 42 Level 18, 25 Old Broad Street, London, EC2N 1HQ
Activities: Hospital activities
Parent: Ramsay Health Care Holdings UK Limited
Officers: Mehdi Erfan, Secretary; Andrew Watkin Jones [1974] Director/Chief Executive Officer; Hiten Mehta [1961] Director

The Random House Group Limited
Incorporated: 12 May 1969 *Employees:* 1,069
Net Worth: £181,461,376 *Total Assets:* £464,781,536
Registered Office: 20 Vauxhall Bridge Road, London, SW1V 2SA
Activities: Book publishing
Parent: Penguin Random House Limited
Officers: Sinead Mary Martin, Secretary; Markus Franz-Joseph Dohle [1968] Director [German]; Mark William Gardiner [1961] Director; Robert Angus Waddington [1970] Sales Director; Thomas Daryl Weldon [1963] Director/Publisher

Rank Foundation Limited (The)
Incorporated: 25 February 1953 *Employees:* 37
Net Worth: £246,651,008 *Total Assets:* £258,116,000
Registered Office: 12 Warwick Square, London, SW1V 2AA
Activities: Other social work activities without accommodation n.e.c.
Officers: Wendy Louise Matthews, Secretary; Nicholas Fowell Buxton [1966] Director/Chartered Accountant; Jason James Chaffer [1962] Director/Recruitment Consultant; Lindsey Anne Clay [1965] Director; Andrew Edward Cowen [1958] Director; Rose Mary Fitzpatrick [1960] Director/Senior Police Officer; Andrew Neil Rithet Fleming [1959] Director/Investment Manager; Joseph Robert Newton [1956] Director/Farmer; Johanna Louise Ropner [1963] Director; Mark Daniel Benjamin Simon [1965] Director/Solicitor; Earl Michael Henry Hicks Beach St Aldwyn [1950] Director/Financial Intermediary; The Hon Caroline Twiston Davies [1960] Director/Mother; William Penfold Wyatt [1968] Director/Investment Manager

R. Raphael & Sons PLC
Incorporated: 1 December 1976 *Employees:* 142
Net Worth: £44,801,000 *Total Assets:* £402,428,992
Registered Office: 19-21 Shaftesbury Avenue, London, W1D 7ED
Activities: Banks
Parent: Lenlyn Holdings Limited
Officers: Richard Charles Wells, Secretary; Mark Keith Adams [1966] Director; Trevor Eric Johnson [1944] Director; Jeremy Parrish [1955] Director; Michael Anthony Redican [1955] Director; Richard Charles Wells [1963] Finance Director

Raphael Freshwater Memorial Association Limited (The)
Incorporated: 28 March 1961
Net Worth: £135,464,000 *Total Assets:* £165,399,008
Registered Office: 158-162 Shaftesbury Avenue, London, WC2H 8HR
Activities: Other service activities n.e.c.
Officers: Mark Roy Mason Jenner, Secretary; David Davis [1935] Director/Chartered Accountant; Richard Fischer [1937] Director/Lecturer Rtd; Benzion Schalom Eliezer Freshwater [1948] Director; Solomon Israel Freshwater [1950] Director

Rapiscan Systems Limited
Incorporated: 13 October 1992 *Employees:* 346
Net Worth: £81,570,984 *Total Assets:* £159,289,440
Registered Office: One New Change, London, EC4M 9AF
Activities: Other business support service activities n.e.c.
Parent: OSI (Holdings) Company Limited
Officers: Tajinder Singh Ghattaure [1955] Director/Service; Ajay Mehra [1962] Director [American]; Alan Leighton Mixer [1982] Director/Accounting [American]; Marc John Stas [1964] Commercial Director; Peter Craig Williamson [1958] Director/Vice President Sales [American]

Rathbone Brothers Public Limited Company
Incorporated: 21 January 1971 *Employees:* 1,147
Net Worth: £363,278,016 *Total Assets:* £2,738,850,048
Registered Office: 8 Finsbury Circus, London, EC2M 7AZ
Activities: Activities of financial services holding companies
Officers: Ali Johnson, Secretary; Colin Martin Clark [1959] Director; James William Dean [1957] Director/Chartered Accountant; Terri Lynn Duhon [1972] Director [American]; Sarah Felicity Gentleman [1970] Director; Philip Luard Howell [1955] Director Financial Services; Mark Patrick Nicholls [1949] Director/Solicitor; James Neilson Pettigrew [1958] Director; Robert Paul Stockton [1965] Director/Chartered Accountant

Rational Foreign Exchange Limited
Incorporated: 8 March 2005 *Employees:* 86
Net Worth: £1,789,231 *Total Assets:* £212,371,088
Registered Office: Floor 32, One Canada Square, London, E14 5AB
Activities: Financial intermediation not elsewhere classified
Major Shareholder: Rajesh Agrawal
Officers: Amir Karmacharya, Secretary; Rajesh Agrawal [1977] Director; Paresh Davdra [1980] Director; Chris Humphrey [1979] Director/Chief Operating Officer

Rational Group Limited
Incorporated: 4 October 2006 *Employees:* 86
Net Worth: £111,693 *Total Assets:* £212,271,904
Registered Office: Floor 32, One Canada Square, London, E14 5AB
Activities: Activities of financial services holding companies
Major Shareholder: Rajesh Agrawal
Officers: Rajesh Agrawal, Secretary [Indian]; Rajesh Agrawal [1977] Director; Paresh Davdra [1980] Director

Ravenseft Properties Limited
Incorporated: 5 August 1949
Net Worth: £1,258,006,016 *Total Assets:* £1,267,293,952
Registered Office: 100 Victoria Street, London, SW1E 5JL
Activities: Development of building projects
Parent: Land Securities Portfolio Management Limited
Officers: Elizabeth Miles [1977] Director/Solicitor

Ravenside Investments Limited
Incorporated: 21 June 1971
Net Worth: £786,324,992 *Total Assets:* £794,372,992
Registered Office: 100 Victoria Street, London, SW1E 5JL
Activities: Development of building projects
Parent: Land Securities Portfolio Management Limited
Officers: Elizabeth Miles [1977] Director/Solicitor

Raymond Estates Ltd
Incorporated: 7 April 2010 *Employees:* 10
Net Worth: £87,472,224 *Total Assets:* £134,571,280
Registered Office: 4th Floor, Cardinal House, 39-40 Albemarle Street, London, W1S 4TE
Activities: Other letting and operating of own or leased real estate
Shareholders: Mark Philip Wyndham Quinn; Michael John Bostelmann; Rosalind Margaret Abrahams
Officers: Robert Davidson Binns [1941] Director; Mark Philip Wyndham Quinn [1964] Director; Howard Wyndham Raymond [1959] Director

Raznoimport (UK) Limited
Incorporated: 7 May 1980 *Employees:* 6
Net Worth: £36,321,544 *Total Assets:* £141,846,352
Registered Office: 3rd Floor, 114a Cromwell Road, London, SW7 4AG
Activities: Other business support service activities n.e.c.
Officers: Oleg Igorevich Gorbatsevitch, Secretary; Mikhail Jeleznikov [1953] Director [Russian]

RBC Europe Limited
Incorporated: 2 December 1970 *Employees:* 611
Net Worth: £1,056,969,024 *Total Assets:* £40,034,942,976
Registered Office: Riverbank House, 2 Swan Lane, London, EC4R 3BF
Activities: Banks
Parent: Royal Bank of Canada
Officers: Alexander Philip Richardson, Secretary; Nadine Ahn [1971] Director/CFO, Wholesale Finance, Royal Bank of Canada [Canadian]; Stephen Rosenstjerne Krag [1959] Director/Chief Financial Officer, Europe; Bruce William Maclaren [1959] Director/Banker [Canadian]; Vernon Troy Maxwell [1965] Director/CFO, RBC Capital Markets [Canadian]; Nicola Jane Mumford [1960] Director/Lawyer; James Neilson Pettigrew [1958] Director; Harry Jacob Samuel [1965] Director/Banker [Canadian]; David Thomas [1965] Director/Banker; Polly Ann Williams [1965] Director

RBS AA Holdings (UK) Limited
Incorporated: 18 May 1992
Net Worth: £777,676,032 *Total Assets:* £879,020,992
Registered Office: 250 Bishopsgate, London, EC2M 4AA
Activities: Activities of head offices
Parent: The Royal Bank of Scotland Group PLC
Officers: Justine Ann Ferguson, Secretary; Scott Kirkby [1977] Director/Bank Official; Richard John Lawrence [1972] Director/Chartered Accountant; Matthew Edward James Waymark [1975] Director/Bank Official

RBS Invoice Finance Limited
Incorporated: 15 June 1960 *Employees:* 501
Net Worth: £42,296,000 *Total Assets:* £5,221,587,968
Registered Office: 250 Bishopsgate, London, EC2M 4AA
Activities: Financial intermediation not elsewhere classified
Shareholders: National Westminster Bank PLC; RBS Invoice Finance (Holdings) Limited
Officers: Christopher William Green [1972] Director/Bank Official; Alan David Parry [1967] Director/Bank Official; Joseph Alexander Pattara [1973] Director/Bank Official; Christian Gerrard Rowden [1970] Director/Bank Official

RBS SME Investments Limited
Incorporated: 5 March 2009
Net Worth: £7,485,716 *Total Assets:* £307,941,952
Registered Office: 1 Princes Street, London, EC2R 8PB
Activities: Financial intermediation not elsewhere classified
Shareholders: RBS AA Holdings (UK) Limited; The Royal Bank of Scotland PLC
Officers: David Generald Harris [1969] Director/Bank Official; Stuart Christopher Johnstone [1972] Director/Bank Official; Scott McFarlane Thomson [1971] Director/Bank Official

RDL Realisation PLC
Incorporated: 25 March 2015
Previous: Ranger Direct Lending Fund PLC
Net Worth: £160,753,904 *Total Assets:* £227,264,160
Registered Office: 6th Floor, 65 Gresham Street, London, EC2V 7NQ
Activities: Activities of investment trusts
Officers: Dominik Dolenec [1973] Director/Investment Professional [British/Slovenian]; Brendan Hawthorne [1968] Director/Accountant; Joseph Anthony Kenary [1964] Finance Director [American]; Brett Lance Miller [1967] Director; Gregory Share [1973] Director/Investment Management [American]

Reach Magazines Publishing PLC
Incorporated: 7 May 1982 *Employees:* 82
Previous: TM Publishing 1 PLC
Net Worth: £124,949,000 *Total Assets:* £619,148,992
Registered Office: One Canary Wharf, London, E14 5AP
Activities: Publishing of consumer and business journals and periodicals
Parent: Reach Network Media Limited
Officers: Simon Richard Fox [1961] Director/Chief Executive; Simon Jeremy Ian Fuller [1977] Director/Chartered Accountant; Vijay Lakhman Vaghela [1966] Director/Accountant

Reach Network Media Limited
Incorporated: 4 October 2000
Previous: Trinity Mirror Network Limited
Net Worth: £442,849,984 *Total Assets:* £947,798,016
Registered Office: One Canary Wharf, London, E14 5AP
Activities: Activities of head offices
Parent: Reach Publishing Group Limited
Officers: Simon Richard Fox [1961] Director/Chief Executive; Simon Jeremy Ian Fuller [1977] Director/Chartered Accountant; Vijay Lakhman Vaghela [1966] Director/Accountant

Reach PLC
Incorporated: 11 November 1904 *Employees:* 5,067
Previous: Trinity Mirror PLC
Net Worth: £666,800,000 *Total Assets:* £1,342,899,968
Registered Office: One Canary Wharf, London, E14 5AP
Activities: Activities of head offices
Officers: Simon Jeremy Fuller, Secretary; Simon Richard Fox [1961] Director/Chief Executive; Simon Jeremy Ian Fuller [1977] Director/Chartered Accountant; Lee Dale Ginsberg [1957] Director; Steven Thomas Hatch [1970] Director; Dr David Thomas Kelly [1963] Director; Nicholas Edward Tucker Prettejohn [1960] Director; Helen Claire Stevenson [1960] Director; Olivia Streatfeild [1978] Director

Reach Printing Services Limited
Incorporated: 17 January 1986 *Employees:* 569
Previous: Trinity Mirror Printing Limited
Net Worth Deficit: £88,788,000 *Total Assets:* £265,234,000
Registered Office: One Canary Wharf, London, E14 5AP
Activities: Printing of newspapers
Parent: MGL2 Limited
Officers: Simon Richard Fox [1961] Director/Chief Executive; Simon Jeremy Ian Fuller [1977] Director/Chartered Accountant; Vijay Lakhman Vaghela [1966] Director/Accountant

Reach Publishing Group Limited
Incorporated: 3 December 1999
Previous: Trinity Mirror Group Limited
Net Worth: £794,000,000 *Total Assets:* £794,000,000
Registered Office: One Canary Wharf, London, E14 5AP
Activities: Activities of head offices
Parent: Reach PLC
Officers: Simon Richard Fox [1961] Director/Chief Executive; Simon Jeremy Ian Fuller [1977] Director/Chartered Accountant; Vijay Lakhman Vaghela [1966] Director/Accountant

Reach Regionals Limited
Incorporated: 3 December 1999 *Employees:* 540
Previous: Trinity Mirror Regionals Limited
Net Worth: £293,472,992 *Total Assets:* £354,289,984
Registered Office: One Canary Wharf, London, E14 5AP
Activities: Activities of head offices
Parent: Reach Publishing Group Limited
Officers: Simon Richard Fox [1961] Director/Chief Executive; Simon Jeremy Ian Fuller [1977] Director/Chartered Accountant; Vijay Lakhman Vaghela [1966] Director/Accountant

Reach Shared Services Limited
Incorporated: 3 December 1999 *Employees:* 39
Previous: Trinity Mirror Shared Services Limited
Net Worth Deficit: £14,743,000 *Total Assets:* £1,677,395,968
Registered Office: One Canary Wharf, London, E14 5AP
Activities: Activities of head offices
Parent: Reach PLC
Officers: Simon Richard Fox [1961] Director/Chief Executive; Simon Jeremy Ian Fuller [1977] Director/Chartered Accountant; Vijay Lakhman Vaghela [1966] Director/Accountant

Real Estate Participation Management Limited
Incorporated: 22 June 2012
Net Worth: £107,270,256 *Total Assets:* £792,962,368
Registered Office: 1 Churchill Place, London, E14 5HP
Activities: Financial intermediation not elsewhere classified
Parent: Barclays Bank PLC
Officers: Christopher Patrick Le Neve Foster [1981] Director/Banker; David James Rothnie [1982] Director/Banker; Carl Thomas Senior [1978] Director/Banker; Patrick Brittain Voisey [1979] Director

Real Estate Participation Services Limited
Incorporated: 22 June 2012
Net Worth: £955,816,704 *Total Assets:* £1,747,502,336
Registered Office: 1 Churchill Place, London, E14 5HP
Activities: Financial intermediation not elsewhere classified
Parent: Barclays Long Island Limited
Officers: Christopher Patrick Le Neve Foster [1981] Director/Banker; David James Rothnie [1982] Director/Banker; Carl Thomas Senior [1978] Director/Banker; Patrick Brittain Voisey [1979] Director

Real Estate Venture Capital Partners LLP
Incorporated: 4 March 2004 *Employees:* 27
Net Worth Deficit: £103,087,656 *Total Assets:* £201,511,952
Registered Office: 105 Wigmore Street, London, W1U 1QY
Officers: William James Killick [1972] Member; Andrew John Pettit [1968] Member; Terence Shelby Cole [1932] LLP Member; Steven Ross Collins [1952] LLP Member; Francois Guiraud [1970] LLP Member; Mark Neil Steinberg [1959] LLP Member; Nicholas Ashley West [1972] LLP Member

Really Useful Theatres Entertainment Limited
Incorporated: 11 August 1988
Net Worth: £10,741,000 *Total Assets:* £114,163,000
Registered Office: 65 Drury Lane, London, WC2B 5SP
Activities: Activities of head offices
Parent: Really Useful Theatres Holding Limited
Officers: Daniel James Freeman [1976] Finance Director; Rebecca Kane Burton [1975] Managing Director; Mark Gregory Wordsworth [1959] Director

Realreed Limited
Incorporated: 10 March 1989 *Employees:* 18
Net Worth: £186,487,088 *Total Assets:* £212,824,672
Registered Office: c/o Chelsea Cloisters, Sloane Avenue, London, SW3 3DW
Activities: Other letting and operating of own or leased real estate
Officers: Charles John William Moran [1989] Director; Christopher John Moran [1948] Director/Financier; Jamie Christopher George Moran [1988] Director; Colin James Reilly [1979] Director/Chartered Accountant [Irish]

Reclaim Fund Ltd
Incorporated: 13 August 2010 *Employees:* 8
Net Worth: £73,713,000 *Total Assets:* £672,713,984
Registered Office: 3rd Floor, 11-12 St James's Square, London, SW1Y 4LB
Activities: Financial intermediation not elsewhere classified
Parent: Angel Square Investments Limited
Officers: Paul Chisnall [1958] Director; Adrian Michael Coles [1954] Director-General, The Building Societies Association; Katherine Angela Garner [1968] Director; Jane Carolyn Hanson [1967] Director/Accountant; James Alexander Hardie [1961] Director; Robert Newton [1950] Director; Adrian Paul Smith [1969] Director/Consultant; Glyn Michael Smith [1952] Director; Mark Andrew Summerfield [1961] Director; Jennifer Watson [1964] Director

Recruit Global Treasury Services AUD Ltd
Incorporated: 16 January 2017
Net Worth: £131,134,584 *Total Assets:* £131,713,040
Registered Office: 75 King William Street, London, EC4N 7BE
Activities: Financial management
Parent: Recruit Global Treasury Services Ltd
Officers: Yasushi Hashimoto [1967] Director [Japanese]; Tomonori Kimura [1974] Director [Japanese]; Yuya Koshigoe [1977] Director [Japanese]

Recruit Global Treasury Services Ltd
Incorporated: 5 January 2017 *Employees:* 2
Net Worth: £650,100,736 *Total Assets:* £1,313,774,464
Registered Office: 75 King William Street, London, EC4N 7BE
Activities: Financial management
Parent: Recruit Holdings Co.,Ltd.
Officers: Yasushi Hashimoto [1967] Director [Japanese]; Tomonori Kimura [1974] Director [Japanese]; Yuya Koshigoe [1977] Director/Officer [Japanese]

Red Bee Media Limited
Incorporated: 23 July 2001 *Employees:* 1,100
Previous: Ericsson Media Services UK Limited
Net Worth Deficit: £37,332,000 *Total Assets:* £133,907,000
Registered Office: Building 1, 566 Chiswick High Road, London, W4 5BE
Activities: Television programming and broadcasting activities
Parent: Telefonaktiebolaget LM Ericsson
Officers: James Matthew Arnold, Secretary; James Matthew Arnold [1968] Director/Accountant; Steve Ricard Sina Nylund [1968] Director [Swedish]; Liam Kieran O'Brien [1973] Director/Accountant [Irish]; Bengt Edward Odevall [1982] Director [Swedish]

Red Star Pub Company (WR III) Limited
Incorporated: 13 October 2000
Net Worth: £93,531,000 *Total Assets:* £634,699,008
Registered Office: Elsley Court, 20-22 Great Titchfield Street, London, W1W 8BE
Activities: Other business support service activities n.e.c.
Parent: Red Star Pub Company (WRH) Limited
Officers: David Michael Forde [1968] Managing Director [Irish]; Christopher John Moore [1970] Director; Lawson John Wembridge Mountstevens [1968] Senior Director on Trade; David James Tannahill [1977] Finance Director

Redcastle (214 Oxford Street) Limited
Incorporated: 4 November 1999
Net Worth: £50,034,000 *Total Assets:* £162,828,992
Registered Office: Colegrave House, 70 Berners Street, London, W1T 3NL
Activities: Other business support service activities n.e.c.
Officers: Rebecca Rose Flaherty, Secretary; Stephen Boyce [1964] Director/Surveyor; Richard Leeroy Burchill [1971] Director/Accountant; Ian Michael Grabiner [1959] Director

Redcastle Limited
Incorporated: 3 May 1996
Net Worth: £337,844,992 *Total Assets:* £386,992,992
Registered Office: Colegrave House, 70 Berners Street, London, W1T 3NL
Activities: Development of building projects
Officers: Rebecca Rose Flaherty, Secretary; Stephen Boyce [1964] Director/Surveyor; Richard Leeroy Burchill [1971] Director/Accountant; Ian Michael Grabiner [1959] Director

Redquince Limited
Incorporated: 10 November 2006 *Employees:* 2
Net Worth: £213,118,384 *Total Assets:* £225,825,200
Registered Office: 8 Bouverie Street, London, EC4Y 8AX
Activities: Non-life insurance
Shareholders: Fantfoot Limited; Fantfoot Limited
Officers: Tim Jonathan Bratton [1972] Director/General Counsel; Sarah Joanne Cooke [1975] Director

Redrock Investment Limited
Incorporated: 1 February 2016
Net Worth Deficit: £4,859,946 *Total Assets:* £226,744,384
Registered Office: 5th Floor, 6 St Andrew Street, London, EC4A 3AE
Activities: Other business support service activities n.e.c.
Parent: The State-Owned Assets Supervision and Administration Commission of China
Officers: Zhang Kaihong [1976] Director/Assistant General Manager - SDIC Power [Chinese]

Redwood Partnership Ventures 2 Limited
Incorporated: 29 March 2011
Net Worth: £12,632,000 *Total Assets:* £413,273,984
Registered Office: 55 Baker Street, London, W1U 8EW
Activities: Activities of head offices
Parent: Infrastructure Investments Holdings Limited
Officers: Jayne Cheadle, Secretary; Nigel William Michael Goddard Chism [1954] Director/Chartered Accountant; Ross William Driver [1981] Director/Corporate Finance; Stewart Orrell [1965] Director; Keith William Pickard [1968] Director/Accountant; Natalia Poupard [1977] Director/Asset Manager; Julian Mark Rudd-Jones [1955] Director/Property Developer

Redwood Partnership Ventures Limited
Incorporated: 15 May 2007
Net Worth Deficit: £51,322,000 *Total Assets:* £245,708,000
Registered Office: 55 Baker Street, London, W1U 8EW
Activities: Activities of head offices
Shareholders: Infrastructure Investments Holdings Limited; Kajima Partnerships Limited
Officers: Jayne Cheadle, Secretary; Nigel William Michael Goddard Chism [1954] Director/Chartered Accountant; Ross William Driver [1981] Director/Corporate Finance; Hiroto Ichiki [1962] Director/Real Estate Developer [Japanese]; Stewart Orrell [1965] Director; Keith William Pickard [1968] Director/Accountant; Natalia Poupard [1977] Director/Asset Manager; Julian Mark Rudd-Jones [1955] Director/Property Developer

Reebok International Limited
Incorporated: 3 October 1983 *Employees:* 204
Net Worth: £697,054,144 *Total Assets:* £770,678,528
Registered Office: 4th Floor, 11-12 Pall Mall, London, SW1Y 5LU
Activities: Activities of other holding companies n.e.c.
Parent: Adidas AG
Officers: Rowan Julia Hughes, Secretary; John William Lynch [1964] Director/Senior Executive [American]; Martin Edmund O'Brien [1960] Director/Accountant; Matthew Hasten O'Toole [1962] Director/Marketing Executive [American]; Katherine Jane Roseveare [1974] Director/Solicitor; Sarah Talbot [1971] Director/Solicitor; Craig Thornton [1977] Director/VP Finance Reebok Brand [American]

Reed Business Information (Holdings) Limited
Incorporated: 2 May 1897
Previous: Formpart (RPL) Limited
Net Worth: £5,007,000 *Total Assets:* £404,247,008
Registered Office: 1-3 Strand, London, WC2N 5JR
Activities: Activities of head offices
Parent: RELX (UK) Limited
Officers: Alan William McCulloch [1966] Director/Chartered Secretary; Henry Adam Udow [1957] Director/Chief Legal Officer

Reed Overseas Corporation Limited
Incorporated: 21 November 1963
Net Worth: £203,844,992 *Total Assets:* £204,028,000
Registered Office: 1-3 Strand, London, WC2N 5JR
Activities: Activities of households as employers of domestic personnel
Parent: RELX (UK) Limited
Officers: Alan William McCulloch [1966] Director/Chartered Secretary; Henry Adam Udow [1957] Director/Chief Legal Officer

Reed Smith LLP
Incorporated: 23 December 2002 *Employees:* 662
Net Worth: £99,505,280 *Total Assets:* £151,831,888
Registered Office: The Broadgate Tower, 20 Primrose Street, London, EC2A 2RS
Officers: Mary Tamara Box [1967] Member; Douglas Earl Cameron [1959] Member; Benoit Charot [1962] Member; Kyriacos Evagora [1968] Member; Catherine Stephanie Ryan [1971] Member; Philip Minchinton Taylor [1966] Member; Alexander Young Thomas [1966] Member; Leith Faisal Abu-Moghli [1983] LLP Member; Gareth John Amdor [1970] LLP Member; Alexander Tudor Collella Andrews [1960] LLP Member; Fernand Makram Arsanios [1977] LLP Member; Kamal Arulvel [1982] LLP Member; David Ian Ashmore [1980] LLP Member; Ana Atallah [1965] LLP Member; Iain Balkwill [1980] LLP Member; Monica Barton [1978] LLP Member; Ranajoy Basu [1978] LLP Member; Patrick Anthony Eric Beale [1966] LLP Member; Gautam Bhattacharyya [1969] LLP Member; Florence Bilger [1967] LLP Member; Christopher Edward Borg [1967] LLP Member; David John Boutcher [1957] LLP Member; Nicholas William Shearwood Brocklesby [1975] LLP Member; Adrian John Catton Brown [1966] LLP Member; George Brown [1957] LLP Member; Ian Claude Brown [1957] LLP Member; Laura Clare Brunnen [1976] LLP Member; Sarah Louise Caldwell [1984] LLP Member; David Andrew Calligan [1959] LLP Member; Margaret Elizabeth Campbell [1956] LLP Member; Chloe Jane Carswell [1976] LLP Member; Joanna Margaret Carter [1975] LLP Member; Peter John Cassidy [1959] LLP Member; Richard Anthony Ceeney [1973] LLP Member; Eleanor Emma Chapman [1982] LLP Member; Douglas Elliott Franklin Cherry [1976] LLP Member; Jeb Anthony Clulow [1973] LLP Member; David Colin [1969] LLP Member; Jean-Pierre Georges Collet [1962] LLP Member; Sarah Louise Cunningham [1980] LLP Member; Delphine Anne Currie [1964] LLP Member; Kevin Paul Deveau [1979] LLP Member; Captain Marcus Piers Dodds [1971] LLP Member; Timothy Patrick Dolan [1976] LLP Member; Jeffrey Ross Drew [1954] LLP Member; Shareena Denice Edmonds [1976] LLP Member; Stephen Edwards [1949] LLP Member; Robert Pearce Falkner [1959] LLP Member; Elizabeth Margaret Farrell [1984] LLP Member; Sian Catherine Fellows [1960] LLP Member; James Barrington Maxwell Fisher [1980] LLP Member; Michael John Fosh [1963] LLP Member; Caspar Lloyd Fox [1972] LLP Member; Marc Fredj [1970] LLP Member; Graham Andrew Green [1973] LLP Member; Richard Malcolm Gunn [1957] LLP Member; Richard Michael Hakes [1983] LLP Member; Peter Alec Hardy [1959] LLP Member; Nicholas Edward Harris [1980] LLP Member; Simon Peace Hartley [1969] LLP Member; Charles Michael Hewetson [1964] LLP Member; Brett Hillis [1973] LLP Member; Guilain Hippolyte [1978] LLP Member; George Richard Alexander Hoare [1981] LLP Member; Marjorie Cecelia Holmes [1956] LLP Member; Jane Elizabeth Howard [1966] LLP Member; William Anthony Howard [1964] LLP Member; Simon Benjamin Hugo [1982] LLP Member; Stephane Pierre Leo Illouz [1968] LLP Member; Robin Bryan Jeffcott [1970] LLP Member; Andrew Philip Jenkinson [1969] LLP Member; Bronwen Clare Jones [1963] LLP Member; Charles Jurd [1981] LLP Member; Daniel Kadar [1971] LLP Member; Panagiotis Katsambas [1977] LLP Member; Rosanne Mary Beatrix Kay [1974] LLP Member; Stephen Andrew Kirkpatrick [1963] LLP Member; Marc Levy [1965] LLP Member; Isabelle MacElhone [1959] LLP Member; Severine Aude Martel [1977] LLP Member; Michael James Maxtone Smith [1962] LLP Member; Andrew Barry Richard Meads [1973] LLP Member; Edward Samuel Miller [1961] LLP Member; Luke Jon Mines [1977] LLP Member; Charlotte Moller Whiting [1974] LLP Member; Brigid Anne North [1978] LLP Member; Cynthia Rose Longo O'Donoghue [1963] LLP Member; Eoin O'Shea [1969] LLP Member; Al-Ali Omar [1981] LLP Member; Petar Orlic [1974] LLP Member; Belinda Louise Paisley [1962] LLP Member; George Constantine Panagopoulos [1968] LLP Member; Antonia Bridget Panayides [1983] LLP Member; Vassiliki Payiataki [1971] LLP Member; Winston Denys Alexander Penhall [1972] LLP Member; Carolyn Ellen Pepper [1972] LLP Member; Jonathan Richard Pike [1958] LLP Member; Anthony Poulopoulos [1969] LLP Member; Leslie Mark Pring [1966] LLP Member; Gregor John Pryor [1975] LLP Member

Reed Specialist Recruitment Limited
Incorporated: 12 May 2009 *Employees:* 2,108
Net Worth: £31,731,000 *Total Assets:* £148,875,008
Registered Office: Academy Court, 94 Chancery Lane, London, WC2A 1DT
Activities: Other activities of employment placement agencies
Parent: Reed Executive Limited
Officers: Karen Louise Jackson [1972] HR Director; Thomas Mark Lovell [1970] Managing Director; James Andrew Reed [1963] Director; Lee Winton Richards [1973] Finance Director

Regent's Place Holding Company Limited
Incorporated: 17 March 2016
Net Worth: £1,936,865,536 *Total Assets:* £1,936,865,536
Registered Office: York House, 45 Seymour Street, London, W1H 7LX
Activities: Development of building projects
Parent: BL Office (Non-City) Holding Company Limited
Officers: Sarah Morrell Barzycki [1958] Director/Head of Finance; David Ian Lockyer [1969] Director/Chartered Surveyor; Timothy Andrew Roberts [1964] Director/Chartered Surveyor; Nigel Mark Webb [1963] Director/Chartered Surveyor

Regus Group Limited
Incorporated: 18 August 2003 *Employees:* 2
Net Worth: £185,279,008 *Total Assets:* £264,931,008
Registered Office: 2 Kingdom Street, London, W2 6BD
Activities: Activities of head offices
Shareholders: IWG PLC; Regus PLC
Officers: Timothy Sean James Donovan Regan, Secretary/Solicitor; Timothy Sean James Donovan Regan [1965] Director/Solicitor; Stephen James Wetherall [1976] Director/Solicitor

Relative Value Investments UK Limited Liability Partnership
Incorporated: 18 February 2009
Net Worth: £3,760,061 *Total Assets:* £2,166,709,248
Registered Office: 1 Churchill Place, London, E14 5HP

Relative Value Trading Limited
Incorporated: 12 February 2009
Net Worth: £357,937 *Total Assets:* £1,365,087,872
Registered Office: 1 Churchill Place, London, E14 5HP
Activities: Financial intermediation not elsewhere classified
Parent: Maloney Investments Limited
Officers: Carl Thomas Senior [1978] Director/Banker; Vishal Shah [1984] Director/Banker; Patrick Brittain Voisey [1979] Director; Jonathan Michael Walthoe [1975] Director/Banker

Reliance Bank Limited
Incorporated: 28 December 1900 *Employees:* 20
Net Worth: £11,404,794 *Total Assets:* £209,158,800
Registered Office: 23-24 Lovat Lane, London, EC3R 8EB
Activities: Banks
Parent: The Salvation Army International Trustee Company
Officers: Kevin Robert Dare, Secretary; Alka Ahuja [1964] Director/Management Accountant; Nigel Wayne Boothroyd [1960] Director; Andrew Martin Brown [1955] Director; Martyn Richard Croft [1952] Director/Retired; Paul William Croucher [1962] Director; Kevin Robert Dare [1974] Director/Accountant; Simon Andrew Featherstone [1968] Director; Julie Nicholson [1965] Director; John Douglas Wainwright [1951] Director/Minister of Religion

RELX (Holdings) Limited
Incorporated: 5 May 2006
Previous: Reed Elsevier (Holdings) Limited
Net Worth: £8,960,448,512 *Total Assets:* £12,146,595,840
Registered Office: 1-3 Strand, London, WC2N 5JR
Activities: Other business support service activities n.e.c.
Parent: RELX Group PLC
Officers: Alan William McCulloch, Secretary; Nicholas Lawrence Luff [1967] Director; Henry Adam Udow [1957] Director/Chief Legal Officer

RELX (Investments) PLC
Incorporated: 9 May 2006
Previous: Reed Elsevier (Investments) PLC
Net Worth: £61,517,000 *Total Assets:* £619,366,016
Registered Office: 1-3 Strand, London, WC2N 5JR
Activities: Other business support service activities n.e.c.
Parent: RELX (Holdings) Limited
Officers: Alan William McCulloch, Secretary; Nicholas Lawrence Luff [1967] Director; Henry Adam Udow [1957] Director/Chief Legal Officer

RELX (UK) Limited
Incorporated: 11 September 1992 *Employees:* 1,251
Previous: Reed Elsevier (UK) Limited
Net Worth: £856,172,032 *Total Assets:* £5,768,024,064
Registered Office: 1-3 Strand, London, WC2N 5JR
Activities: Activities of head offices
Parent: RELX (Holdings) Limited
Officers: Alan William McCulloch, Secretary; Nicholas Lawrence Luff [1967] Director; Henry Adam Udow [1957] Director/Chief Legal Officer

RELX Finance Limited
Incorporated: 27 June 2017
Net Worth: £60,264 *Total Assets:* £403,285,120
Registered Office: 1-3 Strand, London, WC2N 5JR
Activities: Other business support service activities n.e.c.
Parent: RELX (Holdings) Limited
Officers: Alan William McCulloch, Secretary; Nicholas Lawrence Luff [1967] Director; Alan William McCulloch [1966] Director/Company Secretary; Suzanne Michelle Perry [1975] Director/Treasurer; Henry Adam Udow [1957] Director/Chief Legal Officer

RELX Group PLC
Incorporated: 11 September 1992 *Employees:* 3,100
Previous: Reed Elsevier Group PLC
Net Worth: £2,352,999,936 *Total Assets:* £12,282,999,808
Registered Office: 1-3 Strand, London, WC2N 5JR
Activities: Activities of head offices
Parent: RELX PLC
Officers: Alan William McCulloch, Secretary; Nicholas Lawrence Luff [1967] Director; Henry Adam Udow [1957] Director/Chief Legal Officer

RELX Overseas Holdings Limited
Incorporated: 13 March 2015
Net Worth: £739,833,984 *Total Assets:* £1,806,772,992
Registered Office: 1-3 Strand, London, WC2N 5JR
Activities: Activities of head offices
Parent: RELX (Holdings) Limited
Officers: Alan William McCulloch, Secretary; Nicholas Lawrence Luff [1967] Director; Henry Adam Udow [1957] Director/Chief Legal Officer

RELX PLC
Incorporated: 28 May 1903 *Employees:* 31,000
Previous: Reed Elsevier PLC
Net Worth: £2,352,999,936 *Total Assets:* £12,282,999,808
Registered Office: 1-3 Strand, London, WC2N 5JR
Activities: Book publishing
Officers: Henry Adam Udow, Secretary; Erik Engstrom [1963] Director [Swedish]; Sir Anthony John Habgood [1946] Director; Wolfhart Gunnar Hauser [1949] Director [German]; Adrian Hennah [1957] Director/Chief Financial Officer; Nicholas Lawrence Luff [1967] Director; Robert James MacLeod [1964] Director; Carol Geiger Mills [1953] Director [American]; Linda Szabat Sanford [1953] Director [American]; Ben Van Der Veer [1951] Director [Dutch]; Marike Van Lier Lels [1959] Director [Dutch]; Suzanne Wood [1960] Director [American]

Renaissancere Corporate Capital (UK) Limited
Incorporated: 5 March 2009
Net Worth Deficit: £17,406,480 *Total Assets:* £1,508,586,240
Registered Office: 18th Floor, 125 Old Broad Street, London, EC2N 1AR
Activities: Non-life insurance
Parent: Renaissancere Specialty Holdings (UK) Limited
Officers: Leo David Lechmere Barran, Secretary; Hugh Richard Timothy Brennan [1977] Director [Irish]; Ross Arthur Curtis [1972] Director/SVP Group Chief Underwriting Officer; Divyesh Dinesh Upadhyaya [1971] Finance Director

Renault Retail Group UK Limited
Incorporated: 12 October 1988 *Employees:* 900
Net Worth Deficit: £11,055,000 *Total Assets:* £198,159,008
Registered Office: Head Office, Concord Road, Western Avenue, London, W3 0RZ
Activities: Sale of new cars and light motor vehicles
Parent: Renault U.K. Limited
Officers: Scott Kilbourne, Secretary; Leonard Stephen Curran [1959] Director; Mark Fellows [1967] Director; Barry William Jones [1968] Director; Scott Edward Kilbourne [1973] Director

Renbuff Investments Limited
Incorporated: 25 March 2015
Net Worth: £167,281,072 *Total Assets:* £452,034,880
Registered Office: Berkeley House, 304 Regents Park Road, London, N3 2JY
Activities: Buying and selling of own real estate
Officers: Paul Hallam, Secretary; Christopher Charles McGill [1960] Managing Director; William Kenneth Procter [1953] Director/Accountant

Renewable Energy Income Partnership Holdings 1 Limited
Incorporated: 28 February 2017
Net Worth Deficit: £1,096,259 *Total Assets:* £278,375,488
Registered Office: 6th Floor, 33 Holborn, London, EC1N 2HT
Activities: Activities of other holding companies n.e.c.
Parent: Octopus Renewable Energy Income Partnership GP LLP
Officers: Alexander David Kelson Brierley [1978] Director; Thomas James Rosser [1985] Director; Katrina Anne Shenton [1971] Director

Renewable Energy Income Partnership Holdings 2 Limited
Incorporated: 1 March 2017 *Employees:* 3
Net Worth: £1 *Total Assets:* £275,413,152
Registered Office: 6th Floor, 33 Holborn, London, EC1N 2HT
Activities: Activities of other holding companies n.e.c.
Parent: Renewable Energy Income Partnership Holdings 1 Limited
Officers: Alexander David Kelson Brierley [1978] Director; Thomas James Rosser [1985] Director; Katrina Anne Shenton [1971] Director

Renewable Energy Income Partnership Holdings Limited
Incorporated: 1 March 2017 *Employees:* 3
Net Worth Deficit: £406,273 *Total Assets:* £283,285,088
Registered Office: 6th Floor, 33 Holborn, London, EC1N 2HT
Activities: Production of electricity
Parent: Renewable Energy Income Partnership Holdings 2 Limited
Officers: Alexander David Kelson Brierley [1978] Director; Thomas James Rosser [1985] Director; Katrina Anne Shenton [1971] Director

The Renewables Infrastructure Group (UK) Investments Limited
Incorporated: 28 April 2015
Net Worth: £359,740,000 *Total Assets:* £1,081,892,992
Registered Office: 12 Charles II Street, London, SW1Y 4QU
Activities: Other business support service activities n.e.c.
Parent: The Renewables Infrastructure Group (UK) Limited
Officers: Emily Mendes, Secretary; William Richard Crawford [1963] Investment Director; Jonathan Mark Entract [1972] Investment Director; Philip Roger Perkins George [1971] Portfolio Director; Christopher Paul Gill [1957] Director/Merchant Banker

The Renewables Infrastructure Group (UK) Limited
Incorporated: 26 April 2013
Net Worth: £358,152,992 *Total Assets:* £360,944,000
Registered Office: 12 Charles II Street, London, SW1Y 4QU
Activities: Activities of head offices
Parent: The Renewables Infrastructure Group Limited
Officers: Emily Mendes, Secretary; Jaz Bains [1966] Director; William Richard Crawford [1963] Investment Director; Jonathan Mark Entract [1972] Investment Director; Philip Roger Perkins George [1971] Portfolio Director; Christopher Paul Gill [1957] Director/Merchant Banker; Donald Crawford Joyce [1973] Director/Chief Financial Officer; Rachel Ruffle [1967] Director/Chartered Engineer

Rensburg Sheppards PLC
Incorporated: 8 July 1987 *Employees:* 7
Net Worth: £329,488,000 *Total Assets:* £329,575,008
Registered Office: 30 Gresham Street, London, EC2V 7QN
Activities: Activities of head offices
Parent: Investec Bank PLC
Officers: Steven Robert Kilday, Secretary; Stephen Maclaurin Elliott [1954] Director/Banker [South African]; Iain William Hooley [1972] Director/Secretary; Bernard Kantor [1949] Director/Banker [Irish]; Stephen Koseff [1951] Director [South African]; Judith Edna Price [1957] Director; Tomas Haydn Street [1964] Director; Jonathan Peter Wragg [1967] Director

Repsol Sinopec Alpha Limited
Incorporated: 12 June 2003
Previous: Talisman Sinopec Alpha Limited
Net Worth Deficit: £50,772,012 *Total Assets:* £183,322,288
Registered Office: Suite 1, 3rd Floor, 11-12 St James's Square, London, SW1Y 4LB
Activities: Extraction of crude petroleum
Parent: Repsol Sinopec Resources UK Limited
Officers: Gemma Crawford, Secretary; Jose Carlos Vicente Bravo [1965] Executive Director [Spanish]; Manuel Tomas Garcia Blanco [1964] E&P Regional Executive Director, Europe, Africa, [Spanish]; Che Hung Lo [1953] Director [Malaysian]; Dale Kelly Moore [1960] Director/Engineer [Canadian]

Repsol Sinopec North Sea Limited
Incorporated: 18 July 1972
Previous: Talisman Sinopec North Sea Limited
Net Worth Deficit: £558,407,040 *Total Assets:* £557,872,256
Registered Office: Suite 1, 3rd Floor, 11-12 St James's Square, London, SW1Y 4LB
Activities: Extraction of crude petroleum
Parent: Repsol Sinopec Resources UK Limited
Officers: Gemma Crawford, Secretary; Jose Carlos Vicente Bravo [1965] Executive Director [Spanish]; Manuel Tomas Garcia Blanco [1964] E&P Regional Executive Director, Europe, Africa, [Spanish]; Che Hung Lo [1953] Director [Malaysian]; Dale Kelly Moore [1960] Director/Engineer [Canadian]

Repsol Sinopec Oil Trading Limited
Incorporated: 20 October 1988
Previous: Talisman Sinopec Oil Trading Limited
Net Worth Deficit: £477,596,608 *Total Assets:* £449,388,416
Registered Office: Suite 1, 3rd Floor, 11-12 St James's Square, London, SW1Y 4LB
Activities: Extraction of crude petroleum
Parent: Repsol Sinopec North Sea Limited
Officers: Gemma Crawford, Secretary; Jose Carlos Vicente Bravo [1965] Executive Director [Spanish]; Manuel Tomas Garcia Blanco [1964] E&P Regional Executive Director, Europe, Africa, [Spanish]; Che Hung Lo [1953] Director [Malaysian]; Dale Kelly Moore [1960] Director/Engineer [Canadian]

Repsol Sinopec Resources UK Limited
Incorporated: 3 November 1964 *Employees:* 940
Previous: Talisman Sinopec Energy UK Limited
Net Worth Deficit: £868,081,664 *Total Assets:* £2,514,711,808
Registered Office: Suite 1, 3rd Floor, 11-12 St James's Square, London, SW1Y 4LB
Activities: Extraction of crude petroleum
Shareholders: Talisman Colombia Holdco Limited; Addax Petroleum UK Limited
Officers: Gemma Crawford, Secretary; Jose Carlos Vicente Bravo [1965] Executive Director [Spanish]; Manuel Tomas Garcia Blanco [1964] E&P Regional Executive Director, Europe, Africa, [Spanish]; Che Hung Lo [1953] Director [Malaysian]; Dale Kelly Moore [1960] Director/Engineer [Canadian]; Roger Stephen Ramshaw [1949] Director

Residential Mortgage Securities 23 PLC
Incorporated: 4 February 2008
Net Worth: £42,000 *Total Assets:* £144,196,992
Registered Office: 6th Floor, 65 Gresham Street, London, EC2V 7NQ
Activities: Other business support service activities n.e.c.
Parent: RMS Securitisation Holdings Limited
Officers: Sean Peter Martin [1965] Director

Residential Mortgage Securities 25 PLC
Incorporated: 3 September 2010
Net Worth Deficit: £82,000 *Total Assets:* £111,644,000
Registered Office: 6th Floor, 65 Gresham Street, London, EC2V 7NQ
Activities: Other business support service activities n.e.c.
Parent: RMS Securitisation Holdings Limited
Officers: Sean Peter Martin [1965] Director

Residential Mortgage Securities 26 PLC
Incorporated: 24 July 2012
Net Worth: £23,000 *Total Assets:* £133,593,000
Registered Office: 6th Floor, 65 Gresham Street, London, EC2V 7NQ
Activities: Activities of mortgage finance companies
Parent: RMS Securitisation Holdings Limited
Officers: Sean Peter Martin [1965] Director

Residential Mortgage Securities 28 PLC
Incorporated: 13 January 2015
Net Worth Deficit: £505,000 *Total Assets:* £328,656,000
Registered Office: 35 Great St Helen's, London, EC3A 6AP
Activities: Financial intermediation not elsewhere classified
Parent: Residential Mortgage Securities 28 Parent Limited
Officers: Daniel Marc Richard Jaffe [1975] Director

Residential Mortgage Securities 29 PLC
Incorporated: 5 December 2016
Net Worth: £30,000 *Total Assets:* £526,536,000
Registered Office: 6th Floor, 65 Gresham Street, London, EC2V 7NQ
Activities: Activities of mortgage finance companies
Parent: Residential Mortgage Securities 29 Parent Limited
Officers: Sean Peter Martin [1965] Director

Residential Mortgage Securities 30 PLC
Incorporated: 26 May 2017 *Employees:* 3
Net Worth: £24,000 *Total Assets:* £421,236,992
Registered Office: 6th Floor, 65 Gresham Street, London, EC2V 7NQ
Activities: Activities of mortgage finance companies
Parent: Residential Mortgage Securities 30 Parent Limited
Officers: Sean Peter Martin [1965] Director

Resloc UK 2007-1 PLC
Incorporated: 13 February 2007
Net Worth: £3,259,388 *Total Assets:* £470,531,104
Registered Office: Third Floor, 1 King's Arms Yard, London, EC2R 7AF
Activities: Other business support service activities n.e.c.
Parent: Resloc UK Holdings Limited
Officers: Daniel Jonathan Wynne [1970] Director

Resource Solutions Limited
Incorporated: 25 July 1986 *Employees:* 778
Net Worth: £25,261,000 *Total Assets:* £137,035,008
Registered Office: 11 Slingsby Place, St Martin's Courtyard, London, WC2E 9AB
Activities: Other activities of employment placement agencies
Parent: Robert Walters Holdings Limited
Officers: Alan Robert Bannatyne, Secretary/Chartered Accountant; Alan Robert Bannatyne [1970] Director/Chartered Accountant; Giles Philip Daubeney [1961] Director/Deputy Chief Executive Officer; Adam James McDonnell [1977] Finance Director

The Restaurant Group (UK) Limited
Incorporated: 20 December 1966 *Employees:* 9,986
Net Worth: £74,082,000 *Total Assets:* £283,492,992
Registered Office: 5-7 Marshalsea Road, Borough, London, SE1 1EP
Activities: Licenced restaurants
Parent: TRG (Holdings) Limited
Officers: Kirk Dyson Davis [1971] Director; Andrew McCue [1974] Director/Chief Executive Officer [Irish]

Retail Centres V (Sweden) Investment Limited
Incorporated: 12 December 2014 *Employees:* 3
Net Worth: £180,733,552 *Total Assets:* £186,266,512
Registered Office: 70 Grosvenor Street, London, W1K 3JP
Activities: Other business support service activities n.e.c.
Parent: Retail Centres V (Sweden) General Partner Limited
Officers: Lisa Sorrell, Secretary; Robert Richard Davis [1967] Finance Director; Boris Van Warmerdam [1976] Director [Dutch]; David Robert Wright [1981] Director/Accountant

Retina Finance UK Limited
Incorporated: 25 February 2005
Previous: ARM Finance UK Limited
Net Worth: £433,734,016 *Total Assets:* £433,771,008
Registered Office: 69 Grosvenor Street, London, W1K 3JP
Activities: Activities of other holding companies n.e.c.
Parent: ARM Holdings PLC
Officers: Paul Alexander Davison [1988] Director

Retirement Bridge Investments Limited
Incorporated: 15 October 2015 *Employees:* 24
Net Worth Deficit: £4,673,000 *Total Assets:* £327,768,000
Registered Office: 54 Portland Place, London, W1B 1DY
Activities: Other business support service activities n.e.c.
Officers: Ashish Kashyap [1979] Investment Director; Shane Edward Law [1972] Director

Reuters Transaction Services Limited
Incorporated: 13 January 1987
Net Worth: £101,899,416 *Total Assets:* £143,959,552
Registered Office: The Thomson Reuters Building, 30 South Colonnade, Canary Wharf, London, E14 5EP
Activities: Financial intermediation not elsewhere classified
Parent: Reuters Limited
Officers: Carla O'Hanlon, Secretary; Paul Eric Clarke [1967] Director; Christopher Paul Glanvill [1971] Director/Head of Customer Administration - EMEA; Mark Daniel Johnston [1971] Director/Head of Finance; Christopher Leonard-Appleton [1983] Director/Financial Services; Neill Martin Penney [1970] Director; Philip James Wellard [1965] Director/C T O

Revcap Finance Limited
Incorporated: 14 October 2013
Net Worth: £1,124,996 *Total Assets:* £263,825,504
Registered Office: 105 Wigmore Street, London, W1U 1QY
Activities: Activities auxiliary to financial intermediation n.e.c.
Parent: Revcap UK Holdings Limited
Officers: Richard Bruce Mitchell, Secretary; William James Killick [1972] Director/Investment Banker; Andrew John Pettit [1968] Director/Investment Banker; Nicholas Ashley West [1972] Director/Chartered Surveyor

Revcap UK Holdings Limited
Incorporated: 15 December 2003
Net Worth: £114,354,952 *Total Assets:* £220,593,568
Registered Office: 105 Wigmore Street, London, W1U 1QY
Activities: Other letting and operating of own or leased real estate
Parent: Real Estate Venture Capital Partners I LLP
Officers: Richard Bruce Mitchell, Secretary; William James Killick [1972] Director/Investment Banker; Andrew John Pettit [1968] Director/Banker; Stephen John Pettit [1976] Director/Banker

RG Engagement Group 5 Limited
Incorporated: 27 July 2015
Net Worth: £29,564,186 *Total Assets:* £150,111,920
Registered Office: 265 Tottenham Court Road, London, W1T 7RQ
Activities: Other activities of employment placement agencies
Parent: RG Engagement Group 4 Limited
Officers: Robert Alan Boland [1981] Group Director; Douglas Andrew Butler [1964] Director/Executive - Software Services [American]

RG Engagement Group Limited
Incorporated: 27 July 2015 *Employees:* 380
Net Worth Deficit: £46,098,572 *Total Assets:* £181,836,944
Registered Office: 265 Tottenham Court Road, London, W1T 7RQ
Activities: Other activities of employment placement agencies
Officers: Robert Alan Boland [1981] Group Director; Christopher Busby [1975] Director/Private Equity; Douglas Andrew Butler [1964] Director/Executive - Software Services [American]; Drew Loucks [1982] Director/Investment Manager [American]; Matthew Vettel [1967] Director/Private Equity [American]

Rhythmone PLC
Incorporated: 23 April 2007 *Employees:* 474
Previous: Blinkx PLC
Net Worth: £215,845,120 *Total Assets:* £322,566,912
Registered Office: 6th Floor, 65 Gresham Street, London, EC2V 7NQ
Activities: Other service activities n.e.c.
Officers: Amy Melissa Rothstein, Secretary; Mark Joseph Bonney [1954] President, CEO and Director [American]; John Mutch [1956] Director/Founder and Managing Partner of MV Advisors, LLC [American]; Eric Brandon Singer [1974] Director/Founder and Managing Partner of Viex Capital [American]

RI Income UK Holdings Limited
Incorporated: 25 November 2014
Net Worth: £226,354,000 *Total Assets:* £452,668,992
Registered Office: 12 Throgmorton Avenue, London, EC2N 2DL
Activities: Activities of other holding companies n.e.c.
Parent: BRI UK Finance Limited
Officers: Peter George Raftery [1968] Director/Engineer; Stephane Christophe Tetot [1981] Director [French]

Ribbon Acquisition Limited
Incorporated: 8 March 2005
Previous: LRG Acquisition Limited
Net Worth: £621,529,024 *Total Assets:* £624,860,032
Registered Office: 10 Queen Street Place, London, EC4R 1AG
Activities: Buying and selling of own real estate
Parent: Ribbon Bidco Limited
Officers: David Mark Andrew Beveridge [1959] Director; Gideon Efrati [1956] Director [Israeli]; Simon Michael Teasdale [1965] Director

Ribbon Bidco Limited
Incorporated: 6 November 2015
Net Worth: £44,169,000 *Total Assets:* £553,521,024
Registered Office: 10 Queen Street Place, London, EC4R 1AG
Activities: Activities of other holding companies n.e.c.
Parent: Ribbon Midco Limited
Officers: David Mark Andrew Beveridge [1959] Director; Gideon Efrati [1956] Director [Israeli]; Simon Michael Teasdale [1965] Director

Ribbon Holdco Limited
Incorporated: 6 November 2015 *Employees:* 1,960
Net Worth: £116,099,000 *Total Assets:* £685,795,008
Registered Office: 10 Queen Street Place, London, EC4R 1AG
Activities: Activities of other holding companies n.e.c.
Parent: Lapithus Hotels Management UK Limited
Officers: David Mark Andrew Beveridge [1959] Director; Gideon Efrati [1956] Director [Israeli]; Simon Michael Teasdale [1965] Director

Ribbon Mezzco Limited
Incorporated: 6 November 2015
Net Worth: £103,302,000 *Total Assets:* £249,370,000
Registered Office: 10 Queen Street Place, London, EC4R 1AG
Activities: Activities of other holding companies n.e.c.
Parent: Ribbon Holdco Limited
Officers: David Mark Andrew Beveridge [1959] Director; Gideon Efrati [1956] Director [Israeli]; Simon Michael Teasdale [1965] Director

Ribbon Midco Limited
Incorporated: 6 November 2015 *Employees:* 1,960
Net Worth: £115,306,000 *Total Assets:* £685,670,016
Registered Office: 10 Queen Street Place, London, EC4R 1AG
Activities: Activities of other holding companies n.e.c.
Parent: Ribbon Mezzco Limited
Officers: David Mark Andrew Beveridge [1959] Director; Gideon Efrati [1956] Director [Israeli]; Simon Michael Teasdale [1965] Director

Richemont Holdings (UK) Limited
Incorporated: 28 July 1993
Net Worth: £791,281,024 *Total Assets:* £1,137,566,976
Registered Office: 15 Hill Street, London, W1J 5QT
Activities: Activities of head offices
Parent: Richemont International Holding SA
Officers: Shamini Rajah-Barrett, Secretary; Rupert John Brooks [1967] Director/Solicitor; Sheila Mary Henderson [1965] Director/Lawyer; The Duke of Wellington Arthur Charles Valerian Wellesley [1945] Director/Chairman

Rickleford Ltd
Incorporated: 25 July 2012
Net Worth: £172,902,848 *Total Assets:* £196,131,360
Registered Office: Ramillies House, 2 Ramillies Street, London, W1F 7LN
Activities: Other credit granting n.e.c.
Parent: Rickleford Group Limited
Officers: David Sullivan [1949] Director

Ricoh Capital Limited
Incorporated: 14 December 1994 *Employees:* 18
Net Worth: £96,471,000 *Total Assets:* £171,324,992
Registered Office: 20 Triton Street, London, NW1 3BF
Activities: Renting and leasing of office machinery and equipment (including computers)
Officers: Nicola Clare Downing, Secretary; Nicola Clare Downing [1974] Director; David Kemmitt [1962] Finance Director; Timothy Ian Stuart [1975] Director

Ricoh Europe ASP Limited
Incorporated: 20 November 2000
Net Worth: £132,718,496 *Total Assets:* £160,772,160
Registered Office: 20 Triton Street, London, NW1 3BF
Activities: Information technology consultancy activities
Parent: Ricoh Europe Holdings PLC
Officers: Nicola Clare Downing, Secretary; Nicola Clare Downing [1974] Director/Lawyer; Kyoichiro Fujimoto [1966] Director [Japanese]; David Mills [1958] Director

Ricoh Europe Finance Limited
Incorporated: 18 October 1963
Net Worth: £17,777,976 *Total Assets:* £1,556,859,392
Registered Office: 20 Triton Street, London, NW1 3BF
Activities: Financial management
Parent: Ricoh Europe Holdings PLC
Officers: Nicola Clare Downing, Secretary; Masaki Kawakami [1968] Director [Japanese]; Yoshitaka Motomura [1966] Director [Japanese]; Constantia Smith [1972] Director/Lawyer; Timothy Ian Stuart [1975] Director

Ricoh Europe Holdings PLC
Incorporated: 8 June 2007 *Employees:* 15,980
Net Worth: £1,576,000,000 *Total Assets:* £3,065,400,064
Registered Office: 20 Triton Street, London, NW1 3BF
Activities: Activities of head offices
Parent: Ricoh Company, Ltd
Officers: Nicola Clare Downing, Secretary; Kyoichiro Fujimoto [1966] Director [Japanese]; David Mills [1958] Director; Akira Oyama [1961] Director [Japanese]

Rio 587 Limited
Incorporated: 17 January 2008
Net Worth: £291,080,000 *Total Assets:* £314,392,992
Registered Office: The Walbrook Building, 25 Walbrook, London, EC4N 8AW
Activities: Other business support service activities n.e.c.
Parent: Friary Intermediate Limited
Officers: Alistair Charles Peel, Secretary; Matthew William Pike [1964] Director

Rio 588 Limited
Incorporated: 6 February 2008
Net Worth Deficit: £101,592,000 *Total Assets:* £160,050,000
Registered Office: The Walbrook Building, 25 Walbrook, London, EC4N 8AW
Activities: Other business support service activities n.e.c.
Parent: Rio 587 Limited
Officers: Alistair Charles Peel, Secretary; Matthew William Pike [1964] Director

Rio Tinto Australian Holdings Limited
Incorporated: 2 February 1949
Net Worth: £12,556,300,288 *Total Assets:* £12,598,478,848
Registered Office: 6 St James's Square, London, SW1Y 4AD
Activities: Activities of head offices
Parent: Rio Tinto South East Asia Limited
Officers: Richard Alan Avery [1975] Director/Chartered Accountant; Michael Philip Bossick [1960] Director/Chartered Accountant; Paul Ian Hedley [1969] Director/Treasurer

Rio Tinto Diamonds Limited
Incorporated: 21 October 2004
Net Worth: £104,153,952 *Total Assets:* £239,263,200
Registered Office: 6 St James's Square, London, SW1Y 4AD
Activities: Other business support service activities n.e.c.
Parent: Rio Tinto International Holdings Limited
Officers: Alan Kevin Chirgwin [1967] Director/VP Sales & Marketing - Copper & Diamonds [Australian]; Helena Nonka [1975] Director/General Manager - Global Transfer Pricing [Canadian]; Elias Scafidas [1977] Director/Chartered Accountant [Australian]; Arnaud Soirat [1964] Director/Manager [French]

Rio Tinto European Holdings Limited
Incorporated: 29 October 1970
Net Worth: £6,112,731,136 *Total Assets:* £9,062,165,504
Registered Office: 6 St James's Square, London, SW1Y 4AD
Activities: Activities of head offices
Parent: Rio Tinto PLC
Officers: Steven Patrick Allen [1971] Director/Company Secretary; Michael Philip Bossick [1960] Director/Chartered Accountant; Peter Lloyd Cunningham [1966] Director/Accountant; Paul Ian Hedley [1969] Director/Treasurer

Rio Tinto Finance (USA) PLC
Incorporated: 20 June 2007
Net Worth: £57,346 *Total Assets:* £1,341,607,168
Registered Office: 6 St James's Square, London, SW1Y 4AD
Activities: Activities of head offices
Parent: Rio Tinto International Holdings Limited
Officers: Steven Patrick Allen [1971] Director/Company Secretary; Michael Philip Bossick [1960] Director/Chartered Accountant; Peter Lloyd Cunningham [1966] Director/Accountant; Paul Ian Hedley [1969] Director/Treasurer

Rio Tinto Finance PLC
Incorporated: 19 January 1940
Net Worth: £1,580,396,928 *Total Assets:* £31,661,467,648
Registered Office: 6 St James's Square, London, SW1Y 4AD
Activities: Financial intermediation not elsewhere classified
Parent: Rio Tinto International Holdings Limited
Officers: Steven Patrick Allen [1971] Director/Company Secretary; Michael Philip Bossick [1960] Director/Chartered Accountant; Peter Lloyd Cunningham [1966] Director/Accountant; Paul Ian Hedley [1969] Director/Treasurer

Rio Tinto International Holdings Limited
Incorporated: 17 December 1946
Net Worth: £30,446,983,168 *Total Assets:* £41,757,265,920
Registered Office: 6 St James's Square, London, SW1Y 4AD
Activities: Activities of head offices
Parent: Rio Tinto PLC
Officers: Steven Patrick Allen [1971] Director/Company Secretary; Michael Philip Bossick [1960] Director/Chartered Accountant; Peter Lloyd Cunningham [1966] Director/Accountant; Paul Ian Hedley [1969] Director/Treasurer

Rio Tinto London Limited
Incorporated: 26 October 1948 *Employees:* 267
Net Worth: £682,307,968 *Total Assets:* £888,339,008
Registered Office: 6 St James's Square, London, SW1Y 4AD
Activities: Activities of head offices
Parent: Rio Tinto European Holdings Limited
Officers: Steven Patrick Allen [1971] Director/Company Secretary; Michael Philip Bossick [1960] Director/Chartered Accountant; Peter Lloyd Cunningham [1966] Director/Accountant; Paul Ian Hedley [1969] Director/Treasurer

Rio Tinto Metals Limited
Incorporated: 12 April 1917
Net Worth: £8,694,735 *Total Assets:* £183,489,488
Registered Office: 6 St James's Square, London, SW1Y 4AD
Activities: Activities of head offices
Parent: Rio Tinto European Holdings Limited
Officers: Richard Alan Avery [1975] Director/Chartered Accountant; Michael Philip Bossick [1960] Director/Chartered Accountant; Paul Ian Hedley [1969] Director/Treasurer

Rio Tinto Minerals Development Limited
Incorporated: 2 November 1933
Net Worth: £104,775,928 *Total Assets:* £105,142,728
Registered Office: 6 St James's Square, London, SW1Y 4AD
Activities: Activities of head offices
Parent: Rio Tinto European Holdings Limited
Officers: Daniel Linton Brackner [1971] Director/Accountant [American]; Arnaud Jean-Francois Christophe Brion [1969] Director [French]; Dr Kenneth Melbourne Tainton [1966] Director/Exploration Executive

Rio Tinto PLC
Incorporated: 30 March 1962 *Employees:* 46,807
Net Worth: £32,455,720,960 *Total Assets:* £69,487,517,696
Registered Office: 6 St James's Square, London, SW1Y 4AD
Activities: Activities of head offices
Officers: Steven Patrick Allen, Secretary; Dr Megan Elizabeth Clark [1958] Director [Australian]; David Edward Constable [1961] Director [Canadian]; M Ann Frances Godbehere [1955] Director [British/Canadian]; Moya Marguerite Greene [1954] Corporate Director [Canadian]; Simon Peter Henry [1961] Director; Jean Sebastien Dominique Francois Jacques [1971] Director/Deputy Chief Executive; Michael Gerard L'estrange [1952] Director/University Professor [Australian]; William Samuel Hugh Laidlaw [1956] Director; Simon Vincent McKeon [1955] Director [Australian]; Jakob Stausholm [1968] Director/Executive [Danish]; Simon Robert Thompson [1959] Director

Rio Tinto South East Asia Limited
Incorporated: 21 January 1999
Net Worth: £5,941,101,056 *Total Assets:* £23,109,890,048
Registered Office: 6 St James's Square, London, SW1Y 4AD
Activities: Activities of head offices
Parent: Rio Tinto International Holdings Limited
Officers: Michael Philip Bossick [1960] Director/Chartered Accountant; Peter Lloyd Cunningham [1966] Director/Accountant; Paul Ian Hedley [1969] Director/Treasurer; Andrew William Hodges [1967] Director/Chartered Secretary

Rio Tinto Western Holdings Limited
Incorporated: 29 March 1873
Net Worth: £5,883,106,304 *Total Assets:* £5,898,169,856
Registered Office: 6 St James's Square, London, SW1Y 4AD
Activities: Activities of head offices
Parent: Rio Tinto European Holdings Limited
Officers: Michael Philip Bossick [1960] Director/Chartered Accountant; Peter Lloyd Cunningham [1966] Director/Accountant; Andrew William Hodges [1967] Director/Chartered Secretary

Ripon Mortgages PLC
Incorporated: 10 March 2017
Net Worth: £14,120 *Total Assets:* £9,675,343,872
Registered Office: 35 Great St Helen's, London, EC3A 6AP
Activities: Activities of mortgage finance companies
Parent: Ripon Mortgages Holdings Limited
Officers: Susan Iris Abrahams [1957] Director

RIT Capital Partners PLC
Incorporated: 7 May 1987 *Employees:* 67
Net Worth: £2,858,299,904 *Total Assets:* £3,366,299,904
Registered Office: 27 St James's Place, London, SW1A 1NR
Activities: Activities of financial services holding companies
Officers: Philippe Costeletos [1965] Director; Michael John Paul Marks [1941] Director; Andre Perold [1952] Director [American]; Michael Kevin Power [1957] Director/University Professor; The Hon Hannah Mary Rothschild [1962] Director/Film Producer; Lord Nathaniel Charles Jacob Rothschild [1936] Director; Jeremy William Sillem [1950] Director; Amy Stirling [1969] Finance Director; The Duke of Wellington Arthur Charles Valerian Wellesey [1945] Director/Company Chairman

Ritz Hotel (London) Limited (The)
Incorporated: 17 November 1899 *Employees:* 438
Net Worth: £75,583,000 *Total Assets:* £234,716,000
Registered Office: 150 Piccadilly, London, W1V 9DG
Activities: Hotels and similar accommodation
Officers: Aidan Stuart Barclay [1956] Director; Howard Myles Barclay [1959] Financier Director; Ciaran Fahy [1964] Director/General Manager [Irish]; Andrew Michael Love [1941] Director/Chief Executive; Philip Leslie Peters [1957] Banking Director; Michael Seal [1948] Director/Chartered Accountant

The Ritz Hotel, Limited
Incorporated: 29 May 1896 *Employees:* 588
Net Worth Deficit: £112,085,352 *Total Assets:* £435,534,336
Registered Office: 55 Park Lane, London, W1K 1NA
Activities: Hotels and similar accommodation
Major Shareholder: Mohamed Al Fayed
Officers: Pierre Jacques Descours, Secretary; Mohamed Al Fayed [1933] Director [Egyptian]; Omar Alexander Mohamed Al Fayed [1987] Director; Franz Josef Klein [1944] Director/Hotelier [German]; Rene Mauron [1950] Director/Financial Advisor [Swiss]; Heini Jasmine Wathen-Fayed [1955] Director [Finnish]

River Island Clothing Co. Limited
Incorporated: 31 August 1959 *Employees:* 9,880
Net Worth: £581,600,000 *Total Assets:* £735,200,000
Registered Office: Chelsea House, West Gate, London, W5 1DR
Activities: Retail sale of clothing in specialised stores
Parent: River Island Holdings Limited
Officers: Benjamin Joseph Lewis [1967] Director; Bernard Lewis [1926] Director/Draper; Clive Robert Lewis [1956] Director; Vanessa Jane Lewis [1946] Fashion Director

River Island Holdings Limited
Incorporated: 2 December 2014 *Employees:* 3,724
Net Worth: £170,200,000 *Total Assets:* £679,699,968
Registered Office: Chelsea House, West Gate, London, W5 1DR
Activities: Retail sale of clothing in specialised stores
Officers: Benjamin Joseph Lewis [1967] Director; Bernard Lewis [1926] Director; Clive Robert Lewis [1956] Director; Julian Harley Lewis [1954] Director; Vanessa Jane Lewis [1946] Director

Riverland Holdings Limited
Incorporated: 4 June 1993
Net Worth: £63,098,656 *Total Assets:* £115,220,112
Registered Office: 55 Baker Street, London, W1U 7EU
Activities: Activities of head offices
Shareholders: Topland Group PLC; Meridian Commodities Limited
Officers: Cheryl Frances Moharm, Secretary; Meir Hamama [1934] Director/Businessman [Israeli]; MoTI Hamama [1958] Director [Israeli]; Mark Simon Kingston [1965] Director/Real Estate Professional; Cheryl Frances Moharm [1958] Director/Company Secretary

Riverside Resource Recovery Limited
Incorporated: 1 March 1999 *Employees:* 75
Net Worth Deficit: £53,500,000 *Total Assets:* £591,950,016
Registered Office: 2 Coldbath Square, London, EC1R 5HL
Activities: Treatment and disposal of non-hazardous waste
Parent: Cory Riverside (Holdings) Limited
Officers: Tess Bridgman, Secretary; Benjamin James Butler [1981] Director; Andrew Robert Pike [1975] Director; Charles Nicholas Pollard [1958] Director; Julian William Walker [1973] Director/Chief Operating Officer

RKH Group Limited
Incorporated: 4 August 1998 *Employees:* 5
Previous: R K Harrison Holdings Limited
Net Worth: £69,578,000 *Total Assets:* £153,036,992
Registered Office: One Creechurch Place, London, EC3A 5AF
Activities: Activities of financial services holding companies
Parent: Hyperion Insurance Group Limited
Officers: Andrew John Moore, Secretary; Alistair Barrett [1972] Director; Andrew Timothy Bastow [1961] Director/Head of Compliance and Risk; John Charles Birkmire [1954] Director/Accountant; Andrea Bragoli [1964] Director/Insurance Broker; Angus Kenneth Cameron [1957] Director; Sarah Ann Davies [1964] Director/Consultant/Executive Coach; Paul William Nicholas Redgate [1968] Director; Barnaby Douglas Rugge-Price [1969] Director/Insurance Broker

RL Finance Bonds No. 2 PLC
Incorporated: 6 November 2013
Net Worth: £6,647 *Total Assets:* £400,349,536
Registered Office: 55 Gracechurch Street, London, EC3V 0RL
Activities: Other activities auxiliary to insurance and pension funding
Shareholders: The Royal London Mutual Insurance Society Limited; Royal London Mutual Insurance Society Limited
Officers: Timothy Walter Harris [1969] Director; Martin Pierce Lewis [1963] Director

RL Finance Bonds No. 3 PLC
Incorporated: 30 June 2015
Net Worth: £10,631 *Total Assets:* £352,890,784
Registered Office: 55 Gracechurch Street, London, EC3V 0RL
Activities: Other activities auxiliary to insurance and pension funding
Parent: Royal London Mutual Insurance Society Limited
Officers: Timothy Walter Harris [1969] Director; Martin Pierce Lewis [1963] Director

RMC Estates Co. LLP
Incorporated: 13 March 2015
Net Worth: £207,194,784 *Total Assets:* £209,492,800
Registered Office: 6th Floor, Lansdowne House, Berkeley Square, London, W1J 6ER

Road Management Consolidated PLC
Incorporated: 20 June 1995
Net Worth Deficit: £411,000 *Total Assets:* £102,270,000
Registered Office: Cannon Place, 78 Cannon Street, London, EC4N 6AF
Activities: Other business support service activities n.e.c.
Parent: Road Management Group Limited
Officers: David William Bowler [1945] Director/Solicitor; Victor Ensenat Coe [1974] Director/Planning Manager [Spanish]; Matthew James Edwards [1985] Associate Director; Larry Jay Henry [1953] Director [American]; Lee Johnson [1970] Director/Operational Manager; Peter John Meffan [1964] Director/VP Ventures; Javier Carol Vilarasau [1962] Director [Spanish]

Road Management Group Limited
Incorporated: 26 March 1993
Net Worth: £120,451,000 *Total Assets:* £265,700,992
Registered Office: Cannon Place, 78 Cannon Street, London, EC4N 6AF
Activities: Activities of head offices
Shareholders: Abertis Motorways UK Limited; AM Holdco Limited
Officers: David William Bowler [1945] Director/Solicitor; Victor Ensenat Coe [1974] Director/Planning Manager [Spanish]; Matthew James Edwards [1985] Associate Director; Larry Jay Henry [1953] Director [American]; Lee Johnson [1970] Director/Operational Manager; Peter John Meffan [1964] Director/VP Ventures; Javier Carol Vilarasau [1962] Director [Spanish]

Road Management Services (A13) Holdings Limited
Incorporated: 2 February 2000
Net Worth Deficit: £7,309,000 *Total Assets:* £220,472,000
Registered Office: 43 Orchard Place, London, E14 0JW
Activities: Activities of head offices
Officers: Tarenjit Kaur Deshore, Secretary; Michael John Eyles [1955] Director/Civil Engineer; Larry Jay Henry [1953] Director [American]; Nathan Horsman [1980] Proposal Director

Road Management Services (A13) PLC
Incorporated: 2 February 2000
Net Worth Deficit: £7,312,000 *Total Assets:* £220,468,992
Registered Office: 43 Orchard Place, London, E14 0JW
Activities: Construction of roads and motorways
Parent: Road Management Services (A13) Holdings Limited
Officers: Tarenjit Kaur Deshore, Secretary; Michael John Eyles [1955] Director/Civil Engineer; Larry Jay Henry [1953] Director [American]; Nathan Horsman [1980] Proposal Director

Road Management Services (Gloucester) Limited
Incorporated: 11 April 1995
Net Worth: £66,737,000 *Total Assets:* £111,040,000
Registered Office: Cannon Place, 78 Cannon Street, London, EC4N 6AF
Activities: Construction of roads and motorways
Parent: Road Management Group Limited
Officers: David William Bowler [1945] Director/Solicitor; Victor Ensenat Coe [1974] Director/Planning Manager [Spanish]; Matthew James Edwards [1985] Associate Director; Larry Jay Henry [1953] Director [American]; Lee Johnson [1970] Director/Operational Manager; Peter John Meffan [1964] Director/VP Ventures; Javier Carol Vilarasau [1962] Director [Spanish]

Road Management Services (Peterborough) Limited
Incorporated: 26 March 1993
Net Worth: £54,123,000 *Total Assets:* £155,243,008
Registered Office: Cannon Place, 78 Cannon Street, London, EC4N 6AF
Activities: Construction of roads and motorways
Parent: Road Management Group Limited
Officers: David William Bowler [1945] Director/Solicitor; Victor Ensenat Coe [1974] Director/Planning Manager [Spanish]; Matthew James Edwards [1985] Associate Director; Larry Jay Henry [1953] Director [American]; Lee Johnson [1970] Director/Operational Manager; Peter John Meffan [1964] Director/VP Ventures; Javier Carol Vilarasau [1962] Director [Spanish]

Rochester Financing No.2 PLC
Incorporated: 23 December 2015
Net Worth: £14,058 *Total Assets:* £333,255,168
Registered Office: 35 Great St Helen's, London, EC3A 6AP
Activities: Financial intermediation not elsewhere classified
Parent: Rochester Mortgages Holdings No.2 Limited
Officers: Daniel Marc Richard Jaffe [1975] Director

Rock Rail East Anglia PLC
Incorporated: 6 September 2016
Net Worth Deficit: £676,984 *Total Assets:* £333,846,912
Registered Office: Capital Tower, 91 Waterloo Road, London, SE1 8RT
Activities: Renting and leasing of other machinery, equipment and tangible goods n.e.c.
Parent: Rock Rail East Anglia (Holdings) 2 Limited
Officers: Joanne Shepherd, Secretary; Andrew Noel Chivers [1959] Director; Daniel Frank Hobson [1979] Director/Local Government Officer; Roger McDonald [1953] Director/Transport Consultant; Mark Roy Swindell [1960] Director/Chief Executive Officer (CEO); Maciej Tarasiuk [1986] Investment Director

Rock Rail South Western (Holdings) 2 Limited
Incorporated: 3 May 2017 *Employees:* 4
Net Worth Deficit: £519,053 *Total Assets:* £177,925,328
Registered Office: Capital Tower, 91 Waterloo Road, London, SE1 8RT
Activities: Activities of other holding companies n.e.c.
Parent: Rock Rail South Western (Holdings) 1 Limited
Officers: Joanne Shepherd, Secretary; Andrew Noel Chivers [1959] Director; Graeme Kenneth Wilson Dunbar [1977] Investment Director; Roger McDonald [1953] Director/Transport Consultant; Mark Roy Swindell [1960] Director; Maciej Tarasiuk [1986] Investment Director

Rock Rail South Western PLC
Incorporated: 4 May 2017
Net Worth Deficit: £480,668 *Total Assets:* £177,962,208
Registered Office: Capital Tower, 91 Waterloo Road, London, SE1 8RT
Activities: Renting and leasing of other machinery, equipment and tangible goods n.e.c.
Parent: Rock Rail South Western (Holdings) 2 Limited
Officers: Joanne Shepherd, Secretary; Andrew Noel Chivers [1959] Director; Graeme Kenneth Wilson Dunbar [1977] Investment Director; Roger McDonald [1953] Director/Transport Consultant; Mark Roy Swindell [1960] Director; Maciej Tarasiuk [1986] Investment Director

Rockhopper Exploration (Hydrocarbons) Limited
Incorporated: 25 February 2005
Net Worth Deficit: £169,138,720 *Total Assets:* £157,159,328
Registered Office: 4th Floor, 5 Welbeck Street, London, W1G 9YQ
Activities: Extraction of crude petroleum
Parent: Rockhopper Exploration PLC
Officers: Janette Lesley Davies, Secretary; Stewart MacDonald [1981] Director/Chief Financial Officer; Samuel John Moody [1970] Director

Rockhopper Exploration PLC
Incorporated: 5 October 2004 *Employees:* 15
Net Worth: £316,834,656 *Total Assets:* £397,789,088
Registered Office: 4th Floor, 5 Welbeck Street, London, W1G 9YQ
Activities: Extraction of crude petroleum
Officers: Janette Lesley Davies, Secretary; Alison Claire Baker [1971] Director/Chartered Accountant; Timothy Paul Bushell [1959] Director; Keith Geddes Lough [1959] Director; Stewart MacDonald [1981] Finance Director; David McManus [1953] Director/Petroleum Engineer; Samuel John Moody [1970] Director; Dr Arthur John Summers [1955] Director/Geologist

Rockrose UKCS4 Limited
Incorporated: 29 October 1990 *Employees:* 16
Previous: Idemitsu Petroleum UK Ltd.
Net Worth: £62,183,548 *Total Assets:* £255,492,608
Registered Office: Cooley Services Limited, Dashwood House, 69 Old Broad Street, London, EC2M 1QS
Activities: Extraction of crude petroleum
Parent: Rockrose Energy PLC
Officers: Andrew Philip Austin [1965] Director; Richard Alan Benmore [1958] Director

Roder Investments No. 1 Limited
Incorporated: 14 December 2012
Net Worth Deficit: £264,253,648 *Total Assets:* £357,398,944
Registered Office: 1 Churchill Place, London, E14 5HP
Activities: Financial intermediation not elsewhere classified
Parent: Barclays Bank PLC
Officers: Christopher Patrick Le Neve Foster [1981] Director/Banker; Gregor William McMillan [1970] Director/Banker; Carl Thomas Senior [1978] Director/Banker; Jonathan Michael Walthoe [1975] Director/Banker

Roder Investments No. 2 Limited
Incorporated: 14 December 2012
Net Worth Deficit: £264,253,648 *Total Assets:* £357,398,944
Registered Office: 1 Churchill Place, London, E14 5HP
Activities: Financial intermediation not elsewhere classified
Parent: Barclays Bank PLC
Officers: Christopher Patrick Le Neve Foster [1981] Director/Banker; Gregor William McMillan [1970] Director/Banker; Carl Thomas Senior [1978] Director/Banker; Jonathan Michael Walthoe [1975] Director/Banker

Roehampton University
Incorporated: 23 June 2004 *Employees:* 1,061
Net Worth: £59,664,000 *Total Assets:* £202,070,000
Registered Office: Grove House, Roehampton Lane, London, SW15 5PJ
Activities: First-degree level higher education
Officers: Mark Richard Michael Ellul, Secretary; Sir David Charles Maurice Bell [1946] Director and Chairman; Sister Lorna Joyce Marjorie Brockett [1940] Director/Religious Sister; Dr Sultana Choudhry [1982] Director of Research, Dept of Psychology, UEL; Janet Cooper [1959] Director/Lawyer; Professor Ann Rosalind David [1953] Director/University Lecturer; Roger James Dawe [1941] Director/Education Adviser; Sister Christine Anne Edwards [1948] Director/Retired; Dennis Vincent Hone [1958] Finance Director; Reverend Margaret Playford Jones [1945] Director/Retired Methodist Minister; Mark Frost Neale [1957] Director/Public Servant; Sidney Brian Newey [1937] Director/Retired; Chukwuemeka Chika Obinna Goodluck Nwagu [1994] Director/Student; Professor Paul Gerard O'Prey [1956] Director/Vice Chancellor; Professor Laura Lynn Peters [1964] Director/University Principal Lecturer [British/Canadian]; Sheena Pindoria [1974] Director/Chartered Accountant; Nancy Richards [1966] Director/Registry Manager, Higher Education; Kevin Paul Thomas [1967] Director of Corporate Services, Wales Audit Office

Rogers Chapman UK Limited
Incorporated: 30 January 1987
Net Worth: £16,296,167 *Total Assets:* £112,168,856
Registered Office: 30 Warwick Street, London, W1B 5NH
Activities: Real estate agencies
Parent: Jones Lang Lasalle Limited
Officers: Nicolas Guillaume Taylor, Secretary; Richard Henry Webster, Secretary; James Edward Gregory [1975] Director/Chartered Accountant

Rolex Watch Company,Limited (The)
Incorporated: 15 November 1915 *Employees:* 191
Net Worth: £99,164,000 *Total Assets:* £145,143,008
Registered Office: 19 St James's Square, London, SW1Y 4JE
Activities: Wholesale of watches and jewellery
Officers: Deon Alan Parker, Secretary; Richard de Leyser [1962] Managing Director; Bertrand Gros [1950] Director/Lawyer [Swiss]; Deon Alan Parker [1972] Director/Accountant; Catherine Marie France Thomson [1963] Director [French]

Rolls-Royce & Partners Finance Limited
Incorporated: 1 September 1987 *Employees:* 17
Net Worth: £305,192,480 *Total Assets:* £1,439,967,616
Registered Office: 62 Buckingham Gate, London, SW1E 6AT
Activities: Financial intermediation not elsewhere classified
Parent: Alpha Partners Leasing Limited
Officers: Rachel Johnson, Secretary; Mark Brady [1965] Director; Mark Garrett [1969] Managing Director Engine Leasing & Parts Trading; Deborah Ann Golden [1954] Director/Executive Vice President, General Counsel [American]; Paul Sybray Inman [1966] Director; Robert Clair Lyons [1964] Director/CFO Gatx Corp [American]; Donald James Spooner [1962] Director [American]

Rolls-Royce Group PLC
Incorporated: 21 March 2003
Net Worth: £1,914,435,968 *Total Assets:* £2,285,015,040
Registered Office: 62 Buckingham Gate, London, SW1E 6AT
Activities: Activities of head offices
Parent: Rolls-Royce Holdings PLC
Officers: Pamela Mary Coles, Secretary; Stephen Wayne Daintith [1964] Director; David Warren Arthur East [1961] Director

Rolls-Royce Holdings PLC
Incorporated: 10 February 2011 *Employees:* 50,000
Net Worth: £6,167,000,064 *Total Assets:* £30,001,999,872
Registered Office: 62 Buckingham Gate, London, SW1E 6AT
Activities: Activities of head offices
Officers: Pamela Mary Coles, Secretary; Lewis William Killcross Booth [1948] Director; Linda Ruth Cairnie [1953] Director; Sir Frank Joseph Chapman [1953] Director; Stephen Wayne Daintith [1964] Director; Ian Edward Lamert Davis [1951] Director; David Warren Arthur East [1961] Director; Beverly Kenyon Goulet [1954] Director [American]; Hsien Yang Lee [1957] Director [Singaporean]; Nicholas Lawrence Luff [1967] Director; Bradley Singer [1966] Director [American]; Sir Kevin Smith [1954] Director; Jasmin Staiblin [1970] Director [German]

Rolls-Royce PLC
Incorporated: 23 February 1971 *Employees:* 50,000
Net Worth: £7,976,999,936 *Total Assets:* £31,794,999,296
Registered Office: 62 Buckingham Gate, London, SW1E 6AT
Activities: Manufacture of steam generators, except central heating hot water boilers
Parent: Rolls-Royce Group PLC
Officers: Pamela Mary Coles, Secretary; Lewis William Killcross Booth [1948] Director; Linda Ruth Cairnie [1953] Director; Sir Frank Joseph Chapman [1953] Director; Stephen Wayne Daintith [1964] Director; Ian Edward Lamert Davis [1951] Director; David Warren Arthur East [1961] Director; Beverly Kenyon Goulet [1954] Director [American]; Hsien Yang Lee [1957] Director [Singaporean]; Nicholas Lawrence Luff [1967] Director; Bradley Singer [1966] Director [American]; Sir Kevin Smith [1954] Director; Jasmin Staiblin [1970] Director [German]

Rome Bidco Limited
Incorporated: 15 September 2006
Net Worth Deficit: £399,332,992 *Total Assets:* £326,511,008
Registered Office: 9-15 Neal Street, London, WC2H 9QL
Activities: Activities of head offices
Parent: Rome Pikco Limited
Officers: Benedict James Price, Secretary; Dr Generald William Ford [1957] Director/Chairman & CEO [American]; Benedict James Price [1967] Finance Director

Rome PIK Holdco Limited
Incorporated: 15 September 2006
Net Worth: £31,193,000 *Total Assets:* £254,214,000
Registered Office: 9-15 Neal Street, London, WC2H 9QL
Activities: Activities of head offices
Parent: Rome Topco Limited
Officers: Benedict James Price, Secretary; Dr Generald William Ford [1957] Director/Chairman & CEO [American]; Benedict James Price [1967] Finance Director

Rome Topco Limited
Incorporated: 17 November 2006
Previous: Rome Topco Unlimited
Net Worth: £335,646,016 *Total Assets:* £335,646,016
Registered Office: 9-15 Neal Street, London, WC2H 9QL
Activities: Activities of head offices
Parent: Rome Intermediate Holdings SARL
Officers: Benedict James Price, Secretary; Dr Generald William Ford [1957] Director/Chairman & CEO [American]; Benedict James Price [1967] Finance Director

Romulus Holdings Limited
Incorporated: 5 October 1999 *Employees:* 29
Net Worth: £152,202,384 *Total Assets:* £474,067,744
Registered Office: Sandford House, 10 Maynard Close, London, SW6 2DB
Activities: Activities of head offices
Shareholder: Douglas Philip Woolf
Officers: Matthew James Garner, Secretary; Matthew James Garner [1981] Director/Chartered Accountant; Alexander Thomas Woolf [1989] Director; Anne Jillian Woolf [1955] Director; Douglas Philip Woolf [1937] Director; Thomas Alexander Woolf [1991] Director; Wilfred Laurence Joel Woolf [1996] Director

Romulus Securities Limited
Incorporated: 10 May 1972 *Employees:* 1
Net Worth: £71,669,688 *Total Assets:* £154,326,400
Registered Office: Sandford House, 10 Maynard Close, London, SW6 2DB
Activities: Other letting and operating of own or leased real estate
Parent: Romulus Holdings Limited
Officers: Matthew James Garner, Secretary; Matthew James Garner [1981] Director/Chartered Accountant; Anne Jillian Woolf [1955] Director; Douglas Philip Woolf [1937] Director/Chartered Surveyor; Thomas Alexander Woolf [1991] Director

Ronin Trading Europe LLP
Incorporated: 7 July 2010 *Employees:* 3
Net Worth: £80,218,344 *Total Assets:* £2,767,977,472
Registered Office: Tricor Suite, 4th Floor, 50 Mark Lane, London, EC3R 7QR

Rontec Roadside Retail Limited
Incorporated: 14 July 2014 *Employees:* 298
Previous: Rontec Group Limited
Net Worth: £135,216,992 *Total Assets:* £604,984,000
Registered Office: Acre House, 11-15 William Road, London, NW1 3ER
Activities: Other business support service activities n.e.c.
Parent: Snax 24 Garage Properties Limited
Officers: William James Ahearn [1952] Director; Lisa Debra Althasen [1968] Marketing Director; Richard Jonathan Benson [1963] Property Director; Thomas Edward Cookson [1965] Director of Fuels and IT; Alan Irving Goldman [1943] Director; Nicholas James Lowe [1974] Operations Director; Tracy Anne Moloney [1982] Director/Accountant; Ian Samuel George Pogue [1958] Director/Accountant [Irish]; Dame Gail Ronson [1946] Director/Personal Assistant; Generald Maurice Ronson [1939] Director; Nicole Julia Ronson-Allalouf [1972] Director/Show Producer/Entertainment Consultant; Giles Nicholas Taylor [1967] Managing Director

Rooftop Funding Limited
Incorporated: 4 April 2003
Net Worth: £135,373,776 *Total Assets:* £136,982,464
Registered Office: 25 Bank Street, Canary Wharf, London, E14 5JP
Activities: Credit granting by non-deposit taking finance houses and other specialist consumer credit grantors
Officers: Mark Steven Allen [1970] Director/Accountant; John Richard Hobson [1973] Director/Accountant; David Anthony Lehane [1983] Director/Accountant [Irish]

Ropemaker RB Holdings Limited
Incorporated: 16 September 2016
Net Worth: £115,057,520 *Total Assets:* £166,148,720
Registered Office: Ropemaker Place, 28 Ropemaker Street, London, EC2Y 9HD
Activities: Activities of other holding companies n.e.c.
Officers: Helen Louise Everitt, Secretary; Mark Jonathan Dooley [1962] Director/Investment Banker [Australian]; Adam Cade Nancarrow [1975] Director [Australian]; Matthew Porter [1977] Director/Banker

Rosediamond LLP
Incorporated: 27 June 2006
Net Worth: £150,257,232 *Total Assets:* £150,262,224
Registered Office: 3rd Floor, 5 Lloyds Avenue, London, EC3N 3AE
Officers: Francisco Lopes Filho [1935] Member

Rosequake Ltd
Incorporated: 25 July 2012 *Employees:* 16
Net Worth: £187,531,808 *Total Assets:* £449,122,432
Registered Office: Ramillies House, 2 Ramillies Street, London, W1F 7LN
Activities: Activities of other holding companies n.e.c.
Parent: Rosequake Investment Holdings Limited
Officers: David Sullivan [1949] Director

Rosleb Limited
Incorporated: 12 September 2002 *Employees:* 2
Net Worth: £81,275,296 *Total Assets:* £107,043,808
Registered Office: Berkeley House, 304 Regents Park Road, London, N3 2JY
Activities: Buying and selling of own real estate
Parent: Hathber GR Limited
Officers: Paul Hallam, Secretary; Christopher Charles McGill [1960] Managing Director; William Kenneth Procter [1953] Director/Accountant

Rotch Property Group Limited
Incorporated: 1 July 1980 *Employees:* 12
Net Worth: £5,745,049 *Total Assets:* £142,250,432
Registered Office: 5th Floor, Leconfield House, Curzon Street, London, W1J 5JA
Activities: Activities of head offices
Officers: Antony Simon Fitzpatrick, Secretary; Robert Tchenguiz [1960] Director; Vincent Aziz Tchenguiz [1956] Director; Michael David Watson [1958] Director/Chartered Accountant

Rothesay Holdco UK Limited
Incorporated: 29 August 2013 *Employees:* 179
Net Worth: £1,752,999,936 *Total Assets:* £38,373,998,592
Registered Office: Level 25, The Leadenhall Building, 122 Leadenhall Street, London, EC3V 4AB
Activities: Activities of financial services holding companies
Shareholders: Minister for Finance; Stephen Schwarzman
Officers: Phoebe Kathleen Lowri Burnett, Secretary; William Alexander Thomas Gillions, Secretary; Syed Qasim Abbas [1976] Director; Constant Beckers [1952] Director [Belgian]; Melvin Timothy Corbett [1960] Director/Chief Investment Officer [American]; Robin Alexander de Beir Jarratt [1972] Director; Naguib Kheraj [1964] Director; Ray King [1953] Director/Chartered Accountant; Antigone Loudiadis [1963] Managing Director [Greek]; Therese Lynn Miller [1951] Director; Thomas James Pearce [1979] Managing Director; Charles David Pickup [1956] Director/Actuary; William John Robertson [1953] Director; Andrew Mark Stoker [1967] Director/Chief Financial Officer

Rothesay Life PLC
Incorporated: 26 February 2007
Previous: Rothesay Life Limited
Net Worth: £1,651,000,064 *Total Assets:* £38,265,999,360
Registered Office: Level 25, The Leadenhall Building, 122 Leadenhall Street, London, EC3V 4AB
Activities: Life insurance
Parent: Rothesay Holdco UK Limited
Officers: Phoebe Kathleen Lowri Burnett, Secretary; William Alexander Thomas Gillions, Secretary; Syed Qasim Abbas [1976] Director; Constant Beckers [1952] Director [Belgian]; Melvin Timothy Corbett [1960] Director/Chief Investment Officer [American]; Robin Alexander de Beir Jarratt [1972] Director; Naguib Kheraj [1964] Director; Ray King [1953] Director/Chartered Accountant; Antigone Loudiadis [1963] Managing Director [Greek]; Therese Lynn Miller [1951] Director; Thomas James Pearce [1979] Managing Director; Charles David Pickup [1956] Director; William John Robertson [1953] Director; Andrew Mark Stoker [1967] Director/Chief Financial Officer

Rothmans International Enterprises Limited
Incorporated: 5 March 1992
Net Worth: £769,108,992 *Total Assets:* £769,108,992
Registered Office: Globe House, 4 Temple Place, London, WC2R 2PG
Activities: Activities of head offices
Parent: Rothmans International Limited
Officers: Oliver James Martin, Secretary; David Patrick Ian Booth [1974] Director/Group Chief Accountant; Robert James Casey [1948] Director/Attorney [American]; Robert Fergus Heaton [1965] Director/Head of UK Tax

Rothmans International Limited
Incorporated: 6 April 1995
Net Worth: £291,668,992 *Total Assets:* £291,668,992
Registered Office: Globe House, 1 Water Street, London, WC2R 3LA
Activities: Activities of head offices
Parent: Weston Investment Company Limited
Officers: Jonathan Michael Guttridge, Secretary; David Patrick Ian Booth [1974] Director/Group Chief Accountant; Noelle Colfer [1968] Director/Solicitor; Robert Fergus Heaton [1965] Director/Head of UK Tax

Rothschild & Co Continuation Finance PLC
Incorporated: 30 August 2000
Previous: Rothschilds Continuation Finance PLC
Net Worth: £212,711 *Total Assets:* £133,593,280
Registered Office: New Court, St Swithin's Lane, London, EC4N 8AL
Activities: Financial intermediation not elsewhere classified
Parent: N.M. Rothschild & Sons Limited
Officers: Helen Marie Horton, Secretary; Peter William Barbour [1973] Finance Director; Christopher Lewis Coleman [1968] Director/Banker; Mark Leslie Crump [1963] Finance Director

Rothschild & Co Continuation Limited
Incorporated: 31 December 1941
Previous: Rothschilds Continuation Limited
Net Worth: £195,244,000 *Total Assets:* £252,591,008
Registered Office: New Court, St Swithin's Lane, London, EC4N 8AL
Activities: Financial intermediation not elsewhere classified
Parent: Rothschild & Co
Officers: Peter William Barbour [1973] Finance Director; Anthony Leonard Chapman [1946] Director/Merchant Banker; Anthony James Granville Coghlan [1957] Director/Accountant; Andrew Didham [1956] Director/Banker; Bernard Ian Myers [1944] Director/Merchant Banker

Rothschild & Co Holdings UK Limited
Incorporated: 26 February 1997
Previous: N M Rothschild Holdings Limited
Net Worth: £155,591,008 *Total Assets:* £155,591,008
Registered Office: New Court, St Swithin's Lane, London, EC4N 8AL
Activities: Activities of financial services holding companies
Parent: Rothschilds Continuation Limited
Officers: Peter William Barbour [1973] Finance Director; Anthony James Granville Coghlan [1957] Director/Accountant; John Andrew King [1964] Director

N. M. Rothschild & Sons Limited
Incorporated: 1 January 1968 *Employees:* 706
Net Worth: £594,241,024 *Total Assets:* £857,472,000
Registered Office: New Court, St Swithin's Lane, London, EC4N 8AL
Activities: Activities auxiliary to financial intermediation n.e.c.
Parent: N M Rothschild Holdings Limited
Officers: Helen Marie Horton, Secretary; Anthony Joseph Alt [1946] Director/Merchant Banker; Peter William Barbour [1973] Finance Director; Christopher Lewis Coleman [1968] Managing Director; Andrew Didham [1956] Director/Banker; Robert Mark Leitao [1963] Director/Investment Banker; Peter Alan Smith [1946] Director/Chartered Accountant; Jonathan Westcott [1962] Managing Director; Nicholas Hugh Tremayne Wrigley [1955] Director/Merchant Banker

Rothschild Foundation (Hanadiv) Europe
Incorporated: 16 March 2000 *Employees:* 6
Net Worth: £128,338,904 *Total Assets:* £132,054,384
Registered Office: Spencer House, 27 St James Place, London, SW1A 1DR
Activities: Cultural education
Officers: Ludmila Masterton, Secretary; Maurice Victor Blank [1942] Director/Entrepreneur; Nicola Josephine Cobbold [1965] Director/Trustee; Adam Cohen [1980] Director/Entrepreneur; Dr David Landau [1950] Director [Israeli]; Nicola Caren Loftus [1971] Director/Trustee; Beatrice Juliette Ruth Rosenberg [1939] Director [French]; The Honourable Beth Matilda Rothschild [1964] Director; Lord Nathaniel Charles Jacob Rothschild [1936] Director

Rowan Companies PLC
Incorporated: 11 October 2011 *Employees:* 2,762
Net Worth: £1,585,548,288 *Total Assets:* £3,778,735,872
Registered Office: Cannon Place, 78 Cannon Street, London, EC4N 6AF
Activities: Support activities for petroleum and natural gas mining
Officers: Mark Francis Mai, Secretary; Ryan Harrison Tarkington, Secretary; William Eugene Albrecht [1951] Director/Executive [American]; Dr Thomas Peter Horlick Burke [1967] Director/President & CEO; Thomas Russell Hix [1947] Director [American]; Jack Boyd Moore [1953] Director [American]; Suzanne Paquin Nimocks [1959] Director/Business Executive [American]; Thierry Pilenko [1957] Director/Executive Chairman, Technip FMC [French]; John Joseph Quicke [1949] Director/Business Executive [American]; Tore Ingebrigt Sandvold [1947] Director/Business Executive [Norwegian]; Charles Lawrence Szews [1956] Director [American]

Rowan No.1 Limited
Incorporated: 11 April 2012 *Employees:* 3
Net Worth: £2,715,334,400 *Total Assets:* £2,715,499,520
Registered Office: Cannon Place, 78 Cannon Street, London, EC4N 6AF
Activities: Activities of head offices
Parent: Rowan Companies PLC
Officers: Mark Francis Mai, Secretary; Dennis Scott Baldwin [1960] Director/Chief Accounting Officer [American]; Theodore David Gobillot [1965] Director/Attorney [American]; Rui Miguel Silva Gomes [1973] Director/Business Executive [Portuguese]

Rowan No.2 Limited
Incorporated: 11 April 2012 *Employees:* 3
Net Worth: £2,370,541,568 *Total Assets:* £2,370,541,568
Registered Office: Cannon Place, 78 Cannon Street, London, EC4N 6AF
Activities: Activities of head offices
Parent: Rowan Companies PLC
Officers: Mark Francis Mai, Secretary; Dennis Scott Baldwin [1960] Director/Chief Accounting Officer [American]; Theodore David Gobillot [1965] Director/Attorney [American]; Rui Miguel Silva Gomes [1973] Director/Business Executive [Portuguese]

T. Rowe Price International Ltd
Incorporated: 23 March 2000 *Employees:* 512
Net Worth: £406,020,448 *Total Assets:* £649,670,080
Registered Office: 60 Queen Victoria Street, London, EC4N 4TZ
Activities: Security and commodity contracts dealing activities
Officers: David Oestreicher, Secretary; Christopher David Alderson [1962] Director; Emma Hilary Beal [1974] Director/Lawyer; Celine Solange Therese Dufetel [1981] Director/Chief Financial Officer [American]; Jeremy Michael Fisher [1963] Director; Robert Charles Trant Higginbotham [1967] Director/Chairman and CEO

The Royal Automobile Club Limited
Incorporated: 20 May 1998 *Employees:* 580
Net Worth: £86,940,000 *Total Assets:* £121,616,000
Registered Office: Royal Automobile Club, 89-91 Pall Mall, London, SW1Y 5HS
Activities: Activities of other membership organisations n.e.c.
Officers: Miles William Ellis Wade, Secretary; Gordon George Reid Ballard [1959] Director/Engineer; Elizabeth Mary Ann Bishop [1958] Finance Director; Philippa Catherine Natalia Cronk [1979] Director/Management Consultant; Benjamin Piers Cussons [1966] Director, Wholesaler; Christine Ann Gaskell [1959] Director/Personnel Management; Andrew Laird [1955] Commercial Director; Christopher Ellis Moyle [1946] Director/Banker; Peter Graham Read [1956] Director/Chartered Accountant; Peter Tyrie [1946] Director/Hotelier; Graham Peter White [1955] Director/Solicitor

Royal Brompton and Harefield Hospitals Charity
Incorporated: 3 October 2011 *Employees:* 16
Previous: Royal Brompton & Harefield Charity Trustee
Net Worth: £127,651,000 *Total Assets:* £167,691,008
Registered Office: 50 Broadway, London, SW1H 0BL
Activities: Regulation of health care, education, cultural and other social services, not incl. social security
Officers: Caroline Bault [1965] Director/Consultant [French]; Lord Geoffrey Robert James Borwick [1955] Director/Member of The House of Lords; Professor Timothy William Evans [1954] Director/Physician; Prof Duncan Geddes [1942] Director/Doctor; Caroline Anne Greenhalgh [1963] Director; Richard Hugh Hunting CBE [1946] Director/Company Chairman; Sarah Newitt [1964] Director/Freelance Copywriter; Helen Margaret Putter [1960] Director; Raj Rashmikant Shah [1968] Director/Partner - Private Equity; Joanne Louise Thomas [1964] Director; Brenda Vandamme [1960] Director [French]

Royal London Asset Management Limited
Incorporated: 14 April 1988 *Employees:* 199
Net Worth: £112,532,000 *Total Assets:* £168,578,000
Registered Office: 55 Gracechurch Street, London, EC3V 0RL
Activities: Other activities auxiliary to insurance and pension funding
Parent: Royal London Mutual Insurance Society Limited
Officers: Andrew Stewart Carter [1960] Director; Piers Adrian Carlyle Hillier [1968] Director/Chief Investment Officer; Andrew Hunt [1976] Finance Director; Alexander Rudolf Dieter Koslowski [1971] Director [German]; Andrea Gertrude Martha Montague [1975] Director/Accountant; Andrew William Palmer [1953] Director; Catherine Rebecca Read [1980] Director/Chief Operating Officer; Ewan Farquharson Smith [1963] Director; Robert Arthur Daniel Williams [1971] Director

Royal London Management Services Limited
Incorporated: 1 November 1993
Net Worth Deficit: £41,872,000 *Total Assets:* £135,504,992
Registered Office: 55 Gracechurch Street, London, EC3V 0RL
Activities: Other activities auxiliary to insurance and pension funding
Parent: Royal London Mutual Insurance Society Limited
Officers: Matt Blake [1974] Director/Company Secretary; John Davies [1971] Director/Company Secretary; Kenny Fenna [1964] Director; Michelle Anne Hill [1977] Director/Company Secretary; Martin Pierce Lewis [1963] Director; Gurdeep Singh Rai [1981] Director/Company Secretary; Fergus Harry Speight [1964] Director/Solicitor

Royal London Mutual Insurance Society,Limited (The)
Incorporated: 31 July 1908 *Employees:* 4,252
Total Assets: £99,318,996,992
Registered Office: 55 Gracechurch Street, London, EC3V 0RL
Activities: Other activities auxiliary to insurance and pension funding
Officers: Sally Bridgeland [1964] Director/Independent Management Consultant Actuary; Ian Edwin Dilks [1953] Director; Tracey Graham [1965] Director; Timothy Walter Harris [1969] Finance Director; Philip Duncan Loney [1964] Director; Jonathan Mark MacDonald [1972] Director; Andrew William Palmer [1953] Director; David Avery Weymouth [1955] Director

Royal Mail Estates Limited
Incorporated: 5 April 2006
Net Worth: £898,000,000 *Total Assets:* £916,000,000
Registered Office: 100 Victoria Embankment, London, EC4Y 0HQ
Activities: Buying and selling of own real estate
Parent: Royal Mail Group Limited
Officers: Kulbinder Kaur Dosanjh, Secretary; Martin David Gafsen [1961] Director; Jayesh Patel [1974] Director

Royal Mail Group Limited
Incorporated: 10 January 2001 *Employees:* 138,002
Net Worth: £3,812,999,936 *Total Assets:* £6,848,000,000
Registered Office: 100 Victoria Embankment, London, EC4Y 0HQ
Activities: Postal activities under universal service obligation
Parent: Royal Mail PLC
Officers: Kulbinder Kaur Dosanjh, Secretary; Herr Rico Back [1954] Managing Director [German]; Michael John Jeavons [1969] Director/Accountant; Stuart Campbell Simpson [1967] Director of Group Finance

Royal Mail Investments Limited
Incorporated: 19 July 1996
Net Worth: £533,000,000 *Total Assets:* £1,084,999,936
Registered Office: 100 Victoria Embankment, London, EC4Y 0HQ
Activities: Activities of other holding companies n.e.c.
Parent: Royal Mail Group Limited
Officers: Kulbinder Kaur Dosanjh, Secretary; Michael John Jeavons [1969] Director/Accountant; Stuart Campbell Simpson [1967] Director of Group Finance

Royal Mail PLC
Incorporated: 6 September 2013 *Employees:* 158,846
Net Worth: £4,435,999,744 *Total Assets:* £7,256,999,936
Registered Office: 100 Victoria Embankment, London, EC4Y 0HQ
Activities: Activities of other holding companies n.e.c.
Officers: Kulbinder Kaur Dosanjh, Secretary; Herr Rico Back [1954] Managing Director [German]; Rita Elizabeth Griffin [1963] Director [American]; Orna Gabrielle Ni-Chionna [1956] Director [Irish]; Arthur Leslie Owen [1949] Director; Stuart Campbell Simpson [1967] Director of Group Finance; Simon Thompson [1966] Director; Keith Williams [1956] Director

The Royal Marsden Cancer Charity
Incorporated: 12 December 2002 *Employees:* 85
Net Worth: £97,041,000 *Total Assets:* £129,362,000
Registered Office: The Royal Marsden Hospital, 203 Fulham Road, London, SW3 6JJ
Activities: Other human health activities
Officers: Marcus James Thorman, Secretary; Charles Edward Alexander [1953] Director/Chairman; Sir Douglas Jardine Flint [1955] Director Group Chairman of HSBC Holdings; Sir Terence Patrick Leahy [1956] Director/Retired; Richard Oldfield [1955] Director; Caroline Ann Palmer [1958] Director/Chief Executive; Lady Helen Marina Lucy Taylor [1980] Director/Consultant; Richard Turnor [1956] Director/Solicitor

The Royal Masonic Benevolent Institution Care Company
Incorporated: 6 January 1977 *Employees:* 1,009
Previous: The Royal Masonic Benevolent Institution
Net Worth: £123,946,000 *Total Assets:* £127,270,000
Registered Office: 60 Great Queen Street, London, WC2B 5AZ
Activities: Residential nursing care facilities
Officers: Mark Valpy Lloyd, Secretary; John Boyington [1953] Director; Randall Marks [1953] Director/Retired [American]; Ian Charles Arthur Newby [1945] Director; Sushilkumar Chandulal Radia [1953] Managing Director; Dr John William Reuther [1946] Director/University Lecturer Biomedical; Sarah Sheppard [1964] Director/NHS Manager; Sylvia Nina Short [1947] Director/Retired; David William Snowdon [1960] Director/Retired; David Southern [1960] Director; Christopher George White [1958] Director/Retired; Dr Kevin Rhydderch Williams [1957] Director/Doctor of Medicine; Sir Paul Michael Williams [1948] Director/Retired

Royal Mencap Society
Incorporated: 9 June 1955 *Employees:* 8,530
Net Worth: £83,234,000 *Total Assets:* £167,220,000
Registered Office: 123 Golden Lane, London, EC1Y 0RT
Activities: Residential care activities for learning difficulties, mental health and substance abuse
Officers: Oonagh Smyth, Secretary; Geoffrey Giles Alltimes [1948] Director/Retired; Yogendra Amin [1973] Director/Solicitor; Lucy Kathryne Edge [1975] Chief Operating Office and Director; Elaine Hindal [1972] Director/Charity Worker; Katherine Sylvia Hollier [1972] Director/Marketing Manager; Stephen Andrew Jack [1958] Director/Banking Sector; Derek Compton Lewis [1946] Director; Jacqueline Louise Pollock [1983] Director/Technical Lead; Linda Rose Redford [1946] Director/Retired; Graham Timothy Williams [1958] Director/Chartered Accountant; Andrew Wilson [1983] Director; David Noel Wolverson [1952] Director/Retired

Royal Opera House Covent Garden Foundation
Incorporated: 1 April 1950 *Employees:* 1,077
Net Worth: £242,952,992 *Total Assets:* £302,470,016
Registered Office: Royal Opera House, Covent Garden, London, WC2E 9DD
Activities: Artistic creation
Officers: Ivan Luke Daffern, Secretary; Timothy Brian Bunting [1963] Director/Investor; Kirstine Ann Cooper [1964] Director/Solicitor; Dr Genevieve Rachel Davies [1971] Director; Lloyd Marshall Dorfman [1952] Director; Dame Vivien Louise Duffield [1946] Director; Suzanne Elizabeth Heywood [1969] Director/Partner; M Susan Linda Hoyle [1953] Director/Arts and Leadership Consultant; Nicholas Robert Hytner [1956] Theatre Director; John Kingman [1969] Director/Second Permanent Secretary; Julian Metherell [1963] Director; Dr Dr Munira Mirza [1978] Director/Deputy Mayor, Education and Culture; Paul Dring Morrell [1948] Director; Ian Roper Taylor [1956] Director; Laura Katharine Wade-Gery [1965] Executive Director Multi-Channel E-Commerce; Roger William Wright [1956] Director/Chief Executive Snape Maltings; Mr Daniel Charles Wyler [1951] Director [Dutch]

RPOW UK Limited
Incorporated: 31 May 1996 *Employees:* 2
Net Worth: £51,339,004 *Total Assets:* £254,321,424
Registered Office: Hays Galleria, 1 Hays Lane, London, SE1 2RD
Activities: Non-trading company
Parent: RPM International Inc.
Officers: Hilde Maria Eleonora de Backer [1969] Director [Belgian]; Richard Murray Hill [1960] Director; Edward Winslow Moore [1957] Director [American]

RQIH Limited
Incorporated: 20 November 1998
Net Worth: £30,406,000 *Total Assets:* £167,022,000
Registered Office: 71 Fenchurch Street, London, EC3M 4BS
Activities: Management consultancy activities other than financial management
Parent: Randall & Quilter Investment Holdings Ltd.
Officers: Mark Andrew Langridge [1963] Director; Alan Kevin Quilter [1951] Director; Kenneth Edward Randall [1948] Director

RRPF Engine Leasing Limited
Incorporated: 12 December 1991 *Employees:* 2
Net Worth: £265,772,512 *Total Assets:* £1,437,367,168
Registered Office: 62 Buckingham Gate, London, SW1E 6AT
Activities: Renting and leasing of air passenger transport equipment
Parent: Rolls-Royce & Partners Finance Limited
Officers: Rachel Johnson, Secretary; Mark Brady [1965] Director/Commercial Representative; Mark Garrett [1969] Director

RSA Insurance Group PLC
Incorporated: 26 January 1989 *Employees:* 13,363
Net Worth: £3,950,000,128 *Total Assets:* £20,600,000,512
Registered Office: 20 Fenchurch Street, London, EC3M 3AU
Activities: Activities of head offices
Officers: Charlotte Dawn Alethea Heiss, Secretary; Alastair William Stewart Barbour [1953] Director; Sonia Ameena Baxendale [1962] Director [Canadian]; Enrico Tommaso Cucchiani [1950] Director [Italian]; Scott Egan [1971] Director/Chief Financial Officer; Stephen Alan Michael Hester [1960] Director/Chief Executive Officer; Isabel Frances Hudson [1959] Director; Charlotte Claire Jones [1968] Executive Director, Chief Financial Officer; Martin Anthony Scicluna [1950] Director/Chairman; Kathleen Mary Shailer [1963] Director; Joseph Bonifacius Maria Streppel [1949] Director [Dutch]; Martin Strobel [1966] Director [Swiss]

RSL Finance (No. 1) PLC
Incorporated: 5 November 1998
Net Worth: £1,067,000 *Total Assets:* £274,515,008
Registered Office: 6th Floor, 65 Gresham Street, London, EC2V 7NQ
Activities: Financial intermediation not elsewhere classified
Parent: RSL Finance (Holdings) Limited
Officers: Carl Steven Baldry [1966] Director

RSM UK Holdings Limited
Incorporated: 5 September 2006 *Employees:* 3,477
Previous: Baker Tilly UK Holdings Limited
Net Worth: £46,897,000 *Total Assets:* £223,715,008
Registered Office: 6th Floor, 25 Farringdon Street, London, EC4A 4AB
Activities: Activities of head offices
Officers: Patricia Mary O'Flynn, Secretary; Penrose Margaret Helen Foss [1970] Director/Solicitor; David Gwilliam [1963] Director/Chartered Accountant; Simon Michael Reginald Harding-Rolls [1959] IT Director; Elfed Wyn Jarvis [1954] Director/Chartered Accountant; Laurence Peter Longe [1955] Director/Chartered Accountant; Martin Bruce Rodgers [1948] Director/Chartered Accountant; Nigel John Tristem [1960] Director/Chartered Accountant

RTA Holdco 4 Limited
Incorporated: 19 October 2007
Net Worth: £1,029,637,376 *Total Assets:* £2,488,492,032
Registered Office: 6 St James's Square, London, SW1Y 4AD
Activities: Activities of head offices
Parent: Rio Tinto International Holdings Limited
Officers: Richard Alan Avery [1975] Director/Chartered Accountant; Michael Philip Bossick [1960] Director/Chartered Accountant; Paul Ian Hedley [1969] Director/Treasurer

Ruffer LLP
Incorporated: 13 August 2003 *Employees:* 254
Net Worth: £128,306,240 *Total Assets:* £183,574,688
Registered Office: 80 Victoria Street, London, SW1E 5JL
Officers: Miranda Jane Best [1983] Member; Myles Columba Marmion [1959] Member; Henry Maxey [1974] Member; Jonathan Garnier Ruffer [1951] Member; Clementine Mary Vaughan [1981] Member; Dr Paula Walter [1973] Member; Ruchir Asnani [1976] LLP Member; Hamish Michael Baillie [1979] LLP Member; David Christopher Ballance [1960] LLP Member; Michael David Bayliffe [1948] LLP Member; David Adam Benson [1968] LLP Member; Edwina Katherine Heather Russell Blackford [1981] LLP Member; Benjamin Boucher-Ferte [1976] LLP Member; Patrick Desmond Brennan [1967] LLP Member; Harry Charles Buscall [1963] LLP Member; Peter Alan Carew [1953] LLP Member; Edward Robert Samuel Dannatt [1981] LLP Member; Hermione Anne Davies [1958] LLP Member; Jonathan Anthony Dye [1977] LLP Member; Richard Edwards [1978] LLP Member; Sahil Gaba [1980] LLP Member; Luka Gakic [1985] LLP Member; Alexander Grispos [1975] LLP Member; James David Stafford Heal [1967] LLP Member; Jacques Hirsch [1976] LLP Member; Nicholas Horder [1976] LLP Member; Paul Stephen Kennedy [1974] LLP Member; Alexander Samuel Lennard [1985] LLP Member; Annabel MacKenzie [1980] LLP Member; Simon Benedict Martin [1969] LLP Member; Mary Charlotte McBain [1963] LLP Member; Sean Frederick McCreery [1964] LLP Member; Justine McMullan [1978] LLP Member; Philipp Mitterbauer [1978] LLP Member; Philip Estment Morris [1960] LLP Member; Kentaro Nishida [1960] LLP Member; Dominic Edward Pearson [1968] LLP Member; Emma Jane Victoria Potter [1983] LLP Member; Christopher Queree [1965] LLP Member; Steve Russell [1964] LLP Member; Emma Rutter [1977] LLP Member; Louise Mary Stanway [1977] LLP Member; Claire Rebecca Titmarsh [1984] LLP Member; James Russell Verdier [1975] LLP Member; Russell Vickers [1977] LLP Member; Dr Peter James Warburton [1954] LLP Member; Trevor David Wild [1956] LLP Member; Tim Youngman [1955] LLP Member

Ruffer Management Limited
Incorporated: 16 May 1994 *Employees:* 205
Net Worth: £11,004,966 *Total Assets:* £156,156,880
Registered Office: 80 Victoria Street, London, SW1E 5JL
Activities: Activities of financial services holding companies
Shareholder: Lempriere Pringle 2015
Officers: Alexandra Ringer, Secretary; The Right Honourable Robert William Saswalo 14th Earl Ferrers [1952] Director/Chartered Accountant; Myles Columba Marmion [1959] Director/Chief Financial Officer; Robin Crispin William Odey [1959] Director/Investment Management; Jonathan Garnier Ruffer [1951] Director/Chief Executive

Ruspetro Limited
Incorporated: 20 October 2011 *Employees:* 219
Previous: Ruspetro PLC
Net Worth: £731,313 *Total Assets:* £330,735,168
Registered Office: International House, 24 Holborn Viaduct, London, EC1A 2BN
Activities: Extraction of crude petroleum
Officers: Dominic Manley, Secretary; Irina Babirenko [1982] Director/Lawyer [Russian]; Alexander Nikolaevich Chistyakov [1973] Director [Russian]; Vitalii Deev [1979] General Director [Russian]

Charles Russell Speechlys LLP
Incorporated: 24 February 2005 *Employees:* 757
Net Worth: £68,793,000 *Total Assets:* £110,557,000
Registered Office: 5 Fleet Place, London, EC4M 7RD
Officers: David Harold Berry [1960] Member; James William Carter [1965] Member; Andrew McKeown Collins [1966] Member; Keir Watson Gordon [1962] Member; Robin Alexander John Grove [1970] Member; Suzanne Jane Marriott [1969] Member; Adrian George Alan Mayer [1970] Member; Christopher John Page [1958] Member; Erica Augusta Shelton [1957] Member; Jonathan Wright Whitehead [1959] Member; Shona Victoria Rosslyn Alexander [1970] LLP Member; Sarah Therese Anticoni [1963] LLP Member; Paul Malcolm Arathoon [1978] LLP Member; Sally Louise Ashford [1967] LLP Member; Jane Mary Bagnall [1960] LLP Member; Mark Alexander Bailey [1969] LLP Member; Timothy Jocelyn George Ball [1967] LLP Member; Emma Jane Bartlett [1971] LLP Member; Jonathan Michael Bayliss [1958] LLP Member; William James Begley [1971] LLP Member; Trevor Martin Calcutt Bettany [1963] LLP Member; Robert Francis Birchall [1982] LLP Member; Robert Henry Blower [1965] LLP Member; Jon-Wesley Bond [1976] LLP Member; Sarah Jane Boon [1984] LLP Member; James David Wyatt Bradford [1977] LLP Member; Sarah Jane Brostoff [1970] LLP Member; Ian James Brothwood [1963] LLP Member; Stephen Christopher Burns [1974] LLP Member; Andrew Wyndham Armar Cameron [1965] LLP Member; Rose Carey [1977] LLP Member; Steven John Carey [1962] LLP Member; Jamie Cartwright [1981] LLP Member; Sangna Chauhan [1981] LLP Member; Louise Yvette Orledge Clark [1960] LLP Member; Andrew James Joseph Clarke [1962] LLP Member; David Richard Howell Coates [1981] LLP Member; Richard Samuel Coleman [1982] LLP Member; Ian James Cooke [1966] LLP Member; Nicholas Duncan Couchman [1965] LLP Member; Julia Louise Cox [1970] LLP Member; Edward David Crichton Craig [1970] LLP Member; Adam John Crossley [1980] LLP Member; Catherine Ann Drew [1957] LLP Member; George Lindsay Duncan [1955] LLP Member; Fiona Kirstie Edmond [1977] LLP Member; Roger Alec Elford [1979] LLP Member; Duncan William Elson [1960] LLP Member; Simon George Ewing [1974] LLP Member; Claire Suzanne Fallows [1971] LLP Member; James Henry Magnus Fea [1973] LLP Member; Miranda Kate Fisher [1973] LLP Member; Kevin Hugh Forsyth [1969] LLP Member; James David Freeman [1974] LLP Member; William Talbot Garner [1970] LLP Member; Suzanne Michelle Gatward [1978] LLP Member; William Douglas Granger [1965] LLP Member; David Keith Haines [1971] LLP Member; Paul Edward Thomas Henty [1976] LLP Member; Stewart Ratcliffe Hey [1968] LLP Member; David James Hicks [1979] LLP Member; Sarah Dorothy Higgins [1962] LLP Member; Robert Peter Highmore [1957] LLP Member; Mark Howard [1974] LLP Member; Grant Howell [1956] LLP Member; Emma Clare Humphreys [1975] LLP Member; Nicholas Simon Hurley [1968] LLP Member; Charles Robert Hutton [1973] LLP Member; Helen Susannah Hutton [1975] LLP Member; James Hyne [1974] LLP Member; Timothy Paul Jenkins [1971] LLP Member; Michael Mortimer Jones [1971] LLP Member; Paul Alexander Kay [1956] LLP Member; Catherine Jamie McBride Kennaugh [1983] LLP Member; Satish Khandke [1968] LLP Member; Ashley King-Christopher [1968] LLP Member; Graeme Kleiner [1971] LLP Member; Ashley Martin Kopitko [1961] LLP Member; Rupa Lakha [1977] LLP Member; Dominic Geoffrey Lawrance [1974] LLP Member; Peter Levaggi [1965] LLP Member; Michael Robert Lingens [1957] LLP Member; William Fallowfield Longrigg [1960] LLP Member; Jody MacDonald [1981] LLP Member; Malcolm MacDougall [1971] LLP Member; William Alexander Marriott [1979] LLP Member; Christian Broome Massey [1972] LLP Member; Piers Harcourt Master [1976] LLP Member; Jonathan Patrick McDonald [1979] LLP Member; Lee Granville Medlock [1968] LLP Member; Karen Lee Mitchell [1975] LLP Member; Thomas James Moran [1972] LLP Member; Jonathan Nigel Morley [1975] LLP Member; Sarah Louise Morley [1978] LLP Member; Nigel John Morton [1958] LLP Member; William Robert Nash [1969] LLP Member; Naomi Jessica Nettleton [1981] LLP Member; Ngoc Hanh Nguyen [1979] LLP Member; Richard William Fisher Norton [1959] LLP Member; Rhys John Francis Novak [1974] LLP Member

Russneft (UK) Limited
Incorporated: 26 November 2001 *Employees:* 2
Net Worth Deficit: £4,582,298 *Total Assets:* £417,847,072
Registered Office: 71 Queen Victoria Street, London, EC4V 4BE
Activities: Distribution of gaseous fuels through mains
Officers: Stephen John Goldsmith, Secretary; Magomed-Ali Evloev [1976] Director [Russian]; Elena Nikitina [1963] Director [Russian]; Olga Prozorovskaya [1965] Director [Russian]; Igor Vassiliev [1967] Director

Ruthenium Investments Limited
Incorporated: 1 November 2005
Net Worth Deficit: £10,212,070 *Total Assets:* £1,088,129,920
Registered Office: 1 Churchill Place, London, E14 5HP
Activities: Financial intermediation not elsewhere classified
Parent: Barclays Bank PLC
Officers: Carl Thomas Senior [1978] Director/Banker; Vishal Shah [1984] Director/Banker; Patrick Brittain Voisey [1979] Director; Jonathan Michael Walthoe [1975] Director/Banker

Rutherfurd Acquisitions Limited
Incorporated: 3 June 2010
Net Worth Deficit: £132,879,112 *Total Assets:* £375,680,544
Registered Office: Accurist House, 44 Baker Street, London, W1U 7AL
Activities: Activities of head offices
Parent: Emerson Electric Co.
Officers: Bente Bulow Bundgaard-Antoine [1972] Director/Accountant [Danish]; Martin Benedict Fernandez [1959] Director/Treasurer; Victor Andrew Lazzaretti [1964] Director/Lawyer [American]; Derek Shaw [1955] Tax Director; John Anthony Sperino [1970] Director/Attorney [American]

RVT CLO Investments LLP
Incorporated: 1 December 2010
Net Worth: £153,765,504 *Total Assets:* £1,497,573,760
Registered Office: 1 Churchill Place, London, E14 5HP

RW Wentworth UK Limited
Incorporated: 1 August 2014 *Employees:* 250
Net Worth Deficit: £23,678,000 *Total Assets:* £189,490,000
Registered Office: 2nd Floor, 55 Mark Lane, London, EC3R 7NE
Activities: Activities of other holding companies n.e.c.
Major Shareholder: Chanchai Ruayrungruang
Officers: Yi-Chun Lai [1966] Director [Taiwanese]; Dr Chanchai Ruayrungruang [1954] Director [Thai]; Woraphanit Ruayrungruang [1990] Director [Thai]

S & N Angel Investments Ltd.
Incorporated: 30 October 1953
Net Worth: £1,025,386,688 *Total Assets:* £1,721,977,856
Registered Office: Elsley Court, 20-22 Great Titchfield Street, London, W1W 8BE
Activities: Non-trading company
Parent: Heineken UK Limited
Officers: David Michael Forde [1968] Managing Director [Irish]; Sean Michael Paterson [1982] Director/Accountant; Radovan Sikorsky [1967] Finance Director [Slovak]; Kelly Taylor-Welsh [1978] Director/Head of UK Tax

S & N Finland Limited
Incorporated: 14 December 2001
Net Worth: £4,337,999,872 *Total Assets:* £4,606,000,128
Registered Office: Elsley Court, 20-22 Great Titchfield Street, London, W1W 8BE
Activities: Non-trading company
Parent: Heineken UK Limited
Officers: David Michael Forde [1968] Managing Director [Irish]; Sean Michael Paterson [1982] Director/Accountant; Radovan Sikorsky [1967] Finance Director [Slovak]; Kelly Taylor Welsh [1978] Director/Head of UK Tax

S & P Global Commodities UK Limited
Incorporated: 13 April 2001
Previous: McGraw Hill Financial Commodities UK Limited
Net Worth: £210,000,992 *Total Assets:* £424,832,000
Registered Office: 20 Canary Wharf, London, E14 5LH
Activities: Publishing of consumer and business journals and periodicals
Parent: S & P Global Inc.
Officers: Elizabeth Hithersay, Secretary; Catherine Westley, Secretary; James Alexander Douse [1978] Senior Tax Director; Elizabeth Hithersay [1980] Director/Legal Counsel; Ryan Weelson [1980] Director/Assistant EMEA Controller; Kevin Wise [1973] Director of Financial Services

S & P Global Finance Europe Limited
Incorporated: 12 June 2002
Previous: McGraw-Hill Finance Europe Limited
Net Worth: £51,852,000 *Total Assets:* £492,707,008
Registered Office: 20 Canary Wharf, London, E14 5LH
Activities: Activities of head offices
Parent: S & P Global Inc.
Officers: Elizabeth Hithersay, Secretary; Antony Bernard Theodore Montague, Secretary; James Alexander Douse [1978] Senior Director Taxes; Edward Haran [1967] Director/SVP and Treasurer [American]; Elizabeth Hithersay [1980] Director/Legal Counsel; Ryan Weelson [1980] Director/Assistant EMEA Controller; Kevin Wise [1973] Director of Financial Services

S32 Leasing Company Ltd
Incorporated: 14 November 2006
Net Worth Deficit: £7,581,638 *Total Assets:* £311,637,248
Registered Office: Broadwalk House, 5 Appold Street, London, EC2A 2DA
Activities: Renting and leasing of passenger water transport equipment
Parent: Credit Agricole CIB Marine Leasing Holdings Limited
Officers: Simon Alvin Harding [1974] Director/Accountant; Aodhan James Garrett McCarthy [1975] Director/Accountant

Saatchi & Saatchi Holdings Limited
Incorporated: 21 August 1989 *Employees:* 3
Net Worth: £129,395,000 *Total Assets:* £129,396,000
Registered Office: Tooks Court, 40 Chancery Lane, London, WC2A 1JA
Activities: Advertising agencies
Parent: MMS UK Holdings Limited
Officers: Joanne Munis, Secretary; James Joseph Carrigan [1959] Director/Head of UK Tax; Jean-Michel Michel Etienne [1951] Director/Chief Finance Officer [French]; Annette King [1968] Director/Chief Executive Officer

M & C Saatchi PLC
Incorporated: 28 April 2004 *Employees:* 2,483
Net Worth: £57,538,000 *Total Assets:* £264,628,992
Registered Office: 36 Golden Sqaure, London, W1R 4EE
Activities: Activities of head offices
Officers: Andrew Simon Blackstone, Secretary/Accountant; Michael Dobbs [1948] Director; James Neil Terry Hewitt [1959] Director/Accountant; David Andrew Kershaw [1954] Director; William Mortimer Muirhead [1946] Director; Sir Michael Charles Gerrard Peat [1949] Director; Lord Maurice Saatchi [1946] Director; Jeremy Theodorson Sinclair [1946] Director; Lorna Tilbian [1957] Director

Saavi Energia (UK) Ltd
Incorporated: 22 June 2011
Previous: Intergen International (UK) Ltd
Net Worth: £676,772,544 *Total Assets:* £677,936,000
Registered Office: 21 Holborn Viaduct, London, EC1A 2DY
Activities: Activities of head offices
Officers: Melissa Gabrielle Bourgeois [1983] Director/Chartered Secretary; Marco Ivan de La Paz Fuentes [1978] Director [Mexican]; Amy Nicole Lejune [1977] Director [American]; Esmeralda Viramontes Mayorga [1972] Director [Mexican]

Sabah Shell Petroleum Company Limited
Incorporated: 7 July 1938 *Employees:* 813
Net Worth: £152,062,592 *Total Assets:* £1,031,010,176
Registered Office: Shell Centre, London, SE1 7NA
Activities: Extraction of crude petroleum
Parent: The Shell Petroleum Company Limited
Officers: Madam Yit Chan Tai, Secretary; Yuen Ling Tai, Secretary; Jill Chieng Hui Chiun Chieng [1973] Director/General Manager [Malaysian]; Simon George Durkin [1959] Managing Director; Prithipal Singh Jinnil Singh [1977] Director/General Manager [Malaysian]; Mohammad Hilmi Yusof [1975] Director/General Manager [Malaysian]

Sable Holding Limited
Incorporated: 8 October 2003
Net Worth: £9,438,512,128 *Total Assets:* £11,236,747,264
Registered Office: Griffin House, 161 Hammersmith Road, London, W6 8BS
Activities: Activities of head offices
Parent: Cable & Wireless Limited
Officers: Leah Helena Pegg, Secretary; Leah Helena Pegg [1985] Director/Company Secretary; Matthew Edward Read [1977] Director/Treasurer

Sableknight Limited
Incorporated: 8 December 1976 *Employees:* 3
Net Worth: £204,687,840 *Total Assets:* £212,104,368
Registered Office: 22 Chancery Lane, London, WC2A 1LS
Activities: Activities of head offices
Shareholders: Aine Deirdre O'Reilly; Nicholas Peter James Falla; Peter James Howes; Michael Powell
Officers: Thomas Morton West, Secretary; Robin Shedden Broadhurst [1946] Director/Chartered Surveyor; Desmond Roger Wingate Harrison [1933] Director; Rosemary Frances Norris [1961] Director; Ian Christopher Woodward [1959] Director/Chartered Surveyor

Sach 1 Ltd
Incorporated: 23 March 2017 *Employees:* 2
Net Worth: £66,414,000 *Total Assets:* £346,892,992
Registered Office: 3rd Floor, Greener House, 68 Haymarket, London, SW1Y 4RF
Activities: Financial management
Parent: Sirius Minerals PLC
Officers: Nicholas Anthony King, Secretary; Christopher Neil Fraser [1974] Director/Chief Executive Officer; Thomas Jay Staley [1980] Director/Chief Financial Officer [Australian]

Sach 2 Ltd
Incorporated: 30 March 2017 *Employees:* 2
Net Worth: £108,030,000 *Total Assets:* £454,923,008
Registered Office: 3rd Floor, Greener House, 68 Haymarket, London, SW1Y 4RF
Activities: Financial management
Parent: Sirius Minerals PLC
Officers: Nicholas Anthony King, Secretary; Christopher Neil Fraser [1974] Director/Chief Executive Officer; Thomas Jay Staley [1980] Director/Chief Financial Officer [Australian]

Sage Publications Limited
Incorporated: 13 July 1971 *Employees:* 1,020
Net Worth: £53,813,000 *Total Assets:* £122,282,000
Registered Office: 1 Olivers Yard, 55 City Road, London, EC1Y 1SP
Activities: Publishing of consumer and business journals and periodicals
Parent: Sage Publications Inc
Officers: Katharine Mary Jackson, Finance Director; James Stephen Barr [1956] Managing Director; Philip John Denvir [1963] IT Director; Richard Fidczuk [1961] Production Director; Anthony John Histed [1967] Sales Director; Carol Rosemary Irwin [1967] HR Director; Katharine Mary Jackson [1964] Director; Jane Illona Makoff [1966] Marketing Director; Ziyad Paul Marar [1966] Editorial Director; Sara Miller McCune [1941] Director/Publisher [American]; Karen Rosalyn Phillips [1962] Editorial Director; Kiren Shoman [1972] Editorial Director, Pedagogy; Richard Royston Thame [1970] Finance Director

Sager House (Almeida) Limited
Incorporated: 12 March 2001
Net Worth: £38,764,036 *Total Assets:* £247,620,912
Registered Office: 33 Davies Street, London, W1K 4LR
Activities: Buying and selling of own real estate
Major Shareholder: Todd Boehly
Officers: Simon James Brooks [1980] Director/Banker; Jonathan Simon Goldstein [1966] Director; Richard Michael Pilkington [1967] Director/Investment Professional

Sagittarius International Limited
Incorporated: 1 December 2015 *Employees:* 1
Net Worth: £306,218,880 *Total Assets:* £1,728,063,360
Registered Office: First Floor, Stratton House, 5 Stratton Street, Mayfair, London, W1J 8LA
Activities: Other service activities n.e.c.
Parent: Libra International Limited
Officers: Dongshan Zheng [1962] Director [Chinese]

Sahara Hospitality Operations LLP
Incorporated: 23 July 2012 *Employees:* 640
Net Worth: £154,601,616 *Total Assets:* £764,899,008
Registered Office: 6th Floor, 25 Farringdon Street, London, EC4A 4AB

J Sainsbury PLC
Incorporated: 10 November 1922 *Employees:* 121
Net Worth: £7,410,999,808 *Total Assets:* £22,001,000,448
Registered Office: 33 Holborn, London, EC1N 2HT
Activities: Retail sale in non-specialised stores with food, beverages or tobacco predominating
Officers: Timothy Fallowfield, Secretary; Matthew John Brittin [1968] Director; Brian Jude Cassin [1967] Director [Irish]; Michael Andrew Coupe [1960] Trading Director; Jo Nell Harlow [1962] Director [American]; David Wilson Keens [1953] Director; Kevin O'Byrne [1964] Director/Chief Financial Officer [Irish]; Dame Susan Ilene Rice [1946] Director; John Terence Rogers [1968] Director; Martin Anthony Scicluna [1950] Director; Jean Tomlin [1955] Director; David Alan Tyler [1953] Director

Sainsbury Propco A Limited
Incorporated: 5 December 2005
Net Worth Deficit: £67,000,000 *Total Assets:* £2,255,000,064
Registered Office: 33 Holborn, London, EC1N 2HT
Activities: Other letting and operating of own or leased real estate
Parent: Sainsbury Holdco A Limited
Officers: Timothy Fallowfield, Secretary; Dean Clegg [1967] Property Director; Geraint Jamie Cowen [1972] Director/Chartered Surveyor; David Clifford Wheeler [1984] Director

Sainsbury Propco B Limited
Incorporated: 5 December 2005
Net Worth: £389,000,000 *Total Assets:* £1,278,000,000
Registered Office: 33 Holborn, London, EC1N 2HT
Activities: Other letting and operating of own or leased real estate
Parent: Sainsbury Holdco B Limited
Officers: Timothy Fallowfield, Secretary; Dean Clegg [1967] Property Director; Geraint Jamie Cowen [1972] Director/Chartered Surveyor; David Clifford Wheeler [1984] Director

Sainsbury Property Investments Limited
Incorporated: 27 October 1987
Net Worth: £120,289,000 *Total Assets:* £273,072,992
Registered Office: 33 Holborn, London, EC1N 2HT
Activities: Development of building projects
Parent: J Sainsbury PLC
Officers: Timothy Fallowfield, Secretary; Martyn Stephen Burke [1970] Director; Geraint Jamie Cowen [1972] Director/Chartered Surveyor; John Terence Rogers [1968] Director Corporate Finance; David Clifford Wheeler [1984] Director

Sainsbury's Bank PLC
Incorporated: 12 November 1996 *Employees:* 1,477
Net Worth: £943,000,000 *Total Assets:* £7,765,000,192
Registered Office: 33 Holborn, London, EC1N 2HT
Activities: Banks
Parent: J Sainsbury PLC
Officers: Donald Hamish MacLeod McNaughton, Secretary; Gwyn Burr [1963] Customer Director; Carole Vera Butler [1962] Director; Marcia Dominic Campbell [1959] Director; Peter Lawrence Clarke [1959] Director; Roger William John Davis [1956] Director; Graeme Forrester [1964] Director/Chief Risk Officer; Peter Lloyd Griffiths [1958] Director/Chief Executive; David Jones [1974] Director/Chief Customer Office; Michael Larkin [1969] Director/Chief Financial Officer [Irish]; Angela Susan Risley [1958] Group HR Director; John Terence Rogers [1968] Director; Michael Alexander Nunes Ross [1969] Director; William Guy Thomas [1955] Independent Non-Executive Director

Sainsbury's Intermediate Holdings Limited
Incorporated: 14 April 2016
Net Worth: £1,233,517,056 *Total Assets:* £1,233,517,056
Registered Office: 33 Holborn, London, EC1N 2HT
Activities: Activities of other holding companies n.e.c.
Parent: J Sainsbury PLC
Officers: Timothy Fallowfield, Secretary; Michael Andrew Coupe [1960] Director/Chief Executive; John Terence Rogers [1968] Director/Chief Financial Officer

Sainsbury's Supermarkets Ltd
Incorporated: 10 October 1996 *Employees:* 102
Net Worth: £4,712,000,000 *Total Assets:* £10,021,999,616
Registered Office: 33 Holborn, London, EC1N 2HT
Activities: Retail sale in non-specialised stores with food, beverages or tobacco predominating
Parent: J Sainsbury PLC
Officers: Timothy Fallowfield, Secretary; Michael Andrew Coupe [1960] Trading Director; Timothy Fallowfield [1963] Director/Solicitor; Peter Lloyd Griffiths [1958] Director/Chief Executive; Phil Victor Jordan [1968] Director; Nicolas Paul Michael Angelo Mills-Hicks [1971] Director/Chartered Accountant; Clodagh Moriarty [1979] Director [Irish]; Kevin O'Byrne [1964] Director/Chief Financial Officer [Irish]; Angela Susan Risley [1958] Group HR Director; Simon John Roberts [1971] Retail & Operations Director; John Terence Rogers [1968] Director

Saka Indonesia Pangkah Limited
Incorporated: 5 July 1995 *Employees:* 309
Net Worth: £8,501,112 *Total Assets:* £411,649,920
Registered Office: 3rd Floor, 11-12 St James's Square, London, SW1Y 4LB
Activities: Extraction of crude petroleum
Parent: Ministry of State-Owned Enterprises of Republic of Indonesia
Officers: Devi Pradnya Paramita [1977] Director/Chief Finance and Administration [Indonesian]; Tumbur Parlindungan Parlindungan [1968] Director/Saka Employee [Indonesian]; Vincentius Argo Rusdibyo [1966] Director [Indonesian]

Salamander Energy (S.E. Asia) Limited
Incorporated: 12 December 2005
Net Worth: £132,333,208 *Total Assets:* £132,920,504
Registered Office: Level 4, 123 Victoria Street, London, SW1E 6DE
Activities: Extraction of crude petroleum
Parent: Ophir Thailand (E & P) Limited
Officers: Philip Laing, Secretary; Anthony John Mulgrove [1964] Director; Dr Oliver Francis Quinn [1978] Director; Anthony John Rouse [1956] Director

Salamander Energy Group Limited
Incorporated: 29 December 2004
Net Worth: £228,056,288 *Total Assets:* £434,304,288
Registered Office: Level 4, 123 Victoria Street, London, SW1E 6DE
Activities: Extraction of crude petroleum
Parent: Salamander Energy PLC
Officers: Philip Laing, Secretary; Anthony John Mulgrove [1964] Director; Dr Oliver Francis Quinn [1978] Commercial Director; Anthony John Rouse [1956] Director

Salamander Energy PLC
Incorporated: 13 September 2006 *Employees:* 201
Net Worth: £167,984,176 *Total Assets:* £626,995,520
Registered Office: Level 4, 123 Victoria Street, London, SW1E 6DE
Activities: Extraction of crude petroleum
Parent: Ophir Energy PLC
Officers: Philip Laing, Secretary; Alan Booth [1958] Director; Dr Oliver Francis Quinn [1978] Director; Anthony John Rouse [1956] Director

Salesforce.Com EMEA Limited
Incorporated: 5 April 2004 *Employees:* 1,252
Net Worth: £88,423,648 *Total Assets:* £1,577,490,176
Registered Office: Floor 26, Salesforce Tower, 110 Bishopsgate, London, EC2N 4AY
Activities: Other information technology service activities
Parent: Salesforce.Com, Inc.
Officers: Jose Luiz Moura Neto, Secretary; Jose Luiz Moura Neto [1965] Director/Business Executive; Hakan Joachim Wettermark [1966] Director/Business Executive [American]

Salic (UK) Limited
Incorporated: 2 September 2014
Net Worth: £486,925,536 *Total Assets:* £490,574,752
Registered Office: 16th Floor, 125 Old Broad Street, London, EC2N 1AR
Activities: Activities of head offices
Parent: Ministry of Finance (Saudi Arabia)
Officers: Khaled Mohammed Alaboodi [1960] Director [Saudi Arabian]; Abdulrahman Hassan Alhassan [1959] Director/Business Executive - CIO [Saudi Arabian]; Mohammed Tayeb [1984] Director

Salix Finance Ltd
Incorporated: 9 March 2004 *Employees:* 46
Net Worth: £3,520,883 *Total Assets:* £283,619,424
Registered Office: 6th Floor, 25 Farringdon Street, London, EC4A 4AB
Activities: Other professional, scientific and technical activities n.e.c.
Officers: Annie Shepperd, Secretary; John Walter Edmonds [1944] Director/University Research Fellow; Teresa Colomba Graham [1956] Director/Business Advisor; Annie Shepperd [1951] Director/Chief Executive, Salix Finance; Michael Colin Stark [1949] Director/Charity Trustee

Sam UK Investment Holdings Limited
Incorporated: 18 June 2013
Net Worth: £615,188,288 *Total Assets:* £1,494,655,744
Registered Office: 2 Triton Square, Regent's Place, London, NW1 3AN
Activities: Activities of financial services holding companies
Parent: Banco Santander, S.A.
Officers: Harrus Ali, Secretary; Monica Cueva Diaz [1965] Director [Spanish]; Jack Gustaaf Catharina Maria Jules Treunen [1966] Director/Banker [Belgian]

Sampford Underwriting Limited
Incorporated: 22 April 2003
Net Worth Deficit: £83,476,000 *Total Assets:* £240,958,000
Registered Office: c/o Neon Underwriting Limited, 20 Gracechurch Street, London, EC3V 0BG
Activities: Non-life insurance
Parent: Neon Holdings (U.K.) Limited
Officers: Larysa Alla Dlaboha, Secretary; Ian James Harman [1985] Director/Head of Finance; David John Witzgall [1959] Director [American]

Sandown 2012-2 PLC
Incorporated: 20 April 2012
Net Worth: £19,000 *Total Assets:* £734,204,992
Registered Office: 35 Great St Helen's, London, EC3A 6AP
Activities: Financial intermediation not elsewhere classified
Parent: Sandown 2012-2 Holdings Limited
Officers: Daniel Marc Richard Jaffe [1975] Director

Sandown Gold 2012-1 PLC
Incorporated: 3 February 2012
Net Worth: £20,000 *Total Assets:* £694,273,024
Registered Office: 35 Great St Helen's, London, EC3A 6AP
Activities: Financial intermediation not elsewhere classified
Parent: Sandown Gold 2012-1 Holdings Limited
Officers: Daniel Marc Richard Jaffe [1975] Director

Sanne Group (UK) Limited
Incorporated: 29 August 2006
Net Worth: £976,226 *Total Assets:* £191,900,192
Registered Office: 2nd Floor, Asticus Building, 21 Palmer Street, London, SW1H 0AD
Activities: Financial intermediation not elsewhere classified
Parent: Sanne Group PLC
Officers: Coral Suzanne Bidel [1983] Director; Jason Christopher Bingham [1978] Director; Rhea Leom Hood [1981] Director; Martin Charles Schnaier [1977] Director; Beejadhursingh Mahen Surnam [1970] Director; Ian Stephen Venter [1970] Director; Christopher Michael Warnes [1977] Director

Santa Fe Group Limited
Incorporated: 12 December 2005 *Employees:* 69
Net Worth: £78,862,440 *Total Assets:* £114,546,736
Registered Office: Central Way, Park Royal, London, NW10 7XW
Activities: Activities of head offices
Officers: Christian Moller Laursen [1966] Director [Danish]; Martin Thaysen [1971] Director/Chief Executive [Danish]

Santander Asset Finance PLC
Incorporated: 8 December 1980
Net Worth: £212,003,008 *Total Assets:* £1,895,448,960
Registered Office: 2 Triton Square, Regent's Place, London, NW1 3AN
Activities: Financial leasing
Parent: Santander UK PLC
Officers: Stephen David Affleck [1979] Finance Director; Mr George Smith-Salmond Ashworth [1956] Managing Director; Anna Maria Konter [1967] Director [Dutch]

Santander Asset Management UK Holdings Limited
Incorporated: 24 December 1958
Net Worth: £243,117,296 *Total Assets:* £243,189,888
Registered Office: 10 Brock Street, Regent's Place, London, NW1 3FG
Activities: Activities of head offices
Parent: Sam UK Investment Holdings Limited
Officers: Harrus Ali, Secretary; Betsabeh Rais, Secretary; Monica Cueva Diaz [1965] Director [Spanish]; Mehdi Kadhim [1979] Director; Mr Luis Garcia-Izquierdo Ruiz [1966] Director [Spanish]

Santander Lending Limited
Incorporated: 30 May 2006
Net Worth: £197,767,808 *Total Assets:* £451,748,192
Registered Office: 2 Triton Square, Regent's Place, London, NW1 3AN
Activities: Financial intermediation not elsewhere classified
Parent: Santander UK PLC
Officers: Stephen David Affleck [1979] Finance Director; Andrew Ellis Jack Briggs [1962] Director/Bank Manager; Christopher Paul Fallis [1980] Director/Banker

Santander Private Banking UK Limited
Incorporated: 13 February 1991
Net Worth: £254,645,168 *Total Assets:* £258,157,104
Registered Office: 2 Triton Square, Regent's Place, London, NW1 3AN
Activities: Other business support service activities n.e.c.
Parent: Santander UK PLC
Officers: Susan Mary Allen [1966] Director/Banker [Irish]; Jennifer Anne Steven Moodie [1958] Director of Operational Risk; Rachel Jane Morrison [1968] Director/Chartered Accountant

Santander UK Group Holdings PLC
Incorporated: 23 September 2013
Net Worth: £15,800,999,936 *Total Assets:* £314,760,003,584
Registered Office: 2 Triton Square, Regents Place, London, NW1 3AN
Activities: Activities of financial services holding companies
Parent: Banco Santander, S.A
Officers: Gavin Raymond White, Secretary; Susan Mary Allen [1966] Director/Banker [Irish]; Lindsey Tyler Argalas [1974] Director [American]; Nathan Mark Bostock [1960] Director; Ana Patricia Botin-Sanz de Sautuola y O'Shea [1960] Director [Spanish]; Generald Byrne [1956] Director [Irish]; Julie Chakraverty [1971] Director; Annemarie Verna Florence Durbin [1963] Director [British/New Zealander]; Edward Joseph Giera [1962] Director [American]; Christopher Philip Jones [1956] Director; Antonio Roman [1967] Director/Banker [Spanish]; Genevieve Helen Shore [1969] Director; Baroness Shriti Vinodkant Vadera [1962] Director; Jonathan Scott Wheway [1966] Director

Santander UK PLC
Incorporated: 12 September 1988 *Employees:* 19,559
Net Worth: £16,053,000,192 *Total Assets:* £314,764,984,320
Registered Office: 2 Triton Square, Regent's Place, London, NW1 3AN
Activities: Banks
Parent: Santander UK Group Holdings PLC
Officers: Gavin Raymond White, Secretary; Susan Mary Allen [1966] Director/Banker [Irish]; Lindsey Tyler Argalas [1974] Director [American]; Nathan Mark Bostock [1960] Director; Ana Patricia Botin-Sanz de Sautuola y O'Shea [1960] Director [Spanish]; Generald Byrne [1956] Director [Irish]; Julie Chakraverty [1971] Director; Annemarie Verna Florence Durbin [1963] Director [British/New Zealander]; Edward Joseph Giera [1962] Director [American]; Christopher Philip Jones [1956] Director; Antonio Roman [1967] Director/Banker [Spanish]; Genevieve Helen Shore [1969] Director; Baroness Shriti Vinodkant Vadera [1962] Director; Jonathan Scott Wheway [1966] Director

Santos (UK) Limited
Incorporated: 20 June 2013
Net Worth: £120,238,040 *Total Assets:* £135,567,616
Registered Office: 66 Lincoln's Inn Fields, London, WC2A 3LH
Activities: Extraction of crude petroleum
Officers: Kevin Thomas Gallagher [1965] Managing Director and Chief Executive Officer [Australian]; Anthony Neilson [1971] Director/Chief Financial Officer [Australian]; James Thorne [1953] Director/Consultant

Sapient Limited
Incorporated: 8 January 1996 *Employees:* 764
Net Worth: £2,145,000 *Total Assets:* £135,204,992
Registered Office: 1st Floor, 2 Television Centre, 101 Wood Lane, London, W12 7FR
Activities: Other information technology service activities
Parent: MMS UK Holdings Limited
Officers: Joanne Munis, Secretary; Scott Antony Criddle [1972] Director/Group Vice President - UK; Kristen Signore [1974] Director/Chief Financial Officer [Italian]; Nigel Gregory Vaz [1978] Director [American]

Sarti Holdings (UK) Limited
Incorporated: 27 May 2016 *Employees:* 1,247
Net Worth: £29,254,884 *Total Assets:* £161,327,712
Registered Office: Investcorp House, 48 Grosvenor Street, London, W1K 3HW
Activities: Activities of other holding companies n.e.c.
Officers: Andrea Jayne Davis [1965] Managing Director/Banker; Grahame Ivey [1958] Director

Sarum Issuer Holdco Limited
Incorporated: 15 November 2011
Net Worth: £400,449 *Total Assets:* £501,483,392
Registered Office: 35 Great St Helen's, London, EC3A 6AP
Activities: Non-trading company
Parent: Intertrust Corporate Services Limited
Officers: Daniel Marc Richard Jaffe [1975] Director

Satellite Financing (Holdings) Limited
Incorporated: 14 October 2005
Net Worth: £9,007 *Total Assets:* £504,411,232
Registered Office: 35 Great St Helen's, London, EC3A 6AP
Activities: Non-trading company
Parent: Intertrust Corporate Services Limited
Officers: Susan Iris Abrahams [1957] Director

Satellite Financing PLC
Incorporated: 14 October 2005
Net Worth: £21,508 *Total Assets:* £504,411,232
Registered Office: 35 Great St Helen's, London, EC3A 6AP
Activities: Financial intermediation not elsewhere classified
Parent: Satellite Financing (Holding) Limited
Officers: Susan Iris Abrahams [1957] Director

Saturn UK Holdco Limited
Incorporated: 14 August 2015
Net Worth: £334,272,704 *Total Assets:* £334,280,096
Registered Office: Suite 1, 3rd Floor, 11-12 St James's Square, London, SW1Y 4LB
Activities: Activities of head offices
Officers: Laurent Jean-Claude Uberti [1971] Director [French]

Save The Children Fund
Incorporated: 1 December 1921 *Employees:* 1,164
Net Worth: £61,702,000 *Total Assets:* £158,814,000
Registered Office: 1 St John's Lane, London, EC1M 4AR
Activities: Other social work activities without accommodation n.e.c.
Officers: Andrew Charles Willis, Secretary; Gareth Thomas Davies [1965] Director/Auditor; Arabella Elizabeth Duffield [1971] Director and Trustee; Naomi Helen Eisenstadt [1950] Director/Retired; Anne Kathleen Fahy [1960] Director [Irish]; Sebastian Richard Edward Cuthbert James [1966] Director; Dr Sophia Jane Aubrey McCormick [1950] Director/Volunteer; Dianna Patricia Melrose [1952] Director/Retired/Former British Diplomat; David Clement Ripert [1978] Director/Employee [French]; Lisa Rosen [1967] Director/Compliance [British/American]; Babatunde Temitope Soyoye [1968] Director/Managing Partner [British/Nigerian]; Charles Richard Arklay Steel [1975] Director/Investment Professional; Mark Francis Swallow [1967] Director/Finance Executive

Save The Children International
Incorporated: 12 March 1999 *Employees:* 16,495
Net Worth: £59,268,572 *Total Assets:* £278,284,128
Registered Office: St Vincent House, 30 Orange Street, London, WC2H 7HH
Activities: Other social work activities without accommodation n.e.c.
Officers: Clare Louise Canning, Secretary; Inger Ashing [1974] Director [Swedish]; Roy Leonard Caple Hernandez [1961] Director/Business and Communications Consultant [Mexican]; Anne Kathleen Fahy [1960] Director [Irish]; Debra Fine [1960] Director/Investment Manager [American]; Robert Patrick Henry Good [1952] Director/Retired [Irish]; Peter John Hodgson [1955] Director/Chief Executive [Australian]; Tamara Ingram [1960] Director/Global Chair Advertising; Bradley Chapman Irwin [1958] Director/President & CEO [American]; Elizabeth Laura Lule [1951] Director/Global Health Expert [Ugandan]; Sigrun Marie Moegedal [1943] Director/Special Adviser [Norwegian]; Joon Oh [1955] Director/Professor [South Korean]; Jonathan Nicholas Powell [1956] Director; Pernille Spiers-Lopez [1959] Corporate/Non-Profit Director [American]; Dona Young [1954] Consultant and Director [American]

Savers Health and Beauty Limited
Incorporated: 4 December 1987 *Employees:* 4,215
Net Worth: £64,545,000 *Total Assets:* £231,971,008
Registered Office: Hutchison House, 5 Hester Road, Battersea, London, SW11 4AN
Activities: Retail sale of cosmetic and toilet articles in specialised stores
Parent: A S Watson (Health & Beauty UK) Limited
Officers: Edith Shih, Secretary; Richard Alexander Fleming [1971] Finance Director; Dr Alan John Heaton [1962] Director; Dominic Kai Ming Lai [1953] Director [Canadian]; Peter William MacNab [1957] Director

Savills (Overseas Holdings) Limited
Incorporated: 14 November 1988 *Employees:* 16
Net Worth: £7,630,000 *Total Assets:* £181,804,992
Registered Office: 33 Margaret Street, London, W1G 0JD
Activities: Activities of head offices
Officers: Christine Lynn Cox, Secretary; Philip Alexander Ingleby [1965] Director/Chief Operating Officer; Christopher Michael Lee [1965] Director; Danny O'Donnell [1964] Finance Director; John Jeremy Mark Ridley [1962] Director/Surveyor; Simon James Blouet Shaw [1965] Director; James Simon Ward Sparrow [1967] Director; Craig Antony Watson [1962] Financial Director

Savills (UK) Limited
Incorporated: 25 April 1991 *Employees:* 4,026
Net Worth: £85,818,000 *Total Assets:* £362,920,000
Registered Office: 33 Margaret Street, London, W1G 0JD
Activities: Real estate agencies
Officers: Christine Lynn Cox, Secretary; Christopher Michael Lee, Secretary; Peter Allen [1973] Director/Head of Residential Capital Markets; Jeremy Neil Bates [1965] Director; Simon Collett [1968] Director/Head of Professional Services; Stephen Thomas Down [1967] Director; Philip John Gready [1958] Director/Chartered Surveyor; James Alexander Guy Gulliford [1975] Director; Andrew Richard Harle [1963] Director/Chartered Surveyor; Nicholas Peter Herward [1969] Director; Simon Richard Hope [1964] Director; Justin Marking [1958] Director; Timothy Sven Maynard [1961] Director; Philip Ian Pearce [1966] Director; Richard Morgan Rees [1967] Director/Chartered Surveyor; James Simon Ward Sparrow [1967] Director; David John Williams [1962] Director/Chartered Surveyor

Savills Holding Company Limited
Incorporated: 13 February 2008
Net Worth: £288,105,984 *Total Assets:* £474,801,984
Registered Office: 33 Margaret Street, London, W1G 0JD
Activities: Other business support service activities n.e.c.
Officers: Christine Lynn Cox, Secretary; Christopher Michael Lee [1965] Director/Company Secretary; Danny O'Donnell [1964] Finance Director; John Jeremy Mark Ridley [1962] Director/Surveyor; Simon James Blouet Shaw [1965] Director/Chief Financial Officer

Savills PLC
Incorporated: 10 April 1987 *Employees:* 96
Net Worth: £440,200,000 *Total Assets:* £1,270,599,936
Registered Office: 33 Margaret Street, London, W1G 0JD
Activities: Activities of head offices
Officers: Christopher Michael Lee, Secretary; Stacey Cartwright [1963] Director; Nicholas Eustace Haddon Ferguson [1948] Director; Timothy George Freshwater [1944] Director; Elizabeth Anne Hewitt [1956] Director; Charles Senff McVeigh III [1942] Director/Banker; John Jeremy Mark Ridley [1962] Director/Chartered Surveyor; Rupert Hugo Wynne Robson [1961] Director; Simon James Blouet Shaw [1965] Director/Chief Financial Officer

The Savoy Hotel Limited
Incorporated: 12 November 1998 *Employees:* 484
Net Worth Deficit: £157,910,000 *Total Assets:* £410,927,008
Registered Office: c/o CMS Cameron McKenna LLP, 78 Cannon Street, London, EC4N 6AF
Activities: Hotels and similar accommodation
Parent: Dunwilco (1784) Limited
Officers: Benjamin David Cadwell [1982] Director/Executive [American]; Ashley Fernandes [1968] Director [Indian]; Sean Piers Harrison [1971] Director/General Counsel; Kamal Rhazali [1979] Director/General Counsel [French]

SB Energy Holdings Limited
Incorporated: 11 June 2015
Net Worth: £103,861,552 *Total Assets:* £106,514,464
Registered Office: 69 Grosvenor Street, London, W1K 3JP
Activities: Activities of other holding companies n.e.c.
Parent: Softbank Group International Limited
Officers: Ippei Mimura [1968] Director [Japanese]; Shigeki Miwa [1967] Representative Director & CEO [Japanese]; Alok Sama [1962] Director/Chief Strategy & Corporate Development Officer

SB Energy Three Holdings Limited
Incorporated: 22 February 2017
Net Worth: £785,131,776 *Total Assets:* £785,131,904
Registered Office: 69 Grosvenor Street, London, W1K 3JP
Activities: Activities of other holding companies n.e.c.
Parent: SB Energy Holdings Limited
Officers: Shigeki Miwa [1967] Representative Director & CEO [Japanese]; Raman Nanda [1973] Director [Indian]

SB Investment Advisers (UK) Limited
Incorporated: 25 November 2016 *Employees:* 44
Net Worth: £95,843,288 *Total Assets:* £174,971,472
Registered Office: 69 Grosvenor Street, London, W1K 3JP
Activities: Fund management activities
Parent: Softbank Group Corp.
Officers: Rajeev Misra [1962] Director/Company Executive; Saleh Romeih [1967] Director/Portfolio Manager [French]; Ruwan Upendra Weerasekera [1966] Director/Chief Operating Officer

SBWW Investments Asia Limited
Incorporated: 13 September 2017
Net Worth: £536,686,336 *Total Assets:* £536,686,336
Registered Office: c/o Hackwood Secretaries Limited, One Silk Street, London, EC2Y 8HQ
Activities: Activities of other holding companies n.e.c.
Parent: SBWW Investments Limited
Officers: Ayako Adachi Adachi [1987] Director [Spanish]; Ronald D Fisher [1947] Director/Company Executive [American]; Amanda Sanchez-Barry [1982] Director

SBWW Investments Limited
Incorporated: 15 August 2017
Net Worth: £2,836,770,560 *Total Assets:* £2,836,770,560
Registered Office: c/o Hackwood Secretaries Limited, One Silk Street, London, EC2Y 8HQ
Activities: Activities of other holding companies n.e.c.
Shareholder: Softbank Group Capital Limited
Officers: Ayako Adachi Adachi [1987] Director [Spanish]; Ronald D Fisher [1947] Director/Company Executive [American]; Amanda Sanchez-Barry [1982] Director

Scania Finance Great Britain Limited
Incorporated: 6 October 1987 *Employees:* 47
Net Worth: £82,491,000 *Total Assets:* £709,678,976
Registered Office: 55 Baker Street, London, W1U 7EU
Activities: Financial intermediation not elsewhere classified
Parent: Volkswagen AG
Officers: Jean Denise Mitchell, Secretary; Martin Hay [1965] Managing Director; Anders Peter Herlitz [1960] Director/Vice President Scania Financial Services [Swedish]; Alan Rhodes [1960] Director; Per-Olof Gunnar Spjut [1965] Director/Vice President, Scania Financial Services [Swedish]

SCDM Energy Limited
Incorporated: 6 February 2015 *Employees:* 170
Net Worth: £280,222,336 *Total Assets:* £361,823,200
Registered Office: 50 Cannon Street, London, EC4N 6JJ
Activities: Other professional, scientific and technical activities n.e.c.
Officers: Olivier George Rene Bouygues [1950] Director-General [French]

Schawk Wace Group
Incorporated: 9 March 1965
Net Worth: £255,088,624 *Total Assets:* £255,654,624
Registered Office: Second Floor, Angel House, 338-346 Goswell Road, London, EC1V 7LQ
Activities: Activities of head offices
Officers: Joseph Carlo Bartolacci [1960] Director [American]; Steven Francis Nicola [1960] Director [American]; Brian Dixon Walters [1969] Director [American]

Henry Schein Animal Health Holdings Limited
Incorporated: 11 October 2010 *Employees:* 6
Net Worth: £222,008,128 *Total Assets:* £494,477,600
Registered Office: 18 Stanhope Place, London, W2 2HH
Activities: Activities of other holding companies n.e.c.
Officers: Russell Adrian Cooke [1965] Director; Michael Ellis [1959] Director; Graham Michael Rhodes [1962] Director

Schroder & Co. Limited
Incorporated: 27 July 1988 *Employees:* 338
Net Worth: £237,096,992 *Total Assets:* £2,332,116,992
Registered Office: 1 London Wall Place, London, EC2Y 5AU
Activities: Banks
Parent: Schroder Wealth Holdings Limited
Officers: Mary Anne Daly [1957] Director; Susan Elizabeth Harris [1961] Director/Chartered Accountant; Richard John Keers [1963] Director; Annamaria Enrichetta Luisa Koerling [1965] Director; Caspar Alexander Rock [1965] Director/Chief Investment Officer; Carolyn Sims [1965] Director; Jeremy William John Turnbull [1971] Director; Alexander Dudley Whitburn [1960] Director/Banker

Schroder Administration Limited
Incorporated: 18 November 2003
Net Worth: £510,892,992 *Total Assets:* £982,630,976
Registered Office: 1 London Wall Place, London, EC2Y 5AU
Activities: Activities of head offices
Parent: Schroders PLC
Officers: Tim McCann [1973] Director/Group Head of Tax; Wayne Mepham [1973] Director/Head of Financial Reporting; Graham Staples [1961] Director/Chartered Secretary; Nicholas Michael Taylor [1968] Director

Schroder Asian Total Return Investment Company PLC
Incorporated: 6 August 1987
Previous: Asian Total Return Investment Company PLC
Net Worth: £294,425,984 *Total Assets:* £314,976,000
Registered Office: 1 London Wall Place, London, EC2Y 5AU
Activities: Activities of investment trusts
Officers: David Brief [1953] Director; Caroline Margaret Hitch [1959] Director/Investment Banker; Michael John Holt [1960] Director; Sarah Juliet MacAulay [1962] Director

Schroder AsiaPacific Fund PLC
Incorporated: 18 September 1995
Net Worth: £825,041,984 *Total Assets:* £873,598,016
Registered Office: 1 London Wall Place, London, EC2Y 5AU
Activities: Financial intermediation not elsewhere classified
Officers: Keith Robert Craig [1962] Director; Rosemary Jane Morgan [1954] Director; Martin Porter [1957] Director; Nicholas Michael Norman Smith [1951] Director; James Frederick William Williams [1965] Director

Schroder Financial Holdings Limited
Incorporated: 22 July 2015
Net Worth: £247,320,992 *Total Assets:* £250,094,000
Registered Office: 1 London Wall Place, London, EC2Y 5AU
Activities: Activities of financial services holding companies
Parent: Schroder Administration Limited
Officers: Tim McCann [1973] Director/Group Head of Tax; Wayne Mepham [1973] Director; Graham Staples [1961] Director; Nicholas Michael Taylor [1968] Director

Schroder Financial Services Limited
Incorporated: 26 March 1985
Net Worth: £127,693,000 *Total Assets:* £2,348,472,064
Registered Office: 1 London Wall Place, London, EC2Y 5AU
Activities: Financial intermediation not elsewhere classified
Parent: Schroder Financial Holdings Limited
Officers: Tim McCann [1973] Director/Group Head of Tax; Wayne Mepham [1973] Director/Head of Financial Reporting; Nicholas Michael Taylor [1968] Director

Schroder Income Growth Fund PLC
Incorporated: 5 January 1995
Net Worth: £216,740,000 *Total Assets:* £237,619,008
Registered Office: 1 London Wall Place, London, EC2Y 5AU
Activities: Financial intermediation not elsewhere classified
Officers: Ian Christopher Simon Barby [1945] Director/Chairman; Ewen Cameron Watt [1956] Director; David John Causer [1950] Director; Bridget Elisabeth Guerin [1961] Director

Schroder International Holdings Limited
Incorporated: 17 September 1959
Net Worth: £522,192,000 *Total Assets:* £558,392,000
Registered Office: 1 London Wall Place, London, EC2Y 5AU
Activities: Activities of other holding companies n.e.c.
Parent: Schroder Administration Limited
Officers: Tim McCann [1973] Director/Group Head of Tax; Wayne Mepham [1973] Director/Head of Financial Reporting; Graham Staples [1961] Director/Chartered Secretary; Nicholas Michael Taylor [1968] Director

Schroder Investment Company Limited
Incorporated: 19 January 1960
Net Worth: £55,363,000 *Total Assets:* £454,628,000
Registered Office: 1 London Wall Place, London, EC2Y 5AU
Activities: Activities of other holding companies n.e.c.
Parent: Schroder Financial Holdings Limited
Officers: Tim McCann [1973] Director/Group Head of Tax; Wayne Mepham [1973] Director/Head of Financial Reporting; Graham Staples [1961] Director/Chartered Secretary; Nicholas Michael Taylor [1968] Director

Schroder Investment Management Limited
Incorporated: 7 March 1985 *Employees:* 2,071
Net Worth: £443,300,000 *Total Assets:* £787,299,968
Registered Office: 1 London Wall Place, London, EC2Y 5AU
Activities: Financial intermediation not elsewhere classified
Parent: Schroder International Holdings Limited
Officers: John Stewart Carmichael [1965] Director/Chief Technology Officer; Peter Harrison [1966] Director; Richard John Keers [1963] Director; Nicola Jane Richards [1966] Director/Global Head of Equities; John Alexander Troiano [1959] Director/Fund Manager

Schroder Japan Growth Fund PLC
Incorporated: 12 May 1994
Net Worth: £292,268,000 *Total Assets:* £334,451,008
Registered Office: 1 London Wall Place, London, EC2Y 5AU
Activities: Activities of investment trusts
Officers: Anja Maria Balfour [1963] Director; Alan Francis Gibbs [1953] Director; Richard Edgar Greer [1954] Director; Belinda Jane Richards [1958] Director

Schroder Pension Management Limited
Incorporated: 28 October 2005
Net Worth: £40,226,000 *Total Assets:* £10,618,825,728
Registered Office: 1 London Wall Place, London, EC2Y 5AU
Activities: Financial intermediation not elsewhere classified
Parent: Schroder International Holdings Limited
Officers: Graham Kenneth Aslet [1948] Director/Actuary; David James Heathcock [1975] Director/Head of Life Operations; Guy Henriques [1964] Director; Wayne Mepham [1973] Director/Head of Financial Reporting; Calum Thomson [1960] Director; Julian Walker-Hazell [1968] Director/Operations Manager; Derek John Wright [1954] Director

Schroder Private Assets Holdings Limited
Incorporated: 4 April 2017
Net Worth Deficit: £824,000 *Total Assets:* £142,330,000
Registered Office: 1 London Wall Place, London, EC2Y 5AU
Activities: Activities of financial services holding companies
Parent: Schroder Administration Limited
Officers: Tim McCann [1973] Director; Wayne Mepham [1973] Director; Graham Staples [1961] Director; Nicholas Michael Taylor [1968] Director

Schroder Unit Trusts Limited
Incorporated: 2 April 2001
Net Worth: £81,379,000 *Total Assets:* £279,406,016
Registered Office: 1 London Wall Place, London, EC2Y 5AU
Activities: Activities of unit trusts
Parent: Schroder International Holdings Limited
Officers: James Stephen Barker [1978] Portfolio Director; Paul James Chislett [1978] Director/Chartered Management Accountant; Guy Henriques [1964] Director; Philip Robert Middleton [1968] Director/Co-Head of UK Intermediary Business; Calum Thomson [1960] Director; Julian Walker-Hazell [1968] Director/Operations Manager; Howard Williams [1960] Director

Schroder Wealth Holdings Limited
Incorporated: 22 July 2015
Net Worth: £220,976,000 *Total Assets:* £221,148,992
Registered Office: 1 London Wall Place, London, EC2Y 5AU
Activities: Activities of financial services holding companies
Parent: Schroder Administration Limited
Officers: Tim McCann [1973] Director/Group Head of Tax; Wayne Mepham [1973] Director; Graham Staples [1961] Director; Nicholas Michael Taylor [1968] Director

Schroders PLC
Incorporated: 14 January 2000 *Employees:* 4,013
Net Worth: £3,471,000,064 *Total Assets:* £8,501,499,904
Registered Office: 1 London Wall Place, London, EC2Y 5AU
Activities: Activities of head offices
Officers: Graham Staples, Secretary; Robin William Turnbull Buchanan [1952] Business Advisor and Board Director; Sir Damon Marcus Buffini [1962] Director/Investor; Rhian Lynn Davies [1965] Director/Part-Time Senior Adviser; Michael William Romsey Dobson [1952] Director/Banker; Rakhi Goss-Custard [1974] Director [American]; Peter Harrison [1966] Director/Head of Investment; Richard John Keers [1963] Director/Accountant; Ian Graham King [1956] Director/Chief Executive; Philip Stephan Arnold Mallinckrodt [1962] Director/Banker [British/German]; Nichola Pease [1961] Director

Schweppes International Limited
Incorporated: 17 August 1923 *Employees:* 94
Net Worth: £357,152,096 *Total Assets:* £453,451,424
Registered Office: 7 Albemarle Street, London, W1S 4HQ
Activities: Manufacture of soft drinks; production of mineral waters and other bottled waters
Parent: Suntory Beverage & Food Limited
Officers: Patrick David Blake [1977] Finance Director [Irish]; Sylvie Bouvet Ep. Toole [1971] Director/Supply Operations Manager [French]; Diego de Blas Bravo [1963] Director/Chief Legal Officer [Spanish]; Louis-Francois Amand Gombert [1967] Director/Senior General Manager Global Finance [French]; Jaime Antonio Mussons Freixas [1961] Director/Chief Marketing Officer [Spanish]; Jonathan Mark Roberts [1966] Managing Director; Jennegien Willemina Schnieders [1967] Director/Legal Executive [Dutch]; Tetsu Tanaka [1967] Director/Chief of Staff to SBFE CEO [Japanese]

Scimco Limited
Incorporated: 31 January 1996
Net Worth Deficit: £8,989,000 *Total Assets:* £116,849,000
Registered Office: 33 Wigmore Street, London, W1U 1QX
Activities: Activities of other holding companies n.e.c.
Parent: Babcock Support Services (Investments) Limited
Officers: Sally Fiona Brooks [1966] Finance Director; Pieter Esbach [1962] Director; Iain Stuart Urquhart [1965] Director

SCMB Overseas Limited
Incorporated: 25 October 1983
Net Worth: £674,423,808 *Total Assets:* £680,016,128
Registered Office: 1 Basinghall Avenue, London, EC2V 5DD
Activities: Financial intermediation not elsewhere classified
Parent: Standard Chartered Holdings Limited
Officers: Paul Stuart Chambers [1967] Director/Chartered Accountant; Christopher John Daniels [1974] Director; Sandeep Singh Rai [1980] Director

SCMI Limited
Incorporated: 19 October 2012
Net Worth: £12,068,753 *Total Assets:* £402,256,832
Registered Office: Vintners' Place, 68 Upper Thames Street, London, EC4V 3BJ
Activities: Security and commodity contracts dealing activities
Parent: Sumitomo Corporation
Officers: Takuro Haga [1972] Director [Japanese]; Hideyuki Kambayashi [1974] Director [Japanese]; Hironobu Yamamura [1975] Director [Japanese]

SCOR UK Company Limited
Incorporated: 19 October 1977
Net Worth: £130,547,000 *Total Assets:* £1,422,754,048
Registered Office: 10 Lime Street, London, EC3M 7AA
Activities: Non-life insurance
Shareholders: SCOR Holding (UK) Ltd; SCOR (UK) Group Limited
Officers: Gillian Heather Phillips, Secretary; James Alexander Bayfield [1971] Director/Accountant; Thomas Rokeby Conyngham Corfield [1962] Director/Chief Underwriting Officer; Christian Delannes [1958] Director/Insurance Executive [French]; Peter Viktor Eckert [1945] Director/Consultant [Swiss]; Brian James George Hilton [1940] Director/Consultant; Stuart Forbes McMurdo [1971] Director [South African/British]; Malcolm Charles Newman [1958] Director/Chartered Accountant; Victor Yves Peignet [1957] Director [French]; Laurent Rousseau [1979] Director/Insurance [French]; Jane Fields Wicker-Miurin [1958] Director

SCOR Underwriting Limited
Incorporated: 1 October 2001
Net Worth: £3,254,000 *Total Assets:* £1,947,105,024
Registered Office: 10 Lime Street, London, EC3M 7AA
Activities: Non-life insurance
Parent: SCOR Global P & C SE
Officers: Charles Bartlett, Secretary; Charles James Bartlett [1982] Managing Director; James Alexander Bayfield [1971] Director/Chief Financial Officer; Christian Delannes [1958] Director/Insurance Executive [French]; Malcolm Charles Newman [1958] Director/Accountant; Sylvie Anne Van Viet [1961] Director/Head of Underwriting [French]

Scotiabank Europe PLC
Incorporated: 28 August 1964 *Employees:* 103
Net Worth: £1,395,699,968 *Total Assets:* £18,754,246,656
Registered Office: 201 Bishopsgate, London, EC2M 3NS
Activities: Banks
Parent: The Bank of Nova Scotia
Officers: Julian Nicholas James Rhys, Secretary; Julie Louise Currie [1974] Director; Philip Martin Cutts [1955] Director; Peter Heidinger [1963] Director [Canadian]; Fergus James Rupert McDonald [1964] Director; Philip Stephen Watson Smith [1966] Director/Banker [Canadian]; Kerry Madeline Spooner [1961] Director

The Scott Trust Limited
Incorporated: 24 September 2008
Net Worth: £971,299,968 *Total Assets:* £1,055,600,000
Registered Office: P O Box 68164, Kings Place, 90 York Way, London, N1P 2AP
Activities: Activities of head offices
Officers: Stephen John Godsell, Secretary; Emily Jane Bell [1965] Director/Professor; Alexander Graham [1953] Director; Catherine Alice Howarth [1974] Charity Director; David Adetayo Olusoga [1970] Director; David Skipwith Pemsel [1968] Director; Nils Martin Pratley [1967] Director/Journalist; Stuart Graham Proffitt [1961] Director/Book Publisher; Sir Anthony Michael Vaughan Salz [1950] Director; Vivian Luisa Schiller [1961] Director/Media Consultant [American]; Russell James Scott [1969] Director; Ole Jacob Sunde [1954] Director/Entrepreneur [Norwegian]; Katharine Sophie Viner [1971] Director/Journalist

Scottish & Newcastle India Limited
Incorporated: 10 April 1995
Net Worth: £107,743,000 *Total Assets:* £107,743,000
Registered Office: Elsley Court, 20-22 Great Titchfield Street, London, W1W 8BE
Activities: Non-trading company
Parent: Scottish & Newcastle Limited
Officers: David Michael Forde [1968] Managing Director [Irish]; Sean Michael Paterson [1982] Director/Accountant; Radovan Sikorsky [1967] Finance Director [Slovak]; Kelly Taylor-Welsh [1978] Director/Head of UK Tax

Scottish Sea Farms Limited
Incorporated: 10 July 1969 *Employees:* 428
Net Worth: £92,923,000 *Total Assets:* £147,022,000
Registered Office: Condor House, 10 St Paul's Churchyard, London, EC4M 8AL
Activities: Marine aquaculture
Officers: Dermot Anderson, Secretary; Henning Kolbj Beltestad [1968] Director [Norwegian]; James Francis Gallagher [1968] Managing Director; Leif Inge Nordhammer [1958] Director/Chairman Salmar AS [Norwegian]; John Rea [1965] Director/Production Manager; Helge Singelstad [1963] Director [Norwegian]; Gustave Witzoe [1953] Managing Director [Norwegian]

Scottish Widows Limited
Incorporated: 2 May 1996 *Employees:* 2,506
Previous: Clerical Medical Investment Group Limited
Net Worth: £4,752,999,936 *Total Assets:* £147,307,003,904
Registered Office: 25 Gresham Street, London, EC2V 7HN
Activities: Life insurance
Parent: Scottish Widows Group Limited
Officers: Joanne Margaret Jolly, Secretary; Andrea Margaret Blance [1964] Director; Kate Cheetham [1963] Director/Group General Counsel; Mark George Culmer [1962] Finance Director; Jane Elizabeth Mary Curtis [1960] Director; Michael Harris [1965] Director; John Francis Hylands [1951] Director; Antonio Lorenzo [1966] Director [Spanish]; Christopher John George Moulder [1958] Director; Sophie Jane O'Connor [1970] Director; Dr Jakob Pfaudler [1972] Community Banking Director [Austrian]; Nicholas Edward Tucker Prettejohn [1960] Director

SCP Acquisition Bidco Limited
Incorporated: 12 December 2014
Net Worth: £7,703,000 *Total Assets:* £107,581,000
Registered Office: 25 Kingly Street, London, W1B 5QB
Activities: Advertising agencies
Parent: SCP Acquisition Midco Limited
Officers: Tim James Bleakley [1965] Director/Chief Executive Officer; Stephen Zev Joseph [1980] Director/Chief Financial Officer

SCP Acquisition Topco Limited
Incorporated: 12 December 2014
Net Worth Deficit: £20,252,000 *Total Assets:* £148,703,008
Registered Office: 25 Kingly Street, London, W1B 5QB
Activities: Advertising agencies
Parent: SCP OCN Acquisition Lux S.A.R.L
Officers: Andrew McGregor Barron [1965] Director; Tim James Bleakley [1965] Director/Chief Executive Officer; Stephen Zev Joseph [1980] Director/Chief Financial Officer

SDN Limited
Incorporated: 24 January 1997 *Employees:* 2
Net Worth: £536,408,000 *Total Assets:* £546,171,008
Registered Office: 2 Waterhouse Square, 140 Holborn, London, EC1N 2AE
Activities: Television programme production activities
Parent: ITV Holdings (Cayman) Limited
Officers: Ross Appleton [1984] Director; Magnus Hugh Brooke [1971] Director; Timothy Luke Martin Cadbury [1982] Commercial Director

Seadrill Mexico UK Ltd.
Incorporated: 25 October 2013
Net Worth: £93,761,944 *Total Assets:* £450,155,232
Registered Office: 2nd Floor, Building 11, Chiswick Business Park, 566 Chiswick High Road, London, W4 5YS
Activities: Activities of head offices
Parent: Seadrill Limited
Officers: Ricardo Maldonado Yanez [1967] Director [Mexican]; Christian Whamond [1973] Director [Argentinian]; Per Winther Wullf [1960] Director [Danish]; Jon Olav Osthus [1953] Director [Norwegian]

Seadrill UK Ltd.
Incorporated: 18 March 2008 *Employees:* 2
Net Worth: £171,003,424 *Total Assets:* £272,841,344
Registered Office: 2nd Floor, Building 11, Chiswick Business Park, 566 Chiswick High Road, London, W4 5YS
Activities: Renting and leasing of construction and civil engineering machinery and equipment
Parent: Seadrill Rig Holding Company Limited
Officers: Neil Derek Gilliver [1965] Director/Accountant; Harald Thorstein [1979] Director/Business Development [Norwegian]

Searchmap Limited
Incorporated: 18 August 1999 *Employees:* 2
Net Worth: £97,206,000 *Total Assets:* £123,790,000
Registered Office: 29 Albemarle Street, London, W1S 4JA
Activities: Other letting and operating of own or leased real estate
Parent: A E Properties UK Limited
Officers: Bryan Bamberger, Secretary; Francois Xavier Graff [1963] Director/Jeweller; Nicholas Paine [1960] Director

Sears Limited
Incorporated: 15 February 1912
Net Worth: £409,400,000 *Total Assets:* £411,600,000
Registered Office: Third Floor, 86 Jermyn Street, London, SW1Y 6JD
Activities: Non-trading company
Parent: January Investments Limited
Officers: Philip Leslie Peters [1957] Director; Michael Seal [1948] Director/Chartered Accountant

SEC Lighting Services Trading Limited
Incorporated: 23 October 1996
Net Worth Deficit: £50,951,000 *Total Assets:* £378,683,008
Registered Office: 5th Floor, 120 Aldersgate Street, London, EC1A 4JQ
Activities: Electrical installation
Officers: David Thomas Adams, Secretary; Thomas Samuel Cunningham [1975] Director; Amit Rishi Jaysukh Thakrar [1987] Director

Sectormatch Limited
Incorporated: 24 September 1990 *Employees:* 182
Net Worth: £95,901,304 *Total Assets:* £117,013,464
Registered Office: 58 Rochester Row, Westminster, London, SW1P 1JU
Activities: Hotels and similar accommodation
Parent: Globalgrange Limited
Officers: Harpal Singh Matharu, Secretary; Harpal Singh Matharu [1956] Director/Executive; Raj Singh Matharu [1958] Director/Executive; Tejinderpal Singh Matharu [1960] Director/Hotelier

Secure Income REIT PLC
Incorporated: 24 January 2007
Net Worth: £860,577,024 *Total Assets:* £1,872,829,952
Registered Office: Cavendish House, 18 Cavendish Square, London, W1G 0PJ
Activities: Activities of head offices
Officers: Sandra Louise Gumm, Secretary/Chartered Accountant [Australian]; Philip Michael Brown [1960] Director; Leslie Jane Ferrar [1955] Director; Sandra Louise Gumm [1966] Director/Chartered Accountant [Australian]; Jonathan Lawrence Lane [1958] Director; Nicholas Mark Leslau [1959] Director/Chartered Surveyor; Ian Marcus [1959] Director; Martin Richard Moore [1956] Director

Securitas Services Holding UK Limited
Incorporated: 28 March 2006
Net Worth: £91,650,392 *Total Assets:* £133,834,496
Registered Office: St James House, 13 Kensington Square, London, W8 5HD
Activities: Activities of head offices
Parent: Securitas AB
Officers: John Joseph Collins [1958] Director/Accountant; Shaun William Kennedy [1976] Director; Brian Riis Nielsen [1966] Director/Country President [Danish]

Securitisation of Consumer Agreements Limited
Incorporated: 18 March 2016
Net Worth Deficit: £3,371,240 *Total Assets:* £124,123,120
Registered Office: 5th Floor, 6 St Andrew Street, London, EC4A 3AE
Activities: Other business support service activities n.e.c.
Parent: TMF Trustee Limited
Officers: Andrew Wallace [1971] Director/DCS, UK, Management

Sedgwick Morden Acquisitions
Incorporated: 12 May 1998
Previous: Lindsey Morden Acquisitions
Net Worth: £244,187,600 *Total Assets:* £355,240,480
Registered Office: 60 Fenchurch Street, London, EC3M 4AD
Activities: Activities of other holding companies n.e.c.
Parent: Sedgwick UK Holdings II Limited
Officers: Jonathan Sutton, Secretary; Domenick C. di Cicco [1963] Director [American]; Meera Odedra [1960] Finance Director; Jonathan Sutton [1969] Finance Director

Sedgwick Overseas Limited
Incorporated: 16 May 1989
Previous: Cunningham Group Overseas Limited
Net Worth: £258,117,008 *Total Assets:* £342,951,296
Registered Office: 60 Fenchurch Street, London, EC3M 4AD
Activities: Activities of other holding companies n.e.c.
Parent: Sedgwick Morden Acquisitions
Officers: Jonathan Sutton, Secretary; Domenick C. di Cicco [1963] Director [American]; Meera Odedra [1960] Finance Director; Jonathan Sutton [1969] Finance Director

Sedgwick UK Holdings II Limited
Incorporated: 4 December 2007
Previous: Cunningham Lindsey Holdings II (UK) Limited
Net Worth: £46,689,532 *Total Assets:* £562,665,344
Registered Office: 60 Fenchurch Street, London, EC3M 4AD
Activities: Activities of other holding companies n.e.c.
Parent: Sedgwick UK Holdings Limited
Officers: Jonathan Sutton, Secretary; Domenick C. di Cicco [1963] Director [American]; Meera Odedra [1960] Finance Director; Jonathan Sutton [1969] Finance Director

Sedgwick UK Holdings Limited
Incorporated: 4 December 2007
Previous: Cunningham Lindsey Holdings (UK) Limited
Net Worth: £187,772,464 *Total Assets:* £342,694,624
Registered Office: 60 Fenchurch Street, London, EC3M 4AD
Activities: Activities of other holding companies n.e.c.
Parent: CL Intermediate (UK) Limited
Officers: Jonathan Sutton, Secretary; Domenick C. di Cicco [1963] Director [American]; Meera Odedra [1960] Finance Director; Jonathan Sutton [1969] Finance Director

Segro Industrial Estates Limited
Incorporated: 31 October 1947
Net Worth: £244,636,000 *Total Assets:* £245,743,008
Registered Office: Cunard House, 15 Regent Street, London, SW1Y 4LR
Activities: Development of building projects
Parent: Segro Properties Limited
Officers: Elizabeth Ann Blease, Secretary; Andrew Stephen Gulliford [1962] Director/Chartered Surveyor; Alan Michael Holland [1974] Director; Gareth John Osborn [1962] Director; Ann Octavia Peters [1969] Director; Andrew John Pilsworth [1974] Director; Philip Anthony Redding [1968] Director

Segro Overseas Holdings Limited
Incorporated: 15 May 1972
Net Worth: £621,040,000 *Total Assets:* £791,814,016
Registered Office: Cunard House, 15 Regent Street, London, SW1Y 4LR
Activities: Renting and operating of Housing Association real estate
Parent: Segro Public Limited Company
Officers: Elizabeth Ann Blease, Secretary; Soumen Das [1976] Director; Ann Octavia Peters [1969] Director; Andrew John Pilsworth [1974] Director; David John Rivers Sleath [1961] Finance Director

Segro Properties Limited
Incorporated: 31 January 1948
Net Worth: £132,627,000 *Total Assets:* £729,344,000
Registered Office: Cunard House, 15 Regent Street, London, SW1Y 4LR
Activities: Development of building projects
Parent: Segro PLC
Officers: Elizabeth Ann Blease, Secretary; Andrew Stephen Gulliford [1962] Director/Chartered Surveyor; Alan Michael Holland [1974] Director; Gareth John Osborn [1962] Director/Chartered Surveyor; Ann Octavia Peters [1969] Director; Andrew John Pilsworth [1974] Director; Philip Anthony Redding [1968] Director

Segro Public Limited Company
Incorporated: 19 May 1920 *Employees:* 293
Net Worth: £5,585,399,808 *Total Assets:* £7,936,300,032
Registered Office: Cunard House, 15 Regent Street, London, SW1Y 4LR
Activities: Activities of real estate investment trusts
Officers: Elizabeth Ann Blease, Secretary; Mary Elizabeth Barnard [1966] Director; Susan Vivien Clayton [1957] Director; Generald Michael Nolan Corbett [1951] Director; Soumen Das [1976] Director; Carol Ann Fairweather [1961] Director; Christopher Charles Fisher [1953] Director; Andrew Stephen Gulliford [1962] Director/Chartered Surveyor; Martin Richard Moore [1956] Director; Philip Anthony Redding [1968] Director; David John Rivers Sleath [1961] Director; Douglas Russell Webb [1961] Director

SEI Investments (Europe) Ltd
Incorporated: 30 April 1999 *Employees:* 259
Net Worth: £87,699,000 *Total Assets:* £133,589,000
Registered Office: 1st Floor, Alphabeta, 14-18 Finsbury Square, London, EC2A 1BR
Activities: Other business support service activities n.e.c.
Parent: SEI Investments Company
Officers: Connie MacCurrach, Secretary; Patrick William Wynn Disney [1956] Director; William Michael Doran [1940] Director/Lawyer [American]; Robert Andrew Goldspink [1949] Director/Consultant; Ahsan Mallick [1977] Director/Lawyer General Counsel; Robert Allen Nesher [1946] Director/Business Executive [American]; Brett Stuart Powell Williams [1959] Director

Select Service Partner UK Limited
Incorporated: 25 January 2006 *Employees:* 9,035
Net Worth: £428,247,008 *Total Assets:* £540,833,984
Registered Office: 169 Euston Road, London, NW1 2AE
Activities: Take-away food shops and mobile food stands
Parent: SSP Financing UK Limited
Officers: Helen Byrne, Secretary; Neil Stephen Campbell [1974] Director; Miles Eric Collins [1966] Director/Chartered Accountant; Jonathan Owen Davies [1962] Director; Simon Smith [1972] Director

Selectuser Limited
Incorporated: 23 August 1999
Net Worth: £301,110,016 *Total Assets:* £823,937,984
Registered Office: York House, 45 Seymour Street, London, W1H 7JT
Activities: Non-trading company
Parent: Bunzl Overseas Holdings (No.2) Limited
Officers: Paul Nicholas Hussey, Secretary/Solicitor; Andrew James Ball [1963] Finance Director; Paul Nicholas Hussey [1959] Director/Solicitor; Brian Michael May [1964] Finance Director

Selene Holdings Limited
Incorporated: 5 October 2017
Net Worth: £88,047,000 *Total Assets:* £867,201,984
Registered Office: 41-43 Brook Street, Mayfair, London, W1K 4HJ
Activities: Activities of other holding companies n.e.c.
Officers: Fady Bakhos [1971] Director/Legal Counsel [French]; Liam Cunningham [1958] Director [Irish]

Selene Midco Limited
Incorporated: 5 October 2017
Net Worth: £116,796,000 *Total Assets:* £455,049,984
Registered Office: 41-43 Brook Street, Mayfair, London, W1K 4HJ
Activities: Activities of other holding companies n.e.c.
Parent: Selene Holdings Limited
Officers: Fady Bakhos [1971] Director/Legal Counsel [French]; Liam Cunningham [1958] Director [Irish]

Selfridges & Co. Limited
Incorporated: 2 February 1998
Net Worth: £113,000,000 *Total Assets:* £113,000,000
Registered Office: 400 Oxford Street, London, W1A 1AB
Activities: Other retail sale in non-specialised stores
Parent: Selfridges Holdings Limited
Officers: Sarah Hemsley, Secretary; Keith Down [1965] Finance Director; Paul Gerard Kelly [1952] Director/Chief Executive Officer [Irish]; Anne Pitcher [1956] Director; Matthew George Smith [1971] Finance Director; Alannah Elizabeth Weston [1972] Director/Self Employed Consultant [Canadian]; Hilary Weston [1942] Director [Canadian/Irish]; Willard Gordon Galen Weston [1940] Director [Canadian]; Willard Galen Garfield Weston [1972] Director [Canadian]

Selfridges Financing Limited
Incorporated: 7 December 2017
Net Worth: £726,000,000 *Total Assets:* £1,076,700,032
Registered Office: 400 Oxford Street, London, W1A 1AB
Activities: Financial intermediation not elsewhere classified
Officers: Sarah Hemsley, Secretary; Keith Down [1965] Finance Director; Paul Gerard Kelly [1952] Director [Irish]; Timothy Piers Chorley de Walton Reade [1969] Director; Matthew George Smith [1971] Finance Director

Selfridges Holdings Limited
Incorporated: 4 April 2003
Net Worth: £450,500,000 *Total Assets:* £450,700,000
Registered Office: 400 Oxford Street, London, W1A 1AB
Activities: Activities of head offices
Parent: SHEL Holdings Europe Limited
Officers: Sarah Hemsley, Secretary; Keith Down [1965] Finance Director; Norah Hanratty [1973] Director/Business Executive [Irish]; Paul Gerard Kelly [1952] Director [Irish]; Matthew George Smith [1971] Finance Director

Selfridges Properties Limited
Incorporated: 19 November 2003
Net Worth: £726,000,000 *Total Assets:* £1,423,299,968
Registered Office: 400 Oxford Street, London, W1A 1AB
Activities: Development of building projects
Officers: Sarah Hemsley, Secretary; Keith Down [1965] Finance Director; Paul Gerard Kelly [1952] Director/Chief Executive Officer [Irish]; Mr Tim Reade [1969] Director/Chartered Surveyor; Matthew George Smith [1971] Finance Director

Selfridges Retail Limited
Incorporated: 5 March 1908 *Employees:* 3,044
Net Worth: £422,700,000 *Total Assets:* £633,400,000
Registered Office: 400 Oxford Street, London, W1A 1AB
Activities: Other retail sale in non-specialised stores
Parent: Selfridges & Co. Limited
Officers: Sarah Hemsley, Secretary; Simon Forster [1964] Director/Retail; Sarah Hemsley [1976] Director/Company Secretary; Paul Gerard Kelly [1952] Chief Executive Director [Irish]; Anne Pitcher [1956] Director; Matthew George Smith [1971] Finance Director; Meave Wall [1973] Stores Director [Irish]

Selligent Holdings Limited
Incorporated: 6 July 2015 *Employees:* 401
Net Worth: £105,328,816 *Total Assets:* £141,117,888
Registered Office: Second Floor, 45 Folgate Street, London, E1 6GL
Activities: Activities of other holding companies n.e.c.
Officers: John Jospeh Hernandez [1967] Director [American]; Farouk Hussein [1986] Director/Private Equity [Canadian]; Richard Franklin Lawson [1971] Director/Private Equity [American]; Steven Leistner [1985] Director/Investment Professional [American]; Andre Louis Maurice Cyrille Lejeune [1966] Director [Belgian]; Alexander Rayden [1983] Director/Investment Banking

Seminole Hard Rock UK Limited
Incorporated: 7 February 2007 *Employees:* 15
Net Worth: £38,596,000 *Total Assets:* £281,200,992
Registered Office: Cannon Place, 78 Cannon Street, London, EC4N 6AF
Activities: Activities of head offices
Officers: Brian Learned Alexander [1971] Director/Attorney [American]; David Stuart Pellow [1976] Director/Area Vice President

Semperian (Community Health) Limited
Incorporated: 14 November 2006 *Employees:* 2
Net Worth Deficit: £14,156,887 *Total Assets:* £153,490,592
Registered Office: 4th Floor, 1 Gresham Street, London, EC2V 7BX
Activities: Other business support service activities n.e.c.
Parent: Semperian PPP Investment Partners Limited
Officers: Chris Burlton [1973] Director/Accountant; Jonathan Michael Simpson [1973] Director/Accountant

Semperian No.21 Limited
Incorporated: 9 May 2007 *Employees:* 2
Net Worth Deficit: £12,116,638 *Total Assets:* £174,434,896
Registered Office: 4th Floor, 1 Gresham Street, London, EC2V 7BX
Activities: Other business support service activities n.e.c.
Parent: Semperian PPP Investment Partners No.2 Limited
Officers: Chris Burlton [1973] Director/Accountant; Jonathan Michael Simpson [1973] Director/Accountant

Semperian PPP Investment Partners Group Limited
Incorporated: 4 September 2009
Net Worth: £10,420,329 *Total Assets:* £528,796,896
Registered Office: 4th Floor, 1 Gresham Street, London, EC2V 7BX
Activities: Other business support service activities n.e.c.
Parent: Semperian PPP Investment Partners Holdings Limited
Officers: Susan Taberner, Secretary; Colin John Anderson [1963] Director/Solicitor; Alan Edward Birch [1970] Director; Andrew Charles Mutch Rhodes [1970] Director; Jonathan Michael Simpson [1973] Director/Accountant

Semperian PPP Investment Partners Limited
Incorporated: 7 August 2007
Net Worth Deficit: £306,638,016 *Total Assets:* £1,097,780,992
Registered Office: 4th Floor, 1 Gresham Street, London, EC2V 7BX
Activities: Other business support service activities n.e.c.
Parent: Semperian PPP Investment Partners Group Limited
Officers: Susan Taberner, Secretary; Alan Edward Birch [1970] Director; Andrew Charles Mutch Rhodes [1970] Director; Jonathan Michael Simpson [1973] Director/Accountant

Semperian PPP Investment Partners No.2 Limited
Incorporated: 17 May 2007 *Employees:* 3
Net Worth: £116,082,208 *Total Assets:* £821,650,816
Registered Office: 4th Floor, 1 Gresham Street, London, EC2V 7BX
Activities: Other business support service activities n.e.c.
Parent: Semperian PPP Investment Partners Limited
Officers: Alan Edward Birch [1970] Director; Andrew Charles Mutch Rhodes [1970] Director; Jonathan Michael Simpson [1973] Director/Accountant

Semperian Senior Funding PLC
Incorporated: 19 October 2007
Net Worth Deficit: £12,187,178 *Total Assets:* £209,622,752
Registered Office: 35 Great St Helens, London, EC3A 6AP
Activities: Financial intermediation not elsewhere classified
Parent: Intertrust Corporate Services Limited
Officers: Paivi Helena Whitaker [1963] Director/Chartered Secretary [Finnish]

Sensburg Finance Ltd
Incorporated: 22 February 2005
Net Worth Deficit: £84,878,808 *Total Assets:* £152,771,504
Registered Office: Langley House, Park Road, London, N2 8EY
Activities: Other business support service activities n.e.c.
Major Shareholder: Jean Francois Maurice Cordemans
Officers: Michael Thomas Gordon [1954] Director

Sensis Holding II Limited
Incorporated: 14 August 2017
Net Worth: £1,034,139 *Total Assets:* £196,972,896
Registered Office: 100 New Bridge Street, London, EC4V 6JA
Activities: Activities of other holding companies n.e.c.
Parent: Sensis Holding Limited
Officers: Eva Monica Kalawski, Secretary; Ian Michael Stuart Downie [1949] Director/Executive; Eva Monica Kalawski [1955] Director/Executive [American]; Mary Ann Sigler [1954] Director/Executive [American]

Sensis Holding Limited
Incorporated: 13 November 2015 *Employees:* 1,170
Net Worth Deficit: £29,238,672 *Total Assets:* £307,040,544
Registered Office: 100 New Bridge Street, London, EC4V 6JA
Activities: Activities of other holding companies n.e.c.
Officers: Eva Monica Kalawski, Secretary; Ian Michael Stuart Downie [1949] Director/Finance Executive; Eva Monica Kalawski [1955] Director/Executive [American]; Mary Ann Sigler [1954] Director [American]

Seven Capital PLC
Incorporated: 7 September 2009 *Employees:* 13
Net Worth: £16,289,509 *Total Assets:* £217,924,528
Registered Office: 97 Park Lane, Mayfair, London, W1K 7TG
Activities: Buying and selling of own real estate
Major Shareholder: Balbinder Singh Sohal
Officers: Balbinder Singh Sohal, Secretary; Philip John Carlin [1978] Director/Chartered Surveyor; Neil Martin [1972] Director; Damien Anthony Siviter [1978] Director; Balbinder Singh Sohal [1975] Director

Sextant Consolidated Limited
Incorporated: 10 February 2014
Net Worth: £195,959,968 *Total Assets:* £195,960,176
Registered Office: 3rd Floor, 14 Hanover Street, Mayfair, London, W1S 1YH
Activities: Activities of other holding companies n.e.c.
Major Shareholder: Vincenzo Bianchi
Officers: Vincenzo Bianchi [1958] Director [Italian]; Philip Lawrence [1953] Director; Marco Rossi [1964] Director [Italian]

SFP Holdings Limited
Incorporated: 15 January 2018
Net Worth: £726,000,000 *Total Assets:* £1,423,500,032
Registered Office: 400 Oxford Street, London, W1A 1AB
Activities: Activities of other holding companies n.e.c.
Officers: Sarah Hemsley, Secretary; Keith Down [1965] Finance Director; Paul Gerard Kelly [1952] Director [Irish]; Timothy Piers Chorley de Walton Reade [1969] Director; Matthew George Smith [1971] Finance Director

SG (Maritime) Leasing Limited
Incorporated: 16 July 2001
Previous: RBSSAF (26) Limited
Net Worth: £2,419,299 *Total Assets:* £207,173,008
Registered Office: c/o Group Legal, SG House, 41 Tower Hill, London, EC3N 4SG
Activities: Financial leasing
Parent: Societe Generale
Officers: Catherine Marie Madeleine Balinska-Jundzill, Secretary; Stuart Donald Cook [1964] Director/Banker; Christopher Alan Hastings [1969] Director/Banker; Neill Charles Proudfoot [1974] Director/Banker; Paul Shields [1982] Director/Solicitor; Lindsay Ginnette Sides [1976] Director/Solicitor

SG Kleinwort Hambros Bank Limited
Incorporated: 16 October 1969 *Employees:* 447
Previous: SG Hambros Bank Limited
Net Worth: £420,905,984 *Total Assets:* £2,812,984,064
Registered Office: 5th Floor, 8 St James's Square, London, SW1Y 4JU
Activities: Administration of financial markets
Parent: SG Kleinwort Hambros Limited
Officers: Kiran Singh, Secretary; Eric Edmund Barnett [1961] Director/Banker; Stuart William Barnett [1951] Director/Chartered Accountant; Gabrielle Alice Branson [1968] Director/Lawyer; Mouhammed Choukier [1977] Director/Deputy CEO and CIO; Anne Shirley Ewing [1955] Independent Non-Executive Director; Xavier Philippe Lofficial [1972] Director [French]; John Whitaker Maitland [1961] Director/Private Banker; Jean-Francois Mazaud [1967] Director/Banker [French]; Oliver Duplan Meredith [1968] Director/Banker; Michael Peter Newman [1961] Director; Emma Victoria Perez [1970] Director; Sadia Brigitte Ricke [1970] Director [French]; Konstantin Nikolaus Graf Von Schweinitz [1961] Director [German]

SG Kleinwort Hambros Limited
Incorporated: 24 November 1997
Previous: SG Hambros Limited
Net Worth: £506,212,960 *Total Assets:* £506,212,960
Registered Office: 5th Floor, 8 St James's Square, London, SW1Y 4JU
Activities: Financial intermediation not elsewhere classified
Parent: Societe Generale SA
Officers: Kiran Singh, Secretary; John Whitaker Maitland [1961] Director/Private Banker; Jean-Francois Alain Mazaud [1967] Director/Banker [French]; Oliver Duplan Meredith [1968] Financial Director

SG Leasing (Gems) Limited
Incorporated: 9 February 2004
Previous: RBSSAF (19) Limited
Net Worth: £2,569,316 *Total Assets:* £375,521,312
Registered Office: c/o Group Legal SG House, 41 Tower Hill, London, EC3N 4SG
Activities: Financial leasing
Parent: Societe Generale
Officers: Catherine Marie Madeleine Balinska-Jundzill, Secretary; Stuart Donald Cook [1964] Director/Banker; Nicholas Michael Dent [1965] Director/Banker; Stephen Lethbridge Fowler [1969] Director/Banker; Neill Charles Proudfoot [1974] Director/Banker; Paul Shields [1982] Director/Solicitor; Lindsay Ginnette Sides [1976] Director/Solicitor

SG Leasing (March) Limited
Incorporated: 25 September 1963
Net Worth: £16,695,071 *Total Assets:* £5,237,285,376
Registered Office: SG House, 41 Tower Hill, London, EC3N 4SG
Activities: Financial leasing
Parent: Societe Generale Investments (U.K.) Limited
Officers: Catherine Marie Madeleine Balinska-Jundzill, Secretary; Stuart Donald Cook [1964] Director/Banker; Nicholas Michael Dent [1965] Director/Chartered Accountant; Stephen Lethbridge Fowler [1969] Director/Banker; Paul Shields [1982] Director/Solicitor; Lindsay Ginnette Sides [1976] Director/Solicitor

SGO Corporation Limited
Incorporated: 23 December 2010 *Employees:* 448
Net Worth: £97,212,296 *Total Assets:* £124,794,144
Registered Office: 88 Baker Street, London, W1U 6TQ
Activities: Activities of head offices
Officers: David Charles Melville, Secretary; Sir Nigel Graham Knowles [1956] Director; George Mark Lord Malloch-Brown [1953] Director/Consultant; Antonio Jose Mugica Rivero [1974] Director/Smartmatic Group CEO [Venezuelan]; Roger Alejandro Pinate Martinez [1975] Director [Venezuelan]

Shaftesbury AV Investment Limited
Incorporated: 8 January 2015
Net Worth: £287,864,992 *Total Assets:* £287,864,992
Registered Office: 22 Ganton Street, London, W1F 7FD
Activities: Other letting and operating of own or leased real estate
Parent: Shaftesbury PLC
Officers: Penelope Ruth Thomas, Secretary; Brian Bickell [1954] Director/Chief Executive; Simon John Quayle [1958] Director/Chartered Surveyor; Christopher Peter Alan Ward [1968] Director/Chartered Accountant; Thomas James Chisnell Welton [1961] Director/Chartered Surveyor

Shaftesbury AV Limited
Incorporated: 8 January 2015
Net Worth: £472,560,000 *Total Assets:* £745,068,992
Registered Office: 22 Ganton Street, Carnaby, London, W1F 7FD
Activities: Other letting and operating of own or leased real estate
Parent: Shaftesbury AV Investment Limited
Officers: Penelope Ruth Thomas, Secretary; Brian Bickell [1954] Director/Chief Executive; Simon John Quayle [1958] Director/Chartered Surveyor; Christopher Peter Alan Ward [1968] Director/Chartered Accountant; Thomas James Chisnell Welton [1961] Director/Chartered Surveyor

Shaftesbury Carnaby PLC
Incorporated: 18 July 1986
Previous: Shaftesbury Carnaby Limited
Net Worth: £424,014,016 *Total Assets:* £713,144,000
Registered Office: 22 Ganton Street, Carnaby, London, W1F 7FD
Activities: Renting and operating of Housing Association real estate
Parent: Shaftesbury PLC
Officers: Penelope Ruth Thomas, Secretary; Brian Bickell [1954] Director/Chartered Accountant; Simon John Quayle [1958] Director/Chartered Surveyor; Christopher Peter Alan Ward [1968] Finance Director; Thomas James Chisnell Welton [1961] Director/Chartered Surveyor

Shaftesbury Chinatown PLC
Incorporated: 22 January 1988
Previous: Shaftesbury Chinatown Limited
Net Worth: £280,128,992 *Total Assets:* £572,806,976
Registered Office: 22 Ganton Street, Carnaby, London, W1F 7FD
Activities: Renting and operating of Housing Association real estate
Parent: Shaftesbury PLC
Officers: Penelope Ruth Thomas, Secretary; Brian Bickell [1954] Director/Chartered Accountant; Simon John Quayle [1958] Director/Chartered Surveyor; Christopher Peter Alan Ward [1968] Finance Director; Thomas James Chisnell Welton [1961] Director/Chartered Surveyor

Shaftesbury CL Investment Limited
Incorporated: 13 December 2013
Net Worth: £220,000,000 *Total Assets:* £220,000,096
Registered Office: 22 Ganton Street, Carnaby, London, W1F 7FD
Activities: Other letting and operating of own or leased real estate
Parent: Shaftesbury PLC
Officers: Penelope Ruth Thomas, Secretary; Brian Bickell [1954] Director/Chartered Accountant; Simon John Quayle [1958] Director/Chartered Surveyor; Christopher Peter Alan Ward [1968] Finance Director; Thomas James Chisnell Welton [1961] Director/Chartered Surveyor

Shaftesbury CL Limited
Incorporated: 17 August 2004
Net Worth: £415,911,008 *Total Assets:* £573,478,016
Registered Office: 22 Ganton Street, Carnaby, London, W1F 7FD
Activities: Non-trading company
Parent: Shaftesbury CL Investment Limited
Officers: Penelope Ruth Thomas, Secretary; Brian Bickell [1954] Director/Chartered Accountant; Simon John Quayle [1958] Director/Chartered Surveyor; Christopher Peter Alan Ward [1968] Finance Director; Thomas James Chisnell Welton [1961] Director/Chartered Surveyor

Shaftesbury Covent Garden Limited
Incorporated: 2 February 1996
Net Worth: £862,531,008 *Total Assets:* £870,398,016
Registered Office: 22 Ganton Street, Carnaby, London, W1F 7FD
Activities: Development of building projects
Parent: Shaftesbury PLC
Officers: Penelope Ruth Thomas, Secretary; Brian Bickell [1954] Director/Chartered Accountant; Simon John Quayle [1958] Director/Chartered Surveyor; Christopher Peter Alan Ward [1968] Finance Director; Thomas James Chisnell Welton [1961] Director/Chartered Surveyor

Shaftesbury PLC
Incorporated: 13 March 1986 *Employees:* 30
Net Worth: £3,032,999,936 *Total Assets:* £4,022,400,000
Registered Office: 22 Ganton Street, Carnaby, London, W1F 7FD
Activities: Buying and selling of own real estate
Officers: Penelope Ruth Thomas, Secretary; Richard John Akers [1961] Director; Brian Bickell [1954] Director/Chartered Accountant; Jill Caroline Little [1953] Retail Director; Dermot Colin Anthony Mathias [1949] Director; Jonathan Clive Nicholls [1957] Director; Simon John Quayle [1958] Director/Chartered Surveyor; Jennelle Lisa Tilling [1969] Director [Australian]; Sally Elizabeth Walden [1959] Director; Christopher Peter Alan Ward [1968] Finance Director; Thomas James Chisnell Welton [1961] Director/Chartered Surveyor

Shaftesbury Soho Limited
Incorporated: 19 November 2004
Net Worth: £270,753,984 *Total Assets:* £284,689,984
Registered Office: 22 Ganton Street, Carnaby, London, W1F 7FD
Activities: Non-trading company
Parent: Shaftesbury PLC
Officers: Penelope Ruth Thomas, Secretary; Brian Bickell [1954] Director/Chartered Accountant; Simon John Quayle [1958] Director/Chartered Surveyor; Christopher Peter Alan Ward [1968] Finance Director; Thomas James Chisnell Welton [1961] Director/Chartered Surveyor

Shake UK Newco Limited
Incorporated: 19 April 2013 *Employees:* 3
Net Worth: £101,050,968 *Total Assets:* £101,374,040
Registered Office: 10 Chiswick Park, 566 Chiswick High Road, London, W4 5XS
Activities: Activities of other holding companies n.e.c.
Parent: Vue International Bidco PLC
Officers: Stephen Jeremy Knibbs [1961] Director/Chief Operating Officer; Alan Ewart McNair [1955] Director/Chief Financial Officer; James Timothy Richards [1959] Director/Chief Executive Officer

Shams Maan Solar UK Limited
Incorporated: 27 May 2014
Net Worth: £17,126,160 *Total Assets:* £123,360,920
Registered Office: Mid City Place, 71 High Holborn, London, WC1V 6BA
Activities: Production of electricity
Shareholders: The State of Qatar; Jordan Energy Investment 2 Limited; Kawar Solar Investments Limited
Officers: Hussam Jehad Abounahia [1965] Director/Senior Advisor [American]; Khalid Mohd Jolo [1973] Director/Chief Executive [Qatari]; Karim Tawfiq Amin Kawar [1966] Director/Business Owner [Jordanian]; Rudain Tawfiq Kawar [1964] Director/Business Owner [Jordanian]; Yukinori Kodaira [1967] Director [Japanese]; Keiichi Suzuki [1969] Director/Chief Executive [Japanese]

Shanti Hospitality Group Limited
Incorporated: 11 May 2004 *Employees:* 6
Net Worth: £6,767,679 *Total Assets:* £143,324,400
Registered Office: 23 Buckingham Gate, London, SW1E 6LB
Activities: Hotels and similar accommodation
Officers: Satyabhama Pudaruth, Secretary/Compliance Officer [Mauritian]; Bhanu Choudhrie [1978] Director; Dhairya Choudhrie [1982] Director [Indian]; Antoine Georges Corinthios [1947] Director [American]; Sumant Kapur [1952] Director; Corine Montepeque [1968] Business Development Director [Singaporean]; Cherian Padinjarethalakal Thomas [1959] Director

SHC Holdings Limited
Incorporated: 31 October 2001
Net Worth: £504,623,008 *Total Assets:* £546,337,984
Registered Office: 3 Dorset Rise, London, EC4Y 8EN
Activities: Hospital activities
Parent: Spire Healthcare (Holdings) Limited
Officers: Daniel Francis Toner, Secretary; Justinian Joseph Ash [1965] Director/Chief Executive Officer; Peter James Corfield [1971] Director/Chief Commercial Officer; Jitesh Himatlal Sodha [1968] Director/Chief Financial Officer; Daniel Francis Toner [1968] Director/Solicitor

SHEL Holdings Europe Limited
Incorporated: 27 October 2011 *Employees:* 7,313
Net Worth: £1,347,299,968 *Total Assets:* £2,301,700,096
Registered Office: 103 Wigmore Street, London, W1U 1QS
Activities: Activities of head offices
Officers: Emma Howes, Secretary; Keith Down [1965] Finance Director; Norah Hanratty [1973] Director/Business Executive [Irish]; Paul Gerard Kelly [1952] Director/Chief Executive Officer [Irish]

Sheldon Euro Investments 2 Limited
Incorporated: 28 July 2011
Net Worth: £3,546,645,504 *Total Assets:* £3,546,684,672
Registered Office: 3 Sheldon Square, Paddington, London, W2 6PX
Activities: Other business support service activities n.e.c.
Parent: Sheldon Holdings Limited
Officers: Paul Moore, Secretary; Jean-Noel Hughes Roger Groleau [1974] Director [French]; Paul Anthony Moore [1970] Director/Company Secretary

Sheldon Holdings Limited
Incorporated: 22 February 1993
Net Worth: £4,436,802,048 *Total Assets:* £8,861,050,880
Registered Office: 3 Sheldon Square, Paddington, London, W2 6PX
Activities: Activities of head offices
Parent: Kingfisher Holdings Limited
Officers: Paul Moore, Secretary; Jean-Noel Hughes Roger Groleau [1974] Director [French]; Paul Anthony Moore [1970] Director/Company Secretary

Sheldon Poland Investments Limited
Incorporated: 19 February 2013
Net Worth: £479,888,992 *Total Assets:* £480,404,000
Registered Office: 3 Sheldon Square, Paddington, London, W2 6PX
Activities: Non-trading company
Officers: Paul Moore, Secretary; Jean-Noel Hughes Roger Groleau [1974] Director [French]; Paul Anthony Moore [1970] Director/Company Secretary

Sheldon Sterling Investments Limited
Incorporated: 3 May 2001
Net Worth: £1,326,910,976 *Total Assets:* £1,328,867,968
Registered Office: 3 Sheldon Square, Paddington, London, W2 6PX
Activities: Other business support service activities n.e.c.
Officers: Paul Moore, Secretary; Jean-Noel Hughes Roger Groleau [1974] Director [French]; Paul Anthony Moore [1970] Director/Company Secretary

Shell Aviation Limited
Incorporated: 12 August 1997
Net Worth: £3,776,738 *Total Assets:* £343,973,792
Registered Office: Shell Centre, London, SE1 7NA
Activities: Agents involved in the sale of fuels, ores, metals and industrial chemicals
Parent: The Shell Petroleum Company Limited
Officers: Anne Anderson [1969] Director [American]; Thomas de Boer [1975] Director/General Manager, Aviation [Dutch]; Adam Richard Harrison [1969] Director/Oil Company Executive; Neil John Justice [1979] Director/Global Finance Manager, Aviation

Shell Caribbean Investments Limited
Incorporated: 17 December 2001
Net Worth: £141,053,856 *Total Assets:* £141,664,784
Registered Office: Shell Centre, York Road, London, SE1 7NA
Activities: Other business support service activities n.e.c.
Parent: Shell Overseas Holdings Limited
Officers: Mark Gallagher [1959] Director/General Manager; Guus Greve [1964] Director/VP [Dutch]

Shell Chemicals U.K. Limited
Incorporated: 28 March 1946
Net Worth: £111,375,000 *Total Assets:* £178,708,000
Registered Office: Shell Centre, London, SE1 7NA
Activities: Manufacture of other organic basic chemicals
Parent: Shell Holdings (U.K.) Limited
Officers: James Bell [1979] Director/Finance Manager; Thierry Capelle [1963] Director/GM New Business Development [French]; Colin Bruce McKendrick [1958] Director/General Manager; David Bryan Topliffe [1959] Director/Oil Company Executive

Shell China Exploration and Production Company Limited
Incorporated: 9 May 1974 *Employees:* 254
Net Worth: £542,902,208 *Total Assets:* £606,241,920
Registered Office: Shell Centre, London, SE1 7NA
Activities: Extraction of crude petroleum
Shareholders: B.V. Dordtsche Petroleum Maatschappij; Shell China Holding GmbH
Officers: Peng Li, Secretary; Kim Elan Code [1965] Managing Director [Canadian]; Robin Anne Grouette [1974] Director/Oil Company Executive [Canadian]; Hong Zhang [1974] Director/Country Finance Manager China; Xinsheng Zhang [1961] Director/Chief Executive [Canadian]

Shell Clair UK Limited
Incorporated: 18 December 2009
Net Worth: £400,512,992 *Total Assets:* £1,279,323,008
Registered Office: Shell Centre, London, SE1 7NA
Activities: Extraction of crude petroleum
Parent: Enterprise Oil Limited
Officers: Gary James Archibald [1963] Director/Oil Company Executive; Marianne Wold Eide [1969] Director/Oil Company Executive [Norwegian]; Howard Edwin Jones [1978] Director/Oil Company Executive; Shannon Lorraine Ouellette [1969] Director/Oil Company Executive [Canadian]

The Shell Company of Thailand Limited
Incorporated: 11 August 1913 *Employees:* 493
Net Worth: £256,201,824 *Total Assets:* £668,028,480
Registered Office: Shell Centre, London, SE1 7NA
Activities: Wholesale of other fuels and related products
Parent: Shell Overseas Holdings Limited
Officers: Asada Harinsuit [1961] Director/Oil Company Executive [Thai]; Ornuthai Na Chiangmai [1970] Director/Businesswoman [Thai]; Chanida Pincharoen [1972] Director/Businessman [Thai]; Panun Prachuabmoh [1963] Director/Oil Company Executive [Thai]; Veethara Trakulboon [1974] Director/Businesswoman [Thai]

Shell Company of The Philippines Limited (The)
Incorporated: 30 January 1914
Net Worth: £129,391,000 *Total Assets:* £159,611,008
Registered Office: Shell Centre, London, SE1 7NA
Activities: Other letting and operating of own or leased real estate
Parent: The Shell Petroleum Company Limited
Officers: Erwin Reroma Orocio, Secretary; Nina Perpetua Datu Aguas [1952] Director/Insurance Co. Executive [Filipino]; Ramon Damasco Del Rosario [1959] Director/Oil Company Executive [Filipino]; Dennis Gamab [1965] Director/Oil Company Executive [Filipino]; Cesar Grospe Romero [1965] Director/Oil Company Executive [Filipino]; Anthony Lawrence Dadios Yam [1964] Director/Oil Company Executive [Filipino]; Fernando de Ayala Zobel [1960] Director/Business Executive [Filipino]

Shell Energy Europe Limited
Incorporated: 19 February 2001
Net Worth: £1,024,603,712 *Total Assets:* £3,093,540,352
Registered Office: Shell Centre, London, SE1 7NA
Activities: Trade of electricity
Parent: Shell Trading International Limited
Officers: Matthew David Griffiths, Secretary; Sharon Liow [1974] Director/Chartered Accountant [Malaysian]; Herman Johan Stinis [1964] Director/Oil Company Executive [Dutch]; David William Wells [1960] Director/Oil Company Executive

Shell Energy Investments Limited
Incorporated: 5 December 2002
Net Worth: £11,098,505,216 *Total Assets:* £11,099,362,304
Registered Office: Shell Centre, London, SE1 7NA
Activities: Activities of head offices
Parent: Shell Overseas Holdings Limited
Officers: Gary James Archibald [1963] Director/Oil Company Executive; Frances Hinden [1968] Director/Oil Company Executive; Lindsey Jane Ritchie [1972] Director/Tax Advisor

Shell EP Offshore Ventures Limited
Incorporated: 26 November 1982
Net Worth: £404,700,000 *Total Assets:* £1,743,800,064
Registered Office: Shell Centre, London, SE1 7NA
Activities: Extraction of crude petroleum
Parent: Enterprise Oil Limited
Officers: Gary James Archibald [1963] Director/Oil Company Executive; Marianne Wold Eide [1969] Director/Oil Company Executive [Norwegian]; Howard Edwin Jones [1978] Director/Oil Company Executive; Olivier Marie Charles Lazare [1960] Director/Oil Company Executive [French]; Shannon Lorraine Ouellette [1969] Director/Oil Company Executive [Canadian]

Shell Exploration and Production Tanzania Limited
Incorporated: 25 January 2002 *Employees:* 31
Previous: BG Tanzania Limited
Net Worth: £846,927,872 *Total Assets:* £912,468,480
Registered Office: Shell Centre, London, SE1 7NA
Activities: Non-trading company
Parent: BG International Limited
Officers: Marc Den Hartog [1960] Director/Manager [Dutch]; Deepak Khosla [1970] Director/Chartered Accountant; Dirk Nevelsteen [1967] Director/General Manager Commercial [Belgian]; Jonathan Robert Peachey [1965] Director/General Manager, Exploration

Shell Foundation
Incorporated: 31 May 2000 *Employees:* 19
Net Worth: £423,239,296 *Total Assets:* £446,822,048
Registered Office: Shell Centre, London, SE1 7NA
Activities: Activities of other membership organisations n.e.c.
Officers: Malcolm Arthur Brinded [1953] Director/Oil Company Executive; Andrew Brown [1962] Director/Oil Company Executive; Diana Lisa Carney [1965] Director/Economist; Alice Georgina Chapple [1964] Director/Consultant; Professor Margaret Jean Blick Kigozi [1950] Director/Entrepreneur [Ugandan]; Gail Alfreda Klintworth [1963] Business Director [Irish]; Sinead Caitlin Lynch [1971] Director/Oil Company Executive [Irish]; Maarten Wetselaar [1968] Director/Oil Company Executive [Dutch]

Shell Gas Holdings (Malaysia) Limited
Incorporated: 1 July 2002
Net Worth: £208,947,248 *Total Assets:* £244,753,920
Registered Office: Shell Centre, London, SE1 7NA
Activities: Activities of head offices
Parent: Shell U.K. Limited
Officers: Michael James Dawson [1980] Director/Assistant Treasurer; Deepak Khosla [1970] Director/Chartered Accountant

Shell Hasdrubal Limited
Incorporated: 7 August 2007
Previous: BG Hasdrubal Limited
Net Worth: £195,052,288 *Total Assets:* £561,027,392
Registered Office: Shell Centre, London, SE1 7NA
Activities: Extraction of crude petroleum
Parent: Shell Tunisia Upstream Limited
Officers: Khaled Kacem [1969] Director [Tunisian]; Raed Hamade Karame [1974] Director/Oil Company Executive [Venezuelan]; Rozimi Bin Abdul Rahman [1977] Director/Oil Company Executive; Mark Kenneth Tough [1975] Director/Oil Company Executive

Shell Holdings (U.K.) Limited
Incorporated: 17 March 1980
Net Worth: £2,269,499,904 *Total Assets:* £3,559,500,032
Registered Office: Shell Centre, London, SE1 7NA
Activities: Activities of head offices
Parent: The Shell Petroleum Company Limited
Officers: Sarah Joanne Judd [1978] Director/Solicitor; Steven Robert Phimister [1969] Director/Oil Company Executive

Shell International Limited
Incorporated: 29 June 1995 *Employees:* 1,019
Net Worth: £36,482,000 *Total Assets:* £388,148,992
Registered Office: Shell Centre, London, SE1 7NA
Activities: Other business support service activities n.e.c.
Parent: The Shell Petroleum Company Limited
Officers: Simon Alan Constant-Glemas [1969] Director/Oil Company Executive; Frances Hinden [1968] Director/Oil Company Executive; Sinead Caitlin Lynch [1971] Director/Oil Company Executive [Irish]; Alan Daniel McLean [1966] Director/Oil Company Executive; Russell Leslie O'Brien [1974] Director/Oil Company Executive; Martinus Jacobus Ten Brink [1960] Director/Oil Company Executive [Dutch]

Shell International Petroleum Company Limited
Incorporated: 16 February 1959 *Employees:* 870
Net Worth: £316,100,000 *Total Assets:* £771,200,000
Registered Office: Shell Centre, London, SE1 7NA
Activities: Other business support service activities n.e.c.
Parent: The Shell Petroleum Company Limited
Officers: Martin Edward Bambridge [1962] Director/Lawyer; Bjorn Alexander Fermin [1962] Director/Oil Company Executive [Dutch]; Huibert Hans Vigeveno [1969] Director/Executive at Royal Dutch Shell [Dutch]

Shell International Trading and Shipping Company Limited
Incorporated: 26 October 1953 *Employees:* 862
Net Worth: £222,377,568 *Total Assets:* £554,585,280
Registered Office: 80 Strand, London, WC2R 0ZA
Activities: Wholesale of petroleum and petroleum products
Parent: The Shell Petroleum Company Limited
Officers: Philippa Alice May Bounds, Secretary; Jacek Jan Dziembaj [1968] Director/Oil Company Executive [Polish]; Grahaeme Henderson [1954] Director/Oil Company Executive; Alison Ayodele Henwood [1965] Director/Oil Company Executive; Mark Quartermain [1961] Director/Oil Company Executive; Andrew James Smith [1964] Director [Australian]; David William Wells [1960] Director/Oil Company Executive

Shell Malaysia Limited
Incorporated: 28 February 1911 *Employees:* 90
Net Worth: £12,181,886 *Total Assets:* £887,786,304
Registered Office: Shell Centre, London, SE1 7NA
Activities: Other business support service activities n.e.c.
Parent: Shell Overseas Holdings Limited
Officers: Madam Yit Chan Tai, Secretary; Yuen Ling Tai, Secretary; Shairan Huzani Husain [1968] Director/Oil Company Executive [Malaysian]; Iain John Lo [1961] Director/Oil Company Executive [Malaysian]; Mohammad Hilmi Yusof [1975] Director/General Manager [Malaysian]

Shell Overseas Holdings Limited
Incorporated: 30 December 1957
Net Worth: £3,164,853,504 *Total Assets:* £23,419,246,592
Registered Office: Shell Centre, London, SE1 7NA
Activities: Activities of head offices
Parent: The Shell Petroleum Company Limited
Officers: Michael John Ashworth [1961] Director/Oil Company Executive; Bjorn Alexander Fermin [1962] Director/Oil Company Executive [Dutch]; Alan Daniel McLean [1966] Director/Oil Company Executive; Russell Leslie O'Brien [1974] Director/Oil Company Executive; Martinus Jacobus Ten Brink [1960] Director/Oil Company Executive [Dutch]

Shell Pension Reserve Company (UK) Limited
Incorporated: 19 February 2014
Net Worth: £321,690,560 *Total Assets:* £331,726,592
Registered Office: Shell Centre, London, SE1 7NA
Activities: Pension funding
Parent: The Shell Petroleum Company Limited
Officers: Gary James Archibald [1963] Director/Oil Company Executive; Michael John Ashworth [1961] Director/Oil Company Executive; Michael David Clark [1966] Director/Oil Company Executive; Mary Clare Dewitt Corrie [1960] Director/Business Consultant; Timothy Donald Ryan Morrison [1953] Director/Retired Oil Company Executive

Shell Petroleum Company Limited (The)
Incorporated: 29 June 1903
Net Worth: £20,941,326,336 *Total Assets:* £43,931,176,960
Registered Office: Shell Centre, London, SE1 7NA
Activities: Activities of head offices
Officers: Michael John Ashworth [1961] Director/Oil Company Executive; Alan Daniel McLean [1966] Director/Oil Company Executive; Russell Leslie O'Brien [1974] Director/Oil Company Executive; Martinus Jacobus Ten Brink [1960] Director/Oil Company Executive [Dutch]

Shell QGC Holdings Limited
Incorporated: 9 April 2008
Previous: BG 456 Limited
Net Worth: £14,318,409,728 *Total Assets:* £14,394,172,416
Registered Office: Shell Centre, London, SE1 7NA
Activities: Non-trading company
Parent: BG Energy Holdings Limited
Officers: Michael John Ashworth [1961] Director/Oil Company Executive; Frances Hinden [1968] Director/Oil Company Executive

Shell QGC Midstream 1 Limited
Incorporated: 9 April 2008
Previous: BG 789 Limited
Net Worth: £3,673,280,512 *Total Assets:* £3,673,281,536
Registered Office: Shell Centre, London, SE1 7NA
Activities: Non-trading company
Parent: BG 456 Limited
Officers: Gary James Archibald [1963] Director/Oil Company Executive; Meta Hanlon [1980] Director/Lawyer [American]; Lindsey Jane Ritchie [1972] Director/Tax Advisor; David Andrew Warrilow [1969] Director/Chartered Accountant

Shell QGC Upstream 1 Limited
Incorporated: 9 April 2008
Previous: BG 123 Limited
Net Worth: £6,812,773,888 *Total Assets:* £7,750,784,512
Registered Office: Shell Centre, London, SE1 7NA
Activities: Non-trading company
Parent: BG 456 Limited
Officers: Gary James Archibald [1963] Director/Oil Company Executive; Lindsey Jane Ritchie [1972] Director/Tax Advisor; David Andrew Warrilow [1969] Director/Chartered Accountant

Shell Trading International Limited
Incorporated: 14 September 1998 *Employees:* 649
Net Worth: £1,320,586,496 *Total Assets:* £11,342,779,392
Registered Office: Shell Centre, York Road, London, SE1 7NA
Activities: Wholesale of petroleum and petroleum products
Parent: The Shell Petroleum Company Limited
Officers: Simon Ludgate, Secretary; Alison Ayodele Henwood [1965] Director/Oil Company Executive; Alan Daniel McLean [1966] Director/Oil Company Executive; Russell Leslie O'Brien [1974] Director/Oil Company Executive; Andrew James Smith [1964] Director [Australian]

The Shell Transport and Trading Company Limited
Incorporated: 18 October 1897
Net Worth: £4,399,184,896 *Total Assets:* £5,162,565,120
Registered Office: Shell Centre, London, SE1 7NA
Activities: Activities of head offices
Parent: Shell Petroleum N V
Officers: Michael John Ashworth [1961] Director/Oil Company Executive; Alan Daniel McLean [1966] Director/Oil Company Executive; Russell Leslie O'Brien [1974] Director/Oil Company Executive; Martinus Jacobus Ten Brink [1960] Director/Oil Company Executive [Dutch]

Shell Treasury Centre Limited
Incorporated: 12 November 1997 *Employees:* 28
Net Worth: £1,009,236,224 *Total Assets:* £65,824,321,536
Registered Office: Shell Centre, London, SE1 7NA
Activities: Financial intermediation not elsewhere classified
Parent: The Shell Petroleum Company Limited
Officers: Michael James Dawson [1980] Director/Assistant Treasurer; Frances Hinden [1968] Director/Oil Company Executive; Russell Leslie O'Brien [1974] Director/Oil Company Executive; Michael Harvey Pearman [1977] Director/Oil Company Executive

Shell Treasury Dollar Company Limited
Incorporated: 17 November 1997
Net Worth: £876,193,984 *Total Assets:* £41,182,162,944
Registered Office: Shell Centre, London, SE1 7NA
Activities: Financial intermediation not elsewhere classified
Parent: The Shell Petroleum Company Limited
Officers: David Nicholas Gardner [1978] Director/Oil Company Executive; Michael Harvey Pearman [1977] Director/Oil Company Executive; David Andrew Warrilow [1969] Director/Chartered Accountant

Shell Treasury UK Limited
Incorporated: 17 May 2006
Net Worth: £4,447,499,776 *Total Assets:* £4,529,800,192
Registered Office: Shell Centre, York Road, London, SE1 7NA
Activities: Financial intermediation not elsewhere classified
Parent: The Shell Petroleum Company Limited
Officers: Michael John Ashworth [1961] Director/Oil Company Executive; David Nicholas Gardner [1978] Director/Oil Company Executive; Deepak Khosla [1970] Director/Chartered Accountant; David Andrew Warrilow [1969] Director/Chartered Accountant

Shell Trinidad 5(A) Limited
Incorporated: 26 September 2005
Previous: BG Trinidad 5(A) Limited
Net Worth: £44,203,788 *Total Assets:* £246,320,624
Registered Office: Shell Centre, London, SE1 7NA
Activities: Extraction of crude petroleum
Parent: BG International Limited
Officers: Michael John Ashworth [1961] Director/Oil Company Executive; Nicholas William Hermann Blaker [1975] Director/Tax Manager; Rudolph Wilhelmina Johannes Driessen [1963] Director/Oil Company Executive [Dutch]; Robert Joseph Henderson [1962] Director/Oil Company Executive; Derek Hudson [1956] Director/VP

Shell Trinidad and Tobago Limited
Incorporated: 19 May 1989 *Employees:* 422
Previous: BG Trinidad and Tobago Limited
Net Worth Deficit: £340,118,080 *Total Assets:* £321,853,088
Registered Office: Shell Centre, London, SE1 7NA
Activities: Extraction of crude petroleum
Parent: BG North Sea Holdings Limited
Officers: Michael John Ashworth [1961] Director/Oil Company Executive; Nicholas William Hermann Blaker [1975] Director/Tax Manager; Rudolph Wilhelmina Johannes Driessen [1963] Director/Oil Company Executive [Dutch]; Derek Hudson [1956] Director/VP

Shell Tunisia Upstream Limited
Incorporated: 21 September 1992 *Employees:* 379
Previous: BG Tunisia Limited
Net Worth: £485,405,248 *Total Assets:* £1,539,091,072
Registered Office: Shell Centre, London, SE1 7NA
Activities: Extraction of crude petroleum
Parent: BG General Holdings Limited
Officers: Khaled Kacem [1969] Director [Tunisian]; Raed Hamade Karame [1974] Director/Oil Company Executive [Venezuelan]; Rozimi Bin Abdul Rahman [1977] Director/Oil Company Executive; Mark Kenneth Tough [1975] Director/Oil Company Executive

Shell U.K. Limited
Incorporated: 30 April 1915 *Employees:* 2,123
Net Worth: £4,988,000,256 *Total Assets:* £13,854,000,128
Registered Office: Shell Centre, London, SE1 7NA
Activities: Extraction of crude petroleum
Parent: Shell Holdings (U.K.) Limited
Officers: Barbara Frances Maria Blum [1964] Director/Solicitor; Nigel Anthony Hobson [1964] Director/Oil Company Executive; Sarah Joanne Judd [1978] Director/Solicitor; Monika Khullar [1972] Director/Oil Company Executive; Sinead Caitlin Lynch [1971] Director/Oil Company Executive [Irish]; Steven Robert Phimister [1969] Director/Oil Company Executive; Bernadette Williamson [1972] Director/Oil Company Executive

Shell U.K. North Atlantic Limited
Incorporated: 17 June 2003
Net Worth: £38,521,000 *Total Assets:* £396,984,992
Registered Office: Shell Centre, London, SE1 7NA
Activities: Extraction of crude petroleum
Parent: Shell U.K. Limited
Officers: Marianne Wold Eide [1969] Director/Oil Company Executive [Norwegian]; Howard Edwin Jones [1978] Director/Oil Company Executive; Shannon Lorraine Ouellette [1969] Director/Oil Company Executive [Canadian]

Shell Upstream Overseas Services (I) Limited
Incorporated: 3 June 2011
Net Worth: £933,925,696 *Total Assets:* £1,182,359,296
Registered Office: Shell Centre, London, SE1 7NA
Activities: Extraction of crude petroleum
Parent: Enterprise Oil Middle East Limited
Officers: Marianne Wold Eide [1969] Director/Oil Company Executive [Norwegian]; Howard Edwin Jones [1978] Director/Oil Company Executive; Shannon Lorraine Ouellette [1969] Director/Oil Company Executive [Canadian]

Shenda Investment UK Limited
Incorporated: 12 December 2016
Net Worth: £194,065,664 *Total Assets:* £248,003,696
Registered Office: Suite 1, 3rd Floor, 11-12 St James's Square, London, SW1Y 4LB
Activities: Activities of production holding companies
Officers: Lu Zhijun [1970] Director/Vice President [Chinese]

SHG Acquisition (UK) Limited
Incorporated: 10 October 2007 *Employees:* 2,587
Net Worth Deficit: £114,129,000 *Total Assets:* £284,444,000
Registered Office: 72-74 Dean Street, London, W1D 3SG
Activities: Activities of head offices
Major Shareholder: Ronald Wayne Burkle
Officers: James Wyndham Stuart Lawrence, Secretary/Accountant Director; Richard Allan Caring [1948] Director; Nicholas Keith Arthur Jones [1963] Director; Peter Jonathan McPhee [1975] Director [American]

Shine Acquisition Co Limited
Incorporated: 18 July 2017
Net Worth: £482,547,008 *Total Assets:* £761,961,024
Registered Office: 35 Great St Helen's, London, EC3A 6AP
Activities: Activities of other holding companies n.e.c.
Parent: Shine Holdco III Limited
Officers: Thomas Bruce Mangas [1967] Director [American]; Nilesh Kundanlal Pandya [1971] Director/Accountant; Michael Andrew James Smith [1962] Director/Chairman

Shine Holdco I Limited
Incorporated: 18 July 2017 *Employees:* 6
Net Worth: £489,689,984 *Total Assets:* £489,689,984
Registered Office: 35 Great St Helen's, London, EC3A 6AP
Activities: Activities of other holding companies n.e.c.
Parent: Shine Holdco (UK) Limited
Officers: Thomas Bruce Mangas [1967] Director [American]; Nilesh Kundanlal Pandya [1971] Director/Accountant; Michael Andrew James Smith [1962] Director/Chairman

Shine Holdco II Limited
Incorporated: 18 July 2017
Net Worth: £489,689,984 *Total Assets:* £489,689,984
Registered Office: 35 Great St Helen's, London, EC3A 6AP
Activities: Activities of other holding companies n.e.c.
Parent: Shine Holdco I Limited
Officers: Thomas Bruce Mangas [1967] Director [American]; Nilesh Kundanlal Pandya [1971] Director/Accountant; Michael Andrew James Smith [1962] Director/Chairman

Shine Holdco III Limited
Incorporated: 19 July 2017
Net Worth: £489,689,984 *Total Assets:* £489,689,984
Registered Office: 35 Great St Helen's, London, EC3A 6AP
Activities: Activities of other holding companies n.e.c.
Parent: Shine Holdco II Limited
Officers: Thomas Bruce Mangas [1967] Director [American]; Nilesh Kundanlal Pandya [1971] Director/Accountant; Michael Andrew James Smith [1962] Director/Chairman

Shine Limited
Incorporated: 22 May 2000
Net Worth: £141,683,008 *Total Assets:* £254,308,000
Registered Office: Central Legal Department, Shepherds Building, Endemol Shine UK, Charecroft Way, London, W14 0EE
Activities: Television programme production activities
Parent: NC Shine Acquisition Limited
Officers: Richard Robert Johnston [1967] Director; Sophie Henrietta Turner Laing [1960] Director

Shionogi Limited
Incorporated: 10 February 2012 *Employees:* 59
Net Worth: £762,809,152 *Total Assets:* £774,479,232
Registered Office: 33 Kingsway, London, WC2B 6UF
Activities: Other professional, scientific and technical activities n.e.c.
Parent: Shionogi & Co., Ltd.
Officers: Koji Hanasaki [1961] Director [Japanese]; Toshinobu Iwasaki [1963] Director/Corporate Officer, Senior Vice President, Global [Japanese]; John Apeler Keller [1964] Director [American]

Ship Holdco Limited
Incorporated: 29 July 2010
Net Worth: £804,846,976 *Total Assets:* £809,654,016
Registered Office: The Walbrook Building, 25 Walbrook, London, EC4N 8AF
Activities: Other business support service activities n.e.c.
Parent: Worldpay Group Limited
Officers: Rohinton Minoo Kalifa [1961] Director; Jared Michael Warner [1977] Director/Lawyer [American]

Ship Midco Limited
Incorporated: 29 July 2010
Net Worth: £305,772,992 *Total Assets:* £1,511,101,952
Registered Office: The Walbrook Building, 25 Walbrook, London, EC4N 8AF
Activities: Other business support service activities n.e.c.
Parent: Ship Holdco Limited
Officers: Rohinton Minoo Kalifa [1961] Director; Jared Michael Warner [1977] Director/Lawyer [American]

Shire Biopharmaceuticals Holdings
Incorporated: 27 June 2005
Net Worth: £592,063,168 *Total Assets:* £1,441,087,232
Registered Office: 1 Kingdom Street, London, W2 6BD
Activities: Activities of head offices
Parent: Takeda Pharmaceutical Company Limited
Officers: Mark Gibbons [1984] Director/Accountant [South African]; Nicholas Hugh Meryon Insall [1982] Director/Chartered Accountant; Kentaro Shirahata [1976] Director/Accountant [Japanese]

Shire Europe Limited
Incorporated: 10 April 2008
Net Worth: £176,820,080 *Total Assets:* £189,961,200
Registered Office: 1 Kingdom Street, London, W2 6BD
Activities: Other human health activities
Parent: Shire Pharmaceuticals Group
Officers: Sarah Lucy Charsley [1974] Director/Assistant Company Secretary; Mark Gibbons [1984] Director/Accountant [South African]

Shire Global Finance
Incorporated: 8 April 2005
Net Worth: £286,156,544 *Total Assets:* £1,682,692,608
Registered Office: 1 Kingdom Street, London, W2 6BD
Activities: Other business support service activities n.e.c.
Parent: Shire Holdings UK Limited
Officers: Sarah Lucy Charsley [1974] Director/Assistant Company Secretary; Nicholas Hugh Meryon Insall [1982] Director/Chartered Accountant; Kentaro Shirahata [1976] Director/Accountant [Japanese]

Shire Holdings Europe Limited
Incorporated: 13 February 1996
Net Worth: £228,546,208 *Total Assets:* £243,420,304
Registered Office: 1 Kingdom Street, London, W2 6BD
Activities: Activities of head offices
Parent: Shire Europe Limited
Officers: Sarah Lucy Charsley [1974] Director/Assistant Company Secretary; Nicholas Hugh Meryon Insall [1982] Director/Accountant; Kentaro Shirahata [1976] Director/Accountant [Japanese]

Shire Holdings UK Limited
Incorporated: 14 February 2003
Net Worth: £741,714,688 *Total Assets:* £742,684,672
Registered Office: 1 Kingdom Street, London, W2 6BD
Activities: Activities of head offices
Parent: Shire Pharmaceuticals Group
Officers: Sarah Lucy Charsley [1974] Director/Assistant Company Secretary; Mark Gibbons [1984] Director/Accountant [South African]

Shire Pharmaceutical Development Limited
Incorporated: 29 March 1990 *Employees:* 68
Net Worth: £177,422,000 *Total Assets:* £185,380,992
Registered Office: 1 Kingdom Street, London, W2 6BD
Activities: Other research and experimental development on natural sciences and engineering
Parent: Shire Pharmaceuticals Group
Officers: Sarah Lucy Charsley [1974] Director/Assistant Company Secretary; Nicholas Hugh Meryon Insall [1982] Director/Chartered Accountant; Kentaro Shirahata [1976] Director/Accountant [Japanese]

Shire Pharmaceuticals Group
Incorporated: 1 January 1994 *Employees:* 79
Net Worth: £309,542,272 *Total Assets:* £410,338,112
Registered Office: 1 Kingdom Street, London, W2 6BD
Activities: Activities of head offices
Parent: Shire Biopharmaceuticals Holdings
Officers: Damien Rodolphe Edmond Bailly [1966] Commercial Director [French]; Nicholas Hugh Meryon Insall [1982] Director/Chartered Accountant; Kentaro Shirahata [1976] Director/Accountant [Japanese]

Shop Direct Holdings Limited
Incorporated: 1 March 2004 *Employees:* 3,736
Net Worth: £199,800,000 *Total Assets:* £3,280,199,936
Registered Office: 2nd Floor, 14 St George Street, London, W1S 1FE
Activities: Activities of head offices
Officers: Aidan Stuart Barclay [1956] Director; Howard Myles Barclay [1959] Director; Philip Leslie Peters [1957] Director; Michael Seal [1948] Director

Shortline PLC
Incorporated: 15 March 2013
Net Worth Deficit: £19,476,986 *Total Assets:* £367,979,008
Registered Office: 5th Floor, 6 St Andrew Street, London, EC4A 3AE
Activities: Other business support service activities n.e.c.
Parent: TMF Trustee Limited
Officers: Stephen William Spencer Norton [1959] Director

Siblu Holdings Limited
Incorporated: 1 December 2006
Net Worth: £63,349,952 *Total Assets:* £134,535,120
Registered Office: 5th Floor, 6 St Andrew Street, London, EC4A 3AE
Activities: Activities of head offices
Officers: Nigel Anthony Law, Secretary; Laurent Georges Bory [1974] Finance Director [French]; Simon Aeran Crabbe [1973] Director; Leslie Ronald Hurst [1954] Director/Manager; Ian Roy Smith [1956] Operations Director

SIG PLC
Incorporated: 29 December 1970 *Employees:* 9,674
Net Worth: £476,800,000 *Total Assets:* £1,335,800,064
Registered Office: 10 Eastbourne Terrace, London, W2 6LG
Activities: Activities of head offices
Officers: Richard Charles Monro, Secretary; Andrea Abt [1960] Director [German]; Andrew James Allner [1953] Director; Janet Elizabeth Ashdown [1959] Director; Ian Barnet Duncan [1961] Director; Alan Charles Lovell [1953] Director; Nicholas William Maddock [1971] Director; Meinie Oldersma [1959] Director [Dutch]; Cyrille Marie Patrick Ragoucy [1956] Director [French]

Sigma Pharmaceuticals PLC
Incorporated: 15 May 1981 *Employees:* 328
Net Worth: £30,869,000 *Total Assets:* £106,546,000
Registered Office: First Floor, Roxburghe House, 273-287 Regent Street, London, W1B 2HA
Activities: Wholesale of pharmaceutical goods
Shareholder: Orion Holdings (UK) Limited
Officers: Manish Hansraj Shah, Secretary/Chartered Accountant; Bharat Kumar Hansraj Devraj Shah [1949] Director/Pharmacist; Bhavin Manish Shah [1983] Director/Chartered Accountant; Hatul Bharat Kumar Shah [1978] Director/Pharmacist; Jayoti Bharat Shah [1952] Director/Credit Controller; Kalpana Manish Shah [1956] Director/Personnel Manageress; Kamal Hansraj Shah [1959] Director/Office Manager; Manish Hansraj Shah [1955] Director/Chartered Accountant; Nishal Kamal Shah [1991] Director/Doctor; Paras Kamal Shah [1987] Director; Rajiv Bharat Kumar Shah [1985] Director/Pharmacist; Sachin Manish Shah [1986] Director/Dentist

Silchester Capital Limited
Incorporated: 18 December 2015
Net Worth: £602,957,312 *Total Assets:* £609,525,504
Registered Office: Time and Life Building, 1 Bruton Street, London, W1J 6TL
Activities: Financial intermediation not elsewhere classified
Shareholders: Silchester Partners Limited; Silchester Partners Limited
Officers: Stephen Charles Butt [1951] Director/Investment Management; Michael John Julian Cowan [1952] Director/Investment Manager; Timothy John Linehan [1970] Director/Head of Operations [American]

Silchester Partners Limited
Incorporated: 12 December 1994
Net Worth: £401,897,696 *Total Assets:* £454,588,448
Registered Office: Time & Life Building, 1 Bruton Street, London, W1J 6TL
Activities: Financial intermediation not elsewhere classified
Shareholders: Caroline Butt; Stephen Charles Butt
Officers: Stephen Charles Butt [1951] Director/Investment Management; Michael John Julian Cowan [1952] Director/Investment Manager; Timothy John Linehan [1970] Director/Head of Operations [American]

Silverstone Funding (No.1) Limited
Incorporated: 5 June 2008
Net Worth: £80,000 *Total Assets:* £3,761,101,056
Registered Office: Third Floor, 1 King's Arms Yard, London, EC2R 7AF
Activities: Other business support service activities n.e.c.
Parent: Silverstone Securitisation Holdings Limited
Officers: Robert Sutton [1978] Director/Financial Services [American]; Philip Andrew Townsend [1965] Director; Daniel Jonathan Wynne [1970] Director

Silverstone Master Issuer PLC
Incorporated: 5 June 2008
Net Worth Deficit: £2,255,000 *Total Assets:* £4,002,244,096
Registered Office: Third Floor, 1 King's Arms Yard, London, EC2R 7AF
Activities: Other business support service activities n.e.c.
Parent: Silverstone Securitisation Holdings Limited
Officers: Robert Sutton [1978] Director/Financial Services [American]; Philip Andrew Townsend [1965] Director; Daniel Jonathan Wynne [1970] Director

Simca LLP
Incorporated: 9 December 2009 *Employees:* 1
Net Worth: £116,981,616 *Total Assets:* £126,360,168
Registered Office: 15 Regent Street, London, SW1Y 4LR

Simec Lochaber Hydropower 2 Limited
Incorporated: 14 February 1963 *Employees:* 171
Previous: Alcan Aluminium UK Limited
Net Worth: £544,924,032 *Total Assets:* £690,625,984
Registered Office: 7 Hertford Street, London, W1J 7RH
Activities: Aluminium production
Parent: Simec Lochaber Hydropower Ltd
Officers: Rajeev Gandhi [1973] Director [Indian]; Parduman Kumar Gupta [1943] Director [Indian]

Simmons & Simmons LLP
Incorporated: 1 March 2010 *Employees:* 1,407
Net Worth: £101,053,000 *Total Assets:* £244,031,008
Registered Office: Citypoint, One Ropemaker Street, London, EC2Y 9SS
Officers: Jeremy Quentin Hoyland [1967] Member; Colin John Passmore [1959] Member; Andrea Accornero [1966] LLP Member; Hans Hermann Aldenhoff [1969] LLP Member; Robert Charles Kinkead Allen [1978] LLP Member; Ombline Marie Caroline Ancelin [1976] LLP Member; Sarah Evelyn Bailey [1964] LLP Member; Edward James MacDonald Baker [1967] LLP Member; Paul Michael Baker [1979] LLP Member; Charles William Newsom Bankes [1960] LLP Member; Yves Baratte [1977] LLP Member; Romeo Battigaglia [1969] LLP Member; Jayne Gabrielle Bentham [1978] LLP Member; Nicholas John Ormond Benwell [1965] LLP Member; Bastiaan Jan Berghuis Van Woortman [1970] LLP Member; Stefania Bergia [1971] LLP Member; Dr Oliver Beyer [1972] LLP Member; Dr Felix Biedermann [1976] LLP Member; Craig Bisson [1979] LLP Member; Eric Ariel Alain Boillot [1969] LLP Member; Colin John Bole [1975] LLP Member; Fiona Samari Uchenna Sarah Bolton [1977] LLP Member; Christian Bornhorst [1973] LLP Member; Jeroen Johannes Pieter Bos [1977] LLP Member; Timothy John Boyce [1967] LLP Member; Patrick Michael Boyd [1974] LLP Member; John Patrick Boylan [1971] LLP Member; Eucharia Mary Ellen Bragg [1981] LLP Member; Fionan Breathnach [1969] LLP Member; James Harris Bresslaw [1961] LLP Member; Jason Bright [1967] LLP Member; Peter Alan Christopher Zingrich Broadhurst [1971] LLP Member; James Alexander Hugh Brown [1975] LLP Member; Lawrence William Brown [1979] LLP Member; Paul Andrew Browne [1968] LLP Member; Sean Bulmer [1966] LLP Member; Richard James Robert Bunce [1965] LLP Member; Michael Burdon [1963] LLP Member; Ahmed Tahir Butt [1976] LLP Member; Mark Jonathan Carroll [1962] LLP Member; Philippe Cavalieros [1974] LLP Member; Jen Yee Chan [1972] LLP Member; Louis-Mael Cogis [1980] LLP Member; Luc Cohen [1975] LLP Member; Nicholas Stuart Colston [1981] LLP Member; Richard Michael Cook [1974] LLP Member; Adam Jolyon Cooper [1968] LLP Member; James Edward Cotter [1974] LLP Member; Marina Anne Germaine Couste [1952] LLP Member; Nicholas Simon Cronkshaw [1966] LLP Member; Edward James Crosse [1971] LLP Member; Alison Lee Crosthwaite [1977] LLP Member; Willaim Iain Cullen [1953] LLP Member; Mark John Curtis [1966] LLP Member; Davide D'Affronto [1976] LLP Member; Jason Matthew Daniel [1970] LLP Member; David Alan Davies [1961] LLP Member; Mathias Wilhelmus de Koning [1979] LLP Member; Alfredo de Lorenzo [1972] LLP Member; James Thomas Dean [1974] LLP Member; Pollyanna Elizabeth Catriona Deane [1966] LLP Member; Giles Thomas Peter Dennison [1970] LLP Member; Satyen Narendra Dhana [1976] LLP Member; Michael Robert James Dodson [1971] LLP Member; Marieke Driessen [1974] LLP Member; Pierre-Regis Dukmedjian [1974] LLP Member; Iain Andrew Duncan [1979] LLP Member; Stuart Dutson [1969] LLP Member; Francis Richard Ross Dyton [1964] LLP Member; Guillaume-Denis Faure [1971] LLP Member; Alfonso Fernandez-Puebla [1975] LLP Member; Christophe Charles Yves Marie Fichet [1974] LLP Member; Andrea Lindsay Finn [1974] LLP Member; Lucian Christopher John Firth [1980] LLP Member; Darren James Fox [1973] LLP Member; Thomas Alexander Fyfe [1970] LLP Member; Dale Gabbert [1970] LLP Member; Simon Gardiner [1974] LLP Member; Michael Edward Gavey [1976] LLP Member; Stephen Gentle [1964] LLP Member; Patrick Gerry [1969] LLP Member; Leonardo Giani [1978] LLP Member; Simonetta Giordano [1973] LLP Member; Harald Sebastian Glander [1974] LLP Member; Jens Wilhelm Golz [1978] LLP Member; Thierry Gontard [1962] LLP Member; James Edward Laurence Grand [1966] LLP Member; Patrick Michael Graves [1960] LLP Member; Helen Maria Hagan [1978] LLP Member; Ian Russell Hammond [1963] LLP Member; Jonathan Scott Hammond [1969] LLP Member; Helen Mathias Hancock [1964] LLP Member; Dr Boris Handorn [1973] LLP Member; Charles Henry Hawes [1971] LLP Member; Matthew Peter Hebburn [1975] LLP Member; Dr Robert Hendriks [1964] LLP Member; Mark Antony Hewland [1965] LLP Member; Robert Alan Heym [1971] LLP Member; Simon Christopher Reginald Hilditch [1965] LLP Member; Oscar Willem Jan Hoefangels [1972] LLP Member

Simon Group Limited
Incorporated: 24 May 1897 *Employees:* 1
Net Worth: £90,422,192 *Total Assets:* £123,476,264
Registered Office: 2nd Floor, 130 Shaftesbury Avenue, London, W1D 5EU
Activities: Activities of head offices
Officers: Georges Jules Bruers [1934] Director [Belgian]; Patricia Ann Grout [1945] Director/Administrative Assistant; Dirk Jozef Dymphna Hooybergs [1966] Director/Economist [Belgian]

Sinclair Pharma Limited
Incorporated: 29 July 1999 *Employees:* 187
Previous: Sinclair Pharma PLC
Net Worth: £99,183,000 *Total Assets:* £168,876,992
Registered Office: Whitfield Court, 30-32 Whitfield Street, London, W1T 2RQ
Activities: Activities of other holding companies n.e.c.
Parent: Huadong Medicine Co Ltd
Officers: Jayne Katherine Burrell, Secretary; Bo Chen [1972] Director/Manager [Chinese]; Shizheng Duan [1968] Director/Senior Manager [Chinese]; Chengwei Liu [1973] Director [Chinese]; Alan Musgrave Olby [1971] Director/Chartered Accountant; Christopher Paul Spooner [1968] Director

Sinochem International Oil (London) Co., Limited
Incorporated: 30 October 1990 *Employees:* 20
Net Worth: £20,384,180 *Total Assets:* £3,056,467,712
Registered Office: 11th Floor, Westminster Tower, 3 Albert Embankment, London, SE1 7RZ
Activities: Agents involved in the sale of fuels, ores, metals and industrial chemicals
Parent: The State-Owned Assets Supervision and Administration Commission
Officers: Bin Hu, Secretary; Xiaowen Liu [1965] Managing Director [Chinese]; Wenlong Wu [1982] Director [Chinese]; Dan Ye [1967] Director [Chinese]

Sinochem Resources UK Limited
Incorporated: 13 July 2009 *Employees:* 93
Net Worth Deficit: £98,167,600 *Total Assets:* £234,224,496
Registered Office: Seventeenth Floor, New Zealand House, 80 Haymarket, London, SW1Y 4TE
Activities: Activities of head offices
Parent: The Government of The People's Republic of China
Officers: Richard Konn, Secretary; Chenhan Dai [1980] Director/Accountant [Chinese]; Jia-Zhao Lei [1960] Director [Chinese]; Chao Zhang [1970] Director [Chinese]; Guoqing Zhang [1966] Director [Chinese]

SIR ATP Limited
Incorporated: 26 February 2007
Net Worth: £54,375,000 *Total Assets:* £207,650,000
Registered Office: Cavendish House, 18 Cavendish Square, London, W1G 0PJ
Activities: Other letting and operating of own or leased real estate
Parent: Secure Income REIT PLC
Officers: Sandra Louise Gumm, Secretary [Australian]; Philip Michael Brown [1960] Investment Director; Timothy James Evans [1969] Director/Chartered Surveyor; Sandra Louise Gumm [1966] Director/Chartered Accountant [Australian]; Nicholas Mark Leslau [1959] Director/Chartered Surveyor

SIR Healthcare 2 Limited
Incorporated: 17 August 2015
Net Worth: £201,659,008 *Total Assets:* £534,009,984
Registered Office: Cavendish House, 18 Cavendish Square, London, W1G 0PJ
Activities: Activities of other holding companies n.e.c.
Parent: Secure Income REIT PLC
Officers: Sandra Louise Gumm, Secretary; Philip Michael Brown [1960] Investment Director; Timothy James Evans [1969] Director/Chartered Surveyor; Sandra Louise Gumm [1966] Director/Chartered Accountant [Australian]; Nicholas Mark Leslau [1959] Director/Chartered Surveyor

Sir Hospital Holdings Limited
Incorporated: 30 June 2006
Net Worth: £96,890,000 *Total Assets:* £376,676,992
Registered Office: Cavendish House, 18 Cavendish Square, London, W1G 0PJ
Activities: Activities of head offices
Parent: Secure Income REIT PLC
Officers: Sandra Louise Gumm, Secretary/Chartered Accountant [Australian]; Philip Michael Brown [1960] Investment Director; Timothy James Evans [1969] Director/Chartered Surveyor; Sandra Louise Gumm [1966] Director/Chartered Accountant [Australian]; Nicholas Mark Leslau [1959] Director/Chartered Surveyor

SIR Hospitals Propco Limited
Incorporated: 21 March 2003
Net Worth: £535,819,008 *Total Assets:* £762,089,024
Registered Office: Cavendish House, 18 Cavendish Square, London, W1G 0PJ
Activities: Activities of head offices
Parent: Secure Income REIT PLC
Officers: Sandra Louise Gumm, Secretary/Chartered Accountant [Australian]; Philip Michael Brown [1960] Investment Director; Timothy James Evans [1969] Director/Chartered Surveyor; Sandra Louise Gumm [1966] Director/Chartered Accountant [Australian]; Nicholas Mark Leslau [1959] Director/Chartered Surveyor

SIR Hotels 1 Limited
Incorporated: 16 June 2016
Net Worth: £59,552,000 *Total Assets:* £138,648,992
Registered Office: Cavendish House, 18 Cavendish Square, London, W1G 0PJ
Activities: Activities of head offices
Parent: Secure Income REIT PLC
Officers: Philip Michael Brown [1960] Director; Timothy James Evans [1969] Director/Chartered Surveyor; Sandra Louise Gumm [1966] Director/Chartered Accountant [Australian]; Nicholas Mark Leslau [1959] Director

SIR Rivers Limited
Incorporated: 23 March 2007
Net Worth: £57,134,000 *Total Assets:* £153,480,000
Registered Office: Cavendish House, 18 Cavendish Square, London, W1G 0PJ
Activities: Other letting and operating of own or leased real estate
Parent: Secure Income REIT PLC
Officers: Sandra Louise Gumm, Secretary [Australian]; Philip Michael Brown [1960] Investment Director; Timothy James Evans [1969] Director/Chartered Surveyor; Sandra Louise Gumm [1966] Director/Chartered Accountant [Australian]; Nicholas Mark Leslau [1959] Director/Chartered Surveyor

SIR Theme Park Subholdco Limited
Incorporated: 27 September 2006
Net Worth: £127,799,000 *Total Assets:* £605,110,016
Registered Office: Cavendish House, 18 Cavendish Square, London, W1G 0PJ
Activities: Activities of head offices
Parent: Secure Income REIT PLC
Officers: Sandra Louise Gumm, Secretary/Chartered Accountant [Australian]; Philip Michael Brown [1960] Investment Director; Timothy James Evans [1969] Director/Chartered Surveyor; Sandra Louise Gumm [1966] Director/Chartered Accountant [Australian]; Nicholas Mark Leslau [1959] Director/Chartered Surveyor

SIR Theme Parks Limited
Incorporated: 27 February 2007
Net Worth Deficit: £7,309,000 *Total Assets:* £375,456,992
Registered Office: Cavendish House, 18 Cavendish Square, London, W1G 0PG
Activities: Activities of head offices
Parent: Secure Income REIT PLC
Officers: Sandra Louise Gumm, Secretary [Australian]; Philip Michael Brown [1960] Investment Director; Timothy James Evans [1969] Director/Chartered Surveyor; Sandra Louise Gumm [1966] Director/Chartered Accountant [Australian]; Nicholas Mark Leslau [1959] Director/Chartered Surveyor

SIR TP Limited
Incorporated: 26 February 2007
Net Worth: £40,055,000 *Total Assets:* £152,426,000
Registered Office: Cavendish House, 18 Cavendish Square, London, W1G 0PJ
Activities: Other letting and operating of own or leased real estate
Parent: Secure Income REIT PLC
Officers: Sandra Louise Gumm, Secretary [Australian]; Philip Michael Brown [1960] Investment Director; Timothy James Evans [1969] Director/Chartered Surveyor; Sandra Louise Gumm [1966] Director/Chartered Accountant [Australian]; Nicholas Mark Leslau [1959] Director/Chartered Surveyor

SIR Umbrella Limited
Incorporated: 17 August 2015
Net Worth Deficit: £54,813,000 *Total Assets:* £367,551,008
Registered Office: Cavendish House, 18 Cavendish Square, London, W1G 0PJ
Activities: Activities of other holding companies n.e.c.
Parent: Secure Income REIT PLC
Officers: Sandra Louise Gumm, Secretary; Philip Michael Brown [1960] Investment Director; Timothy James Evans [1969] Director/Chartered Surveyor; Sandra Louise Gumm [1966] Director/Chartered Accountant [Australian]; Nicholas Mark Leslau [1959] Director/Chartered Surveyor

Sirius (Korea) Limited
Incorporated: 7 October 1999
Net Worth: £66,035,000 *Total Assets:* £245,060,000
Registered Office: Ground Floor, Building 5, Chiswick Park, 566 Chiswick High Road, London, W4 5YF
Activities: Activities of construction holding companies
Parent: Otis Investments Limited
Officers: Rene Bisson [1971] Managing Director [American]; Robert William Sadler [1967] Director/Solicitor; Maxime Yao [1977] Director

Sirius GR Limited
Incorporated: 3 August 2016 *Employees:* 2
Net Worth: £24,286 *Total Assets:* £179,664,000
Registered Office: Berkeley House, 304 Regents Park Road, London, N3 2JY
Activities: Buying and selling of own real estate
Parent: Turing GR Limited
Officers: Paul Hallam, Secretary; Christopher Charles McGill [1960] Managing Director; William Kenneth Procter [1953] Director/Accountant

Sirius International UK Holdings Ltd
Incorporated: 16 February 2017 *Employees:* 4
Net Worth: £1,306,076,032 *Total Assets:* £1,306,228,608
Registered Office: The St Botolph Building, 138 Houndsditch, London, EC3A 7AR
Activities: Activities of financial services holding companies
Officers: Lars Olof Ek [1952] Finance Director [Swedish]; Robert Ian Charles Harman [1969] Director/Chief Executive Officer; Sheila Elizabeth Nicoll [1955] Director/Senior Vice President [American]; Ralph Anthony Salamone [1966] Director/Senior Vice President [American]

Sirius Minerals Holdings Limited
Incorporated: 10 December 2012
Net Worth: £75,906,000 *Total Assets:* £314,515,008
Registered Office: 3rd Floor, Greener House, 66-68 Haymarket, London, SW1Y 4RF
Activities: Support activities for other mining and quarrying
Parent: Sirius Minerals PLC
Officers: Nicholas Anthony King, Secretary; Christopher Neil Fraser [1974] Director; Nicholas Anthony King [1973] Director/General Counsel; Thomas Jay Staley [1980] Finance Director [Australian]

Sirius Minerals PLC
Incorporated: 30 October 2003 *Employees:* 91
Net Worth: £505,129,984 *Total Assets:* £796,924,992
Registered Office: 3rd Floor, Greener House, 68 Haymarket, London, SW1Y 4RF
Activities: Mining of chemical and fertilizer minerals
Officers: Nicholas Anthony King, Secretary; Keith Edward Clarke [1952] Director; Christopher Neil Fraser [1974] Director; Louise Jane Hardy [1966] Director; Elizabeth Noel Harwerth [1947] Director [British/American]; Lord Hutton of Furness Hutton of Furness [1955] Director; Jane Ann Lodge [1955] Director; Russell John Scrimshaw [1949] Director [Australian]; Thomas Jay Staley [1980] Finance Director [Australian]

SITI 1 Limited
Incorporated: 23 July 2001
Net Worth: £975,936,000 *Total Assets:* £975,936,000
Registered Office: c/o Smiths Group PLC, 4th Floor, 11-12 St James's Square, London, SW1Y 4LB
Activities: Activities of head offices
Parent: Smiths Group International Holdings Limited
Officers: Fiona Margaret Gillespie, Secretary; Alexander St. John Stopford Kenny [1971] Director of Treasury; John Michael Mills [1964] Director/Secretary; George James Montague [1964] Director/Group Financial Controller [American]; Melanie Jane Rowlands [1968] Director/Solicitor

Six Degrees Holdings Limited
Incorporated: 17 December 2010 *Employees:* 278
Previous: Six Degrees Technology Group Limited
Net Worth Deficit: £19,327,000 *Total Assets:* £221,875,008
Registered Office: Commodity Quay, St Katharine Docks, London, E1W 1AZ
Activities: Other telecommunications activities
Parent: CB-SDG Limited
Officers: David Michael Howson [1970] Director; Steven Keith Mitchell [1976] Director

Sixmoor Limited
Incorporated: 21 December 2016 *Employees:* 2
Net Worth: £39,290 *Total Assets:* £153,397,920
Registered Office: Berkeley House, 304 Regents Park Road, London, N3 2JY
Activities: Activities auxiliary to financial intermediation n.e.c.
Parent: Lightyear Estates Holdings Limted
Officers: Paul Hallam, Secretary; Christopher Charles McGill [1960] Managing Director; William Kenneth Procter [1953] Director/Accountant

SK Energy Europe Limited
Incorporated: 10 January 2001 *Employees:* 24
Net Worth: £66,808,944 *Total Assets:* £412,422,336
Registered Office: 3rd Floor, 175-179 Oxford Street, London, W1D 2JS
Activities: Wholesale of other fuels and related products
Officers: Jaeyoung Yang, Secretary; Jaesang Jin [1964] Director [South Korean]; Yeonsoo Lee [1983] Director [South Korean]; Sukhyun Yoon [1970] Managing Director [South Korean]

SK Shipping Europe PLC
Incorporated: 12 July 1999 *Employees:* 3
Net Worth: £39,380,080 *Total Assets:* £148,238,240
Registered Office: 6th Floor, Capital Tower, 91 Waterloo Road, London, SE1 8RT
Activities: Sea and coastal freight water transport
Officers: Se Bin Im [1971] Director [South Korean]; Namho Kim [1965] Director [South Korean]; Sung Ick Kim [1968] Director [South Korean]; Changho Lee [1977] Managing Director [South Korean]; Jang Ho Suh [1964] Director [South Korean]

Skrill Limited
Incorporated: 27 July 2001 *Employees:* 113
Net Worth: £285,144,704 *Total Assets:* £729,160,704
Registered Office: 25 Canada Square, London, E14 5LQ
Activities: Financial intermediation not elsewhere classified
Parent: Skrill Holdings Limited
Officers: Elaine Quine, Secretary; Mohammed Fayyaz Ansari [1970] Director/Financial Controller; Miroslav Bojilov [1974] Director/General Manager [Bulgarian]; Daniel Jay Chazonoff [1963] Director/Chief Operating Officer [Canadian]; Mark Aidan Jeffrey [1958] Director; Lorenzo Pellegrino [1974] Director [Italian]; Elliott Mark Wiseman [1974] Director/Solicitor

Skuld I Limited
Incorporated: 1 October 2010
Net Worth Deficit: £17,662,000 *Total Assets:* £140,800,992
Registered Office: 5th Floor, 40 Gracechurch Street, London, EC3V 0BT
Activities: Non-life insurance
Parent: Skuld Investment Limited
Officers: Stale Lyngvaer Hansen [1975] Director [Norwegian]; Kristian Johan Dekke Loberg [1980] Director/EVP CFO [Norwegian]; Keith Arthur Parker [1966] Director/EVP UK Operations

Sky Holdco Limited
Incorporated: 12 January 2017
Net Worth: £458,186,976 *Total Assets:* £458,186,976
Registered Office: Acre House, 11-15 William Road, London, NW1 3ER
Activities: Other business support service activities n.e.c.
Parent: Canary Midco Limited
Officers: Susan Gillian Boulton [1969] Director; John Eric Fountain-Johnston [1958] Director; Jose Maria Hurtado Carrasco [1972] Director [Spanish]

Skyscanner Holdings Limited
Incorporated: 16 September 2011
Net Worth: £157,726,000 *Total Assets:* £157,814,000
Registered Office: Floor 6, The Avenue, 1 Bedford Avenue, London, WC1B 3AU
Activities: Business and domestic software development
Parent: Ctrip.Com International Ltd
Officers: Carolyn Hay, Secretary; James Jianzhang Liang [1969] Director [Kittitian]; Jane Jie Sun [1968] Director [Singaporean]; Xiaofan Wang [1975] Director [Chinese]; Gareth John Williams [1969] Director/IT Consultant; Xiong Xing [1973] Director [American]

Slate No.1 PLC
Incorporated: 23 September 2014
Net Worth: £15,869 *Total Assets:* £1,170,697,984
Registered Office: 35 Great St Helen's, London, EC3A 6AP
Activities: Financial intermediation not elsewhere classified
Parent: Slate No.1 Mortgage Holdings Limited
Officers: Susan Iris Abrahams [1957] Director

Slate No.2 PLC
Incorporated: 23 September 2014
Net Worth: £15,869 *Total Assets:* £241,276,384
Registered Office: 35 Great St Helen's, London, EC3A 6AP
Activities: Financial intermediation not elsewhere classified
Parent: Slate No.2 Mortgage Holdings Limited
Officers: Susan Iris Abrahams [1957] Director

Slater & Gordon (UK) 1 Limited
Incorporated: 3 January 2012
Net Worth Deficit: £173,680,000 *Total Assets:* £427,860,992
Registered Office: 50-52 Chancery Lane, London, WC2A 1HL
Activities: Activities of head offices
Officers: David John Ludlow Whitmore [1959] Director; Alison Louise Wilford [1965] Director/Chief Financial Officer

Slater & Gordon (UK) 2 LLP
Incorporated: 3 January 2012
Previous: Slater & Gordon (UK) LLP
Net Worth: £149,523,232 *Total Assets:* £245,571,776
Registered Office: 50-52 Chancery Lane, London, WC2A 1HL

Slater and Gordon UK Limited
Incorporated: 1 February 2012 *Employees:* 1,298
Previous: Slater Gordon Solutions Legal Limited
Net Worth Deficit: £203,316,992 *Total Assets:* £160,450,000
Registered Office: 50-52 Chancery Lane, London, WC2A 1HL
Activities: Solicitors
Parent: Slater & Gordon (UK) 1 Limited
Officers: Matthew Paul Jarvis [1978] Managing Director - Personal Injury Services; David John Ludlow Whitmore [1959] Director

Slough Trading Estate Limited
Incorporated: 17 September 1974
Net Worth: £1,227,376,000 *Total Assets:* £1,421,524,992
Registered Office: Cunard House, 15 Regent Street, London, SW1Y 4LR
Activities: Development of building projects
Shareholder: Segro Public Limited Company
Officers: Elizabeth Ann Blease, Secretary; Andrew Stephen Gulliford [1962] Director/Chartered Surveyor; Alan Michael Holland [1974] Director; Gareth John Osborn [1962] Director; Ann Octavia Peters [1969] Director; Andrew John Pilsworth [1974] Director; Philip Anthony Redding [1968] Director

Smart DCC Limited
Incorporated: 7 August 2013 *Employees:* 320
Total Assets: £593,134,016
Registered Office: 30 Berners Street, London, W1T 3LR
Activities: Other service activities n.e.c.
Parent: Capita Business Services Ltd
Officers: David Nicholas Brown [1973] Director; Angus Robert Flett [1964] Director; John James Hemming [1962] Director; Philip Stewart Male [1966] Director; Mark William Mathieson [1966] Director; Richard John McCarthy [1958] Director; William Francis Sebastian Rickett [1953] Director

Smartestenergy Limited
Incorporated: 16 May 2000 *Employees:* 184
Net Worth: £60,414,000 *Total Assets:* £348,436,000
Registered Office: Dashwood House, 69 Old Broad Street, London, EC2M 1QS
Activities: Distribution of electricity
Parent: Marubeni Corporation
Officers: David Martyn Cockshott [1969] Director; Robert Sebastian Groves [1965] Director; Satoru Harada [1967] Director [Japanese]; Tomohiko Hirano [1963] Director [Japanese]; Naoki Ito [1969] Director [Japanese]; Ryuichi Noyama [1972] Director [Japanese]; Hiroyuki Sawada [1963] Director [Japanese]; Takafumi Shigemura [1973] Director [Japanese]

Smartstream Technologies Group Limited
Incorporated: 12 July 2006
Net Worth: £130,466,000 *Total Assets:* £180,135,008
Registered Office: St Helen's, 1 Undershaft, London, EC3A 8EE
Activities: Activities of head offices
Parent: D-Clear Europe
Officers: Claudia Giunta, Secretary; Khalifa Hassan Al Daboos [1967] Director [Emirati]; Thani Abdulla Al Zaffin [1965] Director General [Emirati]; Ahmad Abdulkarim Mohd Julfar [1961] Director/Engineer [Emirati]; Abdulla Abdulrahman Qassem [1963] Director [Emirati]

Smartstream Technologies Limited
Incorporated: 9 August 1988 *Employees:* 138
Net Worth: £101,582,000 *Total Assets:* £163,484,992
Registered Office: St Helen's, 1 Undershaft, London, EC3A 8EE
Activities: Business and domestic software development
Parent: Smartstream Technologies Holdings Limited
Officers: Claudia Giunta, Secretary; Richard William Bowler [1973] Director/Chief Financial Officer; Claudia Giunta [1967] Director/General Counsel [American]; Stephen Paul Thomas [1971] Director/Accountant

SMBC Aviation Capital (UK) Limited
Incorporated: 5 December 2003
Net Worth: £126,097,200 *Total Assets:* £681,355,904
Registered Office: 99 Queen Victoria Street, London, EC4V 4EH
Activities: Financial leasing
Shareholder: Sumitomo Mitsui Financial Group
Officers: Peter John Barrett [1966] Director [Irish]; Lawrence James Butcher [1968] Director; Barry Flannery [1969] Director [Irish]; Koichi Kawamura [1965] Director [Japanese]; Mark Jeremy Rutherford [1965] Director; Koichi Tanaka [1967] Director [Japanese]; Takashi Yamana [1963] Director [Japanese]

SMBC Derivative Products Limited
Incorporated: 4 November 1994 *Employees:* 9
Net Worth: £162,232,864 *Total Assets:* £172,315,616
Registered Office: One New Change, London, EC4M 9AF
Activities: Financial intermediation not elsewhere classified
Shareholders: SMBC Nikko Capital Markets Limited; SMBC Nikko Capital Markets Limited
Officers: Parul Dave, Secretary; Thomas Sedgwick Coleman [1955] Director/Risk Consultant [American]; Roger Stephen McCormick [1951] Director/Solicitor; Augustus Moore [1965] Director/Banker [American]; Naoki Okubo [1965] Director/Banker [Japanese]; Timothy F Quinn [1953] Director/Accountant [American]; Ryoji Sato [1964] Director/Banker [Japanese]; John David Thomas [1961] Director/Banker; Antony Yates [1962] Director/Banker; Takahiro Yazawa [1964] Director/Banker [Japanese]

SMBC Leasing (UK) Limited
Incorporated: 16 May 1986 *Employees:* 16
Net Worth: £5,800,913 *Total Assets:* £363,096,448
Registered Office: 99 Queen Victoria Street, London, EC4V 4EH
Activities: Financial leasing
Officers: Lee Lawrence Barnsley [1960] Director/Banker; Lawrence James Butcher [1968] Director/Banker; Antony Edward Mitton [1967] Director/Chartered Accountant; Mark Jeremy Rutherford [1965] Director/Banker; David Allen Ward [1956] Director/Banker [American]

SMBC Nikko Capital Markets Limited
Incorporated: 30 August 1989 *Employees:* 289
Net Worth: £1,200,954,880 *Total Assets:* £11,464,048,640
Registered Office: One New Change, London, EC4M 9AF
Activities: Security dealing on own account
Officers: Parul Dave, Secretary; Tetsuro Imaeda [1962] Director/Banker [Japanese]; Patricia Doreen Jackson [1952] Director; Hideo Kawafune [1969] Director [Japanese]; Hitoshi Minami [1961] Director [Japanese]; Bungo Miura [1967] Director/Banker [Japanese]; Naoki Okubo [1965] Director/Banker [Japanese]; Stephen Alec Souchon [1960] Director [South African]; John David Thomas [1961] Director/Banker; Antony Yates [1962] Director/Banker; Takahiro Yazawa [1964] Director/Banker [Japanese]

Smith & Nephew (Overseas) Limited
Incorporated: 20 January 1961
Net Worth: £5,385,677,312 *Total Assets:* £5,393,190,912
Registered Office: 15 Adam Street, London, WC2N 6LA
Activities: Activities of head offices
Parent: Smith & Nephew PLC
Officers: Timothy John Allison [1970] Director/Treasurer; Susan Margaret Swabey [1961] Director/Chartered Secretary

Smith & Nephew ARTC Limited
Incorporated: 29 July 2014
Net Worth: £1,757,675,392 *Total Assets:* £1,757,681,536
Registered Office: 15 Adam Street, London, WC2N 6LA
Activities: Non-trading company
Parent: Smith & Nephew (Overseas) Limited
Officers: Timothy John Allison [1970] Director/Accountant; Susan Margaret Swabey [1961] Director/Chartered Secretary

Smith & Nephew Investment Holdings Limited
Incorporated: 24 December 1943
Net Worth: £68,801,000 *Total Assets:* £655,462,016
Registered Office: 15 Adam Street, London, WC2N 6LA
Activities: Activities of head offices
Parent: Smith & Nephew UK Limited
Officers: Timothy John Allison [1970] Director; Susan Margaret Swabey [1961] Director/Chartered Secretary

Smith & Nephew PLC
Incorporated: 17 February 1937 *Employees:* 16,333
Net Worth: £3,371,080,192 *Total Assets:* £5,709,930,496
Registered Office: 15 Adam Street, London, WC2N 6LA
Activities: Manufacture of other chemical products n.e.c.
Officers: Susan Margaret Swabey, Secretary; Graham Timothy Baker [1968] Director/Chief Financial Officer; Vinita Bali [1955] Director [Indian]; Ian Edward Barlow [1951] Director/Chartered Accountant; Baroness Virginia Hilda Brunette Maxwell Bottomley [1948] Director/Executive Search; Roland Daniel Diggelmann [1967] Director [Swiss]; Erik Engstrom [1963] Director [Swedish]; Robin Anthony David Freestone [1958] Finance Director; Michael Allen Friedman [1943] Director [American]; Namal Sasrika Nawana [1970] Director/Chief Executive Officer [Australian/French]; Marc Ellis Owen [1959] Director; Roberto Quarta [1949] Director/Chairman [Italian/American]; Angela Susan Risley [1958] Director

Smith & Nephew Trading Group Limited
Incorporated: 20 January 1961
Net Worth: £200,747,008 *Total Assets:* £200,747,008
Registered Office: 15 Adam Street, London, WC2N 6LA
Activities: Activities of head offices
Parent: Smith & Nephew UK Limited
Officers: Timothy John Allison [1970] Director; Susan Margaret Swabey [1961] Director/Chartered Secretary

Smith & Nephew UK Limited
Incorporated: 19 April 2002 *Employees:* 149
Net Worth: £47,494,000 *Total Assets:* £350,328,992
Registered Office: 15 Adam Street, London, WC2N 6LA
Activities: Activities of head offices
Parent: Smith & Nephew PLC
Officers: Timothy John Allison [1970] Director/Group Treasurer; John Richard Ashworth [1964] Director; Susan Margaret Swabey [1961] Director/Chartered Secretary

Smith & Nephew USD Limited
Incorporated: 21 November 1973 *Employees:* 59
Net Worth: £7,648,556,032 *Total Assets:* £9,945,561,088
Registered Office: 15 Adam Street, London, WC2N 6LA
Activities: Other business support service activities n.e.c.
Parent: TP Limited
Officers: Timothy John Allison [1970] Director; John Richard Ashworth [1964] Director; Victoria Anne Reuben [1978] Director/Company Secretary; Susan Margaret Swabey [1961] Director/Chartered Secretary

Smith & Williamson Holdings Limited
Incorporated: 12 September 2002 *Employees:* 1,722
Net Worth: £270,492,000 *Total Assets:* £1,645,234,048
Registered Office: 25 Moorgate, London, EC2R 6AY
Activities: Activities of financial services holding companies
Shareholder: Blake Charles Goldring
Officers: Deborah Ann Saunders, Secretary; Elizabeth Grace Chambers [1962] Director/Business Executive [American]; David Martin Cobb [1964] Director; Peter Luis Fernandes [1964] Director/Fund Manager; Andrew Charles Fisher [1961] Director; Blake Charles Goldring [1958] Director [Canadian]; Grant Thomas Hotson [1971] Finance Director; Keith Jones [1952] Director; Kevin Peter Stopps [1961] Director/Chartered Accountant; Andrew Francis Sykes [1957] Director

Smith & Williamson Investment Services Limited
Incorporated: 2 April 1970
Net Worth: £43,534,000 *Total Assets:* £1,212,504,064
Registered Office: 25 Moorgate, London, EC2R 6AY
Activities: Banks
Parent: Smith & Williamson Holdings Limited
Officers: Deborah Ann Saunders, Secretary; Elizabeth Grace Chambers [1962] Director/Business Executive [American]; David Martin Cobb [1964] Director; Peter Luis Fernandes [1964] Director/Private Client Fund Manager; Andrew Charles Fisher [1961] Director; Blake Charles Goldring [1958] Director/Executive [Canadian]; Grant Thomas Hotson [1971] Finance Director; Keith Jones [1952] Director; Kevin Peter Stopps [1961] Director/Chartered Accountant; Andrew Francis Sykes [1957] Director

Smith & Williamson LLP
Incorporated: 9 November 2011
Net Worth: £110,644,000 *Total Assets:* £132,956,000
Registered Office: 25 Moorgate, London, EC2R 6AY
Officers: David Martin Cobb [1964] Member; Peter Luis Fernandes [1964] Member; Grant Thomas Hotson [1971] Member; Kevin Peter Stopps [1961] Member; Ray Alexander Abercromby [1967] LLP Member; Timothy James Adams [1980] LLP Member; Stephen John Adshead [1956] LLP Member; David Peter Alexander [1963] LLP Member; Inez Jackson Anderson [1957] LLP Member; John Christopher Appleton [1952] LLP Member; Justin James Arnesen [1985] LLP Member; Lisa Karen Ball [1972] LLP Member; Peter Edwin Ball [1975] LLP Member; Karen Elizabeth Barrow [1955] LLP Member; Garry James Bell [1970] LLP Member; Mark Simon Peter Benka [1973] LLP Member; Philip William Best [1960] LLP Member; Andrew David Bond [1963] LLP Member; Robert Owen Brassington [1958] LLP Member; Luke Brooks [1980] LLP Member; Andrew Peter Buchanan [1980] LLP Member; Christopher James Bulleyment [1976] LLP Member; Karen Elizabeth Campbell [1977] LLP Member; Nicholas John Cartwright [1967] LLP Member; Thomas Clamp [1981] LLP Member; Leonard James Clarke [1955] LLP Member; Rebecca Combes [1973] LLP Member; Wilson Peter Cotton [1956] LLP Member; Patrick Damien Coulter [1957] LLP Member; Martin Ralph Courtney [1958] LLP Member; Martyn Peter Cross [1961] LLP Member; Andrew Ronald Cunnington [1980] LLP Member; Jocelyn Hew Dalrymple [1962] LLP Member; Carl Deane [1967] LLP Member; Helen Veronica Demuth [1954] LLP Member; Stephen David Drew [1967] LLP Member; Paul Duckworth [1969] LLP Member; Andrew John Edmonds [1973] LLP Member; Edward Thomas Crawshaw Emblem [1978] LLP Member; Geoffrey Oliver Everett [1962] LLP Member; Peter Fairchild [1969] LLP Member; Maria Fandrakis [1972] LLP Member; Martyn Stuart Fraser [1975] LLP Member; Paul Frederick Garwood [1955] LLP Member; Daniela Glover [1961] LLP Member; James Gordon [1969] LLP Member; Douglas John Hall [1958] LLP Member; Faye Hall [1973] LLP Member; Nigel James Hardy [1961] LLP Member; Ashley Higgs [1975] LLP Member; John Frederick Hodgson [1958] LLP Member; John Holden [1968] LLP Member; Matthew Rhys Howells [1976] LLP Member; Angela Helen Frances Hughes [1964] LLP Member; Andrew Hunt [1964] LLP Member; Keith Jackman [1953] LLP Member; Nicholas John Jacques [1974] LLP Member; Nicholas James [1963] LLP Member; Mandy Isabel Keane [1963] LLP Member; Angela Kellock [1958] LLP Member; Jamie Nicholas Lane [1983] LLP Member; Penelope Mary Lang [1956] LLP Member; Michael David LEA [1962] LLP Member; Gilbert John Lemon [1956] LLP Member; Richard John Lewis [1975] LLP Member; Brian Keith Livingston [1960] LLP Member; Andrew Sean Lockwood [1967] LLP Member; Margaret Mary Lowe [1963] LLP Member; Iain James Lownes [1971] LLP Member; Simon John Mabey [1952] LLP Member; Peter Damian Maher [1960] LLP Member; Matthew John Maneely [1970] LLP Member; Lindsay Claire Manson [1980] LLP Member; Andrew Stephen McGill [1963] LLP Member; Andrew McKenna [1967] LLP Member; Brian John McLean [1977] LLP Member; Anita Dawn Millar-Neale [1971] LLP Member; Jeffrey Paul Millington [1967] LLP Member; Chetan Mistry [1984] LLP Member; Nicola Claire Mitford-Slade [1967] LLP Member; Philip Edward Moody [1954] LLP Member; John Mark Morris [1974] LLP Member; David John Mouncey [1960] LLP Member; Giles Adam Stuart George Murphy [1969] LLP Member; Christopher James Murray [1955] LLP Member; Michael John Neale [1954] LLP Member; Finbarr Thomas O'Connell [1960] LLP Member; Jacqueline Mary Oakes [1976] LLP Member; Nicholas Charles Osler [1959] LLP Member; Jeremy Nicholas Oswell [1953] LLP Member; Greg Andrew Palfrey [1964] LLP Member; Matthew Edward Pearson [1970] LLP Member; Claire Louise Perrett [1972] LLP Member; Rupert Jeremy Christopher Doble Phelps [1970] LLP Member; Mark John Prior [1963] LLP Member; Andrew Jonathan Pryor [1959] LLP Member; Syed Tasawar Quayum [1970] LLP Member; Philip Aidan Quigley [1959] LLP Member; Julia Ridger [1968] LLP Member

DS Smith Corrugated Packaging Limited
Incorporated: 30 August 1897 *Employees:* 579
Net Worth: £66,069,000 *Total Assets:* £141,236,992
Registered Office: 350 Euston Road, London, NW1 3AX
Activities: Manufacture of other paper and paperboard containers
Parent: DS Smith Display Holding Limited
Officers: Zillah Wendy Stone, Secretary; Paul Jonathan Brown [1971] Director; William Beverley Hicks [1962] Director; Richard Hugh Newman [1968] Director; Stefano Rossi [1967] Director [Italian]

DS Smith Display Holding Limited
Incorporated: 11 September 1943
Net Worth Deficit: £28,419,000 *Total Assets:* £165,900,000
Registered Office: 350 Euston Road, London, NW1 3AX
Activities: Activities of head offices
Parent: DS Smith International Limited
Officers: Zillah Wendy Stone, Secretary; Paul Jonathan Brown [1971] Director; William Beverley Hicks [1962] Director; Stefano Rossi [1967] Director [Italian]

DS Smith Holdings Limited
Incorporated: 3 November 2008
Net Worth: £945,816,000 *Total Assets:* £2,721,798,912
Registered Office: 350 Euston Road, London, NW1 3AX
Activities: Activities of head offices
Parent: DS Smith PLC
Officers: Zillah Wendy Stone, Secretary; William Beverley Hicks [1962] Director; Stefano Rossi [1967] Director [Italian]; Zillah Wendy Stone [1965] Director/Company Secretary

DS Smith International Limited
Incorporated: 9 August 1991
Net Worth: £730,864,000 *Total Assets:* £2,255,659,008
Registered Office: 350 Euston Road, London, NW1 3AX
Activities: Other business support service activities n.e.c.
Parent: DS Smith Holdings Limited
Officers: Zillah Wendy Stone, Secretary; William Beverley Hicks [1962] Director; Stefano Rossi [1967] Director [Italian]; Zillah Wendy Stone [1965] Director/Company Secretary

DS Smith Packaging Limited
Incorporated: 18 June 1959 *Employees:* 2,788
Net Worth: £43,990,000 *Total Assets:* £389,876,000
Registered Office: 350 Euston Road, London, NW1 3AX
Activities: Manufacture of other paper and paperboard containers
Parent: DS Smith (UK) Limited
Officers: Zillah Wendy Stone, Secretary; Paul Jonathan Brown [1971] Director; William Beverley Hicks [1962] Director; Richard Hugh Newman [1968] Director; Stefano Rossi [1967] Director [Italian]

DS Smith Paper Limited
Incorporated: 20 August 1898 *Employees:* 460
Net Worth: £255,287,008 *Total Assets:* £434,996,000
Registered Office: 350 Euston Road, London, NW1 3AX
Activities: Manufacture of paper and paperboard
Shareholders: DS Smith Holdings Limited; DS Smith International Limited
Officers: Zillah Wendy Stone, Secretary; William Beverley Hicks [1962] Director; Colin Stuart McIntyre [1962] Director; Neil Julian Miller [1973] Director

DS Smith Perch Limited
Incorporated: 20 July 2012
Net Worth: £116,554,000 *Total Assets:* £124,230,000
Registered Office: 350 Euston Road, London, NW1 3AX
Activities: Non-trading company
Parent: DS Smith Holdings Limited
Officers: Zillah Wendy Stone, Secretary; William Beverley Hicks [1962] Director; Zillah Wendy Stone [1965] Director/Company Secretary

DS Smith PLC
Incorporated: 7 July 1978 *Employees:* 27,097
Net Worth: £2,108,999,936 *Total Assets:* £6,328,999,936
Registered Office: 350 Euston Road, London, NW1 3AX
Activities: Activities of head offices
Officers: Iain David Cameron Simm, Secretary; Christopher Paul Britton [1957] Director; Gareth Davis [1950] Director; Adrian Ross Thomas Marsh [1966] Director; Jonathan Clive Nicholls [1957] Director; Kathleen Anne O'Donovan [1957] Director; Miles William Roberts [1964] Director; Louise Helen Smalley [1967] Director

DS Smith Recycling UK Limited
Incorporated: 10 July 1926 *Employees:* 423
Net Worth: £67,901,000 *Total Assets:* £139,506,000
Registered Office: 350 Euston Road, London, NW1 3AX
Activities: Recovery of sorted materials
Parent: DS Smith International Limited
Officers: Zillah Wendy Stone, Secretary; Jochen Friedrich Behr [1973] Director [German]; William Beverley Hicks [1962] Director; Colin Stuart McIntyre [1962] Director; Mathew Dafydd Prosser [1961] Director; Jonathan Paul Clason Silk [1976] Director

DS Smith Sudbrook Limited
Incorporated: 1 April 1953
Net Worth Deficit: £7,175,000 *Total Assets:* £318,823,008
Registered Office: 350 Euston Road, London, NW1 3AX
Activities: Non-trading company
Parent: DS Smith International Limited
Officers: Zillah Wendy Stone, Secretary; William Beverley Hicks [1962] Director; Zillah Wendy Stone [1965] Director/Company Secretary

Smithfield Limited
Incorporated: 12 December 1994
Net Worth: £563,150,912 *Total Assets:* £736,334,592
Registered Office: Laurence Pountney Hill, London, EC4R 0HH
Activities: Other business support service activities n.e.c.
Parent: The Prudential Assurance Company Limited
Officers: Trevor John Hankin [1959] Director/Chartered Surveyor; Jonathan James Rowley [1967] Director/Chartered Surveyor; Robert James Tidy [1961] Director/Chartered Surveyor

Smiths Detection Group Limited
Incorporated: 26 May 2004 *Employees:* 56
Net Worth: £803,897,984 *Total Assets:* £949,803,008
Registered Office: 1 Sheldon Square, Paddington, London, W2 6TT
Activities: Activities of head offices
Parent: Smiths Group International Holdings Limited
Officers: Roland Henry Clyne Carter [1967] Director/President Smiths APAC and Smiths Detection; Alain Charles McInnes [1974] Director

Smiths Finance Limited
Incorporated: 20 December 2011
Net Worth: £433,520,992 *Total Assets:* £433,520,992
Registered Office: c/o Smiths Group PLC, 4th Floor, 11-12 St James's Square, London, SW1Y 4LB
Activities: Activities of head offices
Parent: Smiths Group International Holdings Limited
Officers: Fiona Margaret Gillespie, Secretary; Alexander St. John Stopford Kenny [1971] Director of Treasury; John Michael Mills [1964] Director/Secretary; George James Montague [1964] Director/Group Financial Controller [American]

Smiths Group Finance EU Limited
Incorporated: 21 October 2016
Net Worth: £87,779,336 *Total Assets:* £365,820,896
Registered Office: c/o Smiths Detection, 7th Floor West, 1 Sheldon Square, London, W2 6TT
Activities: Activities of head offices
Parent: Smiths Group International Holdings Limited
Officers: Adam David John Ramsay, Secretary; Suzanne Ruth Hardy [1981] Director, Financial Planning & Analysis; Adam David John Ramsay [1968] Director/General Counsel

Smiths Group Finance US Limited
Incorporated: 21 October 2016 *Employees:* 2
Net Worth: £74,490,416 *Total Assets:* £606,636,928
Registered Office: c/o Smiths Detection, 7th Floor West, 1 Sheldon Square, London, W2 6TT
Activities: Activities of head offices
Parent: Smiths Group International Holdings Limited
Officers: Adam David John Ramsay, Secretary; Alexander St. John Stopford Kenny [1971] Director/Treasurer; Liam Peter King [1985] Director; Adam David John Ramsay [1968] Director/General Counsel

Smiths Group International Holdings Limited
Incorporated: 5 December 1972
Net Worth: £1,894,322,048 *Total Assets:* £9,764,216,832
Registered Office: c/o Smiths Group PLC, 4th Floor, 11-12 St James's Square, London, SW1Y 4LB
Activities: Activities of head offices
Parent: Smiths Group PLC
Officers: Fiona Margaret Gillespie, Secretary; Alexander St. John Stopford Kenny [1971] Director of Treasury; John Michael Mills [1964] Director/Company Secretary; George James Montague [1964] Director/Group Financial Controller [American]; Melanie Jane Rowlands [1968] Director/Solicitor

Smiths Group PLC
Incorporated: 15 July 1914 *Employees:* 21,700
Net Worth: £2,272,000,000 *Total Assets:* £5,173,000,192
Registered Office: 4th Floor, 11-12 St James's Square, London, SW1Y 4LB
Activities: Activities of head offices
Officers: John Michael Mills, Secretary; Bruno Francois Jules Angelici [1947] Director [French]; Olivier Jean Bohuon [1959] Director [French]; Sir George William Buckley [1947] Director/International Businessman; Dame Ann Patricia Dowling [1952] Director; Tanya Dianne Fratto [1960] Director [American]; Andrew Reynolds Smith [1966] Director/Chief Executive Officer; William Claire Seeger Jr [1951] Director [American]; Mark Donald Seligman [1956] Director; John Francis Shipsey [1964] Director/Chief Financial Officer; Noel Naval Tata [1956] Director [Irish]

Smyths Toys UK Limited
Incorporated: 12 January 2007 *Employees:* 2,195
Net Worth: £32,578,000 *Total Assets:* £197,444,992
Registered Office: Royds Withy King, 69 Carter Lane, London, EC4V 5EQ
Activities: Retail sale of games and toys in specialised stores
Officers: Anthony Smyth, Secretary/Director [Irish]; Anthony Smyth [1956] Director [Irish]; Liam Smyth [1962] Director [Irish]; Patrick Smyth [1957] Director [Irish]; Thomas Smyth [1958] Director [Irish]

Snacks International Development UK Limited
Incorporated: 28 July 2016 *Employees:* 2
Net Worth: £24,872,620 *Total Assets:* £127,669,168
Registered Office: 308-310 Elveden Road, London, NW10 7ST
Activities: Activities of other holding companies n.e.c.
Officers: Christophe Fenart [1969] Director/Manager [French]

Snap Group Limited
Incorporated: 4 September 2015 *Employees:* 128
Net Worth: £313,628,128 *Total Assets:* £573,907,200
Registered Office: 7-11 Lexington Street, London, W1F 9AF
Activities: Other information technology service activities
Officers: David Morris Abraham Lewis [1979] Director/Solicitor; Amanda Louise Reid [1978] Director/Accountant

Snap International I Limited
Incorporated: 14 November 2016
Net Worth: £1,107,347,200 *Total Assets:* £1,107,347,328
Registered Office: 77 Shaftesbury Avenue, Soho, London, W1D 5DU
Activities: Activities of head offices
Officers: Atul Manilal Porwal [1982] Director/Attorney [American]

Snap International II Limited
Incorporated: 14 November 2016
Net Worth: £1,107,229,184 *Total Assets:* £1,107,267,840
Registered Office: 77 Shaftesbury Avenue, Soho, London, W1D 5DU
Activities: Activities of head offices
Officers: Atul Manilal Porwal [1982] Director/Attorney [American]

SNC Securities Limited
Incorporated: 20 June 1977 *Employees:* 2
Net Worth: £1,301,371,136 *Total Assets:* £1,384,677,760
Registered Office: 2 King Edward Street, London, EC1A 1HQ
Activities: Financial intermediation not elsewhere classified
Parent: Bank of America Corporation
Officers: Jonathan Howard Redvers Lee [1966] Director/Company Executive; Trevor Caleb Martin [1960] Director/Company Executive

Snowdon Leasing Company Limited
Incorporated: 6 November 2007
Net Worth Deficit: £2,457,711 *Total Assets:* £117,300,536
Registered Office: Broadwalk House, 5 Appold Street, London, EC2A 2DA
Activities: Renting and leasing of freight water transport equipment
Parent: Credit Agricole CIB Marine Leasing Holdings Limited
Officers: Michelle Juanita Mahmood [1975] Director/Associate [Australian]; Aodhan James Garrett McCarthy [1975] Director/Accountant

Socar Trading (UK) Limited
Incorporated: 9 February 2015 *Employees:* 34
Net Worth Deficit: £11,620,848 *Total Assets:* £758,045,504
Registered Office: 2 St James's Market, London, SW1Y 4AH
Activities: Security and commodity contracts dealing activities
Parent: State Oil Company of Azerbaijan Republic
Officers: Emil Bayramli [1976] Director/Chief Financial Officer [Azerbaijani]; Vincent Mohy [1978] Director/General Counsel [Belgian]; Mariam Almaszade Prensilevich [1977] Director [Swiss/Azerbaijani]

Societe Generale International Limited
Incorporated: 30 March 2005 *Employees:* 285
Previous: Societe Generale Newedge UK Limited
Net Worth: £1,129,600,000 *Total Assets:* £37,335,166,976
Registered Office: 10 Bishops Square, London, E1 6EG
Activities: Financial intermediation not elsewhere classified
Parent: Societe Generale
Officers: Gerard Alfred Marie de Lambilly, Secretary; Marcia Ina Cantor-Grable [1954] Director; Michael John Collins [1947] Director/Consultant; Bruno Germain [1969] Director/Business Executive [French]; John Charles Fortescue Hitchins [1955] Independent Non-Executive Director; Christophe Bernard Lattuada [1975] Director/Chief Executive [French]; Tara Marie Palmer [1976] Director; Barry John Pearce [1965] Director; Jonathan Simon Whitehead [1966] Director/Global Head of Commodity Markets

Societe Generale Investments (U.K.) Limited
Incorporated: 22 July 1927
Net Worth: £214,449,584 *Total Assets:* £268,892,896
Registered Office: c/o Group Legal, SG House, 41 Tower Hill, London, EC3N 4SG
Activities: Activities of financial services holding companies
Parent: Societe Generale
Officers: Catherine Marie Madeleine Balinska-Jundzill, Secretary; Sarah Jane Linstead [1972] Director/Solicitor; Barry John Pearce [1965] Director/Accountant; Sadia Brigitte Ricke [1970] Director/Banker [French]; Philippe Jacques Michel Robeyns [1961] Director/Chief Operating Officer, EMEA [French]

Soco International PLC
Incorporated: 10 January 1997
Net Worth: £372,580,032 *Total Assets:* £534,689,280
Registered Office: 48 Dover Street, London, W1S 4FF
Activities: Extraction of crude petroleum
Officers: Anthony George Hunter, Secretary; Janice Margaret Brown [1955] Director; Rui Manuel Cabecadas Coelho de Sousa [1955] Director [Portuguese]; Ettore Paolo Michele Contini [1974] Director/Banker [Swiss]; Robert Gresham Gray [1954] Director; John Edward Martin [1949] Director [Australian]; Ambassador Antonio Victor Martins Monteiro [1944] Director/Diplomat [Portuguese]; Edward T Story [1943] Director/President & CEO; Dr Michael John Watts [1956] Director

Sodexo Holdings Limited
Incorporated: 4 November 1994
Net Worth: £531,716,000 *Total Assets:* £940,289,984
Registered Office: One Southampton Row, London, WC1B 5HA
Activities: Activities of head offices
Officers: Gareth Luke Sefton John, Secretary; Laurent Arnaudo [1967] Director [French]; Stuart Anthony Carter [1965] Director; Sean Michael Haley [1970] Director; Angelo Piccirillo [1975] Director [Italian]

Sodexo Limited
Incorporated: 26 March 1965 *Employees:* 36,869
Net Worth: £135,851,008 *Total Assets:* £917,420,992
Registered Office: One Southampton Row, London, WC1B 5HA
Activities: Activities of head offices
Parent: Sodexo Holdings Limited
Officers: Gareth Luke Sefton John, Secretary; Paul Anstey [1972] Director; Laurent Paul Joseph Arnaudo [1967] Director [French]; David Ian Bailey [1966] Director; Christopher John Bray [1971] Director; Stuart Anthony Carter [1965] Director; Sean Michael Haley [1970] Director; Chris James John [1959] Director; Janine Marcelle McDowell [1968] Director; Ian Spence [1971] Director

Sodexo Services Group Limited
Incorporated: 9 June 1992
Net Worth: £275,316,992 *Total Assets:* £319,384,000
Registered Office: One Southampton Row, London, WC1B 5HA
Activities: Non-trading company
Parent: Sodexo Holdings Limited
Officers: Stuart Anthony Carter [1965] Director

Softbank Group Capital Europe Limited
Incorporated: 18 October 1995 *Employees:* 3
Previous: Softbank Group Capital Limited
Net Worth: £1,423,766,784 *Total Assets:* £1,428,270,976
Registered Office: 69 Grosvenor Street, London, W1K 3JP
Activities: Activities of head offices
Parent: Softbank Group Corp
Officers: Alok Sama [1962] Director/Company Executive; Robert S. Townsend [1956] Director/Chief Legal Officer [American]

Softbank Group Capital Limited
Incorporated: 30 April 2015 *Employees:* 9
Net Worth: £25,739,323,392 *Total Assets:* £26,728,237,056
Registered Office: 69 Grosvenor Street, London, W1K 3JP
Activities: Activities of other holding companies n.e.c.
Parent: Softbank Group Corp
Officers: Lidija Mankovskaya [1983] Director [Canadian]; Alok Sama [1962] Director/Company Executive; Sarah Scott Taylor [1973] Director; Robert S. Townsend [1956] Director/Attorney [American]

Soho Estates Holdings Limited
Incorporated: 13 August 2010 *Employees:* 26
Net Worth: £702,764,992 *Total Assets:* £1,039,068,992
Registered Office: 58 Wardour Street, London, W1D 4JQ
Activities: Other letting and operating of own or leased real estate
Parent: FIJ PTC Limited
Officers: Rachel Wood, Secretary; Melvyn John Egglenton [1957] Director; Fawn Ilona James [1986] Director; John James [1953] Director; Rachel Wood [1976] Director/Chartered Certified Accountant

Soho Estates Limited
Incorporated: 5 October 1949 *Employees:* 22
Net Worth: £667,945,024 *Total Assets:* £1,003,897,984
Registered Office: 58 Wardour Street, London, W1D 4JQ
Activities: Other letting and operating of own or leased real estate
Parent: Soho Estates Holdings Limited
Officers: Rachel Wood, Secretary; Melvyn John Egglenton [1957] Director; Fawn Ilona James [1986] Director; John James [1953] Director; Steven John Norris [1945] Director; Philip Lee Thompson [1963] Director; Paul Whalan [1963] Director; Rachel Wood [1976] Director/Certified Chartered Accountant

Soho Estates Portfolio Limited
Incorporated: 9 March 2012
Net Worth: £35,721,000 *Total Assets:* £141,135,008
Registered Office: 58 Wardour Street, London, W1D 4JQ
Activities: Other letting and operating of own or leased real estate
Parent: Soho Estates Limited
Officers: Rachel Wood, Secretary; Melvyn John Egglenton [1957] Director; Fawn Ilona James [1986] Director; John James [1953] Director; Philip Lee Thompson [1963] Director; Paul Whalan [1963] Director; Rachel Wood [1976] Director/Certified Chartered Accountant

Soho House UK Limited
Incorporated: 20 October 1993 *Employees:* 1,939
Net Worth Deficit: £7,843,511 *Total Assets:* £196,620,016
Registered Office: 72-74 Dean Street, London, W1D 3SG
Activities: Licenced restaurants
Parent: Soho House Limited
Officers: Nicholas Keith Arthur Jones [1963] Director; Peter Jonathan McPhee [1975] Director [American]

Sojitz Energy Development Limited
Incorporated: 2 February 2017
Net Worth Deficit: £1,445,357 *Total Assets:* £110,634,936
Registered Office: 7th Floor, 8 Finsbury Circus, London, EC2M 7EA
Activities: Other business support service activities n.e.c.
Parent: Sojitz Corporation
Officers: Takahiro Ebisu [1967] Director/Office Worker [Japanese]; Masahiro Matsuura [1968] Director/Office Worker [Japanese]; Daisuke Yasuda [1969] Director [Japanese]

Sojitz Europe PLC
Incorporated: 1 October 1992 *Employees:* 196
Net Worth: £160,880,000 *Total Assets:* £311,593,984
Registered Office: 7th Floor, 8 Finsbury Circus, London, EC2M 7EA
Activities: Wholesale of other food, including fish, crustaceans and molluscs
Parent: Sojitz Corporation
Officers: John Emmerson, Secretary/Accounting Manager; Osamu Iwai [1959] Director/Businessman [Japanese]; Shigeru Nishihara [1962] Director/Businessman [Japanese]; Satoru Takahama [1960] Director/Businessman [Japanese]

Sojitz Global Finance PLC
Incorporated: 22 December 2015 *Employees:* 2
Net Worth: £15,231,604 *Total Assets:* £249,431,344
Registered Office: 7th Floor, 8 Finsbury Circus, London, EC2M 7EA
Activities: Financial intermediation not elsewhere classified
Parent: Sojitz Corporation
Officers: John Emmerson, Secretary; Tatsuya Maeda [1968] Director/Businessman [Japanese]; Takeshi Sumida [1974] Director/Businessman [Japanese]

SOL Aviation Services Limited
Incorporated: 25 October 2004 *Employees:* 43
Net Worth: £66,419,308 *Total Assets:* £186,393,232
Registered Office: 3 Coach House Yard, Hampstead High Street, London, NW3 1QD
Activities: Agents involved in the sale of fuels, ores, metals and industrial chemicals
Officers: Pierre Patrick Gerard Magnan [1973] Director/Chief Executive Officer [Canadian]; Andrew Albert Niles [1960] Director/Company Executive [Barbadian]; Scott William Stickland [1985] Director/Chief Financial Officer [Canadian]

Solarwinds MSP Holdings Limited
Incorporated: 1 February 2016 *Employees:* 232
Net Worth: £160,224,288 *Total Assets:* £379,050,400
Registered Office: 35 Great St Helen's, London, EC3A 6AP
Activities: Activities of other holding companies n.e.c.
Officers: Joseph Robert Antonio Ciccarello [1975] Director [American]; James Barton Kalsu [1967] Director [American]

Solitaire Group Limited
Incorporated: 9 December 1994
Net Worth: £106,890,552 *Total Assets:* £119,204,560
Registered Office: Berkeley House, 304 Regents Park Road, London, N3 2JY
Activities: Buying and selling of own real estate
Parent: Solitaire Real Estate Holdings Limited
Officers: Paul Hallam, Secretary; Christopher Charles McGill [1960] Managing Director; William Kenneth Procter [1953] Director/Accountant

Sonali Bank (UK) Limited
Incorporated: 15 June 1999 *Employees:* 52
Net Worth: £61,812,092 *Total Assets:* £240,077,552
Registered Office: 29-33 Osborn Street, London, E1 6TD
Activities: Banks
Parent: Government of Bangladesh
Officers: Mohammed Sarwar Hossain, Secretary; Md.Obayed Ullah Al Masud [1960] CEO & Managing Director [Bangladeshi]; Steven George Boult [1965] Chief Risk Officer & Executive Director; Peter John Haines [1959] Director/Chartered Accountant; Fazlul Haque [1960] Director at Sonali Bank Ltd [Bangladeshi]; Mohammed Sarwar Hossain [1959] Director/Chief Executive Officer [Bangladeshi]; Sm Mahmud Hussain [1963] Director and Chairman; Paul Mark Johnson [1966] Director

Songbird Finance Limited
Incorporated: 11 April 2007 *Employees:* 2
Net Worth: £1,893,117,568 *Total Assets:* £1,895,356,800
Registered Office: One Canary Wharf, London, E14 5AB
Activities: Activities of head offices
Parent: Canary Wharf Group Investment Holdings PLC
Officers: John Raymond Garwood, Secretary; Khalifa Khalid Al-Thani [1990] Director [Qatari]; Zachary Bryan Vaughan [1977] Director [Canadian]

Sonic Healthcare Holding Company
Incorporated: 12 December 2001 *Employees:* 5
Net Worth: £93,713,000 *Total Assets:* £170,646,000
Registered Office: The Halo Building, 1 Mabledon Place, London, WC1H 9AX
Activities: Activities of head offices
Officers: Paul Joseph Alexander, Secretary; Thomas George Timothy Amies [1971] Finance Director; David Anthony Byrne [1959] Director; Dr Colin Stephen Goldschmidt [1954] Managing Director [Australian]; Christopher David Wilks [1958] Finance Director [Australian]

Sony Corporate Services Europe Limited
Incorporated: 24 February 1989 *Employees:* 26
Net Worth: £1,073,614,976 *Total Assets:* £1,140,171,008
Registered Office: 100 New Bridge Street, London, EC4V 6JA
Activities: Activities of head offices
Parent: Sony Entertainment Holdings Europe Limited
Officers: Sarah Jayne Fahy [1964] Director/Chartered Accountant; Antony Guy France [1971] Director/Accountant; Karen Lee Halby [1958] Director/Controller [American]; Yutaka Honzawa [1960] Director/Executive [Japanese]

Sony DADC Europe Limited
Incorporated: 30 November 2005 *Employees:* 795
Previous: Sony DADC UK Limited
Net Worth: £400,473,984 *Total Assets:* £524,750,016
Registered Office: Level 5, 2 More London Riverside, London, SE1 2AP
Activities: Reproduction of sound recording
Parent: Sony Entertainment Holdings Europe Limited
Officers: Nicholas Langhorne, Secretary; Mark Khalil [1957] Director/Attorney [American]; Shoji Nemoto [1956] Director/Corporate Executive [Japanese]; Dietmar Tanzer [1964] Director [Austrian]; Russell David Taylor [1976] Director/Chartered Accountant

Sony Entertainment Holdings Europe Limited
Incorporated: 22 July 1998
Net Worth: £1,239,955,968 *Total Assets:* £1,391,933,952
Registered Office: 100 New Bridge Street, London, EC4V 6JA
Activities: Activities of head offices
Parent: Sony Corporation
Officers: Sarah Jayne Fahy [1964] Director/Chartered Accountant; Antony Guy France [1971] Director/Accountant; Karen Lee Halby [1958] Director/Controller [American]; Yutaka Honzawa [1960] Director/Executive [Japanese]

Sony Interactive Entertainment Europe Limited
Incorporated: 13 November 1996 *Employees:* 1,174
Previous: Sony Computer Entertainment Europe Limited
Net Worth: £514,338,016 *Total Assets:* £1,953,571,840
Registered Office: 10 Great Marlborough Street, London, W1F 7LP
Activities: Other information technology service activities
Parent: Sony Corporation
Officers: Marian Toole, Secretary; Tsuyoshi Kodera [1969] Director/President - Sony Network Entertainment [Japanese]; Simon Gerrard Rutter [1967] Director/EVP Marketing and Sales; James George Ryan [1959] Director

Sony Interactive Entertainment Network Europe Limited
Incorporated: 6 December 2006
Previous: Sony Network Entertainment Europe Limited
Net Worth: £81,253,568 *Total Assets:* £1,075,750,144
Registered Office: 10 Great Marlborough Street, London, W1F 7LP
Activities: Other business support service activities n.e.c.
Parent: Sony Interactive Entertainment Europe Limited
Officers: Marian Toole, Secretary; Tsuyoshi Kodera [1969] Director/President-Sony Network Entertainment International LLC [Japanese]; Simon Gerrard Rutter [1967] Director; James George Ryan [1959] Director

Sony Music Entertainment International Limited
Incorporated: 14 May 1986 *Employees:* 94
Net Worth: £568,792,000 *Total Assets:* £1,488,807,040
Registered Office: 9 Derry Street, London, W8 5HY
Activities: Other business support service activities n.e.c.
Parent: Sony Music Entertainment UK Holdings Limited
Officers: Simon Jenkins, Secretary; Stuart Anthony Levene [1977] Director/Solicitor; James Anthony Mullan [1972] Director/Barrister [Irish]; William Patrick Rowe [1961] Director/Chartered Accountant; Julie Swidler [1958] Director [American]

Sony Music Entertainment UK Limited
Incorporated: 4 January 1980 *Employees:* 317
Net Worth: £264,248,000 *Total Assets:* £529,380,000
Registered Office: 9 Derry Street, London, W8 5HY
Activities: Other amusement and recreation activities n.e.c.
Parent: Sony Music Entertainment UK Holdings Limited
Officers: Simon Jenkins, Secretary; William Patrick Rowe [1961] Director/Chartered Accountant; Michael Anthony Smith [1959] Director/Lawyer; Julie Swidler [1958] Director [American]

Sony Pictures Television Production UK Limited
Incorporated: 9 August 1996
Net Worth: £18,103,000 *Total Assets:* £118,343,000
Registered Office: Sony Pictures, Europe House, 25 Golden Square, London, W1F 9LU
Activities: Television programme production activities
Parent: Columbia Pictures Corporation Limited
Officers: Darren Nigel Hopgood, Secretary; Carrie Beth Ferman Smith [1975] Director [American]; Mark Roy Forrester [1976] Finance Director; Dr Wayne Fernley Garvie [1963] Director/President, International Production; Darren Nigel Hopgood [1977] Director/Accountant; Cheryl Lynch [1972] Director/International Business Affairs [American]; Richard John Parsons [1967] Director/Lawyer

Sotheby's
Incorporated: 24 March 1966 *Employees:* 532
Net Worth: £142,780,000 *Total Assets:* £386,742,016
Registered Office: 34-35 New Bond Street, London, W1A 2AA
Activities: Other service activities n.e.c.
Parent: Oatshare Limited
Officers: Natalie Guelfi, Secretary; Clive Graham Lord [1960] Director/C.O.O; Jan Prasens [1974] Managing Director, Europe [Slovak]

South Downs Waste Services Limited
Incorporated: 29 January 2002 *Employees:* 4
Net Worth: £29,305,000 *Total Assets:* £221,548,000
Registered Office: 210 Pentonville Road, London, N1 9JY
Activities: Collection of non-hazardous waste
Parent: Veolia ES Aurora Limited
Officers: Benjamin Peter Lambert, Secretary; Christophe Bellynck [1961] Director [French]; Neil Vincent Gallagher [1963] Finance Director; David Andrew Gerrard [1964] Executive Director; Benjamin Slater [1971] Regional Director

South Eastern Power Networks PLC
Incorporated: 7 April 1995
Net Worth: £912,899,968 *Total Assets:* £3,223,699,968
Registered Office: Newington House, 237 Southwark Bridge Road, London, SE1 6NP
Activities: Distribution of electricity
Parent: UK Power Networks Holdings Limited
Officers: Andrew Charles Pace, Secretary; Kee Ham Chan [1963] Director/Chief Financial Officer; Loi Shun Chan [1962] Director [Chinese]; Hok Shan Chong [1948] Director [Chinese]; Christopher John David Clarke [1950] Director/Solicitor; Andrew John Hunter [1958] Director; Paul Robert Jeffrey [1955] Director; Hing Lam Kam [1946] Director [Chinese]; Duncan Nicholas MacRae [1970] Director; Neil Douglas McGee [1951] Director [Australian]; Mei Fan Ngan [1965] Director [Chinese]; Basil Scarsella [1955] Director [Australian]; Charles Chao Chung Tsai [1957] Director and Chief Officer [Canadian]; Chi Tin Wan [1950] Director [Australian]

South Hook Gas Company Ltd.
Incorporated: 13 November 2003 *Employees:* 19
Net Worth Deficit: £300,264,000 *Total Assets:* £830,753,024
Registered Office: Level 28, The Shard, 32 London Bridge Street, London, SE1 9SG
Activities: Wholesale of other fuels and related products
Shareholders: Qatar Petroleum; ExxonMobil Corporation
Officers: Abdulaziz Al-Khalifa, Secretary; Abdulla Ahmad Al-Hussaini [1982] Director/Executive Vice President, Marketing, QP Marketing [Qatari]; Noora Ali Al-Kharji [1984] Director/Head of LNG Value Chain, Qatar Petroleum [Qatari]; Ali Al-Mana [1983] Director/Manager Portfolio & Assessment and Economic Evaluation [Qatari]; Ebrahim Ahmad Al-Mannai [1971] Director [Qatari]; Rodrigo Eduardo Diaz Lacayo [1969] Director/Oil & Gas Company Executive [Nicaraguan]; Ryan Christopher Ratchford [1976] Director/Oil & Gas Company Executive [American]

South London Church Fund & Southwark Diocesan Board of Finance (The)
Incorporated: 22 January 1929 *Employees:* 53
Net Worth: £287,107,008 *Total Assets:* £302,356,000
Registered Office: Trinity House, 4 Chapel Court, Borough High Street, London, SE1 1HW
Activities: Activities of religious organisations
Officers: Ruth Martin, Secretary; The Venerable Moira Anne Elizabeth Astin [1965] Director/Archdeacon; David Richard Beamish [1952] Director/Retired; John Christopher Thomas Bishop [1951] Director; Dr Nicholas John Burt [1948] Director/Retired Civil Engineer; Rebecca Justine Chapman [1981] Director/Housewife; Rt Revd Dr Richard Ian Cheetham [1955] Director/Bishop; Christopher Thomas James Chessun [1956] Director/Bishop (Church of England); Jonathan Dunnett Clark [1961] Director/Bishop; Alastair Murray Cutting [1960] Director/Archdeacon; Jacqueline Sarah Dean [1965] Director; John Edward Dewhurst [1945] Director/Semi Retired Consultant; Rt Revd Dr Woyin Karowei Dorgu [1958] Director/Bishop of Woolwich; Christopher John Elliott [1945] Director/Retired; Revd Peter James Farley-Moore [1972] Director/Clerk in Holy Orders; Lotwina Sarudzayi Farodoye [1971] Director; Philip John Fletcher [1946] Director/Retired; Despina Francois [1958] Director/Administrator; The Venerable Simon Philip Gates [1960] Director/Archdeacon; Vasanthini Berla Kirubaibai Gnanadoss [1951] Director/Retired; Adrian Douglas Crispin Greenwood [1951] Director; Michael Robert Hartley [1956] Director/Retired; Richard Alexander Helliwell [1989] Director/Tax Advisor; Dr David Clifton Keiller [1949] Director; The Venerable John Kiddle [1958] Director/Archdeacon; Nicholas Kwabena Lebey CA [1982] Director/Church Army Evangelist; Revd Jonathan Edward Gordon Macy [1968] Director/Clerk in Holy Orders; Canon Marlene Rosemarie Mallett [1959] Director/Clerk in Holy Orders; Andrew Stratton McMurtrie [1962] Director/Retired; Solabomi Anike Ogun [1958] Director/Retired; Paul Ronald Milway Parkinson [1961] Director/HR Professional (FCIPD); Colin Richard Plant [1956] Director/Retired; Revd Gregory Stephen Prior [1968] Director/Clerk in Holy Orders [South African]; Alan George Saunders [1949] Director/Retired; The Venerable Christopher John Skilton [1955] Director/Archdeacon; Jane Elizabeth Steen [1964] Director/Archdeacon; Revd Katie Jane Thomas [1971] Director/Clerk in Holy Orders; Revd Alison Janet Way [1961] Director/Clerk in Holy Orders; Revd Leslie John Wells [1961] Director/Clerk in Holy Orders

South32 SA Investments Limited
Incorporated: 13 February 2002 *Employees:* 24
Previous: BHP Billiton SA Investments Limited
Net Worth: £1,340,989,056 *Total Assets:* £2,167,046,144
Registered Office: 4th Floor, 62 Buckingham Gate, London, SW1E 6AJ
Activities: Activities of head offices
Parent: South32 Limited
Officers: Daniel James Chandler [1979] Director; Brian Robert Purdy [1966] Director/Accountant [Australian]; Anna Margarita Wood [1977] Director/Marketing Manager

Southampton Container Terminals Limited
Incorporated: 18 November 1985 *Employees:* 543
Net Worth: £93,418,000 *Total Assets:* £158,175,008
Registered Office: 16 Palace Street, London, SW1E 5JQ
Activities: Cargo handling for water transport activities
Parent: The Peninsular and Oriental Steam Navigation Company
Officers: Mohammad Alhashimy, Secretary; Rashed Ali Hassan Abdulla Al Qahtani Al Qahtani [1971] Director/SVP & MD Europe & Russia [Emirati]; Mantraraj Dipak Budhdev [1986] Director/Solicitor; Francis Christopher Lewis [1954] Managing Director; Nicholas Paul Loader [1962] Director/Accountant; Alan Shaoul [1971] Business Development Director; Dirk Van Den Bosch [1958] Commercial Director [Belgian]; Robert Barclay Woods [1946] Managing Director

Southbank Media Ltd
Incorporated: 15 December 2010
Net Worth: £1,563,655,296 *Total Assets:* £1,567,190,912
Registered Office: One Fleet Place, London, EC4M 7WS
Activities: Activities of other holding companies n.e.c.
Parent: Discovery, Inc.
Officers: Todd Francis Davis [1962] Director/EVP, Senior Tax Counsel [American]; Roanne LEA Weekes [1978] Director/Accountant [Australian]

Southern Pacific Mortgage Limited
Incorporated: 15 October 1996 *Employees:* 4
Net Worth: £295,184,992 *Total Assets:* £1,590,978,944
Registered Office: Hays Galleria, 1 Hays Lane, London, SE1 2RD
Activities: Financial intermediation not elsewhere classified
Parent: Resetfan Limited
Officers: Lee Christopher Brandon [1953] Director

Sova Capital Limited
Incorporated: 19 December 2002 *Employees:* 228
Previous: Otkritie Capital International Limited
Net Worth: £255,812,080 *Total Assets:* £1,113,623,296
Registered Office: 12th Floor, 88 Wood Street, London, EC2V 7RS
Activities: Financial intermediation not elsewhere classified
Major Shareholder: Roman Avdeev
Officers: Oleg Borunov [1979] Financial Services Director [Russian/Cypriot]; Kerim Richard Derhalli [1962] Director/Chief Executive Officer; Nikolay Katorzhnov [1984] Director/Financial Services [Cypriot/Russian]; Michael David Newton [1955] Certified Chartered Accountant & Director; Howard Peter Snell [1955] Financial Services Director; Sergey Sergeevich Sukhanov [1974] Director/Financial Services [Russian]

Sparrows Offshore Services Limited
Incorporated: 14 April 1965 *Employees:* 881
Net Worth: £47,580,000 *Total Assets:* £160,888,992
Registered Office: 30 Crown Place, London, EC2A 4ES
Activities: Other business support service activities n.e.c.
Parent: Sparrows Offshore International Group Ltd.
Officers: Neil Austin Johnson [1969] Director CFO; Ewen Kerr [1968] Director; Stewart Andrew Alan Mitchell [1966] Director

SPIE UK Limited
Incorporated: 24 March 2010
Net Worth: £71,661,000 *Total Assets:* £204,720,000
Registered Office: 2nd Floor, 33 Gracechurch Street, London, EC3V 0BT
Activities: Other business support service activities n.e.c.
Parent: SPIE Operations
Officers: Benjamin Christopher Hancock, Secretary; Denis Chene [1961] Director [French]; Robert Roy Goodhew [1965] Director/Chartered Engineer; Gauthier Louette [1961] Director [French]; Antony David Wilkinson [1966] Director/Chief Financial Officer

Spire Healthcare (Holdings) Limited
Incorporated: 31 October 2001
Net Worth: £579,944,000 *Total Assets:* £648,798,016
Registered Office: 3 Dorset Rise, London, EC4Y 8EN
Activities: Other business support service activities n.e.c.
Parent: Spire Healthcare Holdings 3 Limited
Officers: Daniel Francis Toner, Secretary; Justinian Joseph Ash [1965] Director/Chief Executive Officer; Peter James Corfield [1971] Director/Chief Commercial Officer; Jitesh Himatlal Sodha [1968] Director/Chief Financial Officer; Daniel Francis Toner [1968] Director/Solicitor

Spire Healthcare Finance Limited
Incorporated: 10 June 2014
Net Worth: £1,004,168,000 *Total Assets:* £1,493,936,000
Registered Office: 3 Dorset Rise, London, EC4Y 8EN
Activities: Activities of head offices
Parent: Spire Healthcare Group PLC
Officers: Daniel Francis Toner, Secretary; Justinian Joseph Ash [1965] Director/Chief Executive Officer; Peter James Corfield [1971] Director/Chief Commercial Officer; Jitesh Himatlal Sodha [1968] Director/Chief Financial Officer; Daniel Francis Toner [1968] Director/Solicitor

Spire Healthcare Group PLC
Incorporated: 12 June 2014 *Employees:* 11,344
Net Worth: £1,037,900,032 *Total Assets:* £1,734,099,968
Registered Office: 3 Dorset Rise, London, EC4Y 8EN
Activities: Activities of head offices
Officers: Daniel Francis Toner, Secretary; Adele Helen Anderson [1965] Director; Justinian Joseph Ash [1965] Director/Chief Executive Officer; Peter Richard Bamford [1954] Director; Anthony Rhys Bourne [1953] Director; Professor Dame Janet Elizabeth Husband [1940] Director; Simon Nicholas Rowlands [1957] Director; Jitesh Himatlal Sodha [1968] Director/Chief Financial Officer; Dr Carel Aron Van Der Merwe [1962] Director/Chief Executive Officer [South African]; Garry Watts [1956] Director

Spire Healthcare Group UK Limited
Incorporated: 4 September 2008
Net Worth: £634,851,968 *Total Assets:* £638,585,984
Registered Office: 3 Dorset Rise, London, EC4Y 8EN
Activities: Activities of other holding companies n.e.c.
Parent: Spire Healthcare Finance Limited
Officers: Daniel Francis Toner, Secretary; Justinian Joseph Ash [1965] Director/Chief Executive Officer; Peter James Corfield [1971] Director/Chief Commercial Officer; Jitesh Himatlal Sodha [1968] Director/Chief Financial Officer; Daniel Francis Toner [1968] Director/Solicitor

Spire Healthcare Holdings 1
Incorporated: 14 August 2007
Net Worth: £990,056,000 *Total Assets:* £991,774,016
Registered Office: 3 Dorset Rise, London, EC4Y 8EN
Activities: Activities of head offices
Parent: Spire Healthcare Group UK Limited
Officers: Daniel Francis Toner, Secretary; Justinian Joseph Ash [1965] Director/Chief Executive Officer; Peter James Corfield [1971] Director/Chief Commercial Officer; Jitesh Himatlal Sodha [1968] Director/Chief Financial Officer; Daniel Francis Toner [1968] Director/Solicitor

Spire Healthcare Holdings 2 Limited
Incorporated: 14 August 2007
Net Worth: £709,390,976 *Total Assets:* £709,414,976
Registered Office: 3 Dorset Rise, London, EC4Y 8EN
Activities: Activities of head offices
Parent: Spire Healthcare Holdings 1
Officers: Daniel Francis Toner, Secretary; Justinian Joseph Ash [1965] Director/Chief Executive Officer; Peter James Corfield [1971] Director/Chief Commercial Officer; Jitesh Himatlal Sodha [1968] Director/Chief Financial Officer; Daniel Francis Toner [1968] Director/Solicitor

Spire Healthcare Holdings 3 Limited
Incorporated: 7 June 2007
Net Worth: £1,724,327,936 *Total Assets:* £1,731,436,032
Registered Office: 3 Dorset Rise, London, EC4Y 8EN
Activities: Activities of other holding companies n.e.c.
Parent: Spire Healthcare Holdings 2 Limited
Officers: Daniel Francis Toner, Secretary; Justinian Joseph Ash [1965] Director/Chief Executive Officer; Peter James Corfield [1971] Director/Chief Commercial Officer; Jitesh Himatlal Sodha [1968] Director/Chief Financial Officer; Daniel Francis Toner [1968] Director/Solicitor

Spire Healthcare Limited
Incorporated: 15 October 1980 *Employees:* 8,219
Net Worth: £182,326,000 *Total Assets:* £878,553,984
Registered Office: 3 Dorset Rise, London, EC4Y 8EN
Activities: Hospital activities
Parent: Spire Healthcare (Holdings) Limited
Officers: Daniel Francis Toner, Secretary; Justinian Joseph Ash [1965] Director/Chief Executive Officer; Peter James Corfield [1971] Director/Chief Commercial Officer; Dr Jean Jacques de Gorter [1968] Director [French]; Jitesh Himatlal Sodha [1968] Director/Chief Financial Officer; Daniel Francis Toner [1968] Director/Solicitor

Spire Property 5 Limited
Incorporated: 25 October 2007
Net Worth: £96,958,000 *Total Assets:* £100,384,000
Registered Office: 3 Dorset Rise, London, EC4Y 8EN
Activities: Other business support service activities n.e.c.
Parent: Spire UK Holdco 4 Limited
Officers: Daniel Francis Toner, Secretary; Justinian Joseph Ash [1965] Director/Chief Executive Officer; Peter James Corfield [1971] Director/Chief Commercial Officer; Jitesh Himatlal Sodha [1968] Director/Chief Financial Officer; Daniel Francis Toner [1968] Director/Solicitor

Spire UK Holdco 2A Limited
Incorporated: 13 August 2008
Net Worth: £519,305,984 *Total Assets:* £526,416,000
Registered Office: 3 Dorset Rise, London, EC4Y 8EN
Activities: Activities of head offices
Parent: Spire Healthcare Finance Limited
Officers: Daniel Francis Toner, Secretary; Justinian Joseph Ash [1965] Director/Chief Executive Officer; Peter James Corfield [1971] Director/Chief Commercial Officer; Jitesh Himatlal Sodha [1968] Director/Chief Financial Officer; Daniel Francis Toner [1968] Director/Solicitor

Spire UK Holdco 4 Limited
Incorporated: 14 August 2007
Net Worth: £391,342,016 *Total Assets:* £669,118,976
Registered Office: 3 Dorset Rise, London, EC4Y 8EN
Activities: Activities of head offices
Parent: Spire UK Holdco 2A Limited
Officers: Daniel Francis Toner, Secretary; Justinian Joseph Ash [1965] Director/Chief Executive Officer; Peter James Corfield [1971] Director/Chief Commercial Officer; Jitesh Himatlal Sodha [1968] Director/Chief Financial Officer; Daniel Francis Toner [1968] Director/Solicitor

Spirit Aerosystems (Europe) Limited
Incorporated: 29 December 2005 *Employees:* 897
Net Worth: £267,396,000 *Total Assets:* £493,632,000
Registered Office: Tower Bridge House, St Katharine's Way, London, E1W 1AA
Activities: Manufacture of air and spacecraft and related machinery
Parent: Spirit Aerosystems Holdings Inc.
Officers: Stacy Cozad, Secretary; Allan Russell Bowie [1964] Director/Chartered Accountant; Thomas Hugh Cowan [1976] Finance Director; John Gilson [1971] Director [American]; Scott McLarty [1969] Director

Spirit Issuer Parent Limited
Incorporated: 15 October 2004
Net Worth: £127,000 *Total Assets:* £825,761,984
Registered Office: Third Floor, 1 King's Arms Yard, London, EC2R 7AF
Activities: Other business support service activities n.e.c.
Parent: Wilmington Trust SP Services (London) Limited
Officers: Daniel Jonathan Wynne [1970] Director

Spirit Issuer PLC
Incorporated: 21 October 2004
Net Worth: £164,000 *Total Assets:* £825,761,984
Registered Office: Third Floor, 1 King's Arms Yard, London, EC2R 7AF
Activities: Other business support service activities n.e.c.
Parent: Spirit Issuer Parent Limited
Officers: Daniel Jonathan Wynne [1970] Director

Spitalfields Developments Limited
Incorporated: 5 June 1986
Net Worth: £4,550,000 *Total Assets:* £106,620,000
Registered Office: Kings Place, 90 York Way, London, N1 9GE
Activities: Buying and selling of own real estate
Parent: Spitalfields Holdings Limited
Officers: Andrew John Berger-North [1961] Director/Chartered Surveyor; Peter William Beaumont Cole [1959] Director/Chartered Surveyor

Sponsio Limited
Incorporated: 26 February 2001
Net Worth: £259,596,992 *Total Assets:* £259,806,000
Registered Office: 3rd Floor, One New Change, London, EC4M 9AF
Activities: Other business support service activities n.e.c.
Parent: Ladbrokes Investments Holdings Limited
Officers: Sian Amanda Hoskin, Secretary; Fiona Lorraine Perez, Secretary; Mark Anthony Fowler [1969] Director; Adam Bryce Greenblatt [1974] Director; Ross Martin Sandbach [1977] Finance Director

The Sporting Exchange Limited
Incorporated: 4 May 1999
Net Worth: £127,191,000 *Total Assets:* £374,878,016
Registered Office: Waterfront, Hammersmith Embankment, Chancellors Road, access on Winslow Road, London, W6 9HP
Activities: Other information technology service activities
Parent: Betfair Group Limited
Officers: Pritti Patel, Secretary; Jeremy Peter Jackson [1975] Director; Edward Martin Traynor [1977] Director/General Counsel [Irish]

The Sports Council Trust Company
Incorporated: 27 June 1990
Net Worth: £110,946,000 *Total Assets:* £112,139,000
Registered Office: First Floor, 21 Bloomsbury Street, London, WC1B 3HF
Activities: Operation of sports facilities
Officers: Tanya Van Niekerk, Secretary; Vivien Margaret Blacker [1958] Director/Consultant; David Joseph Cove [1968] Director/Charity Chief Executive; Graeme Ryland Frederick Dell [1964] Director; Helen Martin [1970] Director/Finance and Governance Consultant; Peter William Rowley [1955] Director/Advisor to Charities/Portfolio Non-Executive Appointment; Andrew Loyn Watson [1967] Director

Spotify Finance Limited
Incorporated: 11 April 2011
Net Worth: £1,291,962 *Total Assets:* £172,063,216
Registered Office: 4th Floor, 25 Argyll Street, London, W1F 7TU
Activities: Other business support service activities n.e.c.
Parent: Spotify Technology S.A.
Officers: Thomas Wolfe Tone Connaughton [1979] Director/Business Executive [Irish]; Barry McCarthy Jr [1953] Director [American]; Jens Christian Grejs Svolgaard [1966] Director/Business Executive [Danish]

Spotify Limited
Incorporated: 23 November 2007 *Employees:* 226
Net Worth: £496,689 *Total Assets:* £111,565,200
Registered Office: 4th Floor, 25 Argyll Street, London, W1F 7TU
Activities: Other business support service activities n.e.c.
Parent: Spotify Technology S.A.
Officers: W Barry McCarthy Jr [1953] Director [American]; Thomas Wolfe Tone Connaughton [1979] Director/Business Executive [Irish]; Jens Christian Grejs Svolgaard [1966] Director/Business Executive [Danish]

Spring Group Limited
Incorporated: 6 September 1957
Net Worth: £108,099,000 *Total Assets:* £391,708,000
Registered Office: Millennium Bridge House, 2 Lambeth Hill, London, EC4V 4BG
Activities: Activities of head offices
Parent: Olsten (U.K) Holdings Limited
Officers: Rashida Atinuke Akinjobi, Secretary; Alexandra Helen Bishop [1974] Director; Yann Serge Stephane Halka [1974] Director/Chief Financial Officer [French]; Gavin Kenneth Tagg [1972] Director

Spring Technology Staffing Services Limited
Incorporated: 19 June 1985 *Employees:* 112
Net Worth: £49,116,000 *Total Assets:* £472,331,008
Registered Office: Millennium Bridge House, 2 Lambeth Hill, London, EC4V 4BG
Activities: Temporary employment agency activities
Parent: Spring Group Limited
Officers: Rashida Atinuke Akinjobi, Secretary; Gavin Tagg, Secretary; Alexandra Helen Bishop [1974] Director; Yann Serge Stephane Halka [1974] Director/Chief Financial Officer [French]; Gavin Kenneth Tagg [1972] Director

Springer Nature Holdings Limited
Incorporated: 31 January 1896
Previous: HM Publishers Holdings Limited
Net Worth: £100,806,000 *Total Assets:* £203,584,992
Registered Office: The Campus, 4 Crinan Street, London, N1 9XW
Activities: Book publishing
Shareholders: Stefan von Holtzbrinck; Springer Nature Publishers Holdings Limited
Officers: Gabrielle Mary Williams Hamer, Secretary; Steven Charles Inchcoombe [1964] Executive Director; Rachel Elizabeth Jacobs [1975] Director/Lawyer; Gabrielle Mary Williams Hamer [1958] Director/Company Secretary

Springer Nature Limited
Incorporated: 24 December 1963 *Employees:* 1,359
Previous: Macmillan Publishers Limited
Net Worth: £218,600,000 *Total Assets:* £667,692,992
Registered Office: The Campus, 4 Crinan Street, London, N1 9XW
Activities: Book publishing
Shareholders: Springer Nature (UK) Limited; Stefan von Holtzbrinck
Officers: Gabrielle Mary Williams Hamer, Secretary; Emma Jane Bourne [1969] Director/Publisher; Steven Charles Inchcoombe [1964] Executive Director; Rachel Elizabeth Jacobs [1975] Director/Lawyer; Dr Helmut Ulrich Vest [1963] Director/Chief Financial Officer [German]; Gabrielle Mary Williams Hamer [1958] Director/Company Secretary

Springer Nature One Limited
Incorporated: 15 December 2016
Net Worth: £40,324,140 *Total Assets:* £131,092,760
Registered Office: 4 The Campus, Crinan Street, London, N1 9XW
Activities: Non-trading company
Shareholder: Stefan von Holtzbrinck
Officers: Gabrielle Mary Williams Hamer, Secretary; Steven Charles Inchcoombe [1964] Executive Director; Rachel Elizabeth Jacobs [1975] Director/Lawyer; Dr Helmut Ulrich Vest [1963] Director/Chief Financial Officer [German]; Gabrielle Mary Williams Hamer [1958] Director/Company Secretary

Springer Nature Publishers Holdings Limited
Incorporated: 10 April 1995
Previous: Holtzbrinck Publishers Holdings Limited
Net Worth: £263,432,000 *Total Assets:* £496,536,992
Registered Office: The Campus, 4 Crinan Street, London, N1 9XW
Activities: Book publishing
Shareholder: Stefan von Holtzbrinck
Officers: Gabrielle Mary Williams Hamer, Secretary; Steven Charles Inchcoombe [1964] Director; Rachel Elizabeth Jacobs [1975] Director/Lawyer; Dr Helmut Ulrich Vest [1963] Director/Chief Financial Officer [German]; Gabrielle Mary Williams Hamer [1958] Director/Company Secretary

Springer Nature Two Limited
Incorporated: 15 December 2016
Net Worth: £54,009,448 *Total Assets:* £175,883,840
Registered Office: 4 Crinan Street, London, N1 9XW
Activities: Non-trading company
Shareholders: Stefan von Holtzbrinck; Macmillan Limited
Officers: Gabrielle Mary Williams Hamer, Secretary; Steven Charles Inchcoombe [1964] Executive Director; Rachel Elizabeth Jacobs [1975] Director/Lawyer; Dr Helmut Ulrich Vest [1963] Director/Chief Financial Officer [German]; Gabrielle Mary Williams Hamer [1958] Director/Company Secretary

SPX European Holding Limited
Incorporated: 20 April 2015
Net Worth: £131,972,000 *Total Assets:* £281,107,008
Registered Office: 5th Floor, One New Change, London, EC4M 9AF
Activities: Other service activities n.e.c.
Parent: SPX Corporation
Officers: Kevin Paul Lench [1961] Managing Director; John Nurkin [1969] Director [American]; Scott William Sproule [1969] Director/Vice President, Treasurer & CFO [American]; Lynn Williams [1956] Director/Accountant

Square Enix Limited
Incorporated: 29 March 1984 *Employees:* 228
Net Worth Deficit: £301,297,984 *Total Assets:* £256,988,000
Registered Office: 240 Blackfriars Road, London, SE1 8NW
Activities: Publishing of computer games
Parent: Square Enix Holdings Co., Ltd
Officers: Amit Chokshi, Secretary; Yosuke Matsuda [1963] Director [Japanese]; Philip Timo Rogers [1969] Director

SRE Portfolios UK Ltd
Incorporated: 2 November 2011
Net Worth: £186,662,784 *Total Assets:* £186,668,912
Registered Office: Floor 6, Quadrant House, 4 Thomas More Square, London, E1W 1YW
Activities: Other service activities n.e.c.
Officers: Ian Malcolm Livingstone [1962] Director; Richard John Livingstone [1964] Director; Leonard Kevin Sebastian [1969] Group Managing and Legal Director [Swiss]

SREP Holdings Ltd
Incorporated: 29 August 2014 *Employees:* 190
Net Worth: £221,684,992 *Total Assets:* £341,784,992
Registered Office: Floor 6, Quadrant House, 4 Thomas More Square, London, E1W 1YW
Activities: Activities of other holding companies n.e.c.
Shareholders: Richard John Livingstone; Ian Malcolm Livingstone
Officers: Ian Malcolm Livingstone [1962] Director; Leonard Kevin Sebastian [1969] Group Managing and Legal Director [Swiss]

SSB No. 1 PLC
Incorporated: 8 December 2010
Net Worth: £1,704,786 *Total Assets:* £1,007,020,224
Registered Office: 6th Floor, 65 Gresham Street, London, EC2V 7NQ
Activities: Other business support service activities n.e.c.
Parent: Link Trust Nominees No.1 Limited
Officers: Colin Arthur Benford [1962] Director

SSC Holdco (UK) Limited
Incorporated: 2 December 2016 *Employees:* 4
Net Worth: £207,474,800 *Total Assets:* £424,753,472
Registered Office: Suite 1, 3rd Floor, 11-12 St James's Square, London, SW1Y 4LB
Activities: Manufacture of medical and dental instruments and supplies
Officers: Victor Manuel Diaz [1960] Director/Medical Devices [American]; Daniel Joseph Sutherby [1964] Director/Finance Officer [American]; Lawrence Wang [1977] Director/Finance [American]; Chen Yu [1974] Director/Finance [American]

SSC Intermediateco Limited
Incorporated: 22 December 2016 *Employees:* 4
Net Worth: £214,794,112 *Total Assets:* £214,955,120
Registered Office: Suite 1, 3rd Floor, 11-12 St James's Square, London, SW1Y 4LB
Activities: Manufacture of medical and dental instruments and supplies
Officers: Victor Manuel Diaz [1960] Director/Medical Devices [American]; Daniel Joseph Sutherby [1964] Director/Finance Officer [American]; Lawrence Wang [1977] Director/Finance [American]; Chen Yu [1974] Director/Finance [American]

SSP Euro Holdings Limited
Incorporated: 16 August 2013
Net Worth: £256,144,496 *Total Assets:* £385,417,664
Registered Office: 169 Euston Road, London, NW1 2AE
Activities: Activities of head offices
Parent: SSP Financing Limited
Officers: Helen Byrne, Secretary; Russell Ian Chaplin [1956] Director/Head of Tax; Miles Eric Collins [1966] Director/Group Financial Controller; Jonathan Owen Davies [1962] Finance Director; Christopher McNaughton Wright [1978] Director/Treasurer

SSP Financing Limited
Incorporated: 9 March 2006
Net Worth: £585,462,016 *Total Assets:* £1,697,709,056
Registered Office: 169 Euston Road, London, NW1 2AE
Activities: Activities of head offices
Parent: SSP Group Holdings Limited
Officers: Helen Byrne, Secretary; Russell Ian Chaplin [1956] Director/Head of Tax; Miles Eric Collins [1966] Director/Chartered Accountant; Jonathan Owen Davies [1962] Director; Christopher McNaughton Wright [1978] Director/Treasurer

SSP Financing UK Limited
Incorporated: 9 March 2006 *Employees:* 108
Net Worth: £238,440,992 *Total Assets:* £447,025,984
Registered Office: 169 Euston Road, London, NW1 2AE
Activities: Activities of head offices
Parent: SSP Financing Limited
Officers: Helen Byrne, Secretary; Russell Ian Chaplin [1956] Director/Head of Tax; Miles Eric Collins [1966] Director/Chartered Accountant; Jonathan Owen Davies [1962] Director; Christopher McNaughton Wright [1978] Director/Treasurer

SSP Group Holdings Limited
Incorporated: 9 March 2006
Net Worth: £918,065,024 *Total Assets:* £918,065,024
Registered Office: 169 Euston Road, London, NW1 2AE
Activities: Activities of head offices
Parent: SSP Group PLC
Officers: Helen Byrne, Secretary; Russell Ian Chaplin [1956] Director/Head of Tax; Miles Eric Collins [1966] Director/Chartered Accountant; Jonathan Owen Davies [1962] Director

SSP Group PLC
Incorporated: 9 March 2006 *Employees:* 36,783
Net Worth: £400,300,000 *Total Assets:* £1,443,800,064
Registered Office: 169 Euston Road, London, NW1 2AE
Activities: Activities of head offices
Officers: Helen Byrne, Secretary; Carolyn Jane Bradley [1964] Director; Jonathan Owen Davies [1962] Director; Ian Dyson [1962] Director; Simon Smith [1972] Director; Vagn Ove Soerensen [1959] Director/Chairman of The Board [Danish]; Kathryn Elizabeth Swann [1964] Director; Per Utnegaard [1959] Director [Norwegian]

St Andrew's Insurance PLC
Incorporated: 15 September 1995
Net Worth: £89,400,000 *Total Assets:* £376,388,992
Registered Office: 33 Old Broad Street, London, EC2N 1HZ
Activities: Non-life insurance
Parent: Lloyds Bank General Insurance Holdings Limited
Officers: Joanne Margaret Jolly, Secretary; Andrea Margaret Blance [1964] Director; Kate Cheetham [1963] Director/Group General Counsel; Mark George Culmer [1962] Finance Director; Jane Elizabeth Mary Curtis [1960] Director; Michael Harris [1965] Director; John Francis Hylands [1951] Director; Antonio Lorenzo [1966] Director [Spanish]; Christopher John George Moulder [1958] Director; Sophie Jane O'Connor [1970] Director; Dr Jakob Pfaudler [1972] Community Banking Director [Austrian]; Nicholas Edward Tucker Prettejohn [1960] Director

St Ermin's Property Co.Limited
Incorporated: 2 April 1962 *Employees:* 3
Net Worth: £120,858,608 *Total Assets:* £123,394,552
Registered Office: Ground Floor, 30 City Road, London, EC1Y 2AB
Activities: Buying and selling of own real estate
Shareholders: Mark Andrew Pears; Trevor Steven Pears; Barry Michael Howard Shaw
Officers: William Frederick Bennett, Secretary; David Alan Pears, Secretary; David Alan Pears [1968] Director; Mark Andrew Pears [1962] Director; Sir Trevor Steven Pears [1964] Director

St Martins Healthcare Limited
Incorporated: 1 December 1944 *Employees:* 1,020
Net Worth: £323,344,000 *Total Assets:* £587,046,016
Registered Office: 242 Marylebone Road, London, NW1 6JL
Activities: Hospital activities
Parent: St. Martins Ltd.
Officers: Catherine Mary Jane Vickery, Secretary; John Mozart Franck [1962] Director/Attorney [American]; Michael Thomas Neeb [1962] Director/Chief Executive Officer; Teresa Finch Pritchard [1960] Director [American]; John Michael Reay [1961] Director; Catherine Mary Jane Vickery [1975] Director/Solicitor

St Mungo Community Housing Association
Incorporated: 24 September 2012 *Employees:* 1,475
Net Worth: £17,722,000 *Total Assets:* £115,348,000
Registered Office: 5th Floor, 3 Thomas More Square, London, E1W 1YW
Activities: Other accommodation
Officers: Louise Ann Wykes, Secretary; Tracy Helen Allison [1965] Executive Director; Rolande Jane Anderson [1955] Director/Retired; Alexandra Flora Beidas [1978] Director/Lawyer; Daniel Richard Corry [1959] Director/Chief Executive; Timothy James Gadd [1958] Director/Independent Consultant; John Maxted [1956] Director/Business Consultant; Robert Stewart Napier [1947] Director/Chairman; Mark Andrew Pears [1962] Director; Dr Helen Walters [1966] Director/Doctor; John Watts [1957] Director/Self Employed

St. James Court Hotel Limited
Incorporated: 3 December 1999 *Employees:* 281
Net Worth: £63,043,776 *Total Assets:* £112,399,848
Registered Office: St James Court Hotel, Buckingham Gate, London, SW1E 6AF
Activities: Hotels and similar accommodation
Parent: The Indian Hotels Company Limited
Officers: Piyush Mangal, Secretary; Puneet Chhatwal [1964] Director/Chief Executive [German]; Farrokh Kavarana [1944] Director [Indian]; Chandrasekhar Nagarajan [1963] Director/Management Consultant; Rajesh Nagpal [1968] Director/Hotelier [Indian]; Rajkumar Menghraj Nagpal [1942] Director/Hotelier [Indian]; Sudhir Nagpal [1959] Director [Indian]; Giridhar Sanjeevi [1963] Director/Chief Financial Officer [Indian]

St. John Ambulance
Incorporated: 21 October 1999 *Employees:* 1,799
Net Worth: £130,700,000 *Total Assets:* £154,500,000
Registered Office: St John's Gate, St John's Lane, London, EC1M 4DA
Activities: Other human health activities
Officers: Martin Houghton-Brown, Secretary; Richard James Sims, Secretary; Ann Elizabeth Cable [1953] Director/Headteacher; Margaret Ellen Coleman [1950] Director; Nicholas Arthur Frayling [1944] Director; Lionel John Jarvis [1955] Director; Mohan Mansigani [1957] Director/Accountant; Jayne Elizabeth Mee [1961] Human Resources Director; Michael Messinger [1946] Director/Retired; Professor Sir Keith MacDonald Porter [1948] Director/Professor of Clinical Traumatology; David Alan Reeves [1947] Director/Consultant; David John Springthorpe [1959] Director/Finance Officer; Matt Stevenson-Dodd [1973] Director/Chief Executive

St. Martins Ltd.
Incorporated: 28 October 1999
Net Worth Deficit: £51,404,000 *Total Assets:* £471,756,992
Registered Office: 242 Marylebone Road, London, NW1 6JL
Activities: Hospital activities
Parent: HCA UK Holdings Limited
Officers: Catherine Mary Jane Vickery, Secretary; John Mozart Franck [1962] Director/Attorney [American]; Jeremy Randal Midkiff [1979] Director [American]; Michael Thomas Neeb [1962] Director/Chief Executive Officer; Teresa Finch Pritchard [1960] Director [American]; John Michael Reay [1961] Director; Catherine Mary Jane Vickery [1975] Director/Solicitor

St. Paul's School
Incorporated: 6 March 2007 *Employees:* 300
Net Worth: £108,286,000 *Total Assets:* £133,338,000
Registered Office: St Paul's School, Lonsdale Road, Barnes, London, SW13 9JT
Activities: Primary education
Officers: Sarah Anne Barker [1976] Director/Solicitor; Nicola Jane Doyle [1961] Director/Headteacher; Adam Fenwick [1960] Director/Company Chairman; Sir Simon James Fraser [1958] Director; Lord Anthony Stephen Grabiner QC [1945] Director/Barrister; Professor Rosemary Helen Luckin [1958] Director/University Professor; Alison MacLeod [1958] Director/HR Manager; Alison Jane Palmer [1970] Director/Recruitment Consultant; John Manwaring Robertson [1951] Director; Earl Michael Henry Hicks Beach St Aldwyn [1950] Director/Financial Intermediary; Alistair Generald Summers [1965] Director/Chartered Accountant; Benjamin Victor Robert Thomas [1969] Director; Christopher John Vermont [1959] Managing Director, GuarantCo

St. Stephens Shopping Centre Limited
Incorporated: 14 October 2003
Net Worth: £129,439,584 *Total Assets:* £155,995,776
Registered Office: York House, 45 Seymour Street, London, W1H 7LX
Activities: Development of building projects
Parent: Union Property Holdings (London) Limited
Officers: Sarah Morrell Barzycki [1958] Director/Head of Finance; Timothy Andrew Roberts [1964] Director/Chartered Surveyor; Nigel Mark Webb [1963] Director/Chartered Surveyor

STA Travel International Limited
Incorporated: 20 January 2004 *Employees:* 46
Net Worth: £18,155,776 *Total Assets:* £179,776,960
Registered Office: Priory House, 6 Wrights Lane, London, W8 6TA
Activities: Travel agency activities
Parent: STA Travel Holding AG
Officers: Victoria Parkinson, Secretary; Reinhard Kotzaurek [1965] Director [Austrian]; Nino Alexander Ostertag [1979] Director [German]

The Stage Shoreditch LLP
Incorporated: 31 March 2015
Net Worth: £170,971,488 *Total Assets:* £285,726,496
Registered Office: 33 Davies Street, London, W1K 4LR

The Stage Shoreditch Residential Limited
Incorporated: 23 April 2015
Net Worth Deficit: £8,589,917 *Total Assets:* £179,344,176
Registered Office: 33 Davies Street, London, W1K 4LR
Activities: Buying and selling of own real estate
Parent: The Stage Shoreditch LLP
Officers: Stephen Stuart Solomon Conway [1948] Director; Jonathan Simon Goldstein [1966] Director; Drew McCourt [1981] Director/Real Estate President [American]; Donagh O'Sullivan [1968] Construction Director [Irish]; Richard Michael Pilkington [1967] Managing Director

Stallergenes Greer PLC
Incorporated: 6 December 2013 *Employees:* 16
Net Worth: £392,322,400 *Total Assets:* £473,830,016
Registered Office: Tower Bridge House, St Katharine's Way, London, E1W 1DD
Activities: Other professional, scientific and technical activities n.e.c.
Officers: Nunzio Michele Antonelli [1960] Director [Italian]; Rodolfo Bogni [1947] Director [Italian]; Philip Arthur John Broadley [1961] Director; Jean-Luc Belingard [1948] Director [French]; Stefan Mario Meister [1965] Director [Swiss]; Yvonne Schlaeppi [1960] Director [American/Swiss]; Elmar Schnee [1959] Director [Swiss]

Stamford Properties Three Limited
Incorporated: 17 December 1999
Net Worth: £137,374,992 *Total Assets:* £178,750,048
Registered Office: 33 Holborn, London, EC1N 2HT
Activities: Development of building projects
Parent: J Sainsbury PLC
Officers: Timothy Fallowfield, Secretary; Timothy Fallowfield [1963] Director/Solicitor; David Clifford Wheeler [1984] Director

Stanbic Africa Holdings Limited
Incorporated: 21 May 1965
Net Worth: £924,126,656 *Total Assets:* £929,189,568
Registered Office: 20 Gresham Street, London, EC2V 7JE
Activities: Activities of financial services holding companies
Officers: Arno Daehnke [1967] Group Financial Director [South African]; Olusola Adejoke David-Borha [1960] Director [Nigerian]; Ian Hamish Scott Sinton [1956] Director/General Counsel [South African]; Simpiwe Kenneth Tshabalala [1967] Director/Group, Chief Executive [South African]

Standard Bank London Holdings Limited
Incorporated: 10 May 1988
Net Worth: £533,112,896 *Total Assets:* £533,765,920
Registered Office: 20 Gresham Street, London, EC2V 7JE
Activities: Activities of financial services holding companies
Officers: Susan Caroline Smollett, Secretary; Andrew Hall [1965] Director/Banker; Timothy James Lancaster [1968] Director/Banker; Simon Peter Ridley [1955] Director/Banker [South African]; Susan Caroline Smollett [1961] Director/Chartered Accountant; Gert Marthinus Vogel [1966] Director/Banker

Standard Chartered Apr Limited
Incorporated: 26 August 2004
Net Worth: £50,812,696 *Total Assets:* £194,617,808
Registered Office: 1 Basinghall Avenue, London, EC2V 5DD
Activities: Activities of other holding companies n.e.c.
Parent: Standard Chartered Holdings Limited
Officers: Paul Stuart Chambers [1967] Director/Chartered Accountant; Christopher John Daniels [1974] Director; Yee Mann Hau [1969] Director [Chinese]; Richard Douglas John Staff [1978] Director

Standard Chartered Holdings Limited
Incorporated: 25 September 1989
Net Worth: £21,363,714,048 *Total Assets:* £21,421,469,696
Registered Office: 1 Basinghall Avenue, London, EC2V 5DD
Activities: Financial intermediation not elsewhere classified
Parent: Standard Chartered PLC
Officers: Michelle Amey, Secretary; Tracy Jayne Clarke [1967] Director/Banking Executive; Andrew Nigel Halford [1959] Director; Mark Smith [1961] Director; William Thomas Winters [1961] Director/Group Chief Executive [American]

Standard Chartered I H Limited
Incorporated: 21 February 2013
Net Worth Deficit: £11,965,039 *Total Assets:* £688,096,320
Registered Office: 1 Basinghall Avenue, London, EC2V 5DD
Activities: Activities of financial services holding companies
Parent: Standard Chartered Holdings Limited
Officers: Paul Stuart Chambers [1967] Director/Chartered Accountant; Christopher John Daniels [1974] Director; Sandeep Singh Rai [1980] Director

Standard Chartered NEA Limited
Incorporated: 27 January 2005
Net Worth: £2,070,972,032 *Total Assets:* £2,220,448,256
Registered Office: 1 Basinghall Avenue, London, EC2V 5DD
Activities: Financial intermediation not elsewhere classified
Parent: Standard Chartered Holdings Limited
Officers: Paul Stuart Chambers [1967] Director/Chartered Accountant; Christopher John Daniels [1974] Director; Sandeep Singh Rai [1980] Director

Standard Chartered PLC
Incorporated: 18 November 1969 *Employees:* 86,794
Net Worth: £38,769,115,136 *Total Assets:* £499,812,433,920
Registered Office: 1 Basinghall Avenue, London, EC2V 5DD
Activities: Financial intermediation not elsewhere classified
Officers: Elizabeth Ann Lloyd, Secretary; Louis Chi-Yan Cheung [1963] Director; David Philbrick Conner [1948] Director [American]; Byron Elmer Grote [1948] Director [American]; Andrew Nigel Halford [1959] Director; Christine Mary Hodgson [1964] Director; Gay Huey Evans [1954] Director; Naguib Kheraj [1964] Director; Ngozi Okonjo-Iweala [1954] Director [Nigerian]; Carlson Tong [1954] Director; Jose Maria Vinals Iniguez [1954] Director [Spanish]; Jasmine Mary Whitbread [1963] Director; William Thomas Winters [1961] Director/Group Chief Executive [American]

Charles Stanley & Co. Limited
Incorporated: 9 April 1985 *Employees:* 756
Net Worth: £89,473,000 *Total Assets:* £273,304,992
Registered Office: 55 Bishopsgate, London, EC2N 3AS
Activities: Financial intermediation not elsewhere classified
Parent: Charles Stanley Group PLC
Officers: Julie Ung, Secretary; Paul Andrew Abberley [1959] Director/Chief Executive Officer; Marcia Dominic Campbell [1959] Director; Andrew Didham [1956] Director; Hugh John Grootenhuis [1958] Director; Bridget Elisabeth Guerin [1961] Director; Benjamin Burdett Money-Coutts [1961] Director

Charles Stanley Group PLC
Incorporated: 16 July 1896 *Employees:* 773
Net Worth: £97,762,000 *Total Assets:* £281,575,008
Registered Office: 55 Bishopsgate, London, EC2N 3AS
Activities: Financial intermediation not elsewhere classified
Officers: Julie Ung, Secretary; Paul Andrew Abberley [1959] Director/Chief Executive Officer; Marcia Dominic Campbell [1959] Director; Andrew Didham [1956] Director; Hugh John Grootenhuis [1958] Director; Bridget Elisabeth Guerin [1961] Director; Sir David Howarth Seymour Howard [1945] Director; Benjamin Burdett Money-Coutts [1961] Director; Gary Teper [1973] Director/Solicitor [South African]

Stanlington No. 1 PLC
Incorporated: 12 January 2017
Net Worth: £30,000 *Total Assets:* £223,148,992
Registered Office: 35 Great St Helen's, London, EC3A 6AP
Activities: Activities of mortgage finance companies
Parent: Stanlington No. 1 Holdings Limited
Officers: Paivi Helena Whitaker [1963] Director [Finnish]

Stanlow Receivables Funding Limited
Incorporated: 9 April 2015
Net Worth: £2,411 *Total Assets:* £390,517,856
Registered Office: Third Floor, c/o Wilmington Trust SP Services (London) Limited, 1 Kings Arms Yard, London, EC2R 7AF
Activities: Other business support service activities n.e.c.
Parent: Wilmington Trust SP Services (London) Limited
Officers: Daniel Jonathan Wynne [1970] Director

Star Energy Group Limited
Incorporated: 24 February 2004
Net Worth: £13,199,000 *Total Assets:* £124,864,000
Registered Office: 7 Down Street, London, W1J 7AJ
Activities: Extraction of crude petroleum
Parent: IGas Energy PLC
Officers: John Malcolm Blaymires [1957] Director; Stephen David Bowler [1973] Director/Chief Financial Officer; Julian Lester Tedder [1969] Director/Chief Financial Officer

Star Pubs & Bars (Property) Limited
Incorporated: 23 January 1929
Net Worth: £3,667,000 *Total Assets:* £324,868,000
Registered Office: Elsley Court, 20-22 Great Titchfield Street, London, W1W 8BE
Activities: Non-trading company
Parent: Star Pubs & Bars Limited
Officers: Ruth Carol Hunter, Secretary; David Michael Forde [1968] Managing Director [Irish]; Christopher John Moore [1970] Director; Lawson John Wembridge Mountstevens [1968] Senior Director on Trade; David James Tannahill [1977] Finance Director

Starbucks Coffee Holdings (UK) Limited
Incorporated: 1 April 1997
Net Worth: £292,150,144 *Total Assets:* £292,150,144
Registered Office: Chiswick Park, Building 4, 566 Chiswick High Road, London, W4 5YE
Activities: Retail sale of beverages in specialised stores
Parent: Starbucks Corporation
Officers: Martin Brok [1966] Director [Dutch]; Ralp Duncanson Marshall [1968] Director/VP Technology EMEA

Starbucks EMEA Holdings Ltd
Incorporated: 23 July 2014
Net Worth: £2,935,945,216 *Total Assets:* £2,939,917,056
Registered Office: Chiswick Park, 566 Chiswick High Road, London, W4 5YE
Activities: Activities of head offices
Parent: Starbucks International (Holdings) Ltd
Officers: Martin Brok [1966] Director/Vice President EMEA [Dutch]; Ralph Duncanson Marshall [1968] Director/VP Technology EMEA

Starbucks EMEA Ltd
Incorporated: 12 June 2014 *Employees:* 180
Net Worth: £1,210,425,984 *Total Assets:* £2,004,648,576
Registered Office: Chiswick Park, 566 Chiswick High Road, London, W4 5YE
Activities: Other service activities n.e.c.
Parent: Starbucks EMEA Holdings Ltd
Officers: Martin Brok [1966] Director/Vice President EMEA [Dutch]; Ralph Duncanson Marshall [1968] Director/VP Technology EMEA

Starbucks International (Holdings) Ltd
Incorporated: 11 August 2014
Net Worth: £1,608,121,344 *Total Assets:* £2,365,995,008
Registered Office: Chiswick Park, 566 Chiswick High Road, London, W4 5YE
Activities: Activities of head offices
Officers: Martin Brok [1966] Director/Vice President EMEA [Dutch]; Ralph Duncanson Marshall [1968] Director/VP Technology EMEA

Starr Syndicate Limited
Incorporated: 17 August 2006
Net Worth: £76,957,000 *Total Assets:* £936,635,008
Registered Office: 30 Fenchurch Avenue, London, EC3M 5AD
Activities: Non-life insurance
Officers: Adrian Missen, Secretary; Steven George Blakey [1957] Managing Director; Graham John Lytton Broughton [1977] Financial Director; James Richard Herbert [1953] Director; Richard Nathan Shaak [1964] Director/Insurance Agency President [American]

Starstone Corporate Capital 1 Limited
Incorporated: 4 November 1999
Previous: Torus Underwriting Limited
Net Worth Deficit: £46,548,992 *Total Assets:* £135,595,136
Registered Office: 5th Floor, 88 Leadenhall Street, London, EC3A 3BP
Activities: Non-life insurance
Parent: Enstar Group Limited
Officers: Siobhan Mary Hextall, Secretary; Clare Ellis Traxler, Secretary; Alexandra Louise Cliff [1979] Director/Accountant; Rachel Mary Delhaise [1967] Director

Starstone Finance Limited
Incorporated: 27 November 2007
Previous: Torus Finance Limited
Net Worth: £98,305,824 *Total Assets:* £145,138,672
Registered Office: 5th Floor, 88 Leadenhall Street, London, EC3A 3BP
Activities: Other activities auxiliary to insurance and pension funding
Parent: Enstar Group Limited
Officers: Siobhan Mary Hextall, Secretary; Clare Ellis Traxler, Secretary; Alexandra Louise Cliff [1979] Director/Accountant; David Roy Message [1969] Director; Michael John Summersgill [1969] Director/Head of Operations

State Grid Europe Development (2014) Public Limited Company
Incorporated: 20 November 2014
Net Worth: £49,208 *Total Assets:* £885,205,056
Registered Office: Level 3, 40 Bank Street, London, E14 5NR
Activities: Other business support service activities n.e.c.
Parent: State Grid Europe Limited
Officers: Ying Wang [1964] Director [Chinese]; Hu Yuhai [1963] Director [Chinese]

State Grid Europe Limited
Incorporated: 11 November 2011
Net Worth: £515,081,632 *Total Assets:* £2,667,261,952
Registered Office: Level 3, 40 Bank Street, London, E14 5NR
Activities: Transmission of electricity
Parent: State Grid Corporation of China
Officers: Ying Wang [1964] Director [Chinese]; Hu Yuhai [1963] Director [Chinese]

State Street Europe Limited
Incorporated: 1 August 1997 *Employees:* 60
Previous: State Street Bank Europe Limited
Net Worth: £245,900,000 *Total Assets:* £427,441,984
Registered Office: 20 Churchill Place, London, E14 5HJ
Activities: Financial intermediation not elsewhere classified
Officers: Brian Steven Allis [1968] Managing Director; Dennis Arnum [1953] Director; Christine Moran [1971] Director; Robert Stansbury [1954] Director

State Street Global Advisors Limited
Incorporated: 8 June 1990 *Employees:* 412
Net Worth: £281,111,424 *Total Assets:* £334,152,352
Registered Office: 20 Churchill Place, Canary Wharf, London, E14 5HJ
Activities: Financial intermediation not elsewhere classified
Parent: State Street Corporation
Officers: Vathoulla Sullivan, Secretary; Alex Joseph Castle [1968] Director/Head of Operations; Cuan Farndell Humphrey Coulter [1972] Director/Head of SSGA EMEA [American]; Scott Victor Sanderson [1971] Director/Chartered Accountant; Karen Sharpe [1958] Director; Theodore Thomas Sotir [1958] Director [American/British]; William Derek Russell Street [1968] Director/Head of Investments, EMEA

State Street Global Markets International Limited
Incorporated: 12 August 1997 *Employees:* 17
Net Worth: £8,213,000 *Total Assets:* £184,004,000
Registered Office: 20 Churchill Place, Canary Wharf, London, E14 5HJ
Activities: Security and commodity contracts dealing activities
Parent: State Street Europe Limited
Officers: Dennis Arnum [1953] Director; Christopher Anthony Barrett [1962] Managing Director; Pinar Emirdag-Temelkuran [1972] Director/Banker; David Donald Peter Newns [1974] Director; Olubusola Sodeinde [1977] Finance Director

State Street International Holdings UK Limited
Incorporated: 23 April 2015
Net Worth: £123,662,720 *Total Assets:* £1,824,482,432
Registered Office: 20 Churchill Place, Canary Wharf, London, E14 5HJ
Activities: Activities of financial services holding companies
Parent: State Street Corporation
Officers: Richard Thomas Flood [1958] Director/Risk Manager; Imran Shaffi [1984] Director/Banker

Statkraft UK Ltd
Incorporated: 14 March 2006 *Employees:* 49
Net Worth: £932,585,024 *Total Assets:* £966,356,992
Registered Office: 4th Floor, 41 Moorgate, London, EC2R 6PP
Activities: Other business support service activities n.e.c.
Parent: Statkraft AS
Officers: Oliver Cripps, Secretary; Sergio Patricio Castedo [1968] Director/Engineer [American]; Duncan Dale [1964] Director/Commercial Management; David John Flood [1980] Director/Engineer; Dennis Manuel Geyermann [1978] Director/Electrical Engineer [German]; Sorrel Anne Sorsby [1962] Director/Financial Controller; Emma Elizabeth Voss [1975] Director/Senior Tax Manager

Steamship Mutual Underwriting Association Limited
Incorporated: 16 October 1909
Net Worth: £83,376,512 *Total Assets:* £732,111,168
Registered Office: Aquatical House, 39 Bell Lane, London, E1 7LU
Activities: Non-life insurance
Officers: Arjun Thawani, Secretary; Christopher Barry Adams [1954] Director/Manager - Marine Insurance; Christian Jurgen Ahrenkiel [1952] Director/Shipowning (Foreign) [German]; Clive Bouch [1961] Director/Chartered Accountant; Isabella Grimaldi [1954] Director/Shipping Insurance Manager [Italian]; Carlos Juan Madinabeitia [1960] Director - Commercial Shipping Agent [Spanish]; Stephen James Martin [1954] Director/P&I Club Manager; Armand Pohan [1944] Director/Chairman - Port Imperial Ferry Corp [American]; Lieh Sing Alan Tung [1967] Director/Chief Financial Officer - Maritime Transportation [Chinese]; Raffaele Zagari [1969] Director/Chairman [Italian]

Stemcor Holdings 2 Limited
Incorporated: 12 December 2013 *Employees:* 30
Net Worth: £48,346,000 *Total Assets:* £137,268,992
Registered Office: Longbow House, 14-20 Chiswell Street, London, EC1Y 4TW
Activities: Activities of head offices
Parent: Stemcor Acquisitions Limited
Officers: Andrew John Checketts [1970] Director; Gerard Paul Eyre Craggs [1963] Director; Julian Verden [1958] Director

Stena (UK) Limited
Incorporated: 19 November 1992 *Employees:* 4
Net Worth: £540,613,120 *Total Assets:* £543,296,704
Registered Office: 45 Albemarle Street, London, W1S 4JL
Activities: Activities of other holding companies n.e.c.
Major Shareholder: Dan Sten Olsson
Officers: Thomas Sven Andersson, Secretary; Ian Hampton [1981] Director/HR Manager; Staffan Werner Hultgren [1961] Chief Financial Director [Swedish]; Mauro Mattiuzzo [1957] Director/Consultant; Hans Erik Noren [1957] Managing Director [Swedish]; Michael Hugh Percy [1949] Director/Banker; Mikael Fredrik Stenvaller [1973] Director/Group Chief Accountant [Swedish]

Stena Icemax Limited
Incorporated: 16 April 2012
Net Worth: £155,215,040 *Total Assets:* £671,847,552
Registered Office: 45 Albemarle Street, London, W1S 4JL
Activities: Sea and coastal freight water transport
Major Shareholder: Dan Sten Olsson
Officers: Thomas Sven Andersson, Secretary; Ian Hampton [1981] Director/HR Manager; Staffan Werner Hultgren [1961] Director of Business Management [Swedish]; Mauro Mattiuzzo [1957] Director/Consultant; Hans Erik Noren [1957] Director [Swedish]; Michael Hugh Percy [1949] Director/Banker; Mikael Fredrik Stenvaller [1973] Director/Group Chief Accountant [Swedish]

Stena North Sea Limited
Incorporated: 23 October 2002
Net Worth: £144,260,160 *Total Assets:* £480,460,448
Registered Office: 45 Albemarle Street, London, W1S 4JL
Activities: Sea and coastal passenger water transport
Major Shareholder: Dan Sten Olsson
Officers: Thomas Sven Andersson, Secretary; Ian Hampton [1981] Director/HR Manager; Staffan Warner Hultgren [1967] Director/Chief Financial Controller [Swedish]; Mauro Mattiuzzo [1957] Director/Consultant; Hans Erik Noren [1957] Director [Swedish]; Michael Hugh Percy [1949] Director/Banker; Mikael Fredrik Stenvaller [1973] Director/Group Chief Accountant [Swedish]

Stena Ropax Limited
Incorporated: 25 September 1978 *Employees:* 6
Net Worth: £56,744,000 *Total Assets:* £199,340,000
Registered Office: 45 Albemarle Street, London, W1S 4JL
Activities: Sea and coastal passenger water transport
Major Shareholder: Dan Sten Olsson
Officers: Thomas Sven Andersson, Secretary; Ian Hampton [1981] Director/HR Manager; Staffan Werner Hultgren [1961] Director/Chief Financial Controller [Swedish]; Mauro Mattiuzzo [1957] Director/Consultant; Hans Erik Noren [1957] Managing Director [Swedish]; Michael Hugh Percy [1949] Director/Banker; Mikael Fredrik Stenvaller [1973] Director/Group Chief Accountant [Swedish]

Stena Spey Services Limited
Incorporated: 11 November 2011
Net Worth: £8,946,298 *Total Assets:* £106,191,912
Registered Office: 45 Albemarle Street, London, W1S 4JL
Activities: Support activities for petroleum and natural gas mining
Officers: Stuart Maxwell Wyness, Secretary; Erik Bergsvein Ronsberg [1972] Director; Stuart Maxwell Wyness [1971] Director

Stephenson Harwood LLP
Incorporated: 21 March 2012 *Employees:* 977
Net Worth: £106,500,000 *Total Assets:* £150,000,000
Registered Office: 1 Finsbury Circus, London, EC2M 7SH
Officers: Roland Anthony John Foord [1958] Member; Sean Michael Gibbons [1967] Member; Paul Dwayne Phillips [1964] Member; Alexandra Zoe Pygall [1979] Member; Jamie Stranger [1971] Member; Sharon Tracey White [1960] Member; Warren Allan [1979] LLP Member; Barbara Agnes Ruth Allen [1958] LLP Member; Sean Leonard Angle [1961] LLP Member; Nicholas Barber [1973] LLP Member; Graeme Barton [1981] LLP Member; Alan Stuart Beadnall [1959] LLP Member; Yann Karl Edmond Beckers [1971] LLP Member; Peter George Bennett [1958] LLP Member; Alan Sidney Bercow [1958] LLP Member; Catriona Ann Berman [1977] LLP Member; Helena Louise Berman [1970] LLP Member; Gabriel Boghossian [1984] LLP Member; Nigel Vaughan Bowen-Morris [1961] LLP Member; Simon Don Brading [1979] LLP Member; Catherine Fiona Neil Brearley [1957] LLP Member; Martin James Brown [1979] LLP Member; Julian Adam Cahn [1977] LLP Member; Edward Campbell [1964] LLP Member; Rebecca Louise Carter [1971] LLP Member; Mark David Catchpole [1964] LLP Member; Salem Chalabi [1963] LLP Member; Roy Chan [1976] LLP Member; Rovine Pradeep Chandrasekera [1973] LLP Member; Jonathan Mark Wai Wah Chu [1979] LLP Member; Anthony Clare [1970] LLP Member; Julie Margrethe Clegg [1957] LLP Member; Anthony Noel Concagh [1965] LLP Member; Timothy Cooke [1977] LLP Member; Kate Alice Cordery [1980] LLP Member; Barthelemy Jean Cousin [1964] LLP Member; Jonathan Richard Casbourne Cripps [1963] LLP Member; George Cyriac [1975] LLP Member; Edward Thomas Davis [1975] LLP Member; Gavin Alexander Lloyd Davis [1967] LLP Member; Nicolas Demigneux [1973] LLP Member; Ian Michael Devereux [1956] LLP Member; Andrew John Edge [1968] LLP Member; Anthony Mark Edwards [1971] LLP Member; Elizabeth Helen Elliott [1972] LLP Member; Cristan Evans [1976] LLP Member; Jezamine Fewins [1972] LLP Member; Elizabeth Field [1963] LLP Member; Louis Kruschev Flannery [1963] LLP Member; John Michael Fordham [1948] LLP Member; Stuart John Frith [1957] LLP Member; King Tak Fung [1959] LLP Member; Marta Isabel Garcia [1974] LLP Member; Richard Garcia-Almendros [1979] LLP Member; Alain Paul Alexandre Gautron [1961] LLP Member; Sara Victoria George [1974] LLP Member; Purvis Ghani [1977] LLP Member; Paolo Severino Giorgio Ghirardani [1959] LLP Member; Philip David Goodchild [1970] LLP Member; Sam Jack Gray [1980] LLP Member; Martin James Green [1959] LLP Member; Richard Gwynne [1955] LLP Member; Marc Hammerson [1970] LLP Member; Alexander Iain Haynes [1978] LLP Member; Paul Hayward-Surry [1968] LLP Member; Laurence Chak Ching Ho [1982] LLP Member; Daniel Thomas Holland [1973] LLP Member; Karima Jennifer Hudson [1969] LLP Member; Rob Jacob [1981] LLP Member; Sean Peter Jeffrey [1968] LLP Member; William Hugo Jenney [1965] LLP Member; Gregg Crawford Johnston [1976] LLP Member; Nijoe Joseph [1979] LLP Member; Ingolf Peter Kaiser [1969] LLP Member; Malcolm Bernard Kemp [1954] LLP Member; Kyong Hwa Kim [1966] LLP Member; Jonathan Andrew Kirsop [1977] LLP Member; Menelaos Photiou Kouzoupis [1976] LLP Member; Huay Yee Kwan [1971] LLP Member; David Graham Lacey [1963] LLP Member; Eugene Lai [1970] LLP Member; Voon Keat Lai [1967] LLP Member; Sephen James Laud [1969] LLP Member; Kevin Ming Shih Lee [1958] LLP Member; James Maximilian Lemanski [1977] LLP Member; Edward James Linforth [1972] LLP Member; Kiersten Lucas [1974] LLP Member; Ian Richard Mace [1976] LLP Member; Dora Mace-Kokota [1981] LLP Member; Lisa Michelle Marks [1962] LLP Member; Duncan Eric James McDonald [1954] LLP Member; Jennifer McKeown [1971] LLP Member; Andrew James McLean [1963] LLP Member; Graeme Gibson McLellan [1970] LLP Member; John Meehan [1980] LLP Member; Benedict Gardiner Mercer [1977] LLP Member; Susan Marie Millar [1970] LLP Member; Simon Richard Moore [1976] LLP Member; Susan Wendy Moore [1969] LLP Member; Eifion Wyn Morris [1972] LLP Member

Stepstone UK Holding Limited
Incorporated: 18 June 2013 *Employees:* 35
Net Worth: £258,768,608 *Total Assets:* £259,645,008
Registered Office: Blue Fin, 110 Southwark Street, London, SE1 0TA
Activities: Activities of other holding companies n.e.c.
Officers: Ralf Wilfried Baumann [1956] Director [German]; Nicholas Simon James Gold [1972] Director; Thorsten Otte [1970] Director [German]; Patrick Philip Frank Wehrmann [1970] Director/Manager

Sterling Midco Limited
Incorporated: 16 December 2016
Net Worth: £588,577,024 *Total Assets:* £588,585,024
Registered Office: 2nd Floor, 11 Old Jewry, London, EC2R 8DU
Activities: Activities of other holding companies n.e.c.
Officers: Alan Denis Booth [1981] Director [Irish]; Stuart Roderick Jenkin [1957] Director; Justin Reynolds Skiver [1977] Director [American]

Sterling UK Holdco Limited
Incorporated: 11 June 2014
Net Worth: £938,144,384 *Total Assets:* £943,811,328
Registered Office: 6 Bevis Marks, London, EC3A 7BA
Activities: Activities of financial services holding companies
Shareholder: Dollar Financial U.K. Limited
Officers: Scott Aaron Cohen [1971] Director/Business Executive [American]

Stewardship Services (UKET) Limited
Incorporated: 1 October 1906 *Employees:* 45
Net Worth: £113,268,000 *Total Assets:* £128,446,000
Registered Office: 1 Lamb's Passage, London, EC1Y 8AB
Activities: Activities of patent and copyright agents; other legal activities n.e.c.
Officers: Juliet Maggs, Secretary; Antony Jonathan Ward Barnes [1964] Director of Tax and Treasury; Stephanie Clare Biden [1980] Director/Solicitor; Simon James Blake [1973] Director/Chartered Accountant; Gareth Eoin Burns [1972] Director/Actuary [Irish]; Sandra Elaine Cobbin [1964] Director/Business Consultant; Balram Gidoomal [1950] Director; Heather Anne Woodruff Grizzle [1981] Director/Advisor [American]; Jeremy Samuel John Marshall [1963] Director/Banker; Helen Alice Senior [1967] Director/Chartered Accountant; Ritzema Ryk Steytler [1969] Director/Entrepreneur; Michael John Peirse Wright [1954] Director/I M Manager

SThree Overseas Holdings Limited
Incorporated: 9 September 1996
Net Worth: £180,082,000 *Total Assets:* £234,876,992
Registered Office: 1st Floor, 75 King William Street, London, EC4N 7BE
Activities: Temporary employment agency activities
Parent: SThree PLC
Officers: Steven Colin Hornbuckle [1967] Director/Company Secretary; David MacKay [1971] Director/Tax Manager

SThree PLC
Incorporated: 13 July 1999 *Employees:* 2,856
Net Worth: £80,705,000 *Total Assets:* £273,526,016
Registered Office: 1st Floor, 75 King William Street, London, EC4N 7BE
Activities: Activities of head offices
Officers: Steven Colin Hornbuckle, Chartered Secretary; James Daniel Bilefield [1969] Director; Barrie Christopher Brien [1966] Director; Denise Rosemary Collis [1957] Director; Gary Paul Elden [1967] Director; Anne Kathleen Fahy [1960] Director [Irish]; Edward Justin Hughes [1969] Director; Alex Smith [1965] Director

SThree UK Holdings Limited
Incorporated: 9 July 1999
Net Worth: £122,495,000 *Total Assets:* £122,673,000
Registered Office: 1st Floor, 75 King William Street, London, EC4N 7BE
Activities: Non-trading company
Parent: SThree PLC
Officers: Steven Colin Hornbuckle [1967] Director/Company Secretary; David MacKay [1971] Director/Tax Manager

Stifel Nicolaus Europe Limited
Incorporated: 19 February 1999 *Employees:* 507
Net Worth: £56,175,000 *Total Assets:* £185,580,992
Registered Office: 4th Floor, 150 Cheapside, London, EC2V 6ET
Activities: Security and commodity contracts dealing activities
Parent: Stifel Europe Holdings Limited
Officers: Charles James Ashton [1961] Director/Chief Financial Officer; Spencer Harman [1972] Director/Fixed Income Sales; Robin David Mann [1973] Director/Investment Banker; Thomas Beaulieu Michaud [1964] Director/Investment Banker [American]; Victor John Nesi [1960] Director/Co-President Stifel Financial [American]; Eithne Maria O'Leary [1968] Director [Irish]; John Richard Owen [1960] Director; Clifford Alan Siegel [1957] Director/Vice Chairman; Richard Christopher Wynne-Griffith [1960] Director/Banker

Stobart Holdings Limited
Incorporated: 7 May 2010
Net Worth: £428,700,000 *Total Assets:* £442,312,992
Registered Office: Third Floor, 15 Stratford Place, London, W1C 1BE
Activities: Freight transport by road
Parent: Stobart Group Limited
Officers: Louise Brace, Secretary; Louise Mary Helen Brace [1972] Director/Company Secretary; Warwick Brady [1964] Director

Stockton Retail Park Limited
Incorporated: 23 June 2005
Net Worth: £296,411,840 *Total Assets:* £325,927,136
Registered Office: York House, 45 Seymour Street, London, W1H 7LX
Activities: Development of building projects
Parent: BL Retail Warehousing Holding Company Limited
Officers: Sarah Morrell Barzycki [1958] Director/Head of Finance; Benjamin Toby Grose [1969] Director/Chartered Surveyor; Paul Stuart Macey [1978] Director/Accountant; Jonathan Charles McNuff [1986] Director/Chartered Accountant; Charles John Middleton [1966] Director/Corporate Tax Executive; Timothy Andrew Roberts [1964] Director/Chartered Surveyor; Nigel Mark Webb [1963] Director/Chartered Surveyor

Marie Stopes International
Incorporated: 16 March 1973 *Employees:* 11,612
Net Worth: £107,308,000 *Total Assets:* £198,422,000
Registered Office: 1 Conway Street, Fitzroy Square, London, W1T 6LP
Activities: General medical practice activities
Officers: Amanda Couper, Secretary; Doctor Mohsina Ahsan Bilgrami [1951] Country Director Pakistan [Pakistani]; Franki Nicolas Braeken [1960] Director/Chief Investment Officer [Belgian]; Philip Dow Harvey [1938] Director [American]; Claire Emma Morris [1972] Director/Self Employed; Dr Kristin Anne Rutter [1976] Director/Management Consultant; Timothy Morton Rutter [1940] Director/Obstetrician Gynaecologist; Jessica Search [1969] Director

Stow Real Estate PLC
Incorporated: 16 August 1996 *Employees:* 2
Net Worth: £85,683,080 *Total Assets:* £228,770,512
Registered Office: 86 Brook Street, London, W1K 5AY
Activities: Buying and selling of own real estate
Officers: Shivaji Tony Mainee, Secretary; Shivaji Tony Mainee [1963] Director/Chartered Accountant [Indian]; Colette Massaad [1964] Director/Lawyer [Lebanese]; Julian Richard Milne [1956] Director/Chartered Surveyor

Stradawood Limited
Incorporated: 15 April 2016
Net Worth Deficit: £6,581,103 *Total Assets:* £179,359,520
Registered Office: 35 Albemarle Street, London, W1S 4JD
Activities: Activities of other holding companies n.e.c.
Major Shareholder: Graeme Walter Briggs
Officers: Matthew Martin Farrell [1989] Director; Jonathon Ian Lee McLuskie [1990] Director

Strategic Equity Capital PLC
Incorporated: 10 May 2005
Net Worth: £174,280,992 *Total Assets:* £175,224,000
Registered Office: 1 Finsbury Circus, London, EC2M 7SH
Activities: Activities of investment trusts
Officers: John William Marshall Barlow [1964] Director/Manager; Josephine Dixon [1959] Director; Richard John Hills [1955] Director; Richard Edmund Staniforth Locke [1966] Director; David John Morrison [1959] Director

Stratford City Business District Limited
Incorporated: 28 July 2010
Net Worth: £135,471,008 *Total Assets:* £255,488,992
Registered Office: 20 Triton Street, Regent's Place, London, NW1 3BF
Activities: Development of building projects
Shareholders: LCR Stratford GP Limited; Lendlease Stratford GP Limited
Officers: Mark Boor [1965] Director/Chartered Surveyor; Peter Hawthorne [1966] Finance Director; David Joy [1954] Director/Town Planner; Thomas Lachlan MacKellar [1982] Director/Chief Financial Officer [Australian]; Rebecca Seeley [1980] Finance Director; Raymond Gareth Willis [1969] Director/Town Planner

Stratton Metal Resources Limited
Incorporated: 4 October 2002 *Employees:* 6
Net Worth: £64,851,272 *Total Assets:* £160,976,032
Registered Office: 5th Floor, 6 St Andrew Street, London, EC4A 3AE
Activities: Wholesale of metals and metal ores
Major Shareholder: Keith Spencer Gerard Dunleavy
Officers: Keith Spencer Gerard Dunleavy [1965] Director

Structadene (LBG) Holdings Limited
Incorporated: 14 July 2014
Net Worth: £1 *Total Assets:* £223,737,488
Registered Office: Floor 6, Quadrant House, 4 Thomas More Square, London, E1W 1YW
Activities: Other service activities n.e.c.
Parent: Structadene Limited
Officers: Howard Pearlman, Secretary; Michael Robert Goldberger [1956] Director; David Alan Pearlman [1945] Director; Howard Alan Pearlman [1975] Director/Property Management

Structadene (LBG) Properties Limited
Incorporated: 14 July 2014
Net Worth: £11,913,519 *Total Assets:* £227,176,336
Registered Office: Floor 6, Quadrant House, 4 Thomas More Square, London, E1W 1YW
Activities: Other service activities n.e.c.
Parent: Structadene (LBG) Holdings Limited
Officers: Howard Pearlman, Secretary; Michael Robert Goldberger [1956] Director; David Alan Pearlman [1945] Director; Howard Alan Pearlman [1975] Director/Property Management

Structadene Limited
Incorporated: 2 November 1978 *Employees:* 85
Net Worth: £425,045,728 *Total Assets:* £946,374,912
Registered Office: Floor 6, Quadrant House, 4 Thomas More Square, London, E1W 1YW
Activities: Buying and selling of own real estate
Major Shareholder: David Alan Pearlman
Officers: Howard Alan Pearlman, Secretary; Philip Anthony Colvin [1970] Director; Michael Robert Goldberger [1956] Director; Robert William O'Dwyer [1962] Director/Head of Commercial Property Management; Gulam Mohamed Patel [1948] Director/Chartered Accountant; David Alan Pearlman [1945] Director; Howard Alan Pearlman [1975] Director/Property Management

Student Finance PLC
Incorporated: 1 November 2016
Net Worth: £22,178 *Total Assets:* £215,315,040
Registered Office: 35 Great St Helen's, London, EC3A 6AP
Activities: Financial intermediation not elsewhere classified
Parent: Student Finance Holdings Limited
Officers: Daniel Marc Richard Jaffe [1975] Director

STV News Services Limited
Incorporated: 11 March 1999
Net Worth: £24,906,000 *Total Assets:* £276,295,008
Registered Office: 9 Savoy Street, London, WC2E 7EG
Activities: Television programme production activities
Officers: Jane Elizabeth Anne Tames, Secretary; Simon Jeremy Pitts [1975] Director; William George Watt [1967] Finance Director

Subsea Leasing Limited
Incorporated: 28 October 1988
Net Worth: £61,290,200 *Total Assets:* £272,916,320
Registered Office: 45 Albemarle Street, London, W1S 4JL
Activities: Support activities for petroleum and natural gas mining
Officers: Stuart Maxwell Wyness, Secretary; Peter Claesson [1965] Finance Director [Swedish]; Staffan Werner Hultgren [1961] Director/Chief Controller [Swedish]; Erik Bergsvein Ronsberg [1972] Director; Stuart Maxwell Wyness [1971] Director

Sucden Financial Limited
Incorporated: 14 February 1973 *Employees:* 190
Net Worth: £101,569,152 *Total Assets:* £449,468,544
Registered Office: 3rd Floor, Plantation Place South, 60 Great Tower Street, London, EC3R 5AZ
Activities: Financial intermediation not elsewhere classified
Major Shareholder: Serge Versano
Officers: Marc Richard Bailey [1964] Managing Director; Thierry Bourvis [1957] Director/Financial Manager [French]; Marc Andre Breillout [1954] Director [French]; Sami Erza Demal [1948] Director/General Manager [French]; Tobias Charles Osborne [1967] Finance Director; Michael Overlander [1951] Director; Gavin Trevor Parker [1964] Director; Serge Varsano [1955] Director/President of the Management [French]

Sulawesi LNG Development Limited
Incorporated: 12 February 2010 *Employees:* 6
Net Worth: £566,637,696 *Total Assets:* £566,709,120
Registered Office: Mid City Place, 71 High Holborn, London, WC1V 6BA
Activities: Other business support service activities n.e.c.
Parent: Mitsubishi Corporation
Officers: Hiroto Hyakkoku [1962] Director/Businessman [Japanese]; Keum Woo Lee [1964] Director [South Korean]; Wataru Noguchi [1968] Director [Japanese]

Sumi Agro Europe Limited
Incorporated: 28 June 1995 *Employees:* 615
Net Worth: £67,016,316 *Total Assets:* £232,749,680
Registered Office: Vintners Place, 68 Upper Thames Street, London, EC4V 3BJ
Activities: Manufacture of pesticides and other agrochemical products
Parent: Sumitomo Corporation
Officers: Christopher John White, Secretary; Takahiro Nishihara [1962] Director [Japanese]; Kazuma Suzuki [1969] Director [Japanese]; Kotaro Tameda [1966] Director [Japanese]; Tomoaki Tetsu [1966] Director [Japanese]; Wlodzimierz Jerzy Wleklik [1952] Director [Polish]; Takashi Yamana [1963] Director [Japanese]

Sumisho Osaka Gas Water UK Limited
Incorporated: 21 January 2013 *Employees:* 390
Net Worth: £198,780,992 *Total Assets:* £490,910,016
Registered Office: Vintners' Place, 68 Upper Thames Street, London, EC4V 3BJ
Activities: Activities of other holding companies n.e.c.
Shareholders: Summit Water Limited; Osaka Gas UK, Ltd
Officers: Graham David Holman, Secretary; Toru Kamoi [1963] Director [Japanese]; Seiji Kitajima [1969] Director/General Manager [Japanese]; Masashi Kobayashi [1969] Director/General Manager [Japanese]; Ryuichi Nishida [1965] Managing Director of Osaka Gas UK Ltd [Japanese]

Sumitomo Corporation Capital Europe PLC
Incorporated: 30 December 1985
Net Worth: £176,194,928 *Total Assets:* £1,105,428,224
Registered Office: Vintners Place, 68 Upper Thames Street, London, EC4V 3BJ
Activities: Other business support service activities n.e.c.
Parent: Sumitomo Corporation Europe Limited
Officers: Atsuhiko Murakami [1976] Managing Director [Japanese]; Kimihiko Sato [1962] Director [Japanese]; Toshiyuki Takahashi [1966] Director [Japanese]; Hidetaka Tomita [1975] Director [Japanese]

Sumitomo Corporation Europe Holding Limited
Incorporated: 25 November 1996 *Employees:* 2
Net Worth: £214,097,968 *Total Assets:* £214,714,704
Registered Office: Vintners Place, 68 Upper Thames Street, London, EC4V 3BJ
Activities: Other business support service activities n.e.c.
Parent: Sumitomo Corporation
Officers: Kimihiko Sato, Secretary; Masato Ishida [1960] Director/Chairman of SCEH [Japanese]; Takashi Yamana [1963] Director [Japanese]

Sumitomo Corporation Europe Limited
Incorporated: 11 February 1985 *Employees:* 241
Net Worth: £425,481,664 *Total Assets:* £857,546,112
Registered Office: Vintners' Place, 68 Upper Thames Street, London, EC4V 3BJ
Activities: Non-specialised wholesale trade
Parent: Sumitomo Corporation Europe Holding Limited
Officers: Oliver Henry Hersee, Secretary; Graham David Holman [1966] Director/Solicitor; Kimihiko Sato [1962] Director [Japanese]; Takashi Yamana [1963] Director [Japanese]

Sumitomo Corporation Global Commodities Limited
Incorporated: 16 February 2006 *Employees:* 24
Net Worth: £45,734,544 *Total Assets:* £349,153,696
Registered Office: Vintners' Place, 68 Upper Thames Street, London, EC4V 3BJ
Activities: Security and commodity contracts dealing activities
Parent: Sumitomo Corporation
Officers: Takuro Haga [1972] Director [Japanese]; Eijiro Nagao [1968] Director [Japanese]; Hironobu Yamamura [1975] Director [Japanese]

Sumitomo Electric Finance UK Limited
Incorporated: 19 October 1989 *Employees:* 12
Net Worth: £21,592,160 *Total Assets:* £506,555,808
Registered Office: 125 Old Broad Street, London, EC2N 1AR
Activities: Financial intermediation not elsewhere classified
Parent: Sumitomo Electric Industries Ltd,
Officers: Daiki Kawakami, Secretary; Ryo Hagano [1968] Director [Japanese]; Koji Kimura [1969] Managing Director [Japanese]; Kenichiro Seto [1962] Director [Japanese]; Kenichi Shimada [1964] Director/General Manager [Japanese]; Makoto Tani [1957] Director [Japanese]

Sumitomo Mitsui Banking Corporation Europe Limited
Incorporated: 3 March 2003 *Employees:* 1,050
Net Worth: £3,104,014,336 *Total Assets:* £46,017,851,392
Registered Office: 99 Queen Victoria Street, London, EC4V 4EH
Activities: Banks
Parent: Sumitomo Mitsui Financial Group, Inc
Officers: Mark James Bradley, Secretary; Tetsuro Imaeda [1962] Director [Japanese]; Masaki Kambayashi [1964] Director/Deputy Chief Executive Officer [Japanese]; Hideo Kawafune [1969] Director/General Manager [Japanese]; Alan McAlpine Keir [1958] Director; Charlotte Elisabeth Diana Morgan [1950] Independent Non-Executive Director; Keiichiro Nakamura [1966] Director/General Manager [Japanese]; Laurel Claire Powers-Freeling [1957] Director; Stanislas Roger [1964] Director/General Manager [French]

Summit Exploration and Production Limited
Incorporated: 24 January 2014 *Employees:* 16
Net Worth: £91,569,872 *Total Assets:* £115,015,440
Registered Office: 4th Floor, 23 College Hill, London, EC4R 2RP
Activities: Extraction of crude petroleum
Parent: Sumitomo Corporation
Officers: Masaki Ozawa, Secretary; John Anthony Austin [1956] Director; Akira Kodama [1978] Director [Japanese]; Wataru Sato [1970] Director [Japanese]; Satoru Sugiura [1965] Director [Japanese]

Sunblest Bakeries Limited
Incorporated: 9 January 1940
Net Worth: £57,989,000 *Total Assets:* £510,161,984
Registered Office: Weston Centre, 10 Grosvenor Street, London, W1K 4QY
Activities: Activities of head offices
Parent: A.B.F. Holdings Limited
Officers: Rosalyn Sharon Schofield, Secretary; Rosalyn Sharon Schofield [1956] Director/Solicitor; Andrew Arthur Smith [1972] Director/Chartered Accountant

Sunderland (SHG) Finance PLC
Incorporated: 31 May 2001
Net Worth: £12,500 *Total Assets:* £216,307,760
Registered Office: 4th Floor, 107 Cannon Street, London, EC4N 5AF
Activities: Financial intermediation not elsewhere classified
Parent: Sunderland (SHG) Finance Holdings Limited
Officers: Colin John Burke [1962] Director/Company Secretary; Fenella Jane Edge [1963] Director/Treasurer; John Piers Williamson [1961] Director

The Bernard Sunley Charitable Foundation
Incorporated: 30 March 2005 *Employees:* 3
Net Worth: £112,563,000 *Total Assets:* £116,820,000
Registered Office: 20 Berkeley Square, London, W1J 6LH
Activities: Non-trading company
Officers: Susanne Davies, Secretary; Lucy Pauline Alexandra Evans [1970] Director/Non Practising Solicitor; Anabel Mary Louise Knight [1970] Director; Dr Brian Wardley Martin [1942] Director/Retired; Inigo Paternina [1967] Director [Spanish]; Bella Sunley [1938] Director; Joan Mary Tice [1933] Director; William Tice [1961] Director/Surgeon

Sunshine Finco Limited
Incorporated: 9 December 2013
Net Worth: £74,351,800 *Total Assets:* £132,909,272
Registered Office: 23 Savile Row, London, W1S 2ET
Activities: Activities of head offices
Parent: Sunshine Topco Limited
Officers: Thomas Gareth Hussey [1988] Director/Investor

Sunshine Holdco Limited
Incorporated: 21 February 2014
Net Worth: £132,209,968 *Total Assets:* £132,228,800
Registered Office: 23 Savile Row, London, W1S 2ET
Activities: Activities of head offices
Parent: Sunshine Finco Limited
Officers: Thomas Gareth Hussey [1988] Director/Investor

Sunshine Midco Limited
Incorporated: 9 December 2013 *Employees:* 374
Net Worth: £79,976,688 *Total Assets:* £159,835,936
Registered Office: 23 Savile Row, London, W1S 2ET
Activities: Activities of head offices
Parent: Sunshine Holdco Limited
Officers: Thomas Gareth Hussey [1988] Director/Investor

Sunshine Purchaser Limited
Incorporated: 9 December 2013 *Employees:* 2
Net Worth: £125,528,960 *Total Assets:* £178,874,848
Registered Office: 23 Savile Row, London, W1S 2ET
Activities: Activities of head offices
Parent: Sunshine Midco Limited
Officers: Thomas Gareth Hussey [1988] Director/Investor

Sunshine Topco Limited
Incorporated: 9 December 2013 *Employees:* 374
Net Worth: £79,422,632 *Total Assets:* £159,102,560
Registered Office: 23 Savile Row, London, W1S 2ET
Activities: Activities of head offices
Officers: Jan Michiel Hessels [1942] Director/Special Advisor [Dutch]; Rene Marc Kern [1963] Director/Businessman [American]; Pierre Vincent Samec [1963] Director/Vice-President [French]

Superior Acquisitions Limited
Incorporated: 19 March 2007
Previous: AB Acquisitions Limited
Net Worth: £3,287,000,064 *Total Assets:* £11,281,999,872
Registered Office: 4th Floor, Sedley Place, 361 Oxford Street, London, W1C 2JL
Activities: Activities of head offices
Shareholders: WBAD Holdings Limited; WBA International Limited
Officers: Frank Standish, Company Secretary [Irish]; Aidan Gerard Clare [1966] Director [Irish]; Mark Francis Muller [1964] Director; Frank Standish [1963] Director/Company Secretary [Irish]

Superior Holdings Limited
Incorporated: 4 December 2014
Net Worth: £15,931,039,744 *Total Assets:* £25,416,304,640
Registered Office: 4th Floor, Sedley Place, 361 Oxford Street, London, W1C 2JL
Activities: Activities of other holding companies n.e.c.
Parent: Walgreens Boots Alliance Scottish LP
Officers: Frank Standish, Secretary; Aidan Gerard Clare [1966] Director [Irish]; Martin Christopher Delve [1967] Director; Mark Francis Muller [1964] Director; Frank Standish [1963] Director/Company Secretary [Irish]

Sureserve Group PLC
Incorporated: 28 January 2015 *Employees:* 2,416
Previous: Lakehouse PLC
Net Worth: £50,242,000 *Total Assets:* £153,612,000
Registered Office: 50 Liverpool Street, London, EC2M 7PY
Activities: Activities of head offices
Officers: John William Charles Charlton, Secretary; Robert Holt [1954] Director; Robert William Lindsay Legget [1950] Director; Michael McMahon [1976] Director; Derek Zissman [1944] Director

Surgical Specialties Corporation Limited
Incorporated: 23 February 2017
Net Worth: £148,236,416 *Total Assets:* £246,160,832
Registered Office: Suite 1, 3rd Floor, 11-12 St James's Square, London, SW1Y 4LB
Activities: Manufacture of medical and dental instruments and supplies
Officers: Victor Manuel Diaz [1960] Director/Medical Devices [American]; Daniel Joseph Sutherby [1964] Director/Finance Officer [American]; Lawrence Wang [1977] Director/Finance [American]

Sir Richard Sutton Limited
Incorporated: 18 November 1938 *Employees:* 492
Previous: Sir Richard Sutton Estates Limited
Net Worth: £191,556,992 *Total Assets:* £356,275,008
Registered Office: 14 Bolton Street, Piccadilly, London, W1J 8BF
Activities: Mixed farming
Shareholders: Richard Lexington Sutton; Lady Fiamma Sutton; Peter Lewis Wyman; Christopher Nigel Barrington Lacey; David Robert Sutton
Officers: Nicholas John Campbell Pollock, Secretary; Christopher William Baylis [1976] Director of Farming; Stephen Charles Broome [1951] Director/Hotel Consultant; Robert Henry Cobb [1947] Director/Chartered Surveyor; Robert Howard Dudley [1951] Director/Chartered Accountant; Christopher Nigel Barrington Lacey [1961] Director/Chartered Surveyor; Caroline Victoria Sutton [1965] Director; David Robert Sutton [1960] Director/Farmer; Sir Richard Lexington Sutton [1937] Director/Farmer; Robert Glanville White [1956] Director/Chartered Surveyor; Peter Lewis Wyman [1950] Director/Chartered Accountant

Suzaku Aviation One Limited
Incorporated: 31 July 2015
Net Worth Deficit: £4,422,899 *Total Assets:* £105,291,064
Registered Office: 11 Old Jewry, London, EC2R 8DU
Activities: Renting and leasing of air passenger transport equipment
Parent: Ocorian (UK) Limited
Officers: Stuart Roderick Jenkin [1957] Director; Christopher John Wilson [1962] Director

SVF Holdco (UK) Limited
Incorporated: 16 October 1990
Previous: SVF Holdco (UK) PLC
Net Worth: £215,639,008 *Total Assets:* £215,639,008
Registered Office: c/o Hackwood Secretaries Limited, One Silk Street, London, EC2Y 8HQ
Activities: Other information technology service activities
Parent: SVF Holdings (UK) LLP
Officers: Paul Alexander Davison [1988] Director; James Alves MacDonald [1987] Director; Brian Clayton Wheeler [1975] Director/Attorney (NY and CA-Qualified) [American]

SVF Holdings (UK) LLP
Incorporated: 28 February 2017
Net Worth: £6,136,399,872 *Total Assets:* £9,019,357,184
Registered Office: 69 Grosvenor Street, London, W1K 3JP

SVF Investments (UK) Limited
Incorporated: 13 April 2017
Net Worth: £609,386,112 *Total Assets:* £609,386,112
Registered Office: 69 Grosvenor Street, London, W1K 3JP
Activities: Activities of other holding companies n.e.c.
Parent: SVF Holdings (UK) LLP
Officers: Ayako Adachi Adachi [1987] Director/Attorney (NY Qualified) [Spanish]; Amanda Sanchez-Barry [1982] Director; Brian Clayton Wheeler [1974] Director/Attorney (NY and CA-Qualified) [American]

Swan National Limited
Incorporated: 24 June 1980
Net Worth: £1,489,129 *Total Assets:* £198,463,552
Registered Office: 8 Canada Square, London, E14 5HQ
Activities: Financial leasing
Parent: HSBC Asset Finance (UK) Limited
Officers: Larissa Wilson, Secretary; Crispin Robert John Irvin [1978] Director/Chief Financial Officer; Simon Einar Long [1974] Director/Banker; Gareth Owen Conway [1966] Director/Investment Banking; Jaya Subramaniyan [1962] Director/Accountant [Malaysian]; Okechukwu Uwakwe [1969] Director [Irish]

John Swire & Sons Limited
Incorporated: 1 January 1914 *Employees:* 94,235
Net Worth: £12,677,000,192 *Total Assets:* £38,939,000,832
Registered Office: Swire House, 59 Buckingham Gate, London, SW1E 6AJ
Activities: Activities of head offices
Officers: David Charles Morris, Secretary; Martin Cubbon [1957] Director; Baroness Lydia Selina Dunn [1940] Director; Nicholas Adam Hodnett Fenwick [1960] Director; James Edward Hughes-Hallett [1965] Director/Chartered Accountant; James Wyndham John Hughes-Hallett [1949] Director; Gordon Douglas McCallum [1960] Director; Barnaby Nicholas Swire [1964] Director; John Samuel Swire [1962] Director; Merlin Bingham Swire [1973] Director; Samuel Compton Swire [1980] Director; William John Wemyss [1970] Director

Swire Oilfield Services (Holdings) Limited
Incorporated: 17 December 1999
Net Worth: £85,235,000 *Total Assets:* £189,808,992
Registered Office: Swire House, 59 Buckingham Gate, London, SW1E 6AJ
Activities: Activities of other holding companies n.e.c.
Parent: John Swire & Sons Limited
Officers: David Charles Morris, Secretary; John Bruce Rae-Smith [1963] Director; Dave Duncan Struan Robertson [1949] Director; Martin Humphrey Shaw [1972] Director/Chartered Accountant; Samuel Compton Swire [1980] Director; Manfred Vonlanthen [1970] Director [Swiss]

Swiss Re Services Limited
Incorporated: 7 March 2001 *Employees:* 438
Net Worth: £48,402,000 *Total Assets:* £107,513,000
Registered Office: 30 St Mary Axe, London, EC3A 8EP
Activities: Other business support service activities n.e.c.
Parent: Swiss RE Ltd
Officers: Jennifer Gandy, Secretary; Ian William Haycock [1966] Director/Chief Operating Officer Asset Manager; Simon Jukes [1975] Finance Director; Tavaziva Madzinga [1978] Director [Zimbabwean]; Nicola Jane Parton [1973] Director/Executive Claims Manager [New Zealander]

Swiss Re Specialised Investments Holdings (UK) Limited
Incorporated: 20 May 2002
Net Worth: £27,777,000 *Total Assets:* £628,750,016
Registered Office: 11th Floor, 200 Aldersgate Street, London, EC1A 4HD
Activities: Activities auxiliary to financial intermediation n.e.c.
Parent: Swiss RE Ltd
Officers: Ian Peter Bullock [1976] Director/Chartered Accountant; Stephen Paul Hjorring [1967] Director/Accountant; Damon Mark Lambert [1971] Director/Head of European Taxes; Drew Price [1968] Director/Accountant

Syco Entertainment Limited
Incorporated: 22 March 2010
Net Worth: £38,703,104 *Total Assets:* £149,280,864
Registered Office: 9 Derry Street, London, W8 5HY
Activities: Other amusement and recreation activities n.e.c.
Shareholders: Syco Holdings Limited; Sony Music Entertainment UK Limited
Officers: Simon Jenkins, Secretary; Simon Cowell [1959] Director; Michael Anthony Smith [1959] Director/Lawyer

Syco Holdings Limited
Incorporated: 3 July 2015
Net Worth: £79,141,728 *Total Assets:* £138,807,456
Registered Office: 9 Derry Street, London, W8 5HY
Activities: Other amusement and recreation activities n.e.c.
Parent: Sony Music Entertainment UK Limited
Officers: Simon Jenkins, Secretary; Simon Cowell [1959] Director; Michael Anthony Smith [1959] Director/Lawyer

Symphony Bidco Limited
Incorporated: 14 September 2016 *Employees:* 434
Net Worth Deficit: £196,590 *Total Assets:* £222,767,776
Registered Office: 3rd Floor, 11-12 St James's Square, London, SW1Y 4LB
Activities: Non-trading company
Parent: State-Owned Assets Supervision and Administration Commission of The State Council
Officers: Yusi Dai [1965] Director [Chinese]; Jing Guo [1981] Director [Chinese]; Qinghong Liu [1973] Director [Chinese]; Gary Montgomery [1967] Director/Engineer; Zhen Pang [1964] Director [Chinese]; Tongyu Xu [1968] Director/Vice President of Avicade [Chinese]; Jifeng Zhao [1976] Director [Chinese]

Syncbeam Limited
Incorporated: 16 August 1999 *Employees:* 3
Net Worth: £105,477,032 *Total Assets:* £105,484,032
Registered Office: 3 Grace Court, Totteridge Green, London, N20 8PY
Activities: Security dealing on own account
Shareholders: Moneypitch Company Limited; Brendon Street Investments Limited
Officers: Kamal Somchand Shah, Company Secretary; Gurjit Wernham [1958] Director; Nigel William Wray [1948] Director

SYND Holdco Limited
Incorporated: 13 August 2014
Net Worth: £153,490,000 *Total Assets:* £158,074,000
Registered Office: 27-28 Eastcastle Street, London, W1W 8DH
Activities: Activities of other holding companies n.e.c.
Shareholders: Swiss Life GIO SYND Limited; Greencoat UK Wind Holdco Limited
Officers: Constantin Dogos-Docovitch [1980] Director/Investment Manager [French]; Constance Wing-Yin Lee [1974] Director/Investment Manager; Stephen Bernard Lilley [1968] Director; Adolfo Francisco Pardo de Santayana Montes [1973] Director [Spanish]; Javier Francisco Serrano Alonso [1978] Director/Asset Manager [Spanish]

Synlab BondCo PLC
Incorporated: 23 March 2015 *Employees:* 18,303
Net Worth: £960,976,320 *Total Assets:* £3,797,325,056
Registered Office: 4th Floor, 1 Kingdom Street, London, W2 6BD
Activities: Activities of head offices
Parent: Synlab Unsecured BondCo PLC
Officers: Sami Badarani [1963] Director [French]; Nicholas John Stopford [1972] Director

Synlab Holdco Limited
Incorporated: 4 June 2015
Net Worth: £1,222,616,064 *Total Assets:* £1,222,679,936
Registered Office: 4th Floor, 1 Kingdom Street, London, W2 6BD
Activities: Activities of head offices
Parent: Synlab Limited
Officers: Sami Badarani [1963] Director [French]; Stuart James Quin [1975] Director

Synlab Limited
Incorporated: 9 June 2015 *Employees:* 18,303
Net Worth: £953,283,072 *Total Assets:* £3,792,979,968
Registered Office: 4th Floor, 1 Kingdom Street, London, W2 6BD
Activities: Activities of head offices
Officers: Kimberly Urdahl, Secretary; Peter Anthony Colin Catterall [1968] Director; Pierre Robert Maurice Estrade [1979] Director [French]; Mathieu Olivier Floreani [1967] Director [French]; Alexander Francis Stewart Leslie [1979] Director/Principal; Christian Salling [1973] Director [Danish]; Robert Marvin Teubner [1978] Director [German]; Dr. Bartholomaus Wimmer [1960] Director [German]

Synlab Unsecured BondCo PLC
Incorporated: 4 June 2015
Net Worth: £1,217,102,208 *Total Assets:* £1,546,060,544
Registered Office: 4th Floor, 1 Kingdom Street, London, W2 6BD
Activities: Activities of head offices
Parent: Synlab Holdco Limited
Officers: Sami Badarani [1963] Director [French]; Nicholas John Stopford [1972] Director

T & L Sugars Limited
Incorporated: 19 July 2010 *Employees:* 611
Net Worth: £210,534,416 *Total Assets:* £412,118,432
Registered Office: Thames Refinery, Factory Road, London, E16 2EW
Activities: Manufacture of sugar
Officers: Paul Stebbings, Secretary; Tarun Arora [1979] Finance Director [Indian]; Gabriel Buenaventura [1975] Director/Corporate Executive [Spanish]; Andrew Jones [1969] Sales & Marketing Director; Generald Mason [1974] Director/Executive; Armando Tabernilla [1959] Director/Attorney/Executive [American]

T-Systems Limited
Incorporated: 1 October 1982 *Employees:* 572
Net Worth: £11,033,000 *Total Assets:* £151,955,008
Registered Office: Sixth Floor, 20 Rathbone Place, Fitzrovia, London, W1T 1HY
Activities: Other telecommunications activities
Parent: T-Systems International GmbH
Officers: Jeevan Joseph Leonard D Silva, Secretary; Alison Dodd [1968] Managing Director [Australian]; Isabelle Sylvie Sabaud [1965] Director [French]

T.H.F.C. (Capital) PLC
Incorporated: 13 March 2001
Net Worth: £31,000 *Total Assets:* £564,777,024
Registered Office: 4th Floor, 107 Cannon Street, London, EC4N 5AF
Activities: Financial intermediation not elsewhere classified
Parent: T.H.F.C. (Services) Limited
Officers: Colin John Burke, Secretary; Scott Lee Bottles [1956] Director [American]; Colin John Burke [1962] Director; Fenella Jane Edge [1963] Director/Treasurer; Keith Philip Exford [1954] Director/Chief Executive; John Henry Parker [1949] Director; Gillian Caroline Sarah Payne [1963] Director; Ian Rex Peacock [1947] Director; William Richard Perry [1978] Director; Deborah Frances Shackleton [1952] Director/Chief Executive; Shirley Diana Smith [1960] Director; John Piers Williamson [1961] Director/Chief Executive

T.H.F.C. (Funding No. 1) PLC
Incorporated: 18 November 2004
Net Worth: £12,500 *Total Assets:* £253,020,928
Registered Office: 4th Floor, 107 Cannon Street, London, EC4N 5AF
Activities: Financial intermediation not elsewhere classified
Parent: T.H.F.C. (Services) Limited
Officers: Colin John Burke [1962] Director/Company Secretary; Fenella Jane Edge [1963] Director/Treasurer; John Piers Williamson [1961] Director/Chief Executive

T.H.F.C. (Funding No.2) PLC
Incorporated: 3 June 2009
Net Worth: £12,500 *Total Assets:* £402,146,176
Registered Office: 4th Floor, 107 Cannon Street, London, EC4N 5AF
Activities: Financial intermediation not elsewhere classified
Parent: T.H.F.C. (Services) Limited
Officers: Colin John Burke [1962] Director/Company Secretary; Fenella Jane Edge [1963] Director/Treasurer; John Piers Williamson [1961] Director/Chief Executive

T.H.F.C. (Funding No.3) PLC
Incorporated: 7 September 2011
Net Worth: £12,500 *Total Assets:* £788,900,224
Registered Office: 4th Floor, 107 Cannon Street, London, EC4N 5AF
Activities: Financial intermediation not elsewhere classified
Parent: T.H.F.C. (Services) Limited
Officers: Colin John Burke [1962] Director/Company Secretary; Fenella Jane Edge [1963] Director; John Piers Williamson [1961] Director/Chief Executive

TA I Limited
Incorporated: 25 June 1998
Net Worth: £7,426,376,192 *Total Assets:* £11,025,833,984
Registered Office: 51 Lime Street, London, EC3M 7DQ
Activities: Activities of head offices
Parent: Willis Investment UK Holdings Limited
Officers: Marcus Philip Dowding, Secretary; Steven James Alcock [1979] Director/Certified Accountant; Shirley Marie Girling [1969] Director/In-House Solicitor; Andrew Krasner [1975] Director [American]; Jonathan David Rand [1973] Director

TA Mfg Limited
Incorporated: 17 January 1986 *Employees:* 4
Net Worth: £582,351,424 *Total Assets:* £947,218,496
Registered Office: 5 New Street Square, London, EC4A 3TW
Activities: Non-specialised wholesale trade
Officers: Stephen Nolan [1969] Director [American]; Curtis Carl Reusser [1960] Director/President and Chief Executive Officer [American]; Albert Scott Yost [1965] Director/Group Vice President [American]

Tabletop London Limited
Incorporated: 20 December 2007 *Employees:* 31
Net Worth: £325,779,584 *Total Assets:* £426,151,552
Registered Office: New Burlington House, 1075 Finchley Road, London, NW11 0PU
Activities: Activities of head offices
Shareholders: Abraham Klein; Berish Berger; Vivian Naftali Vernick
Officers: Pessie Berger, Secretary; Sarah Rachel Klein, Secretary; Berish Berger [1956] Director; Abraham Klein [1962] Director [American]; Joshua Sternlicht [1965] Director

TAI Investments Limited
Incorporated: 29 June 1988
Net Worth: £352,400,000 *Total Assets:* £352,400,000
Registered Office: 40 Broadway, London, SW1H 0BT
Activities: Activities of other holding companies n.e.c.
Parent: Intu Properties PLC
Officers: Susan Marsden, Secretary; David Andrew Fischel [1958] Director/Chartered Accountant; Gary Richard Hoskins [1971] Director/Chartered Accountant

Taikoo Limited
Incorporated: 13 October 1989
Net Worth: £291,980,000 *Total Assets:* £292,812,000
Registered Office: Swire House, 59 Buckingham Gate, London, SW1E 6AJ
Activities: Activities of head offices
Parent: John Swire & Sons Limited
Officers: David Charles Morris, Secretary; Barnaby Nicholas Swire [1964] Director; Samuel Compton Swire [1980] Director

Take-Two Interactive Software UK Limited
Incorporated: 22 April 2015 *Employees:* 19
Net Worth: £13,791,317 *Total Assets:* £353,369,696
Registered Office: Hanover House, 14 Hanover Square, London, W1S 1HP
Activities: Other software publishing
Parent: Take Two Interactive Software Inc.
Officers: John Sebastian Belcher [1970] Director/Lawyer; Andrew John Wood [1962] Director/Accountant

Talbot 2002 Underwriting Capital Ltd
Incorporated: 23 July 2001
Net Worth: £5,724,184 *Total Assets:* £1,820,064,768
Registered Office: 60 Threadneedle Street, London, EC2R 8HP
Activities: Non-life insurance
Parent: American International General, Inc
Officers: Marie-Claire Gallagher, Secretary; Julian Graeme Ross [1965] Director/Actuary; James Edward Skinner [1961] Director/Insurance Underwriter; Nigel David Wachman [1958] Director/Accountant

Talisman Colombia Holdco Limited
Incorporated: 7 July 2010
Net Worth: £675,090,880 *Total Assets:* £677,987,456
Registered Office: Suite 1, 3rd Floor, 11-12 St James's Square, London, SW1Y 4LB
Activities: Other business support service activities n.e.c.
Parent: Repsol S.A.
Officers: Jose Luis Munoz Vega, Secretary; Jose Carlos Vicente Bravo [1965] Executive Director [Spanish]; Pablo Hernando [1970] Director/Executive [Spanish]; Jose Luis Munoz Vega [1979] Director; Jose Luis Munoz Vega [1979] Director/Economist [Spanish]

Talktalk Brands Limited
Incorporated: 8 June 2006
Net Worth Deficit: £322,553,984 *Total Assets:* £138,647,008
Registered Office: 11 Evesham Street, London, W11 4AR
Activities: Other telecommunications activities
Parent: Talktalk Telecom Holdings Limited
Officers: Timothy Simon Morris, Secretary; Kate Ferry [1973] Director; Tristia Adele Harrison [1973] Director/Chief Executive

Talktalk Communications Limited
Incorporated: 28 September 1999
Net Worth: £260,672,000 *Total Assets:* £1,216,727,040
Registered Office: 11 Evesham Street, London, W11 4AR
Activities: Other telecommunications activities
Parent: Talktalk Group Limited
Officers: Timothy Simon Morris, Secretary/Solicitor; Kate Ferry [1973] Director/Chief Financial Officer; Tristia Adele Harrison [1973] Director; Gary Steen [1971] Director

Talktalk Group Limited
Incorporated: 13 March 2008 *Employees:* 2,226
Net Worth: £563,201,984 *Total Assets:* £1,113,172,992
Registered Office: 11 Evesham Street, London, W11 4AR
Activities: Other telecommunications activities
Parent: Talktalk Telecom Holdings Limited
Officers: Timothy Simon Morris, Secretary; Sir Charles William Dunstone [1964] Director; Kate Ferry [1973] Director/Chief Financial Officer; Tristia Adele Harrison [1973] Director

Talktalk Telecom Group PLC
Incorporated: 15 December 2009 *Employees:* 2,288
Net Worth: £212,000,000 *Total Assets:* £1,542,000,000
Registered Office: 11 Evesham Street, London, W11 4AR
Activities: Other telecommunications activities
Officers: Timothy Simon Morris, Secretary; Charles John Allwood [1951] Director; Sir Charles William Dunstone [1964] Director; Kate Ferry [1973] Director/Chief Financial Officer; John Gildersleeve [1944] Director; Tristia Adele Harrison [1973] Director; Phil Victor Jordan [1968] Director/Chief Information Officer; Catherine Jane Keers [1965] Director; Nigel Jeremy Langstaff [1968] Director; Sir Howard Stringer [1942] Director [British/American]; Roger William Taylor [1964] Director; Ian Christopher West [1964] Director

Talktalk Telecom Holdings Limited
Incorporated: 23 September 1996
Net Worth: £485,200,992 *Total Assets:* £486,219,008
Registered Office: 11 Evesham Street, London, W11 4AR
Activities: Other telecommunications activities
Parent: Talktalk Telecom Group PLC
Officers: Timothy Simon Morris, Secretary; Kate Ferry [1973] Director/Chief Financial Officer; Tristia Adele Harrison [1973] Director

Talktalk Telecom Limited
Incorporated: 10 January 2003
Net Worth: £162,868,992 *Total Assets:* £1,012,142,976
Registered Office: 11 Evesham Street, London, W11 4AR
Activities: Other telecommunications activities
Parent: Talktalk Group Limited
Officers: Timothy Simon Morris, Secretary; Kate Ferry [1973] Director/Chief Financial Officer; Tristia Adele Harrison [1973] Director

Tallwood Investments Ltd
Incorporated: 10 March 2017
Net Worth Deficit: £3,093,720 *Total Assets:* £190,124,000
Registered Office: 5th Floor, Crowne House, 56-58 Southwark Street, London, SE1 1UN
Activities: Activities of financial services holding companies
Major Shareholder: Marquess of Bute John Colum Bute
Officers: Chiquita Harding, Secretary; John Colum Bute [1958] Director/Businessman

Tallwood Limited
Incorporated: 27 January 2000 *Employees:* 1
Net Worth: £24,056,908 *Total Assets:* £103,910,400
Registered Office: 5th Floor, Crown House, 56-58 Southwark Street, London, SE1 1UN
Activities: Other letting and operating of own or leased real estate
Shareholder: John Colum Bute
Officers: Stephen Hudson Jenkins, Secretary; John Colum Bute [1958] Director; Cathleen Crichton-Stuart [1986] Director; John Bryson Dumfries [1989] Director; Stephen Hudson Jenkins [1956] Director

Tam Investment Limited
Incorporated: 21 January 2009
Net Worth: £406,902,080 *Total Assets:* £406,943,456
Registered Office: Cannon Place, 78 Cannon Street, London, EC4N 6AG
Activities: Financial intermediation not elsewhere classified
Parent: Ameriprise Financial, Inc.
Officers: Alan Kaye, Secretary; John Borg [1951] Director/Certified Public Accountant [Maltese]; Edward Carbone [1942] Director/Management Consultant [Maltese]; David Hal Weiser [1960] Director/Attorney [American]; Bernard Joseph Zammit [1961] Director/Certified Public Accountant [Maltese]

Tam UK Holdings Limited
Incorporated: 23 December 2008
Net Worth: £332,022,016 *Total Assets:* £332,051,008
Registered Office: Cannon Place, 78 Cannon Street, London, EC4N 6AG
Activities: Activities of financial services holding companies
Parent: Threadneedle Holdings Limited
Officers: Alan Kaye, Secretary; Peter Stone [1965] Director/Accountant

Tamoa Limited
Incorporated: 9 August 1972
Net Worth: £113,930,928 *Total Assets:* £118,464,464
Registered Office: 16 Hans Road, London, SW3 1RT
Activities: Non-trading company
Officers: Manfred Stanley Gorvy [1938] Director/Chartered Accountant; Dr Sean Gorvy [1963] Director/Executive; John Patrick Kennedy [1957] Director [Irish]; Alan Jay Leibowitz [1952] Director/Surveyor; Trevor Moross [1948] Director/Chartered Surveyor

Tandem Bank Limited
Incorporated: 4 June 1969 *Employees:* 109
Previous: Harrods Bank Limited
Net Worth: £55,180,644 *Total Assets:* £492,037,600
Registered Office: 123 Pentonville Road, London, N1 9LG
Activities: Banks
Parent: Tandem Money Limited
Officers: Edward Charles Freeman, Secretary; Michael Lester Amato [1956] Director [American]; Matthew Jonathan Cooper [1966] Director [American]; Michael Klimbacher [1980] Director Investments and M&A [Austrian]; Frederick Samuel Knox [1975] Director [American]; Jeffrey John Pritchard [1963] Director; Jevgenijs Zagorovskis [1979] Associate Director, QIA

Tangguh Hiri Finance Limited
Incorporated: 21 November 2007
Net Worth: £5,803,835 *Total Assets:* £126,913,568
Registered Office: c/o Teekay Shipping (UK) Limited, 2nd Floor, 86 Jermyn Street, London, SW1Y 6JD
Activities: Service activities incidental to water transportation
Parent: Teekay LNG Partners L.P.
Officers: John Adams [1955] Director; Anne Elizabeth Liversedge [1968] Director/Attorney; Anthony Budiawan Oen [1961] Director [Indonesian]; Iain Relf [1959] Director/Vice President, Gas Fleet Operations; Siana Anggraeni Surya [1967] Director [Indonesian]

Tangguh Sago Finance Limited
Incorporated: 21 November 2007
Net Worth: £2,517,834 *Total Assets:* £125,751,456
Registered Office: c/o Teekay Shipping (UK) Limited, 2nd Floor, 86 Jermyn Street, London, SW1Y 6JD
Activities: Service activities incidental to water transportation
Parent: Teekay LNG Partners L.P.
Officers: John Adams [1955] Director; Anne Elizabeth Liversedge [1968] Director/Attorney; Anthony Budiawan Oen [1961] Director [Indonesian]; Iain Relf [1959] Director/Vice President, Gas Fleet Operations; Siana Anggraeni Surya [1967] Director [Indonesian]

The Tannen Group Limited
Incorporated: 15 April 1958 *Employees:* 14
Net Worth: £45,733,000 *Total Assets:* £219,398,000
Registered Office: Sutherland House, 70-78 West Hendon Broadway, London, NW9 7BT
Activities: Buying and selling of own real estate
Shareholders: Martin Irving Tannen; Daniel Asher Tannen
Officers: Jonathan Mark Miller, Secretary; Daniel Asher Tannen [1957] Director; David Tannen [1929] Director; Martin Irving Tannen [1955] Director; Miriam Tannen [1932] Director

Tanqueray Gordon and Company Limited
Incorporated: 11 January 1898
Net Worth: £73,627,000 *Total Assets:* £1,730,615,040
Registered Office: Lakeside Drive, Park Royal, London, NW10 7HQ
Activities: Other business support service activities n.e.c.
Parent: Diageo PLC
Officers: James Matthew Crayden Edmunds [1974] Director/Solicitor; Gabor Kovacs [1980] Director [Hungarian]; Kara Elizabeth Major [1977] Director [American]; Edward Worsley Pilkington [1967] Marketing and Innovation Director

Taqa Bratani Limited
Incorporated: 23 October 2006 *Employees:* 545
Net Worth Deficit: £408,058,720 *Total Assets:* £1,909,399,680
Registered Office: Cannon Place, 78 Cannon Street, London, EC4N 6AF
Activities: Extraction of crude petroleum
Officers: Alexander Burnett Hutchison, Secretary; Mohammed Abdulla Falah Jaber Al Ahbabi [1981] Director [Emirati]; Awad Saeed Bakhit Saeed Alketbi [1979] Director/Acting Executive VP of Business Support [Emirati]; Neil Morgan Fowler [1960] HSSEQ Director; Vivek Gambhir [1963] Director/General Counsel; David Gibson [1965] Technical Director; Alexander Burnett Hutchison [1978] Director/Solicitor; Donald Niven Taylor [1961] Operations Director

Tarsus Group Limited
Incorporated: 14 March 1986 *Employees:* 24
Net Worth: £20,056,484 *Total Assets:* £276,295,744
Registered Office: 9th Floor, Metro Building, 1 Butterwick, London, W6 8DL
Activities: Activities of other holding companies n.e.c.
Parent: Tarsus Luzhniki Limited
Officers: Simon Joseph Smith, Secretary; James Douglas Emslie [1966] Director/Chartered Accountant; Daniel Philip O'Brien [1967] Director/Chartered Accountant; Simon Joseph Smith [1976] Director/Chartered Secretary

Tarsus Holdings Limited
Incorporated: 30 September 2004
Net Worth: £114,085,160 *Total Assets:* £185,500,352
Registered Office: 9th Floor, Metro Building, 1 Butterwick, Hammersmith, London, W6 8DL
Activities: Activities of head offices
Parent: Tarsus Group Limited
Officers: Simon Joseph Smith, Secretary; James Douglas Emslie [1966] Director/Chartered Accountant; Daniel Philip O'Brien [1967] Director/Chartered Accountant; Simon Joseph Smith [1976] Director/Chartered Secretary

Taste Bidco Limited
Incorporated: 24 June 2015
Net Worth: £129,739,000 *Total Assets:* £256,824,000
Registered Office: 2nd Floor, 61 Berners Street, London, W1T 3NJ
Activities: Activities of head offices
Parent: Taste Midco 2 Limited
Officers: Kristina Zienko, Secretary; Alexander Rupert Gauvain Scrimgeour [1971] Director; Strahan Leonard Arthur Wilson [1975] Director

Taste Midco 2 Limited
Incorporated: 24 June 2015 *Employees:* 3,226
Net Worth: £76,762,000 *Total Assets:* £243,928,000
Registered Office: 2nd Floor, 61 Berners Street, London, W1T 3NJ
Activities: Activities of head offices
Parent: Taste Midco 1 Limited
Officers: Kristina Zienko, Secretary; Alexander Rupert Gauvain Scrimgeour [1971] Director; Strahan Leonard Arthur Wilson [1975] Director

Tata Steel Europe Limited
Incorporated: 5 October 2006 *Employees:* 21,100
Net Worth Deficit: £2,318,000,128 *Total Assets:* £7,632,000,000
Registered Office: 30 Millbank, London, SW1P 4WY
Activities: Activities of head offices
Officers: Helen Lochhead Matheson Avontuur, Secretary; Petrus Matthias Marie Blauwhoff [1953] Director [Dutch]; Koushik Chatterjee [1968] Director [Indian]; Dr Johannes Ludwig Maria Fischer [1956] Director/Chief Executive [German]; Narendra Kumar Misra [1956] Executive Director Finance [Indian]; Thachat Viswanath Narendran [1965] Managing Director, India and South East Asia [Indian]; Andrew MacKenzie Robb [1942] Director

Tata Steel UK Holdings Limited
Incorporated: 26 July 2006 *Employees:* 1,681
Net Worth Deficit: £2,008,000,000 *Total Assets:* £7,656,999,936
Registered Office: 30 Millbank, London, SW1P 4WY
Activities: Manufacture of basic iron and steel and of ferro-alloys
Parent: Tulip UK Holdings (No. 3) Limited
Officers: Sharone Vanessa Gidwani, Secretary; Dibyendu Dutta [1967] Director/Group Head - M & A And Treasury [Indian]; Narendra Kumar Misra [1956] Executive Director, Finance [Indian]

Tata Steel UK Limited
Incorporated: 26 July 1988
Net Worth Deficit: £88,000,000 *Total Assets:* £4,328,000,000
Registered Office: 30 Millbank, London, SW1P 4WY
Activities: Manufacture of basic iron and steel and of ferro-alloys
Parent: Corus Group Limited
Officers: Sharone Vanessa Gidwani, Secretary; Dr Henrik Adam [1964] Director/Engineer [German]; Torquil John Farquhar [1965] Executive Director, Human Resources; Dr Hans Fischer [1956] Director/Chief Technical Officer [German]; Ernst Hoogenes [1961] Director/Chief Technical Officer [Dutch]; Helen Lochhead Matheson Avontuur [1964] Director, Legal; Narendra Kumar Misra [1956] Executive Director Finance [Indian]; John Phillips [1969] Finance Director

Tate & Lyle Industries Limited
Incorporated: 21 July 1961 *Employees:* 3
Net Worth: £267,000,000 *Total Assets:* £312,000,000
Registered Office: 1 Kingsway, London, WC2B 6AT
Activities: Other business support service activities n.e.c.
Parent: Tate & Lyle Investments Limited
Officers: Jaime Tham, Secretary; Rowan Daniel Justin Adams [1967] Director/Chartered Secretary; Lindsay Claire Beardsell [1976] Director/Solicitor; Christopher Mark McLeish [1970] Director/Accountant

Tate & Lyle International Finance PLC
Incorporated: 16 January 1970
Net Worth: £128,052,000 *Total Assets:* £2,089,197,056
Registered Office: 1 Kingsway, London, WC2B 6AT
Activities: Financial intermediation not elsewhere classified
Parent: Tate & Lyle PLC
Officers: Jaime Tham, Secretary; Barry John Cannings [1956] Director/Accountant [Australian]; Christopher Mark McLeish [1970] Director/Accountant; Imran Nawaz [1973] Director/Chief Financial Officer [Luxembourger]; James Anthony Quinn [1963] Director/Chief Trader; Oliver Andrew Whiddett [1976] Director/Treasurer

Tate & Lyle Investments Limited
Incorporated: 15 May 1935
Net Worth: £1,308,670,976 *Total Assets:* £2,882,418,944
Registered Office: 1 Kingsway, London, WC2B 6AT
Activities: Activities of other holding companies n.e.c.
Parent: Tate & Lyle PLC
Officers: Jaime Tham, Secretary; Rowan Daniel Justin Adams [1967] Director/Chartered Secretary; Lindsay Claire Beardsell [1976] Director/Solicitor; Christopher Mark McLeish [1970] Director/Accountant

Tate & Lyle Public Limited Company
Incorporated: 27 February 1903 *Employees:* 4,189
Net Worth: £1,367,000,064 *Total Assets:* £2,571,000,064
Registered Office: 1 Kingsway, London, WC2B 6AT
Activities: Activities of head offices
Officers: Claire-Marie O'Grady, Secretary; Paul Anthony Foreman [1965] Director; Lars Vinge Frederiksen [1958] Director [Danish]; Anthony Nicholas Seymour Hampton [1967] Director/Accountant; Douglas Malcolm Hurt [1956] Director; Anne Elizabeth Minto [1953] Director; Gerard Martin Murphy [1955] Director [Irish]; Imran Nawaz [1973] Director/Chief Financial Officer [Luxembourger]; Dr Ajai Puri [1953] Director [American]; Sybella Jane Stanley [1961] Director; Warren Tucker [1962] Director

Tate & Lyle Technology Limited
Incorporated: 10 November 2006
Net Worth: £207,246,000 *Total Assets:* £208,627,008
Registered Office: 1 Kingsway, London, WC2B 6AT
Activities: Other business support service activities n.e.c.
Parent: Tate & Lyle PLC
Officers: Jaime Tham, Secretary; Rowan Daniel Justin Adams [1967] Director/Chartered Secretary; Lindsay Claire Beardsell [1976] Director/Solicitor; Christopher William Edward Darwen [1961] Director; Christopher Mark McLeish [1970] Director/Accountant

Taveta Investments (No.2) Limited
Incorporated: 25 May 2004
Net Worth: £487,828,992 *Total Assets:* £2,525,287,936
Registered Office: Colegrave House, 70 Berners Street, London, W1T 3NL
Activities: Other business support service activities n.e.c.
Shareholder: Taveta Investments Limited
Officers: Michelle Jane Gammon, Secretary; Ian Michael Grabiner [1959] Director; Gillian Anne Hague [1965] Director/Group Financial Controller

Taveta Investments Limited
Incorporated: 19 June 2002 *Employees:* 23,424
Net Worth Deficit: £78,386,000 *Total Assets:* £1,415,104,000
Registered Office: Colegrave House, 70 Berners Street, London, W1T 3NL
Activities: Other business support service activities n.e.c.
Major Shareholder: Lady Cristina Stuart Green
Officers: Michelle Jane Gammon, Secretary; Baroness Karren Rita Brady [1969] Director/Vice Chairman of West Ham United Football Club; Sharon Brown [1968] Director; Siobhan Forey [1972] Director/Chief Operating Officer; Ian Michael Grabiner [1959] Director; Sir Philip Nigel Ross Green [1952] Director; Gillian Anne Hague [1965] Director/Group Financial Controller; Brett Alexander Palos [1974] Director; David St John Shepherd [1963] Director/Chief Operating Officer

Tay Valley Lighting (Hampshire) Limited
Incorporated: 7 September 2009
Net Worth Deficit: £34,957,000 *Total Assets:* £131,071,000
Registered Office: 5th Floor, 120 Aldersgate Street, London, EC1A 4JQ
Activities: Other service activities n.e.c.
Parent: Tay Valley Lighting (Hampshire) Holdings Limited
Officers: Jonjo Benjamin Challands, Secretary; Thomas Samuel Cunningham [1975] Director; Amit Rishi Jaysukh Thakrar [1987] Director

Taylor Clark Limited
Incorporated: 27 May 1938 *Employees:* 9
Net Worth: £188,568,000 *Total Assets:* £192,220,992
Registered Office: 20 York Street, London, W1U 6PU
Activities: Activities of investment trusts
Shareholder: Colin Clark
Officers: Michele Judge, Secretary; Richard Bennison [1958] Director and Trustee; Reginald John Harvey [1950] Director/General Manager; Caroline Elizabeth Madelin [1978] Director/Accountant

Taylor Nelson Sofres International Limited
Incorporated: 7 October 1985 *Employees:* 4
Net Worth: £730,969,024 *Total Assets:* £776,883,968
Registered Office: Sea Containers, 18 Upper Ground, London, SE1 9GL
Activities: Activities of head offices
Parent: TNS Group Holdings Limited
Officers: Robert James Bowtell [1959] Director; David Grant Errington [1954] Director; Charles Ward Van Der Welle [1959] Director of Treasury

TBL (Milton Keynes) Limited
Incorporated: 6 October 1999
Net Worth: £96,645,584 *Total Assets:* £165,782,672
Registered Office: York House, 45 Seymour Street, London, W1H 7LX
Activities: Development of building projects
Parent: TBL Properties Limited
Officers: Sarah Morrell Barzycki [1958] Director/Head of Finance; Bryan Lewis [1967] Director/Chartered Surveyor; Charles Sheridan Alexander Maudsley [1964] Director; Timothy Andrew Roberts [1964] Director/Chartered Surveyor

TBL (Peterborough) Limited
Incorporated: 7 October 1999
Net Worth: £69,689,552 *Total Assets:* £153,614,160
Registered Office: York House, 45 Seymour Street, London, W1H 7LX
Activities: Development of building projects
Parent: TBL Properties Limited
Officers: Sarah Morrell Barzycki [1958] Director/Corporate Services Executive; Bryan Lewis [1967] Director/Chartered Surveyor; Charles Sheridan Alexander Maudsley [1964] Director; Timothy Andrew Roberts [1964] Director/Chartered Surveyor

TBWA EMEA Limited
Incorporated: 31 October 2014
Net Worth: £187,192,032 *Total Assets:* £187,193,536
Registered Office: Bankside 3, 90-100 Southwark Street, London, SE1 0SW
Activities: Activities of head offices
Parent: Omnicom EMEA Holdings Limited
Officers: Sally-Ann Bray, Secretary; Stephen Christopher Nigel Medhurst [1960] Director; Anthony Peter Phipkin [1957] Director/Accountant

TBWA UK Group Limited
Incorporated: 30 November 2001 *Employees:* 446
Net Worth: £40,836,200 *Total Assets:* £107,099,520
Registered Office: Bankside 3, 90-100 Southwark Street, London, SE1 0SW
Activities: Activities of head offices
Parent: TBWA EMEA Limited
Officers: Sally Ann Bray, Secretary; Philip Russell Franklin Brett [1969] Director/Advertising; Gary John Smith [1967] Director

TC Financing Limited
Incorporated: 10 December 2010
Net Worth: £40,448,000 *Total Assets:* £197,476,000
Registered Office: Cannon Place, 78 Cannon Street, London, EC4N 6AG
Activities: Activities of financial services holding companies
Parent: Threadneedle Asset Management Holdings Limited
Officers: Alan Kaye, Secretary; Peter Stone [1965] Director/Accountant

TC Ormonde OFTO Limited
Incorporated: 1 December 2010
Net Worth: £10,010,000 *Total Assets:* £125,122,000
Registered Office: 3 More London Riverside, London, SE1 2AQ
Activities: Transmission of electricity
Parent: Ofto Superholdco Limited
Officers: Amanda Elizabeth Woods, Secretary; Simon Fennell [1980] Director/Chartered Accountant; Giles James Frost [1962] Director/Solicitor; Michael John Gregory [1968] Director/Chartered Builder

TCI Fund Holdings Limited
Incorporated: 25 February 2010 *Employees:* 37
Net Worth: £775,257,600 *Total Assets:* £867,146,048
Registered Office: 7 Clifford Street, London, W1S 2FT
Activities: Activities of head offices
Major Shareholder: Christopher Anthony Hohn
Officers: Christopher Anthony Hohn [1966] Director/Fund Manager

TD Bank Europe Limited
Incorporated: 27 July 1992 *Employees:* 7
Net Worth: £536,704,000 *Total Assets:* £2,047,341,952
Registered Office: 60 Threadneedle Street, London, EC2R 8AP
Activities: Financial intermediation not elsewhere classified
Officers: Daksha Hirani, Secretary; John Henry Godfrey [1966] Director/Chief Executive [American]; Jane Jon [1977] Director [Canadian]; Patrice McDonald [1969] Director [Irish]; Andrea Marianne Jane Minton Beddoes [1970] Communications Director; Kevin Taylor [1967] Director; Peter Michael Cumnor Walker [1971] Director/Chief Executive

Technicolor Disc Services International Limited
Incorporated: 18 December 2000 *Employees:* 46
Net Worth: £102,211,000 *Total Assets:* £129,710,000
Registered Office: 16 Great Queen Street, Covent Garden, London, WC2B 5AH
Activities: Other professional, scientific and technical activities n.e.c.
Parent: Technicolor Videocassette Holdings (UK) Limited
Officers: Sophie Ida Jacqueline Le Menaheze, Secretary; Patricia Ann Dave [1968] Director/Chief Finance Officer/SVP [American]; Roy Charles Fossett [1953] Director/Company Executive; Simon Marshall Hibbins [1964] Director/Chief Executive [Australian]; Rafal Grzegorz Krawczyk [1970] Director [Polish]

Technip UK Limited
Incorporated: 27 August 1924 *Employees:* 748
Net Worth: £463,041,984 *Total Assets:* £1,277,932,032
Registered Office: One St Paul's Churchyard, London, EC4M 8AP
Activities: Support activities for petroleum and natural gas mining
Parent: TechnipFMC PLC
Officers: Brenda Janette Mennie, Secretary; Knut Boe [1958] Director/Executive Vice President [Norwegian]; William Edgar Morrice [1964] Managing Director; Kevin Murray Thomson [1976] Director/Vice President One Fleet (TMOS); Helen Urquhart [1967] Finance Director

Technip-Coflexip UK Holdings Limited
Incorporated: 19 September 1989
Net Worth: £86,168,000 *Total Assets:* £181,336,992
Registered Office: One St Paul's Churchyard, London, EC4M 8AP
Activities: Activities of head offices
Parent: TechnipFMC PLC
Officers: Brenda Janette Mennie, Secretary; Knut Boe [1958] Director/Senior Vice President NSC Region [Norwegian]; William Edgar Morrice [1964] Managing Director; Stephen Siegel [1976] Legal Director Corporate & Restructuring [French]; Helen Urquhart [1967] Finance Director

TechnipFMC Holdings Limited
Incorporated: 19 October 2016
Net Worth: £7,334,835,712 *Total Assets:* £9,496,069,120
Registered Office: 1 St Paul's Churchyard, London, EC4M 8AP
Activities: Non-trading company
Parent: TechnipFMC PLC
Officers: Jose Santos Cadena [1964] Director/Tax Attorney [American]; Barry Allen Glickman [1968] Director/Business Executive [American]

TechnipFMC Umbilicals Ltd
Incorporated: 3 July 1989 *Employees:* 378
Previous: Technip Umbilicals Ltd
Net Worth: £26,775,000 *Total Assets:* £271,892,000
Registered Office: One St Paul's Churchyard, London, EC4M 8AP
Activities: Other manufacturing n.e.c.
Parent: TechnipFMC PLC
Officers: Brenda Janette Mennie, Secretary; Tomas Svanes Bille [1972] Director/Vice President Legal Operations [Norwegian]; Knut Boe [1958] Director/Senior VP Region North Sea Canada [Norwegian]; Sarah Catherine Cridland [1970] Managing Director; Helen Urquhart [1967] Finance Director

Teesside Gas & Liquids Processing
Incorporated: 25 November 1992 *Employees:* 3
Net Worth: £9,697,000 *Total Assets:* £186,182,000
Registered Office: Suite 1, 3rd Floor, 11-12 St James's Square, London, SW1Y 4LB
Activities: Support activities for petroleum and natural gas mining
Parent: TGPP 1 Limited
Officers: Andrew Robert William Heppel [1971] Director/Energy Executive; Piotr Lukasz Sochocki [1982] Director/Investment Professional [Polish]; Sara Murtadha Jaffar Sulaiman [1977] Director [Omani]; Gareth Williams [1974] Finance Director

Telecom New Zealand (UK) Enterprises Limited
Incorporated: 17 September 1990
Net Worth: £594,391,104 *Total Assets:* £604,340,992
Registered Office: Suite 1, 3rd Floor, 11-12 St James's Square, London, SW1Y 4LB
Activities: Dormant company
Officers: Francis Thomas Evett [1971] Director [New Zealander]; Matthew Peter Floyd Sheppard [1967] Director [New Zealander]

Telecom Plus PLC
Incorporated: 9 October 1996 *Employees:* 1,177
Net Worth: £227,015,008 *Total Assets:* £437,920,000
Registered Office: Network HQ, 508 Edgware Road, The Hyde, London, NW9 5AB
Activities: Other telecommunications activities
Officers: David William Baxter, Secretary; Andrew Mark Blowers [1960] Director; Beatrice Hannah Millicent Hollond [1960] Director; Melvin Anthony Lawson [1958] Director; Andrew Lindsay [1977] Director; Julian Dominic Schild [1959] Director/Chartered Accountant; Nicholas Jakub Schoenfeld [1970] Financial Director; The Honorable Charles Francis Wigoder [1960] Director

Telegraph Media Group Limited
Incorporated: 31 March 1948 *Employees:* 1,084
Net Worth: £133,800,000 *Total Assets:* £219,600,000
Registered Office: 111 Buckingham Palace Road, London, SW1W 0DT
Activities: Publishing of newspapers
Officers: Aidan Stuart Barclay [1956] Director; Howard Myles Barclay [1959] Director/Financier; Nicholas Daniel Hugh [1975] Director/Chief Executive; Murdoch MacLennan [1949] Director/Deputy Chairman; Rigel Kent Mowatt [1948] Director; Philip Leslie Peters [1957] Company Banking Director; Michael Seal [1948] Director/Chartered Accountant

Telehouse Holdings Limited
Incorporated: 5 May 1993 *Employees:* 282
Net Worth: £438,824,992 *Total Assets:* £650,107,008
Registered Office: Coriander Avenue, London, E14 2AA
Activities: Other information technology service activities
Parent: Kddi Corporation
Officers: Kouhei Ohno [1975] Deputy Managing Director [Japanese]; Ken Sakai [1964] Managing Director [Japanese]

Telehouse International Corporation of Europe Ltd
Incorporated: 8 June 1987 *Employees:* 205
Net Worth: £376,649,984 *Total Assets:* £542,392,000
Registered Office: Coriander Avenue, London, E14 2AA
Activities: Other information technology service activities
Parent: Kddi Corporation
Officers: Kouhei Ohno [1975] Deputy Managing Director [Japanese]; Ken Sakai [1964] Managing Director [Japanese]; Yasuhiko Shiozaki [1960] Director [Japanese]

Telenor (UK) Limited
Incorporated: 22 April 1996 *Employees:* 22
Net Worth: £12,832,907,264 *Total Assets:* £14,483,332,096
Registered Office: 40 Bernard Street, London, WC1N 1LE
Activities: Satellite telecommunications activities
Officers: Julian Paul Crudge, Secretary; Julian Paul Crudge [1964] Director/Chartered Accountant; Martin Alexander Foss [1967] Director [Norwegian]; Morten Tengs [1961] Director [Norwegian]

Telereal (London Wall) Limited
Incorporated: 1 December 2014 *Employees:* 6
Net Worth Deficit: £141,304,992 *Total Assets:* £194,176,992
Registered Office: 140 London Wall, London, EC2Y 5DN
Activities: Management of real estate on a fee or contract basis
Parent: Telereal (LW) Holdings Limited
Officers: Aaron Jon Burns, Secretary; Adam Dakin [1962] Director; Graham Henry Edwards [1964] Director/Chief Executive Officer; Russell Charles Gurnhill [1970] Director; Michael Akiva Hackenbroch [1973] Director; Graeme Richard William Hunter [1963] Director

Telereal 112 Investments Limited
Incorporated: 2 September 2013
Net Worth: £100,424,000 *Total Assets:* £351,784,000
Registered Office: 140 London Wall, London, EC2Y 5DN
Activities: Management of real estate on a fee or contract basis
Parent: The Bank of N.T Butterfield & Son Limited
Officers: Aaron Jon Burns, Secretary; Adam Dakin [1962] Director; Graham Henry Edwards [1964] Director/Chief Executive Officer; Russell Charles Gurnhill [1970] Director; Michael Akiva Hackenbroch [1973] Director; Graeme Richard William Hunter [1963] Director

Telereal 112 Limited
Incorporated: 8 March 2001
Net Worth: £150,332,992 *Total Assets:* £401,929,984
Registered Office: 140 London Wall, London, EC2Y 5DN
Activities: Renting and operating of Housing Association real estate
Parent: Telereal 112 Holdings Limited
Officers: Aaron Jon Burns, Secretary; Adam Dakin [1962] Director/Chief Operating Officer; Graham Henry Edwards [1964] Director/Chief Executive Officer; Russell Charles Gurnhill [1970] Director; Michael Akiva Hackenbroch [1973] Director; Graeme Richard William Hunter [1963] Director

Telereal Secured Finance Holdings Limited
Incorporated: 28 June 2013
Net Worth: £4,000 *Total Assets:* £401,185,984
Registered Office: 140 London Wall, London, EC2Y 5DN
Activities: Non-trading company
Parent: Wilmington Trust SP Services (London) Limited
Officers: Aaron Jon Burns, Secretary; Adam Dakin [1962] Director; Graham Henry Edwards [1964] Director; Russell Charles Gurnhill [1970] Director; Michael Akiva Hackenbroch [1973] Director

Telereal Secured Finance PLC
Incorporated: 28 June 2013
Net Worth: £17,000 *Total Assets:* £401,183,008
Registered Office: 140 London Wall, London, EC2Y 5DN
Activities: Financial intermediation not elsewhere classified
Parent: Telereal Secured Finance Holdings Limited
Officers: Aaron Jon Burns, Secretary; Adam Dakin [1962] Director; Graham Henry Edwards [1964] Director; Russell Charles Gurnhill [1970] Director; Michael Akiva Hackenbroch [1973] Director

Telereal Securitisation Holdings Limited
Incorporated: 22 May 2001
Net Worth Deficit: £212,852,992 *Total Assets:* £3,218,255,104
Registered Office: 140 London Wall, London, EC2Y 5DN
Activities: Non-trading company
Parent: Wilmington Trust SP Services (London) Limited
Officers: Aaron Jon Burns, Secretary; Adam Dakin [1962] Director/Chief Operating Officer; Graham Henry Edwards [1964] Director/Chief Executive Officer; Russell Charles Gurnhill [1970] Director; Michael Akiva Hackenbroch [1973] Director

Telereal Securitisation PLC
Incorporated: 22 May 2001
Net Worth Deficit: £212,855,008 *Total Assets:* £3,218,255,104
Registered Office: 140 London Wall, London, EC2Y 5DN
Activities: Financial intermediation not elsewhere classified
Parent: Telereal Securitisation Holdings Limited
Officers: Aaron Jon Burns, Secretary; Adam Dakin [1962] Director/Chief Operating Officer; Graham Henry Edwards [1964] Director/Chief Executive Officer; Russell Charles Gurnhill [1970] Director; Michael Akiva Hackenbroch [1973] Director

Telereal Services Limited
Incorporated: 8 March 2001 *Employees:* 113
Net Worth: £26,528,000 *Total Assets:* £446,231,008
Registered Office: 140 London Wall, London, EC2Y 5DN
Activities: Management of real estate on a fee or contract basis
Parent: Telereal Holdings Limited
Officers: Aaron Jon Burns, Secretary; Michael Terence Baker [1961] Director; Adam Dakin [1962] Director/Chief Operating Officer; Graham Henry Edwards [1964] Director/Chief Executive Officer; Russell Charles Gurnhill [1970] Director; Michael Akiva Hackenbroch [1973] Director; Graeme Richard William Hunter [1963] Director

Telesat International Limited
Incorporated: 21 December 2001
Previous: Telesat Network Services (Europe) Limited
Net Worth: £50,787,948 *Total Assets:* £415,014,688
Registered Office: 55 Baker Street, London, W1U 7EU
Activities: Satellite telecommunications activities
Parent: Telesat (IOM) Holdings Limited
Officers: Christopher Difrancesco, Secretary; Christopher Stephen Difrancesco [1963] Director/Lawyer [Canadian]; Nicolas Pascal Edwards [1965] Director; Clarissa Offwood [1970] Sales Director

Telit Communications PLC
Incorporated: 30 November 2004 *Employees:* 1,076
Net Worth: £94,745,528 *Total Assets:* £256,675,536
Registered Office: Cannon Place, 78 Cannon Street, London, EC4N 6AF
Activities: Other telecommunications activities
Officers: Shiri Miller, Secretary; Yariv Dafna [1974] Finance Director [Israeli]; Paolo Carlo Renato Dal Pino [1962] Director [Italian]; Simon Patrick Duffy [1949] Director; Suvi Helmi Tellervo Linden [1962] Director [Finnish]; Adam Nicholas Power [1969] Director [British/Australian]; Harald Roesch [1968] Director [German]; Gil Sharon [1963] Director [Israeli]

Telstra Limited
Incorporated: 24 August 1999 *Employees:* 187
Net Worth: £47,543,000 *Total Assets:* £172,111,008
Registered Office: 2nd Floor, Blue Fin, 110 Southwark Street, London, SE1 0TA
Activities: Wired telecommunications activities
Parent: Telstra Global Limited
Officers: Thomas Luke Homer [1968] Managing Director; Douglas James Rogerson [1975] Finance Director

Temese Funding 2 PLC
Incorporated: 8 August 2014
Net Worth: £26,000 *Total Assets:* £667,886,976
Registered Office: 35 Great St Helen's, London, EC3A 6AP
Activities: Financial intermediation not elsewhere classified
Parent: Temese Funding 2 Holdings Limited
Officers: Daniel Marc Richard Jaffe [1975] Director

Temple Bar Investment Trust PLC
Incorporated: 24 June 1926
Net Worth: £936,366,016 *Total Assets:* £1,051,443,968
Registered Office: Woolgate Exchange, 25 Basinghall Street, London, EC2V 5HA
Activities: Activities of investment trusts
Officers: Arthur Tyrer Copple [1954] Director; June Frances de Moller [1947] Director; Richard Wilson Jewson [1944] Director; Lesley Rowena Sherratt [1962] Director; Richard Edward John Wyatt [1959] Director

Tenecom Limited
Incorporated: 4 December 1972
Net Worth: £31,095,384 *Total Assets:* £349,472,256
Registered Office: 4th Floor, 8 Fenchurch Place, London, EC3M 4AJ
Activities: Non-life insurance
Officers: Colleen Martin, Company Secretary; Karen Lesley Amos [1959] Director; Christopher Peter Hare [1947] Director; Vijay Anantray Mavani [1962] Director/Reinsurance; Brian Gerard Snover [1962] Director/Senior Vice President and Legal Counsel [American]; Andrew Wilson [1967] Director/Accountant

Tennants Consolidated Limited
Incorporated: 23 September 1930 *Employees:* 1,219
Net Worth: £257,848,992 *Total Assets:* £383,999,008
Registered Office: 12 Upper Belgrave Street, London, SW1X 8BA
Activities: Activities of head offices
Officers: Sean William Sloan, Secretary; Duncan James Alexander [1956] Director; Stuart Edward Ritchie Alexander [1955] Director; William Paul Alexander [1954] Director; Jonathan Harry Cartwright [1953] Director; Andrew Clive Gingell [1954] Director/Chemist; Paul Colin Hancock [1957] Director/Financier; Michael Gary Hughes [1968] Director; Kevin Garth Jones [1956] Director; Andrew Fraser John Mitchell [1953] Director

Tenneco Management (Europe) Limited
Incorporated: 14 November 1994 *Employees:* 1
Net Worth: £78,971,000 *Total Assets:* £112,064,000
Registered Office: 7 Albemarle Street, London, W1S 4HQ
Activities: Financial intermediation not elsewhere classified
Parent: Walker Limited
Officers: Steven Kenneth Evans [1963] Operations Director; Carol Avril Jones [1957] Director/Accountant

Terido LLP
Incorporated: 4 September 2012
Net Worth: £231,868,912 *Total Assets:* £234,794,560
Registered Office: 6th Floor, 33 Holborn, London, EC1N 2HT

TES Finance Limited
Incorporated: 23 June 2014
Previous: TES Finance PLC
Net Worth Deficit: £7,513,000 *Total Assets:* £350,660,000
Registered Office: 26 Red Lion Square, London, WC1R 4HQ
Activities: Activities of head offices
Parent: TES Global Holdings Limited
Officers: Paul Simpson, Secretary; Robert Ian Grimshaw [1971] Director; Paul Simpson [1968] Director/Chief Financial Officer

TES Global Group Limited
Incorporated: 1 July 2013
Net Worth Deficit: £96,321,000 *Total Assets:* £104,998,000
Registered Office: 26 Red Lion Square, London, WC1R 4HQ
Activities: Activities of head offices
Parent: TES Acquisition Limited
Officers: Robert Ian Grimshaw [1971] Director; Edward Frederick Llywelyn Hughes [1982] Director; Dany Rammal [1974] Director [French]; Paul Simpson [1968] Director/Chief Financial Officer

TES Global Holdings Direct Limited
Incorporated: 1 July 2013 *Employees:* 644
Net Worth Deficit: £106,127,000 *Total Assets:* £481,471,008
Registered Office: 26 Red Lion Square, London, WC1R 4HQ
Activities: Activities of head offices
Officers: Antonio Capo [1970] Director/Investment Professional [Italian]; Malte Johannes Janzarik [1980] Director/Investor [German]; Karl Ivar Peterson [1970] Director/Investor [American]

TES Global Holdings Limited
Incorporated: 6 March 2007 *Employees:* 644
Net Worth Deficit: £161,618,000 *Total Assets:* £198,426,000
Registered Office: 26 Red Lion Square, London, WC1R 4HQ
Activities: Activities of head offices
Parent: TES Global Group Limited
Officers: Paul Simpson, Secretary; Robert Ian Grimshaw [1971] Director; Paul Simpson [1968] Director/Chief Financial Officer

TES Global Limited
Incorporated: 7 May 1986 *Employees:* 367
Net Worth: £194,698,000 *Total Assets:* £242,991,008
Registered Office: 26 Red Lion Square, London, WC1R 4HQ
Activities: Publishing of consumer and business journals and periodicals
Parent: TSL Education SPV 2 Limited
Officers: Paul Simpson, Secretary; Robert Ian Grimshaw [1971] Director; Paul Simpson [1968] Director/Chief Financial Officer

Tesco Property Finance 2 PLC
Incorporated: 28 August 2009
Net Worth: £289,489 *Total Assets:* £725,238,144
Registered Office: 35 Great St Helen's, London, EC3A 6AP
Activities: Financial intermediation not elsewhere classified
Parent: Atrato Issuer Holdco Limited
Officers: Daniel Marc Richard Jaffe [1975] Director

Tesco Property Finance 3 PLC
Incorporated: 12 May 2010
Net Worth: £806,106 *Total Assets:* £1,090,515,712
Registered Office: 35 Great St Helen's, London, EC3A 6AP
Activities: Financial intermediation not elsewhere classified
Parent: Passaic Issuer Holdco Limited
Officers: Daniel Marc Richard Jaffe [1975] Director

Tesco Property Finance 4 PLC
Incorporated: 30 November 2010
Net Worth: £588,070 *Total Assets:* £702,495,488
Registered Office: 35 Great St Helen's, London, EC3A 6AP
Activities: Financial intermediation not elsewhere classified
Parent: Navona Issuer Holdco Limited
Officers: Daniel Marc Richard Jaffe [1975] Director

Tesco Property Finance 5 PLC
Incorporated: 15 November 2011
Net Worth: £400,448 *Total Assets:* £501,483,392
Registered Office: 35 Great St Helen's, London, EC3A 6AP
Activities: Financial intermediation not elsewhere classified
Parent: Sarum Issuer Holdco Limited
Officers: Daniel Marc Richard Jaffe [1975] Director

Tesco Property Finance 6 PLC
Incorporated: 25 September 2012
Net Worth: £261,411 *Total Assets:* £548,355,264
Registered Office: 35 Great St Helen's, London, EC3A 6AP
Activities: Financial intermediation not elsewhere classified
Parent: Dorney Issuer Holdco Limited
Officers: Daniel Marc Richard Jaffe [1975] Director

Tesnik Holdings Limited
Incorporated: 13 May 2016 *Employees:* 3,304
Net Worth: £25,108,680 *Total Assets:* £1,246,130,688
Registered Office: 35 Great St Helen's, London, EC3A 6AP
Activities: Activities of other holding companies n.e.c.
Officers: Sajid Mahmood Ataullah [1967] Director; Sarbjit Singh Basi [1968] Director; Clifford Andrew Bottomley [1970] Director Treasury, Europe; Emma Elizabeth Mowbray Clifton [1972] Director; Sebastian Cordova Moyano [1973] Director/Attorney [Argentinian]; Gustavo D'Alessandro [1965] Director [Argentinian]; Laura Edith Ferrari [1972] Director [Argentinian]; Khalid Ikram [1967] Director; Luis Pablo Rogelio Pagano [1953] Director/Businessman [Argentinian]

TFG Brands (London) Limited
Incorporated: 8 January 2015
Net Worth Deficit: £18,206,000 *Total Assets:* £227,236,992
Registered Office: 55 Kimber Road, London, SW18 4NX
Activities: Retail sale of clothing in specialised stores
Parent: Dress Holdco A Limited
Officers: Stuart Andrew Baird [1965] Retail Director [South African]; Benjamin Lawrence Maximilian Barnett [1979] Director; Lee Eric Harlow [1971] Director; Catherine Ann Lambert [1965] Director/Chief Financial Officer; Alexander Douglas Murray [1957] Director; Bongiwe Ntuli [1977] Director [South African]; Anthony Edward Thunstrom [1970] Director [South African]

TFS Derivatives Limited
Incorporated: 14 August 2000 *Employees:* 51
Net Worth: £12,071,000 *Total Assets:* £240,331,008
Registered Office: Beaufort House, 15 St Botolph Street, London, EC3A 7QX
Activities: Financial intermediation not elsewhere classified
Shareholders: Tradition Financial Services Ltd; Compagnie Financial Tradition SA
Officers: Peter Francis Weston, Secretary; Martin Abbott [1960] Director/Executive; Michael Jon Anderson [1961] Director/Executive; Christian Marcel Michel Baillet [1950] Director/Executive [French]; Francois Brisebois [1974] Group Consolidation Director [Canadian]; Herve Pierre Benoit Carmen de Carmoy [1937] Director/Executive [French]; Michael Saul Leibowitz [1965] Director/Executive [American]; Daniel Craig Marcus [1973] Director/Executive; Malcolm Graham McCaig [1955] Director; Stevan Vjestica [1964] Director/Executive; William Pierre Francois Norbert Wostyn [1973] Director/Lawyer [French]

TH Holdings Limited
Incorporated: 10 November 2006 *Employees:* 1,342
Previous: Tonstate (Hotels) Limited
Net Worth Deficit: £55,806,000 *Total Assets:* £509,678,016
Registered Office: 3 Park Place, St James's, London, SW1A 1LP
Activities: Activities of head offices
Shareholders: Arthur Matyas; Edward Oded Wojakovski
Officers: Dr Edward Oded Wojakovski, Secretary; Arthur Matyas [1932] Director; Dr Edward Oded Wojakovski [1969] Director

Thames Quay Properties Holdings Limited
Incorporated: 22 November 2013
Net Worth Deficit: £558,000 *Total Assets:* £109,986,000
Registered Office: 3rd Floor, Walbrook Building, 195 Marsh Wall, London, E14 9SG
Activities: Buying and selling of own real estate
Major Shareholder: Allirajah Subaskaran
Officers: Aiadurai Sivasamy Premananthan, Secretary; Aiadurai Sivasamy Premananthan [1963] Director/Businessman; Allirajah Subaskaran [1972] Director/Businessman

Thames Quay Properties II Limited
Incorporated: 29 October 2013
Net Worth Deficit: £574,000 *Total Assets:* £109,986,000
Registered Office: 3rd Floor, Walbrook Building, 195 Marsh Wall, London, E14 9SG
Activities: Buying and selling of own real estate
Parent: Thames Quay Properties Limited
Officers: Aiadurai Sivasamy Premananthan, Secretary; Aiadurai Sivasamy Premananthan [1963] Director/Businessman; Allirajah Subaskaran [1972] Director/Businessman

Thames Quay Properties III Limited
Incorporated: 22 November 2013
Net Worth Deficit: £557,000 *Total Assets:* £109,986,000
Registered Office: 3rd Floor, Walbrook Building, 195 Marsh Wall, London, E14 9SG
Activities: Buying and selling of own real estate
Parent: Thames Quay Properties Holdings Limited
Officers: Aiadurai Sivasamy Premananthan, Secretary; Aiadurai Sivasamy Premananthan [1963] Director/Businessman; Allirajah Subaskaran [1972] Director/Businessman

Thames Quay Properties Limited
Incorporated: 1 July 2013
Net Worth Deficit: £574,000 *Total Assets:* £109,986,000
Registered Office: 3rd Floor, Walbrook Building, 195 Marsh Wall, London, E14 9SG
Activities: Buying and selling of own real estate
Parent: Thames Quay Properties III Limited
Officers: Aiadurai Sivasamy Premananthan, Secretary; Aiadurai Sivasamy Premananthan [1963] Director/Businessman; Allirajah Subaskaran [1972] Director/Businessman

Thameswey Housing Limited
Incorporated: 27 April 2005
Net Worth: £40,380,528 *Total Assets:* £158,349,888
Registered Office: The St Botolph Building, 138 Houndsditch, London, EC3A 7AR
Activities: Development of building projects
Parent: Thameswey Limited
Officers: David John Bittleston [1957] Director/Businessman; Peter Nigel Bryant [1956] Director/Solicitor; Colin Sidney Kemp [1959] Director/Councillor; Dr Barry Martin Maunders [1956] Director/Independent Consultant; Terry Price [1954] Director/Accountant

Thameswey Limited
Incorporated: 27 January 1999 *Employees:* 33
Net Worth: £27,438,288 *Total Assets:* £257,317,360
Registered Office: The St Botolph Building, 138 Houndsditch, London, EC3A 7AR
Activities: Activities of head offices
Officers: David John Bittleston [1957] Director/Businessman; Peter Nigel Bryant [1956] Director/Solicitor; Councillor Beryl Ann Hunwicks [1946] Director; Dr Barry Martin Maunders [1956] Director/Independent Consultant; Raymond Nigel Morgan [1953] Director/Chief Executive; William Prescott [1952] Project Development Director; Terry Price [1954] Director/Accountant; Douglas James Spinks [1955] Director/Deputy Chief Executive

Thanet Offshore Wind Limited
Incorporated: 15 August 2002
Net Worth: £496,200,000 *Total Assets:* £618,955,008
Registered Office: First Floor, 1 Tudor Street, London, EC4Y 0AH
Activities: Production of electricity
Shareholders: Vattenfall Wind Power Ltd; Vattenfall Vindkraft AB
Officers: Frederik Bernard Hendrik Hiensch [1974] Director [Dutch]; Jonas Van Mansfeld [1976] Director [Dutch]; Klemens Millonig [1970] Director [Austrian]

Thanet OFTO Holdco Limited
Incorporated: 30 July 2010
Net Worth Deficit: £11,055,000 *Total Assets:* £190,670,000
Registered Office: Balfour Beatty Capital Limited, 6th Floor, 350 Euston Road, London, NW1 3AX
Activities: Activities of head offices
Parent: Equitix Infrastructure 3 Limited
Officers: Saiema Ibrahim, Secretary; Rebecca Collins [1971] Director; John Sinclair [1962] Director; Nathan John Wakefield [1974] Director; Brian Roland Walker [1955] Director/Quantity Surveyor

Thanet OFTO Limited
Incorporated: 12 August 2010
Net Worth Deficit: £11,055,000 *Total Assets:* £190,670,000
Registered Office: Balfour Beatty Capital Limited, 6th Floor, 350 Euston Road, London, NW1 3AX
Activities: Transmission of electricity
Officers: Saiema Ibrahim, Secretary; Rebecca Collins [1971] Director; John Sinclair [1962] Director; Nathan John Wakefield [1974] Director; Brian Roland Walker [1955] Director/Quantity Surveyor

Theatre (Hospitals) No.1 PLC
Incorporated: 25 January 2007
Net Worth: £50,751 *Total Assets:* £258,527,664
Registered Office: 35 Great St Helen's, London, EC3A 6AP
Activities: Financial intermediation not elsewhere classified
Parent: Intertrust Corporate Services Limited
Officers: Susan Iris Abrahams [1957] Director

Theatre (Hospitals) No.2 PLC
Incorporated: 25 January 2007
Net Worth: £43,470 *Total Assets:* £172,415,632
Registered Office: 35 Great St Helen's, London, EC3A 6AP
Activities: Financial intermediation not elsewhere classified
Parent: Intertrust Corporate Services Limited
Officers: Susan Iris Abrahams [1957] Director

Thinc UK Group Limited
Incorporated: 15 September 2006
Previous: Bluefin Group Limited
Net Worth: £92,302,000 *Total Assets:* £104,136,000
Registered Office: 5 Old Broad Street, London, EC2N 1AD
Activities: Activities of other holding companies n.e.c.
Parent: Axa UK PLC
Officers: Jeremy Peter Small, Secretary; Christopher Graham Bobby [1966] Director; Susan Nicola Teale [1962] Director

Third New Court Limited
Incorporated: 21 January 2008
Net Worth: £11,025,573 *Total Assets:* £166,222,432
Registered Office: New Court, St Swithin's Lane, London, EC4N 8AL
Activities: Other letting and operating of own or leased real estate
Parent: Rothschild & Co
Officers: Peter William Barbour [1973] Finance Director; Anthony Leonard Chapman [1946] Director; Anthony James Granville Coghlan [1957] Director/Accountant; Mark Leslie Crump [1963] Finance Director

Third Point RE (UK) Holdings Ltd
Incorporated: 21 November 2014
Net Worth: £122,210,576 *Total Assets:* £122,350,792
Registered Office: 7th Floor, 1 Minster Court, Mincing Lane, London, EC3R 7AA
Activities: Other activities auxiliary to insurance and pension funding
Parent: Third Point Reinsurance Ltd
Officers: James Robert Bredahl [1963] Director/Insurance Executive [American]; Christopher Stanley Coleman [1973] Director [American]

Thistle Investments (AMC) Limited
Incorporated: 3 October 2016
Net Worth: £3,643,000 *Total Assets:* £424,992,000
Registered Office: 35 Great St Helen's, London, EC3A 6AP
Activities: Financial intermediation not elsewhere classified
Parent: Intertrust Corporate Services Limited
Officers: Daniel Marc Richard Jaffe [1975] Director

Thistle Investments (ERM) Limited
Incorporated: 17 September 2014
Net Worth: £13,348,000 *Total Assets:* £241,243,008
Registered Office: 35 Great St Helen's, London, EC3A 6AP
Activities: Non-trading company
Parent: Intertrust Corporate Services Limited
Officers: Daniel Marc Richard Jaffe [1975] Director

Thistleclub Limited
Incorporated: 21 September 1988
Net Worth: £3,612,596,992 *Total Assets:* £3,614,221,056
Registered Office: Sea Containers House, 18 Upper Ground, London, SE1 9GL
Activities: Activities of head offices
Parent: Line Exchange Limited
Officers: Charles Ward Van Der Welle [1959] Director of Treasury; Steve Richard Winters [1968] Director/Chartered Accountant

J. Walter Thompson Group Limited
Incorporated: 27 August 1982 *Employees:* 267
Net Worth: £96,342,000 *Total Assets:* £141,492,000
Registered Office: 1 Knightsbridge Green, London, SW1X 7NW
Activities: Advertising agencies
Officers: Peter Howard Dipple, Secretary; Christopher Henry St J Hoare [1960] Director/Executive Chairman; Sally Sharon Bird Spensley [1958] Director/Chief Financial Officer; Keith Kelley Wilkins [1951] Director/Advertising Executive; Ngen Siak Yap [1977] Finance Director [Malaysian]

Thomson Business Information Holdings Limited
Incorporated: 10 October 1994
Net Worth: £353,200,736 *Total Assets:* £356,915,072
Registered Office: The Thomson Reuters Building, 30 South Colonnade, Canary Wharf, London, E14 5EP
Activities: Dormant company
Parent: The Thomson Organisation (No. 23)
Officers: Stuart Nicholas Corbin [1964] Director/International Treasurer; Kimberley Major [1985] Director/Chartered Accountant

Thomson Information & Publishing Holdings Limited
Incorporated: 21 November 1994
Net Worth: £133,493,960 *Total Assets:* £133,493,960
Registered Office: The Thomson Reuters Building, 30 South Colonnade, Canary Wharf, London, E14 5EP
Activities: Dormant company
Parent: Thomson Publishing Group Limited
Officers: Stuart Nicholas Corbin [1964] Director/International Treasurer; Kimberley Major [1985] Director/Chartered Accountant

Thomson Legal & Professional Group Limited
Incorporated: 9 June 1980
Net Worth: £385,656,992 *Total Assets:* £386,249,568
Registered Office: The Thomson Reuters Building, 30 South Colonnade, London, E14 5EP
Activities: Activities of head offices
Parent: Thomson Business Information Holdings Limited
Officers: Stuart Nicholas Corbin [1964] Director/International Treasurer; Kimberley Major [1985] Director/Chartered Accountant

The Thomson Organisation (No.23)
Incorporated: 25 May 1989
Net Worth Deficit: £12,038,979 *Total Assets:* £384,252,320
Registered Office: The Thomson Reuters Building, 30 South Colonnade, Canary Wharf, London, E14 5EP
Activities: Dormant company
Shareholders: TR Organisation Limited; TTC (1994) Limited
Officers: Stuart Nicholas Corbin [1964] Director/International Treasurer; Kimberley Major [1985] Director/Chartered Accountant

Thomson Reuters (Professional) UK Limited
Incorporated: 17 November 1982 *Employees:* 1,548
Net Worth: £487,652,000 *Total Assets:* £706,771,968
Registered Office: Five Canary Wharf, London, E14 5AQ
Activities: Activities of head offices
Parent: TR Professional Holdings Limited
Officers: Barbara Abena Boateng, Secretary; Matthew Bryan Keen [1978] Director/Chartered Accountant; Kimberley Major [1985] Director/Chartered Accountant

Threadneedle Asset Management Finance Limited
Incorporated: 30 September 2005
Net Worth: £31,823,000 *Total Assets:* £169,256,992
Registered Office: Cannon Place, 78 Cannon Street, London, EC4N 6AG
Activities: Financial intermediation not elsewhere classified
Parent: Threadneedle Asset Management Holdings Limited
Officers: Alan Kaye, Secretary; Peter Stone [1965] Director/Accountant

Threadneedle Asset Management Holdings Limited
Incorporated: 22 April 1998 *Employees:* 488
Net Worth: £307,160,992 *Total Assets:* £530,095,008
Registered Office: Cannon Place, 78 Cannon Street, London, EC4N 6AG
Activities: Activities of head offices
Parent: Tam UK Holdings Limited
Officers: Alan Kaye, Secretary; Mark Andrew Burgess [1964] Director/Chief Investment Officer; Michelle Sylvia Scrimgeour [1963] Director/Chief Executive Officer; Peter Stone [1965] Director/Accountant

Threadneedle Asset Management Limited
Incorporated: 22 October 1956 *Employees:* 173
Net Worth: £132,850,000 *Total Assets:* £244,072,992
Registered Office: Cannon Place, 78 Cannon Street, London, EC4N 6AG
Activities: Security and commodity contracts dealing activities
Parent: TC Financing Limited
Officers: Alan Kaye, Secretary; Mark Andrew Burgess [1964] Director/Chief Investment Officer; Michelle Sylvia Scrimgeour [1963] Director/Chief Executive Officer; Peter Stone [1965] Director/Accountant

Threadneedle Holdings Limited
Incorporated: 6 October 2010
Net Worth: £101,409,000 *Total Assets:* £354,388,000
Registered Office: Cannon Place, 78 Cannon Street, London, EC4N 6AG
Activities: Activities of head offices
Parent: Ameriprise Financial, Inc.
Officers: Alan Kaye, Secretary; Peter Stone [1965] Director/Accountant

Threadneedle Investment Services Limited
Incorporated: 26 January 1999 *Employees:* 110
Net Worth: £121,564,000 *Total Assets:* £519,276,000
Registered Office: Cannon Place, 78 Cannon Street, London, EC4N 6AG
Activities: Financial intermediation not elsewhere classified
Parent: TC Financing Limited
Officers: Alan Kaye, Secretary; Ann Lindsay Roughead [1962] Director/Consultant; Michelle Sylvia Scrimgeour [1963] Director/Chief Executive Officer; Kathleen Mary Shailer [1963] Director; Peter Stone [1965] Director/Accountant; Laura Mary Weatherup [1975] Director/Head of Investment Operations, EMEA

Threadneedle Pensions Limited
Incorporated: 9 July 1970
Net Worth: £24,418,000 *Total Assets:* £3,595,792,896
Registered Office: Cannon Place, 78 Cannon Street, London, EC4N 6AG
Activities: Life insurance
Parent: Threadneedle Asset Management Holdings Limited
Officers: Alan Kaye, Secretary; Andrew James Nicoll [1969] Director/Global Head of Insurance; Ann Lindsay Roughead [1962] Director/Consultant; Michelle Sylvia Scrimgeour [1963] Director/Chief Executive Officer; Kathleen Mary Shailer [1963] Director; Peter Stone [1965] Director/Accountant; William Frederick Truscott [1960] Director/Executive [American]

Throgmorton Assets PLC
Incorporated: 11 June 2014
Net Worth: £162,448,752 *Total Assets:* £191,411,504
Registered Office: Drapers' Hall, Throgmorton Avenue, London, EC2N 2DQ
Activities: Other letting and operating of own or leased real estate
Parent: The Drapers' Company
Officers: David Michael Sumner, Secretary; Patrick Alexander Beddows [1961] Director/Chartered Surveyor; William Francis Charnley [1960] Director/Solicitor; John William Giffard [1952] Director; David Michael Sumner [1971] Director/Chartered Accountant; Richard Dirdoe Winstanley [1964] Director

Thrones 2014-1 PLC
Incorporated: 30 June 2014
Net Worth Deficit: £776,159 *Total Assets:* £239,963,856
Registered Office: 35 Great St Helen's, London, EC3A 6AP
Activities: Financial intermediation not elsewhere classified
Parent: Intertrust Corporate Services Limited
Officers: Daniel Marc Richard Jaffe [1975] Managing Director

Thrones 2015-1 PLC
Incorporated: 15 July 2015
Net Worth Deficit: £11,392,166 *Total Assets:* £252,474,016
Registered Office: 35 Great St Helen's, London, EC3A 6AP
Activities: Financial intermediation not elsewhere classified
Parent: Intertrust Corporate Services Limited
Officers: Daniel Marc Richard Jaffe [1975] Managing Director

TI Atlantic Europe Holdings Limited
Incorporated: 12 June 2012
Previous: Time Atlantic Europe Holdings Limited
Net Worth: £26,874,096 *Total Assets:* £102,559,912
Registered Office: 6th Floor, 60 Gracechurch Street, London, EC3V 0HR
Activities: Activities of head offices
Parent: Time European Holdings Limited
Officers: Joseph Henry Ceryanec [1961] Director [American]; John Stanley Zieser [1959] Director [American]

TI European Holdings Limited
Incorporated: 2 April 2014
Previous: Time European Holdings Limited
Net Worth Deficit: £31,370,104 *Total Assets:* £104,088,248
Registered Office: 6th Floor, 60 Gracechurch Street, London, EC3V 0HR
Activities: Activities of head offices
Parent: Time Inc.
Officers: Joseph Henry Ceryanec [1961] Director [American]; John Stanley Zieser [1959] Director [American]

TI Magazines (UK) Limited
Incorporated: 18 December 1997
Previous: IPC Magazines (UK) Limited
Net Worth: £91,036,000 *Total Assets:* £312,147,008
Registered Office: 6th Floor, 60 Gracechurch Street, London, EC3V 0HR
Activities: Activities of other holding companies n.e.c.
Parent: Time UK Publishing Holdings Limited
Officers: Joseph Henry Ceryanec [1961] Director/Chief Financial Officer, Meredith Corporation [American]; John Stanley Zieser [1959] Director/CDO, GC & Secretary, Meredith Corporation [American]

TI Magazines Holdings Limited
Incorporated: 13 November 1997
Previous: IPC Magazines Holdings Limited
Net Worth: £294,248,992 *Total Assets:* £395,024,000
Registered Office: 6th Floor, 60 Gracechurch Street, London, EC3V 0HR
Activities: Activities of other holding companies n.e.c.
Parent: International Publishing Corporation Limited
Officers: Joseph Henry Ceryanec [1961] Director [American]; John Stanley Zieser [1959] Director [American]

TI Media Limited
Incorporated: 5 August 1897 *Employees:* 1,204
Previous: Time Inc. (UK) Ltd
Net Worth: £37,285,000 *Total Assets:* £144,431,008
Registered Office: 3rd Floor, 161 Marsh Wall, London, E14 9AP
Activities: Publishing of consumer and business journals and periodicals
Parent: Sapphire Bidco Limited
Officers: Rachel Addison [1970] Director; Samuel Peter Finlay [1972] Director; Adrian John Hughes [1971] Director; Marcus Alvin Rich [1959] Director; Neil Simon Robinson [1972] Director

TI UK Publishing Holdings Limited
Incorporated: 23 April 2001 *Employees:* 3
Previous: Time UK Publishing Holdings Limited
Net Worth: £97,620,000 *Total Assets:* £209,391,008
Registered Office: 6th Floor, 60 Gracechurch Street, London, EC3V 0HR
Activities: Activities of head offices
Parent: Time Atlantic Europe Holdings Limited
Officers: Joseph Henry Ceryanec [1961] Director/Chief Financial Officer, Meredith Corporation [American]; John Stanley Zieser [1959] Director/CDO, GC & Secretary, Meredith Corporation [American]

TIAA International Holdings 2 Limited
Incorporated: 19 September 2013 *Employees:* 295
Net Worth: £206,907,264 *Total Assets:* £241,177,152
Registered Office: 150 Aldersgate Street, London, EC1A 4AB
Activities: Other service activities n.e.c.
Officers: Glenn Eugene Brightman [1972] Director/Executive Vice President, Chief Financial Officer [American]; Michael John Lawson Sales [1964] Director/Chief Executive Officer

TIAA International Holdings 3 Limited
Incorporated: 20 September 2013
Net Worth: £204,648,176 *Total Assets:* £205,911,488
Registered Office: 150 Aldersgate Street, London, EC1A 4AB
Activities: Other service activities n.e.c.
Parent: TIAA International Holdings 2 Limited
Officers: John Leland MacCarthy [1959] Director/Finance [American]

Tianqi UK Limited
Incorporated: 26 March 2014
Net Worth: £316,664,576 *Total Assets:* £316,678,528
Registered Office: 5th Floor, 6 St Andrew Street, London, EC4A 3AE
Activities: Non-trading company
Major Shareholder: Weiping Jiang
Officers: Stephen William Spencer Norton [1959] Director; Wei Wu [1974] Director/Company Executive [Chinese]

Tibra Equities Europe Limited
Incorporated: 14 June 2010 *Employees:* 7
Net Worth: £54,240,140 *Total Assets:* £453,772,128
Registered Office: Level 11, 5 Aldermanbury Square, London, EC2V 7HR
Activities: Activities of financial services holding companies
Officers: Timothy Edward Knipe, Secretary; Hugo Hesse [1982] Director [Australian]; Campbell Terence Norwood [1977] Director/Head of Strategy [Australian]; Gary Ngunjiri Richard Pickwell [1967] Director/Global Head of Finance [Australian]; Christopher Alfred Udy [1977] Director/Global General Manager [New Zealander]

Ticketmaster Europe Holdco Limited
Incorporated: 23 September 2008
Net Worth: £113,574,992 *Total Assets:* £283,597,504
Registered Office: 2nd Floor, Regent Arcade House, 19-25 Argyll Street, London, W1F 7TS
Activities: Activities of head offices
Parent: Live Nation Entertainment, Inc
Officers: David Nicholas Hamilton, Secretary; Christopher James Edmonds [1959] Managing Director; Selina Holliday Emeny [1968] Director/Solicitor; David Nicholas Hamilton [1962] Finance Director; Kjell Arne Orseth [1968] Director/EVP Business Operations Ticketmaster International [Norwegian]; Mark Jeffery Yovich [1974] Director/President Ticketmaster International

Ticketmaster UK Limited
Incorporated: 13 November 1991 *Employees:* 674
Net Worth: £103,208,000 *Total Assets:* £197,638,000
Registered Office: 2nd Floor, Regent Arcade House, 19-25 Argyll Street, London, W1F 7TS
Activities: Retail sale via mail order houses or via Internet
Parent: TM Number One Limited
Officers: David Nicholas Hamilton, Finance Director; Christopher James Edmonds [1959] Managing Director; Selina Holliday Emeny [1968] Director/Solicitor; David Nicholas Hamilton [1962] Finance Director; Andrew John Parsons [1975] Managing Director; Mark Jeffery Yovich [1974] Director/President Ticketmaster International

Tiffany & Co. (UK) Holdings Limited
Incorporated: 11 February 2008 *Employees:* 49
Net Worth: £155,189,248 *Total Assets:* £295,855,232
Registered Office: 25 Old Bond Street, London, W1S 4QB
Activities: Activities of head offices
Parent: Tiffany & Co.
Officers: Leigh Marie Harlan, Secretary; Mark Erceg [1969] Director/Executive Vice President - Chief Financial Officer [American]; Leigh Marie Harlan [1976] Director [American]; Marc Jacheet [1972] Director/GVP-Europe, Mid East, Africa [French]

TIGI Holdings Limited
Incorporated: 8 July 1992
Net Worth: £146,858,000 *Total Assets:* £147,452,992
Registered Office: Unilever House, 100 Victoria Embankment, London, EC4Y 0DY
Activities: Activities of head offices
Parent: Unilever Overseas Holdings Limited
Officers: James Oliver Earley, Secretary; Richard Clive Hazell, Secretary; Anna Jo Karen Elphick [1975] Director/Accountant; Richard Clive Hazell [1966] Director/Solicitor; Amanda Louise King [1973] UK & Ireland Tax Director

Tilbury Green Power Limited
Incorporated: 14 December 2007
Net Worth Deficit: £17,471,306 *Total Assets:* £203,592,352
Registered Office: Tricor Services Europe LLP, 4th Floor, 50 Mark Lane, London, EC3R 7QR
Activities: Production of electricity
Parent: Tilbury Green Power Holdings Limited
Officers: Dr John Healy, Secretary; Jim Caplis [1972] Director/Accountant [Irish]; Seamus Deeny [1954] Director/Engineer [Irish]; Christian Grundtvig [1959] Director [Danish]; Andrew Horsley Clifford Hartley [1958] Director; Peter Knott [1964] Director

Tilfen Land Limited
Incorporated: 18 December 1998
Net Worth: £79,762,000 *Total Assets:* £102,415,000
Registered Office: 45 Westminster Bridge Road, London, SE1 7JB
Activities: Remediation activities and other waste management services
Officers: Penelope McKelvey, Secretary; Phillipa Anne Aitken [1952] Director [Australian]; Jennifer Daly [1970] Director of Planning; Ian Peters [1958] Director; Catherine Ann Shaw [1972] Director/Deputy Chief Executive; Peter Sean Vernon [1959] Director/Chief Executive

Tilney Group Limited
Incorporated: 21 October 2013 *Employees:* 1,227
Previous: Tilney Bestinvest Group Limited
Net Worth: £434,342,016 *Total Assets:* £948,124,992
Registered Office: 6 Chesterfield Gardens, London, W1J 5BQ
Activities: Activities of head offices
Parent: Violin Equityco Limited
Officers: Rehana Hasan, Secretary; Jonathan Paul Asquith [1956] Director; Andrew Martin Baddeley [1964] Director; Breon Thomas Corcoran [1971] Director [Irish]; James Annand Fraser [1965] Director/Partner; Philip Sebastian Muelder [1974] Director/Partner [German]; William Meredith Samuel [1952] Director/Chairman; Christopher Woodhouse [1961] Director/Chief Executive Officer

Time Out Group PLC
Incorporated: 15 November 2010 *Employees:* 426
Previous: Time Out Group Limited
Net Worth: £98,829,000 *Total Assets:* £131,047,000
Registered Office: 77 Wicklow Street, London, WC1X 9JY
Activities: Public relations and communications activities
Shareholders: Peter Adam Daiches Dubens; Ian Patrick Pilgrim; Robert Paul Harold Stevenson
Officers: Anne Olivia Crompton, Secretary; Julio Bruno Castellanos [1965] Director [Spanish/American]; Alexander Fiske Collins [1971] Director/Corporate Finance [Italian]; Peter Adam Daiches Dubens [1966] Director/Entrepreneur; Anthony Michael Manton Elliott [1947] Director; Matthew Robinson Riley [1974] Director; Stuart Alan Ransom Rose [1949] Director; Adam Silver [1975] Director

Time Warner Entertainment Limited
Incorporated: 6 May 1992 *Employees:* 5
Net Worth: £112,660,000 *Total Assets:* £112,660,000
Registered Office: 16 Great Marlborough Street, London, W1F 7HS
Activities: Activities of head offices
Parent: Time Warner Limited
Officers: Billy Wilkins, Secretary; Bronwen Elizabeth Stuart Jones [1959] Executive Director; Steven William Mertz [1957] Director/Lawyer [American]; Tracey Waring Mundy [1968] Finance Director; Joseph Wilkins [1973] Tax Director

Time Warner Holdings Limited
Incorporated: 18 October 1995
Net Worth: £957,379,008 *Total Assets:* £957,379,008
Registered Office: 16 Great Marlborough Street, London, W1F 7HS
Activities: Activities of head offices
Parent: Time Warner Inc.
Officers: William Wilkins, Secretary; Bronwen Elizabeth Stuart Jones [1959] Executive Director; Tracey Waring Mundy [1968] Finance Director; Joseph Wilkins [1973] Tax Director

Time Warner International Finance Limited
Incorporated: 11 October 2005
Net Worth: £42,916,508 *Total Assets:* £885,070,912
Registered Office: 16 Great Marlborough Street, London, W1F 7HS
Activities: Financial management
Parent: Time Warner Inc.
Officers: Janice Canon, Secretary [American]; William Wilkins, Secretary; Bronwen Elizabeth Stuart Jones [1959] Company Secretary/Director; Tracey Waring-Mundy [1968] Director International Treasury; Joe Wilkins [1973] Tax Director

Time Warner London Limited
Incorporated: 1 October 2003 *Employees:* 4
Net Worth: £806,510,976 *Total Assets:* £1,437,228,032
Registered Office: 16 Great Marlborough Street, London, W1F 7HS
Activities: Activities of head offices
Parent: Time Warner Holdings Limited
Officers: William Wilkins, Secretary; Bronwen Elizabeth Stuart Jones [1959] Director; Tracey Waring Mundy [1968] Finance Director; Joseph Wilkins [1973] Tax Director

Tintagel Castle Limited
Incorporated: 22 December 2009
Net Worth: £68,698,216 *Total Assets:* £279,398,208
Registered Office: 33 Holborn, London, EC1N 2HT
Activities: Activities of other holding companies n.e.c.
Parent: J Sainsbury PLC
Officers: Timothy Fallowfield, Secretary; Duncan John Cooper [1979] Director/Chartered Accountant

Tiso Blackstar Group SE
Incorporated: 30 June 2017 *Employees:* 3,773
Net Worth: £181,747,936 *Total Assets:* £414,774,240
Registered Office: Berkeley Square House, Berkeley Square, Mayfair, London, W1J 6BD
Activities: Other information service activities n.e.c.
Officers: David Kwame Tandoh Adomakoh [1965] Member/Non-Executive Chairman; Andrew David Bonamour [1971] Member/Non-Executive Director [South African]; Harishkumar Kantilal Mehta [1950] Member/Non-Executive Director [South African]; John Broadhurst Mills [1969] Member/Non-Executive Deputy Chairman [Irish]; Nkululeko Leonard Sowazi [1963] Member/Non-Executive Director [South African]

Tiso Blackstar Holdings SE
Incorporated: 9 May 2017
Net Worth: £165,160,480 *Total Assets:* £195,748,336
Registered Office: Berkeley Square House, Berkeley Square, Mayfair, London, W1J 6BD
Activities: Other information service activities n.e.c.
Officers: David Kwame Tandoh Adomakoh [1965] Member/Non-Executive Chairman; Andrew David Bonamour [1971] Member/Non-Executive Director [South African]; Harishkumar Kantilal Mehta [1950] Member/Non-Executive Director [South African]; John Broadhurst Mills [1969] Member/Non-Executive Deputy Chairman [Irish]; Nkululeko Leonard Sowazi [1963] Member/Non-Executive Director [South African]

Titan Acquisition Holdco Limited
Incorporated: 6 May 2016
Net Worth: £93,572 *Total Assets:* £207,284,576
Registered Office: Floor 6, Quadrant House, 4 Thomas More Square, London, E1W 1YW
Activities: Other service activities n.e.c.
Parent: Titan Financing Limited
Officers: Leonard Kevin Sebastian [1969] Group Managing and Legal Director [Swiss]

Titan Acquisition Limited
Incorporated: 9 May 2016 *Employees:* 1
Net Worth Deficit: £696,307 *Total Assets:* £517,767,648
Registered Office: Floor 6, Quadrant House, 4 Thomas More Square, London, E1W 1YW
Activities: Other service activities n.e.c.
Parent: Titan Acquisition Holdco Limited
Officers: Leonard Kevin Sebastian [1969] Group Managing and Legal Director [Swiss]

Titan Financing Holdco Limited
Incorporated: 5 May 2016 *Employees:* 1,425
Net Worth: £87,309,472 *Total Assets:* £725,359,936
Registered Office: Floor 6, Quadrant House, 4 Thomas More Square, London, E1W 1YW
Activities: Other service activities n.e.c.
Parent: London & Regional Group Trading No.3 Limited
Officers: Leonard Kevin Sebastian [1969] Group Managing and Legal Director [Swiss]; Desmond Louis Mildmay Taljaard [1961] Director

Titan Financing Limited
Incorporated: 6 May 2016
Net Worth Deficit: £181,708 *Total Assets:* £207,556,592
Registered Office: Floor 6, Quadrant House, 4 Thomas More Square, London, E1W 1YW
Activities: Other service activities n.e.c.
Parent: Titan Financing Holdco Limited
Officers: Leonard Kevin Sebastian [1969] Group Managing and Legal Director [Swiss]

Titanium UK Holdco 1 Limited
Incorporated: 18 January 2016
Net Worth: £320,770,336 *Total Assets:* £527,658,304
Registered Office: Peterborough Court, 133 Fleet Street, London, EC4A 2BB
Activities: Activities of financial services holding companies
Parent: ELQ Investors VIII Ltd
Officers: Thomas Kelly, Secretary; Mark Desmond Charles Olivier [1974] Managing Director; Natalia Ross [1972] Director/Accountant [Polish]; Richard James Spencer [1974] Director

Tizir Limited
Incorporated: 3 August 2011 *Employees:* 908
Net Worth: £233,653,536 *Total Assets:* £706,950,784
Registered Office: Suite 1, 3rd Floor, 11-12 St James's Square, London, SW1Y 4LB
Activities: Mining of other non-ferrous metal ores
Officers: Kleber de Souza E Silva [1963] Director/Deputy CEO; Thomas Claude Roland Devedjian [1971] Director/Chief Financial Officer of ERAMET [French]; Jean - Michel Jacques Francois Fourcade [1958] Director [French]; Anne-Marie Claude Marthe Le Maignan [1960] Director/Vice President Human Resources ERAMET Manganese [French]; Charles Hubert Nouel [1967] Director/Vice President Ore Market [French]; Jean-Michel Olivier Tajan [1964] Director/Vice President Legal for Financing ERAMET SA [French]

TKG-Storagemart Partners UK Limited
Incorporated: 22 September 2016 *Employees:* 54
Net Worth: £33,510,456 *Total Assets:* £128,012,696
Registered Office: 5th Floor, 6 St Andrew Street, London, EC4A 3AE
Activities: Activities of other holding companies n.e.c.
Major Shareholder: Stanley Kroenke
Officers: Michael G Burnam [1953] Director/Chief Executive Officer [American]; E Stanley Kroenke [1947] Director/Real Estate [American]; Otto Maly [1956] Director [American]

TM Media Holdings Limited
Incorporated: 9 November 2000 *Employees:* 3
Previous: Northern & Shell Media Holdings Limited
Net Worth: £212,583,008 *Total Assets:* £348,332,992
Registered Office: One Canary Wharf, London, E14 5AP
Activities: Activities of head offices
Parent: Trinity Mirror Media Limited
Officers: Simon Richard Fox [1961] Director/Chief Executive; Simon Jeremy Ian Fuller [1977] Director/Chartered Accountant; Vijay Lakhman Vaghela [1966] Director/Accountant

TNS Group Holdings Limited
Incorporated: 7 August 1967 *Employees:* 4
Net Worth: £310,478,016 *Total Assets:* £503,308,000
Registered Office: TNS House, Westgate, London, W5 1UA
Activities: Activities of head offices
Parent: WPP Jubilee Limited
Officers: Andrea Jane Harris, Secretary; Robert James Bowtell [1959] Director; David Grant Errington [1954] Director; Eric Ralph Salama [1961] Director; Charles Ward Van Der Welle [1959] Director of Treasury

TNS UK Holdings Limited
Incorporated: 5 April 2007 *Employees:* 2
Net Worth: £199,992,000 *Total Assets:* £200,000,000
Registered Office: TNS House, West Gate, London, W5 1UA
Activities: Activities of head offices
Parent: TNS Group Holdings Limited
Officers: Robert James Bowtell [1959] Director; David Grant Errington [1957] Director

TNS-NFO UK Limited
Incorporated: 29 July 2005 *Employees:* 3
Net Worth: £251,560,288 *Total Assets:* £253,229,776
Registered Office: 27 Farm Street, London, W1J 5RJ
Activities: Non-trading company
Parent: Taylor Nelson Sofres International Limited
Officers: Robert James Bowtell [1959] Director; Charles Ward Van Der Welle [1959] Director of Treasury

Together Asset Backed Securitisation 1 PLC
Incorporated: 17 May 2017
Net Worth: £50,810 *Total Assets:* £236,310,448
Registered Office: 6th Floor, 65 Gresham Street, London, EC2V 7NQ
Activities: Financial intermediation not elsewhere classified
Parent: Together Asset Backed Securitisation 1 Holdings Limited
Officers: Colin Arthur Benford [1962] Director

Tokai Tokyo Securities Europe Limited
Incorporated: 1 September 2006 *Employees:* 10
Net Worth: £11,286,853 *Total Assets:* £208,778,224
Registered Office: 4th Floor, Salisbury House, London Wall, London, EC2M 5QQ
Activities: Security dealing on own account
Parent: Tokai Tokyo Financial Holdings Inc.
Officers: Koki Ukebe, Secretary; Yuji Ban [1964] Director/Executive Officer [Japanese]; Shinya Kada [1957] Director/Senior Managing Executive Officer [Japanese]; Yoshihiko Kasahara [1958] Director/Chief Executive [Japanese]; Hiroshi Maezono [1960] Director/Senior Managing Executive Officer [Japanese]

Tokio Marine HCC Insurance Holdings (International) Limited
Incorporated: 22 June 1989
Previous: Pepys Holdings Limited
Net Worth: £182,558,320 *Total Assets:* £183,125,744
Registered Office: 1 Aldgate, London, EC3N 1RE
Activities: Activities of financial services holding companies
Parent: Tokio Marine Holdings, Inc.
Officers: Jenna Louise Holliday, Secretary; Barry John Cook [1960] Director/Insurance Executive; Brad Terry Irick [1966] Director/Chief Financial Officer [American]; Katherine Lee Letsinger [1962] Director/Chief Financial Officer

Tokio Marine Kiln Group Limited
Incorporated: 11 July 1994 *Employees:* 260
Net Worth: £360,479,008 *Total Assets:* £1,066,392,000
Registered Office: 20 Fenchurch Street, London, EC3M 3BY
Activities: Activities of head offices
Parent: Tokio Marine & Nichido Fire Insurance Co. Limited
Officers: Fiona Jane Molloy, Secretary; Richard Bennison [1958] Director; Charles Anthony Stapleton Franks [1962] Director; Kiichiro Hatakeyama [1967] Director [Japanese]; Brad Terry Irick [1966] Director [American]; Ichiro Ishii [1955] Director [Japanese]; Reeken Patel [1979] Director; Shinji Urano [1963] Director [Japanese]; Christopher John Bodman Williams [1956] Director/Insurance Executive [American]

Tokio Marine Kiln Insurance Limited
Incorporated: 15 September 1970 *Employees:* 116
Net Worth: £107,957,000 *Total Assets:* £587,022,016
Registered Office: 20 Fenchurch Street, London, EC3M 3BY
Activities: Non-life insurance
Parent: Tokio Marine Kiln Group Limited
Officers: Fiona Jane Molloy, Secretary; Richard Bennison [1958] Director; David Andrew Constable [1957] Director; Paul Michael Culham [1965] Director/Underwriter; Charles Anthony Stapleton Franks [1962] Chief Executive and Non-Executive Director; Rosemary Harris [1958] Director; Anna McNamara [1978] Director; Reeken Patel [1979] Director; Vivek Syal [1983] Director; David Andrew Torrance [1953] Director; Shinji Urano [1963] Director [Japanese]

Tokio Marine Underwriting Limited
Incorporated: 27 October 2008
Net Worth: £144,068,992 *Total Assets:* £2,147,926,016
Registered Office: 20 Fenchurch Street, London, EC3M 3BY
Activities: Non-life insurance
Parent: Tokio Marine & Nichido Fire Insurance Limited
Officers: Fiona Jane Molloy, Secretary; Charles Anthony Stapleton Franks [1962] Director; Kiichiro Hatakeyama [1967] Director [Japanese]; Hideyuki Ishii [1971] Director [Japanese]

Tokio Millennium RE (UK) Limited
Incorporated: 30 October 1990 *Employees:* 16
Net Worth: £204,523,008 *Total Assets:* £431,465,984
Registered Office: 20 Fenchurch Street, London, EC3M 3BY
Activities: Non-life reinsurance
Parent: Tokio Marine & Nichido Fire Insurance Co. Ltd.
Officers: Elliot John Dunseath, Secretary; David John Finch [1952] Director/Accountant; Ken Hatakeyama [1967] Director/Reinsurance Executive [Japanese]; Mark James Phillip Julian [1972] Director/Insurance Company CEO; Maurice Stephen Kane [1972] Director/Chief Financial Officer, Reinsurance [Irish]; Clemens Von Bechtolsheim [1945] Director/Insurance Executive [German]

Tolmar Holding Limited
Incorporated: 8 October 2015 *Employees:* 737
Net Worth: £148,021,376 *Total Assets:* £284,213,632
Registered Office: Third Floor, 20 Old Bailey, London, EC4M 7AN
Activities: Other business support service activities n.e.c.
Officers: Fernando Ariel German [1975] Director [Argentinian]

Tomahawk Capital Partners I LLP
Incorporated: 16 December 2013
Net Worth: £209,613,776 *Total Assets:* £209,683,968
Registered Office: 105 Wigmore Street, London, W1U 1QY

Tombac No.1 PLC
Incorporated: 11 February 2014
Net Worth: £26,000 *Total Assets:* £1,146,140,032
Registered Office: Third Floor, c/o Wilmington Trust SP Services (London) Limited, 1 King's Arms Yard, London, EC2R 7AF
Activities: Other business support service activities n.e.c.
Parent: Tombac No.1 Mortgage Holdings Limited
Officers: Daniel Jonathan Wynne [1970] Director

Tombac No.2 PLC
Incorporated: 27 October 2015
Net Worth Deficit: £1,113,000 *Total Assets:* £676,579,008
Registered Office: c/o Wilmington Trust SP Services (London) Limited, Third Floor, 1 Kings Arms Yard, London, EC2R 7AF
Activities: Other business support service activities n.e.c.
Parent: Tombac No.2 Mortgage Holdings Limited
Officers: Daniel Jonathan Wynne [1970] Director

Tomkins Engineering Limited
Incorporated: 5 March 1914
Net Worth: £201,956,000 *Total Assets:* £233,224,000
Registered Office: 35 Great St Helen's, London, EC3A 6AP
Activities: Activities of head offices
Parent: Gates Finance Limited
Officers: Nathan Andrew Rogers [1964] Director [American]; Jamey Susan Seely [1971] Director/Executive Vice President [American]; Marc Gregory Swanson [1969] Director/Vice President, Global Tax [American]

Tomkins Overseas Investments Limited
Incorporated: 26 March 1934
Net Worth: £641,996,480 *Total Assets:* £644,658,432
Registered Office: 35 Great St Helen's, London, EC3A 6AP
Activities: Activities of head offices
Parent: Gtaes Finance Limited
Officers: Nathan Andrew Rogers [1964] Director [American]; Jamey Susan Seely [1971] Director/Executive Vice President [American]; Marc Gregory Swanson [1969] Director/Vice President, Global Tax [American]

Tomori E & P Limited
Incorporated: 13 November 2009 *Employees:* 10
Net Worth: £299,566,688 *Total Assets:* £328,864,192
Registered Office: Mid City Place, 71 High Holborn, London, WC1V 6BA
Activities: Extraction of crude petroleum
Parent: Mitsubishi Corporation
Officers: Keum Woo Lee [1964] Director [South Korean]; Kazuki Nishida [1985] Director [Japanese]; Wataru Noguchi [1968] Director/Office Worker [Japanese]; Sang Hak Yun [1970] Director [South Korean]

Tonicstar Limited
Incorporated: 6 September 2000
Net Worth: £35,832,000 *Total Assets:* £209,659,008
Registered Office: 4th Floor, 8 Fenchurch Place, London, EC3M 4AJ
Activities: Non-life insurance
Officers: Colleen Martin, Company Secretary; Guy Edward Finney [1966] Finance Director; Stephen Andrew Michael [1961] Managing Director; Andrew Wilson [1967] Director

Tonstate Metropole Hotels Limited
Incorporated: 7 August 2006
Net Worth Deficit: £234,738,176 *Total Assets:* £442,838,848
Registered Office: 3 Park Place, St James's, London, SW1A 1LP
Activities: Activities of head offices
Parent: Annie Property Investments Limited
Officers: Dr Edward Oded Wojakovski, Secretary; Arthur Matyas [1932] Director; Dr Edward Oded Wojakovski [1969] Director

Top Shop / Top Man Properties Limited
Incorporated: 19 June 2002
Net Worth Deficit: £19,035,000 *Total Assets:* £127,400,000
Registered Office: Colegrave House, 70 Berners Street, London, W1T 3NL
Activities: Buying and selling of own real estate
Parent: Top Shop/Top Man Limited
Officers: Rebecca Rose Flaherty, Secretary; Stephen Boyce [1964] Director/Surveyor; Richard Leeroy Burchill [1971] Director/Accountant; Ian Michael Grabiner [1959] Director

Top Shop/Top Man Limited
Incorporated: 15 November 1988 *Employees:* 8,519
Net Worth: £643,033,984 *Total Assets:* £1,279,303,936
Registered Office: Colegrave House, 70 Berners Street, London, W1T 3NL
Activities: Retail sale of clothing in specialised stores
Parent: Top Shop/ Top Man (Holdings) Limited
Officers: Michelle Jane Gammon, Secretary; Siobhan Forey [1972] Director/Chief Operating Officer; Ian Michael Grabiner [1959] Director; Sir Philip Nigel Ross Green [1952] Director; Adam Thomas Levyn [1983] Director/Principal [American]; Paul Stephen Price [1962] Director/CEO Topshop/Topman; Jon Richens [1969] Director; Jonathan Sokoloff [1957] Director [American]

Topland Group PLC
Incorporated: 28 May 1991 *Employees:* 40
Net Worth Deficit: £14,278,824 *Total Assets:* £834,398,336
Registered Office: 55 Baker Street, London, W1U 7EU
Activities: Development of building projects
Major Shareholder: Haim Judah Michael Levy
Officers: Cheryl Frances Moharm, Secretary; Moshe Jaacov Anahory [1970] Director/Barrister-at-Law; Thomas Richard Betts [1966] Director/Real Estate Finance; Mark Simon Kingston [1965] Director/Real Estate Professional; Simon Levick Garth Wilson [1974] Director/Accountant; Eddie Zakay [1950] Director; Sol Zakay [1952] Director

Topland Jupiter Limited
Incorporated: 14 December 2010
Net Worth: £2,153,058 *Total Assets:* £228,901,472
Registered Office: 55 Baker Street, London, W1U 7EU
Activities: Other business support service activities n.e.c.
Shareholders: Haim Judah Michael Levy; Christopher George White
Officers: Cheryl Frances Moharm, Secretary; Thomas Richard Betts [1966] Director/Real Estate Finance; Mark Simon Kingston [1965] Director/Real Estate Professional; Cheryl Frances Moharm [1958] Director/Company Secretary; Simon Levick Garth Wilson [1974] Director/Accountant; Eddie Zakay [1950] Director

Toscafund Limited
Incorporated: 15 May 2000
Net Worth: £286,409,440 *Total Assets:* £384,173,728
Registered Office: 7th Floor, 90 Long Acre, London, WC2E 9RA
Activities: Security dealing on own account
Major Shareholder: Martin Brian Hughes
Officers: Martin James McKay, Secretary/Accountant; Martin Brian Hughes [1961] Director/Bank Analyst

Total E & P International K2 Ltd.
Incorporated: 30 October 2015
Previous: Maersk Oil Exploration International K2 Ltd
Net Worth: £184,130,576 *Total Assets:* £251,288,736
Registered Office: 18th Floor, 10 Upper Bank Street, Canary Wharf, London, E14 5BF
Activities: Extraction of crude petroleum
Parent: Total E & P International Ltd.
Officers: Karen Dyrskjot Boesen [1971] Finance Director [Danish]; Kevin Francis Boyne [1959] Director; Jean-Luc Guiziou [1961] Director/Engineer [French]; Khaled Mohamed Kouki [1970] Director/VP, Exploration West Africa & Kenya [French]; Joao Peres Do Amaral [1960] Director/VP Africa - Exploration Subsidiaries [French]

Total E & P International K3 Ltd.
Incorporated: 30 October 2015
Previous: Maersk Oil Exploration International K3 Ltd
Net Worth: £145,144,912 *Total Assets:* £173,341,296
Registered Office: 18th Floor, 10 Upper Bank Street, Canary Wharf, London, E14 5BF
Activities: Extraction of crude petroleum
Parent: Total E & P International Ltd.
Officers: Karen Dyrskjot Boesen [1971] Finance Director [Danish]; Kevin Francis Boyne [1959] Director; Jean-Luc Guiziou [1961] Director/Engineer [French]; Khaled Mohamed Kouki [1970] Director/VP, Exploration West Africa & Kenya [French]; Joao Peres Do Amaral [1960] Director/VP Africa - Exploration Subsidiaries [French]

Total E & P International Ltd.
Incorporated: 7 October 2015
Previous: Maersk Oil Exploration International Ltd
Net Worth: £411,791,264 *Total Assets:* £418,298,912
Registered Office: 18th Floor, 10 Upper Bank Street, Canary Wharf, London, E14 5BF
Activities: Activities of production holding companies
Parent: Total E & P Danmark A/S
Officers: Karen Dyrskjot Boesen [1971] Finance Director [Danish]; Kevin Francis Boyne [1959] Director; Jean-Luc Guiziou [1961] Director/Engineer [French]; Alan Thomas McInally [1969] Director/Head of Exploration Held Assets; Joao Peres Do Amaral [1960] Director/VP Africa - Exploration Subsidiaries [French]

Total E & P North Sea UK Limited
Incorporated: 11 December 1998 *Employees:* 619
Previous: Maersk Oil North Sea UK Limited
Net Worth: £1,471,684,480 *Total Assets:* £3,306,544,384
Registered Office: 18th Floor, 10 Upper Bank Street, Canary Wharf, London, E14 5BF
Activities: Extraction of crude petroleum
Parent: Total Oil GB Limited
Officers: Bryan Wilson, Secretary; Karen Dyrskjot Boesen [1971] Finance Director [Danish]; Michael Simon Borrell [1962] Director/SVP North Sea and Russia; Kevin Francis Boyne [1959] Director/Oil and Gas Manager; Jean-Baptiste Pierre Faget [1971] Technical Director North Sea and Russia [French]; Jean-Luc Guiziou [1961] Director/Engineer [French]

Total E & P UK Limited
Incorporated: 8 July 1964 *Employees:* 586
Net Worth Deficit: £84,333,000 *Total Assets:* £3,227,180,032
Registered Office: 18th Floor, 10 Upper Bank Street, Canary Wharf, London, E14 5BF
Activities: Extraction of crude petroleum
Parent: Total Upstream UK Limited
Officers: Bryan Wilson, Secretary; Frederic Agnes [1971] Director [French]; Karen Dyrskjot Boesen [1971] Director/Chief Financial Officer [Danish]; Michael Simon Borrell [1962] Director; Jean-Luc Guiziou [1961] Director/Engineer [French]

Total Energy (MEUK) Ltd.
Incorporated: 3 June 2005
Previous: Maersk Energy UK Ltd.
Net Worth: £1,103,911,680 *Total Assets:* £1,103,911,680
Registered Office: 18th Floor, 10 Upper Bank Street, Canary Wharf, London, E14 5BF
Activities: Activities of production holding companies
Parent: Total E & P Danmark A/S
Officers: Bryan Wilson, Secretary; Karen Dyrskjot Boesen [1971] Finance Director [Danish]; Michael Simon Borrell [1962] Director/SVP North Sea and Russia; Kevin Francis Boyne [1959] Director/Oil and Gas Manager; Jean-Baptiste Pierre Faget [1971] Technical Director North Sea and Russia [French]; Jean-Luc Guiziou [1961] Director/Engineer [French]

Total Gas & Power Limited
Incorporated: 30 September 1987 *Employees:* 527
Net Worth: £1,710,768,000 *Total Assets:* £3,668,352,000
Registered Office: 13th Floor, 10 Upper Bank Street, Canary Wharf, London, E14 5BF
Activities: Distribution of electricity
Parent: Total Midstream Holdings UK Limited
Officers: Stephen Douglas Allen Bird, Secretary; Simon Binet [1969] Finance Director; Philippe Camille Chauvain [1963] Director/Vice President Risk Control [French]; David Anthony Cranfield [1964] Director/General Manager UKM; Antoine Larenaudie [1959] Finance Director [French]; Philippe Rene Pierre Lautard [1961] Director/Vice President New Ventures [French]; Gregoire Natta [1961] Director/Vice President, GRP [French]; Jean-Marc Simandoux [1967] Director/Acting Head of Front Office [French]; Laurent Vivier [1970] Director/President Gas [French]

Total Holdings UK Limited
Incorporated: 10 May 1983
Net Worth: £1,642,649,984 *Total Assets:* £1,644,979,968
Registered Office: 18th Floor, 10 Upper Bank Street, Canary Wharf, London, E14 5BF
Activities: Activities of head offices
Parent: Total S.A.
Officers: Bryan Wilson, Secretary; Karen Dyrskjot Boesen [1971] Director/Chief Financial Officer [Danish]; Michael Simon Borrell [1962] Director; Jean-Marc Durand [1972] Director/General Manager Total Lindsey Oil Refinery [French]; Jean Francois Good [1972] Director/SVP Refining Petrochemicals Orient [French]; Jean-Luc Guiziou [1961] Director/Engineer [French]; Laurent Vivier [1970] Director/President - Gas [French]

Total Midstream Holdings UK Limited
Incorporated: 10 April 1991
Net Worth: £151,348,992 *Total Assets:* £151,348,992
Registered Office: 13th Floor, 10 Upper Bank Street, London, E14 5BF
Activities: Activities of head offices
Parent: Elf Petroleum UK Limited
Officers: Stephen Douglas Allen Bird, Secretary; Simon Binet [1969] Finance Director; Jean-Luc Guiziou [1961] Managing Director [French]; Jean-Marc Simandoux [1967] Director/Acting Head of Front Office [French]; Laurent Vivier [1970] Director/President, Gas [French]

Total Oil GB Limited
Incorporated: 19 March 1998
Previous: Maersk Oil GB Limited
Net Worth: £543,382,656 *Total Assets:* £952,974,016
Registered Office: 18th Floor, 10 Upper Bank Street, Canary Wharf, London, E14 5BF
Activities: Extraction of crude petroleum
Parent: Total Energy (MEUK) Ltd.
Officers: Bryan Wilson, Secretary; Karen Dyrskjot Boesen [1971] Finance Director [Danish]; Michael Simon Borrell [1962] Director/SVP North Sea and Russia; Kevin Francis Boyne [1959] Director/Oil & Gas Manager; Jean-Baptiste Pierre Faget [1971] Technical Director North Sea & Russia [French]; Jean-Luc Guiziou [1961] Director/Engineer [French]

Total Oil UK Limited
Incorporated: 30 January 1969
Previous: Maersk Oil UK Limited
Net Worth Deficit: £77,732,120 *Total Assets:* £465,144,512
Registered Office: 18th Floor, 10 Upper Bank Street, Canary Wharf, London, E14 5BF
Activities: Extraction of crude petroleum
Parent: Total Oil GB Limited
Officers: Bryan Wilson, Secretary; Karen Dyrskjot Boesen [1971] Finance Director [Danish]; Michael Simon Borrell [1962] Director/SVP North Sea and Russia; Kevin Francis Boyne [1959] Director/Oil & Gas Manager; Jean-Baptiste Pierre Faget [1971] Technical Director North Sea & Russia [French]; Jean-Luc Guiziou [1961] Director/Engineer [French]

Total UK Finance Limited
Incorporated: 9 May 2000
Net Worth: £64,543,000 *Total Assets:* £3,864,538,880
Registered Office: 18th Floor, 10 Upper Bank Street, Canary Wharf, London, E14 5BF
Activities: Credit granting by non-deposit taking finance houses and other specialist consumer credit grantors
Parent: Total S.A.
Officers: Bryan Wilson, Secretary; Karen Dyrskjot Boesen [1971] Director/Chief Financial Officer [Danish]; Jean-Luc Guiziou [1961] Director/Engineer [French]; Frederic Joseph Maupetit [1986] Director/Corporate and Project Finance Manager [French]

Total UK Limited
Incorporated: 19 August 1955 *Employees:* 136
Net Worth: £7,000,000 *Total Assets:* £224,000,000
Registered Office: 183 Eversholt Street, London, NW1 1BU
Activities: Other treatment of petroleum products (excluding petrochemicals manufacture)
Shareholders: Total Marketing Services SA; Total SA
Officers: Calum James Stacey, Secretary; Jonathan David Milton [1970] Director/Oil Company Executive; Alexis Rouxelin [1975] Director/Financial Controller [French]; Anna Gabrielle Whitehouse [1964] Director/Oil Company Executive [Irish]; John Gredal Wilson [1967] Director/Company Executive

Total Upstream UK Limited
Incorporated: 16 August 1989
Net Worth: £119,971,000 *Total Assets:* £120,015,000
Registered Office: 18th Floor, 10 Upper Bank Street, Canary Wharf, London, E14 5BF
Activities: Activities of head offices
Parent: Elf Petroleum UK Limited
Officers: Bryan Wilson, Secretary; Frederic Agnes [1971] Director [French]; Karen Dyrskjot Boesen [1971] Director/Chief Financial Officer [Danish]; Michael Simon Borrell [1962] Director; Jean-Luc Guiziou [1961] Director/Engineer [French]; Philippe Pascal Hergaux [1969] Director/Engineer [French]; Jean-Pierre Gerard Claude Sbraire [1965] Director/Treasurer [French]; Laurent Vivier [1970] Director/President - Gas [French]

Tottenham Hotspur Limited
Incorporated: 14 March 1983 *Employees:* 439
Net Worth: £227,240,992 *Total Assets:* £840,729,984
Registered Office: Lilywhite House, 782 High Road, London, N17 0BX
Activities: Operation of sports facilities
Major Shareholder: Joseph Charles Lewis
Officers: Matthew John Collecott, Secretary; Rebecca Anne Caplehorn [1975] Director/Chartered Accountant; Matthew John Collecott [1968] Director/Chartered Accountant; Donna-Maria Cullen [1963] Director; Daniel Philip Levy [1962] Managing Director; Ronald Alexander Robson [1963] Director

Tottenham Hotspur Stadium Development Limited
Incorporated: 26 April 2016
Net Worth: £230,498,896 *Total Assets:* £230,498,896
Registered Office: Lilywhite House, 782 High Road, Tottenham, London, N17 0BX
Activities: Other letting and operating of own or leased real estate
Parent: Tottenham Hotspur Limited
Officers: Matthew John Collecott, Secretary; Rebecca Anne Caplehorn [1975] Director; Matthew John Collecott [1968] Director; Donna-Maria Cullen [1963] Director; Daniel Philip Levy [1962] Director

Tottenham Hotspur Stadium Limited
Incorporated: 27 April 2016
Net Worth: £230,469,952 *Total Assets:* £393,239,424
Registered Office: Lilywhite House, 782 High Road, Tottenham, London, N17 0BX
Activities: Operation of sports facilities
Parent: Tottenham Hotspur Stadium Development Limited
Officers: Matthew John Collecott, Secretary; Rebecca Anne Caplehorn [1975] Director; Matthew John Collecott [1968] Director; Donna-Maria Cullen [1963] Director; Daniel Philip Levy [1962] Director

Touchstone Innovations Businesses LLP
Incorporated: 19 December 2007
Previous: Imperial Innovations Businesses LLP
Net Worth: £564,527,360 *Total Assets:* £584,473,088
Registered Office: The Walbrook Building, 25 Walbrook, London, EC4N 8AF
Officers: Anjum Mazahar Ahmad [1968] LLP Member; Daniel Gonzalez Bach [1974] LLP Member; Robert Harold Bahns [1964] LLP Member; Dr Andrew Joseph Barber [1949] LLP Member; Maina Bhaman [1972] LLP Member; Justin Bowen [1970] LLP Member; Mario Branciforti [1974] LLP Member; Nichola Carter [1971] LLP Member; Diana Crisp [1967] LLP Member; Russell Cummings [1964] LLP Member; Inga Deakin [1983] LLP Member; Jonathan Adrien Edington [1970] LLP Member; Brian Clive Graves [1955] LLP Member; Laura Guida [1966] LLP Member; Dr Christopher David Haley [1975] LLP Member; Dr Anthony Charles Hickson [1968] LLP Member; Dayle Spencer Hogg [1976] LLP Member; John Peter Stefano Holden [1966] LLP Member; Jan Singleton Huisamen [1974] LLP Member; Simon Christopher Kerr [1957] LLP Member; Kamila Paola Kirby Green [1975] LLP Member; Eva Lauren Kirkby Leary [1982] LLP Member; Maija Katriina Kontto [1975] LLP Member; Adaku Amowie Lawrence [1976] LLP Member; Ross Llewelyn Manning [1979] LLP Member; Paul Graham May [1959] LLP Member; Richard May [1972] LLP Member; Lynne Maureen McGregor [1957] LLP Member; Andrew Eoin Murphy [1970] LLP Member; Kathryn Owen [1979] LLP Member; Jonathan Heeley Page [1967] LLP Member; Dr Hugh Alan Penfold [1952] LLP Member; Govind Keshavji Pindoria [1964] LLP Member; Nigel Aaron Pitchford [1969] LLP Member; William Nicholas Rayner [1972] LLP Member; Simone Reid [1982] LLP Member; Ushasri Sarma [1971] LLP Member; Susan Jane Searle [1963] LLP Member; Kelsey Bircher Lynn Skinner [1982] LLP Member; Julian Matthew Smith [1965] LLP Member; Bobby G. Soni [1971] LLP Member; Jonathan Leslie Tobin [1982] LLP Member; Dr Jonathan Frome Wilkinson [1969] LLP Member; Dr Robbie Woodman [1977] LLP Member

Touchstone Innovations Investments Limited
Incorporated: 25 January 2007
Previous: Imperial Innovations Investments Limited
Net Worth: £298,818 *Total Assets:* £154,591,216
Registered Office: The Walbrook Building, 25 Walbrook, London, EC4N 8AF
Activities: Activities of financial services holding companies
Parent: Touchstone Innovations PLC
Officers: Alan John Aubrey [1961] Director; David Graham Baynes [1964] Director; Gregory Simon Smith [1978] Director; Michael Charles Nettleton Townend [1962] Director

Touchstone Innovations PLC
Incorporated: 26 April 2006 *Employees:* 68
Previous: Imperial Innovations Group PLC
Net Worth: £503,534,016 *Total Assets:* £607,612,992
Registered Office: The Walbrook Building, 25 Walbrook, London, EC4N 8AF
Activities: Activities of head offices
Parent: IP Group PLC
Officers: Angela Leach, Secretary; Alan John Aubrey [1961] Director; David Graham Baynes [1964] Director; Gregory Simon Smith [1978] Director; Michael Charles Nettleton Townend [1962] Director

Towd Point Mortgage Funding 2016 - Auburn 10 PLC
Incorporated: 22 July 2015
Net Worth: £32,000 *Total Assets:* £1,140,260,992
Registered Office: Third Floor, 1 Kings Arms Yard, London, EC2R 7AF
Activities: Other business support service activities n.e.c.
Parent: Towd Point Mortgage Funding 2016-Auburn 10 Holdings Limited
Officers: Daniel Jonathan Wynne [1970] Director

Towd Point Mortgage Funding 2016-Granite1 PLC
Incorporated: 3 February 2016
Net Worth: £18,000 *Total Assets:* £4,730,587,136
Registered Office: Third Floor, c/o Wilmington Trust SP Services (London) Limited, 1 Kings Arms Yard, London, EC2R 7AF
Activities: Other business support service activities n.e.c.
Parent: Towd Point Mortgage Funding 2016-Granite1 Holdings Limited
Officers: Daniel Jonathan Wynne [1970] Director

Towd Point Mortgage Funding 2016-Granite2 PLC
Incorporated: 20 October 2016
Net Worth: £17,000 *Total Assets:* £362,950,016
Registered Office: Third Floor, c/o Wilmington Trust SP Services (London) Limited, 1 Kings Arms Yard, London, EC2R 7AF
Activities: Other business support service activities n.e.c.
Parent: Towd Point Mortgage Funding 2016-Granite2 Holdings Limited
Officers: Eileen Marie Hughes [1966] Director/Head of Structured Products UK [American]; Daniel Jonathan Wynne [1970] Director

Towd Point Mortgage Funding 2016-Granite3 PLC
Incorporated: 20 October 2016
Net Worth: £17,000 *Total Assets:* £200,714,000
Registered Office: Third Floor, c/o Wilmington Trust SP Services (London) Limited, 1 Kings Arms Yard, London, EC2R 7AF
Activities: Other business support service activities n.e.c.
Parent: Towd Point Mortgage Funding 2016-Granite3 Holdings Limited
Officers: Eileen Marie Hughes [1966] Director/Head of Structured Products UK [American]; Daniel Jonathan Wynne [1970] Director

Towd Point Mortgage Funding 2016-Vantage1 PLC
Incorporated: 4 November 2016
Net Worth: £17,000 *Total Assets:* £741,123,008
Registered Office: c/o Wilmington Trust SP Services (London) Limited, Third Floor, 1 King's Arms Yard, London, EC2R 7AF
Activities: Other business support service activities n.e.c.
Parent: Towd Point Mortgage Funding 2016-Vantage1 Holdings Limited
Officers: Eileen Marie Hughes [1966] Director/Head of Structured Products UK [American]; Daniel Jonathan Wynne [1970] Director

Towd Point Mortgage Funding 2017 - Auburn 11 PLC
Incorporated: 23 December 2016
Net Worth: £30,000 *Total Assets:* £959,894,976
Registered Office: Third Floor, 1 King's Arms Yard, London, EC2R 7AF
Activities: Activities of mortgage finance companies
Parent: Towd Point Mortgage Funding 2017-Auburn 11 Holdings Limited
Officers: Daniel Jonathan Wynne [1970] Director/Banker

Tower Bridge Funding No.1 PLC
Incorporated: 2 June 2017
Net Worth Deficit: £1,631,984 *Total Assets:* £241,896,928
Registered Office: 35 Great St Helen's, London, EC3A 6AP
Activities: Activities of mortgage finance companies
Parent: Tower Bridge Funding No.1 Holdings Limited
Officers: Paivi Helena Whitaker [1963] Director [Finnish]

The Tower Hotel (London) Limited
Incorporated: 22 March 1949 *Employees:* 200
Net Worth: £228,886,000 *Total Assets:* £236,366,000
Registered Office: 110 Central Street, London, EC1V 8AJ
Activities: Hotels and similar accommodation
Shareholder: GLH Hotels Limited
Officers: Susan Lim Geok Mui, Secretary; Neil Gallagher [1973] Director/Chief Financial Officer; Peter Michael Herbert [1980] Director/Chief Financial Officer; Kah Meng Ho [1966] Executive Director [Malaysian]

Toyota Tsusho Metals Limited
Incorporated: 25 November 1998 *Employees:* 29
Net Worth: £39,514,000 *Total Assets:* £161,736,000
Registered Office: 88 Wood Street, London, EC2V 7DA
Activities: Wholesale of metals and metal ores
Parent: Toyota Tsusho Corporation
Officers: Hiroto Nakane, Secretary; Takeo Fujihara [1969] Director/Manager [Japanese]; Paul Marney [1966] Trading Director; Hiroto Nakane [1964] Managing Director [Japanese]; Shigeru Nakashima [1968] Director/General Manager [Japanese]; John Frederic James Wilkes [1956] Director

TP Holdings Limited
Incorporated: 26 October 1995
Net Worth: £756,340,992 *Total Assets:* £756,340,992
Registered Office: Floor 2, 155 Bishopsgate, London, EC2M 3TQ
Activities: Activities of financial services holding companies
Parent: Tullett Prebon Group Holdings PLC
Officers: Giles Martin [1965] Director/Financier; Philip Price [1965] Director/Group General Counsel; Robin James Stewart [1967] Director

TP ICAP PLC
Incorporated: 5 May 2006 *Employees:* 5,128
Previous: Tullett Prebon PLC
Net Worth: £1,820,000,000 *Total Assets:* £37,373,001,728
Registered Office: Floor 2, 155 Bishopsgate, London, EC2M 3TQ
Activities: Activities of financial services holding companies
Officers: Richard Cordeschi, Secretary; Nicolas Noel Andre Breteau [1968] Director [French]; Michael Christopher Heaney [1964] Director [American]; Angela Ann Knight [1950] Director; Edmund Chin Hang NG [1963] Director/Chief Investment Officer [Canadian]; Roger Kitson Perkin [1948] Director; Philip Price [1965] Director/Group General Counsel; Stephen Jeffrey Pull [1956] Director; Rupert Hugo Wynne Robson [1961] Director; David Peter Shalders [1967] Director/Insurance Broking; Robin James Stewart [1967] Director; Margaret Lorraine Trainer [1952] Director

TPD Investments Limited
Incorporated: 14 November 2006 *Employees:* 1,210
Net Worth Deficit: £79,184,000 *Total Assets:* £454,883,008
Registered Office: 3 Park Place, St James's, London, SW1A 1LP
Activities: Activities of head offices
Parent: TH Holdings Limited
Officers: Dr Edward Oded Wojakovski, Secretary; Arthur Matyas [1932] Director; Dr Edward Oded Wojakovski [1969] Director

TR European Growth Trust PLC
Incorporated: 10 July 1990
Net Worth: £574,590,976 *Total Assets:* £628,348,032
Registered Office: 201 Bishopsgate, London, EC2M 3AE
Activities: Activities of investment trusts
Officers: Christopher Michael Casey [1955] Director; Simona Heidempergher [1968] Director [Italian]; Andrew Everard Martin Smith [1952] Director; Alexander Mettenheimer [1952] Independent Director [German]; Audley William Twiston Davies [1950] Director/Investment Fund Manager

TR Property Investment Trust PLC
Incorporated: 5 May 1905
Net Worth: £1,255,559,040 *Total Assets:* £1,366,977,024
Registered Office: 3rd Floor, 11-12 Hanover Street, London, W1S 1YQ
Activities: Financial intermediation not elsewhere classified
Officers: Timothy Nicholas Gillbanks [1966] Director; Simon Wilson Marrison [1964] Director/Chartered Surveyor; Hugh Richard Seaborn [1962] Director; David Kenneth Watson [1959] Director

Tradition London Clearing Limited
Incorporated: 17 September 1998 *Employees:* 12
Net Worth: £5,141,000 *Total Assets:* £392,339,008
Registered Office: Beaufort House, 15 St Botolph, London, EC3A 7QX
Activities: Financial intermediation not elsewhere classified
Parent: Compagnie Financial Tradition SA
Officers: Stefan Lewis Green, Secretary; Catherine Bienstock [1954] Director [French]; Francois Brisebois [1974] Finance Director [Canadian]; Tristan de Saint Ouen [1974] Director/Chief Executive Officer; William Pierre Francois Norbert Wostyn [1973] Director/Lawyer [French]

The Trafford Centre Limited
Incorporated: 18 July 1995
Net Worth: £1,666,800,000 *Total Assets:* £2,740,600,064
Registered Office: 40 Broadway, London, SW1H 0BT
Activities: Buying and selling of own real estate
Parent: The Trafford Centre Holdings Limited
Officers: Susan Marsden, Secretary; Martin Richard Breeden [1967] Director/Chartered Surveyor; David Andrew Fischel [1958] Director/Chartered Accountant; Colin Flinn [1969] Director; Hugh Michael Ford [1967] Director/General Corporate Counsel; Barbara Gibbes [1975] Director/Accountant; Kathryn Anne Grant [1973] Director/Chartered Surveyor; Trevor Pereira [1965] Director; Edward Matthew Giles Roberts [1963] Finance Director; Nick Round [1962] Director; Rebecca Mary Sarah Elizabeth Ryman [1975] Regional Director; Julian Nicholas Wilkinson [1963] Director/Chartered Surveyor

Trailfinders Group Limited
Incorporated: 19 December 2001 *Employees:* 1,090
Net Worth: £300,924,992 *Total Assets:* £501,131,008
Registered Office: 48 Earls Court Road, London, W8 6FT
Activities: Non-trading company
Major Shareholder: Michael David William Gooley
Officers: Elodie Deborah Marechal, Secretary; Michael David William Gooley [1936] Director/Travel Agent; Edwin Robert Lee [1949] Director/Solicitor

Trailfinders Limited
Incorporated: 11 March 1971 *Employees:* 990
Net Worth: £272,180,000 *Total Assets:* £490,404,992
Registered Office: 48 Earls Court Road, London, W8 6FT
Activities: Travel agency activities
Parent: Trailfinders Group Limited
Officers: Elodie Deborah Marechal, Secretary; Nikki Davies [1968] Director/PR & Marketing; Gareth Dyer [1961] Director/Travel Agent; Fiona Kathleen Gooley [1962] Director; Michael David William Gooley [1936] Director/Travel Agent; Tristan Patrick Gooley [1973] Director/Travel Agent; Toby Michael Kelly [1974] Sales Director; Edwin Robert Lee [1949] Director/Solicitor; Russell McHardy [1967] Director/Travel Agent; David Andrew Ness [1977] Cruise Director; Matthew Charles Raymond [1962] Systems Director; Ross Simpson [1979] Premium Travel Director; Mark William West [1971] Property Director

Trainline Group Investments Limited
Incorporated: 19 May 2006
Net Worth Deficit: £24,915,000 *Total Assets:* £180,560,000
Registered Office: 120 Holborn, London, EC1N 2TD
Activities: Activities of head offices
Parent: Trainline Junior Mezz Limited
Officers: Neil Anthony Murrin, Secretary/Solicitor; Clare Gilmartin [1975] Director [Irish]; Robin Hancock [1972] Director; Mark Holt [1972] Director; Shaun McCabe [1968] Finance Director

Trainline Holdings Limited
Incorporated: 25 November 1999
Net Worth: £114,132,000 *Total Assets:* £165,575,008
Registered Office: 120 Holborn, London, EC1N 2TD
Activities: Activities of head offices
Parent: Trainline Group Investments Limited
Officers: Neil Anthony Murrin, Secretary/Solicitor; Clare Gilmartin [1975] Director [Irish]; Robin Hancock [1972] Director; Mark Holt [1972] Director; Shaun McCabe [1968] Finance Director

Trainline Investments Holdings Limited
Incorporated: 10 April 2006
Net Worth Deficit: £20,600,000 *Total Assets:* £151,338,000
Registered Office: 120 Holborn, London, EC1N 2TD
Activities: Activities of head offices
Parent: Victoria Investments Newco Limited
Officers: Neil Anthony Murrin, Secretary/Solicitor; Clare Gilmartin [1975] Director [Irish]; Robin Hancock [1972] Director; Mark Holt [1972] Director/Chief Technology Officer; Shaun McCabe [1968] Finance Director; Douglas Stuart McCallum [1966] Director

Trainline.Com Limited
Incorporated: 17 September 1999 *Employees:* 478
Net Worth: £128,924,000 *Total Assets:* £320,743,008
Registered Office: 120 Holborn, London, EC1N 2TD
Activities: Other information technology service activities
Parent: Trainline Holdings Limited
Officers: Neil Anthony Murrin, Secretary/Solicitor; Clare Gilmartin [1975] Director [Irish]; Robin Hancock [1972] Director; Mark Holt [1972] Director; Shaun McCabe [1968] Finance Director

Tramlink Nottingham (Holdings) Limited
Incorporated: 7 April 2011
Net Worth Deficit: £96,950,000 *Total Assets:* £424,684,992
Registered Office: 4th Floor, 105 Piccadilly, London, W1J 7NJ
Activities: Urban and suburban passenger railway transportation by underground, metro and similar systems
Shareholder: Meridiam Infrastructure Net S.A.R.L
Officers: Richard Mark Ashcroft [1967] Director/Chief Executive; Arnaud de Monts de Savasse [1956] Senior Director Alstom Transport SA [French]; Ian David Hudson [1964] Director/Chartered Accountant; Brian Robert King [1944] Director; Frederic Long [1979] Director/Investment Manager [French]; Peter Richardson [1952] Director; Julien Georges Louis Wolff [1980] Director/Head of Financing and Treasury of Keolis Group [French]

Tramlink Nottingham Limited
Incorporated: 11 April 2011
Net Worth Deficit: £96,950,000 *Total Assets:* £424,684,992
Registered Office: 4th Floor, 105 Piccadilly, London, W1J 7NJ
Activities: Urban and suburban passenger railway transportation by underground, metro and similar systems
Parent: Tramlink Nottingham (Holdings) Limited
Officers: Richard Mark Ashcroft [1967] Director/Chief Executive; Ludovic Edward Both [1973] Director/Asset Manager OFI InfraVia [French]; Arnaud de Monts de Savasse [1956] Senior Director Alstom Transport SA [French]; Ian David Hudson [1964] Director/Chartered Accountant; Brian Robert King [1944] Director; Frederic Long [1979] Director/Investment Manager [French]; Peter Richardson [1952] Director; Julien Georges Louis Wolff [1980] Director/Head of Financing and Treasury of Keolis Group [French]

Tramtrack Croydon Limited
Incorporated: 17 August 1995
Net Worth Deficit: £16,387,000 *Total Assets:* £171,624,000
Registered Office: 55 Broadway, London, SW1H 0BD
Activities: Urban and suburban passenger railway transportation by underground, metro and similar systems
Parent: Transport Trading Limited
Officers: Howard Ernest Carter, Secretary; Jill Louise Collis [1968] Director of Health Safety & Environment; Patrick Doig [1982] Director/Planning & Reporting Controller; Jonathan Fox [1964] Director; Gareth William Powell [1976] Director of Strategy

TransDigm European Holdings Limited
Incorporated: 6 March 2001 *Employees:* 2
Previous: Technical Airborne Components Limited
Net Worth: £484,500,576 *Total Assets:* £615,044,288
Registered Office: Suite 1, 3rd Floor, 11-12 St James's Square, London, SW1Y 4LB
Activities: Non-trading company
Parent: TransDigm UK Holding PLC
Officers: Jonathan David Crandall [1977] Director [American]; Sarah Louise Wynne [1973] Director

TransDigm UK Holdings PLC
Incorporated: 2 April 2015 *Employees:* 2
Previous: TransDigm UK Holdings Limited
Net Worth: £474,105,696 *Total Assets:* £474,105,696
Registered Office: Suite 1, 3rd Floor, 11-12 St James's Square, London, SW1Y 4LB
Activities: Non-trading company
Parent: McKechnie Aerospace (Europe) Ltd
Officers: Jonathan David Crandall [1977] Director [American]; Sarah Louise Wynne [1973] Director

Transfercom Limited
Incorporated: 6 April 2006
Net Worth: £40,760,744 *Total Assets:* £289,822,144
Registered Office: 4th Floor, 8 Fenchurch Place, London, EC3M 4AJ
Activities: Non-life insurance
Officers: Colleen Martin, Company Secretary; Karen Lesley Amos [1959] Director; Christopher Peter Hare [1947] Director; Vijay Anantray Mavani [1962] Director Reinsurance; Brian Gerard Snover [1962] Director/Senior Vice President and Legal Counsel [American]; Andrew Wilson [1967] Director/Accountant

Transkey Limited
Incorporated: 6 June 2013
Previous: Transkey PLC
Net Worth: £199,963,472 *Total Assets:* £207,157,712
Registered Office: 2nd Floor, 13 John Princes Street, London, W1G 0JR
Activities: Freight transport by road
Major Shareholder: Andrey Klyucharev
Officers: Keith Robert Ridgway [1950] Managing Director

Transocean UK Limited
Incorporated: 20 June 2000
Net Worth: £3,671,701 *Total Assets:* £180,771,296
Registered Office: 15 Appold Street, London, EC2A 2HB
Activities: Extraction of crude petroleum
Parent: Transocean Ltd.
Officers: Anne Bolkow [1980] Director/Team Leader [German]; Stephen Lowry Hayes [1958] Director/Business Executive [American]; Fabrice Maire [1969] Director/Businessman [French/Luxembourger]; Charles Stephen McFadin [1957] Director/Businessman [American]

Transport for London Finance Limited
Incorporated: 10 November 2008
Net Worth Deficit: £81,892,000 *Total Assets:* £1,702,926,976
Registered Office: 55 Broadway, London, SW1H 0BD
Activities: Activities auxiliary to financial intermediation n.e.c.
Parent: Transport Trading Limited
Officers: Howard Ernest Carter, Secretary/General Counsel; Sarah Elizabeth Bradley [1967] Director; Howard Ernest Carter [1967] Director/General Counsel; Simon David Kilonback [1974] Director

Transport Trading Limited
Incorporated: 24 January 2000 *Employees:* 21,331
Net Worth: £10,371,200,000 *Total Assets:* £36,950,999,040
Registered Office: 55 Broadway, London, SW1H 0BD
Activities: Urban and suburban passenger railway transportation by underground, metro and similar systems
Parent: Transport for London
Officers: Howard Ernest Carter, Secretary; Michael William Tuke Brown [1964] Managing Director; Howard Ernest Carter [1967] Director/General Counsel; Simon David Kilonback [1974] Director; Gareth William Powell [1976] Director/MD Surface Transport

Transre London Limited
Incorporated: 26 April 2013
Net Worth: £376,795,872 *Total Assets:* £1,267,958,016
Registered Office: Corn Exchange, 55 Mark Lane, London, EC3R 7NE
Activities: Non-life reinsurance
Parent: Alleghany Corporation
Officers: Paul Andre Bonny [1956] Director/Reinsurance; Stewart Keith Laderman [1956] Director; Geoffrey Neville Peach [1959] Director/Reinsurance; David Charles Radford [1962] Director/Chartered Accountant; Michael Sapnar [1966] Director/President and CEO [American]; Gary Allen Schwartz [1960] Director/EVP and General Counsel [American]; Thomas Mark Stephen [1957] Director/Chartered Accountant; Mark Winlow [1962] Director

Transworld Petroleum (U.K.) Limited
Incorporated: 11 May 1971
Net Worth Deficit: £43,353,920 *Total Assets:* £205,773,136
Registered Office: Suite 1, 3rd Floor, 11-12 St James's Square, London, SW1Y 4LB
Activities: Extraction of crude petroleum
Parent: Repsol Sinopec North Sea Limited
Officers: Gemma Crawford, Secretary; Jose Carlos Vicente Bravo [1965] Executive Director [Spanish]; Manuel Tomas Garcia Blanco [1964] E&P Regional Executive Director, Europe, Africa, [Spanish]; Che Hung Lo [1953] Director [Malaysian]; Dale Kelly Moore [1960] Director/Engineer [Canadian]

Travel Document Service
Incorporated: 14 June 1934
Net Worth: £248,644,992 *Total Assets:* £248,644,992
Registered Office: 3rd Floor, One New Change, London, EC4M 9AF
Activities: Activities of other holding companies n.e.c.
Parent: Ladbrokes Investments Holdings Limited
Officers: Stuart John Smith [1981] Director/Accountant; Charles Alexander Sutters [1980] Director

Travelers Insurance Company Limited
Incorporated: 10 December 1971
Net Worth: £445,476,992 *Total Assets:* £1,256,849,024
Registered Office: 23-27 Alie Street, London, E1 8DS
Activities: Non-life insurance
Parent: The Travelers Companies, Inc
Officers: John Matthew Abramson, Secretary; Sir John Gordon Thomas Carter [1937] Director; Anthony Gerrard Coughlan [1957] Director/Accountant [American]; Gary Stewart Dibb [1950] Director/Chief Administrative Officer; Paul Howard Eddy [1955] Director/Attorney [American]; Michael John Gent [1964] Director/Chartered Accountant; Graham John McKean [1941] Director/Insurance Broker Retired; Kevin Christopher Smith [1961] Director/President of International Division [American]; Matthew Liam Wilson [1969] Director/Lawyer

Travelex Banknotes Limited
Incorporated: 16 March 2005 *Employees:* 175
Net Worth: £22,565,000 *Total Assets:* £256,947,008
Registered Office: 4th Floor, Kings Place, 90 York Way, London, N1 9AG
Activities: Other business support service activities n.e.c.
Parent: Travelex Limited
Officers: Victoria Benis-Lonsdale, Secretary; Philip Jon Barter [1975] Director; Nathan John Best [1974] Director; Clare Leanne Hall [1976] Director; Daryl Norman [1972] Risk and Compliance Director

Travelex Central Services Limited
Incorporated: 16 March 2005 *Employees:* 255
Net Worth Deficit: £76,186,000 *Total Assets:* £113,746,000
Registered Office: 4th Floor, Kings Place, 90 York Way, London, N1 9AG
Activities: Other business support service activities n.e.c.
Parent: Travelex Limited
Officers: Victoria Benis-Lonsdale, Secretary; James Edward Sullivan Birch [1964] Director; Roderick Barry Suckling [1968] Director

Travelex Financing PLC
Incorporated: 12 June 2013
Net Worth Deficit: £1,500,000 *Total Assets:* £313,600,000
Registered Office: 4th Floor, Kings Place, 90 York Way, London, N1 9AG
Activities: Other business support service activities n.e.c.
Parent: Travelex Holdings Limited
Officers: Victoria Benis-Lonsdale, Secretary; James Edward Sullivan Birch [1964] Director/General Counsel; Anthony Francis D'Souza [1971] Director; Roderick Barry Suckling [1968] Director

Travelex Group Investments Limited
Incorporated: 26 January 1961
Net Worth: £141,400,000 *Total Assets:* £143,500,000
Registered Office: 4th Floor, Kings Place, 90 York Way, London, N1 9AG
Activities: Other business support service activities n.e.c.
Parent: Travelex Limited
Officers: Victoria Benis-Lonsdale, Secretary; James Edward Sullivan Birch [1964] Director/General Counsel; Roderick Barry Suckling [1968] Director

Travelex Holdings Limited
Incorporated: 8 February 2005 *Employees:* 7,593
Net Worth Deficit: £809,900,032 *Total Assets:* £1,329,500,032
Registered Office: 4th Floor, Kings Place, 90 York Way, London, N1 9AG
Activities: Other business support service activities n.e.c.
Major Shareholder: Bavaguthu Raghuram Shetty
Officers: Victoria Benis Lonsdale, Secretary; Khaleefa Butti Omair Yousif Al Muhairi [1979] Director [Emirati]; Abdulrahman Sadiq Salim Basaddiq [1948] Director [Kenyan]; James Edward Sullivan Birch [1964] Director/General Counsel; Jonathon Galton Bomford [1948] Director; Hani Buttikhi [1984] Director; Anthony Francis D'Souza [1971] Director; Gavin Crawford Laws [1957] Director; Karim Aly Awad Saleh Salama [1976] Director [Egyptian]; Dr Bavaguthu Raghuram Shetty [1942] Director [Indian]; Binay Raghuram Shetty [1983] Director [Indian]

Travelex Limited
Incorporated: 25 May 2000 *Employees:* 230
Net Worth: £214,060,000 *Total Assets:* £1,034,035,968
Registered Office: 4th Floor, Kings Place, 90 York Way, London, N1 9AG
Activities: Other business support service activities n.e.c.
Parent: Travelex Holdings Limited
Officers: Victoria Benis-Lonsdale, Secretary; James Edward Sullivan Birch [1964] Director/Solicitor; Anthony Francis D'Souza [1971] Director; Roderick Barry Suckling [1968] Director

Traveljigsaw Limited
Incorporated: 14 July 2004 *Employees:* 1,526
Net Worth: £12,192,000 *Total Assets:* £337,835,008
Registered Office: 100 New Bridge Street, London, EC4V 6JA
Activities: Other business support service activities n.e.c.
Parent: Traveljigsaw Holdings Limited
Officers: James Victor Adams [1983] Product & Commercial Director; Jonathan Neil Barnes [1965] Director/Accountant; Ian Anthony Brown [1974] Director

Trayport Holdings Limited
Incorporated: 25 January 2008
Previous: GFI TP Ltd.
Net Worth: £130,013,032 *Total Assets:* £130,080,504
Registered Office: 7th Floor, 9 Appold Street, London, EC2A 2AP
Activities: Financial intermediation not elsewhere classified
Parent: TMX Group Limited
Officers: Elliott John Pickard, Secretary; Amer Chaudhry [1970] Director [Canadian/Pakistani]; Peter Conroy [1969] Director [Canadian]; John McKenzie [1972] Director [Canadian]; Jayakumar Rajarathinam [1975] Director/Chief Technology Officer [American]

Trebuchet Investments (UK) Limited
Incorporated: 7 December 2016 *Employees:* 145
Net Worth: £14,384,000 *Total Assets:* £159,480,992
Registered Office: 20 Old Broad Street, London, EC2N 1DP
Activities: Activities of financial services holding companies
Officers: Brad Scott Huntington [1959] Director/Chairman & CEO; Doreen Pauline Elizabeth Richards [1948] Director/Chief Operating Officer; John Caldicott Williams [1958] Director/President

Treimco Limited
Incorporated: 30 October 2009
Net Worth Deficit: £30,000 *Total Assets:* £258,423,008
Registered Office: c/o Mr J Mocatta, 5th Floor, 40 Gracechurch Street, London, EC3V 0BT
Activities: Non-life insurance
Officers: Paul Andre Bonny [1956] Director/EVP & President International Operations; Geoffrey Neville Peach [1959] Director/SVP & CEO Europe Operations; David Charles Radford [1962] Director/SVP Operations & Financial Controller International Operations; David Wilson Sinclair [1966] Director/VP & Financial Risks U/W Manager

Tremco Illbruck Limited
Incorporated: 10 October 1930 *Employees:* 189
Previous: Tremco Illbruck Coatings Limited
Net Worth: £64,921,908 *Total Assets:* £117,303,544
Registered Office: Hays Galleria, 1 Hays Lane, London, SE1 2RD
Activities: Manufacture of paints, varnishes and similar coatings, mastics and sealants
Parent: RPM International Inc.
Officers: John William Gordon [1971] Director; Richard Murray Hill [1960] Director; Daniel Matthew Johnson [1980] Director

Trendcycle Limited
Incorporated: 24 October 2002
Net Worth: £112,679,000 *Total Assets:* £811,398,976
Registered Office: Saffron Court, 14b St Cross Street, London, EC1N 8XA
Activities: Activities of head offices
Parent: Primepanel Limited
Officers: Aaron Campbell, Secretary; Hiroyasu Matsui [1965] Director [Japanese]; Jonathan Paul Scott [1961] Director/Accountant

Trenport Property Holdings Limited
Incorporated: 2 February 2015 *Employees:* 17
Net Worth: £124,300,000 *Total Assets:* £221,800,000
Registered Office: 2nd Floor, 14 St George Street, London, W1S 1FE
Activities: Activities of other holding companies n.e.c.
Parent: Shop Direct Holdings Limited
Officers: Aidan Stuart Barclay [1956] Director; Howard Myles Barclay [1959] Director; Christopher Derek Hall [1958] Director/Town Planner; Richard John Hall [1969] Director/Chartered Surveyor; Selwyn Heycock [1947] Director/Accountant; Nicholas John Hopper [1954] Director/Chartered Certified Accountant; Philip Leslie Peters [1957] Director; Michael Seal [1948] Director/Chartered Accountant

TRG (Holdings) Limited
Incorporated: 7 September 2005
Net Worth: £193,779,280 *Total Assets:* £260,793,040
Registered Office: 5-7 Marshalsea Road, Borough, London, SE1 1EP
Activities: Activities of head offices
Parent: The Restaurant Group PLC
Officers: Kirk Dyson Davis [1971] Director; Andrew McCue [1974] Director/Chief Executive Officer [Irish]

Triathlon Homes LLP
Incorporated: 29 January 2008
Net Worth Deficit: £1,997,000 *Total Assets:* £245,935,008
Registered Office: Fleet House, 59-61 Clerkenwell Road, London, EC1M 5LA

Tribeca Square LLP
Incorporated: 26 November 2013
Net Worth: £195,809,920 *Total Assets:* £311,086,624
Registered Office: 6th Floor, Lansdowne House, Berkeley Square, London, W1J 6ER

Triland Metals Limited
Incorporated: 19 May 1971 *Employees:* 59
Net Worth: £58,788,684 *Total Assets:* £653,182,592
Registered Office: Midcity Place, 71 High Holborn, London, WC1V 6BA
Activities: Financial intermediation not elsewhere classified
Parent: Mitsubishi Corporation
Officers: Nicholas Michael Currie, Secretary; Guy Usher, Secretary; Christopher Michael Bond [1943] Director; Isao Kano [1960] Director [Japanese]; Kazuyoshi Kawakami [1969] Director [Japanese]; Vineet Kohli [1971] Director [Indian]; Koichiro Murata [1966] Director [Japanese]; Junya Nagase [1963] Director [Japanese]; Martin Joel Pratt [1972] Director; Toshiro Sakai [1960] Director [Japanese]; Keiichi Shiobara [1963] Director [Japanese]; John William Smillie [1952] Director; Shinsuke Takahashi [1964] Director [Japanese]

Trillium (Prime) Holdings Limited
Incorporated: 25 April 2000
Net Worth: £322,737,984 *Total Assets:* £322,815,008
Registered Office: 140 London Wall, London, EC2Y 5DN
Activities: Management of real estate on a fee or contract basis
Parent: Trillium Holdings Limited
Officers: Aaron Jon Burns, Secretary; Adam Dakin [1962] Director; Graham Henry Edwards [1964] Director/Chief Executive Officer; Russell Charles Gurnhill [1970] Director; Michael Akiva Hackenbroch [1973] Director; Graeme Richard William Hunter [1963] Director

Trillium (Prime) Project Holdings Limited
Incorporated: 20 May 1998
Net Worth: £300,000,000 *Total Assets:* £300,000,000
Registered Office: 140 London Wall, London, EC2Y 5DN
Activities: Management of real estate on a fee or contract basis
Parent: Trillium (Prime) Holdings Limited
Officers: Aaron Jon Burns, Secretary; Adam Dakin [1962] Director; Graham Henry Edwards [1964] Director/Chief Executive Officer; Russell Charles Gurnhill [1970] Director; Michael Akiva Hackenbroch [1973] Director; Graeme Richard William Hunter [1963] Director

Trillium (Prime) Property GP Limited
Incorporated: 19 August 1997
Net Worth: £823,721,024 *Total Assets:* £996,601,024
Registered Office: 140 London Wall, London, EC2Y 5DN
Activities: Management of real estate on a fee or contract basis
Parent: Trillium (Prime) Project Holdings Limited
Officers: Aaron Jon Burns, Secretary; Adam Dakin [1962] Director; Graham Henry Edwards [1964] Director/Chief Executive Officer; Russell Charles Gurnhill [1970] Director; Michael Akiva Hackenbroch [1973] Director; Graeme Richard William Hunter [1963] Director

Trillium Holdings Limited
Incorporated: 23 December 1997 *Employees:* 241
Net Worth: £998,552,000 *Total Assets:* £1,823,208,960
Registered Office: 140 London Wall, London, EC2Y 5DN
Activities: Management of real estate on a fee or contract basis
Parent: London Wall Outsourcing Limited
Officers: Aaron Jon Burns, Secretary; Adam Dakin [1962] Director; Graham Henry Edwards [1964] Director/Chief Executive Officer; Russell Charles Gurnhill [1970] Director; Michael Akiva Hackenbroch [1973] Director; Graeme Richard William Hunter [1963] Director

Trinity Acquisition PLC
Incorporated: 25 June 1998
Previous: Trinity Acquisition Limited
Net Worth: £8,268,173,312 *Total Assets:* £12,031,638,528
Registered Office: 51 Lime Street, London, EC3M 7DQ
Activities: Activities of head offices
Parent: Willis Towers Watson UK Holdings Limited
Officers: Marcus Philip Dowding, Secretary; Steven James Alcock [1979] Director/Certified Accountant; Andrew Krasner [1975] Director [American]; Jonathan David Rand [1973] Director

Trinity Financing PLC
Incorporated: 12 November 2008
Net Worth: £47,000 *Total Assets:* £556,001,024
Registered Office: 35 Great St Helen's, London, EC3A 6AP
Activities: Financial intermediation not elsewhere classified
Parent: Trinity Financing Holdings Limited
Officers: Daniel Marc Richard Jaffe [1975] Director

Trinity Mirror Finance Limited
Incorporated: 2 November 2001
Previous: Northern and Shell Finance Limited
Net Worth Deficit: £294,000 *Total Assets:* £265,186,000
Registered Office: One Canary Wharf, London, E14 5AP
Activities: Other business support service activities n.e.c.
Parent: Reach Network Media Limited
Officers: Simon Richard Fox [1961] Director/Chief Executive; Simon Jeremy Ian Fuller [1977] Director/Chartered Accountant; Vijay Lakhman Vaghela [1966] Director/Accountant

Trinity Mirror Media Limited
Incorporated: 7 November 2000
Previous: Northern & Shell Media Limited
Net Worth: £288,795,008 *Total Assets:* £289,183,008
Registered Office: One Canary Wharf, London, E14 5AP
Activities: Activities of head offices
Parent: Reach Network Media Limited
Officers: Simon Richard Fox [1961] Director/Chief Executive; Simon Jeremy Ian Fuller [1977] Director/Chartered Accountant; Vijay Lakhman Vaghela [1966] Director/Accountant

Trinity Square 2015-1 PLC
Incorporated: 1 October 2015
Net Worth: £34,000 *Total Assets:* £1,168,448,000
Registered Office: 35 Great St Helen's, London, EC3A 6AP
Activities: Financial intermediation not elsewhere classified
Parent: Trinity Square 2015-1 Holdings Limited
Officers: Daniel Marc Richard Jaffe [1975] Director

Tripadvisor Limited
Incorporated: 4 November 2005 *Employees:* 283
Net Worth: £152,703,360 *Total Assets:* £213,870,272
Registered Office: 7 Soho Square, London, W1D 3QB
Activities: Travel agency activities
Parent: Tripadvisor, Inc.
Officers: Joseph Deangelo [1961] Director/VP, Tax Tripadvisor Inc [American]; Seth Kalvert [1969] Director [American]; Matthew Craig Strathdee [1974] Director/Lawyer [Australian]; Sarah Jo Wellman [1978] Director/Lawyer

Tripadvisor UK Holdco Limited
Incorporated: 2 November 2012
Net Worth: £1,656,850,560 *Total Assets:* £2,431,966,208
Registered Office: 7 Soho Square, London, W1D 3QB
Activities: Ready-made interactive leisure and entertainment software development
Parent: Tripadvisorinc.
Officers: Joe Deangelo [1961] Director/Accountant [American]; Seth Jonathan Kalvert [1969] Director/Attorney/General Counsel [American]; Matthew Craig Strathdee [1974] Director/Lawyer [Australian]; Sarah Jo Wellman [1978] Director/Lawyer

Triple Point Social Housing REIT PLC
Incorporated: 12 June 2017
Net Worth: £201,672,000 *Total Assets:* £208,699,008
Registered Office: 1 King William Street, London, EC4N 7AF
Activities: Activities of real estate investment trusts
Officers: Peter John Coward [1956] Director; Tracey Fletcher [1964] Director; Paul Francis Oliver [1955] Director; Christopher Robin Leslie Phillips [1950] Director; Ian William Reeves [1944] Director

Triplereason Limited
Incorporated: 17 April 1991
Net Worth: £293,218,624 *Total Assets:* £293,268,352
Registered Office: Winchester House, 1 Great Winchester Street, London, EC2N 2DB
Activities: Activities of head offices
Parent: Deutsche Bank Aktiengesellschaft
Officers: Joanne Louise Bagshaw, Secretary; Andrew William Bartlett, Secretary; Ross Daniel Cloney [1976] Director/Banker; Christopher Charles Snailham [1976] Director/Accountant

Triplog Holdings Limited
Incorporated: 5 May 2017
Net Worth: £101,723,408 *Total Assets:* £227,880,032
Registered Office: Investcorp House, 48 Grosvenor Street, London, W1K 3HW
Activities: Other service activities n.e.c.
Parent: Dauphine Holdings (UK) Limited
Officers: Andrea Jayne Davis [1965] Managing Director; Grahame Ivey [1958] Director/Chartered Accountant

Tritax REIT Acquisition 16 Limited
Incorporated: 3 December 2014
Net Worth: £55,520,000 *Total Assets:* £107,710,048
Registered Office: Fourth Floor, Standbrook House, 2-5 Old Bond Street, London, W1S 4PD
Activities: Other letting and operating of own or leased real estate
Parent: Tritax Big Box REIT PLC
Officers: Mark Glenn Bridgman Shaw, Secretary; Petrina Marie Austin [1974] Director/Surveyor; Henry Bell Franklin [1973] Director; Colin Richard Godfrey [1965] Director/Surveyor; Bjorn Dominic Hobart [1979] Director/Surveyor; Mark Glenn Bridgman Shaw [1947] Director

Tronox International Finance LLP
Incorporated: 8 May 2012
Net Worth: £2,826,848,768 *Total Assets:* £2,828,649,472
Registered Office: 7 Albemarle Street, London, W1S 4HQ

Tronox Sands Investment Funding Limited
Incorporated: 9 May 2012 *Employees:* 1
Net Worth Deficit: £81,519,024 *Total Assets:* £284,691,712
Registered Office: 7 Abermarle Street, London, W1S 4HQ
Activities: Activities of other holding companies n.e.c.
Parent: Tronox Sands UK Holdings Limited
Officers: Timothy Craig Carlson [1965] Director/Chief Financial Officer [American]; Steven Andrew Kaye [1976] Director/Lawyer/Attorney [American]

Tronox Sands LLP
Incorporated: 8 May 2012
Net Worth: £379,432,512 *Total Assets:* £379,758,784
Registered Office: 7 Albemarle Street, London, W1S 4HQ

Tronox Sands UK Holdings Limited
Incorporated: 21 December 2016
Net Worth: £401,111,040 *Total Assets:* £401,132,896
Registered Office: 7 Albemarle Street, London, W1S 4HQ
Activities: Activities of financial services holding companies
Parent: Tronox Sands LLP
Officers: Ian Lambert [2000] Independent Director; Nicholas John Rafford Watkins [1968] Independent Director

Tronox UK Finance Limited
Incorporated: 9 May 2012
Net Worth: £405,773,824 *Total Assets:* £410,245,984
Registered Office: 7 Abermarle Street, London, W1S 4HQ
Activities: Activities of other holding companies n.e.c.
Parent: Tronox Sands Investment Funding Limited
Officers: Timothy Craig Carlson [1965] Director/Chief Financial Officer [American]; Steven Andrew Kaye [1976] Director/Lawyer/Attorney [American]

Tronox UK Holdings Limited
Incorporated: 21 December 2016
Net Worth: £2,110,148,352 *Total Assets:* £2,799,163,904
Registered Office: 7 Albemarle Street, London, W1S 4HQ
Activities: Activities of financial services holding companies
Parent: Tronox Limited
Officers: Timothy Craig Carlson [1965] Director/Chief Financial Officer [American]; Shirley Fodor [1977] Director/General Counsel [South African]; Steven Andrew Kaye [1976] Director/Attorney [American]; Jeffrey Nathan Neuman [1961] Director/Attorney/General Counsel [American]

Tronox UK Limited
Incorporated: 8 March 2017
Net Worth: £443,276,352 *Total Assets:* £443,276,352
Registered Office: 7 Albemarle Street, London, W1S 4HQ
Activities: Activities of financial services holding companies
Parent: Tronox UK Holdings Limited
Officers: Timothy Craig Carlson [1965] Director/Chief Financial Officer [American]; Steven Kaye [1976] Director/Attorney [American]

TRS Group (UK) Limited
Incorporated: 28 June 2011 *Employees:* 233
Net Worth: £91,373,448 *Total Assets:* £100,450,704
Registered Office: 29 Welbeck Street, London, W1G 8DA
Activities: Activities of other holding companies n.e.c.
Officers: Fakhruddin Taherally Suterwalla [1938] Director; Hatim Taherally Suterwalla [1940] Director; Iqbal Taherally Suterwalla [1950] Director; Mansoor Taherally Suterwalla [1945] Director; Siraj Taherally Suterwalla [1944] Director

TRU Taj Holdings 2 Limited
Incorporated: 23 June 2016
Net Worth: £752,862,016 *Total Assets:* £752,862,016
Registered Office: c/o CMS Cameron McKenna LLP, Cannon Place, 78 Cannon Street, London, EC4N 6AF
Activities: Other business support service activities n.e.c.
Officers: Timothy Sean James Donovan Regan [1965] Director/Lawyer

Trustees of The London Clinic Limited
Incorporated: 28 November 1935 *Employees:* 1,196
Net Worth: £170,754,000 *Total Assets:* £261,098,000
Registered Office: 20 Devonshire Place, London, W1G 6BW
Activities: Hospital activities
Officers: Georgina Holtby, Secretary; Manish Jayantilal Chande [1956] Director/Chief Executive; Professor John Gribben [1955] Director/Doctor [British/American]; Ian Hamish Leslie Melville [1944] Director/Banker; Nicholas James Anthony Melhuish [1969] Director/Investment Manager; Helen Margaret Otton [1944] Director/Trustee

Truworths UK Holdco 1 Limited
Incorporated: 16 July 2015 *Employees:* 2,897
Net Worth: £197,388,992 *Total Assets:* £345,216,992
Registered Office: Classic House, Martha's Buildings, 180 Old Street, London, EC1V 9BP
Activities: Non-trading company
Parent: Truworths International Limited
Officers: Michael Samuel Mark [1952] Director/Chief Executive Officer [South African]; David Brian Pfaff [1965] Director [South African]; Kerry-Lee Anne Van Der Merwe [1976] Director

Truworths UK Holdco 2 Limited
Incorporated: 14 August 2015 *Employees:* 2,897
Net Worth: £218,231,008 *Total Assets:* £344,678,016
Registered Office: Classic House, Martha's Buildings, 180 Old Street, London, EC1V 9BP
Activities: Non-trading company
Parent: Truworths UK Holdco 1 Limited
Officers: Michael Samuel Mark [1952] Director/Chief Executive Officer [South African]; Lorenzo Giovanni Moretti [1970] Director/Chief Executive Officer; David Brian Pfaff [1965] Director [South African]; Kerry-Lee Anne Van Der Merwe [1976] Director

Truworths UK Holdco 3 Limited
Incorporated: 2 November 2015 *Employees:* 6
Net Worth: £151,764,000 *Total Assets:* £269,256,000
Registered Office: Classic House, Martha's Buildings, 180 Old Street, London, EC1V 9BP
Activities: Non-trading company
Parent: Truworths UK Holdco 2 Limited
Officers: Michael Samuel Mark [1952] Director/Chief Executive Officer [South African]; Lorenzo Giovanni Moretti [1970] Director/Chief Executive Officer; David Brian Pfaff [1965] Director [South African]; Kerry-Lee Anne Van Der Merwe [1976] Director

TS Property Lending Limited
Incorporated: 16 July 2012
Previous: Titlestone Property Lending Limited
Net Worth: £37,507,440 *Total Assets:* £313,885,600
Registered Office: Oaktree Capital Management LLP, 10 Bressenden Place, London, SW1E 5DH
Activities: Credit granting by non-deposit taking finance houses and other specialist consumer credit grantors
Parent: Oaktree Capital Group LLC
Officers: Samuele Cappelletti [1980] Director [Italian]; Nael Khatoun [1977] Director [French]

TS Real Estate Limited
Incorporated: 7 October 2013
Previous: Titlestone Real Estate Limited
Net Worth: £25,874,016 *Total Assets:* £136,248,768
Registered Office: Oaktree Capital Management, 10 Bressenden Place, London, SW1E 5DH
Activities: Other credit granting n.e.c.
Parent: Oaktree Capital Group, LLC
Officers: Samuele Cappelletti [1980] Director [Italian]; Nael Khatoun [1977] Director/Investment Professional [French]

TS Structured Finance Limited
Incorporated: 9 September 2015
Previous: Titlestone Structured Finance Limited
Net Worth: £14,005,382 *Total Assets:* £154,569,392
Registered Office: Oaktree Capital Management, 10 Bressenden Place, London, SW1E 5DH
Activities: Credit granting by non-deposit taking finance houses and other specialist consumer credit grantors
Parent: Oaktree Capital Group, LLC
Officers: Samuele Cappelletti [1980] Director [Italian]; Nael Khatoun [1977] Director/Investment Professional [French]

TSB Banking Group PLC
Incorporated: 31 January 2014
Net Worth: £1,864,000,000 *Total Assets:* £41,161,601,024
Registered Office: 20 Gresham Street, London, EC2V 7JE
Activities: Activities of head offices
Parent: Banco de Sabadell, S.A.
Officers: Carlos Bas Short, Secretary; Keith Graham Hawkins, Secretary; Paulina Beato Blanco [1946] Director [Spanish]; Ralph Coates [1972] Director/Chief Financial Officer; Dame Sandra June Dawson [1946] Director/Academic Professor; Richard Graeme Barclay Hardie [1961] Director/Banking; Richard Henry Meddings [1958] Director; Miquel Montes Guell [1960] Director/Banking Industry Executive [Spanish]; Dr Stephen Dowland Page [1961] Director [Australian]; Andrew Warwick Simmonds [1956] Director; Tomas Varela Muina [1960] Director/Banking Industry Executive [Spanish]; Polly Ann Williams [1965] Director

TSL Education SPV 2 Limited
Incorporated: 6 March 2007
Net Worth Deficit: £391,695,008 *Total Assets:* £118,889,000
Registered Office: 26 Red Lion Square, London, WC1R 4HQ
Activities: Activities of head offices
Parent: TES Global Holdings Limited
Officers: Paul Simpson, Secretary; Robert Ian Grimshaw [1971] Director; Paul Simpson [1968] Director/Chief Financial Officer

TSMUK Ltd
Incorporated: 23 September 2010 *Employees:* 107
Previous: Tata Steel Minerals UK Limited
Net Worth: £61,796,128 *Total Assets:* £635,094,080
Registered Office: 18 Grosvenor Place, London, SW1X 7HS
Activities: Activities of financial services holding companies
Officers: Farroakh Parekh, Secretary; Sandip Biswas [1968] Director [Indian]; Dibyendu Bose [1961] Director/Service [Indian]; Narendra Kumar Misra [1956] Executive Director Finance Europe [Indian]

TT Club Mutual Insurance Limited
Incorporated: 24 October 1991
Net Worth: £48,037,664 *Total Assets:* £377,373,248
Registered Office: 90 Fenchurch Street, London, EC3M 4ST
Activities: Non-life insurance
Officers: Ulrike Baum [1966] Director [German]; Ehsan Saif Chowdhury [1969] Director; Charles Edward Fenton [1964] Director; Ulrich Kranich [1950] Director [German]; Josef Johann Kuttel [1952] Director [Swiss]; Michael Leonard Onslow [1959] Director; David John Robinson [1964] Director; Niels Smedegaard [1962] Director [Danish]

TT Games Limited
Incorporated: 24 January 2005 *Employees:* 27
Net Worth: £103,823,032 *Total Assets:* £155,408,512
Registered Office: Warner House, 98 Theobalds Road, London, WC1X 8WB
Activities: Activities of head offices
Parent: WB/TT Holdings Limited
Officers: Thomas Hugh Creighton [1964] Director/Accountant; Jonathan Trevor Smith [1972] Director/Videogame Producer; Thomas Sidney Stone [1956] Director

TTL Earls Court Properties Limited
Incorporated: 20 March 2014
Net Worth Deficit: £350,000 *Total Assets:* £448,424,992
Registered Office: 55 Broadway, London, SW1H 0BD
Activities: Other letting and operating of own or leased real estate
Parent: TTL Properties Limited
Officers: Howard Ernest Carter, Secretary; Howard Ernest Carter [1967] Director/General Counsel; Graeme Kenneth Craig [1968] Director of Commercial Development; Lester Paul Hampson [1961] Director

TTT Moneycorp Limited
Incorporated: 25 October 1962 *Employees:* 289
Net Worth: £70,915,000 *Total Assets:* £435,222,016
Registered Office: Floor 5, Zig Zag Building, 70 Victoria Street, London, SW1E 6SQ
Activities: Financial intermediation not elsewhere classified
Parent: Bridgepoint Europe (SGP) Limited
Officers: Stephen Nathaniel Green [1963] Bridgepoint - Director; Nicholas John Haslehurst [1972] Director/Accountant; Mark Horgan [1966] Director; Robert Patrick Moores [1962] Director

Tube Lines Limited
Incorporated: 7 February 2000 *Employees:* 1,084
Net Worth: £54,100,000 *Total Assets:* £326,500,000
Registered Office: 55 Broadway, London, SW1H 0BD
Activities: Construction of other civil engineering projects n.e.c.
Parent: Transport Trading Limited
Officers: Howard Ernest Carter, Secretary; Tanya Louise Coff [1962] Finance Director; Jill Louise Collis [1968] Director of Health Safety & Environment; David Emrys Hughes [1970] Director of Strategy & Network Development; Peter McNaught [1973] Director of Asset Operations

Tudehope Ltd
Incorporated: 16 December 2010
Net Worth: £24,615,992 *Total Assets:* £107,169,504
Registered Office: Imperial Hotel, 61-66 Russell Square, London, WC1B 5BB
Activities: Other letting and operating of own or leased real estate
Parent: Imperial London Properties Ltd
Officers: Alexander Harold Edward Peter Walduck [1971] Director/Accountant; Hugh Richard Walduck [1941] Director/Hotelier; Jason Alexander George Walduck [1970] Director/Hotelier; Nicholas Stanley Richard David Walduck [1972] Director/Hotelier; Stephen Howard Walduck [1947] Director/Hotelier; Katharine Tanya Waller [1970] Director/Hotelier; Candida Stephanie Walton [1976] Director/Hotelier

Tudor Minstrel
Incorporated: 1 April 1999
Net Worth: £4,506,649,088 *Total Assets:* £5,633,908,224
Registered Office: 81 Newgate Street, London, EC1A 7AJ
Activities: Non-trading company
Parent: BT SLE USD Limited
Officers: Mark Philip Genikis [1961] Director/Accountant; Michael Joseph Mohun [1990] Director/Company Secretary Manager [Australian]; Christina Bridget Ryan [1960] Director/Company Secretary [Irish]

The Tudor Trust
Incorporated: 3 August 2004 *Employees:* 19
Net Worth: £246,312,992 *Total Assets:* £265,531,008
Registered Office: 7 Ladbroke Grove, London, W11 3BD
Activities: Other social work activities without accommodation n.e.c.
Officers: Fiona Denise Young, Secretary; Catherine Mary Antcliff [1960] Director/Musician; Holly Anya Baxter Baine [1985] Director/Project Manager; Dr Monica Anne Barlow [1958] Director/Research Consultant; Jonathan Anthony Bell [1965] Director/Investment Manager; Penelope Jane Buckler [1956] Director/Farmer; Louise Katherine Collins [1960] Director/Farmer; Elizabeth Helen Crawshaw [1962] Director/Housewife; Benjamin Hugh Dunwell [1969] Director/Writer; Matthew Stephen Dunwell [1963] Director/Farmer; Rosalind Helen Dunwell [1957] Director; James William Davenport Long [1949] Director/Author; Francis Arthur Runacres [1959] Director/Accountant; Shilpa Shah [1982] Director/Freelance Facilitator; Carey Rose Weeks [1987] Director/Regional Sponsorship Manager

Tulip UK Holdings (No.3) Limited
Incorporated: 14 September 2006
Net Worth Deficit: £2,446,000,128 *Total Assets:* £2,267,000,064
Registered Office: 30 Millbank, London, SW1P 4WY
Activities: Activities of head offices
Parent: Tulip UK Holdings (No.2) Limited
Officers: Sharone Vanessa Gidwani, Secretary; Dibyendu Dutta [1967] Director/Group Head - M & A And Treasury [Indian]; Narendra Kumar Misra [1956] Director [Indian]

Tullett Prebon (Europe) Limited
Incorporated: 19 November 1969 *Employees:* 454
Net Worth: £88,398,000 *Total Assets:* £423,468,000
Registered Office: Floor 2, 155 Bishopsgate, London, EC2M 3TQ
Activities: Security dealing on own account
Parent: Tullett Prebon Investment Holdings Limited
Officers: Paul James Ashley [1978] Finance Director; Paul Simon Dunkley [1964] Director/Broker; David Michael Daniele Goodchild [1974] Director/Head of Risk-EMEA; Giles Martin [1965] Director/Financier; Kevin Fergus McDermott [1970] Director; Andrew Aristotle Polydor [1962] Managing Director; Nicholas James Justin Potter [1965] Director/Moneybroker

Tullett Prebon (No. 1)
Incorporated: 16 May 2007
Net Worth: £28,669,880 *Total Assets:* £142,296,448
Registered Office: Floor 2, 155 Bishopsgate, London, EC2M 3TQ
Activities: Activities of financial services holding companies
Parent: Tullett Prebon Investment Holdings Limited
Officers: Giles Martin [1965] Director/Financier; David Huw Williams [1962] Director/Accountant

Tullett Prebon (No. 3) Limited
Incorporated: 29 May 2007
Net Worth: £115,839,424 *Total Assets:* £117,176,320
Registered Office: Floor 2, 155 Bishopsgate, London, EC2M 3TQ
Activities: Financial intermediation not elsewhere classified
Parent: Tullett Prebon Investment Holdings Limited
Officers: Giles Martin [1965] Director/Financier; David Huw Williams [1962] Director/Accountant

Tullett Prebon (Securities) Limited
Incorporated: 12 December 1991 *Employees:* 145
Net Worth: £55,640,000 *Total Assets:* £1,133,606,016
Registered Office: Floor 2, 155 Bishopsgate, London, EC2M 3TQ
Activities: Financial intermediation not elsewhere classified
Parent: Tullett Prebon Investment Holdings Limited
Officers: Paul James Ashley [1978] Finance Director; Nicolas Noel Andre Breteau [1968] Director [French]; Paul Simon Dunkley [1964] Director/Broker; David Michael Daniele Goodchild [1974] Director/Head of Risk-EMEA; Giles Martin [1965] Director/Financier; Kevin Fergus McDermott [1970] Director; Andrew Aristotle Polydor [1962] Managing Director; Nicholas James Justin Potter [1965] Director/Moneybroker

Tullett Prebon Group Holdings PLC
Incorporated: 11 January 2000
Net Worth: £1,015,707,008 *Total Assets:* £1,015,715,968
Registered Office: Floor 2, 155 Bishopsgate, London, EC2M 3TQ
Activities: Activities of financial services holding companies
Parent: TP ICAP PLC
Officers: Richard Cordeschi, Secretary; Philip Price [1965] Director/Group General Counsel; Robin James Stewart [1967] Director

Tullett Prebon Group Limited
Incorporated: 30 March 1973 *Employees:* 1,094
Net Worth: £869,881,024 *Total Assets:* £997,297,024
Registered Office: Floor 2, 155 Bishopsgate, London, EC2M 3TQ
Activities: Activities of financial services holding companies
Parent: TP Holdings Limited
Officers: Richard Cordeschi, Secretary; Philip Price [1965] Director/Group General Counsel; Robin James Stewart [1967] Director

Tullett Prebon Investment Holdings Limited
Incorporated: 14 October 2009
Net Worth: £875,200,000 *Total Assets:* £958,499,968
Registered Office: Floor 2, 155 Bishopsgate, London, EC2M 3TQ
Activities: Activities of financial services holding companies
Parent: Tullett Prebon Group Limited
Officers: Philip Price [1965] Director/Group General Counsel; Robin James Stewart [1967] Director

Tullow Group Services Limited
Incorporated: 21 December 2005 *Employees:* 439
Net Worth: £61,638,608 *Total Assets:* £207,573,280
Registered Office: 9 Chiswick Park, 566 Chiswick High Road, London, W4 5XT
Activities: Extraction of crude petroleum
Parent: Tullow Oil PLC
Officers: Kevin Massie, Secretary; Kevin Michael Massie [1980] Director/Lawyer [Canadian]; Paul McDade [1963] Director; Richard David Miller [1983] Director/Accountant; Rupert Richmond Rowland-Clark [1975] Director/Solicitor; George Leslie Wood [1962] Director/Chief Finance Officer

Tullow Oil Finance Limited
Incorporated: 15 June 2012
Net Worth Deficit: £354,115,648 *Total Assets:* £601,784,064
Registered Office: 9 Chiswick Park, Chiswick High Road, London, W4 5XT
Activities: Extraction of crude petroleum
Parent: Tullow Oil PLC
Officers: Kevin Massie, Secretary; Kevin Michael Massie [1980] Director/Lawyer [Canadian]; Paul McDade [1963] Director; Richard David Miller [1983] Director/Accountant; Rupert Richmond Rowland-Clark [1975] Director/Solicitor; George Leslie Wood [1962] Director/Chief Finance Officer

Tullow Oil PLC
Incorporated: 4 February 2000 *Employees:* 1,172
Net Worth: £1,928,311,808 *Total Assets:* £7,858,975,232
Registered Office: 9 Chiswick Park, 566 Chiswick High Road, London, W4 5XT
Activities: Extraction of crude petroleum
Officers: Adam Holland, Secretary; Kofi Tutu Agyare [1963] Director/Asset Manager; Stephen Charles Burrard-Lucas [1954] Director; Michael Christopher Daly [1953] Director/Geologist; Angus Murray McCoss [1961] Director/Geologist; Paul McDade [1963] Director; Dorothy Carrington Thompson [1960] Director; Jeremy Richard Wilson [1964] Director/Self Employed; George Leslie Wood [1962] Director

Tullow Oil SK Limited
Incorporated: 16 November 2004
Net Worth Deficit: £117,704,000 *Total Assets:* £137,587,008
Registered Office: 9 Chiswick Park, 566 Chiswick High Road, London, W4 5XT
Activities: Extraction of crude petroleum
Parent: Tullow Oil PLC
Officers: Kevin Massie, Secretary; Kevin Michael Massie [1980] Director/Lawyer [Canadian]; Paul McDade [1963] Director; Richard David Miller [1983] Director/Accountant; Rupert Richmond Rowland-Clark [1975] Director/Solicitor; George Leslie Wood [1962] Director/Chief Finance Officer

Tullow Oil SPE Limited
Incorporated: 5 December 2002
Net Worth: £195,703,392 *Total Assets:* £270,039,936
Registered Office: 9 Chiswick Park, 566 Chiswick High Road, London, W4 5XT
Activities: Extraction of crude petroleum
Parent: Tullow Oil PLC
Officers: Kevin Massie, Secretary; Kevin Michael Massie [1980] Director/Lawyer [Canadian]; Paul McDade [1963] Director; Richard David Miller [1983] Director/Accountant; Rupert Richmond Rowland-Clark [1975] Director/Solicitor; George Leslie Wood [1962] Director/Chief Finance Officer

Tungsten Corporation PLC
Incorporated: 2 February 2012 *Employees:* 331
Net Worth: £121,461,000 *Total Assets:* £143,247,008
Registered Office: Pountney Hill House, 6 Laurence Pountney Hill, London, EC4R 0BL
Activities: Financial intermediation not elsewhere classified
Officers: Patrick Thomas Clark, Secretary; Anthony Sebastian Bromovsky [1948] Director; Andrew Spencer Doman [1951] Director [British/Australian]; Duncan Erling Goldie-Morrison [1955] Director; Vivienne Katherine MacLachlan [1978] Director/Chief Financial Officer; David Michael Williams [1977] Director/Chartered Accountant

Turbo Finance 6 PLC
Incorporated: 22 September 2015
Net Worth: £5,450,125 *Total Assets:* £182,386,352
Registered Office: 35 Great St Helen's, London, EC3A 6AP
Activities: Financial intermediation not elsewhere classified
Parent: Intertrust Corporate Services Limited
Officers: Paivi Helena Whitaker [1963] Director [Finnish]

Turbo Finance 7 PLC
Incorporated: 2 September 2016
Net Worth: £11,213,230 *Total Assets:* £349,453,824
Registered Office: 35 Great St Helen's, London, EC3A 6AP
Activities: Financial intermediation not elsewhere classified
Parent: Intertrust Corporate Services Limited
Officers: Paivi Helena Whitaker [1963] Director [Finnish]

Turkish Bank (UK) Limited
Incorporated: 4 September 1991 *Employees:* 82
Net Worth: £26,647,000 *Total Assets:* £177,603,008
Registered Office: 84-86 Borough High Street, London, SE1 1LN
Activities: Banks
Parent: Turk Bankasi Limited
Officers: Murat Arig [1960] Director/Banker [Turkish]; Steven Mark Bennett [1970] Director/Banker; Steven Betteridge [1955] Director; Ibrahim Hakan Bortecene [1958] Director/Banker [Turkish]; James Gillan [1957] Director [Irish]; Jeremy William Charles Heales [1966] Director; Mehmet Ali Yunus Rahmioglu [1955] Director/Banker [Cypriot]

Turner Broadcasting System Europe Limited
Incorporated: 2 July 1985 *Employees:* 491
Net Worth: £330,945,792 *Total Assets:* £476,681,056
Registered Office: Turner House, 16 Great Marlborough Street, London, W1F 7HS
Activities: Television programme production activities
Parent: Turner Broadcasting System Holdings (Europe) Ltd
Officers: Eleanor Caroline Browne, Secretary; Eleanor Caroline Browne [1970] Director/Solicitor; Robert James Friend [1981] Director; Giorgio Stock [1964] Director/President, Europe/Middle East/Africa [German]

Glen Turner Company Limited
Incorporated: 4 November 1981 *Employees:* 127
Net Worth: £250,004,000 *Total Assets:* £302,870,016
Registered Office: 2nd Floor, Regis House, 45 King William Street, London, EC4R 9AN
Activities: Wholesale of wine, beer, spirits and other alcoholic beverages
Officers: Jean Pierre Cayard [1942] Director [French]

R.Twining and Company Limited
Incorporated: 27 October 1953 *Employees:* 396
Net Worth: £177,000,992 *Total Assets:* £228,972,000
Registered Office: Weston Centre, 10 Grosvenor Street, London, W1K 4QY
Activities: Wholesale of coffee, tea, cocoa and spices
Parent: Twining Crosfield & Co. Limited
Officers: Rosalyn Sharon Schofield, Secretary; George Thomson McCallum [1963] Regional Director; Nicholas Stephen Revett [1960] Commodities Director; Robert Edward Tavener [1964] Director/Chief Executive

Tyman Financial Services Limited
Incorporated: 25 January 2017 *Employees:* 3
Net Worth: £3,749,000 *Total Assets:* £124,001,000
Registered Office: 29 Queen Anne's Gate, London, SW1H 9BU
Activities: Financial intermediation not elsewhere classified
Parent: Jasper Acquisition Holdings Limited
Officers: Carolyn Ann Gibson, Secretary; James Edward Brotherton [1969] Director/Accountant; Louis Leslie Alexander Eperjesi [1962] Director [British/Canadian]; Kevin O'Connell [1960] Director/Accountant [Irish]

Tyman PLC
Incorporated: 1 April 1993 *Employees:* 3,904
Net Worth: £364,515,008 *Total Assets:* £697,913,984
Registered Office: 29 Queen Anne's Gate, London, SW1H 9BU
Activities: Activities of head offices
Officers: Carolyn Ann Gibson, Secretary; Pamela Ann Bingham [1969] Director; James Edward Brotherton [1969] Director/Chartered Accountant; Helen Frances Clatworthy [1961] Director; Louis Leslie Alexander Eperjesi [1962] Director [British/Canadian]; Mark Rollins [1962] Director; Martin George Towers [1952] Director

Tyrion Security Bidco Limited
Incorporated: 14 April 2014 *Employees:* 19
Net Worth: £48,550,000 *Total Assets:* £167,042,000
Registered Office: Third Floor, International Buildings, 71 Kingsway, London, WC2B 6ST
Activities: Activities of other holding companies n.e.c.
Parent: Tyrion Security Midco Limited
Officers: Suzanne Claire Hardyman, Secretary; Darron William Cavanagh [1976] Director; Suzanne Claire Hardyman [1979] Director/Solicitor; Richard Jones [1972] Director; Lee Jon Newman [1973] Director

Tyrion Security Midco Limited
Incorporated: 14 April 2014 *Employees:* 1,699
Net Worth Deficit: £86,798,000 *Total Assets:* £138,040,992
Registered Office: Third Floor, International Buildings, 71 Kingsway, London, WC2B 6ST
Activities: Activities of other holding companies n.e.c.
Parent: Tyrion Security Debtco Limited
Officers: Suzanne Claire Hardyman, Secretary; Darron William Cavanagh [1976] Director; Suzanne Claire Hardyman [1979] Director/Solicitor; Richard Jones [1972] Director; Lee Jon Newman [1973] Director

Tyrion Security Topco Limited
Incorporated: 4 March 2014 *Employees:* 1,699
Net Worth Deficit: £86,285,000 *Total Assets:* £137,823,008
Registered Office: Third Floor, International Buildings, 71 Kingsway, London, WC2B 6ST
Activities: Activities of other holding companies n.e.c.
Parent: Targaryen Security 1 S.A.R.L
Officers: Suzanne Claire Hardyman, Secretary; Christopher Marc Afors [1979] Director [Swedish]; Darron William Cavanagh [1976] Director; David Stewart Downie [1965] Director; Fabrice Fouletier [1975] Director/Partner [French]; Suzanne Claire Hardyman [1979] Director/Solicitor; Richard Jones [1972] Director; Gerard Christopher Loftus [1960] Director; Lee Jon Newman [1973] Director; Colm Paul O'Sullivan [1967] Director [Irish]

Charles Tyrwhitt Shirts Limited
Incorporated: 31 March 1994 *Employees:* 186
Previous: Wheeler Higgins Limited
Net Worth: £128,509,000 *Total Assets:* £208,734,000
Registered Office: First Floor, Cottons Centre, Cottons Lane, London, SE1 2QG
Activities: Retail sale of clothing in specialised stores
Major Shareholder: Nicholas Charles Tyrwhitt Wheeler
Officers: Peter John Higgins, Secretary; Peter John Higgins [1962] Director; Nicholas Charles Tyrwhitt Wheeler [1965] Director

U and I Group PLC
Incorporated: 18 November 1980 *Employees:* 119
Previous: Development Securities PLC
Net Worth: £379,280,992 *Total Assets:* £664,147,968
Registered Office: 7a Howick Place, London, SW1P 1DZ
Activities: Activities of other holding companies n.e.c.
Officers: Chris Barton, Secretary; Barry John Bennett [1951] Director [Irish]; Rosaleen Clare Kerslake [1957] Director/Chief Executive; Lynette Gillian Krige [1966] Director/Chartered Accountant (SA) [South African]; Marcus Owen Shepherd [1965] Director; Nicholas Howard Thomlinson [1953] Director/Chartered Surveyor; Richard Upton [1967] Director; Matthew Simon Weiner [1970] Director/Chartered Surveyor; Peter Wodehouse Williams [1953] Director

U-Pol Holdings Limited
Incorporated: 29 July 2010 *Employees:* 326
Net Worth Deficit: £44,760,000 *Total Assets:* £117,569,000
Registered Office: The Grange, 100 High Street, London, N14 6BN
Activities: Manufacture of paints, varnishes and similar coatings, mastics and sealants
Shareholder: Gaphite Capital General Partner V11 LLP
Officers: Michael John Coombes [1963] Director; Guy Hampson Williams [1967] Director

U.K.& European Investments Limited
Incorporated: 16 March 1964 *Employees:* 618
Net Worth: £286,900,000 *Total Assets:* £809,400,000
Registered Office: Chelsea House, West Gate, London, W5 1DR
Activities: Activities of head offices
Parent: Lewis Trust Group Limited
Officers: Bernard Lewis [1926] Director; Clive Robert Lewis [1956] Director; Julian Harley Lewis [1954] Director; Michael Henry Rosehill [1960] Director/Chartered Accountant [Irish]

UBM (GP) No1 Limited
Incorporated: 4 October 1996
Net Worth: £354,592,992 *Total Assets:* £377,396,000
Registered Office: 5 Howick Place, London, SW1P 1WG
Activities: Activities of head offices
Parent: UBMG Limited
Officers: Emma Louise Morgan [1981] Director/Accountant

UBM (UK) Limited
Incorporated: 19 November 1941 *Employees:* 452
Net Worth: £241,136,000 *Total Assets:* £3,795,151,872
Registered Office: 5 Howick Place, London, SW1P 1WG
Activities: Other business support service activities n.e.c.
Parent: UBMG Holdings
Officers: Simon James Parker [1966] Director; Alex James Simm [1978] Director/EMEA Chief Financial Officer; Andrew Nicholas Williams [1966] Global Brand Director

UBM Shared Services Limited
Incorporated: 7 November 2003 *Employees:* 123
Net Worth: £84,980,000 *Total Assets:* £364,011,008
Registered Office: 5 Howick Place, London, SW1P 1WG
Activities: Non-trading company
Parent: UBMG Holdings
Officers: Carl Sheldon Adrian [1972] Director/Accountant; Ian Branch [1968] Director; Simon Peter Hollins [1963] Director/Chief Information Officer; Zoe Miller [1974] Director/Accountant

UBMG Holdings
Incorporated: 18 December 1918
Net Worth Deficit: £198,000,000 *Total Assets:* £5,912,000,000
Registered Office: 5 Howick Place, London, SW1P 1WG
Activities: Activities of head offices
Officers: Simon Robert Bane [1971] Director/Solicitor; Rupert John Joseph Hopley [1969] Director/Solicitor; Nicholas Michael Perkins [1969] Tax Director; Gareth Richard Wright [1972] Director/Accountant [Australian]

UBMG Limited
Incorporated: 21 January 1983 *Employees:* 97
Net Worth: £696,112,000 *Total Assets:* £5,385,268,224
Registered Office: 5 Howick Place, London, SW1P 1WG
Activities: Activities of head offices
Parent: UBMG Holdings
Officers: Carl Sheldon Adrian [1972] Director/Accountant

UBMG Services Limited
Incorporated: 12 November 1998
Net Worth: £345,750,016 *Total Assets:* £381,823,008
Registered Office: 5 Howick Place, London, SW1P 1WG
Activities: Activities of head offices
Parent: UBMG Limited
Officers: Rupert John Joseph Hopley [1969] Director/Solicitor

UBS Asset Management (UK) Ltd
Incorporated: 19 February 1981
Previous: UBS Global Asset Management (UK) Ltd
Net Worth: £162,190,000 *Total Assets:* £214,412,000
Registered Office: 5 Broadgate, London, EC2M 2QS
Activities: Security and commodity contracts dealing activities
Parent: UBS Asset Management Holding Ltd
Officers: Ruth Beechey [1972] Director/Chief of Staff; Luke Richard Tyrrill Browne [1973] Director/Deputy Global Head of Structured Solutions; Eric Charles Sprague Byrne [1968] Director/Head of Asset Management UK & Ireland; Priscilla Ann Davies [1971] Director; Keith Martin Jecks [1957] Director

UBS Asset Management Holding (No.2) Ltd
Incorporated: 17 March 1998
Previous: UBS Global Asset Management Holding (No.2) Ltd
Net Worth: £181,499,008 *Total Assets:* £181,616,992
Registered Office: 5 Broadgate, London, EC2M 2QS
Activities: Other business support service activities n.e.c.
Parent: UBS Group AG
Officers: Luke Richard Tyrrill Browne [1973] Director/Deputy Global Head of Structured Solutions; Eric Charles Sprague Byrne [1968] Director/Head of Asset Management UK & Ireland

UBS Asset Management Holding Ltd
Incorporated: 5 May 1988 *Employees:* 341
Previous: UBS Global Asset Management Holding Ltd
Net Worth: £151,230,000 *Total Assets:* £197,776,000
Registered Office: 5 Broadgate, London, EC2M 2QS
Activities: Activities of head offices
Parent: UBS Asset Management Holding (No.2) Ltd
Officers: Luke Richard Tyrrill Browne [1973] Director/Deputy Global Head of Structured Solutions; Eric Charles Sprague Byrne [1968] Director/Head of Asset Management UK & Ireland

UBS Asset Management Life Ltd
Incorporated: 19 November 1996
Previous: UBS Global Asset Management Life Ltd
Net Worth: £31,310,000 *Total Assets:* £8,780,994,560
Registered Office: 5 Broadgate, London, EC2M 2QS
Activities: Life insurance
Parent: UBS Asset Management Holding Ltd
Officers: Ruth Beechey [1972] Director/Chief of Staff; Eric Charles Sprague Byrne [1968] Director/Head of Asset Management UK & Ireland; Peter Davis [1960] Director; Malcolm Gordon [1973] Director/Head of UK Institutional; John Charles Stannard [1956] Director

UBS UK Properties Limited
Incorporated: 11 June 1980
Net Worth: £109,021,000 *Total Assets:* £153,223,008
Registered Office: 5 Broadgate, London, EC2M 2QS
Activities: Development of building projects
Parent: UBS Group AG
Officers: Harriet Helen Lucinda Charles, Secretary; Robert Paul Bullough [1970] Director/Real Estate Management; Matthew James Cartledge [1975] Director/Chartered Accountant; Craig Alan Goldband [1975] Director/Financial Analyst [American]; John Quarmby [1968] Director/Chartered Tax Adviser

UCC Europe Limited
Incorporated: 3 April 2012 *Employees:* 1,400
Net Worth: £257,473,360 *Total Assets:* £500,802,848
Registered Office: 5th Floor, 6 St Andrew Street, London, EC4A 3AE
Activities: Production of coffee and coffee substitutes
Officers: Tsukasa Sato [1974] Director/Company Executive [Japanese]; Yasumasa Shimura [1952] Director/Company Executive [Japanese]; Kazuhiro Tashiro [1978] Executive Director [Japanese]; Gota Ueshima [1968] Director/Company Executive [Japanese]; Masaro Ueshima [1970] Director/Company Executive [Japanese]; Seisuke Ueshima [1973] Director [Japanese]; Hideyuki Yasuda [1967] Director of International Business Development [Japanese]

UD Europe Limited
Incorporated: 26 October 2009 *Employees:* 3
Net Worth: £137,025,920 *Total Assets:* £255,606,656
Registered Office: 1st Floor, 1 King William Street, London, EC4N 7AR
Activities: Development of building projects
Parent: Nippon Telegraph and Telephone Corporation
Officers: Toru Kinoshita [1973] Director [Japanese]; Seiji Okinaga [1964] Director [Japanese]; Toshiaki Tanaka [1967] Director [Japanese]

UDV (SJ) Holdings Limited
Incorporated: 15 December 2008
Net Worth: £2,827,000 *Total Assets:* £10,873,380,864
Registered Office: Lakeside Drive, Park Royal, London, NW10 7HQ
Activities: Activities of head offices
Parent: Diageo PLC
Officers: James Matthew Crayden Edmunds [1974] Director/Solicitor; Gabor Kovacs [1980] Director [Hungarian]; Kara Elizabeth Major [1977] Director [American]

UDV (SJ) Limited
Incorporated: 11 September 1970
Net Worth: £42,667,999,232 *Total Assets:* £51,027,001,344
Registered Office: Lakeside Drive, Park Royal, London, NW10 7HQ
Activities: Activities of head offices
Parent: Grand Metropolitan International Holdings Limited
Officers: James Matthew Crayden Edmunds [1974] Director/Solicitor; Kara Elizabeth Major [1977] Director [American]; Monika Pais [1973] Director [Hungarian]; Vinod Rao [1962] Director [Indian]; Prabhaharan Viswanathan [1972] Director [Australian]

UIG Holdings (No 4) Ltd
Incorporated: 15 January 2016 *Employees:* 3
Previous: LCCG UK Holdings Limited
Net Worth: £187,658,944 *Total Assets:* £188,285,200
Registered Office: Devonshire House, 1 Devonshire Street, London, W1W 5DR
Activities: Activities of head offices
Parent: Oaktree Capital Group LLC
Officers: Chris Helmut Boehringer [1971] Director [British/Canadian]; Ian Graham Maidens [1964] Director; Henry Edward Frederick Smith [1982] Director; Andrew Paul Thompson [1962] Director

UK Green Investment Gwynt y Mor Limited
Incorporated: 6 July 2015
Net Worth: £69,922,760 *Total Assets:* £202,671,216
Registered Office: 18 St Swithin's Lane, London, EC4N 8AD
Activities: Activities of other holding companies n.e.c.
Parent: UK Green Investment (OSW) GP Limited
Officers: Dominic Tan, Secretary; Karl Ben Smith [1977] Director/Banker; Partha Vasudev [1976] Director/Banker

UK Green Investment Gym Participant Limited
Incorporated: 23 April 2010
Previous: RWE Innogy Gym 1 Limited
Net Worth: £47,399,328 *Total Assets:* £194,683,184
Registered Office: 18 St Swithin's Lane, London, EC4N 8AD
Activities: Activities of other holding companies n.e.c.
Parent: UK Green Investment Gwynt y Mor Limited
Officers: Dominic Tan, Secretary; Karl Ben Smith [1977] Director/Banker; Partha Vasudev [1976] Director/Banker

UK Green Investment Lid Limited
Incorporated: 29 January 2016
Net Worth: £67,923,664 *Total Assets:* £223,881,440
Registered Office: 18 St Swithin's Lane, London, EC4N 8AD
Activities: Activities of other holding companies n.e.c.
Parent: UK Green Investment (OSW) GP Limited
Officers: Dominic Tan, Secretary; Karl Ben Smith [1977] Director/Banker; Alexis Eduardo Ulens [1967] Fund Director [Belgian]

UK Green Investment Lyle Limited
Incorporated: 22 December 2016
Net Worth: £58,605,336 *Total Assets:* £295,997,216
Registered Office: 18 St Swithin's Lane, London, EC4N 8AD
Activities: Activities of other holding companies n.e.c.
Parent: Clyde SPV Limited
Officers: Dominic Tan, Secretary; Richard Abel [1970] Director/Investment Banking; Serkan Bahceci [1972] Director; Stephen Alan John Deeley [1980] Director/Investment Manager; Erin Kate Eisenberg [1978] Director [American]; Charles Hazelwood [1963] Director; Tom Kelly [1989] Director/Investment Manager [Irish]; Gordon Ian Winston Parsons [1967] Director/Accountant; David Paul Tilstone [1969] Director/Banker

UK Green Investment Sheringham Shoal Limited
Incorporated: 19 November 2014
Net Worth: £176,546,176 *Total Assets:* £228,822,144
Registered Office: 18 St Swithin's Lane, London, EC4N 8AD
Activities: Activities of other holding companies n.e.c.
Parent: UK Green Investment (OSW) GP Limited
Officers: Dominic Tan, Secretary; Karl Ben Smith [1977] Director/Banker; Alexis Eduardo Ulens [1967] Fund Director [Belgian]

UK Group Finance Holdco Limited
Incorporated: 5 January 2016
Net Worth: £561,490,688 *Total Assets:* £561,500,800
Registered Office: 1 Finsbury Circus, London, EC2M 7SH
Activities: Activities of other holding companies n.e.c.
Parent: Urban Outfitters, Inc.
Officers: Francis John Conforti [1976] Director/Chief Financial Officer [American]; Azeez Hayne [1977] Director/General Counsel [American]; Richard Allan Hayne [1947] Director/Chairman & Chief Executive Officer [American]

UK Group of Hotels PLC
Incorporated: 26 April 2004 *Employees:* 2,270
Net Worth Deficit: £166,112,000 *Total Assets:* £227,820,992
Registered Office: The Shard, 32 London Bridge Street, London, SE1 9SG
Activities: Hotels and similar accommodation
Officers: Peter Procopis, Secretary; Michael Edward Jourdain [1964] Director; Peter Procopis [1966] Finance Director [Australian]

UK Holdings CAP (Commonwealth, Asia and Pacific) Limited
Incorporated: 8 November 2005
Net Worth: £2,387,179,264 *Total Assets:* £2,387,190,784
Registered Office: 100 New Bridge Street, London, EC4V 6JA
Activities: Activities of head offices
Parent: Danone Holdings (UK)
Officers: Paul Leslie Avis [1974] Director/Accountant; Stuart Richard Boyce [1971] Finance Director [New Zealander]; Sudip Dasgupta [1964] Finance Director [Indian]; Dr Roger David John Phillips [1955] Director/VP Medical Business

UK Power Networks (Operations) Limited
Incorporated: 3 November 1999 *Employees:* 5,143
Net Worth: £23,700,000 *Total Assets:* £349,600,000
Registered Office: Newington House, 237 Southwark Bridge Road, London, SE1 6NP
Activities: Production of electricity
Parent: UK Power Networks Holdings Limited
Officers: Andrew Charles Pace, Secretary; Kee Ham Chan [1963] Director/Chief Financial Officer; Loi Shun Chan [1962] Director [Chinese]; Andrew John Hunter [1958] Director; Neil Douglas McGee [1951] Director [Australian]; Basil Scarsella [1955] Director [Australian]

UK Power Networks Holdings Limited
Incorporated: 21 June 2010 *Employees:* 6,052
Net Worth: £3,348,800,000 *Total Assets:* £13,513,100,288
Registered Office: Newington House, 237 Southwark Bridge Road, London, SE1 6NP
Activities: Production of electricity
Shareholders: CKI Number 2 Limited; CKI Number 3 Limited
Officers: Andrew Charles Pace, Secretary; Kee Ham Chan [1963] Director/Chief Financial Officer; Loi Shun Chan [1962] Director/Accountant [Chinese]; Hok Shan Chong [1948] Director [Chinese]; Andrew John Hunter [1958] Director; Hing Lam Kam [1946] Director [Chinese]; Duncan Nicholas MacRae [1970] Director; Neil Douglas McGee [1951] Director [Australian]; Mei Fan Ngan [1965] Director [Chinese]; Basil Scarsella [1955] Director [Australian]; Wendy Wai Che Tong-Barnes [1960] Director/Business Executive; Charles Chao Chung Tsai [1957] Director and Chief Executive Officer [Canadian]; Chi Tin Wan [1950] Director [Australian]

UK Power Networks Services (Contracting) Limited
Incorporated: 8 March 1988 *Employees:* 99
Net Worth: £215,138,000 *Total Assets:* £399,351,008
Registered Office: Newington House, 237 Southwark Bridge Road, London, SE1 6NP
Activities: Production of electricity
Parent: UK Power Networks Services Holdings Limited
Officers: Andrew Charles Pace, Secretary; Loi Shun Chan [1962] Director [Chinese]; Andrew John Hunter [1958] Director; Basil Scarsella [1955] Director [Australian]

UK Power Networks Services (Development) Limited
Incorporated: 18 April 1996
Net Worth: £920,038,016 *Total Assets:* £920,038,016
Registered Office: Newington House, 237 Southwark Bridge Road, London, SE1 6NP
Activities: Activities of head offices
Parent: UK Power Networks Services (South East) Limited
Officers: Andrew Charles Pace, Secretary; Loi Shun Chan [1962] Director [Chinese]; Andrew John Hunter [1958] Director; Basil Scarsella [1955] Director [Australian]

UK Power Networks Services (South East) Limited
Incorporated: 1 April 1989
Net Worth: £239,600,000 *Total Assets:* £1,238,899,968
Registered Office: Newington House, 237 Southwark Bridge Road, London, SE1 6NP
Activities: Activities of head offices
Parent: UK Power Networks Services Holdings Limited
Officers: Andrew Charles Pace, Secretary; Loi Shun Chan [1962] Director [Chinese]; Andrew John Hunter [1958] Director; Basil Scarsella [1955] Director [Australian]

UK Power Networks Services Holdings Limited
Incorporated: 6 July 2010 *Employees:* 229
Net Worth: £260,000,000 *Total Assets:* £706,000,000
Registered Office: Newington House, 237 Southwark Bridge Road, London, SE1 6NP
Activities: Production of electricity
Parent: UK Power Networks Holdings Limited
Officers: Andrew Charles Pace, Secretary; Kee Ham Chan [1963] Director/Chief Financial Officer; Loi Shun Chan [1962] Director [Chinese]; Hok Shan Chong [1948] Director [Chinese]; Andrew John Hunter [1958] Director; Hing Lam Kam [1946] Director [Chinese]; Duncan Nicholas MacRae [1970] Director; Neil Douglas McGee [1951] Director [Australian]; Mei Fan Ngan [1965] Director [Chinese]; Basil Scarsella [1955] Director [Australian]; Charles Chao Chung Tsai [1957] Director and Chief Executive Officer [Canadian]; Chi Tin Wan [1950] Director [Australian]

UK Renewable Holdco 1 Limited
Incorporated: 14 September 2015 *Employees:* 67
Net Worth: £104,691,832 *Total Assets:* £1,070,545,280
Registered Office: 3 More London Riverside, London, SE1 2AQ
Activities: Activities of financial services holding companies
Officers: Loi Shun Chan [1962] Director [Chinese]; Mark John Horsley [1959] Director/Chief Executive Officer; Andrew John Hunter [1958] Director; Hing Lam Kam [1946] Director [Chinese]; Basil Scarsella [1955] Director [Australian]; Chao Chung Charles Tsai [1957] Director [Canadian]

UK Renewable Holdco 2 Limited
Incorporated: 14 September 2015 *Employees:* 6
Net Worth: £294,514,976 *Total Assets:* £301,524,128
Registered Office: 3 More London Riverside, London, SE1 2AQ
Activities: Activities of financial services holding companies
Parent: UK Renewable Holdco 1 Limited
Officers: Loi Shun Chan [1962] Director [Chinese]; Mark John Horsley [1959] Director/Chief Executive Officer; Andrew John Hunter [1958] Director; Hing Lam Kam [1946] Director [Chinese]; Basil Scarsella [1955] Director [Australian]; Chao Chung Charles Tsai [1957] Director [Canadian]

UK Renewable Holdco 3 Limited
Incorporated: 14 September 2015 *Employees:* 6
Net Worth: £283,076,032 *Total Assets:* £290,605,152
Registered Office: 3 More London Riverside, London, SE1 2AQ
Activities: Activities of financial services holding companies
Parent: UK Renewable Holdco 2 Limited
Officers: Loi Shun Chan [1962] Director [Chinese]; Mark John Horsley [1959] Director/Chief Executive Officer; Andrew John Hunter [1958] Director; Hing Lam Kam [1946] Director [Chinese]; Basil Scarsella [1955] Director [Australian]; Chao Chung Charles Tsai [1957] Director [Canadian]

UK SPV Credit Finance PLC
Incorporated: 24 January 2007
Net Worth Deficit: £266,108,752 *Total Assets:* £116,083,512
Registered Office: 5th Floor, 6 St Andrew Street, London, EC4A 3AE
Activities: Other business support service activities n.e.c.
Parent: UK Credit Finance Limited
Officers: Stephen William Spencer Norton [1959] Finance Director

UKEI (Finance) Limited
Incorporated: 6 March 2013
Net Worth: £226,336,240 *Total Assets:* £226,623,104
Registered Office: Chelsea House, West Gate, London, W5 1DR
Activities: Financial intermediation not elsewhere classified
Parent: U.K.& European Investments Limited
Officers: Clive Robert Lewis [1956] Director; Julian Harley Lewis [1954] Director; Michael Henry Rosehill [1960] Director/Chartered Accountant [Irish]

UKTV Media Holdings Limited
Incorporated: 7 April 2011 *Employees:* 274
Net Worth: £55,150,000 *Total Assets:* £234,824,992
Registered Office: 10 Hammersmith Grove, London, W6 7AP
Activities: Television programming and broadcasting activities
Shareholders: BBC Studios Distribution Limited; Southbank Media Limited
Officers: Patricia Edmondson, Secretary; Marcus Peter Arthur [1966] Director; Bruce Loren Campbell [1967] Director/Chief Development, Distribution & Legal Officer [American]; Stephen Thomas Davies [1968] Director; Thomas Cyrus Fussell [1970] Director/Chief Financial Officer; Jean-Briac Julien Perrette [1971] Director/President & CEO [French]

UKTV Media Limited
Incorporated: 7 August 2001 *Employees:* 274
Net Worth: £55,135,000 *Total Assets:* £234,824,992
Registered Office: 10 Hammersmith Grove, London, W6 7AP
Activities: Television programming and broadcasting activities
Shareholders: BBC Studios Distribution Limited; Southbank Media Limited; UKTV Media Holdings Limited
Officers: Patricia Edmondson, Secretary; Marcus Peter Arthur [1966] Director; Bruce Loren Campbell [1967] Director/Chief Development, Distribution & Legal Officer [American]; Stephen Thomas Davies [1968] Director; Thomas Cyrus Fussell [1970] Director/Chief Financial Officer; Jean-Briac Julien Perrette [1971] Director/President & CEO [French]

ULiving@Hertfordshire Holdco Limited
Incorporated: 9 October 2012
Net Worth Deficit: £10,255,000 *Total Assets:* £201,738,000
Registered Office: 4th Floor, 105 Piccadilly, London, W1J 7NJ
Activities: Development of building projects
Parent: Meridiam Infrastructure Finance II S.A R.L.
Officers: Richard Mark Ashcroft [1967] Director/Chief Executive; Axel Francois Cornelis Boutrolle [1969] Director [French]; Professor Ian Gordon Campbell [1963] Director/Deputy Vice-Chancellor; Susan Carol Grant [1961] Director/Academic Registrar; Charles-Henry Jaques Joseph Lecointe [1979] Director/Investment Manager [French/British]; Peter Marlon McCormack [1956] Director/Chief Executive; Clive Harry Pitt [1963] Director/Head of Finance; Matthew Thomas Rickards [1986] Director/Group Accountant; Martin John Smith [1962] Director

ULiving@Hertfordshire PLC
Incorporated: 17 December 2012 *Employees:* 9
Net Worth Deficit: £10,255,000 *Total Assets:* £201,738,000
Registered Office: 4th Floor, 105 Piccadilly, London, W1J 7NJ
Activities: Other accommodation
Parent: ULiving@Hertfordshire Holdco Limited
Officers: Richard Mark Ashcroft [1967] Director/Chief Executive; Axel Francois Cornelis Boutrolle [1969] Director [French]; Professor Ian Gordon Campbell [1963] Director/Deputy Vice-Chancellor; Susan Carol Grant [1961] Director/Academic Registrar; Charles-Henry Jaques Joseph Lecointe [1979] Director/Investment Manager [French/British]; Peter Marlon McCormack [1956] Director/Chief Executive; Clive Harry Pitt [1963] Director/Head of Finance; Matthew Thomas Rickards [1986] Director/Group Accountant; Martin John Smith [1962] Director

Unifund PLC
Incorporated: 9 March 2007
Net Worth: £17,560 *Total Assets:* £136,634,944
Registered Office: 6th Floor, 65 Gresham Street, London, EC2V 7NQ
Activities: Other business support service activities n.e.c.
Parent: Link Trust Nominees No.1 Limited
Officers: Colin Arthur Benford [1962] Director

Unilever Australia Investments Limited
Incorporated: 12 September 1914
Net Worth: £187,936,992 *Total Assets:* £187,936,992
Registered Office: Unilever House, 100 Victoria Embankment, London, EC4Y 0DY
Activities: Activities of head offices
Parent: Brooke Bond Group Limited
Officers: James Oliver Earley, Secretary; Richard Clive Hazell, Secretary; Anna Jo Karen Elphick [1975] Director/Accountant; Richard Clive Hazell [1966] Director/Solicitor; Amanda Louise King [1973] UK & Ireland Tax Director

Unilever Australia Partnership Limited
Incorporated: 17 June 1936
Net Worth: £187,919,008 *Total Assets:* £187,919,008
Registered Office: Unilever House, 100 Victoria Embankment, London, EC4Y 0DY
Activities: Activities of head offices
Parent: Brooke Bond Group Limited
Officers: James Oliver Earley, Secretary; Richard Clive Hazell, Secretary; Anna Jo Karen Elphick [1975] Director/Accountant; Richard Clive Hazell [1966] Director/Solicitor; Amanda Louise King [1973] UK & Ireland Tax Director

Unilever Overseas Holdings Limited
Incorporated: 4 April 1921
Net Worth: £423,004,992 *Total Assets:* £1,739,591,936
Registered Office: Unilever House, 100 Victoria Embankment, London, EC4Y 0DY
Activities: Activities of head offices
Parent: Unilever PLC
Officers: James Oliver Earley, Secretary; Richard Clive Hazell, Secretary; Anna Jo Karen Elphick [1975] Director/Accountant; Richard Clive Hazell [1966] Director/Solicitor; Amanda Louise King [1973] UK & Ireland Tax Director

Unilever U.K. Central Resources Limited
Incorporated: 13 June 1889 *Employees:* 3,419
Net Worth Deficit: £1,006,169,024 *Total Assets:* £9,612,857,344
Registered Office: Unilever House, 100 Victoria Embankment, London, EC4Y 0DY
Activities: Other research and experimental development on natural sciences and engineering
Parent: Unilever U.K. Holdings Limited
Officers: James Oliver Earley, Secretary; Richard Clive Hazell, Secretary; Julia Helen Fentem [1966] Director/R&D Leader/Global Head of Product Safety; Cameron William Jones [1965] Director/VP RD Hair and Head of Lab; Placid Oriol Jover Goma [1981] Director/VP HR UK & Ireland [Spanish]; Roger John Seabrook [1962] Director/Finance

Unilever U.K. Holdings Limited
Incorporated: 8 July 1882
Net Worth: £506,185,984 *Total Assets:* £1,262,872,960
Registered Office: Unilever House, 100 Victoria Embankment, London, EC4Y 0DY
Activities: Activities of head offices
Parent: Unilever PLC
Officers: James Oliver Earley, Secretary; Richard Clive Hazell, Secretary; Lucy Alice Beaumont [1982] Director/Solicitor; Julia Eisenstadt [1987] Director/Controller UKI [German]; Richard Clive Hazell [1966] Director/Solicitor; Amanda Louise King [1973] UK & Ireland Tax Director

Unilever UK & CN Holdings Limited
Incorporated: 2 July 1903
Net Worth: £1,645,604,992 *Total Assets:* £2,183,439,872
Registered Office: Unilever House, 100 Victoria Embankment, London, EC4Y 0DY
Activities: Activities of head offices
Parent: Unilever U.K. Holdings Limited
Officers: James Oliver Earley, Secretary; Richard Clive Hazell, Secretary; Lucy Alice Beaumont [1982] Director/Solicitor; Anna Jo Karen Elphick [1975] Director/Accountant; Amanda Louise King [1973] UK & Ireland Tax Director

Unilever UK Group Limited
Incorporated: 22 March 2012
Net Worth: £1,364,880,000 *Total Assets:* £1,364,880,000
Registered Office: Unilever House, 100 Victoria Embankment, London, EC4Y 0DY
Activities: Activities of head offices
Shareholders: Unilever UK & CN Holdings Limited; Alberto-Culver UK Holdings Limited
Officers: James Oliver Earley, Secretary; Richard Clive Hazell, Secretary; Anna Jo Karen Elphick [1975] Director/Accountant; Richard Clive Hazell [1966] Director/Solicitor; Amanda Louise King [1973] UK & Ireland Tax Director

Unilever US Investments Limited
Incorporated: 10 June 2004
Net Worth: £7,540,713,984 *Total Assets:* £8,564,141,056
Registered Office: Unilever House, 100 Victoria Embankment, London, EC4Y 0DY
Activities: Activities of head offices
Parent: Unilever PLC
Officers: James Oliver Earley, Secretary; Richard Clive Hazell, Secretary; Anna Jo Karen Elphick [1975] Director/Accountant; Richard Clive Hazell [1966] Director/Solicitor; Amanda Louise King [1973] UK & Ireland Tax Director

Union Bank UK PLC
Incorporated: 10 February 2003 *Employees:* 40
Net Worth: £58,752,544 *Total Assets:* £328,466,304
Registered Office: 1 Kings Arms Yard, London, EC2R 7AF
Activities: Banks
Parent: Union Bank of Nigeria PLC
Officers: Paul Hartley, Secretary; Albert Chukwuemeka Emuwa [1961] Director/Banker [Nigerian]; David John Forster [1957] Director/Banker; Suzanne Olufunke Iroche [1959] Director/Financial Consultant [Nigerian]; Kandolo Symphorien Kasongo [1955] Director/Banker [Congolese]; Gavin Crawford Laws [1957] Director/Banker; Godson Chukwuemeka Okonkwo [1965] Director/Banker [Nigerian]; Nigel John Richards [1958] Director/Banker

Union Lifestyle Holdings Limited
Incorporated: 21 July 2016 *Employees:* 2,045
Net Worth: £40,074,532 *Total Assets:* £103,947,872
Registered Office: 95 Victoria Road, London, NW10 6DJ
Activities: Other business support service activities n.e.c.
Parent: Bluegem II General Partner LLP
Officers: Marco Anatriello [1981] Director [Italian]; Marco Capello [1960] Director [Italian]; Suzanne Marie Harlow [1966] Director

Union Property Corporation Limited
Incorporated: 12 July 1960
Net Worth: £1,037,218,496 *Total Assets:* £1,037,218,496
Registered Office: York House, 45 Seymour Street, London, W1H 7LX
Activities: Development of building projects
Parent: BL Retail Holding Company Limited
Officers: Sarah Morrell Barzycki [1958] Director/Head of Finance; Paul Stuart Macey [1978] Director/Accountant; Jonathan Charles McNuff [1986] Director/Chartered Accountant; Charles John Middleton [1966] Director/Corporate Tax Executive; Timothy Andrew Roberts [1964] Director/Chartered Surveyor; Nigel Mark Webb [1963] Director/Chartered Surveyor

Union Property Holdings (London) Limited
Incorporated: 16 November 1946
Net Worth: £2,020,119,424 *Total Assets:* £2,027,437,568
Registered Office: York House, 45 Seymour Street, London, W1H 7LX
Activities: Development of building projects
Parent: BL Retail Holding Company Limited
Officers: Sarah Morrell Barzycki [1958] Director/Head of Finance; Paul Stuart Macey [1978] Director/Accountant; Jonathan Charles McNuff [1986] Director/Chartered Accountant; Charles John Middleton [1966] Director/Corporate Tax Executive; Timothy Andrew Roberts [1964] Director/Chartered Surveyor; James Fielding Taylor [1974] Director/Chartered Surveyor/Asset Manager; Nigel Mark Webb [1963] Director/Chartered Surveyor

Uniqlo Europe Ltd
Incorporated: 24 July 2003 *Employees:* 2,673
Net Worth: £26,175,272 *Total Assets:* £345,626,208
Registered Office: 6th Floor, 1 Kingsway, London, WC2B 6AN
Activities: Retail sale of clothing in specialised stores
Parent: Fast Retailing Co. Ltd.
Officers: Taku Morikawa, Secretary; Taku Morikawa [1974] Director/Chief Executive Officer [Japanese]; Tadashi Yanai [1949] Director/Chairman [Japanese]

Unisys Europe Limited
Incorporated: 29 September 2015 *Employees:* 64
Net Worth: £181,576,384 *Total Assets:* £278,650,976
Registered Office: 1st Floor, Building 6, Chiswick Park, 566 Chiswick High Road, London, W4 5HR
Activities: Business and domestic software development
Officers: Gwyn Reeves, Secretary; Martin Richard Godfrey [1967] Human Resources Director; Thomas Martin Higgins [1965] Director/VP and General Manager, Enterprise Solutions, EMEA [Irish]; Matthew Roy Piercy [1961] Finance Director

Unisys Finance Limited
Incorporated: 5 May 1998
Net Worth: £34,584,068 *Total Assets:* £133,671,704
Registered Office: 1st Floor, Building 6, Chiswick Park, 566 Chiswick High Road, London, W4 5HR
Activities: Financial intermediation not elsewhere classified
Officers: Gwyn Reeves, Secretary; Franco Paul Mallia [1963] Finance Director; Matthew Roy Piercy [1961] Finance Director; Gary Edward Purvey [1962] Director/Treasurer

Unisys Limited
Incorporated: 26 June 1909 *Employees:* 457
Net Worth: £46,258,000 *Total Assets:* £408,195,008
Registered Office: 1st Floor, Building 6, Chiswick Park, 566 Chiswick High Road, London, W4 5HR
Activities: Business and domestic software development
Parent: BMX Information Systems (UK) Limited
Officers: Gwyn Reeves, Secretary; Martin Richard Godfrey [1967] Human Resources Director; Franco Paul Mallia [1963] Finance Director; Matthew Roy Piercy [1961] Finance Director; Martin Walker [1965] Director

Unite (USAF) II PLC
Incorporated: 14 May 2013
Net Worth: £20,000 *Total Assets:* £697,769,984
Registered Office: 6th Floor, 65 Gresham Street, London, EC2V 7NQ
Activities: Financial intermediation not elsewhere classified
Parent: USAF Issuer Holdings II Limited
Officers: Colin Arthur Benford [1962] Director

United Bank for Africa (UK) Limited
Incorporated: 21 September 1995 *Employees:* 27
Previous: UBA Capital (Europe) Limited
Net Worth: £34,319,304 *Total Assets:* £112,132,800
Registered Office: 36 Queen Street, London, EC4R 1BN
Activities: Banks
Officers: Olufunmilayo Itinuola Dele-Giwa, Secretary; Adeleke Surajudeen Adeyemi [1969] Director/Accountant [Nigerian]; Clive David Carpenter [1951] Director/International Banker Consultant; John Coulter [1961] Director/Banker [Irish]; Patrick Rudolf Gutmann [1973] Director/Banker [Swiss]; Rose Ada Okwechime [1947] Director [Nigerian]; Samuel Oni [1954] Director/Consultant [Nigerian]; Victor Aiminogho Osadolor [1965] Director/Banker [Nigerian]; Alexander Knyvett Romer-Lee [1953] Director

United Cinemas International (UK) Limited
Incorporated: 15 June 1983 *Employees:* 1,429
Net Worth: £208,466,000 *Total Assets:* £249,984,000
Registered Office: St Albans House, 57-59 Haymarket, London, SW1Y 4QX
Activities: Motion picture distribution activities
Parent: Odeon Cinemas Holdings Limited
Officers: Christopher Thomas, Secretary; Andrew Stephen Alker [1966] Director/Accountant; Jan Bernhardsson [1962] Director [Swedish]; Mark Jonathan Way [1971] Director/Chartered Accountant; Carol Ann Welch [1970] Managing Director; Neil James Williams [1971] Director/Accountant

United Cinemas International Acquisitions Limited
Incorporated: 23 January 2004
Net Worth: £157,100,000 *Total Assets:* £242,300,000
Registered Office: St Albans House, 57-59 Haymarket, London, SW1Y 4QX
Activities: Motion picture projection activities
Parent: Odeon and UCI Cinemas Holdings Limited
Officers: Christopher Thomas, Secretary; Andrew Stephen Alker [1966] Director/Accountant; Jan Bernhardsson [1962] Director [Swedish]; Mark Jonathan Way [1971] Director/Chartered Accountant

United Dominions Leasing Limited
Incorporated: 26 October 1964
Net Worth: £4,463,000 *Total Assets:* £379,001,984
Registered Office: 25 Gresham Street, London, EC2V 7HN
Activities: Financial intermediation not elsewhere classified
Parent: Black Horse Finance Holdings Limited
Officers: David Dermot Hennessey, Secretary; Bertil Derrick Bos [1974] Director [Dutch]

United Dominions Trust Limited
Incorporated: 3 October 1922
Net Worth: £2,106,000 *Total Assets:* £1,140,125,056
Registered Office: 25 Gresham Street, London, EC2V 7HN
Activities: Financial intermediation not elsewhere classified
Parent: Black Horse Finance Holdings Limited
Officers: David Dermot Hennessey, Secretary; Richard Andrew Jones [1972] Marketing Director; Raymond John Hildreth Milne [1959] Business Risk Director

United Finance Limited
Incorporated: 26 February 1969
Net Worth: £66,988,000 *Total Assets:* £7,359,420,928
Registered Office: 5 Howick Place, London, SW1P 1WG
Activities: Activities of head offices
Parent: UBMG Holdings
Officers: Simon Robert Bane [1971] Director/Solicitor; Rupert John Joseph Hopley [1969] Director/Solicitor; Nicholas Michael Perkins [1969] Tax Director; Gareth Richard Wright [1972] Director/Accountant [Australian]

The United Kingdom Mutual Steam Ship Assurance Association (Europe) Limited
Incorporated: 18 February 1886
Net Worth: £152,710,032 *Total Assets:* £1,000,043,136
Registered Office: 90 Fenchurch Street, London, EC3M 4ST
Activities: Non-life insurance
Officers: Kieran Patrick Halpenny, Secretary; Randy Chen [1973] Director [American]; Nigel Christopher de Silva [1976] Director; Harley Vincent Franco [1952] Director [American]; Roger Charles Gillett [1952] Director; Nikolaos Inglessis [1955] Director [Greek]; Anastasios Margaronis [1955] Director [Greek]; Hans Nikolaus Schues [1965] Director [German]; Nigel Hugh Hamilton Smith [1949] Director; Andrew John Taylor [1970] Director; Paul Anthony Wogan [1962] Director

United National Bank Limited
Incorporated: 24 January 2001 *Employees:* 119
Net Worth: £83,812,608 *Total Assets:* £522,062,240
Registered Office: 2 Brook Street, London, W1S 1BQ
Activities: Banks
Shareholder: Government of Pakistan
Officers: Toby George Varkey, Secretary; Brian Gilbert Firth [1967] Director/Chief Executive Officer; Muhammad Faraz Haider [1970] Director/Banking (Compliance) [Pakistani]; Bande Hasan [1942] Director/Retired; Syed Zia Ijaz [1968] Director/Banker [Pakistani]; Sima Kamil [1957] Director/Banker [Pakistani]; Muhammad Naeem [1942] Director [Pakistani]; Richard Brian Wilton [1951] Director/Retired

United Trust Bank Limited
Incorporated: 23 May 1955 *Employees:* 155
Net Worth: £106,315,000 *Total Assets:* £1,013,899,008
Registered Office: 28th Floor, One Ropemaker Street, London, EC2Y 9AW
Activities: Banks
Parent: UTB Partners Limited
Officers: Shane Clement Bannerton, Secretary; Alice Helene Ernesta Renee Altemaire [1977] Director [French]; Jonathan James Ayres [1971] Director/Chartered Accountant; Tracy Marie Blackwell [1967] Director [Irish]; Graham Harold Davin [1956] Director/Chief Executive Officer [South African]; Andrew William Herd [1958] Director; Harley Farrell Kagan [1969] Managing Director; Michael Lewis [1959] Director; Stephen John Lockley [1958] Director/Chief Financial Officer; Anthony Noel Meredith [1955] Director of Sales; Richard Andrew Murley [1957] Director

Universal Coal PLC
Incorporated: 11 July 2002 *Employees:* 168
Net Worth: £57,289,896 *Total Assets:* £152,829,088
Registered Office: 6th Floor, 60 Gracechurch Street, London, EC3V 0HR
Activities: Other mining and quarrying n.e.c.
Officers: Ben Harber, Secretary; Carlo Baravalle [1961] Director [Italian]; Hendrik Willem Bonsma [1968] Director/Lawyer [South African]; Andries Johannes Marthinus Englebrecht [1973] Director [South African]; John David Hopkins [1950] Director [Australian]; Shammy Arewanga Luvhengo [1974] Director [South African]; Nonkululeko Merina Cheryl Nyembezi [1960] Director [South African]; David Twist [1953] Director; Anton Weber [1971] Director [South African]

Universal Music (UK) Holdings Limited
Incorporated: 9 June 1997
Net Worth: £1,212,505,984 *Total Assets:* £1,529,686,016
Registered Office: 4 Pancras Square, London, N1C 4AG
Activities: Activities of head offices
Parent: Universal Music Holdings Limited
Officers: Abolanle Abioye, Secretary; Simon Lloyd Carmel [1973] Director/Solicitor; Paramjit Jassal [1963] Director/Chief Financial Officer - Finance Operations; Boyd Johnston Muir [1959] Director/EVO & CFO

Universal Music Holdings Limited
Incorporated: 27 January 2005 *Employees:* 1,233
Net Worth Deficit: £12,523,000 *Total Assets:* £2,462,113,024
Registered Office: 4 Pancras Square, London, N1C 4AG
Activities: Activities of head offices
Parent: Vivendi S.A
Officers: Abolanle Abioye, Secretary; Simon Lloyd Carmel [1973] Director/Solicitor; Paramjit Jassal [1963] Director/Chief Financial Officer - Finance Operations; Boyd Johnston Muir [1959] Director/EVO & CFO

Universal Music Leisure Limited
Incorporated: 10 June 1997
Net Worth: £200,043,008 *Total Assets:* £312,329,984
Registered Office: 4 Pancras Square, London, N1C 4AG
Activities: Activities of head offices
Parent: Universal Music (UK) Holdings Limited
Officers: Abolanle Abioye, Secretary; Simon Lloyd Carmel [1973] Director/Solicitor; Paramjit Jassal [1963] Director/Chief Financial Officer - Finance Operations; Boyd Johnston Muir [1959] Director/EVO & CFO

Universal Music Operations Limited
Incorporated: 18 March 1969
Net Worth: £69,903,000 *Total Assets:* £2,048,248,064
Registered Office: 4 Pancras Square, London, N1C 4AG
Activities: Other service activities n.e.c.
Parent: Universal Music Leisure Limited
Officers: Abolanle Abioye, Secretary; Adam Martin Barker [1968] Director/Lawyer; David Spencer Joseph [1968] Director/Chairman & CEO; David Richard James Sharpe [1967] Director/Chief Operating Officer [Irish]

Universal Music Publishing International Limited
Incorporated: 28 August 1986
Net Worth: £13,136,000 *Total Assets:* £527,726,016
Registered Office: 4 Pancras Square, London, N1C 4AG
Activities: Sound recording and music publishing activities
Parent: Universal Music Leisure Limited
Officers: Abolanle Abioye, Secretary; Jacqueline Gay Alway [1966] Director of Legal & Business Affair; Robert John Morris [1972] Finance Director

Universal Music Publishing Limited
Incorporated: 29 September 1965
Net Worth: £9,873,000 *Total Assets:* £512,600,992
Registered Office: 4 Pancras Square, London, N1C 4AG
Activities: Sound recording and music publishing activities
Parent: Universal Music Leisure Limited
Officers: Abolanle Abioye, Secretary; Abolanle Abioye [1960] Director/Company Secretary; Jacqueline Gay Alway [1966] Director of Legal & Business Affair; Simon Neal Baker [1963] Finance Director; Robert John Morris [1972] Finance Director

Universal Music Publishing MGB Limited
Incorporated: 17 July 1967
Net Worth: £143,500,992 *Total Assets:* £234,824,000
Registered Office: 4 Pancras Square, London, N1C 4AG
Activities: Other publishing activities
Parent: Universal Music Publishing MGB Holding UK Limited
Officers: Abolanle Abioye, Secretary; Jacqueline Gay Alway [1966] Director; Robert John Morris [1972] Finance Director

Universal Publishing Production Music Limited
Incorporated: 17 June 1981
Net Worth: £19,576,000 *Total Assets:* £127,741,000
Registered Office: 4 Pancras Square, London, N1C 4AG
Activities: Other publishing activities
Parent: Universal Music Publishing MGB Limited
Officers: Abolanle Abioye, Secretary; Jacqueline Gay Alway [1966] Director; Robert John Morris [1972] Finance Director

Universal Studios Limited
Incorporated: 6 June 2014 *Employees:* 114
Net Worth: £1,258,074,496 *Total Assets:* £2,069,363,328
Registered Office: 1 Central St Giles, St Giles High Street, London, WC2H 8NU
Activities: Motion picture distribution activities
Parent: Comcast Corporation
Officers: Alison Mansfield, Secretary; Marisa Montis, Secretary; Jason Jon Beesley [1976] Director/SVP & CFO, Universal International [American]; Duncan John Timothy Bratchell [1958] Director/Chartered Accountant; Oliver Canning [1970] Director/Solicitor; Duncan Cameron Clark [1952] Director/President, International Theatrical; Tracy Lockhart [1970] Director/SVP & Group Financial Controller International; Marc Mathew Low [1966] Director/SVP International Consumer Products [American/Dutch]; Kevin Michael MacLellan [1967] Director/Media Executive [American]; Belinda Elvira Menendez [1954] Director/President & CRO of Global Distribution [American/British]; John William Revill [1971] Director/Regional MD & SVP, Sales, Catalogue & Marketing; Carolyn Stalins-Fussman [1966] Director/SVP Distribution, EMEA [French]

University of Greenwich
Incorporated: 12 August 1970 *Employees:* 2,253
Net Worth: £100,011,000 *Total Assets:* £372,940,992
Registered Office: Old Royal Naval College, Park Row, Greenwich, London, SE10 9LS
Activities: First-degree level higher education
Officers: Peter Douglas Garrod, Secretary; Simon Gass [1956] Director; Peter Frank Hazell [1948] Director; Bronwyn Mary Hill [1960] Director; Meike Imberg [1992] Director/President Students Union [German]; Marianne Laing Ismail [1952] Director; Diane Khanna [1968] Director/Headteacher; Patricia Anne King [1961] Director/Vice President Case Education Charity; Denise Larnder [1960] Director/Accountant; Professor David John Maguire [1958] Director/Vice-Chancellor; Craig David McWilliam [1972] Director/Chief Executive; Murray Leonard Orr [1958] Director/Banker [Irish]; Winnie Yi-Chen Palmer [1974] Director/Marketing Consultant; Sara Ragab [1968] Director/University Administrator; Elizabeth Ellen Sideris [1953] Director; Julie Louise Wood [1960] Director of Ove Arup & Partners

The University of Westminster
Incorporated: 22 April 1970 *Employees:* 1,900
Net Worth: £224,055,008 *Total Assets:* £458,990,016
Registered Office: 309 Regent Street, London, W1B 2HW
Activities: Other research and experimental development on natural sciences and engineering
Officers: John Bernard James Cappock, Secretary; Robert Digby Phillips Barnes [1957] Director/Chartered Surveyor; John David Begg [1963] Director/Senior Lecturer; Christiana Adeola Bernard [1964] Director/Executive Headhunter; Dr Peter William Bonfield [1963] Director/Vice Chancellor; Nicholas Robert Catterall [1981] Director/Senior Compliance and Development Manager; David Stewart Cheeseman [1963] Director; Geoffrey Laurence Davies [1954] Director/Principal Lecturer; Dame Karen Hope Dunnell [1946] Director/Retired; Mary Clare Hogg [1947] Director/Barrister; Professor Alexandra Hughes [1960] Director/Deputy Vice-Chancellor; Vanessa Ruth James [1973] Director/Solicitor; Gary Cornwell Morley [1957] Director/Chartered Accountant; Philip Robert Murphy [1948] Director; Lareb Naseem [1995] Director/Students' Union President; Helen Lindsay Bland Owen [1959] Director; Linda Phillips [1961] Director; Matthew James Smith [1976] Director/Barrister; Canon David Stanton [1960] Director/Canon of Westminster; Philomine Frances Wales [1950] Director/Architect (Retired); Simon Bryant Wylie [1960] Director/Consultant; Diane Helen Yeo [1945] Director/Charity

Unlimited Marketing Group Ltd
Incorporated: 8 November 2016 *Employees:* 781
Net Worth: £8,178,000 *Total Assets:* £108,474,000
Registered Office: Unlimited House, 10 Great Pulteney Street, London, W1F 9NB
Activities: Activities of other holding companies n.e.c.
Officers: Olivia Alexandra Walker, Secretary; Michael Jordan Branigan [1956] Director; Iain Fraser Ferguson [1957] Director; Timothy John Pennington Hancock [1955] Director; Nicholas James Hargrave [1978] Investment Director; Michael Andrew Haxby [1972] Director; Kathryn Louise Herrick [1966] Director CFO; James Michael Mara [1946] Director/Finance [American]; Michael John Richards [1964] Managing Director

Upfield Foods UK Limited
Incorporated: 1 April 2015 *Employees:* 179
Previous: Unilever BCS UK Limited
Net Worth: £79,120,000 *Total Assets:* £108,406,800
Registered Office: Thomas House, 84 Ecclestone Square, London, SW1V 1PX
Activities: Butter and cheese production
Parent: Upfield Spreads UK Limited
Officers: Anthony William Barratt, Secretary; Daniel James Balmer [1978] Director; Steven James Hermiston [1972] Director; David John Salkeld [1956] Director/Executive Vice President

Upfield Spreads UK Limited
Incorporated: 25 November 2014
Previous: Unilever BCS Limited
Net Worth: £964,864,000 *Total Assets:* £1,241,015,040
Registered Office: Thomas House, 84 Ecclestone Square, London, SW1V 1PX
Activities: Manufacture of margarine and similar edible fats
Officers: Anthony William Barratt, Secretary; Paul Francis O'Neill [1978] Director [Irish]; Francisco Javier Tena Unna [1975] Director/CFO BCS [Dutch]

UPP (Broadgate Park) Holdings Limited
Incorporated: 24 January 2003 *Employees:* 57
Net Worth: £13,352,000 *Total Assets:* £104,556,000
Registered Office: 40 Gracechurch Street, London, EC3V 0BT
Activities: Other letting and operating of own or leased real estate
Parent: UPP Bond 1 Limited
Officers: Richard Antoine Bienfait [1967] Director; Henry Barnaby Gervaise Jones [1980] Director/Accountant; Mark Swindlehurst Swindlehurst [1969] Managing Director

UPP (Cartwright Gardens) Holdings Limited
Incorporated: 13 February 2014 *Employees:* 24
Net Worth: £10,135,000 *Total Assets:* £163,999,008
Registered Office: 40 Gracechurch Street, London, EC3V 0BT
Activities: Activities of head offices
Parent: UPP Group Limited
Officers: Dr Ghazwa Alwani-Starr [1963] University Director; Richard Antoine Bienfait [1967] Director; Henry Barnaby Gervaise Jones [1980] Director/Accountant; Mark Swindlehurst Swindlehurst [1969] Managing Director

UPP (Duncan House) Holdings Limited
Incorporated: 13 July 2016 *Employees:* 5
Net Worth: £1,046,000 *Total Assets:* £112,697,000
Registered Office: 40 Gracechurch Street, London, EC3V 0BT
Activities: Activities of head offices
Parent: UPP Group Limited
Officers: Dr Ghazwa Alwani-Starr [1963] University Director; Richard Antoine Bienfait [1967] Director; Henry Barnaby Gervaise Jones [1980] Director/Accountant; Mark Swindlehurst Swindlehurst [1969] Managing Director

UPP (Duncan House) Limited
Incorporated: 13 July 2016 *Employees:* 5
Net Worth: £1,046,000 *Total Assets:* £112,696,000
Registered Office: 40 Gracechurch Street, London, EC3V 0BT
Activities: Development of building projects
Parent: UPP (Duncan House) Holdings Limited
Officers: Dr Ghazwa Alwani-Starr [1963] University Director; Richard Antoine Bienfait [1967] Director; Henry Barnaby Gervaise-Jones [1980] Director/Accountant; Mark Swindlehurst Swindlehurst [1969] Managing Director

UPP (Exeter) Limited
Incorporated: 23 April 2009 *Employees:* 63
Net Worth: £3,654,000 *Total Assets:* £143,560,000
Registered Office: 40 Gracechurch Street, London, EC3V 0BT
Activities: Other letting and operating of own or leased real estate
Parent: UPP Bond 1 Limited
Officers: Richard Antoine Bienfait [1967] Director; Henry Barnaby Gervaise-Jones [1980] Director/Accountant; Mark Swindlehurst Swindlehurst [1969] Managing Director

UPP (Hull) Holdings Limited
Incorporated: 24 January 2017 *Employees:* 11
Net Worth: £1,070,000 *Total Assets:* £166,520,000
Registered Office: 40 Gracechurch Street, London, EC3V 0BT
Activities: Activities of head offices
Parent: UPP Group Limited
Officers: Richard Antoine Bienfait [1967] Director; Henry Barnaby Gervaise Jones [1980] Director/Accountant; Mark Swindlehurst Swindlehurst [1969] Managing Director; Trudi Jane Vout [1965] Director

UPP (Hull) Limited
Incorporated: 25 January 2017 *Employees:* 11
Net Worth: £1,019,000 *Total Assets:* £166,468,992
Registered Office: 40 Gracechurch Street, London, EC3V 0BT
Activities: Development of building projects
Parent: UPP (Hull) Holdings Limited
Officers: Richard Antoine Bienfait [1967] Director; Henry Barnaby Gervaise-Jones [1980] Director/Accountant; Mark Swindlehurst Swindlehurst [1969] Director/Managing; Trudi Jane Vout [1965] Director

UPP (Lancaster) Holdings Limited
Incorporated: 24 January 2003 *Employees:* 17
Net Worth Deficit: £54,021,000 *Total Assets:* £215,271,008
Registered Office: 40 Gracechurch Street, London, EC3V 0BT
Activities: Activities of head offices
Parent: UPP Group Limited
Officers: Richard Antoine Bienfait [1967] Director; Henry Barnaby Gervaise Jones [1980] Director/Accountant; Mark Swindlehurst Swindlehurst [1969] Managing Director

UPP (Lancaster) Limited
Incorporated: 16 May 2002 *Employees:* 17
Net Worth Deficit: £54,007,000 *Total Assets:* £215,283,008
Registered Office: 40 Gracechurch Street, London, EC3V 0BT
Activities: Other letting and operating of own or leased real estate
Parent: UPP (Lancaster) Holdings Limited
Officers: Richard Antoine Bienfait [1967] Director; Henry Barnaby Gervaise-Jones [1980] Director/Accountant; Mark Swindlehurst Swindlehurst [1969] Managing Director

UPP (Nottingham) Ltd
Incorporated: 18 September 2001 *Employees:* 112
Net Worth: £8,365,000 *Total Assets:* £111,490,000
Registered Office: 40 Gracechurch Street, London, EC3V 0BT
Activities: Other letting and operating of own or leased real estate
Parent: UPP Bond 1 Limited
Officers: Richard Antoine Bienfait [1967] Director; Stephen John Denton [1965] Director/Chief Operating Officer; Henry Barnaby Gervaise-Jones [1980] Director/Accountant; Mark Swindlehurst Swindlehurst [1969] Managing Director

UPP (Reading I) Holdings Limited
Incorporated: 17 May 2011 *Employees:* 168
Net Worth: £48,016,000 *Total Assets:* £350,255,008
Registered Office: 40 Gracechurch Street, London, EC3V 0BT
Activities: Activities of head offices
Parent: UPP (Midco) Limited
Officers: Richard Antoine Bienfait [1967] Director; Henry Barnaby Gervaise-Jones [1980] Director/Accountant; Mark Swindlehurst Swindlehurst [1969] Managing Director; Matthew James White [1970] Director of Campus Commerce

UPP (Reading I) Limited
Incorporated: 17 May 2011 *Employees:* 140
Net Worth: £121,532,000 *Total Assets:* £340,072,992
Registered Office: 40 Gracechurch Street, London, EC3V 0BT
Activities: Other letting and operating of own or leased real estate
Parent: UPP (Reading I) Holdings Limited
Officers: Richard Antoine Bienfait [1967] Director; Henry Barnaby Gervaise-Jones [1980] Director/Accountant; Dr Timothy John Gerard Lees [1980] Director/Academic (Associate Professor); David Marsden [1975] Director/Chartered Surveyor; Mark Swindlehurst Swindlehurst [1969] Managing Director; Karen Louise Thomas [1972] Contract Director; Matthew James White [1970] Director of Campus Commerce

UPP Bond 1 Holdings Limited
Incorporated: 15 October 2012 *Employees:* 306
Net Worth: £39,805,000 *Total Assets:* £740,257,024
Registered Office: 40 Gracechurch Street, London, EC3V 0BT
Activities: Activities of other holding companies n.e.c.
Parent: UPP Group Limited
Officers: Richard Antoine Bienfait [1967] Director; Henry Barnaby Gervaise Jones [1980] Director/Accountant; Mark Swindlehurst Swindlehurst [1969] Managing Director

UPP Bond 1 Issuer PLC
Incorporated: 16 October 2012
Net Worth: £5,777,000 *Total Assets:* £543,244,992
Registered Office: 40 Gracechurch Street, London, EC3V 0BT
Activities: Activities of other holding companies n.e.c.
Parent: UPP Bond 1 Limited
Officers: Richard Antoine Bienfait [1967] Director; Henry Barnaby Gervaise-Jones [1980] Director/Accountant

UPP Bond 1 Limited
Incorporated: 16 October 2012
Net Worth: £48,457,000 *Total Assets:* £256,740,000
Registered Office: 40 Gracechurch Street, London, EC3V 0BT
Activities: Activities of other holding companies n.e.c.
Parent: UPP Bond 1 Holdings Limited
Officers: Richard Antoine Bienfait [1967] Director; Henry Barnaby Gervaise-Jones [1980] Director/Accountant

UPP Group Holdings Limited
Incorporated: 15 January 2004 *Employees:* 777
Net Worth: £120,964,000 *Total Assets:* £2,126,075,008
Registered Office: 40 Gracechurch Street, London, EC3V 0BT
Activities: Activities of head offices
Shareholder: State Administration of Foreign Exchange
Officers: Richard Antoine Bienfait [1967] Director; Michael Andrew Bryan [1969] Director/Senior Investment Manager; Irina Anatoljevna Frolova [1971] Director/Senior Investment Manager [Dutch]; Henry Barnaby Gervaise-Jones [1980] Director/Accountant; Hendrik Luitje Huizing [1954] Director [Dutch]; Robert Sean McClatchey [1965] Director/Venture Capitalist; Paul Edward Milner [1965] Managing Director; Andrew William Percival [1972] Managing Director; Mark Swindlehurst Swindlehurst [1969] Managing Director; Andrew Scott Wilkie [1983] Director/Infrastructure Investment Management [Australian]

UPP Group Limited
Incorporated: 19 April 2007 *Employees:* 69
Net Worth: £266,038,000 *Total Assets:* £497,760,000
Registered Office: 40 Gracechurch Street, London, EC3V 0BT
Activities: Activities of head offices
Parent: UPP Group Holdings Limited
Officers: Richard Antoine Bienfait [1967] Director; Michael Eady [1957] Health and Safety Director; Henry Barnaby Gervaise-Jones [1980] Director/Accountant; Dr Paul Michael Marshall [1973] Director; Paul Edward Milner [1965] Managing Director; Andrew William Percival [1972] Managing Director; Kelly Stafford [1969] HR Director; Mark Swindlehurst Swindlehurst [1969] Managing Director

Urban & Civic Alconbury Limited
Incorporated: 7 April 2014 *Employees:* 4
Net Worth: £132,841,520 *Total Assets:* £243,914,512
Registered Office: 50 New Bond Street, London, W1S 1BJ
Activities: Development of building projects
Parent: Urban & Civic Alconbury S.A.R.L
Officers: Robin Elliott Butler [1959] Director; William Nigel Hugill [1958] Director; Philip Alexander Jeremy Leech [1963] Property Director; David Lewis Wood [1971] Director

Urban & Civic Central Funding Limited
Incorporated: 27 May 1999
Previous: PCG Residential Lettings Limited
Net Worth: £310,762,784 *Total Assets:* £333,050,432
Registered Office: 50 New Bond Street, London, W1S 1BJ
Activities: Buying and selling of own real estate
Parent: Urban & Civic PLC
Officers: Robin Elliott Butler [1959] Director; William Nigel Hugill [1958] Director; Philip Alexander Jeremy Leech [1963] Director; David Lewis Wood [1971] Director

Urban Exposure PLC
Incorporated: 10 April 2018
Net Worth: £157,858,000 *Total Assets:* £157,940,992
Registered Office: 6 Duke Street, St James's, London, SW1Y 6BN
Activities: Activities of other holding companies n.e.c.
Officers: Andrew Martin Baddeley [1964] Director; Trevor Keith Dacosta [1964] Director; Nigel Peter Greenaway [1960] Director; William Arthur McKee [1942] Director; Randeesh Singh Sandhu [1977] Director; Rabinder Singh Takhar [1965] Director

URBN Holdings UK Limited
Incorporated: 24 June 2015
Net Worth: £163,369,488 *Total Assets:* £163,606,176
Registered Office: 1 Finsbury Circus, London, EC2M 7SH
Activities: Activities of other holding companies n.e.c.
Parent: UK Group Finance Holdco Limited
Officers: Francis John Conforti [1976] Director/Chief Financial Officer [American]; Azeez Hayne [1977] Director/General Counsel [American]; Richard Allan Hayne [1947] Director/Chairman and Chief Executive Officer [American]

URBN International Operations Limited
Incorporated: 24 June 2015
Net Worth: £140,407,808 *Total Assets:* £140,417,920
Registered Office: 1 Finsbury Circus, London, EC2M 7SH
Activities: Activities of other holding companies n.e.c.
Parent: URBN Holdings UK Limited
Officers: Francis John Conforti [1976] Director/Chief Financial Officer [American]; Azeez Hayne [1977] Director/General Counsel [American]; Richard Allan Hayne [1947] Director/Chairman and Chief Executive Officer [American]

URBN UK Limited
Incorporated: 9 November 1995 *Employees:* 1,835
Net Worth: £93,702,200 *Total Assets:* £143,220,672
Registered Office: 1 Finsbury Circus, London, EC2M 7SH
Activities: Retail sale of clothing in specialised stores
Parent: URBN International Operations Limited
Officers: Elizabeth Field, Secretary; Francis John Conforti [1976] Director/Chief Financial Officer [American]; Azeez Hayne [1977] Director/General Counsel [American]; Richard Allan Hayne [1947] Director/Chairman President and Chief Executive [American]

Uropa Assets No. 1 Limited
Incorporated: 2 April 2007
Net Worth: £1,000 *Total Assets:* £364,286,016
Registered Office: 35 Great St Helen's, London, EC3A 6AP
Activities: Financial intermediation not elsewhere classified
Parent: Intertrust Corporate Services Limited
Officers: Paivi Helena Whitaker [1963] Director/Chartered Secretary [Finnish]

Uropa Assets No.2 Limited
Incorporated: 21 July 2008
Total Assets: £254,236,000
Registered Office: 35 Great St Helen's, London, EC3A 6AP
Activities: Non-trading company
Parent: Intertrust Corporate Services Limited
Officers: Paivi Helena Whitaker [1963] Director of SPVS [Finnish]

Uropa Holdings Limited
Incorporated: 2 April 2007
Net Worth: £1,000 *Total Assets:* £520,148,000
Registered Office: 35 Great St Helen's, London, EC3A 6AP
Activities: Non-trading company
Parent: Intertrust Corporate Services Limited
Officers: Paivi Helena Whitaker [1963] Director/Chartered Secretary [Finnish]

Uropa Securities PLC
Incorporated: 19 March 2007
Net Worth: £13,000 *Total Assets:* £520,148,000
Registered Office: 35 Great St Helen's, London, EC3A 6AP
Activities: Financial intermediation not elsewhere classified
Parent: Uropa Holdings Limited
Officers: Paivi Helena Whitaker [1963] Director/Chartered Secretary [Finnish]

URS Corporation Group Limited
Incorporated: 29 November 2005
Net Worth: £174,936,000 *Total Assets:* £207,976,000
Registered Office: St George's House, 5 St George's Road, Wimbledon, London, SW19 4DR
Activities: Activities of head offices
Parent: Universe Bidco Limited
Officers: Bolaji Moruf Taiwo, Secretary; Cheryl Rosalind McCall [1974] Director/Accountant; David John Price [1970] Director

US Real Estate Holdings No.1 Limited
Incorporated: 19 January 2016
Net Worth: £628,257,600 *Total Assets:* £634,552,512
Registered Office: 1 Churchill Place, London, E14 5HP
Activities: Buying and selling of own real estate
Parent: Real Estate Participation Services Limited
Officers: Neil Malcolm Grassie [1963] Director/Architect; Andrea Megnin [1975] Director/Project Manager [American]; Michelle Shu [1975] Director/Financial Controller [American]; Jai Westwood [1971] Director/Banking [American]; Neil Andrew Woodger [1969] Project Director

USAA Limited
Incorporated: 23 July 1962 *Employees:* 115
Net Worth: £93,589,000 *Total Assets:* £223,315,008
Registered Office: 4th Floor, Fitzwilliam House, 10 St Mary Axe, London, EC3A 8AE
Activities: Non-life insurance
Officers: Karen Morris, Secretary; Laura Ann Bishop [1961] Director/Accountant [American]; Michael Joseph Gaughan [1963] Director/Marketing Consultant [Irish]; Karen Elizabeth Graves [1965] Director; Simon Patrick Kendall Keith [1966] Director/General Manager; Jennifer MacNaughton [1964] Director/Vice President International Operations [American]; Steven Wayne Peacock [1958] Director/President USA Property and Casualty Group [American]; Craig Anthony Scarr [1962] Director/Chartered Accountant

UTB Partners Limited
Incorporated: 14 October 2003 *Employees:* 155
Net Worth: £106,344,000 *Total Assets:* £1,013,899,008
Registered Office: 28th Floor, One Ropemaker Street, London, EC2Y 9AW
Activities: Activities of financial services holding companies
Parent: Accuro Fiduciary Limited
Officers: Shane Clement Bannerton, Secretary; Alice Helene Ernesta Renee Altemaire [1977] Director [French]; Jonathan James Ayres [1971] Director; Tracy Marie Blackwell [1967] Director [Irish]; Nicholas Peter Clegg [1936] Director; Graham Harold Davin [1956] Director [South African]; Andrew William Herd [1958] Director; Harley Farrell Kagan [1969] Director; Michael Lewis [1959] Director; Stephen John Lockley [1958] Director; Ehsan Mani [1945] Director [Pakistani]; Anthony Noel Meredith [1955] Director of Sales; Richard Andrew Murley [1957] Director; Charles Roger Tidyman [1949] Director; Giles Alistair White [1975] Director/Investment Manager

V Acquisition Limited
Incorporated: 5 March 2015
Net Worth: £93,801,000 *Total Assets:* £1,615,800,960
Registered Office: Level 13, Broadgate Tower, 20 Primrose Street, London, EC2A 2EW
Activities: Activities of other holding companies n.e.c.
Parent: Verisk UK Holdco Limited
Officers: Kenneth Edward Thompson [1959] Director/Attorney [American]

V2 Music Group Limited
Incorporated: 30 May 1996
Net Worth: £942,196,992 *Total Assets:* £1,008,476,032
Registered Office: 4 Pancras Square, London, N1C 4AG
Activities: Reproduction of sound recording
Parent: Universal Music Holdings Limited
Officers: Abolanle Abioye, Secretary; Adam Martin Barker [1968] Director/Lawyer; David Richard James Sharpe [1967] Director/Chief Operating Officer [Irish]

Vacant Property Security Limited
Incorporated: 5 March 1993 *Employees:* 2
Net Worth: £38,291,000 *Total Assets:* £148,160,000
Registered Office: Third Floor, International Buildings, 71 Kingsway, London, WC2B 6ST
Activities: Activities of other holding companies n.e.c.
Parent: VPS Holdings Limited
Officers: Suzanne Claire Hardyman, Secretary; Darron William Cavanagh [1976] Director; Suzanne Claire Hardyman [1979] Director/Solicitor; Richard Jones [1972] Director; Lee Jon Newman [1973] Director

Val TM (Holdings) Limited
Incorporated: 30 January 2014 *Employees:* 5
Net Worth: £173,095,008 *Total Assets:* £173,100,992
Registered Office: The Battleship Building, 179 Harrow Road, London, W2 6NB
Activities: Non-trading company
Shareholders: Delta Air Lines, Inc; VEL Holdings Limited
Officers: Jefferey Allen Arinder [1970] Director [American]; William Carroll [1957] Director [American]; Peter Michael Russell Norris [1955] Director/Self Employed; Lisa Victoria Thomas [1967] Director/Marketing; Ian Philip Woods [1974] Director/Solicitor

Val TM Limited
Incorporated: 29 January 2014 *Employees:* 5
Net Worth: £176,796,992 *Total Assets:* £178,974,000
Registered Office: The Battleship Building, 179 Harrow Road, London, W2 6NB
Activities: Non-trading company
Parent: Val TM (Holdings) Limited
Officers: Jefferey Allen Arinder [1970] Director [American]; William Carroll [1957] Director [American]; Peter Michael Russell Norris [1955] Director/Self Employed; Lisa Victoria Thomas [1967] Director/Marketing; Ian Philip Woods [1974] Director/Solicitor

Vale Europe Limited
Incorporated: 22 July 1914 *Employees:* 304
Net Worth: £13,544,000 *Total Assets:* £205,186,000
Registered Office: Suite 1, 3rd Floor, 11-12 St James's Square, London, SW1Y 4LB
Activities: Other non-ferrous metal production
Parent: Vale Inco Europe Holdings
Officers: Michael James Cox [1967] Director/General Manager; Michael Edward McCann [1967] Director [Canadian]; Stephen Dennis Stacey [1960] Director/Refinery Manager; Dr Christopher Boyd Thomson [1967] Director/Refinery Manager; Benjamin Gareth Tipping [1982] Director/Finance Manager

Vale Inco Europe Holdings
Incorporated: 22 December 1999
Net Worth: £108,081,000 *Total Assets:* £108,081,000
Registered Office: Suite 1, 3rd Floor, 11-12 St James's Square, London, SW1Y 4LB
Activities: Non-trading company
Officers: Michael James Cox [1967] Director/General Manager; Michael Edward McCann [1967] Director [Canadian]

Valeo Foods UK Limited
Incorporated: 13 February 2014 *Employees:* 4
Net Worth: £144,002,000 *Total Assets:* £323,568,000
Registered Office: 35 Great St Helen's, London, EC3A 6AP
Activities: Activities of other holding companies n.e.c.
Officers: Ian Christopher Ainsworth [1963] Director; Penelope Kate Briant [1971] Director/Partner; Othmane Khelladi [1986] Director [French]; Jason Simon Rodrigues [1982] Director/Principal

Valero Energy Ltd
Incorporated: 12 June 2013 *Employees:* 702
Net Worth: £2,166,000,128 *Total Assets:* £3,494,400,000
Registered Office: 5th Floor, 100 Wood Street, London, EC2V 7EX
Activities: Activities of other holding companies n.e.c.
Parent: Valero Holdco UK Limited
Officers: Matthew Alan Dooley [1974] Director [American]; Eric Ashley Fisher [1968] Director [American]; Nicholas Elis Vaughan Roberts [1965] Director; Edward Tomp [1959] Director

Valero Energy UK Ltd
Incorporated: 31 October 1916
Net Worth: £123,803,000 *Total Assets:* £141,668,000
Registered Office: 5th Floor, 100 Wood Street, London, EC2V 7EX
Activities: Activities of other holding companies n.e.c.
Parent: Valero Energy Ltd
Officers: Matthew Alan Dooley [1974] Director [American]; Nicholas Elis Vaughan Roberts [1965] Director/Accountant

Valero Holdco UK Ltd
Incorporated: 24 February 2011
Net Worth: £651,886,016 *Total Assets:* £1,428,976,000
Registered Office: 5th Floor, 100 Wood Street, London, EC2V 7EX
Activities: Activities of financial services holding companies
Officers: Matthew Alan Dooley [1974] Director [American]; Nicholas Elis Vaughan Roberts [1965] Director/Energy Executive

Valero Logistics UK Ltd
Incorporated: 28 June 2013 *Employees:* 63
Net Worth: £67,429,000 *Total Assets:* £134,712,000
Registered Office: 5th Floor, 100 Wood Street, London, EC2V 7EX
Activities: Activities of other holding companies n.e.c.
Parent: Valero Energy Ltd
Officers: Matthew Alan Dooley [1974] Director [American]; Nicholas Elis Vaughan Roberts [1965] Director/Energy Executive; Edward Tomp [1959] Director/Vice President and General Manager; Neil Richard Watkins [1970] Director

Validus Holdings (UK) Ltd
Incorporated: 2 February 2012
Previous: Validus Holdings (UK) PLC
Net Worth: £878,765,504 *Total Assets:* £1,082,492,288
Registered Office: 60 Threadneedle Street, London, EC2R 8HP
Activities: Activities of head offices
Parent: American International General, Inc
Officers: Jane Sarah Clouting [1957] Director; Nigel David Wachman [1958] Director/Accountant

VAM Bidco Limited
Incorporated: 25 April 2014
Net Worth: £209,409,136 *Total Assets:* £809,517,184
Registered Office: Suite 1, 3rd Floor, 11-12 St James's Square, London, SW1Y 4LB
Activities: Activities of financial services holding companies
Parent: Affiliated Managers Group, Inc.
Officers: David Michael Billings [1962] Director [American]; Dean Aaron Maines [1970] Director [American]

Vancor Ltd
Incorporated: 2 November 2011
Net Worth: £178,859,360 *Total Assets:* £287,055,392
Registered Office: 2nd Floor, Whitehall House, 41 Whitehall, London, SW1A 2BY
Activities: Other professional, scientific and technical activities n.e.c.
Parent: Vancor Holding Limited
Officers: Giacomo Carcangiu [1961] Director [Italian]; Armin Poernbacher [1977] Director [Italian]

Vancouver Topco Limited
Incorporated: 13 May 2011 *Employees:* 1,093
Net Worth Deficit: £9,266,000 *Total Assets:* £139,754,000
Registered Office: Vineyard House, 44 Brook Green, Hammersmith, London, W6 7BT
Activities: Other publishing activities
Major Shareholder: Hubert Dietrich Burda
Officers: Katherine Conlon, Secretary; Thomas Pierre Bureau [1968] Director/C.E.O; Kevin Donald Langford [1964] Director/Accountant; Martin Weiss [1967] Managing Director [German]

Vanguard Asset Services, Ltd.
Incorporated: 4 May 2010 *Employees:* 404
Net Worth: £60,908,000 *Total Assets:* £145,336,000
Registered Office: 4th Floor, The Walbrook Building, 25 Walbrook, London, EC4N 8AF
Activities: Fund management activities
Officers: Katie Smith, Secretary; Nicholas Blake [1965] Director; Sean Patrick Hagerty [1961] Director [American]; Cynthia Lui [1970] Director [Australian]; James Maurice Norris [1963] Director [American]; Frank Lord Satterthwaite [1962] Director/Chief Financial Officer [American]

Vanta Education Holdings Limited
Incorporated: 1 June 2009
Previous: Apollo UK Acquisition Company Limited
Net Worth: £268,018,672 *Total Assets:* £322,304,160
Registered Office: One Wood Street, London, EC2V 7WS
Activities: Activities of head offices
Parent: Socrates Global Holdco Limited
Officers: Gregory Cappelli [1967] Director [American]; Mary Folline Morris Cullen [1966] Director/Finance Executive [American]

Vattenfall Wind Power Ltd
Incorporated: 10 April 2007 *Employees:* 226
Net Worth: £898,966,016 *Total Assets:* £998,950,976
Registered Office: First Floor, 1 Tudor Street, London, EC4Y 0AH
Activities: Production of electricity
Parent: Vattenfall Vindkraft AB
Officers: Sandra Leece, Secretary; Gunnar Groebler [1972] Director/Head of BU Renewables [German]; Danielle Claire Lane [1975] Director; Jonas Van Mansfeld [1976] Director Central Controlling [Dutch]; Robert Zurawski [1976] Director [German]

Vaultex UK Limited
Incorporated: 30 August 2007 *Employees:* 1,834
Net Worth: £14,878,000 *Total Assets:* £223,322,000
Registered Office: All Saints Triangle, Caledonian Road, London, N1 9UT
Activities: Activities auxiliary to financial intermediation n.e.c.
Shareholders: HSBC UK Bank PLC; Barclays Bank UK PLC
Officers: Mary Margaret McIntosh [1973] Director/Banker; Andrew Nash [1957] Director/Chairman; Christine Smith [1972] Director/Segments FD, Barclays; Philip Leslie Vaughan [1964] Director; Emanuele Vignoli [1971] Director/Banker [British/Italian]; Caroline Wallis [1976] Director/Regional Head of Operations, Europe

Vauxhall Square (Nominee 1) Limited
Incorporated: 8 February 2017
Net Worth Deficit: £2,526,351 *Total Assets:* £168,955,008
Registered Office: 3rd & 5th Floor, Sky Gardens Nine Elms, 153 Wandsworth Road, London, SW8 2GB
Activities: Other letting and operating of own or leased real estate
Parent: R & F Properties VS (UK) Co., Ltd.
Officers: Sze Lim Li [1957] Director [Chinese]; Ning Xia [1978] Director/Architect [Chinese]

Vector Industries Limited
Incorporated: 10 August 1993 *Employees:* 5
Net Worth: £85,295,000 *Total Assets:* £159,312,992
Registered Office: 8-12 York Gate, London, NW1 4QG
Activities: Non-trading company
Parent: Finance Holdings Limited
Officers: Jonathan Charles Richardson, Secretary/Director; Joseph Boucher [1983] Director/Chartered Accountant; Andrew Olaf Fischer [1964] Director [German]; Ian Fisher [1950] Director; Alan Thomas Fletcher [1934] Director; Jonathan Charles Richardson [1960] Director

Vectura Group Services Limited
Incorporated: 18 February 1910 *Employees:* 8
Previous: Skyepharma Limited
Net Worth: £228,000,000 *Total Assets:* £229,000,000
Registered Office: 46-48 Grosvenor Gardens, London, SW1W 0EB
Activities: Other business support service activities n.e.c.
Parent: Vectura Group PLC
Officers: John Murphy, Secretary; John Murphy [1953] Director/General Counsel; James Ward-Lilley [1965] Director/Chief Executive

Vedanta Finance UK Limited
Incorporated: 8 January 2014 *Employees:* 3
Net Worth: £232,784,096 *Total Assets:* £232,788,144
Registered Office: 5th Floor, 6 St Andrew Street, London, EC4A 3AE
Activities: Other business support service activities n.e.c.
Parent: Vedanta Resources Finance Limited
Officers: Deepak Kumar, Secretary; Deepak Kumar [1975] Director/Company Secretary; Mansoor Siddiqi [1953] Group Director - Projects [Indian]

Vedanta Resources Finance Limited
Incorporated: 25 November 2004 *Employees:* 2
Net Worth: £439,184,608 *Total Assets:* £440,369,376
Registered Office: 5th Floor, 6 St Andrew Street, London, EC4A 3AE
Activities: Other business support service activities n.e.c.
Parent: Vedanta Resources Holdings Limited
Officers: Deepak Kumar, Secretary; Deepak Kumar [1975] Director/Company Secretary; Mansoor Siddiqi [1953] Group Director - Projects [Indian]

Vedanta Resources Holdings Limited
Incorporated: 12 May 2003 *Employees:* 2
Net Worth: £913,821,248 *Total Assets:* £3,290,351,360
Registered Office: 5th Floor, 6 St Andrew Street, London, EC4A 3AE
Activities: Activities of head offices
Parent: Vedanta Resources Limited
Officers: Deepak Kumar, Secretary; Deepak Kumar [1975] Director/Company Secretary; Mansoor Siddiqi [1953] Group Director - Projects [Indian]

Vedanta Resources Limited
Incorporated: 22 April 2003 *Employees:* 25,083
Previous: Vedanta Resources PLC
Net Worth Deficit: £259,756,192 *Total Assets:* £22,416,928,768
Registered Office: 5th Floor, 6 St Andrew Street, London, EC4A 3AE
Activities: Other mining and quarrying n.e.c.
Officers: Deepak Kumar, Secretary; Anil Agarwal [1952] Director/Chairman [Indian]; Navin Agarwal [1961] Director/Industrialist [Indian]; Dr Geoffrey Stephen Green [1949] Director/Lawyer; Edward T Story Jnr [1943] Director/President/Chief Executive Officer [American]; Deepak Parekh [1944] Director Chairman [Indian]; Ravi Rajagopal [1953] Director/Consultant; Srinivasan Venkatakrishnan [1965] Director/Chief Executive Officer; Ekaterina Nikolaevna Zotova [1978] Director [Dutch]

VEL Holdings Limited
Incorporated: 4 January 2005
Net Worth: £406,824,000 *Total Assets:* £406,824,000
Registered Office: The Battleship Building, 179 Harrow Road, London, W2 6NB
Activities: Activities of other holding companies n.e.c.
Parent: Virgin Management Limited
Officers: Barry Alexander Ralph Gerrard, Secretary; Robert Pieter Blok [1976] Director/Lawyer; Matthew Downie Bridge [1978] Director/Investment Management; Amy Stirling [1969] Director; Ian Philip Woods [1974] Director/Solicitor

Veladail Hotels Limited
Incorporated: 13 September 1971 *Employees:* 292
Net Worth: £80,123,872 *Total Assets:* £171,877,040
Registered Office: 7-12 Half Moon Street, London, W1J 7BH
Activities: Hotels and similar accommodation
Shareholder: Satinder Kishore Gulhati
Officers: Sudha Gulhati, Secretary; Satinder Kishore Gulhati [1944] Director/Hotelier; Shagun Kishor Gulhati [1981] Director/Hotelier; Sudha Gulhati [1949] Director/Secretary

Venaglass Limited
Incorporated: 12 May 1976 *Employees:* 11
Net Worth: £92,202,464 *Total Assets:* £110,882,160
Registered Office: 3rd Floor, 12 Gough Square, London, EC4A 3DW
Activities: Buying and selling of own real estate
Shareholders: Bryan Anthony Joseph Radcliffe; Bracs (UK) Limited
Officers: Luke Robinson Orlando Bridgeman [1971] Director; Bryan Anthony Joseph Radcliffe [1941] Director/Solicitor; Jerome Henry Vaughan [1973] Director; John Francis Vaughan [1976] Director/Chartered Surveyor; Lorna Patricia Vaughan [1945] Director/Secretary; Patrick Vaughan [1943] Director/Chartered Surveyor

Ventient Energy Limited
Incorporated: 1 February 2017 *Employees:* 24
Net Worth: £195,070,000 *Total Assets:* £1,232,311,040
Registered Office: c/o Morton Fraser, St Martins House, 16 St Martin's-le-Grand, London, EC1A 4EN
Activities: Non-trading company
Parent: Mobius Renewables Holdco Limited
Officers: Leanne Marie Bell [1960] Director [American]; Mark Richard Jones [1966] Director; Olov Mikael Kramer [1953] Director [Swedish]; Andrew William Lee [1957] Director/Chartered Accountant; Steen Stavnsbo [1964] Director [Danish]; Mark Alan Walters [1979] Director

Veolia Environmental Services (UK) PLC
Incorporated: 1 February 1988 *Employees:* 12,573
Net Worth: £602,427,008 *Total Assets:* £2,317,003,008
Registered Office: 210 Pentonville Road, London, N1 9JY
Activities: Activities of head offices
Parent: Veolia ES Holdings (UK) Limited
Officers: Celia Rosalind Gough, Secretary; John Patrick Abraham [1968] Director; Estelle Karine Brachlianoff [1972] Executive Director [French]; David Andrew Gerrard [1964] Executive Director; Celia Rosalind Gough [1975] Director/Solicitor; Gavin Howard Graveson [1963] Executive Director; Kevin Anthony Hurst [1958] Director/Chief Operations Officer, Industrial Customers; Carine Isabelle Kraus [1979] Director/Chief of Staff to The Chairman & CEO [French]

Veolia ES (UK) Limited
Incorporated: 16 March 1990 *Employees:* 9,931
Net Worth: £78,579,000 *Total Assets:* £598,864,000
Registered Office: 210 Pentonville Road, London, N1 9JY
Activities: Activities of other holding companies n.e.c.
Parent: Veolia Environmental Services (UK) PLC
Officers: Celia Rosalind Gough, Secretary; John Patrick Abraham [1968] Director; David Andrew Gerrard [1964] Executive Director; Celia Rosalind Gough [1975] Director/Solicitor; Gavin Howard Graveson [1963] Executive Director; Kevin Anthony Hurst [1958] Director/Chief Operations Officer, Industrial Customers; Marguerite Alice Ulrich [1961] HR Director [American]

Veolia ES Holdings (UK) Limited
Incorporated: 28 May 1997 *Employees:* 7
Net Worth: £204,584,000 *Total Assets:* £1,007,881,984
Registered Office: 210 Pentonville Road, London, N1 9JY
Activities: Activities of other holding companies n.e.c.
Parent: Veolia UK Limited
Officers: Celia Rosalind Gough, Secretary; John Patrick Abraham [1968] Director; Estelle Karine Brachlianoff [1972] Executive Director [French]; David Andrew Gerrard [1964] Executive Director; Celia Rosalind Gough [1975] Director/Solicitor; Gavin Howard Graveson [1963] Executive Director; Kevin Anthony Hurst [1958] Director/Chief Operations Officer, Industrial Customers

Veolia ES Landfill Limited
Incorporated: 22 December 1970 *Employees:* 151
Net Worth: £27,140,000 *Total Assets:* £205,944,000
Registered Office: 210 Pentonville Road, London, N1 9JY
Activities: Other business support service activities n.e.c.
Parent: Veolia Environmental Services (UK) PLC
Officers: James Thomas Condliffe, Secretary; Neil Vincent Gallagher [1963] Finance Director; David Andrew Gerrard [1964] Executive Director; Celia Rosalind Gough [1975] Director/Solicitor; Gavin Howard Graveson [1963] Managing Director; Donald John Fraser MacPhail [1967] Regional Director

Veolia ES Leeds Limited
Incorporated: 9 December 2011 *Employees:* 66
Net Worth Deficit: £3,523,000 *Total Assets:* £150,388,000
Registered Office: 210 Pentonville Road, London, N1 9JY
Activities: Collection of non-hazardous waste
Parent: Veolia ES Aurora Limited
Officers: James Thomas Condliffe, Secretary; Christophe Bellynck [1961] Director [French]; Neil Vincent Gallagher [1963] Finance Director; David Andrew Gerrard [1964] Director; Philip Gilmour [1959] Regional Director

Veolia ES Shropshire Limited
Incorporated: 23 May 2007 *Employees:* 313
Net Worth: £28,252,000 *Total Assets:* £124,645,000
Registered Office: 210 Pentonville Road, London, N1 9JY
Activities: Collection of non-hazardous waste
Parent: Veolia ES Aurora Limited
Officers: James Thomas Condliffe, Secretary; Christophe Bellynck [1961] Director [French]; Neil Vincent Gallagher [1963] Finance Director; David Andrew Gerrard [1964] Executive Director; Donald John Fraser MacPhail [1967] Regional Director

Veolia ES Staffordshire Limited
Incorporated: 19 May 2010 *Employees:* 40
Net Worth: £25,321,000 *Total Assets:* £217,980,000
Registered Office: 210 Pentonville Road, London, N1 9JY
Activities: Collection of non-hazardous waste
Parent: Veolia ES Aurora Limited
Officers: James Thomas Condliffe, Secretary; Christophe Bellynck [1961] Director [French]; Neil Vincent Gallagher [1963] Finance Director; David Andrew Gerrard [1964] Financial Director; Donald John Fraser MacPhail [1967] Regional Director

Veolia UK Limited
Incorporated: 21 November 1991 *Employees:* 7
Previous: Veolia Environnement UK Limited
Net Worth: £807,520,000 *Total Assets:* £3,350,782,976
Registered Office: 210 Pentonville Road, London, N1 9JY
Activities: Activities of head offices
Parent: Veolia Environnement SA
Officers: Celia Rosalind Gough, Secretary; Estelle Karine Brachlianoff [1972] Executive Director [French]; David Andrew Gerrard [1964] Director/Chief Financial Officer; Gavin Howard Graveson [1963] Executive Director; Claude Olivier Francois Laruelle [1967] Director of Global Enterprises [French]; Jean-Francois Andre Nogrette [1968] Managing Director, Veolia Water Technologies [French]; Helene Petit [1967] Director [French]

Veolia Water Enterprise Limited
Incorporated: 26 November 2007 *Employees:* 4
Net Worth: £197,000 *Total Assets:* £160,223,008
Registered Office: 210 Pentonville Road, London, N1 9JY
Activities: Activities of head offices
Parent: Veolia Water UK Limited
Officers: Celia Rosalind Gough, Secretary; John Patrick Abraham [1968] Director; David Andrew Gerrard [1964] Executive Director; Celia Rosalind Gough [1975] Director/Solicitor

Veolia Water Outsourcing Limited
Incorporated: 4 July 1990 *Employees:* 249
Net Worth: £65,305,000 *Total Assets:* £138,582,000
Registered Office: 210 Pentonville Road, London, N1 9JY
Activities: Water collection, treatment and supply
Parent: Veolia Water Enterprise Limited
Officers: Elaine Margaret Aitken, Secretary; John Patrick Abraham [1968] Director; Xavier Aragon [1970] Director/Engineer [French]; Caroline Garrett [1976] Director/Solicitor; David Andrew Gerrard [1964] Executive Director; Celia Rosalind Gough [1975] Director/Solicitor; Tracy Jayne Knipe [1968] Finance Director; Dr Adrian Graham Mercer [1969] Technical Director, Water; Sinead Isobel Patton [1975] Finance Director [Irish]; Mark Andrew Wilson [1968] Northern Director

Veolia Water UK Limited
Incorporated: 1 May 1987 *Employees:* 28
Net Worth: £139,840,000 *Total Assets:* £189,986,000
Registered Office: 210 Pentonville Road, London, N1 9JY
Activities: Activities of head offices
Parent: Veolia UK Limited
Officers: Celia Rosalind Gough, Secretary; John Patrick Abraham [1968] Director; Estelle Karine Brachlianoff [1972] Executive Director [French]; David Andrew Gerrard [1964] Executive Director; Celia Rosalind Gough [1975] Director/Solicitor; Gavin Howard Graveson [1963] Executive Director

Verbena Investment Limited
Incorporated: 20 December 2013 *Employees:* 2
Net Worth: £107,563,952 *Total Assets:* £107,566,376
Registered Office: Hill House, 1 Little New Street, London, EC4A 3TR
Activities: Other service activities n.e.c.
Major Shareholder: Henri Biard
Officers: Karl Guenard [1967] Director/Company Secretary [French]; Didier Sabbatucci [1971] Director/Solicitor [French]

Verdoso Holdings Limited
Incorporated: 19 May 2000 *Employees:* 2
Net Worth: £76,489,808 *Total Assets:* £111,656,312
Registered Office: Connect House, 133-137 Alexandra Road, Wimbledon, London, SW19 7JY
Activities: Activities of investment trusts
Major Shareholder: Franck Ullmann-Hamon
Officers: Anne-Luce Julsaint-Buonomo, Secretary; Vincent Fahmy [1974] Director/Company Administrator [French]; Franck Ullmann Hamon [1953] Director [French]

Verisk UK Holdco Limited
Incorporated: 1 May 2015
Net Worth: £404,982,016 *Total Assets:* £573,934,976
Registered Office: Level 13, Broadgate Tower, 20 Primrose Street, London, EC2A 2EW
Activities: Activities of other holding companies n.e.c.
Parent: Verisk Analytics, Inc
Officers: Kenneth Edward Thompson [1959] Director/Attorney [American]

Versum Materials UK Limited
Incorporated: 11 November 2015
Net Worth: £157,788,000 *Total Assets:* £351,856,992
Registered Office: 5th Floor, 6 St Andrew Street, London, EC4A 3AE
Activities: Wholesale of chemical products
Officers: Michael Valente, Secretary; John Frederick Buckwalter [1966] Director/Accountant [American]; Stuart Richard Ryder [1961] Sales Director [Irish]; Arnoud Stibane [1979] Director/General Manager [Dutch]; Michael Valente [1968] Director/Attorney [American]

Vertex Pharmaceuticals (Europe) Limited
Incorporated: 11 March 1994 *Employees:* 241
Net Worth: £692,181,248 *Total Assets:* £1,581,478,144
Registered Office: 2 Kingdom Street, London, W2 6BD
Activities: Other research and experimental development on natural sciences and engineering
Parent: Vertex Pharmaceuticals Incorporated
Officers: Michele Bellandi [1967] Director/Pharmaceutical Executive [Italian]; Simon Kempin Lem [1973] Director/Country Manager; Ian Frederick Smith [1966] Director/CFO of Vertex Pharmaceuticals Inc

Vertice Pharma UK Parent Limited
Incorporated: 21 October 2015 *Employees:* 178
Net Worth: £66,713,376 *Total Assets:* £224,279,200
Registered Office: 25 Moorgate, London, EC2R 6AY
Activities: Activities of other holding companies n.e.c.
Officers: Don Degolyer, Secretary; Cem Behmoaram de Toledo [1986] Director/Investment Professional [Spanish]; Ruoxi Chen [1983] Director/Investment Professional [American]; Don Degolyer [1981] Director/General Manager [American]; Rianne Caroline Schipper [1991] Director/Investment Professional [Dutch]

Vertus NFL Limited
Incorporated: 27 February 2015 *Employees:* 3
Net Worth Deficit: £38,236,496 *Total Assets:* £247,151,248
Registered Office: One Canary Wharf, London, E14 5AB
Activities: Development of building projects
Parent: Vertus NFL Properties Limited
Officers: John Raymond Garwood, Secretary; Peter a Anderson II [1953] Director/Real Estate Executive [American]; George Iacobescu [1945] Director; Russell James John Lyons [1961] Director

Vesuvius Ceramics Limited
Incorporated: 30 April 1919
Previous: Cookson Ceramics Limited
Net Worth: £208,358,000 *Total Assets:* £208,358,000
Registered Office: 165 Fleet Street, London, EC4A 2AE
Activities: Activities of other holding companies n.e.c.
Parent: Wilkes-Lucas Limited
Officers: Jennifer Smith, Secretary; Henry James Knowles [1969] Director/General Counsel and Company Secretary; Ian James Lawson [1968] Director/Accountant; Simon Christopher Upcott [1958] Director/Tax Manager

Vesuvius Holdings Limited
Incorporated: 12 November 1930 *Employees:* 33
Net Worth: £2,192,086,016 *Total Assets:* £3,621,038,080
Registered Office: 165 Fleet Street, London, EC4A 2AE
Activities: Activities of head offices
Parent: Vesuvius PLC
Officers: Jennifer Smith, Secretary; Patrick Georges Felix Andre [1963] Director/Chief Executive [French]; Euan Gunn Drysdale [1977] Director/Group Head of Corporate Finance; Henry James Knowles [1969] Director/General Counsel and Company Secretary; Ian James Lawson [1968] Director/Accountant; Agnieszka Tomczak [1966] Director/Chief Human Resources Officer [Polish]; Simon Christopher Upcott [1958] Director/Tax Manager; Guy Franklin Young [1969] Director/Chief Financial Officer [South African]

Vesuvius Investments Limited
Incorporated: 30 December 1949 *Employees:* 3
Previous: Cookson Investments Limited
Net Worth: £340,753,984 *Total Assets:* £340,753,984
Registered Office: 165 Fleet Street, London, EC4A 2AE
Activities: Activities of other holding companies n.e.c.
Parent: Vesuvius Overseas Limited
Officers: Jennifer Smith, Secretary; Henry James Knowles [1969] Director/General Counsel and Company Secretary; Ian James Lawson [1968] Director/Accountant; Simon Christopher Upcott [1958] Director/Tax Manager

Vesuvius Overseas Limited
Incorporated: 20 January 1928
Previous: Cookson Overseas Limited
Net Worth: £984,673,984 *Total Assets:* £1,155,239,040
Registered Office: 165 Fleet Street, London, EC4A 2AE
Activities: Activities of other holding companies n.e.c.
Parent: Vesuvius Holdings Limited
Officers: Jennifer Smith, Secretary; Henry James Knowles [1969] Director/General Counsel and Company Secretary; Ian James Lawson [1968] Director/Accountant; Simon Christopher Upcott [1958] Director/Tax Manager

Vesuvius PLC
Incorporated: 17 September 2012 *Employees:* 10,974
Net Worth: £1,028,700,032 *Total Assets:* £2,072,400,000
Registered Office: 165 Fleet Street, London, EC4A 2AE
Activities: Activities of head offices
Officers: Henry James Knowles, Secretary; Patrick Georges Felix Andre [1963] Director/Chief Executive [French]; Christer Goran Harald Gardell [1960] Director [Swedish]; Hock Goh [1955] Director/Engineer [Singaporean]; Ida Jane Hinkley [1950] Director; Douglas Malcolm Hurt [1956] Director; Holly Keller Koeppel [1958] Director [American]; John McDonough [1951] Director; Guy Franklin Young [1969] Director/Chief Financial Officer [South African]

Vetco Gray Holding
Incorporated: 31 October 2006
Net Worth: £515,325,280 *Total Assets:* £559,470,912
Registered Office: The Arc, 201 Talgarth Road, Hammersmith, London, W6 8BJ
Activities: Activities of head offices
Parent: GE Industrial (UK) Holdings
Officers: Alasdair Murray Campbell Sloan [1967] Director

Vetco International Holding 4
Incorporated: 9 July 2003
Net Worth: £558,971,840 *Total Assets:* £558,971,840
Registered Office: The Arc, 201 Talgarth Road, Hammersmith, London, W6 8BJ
Activities: Activities of head offices
Parent: Vetco Gray Holding
Officers: Alasdair Murray Campbell Sloan [1967] Director

Viacom Camden Lock Limited
Incorporated: 28 January 2010 *Employees:* 15
Net Worth: £3,141,606,912 *Total Assets:* £5,074,217,984
Registered Office: 17-29 Hawley Crescent, London, NW1 8TT
Activities: Other letting and operating of own or leased real estate
Parent: Viacom Inc.
Officers: James Robert Currell [1971] Director/Accountant; Paul Dunthorne [1967] Director/Chief Operating Officer; Timothy Stevenson [1954] Director/Corporate Real Estate [American]

Vibe Corporate Member Limited
Incorporated: 6 November 2006
Net Worth Deficit: £22,728,000 *Total Assets:* £246,222,000
Registered Office: 90 Fenchurch Street, London, EC3M 4ST
Activities: Non-life insurance
Parent: Niro Underwriting Limited
Officers: Paul Ernest Box, Secretary; Paul Stephen Donovan [1974] Director/Chief Operating Officer; Dr Alex Anatol Fridlyand [1967] Director/Banker [American]; Alexander Edward Williams [1975] Director/Chartered Accountant

Victoria Asset Finance Limited
Incorporated: 20 March 2015
Net Worth Deficit: £4,385,000 *Total Assets:* £216,208,992
Registered Office: Camelford House, 89 Albert Embankment, London, SE1 7TP
Activities: Financial leasing
Parent: LC Asset 1 S.A.R.L
Officers: Selina Lee Burdell [1969] Director; Adrian Richard Cloake [1975] Director/Accountant; Hitesh Shah [1979] Director/Investment Manager

Victoria Investments Bidco Limited
Incorporated: 19 January 2015
Net Worth: £347,508,992 *Total Assets:* £644,963,968
Registered Office: 120 Holborn, London, EC1N 2TD
Activities: Activities of head offices
Parent: Victoria Investments Midco Limited
Officers: Neil Anthony Murrin, Secretary; Philipp Freise [1973] Director [German]; Clare Gilmartin [1975] Director [Irish]; Franziska Kayser [1987] Director/Private Equity [German]; Shaun McCabe [1968] Finance Director; Douglas Stuart McCallum [1966] Director; Martin Mignot [1984] Director [French]; Andrew James Phillipps [1968] Director; Lucian Schonefelder [1979] Director [German]

Victoria Investments Finco Limited
Incorporated: 19 January 2015 *Employees:* 553
Net Worth Deficit: £132,694,000 *Total Assets:* £677,012,992
Registered Office: 120 Holborn, London, EC1N 2TD
Activities: Activities of head offices
Parent: Victoria Intermediate Topco Limited
Officers: Neil Murrin, Secretary; Franziska Kayser [1987] Director/Private Equity [German]; Shaun McCabe [1968] Finance Director; Lucian Schonefelder [1979] Director [German]

Victoria Investments Intermediate Holdco Limited
Incorporated: 20 February 2015
Net Worth: £341,142,016 *Total Assets:* £367,176,000
Registered Office: 120 Holborn, London, EC1N 2TD
Activities: Activities of head offices
Parent: Victoria Investments Finco Limited
Officers: Neil Murrin, Secretary; Philipp Freise [1973] Director [German]; Clare Gilmartin [1975] Director [Irish]; Franziska Kayser [1987] Director/Private Equity [German]; Shaun McCabe [1968] Finance Director; Douglas Stuart McCallum [1966] Director; Martin Mignot [1984] Director [French]; Andrew James Phillipps [1968] Director; Lucian Schonefelder [1979] Director [German]

Victoria Investments Midco Limited
Incorporated: 19 January 2015
Net Worth: £366,734,016 *Total Assets:* £423,276,000
Registered Office: 120 Holborn, London, EC1N 2TD
Activities: Activities of head offices
Parent: Victoria Investments PIKco Limited
Officers: Neil Murrin, Secretary; Franziska Kayser [1987] Director/Private Equity [German]; Shaun McCabe [1968] Finance Director; Lucian Schonefelder [1979] Director [German]

Victoria Investments PIKco Limited
Incorporated: 28 January 2016
Net Worth: £83,487,000 *Total Assets:* £143,482,000
Registered Office: 120 Holborn, London, EC1N 2TD
Activities: Other business support service activities n.e.c.
Parent: Victoria Investments Intermediate Holdco Limited
Officers: Neil Murrin, Secretary; Franziska Kayser [1987] Director/Private Equity [German]; Shaun McCabe [1968] Finance Director; Lucian Schoenefelder [1979] Director [German]

Victoria Oil & Gas PLC
Incorporated: 27 May 2004 *Employees:* 164
Net Worth: £82,749,528 *Total Assets:* £117,908,848
Registered Office: 200 Strand, London, WC2R 1DJ
Activities: Extraction of natural gas
Officers: Leena Nagrecha, Secretary; John Bryant [1946] Director; Andrew Lee Diamond [1975] Director/Chartered Accountant; Ahmet Dik [1973] Director [Australian]; Kevin Alfred Foo [1949] Director [Australian]; Roger Cameron Kennedy [1963] Director [American]

Victoria's Secret UK Limited
Incorporated: 9 June 2010 *Employees:* 1,254
Net Worth: £85,673,000 *Total Assets:* £131,980,000
Registered Office: 16 Garrick Street, London, WC2E 9BA
Activities: Other letting and operating of own or leased real estate
Parent: Intimate Brands Management Limited
Officers: Timothy James Faber [1961] Director/Business Executive [American]; Todd Gregory Helvie [1963] Director/Tax Executive [American]; Mark R Koenig [1964] Director [American]

Viking Consortium Acquisition Limited
Incorporated: 25 January 2007 *Employees:* 290
Net Worth Deficit: £173,748,992 *Total Assets:* £608,558,976
Registered Office: 2 Coldbath Square, London, EC1R 5HL
Activities: Activities of head offices
Parent: Denmark Holdco Limited
Officers: Tess Bridgman, Secretary; Benjamin James Butler [1981] Director; Andrew Robert Pike [1975] Director; Charles Nicholas Pollard [1958] Director; Julian William Walker [1973] Director/Chief Operating Officer

VIL Ltd
Incorporated: 28 April 2015 *Employees:* 2,854
Net Worth: £139,832,768 *Total Assets:* £265,902,832
Registered Office: 6th Floor, 2 Kingdom Street, London, W2 6JP
Activities: Wholesale of household goods (other than musical instruments) n.e.c
Officers: Roger David Box [1978] Director/Marketing [Australian]; Sophie Campeau [1976] Director/Chief Financial Officer [Canadian]; Thomas James Denny Cripps [1979] Director, Venture Capitalist, Real Estate Investor [Australian]; Benjamin Daniel John Lucas [1973] Director/Chief Investment Officer; Jeffery Michael Malcolm [1954] Director [American]; Peter Albert Pelletier [1947] Director [American]; Amy Louise Tennent [1977] Director/Executive Vice President [Australian]

Vine Acquisitions Limited
Incorporated: 8 December 2016 *Employees:* 4
Net Worth Deficit: £1,154,000 *Total Assets:* £113,883,000
Registered Office: 54 Portland Place, London, W1B 1DY
Activities: Other business support service activities n.e.c.
Officers: Edward Michael Bashforth, Secretary; Noah Aaron Bulkin [1977] Director; Gautam Chhabra [1983] Director; Stephen Edward Timothy Green [1967] Director; Shane Edward Law [1972] Director

Viners Energy Limited
Incorporated: 23 June 2015
Net Worth Deficit: £66,234,000 *Total Assets:* £696,017,024
Registered Office: 6th Floor, 33 Holborn, London, EC1N 2HT
Activities: Activities of head offices
Parent: Elios Renewable Energy Limited
Officers: Jonathan Charles Nigel Digges [1970] Director; David Hastings [1966] Director; Paul Stephen Latham [1956] Director; Matthew George Setchell [1977] Director

Violin Debtco Limited
Incorporated: 21 October 2013
Net Worth: £452,328,992 *Total Assets:* £452,353,984
Registered Office: 6 Chesterfield Gardens, London, W1J 5BQ
Activities: Activities of head offices
Parent: Violin Topco Limited
Officers: Rehana Hasan, Secretary; Paul Richard Armstrong [1973] Director/Finance Executive; Andrew Martin Baddeley [1964] Director; Christopher Jon Pell [1978] Director/Finance Executive; Christopher Woodhouse [1961] Director/Chief Executive Officer

Violin Equityco Limited
Incorporated: 21 October 2013
Net Worth: £445,712,000 *Total Assets:* £445,712,000
Registered Office: 6 Chesterfield Gardens, London, W1J 5BQ
Activities: Activities of head offices
Parent: Violin Debtco Limited
Officers: Rehana Hasan, Secretary; Andrew Martin Baddeley [1964] Director; Philip Sebastian Muelder [1974] Director/Partner [German]; Christopher Jon Pell [1978] Director/Finance Executive; Christopher Woodhouse [1961] Director/Chief Executive Officer

Violin Topco Limited
Incorporated: 21 October 2013 *Employees:* 1,227
Net Worth: £435,487,008 *Total Assets:* £944,281,024
Registered Office: 6 Chesterfield Gardens, London, W1J 5BQ
Activities: Activities of head offices
Shareholders: Alexlux S.A.R.L; Carey Pensions and Benefits Limited
Officers: Rehana Hasan, Secretary; Andrew Martin Baddeley [1964] Director; Philip Sebastian Muelder [1974] Director/Partner [German]; Christopher Jon Pell [1978] Director/Finance Executive; Christopher Woodhouse [1961] Director/Chief Executive Officer

Virgin Active Group Investments Limited
Incorporated: 8 January 2002
Net Worth: £581,766,976 *Total Assets:* £581,766,976
Registered Office: 100 Aldersgate Street, London, EC1A 4LX
Activities: Operation of sports facilities
Shareholders: Virgin Active Health Club Holdings Limited; Virgin Active Group Limited
Officers: Ashley John Aylmer, Secretary; Matthew William Bucknall [1960] Director; Johanna Ruth Hartley [1975] Director

Virgin Active Group Limited
Incorporated: 20 November 1991
Net Worth: £657,038,976 *Total Assets:* £663,260,032
Registered Office: 100 Aldersgate Street, London, EC1A 4LX
Activities: Activities of head offices
Parent: Virgin Active Health Club Holdings Limited
Officers: Ashley John Aylmer, Secretary; Matthew William Bucknall [1960] Director; Johanna Ruth Hartley [1975] Director

Virgin Active Health Club Holdings Limited
Incorporated: 2 August 2011
Net Worth: £272,432,000 *Total Assets:* £934,118,016
Registered Office: 100 Aldersgate Street, London, EC1A 4LX
Activities: Activities of head offices
Parent: Virgin Active International Limited
Officers: Ashley John Aylmer, Secretary; Matthew William Bucknall [1960] Director; Johanna Ruth Hartley [1975] Director

Virgin Active Holdings Limited
Incorporated: 11 August 1998
Net Worth: £156,752,000 *Total Assets:* £501,740,992
Registered Office: 100 Aldersgate Street, London, EC1A 4LX
Activities: Activities of head offices
Parent: Virgin Active Investment Holdings Limited
Officers: Ashley John Aylmer, Secretary; Matthew William Bucknall [1960] Director; Johanna Ruth Hartley [1975] Director

Virgin Active International Limited
Incorporated: 2 August 2011 *Employees:* 11,238
Previous: Virgin Active Health Fitness & Racquets Limited
Net Worth Deficit: £77,400,000 *Total Assets:* £944,099,968
Registered Office: 100 Aldersgate Street, London, EC1A 4LX
Activities: Activities of head offices
Parent: Brait SE
Officers: Ashley John Aylmer, Secretary; Matthew William Bucknall [1960] Director; Johanna Ruth Hartley [1975] Director

Virgin Active Investment Holdings Limited
Incorporated: 10 September 2007
Net Worth: £524,923,008 *Total Assets:* £524,923,008
Registered Office: 100 Aldersgate Street, London, EC1A 4LX
Activities: Activities of head offices
Parent: Virgin Active Group Investments Limited
Officers: Ashley John Aylmer, Secretary; Matthew William Bucknall [1960] Director; Johanna Ruth Hartley [1975] Director

Virgin Active Limited
Incorporated: 13 October 1997 *Employees:* 4,999
Net Worth: £161,694,000 *Total Assets:* £360,310,016
Registered Office: 100 Aldersgate Street, London, EC1A 4LX
Activities: Other amusement and recreation activities n.e.c.
Parent: Virgin Active Holdings Limited
Officers: James Hugh Culver Archibald, Secretary; Matthew William Bucknall [1960] Director; David Anthony Rowland Carter [1970] Finance Director; Robert Barclay Cook [1966] UK Managing Director; Johanna Ruth Hartley [1975] Director

Virgin Active South Africa Holdings Limited
Incorporated: 24 November 2011
Net Worth: £268,690,464 *Total Assets:* £296,040,544
Registered Office: 100 Aldersgate Street, London, EC1A 4LX
Activities: Activities of head offices
Parent: Virgin Active Gyms
Officers: Ashley John Aylmer, Secretary; Ross Andrew Faragher-Thomas [1967] Managing Director [Irish]; Norman Mark Field [1970] Finance Director [South African]

Virgin Gyms Limited
Incorporated: 27 June 2006
Net Worth: £185,587,488 *Total Assets:* £292,941,664
Registered Office: 100 Aldersgate Street, London, EC1A 4LX
Activities: Activities of head offices
Parent: Virgin Active Health Club Holdings Limited
Officers: Ashley John Aylmer, Secretary; Matthew William Bucknall [1960] Director; Johanna Ruth Hartley [1975] Director

Virgin Holdings Limited
Incorporated: 29 July 1998 *Employees:* 9,760
Net Worth: £323,000,000 *Total Assets:* £892,000,000
Registered Office: The Battleship Building, 179 Harrow Road, London, W2 6NB
Activities: Activities of other holding companies n.e.c.
Parent: Classboss Limited
Officers: Barry Alexander Ralph Gerrard, Secretary; Robert Pieter Blok [1976] Director/Lawyer; Matthew Downie Bridge [1978] Director/Investment Management; Amy Stirling [1969] Director; Ian Philip Woods [1974] Director/Solicitor

Virgin Management Limited
Incorporated: 18 June 1981 *Employees:* 127
Net Worth: £1,310,472,960 *Total Assets:* £1,328,526,976
Registered Office: The Battleship Building, 179 Harrow Road, London, W2 6NB
Activities: Activities of other holding companies n.e.c.
Parent: Virgin Holdings Limited
Officers: Barry Alexander Ralph Gerrard, Secretary; Robert Pieter Blok [1976] Director/Lawyer; Amy Stirling [1969] Director; Lisa Victoria Thomas [1967] Director/Marketing; Ian Philip Woods [1974] Director/Solicitor

Virgin Models Limited
Incorporated: 27 April 1989
Net Worth: £1,040,396,032 *Total Assets:* £1,041,555,968
Registered Office: The Battleship Building, 179 Harrow Road, London, W2 6NB
Activities: Activities of other holding companies n.e.c.
Parent: Virgin Group Limited
Officers: Barry Alexander Ralph Gerrard, Secretary; Robert Pieter Blok [1976] Director/Lawyer; Ian Philip Woods [1974] Director/Solicitor

Virgin Music Group
Incorporated: 17 May 1988
Net Worth Deficit: £2,126,526,976 *Total Assets:* £4,610,822,144
Registered Office: 4 Pancras Square, London, N1C 4AG
Activities: Artistic creation
Parent: EMI Group Limited
Officers: Abolanle Abioye, Secretary; Simon Lloyd Carmel [1973] Director/Solicitor; Paramjit Jassal [1963] Director/Chief Financial Officer - Finance Operations; Boyd Johnston Muir [1959] Director/EVP & CFO

Virgin Rail Group Holdings Limited
Incorporated: 9 April 2001 *Employees:* 3,289
Net Worth: £55,895,000 *Total Assets:* £172,272,000
Registered Office: The Battleship Building, 179 Harrow Road, London, W2 6NB
Activities: Passenger rail transport, interurban
Shareholders: Virgin Holdings Limited; Stagecoach Rail Holdings Limited
Officers: Barry Alexander Ralph Gerrard, Secretary; Peter James Broadley [1971] Customer, Operations and Safety Director; Sarah Jane Copley [1973] Executive Director, Commercial; Martin Andrew Griffiths [1966] Finance Director; Caroline Suzanne Marsh [1963] International Development Director; Patrick Charles Kingdon McCall [1964] Corporate Operations Director; Ross John Paterson [1971] Director/Accountant; Mark Edward Whitehouse [1979] Executive Director Finance; Philip Whittingham [1971] Finance Director

Virgin Records Limited
Incorporated: 8 September 1972
Net Worth: £991,222,976 *Total Assets:* £1,039,337,024
Registered Office: 4 Pancras Square, London, N1C 4AG
Activities: Artistic creation
Parent: Virgin Music Group
Officers: Abolanle Abioye, Secretary; Adam Martin Barker [1968] Director/Lawyer; Emma Jane Berkeley [1973] Director/Accountant; Edward John Cockle [1972] Director/Co-President; Boyd Johnston Muir [1959] Director/EVP & CFO; David Richard James Sharpe [1967] Director/Chief Operating Officer [Irish]

Virgin Records Overseas Limited
Incorporated: 5 January 1938
Net Worth: £301,772,992 *Total Assets:* £556,294,016
Registered Office: 4 Pancras Square, London, N1C 4AG
Activities: Activities of head offices
Parent: EMI Group Worldwide
Officers: Abolanle Abioye, Secretary; Simon Lloyd Carmel [1973] Director/Solicitor; Paramjit Jassal [1963] Director/Chief Financial Officer - Finance Operations; Boyd Johnston Muir [1959] Director/EVP & CFO

Virgin UK Holdings Limited
Incorporated: 19 February 1996 *Employees:* 9,760
Previous: Virgin Wings Limited
Net Worth: £520,000,000 *Total Assets:* £1,082,000,000
Registered Office: The Battleship Building, 179 Harrow Road, London, W2 6NB
Activities: Activities of other holding companies n.e.c.
Major Shareholder: Richard Charles Nicholas Branson
Officers: Barry Alexander Ralph Gerrard, Secretary; Joshua Bayliss [1973] Director; Evan McCulloch Lovell [1969] Director/Partner [American]; Patrick Charles Kingdon McCall [1964] Corporate Operations Director; Peter Michael Russell Norris [1955] Director/Self Employed; Amy Stirling [1969] Director; Lisa Victoria Thomas [1967] Director/Marketing; Ian Philip Woods [1974] Director/Solicitor

Virtus Holdco Limited
Incorporated: 15 June 2011 *Employees:* 42
Net Worth: £41,994,000 *Total Assets:* £302,497,984
Registered Office: Kent House, 14-17 Market Place, London, W1W 8AJ
Activities: Other information technology service activities
Officers: Lim Ah DOO [1949] Director [Singaporean]; Zulkifli Bin Baharudin [1959] Director [Singaporean]; Neil David Cresswell [1965] Director; Bruno Lopez [1964] Director [Singaporean]; Stephen Geoffrey Miller [1963] Director [Australian]; Sio Tat Hiang [1947] Director [Singaporean]

Virtus IMH 2 Limited
Incorporated: 2 September 2015
Net Worth Deficit: £53,365,000 *Total Assets:* £153,124,992
Registered Office: Kent House, 14-17 Market Place, London, W1W 8AJ
Activities: Other information technology service activities
Parent: Virtus Data Centres Properties Limited
Officers: Neil Cresswell [1965] Director; Jonathan Allen King [1976] Director/Chief Operating Officer [Australian]; Nelson Lim Yueh Hua [1970] Director [Singaporean]; Bruno Lopez [1964] Director [Singaporean]; Daryl Robert Leslie Seaton [1973] Director/Chief Financial Officer; Nicholas Toh Lik Hau [1981] Director/Vice President [Australian]

Virtus IMH Limited
Incorporated: 18 April 2012
Net Worth Deficit: £45,167,000 *Total Assets:* £128,266,000
Registered Office: Kent House, 14-17 Market Place, London, W1W 8AJ
Activities: Other information technology service activities
Parent: Virtus Data Centres Properties Limited
Officers: Neil Cresswell [1965] Director; Jonathan Allen King [1976] Director [Australian]; Nelson Lim Yueh Hua [1970] Director [Singaporean]; Bruno Lopez [1964] Director [Singaporean]; Daryl Robert Leslie Seaton [1973] Director/Chief Financial Officer; Nicholas Toh Lik Hau [1981] Director/Vice President [Australian]

Visa Europe Limited
Incorporated: 27 May 2004 *Employees:* 1,581
Net Worth: £2,755,492,096 *Total Assets:* £4,939,637,760
Registered Office: 1 Sheldon Square, London, W2 6TT
Activities: Financial intermediation not elsewhere classified
Parent: Visa International Holdings Limited
Officers: Prini Pithouse, Secretary; Deborah Alison Hewitt [1963] Independent Non-Executive Director; Charlotte Mary Hogg [1970] Director/Chief Executive Officer; Mary Ellen Richey [1949] Director [American]; William Morgan Sheedy [1967] Director/Global Executive [American]; Jose Manuel Souto Gonzalez [1967] Director [American]

Visa International Holdings Limited
Incorporated: 11 November 2016
Net Worth: £8,483,158,016 *Total Assets:* £17,259,573,248
Registered Office: 10 Norwich Street, London, EC4A 1BD
Activities: Non-trading company
Parent: Visa Inc.
Officers: Prini Patel Pithouse, Secretary; Charlotte Mary Hogg [1970] Director/Chief Executive Officer; Jose Manuel Souto Gonzalez [1967] Director/CFO Visa Europe [American]

Vitality Health Insurance Limited
Incorporated: 15 April 1987
Net Worth: £332,492,000 *Total Assets:* £332,577,984
Registered Office: 3 More London Riverside, London, SE1 2AQ
Activities: Non-life insurance
Officers: Jennifer Thorn, Secretary; Nicholas Michael Caplan [1959] Director; Lord Sebastian Newbold Coe [1956] Director; Andrew Michael Crossley [1956] Director/Chief Financial Officer; Sir Andrew William Foster [1944] Director; Adrian Gore [1964] Director/Actuary [South African]; Rosemary Hilary [1955] Director; Monty Isidore Hilkowitz [1940] Director [Israeli]; Neville Stanley Koopowitz [1964] Director/Chief Executive Officer Pru Health [South African]; Ayanda Ntsaluba [1960] Director [South African]; Stephen John Sarjant [1960] Director

Vitality Health Limited
Incorporated: 20 February 2004
Net Worth: £228,356,000 *Total Assets:* £667,292,992
Registered Office: 3 More London Riverside, London, SE1 2AQ
Activities: Non-life insurance
Officers: Jennifer Thorn, Secretary; Nicholas Michael Caplan [1959] Director; Lord Sebastian Newbold Coe [1956] Director; Andrew Michael Crossley [1956] Director/Chief Executive Officer; Sir Andrew William Foster [1944] Director; Adrian Gore [1964] Director/Actuary [South African]; Rosemary Hilary [1955] Director; Monty Isidore Hilkowitz [1940] Director [Israeli]; Neville Stanley Koopowitz [1964] Director/Chief Executive Officer Pru Health [South African]; Alastair David Lyons [1953] Independent Non-Executive Director; Ayanda Nstaluba [1960] Director [South African]; Stephen John Sarjant [1960] Director; Joanne Mary Shaw [1963] Independent Non-Executive Director

Vitol Services Limited
Incorporated: 26 October 1999
Net Worth Deficit: £1,191,502 *Total Assets:* £226,713,120
Registered Office: 4th Floor, Nova South, 160 Victoria Street, London, SW1E 5LB
Activities: Other business support service activities n.e.c.
Officers: John Kerr Martin, Secretary/Oil Executive; Diane Cook [1949] Director/Oil Executive; Mark Adrian Hayward [1971] Director/Broker; Jonathan Robert Marsh [1968] Director/Lawyer; John Kerr Martin [1957] Director/Oil Executive

Vivo Energy Namibia Limited
Incorporated: 29 May 1975 *Employees:* 85
Net Worth: £426,360,000 *Total Assets:* £882,790,976
Registered Office: 5th Floor, The Peak, 5 Wilton Road, London, SW1V 1AN
Activities: Wholesale of other fuels and related products
Officers: Johan Depraetere, Secretary; Christophe Dia [1971] Director [Senegalese]; Nicolaas Johannes Grobbelaar [1971] Director [Namibian]; David Muraguri Muriithi [1963] Director [Kenyan]; Edward Ronald Walugembe [1971] Director [Ugandan]

Vivo Energy PLC
Incorporated: 12 March 2018
Net Worth: £1,362,452,608 *Total Assets:* £1,378,502,144
Registered Office: 5th Floor, The Peak, 5 Wilton Road, London, SW1V 1AN
Activities: Activities of head offices
Officers: Ben Walker, Secretary; Gawad Abaza [1963] Director [Egyptian]; Javed Ahmed [1969] Director; Carol Ann Arrowsmith [1954] Director; Christian Georges Chammas [1954] Director [French]; John Patrick Daly [1956] Director [Irish]; Johan Stefaan Edgard Depraetere [1967] Director [Belgian]; Temitope Olugbeminiyi Lawani [1970] Director/Managing Partner [Nigerian]; Hixonia Thembalihle Nyasulu [1954] Director [South African]; Chris Rogers [1960] Director

VM Receivables Financing PLC
Incorporated: 16 September 2016
Net Worth: £14,272 *Total Assets:* £121,323,632
Registered Office: 5th Floor, 6 St Andrew Street, London, EC4A 3AE
Activities: Other business support service activities n.e.c.
Parent: TMF Trustee Limited
Officers: Nita Ramesh Savjani [1980] Director

Vocalink Holdings Limited
Incorporated: 20 February 2007
Net Worth: £151,100,000 *Total Assets:* £164,300,000
Registered Office: 1 Angel Lane, London, EC4R 3AB
Activities: Data processing, hosting and related activities
Parent: Mastercard UK Holdco Ltd
Officers: Jacqueline Panayi, Secretary; Mark David Ashley Barnett [1967] Director; Ajay Bhalla [1966] Director [Singaporean]; Sir Edward John Watson Gieve [1950] Director & Consultant; Daniel Meredith Jones [1971] Director; Marion King [1958] Director; Edward Grunde McLaughlin [1965] Director [American]; Michael Miebach [1967] Director [German]; Paul Roy Stoddart [1974] Director; David Gregg Yates [1962] Director [Irish]

Vocalink Limited
Incorporated: 20 February 2007 *Employees:* 962
Net Worth: £41,500,000 *Total Assets:* £266,700,000
Registered Office: 1 Angel Lane, London, EC4R 3AB
Activities: Other business support service activities n.e.c.
Parent: Vocalink Holdings Limited
Officers: Jacqueline Panayi, Secretary; Mark David Ashley Barnett [1967] Director; Ajay Bhalla [1966] Director [Singaporean]; Edward Grunde McLaughlin [1965] Director [American]; Michael Miebach [1967] Director [German]; Paul Roy Stoddart [1974] Director; David Gregg Yates [1962] Director [Irish]

Voice Topco Limited
Incorporated: 4 August 2015 *Employees:* 124
Net Worth Deficit: £18,009,386 *Total Assets:* £106,773,224
Registered Office: 16 Upper Woburn Place, London, WC1H 0BS
Activities: Activities of other holding companies n.e.c.
Parent: Vitruvian Partners LLP
Officers: Jens Meggers [1970] Director [American]; Itay Rosenfeld [1976] Director/Chief Executive Officer [Belgian]

Vosper Thornycroft (UK) Limited
Incorporated: 22 May 1901
Net Worth: £1,014,480,000 *Total Assets:* £2,157,466,112
Registered Office: 33 Wigmore Street, London, W1U 1QX
Activities: Building of ships and floating structures
Shareholders: Babcock Southern Holdings Limited; Babcock2 Limited
Officers: Nicholas James William Borrett [1967] Director/Group Company Secretary and General Counsel; Franco Martinelli [1960] Director/Chartered Accountant; Iain Stuart Urquhart [1965] Director

Vouvray Acquisition Limited
Incorporated: 14 July 2011
Net Worth Deficit: £182,927,552 *Total Assets:* £131,961,384
Registered Office: 1st Floor, 63 Queen Victoria Street, London, EC4N 4UA
Activities: Activities of head offices
Parent: Vouvray Midco Limited
Officers: Deborah Grimason [1963] Director/General Counsel & Company Secretary; Ian Vallance [1969] Director/Chartered Accountant

Vouvray Finance Limited
Incorporated: 15 September 2010
Net Worth Deficit: £10,769,454 *Total Assets:* £237,180,608
Registered Office: 1st Floor, 63 Queen Victoria Street, London, EC4N 4UA
Activities: Service activities incidental to water transportation
Officers: Deborah Grimason [1963] Director/General Counsel & Company Secretary; Ian Vallance [1969] Director/Chartered Accountant

Vouvray Midco Limited
Incorporated: 14 July 2011
Net Worth: £239,605,840 *Total Assets:* £239,769,888
Registered Office: 1st Floor, 63 Queen Victoria Street, London, EC4N 4UA
Activities: Activities of head offices
Parent: Vouvray Finance Limited
Officers: Deborah Grimason [1963] Director/General Counsel & Company Secretary; Ian Vallance [1969] Director/Chartered Accountant

VPC Specialty Lending Investments PLC
Incorporated: 12 January 2015
Net Worth: £339,401,024 *Total Assets:* £397,013,376
Registered Office: 6th Floor, 65 Gresham Street, London, EC2V 7NQ
Activities: Activities of investment trusts
Officers: Kevin Ingram [1954] Director; Richard Levy [1972] Director/Chief Executive [American]; Elizabeth Susan Passey [1972] Director; Clive Richard Peggram [1959] Director

VPI Holding Limited
Incorporated: 11 April 2013 *Employees:* 68
Net Worth: £115,837,000 *Total Assets:* £710,097,024
Registered Office: 4th Floor, Nova South, 160 Victoria Street, London, SW1E 5LB
Activities: Production of electricity
Officers: Elizabeth Essex, Secretary; Javed Ahmed [1969] Director/Global Head of Investments; Russell David Hardy [1965] Director; Mark Longstreth [1982] Director [American]

VPI Immingham LLP
Incorporated: 15 November 2001 *Employees:* 68
Net Worth: £228,900,992 *Total Assets:* £678,916,992
Registered Office: 4th Floor, Nova South, 160 Victoria Street, London, SW1E 5LB

VTB Capital PLC
Incorporated: 18 October 1919 *Employees:* 261
Net Worth: £625,775,488 *Total Assets:* £5,084,092,416
Registered Office: 14 Cornhill, London, EC3V 3ND
Activities: Banks
Officers: Roger Poindexter Munger, Secretary; Philip John Dayer [1951] Director; John Elliott Hooper [1961] Director; Nicholas Jonathan Marc Hutt [1975] Director/Chief Executive; Nicholas Joseph [1963] Director/Global Chief Risk Officer; Jonathan Simon Klus [1963] Director/Chief Financial Officer; Roger Poindexter Munger [1961] Director/Lawyer; Peter Mark Richardson [1966] Director/Global Head-Equity Derivatives/Global Markets International; Thierry Jean Philippe Sciard [1956] Senior Independent Director [French]

VTB Capital Trading Limited
Incorporated: 2 February 2006 *Employees:* 16
Net Worth: £48,933,056 *Total Assets:* £780,438,016
Registered Office: 14 Cornhill, London, EC3V 3ND
Activities: Agents involved in the sale of fuels, ores, metals and industrial chemicals
Officers: Graham Ian Hindle [1957] Director/Chief Executive Officer; Sean Tiwari [1969] Director/Lawyer

Vue Entertainment Holdings (UK) Limited
Incorporated: 23 July 1999 *Employees:* 3
Net Worth: £76,397,000 *Total Assets:* £232,246,000
Registered Office: 10 Chiswick Park, 566 Chiswick High Road, London, W4 5XS
Activities: Activities of other holding companies n.e.c.
Parent: Vue Entertainment Holdings Limited
Officers: Euan Sutton, Secretary; Stephen Jeremy Knibbs [1961] Director/Chief Operating Officer; Alan Ewart McNair [1955] Director/Chief Financial Officer; James Timothy Richards [1959] Director/Chief Executive Officer

Vue Entertainment Investment Limited
Incorporated: 11 May 2006 *Employees:* 3
Net Worth Deficit: £369,375,008 *Total Assets:* £241,616,000
Registered Office: 10 Chiswick Park, 566 Chiswick High Road, London, W4 5XS
Activities: Activities of head offices
Parent: Vue Holdings (UK) Limited
Officers: Euan Sutton, Secretary; Stephen Jeremy Knibbs [1961] Director/Chief Operating Officer; Alan Ewart McNair [1955] Director/Chief Financial Officer; James Timothy Richards [1959] Director/Chief Executive Officer

Vue Entertainment Limited
Incorporated: 17 March 2003 *Employees:* 3,243
Net Worth: £309,148,000 *Total Assets:* £632,769,984
Registered Office: 10 Chiswick Park, 566 Chiswick High Road, London, W4 5XS
Activities: Motion picture projection activities
Parent: Vue Entertainment Holdings (UK) Limited
Officers: Euan Sutton, Secretary; Stephen Jeremy Knibbs [1961] Director/Chief Operating Officer; Alan Ewart McNair [1955] Director/Chief Financial Officer; James Timothy Richards [1959] Director/Chief Executive Officer

Vue Holdings (UK) Limited
Incorporated: 28 October 2010 *Employees:* 3
Net Worth Deficit: £131,479,000 *Total Assets:* £768,684,992
Registered Office: 10 Chiswick Park, 566 Chiswick High Road, London, W4 5XS
Activities: Activities of other holding companies n.e.c.
Parent: Vougeot Bidco P.L.C.
Officers: Euan Sutton, Secretary; Stephen Jeremy Knibbs [1961] Director/Chief Operating Officer; Alan Ewart McNair [1955] Director/Chief Financial Officer; James Timothy Richards [1959] Director/Chief Executive Officer

Vue International Bidco PLC
Incorporated: 2 May 2013 *Employees:* 9,714
Previous: Vougeot Bidco P.L.C.
Net Worth Deficit: £385,480,992 *Total Assets:* £1,431,779,968
Registered Office: 10 Chiswick Park, 566 Chiswick High Road, London, W4 5XS
Activities: Activities of other holding companies n.e.c.
Parent: Vue International Midco Limited
Officers: Euan Sutton, Secretary; Simon Philip Jones [1982] Director/Private Equity Executive; Stephen Jeremy Knibbs [1961] Director/Chief Operating Officer; Alan Ewart McNair [1955] Director/Chief Financial Officer; Jason Anthony Dean Peters [1976] Director [Canadian]; Michael Mark Redman [1968] Director/Private Equity Executive; James Timothy Richards [1959] Director/Chief Executive Officer; Peter James Teti [1967] Director/Senior Vice President, Private Equity [Canadian]

Vue International Finco Limited
Incorporated: 2 May 2013 *Employees:* 7
Previous: Vougeot Finco Limited
Net Worth: £3,519,000 *Total Assets:* £737,393,984
Registered Office: 10 Chiswick Park, 566 Chiswick High Road, London, W4 5XS
Activities: Activities of other holding companies n.e.c.
Officers: Euan Sutton, Secretary; Adam Golebiowski [1981] Director [Swiss]; Simon Philip Jones [1982] Director/Private Equity Executive; Stephen Jeremy Knibbs [1961] Director/Chief Operating Officer; Alan Ewart McNair [1955] Director/Chief Financial Officer; Michael Mark Redman [1968] Director/Private Equity Executive; James Timothy Richards [1959] Director/Chief Executive Officer; Kevin Benjamin Roseke [1982] Director/Private Equity Executive [Canadian]

Vue International Midco Limited
Incorporated: 2 May 2013 *Employees:* 7
Previous: Vougeot Midco Limited
Net Worth: £6,615,000 *Total Assets:* £738,563,008
Registered Office: 10 Chiswick Park, 566 Chiswick High Road, London, W4 5XS
Activities: Activities of other holding companies n.e.c.
Parent: Vue International Finco Limited
Officers: Euan Sutton, Secretary; Adam Golebiowski [1981] Director [Swiss]; Simon Philip Jones [1982] Director/Private Equity Executive; Stephen Jeremy Knibbs [1961] Director/Chief Operating Officer; Alan Ewart McNair [1955] Director/Chief Financial Officer; Michael Mark Redman [1968] Director/Private Equity Executive; James Timothy Richards [1959] Director/Chief Executive Officer; Kevin Benjamin Roseke [1982] Director/Private Equity Executive [Canadian]

Louis Vuitton UK Limited
Incorporated: 5 May 1982 *Employees:* 472
Net Worth: £63,281,000 *Total Assets:* £106,022,000
Registered Office: c/o Browne Jacobson LLP, 6 Bevis Marks, London, EC3A 7BA
Activities: Retail sale of clothing in specialised stores
Parent: LVMH Moet Hennessy Louis Vuitton
Officers: Gaetan Guillaume Louis Fabry [1979] Director [French]; Alessandro Valenti [1972] Director [Italian]

VUR Holdings (UK) Limited
Incorporated: 27 October 2014 *Employees:* 4,110
Net Worth: £204,134,000 *Total Assets:* £671,553,984
Registered Office: One Fleet Place, London, EC4M 7WS
Activities: Activities of other holding companies n.e.c.
Officers: Coley James Brenan [1978] Director/Investor [American]; Steven Siegel [1962] Director [American]; Richard Weissmann [1962] Director/Partner [American]

VUR Investment (UK) Limited
Incorporated: 27 October 2014 *Employees:* 4,110
Net Worth: £329,969,984 *Total Assets:* £1,344,334,976
Registered Office: One Fleet Place, London, EC4M 7WS
Activities: Activities of other holding companies n.e.c.
Parent: VUR Mezzanine II (UK) Limited
Officers: Coley James Brenan [1978] Director/Investor [American]; Steven Siegel [1962] Director [American]; Richard Weissmann [1962] Director/Partner [American]

VUR Mezzanine I (UK) Limited
Incorporated: 27 October 2014 *Employees:* 3
Net Worth: £186,082,000 *Total Assets:* £197,886,000
Registered Office: One Fleet Place, London, EC4M 7WS
Activities: Activities of other holding companies n.e.c.
Parent: VUR Holdings (UK) Limited
Officers: Coley James Brenan [1978] Director/Investor [American]; Steven Siegel [1962] Director [American]; Richard Weissmann [1962] Director/Partner [American]

VUR Mezzanine II (UK) Limited
Incorporated: 27 October 2014
Net Worth: £196,000,000 *Total Assets:* £196,824,000
Registered Office: One Fleet Place, London, EC4M 7WS
Activities: Activities of other holding companies n.e.c.
Parent: VUR Mezzanine I (UK) Limited
Officers: Coley James Brenan [1978] Director/Investor [American]; Steven Siegel [1962] Director [American]; Richard Weissmann [1962] Director/Partner [American]

Wagamama Finance PLC
Incorporated: 16 January 2015
Net Worth Deficit: £29,619,000 *Total Assets:* £227,991,008
Registered Office: 76 Wardour Street, London, W1F 0UR
Activities: Activities of other holding companies n.e.c.
Parent: Mabel Bidco Limited
Officers: John Wilfred Rooney, Secretary; Kirk Dyson Davis [1971] Director; Andrew McCue [1974] Director [Irish]; Nicholas Charles Fraser Taylor [1974] Director; Emma Margaret Woods [1968] Director

Wagamama Limited
Incorporated: 29 April 1991 *Employees:* 5,420
Net Worth: £156,775,008 *Total Assets:* £215,190,000
Registered Office: 76 Wardour Street, London, W1F 0UR
Activities: Licenced restaurants
Parent: Wagamama Group Limited
Officers: John Wilfred Rooney, Secretary; Kirk Dyson Davis [1971] Director; Andrew McCue [1974] Director [Irish]; Nicholas Charles Fraser Taylor [1974] Director; Emma Margaret Woods [1968] Director

Waitrose Limited
Incorporated: 3 September 1908 *Employees:* 52,590
Net Worth: £841,500,032 *Total Assets:* £2,839,099,904
Registered Office: 171 Victoria Street, London, SW1E 5NN
Activities: Retail sale in non-specialised stores with food, beverages or tobacco predominating
Parent: John Lewis PLC
Officers: Peter Simpson, Secretary; Robert Collins [1970] Managing Director; John Patrick Lewis [1965] Director/Retailer; Sir Andrew Charles Mayfield [1966] Director

Waldorf Hotel Investment Limited
Incorporated: 15 May 2001
Net Worth: £74,483,000 *Total Assets:* £235,574,000
Registered Office: 14 Chester Terrace, London, NW1 4ND
Activities: Other letting and operating of own or leased real estate
Parent: Choicezone Limited
Officers: Jitendra Patel, Secretary; Gulshan Bhatia [1933] Director; Nimet Esmail [1958] Sales Director; Shelina Jetha [1961] Marketing Director

Walgreens Boots Alliance Limited
Incorporated: 19 March 2007
Previous: Alliance Boots Limited
Net Worth: £4,081,999,872 *Total Assets:* £4,097,999,872
Registered Office: 4th Floor, Sedley Place, 361 Oxford Street, London, W1C 2JL
Activities: Activities of head offices
Parent: WBA Acquisitions UK Topco Limited
Officers: Frank Standish, Company Secretary [Irish]; Aidan Gerard Clare [1966] Director [Irish]; Mark Francis Muller [1964] Director; Frank Standish [1963] Director/Company Secretary [Irish]

Wallis Retail Limited
Incorporated: 12 July 2001 *Employees:* 1,467
Net Worth: £155,158,000 *Total Assets:* £179,298,000
Registered Office: Colegrave House, 70 Berners Street, London, W1T 3NL
Activities: Other business support service activities n.e.c.
Parent: Arcadia Group Limited
Officers: Rebecca Rose Flaherty, Secretary; Ian Michael Grabiner [1959] Director; Gillian Anne Hague [1965] Director/Group Financial Controller; David St John Shepherd [1963] Director/Chief Operating Officer

Walney (UK) Offshore Windfarms Limited
Incorporated: 30 September 2004
Net Worth: £638,901,632 *Total Assets:* £756,060,160
Registered Office: 5 Howick Place, London, SW1P 1WG
Activities: Production of electricity
Shareholders: Orsted Power (UK) Limited; SSE Renewables Walney (UK) Limited
Officers: Philip Henry de Villiers [1975] Director; Neil Lannen [1968] Director/Civil Engineer; David Murray [1983] Director/Accountant [Irish]; Dennis Van Alphen [1968] Director/Senior Investment Manager [Dutch]; Cornelia Bernadette Maria Van Heijningen [1971] Alternate Director to D. Van Alphen [Dutch]; Hugh Alistair Yendole [1968] Director/Asset Manager

Walney Extension Holdings Limited
Incorporated: 4 August 2017
Net Worth: £534,640,576 *Total Assets:* £1,308,828,032
Registered Office: 5 Howick Place, London, SW1P 1WG
Activities: Other business support service activities n.e.c.
Shareholders: Anno 2017 Joint Holding (UK) Limited; Orsted Walney Extension Holdings Limited
Officers: Ulrik Palliso Borno [1981] Alternate Director of Domenico Tripodi [Danish]; Nicolai Eberhard [1974] Director [Danish]; Christian Krogsgaard [1974] Director [Danish]; Jacob Lise Lyngsgaard [1981] Alternate Director of Christian Krogsgaard [Danish]; Benjamin John Sykes [1965] Director; Domenico Tripodi [1984] Director [Italian]

Walney Extension Limited
Incorporated: 7 July 2010
Previous: Dong Energy Walney Extension (UK) Ltd
Net Worth: £575,235,712 *Total Assets:* £1,752,125,696
Registered Office: 5 Howick Place, London, SW1P 1WG
Activities: Other business support service activities n.e.c.
Parent: Walney Extension Holdings Limited
Officers: Ulrik Palliso Borno [1981] Alternate Director of Domenico Tripodi [Danish]; Nicolai Eberhard [1974] Director [Danish]; Christian Krogsgaard [1974] Director [Danish]; Jacob Lise Lyngsgaard [1981] Alternate Director of Christian Krogsgaard [Danish]; Benjamin John Sykes [1965] Director/UK Country Manager; Domenico Tripodi [1984] Director [Italian]

Robert Walters PLC
Incorporated: 24 March 2000 *Employees:* 3,554
Net Worth: £121,808,000 *Total Assets:* £323,680,000
Registered Office: 11 Slingsby Place, St Martin's Courtyard, London, WC2E 9AB
Activities: Temporary employment agency activities
Officers: Alan Robert Bannatyne, Secretary/Accountant; Alan Robert Bannatyne [1970] Director/Chartered Accountant; Steven Cooper [1970] Director; Giles Philip Daubeney [1961] Deputy Chief Executive Director; Tanith Dodge [1960] HR Director; Carol Hui [1956] Director/Lawyer; Brian David McArthur-Muscroft [1963] Finance Director; Robert Charles Walters [1954] Director/Chief Executive

Walworth Investment Properties Limited
Incorporated: 27 February 2013
Net Worth: £118,469,504 *Total Assets:* £214,502,032
Registered Office: 16 Hans Road, London, SW3 1RT
Activities: Other letting and operating of own or leased real estate
Parent: Dorrington Investment PLC
Officers: Anthony Mark Barber [1980] Director/Chartered Surveyor; Andrew Richard Giblin [1978] Director; John Patrick Kennedy [1957] Director [Irish]; Alan Jay Leibowitz [1952] Director; Duncan James Salvesen [1957] Director/Chartered Surveyor

Warner Bros. Entertainment UK Limited
Incorporated: 15 October 1931 *Employees:* 475
Net Worth: £221,678,000 *Total Assets:* £367,608,992
Registered Office: Warner House, 98 Theobalds Road, London, WC1X 8WB
Activities: Motion picture distribution activities
Parent: AT & T Inc.
Officers: Joshua Adam Berger [1966] President and Managing Director [American/British]; Thomas Hugh Creighton [1964] Director/Accountant; Steven William Mertz [1957] Director/Lawyer [American]

Warner Bros. Studios Leavesden Limited
Incorporated: 16 August 1937 *Employees:* 464
Net Worth: £146,656,000 *Total Assets:* £239,048,000
Registered Office: Warner House, 98 Theobalds Road, London, WC1X 8WB
Activities: Motion picture production activities
Parent: Time Warner Entertainment Limited
Officers: David Bisoni, Secretary; David Bisoni [1968] Director/Lawyer; Thomas Hugh Creighton [1964] Director/Accountant; Daniel Christian Dark [1964] Senior Vice President and Managing Director

Warner Media International Limited
Incorporated: 6 May 1992 *Employees:* 55
Previous: Time Warner Limited
Net Worth: £890,083,968 *Total Assets:* £893,763,968
Registered Office: 16 Great Marlborough Street, London, W1F 7HS
Activities: Activities of head offices
Parent: Time Warner London Limited
Officers: William Wilkins, Secretary; Bronwen Elizabeth Stuart Jones [1959] Director; Tracey Waring Mundy [1968] Finance Director; Joseph Wilkins [1973] Tax Director

Warner Music International Services Limited
Incorporated: 16 May 1988 *Employees:* 195
Net Worth: £133,169,000 *Total Assets:* £148,956,000
Registered Office: Cannon Place, 78 Cannon Street, London, EC4N 6AF
Activities: Activities of other holding companies n.e.c.
Parent: WMG Acquisition (UK) Limited
Officers: Roger Denys Booker [1946] Director; Kathryn Le Gassick [1973] Director/Solicitor; Paul Martin Robinson [1958] Director/Attorney [American]

Warner Music UK Limited
Incorporated: 13 January 1961 *Employees:* 216
Net Worth: £11,118,000 *Total Assets:* £147,519,008
Registered Office: Cannon Place, 78 Cannon Street, London, EC4N 6AF
Activities: Wholesale of audio tapes, records, CDs and video tapes and the equipment on which these are played
Parent: Warner Music International Services Limited
Officers: Roger Denys Booker [1946] Director; Peter David Breeden [1964] Director; Paul Martin Robinson [1958] Director/Attorney [American]

Warwick & Esplen Limited
Incorporated: 18 September 1912 *Employees:* 8
Net Worth: £55,452,288 *Total Assets:* £164,788,736
Registered Office: Fourth Floor, 117-119 Houndsditch, London, EC3A 7BT
Activities: Activities of head offices
Officers: Robert Amyon John Templeman Chaffey, Secretary; Belinda Arthur [1961] Director; Angela Mary Hood [1930] Director/Shipping; Paul George Mersham Lewis [1976] Director; Iona Clare FitzGenerald Parker [1964] Director/Solicitor; James Walter FitzGenerald Warwick [1966] Director/Ship Broker

Warwick Finance Residential Mortgages Number One PLC
Incorporated: 28 August 2014
Net Worth: £39,521,240 *Total Assets:* £1,188,629,504
Registered Office: 35 Great St Helen's, London, EC3A 6AP
Activities: Financial intermediation not elsewhere classified
Parent: Warwick Finance Residential Mortgages Holdings Limited
Officers: Daniel Marc Richard Jaffe [1975] Director

Warwick Finance Residential Mortgages Number Two PLC
Incorporated: 17 April 2015
Net Worth: £31,727,580 *Total Assets:* £1,325,796,992
Registered Office: 35 Great St Helen's, London, EC3A 6AP
Activities: Financial intermediation not elsewhere classified
Parent: Warwick Finance Residential Mortgages Holdings Number Two Limited
Officers: Daniel Marc Richard Jaffe [1975] Director

Watch Tower Bible and Tract Society of Britain
Incorporated: 8 October 1999
Net Worth: £131,352,200 *Total Assets:* £147,207,760
Registered Office: IBSA House, The Ridgeway, London, NW7 1RN
Activities: Other publishing activities
Officers: Peter Phillip Bell [1950] Director/Minister of Religion; Robert Li [1972] Director/Minister; Andrew Jeffery Llewellyn [1966] Director/Minister; Giosue Maraia [1975] Director/Minister of Religion; Stephen John Morice [1954] Director/Minister; Jonathan Rastall [1963] Director/Minister

Waterstones Booksellers Limited
Incorporated: 22 August 1958 *Employees:* 3,123
Net Worth: £18,496,000 *Total Assets:* £188,808,000
Registered Office: 203-206 Piccadilly, London, W1J 9HD
Activities: Retail sale of books in specialised stores
Parent: Book Retail Bidco Limited
Officers: Alison Campbell, Secretary; Paul Best [1978] Director/Investment Manager; Achilles James Daunt [1963] Director/Bookseller; Jane Molloy [1976] Director/Accountant

Wates City of London Properties Limited
Incorporated: 2 February 1984
Net Worth: £328,102,112 *Total Assets:* £328,102,112
Registered Office: York House, 45 Seymour Street, London, W1H 7LX
Activities: Development of building projects
Parent: Pillar City PLC
Officers: Benjamin Toby Grose [1969] Director/Chartered Surveyor; Jonathan Charles McNuff [1986] Director/Chartered Accountant; Charles John Middleton [1966] Director/Corporate Tax Executive

A.S. Watson (Health & Beauty UK) Limited
Incorporated: 8 August 2000 *Employees:* 19,529
Net Worth: £446,476,992 *Total Assets:* £1,267,885,056
Registered Office: Hutchison House, 5 Hester Road, Battersea, London, SW11 4AN
Activities: Activities of head offices
Officers: Edith Shih, Secretary; Richard Alexander Fleming [1971] Finance Director; Dr Alan John Heaton [1962] Director; Dominic Kai Ming Lai [1953] Director; Jonathan Theodore Miller [1971] Director; Dr Christian Nicolas Roger Salbaing [1950] Director [French]; Edith Shih [1952] Director/Solicitor

A.S. Watson (P & C UK) Ltd
Incorporated: 8 March 2005
Net Worth: £20,761,584 *Total Assets:* £225,150,528
Registered Office: Hutchison House, 5 Hester Road, London, SW11 4AN
Activities: Activities of head offices
Parent: A. S. Watson (Health & Beauty UK) Limited
Officers: Edith Shih, Secretary; Richard Alexander Fleming [1971] Finance Director; Dr Alan John Heaton [1962] Director; Dominic Kai Ming Lai [1953] Director; Christian Nicolas Roger Salbaing [1950] Director [French]; Frank John Sixt [1951] Director [Canadian]; Gillian Greig Smith [1966] Finance Director

Wavemaker Limited
Incorporated: 26 September 2000 *Employees:* 464
Previous: Mediaedge:cia UK Limited
Net Worth: £30,605,000 *Total Assets:* £154,024,992
Registered Office: Sea Containers, 18 Upper Ground, London, SE1 9ET
Activities: Advertising agencies
Parent: WPP Samson Limited
Officers: Anna Hickey [1976] Director; Paul Hutchison [1975] Director/Chief Operations Officer; Shil Patel [1977] Director

Waymark Asset Investments Limited
Incorporated: 28 November 2012
Net Worth: £10,401,000 *Total Assets:* £2,818,491,904
Registered Office: 25 Gresham Street, London, EC2V 7HN
Activities: Financial intermediation not elsewhere classified
Parent: Lloyds Bank Financial Services (Holdings) Limited
Officers: Alyson Elizabeth Mulholland, Secretary; Mark Bradshaw [1969] Director; Gavin Stuart Parker [1968] Director; Richard Douglas Shrimpton [1970] Director

WB/TT Holdings Limited
Incorporated: 1 November 2007
Net Worth: £292,796,128 *Total Assets:* £292,805,344
Registered Office: Warner House, 98 Theobalds Road, London, WC1X 8WB
Activities: Activities of head offices
Parent: Time Warner Holdings Limited
Officers: Thomas Hugh Creighton [1964] Director/Accountant; Steven William Mertz [1957] Director [American]

WBA Acquisitions UK Holdco 2 Limited
Incorporated: 16 April 2007
Previous: AB Acquisitions UK Holdco 2 Limited
Net Worth: £197,940,992 *Total Assets:* £197,946,000
Registered Office: 4th Floor, Sedley Place, 361 Oxford Street, London, W1C 2JL
Activities: Activities of head offices
Officers: Frank Standish, Company Secretary [Irish]; Aidan Gerard Clare [1966] Director [Irish]; Mark Francis Muller [1964] Director; Frank Standish [1963] Director/Company Secretary [Irish]

WBA Acquisitions UK Holdco 5 Limited
Incorporated: 6 October 2010
Previous: AB Acquisitions UK Holdco 5 Limited
Net Worth: £166,370,000 *Total Assets:* £355,188,992
Registered Office: 4th Floor, Sedley Place, 361 Oxford Street, London, W1C 2JL
Activities: Activities of other holding companies n.e.c.
Parent: Alliance Boots Holdings Limited
Officers: Frank Standish, Secretary; Aidan Gerard Clare [1966] Director [Irish]; Mark Francis Muller [1964] Director; Frank Standish [1963] Director [Irish]

WBA Acquisitions UK Holdco 7 Limited
Incorporated: 24 July 2012
Previous: AB Acquisitions UK Holdco 7 Limited
Net Worth: £8,795,199,488 *Total Assets:* £13,294,699,520
Registered Office: 4th Floor, Sedley Place, 361 Oxford Street, London, W1C 2JL
Activities: Activities of head offices
Parent: Superior Acquisitions Limited
Officers: Frank Standish, Secretary; Aidan Gerard Clare [1966] Director [Irish]; Mark Francis Muller [1964] Director; Frank Standish [1963] Director [Irish]

WBA Acquisitions UK Topco Limited
Incorporated: 19 March 2007
Previous: AB Acquisitions UK Topco Limited
Net Worth: £2,824,059,904 *Total Assets:* £2,824,169,984
Registered Office: 4th Floor, Sedley Place, 361 Oxford Street, London, W1C 2JL
Activities: Activities of head offices
Parent: Superior Holdings Limited
Officers: Frank Standish, Company Secretary [Irish]; Aidan Gerard Clare [1966] Director [Irish]; Mark Francis Muller [1964] Director; Frank Standish [1963] Director/Company Secretary [Irish]

WBA Finance 1 Limited
Incorporated: 10 March 2015
Net Worth: £113,530,776 *Total Assets:* £113,748,552
Registered Office: Sedley Place, Oxford Street, London, W1C 2JL
Activities: Activities of financial services holding companies
Parent: Walgreens Boots Alliance Scottish LP
Officers: Frank Standish, Secretary; Aidan Gerard Clare [1966] Director [Irish]; Mark Francis Muller [1964] Director; Frank Standish [1963] Director [Irish]

WBA Finance 2 Limited
Incorporated: 14 July 2015
Net Worth: £2,735,119,104 *Total Assets:* £2,756,532,992
Registered Office: 4th Floor, Sedley Place, 361 Oxford Street, London, W1C 2JL
Activities: Activities of other holding companies n.e.c.
Parent: Superior Holdings Limited
Officers: Frank Standish, Secretary; Aidan Gerard Clare [1966] Director [Irish]; Mark Francis Muller [1964] Director; Frank Standish [1963] Director [Irish]

WBA Financial Limited
Incorporated: 15 December 2014
Net Worth: £2,291,666,688 *Total Assets:* £8,908,972,032
Registered Office: 4th Floor, Sedley Place, 361 Oxford Street, London, W1C 2JL
Activities: Other business support service activities n.e.c.
Parent: Walgreens Boots Alliance, Inc
Officers: Frank Standish, Secretary; Aidan Gerard Clare [1966] Director [Irish]; Mark Francis Muller [1964] Director; Frank Standish [1963] Director [Irish]

WBA Financial Services Limited
Incorporated: 15 December 2014
Net Worth: £8,992,450,560 *Total Assets:* £9,258,130,432
Registered Office: 4th Floor, Sedley Place, 361 Oxford Street, London, W1C 2JL
Activities: Other business support service activities n.e.c.
Parent: WBA Financial Limited
Officers: Frank Standish, Secretary; Aidan Gerard Clare [1966] Director [Irish]; Mark Francis Muller [1964] Director; Frank Standish [1963] Director [Irish]

WBA Holdings 1 Limited
Incorporated: 2 July 1990
Previous: Alliance Boots Holdings 1 Limited
Net Worth: £153,600,000 *Total Assets:* £153,700,000
Registered Office: 4th Floor, Sedley Place, 361 Oxford Street, London, W1C 2JL
Activities: Activities of head offices
Parent: Alliance Boots Holdings Limited
Officers: Frank Standish, Company Secretary [Irish]; Aidan Gerard Clare [1966] Director [Irish]; Mark Francis Muller [1964] Director; Frank Standish [1963] Director/Company Secretary [Irish]

WBA International Limited
Incorporated: 19 March 2007
Previous: Alliance Boots International Limited
Net Worth: £5,024,099,840 *Total Assets:* £5,027,800,064
Registered Office: 4th Floor, Sedley Place, 361 Oxford Street, London, W1C 2JL
Activities: Activities of head offices
Parent: Walgreens Boots Alliance Limited
Officers: Frank Standish, Company Secretary [Irish]; Aidan Gerard Clare [1966] Director [Irish]; Mark Francis Muller [1964] Director; Frank Standish [1963] Company Secretary/Director [Irish]

WBA Latin America Limited
Incorporated: 23 November 2012
Previous: Alliance Boots Latin America Limited
Net Worth: £354,461,216 *Total Assets:* £365,959,936
Registered Office: 4th Floor, Sedley Place, 361 Oxford Street, London, W1C 2JL
Activities: Dormant company
Parent: Alliance Boots Holdings Limited
Officers: Frank Standish, Secretary; Aidan Gerard Clare [1966] Director [Irish]; Mark Francis Muller [1964] Director; Frank Standish [1963] Director/Company Secretary [Irish]

WBA Propco C LLP
Incorporated: 5 September 2007
Previous: Alliance Boots Propco C LLP
Net Worth: £289,352,000 *Total Assets:* £289,744,992
Registered Office: 4th Floor, Sedley Place, 361 Oxford Street, London, W1C 2JL

WBA UK Finance Limited
Incorporated: 11 December 2014
Net Worth: £401,785,728 *Total Assets:* £405,197,440
Registered Office: 4th Floor, 361 Oxford Street, London, W1C 2JL
Activities: Other business support service activities n.e.c.
Parent: Superior Holdings Limited
Officers: Frank Standish, Secretary; Aidan Gerard Clare [1966] Director [Irish]; Mark Francis Muller [1964] Director; Frank Standish [1963] Director [Irish]

WBAD Holdings Limited
Incorporated: 15 December 2014
Net Worth: £5,464,358,400 *Total Assets:* £5,464,866,304
Registered Office: 4th Floor, Sedley Place, 361 Oxford Street, London, W1C 2JL
Activities: Other business support service activities n.e.c.
Parent: Superior Holdings Limited
Officers: Frank Standish, Secretary; Aidan Gerard Clare [1966] Director [Irish]; Mark Francis Muller [1964] Director; Frank Standish [1963] Director [Irish]

Webhelp UK Holdings Ltd
Incorporated: 20 November 2012 *Employees:* 9,293
Net Worth: £29,570,000 *Total Assets:* £141,452,000
Registered Office: 48-49 St James's Street, London, SW1A 1JT
Activities: Other telecommunications activities
Parent: Webhelp SAS
Officers: Oliver Fabrice Duha [1969] Director/Outsourced Telecommunications Services [French]; Dean Robert Hartley [1973] Director/Outsourced Telecommunications Services; Frederic Andre Jousset [1970] Director [French]; David John Turner [1960] Director/Outsourced Telecommunications Services

Wedco EMEA Ventures Limited
Incorporated: 26 June 2014
Net Worth: £947,902,976 *Total Assets:* £947,934,016
Registered Office: 3 Queen Caroline Street, Hammersmith, London, W6 9PE
Activities: Activities of other holding companies n.e.c.
Parent: Wedco Global Ventures LLP
Officers: Zelda Hansson [1976] Director/Finance Executive; Peter Lloyd Wiley [1968] Director/Lawyer

Weldcure Limited
Incorporated: 4 August 1998
Net Worth: £1,040,288,000 *Total Assets:* £1,063,419,008
Registered Office: 6th Floor, 322 High Holborn, London, WC1V 7PB
Activities: Other business support service activities n.e.c.
Parent: Charter Overseas Holdings Limited
Officers: William Flexon [1963] Director/Chartered Accountant [American]; Mark Paul Lehman [1967] Director/Solicitor [American]; Eileen Annabelle Raperport [1951] Director/Pensions Co-ordinator; Guy Rostron [1960] Director/Chartered Accountant

Wellcome Trust Finance PLC
Incorporated: 26 June 2006
Net Worth: £137,500,000 *Total Assets:* £963,444,672
Registered Office: Gibbs Building, 215 Euston Road, London, NW1 2BE
Activities: Other service activities n.e.c.
Parent: The Wellcome Trust Limited, as Trustee of The Wellcome Trust
Officers: Christopher Bird, Secretary; Nicholas David Moakes [1964] Director/Managing Partner; Peter John Pereira Gray [1963] Director/Managing Partner; Fabian Thehos [1981] Director/Investment Principal [German]

Wellcome Trust Investments 1 Unlimited
Incorporated: 24 January 2008
Net Worth: £330,852,608 *Total Assets:* £353,874,720
Registered Office: Gibbs Building, 215 Euston Road, London, NW1 2BE
Activities: Other service activities n.e.c.
Parent: The Wellcome Trust Limited
Officers: Carolyn Kloet, Secretary; Elaina Tatem Elzinga [1984] Director/Investment Principal; Nicholas David Moakes [1964] Director/Managing Partner; Lisha Nagin Patel [1980] Director/Head of Direct Transactions; Peter John Pereira Gray [1963] Director/Managing Partner

Wellcome Trust Investments 2 Unlimited
Incorporated: 24 April 2008
Net Worth: £327,448,448 *Total Assets:* £350,151,584
Registered Office: Gibbs Building, 215 Euston Road, London, NW1 2BE
Activities: Other service activities n.e.c.
Officers: Carolyn Kloet, Secretary; Elaina Tatem Elzinga [1984] Director/Investment Principal; Nicholas David Moakes [1964] Director/Managing Partner; Lisha Nagin Patel [1980] Director/Head of Direct Transactions; Peter John Pereira Gray [1963] Director/Managing Partner

Wellcome Trust Residential 1 Limited
Incorporated: 30 May 2007
Net Worth: £125,971,320 *Total Assets:* £130,192,656
Registered Office: Gibbs Building, Euston Road, London, NW1 2BE
Activities: Other service activities n.e.c.
Officers: Carolyn Kloet, Secretary; Robert Henry Dewes Coke [1972] Director/Investor; Elaina Tatem Elzinga [1984] Director/Investment Principal; Nicholas David Moakes [1964] Director/Managing Partner; Lisha Nagin Patel [1980] Director/Head of Direct Transactions; Peter John Pereira Gray [1963] Director/Managing Partner

Wellington Management International Limited
Incorporated: 7 September 2001 *Employees:* 300
Net Worth: £112,408,000 *Total Assets:* £165,862,000
Registered Office: Cardinal Place, 80 Victoria Street, London, SW1E 5JL
Activities: Fund management activities
Officers: Susanne Ballauff [1966] Director/Business Development Manager [German]; Natasha Louise Brook-Walters [1974] Director; Yolanda Cristina Courtines [1969] Director/Portfolio Manager; Carl Dirk Enderlein [1973] Director [German]; Stefan Kurt Haselwandter [1976] Director/Business Executive [Austrian]; Jr Helfer [1960] Director [American]; Amy Beth Kramer [1978] Director/Senior Executive, Fund Business [American]; Lucinda Maria Marrs [1962] Director [American]; John Peter Parsons [1964] Director/Investment Portfolio Manager [Irish]; Phillip H Perelmuter [1961] Director of Investment Research [American]; Edward Joseph Steinborn [1962] Director/C F O [American]; Luke Barnaby Stellini [1975] Director

Wellington Pub Company PLC
Incorporated: 22 July 1997
Net Worth: £337,750,016 *Total Assets:* £492,552,000
Registered Office: 73 Cornhill, London, EC3V 3QQ
Activities: Public houses and bars
Parent: Wellington Investments Limited
Officers: Anne Benjamin, Secretary; Stephane Abraham Joseph Nahum [1975] Director/Investment Advisor [French]; Eileen Marie Sawyer [1979] Director/Accountant; Malcolm Robin Turner [1935] Director

Wells Fargo Capital Finance (UK) Limited
Incorporated: 21 October 1991 *Employees:* 58
Previous: Burdale Financial Limited
Net Worth: £110,043,704 *Total Assets:* £774,174,656
Registered Office: 33 King William Street, London, EC4R 9AT
Activities: Credit granting by non-deposit taking finance houses and other specialist consumer credit grantors
Parent: Wells Fargo & Co
Officers: Steven Jonathan Chait [1965] Director/Chartered Accountant; Nigel Broadbery Hogg [1960] Director/Chartered Accountant; Kurt Richard Marsden [1969] Director/Banker [American]; Christine Brooke Meyers [1965] Director/Banker [American]

Wells Fargo Securities International Limited
Incorporated: 1 September 1997 *Employees:* 31
Net Worth: £375,190,528 *Total Assets:* £4,601,052,160
Registered Office: 33 King William Street, London, EC4R 9AT
Activities: Financial intermediation not elsewhere classified
Parent: Wells Fargo & Company
Officers: Patricia McGuinness, Secretary; Thomas Christopher Sermon, Secretary; Nicholas Charles George Andrews [1959] Director/Consultant; Paola Bergamaschi Broyd [1961] Director [Italian]; Walter Ernesto Dolhare [1966] Director/Banker [Argentinian]; Christine Brooke Meyers [1965] Director/Regional Risk Executive [American]; Bryn Eiron Owen [1961] Director/Accountant; Francis Anthony Pizzo [1956] Director/Banker [American]; Francisco Rey Alegria [1967] Director [Spanish]; Alicia Reyes Revuelta [1972] Director/Investment Banker [Spanish]

Wembley Park Limited
Incorporated: 22 August 1927 *Employees:* 3
Net Worth Deficit: £213,045,664 *Total Assets:* £298,687,008
Registered Office: 180 Great Portland Street, London, W1W 5QZ
Activities: Development of building projects
Parent: Chesterfield (No.40) Limited
Officers: Frances Victoria Heazell, Secretary; Angus Alexander Dodd [1967] Senior Managing Director; Michael Ben Jenkins [1972] Director [British/Australian]; James Michael Edward Saunders [1966] Director

Werner European Holding Limited
Incorporated: 16 June 2017
Net Worth: £189,641,184 *Total Assets:* £395,419,008
Registered Office: Suite 1, 3rd Floor, 11-12 St James's Square, London, SW1Y 4LB
Activities: Activities of other holding companies n.e.c.
Officers: James Timothy Caudill [1967] Director/Chief Executive Officer [American]; Geoffrey Robert Hartenstein [1961] Director [American]

Werner US Holding Limited
Incorporated: 16 June 2017
Net Worth: £108,119,296 *Total Assets:* £108,119,296
Registered Office: Suite 1, 3rd Floor, 11-12 St James's Square, London, SW1Y 4LB
Activities: Activities of other holding companies n.e.c.
Officers: James Timothy Caudill [1967] Director/Chief Executive Officer [American]; Geoffrey Robert Hartenstein [1961] Director [American]

West Coast Trains Limited
Incorporated: 10 January 1995 *Employees:* 3,289
Net Worth: £55,380,000 *Total Assets:* £171,311,008
Registered Office: The Battleship Building, 179 Harrow Road, London, W2 6NB
Activities: Passenger rail transport, interurban
Parent: Virgin Rail Group Limited
Officers: Barry Alexander Ralph Gerrard, Secretary; Peter James Broadley [1971] Customer, Operations and Safety Director; Sarah Jane Copley [1973] Executive Director, Commercial; Mark Edward Whitehouse [1979] Executive Director Finance; Philip Whittingham [1971] Finance Director

West Ham United Football Club Limited
Incorporated: 5 July 1900 *Employees:* 435
Net Worth Deficit: £50,836,000 *Total Assets:* £184,198,000
Registered Office: London Stadium, Queen Elizabeth Olympic Park, London, E20 2ST
Activities: Activities of sport clubs
Parent: West Ham United Limited
Officers: Andrew John Mollett, Secretary; Baroness Karren Rita Brady [1969] Director; David Gold [1937] Director; Andrew John Mollett [1961] Director/Chartered Accountant; J Albert Smith [1965] Director [American]; David Sullivan [1949] Director; Tara Warren [1978] Executive Director-Marketing and Communications

West India Quay (Eastern) Limited
Incorporated: 1 August 1997 *Employees:* 162
Net Worth: £123,858,776 *Total Assets:* £173,968,016
Registered Office: 6th Floor, Charles House, 108-110 Finchley Road, London, NW3 5JJ
Activities: Hotels and similar accommodation
Parent: Yianis Docklands Hotels Limited
Officers: Yiannakis Theophani Christodoulou [1965] Director; Lambros Hadjiioannou [1978] Director

West London & Suburban Property Investments Limited
Incorporated: 16 September 1954
Net Worth: £234,115,136 *Total Assets:* £240,080,768
Registered Office: 25 Savile Row, London, W1S 2ER
Activities: Buying and selling of own real estate
Parent: Derwent Valley Limited
Officers: David Andrew Lawler, Secretary; John David Burns [1944] Director; Nigel Quentin George [1963] Director; Simon Paul Silver [1950] Director; David Gary Silverman [1969] Director; Paul Malcolm Williams [1960] Director/Surveyor; Damian Mark Alan Wisniewski [1961] Director

West Quay Shopping Centre Limited
Incorporated: 30 November 1959
Net Worth: £224,903,008 *Total Assets:* £225,128,992
Registered Office: Kings Place, 90 York Way, London, N1 9GE
Activities: Management of real estate on a fee or contract basis
Parent: Hammerson UK Properties PLC
Officers: Warren Stuart Austin [1966] Director/Chartered Accountant; Mark Richard Bourgeois [1968] Managing Director UK and Ireland; Peter Frank Cooper [1963] Director/Chartered Surveyor; Richard Geoffrey Shaw [1973] Director/Accountant

West-Ward Holdings Limited
Incorporated: 16 July 2015
Net Worth: £390,027,360 *Total Assets:* £390,027,360
Registered Office: 1 New Burlington Place, London, W1S 2HR
Activities: Other business support service activities n.e.c.
Parent: Hikma UK Limited
Officers: Peter Alexander Speirs, Secretary; Gurpal Singh Atwal [1964] Tax Director; Peter Alexander Speirs [1979] Director/Company Secretary

Westark Properties Limited
Incorporated: 26 April 2004
Net Worth: £55,971,000 *Total Assets:* £190,420,000
Registered Office: 41-43 Brook Street, Mayfair, London, W1K 4HJ
Activities: Activities of head offices
Parent: Coroin Limited
Officers: Liam Cunningham [1958] Director [Irish]; Mahmoud Raafat [1973] Director [Egyptian]; Marc Socker [1976] Director

The Westbury Hotel Limited
Incorporated: 10 September 2001 *Employees:* 302
Net Worth Deficit: £3,422,000 *Total Assets:* £152,935,008
Registered Office: Flat 1, 1-2 Coach and Horses Yard, London, W1S 2EH
Activities: Hotels and similar accommodation
Parent: Cola Holdings Limited
Officers: Azad Bakir Ali Cola, Secretary/Director; Azad Bakir Ali Cola [1979] Director

Westermost Rough (Holding) Limited
Incorporated: 20 February 2014
Net Worth: £442,619,200 *Total Assets:* £442,623,872
Registered Office: 5 Howick Place, London, SW1P 1WG
Activities: Activities of other holding companies n.e.c.
Shareholders: WMR JV Investco Limited; Orsted Westermost Rough Limited
Officers: Serkan Bahceci [1972] Director; Philip Henry de Villiers [1975] Director/Asset Manager; Mairi Dudley [1988] Alternate Director of Philip H. de Villiers; Kasper Holst Skyttegaard-Nielsen [1979] Director [Danish]; David Paul Tilstone [1969] Director

Westermost Rough Limited
Incorporated: 1 May 2007
Net Worth: £479,295,136 *Total Assets:* £513,143,840
Registered Office: 5 Howick Place, London, SW1P 1WG
Activities: Production of electricity
Parent: Westermost Rough (Holding) Limited
Officers: Serkan Bahceci [1972] Director; Philip Henry de Villiers [1975] Director/Asset Manager; Mairi Dudley [1988] Alternate Director of Philip de Villiers; Kasper Holst Skyttegaard-Nielsen [1979] Director [Danish]; David Paul Tilstone [1969] Director

Western Union Business Solutions (UK) Limited
Incorporated: 14 September 1993 *Employees:* 285
Net Worth: £53,430,000 *Total Assets:* £146,196,992
Registered Office: 200 Hammersmith Road, London, W6 7DL
Activities: Financial intermediation not elsewhere classified
Parent: The Western Union Company
Officers: Andrew Summerill [1973] Director/Vice President, Finance; Fedde Tristan Van Der Vijver [1978] Director/Head of Compliance [Dutch]; Bradley Allen Windbigler [1976] Director/Group Treasurer [American]

Westfield Europe Limited
Incorporated: 24 January 2000 *Employees:* 504
Net Worth: £36,462,000 *Total Assets:* £498,988,992
Registered Office: 4th Floor, 1 Ariel Way, London, W12 7SL
Activities: Development of building projects
Parent: Unibail-Rodamco SE
Officers: Gillian Claire Houinato, Secretary; Thomas David Merrifield, Secretary; Amanda Beattie [1973] Director/Solicitor; Jonathan Andrew Hodes [1968] Director/Chartered Accountant and Chartered Tax Advisor; Peter Howard Miller [1965] Director

Westfield Stratford City Finance PLC
Incorporated: 20 June 2014
Net Worth Deficit: £15,114,462 *Total Assets:* £753,980,544
Registered Office: Suite 2, 3rd Floor, 11-12 St James's Square, London, SW1Y 4LB
Activities: Other letting and operating of own or leased real estate
Officers: Sunil Masson, Secretary; Julius Manuel Bozzino [1970] Director; Sunil Masson [1971] Director

Westfield UK & Europe Finance PLC
Incorporated: 6 June 2012
Net Worth: £4,354,660 *Total Assets:* £827,535,872
Registered Office: 4th Floor, 1 Ariel Way, London, W12 7SL
Activities: Other business support service activities n.e.c.
Parent: Unibail-Rodamco SE
Officers: Gillian Claire Houinato, Secretary; Thomas David Merrifield, Secretary; Jonathan Andrew Hodes [1968] Director/Chartered Accountant and Chartered Tax Advisor; Peter Howard Miller [1965] Director

Westfield UK Acquisitions Finance Limited
Incorporated: 8 June 2004
Net Worth: £436,907,744 *Total Assets:* £581,109,568
Registered Office: 4th Floor, 1 Ariel Way, London, W12 7SL
Activities: Other business support service activities n.e.c.
Parent: Unibail-Rodamco SE
Officers: Gillian Claire Houinato, Secretary; Thomas David Merrifield, Secretary; Amanda Beattie [1973] Director/Solicitor; Jonathan Andrew Hodes [1968] Director/Chartered Accountant and Chartered Tax Advisor; Peter Howard Miller [1965] Director

Westfield UK Finance Limited
Incorporated: 18 February 2008
Net Worth: £304,238 *Total Assets:* £602,275,712
Registered Office: 4th Floor, 1 Ariel Way, London, W12 7SL
Activities: Other business support service activities n.e.c.
Parent: Unibail-Rodamco SE
Officers: Gillian Claire Houinato, Secretary; Thomas David Merrifield, Secretary; Jonathan Andrew Hodes [1968] Director/Chartered Accountant and Chartered Tax Advisor; Peter Howard Miller [1965] Director

Westminster Acquisition Limited
Incorporated: 28 March 2017 *Employees:* 1,214
Net Worth: £797,091,008 *Total Assets:* £1,618,704,000
Registered Office: 100 New Bridge Street, London, EC4V 6JA
Activities: Activities of other holding companies n.e.c.
Parent: Post Holdings, Inc.
Officers: Diedre Johnston Gray, Secretary; Sally Jane Abbott [1967] Director; Richard William Thomas Martin [1962] Director

Westminster Topco Limited
Incorporated: 12 November 2014 *Employees:* 692
Net Worth Deficit: £25,253,000 *Total Assets:* £125,833,000
Registered Office: 222 Bishopsgate, London, EC2M 4QD
Activities: Activities of head offices
Shareholder: Timothy James Cook
Officers: Graham John Anthony Dolan, Secretary; Andrew Jeremy Burchall [1964] Director; Timothy James Cook [1968] Director; Adam Herron [1973] Director; Geoffrey William Lloyd [1948] Director

Weston (2009) Limited
Incorporated: 6 November 2009
Net Worth: £29,966,981,120 *Total Assets:* £33,144,428,544
Registered Office: Globe House, 4 Temple Place, London, WC2R 2PG
Activities: Activities of other holding companies n.e.c.
Parent: British American Tobacco (2009) Limited
Officers: Oliver James Martin, Secretary; Jerome Bruce Abelman [1963] Director/Lawyer [American]; Jack Bowles [1963] Director, Asia-Pacific [French]; Nicandro Durante [1956] Director/Economist [Brazilian]; John Benedict Stevens [1959] Finance Director

Weston Aerospace Limited
Incorporated: 22 April 2003 *Employees:* 459
Net Worth: £178,486,000 *Total Assets:* £235,542,000
Registered Office: 5 New Street Square, London, EC4A 3TW
Activities: Manufacture of other special-purpose machinery n.e.c.
Parent: Esterline Technologies Europe Limited
Officers: Stephen Nolan [1969] Director [American]; Curtis Carl Reusser [1960] Director/President and Chief Executive Officer [American]; Roger Alan Ross [1968] Director [American]; Pierre Rossignol [1968] Director/EAS President [French]

Weston Investment Company Limited
Incorporated: 24 January 1922
Net Worth: £13,758,508,032 *Total Assets:* £14,743,345,152
Registered Office: Globe House, 4 Temple Place, London, WC2R 2PG
Activities: Activities of head offices
Parent: Weston (2009) Limited
Officers: Jonathan Michael Guttridge, Secretary; Jerome Bruce Abelman [1963] Director/General Counsel [American]; Andrew James Barrett [1974] Director/Group Financial Controller; Robert James Casey [1948] Director/Attorney [American]; Steven Glyn Dale [1967] Director/Tax Adviser; John Benedict Stevens [1959] Director/Tobacco Manufacturer; Neil Arthur Wadey [1964] Director/Treasurer

Westone Hotel Acquisitions Company
Incorporated: 3 April 1998
Net Worth: £228,996,000 *Total Assets:* £237,096,000
Registered Office: 41-43 Brook Street, Mayfair, London, W1K 4HJ
Activities: Activities of other holding companies n.e.c.
Parent: Raglan Real Estate Acquisition Company
Officers: Liam Cunningham [1958] Director [Irish]; Mahmoud Raafat [1973] Director [Egyptian]; Marc Socker [1976] Director

Westpac Europe Limited
Incorporated: 21 December 2005
Net Worth: £47,753,212 *Total Assets:* £265,950,128
Registered Office: Camomile Court, 23 Camomile Street, London, EC3A 7LL
Activities: Banks
Officers: Leisha White, Secretary; Christopher Ian Bannister [1967] Director; Anthony Murray Belchambers [1947] Director; Christopher Jonathan Lloyd Burgess [1964] Director/Banker; Rodney Maxwell Jackson [1958] Director/Banker [Australian]; Brian David Stevenson [1953] Director/Banker

Wework International Limited
Incorporated: 24 October 2014 *Employees:* 198
Previous: Wework UK Limited
Net Worth Deficit: £52,628,096 *Total Assets:* £307,729,440
Registered Office: c/o Legalinx Ltd, One Fetter Lane, London, EC4A 1BR
Activities: Other letting and operating of own or leased real estate
Officers: Abraham Joseph Safdie [1973] Director/Attorney [American]; Anthony Yazbeck [1978] Director/Deputy Head of Region [French/Lebanese]

WEX Europe UK Limited
Incorporated: 18 November 2016 *Employees:* 2
Net Worth Deficit: £380,893 *Total Assets:* £102,597,920
Registered Office: Fourth Floor, East Building, 1 London Bridge, London, SE1 9BG
Activities: Other business support service activities n.e.c.
Parent: Wright Express International Holdings Limited
Officers: Anant Ramanbhai Patel [1974] Managing Director; Bruce Selwyn Underwood [1969] Director

Weybourne Finance Limited
Incorporated: 14 March 2013
Previous: Bacton Finance Limited
Net Worth: £122,793,000 *Total Assets:* £520,072,992
Registered Office: Minerva House, 5 Montague Close, London, SE1 9BB
Activities: Financial intermediation not elsewhere classified
Parent: Weybourne Group Limited
Officers: Sir James Jeffrey Corfield Bucknall [1958] Director; Ian William Hubbard [1967] Director/Accountant; Caroline Jane Tucker [1980] Director/Chief Financial Officer; Ben Wiseman [1969] Director/Chartered Accountant

Weybourne Group Limited
Incorporated: 14 March 2013 *Employees:* 9,243
Previous: Holkham Group Limited
Net Worth: £2,380,999,936 *Total Assets:* £4,112,000,000
Registered Office: Minerva House, 5 Montague Close, London, SE1 9BB
Activities: Activities of other holding companies n.e.c.
Major Shareholder: James Dyson
Officers: Sir James Jeffrey Corfield Bucknall [1958] Director; Anthony David Buffin [1971] Director; Jacob Dyson [1972] Director; Sir James Dyson [1947] Director/Inventor/Entrepreneur; Samuel Dyson [1978] Director; Emily Dyson Paley [1971] Director; Edward David Fursdon [1952] Director; Anthony John Hobson [1947] Director; Ian Stuart Robertson [1958] Director; Mark William Slater [1969] Director; Ian Roper Taylor [1956] Director/President and CEO; Caroline Jane Tucker [1980] Director/Chief Financial Officer; Ben Wiseman [1969] Director/Chartered Accountant

WFL (UK) Limited
Incorporated: 20 November 1957 *Employees:* 825
Net Worth: £42,916,000 *Total Assets:* £237,782,000
Registered Office: Third Floor, The Broadgate Tower, 20 Primrose Street, London, EC2A 2RS
Activities: Wholesale of petroleum and petroleum products
Parent: WFS UK Holding Company III Limited
Officers: Claire Jean Bishop [1967] Finance Director; Grant Scott Roberts [1970] Director; Robert Taylor [1962] Managing Director; Paul Thomas Vian [1971] Director/SVP, EMEA Land

WFS UK Holding Company II Limited
Incorporated: 9 December 2010
Net Worth: £485,350,624 *Total Assets:* £811,068,544
Registered Office: Third Floor, The Broadgate Tower, 20 Primrose Street, London, EC2A 2RS
Activities: Other business support service activities n.e.c.
Parent: World Fuel Services Corporation
Officers: Maria Charash Koundina [1977] Director/VP M&A EMEA; Richard Donald McMichael [1962] Director/SVP-Finance (Aviation) [Canadian]

WFS UK Holding Company III Limited
Incorporated: 26 February 2014
Net Worth: £15,291,974 *Total Assets:* £164,162,816
Registered Office: Third Floor, The Broadgate Tower, 20 Primrose Street, London, EC2A 2RS
Activities: Other business support service activities n.e.c.
Parent: World Fuel Services Corporation
Officers: Richard Donald McMichael [1962] Director/SVP-Finance (Aviation) [Canadian]

WGA (UK) Holdings Limited
Incorporated: 18 May 2005 *Employees:* 250
Net Worth Deficit: £5,825,000 *Total Assets:* £158,320,000
Registered Office: 31 Hill Street, London, W1J 5LS
Activities: Activities of head offices
Parent: RW Wentworth Limited
Officers: Robert Lai [1966] Director [Chinese]; Woraphanit Ruayrungruang [1990] Director [Thai]

WGC (UK) Finance Limited
Incorporated: 17 December 2012 *Employees:* 1
Net Worth: £77,867,744 *Total Assets:* £228,504,176
Registered Office: 10 Old Bailey, London, EC4M 7NG
Activities: Other business support service activities n.e.c.
Parent: WGC (UK) Limited
Officers: Terence Heymann [1977] Director/CFO, World Gold Council

WGC (UK) Limited
Incorporated: 1 December 2011 *Employees:* 10
Net Worth: £276,336,736 *Total Assets:* £298,472,736
Registered Office: 10 Old Bailey, London, EC4M 7NG
Activities: Other business support service activities n.e.c.
Officers: Terence Heymann [1977] Director/CFO, World Gold Council; Aram Edward Shishmanian [1951] Director

WGSN Group Limited
Incorporated: 17 October 2012
Net Worth: £732,000 *Total Assets:* £222,760,992
Registered Office: c/o Ascential Group Limited, The Prow, 1 Wilder Walk, London, W1B 5AP
Activities: Activities of other holding companies n.e.c.
Parent: Ascential Information Services Limited
Officers: Shanny Looi, Secretary; Louise Meads, Secretary; Amanda Jane Gradden [1968] Director; Duncan Anthony Painter [1970] Director

WH Holding Limited
Incorporated: 9 November 2006 *Employees:* 435
Net Worth: £7,813,000 *Total Assets:* £184,198,000
Registered Office: London Stadium, Queen Elizabeth Olympic Park, London, E20 2ST
Activities: Operation of sports facilities
Shareholders: David Sullivan; David Gold
Officers: Andrew John Mollett, Secretary; Baroness Karren Rita Brady [1969] Director; David Gold [1937] Director; Daniel Bruce Harris [1960] Director; Andrew John Mollett [1961] Director/Chartered Accountant; J.Albert Smith [1965] Director [American]; David Sullivan [1949] Director

Wheel Bidco Limited
Incorporated: 4 February 2014 *Employees:* 999
Net Worth Deficit: £111,065,720 *Total Assets:* £454,691,840
Registered Office: 7th Floor, Warwick Court, Paternoster Square, London, EC4M 7DX
Activities: Other business support service activities n.e.c.
Officers: Luigi Del Monaco [1964] Director [Italian]; Giuseppe Prestia [1975] Director/Investment Manager [Italian]

White City Acquisitions Limited
Incorporated: 7 March 1996
Net Worth: £680,598,016 *Total Assets:* £1,915,339,008
Registered Office: 4th Floor, 1 Ariel Way, London, W12 7SL
Activities: Development of building projects
Parent: Unibail-Rodamco SE
Officers: Gillian Claire Houinato, Secretary; Thomas David Merrifield, Secretary; Amanda Beattie [1973] Director/Solicitor; Jonathan Andrew Hodes [1968] Director/Chartered Accountant and Chartered Tax Advisor; Peter Howard Miller [1965] Director

White City Property Finance PLC
Incorporated: 26 January 2005
Net Worth Deficit: £29,863,038 *Total Assets:* £381,210,336
Registered Office: 35 Great St Helen's, London, EC3A 6AP
Activities: Financial intermediation not elsewhere classified
Parent: White City Property Holdings Limited
Officers: Susan Iris Abrahams [1957] Director

White City Property Holdings Limited
Incorporated: 26 January 2005
Net Worth Deficit: £29,875,540 *Total Assets:* £381,197,856
Registered Office: 35 Great St Helen's, London, EC3A 6AP
Activities: Non-trading company
Parent: Intertrust Corporate Services Limited
Officers: Susan Iris Abrahams [1957] Director

Whiteacre Resources Ltd
Incorporated: 15 March 2006
Net Worth: £109,741,480 *Total Assets:* £109,755,680
Registered Office: 4th Floor, 1 Knightrider Court, London, EC4V 5BJ
Activities: Activities of other holding companies n.e.c.
Officers: Anna Nydegger [1979] Director/Businesswoman [Swiss]

Whitewell UK Investments 1 Limited
Incorporated: 24 December 2015
Net Worth: £1,084,328,960 *Total Assets:* £1,492,259,968
Registered Office: Fifth Floor, 80 Hammersmith Road, London, W14 8UD
Activities: Activities of other holding companies n.e.c.
Parent: Whitewell UK Holding Company 1 Limited
Officers: David James Hall, Secretary; Christopher Lee Howard [1966] Director [American]; Nigel Myers [1966] Director; Debra Kay Osteen [1955] Director/Chief Executive [American]; Trevor Michael Torrington [1961] Director

WIC (UK) Ltd
Incorporated: 24 November 2014
Net Worth: £101,818,784 *Total Assets:* £101,821,696
Registered Office: 5th Floor, 1 Lumley Street, London, W1K 6JE
Activities: Non-trading company
Officers: Ian Henry Anderson [1961] Director; Juan Luis Medina [1966] Director; Christopher Stephen Smith [1972] Director

WIG Holdings I Limited
Incorporated: 12 January 2016 *Employees:* 50
Net Worth Deficit: £9,894,000 *Total Assets:* £366,838,016
Registered Office: Level 13, Broadgate Tower, 20 Primrose Street, London, EC2A 2EW
Activities: Wireless telecommunications activities
Parent: 3i WIG Limited
Officers: Matthew Giles Barker [1985] Director, Infrastructure, 31 PLC; John Ivor Cavill [1972] Director/Investment Manager; Scott Terrence Coates [1971] Director; Kingsley John Neville Meek [1955] Director; Nigel Moss [1975] Director; Philip Joseph White [1962] Director/Managing Partner

WIG Holdings II Limited
Incorporated: 12 January 2016 *Employees:* 6
Net Worth Deficit: £5,722,000 *Total Assets:* £203,500,000
Registered Office: Level 13, Broadgate Tower, 20 Primrose Street, London, EC2A 2EW
Activities: Wireless telecommunications activities
Parent: WIG Holdings I Limited
Officers: Matthew Giles Barker [1985] Director; John Ivor Cavill [1972] Director/Investment Manager; Scott Terrence Coates [1971] Director; Nigel Moss [1975] Director; Philip Joseph White [1962] Director/Managing Partner

Wilhunter (UK) Limited
Incorporated: 30 December 2009
Net Worth Deficit: £14,525,033 *Total Assets:* £224,941,344
Registered Office: 3rd Floor, 11-12 St James's Square, London, SW1Y 4LB
Activities: Support activities for petroleum and natural gas mining
Parent: Awilco Drilling PLC
Officers: Jon Oliver Sinclair Bryce [1968] Director; Jan Borge Usland [1960] Director/Commercial Advisor [Norwegian]

Wilkes-Lucas Limited
Incorporated: 18 July 1941 *Employees:* 3
Net Worth: £292,044,992 *Total Assets:* £738,737,984
Registered Office: 165 Fleet Street, London, EC4A 2AE
Activities: Activities of other holding companies n.e.c.
Parent: Vesuvius Investments Limited
Officers: Jennifer Smith, Secretary; Henry James Knowles [1969] Director/General Counsel and Company Secretary; Ian James Lawson [1968] Director; Simon Christopher Upcott [1958] Director/Tax Manager

Williams Lea Group Limited
Incorporated: 7 April 1982
Net Worth: £143,655,008 *Total Assets:* £326,702,016
Registered Office: 55 Wells Street, London, W1A 3AE
Activities: Other business support service activities n.e.c.
Parent: Williams Lea Holdings Limited
Officers: David Nicholas Kassler [1966] Director [British/American]; Benedict James Smith [1969] Director

Williams Lea Holdings Limited
Incorporated: 3 February 2006
Net Worth: £293,079,584 *Total Assets:* £344,531,296
Registered Office: 55 Wells Street, London, W1A 3AE
Activities: Activities of head offices
Parent: Wertheimer UK Limited
Officers: David Nicholas Kassler [1966] Director [British/American]; Jonathan Andrew Simpson-Dent [1966] Director

Williams Lea Limited
Incorporated: 3 April 1987 *Employees:* 2,391
Net Worth: £38,065,000 *Total Assets:* £156,864,000
Registered Office: 55 Wells Street, London, W1A 3AE
Activities: Other business support service activities n.e.c.
Parent: Williams Lea Group Limited
Officers: Roger Stuart Howl [1962] Director/Accountant; David Nicholas Kassler [1966] Director [British/American]; Jonathan Andrew Simpson-Dent [1966] Director

Willis Faber Limited
Incorporated: 1 September 1978
Net Worth: £856,000,000 *Total Assets:* £884,000,000
Registered Office: 51 Lime Street, London, EC3M 7DQ
Activities: Other business support service activities n.e.c.
Parent: Willis Group Limited
Officers: Marcus Philip Dowding, Secretary; Steven James Alcock [1979] Director/Certified Accountant

Willis Group Limited
Incorporated: 25 February 1959
Net Worth: £5,327,591,424 *Total Assets:* £5,745,924,096
Registered Office: 51 Lime Street, London, EC3M 7DQ
Activities: Other business support service activities n.e.c.
Parent: Trinity Acquisition PLC
Officers: Marcus Philip Dowding, Secretary; Steven James Alcock [1979] Director; Andrew Krasner [1975] Director [American]; Catherine Roy [1965] Director

Willis Group Services Limited
Incorporated: 1 October 1979 *Employees:* 604
Net Worth: £66,000,000 *Total Assets:* £708,000,000
Registered Office: 51 Lime Street, London, EC3M 7DQ
Activities: Other business support service activities n.e.c.
Parent: Willis Faber Limited
Officers: Richard Goff [1973] Director/Accountant; John Christopher Lewis [1965] Director/Finance Professional; Iain Vyvyan Pocock [1966] Director

Willis GS UK Holdings Limited
Incorporated: 7 October 2015
Net Worth: £325,443,776 *Total Assets:* £696,611,072
Registered Office: 51 Lime Street, London, EC3M 7DQ
Activities: Activities of other holding companies n.e.c.
Shareholders: Willis Overseas Investments Limited; Willis International Limited
Officers: Pamela Jane Thomson-Hall [1968] Programme Director and General Counsel

Willis GS UK Limited
Incorporated: 7 October 2015
Net Worth: £699,180,544 *Total Assets:* £707,781,952
Registered Office: 51 Lime Street, London, EC3M 7DQ
Activities: Non-trading company
Parent: Willis GS UK Holdings Limited
Officers: Pamela Jane Thomson-Hall [1968] Programme Director and General Counsel

Willis International Limited
Incorporated: 20 November 1975
Net Worth: £153,000,000 *Total Assets:* £498,000,000
Registered Office: 51 Lime Street, London, EC3M 7DQ
Activities: Activities of head offices
Parent: Willis Faber Limited
Officers: Adam Laird Garrard [1965] Director; Pamela Jane Thomson-Hall [1968] Director/Legal Counsel

Willis Investment UK Holdings Limited
Incorporated: 20 August 2008
Net Worth: £4,486,706,176 *Total Assets:* £9,730,360,320
Registered Office: 51 Lime Street, London, EC3M 7DQ
Activities: Activities of head offices
Parent: Willis Towers Watson Public Limited Company
Officers: Marcus Philip Dowding, Secretary; Steven James Alcock [1979] Director/Certified Accountant; Shirley Marie Girling [1969] Director/In-House Solicitor; Andrew Krasner [1975] Director [American]; Jonathan David Rand [1973] Director

Willis Limited
Incorporated: 12 April 1922 *Employees:* 3,243
Net Worth: £911,004,672 *Total Assets:* £5,299,796,992
Registered Office: 51 Lime Street, London, EC3M 7DQ
Activities: Non-life insurance
Parent: Willis Faber Limited
Officers: Marcus Philip Dowding, Secretary; Nicolas Aubert [1965] Director [French]; Rodney Pennington Baker-Bates [1944] Director; Peter James Carter [1970] Director; Rosemary Hilary [1955] Director; James Edward Kent [1967] Director; Eloise Marnie Martin [1975] Director; Dr Brendan Richard O'Neill [1948] Director; Catherine Roy [1965] Director; Peter Anderson Shaw [1959] Director; Alastair John Pardoe Swift [1970] Director/Insurance Broker; Sarah Joan Turvill [1953] Director; James Henry Willens [1956] Director

Willis Overseas Investments Limited
Incorporated: 22 August 1997
Net Worth: £120,000,000 *Total Assets:* £184,000,000
Registered Office: 51 Lime Street, London, EC3M 7DQ
Activities: Activities of head offices
Parent: Willis International Limited
Officers: Katherine Louise Clark [1970] Director/Accountant

Willis Towers Watson UK Holdings Limited
Incorporated: 20 September 2016
Net Worth: £8,311,111,168 *Total Assets:* £8,311,111,168
Registered Office: 51 Lime Street, London, EC3M 7DQ
Activities: Activities of other holding companies n.e.c.
Parent: TA I Limited
Officers: Marcus Philip Dowding, Secretary; Steven James Alcock [1979] Director; Shirley Marie Girling [1969] Director/In-House Solicitor; Andrew Krasner [1975] Director [American]; Jonathan David Rand [1973] Director

Wilmington PLC
Incorporated: 30 January 1995 *Employees:* 849
Previous: Wilmington Group PLC
Net Worth: £42,434,000 *Total Assets:* £150,780,992
Registered Office: 5th Floor, 10 Whitechapel High Street, London, E1 8QS
Activities: Activities of head offices
Officers: Daniel Carl Barton, Secretary; Richard John Amos [1967] Director; Derek Raymond Anthony Carter [1949] Director; Paul Bernard Dollman [1956] Director; Martin William Howard Morgan [1950] Director; Nathalie Esther Schwarz [1970] Director

Wilphoenix (UK) Limited
Incorporated: 30 December 2009
Net Worth: £121,948,936 *Total Assets:* £355,793,152
Registered Office: 3rd Floor, 11-12 St James's Square, London, SW1Y 4LB
Activities: Support activities for petroleum and natural gas mining
Parent: Awilco Drilling PLC
Officers: Jon Oliver Sinclair Bryce [1968] Director; Jan Borge Usland [1960] Director/Commercial Advisor [Norwegian]

Wilsonart Limited
Incorporated: 23 August 2012 *Employees:* 131
Net Worth: £54,780,016 *Total Assets:* £138,668,176
Registered Office: 100 New Bridge Street, London, EC4V 6JA
Activities: Activities of head offices
Major Shareholder: Donald Gogel
Officers: William Joseph Thesing, Secretary; Jeffrey Scott Lee [1969] Director/Business Executive [American]; Timothy John O'Brien [1963] Director/Chief Executive Officer [American]; Alan Timothy Pearson [1969] Director/Western Europe President; Jeffrey Hugh Robb [1967] Finance Director

Wind UK Invest Limited
Incorporated: 15 January 2014
Net Worth: £144,774,000 *Total Assets:* £309,574,016
Registered Office: 4th Floor, 41 Moorgate, London, EC2R 6PP
Activities: Activities of head offices
Shareholders: Statkraft UK Limited; State Administration of Foreign Exchange
Officers: Luke James Freeman, Secretary; David John Flood [1980] Director/VP; Jingshen Hu [1980] Director/Deputy CEO [Chinese]; Andrew Scott Wilkie [1983] Director/Investment Manager [Australian]; Bjorn Fredrik Mo Ostgren [1966] Director/Vice President [Swedish]

Winterflood Securities Limited
Incorporated: 8 April 1988 *Employees:* 265
Net Worth: £71,064,368 *Total Assets:* £688,042,752
Registered Office: The Atrium Building, Cannon Bridge, 25 Dowgate, London, EC4R 2GA
Activities: Financial intermediation not elsewhere classified
Parent: Close Brothers Holdings Limited
Officers: James Stapleton, Secretary; Grant Michael Davidson [1973] Director; Bradley Terence Dyer [1969] Director; Michael Bartlett Morgan [1965] Director; Preben Prebensen [1956] Director/Chairman; Simon Mark Rafferty [1972] Director/Secretary; Alexander Matthew Skrine [1977] Director; Joseph Daniel David Winkley [1973] Director; Philip James Yarrow [1968] Director/Accountant

Winton Capital Management Limited
Incorporated: 3 February 1997 *Employees:* 375
Net Worth: £136,000,000 *Total Assets:* £222,671,008
Registered Office: Third Floor, 20 Old Bailey, London, EC4M 7AN
Activities: Security and commodity contracts dealing activities
Parent: Winton Group Limited
Officers: David Winton Harding [1961] Director/Fund Manager; Andrew Moss [1975] Director; Amy Brigid Ann Rentoul [1961] Director/Lawyer

Winton Group Limited
Incorporated: 4 October 2013 *Employees:* 453
Previous: Winton Capital Group Limited
Net Worth: £228,419,008 *Total Assets:* £314,668,000
Registered Office: Third Floor, 20 Old Bailey, London, EC4M 7AN
Activities: Other business support service activities n.e.c.
Major Shareholder: David Winton Harding
Officers: Amy Brigid Ann Rentoul, Secretary; Anthony Daniell [1954] Director/Vice Chairman; David Winton Harding [1961] Director/Fund Manager; The Hon Martin John Hunt [1962] Director/Fund Manager; Amal Osman Murgian [1967] Director [Kenyan/American]; Amy Brigid Ann Rentoul [1961] Director/Lawyer; Isobel Nicol Sharp [1956] Director/Chartered Accountant; Sir David Alan Walker [1939] Director

Wipro Holdings (UK) Limited
Incorporated: 9 December 2002
Net Worth: £32,232,928 *Total Assets:* £115,971,912
Registered Office: Devonshire House, 60 Goswell Road, London, EC1M 7AD
Activities: Other business support service activities n.e.c.
Parent: Wipro Limited
Officers: Nallathur Saravanan Balasubramanian [1965] Director [Indian]; Ramesh Phillips [1970] Director/Head of Operations-Europe

The Wireless Infrastructure Company Limited
Incorporated: 24 January 1997 *Employees:* 5
Net Worth: £23,577,598 *Total Assets:* £136,674,320
Registered Office: Level 13, The Broadgate Tower, Primrose Street, London, EC2A 2EW
Activities: Wireless telecommunications activities
Parent: The Wireless Resources Company Limited
Officers: Bryan Doak, Secretary; Scott Terrence Coates [1971] Managing Director; Bryan Doak [1968] Director/Chartered Accountant; James Michael Fowkes [1976] Director/Chartered Surveyor; Richard David Grimes [1975] Director/Chartered Surveyor; Nigel Moss [1975] Director

Wireless Infrastructure Group Limited
Incorporated: 26 April 2005 *Employees:* 4
Net Worth: £1,267,000 *Total Assets:* £131,551,000
Registered Office: Level 13, The Broadgate Tower, Primrose Street, London, EC2A 2EW
Activities: Activities of head offices
Parent: UK Wig II Limited
Officers: Bryan Doak, Secretary; Scott Terrence Coates [1971] Director; Bryan Doak [1968] Director/Chartered Accountant; Nigel Moss [1975] Director

Wisdom Profit (UK) Development Limited
Incorporated: 20 October 2014
Net Worth: £106,212,040 *Total Assets:* £106,229,608
Registered Office: 3rd Floor, 11-12 St James's Square, London, SW1Y 4LB
Activities: Other food services
Shareholders: Wisdom Profit Development Limited; Shanghai State-Owned Assets Supervision and Administration Commission of The State Council
Officers: Min Fang [1967] Director [Chinese]; Bo Jin [1974] Director/General Manager [Chinese]; Yingfei Li [1986] Director/Investment Manager [German]; Tonghong Wu [1974] Director/President [Chinese]

Wise Conclusion
Incorporated: 3 August 1994
Net Worth: £138,730,000 *Total Assets:* £154,083,008
Registered Office: Sea Containers House, 18 Upper Ground, London, SE1 9GL
Activities: Activities of head offices
Parent: Belgrave Square
Officers: Charles Ward Van Der Welle [1959] Director/Group Treasurer; Steve Richard Winters [1968] Director/Chartered Accountant

Witan Investment Trust PLC
Incorporated: 17 February 1909
Net Worth: £1,980,520,960 *Total Assets:* £2,230,278,912
Registered Office: 14 Queen Annes Gate, London, SW1H 9AA
Activities: Activities of investment trusts
Officers: Andrew Leighton Craig Bell [1955] Director/CEO Investment Trust Company; Henry Merton Henderson [1952] Director/Stockbroker; Suzy Anne Efua Gloria Neubert [1965] Director; Richard John Oldfield [1955] Director; John Scott Perry [1954] Director; Benjamin Charlton Rogoff [1972] Director/Fund Manager; Anthony Watson [1945] Director; Paul Tennant Yates [1957] Director

Wittington Investments (Properties) Limited
Incorporated: 24 February 2009 *Employees:* 2
Net Worth: £46,962,412 *Total Assets:* £204,649,504
Registered Office: Weston Centre, 10 Grosvenor Street, London, W1K 4QY
Activities: Other business support service activities n.e.c.
Parent: Wittington Investments Limited
Officers: Amanda Geday, Secretary; Kevin Martin Boylan [1970] Director; Helen Victoria Gibson [1967] Director; Martin Edward Michael Hattrell [1961] Director; Charles Daniel Edward Mason [1966] Director; George Garfield Weston [1964] Director [Canadian]; Guy Howard Weston [1960] Director

Wittington Investments Finance Limited
Incorporated: 12 March 2014
Net Worth: £646,521,984 *Total Assets:* £737,468,992
Registered Office: Weston Centre, 10 Grosvenor Street, London, W1K 4QY
Activities: Non-trading company
Parent: Wittington Investments Limited
Officers: Amanda Susan Millett Geday, Secretary; Kate Hobhouse [1962] Director [Canadian]; Charles Daniel Edward Mason [1966] Director/Chief Investment Officer; George Garfield Weston [1964] Director [Canadian]; Guy Howard Weston [1960] Director

Wittington Investments Limited
Incorporated: 22 March 1941 *Employees:* 133,913
Net Worth: £5,966,000,128 *Total Assets:* £14,330,000,384
Registered Office: Weston Centre, 10 Grosvenor Street, London, W1K 4QY
Activities: Manufacture of other food products n.e.c.
Shareholders: Camilla Dalglish; Kate Hobhouse; Jana Ruth Khayat; Sophia Mary Mason; Eliza Mitchell; Melissa Baron Murdoch; Guy Howard Weston; George Garfield Weston; Galen Weston
Officers: Amanda Geday, Secretary; Emma Susan Adamo [1963] Director [Canadian]; Sir Harry Arieh Simon Djanogly [1938] Director; Martin Edward Michael Hattrell [1961] Director; Anna Catrina Hobhouse [1962] Director; Charles Daniel Edward Mason [1966] Director; Garth John Weston [1969] Managing Director; George Garfield Weston [1964] Director [Canadian]; George Grainger Weston [1923] Director [Canadian]; Guy Howard Weston [1960] Director; Willard Gordon Galen Weston [1940] Director [Canadian]

WM SA Investments Limited
Incorporated: 25 February 2011 *Employees:* 3
Net Worth: £339,891,552 *Total Assets:* £945,702,336
Registered Office: c/o Clarusone Sourcing Services, Russell Square, London, WC1B 5EH
Activities: Other business support service activities n.e.c.
Parent: Walmart, Inc.
Officers: Matthew William Allen [1976] Director [American]; John Caraway McDowell [1964] Director [American]; Chase Nicholas Tacker [1983] Director [American]

WMG Acquisition (UK) Limited
Incorporated: 8 December 2003
Net Worth: £107,340,000 *Total Assets:* £755,628,032
Registered Office: Cannon Place, 78 Cannon Street, London, EC4N 6AF
Activities: Activities of head offices
Major Shareholder: Leonard Blavatnik
Officers: Roger Denys Booker [1946] Director; Kathryn Le Gassick [1973] Director/Solicitor; Paul Martin Robinson [1958] Director/Attorney [American]

WMG Finance Limited
Incorporated: 20 November 2012
Previous: PLG Holdco Limited
Net Worth: £58,888,304 *Total Assets:* £342,334,880
Registered Office: Cannon Place, 78 Cannon Street, London, EC4N 6AF
Activities: Activities of other holding companies n.e.c.
Parent: Warner Music Holdings Limited
Officers: Roger Denys Booker [1946] Director/VP International Tax and Treasury; Vince Capurso [1954] Director/SVP, Global Tax - WMG [American]; Frank Vincent Kimick [1966] Director/Treasurer [American]; Eric Levin [1962] Director/EVP and Chief Financial Officer - WMG [American]

WMR Holdco Limited
Incorporated: 22 November 2016
Net Worth Deficit: £5,064,960 *Total Assets:* £115,739,320
Registered Office: 18 St Swithin's Lane, London, EC4N 8AD
Activities: Activities of other holding companies n.e.c.
Parent: OSW Co Holdings 2 Limited
Officers: Dominic Tan, Secretary; Richard Abel [1970] Director/Investment Banking; Stephen Alan John Deeley [1980] Director/Investment Manager; Mark Jonathan Dooley [1962] Director/Investment Banker [Australian]; Erin Kate Eisenberg [1978] Director [American]; Tom Kelly [1989] Director/Investment Manager [Irish]; Gordon Ian Winston Parsons [1967] Director/Accountant; Roberto Purcaro [1978] Senior Managing Director [Italian]; David Paul Tilstone [1969] Director/Banker

WMR JV Holdco Limited
Incorporated: 4 March 2014 *Employees:* 4
Net Worth: £112,636,304 *Total Assets:* £454,693,504
Registered Office: Two London Bridge, London, SE1 9RA
Activities: Activities of other holding companies n.e.c.
Shareholders: WMR Holdco Limited; Fuujin Power Limited
Officers: Serkan Bahceci [1972] Director/Banker; Charles John Gore Hazelwood [1963] Director/Banker; David Paul Tilstone [1969] Director/Investment Banker; Anthony James Wort [1977] Director/Banker

WMR JV Investco Limited
Incorporated: 4 March 2014
Net Worth: £112,636,296 *Total Assets:* £454,693,504
Registered Office: Two London Bridge, London, SE1 9RA
Activities: Trade of electricity
Parent: WMR JV Holdco Limited
Officers: Serkan Bahceci [1972] Director/Banker; Charles John Gore Hazelwood [1963] Director/Banker; David Paul Tilstone [1969] Director/Investment Banker; Anthony James Wort [1977] Director/Banker

The Wolfson Foundation
Incorporated: 6 March 2014 *Employees:* 8
Net Worth: £807,776,000 *Total Assets:* £808,065,984
Registered Office: 8 Queen Anne Street, London, W1G 9LD
Activities: Other credit granting n.e.c.
Officers: Paul Benjamin Ramsbottom, Secretary; Professor Sir Eric Albert Ash [1928] Director/Emeritus Professor; Professor Sir David Nicholas Cannadine [1950] Director/Professor; Dame Hermione Lee [1948] Director/President Wolfson College; Rebecca Sarah Marks [1974] Director/Film Producer; Lord Ian McColl of Dulwich [1933] Director/Emeritus Professor; Sir Michael Pepper [1942] Director/Professor; Sir Peter John Ratcliffe [1954] Director/Nuffield Professor of Clinical Medicine; Dame Jean Olwen Thomas [1942] Director/Master, St Catharine's College; Lord Leslie Arnold Turnberg [1934] Director/Retired Physician; Janet Frances Wolfson de Botton [1952] Director/Chairman of Charity; Charles Ralph Wolfson Townsley [1984] Director/Investment Management; Laura Helen Wolfson Townsley [1954] Director/Chairman of Charity

Woodside Energy Holdings (Senegal) Limited
Incorporated: 22 June 2016
Net Worth: £415,598,752 *Total Assets:* £415,598,752
Registered Office: 1st Floor, Sackville House, 143-149 Fenchurch Street, London, EC3M 6BN
Activities: Activities of other holding companies n.e.c.
Parent: Woodside Energy (UK) Limited
Officers: Robert James Edwardes [1945] Director/Executive [Australian]

Workspace 12 Limited
Incorporated: 31 March 2006
Net Worth: £263,900,976 *Total Assets:* £292,848,896
Registered Office: Canterbury Court, Kennington Park, 1-3 Brixton Road, London, SW9 6DE
Activities: Other letting and operating of own or leased real estate
Parent: Workspace Group PLC
Officers: Carmelina Carfora, Secretary; Angus Robert Boag [1959] Development Director; Graham Colin Clemett [1960] Director; Jameson Paul Hopkins [1968] Director; Dr Christopher John Pieroni [1958] Operations Director; John Robson [1977] Asset Management Director

Workspace 13 Limited
Incorporated: 1 June 2006
Net Worth: £455,509,248 *Total Assets:* £463,794,240
Registered Office: Canterbury Court, Kennington Park, 1-3 Brixton Road, London, SW9 6DE
Activities: Other letting and operating of own or leased real estate
Parent: Workspace Group PLC
Officers: Carmelina Carfora, Secretary; Angus Robert Boag [1959] Development Director; Graham Colin Clemett [1960] Director; Jameson Paul Hopkins [1968] Director; Dr Christopher John Pieroni [1958] Operations Director; John Robson [1977] Asset Management Director

Workspace 14 Limited
Incorporated: 1 June 2006
Net Worth: £909,258,496 *Total Assets:* £1,389,096,064
Registered Office: Canterbury Court, Kennington Park, 1-3 Brixton Road, London, SW9 6DE
Activities: Other letting and operating of own or leased real estate
Parent: Workspace Group PLC
Officers: Carmelina Carfora, Secretary; Angus Robert Boag [1959] Development Director; Graham Colin Clemett [1960] Director; Jameson Paul Hopkins [1968] Director; Dr Christopher John Pieroni [1958] Operations Director; John Robson [1977] Asset Management Director

Workspace Group PLC
Incorporated: 29 July 1986 *Employees:* 217
Net Worth: £1,712,899,968 *Total Assets:* £2,339,200,000
Registered Office: Canterbury Court, Kennington Park, 1-3 Brixton Road, London, SW9 6DE
Activities: Other letting and operating of own or leased real estate
Officers: Carmelina Carfora, Secretary; Graham Colin Clemett [1960] Director; Christopher Francis Girling [1954] Director; Jameson Paul Hopkins [1968] Director; Stephen Arthur Hubbard [1952] Director; Daniel John Kitchen [1952] Director; Ishbel Jean Stewart Macpherson [1960] Director; Dr Maria Victoria Moloney [1951] Director; Damon James Russell [1965] Director

World Fuel Services Europe, Ltd.
Incorporated: 28 July 2003 *Employees:* 253
Net Worth: £71,066,144 *Total Assets:* £1,190,469,888
Registered Office: Third Floor, The Broadgate Tower, 20 Primrose Street, London, EC2A 2RS
Activities: Wholesale of petroleum and petroleum products
Parent: WFS UK Holding Company II Limited
Officers: Richard Donald McMichael [1962] Director/Businessman [Canadian]; Michael John Ranger [1964] Director/Senior Vice President, Supply EMEAA Aviation; Paul Thomas Vian [1971] Director/SVP, EMEA Land

World Fuel Services European Holding Company I, Ltd.
Incorporated: 21 July 2003
Net Worth Deficit: £18,972,988 *Total Assets:* £127,679,784
Registered Office: Third Floor, The Broadgate Tower, 20 Primrose Street, London, EC2A 2RS
Activities: Activities of head offices
Parent: World Fuel Services Corporation
Officers: Richard Donald McMichael [1962] Director/Businessman [Canadian]

Worldline IT Services UK Limited
Incorporated: 2 May 2013 *Employees:* 516
Net Worth: £58,720,000 *Total Assets:* £170,230,000
Registered Office: Second Floor, Mid City Place, 71 High Holborn, London, WC1V 6EA
Activities: Information technology consultancy activities
Parent: Worldline SA
Officers: James Terence John Loughrey, Secretary; Helen Lisa Coleman [1968] Director; Marc-Henri Desportes [1972] Director/General Manager of Worldline [French]

Worldpay (UK) Limited
Incorporated: 15 July 2010 *Employees:* 3,354
Net Worth: £1,434,499,968 *Total Assets:* £3,931,000,064
Registered Office: The Walbrook Building, 25 Walbrook, London, EC4N 8AF
Activities: Other business support service activities n.e.c.
Parent: Worldpay Finance PLC
Officers: Christiaan Thomas Allen [1977] Finance Director; Rohinton Minoo Kalifa [1961] Director; Steven John Newton [1975] Director

Worldpay AP Ltd.
Incorporated: 14 October 2005 *Employees:* 15
Net Worth: £62,656,000 *Total Assets:* £448,169,984
Registered Office: The Walbrook Building, 25 Walbrook, London, EC4N 8AF
Activities: Financial intermediation not elsewhere classified
Parent: Worldpay Ecommerce Limited
Officers: Joanne Louise Bates [1971] Director; Mordechay Bring [1973] Director; Rohinton Minoo Kalifa [1961] Director; Stephen Lavaughn McKnight [1969] Director/Accountant [American]

Worldpay Ecommerce Limited
Incorporated: 26 August 2010
Net Worth: £343,380,000 *Total Assets:* £474,294,016
Registered Office: The Walbrook Building, 25 Walbrook, London, EC4N 8AF
Activities: Other business support service activities n.e.c.
Parent: Worldpay Finance PLC
Officers: Mordechay Bring [1973] Director; Rohinton Minoo Kalifa [1961] Director

Worldpay Finance PLC
Incorporated: 30 September 2010
Previous: Worldpay Finance Limited
Net Worth: £1,458,830,976 *Total Assets:* £2,807,803,904
Registered Office: The Walbrook Building, 25 Walbrook, London, EC4N 8AF
Activities: Other business support service activities n.e.c.
Parent: Ship Midco Limited
Officers: Nelson Greene, Secretary; Rohinton Minoo Kalifa [1961] Director; Steven John Newton [1975] Director/Chief Operating Officer

Worldpay Group Limited
Incorporated: 5 November 2013 *Employees:* 5,211
Previous: Worldpay Group PLC
Net Worth: £960,499,968 *Total Assets:* £8,142,600,192
Registered Office: The Walbrook Building, 25 Walbrook, London, EC4N 8AF
Activities: Other business support service activities n.e.c.
Parent: Worldpay International Limited
Officers: Nelson Greene [1963] Director/Chief Legal Officer & Corporate Secretary [American]; Jared Michael Warner [1977] Director/Deputy General Counsel [American]

Worldpay Limited
Incorporated: 26 August 1997 *Employees:* 8
Net Worth: £178,584,992 *Total Assets:* £461,369,984
Registered Office: The Walbrook Building, 25 Walbrook, London, EC4N 8AF
Activities: Other business support service activities n.e.c.
Parent: Worldpay Ecommerce Limited
Officers: Joanne Louise Bates [1971] Director; Mordechay Bring [1973] Director; Rohinton Minoo Kalifa [1961] Director/Chief Executive Officer; Stephen Lavaughn McKnight [1969] Director/Accountant [American]; Steven John Newton [1975] Director/Chief Operating Officer

Worldwide Healthcare Trust PLC
Incorporated: 14 February 1995
Net Worth: £1,202,188,032 *Total Assets:* £1,311,150,976
Registered Office: 1 Wood Street, London, EC2V 7WS
Activities: Activities of investment trusts
Officers: Sarah Catherine Bates [1959] Director; Sven Heinz Borho [1967] Director/Portfolio Manager [American]; David Mark Anthony Holbrook [1960] Director/Venture Capitalist; Douglas Fraser McCutcheon [1964] Director/President, Gormley Limited [Canadian]; Sir Martin Gregory Smith [1943] Director; Humphrey Van Der Klugt [1953] Director

WP R Holdco Limited
Incorporated: 21 March 2016
Net Worth: £131,287,824 *Total Assets:* £203,222,624
Registered Office: Reiss Building, 12 Picton Place, London, W1U 1BW
Activities: Activities of distribution holding companies
Parent: WP R Midco 2 Limited
Officers: Christos Angelides [1963] Director; Jonathan Neil Blanchard [1965] Director; Flavio Porciani [1985] Director/Investment Professional [German]; Daniel Zilberman [1973] Managing Director [American]

WP R Midco 1 Limited
Incorporated: 21 March 2016 *Employees:* 1,377
Net Worth: £100,517,000 *Total Assets:* £226,974,000
Registered Office: Reiss Building, 12 Picton Place, London, W1U 1BW
Activities: Activities of distribution holding companies
Officers: Christos Angelides [1963] Director; Jonathan Neil Blanchard [1965] Director; Flavio Porciani [1985] Director/Investment Professional [German]; Daniel Zilberman [1973] Managing Director [American]

WP R Midco 2 Limited
Incorporated: 21 March 2016
Net Worth: £138,320,288 *Total Assets:* £143,381,936
Registered Office: Reiss Building, 12 Picton Place, London, W1U 1BW
Activities: Activities of distribution holding companies
Parent: WP R Midco 1 Limited
Officers: Christos Angelides [1963] Director; Jonathan Neil Blanchard [1965] Director; Flavio Porciani [1985] Director/Investment Professional [German]; Daniel Zilberman [1973] Managing Director [American]

WPG Finance Limited
Incorporated: 8 April 2013 *Employees:* 7
Net Worth: £928,552,384 *Total Assets:* £933,070,208
Registered Office: Ground Floor, 30 City Road, London, EC1Y 2AB
Activities: Other credit granting n.e.c.
Parent: William Pears Group Limited
Officers: William Frederick Bennett, Secretary; David Alan Pears [1968] Director; Mark Andrew Pears [1962] Director; Sir Trevor Steven Pears [1964] Director

WPG Treasury Limited
Incorporated: 8 April 2013
Net Worth: £134,432,736 *Total Assets:* £288,321,600
Registered Office: Ground Floor, 30 City Road, London, EC1Y 2AB
Activities: Other credit granting n.e.c.
Parent: The William Pears Group of Companies Limited
Officers: William Frederick Bennett, Secretary; David Alan Pears [1968] Director; Mark Andrew Pears [1962] Director; Sir Trevor Steven Pears [1964] Director

WPP 1178
Incorporated: 12 December 1991
Net Worth: £4,254,933,248 *Total Assets:* £4,266,067,712
Registered Office: Sea Containers House, 18 Upper Ground, London, SE1 9GL
Activities: Non-trading company
Parent: WPP Beans Limited
Officers: Charles Ward Van Der Welle [1959] Director/Group Treasurer; Steve Richard Winters [1968] Director/Chartered Accountant

WPP 2005 Limited
Incorporated: 1 March 1971 *Employees:* 224
Net Worth: £3,207,300,096 *Total Assets:* £4,518,000,128
Registered Office: Sea Containers House, 18 Upper Ground, London, SE1 9GL
Activities: Activities of head offices
Shareholders: WPP Madrid Square Limited; WPP Jubilee Limited
Officers: Marie Winifred Capes, Secretary; Mark Julian Read [1966] Director/Chief Executive; Andrew Grant Balfour Scott [1968] Director/Chief Operating Officer; Charles Ward Van Der Welle [1959] Director of Treasury; Steve Richard Winters [1968] Director/Chartered Accountant

WPP 2318 Limited
Incorporated: 11 May 2001
Net Worth: £358,289,536 *Total Assets:* £358,289,536
Registered Office: Sea Containers House, 18 Upper Ground, London, SE1 9GL
Activities: Activities of head offices
Parent: WPP 2323 Limited
Officers: Charles Ward Van Der Welle [1959] Director/Group Treasurer; Steve Richard Winters [1968] Director/Chartered Accountant

WPP 2323 Limited
Incorporated: 10 May 2001
Net Worth: £864,050,560 *Total Assets:* £864,050,560
Registered Office: Sea Containers House, 18 Upper Ground, London, SE1 9GL
Activities: Non-trading company
Parent: WPP Madrid Square Limited
Officers: Charles Ward Van Der Welle [1959] Director/Group Treasurer; Steve Richard Winters [1968] Director/Chartered Accountant

WPP 2709 Limited
Incorporated: 16 December 2003
Net Worth: £251,386,000 *Total Assets:* £251,386,000
Registered Office: Sea Containers House, 18 Upper Ground, London, SE1 9GL
Activities: Non-trading company
Parent: Intact Limited
Officers: Charles Ward Van Der Welle [1959] Director/Group Treasurer; Steve Richard Winters [1968] Director/Chartered Accountant

WPP Beans Limited
Incorporated: 20 September 1999
Net Worth: £3,769,989,120 *Total Assets:* £3,770,113,024
Registered Office: Sea Containers House, 18 Upper Ground, London, SE1 9GL
Activities: Non-trading company
Parent: WPP Pearls Limited
Officers: Andrew Robertson Payne [1957] Director; Charles Ward Van Der Welle [1959] Director of Treasury; Steve Richard Winters [1968] Director/Chartered Accountant

WPP Brands Development Holdings (UK) Limited
Incorporated: 1 March 1999
Previous: Young & Rubicam Development (Holdings) Limited
Net Worth: £493,494,016 *Total Assets:* £493,630,016
Registered Office: Greater London House, Hampstead Road, London, NW1 7QP
Activities: Other business support service activities n.e.c.
Shareholders: WPP Russell UK Two Limited; WPP Jubilee Ltd
Officers: Helina Mazur, Secretary; David Julian Gladwell [1970] Director/Accountant; Ian Gary Paul [1963] Director/Accountant; Ignacio Cabezon Pinilla [1956] Director/CFO/COO [Spanish]

WPP Brands Holdings (UK) Limited
Incorporated: 29 December 1980
Previous: Young & Rubicam Holdings (U.K.) Limited
Net Worth: £214,995,008 *Total Assets:* £214,995,008
Registered Office: Greater London House, Hampstead Road, London, NW1 7QP
Activities: Non-trading company
Parent: Young & Rubicam Development (Holdings) Ltd
Officers: Helina Mazur, Secretary; David Julian Gladwell [1970] Director/Accountant; Ian Gary Paul [1963] Director/Accountant; Ignacio Cabezon Pinilla [1956] Director/CFO/COO [Spanish]

WPP Compete
Incorporated: 3 October 2005
Net Worth: £2,848,218,880 *Total Assets:* £2,848,218,880
Registered Office: Sea Containers House, 18 Upper Ground, London, SE1 9GL
Activities: Non-trading company
Parent: WPP Jubilee Limited
Officers: Charles Ward Van Der Welle [1959] Director of Treasury; Steve Richard Winters [1968] Director/Chartered Accountant

WPP Dutch Holdings Limited
Incorporated: 11 August 1998
Net Worth: £3,199,511,040 *Total Assets:* £3,199,870,976
Registered Office: Sea Containers House, 18 Upper Ground, London, SE1 9GL
Activities: Non-trading company
Parent: Eaton Square Limited
Officers: Charles Ward Van Der Welle [1959] Director/Group Treasurer; Steve Richard Winters [1968] Director/Chartered Accountant

WPP Finance 2010
Incorporated: 26 October 2010
Net Worth: £11,824,482 *Total Assets:* £2,185,954,816
Registered Office: Sea Containers House, 18 Upper Ground, London, SE1 9GL
Activities: Activities of other holding companies n.e.c.
Shareholders: WPP Group (Nominees) Ltd; WPP Finance (UK)
Officers: Charles Ward Van Der Welle [1959] Director of Treasury; Steve Richard Winters [1968] Director/Chartered Accountant

WPP Finance 2013
Incorporated: 30 October 2013
Net Worth: £22,694,832 *Total Assets:* £2,104,328,704
Registered Office: Sea Containers House, 18 Upper Ground, London, SE1 9GL
Activities: Other business support service activities n.e.c.
Parent: WPP Group (UK) Ltd
Officers: Charles Ward Van Der Welle [1959] Director; Steve Richard Winters [1968] Director/Chartered Accountant

WPP Finance Co. Limited
Incorporated: 16 March 2000
Net Worth: £1,461,809,024 *Total Assets:* £2,985,154,048
Registered Office: Sea Containers House, 18 Upper Ground, London, SE1 9GL
Activities: Other business support service activities n.e.c.
Parent: WPP LN Limited
Officers: Charles Ward Van Der Welle [1959] Director of Treasury; Steve Richard Winters [1968] Director/Chartered Accountant

WPP Fitzroy Square
Incorporated: 24 March 2017
Net Worth: £671,606,720 *Total Assets:* £671,606,720
Registered Office: Sea Containers House, 18 Upper Ground, London, SE1 9GL
Activities: Activities of head offices
Parent: WPP Jubilee Limited
Officers: Charles Ward Van Der Welle [1959] Director of Treasury; Steve Richard Winters [1968] Director/Chartered Accountant

WPP Global
Incorporated: 28 June 2007
Net Worth: £10,027,395,072 *Total Assets:* £10,027,397,120
Registered Office: Sea Containers House, 18 Upper Ground, London, SE1 9GL
Activities: Activities of head offices
Parent: WPP Jubilee Limited
Officers: Charles Ward Van Der Welle [1959] Director of Treasury; Steve Richard Winters [1968] Director/Chartered Accountant

WPP Group (UK) Ltd
Incorporated: 12 December 1991
Net Worth: £4,261,128,960 *Total Assets:* £4,558,473,216
Registered Office: Sea Containers House, 18 Upper Ground, London, SE1 9GL
Activities: Non-trading company
Shareholders: WPP Jubilee Limited; WPP LN Limited
Officers: Charles Ward Van Der Welle [1959] Director of Treasury; Steve Richard Winters [1968] Director/Chartered Accountant

WPP Group Holdings Limited
Incorporated: 5 December 1991
Net Worth: £262,970,000 *Total Assets:* £634,384,000
Registered Office: Sea Containers House, 18 Upper Ground, London, SE1 9GL
Activities: Non-trading company
Shareholders: WPP Russell UK Two Limited; WPP 2709 Limited
Officers: Kevin Farewell [1954] Director/Senior Tax Counsel [American]; Charles Ward Van Der Welle [1959] Director/Group Treasurer; Steve Richard Winters [1968] Director/Chartered Accountant

WPP Headline
Incorporated: 17 May 2007
Net Worth: £2,477,142,528 *Total Assets:* £2,477,144,064
Registered Office: Sea Containers House, 18 Upper Ground, London, SE1 9GL
Activities: Activities of head offices
Parent: WPP Jubilee Limited
Officers: Charles Ward Van Der Welle [1959] Director of Treasury; Steve Richard Winters [1968] Director/Chartered Accountant

WPP Jubilee Limited
Incorporated: 8 November 2012 *Employees:* 134,413
Net Worth: £14,804,100,096 *Total Assets:* £40,654,798,848
Registered Office: Sea Containers House, 18 Upper Ground, London, SE1 9GL
Activities: Activities of head offices
Officers: Charles Ward Van Der Welle [1959] Director of Treasury; Steve Richard Winters [1968] Director/Chartered Accountant

WPP LN Limited
Incorporated: 9 August 2000
Net Worth: £5,579,222,016 *Total Assets:* £5,582,645,760
Registered Office: Sea Containers House, 18 Upper Ground, London, SE1 9GL
Activities: Non-trading company
Parent: WPP 2005 Limited
Officers: Charles Ward Van Der Welle [1959] Director/Group Treasurer; Steve Richard Winters [1968] Director/Chartered Accountant

WPP Magic Limited
Incorporated: 19 December 2002
Net Worth: £2,598,273,024 *Total Assets:* £3,531,806,976
Registered Office: Sea Containers House, 18 Upper Ground, London, SE1 9GL
Activities: Non-trading company
Parent: WPP Sparky Limited
Officers: Charles Ward Van Der Welle [1959] Director/Group Treasurer; Steve Richard Winters [1968] Director/Chartered Accountant

WPP Marketing Communications Spain
Incorporated: 16 March 2001 *Employees:* 4
Net Worth: £151,610,128 *Total Assets:* £344,875,680
Registered Office: Sea Containers House, 18 Upper Ground, London, SE1 9GL
Activities: Non-trading company
Parent: WPP 2318 Limited
Officers: Charles Ward Van Der Welle [1959] Director of Treasury; Steve Richard Winters [1968] Director/Chartered Accountant

WPP North Atlantic Limited
Incorporated: 12 December 1991
Net Worth: £3,416,218,112 *Total Assets:* £3,416,218,112
Registered Office: Sea Containers House, 18 Upper Ground, London, SE1 9GL
Activities: Non-trading company
Parent: WPP Dutch Holdings Limited
Officers: Charles Ward Van Der Welle [1959] Director/Group Treasurer; Steve Richard Winters [1968] Director/Chartered Accountant

WPP Pearls Limited
Incorporated: 20 September 1999
Net Worth: £3,361,861,888 *Total Assets:* £3,361,861,888
Registered Office: Sea Containers House, 18 Upper Ground, London, SE1 9GL
Activities: Non-trading company
Parent: WPP North Atlantic Limited
Officers: Charles Ward Van Der Welle [1959] Director of Treasury; Steve Richard Winters [1968] Director/Chartered Accountant

WPP Rocky Ltd
Incorporated: 13 December 2007
Net Worth: £230,320,992 *Total Assets:* £230,320,992
Registered Office: Sea Containers House, 18 Upper Ground, London, SE1 9GL
Activities: Advertising agencies
Parent: WPP Jubilee Limited
Officers: Charles Ward Van Der Welle [1959] Director of Treasury; Steve Richard Winters [1968] Director/Chartered Accountant

WPP Sparky Limited
Incorporated: 19 December 2001
Net Worth: £2,497,462,016 *Total Assets:* £2,497,462,016
Registered Office: Sea Containers House, 18 Upper Ground, London, SE1 9GL
Activities: Non-trading company
Shareholders: WPP Spike Limited; WPP Group (UK) Ltd
Officers: Charles Ward Van Der Welle [1959] Director/Group Treasurer; Steve Richard Winters [1968] Director/Chartered Accountant

WPP Sphinx Limited
Incorporated: 27 November 2013
Net Worth: £8,692,347,904 *Total Assets:* £8,692,347,904
Registered Office: Sea Containers House, 18 Upper Ground, London, SE1 9GL
Activities: Other business support service activities n.e.c.
Parent: WPP Jubilee Limited
Officers: Charles Ward Van Der Welle [1959] Director; Steve Richard Winters [1968] Director/Chartered Accountant

WPP Spike Limited
Incorporated: 19 December 2001
Net Worth: £1,461,248,000 *Total Assets:* £1,461,515,008
Registered Office: Sea Containers House, 18 Upper Ground, London, SE1 9GL
Activities: Non-trading company
Parent: WPP Group (UK) Ltd
Officers: Charles Ward Van Der Welle [1959] Director/Group Treasurer; Steve Richard Winters [1968] Director/Chartered Accountant

WPP Toronto Ltd
Incorporated: 13 December 2007
Net Worth: £357,804,000 *Total Assets:* £359,520,000
Registered Office: Sea Containers House, 18 Upper Ground, London, SE1 9GL
Activities: Activities of head offices
Parent: WPP Rocky Ltd
Officers: Charles Ward Van Der Welle [1959] Director of Treasury; Steve Richard Winters [1968] Director/Chartered Accountant

WPP UK Germany Holdings
Incorporated: 24 March 2017
Net Worth: £284,348,800 *Total Assets:* £284,348,800
Registered Office: Sea Containers House, 18 Upper Ground, London, SE1 9GL
Activities: Activities of head offices
Parent: WPP Jubilee Limited
Officers: Charles Ward Van Der Welle [1959] Director of Treasury; Steve Richard Winters [1968] Director/Chartered Accountant

WPP UK Torre
Incorporated: 18 May 2017
Net Worth: £575,240,384 *Total Assets:* £575,240,384
Registered Office: Sea Containers House, 18 Upper Ground, London, SE1 9GL
Activities: Activities of head offices
Parent: WPP US Investments Limited
Officers: Charles Ward Van Der Welle [1959] Director of Treasury; Steve Richard Winters [1968] Director/Chartered Accountant

WPP Unicorn Limited
Incorporated: 15 July 2002
Net Worth: £323,854,016 *Total Assets:* £323,854,016
Registered Office: Sea Containers House, 18 Upper Ground, London, SE1 9GL
Activities: Non-trading company
Parent: Cockpit Holdings Limited
Officers: Charles Ward Van Der Welle [1959] Director/Group Treasurer; Steve Richard Winters [1968] Director/Chartered Accountant

WPP US Investments Limited
Incorporated: 28 November 2012
Net Worth: £10,805,979,136 *Total Assets:* £11,302,666,240
Registered Office: Sea Containers House, 18 Upper Ground, London, SE1 9GL
Activities: Activities of head offices
Parent: WPP Jubilee Limited
Officers: Charles Ward Van Der Welle [1959] Director of Treasury; Steve Richard Winters [1968] Director/Chartered Accountant

WR Midco Limited
Incorporated: 15 November 2016
Net Worth: £114,520,792 *Total Assets:* £114,531,816
Registered Office: 2nd Floor, 11 Old Jewry, London, EC2R 8DU
Activities: Residential nursing care facilities
Parent: Welltower, Inc
Officers: Stuart Roderick Jenkin [1957] Director; Justin Reynolds Skiver [1977] Director [American]

WRBC Corporate Member Limited
Incorporated: 7 November 2001
Net Worth Deficit: £37,226,100 *Total Assets:* £369,292,352
Registered Office: 14th Floor, 52 Lime Street, London, EC3M 7AF
Activities: Non-life insurance
Parent: W. R. Berkley Syndicate Holdings Limited
Officers: Ira Seth Lederman, Secretary/Senior Vice President [American]; William Robert Jr Berkley [1945] Director [American]; William Robert Jr Berkley [1972] Director/Executive Vice President [American]; Alastair Blades [1966] Director; James Patrick Bronner [1961] Director/E.V.P [American]; Ira Seth Lederman [1953] Director and Secretary [American]; Steven William Taylor [1959] Director and Insurance Executive

Wright Express International Holdings Limited
Incorporated: 27 March 2012 *Employees:* 2
Net Worth: £143,625,216 *Total Assets:* £366,444,832
Registered Office: Fourth Floor, East Building, 1 London Bridge, London, SE1 9BG
Activities: Activities of other holding companies n.e.c.
Parent: WEX Inc
Officers: Anant Ramanbhai Patel [1974] Director/Vice President; Roberto Simon Rabanal [1974] Director [Spanish/American]; Hilary Ann Rapkin [1966] Director/SVP of Legal, General Counsel and Corporate Secretary [American]

WSP Group Holdings Limited
Incorporated: 14 September 2011
Net Worth: £402,982,016 *Total Assets:* £472,518,016
Registered Office: WSP House, 70 Chancery Lane, London, WC2A 1AF
Activities: Activities of other holding companies n.e.c.
Parent: WSP Group Limited
Officers: Karen Anne Sewell, Secretary; Miles Lawrence Barnard [1966] Finance Director; Mark William Naysmith [1966] Director/Civil Engineer

WSP Group Limited
Incorporated: 1 June 1987
Net Worth: £293,068,992 *Total Assets:* £332,639,008
Registered Office: WSP House, 70 Chancery Lane, London, WC2A 1AF
Activities: Activities of other holding companies n.e.c.
Parent: WSP Holding UK Limited
Officers: Karen Anne Sewell, Secretary; Miles Lawrence Barnard [1966] Finance Director; Paul Kenneth Edward Dollin [1971] Director

WSP UK Limited
Incorporated: 11 August 1978 *Employees:* 4,530
Net Worth: £212,523,008 *Total Assets:* £508,828,000
Registered Office: WSP House, 70 Chancery Lane, London, WC2A 1AF
Activities: Engineering related scientific and technical consulting activities
Parent: WSP Group Holding AB
Officers: Karen Anne Sewell, Secretary; Miles Lawrence Barnard [1966] Finance Director; Mark William Naysmith [1966] Director/Civil Engineer; Michael Patrick Rogerson [1966] Director/Chartered Structural Engineer

WTI Ferrybridge Limited
Incorporated: 20 March 2017
Net Worth: £6,713,844 *Total Assets:* £248,105,824
Registered Office: 8th Floor, Portland House, Bressenden Place, London, SW1E 5BH
Activities: Treatment and disposal of non-hazardous waste
Parent: WTI Ferrybridge Holdings Limited
Officers: Jessica Gray [1978] Director/Solicitor; Paul Alexander William Green [1967] Managing Director; Mark Richard Haselhurst [1981] Finance Director; Michael Francis O'Friel [1960] Director/Vice President and General Counsel [American]

WTI/EFW Holdings Ltd
Incorporated: 6 April 2011
Net Worth: £153,691,920 *Total Assets:* £519,338,400
Registered Office: Cannon Place, 78 Cannon Street, London, EC4N 6AF
Activities: Combined office administrative service activities
Officers: Robert Boucher [1965] Director/CEO Wheelabrator Technologies Inc [American]; Alan Patrick Dunlea [1969] Director/Chief Financial Officer [American]; Jessica Gray [1978] Director/Solicitor; Paul Alexander William Green [1967] Managing Director; Mark Richard Haselhurst [1981] Finance Director; Michael Francis O'Friel [1960] Director/Executive [American]

Wyelands Holdings Limited
Incorporated: 11 December 2015 *Employees:* 30
Net Worth: £97,759,000 *Total Assets:* £610,633,024
Registered Office: 7 Hertford Street, London, W1J 7RH
Activities: Activities auxiliary to financial intermediation n.e.c.
Parent: SKG Financial Holdings PTE Limited
Officers: Ben Howard, Secretary; John David Crompton [1963] Director/Corporate Adviser; Ian Pierre Gomes [1957] Director/Chartered Accountant; Simon James Grenfell [1972] Director/Banker [Australian]; George Jay Hambro [1974] Director; John David Howland Jackson [1949] Director/Barrister; Iain Mark Hunter [1970] Director/Banking Services; Stephen John Kent Reid [1963] Director/Banker; Neil John Sawbridge [1963] Director/Accountant; David John Smith [1953] Director/Consultant

Oliver Wyman Limited
Incorporated: 28 November 1994 *Employees:* 573
Net Worth: £136,820,992 *Total Assets:* £318,327,008
Registered Office: 1 Tower Place West, Tower Place, London, EC3R 5BU
Activities: Other service activities n.e.c.
Parent: MMOW Limited
Officers: Sallie Ellis, Secretary; Matthew John Cunningham [1968] Director/Chief Financial Officer [American]; Dr Jean-Paul D'Offay [1972] Director/Chartered Accountant; Thomas Scott McDonald [1967] Director/Management Consultant [Canadian/British]; Davide Giacomo Taliente [1967] Director/Management Consultant [Italian]

XDG Limited
Incorporated: 18 March 1954
Net Worth: £208,075,008 *Total Assets:* £213,344,992
Registered Office: c/o Smiths Group PLC, 4th Floor, 11-12 St James's Square, London, SW1Y 4LB
Activities: Activities of head offices
Parent: Smiths Group PLC
Officers: Fiona Margaret Gillespie, Secretary; Marc Furlonger [1972] Director of Financial Controller; Fiona Margaret Gillespie [1969] Director/Company Secretary

Xerium Technologies Limited
Incorporated: 24 June 2004 *Employees:* 2
Net Worth: £171,804,624 *Total Assets:* £257,579,040
Registered Office: Eighth Floor, Ten Bishops Square, London, E1 6EG
Activities: Activities of head offices
Officers: Michael Francis Bly [1966] Director [American]; Harald Weimer [1964] Director [German]

XL Catlin Insurance Company UK Limited
Incorporated: 10 January 2005
Previous: Catlin Insurance Company (UK) Ltd.
Net Worth: £206,478,000 *Total Assets:* £1,525,981,056
Registered Office: 20 Gracechurch Street, London, EC3V 0BG
Activities: Non-life insurance
Parent: Catlin Insurance Company (UK) Holdings Ltd.
Officers: Marie Louise Rees, Secretary; Mark Rankin Cummings [1974] Director; Paul Greensmith [1975] Underwriting Director UK/Ireland; Claire Aimie Clara Ighodaro [1953] Director; Bryan Ruthven Joseph [1959] Director/Actuary [British/Trinidadian/Tobagonian]; Robert David Littlemore [1968] Director/Chief Executive, London Reinsurance; Sir John Michael Medlicott Vereker [1944] Director; Paul Wilson [1951] Director

XL Gracechurch Limited
Incorporated: 7 April 2003
Net Worth: £750,592,128 *Total Assets:* £750,604,096
Registered Office: 20 Gracechurch Street, London, EC3V 0BG
Activities: Activities of financial services holding companies
Parent: Axa SA
Officers: Marie Louise Rees, Secretary; Clynton Jacobus Luttig [1973] Director; Juliet Phillips [1972] Director/Chartered Accountant

XL Insurance (UK) Holdings Limited
Incorporated: 1 May 2001
Net Worth: £750,382,016 *Total Assets:* £777,950,016
Registered Office: 20 Gracechurch Street, London, EC3V 0BG
Activities: Activities of financial services holding companies
Parent: XL Gracechurch Limited
Officers: Marie Louise Rees, Secretary; Paul Richard Bradbrook [1976] Finance Director; Clynton Luttig [1973] Director/Group/Enterprise Expense & Allocations Controller; Juliet Phillips [1972] Director/Chartered Accountant

XL London Market Group Limited
Incorporated: 29 August 1984
Net Worth: £238,114,000 *Total Assets:* £244,859,008
Registered Office: 20 Gracechurch Street, London, EC3V 0BG
Activities: Non-life insurance
Parent: Axa SA
Officers: Marie Louise Rees, Secretary; Paul Richard Bradbrook [1976] Finance Director; Neil Donald Robertson [1968] Director/Insurance Executive

Xstrata Limited
Incorporated: 31 December 2001
Net Worth: £23,069,845,504 *Total Assets:* £24,004,446,208
Registered Office: 50 Berkeley Street, London, W1J 8HD
Activities: Other business support service activities n.e.c.
Parent: Glencore Services (UK) Ltd
Officers: Nicholas James Reid, Secretary; John William Burton [1965] Director/Solicitor; Martin William Haering [1964] Director/Accountant [Swiss]; Andreas Peter Hubmann [1966] Director/Accountant [Swiss]; Carlos Perezagua Marin [1974] Director/Manager [Spanish]

XTX Markets Limited
Incorporated: 30 January 2015 *Employees:* 47
Net Worth: £207,178,000 *Total Assets:* £258,720,992
Registered Office: R7, 14-18 Handyside Street, London, N1C 4DN
Activities: Security dealing on own account
Major Shareholder: Alexander Gerko
Officers: Mathieu Freville, Secretary; Dr Zarthustra Jal Amrolia [1963] Director; Nicola Beattie [1966] Director; Alexander Gerko [1979] Director [British/Russian]

XXIII Capital A Limited
Incorporated: 11 October 2016
Net Worth Deficit: £3,150,977 *Total Assets:* £192,074,736
Registered Office: 4th Floor, Welbeck Works, 33 Welbeck Street, London, W1G 8EX
Activities: Other business support service activities n.e.c.
Parent: XXIII Capital Limited
Officers: Andrew Bray [1976] Director/Accountant; Nicholas Gonella [1964] Director; Jason Traub [1975] Director/Financier

Yianis Docklands Hotels Limited
Incorporated: 8 May 2006
Net Worth Deficit: £36,464,340 *Total Assets:* £133,626,960
Registered Office: 6th Floor, Charles House, 108-110 Finchley Road, London, NW3 5JJ
Activities: Hotels and similar accommodation
Parent: Gold Quay Assets Limited
Officers: Yiannakis Theophani Christodoulou [1965] Director; Lambros Hadjiioannou [1978] Director

Yianis Holdings Limited
Incorporated: 26 November 2003 *Employees:* 253
Net Worth: £514,351,136 *Total Assets:* £887,897,344
Registered Office: 6th Floor, Charles House, 108-110 Finchley Road, London, NW3 5JJ
Activities: Activities of other holding companies n.e.c.
Major Shareholder: Yiannakis Christodoulou
Officers: Yiannakis Theophani Christodoulou [1965] Director; Lambros Hadjiioannou [1978] Director

Yianis Hotels Limited
Incorporated: 27 July 2005
Net Worth: £94,445,904 *Total Assets:* £199,508,240
Registered Office: 6th Floor, Charles House, 108-110 Finchley Road, London, NW3 5JJ
Activities: Hotels and similar accommodation
Parent: Gold Quay Assets Limited
Officers: Yiannakis Theophani Christodoulou [1965] Director; Christopher Christou [1961] Director/Solicitor; Lambros Hadjiioannou [1978] Director

Yianis Investments Limited
Incorporated: 19 January 2007
Net Worth: £97 *Total Assets:* £161,298,496
Registered Office: 6th Floor, Charles House, 108-110 Finchley Road, London, NW3 5JJ
Activities: Dormant company
Parent: Yianis Holdings Limited
Officers: Yiannakis Theophani Christodoulou [1965] Director; Lambros Hadjiioannou [1978] Director

YOA Holdco Limited
Incorporated: 24 April 2014
Net Worth: £264,134,400 *Total Assets:* £264,146,400
Registered Office: 163 Eversholt Street, London, NW1 1BU
Activities: Activities of other holding companies n.e.c.
Parent: Casual Dining Group Limited
Officers: Giles Matthew Oliver David, Secretary; Giles Matthew Oliver David [1967] Director/Accountant; Stephen Richards [1967] Director

York House W1 Limited
Incorporated: 18 November 1993
Net Worth: £174,002,112 *Total Assets:* £190,038,064
Registered Office: York House, 45 Seymour Street, London, W1H 7LX
Activities: Development of building projects
Parent: BL Office (Non-City) Holding Company Limited
Officers: Sarah Morrell Barzycki [1958] Director/Head of Finance; Paul Stuart Macey [1978] Director/Accountant; Jonathan Charles McNuff [1986] Director/Chartered Accountant; Charles John Middleton [1966] Director/Corporate Tax Executive; Timothy Andrew Roberts [1964] Director/Chartered Surveyor; Nigel Mark Webb [1963] Director/Chartered Surveyor

York Potash Holdings Limited
Incorporated: 10 December 2012
Net Worth: £76,661,000 *Total Assets:* £314,510,016
Registered Office: 3rd Floor, Greener House, 66-68 Haymarket, London, SW1Y 4RF
Activities: Support activities for other mining and quarrying
Parent: Sirius Minerals Holdings Limited
Officers: Nicholas Anthony King, Secretary; Christopher Neil Fraser [1974] Director; Nicholas Anthony King [1973] Director/General Counsel; Thomas Jay Staley [1980] Finance Director [Australian]

York Potash Ltd
Incorporated: 12 May 2010 *Employees:* 51
Net Worth Deficit: £25,521,000 *Total Assets:* £372,072,992
Registered Office: 3rd Floor, Greener House, 68 Haymarket, London, SW1Y 4RF
Activities: Mining of chemical and fertilizer minerals
Parent: York Potash Holdings Limited
Officers: Nicholas Anthony King, Secretary; Simon Anthony Carter [1956] Development Director; Graham Clarke [1963] Director; Christopher Neil Fraser [1974] Director [British/Australian]; Thomas Jay Staley [1980] Finance Director [Australian]

York UK Holdco International Limited
Incorporated: 7 June 2012
Net Worth: £1,074,479,872 *Total Assets:* £1,457,842,560
Registered Office: 34 New Bond Street, London, W1A 2AA
Activities: Other business support service activities n.e.c.
Parent: Sotheby's
Officers: Natalie Guelfi, Secretary; Michael Fenton Goss [1959] Director/Chief Financial Officer [American]; Henry Koon Hung Li [1958] Finance Director [Canadian]; Clive Graham Lord [1960] Director/Chief Operating Officer; Jan Prasens [1974] Managing Director, Europe [Slovak]

Yorker Holdings PKR Limited
Incorporated: 20 November 2006
Net Worth Deficit: £86,857,000 *Total Assets:* £153,723,008
Registered Office: 12 Charles II Street, London, SW1Y 4QU
Activities: Activities of other holding companies n.e.c.
Parent: Infrastructure Investments Holdings Limited
Officers: Emily Mendes, Secretary; Keith William Pickard [1968] Portfolio Director; Natalia Poupard [1977] Director/Asset Manager; Harry Edward Charles Seekings [1973] Director/Financier

Yorse No. 3 Limited
Incorporated: 15 November 1988
Net Worth Deficit: £17,861,936 *Total Assets:* £658,830,720
Registered Office: York House, 45 Seymour Street, London, W1H 7JT
Activities: Non-trading company
Parent: Bunzl Public Limited Company
Officers: Paul Nicholas Hussey, Secretary; Andrew James Ball [1963] Finance Director; Paul Nicholas Hussey [1959] Director/Solicitor; Brian Michael May [1964] Finance Director

Yougov PLC
Incorporated: 30 July 1998 *Employees:* 816
Net Worth: £92,071,000 *Total Assets:* £144,754,000
Registered Office: 50 Featherstone Street, London, EC1Y 8RT
Activities: Market research and public opinion polling
Officers: Tilly Claire Heald, Secretary; Sundip Singh Chahal [1975] Director/Chief Operating Officer; Benjamin William Elliot [1975] Director/Entrepreneur; Jonathan Nicholas Jones [1965] Director/CFO at Achilles Group; Rosemary Blaire Leith [1961] Director; Ashley Graham Martin [1958] Director; Alexander George McIntosh [1977] Director/Chief Financial Officer; Andrea Clare Newman [1971] Director; Roger George Parry [1953] Director; Stephan Shakespeare [1957] Director

Young & Co's Brewery PLC
Incorporated: 17 November 1890 *Employees:* 3,990
Net Worth: £549,200,000 *Total Assets:* £800,600,000
Registered Office: Riverside House, 26 Osiers Road, Wandsworth, London, SW18 1NH
Activities: Hotels and similar accommodation
Officers: Anthony Ian Schroeder, Secretary; Patricia Ann Corzine [1957] Director; Patrick Anthony Dardis [1959] Director [Irish]; Tracy Janice Dodd [1969] Director; Stephen Frederick Goodyear [1955] Director/Chief Executive; Roger Mark Uvedale Lambert [1959] Director; Ian Philip McHoul [1960] Director; Nick Brian Miller [1965] Director; Torquil Charles Fflorance Barrow Sligo-Young [1959] Director

Young Street Holdings Limited
Incorporated: 15 July 2002
Net Worth: £260,710,928 *Total Assets:* £260,710,928
Registered Office: Northcliffe House, 2 Derry Street, London, W8 5TT
Activities: Activities of head offices
Parent: Ralph US Holdings
Officers: Frances Louise Sallas, Secretary; William Richard Flint [1969] Director/Accountant; Frances Louise Sallas [1977] Director/Company Secretary

Yunnan Limited
Incorporated: 16 November 2012 *Employees:* 3
Net Worth: £179,039,008 *Total Assets:* £327,691,296
Registered Office: Winnington House, 2 Woodberry Grove, London, N12 0DR
Activities: Activities of financial services holding companies
Officers: Andrea Aimar [1983] Director [Italian]; John Charles Higgins [1954] Director/Chairman [Australian]; Allan James Myers [1947] Director/Barrister [Australian]

Zara U.K. Limited
Incorporated: 20 April 1988 *Employees:* 3,198
Net Worth: £57,277,000 *Total Assets:* £148,931,008
Registered Office: Lumina House, 89 New Bond Street, London, W1S 1DA
Activities: Retail sale of clothing in specialised stores
Parent: Inditex S.A.
Officers: Alvaro Canete Diaz [1962] Director [Spanish]; Ramon Renon Tunez [1942] Director [Spanish]; Jose Manuel Romay de La Colina [1960] Director [Spanish]

Zavarco PLC
Incorporated: 29 June 2011 *Employees:* 113
Net Worth: £75,506,720 *Total Assets:* £205,853,232
Registered Office: Suite A, 6 Honduras Street, London, EC1Y 0TH
Activities: Wired telecommunications activities
Officers: Tunku Mazlina Binti Tunku Abd Aziz [1974] Director [Malaysian]; Teoh Hock Peng [1969] Director [Malaysian]

Zayo Group International Limited
Incorporated: 13 May 1999 *Employees:* 3
Net Worth: £57,658,000 *Total Assets:* £350,401,984
Registered Office: 100 New Bridge Street, London, EC4V 6JA
Activities: Other information technology service activities
Parent: Zayo Group Holdings, Inc.
Officers: Hans Andreas Lehmann [1974] Director/Business Executive [Danish/Canadian]; Robert Louis Merkel [1965] Director/VP Tax [American]; W Matthew Steinfort [1970] Director/Business Executive [American]

Zayo Group UK Limited
Incorporated: 4 March 1999 *Employees:* 107
Net Worth: £96,539,000 *Total Assets:* £141,668,992
Registered Office: 100 New Bridge Street, London, EC4V 6JA
Activities: Other information technology service activities
Parent: Zayo Group International Limited
Officers: Hans Andreas Lehmann [1974] Director/Business Executive [Danish/Canadian]; Robert Louis Merkel [1965] Director/VP Tax [American]; W Matthew Steinfort [1970] Director/Business Executive [American]

Zeal Network SE
Incorporated: 7 February 2014 *Employees:* 274
Net Worth: £94,989,312 *Total Assets:* £125,722,560
Registered Office: 5th Floor, One New Change, London, EC4M 9AF
Activities: Gambling and betting activities
Officers: Dr Helmut Wilhelm Becker [1969] Member/Chief Marketing Officer [German]; Jonas Mattsson [1965] Member/Chief Financial Officer [Swedish]; Thorsten Hauke Hehl [1972] Member/Investment Manager [German]; Oliver Jaster [1970] Member/Managing Director [German]; Leslie-Ann Reed [1959] Member/Chartered Accountant; Bernd Schiphorst [1943] Member/Business Consultant [German]; Jens Georg Schumann [1973] Member/Lawyer [German]; Peter Steiner [1959] Member/Auditor and Tax Advisor [German]

Zealburg Holdings Limited
Incorporated: 20 November 2006
Net Worth Deficit: £54,785,000 *Total Assets:* £171,712,000
Registered Office: 12 Charles II Street, London, SW1Y 4QU
Activities: Activities of other holding companies n.e.c.
Parent: Infrastructure Investments Holdings Limited
Officers: Emily Mendes, Secretary; Keith William Pickard [1968] Portfolio Director; Natalia Poupard [1977] Director/Asset Manager; Harry Edward Charles Seekings [1973] Director/Financier

Zegona Communications PLC
Incorporated: 19 January 2015 *Employees:* 10
Net Worth: £172,044,384 *Total Assets:* £174,181,728
Registered Office: 20 Buckingham Street, London, WC2N 6EF
Activities: Activities of other holding companies n.e.c.
Officers: Mark Irvine John Brangstrup Watts [1974] Director; Ashley Graham Martin [1958] Director/Chartered Accountant; Eamonn Francis O'Hare [1963] Director [Irish]; Robert Walter Samuelson [1964] Director; Murray John Scott [1962] Director/Chartered Accountant; Richard James Williams [1972] Director

Zenith Bank (UK) Limited
Incorporated: 17 February 2006 *Employees:* 82
Net Worth: £150,106,928 *Total Assets:* £1,216,435,968
Registered Office: 39 Cornhill, London, EC3V 3ND
Activities: Banks
Shareholders: Zenith Bank PLC; Zenith Bank PLC
Officers: Nicholas John Hornsey, Secretary; Peter Amangbo [1965] Director/Accountant [Nigerian]; Jeffrey Christopher Efeyini [1946] Director [British/Nigerian]; Andrew Gamble [1953] Director/Lawyer; Ian Douglas Francis Ogilvie [1959] Director; James Ovia [1951] Director/Banker [Nigerian]; David Somers [1948] Director/FCCA; Anthony Uchenna Uzoebo [1968] Director/Banker [Nigerian]; Pamela Mimi Yough [1962] Director/Chief Executive [Nigerian]

Zenith UK (Media) Limited
Incorporated: 11 June 1985 *Employees:* 488
Previous: Zenithoptimedia Ltd
Net Worth: £2,653,000 *Total Assets:* £134,800,992
Registered Office: 1st Floor, 2 Television Centre, 101 Wood Lane, London, W12 7FR
Activities: Advertising agencies
Parent: Publicis Media Limited
Officers: Joanne Munis, Secretary; Gerard Paul Boyle [1971] Director/Chief Executive Officer - APAC & EMEA; Natalie Cummins [1975] Director; Adrian Carl Sayliss [1960] Director

Zero Bypass (Holdings) Limited
Incorporated: 24 May 2016 *Employees:* 8
Net Worth: £12,038,307 *Total Assets:* £190,867,152
Registered Office: Cannon Place, 78 Cannon Street, London, EC4N 6AF
Activities: Activities of head offices
Shareholders: Parachute Investments Limited; Cintra Slovakia Ltd.
Officers: Gabriel Gutierrez Arnaiz [1971] Director/Assets Manager [Spanish]; Wolfgang Kainzmeier [1982] Director [Austrian]; Alexander Cheasty Kornman [1982] Director/Senior Vice President [American]; Yann Ottenwaelder [1981] Director/Senior Investment Manager [French]; Jose Angel Tamariz-Martel Goncer [1968] Director for Europe and New Markets at Cintra [Spanish]

Zero Bypass Limited
Incorporated: 7 December 2015 *Employees:* 8
Net Worth: £12,038,307 *Total Assets:* £190,867,152
Registered Office: Cannon Place, 78 Cannon Street, London, EC4N 6AF
Activities: Other professional, scientific and technical activities n.e.c.
Parent: Zero Bypass (Holdings) Limited
Officers: Wolfgang Kainzmeier [1982] Director [Austrian]; Alexander Cheasty Kornman [1982] Director/Senior Vice President [American]; Yann Ottenwaelder [1981] Director/Senior Investment Manager [French]; Juan Ramon Perez Perez [1966] Director/Manager [Spanish]; Jose Angel Tamariz-Martel Goncer [1968] Director for Europe and New Markets at Cintra [Spanish]

Zetar Limited
Incorporated: 8 December 2004 *Employees:* 1,582
Net Worth: £35,824,000 *Total Assets:* £139,816,000
Registered Office: 1000 Highgate Studios, 53-79 Highgate Road, London, NW5 1TL
Activities: Manufacture of cocoa and chocolate confectionery
Parent: Zertus UK Holding Limited
Officers: Clive Henry Beecham [1953] Director; Christian Diekmann [1965] Director [German]

Zeus Land Investments Limited
Incorporated: 25 March 1958
Net Worth: £1,310,857,984 *Total Assets:* £1,610,893,952
Registered Office: 3 Sheldon Square, Paddington, London, W2 6PX
Activities: Development of building projects
Parent: Sheldon Holdings Limited
Officers: Paul Moore, Secretary; Jean-Noel Hughes Roger Groleau [1974] Director [French]; Paul Anthony Moore [1970] Director/Company Secretary

Zeuss Childcare Limited
Incorporated: 14 December 2015
Net Worth: £169,390,272 *Total Assets:* £169,438,880
Registered Office: 5th Floor, 6 St Andrew Street, London, EC4A 3AE
Activities: Financial intermediation not elsewhere classified
Officers: Andrew MacCormick Campbell [1976] Director; Florian Rolf Marquis [1978] Director/Senior Investment Professional [German]; Sam Rozati [1984] Director

Zoopla Limited
Incorporated: 30 January 2007 *Employees:* 319
Previous: ZPG Limited
Net Worth: £110,496,000 *Total Assets:* £146,314,000
Registered Office: The Cooperage, 5 Copper Row, London, SE1 2LH
Activities: Other information technology service activities
Parent: ZPG Property Services Holdings Services UK Limited
Officers: Andrew James Botha [1967] Director; Charles Roy Bryant [1970] Director

ZPG Limited
Incorporated: 22 April 2014 *Employees:* 850
Previous: ZPG PLC
Net Worth: £239,940,992 *Total Assets:* £615,939,968
Registered Office: The Cooperage, 5 Copper Row, London, SE1 2LH
Activities: Web portals
Parent: Zephyr Bidco Limited
Officers: Andrew James Botha [1967] Director; Ulf Helge Pagenkopf [1985] Director; Simon Iain Patterson [1973] Director

This page is intentionally left blank

Standard Industrial Classification

01500 Mixed farming

Farmcare Trading Limited
Sir Richard Sutton Limited

01610 Support activities for crop production

Frontier Agriculture Limited

01630 Post-harvest crop activities

Frontier Agriculture Limited

03210 Marine aquaculture

Scottish Sea Farms Limited

06100 Extraction of crude petroleum [134]

Apache North Sea Limited
BG Global Energy Limited
BG Great Britain Limited
BG Group Limited
BG International Limited
BG Karachaganak Limited
BG North Sea Holdings Limited
BG Rosetta Limited
BG Trinidad LNG Limited
BHP Billiton Petroleum Great Britain
Borders & Southern Petroleum PLC
Bridge Petroleum 3 Limited
Bridge Petroleum 4 Limited
Burlington Resources (Irish Sea) Ltd
CNR International (U.K.) Developments
CNR International (U.K.) Investments
CNR International (U.K.) Ltd
Chevron North Sea Limited
Chrysaor E & P Finance Limited
Chrysaor E & P Services Ltd
Chrysaor Limited
Chrysaor North Sea Limited
ConocoPhillips (U.K.) Limited
ConocoPhillips (U.K.) Sigma Ltd
ConocoPhillips (U.K.) Theta Ltd
ConocoPhillips Petroleum Company U.K.
Cove Energy Limited
Dana Petroleum (BvUK) Limited
Dana Petroleum (E & P) Limited
Diamond Offshore Drilling (UK) Ltd
Diamond Offshore Limited
E. F. Oil and Gas Limited
EMP Exploration (Kangean) Ltd
ENI AEP Limited
ENI Australia Limited
ENI Elgin/Franklin Limited
ENI Lasmo PLC
ENI Oil Algeria Limited
ENI Pakistan Limited
ENI UK Limited
ENI ULX Limited
Encore Oil Limited
Endeavour Energy UK Limited
Energean Oil & Gas PLC
Enquest Britain Limited
Enquest ENS Limited
Enquest Global Limited
Enquest Heather Leasing Ltd
Enquest Heather Limited
Enquest NNS Limited
Enquest PLC
Enterprise Oil Limited
Enterprise Oil Middle East Ltd
Enterprise Oil U.K. Limited
Equion Energia Limited
Faroe Petroleum (U.K.) Limited
Faroe Petroleum PLC
Hess Finance
Hess Limited
Hess Malaysia and Thailand Ltd
IGas Energy PLC
INEOS E & P (UK) Limited
Inpex Angola Block 14 Ltd.
Island Gas Limited
JX Nippon Exploration and Production (U.K.)
Kufpec UK Limited
MCX Dunlin (UK) Limited
MCX Osprey (UK) Limited
Marathon Oil West of Shetlands Ltd
Marubeni North Sea Limited
Marubeni Oil & Gas (U.K.) Ltd
Mitsui E & P UK Limited
National Grid Grain LNG Ltd
Nautical Petroleum Limited
Neptune E & P UKCS Limited
Nobel Oil E & P (UK) Limited
Noble Corporation PLC
Noble Holding Land Support Ltd
Nostrum Oil & Gas PLC
Ophir Energy PLC
Ophir Holdings & Ventures Ltd
Ophir Thailand (E & P) Limited
Oranje-Nassau Energie Resources Ltd
PP Oil & Gas (Indonesia-Jabung) Ltd
PTTEP SP Limited
Perenco Rang Dong Limited
Petroceltic Resources Limited
Petrofac (Malaysia-PM 304) Ltd
Phoenix Global Resources PLC
Premier Oil E & P UK EU Ltd
Premier Oil E & P UK Limited
Premier Oil Exploration and Production
Repsol Sinopec Alpha Limited
Repsol Sinopec North Sea Ltd
Repsol Sinopec Oil Trading Ltd
Repsol Sinopec Resources UK Ltd
Rockhopper Exploration (Hydrocarbons)
Rockhopper Exploration PLC
Rockrose UKCS4 Limited
Ruspetro Limited
Sabah Shell Petroleum Co Ltd
Saka Indonesia Pangkah Limited
Salamander Energy (S.E. Asia) Ltd
Salamander Energy Group Ltd
Salamander Energy PLC
Santos (UK) Limited
Shell China Exploration and Production Co
Shell Clair UK Limited
Shell EP Offshore Ventures Ltd
Shell Hasdrubal Limited
Shell Trinidad 5(A) Limited
Shell Trinidad and Tobago Ltd
Shell Tunisia Upstream Limited
Shell U.K. Limited
Shell U.K. North Atlantic Ltd
Shell Upstream Overseas Services (I)
Soco International PLC
Star Energy Group Limited
Summit Exploration and Production
Taqa Bratani Limited
Tomori E & P Limited
Total E & P International K2 Ltd.
Total E & P International K3 Ltd.
Total E & P North Sea UK Ltd
Total E & P UK Limited
Total Oil GB Limited
Total Oil UK Limited
Transocean UK Limited
Transworld Petroleum (U.K.) Ltd
Tullow Group Services Limited
Tullow Oil Finance Limited
Tullow Oil PLC
Tullow Oil SK Limited
Tullow Oil SPE Limited

06200 Extraction of natural gas [68]

BG Group Limited
BG LNG Investments Limited
CNR International (U.K.) Developments
CNR International (U.K.) Investments
CNR International (U.K.) Ltd
Chrysaor E & P Finance Limited
Chrysaor E & P Services Ltd
Chrysaor Limited
Chrysaor North Sea Limited
Cove Energy Limited
ENI AEP Limited
ENI Australia Limited
ENI Elgin/Franklin Limited
ENI JPDA 03-13 Limited
ENI Oil Algeria Limited
ENI Pakistan Limited
ENI UK Limited
ENI ULX Limited
Encore Oil Limited
Endeavour Energy UK Limited
Energean Oil & Gas PLC
Equinor UK Limited
Equion Energia Limited
Hess Finance
Hess Limited
Hess Malaysia and Thailand Ltd
INEOS E & P (UK) Limited
INEOS Offshore BCS Limited
INEOS UK SNS Limited
Inpex Angola Block 14 Ltd.
Iranian Oil Company (U.K.) Ltd
Island Gas Limited
JX Nippon Exploration and Production (U.K.)
MCX Dunlin (UK) Limited
MCX Osprey (UK) Limited
Marathon Oil West of Shetlands Ltd
Mitsui E & P Mozambique Area 1 Ltd
Mitsui E & P UK Limited
Neptune E & P UKCS Limited
Nostrum Oil & Gas PLC
Ophir Energy PLC
Ophir Holdings & Ventures Ltd
Oranje-Nassau Energie Resources Ltd
PP Oil & Gas (Indonesia-Jabung) Ltd
PTTEP SP Limited
Perenco CUU Long Limited
Petroceltic Resources Limited
Phoenix Global Resources PLC
Premier Oil E & P UK EU Ltd
Premier Oil E & P UK Limited
Premier Oil Exploration and Production
Repsol Sinopec Alpha Limited
Repsol Sinopec North Sea Ltd
Repsol Sinopec Oil Trading Ltd
Repsol Sinopec Resources UK Ltd
Saka Indonesia Pangkah Limited
Salamander Energy PLC
Star Energy Group Limited
Summit Exploration and Production
Tomori E & P Limited
Total E & P North Sea UK Ltd
Total Oil GB Limited
Total Oil UK Limited

Transworld Petroleum (U.K.) Ltd
Tullow Group Services Limited
Tullow Oil Finance Limited
Tullow Oil SPE Limited
Victoria Oil & Gas PLC

07100 Mining of iron ores

Eurasian Natural Resources Corporation
Ferrexpo PLC

07290 Mining of other non-ferrous metal ores

Fresnillo PLC
Hochschild Mining Holdings Ltd
Hochschild Mining PLC
Tizir Limited

08910 Mining of chemical and fertilizer minerals

Kore Potash PLC
Sirius Minerals PLC
York Potash Ltd

08990 Other mining and quarrying n.e.c. [14]

Acacia Mining PLC
Anglo American PLC
Anglo Asian Mining PLC
Anglo Pacific Group PLC
Antofagasta PLC
BHP Group PLC
Firestone Diamonds PLC
Gemfields Limited
Marubeni Copper Holdings Ltd
Metals Exploration PLC
Pan African Resources PLC
Petropavlovsk PLC
Universal Coal PLC
Vedanta Resources Limited

09100 Support activities for petroleum and natural gas mining [31]

Awilco Drilling PLC
BG Delta Limited
BG Overseas Limited
Baker Hughes Limited
Borders & Southern Falkland Islands
Dolphin Drilling Limited
Ensco Deepwater Drilling Ltd
Ensco Finance Limited
Ensco Offshore U.K. Limited
Ensco PLC
Ensco U.K. Limited
Ensco Universal Limited
Ensco Worldwide Investments Ltd
Fortune Oil Limited
Halliburton Manufacturing and Services
Hydrasun Group Acquisitions Ltd
Hydrasun Group Finance Ltd
Hydrasun Group Holdings Ltd
IGas Energy PLC
Noble Holding UK Limited
Ophir Thailand (E & P) Limited
Premier Oil Holdings Limited
Rowan Companies PLC
Salamander Energy Group Ltd
Salamander Energy PLC
Stena Spey Services Limited
Subsea Leasing Limited
Technip UK Limited
Teesside Gas & Liquids Processing
Wilhunter (UK) Limited
Wilphoenix (UK) Limited

09900 Support activities for other mining and quarrying

MC Resource Development Ltd.
Sirius Minerals Holdings Ltd
York Potash Holdings Limited

10200 Processing and preserving of fish, crustaceans and molluscs

Lur Berri International Ltd

10320 Manufacture of fruit and vegetable juice

Innocent Limited

10390 Other processing and preserving of fruit and vegetables

Innocent Limited

10420 Manufacture of margarine and similar edible fats

Upfield Spreads UK Limited

10512 Butter and cheese production

Upfield Foods UK Limited

10611 Grain milling

Food Investments Limited

10710 Manufacture of bread; manufacture of fresh pastry goods and cakes

ABF Grain Products Limited

10810 Manufacture of sugar

British Sugar PLC
T & L Sugars Limited

10821 Manufacture of cocoa and chocolate confectionery

Zetar Limited

10831 Tea processing

Finlay Extracts & Ingredients UK Ltd

10832 Production of coffee and coffee substitutes

UCC Europe Limited

10840 Manufacture of condiments and seasonings

Mizkan Euro Ltd.

10850 Manufacture of prepared meals and dishes

Bakkavor Foods Limited

10890 Manufacture of other food products n.e.c.

H.J. Heinz Manufacturing UK Ltd
Innocent Limited
Wittington Investments Limited

10910 Manufacture of prepared feeds for farm animals

AB Agri Limited

11010 Distilling, rectifying and blending of spirits

Diageo Great Britain Limited
Glen Scotia Distillery Co Ltd
Justerini & Brooks,Limited
Loch Lomond Distillers Limited
Loch Lomond Distillery Co Ltd

11030 Manufacture of cider and other fruit wines

H P Bulmer Limited

11060 Manufacture of malt

Guinness Limited
Justerini & Brooks,Limited

11070 Manufacture of soft drinks; production of mineral waters and other bottled waters

Diageo Great Britain Limited
Schweppes International Ltd

12000 Manufacture of tobacco products

B.A.T (U.K. and Export) Ltd
B.A.T. China Limited
British American Tobacco Western Europe
Commercial Trading

13100 Preparation and spinning of textile fibres

G. Modiano Limited

13921 Manufacture of soft furnishings

Burberry Limited

13950 Manufacture of non-wovens and articles made from non-wovens, except apparel

Fiberweb Limited
PGI Acquisition Limited

14132 Manufacture of other women's outerwear

Burberry Limited

14190 Manufacture of other wearing apparel and accessories n.e.c.

Fred Perry Limited

17120 Manufacture of paper and paperboard

DS Smith Paper Limited

17219 Manufacture of other paper and paperboard containers

DS Smith Corrugated Packaging Ltd
DS Smith Packaging Limited
DS Smith Paper Limited

18110 Printing of newspapers

MGN Limited
Reach Printing Services Ltd

18201 Reproduction of sound recording
Sony DADC Europe Limited
V2 Music Group Limited

18202 Reproduction of video recording
Sony DADC Europe Limited

18203 Reproduction of computer media
Centurycomm Limited

19201 Mineral oil refining
Norsea Pipeline Limited
Phillips 66 Limited

19209 Other treatment of petroleum products (excluding petrochemicals manufacture)
Total UK Limited

20130 Manufacture of other inorganic basic chemicals
Petroineos Europe Limited

20140 Manufacture of other organic basic chemicals
Shell Chemicals U.K. Limited

20200 Manufacture of pesticides and other agrochemical products
Sumi Agro Europe Limited

20301 Manufacture of paints, varnishes and similar coatings, mastics and sealants
Tremco Illbruck Limited
U-Pol Holdings Limited

20590 Manufacture of other chemical products n.e.c.
Johnson Matthey PLC
Smith & Nephew PLC
Tremco Illbruck Limited

21100 Manufacture of basic pharmaceutical products
Hikma Pharmaceuticals PLC
Hikma UK Limited
Mercury Pharma Group Limited
Smith & Nephew PLC

24100 Manufacture of basic iron and steel and of ferro-alloys
EVRAZ PLC
Tata Steel UK Holdings Limited
Tata Steel UK Limited

24410 Precious metals production
Johnson Matthey PLC
Johnson Matthey Precious Metals Ltd

24420 Aluminium production
Simec Lochaber Hydropower 2 Ltd

24450 Other non-ferrous metal production
Vale Europe Limited

25300 Manufacture of steam generators, except central heating hot water boilers
Rolls-Royce PLC

25400 Manufacture of weapons and ammunition
BAE Systems PLC

25620 Machining
Cummins Power Generation Ltd
Rolls-Royce PLC

25910 Manufacture of steel drums and similar containers
Greif UK International Holding Ltd

26110 Manufacture of electronic components
Dialight PLC

26200 Manufacture of computers and peripheral equipment
Atos IT Services UK Limited

26301 Manufacture of telegraph and telephone apparatus and equipment
Capita Secure Information Solutions

26400 Manufacture of consumer electronics
Capita Secure Information Solutions

26600 Manufacture of irradiation, electromedical and electrotherapeutic equipment
Livanova PLC

26800 Manufacture of magnetic and optical media
Sony DADC Europe Limited

27400 Manufacture of electric lighting equipment
Dialight PLC

28110 Manufacture of engines and turbines, except aircraft, vehicle and cycle engines
Cummins Ltd.
Rolls-Royce PLC

28120 Manufacture of fluid power equipment
Hydrasun Group Acquisitions Ltd
Hydrasun Group Finance Ltd
Hydrasun Group Holdings Ltd

28220 Manufacture of lifting and handling equipment
Ascend Overseas Limited
Otis Limited

28990 Manufacture of other special-purpose machinery n.e.c.
Aker Solutions Limited
Cameron Flow Control Technology (UK)
Onesubsea UK Limited
Weston Aerospace Limited

29100 Manufacture of motor vehicles
BAE Systems PLC

29201 Manufacture of bodies (coachwork) for motor vehicles (except caravans)
Lear Corporation (UK) Limited

29310 Manufacture of electrical and electronic equipment for motor vehicles and their engines
Ixellion Technologies Ltd

29320 Manufacture of other parts and accessories for motor vehicles
Auria Solutions UK I Ltd.
Johnson Matthey PLC

30110 Building of ships and floating structures
BAE Systems PLC
Vosper Thornycroft (UK) Ltd

30200 Manufacture of railway locomotives and rolling stock
Agility Trains East Limited
Agility Trains West Limited
Alstom Transport UK Limited
Bombardier Transportation (Global Holding) UK
Bombardier Transportation (Investment) UK
Bombardier UK Holding Limited

30300 Manufacture of air and spacecraft and related machinery
BAE Systems PLC
L3 Commercial Training Solutions Ltd
Ontic Engineering & Manufacturing UK
Spirit Aerosystems (Europe) Ltd

32120 Manufacture of jewellery and related articles
Graff Diamonds Limited
David Morris International Ltd

32500 Manufacture of medical and dental instruments and supplies
Gyrus Group Limited
Livanova PLC
SSC Holdco (UK) Limited
SSC Intermediateco Limited
Smith & Nephew PLC
Surgical Specialties Corporation Ltd

32990 Other manufacturing n.e.c.
Emerson Electric U.K. Limited
Gulf Marine Services PLC
Hydrasun Group Acquisitions Ltd
Hydrasun Group Finance Ltd
Hydrasun Group Holdings Ltd
TechnipFMC Umbilicals Ltd
Weston Aerospace Limited

33120 Repair of machinery
Mitsubishi Hitachi Power Systems Europe, Ltd.

33170 Repair and maintenance of other transport equipment n.e.c.

Alstom Transport UK Limited
Braddell Limited

35110 Production of electricity [55]

APR Energy Holdings Limited
Abengoa Concessions Investments Ltd
Beaufort Wind Limited
CGN Europe Energy Green Power Holding
CGN Europe Energy UK Holding Ltd
Carrington Power Limited
Cubico Sustainable Investments Holdings
Cubico Sustainable Investments Ltd
Diamond Generating Europe Ltd
Dudgeon Offshore Wind Limited
EDF Development Co Ltd
EDF Energy (Cottam Power) Ltd
EDF Energy (Energy Branch) Ltd
EDF Energy (Thermal Generation) Ltd
EDF Energy Limited
ENI Australia Limited
EP Langage Limited
EP SHB Limited
ESB Asset Development UK Ltd
ESB Group (UK) Limited
East Anglia One Limited
Elios Energy Holdings 3 Ltd
Elios Energy Holdings Limited
Elios Renewable Energy Limited
First Hydro Company
Gunfleet Sands Limited
IPM Energy Trading Limited
International Power Ltd.
Lightsource BP Renewable Energy Investments
Lightsource Pumbaa Limited
Lightsource Pumpkin 4 Limited
Lightsource Radiate 2 Limited
Lightsource Simba Limited
Lightsource Timon Limited
NNB Generation Company (HPC) Ltd
Ormonde Energy Limited
Orsted London Array Limited
Orsted Power (UK) Limited
Orsted Race Bank (Holding) Ltd
Orsted West of Duddon Sands (UK) Ltd
Perpetual Power (UK) Limited
Race Bank Wind Farm (Holding) Ltd
Race Bank Wind Farm Limited
Renewable Energy Income Partnership Holdings
Shams Maan Solar UK Limited
Thanet Offshore Wind Limited
Tilbury Green Power Limited
UK Power Networks (Operations) Ltd
UK Power Networks Holdings Ltd
UK Power Networks Services (Contracting)
UK Power Networks Services Holdings
VPI Holding Limited
Vattenfall Wind Power Ltd
Walney (UK) Offshore Windfarms Ltd
Westermost Rough Limited

35120 Transmission of electricity [16]

Abengoa Concessions Investments Ltd
Blue Transmission London Array Ltd
Blue Transmission Walney 1 Ltd
Britned Development Limited
Diamond Transmission Corporation Ltd
Greater Gabbard OFTO PLC
Gwynt y Mor OFTO Holdings Ltd
Gwynt y Mor OFTO PLC
Humber Gateway OFTO Holdings Ltd
Humber Gateway OFTO Limited
National Grid Electricity Transmission
National Grid Interconnectors Ltd
State Grid Europe Limited
TC Ormonde OFTO Limited
Thanet OFTO Limited
Thanet Offshore Wind Limited

35130 Distribution of electricity [10]

EDF Energy Customers Limited
Eastern Power Networks PLC
Gazprom Marketing & Trading Retail
London Power Networks PLC
Public Power Corporation Finance PLC
Smartestenergy Limited
South Eastern Power Networks PLC
State Grid Europe Limited
Thanet Offshore Wind Limited
Total Gas & Power Limited

35140 Trade of electricity

E D F Trading Limited
Gazprom Marketing & Trading Ltd
MC GFS Investment Co Ltd
Melton Renewable Energy UK Ltd
Shell Energy Europe Limited
Total Gas & Power Limited
WMR JV Investco Limited

35210 Manufacture of gas

Cove Energy Limited
National Grid Gas PLC

35220 Distribution of gaseous fuels through mains

EDF Energy Customers Limited
Firmus Energy (Distribution) Ltd
Gazprom Marketing & Trading Retail
Russneft (UK) Limited
Total Gas & Power Limited

35230 Trade of gas through mains

Gazprom Marketing & Trading Ltd
National Grid Metering Limited
Orsted Sales (UK) Limited
Petronas Energy Trading Ltd
Shell Energy Europe Limited
Total Gas & Power Limited

36000 Water collection, treatment and supply

Veolia Water Outsourcing Ltd

38110 Collection of non-hazardous waste

Hampshire Waste Services Ltd
South Downs Waste Services Ltd
Veolia ES Leeds Limited
Veolia ES Shropshire Limited
Veolia ES Staffordshire Ltd

38210 Treatment and disposal of non-hazardous waste

Hampshire Waste Services Ltd
Riverside Resource Recovery Ltd
South Downs Waste Services Ltd
Veolia ES Leeds Limited
Veolia ES Shropshire Limited
Veolia ES Staffordshire Ltd
WTI Ferrybridge Limited

38220 Treatment and disposal of hazardous waste

Riverside Resource Recovery Ltd
Veolia ES Shropshire Limited

38320 Recovery of sorted materials

Hampshire Waste Services Ltd
DS Smith Recycling UK Limited
Veolia ES Leeds Limited
Veolia ES Shropshire Limited
Veolia ES Staffordshire Ltd

39000 Remediation activities and other waste management services

Glen Water Limited
Tilfen Land Limited

41100 Development of building projects [211]

1 & 4 & 7 Triton Limited
10 Brock Street Limited
10 Triton Street Limited
20 Triton Street Limited
334 Ramsbury Oxford Limited
338 Euston Road Limited
350 Euston Road Limited
A2dominion Developments Ltd
Adamant Investment Corporation Ltd
Aitch Group Limited
B.L.Holdings Limited
BF Properties (No.4) Ltd
BF Properties (No.5) Ltd
BL Bluebutton 2014 Limited
BL CW Holdings Limited
BL Chess Limited
BL City Offices Holding Co Ltd
BL Department Stores Holding Co Ltd
BL Ealing Limited
BL HB Investments Limited
BL Intermediate Holding Co Ltd
BL Leisure and Industrial Holding Co Ltd
BL Office (Non-City) Holding Co Ltd
BL Office Holding Co Ltd
BL Piccadilly Residential Ltd
BL Residual Holding Co Ltd
BL Retail Holding Co Ltd
BL Retail Investments Limited
BL Retail Warehousing Holding Co Ltd
BL Sainsbury Superstores Ltd
BL Superstores (Funding) Ltd
BL Superstores Finance PLC
BL Superstores Holding Co Ltd
BLD Property Holdings Limited
BLSSP Property Holdings Ltd
Ballymore Properties Limited
Barts Square First Limited
Bayeast Property Co Limited
Berkley Estates London Limited
Birch Sites Limited
Bluebutton (5 Broadgate) UK Ltd

Bluebutton Properties UK Ltd
Bouygues (U.K.) Limited
British Land (Joint Ventures) Ltd
British Land Acquisitions Ltd
British Land Broadgate 2005 Ltd
British Land Company PLC
British Land Department Stores Ltd
British Land Fund Management Ltd
British Land Industrial Ltd
British Land Leisure Limited
British Land in Town Retail Ltd
Brixton (Metropolitan Park) 1 Ltd
Brixton (Origin) Limited
Brixton Greenford Park Limited
Brixton Limited
Brixton Premier Park Limited
Broadgate (Funding) 2005 Ltd
Broadgate (PHC 11) 2005 Ltd
Broadgate (PHC 14) Limited
Broadgate (PHC 15A) Limited
Broadgate (PHC 16) 2005 Ltd
Broadgate (PHC 2) Limited
Broadgate (PHC 3) Limited
Broadgate (PHC 5) 2005 Limited
Broadgate (PHC 6) 2005 Limited
Broadgate (PHC 7) Limited
Broadgate (PHC 8) 2008 Limited
Broadgate (PHC 9) Limited
Broadgate Financing PLC
Broadgate PHC 2010 Limited
Broadgate Property Holdings Ltd
CBRE Limited
CIB Properties Limited
CWG (Wood Wharf Two) Limited
Canary Wharf Developments Ltd
Canary Wharf Investments (BP4) Ltd
Canary Wharf Investments (Three)
Canary Wharf Limited
Capital & Regional Holdings Ltd
Centremanor Limited
Chesterfield Properties Ltd
Circadian Limited
City of London Real Property Co Ltd
Cobalt Data Centres Limited
Conegate Developments Limited
Consolidated Developments Ltd
Convoys Properties Limited
Dashwood House Limited
Debenhams Properties Limited
Derwent Central Cross Limited
Derwent London Oliver's Yard Ltd
Derwent London PLC
Deutsche Alternative Asset Management (UK)
Earls Court Partnership Ltd
Euston Tower Limited
Farmont Baker Street Limited
Flodrive Holdings Limited
Frasers Property (UK) Limited
GS Finco Limited
Gazeley Limited
Gazeley UK Limited
Giltbrook Retail Park Nottingham Ltd
Goldman Sachs Property Management
Grantchester Limited
Great Portland Estates P L C
Greenland (United Kingdom) Investment
Greenland Hertsmere (London) Ltd
Greenland Ram (London) Limited
HQCB Investments Limited
Hammerson (60 Threadneedle Street)
Hammerson (Brent Cross) Ltd
Hammerson (Bristol Investments) Ltd
Hammerson (Leeds Investments) Ltd
Hammerson (Leicester) Limited.
Hammerson (Merthyr) Limited
Hammerson (Rugby) Limited
Hammerson (Value Retail Investments)
Hammerson Bull Ring Limited
Hammerson Oracle Investments Ltd
Hammerson PLC
Hammerson UK Properties PLC
Happybadge Projects Limited
Hectagon Assets Limited
Helical PLC
Hestok Limited
The Robert Hitchins Group Ltd
Hotel (PL Property) Holding Ltd
Kajima Europe Limited
Kenmin (HP) Limited
Knight Dragon Developments Ltd
Knight Dragon Investments Ltd
LS 1 New Street Square Limited
LS 62 Buckingham Gate Limited
LS City & West End Limited
LS Harbour Exchange Option Ltd
LS Lewisham Limited
LS Retail Warehouses Limited
LS Shepherds Bush Limited
Land Securities P L C
Legal & General Homes Communities
Lendlease (Elephant & Castle) Ltd
Linestair Limited
London & Regional Group Holdings Ltd
Longmartin Properties Limited
Luminus Group Limited
MSC Property Intermediate Holdings
Mace Limited
Martin's Properties Holdings Ltd
Mary Street Estate Limited
Meadowhall Centre (1999) Ltd
Meadowhall Finance PLC
Meadowhall Shopping Centre Ltd
Meadowhall Shopping Centre Property Holdings
Morgan Sindall Group PLC
Mount Anvil Group Limited
Mount Anvil New Holdings Ltd
National Grid Property Holdings Ltd
Network Rail Infrastructure Ltd
North Colonnade Limited
Nugent Shopping Park Limited
O & H Capital Limited
O & H Properties Limited
O & H Q7 Limited
Octagon Assets Limited
Orbital Shopping Park Swindon Ltd
Osnaburgh Street Limited
Percy Village Limited
Pillar City PLC
Pillar Denton Limited
Pillar Property Group Limited
Places for People Developments Ltd
Primary Medical Property Investments
Pulford Trading Limited
Quadrant Construction Services Ltd
Quintain Limited
R & F One (UK) Limited
Ravenseft Properties Limited
Ravenside Investments Limited
Redcastle Limited
Regent's Place Holding Co Ltd
Sainsbury Property Investments Ltd
Segro Industrial Estates Ltd
Segro Properties Limited
Selfridges Properties Limited
Shaftesbury Covent Garden Ltd
Slough Trading Estate Limited
St. Stephens Shopping Centre Ltd
Stamford Properties Three Ltd
Stockton Retail Park Limited
Stratford City Business District Ltd
TBL (Milton Keynes) Limited
TBL (Peterborough) Limited
Thameswey Housing Limited
Tilfen Land Limited
Topland Group PLC
UBS UK Properties Limited
UD Europe Limited
ULiving@Hertfordshire Holdco Ltd
UPP (Duncan House) Limited
UPP (Hull) Limited
Union Property Corporation Ltd
Union Property Holdings (London) Ltd
Urban & Civic Alconbury Ltd
Vertus NFL Limited
Wates City of London Properties Ltd
Wembley Park Limited
Westfield Europe Limited
White City Acquisitions Ltd
York House W1 Limited
Zeus Land Investments Limited

41201 Construction of commercial buildings [18]

Ardmore Construction Limited
Ardmore Group Limited
Balfour Beatty Group Limited
Barnsley SPV Three Limited
Bouygues (U.K.) Limited
Canary Wharf (North Quay) Ltd
Canary Wharf Contractors Ltd
Canary Wharf Properties (Crossrail)
Canary Wharf Properties (RT5) Ltd
ISG Construction Limited
ISG Fit Out Limited
Lendlease Construction (Europe) Ltd
Lovell Partnerships Limited
Luminus Group Limited
Mace Limited
Morgan Sindall Construction & Infrastructure
O & H Capital Limited
Overbury PLC

41202 Construction of domestic buildings

Bouygues (U.K.) Limited
Build King Construction Ltd
Hodson Holdings (Ashford) Ltd
Mount Anvil Limited

42110 Construction of roads and motorways

Connect M1-A1 Holdings Limited
Connect M1-A1 Limited
Connect M77/GSO PLC
Ferrovial Agroman (UK) Limited
Ferrovial Agroman Limited
John Laing Infrastructure Ltd
Road Management Services (A13) PLC
Road Management Services (Gloucester)
Road Management Services (Peterborough)

42120 Construction of railways and underground railways

Alstom Transport UK Limited
Build King Construction Ltd
Colas Rail Limited
Crossrail Limited
Ferrovial Agroman (UK) Limited

42130 Construction of bridges and tunnels

Build King Construction Ltd
Ferrovial Agroman (UK) Limited
Ferrovial Agroman Limited

42210 Construction of utility projects for fluids

Glen Water Limited

42220 Construction of utility projects for electricity and telecommunications

BIG Legolas Holdings Limited
BIH Holdings Limited
Bioenergy Infrastructure Ltd
Nemo Link Limited

42990 Construction of other civil engineering projects n.e.c. [12]

Bazalgette Equity Limited
Bazalgette Holdings Limited
Bazalgette Tunnel Limited
Bazalgette Ventures Limited
Bechtel Limited
Build King Construction Ltd
CB & I UK Limited
Ferrovial Agroman (UK) Limited
Ferrovial Agroman Limited
J. Murphy & Sons Limited
Origin Invest Limited
Tube Lines Limited

43210 Electrical installation

Balfour Beatty Group Limited
T Clarke PLC
SEC Lighting Services Trading Ltd

43220 Plumbing, heat and air-conditioning installation

Balfour Beatty Group Limited
T Clarke PLC
Integral UK Limited

43999 Other specialised construction activities n.e.c.

Balfour Beatty Group Limited
European Investments Solar Holdings
Legal & General Homes Communities (Crowthorne)
Multiplex Construction Europe Ltd
Permasteelisa (UK) Limited

45111 Sale of new cars and light motor vehicles

Glyn Hopkin Limited
H.R.Owen PLC
Renault Retail Group UK Ltd

45112 Sale of used cars and light motor vehicles

Car Giant Limited
Glyn Hopkin Limited
H.R.Owen PLC

45200 Maintenance and repair of motor vehicles

BT Fleet Limited
H.R.Owen PLC

45310 Wholesale trade of motor vehicle parts and accessories

121222 Holdco Limited
121333 Limited
Alliance Automotive Procurement Ltd
PA Group Holdings Limited
PA Topco Limited

45320 Retail trade of motor vehicle parts and accessories

H.R.Owen PLC

46120 Agents involved in the sale of fuels, ores, metals and industrial chemicals

BASF Metals Limited
Concord Resources Limited
E D F Trading Limited
OMV Supply & Trading Limited
SOL Aviation Services Limited
Shell Aviation Limited
Sinochem International Oil (London) Co.,
VTB Capital Trading Limited

46180 Agents specialised in the sale of other particular products

Christie's Private Sales Ltd
E D & F Man Sugar Limited

46190 Agents involved in the sale of a variety of goods

CLDN UK Limited
Mitsubishi Corporation International (Europe)

46210 Wholesale of grain, unmanufactured tobacco, seeds and animal feeds

British American Tobacco (GLP) Ltd
Holbud Limited

46341 Wholesale of fruit and vegetable juices, mineral water and soft drinks

Burlingtown UK Limited

46342 Wholesale of wine, beer, spirits and other alcoholic beverages

Angus Dundee Distillers PLC
BB & R Limited
Diageo Great Britain Limited
Glen Scotia Distillery Co Ltd
Justerini & Brooks,Limited
Loch Lomond Distillers Limited
Loch Lomond Distillery Co Ltd
Pernod Ricard UK Limited
Glen Turner Co Ltd

46370 Wholesale of coffee, tea, cocoa and spices

ECOM Agrotrade Holdings Ltd
ECOM Agrotrade Limited
Finlay Extracts & Ingredients UK Ltd
R.Twining and Co Ltd

46380 Wholesale of other food, including fish, crustaceans and molluscs

HP Foods Limited
H.J. Heinz Co Ltd
H.J. Heinz Foods UK Limited
Sojitz Europe PLC

46390 Non-specialised wholesale of food, beverages and tobacco

Bestway (Holdings) Limited
Bestway Northern Limited
Bestway Wholesale Limited

46420 Wholesale of clothing and footwear

All Saints Retail Limited
Ted Baker PLC
Burberry Limited
Chanel Limited
J. Choo Limited
Daisy 2015 Holdco Limited
Daisy 2015 Topco Limited
No Ordinary Designer Label Ltd

46431 Wholesale of audio tapes, records, CDs and video tapes and the equipment on which these are played

Warner Music UK Limited

46450 Wholesale of perfume and cosmetics

Chanel Limited
L'Oreal (U.K.) Limited
Estee Lauder Cosmetics Ltd

46460 Wholesale of pharmaceutical goods

Baxalta UK Investments Ltd.
Leadiant Biosciences Limited
McKesson Global Procurement & Sourcing
McKesson Global Sourcing UK Ltd
Sigma Pharmaceuticals PLC

46480 Wholesale of watches and jewellery

Chanel Limited
Graff Diamonds International Ltd
Graff Diamonds Limited
Pandora Jewellery UK Limited
Rolex Watch Co Ltd

46499 Wholesale of household goods (other than musical instruments) n.e.c

Moussaieff Jewellers Limited
VIL Ltd

46510 Wholesale of computers, computer peripheral equipment and software

Lombard Technology Services Ltd

46520 Wholesale of electronic and telecommunications equipment and parts

Motorola Solutions UK Limited
NTT Europe Ltd.

46711 Wholesale of petroleum and petroleum products

Cosmo Oil (U.K.) Limited
OMV Supply & Trading Limited
PTT International Trading London Ltd
Shell International Trading and Shipping Co
Shell Trading International Ltd
Total UK Limited
WFL (UK) Limited
World Fuel Services Europe, Ltd.

46719 Wholesale of other fuels and related products [14]

Chevron Products UK Limited
Greenergy Fuels Limited
IOCL Exploration and Production Oman
Mabanaft Limited
OMV Supply & Trading Limited
Petroineos Fuels Limited
Private Oil Holdings Oman Ltd
SK Energy Europe Limited
Shell Company of Thailand Ltd
Sojitz Europe PLC
South Hook Gas Co Ltd.
Total UK Limited
Vivo Energy Namibia Limited
World Fuel Services Europe, Ltd.

46720 Wholesale of metals and metal ores

Amalgamated Metal Corporation PLC
Edgen Murray Europe Limited
KAZ Minerals PLC
KAZ Minerals Sales Limited
Liberty Commodities Limited
Minmetals (U.K) Limited
Nexa Resources UK Limited
Stratton Metal Resources Ltd
Toyota Tsusho Metals Limited

46730 Wholesale of wood, construction materials and sanitary equipment

Citywide Trading (UK) Limited

46750 Wholesale of chemical products

Elementis UK Limited
Itochu Fibre Limited
Sojitz Europe PLC
Versum Materials UK Limited

46760 Wholesale of other intermediate products

Itochu Fibre Limited
Koch Fertilizer International Ltd
Menzies Distribution Limited

46900 Non-specialised wholesale trade [14]

AH UK Animal Health (PVT) Ltd
Bunzl Retail & Healthcare Supplies
Bunzl UK Limited
Colart International Holdings Ltd
Eastlink Lanker PLC
Liberty Commodities Limited
Marubeni Europe PLC
Metdist Limited
Mitsui & Co. Europe PLC
Noble Clean Fuels Limited
Noble Resources UK Limited
Sojitz Europe PLC
Sumitomo Corporation Europe Ltd
TA Mfg Limited

47110 Retail sale in non-specialised stores with food, beverages or tobacco predominating

Pam Acquisitionco Limited
Pret A Manger (Europe) Limited
J Sainsbury PLC
Sainsbury's Supermarkets Ltd
Waitrose Limited

47190 Other retail sale in non-specialised stores

Harrods Limited
Harvey Nichols and Co Ltd
John Lewis PLC
Marks and Spencer Group P.L.C.
Marks and Spencer P.L.C.
PTT International Trading London Ltd
Selfridges & Co. Limited
Selfridges Retail Limited

47250 Retail sale of beverages in specialised stores

BB & R Limited
Starbucks Coffee Holdings (UK) Ltd

47260 Retail sale of tobacco products in specialised stores

British American Tobacco Global Travel Retail

47290 Other retail sale of food in specialised stores

Pret A Manger (Europe) Limited
Starbucks Coffee Holdings (UK) Ltd

47421 Retail sale of mobile telephones

Carphone Warehouse Limited
Phone House Holdings (UK) Ltd

47510 Retail sale of textiles in specialised stores

Laura Ashley Limited

47540 Retail sale of electrical household appliances in specialised stores

DSG Retail Limited

47599 Retail of furniture, lighting, and similar (not musical instruments or scores) in specialised store

Laura Ashley Limited
Howden Joinery Limited

47610 Retail sale of books in specialised stores

Waterstones Booksellers Ltd

47650 Retail sale of games and toys in specialised stores

Smyths Toys UK Limited

47710 Retail sale of clothing in specialised stores [26]

A.G. Clothing Limited
All Saints Retail Limited
Arcadia Group Limited
Laura Ashley Limited
Ted Baker PLC
Burberry Limited
Chanel Limited
Coach Stores Limited
Debenhams Retail PLC
Dress Holdco 4 Limited
Dress Holdco A Limited
Dress Holdco C Limited
GPS (Great Britain) Limited
H & M Hennes & Mauritz UK Ltd
Monsoon Accessorize Limited
No Ordinary Designer Label Ltd
Primark Stores Limited
River Island Clothing Co. Ltd
River Island Holdings Limited
TFG Brands (London) Limited
Top Shop/Top Man Limited
Charles Tyrwhitt Shirts Ltd
URBN UK Limited
Uniqlo Europe Ltd
Louis Vuitton UK Limited
Zara U.K. Limited

47721 Retail sale of footwear in specialised stores [12]

Ted Baker PLC
J. Choo Limited
Coach Stores Limited
Debenhams Retail PLC
GPS (Great Britain) Limited
Kurt Geiger Limited
KG Group Holdings Limited
No Ordinary Designer Label Ltd
Office Holdings Limited
Office Retail Limited
Uniqlo Europe Ltd
Louis Vuitton UK Limited

47722 Retail sale of leather goods in specialised stores

J. Choo Limited
Coach Stores Limited
Mercury Acquisitions Limited
Mercury Midco 1 Limited
Mercury Midco 2 Limited
Louis Vuitton UK Limited

47750 Retail sale of cosmetic and toilet articles in specialised stores

GPS (Great Britain) Limited
L'Oreal (U.K.) Limited
Perfume Shop Limited
Savers Health and Beauty Ltd

47770 Retail sale of watches and jewellery in specialised stores

Graff Diamonds Limited
David Morris International Ltd
Pandora Jewellery UK Limited
Louis Vuitton UK Limited

47781 Retail sale in commercial art galleries

Eclectic Capital Limited

47789 Other retail sale of new goods in specialised stores (not commercial art galleries and opticians)

Cath Kidston Group Limited

47910 Retail sale via mail order houses or via Internet [10]

Laura Ashley Limited
Asos.Com Limited
Ted Baker PLC
J.P. Boden & Co. Limited
Farfetch UK Limited
Cath Kidston Group Limited
Net-a-Porter Group Limited
No Ordinary Designer Label Ltd
QVC UK
Ticketmaster UK Limited

47990 Other retail sale not in stores, stalls or markets

Nine United Properties UK Ltd

49100 Passenger rail transport, interurban [11]

Antofagasta PLC
Antofagasta Railway Company PLC
Eurostar International Limited
Hitachi Rail Europe Limited
Network Rail (High Speed) Ltd
Network Rail Infrastructure Ltd
Network Rail Limited
Rail Settlement Plan Limited
Rail for London Limited
Virgin Rail Group Holdings Ltd
West Coast Trains Limited

49200 Freight rail transport

Freightliner Heavy Haul Ltd
Freightliner Limited
GB Railfreight Limited
Management Consortium Bid Ltd
Network Rail (High Speed) Ltd
Network Rail Infrastructure Ltd

49311 Urban and suburban passenger railway transportation by underground, metro and similar systems

Alstom NL Service Provision Ltd
Docklands Light Railway Ltd
London Underground Limited
Tramlink Nottingham (Holdings) Ltd
Tramlink Nottingham Limited
Tramtrack Croydon Limited
Transport Trading Limited

49319 Other urban, suburban or metropolitan passenger land transport (not underground, metro or similar)

HS1 Limited
Metroline Limited
Metroline Travel Limited

49320 Taxi operation

Addison Lee Limited

49390 Other passenger land transport

Braddell Limited
London Bus Services Limited

49410 Freight transport by road

Freightliner Limited
Stobart Holdings Limited
Transkey Limited

49500 Transport via pipeline

CLH Pipeline System (CLH-PS) Ltd
GNI (UK) Limited
Interconnector (UK) Limited

50100 Sea and coastal passenger water transport

Magical Cruise Company, Ltd
Norwegian Compass Ltd
Norwegian Sextant Ltd
Fred. Olsen Cruise Lines Ltd
Stena North Sea Limited
Stena Ropax Limited

50200 Sea and coastal freight water transport [14]

BG Gas Marketing Ltd
Evergreen Marine (UK) Limited
Fleet Trade & Transport Ltd
Gulfmark North Sea Limited
Gulfmark UK Ltd
ISS Group Holdings Limited
Inchcape Shipping Services Holdings
K Line Bulk Shipping (UK) Ltd
K Line LNG Shipping (UK) Ltd
Methane Services Limited
SK Energy Europe Limited
SK Shipping Europe PLC
Shell International Trading and Shipping Co
Stena Icemax Limited

51101 Scheduled passenger air transport

Docklands Aviation Group Ltd
London City Airport Limited
London Southend Airport Co Ltd
World Fuel Services Europe, Ltd.

51102 Non-scheduled passenger air transport

Babcock Mission Critical Services Ltd
Docklands Aviation Group Ltd

51210 Freight air transport

World Fuel Services Europe, Ltd.

52101 Operation of warehousing and storage facilities for water transport activities

Phillips 66 CS Limited

52103 Operation of warehousing and storage facilities for land transport activities

Book Service Limited
Iron Mountain (UK) PLC
London Southend Airport Co Ltd
Sony DADC Europe Limited

52212 Operation of rail passenger facilities at railway stations

Rail Settlement Plan Limited

52219 Other service activities incidental to land transportation, n.e.c.

Eversholt Rail Limited
Iron Mountain (UK) PLC
National Car Parks Limited
SK Shipping Europe PLC

52220 Service activities incidental to water transportation

London Gateway Port Limited
SK Shipping Europe PLC
Tangguh Hiri Finance Limited
Tangguh Sago Finance Limited
Vouvray Finance Limited

52230 Service activities incidental to air transportation

BBA Aviation PLC
Boeing Commercial Aviation Services Europe

52241 Cargo handling for water transport activities

Evergreen Marine (UK) Limited
Southampton Container Terminals Ltd

52242 Cargo handling for air transport activities

London Gateway Port Limited

52243 Cargo handling for land transport activities

Evergreen Marine (UK) Limited

52290 Other transportation support activities

Big Bus Tours Limited
Braemar Shipping Services PLC
Marken Limited

53100 Postal activities under universal service obligation

Post Office Limited
Royal Mail Group Limited

53201 Licensed carriers

Addison Lee Limited

55100 Hotels and similar accommodation [73]

4 Howley Place Limited
Accor Hotelservices UK Limited
Accor UK Business & Leisure Hotels
Accor UK Economy Hotels Ltd
Admiral Taverns (780) Limited
Amyn Hotels Limited
Berkeley Hotel Limited
Blue Manchester Limited
Breezeroad Limited
Capital Hill Hotels Group Europe Ltd
Capital Hill Hotels Group London Ltd
Carolia Tower Hotel Limited
Carolia Westminster Hotel Ltd
Cavendish Hotel (London) Ltd
Claridge's Hotel Limited
Cola Holdings Limited
Connaught Hotel Limited
Constellation Barclay UK Ltd
Cranefield Limited
Dorchester Hotel Limited
Doyle London Hotels Limited
Dragonglass UK Holding Limited
Dunwilco (1783) Limited
Dunwilco (1784) Limited
Dunwilco (1847) Limited
Firmdale Hotels PLC
Firoka (Kings Cross) Limited
Flemings Hotel Mayfair Ltd
Rocco Forte & Family (London) Ltd
Rocco Forte Hotels Limited
Fuller Smith & Turner PLC
Globalgrange Limited
Gracechurch Bellyard Limited
Grange (Prescot Street) Ltd
HICP Holdings Limited
HPI UK Holding Ltd.
Ham Yard Investment Limited
Havana Holdings (UK) Limited
Imperial London Hotels Limited
Inn on BW (UK) Limited
Inn on the Park (London) Ltd
International Hoteliers (UK) Ltd
Jurys Inns (UK) Limited
Kensington Close Hotel Limited
LGH Hotels Management Limited
Lancaster Landmark Hotel Co Ltd
Landmark Hotel London Limited
Laser Tradeco Limited
London Kensington Hotel Ltd
Malmaison Hotel du Vin Brand Services
Mandarin Oriental Hyde Park (Investment)
Mandarin Oriental Hyde Park Ltd
Marble Arch Hotel (London) Ltd
Marlbray Limited
Meurice Limited
Muirgold Limited
PL Hotel Limited
Primeairo Limited
Ritz Hotel (London) Limited
Ritz Hotel, Limited
Savoy Hotel Limited
Sectormatch Limited
Shanti Hospitality Group Ltd
St. James Court Hotel Limited
Sir Richard Sutton Limited
Tower Hotel (London) Limited
UK Group of Hotels PLC
Veladail Hotels Limited
West India Quay (Eastern) Ltd
Westbury Hotel Limited
Yianis Docklands Hotels Ltd
Yianis Hotels Limited
Young & Co's Brewery PLC

55900 Other accommodation

Constitution Bidco 2 Limited
Goodenough College
LHA London Ltd
Onefinestay (Holdings) Limited
St Mungo Community Housing Association
ULiving@Hertfordshire PLC

56101 Licenced restaurants [13]

Admiral Taverns Limited
Azzurri Restaurants Limited
Casual Dining Bidco Limited
Eclectic Capital Limited
Hakkasan Limited
Hard Rock International Ltd
Harvey Nichols and Co Ltd
Nando's Chickenland Limited
Nando's Limited
Restaurant Group (UK) Limited
Soho House UK Limited
St. James Court Hotel Limited
Wagamama Limited

56102 Unlicenced restaurants and cafes

McDonald's Restaurants Limited
Nero Holdings Limited

56103 Take-away food shops and mobile food stands

Select Service Partner UK Ltd

56290 Other food services

Nando's Limited
Wisdom Profit (UK) Development Ltd

56302 Public houses and bars

Admiral Taverns (780) Limited
Admiral Taverns Limited
Fuller Smith & Turner PLC
Harvey Nichols and Co Ltd
Punch Partnerships (PTL) Ltd
Wellington Pub Company PLC
Young & Co's Brewery PLC

58110 Book publishing [19]

Bloomsbury Publishing PLC
EMI Music Publishing Finance (UK)
EMI Music Publishing Limited
EMI Songs Limited
Economist Intelligence Unit Ltd
Economist Newspaper Limited
Hachette UK Limited
Informa Telecoms & Media Ltd
Informa UK Limited
Music Sales Group Limited
Pearson Education Limited
Penguin Books Limited
Penguin Random House Limited
Quarto Publishing PLC
RELX PLC
Random House Group Limited
Springer Nature Holdings Ltd
Springer Nature Limited
Springer Nature Publishers Holdings

58130 Publishing of newspapers [14]

Associated Newspapers Limited
Centurycomm Limited
Eclectic Capital Limited
Economist Newspaper Limited
Express Newspapers
Financial Times Limited
Guardian Media Group PLC
Guardian News & Media Limited
Informa UK Limited
MGN Limited
News Corp UK & Ireland Limited
News Group Newspapers Limited
Reach Printing Services Ltd
Telegraph Media Group Limited

58141 Publishing of learned journals

Biomed Central Limited

58142 Publishing of consumer and business journals and periodicals [14]

Economist Intelligence Unit Ltd
Economist Newspaper Limited
Euromoney Institutional Investor PLC
Informa UK Limited
National Magazine Co Ltd
RELX PLC
Reach Magazines Publishing PLC
S & P Global Commodities UK Ltd
Sage Publications Limited
Springer Nature Holdings Ltd
Springer Nature Limited
Springer Nature Publishers Holdings
TES Global Limited
TI Media Limited

58190 Other publishing activities [24]

Argus Media Limited
Bloomsbury Publishing PLC
Conde Nast International Ltd
Conde Nast Publications Ltd
Economist Newspaper Limited
Fleet Bidco Limited
Fleet Finco Limited
Fleet Midco I Limited
Fleet Midco II Limited
Fleet Midco Limited
Hachette UK (Holdings) Limited
Immediate Media Co Ltd
Informa Telecoms & Media Ltd
MSCI Limited
McGraw-Hill Education (UK) Ltd
Mergermarket Limited
Oath (UK) Limited
Pearson PLC
RELX PLC
S & P Global Commodities UK Ltd
Universal Music Publishing MGB Ltd
Universal Publishing Production Music
Vancouver Topco Limited
Watch Tower Bible and Tract Society of Britain

58210 Publishing of computer games

Square Enix Limited

58290 Other software publishing [12]

Bloomsbury Publishing PLC
CACI Limited
Capita PLC
Finastra Global Limited
Finastra Group Holdings Ltd
Finastra International Limited
Finastra UK Limited
Fujitsu Services Holdings PLC
Fujitsu Services Limited
Misys International Limited
RELX PLC
Take-Two Interactive Software UK Ltd

59111 Motion picture production activities

Assembled Productions III UK Ltd
Discovery Lightning Investments Ltd
Entertainment One UK Limited
Paramount British Pictures Ltd
Warner Bros. Studios Leavesden Ltd

59113 Television programme production activities [26]

21CF Shine Holdings UK Limited
All3media Limited
All3media USA Limited
BBC Studios Distribution Ltd
Carnival Film & Television Ltd
Channel 5 Broadcasting Limited
Discovery Communications Europe Ltd
Discovery Networks International Holdings
Endemol Shine Group Holding UK Ltd
Endemol Shine UK Limited
Eros International Limited
Fremantlemedia Limited
IMG Media Limited
ITV Broadcasting Limited
ITV Digital Channels Limited
ITV Global Entertainment Ltd
ITV Studios Limited
ITV2 Limited
NC Shine Acquisition Ltd.
NGC UK Holdings Co Ltd
QVC UK
SDN Limited
STV News Services Limited
Shine Limited
Sony Pictures Television Production UK
Turner Broadcasting System Europe

59131 Motion picture distribution activities [10]

Colgems Productions Limited
Columbia Pictures Corporation Ltd
Entertainment One UK Limited
Eros International Limited
Fremantlemedia Limited
Lions Gate International Media Ltd
Odeon Cinemas Limited
United Cinemas International (UK)
Universal Studios Limited
Warner Bros. Entertainment UK Ltd

59132 Video distribution activities

Amazon Video Limited
Universal Studios Limited

59133 Television programme distribution activities

AMC Networks International Zone Holdings
Bein IP Limited
Columbia Pictures Corporation Ltd
Iridium Midco Limited
Turner Broadcasting System Europe
Universal Studios Limited

59140 Motion picture projection activities

Odeon Cinemas Limited
United Cinemas International Acquisitions
Vue Entertainment Limited

59200 Sound recording and music publishing activities

BW Publishing Limited
MP Granite Ltd
Phonographic Performance Ltd
Universal Music Publishing International
Universal Music Publishing Ltd
Universal Music Publishing MGB Ltd
Universal Publishing Production Music
V2 Music Group Limited
Warner Music UK Limited

60100 Radio broadcasting

GWR Group Limited
Global Radio Holdings Limited
Global Radio Limited

60200 Television programming and broadcasting activities [13]

4 Ventures Limited
AMC Networks International Broadcasting
Chello Zone Holdings Limited
Discovery Communications Europe Ltd
Formula One World Championship Ltd
Fox Networks Group (UK) Ltd
NGC Europe Limited
NGC UK Holdings Co Ltd
Nordic Entertainment Group UK Ltd
Red Bee Media Limited
Turner Broadcasting System Europe
UKTV Media Holdings Limited
UKTV Media Limited

61100 Wired telecommunications activities

CenturyLink EMEA Holdings Ltd
Interoute Managed Services UK Ltd
Telstra Limited
Zavarco PLC

61200 Wireless telecommunications activities

Docomo Digital Limited
Mavenir Private Finance Ltd
Telstra Limited
WIG Holdings I Limited
WIG Holdings II Limited
Wireless Infrastructure Co Ltd

61300 Satellite telecommunications activities

Avanti Communications Group PLC
Avanti Hylas 2 Limited
Inmarsat Finance PLC
Inmarsat Holdings Limited
Intelsat Global Sales & Marketing Ltd.
Telenor (UK) Limited
Telesat International Limited

61900 Other telecommunications activities [48]

Airwave Solutions Limited
BT Global Services Limited
BT Group PLC
BT Limited
Babcock Communications Limited
British Telecommunications PLC
Cable & Wireless International HQ
Cable & Wireless Limited
Cable and Wireless (West Indies) Ltd
Carphone Warehouse Limited
CenturyLink Communications Europe
CenturyLink Communications UK Ltd
Cityfibre Holdings Limited
Cityfibre Infrastructure Holdings
Cityfibre Limited
Colt Technology Services
Colt Technology Services Europe Ltd
Colt Technology Services Group Ltd
Colt Telecom Finance Euro
Colt Telecom Finance Switzerland
Colt Telecom Holdings Limited
Communications Networking Services (UK)
Eunetworks Fiber UK Limited
Inmarsat Global Limited
Interoute Communications Holdings
Interoute Communications Ltd
Interoute Managed Services UK Ltd
Kddi Europe Limited
Lebara Limited
Lycamobile UK Limited
Motorola Solutions UK Limited
NTT Europe Ltd.
Orange Brand Services Limited
Orange Participations UK Ltd
Phone House Holdings (UK) Ltd
Qwest Communications International Ltd.
Six Degrees Holdings Limited
T-Systems Limited
Talktalk Brands Limited
Talktalk Communications Ltd
Talktalk Group Limited
Talktalk Telecom Group PLC
Talktalk Telecom Holdings Ltd
Talktalk Telecom Limited
Telecom Plus PLC
Telit Communications PLC
Telstra Limited
Webhelp UK Holdings Ltd

62011 Ready-made interactive leisure and entertainment software development

Gamesys Limited
Tripadvisor UK Holdco Limited

62012 Business and domestic software development [14]

Atlassian (Australia) Limited
Atlassian (UK) Limited

Atlassian Corporation PLC
Aztech Advantage Ltd
Canonical Group Limited
I-Logic Holdings Limited
I-Logic Technologies Bidco Ltd
Nintex Global Limited
Nintex UK Limited
Openbet Technologies Limited
Skyscanner Holdings Limited
Smartstream Technologies Ltd
Unisys Europe Limited
Unisys Limited

62020 Information technology consultancy activities [19]

Amdocs (UK) Limited
Avanade Europe Holdings Ltd.
CACI Limited
CDW Finance Bidco Limited
CGI IT UK Limited
Canyon UK Investments Ltd.
Capita Business Services Ltd
Cognizant Worldwide Limited
Fair Isaac UK International Holdings Ltd.
Fujitsu Services Holdings PLC
Fujitsu Services Limited
Kaspersky Lab UK Limited
Kaspersky Labs Limited
Mavenir Private Finance Ltd
Openbet Technologies Limited
Ricoh Europe ASP Limited
Smartstream Technologies Ltd
Unisys Europe Limited
Worldline IT Services UK Ltd

62090 Other information technology service activities [52]

Agilisys Holdings Limited
Apple (UK) Limited
Atos IT Services UK Limited
Atos UK IT Limited
Avanade Europe Services Ltd.
Betfair Group Limited
British American Shared Services (GSD)
Campaign Monitor (UK) Limited
Campaign Monitor Holdings (UK) Ltd
Capita Secure Information Solutions
Centurycomm Limited
Cerner Limited
Civica Group Limited
Civica UK Limited
Claranet Group Limited
Claranet Limited
Cognizant Worldwide Limited
Fujitsu Services Limited
Gamma Communications PLC
JS Information Systems Limited
Kaspersky Labs Limited
Kingfisher Information Technology Services (UK)
LSEG Business Services Limited
Mastercard Payment Gateway Services
Match.Com Europe Limited
Match.Com Foreign Holdings Ltd
Midasplayer.Com Ltd.
Mphasis UK Limited
NCR Limited
NTT Europe Ltd.
Openbet Technologies Limited
SVF Holdco (UK) Limited
Salesforce.Com EMEA Limited
Sapient Limited
Smartstream Technologies Ltd
Snap Group Limited
Sony Interactive Entertainment Europe
Sporting Exchange Limited
T-Systems Limited
TES Global Limited
Telehouse Holdings Limited
Telehouse International Corporation of Europe
Ticketmaster UK Limited
Trainline.Com Limited
Unisys Europe Limited
Virtus Holdco Limited
Virtus IMH 2 Limited
Virtus IMH Limited
Worldline IT Services UK Ltd
Zayo Group International Ltd
Zayo Group UK Limited
Zoopla Limited

63110 Data processing, hosting and related activities [11]

CACI Limited
Capita Customer Management Ltd
Conduent Business Process Solutions
Donnelley Financial Solutions Holdings UK
Mastercard Payment Gateway Services Group
NTT Europe Ltd.
Paragon Group Limited
Pharm Research Associates (UK) Ltd
S & P Global Commodities UK Ltd
Vocalink Holdings Limited
Zoopla Limited

63120 Web portals [10]

Allied SX Ltd
Just Eat Holding Limited
Just Eat PLC
Just Eat.co.uk Ltd
Oath (UK) Limited
Paragon Group Limited
TES Global Limited
Turner Broadcasting System Europe
ZPG Limited
Zoopla Limited

63990 Other information service activities n.e.c. [20]

Awin Ltd
CDW International Holdings Ltd
CDW Limited
Calypso FX EUR Limited
Calypso FX USD Limited
Calypso Group UK Limited
Marie Curie
FTSE International Limited
Factset Europe Limited
Internetq Group Limited
Moody's Analytics UK Limited
Moody's Group Finance Limited
Moody's Group UK Ltd
Moody's International (UK) Ltd
Moody's Investors Service Ltd
NTT Data EMEA Ltd.
Paragon Group Limited
Tiso Blackstar Group SE
Tiso Blackstar Holdings SE
Worldline IT Services UK Ltd

64110 Central banking

Bank of England Asset Purchase Facility Fund
Barclays Bank PLC
Barclays PLC
Coutts & Company
Punjab National Bank (International)

64191 Banks [88]

ADIB (UK) Limited
Ahli United Bank (UK) PLC
Al Rayan Bank PLC
Alpha Bank London Limited
Axis Bank UK Limited
Bank Leumi (U.K.) P.L.C.
Bank Mandiri (Europe) Limited
Bank Saderat PLC
Bank Sepah International PLC
Bank and Clients PLC
Bank of Beirut (UK) Ltd
Bank of China (UK) Limited
Bank of Ireland (UK) PLC
Bank of London and The Middle East PLC
British Arab Commercial Bank PLC
Brown Shipley & Co. Limited
CIBC World Markets PLC
Canada Square Operations Ltd
Cater Allen Limited
Charter Central Finance Ltd
Clydesdale Financial Services Ltd
Commerzbank Finance Limited
ConocoPhillips Treasury Ltd
Credit Suisse International
Cynergy Bank Limited
DNB (UK) Limited
DSG Card Handling Services Ltd
Diamond Bank (UK) PLC
EFG Private Bank Limited
Europe Arab Bank PLC
FBN Bank (UK) Limited
Fosse Funding (No.1) Limited
Fosse Master Issuer PLC
Gatehouse Bank PLC
Ghana International Bank PLC
Goldman Sachs Asset Management International
Goldman Sachs International Bank
Guaranty Trust Bank (UK) Ltd
Gulf International Bank (UK) Ltd
HBL Bank UK Limited
HGI Group Limited
HSBC Bank PLC
HSBC Private Bank (UK) Limited
Habib Bank Zurich PLC
Hampshire Trust Bank PLC
Havin Bank Ltd
Henderson Global Investors Asset Management
C. Hoare & Co.
ICBC (London) PLC
ICBC Standard Bank PLC
Investec Bank PLC
Itau BBA International PLC
Jordan International Bank PLC
Kexim Bank (UK) Limited
Kookmin Bank International Ltd
Lloyds Bank PLC
Melli Bank PLC
Metro Bank PLC
Mizuho International PLC
J.P. Morgan Limited

J.P. Morgan Securities PLC
Morgan Stanley Bank International
National Bank of Egypt (UK) Ltd
National Bank of Kuwait (International)
Nomura Bank International PLC.
Oaknorth Bank PLC
P & O Property Accounts Ltd
Persia International Bank PLC
QIB (UK) PLC
RBC Europe Limited
R. Raphael & Sons PLC
Reliance Bank Limited
Sainsbury's Bank PLC
Santander UK PLC
Schroder & Co. Limited
Scotiabank Europe PLC
Smith & Williamson Investment Services
Sonali Bank (UK) Limited
Sumitomo Mitsui Banking Corporation Europe
Tandem Bank Limited
Turkish Bank (UK) Limited
Union Bank UK PLC
United Bank for Africa (UK) Ltd
United National Bank Limited
United Trust Bank Limited
VTB Capital PLC
Westpac Europe Limited
Zenith Bank (UK) Limited

64192 Building societies

ICICI Bank UK PLC

64201 Activities of agricultural holding companies

Chiquita Holdings Limited
Lonrho Limited
P & P Spearhead UK Holdings, Ltd

64202 Activities of production holding companies [17]

Alberto-Culver Group Limited
Alberto-Culver UK Products Ltd
Apple Bidco Limited
Avara Pharma Services Ltd
Cubico Holdings (UK) 2 Limited
Equitix Offshore 2 Limited
Equitix Offshore 3 Limited
Equitix Offshore 4 Limited
Equitix Offshore 5 Limited
Great Beer Co Ltd
Gunfleet Sands Holding Ltd
Loch Lomond Holdings 1 Limited
MBC Europe Limited
Marfrig NBM Holdings Limited
Shenda Investment UK Limited
Total E & P International Ltd.
Total Energy (MEUK) Ltd.

64203 Activities of construction holding companies [13]

Bechtel Holdings Limited
CWG Newco Limited
Cathexis UK Holdings Limited
Drilton Limited
Equitix Orbital Holdings Ltd
Lendlease Europe Holdings Ltd
Mace Finance Limited
Mace Limited
McLaren Construction Group PLC
Multiplex Construction Europe Holding
Multiplex Europe Limited
Multiplex Global Limited
Sirius (Korea) Limited

64204 Activities of distribution holding companies

Diageo UK Turkey Holdings Ltd
Great Beer Co Ltd
Le Creuset Holding Limited
Stobart Holdings Limited
WP R Holdco Limited
WP R Midco 1 Limited
WP R Midco 2 Limited

64205 Activities of financial services holding companies [204]

AMG Plymouth UK Holdings (1) Ltd
AON Benfield Limited
AON Delta UK Limited
AON Global Operations PLC
AON Overseas Holdings Limited
AON UK Group Limited
AON UK Holdings Intermediaries Ltd
AON US & International Holdings Ltd
Aberdeen Asset Investments Ltd
Aberdeen Infrastructure (No.3) Ltd
Aberdeen Investments Limited
Ace European Holdings Limited
Aether IOS Limited
Airport Group Investments Ltd
American Express Holdings Ltd
Ashmore Group PLC
Ashmore Investments (UK) Ltd
Australian Gas Networks UK Ltd
Aviva Europe SE
Aviva Investors Holdings Ltd
Aviva Investors Realm Infrastructure No.1
Axa Equity & Law PLC
Axa Insurance PLC
Axa PPP Healthcare Group Ltd
BBP Bandenia PLC
BC Capital Management Services Ltd
BGEO Group Limited
BLME Holdings PLC
BMO Global Asset Management (Europe)
Baltic Sea Offshore Holdco Ltd
Bank of Montreal Capital Markets (Holdings)
Barclays Capital Asia Holdings Ltd
Barclays Capital Japan Securities Holdings
Barclays Principal Investments Ltd
Blackrock Group Limited
Blackrock UK (Alpha) Limited
Blue Finco Limited
Brightsphere Investment Group PLC
Brightsphere UK, Ltd.
Brokertec Investments
Burberry Beauty Limited
Caledonia Thames Holdings Ltd
Catalina Echo Limited
Catalina Holdings UK Limited
Cathedral Capital Limited
Chubb Market Co Ltd
Cigna Chestnut Holdings, Ltd
Cigna Walnut Holdings, Ltd.
Circle Anglia Social Housing 2 PLC
Circle Anglia Social Housing PLC
Conning Holdings Limited
Creditex Holdco Limited
D & P International Holdings (UK)
DHCM Holdco Limited
Diageo UK Turkey Limited
Digital River UK Holdings II Ltd
Dollar Financial UK Holding Ltd
EBS Group Limited
EBS Investments
ERS DGB Limited
Electricity First Limited
Endowment Investment Holdings Ltd
Equitix Infrastructure 4 Ltd
Euroclear UK & Ireland Limited
European Financial Services Ltd
European Legacy Holdings Ltd
FIL Holdings (UK) Limited
GFI EMEA Holdings Limited
GFI Holdings Limited
GFI Markets Limited
GLIL Corporate Holdings Ltd
Gam (U.K.) Limited
Garban Group Holdings Limited
Garban-Intercapital (2001) Ltd
Global Reach Group Ltd
Goldman Sachs Funding International
Great Beer Co Ltd
Guardian Royal Exchange PLC
HGI Asset Management Group Ltd
HSBC Asia Holdings (UK) Ltd
HSBC Asia Pacific Holdings (UK) Ltd
HSBC Finance (Netherlands)
HSBC Global Asset Management Ltd
HSBC Global Services (China) Holdings
HSBC Investment Bank Holdings Ltd
HSBC Overseas Holdings (UK) Ltd
HSIL Investments Limited
Habib Allied Holding Limited
J O Hambro Capital Management Holdings
Henderson Group Holdings Asset Management
Hoggant Limited
Houlihan Lokey Capital (Holdings)
Hurricane Bidco Limited
Hurricane Cleanco Limited
Hurricane Noteco Limited
ICAP America Investments Ltd
ICAP Global Broking Finance Ltd
ICAP Global Broking Holdings Ltd
ICAP Global Broking Investments
ICAP Holdings (UK) Limited
ICAP Holdings Limited
ICE Asia Holdings Limited
IG Group Holdings PLC
Ice Europe Parent Limited
Infrastructure Investments (Affinity)
Infrastructure Investments (Colorado)
Intercontinentalexchange Holdings
Investec 1 Limited
Investec Holding Co Ltd
Investec PLC
JC No. 3 (UK) Limited
LBG Capital Holdings Limited
LMS Capital Group Limited
LMS Capital Holdings Limited
Lazard & Co., Holdings Limited
Legal & General Capital Investments
Legal & General Group PLC
Legal & General Insurance Holdings
Legal & General Insurance Holdings No.2
Legal & General International (Holdings)
Legal & General International Ltd
Legal & General Investment Management (Holdings)
Legal & General Overseas Holdings
Legal & General Overseas Operations

Legal & General RE Holdings Ltd
Lion-Shoes Midco Limited
MC GIP-UK Ltd.
MGM Advantage Holdings Limited
Mercury UK Holdco Limited
Midcorp Limited
N.B.S.A. Limited
NEX Markets Limited
NEX Optimisation Limited
NYK International PLC
NYSE Holdings UK Limited
Nomura Europe Holdings PLC
Nuveen FCACO Limited
Nuveen Real Estate Limited
OM Zimbabwe Holdco Limited
Old Oak Holdings Limited
PCF Group PLC
PGIM Financial Limited
Pace Topco Limited
Pendal UK Limited
Picture Holdco Limited
Polar Capital Holdings PLC.
Principal Financial Services II (UK) Ltd
Principal Financial Services III (UK)
Principal Financial Services Latin America
Principal International Latin America
Principal International South America I
Principal International South America II
Prudential (US Holdco 1) Ltd
Prudential Capital Holding Co Ltd
Prudential Financial Services Ltd
Quilter Cheviot Holdings Ltd
RIT Capital Partners PLC
RKH Group Limited
Rathbone Brothers PLC
Rational Group Limited
Rothesay Holdco UK Limited
Rothschild & Co Holdings UK Ltd
Ruffer Management Limited
Sam UK Investment Holdings Ltd
Santander UK Group Holdings PLC
Schroder Financial Holdings Ltd
Schroder Private Assets Holdings Ltd
Schroder Wealth Holdings Ltd
Sirius International UK Holdings Ltd
Smith & Williamson Holdings Ltd
Societe Generale Investments (U.K.)
Stanbic Africa Holdings Ltd
Standard Bank London Holdings Ltd
Standard Chartered I H Limited
State Street International Holdings UK
Sterling UK Holdco Limited
TC Financing Limited
TP Holdings Limited
TP ICAP PLC
TSMUK Ltd
Tallwood Investments Ltd
Tam UK Holdings Limited
Tibra Equities Europe Limited
Titanium UK Holdco 1 Limited
Tokio Marine HCC Insurance Holdings (International)
Touchstone Innovations Investments
Trebuchet Investments (UK) Ltd
Tronox Sands UK Holdings Ltd
Tronox UK Holdings Limited
Tronox UK Limited
Tullett Prebon (No. 1)
Tullett Prebon Group Holdings PLC
Tullett Prebon Group Limited
Tullett Prebon Investment Holdings
UK Renewable Holdco 1 Limited
UK Renewable Holdco 2 Limited
UK Renewable Holdco 3 Limited
UTB Partners Limited
VAM Bidco Limited
Valero Holdco UK Ltd
WBA Finance 1 Limited
XL Gracechurch Limited
XL Insurance (UK) Holdings Ltd
Yunnan Limited

64209 Activities of other holding companies n.e.c. [742]

A V Co 1 Limited
A-Gas Bidco Limited
A-Gas Group Limited
AAA UK Acquisition Co. Limited
AAA UK Holding Co. Limited
ABP Acquisitions UK Limited
ABP Bonds UK Limited
ABP Finance PLC
ABPA Holdings Limited
AI Mistral Holdco Limited
AI Mistral Limited
AI Mistral Parentco Limited
AI Mistral Topco Limited
AMS Bidco Ltd
AMS Holdco Ltd
AMS Midco Ltd
APG (KE) Ltd.
APR Energy Limited
ASOS Intermediate Holdings Ltd
Accor Hotelinvest UK Limited
Accord Bidco Limited
Accord Topco Limited
Addison Lee Financing Limited
Addison Lee Group Limited
Addison Lee Holdings Limited
Addison Lee Midco II Limited
Agility Trains East (Holdings) Ltd
Agility Trains West (Holdings) Ltd
Agman Holdings Limited
Aldea UK Holdco Limited
Aldwych Finance Limited
Allianz Europe Limited
Almacantar (Centre Point) Ltd
Amber Infrastructure Group Holdings
Annington Homes Limited
Annington Limited
Annington Rentals (Holdings) Ltd
Annington Subsidiary Holdings Ltd
Arca Bidco Limited
Arca Holdco Limited
Arca Midco Limited
Arca Topco Limited
Arches Holdings Limited
Ardonagh Midco 3 PLC
Argo International Holdings Ltd
Argo Underwriting Agency Ltd
Arrow Bidco Limited
Ascential Group Limited
Ascential UK Holdings Limited
Ashtead Group PLC
Autovista Group Limited
Autovista Holdco UK Limited
Autovista Limited
Axel Springer International Ltd
BCI UK Holdings Limited
BCP IV UK Fuel Holdings II Ltd
BCP IV UK Fuel Holdings III Ltd
BCP IV UK Fuel Holdings IV Ltd
BCP IV UK Fuel Holdings V Ltd
BHP Billiton Marketing UK Ltd
BIS (Postal Services Act 2011) Co Ltd
BMI Group Holdings UK Limited
BNY Mellon International Asset Management (Holdings)
BNY Mellon International Asset Management (Holdings) No. 1
BNY Mellon Investment Management (Europe)
BNY Mellon Investment Management Seed Capital
BPG Global Holdings UK Limited
BT (International) Holdings Ltd
BT European Investments Ltd
BT Fifty-One
BT Fifty-Three Limited
BT Holdings Limited
BT SLE Euro Limited
BT SLE USD Limited
BTG Pactual UK Holdco Limited
BTGP-BSI Limited
Babcock (UK) Holdings Limited
Babcock Aviation Services (Holdings)
Babcock Brazil Investments Ltd
Babcock Holdings Limited
Babcock International Support Services
Babcock Management Limited
Babcock Marine & Technology Holdings
Babcock Mission Critical Services Topco
Babcock Mission Critical Services UK
Babcock Southern Holdings Ltd
Babcock US Investments Limited
Barchester Finco 2017 UK Ltd
Barfair Limited
Beaubien Finance Limited
Beaubien UK Finance Limited
Benton Finance Limited
Beta Holdings Limited
Betjeman Holdings JVCO Limited
Betjeman Holdings Limited
Betjeman Holdings Midco Ltd
Big Box Midco UK Limited
Big Bus Tours Group Holdings Ltd
Big Bus Tours Group Limited
Big Bus Tours Holdings 1 Ltd
Big Bus Tours Holdings 2 Ltd
Big Society Trust
Biocon Biologics Limited
Birchgree Limited
Black Star Holdings Limited
Bluebottle UK Limited
Bluefin Insurance Group Ltd
Boeing European Holdings Ltd
Bombardier Aerospace (Holdings) UK
Bond Mission Critical Services PLC
Bristol Water Group Limited
British American Tobacco (2009 Pca)
British American Tobacco (2009) Ltd
British American Tobacco Italy Investments
British American Tobacco Peru Holdings
British Land Company PLC
Brookfield BBP UK Holdings II Ltd
Brookfield BBP UK Holdings III Ltd
Brookfield Global Corporate Investments
Brookfield Global Subinvestments Ltd
Brookfield Renewable UK Hydro Ltd
Building & Property (Holdings) Ltd
Building Energy 1 Holdings PLC
Building Energy Ltd
Bunge Corporation Limited
Bupa Care Homes (Holdings) Ltd
Burberry Haymarket Limited
Burberry International Holdings Ltd

Burbo Extension Holding Ltd
Burlingtown UK Limited
Burren Energy PLC
C & C Bidco Limited
C & C Properties UK Limited
C & C Topco Limited
CFC Group Limited
CGI Corporate Holdings Limited
CGI Finance Holdco Two Limited
CGI Group Holdings Europe Ltd
CGI Nordic Holdings Limited
CGI Nordic Investments Limited
CII Holdco Ltd
CKI Gas Infrastructure Limited
CL Intermediate (UK) Limited
CLS One Limited
Cambian Education Services Ltd
Cambian Heritage I Limited
Cambian Properties (U.K.) Ltd
Camelot UK Bidco Limited
Camelot UK Holdco Limited
Camelot UK Top Holdco Limited
Cameron Petroleum (UK) Limited
Canary Wharf Holdings (PB) Ltd
Capital & Counties Limited
Capital & Counties Properties PLC
Capital Hill Hotels Limited
Carros Sensors Topco Limited
Cascade Regional Holdings Ltd
Casper UK Bidco Limited
Cayzer Trust Co Ltd
Chapelfield LP Limited
Chaucer Capital Investments Ltd
Chaucer Holdings Limited
Chelsea Harbour Estates Ltd
China Navigation Co Ltd
Jimmy Choo (Holdings) Limited
Jimmy Choo Group Limited
Choo Luxury Finance Limited
Choo Luxury Holdings Limited
Christie Manson & Woods Ltd
Christie's International PLC
City Football Group Limited
Classboss Limited
Clearmoon Commercial Ltd
Cleveland Clinic UK Holdings Ltd
Cloudreach Acquisitions Ltd
Collins Stewart Former Holdings Ltd
Comet Midco Limited
Compart Systems Limited
Conduit Insurance Holdings Ltd
Connect Bidco Limited
Connect Midco Limited
Consolidated Holdings Limited
Consort Healthcare (Birmingham) Holdings
ContourGlobal PLC
Corob Consolidated Limited
Covent Garden Group Holdings Ltd
Crops Holdings (UK) Limited
Cubico Holdings (UK) 4 Limited
Cummins EMEA Holdings Limited
Cummins PGI Holdings Ltd
Cushman & Wakefield UK USD Holdco
Czarnikow Group Limited
C. Czarnikow Limited
D B Investments (GB) Limited
DB UK Holdings Limited
DCC Energy Finance UK Limited
DCC Holdings (UK) Limited
DCC Limited
DCC Technology Limited
DEKA Energy Associates Limited
DEKA Energy Enterprises Ltd
DIF Tamblin Limited
DNI Europe Holdings Limited
DNI Foreign Holdings Limited
DTEK Finance PLC
DTEK Investments Limited
DTZ UK Bidco 2 Limited
DTZ UK Bidco Limited
DTZ UK Guarantor Limited
DTZ UK Holdco Limited
DTZ UK Newco Limited
Dauphine Holdings (UK) Limited
Daytona Midco 1 Limited
Deltatre Holdings Limited
Derwent Valley Limited
Deutsche Holdings Limited
Deutsche Morgan Grenfell Group PLC
Diamond Bidco Limited
Diamond Midco Limited
Diamond Topco Limited
Digital River UK Holdings I Ltd
Divisional Finance UK Limited
Dixons Carphone Holdings Ltd
Dobbies Garden Centres Group Ltd
Donnelley Financial Solutions Group UK
Doubleplay II Limited
Doubleplay III Limited
Dreof II Europe Holdings Ltd
Drillgreat Limited
EDM Business Services Holdings Ltd
EI Ventures Limited
EMI Group (Newco) Limited
EMI Group Global Limited
EMT 2 Holdings Limited
EMT Holdings Limited
ENI Investments PLC
ENI Lasmo PLC
ENI UK Holding PLC
ENI ULT Limited
ENRC Finance Limited
ERPE Finco Limited
ERPE Topco Limited
ESBII UK Limited
EVRAZ North America PLC
East Slope Residencies PLC
Eastern & Oriental PLC
Economist Group (US Holdings) Ltd
Electricinvest Acquisitions Ltd
Electricinvest Holding Co Ltd
Element Materials Technology Group Holdings CC1
Element Materials Technology Group Holdings CC2
Element Materials Technology Group Holdings
Element Materials Technology Group
Element Materials Technology Ltd
Emerald Acquisition Limited
Enbridge Rampion UK Ltd
Enbridge UK Holdings Ltd
Endeavour Acquisition UK Ltd
Engelhart CTP Group (UK) Ltd
Engelhart CTP Holding (UK) Ltd
Enrichment Holdings Ltd.
Enrichment Investments Limited
Ensono Opco Holdings Limited
Envol Investments Limited
Envol Midco Limited
Equitix Healthcare Limited
Equitix MA 2 Capital Eurobond Ltd
European Fintyre Distribution Ltd
Exova 2014 Limited
Exterion Holdings (UK) Limited
Extraclick Limited
FC Skyfall Bidco Ltd
FC Skyfall TA Limited
FC Skyfall Upper Midco Ltd
FET Global Holdings Limited
FIS UK Holdings Limited
Fair Isaac Software Holdings Ltd
Fair Isaac UK Group Limited
Ferrari Group Limited
Financial Times Group Limited
Finco Omaha Ltd
Fisher Island Limited
Flavia Holdco Limited
Flint Nominees Limited
Folgate Holdings Limited
Forum Worldwide Holdings Ltd
Foseco Holding Limited
Foseco Limited
Foster + Partners Group Ltd
Foundry Bidco No.2 Limited
Foundry Holdco Limited
Foundry Midco 3 Limited
Foundry Topco No.2 Limited
Fox Healthcare Holdco 2 Ltd
Friary Court Investments Ltd
Fujitsu Services Holdings PLC
G4S Finance Limited
G4S International Finance PLC
G4S International Holdings Ltd
G4S Investment London Limited
G4S UK Holdings Limited
G4S US Holdings Limited
G4S US Investments Limited
GFG UK 1 Limited
GFS Renewable Energy Limited
GH Holdings 1 Limited
GH Holdings 2 Limited
GHG 1 (Hospital Operations) Ltd
GHG Intermediate Holdings Ltd
GIP II (Vista) Holdco 1, Ltd
GWI UK Acquisition Co Ltd
GWI UK Holding Limited
GWW UK Holdings Ltd
Gain Capital Holdings Ltd
Galaxy Group Midco Limited
Galloper Holdco Limited
Gardaworld Consulting (UK) Ltd
Garden Finance Limited
Garden Midco 1 Limited
Garden Midco 2 Limited
Gazeley Blue UK Limited
Gazeley Holdings UK Limited
Genel Energy Miran Bina Bawi Ltd
General Alumina Holdings Ltd
General Dynamics European Finance
General Healthcare Holdings (2) Ltd
General Healthcare Holdings (3) Ltd
General Healthcare Holdings (4) Ltd
Genting Americas Holdings Ltd
Get Living London EV2 Holdco Ltd
Global Fashion Group Middle East Holdings (UK)
Global Fashion Group UK Finance Ltd
Gold Quay Assets Limited
Great Beer Co Ltd
Greencoat Solar Assets I Ltd
Greencoat Solar Assets II Ltd
Greencoat UK Wind Holdco Ltd
Greenrock Bidco Limited
Greenrock Topco Limited
Group Miki Holdings Limited

HKEX Investment (UK) Limited
HM Treasury UK Sovereign Sukuk PLC
HNVR Holdco Limited
HNVR Midco Limited
HNVR Topco Limited
Halliburton Global Holdings Ltd
Hanover Insurance International Holdings
Hays International Holdings Ltd
Hector Rail Holding UK Limited
Helix Acquisition Limited
Helix Bufferco Limited
Helix Midco Limited
Hellen Holdings Limited
Henwick Ventures Ltd
Hess NWE Holdings
Hikma Acquisitions (UK) Ltd
Hikma Holdings (UK) Limited
Holbud Group Limited
Homebase (UK & I) Holdings Ltd
Horizon Debtco Limited
Horizon Groupco Limited
Horizon Midco Limited
Hostelworld Group PLC
Howard de Walden Estates Holdings
Howden Joinery Holdings Ltd
IDCO Overseas Holdings Limited
IDCO Worldwide Holdings Ltd
IEP Infrastructure Holdco Ltd
IP Fibre Devices (UK) Limited
IPGL (Holdings) Limited
IPGL Limited
IPP Gas Holdings Limited
IQVIA Solutions Finance UK I Ltd.
IQVIA Solutions Finance UK II Ltd.
IQVIA Solutions Finance UK V Ltd.
IQVIA Solutions Global Holdings UK Ltd.
ISG PLC
Icebox Bidco Limited
Indigo Cleanco Limited
Indigo Intermediate Limited
Indigo Parent Limited
Infopro Digital Holding (UK) Ltd
Ingenious Media Holdings Ltd
Inremco 26 Limited
Insight Investment Management Ltd
Integrafin Holdings PLC
International Publishing Corporation
Interservefm (Holdings) Ltd
Intu (SGS) Holdco Limited
Intu Potteries Limited
Intu Properties Investments Ltd
Intu Trafford Centre Group (UK) Ltd
Iron Mountain Europe (Group) Ltd
Ivy Holdco Limited
JLEAG Wind Holding Limited
JLEAG Wind Limited
JLIF Holdings (Barcelona Metro) Ltd
James River Group Holdings UK Ltd
Jester Bidco Limited
Jester Debtco Limited
Jester Midco Limited
Johnson Matthey Investments Ltd
Jupiter Acquisitions (Holdings) Ltd
Jupiter Properties 2011 UK Ltd
Just Eat (Acquisitions) Holding Ltd
Just Eat Central Holdings Ltd
Kazphosphate Limited
A.T. Kearney Holdings Limited
Kellas Holdco Limited
Kellas Topco Limited
Keller Holdings Limited
Kenon Limited

Kensington & Global Limited
Cath Kidston Acquisitions Ltd
Kingfisher Holdings Limited
Knightsbridge Asset Management Ltd
Korn Ferry GH1 Limited
Korn Ferry Global Holdings (UK) Ltd
L-3 Communications Limited
L-3 Global Holding UK Ltd
LEH Global Ltd
LHC4 (UK) Limited
LIH Financing Limited
Ladbroke & Co., Limited
Ladbroke Group
Ladbroke US Investments Ltd
Ladbrokes Investments Holdings Ltd
John Laing Environmental Assets Group (UK)
Land Securities Portfolio Management
Land Securities Property Holdings
Lazari Financial Holdings Ltd
Lazari Investments Limited
Leopard UK Kensington Propco Ltd
Lewis Trust Holdings Limited
Liberty GR Acquisition Co Ltd
Liberty GR Holding Co Ltd
Liberty International Holdings Ltd
Liberty Living Investments II Holdco 2
Liberty Living Investments II Ltd
Liberty Living Investments Ltd
Lion/Heaven UK II Limited
Lion/Heaven UK Limited
Lion/Jenga Midco Limited
Liquid Telecommunications Financing PLC
Liquid Telecommunications Investments
Livn UK Holdco Limited
Lloyd's Register Foundation
Lloyd's Register Group Limited
Logica Limited
London & Birmingham Hotels Ltd
London Merchant Securities Ltd
London and City Group Holdings Ltd
Lonrho Limited
Luxtail Limited
Lynwood Retail UK Limited
MC Ocean Holdings Limited
MCD Europe Limited
MCD Global Franchising Limited
MHDV Holdings (UK) Limited
MHG Senior Borrower Limited
MMC International Limited
MMC Middle East Holdings Ltd
MMC UK Group Limited
MSCI UK Holdings Limited
MV Werften Holdings Limited
MYI UK Holdings (No.1) Limited
Mabel Bidco Limited
Mabel Mezzco Limited
Mabel Midco Limited
Mabel Topco Limited
Macquarie Aerospace Holdings UK Ltd
Macquarie Commodities Finance (UK)
Macquarie European Investment Holdings
Maestro (Holdings 1) Limited
Maestro (Holdings 2) Limited
Malmaison Hotel du Vin Holdings Ltd
Maref Topco Ltd
Margolis and Ridley Limited
Marken Services Limited
Marsh & McLennan Companies Acquisition
Martin's Family Holdings Ltd
Masdar Offshore Wind UK Ltd
Mastercard UK Holdco Limited

Matthey Finance Limited
Mavenir Private Holdings I Ltd
Mavenir Private Holdings II Ltd
Medical Centre Holdings Ltd
Mergermarket Bidco Limited
Mergermarket Midco 1 Limited
Mergermarket Midco 2 Limited
Mergermarket Topco Limited
Mezqual Limited
Miller 2015 Limited
Miracle Nova (UK) Limited
Mitie Security Holdings Ltd
Mitie Technical Facilities Management Holdings
Mizkan Euro Holdings Limited
Mobius Life Holdings Limited
Mobius Wind Holdings Limited
Monsoon Holdings (No.1) Ltd
Moody's Group (Holdings) Unlimited
J.P. Morgan Capital Holdings Ltd
Motorola Solutions UK Acquisition Co Ltd
Mountain Warehouse International Ltd
Nadezhda Limited
National Grid Interconnector Holdings
Navigator Gas Invest Limited
Neo (BC) UK Limited
New Green Interim Holdco Ltd
New Ventures II (UK) Limited
Newday BondCo PLC
Newday UK Limited
Nexteer UK Holding Ltd.
Nextenergy Solar Holdings Ltd
Nextpower Radius Limited
Nimbus Acquisitions Holdings Ltd
Nimbus Acquisitions Midco 1 Ltd
Nimbus Acquisitions Midco Ltd
Nobel Oil Services (UK) Ltd
Noble Resources UK Holdings Ltd
OHI UK Healthcare Properties Ltd
OSW Co Holdings 1 Limited
OSW Co Holdings 2 Limited
OSW LP Holdco Limited
Oikia (UK) Limited
Omnicom EMEA Investments Ltd
Omnicom Europe Subholdings Ltd
Onesubsea Investments UK Ltd
Ophir Thailand (E & P) Limited
Orosi (UK) 2 Limited
Orsted Burbo Extension Holding Ltd
Osaka Gas UK, Ltd.
Outsourcing UK Limited
PA Consulting Management Services
PE Pioneer Holding II Limited
PE QIQ Holding Limited
PRACCL Limited
PSP Britannia Ltd
Patriot Topco Limited
Pearl Income Holdings UK Ltd
Pearl Income Investments II UK Ltd
Pearl Income Investments UK Ltd
William Pears Group Investments Ltd
William Pears Group Limited
Pearson Australia Finance Unlimited
Pearson Dollar Finance PLC
Pearson Dollar Finance Two Ltd
Pearson Education Investments Ltd
Pearson Funding Five PLC
Pearson Funding Four PLC
Pearson International Finance Ltd
Pearson Loan Finance Unlimited
Pearson Management Services Ltd
Pearson Overseas Holdings Ltd

Pearson PRH Holdings Limited
Pearson Services Limited
Perpetual Power (UK) Limited
Petroceltic Holdings Limited
Pharmadeals Limited
Photobox Holdco Alpha Limited
Photobox Holdco Beta Limited
Pinnacle Resources Limited
Poplar HARCA Capital PLC
Praesidiad Group Limited
Praesidiad Limited
Priory Group No. 1 Limited
Priory Group No. 3 Limited
Project Lake Holdings Limited
Project Leopard Acquireco Ltd
Project Leopard Intermediateco Ltd
Project Leopard Topco Limited
Project Quill Holding Limited
Promontoria Gyle Holding Ltd
Promontoria Gyle Holdings (2) Ltd
Promontoria Gyle Top Holding Ltd
Proserv Operations Limited
Prudential Corporation Holdings Ltd
Prudential Group Holdings Ltd
Puente Holding Limited
Punch Taverns (Chiltern) Ltd
Q Holdco Limited
Q Intermediate Holdco Limited
QDD Athletes Village UK Ltd
Qatar Airways Investments (UK) Ltd
Quadgas Investments Bidco Ltd
Quest Diagnostics Holdings Ltd.
Quest Diagnostics Subsidiary Holdings Ltd.
RI Income UK Holdings Limited
RW Wentworth UK Limited
Rampion Investco Limited
Reebok International Limited
Renewable Energy Income Partnership Holdings 1
Renewable Energy Income Partnership Holdings 2
Retina Finance UK Limited
Ribbon Bidco Limited
Ribbon Holdco Limited
Ribbon Mezzco Limited
Ribbon Midco Limited
Rock Rail South Western (Holdings) 2
Ropemaker RB Holdings Limited
Rosequake Ltd
Royal Mail Investments Limited
Royal Mail PLC
SB Energy Holdings Limited
SB Energy Three Holdings Ltd
SBWW Investments Asia Limited
SBWW Investments Limited
SFP Holdings Limited
SIR Healthcare 2 Limited
SIR Umbrella Limited
SREP Holdings Ltd
SVF Investments (UK) Limited
SYND Holdco Limited
Sainsbury's Intermediate Holdings
Sarti Holdings (UK) Limited
Henry Schein Animal Health Holdings
Schroder International Holdings Ltd
Schroder Investment Co Ltd
Scimco Limited
Sedgwick Morden Acquisitions
Sedgwick Overseas Limited
Sedgwick UK Holdings II Ltd
Sedgwick UK Holdings Limited
Selene Holdings Limited
Selene Midco Limited
Selligent Holdings Limited
Sensis Holding II Limited
Sensis Holding Limited
Sextant Consolidated Limited
Shake UK Newco Limited
Shine Acquisition Co Limited
Shine Holdco I Limited
Shine Holdco II Limited
Shine Holdco III Limited
Sinclair Pharma Limited
Snacks International Development UK
Softbank Group Capital Limited
Solarwinds MSP Holdings Ltd
Southbank Media Ltd
Spire Healthcare Group UK Ltd
Spire Healthcare Holdings 3 Ltd
Standard Chartered Apr Limited
Stena (UK) Limited
Stepstone UK Holding Limited
Sterling Midco Limited
Stradawood Limited
Sumisho Osaka Gas Water UK Ltd
Superior Holdings Limited
Sir Richard Sutton Limited
Swire Oilfield Services (Holdings)
TAI Investments Limited
TI Magazines (UK) Limited
TI Magazines Holdings Limited
TKG-Storagemart Partners UK Ltd
TRS Group (UK) Limited
Tarsus Group Limited
Tate & Lyle Investments Ltd
Tesnik Holdings Limited
Thinc UK Group Limited
Tintagel Castle Limited
Travel Document Service
Trenport Property Holdings Ltd
Tronox Sands Investment Funding Ltd
Tronox UK Finance Limited
Tyrion Security Bidco Limited
Tyrion Security Midco Limited
Tyrion Security Topco Limited
U and I Group PLC
UK Green Investment Gwynt y Mor Ltd
UK Green Investment Gym Participant
UK Green Investment Lid Ltd
UK Green Investment Lyle Ltd
UK Green Investment Sheringham Shoal
UK Group Finance Holdco Ltd
UPP Bond 1 Holdings Limited
UPP Bond 1 Issuer PLC
UPP Bond 1 Limited
URBN Holdings UK Limited
URBN International Operations Ltd
Unlimited Marketing Group Ltd
Urban Exposure PLC
V Acquisition Limited
VEL Holdings Limited
VIL Ltd
VUR Holdings (UK) Limited
VUR Investment (UK) Limited
VUR Mezzanine I (UK) Limited
VUR Mezzanine II (UK) Limited
Vacant Property Security Ltd
Valeo Foods UK Limited
Valero Energy Ltd
Valero Energy UK Ltd
Valero Logistics UK Ltd
Veolia ES (UK) Limited
Veolia ES Holdings (UK) Ltd
Verisk UK Holdco Limited
Vertice Pharma UK Parent Ltd
Vesuvius Ceramics Limited
Vesuvius Investments Limited
Vesuvius Overseas Limited
Virgin Holdings Limited
Virgin Management Limited
Virgin Models Limited
Virgin UK Holdings Limited
Voice Topco Limited
Vue Entertainment Holdings (UK) Ltd
Vue Holdings (UK) Limited
Vue International Bidco PLC
Vue International Finco Ltd
Vue International Midco Ltd
WBA Acquisitions UK Holdco 5 Ltd
WBA Finance 2 Limited
WGSN Group Limited
WMG Finance Limited
WMR Holdco Limited
WMR JV Holdco Limited
WPP Finance 2010
WSP Group Holdings Limited
WSP Group Limited
Wagamama Finance PLC
Warner Music International Services
Wedco EMEA Ventures Limited
Werner European Holding Ltd
Werner US Holding Limited
Westermost Rough (Holding) Ltd
Westminster Acquisition Ltd
Weston (2009) Limited
Westone Hotel Acquisitions Company
Weybourne Group Limited
Whiteacre Resources Ltd
Whitewell UK Investments 1 Ltd
Wilkes-Lucas Limited
Willis GS UK Holdings Limited
Willis Towers Watson UK Holdings Ltd
Woodside Energy Holdings (Senegal)
Wright Express International Holdings
YOA Holdco Limited
Yianis Docklands Hotels Ltd
Yianis Holdings Limited
Yorker Holdings PKR Limited
Zealburg Holdings Limited
Zegona Communications PLC

64301 Activities of investment trusts [70]

Aberdeen Japan Investment Trust PLC
Aberdeen New Dawn Investment Trust PLC
Aberdeen New India Investment Trust PLC
Aberdeen New Thai Investment Trust PLC
Aberdeen Standard Asia Focus PLC
Aberdeen Standard European Logistics Income
Aberforth Split Level Income Trust PLC
Artemis Alpha Trust PLC
Australian Gas Networks UK 2 Ltd
Baillie Gifford UK Growth Fund PLC
Bankers Investment Trust PLC
Baronsmead Second Venture Trust PLC
Baronsmead Venture Trust PLC
Biotech Growth Trust PLC
Blackrock Frontiers Investment Trust PLC
Blackrock Greater Europe Investment Trust
Blackrock Latin American Investment Trust
Blackrock North American Income Trust
Blackrock Throgmorton Trust PLC
Blackrock World Mining Trust PLC
Caledonia Investments PLC
City of London Investment Trust PLC
Ecofin Global Utilities and Infrastructure Trust

Electra Private Equity PLC
FFP Investment UK Ltd
Fundsmith Emerging Equities Trust PLC
Gabelli Value Plus + Trust PLC
Ground Rents Income Fund PLC
Hansa Trust PLC
Henderson Diversified Income Trust PLC
Henderson European Focus Trust PLC
Henderson Eurotrust PLC
Henderson High Income Trust PLC
Henderson International Income Trust PLC
Henderson Smaller Companies Investment Trust
Herald Investment Trust PLC
ICG Enterprise Trust PLC
Impax Environmental Markets PLC
International Biotechnology Trust PLC
Ipek Investment Limited
JPMorgan Elect PLC
JPMorgan European Smaller Companies Trust
JPMorgan Global Emerging Markets Income Trust
JPMorgan Japan Smaller Companies Trust
JPMorgan Japanese Investment Trust PLC
Jupiter Emerging & Frontier Income Trust
Jupiter European Opportunities Trust PLC
Jupiter US Smaller Companies PLC
Lowland Investment Company P L C
MPI (London) Limited
Majedie Investments PLC
Monks Investment Trust PLC
North Atlantic Smaller Companies Investment Trust
P2P Global Investments PLC
Pacific Horizon Investment Trust PLC
Polar Capital Global Financials Trust
Polar Capital Global Healthcare Trust
Polar Capital Technology Trust PLC
RDL Realisation PLC
RIT Capital Partners PLC
Schroder Asian Total Return Investment Company
Schroder Japan Growth Fund PLC
Strategic Equity Capital PLC
TR European Growth Trust PLC
Taylor Clark Limited
Temple Bar Investment Trust PLC
VPC Specialty Lending Investments PLC
Verdoso Holdings Limited
Witan Investment Trust PLC
Worldwide Healthcare Trust PLC

64302 Activities of unit trusts

Legal & General (Unit Trust Managers)
Schroder Unit Trusts Limited

64303 Activities of venture and development capital companies

Business Growth Fund Limited
CDC Group PLC
Diageo DV Limited
IP Group PLC
Peabody Capital No 2 PLC

64304 Activities of open-ended investment companies

Allianz Renewable Energy Partners V PLC
Allianz Renewable Energy Partners VI
Axiata Investments (UK) Ltd
DTZ UK Bidco 2 Limited
Flint Nominees Limited
Legal & General (Unit Trust Managers)
PG (April) Limited
Portobar Capital Limited

64306 Activities of real estate investment trusts [13]

AEW UK REIT PLC
Ediston Property Investment Company PLC
Epic (No. 1) Limited
Impact Healthcare REIT PLC
Intu Properties PLC
LXI Property Holdings 1 Ltd
LXI REIT PLC
Land Securities Group PLC
M7 Real Estate Investment Holdings Holdco
Segro PLC
Triple Point Social Housing REIT PLC
Verdoso Holdings Limited
Zavarco PLC

64910 Financial leasing [32]

A & L CF June (3) Limited
Al Rayan Bank PLC
Alpha Partners Leasing Limited
BBP Bandenia PLC
Bal Global Finance (UK) Ltd
Bank of Scotland Structured Asset Finance
Barclays Mercantile Business Finance
CWCB Finance Leasing (DS7B) Ltd
Caledonian Rail Leasing Ltd
Coutts Finance Co.
Eversholt Rail Leasing Limited
Halifax Leasing (September) Ltd
Macquarie European Rail Ltd
Macquarie Meters 3 (UK) Ltd
Mercantile Leasing Company (No.132)
Mithras Leasing (No.1) Ltd
Mithras Leasing (No.4) Limited
Motability Operations Limited
National Australia Finance (Vessel Leasing No.5)
Omega Leasing (No. 12) Limited
Omega Leasing (No.10) Limited
Omega Leasing (No.11) Limited
Omega Leasing (No.9) Limited
QW Rail Leasing Limited
SG (Maritime) Leasing Limited
SG Leasing (Gems) Limited
SG Leasing (March) Limited
SMBC Aviation Capital (UK) Ltd
SMBC Leasing (UK) Limited
Santander Asset Finance PLC
Swan National Limited
Victoria Asset Finance Limited

64921 Credit granting by non-deposit taking finance houses and other specialist consumer credit grantors [16]

BBP Bandenia PLC
CW Lending II Limited
Dunbar Assets PLC
FGIC UK Limited
GB Social Housing PLC
India Infrastructure Finance Company (UK)
Instant Cash Loans Limited
Kensington Mortgage Securities PLC
Morgan Stanley Bank International
Privilege Project Finance Ltd
Rooftop Funding Limited
Schroder & Co. Limited
TS Property Lending Limited
TS Structured Finance Limited
Total UK Finance Limited
Wells Fargo Capital Finance (UK) Ltd

64922 Activities of mortgage finance companies [16]

Belmont Green Funding 1 Ltd
Belmont Green Funding 3 Ltd
Castle Trust Capital PLC
Finsbury Square 2017-1 PLC
Friary No.4 PLC
Harben Finance 2017-1 PLC
Lazari Finance Limited
Lazari Financial Holdings Ltd
Privilege Project Finance Ltd
Residential Mortgage Securities 26 PLC
Residential Mortgage Securities 29 PLC
Residential Mortgage Securities 30 PLC
Ripon Mortgages PLC
Stanlington No. 1 PLC
Towd Point Mortgage Funding 2017 - Auburn 11
Tower Bridge Funding No.1 PLC

64929 Other credit granting n.e.c. [15]

CPB Residential Finance Ltd
Chiquita Finance Co Ltd
Crown Financial & Merchant Bank PLC
DVB Transport Finance Limited
Genting Worldwide Services Ltd
Honeycomb Investment Trust PLC
Interoute Finco Limited
Olekit Investments Ltd
P2P BL-3 PLC
Prepaid Financial Services Ltd
Rickleford Ltd
TS Real Estate Limited
WPG Finance Limited
WPG Treasury Limited
Wolfson Foundation

64991 Security dealing on own account [22]

AV Equity Trading Limited
Arunvill Global Equity Trading Ltd
C.C. Licensing
Citadel Securities (Europe) Ltd
EGX Credit Liquidity Ltd
Eclectic Capital Limited
Finantia UK Limited
Fox Investments Limited
ICBC (London) PLC
Jane Street Europe Limited
Jane Street Financial Limited
Jump Trading International Ltd
MUFG Securities EMEA PLC
Maven Investment Partners Ltd
Milton Magna Limited
RIT Capital Partners PLC
SMBC Nikko Capital Markets Ltd
Syncbeam Limited
Tokai Tokyo Securities Europe Ltd
Toscafund Limited
Tullett Prebon (Europe) Ltd
XTX Markets Limited

64992 Factoring

BBP Bandenia PLC
Macquarie Commodities (UK) Ltd
Macquarie Factoring (UK) Ltd

64999 Financial intermediation not elsewhere classified [547]

3i Group PLC
3i PLC
ABC International Bank PLC
AD (Europe) Finance
AD Fin Services Limited
ADM Investor Services International
Abbey National Property Investments
Abbey National Treasury Services Overseas Holdings
Abbey National Treasury Services PLC
Aberdeen Infrastructure II Ltd
Aberdeen Infrastructure Ltd
Aberdeen Standard Equity Income Trust
Aequor Investments Limited
Affinity Sutton Capital Markets PLC
Affinity Sutton Funding Ltd
Affordable Housing Finance PLC
Aggregator Vehicle PLC
Aggregator of Loans Backed By Assets 2015-1
Airbnb Payments UK Limited
Albion No.3 PLC
Allianz Renewable Energy Partners II
Allianz Renewable Energy Partners IV
Allianz Renewable Energy Partners VIII
Allianz Technology Trust PLC
Allied SX Ltd
Anglo American Prefco Limited
Anzef Limited
Arbuthnot Banking Group PLC
Arbuthnot Latham & Co., Ltd
Arsenal Securities PLC
Artesian Finance III PLC
Ascential Financing Limited
Ascential Prefco Limited
Auto ABS UK Loans 2017 PLC
Auto ABS UK Loans PLC
Aviva Investors UK Fund Services Ltd
B.A.T. International Finance P.L.C.
BBA Aviation Finance
BBA Finance
BBA Finance No. 4 Limited
BBA Finance No.1
BBA Holdings Limited
BCS Prime Brokerage Limited
BG Atlantic Finance Limited
BMCE Bank International PLC
BMO AM Holdings Limited
BMO Capital Markets Limited
BMO Capital and Income Investment Trust
BMO Global Smaller Companies PLC
BNP Paribas Commodity Futures Ltd
BNP Paribas U.K. Holdings Ltd
BNP Paribas UK Limited
BNY Mellon Fund Managers Ltd
BNY Mellon Investment Management EMEA
BTIG Limited
Balderton Aviation Holdings Ltd
Bank of New York Mellon (International)
Barbados Enterprises PLC
Barclays (Barley) Limited
Barclays Aldersgate Investments Ltd
Barclays Capital Securities Ltd
Barclays Funds Investments Ltd
Barclays Investment Management Ltd
Barclays Long Island Limited
Batif Dollar Limited
Bear Stearns Holdings Limited
Belmont Green Funding 1 Ltd
Belmont Green Funding 3 Ltd
Bitstamp Limited
Black Horse Finance Holdings Ltd
Black Horse Limited
Blackrock Advisors (UK) Ltd
Blackrock Finco UK Ltd
Blackrock Fund Managers Ltd
Blackrock Group Limited
Blackrock Investment Management (UK)
Blackrock UK Holdco Limited
Bodiam Hill Limited
Boreas (Investment) Limited
Boreas Holdco Limited
Brewin Dolphin Limited
Bridgepoint Funding III A Ltd
Brit Group Finance Limited
Broad Street Principal Investments UK
Brook Funding (No.1) Limited
Brunner Investment Trust PLC
Bumper 8 (UK) Finance PLC
Burford Investments Limited
CMC Markets Holdings Limited
CMC Markets PLC
CMC Markets UK Holdings Ltd
CMC Markets UK PLC
CNH Industrial UK Limited
CTRL Section 1 Finance PLC
CWBC Finance (BP1) Limited
CWBC Finance Two (BP1) Limited
Caledonian Rail Leasing Ltd
Canaccord Genuity Limited
Canary Wharf Finance Leasing (BP1)
Cantor Fitzgerald Europe
Capco Group Treasury Limited
Capita Customer Management Ltd
Capita Life & Pensions Regulated Services
Care Homes 1 Limited
Care Homes 2 Limited
Care Homes 3 Limited
Castile Acquisitions Ltd
Castle Trust Direct PLC
Castle Trust Finance Limited
Castle Trust Treasury Limited
Catalyst Finance Limited
Chapelcrest Investments Ltd
Charter Mortgage Funding 2017-1 PLC
Chepstow Blue PLC
China Construction Bank (London) Ltd
Citifinancial Europe Limited
Citigroup Participation Luxembourg
Clavis Securities PLC
Cliffrange Limited
Close Brothers Finance PLC
Close Brothers Limited
Close Invoice Finance Limited
Cofunds Limited
Commercial Acceptances Limited
Commerzbank Finance Limited
Community Finance Company 1 PLC
Corbiere Asset Investments Ltd
Corfe Hill Limited
Credit Suisse (UK) Limited
Credit Suisse Asset Management (UK) Holding
Credit Suisse Asset Management Ltd
Credit Suisse Securities (Europe)
Crown Financial & Merchant Bank PLC
Currencies Direct Holdings Ltd
Cyan Auto Receivables Limited
DB UK Bank Limited
DWS Alternatives Global Ltd
DWS Group Services UK Limited
Daily Mail International Ltd
Daiwa Capital Markets Europe Ltd
Darrowby No. 3 PLC
Darrowby No. 4 PLC
Daunus Limited
Debussy DTC PLC
Delamare Finance PLC
Derwent Valley Finance Limited
Deutsche Alternative Asset Management (UK)
Deutsche Holdings No.2 Limited
Deutsche Holdings No.3 Limited
Deutsche Holdings No.4 Limited
Deva Financing PLC
Diageo US Holdings
Dinosaur Merchant Bank Limited
Dukinfield II PLC
Dukinfield PLC
Duncan Funding 2015-1 PLC
Duncan Funding 2016-1 PLC
E-Carat 6 PLC
E-Carat 7 PLC
E-Carat 8 PLC
ELQ Holdings (UK) Ltd
ELQ Investors II Ltd
ELQ Investors IX Ltd
ELQ Investors VI Ltd
ELQ Investors VII Ltd
ELQ Investors VIII Ltd
ELQ Investors, Ltd
ELQ Omega UK Ltd
EMI Group Finance Limited
Eagle Financial and Leasing Services (UK)
East Finance PLC
Edgbaston RMBS 2010-1 PLC
Equitix Capital Eurobond 3 Ltd
Equitix Capital Eurobond Ltd
Equitix Infrastructure 3 Ltd
Eurasia Finance Management Ltd
Euroclear Limited
Eurohome UK Mortgages 2007 - 1 PLC
Eurohome UK Mortgages 2007-2 PLC
European Wind Investments Group Ltd
Exane Limited
Exelvia Company
F & C Investment Trust PLC
FGIC UK Limited
Feldspar 2016-1 PLC
Finantia UK Limited
Finsbury Square 2016-1 PLC
Finsbury Square 2017-1 PLC
Finventures UK Limited
First State Investment Services (UK)
First State Investments (UK) Ltd
Firstplus Financial Group Ltd
Fitch Ratings Ltd
Fitch Solutions Group Limited
Friary No.2 PLC
Friary No.3 PLC
Friary No.4 PLC
Fujitsu EMEA PLC
GF Financial Markets (UK) Ltd
GFI Securities Limited
GS Funding Europe
GS Funding Europe III Ltd
GS Funding Europe V Limited
GS Sapphire Investment Limited
Gatehouse Bank PLC
Global Prime Partners Ltd
Global Reach Partners Limited
Goldman Sachs Group U.K. Finance Ltd
Goldman Sachs International
Goldman Sachs International Investments

Google Payment Limited
HCUK Auto Funding 2017-1 Ltd
HSBC (BGF) Investments Limited
HSBC Asset Finance (UK) Ltd
HSBC Equipment Finance (UK) Ltd
HSBC Securities (Japan) Ltd
HSBC Specialist Investments Ltd
HSBC Trust Company (UK) Ltd
J O Hambro Capital Management Ltd
Harbour Funding PLC
Harewood Helena 2 Limited
Harewood Holdings Limited
Harwood Capital Management Ltd
Haven Funding PLC
Hawkins Funding Limited
Hawksmoor Mortgages 2016-1 PLC
Hawksmoor Mortgages 2016-2 PLC
Henderson Investment Funds Ltd
Hermes Fund Managers Limited
HgCapital Trust PLC
Holmes Funding Limited
Holmes Master Issuer PLC
Howard Investments Limited
IBM Global Asset Management Ltd
ICG Carbon Funding Limited
ICG Global Investment UK Ltd
IG Finance Three
IG Finance Two
IG Index Limited
IHS Markit Group Holdings Ltd
Idex UK Ltd.
Inchcape Finance PLC
Income Contingent Student Loans 1 (2002-2006)
Infrastructure Investments (A63) Holdings
Infrastructure Investments Betjeman
Infrastructure Investments Trafalgar
Instant Cash Loans Limited
Intelligent Processing Solutions Ltd
Intermediate Capital Group PLC
Intu (SGS) Finance PLC
Intu Metrocentre Finance PLC
Investec Wealth & Investment Ltd
Itochu Treasury Centre Europe PLC
JPMorgan American Investment Trust PLC
JPMorgan Asian Investment Trust PLC
JPMorgan Asset Management (UK) Ltd
JPMorgan Asset Management Holdings (UK)
JPMorgan Chinese Investment Trust PLC
JPMorgan Claverhouse Investment Trust
JPMorgan Emerging Markets Investment Trust
JPMorgan European Investment Trust PLC
JPMorgan Global Growth & Income PLC
JPMorgan Indian Investment Trust PLC
JPMorgan Mid Cap Investment Trust PLC
JPMorgan Russian Securities PLC
JPMorgan Smaller Companies Investment Trust
JPMorgan US Smaller Companies Investment Trust
Jasper Acquisition Limited
Jefferies International Ltd
Johnson & Johnson Swiss Finance Co Ltd
Jupiter Asset Management Group Ltd
Jupiter Asset Management Ltd
Jupiter Fund Management Group Ltd
Jupiter Fund Management PLC
Jupiter Unit Trust Managers Ltd
Juturna (European Loan Conduit No. 16)
King & Shaxson Limited
Koch Metals Trading Limited

Kypris Acquisitions Ltd
LCR Finance PLC
LMS Capital PLC
LMS Finance Limited
LTG International Limited
LYB Treasury Services Ltd.
John Laing Infrastructure Ltd
John Laing Social Infrastructure
Lanark Funding Limited
Lanark Master Issuer PLC
Landmark Mortgage Securities No.2 PLC
Landmark Mortgage Securities No.3 PLC
Langton Funding (No.1) Limited
Langton Securities (2008-1) PLC.
Langton Securities (2010-1) PLC
Lannraig Master Issuer PLC
Law Debenture Corporation PLC
Lazard & Co., Limited
Leadenhall Securities Corporation
Lendlease Europe Finance PLC
Liberty International Group Treasury
Lingfield 2014 I PLC
Link Fund Solutions Limited
Lloyds Bank Asset Finance Ltd
Lloyds UDT Limited
Lochside Asset Purchaser No.1 PLC
Lombard Business Leasing Ltd
Lombard North Central PLC
London Forfaiting Co Ltd
Long Island Assets Limited
Longstone Finance PLC
Ludgate Funding PLC
Luminus Finance Limited
M & G Group Limited
M & G. Securities Limited
ML Invest Holdings
ML UK Capital Holdings Limited
MLEIH Funding
MMC International Treasury Centre
MUFG Securities EMEA PLC
Macquarie Bank International Ltd
Macquarie Capital (Europe) Ltd
Macquarie Commodities (UK) Ltd
Macquarie Euro Limited
Macquarie Group Investments (UK) No.2
Macquarie Investments (UK) Ltd
Malt Hill No.1 PLC
Mansard Mortgages 2006-1 PLC
Mansard Mortgages 2007-2 PLC
Marex Financial
Marex Spectron Group Limited
Markit Group Limited
Markitserv Holdings Limited
Marks and Spencer Investments
Marsh Treasury Services Ltd
Marubeni Finance Europe PLC
Max Recovery Limited
Mercantile Investment Trust PLC
Merchants Trust PLC
Mercia No.1 PLC
Merrill Lynch (Camberley) Ltd
Merrill Lynch Europe Limited
Merrill Lynch International
Merrill Lynch UK Finance
Metinvest Capital UK Limited
Metinvest Investments Limited
Millennium Capital Management Ltd.
Mithras Leasing (No.1) Ltd
Mithras Leasing (No.4) Limited
Mitsubishi Corporation Finance PLC
Mitsui & Co. Financial Services (Europe)
Mizuho International PLC

Molineux RMBS 2016-1 PLC
Monecor (London) Limited
Monex Europe Limited
Montserrat Acquisitions Ltd
J.P. Morgan Capital Financing Ltd
J.P. Morgan Chase International Financing
J.P. Morgan Markets Limited
Morgan Stanley Corporate Trader
Morgan Stanley Employment Services UK
Morgan Stanley Gamma Investments
Morgan Stanley Langton Limited
Morgan Stanley Longcross Ltd
Morgan Stanley Swallow Limited
Morgan Stanley UK Group
Motor 2015-1 PLC
Motor 2017-1 PLC
Motor Oil Finance PLC
Mountsfield Park Finance Ltd
NBG Finance (Dollar) PLC
NYK Investments Limited
Naxos Investments Limited
Network Rail Infrastructure Finance PLC
Neuberger Berman Europe Ltd
Newday Funding 2015-1 PLC
Newday Funding 2015-2 PLC
Newday Funding 2016-1 PLC
Newday Funding 2017-1 PLC
Newday Partnership Funding 2015-1 PLC
Newfound Bay Limited
Newgate Funding PLC
Nomura Capital Markets Limited
Nomura European Investment Ltd
Nomura International PLC
Northern Trust Holdings Ltd
Northern Trust Management Services
Northstar Holding Limited
Northstar Investments Limited
Northstar Midco Limited
Northwharf Investments Limited
Novae Corporate Underwriting Ltd
Numis Securities Limited
OCHL (Globe) Limited
Oak No.1 PLC
Oat Hill No.1 PLC
Octopus AIM VCT PLC
Octopus Apollo VCT PLC
Octopus Titan VCT PLC
Offa No.1 PLC
Oncilla Mortgage Funding 2016-1 PLC
Optimum Three Limited
PGIM Limited
PHP SB Limited
PIP Infrastructure Investments (No 6)
Pacific Quay Finance PLC
Pacific Quay Holdings Limited
Pangaea Funding 1 PLC
Park Tower Investments Limited
Peabody Capital PLC
Penarth Master Issuer PLC
Permanent Funding (No.2) Ltd
Permanent Master Issuer PLC
Petra Diamonds UK Treasury Ltd
Petra Diamonds US$ Treasury PLC
Phillips 66 Treasury Limited
Pictet Asset Management Ltd
Pips Asset Investments Limited
Post Office Limited
Precise Mortgage Funding 2015-2B PLC
Precise Mortgage Funding 2015-3R PLC
Precise Mortgage Funding 2017-1B PLC
Premiertel PLC
Prudential Capital PLC

Prutec Limited
Pyrenees Acquisitions Limited
QW Rail Leasing Limited
Quilter Cheviot Limited
RBS Invoice Finance Limited
RBS SME Investments Limited
RSL Finance (No. 1) PLC
Rational Foreign Exchange Ltd
Real Estate Participation Management
Real Estate Participation Services
Reclaim Fund Ltd
Relative Value Trading Limited
Residential Mortgage Securities 28 PLC
Residential Mortgage Securities 29 PLC
Residential Mortgage Securities 30 PLC
Reuters Transaction Services Ltd
Rio Tinto Finance PLC
Ripon Mortgages PLC
Rochester Financing No.2 PLC
Roder Investments No. 1 Ltd
Roder Investments No. 2 Ltd
Rolls-Royce & Partners Finance Ltd
Rothschild & Co Continuation Finance PLC
Rothschild & Co Continuation Ltd
Ruthenium Investments Limited
SCMB Overseas Limited
SG Kleinwort Hambros Limited
SMBC Derivative Products Ltd
SMBC Leasing (UK) Limited
SNC Securities Limited
Sandown 2012-2 PLC
Sandown Gold 2012-1 PLC
Sanne Group (UK) Limited
Santander Lending Limited
Satellite Financing PLC
Scania Finance Great Britain Ltd
Schroder & Co. Limited
Schroder AsiaPacific Fund PLC
Schroder Financial Services Ltd
Schroder Income Growth Fund PLC
Schroder Investment Management Ltd
Schroder Pension Management Ltd
Selfridges Financing Limited
Semperian Senior Funding PLC
Shell Treasury Centre Limited
Shell Treasury Dollar Co Ltd
Shell Treasury UK Limited
Silchester Capital Limited
Silchester Partners Limited
Skrill Limited
Slate No.1 PLC
Slate No.2 PLC
Societe Generale International Ltd
Societe Generale Investments (U.K.)
Sojitz Global Finance PLC
Southern Pacific Mortgage Ltd
Sova Capital Limited
Standard Chartered Holdings Ltd
Standard Chartered NEA Limited
Standard Chartered PLC
Charles Stanley & Co. Limited
Charles Stanley Group PLC
State Street Europe Limited
State Street Global Advisors Ltd
Student Finance PLC
Sucden Financial Limited
Sumitomo Electric Finance UK Ltd
Sunderland (SHG) Finance PLC
T.H.F.C. (Capital) PLC
T.H.F.C. (Funding No. 1) PLC
T.H.F.C. (Funding No.2) PLC
T.H.F.C. (Funding No.3) PLC
TD Bank Europe Limited
TFS Derivatives Limited
TR Property Investment Trust PLC
TTT Moneycorp Limited
Tam Investment Limited
Tate & Lyle International Finance PLC
Telereal Secured Finance PLC
Telereal Securitisation PLC
Temese Funding 2 PLC
Tenneco Management (Europe) Ltd
Tesco Property Finance 2 PLC
Tesco Property Finance 3 PLC
Tesco Property Finance 4 PLC
Tesco Property Finance 5 PLC
Tesco Property Finance 6 PLC
Theatre (Hospitals) No.1 PLC
Theatre (Hospitals) No.2 PLC
Thistle Investments (AMC) Ltd
Threadneedle Asset Management Finance
Threadneedle Investment Services Ltd
Thrones 2014-1 PLC
Thrones 2015-1 PLC
Together Asset Backed Securitisation 1
Tower Bridge Funding No.1 PLC
Tradition London Clearing Ltd
Trayport Holdings Limited
Triland Metals Limited
Trinity Financing PLC
Trinity Square 2015-1 PLC
Tullett Prebon (No. 3) Limited
Tullett Prebon (Securities) Ltd
Tungsten Corporation PLC
Turbo Finance 6 PLC
Turbo Finance 7 PLC
Tyman Financial Services Ltd
UKEI (Finance) Limited
Unisys Finance Limited
Unite (USAF) II PLC
United Dominions Leasing Ltd
United Dominions Trust Limited
Uropa Assets No. 1 Limited
Uropa Securities PLC
Visa Europe Limited
Warwick Finance Residential Mortgages Number One
Warwick Finance Residential Mortgages Number Two
Waymark Asset Investments Ltd
Wells Fargo Securities International
Western Union Business Solutions (UK)
Weybourne Finance Limited
White City Property Finance PLC
Winterflood Securities Limited
Worldpay AP Ltd.
Zeuss Childcare Limited

65110 Life insurance [15]

AIG Life Limited
Aviva Investors Pensions Ltd
Beazley Group Limited
HSBC Life (UK) Limited
ICP Holdings Limited
Integralife UK Limited
JPMorgan Life Limited
Legal and General Assurance (Pensions Management)
Legal and General Assurance Society
Mobius Life Limited
Partnership Life Assurance Co Ltd
Rothesay Life PLC
Scottish Widows Limited
Threadneedle Pensions Limited
UBS Asset Management Life Ltd

65120 Non-life insurance [146]

AGF Insurance Limited
AMT Mortgage Insurance Limited
ANV Corporate Name Limited
Advent Capital (No. 3) Limited
Aegis Electric & Gas International Services
Aegis London Holdings Limited
Aetna Insurance Co Ltd
Ambac Assurance UK Limited
Amtrust Corporate Member Ltd
Antares Underwriting Limited
Arch Insurance Company (Europe) Ltd
Arch Syndicate Investments Ltd
Argo (Alpha) Limited
Argo (No. 604) Limited
Argo (No. 703) Limited
Ariel Corporate Member Limited
Ark Corporate Member Limited
Ascot Corporate Name Limited
Ascot Underwriting Group Ltd
Aspen (UK) Holdings Limited
Aspen European Holdings Ltd
Aspen Insurance UK Limited
Aspen Managing Agency Limited
Aspen Underwriting Limited
Assured Guaranty (Europe) PLC
Aston Lark (Bidco) Limited
Aston Lark (Topco) Limited
Atrium 5 Limited
Aviva International Insurance Ltd
Axa Insurance UK PLC
Axa PPP Healthcare Limited
Barbican Corporate Member Ltd
Beaufort Dedicated No 2 Ltd
Beazley Management Limited
Beazley Underwriting Limited
Berkshire Hathaway International Insurance
Bluefin Insurance Services Ltd
Brit Insurance Holdings Ltd
Brit Limited
Brit UW Limited
Britannia Steam Ship Insurance Association
Bupa Insurance Limited
CNA Europe Holdings Limited
CNA Insurance Co Ltd
Catlin Syndicate 6112 Limited
Catlin Syndicate Limited
Chaucer Holdings Limited
Chubb Capital I Limited
Chubb Capital Ltd
Chubb Capital V Limited
Discovery Holdings Europe Ltd
Domestic & General Insurance PLC
Domestic & General Services Ltd
Dornoch Limited
ED Broking Group Limited
ED Broking Holdings (London) Ltd
ERS Corporate Member Limited
Endurance Corporate Capital Ltd
Endurance Worldwide Insurance Ltd
FGIC UK Limited
Fidelis Underwriting Limited
Flectat Limited
GAI Indemnity, Ltd.
Arthur J. Gallagher (UK) Ltd
Arthur J. Gallagher Holdings (UK)
Global Aerospace Underwriting Managers
Great Lakes Reinsurance (UK) SE
Griffin Insurance Association Ltd
HCC International Insurance Company PLC

HIG Finance Limited
HLG Holdings Limited
HSB Engineering Insurance Ltd
Hardy Underwriting Limited
Helios Underwriting PLC
Hiscox Dedicated Corporate Member
Hiscox Insurance Co Ltd
Hiscox PLC
Hiscox Underwriting Ltd
Howden Broking Group Limited
Howden UK Group Limited
Hyperion Development UK Ltd
Hyperion Insurance Group Ltd
ICP Capital Limited
ICP Holdings Limited
International General Insurance Company (UK)
International Transport Intermediaries Club
JLT Insurance Group Holdings Ltd
JLT Reinsurance Brokers Ltd
JLT Specialty Limited
Labuan RE Underwriting Limited
Lancashire Insurance Company (UK)
Lavenham Underwriting Limited
Legal & General Insurance Ltd
Liberty Corporate Capital (Two) Ltd
Liberty Corporate Capital Ltd
Liberty Managing Agency Ltd
Lloyds Bank General Insurance Ltd
Lloyds Bank Insurance Services Ltd
London and Overseas Insurance Co Ltd
MAP Capital Limited
MS Amlin Corporate Member Ltd
MS Amlin PLC
MS Amlin Underwriting Limited
MSI Corporate Capital Limited
Markel Capital Limited
Markel International Insurance Co Ltd
Mitsui Sumitomo Insurance Company (Europe),
Munich RE Capital Limited
NRG Victory Reinsurance Ltd
Nameco (No.808) Limited
Navigators Corporate Underwriters
Newline Corporate Name Limited
Newline Insurance Co Ltd
OIC Run-Off Limited
Ocean Marine Insurance Co Ltd
QBE Corporate Limited
QBE RE (Europe) Limited
QBE UK Limited
Redquince Limited
Renaissancere Corporate Capital (UK)
SCOR UK Co Ltd
SCOR Underwriting Limited
Sampford Underwriting Limited
Skuld I Limited
St Andrew's Insurance PLC
Starr Syndicate Limited
Starstone Corporate Capital 1 Ltd
Steamship Mutual Underwriting Association
TT Club Mutual Insurance Ltd
Talbot 2002 Underwriting Capital Ltd
Tenecom Limited
Tokio Marine Kiln Insurance Ltd
Tokio Marine Underwriting Ltd
Tonicstar Limited
Transfercom Limited
Travelers Insurance Co Ltd
Treimco Limited
USAA Limited
United Kingdom Mutual Steam Ship Assurance Association (Europe)
Vibe Corporate Member Limited
Vitality Health Insurance Ltd
Vitality Health Limited
WRBC Corporate Member Limited
Willis Limited
XL Catlin Insurance Company UK Ltd
XL London Market Group Limited

65201 Life reinsurance

Beazley Group Limited
Mobius Life Limited
Pacific Life RE Limited
Prudential Assurance Co Ltd
Prudential Pensions Limited

65202 Non-life reinsurance [49]

AMT Mortgage Insurance Limited
Aetna Insurance Co Ltd
Antares Underwriting Limited
Aspen (UK) Holdings Limited
Aspen European Holdings Ltd
Aspen Insurance UK Limited
Aspen Managing Agency Limited
Aspen Underwriting Limited
Beaufort Dedicated No 2 Ltd
Beazley Management Limited
Beazley Underwriting Limited
Brit Limited
Chaucer Holdings Limited
China RE UK Limited
Domestic & General Insurance PLC
Domestic & General Services Ltd
Dornoch Limited
ED Broking Group Limited
ED Broking Holdings (London) Ltd
Endurance Corporate Capital Ltd
Equitas Limited
Equitas Reinsurance Limited
Fidelis Underwriting Limited
Friary Intermediate Limited
GAI Indemnity, Ltd.
HSB Engineering Insurance Ltd
Helios Underwriting PLC
ICP Capital Limited
International General Insurance Company (UK)
Lavenham Underwriting Limited
Legal & General Pensions Ltd
Liberty Corporate Capital Ltd
Liberty Managing Agency Ltd
MS Amlin PLC
MSI Corporate Capital Limited
Nameco (No.808) Limited
Navigators Corporate Underwriters
Pool Reinsurance Co Ltd
QBE UK Limited
Renaissancere Corporate Capital (UK)
Sampford Underwriting Limited
Skuld I Limited
Tokio Marine Kiln Insurance Ltd
Tokio Marine Underwriting Ltd
Tokio Millennium RE (UK) Ltd
Transre London Limited
Treimco Limited
Willis Limited
XL London Market Group Limited

65300 Pension funding

Aberdeen Asset Management Life and Pensions
Capita Employee Benefits Ltd
Managed Pension Funds Limited
Partnership Life Assurance Co Ltd
Shell Pension Reserve Company (UK)

66110 Administration of financial markets

AD European Investments Ltd
Burford Capital PLC
Crown Financial & Merchant Bank PLC
Ice Clear Europe Limited
LME Clear Limited
London Stock Exchange PLC
PhillipCapital UK Ltd
SG Kleinwort Hambros Bank Ltd

66120 Security and commodity contracts dealing activities [50]

Alcentra Limited
Axa Investment Managers UK Ltd
BOCI Global Commodities (UK) Ltd
Sanford C. Bernstein Limited
CLSA (UK)
Canaccord Genuity Limited
China Merchants Securities (UK) Ltd
Citigroup Global Markets Ltd
Forex Capital Markets Limited
G.H. Financials Limited
Gatehouse Bank PLC
Glencore Commodities Ltd
Glencore Energy UK Ltd.
Glencore UK Ltd.
Henderson Global Investors Ltd
ICAP Securities Limited
ICAP WCLK Limited
INTL FCStone Ltd
Insight Investment Management (Global)
Instinet Europe Limited
Interactive Brokers (U.K.) Ltd
Intermediate Capital Managers Ltd
Investcorp Credit Management EU Ltd
KCG Europe Limited
Koch Commodities Europe Ltd
Koch Industries International Ltd
London Metal Exchange
M & G Investment Management Ltd
Macsco 22 Limited
Majedie Asset Management Ltd
E D & F Man Capital Markets Ltd
Mitsui Bussan Commodities Ltd
Morgan Stanley & Co. International PLC
Octopus AIM VCT PLC
Octopus Capital Limited
Parvus Asset Management Ltd
PhillipCapital UK Ltd
T. Rowe Price International Ltd
SCMI Limited
Shell International Trading and Shipping Co
Shell Trading International Ltd
Smith & Williamson Investment Services
Socar Trading (UK) Limited
State Street Global Markets International
Stifel Nicolaus Europe Limited
Sumitomo Corporation Global Commodities
Threadneedle Asset Management Ltd
Toyota Tsusho Metals Limited
UBS Asset Management (UK) Ltd
Winton Capital Management Ltd

66190 Activities auxiliary to financial intermediation n.e.c. [25]

ANZ Europe Limited
AWP Assistance UK Ltd
Caledonia Thames Acquisitions Ltd
Caledonia Thames Group Limited
Capita Employee Benefits Ltd
Citigroup Capital UK Limited
EBS Dealing Resources International
EFL Futures Limited
European Policy Exchange Ltd
FTSE Global Debt Capital Markets Ltd
Gatehouse Bank PLC
ICE Overseas Limited
Lazard & Co., Limited
E D & F Man Capital Markets Treasury Management
National Westminster Bank PLC
Paysafe Financial Services Ltd
Phoenix Natural Gas PP Finance PLC
Reuters Transaction Services Ltd
Revcap Finance Limited
N. M. Rothschild & Sons Ltd
Sixmoor Limited
Swiss Re Specialised Investments Holdings (UK)
Transport for London Finance Ltd
Vaultex UK Limited
Wyelands Holdings Limited

66210 Risk and damage evaluation

FFI Holdings PLC

66220 Activities of insurance agents and brokers

AON UK Limited
AWP Assistance UK Ltd
Cathedral Capital Holdings Ltd
ICP Holdings Limited
Integro Insurance Brokers Holdings
Integro Insurance Brokers Ltd
Marsh Limited

66290 Other activities auxiliary to insurance and pension funding [32]

Additional Securities Limited
Arig Capital Limited
Axis Corporate Capital UK Ltd
Axis Specialty Finance PLC
Blackrock Life Limited
Capita Employee Benefits Ltd
Cathedral Capital (1998) Ltd
Cathedral Capital Holdings Ltd
Chaucer Corporate Capital (No. 3)
Crawford & Company EMEA/A-P Holdings
Crawford & Company Risk Services Investments
Endurance Worldwide Holdings Ltd
Faraday Capital Limited
Hardy Underwriting Group Ltd
JLT Benefit Solutions Limited
Lancashire Insurance Holdings (UK)
Mobius Life Limited
PRA Corporate Capital Limited
Pacific Life RE Services Ltd
Partnership Assurance Group Ltd
Pension Insurance Corporation Group
Pension Insurance Corporation PLC
Phillips 66 UK Funding Limited
Pic Holdings Limited
Principal Financial Services V (UK) Ltd
RL Finance Bonds No. 2 PLC
RL Finance Bonds No. 3 PLC
Royal London Asset Management Ltd
Royal London Management Services Ltd
Royal London Mutual Insurance Society,Limited
Starstone Finance Limited
Third Point RE (UK) Holdings Ltd

66300 Fund management activities [40]

Acquisition Fine Art
Alliancebernstein Limited
Ashmore Investment Management Ltd
Aspect Capital Limited
Aviva Investors Global Services Ltd
Aviva Investors Realm Infrastructure No.5
Axa Investment Managers UK Ltd
BGF Group PLC
Big Society Capital Limited
Blackrock Advisors (UK) Ltd
Blackrock Investment Management (UK)
Bluebay Asset Management (Services) Ltd
Crown Financial & Merchant Bank PLC
DIF Infra 3 UK Limited
Doughty Hanson & Co Managers Ltd
FIL Investment Management Ltd
Foresight VCT PLC
GAM Systematic Holding Limited
HSBC Global Asset Management (UK)
IDR Finance UK II Limited
Investec Asset Management Ltd
Legal & General Investment Management
Morgan Stanley Investment Management
Newton Investment Management Ltd
Newton Management Limited
Nuveen Real Estate Management Ltd
PIMCO Europe Ltd
Pace Bidco Limited
Pelham Capital Investments Ltd
PhillipCapital UK Ltd
Reclaim Fund Ltd
Royal London Asset Management Ltd
SB Investment Advisers (UK) Ltd
Schroder Investment Management Ltd
Threadneedle Asset Management Ltd
Threadneedle Pensions Limited
Vanguard Asset Services, Ltd.
Verdoso Holdings Limited
Wellington Management International
Zeuss Childcare Limited

68100 Buying and selling of own real estate [149]

Aberdeen Standard European Logistics Income
Almack Ltd
Area Estates Limited
Arlington House Investments Ltd
Atrium 100 Properties Limited
Bampton Property Group Limited
Bestway (Holdings) Limited
Beta Centauri Limited
Betelgeuse Limited
Better Properties Limited
Birch Sites Limited
Boots Propco B Limited
Braehead Glasgow Limited
Braehead Park Investments Ltd
CF Sparks Limited
CGIS Group (No. 3) Limited
Canary Wharf Investments (DS8) Ltd
Capital & Regional PLC
Central London Commercial Estates
Chesterfield Properties Ltd
City and Country Properties Ltd
Collin Estates Limited
Conegate Developments Limited
Conygar Investment Company PLC
Daejan Holdings PLC
Daejan Investments (Grove Hall) Ltd
Daejan Investments Limited
Daejan Properties Limited
Daejan Traders Limited
Henry Davies (Holborn) Ltd
Dellmes GR Limited
Derwent London Angel Square Ltd
Derwent London Farringdon Ltd
Derwent London Page Street Ltd
Derwent Valley Central Limited
Derwent Valley London Limited
Derwent Valley Property Developments
Derwent Valley Property Investments
Dorrington Investment P L C
Dorrington PLC
Dorrington Properties PLC
Drift Properties Limited
Due West Investments Limited
Eaton Square Properties Ltd
Endell Properties Limited
FPI (UK) 1 Limited
Fairhold Finance Limited
Fairhold Homes (No.2) Limited
Fairhold Homes (No.6) Limited
Fairhold Homes (No.7) Limited
Fairhold Homes (No.9) Limited
Fairhold Homes Investment (No.16) AL
Fairhold Homes Limited
Farmont Baker Street Limited
Frenchgate Interchange Limited
GMS Estates Limited
Grand Metropolitan Estates Ltd
Great Portland Estates P L C
Greenland Hertsmere (London) Ltd
Greenland Ram (London) Limited
Grosvenor Properties
Grosvenor West End Properties
HQCB Properties (HQ5 (2)) Ltd
Hammerson (Value Retail Investments)
Hammerson Bull Ring Limited
Hammerson PLC
Hammerson UK Properties PLC
Hanover & Oxford Property Ltd
Hanover House Limited
Hathber GR Limited
Hectagon Assets Limited
Helical PLC
Heven Limited
Highdorn Co. Limited
Knighton Estates Limited
L & Q New Homes Limited
LMS (City Road) Limited
LMS Offices Limited
LR Skipton House Limited
LXI Property Holdings 2 Ltd
Launcelot Investments (UK) Ltd
Leathbond Limited
Lendlease Europe Limited
J. Leon & Co Ltd
John Lewis Properties PLC
Lexadon Limited
Lexton Investments Limited
Littonace HMF Limited

London & Associated Properties PLC
London & Continental Railways Ltd
London & Regional Hotel Finance Ltd
Londonmetric Property PLC
Longmartin Properties Limited
MacTaggart Heritable Limited
Maurice Investments Limited
Metric Property Investments Ltd
Metropolitan Properties Co. (F.G.C.)
Metropolitan Properties Co Ltd
Mitsubishi Estate London Ltd
Mountview Estates PLC
Network Rail Infrastructure Ltd
New River Co Ltd
Newriver REIT PLC
O & H (NBS) Limited
O & H Capital Limited
O & H Holdings Limited
C J O'Shea Group Limited
Octagon Assets Limited
Old Hall Street Properties Ltd
PLJ Chelsea Limited
Palmbest Limited
Pontegadea UK Ltd
Pontsarn Investments Limited
Portman Investments (Baker Street)
Proxima GR Properties Limited
Questor Properties Ltd
Quintain Limited
Ramchez GR Limited
Renbuff Investments Limited
Ribbon Acquisition Limited
Rosequake Ltd
Rosleb Limited
Royal Mail Estates Limited
Sager House (Almeida) Limited
Segro PLC
Seven Capital PLC
Shaftesbury Covent Garden Ltd
Shaftesbury PLC
Sirius GR Limited
Solitaire Group Limited
Spitalfields Developments Ltd
St Ermin's Property Co.Limited
Stage Shoreditch Residential Ltd
Stow Real Estate PLC
Structadene Limited
Tannen Group Limited
Thames Quay Properties Holdings Ltd
Thames Quay Properties II Ltd
Thames Quay Properties III Ltd
Thames Quay Properties Limited
Tilfen Land Limited
Top Shop / Top Man Properties Ltd
Trafford Centre Limited
UD Europe Limited
US Real Estate Holdings No.1 Ltd
Urban & Civic Central Funding Ltd
Venaglass Limited
Wembley Park Limited
West London & Suburban Property Investments

68201 Renting and operating of Housing Association real estate [37]

Abbey Commercial Ltd
Antham 1 Limited
Atrium 100 Properties Limited
Bana One Limited
Birch Sites Limited
Brent Co-Efficient Limited
CW Properties DS7B Limited
CWCB Properties (DS6) Limited
Cabot Place Holdings Limited
Canary Wharf Investments Ltd
Capita Property and Infrastructure Holdings
Castle Lane Securities Limited
Chesterfield Properties Ltd
Daejan (UK) Limited
Daejan (US) Limited
East End Homes Limited
Hammerson PLC
Hammerson UK Properties PLC
Kirkglade Limited
LS Buchanan Limited
Lanesborough Management Ltd
Larch Life No.1 (UK) Ltd
John Lewis Properties PLC
Lexton Investments Limited
Ludgate Northumberland Holdings Ltd
MEPC (1946) Limited
Newport Holdings Limited
Origin Finance Limited
P & O Property Holdings Ltd
PHP Investments No.2 Limited
Segro Overseas Holdings Ltd
Shaftesbury Carnaby PLC
Shaftesbury Chinatown PLC
St Mungo Community Housing Association
Telereal 112 Limited
Thameswey Housing Limited
Top Shop / Top Man Properties Ltd

68202 Letting and operating of conference and exhibition centres

Business Design Centre Limited

68209 Other letting and operating of own or leased real estate [186]

2 & 3 Triton Limited
6 Bevis Marks Limited
Aberdeen Standard European Logistics Income
Akelius UK One Limited
Annington Property Limited
Annington Rentals (No. 6) Ltd
Arlington House Investments Ltd
Arsenal (Emirates Stadium) Ltd
Ash8 Group Holdings Limited
Ash8 Group Limited
Bath Road Cheltenham Limited
Batleys Properties Limited
Bedford Estates Bloomsbury Ltd
Belvedere Realty Investments Ltd
Bestway (Holdings) Limited
C.I. Property & Investments Ltd
CLS Spring Gardens Limited
CP Co 3 Limited
CP Co 7 Limited
CP Co Borrower Limited
Cadogan Estates Limited
Cadogan Holdings Limited
Cambian Heritage II Limited
Canada Square Investments Ltd
Central London Commercial Estates
Centro Asset Management Ltd
Chelsea Harbour Limited
Choicezone Limited
Conegate Developments Limited
Conygar Investment Company PLC
Cubcall Limited
Daejan Holdings PLC
Danataugusta Propco1 Limited
Danataugusta Propco3 Limited
Derwent London Angel Square Ltd
Derwent London Farringdon Ltd
Derwent London Page Street Ltd
Derwent Valley Central Limited
Derwent Valley London Limited
Derwent Valley Property Developments
Derwent Valley Property Investments
Dorrington London Flats Ltd
Dynamic Estates Limited
E & A Property Investment Co Ltd
Empiric Investments (Four) Ltd
Empiric Investments (One) Ltd
Empiric Student Property PLC
Eskmuir Properties Limited
Eskmuir Securities Limited
Estates & Agency Holdings Ltd
Folgate Estates Limited
Folio London Limited
Frasers Hospitality UK Holdings Ltd
GLA Land and Property Limited
GMS Estates Limited
Gabriel International Assets Ltd
Gabriel International Limited
Get Living London EV N01 Ltd
Get Living London EV N07 Ltd
Graff Diamonds International Ltd
Grainmarket Properties Limited
Greater London Authority Holdings
HHT PLC
Hammerson Bull Ring Limited
Hansteen Property Investments Ltd
Harrods Commercial Property Ltd
Harrods Property Limited
Helical PLC
Howard de Walden Estates Ltd
Intu Eldon Square Limited
Intu Investments Limited
Intu Lakeside Limited
Intu Metrocentre Limited
Intu Milton Keynes Limited
Intu Shopping Centres PLC
Intu The Hayes Limited
Intu Watford Limited
L & Q PRS Co Limited
LMS (City Road) Limited
LMS Offices Limited
LS Ashdown Limited
LS Cardiff Limited
LS Hill House Limited
LS Mirage Limited
LS One New Change Limited
LS Zig Zag Limited
Lakenorth Limited
Land Securities (Hotels) Ltd
Land Securities Buchanan Street Developments
Lazari Investments Limited
Lazari Properties 1 Limited
Lazari Properties 2 Limited
Lazari Properties 3 Limited
Lazari Properties 5 Limited
Lazari Properties 7 Limited
Leathbond Limited
Leconport Estates
J. Leon & Co Ltd
Lexadon Limited
Liberty Plaza (London) Limited
London Leasehold Flats Limited
Londonmetric Retail Distribution I
Londonmetric Saturn Limited
Malmaison and Hotel du Vin Property

Holdings
Marston Properties Limited
Metric Property Investments Ltd
Monopro Limited
Christopher Moran Holdings Ltd
New Printing House Square Ltd
New River Co Ltd
Newriver REIT PLC
Nine United Properties UK Ltd
Nomura Properties PLC
Nyraff Limited
Ocubis Limited
One Fleet Realty Ltd
Onyx Germany (1) Ltd
Onyx Germany (2) Ltd
Orchard Street UK Prime Property GP
PHP Glen Spean Limited
PHP Primary Properties Limited
Palace Capital PLC
Pall Mall 3 Limited
Pall Mall Investments (London) Ltd
Palmbest Limited
Peer Group PLC
Pipesafe Limited
Portman Investments (Baker Street)
Prestmade Limited
Primary Health Investment Properties
Primary Health Properties PLC
Queensgate Bow Opco Limited
Queensgate Bow UK Midco Ltd
Queensgate Bow UK Parent Ltd
Queensgate Bow UK Topco Ltd
R.B. Bishopsgate Investments Ltd
Raymond Estates Ltd
Realreed Limited
Revcap UK Holdings Limited
Romulus Securities Limited
Rosequake Ltd
Royal Mail Estates Limited
SIR ATP Limited
SIR Rivers Limited
SIR TP Limited
Sainsbury Propco A Limited
Sainsbury Propco B Limited
Searchmap Limited
Shaftesbury AV Investment Ltd
Shaftesbury AV Limited
Shaftesbury CL Investment Ltd
Shell Company of The Philippines Ltd
Soho Estates Holdings Limited
Soho Estates Limited
Soho Estates Portfolio Limited
Sir Richard Sutton Limited
TTL Earls Court Properties Ltd
Tallwood Limited
Third New Court Limited
Throgmorton Assets PLC
Tilfen Land Limited
Tottenham Hotspur Stadium Development
Trafford Centre Limited
Tritax REIT Acquisition 16 Ltd
Tudehope Ltd
U and I Group PLC
UD Europe Limited
UPP (Broadgate Park) Holdings Ltd
UPP (Duncan House) Limited
UPP (Exeter) Limited
UPP (Hull) Limited
UPP (Lancaster) Limited
UPP (Nottingham) Ltd
UPP (Reading I) Limited
Vauxhall Square (Nominee 1) Ltd
Viacom Camden Lock Limited
Victoria's Secret UK Limited
Waldorf Hotel Investment Ltd
Walworth Investment Properties Ltd
West London & Suburban Property
Investments
Westfield Stratford City Finance PLC
Wework International Limited
Workspace 12 Limited
Workspace 13 Limited
Workspace 14 Limited
Workspace Group PLC

68310 Real estate agencies [13]

Blueco Limited
CB/TCC Global Holdings Limited
CBRE Limited
Colliers International EMEA Holdings
Cushman & Wakefield Debenham Tie Leung
JLL 2002
Jones Lang Lasalle Capital Investments,
Jones Lang Lasalle Europe Ltd
Jones Lang Lasalle European Holdings
Jones Lang Lasalle Limited
Ocubis Financing Limited
Rogers Chapman UK Limited
Savills (UK) Limited

68320 Management of real estate on a fee or contract basis [48]

Admiral Taverns (Chester) Ltd
Akelius Residential Limited
Atrium 100 Properties Limited
Birch Sites Limited
Busyexport Limited
CBRE Global Investors Europe Holdings
CBRE Limited
Canary Wharf Properties (WF9) Ltd
Debenhams Properties Limited
Elite Gemstones Properties Ltd
Fairhold Services Limited
First Property Group PLC
Grantchester Limited
Hammerson (Brent Cross) Ltd
Hammerson PLC
Hammerson UK Properties PLC
Intu Shopping Centres PLC
JLL 2002
Jones Lang Lasalle Capital Investments,
Jones Lang Lasalle Dorchester Ltd
Jones Lang Lasalle Europe Ltd
Jones Lang Lasalle European Holdings
Jones Lang Lasalle Limited
LS Cardinal Limited
Land Securities Properties Ltd
London & Regional (Baker Street) Holdings
London Wall Outsourcing Freeholds
London and Regional Properties Ltd
Luminus Group Limited
Marks & Spencer Simply Foods Ltd
Marks and Spencer (Bradford) Ltd
NHS Property Services Limited
National Car Parks Limited
Old Hall Street Properties Ltd
Prestbury Investment Holdings Ltd
Redcastle Limited
Rogers Chapman UK Limited
Savills (UK) Limited
Telereal (London Wall) Limited
Telereal 112 Investments Ltd
Telereal Services Limited
Trillium (Prime) Holdings Ltd
Trillium (Prime) Project Holdings
Trillium (Prime) Property GP Ltd
Trillium Holdings Limited
Viacom Camden Lock Limited
West Quay Shopping Centre Ltd
Zeus Land Investments Limited

69102 Solicitors

Land Securities Capital Markets PLC
Slater and Gordon UK Limited

69109 Activities of patent and copyright agents; other legal activities n.e.c.

Stewardship Services (UKET) Ltd

69201 Accounting and auditing activities

Deloitte MCS Limited
EY Global Services Limited
Ernst & Young (Asia-Pacific) Services
Ernst & Young (EMEIA) Services Ltd
Stewardship Services (UKET) Ltd

70100 Activities of head offices [1170]

111 Group Holdings Limited
3i Holdings PLC
3i International Holdings
4 Imprint USA Limited
4imprint UK Holdings Limited
A.B.F.Holdings Limited
AB Mauri (UK) Limited
ABF Investments PLC
ABF Overseas Limited
ABF US Holdings Limited
ABP Subholdings UK Limited
AD INV Limited
AD Overseas (Europe) Limited
AECOM Corporation Holdings (UK) Ltd
AECOM Holdings Limited
AON Global Holdings Limited
AON PLC
ASOS PLC
Abbey National Treasury Services Overseas Holdings
Abbey National Treasury Services PLC
Abbott Mead Vickers Group Ltd
Acturis Group Limited
Acturis International Limited
Admiral Taverns Bidco Limited
Aegis Finance
Aegis GPS Holdings Limited
Aegis Group Holdings Limited
Aegis Group Participations Ltd
Aegis International Limited
Aegis Media Pacific Ltd
Aegis Triton Limited
Aegon Holdings (UK) Limited
Aegon UK PLC
Alberto-Culver (Europe) Ltd
Alberto-Culver UK Holdings Ltd
Algeco Global Finance PLC
Allen & Ginter (UK) Limited
Alliance Boots Holdings Ltd
Allied Domecq (Holdings) Ltd
Allied Domecq Limited
Allied Domecq Spirits & Wine Holdings
Alopuc Limited
Alpha Plus Holdings PLC
Alpha Prema UK Limited
Alstom Transport UK (Holdings) Ltd

Amalgamated Metal Corporation PLC
Amarin Corporation PLC
Amber Bidco Limited
Amco Investments Limited
Amesbury Holdings Limited
Amore Group (Holdings) Limited
Angel Trains Group Limited
Anglo American Diamond Holdings Ltd
Anglo American Holdings Ltd
Anglo American International Holdings
Anglo-Eastern Plantations PLC
Anmercosa Finance Limited
Ansell (U.K.) Limited
Antalis Group
Antalis Group (Holdings) Ltd
Antalis Holdings Limited
Antalis Limited
Anthology Group Limited
Antofagasta Railway Company PLC
Anyslam Investments
Anyslam Limited
Arcadia Group Limited
Arcadis UK (Holdings) Limited
Argent Foods Limited
Argenta Holdings Limited
Arup Group Limited
Ascential Group Limited
Ascential PLC
Ascential UK Holdings Limited
Laura Ashley Holdings PLC
Aspers Group Limited
Associated British Foods PLC
Associated British Ports Holdings
Aston Bidco Limited
Atos International IT Holdings Ltd
Atos UK Holdings Limited
Atos UK IT Holdings Limited
Avation PLC
Aviva Group Holdings Limited
Aviva International Holdings Ltd
Aviva PLC
Axa Partners CLP UK Holdings Ltd
Axa Partners Holdings Limited
Axa UK PLC
Azzurri Trading Limited
B.A.T Industries P.L.C.
B.A.T Uzbekistan (Investments) Ltd
BBA Overseas Holdings Limited
BBC Commercial Holdings Ltd
BBC Studios Limited
BBDO European Holdings Limited
BCG UK1 Limited
BDCG Holdings Limited
BG Energy Holdings Limited
BG General Holdings Limited
BG Overseas Holdings Limited
BG Overseas Investments Ltd
BG Singapore Limited
BG UK Holdings Limited
BGEO Group Limited
BHF Group UK Limited
BHP Billiton (UK) Limited
BHP Billiton Group Limited
BHP Billiton Holdings Limited
BM Manchester Limited
BMG Rights Management (UK) Ltd
BMO AM Group (Holdings) Ltd
BMO AM Group (Management) Ltd
BNP PUK Holding Limited
BP P.L.C.
BPP Holdings Limited
BT Group Investments Limited
BTC Islands Limited
BTG Management Services Ltd
Babcock International Limited
Babcock Investments (Number Four)
Babcock Investments (Number Three)
Babcock Marine Holdings (UK) Ltd
Babcock Mission Critical Services Design and Completions
Babcock Support Services (Investments)
Bakkavor (London) Limited
Bakkavor Group PLC
Bakkavor Holdings Limited
Balfour Beatty Infrastructure Investments
Balfour Beatty Investment Holdings
Balfour Beatty Overseas Investments
Balfour Beatty PLC
Barchester Healthcare Limited
Barclays Mercantile Business Finance
Barclays PLC
Beazley Furlonge Holdings Ltd
Beefeater Gin Limited
W. R. Berkley London Holdings, Ltd
Berry Bros. & Rudd Limited
Bertelsmann UK Limited
Besso Insurance Group Limited
Best Buy Distributions Limited
Bestway (Holdings) Limited
Bestway Securities Limited
Bestway UK Holdco Limited
Beta Central Profits Limited
Blackmead Infrastructure Ltd
Bond Aviation Topco Limited
Bracken Holdings Limited
Robert Brett & Sons Limited
Brewin Dolphin Holdings PLC
Brit Limited
British Alcan Aluminium Ltd
British American Tobacco (1998) Ltd
British American Tobacco (2012) Ltd
British American Tobacco (AIT) Ltd
British American Tobacco (Brands)
British American Tobacco (Investments)
British American Tobacco (NGP) Ltd
British American Tobacco China Holdings
British American Tobacco International Holdings (UK)
British American Tobacco Malaysia (Investments)
British American Tobacco P.L.C.
British Land (Joint Ventures) Ltd
British Sugar (Overseas) Ltd
British-American Tobacco (Holdings)
Brixton (Axis Park) Limited
Broad Gain (UK) Limited
Brooke Bond Assam Estates Ltd
Brooke Bond South India Estates Ltd
Brooks MacDonald Group PLC
Bunzl Finance PLC
Bunzl PLC
Bupa Care Homes (CFG) PLC
Bupa Global Holdings Limited
Burberry Group PLC
Burford Capital Holdings (UK) Ltd
Burford Global Investments Ltd
C & C Alpha Group Limited
CAN Holdings Limited
CBRE Global Investors Europe Holdings
CD & R Firefly 2 Limited
CD & R Firefly 4 Limited
CD & R Firefly Holdco Limited
CDCH Limited
CE Acquisition 1 Limited
CEVA Group PLC
CKI Number 1 Limited
CKI Number 2 Limited
CKI Number 3 Limited
CLS Holdings PLC
CPA Global Management Services Ltd
CWCB Investments (Rt2) Limited
CWIGroup Limited
Cable & Wireless Communications Ltd
Cadogan Group Limited
Cadogan Settled Estates Ltd
Caesars Entertainment UK Ltd
Caffe Nero Group Holdings Ltd
Cambian Group Holdings Limited
Cambian Group Limited
Canary Wharf Finance II PLC
Canary Wharf Holdings Limited
Canonsfield Estates Limited
Caparo Holdings (US) Limited
Capita Holdings Limited
Capita Justice & Secure Services Holdings
Capital & Counties Properties PLC
Cardinia Europe Limited
Carestream Dental Technology Holdings 1
Carestream Dental Technology Holdings 2
Carlton Communications Limited
Carnival Film & Television Ltd
Carphone Warehouse Europe Ltd
Casual Dining Group Limited
Casual Dining Limited
Catlin (North American) Holdings Ltd
Catlin Holdings Limited
Catlin Insurance Company (UK) Holdings Ltd.
Cavendish Fluor Partnership Ltd
Cboe Worldwide Holdings Ltd
Cello Health PLC
Centaur Media PLC
Central Asia Metals PLC
Centro Holdings (UK) Limited
CenturyLink Impsat Holdings I Ltd
CenturyLink Impsat Holdings II Ltd
Ceridian Global UK Holding Co Ltd
Chambertin (Holdings) Limited
Chambertin Acquisition Limited
Chambertin Finance Limited
Chambertin Midco Limited
Charter Consolidated Limited
Charter Limited
Chelsea FC PLC
Chelsea Harbour Estates Ltd
Chelsea Land Limited
Chelwood Trading & Investment Co Ltd
Chesterlodge Limited
Chilean Northern Mines Limited
Chime Communications Limited
Chime Finance Limited
Chime Group Limited
Chivas Atlantic Holdings Ltd
Chivas Brothers (Holdings) Ltd
Christie Manson & Woods Ltd
Chugai Pharma Europe Limited
Citibank Investments Limited
Citigroup Global Markets Europe Finance
Civica Holdings Limited
Claridge's Hotel Holdings Ltd
Clarion Acquisition Limited
Clarion UK Holdco Limited
Clarion UK Midco Limited
Clarion UK Topco Limited
Clarkson PLC
Close Asset Management Holdings Ltd

Close Brothers Group PLC
Close Brothers Holdings Ltd
Coca-Cola Holdings (United Kingdom)
Colfax UK Finance Ltd
Colfax UK Holdings Ltd
Collinson International Ltd
Colt Technology Services Group Ltd
Commerzbank Finance Limited
Computer Patent Annuities International
Connect M1-A1 Holdings Limited
Connect M77/GSO Holdings Ltd
ConocoPhillips (U.K.) Zeta Ltd
ConocoPhillips Holdings Ltd
Consolidated Insurance Group Ltd
Conygar Investment Company PLC
Thomas Cook Group PLC
Coral Eurobet Holdings Limited
Coral Eurobet Limited
Coral Group Limited
Coral Group Trading Limited
Coral Limited
Coralglade Limited
Cornwall Bidco Limited
Cornwall Midco Limited
Coroin Limited
Corus Group Limited
Corus International (Overseas Holdings)
Corus International Limited
Cory Environmental Holdings Ltd
Cory Riverside (Holdings) Ltd
Cory Riverside Energy Finance Ltd
Cory Riverside Energy Holdings Ltd
G. Costa (Holdings) Limited
Cote Group (Bidco) Limited
Cote Group (Financing) Limited
Cote Restaurants Group Holdings Ltd
Craegmoor Group (No.3) Limited
Craegmoor Group (No.6) Limited
Craegmoor Group Limited
Craegmoor Limited
Credit Suisse Investment Holdings (UK)
Credit Suisse Investments (UK)
D-Clear Europe Limited
DDB UK Investments Limited
DHE Regional Limited
DIVX Express Limited
DLG Acquisitions Limited
DLJ Group
DLJ International Group Ltd
DLJ UK Holding
DLJ UK Investment Holdings Ltd
DMG Atlantic Limited
DMG Charles Limited
DMG Investment Holdings Ltd
DMGB Limited
DMGV Limited
DMGZ Limited
DSG International Holdings Ltd
DSG Overseas Investments Ltd
Dagger Holdings Limited
Daily Mail and General Holdings Ltd
Daily Mail and General Investments
Daily Mail and General Trust P L C
Dan Regents Place Finance Ltd
Danone Financing UK Limited
Danone Holdings (UK)
De Beers Jewellers Limited
De Facto 1341 Limited
Dealogic (Holdings) Limited
Debenhams Group Holdings Ltd
Debenhams PLC
Debenhams Retail PLC

Delta 3 (UK) Limited
J. & J. Denholm Limited
Dentsu Aegis Network Ltd.
Diageo Great Britain Limited
Diageo Holdings Limited
Diageo PLC
Dialog Semiconductor PLC
Digital Appliance Controls (UK) Ltd
Diploma Holdings PLC
Diploma PLC
Discovery Finance Company Europe Ltd
Discovery Group Europe Limited
Diversified Agency Services Ltd
Dixons Retail Group Limited
Dollar Financial U.K. Limited
Domestic & General Acquisitions 1
Dorchester Group Limited
Dudgeon Holdings Ltd
EDF Energy (Energy Branch) Ltd
EDF Energy (UK) Limited
EDF Energy Group Holdings Ltd
EDF Energy Holdings Limited
EDF Energy Lake Limited
EII (Ventures) Limited
EIS Group PLC
EMGH Limited
EMI Group Limited
EMI Group Worldwide
EMI Group Worldwide Holdings Ltd
ERM Emilion Limited
ERM Worldwide Group Limited
Eagle 3 Limited
Eagle 4 Limited
Eaton Towers Limited
Ebiquity PLC
Economist Overseas (Holdings) Ltd
Elbon Holdings (1) Limited
Elbon Holdings (2) Limited
Elbon Holdings (3) Limited
Electrocomponents PLC
Electrocomponents U.K. Limited
Element Materials Technology Holding UK
Elementis Holdings Limited
Elementis PLC
Elf Petroleum UK Limited
Ellerman Investments Limited
Elm Trading Limited
Emerald 2 Limited
Emerald 3 Limited
Emerson Holding Co Ltd
Emerson USD Finance Co Ltd
Endeavour Company Holdings Ltd
Endeavour Resources Limited
Energy Power Resources Limited
Engine Acquisition Limited
Enovert Management Limited
Ensco Holdco Limited
Entertainment One UK Holdings Ltd
Eponymousco Limited
Equinor New Energy Limited
Equitas Holdings Limited
Equitix Capital Eurobond 2 Ltd
Equitix Healthcare 2 Limited
Equitix Highways 2 Limited
Esab Holdings Limited
Essar Energy Limited
Esterline Technologies Europe Ltd
Esterline Technologies Global Ltd
Esterline Technologies Holdings Ltd
Esterline Technologies Limited
Eucalyptus Energy Holdings Ltd
Eucalyptus Energy Limited

Euromoney Canada Limited
Euromoney Charles Limited
Euromoney Consortium 2 Limited
Euromoney Consortium Limited
Euromoney Trading Limited
European Ferries Limited
Exova Treasury Limited
FDL Holdings Limited
FHH No.1 Limited
FS Debtco Limited
FS Holdco 2 Limited
FS Holdco Limited
Factset UK Limited
Fantfoot Limited
Fern Trading Limited
Fevertree Drinks PLC
Fidessa Group Holdings Limited
Finance Holdings Limited
Finlay Group Limited
Fintry 3 Limited
First Hydro Finance PLC
First Hydro Holdings Company
First Olsen (Holdings) Limited
First Rail Holdings Limited
FirstGroup Holdings Limited
Firstbus (North) Limited
Firstbus Investments Limited
Fletcher Bay Group Limited
Flodrive Holdings Limited
Food Investments Limited
Fordstam Limited
Fox Healthcare Acquisitions Ltd
Foxtons Group PLC
Foxtons Intermediate Holdings Ltd
Fremantlemedia Group Limited
Fujitsu Services Holdings PLC
G4S Corporate Services Limited
G4S Regional Management (UK & I) Ltd
GAP (UK Holdings) Limited
GBG International Holding Co Ltd
GCM Global Energy PLC
GCP (UK) Holdings Limited
GLH Hotels Limited
GMR Capital Limited
Gabriel International Holdings Ltd
Gallagher Holdings (UK) Ltd
Gartmore Investment Management Ltd
Gates Acquisitions Limited
Gates European Holdings Ltd
Gates Finance Limited
Gates Holdings Limited
Gates Worldwide Limited
General Dynamics Global Holdings Ltd
General Healthcare Group Ltd
Georgia Healthcare Group PLC
Glen Water (Holdings) Limited
Global Media & Entertainment Ltd
Global Ports Holding PLC
Global Radio Acquisitions Ltd
Globaldata PLC
Goal Acquisitions (Holdings) Ltd
Gorkana Group Holdings Limited
Grand Metropolitan Capital Co Ltd
Grand Metropolitan International Holdings
Grand Metropolitan Limited
Grantchester Holdings Limited
Greater Gabbard OFTO Holdings Ltd
Green Bidco Limited
Green Midco Limited
Grey Communications Group Ltd
Grosvenor Americas Holdings Ltd
Grosvenor Continental Europe Holdings

Grosvenor Estate Holdings
Grosvenor Europe Limited
Grosvenor Group Limited
Grosvenor Limited
Grosvenor Overseas Holdings Ltd
Guardian Digital Communications Ltd
Guthrie Corporation Limited
Guthrie Overseas Investments Ltd
HBOS Financial Services Ltd
HBOS Insurance & Investment Group
HCA International Holdings Ltd
HCA UK Capital Limited
HGPE FRWL Holdco Limited
HSBC Global Services Limited
HSBC Holdings PLC
HSBC Latin America Holdings (UK) Ltd
Hadley Shipping Group Limited
Halcrow Holdings Limited
Paul Hamlyn Foundation
Hammerson International Holdings Ltd
Hanover Acceptances Limited
Hansteen Holdings PLC
HarperCollins (UK)
Harrods (UK) Limited
Harrods Corporate Management Ltd
Harrods Group (Holding) Ltd
Harrods Holdings Limited
Harvey Nichols Group Limited
Hayabusa Limited
Hays PLC
Henderson Administration Ltd
Henderson Asset Management Ltd
Henderson Global Investors (Holdings)
Henderson Holdings Limited
Heron Corporation
Heron International Holdings
Heron Property Corporation Ltd
Hinduja Automotive Limited
Hines Europe Limited
Hiscox Holdings Limited
Holidaybreak Limited
Horizon Holdco Limited
House of Fraser (UK & Ireland) Acquisitions
Howard de Walden Estates Holdings
Howden Broking Group Limited
Howden Group Limited
Howden Holdings Limited
Howden Joinery Group PLC
Hubbell Holdings Europe Ltd
Hunt Amber London 1 Ltd
Hunt Amber London 2 Ltd
Hunting Energy Holdings Ltd
Hunting Oil Holdings Limited
Hunting PLC
Huntsworth Holdings Limited
Huntsworth PLC
Hyperion Insurance Group Ltd
I2 Bidco Limited
I2 Holdco 2 Limited
I2 Holdco Limited
IBC Fourteen Limited
IBM Global Financing UK Company
IBM North Region Holdings
ICAP Management Services Ltd
ICG FMC Limited
IG Communications Limited
IG Group Limited
IIR Management Limited
INCJ SJ Investment Limited
IP Karugamo Holdings (UK) Ltd
IPC Information Systems UK Ltd
IPG Holdings (UK) Limited
IPM Holdings (UK) Limited
IPP Bond Limited
IQVIA Holdings (UK) Ltd.
IQVIA Solutions HQ Ltd.
ISG Central Services Limited
ITE Group PLC
ITE Holdings Limited
ITV Consumer Limited
ITW UK
ITWP Acquisitions Limited
Idex UK Investment Ltd
Imagination Industries Ltd
Imperial London Hotels Group Ltd
Inchcape Corporate Services Ltd
Inchcape International Holdings Ltd
Inchcape PLC
Indigo Bidco Limited
Informa Group Limited
Informa PLC
Inmarsat Group Limited
Inmarsat Investments Limited
Inmarsat PLC
Inmarsat Solutions Limited
Insight Group Limited
Instinet International Limited
Intercapital Limited
Intergen Holdings (UK) Limited
Interior Services Group (UK Holdings)
International Game Technology PLC
International Power (Fawkes)
International Power (Zebra) Ltd
International Power Australia Holdings (1)
International Power Australia Holdings
International Power Consolidated Holdings
International Power Holdings Ltd
International Power Luxembourg Finance
Interpublic Limited
Interservefm Ltd
Intertek Group PLC
Intu (SGS) Finco Limited
Intu Debenture PLC
Intu Finance MH Limited
Iron Mountain Europe Limited
Istithmar P & O Estates (UK) Ltd
Ivy Bidco Limited
JIB Group Holdings Limited
JIB Group Limited
JIB Overseas Holdings Limited
JIB UK Holdings Limited
JKX Oil & Gas PLC
JLIF Investments Limited
JLT Management Services Ltd
JLT UK Investment Holdings Ltd
Jardine Lloyd Thompson Group PLC
Jasper Acquisition Holdings Ltd
Jockey Club Racecourses (Holdings)
Just Eat PLC
KAS No.2 Limited
KAZ Minerals Investments Ltd
Kas No.8 Limited
Kellen Acquisitions Limited
Kellen Investments Limited
Keller Group PLC
Kin and Carta Marketing Services Ltd
Kin and Carta PLC
Kingfisher International Holdings
Kingfisher PLC
Kobalt Music Group Limited
Michael Kors (UK) Holdings Ltd
Michael Kors (UK) Intermediate Ltd.
L51N Limited
LCH Group Holdings Limited
LCI Helicopters (UK) Limited
LIH UK Topco Limited
LMS Capital PLC
LN-Gaiety Holdings Limited
LW Theatres Holdings Limited
Labcorp UK Holdings, Ltd.
John Laing Group PLC
John Laing Holdco Limited
John Laing Infrastructure Ltd
John Laing Investments Ltd
John Laing Investments Overseas Holdings
John Laing Limited
John Laing Social Infrastructure
Laird (Finance) Limited
Laird Asia Holdings Limited
Laird Limited
Laird Overseas Holdings Ltd
Lake Acquisitions Limited
Lanespace Limited
Largenta Limited
Laser Hotels One Limited
Lattice Group Limited
Laudico Limited
Lazard Asset Management (UK) Holdings
Legal & General Resources Ltd
Lendlease Construction Holdings (Europe)
Lendlease Europe Holdings Ltd
Lendlease Residential (CG) Ltd
Lenlyn Holdings Limited
John Lewis PLC
John Lewis Partnership PLC
Lewis Trust Group Limited
Liberty Global Broadband I Ltd
Liberty Global Europe 2 Ltd
Liberty Global Finance I (UK) Ltd
Liberty Global Incorporated Ltd
Liberty Global PLC
Liberty International Financial Services
Lifeways Finance Limited
Lionrai Investments No.1 Ltd
Lionrai Investments No.2 Ltd
Listrac Bidco Limited
Listrac Finance Limited
Listrac Midco Limited
Live Nation Limited
Lloyds Bank Financial Services (Holdings)
Lloyds Bank Hill Samuel Holding Co Ltd
Lloyds Bank Subsidiaries Ltd
Lockfold Communications Ltd
Lockton International Holdings Ltd
Lockton International Limited
London Clubs Management Ltd
London International Exhibition Centre Holdings
London Power Networks PLC
London Stock Exchange Group PLC
London Town Group of Companies Holdings
London Town Group of Companies Ltd
London Wall Outsourcing Ltd
Longman Group (Overseas Holdings)
Lonmin PLC
Lonrho Africa (Holdings) Ltd
Lonrho Holdings Limited
Lonrho Limited
Lotus Group Ltd
Louisville Securities Limited
Ludgate Northumberland Holdings Ltd
M & G Limited
M I Investment Holding Limited
MAN Group Holdings Limited
MAN Group PLC
MAN Mash Limited

MAN Strategic Holdings Limited
MCD Investments Limited
MEIF II CP Holdings 1 Limited
MEIF II CP Holdings 3 Limited
MEIF II CP SPV 2 Limited
MGL2 Limited
MMC Holdings (UK) Limited
MMC Treasury Holdings (UK) Ltd
MPS Group International Ltd
MS Amlin Corporate Services Ltd
Macquarie Holdings (UK) No.1 Ltd
Macquarie International Holdings Ltd
Macquarie Internationale Investments
Macsco 22 Limited
Maintel Holdings PLC
Majority Kingdom Investment Ltd
E D & F Man Holdings Limited
E D & F Man Limited
Alexander Mann Group Limited
Markel Capital Holdings Ltd
Marken Services Limited
Marks and Spencer International Holdings
Marsh & McLennan Companies UK Ltd
Marston Properties Holdings Ltd
Mastercard/Europay U.K. Ltd
Maybourne Hotels Limited
McKesson UK Finance I Limited
McKesson UK Finance II Limited
McKesson UK Finance IV Limited
Mediaedge:cia (UK) Holdings Ltd
Meininger Hotels Limited
Merchant Retail Group Limited
Mercury Holding Limited
Metallon Corporation Limited
Meteogroup Limited
Minerva Corporation Limited
Minerva Limited
Minova Insurance Holdings Ltd
Mitsubishi Estate Europe Ltd
Moly-Cop UK Holdings Limited
Morgan Sindall Group PLC
Morgan Stanley Group (Europe)
Morgan Stanley International Ltd
Morgan Stanley Investments (UK)
Morgan Stanley Mallard Investments
Morgan Stanley Montgomerie Investments
NEX Group Holdings Limited
NEX International Limited
NEX Services Limited
NNB Holding Company (HPC) Ltd
NRG Victory Holdings Limited
NSC Europe Limited
Nakano Asset Global Ltd.
Nando's Finance Limited
Nando's Group Holdings Limited
Nando's Group Limited
National Grid Commercial Holdings
National Grid Gas Holdings Ltd
National Grid Holdings One PLC
National Grid International Ltd
National Grid PLC
National Grid Thirty Five Ltd
National Power International Holdings
Nbcuniversal International Ltd
Neon Capital Limited
New Topco Limited
News Corp Holdings UK & Ireland
News Corp Investments UK & Ireland
Nicoventures Holdings Limited
Nord Anglia Education (UK) Holdings PLC
Nord Anglia Education Limited
Nordson London Limited
Norland Holdings Ltd
Northern & Shell PLC
Northern & Shell Properties Ltd
Northrop Grumman Global Holdings Ltd
Novae Group Limited
Numis Corporation PLC
OM Group (UK) Limited
OM Residual UK Limited
Oath (UK) Limited
Octagon Overseas Limited
Odeon Cinemas Group Limited
Odeon Cinemas Holdings Limited
Odeon and UCI Cinemas Holdings Ltd
Ofto Superholdco Limited
Old Mutual Business Services Ltd
Fred. Olsen Renewables Ltd
Fred. Olsen Wind Holdings Ltd
Fred. Olsen Wind Limited
Olsten (U.K.) Holdings Limited
Omnicom DDB Holdings Limited
Omnicom EMEA Holdings Limited
Omnicom Europe Limited
Omnicom Holdings Limited
Omnicom Latam Holdings Limited
Omnicom Management Europe
Omnicom Network Holdings Ltd
Ophir Energy PLC
Otter Ports I Limited
Otter Ports II Limited
Otter Ports Limited
Oval (2041) Limited
PA Consulting Group Limited
PA Consulting Holdings Limited
PA Holdings Limited
PA International Consulting Group
PA Overseas Holdings Limited
PACG2 Limited
PAH Gas Infrastructure Limited
PR Goal 3 Limited
Pacific Life RE Holdings Ltd
Pacific Life RE Services Ltd
Pam Group Limited
Partnership Group Holdings Ltd
Partnership Holdings Limited
William Pears Group of Companies
Pearson Education Holdings Ltd
Pelican Point Power Limited
Pentland Group PLC
Perenco Overseas Holdings Ltd
Perenco UK Limited
Fred Perry (Holdings) Limited
Petropavlovsk PLC
Phillips 66 UK Holdings Ltd
Phoenix Distribution Holdings Ltd
Phoenix Energy Holdings Ltd
Places for People Group Ltd
Places for People Ventures Ltd
Portman Square US Holdings Ltd
Precis (1789) Limited
Precis (1814) Limited
Premier Lotteries Investments UK Ltd
Premier Oil E & P UK Limited
Premier Oil Group Holdings Ltd
Press Acquisitions Limited
Prestbury Investment Holdings Ltd
Priceline.Com Holdco U.K. Ltd
Principal Global Financial Services (Europe) II
Priory Group Limited
Priory Securitisation Holdings Ltd
Privilege Holdings Limited
Prophaven Limited
Prudential PLC
Punter Southall Group Limited
QBE European Operations PLC
QBE Holdings (EO) Limited
QBE Management Services (UK) Ltd
QH Participations Limited
QH Partners Limited
QHotels Holdings Limited
QHotels Services Limited
QVC UK Holdings Limited
Quilter PLC
Quintain Limited
RBS AA Holdings (UK) Limited
RELX (UK) Limited
RELX Group PLC
RELX Overseas Holdings Limited
RSA Insurance Group PLC
RSM UK Holdings Limited
RTA Holdco 4 Limited
Rabai Power Holdings Limited
Radianz Limited
Ralph US Holdings
Ramsay Health Care (UK) Ltd
Reach Network Media Limited
Reach PLC
Reach Printing Services Ltd
Reach Publishing Group Limited
Reach Regionals Limited
Reach Shared Services Limited
Really Useful Theatres Entertainment
Redwood Partnership Ventures 2 Ltd
Redwood Partnership Ventures Ltd
Reed Business Information (Holdings)
Regus Group Limited
Renewables Infrastructure Group (UK)
Rensburg Sheppards PLC
Richemont Holdings (UK) Ltd
Ricoh Europe Holdings PLC
Rio Tinto Australian Holdings Ltd
Rio Tinto European Holdings Ltd
Rio Tinto Finance (USA) PLC
Rio Tinto International Holdings Ltd
Rio Tinto London Limited
Rio Tinto Metals Limited
Rio Tinto Minerals Development Ltd
Rio Tinto PLC
Rio Tinto South East Asia Ltd
Rio Tinto Western Holdings Ltd
Riverland Holdings Limited
Road Management Group Limited
Road Management Services (A13) Holdings
Rolls-Royce Group PLC
Rolls-Royce Holdings PLC
Rome Bidco Limited
Rome PIK Holdco Limited
Rome Topco Limited
Romulus Holdings Limited
Rotch Property Group Limited
Rothmans International Enterprises
Rothmans International Limited
Rowan No.1 Limited
Rowan No.2 Limited
Rutherfurd Acquisitions Ltd
S & P Global Finance Europe Ltd
SGO Corporation Limited
SHEL Holdings Europe Limited
SHG Acquisition (UK) Limited
SIG PLC
SIR Hospitals Propco Limited
SIR Hotels 1 Limited
SIR Theme Park Subholdco Ltd
SIR Theme Parks Limited

SITI 1 Limited
SSP Euro Holdings Limited
SSP Financing Limited
SSP Financing UK Limited
SSP Group Holdings Limited
SSP Group PLC
SThree PLC
M & C Saatchi PLC
Saavi Energia (UK) Ltd
Sable Holding Limited
Sableknight Limited
Salic (UK) Limited
Santa Fe Group Limited
Santander Asset Management UK Holdings
Saturn UK Holdco Limited
Savills (Overseas Holdings) Ltd
Savills PLC
Schawk Wace Group
Schroder Administration Ltd
Schroders PLC
Scott Trust Limited
Seadrill Mexico UK Ltd.
Secure Income REIT PLC
Securitas Services Holding UK Ltd
Segro PLC
Selfridges Holdings Limited
Seminole Hard Rock UK Limited
Sheldon Holdings Limited
Shell Energy Investments Ltd
Shell Gas Holdings (Malaysia) Ltd
Shell Holdings (U.K.) Limited
Shell Overseas Holdings Ltd
Shell Petroleum Co Ltd
Shell Transport and Trading Co Ltd
Shire Biopharmaceuticals Holdings
Shire Holdings Europe Limited
Shire Holdings UK Limited
Shire Pharmaceuticals Group
Shop Direct Holdings Limited
Siblu Holdings Limited
Simon Group Limited
Sinochem Resources UK Limited
Sir Hospital Holdings Limited
Slater & Gordon (UK) 1 Limited
Smartstream Technologies Group Ltd
Smith & Nephew (Overseas) Ltd
Smith & Nephew Investment Holdings
Smith & Nephew PLC
Smith & Nephew Trading Group Ltd
Smith & Nephew UK Limited
DS Smith Display Holding Ltd
DS Smith Holdings Limited
DS Smith PLC
Smiths Detection Group Limited
Smiths Finance Limited
Smiths Group Finance EU Ltd
Smiths Group Finance US Ltd
Smiths Group International Holdings
Smiths Group PLC
Snap International I Limited
Snap International II Limited
Sodexo Holdings Limited
Sodexo Limited
Softbank Group Capital Europe Ltd
Songbird Finance Limited
Sonic Healthcare Holding Company
Sony Corporate Services Europe Ltd
Sony Entertainment Holdings Europe
South32 SA Investments Limited
Spire Healthcare Finance Ltd
Spire Healthcare Group PLC
Spire Healthcare Holdings 1
Spire Healthcare Holdings 2 Ltd
Spire UK Holdco 2A Limited
Spire UK Holdco 4 Limited
Spring Group Limited
Starbucks EMEA Holdings Ltd
Starbucks International (Holdings) Ltd
Stemcor Holdings 2 Limited
Sumi Agro Europe Limited
Sunblest Bakeries Limited
Sunshine Finco Limited
Sunshine Holdco Limited
Sunshine Midco Limited
Sunshine Purchaser Limited
Sunshine Topco Limited
Superior Acquisitions Limited
Sureserve Group PLC
John Swire & Sons Limited
Synlab BondCo PLC
Synlab Holdco Limited
Synlab Limited
Synlab Unsecured BondCo PLC
TA I Limited
TBWA EMEA Limited
TBWA UK Group Limited
TCI Fund Holdings Limited
TES Finance Limited
TES Global Group Limited
TES Global Holdings Direct Ltd
TES Global Holdings Limited
TH Holdings Limited
TI Atlantic Europe Holdings Ltd
TI European Holdings Limited
TI UK Publishing Holdings Ltd
TIGI Holdings Limited
TM Media Holdings Limited
TNS Group Holdings Limited
TNS UK Holdings Limited
TPD Investments Limited
TRG (Holdings) Limited
TSB Banking Group PLC
TSL Education SPV 2 Limited
TT Games Limited
Tabletop London Limited
Taikoo Limited
Tarsus Holdings Limited
Taste Bidco Limited
Taste Midco 2 Limited
Tata Steel Europe Limited
Tate & Lyle PLC
Taylor Clark Limited
Taylor Nelson Sofres International
Technip-Coflexip UK Holdings Ltd
Tennants Consolidated Limited
Thameswey Limited
Thanet OFTO Holdco Limited
Thistleclub Limited
Thomson Legal & Professional Group
Thomson Reuters (Professional) UK
Threadneedle Asset Management Holdings
Threadneedle Holdings Limited
Ticketmaster Europe Holdco Ltd
Tiffany & Co. (UK) Holdings Ltd
Tilney Group Limited
Time Warner Entertainment Ltd
Time Warner Holdings Limited
Time Warner London Limited
Tokio Marine Kiln Group Ltd
Tomkins Engineering Limited
Tomkins Overseas Investments Ltd
Tonstate Metropole Hotels Ltd
Topland Group PLC
Total Holdings UK Limited
Total Midstream Holdings UK Ltd
Total UK Limited
Total Upstream UK Limited
Touchstone Innovations PLC
Trainline Group Investments Ltd
Trainline Holdings Limited
Trainline Investments Holdings Ltd
Trendcycle Limited
Trinity Acquisition PLC
Trinity Mirror Media Limited
Triplereason Limited
Tulip UK Holdings (No.3) Ltd
Tyman PLC
U.K.& European Investments Ltd
UBM (GP) No1 Limited
UBMG Holdings
UBMG Limited
UBMG Services Limited
UBS Asset Management Holding Ltd
UDV (SJ) Holdings Limited
UDV (SJ) Limited
UIG Holdings (No 4) Ltd
UK Holdings CAP (Commonwealth, Asia and Pacific)
UK Power Networks Services (Development)
UK Power Networks Services (South East)
UPP (Cartwright Gardens) Holdings
UPP (Duncan House) Holdings Ltd
UPP (Hull) Holdings Limited
UPP (Lancaster) Holdings Ltd
UPP (Reading I) Holdings Ltd
UPP Group Holdings Limited
UPP Group Limited
URS Corporation Group Limited
Unilever Australia Investments Ltd
Unilever Australia Partnership Ltd
Unilever Overseas Holdings Ltd
Unilever U.K. Holdings Limited
Unilever UK & CN Holdings Ltd
Unilever UK Group Limited
Unilever US Investments Ltd
United Finance Limited
Universal Music (UK) Holdings Ltd
Universal Music Holdings Ltd
Universal Music Leisure Ltd
Universal Studios Limited
VIL Ltd
Validus Holdings (UK) Ltd
Vanta Education Holdings Ltd
Vedanta Resources Holdings Ltd
Veolia Environmental Services (UK) PLC
Veolia UK Limited
Veolia Water Enterprise Ltd
Veolia Water UK Limited
Vesuvius Holdings Limited
Vesuvius PLC
Vetco Gray Holding
Vetco International Holding 4
Victoria Investments Bidco Ltd
Victoria Investments Finco Ltd
Victoria Investments Intermediate Holdco
Victoria Investments Midco Ltd
Viking Consortium Acquisition Ltd
Viners Energy Limited
Violin Debtco Limited
Violin Equityco Limited
Violin Topco Limited
Virgin Active Group Limited
Virgin Active Health Club Holdings
Virgin Active Holdings Limited
Virgin Active International Ltd
Virgin Active Investment Holdings

Virgin Active South Africa Holdings
Virgin Gyms Limited
Virgin Records Overseas Ltd
Vivo Energy PLC
Vouvray Acquisition Limited
Vouvray Midco Limited
Vue Entertainment Investment Ltd
WB/TT Holdings Limited
WBA Acquisitions UK Holdco 2 Ltd
WBA Acquisitions UK Holdco 7 Ltd
WBA Acquisitions UK Topco Ltd
WBA Holdings 1 Limited
WBA International Limited
WGA (UK) Holdings Limited
WGSN Group Limited
WMG Acquisition (UK) Limited
WPP 2005 Limited
WPP 2318 Limited
WPP Fitzroy Square
WPP Global
WPP Headline
WPP Jubilee Limited
WPP Toronto Ltd
WPP UK Germany Holdings
WPP UK Torre
WPP US Investments Limited
Walgreens Boots Alliance Ltd
Warner Media International Ltd
Warwick & Esplen Limited
A.S. Watson (Health & Beauty UK)
A.S. Watson (P & C UK) Ltd
Westark Properties Limited
Westfield Europe Limited
Westminster Topco Limited
Weston Investment Co Ltd
Williams Lea Holdings Limited
Willis International Limited
Willis Investment UK Holdings Ltd
Willis Overseas Investments Ltd
Wilmington PLC
Wilsonart Limited
Wind UK Invest Limited
Wireless Infrastructure Group Ltd
Wise Conclusion
Wittington Investments Limited
World Fuel Services European Holding Company I, Ltd.
XDG Limited
Xerium Technologies Limited
Young Street Holdings Limited
Zero Bypass (Holdings) Limited
Zetar Limited
Zeus Land Investments Limited

70210 Public relations and communications activities

Engine Group Limited
Next Fifteen Communications Group PLC
M & C Saatchi PLC
Time Out Group PLC

70221 Financial management [27]

ABP Mezzanine Holdco UK Ltd
Arup Treasury Limited
Belmond Dollar Treasury Ltd
Clarion Treasury Limited
Collinson Finance Limited
Core Laboratories Interests One Ltd
Core Laboratories Interests Two Ltd
DCC Treasury 2014 Limited
Emerson USD Finance Co Ltd
Fence Bidco Limited
Fence Topco Limited
Ferrexpo Finance PLC
Informa Finance UK Limited
Informa Finance USA Limited
L-3 Technology & Services UK Ltd
LTG Treasury Limited
Legal & General Finance PLC
Mondrian Investment Partners Ltd
ODH Investments Limited
Premier Oil Holdings Limited
Recruit Global Treasury Services AUD Ltd
Recruit Global Treasury Services Ltd
Ricoh Europe Finance Limited
Sach 1 Ltd
Sach 2 Ltd
Time Warner International Finance
Wellington Management International

70229 Management consultancy activities other than financial management [21]

AON Hewitt Limited
Accenture (UK) Limited
Acturis Group Limited
Acturis International Limited
Alixpartners Ltd
Atos IT Services UK Limited
Avanti Communications Infrastructure
Capita PLC
Deloitte MCS Limited
Deltatre Group Limited
Dunnhumby Limited
Economist Intelligence Unit Ltd
G.I. Globinvestment Limited
GLH Hotels Holdings Limited
Horizon Bidco Limited
IP2IPO Limited
Informa Telecoms & Media Ltd
Mace Limited
Maxwell Asset Management Ltd
PA Consulting Services Limited
RQIH Limited

71111 Architectural activities

Foster + Partners Limited

71121 Engineering design activities for industrial process and production

CB & I UK Limited
Johnson Matthey PLC
Primetals Technologies, Ltd

71122 Engineering related scientific and technical consulting activities

AECOM Limited
NH2 Limited
Ove Arup & Partners Hong Kong Ltd
Ove Arup & Partners International
WSP UK Limited

71129 Other engineering activities

Babcock International Group PLC
Bechtel Limited
Capita Property and Infrastructure
Dialog Semiconductor (UK) Ltd

71200 Technical testing and analysis

Clearstone Holdings (International) Ltd
Mastercard Europe Services Ltd

72110 Research and experimental development on biotechnology

Biocon Biologics Limited
CRF Health Group Limited
Genome Research Limited
Puretech Health PLC

72190 Other research and experimental development on natural sciences and engineering

BTG International Limited
BTG PLC
Institute of Cancer Research: Royal Cancer Hospital
Ixellion Technologies Ltd
Kennedy Trust for Rheumatology Research
Shire Pharmaceutical Development Ltd
Unilever U.K. Central Resources Ltd
University of Westminster
Vertex Pharmaceuticals (Europe) Ltd

72200 Research and experimental development on social sciences and humanities

Nesta
University of Westminster

73110 Advertising agencies [33]

Awin Ltd
Clear Channel Holdings Limited
Clear Channel International Ltd
Clear Channel Overseas Limited
Clear Channel UK Limited
Cordiant Communications Group Ltd
Dentsu Aegis London Limited
Engine Group Limited
Exterion Media (UK) Limited
Facebook UK Ltd
IPG Holdings (UK) Limited
IQVIA Solutions UK Limited
Kantar Media UK Ltd
MMS UK Holdings Limited
Mastercard Europe Services Ltd
Maxus Communications (UK) Ltd
Mediacom UK Limited
Mindshare Media UK Limited
Mission Marketing Group PLC
OMD EMEA Limited
Ogilvy & Mather Group (Holdings) Ltd
Omnicom Media Group UK Limited
PG Media Services Limited
PHD Media Limited
Publicis Media Limited
SCP Acquisition Bidco Limited
SCP Acquisition Topco Limited
Saatchi & Saatchi Holdings Ltd
M & C Saatchi PLC
J. Walter Thompson Group Ltd
WPP Rocky Ltd
Wavemaker Limited
Zenith UK (Media) Limited

73120 Media representation services

Mastercard Europe Services Ltd
Oath (UK) Limited
Redquince Limited
M & C Saatchi PLC

73200 Market research and public opinion polling

CACI Limited
E-Rewards Bidco Limited
IQVIA Holdings (UK) Ltd.
IQVIA Solutions UK Limited
Ipsos EMEA Holdings Ltd
Mastercard Europe Services Ltd
Yougov PLC

74100 Specialised design activities

Babcock Mission Critical Services Design and Completions

74901 Environmental consulting activities

ERM Emilion Limited
ERM Worldwide Group Limited
Origin Invest Limited

74909 Other professional, scientific and technical activities n.e.c. [37]

Advantage Sales & Marketing Ltd
Amdipharm Mercury UK Limited
Anasuria Hibiscus UK Limited
Arndale Properties Limited
British American Tobacco Italy Ltd
British Medical Association
CMI Canada Financing Ltd
Enbridge UK Holdings Ltd
Exova Group Limited
Faist Limited
Falck Renewables Wind Limited
Hartree Partners Power & Gas Company (UK)
Hubbell (UK) Gulfmex Limited
I-Environment Investments Ltd
IFG UK Holdings Limited
IP2IPO Innovations Limited
Irobot UK Ltd.
Ixellion Technologies Ltd
Kinapse Bidco Limited
Kinapse Holdco Limited
Kinapse Midco Limited
Kinapse Topco Limited
Low Carbon Contracts Co Ltd
MPG Finco Limited
Nectar Loyalty Limited
Noble Europe Limited
P1 Reversions Limited
Paragon Group Limited
Ping Petroleum UK Limited
SCDM Energy Limited
Salix Finance Ltd
Shionogi Limited
Shop Direct Holdings Limited
Stallergenes Greer PLC
Technicolor Disc Services International
Vancor Ltd
Zero Bypass Limited

74990 Non-trading company [219]

AMV BBDO Investments Limited
Abbotstar Trading Ltd
Accantia Group Holdings
Agman Investments Limited
Agrichrome Limited
Atos International IT Limited
Atrato Issuer Holdco Limited
Avaya UK Holdings Limited
Azzurri Group Limited
Azzurri Midco 1 Limited
BGC Global Limited
BMA Investments Limited
BMO AM Treasury Limited
Babcock Corporate Services Ltd
Babcock Investments (Number Eight)
Babcock Investments Limited
Babcock UK Finance
Babcock2 Limited
Bear Stearns UK Holdings Ltd
Bunzl American Holdings (No.1) Ltd
Bunzl American Holdings (No.2) Ltd
Bunzl Overseas Holdings (No. 2) Ltd
Bunzl Overseas Holdings (No. 3) Ltd
Bunzl Overseas Holdings Ltd
CB-SDG Holdco Limited
CB-SDG Limited
CB-SDG Midco Limited
CB-SDG Topco Limited
CGI Eurofin UK Limited
CGI Finance (UK) Limited
CWBC Properties (BP1) Limited
CWCB Finance II Limited
CWCB Leasing (DS6) Limited
Canary Wharf Retail Funding Ltd
Canyon UK Americas Limited
Capita IT Services Holdings Ltd
Cars Alliance UK 2015 Limited
Cast Limited
Centro Europe Limited
Charcoal Midco 2 Limited
Charter Consolidated Holdings Ltd
Chime Holdco Limited
Coral (Holdings) Limited
Creation Communications Ltd
Crosby Worldwide Limited
DMG Information Limited
DMG Loanco Limited
DMG Media Limited
Delamare Group Holdings Ltd
Diageo Investment Holdings Ltd
Diageo Overseas Holdings Ltd
Dorney Issuer Holdco Limited
Doubleplay I Limited
EMGH Limited
Eaton Square Limited
Eddystone Finance Holdings Ltd
Elementis US Limited
Ember Overseas Holdings Ltd
FIA Foundation
Finastra Holdings Limited
FirstGroup Canadian Finance Ltd
Fitzroy Property Limited
Foresight Solar (UK Holdco) Ltd
Frontier Finance PLC
GTA Holdco Limited
General Dynamics Global Holdings Ltd
Granada Group Limited
Granada Limited
Granada Media Limited
Granada Television Overseas Ltd
Granada UK Rental and Retail Ltd
Greenham Trading Limited
Griffon Funding Limited
Gunwharf Quays Limited
Henares Limited
Henderson Holdings Group Ltd
Horizon RE Limited
IAG UK Holdings Limited
IPM Peacock Limited
IQVIA Solutions Finance UK I Ltd.
IQVIA Solutions Finance UK II Ltd.
IQVIA Solutions Finance UK V Ltd.
IQVIA Solutions Global Holdings UK Ltd.
ITV Enterprises Limited
ITV Holdings Limited
ITV Rights Limited
ITW Holdings UK
Informa US Holdings Limited
Insight Group Limited
International Power (Genco) Ltd
Investec Group (UK) Limited
Investec Investments (UK) Ltd
KMC Stirling Square Limited
LGPL Cornwall Limited
LS (Finchley Road) Limited
LS Ludgate (No.1) Limited
LS Ludgate (No.2) Limited
LS QAM Limited
LS White Rose Limited
LSEG (M) Financing Limited
Lannraig Funding Limited
Lapsent Limited
Liberty UK and Europe Holdings Ltd
Livanova IP Limited
Livn UK 2 Co Limited
Livn UK 3 Co Limited
London & Regional Overseas Ltd
London Stock Exchange (C) Ltd
London Stock Exchange Group Holdings (Italy)
London Stock Exchange Group Holdings
MF Bidco Limited
MF Debtco Limited
MF Finco1 Limited
MF Intermediate Limited
MF Midco Limited
MIPL Group Limited
MIPL Holdings Limited
Macquarie Infrastructure and Real Assets Core
Macquarie Infrastructure and Real Assets Investments
Maritime Drilling Holdings Ltd
McKechnie Aerospace (Europe) Ltd
Mediaedge:cia (UK) Holdings Ltd
Mercer Africa Limited
Mesoblast UK Limited
Mitie Holdings Limited
Mortar No.1 Limited
National Grid Twenty-Five Ltd
National Grid William Limited
Navona Issuer Holdco Limited
New England Paint Co Ltd
New Star Asset Management Group Ltd
Newday Funding Loan Note Issuer Ltd
Newday Partnership Loan Note Issuer Ltd
Newsprinters (Broxbourne) Ltd
OTPPB Investments (U.K.) Ltd
Otis Investments Limited
Otis UK Holding Limited
P & O Dover (Holdings) Limited
P & O Overseas Holdings Ltd
Passaic Issuer Holdco Limited
Primepanel Limited
Priory Securitisation Limited
Punch Taverns Holdco (A) Ltd
Punch Taverns Holdings Limited
Punch Taverns Intermediate Holdco (A)
RPOW UK Limited
S & N Angel Investments Ltd.
S & N Finland Limited
SThree UK Holdings Limited
Sarum Issuer Holdco Limited

Satellite Financing (Holdings) Ltd
Scottish & Newcastle India Ltd
Sears Limited
Selectuser Limited
Shaftesbury CL Limited
Shaftesbury Carnaby PLC
Shaftesbury Chinatown PLC
Shaftesbury Soho Limited
Sheldon Poland Investments Ltd
Shell Exploration and Production Tanzania
Shell QGC Holdings Limited
Shell QGC Midstream 1 Limited
Shell QGC Upstream 1 Limited
Smith & Nephew ARTC Limited
DS Smith Perch Limited
DS Smith Sudbrook Limited
Sodexo Services Group Limited
Springer Nature One Limited
Springer Nature Two Limited
Star Pubs & Bars (Property) Ltd
Sunblest Bakeries Limited
The Bernard Sunley Charitable Foundation
Symphony Bidco Limited
TNS-NFO UK Limited
Tamoa Limited
TechnipFMC Holdings Limited
Telereal Secured Finance Holdings
Telereal Securitisation Holdings Ltd
Thistle Investments (ERM) Ltd
Tianqi UK Limited
Trailfinders Group Limited
TransDigm European Holdings Ltd
TransDigm UK Holdings PLC
Truworths UK Holdco 1 Limited
Truworths UK Holdco 2 Limited
Truworths UK Holdco 3 Limited
Tudor Minstrel
UBM Shared Services Limited
Uropa Assets No.2 Limited
Uropa Holdings Limited
Val TM (Holdings) Limited
Val TM Limited
Vale Inco Europe Holdings
Vector Industries Limited
Ventient Energy Limited
Visa International Holdings Ltd
WIC (UK) Ltd
WPP 1178
WPP 2323 Limited
WPP 2709 Limited
WPP Beans Limited
WPP Brands Holdings (UK) Ltd
WPP Compete
WPP Dutch Holdings Limited
WPP Group (UK) Ltd
WPP Group Holdings Limited
WPP LN Limited
WPP Magic Limited
WPP Marketing Communications Spain
WPP North Atlantic Limited
WPP Pearls Limited
WPP Sparky Limited
WPP Spike Limited
WPP Unicorn Limited
Westminster Topco Limited
White City Property Holdings Ltd
Willis GS UK Limited
Wittington Investments Finance Ltd
Yorse No. 3 Limited

77110 Renting and leasing of cars and light motor vehicles

Lex Autolease Limited
Motability Operations Group PLC

77320 Renting and leasing of construction and civil engineering machinery and equipment

Ashtead Plant Hire Co Ltd
Seadrill UK Ltd.

77330 Renting and leasing of office machinery and equipment (including computers)

Ricoh Capital Limited

77341 Renting and leasing of passenger water transport equipment

S32 Leasing Co Ltd

77342 Renting and leasing of freight water transport equipment

Snowdon Leasing Co Ltd

77351 Renting and leasing of air passenger transport equipment

Alpha Partners Leasing Limited
Macquarie Aerospace Finance UK Ltd
Omega Leasing (No. 12) Limited
Omega Leasing (No.10) Limited
Omega Leasing (No.11) Limited
Omega Leasing (No.9) Limited
RRPF Engine Leasing Limited
Suzaku Aviation One Limited

77390 Renting and leasing of other machinery, equipment and tangible goods n.e.c. [10]

Angel Leasing Co Ltd
Angel Trains Limited
Babcock Mission Critical Services Leasing
Beacon Rail Finance (Europe) Ltd
Great Rolling Stock Co Ltd
RRPF Engine Leasing Limited
Rock Rail East Anglia PLC
Rock Rail South Western PLC
Santander Asset Finance PLC
Seadrill Mexico UK Ltd.

77400 Leasing of intellectual property and similar products, except copyright works

Axelos Limited

78109 Other activities of employment placement agencies

Independent Clinical Services Ltd
Pontoon Europe Limited
RG Engagement Group 5 Limited
RG Engagement Group Limited
Reed Specialist Recruitment Ltd
Resource Solutions Limited

78200 Temporary employment agency activities [10]

Adecco UK Limited
Capita Resourcing Limited
Experis Limited
Hays Specialist Recruitment Ltd
Pontoon Europe Limited
Progressive Global Energy Kurdistan
Reed Specialist Recruitment Ltd
SThree Overseas Holdings Ltd
Spring Technology Staffing Services
Robert Walters PLC

78300 Human resources provision and management of human resources functions

Agman Holdings Limited
Balfour Beatty Group Employment Ltd
ING Services Limited
KPMG UK Limited
Alexander Mann Solutions Ltd
Pearson Education Limited

79110 Travel agency activities [10]

Belmond Finance Services Ltd
GBT Travel Services UK Limited
Miki Travel Limited
Opodo Limited
Priceline. Com International Ltd
Prometheon Enterprise Limited
Prometheon Holdings (UK) Ltd
STA Travel International Ltd
Trailfinders Limited
Tripadvisor Limited

79120 Tour operator activities

Kuoni Holdings Limited
Miki Travel Limited
Trailfinders Limited

79909 Other reservation service activities n.e.c.

Chime Group Holdings Limited
Chime Midco Limited
Kuoni Holdings Limited
Miki Travel Limited

80100 Private security activities

Control Risks Capital Limited
G4S PLC
Gardaworld Consulting (UK) Ltd

80300 Investigation activities

Financial Conduct Authority

81100 Combined facilities support activities

CBRE GWS Limited
Interserve (Defence) Ltd
Interserve (Facilities Management) Ltd

81210 General cleaning of buildings

Interserve (Facilities Management) Ltd

81221 Window cleaning services

Interserve (Facilities Management) Ltd

82110 Combined office administrative service activities

Bakkavor Finance (1) Limited
Bakkavor Finance (2) Limited
Bakkavor Finance (3) Limited
Bakkavor Invest Limited
WTI/EFW Holdings Ltd

82200 Activities of call centres

Luminus Group Limited
Ticketmaster UK Limited

82301 Activities of exhibition and fair organisers

Clarion Events Limited
PSPA Finance Limited
PSPA Holdco Limited
PSPA Midco Limited
PSPA Topco Limited

82990 Other business support service activities n.e.c. [760]

10 Trinity Square Residences Ltd
12 Smithfield General Partner Ltd
280 Bishopsgate Finance Ltd
80 Charlotte Street Limited
A & N Media Finance Services Ltd
A2D Funding II PLC
A2D Funding PLC
AB Acquisitions FX Inter Ltd
ABF (No.1) Limited
ABF Funding
ABF HK Finance Limited
ABF Overseas Limited
AD Atlantic Finance Limited
AD Investment Holdings Limited
AD Westport Limited
ADCG (UK) Limited
ADIUK
ADSW Investment Holdings Ltd
AIB UK Loan Management Limited
AIG Holdings Europe Limited
AIG Transaction Execution Ltd
APS Financial Limited
ATK Finance Limited
Accorinvest UK BCT Limited
Acquisition Company Finance Ltd
Aegon UK PLC
Alba 2006-1 PLC
Alba 2006-2 PLC
Alba 2007-1 PLC
Aldermanbury Investments Ltd
All3media Finance Limited
Allied Domecq Spirits & Wine Ltd
Allied World Capital (Europe) Ltd
Alpha Offshore International Leasing
Alpha Shipping Finance Limited
Amazon UK Services Ltd.
Ambassador Square
American Express Group Services Ltd
American Express Payment Services
American Express Services Europe Ltd
Anglo American (London)
Anglo American Capital PLC
Anglo American Investments (UK) Ltd
Anglo American Marketing Ltd
Anglo American Services (UK) Ltd.
Anglo Platinum Marketing Ltd
Annington Funding PLC
Ansco Finance 2011 Limited
Ansco UK Finance Co. 2 Ltd.
Apache UK Investment Limited
Apple Europe Limited
Apple Retail UK Limited
Aprilgrange Limited
Arena Leisure Limited
Arena Racing Corporation Ltd
Artesian Finance II PLC
Artesian Finance PLC
Ashtead Financing Limited
Ashtead Holdings PLC
Atos IT Services Limited
Auburn Securities 9 PLC
Avenell Property PLC
Axa Services Limited
Axia Finance PLC
Axia III APC Limited
Axia III Finance PLC
BBDO EMEA Limited
BG Energy Capital PLC
BG Gas Supply (UK) Limited
BG Netherlands
BG Netherlands Financing Unlimited
BGL Receivables Financing (1) Ltd
BIIF Bidco Limited
BIIF Holdco III Limited
BIIF Holdco Limited
BIIF Issuerco Limited
BIIF Parentco Limited
BMCE International (Holdings) PLC
BMI Healthcare Holdings Ltd
BMO Asset Management Limited
BNY Mellon International Asset Management Group
BOC Aviation (UK) Limited
BT Sixty-Four Limited
Babcock Group International Ltd
Babcock IP Management (Number Two)
Babcock Overseas Investments Ltd
Babcock Services Group Limited
Babcock Training Limited
Bakethin Finance PLC
Bakkavor Limited
Barclaycard Funding PLC
Barclays Services Limited
Bavarian Sky UK 1 PLC
Be Offices Limited
Belgrave Square
Bendler Investments II Ltd
Berrington UK
Beverage Services Limited
Bifurcate Funding Limited
Biz Finance PLC
Black Horse Group Limited
Blackrock Life Limited
Bluefin Insurance Group Ltd
Borealis Infrastructure Europe (UK)
Bounty Brands Holdings Limited
Bowbell No. 1 PLC
Bradley Hall Holdings Limited
Brass No.3 PLC
Brass No.4 PLC
Brass No.5 PLC
Brass No.6 PLC
Brown-Forman Beverages, Europe, Ltd
Brunel Residential Mortgage Securitisation No. 1
Bruning Limited
Bupa Finance PLC.
Bupa Insurance Services Ltd
Bupa Investments Limited
Bupa Investments Overseas Ltd
Burbo Extension Ltd
Burlington Resources (UK) Holdings
Business Design Centre Limited
Business Mortgage Finance 6 PLC
CBRE Acquisition Company 2 Ltd
CBRE Acquisition Company 3 Ltd
CBRE Holdings Limited
CBRE Managed Services Limited
CBRE UK Acquisition Co Ltd
CFL Auto Receivables Limited
CK William Midco 2 Limited
CK William Midco 3 Limited
CKH Gas Infrastructure Limited
CLEF Holdings Limited
CLS UK Intermediate Holdings Ltd.
CMS Distribution Limited
COFCO Holdings 1 Limited
COP Holdings Limited
CWCB Properties (DS7) Limited
CWE SPV HCO Limited
Cadogan Settled Estates Ltd
Caledonian Rail Leasing Ltd
Canary Finco Limited
Canary Holdco Limited
Canary Wharf Estate Limited
Canary Wharf Group Investment Holdings
Canary Wharf Group PLC
Canary Wharf Properties (FC2) Ltd
Canary Wharf Properties (FC4) Ltd
Capita International Limited
Capita PLC
Capita Secure Information Solutions
Cardnet Merchant Services Ltd
Casper UK Bidco Limited
Castell 2017-1 PLC
Catlin Finance (UK) Ltd.
Cavendish Nuclear Limited
Cedar Project Bidco Limited
Cedar Project Holdco Limited
Cedar Project Midco Limited
Charles Street Conduit Asset Backed Securitisation 1
Chemchina UK Limited
Chevron Energy Limited
Childcare Vouchers Limited
Christie Manson & Woods Ltd
Chubb Services UK Limited
Citadel Enterprise Europe Ltd
Clifford Chance London Limited
Close PF Funding I Limited
Closerstill Acquisitions Ltd
Closerstill Finance Limited
Closerstill Media Holdings Ltd
Clydesdale Financial Services Ltd
Cone Investments UK Limited
Consolidated Developments Holdings
Control Risks Group Holdings Ltd
Cranemere Group Limited
Czarnikow Group Limited
DB Group Services (UK) Limited
DLG Financing 1 Limited
DLG Financing 2 Limited
DMEP Holdco Limited
DSG European Investments Ltd
DTZ UK Bidco Limited
DTZ UK Guarantor Limited
DTZ UK Holdco Limited
Dana Petroleum Limited
Das Europe Limited
De Beers UK Limited
Deco 11 - UK Conduit 3 P.L.C.
Deco 8 - UK Conduit 2 PLC

Delamare Cards Funding 1 Ltd
Delamare Cards MTN Issuer PLC
Deloitte Global Services Holdings
Deloitte Global Services Ltd
Deloitte MCS Limited
Device Finance Collections Ltd
Diageo Eire Finance & Co
Diageo Finance PLC
Diageo Finance US Limited
Diageo Financing Turkey Ltd
Diageo US Investments
Diamond Offshore Enterprises Ltd
Diamond Rig Investments Ltd
Digital London Limited
Disney Magic Co Ltd
Dixons Carphone PLC
Dow Jones Business Interactive (U.K.),
Dunhill Tobacco of London Ltd
EC Finance PLC
EFT International Investments Holdings
EFT Investments SE
EMF-UK 2008-1 PLC
EMI Group Limited
EY Global Services Limited
Ebay KTA (UK) Ltd
Economist Intelligence Unit Ltd
Edenred (UK Group) Limited
Electra Investments Limited
Electrocomponents US Finance Ltd
Elegant Hotels Group PLC
Elementis Securities Limited
Elexon Limited
Emperador Holdings (GB) Ltd
Epihiro PLC
Equifax EUA Limited
Equinix (UK) Limited
Equitix Capital Eurobond 4 Ltd
Equity Release Funding (No.1) PLC
Equity Release Funding (No.2) PLC
Equity Release Funding (No.3) PLC
Equity Release Funding (No.4) PLC
Equity Release Funding (No.5) PLC
Equity Release Holdings (No. 5) Ltd
Equity Release Holdings Ltd
Ernst & Young (EMEIA) Services Ltd
Esselco Estates Limited
Esselco Group Limited
Estia Mortgage Finance II PLC
European Express Enterprises Ltd
Eurosail 2006-1 PLC
Eurosail 2006-2BL PLC
Eurosail 2006-3NC PLC
Eurosail 2006-4NP PLC
Eurosail Prime-UK 2007-A PLC
Eurosail-UK 2007-1NC PLC
Eurosail-UK 2007-2NP PLC
Eurosail-UK 2007-3BL PLC
Eurosail-UK 2007-4BL PLC
Eurosail-UK 2007-5NP PLC
Eurosail-UK 2007-6NC PLC
Eversholt Funding PLC
Eversholt UK Rails (Holding) Ltd
Eversholt UK Rails Limited
Expedia.Com Limited
F & G UK Underwriters Limited
FIA UK Funding Limited
FS JV Co Limited
FS Senior Co Limited
Facebook UK Ltd
Fern Renewable Energy Limited
Ferrexpo Finance PLC
Fidessa Group Holdings Limited
Finance for Higher Education Ltd
Finance for Residential Social Housing
Financial Services Compensation Scheme
Firmdale Holdings Limited
Firmdale Property Investments Ltd
First Corporate Consultants Ltd
Firstclear Limited
Formpart (HPL) Limited
Rocco Forte & Family (Luxury Hotels)
Foxland 20FS (UK) Limited
Freepoint Commodities Enterprises Ltd.
Freepoint Commodities Holdings Ltd
Fujitsu EMEA PLC
Funding Circle Holdings PLC
G4S Facilities Management (UK) Ltd
G4S Regional Management (UK & I) Ltd
GESB PLC
GGR Capital Limited
GM Global Treasury Centre Ltd
Gazprom Global LNG Limited
GenFinance II PLC
General Dynamics Swiss Financial Management
General Motors Europe Limited
Global Radio Services Limited
Global Switch Estates 1 Ltd
Global Switch Estates 2 Ltd
Global Switch Limited
Globaldrive Auto Receivables UK 2016-A
Globaldrive Auto Receivables UK 2017 -A
Goldman Sachs Group Holdings (U.K.)
Goldman Sachs Group UK Limited
Google UK Limited
Gosforth Funding 2014-1 PLC
Gosforth Funding 2015-1 PLC
Gosforth Funding 2016-1 PLC
Gosforth Funding 2016-2 PLC
Gosforth Holdings 2014-1 Ltd
Gosforth Holdings 2015-1 Ltd
Gosforth Holdings 2016-2 Ltd
Gracechurch Card Programme Funding PLC
Great Hall Mortgages No.1 PLC
Greencoat UK Wind PLC
Greene King Finance PLC
Greene King Finance Parent Ltd
Greenergy Fuels Holdings Ltd
Greenergy Fuels Limited
Greenergy International Ltd
Greenway Infrastructure Capital PLC
Gresham Receivables (No. 15) UK Ltd
Gresham Receivables (No. 19) UK Ltd
Gresham Receivables (No. 26) UK Ltd
Gresham Receivables (No. 30) UK Ltd
Gresham Receivables (No. 31) UK Ltd
Gresham Receivables (No. 32) UK Ltd
Gresham Receivables (No. 33) UK Ltd
Gresham Receivables (No. 34) UK Ltd
Gresham Receivables (No.11) UK Ltd
Gresham Receivables (No.16) UK Ltd
Gresham Receivables (No.27) UK Ltd
Gresham Receivables (No.36) UK Ltd
Gresham Receivables (No.37) UK Ltd
Gresham Receivables (No.38) UK Ltd
Gresham Receivables (No.39) UK Ltd
Gresham Receivables (No.40) UK Ltd
Gresham Receivables (No.45) UK Ltd
Gresham Receivables (No.46) UK Ltd
Grifonas Finance No.1 PLC
Grifonas Holdings Limited
Grosvenor Europe Investments Ltd
Grosvenor UK Finance PLC
Guildford No.1 PLC
Guildhall Asset Purchasing Company (No.11) UK
Guinness Overseas Limited
H.A. Funding Limited
HCA UK Capital Limited
HCA UK Holdings Limited
HGHL Holdings Ltd
Halcyon Finance Limited
Harben Finance 2017-1 PLC
Harding Midco Limited
Hatton Garden Properties Ltd
Haut Investments Limited
Hawk Newco Limited
Hawthorn Asset Co Limited
Heineken (Orange) 1 Limited
Heineken (Orange) 2 Limited
Heineken (Orange) 3 Limited
H.J. Heinz Finance UK PLC
Hellenic Petroleum Finance PLC
Heron Quays Investments (RT3) Ltd
Heron Treasury Services Ltd
High Speed Rail Finance (1) PLC
High Speed Rail Finance PLC
Hindwain Limited
Hines Europe Limited
Hirecorp Limited
Homer Newco Limited
Honours (Holdings) Limited
Glyn Hopkin Holdings Limited
Hotel (PL Property) Holdco Ltd
Housing Association Funding PLC
Howden Joinery Corporate Services
Huawei Global Finance (UK) Ltd
Hull Esteem Consortium PSP Ltd
Hunter Up 1 Limited
Hunting Knightsbridge Holdings Ltd
Hutchison Whampoa Finance UK PLC
IBC (Ten) Limited
IBM Global Financing UK Company
IG Finance
IG Markets Limited
IQVIA Solutions UK Limited
ITV PLC
ITV Services Limited
ITW CS (UK) Ltd
ITW UK Finance Limited
IW Group Services (UK) Limited
Informa Group Holdings Limited
Infrared Infrastructure Yield Holdings
Infrastructure Investments Holdings
Ingenious Media Limited
Inmarsat Global Limited
Inspired Education Holdings Ltd
Instant Cash Loans Limited
Instinet Global Services Ltd
Intact Limited
Intelsat UK Financial Services Ltd.
Intergen Projects (UK) Limited
International Trade and Exhibitions Overseas
Investors in Private Capital Ltd
Irida PLC
Ivy Midco Limited
Ixellion Technologies Ltd
JC Overseas Ltd
JLIF Investments Limited
JLT EB Holdings Limited
JPMorgan Asset Management International
Johnson Matthey (CM) Limited
Jupiter Hotels Limited
KAZ Minerals Aktogay Finance Ltd
KAZ Minerals Aktogay Project Finance
KAZ Minerals Copper Finance Ltd

KAZ Minerals Finance PLC
KAZ Minerals Projects Finance Ltd
KRF Holdings Limited
Karta II PLC
Katanalotika PLC
Keele Residential Funding PLC
Kellas Midstream Limited
Kili Topco Limited
Kingfisher France Limited
Kingfisher UK Limited
Kirkbi Burbo Extension Holding (UK)
Koch Metals Trading Limited
Kusuma Trust UK
LCH Limited
LDC (Care Homes) Finco Limited
LDC (Managers) Limited
LR (Baker St) Limited
LR (City Road) Ltd
LR Baker St Mezz Borrower Ltd
LR Baker St Mezz Holdco Ltd
LR Baker St Senior Holdco Ltd
LR Office Developments Limited
LS London Holdings One Limited
LS Property Finance Co Ltd
LS Victoria Circle Lp1 Limited
LS Victoria Circle Lp2 Limited
LS Victoria Properties Limited
Ladbrokes Group Finance PLC
John Laing Investments Ltd
Lakeside Asset Backed Securitisation 1
Land Securities (Finance) Ltd
Land Securities Management Ltd
Land Securities Trinity Ltd
Landesk Holdco UK Ltd
Lanterndew Limited
Larch (Nursing Homes) Holdco Ltd
Larch (Nursing Homes) Ltd
Larch Funding (UK) Ltd
Law Debenture Corporation PLC
Lendlease Construction Holdings (Europe)
Lex Autolease Limited
Liberty Theta Limited
Liberty Zeta Limited
Lime Street (Funding) Limited
Limited Life Assets Issuance PLC
Limited Life Assets Master Ltd
Limited Life Assets Services Ltd
Linklaters Business Services
Lloyd's Register Group Services Ltd
Lloyd's Register Inspection Ltd
Lloyds Bank Corporate Asset Finance (No. 1)
Lloyds Bank Corporate Asset Finance (No. 4)
Lloyds Bank Equipment Leasing (No. 1)
Lloyds Bank Equipment Leasing (No. 7)
Lloyds Bank General Leasing (No. 3)
Lloyds Bank Leasing Limited
Lloyds Development Capital (Holdings)
Lloyds General Leasing Limited
London & Regional (Baker Street) Ltd
London & Regional (Empire) Ltd
London & Regional (HC Properties)
London & Regional (St. Georges Court)
London & Regional Dormant Holdings
London & Regional Group Investments
London & Regional Group Securitisation No.1
London & Regional Group Trading No.3
London & Regional Portfolio Finance
London & Regional Trading Holdings
London International Exhibition Centre
London Southend Airport Co Ltd
London Wall Investment Warehouse 01
London Wall Mortgage Capital PLC
London and Regional Group Finance
Loopsign No.2 Limited
Ly Holding Limited
M7 Real Estate Ltd
MAN Group UK Limited
MAN Investments Finance Ltd
MAN Investments Holdings Ltd
MAN Investments Limited
MAN UK Strategies Limited
MDU Investments Limited
MF White Television City Ltd
Mabanaft Limited
Macquarie (UK) Group Services Ltd
Macquarie Commodities Factoring Holdings (UK)
Macquarie UK Passenger Leasing Ltd
E D & F Man Treasury Management PLC
Marble Arch Residential Securitisation No. 4
Market Data Limited
Marsh Corporate Services Ltd
Marsh Services Limited
Marston's Issuer PLC
Martin Pecheur Sterling Investments
Masdar Energy UK Limited
Mastcraft Limited
Matthey Holdings Limited
Max Credit Investment Limited
McDonald's Real Estate Company No.1
Medical Defence Union Limited
Mercer Limited
Miller Freeman Worldwide Ltd
Millward Brown No.2337 Limited
Mirion Technologies (Global), Ltd.
Mirion Technologies (HoldingRep), Ltd.
Mirion Technologies (HoldingSub1), Ltd.
Mirion Technologies (HoldingSub2), Ltd.
Mithras Leasing (No.1) Ltd
Mithras Leasing (No.4) Limited
Mitie Limited
Mitsui Fudosan (U.K.) Ltd.
Mixhold Investments Limited
Modernelite Limited
Monument Containers Limited
Moorgate Funding 2014-1 PLC
J.P. Morgan Europe Limited
J.P. Morgan Securities PLC
Morgan Stanley UK Limited
Mortgage Funding 2008-1 PLC
Motability Tenth Anniversary Trust
Motorola Solutions Finance EMEA Ltd
Motorola Solutions International Holding
Murderme Limited
Mycitydeal Limited
NCR UK Group Limited
NGG Finance PLC
Natgrid One Limited
NatgridTW1 Limited
National Grid (US) Holdings Ltd
National Grid (US) Investments 2 Ltd
National Grid (US) Investments 4 Ltd
National Grid (US) Partner 1 Ltd
National Grid Holdings Limited
National Grid Seventeen Ltd
National Grid Twelve Limited
National Grid Twenty Seven Ltd
National Grid Twenty Three Ltd
Newco NHL UK (17) Limited
Newday Funding Transferor Ltd
Newday Partnership Transferor PLC
News Corp Investments II Ltd
News UK & Ireland Limited
Nixes Six PLC
Norlake Hospitality Limited
North Row Estates Limited
OMD Group Limited
OMFS (GGP) Limited
OMV Supply & Trading Limited
OTE PLC
Oakwood Global Assets Limited
Office Group Holdings Limited
Office Group Midco Limited
Office Group Properties Ltd
Oikia (UK) Limited
Old Mutual Financial Services (UK)
Olympus Finance UK Limited
Omnicom Finance Brazil Limited
Omnicom Finance Limited
Omnicom Media Group Europe Ltd
Orbita Funding 2017-1 PLC
Orsted Burbo (UK) Limited
Orsted Lincs (UK) Ltd
Orsted London Array II Limited
Orsted Power (Gunfleet Sands) Ltd
Orsted Westermost Rough Ltd
Oxhauth Limited
PA Group Treasury Services Ltd
PA Netherlands Treasury Services Ltd
PCL Asset Trustee Limited
PCL Funding I Limited
PFI Infrastructure Finance Ltd
PFI Senior Funding Limited
PKA Burbo Extension Holding (UK) Ltd
PKA Teesrep Holding (UK) Ltd
PRS for Music Limited
Paramount Pictures International Ltd
Partnerships in Care Property 1 Ltd
Paysafe Holdings UK Limited
Paysafe Processing Limited
Pearl Group Holdings (No. 1) Ltd
William Pears Group of Companies
Pearson Shared Services Ltd
Perenco Oil and Gas Colombia Ltd
Petrochina International (London) Co.,
Petropavlovsk Mining Treasury UK Ltd
Pisti 2010-1 PLC
Point Dume Holdings Limited
Portswood Investments Limited
Praxis I Finance PLC
Praxis II APC Limited
Praxis II Finance PLC
Premier Place Finance Limited
Prepaid Services Co Ltd
Prepay Technologies Limited
Pricewaterhousecoopers Services Ltd
Promontoria Gyle 2 Ltd
Prudential Services Limited
Psygnosis Limited
QBE Management Services (UK) Ltd
QW Rail Leasing Limited
Quilter Investors Limited
R & Q Capital No. 6 Limited
R.E.A. Holdings PLC
RELX (Holdings) Limited
RELX (Investments) PLC
RELX Finance Limited
Rapiscan Systems Limited
Raznoimport (UK) Limited
Reach Publishing Group Limited
Reach Shared Services Limited
Red Star Pub Company (WR III) Ltd
Redcastle (214 Oxford Street) Ltd
Redrock Investment Limited
Reebok International Limited

Renewables Infrastructure Group (UK) Investments
Residential Mortgage Securities 23 PLC
Residential Mortgage Securities 25 PLC
Resloc UK 2007-1 PLC
Retail Centres V (Sweden) Investment
Retirement Bridge Investments Ltd
Rio 587 Limited
Rio 588 Limited
Rio Tinto Diamonds Limited
Road Management Consolidated PLC
Rontec Roadside Retail Limited
SEI Investments (Europe) Ltd
SMBC Leasing (UK) Limited
SPIE UK Limited
SSB No. 1 PLC
Saavi Energia (UK) Ltd
Santander Private Banking UK Ltd
Santander UK PLC
Savills Holding Co Ltd
Schroder Financial Services Ltd
Securitisation of Consumer Agreements
Semperian (Community Health) Ltd
Semperian No.21 Limited
Semperian PPP Investment Partners Group
Semperian PPP Investment Partners
Semperian PPP Investment Partners No.2
Sensburg Finance Ltd
Sheldon Euro Investments 2 Ltd
Sheldon Sterling Investments Ltd
Shell Caribbean Investments Ltd
Shell International Limited
Shell International Petroleum Co Ltd
Shell Malaysia Limited
Ship Holdco Limited
Ship Midco Limited
Shire Global Finance
Shortline PLC
Silverstone Funding (No.1) Ltd
Silverstone Master Issuer PLC
Sky Holdco Limited
Smith & Nephew USD Limited
DS Smith International Ltd
Smithfield Limited
Sojitz Energy Development Ltd
Sony Interactive Entertainment Network Europe
Sony Music Entertainment International
Sparrows Offshore Services Ltd
Spire Healthcare (Holdings) Ltd
Spire Property 5 Limited
Spirit Issuer PLC
Spirit Issuer Parent Limited
Sponsio Limited
Spotify Finance Limited
Spotify Limited
Stanlow Receivables Funding Ltd
State Grid Europe Development (2014) PLC
Statkraft UK Ltd
Sulawesi LNG Development Ltd
Sumitomo Corporation Capital Europe PLC
Sumitomo Corporation Europe Holding
Swiss Re Services Limited
TRU Taj Holdings 2 Limited
Talisman Colombia Holdco Ltd
Tanqueray Gordon and Co Ltd
Tate & Lyle Industries Limited
Tate & Lyle Technology Limited
Taveta Investments (No.2) Ltd
Taveta Investments Limited
Thameswey Limited
Thomson Reuters (Professional) UK
Tolmar Holding Limited
Tombac No.1 PLC
Tombac No.2 PLC
Topland Jupiter Limited
Towd Point Mortgage Funding 2016 - Auburn 10
Towd Point Mortgage Funding 2016-Granite1
Towd Point Mortgage Funding 2016-Granite2
Towd Point Mortgage Funding 2016-Granite3
Towd Point Mortgage Funding 2016-Vantage1
Travelex Banknotes Limited
Travelex Central Services Ltd
Travelex Financing PLC
Travelex Group Investments Ltd
Travelex Holdings Limited
Travelex Limited
Traveljigsaw Limited
Trinity Mirror Finance Limited
UBM (UK) Limited
UBS Asset Management Holding (No.2) Ltd
UK SPV Credit Finance PLC
Unifund PLC
Unilever U.K. Central Resources Ltd
Union Lifestyle Holdings Ltd
VM Receivables Financing PLC
Vectura Group Services Limited
Vedanta Finance UK Limited
Vedanta Resources Finance Ltd
Venaglass Limited
Veolia ES Landfill Limited
Victoria Investments PIKco Ltd
Vine Acquisitions Limited
Vitol Services Limited
Vocalink Limited
Vosper Thornycroft (UK) Ltd
WBA Financial Limited
WBA Financial Services Limited
WBA UK Finance Limited
WBAD Holdings Limited
WEX Europe UK Limited
WFS UK Holding Company II Ltd
WFS UK Holding Company III Ltd
WGC (UK) Finance Limited
WGC (UK) Limited
WM SA Investments Limited
WPP Brands Development Holdings (UK)
WPP Finance 2013
WPP Finance Co. Limited
WPP Sphinx Limited
Wallis Retail Limited
Walney Extension Holdings Ltd
Walney Extension Limited
Weldcure Limited
West-Ward Holdings Limited
Westfield UK & Europe Finance PLC
Westfield UK Acquisitions Finance
Westfield UK Finance Limited
Wheel Bidco Limited
Williams Lea Group Limited
Williams Lea Limited
Willis Faber Limited
Willis Group Limited
Willis Group Services Limited
Winton Group Limited
Wipro Holdings (UK) Limited
Wittington Investments (Properties)
Worldpay (UK) Limited
Worldpay Ecommerce Limited
Worldpay Finance PLC
Worldpay Group Limited
Worldpay Limited
XXIII Capital A Limited
Xstrata Limited
York UK Holdco International Ltd

84110 General public administration activities

Financial Conduct Authority
Greenwich BSF SPV Limited

84120 Regulation of health care, education, cultural and other social services, not incl. social security

Royal Brompton and Harefield Hospitals Charity

84130 Regulation of and contribution to more efficient operation of businesses

Financial Conduct Authority

84220 Defence activities

Babcock DSG Ltd
Babcock Land Limited
Boeing Defence UK Limited
General Dynamics United Kingdom Ltd

84230 Justice and judicial activities

G4S Care and Justice Services (UK)

85100 Pre-primary education

Alpha Plus Group Limited
Ark Schools
Girls' Day School Trust

85200 Primary education

Academies Enterprise Trust
Alpha Plus Group Limited
Ark Schools
Creative Education Trust
Girls' Day School Trust
Oasis Charitable Trust
Oasis Community Learning
St. Paul's School

85310 General secondary education [10]

Academies Enterprise Trust
Alpha Plus Group Limited
Ark Schools
Babcock Training Limited
Creative Education Trust
Girls' Day School Trust
Oasis Charitable Trust
Oasis Community Learning
Priory Education Services Ltd
St. Paul's School

85320 Technical and vocational secondary education

Academies Enterprise Trust
Pearson Education Limited

85410 Post-secondary non-tertiary education

Academies Enterprise Trust

85421 First-degree level higher education

London Metropolitan University
London School of Economics & Political Science
London South Bank University
Roehampton University
University of Greenwich
University of Westminster

85422 Post-graduate level higher education

London Metropolitan University
London School of Economics & Political Science
London South Bank University
Roehampton University
University of Greenwich
University of Westminster

85520 Cultural education

Rothschild Foundation (Hanadiv) Europe

85590 Other education n.e.c.

BPP Services Limited
Children's Investment Fund Foundation (UK)
E-Act

85600 Educational support services

Alpha Plus Group Limited
Alpha Plus Holdings PLC
Campden Charities Trustee
Education Endowment Foundation
International Schools Partnership
Kusuma Trust UK
Methodist Independent Schools Trust
NYOP Education (Aberdeen) Ltd
Pearson Education Limited

86101 Hospital activities [23]

BMI Healthcare Limited
Cleveland Clinic UK Holdings Ltd
Congregation of The Daughters of The Cross of Liege
Consort Healthcare (Birmingham) Funding
Consort Healthcare (Birmingham) Ltd
Georgia Healthcare Group PLC
HCA International Holdings Ltd
HCA International Limited
HCA UK Services Limited
Macmillan Cancer Support
Mediclinic International PLC
NMC Health PLC
Partnerships in Care Investments 1
Partnerships in Care Limited
Partnerships in Care Property 1 Ltd
Priory Group UK 1 Limited
Priory Group UK 2 Limited
Ramsay Health Care UK Operations Ltd
SHC Holdings Limited
Spire Healthcare Limited
St Martins Healthcare Limited
St. Martins Ltd.
Trustees of The London Clinic Ltd

86102 Medical nursing home activities

Marie Curie

86210 General medical practice activities

Marie Stopes International

86220 Specialists medical practice activities

BMI Healthcare Limited

86230 Dental practice activities

BMI Healthcare Limited

86900 Other human health activities [26]

Atos IT Services UK Limited
BMI Healthcare Limited
Barchester Healthcare Homes Ltd
British Heart Foundation
British United Provident Association
Bupa Care Homes (CFChomes) Ltd
Bupa Care Homes (Cfhcare) Ltd
Cancer Research UK
Leonard Cheshire Disability
Children's Investment Fund Foundation (UK)
Clearstone Holdings (International) Ltd
Concordia Investment Holdings (UK)
Craegmoor Group (No.5) Limited
Marie Curie
Dayshape Limited
Doctors Laboratory Limited
Dunhill Medical Trust
Great Ormond Street Hospital Children's Charity
Guy's and St Thomas' Charity
Health Foundation
Macmillan Cancer Support
Parkcare Homes (No.2) Limited
Thomas Pocklington Trust
Royal Marsden Cancer Charity
Shire Europe Limited
St. John Ambulance

87100 Residential nursing care facilities

CX Holdco Limited
Leonard Cheshire Disability
GA HC REIT II CH U.K. Senior Housing Portfolio
Royal Masonic Benevolent Institution Care Company
WR Midco Limited

87200 Residential care activities for learning difficulties, mental health and substance abuse

Leonard Cheshire Disability
Royal Mencap Society

87300 Residential care activities for the elderly and disabled

Anchor Carehomes Limited
Blind Veterans UK
Bond Propco Limited
Leonard Cheshire Disability
Congregation of The Daughters of The Cross of Liege
Jewish Care
St Mungo Community Housing Association

87900 Other residential care activities n.e.c.

Oasis Charitable Trust

88990 Other social work activities without accommodation n.e.c. [14]

Benesco Charity Limited
Charity Projects
E-Act
Gosling Foundation Limited
Khodorkovsky Foundation
Lankellychase Foundation
Local Trust
Mayfair Charities Limited
Oasis Charitable Trust
Rank Foundation Limited
Save The Children Fund
Save The Children International
St Mungo Community Housing Association
Tudor Trust

90010 Performing arts

International Entertainment Finance
International Entertainment Holdings
International Entertainment Midco
Live Nation (Music) UK Limited

90020 Support activities to performing arts

International Entertainment Investments
Live Nation (Music) UK Limited

90030 Artistic creation [16]

BBC Studios Distribution Ltd
Delfont Mackintosh Theatres Ltd
Walt Disney Co Ltd
EMI Group International Holdings Ltd
EMI Music Publishing Finance (UK)
EMI Music Publishing Limited
Endemol Shine UK Limited
Entertainment One UK Limited
Cameron Mackintosh Limited
Northern & Shell Enterprises Ltd
PIAS Holding (UK) Limited
Performing Right Society,Limited
Royal Opera House Covent Garden Foundation
Universal Music Holdings Ltd
Virgin Music Group
Virgin Records Limited

90040 Operation of arts facilities

LW Theatres Group Limited
Live Nation (Music) UK Limited
Royal Opera House Covent Garden Foundation

91020 Museums activities

British Museum Trust Limited

92000 Gambling and betting activities [12]

Betfair Limited
Coral Racing Limited
William Hill Holdings Limited
William Hill Investments Ltd
Will Hill Limited
William Hill Organization Ltd
William Hill PLC
Ladbrokes Betting & Gaming Ltd
Ladbrokes Coral Group Limited
Power Leisure Bookmakers Ltd
Sporting Exchange Limited
Zeal Network SE

93110 Operation of sports facilities [10]

All England Lawn Tennis Ground PLC
Arena Leisure Racing Limited
Jockey Club Racecourses Ltd
Sports Council Trust Company
Tottenham Hotspur Limited
Tottenham Hotspur Stadium Ltd
Virgin Active Group Investments Ltd
Virgin Active Health Club Holdings
Virgin Active International Ltd
WH Holding Limited

93120 Activities of sport clubs

All England Lawn Tennis & Croquet Club
Arsenal Football Club PLC
Arsenal Holdings Limited
Chelsea Football Club Limited
Palace Holdco UK Limited
Palace Midco UK Limited
Virgin Active Group Investments Ltd
West Ham United Football Club Ltd

93130 Fitness facilities

Esporta Health & Fitness Ltd

93199 Other sports activities

Football Association Premier League
Formula One World Championship Ltd
Lawn Tennis Association Ltd

93290 Other amusement and recreation activities n.e.c.

Ansco Arena Limited
Fremantlemedia Limited
La Perla Global Management (UK) Ltd
Sony Music Entertainment UK Ltd
Syco Entertainment Limited
Syco Holdings Limited
Virgin Active Group Investments Ltd
Virgin Active Limited

94110 Activities of business and employers membership organisations

Hiscox Underwriting Group Services

94120 Activities of professional membership organisations

Medical Protection Society Ltd

94200 Activities of trade unions

British Medical Association

94910 Activities of religious organisations

Congregation of The Daughters of The Cross of Liege
Council for World Mission (UK)
International Bible Students Association
London Diocesan Fund
South London Church Fund & Southwark Diocesan Board of Finance
Stewardship Services (UKET) Ltd

94990 Activities of other membership organisations n.e.c.

Clothworkers' Foundation
Financial Ombudsman Service Ltd
Pall Mall and Woodcote Park Clubhouses
Priority Pass Limited
Royal Automobile Club Limited
SCOR Underwriting Limited
Shell Foundation

95110 Repair of computers and peripheral equipment

Fujitsu Services Limited

96020 Hairdressing and other beauty treatment

TIGI Holdings Limited

96030 Funeral and related activities

Golden Charter Trust Limited

96090 Other service activities n.e.c. [105]

Aamby Valley (UK) Limited
Advanced Payment Solutions Ltd
Advent Capital (Holdings) Ltd
Amcol (Holdings) Ltd.
Aviva Employment Services Ltd
BTG International (Holdings) Ltd
BTG International Healthcare Ltd
Babcock Integrated Technology Ltd
Babcock Mission Critical Services Ltd
Babcock Rail Limited
Bonhams 1793 Limited
Brookfield Global Property Advisor
Bupa Care Homes (ANS) Limited
CBI UK Cayman Acquisition Ltd
Cheetah Bidco Limited
Cheetah Holdco Limited
Comet Bidco Limited
Concierge Holding Co Ltd
Constantin Investment Limited
Corsair Mint III Limited
The Francis Crick Institute Ltd
Donvand Limited
EDF Energy Services Limited
Entertainment One UK Limited
Financial Models Corporation Ltd
Financial Services Compensation Scheme
First Corporate Shipping Ltd
Foundation for Social Entrepreneurs
Global Radio Services Limited
Global Starnet Limited
Gower Place Investments Ltd
IIR Exhibitions Limited
ITW UK Finance Beta Limited
ITW UK Finance Gamma Limited
Instron International Limited
International Bible Students Association
International Finance Facility for Immunisation Company
International Nuclear Investment Ltd
Interpayment Services Limited
Itochu Europe PLC
Jac Travel Group (Holdings) Ltd
Jeco 2 Ltd
KAZ Minerals PLC
Kantar UK Limited
Khoo Teck Puat UK Foundation
Kiwara UK Limited
L.E.K. Consulting Group Ltd
L.E.K. International Group Ltd
Lancer Square Limited
Libra International Limited
Lok'n Store Limited
Macmillan Cancer Support
Marfrig Beef (UK) Limited
Marfrig Beef International Ltd
Maxwell Asset Management Ltd
Miki Travel Limited
Mitie Technical Facilities Management
Mitie Treasury Management Ltd
Monaco Bidco Limited
Monaco Topco Limited
Muse Developments Limited
NM Money Holdings Limited
Harvey Nash Group Limited
Oceaneering International Services
Opet International Limited
Oxhauth Limited
P & O Properties International Ltd
PA Group Limited
Pepsico Holdings
Pepsico International Limited
Polyus Finance PLC
Primetals Technologies Financial Services
Primetals Technologies, Ltd
Quantoil Limited
Queensgate Bow Propco Limited
Raphael Freshwater Memorial Association
Regus Group Limited
Rhythmone PLC
Road Management Services (A13) Holdings
Road Management Services (A13) PLC
SPX European Holding Limited
SRE Portfolios UK Ltd
Sagittarius International Ltd
Smart DCC Limited
Sotheby's
Starbucks EMEA Ltd
Structadene (LBG) Holdings Ltd
Structadene (LBG) Properties Ltd
TIAA International Holdings 2 Ltd
TIAA International Holdings 3 Ltd
Tay Valley Lighting (Hampshire) Ltd
Titan Acquisition Holdco Ltd
Titan Acquisition Limited
Titan Financing Holdco Limited
Titan Financing Limited
Triplog Holdings Limited
Universal Music Operations Ltd
Veolia ES (UK) Limited
Veolia Environmental Services (UK) PLC
Verbena Investment Limited
Wellcome Trust Finance PLC
Wellcome Trust Investments 1 Unlimited
Wellcome Trust Investments 2 Unlimited
Wellcome Trust Residential 1 Ltd
Oliver Wyman Limited

97000 Activities of households as employers of domestic personnel

Interserve FS (UK) Limited
Reed Overseas Corporation Ltd

98000 Residents property management

A2dominion Residential Limited
A2dominion Treasury Limited
LS White Rose Limited

98100 Undifferentiated goods-producing activities of private households for own use

GroupBT Limited

99999 Dormant company [17]

Blaxmill (Ten) Limited
Blue Transmission Sheringham Shoal
Blue Transmission Walney 2 Ltd
CLS UK Properties PLC
DMG Loanco Limited
Garban-Intercapital US Investments (Holdings)
Garban-Intercapital US Investments (No 1)
Global World-Check
Mediaedge:cia (UK) Holdings Ltd
Telecom New Zealand (UK) Enterprises
Thomson Business Information Holdings
Thomson Information & Publishing Holdings
Thomson Legal & Professional Group
Thomson Organisation (No.23)
WBA Latin America Limited
WPP 2323 Limited
Yianis Investments Limited

This page is intentionally left blank

Printed in 8pt Nimbus Sans L

Designed by URW++ Design and Development GmbH

Dellam Publishing Limited

2 Heath Drive, Sutton, Surrey, SM2 5RP

Fax: 020 8770 7478 email: enquiries@dellam.com

SAN: 0177881 EAN/GLN: 5030670177882

www.ingramcontent.com/pod-product-compliance
Lightning Source LLC
LaVergne TN
LVHW082004200926
848481LV00010B/2799